GENERAL MOTORS CALAIS/GRAN[illegible] 1985-92 REPAIR MANUAL

CHILTON'S

President, Chilton Enterprises — David S. Loewith
Senior Vice President — Ronald A. Hoxter

Publisher and Editor-In-Chief — Kerry A. Freeman, S.A.E.
Managing Editors — Peter M. Conti, Jr. □ W. Calvin Settle, Jr., S.A.E.
Assistant Managing Editor — Nick D'Andrea
Senior Editors — Debra Gaffney □ Ken Grabowski, A.S.E., S.A.E. Michael L. Grady □ Richard J. Rivele, S.A.E. Richard T. Smith □ Jim Taylor Ron Webb
Director of Manufacturing — Mike D'Imperio
Editors — Steve Horner □ John Rutter

CHILTON BOOK COMPANY
*ONE OF THE **DIVERSIFIED PUBLISHING COMPANIES,** A PART OF **CAPITAL CITIES/ABC, INC.***

Manufactured in USA

Chilton Way, Radnor, PA 19089
ISBN 0-8019-8257-X
Library of Congress Catalog Card No. 91-058823
4567890123 4321098765

Contents

Contents

SAFETY NOTICE

Proper service and repair procedures are vital to the safe, reliable operation of all motor vehicles, as well as the personal safety of those performing repairs. This manual outlines procedures for servicing and repairing vehicles using safe, effective methods. The procedures contain many NOTES, CAUTIONS and WARNINGS which should be followed along with standard safety procedures to eliminate the possibility of personal injury or improper service which could damage the vehicle or compromise its safety.

It is important to note that the repair procedures and techniques, tools and parts for servicing motor vehicles, as well as the skill and experience of the individual performing the work vary widely. It is not possible to anticipate all of the conceivable ways or conditions under which vehicles may be serviced, or to provide cautions as to all of the possible hazards that may result. Standard and accepted safety precautions and equipment should be used when handling toxic or flammable fluids, and safety goggles or other protection should be used during cutting, grinding, chiseling, prying, or any other process that can cause material removal or projectiles.

Some procedures require the use of tools specially designed for a specific purpose. Before substituting another tool or procedure, you must be completely satisfied that neither your personal safety, nor the performance of the vehicle will be endangered.

Although information in this manual is based on industry sources and is complete as possible at the time of publication, the possibility exists that some car manufacturers made later changes which could not be included here. While striving for total accuracy, Chilton Book Company cannot assume responsibility for any errors, changes or omissions that may occur in the compilation of this data.

PART NUMBERS

Part numbers listed in this reference are not recommendations by Chilton for any product by brand name. They are references that can be used with interchange manuals and aftermarket supplier catalogs to locate each brand supplier's discrete part number.

SPECIAL TOOLS

Special tools are recommended by the vehicle manufacturer to perform their specific job. Use has been kept to a minimum, but where absolutely necessary, they are referred to in the text by the part number of the tool manufacturer. These tools can be purchased, under the appropriate part number, from your General Motors dealer or regional distributor, or an equivalent tool can be purchased locally from a tool supplier or parts outlet. Before substituting any tool for the one recommended, read the SAFETY NOTICE at the top of this page.

ACKNOWLEDGMENTS

The Chilton Book Company expresses appreciation to General Motors Corp., Detroit, Michigan for their generous assistance.

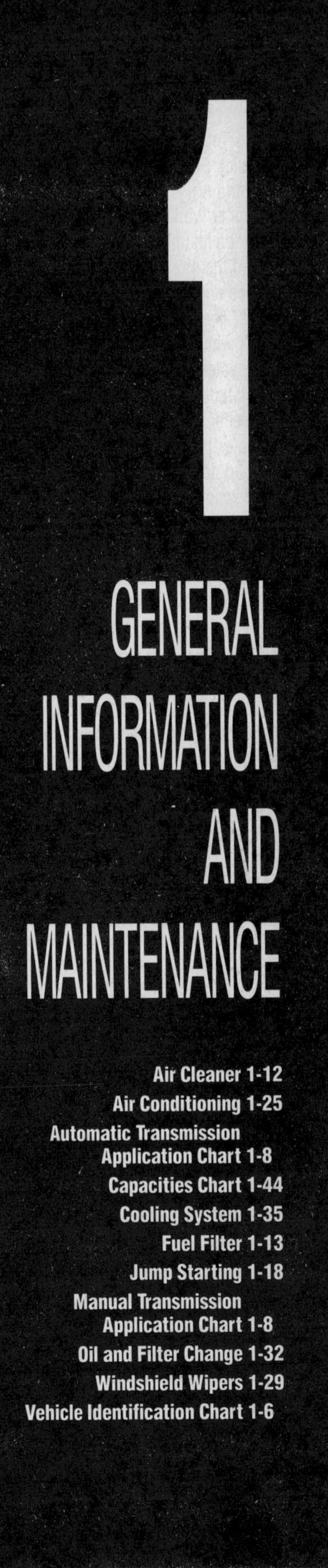

1
GENERAL
INFORMATION
AND
MAINTENANCE
Air Cleaner 1-12
Air Conditioning 1-25
Automatic Transmission Application Chart 1-8
Capacities Chart 1-44
Cooling System 1-35
Fuel Filter 1-13
Jump Starting 1-18
Manual Transmission Application Chart 1-8
Oil and Filter Change 1-32
Windshield Wipers 1-29
Vehicle Identification Chart 1-6

HOW TO USE THIS BOOK

Chilton's Total Car Care manual for Buick Skylark, Buick Somerset, Oldsmobile Calais and Pontiac Grand Am is intended to teach you more about the inner workings of your car and save you money on its upkeep. The first two Sections will be used the most, since they contain maintenance and tune-up information and procedures. The following Sections concern themselves with the more complex systems. Operating systems from engine through brakes are covered to the extent that we feel the average do-it-yourselfer should get involved as well as more complex procedures that will benefit both the advanced do-it-yourselfer mechanic as well as the professional.

A secondary purpose of this book is as a reference for owners who want to understand their car and/or their mechanics better. In this case, no tools at all are required.

Before attempting any repairs or service on your car, read through the entire procedure outlined in the appropriate Section. This will give you the overall view of what tools and supplies will be required. There is nothing more frustrating than having to walk to the bus stop on Monday morning because you were short one gasket on Sunday afternoon. So read ahead and plan ahead. Each operation should be approached logically and all procedures thoroughly understood before attempting any work. Some special tools that may be required can often be rented from local automotive jobbers or places specializing in renting tools and equipment. Check the yellow pages of your phone book.

All Sections contain adjustments, maintenance, removal and installation procedures, and overhaul procedures. When overhaul is not considered practical, we tell you how to remove the failed part and then how to install the new or rebuilt replacement. In this way, you at least save the labor costs. Backyard overhaul of some components is just not practical, but the removal and installation procedure is often simple and well within the capabilities of the average car owner.

Two basic mechanic's rules should be mentioned here. First, whenever the LEFT side of the car or engine is referred to, it is meant to specify the DRIVER'S side of the car. Conversely, the RIGHT side of the car means the PASSENGER'S side. Second, all screws and bolts are removed by turning counterclockwise, and tightened by turning clockwise, unless otherwise noted.

Safety is always the most important rule. Constantly be aware of the dangers involved in working on or around an automobile and take proper precautions to avoid the risk of personal injury or damage to the vehicle. See the section in this Section, Servicing Your Vehicle Safely, and the SAFETY NOTICE on the acknowledgment page before attempting any service procedures and pay attention to the instructions provided. There are 3 common mistakes in mechanical work:

1. Incorrect order of assembly, disassembly or adjustment. When taking something apart or putting it together, doing things in the wrong order usually just costs you extra time; however it CAN break something. Read the entire procedure before beginning disassembly. Do everything in the order in which the instructions say you should do it, even if you can't immediately see a reason for it. When you're taking apart something that is very intricate, you might want to draw a picture of how it looks when assembled at one point in order to make sure you get everything back in its proper position. We will supply exploded views whenever possible, but sometimes the job requires more attention to detail than an illustration provides. When making adjustments (especially tune-up adjustments), do them in order. One adjustment often affects another and you cannot expect satisfactory results unless each adjustment is made only when it cannot be changed by any other.

2. Overtorquing (or undertorquing) nuts and bolts. While it is more common for overtorquing to cause damage, undertorquing can cause a fastener to vibrate loose and cause serious damage, especially when dealing with aluminum parts. Pay attention to torque specifications and utilize a torque wrench in assembly. If a torque figure is not available remember that, if you are using the right tool to do the job, you will probably not have to strain yourself to get a fastener tight enough. The pitch of most threads is so slight that the tension you put on the wrench will be multiplied many times in actual force on what you are tightening. A good example of how critical torque is can be seen in the case of spark plug installation, especially where you are putting the plug into an aluminum cylinder head. Too little torque can fail to crush the gasket, causing leakage of combustion gases and consequent overheating of the plug and engine parts. Too much torque can damage the threads or distort the plug, which changes the spark gap at the electrode. Since more and more manufacturers are using aluminum in their engine and chassis parts to save weight, a torque wrench should be in any serious do-it-yourselfer's tool box.

There are many commercial chemical products available for ensuring that fasteners won't come loose, even if they are not torqued just right (a very common brand is Loctite®). If you're worried about getting something together tight enough to hold, but loose enough to avoid mechanical damage during assembly, one of these products might offer substantial insurance. Read the label on the package and make sure the product is compatible with the materials, fluids, etc. involved before choosing one.

3. Crossthreading. This occurs when a part such as a bolt is screwed into a nut or casting at the wrong angle and forced, causing the threads to become damaged. Crossthreading is more likely to occur if access is difficult. It helps to clean and lubricate fasteners, and to start threading with the part to be installed going straight in, using your fingers. If you encounter resistance, unscrew the part and start over again at a different angle until it can be inserted and turned several times without much effort. Keep in mind that many parts, especially spark plugs, use tapered threads so that gentle turning will automatically bring the part you're threading to the proper angle if you don't force it or resist a change in angle. Don't put a wrench on the part until it's been turned in a couple of times by hand. If you suddenly encounter resistance and the part has not seated fully, don't force it. Pull it back out and make sure it's clean and threading properly.

Always take your time and be patient; once you have some experience, working on your car will become an enjoyable hobby.

TOOLS AND EQUIPMENT

Naturally, without the proper tools and equipment it is impossible to properly service your vehicle. It would be impossible to catalog each tool that you would need to perform each or every operation in this book. It would also be unwise for the amateur to rush out and buy an expensive set of tools an the theory that he may need one or more of them at sometime.

The best approach is to proceed slowly, gathering together a good quality set of those tools that are used most frequently. Don't be misled by the low cost of bargain tools. It is far better to spend a little more for better quality. Forged wrenches, 6- or 12-point sockets and fine tooth ratchets are by far preferable to their less expensive counterparts. As any good mechanic can tell you, there are few worse experiences than trying to work on a truck with bad tools. Your monetary savings will be far outweighed by frustration and mangled knuckles.

Certain tools, plus a basic ability to handle tools, are required to get started. A basic mechanics tool set, a torque wrench, and a Torx bits set. Torx bits are hexlobular drivers which fit both inside and outside on special Torx head fasteners used in various places on your vehicle.

Begin accumulating those tools that are used most frequently; those associated with routine maintenance and tune-up.

In addition to the normal assortment of screwdrivers and pliers you should have the following tools for routine maintenance jobs (your vehicle, depending on the model year, uses both SAE and metric fasteners):

1. SAE/Metric wrenches, sockets and combination open end/box end wrenches in sizes from 1/8 in. (3mm) to 3/4 in. (19mm); and a spark plug socket (13/16 in.) If possible, buy various length socket drive extensions. One break in this department is that the metric sockets available in the U.S. will all fit the ratchet handles and extensions you may already have (1/4 in., 3/8 in., and 1/2 in. drive).
2. Jackstands for support
3. Oil filter wrench
4. Oil filter spout for pouring oil
5. Grease gun for chassis lubrication
6. Hydrometer for checking the battery
7. A container for draining oil
8. Many rags for wiping up the inevitable mess.

In addition to the above items there are several others that are not absolutely necessary, but handy to have around. These include oil-dry (cat box litter works just as well and may be cheaper), a transmission funnel and the usual supply of lubricants, antifreeze and fluids, although these can be purchased as needed. This is a basic list for routine maintenance, but only your personal needs and desires can accurately determine your list of necessary tools.

The second list of tools is for tune-ups. While the tools involved here are slightly more sophisticated, they need not be outrageously expensive. There are several inexpensive tach/dwell meters on the market that are every bit as good for the average mechanic as a $100.00 professional model. Just be sure that it goes to at least 1,200–1,500 rpm on the tach scale and that it works on 4, 6 and 8 cylinder engines. A basic list of tune-up equipment could include:

1. Tach-dwell meter
2. Spark plug wrench
3. Timing light (a DC light that works from the vehicle's battery is best, although an AC light that plugs into 110V house current will suffice at some sacrifice in brightness)
4. Wire spark plug gauge/adjusting tools

In addition to these basic tools, there are several other tools and gauges you may find useful. These include:

1. A compression gauge. The screw-in type is slower to use, but eliminates the possibility of a faulty reading due to escaping pressure
2. A manifold vacuum gauge
3. A test light
4. An induction meter. This is used for determining whether or not there is current in a wire. These are handy for use if a wire is broken somewhere in a wiring harness.

Normally, the use of special factory tools is avoided for repair procedures, since these are not readily available for the do-it-yourself mechanic. When it is possible to perform the job with more commonly available tools, it will be pointed out, but occasionally, a special tool was designed to perform a specific function and should be used. Before substituting another tool, you should be convinced that neither your safety nor the performance of the vehicle will be compromised.

When a special tool is indicated, it will be referred to by the manufacturer's part number. Some special tools are available commercially from major tool manufacturers. Others for your car can be purchased from your GM dealer.

As a final note, you will probably find a torque wrench necessary for all but the most basic work. The beam type models are perfectly adequate, although the newer click (breakaway) type are more precise, and you don't have to crane your neck to see a torque reading in awkward situations. The breakaway torque wrenches are more expensive and should be recalibrated periodically.

Torque specification for each fastener will be given in the procedure in any case that a specific torque value is required. If no torque specifications are given, use the following values as a guide, based upon fastener size:

Bolts marked 6T

6mm bolt/nut – 5–7 ft. lbs.
8mm bolt/nut – 12–17 ft. lbs.
10mm bolt/nut – 23–34 ft. lbs.
12mm bolt/nut – 41–59 ft. lbs.
14mm bolt/nut – 56–76 ft. lbs.

Bolts marked 8T

6mm bolt/nut – 6–9 ft. lbs.
8mm bolt/nut – 13–20 ft. lbs.
10mm bolt/nut – 27–40 ft. lbs.
12mm bolt/nut – 46–69 ft. lbs.
14mm bolt/nut – 75–101 ft. lbs.

SERVICING YOUR VEHICLE SAFELY

It is virtually impossible to anticipate all of the hazards involved with automotive maintenance and service but care and common sense will prevent most accidents.

The rules of safety for mechanics range from "don't smoke around gasoline," to "use the proper tool for the job." The trick to avoid injuries is to develop safe work habits and take every possible precaution.

Do's

• Do keep a fire extinguisher and first aid kit within easy reach.

• Do wear safety glasses or goggles when cutting, drilling, grinding or prying. If you wear glasses for the sake of vision, then they should be made of hardened glass that can serve also as safety glasses, or wear safety goggles over your regular glasses.

• Do wear safety glasses whenever you work around the battery. Batteries contain sulphuric acid. In case of contact with the eyes or skin, flush the area with water or a mixture of water and baking soda and get medical attention immediately.

• Do use safety stands for any under-car service. Jacks are for raising vehicles; safety stands are for making sure the vehicle stays raised until you want it to come down. Whenever the vehicle is raised, block the wheels remaining on the ground and set the parking brake.

• Do use adequate ventilation when working with any chemicals. Asbestos dust resulting from brake lining wear can cause cancer.

• Do disconnect the negative battery cable when working on the electrical system. The primary ignition system can contain up to 40,000 volts.

• Do follow manufacturer's directions whenever working with potentially hazardous materials. Both brake fluid and antifreeze are poisonous if taken internally.

• Do properly maintain your tools. Loose hammerheads, mushroomed punches and chisels, frayed or poorly grounded electrical cords, excessively worn screwdriver, spread wrenches (open end), cracked sockets can cause accidents.

• Do use the proper size and type of tool for the job being done.

• Do when possible, pull on a wrench handle rather than push on it, and adjust your stance to prevent a fall.

• Do be sure that adjustable wrenches are tightly adjusted on the nut or bolt and pulled so that the face is on the side of the fixed jaw.

• Do select a wrench or socket that fits the nut or bolt. The wrench or socket should sit straight, not cocked.

• Do strike squarely with a hammer to avoid glancing blows.

• Do set the parking brake and block the drive wheels if the work requires that the engine

Don'ts

• Don't run an engine in a garage or anywhere else without proper ventilation — EVER! Carbon monoxide is poisonous. It is absorbed by the body 400 times faster than oxygen. It takes a long time to leave the human body and you can build up a deadly supply of it in you system by simply breathing in a little every day. You may not realize you are slowly poisoning yourself. Always use power vents, windows, fans or open the garage doors.

• Don't work around moving parts while wearing a necktie or other loose clothing. Short sleeves are much safer than long, loose sleeves. Hard-toed shoes with neoprene soles protect your toes and give a better grip on slippery surfaces. Jewelry such as watches, fancy belt buckles, beads or body adornment of any kind is not safe working around a car. Long hair should be hidden under a hat or cap.

• Don't use pockets for tool boxes. A fall or bump can drive a screwdriver deep into you body. Even a wiping cloth hanging from the back pocket can wrap around a spinning shaft or fan.

• Don't smoke when working around gasoline, cleaning solvent or other flammable material.

• Don't smoke when working around the battery. When the battery is being charged, it gives off explosive hydrogen gas.

• Don't use gasoline to wash your hands. There are excellent soaps available. Gasoline may contain lead, and lead can enter the body through a cut, accumulating in the body until you are very ill. Gasoline also removes all the natural oils from the skin so that bone dry hands will suck up oil and grease.

• Don't service the air conditioning system unless you are equipped with the necessary tools and training. Do wear safety glasses, the refrigerant, is extremely cold and when exposed to the air, will instantly freeze any surface it comes in contact with, including your eyes. Although the refrigerant is normally nontoxic, it becomes a deadly poisonous gas in the presence of an open flame. One good whiff of the vapors from burning refrigerant can be fatal.

MODEL IDENTIFICATION

General Motors introduced the N body line of vehicles in 1985 to three of its divisions: Buick, Oldsmobile and Pontiac. The Buick models included the Somerset and Skylark. The Somerset was discontinued after 1987. The Oldsmobile version was the Cutlass Calais until 1992 and the Pontiac model remains the Grand Am. General Motors did a body redesign for all three N body vehicles in 1992, with the Oldsmobile model changing its name from Cutlass Calais to Achieva.

SERIAL NUMBER IDENTIFICATION

Vehicle

SEE FIG. 1

The VIN plate which contains the Vehicle Identification Number (VIN) is located at the top and back of the instrument panel on the left side and is visible from outside the vehicle on the lower left (driver's) side of the windshield. The VIN consists of 17 characters which represent codes supplying important information about your vehicle. The first character represents the nation of origin. The second character identifies the manufacturer. The third character represents a code used by the manufacturer to identify the division. The fourth character represents a code used to establish the car line or series. The fifth character is a code which identifies the model. On vehicles from model years 1985–87, the sixth and seventh characters combined represent a code which identifies the body type. On vehicles from model years 1988–92, the sixth character is a code which identifies the body type and the seventh character identifies the type of restraint system used on the vehicle. The eighth character represents the engine code. The ninth character is a check digit. The tenth character is a code which represents the model year of the vehicle. The eleventh character is a code which represents the plant in which the vehicle was assembled. Characters twelve through seventeen are the plant sequence number or the number of the vehicle of that model produced at that plant for the model year.

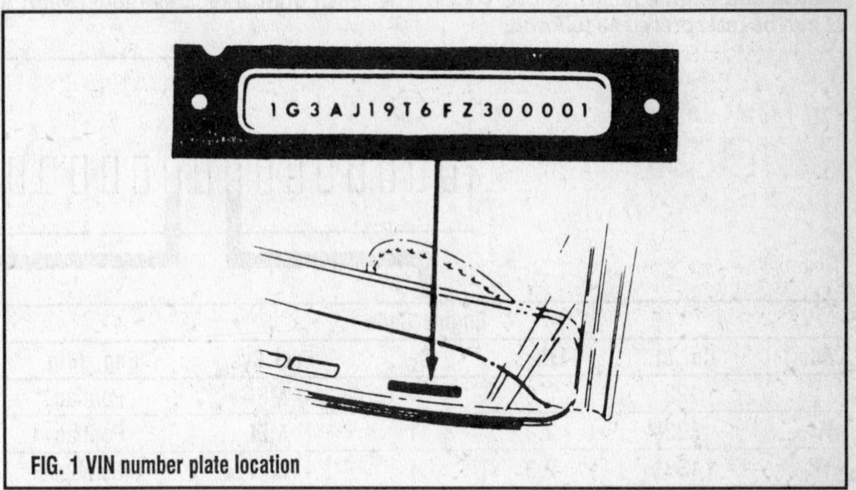

FIG. 1 VIN number plate location

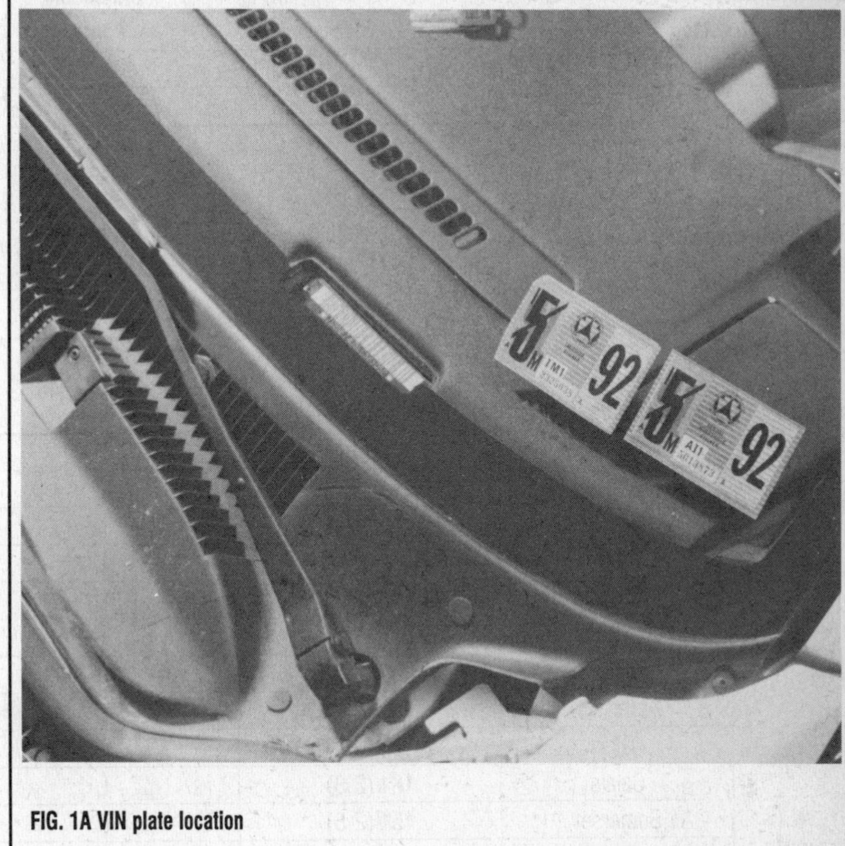

FIG. 1A VIN plate location

VEHICLE IDENTIFICATION CHART

It is important for servicing and ordering parts to be certain of the vehicle and engine identification. The VIN (vehicle identification number) is a 17 digit number visible through the windshield on the driver's side of the dash and contains the vehicle and engine identification codes. The tenth digit indicates model year, and the eighth digit indicates engine code. It can be interpreted as follows:

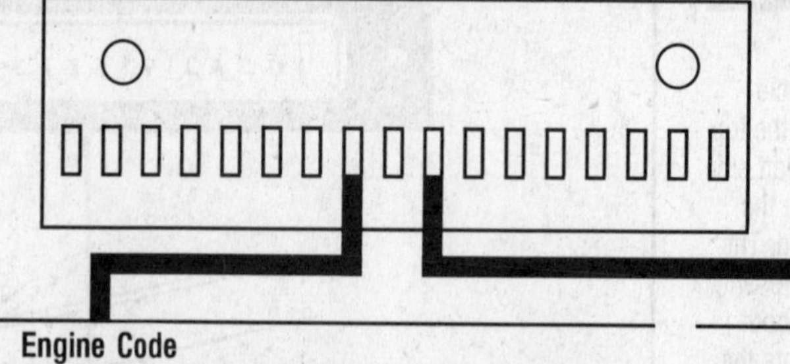

Engine Code

Code	Cu. In.	Liters	Cyl.	Fuel Sys.	Eng. Mfg.
K	122	2.0	4	MFI	Pontiac
M ①	122	2.0	4	MFI	Pontiac
A ②	138	2.3	4	MFI	Oldsmobile
D ②	138	2.3	4	MFI	Oldsmobile
3 ③	138	2.3	4	MFI	Oldsmobile
U	151	2.5	4	TBI	Pontiac
L	181	3.0	6	MFI	Buick
N	204	3.3	6	MFI	Buick

TBI—Throttle Body Injection
MFI—Multi-port Fuel Injection
① Turbo
② Quad-4 engine
③ Single Overhead Cam

Model Year

Code	Year
F	1985
G	1986
H	1987
J	1988
K	1989
L	1990
M	1991
N	1992

ENGINE IDENTIFICATION

Year	Model	Engine Displacement cu. in. (liter)	Engine Series Identification (VIN)	No. of Cylinders	Engine Type
1985	Grand Am	151 (2.5)	U	4	OHV
	Grand Am	181 (3.0)	L	6	OHV
	Calais	151 (2.5)	U	4	OHV
	Calais	181 (3.0)	L	6	OHV
	Somerset	151 (2.5)	U	4	OHV
	Somerset	181 (3.0)	L	6	OHV
1986	Grand Am	151 (2.5)	U	4	OHV
	Grand Am	181 (3.0)	L	6	OHV
	Calais	151 (2.5)	U	4	OHV
	Calais	181 (3.0)	L	6	OHV
	Somerset	151 (2.5)	U	4	OHV
	Somerset	181 (3.0)	L	6	OHV
	Skylark	151 (2.5)	U	4	OHV
	Skylark	181 (3.0)	L	6	OHV
1987	Grand Am	122 (2.0)	K	4	OHC
	Grand Am	122 (2.0)	M	4	OHC Turbo
	Grand Am	151 (2.5)	U	4	OHV
	Grand Am	181 (3.0)	L	6	OHV

ENGINE IDENTIFICATION

Year	Model	Engine Displacement cu. in. (liter)	Engine Series Identification (VIN)	No. of Cylinders	Engine Type
1987	Calais	151 (2.5)	U	4	OHV
	Calais	181 (3.0)	L	6	OHV
	Somerset	151 (2.5)	U	4	OHV
	Somerset	181 (3.0)	L	6	OHV
	Skylark	151 (2.5)	U	4	OHV
	Skylark	181 (3.0)	L	6	OHV
1988	Grand Am	122 (2.0)	M	4	OHC Turbo
	Grand Am	138 (2.3)	D	4	DOHC
	Grand Am	151 (2.5)	U	4	OHV
	Calais	138 (2.3)	D	4	DOHC
	Calais	151 (2.5)	U	4	OHV
	Calais	181 (3.0)	L	6	OHV
	Skylark	138 (2.3)	D	4	DOHC
	Skylark	151 (2.5)	U	4	OHV
	Skylark	181 (3.0)	L	6	OHV
1989	Grand Am	122 (2.0)	M	4	OHC Turbo
	Grand Am	138 (2.3)	D	4	DOHC
	Grand Am	138 (2.3)	A	4	DOHC-HO
	Grand Am	151 (2.5)	U	4	OHV
	Calais	138 (2.3)	D	4	DOHC
	Calais	138 (2.3)	A	4	DOHC-HO
	Calais	151 (2.5)	U	4	OHV
	Calais	204 (3.3)	N	6	OHV
	Skylark	138 (2.3)	D	4	DOHC
	Skylark	151 (2.5)	U	4	OHV
	Skylark	204 (3.3)	N	6	OHV
1990	Grand Am	138 (2.3)	D	4	DOHC
	Grand Am	138 (2.3)	A	4	DOHC-HO
	Grand Am	151 (2.5)	U	4	OHV
	Calais	138 (2.3)	D	4	DOHC
	Calais	138 (2.3)	A	4	DOHC-HO
	Calais	151 (2.5)	U	4	OHV
	Calais	204 (3.3)	N	6	OHV
	Skylark	138 (2.3)	D	4	DOHC
	Skylark	151 (2.5)	U	4	OHV
	Skylark	204 (3.3)	N	6	OHV
1991	Grand Am	138 (2.3)	D	4	DOHC
	Grand Am	138 (2.3)	A	4	DOHC-HO
	Grand Am	151 (2.5)	U	4	OHV
	Calais	138 (2.3)	D	4	DOHC
	Calais	138 (2.3)	A	4	DOHC-HO
	Calais	151 (2.5)	U	4	OHV
	Calais	204 (3.3)	N	6	OHV
	Skylark	138 (2.3)	D	4	DOHC

ENGINE IDENTIFICATION

Year	Model	Engine Displacement cu. in. (liter)	Engine Series Identification (VIN)	No. of Cylinders	Engine Type
1991	Skylark	151 (2.5)	U	4	OHV
	Skylark	204 (3.3)	N	6	OHV
1992	Grand Am	138 (2.3)	3	4	SOHC
	Grand Am	138 (2.3)	D	4	DOHC
	Grand Am	138 (2.3)	A	4	DOHC-HO
	Grand Am	151 (2.5)	U	4	OHV
	Achieva	138 (2.3)	3	4	SOHC
	Achieva	138 (2.3)	D	4	DOHC
	Achieva	138 (2.3)	A	4	DOHC-HO
	Achieva	151 (2.5)	U	4	OHV
	Achieva	204 (3.3)	N	6	OHV
	Skylark	138 (2.3)	3	4	SOHC
	Skylark	138 (2.3)	D	4	DOHC
	Skylark	151 (2.5)	U	4	OHV
	Skylark	204 (3.3)	N	6	OHV

DOHC—Double Overhead Cam
OHV—Overhead Valve
HO—High Output
SOHC—Single Overhead Cam

TRANSAXLE IDENTIFICATION CHART

Year	Engine Liter (cu. in.)	Transaxle Model Manual 4-Spd.	Transaxle Model Manual 5-Spd.	Automatic
1987-89	2.0 (122)	—	HM-282	125C
1988-89	2.3 (138)	—	HM-282	
1990-92	2.3 (138)	—	5T40	
1988-89	2.3 (138)	—	—	125C
1990-92	2.3 (138)	—	—	3T40
1985-92	2.5 (151)		Isuzu 76 MM	
1985-89	2.5 (151)	—	—	125C
1990-92	2.5 (151)	—	—	3T40
1985-88	3.0 (181)	—	—	125C
1989	3.3 (204)	—	—	125C
1990-92	3.3 (204)	—	—	3T40

Engine

➧ SEE FIGS. 2–8

The engine code is represented by the eighth character in the VIN and identifies the engine type, displacement, fuel system type and manufacturing division.

The engine identification code is either stamped onto the engine block or found on a label affixed to the engine. This code supplies information about the manufacturing plant location and time of manufacture. The location for a particular engine is shown in the illustrations.

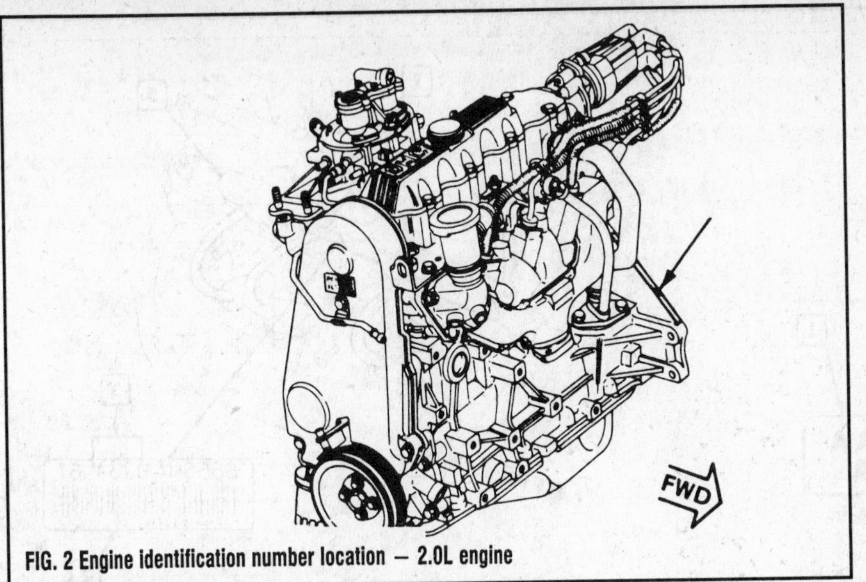

FIG. 2 Engine identification number location – 2.0L engine

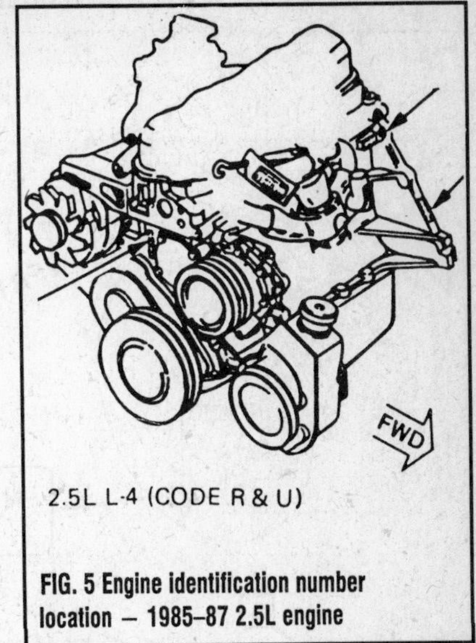

FIG. 5 Engine identification number location – 1985–87 2.5L engine

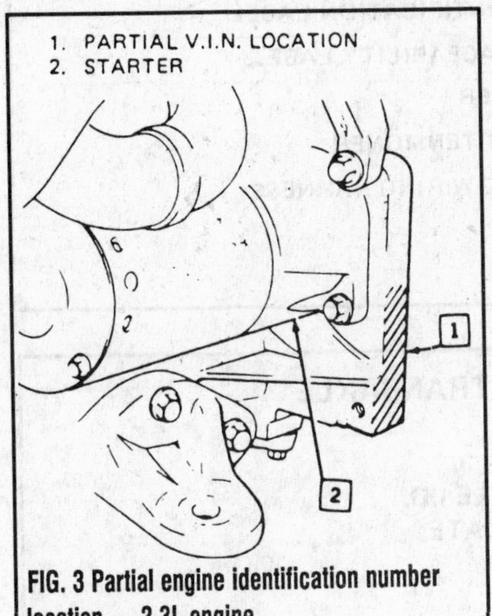

FIG. 3 Partial engine identification number location – 2.3L engine

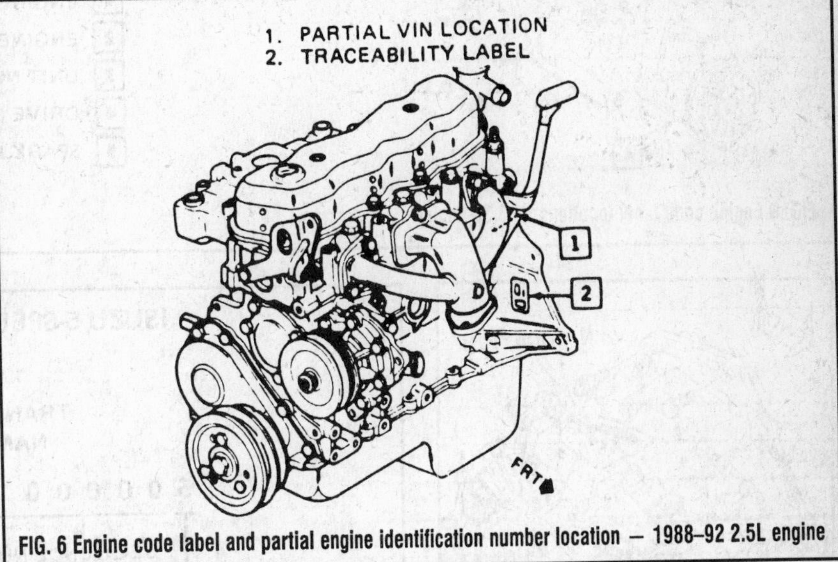

FIG. 6 Engine code label and partial engine identification number location – 1988–92 2.5L engine

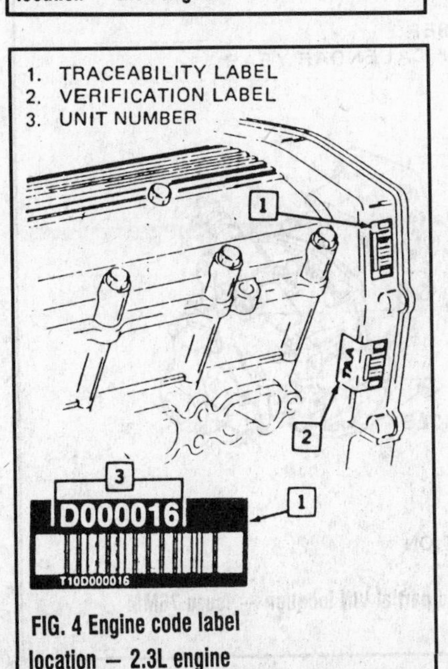

FIG. 4 Engine code label location – 2.3L engine

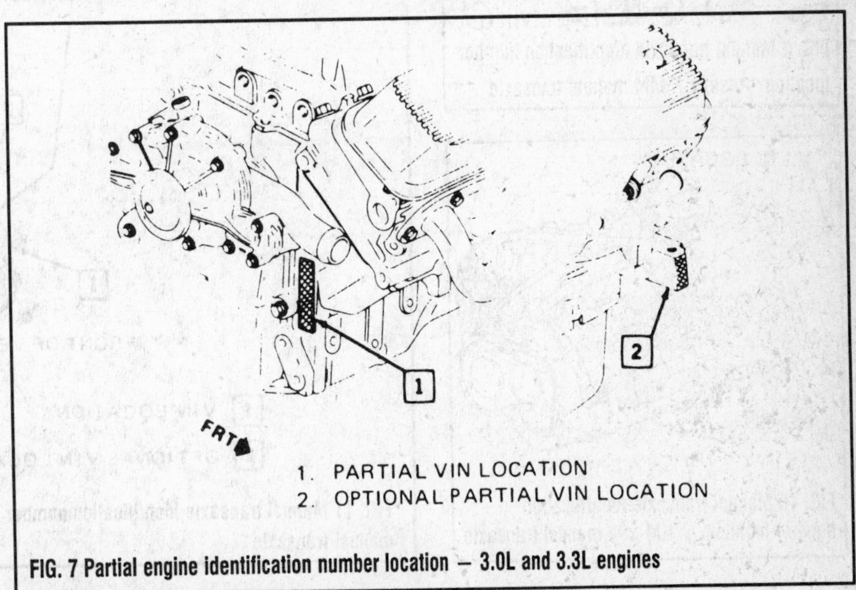

FIG. 7 Partial engine identification number location – 3.0L and 3.3L engines

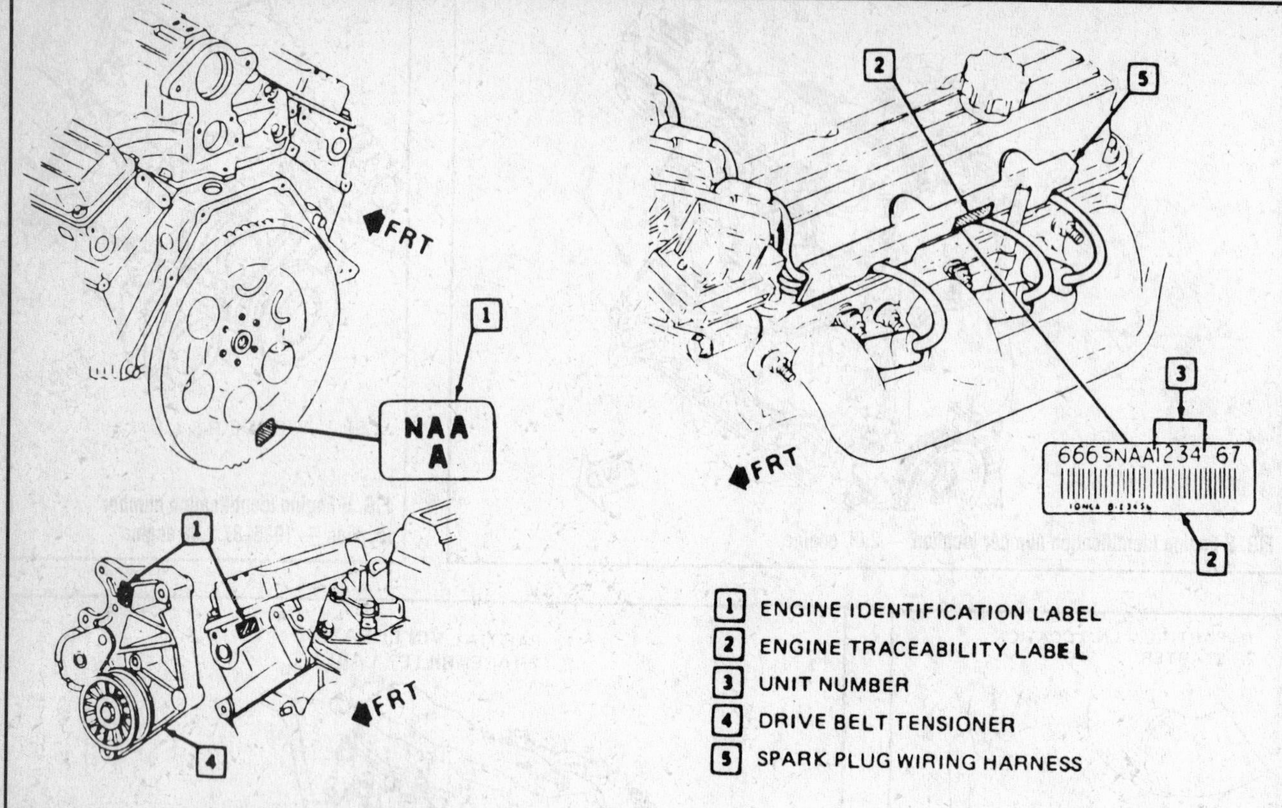

FRT

NAA
A

6665NAA1234 67

1 ENGINE IDENTIFICATION LABEL
2 ENGINE TRACEABILITY LABEL
3 UNIT NUMBER
4 DRIVE BELT TENSIONER
5 SPARK PLUG WIRING HARNESS

FIG. 8 Engine code label locations — 3.3L engine

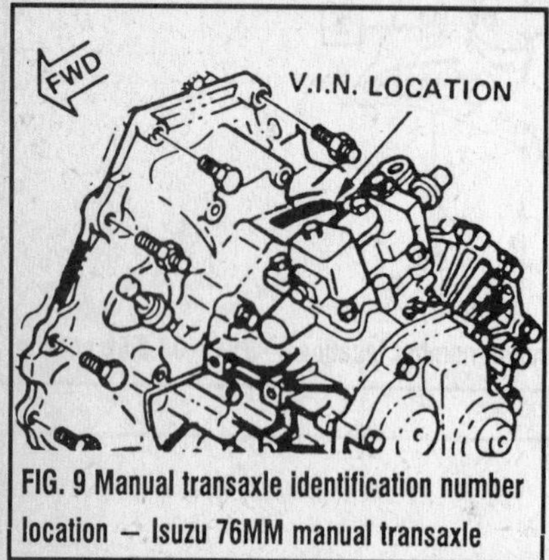

FIG. 9 Manual transaxle identification number location — Isuzu 76MM manual transaxle

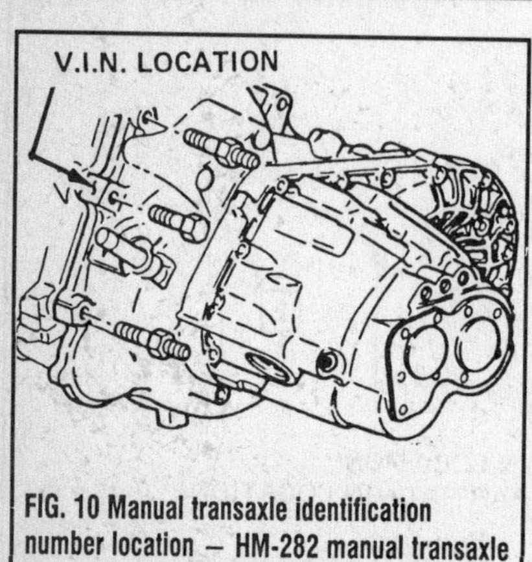

FIG. 10 Manual transaxle identification number location — HM-282 manual transaxle

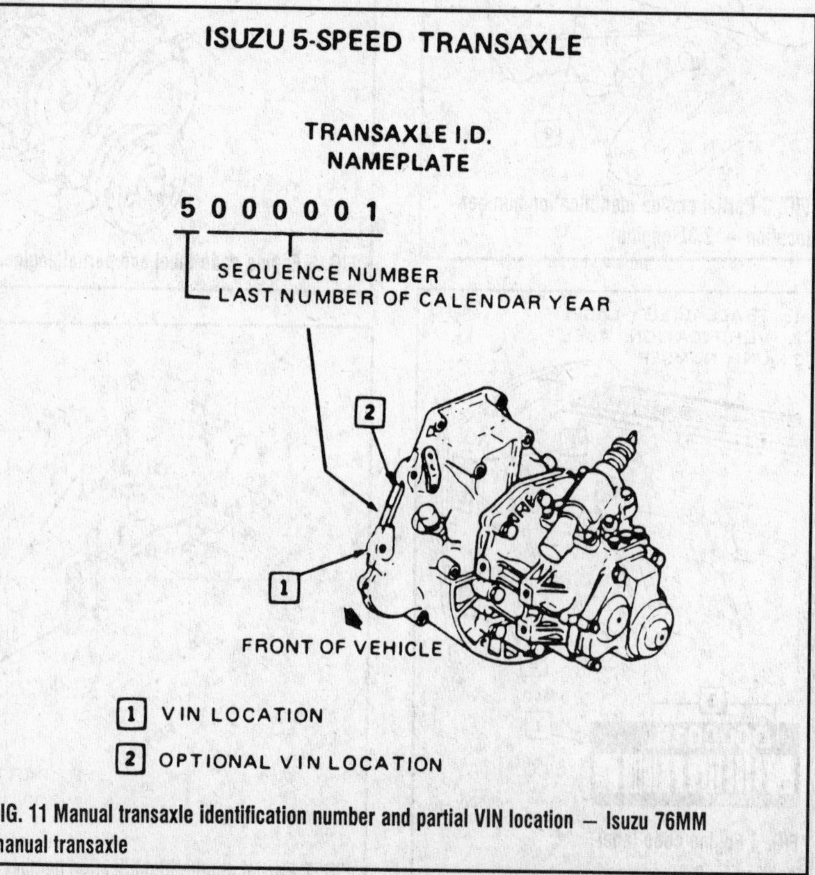

FIG. 11 Manual transaxle identification number and partial VIN location — Isuzu 76MM manual transaxle

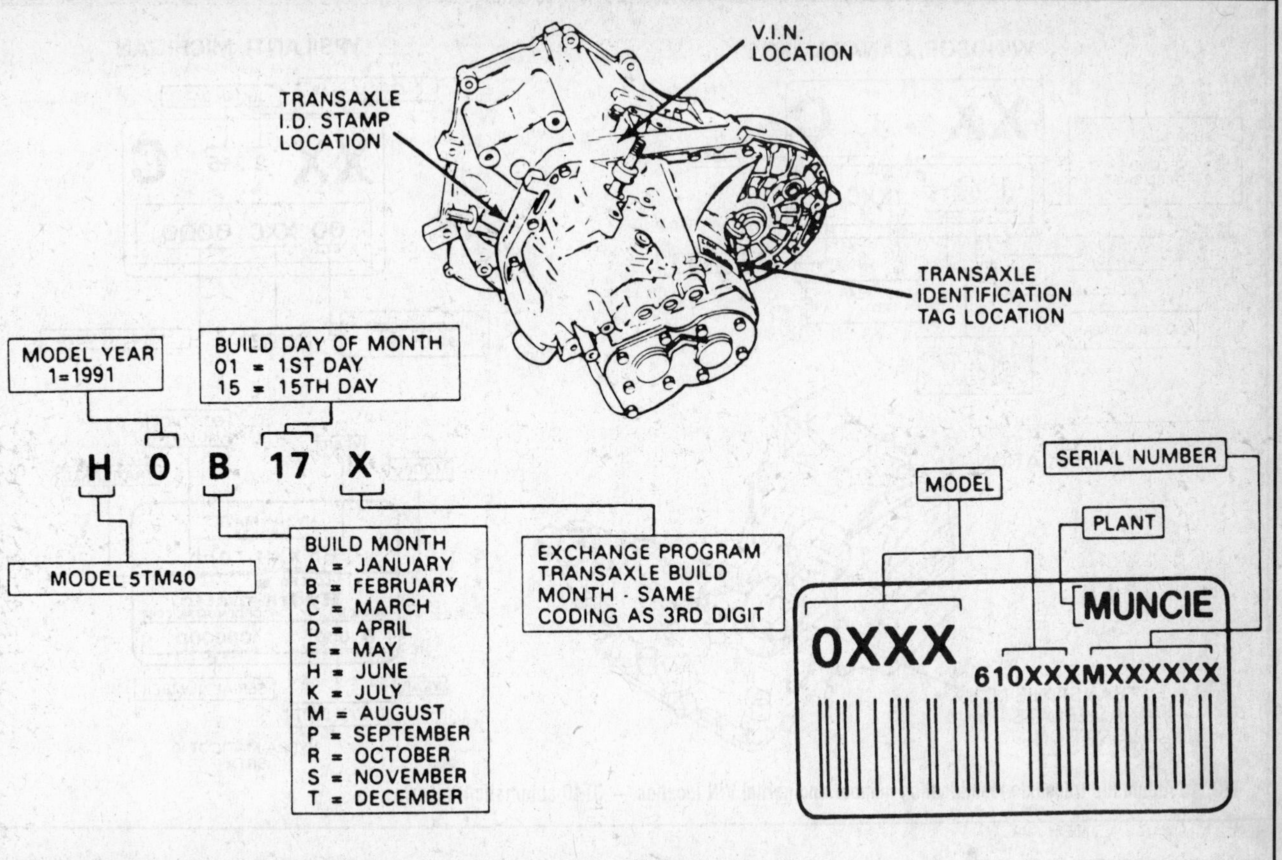

V.I.N.
LOCATION
TRANSAXLE
I.D. STAMP
LOCATION
TRANSAXLE
IDENTIFICATION
TAG LOCATION
MODEL YEAR
1=1991
BUILD DAY OF MONTH
01 = 1ST DAY
15 = 15TH DAY
H 0 B 17 X
MODEL 5TM40
BUILD MONTH
A = JANUARY
B = FEBRUARY
C = MARCH
D = APRIL
E = MAY
H = JUNE
K = JULY
M = AUGUST
P = SEPTEMBER
R = OCTOBER
S = NOVEMBER
T = DECEMBER
EXCHANGE PROGRAM
TRANSAXLE BUILD
MONTH - SAME
CODING AS 3RD DIGIT
SERIAL NUMBER
MODEL
PLANT
MUNCIE
0XXX
610XXXMXXXXXX

FIG. 12 Manual transaxle identification number and partial VIN location — 5T40 manual transaxle

Transaxle

➧ SEE FIGS. 9–14

Similar the engine identification code, the transaxle identification code supplies information about the transaxle such as manufacturing plant, Julian date of manufacture, shift number and model. The location for the transaxle code is shown in the illustrations.

OPTIONAL
VIN LOCATION
FWD
MODEL
CODE
LOCATION
VIN
LOCATION

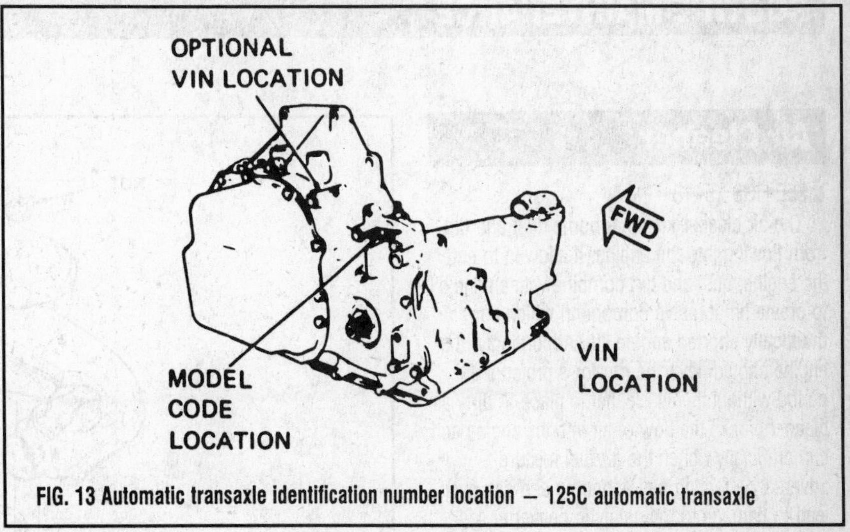

FIG. 13 Automatic transaxle identification number location — 125C automatic transaxle

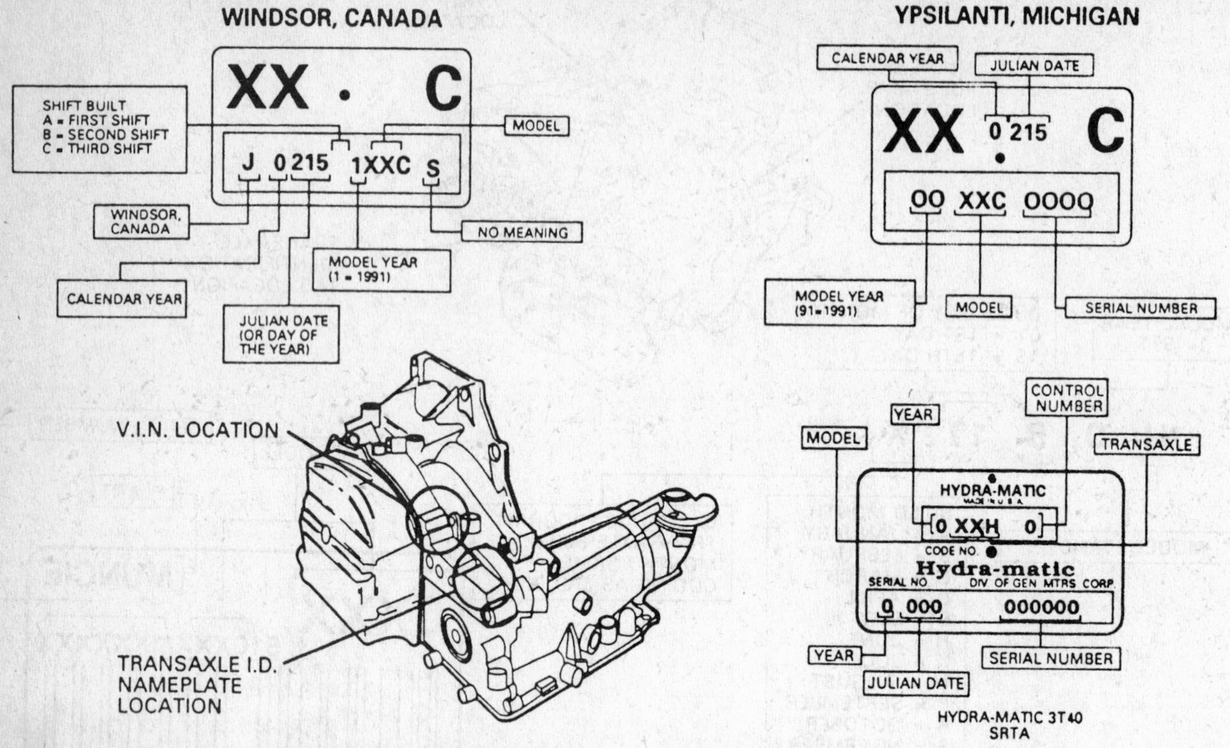

FIG. 14 Automatic transaxle identification number and partial VIN location — 3T40 automatic transaxle

ROUTINE MAINTENANCE

Air Cleaner

➧ SEE FIGS 15–18

The air cleaner keeps airborne dust and dirt from flowing into the engine. If allowed to enter the engine, dust and dirt combine with engine oil to create an abrasive compound which can drastically shorten engine life. Accordingly, the engine should never be run for a prolonged period without the air cleaner in place. A dirty air cleaner blocks the flow of air into the engine and can artificially richen the air/fuel mixture adversely affecting fuel economy and can even lead to damage to the catalytic converter.

The air cleaner should be checked periodically and replaced at least every 30,000 miles, more frequently in dusty driving conditions. Be sure the replacement air cleaner provides a proper fit and is not loose so that air is able to flow around the air cleaner instead of through it.

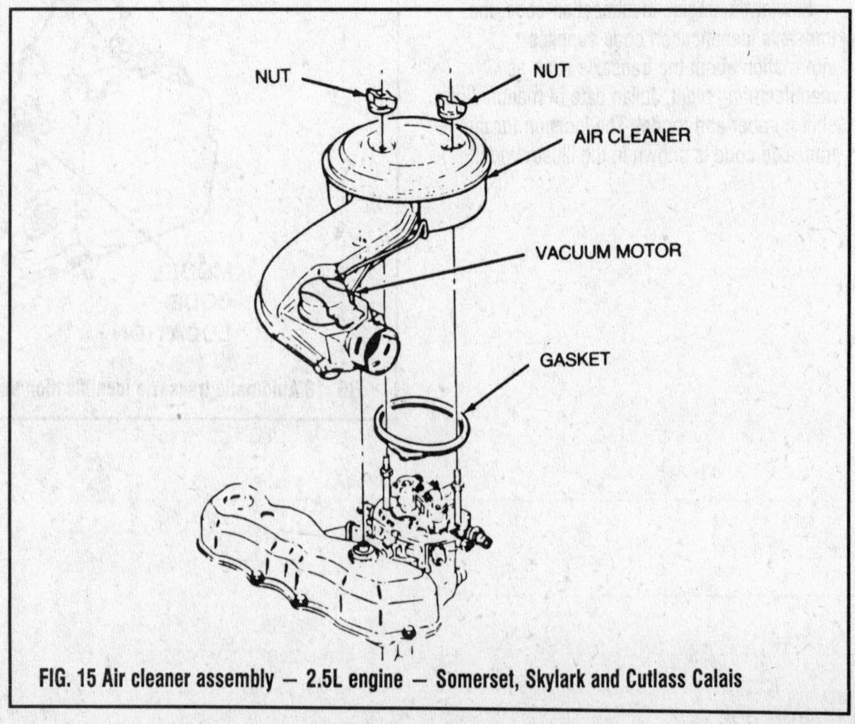

FIG. 15 Air cleaner assembly — 2.5L engine — Somerset, Skylark and Cutlass Calais

FIG. 15A Replacing air cleaner element – 2.5L engine shown

FIG. 15B Replacing crankcase breather filter

REMOVAL & INSTALLATION

2.0L (VIN K and M), 2.5 (VIN U)

1. Remove the wing nut(s) and the air cleaner cover.
2. Remove the old air cleaner element.
3. Wipe remaining dirt from the air cleaner housing.

To install:

4. Install the new air cleaner element
5. Install the air cleaner cover and wing nut(s).

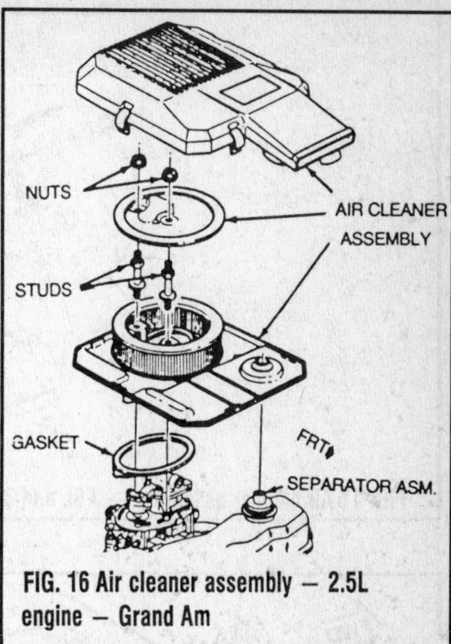

FIG. 16 Air cleaner assembly – 2.5L engine – Grand Am

2.3L (VIN D and A)

1. Remove the upper and lower duct clamps.
2. Disconnect the intake duct-to-oil/air separator hose.
3. Disconnect the air duct from the throttle body and air filter housing.
4. Remove the 2 hold-down clips on the air filter housing to cover and separate.
5. Remove the old air cleaner element and clean the air cleaner housing to remove remaining dirt.

To install:

6. Install the new air cleaner element into the air cleaner housing.
7. Install the air cleaner housing cover.
8. Install the 2 hold-down clips to the cover.
9. Connect the upper air filter duct with clamps to the air filter housing inlet and throttle body.
10. Connect the intake duct-to-oil/air separator hose.
11. Install the upper and lower duct clamps.

3.0L (VIN L) and 3.3L (VIN N)

1. Remove the air cleaner cover.
2. Remove the old air cleaner element
3. Wipe the inside of the air cleaner housing to remove dirt.

To install:

4. Install the new air cleaner element.
5. Install the air cleaner cover.

Fuel Filter

The fuel filter is located near the rear of the vehicle, forward of the fuel tank.

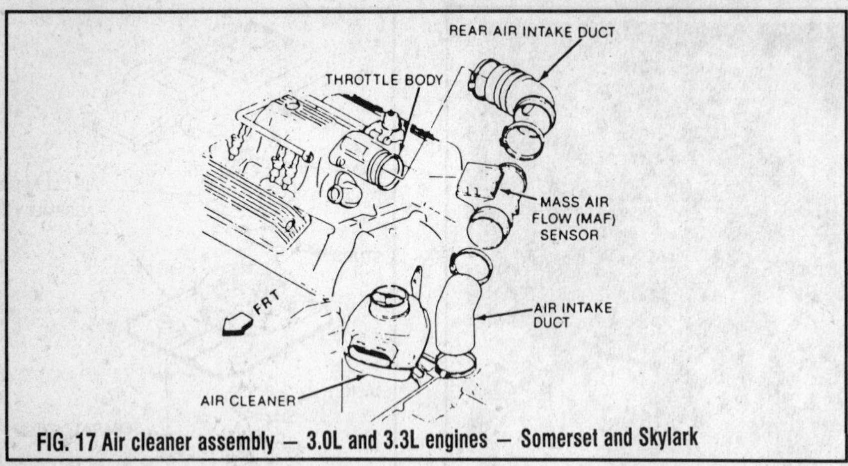

FIG. 17 Air cleaner assembly — 3.0L and 3.3L engines — Somerset and Skylark

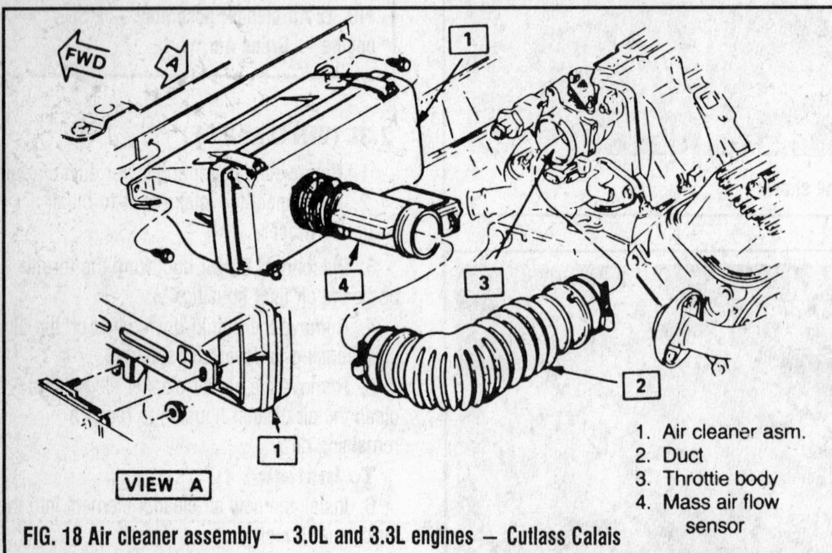

FIG. 18 Air cleaner assembly — 3.0L and 3.3L engines — Cutlass Calais

REMOVAL & INSTALLATION

➧ SEE FIG. 19

1. Relieve the fuel system pressure.
2. Raise and safely support the vehicle.
3. Using a backup wrench, remove the fuel line fittings from the fuel filter.
4. Remove the fuel filter mounting screws and remove the filter from the vehicle.
5. Discard the fuel line O-rings.

To install:

6. Install new O-rings to the fuel line fittings.
7. Connect the fuel lines to the fuel filter.
8. Using a backup wrench, tighten the fuel lines to 20–22 ft. lbs. (27–30 Nm).
9. Install the fuel filter mounting screws.
10. Lower the vehicle.
11. Start the engine and check for leaks.

PCV Valve

Vehicles equipped with 2.3L engines (VIN D and A) for all years or the 2.5L engine (VIN U) for 1991–92 use a crankcase breather system that does not use a PCV valve. The 2.3L engines (VIN D and A) are equipped with an oil/air separator that does not require service. Should the oil/air separator become clogged, the unit must be replaced. In the 2.5L engine (VIN U) in 1991–92 the standard PCV valve is replaced with a constant bleed orifice. If the orifice becomes clogged, clear if possible or replace.

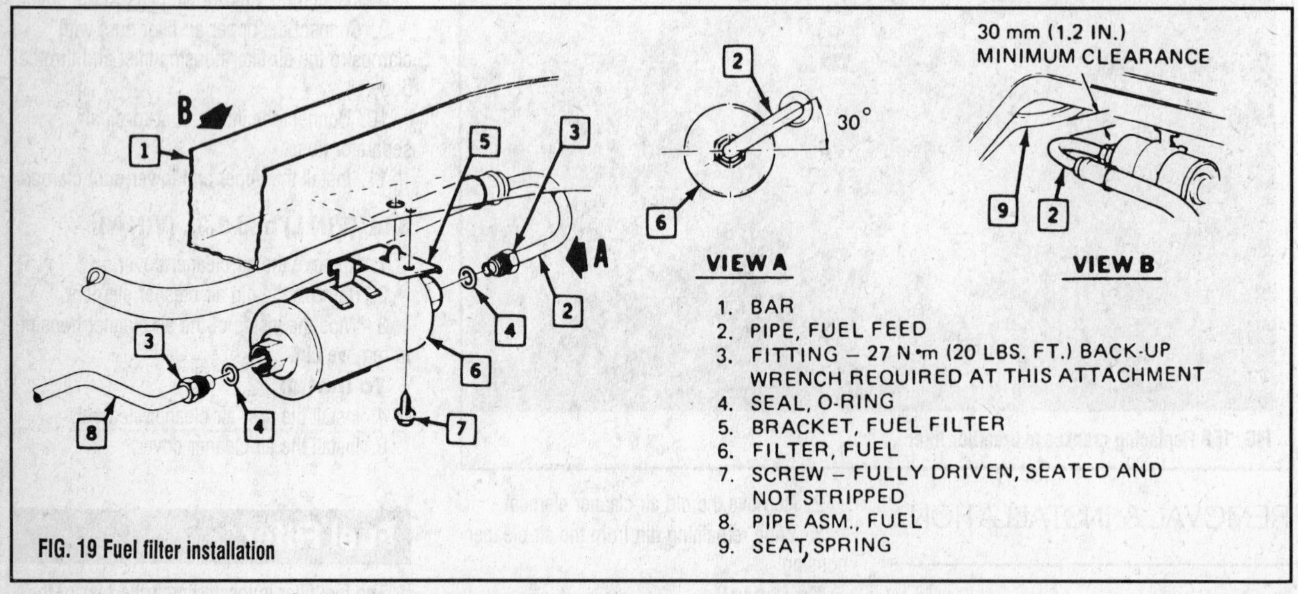

FIG. 19 Fuel filter installation

FIG. 19A Replacing fuel filter

FIG. 20A Replacing PCV valve

2. Remove the PCV valve from the breather hose.

To install:

3. Install the new PCV valve into the breather hose.
4. Install the PCV valve into the grommet in the valve cover.

REMOVAL & INSTALLATION

SEE FIGS. 20 AND 21

1. Remove the PCV valve from the grommet in the valve cover.

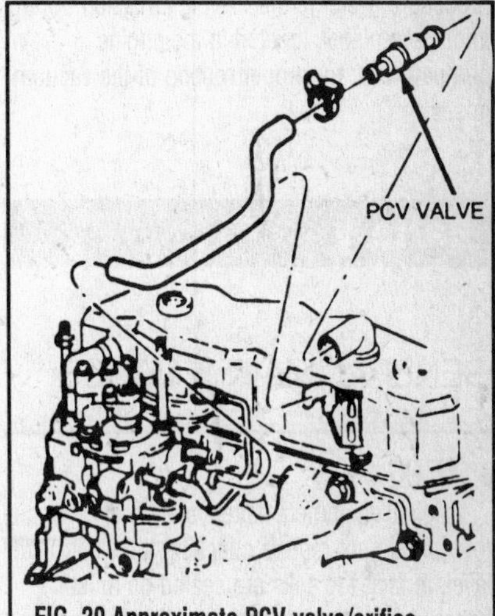

FIG. 20 Approximate PCV valve/orifice location — 2.0L and 2.5L engines

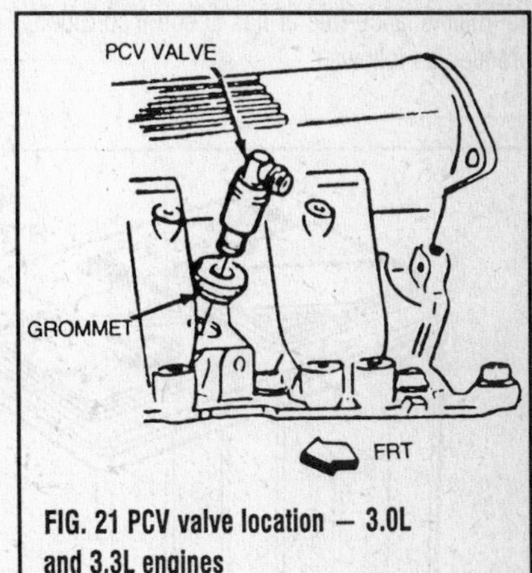

FIG. 21 PCV valve location — 3.0L and 3.3L engines

Evaporative Canister

REMOVAL & Installation

➧ SEE FIG. 22

1. Label and disconnect the hoses from the canister.
2. Remove the charcoal canister retaining nut.
3. Remove the canister from the vehicle.
4. Installation is the reverse of the removal procedure. Refer to the Vehicle Emission Control Information label, located in the engine compartment, for proper routing of the vacuum hoses.

1. TBI
2. Canister purge port
3. Vacuum signal
4. Purge valve
5. Vapor storage canister
6. Purge air
7. Fuel tank
8. Fuel
9. Vapor
10. Pressure-vacuum relief gas cap
11. Vent restricter
12. Fuel tank vent
13. Purge line

PURGE SOLENOID
CANISTER
CONNECTOR

FIG. 22 Typical TBI evaporative control system

Battery

GENERAL MAINTENANCE

➧ SEE FIG. 23–25

Original equipment batteries are maintenance-free and do not require checking the electrolyte level. In fact, the cells are sealed on most batteries. As a result, there should be little or no build-up of corrosion on the battery posts, terminals or cables.

If equipped with a replacement battery that is not maintenance-free or has become corroded, proceed as follows.

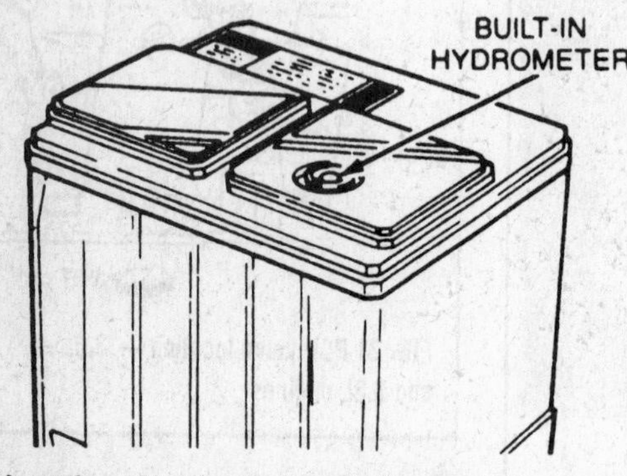

Location of indicator on sealed battery

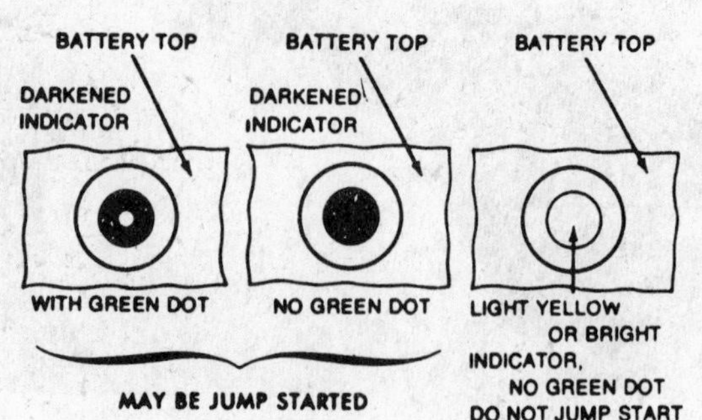

Check the appearance of the charge indicator on top of the battery before attempting a jump start; if it's not green or dark, do not jump start the car

FIG. 23 Original equipment maintenance-free battery with built-in hydrometer

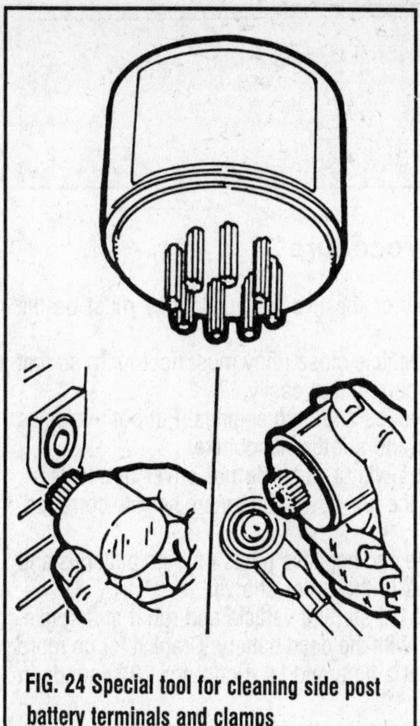

FIG. 24 Special tool for cleaning side post battery terminals and clamps

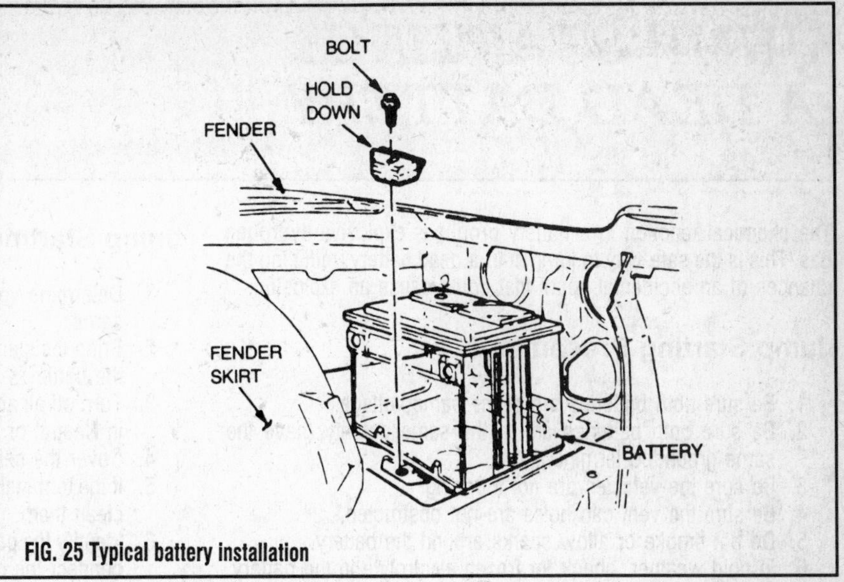

FIG. 25 Typical battery installation

FLUID LEVEL

1. Remove the cell caps from the top of the battery.
2. Check the electrolyte level and add distilled water as necessary to bring the level up to the bottom of the cell filler opening. Some batteries have a fill level marking or a split ring inside the opening.
3. Replace the cell caps, making sure they are properly seated.
4. Wipe up any spilled electrolyte with a shop towel and dispose of the towel in case some of the electrolyte became mixed with the water and was absorbed by the towel.

CABLES

Always use a terminal clamp puller to disconnect the cables from the battery. Attempting to remove the clamp from the battery terminal by prying could crack the battery case.

Clean the cables thoroughly using a terminal brush until the metal is shiny and completely free of corrosion. Special brushes are available to properly clean side-post batteries. If the cables are heavily corroded, they may be cleaned using with a solution of baking soda and water.

Disconnect both battery cables from the battery before using this method. Immerse the cable in the solution until it stops bubbling.

➡ If the cell caps are removable, make sure none of the baking soda solution is allowed to enter the battery. This could neutralize the electrolyte and destroy the battery.

Rinse well with water and allow to dry thoroughly before reconnecting.

Before reconnecting the cables, it is a good idea to remove the battery and inspect the condition of the battery tray. Remove any debris that may have collected under the battery. If the battery tray shows signs of corrosion, remove using a wire brush and apply a coat of acid-resistant paint to protect the tray.

After the cables have been reconnected, apply a thin coat of non-conductive grease to the terminal connection to retard corrosion.

TESTING

Some maintenance-free batteries are equipped with a built-in hydrometer. To check the condition of the battery, observe the "eye" on the top of the battery case for the following conditions:

1. If the indicator is dark, the battery has enough fluid. If the eye is light, the electrolyte level is low and the battery must be replace.
2. If the indicator is green, the battery is sufficiently charged. Proceed to Step 4. If the green dot is not visible, charge the battery as outlined in Step 3.
3. Charge the battery as described below.

➡ Do not charge the battery for more than 50 amp-hours. If the green dot appears or if the electrolyte squirts out of the vent hole, stop the charge and proceed to Step 4.

It may be necessary to tip the battery from side-to-side in order to get the green dot to appear after charging.

⁂ WARNING

When charging the battery, the electrical system and control unit can be quickly damaged by improper connections, high output battery chargers or incorrect service procedures.

4. Connect a battery load tester and a voltmeter across the battery terminals (the battery cable should be disconnected from the battery). Apply a 300 amp load to the battery for 15 seconds to remove the surface charge. Remove the load.
5. Wait 15 seconds to allow the battery to recover. Apply the appropriate test load for 15 seconds while reading the voltage. Disconnect the load.
6. Check the results against specifications. If the voltage is at or above the specified voltage for the temperature listed, the battery is good. If the voltage falls below specification, the battery should be replace.

JUMP STARTING A DEAD BATTERY

The chemical reaction in a battery produces explosive hydrogen gas. This is the safe way to jump start a dead battery, reducing the chances of an accidental spark that could cause an explosion.

Jump Starting Precautions

1. Be sure both batteries are of the same voltage.
2. Be sure both batteries are of the same polarity (have the same grounded terminal).
3. Be sure the vehicles are not touching.
4. Be sure the vent cap holes are not obstructed.
5. Do not smoke or allow sparks around the battery.
6. In cold weather, check for frozen electrolyte in the battery. Do not jump start a frozen battery.
7. Do not allow electrolyte on your skin or clothing.
8. Be sure the electrolyte is not frozen.

CAUTION: Make certin that the ignition key, in the vehicle with the dead battery, is in the OFF position. Connecting cables to vehicles with on-board computers will result in computer destruction if the key is not in the OFF position.

Jump Starting Procedure

1. Determine voltages of the two batteries; they must be the same.
2. Bring the starting vehicle close (they must not touch) so that the batteries can be reached easily.
3. Turn off all accessories and both engines. Put both vehicles in Neutral or Park and set the handbrake.
4. Cover the cell caps with a rag—do not cover terminals.
5. If the terminals on the run-down battery are heavily corroded, clean them.
6. Identify the positive and negative posts on both batteries and connect the cables in the order shown.
7. Start the engine of the starting vehicle and run it at fast idle. Try to start the car with the dead battery. Crank it for no more than 10 seconds at a time and let it cool for 20 seconds in between tries.
8. If it doesn't start in 3 tries, there is something else wrong.
9. Disconnect the cables in the reverse order.
10. Replace the cell covers and dispose of the rags.

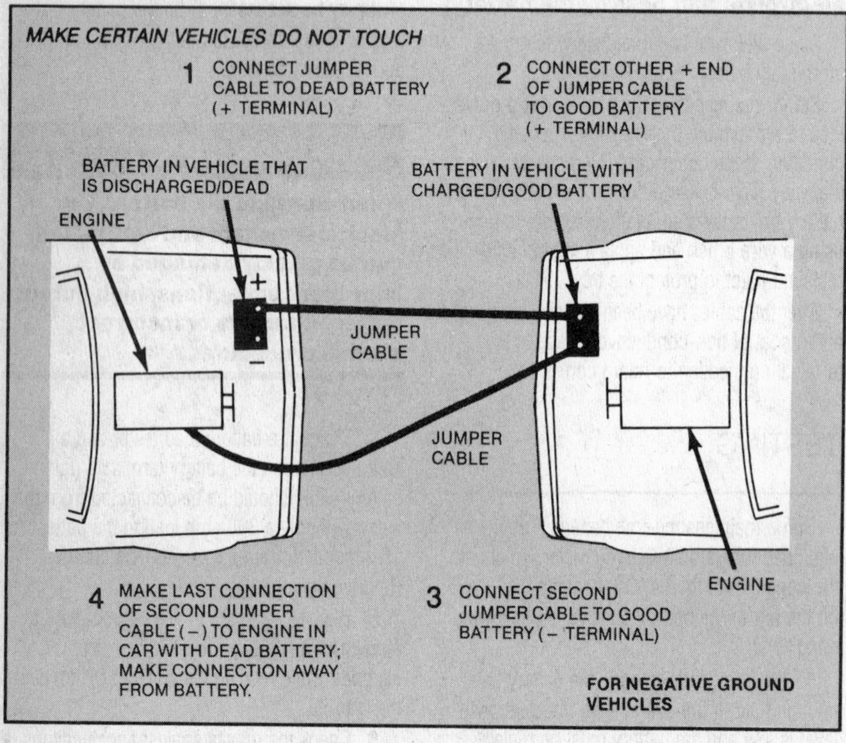

Side terminal batteries occasionally pose a problem when connecting jumper cables. There frequently isn't enough room to clamp the cables without touching sheet metal. Side terminal adaptors are available to alleviate this problem and should be removed after use

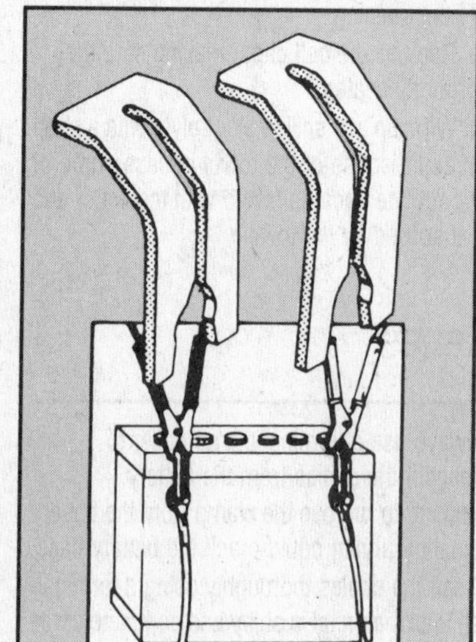

CHARGING

CAUTION

Batteries give off hydrogen gas, which is explosive. DO NOT SMOKE around the battery while it is being charged. The battery electrolyte contains sulfuric acid. If any of the electrolyte should come in contact with the eyes or skin, flush with plenty of clear water and seek medical attention immediately.

The best method for charging a battery is slow charging (often called "trickle charging"), with a low amperage charger. Quick charging a battery can actually cook the battery, damage the plates inside and decreasing the life of the battery. Any charging should be done in a well ventilated area away from the possibility of sparks or open flame. The cell caps (not found on maintenance-free batteries) should be loosened but not removed.

If the battery must be quick-charged, check the cell voltages and the color of the electrolyte a few minutes after the charge is begun. if the cell voltages are not uniform or if the electrolyte is discolored with brown sediment, stop the quick charging in favor of a trickle charge. A common indicator of an overcharged battery is the frequency need to add water to the battery.

REPLACEMENT

If the battery is to be removed or replaced always disconnect the negative cable from the battery first using a battery clamp puller. Disconnect the positive cable next. Remove the battery hold-down clamp. Using a battery puller, remove the battery from the vehicle.

Charge the replacement battery, as required, using the slow charge method discussed above. Inspect the battery terminals and cables, and service as required.

Install the battery into the vehicle and install the battery hold-down clamp, making sure not to overtighten the clamp. Overtightening the battery hold-down clamp could crack the battery case.

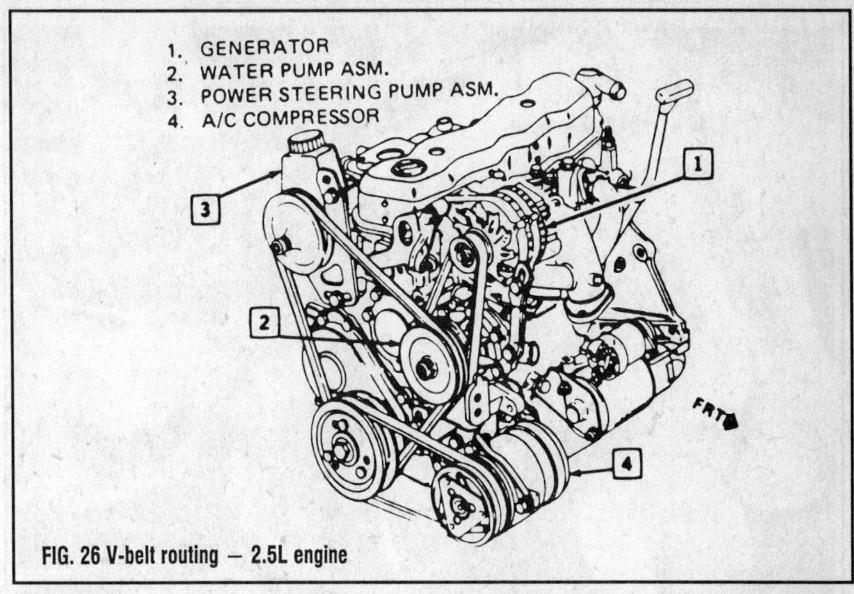

FIG. 26 V-belt routing — 2.5L engine

Connect the positive battery cable to the positive battery post and tighten the clamp.

➡ **Once the negative battery cable has been connected, do not go back to retighten the positive post. Since the electrical path is now complete, should you accidentally touch the body of the vehicle while touching the positive post an electrical short will occur.**

Connect the negative battery cable and tighten the clamp.

Belts

INSPECTION

Belt tension and condition should be checked at least every 30,000 miles or 24 month. Check the condition of both serpentine and V-belts for cracking, fraying and splitting on the inside of the belt.

A quick check for V-belt tension is to grasp the belt with the thumb and forefinger at the mid-point of the longest belt run and twist the belt. The belt should rotate no more than 90°. To properly check V-belt tension use a belt tension gauge and adjust to the specified tension.

Serpentine belts use a spring-loaded tensioner and do not need periodic adjustment.

ADJUSTING

➧ SEE FIG. 26

V-Belt

1. Loosen the alternator mounting bolts.
2. Using a standard belt tension gauge, install it to the center of the longest span of the drive belt.
3. Use a medium prybar on the adjustment lug of the accessory (alternator, compressor or power steering pump) to adjust the belt tension to specification. Tighten the mounting and adjusting bolts.
4. Adjust the V-belts on the 2.5L (VIN U) engine as follows:
   • Alternator — 90–100 lbs. (41–45 kg) for a used belt or 165–175 lbs. (77–79 kg) for a new belt.
   • Power steering/coolant pumps — 90–100 lbs. (41–45 kg) for a used belt or 180 lbs. (81 kg) for a new belt.
   • Air conditioning compressor — 90–100 lbs. (41–45 kg) for a used belt or 165 lbs. (77 kg) for a new belt.

FIG. 26A Replacing V-belt

Serpentine Belt

➧ SEE FIGS. 27–29

A single serpentine belt may be used to drive engine-mounted accessories. Drive belt tension is maintained by a spring loaded tensioner. The drive belt tensioner can control belt tension over a broad range of belt lengths, however, there are limits to the tensioner's ability to compensate.

A belt squeak when the engine in started or stopped is normal and does not necessarily indicate a worn belt. If the squeak persists or worsens, inspect the belt for wear and replace as necessary.

1. Inspect the tensioner markings to see if the belt is within operating lengths. Replace the belt if the belt is excessively worn or is outside of the tensioner's operating range.

2. Run the engine until operating temperature is reached. Be sure all accessories are off. Turn the engine off and read the belt tension using a belt tension gauge tool placed halfway between the alternator and the air conditioning compressor. If not equipped with air conditioning, read the tension between the power steering pump and crankshaft pulley. Remove the tool.

3. Run the engine for 15 seconds and turn it off. Using a box-end wrench, apply clockwise force to tighten to the tensioner pulley bolt. Release the force and immediately take a tension reading without disturbing belt tensioner position.

4. Using the same wrench, apply a counterclockwise force to the tensioner pulley bolt and raise the pulley to its fully raised position. Slowly lower the pulley to engage the belt. Take a tension reading without disturbing the belt tensioner position.

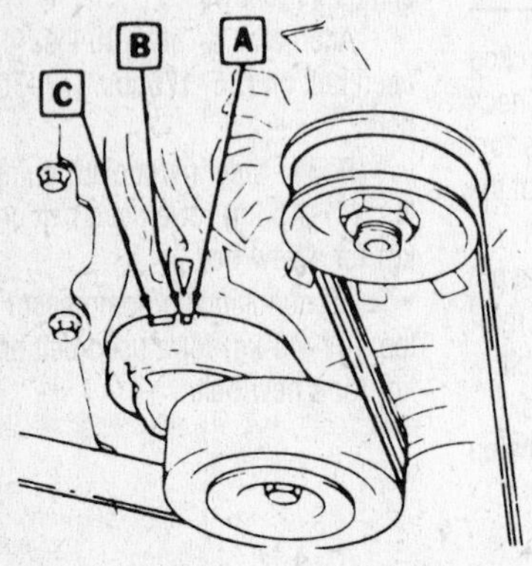

THE INDICATOR MARK ON THE STATIONARY PORTION OF THE TENSIONER MUST BE WITHIN THE LIMITS OF THE SLOTTED AREA ON THE MOVEABLE PORTION OF THE TENSIONER. ANY READING OUTSIDE THESE LIMITS INDICATES EITHER A FAULTY BELT OR TENSIONER.

A MINIMUM BELT LENGTH

B NORMAL BELT LENGTH

C MAXIMUM (REPLACE) BELT LENGTH

FIG. 27 Serpentine drive belt tensioner markings

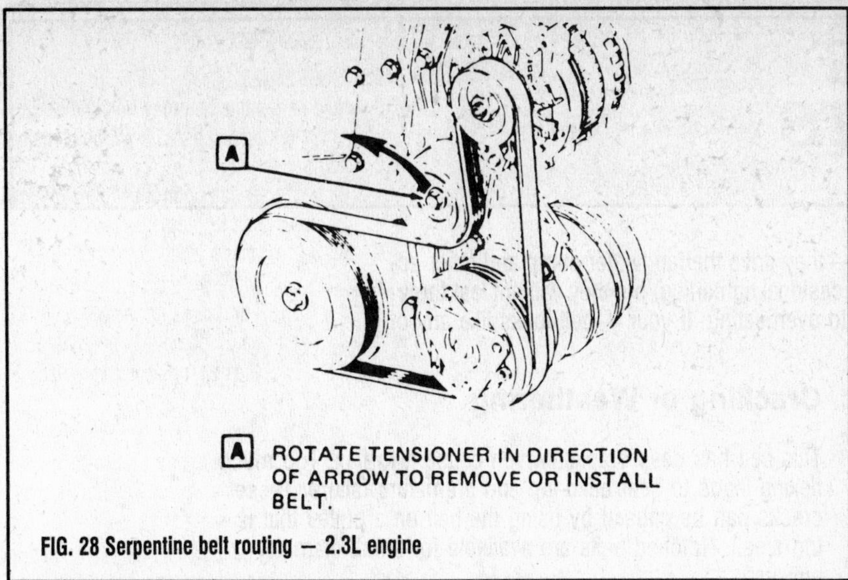

FIG. 28 Serpentine belt routing — 2.3L engine

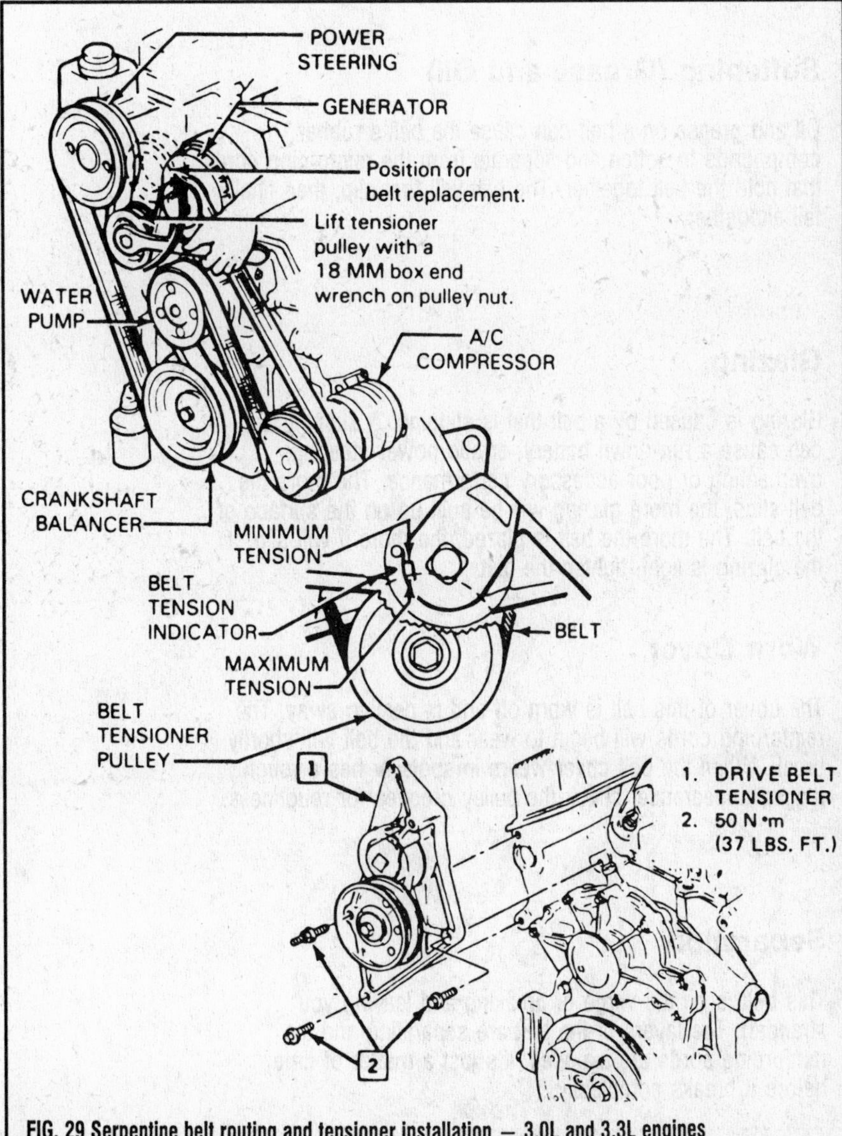

FIG. 29 Serpentine belt routing and tensioner installation — 3.0L and 3.3L engines

5. Average the 3 readings. If their average is lower than specifications, replace the tensioner:
- 2.0L and 2.3L engines — 50 lbs. (23 kg)
- 3.0L engine — 79 lbs. (36 kg)
- 3.3L engine — 67 lbs. (30 kg)

REMOVAL AND INSTALLATION

V-belt

1. Loosen the accessory-to-mounting bracket bolt(s) and adjusting bolt.
2. Rotate the accessory to relieve the belt tension.
3. Slip the drive belt from the accessory pulley and remove it from the engine.

➡ If the engine uses more than 1 belt, it may be necessary to remove belts that are in front of the belt being removed.

To install:

4. Place the new belt over the crankshaft or drive pulley and stretch over the driven (accessory) pulley.
5. If removed, install the other belts in the same way.
6. Adjust the belts to the proper tension.
7. Tighten the adjusting and mounting bolts.

Serpentine Belt

1. Insert a 1/2 in. drive breaker bar into the adjuster arm on the tensioner pulley. Later models require an 18mm box end wrench.

➡ Make sure the drive end of the breaker bar is long enough to fully seat in the tensioner pulley and that both the breaker bar and box wrench are long enough to provide the proper leverage.

2. Rotate the tensioner to the left (counterclockwise) and remove the belt.
3. Slowly rotate the tensioner to the right (clockwise) to release the tension.

To install:

4. Route the belt over the pulleys following the diagram found in the engine compartment.
5. Rotate the tensioner to the left (counterclockwise) and install the belt over the remaining pulley.
6. Inspect the belt positioning over each pulley to ensure the belt is seated properly in all the grooves.

HOW TO SPOT WORN V-BELTS

V–Belts are vital to efficient engine operation—they drive the fan, water pump and other accessories. They require little maintenance (occasional tightening) but they will not last forever. Slipping or failure of the V–belt will lead to overheating. If your V–belt looks like any of these, it should be replaced.

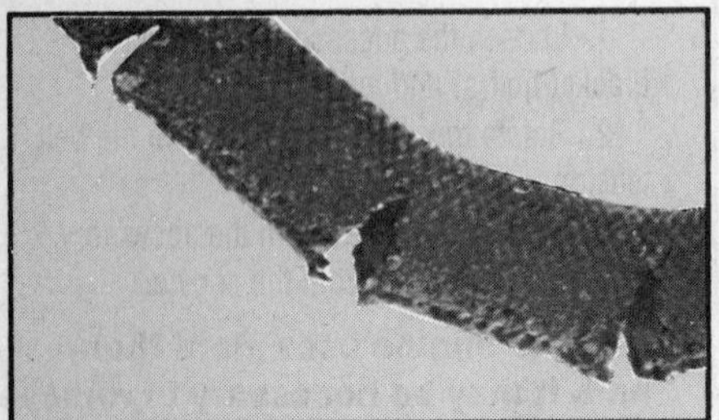

Cracking or Weathering

This belt has deep cracks, which cause it to flex. Too much flexing leads to heat build–up and premature failure. These cracks can be caused by using the belt on a pulley that is too small. Notched belts are available for small diameter pulleys.

Softening (Grease and Oil)

Oil and grease on a belt can cause the belt's rubber compounds to soften and separate from the reinforcing cords that hold the belt together. The belt will first slip, then finally fail altogether.

Glazing

Glazing is caused by a belt that is slipping. A slipping belt can cause a run-down battery, erratic power steering, overheating or poor accessory performance. The more the belt slips, the more glazing will be built up on the surface of the belt. The more the belt is glazed, the more it will slip. If the glazing is light, tighten the belt.

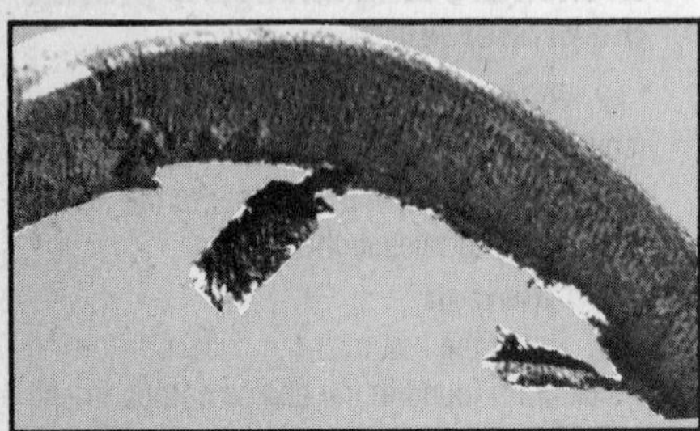

Worn Cover

The cover of this belt is worn off and is peeling away. The reinforcing cords will begin to wear and the belt will shortly break. When the belt cover wears in spots or has a rough jagged appearance, check the pulley grooves for roughness.

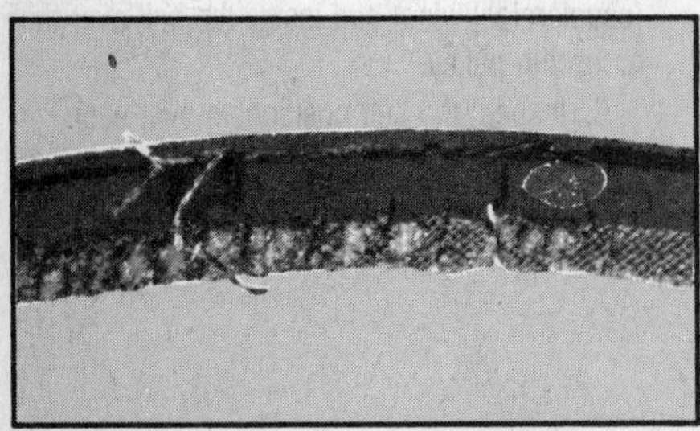

Separation

This belt is on the verge of breaking and leaving you stranded. The layers of the belt are separating and the reinforcing cords are exposed. It's just a matter of time before it breaks completely.

Hoses

The hoses should be checked for deterioration, leaks and loose hose clamps every 12,000 miles or 12 months.

REMOVAL & INSTALLATION

➧ SEE FIGS. 30–32

1. Drain the cooling system into a clean container to a level that is below the hose being removed. Save the coolant for reuse.
2. Loosen the hose clamps.
3. Disconnect the inlet hose from the radiator and thermostat housing.
4. Disconnect the outlet hose from the radiator and coolant pump or cylinder block.

To install:

➡ If installing original equipment hoses, make sure to align the reference marks on the hose with the marks on the radiator. A twist in the hose will place a strain on the radiator fitting and could cause the fitting to crack or break.

5. Connect the outlet hose to the radiator and coolant pump or cylinder block.
6. Connect the radiator hose to the radiator and thermostat.
7. Refill the cooling system to a level just below the filler neck. Install the radiator cap.

➡ The cooling systems on later models may use a surge tank instead of an overflow bottle. The overflow bottle has 1 small hose coming from the radiator filler neck. The surge tank can be

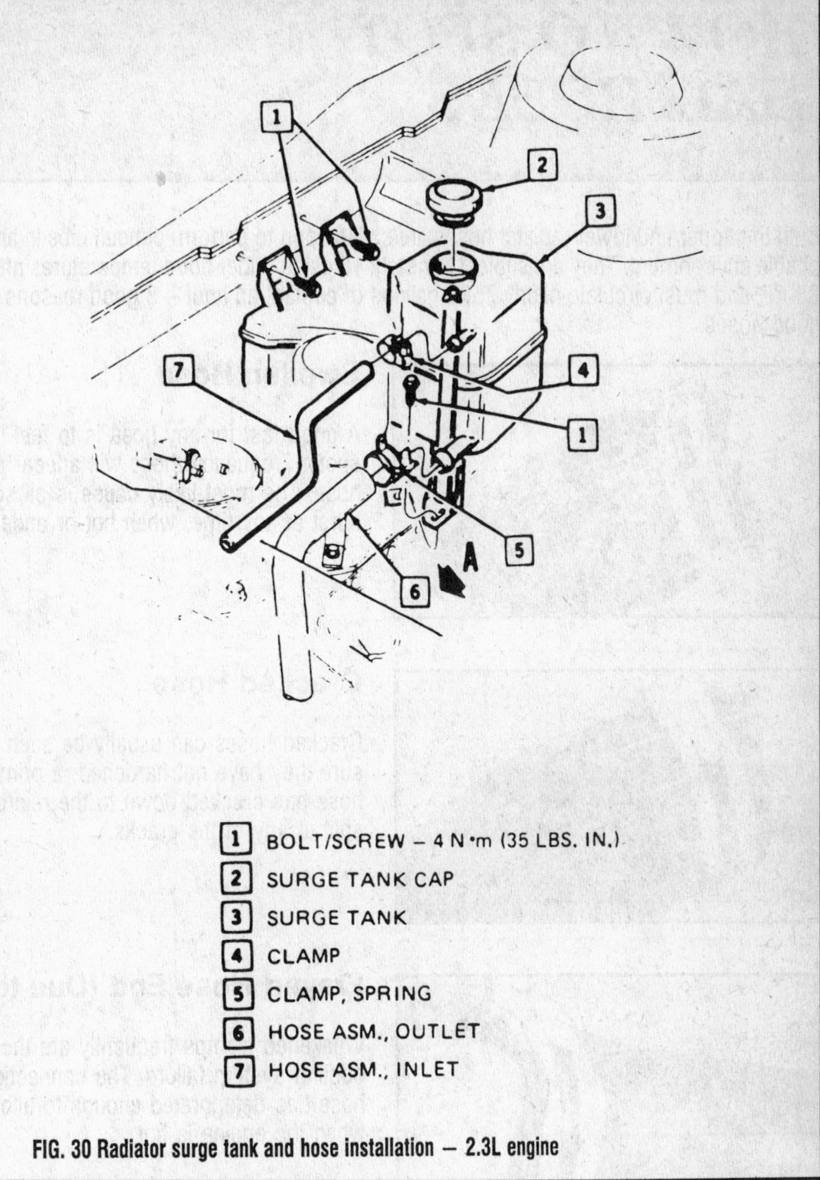

FIG. 30 Radiator surge tank and hose installation – 2.3L engine

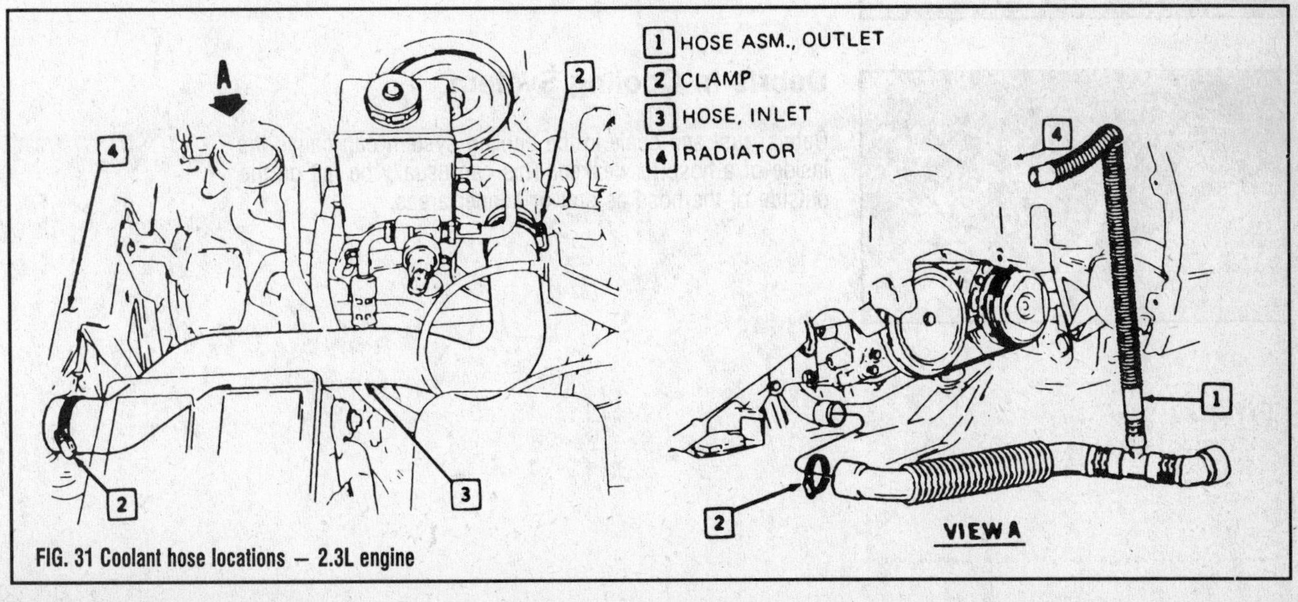

FIG. 31 Coolant hose locations – 2.3L engine

HOW TO SPOT BAD HOSES

Both the upper and lower radiator hoses are called upon to perform difficult jobs in an inhospitable environment. They are subject to nearly 18 psi at under hood temperatures often over 280°F, and must circulate nearly 7500 gallons of coolant an hour — 3 good reasons to have good hoses.

Swollen Hose

A good test for any hose is to feel it for soft or spongy spots. Frequently these will appear as swollen areas of the hose. The most likely cause is oil soaking. This hose could burst at any time, when hot or under pressure.

Cracked Hose

Cracked hoses can usually be seen but feel the hoses to be sure they have not hardened; a prime cause of cracking. This hose has cracked down to the reinforcing cords and could split at any of the cracks.

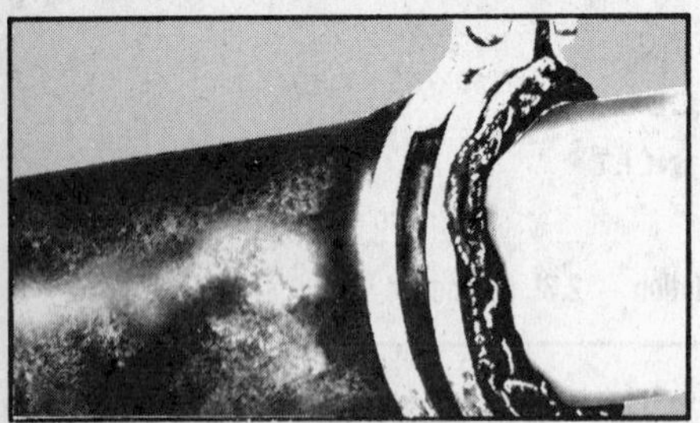

Frayed Hose End (Due to Weak Clamp)

Weakened clamps frequently are the cause of hose and cooling system failure. The connection between the pipe and hose has deteriorated enough to allow coolant to escape when the engine is hot.

Debris in Cooling System

Debris, rust and scale in the cooling system can cause the inside of a hose to weaken. This can usually be felt on the outside of the hose as soft or thinner areas.

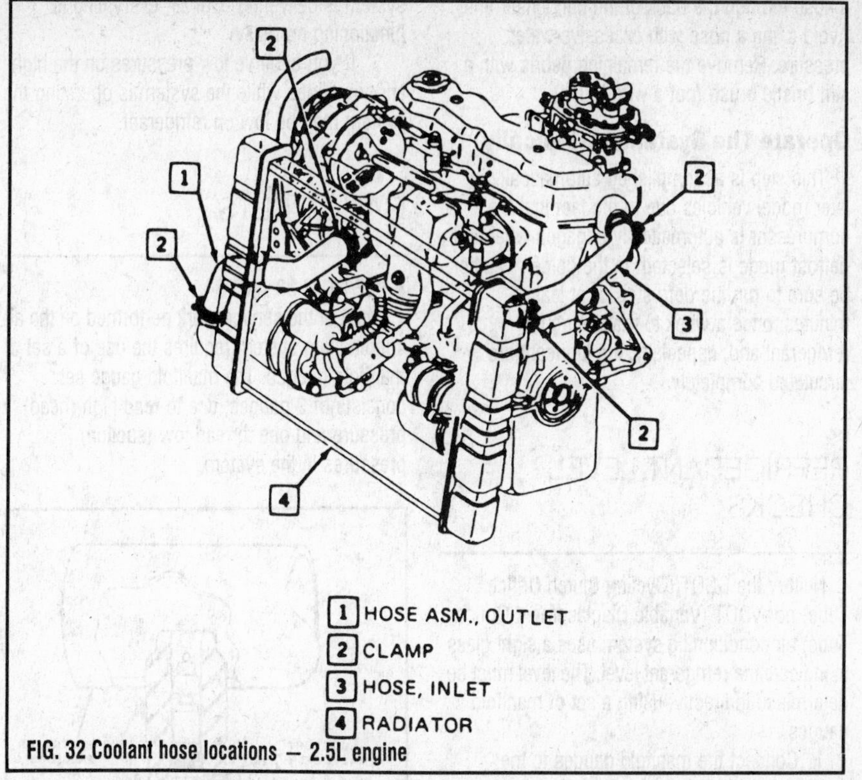

FIG. 32 Coolant hose locations — 2.5L engine

recognized by the presence of 2 hoses, 1 from the radiator cap and 1 outlet to the lower radiator hose. The surge tank is also mounted above the level of the radiator cap, making it the highest point in the cooling system.

8. If equipped with an overflow bottle, perform the following:
   a. Fill the overflow bottle to the "Full Hot" mark.
   b. Start the engine and allow to come to normal operating temperature.
   c. Stop the engine and refill the overflow bottle to the "Full Hot" mark.
   d. Check the coolant level frequently over the next couple of days.
9. If equipped with a surge tank, perform the following:
   a. Fill the surge tank to the base of the filler neck.
   b. Install the pressure cap on the surge tank. Start the engine and allow to come to normal operating temperature or until the upper radiator hose is hot.
   c. Stop the engine and check the level of coolant in the surge tank. If the level is not above the "full" line, allow the engine to cool enough to slowly remove the pressure cap.
   d. Add coolant to bring the level up to the "full" line.
   e. Install the pressure cap. Make sure the arrows on the cap line up with the overflow hose.

Air Conditioning System

SAFETY WARNINGS

Working on automotive air conditioning systems requires a great deal of care due to the nature of the refrigerant and the system pressures (both operating and static). Review the safety precautions listed below before attempting work on the air conditioning system.

- **Always wear safety goggles that completely cover the eyes** when working on the air conditioning system. Do not trust safety glasses or prescription glasses with safety lens to adequately protect the eyes. Refrigerant, released under pressure, contacting the eyes could freeze the eyes causing permanent eye damage. If refrigerant should contact the eyes, seek medical attention immediately.
- If is determined to be necessary to discharge the system, every effort should be made to use an SAE approved R-12 Recovery/Recycling machine so as to avoid discharging the refrigerant to the atmosphere. That could include having a service station remove the refrigerant from the system prior to beginning work.
- Avoid contact with a charged refrigeration system, even when working on another part of the air conditioning system or vehicle. If a heavy tool or sharp object should come in contact with a section of the tubing or heat exchanger, a rupture could occur.
- When it is necessary to apply force to a fitting which contains refrigerant, as when checking that all system couplings are tightened securely, use a backup wrench whenever possible. This will avoid undue torque on the refrigerant tubing. It is advisable, whenever possible, to use tube or line wrenches when tightening these fittings. In the absence of a line wrench, make sure the open end wrench has a firm "bite" on the fitting before tightening.
- DO NOT attempt to discharge the system by merely loosening a fitting or removing the service valve caps and cracking these valves. Precise control is possible only when using the service gauges. If unable to use an approved R-12 Recovery/Recycling machine to remove the refrigerant, place a rag under the open end of the center charging hose to capture any liquid drops that may escape. **Always** wear protective goggles when connecting or disconnecting the service gauge hoses.
- Discharge the system only in a well ventilated area, as high concentrations of the refrigerant can exclude oxygen, which could lead to a loss of consciousness. When leak testing or soldering this precaution is particularly important as toxic gas is formed when R-12 refrigerant comes into contact with a flame.
- Never start a system without first verifying that both service valves are back-seated (if equipped) and that all fittings throughout the system are snugly connected.
- Avoid applying heat to any refrigerant line or storage vessel. Charging may be aided by using water heated to less than 125°F (52°C) to warm the refrigerant container. Never allow a refrigerant storage container to sit in the sun or near any other heat source, such as a radiator.
- Frostbite from liquid refrigerant should be treated by first warming the area gradually with cool water and then gently applying petroleum jelly. Seek medical attention as soon as possible.
- Always keep the refrigerant container fittings capped when not in use. Avoid any

sudden shock to the container, which might occur from dropping it or from banging a heavy tool against it. Never carry a refrigerant container in the passenger compartment of a vehicle.

• Always discharge the system completely if the vehicle is to be painted using a baked-on finish or before welding anywhere near the refrigerant lines.

SYSTEM INSPECTION

Checking For Oil Leaks

Refrigerant leaks show up as oily areas on the various components because the compressor oil is transported through the entire system along with the refrigerant. Look for oily spots on all the hoses and lines, especially on the hose and tubing connections. If there are oily deposits, the system may have a leak. The diagnosis should be confirmed by an experienced repair person.

➡ A small area of oil on the front of the compressor is normal and no cause for alarm.

Checking The Compressor Belt

Refer to the Belts portion of this section. Beginning in 1987, except for the 2.5L (VIN U), a serpentine belt is used to drive all engine accessories. The tension is maintained automatically and not adjustment is needed.

Keep The Condenser Clear

Periodically, inspect the front of the condenser for bent fins or foreign matter, such as dirt, leaves, cigarette butts, etc. Straighten bent fins carefully using the edge of a small slotted screwdriver or purchase a coil comb. Remove any debris by first directing water from a hose through the back of the condenser fins. Avoid using a hose with excessive water pressure. Remove the remaining debris with a stiff bristle brush (not a wire brush).

Operate The System Periodically

This step is accomplished automatically in later model vehicles due to the fact that the compressor is automatically engaged when the defrost mode is selected. In the colder weather, be sure to run the defroster for at least 5 minutes, once a week to make sure the refrigerant and, especially, the lubricant are circulated completely.

REFRIGERANT LEVEL CHECKS

Neither the CCOT (Cycling Clutch Orifice Tube) nor VDOT (Variable Displacement Orifice Tube) air conditioning system uses a sight glass to indicate the refrigerant level. The level must be determined indirectly, using a set of manifold gauges.

1. Connect the manifold gauges to the system. Start the engine and run the air conditioning system. Observe the gauge pressures. if the air conditioner is working properly, the pressures will fall within the specifications shown in the performance chart.

2. Cycle the air conditioner **ON** and **OFF** to make sure you are seeing actual pressures in the system. Turn the system **OFF** and watch the manifold gauges. If there is refrigerant in the system, you should see the low side pressure rise and the high side pressure fall during the **OFF** cycle. If the system pressures are fluctuating when the compressor cycles and the operating pressure is within specification and the system is delivering cool air, everything is functioning normally.

3. If you observe low pressures on the high and low sides while the system is operating the system may be low on refrigerant.

GAUGE SETS

➧ SEE FIGS. 33 AND 34

Most of the service work performed on the air conditioning system requires the use of a set of manifold gauges. The manifold gauge set consists of 2 gauges, one to read high (head) pressure and one to read low (suction) pressures in the system.

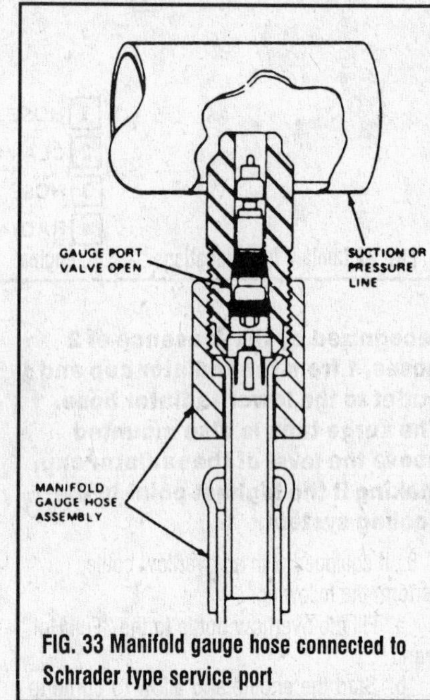

FIG. 33 Manifold gauge hose connected to Schrader type service port

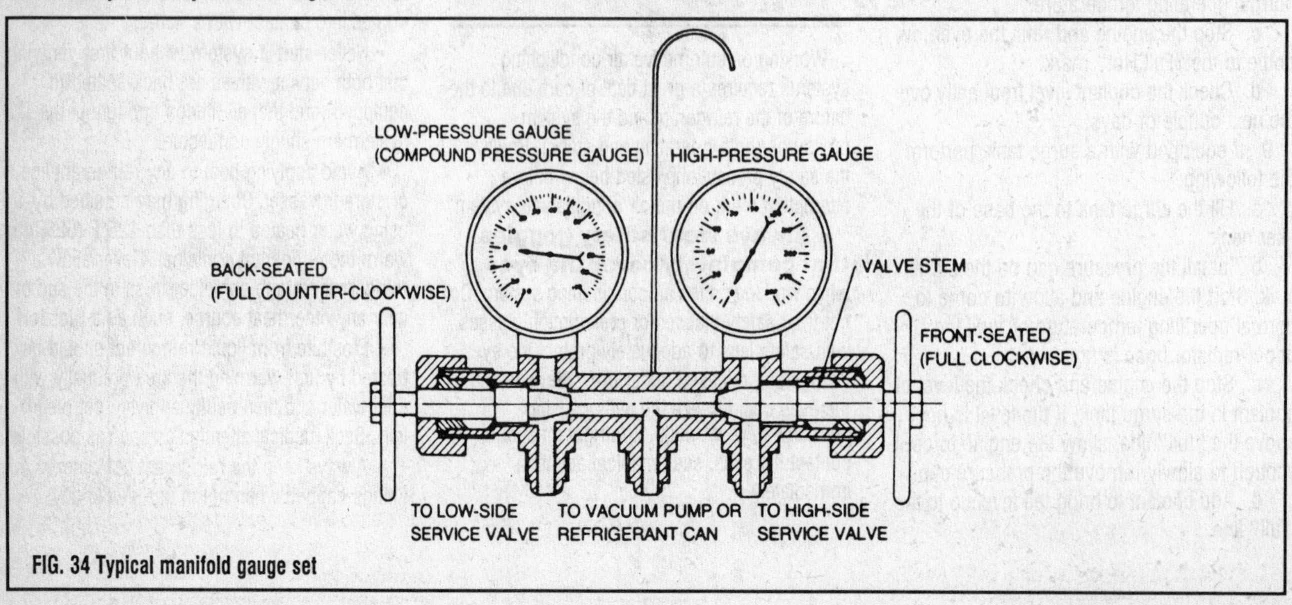

FIG. 34 Typical manifold gauge set

FIG. 33A Accumulator with low side fitting

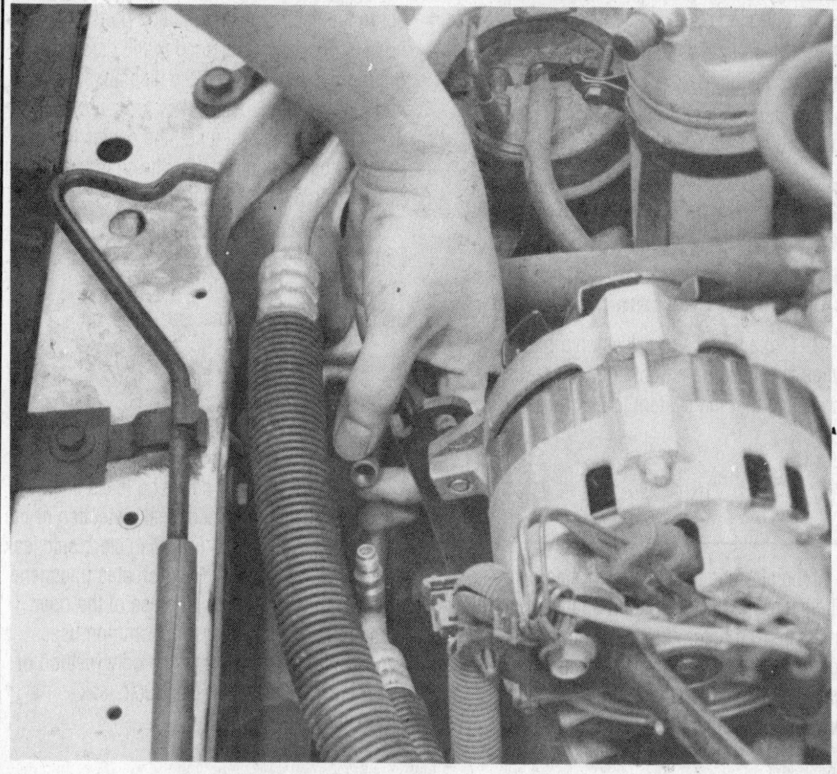
FIG. 33B Removing dust cap from high side fitting

The low side gauge registers both pressure and vacuum readings. The low side scale registers from 0–60 psi (414kpa) and vacuum readings from 0–30 in. Hg.

The high side gauge measures pressure from 0–300 psi (2100kpa).

Both gauges are threaded into a manifold that contains 2 hand shut-off valves. Proper set-up of these valves and the use of the attached test hoses allow the user to perform the following services:

1. Test high and low side pressures.
2. Evacuate air, moisture and/or contaminated refrigerant from the system.
3. Purge the system of refrigerant.
4. Charge the system with refrigerant.

The manifold valves are designed so they have no direct effect on the gauge readings but serve only to provide for or cut off the flow of refrigerant through the manifold. During all testing and hook-up operations, the valves are kept in a closed position to avoid disturbing the refrigerant system. System pressures may be observed without opening the valves. The valves are opened ONLY to discharge, evacuate and charge the system.

When purging the system, the center hose is uncapped at the lower end and both valves are cracked (opened) slightly with the engine not running. This allows the refrigerant pressure to force the entire contents of the system out through the center hose. During evacuation, both valves are opened to allow the vacuum pump to remove all air and moisture from the system before charging. During recharging, the valve on the high system is closed and the low side valve is cracked open. Under these conditions, the low pressure in the evaporator will draw refrigerant from the relatively warm refrigerant storage container into the system.

Service Valves

To diagnose an air conditioning system problem, the system must be entered in order to read the system pressures. The air conditioning systems on General Motors vehicles use Schrader type valves, similar to the valves used on automobile tires. The process of connecting the gauge lines set to the system is the same as threading a tire pump outlet hose onto a bicycle tire valve. As the test hose is threaded onto the service port the valve core is depressed, allowing the refrigerant to enter the test hose outlet. When the test hose is removed, the pressure in the system pushes the valve closed.

**** CAUTION**

Wear protective goggles whenever working on the air conditioning system.

Do NOT remove the gauge hoses while the engine is running. Always turn the engine OFF and allow the system pressure to stabilize before removing the gauge set test hose.

✽✽ CAUTION

Extreme caution must be observed when removing test hoses from the Schrader valves as some refrigerant will normally escape, usually under high pressure. Observe safety precautions.

Using The Manifold Gauges

The following step-by-step procedure should be used to correctly connect the gauge set to the system.

1. Engine NOT running.
2. Remove the caps from the high and low side service ports. Make sure both gauge valves are closed.
3. Connect the blue low side test hose to the service valve on or near the accumulator (large aluminum can).
4. Connect the red high side test hose to the service valve on the refrigerant line that leads from the compressor to the condenser (looks similar to the radiator, mounted in front of the radiator).
5. Start the engine and allow to come to normal operating temperature. All testing and charging of the system should be done at normal operating temperature.
6. Adjust the air conditioner controls to **Max Cold**.
7. Observe the gauge readings.

Storage Of The Gauge Set

When the gauges are not in use, thread the test end of the gauge hoses onto the treaded blank fittings on the manifold assembly. This will keep dirt and especially moisture out of the hoses and manifold. If the gauge set has extra fittings, cap or plug them.

If air and moisture have gotten into the gauges, purge the hoses by supplying refrigerant under pressure to the center hose with both gauge valves open and all openings unplugged. Crack each hose slightly, one at a time, until refrigerant comes out. This will purge the air and moisture from the hoses. Immediately cap the lines as described above.

DISCHARGING THE SYSTEM

➡ R-12 refrigerant is a chlorofluorocarbon which, when released into the atmosphere, can contribute to the depletion of the ozone layer in the upper atmosphere. Ozone filters out harmful radiation from the sun. If possible, an approved R-12 Recovery/Recycling machine that meets SAE standards should be employed when discharging the system. Follow the operating instructions provided with the approved equipment exactly to properly discharge the system.

✽✽ CAUTION

Be sure to perform the operation in a well ventilated area.

1. If the system has a charge and the compressor can be operated, run for at least 10 minutes. Turn the engine OFF.
2. Attach the gauges.
3. Place a container or rag at the outlet of the center charging hose. The refrigerant will be discharged there and this precaution will avoid its uncontrolled release.
4. Open the low side hand valve on the manifold slightly.
5. Open the high side hand valve on the manifold slightly.

➡ If the system is discharged too rapidly, an oily foam will appear in the receiving rag or container. Should this occur, close the valves slowly until the foaming stops.

6. Close both hand valves on the manifold when the pressure on both gauges reads **0**, indicating that the system is discharged.

EVACUATING

If the air conditioning system has been opened to the atmosphere, it should be air and moisture free before being recharged with refrigerant. Moisture and air mixed with refrigerant will raise the compressor head pressure, possibly damage the system's components and will reduce the performance of the system. In addition, air and moisture in the system can lead to internal corrosion of the system components. Moisture will boil at normal room temperature when exposed to a vacuum. To evacuate, or rid the system of air and moisture:

1. Leak test the system and repair any leaks found.
2. Connect an approved charging station, Recovery/Recycling machine or manifold gauge set and vacuum pump to the discharge and suction ports.
3. Open the discharge and suction ports and start the vacuum pump. If the pump is not able to pull at least 26 in. Hg of vacuum there is a leak that must be repaired before evacuation can occur.
4. Once the system has reached at least 26 in. Hg of vacuum, allow the system to evacuate for at least 10 minutes. The longer the system is evacuated, the more moisture will be removed.
5. Close all valves and turn the pump off. If the system loses more than 2 in. Hg of vacuum after 15 minutes, there is a leak that should be repaired.

SYSTEM CHARGING

1. Connect an approved charging station, Recovery/Recycling machine or manifold gauge set to the discharge and suction ports. The red hose is normally connected to the discharge (high pressure) line, and the blue hose is connected to the suction (low pressure) line. If using a manifold gauge set, the center (usually yellow) hose is connected to the charging station or Recovery/Recycling machine.
2. Follow the instructions provided with the equipment and charge the system with the specified amount of refrigerant.
3. Perform a leak test.

LEAK TESTING

There 2 methods of detecting leaks in an air conditioning system: halide leak detection or the open flame method and use of an electronic leak detector. Since burning R-12 creates phosgene gas, which is poisonous, the use of the open flame method is no longer in common use, although it was at one time the only method of leak detection available. Electronic leak detectors are much safer and more accurate, although an electronically created spark is used to detect the presence of refrigerant.

The halide leak detector is a torch-like device which produces a yellow-green color when refrigerant is introduced into the flame at the burner. A purple or violet color indicates the presence of large amounts of refrigerant at the burner.

A electronic leak detector is a small portable device with an extended probe. With the unit activated, the probe is passed along the components of the system which contain refrigerant. Since R-12 refrigerant is heavier than air, passing the probe along the bottom or under the component being tested is a more accurate means of leak detection. If a leak is detected, the unit will sound and alarm signal or activate a display signal depending on the manufacturer's design. Follow the manufacturers's instructions as the design and function of the detector may vary significantly.

**** CAUTION**

Caution should be taken to operate either type of detector in a well ventilated area, so as to reduce the chance of personal injury, which may result from coming into contact with poisonous gases produced when R-12 is exposed to flame or electric spark.

Windshield Wipers

Intense heat from the sun, snow and ice, road oils and the chemicals used in windshield washer solvents combine to deteriorate the rubber wiper refills. The refills should be replaced about twice a year or whenever the blades begin to streak or chatter.

For maximum effectiveness and longest element life, the windshield and wiper blades should be kept clean. Dirt, tree sap, road tar and so on will cause streaking, smearing and blade deterioration if left on the glass. It is advisable to wash the windshield carefully with a commercial glass cleaner at least once a month. Wipe off the rubber blades with the wet rag afterwards. Do not attempt to move the wipers by hand as damage to the motor and drive mechanism will result.

If the blades are found to be cracked, broken or torn, they should be replaced immediately. Replacement intervals will vary with usage, although ozone deterioration usually limits blade life to about 1 year at the maximum. If the wiper pattern is smeared or streaked, or if the blade chatters across the glass, the elements should be replaced. It is easiest and most sensible to replace the elements in pairs.

There are 3 different types of refills, which differ in their method of replacement. One type has 2 release buttons, approximately 1/3 of the way up from each end of the blade frame. Pushing the buttons down releases a lock and allows the rubber filler to be removed from the frame. The new blade slides back into the frame and locks into place.

The second type of refill has 2 metal tabs which are unlocked by squeezing them together. The rubber blade can then be withdrawn from the frame jaws. A new refill is installed by inserting the refill into the front frame jaws and sliding it rearward to engage the remaining frame jaws. There are usually 4 jaws. Be certain when installing that the refill is engaged in all of them. At the end of its travel, the tabs will lock into place on the front jaws of the wiper blade frame.

The third type is a refill made from polycarbonate. The refill has a simple locking device at 2 end which flexes downward out of the groove into which the jaws of the holder fit, allowing easy release. By sliding the new refill through all the jaws and pushing through the slight resistance when it reaches the end of its travel, the refill will lock into position.

Regardless of the type of refill used, make sure that all of the frame jaws are engaged as the refill is pushed into place and locked. The metal blade holder and frame will scratch the glass if allowed to touch it.

WIPER REFILL REPLACEMENT

Normally, if the wipers are not cleaning the windshield properly, only the refill has to be replaced. The blade and arm usually require replacement only in the event of damage. It is only necessary to remove the arm or blade to replace the refill (except on Tridon® refills). The job may be made easier by turning the ignition switch to the **ON** position, then turn the wiper switch **ON**. When the wiper arms reach the center of the windshield, turn the ignition switch to the **OFF** position.

There are several types of refills and your vehicle could have any king, since aftermarket blades and arms may not use exactly the same type of refill as the original equipment.

The original equipment wiper elements can be replaced as follows:

1. Lift the wiper arm off the glass.
2. Depress the release lever on the center bridge and remove the blade from the arm.
3. Lift the tab and pinch the end bridge to release it from the center bridge.
4. Slide the end bridge from the wiper blade and the wiper blade from the opposite end bridge.
5. Install a new element and be sure the tab on the end bridge is down to lock the element into place. Check each release point for positive engagement.

Tires and Wheels

TIRE ROTATION

➧ SEE FIGS. 36 AND 37

Tire wear can be equalized by switching the position of the tires at 6000 miles for new tires and then every 15,000 miles. Including a conventional spare in the rotation pattern can give up to 20% more life to a set of tires.

**** CAUTION**

DO NOT include the temporary use spare in the rotation pattern.

There are certain exceptions to tire rotation, however. Studded snow tires should not be rotated. Radials should be kept on the same side of the vehicle (maintain the same direction or rotation). The belts on radial tires develop a set pattern. If the direction of rotation is reversed, it can cause a rough ride and vibration.

➡ When radials or studded snows are removed for the season, mark them so they can be reinstalled on the same side of the vehicle.

TIRE DESIGN

For maximum service life tires should be used in sets of five, except on vehicles equipped with a space-saver spare tire. Do not mix tires of different designs, such as steel belted radial,

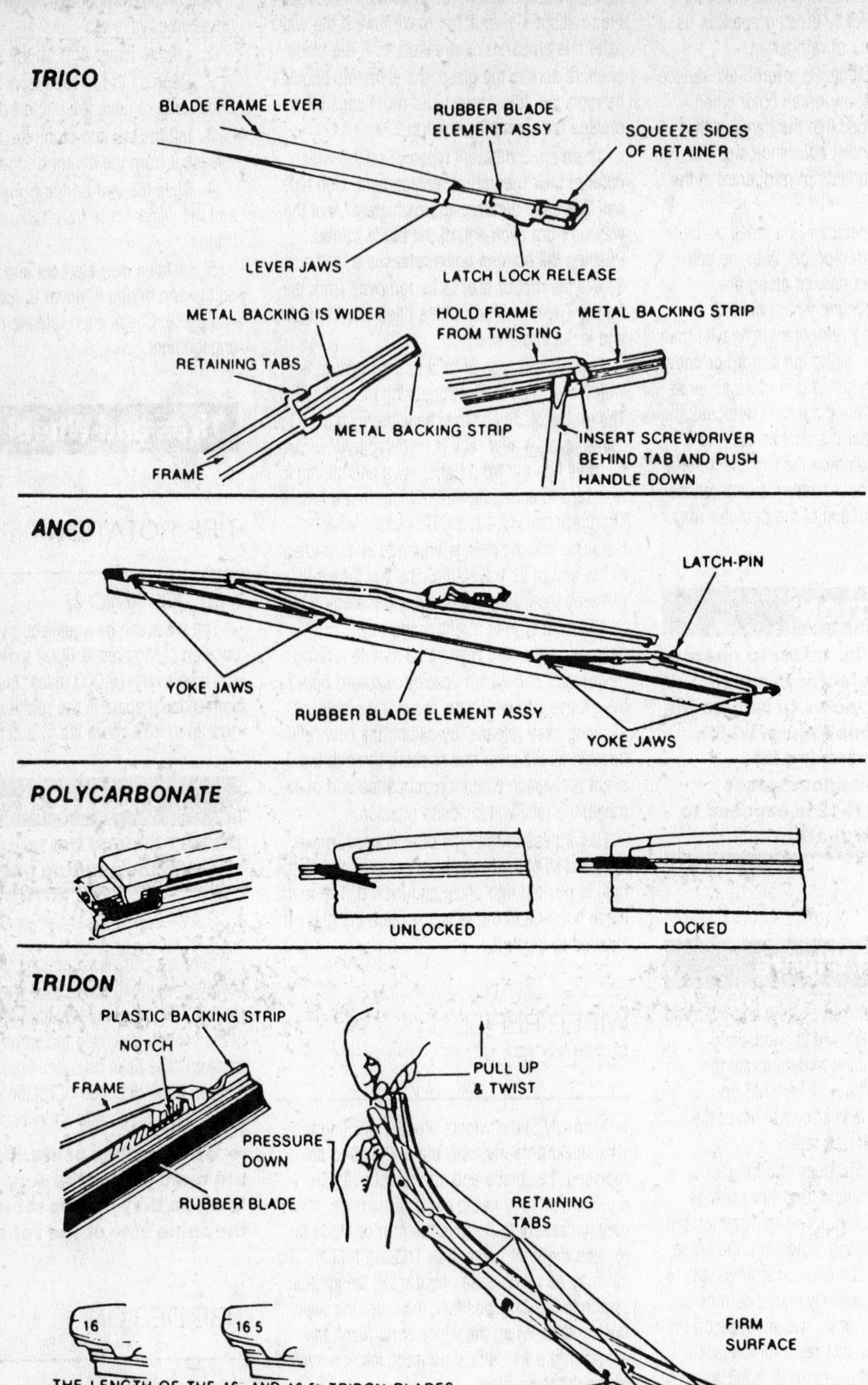

FIG. 35 Wiper insert replacement

fiberglass belted or bias/belted, or tires of different sizes, such as P165SR–14 and P185SR–14.

Conventional bias ply tires are constructed so that the cords run bead-to-bead at an angle (bias). Alternate plies run at an opposite angle. This type of construction gives rigidity to both tread and sidewall. Bias/belted tires are similar in construction to conventional bias ply tires. Belts run at an angel and also at a 90° angle to the bead, as in the radial tire. Tread life in improved considerably over the conventional bias tire. The radial tire differs in construction, but instead of the carcass plies running at an angle of 90° to each other, they run at an angle of 90° to the bead. This gives the tread a great deal of rigidity and the sidewall a great deal of flexibility and accounts for the characteristic bulge associated with radial tires.

All General Motors vehicles are capable of using radial tires and they are the recommended type for all years. If radial tires are used, tires sizes and wheel diameters should be selected to maintain ground clearance and tire load capacity equivalent to the minimum specified tire. Radial tires should always be used in sets of 5 if the spare is a conventional tire. In an emergency, radial tires can be used with caution on the rear axle only. If this is done, both tires on the rear should be of radial design.

➡ **Radial tires should never be used on only the front axle as they can adversely effect steering if tires of different designs are mixed.**

TIRE STORAGE

Store the tires at the proper inflation pressures, if they are mounted. All tires should be stored in a cool, dry place. If the tires are stored in a garage or basement, DO NOT, let them stand on a concrete floor. Instead, set them on blocks of wood.

TIRE INFLATION

Factory installed wheels and tires are designed to handle loads up to and including their rated load capacity when inflated to the recommended inflation pressures. Correct tire pressure and driving techniques have an important influence on tire life. Heavy cornering, excessively rapid acceleration and unnecessary braking increase tire wear. Underinflated tires can cause handling problems, poor fuel economy, shortened tire life and tire overloading.

Maximum axle load must never exceed the value shown on the side of the tire. The inflation pressure should never exceed the value shown on the side of the tire, usually 35 psi (241kpa) for conventional tires or 60 psi (414kpa) for a compact spare tire. The pressure shown on the tire is NOT the recommended operating pressure for the tire or vehicle. In most cases, that pressure is far too high and will result in a rough ride and accelerated tire wear. It is the maximum pressure the tire manufacturer has determined that tire can handle under extreme load circumstances. The correct operating tire inflation pressures are listed on the tire placard located on the side of the driver's door.

Check tire inflation at least once a month.

CARE OF SPECIAL WHEELS

If the vehicle is equipped with aluminum alloy wheels, be very careful when using any type of cleaner on either the wheels or tires. Read the label on the package of the cleaner to make sure that it will not damage aluminum.

RECOMMENDED ROTATION PATTERN
FOR FRONT WHEEL DRIVE CARS

LF RF

LR RR

DO NOT INCLUDE "TEMPORARY USE ONLY" SPARE TIRE IN ROTATION

FIG. 36 Possible tire rotation pattern

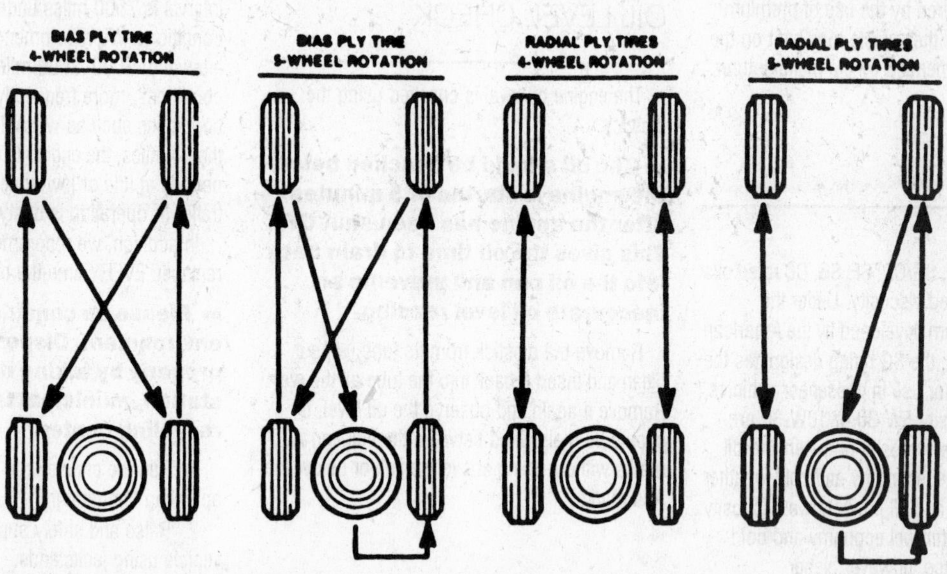

FIG. 37 Tire rotation patterns; note that some manufacturers recommend that radials not be cross-switched

FLUIDS AND LUBRICANTS

Fuel and Engine Oil Recommendations

FUEL

➡ **Some fuel additives contain chemicals that can damage the catalytic converter and/or oxygen sensor. Read all of the labels carefully before using any additive in the engine or fuel system.**

All engines require the use of unleaded fuel only. The octane rating required will vary according to the compression ratio of the engine. For the most part, if the compression ration is 9.0:1 or lower, the vehicle will perform satisfactorily on regular unleaded gasoline. If the compression ratio is greater than 9.0:1, premium unleaded is required. Check the owner's manual for specific guidelines for the engine in your vehicle.

Fuel should be selected for the brand and octane which performs best in your engine. Judge a gasoline by its ability to prevent ping, its engine starting capabilities (both cold and hot) and general all weather performance.

In general, choose the octane the manufacturer recommends. Regardless of the claims made by advertisers as to the improved performance delivered by the use of premium fuel, in most cases the vehicle runs best on the octane fuel recommended by the manufacturer.

OIL

➧ SEE FIG. 38

Use only SG/CC, SG/CD, SF, SG, CC rated oils of the recommended viscosity. Under the classification system developed by the American Petroleum Institute, the SG rating designates the highest quality oil for use in passenger vehicles. Oils with the viscosity 5W-30 or 10W-30 are recommended. The viscosity of the engine oil has an effect on fuel economy and cold weather operation (starting and oil flow). Lower viscosity oil can provide better fuel economy and cold weather performance, however higher temperature weather conditions require higher viscosity engine oils for satisfactory lubrication.

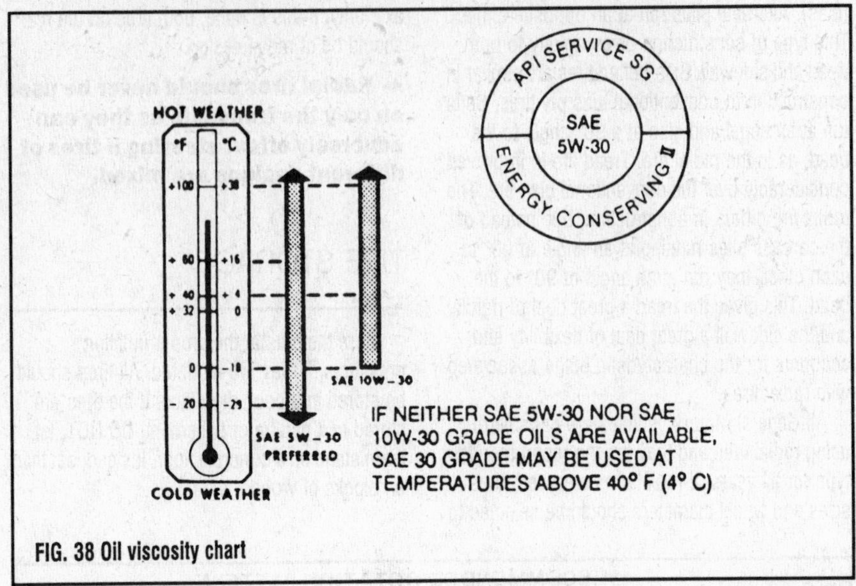

FIG. 38 Oil viscosity chart

Choose your oil with regard to the anticipated temperatures during the period before the next oil change. Using the accompanying chart, choose the oil viscosity of the lowest expected temperature.

Engine

OIL LEVEL CHECK

The engine oil level is checked using the dipstick.

➡ **The oil should be checked before the engine is started or 5 minutes after the engine has been shut OFF. This gives the oil time to drain back into the oil pan and prevents an inaccurate oil level reading.**

Remove the dipstick from its tube, wipe it clean and insert it back into the tube all the way. Remove it again and observe the oil level. It should be maintained between the Full and Add marks without going above the Full or below the Add marks.

⁂ WARNING

DO NOT overfill the crankcase. It may result in oil-fouled spark plugs, oil leaks cause by oil seal failure or engine damage due to oil foaming.

OIL AND FILTER CHANGE

The manufacturer's recommended oil change interval is 7500 miles under normal operating conditions. We recommend an oil change interval of 3000–3500 miles under normal conditions; more frequently under severe conditions such as when the average trip is less than 4 miles, the engine is operated for extended periods at idle or low-speed, when towing a trailer or operating is dusty areas.

In addition, we recommend that the filter be replaced EVERY time the oil is changed.

➡ **Please be considerate of the environment. Dispose of waste oil properly by taking it to a service station, municipal facility or recycling center.**

1. Run the engine until it reaches normal operating temperature.
2. Raise and safely support the front of the vehicle using jackstands.

FIG. 38A Engine oil level dipstick location — 2.5L engine shown

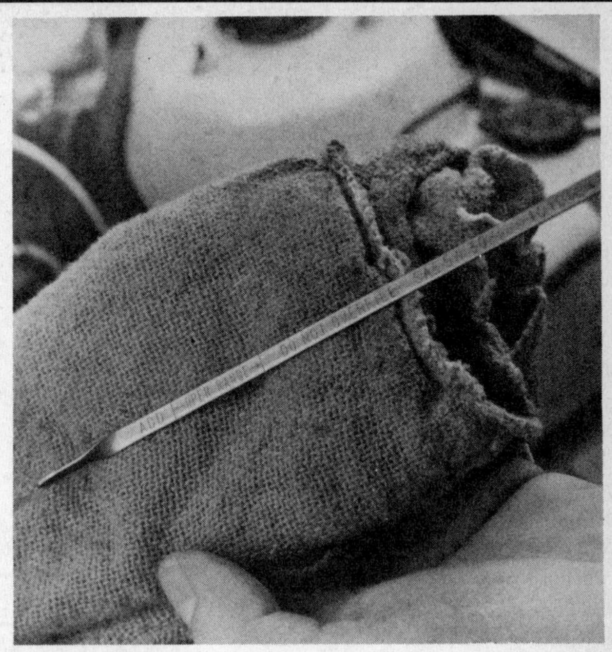
FIG. 38B Engine oil level dipstick markings — keep oil level between lines

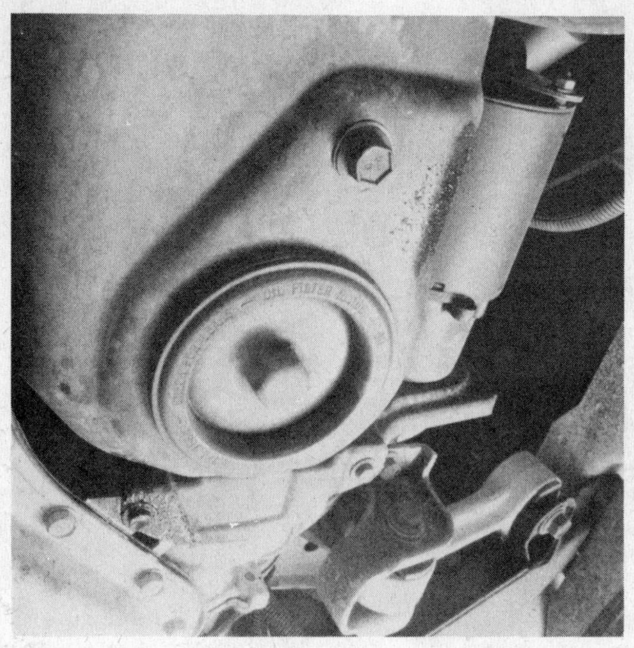
FIG. 38C Engine oil filter mounting location — 2.5L engine shown

FIG. 38D Engine oil fill location — 2.5L engine shown

3. Slide a drain pan of at least 5 quarts capacity under the oil pan.
4. Loosen the drain plug. Turn it out by hand by keeping an inward pressure on the plug as you unscrew it. This will prevent hot oil from escaping past the threads until the plug is completely out of the threads.
5. Allow the oil to drain completely and then reinstall the drain plug. Do not overtighten the plug.
6. Using an oil filter wrench, remove the oil filter. Be aware, that the filter contains about 1 quart of hot, dirty oil.
7. Empty the old oil filter into the drain pan and dispose of the filter properly.
8. Using a clean shop towel, wipe off the filter adapter on the engine block. Be sure the towel does not leave any lint which could clog an oil passage.
9. Coat the rubber gasket on the new filter with fresh oil. Spin the filter onto the adapter by hand until it contacts the mounting surface. Tighten the filter 3/4 to 1 full turn.
10. Refill the crankcase with the specified amount of engine oil.
11. Crank the engine over several times, then start it. After approximately 3–5 seconds, if the pressure gauge shows zero or the oil pressure warning indicator fails to go out, shut the engine OFF and investigate the problem.
12. If the oil pressure is OK and there are no leaks, shut the engine OFF and lower the vehicle.
13. Wait for a few minutes and check the oil level. Add oil, as necessary, to bring the level up to the **FULL** mark.

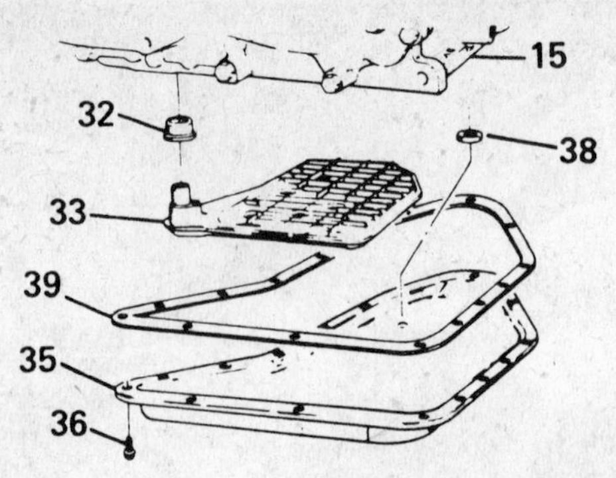

1. Transaxle assembly
2. Seal
3. Transaxle fluid strainer
4. Transaxle fluid pan
5. Transaxle fluid pan screw
6. Chip collector magnet
7. Transaxle fluid pan gasket

FIG. 39 Automatic transaxle pan, screen and gasket installation

FIG. 39A Adding automatic transaxle fluid

Manual Transaxle

FLUID RECOMMENDATIONS

The recommended fluid is synchromesh transaxle fluid. The manual transaxle fluid does not require changing.

LEVEL CHECK

Check fluid level only when the engine is OFF, the vehicle is level and the transaxle is cold. To check the fluid level, remove and read the fluid level indicator/filler plug. If the indicator reads low, add the appropriate amount of synchromesh transaxle fluid to fill the transaxle to the FULL level.

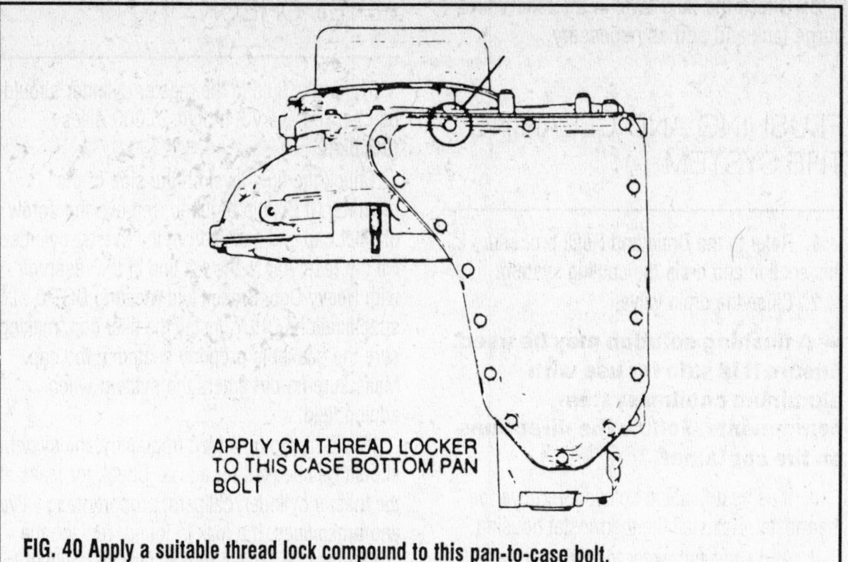

FIG. 40 Apply a suitable thread lock compound to this pan-to-case bolt.

Automatic Transaxle

FLUID RECOMMENDATIONS

When adding fluid or refilling the transaxle, use Dexron®II automatic transmission fluid.

LEVEL CHECK

1. Start the engine and drive the vehicle for a minimum of 15 miles.

➡ **The automatic transmission fluid level must be checked with the vehicle at normal operating temperature; 180-200°F (82-93°C). Temperature will greatly affect transaxle fluid level.**

2. Park the vehicle on a level surface.
3. Place the transaxle gear selector in **P**.
4. Apply the parking brake and block the drive wheels.
5. Let the vehicle idle for 3 minutes with the accessories OFF.
6. With the engine running, check the fluid level, color and condition.
7. Inaccurate fluid level readings may result if the fluid is checked immediately after the vehicle has been operated under any or all of the following conditions:
   a. In high ambient temperatures above 90°F (32°C).
   b. At sustained high speeds.
   c. In heavy city traffic during hot weather.
   d. As a towing vehicle.
   e. In commercial service (taxi or police use).
8. If the vehicle has been operated under these conditions, shut the engine OFF and allow the vehicle to cool for 30 minutes. After the cooldown period, restart the vehicle and continue from Step 2 above.

DRAIN AND REFILL

➧ SEE FIGS. 39 AND 40

1. Raise and safely support the vehicle.
2. Place the drain pan under the transaxle fluid pan.
3. Remove the fluid pan bolts from the front and sides only.
4. Loosen, but do not remove the 4 bolts at the rear of the fluid pan.

➡ **Do not damage the transaxle case or fluid pan sealing surfaces.**

5. Lightly tap the fluid pan with a rubber mallet or pry to allow the fluid to partially drain from the pan.
6. Remove the remaining fluid pan bolts, fluid pan and gasket.

To install:

7. Install a new gasket to the fluid pan.
8. Install the fluid pan to the transaxle.

➡ **Apply a suitable sealant compound to the bolt shown in the illustration to prevent fluid leaks.**

9. Install the pan bolts. Tighten to 133 inch lbs. (11 Nm).
10. Lower the vehicle.
11. Fill the transaxle to the proper level with Dexron® II fluid. Check cold level reading. Do not overfill.
12. Follow the fluid check procedure in this section.
13. Check the pan for leaks.

PAN AND FILTER SERVICE

1. With the pan removed from the vehicle and the fluid completely drained, thoroughly clean the inside of the pan to remove all old fluid and residue.
2. Inspect the gasket sealing surface on the fluid pan and remove any remaining gasket fragments with a scraper.
3. Remove the fluid filter, O-ring and seal from the case.

To install:

4. Apply a small amount of Transjel to the new seal and install the seal.
5. Install a new filter O-ring and filter.
6. Install the new gasket to the pan.

Cooling System

FLUID RECOMMENDATIONS

The cooling system should be inspected, flushed and refilled with fresh coolant at least every 30,000 miles or 24 months. If the coolant is left in the system too long, it loses its ability to prevent rust and corrosion.

When the coolant is being replaced, use a good quality ethylene glycol antifreeze that is safe to be used with aluminum cooling system components. The ratio of ethylene glycol to water should always be a 50/50 mixture. This ratio will ensure the proper balance of cooling ability, corrosion protection and antifreeze protection. At this ratio, the antifreeze protection should be good to –34°F (–37°C). If greater antifreeze protection is needed, the ratio should not exceed 70% antifreeze.

LEVEL CHECK

➡ **When checking the coolant level, the radiator cap need not be removed. Simply check the coolant level in the recovery bottle or surge tank.**

Check the coolant level in the recovery bottle or surge tank, usually mounted on the inner fender. With the engine cold, the coolant level should be at the ADD or COLD level. With the engine at normal operating temperature, the coolant level should be at the FULL mark. Add coolant, as necessary.

DRAIN AND REFILL

CAUTION

When draining the coolant, keep in mind that cats and dogs are attracted by the ethylene glycol antifreeze and are quite likely to drink any that is left in an uncovered container or in puddles on the ground. This will prove fatal in sufficient quantity. Always drain the coolant into a sealable container. Coolant should be reused unless it is contaminated or several years old. To avoid injuries from scalding fluid and steam, DO NOT remove the radiator cap while the engine and radiator are still HOT.

1. With the engine cool, remove the radiator cap by performing the following:
   a. Slowly rotate the cap counterclockwise to the detent.
   b. If any residual pressure is present, WAIT until the hissing stops.
   c. After the hissing noise has ceased, press down on the cap and continue rotating it counterclockwise to remove it.
2. Place a fluid catch pan under the radiator, open the radiator drain valve and drain the coolant from the system.
3. Close the drain valve.
4. Empty the coolant reservoir or surge tank and flush it.
5. Using the correct mixture of antifreeze, fill the radiator to the bottom of the filler neck and the coolant tank to the FULL mark.
6. Install the radiator cap, making sure the arrows line up over the overflow tube leading the reservoir or surge tank.
7. Start the engine. Select heat on the climate control panel and turn the temperature valve to full warm. Run the engine until it reaches normal operating temperature. Check to make sure there is hot air flowing from the floor ducts.
8. Check the fluid level in the reservoir or surge tank and add as necessary.

FLUSHING AND CLEANING THE SYSTEM

1. Refer to the Drain and Refill procedure in this section and drain the cooling system.
2. Close the drain valve.

➡ A flushing solution may be used. Ensure it is safe for use with aluminum cooling system components. Follow the directions on the container.

3. If using a flushing solution, remove the thermostat. Reinstall the thermostat housing.
4. Add sufficient water to fill the system.
5. Start the engine and run for a few minutes. Drain the system.

➡ This next step can get messy, so perform the work in a place where the water can drain away easily.

6. If using a flushing solution, disconnect the heater hose that connects the cylinder head to the heater core (that end of the hose will clamp to a fitting on the firewall. Connect a water hose to the end of the heater hose that runs to the cylinder head and run water into the system until it begins to flow out of the top of the radiator.
7. Allow the water to flow out of the radiator until it is clear.
8. Reconnect the heater hose.
9. Drain the cooling system.
10. Reinstall the thermostat.
11. Empty the coolant reservoir or surge tank and flush it.
12. Fill the cooling system, using the correct ratio of antifreeze and water, to the bottom of the filler neck. Fill the reservoir or surge tank to the FULL mark.
13. Install the radiator cap, making sure that the arrows align with the overflow tube.

Brake Master Cylinder

FLUID RECOMMENDATION

Use only Heavy Duty Brake Fluid meeting DOT 3 specifications. Do NOT use any other fluid because severe brake system damage will result.

LEVEL CHECK

The brake fluid in the master cylinder should be checked every 6 months/6,000 miles (9656km).

Check the fluid level on the side of the reservoir. If fluid is required, remove the screw on filler cap and gasket from the master cylinder. Fill the reservoir to the full line in the reservoir with Heavy Duty Brake Fluid meeting DOT 3 specifications ONLY. Install the filler cap, making sure the gasket is properly seated in the cap. Make sure no dirt enters the system when adding fluid.

If fluid has to be added frequently, the system should be checked for a leak. Check for leaks at the master cylinder, calipers, proportioning valve and brake lines. If a leak is found, replace the component and bleed the system as outlined in Section 9.

Clutch Master Cylinder

FLUID RECOMMENDATION

Use only Heavy Duty Brake Fluid meeting DOT 3 specifications. Do NOT use any other fluid because severe clutch system damage will result.

LEVEL CHECK

The clutch system fluid in the master cylinder should be checked every 6 months/6,000 miles.

The clutch master cylinder reservoir is located on top of the left (driver) strut tower. Check the fluid level on the side of the reservoir. If fluid is required, remove the screw on filler cap and gasket from the master cylinder. Fill the reservoir to the full line in the reservoir with Heavy Duty Brake Fluid meeting DOT 3 specifications ONLY. Install the filler cap, making sure the gasket is properly seated in the cap. Make sure no dirt enters the system when adding fluid.

If fluid has to be added frequently, the system should be checked for a leak. Check for leaks at the master cylinder, slave cylinder and hose. If a leak is found, replace the component and bleed the system as outlined in Section 7.

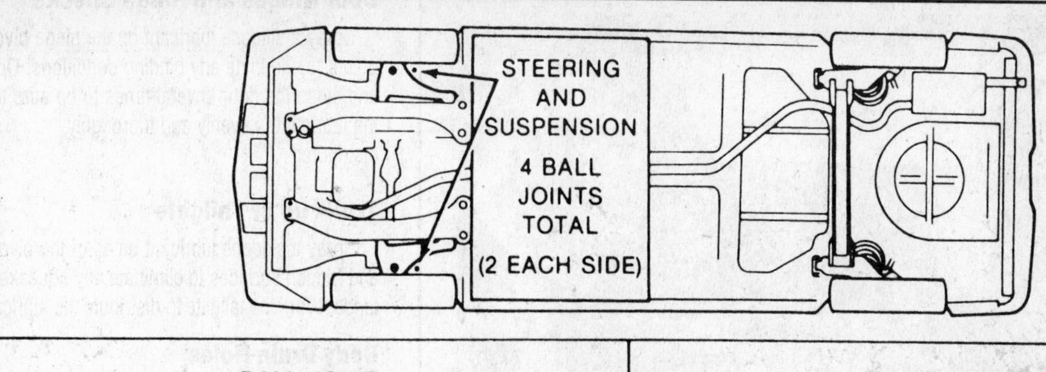

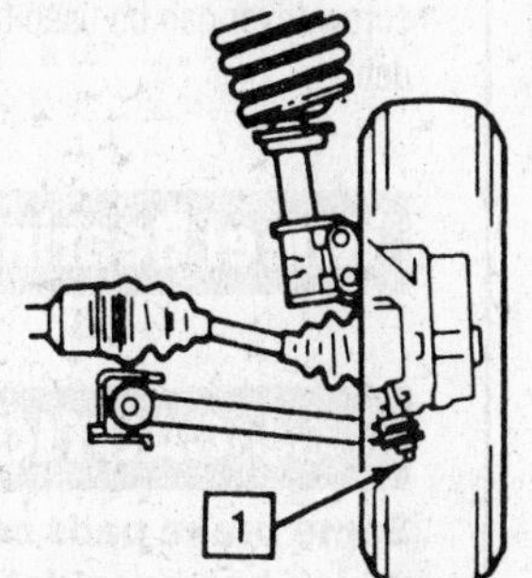

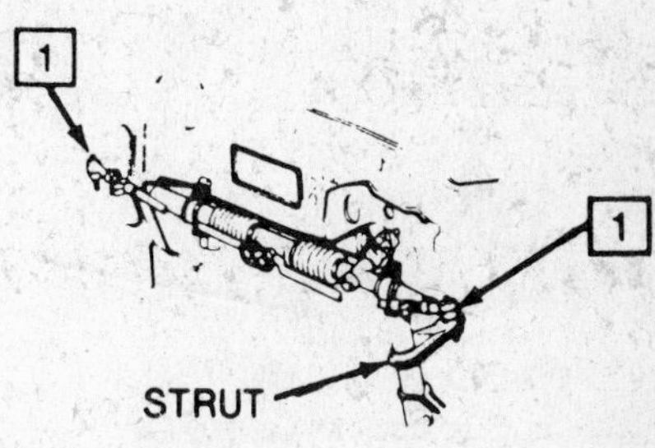

FIG. 41 Lubrication points

Power Steering

FLUID RECOMMENDATIONS

When adding fluid or making a complete fluid change, always use GM P/N 1050017 power steering fluid or equivalent. Do NOT use automatic transmission fluid. Failure to use the proper fluid may cause hose and seal damage and fluid leaks.

LEVEL CHECK

The power steering fluid reservoir is directly above the steering pump. The pump is located on top of the engine on the right (passenger's) side.

Power steering fluid level is indicated either by marks on a see through reservoir or by marks on a fluid level indicator in the reservoir cap.

If the fluid is warmed up (about 150°F), the level should be between the HOT and COLD marks.

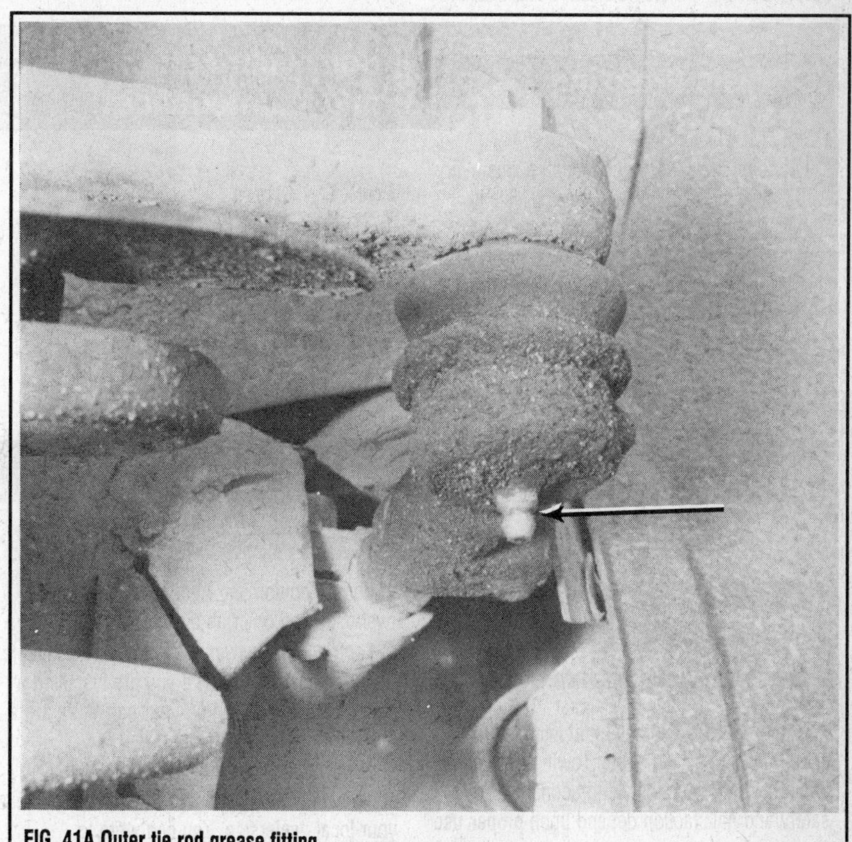

FIG. 41A Outer tie rod grease fitting

FIG. 41B Lower ball joint grease fitting

If the fluid is cooler than above, the level should be between the ADD and COLD marks.

Chassis Greasing

➧ SEE FIG. 41

Lubricate the chassis lubrication points every 7,500 miles or 12 months. If your vehicle is equipped with grease fittings, lubricate the suspension and steering linkage with heavy duty chassis grease. Lubricate the transaxle shift linkage, parking cable guides, under body contact points and linkage with white lithium grease.

Body Lubrication and Maintenance

Lock Cylinders

Apply graphite lubricant sparingly through the key slot. Insert the key and operate the lock several times to be sure that the lubricant is worked into the lock cylinder.

Door Hinges and Hinge Checks

Spray a silicone lubricant on the hinge pivot points to eliminate any binding conditions. Open and close the door several times to be sure that the lubricant is evenly and thoroughly distributed.

Trunk lid or Tailgate

Spray a silicone lubricant on all of the pivot and friction surfaces to eliminate any squeaks or binds. Work the tailgate to distribute the lubricant

Body Drain Holes

Be sure that the drain holes in the doors and rocker panels are cleared of obstruction. A small screwdriver can be used to clear them of any debris.

Wheel Bearings (Rear)

⁂ CAUTION

Some brake pads contain asbestos, which has been determined to be a cancer causing agent. Never clean the brake surfaces with compressed air! Avoid inhaling any dust from any brake surface! When cleaning brake surfaces, use a commercially available brake cleaning fluid.

The N body models are equipped with sealed hub and bearing assemblies for the rear wheels. The hub and bearing assemblies are nonserviceable. If the assembly is damaged, the complete unit must be replaced. Refer to Section 8 for the hub and bearing removal and installation procedure.

TRAILER TOWING

General Recommendations

Your vehicle is designed and intended to be used mainly to carry people. Towing a trailer will affect handling, durability and economy. Your safety and satisfaction depend upon proper use of correct equipment. Also, you should avoid overloads and other abusive use.

Factory trailer towing packages are available on most cars. However, if you are installing a trailer hitch and wiring on your car, there are a few things you should know.

Information on trailer towing, special equipment and optional equipment is available at your local dealership. You can write to Oldsmobile Customer Service Department, P.O. Box 30095, Lansing, MI 48909. In Canada, General Motors of Canada Limited, Customer Service Department, Oshawa, Ontario L1J 5Z6.

Trailer Weight

Trailer weight is the first, and most important,

factor in determining whether or not your vehicle is suitable for towing the trailer you have in mind. The horsepower-to-weight ratio should be calculated. The basic standard is a ratio of 35:1. That is, 35 pounds of GVW (gross vehicle weight) for every horsepower.

To calculate this ratio, multiply you engine's rated horsepower by 35, then subtract the weight of the vehicle, including passengers and luggage. The resulting figure is the ideal maximum trailer weight that you can tow.

Hitch Weight

There are three kinds of hitches: bumper mounted, frame mounted, and load equalizing.

Bumper mounted hitches are those which attach solely to the vehicle's bumper. Many states prohibit towing with this type of hitch, when it attaches to the vehicle's stock bumper, since it subjects the bumper to stresses for which it was not designed. Aftermarket rear step bumpers, designed for trailer towing, are acceptable for use with bumper mounted hitches.

➡ Do NOT attach any hitch to the bumper bar on the vehicle. A hitch attachment may be made through the bumper mounting locations, but only if an additional attachment is also made. Frame mounted hitches can be of the type which bolts to two or more points on the frame, plus the bumper, or just to several points on the frame. Frame mounted hitches can also be of the tongue type, for Class I towing, or, of the receiver type, for classes II and III.

Load equalizing hitches are usually used for large trailers. Most equalizing hitches are welded in place and use equalizing bars and chains to level the vehicle after the trailer is hooked up.

The bolt-on hitches are the most common, since they are relatively easy to install.

Check the gross weight rating of your trailer. Tongue weight is usually figured as 10% of gross trailer weight. Therefore, a trailer with a maximum gross weight of 2,000 lbs. (907 kg) will have a maximum tongue weight of 200 lbs. (91 kg) Class I trailers fall into this category. Class II trailers are those with a gross weight rating of 2,000–3,500 lbs. (907–1588 kg), while Class III trailers fall into the 3,500–6,000 lbs. (1588–2722 kg) category. Class IV trailers are those over 6,000 lbs. (2722 kg) and are for use with fifth wheel trucks, only.

When you have determined the hitch that you'll need, follow the manufacturer's installation instructions, exactly, especially when it comes to fastener torques. The hitch will subjected to a lot of stress and good hitches come with hardened bolts. Never substitute an inferior bolt for a hardened bolt.

Wiring

Wiring the car for towing is fairly easy. There are a number of good wiring kits available and these should be used, rather than trying to design your own. All trailers will need brake lights and turn signals as well as tail lights and side marker lights. Most states require extra marker lights for overly wide trailers. Also, most states have recently required back-up lights for trailers, and most trailer manufacturers have been building trailers with back-up lights for several years.

Additionally, some Class I, most Class II and just about all Class III trailers will have electric brakes.

Add to this number an accessories wire, to operate trailer internal equipment or to charge the trailer's battery, and you can have as many as seven wires in the harness.

Determine the equipment on your trailer and buy the wiring kit necessary. The kit will contain all the wires needed, plus a plug adapter set which included the female plug, mounted on the bumper or hitch, and the male plug, wired into, or plugged into the trailer harness.

When installing the kit, follow the manufacturer's instructions. The color coding of the wires is standard throughout the industry.

One point to note is that some domestic vehicles, and most imported vehicles, have separate turn signals. On most domestic vehicles, the brake lights and rear turn signals operate with the same bulb. For those vehicles with separate turn signals, you can purchase an isolation unit so that the brake lights won't blink whenever the turn signals are operated, or, you can go to your local electronics supply house and buy four diodes to wire in series with the brake and turn signal bulbs. Diodes will isolate the brake and turn signals. The choice is yours. The isolation units are simple and quick to install, but far more expensive than the diodes. The diodes, however, require more work to install properly, since they require the cutting of each bulb's wire and soldering the diode in place.

One final point, the best kits are those with a spring loaded cover on the vehicle mounted socket. This cover prevents dirt and moisture from corroding the terminals. Never let the vehicle socket hang loosely. Always mount it securely to the bumper or hitch.

PUSHING AND TOWING

⁂ WARNING

Push starting is not recommended for cars equipped with a catalytic converter, which represents ALL N Body cars. Raw gas collecting in the converter may cause damage. Jump starting is recommended.

To push start your manual transaxle-equipped car (automatic transaxle-equipped models cannot be push started), make sure of bumper alignment. If the bumper of the car pushing does not match with your car's bumper, it would be wise to tie an old tire either on the back of your car, or on the front of the pushing car. Switch the ignition to ON and depress the clutch pedal. Shift the transaxle to third gear and hold the accelerator pedal about halfway down. Signal the push car to proceed. When the car speed reaches about 10 mph, signal the push car to brake. When your car has coasted a safe distance ahead, gradually release the clutch pedal. The engine should start, if not have the car towed.

Towing the vehicle on a flat bed ("roll back") truck is the most desirable option. The car is safest and the wheels do not have to turn. It is also the most expensive way to tow and not always available.

The second best way to tow the vehicle is with the drive wheels OFF the ground.

Sometimes it is impossible to tow with the opposite wheels on ground. In that case, if the transaxle is in proper working order, the car can be towed with the front wheels on the ground (front wheel drive) for distances under 15 miles at speeds no greater then 30 mph. If the transaxle is known to be damaged or if the car has to be towed over 15 miles or over 30 mph the car must be dollied or towed with the rear wheels raised and the steering wheel secured so that the front wheels remain in the straight-ahead position. The steering wheel must be clamped with a special clamping device designed for towing service. If the key-controlled lock is in the locked position, damage to the lock and steering column may result.

JACKING

➧ SEE FIGS. 42 AND 43

The jack that is furnished with the vehicle is ONLY to be used in an emergency to remove a flat tire. Never get beneath the car or, start or run the engine while the vehicle is supported by the jack. Front wheel drive cars have a center line of gravity that is far forward. Take the proper precautions to make sure the car does not fall forward while it is suspended. Personal injury may result if these procedures are not followed exactly.

When using a floor jack to lift the front of the car, lift from the center of the front crossmember. When using floor jack to lift the rear of the car, lift from the center of the rear jack pad.

After lifting the car, place jackstands under the body side pinch welds or similar strong and stable structure. Lower the car onto the jackstands slowly and carefully and check for stability before getting under the car.

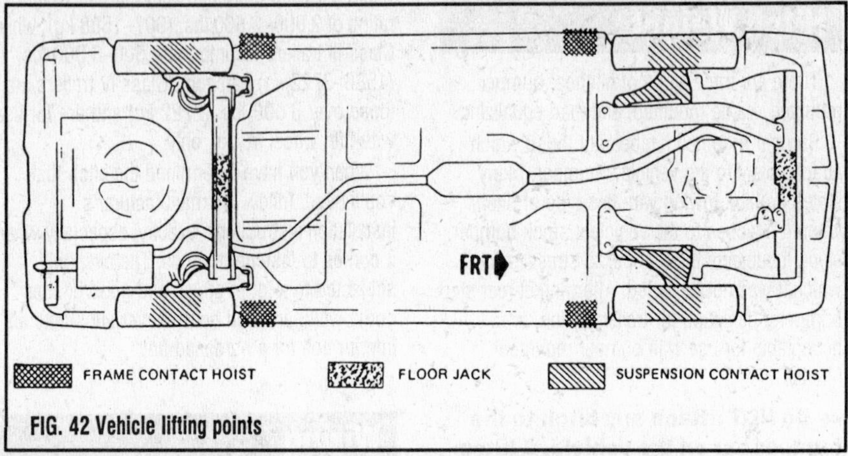

FIG. 42 Vehicle lifting points

FIG. 42A Vehicle lift point—front crossmember

CHANGING A FLAT TIRE

1. Park on a level surface and apply the parking brake firmly.
2. If you are in a public or in a potentially dangerous location, turn the 4-way hazard flashers ON.
3. Shift the transaxle gear selector into the PARK position.
4. Remove the jacking tools and spare tire from the stowage area.
5. Connect the socket with side of ratchet marked UP/ON. Raise the jack slowly.
6. Position the jack head under the vehicle closest to the tire to be changed.
7. Raise the jack until the lift head mates with the vehicle notches as shown in the jacking previous illustration. Do NOT raise the vehicle.

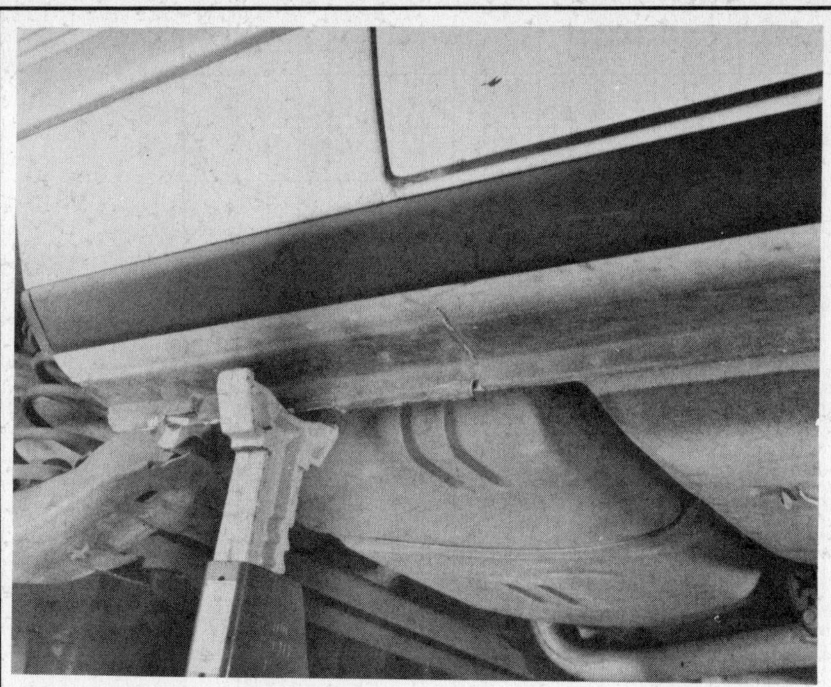

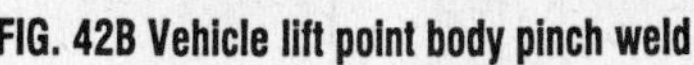

FIG. 42B Vehicle lift point body pinch weld

FIG. 42C Vehicle lift point—rear axle assembly

8. Remove the wheel cover using the wedge end of ratchet. Connect the DOWN/OFF side of the ratchet to the socket and loosen, but do not remove the wheel nuts.

9. Connect the UP/ON side of the ratchet to the jack.

10. Raise the vehicle so the inflated spare will clear the surface when installed.

11. Remove the wheel nuts and wheel.

To install:

12. Install the spare tire and loosely tighten the wheel nuts.

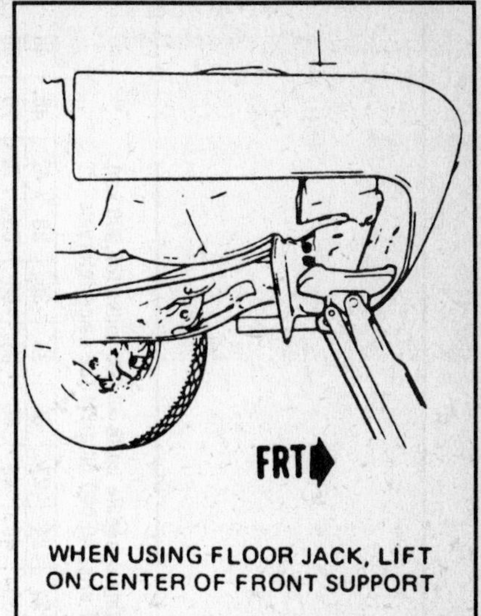

FIG. 43 Lift point for the front of the vehicle

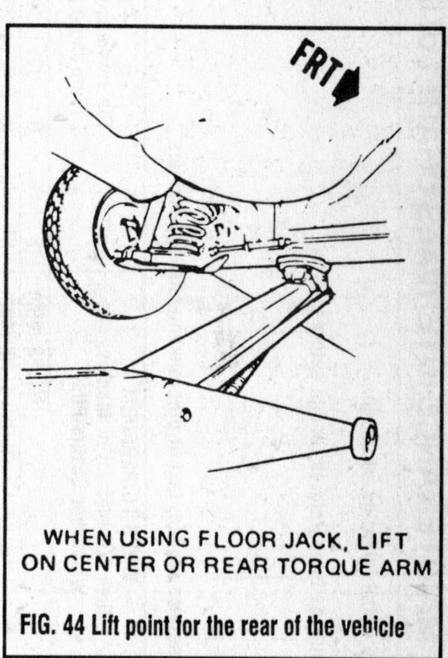

FIG. 44 Lift point for the rear of the vehicle

13. Connect the UP/ON side of the ratchet to the socket and tighten the wheel nuts in a criss-cross sequence.

14. Lower the vehicle and remove the jack.

15. Retighten the wheel nuts securely to 100 ft. lbs. (140 Nm).

16. Install the wheel cover and securely store all jacking equipment.

17. Start driving the vehicle slowly to see if everything is secure.

MAINTENANCE INTERVALS CHART I of II

Follow Schedule I if the car is mainly operated under one or more of the following conditions:

- **When most trips are less than 4 miles (6 kilometers).**
- **When most trips are less than 10 miles (16 kilometers) and outside temperatures remain below freezing.**
- **Idling and/or low-speed operation in stop-and-go traffic.**
- **Towing a trailer**
- **Operating in dusty areas.**

Schedule I should also be followed if the car is used for delivery service, police, taxi or other commercial applications.

ITEM NO.	TO BE SERVICED	WHEN TO PERFORM Miles (Kilometers) or Months, Whichever Occurs First	The services shown in this schedule up to 48,000 miles (80,000 km) are to be performed after 48,000 miles at the same intervals															
		MILES (000)	3	6	9	12	15	18	21	24	27	30	33	36	39	42	45	48
		KILOMETERS (000)	5	10	15	20	25	30	35	40	45	50	55	60	65	70	75	80
1	Engine Oil & Filter Change*	Every 3,000 (5,000 km) or 3 mos.	●	●	●	●	●	●	●	●	●	●	●	●	●	●	●	●
2	Chassis Lubrication	Every other oil change		●		●		●		●		●		●		●		●
3	Carb. Choke & Hose Insp.* (If Equipped)††	At 6,000 mi. (10,000 km) and then every 30,000 mi. (50,000 km)		●								●						
4	Carb. or Throttle Body Mount Bolt Torque (Some Models)*	At 6,000 mi. (10,000 km) only		●														
5	Eng. Idle Speed Adj. (Some Models)*			●														
6	Tire & Wheel Insp. and Rotation	At 6,000 mi. (10,000 km) and then every 15,000 mi. (25,000 km)		●					●					●				
7	Vac. or Air Pump Drive Belt Insp.*	Every 30,000 mi. (50,000 km) or 24 mos.										●						
8	Cooling System Service*											●						
9	Wheel Brg. Repack (Rear-Wheel-Drive Cars Only)	See explanation for service interval																
10	Transmission/Transaxle Service																	
11	Spark Plug Service*	Every 30,000 mi. (50,000 km)										●						
12	Spark Plug Wire Insp. (Some Models)*											●						
13	PCV Valve Insp. (Some Models)*††											●						
14	EGR System Insp.*††	Every 30,000 mi. (50,000 km) or 36 mos.										●						
15	Air Cleaner & PCV Filter Rep.*											●						
16	Eng. Timing Check (Some Models)*	Every 30,000 (50,000 km)										●						
17	Fuel Tank, Cap & Lines Insp.*††											●						
18	Thermostatically Controlled Air Cleaner Insp. (Some Models)*											●						

FOOTNOTES: * An Emission Control Service

†† The U.S. Environmental Protection Agency has determined that the failure to perform this maintenance item will not nullify the emission warranty or limit recall liability prior to the completion of vehicle useful life. General Motors, however, urges that all recommended maintenance services be performed at the indicated intervals and the maintenance be recorded in Section C of the owner's maintenance schedule.

MAINTENANCE INTERVALS CHART II of II

Follow Schedule II if, as a general rule, the car is driven on a daily basis for several miles (km) and none of the above conditions apply.

ITEM NO.	TO BE SERVICED	WHEN TO PERFORM Miles (Kilometers) or Months, Whichever Occurs First	The services shown in this schedule up to 45,000 miles (75,000 km) are to be performed after 45,000 miles at the same intervals					
		MILES (000)	7.5	15	22.5	30	37.5	45
		KILOMETERS (000)	12.5	25	37.5	50	62.5	75
1	Engine Oil & Filter Change*	Every 7,500 mi. (12,500 km) or 12 mos.	●	●	●	●	●	●
	Filter Change*	At first and every other oil change or 12 mos.	●		●		●	
2	Chassis Lubrication	Every 7,500 mi. (12,500 km) or 12 mos.	●	●	●	●	●	●
3	Carb. Choke & Hose Insp.* (If Equipped)††	At 7,500 mi. (12,500 km) and then at each 30,000 mi. (50,000 km) interval	●			●		
4	Carb. or Throttle Body Mount Bolt Torque (Some Models)*	At 7,500 mi. (12,500 km) only	●					
5	Eng. Idle Speed Adj. (Some Models)*		●					
6	Tire & Wheel Insp. and Rotation	At 7,500 mi. (12,500 km) and then every 15,000 mi. (25,000 km)	●		●		●	
7	Vac. or Air Pump Drive Belt Insp.*	Every 30,000 mi. (50,000 km) or 24 mos.				●		
8	Cooling System Service*					●		
9	Wheel Brg. Repack (Rear-Wheel-Drive Cars Only)	Every 30,000 mi. (50,000 km)				●		
10	Transmission/Transaxle Service	See explanation for service interval						
11	Spark Plug Service*	Every 30,000 mi. (50,000 km)				●		
12	Spark Plug Wire Insp. (Some Models)*					●		
13	PCV Valve Insp. (Some Models)*††					●		
14	EGR System Insp.*††	Every 30,000 mi. (50,000 km) or 36 mos.				●		
15	Air Cleaner & PCV Filter Rep.*					●		
16	Eng. Timing Check (Some Models)*	Every 30,000 (50,000 km)				●		
17	Fuel Tank, Cap & Lines Insp.*††					●		
18	Thermostatically Controlled Air Cleaner Insp. (Some Models)*					●		

FOOTNOTES: * An Emission Control Service
†† The U.S. Environmental Protection Agency has determined that the failure to perform this maintenance item will not nullify the emission warranty or limit recall liability prior to the completion of vehicle useful life. General Motors, however, urges that all recommended maintenance services be performed at the indicated intervals and the maintenance be recorded in Section C of the owner's maintenance schedule.

CAPACITIES

Year	Model	VIN	No. Cylinder Displacement cu. in. (liter)	Engine Crankcase with Filter	Transmission (pts.)		Drive Axle (pts.)	Fuel Tank (gal.)	Cooling System (qts.)
					5-Spd	Auto.			
1985	Grand Am	U	151 (2.5)	3.5	5.4	11.7	—	13.6	7.9①
	Grand Am	L	181 (3.0)	4.5	—	18.0	—	13.6	10.3
	Calais	U	151 (2.5)	3.5	5.4	11.7	—	13.6	7.9①
	Calais	L	181 (3.0)	4.5	—	18.0	—	13.6	10.3
	Somerset	U	151 (2.5)	3.5	5.4	11.7	—	13.6	7.9①
	Somerset	L	181 (3.0)	4.5	—	18.0	—	13.6	10.3
1986	Grand Am	U	151 (2.5)	3.5	5.4	11.7	—	13.6	7.9①
	Grand Am	L	181 (3.0)	4.5	—	18.0	—	13.6	10.3
	Calais	U	151 (2.5)	3.5	5.4	11.7	—	13.6	7.9①
	Calais	L	181 (3.0)	4.5	—	18.0	—	13.6	10.3
	Somerset	U	151 (2.5)	3.5	5.4	11.7	—	13.6	7.9①
	Somerset	L	181 (3.0)	4.5	—	18.0	—	13.6	10.3
	Skylark	U	151 (2.5)	3.5	5.4	11.7	—	13.6	7.9①
	Skylark	L	181 (3.0)	4.5	—	18.0	—	13.6	10.3
1987	Grand Am	K	122 (2.0)	4.0	6.0	11.0	—	13.6	7.8①
	Grand Am	M	122 (2.0)	4.0	6.0	11.0	—	13.6	7.8①
	Grand Am	U	151 (2.5)	3.5	5.4	11.7	—	13.6	7.9
	Grand Am	L	181 (3.0)	4.5	—	18.0	—	13.6	10.3
	Calais	U	151 (2.5)	3.5	5.4	11.7	—	13.6	7.9①
	Calais	L	181 (3.0)	4.5	—	18.0	—	13.6	10.3
	Somerset	U	151 (2.5)	3.5	5.4	11.7	—	13.6	7.9①
	Somerset	L	181 (3.0)	4.5	—	18.0	—	13.6	10.3
	Skylark	U	151 (2.5)	3.5	5.4	11.7	—	13.6	7.9①
	Skylark	L	181 (3.0)	4.5	—	18.0	—	13.6	10.3
1988	Grand Am	M	4-122 (2.0)	4	4	8	—	13.6	8
	Grand Am	D	4-138 (2.3)	4	4	8	—	13.6	8
	Grand Am	U	4-151 (2.5)	4	5.3	8	—	13.6	8
	Calais	D	4-138 (2.3)	4	4	8	—	13.6	8
	Calais	U	4-151 (2.5)	4	5.3	8	—	13.6	8
	Calais	L	6-181 (3.0)	4	—	8	—	13.6	10
	Skylark	D	4-138 (2.3)	4	—	8	—	13.6	8
	Skylark	U	4-151 (2.5)	4	—	8	—	13.6	8
	Skylark	L	6-181 (3.0)	4	—	8	—	13.6	10
1989	Grand Am	M	4-122 (2.0)	4	4	8	—	13.6	8
	Grand Am	A	4-138 (2.3)	4	4	—	—	13.6	8
	Grand Am	D	4-138 (2.3)	4	4	8	—	13.6	8
	Grand Am	U	4-151 (2.5)	4	4	8	—	13.6	8
	Calais	A	4-138 (2.3)	4	4	—	—	13.6	8
	Calais	D	4-138 (2.3)	4	4	8	—	13.6	8
	Calais	U	4-151 (2.5)	4	4	8	—	13.6	8
	Calais	N	6-204 (3.3)	4	—	8	—	13.6	10
	Skylark	D	4-138 (2.3)	4	—	8	—	13.6	8
	Skylark	U	4-151 (2.5)	4	—	8	—	13.6	8
	Skylark	N	6-204 (3.3)	4	—	8	—	13.6	10

CAPACITIES

Year	Model	VIN	No. Cylinder Displacement cu. in. (liter)	Engine Crankcase with Filter	Transmission (pts.) 5-Spd	Transmission (pts.) Auto.	Drive Axle (pts.)	Fuel Tank (gal.)	Cooling System (qts.)
1990	Grand Am	A	4-138 (2.3)	4	4	—	—	13.6	8
	Grand Am	D	4-138 (2.3)	4	4	8	—	13.6	8
	Grand Am	U	4-151 (2.5)	4	4	8	—	13.6	8
	Calais	A	4-138 (2.3)	4	4	—	—	13.6	8
	Calais	D	4-138 (2.3)	4	4	8	—	13.6	8
	Calais	U	4-151 (2.5)	4	4	8	—	13.6	8
	Calais	N	6-204 (3.3)	4	—	8	—	13.6	10
	Skylark	D	4-138 (2.3)	4	—	8	—	13.6	8
	Skylark	U	4-151 (2.5)	4	—	8	—	13.6	8
	Skylark	N	6-204 (3.3)	4	—	8	—	13.6	10
1991	Grand Am	A	4-138 (2.3)	4	4	8	—	13.6	10.4
	Grand Am	D	4-138 (2.3)	4	4	8	—	13.6	10.4
	Grand Am	U	4-151 (2.5)	4	4	8	—	13.6	10.7
	Calais	A	4-138 (2.3)	4	4	—	—	13.6	10.4
	Calais	D	4-138 (2.3)	4	4	8	—	13.6	10.4
	Calais	U	4-151 (2.5)	4	4	8	—	13.6	10.7
	Calais	N	6-204 (3.3)	4	—	8	—	13.6	12.7
	Skylark	D	4-138 (2.3)	4	—	8	—	13.6	10.4
	Skylark	U	4-151 (2.5)	4	—	8	—	13.6	10.7
	Skylark	N	6-204 (3.3)	4	—	8	—	13.6	12.7
1992	Grand Am	A	4-138 (2.3)	4	4	8	—	13.6	10.4
	Grand Am	D	4-138 (2.3)	4	4	8	—	13.6	10.4
	Grand Am	U	4-151 (2.5)	4	4	8	—	13.6	10.7
	Achieva	A	4-138 (2.3)	4	4	—	—	13.6	10.4
	Achieva	D	4-138 (2.3)	4	4	8	—	13.6	10.4
	Achieva	3	4-138 (2.3)	4	4	8	—	13.6	10.4
	Achieva	N	6-204 (3.3)	4	—	8	—	13.6	12.7
	Skylark	3	4-138 (2.3)	4	—	8	—	13.6	10.4
	Skylark	N	6-204 (3.3)	4	—	8	—	13.6	12.7

Troubleshooting Basic Air Conditioning Problems

Problem	Cause	Solution
There's little or no air coming from the vents (and you're sure it's on)	• The A/C fuse is blown • Broken or loose wires or connections • The on/off switch is defective	• Check and/or replace fuse • Check and/or repair connections • Replace switch
The air coming from the vents is not cool enough	• Windows and air vent wings open • The compressor belt is slipping • Heater is on • Condenser is clogged with debris • Refrigerant has escaped through a leak in the system • Receiver/drier is plugged	• Close windows and vent wings • Tighten or replace compressor belt • Shut heater off • Clean the condenser • Check system • Service system
The air has an odor	• Vacuum system is disrupted • Odor producing substances on the evaporator case • Condensation has collected in the bottom of the evaporator housing	• Have the system checked/repaired • Clean the evaporator case • Clean the evaporator housing drains
System is noisy or vibrating	• Compressor belt or mountings loose • Air in the system	• Tighten or replace belt; tighten mounting bolts • Have the system serviced
Sight glass condition		
Constant bubbles, foam or oil streaks	• Undercharged system	• Charge the system
Clear sight glass, but no cold air	• No refrigerant at all	• Check and charge the system
Clear sight glass, but air is cold	• System is OK	
Clouded with milky fluid	• Receiver drier is leaking dessicant	• Have system checked
Large difference in temperature of lines	• System undercharged	• Charge and leak test the system
Compressor noise	• Broken valves • Overcharged • Incorrect oil level • Piston slap • Broken rings • Drive belt pulley bolts are loose	• Replace the valve plate • Discharge, evacuate and install the correct charge • Isolate the compressor and check the oil level. Correct as necessary. • Replace the compressor • Replace the compressor • Tighten with the correct torque specification
Excessive vibration	• Incorrect belt tension • Clutch loose • Overcharged • Pulley is misaligned	• Adjust the belt tension • Tighten the clutch • Discharge, evacuate and install the correct charge • Align the pulley
Condensation dripping in the passenger compartment	• Drain hose plugged or improperly positioned • Insulation removed or improperly installed	• Clean the drain hose and check for proper installation • Replace the insulation on the expansion valve and hoses

Troubleshooting Basic Air Conditioning Problems (cont.)

Problem	Cause	Solution
Frozen evaporator coil	• Faulty thermostat • Thermostat capillary tube improperly installed • Thermostat not adjusted properly	• Replace the thermostat • Install the capillary tube correctly • Adjust the thermostat
Low side low—high side low	• System refrigerant is low • Expansion valve is restricted	• Evacuate, leak test and charge the system • Replace the expansion valve
Low side high—high side low	• Internal leak in the compressor—worn	• Remove the compressor cylinder head and inspect the compressor. Replace the valve plate assembly if necessary. If the compressor pistons, rings or
Low side high—high side low (cont.)		cylinders are excessively worn or scored replace the compressor
	• Cylinder head gasket is leaking • Expansion valve is defective • Drive belt slipping	• Install a replacement cylinder head gasket • Replace the expansion valve • Adjust the belt tension
Low side high—high side high	• Condenser fins obstructed • Air in the system • Expansion valve is defective • Loose or worn fan belts	• Clean the condenser fins • Evacuate, leak test and charge the system • Replace the expansion valve • Adjust or replace the belts as necessary
Low side low—high side high	• Expansion valve is defective • Restriction in the refrigerant hose	• Replace the expansion valve • Check the hose for kinks—replace if necessary
Low side low—high side high	• Restriction in the receiver/drier • Restriction in the condenser	• Replace the receiver/drier • Replace the condenser
Low side and high normal (inadequate cooling)	• Air in the system • Moisture in the system	• Evacuate, leak test and charge the system • Evacuate, leak test and charge the system

Troubleshooting Basic Wheel Problems

Problem	Cause	Solution
The car's front end vibrates at high speed	• The wheels are out of balance • Wheels are out of alignment	• Have wheels balanced • Have wheel alignment checked/adjusted
Car pulls to either side	• Wheels are out of alignment • Unequal tire pressure • Different size tires or wheels	• Have wheel alignment checked/adjusted • Check/adjust tire pressure • Change tires or wheels to same size
The car's wheel(s) wobbles	• Loose wheel lug nuts • Wheels out of balance • Damaged wheel • Wheels are out of alignment • Worn or damaged ball joint • Excessive play in the steering linkage (usually due to worn parts) • Defective shock absorber	• Tighten wheel lug nuts • Have tires balanced • Raise car and spin the wheel. If the wheel is bent, it should be replaced • Have wheel alignment checked/adjusted • Check ball joints • Check steering linkage • Check shock absorbers
Tires wear unevenly or prematurely	• Incorrect wheel size • Wheels are out of balance • Wheels are out of alignment	• Check if wheel and tire size are compatible • Have wheels balanced • Have wheel alignment checked/adjusted

Troubleshooting Basic Tire Problems

Problem	Cause	Solution
The car's front end vibrates at high speeds and the steering wheel shakes	• Wheels out of balance • Front end needs aligning	• Have wheels balanced • Have front end alignment checked
The car pulls to one side while cruising	• Unequal tire pressure (car will usually pull to the low side) • Mismatched tires • Front end needs aligning	• Check/adjust tire pressure • Be sure tires are of the same type and size • Have front end alignment checked
Abnormal, excessive or uneven tire wear See "How to Read Tire Wear"	• Infrequent tire rotation • Improper tire pressure • Sudden stops/starts or high speed on curves	• Rotate tires more frequently to equalize wear • Check/adjust pressure • Correct driving habits
Tire squeals	• Improper tire pressure • Front end needs aligning	• Check/adjust tire pressure • Have front end alignment checked

Tire Size Comparison Chart

"Letter" sizes			Inch Sizes	Metric-inch Sizes		
"60 Series"	"70 Series"	"78 Series"	1965–77	"60 Series"	"70 Series"	"80 Series"
			5.50-12, 5.60-12	165/60-12	165/70-12	155-12
		Y78-12	6.00-12			
		W78-13	5.20-13	165/60-13	145/70-13	135-13
		Y78-13	5.60-13	175/60-13	155/70-13	145-13
			6.15-13	185/60-13	165/70-13	155-13, P155/80-13
A60-13	A70-13	A78-13	6.40-13	195/60-13	175/70-13	165-13
B60-13	B70-13	B78-13	6.70-13	205/60-13	185/70-13	175-13
			6.90-13			
C60-13	C70-13	C78-13	7.00-13	215/60-13	195/70-13	185-13
D60-13	D70-13	D78-13	7.25-13			
E60-13	E70-13	E78-13	7.75-13			195-13
			5.20-14	165/60-14	145/70-14	135-14
			5.60-14	175/60-14	155/70-14	145-14
			5.90-14			
A60-14	A70-14	A78-14	6.15-14	185/60-14	165/70-14	155-14
	B70-14	B78-14	6.45-14	195/60-14	175/70-14	165-14
	C70-14	C78-14	6.95-14	205/60-14	185/70-14	175-14
D60-14	D70-14	D78-14				
E60-14	E70-14	E78-14	7.35-14	215/60-14	195/70-14	185-14
F60-14	F70-14	F78-14, F83-14	7.75-14	225/60-14	200/70-14	195-14
G60-14	G70-14	G77-14, G78-14	8.25-14	235/60-14	205/70-14	205-14
H60-14	H70-14	H78-14	8.55-14	245/60-14	215/70-14	215-14
J60-14	J70-14	J78-14	8.85-14	255/60-14	225/70-14	225-14
L60-14	L70-14		9.15-14	265/60-14	235/70-14	
	A70-15	A78-15	5.60-15	185/60-15	165/70-15	155-15
B60-15	B70-15	B78-15	6.35-15	195/60-15	175/70-15	165-15
C60-15	C70-15	C78-15	6.85-15	205/60-15	185/70-15	175-15
	D70-15	D78-15				
E60-15	E70-15	E78-15	7.35-15	215/60-15	195/70-15	185-15
F60-15	F70-15	F78-15	7.75-15	225/60-15	205/70-15	195-15
G60-15	G70-15	G78-15	8.15-15/8.25-15	235/60-15	215/70-15	205-15
H60-15	H70-15	H78-15	8.45-15/8.55-15	245/60-15	225/70-15	215-15
J60-15	J70-15	J78-15	8.85-15/8.90-15	255/60-15	235/70-15	225-15
	K70-15		9.00-15	265/60-15	245/70-15	230-15
L60-15	L70-15	L78-15, L84-15	9.15-15			235-15
	M70-15	M78-15				255-15
		N78-15				

NOTE: Every size tire is not listed and many size comaprisons are approximate, based on load ratings. Wider tires than those supplied new with the vehicle should always be checked for clearance

2
ENGINE PERFORMANCE AND TUNE-UP
Computer Controlled Coil Ignition 2-27
Direct Ignition System 2-26
Electronic Ignition 2-28
Firing Orders 2-7
HEI Ignition System 2-8
Idle Speed and Mixture Adjustment 2-31
Ignition Timing 2-30
Integrated Direct Ignition System 2-16
Tune-up Charts 2-2
Valve Lash Adjustment 2-31

TUNE-UP SPECIFICATIONS

Year	VIN	No. Cylinder Displacement cu. in. (liter)	Spark Plugs Gap (in.)	Ignition Timing (deg.) MT	Ignition Timing (deg.) AT	Fuel Pump (psi)	Idle Speed (rpm) MT	Idle Speed (rpm) AT	Valve Clearance In.	Valve Clearance Ex.
1985	U	4-151 (2.5)	0.060	8B	8B	12	①	①	Hyd.	Hyd.
	L	6-181 (3.0)	0.040	15B	15B	34–44	①	①	Hyd.	Hyd.
1986	U	4-151 (2.5)	0.060	8B	8B	12	①	①	Hyd.	Hyd.
	L	6-181 (3.0)	0.040	15B	15B	34–44	①	①	Hyd.	Hyd.
1987	K	4-122 (2.0) ④	0.035	8B	8B	—	①	①	Hyd.	Hyd.
	M	4-122 (2.0) ②	0.035	8B	8B	—	①	①	Hyd.	Hyd.
	D	4-138 (2.3)	0.035	—	—	34–44	—	—	Hyd.	Hyd.
	U	4-151 (2.5)	0.060	8B	8B	12	①	①	Hyd.	Hyd.
	L	6-181 (3.0)	0.040	15B	15B	34–44	①	①	Hyd.	Hyd.
1988	K	4-122 (2.0) ④	0.035	8B	8B	—	①	①	Hyd.	Hyd.
	M	4-122 (2.0) ②	0.035	8B	8B	—	①	①	Hyd.	Hyd.
	D	4-138 (2.3)	0.035	—	—	34–44	—	—	Hyd.	Hyd.
	U	4-151 (2.5)	0.060	—	—	9–13	①	①	Hyd.	Hyd.
	L	6-181 (3.0)	0.045	③	③	34–44	①	①	Hyd.	Hyd.
1989	M	4-122 (2.0) ②	0.035	8B	8B	—	①	①	Hyd.	Hyd.
	A	4-138 (2.3)	0.035	—	—	34–44	①	—	Hyd.	Hyd.
	D	4-138 (2.3)	0.035	—	—	34–44	—	—	Hyd.	Hyd.
	U	4-151 (2.5)	0.060	—	—	9–13	①	①	Hyd.	Hyd.
	N	6-204 (3.3)	0.060	—	—	36–43	①	①	Hyd.	Hyd.
1990	A	4-138 (2.3)	0.035	⑤	⑤	⑦	⑥	⑥	Hyd.	Hyd.
	D	4-138 (2.3)	0.035	⑤	⑤	⑦	⑥	⑥	Hyd.	Hyd.
	U	4-151 (2.5)	0.060	⑤	⑤	9–13	⑥	⑥	Hyd.	Hyd.
	N	6-204 (3.3)	0.060	—	⑤	⑦	—	⑥	Hyd.	Hyd.
1991	A	4-138 (2.3)	0.035	⑤	⑤	⑦	⑥	⑥	Hyd.	Hyd.
	D	4-138 (2.3)	0.035	⑤	⑤	⑦	⑥	⑥	Hyd.	Hyd.
	U	4-151 (2.5)	0.060	⑤	⑤	9–13	⑥	⑥	Hyd.	Hyd.
	N	6-204 (3.3)	0.060	—	⑤	⑦	⑥	⑥	Hyd.	Hyd.
1992	A	4-138 (2.3)	0.035	⑤	⑤	⑦	⑥	⑥	Hyd.	Hyd.
	D	4-138 (2.3)	0.035	⑤	⑤	⑦	⑥	⑥	Hyd.	Hyd.
	3	4-138 (2.3)	0.035	⑤	⑤	⑦	⑥	⑥	Hyd.	Hyd.
	U	4-151 (2.5)	0.060	⑤	⑤	9–13	⑥	⑥	Hyd.	Hyd.
	N	6-204 (3.3)	0.060	—	⑤	⑦	—	⑥	Hyd.	Hyd.

NOTE: The Underhood Specifications sticker often reflects tune-up specification changes in production. Sticker figures must be used if they disagree with those in this chart.

B—Before Top Dead Center
Hyd.—Hydraulic
① See Underhood Specifications sticker
② Turbocharged
③ No timing adjustment required with C³I ignition
④ Non-Turbocharged
⑤ Ignition timing is controlled by the ECM and is not adjustable
⑥ Idle speed is controlled by the ECM and is not adjustable
⑦ 1—Connect fuel pressure gauge, engine at normal operating temperature.
2—Turn ignition switch on.
3—After approx. 2 seconds; pressure should read 41–47 psi and hold steady.
4—Start engine and idle; pressure should drop 3–10 psi fropm static pressure.

TUNE-UP PROCEDURES

To get the best performance and fuel economy, it is essential that the engine be properly tuned at regular intervals. A periodic tune-up will keep your vehicle's engine running smoothly and will prevent annoying minor breakdowns and poor performance associated with a poorly tuned engine.

Before the days of unleaded fuel, electronic fuel injection, and electronically controlled ignition systems which, initially, did away with mechanical breaker points and has, on most of the newer engines, done away with the distributor altogether, the tune-up was a much more involved process, requiring a delicate ear and just the right touch in order to fine tune an engine. On today's engines, ignition timing, and idle speed and mixture are controlled electronically, by the Electronic Control Module (ECM) and are not adjustable. The choke function has been incorporated into the fuel injection system and is no longer a separate component requiring periodic service and adjustment. In addition, with the advent of unleaded fuel and improved manufacturing techniques, spark plugs last longer. In fact, if your vehicle is equipped with the 2.3L engine, the Integrated Direct Ignition (IDI) system has even eliminated the spark plugs wires, and with them, the need for periodic inspection and replacement. Accordingly, whereas in the 'old days' the engine might have received a seasonal tune-up, one for the winter months and another for summer, the tune-up now consists of replacing the spark plugs, changing the air, fuel and PCV breather filters and performing a detailed visual inspection of the spark plug wires (if equipped!), vacuum, fuel and air lines and coolant hoses every 30,000 miles (48,300km).

This Section will include information about the ignition systems for the engines that may be installed in your Skylark, Somerset, Calais, Achieva or Grand Am. Although, as mentioned, not much of what you will read about is dealt with in the tune-up.

Under normal driving conditions, the tune-up should be performed every 30,000 miles (48,300km). This interval should be halved if the vehicle is operated under severe conditions, such as trailer towing, prolonged idling, continual stop and start driving, or if starting or running problems are noticed. It is assumed that the routine maintenance described in Section 1 has been kept up, as this will have a decided effect on the results of a tune-up. Follow the tune-up steps in order.

If the specifications listed in the on the Tune-Up Specifications chart in this Section differ from those found on the Vehicle Emission Control Information (VECI) label located in the engine compartment (usually on the radiator support) follow the specs on the VECI label. The VECI label often reflects changes made during the production run.

Spark Plugs

A typical spark plug consists of a metal shell surrounding a ceramic insulator. A metal electrode extends downward through the center of the insulator and protrudes a small distance. Located at the end of the plug and attached to the side of the outer metal shell is the side electrode. The side electrode bends in at a 90 angle so that its tip is even with, and parallel to, the tip of the center electrode. The distance between these two electrodes (measured in thousandths of an inch or hundreths of a millimeter) is called the spark plug gap.

The spark plug in no way produces a spark but merely provides a gap across which the current can arc. The coil produces 20,000–40,000 volts or more, which travels from the coils, through the spark plug wires to the spark plugs. The current passes along the center electrode and jumps the gap to the side electrode, and, in so doing, ignites the air/fuel mixture in the combustion chamber.

SPARK PLUG HEAT RANGE

Spark plug heat range is the ability of the plug to dissipate heat. The longer the insulator (or the farther it extends into the engine), the hotter the plug will operate; the shorter the insulator the cooler it will operate. A plug that absorbs little heat and remains too cool will quickly accumulate deposits of oil and carbon since it is not hot enough to burn them off. This leads to plug fouling and consequently to misfiring. A plug that absorbs too much heat may have deposits also, but due to the higher temperatures, the electrodes will burn away quickly. In some instances, the higher temperatures may lead to preignition. Preignition takes place when plug tips get so hot that they glow sufficiently to ignite the fuel/air mixture before the actual spark occurs. This early ignition will usually result in the 'pinging' experienced during low speeds and heavy loads.

The general rule of thumb for choosing the correct heat range when picking a spark plug is, if most of your driving is long distance, high speed travel, use a colder plug; if most of your driving is stop and go, use a hotter plug. In general, however, unless you are experiencing a problem use the factory recommended spark plugs.

A set of spark plugs usually requires replacement after about 30,000 miles (48,300km) on cars with electronic ignition, depending on your style of driving. In normal operation, plug gap increases about 0.001 in. (0.0254mm) for every 1,000–2,500 miles (1600–4000km). As the gap increases, the plug's voltage requirement also increases. It requires a greater voltage to jump the wider gap and about two to three times as much voltage to fire a plug at high speeds than at idle.

REMOVAL & INSTALLATION

➧ SEE FIGS. 1–5

2.0L (VIN K and M) Engine

➡ To avoid engine damage, do NOT remove spark plugs when the engine is warm. When you're removing spark plugs, you should work on one at a time. Don't start by removing the plug wires all at once, because unless you number them, they may become mixed up. Take a minute before you begin and number the wires with tape. The best location for numbering is as near as possible to the spark plug boot.

1. Disconnect the negative battery cable.
2. Remove air cleaner components in order to gain access to the spark plugs.
3. Remove the first spark plug cable by pulling and twisting the boot; then remove the spark plug.
4. The 2.0L (VIN K and M) engines use AC Type R42XLS plugs. Properly gap them to 0.035 in. (0.89mm) prior to installation.
5. Lubricate the threads lightly with an anti-seize compound and install the spark plug. Torque to 20 ft. lbs. (27 Nm). Install the cable on the plug. Make sure it snaps in place.
5. Repeat for the remaining spark plugs.
6. Install the air cleaner components.
7. Connect the negative battery cable.

2.3L Engine

The spark plugs on this engine are located under the ignition coil and module assembly. To gain access to the spark plugs, the coil and module assembly must be removed.

➡ **To avoid engine damage, do NOT remove spark plugs when the engine is warm. When you're removing spark plugs, you should work on one at a time. Don't start by removing the plug wires all at once, because unless you number them, they may become mixed up. Take a minute before you begin and number the wires with tape. The best location for numbering is as near as possible to the spark plug boot.**

1. Disconnect the negative battery cable.
2. Remove the air cleaner assembly.
3. Remove the four ignition cover-to-cylinder head bolts.
4. If the spark plug boot sticks, use a spark plug connector removing tool J-36011 or equivalent to remove with a twisting motion.
5. Remove the ignition cover and set aside.
6. Clean any dirt away from the spark plug recess area.
7. Remove the spark plugs with a spark plug socket.

To install:

8. The 2.3L engine uses AC Type FR3LS plugs. Properly gap them to 0.035 in. (0.89mm) prior to installation.
9. Lubricate the threads lightly with an anti-seize compound and install the four spark plugs. Tighten the plugs to 17 ft. lbs. (23 Nm).
10. If removed, install the plug boots and retainers-to-ignition cover.
11. Apply dielectric compound to the plug boot.
12. Install the ignition cover-to-engine while carefully aligning the boots with the spark plug terminals.
13. Apply Loctite® thread locking compound, or equivalent to the ignition cover bolts. Install the bolts and tighten to 15 ft. lbs. (20 Nm).
14. If removed, connect the ignition cover electrical connectors.
15. Install the air cleaner and connect the negative battery cable.

2.5L Engine

1. Disconnect the negative battery cable.
2. Remove air cleaner components in order to gain access to the spark plugs.
3. Remove the first spark plug cable by pulling and twisting the boot; then remove the spark plug.

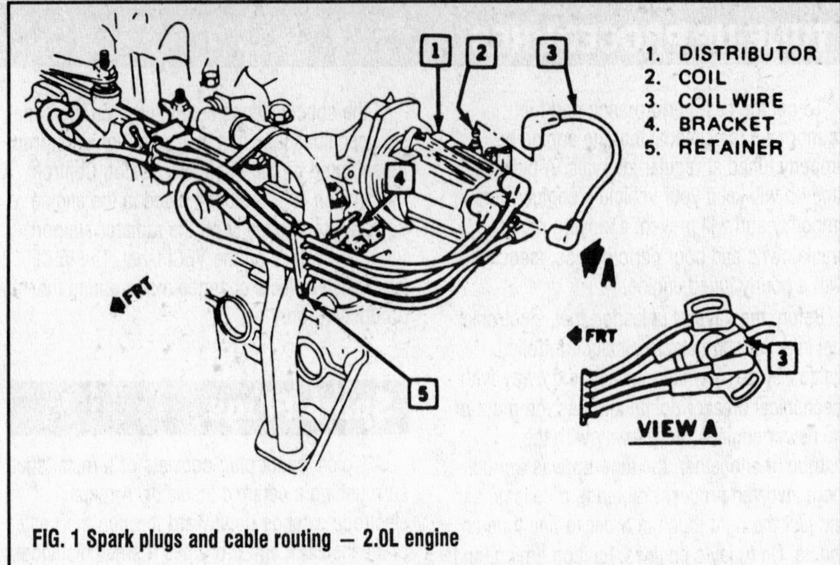

FIG. 1 Spark plugs and cable routing — 2.0L engine

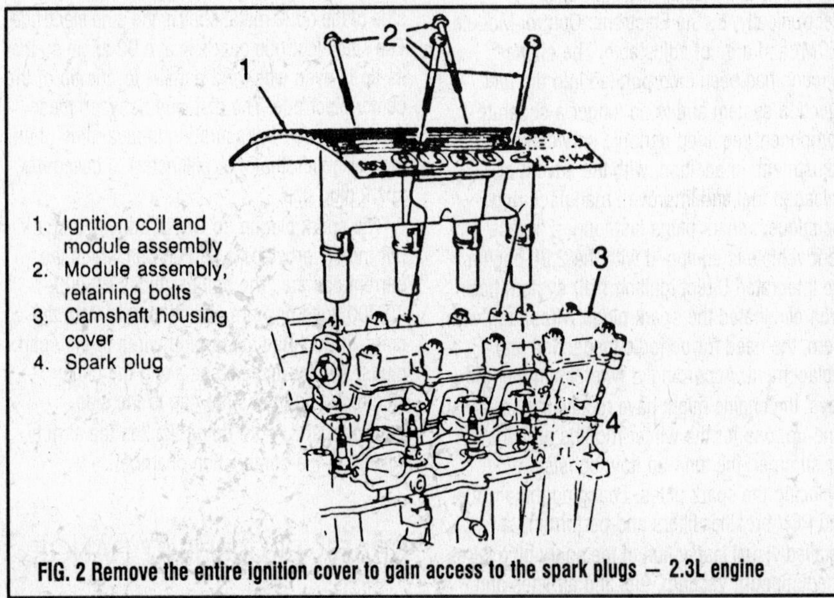

FIG. 2 Remove the entire ignition cover to gain access to the spark plugs — 2.3L engine

4. The 2.5L engine uses AC Type R43TSX or R43TS6 plugs. Properly gap them to 0.060 in. (1.5mm) prior to installation.
5. Lubricate the threads lightly with an anti-seize compound and install the spark plug. Torque to 20 ft. lbs. (27 Nm). Install the cable on the plug. Make sure it snaps in place.
5. Repeat for the remaining spark plugs.
6. Install the air cleaner components.
7. Connect the negative battery cable.

3.0L (VIN L) and 3.3L (VIN N) Engines

1. Disconnect the negative battery cable.
2. Remove the first spark plug cable by twisting the boot half a turn, then pulling up.
3. Remove the spark plug.
4. The 3.0L (VIN L) engine uses AC Type R44LTS plugs and they should be gapped to 0.045 in. (1.1mm) prior to installation. The 3.3L (VIN N) engine uses AC Type R44LTS6 plugs for 1989–90 and R45LTS6 plugs for 1991–92. Gap both types to 0.060 in. (1.5mm).
5. Lubricate the threads lightly with an anti-seize compound and install the spark plug. Torque to 20 ft. lbs. (27 Nm).
6. Install the cable to the plug and snap it in place.
7. Repeat for the remaining spark plugs.
8. Connect the negative battery cable.

CHECKING AND REPLACING SPARK PLUG CABLES

Your vehicle is equipped with an electronic ignition system which utilizes 8mm wires to conduct the hotter spark produced (except 2.3L engine). The boots on these wires are designed to cover the spark plug cavities on the cylinder head. The 2.3L doesn't use spark plug wires. The coil assembly is connected directly to the spark plug with rubber connectors.

Visually inspect the spark plug cables for burns, cuts, or breaks in the insulation. Check the spark plug boots and the nipples on the distributor cap and coil. Replace any damaged wiring. If no physical damage is obvious, the wires can be checked with an ohmmeter for excessive resistance or an open. The resistance specification is 30,000 ohms or less. Always coat the terminals of any wire removed or replaced with a thin layer of dielectric compound.

When installing a new set of spark plug cables, replace the cables one at a time so there will be no mix-up. Start by replacing the longest cable first. Install the boot firmly over the spark plug. Route the wire exactly the same as the original, through all convolute tubing. Make sure the wire is clamped in all holders. Make sure ends snap into place. Repeat the process for each cable.

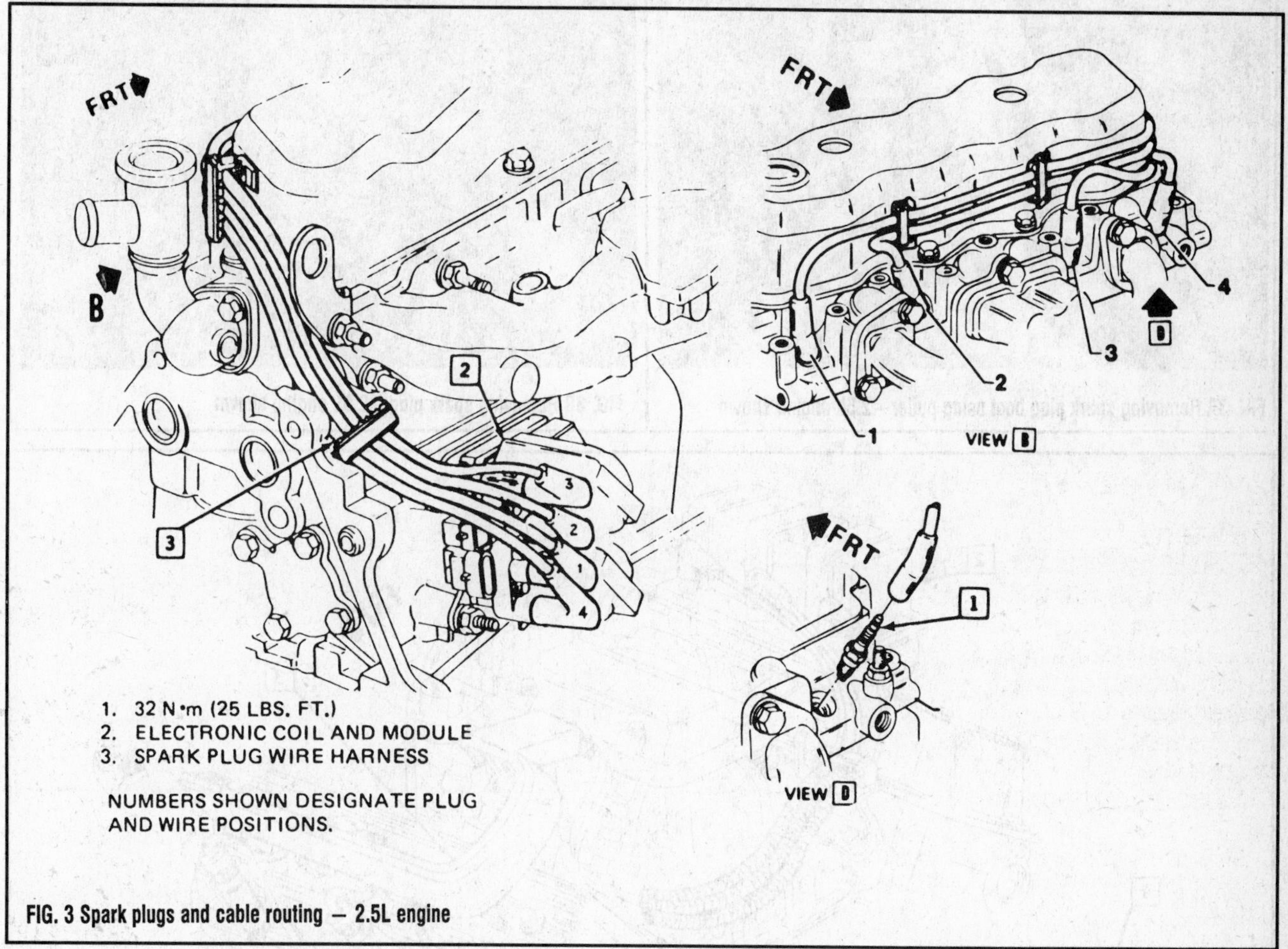

FIG. 3 Spark plugs and cable routing — 2.5L engine

FIG. 3A Removing spark plug boot using puller – 2.5L engine shown

FIG. 3B Removing spark plug – 2.5L engine shown

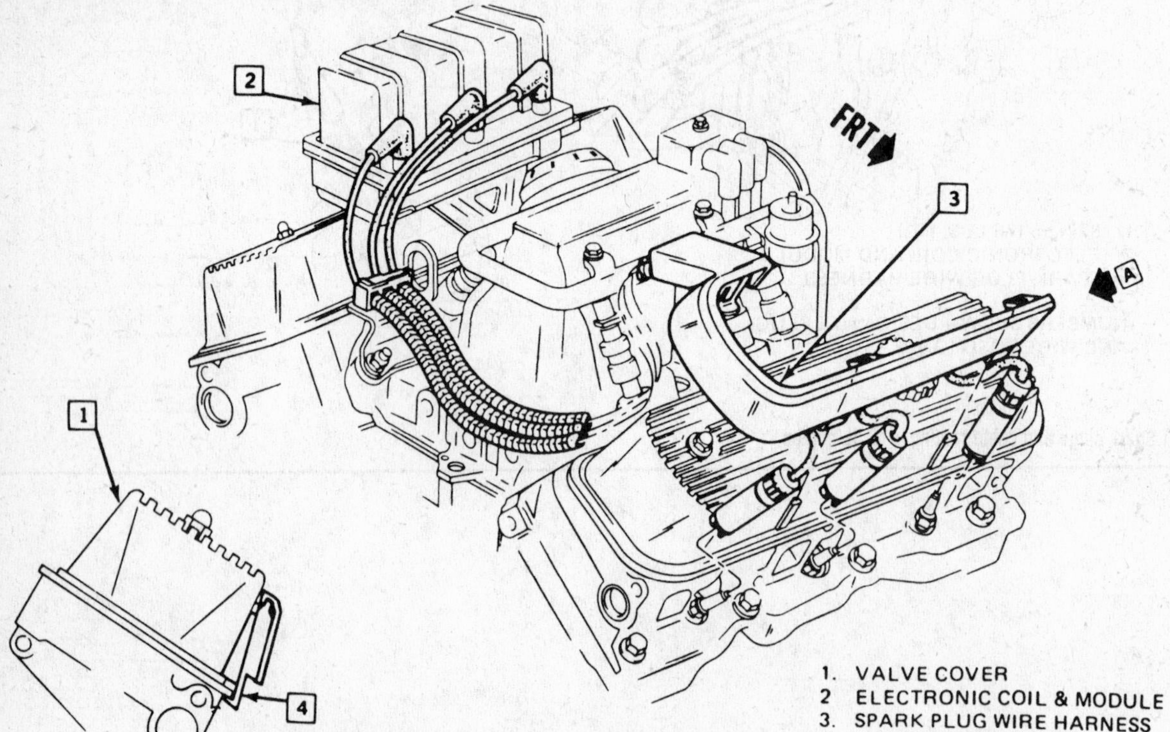

2
FRT
3
A
1
4
VIEW A

TO COMPLETE INSTALLATION, TABS MUST BE FULLY ENGAGED UNDER LOWER EDGE OF VALVE COVER.

1. VALVE COVER
2 ELECTRONIC COIL & MODULE
3. SPARK PLUG WIRE HARNESS
4. HARNESS ASM. TAB

FIG. 4 Spark plugs and cable routing – 3.0L and 3.3L engines

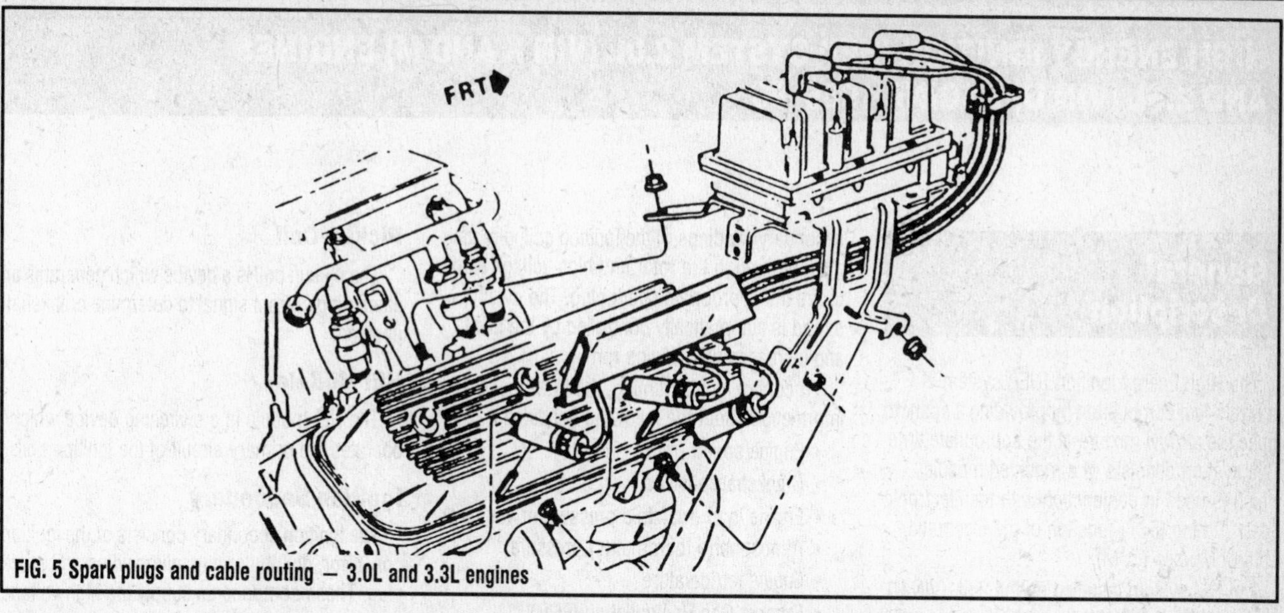

FIG. 5 Spark plugs and cable routing — 3.0L and 3.3L engines

FIRING ORDERS

➧ SEE FIGS. 6–10

➡ **To avoid confusion label, remove, and replace spark plug cables one at a time.**

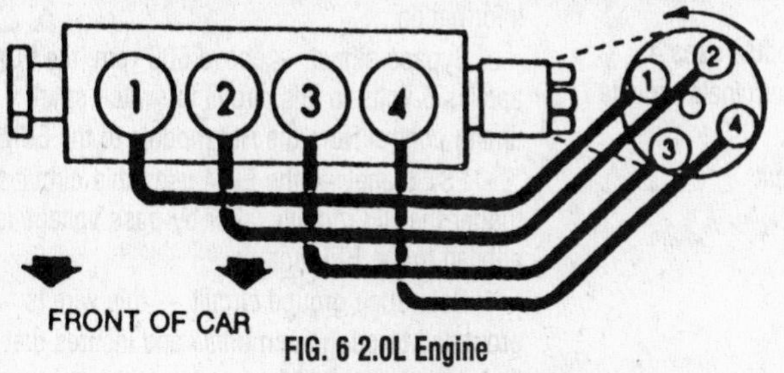

1 2 3 4
1 2 3 4
FRONT OF CAR

FIG. 6 2.0L Engine
Engine Firing Order: 1 – 3 – 4 – 2
Distributor Rotation: Counterclockwise

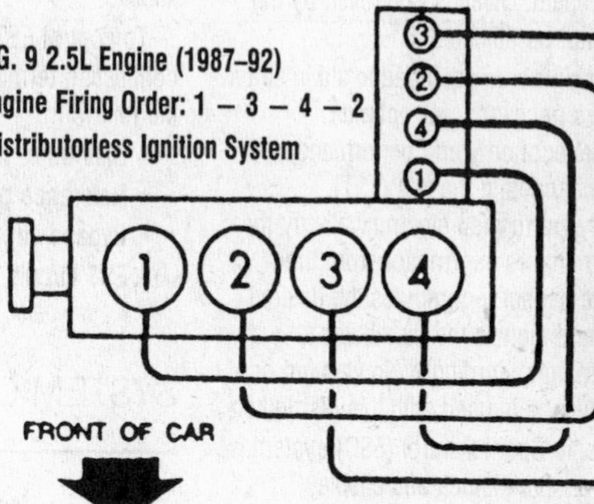

3 2 4 1
1 2 3 4
FRONT OF CAR

FIG. 9 2.5L Engine (1987–92)
Engine Firing Order: 1 – 3 – 4 – 2
Distributorless Ignition System

1 2 3 4
FRONT OF CAR

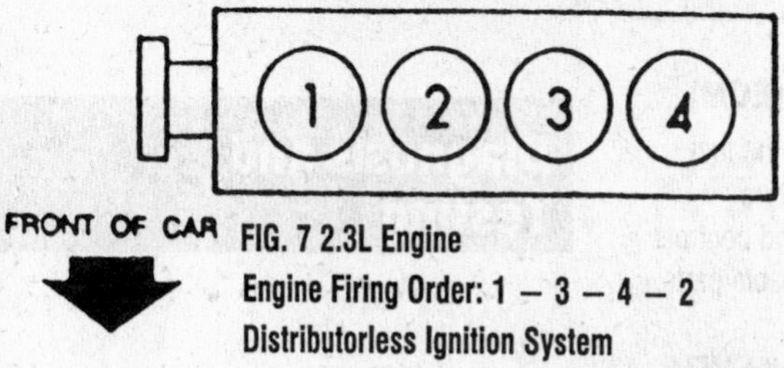

FIG. 7 2.3L Engine
Engine Firing Order: 1 – 3 – 4 – 2
Distributorless Ignition System

4 2 3 1
FRONT OF ENGINE
1 2 3 4
Front of car

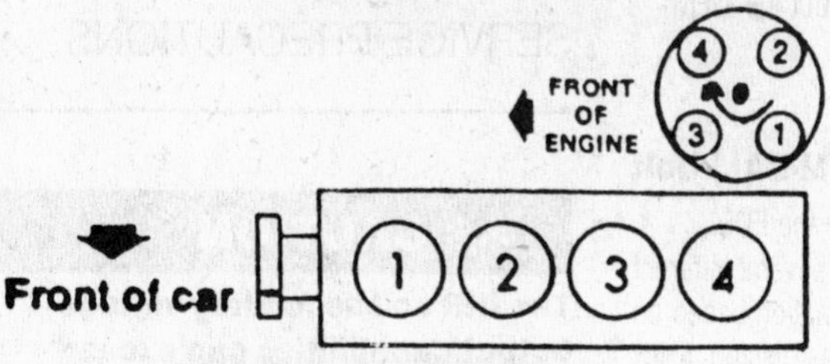

FIG. 8 2.5L Engine (1985–86)
Engine Firing Order: 1 – 3 – 4 – 2
Distributor Rotation: Clockwise

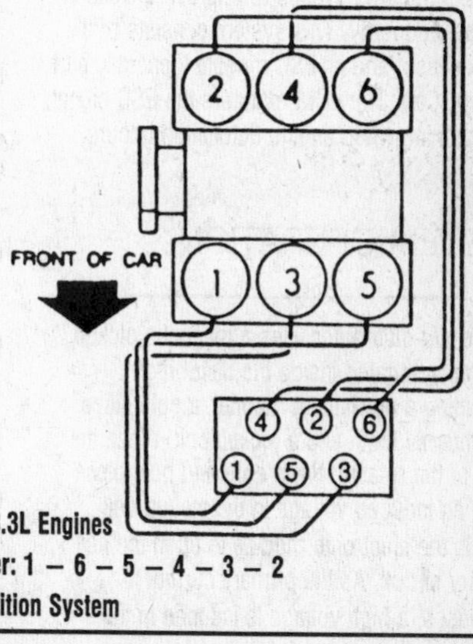

2 4 6
1 3 5
FRONT OF CAR
4 2 6
1 5 3

FIG. 10 3.0L and 3.3L Engines
Engine Firing Order: 1 – 6 – 5 – 4 – 3 – 2
Distributorless Ignition System

HIGH ENERGY IGNITION (HEI) SYSTEM 2.0L (VIN K AND M) ENGINES AND 2.5L (VIN U) ENGINE 1985–86

General Description

The High Energy Ignition (HEI) system controls fuel combustion by providing a spark to ignite the air/fuel mixture at the appropriate time. This system consists of a modified module, which is used in conjunction with the Electronic Spark Timing (EST) function of the Electronic Control Module (ECM).

The HEI system installed on the 2.5L (VIN U) engine is equipped with an externally mounted ignition coil.

The HEI system features a longer spark duration which is essential in firing lean and EGR-diluted air/fuel mixtures. The condenser (capacitor) located within the HEI distributor is provided for noise (static) suppression purposes only and is not a regularly replaced ignition system component. Dwell is controlled by the ECM and cannot be adjusted.

The HEI distributor is equipped to aid in spark timing changes necessary for optimum emissions, fuel economy and performance. All spark timing changes in the HEI (EST) distributors are performed electronically by the ECM, which monitors information from the various engine sensors, computes the desired spark timing and signals the distributor to change the timing accordingly. No vacuum or centrifugal advance is used with this distributor.

The Electronic Spark Control (ESC) system is used to control spark knock and enable maximum spark advance to improve driveability and fuel economy. This system consists of a knock sensor and an ESC module (generally part of Mem-Cal). The ECM monitors the ESC signal to determine when engine detonation occurs.

SYSTEM OPERATION

The HEI distributor uses a magnetic pickup assembly, located inside the distributor containing a permanent magnet, a pole piece with internal teeth and a pickup coil. When the teeth of the rotating timer core and pole piece align, an induced voltage in the pickup coil signals the electronic module to open the coil primary circuit. As the pfimary current decreases, a high voltage is induced in the secondary windings of the ignition coil, directing a spark through the rotor and high voltage leads to fire the appropriate spark plug. The dwell period is automatically controlled by the ECM and increases with engine rpm.

To control ignition timing, the ECM receives information about the following conditions:

- Engine speed (rpm)
- Crankshaft position
- Engine load (manifold pressure or vacuum)
- Atmospheric (barometric) pressure
- Engine temperature
- Exhaust Gas Recirculation (EGR)

The ESC system is designed to retard spark timing 8–10° to reduce spark knock in the engine. When the knock sensor detects spark knock in the engine, it sends an AC voltage signal to the ECM, which increases with the severity of the knock. The ECM then signals the ESC circuit to adjust timing to reduce spark knock.

To control EST, the HEI module uses 4 connecting terminals. These terminals provide the following:

- Distributor reference circuit
- Reference ground circuit
- Bypass circuit
- EST circuit

SYSTEM COMPONENTS

Electronic Control Module (ECM)

The ECM is the control center of the fuel injection system. It constantly monitors information from various sensors and controls the system. The ECM has 2 replaceable parts. These parts are as follows:

- The controller — ECM without the MEM-CAL.
- The MEM-CAL.

Memory Calibration (MEM-CAL) Unit

The MEM-CAL, located inside the ECM, allows the ECM to be installed in several different vehicles. It has calibration information based on the vehicle's weight, engine, transmission, axle ratio and several other factors.

Pickup Coil

The pickup coil is a device which generates an alternating current signal to determine crankshaft position.

HEI Module

The HEI module is a switching device which operates the primary circuit of the ignition coil.

Ignition Secondary

The ignition secondary consists of the ignition coil, rotor, distributor cap, plugs wires and spark plug. These components supply the high voltage to fire the spark plugs.

Electronic Spark Timing (EST)

The EST system consists of the distributor module, ECM and connecting wires. This system includes the following circuits:

- Distributor reference circuit — provides the ECM with rpm and crankshaft position information.
- Bypass signal — above 500 rpm, the ECM applies 5 volts to this circuit to switch spark timing control from the HEI module to the ECM.
- EST signal — the ECM uses this circuit to trigger the HEI module, after by-pass voltage is applied to the HEI module.
- Reference ground circuit — this wire is grounded through the module and insures that the ground circuit has no voltage drop between the ignition module and the ECM which could affect performance.

Diagnosis and Testing

SERVICE PRECAUTIONS

CAUTION

The HEI coil secondary voltage output capabilities can exceed 40,000 volts. Avoid body contact with the HEI high voltage

secondary components when the engine is running, or personal injury may result.

➡ To avoid damage to the ECM or other ignition system components, do not use electrical test equipment such as battery or AC powered voltmeter, ohmmeter, etc. or any type of tester other than specified.

• When making compression checks, disconnect the ignition switch feed wire at the distributor.

• Never allow the tachometer terminal to touch ground, as damage to the module and/or ignition coil can result.

• To prevent Electrostatic Discharge damage, when working with the ECM, do not touch the connector pins or soldered components on the circuit board.

• When handling a PROM, CAL-PAK or MEM-CAL, do not touch the component leads. Also, do not remove the integrated circuit from the carrier.

• Never allow welding cables to lie on, near or across any vehicle electrical wiring.

• Leave new components and modules in the shipping package until ready to install them.

• When performing electrical tests on the system, use a high impedance multimeter, digital voltmeter (DVM) J-34029-A or equivalent.

• Never pierce a high tension lead or boot for any testing purpose; otherwise, future problems are guaranteed.

READING CODES

The Assembly Line Diagnostic Link (ALDL) connector is used for communicating with the ECM. It is usually located under the instrument panel and is sometimes covered by a plastic cover labeled DIAGNOSTIC CONNECTOR. Codes stored in the ECM's memory can be read through a hand-held diagnostic scanner plugged into the ALDL connector. Codes can also be read by connecting a jumper wires between terminals A and B of the ALDL connector and counting the number of flashes of the SERVICE ENGINE SOON light, with the ignition switch turned **ON** and the engine NOT running.

CLEARING CODES

To clear codes from the ECM memory, the ECM power feed must be disconnected for at least 30 seconds. Depending on the vehicle, the ECM power feed can be disconnected at the positive battery terminal pigtail, the inline fuseholder that originates at the positive connection at the battery or the ECM fuse in the fuse block. The negative battery cable may also be disconnected; however, other on-board memory data, such as radio station presets will also be lost.

SYMPTOM DIAGNOSIS

An open or ground in the EST circuit, will set a Code 42 and cause the engine to run on the HEI module timing. This will cause poor performance and poor fuel economy.

Loss of the ESC signal, to the ECM, would cause the ECM to constantly retard the EST. This could result in sluggish performance and cause a Code 43 to set.

ENGINE CRANKS BUT WILL NOT RUN

1. Check that the fuel quantity is ok.
2. Turn the ignition switch **ON**. Verify that the SERVICE ENGINE SOON light is ON.
3. Install the scan tool and check the following:

   Throttle Position Sensor (TPS) — if over 2.5 volts, at closed throttle, check TPS for intermittent, open or short to ground, or faulty TPS.

   Coolant — if less than 86°F (30°C), check Coolant Temperature Sensor (CTS) for intermittent, open or short to ground, or faulty CTS.
4. Connect spark checker, J 26792 or equivalent, and check for spark while cranking. Check at least 2 wires.
   a. If spark occurs, reconnect the spark plug wires and check for fuel spray at the injector(s) while cranking. If no spark is visible, go to the fuel system section in this manual.
   b. If no spark occurs, check for battery voltage to the ignition system. If ok, use the ignition diagnosis chart.

ELECTRONIC SPARK TIMING (EST) CIRCUIT

TESTING

1. Clear codes.
2. Idle the engine for approximately 1 minute or until Code 42 sets. If Code 42 does not set, Code 42 is intermittent.
3. If Code 42 sets, turn the ignition **OFF** and disconnect the ECM connectors.
   a. Turn the ignition switch **ON**.
   b. Using an ohmmeter to ground, probe the ECM harness connector, at the EST circuit. Place the ohmmeter selector switch in the 1000–2000 ohms range. The meter should read less than 1000 ohms.
4. If not, check for a faulty connection, open circuit or faulty ignition module.
5. If ok, probe the bypass circuit with a test light to battery voltage.
6. If the test light is ON, disconnect the ignition 4-way connector and observe the test light.
   a. If the test light goes OFF, the problem is a faulty ignition module.
   b. If the test light stays ON, the bypass circuit is shorted to ground.
7. If the test light remains OFF, from Step 5, again probe the bypass circuit with the test light connected to battery voltage, and the ohmmeter still connected to the EST circuit and ground. As the test light contacts the bypass circuit, resistance should switch from under 1000 to over 2000 ohms.
   a. If it does, reconnect the ECM and idle the engine for approximately 1 minute or until Code 42 sets. If Code 42 sets, its a faulty ECM.
   b. If not, Code 42 is intermittent.
8. If the results are not as indicated in Step 7, disconnect the distributor 4-way connector. With the ohmmeter still connected to the bypass circuit, resistance should have gone high (open circuit).
9. If not, the EST circuit is shorted to ground.
10. If ok, the bypass circuit is open, faulty connections or faulty ignition module.

➡ When the problem has been corrected, clear codes and confirm Closed Loop operation and no SERVICE ENGINE SOON light.

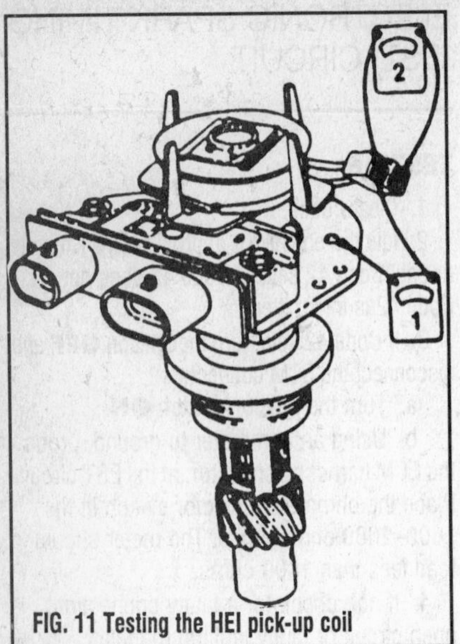
FIG. 11 Testing the HEI pick-up coil

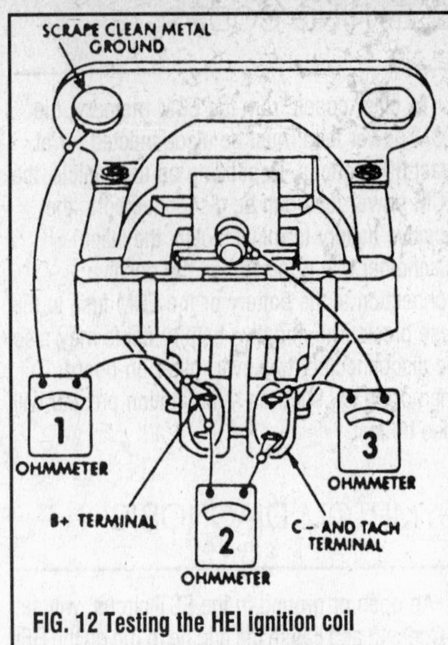

FIG. 12 Testing the HEI ignition coil

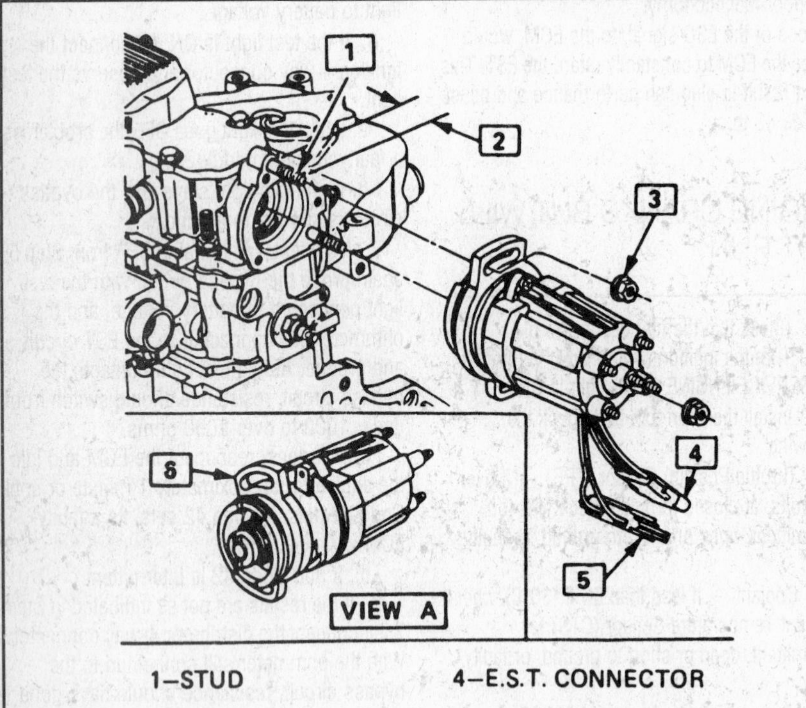

FIG. 13 Distributor installation – 2.0L engine

PICKUP COIL

➧ SEE FIG. 11

1. Remove the rotor and pickup coil leads from the module.
2. Using an ohmmeter, test as follow:
   a. Connect 1 lead of the ohmmeter between the distributor housing and 1 of the pickup coil lead. Meter should read infinity. Flex the leads by hand while observing the ohmmeter, to check for intermittent opens.
   b. Connect the ohmmeter between leads between both of the pickup coil leads. Meter should read a steady value between 500–1500 ohms.
3. If the readings are not as specified, the pickup coil is defective and should be replaced.

IGNITION COIL

➧ SEE FIG. 12

1. Remove the ignition coil and check the coil with an ohmmeter for an open or ground.
2. Connect the meter as indicated in Step 1 (meter on the high scale). Should read very high or infinite. If not, replace the coil.
3. Connect the meter as indicated in Step 2 (meter on the low scale). Should read low or zero ohms. If not, replace the coil.
4. Connect the meter as indicated in Step 3 (meter on the high scale). Should not read infinite. If it does, replace the coil.

Parts Replacement

CAPACITOR

The capacitor, if equipped, is part of the coil wire harness assembly. The capacitor is used only for radio noise suppression, it will seldom need replacement.

HEI DISTRIBUTOR

2.0L Engine

➧ SEE FIG. 13

1. Disconnect the negative battery cable.
2. Label and disconnect the coil and spark plug wires from the distributor cap.
3. Disconnect the coil and EST connectors.
4. Remove the distributor to cam carrier nuts.

5. Remove the distributor, marking the tang drive and camshaft for correct positioning upon reassembly.

To install:

6. Align the tang drive to the camshaft markings made upon removal.
7. Install the distributor-to-cam carrier nuts. Tighten to 13 ft. lbs. (18 Nm).
8. Connect the coil and EST connectors.
9. Connect the coil and spark plug wires to the cap.
10. Connect the negative battery cable.
11. Check and adjust ignition timing, as required.

2.5L Engine

1. Disconnect the negative battery cable.
2. Remove the air cleaner assembly.
3. Disconnect the 2 electrical connectors from the side of the distributor.
4. Remove the distributor cover and wire retainer, if equipped. Turn the retaining screws counterclockwise and remove the cap.
5. Mark the relationship of the rotor to the distributor housing and the housing relationship to the engine.
6. Remove the distributor retaining bolt and hold-down clamp.
7. Pull the distributor up until the rotor just stops turning counterclockwise and again note the position of the rotor.
8. Remove the distributor from the engine.

To install:

9. Insert the distributor into the engine, with the rotor aligned to the marks made previously.
10. Install the distributor hold-down clamp and retaining bolt.
11. If removed, install the wiring harness retainer and secondary wires.
12. Install the distributor cap.
13. Reconnect the 2 connectors to the side of the distributor. Make certain the connectors are fully seated and latched.
14. Reconnect the negative battery cable.

➡ If the engine was accidentally cranked after the distributor was removed, the following procedure can be used during installation.

15. Remove the No. 1 spark plug.
16. Place a finger over the spark plug hole and have a helper crank the engine slowly until compression is felt.
17. Align the timing mark on the pulley to **0** on the engine timing indicator. This will indicate that the engine is near TDC of the compression stroke.
18. Turn the rotor to point between No. 2 and No. 1 spark plug towers on the distributor cap.
19. Install the distributor assembly in the engine.
20. Install the cap and spark plug wires.
21. Check and adjust engine timing.

HEI MODULE

1. Disconnect the negative battery cable.
2. Remove the air cleaner assembly.
3. Remove the distributor cap and rotor.
4. Remove the module retaining screws, then lift the stamped sheet metal shield and module upwards.
5. Disconnect the module leads. Note the color code on the leads, as these cannot be interchanged.

➡ Do not wipe the grease from the module or distributor base, if the same module is to be replaced.

To install:

6. Spread the silicone grease, included in package, on the metal face of the module and on the distributor base where the module seats.
7. Fit the module leads to the module. Make certain the leads are fully seated and latched. Seat the module and metal shield into the distributor and install the retaining screws.
8. Install the rotor and cap.
9. Install the air cleaner assembly.
10. Reconnect the negative battery cable.

PICKUP COIL

1. Disconnect the negative battery cable.
2. Remove the distributor assembly.
3. Support the distributor assembly in a vice and drive the roll pin from the gear. Remove the shaft assembly.
4. To remove the pickup coil, remove the retainer and shield.
5. Lift the pickup coil assembly straight up to remove from the distributor.

To install:

6. Assembly the pickup coil, shield and retainer.
7. Install the shaft.
8. Install the gear and roll pin to the shaft. Make certain the matchmarks are aligned.
9. Spin the shaft and verify that the teeth do not touch the pole piece.
10. Reinstall the distributor.
11. Reconnect the negative battery cable.

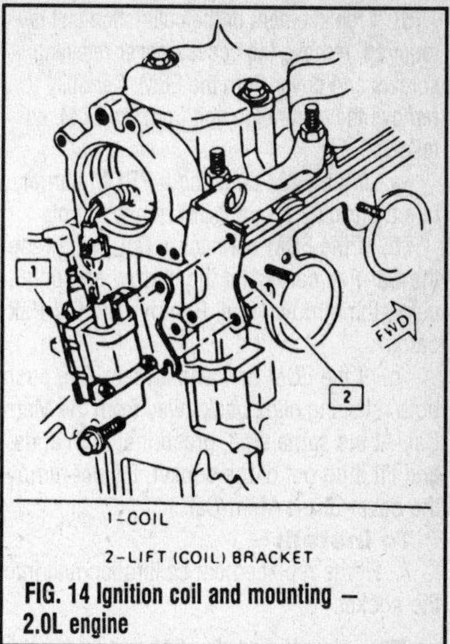

FIG. 14 Ignition coil and mounting — 2.0L engine

IGNITION COIL

1. Disconnect the negative battery cable.
2. Remove the secondary coil lead. Pull on the boot while a twisting.
3. Disconnect the harness connectors from the coil.
4. Remove the coil mounting screws.
5. Remove the ignition coil. If necessary, drill and punch out the rivets holding the coil to the bracket.

To install:

6. Place the ignition coil into position and install the mounting screws.
7. Reconnect the harness connector to the coil. Make certain the connectors are fully seated and latched.
8. Install the secondary lead to the coil tower.
9. Reconnect the negative battery cable.

ELECTRONIC CONTROL MODULE (ECM) PROM CARRIER, CAL-PAK OR MEM-CAL

Removal and Installation

1. Turn the ignition switch **OFF**.
2. Disconnect the negative battery cable.
3. Remove the right side hush panel, as required.
4. Disconnect the harness connectors from the ECM.
5. Remove the ECM-to-bracket retaining screws and remove the ECM.

6. If replacement of the calibration unit is required, remove the access cover retaining screws and cover from the ECM. Carefully remove the calibration unit from the ECM, as follows:

a. If the ECM contains a PROM carrier, use the rocker type PROM removal tool.

b. If the ECM contains a Cal-Pak, grasp the Cal-Pak carrier (at the narrow end only), using the removal tool. Remove the Cal-Pak carrier.

c. If the ECM contains a Mem-Cal, push both retaining clips back away from the Mem-Cal. At the same time, grasp it at both ends and lift it up out of the socket. Do not remove the cover of the Mem-Cal.

To install:

7. Fit the replacement calibration unit into the socket.

➡ The small notch of the carrier should be aligned with the small notch in the socket. Press on the ends of the carrier until it is firmly seated in the socket. Do not press on the calibration unit, only the carrier.

8. Install the access cover and retaining screws.

9. Position the ECM in the vehicle and install the ECM-to-bracket retaining screws.

10. Reconnect the ECM harness connectors.

11. Install the right side hush panel, as required.

12. Check that the ignition switch is **OFF**. Then reconnect the negative battery cable.

➡ Before replacement of a defective ECM first check the resistance of each ECM controlled solenoid. This can be done at the ECM connector, using an ohmmeter and the ECM connector wiring diagram. Any ECM controlled device with low resistance will damage the replacement ECM due to high current flow through the ECM internal circuits.

PROGRAMMABLE READ ONLY MEMORY (PROM)

Functional Check

1. Turn the ignition switch **ON**.

2. Enter diagnostics, by grounding the appropriate ALDL terminals.

a. Allow Code 12 to flash 4 times to verify that no other codes are present. This indicates the PROM is installed properly.

b. If trouble Code 51 is present or if the SERVICE ENGINE SOON light is ON constantly with no codes, the PROM is not fully seated, installed backward, has bent pins or is defective.

➡ Anytime the calibration unit is installed backward and the ignition switch is turned ON, the unit is destroyed.

ESC KNOCK SENSOR

Removal and Installation

1. Disconnect the negative battery cable.

2. Raise and support the vehicle safely.

3. Disconnect the ESC wiring harness connector from the ESC sensor.

4. Remove the ESC sensor from the engine block.

To install:

5. Install the ESC sensor into the engine block. Tighten and torque to 14 ft. lbs. (19 Nm).

6. Reconnect the ESC wiring harness connector to the ESC sensor.

7. Lower the vehicle.

8. Reconnect the negative battery cable.

INTEGRATED DIRECT IGNITION SYSTEM (IDI) 2.3L ENGINE

General Description

➧ SEE FIG. 15

The IDI ignition system features a distributorless ignition engine. The IDI system consists of 2 separate ignition coils, an ignition module and a secondary conductor housing mounted to an aluminum cover plate. The system also consists of a crankshaft sensor, connecting wires and the Electronic Spark Timing (EST) portion of the Electronic Control Module (ECM).

The IDI ignition system uses a magnetic crankshaft sensor (mounted remotely from the ignition module) and a reluctor to determine crankshaft position and engine speed. The reluctor is a special wheel cast into the crankshaft, with 7 slots machined into it. Six of the slots are equally spaced 60° apart and the seventh slot is spaced 10° from 1 of the other slots. This seventh slot is used to generate a sync-pulse.

The IDI system uses the same Electronic Spark Timing (EST) circuits as the distributor-type ignition. The ECM uses the EST circuit to control spark advance and ignition dwell, when the ignition system is operating in the EST mode.

The Electronic Spark Control (ESC) system is used to control spark knock and enable maximum spark advance to improve driveability and fuel economy, . This system consists of a knock sensor and an ESC module (part of Mem-Cal). The ECM monitors the ESC signal to determine when engine detonation occurs.

System Operation

The IDI ignition system uses a waste spark distribution method. Each cylinder is paired with the cylinder opposite it (i.e. 1–4, 2–3). The end of each coil secondary is attached to a spark plug. These 2 plugs are on companion cylinders, meaning they are at top dead center at the same time. The one that is on compression is said to be the event cylinder and the one on the exhaust stroke, the waste cylinder. When the coil discharges, both plugs fire at the same time to complete the series circuit.

Since the polarity of the primary and the secondary windings are fixed, one plug always fires in a forward direction and the other in reverse. This differs from a conventional system in which all plugs fire in the same direction each time. Because of the demand for additional energy; the coil design, saturation time and primary current flow are also different. This redesign of the system allows higher energy to be available from the distributorless coils, greater than 40 kilovolts at all rpm ranges.

The IDI ignition system uses a magnetic crankshaft sensor mounted remotely from the ignition module. It protrudes into the block to within approximately 0.050 in. (1.3mm) of the crankshaft reluctor. As the crankshaft rotates, the slots of the reluctor cause a changing magnetic field at the crankshaft sensor, creating an induced voltage pulse.

The IDI module sends reference signals to the ECM, based on the crankshaft sensor pulses, which are used to determine crankshaft position and engine speed. Reference pulses to the ECM occur at a rate of 1 per each 180° of crankshaft rotation. This signal is called the 2X reference because it occurs 2 times per crankshaft revolution.

A second reference signal is sent to the ECM which occurs at the same time as the sync-pulse, from the crankshaft sensor. This signal is called the 1X reference because it occurs 1 time per crankshaft revolution.

By comparing the time between the 1X and 2X reference pulses, the ignition module can recognize the sync-pulse (the seventh slot) which starts the calculation of the ignition coil sequencing. The second crank pulse following the sync-pulse signals the ignition module to fire No. 2–3 ignition coil and the fifth crank pulse signals the module to fire the No. 1–4 ignition coil.

During cranking, the ignition module monitors the sync-pulse to begin the ignition firing sequence and below 700 rpm the module controls spark advance by triggering each of the 2 coils at a pre-determined interval based on engine speed only. Above 700 rpm, the ECM controls the spark timing (EST) and compensates for all driving conditions. The ignition module must receive a sync-pulse and then a crank signal in that order to enable the engine to start.

To control EST the ECM uses the following inputs:

- Crankshaft position
- Engine speed (rpm)
- Engine coolant temperature
- Manifold air temperature
- Engine load (manifold pressure or vacuum)

The ESC system is designed to retard spark timing up to 15° to reduce spark knock in the engine. When the knock sensor detects spark knocking in the engine, it sends an AC voltage signal to the ECM, which increases with the severity of the knock. The ECM then adjusts the EST to reduce spark knock.

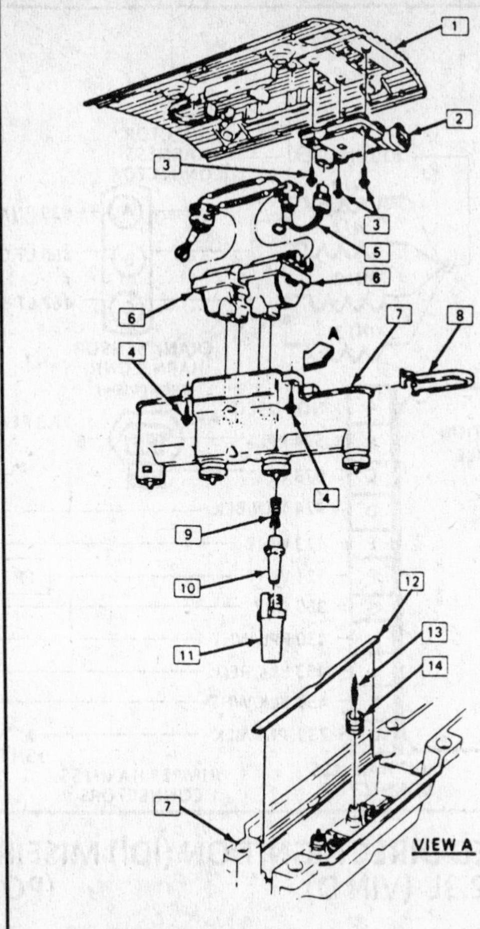

FIG. 15 Exploded view of the IDI assembly — 2.3L engine. The entire unit is removed as an assembly

SYSTEM COMPONENTS

Crankshaft Sensor

The crankshaft sensor, mounted remotely from the ignition module on an aluminum cover plate, is used to determine crankshaft position and engine speed.

Ignition Coil

The ignition coil assemblies are mounted inside the module assembly housing. Each coil distributes the spark for 2 plugs simultaneously.

Electronic Spark Timing (EST)

The EST system is basically the same EST to ECM circuit used on the distributor type ignition systems with EST. This system includes the following circuits:

- Reference circuit — provides the ECM with rpm and crankshaft position information from the IDI module. The IDI module receives this signal from the crank sensor.
- Bypass signal — above 700 rpm, the ECM applies 5 volts to this circuit to switch spark timing control from the IDI module to the ECM.
- EST signal — reference signal is sent to the ECM via the DIS module during cranking. Under 700 rpm, the IDI module controls the ignition timing. Above 700 rpm, the ECM applies 5 volts to the bypass line to switch the timing to the ECM control.
- Reference ground circuit — this wire is grounded through the module and insures that the ground circuit has no voltage drop between the ignition module and the ECM which could affect performance.

ESC Sensor

The ESC sensor, mounted in the engine block near the cylinders, detects abnormal vibration (spark knock) in the engine.

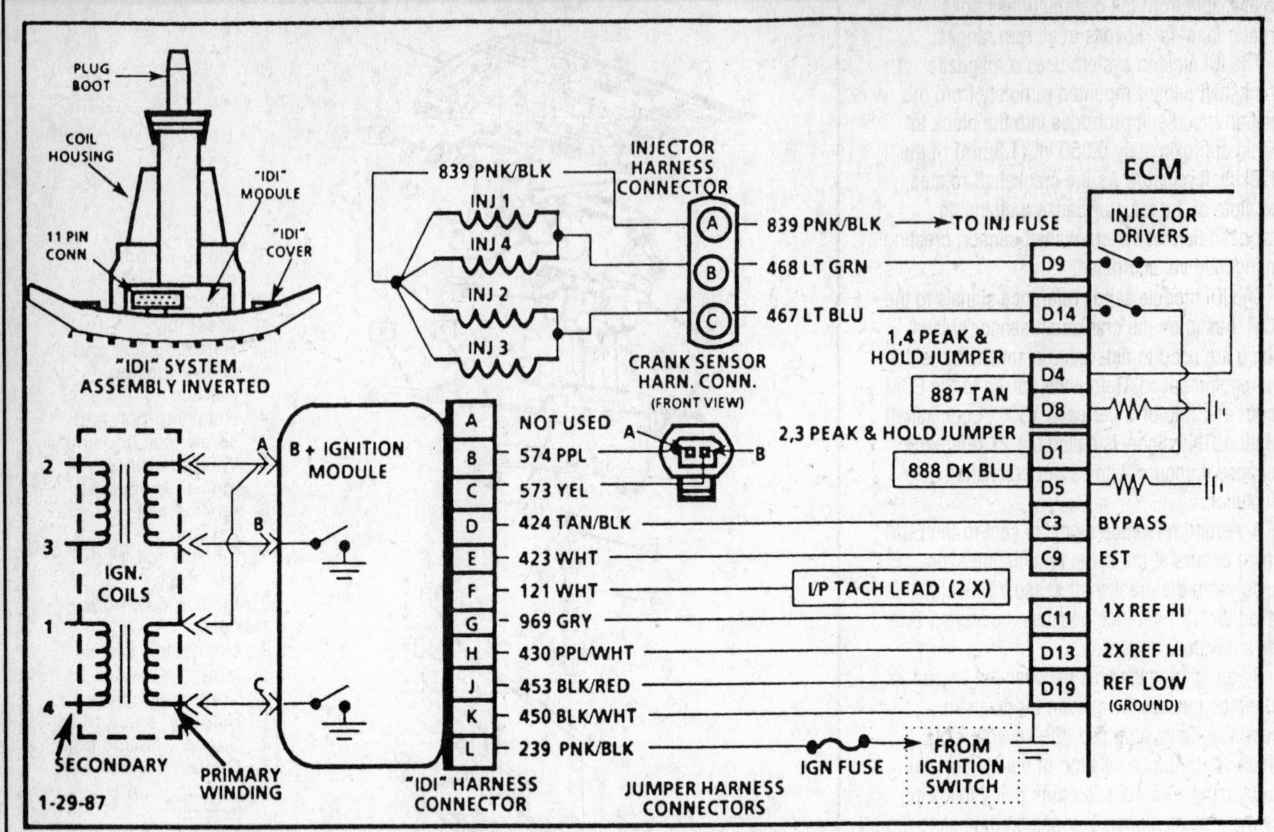

INTEGRATED DIRECT IGNITION (IDI) MISFIRE DIAGNOSIS
2.3L (VIN D) (PORT)

Circuit Description:

The "Integrated Direct Ignition" (IDI) system uses a waste spark method of distribution. In this type of system the ignition module triggers the #1-4 coil pair resulting in both #1 and #4 spark plugs firing at the same time. #1 cylinder is on the compression stroke at the same time #4 is on the exhaust stroke, resulting in a lower energy requirement to fire # 4 spark plug. This leaves the remainder of the high voltage to be used to fire #1 spark plug. On this application, the crank sensor is mounted to, and protrudes through the block to within approximately 0.050" of the crankshaft reluctor. Since the reluctor is a machined portion of the crankshaft and the sensor is mounted in a fixed position on the block, timing adjustments are not possible or necessary.

Test Description: Numbers below refer to circled numbers on the diagnostic chart.

1. This checks for equal relative power output between the cylinders. Any injector which when disconnected did not result in an rpm drop approximately equal to the others, is located on the misfiring cylinder.
2. If a plug boot is burned, the other plug on that coil may still fire at idle. This step tests the system's ability to produce at least 25,000 volts at each spark plug.
3. No spark, on one coil, may be caused by an open secondary circuit. Therefore, the coil's secondary resistance should be checked. Resistance readings above 20,000 ohms, but not infinite, will probably not cause a no start but may cause an engine miss under certain conditions.
4. If the no spark condition is caused by coil connections, a coil or a secondary boot assembly, the test light will blink. If the light does not blink, the fault is module connections or the module.
5. Checks for ignition voltage feed to injector and for an open injector driver circuit.
6. An injector driver circuit shorted to ground would result in the test light "ON" steady, and possibly a flooded condition which could damage engine. A shorted injector (less than 2 ohms) could cause incorrect ECM operation.

Diagnostic Aid:

Verify IDI connector terminal "K", CKT 450 resistance to ground is less than .5 ohm.

FIG. 16 Ignition system diagnosis — 2.3L engine

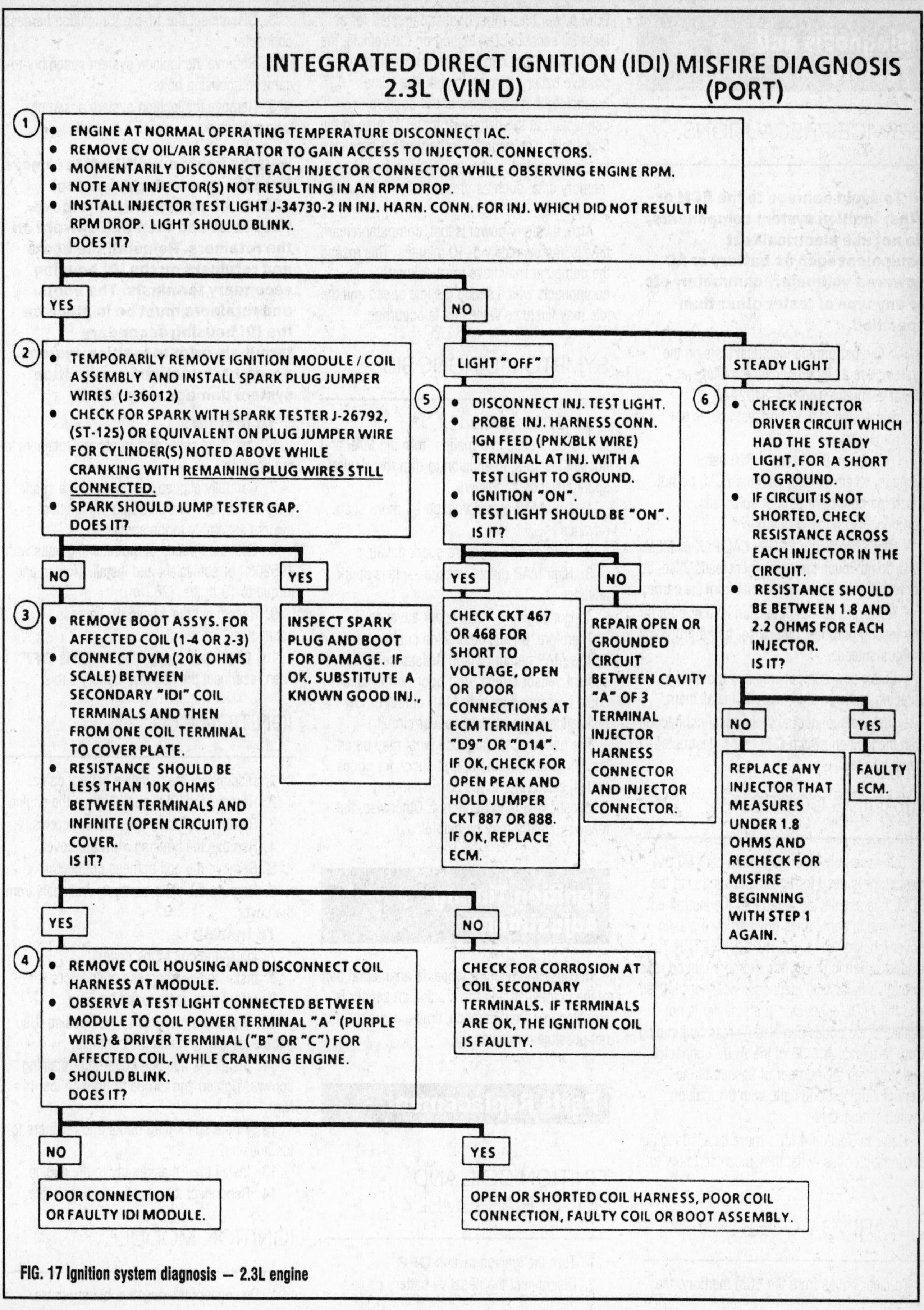

FIG. 17 Ignition system diagnosis — 2.3L engine

Diagnosis and Testing

SERVICE PRECAUTIONS

➡ To avoid damage to the ECM or other ignition system components, do not use electrical test equipment such as battery or AC powered voltmeter, ohmmeter, etc. or any type of tester other than specified.

- When performing electrical tests on the system, use a high impedance multimeter, digital voltmeter (DVM) J–34029–A or equivalent. Use of a 12 volt test light is not recommended.
- To prevent Electrostatic Discharge damage, when working with the ECM, do not touch the connector pins or soldered components on the circuit board.
- When handling a PROM, CAL-PAK or MEM-CAL, do not touch the component leads. Also, do not remove the integrated circuit from the carrier.
- Never pierce a high tension lead or boot for any testing purpose; otherwise, future problems are guaranteed.
- Leave new components and modules in the shipping package until ready to install them.
- Never disconnect any electrical connection with the ignition switch **ON** unless instructed to do so in a test.

READING CODES

The Assembly Line Diagnostic Link (ALDL) connector is used for communicating with the ECM. It is usually located under the instrument panel and is sometimes covered by a plastic cover labeled "DIAGNOSTIC CONNECTOR." Codes stored in the ECM's memory can be read through a hand-held diagnostic scanner plugged into the ALDL connector. If a scanner is not available, the codes can also be read by jumping from terminals **A** to **B** of the ALDL connector and counting the number of flashes of the Service Engine Soon light, with the ignition switch turned **ON**.

Refer to Section 4 for a more detailed look at diagnostic codes, what they mean and how to diagnose them.

CLEARING CODES

To clear codes from the ECM memory, the ECM power feed must be disconnected for at least 30 seconds. Depending on the vehicle, the ECM power feed can be disconnected at the positive battery terminal pigtail, the inline fuseholder that originates at the positive connection at the battery or the ECM fuse in the fuse block. The negative battery cable may also be disconnected; however, other on-board memory data, such as preset radio tuning, will also be lost.

Also, if battery power is lost, computer relearn time is approximately 5–10 minutes. This means the computer may have to re-calibrate components which set up the idle speed and the idle may fluctuate while this is occurring.

SYMPTOM DIAGNOSIS

➧ SEE FIGS. 16 AND 17

The ECM uses information from the MAP and coolant sensors, in addition to rpm to calculate spark advance as follows:

1. Low MAP output voltage — more spark advance
2. Cold engine — more spark advance
3. High MAP output voltage — less spark advance
4. Hot engine — less spark advance

Therefore, briefly, detonation could be caused by low MAP output or high resistance in the coolant sensor circuit. And poor performance could be caused by high MAP output or low resistance in the coolant sensor circuit.

The best way to diagnose what may be an ignition-related problem, first check for codes. If codes, exist, refer to the corresponding diagnostic charts in Section 4. Otherwise, the following charts may be helpful.

Ignition Timing Adjustment

Because the reluctor wheel is an integral part of the crankshaft and the crankshaft sensor is mounted in a fixed position, timing adjustment is not possible or necessary.

Parts Replacement

IGNITION COIL AND MODULE ASSEMBLY

1. Turn the ignition switch **OFF**.
2. Disconnect the negative battery cable.
3. Disconnect the 11-pin IDI ignition harness connector.
4. Remove the ignition system assembly-to-camshaft housing bolts.
5. Remove the ignition system assembly from the engine.

➡ If the boots are difficult to remove from the spark plugs, use tool J36011 or equivalent, to remove. First twist and then pull upward on the retainers. Reinstall the boots and retainers on the IDI housing secondary terminals. The boots and retainers must be in place on the IDI housing secondary terminals prior to ignition system assembly installation or ignition system damage may result.

To install:

6. Install the spark plug boots and retainers to the housing.
7. Carefully aligned the boots to the spark plug terminals, while installing the ignition system assembly to the engine.
8. Coat the threads of the retaining bolts with 1052080 or equivalent and install. Tighten and torque to 19 ft. lbs. (26 Nm).
9. Reconnect the 11-pin IDI harness connector.
10. Check that the ignition switch is **OFF**. Then reconnect the negative battery cable.

IGNITION COIL

1. Disconnect the negative battery cable.
2. Remove the IDI assembly from the engine.
3. Remove the housing to cover screws.
4. Remove the housing from the cover.
5. Remove the coil harness connector.
6. Remove the coils, contacts and seals from the cover.

To install:

7. Install the coil to the cover.
8. Install the coil harness connectors.
9. Install new seals to the housing.
10. Install the contacts to the housing. Use petroleum jelly to retain the contacts.
11. Install the housing cover and retaining screws. Tighten and torque to 35 inch lbs. (4 Nm).
12. Fit the spark plug boots and retainers to the housing.
13. Install the IDI assembly to the engine.
14. Reconnect the negative battery cable.

IGNITION MODULE

1. Disconnect the negative battery cable.

2. Remove the IDI assembly from the engine.
3. Remove the housing to cover screws.
4. Remove the housing from the cover.
5. Remove the coil harness connector from the module.
6. Remove the module-to-cover retaining screws and remove the module from the cover.

➡ **Do not wipe the grease from the module or coil, if the same module is to be replaced. If a new module is to be installed, spread the grease (included in package) on the metal face of the new module and on the cover where the module seats. This grease is necessary from module cooling.**

To install:

7. Position the module to the cover and install the retaining screws. Tighten and torque to 35 inch lbs. (4 Nm).
8. Reconnect the coil harness connector to the module.
9. Install the housing cover and retaining screws. Tighten and torque to 35 inch lbs. (4 Nm).
10. Fit the spark plug boots and retainers to the housing.
11. Install the IDI assembly to the engine.
12. Reconnect the negative battery cable.

CRANKSHAFT SENSOR

➧ SEE FIG. 18

1. Disconnect the negative battery cable.
2. Disconnect the sensor harness connector at the sensor.
3. Remove the sensor retaining bolts and pull the sensor from the engine.

To install:

4. Fit a new O-ring to the sensor and lubricate with engine oil. Install the sensor into the engine.
5. Install the sensor retaining bolt. Tighten and torque to 88 inch lbs. (10 Nm).
6. Reconnect the sensor harness connector.
7. Reconnect the negative battery cable.

ELECTRONIC CONTROL MODULE (ECM) OR MEM-CAL

1. Turn the ignition switch **OFF**.
2. Disconnect the negative battery cable.
3. Remove the right side hush panel.
4. Disconnect the harness connectors from the ECM.
5. Remove the ECM-to-bracket retaining screws and remove the ECM.

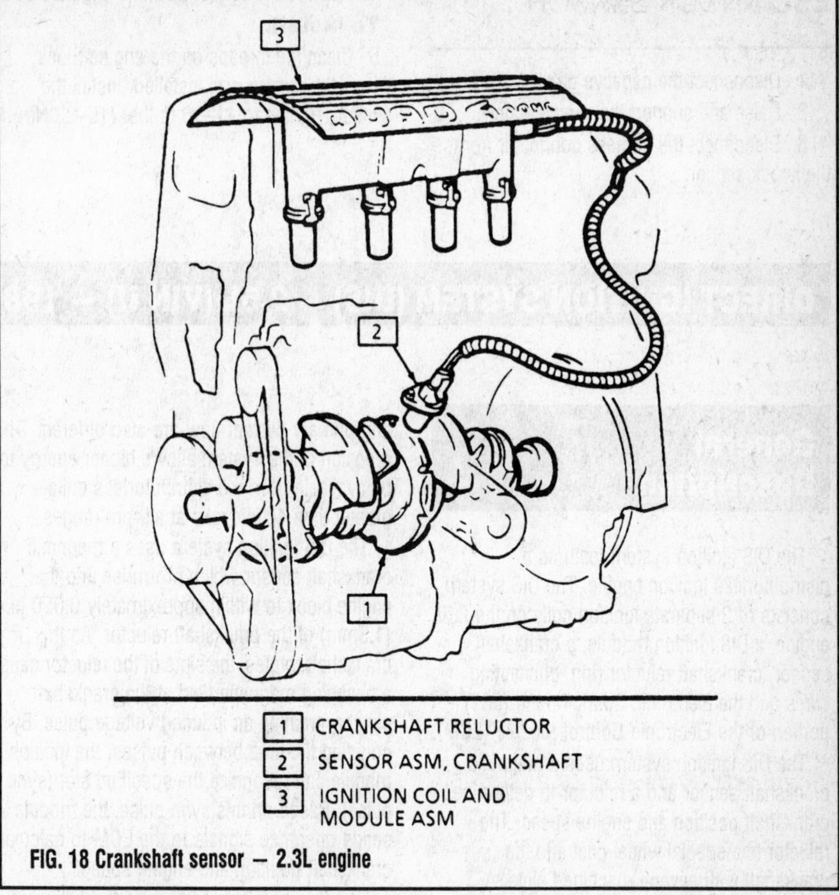

FIG. 18 Crankshaft sensor — 2.3L engine

➡ **Before replacement of a defective ECM first check the resistance of each ECM controlled solenoid. This can be done at the ECM connector, using an ohmmeter and the ECM connector wiring diagram. Any ECM controlled device with low resistance will damage the replacement ECM due to high current flow through the ECM internal circuits.**

6. If replacement of the Mem-Cal is required, remove the access cover retaining screws and cover from the ECM. Note the position of the Mem-Cal for proper installation in the new ECM. Using 2 fingers, carefully push both retaining clips back away from the Mem-Cal. At the same time, grasp it at both ends and lift it up out of the socket. Do not remove the cover of the Mem-Cal.

To install:

7. Fit the replacement Mem-Cal into the socket.

➡ **The small notches in the Mem-Cal must be aligned with the small notches in the socket. Press only on the ends of the Mem-Cal until the retaining clips snap into the ends of the Mem-Cal. Do not press on the middle of the Mem-Cal, only the ends.**

8. Install the access cover and retaining screws.
9. Position the ECM in the vehicle and install the ECM-to-bracket retaining screws.
10. Reconnect the ECM harness connectors.
11. Install the hush panel.
12. Check that the ignition switch is **OFF**. Then reconnect the negative battery cable.

Functional Check

1. Turn the ignition switch **ON**.
2. Enter diagnostics.
   a. Allow Code 12 to flash 4 times to verify no other codes are present. This indicates the Mem-Cal is installed properly and the ECM is functioning.
   b. If trouble Codes 42, 43 or 51 occur, or if the Service Engine Soon light is ON constantly with no codes, the Mem-Cal is not fully seated or is defective.
   c. If it is not fully seated, press firmly on the ends of the Mem-Cal.

ESC KNOCK SENSOR

1. Disconnect the negative battery cable.
2. Raise and support the vehicle safely.
3. Disconnect the harness connector from the knock sensor.
4. Remove the sensor from the engine block.

To install:

5. Clean the threads on the engine block, where the sensor was installed. Install the sensor. Tighten to 11–16 ft. lbs. (15–22 Nm).
6. Reconnect the harness connector to the knock sensor.
7. Lower the vehicle.
8. Reconnect the negative battery cable.

DIRECT IGNITION SYSTEM (DIS) – 2.5L (VIN U) – 1987-92 ENGINE

General Description

The DIS ignition system features a distributorless ignition engine. The DIS system consists of 2 separate ignition coils on the 2.5L engine, a DIS ignition module, a crankshaft sensor, crankshaft reluctor ring, connecting wires and the Electronic Spark Timing (EST) portion of the Electronic Control Module (ECM).

The DIS ignition system uses a magnetic crankshaft sensor and a reluctor to determine crankshaft position and engine speed. The reluctor is a special wheel cast into the crankshaft with several machined slots. A specific slot, on the reluctor wheel, is used to generate a sync-pulse.

The DIS system uses the same Electronic Spark Timing (EST) circuits as the distributor-type ignition. The ECM uses the EST circuit to control spark advance and ignition dwell, when the ignition system is operating in the EST mode.

System Operation

The DIS ignition system uses a waste spark distribution method. Each cylinder is paired with its companion cylinder (i.e. 1–4, 2–3. on a 4-cylinder engine). The end of each coil secondary is attached to a spark plug. These 2 plugs, being companion cylinders, are at top dead center at the same time. The one that is on compression is said to be the event cylinder and the one on the exhaust stroke, the waste cylinder. When the coil discharges, both plugs fire at the same time to complete the series circuit.

Since the polarity of the primary and the secondary windings are fixed, one plug always fires in a forward direction and the other in reverse. This is differs from a conventional system in which all plugs fire in the same direction each time. Because of the demand for additional energy; the coil design, saturation time and primary current flow are also different. This redesign of the system allows higher energy to be available from the distributorless coils, greater than 40 kilovolts at all rpm ranges.

The DIS ignition system uses a magnetic crankshaft sensor which protrudes into the engine block to within approximately 0.050 in. (1.3mm) of the crankshaft reluctor. As the crankshaft rotates, the slots of the reluctor cause a changing magnetic field at the crankshaft sensor, creating an induced voltage pulse. By counting the time between pulses, the ignition module can recognize the specified slot (sync pulse). Based on this sync pulse, the module sends reference signals to the ECM to calculate crankshaft position and engine speed.

To control EST the ECM uses the following inputs:

- Crankshaft position
- Engine Speed (rpm)
- Engine temperature
- Manifold air temperature
- Atmospheric (barometric) pressure
- Engine load (manifold pressure or vacuum)

SYSTEM COMPONENTS

Crankshaft Sensor

The crankshaft sensor is mounted to the bottom of the DIS module. It is used determine crankshaft position and engine speed.

Ignition Coils

The ignition coil assemblies are mounted on the DIS module. Each coil distributes the spark for 2 plugs simultaneously.

Electronic Spark Timing (EST)

The EST system is basically the same EST to ECM circuit use on the distributor type ignition systems with EST. This system includes the following circuits:

- DIS reference circuit – provides the ECM with rpm and crankshaft position information from the DIS module. The DIS module receives this signal from the crank sensor.
- Bypass signal – above 400 rpm, the ECM applies 5 volts to this circuit to switch spark timing control from the DIS module to the ECM.
- EST signal – reference signal is sent to the ECM via the DIS module during cranking. Under 400 rpm, the DIS module controls the ignition timing. Above 400 rpm, the ECM applies 5 volts to the bypass line to switch the timing to the ECM control.
- Reference ground circuit – this wire is grounded through the module and insures that the ground circuit has no voltage drop between the ignition module and the ECM which could affect performance.

Diagnosis and Testing

SERVICE PRECAUTIONS

➡ To avoid damage to the ECM or other ignition system components, do not use electrical test equipment such as battery or AC powered voltmeter, ohmmeter, etc. or any type of tester other than specified.

- When performing electrical tests on the system, use a high impedance multimeter or quality digital voltmeter (DVM). Use of a 12 volt test light is not recommended.
- To prevent electrostatic discharge damage, when working with the ECM, do not touch the connector pins or soldered components on the circuit board.

• When handling a PROM, CAL-PAK or MEM-CAL, do not touch the component leads. Also, do not remove the integrated circuit from the carrier.

• When performing electrical tests on the system, use a high impedance multimeter, digital voltmeter (DVM) J–34029–A or equivalent.

• Never pierce a high tension lead or boot for any testing purpose; otherwise, future problems are guaranteed.

• Leave new components and modules in the shipping package until ready to install them.

• Never disconnect any electrical connection with the ignition switch **ON** unless instructed to do so in a test.

READING CODES

➧ SEE FIG. 19

The Assembly Line Diagnostic Link (ALDL) connector is used for communicating with the ECM. It is usually located under the instrument panel and is sometimes covered by a plastic cover labeled "DIAGNOSTIC CONNECTOR." Codes stored in the ECM's memory can be read through a hand-held diagnostic scanner plugged into the ALDL connector. If a scanner is not available, the codes can also be read by jumping from terminals **A** to **B** of the ALDL connector and counting the number of flashes of the Service Engine Soon light, with the ignition switch turned **ON**.

Refer to Section 4 for a more detailed look diagnostic codes, what they mean and how to diagnose them.

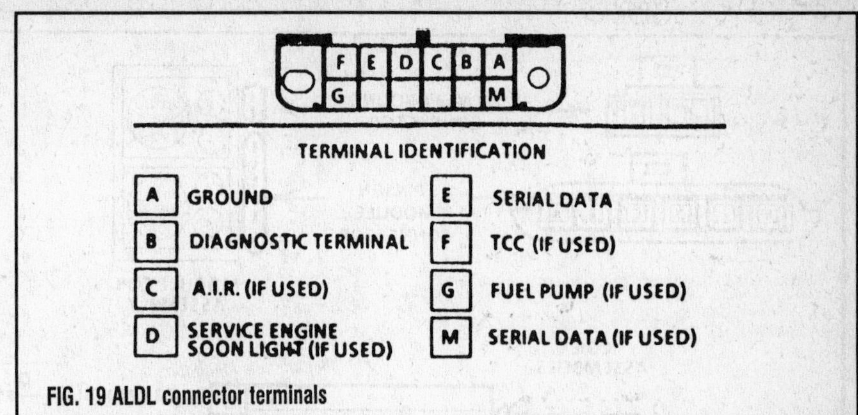

FIG. 19 ALDL connector terminals

CLEARING CODES

To clear codes from the ECM memory, the ECM power feed must be disconnected for at least 30 seconds. Depending on the vehicle, the ECM power feed can be disconnected at the positive battery terminal pigtail, the inline fuseholder that originates at the positive connection at the battery or the ECM fuse in the fuse block. The negative battery cable may also be disconnected; however, other on-board memory data, such as radio station presets, will also be lost.

SYMPTOM DIAGNOSIS

➧ SEE FIGS. 20–23

The ECM uses information from the MAP and coolant sensors, in addition to rpm to calculate spark advance as follows:

1. Low MAP output voltage — more spark advance
2. Cold engine — more spark advance
3. High MAP output voltage — less spark advance
4. Hot engine — less spark advance

Therefore, briefly, detonation could be caused by low MAP output or high resistance in the coolant sensor circuit. And poor performance could be caused by high MAP output or low resistance in the coolant sensor circuit.

The best way to diagnose what may be an ignition-related problem, first check for codes. If codes, exist, refer to the corresponding diagnostic charts in Section 4. Otherwise, the following charts may be helpful.

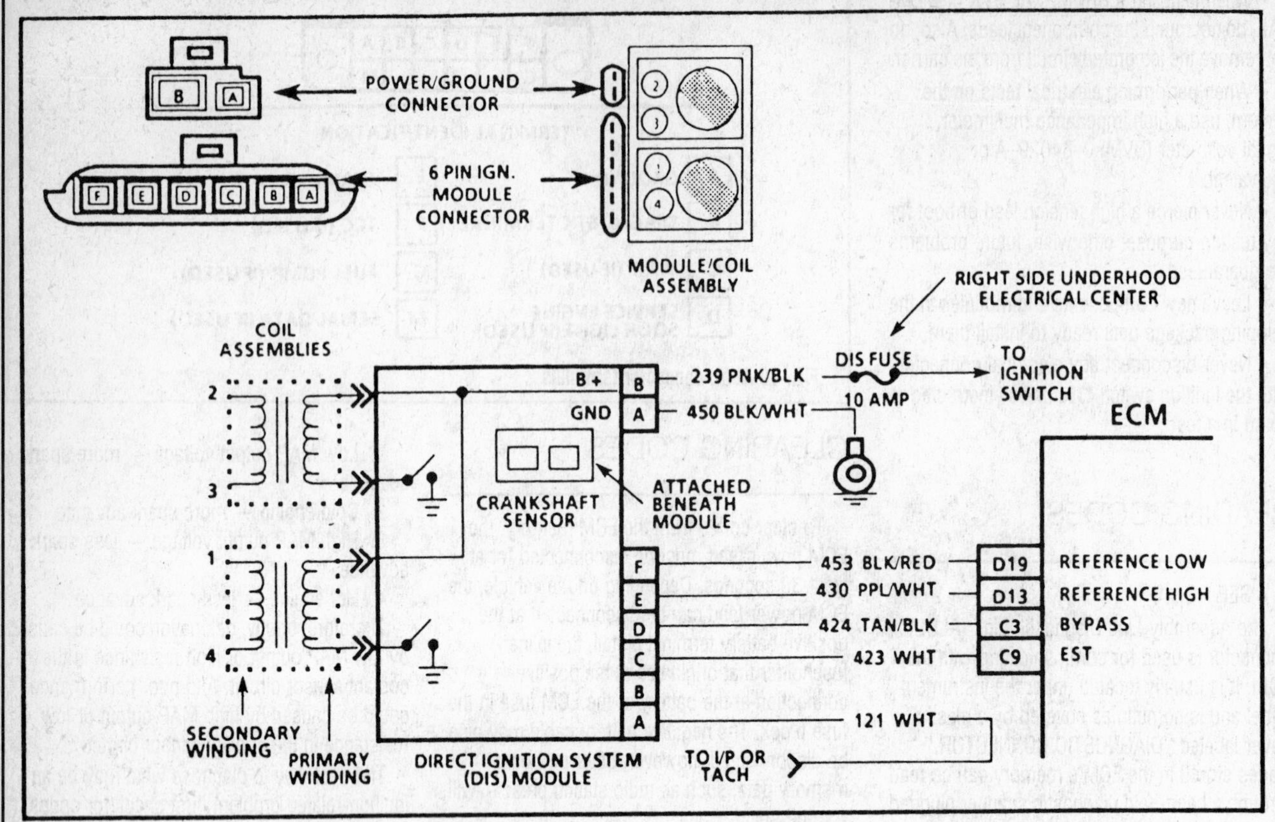

"DIS" MISFIRE UNDER LOAD
2.5L (VIN R) (TBI)

Circuit Description:

The Direct Ignition System (DIS) uses a waste spark method of distribution. In this type of system, the ignition module triggers a dual coil, resulting in both connected spark plugs firing at the same time. One cylinder is on its compression stroke at the same time that the other is on the exhaust stroke, resulting in a lower energy requirement to fire the spark plug in the cylinder on its exhaust stroke. This leaves the remainder of the high voltage to be used to fire the spark plug which is in the cylinder on its compression stroke. On this application, the crank sensor is mounted to the bottom of the coil/module assembly and protrudes through the block to within approximately .050" of the crankshaft reluctor. Since the reluctor is a machined portion of the crankshaft and the crank sensor is mounted in a fixed position on the block, timing adjustments are not possible or necessary.

Test Description: Number(s) below refer to circled number(s) on the diagnostic chart.

1. If the "Misfire" complaint exists at idle only, CHART C-4D-1 must be used. Engine rpm should drop approximately equally on all plug leads. A spark tester such as a ST-125 must be used because it is essential to verify adequate available secondary voltage at the spark plug (25,000 volts).
2. If the spark jumps the test gap after grounding the opposite plug wire, it indicates excessive resistance in the plug which was bypassed. A faulty or poor connection at that plug could also result in the miss condition. Also check for carbon deposits inside the spark plug boot.
3. If carbon tracking is evident, replace coil and be sure plug wires relating to that coil are clean and tight. Excessive wire resistance or faulty connections could have caused the coil to be damaged.
4. If the no spark condition follows the suspected coil, that coil is faulty. Otherwise, the ignition module is the cause of no spark. This test could also be performed by substituting a known good coil for the one causing the no spark condition.

FIG. 20 Ignition system diagnosis — 2.5L engine

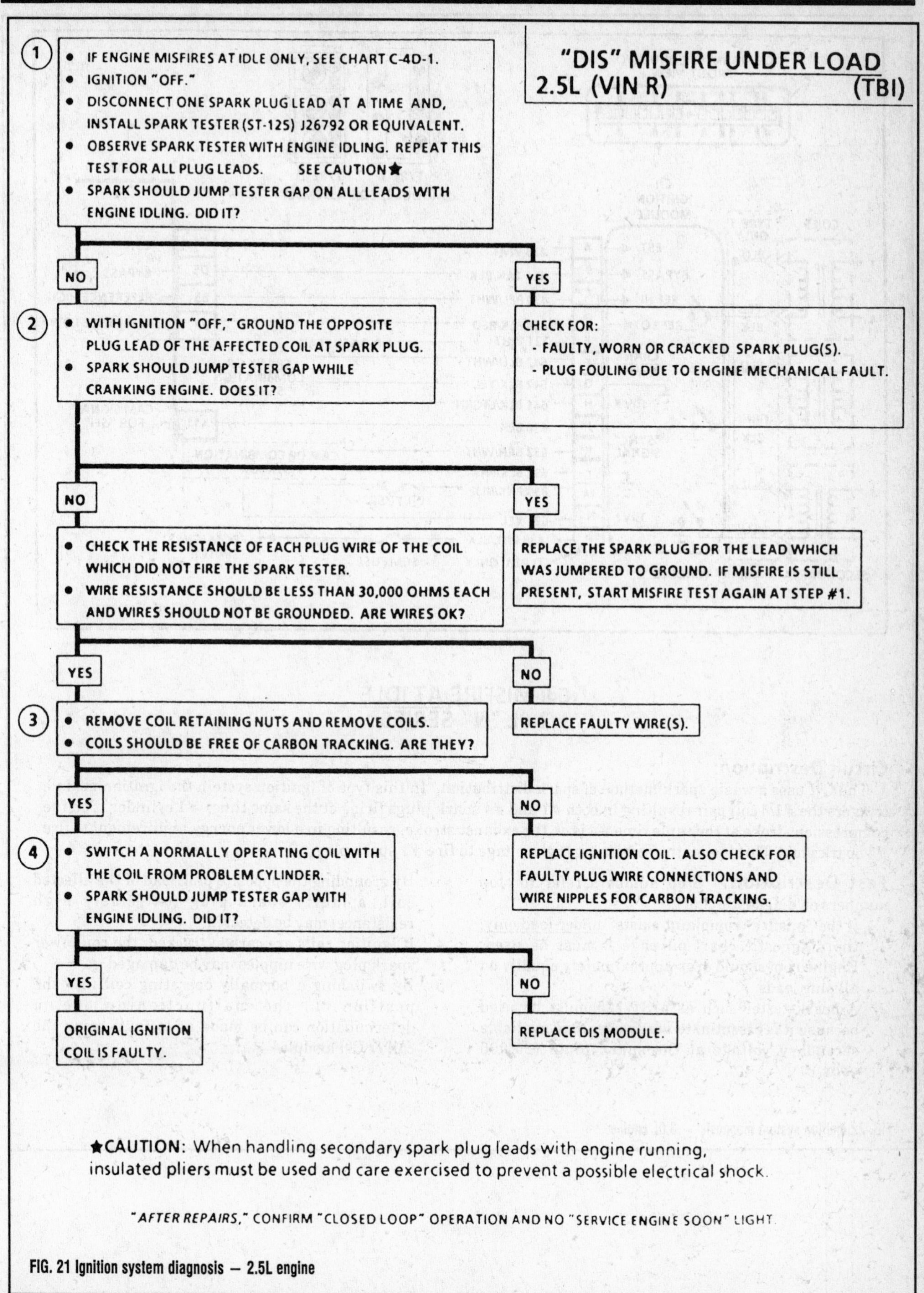

FIG. 21 Ignition system diagnosis — 2.5L engine

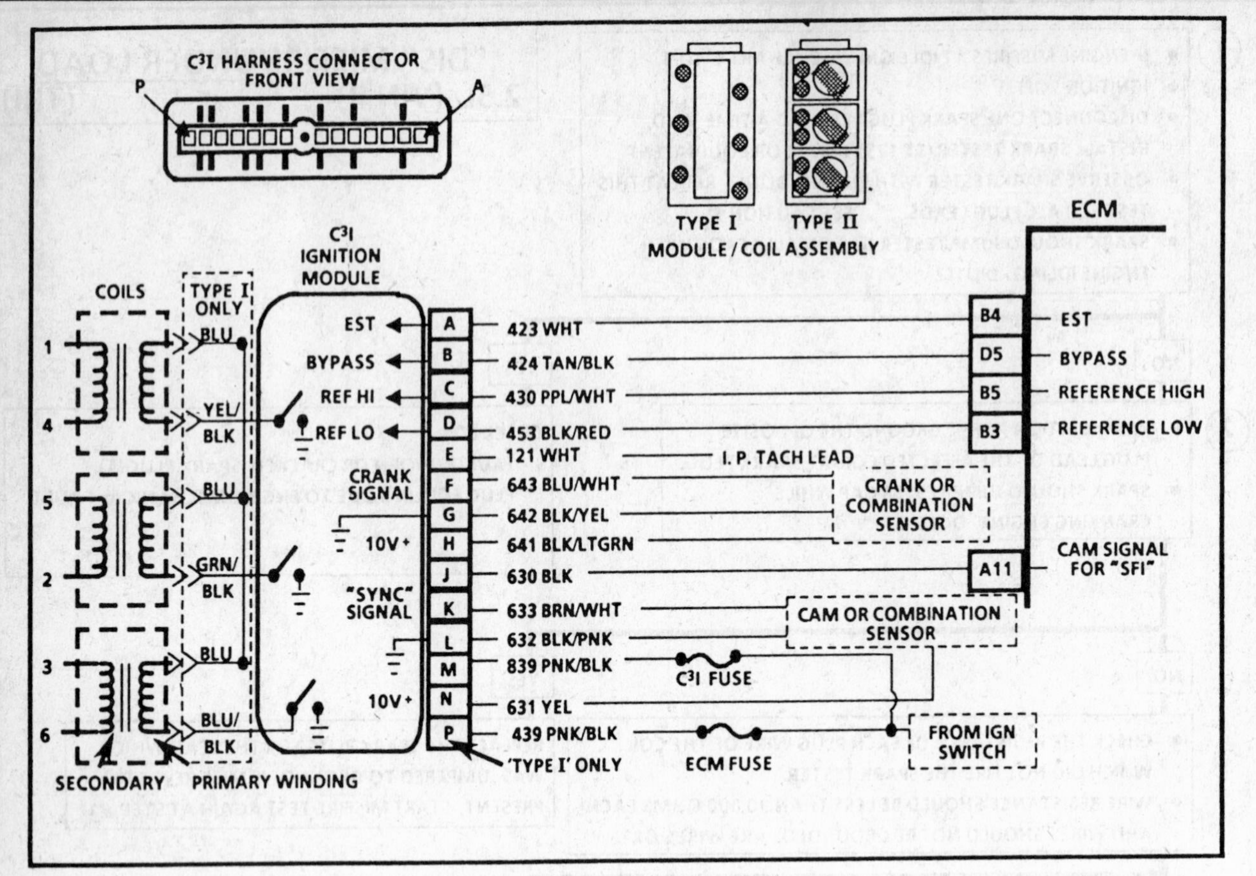

C^3I MISFIRE AT IDLE
3.0L "N" SERIES

Circuit Description:

The C^3I uses a waste spark method of spark distribution. In this type of ignition system the ignition module triggers the #1/4 coil pair resulting in both #1 and #4 spark plugs firing at the same time. #1 cylinder is on the compression stroke at the same time #4 is on the exhaust stroke, resulting in a lower energy requirement to fire #4 spark plug. This leaves the remaining high voltage to fire #1 spark plug.

Test Description: Step numbers refer to step numbers on diagnostic chart.

1. If the "misfire" complaint exists under load only, the diagnostic chart on page 2 must be used. Engine rpm should drop approximately equally on all plug leads.
2. A spark tester such as a ST-125 must be used because it is essential to verify adequate available secondary voltage at the spark plug. (25,000 volts.).
3. By grounding the opposite plug lead of the affected coil, a faulty spark plug (extremely high resistance) may be detected.
4. If ignition coils are carbon tracked, the coil tower spark plug wire nipples may be damaged.
5. By switching a normally operating coil into the position of the malfunctioning one, a determination can be made as to fault being the coil or C^3I module.

FIG. 22 Ignition system diagnosis — 3.0L engine

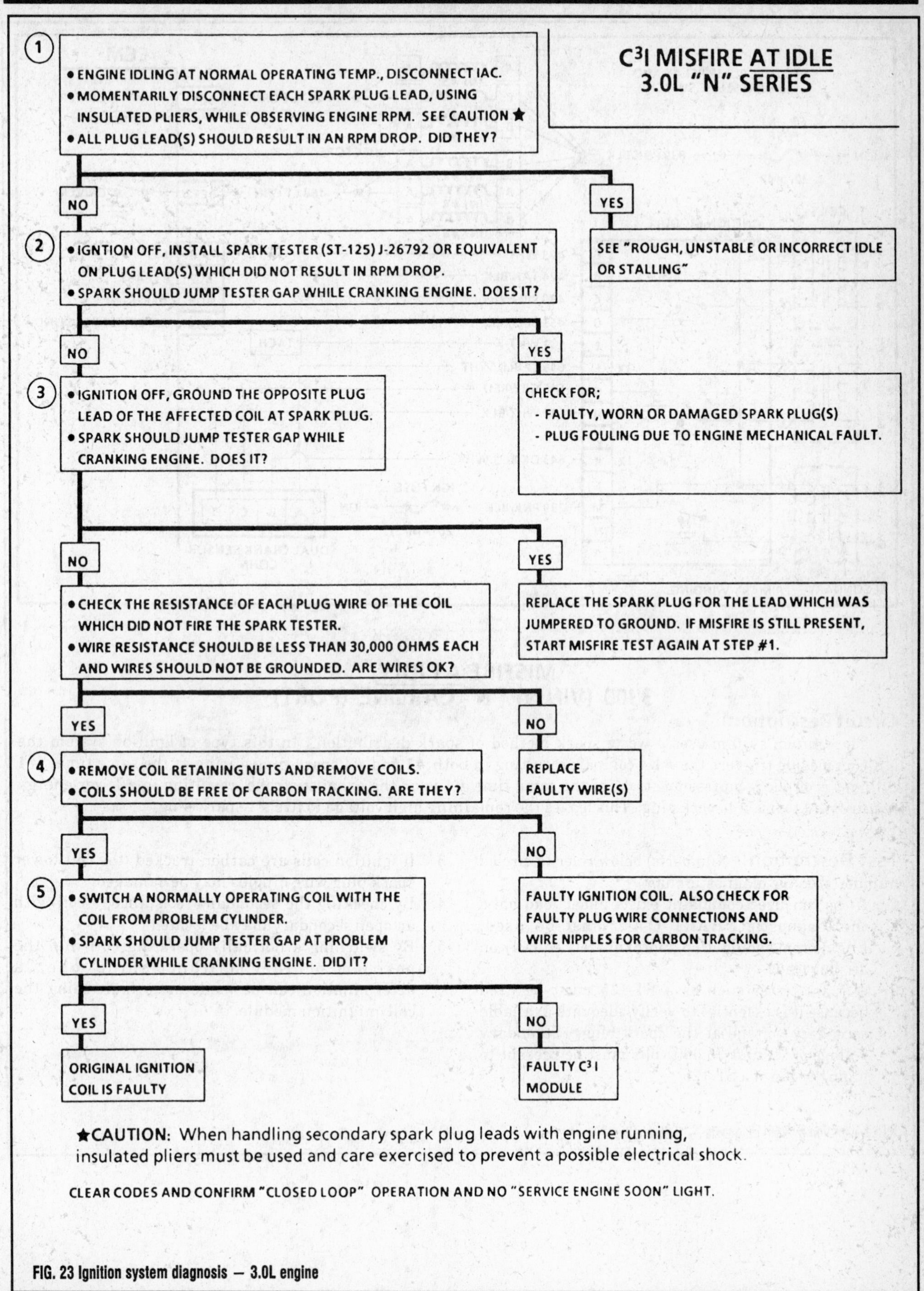

FIG. 23 Ignition system diagnosis — 3.0L engine

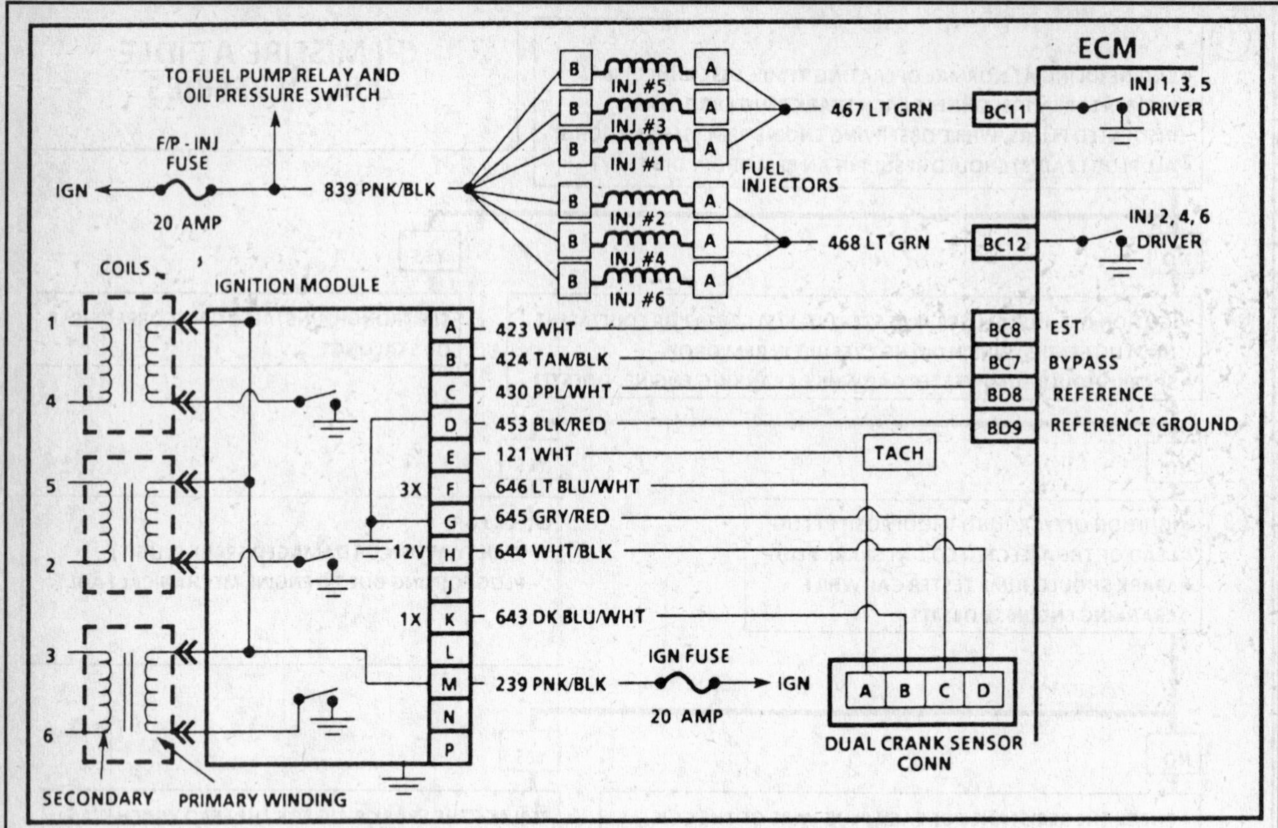

MISFIRE AT IDLE
3300 (VIN N) "N" CARLINE (PORT)

Circuit Description:

The ignition system uses a waste spark method of spark distribution. In this type of ignition system the ignition module triggers the #1/4 coil pair resulting in both #1 and #4 spark plugs firing at the same time. #1 cylinder is on the compression stroke at the same time #4 is on the exhaust stroke, resulting in a lower energy requirement to fire #4 spark plug. This leaves the remaining high voltage to fire #1 spark plug.

Test Description: Number(s) below refer to circled number(s) on the diagnostic chart.

1. If the "misfire" complaint exists under load only, the diagnostic CHART C-4-2 must be used. Engine rpm should drop approximately equally on all plug leads.
2. A spark tester such as a ST-125 must be used because it is essential to verify adequate available secondary voltage at the spark plug. Secondary voltage of at least 25,000 volts must be present to jump the gap of a ST-125.
3. If ignition coils are carbon tracked, the coil tower spark plug wire nipples may be damaged.
4. By checking the secondary resistance, a coil with an open secondary may be located.
5. By switching a normally operating coil into the position of the malfunctioning one, a determination can be made as to fault being the coil or ignition module.

FIG. 24 Ignition system diagnosis — 3.3L engine

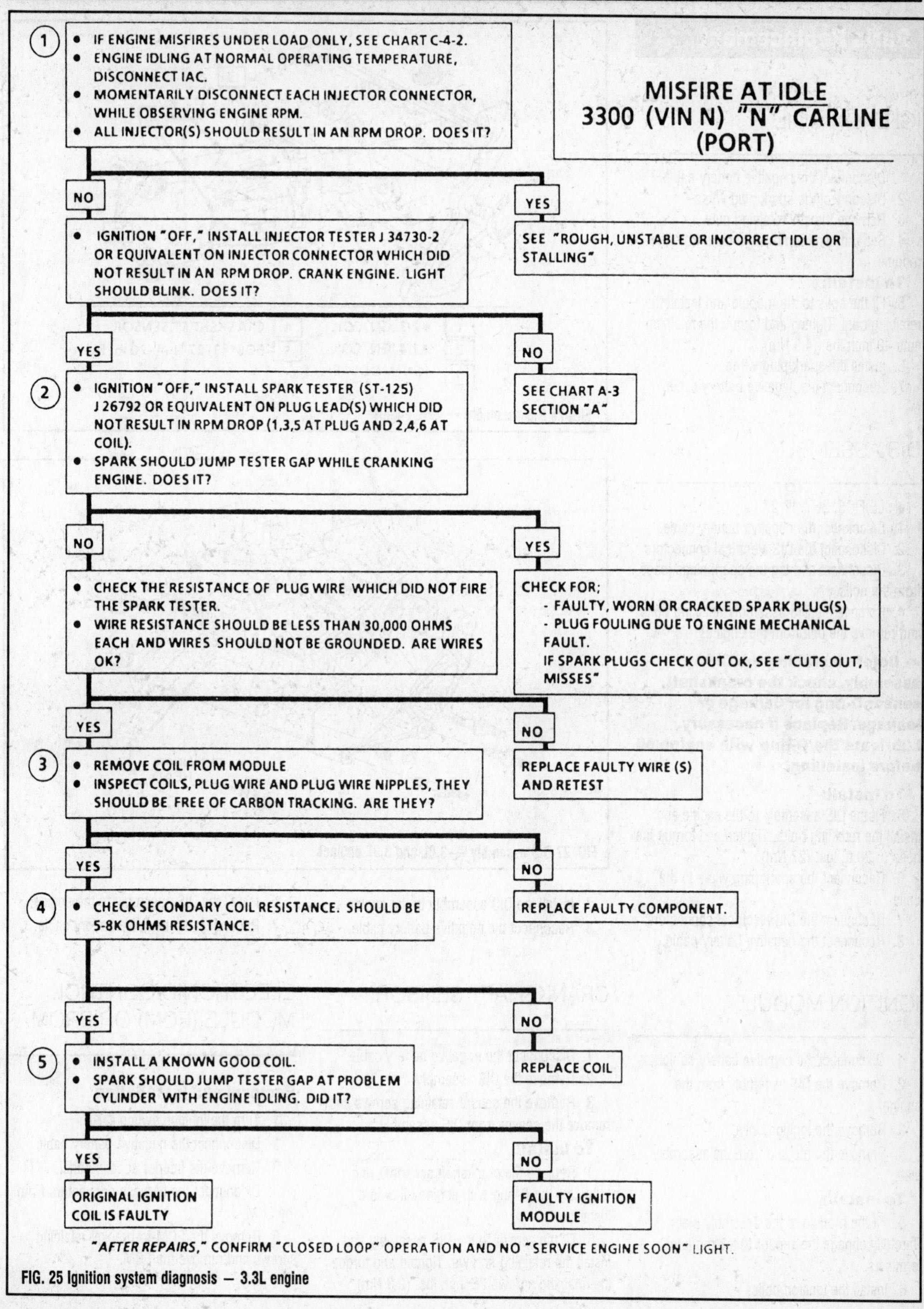

FIG. 25 Ignition system diagnosis — 3.3L engine

Parts Replacement

IGNITION COIL

1. Disconnect the negative battery cable.
2. Disconnect the spark plug wires.
3. Remove the coil retaining nuts.
4. Separate and remove the coils from the module.

To install:

5. Fit the coils to the module and install the retaining nuts. Tighten and torque the retaining nuts 40 inch lbs. (4.5 Nm).
6. Install the spark plug wires.
7. Reconnect the negative battery cable.

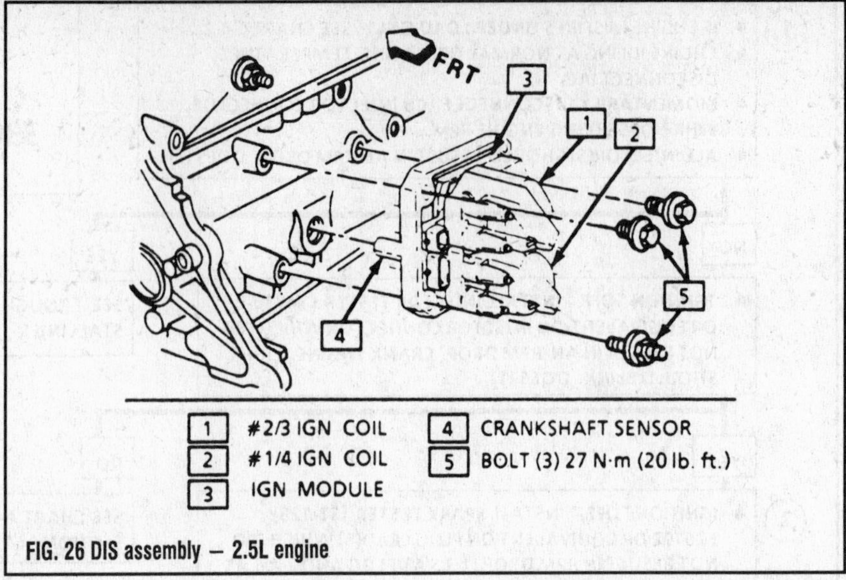

FIG. 26 DIS assembly — 2.5L engine

DIS ASSEMBLY

➧ SEE FIGS. 26 AND 27

1. Disconnect the negative battery cable.
2. Disconnect the DIS electrical connectors.
3. Disconnect and tag the spark plugs leads from the coils.
4. Remove the DIS assembly retaining bolts and remove the unit from the engine.

➡ **Before installing the DIS assembly, check the crankshaft sensor O-ring for damage or leakage. Replace if necessary. Lubricate the O-ring with engine oil before installing.**

To install:

5. Fit the DIS assembly to the engine and install the retaining bolts. Tighten and torque the bolts to 20 ft. lbs. (27 Nm).
6. Reconnect the spark plug wires to the coils.
7. Reconnect the DIS electrical connectors.
8. Reconnect the negative battery cable.

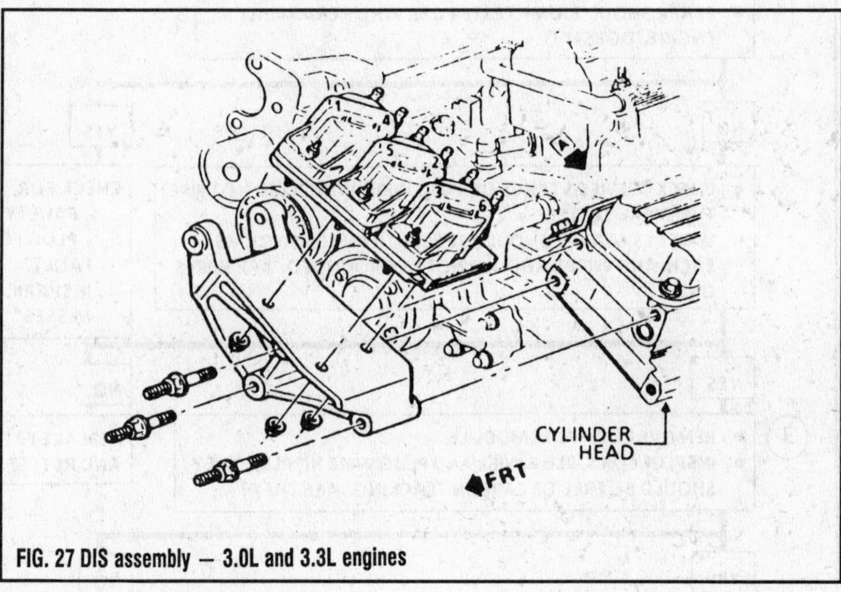

FIG. 27 DIS assembly — 3.0L and 3.3L engines

IGNITION MODULE

1. Disconnect the negative battery cable.
2. Remove the DIS assembly from the engine.
3. Remove the ignition coils.
4. Remove the module from the assembly plate.

To install:

5. Fit the module to the assembly plate. Carefully engage the sensor to the module terminals.
6. Install the ignition coils.
7. Install the DIS assembly to the engine.
8. Reconnect the negative battery cable.

CRANKSHAFT SENSOR

1. Disconnect the negative battery cable.
2. Remove the DIS assembly.
3. Remove the sensor retaining screws and remove the sensor from DIS assembly.

To install:

4. Replace the crankshaft sensor O-ring. Lubricate the O-ring with engine oil before installing.
5. Fit the sensor to the DIS assembly and install the retaining screws. Tighten and torque the retaining screws 20 inch lbs. (2.3 Nm).
6. Install the DIS assembly to the engine.
7. Reconnect the negative battery cable.

ELECTRONIC CONTROL MODULE (ECM) OR PROM

Removal and Installation

1. Turn the ignition switch **OFF**.
2. Disconnect the negative battery cable.
3. Remove the interior access panel.
4. Disconnect the harness connectors from the ECM.
5. Remove the ECM-to-bracket retaining screws and remove the ECM.

6. If PROM replacement is required, remove the access cover retaining screws and cover from the ECM. Carefully remove the PROM carrier assembly from the ECM, using the rocker type PROM removal tool.

To install:

7. Fit the replacement PROM carrier assembly into the PROM socket.

➡ **The small notch of the carrier should be aligned with the small notch in the socket. Press on the PROM carrier until it is firmly seated in the socket. Do not press on the PROM, only the carrier.**

8. Install the access cover and retaining screws.

9. Position the ECM in the vehicle and install the ECM-to-bracket retaining screws.

10. Reconnect the ECM harness connectors.

11. Install the interior access panel.

➡ **Before replacement of a defective ECM first check the resistance of each ECM controlled solenoid. This can be done at the ECM connector, using an ohmmeter and the ECM connector wiring diagram. Any ECM controlled device with low resistance will damage the replacement ECM due to high current flow through the ECM internal circuits.**

12. Check that the ignition switch is **OFF**. Then, reconnect the negative battery cable.

COMPUTER CONTROLLED COIL IGNITION (C^3I) SYSTEM – 3.0L (VIN L) AND 3.3L (VIN N) ENGINES

General Description

The Computer Controlled Coil Ignition (C^3I) system features a distributorless ignition engine. The C^3I system consists of 3 ignition coils, a C^3I ignition module, a dual crank sensor, camshaft sensor, connecting wires, and the Electronic Spark Timing (EST) portion of the Electronic Control Module (ECM).

The C^3I system uses the same Electronic Spark Timing (EST) circuits as the distributor-type ignition. The ECM uses the EST circuit to control spark advance and ignition dwell, when the ignition system is operating in the EST mode. There are 2 modes of ignition system operation. These modes are as follows:

- Module mode — the ignition system operates independently of the ECM, with module mode spark advance always at 10° BTDC. The ECM have no control of the ignition system when in this mode.
- EST mode — the ignition spark timing and ignition dwell time is fully controlled by the ECM. EST spark advance and ignition dwell is calculated by the ECM.

To control spark knock, and enable maximum spark advance to improve driveability and fuel economy, an Electronic Spark Control (ESC) system is used. This system is consists of a knock sensor and an ESC module (part of Mem-Cal). The ECM monitors the ESC signal to determine when engine detonation occurs.

System Operation

The C^3I system uses a waste spark distribution method. Each cylinder is paired with the cylinder opposite it (i.e. 1–4, 2–5, 3–6). The ends of each coil secondary is attached to a spark plug. These 2 plugs, being on companion cylinders, are at top dead center at the same time. The one that is on compression is said to be the event cylinder and the one on the exhaust stroke, the waste cylinder. When the coil discharges, both plugs fire at the same time to complete the series circuit. Therefore, each pair of cylinders is fired for each crankshaft revolution.

Since the polarity of the primary and the secondary windings are fixed, one plug always fires in a forward direction and the other in reverse. This differs from a conventional system in which all plugs fire in the same direction each time. Because of the demand for additional energy; the coil design, saturation time and primary current flow are also different. This redesign of the system allows higher energy to be available from the distributorless coils, greater than 40 kilovolts at all rpm ranges.

During cranking, when the engine speed is beneath 400 rpm, the C^3I module monitors the dual crank sensor sync signal. The sync signal is used to determine the correct pair of cylinders to be sparked first. Once the sync signal has been processed by the ignition module, it sends a fuel control reference pulse to the ECM.

During the cranking period, the ECM will also receive a cam pulse signal and will operate the injectors sequentially, based on true camshaft position only.

The sync signal, or pulse, is used only by the ignition module. It is used for spark synchronization at start-up only.

When the engine speed is beneath 400 rpm (during cranking), the C^3I module controls the spark timing. Once the engine speed exceeds 400 rpm (engine running) spark timing is controlled by the EST signal from the ECM. To control EST the ECM uses the following inputs:

- Crankshaft position
- Engine speed (rpm)
- Engine coolant (Coolant Temperature Sensor — CTS)
- Intake air (Mass Air Flow — MAF)
- Throttle valve position (Throttle Position Sensor — TPS)
- Gear shift lever position (Park/Neutral Switch — P/N)
- Vehicle speed (Vehicle Speed Sensor — VSS)
- ESC signal (Knock Sensor)

The C^3I ignition module provides proper ignition coil sequencing during both the module and the EST modes.

The ESC system is designed to retard spark

timing up to 10° to reduce spark knock in the engine. When the knock sensor detects spark knocking in the engine, it sends an AC voltage signal to the ECM, which increases with the severity of the knock. The ECM then adjusts the EST to reduce spark knock.

SYSTEM COMPONENTS

C³I Module

The C³I module monitors the sync-pulse and the crank signal. During cranking the C³I module monitors the sync-pulse to begin the ignition firing sequence. During this time, each of the 3 coils are fired at a pre-determined interval based on engine speed only. Above 400 rpm, the C³I module is only use as a reference signal.

Ignition Coil

The ignition coil assemblies are mounted on the C³I module. Each coil distributes the spark for 2 plugs simultaneously.

Electronic Spark Control (ESC)

The ESC system incorporates a knock sensor and the ECM. The knock sensor detects engine detonation. When engine detonation occurs, the ECM receives the ESC signal and retards EST to reduce detonation.

Electronic Spark Timing (EST)

The EST system is basically the same EST to ECM circuit use on the distributor type ignition systems with EST. This system includes the following circuits:

- Reference circuit — provides the ECM with rpm and crankshaft position information from the C³I module. The C³I module receives this signal from the crank sensor hall-effect switch.
- Bypass signal — above 400 rpm, the ECM applies 5 volts to this circuit to switch spark timing control from the C³I module to the ECM.
- EST signal — reference signal is sent to the ECM via the CúI module during cranking. Under 400 rpm, the C³I module controls the ignition timing. Above 400 rpm, the ECM applies 5 volts to the bypass line to switch the timing to the ECM control.

Electronic Control Module (ECM)

The ECM is responsible for maintaining proper spark and fuel injection timing for all driving conditions.

Dual Crank Sensor

The dual crank sensor is mounted in a pedestal on the front of the engine near the harmonic balancer. The sensor consists of 2 hall-effect switches, which depend on 2 metal interrupter rings mounted on the balancer to activate them. Windows in the interrupters activate the hall-effect switches as they provide a path for the magnetic field between the switches transducers and magnets.

Diagnosis and Testing

SERVICE PRECAUTIONS

⁂ CAUTION

The ignition coil's secondary voltage output capabilities can exceed 40,000 volts. Avoid body contact with the C³I high voltage secondary components when the engine is running, or personal injury may result.

➡ To avoid damage to the ECM or other ignition system components, do not use electrical test equipment such as battery or AC-powered voltmeter, ohmmeter, etc. or any type of tester other than specified.

- To properly diagnosis the ignition systems and their problems, it will be necessary to refer to the diagnostic charts in the fuel injection section.
- When performing electrical tests on the system, use a high impedance multimeter or quality digital voltmeter (DVM). Use of a 12 volt test light is not recommended.
- To prevent electrostatic discharge damage, when working with the ECM, do not touch the connector pins or soldered components on the circuit board.
- When handling a PROM, CAL-PAK or MEM-CAL, do not touch the component leads. Also, do not remove the integrated circuit from the carrier.
- Never pierce a high tension lead or boot for any testing purpose; otherwise, future problems are guaranteed.
- Do not allow extension cords for power tools or droplights to lie on, near or across any vehicle electrical wiring.
- Leave new components and modules in the shipping package until ready to install them.

READING CODES

The Assembly Line Diagnostic Link (ALDL) connector is used for communicating with the ECM. It is usually located under the instrument panel and is sometimes covered by a plastic cover labeled "DIAGNOSTIC CONNECTOR." Codes stored in the ECM's memory can be read through a hand-held diagnostic scanner plugged into the ALDL connector. If a scanner is not available, the codes can also be read by jumping from terminal **A** to **B** of the ALDL connector and counting the number of flashes of the Service Engine Soon light, with the ignition switch turned **ON**.

Refer to Section 4 for a more detailed look diagnostic codes, what they mean and how to diagnose them.

CLEARING CODES

To clear codes from the ECM memory, the ECM power feed must be disconnected for at least 30 seconds. Depending on the vehicle, the ECM power feed can be disconnected at the positive battery terminal pigtail, the inline fuseholder that originates at the positive connection at the battery or the ECM fuse in the fuse block. The negative battery cable may also be disconnected; however, other on-board memory data, such as radio station presets, will also be lost.

Also, if battery power is lost, computer relearn time is approximately 5–10 minutes. This means the computer may have to re-calibrate components which set up the idle speed and the idle may fluctuate while this is occurring.

BASIC IGNITION SYSTEM CHECK

1. Check for codes. If any are found, refer to the appropriate chart in Section 4.
2. Turn the ignition switch **ON**. Verify that the Service Engine Soon light is ON.
3. Install the scan tool and check the following:

Throttle Position Sensor (TPS) — if over 2.5 volts, at closed throttle, check the TPS and circuit.

Coolant — if not between −22°F (−30°C) and 266°F (130°C), check the sensor and circuit.

4. Disconnect all injector connectors and install injector test light (J-34730-2 or equivalent) in injector harness connector. Test light should be OFF.

➡ **Perform this test on 1 injector from each bank.**

5. Connect spark checker, (J 26792 or equivalent), and check for spark while cranking. Check at least 2 wires.

a. If spark occurs, reconnect the spark plug wires and check for fuel spray at the injector(s) while cranking.

b. If no spark occurs, check for battery voltage to the ignition system. If OK, substitute known good parts for possible faulty ignition parts. If not, refer to the wiring diagrams to track down loss of voltage.

Parts Replacement

IGNITION COIL

1. Disconnect the negative battery cable.
2. Disconnect the spark plug wires.
3. Remove the 2 retaining screws securing the coil to the ignition module.
4. Remove the coil assembly.

To install:

5. Fit the coil assembly to the ignition module.
6. Install the retaining screws and torque to 40 inch lbs. (4–5 Nm).
7. Install the spark plug wires.
8. Reconnect the negative battery cable.

C3I MODULE

1. Disconnect the negative battery cable.
2. Disconnect the 14-way connector at the ignition module.
3. Disconnect the spark plug wires at the coil assembly.
4. Remove the nuts and washers that retains the module to the bracket.
5. Remove the coil-to-module retaining bolts.
6. Note the lead colors or mark for reassembly.
7. Disconnect the connectors between the coil and ignition module.
8. Remove the ignition module.

To install:

9. Fit the coils and connectors to the ignition module and install the retaining bolts. Tighten and torque the retaining bolts to 27 inch lbs. (3 Nm).
10. Fit the module assembly to the bracket and install the nuts and washers.
11. Reconnect the 14-way connector to the module.
12. Reconnect the negative battery cable.

DUAL CRANK SENSOR

➧ SEE FIGS. 28–30

1. Disconnect the negative battery cable.
2. Remove the belt(s) from the crankshaft pulley.
3. Raise and support the vehicle safely.
4. Remove the right front wheel and inner fender access cover.
5. Remove the crankshaft harmonic balancer retaining bolt, then remove the harmonic balancer.
6. Disconnect the sensor electrical connector.
7. Remove the sensor and pedestal from the engine block, then separate the sensor from the pedestal.

To install:

8. Loosely install the crankshaft sensor to the pedestal.
9. Using tool J-37089 or equivalent, position the sensor with the pedestal attached, on the crankshaft.

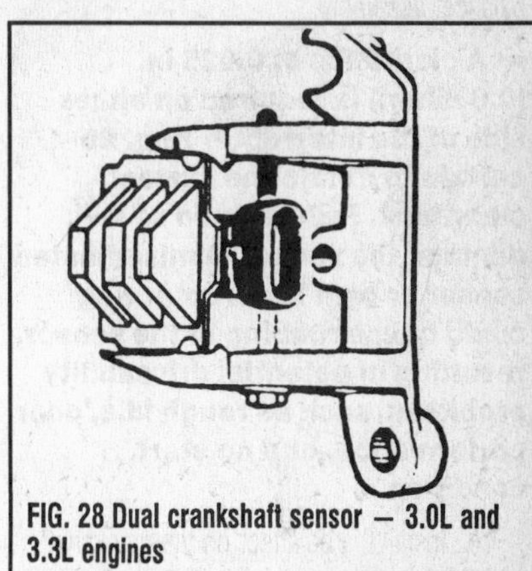

FIG. 28 Dual crankshaft sensor — 3.0L and 3.3L engines

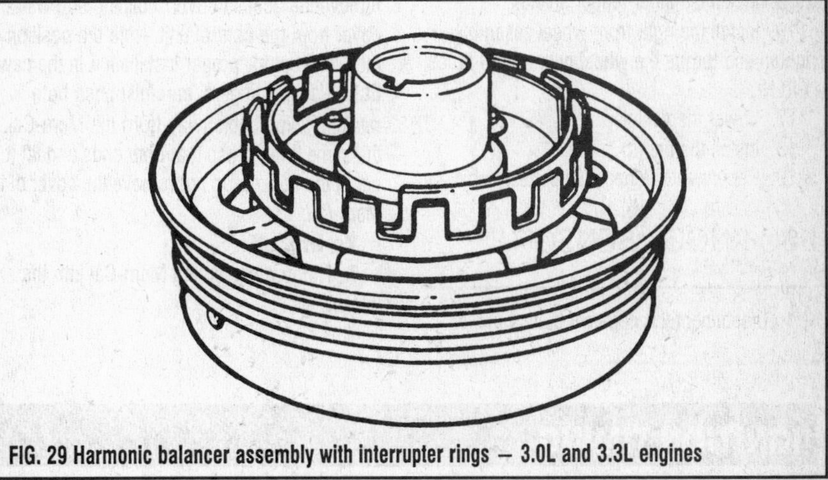

FIG. 29 Harmonic balancer assembly with interrupter rings — 3.0L and 3.3L engines

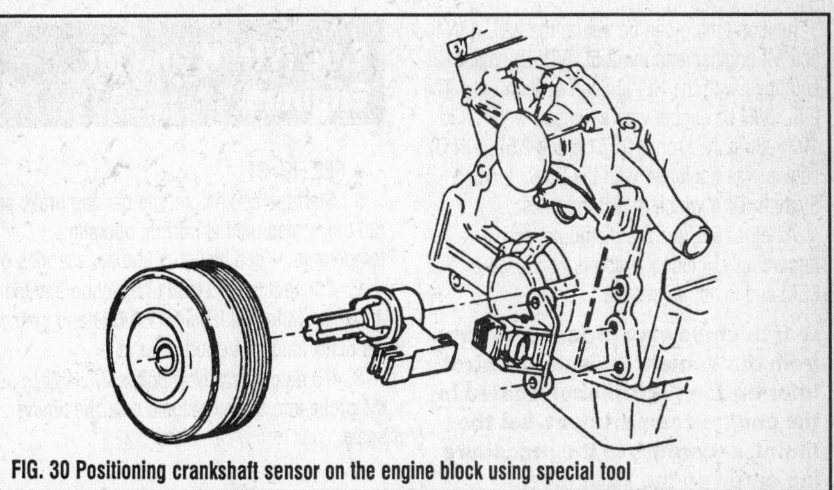

FIG. 30 Positioning crankshaft sensor on the engine block using special tool

10. Install the pedestal-to-block retaining bolts. Tighten and torque to 14–28 ft. lbs. (20–40 Nm).

11. Torque the pedestal pinch bolt 30–35 inch lbs. (20–40 Nm).

12. Remove tool J–37089 or equivalent.

13. Place tool J–37089 or equivalent, on the harmonic balancer and turn. If any vane of the harmonic balancer touches the tool, replace the balancer assembly.

➡ **A clearance of 0.025 in. (0.635mm) is required on either side of the interrupter ring. Be certain to obtain the correct clearance. Failure to do so will damage the sensor. A misadjusted sensor or bent interrupter ring could cause rubbing of the sensor, resulting in potential driveability problems, such as rough idle, poor performance, or a no start condition.**

14. Install the balancer on the crankshaft. Install the balancer retaining bolt. Tighten and torque the retaining bolt to 200–239 ft. lbs. (270–325 Nm).

15. Install the inner fender shield.

16. Install the right front wheel assembly. Tighten and torque the wheel nuts to 100 ft. lbs. (140 Nm).

17. Lower the vehicle.

18. Install the belt(s).

19. Reconnect the negative battery cable.

ESC KNOCK SENSOR

1. Disconnect the negative battery cable.

2. Raise and support the vehicle safely.

3. Disconnect the harness connector from the knock sensor.

4. Remove the sensor from the engine block.

To install:

5. Clean the threads on the engine block, where the sensor was installed. Install the sensor. Tighten to 11–16 ft. lbs. (15–22 Nm).

6. Reconnect the harness connector to the knock sensor.

7. Lower the vehicle.

8. Reconnect the negative battery cable.

ELECTRONIC CONTROL MODULE (ECM) AND/OR MEM-CAL

1. Turn the ignition switch **OFF**.

2. Disconnect the negative battery cable.

3. Remove the right side hush panel.

4. Disconnect the harness connectors from the control unit.

5. Remove the control unit-to-bracket retaining screws and remove the control unit.

6. If replacement of the Mem-Cal is required, remove the access cover retaining screws and cover from the control unit. Note the position of the Mem-Cal for proper installation in the new ECM. Using 2 fingers, carefully push both retaining clips back away from the Mem-Cal. At the same time, grasp it at both ends and lift it up out of the socket. Do not remove the cover of the Mem-Cal.

To install:

7. Fit the replacement Mem-Cal into the socket.

➡ **The small notches in the Mem-Cal must be aligned with the small notches in the socket. Press only on the ends of the Mem-Cal until the retaining clips snap into the ends of the Mem-Cal. Do not press on the middle of the Mem-Cal, only the ends.**

8. Install the access cover and retaining screws.

9. Position the control unit in the vehicle and install the control unit-to-bracket retaining screws.

10. Reconnect the control unit harness connectors.

11. Install the hush panel.

12. Check that the ignition switch is **OFF**. Then reconnect the negative battery cable.

Functional Check

1. Turn the ignition switch **ON**.

2. Enter diagnostics.

a. Allow Code 12 to flash 4 times to verify no other codes are present. This indicates the Mem-Cal is installed properly and the control unit is functioning.

b. If trouble Codes 42, 43 or 51 occur, or if the Service Engine Soon light is ON constantly with no codes, the Mem-Cal is not fully seated or is defective.

c. If it is not fully seated, press firmly on the ends of the Mem-Cal.

IGNITION TIMING

Ignition timing can be set on the 2.0L (VIN K and M) engines and the 2.5L (VIN U) engine equipped with the HEI ignition system only. The 2.5L (VIN U) engine was equipped with HEI in 1985–86 only. From 1987 on, the 2.5L (VIN U) engine was equipped with the Direct Ignition System (DIS) which is distributorless.

All other engines are distributorless. Accordingly, ignition timing is controlled by the ECM and is not adjustable.

➡ **If the following procedures vary from the Vehicle Emission Control Information (VECI) label located in the engine compartment, set the timing according to the procedure indicated on the VECI label.**

2.0L (VIN K and M) Engines

➧ SEE FIG. 31

1. Start the engine, set the parking brake and run the engine until at normal operating temperature. Keep all lights and accessories off.

2. Connect the red lead of a tachometer to the terminal of the coil labeled **TACH** and connect the black lead to a good ground.

3. If a magnetic timing unit is available, insert the probe into the receptacle near the timing scale.

4. If a magnetic timing unit is not available, connect a conventional power timing light to the No. 1 cylinder spark plug wire.

5. With parking brake safely set, place automatic transaxle in **D** or leave manual transaxle in neutral.

6. Ground the ALDL connector under the dash by installing a jumper wire between the **A** and **B** terminals. The check engine light should begin flashing.

7. Aim the timing light at the timing scale or read the magnetic timing unit. Record the reading.

8. Repeat Steps 3–6 using the No. 4 spark plug wire. Record the reading.

9. Use the average of the 2 readings to derive an average timing value.
10. Loosen the distributor hold-down nuts so the distributor can be rotated.
11. Using the average timing value, turn the distributor in the proper direction until the specified timing according to the Vehicle Emission Control Information label is reached.
12. Tighten the hold-down nuts and recheck the timing values.
13. Remove the jumper wire from the ALDL connector. To clear the ECM memory, disconnect the ECM harness from the positive battery pigtail for 10 seconds with the key in the OFF position.

2.5L (VIN U) Engine

1985–86

1. Place transmission in **P**, set parking brake and block wheels.
2. Bring engine to normal operating temperature.
3. Turn air conditioning **OFF**.
4. Connect a jumper between terminals A and B of the ALDL connector.
5. Connect an inductive timing light to the coil wire and check the ignition timing. Compare the reading to the specified setting on the VECI label.
6. If adjustment is necessary, loosen the distributor hold-down bolt and adjust the timing by rotating the distributor while observing the timing light.
7. When the timing is set to specification, tighten the hold-down bolt.
8. Disconnect the timing light.
9. Remove jumper wire.

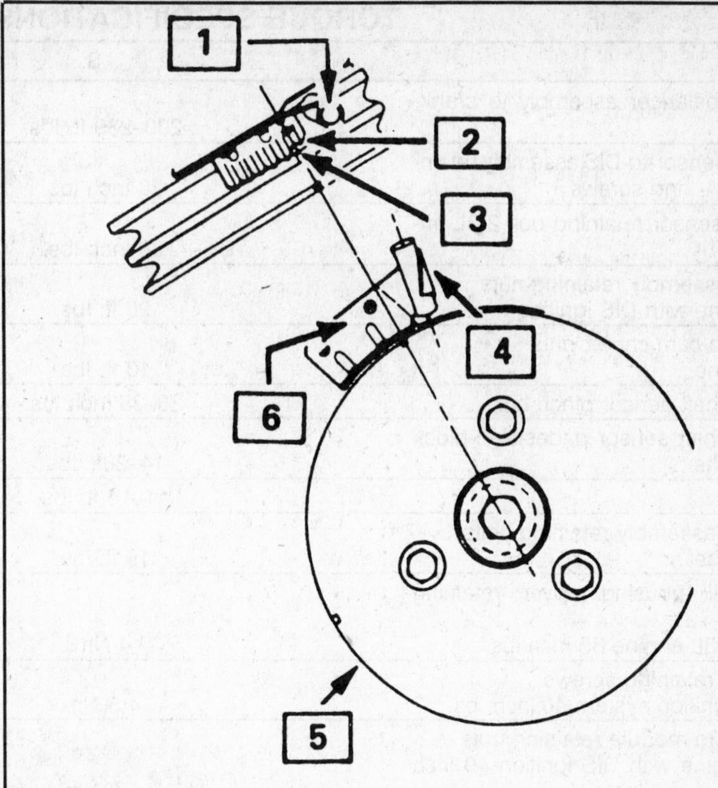

1—MAGNETIC TIMING PROBE HOLE

2—"O" STAMP ON POINTER

3—NOTCH IN PULLEY

4—MAGNETIC TIMING PROBE HOLE ASM.

5—PULLEY

6—ASM. MOUNTED TO FRONT COVER

FIG. 31 Typical ignition timing marker with magnetic pick-up

VALVE LASH

All engines used in N body cars are equipped with hydraulic valve lifters that do not require valve lash adjustment. Adjustment to zero lash is maintained automatically by hydraulic pressure in the lifters.

IDLE SPEED AND MIXTURE ADJUSTMENTS

Idle speed and mixture for all engines is electronically controlled by the computerized fuel injection system. Adjustment are neither necessary or possible. All threaded throttle stop adjusters are factory set and capped to discourage any tampering; in some areas, tampering is illegal. In most cases, proper diagnosis and parts replacement will straighten out any problems concerning this subject.

TORQUE SPECIFICATIONS

Component	U.S.	Metric
Crankshaft balancer assembly to crankshaft	200–239 ft. lbs.	270–325Nm
Crankshaft sensor-to-DIS assembly retaining screws	20 inch lbs.	2 3 Nm
Crankshaft sensor retaining bolt 2 3L engine	88 inch lbs.	10 Nm
DIS assembly retaining nuts 2 5L engine with DIS ignition	20 ft. lbs.	27 Nm
Distributor-to-cam carrier nuts 2 0L engine	13 ft. lbs.	18 Nm
Dual crankshaft sensor pinch bolt	30–35 inch lbs.	20–40 Nm
Dual crankshaft sensor pedestal-to-block retaining bolts	14–28ft. lbs.	20–40 Nm
ESC sensor	11–16 ft. lbs.	15–22 Nm
IDA system assembly retaining bolts 2 3L engine	19 ft. lbs.	26 Nm
Ignition coil housing cover retaining screws 2 3L engine 35 inch lbs.	4 Nm	
Ignition coil retaining screws C^3I Ignition system 40 inch lbs.	4 5 Nm	
Ignition coil-to-module retaining nuts 2 5L engine with DIS ignition 40 inch lbs.	4 5 Nm	
Ignition cover bolts 2 3L engine	15 ft. lbs.	20 Nm
Ignition module retaining bolts C^3I Ignition system 27 inch lbs.	3 Nm	
Lug nuts	100 ft. lbs.	140 Nm
Spark plugs 2 0L, 2 5L 3 0L and 3 3L engines 2 3L engine	 20 ft. lbs. 17 ft. lbs.	 27 Nm 23 Nm

3

ENGINE AND ENGINE OVERHAUL

ENGINE ELECTRICAL

Understanding the Engine Electrical System

The engine electrical system can be broken down into three systems:

1. The starting system.
2. The charging system.
3. The ignition system.

BATTERY AND STARTING SYSTEM

Basic Operating Principles

The battery is the first link in the chain of mechanisms which work together to provide cranking of the automobile engine. In most modern cars, the battery is a lead/acid electrochemical device consisting of six 2v subsections connected in series so the unit is capable of producing approximately 12v of electrical pressure. Each subsection, or cell, consists of a series of positive and negative plates held a short distance apart in a solution of sulfuric acid and water. The two types of plates are of dissimilar metals. This causes a chemical reaction to be set up, and it is this reaction which produces current flow from the battery when its positive and negative terminals are connected to an electrical appliance such as a lamp or motor. The continued transfer of electrons would eventually convert the sulfuric acid in the electrolyte to water, and make the two plates identical in chemical composition. As electrical energy is removed from the battery, its voltage output tends to drop. Thus, measuring battery voltage and battery electrolyte composition are two ways of checking the ability of the unit to supply power. During the starting of the engine, electrical energy is removed from the battery. However, if the charging circuit is in good condition and the operating conditions are normal, the power removed from the battery will be replaced by the generator (or alternator) which will force electrons back through the battery, reversing the normal flow, and restoring the battery to its original chemical state.

The battery and starting motor are linked by very heavy electrical cables designed to minimize resistance to the flow of current. Generally, the major power supply cable that leaves the battery goes directly to the starter, while other electrical system needs are supplied by a smaller cable. During starter operation, power flows from the battery to the starter and is grounded through the car's frame and the battery's negative ground strap.

The starting motor is a specially designed, direct current electric motor capable of producing a very great amount of power for its size. One thing that allows the motor to produce a great deal of power is its tremendous rotating speed. It drives the engine through a tiny pinion gear (attached to the starter's armature), which drives the very large flywheel ring gear at a greatly reduced speed. Another factor allowing it to produce so much power is that only intermittent operation is required of it. This, little allowance for air circulation is required, and the windings can be built into a very small space.

The starter solenoid is a magnetic device which employs the small current supplied by the starting switch circuit of the ignition switch. This magnetic action moves a plunger which mechanically engages the starter and electrically closes the heavy switch which connects it to the battery. The starting switch circuit consists of the starting switch contained within the ignition switch, a transmission neutral safety switch or clutch pedal switch, and the wiring necessary to connect these in series with the starter solenoid or relay.

A pinion, which is a small gear, is mounted to a one-way drive clutch. This clutch is splined to the starter armature shaft. When the ignition switch is moved to the **start** position, the solenoid plunger slides the pinion toward the flywheel ring gear via a collar and spring. If the teeth on the pinion and flywheel match properly, the pinion will engage the flywheel immediately. If the gear teeth butt one another, the spring will be compressed and will force the gears to mesh as soon as the starter turns far enough to allow them to do so. As the solenoid plunger reaches the end of its travel, it closes the contacts that connect the battery and starter and then the engine is cranked.

As soon as the engine starts, the flywheel ring gear begins turning fast enough to drive the pinion at an extremely high rate of speed. At this point, the one-way clutch begins allowing the pinion to spin faster than the starter shaft so that the starter will not operate at excessive speed. When the ignition switch is released from the starter position, the solenoid is de-energized, and a spring contained within the solenoid assembly pulls the gear out of mesh and interrupts the current flow to the starter.

Some starter employ a separate relay, mounted away from the starter, to switch the motor and solenoid current on and off. The relay thus replaces the solenoid electrical switch, buy does not eliminate the need for a solenoid mounted on the starter used to mechanically engage the starter drive gears. The relay is used to reduce the amount of current the starting switch must carry.

THE CHARGING SYSTEM

Basic Operating Principles

The automobile charging system provides electrical power for operation of the vehicle's ignition and starting systems and all the electrical accessories. The battery services as an electrical surge or storage tank, storing (in chemical form) the energy originally produced by the engine driven generator. The system also provides a means of regulating generator output to protect the battery from being overcharged and to avoid excessive voltage to the accessories.

The storage battery is a chemical device incorporating parallel lead plates in a tank containing a sulfuric acid/water solution. Adjacent plates are slightly dissimilar, and the chemical reaction of the two dissimilar plates produces electrical energy when the battery is connected to a load such as the starter motor. The chemical reaction is reversible, so that when the generator is producing a voltage (electrical pressure) greater than that produced by the battery, electricity is forced into the battery, and the battery is returned to its fully charged state.

The vehicle's generator is driven mechanically, through V-belts, by the engine crankshaft. It consists of two coils of fine wire, one stationary (the stator), and one movable (the rotor). The rotor may also be known as the armature, and consists of fine wire wrapped around an iron core which is mounted on a shaft. The electricity which flows through the two coils of wire (provided initially by the battery in some cases) creates an intense magnetic field around both rotor and stator, and the interaction between the two fields creates voltage, allowing the generator to power the accessories and charge the battery.

There are two types of generators: the earlier is the direct current (DC) type. The current produced by the DC generator is generated in the armature and carried off the spinning armature by stationary brushes contacting the commutator. The commutator is a series of smooth metal contact plates on the end of the armature. The commutator is a series of smooth metal contact plates on the end of the armature. The commutator plates, which are separated from one another by a very short gap, are connected to the armature circuits so that current will flow in one directions only in the wires carrying the generator output. The generator stator consists of two stationary coils of wire which draw some of the output current of the generator to form a powerful magnetic field and create the interaction of fields which generates the voltage. The generator field is wired in series with the regulator.

Newer automobiles use alternating current generators or alternators, because they are more efficient, can be rotated at higher speeds, and have fewer brush problems. In an alternator, the field rotates while all the current produced passes only through the stator winding. The brushes bear against continuous slip rings rather than a commutator. This causes the current produced to periodically reverse the direction of its flow. Diodes (electrical one-way switches) block the flow of current from traveling in the wrong direction. A series of diodes is wired together to permit the alternating flow of the stator to be converted to a pulsating, but unidirectional flow at the alternator output. The alternator's field is wired in series with the voltage regulator.

The regulator consists of several circuits. Each circuit has a core, or magnetic coil of wire, which operates a switch. Each switch is connected to ground through one or more resistors. The coil of wire responds directly to system voltage. When the voltage reaches the required level, the magnetic field created by the winding of wire closes the switch and inserts a resistance into the generator field circuit, thus reducing the output. The contacts of the switch cycle open and close many times each second to precisely control voltage.

While alternators are self-limiting as far as maximum current is concerned, DC generators employ a current regulating circuit which responds directly to the total amount of current flowing through the generator circuit rather than to the output voltage. The current regulator is similar to the voltage regulator except that all system current must flow through the energizing coil on its way to the various accessories.

Ignition Coil

➧ SEE FIGS. 1–4

TESTING

Check the ignition coil for opens and ground with an ohmmeter.

1. Connect the negative lead of the ohmmeter, set at a high scale to a good metal ground and the positive lead to the B+ terminal

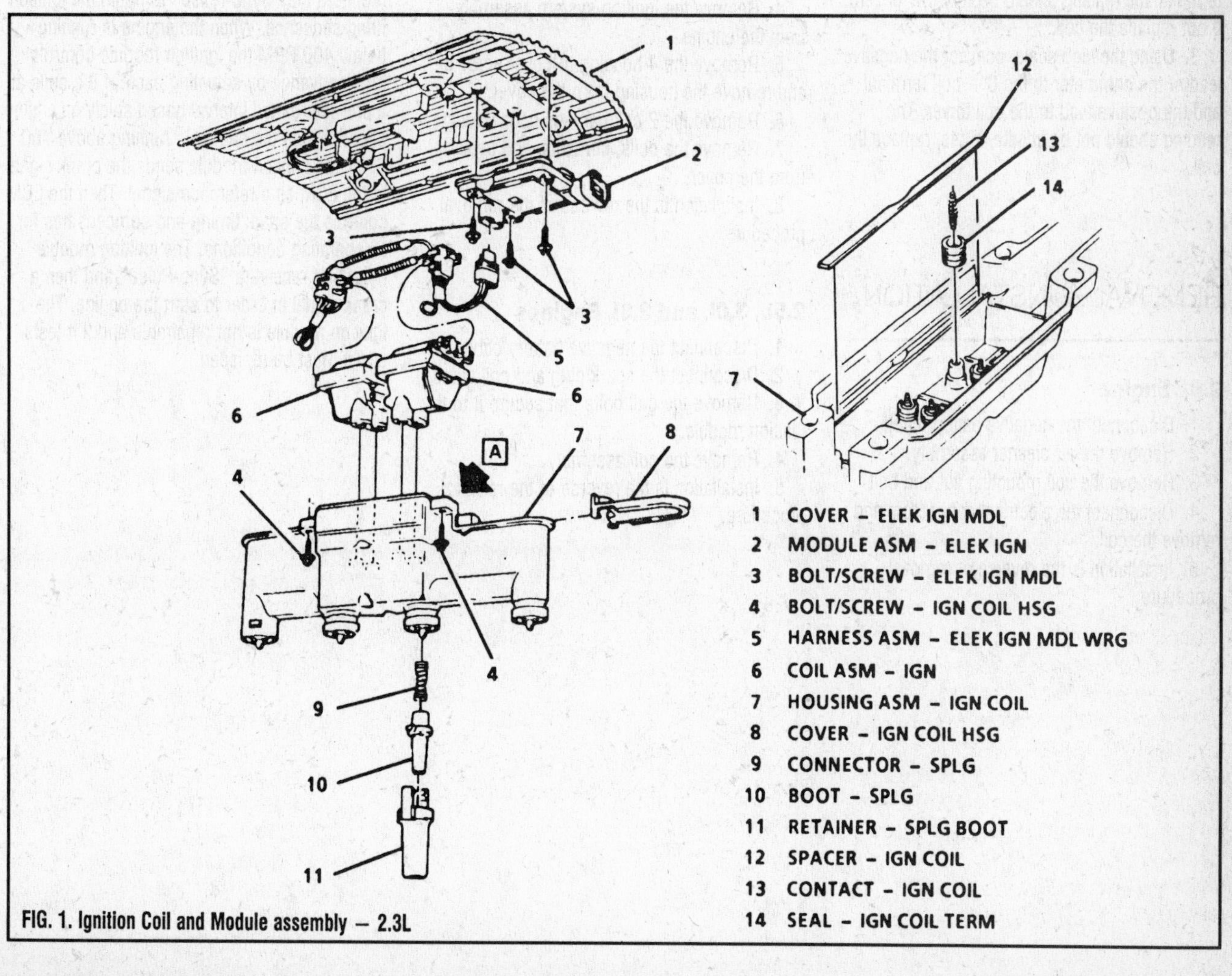

FIG. 1. Ignition Coil and Module assembly — 2.3L

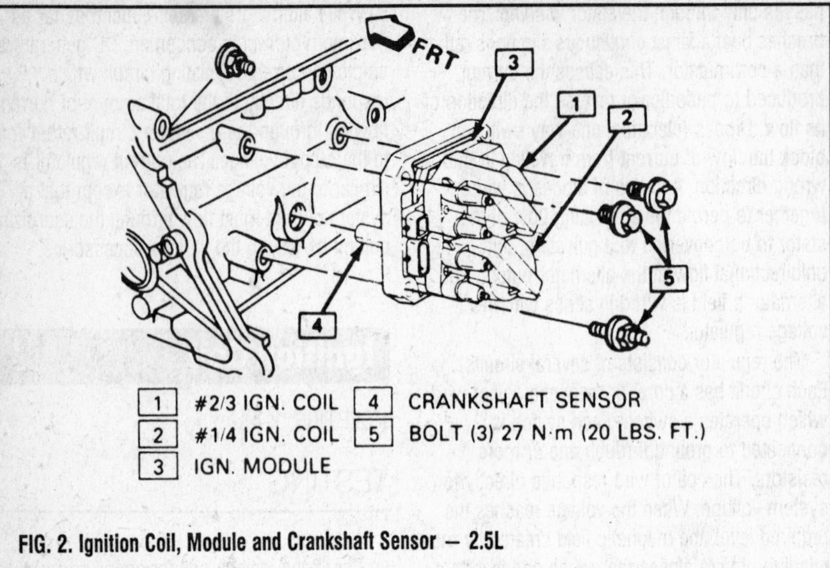

FIG. 2. Ignition Coil, Module and Crankshaft Sensor — 2.5L

of the coil. The reading should be infinite, if not replace the coil.

2. Use the low scale and connect the negative lead of the ohmmeter to the B- terminal of the coil. Connect the positive lead to the C-/tach terminal. the reading should be very low or zero. If not replace the coil.

3. Using the high scale, connect the negative lead of the ohmmeter to the C+ coil terminal and the positive lead to the coil tower. The reading should not be infinite, if it is, replace the coil.

REMOVAL & INSTALLATION

2.0L Engine

1. Disconnect the negative battery cable.
2. Remove the air cleaner assembly.
3. Remove the coil mounting nut and bolt.
4. Disconnect the electrical connectors and remove the coil.
5. Installation is the reverse of removal procedure.

2.3L Engine

1. Disconnect the negative battery cable.
2. Disconnect the 11 pin harness connector.
3. Remove the 4 ignition assembly to cam housing bolts.
4. Remove the ignition system assembly from the engine.
5. Remove the 4 housing to cover screws and remove the housing from the cover.
6. Remove the 2 coil harness connectors.
7. Remove the coils, contacts, and seals from the cover.
8. Installation is the reverse of the removal procedure.

2.5L, 3.0L and 3.3L Engines

1. Disconnect the negative battery cable.
2. Disconnect the spark plug and coil wires.
3. Remove the coil bolts that secure it to the ignition module.
4. Remove the coil assembly.
5. Installation is the reverse of the removal procedure.

Ignition Module

REMOVAL & INSTALLATION

1. Disconnect the negative battery cable.
2. Disconnect the 14-pin connector at the ignition module.
3. Remove the spark plug wires at the coil assembly.
4. Remove the nuts and washers securing the ignition module assembly to the mounting bracket.
5. Remove the screws securing the ignition module to the coil.
6. Tilt the coil and disconnect the coil to module connectors.
7. Separate the coil and module.
8. Installation is the reverse of removal.

The ignition module on the N-Body engines monitors the crank signals and the "Sync-Pulse". The ECM then receives this information and makes adjustments so that the spark and fuel injector timing is correct for all driving conditions. While cranking, the ignition module monitors the "Sync-Pulse" to begin the ignition firing sequence. When the engine is running below 400 RPM the ignition module controls spark advance by actuating each of the coils at a pre-determined interval based solely on engine speed. When the engine is running above 400 RPM, the ignition module sends the crank signal to the ECM as a reference signal. Then the ECM controls the spark timing and compensates for all operating conditions. The ignition module must first receive a "Sync-Pulse" and then a crank signal in order to start the engine. The ignition module is not repairable and if it tests bad it must be replaced.

Computer Controlled Coil Ignition (C³I)

COMPONENT REMOVAL

V6 Engines

IGNITION COIL

1. Disconnect the negative battery cable.
2. Remove the spark plug wires.
3. Remove the screws holding the coil to the ignition module.
4. Tilt the coil assembly to the rear and remove the coil to module connectors.
5. Remove the coil assembly.
6. Installation is the reverse of removal.

IGNITION MODULE

1. Disconnect the negative battery cable.
2. Disconnect the 14-pin connector at the ignition module.
3. Remove the spark plug wires at the coil assembly.
4. Remove the nuts and washers securing the ignition module assembly to the mounting bracket.
5. Remove the screws securing the ignition module to the coil.
6. Tilt the coil and disconnect the coil to module connectors.
7. Separate the coil and module.
8. Installation is the reverse of removal.

CRANKSHAFT SENSOR

➡ It is not necessary to remove the sensor bracket.

1. Disconnect the negative battery cable.
2. Disconnect the sensor 3-way connector.
3. Raise the vehicle and support it safely.
4. Rotate the harmonic balancer so the slot in the disc is aligned with the sensor.
5. Loosen the sensor retaining bolt.
6. Slide the sensor outboard and remove through the notch in the sensor housing.
7. Install the new sensor in the housing and rotate the harmonic balancer so that the disc is positioned in the sensor.

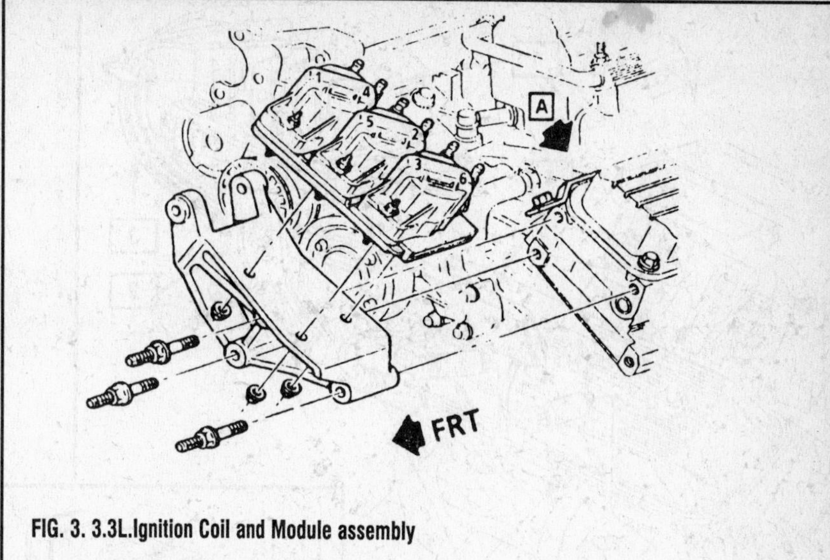

FIG. 3. 3.3L.Ignition Coil and Module assembly

8. Adjust the sensor so that there is an equal distance on each side of the disc. There should be approximately .030 in. (.76mm) clearance between the disc and the sensor.
9. Tighten the retaining bolt and recheck the clearance.
10. Install remaining components in the reverse order of removal.

CAMSHAFT POSITION SENSOR

➡ If only the camshaft sensor is being replaced, it is not necessary to remove the entire assembly. The sensor is replaceable separately.

1. Disconnect the negative battery cable.
2. Disconnect the ignition module 14-pin connector.
3. Remove the spark plug wires at the coil assembly.
4. Remove the ignition module bracket assembly.
5. Disconnect the sensor 3-way connector.
6. Remove the sensor mounting screws, then remove the sensor.
7. Installation is the reverse of removal.

CAMSHAFT POSITION SENSOR DRIVE ASSEMBLY

1. Follow steps 1–6 of the cam sensor removal procedure. Note the position of the slot in the rotating vane.
2. Remove the bolt securing the drive assembly to the engine.
3. Remove the drive assembly.
4. Install the drive assembly with the slot in the vane. Install mounting bolt.
5. Install the camshaft sensor.
6. Rotate the engine to set the No. 1 cylinder at TDC/compression.
7. Mark the harmonic balancer and rotate the engine to 25 degrees after top dead center.
8. Remove the plug wires from the coil assembly.
9. Using weather pack removal tool J-28742-A, or equivalent, remove terminal B of the sensor 3-way connector on the module side.
10. Probe terminal B by installing a jumper and reconnecting the wire removed to the jumper wire.
11. Connect a voltmeter between the jumper wire and ground.
12. With the key ON and the engine stopped, rotate the camshaft sensor counterclockwise until the sensor switch just closes. This is indicated by the voltage reading going from a high 5–12 volts to a low 0–2 volts. The low voltage indicates the switch is closed.
13. Tighten the retaining bolt and reinstall the wire into terminal B.
14. Install remaining components.

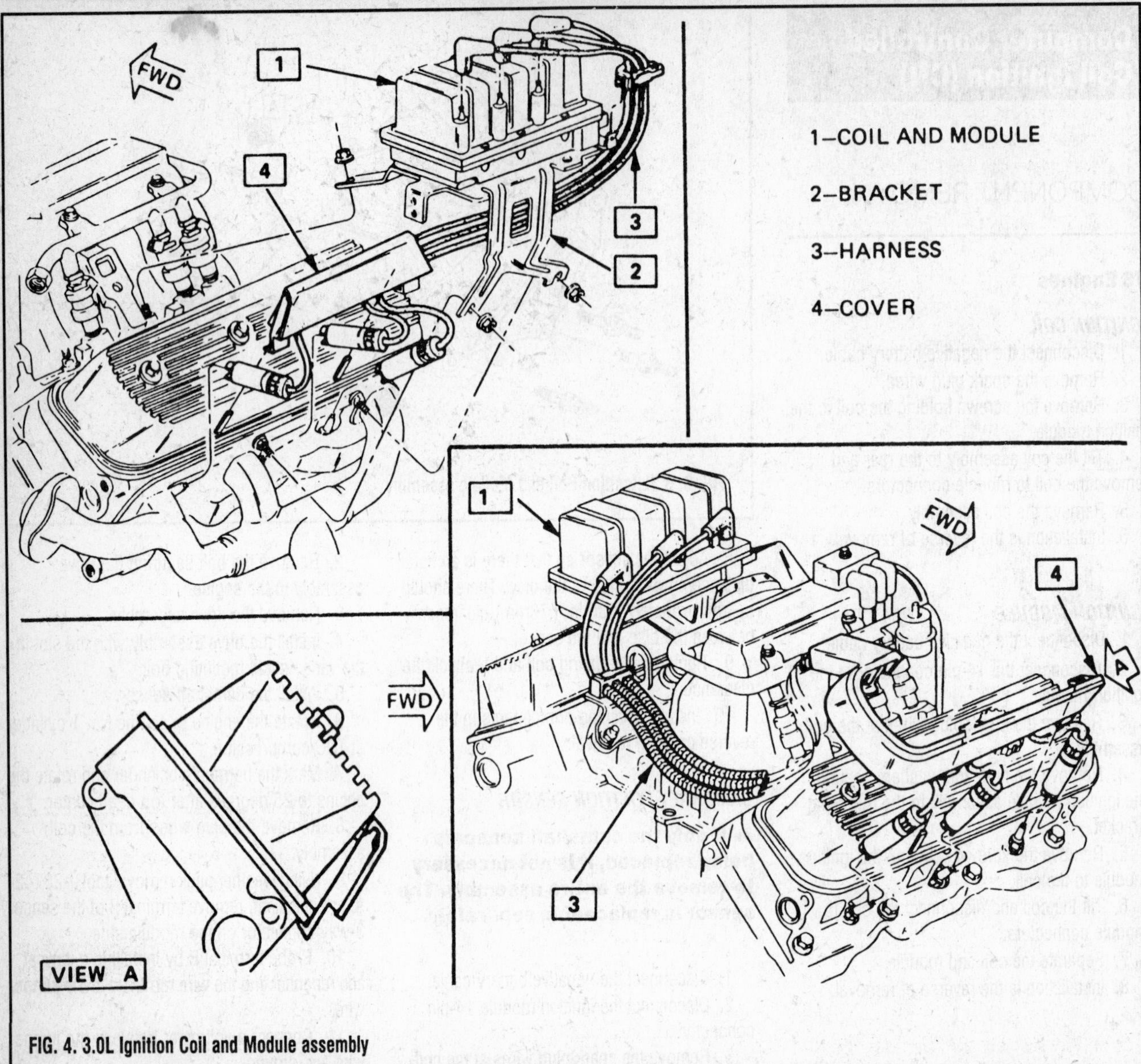

FIG. 4. 3.0L Ignition Coil and Module assembly

Distributor

➧ SEE FIG. 6

REMOVAL

2.0L ENGINE

1. Disconnect the negative battery cable.
2. Disconnect the coil and Electronic Spark Timing (EST) connectors.
3. Remove the coil wire. Unscrew the distributor cap hold-down screws and lift off the distributor cap with all ignition wires still connected.
4. Matchmark the rotor to the distributor housing and the distributor housing to the cam carrier.

➡ Do not crank the engine during this procedure. If the engine is cranked, the rotor's matchmark must be disregarded.

5. Remove the hold-down nuts.
6. Remove the distributor from the engine.

INSTALLATION

TIMING NOT DISTURBED

1. Install a new distributor housing O-ring.
2. Install the distributor in the cam carrier so the rotor is aligned with the matchmark on the housing and the housing is aligned with the matchmark on the cam carrier. Make sure the distributor is fully seated and the distributor tang drive is fully engaged.
3. Install the hold-down nuts.
4. Install the distributor cap and attaching screws. Install the coil wire.
5. Connect the coil and EST connectors.
6. Connect the negative battery cable.
7. Adjust the ignition timing and tighten the hold-down nuts.

TIMING DISTURBED

1. Install a new distributor housing O-ring.
2. Position the engine so the No. 1 piston is at TDC of the compression stroke and the mark on the vibration damper is aligned with **0** on the timing indicator.
3. Install the distributor in the cam carrier so the rotor is aligned with the matchmark on the housing and the housing is aligned with the

matchmark on the cam carrier. Make sure the distributor is fully seated and the distributor tang drive is fully engaged.

4. Install the hold-down nuts.
5. Install the distributor cap and attaching screws. Install the coil wire.
6. Connect the coil and EST connectors.
7. Connect the negative battery cable.
8. Adjust the ignition timing and tighten the hold-down nuts.

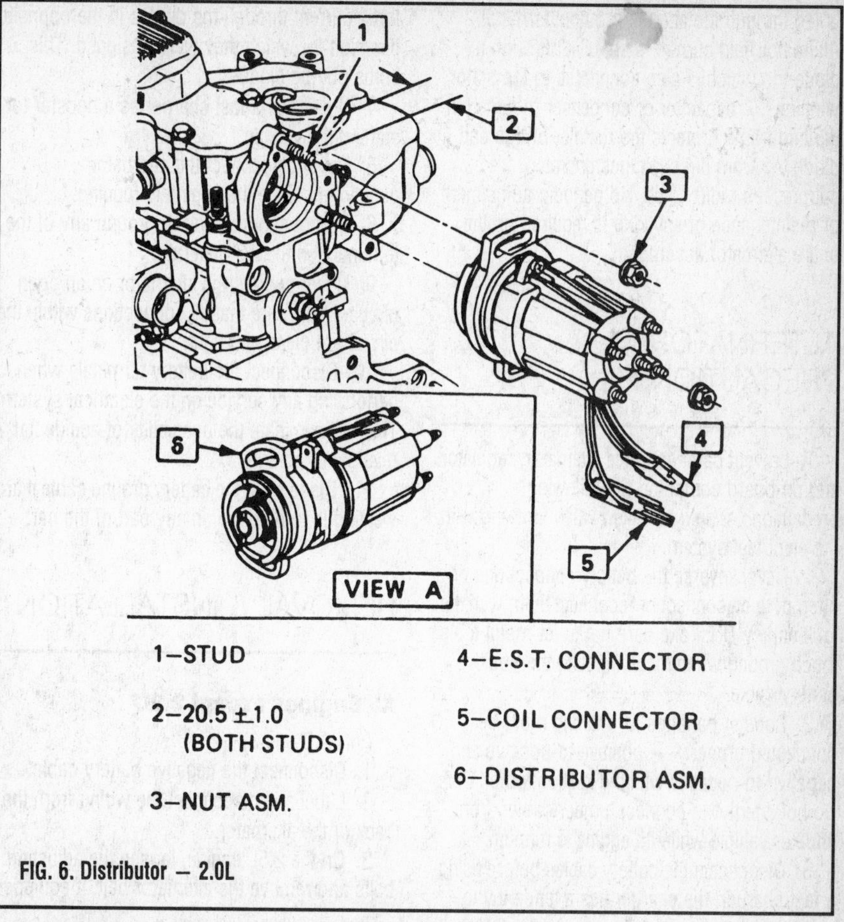

FIG. 6. Distributor – 2.0L

HEI Distributor

REMOVAL & INSTALLATION

2.5L Engine

1. Disconnect the ignition switch battery feed wire from the distributor.
2. Remove the distributor cap with the spark plug wires attached by releasing the two locking tabs and removing the coil wire. Move the cap out of the way.
3. Disconnect the 4-terminal ECM harness connector from the distributor. Release the locking tabs and remove the coil connector from the distributor.
4. Remove the distributor clamp screw and hold-down clamp.
5. Note the position of the rotor and scribe an alignment mark on the distributor base. Pull the distributor slowly up until the rotor stops turning counterclockwise and again scribe an alignment mark on the distributor base.
6. Installation is the reverse of removal. Set the rotor at the second alignment mark and lower the distributor into the engine. The rotor should rotate clockwise to the first alignment mark when the distributor is installed.

➡ The engine should not be rotated while the distributor is removed. If the engine was accidentally cranked with the distributor out, proceed as follows.

7. Remove the No. 1 spark plug.
8. Place your finger over the No. 1 spark plug hole and rotate the engine slowly in the normal direction or rotation until compression is felt.
9. Align the timing mark on the pulley to TDC (0) on the engine timing indicator.
10. Turn the distributor rotor so it points between the No. 1 and No. 3 spark plug towers.
11. Install the distributor and connect all wiring, then install the distributor cap.
12. Start the engine and check the timing as outlined in Section 2.

Distributorless Ignition

REMOVAL & INSTALLATION

2.3L Engine

INTEGRATED DIRECT IGNITION (IDI) COIL AND MODULE ASSEMBLY

1. Disconnect the negative battery cable.
2. Disconnect 11-pin IDI harness connector.
3. Remove the bolts that fasten the assembly to the camshaft housing.
4. Remove the IDI assembly. If the boots adhere to the spark plugs, remove them by twisting and pulling up on the retainers.

To install:

5. Install the boots and retainers to the housing, if they were separated during removal.
6. Align the spark plug boots with the plugs and place the assembly on the camshaft housing.
7. Install the mounting bolts and tighten to 19 ft. lbs. (26 Nm).
8. Connect the harness connector.
9. Connect the negative battery cable and check for proper operation.

Alternator

➧ SEE FIGS. 9–15

All N-Body models use a Delco SI integral regulator charging system. Although several models of alternators are available with different idle and maximum outputs, their basic operating principles are the same.

A solid state regulator is mounted inside the alternator. All regulator components are mounted in a solid mold and this unit along with the brush holder assembly is attached to the slip ring end frame. The regulator voltage cannot be adjusted. If found to be defective, the regulator must be replaced as an assembly.

The alternator rotor bearings contain enough grease to eliminate the need for periodic lubrication. Two brushes carry current through two slip rings to the field coil mounted on the rotor. Stator windings are assembled inside a laminated core that forms part of the alternator frame. A rectifier bridge connected to the stator windings contains six diodes and electrically changes stator AC voltage to DC voltage, which is fed through the alternator output terminal. Alternator field current is supplied through a diode trio which is also connected to the stator windings. A capacitor or condenser mounted in the end frame protects the rectifier bridge and diode trio from high voltages and also suppresses radio noise. No periodic adjustment or maintenance of any kind is required on the entire alternator assembly.

ALTERNATOR PRECAUTIONS

To prevent damage to the alternator, regulator and on-board computer, the following precautions should be taken when working with the electrical system.

1. Never reverse the battery connections or attempt to disconnect or reconnect them with the ignition key ON. Take care not to let metal tools touch ground when disconnecting the positive battery cable.
2. Booster batteries for starting must be connected properly — positive-to-positive and negative-to-negative with the ignition turned OFF. Do not attempt to connect jumper cables from another vehicle while its engine is running.
3. Disconnect the battery cables before using a fast charger; the charger has a tendency to force current through the diodes in the opposite direction for which they were designed. This burns out the diodes.
4. Never use a fast charger as a booster for starting the vehicle.
5. Never disconnect the alternator connectors while the engine is running.
6. Do not short across or ground any of the terminals on the AC generator.
9. Never operate the alternator on an open circuit. Make sure that all connections within the circuit are clean and tight.
10. Disconnect the battery terminals when performing any service on the electrical system. This will eliminate the possibility of accidental reversal of polarity.
11. Disconnect the battery ground cable if arc welding is to be done on any part of the car.

REMOVAL & INSTALLATION

All Engines except 2.3L

(VIN A,D and 3)

1. Disconnect the negative battery cable.
2. Label and disconnect the wiring from the back of the alternator.
3. On the 2.5L engine, loosen the adjusting bolts and remove the alternator belt. If equipped with a serpentine belt, loosen the tensioner and turn it counterclockwise to remove the belt.
4. Remove the alternator mounting bolts and lift the alternator clear.
5. Installation is the reverse of the removal procedure.
6. Check and/or adjust the belt tesion.
7. Connect the negative battery cable and check the alternator for proper operation.

2.3L (VIN A,D and 3) Engines

1. Disconnect the negative battery cable.
2. Loosen the tensioner pulley bolt, turn the pulley counterclockwise and remove the belt from the alternator pulley.
3. Label and disconnect the two vacuum lines at the front of the engine.
4. Disconnect the vacuum line bracket and push to the side.
5. Disconnect the injector harness connector and the alternator electrical connectors.
6. Remove the two rear alternator mounting bolts.
7. Remove the front alternator mounting bolt and engine harness clip.
8. Lift the alternator out, being careful not to damage the A/C lines.

To install:

9. Install the alternator into the engine compartment and hand tighten the front bolt.

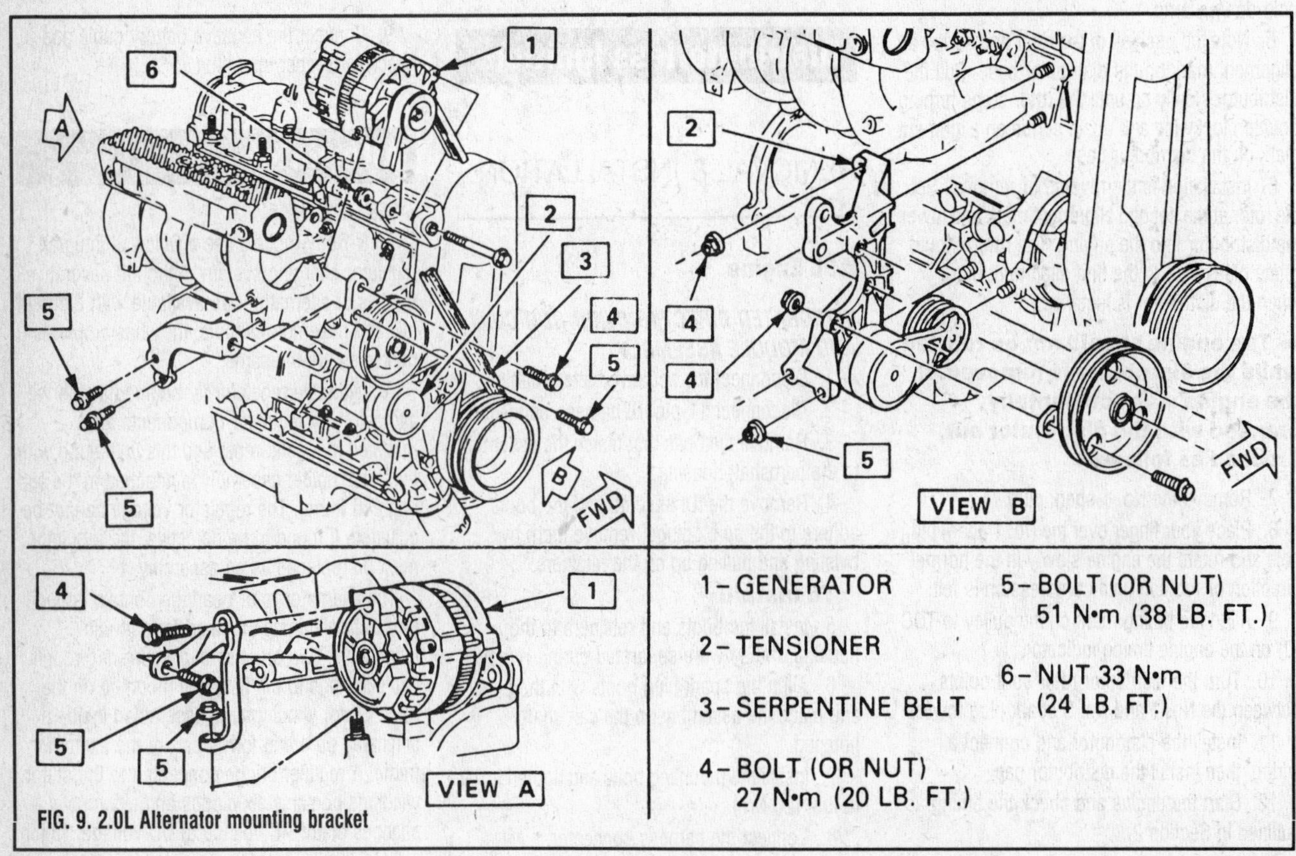

FIG. 9. 2.0L Alternator mounting bracket

10. Connect the front harness clip and install the two rear alternator bolts. Tighten the bolts to 20 ft. lbs. (26 Nm)
11. Tighten the front alternator bolt to 37 ft. lbs. (50 Nm) and install the serpentine belt.
12. Connect the electrical connectors and install the vacuum harness and retaining clip.
13. Connect the two hoses to the vacuum harness and connect the negative battery cable.

➡ When adjusting belt tension, apply pressure at the center of the alternator, not against either end frame.

FIG. 9A Alternator drive belt tension adjusting bolt

Regulator

The alternator used in this vehicle has an internal regulator. The alternator is serviced as a complete unit and cannot be overhauled.

Battery

REMOVAL & INSTALLATION

➡ Always turn off the ignition switch when connecting or disconnecting the battery cables or a battery charger. Failure to do so could damage the ECM or other electronic components. Disconnecting the battery cable may interfere with the functions of the on board computer systems and may require the computer to undergo a complete relearning process once the negative battery cable is connected. Refer to Section 1 for details on battery maintenance.

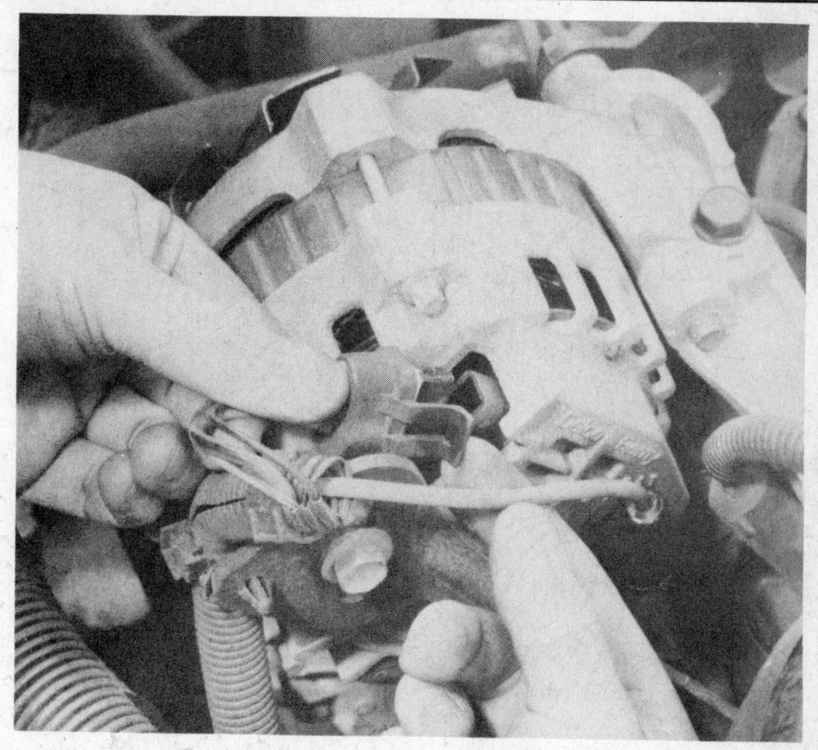

FIG. 9B Disconnecting alternator electrical terminal

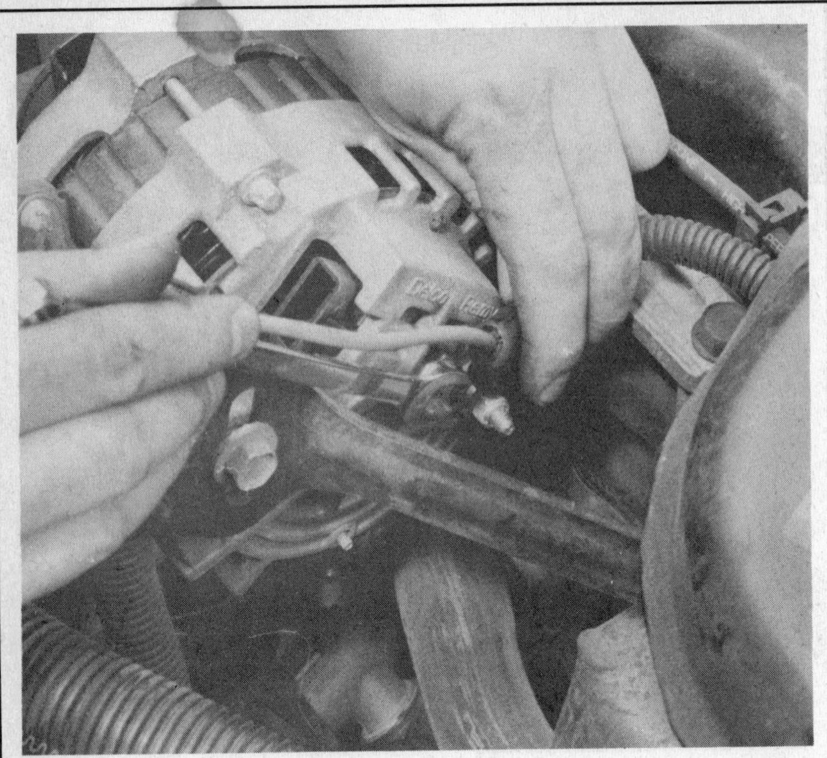

FIG. 9C Removing alternator battery positive connector nut

1. Disconnect the negative (ground) cable from the terminal and then the positive cable. Special pullers are available to remove the cable clamps. To avoid sparks, always disconnect the ground cable first and connect it last.
2. Remove the battery holddown clamp.
3. Remove the battery, being careful not to spill the acid.

➡ Spilled acid can be neutralized with a baking soda/water solution. If you somehow get acid into your eyes, flush it out with lots of water and get to a doctor.

4. Clean the battery posts thoroughly before reinstalling or when installing a new battery.
5. Clean the cable clamps, using a wire brush, both inside and out.
6. Install the battery and the holddown clamp or strap. Connect the positive, and then the negative cable. DO NOT hammer them in place.

➡ The terminals should be coated lightly (externally) with a petroleum type jelly to prevent corrosion. Make absolutely sure that the battery is connected properly before you turn on the ignition switch. Reversed polarity can burn out your alternator and regulator within a matter of a split second.

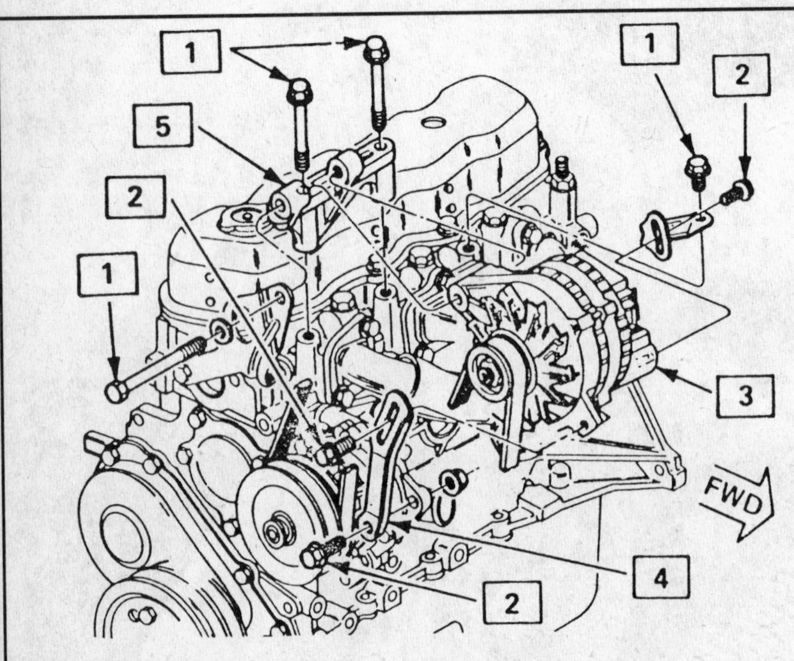

FIG. 10. 2.3L Alternator mounting bracket (VIN U)

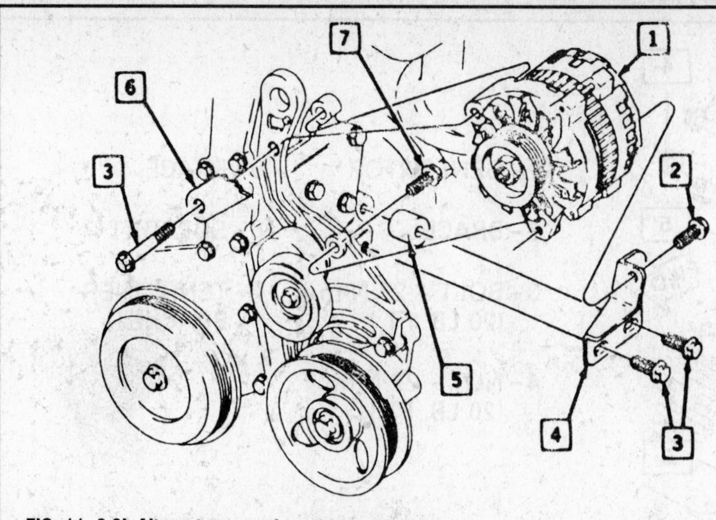

FIG. 11. 2.3L Alternator mounting without A/C (VIN D)

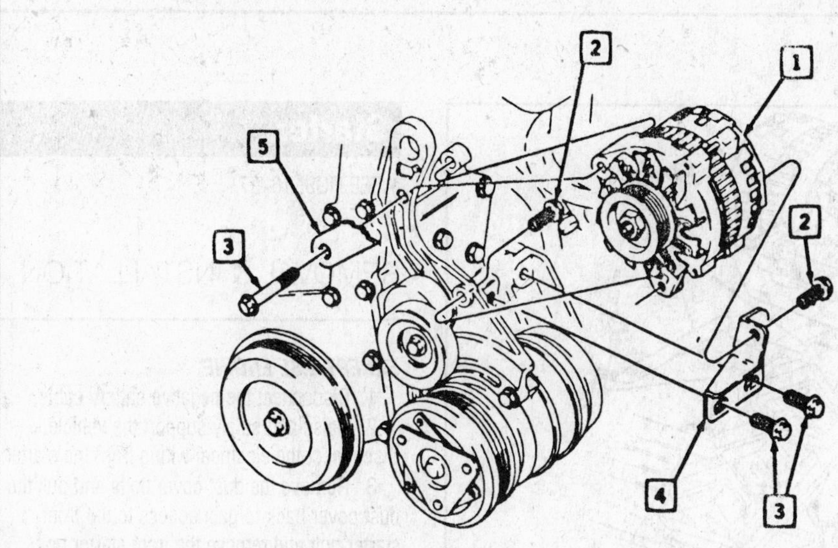

FIG. 12. 2.3L Alternator mounting with A/C (VIN D)

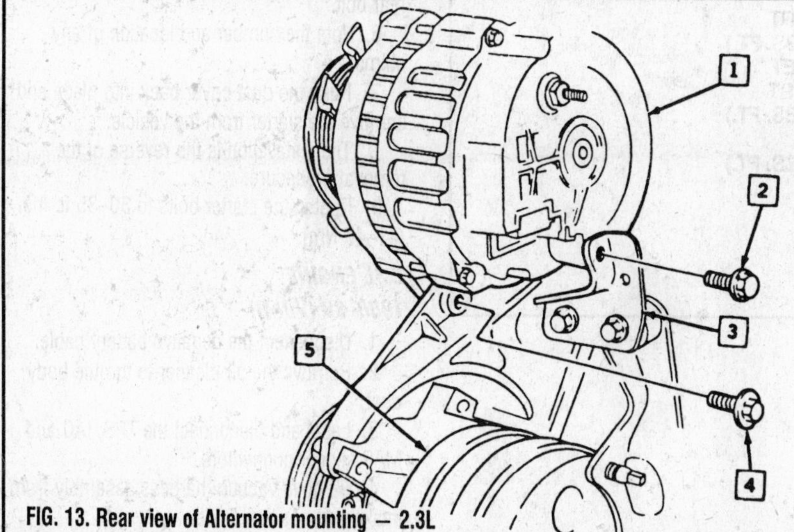

FIG. 13. Rear view of Alternator mounting — 2.3L

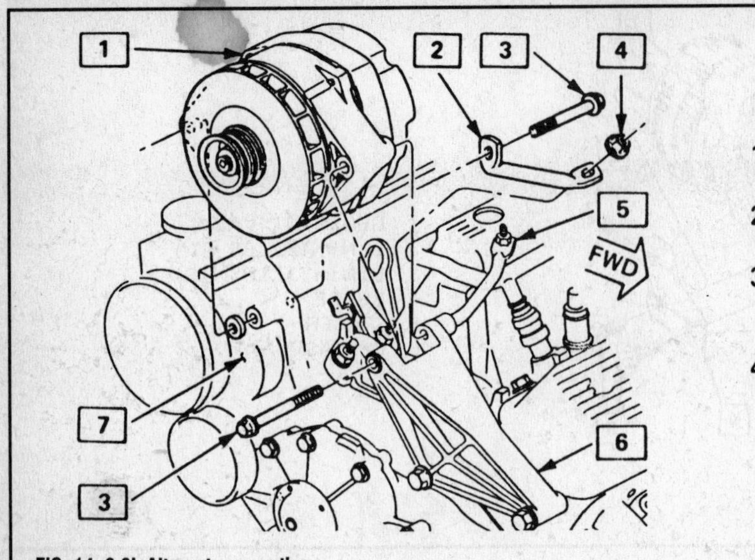

FIG. 14. 3.0L Alternator mounting

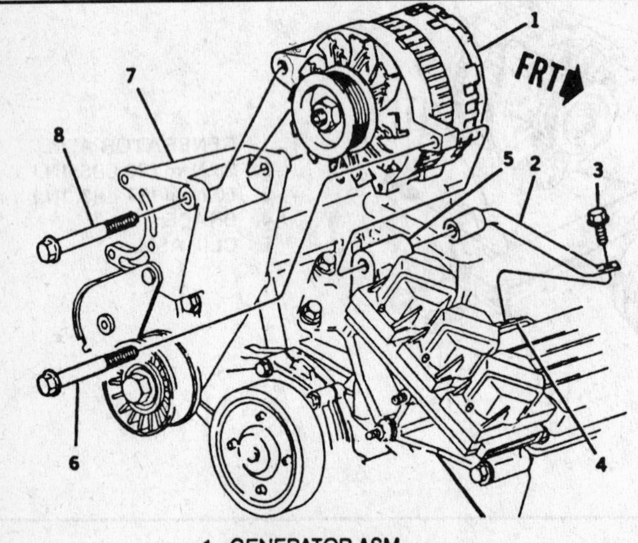

FIG. 15. 3.3L Alternator mounting

Starter

➧ SEE FIGS. 16–27

REMOVAL & INSTALLATION

EXCEPT 2.3L ENGINE

1. Disconnect the negative battery cable.
2. Raise and safely support the vehicle. Disconnect the electrical wiring from the starter.
3. Remove the dust cover bolts and pull the dust cover back to gain access to the front starter bolt and remove the front starter bolt.
4. Remove the rear support bracket.
5. Pull the rear dust cover back to gain access to the rear starter bolt and remove the rear bolt.
6. Note the number and location of any shims.
7. Push the dust cover back into place and remove the starter from the vehicle.
8. The installation is the reverse of the removal procedure.
9. Tighten the starter bolts to 30–35 ft. lbs. (41–47 Nm).

2.3L ENGINE

1988–89 (VIN D)

1. Disconnect the negative battery cable.
2. Remove the air cleaner to throttle body duct.
3. Label and disconnect the TPS, IAC and MAP sensor connectors.
4. Remove vacuum harness assembly from intake and position aside.

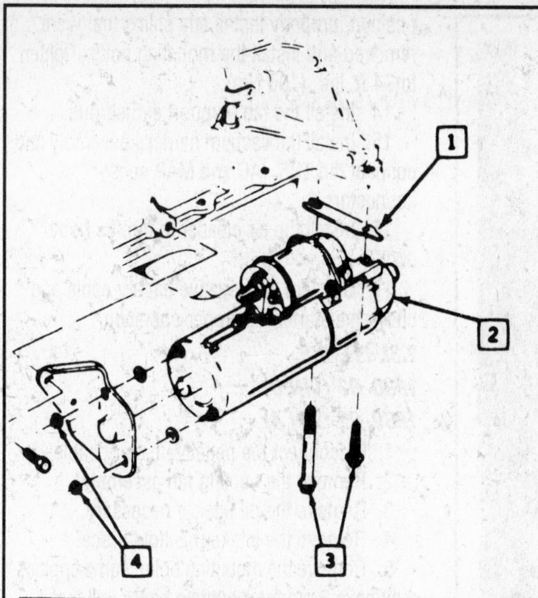

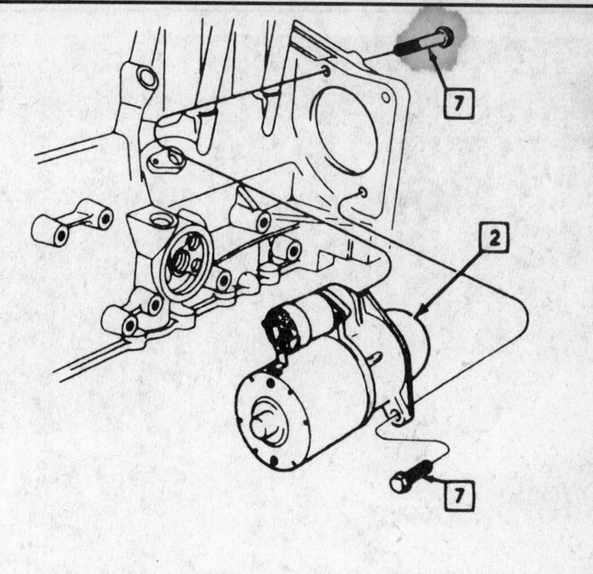

1. SHIM, STARTER
2. STARTER MOTOR
3. BOLT – 43 N·m (32 LBS. FT.)
4. NUT – 8 N·m (71 LBS. IN.)
5. BOLT – 50 N·m (37 LBS. FT.)
6. SUPPORT, STARTER MOTOR
7. BOLT – 100 N·m (74 LBS. FT.)

STARTER NOISE DIAGNOSTIC PROCEDURE

STARTER NOISE DURING CRANKING: REMOVE 1 – .015" DOUBLE SHIM OR ADD SINGLE .015" SHIM TO OUTER BOLT ONLY.

HIGH PITCHED WHINE AFTER ENGINE FIRES: ADD .015" DOUBLE SHIMS UNTIL NOISE DISAPPEARS (NOT TO EXCEED .045").

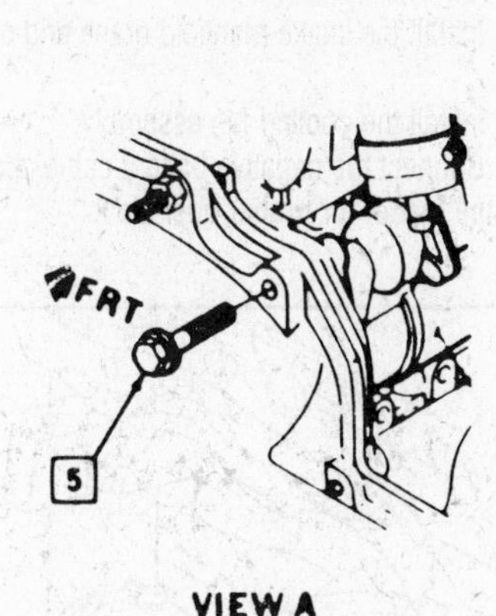

A
FRT
6
5
4
3
2

FIG. 16. VIN U, D, M Starter mounting

5. Remove cooling fan shroud attaching bolts and remove the shroud.
6. Remove upper radiator support.
7. Disconnect the connector from the cooling fan and remove the fan assembly. Do not damage the lock tang on the TPS with the fan bracket.
8. Remove the starter mounting bolts.
9. Tilt the rear of starter towards the radiator, pull the starter out and rotate solenoid towards the radiator to gain access to the electrical connections.

➡ **If present, do not to damage the crank sensor mounted directly to the rear of the starter.**

10. Disconnect the connectors from the solenoid.
11. Move the starter toward the driver's side of the vehicle and remove.

To install:

12. Lower the starter and connect the solenoid connectors.
13. Rotate the starter into installation

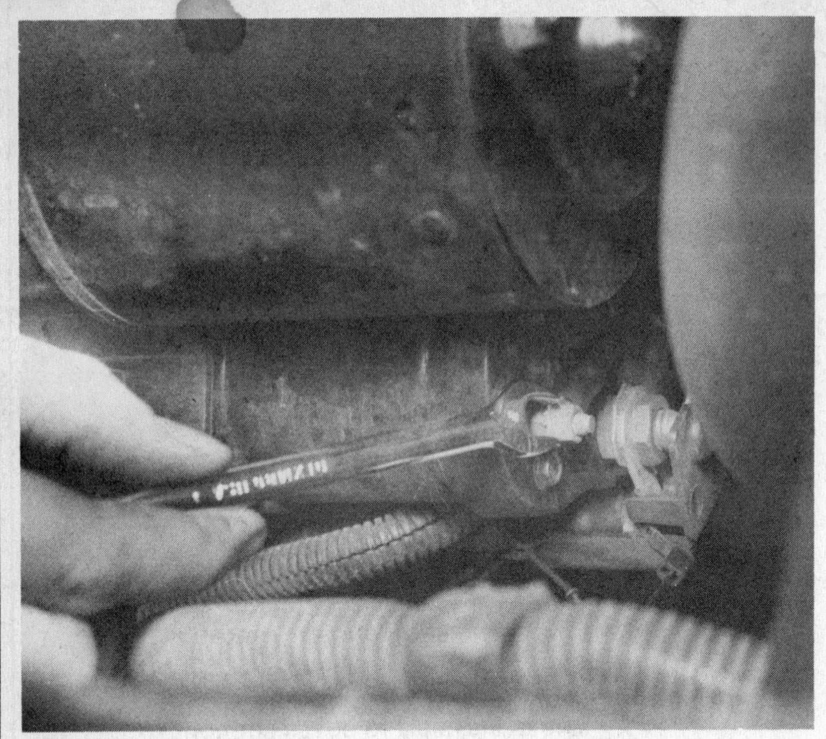
FIG. 16A Removing starter solenoid terminal nut

FIG. 16B Removing starter attaching bolts

position, properly install any shims that were removed and install the mounting bolts. Tighten to 74 ft. lbs. (100 Nm).

14. Install the fan, support and shroud.
15. Install the vacuum harness assembly and connect the TPS, IAC and MAP sensor connectors.
16. Install the air cleaner to throttle body duct.
17. Connect the negative battery cable and check the starter for proper operation.

2.3L ENGINE

1990–92 (VIN D)

1989–92 (VIN A)

1. Disconnect the negative battery cable.
2. Remove the cooling fan assembly.
3. Remove the oil filter, if necessary.
4. Remove the intake manifold brace.
5. Remove the mounting bolts; some engines may have 3 starter mounting bolts. Pull the starter out of the hole and move toward the front of the vehicle.
6. Disconnect the wiring from the solenoid.
7. Remove the starter by lifting it between the intake manifold and the radiator.

To install:

8. Lower the starter between the intake manifold and the radiator and connect the wiring to the solenoid.
9. Rotate the starter into installation position and install the mounting bolts. Tighten to 74 ft. lbs. (100 Nm).
10. Install the intake manifold brace and oil filter.
11. Install the cooling fan assembly.
12. Connect the negative battery cable and check the starter for proper operation.

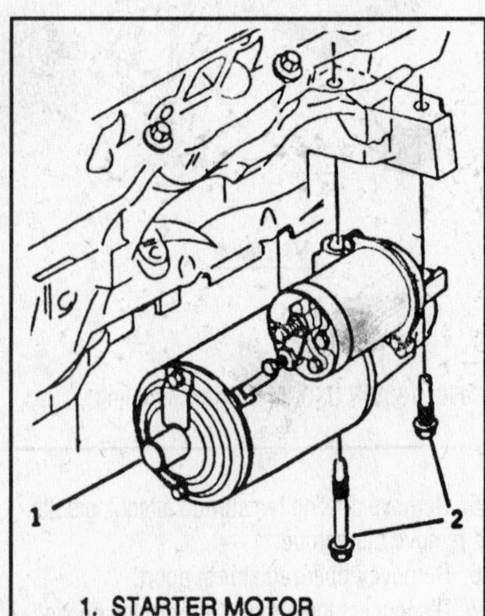

FIG. 17. 3.3L Starter mounting

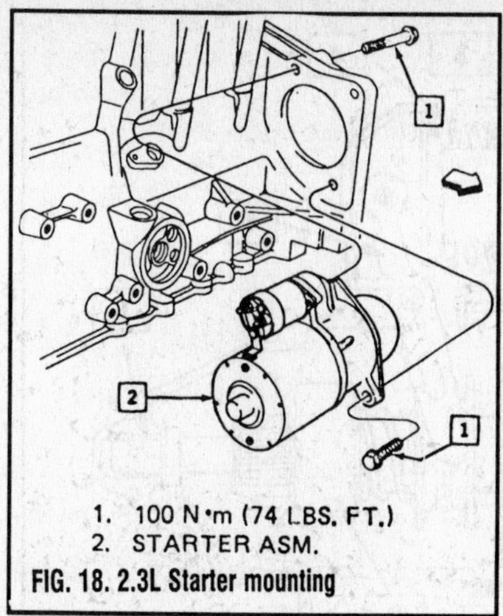

1. 100 N·m (74 LBS. FT.)
2. STARTER ASM.

FIG. 18. 2.3L Starter mounting

STARTER OVERHAUL

Drive Replacement

1. Disconnect the field coil straps from the solenoid.
2. Remove the thru-bolts and separate the commutator end frame, field frame assembly, drive housing and armature assembly from each other.
3. Slide the two piece thrust collar off the end of the armature shaft.
4. Slide a suitably sized metal cylinder (such as a standard $^1/_2$ in. pipe coupling or an old pinion) on the shaft so that the end of the coupling or pinion butts up against the edge of the pinion retainer.
5. Support the lower end of the armature securely on a soft surface, such as a wooden block, and tap the end of the coupling or pinion, driving the retainer towards the armature end of the snap ring.
6. Remove the snap ring from the groove in the armature shaft with a pair of pliers, then slide the retainer and starter drive from the shaft.
7. To reassemble, lubricate the drive end of the armature shaft with silicone lubricant and then slide the starter drive onto the shaft with the pinion facing outward. Slide the retainer onto the shaft with the cupped surface facing outward.
8. Again support the armature on a soft surface, with the pinion at the upper end. Center the snap ring on the top of the shaft, using a new snap ring if the original was damaged during removal. Gently place a block of wood flat on top of the snap ring so as not to move it from a centered position. Tap the wooden block with a hammer in order to force the snap ring around the shaft, then slide the ring down into the snap ring groove.
9. Lay the armature down flat on the surface you're working on. Slide the retainer close up onto the shaft and position it and the thrust collar next to the snap ring. Using two pairs of pliers on opposite sides of the shaft, squeeze the thrust collar and the retainer together until the snap ring is forced into the retainer.
10. Lube the drive housing bushing with a silicone lubricant, then install the armature and clutch assembly into the drive housing, engaging the solenoid shift lever with the clutch and positioning the front end of the armature shaft into the bushing.
11. Apply a sealing compound approved for this application onto the drive housing, then position the field frame around the armature shaft and against the drive housing. Work slowly

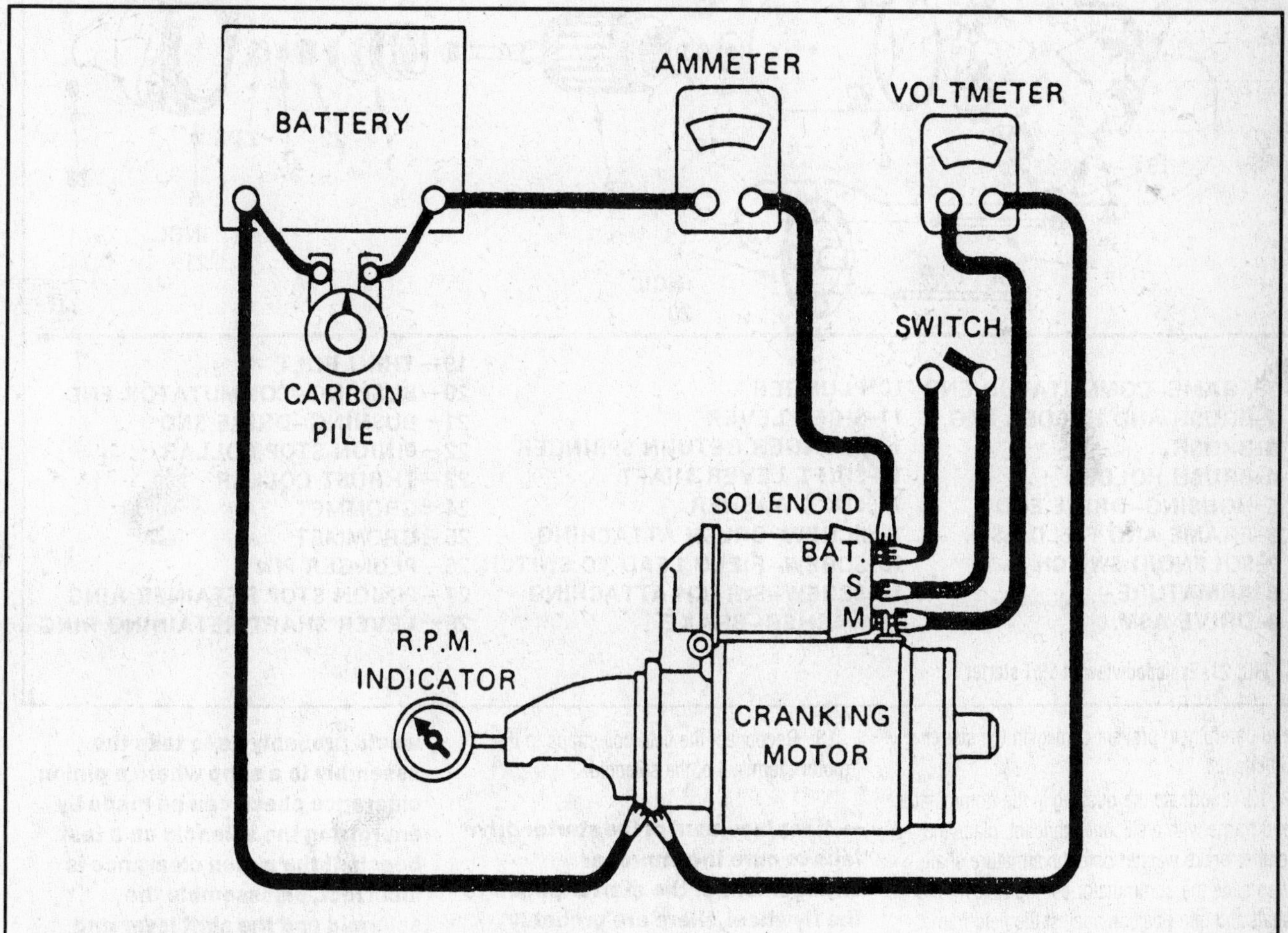

FIG. 19. NO-LOAD testing connections

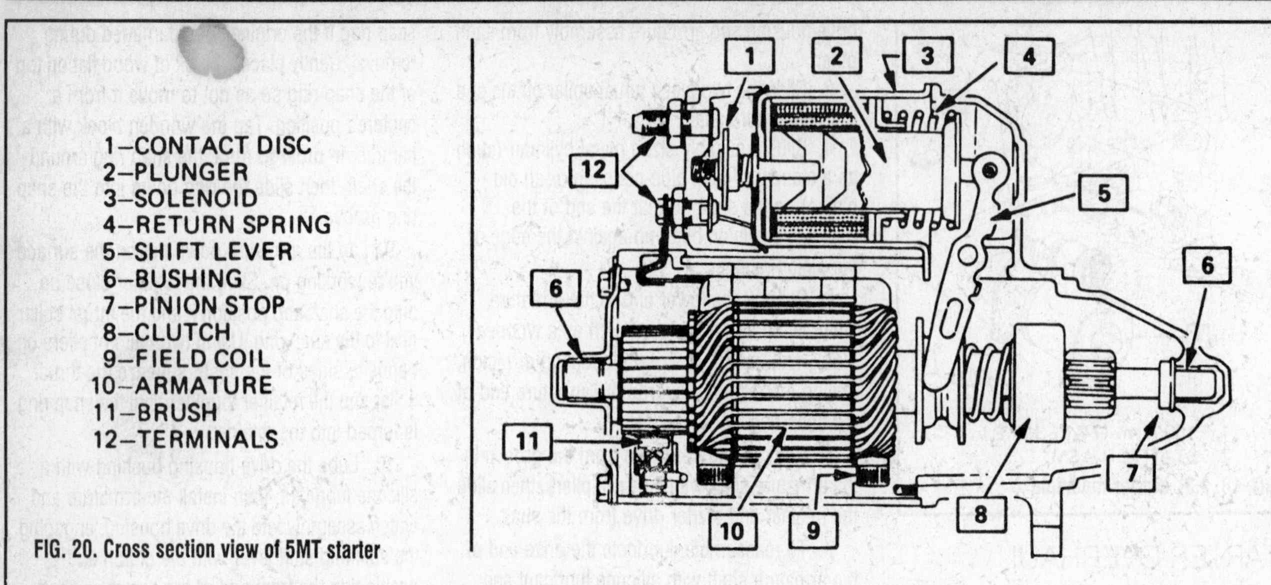

FIG. 20. Cross section view of 5MT starter

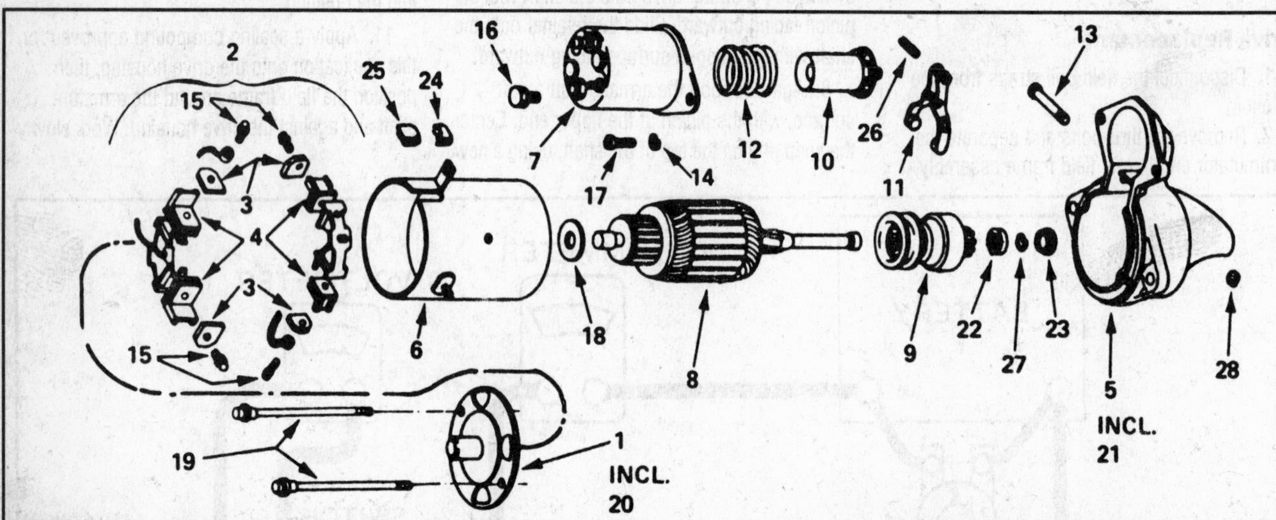

FIG. 21. Exploded view of 5MT starter

and carefully to prevent damaging the starter brushes.

12. Lubricate the bushing in the commutator end frame with a silicone lubricant, place the leather brake washer onto the armature shaft, then slide the commutator end frame over the shaft and into position against the field frame. Line up the bolt holes, then install and tighten the thru-bolts.

13. Reconnect the field coil straps to the "motor" terminal of the solenoid.

➡ **If replacement of the starter drive fails to cure the improper engagement of the starter pinion to the flywheel, there are probably defective parts in the solenoid and/or shift lever. The best procedure would probably be to take the assembly to a shop where a pinion clearance check can be made by energizing the solenoid on a test bench. If the pinion clearance is incorrect, disassemble the solenoid and the shift lever and replace any worn parts.**

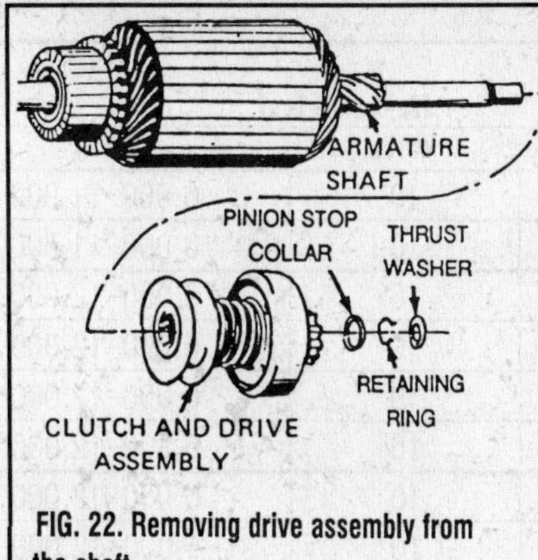

FIG. 22. Removing drive assembly from the shaft

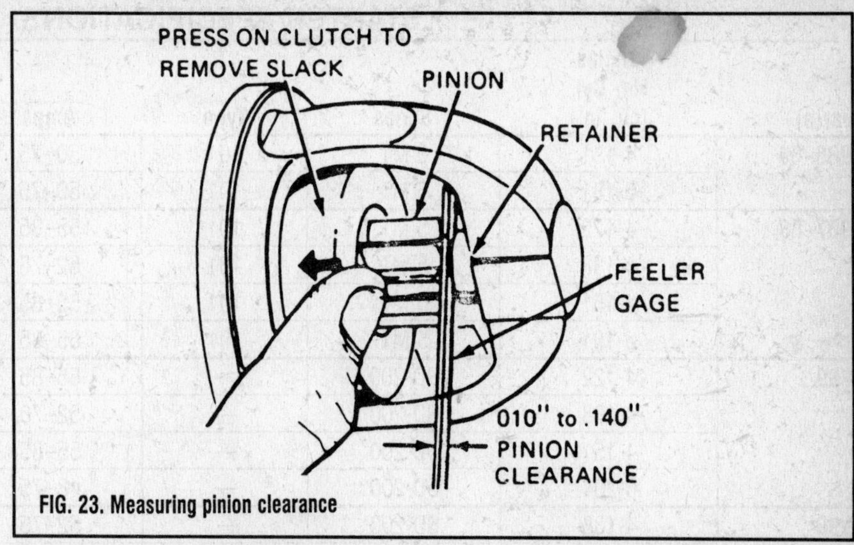

FIG. 23. Measuring pinion clearance

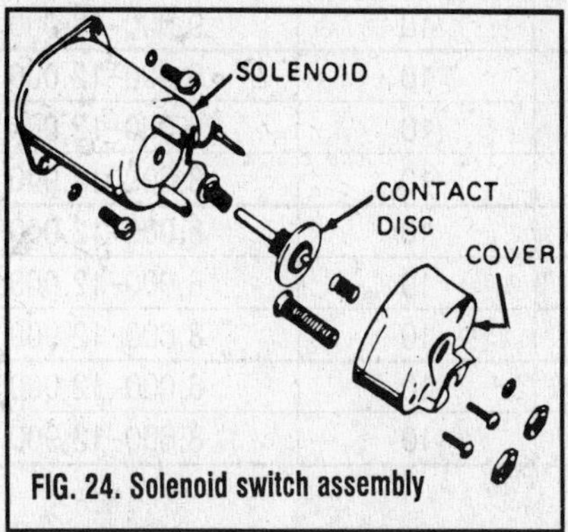

FIG. 24. Solenoid switch assembly

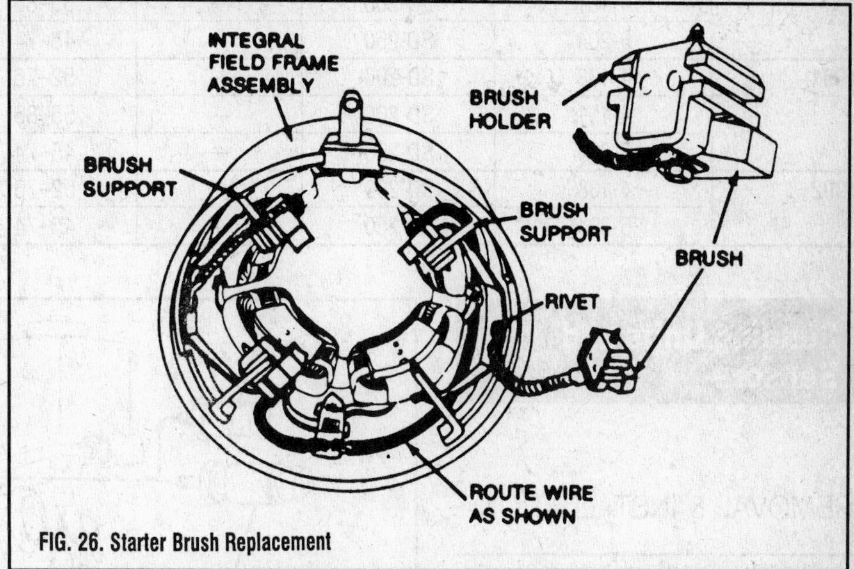

FIG. 26. Starter Brush Replacement

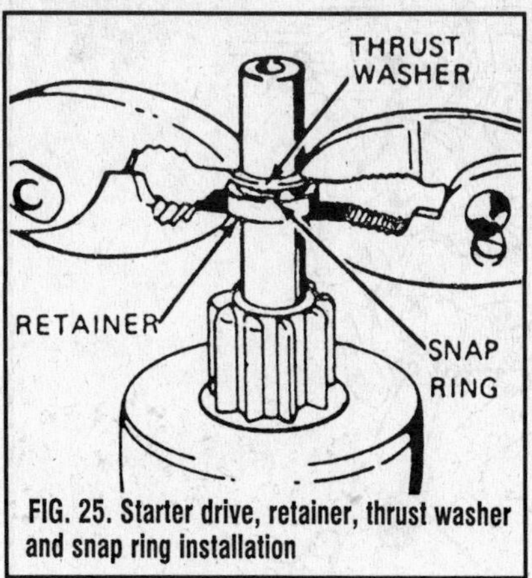

FIG. 25. Starter drive, retainer, thrust washer and snap ring installation

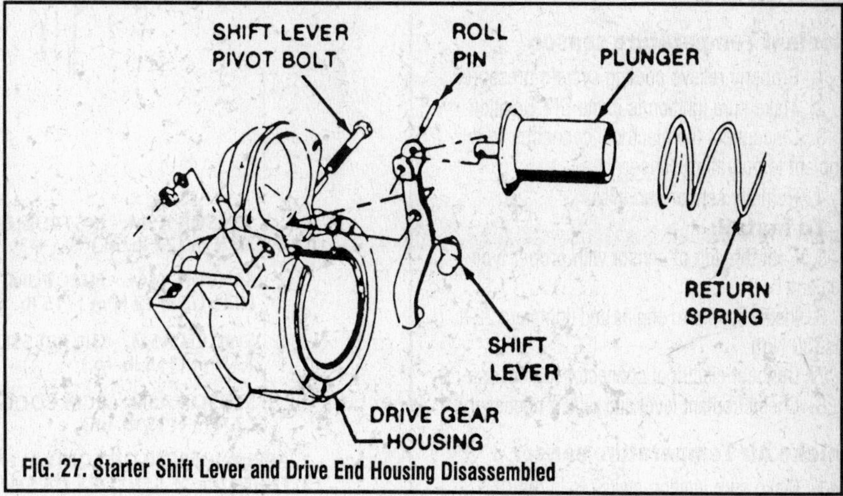

FIG. 27. Starter Shift Lever and Drive End Housing Disassembled

Brush Replacement

1. After removing the starter from the engine, disconnect the field coil from the motor solenoid terminal.
2. Remove the starter thru-bolts and remove the commutator end frame and washer.
3. Remove the field frame and the armature assembly from the drive housing.
4. Remove the brush holder pivot pin which positions one insulated and one grounded brush.
5. Remove the brush springs.
6. Remove the brushes.
7. Installation is the reverse of removal.

STARTER SPECIFICATIONS

Year(s)	Engine No. Cyl. (cu. in.)	Series	Type	Amps	No-Load Test Volts	RPM
1985-86	4-151	5 MT	101	50-75	10	6,000-11,900
	6-181	5 MT	101	50-75	10	6,000-11,900
1987-88	4-122	5 MT	101	55-85	10	6,000-12,000
	4-138	5 MT	101	52-76	10	6,000-12,000
	4-151	5 MT	101	55-85	10	6,000-12,000
	6-181	5 MT	101	55-85	10	6,000-12,000
1989	4-122	SD-200	—	55-85	10	6,000-12,000
	4-138	SD-200	—	52-76	10	6,000-12,000
	4-151	SD-200	—	55-85	10	6,000-12,000
	6-204	SD-200	—	48-75	10	9,000-13,000
1990	4-138	SD-200	—	52-76	10	6,000-12,000
	4-151	SD-200	—	55-85	10	6,000-12,000
	6-204	SD-250	—	45-74	10	8,600-12,900
1991	4-138	SD-200	—	52-76	10	6,000-12,000
	4-151	SD-200	—	55-85	10	6,000-12,000
	6-204	SD-250	—	45-74	10	8,600-12,900
1992	4-138	SD-200	—	52-76	10	6,000-12,000
	6-204	SD-250	—	45-74	10	8,600-12,900

Sending Units and Sensors

REMOVAL & INSTALLATION

➧ SEE FIGS. 28-32

Coolant Temperature sensor

1. Properly relieve cooling system pressure.
2. Make sure ignition is in the OFF position.
3. Disconnect the electrical connector to the coolant temperature sensor.
4. Remove sensor carefully.

To install:

5. Coat threads of sensor with proper type sealant.
6. Install sensor to engine and tighten to 22 ft. lbs.(30 Nm).
7. Connect electrical connector to sensor.
8. Check coolant level and refill if necessary.

Intake Air Temperature sensor

1. Make sure ignition switch is in the OFF position.
2. Disconnect the electrical connector to the IAT sensor.

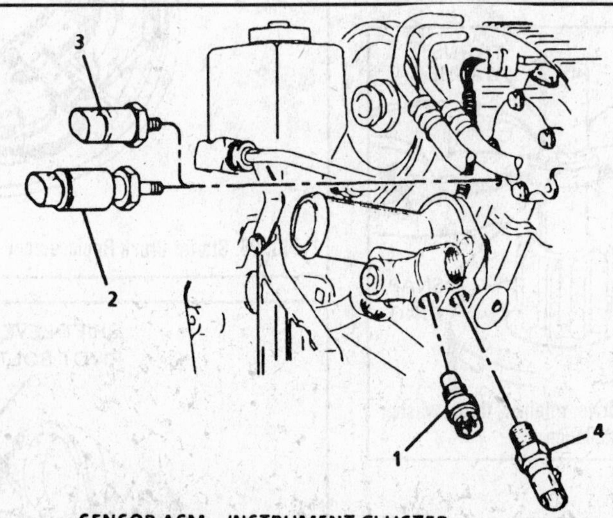

1 SENSOR ASM. - INSTRUMENT CLUSTER 30 N·m (22 lb. in.)
2 SENSOR ASM. - FUEL PUMP SWITCH AND OIL PRESSURE (U21/U52) 13 N·m (115 lb. in.)
3 SWITCH ASM. - OIL PRESSURE (EXC. U21/U52) 13 N·m (115 lb. in.)
4 SENSOR ASM. - ECM COOLANT TEMP. 13 N·m (115 lb. in.)

APPLY 1052080 OR EQUIVALENT TO THREADS OF SENSORS OR SWITCH

FIG. 28. Coolant Sensor

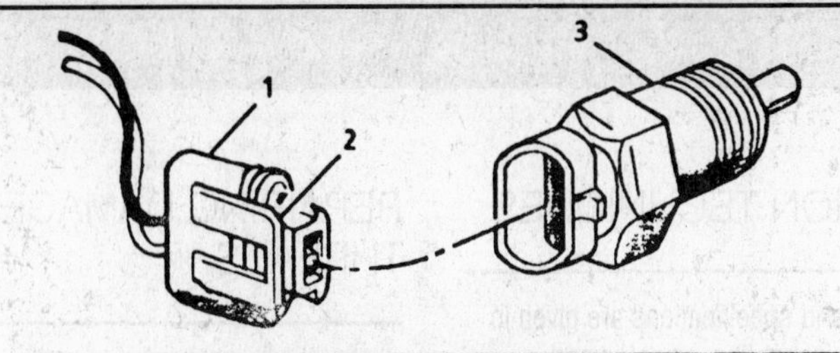

FIG. 29. Intake Air Temperature Sensor

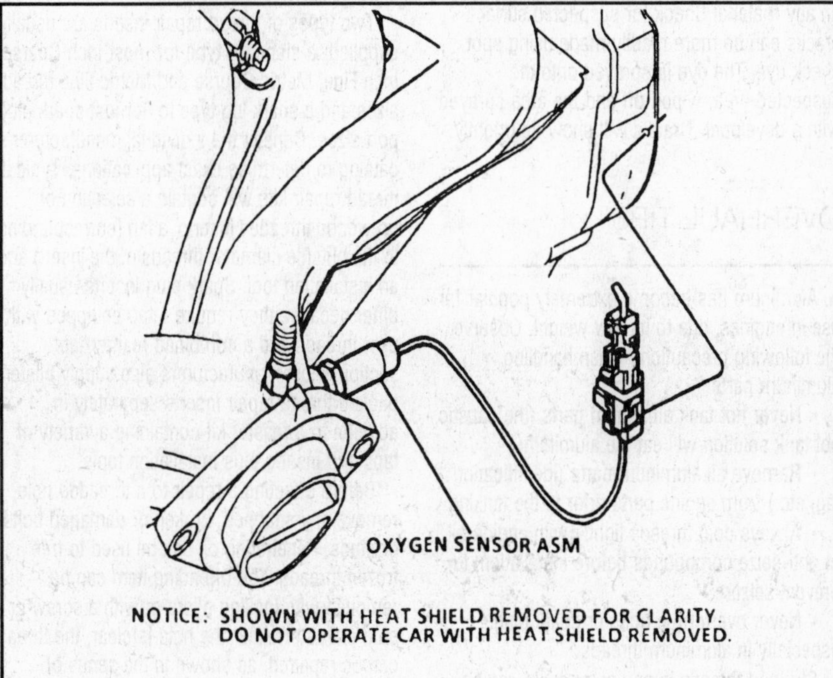

FIG. 30. Oxygen Sensor

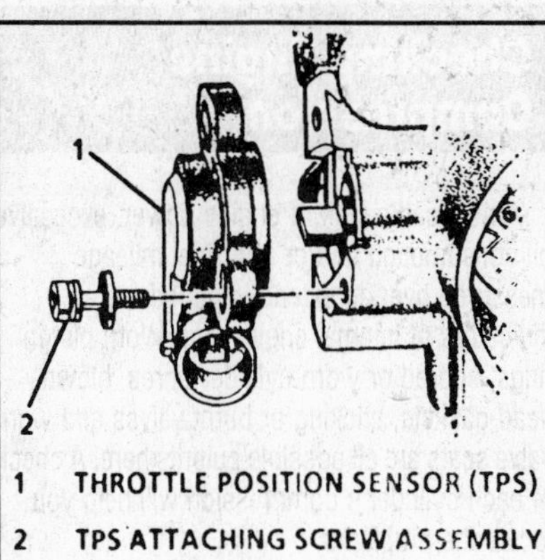

FIG. 31. Throttle Position Sensor

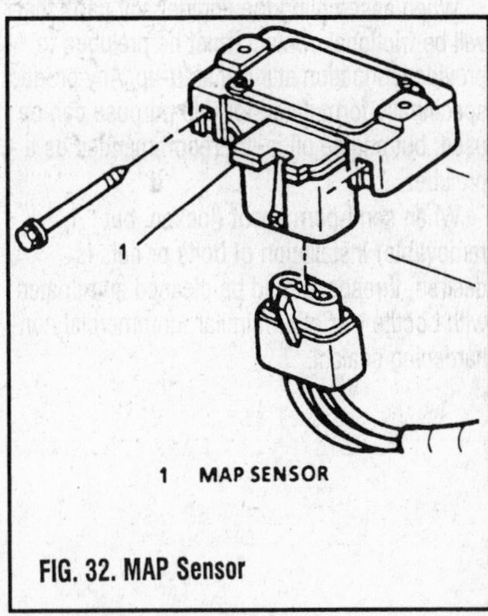

FIG. 32. MAP Sensor

3. Carefully remove the sensor from the intake manifold.

To install:

4. Install the IAT sensor in the intake manifold.
5. Tighten the sensor to 6 ft. lbs.(8 Nm)
6. Connect the electrical connector to the sensor.

Oxygen sensor

1. Make sure ignition is OFF. Disconnect sensor connector.
2. Remove sensor assembly very carefully.

➡ **NOTE:Excessive force may damage the threads in the intake manifold or exhaust pipe.**

To install:

3. Coat threads of Oxygen sensor with Anti-seize compound.
4. Install sensor and torque to 30 ft. lbs.(41 Nm.)
5. Connect electrical connector.

Throttle Position sensor

1. Disconnect the throttle cable.
2. Remove the throttle body air duct.
3. Disconnect the throttle body vacuum line connector.
4. Disconnect the sensor connector.
5. Remove the throttle cable bracket and the throttle body bolts.
6. Lift the throttle body until the TPS clears the fuel line.
7. Remove the TPS attaching screws and retainers.
8. Remove the sensor.

To install:

9. Make sure the throttle valve is in the CLOSED position and install the sensor. The remaining steps are the reversal of the removal procedure.

MAP sensor

1. Disconnect the vacuum hose.
2. Disconnect the electrical connector and remove the attaching screws.
3. Remove the sensor.

To install:

4. Installation is the reverse of the removal procedure.

ENGINE MECHANICAL

Engine Overhaul Tips

Most engine overhaul procedures are fairly standard. In addition to specific parts replacement procedures and complete specifications for your individual engine, this Section also is a guide to accept rebuilding procedures. Examples of standard rebuilding practice are shown and should be used along with specific details concerning your particular engine.

Competent and accurate machine shop services will ensure maximum performance, reliability and engine life.

In most instances it is more profitable for the do-it-yourself mechanic to remove, clean and inspect the component, buy the necessary parts and deliver these to a shop for actual machine work.

On the other hand, much of the rebuilding work (crankshaft, block, bearings, piston rods, and other components) is well within the scope of the do-it-yourself mechanic.

TOOLS

The tools required for an engine overhaul or parts replacement will depend on the depth of your involvement. With a few exceptions, they will be the tools found in a mechanic's tool kit (see Section 1). More in-depth work will require any or all of the following:

- a dial indicator (reading in thousandths) mounted on a universal base
- micrometers and telescope gauges
- jaw and screw-type pullers
- scraper
- valve spring compressor
- ring groove cleaner
- piston ring expander and compressor
- ridge reamer
- cylinder hone or glaze breaker
- Plastigage®
- engine stand

The use of most of these tools is illustrated in this Section. Many can be rented for a one-time use from a local parts jobber or tool supply house specializing in automotive work.

Occasionally, the use of special tools is called for. See the information on Special Tools and Safety Notice in the front of this book before substituting another tool.

INSPECTION TECHNIQUES

Procedures and specifications are given in this Section for inspecting, cleaning and assessing the wear limits of most major components. Other procedures such as Magnaflux® and Zyglo® can be used to locate material flaws and stress cracks. Magnaflux® is a magnetic process applicable only to ferrous materials. The Zyglo® process coats the material with a fluorescent dye penetrant and can be used on any material Check for suspected surface cracks can be more readily made using spot check dye. The dye is sprayed onto the suspected area, wiped off and the area sprayed with a developer. Cracks will show up brightly.

OVERHAUL TIPS

Aluminum has become extremely popular for use in engines, due to its low weight. Observe the following precautions when handling aluminum parts:

- Never hot tank aluminum parts (the caustic hot tank solution will eat the aluminum.
- Remove all aluminum parts (identification tag, etc.) from engine parts prior to the tanking.
- Always coat threads lightly with engine oil or anti-seize compounds before installation, to prevent seizure.
- Never overtorque bolts or spark plugs especially in aluminum threads.

Stripped threads in any component can be repaired using any of several commercial repair kits (Heli-Coil®, Microdot®, Keenserts®, etc.).

When assembling the engine, any parts that will be frictional contact must be prelubed to provide lubrication at initial start-up. Any product specifically formulated for this purpose can be used, but engine oil is not recommended as a prelube.

When semi-permanent (locked, but removable) installation of bolts or nuts is desired, threads should be cleaned and coated with Loctite® or other similar, commercial non-hardening sealant.

REPAIRING DAMAGED THREADS

Several methods of repairing damaged threads are available. Heli-Coil® (shown here), Keenserts® and Microdot® are among the most widely used. All involve basically the same principle — drilling out stripped threads, tapping the hole and installing a prewound insert — making welding, plugging and oversize fasteners unnecessary.

Two types of thread repair inserts are usually supplied: a standard type for most Inch Coarse, Inch Fine, Metric Course and Metric Fine thread sizes and a spark lug type to fit most spark plug port sizes. Consult the individual manufacturer's catalog to determine exact applications. Typical thread repair kits will contain a selection of prewound threaded inserts, a tap (corresponding to the outside diameter threads of the insert) and an installation tool. Spark plug inserts usually differ because they require a tap equipped with pilot threads and a combined reamer/tap section. Most manufacturers also supply blister-packed thread repair inserts separately in addition to a master kit containing a variety of taps and inserts plus installation tools.

Before effecting a repair to a threaded hole, remove any snapped, broken or damaged bolts or studs. Penetrating oil can be used to free frozen threads. The offending item can be removed with locking pliers or with a screw or stud extractor. After the hole is clear, the thread can be repaired, as shown in the series of accompanying illustrations.

Checking Engine Compression

A noticeable lack of engine power, excessive oil consumption and/or poor fuel mileage measured over an extended period are all indicators of internal engine war. Worn piston rings, scored or worn cylinder bores, blown head gaskets, sticking or burnt valves and worn valve seats are all possible culprits here. A check of each cylinder's compression will help you locate the problems.

As mentioned in the Tools and Equipment section of Section 1, a screw-in type compression gauge is more accurate that the type you simply hold against the spark plug hole, although it takes slightly longer to use. It's worth it to obtain a more accurate reading. Follow the procedures below.

Testing the compression on diesel engines requires the use of special adapters and pressure gauges. Consult a tool distributor or dealership for the proper tools.

GENERAL ENGINE SPECIFICATIONS

Year	Engine VIN	Engine Displacement cu. in. (Liters)	Fuel System Type	Net Horsepower @ rpm	Net Torque @ rpm (ft. lbs.)	Bore × Stroke (in.)	Com-pression Ratio	Oil Pressure @ rpm
1985-86	U	151 (2.5)	TBI	92 @ 4500	138 @ 2400	4.00 × 3.00	9.0:1	36-41 @ 2000
	L	181 (3.0)	MFI	125 @ 4900	150 @ 2400	3.80 × 2.66	8.45:1	37 @ 2400
1987	M	122 (2.0)	Turbo	167 @ 4500	175 @ 4000	3.40 × 3.40	8.0:1	NA
	D	138 (2.3)	PFI	150 @ 5200	160 @ 4000	3.62 × 3.35	9.5:1	30 @ 2000
	U	151 (2.5)	TBI	98 @ 4300	135 @ 3200	4.00 × 3.00	8.3:1	37 @ 2000
	L	181 (3.0)	PFI	125 @ 4900	150 @ 2400	3.80 × 2.70	9.0:1	37 @ 2400
1988	M	122 (2.0)	Turbo	167 @ 4500	175 @ 4000	3.40 × 3.40	8.0:1	NA
	D	138 (2.3)	PFI	150 @ 5200	160 @ 4000	3.62 × 3.35	9.5:1	30 @ 2000
	U	151 (2.5)	TBI	98 @ 4300	135 @ 3200	4.00 × 3.00	8.3:1	37 @ 2000
	L	181 (3.0)	PFI	125 @ 4900	150 @ 2400	3.80 × 2.70	9.0:1	37 @ 2400
1989	M	122 (2.0)	Turbo	167 @ 4500	175 @ 4000	3.40 × 3.40	8.0:1	NA
	A	138 (2.3)	PFI	180 @ 6200	160 @ 5200	3.62 × 3.35	10.0:1	30 @ 2000
	D	138 (2.3)	PFI	160 @ 6200	155 @ 5200	3.62 × 3.35	9.5:1	30 @ 2000
	U	151 (2.5)	TBI	110 @ 5200	135 @ 3200	4.00 × 3.00	8.3:1	37 @ 2000
	N	204 (3.3)	PFI	160 @ 5200	185 @ 3200	3.70 × 3.16	9.0:1	45 @ 2000
1990	A	138 (2.3)	PFI	180 @ 6200	160 @ 5200	3.62 × 3.35	10.0:1	30 @ 2000
	D	138 (2.3)	PFI	160 @ 6200	155 @ 5200	3.62 × 3.35	9.5:1	30 @ 2000
	U	151 (2.5)	TBI	110 @ 5200	135 @ 3200	4.00 × 3.00	8.3:1	37 @ 2000
	N	204 (3.3)	PFI	160 @ 5200	185 @ 3200	3.70 × 3.16	9.0:1	45 @ 2000
1991	A	138 (2.3)	PFI	180 @ 6200	160 @ 5200	3.62 × 3.35	10.0:1	30 @ 2000
	D	138 (2.3)	PFI	160 @ 6200	155 @ 5200	3.62 × 3.35	9.5:1	30 @ 2000
	U	151 (2.5)	TBI	110 @ 5200	135 @ 3200	4.00 × 3.00	8.3:1	26 @ 800
	N	204 (3.3)	PFI	160 @ 5200	185 @ 3200	3.70 × 3.16	9.0:1	60 @ 1850
1992	3	138 (2.3)	PFI	180 @ 6200	160 @ 5200	3.62 × 3.35	9.5:1	30 @ 2000
	A	138 (2.3)	PFI	180 @ 6200	160 @ 5200	3.62 × 3.35	10.0:1	30 @ 2000
	D	138 (2.3)	PFI	160 @ 6200	155 @ 5200	3.62 × 3.35	9.5:1	30 @ 2000
	N	204 (3.3)	PFI	160 @ 5200	185 @ 3200	3.70 × 3.16	9.0:1	60 @ 1850

NOTE: Horsepower and torque are SAE net figures. They are measured at the rear of the transmission with all accessories installed and operating. Since the figures vary when a given engine is installed in different models, some are representative rather than exact.

TBI—Throttle Body Injection
MFI—Multi-Port Fuel Injection
PFI—Port Fuel Injection
Turbo—Turbocharged

VALVE SPECIFICATIONS

Year	VIN	No. Cylinder Displacement cu. in. (Liters)	Seat Angle (deg.)	Face Angle (deg.)	Spring Test Pressure (lbs. @ in.)	Spring Installed Height (in.)	Stem-to-Guide Clearance (in.)		Stem Diameter (in.)	
							Intake	Exhaust	Intake	Exhaust
1985	U	4-151 (2.5)	46	45	82 @	1.66	0.0010–0.0027	0.0010–0.0027	0.3420–0.3430	0.3420–0.3430
	L	6-181 (3.0)	45	45	220 @	1.34	0.0015–0.0035	0.0015–0.0032	0.3401–0.3412	0.3401–0.3412
1986	U	4-151 (2.5)	46	45	82 @	1.66	0.0010–0.0027	0.0010–0.0027	0.3130–0.3140	0.3120–0.3130
	L	6-181 (3.0)	45	45	220 @	1.34	0.0015–0.0035	0.0015–0.0032	0.3401–0.3412	0.3405–0.3412
1987-88	M	4-122 (2.0)	45	46	NA	NA	0.0006–0.0020	0.0010–0.0024	—	—
	D	4-138 (2.3)	45	44	64–70 @ 1.4370 in.	1.423–1.443	0.0009–0.0027	0.0015–0.0032	0.2751–0.2744	0.2754–0.2739
	U	4-151 (2.5)	46	45	158–170 @ 1.040 in.	1.44	0.0010–0.0026	0.0013–0.0041	0.3130–0.3140	0.3120–0.3130
	L	6-181 (3.0)	45	45	175–195 @ 1.340 in.	1.73	0.0015–0.0035	0.0015–0.0032	0.3401–0.3412	0.3405–0.3412
1989	M	4-122 (2.0)	45	46	165–179 @ 1.043 in.	NA	0.0006–0.0017	0.0010–0.0024	0.2755–0.2760	0.2747–0.2753
	A	4-138 (2.3)	45	①	188–202 @ 1.043 in.	1.42–1.44	0.0009–0.0027	0.0015–0.0032	0.2744–0.2751	0.2740–0.2747
	D	4-138 (2.3)	45	①	159–173 @ 1.043 in.	1.42–1.44	0.0009–0.0027	0.0015–0.0032	0.2744–0.2751	0.2740–0.2747
	U	4-151 (2.5)	46	45	173 @ 1.24 in.	1.68	0.0010–0.0026	0.0013–0.0041	NA	NA
	N	6-204 (3.3)	45	45	200–220 @ 1.315 in.	1.69–1.75	0.0015–0.0035	0.0015–0.0032	NA	NA
1990	A	4-138 (2.3)	45	①	193–207 @ 1.043 in.	1.42–1.44	0.0009–0.0027	0.0015–0.0032	0.2744–0.2751	0.2740–0.2747
	D	4-138 (2.3)	45	①	193–207 @ 1.043 in.	1.42–1.44	0.0009–0.0027	0.0015–0.0032	0.2744–0.2751	0.2740–0.2747
	U	4-151 (2.5)	46	45	173 @ 1.24 in.	1.68	0.0010–0.0026	0.0013–0.0041	NA	NA
	N	6-204 (3.3)	45	45	200–220 @ 1.315 in.	1.69–1.75	0.0015–0.0035	0.0015–0.0032	NA	NA
1991	A	4-138 (2.3)	45	44	193–207 @ 1.043 in.	0.98–1.00 ②	0.0010–0.0027	0.0015–0.0032	0.2744–0.2751	0.2740–0.2747
	D	4-138 (2.3)	45	44	193–207 @ 1.043 in.	0.98–1.00 ②	0.0010–0.0027	0.0015–0.0032	0.2744–0.2751	0.2740–0.2747
	U	4-151 (2.5)	46	45	173 @ 1.24 in.	1.68	0.0010–0.0026	0.0013–0.0041	NA	NA
	N	6-204 (3.3)	45	45	210 @ 1.315 in.	1.69–1.72	0.0015–0.0035	0.0015–0.0035	NA	NA

VALVE SPECIFICATIONS

Year	VIN	No. Cylinder Displacement cu. in. (Liters)	Seat Angle (deg.)	Face Angle (deg.)	Spring Test Pressure (lbs. @ in.)	Spring Installed Height (in.)	Stem-to-Guide Clearance (in.)		Stem Diameter (in.)	
							Intake	Exhaust	Intake	Exhaust
1992	A	4-138 (2.3)	45	44	193–207 @ 1.043 in.	0.98–1.00 ②	0.0015–0.0032	0.0015–0.0032	0.2740–0.2747	0.2740–0.2747
	D	4-138 (2.3)	45	44	193–207 @ 1.043 in.	0.98–1.00 ②	0.0015–0.0032	0.0015–0.0032	0.2740–0.2747	0.2740–0.2747
	3	4-138 (2.3)	45	44	193–207 @ 1.043 in.	0.98–1.00 ②	0.0015–0.0032	0.0015–0.0032	0.2740–0.2747	0.2740–0.2747
	N	6-204 (3.3)	45	45	210 @ 1.315 in.	1.69–1.72	0.0015–0.0032	0.0015–0.0035	NA	NA

① Intake: 45°
Exhaust: 44.5°
② Measured from top of valve stem to top of camshaft housing mounting surface

CAMSHAFT SPECIFICATIONS

All measurements given in inches.

Year	Engine ID/VIN	Engine Displacement Liters (cc)	Journal Diameter 1	2	3	4	5	Elevation In.	Ex.	Bearing Clearance	Camshaft End Play
1985–86	U	4-151 (2.5)	1.8690	1.8690	1.8690	1.8690	1.8690	0.3980	0.3980	0.0007–0.0027	0.0015–0.0050
	L	6-181 (3.0)	1.7850–1.7860	1.7850–1.7860	1.7850–1.7860	1.7850–1.7860	—	0.3580	0.3840	0.0005–0.0025	NA
1987–88	M	4-122 (2.0)	1.6714–1.6720	1.6812–1.6816	1.6911–1.6917	1.7009–1.7015	1.7108–1.7114	0.2409	NA	0.0008	0.0016–0.0064
	D	4-138 (2.3)	1.3751–1.3760	1.3751–1.3760	1.3751–1.3760	1.3751–1.3760	1.3751–1.3760	0.3400	0.3500	0.0019–0.0043	0.0014–0.0060
	U	4-151 (2.5)	1.8690	1.8690	1.8690	1.8690	1.8690	0.3980	0.3980	0.0007–0.0027	0.0015–0.0050
	L	6-181 (3.0)	1.7850–1.7860	1.7850–1.7860	1.7850–1.7860	1.7850–1.7860	—	0.3580	0.3840	0.0005–0.0025	NA
1989	M	4-122 (2.0)	1.6706–1.6712	1.6812–1.6818	1.6911–1.6917	1.7009–1.7015	1.7100–1.7106	0.2625	0.2625	0.0011–0.0035	0.0016–0.0064
	D	4-138 (2.3)	1.3751–1.3760	1.3751–1.3760	1.3751–1.3760	1.3751–1.3760	1.3751–1.3760	0.3400	0.3500	0.0019–0.0043	0.0014–0.0060
	A	4-138 (2.3)	1.3751–1.3760	1.3751–1.3760	1.3751–1.3760	1.3751–1.3760	1.3751–1.3760	0.4100	0.4100	0.0019–0.0043	0.0014–0.0060
	U	4-151 (2.5)	1.8690	1.8690	1.8690	1.8690	1.8690	0.2480	0.2480	0.0007–0.0027	0.0020–0.0090
	N	6-204 (3.3)	1.7850–1.7860	1.7850–1.7860	1.7850–1.7860	1.7850–1.7860	—	0.2500	0.2550	0.0005–0.0035	NA
1990	D	4-138 (2.3)	1.5720–1.5728	1.3751–1.3760	1.3751–1.3760	1.3751–1.3760	1.3751–1.3760	0.3400	0.3500	0.0019–0.0043	0.0014–0.0060
	A	4-138 (2.3)	1.5720–1.5728	1.3751–1.3760	1.3751–1.3760	1.3751–1.3760	1.3751–1.3760	0.4100	0.4100	0.0019–0.0043	0.0014–0.0060
	U	4-151 (2.5)	1.8690	1.8690	1.8690	1.8690	1.8690	0.2480	0.2480	0.0007–0.0027	0.0020–0.0090
	N	6-204 (3.3)	1.7850–1.7860	1.7850–1.7860	1.7850–1.7860	1.7850–1.7860	—	0.2500	0.2550	0.0005–0.0035	NA

CAMSHAFT SPECIFICATIONS

All measurements given in inches.

Year	Engine ID/VIN	Engine Displacement Liters (cc)	Journal Diameter 1	2	3	4	5	Elevation In.	Ex.	Bearing Clearance	Camshaft End Play
1991	D	4-138 (2.3)	1.5720–1.5728	1.3751–1.3760	1.3751–1.3760	1.3751–1.3760	1.3751–1.3760	0.3750	0.3750	0.0019–0.0043	0.0009–0.0088
	A	4-138 (2.3)	1.5720–1.5728	1.3751–1.3760	1.3751–1.3760	1.3751–1.3760	1.3751–1.3760	0.4100	0.4100	0.0019–0.0043	0.0009–0.0088
	U	4-151 (2.5)	1.8690	1.8690	1.8690	1.8690	1.8690	0.2480	0.2480	0.0007–0.0027	0.0020–0.0090
	N	6-204 (3.3)	1.7850–1.7860	1.7850–1.7860	1.7850–1.7860	1.7850–1.7860	—	0.2500	0.2550	0.0005–0.0035	NA
1992	A	4-138 (2.3)	1.5720–1.5728	1.3751–1.3760	1.3751–1.3760	1.3751–1.3760	1.3751–1.3760	0.4100	0.4100	0.0019–0.0043	0.0009–0.0088
	D	4-138 (2.3)	1.5720–1.5728	1.3751–1.3760	1.3751–1.3760	1.3751–1.3760	1.3751–1.3760	0.3750	0.3750	0.0019–0.0043	0.0009–0.0088
	3	4-138 (2.3)	1.5720–1.5728	1.3751–1.3760	1.3751–1.3760	1.3751–1.3760	1.3751–1.3760	0.4100	0.4100	0.0019–0.0043	0.0009–0.0088
	N	6-204 (3.3)	1.7850–1.7860	1.7850–1.7860	1.7850–1.7860	1.7850–1.7860	—	0.2500	0.2550	0.0005–0.0035	NA

CRANKSHAFT AND CONNECTING ROD SPECIFICATIONS

All measurements are given in inches.

Year	Engine ID/VIN	Engine Displacement Liters (cc)	Crankshaft Main Brg. Journal Dia.	Main Brg. Oil Clearance	Shaft End-play	Thrust on No.	Connecting Rod Journal Diameter	Oil Clearance	Side Clearance
1985–86	U	4-151 (2.5)	2.3000	0.0005–0.0022	0.0035–0.0085	5	2.0000	0.0005–0.0022	0.0060–0.0020
	L	6-181 (3.0)	2.4995	0.0003–0.0018	0.0030–0.0150	2	2.4870	0.0005–0.0026	0.0030–0.0150
1987	M	4-122 (2.0)	2.2830–2.2833 ①	0.0006–0.0016	0.0030–0.0120	3	1.9278–1.9286	0.0007–0.0024	0.0027–0.0095
	D	4-138 (2.3)	2.0470–2.0474	0.0005–0.0020	0.0034–0.0095	3	1.8887–1.8897	0.0005–0.0025	0.0059–0.0177
	U	4-151 (2.5)	2.3000	0.0005–0.0022	0.0035–0.0085	5	2.0000	0.0005–0.0022	0.0060–0.0220
	L	6-181 (3.0)	2.4995	0.0003–0.0018	0.0030–0.0085	2	2.4870	0.0005–0.0026	0.0030–0.0150
1988	M	4-122 (2.0)	2.2830–2.2833 ①	0.0006–0.0016	0.0030–0.0120	3	1.9278–1.9286	0.0007–0.0024	0.0027–0.0095
	D	4-138 (2.3)	2.0470–2.0474	0.0005–0.0022	0.0034–0.0095	3	1.8887–1.8897	0.0005–0.0025	0.0059–0.0177
	U	4-151 (2.5)	2.3000	0.0005–0.0022	0.0035–0.0085	5	2.0000	0.0005–0.0026	0.0060–0.0220
	L	6-181 (3.0)	2.4988–2.4998	0.0003–0.0018	0.0030–0.0110	2	2.2487–2.2495	0.0003–0.0028	0.0030–0.0150

CRANKSHAFT AND CONNECTING ROD SPECIFICATIONS

All measurements are given in inches.

			Crankshaft				Connecting Rod		
Year	Engine ID/VIN	Engine Displacement Liters (cc)	Main Brg. Journal Dia.	Main Brg. Oil Clearance	Shaft End-play	Thrust on No.	Journal Diameter	Oil Clearance	Side Clearance
1989	M	4-122 (2.0)	2.2828–2.2833 ①	0.0006–0.0016	0.0028–0.0118	3	1.9279–1.9287	0.0007–0.0025	0.0028–0.0095
	A	4-138 (2.3)	2.0470–2.0480	0.0005–0.0023	0.0034–0.0095	3	1.8887–1.8897	0.0005–0.0020	0.0059–0.0177
	D	4-138 (2.3)	2.0470–2.0480	0.0005–0.0023	0.0034–0.0095	3	1.8887–1.8897	0.0005–0.0020	0.0059–0.0177
	U	4-151 (2.5)	2.3000	0.0005–0.0020	0.0006–0.0110	5	2.0000	0.0005–0.0030	0.0060–0.0240
	N	6-204 (3.3)	2.4988–2.4998	0.0003–0.0018	0.0030–0.0110	2	2.2487–2.2499	0.0003–0.0026	0.0030–0.0150
1990	A	4-138 (2.3)	2.0470–2.0480	0.0005–0.0023	0.0034–0.0095	3	1.8887–1.8897	0.0005–0.0020	0.0059–0.0177
	D	4-138 (2.3)	2.0470–2.0480	0.0005–0.0023	0.0034–0.0095	3	1.8887–1.8897	0.0005–0.0020	0.0059–0.0177
	U	4-151 (2.5)	2.3000	0.0005–0.0020	0.0006–0.0110	5	2.0000	0.0005–0.0030	0.0060–0.0240
	N	6-204 (3.3)	2.4988–2.4998	0.0003–0.0018	0.0030–0.0110	2	2.2487–2.2499	0.0003–0.0026	0.0030–0.0150
1991	A	4-138 (2.3)	2.0470–2.0480	0.0005–0.0023	0.0034–0.0095	3	1.8887–1.8897	0.0005–0.0020	0.0059–0.0177
	D	4-138 (2.3)	2.0470–2.0480	0.0005–0.0023	0.0034–0.0095	3	1.8887–1.8897	0.0005–0.0020	0.0059–0.0177
	U	4-151 (2.5)	2.3000	0.0005–0.0022	0.0059–0.0110	5	2.0000	0.0005–0.0030	0.0060–0.0240
	N	6-204 (3.3)	2.4988–2.4998	0.0003–0.0018	0.0030–0.0110	2	2.2487–2.2499	0.0003–0.0026	0.0030–0.0150
1992	A	4-138 (2.3)	2.0470–2.0480	0.0005–0.0023	0.0034–0.0095	3	1.8887–1.8897	0.0005–0.0020	0.0059–0.0177
	D	4-138 (2.3)	2.0470–2.0480	0.0005–0.0023	0.0034–0.0095	3	1.8887–1.8897	0.0005–0.0020	0.0059–0.0177
	3	4-138 (2.3)	2.0470–2.0480	0.0005–0.0023	0.0034–0.0095	3	1.8887–1.8897	0.0005–0.0020	0.0059–0.0177
	N	6-204 (3.3)	2.4988–2.4998	0.0003–0.0018	0.0030–0.0110	2	2.2487–2.2499	0.0003–0.0026	0.0030–0.0150

① Brown: 2.2830–2.2833
Green: 2.2827–2.2830

PISTON AND RING SPECIFICATIONS

All measurements are given in inches.

Year	VIN	No. Cylinder Displacement cu. in. (Liters)	Piston Clearance	Ring Gap Top Compression	Ring Gap Bottom Compression	Ring Gap Oil Control	Ring Side Clearance Top Compression	Ring Side Clearance Bottom Compression	Ring Side Clearance Oil Control
1985	U	4-151 (2.5)	0.0014–0.0022 ①	0.0100–0.0200	0.0100–0.0200	0.0200–0.0600	0.00200–0.00300	0.00100–0.00300	0.01500–0.05500
	L	6-181 (3.0)	0.0008–0.0020 ②	0.0130–0.0280	0.0130–0.0230	0.0150–0.0350	0.00300–0.00500	0.00300–0.00500	0.00350
1986	U	4-151 (2.5)	0.0014–0.0022 ①	0.0100–0.0200	0.0100–0.0200	0.0200–0.0600	0.00200–0.00300	0.00100–0.00300	0.01500–0.05500
	L	6-181 (3.0)	0.0008–0.0020 ②	0.0130–0.0280	0.0130–0.0230	0.0150–0.0350	0.00300–0.00500	0.00300–0.00500	0.00350
1987	M	4-122 (2.0)	0.0012–0.0020	0.0120–0.0200	0.0120–0.0200	0.0160–0.0550	0.00200–0.00300	0.00100–0.00240	—
	D	4-138 (2.3)	0.0007–0.0020	0.0160–0.0250	0.0160–0.0250	0.0160–0.0550	0.00200–0.00350	0.00160–0.00310	—
	U	4-151 (2.5)	0.0014–0.0022 ①	0.0100–0.0200	0.0100–0.0200	0.0200–0.0600	0.00200–0.00300	0.00100–0.00300	0.01500–0.05500
	L	6-181 (3.0)	0.0008–0.0020 ②	0.0130–0.0280	0.0130–0.0230	0.0150–0.0350	0.00300–0.00500	0.00300–0.00500	0.00350
1988	M	4-122 (2.0)	0.0012–0.0020	0.0120–0.0200	0.0120–0.0200	0.0160–0.0550	0.00200–0.00300	0.00100–0.00300	NA
	D	4-138 (2.3)	0.0007–0.0020	0.0160–0.0250	0.0160–0.0250	0.0160–0.0550	0.00200–0.00400	0.00160–0.00310	NA
	U	4-151 (2.5)	0.0014–0.0022	0.0100–0.0200	0.0100–0.0200	0.0200–0.0600	0.00200–0.00300	0.00100–0.00300	0.01500–0.05500
	L	6-181 (3.0)	0.0010–0.0045	0.0100–0.0200	0.0100–0.0220	0.0150–0.0550	0.00100–0.00300	0.00100–0.00300	0.00050–0.00650
1989	M	4-122 (2.0)	0.0012–0.0020	0.0100–0.0200	0.0120–0.0200	0.0160–0.0550	0.00200–0.00400	0.00200–0.00300	NA
	A	4-138 (2.3)	0.0007–0.0020	0.0140–0.0240	0.0160–0.0260	0.0160–0.0550	0.00200–0.00400	0.00200–0.00300	NA
	D	4-138 (2.3)	0.0007–0.0020	0.0140–0.0240	0.0160–0.0260	0.0160–0.0550	0.00200–0.00400	0.00200–0.00300	NA
	U	4-151 (2.5)	0.0014–0.0022	0.0100–0.0200	0.0100–0.0200	0.0200–0.0600	0.00200–0.00300	0.00100–0.00300	0.01500–0.05500
	N	6-204 (3.3)	0.0004–0.0022	0.0100–0.0250	0.0100–0.0250	0.0100–0.0400	0.00100–0.00300	0.00100–0.00300	0.00100–0.00800
1990	A	4-138 (2.3)	0.0007–0.0020	0.0140–0.0240	0.0160–0.0260	0.0160–0.0550	0.00300–0.00500	0.00200–0.00300	NA
	D	4-138 (2.3)	0.0007–0.0020	0.0140–0.0240	0.0160–0.0260	0.0160–0.0550	0.00200–0.00400	0.00200–0.00300	NA
	U	4-151 (2.5)	0.0014–0.0022	0.0100–0.0200	0.0100–0.0200	0.0200–0.0600	0.00200–0.00300	0.00100–0.00300	0.01500–0.05500
	N	6-204 (3.3)	0.0004–0.0022	0.0100–0.0250	0.0100–0.0250	0.0100–0.0400	0.00100–0.00300	0.00100–0.00300	0.00100–0.00800

PISTON AND RING SPECIFICATIONS

All measurements are given in inches.

Year	VIN	No. Cylinder Displacement cu. in. (Liters)	Piston Clearance	Ring Gap Top Compression	Ring Gap Bottom Compression	Ring Gap Oil Control	Ring Side Clearance Top Compression	Ring Side Clearance Bottom Compression	Ring Side Clearance Oil Control
1991	A	4-138 (2.3)	0.0007–0.0020	0.0140–0.0240	0.0160–0.0260	0.0160–0.0550	0.00300–0.00500	0.00200–0.00300	NA
	D	4-138 (2.3)	0.0007–0.0020	0.0140–0.0240	0.0160–0.0260	0.0160–0.0550	0.00200–0.00400	0.00200–0.00300	NA
	U	4-151 (2.5)	0.0014–0.0022	0.0100–0.0200	0.0100–0.0200	0.0200–0.0600	0.00200–0.00300	0.00100–0.00300	0.01500–0.05500
	N	6-204 (3.3)	0.0004–0.0022 ①	0.0100–0.0250	0.0100–0.0250	0.0100–0.0400	0.00100–0.00300	0.00100–0.00300	0.00100–0.00800
1992	D	4-138 (2.3)	0.0007–0.0020	0.0138–0.0236	0.0157–0.0256	0.0157–0.0551	0.00197–0.00394	0.00157–0.00315	0.01957–0.02060
	A	4-138 (2.3)	0.0007–0.0020	0.0138–0.0236	0.0157–0.0256	0.0157–0.0551	0.00270–0.00470	0.00157–0.00315	0.01957–0.02060
	3	4-138 (2.3)	0.0007–0.0020	0.0138–0.0236	0.0157–0.0256	0.0157–0.0551	0.00197–0.00394	0.00157–0.00315	0.01957–0.02060
	N	6-204 (3.3)	0.0004–0.0022	0.0100–0.0250	0.0100–0.0250	0.0150–0.0550	0.00130–0.00310	0.00130–0.00310	0.00110–0.00810

NA—Not available
① Measured 1.8 in. (44mm) down from top of piston
② Measured at top of piston skirt

TORQUE SPECIFICATIONS

All readings in ft. lbs.

Year	VIN	No. Cylinder Displacement cu. in. (Liters)	Cylinder Head Bolts	Main Bearing Bolts	Rod Bearing Bolts	Crankshaft Pulley Bolts	Flywheel Bolts	Manifold Intake	Manifold Exhaust	Spark Plugs
1985	U	4-151 (2.5)	92	70	32	200	44	38	44	15
	L	6-181 (3.0)	80	100	40	200	60	45	25	15
1986	U	4-151 (2.5)	92	70	32	162	44	38	44	15
	L	6-181 (3.0)	80	100	40	225	60	45	25	15
1987	U	4-151 (2.5)	92	70	32	162	44	38	44	15
	M	4-122 (2.0)	①	44 ②	26 ⑯	34	48	16	16	15
	D	4-140 (2.3)	—	—	—	—	—	—	—	—
	L	6-181 (3.0)	80	100	40	225	60	45	25	15
1988	M	4-122 (2.0)	①	44 ②	26 ②	20	48 ③	16	16	15
	D	4-140 (2.3)	④	15 ⑤	15 ⑥	74 ⑤	22 ②	18	27	17
	U	4-151 (2.5)	⑫	70	32	162	⑨	25	⑩	15
	L	6-181 (3.0)	⑪	100	45	219	60	32	37	20
1989	M	4-122 (2.0)	①	44 ②	26 ②	20	63 ③	18	10	15
	A	4-138 (2.3)	④	15 ⑤	18 ⑬	74 ⑤	22 ②	18	27	17
	D	4-138 (2.3)	④	15 ⑤	18 ⑬	74 ⑤	22 ②	18	27	17
	U	4-151 (2.5)	⑫	65	29	162	⑨	25	⑩	15
	N	6-204 (3.3)	⑭	90	20 ②	219	61	7	30	20

TORQUE SPECIFICATIONS

All readings in ft. lbs.

Year	VIN	No. Cylinder Displacement cu. in. (Liters)	Cylinder Head Bolts	Main Bearing Bolts	Rod Bearing Bolts	Crankshaft Pulley Bolts	Flywheel Bolts	Manifold Intake	Manifold Exhaust	Spark Plugs
1990	A	4-138 (2.3)	⑮	15⑤	18⑬	74⑤	22②	18	⑦	17
	D	4-138 (2.3)	⑮	15⑤	18⑬	74⑤	22②	18	⑦	17
	U	4-151 (2.5)	⑫	65	29	162	⑨	25	⑩	15
	N	6-204 (3.3)	⑭	90	20②	219	61	7	30	20
1991	A	4-138 (2.3)	⑮	15⑤	18⑬	74⑤	22②	18	⑦	17
	D	4-138 (2.3)	⑮	15⑤	18⑬	74⑤	22②	18	⑦	17
	U	4-151 (2.5)	⑫	65	29	162	⑨	25	⑩	15
	N	6-204 (3.3)	⑭	26⑯	20②	105⑰	89⑧⑤	89⑧	41	20
1992	A	4-138 (2.3)	⑮	15⑤	18⑬	74⑤	22②	18	⑦	17
	D	4-138 (2.3)	⑮	15⑤	18⑬	74⑤	22②	18	⑦	17
	3	4-138 (2.3)	⑮	15⑤	18⑬	74⑤	22②	18	⑦	17
	N	6-204 (3.3)	⑭	26⑯	20②	105⑰	89⑧⑤	89⑧	41	20

① Step 1: 18 ft. lbs.
Step 2: 3 rounds of 60° turns in sequence
Step 3: An additional 30-50° turn after engine warm up
② Plus an additional 40–50° turn
③ Plus an additional 30° turn
④ Short bolts: 26 ft. lbs. plus an additional 80° turn
Long bolts: 26 ft. lbs. plus an additional 90° turn
⑤ Plus an additional 90° turn
⑥ Plus an additional 75° turn
⑦ Nuts: 27 ft. lbs.
Studs: 106 inch lbs.
⑧ Inch lbs.
⑨ Manual transaxle: 69 ft. lbs.
Automatic transaxle: 55 ft. lbs.
⑩ Outer bolts: 26 ft. lbs.
Inner bolts: 37 ft. lbs.
⑪ Step 1: 25 ft. lbs.
Step 2: 2 rounds of 90° turns in sequence, not to exceed 60 ft. lbs.
⑫ Step 1: 18 ft. lbs.
Step 2: 26 ft.lbs., except front bolt/stud
Step 3: Front bolt/stud to 18 ft. lbs.
Step 4: An additional 90° turn
⑬ Plus an additional 80° turn
⑭ Step 1: 35 ft. lbs.
Step 2: An additional 130° turn
Step 3: An additional 30° turn on center 4 bolts
⑮ Short bolts: 26 ft. lbs. plus an additional 100° turn
Long bolts: 26 ft. lbs. plus an additional 110° turn
⑯ Plus an additional 45° turn
⑰ Plus an additional 56° turn

Engine

REMOVAL & INSTALLATION

SEE FIGS. 33–46

CAUTION

When draining the coolant, keep in mind that cats and dogs are attracted by the ethylene glycol antifreeze, and are quite likely to drink any that is left in an uncovered container or in puddles on the ground. This will prove fatal in sufficient quantity. Always drain the coolant into a sealable container. Coolant should be reused unless it is contaminated or several years old.

2.0L AND 2.5L ENGINES

1. Relieve the fuel system pressure.
2. Disconnect both battery cables and ground straps.
3. Drain the cooling system and remove the cooling fan.
4. Remove the air cleaner assembly.
5. Disconnect the ECM connections and feed harness through the bulkhead. Lay the harness across the engine.
6. Label and disconnect the engine wiring harness and all engine-related connectors and lay across the engine.
7. Label and disconnect the radiator hoses and vacuum lines. Disconnect and plug the fuel lines.
8. On 2.5L engine, remove the air conditioning compressor from the engine and lay it aside, without disconnecting the refrigerant lines. Remove the transaxle struts.
9. If equipped with power steering, remove the power steering pump from its mount and lay it aside. Remove the power steering pump bracket from the engine.
10. If equipped with a manual transaxle, disconnect the clutch and transaxle linkage. Remove the throttle cable from the throttle body.
11. If equipped with an automatic transaxle, disconnect the transaxle cooler lines, shifter linkage, down shift cable and throttle cable from the throttle body.
12. Raise and safely support the vehicle.
13. Disconnect all wiring from the transaxle.
14. On 2.0L engine, properly discharge the air conditioning system and remove the compressor. Remove the transaxle strut(s).
15. Disconnect the exhaust pipe from the exhaust manifold and hangers.
16. Disconnect the heater hoses from the heater core tubes and plug them.
17. Remove the front wheels. Remove the calipers and wire them up aside. Remove the brake rotors.
18. Matchmark and remove the knuckle-to-strut bolts.
19. Remove the body-to-cradle bolts at the lower control arms. Loosen the remaining body-to-cradle bolts. Remove a bolt at each cradle side, leaving 1 bolt per corner.
20. Using the proper equipment, support the vehicle under the radiator frame support.
21. Position a jack to the rear of the body pan with a 4 in. (102mm) × 4 in. (102mm) × 6 ft. (1.8m) timber spanning the vehicle.
22. Raise the vehicle enough to remove the support equipment.
23. Position a dolly under the engine/transaxle assembly with 3 blocks of wood for additional support.
24. Lower the vehicle slightly, allowing the engine/transaxle assembly to rest on the dolly.
25. Remove all engine and transaxle mount bolts and brackets. Remove the remaining cradle-to-body bolts.
26. Raise the vehicle, leaving engine and transaxle assembly with the suspension on the dolly.
27. Separate the engine and transaxle.

To install:

28. Assemble the engine and transaxle assembly and position on the dolly.
29. Raise and safely support the vehicle. Roll the assembly to the installation position and lower the vehicle over the assembly.

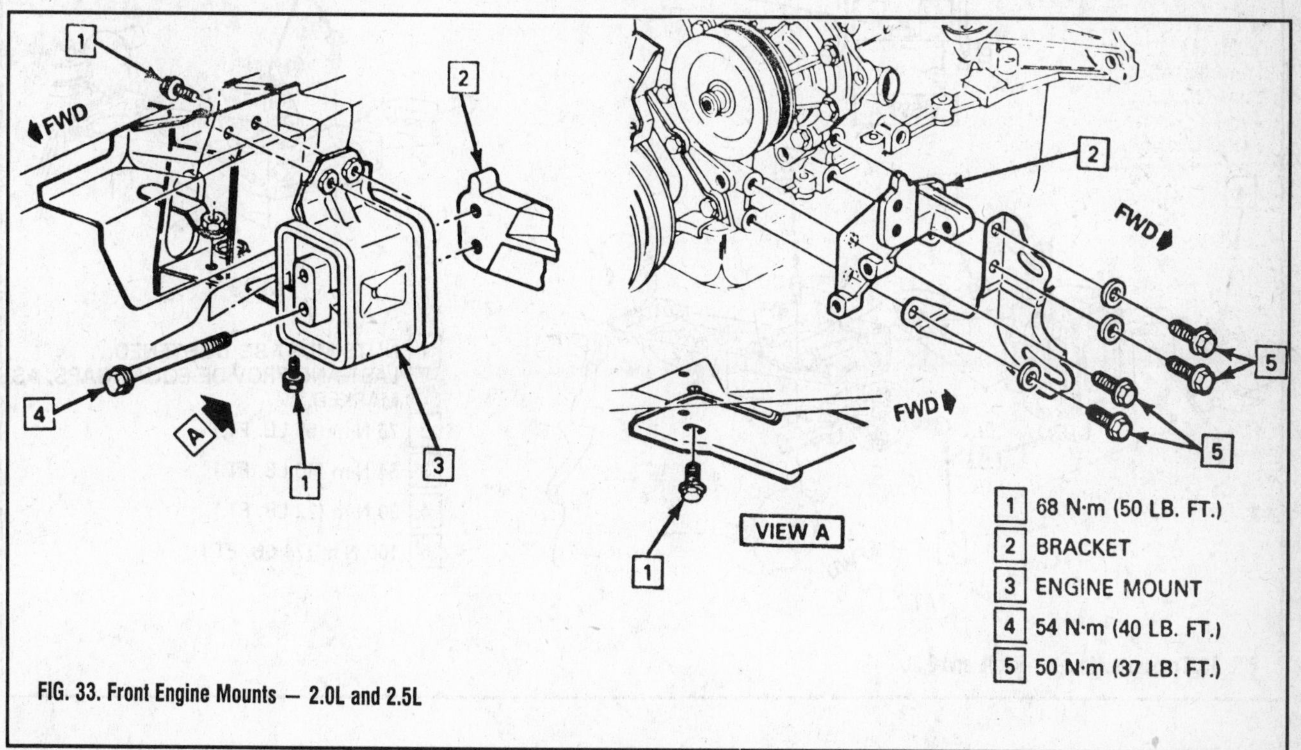

FIG. 33. Front Engine Mounts — 2.0L and 2.5L

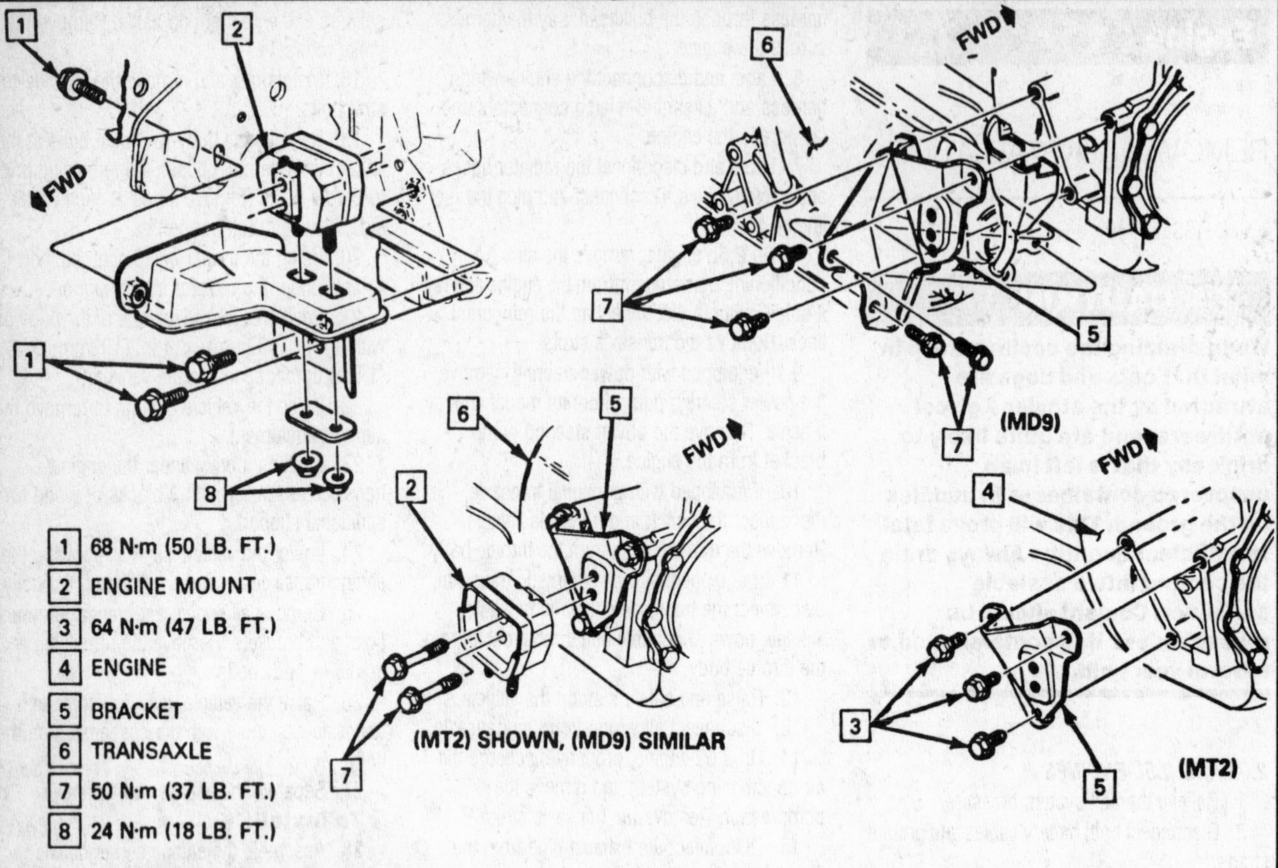

(MT2) SHOWN, (MD9) SIMILAR

(MD9)

(MT2)

1. 68 N·m (50 LB. FT.)
2. ENGINE MOUNT
3. 64 N·m (47 LB. FT.)
4. ENGINE
5. BRACKET
6. TRANSAXLE
7. 50 N·m (37 LB. FT.)
8. 24 N·m (18 LB. FT.)

FIG. 34. Rear Engine Mounts — 2.0L and 2.5L

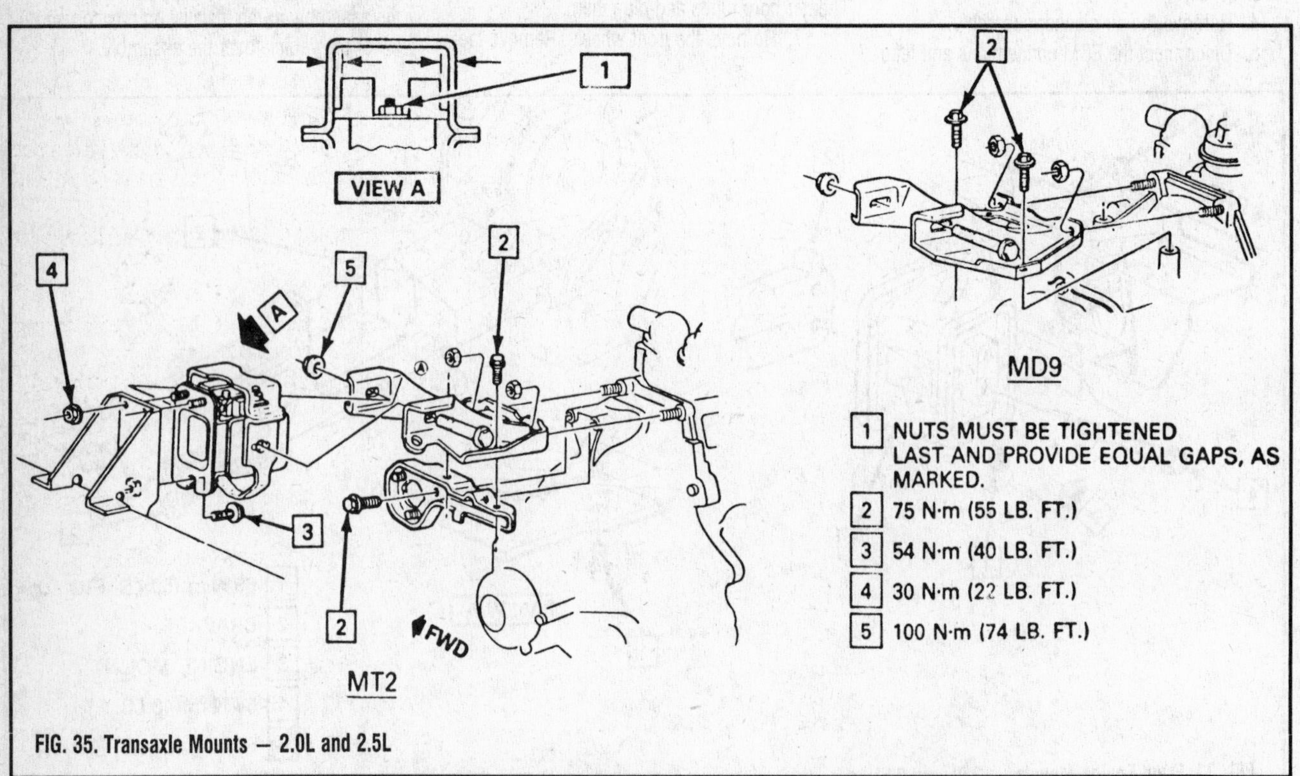

FIG. 35. Transaxle Mounts — 2.0L and 2.5L

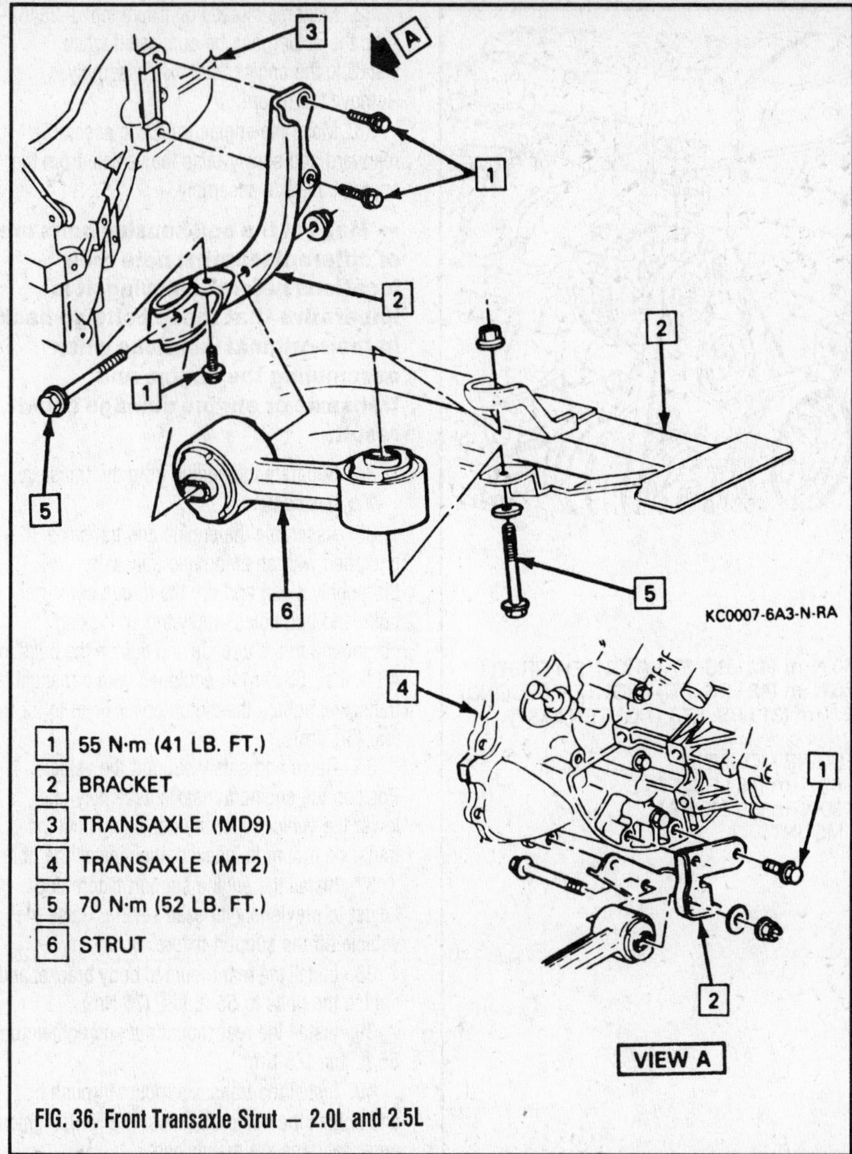

FIG. 36. Front Transaxle Strut — 2.0L and 2.5L

FWD

1 55 N·m (41 LB. FT.)
2 STRUT
3 TRANSAXLE

FIG. 37. Automatic Transaxle Strut — 2.0L and 2.5L

30. Install all engine, transaxle and suspension mounting bolts. Tighten all cradle mounting bolts to 65 ft. lbs. (88 Nm). Connect the wiring to the transaxle.

31. Install the knuckle-to-strut bolts and assemble the brakes.

32. Connect the exhaust pipe to the exhaust manifold and hangers.

33. Connect the heater hoses to the heater core tubes.

34. If equipped with the 2.0L engine, install the air conditioning compressor.

35. Install the wheels and lower the vehicle.

36. If equipped with the 2.5L engine, install the air conditioning compressor.

37. Install the power steering pump and related parts.

38. If equipped with a manual transaxle, connect the clutch and transaxle linkage. Connect the throttle cable to the throttle body.

39. If equipped with an automatic transaxle, connect the transaxle cooler lines, shifter linkage, down shift cable and throttle cable to the throttle body.

40. Connect the radiator hoses, vacuum lines and fuel lines.

41. Connect the engine wiring harness and all engine-related connectors. Feed the ECM connections through the bulkhead and connect.

42. Install the air cleaner assembly.

43. Fill all fluids to their proper levels.

44. Connect the battery cables, start the engine and set the timing, if necessary. Check for leaks.

2.3L ENGINE

1. Relieve the fuel system pressure.

2. Disconnect both battery cables and ground straps from the front engine mount bracket and the transaxle.

3. Drain the cooling system and remove the cooling fan.

4. Remove the air cleaner duct.

5. Disconnect the heater and radiator hoses from the thermostat housing.

6. Properly discharge the air conditioning system and disconnect the hoses from the compressor.

7. Remove the upper radiator support.

8. Disconnect the 2 vacuum hoses from the front of the engine.

9. Label and disconnect all electrical connectors from engine and transaxle-mounted devices.

10. Unplug the wires at the starter solenoid.

11. Disconnect the power brake vacuum hose from the throttle body.

12. Disconnect the throttle cable and remove the bracket.

13. Remove the power steering pump bracket and lay the pump aside with the lines attached.

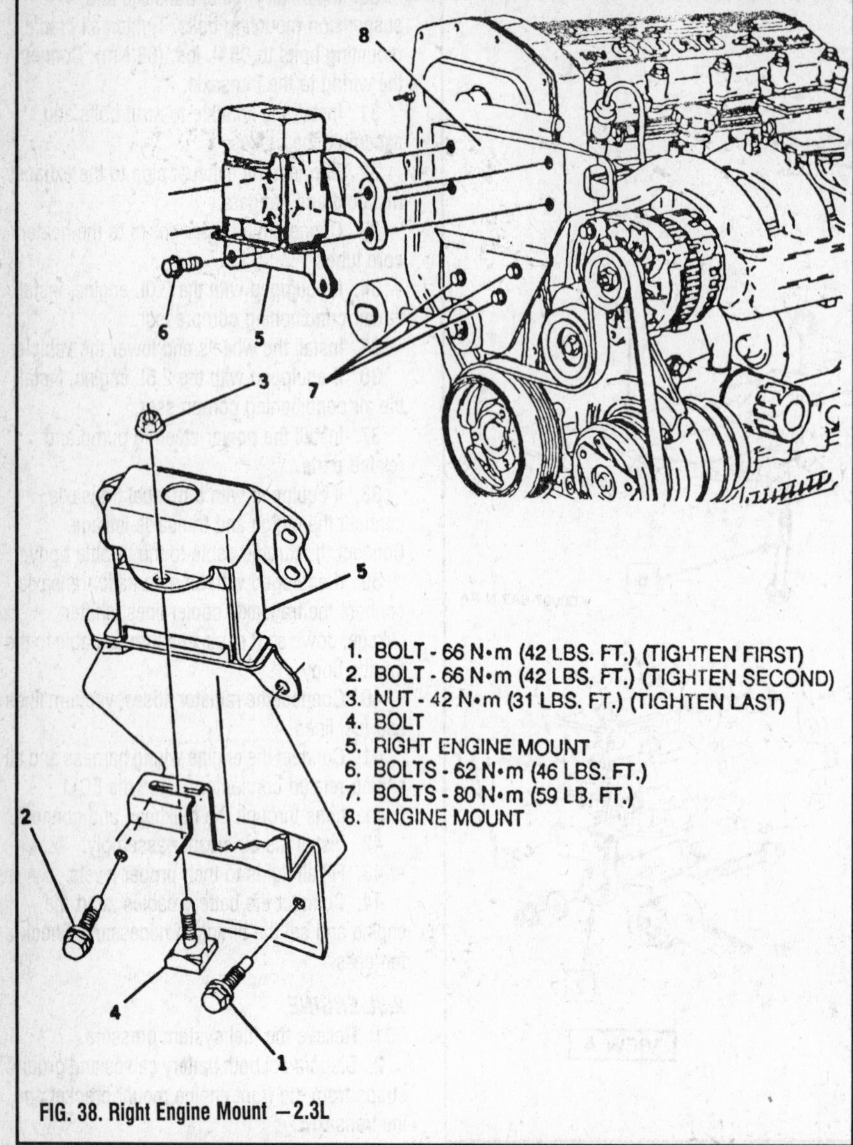

FIG. 38. Right Engine Mount – 2.3L

14. Disconnect and plug the fuel lines.
15. If equipped with a manual transaxle, disconnect the shifter cables and the clutch actuator cylinder.
16. If equipped with an automatic transaxle, disconnect the shift and TV cables.
17. Disconnect the transaxle and engine oil cooler pipes, if equipped.
18. Remove the exhaust manifold and heat shield.
19. Remove the lower radiator hose and front engine mount.
20. Install engine support fixture tool J–28467–A.
21. Raise and safely support the vehicle.
22. Remove the wheels, right side splash shield and radiator air deflector.
23. Separate the ball joints from the steering knuckles.
24. Using the proper equipment, support the suspension supports, crossmember and stabilizer shaft. Remove the attaching bolts and remove as an assembly.
25. Disconnect the heater hose from the radiator outlet pipe.
26. Remove the halfshafts from the transaxle.
27. Remove the nut from the transaxle mount through bolt.
28. Remove the nut from the rear engine mount through bolt.
29. Remove the rear engine mount body bracket.
30. Position a suitable support fixture below the engine/transaxle assembly and lower the vehicle so the weight of the engine/transaxle assembly is on the support fixture.
31. Remove the transaxle mount through bolt.
32. Mark the threads on fixture tool J–28467–A so the setting can be duplicated when installing the engine/transaxle assembly. Remove the fixture.
33. Move the engine/transaxle assembly rearward and slowly raise the vehicle from the engine/transaxle assembly.

➡ **Many of the bell housing bolts are of different lengths; note their locations before removing. It is imperative that these bolts go back in their original locations when assembling the engine and transaxle or engine damage could result.**

34. Separate the engine from the transaxle.

To install:

35. Assemble the engine and transaxle. If equipped with an automatic transaxle, thoroughly clean and dry the torque converter bolts and bolt holes, apply thread locking compound to the threads and tighten the bolts to 46 ft. lbs. (63 Nm). If equipped with a manual transaxle, tighten the clutch cover bolts to 22 ft. lbs. (30 Nm).
36. Raise and safely support the vehicle. Position the engine/transaxle assembly and lower the vehicle over the assembly until the transaxle mount is indexed, then install the bolt.
37. Install the engine support fixture and adjust to previously indexed setting. Raise the vehicle off the support fixture.
38. Install the rear mount to body bracket and tighten the bolts to 55 ft. lbs. (75 Nm).
39. Install the rear mount nut and tighten to 55 ft. lbs. (75 Nm).
40. Install the transaxle mount through bolt and tighten the nut to 55 ft. lbs. (75 Nm). Tighten so equal gaps are maintained.
41. Install the halfshafts.
42. Connect the heater hose to the the radiator outlet pipe.
43. Install the suspension supports, crossmember and stabilizer shaft assembly. Tighten the center bolts first, then front, then rear, to 65 ft. lbs. (90 Nm).
44. Install the ball joints and tighten the nuts to a maximum of 50 ft. lbs. (68 Nm).
45. Install the radiator air deflector and splash shield.
46. Install the wheels and lower the vehicle.
47. Install the front engine mount nut and tighten to 41 ft. lbs. (56 Nm). Remove the engine support fixture. Connect the lower radiator hose.
48. Install the exhaust manifold and heat shield.
49. Connect the transaxle and engine oil cooler pipes, if equipped.

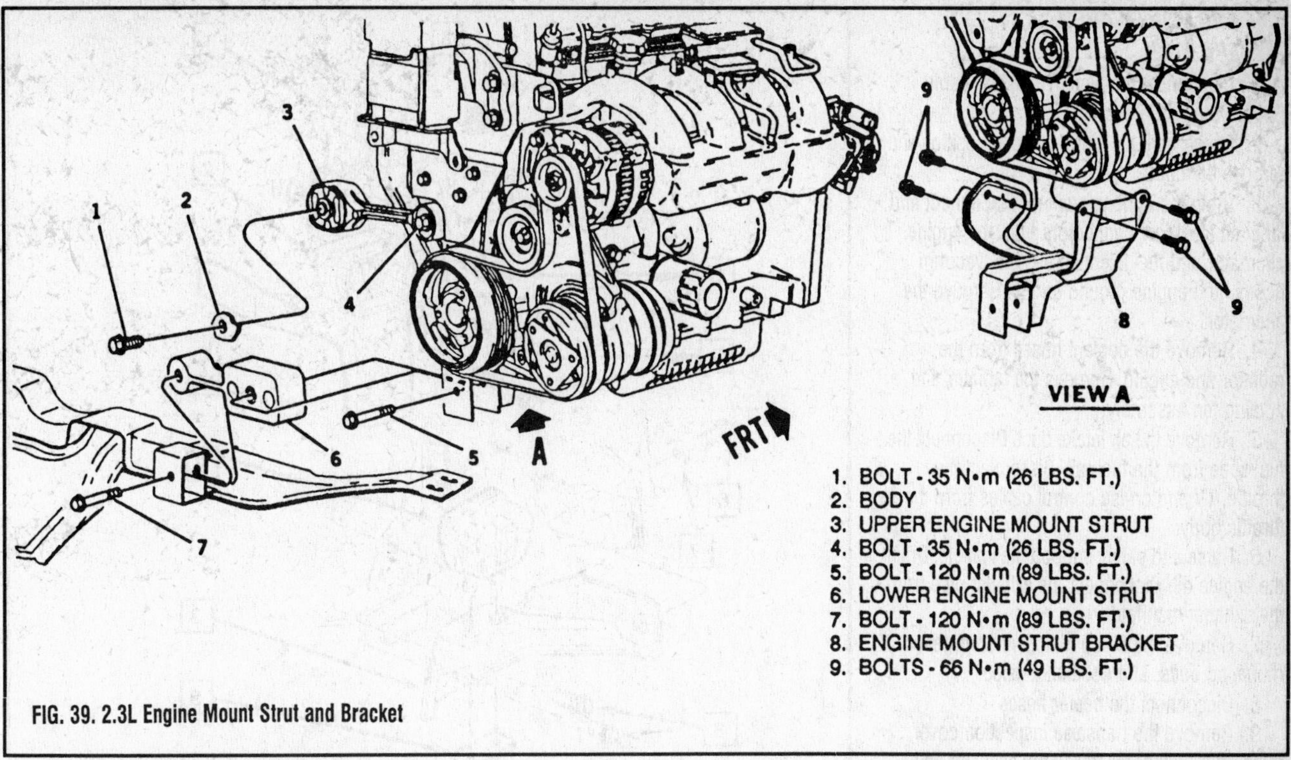

FIG. 39. 2.3L Engine Mount Strut and Bracket

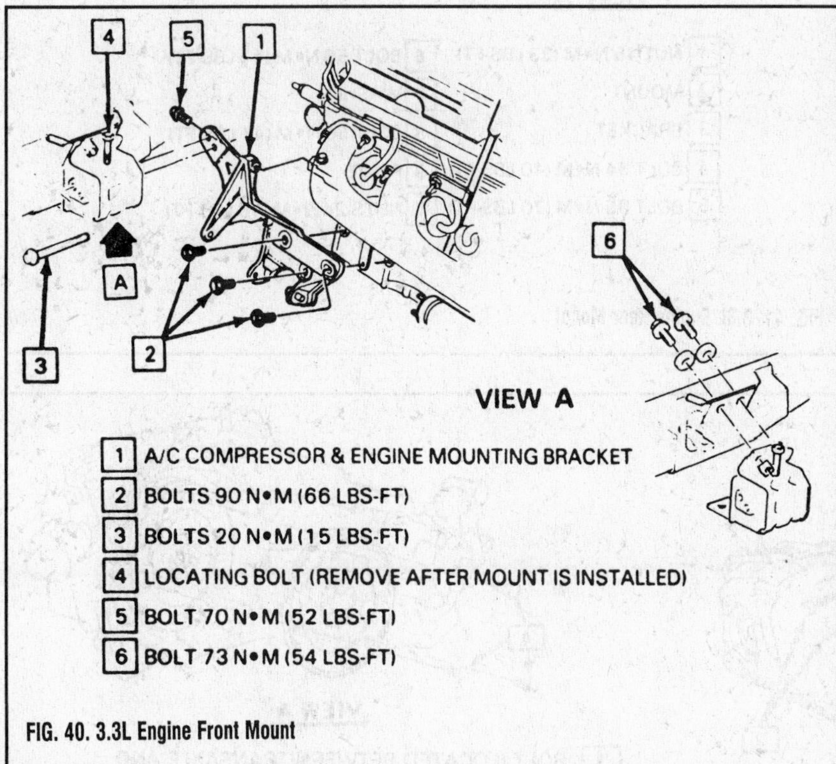

FIG. 40. 3.3L Engine Front Mount

50. If equipped with a manual transaxle, connect the shifter cables and the clutch actuator cylinder.
51. If equipped with an automatic transaxle, connect the shift and TV cables.
52. Connect the fuel lines.
53. Install the power steering pump and related parts.
54. Connect the throttle cable and install the bracket.
55. Connect the power brake vacuum hose to the throttle body.
56. Connect the starter wires.
57. Connect all electrical connectors and cables to the proper engine and transaxle-mounted devices.
58. Connect the 2 vacuum hoses at the front of the engine.
59. Install the upper radiator support.
60. Using new seals, connect the air conditioning hoses to the compressor.
61. Connect the heater and radiator hoses at the thermostat housing.
62. Install the air cleaner duct.
63. Fill all fluids to their proper levels.
64. Connect the battery cables, start the engine and check for leaks.

3.0L AND 3.3L ENGINES (EXCEPT 1992)

1. Disconnect the negative battery cable. Relieve the fuel pressure.
2. Matchmark the hinge-to-hood position and remove the hood.
3. Drain the cooling system. Disconnect and label all electrical connectors from the engine, alternator and fuel injection system, vacuum hoses, and engine ground straps. Remove the alternator.
4. Remove the coolant hoses from the radiator and engine. Remove the radiator and cooling fan assembly.
5. Remove the air intake duct. Disconnect the fuel lines from the fuel rail. Disconnect the throttle, TV and cruise control cables from the throttle body.
6. Raise and safely support the vehicle. Drain the engine oil. Disconnect the exhaust pipe from the exhaust manifold.
7. Remove the air conditioning compressor mounting bolts, and position it aside.
8. Disconnect the heater hoses.
9. Remove the transaxle inspection cover, matchmark the converter to the flexplate and remove the torque converter bolts.
10. Remove the rear engine mount bolts.
11. Remove the lower bell housing bolts. Label and disconnect the starter motor wiring and remove the starter motor from the engine.
12. Lower the vehicle. Remove the power steering pump mounting bolts and set the pump aside.
13. Support the transaxle with a floor jack or equivalent. Attach an engine lifting device to the engine.
14. Remove the upper bell housing bolts.
15. Remove the front engine mount bolts.

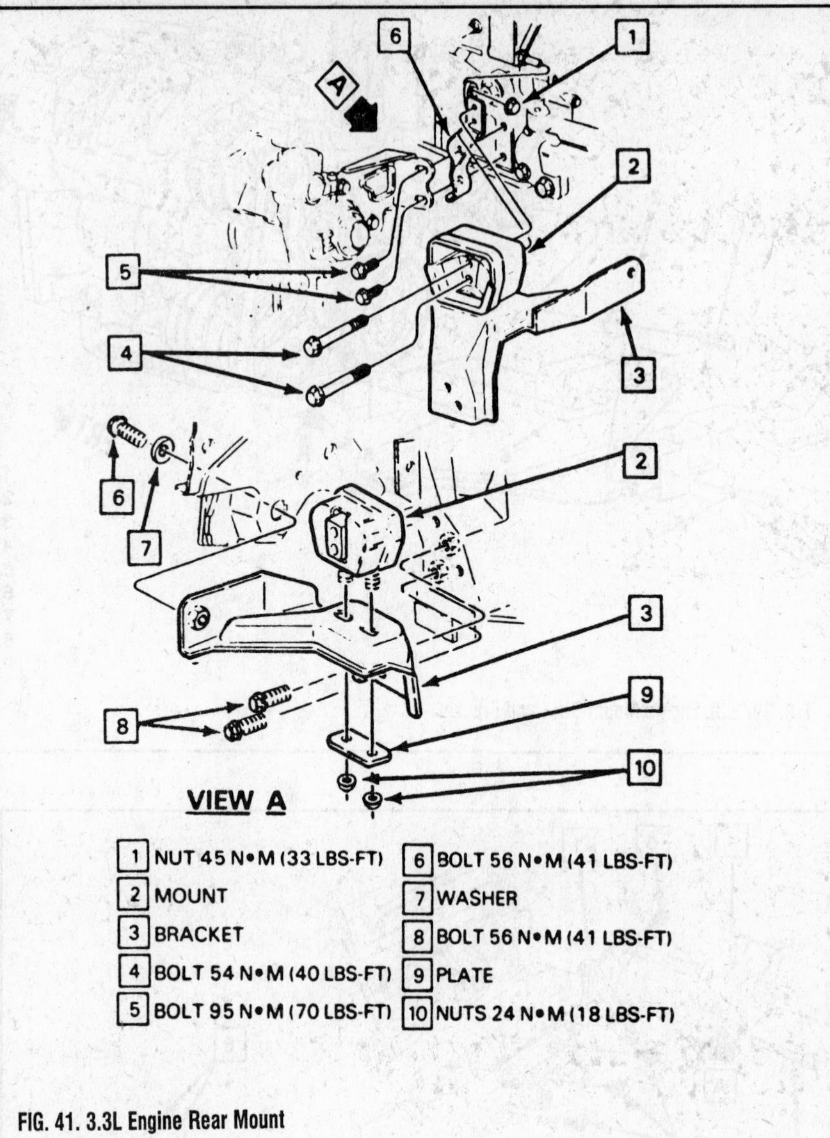

FIG. 41. 3.3L Engine Rear Mount

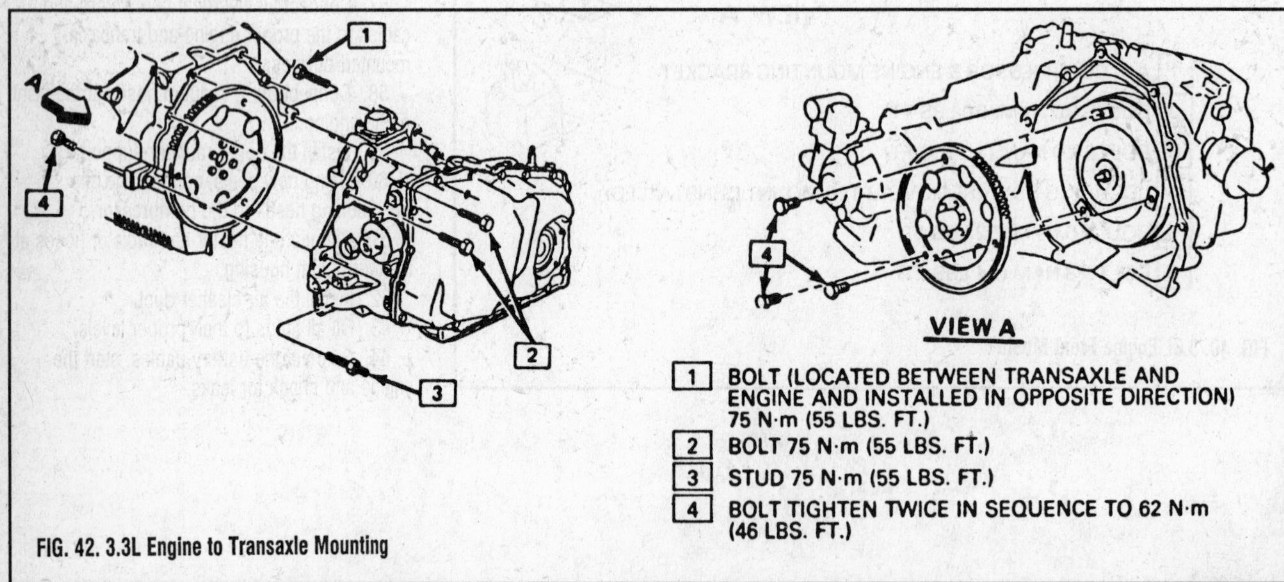

FIG. 42. 3.3L Engine to Transaxle Mounting

16. Lift and remove the engine from the vehicle. If the master cylinder is preventing removal, remove it and plug the brake lines.

To install:

17. Lower the engine into the engine compartment. Align the engine mounts and install the bolts. Tighten the bolts to their proper values:

- Front engine mount bracket to block — 66 ft. lbs. (90 Nm)
- Front engine mount to underbody — 54 ft. lbs. (73 Nm)
- Front engine mount to engine bracket — 15 ft. lbs. (20 Nm)
- Rear engine mount to bracket — 18 ft. lbs. (24 Nm)
- Rear engine mount bracket to underbody — 41 ft. lbs. (56 Nm)
- Rear engine mount to engine bracket — 40 ft. lbs. (54 Nm)

18. Install the upper transaxle-to-engine mounting bolts and tighten to 55 ft. lbs. (75 Nm). Remove the engine lifting fixture from the engine.

19. Raise and safely support the vehicle.

20. Align the converter marks, install the torque converter bolts and tighten to 46 ft. lbs. (63 Nm). Install the transaxle inspection cover.

21. Connect the exhaust pipe to the exhaust manifold. Install the starter motor and connect the wiring.

22. Install the air conditioning compressor. Connect the heater hoses.

23. Lower the vehicle. Install the power steering pump.

24. Install the alternator and belt.

25. Connect all vacuum hoses and electrical connectors to the engine.

26. Connect the fuel lines and all cables to the throttle body. Install the air intake duct.

27. Install the radiator and fan assembly. Connect the fan motor wiring. Connect the radiator hoses and refill the cooling system.

28. Fill all fluids to their proper levels.

29. Connect the battery cables, start the engine and check for leaks.

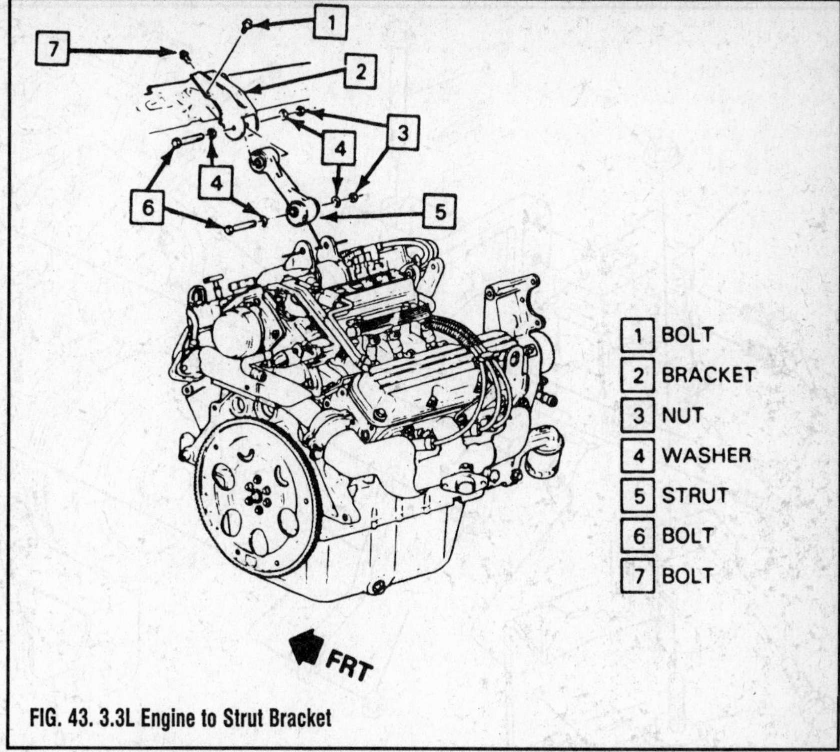

FIG. 43. 3.3L Engine to Strut Bracket

1992 3.3L ENGINE

1. Disconnect the negative battery cable. Relieve the fuel pressure and disconnect the fuel line to the fuel rail.

2. Matchmark the hinge-to-hood position and remove the hood.

3. Support the engine using a proper type engine support tool. Disconnect the exhaust pipe from the manifold.

4. Drain the cooling system. Disconnect and label all electrical connectors from the engine, alternator and fuel injection system, vacuum hoses, and engine ground straps.

5. Remove the coolant hoses from the radiator and engine. Remove the radiator and cooling fan assembly.

6. Remove the air intake duct. Disconnect the fuel lines from the fuel rail. Disconnect the throttle, TV and cruise control cables from the throttle body.

7. Disconnect the vacuum lines from the brake power booster and the evaporative canister.

8. Remove the accessory drive belt and disconnect the power steering pump and place to the side.

9. Remove the upper transaxle to engine bolts.

10. Raise and safely support the vehicle. Drain the engine oil. Disconnect the exhaust pipe from the exhaust manifold.

11. Remove the air conditioning compressor mounting bolts, and position it aside.

12. Remove the right engine mount and engine mount torque strut assembly.

13. Remove the transaxle inspection cover, matchmark the converter to the flexplate and remove the flywheel to converter bolts.

14. Lower the engine and remove the transaxle bolts.

➡ NOTE: One of the transaxle bolts is located between the transaxle case and the engine block. This bolt is installed in the opposite direction.

15. Lower the vehicle and remove the engine assembly.

To install:

16. Lower the engine into the engine compartment. Align the engine with the transaxle and install the bolts. Tighten the bolts to 55 ft. lbs. (75 Nm)

17. Raise and safely support the vehicle.

18. Align and install the flywheel to converter bolts and tighten to 46 ft. lbs. (62 Nm).

19. Install the right engine mount and torque strut. Tighten the bolts to 89 ft. lbs. (120 Nm) Install the transaxle inspection cover.

20. Install the air conditioning compressor. Connect the heater hoses.

21. Connect the exhaust pipe to the exhaust manifold. Install the starter motor and connect the wiring.

22. Lower the vehicle. Install the power steering pump.

23. Install the alternator and belt.

24. Connect all vacuum hoses and electrical connectors to the engine.

25. Connect the fuel lines and all cables to the throttle body. Install the air intake duct.

26. Install the radiator and fan assembly. Connect the fan motor wiring. Connect the radiator hoses and refill the cooling system.

27. Fill all fluids to their proper levels.

28. Connect the battery cables, start the engine and check for leaks.

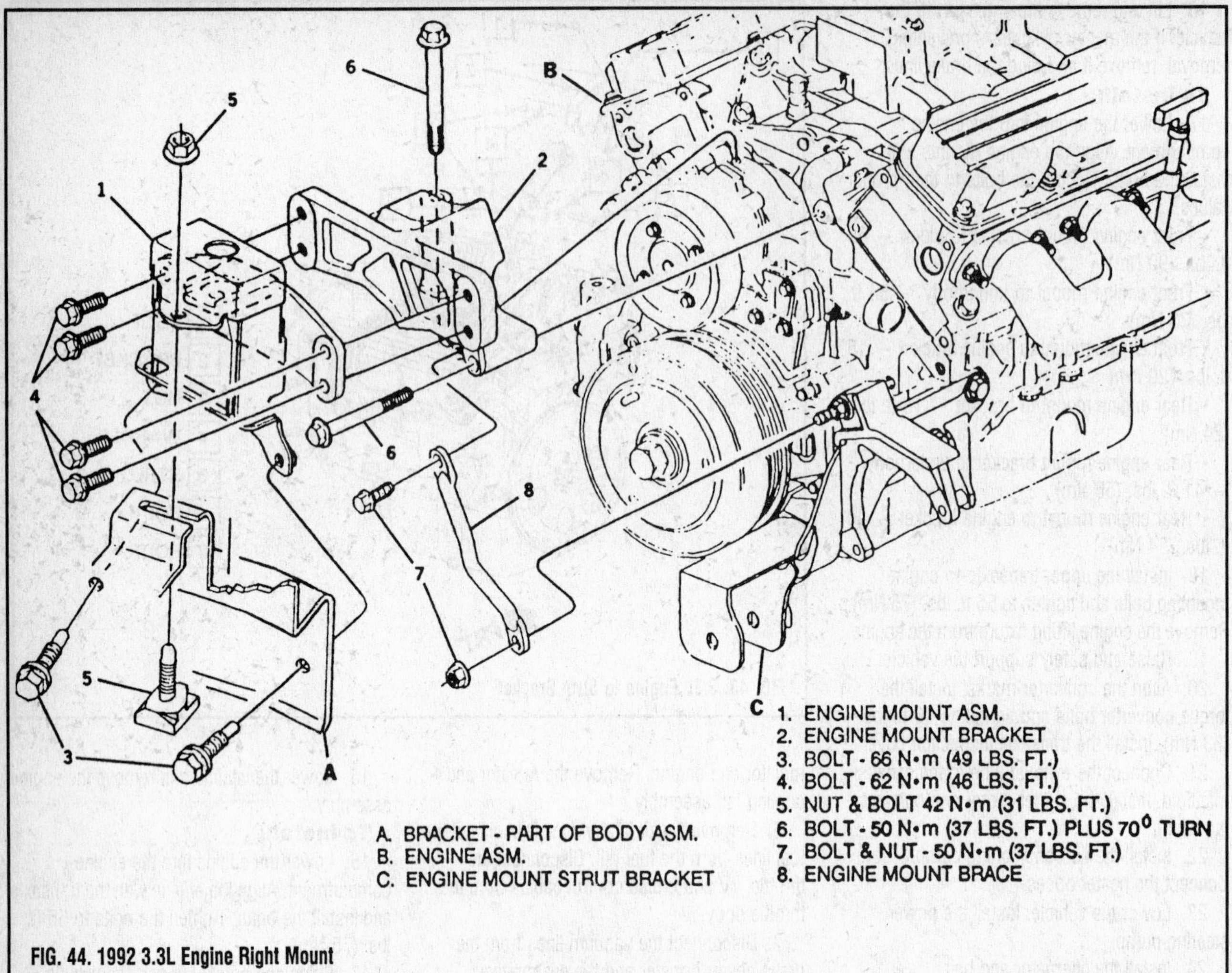

1
2
3
4
5
6
7
8
A
B
C
1. ENGINE MOUNT ASM.
2. ENGINE MOUNT BRACKET
3. BOLT - 66 N•m (49 LBS. FT.)
4. BOLT - 62 N•m (46 LBS. FT.)
5. NUT & BOLT 42 N•m (31 LBS. FT.)
6. BOLT - 50 N•m (37 LBS. FT.) PLUS 70° TURN
7. BOLT & NUT - 50 N•m (37 LBS. FT.)
8. ENGINE MOUNT BRACE
A. BRACKET - PART OF BODY ASM.
B. ENGINE ASM.
C. ENGINE MOUNT STRUT BRACKET

FIG. 44. 1992 3.3L Engine Right Mount

FRT
1
2
3
4
5
6
A
B
A. FRONT SUSPENSION SUPPORT
B. ENGINE ASM.
1. ENGINE MOUNT STRUT ASSEMBLY
2. ENGINE MOUNT STRUT BRACKET ASM.
3. A/C COMPRESSOR BRACKET ASM.
4. STUD - 50 N•m (37 LBS. FT.)
5. BOLT - 120 N•m (89 LBS. FT.)
6. BOLT - 90 N•m (66 LBS. FT.)

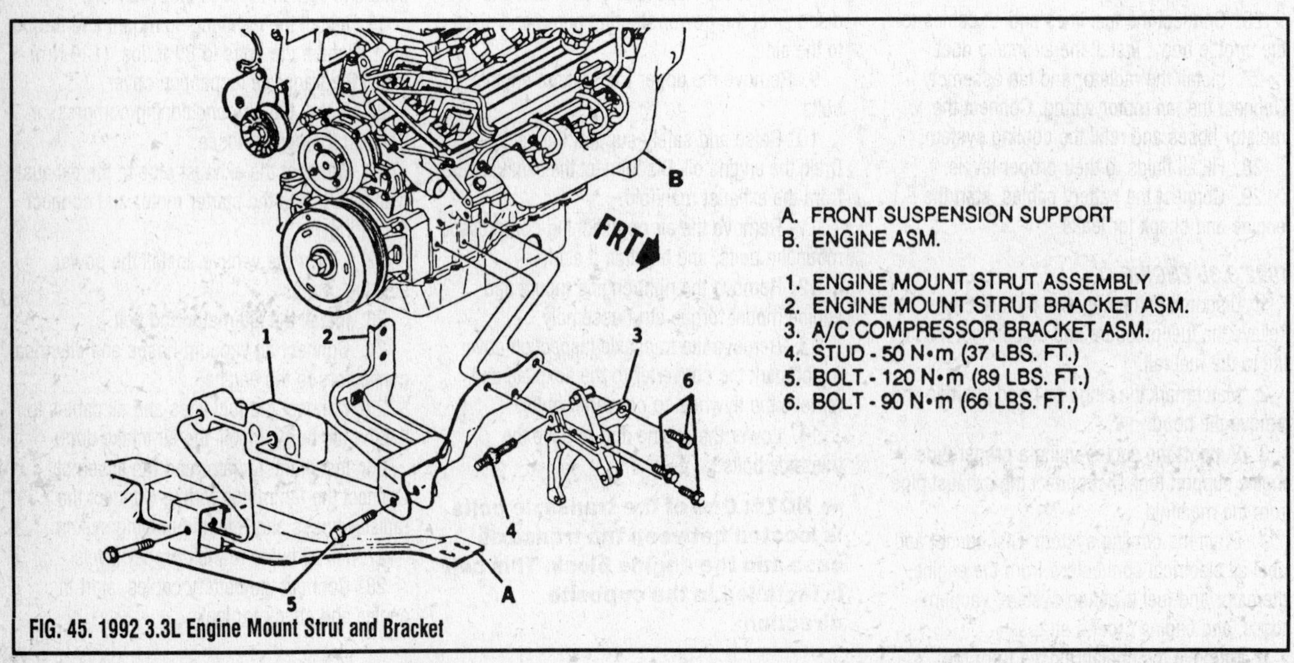

FIG. 45. 1992 3.3L Engine Mount Strut and Bracket

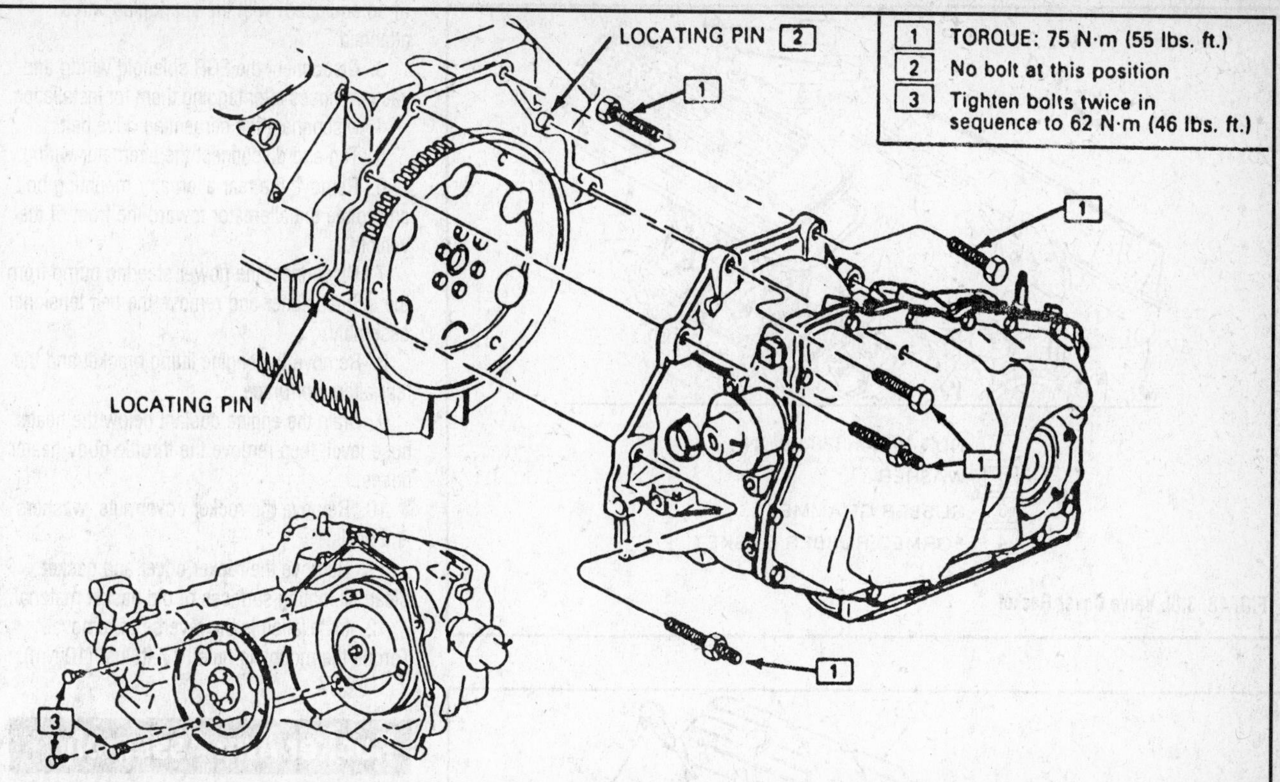

LOCATING PIN 2
1
LOCATING PIN
1 TORQUE: 75 N·m (55 lbs. ft.)
2 No bolt at this position
3 Tighten bolts twice in sequence to 62 N·m (46 lbs. ft.)
1
1
1
3

FIG. 46. 1992 3.3L Engine to Transaxle Mounting

Rocker Arm Cover

➧ SEE FIGS. 47–49

REMOVAL & INSTALLATION

✲✲ CAUTION

When draining the coolant, keep in mind that cats and dogs are attracted by the ethylene glycol antifreeze, and are quite likely to drink any that is left in an uncovered container or in puddles on the ground. This will prove fatal in sufficient quantity. Always drain the coolant into a sealable container. Coolant should be reused unless it is contaminated or several years old.

2.5L Engine

1. Remove the air cleaner.
2. Disconnect the PCV valve and hose.
3. Disconnect the EGR valve.

ROCKER ARM COVER
APPLY A CONTINUOUS 3/16" DIAMETER BEAD OF RTV AS SHOWN
PUSH ROD COVER
APPLY A CONTINUOUS 3/16" DIAMETER BEAD OF RTV AS SHOWN

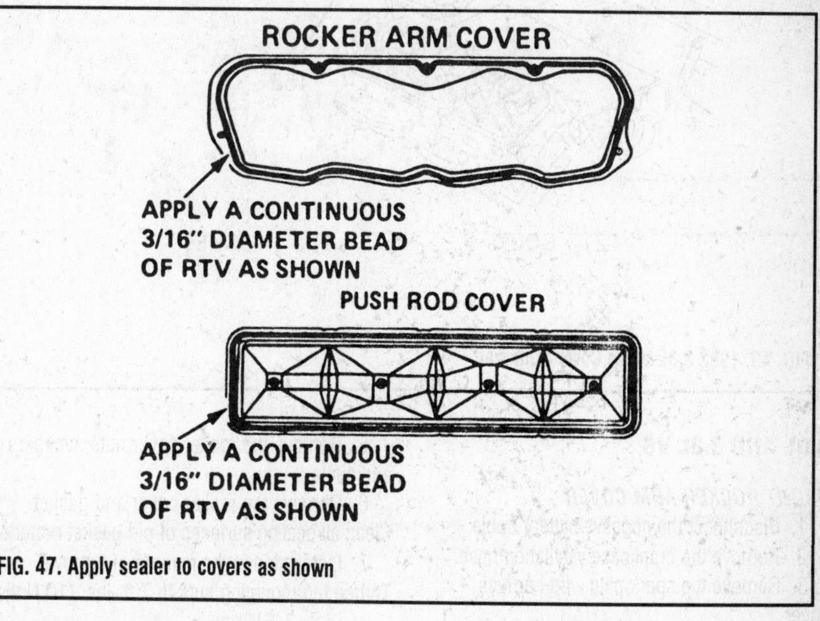

FIG. 47. Apply sealer to covers as shown

4. Remove the rocker arm cover bolts.
5. Remove the spark plug wires from the spark plugs and clips.
6. Tap the rocker arm cover gently with a rubber mallet to break the gasket loose then remove the cover. Do not pry on the cover or damage to the sealing surfaces may result.
7. Clean the sealing surfaces of all old gasket material.
8. Installation is the reverse of removal. Apply a continuous $\frac{3}{16}$ in. (5mm) bead of RTV sealant around the cylinder head sealing surface inboard at the bolt holes. Keep sealant out of the bolt holes. Torque the rocker arm cover mounting bolts to 6 ft. lbs. (8 Nm).

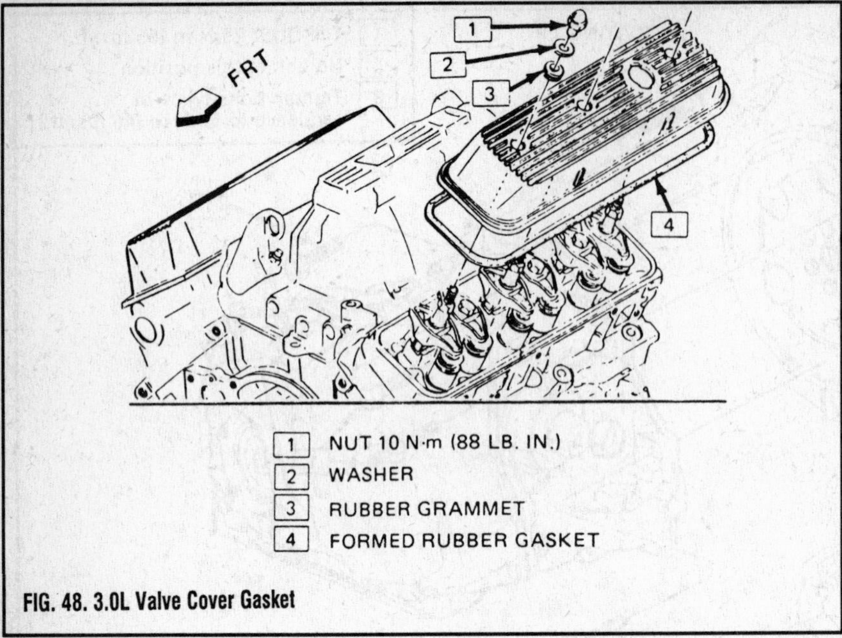

FIG. 48. 3.0L Valve Cover Gasket

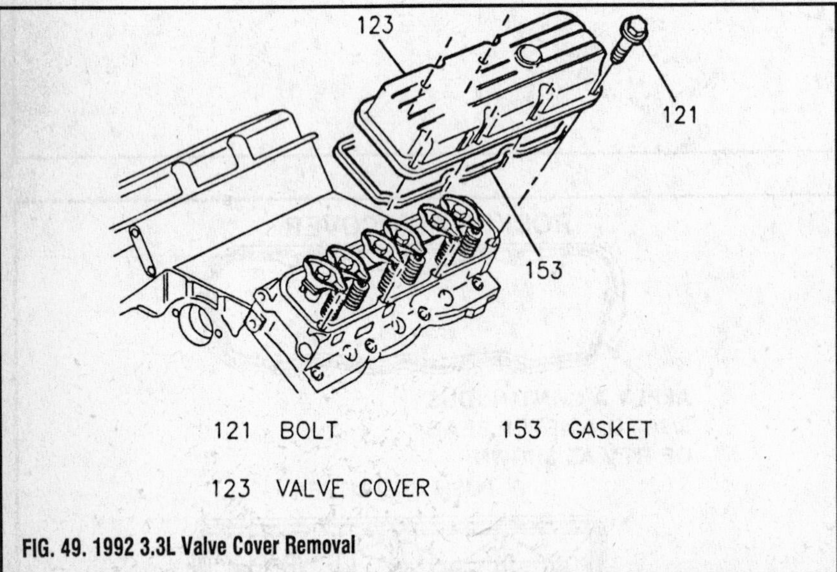

FIG. 49. 1992 3.3L Valve Cover Removal

3.0L AND 3.3L V6

FRONT ROCKER ARM COVER

1. Disconnect the negative battery cable.
2. Remove the crankcase ventilation hose.
3. Remove the spark plug wire harness cover.
4. Tag and disconnect the spark plug wires at the plugs.
5. Remove the rocker cover nuts, washers and seals.
6. Remove the rocker cover and gasket. Clean all sealing surfaces of old gasket material.
7. Installation is the reverse of removal. Torque the mounting nuts to 7 ft. lbs. (10 Nm).

REAR ROCKER COVER

1. Disconnect the negative battery cable.
2. Remove the C3I ignition coil and module (if so equipped) with the spark plug wires attached.
3. Disconnect the EGR solenoid wiring and vacuum hoses after tagging them for installation.
4. Disconnect the serpentine drive belt.
5. Tag and disconnect the alternator wiring.
6. Remove the rear alternator mounting bolt and rotate the alternator toward the front of the vehicle.
7. Disconnect the power steering pump from the belt tensioner and remove the belt tensioner assembly.
8. Remove the engine lifting bracket and the rear alternator brace.
9. Drain the engine coolant below the heater hose level, then remove the throttle body heater hoses.
10. Remove the rocker cover nuts, washers and seals.
11. Remove the rocker cover and gasket. Clean all mating surfaces of old gasket material.
12. Installation is the reverse of removal. Torque the mounting nuts to 7 ft. lbs. (10 Nm).

Rocker Arm Assembly

REMOVAL & INSTALLATION

➧ SEE FIGS. 50, 51

2.0L Engine

1. Disconnect the negative battery cable. Remove the camshaft carrier cover.
2. Hold the valves in place with compressed air, using an air adapter in the spark plug hole.
3. Compress the valve springs using a suitable valve spring compressor.
4. Remove rocker arms. Keep them in order if they are being reused.
5. The installation is the reverse of the removal procedure.
6. Connect the negative battery cable and check for proper operation.

2.5L Engine

1. Remove the rocker arm cover.
2. Remove the rocker arm bolt and ball. If replacing the pushrod only, loosen the rocker arm bolt and swing the arm clear of the pushrod.
3. Remove the rocker arm, pushrod and guide. Store all components in order so they can be reassembled in their original location. Pushrod guides are different and must be reassembled in the previous location.
4. Installation is the reverse of removal. When new rocker arms or balls are used, coat the bearing surfaces with Molykote® or equivalent. Torque the rocker arm bolt to 20 ft. lbs. (27 Nm).

3.0L and 3.3L V6

1. Remove the rocker arm cover as previously described.
2. Remove the rocker arm pedestal retaining bolts.
3. Remove the rocker arm and pedestal assembly. Note the position of the double ended bolts for reassembly. Store all components on a clean surface in order so they may be installed in their original locations.
4. Installation is the reverse of removal. Replace any components that show signs of unusual wear.

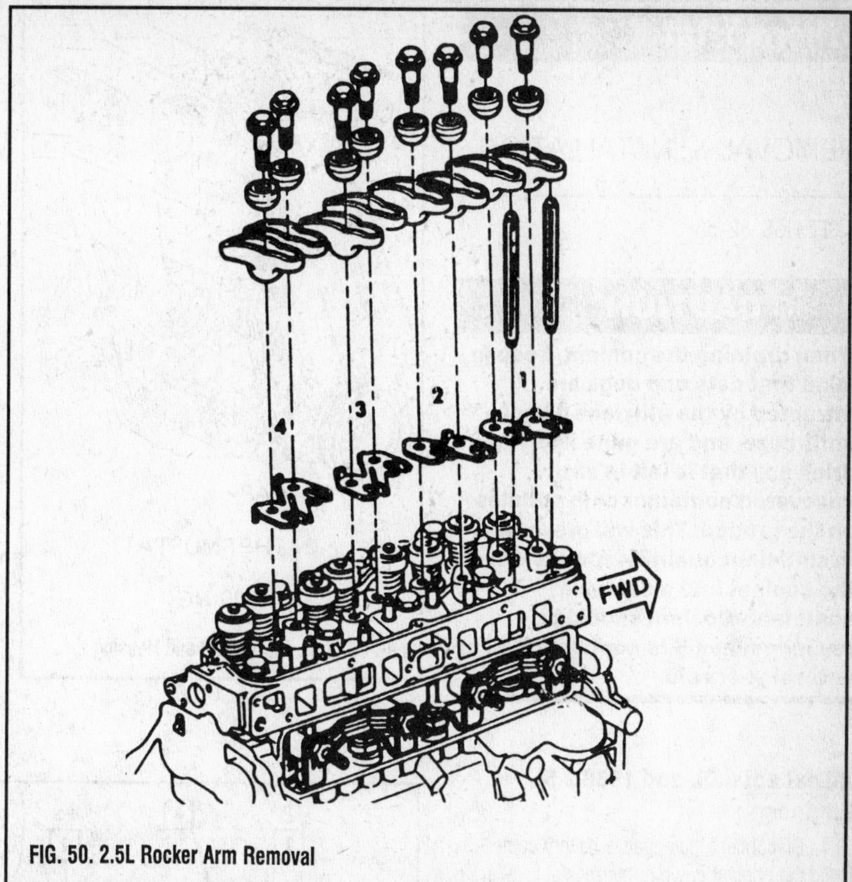

FIG. 50. 2.5L Rocker Arm Removal

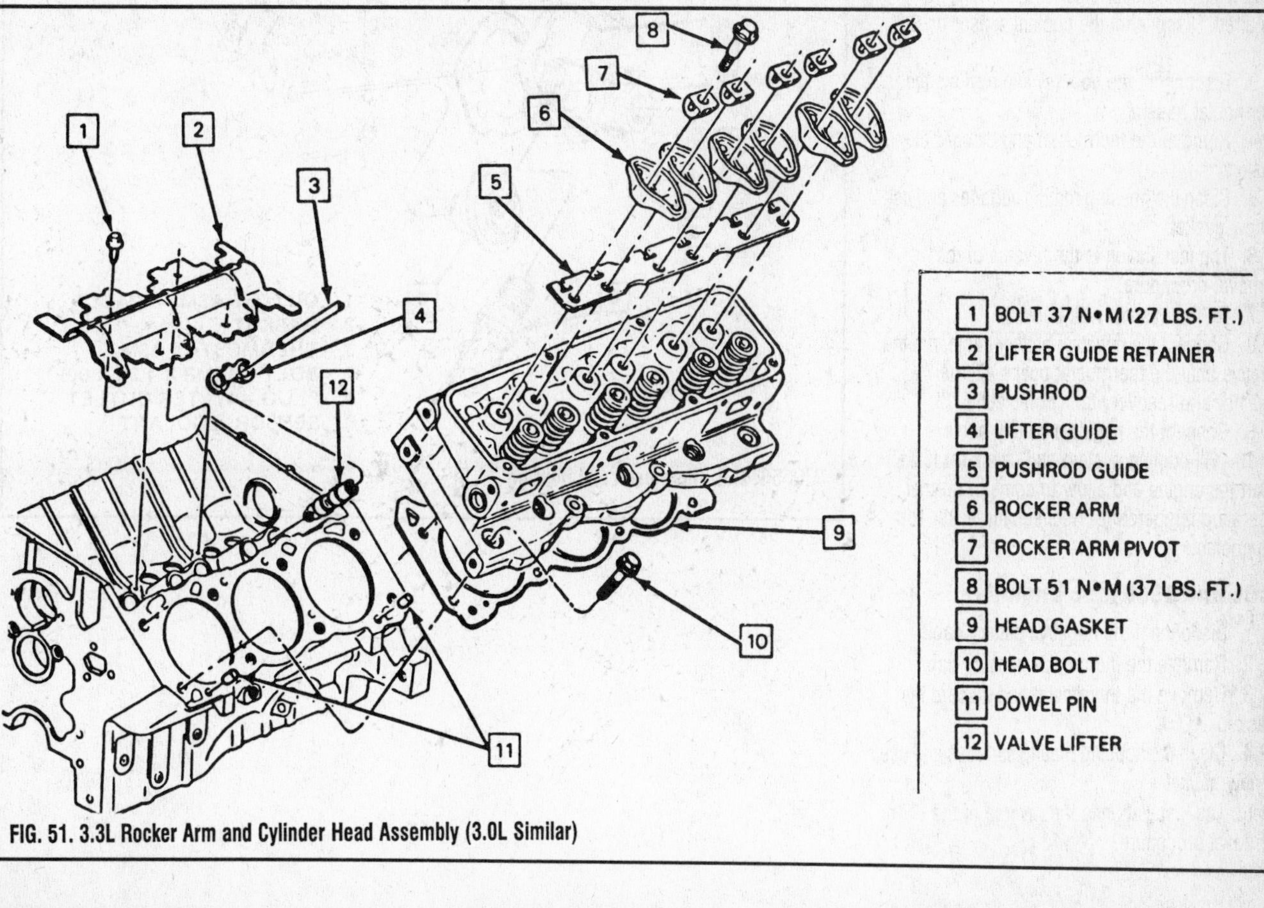

1 BOLT 37 N•M (27 LBS. FT.)
2 LIFTER GUIDE RETAINER
3 PUSHROD
4 LIFTER GUIDE
5 PUSHROD GUIDE
6 ROCKER ARM
7 ROCKER ARM PIVOT
8 BOLT 51 N•M (37 LBS. FT.)
9 HEAD GASKET
10 HEAD BOLT
11 DOWEL PIN
12 VALVE LIFTER

FIG. 51. 3.3L Rocker Arm and Cylinder Head Assembly (3.0L Similar)

Thermostat

REMOVAL & INSTALLATION

➧ SEE FIGS. 52–56

✻✻ CAUTION

When draining the coolant, keep in mind that cats and dogs are attracted by the ethylene glycol antifreeze, and are quite likely to drink any that is left in an uncovered container or in puddles on the ground. This will prove fatal in sufficient quantity. Always drain the coolant into a sealable container. Coolant should be reused unless it is contaminated or several years old.

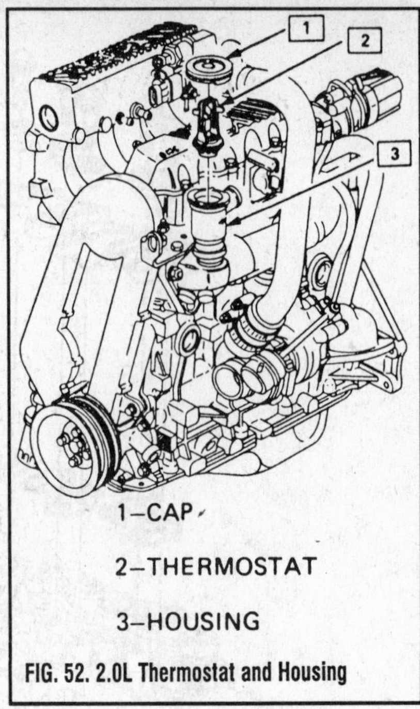

FIG. 52. 2.0L Thermostat and Housing

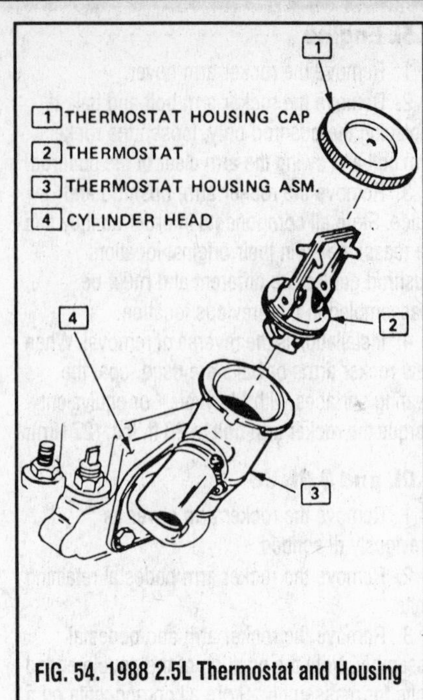

FIG. 54. 1988 2.5L Thermostat and Housing

All except 2.0L and 1988 2.5L Engines

1. Disconnect the negative battery cable. Drain the coolant down to thermostat level or below.
2. Remove the air cleaner assembly, as required. Disconnect the coolant sensor on 2.3L engine.
3. Disconnect the hose(s) and remove the thermostat housing.
4. Remove the thermostat and discard the gasket.
5. Clean the housing mating surfaces and use a new gasket.
6. The installation is the reverse of the removal procedure.
7. Fill the system with coolant.
8. Connect the negative battery cable, run the vehicle until the thermostat opens, fill the radiator and recovery tank completely.
9. Connect the negative battery cable.
10. Fill cooling system and check for leaks. Start the engine and allow to come to normal operating temperature. Recheck for leaks. Top-up coolant.

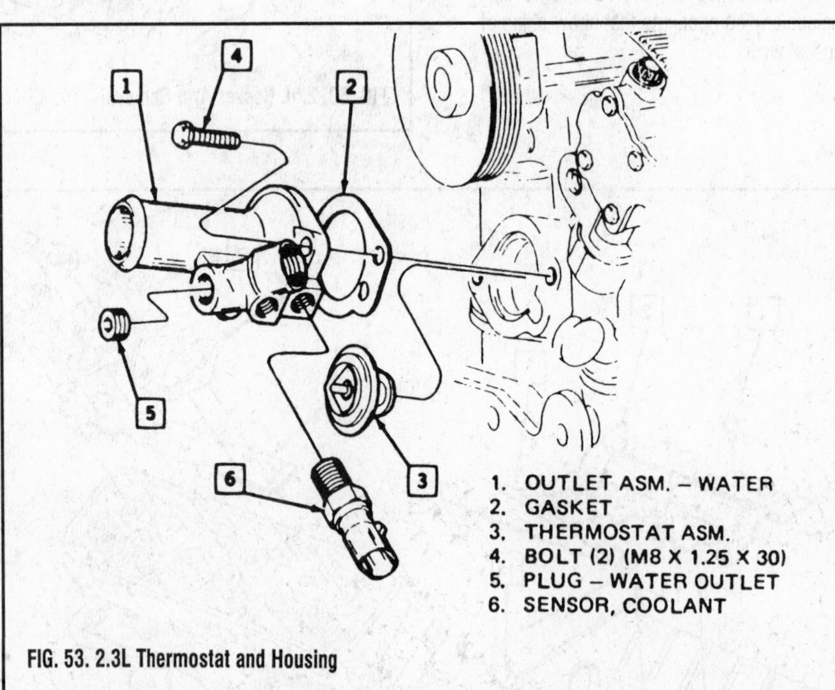

FIG. 53. 2.3L Thermostat and Housing

2.0L and 1988 2.5L Engines

1. Disconnect the negative battery cable.
2. Remove the thermostat housing cap.
3. Remove the thermostat and discard the gasket.
4. Clean the housing mating surfaces and use a new gasket.
5. The installation is the reverse of the removal procedure.

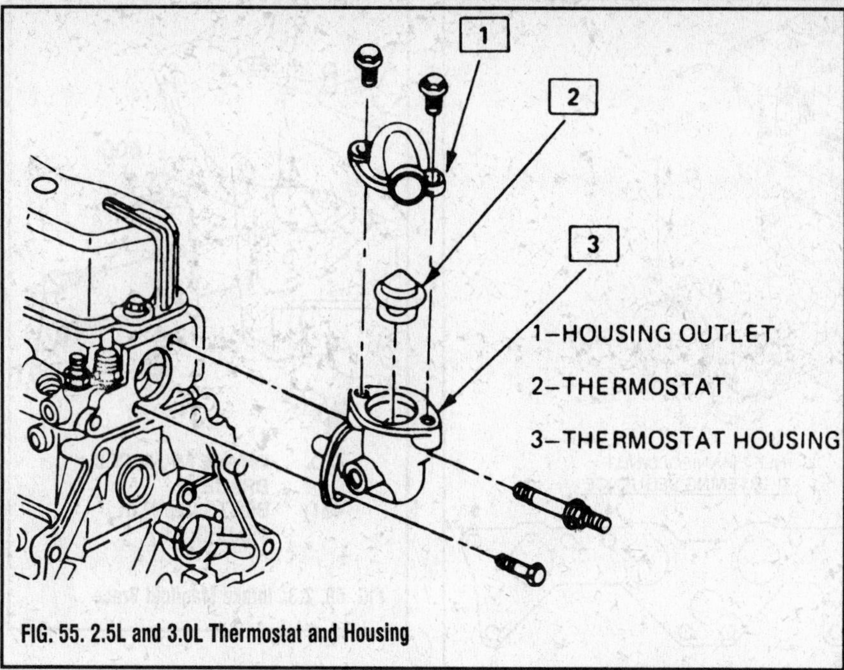

FIG. 55. 2.5L and 3.0L Thermostat and Housing

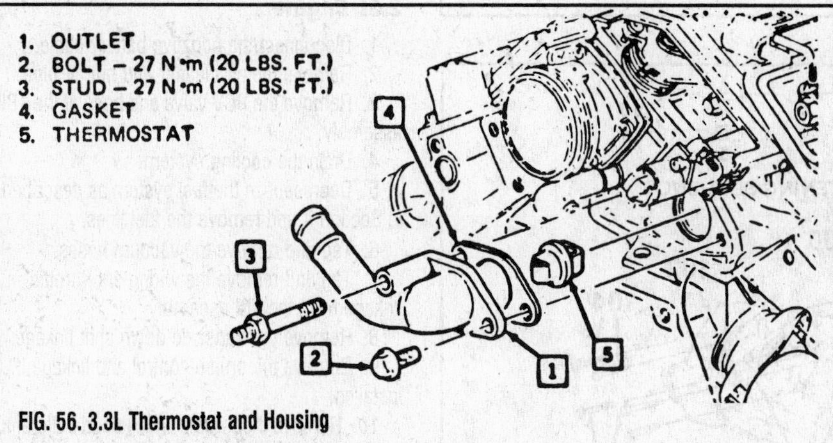

FIG. 56. 3.3L Thermostat and Housing

Intake Manifold

REMOVAL & INSTALLATION

➧ SEE FIGS. 57–62

CAUTION

When draining the coolant, keep in mind that cats and dogs are attracted by the ethylene glycol antifreeze, and are quite likely to drink any that is left in an uncovered container or in puddles on the ground. This will prove fatal in sufficient quantity. Always drain the coolant into a sealable container. Coolant should be reused unless it is contaminated or several years old.

2.0L Engine

1. Remove the air cleaner and drain the engine coolant.
2. Remove the alternator and bracket.
3. Disconnect the power steering pump and place to the side.
4. Remove the coil and disconnect the throttle cable from the intake manifold bracket.
5. Disconnect the throttle, TV cables and wiring from the TBI.
6. Disconnect the inlet and return fuel lines.
7. Disconnect the coolant hoses at the water pump and intake manifold.
8. Disconnect the ECM harness and remove the manifold retaining nuts.
9. Remove the intake manifold and remove all gasket material.

To Install:

10. Install the manifold with a new gasket.
11. Install the nuts and washers and tighten to 16 ft. lbs.(22 Nm).
12. Connect the ECM harness and coolant hoses.
13. Connect the fuel lines and wiring to the TBI.
14. Connect the throttle and TV cables.
15. Install the ignition coil.
16. Install the power steering bracket and power steering pump.
17. Install the alternator and the bracket.
18. Refill the coolant and install the air cleaner.

2.3L Engine

1. Disconnect the negative battery cable.
2. Drain the cooling system.
3. Disconnect the vacuum hose and electrical connector from the MAP sensor.
4. Disconnect the electrical connectors from the MAT sensor and the Purge solenoid.
5. Disconnect the fuel injector harness and place to the side.
6. Disconnect the vacuum hoses from the intake manifold and the hose at the fuel regulator and purge solenoid to the canister.
7. Disconnect the throttle body and vent tube to air cleaner ducts.
8. Disconnect the throttle cable bracket.
9. Disconnect the power brake vacuum line and place to the side.
10. Disconnect the coolant lines from the throttle body.
11. Remove the oil/air separator and leave the hoses connected.
12. Remove the oil fill cap and oil level indicator assembly.
13. Remove the oil fill tube bolt/screw and pull tube upward to remove.
14. Disconnect the injector harness connector.
15. Remove the intake manifold support brace and manifold retaining nuts and bolts.
16. Remove the intake manifold.

To Install:

17. Install the manifold with a new gasket.

➡ Make sure that the numbers stamped on the gasket are facing towards the manifold surface.

18. Follow the tightening sequence and tighten the bolts/nuts to 18 ft. lbs.(25 Nm).

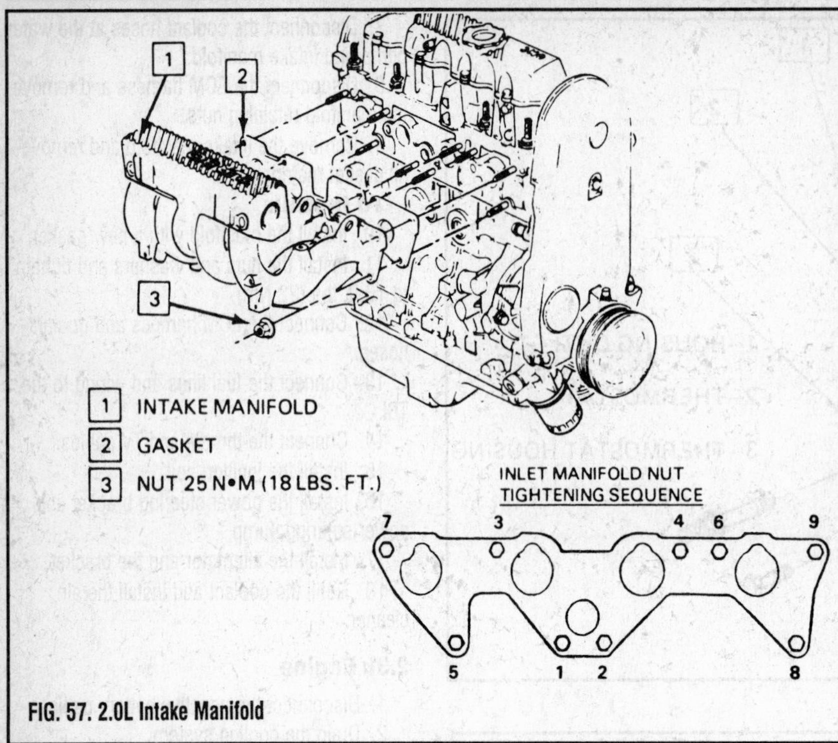

FIG. 57. 2.0L Intake Manifold

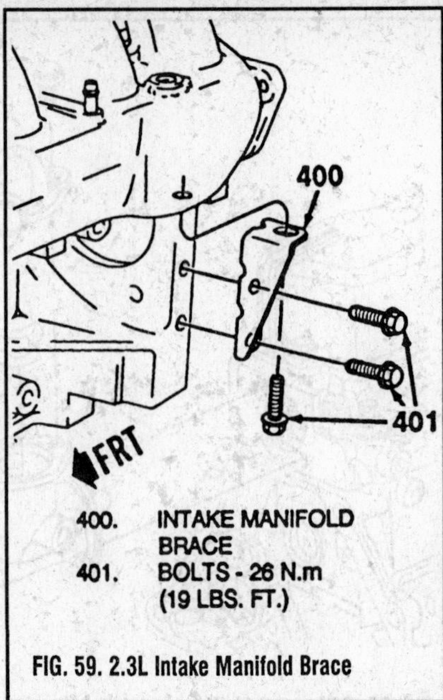

FIG. 59. 2.3L Intake Manifold Brace

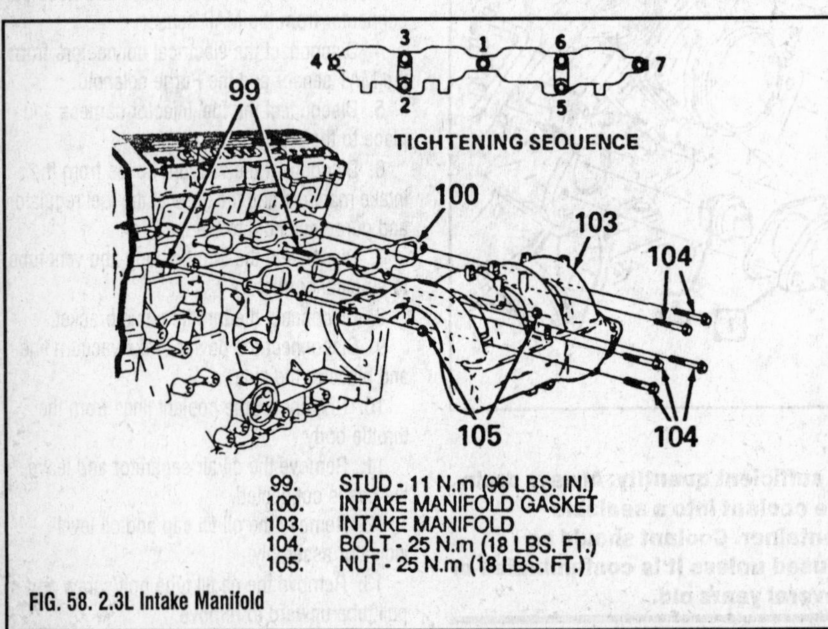

FIG. 58. 2.3L Intake Manifold

19. Install the intake manifold brace and retainers.
20. Lubricate a new oil fill tube O-ring with engine oil and install tube down between intake manifold.
21. Place oil fill tube into it's normal position and press downward until it becomes properly seated.
22. Install the oil/air separator assembly and connect all hoses.
23. Install the oil fill tube bolt/screw.
24. Install the throttle body to the intake manifold using a new gasket.
25. Connect the coolant lines to the throttle body.
26. Connect the power brake vacuum hose and secure bracket.
27. Install the throttle cable bracket.
28. Connect the vacuum hoses to the intake manifold and connect the fuel regulator hose.
29. Connect all electrical connectors.
30. Install the coolant recovery tank and refill the coolant to it's proper level.
31. Connect the negative battery cable.

2.5L Engine

1. Disconnect the negative battery cable.
2. Remove the air cleaner and hot air pipe.
3. Remove the PCV valve and hose at the TBI assembly.
4. Drain the cooling system.
5. Depressurize the fuel system as described in Section 4 and remove the fuel lines.
6. Tag and remove the vacuum hoses.
7. Tag and remove the wiring and throttle linkage from the TBI assembly.
8. Remove the transaxle down shift linkage.
9. Remove the cruise control and linkage if installed.
10. Remove the throttle linkage and bellcrank and lay aside for clearance.
11. Disconnect the heater hose.
12. Remove the upper power steering pump bracket.
13. Remove the ignition coil.
14. Remove the retaining bolts and lift off the intake manifold. Clean all gasket mating surfaces on the intake manifold and cylinder head.
15. Installation is the reverse of removal. Torque the intake manifold retaining bolts to 25 ft. lbs. (34 Nm) in the sequence illustrated. Note that the No. 7 bolt is torqued to 37 ft. lbs. (50 Nm).

3.0L V6

➡ A special bolt wrench J-24394 or equivalent is required for this procedure.

1. Disconnect the negative battery cable.
2. Remove the mass air flow sensor and air intake duct.

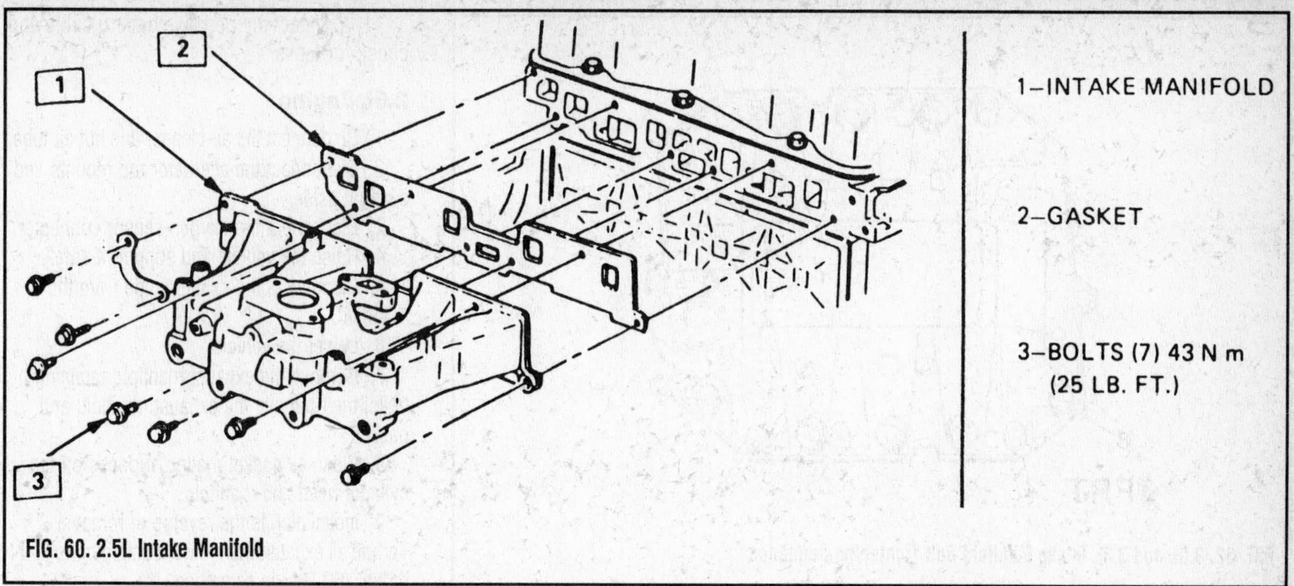

FIG. 60. 2.5L Intake Manifold

3. Remove the serpentine accessory drive belt, alternator and bracket.
4. Remove the C3I ignition module with the spark plug cables attached. Tag all wiring connectors before disconnecting.
5. Tag and disconnect all vacuum lines and wiring connectors as necessary to gain clearance to remove the manifold.
6. Remove the throttle, cruise control and T.V. cables from the throttle body.
7. Drain the cooling system.
8. Remove the heater hoses from the throttle body.
9. Remove the upper radiator hose.
10. Depressurize the fuel system as described in Section 4, then remove the fuel lines, fuel rail and injectors.
11. Remove the intake manifold bolts. Loosen in reverse of the torque sequence to prevent manifold warping. Remove the intake manifold and gasket.
12. Installation is the reverse of removal. Clean all gasket mating surfaces and apply sealer No. 1050026 or equivalent if a steel gasket is used. Torque all manifold bolts in sequence to 32 ft. lbs. (44 Nm).

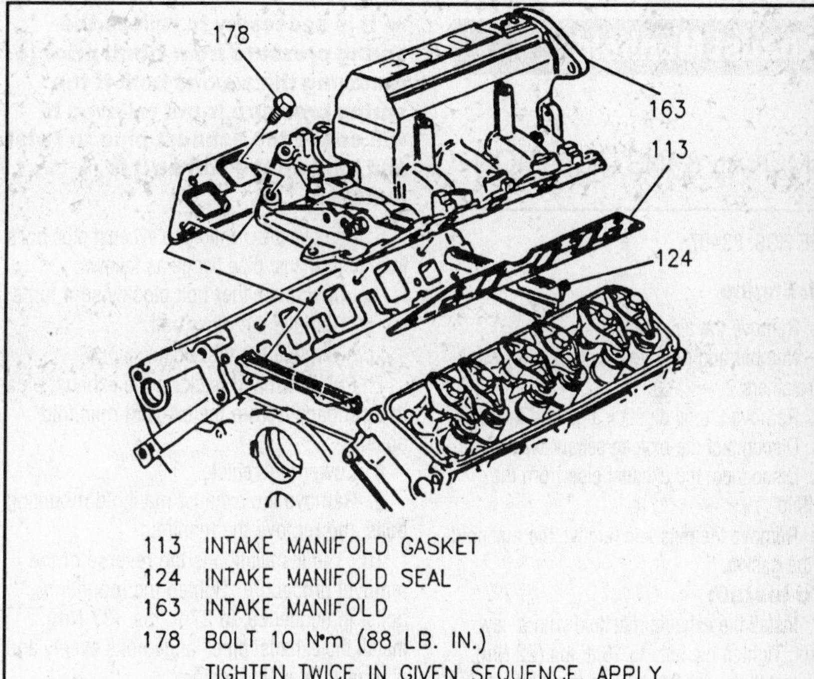

FIG. 61. 3.3L Intake Manifold (3.0L Similar)

3.3L Engine

1. Disconnect the negative battery cable.
2. Depressurize and disconnect the fuel lines from the fuel rail.
3. Drain the coolant.
4. Disconnect the drive belt.
5. Remove the alternator and the supports.
6. Disconnect the power steering pump and the supports.
7. Disconnect the coolant bypass hose, the heater pipe and the upper radiator hose.
8. Disconnect the air inlet duct.
9. Remove the throttle cable bracket and remove the cables from the throttle body.
10. Remove the vacuum hoses from the intake manifold.
11. Disconnect the electrical connectors and remove the fuel rail.
12. Disconnect the vapor canister purge line and the heater hose from the throttle body.
13. Disconnect the rear spark plug wires.
14. Remove the intake manifold bolts and remove the manifold.
15. Installation is the reverse of the removal procedure. Clean cylinder block, heads and intake manifold surfaces of all oil.
16. Apply RTV type sealer to the ends of the manifold seals.
17. Clean the intake manifold bolts and bolt holes of all adhesive compound.
18. Apply thread locking compound to the intake manifold bolts and tighten TWICE to 88 inch lbs.(10 Nm) in the proper sequence.

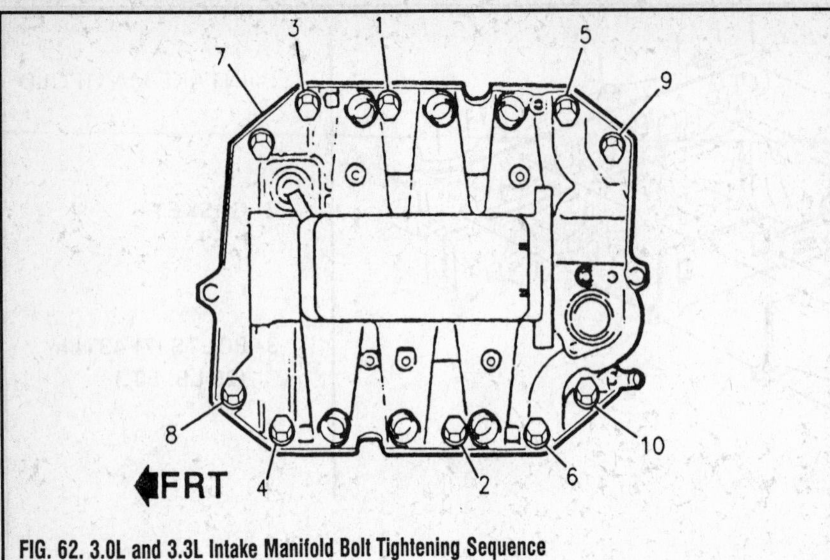

FIG. 62. 3.0L and 3.3L Intake Manifold Bolt Tightening Sequence

Exhaust Manifold

REMOVAL & INSTALLATION

➧ SEE FIGS. 63–67

2.0L Engine

1. Remove the air cleaner.
2. Number and remove the spark plug wires and retainers.
3. Remove the oil dipstick tube and breather.
4. Disconnect the oxygen sensor wire.
5. Disconnect the exhaust pipe from the manifold.
6. Remove the nuts and remove the manifold and the gasket.

To Install:

7. Install the exhaust manifold with a new gasket. Tighten the nuts to 16 ft. lbs.(22 Nm).
8. Install the exhaust pipe to the exhaust manifold and tighten the nuts to 19 ft. lbs.(25 Nm).
9. Connect the wire to the oxygen sensor.
10. Install the oil dipstick tube and breather.
11. Install the spark plug wires and retainers.
12. Install the air cleaner.

2.3L ENGINE

1. Disconnect the negative battery cable and oxygen sensor connector.
2. Remove upper and lower exhaust manifold heat shields.
3. Remove the bolt that attaches the exhaust manifold brace to the manifold.
4. Break loose the manifold to exhaust pipe spring loaded bolts using a 13mm box wrench.
5. Raise and safely support the vehicle.

➡ It is necessary to relieve the spring pressure from 1 bolt prior to removing the second bolt. If the spring pressure is not relieved it will cause the exhaust pipe to twist and bind up the bolt as it is removed.

6. Remove the manifold to exhaust pipe bolts from the exhaust pipe flange as follows:
   a. Unscrew either bolt clockwise 4 turns.
   b. Remove the other bolt.
   c. Remove the first bolt.
7. Pull down and back on the exhaust pipe to disengage it from the exhaust manifold bolts.
8. Lower the vehicle.
9. Remove the exhaust manifold mounting bolts and remove the manifold.
10. The installation is the reverse of the removal procedure. Tighten the mounting bolts, in sequence, to 27 ft. lbs. (37 Nm). Install the exhaust pipe flange bolts evenly and gradually to avoid binding.
11. Connect the negative battery cable and check for leaks.

2.5L Engine

1. Disconnect the air cleaner and hot air tube.
2. Disconnect the alternator top mounts and swing it aside.
3. Disconnect the oxygen sensor connector.
4. Raise the vehicle and support it safely.
5. Disconnect the exhaust pipe from the manifold.
6. Lower the vehicle.
7. Remove the exhaust manifold retaining bolts, then remove the exhaust manifold and gasket.
8. Clean all gasket mating surfaces on the cylinder head and manifold.
9. Installation is the reverse of removal. Torque all exhaust manifold mounting bolts to 44 ft. lbs. (60 Nm) in sequence.

3.0L Engine

1. Disconnect the negative battery cable.
2. Raise and support the vehicle safely.
3. Remove the bolts attaching the exhaust pipe to the manifold.
4. Lower the vehicle.
5. Disconnect the oxygen sensor connector.
6. Remove the spark plug wires. Tag them for installation.
7. Remove the two nuts retaining the crossover pipe to the manifold.
8. Remove the bolts attaching the exhaust manifold and remove the exhaust manifold from the engine.
9. Installation is the reverse of removal. Clean all gasket mating surfaces and torque the exhaust manifold bolts to 37 ft. lbs. (50 Nm).

3.3L Engine

Front

1. Disconnect the negative battery cable.
2. Disconnect the air cleaner inlet duct and disconnect the spark plug wires.
3. Remove the exhaust crossover pipe to manifold bolts.

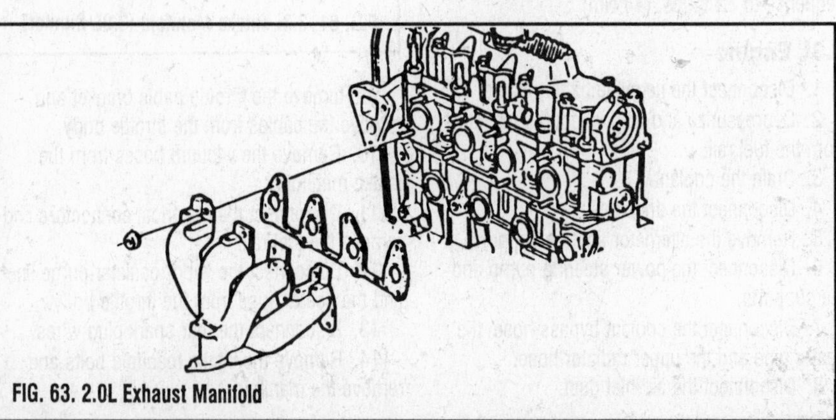
FIG. 63. 2.0L Exhaust Manifold

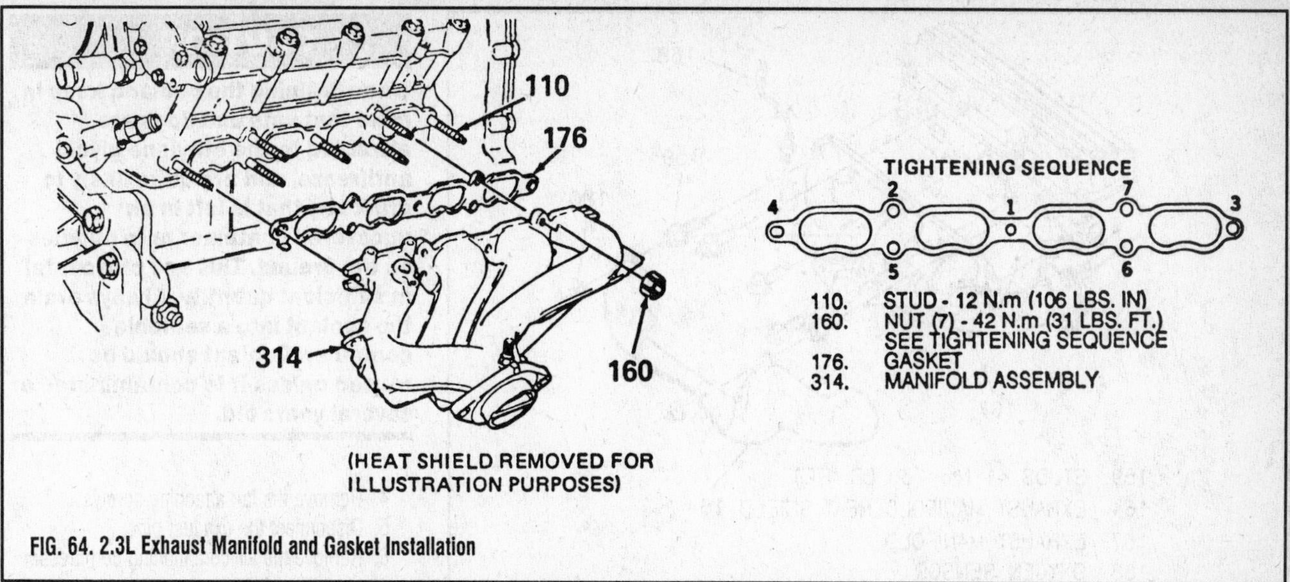

FIG. 64. 2.3L Exhaust Manifold and Gasket Installation

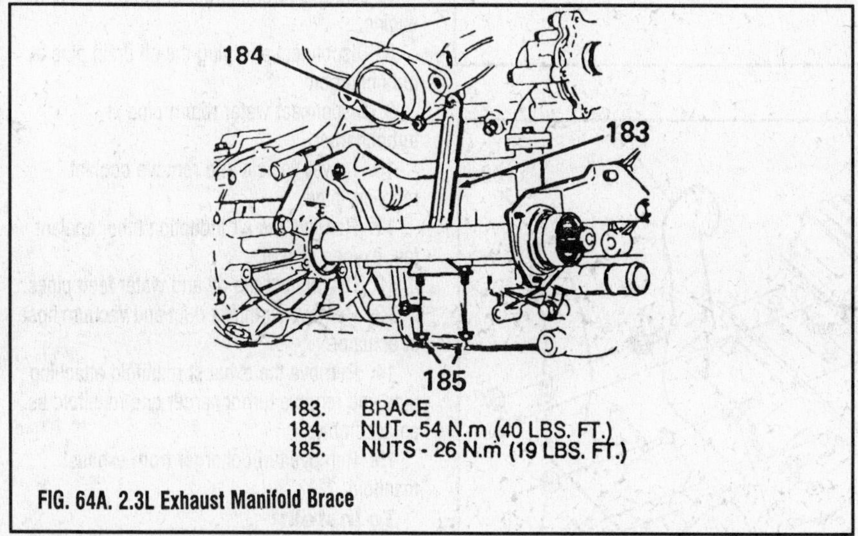

FIG. 64A. 2.3L Exhaust Manifold Brace

4. Remove the engine lift hook and manifold heat shield.
5. Remove the oil level indicator tube and the indicator.
6. Remove the manifold studs and remove the manifold.
7. Installation is the reverse of the removal procedure.

Rear

1. Disconnect the negative battery cable.
2. Disconnect the spark plug wires.
3. Disconnect the wire from the oxygen sensor.
4. Remove the throttle cable bracket and remove the cables from the throttle body.
5. Remove the brake booster hose from the manifold.

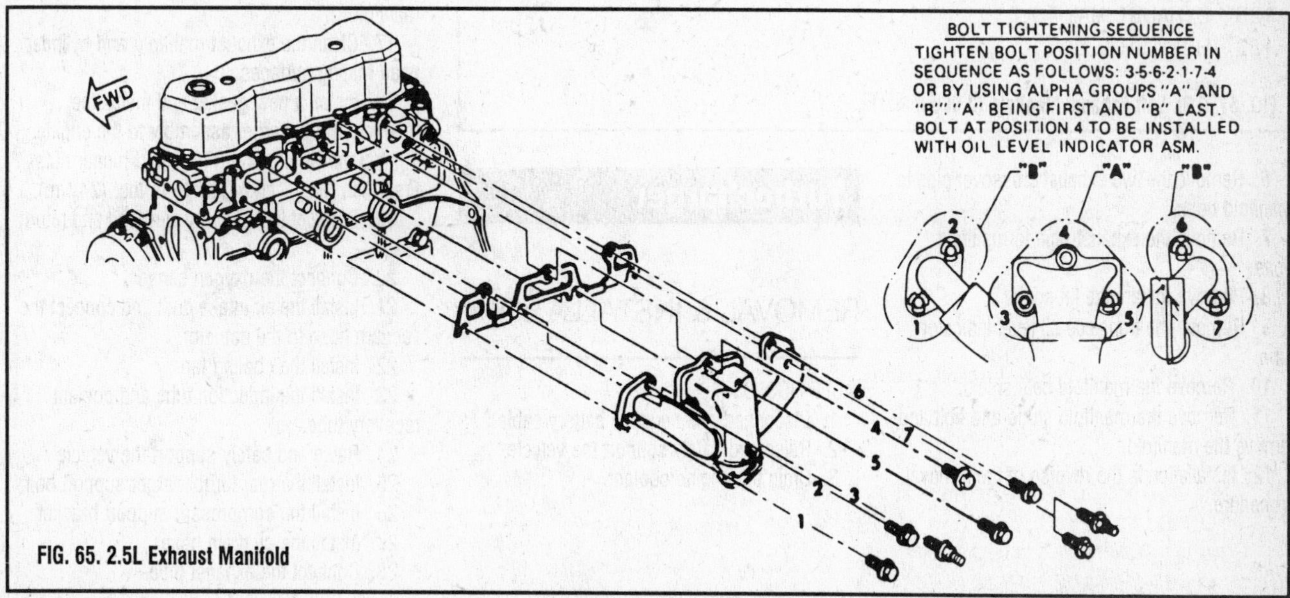

FIG. 65. 2.5L Exhaust Manifold

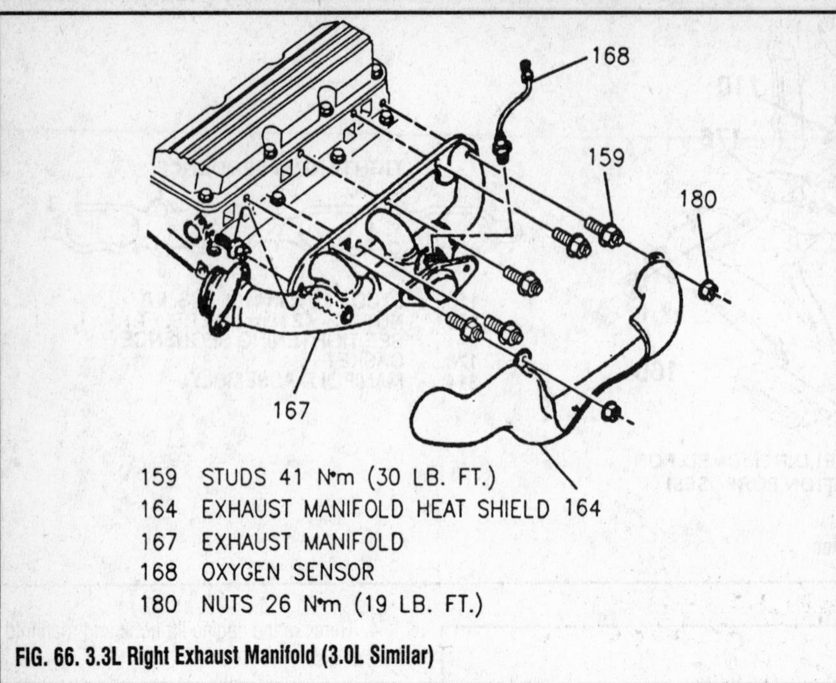

FIG. 66. 3.3L Right Exhaust Manifold (3.0L Similar)

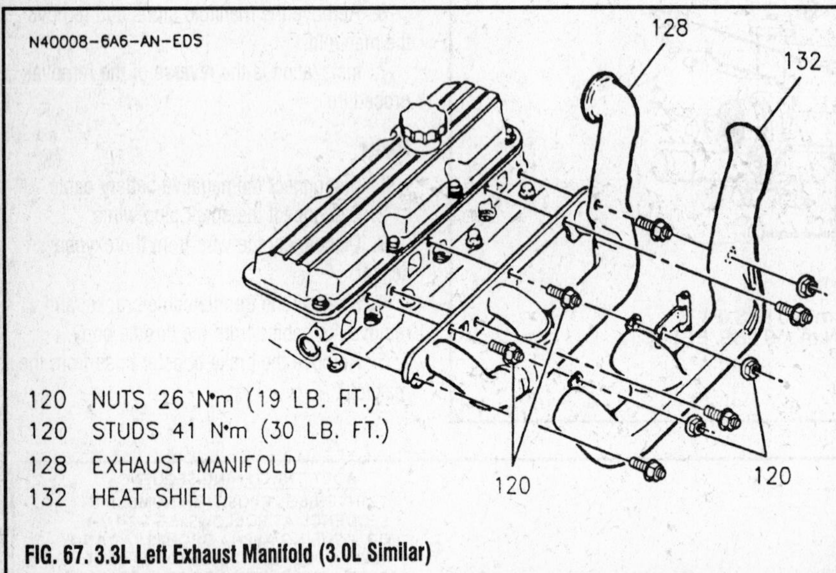

FIG. 67. 3.3L Left Exhaust Manifold (3.0L Similar)

6. Remove the two exhaust crossover pipe to manifold bolts.
7. Remove the exhaust pipe to manifold bolts.
8. Remove the engine lift hook.
9. Remove the transaxle oil level indicator tube.
10. Remove the manifold heat shield.
11. Remove the manifold studs and bolt and remove the manifold.
12. Installation is the reverse of the removal procedure.

Turbocharger

REMOVAL & INSTALLATION

➧ SEE FIGS. 68–70

1. Disconnect the negative battery cable.
2. Raise and safely support the vehicle.
3. Drain the engine coolant.

✲✲ CAUTION

When draining the coolant, keep in mind that cats and dogs are attracted by the ethylene glycol antifreeze, and are quite likely to drink any that is left in an uncovered container or in puddles on the ground. This will prove fatal in sufficient quantity. Always drain the coolant into a sealable container. Coolant should be reused unless it is contaminated or several years old.

4. Remove the fan attaching screws.
5. Disconnect the exhaust pipe.
6. Remove the air conditioning compressor rear support bracket.
7. Remove turbocharger support bracket to engine.
8. Disconnect and plug the oil drain pipe at turbocharger.
9. Disconnect water return pipe at turbocharger.
10. Lower vehicle and remove coolant recovery pipe.
11. Remove the air induction tube, coolant fan, oxygen sensor.
12. Disconnect the oil and water feed pipes.
13. Remove air intake duct and vacuum hose at actuator.
14. Remove the exhaust manifold attaching nuts and remove turbocharger and manifold as an assembly.
15. Remove turbocharger from exhaust manifold.

To install:

16. Assemble the turbocharger and exhaust manifold.
17. Clean the exhaust manifold and cylinder head mating surfaces.
18. Install a new gasket and install the manifold/turbocharger assembly to the engine. Tighten the Nos. 2 and 3 manifold runner nuts first, then Nos. 1 and 4, to 18 ft. lbs. (24 Nm).
19. Connect the oil and water feed and return lines.
20. Connect the oxygen sensor.
21. Install the air intake duct and connect the vacuum hose to the actuator.
22. Install the cooling fan.
23. Install the induction tube and coolant recovery tube.
24. Raise and safely support the vehicle.
25. Install the rear turbocharger support bolt.
26. Install the compressor support bracket.
27. Install the oil drain hose.
28. Connect the exhaust pipe.

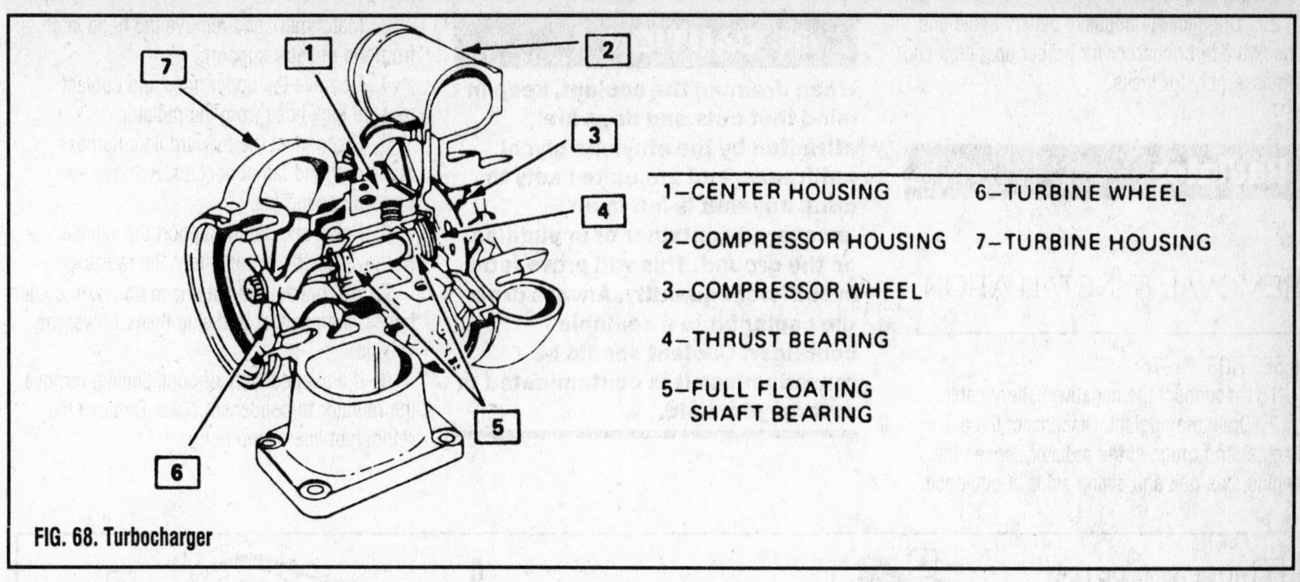

FIG. 68. Turbocharger

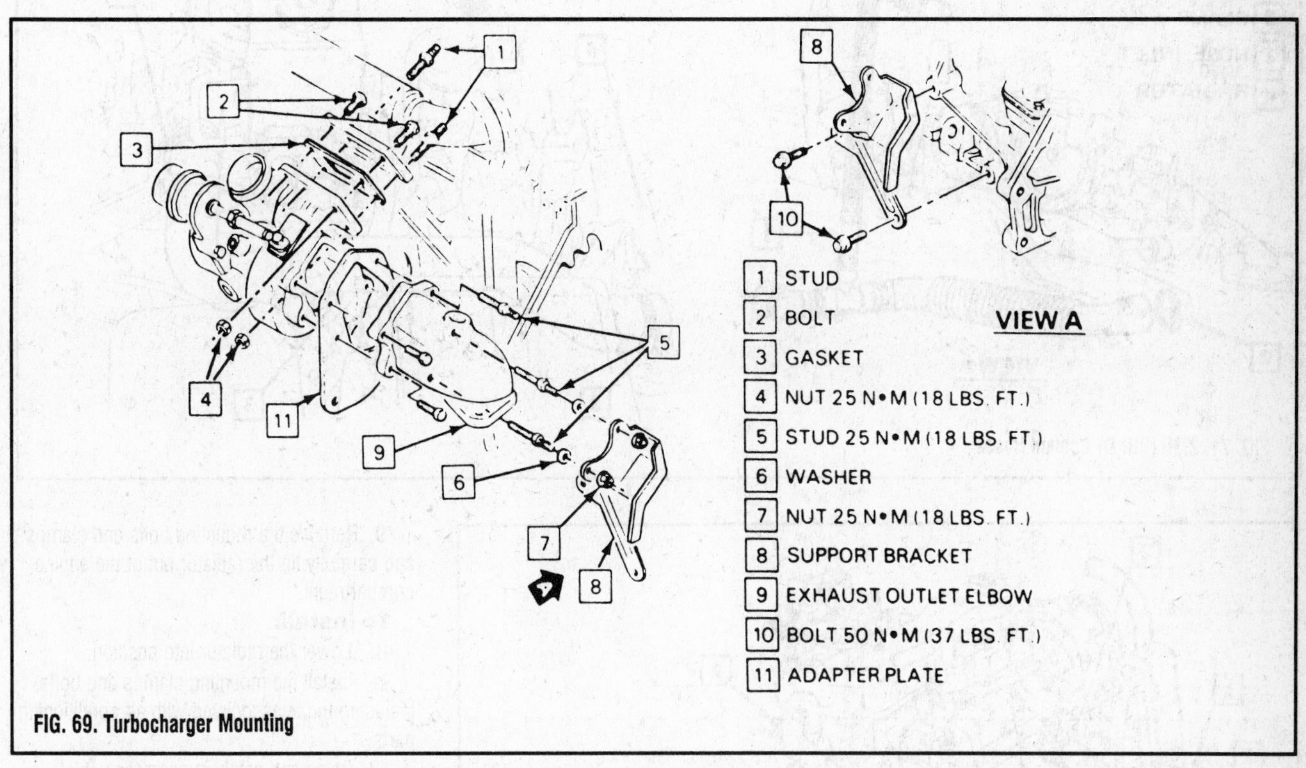

FIG. 69. Turbocharger Mounting

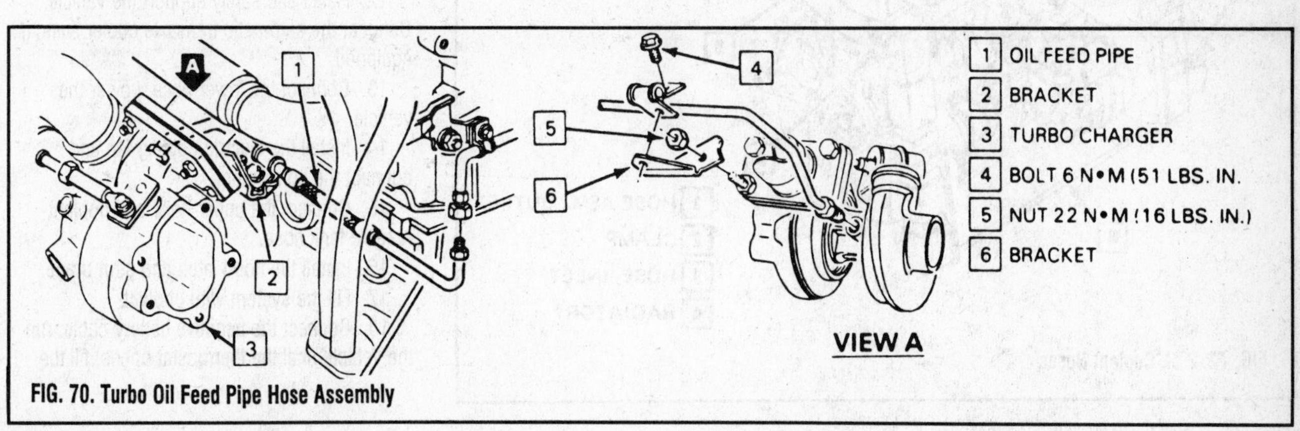

FIG. 70. Turbo Oil Feed Pipe Hose Assembly

29. Connect the negative battery cable and check the turbocharger for proper operation and the assembly for leaks.

Radiator

REMOVAL & INSTALLATION

SEE FIGS. 71–76

1. Disconnect the negative battery cable.
2. Drain the coolant. Disconnect the the engine strut brace at the radiator, loosen the engine side bolt and swing aside, if equipped.

CAUTION

When draining the coolant, keep in mind that cats and dogs are attracted by the ethylene glycol antifreeze, and are quite likely to drink any that is left in an uncovered container or in puddles on the ground. This will prove fatal in sufficient quantity. Always drain the coolant into a sealable container. Coolant should be reused unless it is contaminated or several years old.

3. Matchmark and remove the hood latch from the radiator support.
4. Remove the upper hose and coolant reserve tank hose from the radiator.
5. Disconnect the forward light harness connector and fan connector. Remove the electric cooling fan.
6. Raise and safely support the vehicle. Remove the lower hose from the radiator.
7. Disconnect the automatic transaxle cooler hoses, if equipped, and plug them. Lower the vehicle.
8. If equipped with air conditioning, remove the radiator to condenser bolts. Remove the refrigerant line clamp bolt.

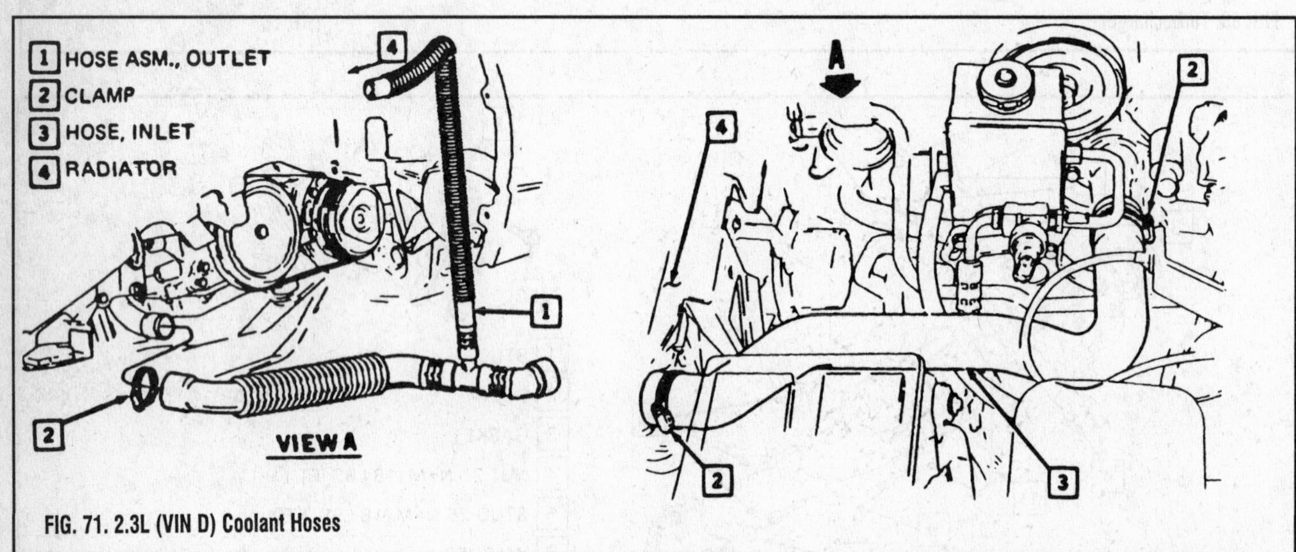

FIG. 71. 2.3L (VIN D) Coolant Hoses

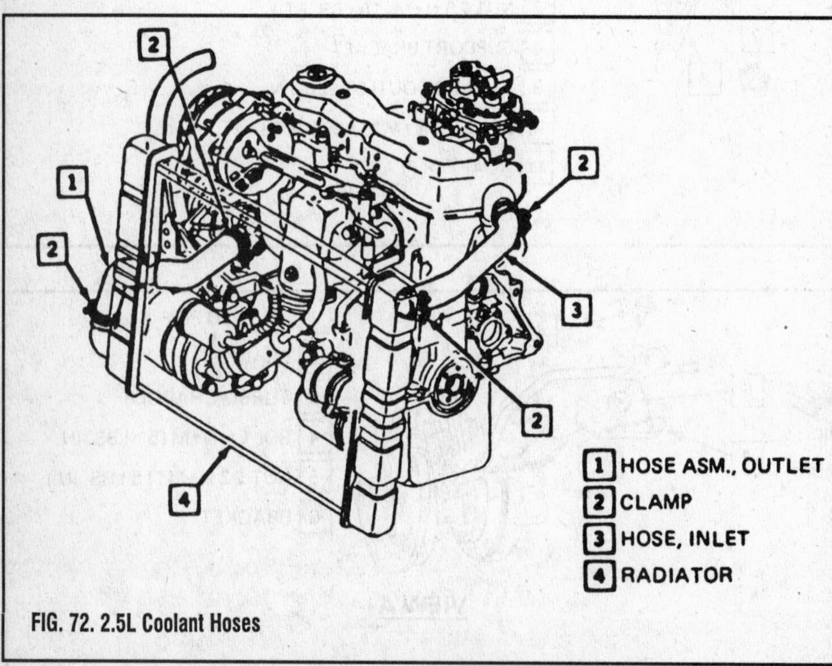

FIG. 72. 2.5L Coolant Hoses

9. Remove the mounting bolts and clamps and carefully lift the radiator out of the engine compartment.

To install:

10. Lower the radiator into position.
11. Install the mounting clamps and bolts, including those associated with air conditioning parts.
12. Raise and safely support the vehicle. Connect the automatic transaxle cooler lines, if equipped.
13. Connect the lower hose. Lower the vehicle.
14. Install the electric cooling fan and connect the connectors.
15. Connect the upper hose and coolant reserve tank hose.
16. Install the hood latch and strut brace.
17. Fill the system with coolant.
18. Connect the negative battery cable, run the vehicle until the thermostat opens, fill the

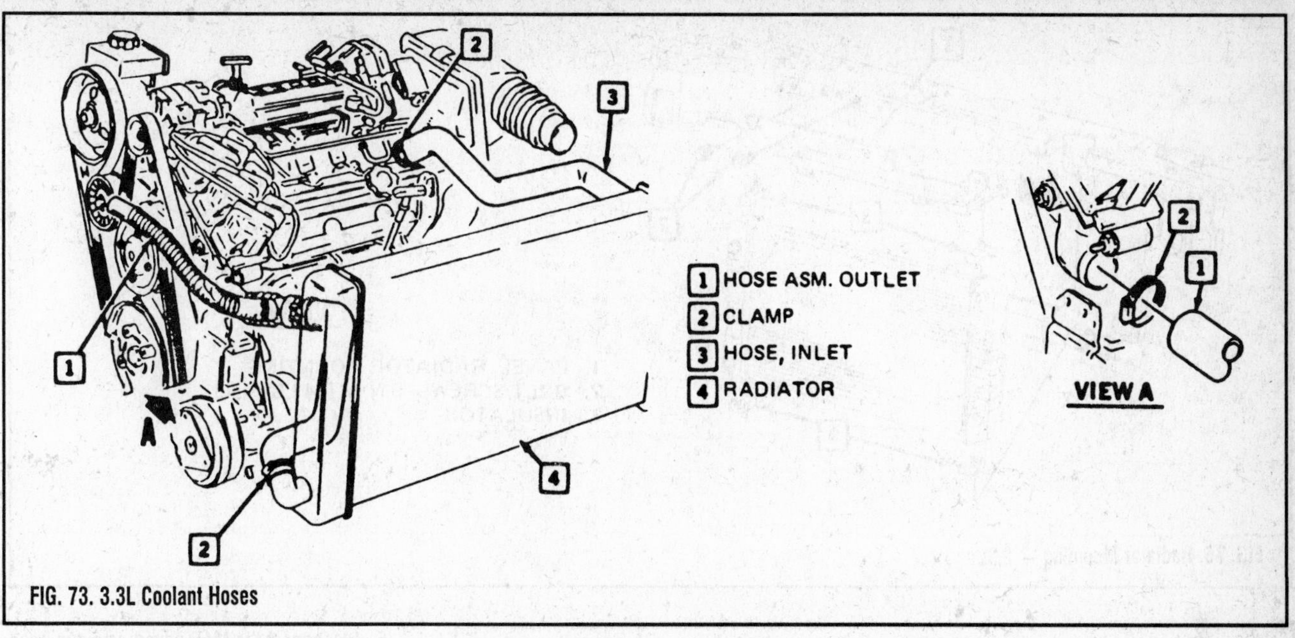

FIG. 73. 3.3L Coolant Hoses

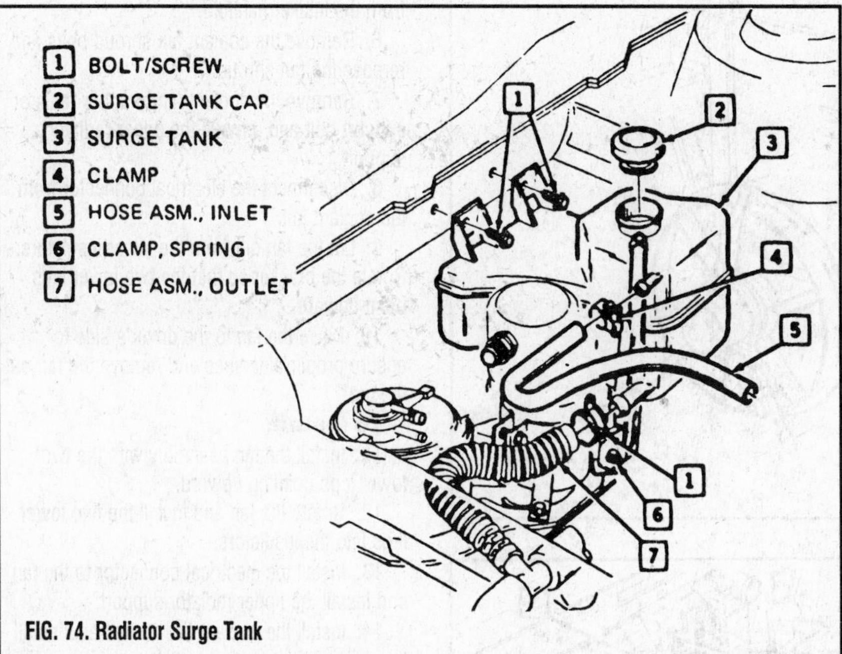

FIG. 74. Radiator Surge Tank

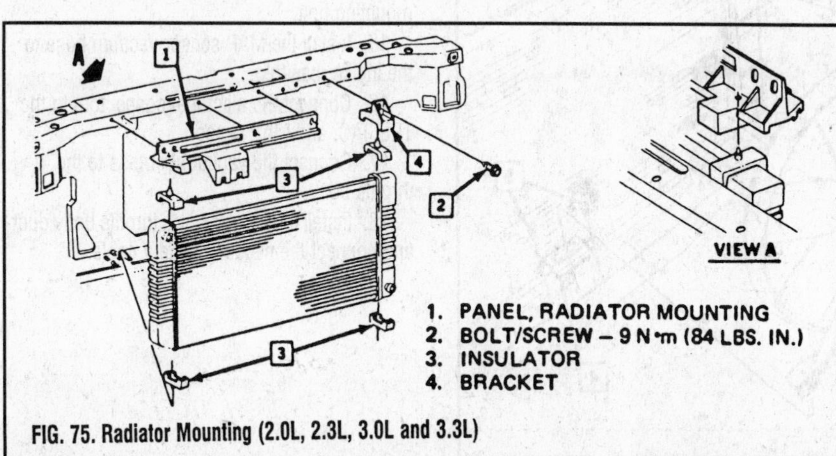

FIG. 75. Radiator Mounting (2.0L, 2.3L, 3.0L and 3.3L)

radiator and recovery tank completely and check the automatic transaxle fluid level.

19. Once the vehicle has cooled, recheck the coolant level.

Engine Fan

REMOVAL & INSTALLATION

➧ SEE FIGS. 77–83

All except 2.3L (VIN D)

1. Disconnect the negative battery cable.
2. Disconnect the wiring harness from the motor and from the fan frame.
3. Remove the fan guard and hose support if necessary.
4. Remove the fan assembly from the radiator support.
5. Installation is the reverse of the removal procedure.

2.3L Engine (VIN D)

1. Disconnect the negative battery cable.
2. Disconnect the air cleaner to the throttle body duct.
3. Disconnect the TPS, IAC, and MAP sensor connectors and position the harness off to the side.
4. Disconnect the vacuum harness assembly from the throttle body and place to the side.

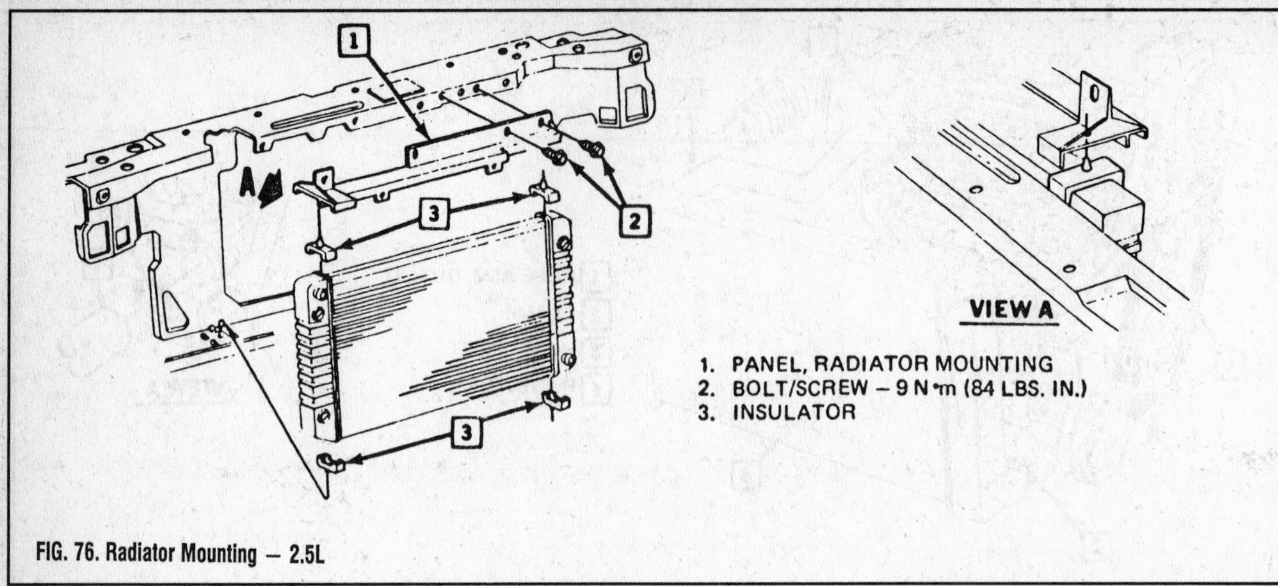

FIG. 76. Radiator Mounting – 2.5L

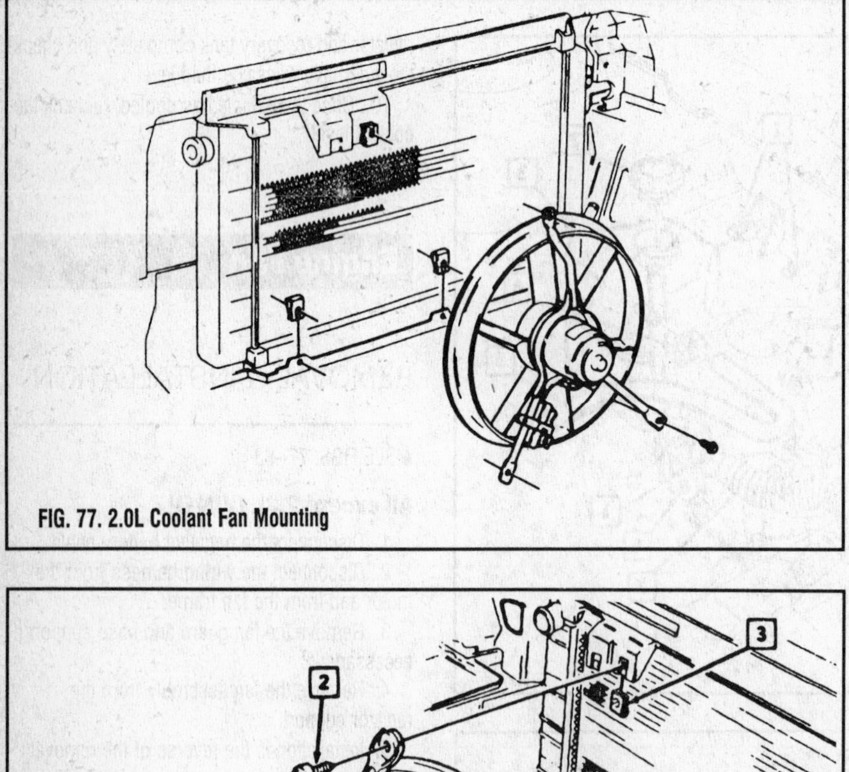

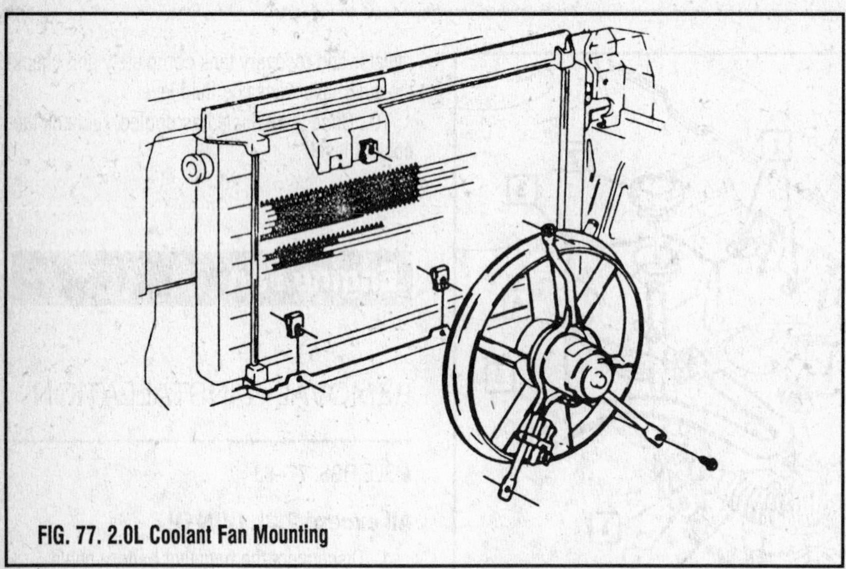

FIG. 77. 2.0L Coolant Fan Mounting

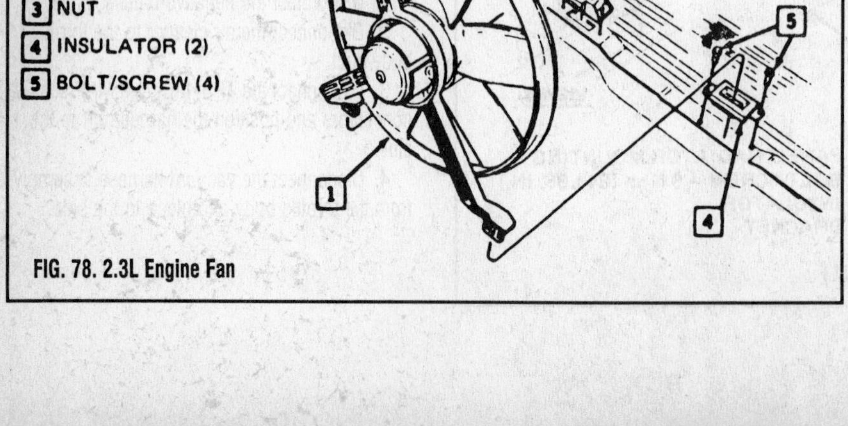

1 FAN ASM.
2 BOLT – 9 N·m (80 LBS. IN.)
3 NUT
4 INSULATOR (2)
5 BOLT/SCREW (4)

FIG. 78. 2.3L Engine Fan

5. Disconnect the MAP sensor vacuum hose from the intake manifold.

6. Remove the coolant fan shroud bolts and remove the fan shroud.

7. Remove the coolant fan to upper radiator support bolt and remove the upper radiator support.

8. Disconnect the electrical connector from the coolant fan.

9. Lift the fan out from the lower insulators. Rotate the bracket so that the two lower legs point upward.

10. Move the fan to the driver's side to ensure proper clearance and remove the fan out the top.

To install:

11. Install the fan assembly with the two lower legs pointing upward.

12. Rotate the fan and install the two lower legs into the insulators.

13. Install the electrical connector to the fan and install the upper radiator support.

14. Install the coolant fan shroud and install the coolant fan to upper radiator support mounting bolt.

15. Install the MAP sensor vacuum hose to the intake manifold.

16. Connect the electrical connectors to the TPS, IAC, and MAP sensor.

17. Connect the vacuum harness to the throttle body.

18. Install the air cleaner to throttle body duct and connect the negative battery cable.

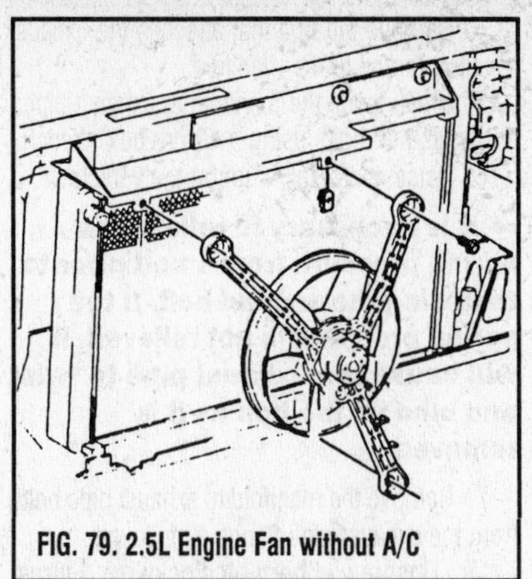
FIG. 79. 2.5L Engine Fan without A/C

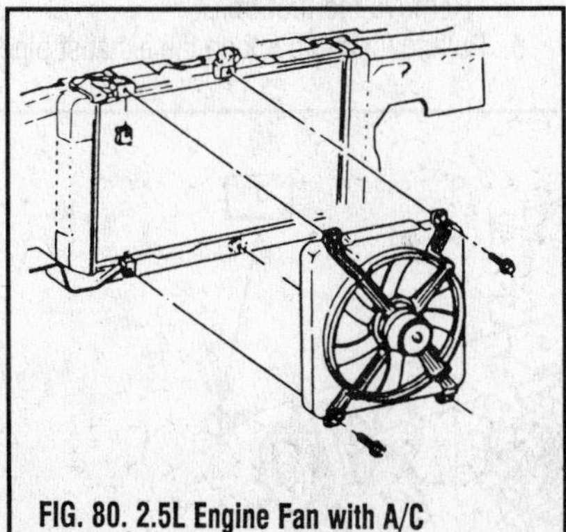
FIG. 80. 2.5L Engine Fan with A/C

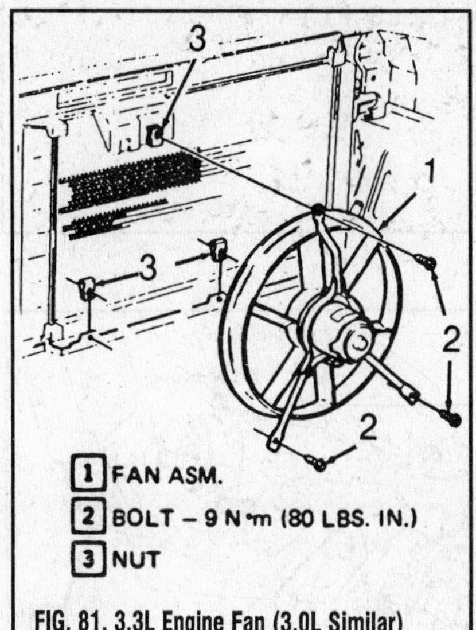

FIG. 81. 3.3L Engine Fan (3.0L Similar)

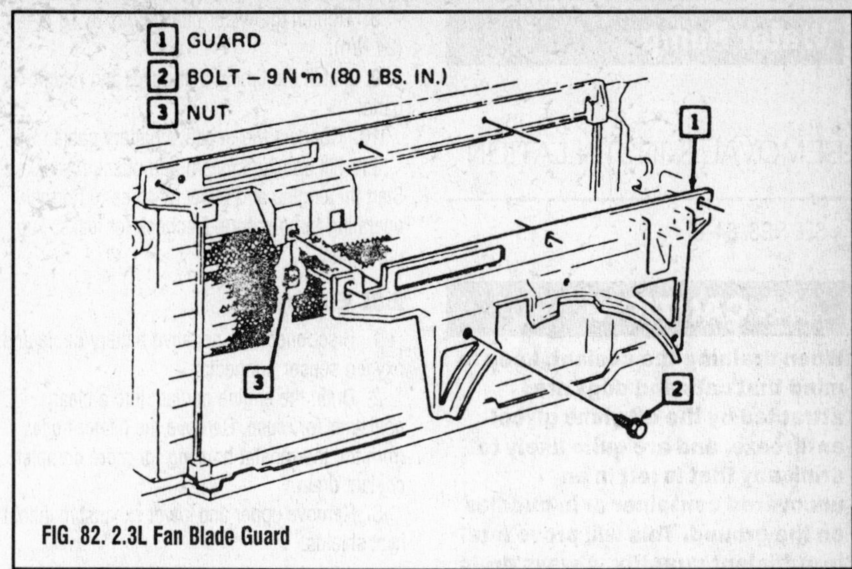

FIG. 82. 2.3L Fan Blade Guard

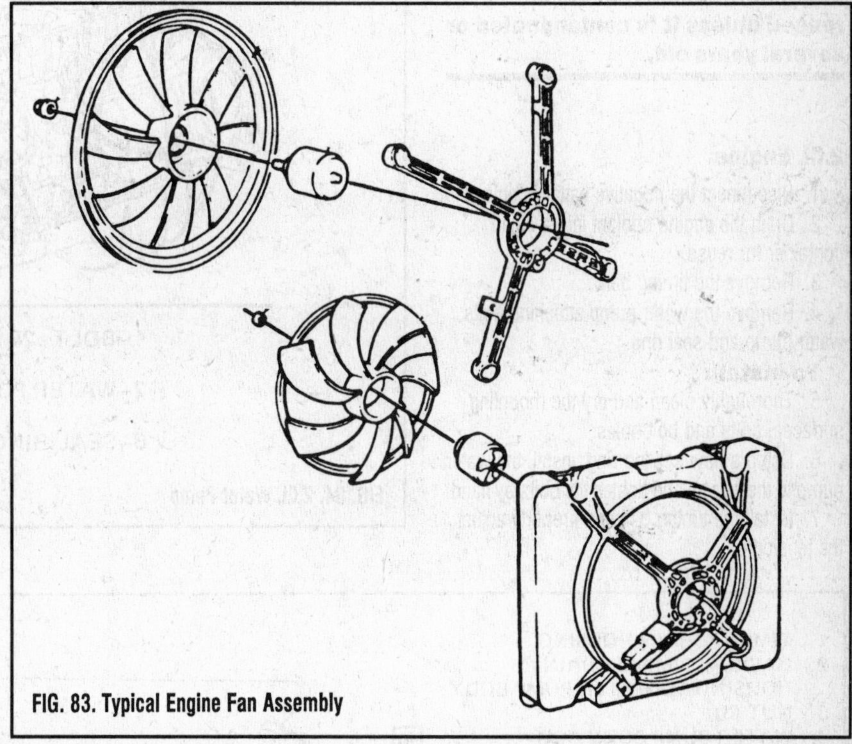
FIG. 83. Typical Engine Fan Assembly

Water Pump

REMOVAL & INSTALLATION

➧ SEE FIGS. 84–87

✲✲ CAUTION

When draining the coolant, keep in mind that cats and dogs are attracted by the ethylene glycol antifreeze, and are quite likely to drink any that is left in an uncovered container or in puddles on the ground. This will prove fatal in sufficient quantity. Always drain the coolant into a sealable container. Coolant should be reused unless it is contaminated or several years old.

2.0L Engine

1. Disconnect the negative battery cable.
2. Drain the engine coolant into a clean container for reuse.
3. Remove the timing belt.
4. Remove the water pump attaching bolts, water pump and seal ring.

To install:

5. Thoroughly clean and dry the mounting surfaces, bolts and bolt holes.
6. Using a new sealing ring, install the water pump to the engine and tighten the bolts by hand.
7. Install the timing belt and properly adjust the tension.
8. Tighten the water pump bolts to 18 ft. lbs. (24 Nm).
9. Install the timing belt cover and related parts.
10. Connect the negative battery cable.
11. Fill cooling system and check for leaks. Start the engine and allow to come to normal operating temperature. Recheck for leaks. Top-up coolant.

2.3L Engine

1. Disconnect the negative battery cable and oxygen sensor connector.
2. Drain the engine coolant into a clean container for reuse. Remove the heater hose from the thermostat housing for more complete coolant drain.
3. Remove upper and lower exhaust manifold heat shields.
4. Remove the bolt that attaches the exhaust manifold brace to the manifold.
5. Break loose the manifold to exhaust pipe spring loaded bolts using a 13mm box wrench.
6. Raise and safely support the vehicle.

➡ It is necessary to relieve the spring pressure from 1 bolt prior to removing the second bolt. If the spring pressure is not relieved, it will cause the exhaust pipe to twist and bind up the bolt as it is removed.

7. Remove the manifold to exhaust pipe bolts from the exhaust pipe flange as follows:
   a. Unscrew either bolt clockwise 4 turns.
   b. Remove the other bolt.
   c. Remove the first bolt.
8. Pull down and back on the exhaust pipe

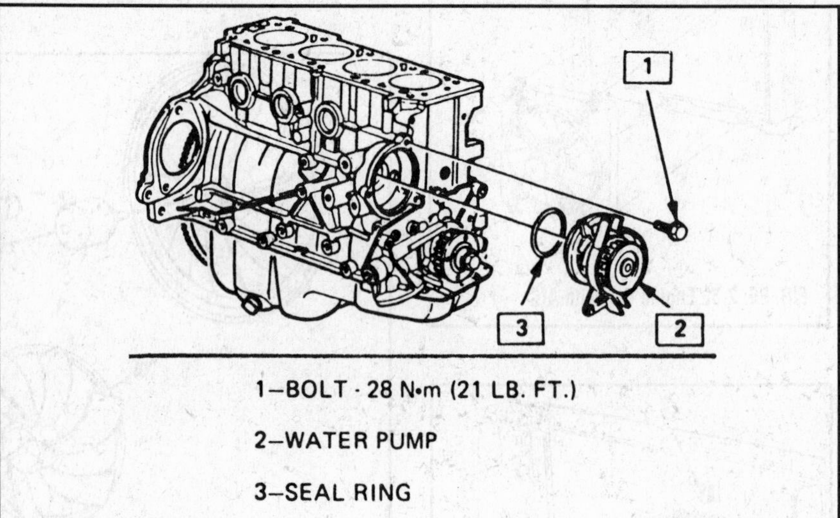

FIG. 84. 2.0L Water Pump

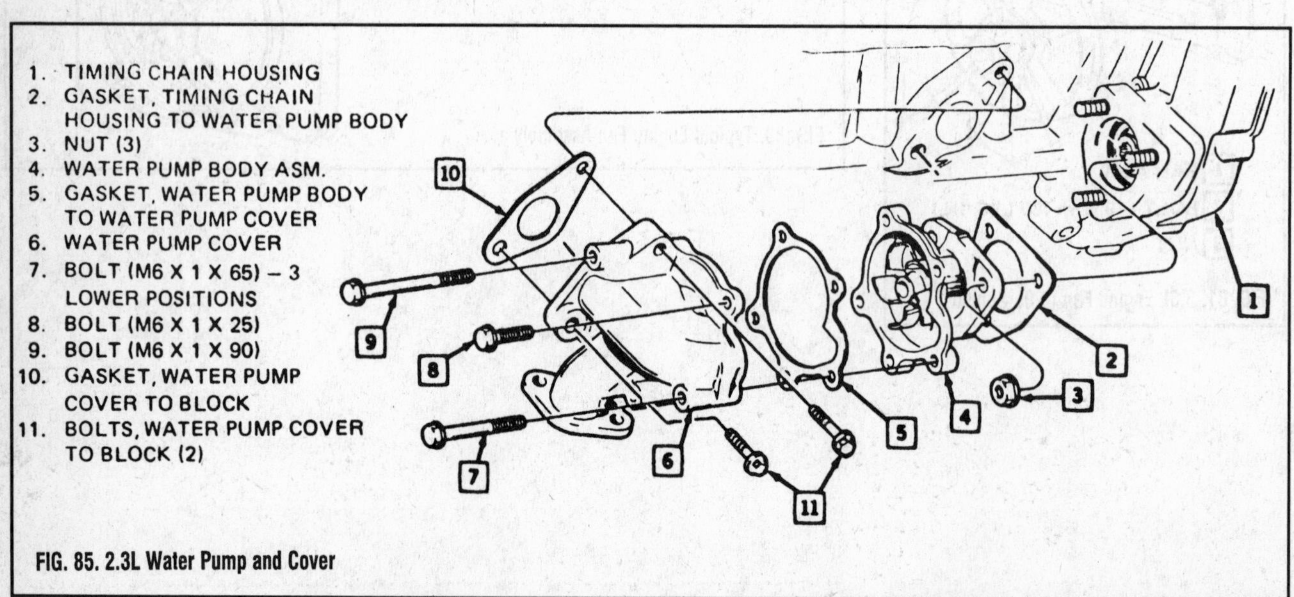

FIG. 85. 2.3L Water Pump and Cover

to disengage it from the exhaust manifold bolts.

9. Remove the radiator outlet pipe from the oil pan and transaxle. If equipped with a manual transaxle, remove the exhaust manifold brace. Leave the lower radiator hose attached and pull down on the outlet pipe to remove it from the water pump.

10. Lower the vehicle.

11. Remove the exhaust manifold, seals and gaskets.

12. Loosen and reposition the rear engine mount and bracket for clearance, as required.

13. Remove the water pump mounting bolts and nuts. Remove the water pump and cover assembly and separate the 2 pieces.

To install:

14. Thoroughly clean and dry all mounting surfaces, bolts and bolt holes. Using a new gasket, install the water pump to the cover and tighten the bolts finger tight.

15. Lubricate the splines of the water pump with clean grease and install the assembly to the engine using new gaskets. Install the mounting bolts and nuts finger tight.

16. Lubricate the radiator outlet pipe O-ring with antifreeze and install to the water pump with the bolts finger tight.

17. With all gaps closed, tighten the bolts, in the following sequence, to the proper values:

a. Pump assembly to chain housing nuts — 19 ft. lbs. (26 Nm).

b. Pump cover to pump assembly — 106 inch lbs. (12 Nm).

c. Cover to block, bottom bolt first — 19 ft. lbs. (26 Nm).

d. Radiator outlet pipe assembly to pump cover — 125 inch lbs. (14 Nm).

18. Install the exhaust manifold.

19. Raise and safely support the vehicle.

20. Install the exhaust pipe flange bolts evenly and gradually to avoid binding.

21. Connect the radiator outlet pipe to the transaxle and oil pan. Install the exhaust manifold brace, if removed. Lower the vehicle.

22. Install the bolt that attaches the exhaust manifold brace to the manifold.

23. Install the heat shields.

24. Connect the oxygen sensor connector.

25. Fill the radiator with coolant until it comes out the heater hose outlet at the thermostat housing. Then connect the heater hose.

26. Connect the negative battery cable, run the vehicle until the thermostat opens, fill the radiator and recovery tank completely.

27. Once the vehicle has cooled, recheck the coolant level.

2.5L Engine

1. Disconnect the negative battery cable.

2. Drain the engine coolant into a clean container for reuse.

3. Remove the drive belts, alternator and air conditioning compressor, as required.

4. Remove the water pump mounting bolts and remove the water pump from the vehicle.

To install:

5. Transfer the water pump pulley to the new pump using the proper pulley removal and installation tools.

6. Thoroughly clean and dry the mounting surfaces, bolts and bolt holes. Place a 1/8 in. (3mm) bead of RTV sealant on the pump's sealing surface.

7. Install the pump to the engine and coat the bolt threads with sealant as they are installed. Tighten the bolts to 25 ft. lbs. (34 Nm).

8. Install the alternator and/or air conditioning compressor. Install and adjust the drive belts.

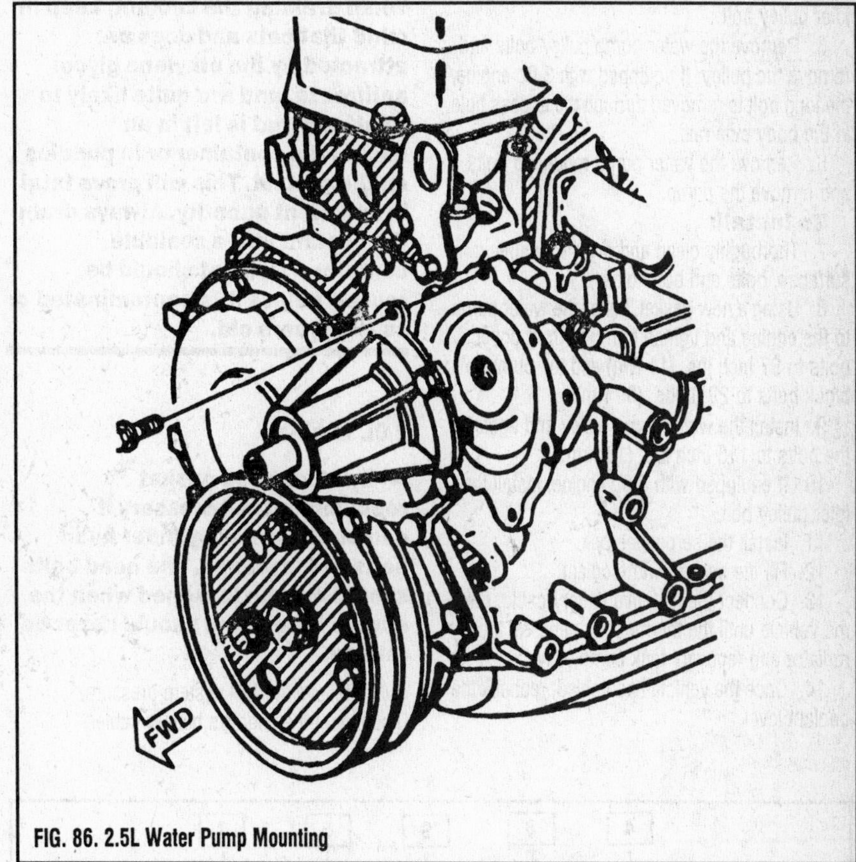

FIG. 86. 2.5L Water Pump Mounting

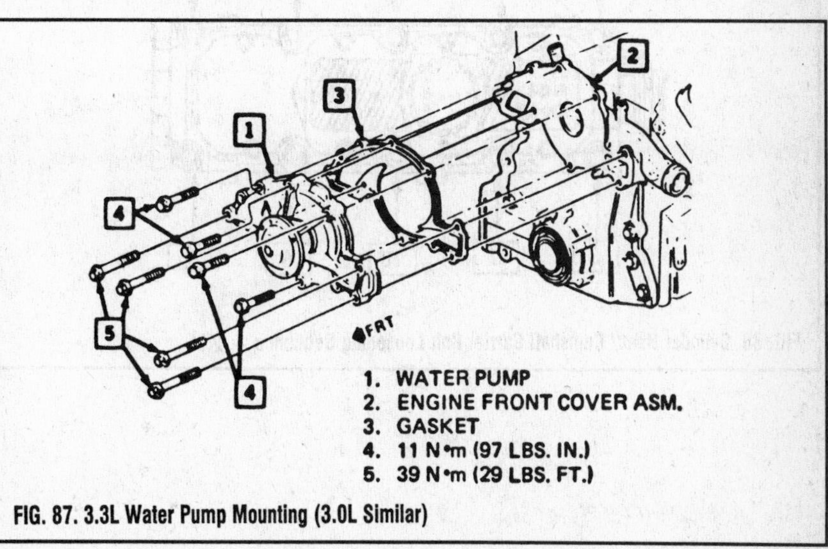

FIG. 87. 3.3L Water Pump Mounting (3.0L Similar)

9. Connect the negative battery cable.

10. Fill cooling system and check for leaks. Start the engine and allow to come to normal operating temperature. Recheck for leaks. Top off coolant level.

3.0L and 3.3L Engines

1. Disconnect the negative battery cable.
2. Drain the engine coolant into a clean container for reuse.
3. Remove the serpentine belt.
4. If equipped with 3.3L engine, remove the idler pulley bolt.
5. Remove the water pump pulley bolts and remove the pulley. If equipped with 3.0L engine, the long bolt is removed through the access hole in the body side rail.
6. Remove the water pump mounting bolts and remove the pump.

To install:

7. Thoroughly clean and dry the mounting surfaces, bolts and bolt holes.
8. Using a new gasket, install the water pump to the engine and tighten pump to front cover bolts to 97 inch lbs. (11 Nm) and the pump to block bolts to 29 ft. lbs. (39 Nm).
9. Install the water pump pulley and tighten the bolts to 115 inch lbs. (13 Nm).
10. If equipped with 3.3L engine, install the idler pulley bolt.
11. Install the serpentine belt.
12. Fill the system with coolant.
13. Connect the negative battery cable, run the vehicle until the thermostat opens, fill the radiator and recovery tank completely.
14. Once the vehicle has cooled, recheck the coolant level.

Cylinder Head

REMOVAL & INSTALLATION

➧ SEE FIGS. 88–90

✲✲ CAUTION

When draining the coolant, keep in mind that cats and dogs are attracted by the ethylene glycol antifreeze, and are quite likely to drink any that is left in an uncovered container or in puddles on the ground. This will prove fatal in sufficient quantity. Always drain the coolant into a sealable container. Coolant should be reused unless it is contaminated or several years old.

2.0L Engine

➡ Cylinder head gasket replacement is necessary if camshaft carrier/cylinder head bolts are loosened. The head bolts should only be loosened when the engine is cold and should never be reused.

1. Relieve the fuel system pressure. Disconnect the negative battery cable.
2. Drain the coolant. Remove the induction tube.
3. Remove the alternator and bracket.
4. Remove the ignition coil.
5. Matchmark the rotor to the distributor housing and the distributor housing to the cam carrier. Remove the distributor and spark plug wires.
6. Disconnect all cables from the throttle body.
7. Disconnect and tag all electrical connections from the throttle body and intake manifold.
8. Disconnect all vacuum lines and heater hoses.
9. Disconnect and plug the fuel lines.
10. Remove the breather from the camshaft carrier.
11. Remove the upper radiator support.
12. Disconnect the exhaust manifold from the turbocharger and disconnect the oxygen sensor.
13. Label and disconnect wiring at engine harness and thermostat housing.
14. Remove the timing belt.
15. Remove the camshaft carrier/cylinder head bolts in the reverse order of the installation sequence.
16. Remove camshaft carrier, rocker arms and valve lifters.
17. Remove cylinder head and manifolds as an assembly. Remove the head gasket.

To install:

18. Thoroughly clean and dry the mating surfaces and bolt holes. Apply a continuous bead of RTV sealant to the sealing surface of camshaft carrier.
19. Install a new head gasket and position the head on the engine block. Tighten the new head bolts in sequence as follows:
   - Step 1 — Tighten to 18 ft. lbs. (25 Nm).
   - Step 2 — Using a torque angle meter, tighten an additional 60 degrees.
   - Step 3 — Tighten another additional 60 degrees.
   - Step 4 — Tighten a third additional 60 degrees.
   - Step 5 — Tighten and additional 30–50 degrees turn after engine warm up.
20. Install the rear cover and timing belt.
21. Connect all wiring to the engine harness and thermostat housing.
22. Install the exhaust manifold to turbo connection and connect the oxygen sensor.
23. Install the upper radiator support.
24. Install the breather on the camshaft carrier.
25. Connect all vacuum and fuel lines.
26. Connect the heater hoses.
27. Connect all electrical connectors to the throttle body and intake manifold.

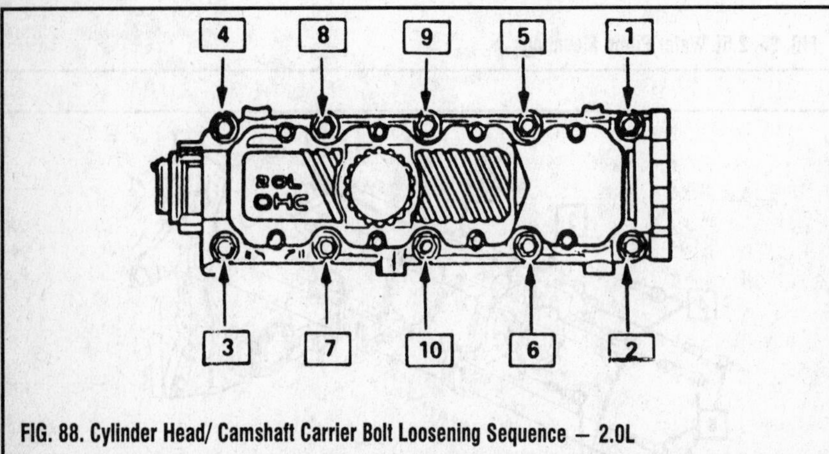

FIG. 88. Cylinder Head/ Camshaft Carrier Bolt Loosening Sequence — 2.0L

28. Connect all cables to the throttle body.
29. Install the distributor and spark plug wires, aligning the matchmarks.
30. Install the ignition coil.
31. Install the alternator and bracket.
32. Fill all fluids to their proper levels.
33. Connect the battery cable, start the engine and check for leaks.
34. Tighten all head bolts another additional 30–50 degrees, in sequence, after full engine warm up.

FIG. 89. Applying Sealer to Camshaft Carrier — 2.0L

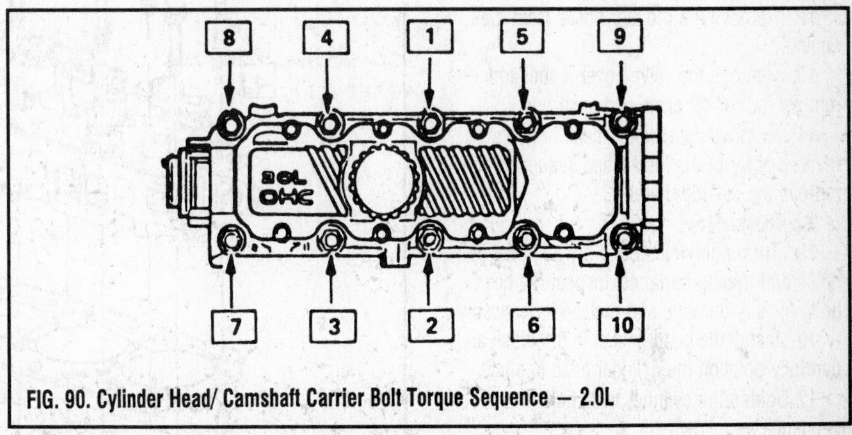

FIG. 90. Cylinder Head/ Camshaft Carrier Bolt Torque Sequence — 2.0L

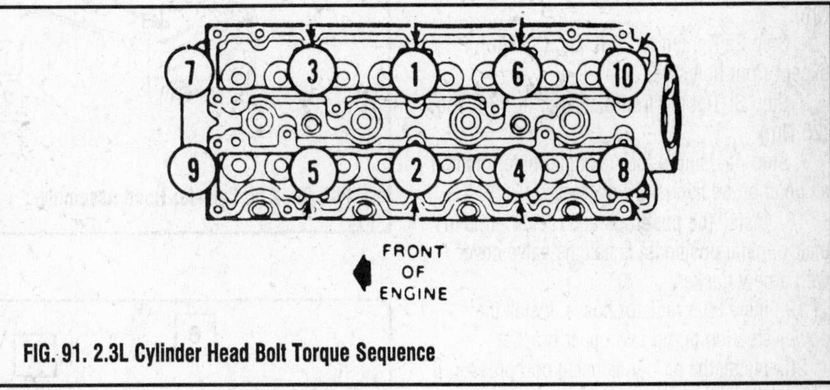

FIG. 91. 2.3L Cylinder Head Bolt Torque Sequence

2.3L Engine

1. Relieve the fuel system pressure. Disconnect the negative battery cable and drain cooling system.
2. Disconnect heater inlet and throttle body heater hoses from water outlet. Disconnect the upper radiator hose from the water outlet.
3. Remove the exhaust manifold.
4. Remove the intake and exhaust camshaft housings.
5. Remove the oil cap and dipstick. Pull oil fill tube upward to unseat from block.
6. Label and disconnect the injector harness electrical connector.
7. Disconnect the throttle body air intake duct. Disconnect the cables and bracket and position aside.
8. Remove the throttle body from the intake manifold.
9. Matchmark and disconnect the vacuum hose from intake manifold.
10. Remove intake manifold bracket to block bolt.
11. Disconnect the coolant sensor connectors.
12. Remove the cylinder head bolts in reverse order of the installation sequence.
13. Remove the cylinder head and gasket. Inspect the oil flow check valve for freedom of movement.

To Install:

14. Thoroughly clean and dry all bolts, bolt holes and mating surfaces. Inspect the head bolts for any damage and replace, if necessary.
15. Install the cylinder head gasket to the cylinder block and carefully position the cylinder head in place.
16. Coat the head bolt threads with clean engine oil and allow the oil to drain off before installing.
17. On 1988–89 engines, tighten the cylinder head bolts in sequence as follows:
   - Step 1 — Tighten all head bolts to 26 ft. lbs. (35 Nm).
   - Step 2 — Using a torque angle meter, tighten the short bolts an additional 80 degrees and the long bolts an additional 90 degrees.
18. On 1990–92 engines, tighten the cylinder head bolts in sequence as follows:
   - Step 1 — Tighten all head bolts to 26 ft. lbs. (35 Nm).
   - Step 2 — Using a torque angle meter, tighten the short bolts an additional 100 degrees and the long bolts an additional 110 degrees.
19. Install the intake manifold bracket.
20. Connect the MAP sensor vacuum hose to the intake manifold.
21. Install the throttle body to the intake manifold.
22. Connect the throttle body air intake duct. Install the throttle cable and bracket.
23. Connect the injector harness electrical connector.
24. Connect the 2 coolant sensor connections.
25. Install the oil cap and dipstick. Install the oil fill tube into the block.
26. Install the exhaust and intake camshaft housings.
27. Install the exhaust manifold.
28. Connect the heater inlet and throttle body heater hoses to the water outlet. Connect the upper radiator hose to the water outlet.
29. Fill all fluids to their proper levels.
30. Connect the battery cable, start the engine and check for leaks.

2.5L Engine

1. Relieve the fuel system pressure.
2. Disconnect the negative battery cable.
3. Drain the coolant and remove the oil dipstick tube.
4. Remove the air cleaner assembly.
5. Raise and safely support the vehicle. Disconnect the exhaust pipe from the manifold.
6. Lower the vehicle.
7. Label and disconnect the electrical wiring and throttle linkage from the throttle body assembly.
8. Disconnect the heater hose from the intake manifold.

9. Remove the ignition coil. Label and disconnect the electrical wiring connectors from the intake manifold and the cylinder head. Remove the alternator.

10. If equipped with a top-mounted air conditioning compressor, remove the compressor and lay it aside.

11. If equipped with power steering, remove the upper bracket from the power steering pump.

12. Remove the radiator hoses from the engine.

13. Remove the valve cover. Label and remove the rocker arms and pushrods.

14. Remove the cylinder head bolts in reverse order of the installation sequence and remove the cylinder head.

To install:

15. Thoroughly clean and dry all bolts, bolt holes and mating surfaces. Inspect the head bolts for any damage and replace if necessary.

16. Install the head gasket to the block and carefully position the cylinder head in place.

17. Tighten the cylinder head bolts in sequence as follows:

- Step 1: Tighten all bolts to 18 ft. lbs. (25 Nm).
- Step 2: Tighten to 26 ft. lbs. (35 Nm), except front bolt/stud.
- Step 3: Tighten front bolt/stud to 18 ft. lbs. (25 Nm).
- Step 4: Using a torque angle meter, tighten all bolts an additional 90 degrees.

18. Install the pushrods and rocker arms in their original positions. Install the valve cover with a new gasket.

19. Install the radiator hoses. Install the power steering pump and upper bracket.

20. Install the air conditioning compressor, if removed.

21. Install the ignition coil and connect the electrical wiring connectors to the intake manifold and the cylinder head.

22. Install the alternator.

23. Install the heater hose to the intake manifold.

24. Connect the electrical wiring and throttle linkage to the throttle body assembly.

25. Raise and safely support the vehicle.

26. Install the exhaust pipe to the manifold.

27. Install the air cleaner assembly.

28. Adjust all belt tensions and fill all fluids to their proper levels.

29. Connect the battery cable, start the engine and check for leaks.

3.0L and 3.3L Engines

1. Relieve the fuel system pressure.

2. Disconnect the negative battery cable and drain the coolant.

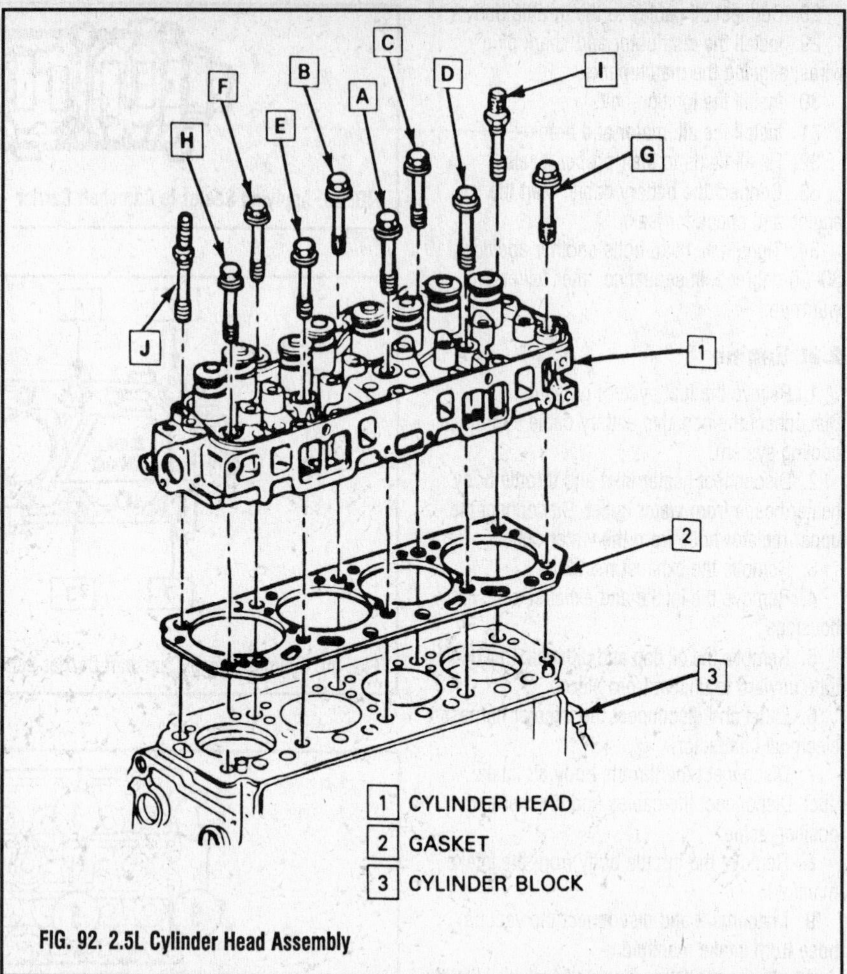

FIG. 92. 2.5L Cylinder Head Assembly

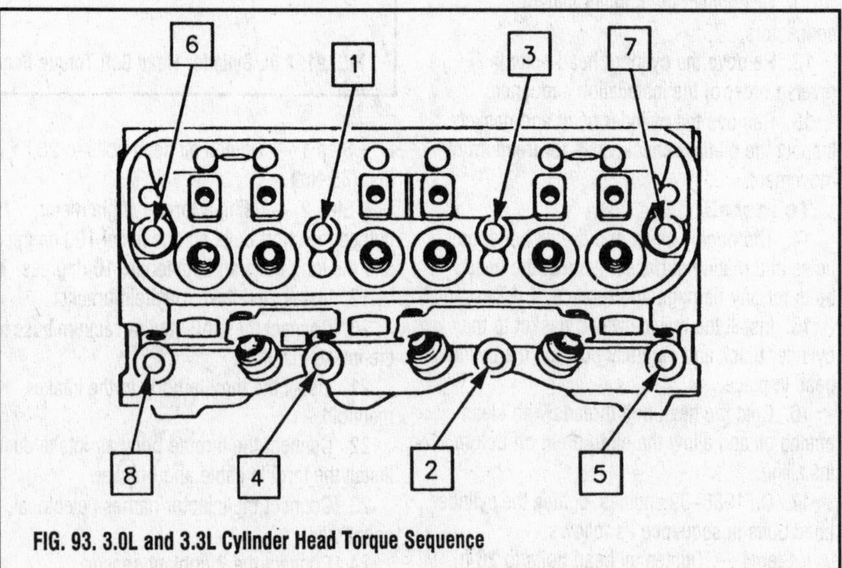

FIG. 93. 3.0L and 3.3L Cylinder Head Torque Sequence

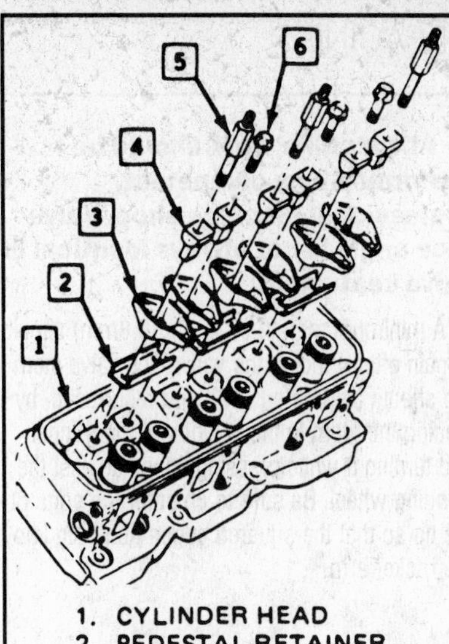

FIG. 94. 3.0L Cylinder Head Assembly

3. Remove the mass air flow sensor and the air intake duct.
4. Remove ignition module and wiring.
5. Remove the serpentine drive belt, the alternator and bracket.
6. Label and remove all necessary vacuum lines and electrical connections.
7. Remove the fuel lines, the fuel rail and the spark plug wires.
8. Remove the heater/radiator hoses from the throttle body and intake manifold. Remove the cooling fan and the radiator.
9. Remove the intake manifold.
10. Remove the valve covers. Label and remove the rocker arms, pedestals and pushrods.
11. Remove the left side exhaust manifold.
12. Remove the power steering pump. Remove the dipstick and dipstick tube.
13. Remove the left side head bolts in reverse order of the installation sequence and lift the left cylinder head from the engine.
14. Raise and safely support the vehicle. Remove the right exhaust manifold-to-engine bolts.
15. Remove the right cylinder head-to-engine bolts in reverse of the installation sequence and lift the right cylinder head from the engine.

To install:

16. Thoroughly clean and dry all bolts, bolt holes and mating surfaces. Inspect the head bolts for any damage and replace if necessary.
17. Install the head gasket to the block and carefully position the cylinder head in place.
18. On the 3.0L engine, tighten the cylinder head bolts, in sequence, as follows:
- Step 1: Tighten to 25 ft. lbs. (34 Nm).
- Step 2: Using a torque angle meter, tighten an additional 90 degrees.
- Step 3: Tighten another additional 90 degrees, to a maximum of 60 ft. lbs. (81 Nm).

19. On the 3.3L engine, tighten the cylinder head bolts, in sequence, as follows:
- Step 1: Tighten to 35 ft. lbs. (47 Nm).
- Step 2: Using a torque angle meter, tighten an additional 130 degrees.
- Step 3: Tighten the 4 center bolts an additional 30 degrees.

20. Install the intake manifold. Raise and safely support the vehicle. Install the exhaust manifold. Lower the vehicle.
21. Install the power steering pump. Install the dipstick and dipstick tube.
22. Install new valve cover gaskets and install the valve covers.
23. Install the rocker arms, pedestals and bolts. Tighten pedestal bolts to 43 ft. lbs. (58 Nm) for the 3.0L engine or 28 ft. lbs. (38 Nm) for the 3.3L engine.
24. Install the intake manifold assembly.
25. Install the heater and radiator hoses to the throttle body and intake manifold.
26. Install the cooling fan and the radiator.
27. Install the fuel lines, the fuel rail and the spark plug wires.
28. Install all vacuum lines and electrical connections.
29. Install the serpentine drive belt, the alternator and bracket.
30. Install the ignition module and wiring.
31. Install the mass air flow sensor and the air intake duct.
32. Fill all fluids to their proper levels.
33. Connect the battery cable, start the engine and check for leaks.

Valves

REMOVAL & INSTALLATION

➧ SEE FIGS. 95–99

1. Disconnect the negative battery cable.
2. Remove the cylinder head and gasket as previously outlined.
3. Using a valve spring compressing tool, compress the valve spring and remove the valve keys.
4. Remove the retainer and spring.
5. Remove the valve seal, using tool J36017 or equivalent.
6. Remove the rotator and the valve.

➡ **Make sure to keep all valve train components together and in order so that they may be reinstalled to their original position.**

To install:

7. Install the valve and rotator.
8. Install the valve seal and properly seat it, using tool J36007 or equivalent.
9. Install the spring and the retainer.
10. Using a valve spring compressing tool,

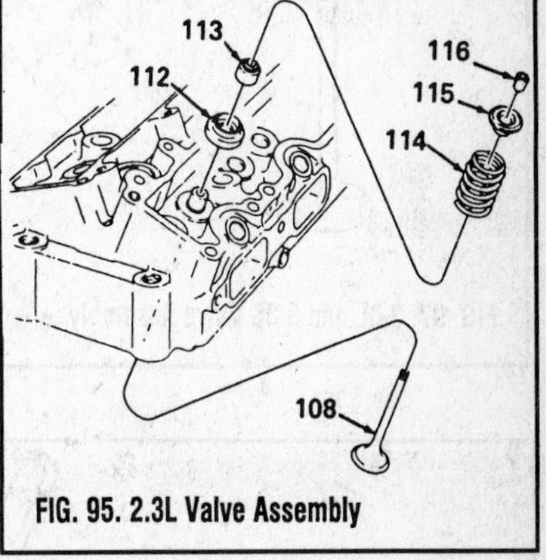

FIG. 95. 2.3L Valve Assembly

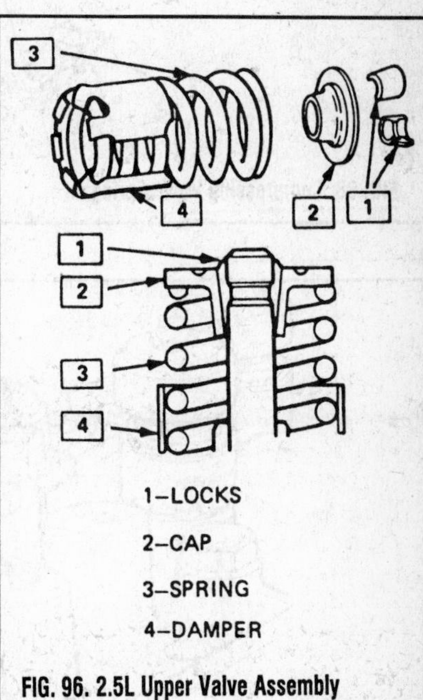

FIG. 96. 2.5L Upper Valve Assembly

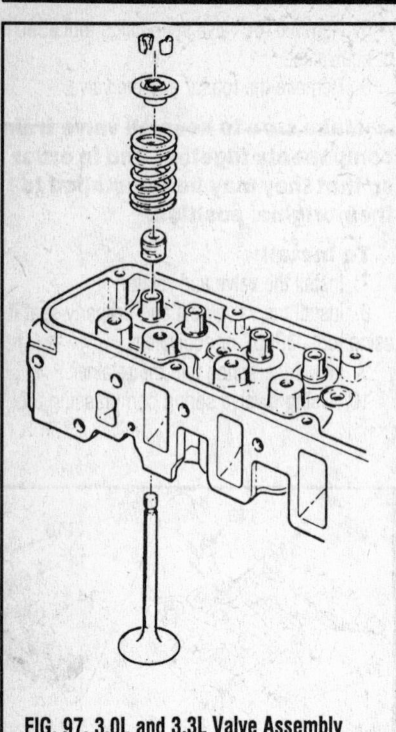

FIG. 97. 3.0L and 3.3L Valve Assembly

compress the valve spring and install the valve keys.

11. Install cylinder head and gasket.
12. Connect the negative battery cable.

INSPECTION

➧ SEE FIG. 100

1. Inspect the valve stem tip for wear.
2. Inspect the lock/keeper grooves for chipping or wear. Replace the valve if chipped or severely worn.
3. Inspect the valve face for burn marks or cracks.
4. Inspect the valve stem for burrs and scratches. Minor scratches can be removed with an oil stone.
5. Inspect the valve stem for straightness. Bent valves must be replaced.
6. Inspect the valve face for grooves. If excessively grooved, the valve must be replaced.
7. If grinding the valves, measure the valve margin when done. If the margin is less that the minimum, replace the valve.

REFACING

➡ All machine work should be performed by a competent, professional machine shop. Valve face angle is not always identical to valve seat angle.

A minimum margin of $\frac{1}{32}$ in. (0.8mm) should remain after grinding the valve. The valve stem top should also be squared and resurfaced, by placing the stem in the V-block of the grinder, and turning it while pressing lightly against the grinding wheel. Be sure to chamfer the edge of the tip so that the squared edges don't dig into the rocker arm.

LAPPING

This procedure should be performed after the valves and seats have been machined, to insure that each valve mates to each seat precisely.

1. Invert the cylinder head, lightly lubricate the valve stems, and install the valves in the head as numbered.
2. Coat valve seats with fine grinding compound, and attach the lapping tool suction cup to a valve head. Moisten the suction cup.
3. Rotate the tool between your palms, changing position and lifting the tool often to prevent grooving.
4. Lap the valve until a smooth, polished seat is evident.
5. Remove the valve and tool, and rinse away all traces of grinding compound.

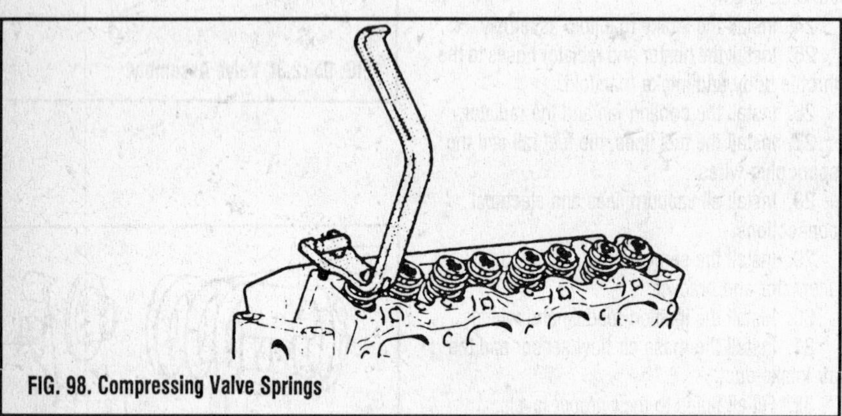

FIG. 98. Compressing Valve Springs

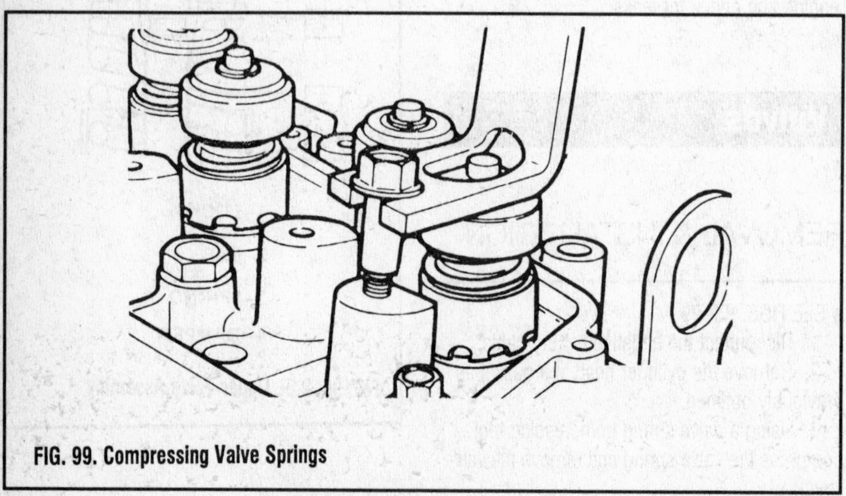

FIG. 99. Compressing Valve Springs

Valve Guide Service

The valve guides used in these engines are integral with the cylinder head, that is, they cannot be replaced. Refer to the previous "Valves — Removal and Installation" to check the valve guides for wear.

Valve guides are most accurately repaired using the bronze wall rebuilding method. In this operation, "threads" are cut into the bore of the valve guide and bronze wire is turned into the threads. The bronze "wall" is then reamed to the proper diameter. This method is well received for a number of reasons: it is relatively inexpensive, it offers better valve lubrication (the wire forms channels which retain oil), it offers less valve friction, and it preserves the original valve guide-to-seat relationship.

Another popular method of repairing valve guides is to have the guides "knurled." Knurling entails cutting into the bore of the valve guide

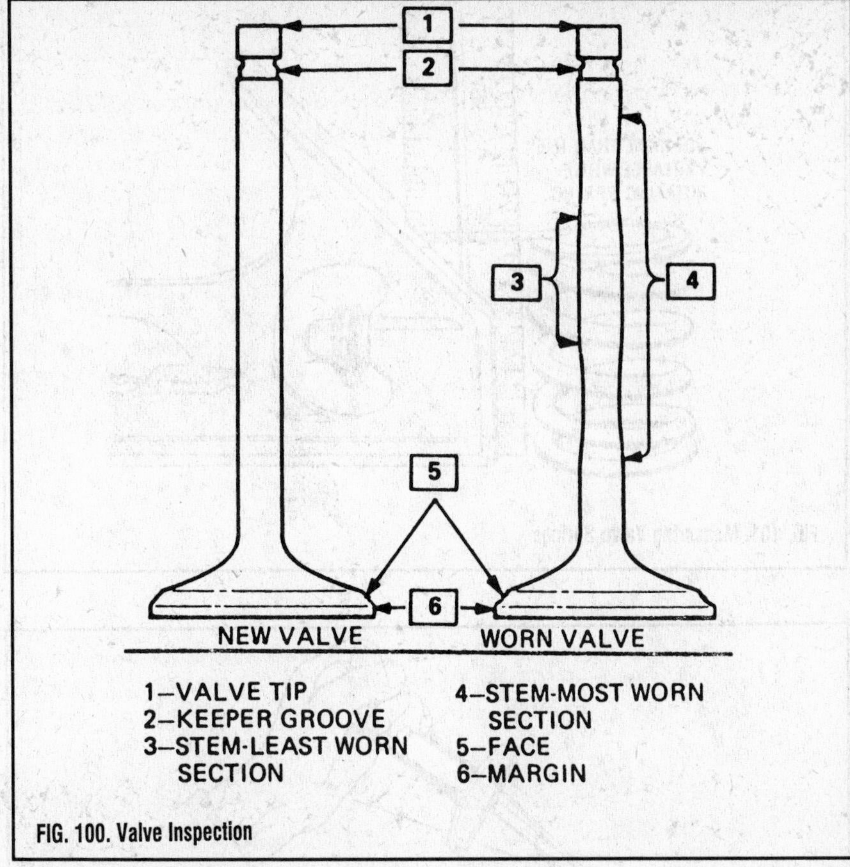

FIG. 100. Valve Inspection

with a special tool The cutting action "raises" metal off of the guide bore which actually narrows the inner diameter of the bore, thereby reducing the clearance between the valve guide bore and the valve stem. This method offers the same advantages as the bronze wall method, but will generally wear faster.

Either of the above services must be performed by a professional machine shop which has the specialized knowledge and tools necessary to perform the service.

Valve Springs and Valve Stem Seals

REMOVAL & INSTALLATION (WITH HEAD ON ENGINE)

2.0L Engine

1. Remove the camshaft carrier cover.
2. Remove the spark plugs.
3. Using air line adapter J22794 or equivalent, apply air pressure to cylinder to hold valve in place.
4. Remove the rocker arms.
5. Using valve spring compressing tool J33302-25 or equivalent, compress the valve spring.
6. Remove the valve lash compensators, valve locks, and valve spring.
7. Using tool J36017 or equivalent, remove the valve seal.

To install:

8. Install the plastic sleeve to the valve stem and lubricate with engine oil.
9. Install the new oil seal over the stem and install the seat over the valve guide. Remove the plastic sleeve.
10. Using tool J33302-25, install the valve springs, caps and locks.
11. Install the rocker arms and valve lash compensators to their original positions.
12. Remove the air line adapter J22794 or equivalent and install the spark plug.
13. Install the camshaft carrier cover.

2.3L Engine

1. Disconnect the negative battery cable.
2. Remove the intake camshaft housing assembly.
3. Remove the exhaust camshaft housing assembly.
4. Remove the spark plugs.
5. Using the proper adapter, apply continuous air pressure to the cylinder.
6. Using a valve spring compressing tool, compress the valve spring.
7. Remove the valve keys, retainer and spring.
8. Using tool J36017 or equivalent, remove the valve seal.
9. Remove the rotator assembly.

To install:

10. Install the rotator and a new valve seal, using tool J36007 or equivalent.
11. Install the spring and retainer.
12. Using a valve spring compressing tool, compress the valve spring and install the valve keys.
13. Remove the air pressure line and install the spark plugs.
14. Install the exhaust camshaft and housing.
15. Install the intake camshaft and housing.
16. Connect the negative battery cable.
17. Start the car and inspect for any oil leakage.

3.0L and 3.3L Engine

1. Remove the negative battery cable.
2. Remove the valve cover.
3. Remove the rocker arm assemblies.
4. Remove the spark plugs.
5. Using an adaptor apply air pressure to the cylinder to hold the valve closed.
6. Using a valve spring compressing tool, compress the valve spring.
7. Remove the valve keys, retainer and spring.
8. Using tool J36017 or equivalent, remove the valve seal.

To install:

10. Install the new valve seal, using tool J36007 or equivalent.
11. Install the spring and retainer.
12. Using a valve spring compressing tool, compress the valve spring and install the valve keys.
13. Remove the air pressure line and install the spark plugs.
14. Install the spark plugs.
15. Install the rocker arm assemblies and the valve cover.
16. Connect the negative battery cable.

REMOVAL & INSTALLATION (WITH HEAD OFF ENGINE)

1. Using a valve spring compressing tool, compress the valve spring and remove the valve keys.
2. Remove the retainer and spring.
3. Remove the valve seal, using tool J36017 or equivalent.
4. Remove the rotator.

To install:

5. Install the rotator and install the valve seal, using tool J36007 or equivalent.
6. Install the spring and the retainer.
7. Using a valve spring compressing tool, compress the valve spring and install the valve keys.

Valve Springs

INSPECTION

SEE FIGS. 101–102

1. Inspect the valve springs at their expanded height.
2. Inspect the spring ends, if not parallel, replace the spring.
3. Using tension tester tool J8056 or equivalent, check the spring tension. If not within specifications, replace the spring.

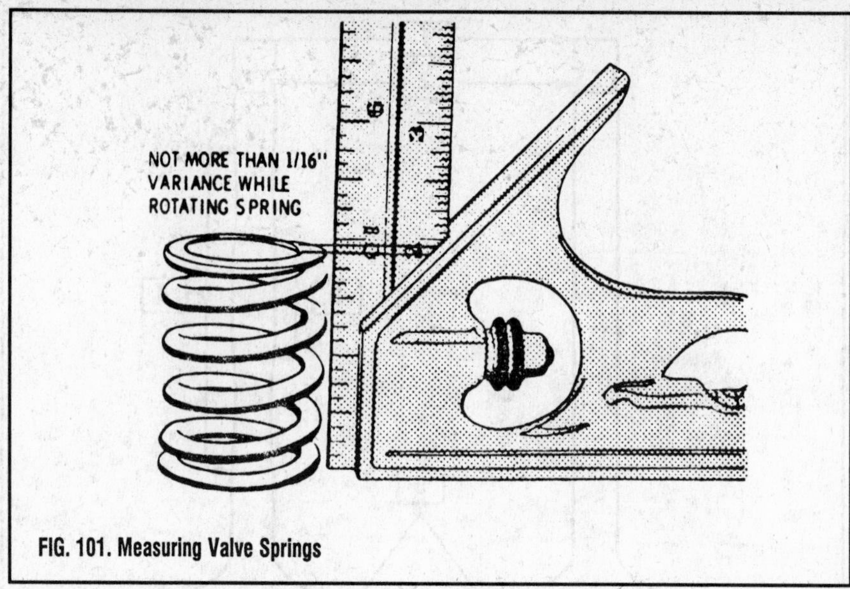

FIG. 101. Measuring Valve Springs

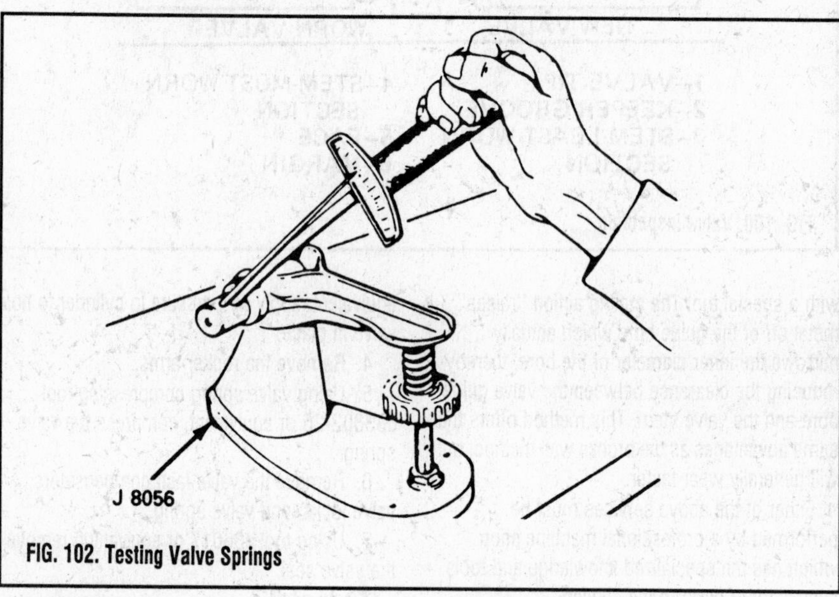

FIG. 102. Testing Valve Springs

Valve Lifters

REMOVAL & INSTALLATION

CAUTION

When draining the coolant, keep in mind that cats and dogs are attracted by the ethylene glycol antifreeze, and are quite likely to drink any that is left in an uncovered container or in puddles on the ground. This will prove fatal in sufficient quantity. Always drain the coolant into a sealable container. Coolant should be reused unless it is contaminated or several years old.

2.0L Engine

1. Disconnect the negative battery cable. Remove the camshaft carrier cover.
2. Hold the valves in place with compressed air, using an air adapter in the spark plug hole.
3. Compress the valve springs using a valve spring compressor.
4. Remove rocker arms; keep them in order for reassembly.
5. Remove the lifters.
6. The installation is the reverse of the removal procedure. Soak the lifters in clean engine oil prior to installation.
7. Connect the negative battery cable and check the lifters for proper operation.

2.3L Engine

1. Disconnect the negative battery cable.
2. Remove the camshafts.
3. Remove the lifters from their bores.
4. The installation is the reverse of the removal procedure. Soak the lifters in clean engine oil prior to installation.
5. Connect the negative battery cable and check the lifters for proper operation.

2.5L Engine

1. Relieve the fuel system pressure.
2. Disconnect the negative battery cable.
3. Remove the valve cover and intake manifold.
5. Remove the side pushrod cover.

6. Loosen the rocker arms in pairs and rotate them in order to clear the pushrods.
7. Remove the pushrods, retainer and guide from each cylinder.
8. Remove the valve lifters.
9. The installation is the reverse of the removal procedure. Soak the lifters in clean engine oil prior to installation.
10. Connect the negative battery cable and check the lifters for proper operation.

3.0L and 3.3L Engines

1. Relieve the fuel system pressure.
2. Disconnect the negative battery terminal.
3. Disconnect and remove the fuel rail and the throttle body from the intake manifold.
4. Drain the cooling system.
5. Remove valve covers and the intake manifold.
6. Remove the rocker arms, pedestals and pushrods. Keep these components in order for accurate installation.
7. Remove the valve lifters.
8. The installation is the reverse of the removal procedure. Soak the lifters in clean engine oil prior to installation.
9. Connect the negative battery cable and check the lifters for proper operation.

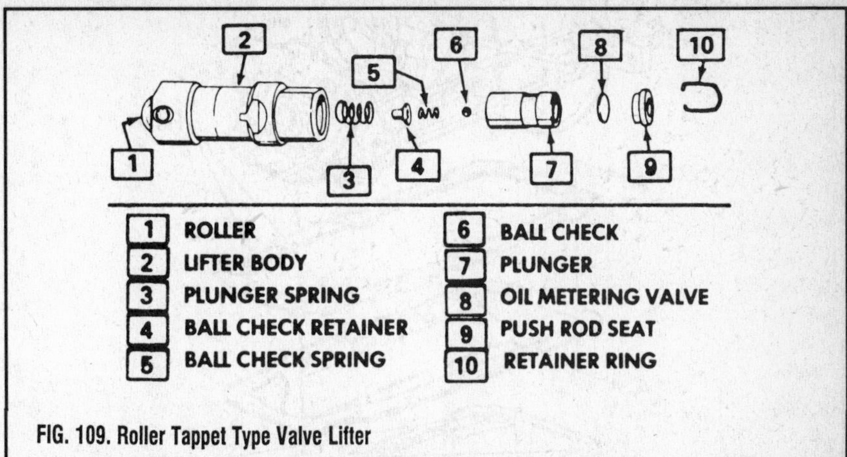

FIG. 109. Roller Tappet Type Valve Lifter

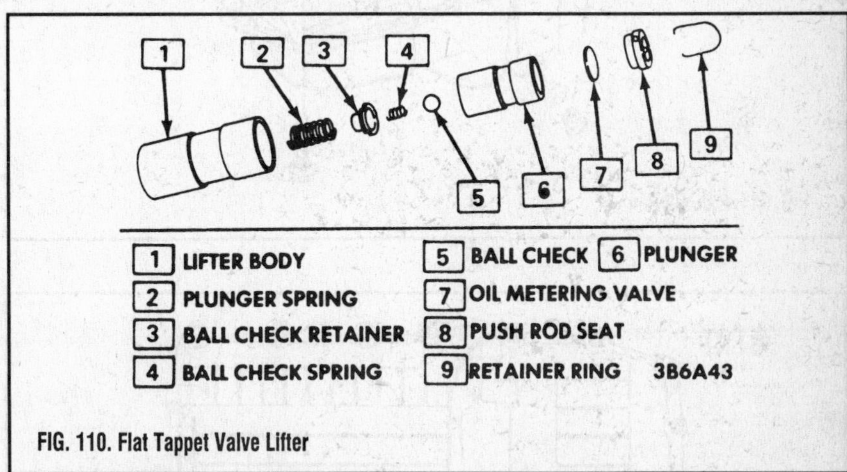

FIG. 110. Flat Tappet Valve Lifter

OVERHAUL

➧ SEE FIGS. 109–110

1. Remove the push rod seat retainer by holding the plunger down and removing the retainer with a small screwdriver.
2. Remove the push rod seat and the metering valve.
3. Remove the plunger. If plunger is stuck, tap the lifter upside down on a flat surface, if still stuck, soak in parts cleaning solvent.
4. Remove the ball check valve assembly.
5. Remove the plunger spring.
6. Clean lifter of all sludge and varnish build-up.
7. Inspect for excessive wear and scuffing. Replace if excessively worn or scuffed.
8. Inspect for flat spots on the bottom. If worn flat, replace the lifter.
9. If equipped with roller, inspect for freedom of movement, looseness, flat spots or pitting. If any detected, replace the lifter.
10. Install the check ball to the small hole in the bottom of the plunger.
11. Place ball retainer and spring over check ball and press into place using a small screwdriver.
12. Install the plunger spring over the ball retainer.
13. Install the lifter body over the spring and plunger. Make sure the oil holes in the lifter body and in the plunger line up.
14. Using a $^{1}/_{8}$ in. (3mm) drift pin, push the plunger down until the oil holes in the lifter body and plunger are aligned.
15. Insert a $^{1}/_{16}$ in. (1.6mm) pin through the oil holes to lock the plunger down.
16. Remove the $^{1}/_{8}$ in. (3mm) pin and fill the lifter with engine oil.
17. Install the metering valve, push rod seat and push rod seat retainer.
18. Push down on the push rod seat to relieve the spring pressure and remove the $^{1}/_{16}$ in. (1.6mm) pin.

Oil Pan

REMOVAL & INSTALLATION

➧ SEE FIGS. 111–114

2.0L Engine

1. Disconnect the negative battery cable.
2. Raise and safely support the vehicle. Remove the right front wheel assembly and the splash shield.
3. Drain the engine oil.
4. Remove the exhaust pipe from the turbocharger.
5. Remove the flywheel inspection cover.
6. Remove the oil pan attaching bolts and remove the oil pan, scraper and gasket.
7. The installation is the reverse of the removal procedure. Use a new gasket and apply sealant at the 4 engine block seams. Use thread locking compound on the bolt threads and tighten to 4 ft. lbs. (6 Nm), starting from the middle and working outward.
8. Fill the crankcase with oil to specification.
9. Connect the negative battery cable and check for leaks.

2.3L Engine

1. Disconnect the negative battery cable. Raise and safely support the vehicle.
2. Remove the flywheel inspection cover.
3. Remove the splash shield-to-suspension support bolt. Remove the exhaust manifold brace, if equipped.

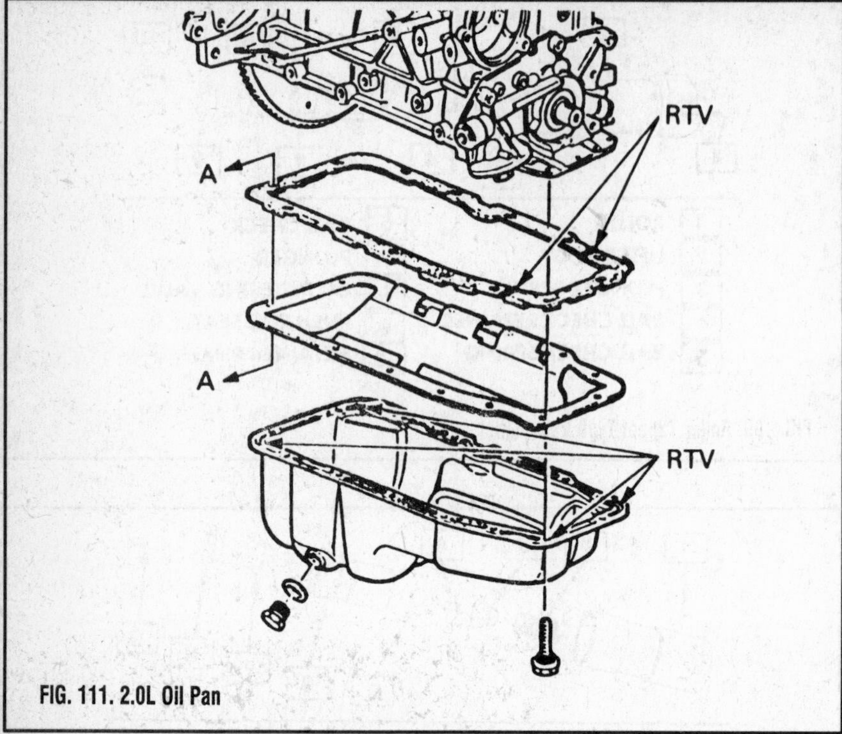

FIG. 111. 2.0L Oil Pan

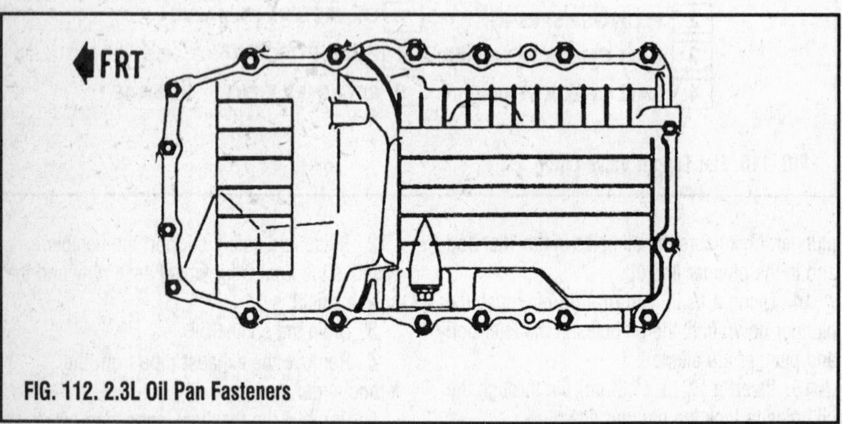

FIG. 112. 2.3L Oil Pan Fasteners

4. Remove the radiator outlet pipe-to-oil pan bolt.

5. Remove the transaxle-to-oil pan nut and stud using a 7mm socket.

6. Gently pry the spacer out from between oil pan and transaxle.

7. Remove the oil pan bolts. Rotate the crankshaft, if necessary, and remove the oil pan and gasket from the engine.

8. Inspect the silicone strips across the top of the aluminum carrier at the oil pan-cylinder block-seal housing 3-way joint. If damaged, these strips must be repaired with silicone sealer. Use only enough sealer to restore the strips to their original dimension; too much sealer could cause leakage.

To install:

9. Thoroughly clean and dry the mating surfaces, bolts and bolt holes. Install the oil pan with a new gasket; do not uses sealer on the gasket. Loosely install the pan bolts.

10. Place the spacer in its approximate installed position but allow clearance to tighten the pan bolt above it.

11. Tighten the pan to block bolts to 17 ft. lbs. (24 Nm) and the remaining bolts to 106 inch lbs. (12 Nm).

12. Install the spacer and stud.

13. Install the oil pan transaxle nut and bolt.

14. Install the slash shield to suspension support.

15. Install the radiator outlet pipe bolt.

16. Install the exhaust manifold brace, if removed.

17. Install the flywheel inspection cover.

18. Fill the crankcase with the proper oil.

19. Connect the negative battery cable and check for leaks.

2.5L Engine

1. Disconnect the negative battery cable.

2. Raise and safely support the vehicle. Drain the engine oil.

3. Disconnect the exhaust pipe and hangers from the exhaust manifold and allow it to swing aside.

4. Disconnect electrical connectors from the starter. Remove the starter-to-engine bolts, the starter and the flywheel housing inspection cover from the engine.

5. Remove the oil pan-to-engine bolts and the oil pan.

To install:

6. Thoroughly clean the mating surfaces, bolts and bolt holes.

7. Apply sealant to the oil pan flange, surrounding all bolt holes. Also, apply sealant to the engine at the front and rear seams.

8. Install the oil pan and tighten the bolts to 20 ft. lbs. (27 Nm) for 1988 vehicles or 89 inch lbs. (10 Nm) for 1989–92 vehicles.

9. Install the flywheel housing cover and exhaust pipe.

10. Fill the crankcase with oil to specification.

11. Connect the negative battery cable and check for leaks.

3.0L and 3.3L Engines

1. Disconnect the negative battery cable.

2. Raise and safely support the vehicle.

3. Drain the engine oil and remove the oil filter.

4. Remove the flywheel cover and the starter.

5. Remove the oil pan, tensioner spring and formed rubber gasket.

6. The installation is the reverse of the removal procedure. Tighten the oil pan-to-engine bolts to 88 inch lbs. (10 Nm) for the 3.0L engine or 124 inch lbs. (14 Nm) for the 3.3L engine.

7. Fill the crankcase with the proper oil.

8. Connect the negative battery cable and check for leaks.

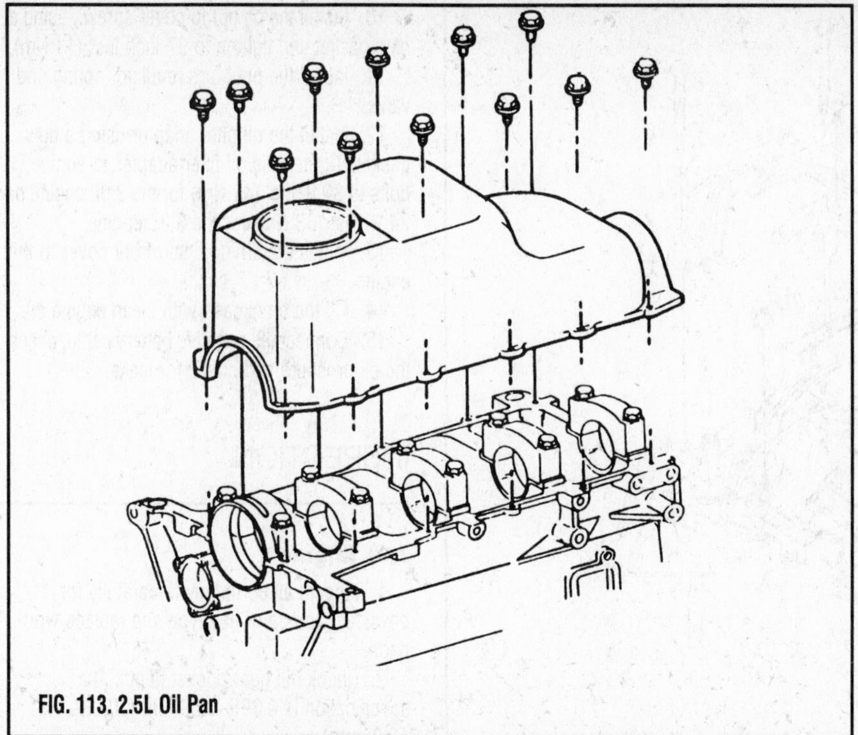
FIG. 113. 2.5L Oil Pan

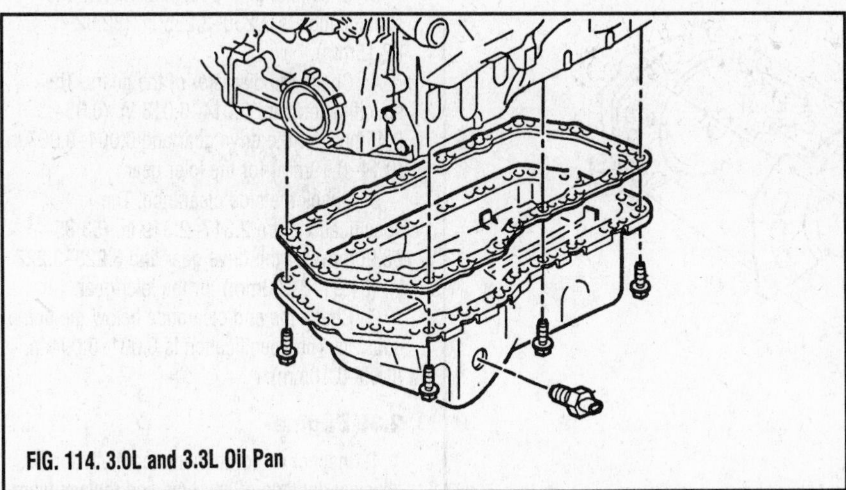
FIG. 114. 3.0L and 3.3L Oil Pan

Oil Pump

REMOVAL & INSTALLATION

➧ SEE FIGS. 115–119

2.0L Engine

1. Disconnect negative battery cable.
2. Remove the timing belt and crankshaft sprocket.
3. Remove the rear timing belt cover.
4. Disconnect oil pressure sending unit connector.
5. Raise and safely support the vehicle.
6. Drain the engine oil.
7. Remove the oil pan and oil filter.
8. Remove the oil pump mounting bolts and remove the pump and pickup tube.

To install:

9. Prime the pump by pouring fresh oil into the pump intake and turning the driveshaft until oil comes out the pressure port. Repeat a few times until no air bubbles are present.
10. The installation is the reverse of the removal procedure. Use a new gasket and seal and tighten the oil pump bolts to 5 ft. lbs. (7 Nm). Use a new ring for the pickup tube.
11. Fill the crankcase with the proper oil.
12. Connect the negative battery cable, check the oil pressure and check for leaks.

2.3L Engine

1. Disconnect the negative battery cable.
2. Raise and safely support the vehicle.
3. Drain the engine oil and remove the oil pan.
4. Remove the oil pump attaching bolts and nut.
5. Remove the oil pump assembly, shims if equipped, and screen.

To install:

6. With the oil pump assembly off the engine, remove 3 attaching bolts and separate the driven gear cover and screen assembly from the oil pump.
7. Install the oil pump on the block using the original shims, if equipped. Tighten the bolts to 33 ft. lbs. (45 Nm).
8. Mount a dial indicator assembly to measure backlash between oil pump to drive gear.
9. Record oil pump drive to driven gear backlash. Proper backlash is 0.010–0.018 in. (0.254–0.457mm). When measuring, do not allow the crankshaft to move.
10. If equipped with shims, remove shims to decrease clearance and add shims to increase clearance. If no shims were present, replace the assembly if proper backlash cannot be obtained.
11. When the proper clearance is reached, rotate crankshaft 1/2 turn and recheck clearance.
12. Remove oil pump from block, fill the cavity with petroleum jelly and reinstall driven gear cover and screen assembly to pump. Tighten the bolts to 106 inch lbs. (13 Nm).
13. Reinstall the pump assembly to the block. Tighten oil pump-to-block bolts 33 ft. lbs. (45 Nm).
14. Install the oil pan.
15. Fill the crankcase with the proper oil.
16. Connect the negative battery cable, check the oil pressure and check for leaks.

2.5L Engine

1. Disconnect the negative battery cable.
2. Drain the engine oil and remove the oil pan.
3. Remove the oil filter.
4. Remove the oil pump cover assembly.
5. Remove the gerotor pump gears.

✻✻ CAUTION

The pressure regulator valve spring is under pressure. Exercise caution when removing the pin or personal injury may result!

6. Remove the pressure regulator pin, spring and valve.

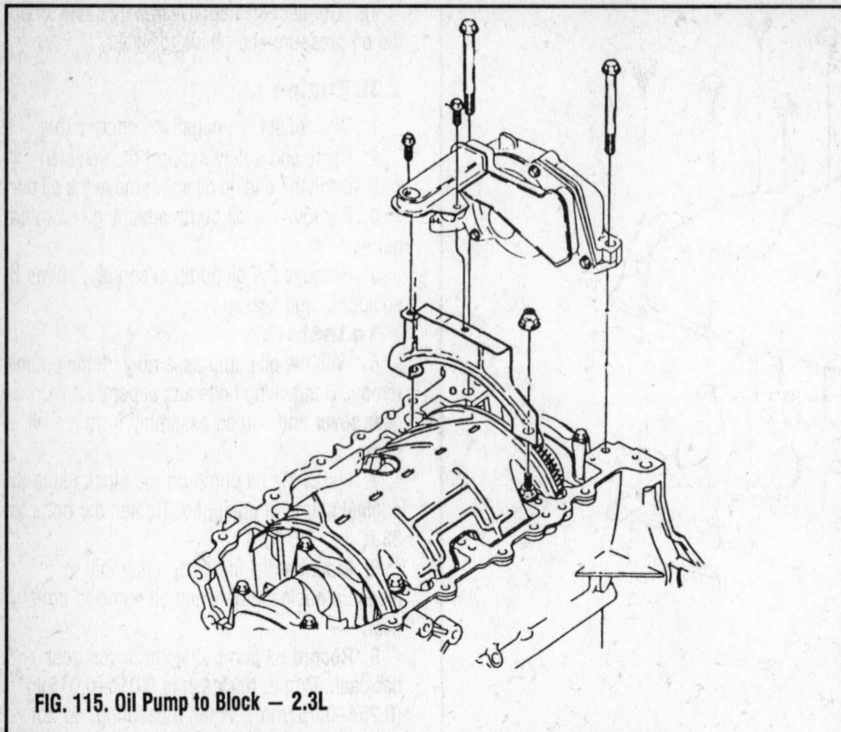
FIG. 115. Oil Pump to Block — 2.3L

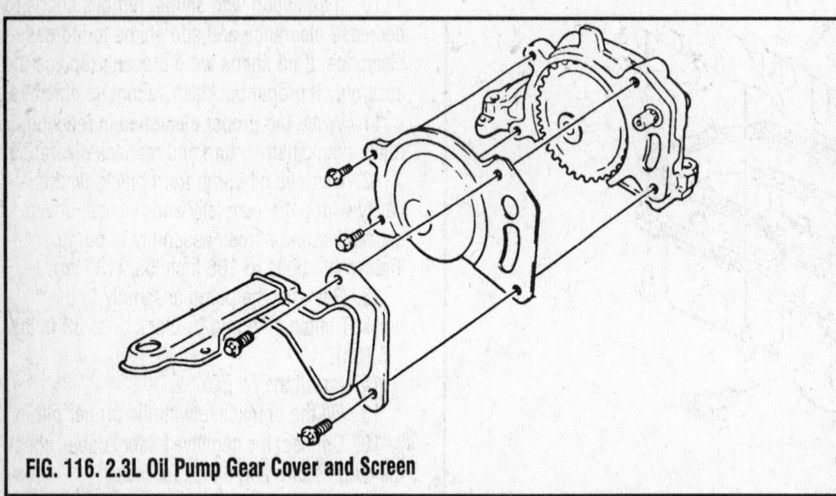
FIG. 116. 2.3L Oil Pump Gear Cover and Screen

To install:

7. Lubricate all internal parts with clean engine oil and fill all pump cavities with petroleum jelly.
8. Install the pressure regulator valve, spring and secure the pin.
9. Install the gerotor gears.
10. Install the pump cover and tighten the screws to 10 ft. lbs. (14 Nm).
11. Install the oil filter.
12. Install the oil pan.
13. Fill the crankcase with oil to specification.
14. Connect the negative battery cable, check the oil pressure and check for leaks.

3.0L and 3.3L Engines

1. Disconnect the negative battery cable.
2. Remove the timing chain front cover.
3. Raise and safely support the vehicle.
4. Drain the engine oil. Lower the vehicle.
5. Remove the oil filter adapter, the pressure regulator valve and the valve spring.
6. Remove the oil pump cover-to-oil pump screws and remove the cover.
7. Remove the oil pump gears.

To install:

8. Lubricate the oil pump gears with clean engine oil.
9. Pack the pump cavity with petroleum jelly.
10. Install the oil pump cover screws using a new gasket and tighten to 97 inch lbs. (11 Nm).
11. Install the pressure regulator spring and valve.
12. Install the oil filter adaptor using a new gasket. Tighten the oil filter adapter-to-engine bolts to 30 ft. lbs. (41 Nm) for the 3.0L engine or 24 ft. lbs. (33 Nm) for the 3.3L engine.
13. Install the timing chain front cover to the engine.
14. Fill the crankcase with clean engine oil.
15. Connect the negative battery cable, check the oil pressure and check for leaks.

INSPECTION

2.0L Engine

1. Inspect all components carefully for physical damage of any type and replace worn parts.
2. Check the gear pocket depth. The specification is 0.395–0.397 in. (10.03–10.08mm).
3. Check the gear pocket diameter. The specification is 3.230–3.235 in. (82.02–82.15mm).
4. Check the diameter of the gears. The specifications are 0.014–0.018 in. (0.35–0.45mm) for the drive gear and 0.004–0.007 in. (0.11–0.19mm) for the idler gear.
5. Check the side clearance. The specifications are 2.317–2.319 in. (58.85–58.90mm) for the drive gear and 3.225–3.227 in. (81.91–81.96mm) for the idler gear.
6. Check the end clearance below the pump housing. The specification is 0.001–0.004 in. (0.03–0.10mm).

2.3L Engine

1. Inspect all components carefully for physical damage of any type and replace worn parts.
2. Check the gerotor cavity depth. The specification for 1988 is 0.689–0.691 in. (17.50–17.55mm). The specification for 1989–92 is 0.674–0.676 in. (17.11–17.16mm).
3. Check the gerotor cavity diameter. The specification for 1988 is 2.010–2.012 in. (51.054–51.104mm). The specification for 1989–92 is 2.127–2.129 in. (53.95–54.00mm).
4. Check the inner gerotor tip clearance. The maximum clearance is 0.006 in. (15mm).
5. Check the outer gerotor diameter clearance. The specification is 0.010–0.014 in. (0.254–0.354mm).

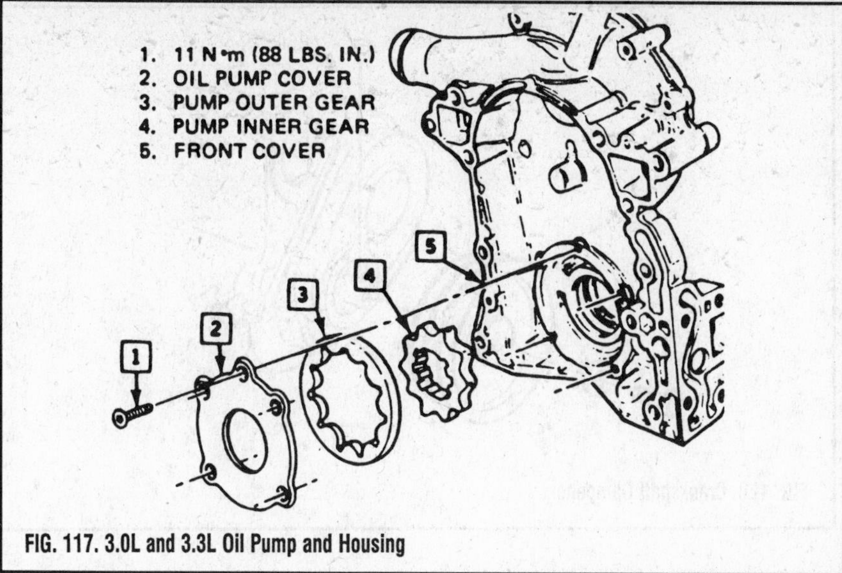

FIG. 117. 3.0L and 3.3L Oil Pump and Housing

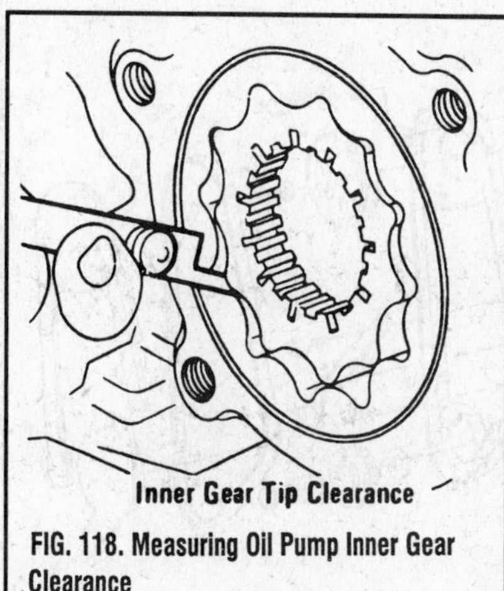

FIG. 118. Measuring Oil Pump Inner Gear Clearance

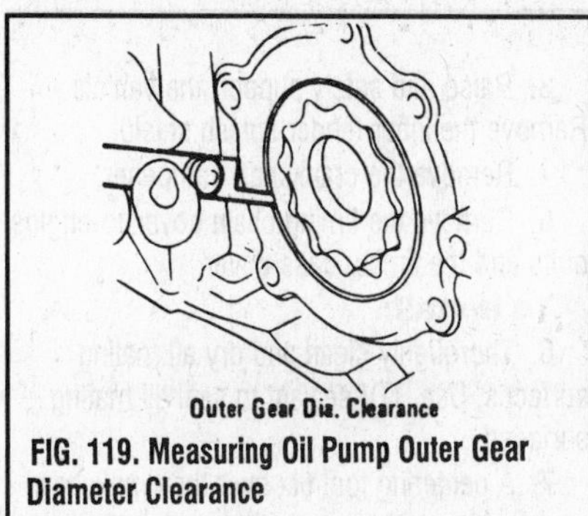

FIG. 119. Measuring Oil Pump Outer Gear Diameter Clearance

2.5L Engine

1. Inspect all components carefully for physical damage of any type and replace worn parts.
2. Check the gerotor cavity depth. The specification for 1988 is 0.995–0.998 in. (25.27–25.35mm). The specification for 1989–92 is 0.514–0.516 in. (13.05–13.10mm).
3. Check the gear lash. The specification is 0.009–0.015 in. (0.23–0.38mm).
4. Check the clearance of both gears. The maximum clearance is 0.004 in. (0.10mm).

3.0L and 3.3L Engines

1. Inspect all components carefully for physical damage of any type and replace worn parts.
2. Check the gear pocket depth. The specification is 0.461–0.463 in. (11.71–11.75mm).
3. Check the gear pocket diameter. The specification is 3.508–3.512 in. (89.10–89.20mm).
4. Check the inner gear tip clearance. The maximum clearance is 0.006 in. (0.152mm).
5. Check the outer gear diameter clearance. The specification is 0.008–0.015 in. (0.025–0.089mm).

OVERHAUL

1. Remove the oil pan or front engine cover to gain access to the oil pump as previously described.
2. Remove the oil pump cover.
3. Remove the oil pump gears.
4. Remove the cotter pin or unscrew the plug from the pressure regulator valve bore and then remove the the spring and pressure regulator valve.

**** CAUTION**

The pressure regulator valve spring is under tension. Use extreme caution when removing the cotter pin or unscrewing the plug or bodily injury may result.

5. Soak all oil pump parts in carburetor cleaning solvent to remove sludge, oil and varnish build-up.
6. Check the pump housing for cracks, scoring, damaged threads or casting flaws.
7. Check the oil pump gears for chipping, galling or wear and replace if necessary.
8. Install the gears to the oil pump housing and check clearances.
9. Lubricate all oil pump parts with clean engine oil and pack all oil pump cavities with petroleum jelly before final assembly to insure oil pump priming.
10. Install oil pump cover and screws. Torque screws to 97 inch lbs.
11. Install pressure regulator spring and valve.
12. Install oil filter adapter with new gasket and install front engine cover.

Crankshaft Dampener

REMOVAL & INSTALLATION

➧ SEE FIG. 120

1. Properly raise and support the vehicle.
2. Remove the crankshaft dampener bolt and washer.
3. Remove the dampener and key.
4. Installation is the reverse of the removal procedure.
5. Tighten the dampener bolt to proper torque specifications.

Timing Belt Front Cover

REMOVAL & INSTALLATION

➧ SEE FIG. 121

2.0L Engine

1. Disconnect negative battery cable.

2. Remove tensioner and bolt.
3. Remove serpentine belt.
4. Unsnap upper and lower cover.
5. The installation is the reverse of the removal procedure.

Oil Seal Replacement

1. Disconnect the negative battery cable.
2. Remove the timing belt sprockets and the inner cover. Remove the crankshaft key and thrust washer.
3. Using a small prybar, pry out the old oil seal.

➡ Use care to avoid damage to seal bore and crankshaft.

4. Thoroughly clean and dry the oil seal mounting surface.
5. Use the appropriate installation tool and drive the oil seal into the front cover.
6. The installation is the reverse of the removal procedure.
7. Connect the negative battery cable and check for leaks.

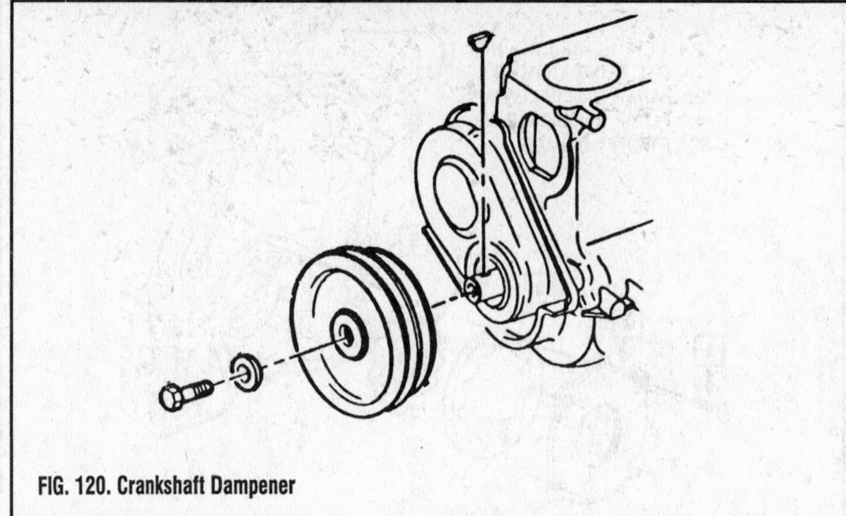

FIG. 120. Crankshaft Dampener

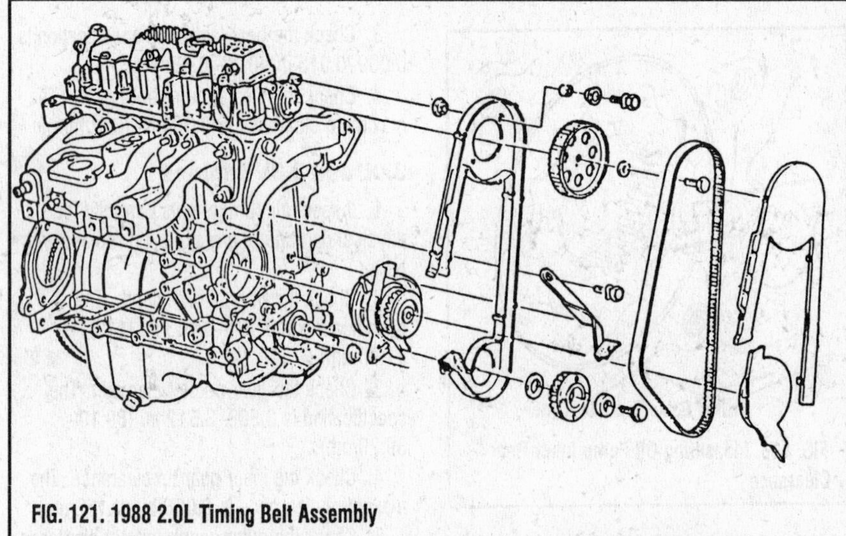

FIG. 121. 1988 2.0L Timing Belt Assembly

Timing Chain Front Cover

REMOVAL & INSTALLATION

➧ SEE FIGS. 122–123

✲✲ CAUTION

When draining the coolant, keep in mind that cats and dogs are attracted by the ethylene glycol antifreeze, and are quite likely to drink any that is left in an uncovered container or in puddles on the ground. This will prove fatal in sufficient quantity. Always drain the coolant into a sealable container. Coolant should be reused unless it is contaminated or several years old.

2.3L Engine

1. Disconnect the negative battery cable. Remove the coolant recovery reservoir.
2. Remove the serpentine drive belt using a 13mm wrench that is at least 24 in. (61cm) long.
3. Remove upper cover fasteners.
4. Raise and safely support the vehicle.
5. Remove the right front wheel assembly and lower splash shield.
6. Remove the crankshaft balancer assembly.

➡ Do not install an automatic transaxle-equipped engine balancer on a manual-transaxle equipped engine or vice-versa.

7. Remove lower cover fasteners and lower the vehicle.
8. Remove the front cover.
9. The installation is the reverse of the removal procedure. Tighten the balancer attaching bolt to 74 ft. lbs. (100 Nm).

1990–92 2.5L ENGINE

1. Disconnect the negative battery cable.
2. Remove the belts. Remove the power steering pump mounting bolts and position it aside.
3. Raise and safely support the vehicle. Remove the inner fender splash shield.
4. Remove the crankshaft dampener.
5. Remove the timing chain cover-to-engine bolts and the timing case cover.

To install:

6. Thoroughly clean and dry all mating surfaces. Use RTV sealant to seal all mating surfaces.
7. A centering tool fits over the crankshaft seal and is used to correctly position the timing case cover during installation. Install the cover and partially tighten the 2 opposing timing case cover screws.
8. Tighten the remaining cover screws and remove the centering tool from the timing case cover. Tighten to 89 inch lbs. (10 Nm).
9. Install the harmonic balancer and tighten the bolt to 162 ft. lbs. (220 Nm). Install the belts and the power steering pump.

10. Install the splash shield.
11. Connect the negative battery cable and check for leaks.

3.0L and 3.3L Engines

1. Disconnect the negative battery cable.
2. Drain the coolant and the engine oil. Remove the oil filter.
3. Loosen the water pump pulley bolts but do not remove them. Remove the serpentine drive belt and the pulley. Remove the water pump-to-engine bolts and the water pump.
4. Raise and safely support the vehicle. Remove the right front wheel assembly and the right inner fender splash shield.
5. Remove the crankshaft harmonic balancer and the crankshaft sensor.
6. Remove the radiator and heater hoses.
7. Remove the timing case cover-to-engine bolts, the timing case cover and the gasket.
8. Clean the gasket mounting surfaces. Replace the front oil seal.
9. The installation is the reverse of the removal procedure. Coat all timing case cover bolts with thread sealer prior to installation.
10. Fill all fluids to their proper levels.
11. Connect the negative battery cable and check for leaks.

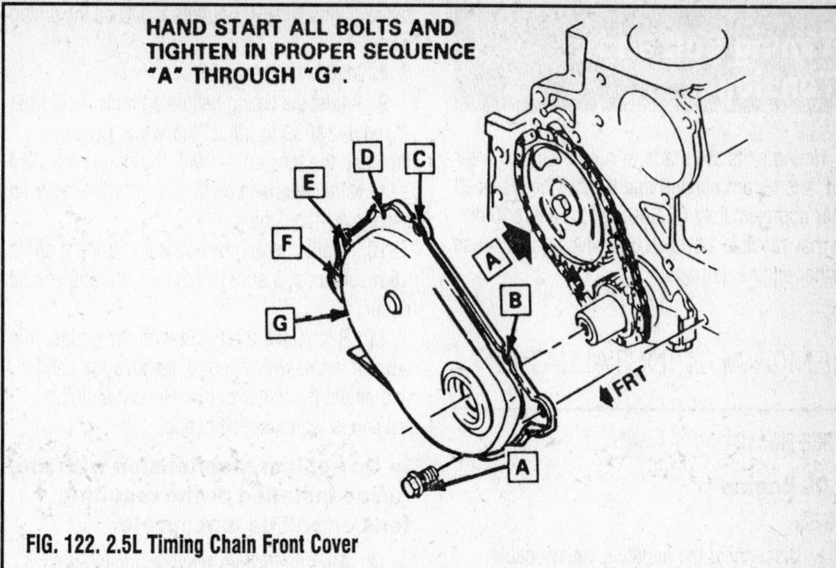

FIG. 122. 2.5L Timing Chain Front Cover

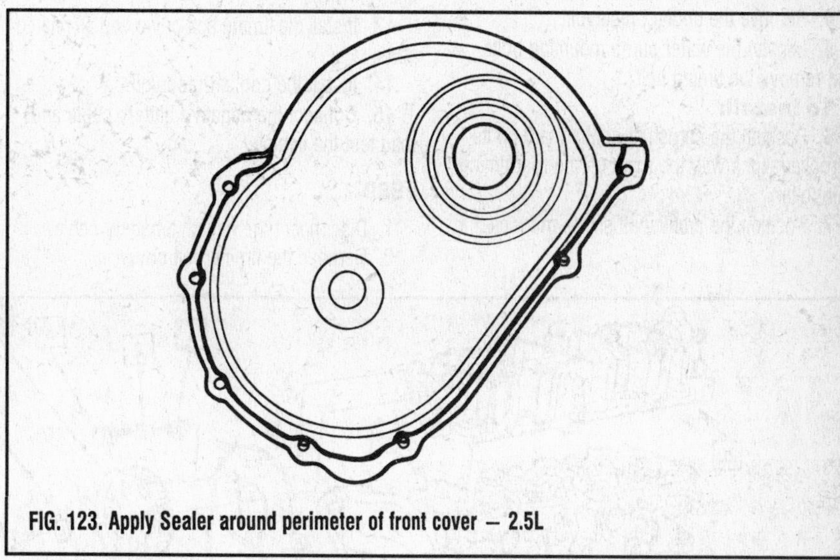
FIG. 123. Apply Sealer around perimeter of front cover – 2.5L

Timing Gear Front Cover

REMOVAL & INSTALLATION

1988–89 2.5L ENGINE

1. Disconnect the negative battery cable.
2. Remove the belts.
3. Raise and safely support the vehicle. Remove the inner fender splash shield.
4. Remove the harmonic balancer.
5. Remove the cover-to-engine bolts and the timing cover.

To install:

6. Thoroughly clean and dry all mating surfaces. Use RTV sealant to seal all mating surfaces.
7. A centering tool fits over the crankshaft seal and is used to correctly position the timing case cover during installation. Install the cover and partially tighten the 2 opposing timing case cover screws.
8. Tighten the remaining cover screws and remove the centering tool from the timing case cover. Final torque of all screws should be 89 inch lbs. (10 Nm).
9. Install the harmonic balancer and tighten the bolt to 162 ft. lbs. (220 Nm). Install the belts and the power steering pump.
10. Install the splash shield.
11. Connect the negative battery cable and check for leaks.

Front Cover Oil Seal

REPLACEMENT

1. Disconnect the negative battery cable.
2. Remove the front cover.
3. Using a small prybar, pry out the old oil seal.

➡ **Use care to avoid damage to seal bore or seal contact surfaces.**

4. Thoroughly clean and dry the oil seal mounting surface.
5. Use the appropriate installation tool and drive the oil seal into the front cover.
6. Lubricate balancer and seal lip with clean engine oil.
7. The installation is the reverse of the removal procedure.
8. Connect the negative battery cable and check for leaks.

Timing Belt and Tensioner

Timing belts are made of rubber and do wear out. It is recommended that the belt be replaced after approximately 60,000 miles. Failure to do so may result in a broken belt which could cause further engine damage.

REMOVAL & INSTALLATION

➧ SEE FIG. 124

2.0L Engine

1988

1. Disconnect the negative battery cable.
2. Remove the timing belt cover.
3. Remove the crankshaft pulley.
4. Remove the coolant reservoir.
5. Loosen the water pump mounting bolts and remove the timing belt.

To install:

6. Position the camshaft so the mark on its sprocket aligns with the mark on the rear timing belt cover.
7. Position the crankshaft so the mark on the pulley aligns with 10 degrees BTDC on the timing scale.
8. Install the timing belt.
9. Adjust the timing belt using tools J–26486–A and J–33039 to adjust the water pump. Increase the tension — with the gauge installed — to within the band on the gauge will ensure an initial over-tensioning.
10. Crank the engine without starting it about 10 revolutions; a substantial tension loss should occur.
11. Recheck the tension with the gauge. If a tension increase is needed, remove the gauge and adjust the water pump. Repeat until the tension is within specification.

➡ Do not increase tension with the gauge installed or the resulting tension will be inaccurate.

12. After the proper tension has been reached, tighten the water pump bolts to 19 ft. lbs. (25 Nm).
13. Install the timing belt cover and all related parts.
14. Install the coolant reservoir.
15. Connect the negative battery cable and road test the vehicle.

1989

1. Disconnect the negative battery cable.
2. Remove the timing belt cover.
3. Remove the crankshaft pulley.
4. Loosen the water pump mounting bolts and relieve the tension using tool J–33039.
5. Remove the timing belt.

To install:

6. Position the camshaft and crankshaft so the marks on their sprockets aligns with the marks on the rear cover.
7. Install the timing belt so the portion between the camshaft and crankshaft has no slack.
8. Adjust the timing belt using tool J–33039 to turn the water pump eccentric clockwise until the tensioner contacts the high torque stop. Temporarily tighten the water to prevent movement.
9. Turn the engine 2 revolutions to fully seat the belt into the gear teeth.
10. Turn the water pump eccentric counterclockwise until the hole in the tensioner arm is aligned with the hole in the base.
11. Tighten the water pump bolts to 19 ft. lbs. (25 Nm), making sure the tensioner hole remains aligned as in Step 10.
12. Install the timing belt cover and all related parts.
13. Install the crankshaft pulley.
14. Install the timing belt cover and all related parts.
15. Connect the negative battery cable and road test the vehicle.

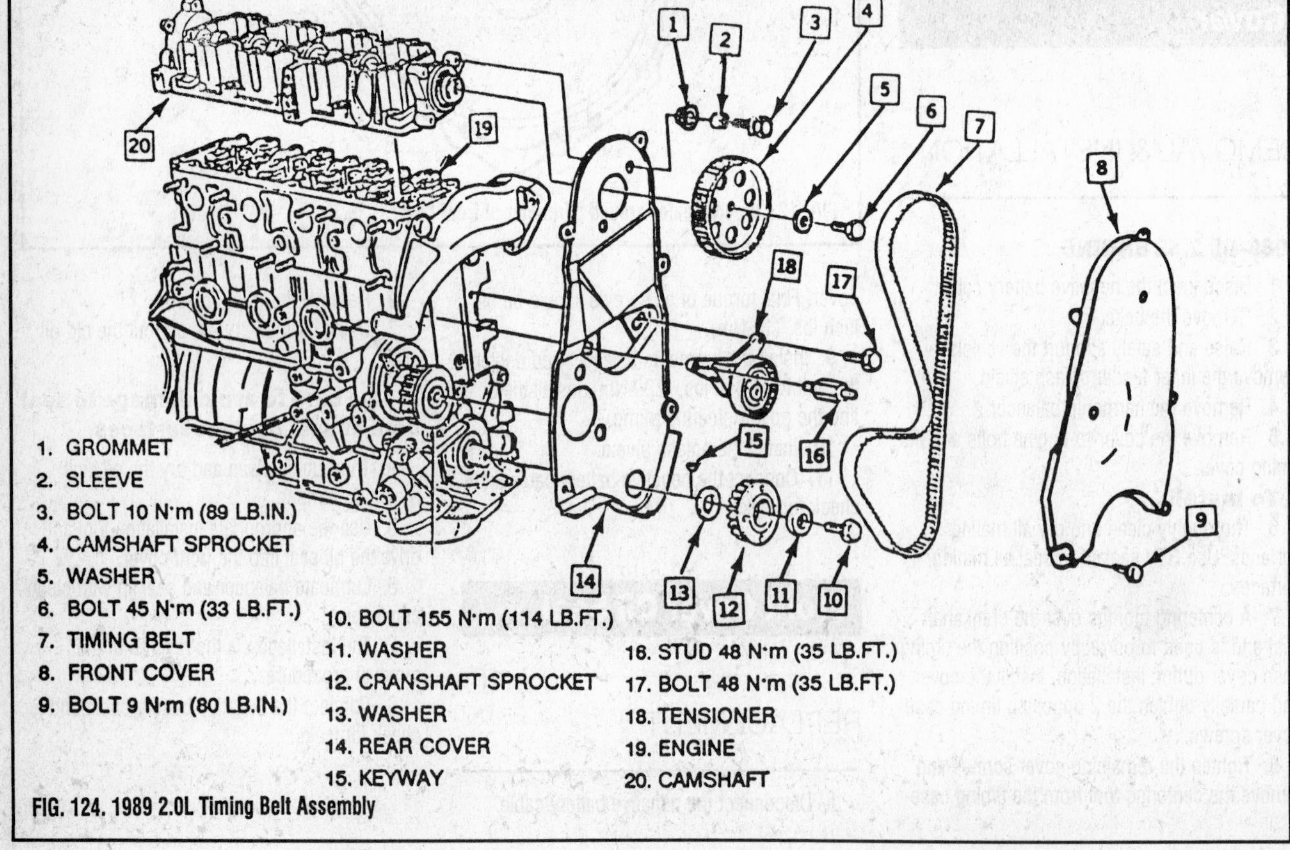

FIG. 124. 1989 2.0L Timing Belt Assembly

Timing Chain and Sprockets

REMOVAL & INSTALLATION

➧ SEE FIGS. 125–126

✻✻ CAUTION

When draining the coolant, keep in mind that cats and dogs are attracted by the ethylene glycol antifreeze, and are quite likely to drink any that is left in an uncovered container or in puddles on the ground. This will prove fatal in sufficient quantity. Always drain the coolant into a sealable container. Coolant should be reused unless it is contaminated or several years old.

2.3L Engine

➡ It is recommended that the entire procedure be reviewed before attempting to service the timing chain.

1. Disconnect the negative battery cable.
2. Remove the front timing chain cover and crankshaft oil slinger.
3. Rotate the crankshaft clockwise, as viewed from front of engine (normal rotation) until the camshaft sprocket's timing dowel pin holes align with the holes in the timing chain housing. The mark on the crankshaft sprocket should align with the mark on the cylinder block. The crankshaft sprocket keyway should point upwards and align with the centerline of the cylinder bores. This is the normal timed position.
4. Remove the 3 timing chain guides.
5. Raise and safely support the vehicle.
6. Gently pry off timing chain tensioner spring retainer and remove spring.

➡ Two styles of tensioner are used. Early production engines will have a spring post and late production ones will not. Both styles are identical in operation and are interchangeable.

7. Remove the timing chain tensioner shoe retainer.
8. Make sure all the slack in the timing chain is above the tensioner assembly; remove the chain tensioner shoe. The timing chain must be disengaged from the wear grooves in the tensioner shoe in order to remove the shoe. Slide a prybar under the timing chain while pulling shoe outward.

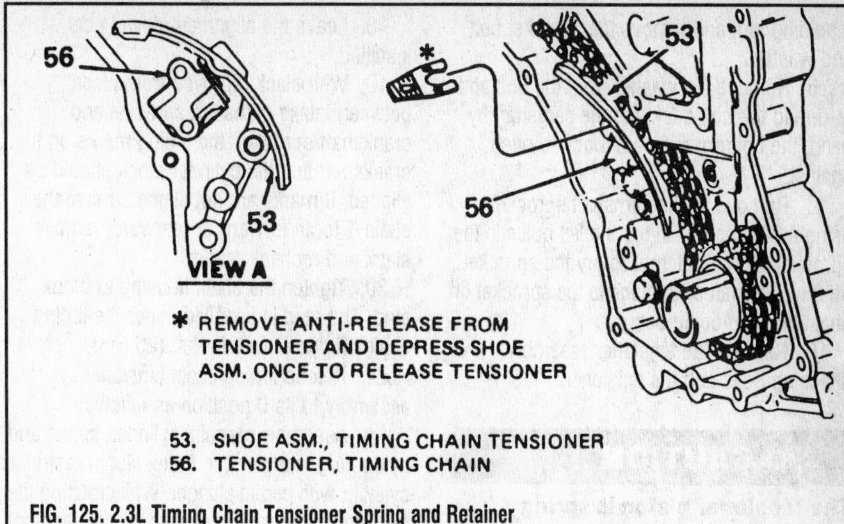

FIG. 125. 2.3L Timing Chain Tensioner Spring and Retainer

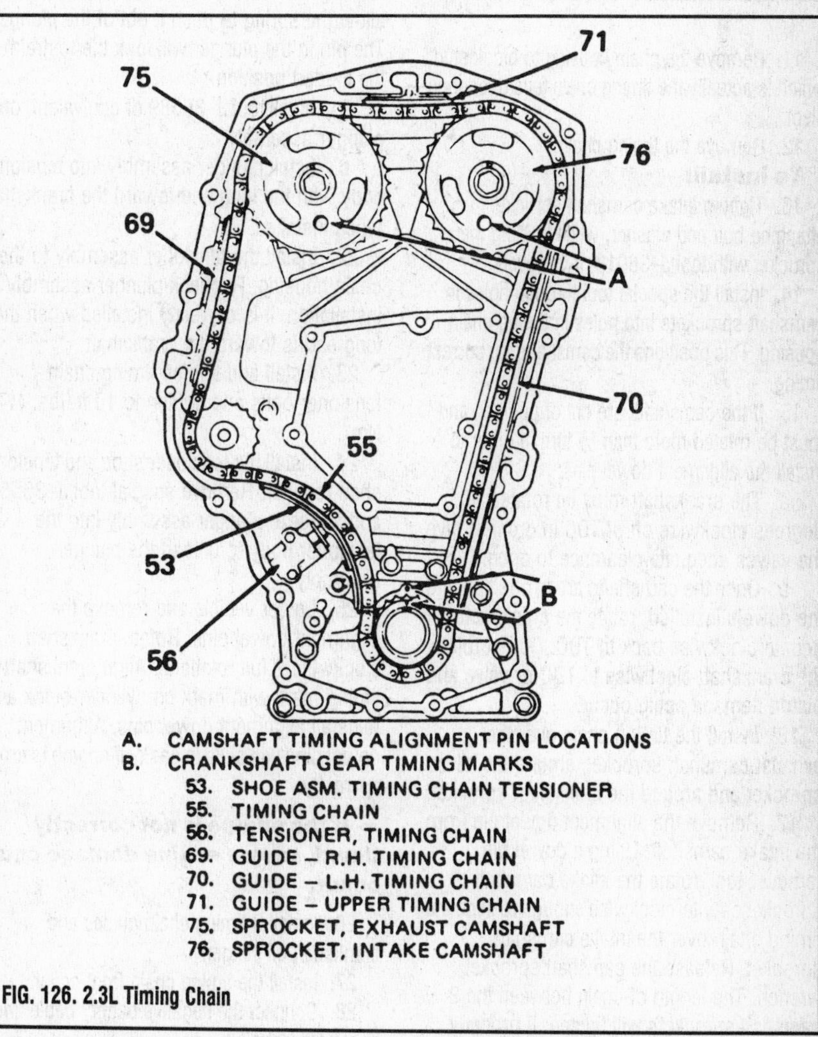

FIG. 126. 2.3L Timing Chain

9. If difficulty is encountered removing chain tensioner shoe, proceed as follows:
   a. Lower the vehicle.
   b. Hold the intake camshaft sprocket with

a holding tool and remove the sprocket bolt and washer.

c. Remove the washer from the bolt and re-thread the bolt back into the camshaft by hand, the bolt provides a surface to push against.

d. Remove intake camshaft sprocket using a 3-jaw puller in the 3 relief holes in the sprocket. Do not attempt to pry the sprocket off the camshaft or damage to the sprocket or chain housing could occur.

10. Remove the tensioner assembly attaching bolts and the tensioner.

CAUTION

The tensioner piston is spring loaded and could fly out causing personal injury.

11. Remove the chain housing to block stud, which is actually the timing chain tensioner shoe pivot.

12. Remove the timing chain.

To install:

13. Tighten intake camshaft sprocket attaching bolt and washer, while holding the sprocket with tool J–36013, if removed.

14. Install the special tool through holes in camshaft sprockets into holes in timing chain housing. This positions the camshafts for correct timing.

15. If the camshafts are out of position and must be rotated more than $^1/_8$ turn in order to install the alignment dowel pins:

a. The crankshaft must be rotated 90 degrees clockwise off of TDC in order to give the valves adequate clearance to open.

b. Once the camshafts are in position and the dowels installed, rotate the crankshaft counterclockwise back to TDC. Do not rotate the crankshaft clockwise to TDC or valve and piston damage could occur.

16. Install the timing chain over the exhaust camshaft sprocket, around the idler sprocket and around the crankshaft sprocket.

17. Remove the alignment dowel pin from the intake camshaft. Using a dowel pin remover tool, rotate the intake camshaft sprocket counterclockwise enough to slide the timing chain over the intake camshaft sprocket. Release the camshaft sprocket wrench. The length of chain between the 2 camshaft sprockets will tighten. If properly timed, the intake camshaft alignment dowel pin should slide in easily. If the dowel pin does not fully index, the camshafts are not timed correctly and the procedure must be repeated.

18. Leave the alignment dowel pins installed.

19. With slack removed from chain between intake camshaft sprocket and crankshaft sprocket, the timing marks on the crankshaft and the cylinder block should be aligned. If marks are not aligned, move the chain 1 tooth forward or rearward, remove slack and recheck marks.

20. Tighten the chain housing to block stud. The stud is installed under the timing chain. Tighten to 19 ft. lbs. (26 Nm).

21. Reload timing chain tensioner assembly to its 0 position as follows:

a. Assemble restraint cylinder, spring and nylon plug into plunger. Index slot in restraint cylinder with peg in plunger. While rotating the restraint cylinder clockwise, push the restraint cylinder into the plunger until it bottoms. Keep rotating the restraint cylinder clockwise but allow the spring to push it out of the plunger. The pin in the plunger will lock the restraint in the loaded position.

b. Install tool J–36589 or equivalent, onto plunger assembly.

c. Install plunger assembly into tensioner body with the long end toward the crankshaft when installed.

22. Install the tensioner assembly to the chain housing. Recheck plunger assembly installation. It is correctly installed when the long end is toward the crankshaft.

23. Install and tighten timing chain tensioner bolts and tighten to 10 ft. lbs. (14 Nm).

24. Install the tensioner shoe and tensioner shoe retainer. Remove special tool J–36589 and squeeze plunger assembly into the tensioner body to unload the plunger assembly.

25. Lower vehicle and remove the alignment dowel pins. Rotate crankshaft clockwise 2 full rotations. Align crankshaft timing mark with mark on cylinder block and reinstall alignment dowel pins. Alignment dowel pins will slide in easily if engine is timed correctly.

➡ **If the engine is not correctly timed, severe engine damage could occur.**

26. Install 3 timing chain guides and crankshaft oil slinger.

27. Install the timing chain front cover.

28. Connect the negative battery cable and check for leaks.

3.0L, 3.3L AND 1990–92 2.5L ENGINES

1. Disconnect the negative battery cable.

2. Drain the cooling system. Disconnect the cooling hose from the water pump.

3. Raise and safely support the vehicle.

4. Remove the inner fender splash shield.

5. Remove the serpentine drive belt.

6. Remove the crankshaft pulley bolt and slide the pulley from the crankshaft.

7. Remove the front cover.

8. Rotate the crankshaft to align the timing marks on the sprockets. Remove the chain dampener assembly.

9. Remove the camshaft sprocket-to-camshaft bolt(s), remove the camshaft sprocket and chain and thrust bearing.

10. Remove the crankshaft gear by sliding it forward.

11. Clean the gasket mounting surfaces. Inspect the timing chain and the sprockets for damage and/or wear and replace damaged parts.

To install:

12. Position the crankshaft so the No. 1 piston is at TDC of its compression stroke. Install the thrust bearing on 2.5L engine.

13. Temporarily install the gear on the camshaft and position the camshaft so the timing mark on the gear is pointing straight down.

14. Assemble the timing chain to the gears so the timing marks are aligned, mark-to-mark.

15. Install the camshaft sprocket attaching bolt(s).

16. Install the camshaft thrust bearing, if not already done.

17. Install the timing chain dampener.

18. Install the front cover and all related parts.

19. Connect the negative battery cable and check for leaks.

Timing Gears

REMOVAL & INSTALLATION

1988–89 2.5L Engine

➡ **If the camshaft gear is to be replaced, the engine must be removed from the vehicle. The crankshaft gear may be replaced with the engine in the vehicle.**

1. Disconnect the negative battery cable.
2. Raise and safely support the vehicle.
3. Remove the inner fender splash shield.
4. Remove the accessory drive belts.

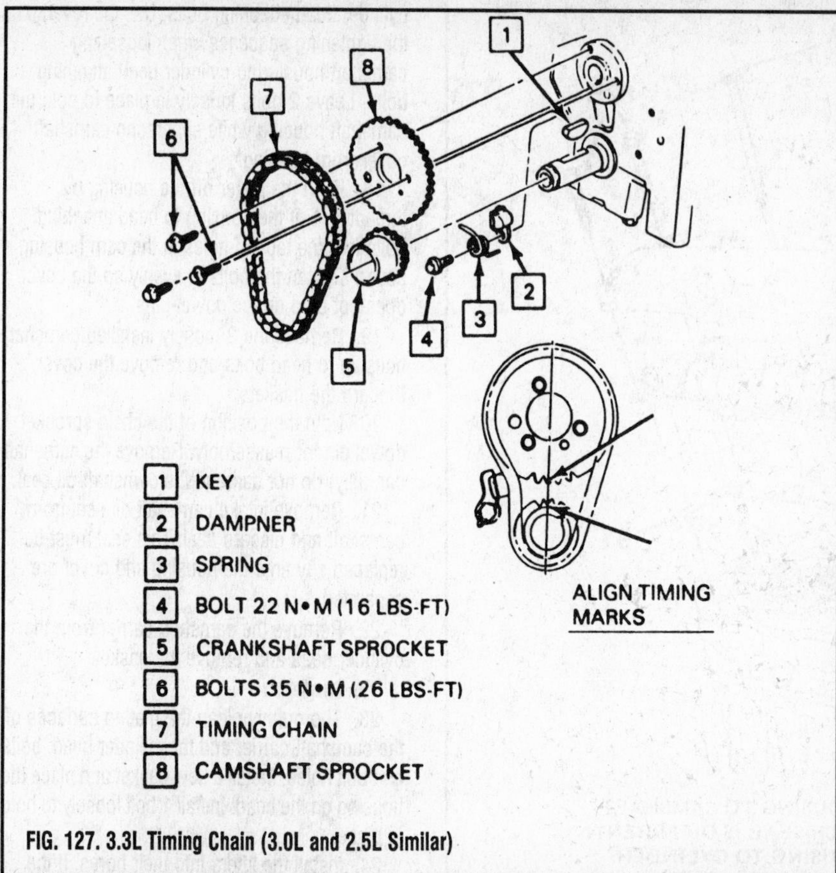

FIG. 127. 3.3L Timing Chain (3.0L and 2.5L Similar)

Remove the crankshaft pulley-to-crankshaft pulley bolt and slide the pulley from the crankshaft.

5. If replacing the camshaft gear, perform the following procedures:
   a. Remove the engine from the vehicle and secure it onto a suitable holding fixture.
   b. Remove the camshaft from the engine.
   c. Using an arbor press, press the camshaft gear from the camshaft.
   d. To install the camshaft gear onto the camshaft, press the gear onto the shaft until a thrust clearance of 0.0015–0.0050 in. (0.0381–0.127mm) exists.
6. If removing the crankshaft gear, perform the following procedures:
   a. Remove the front cover-to-engine bolts.
   b. Remove the attaching bolt and slide the crankshaft gear forward off the crankshaft.
7. Clean the gasket mounting surfaces. Inspect the parts for damage and/or wear and replace damaged parts.
8. The installation is the reverse of the removal procedure. Make sure the timing marks are aligned mark-to-mark when installing.

Timing Sprockets

REMOVAL & INSTALLATION

1. Disconnect the negative battery cable.
2. If removing the camshaft sprocket, remove the camshaft carrier cover.
3. Remove the timing belt cover.
4. Position the engine so the timing marks are aligned for belt installation.
5. Remove the timing belt.
6. If removing the camshaft sprocket, hold the camshaft with an open-end wrench.
7. Remove the camshaft or crankshaft sprocket attaching bolt, washer and the sprocket.
8. The installation is the reverse of the removal procedure. Tighten the camshaft sprocket bolt to 34 ft. lbs. (45 Nm). Tighten the crankshaft sprocket bolt to 114 ft. lbs. (155 Nm).
9. Connect the negative battery cable and road test the vehicle.

Camshaft

REMOVAL & INSTALLATION

➧ SEE FIG. 128

2.0L Engine

1. Relieve the fuel system pressure.
2. Disconnect the negative battery cable.
3. Remove the camshaft carrier cover.
4. Hold the valves in place with compressed air, using air adapters in the spark plug holes.
5. Compress the valve springs with the special valve spring compressing tool.
6. Remove the rocker arms and lifters and keep them in order for reassembly. Hold the camshaft with an open-end wrench and remove the camshaft sprocket. Try to keep the valve timing by using a rubber cord, if possible. If the timing cannot be kept intact, the timing belt will have to be reset.
7. Matchmark and remove the distributor.
8. Remove the camshaft thrust plate from the rear of the carrier.
9. Remove the camshaft by sliding it toward the rear. Remove the front carrier seal.

To install:

10. Install a new carrier seal.
11. Thoroughly lubricate the camshaft and journals with clean oil and install the camshaft.
12. Install the rear thrust plate and tighten the bolts to 70 inch lbs. (8 Nm).
13. Install camshaft sprocket, timing belt and cover.
14. Install the distributor.
15. Hold the valves in place with compressed air as in Step 4, compress the valve springs and install the lifters and rocker arms.
16. Apply sealer to the camshaft carrier cover and install.
17. Connect the negative battery cable and road test the vehicle.

2.3L Engine

INTAKE CAMSHAFT

➡ Any time the camshaft housing to cylinder head bolts are loosened or removed, the camshaft housing to cylinder head gasket must be replaced.

1. Relieve the fuel system pressure. Disconnect the negative battery cable.
2. Label and disconnect the ignition coil and module assembly electrical connections.

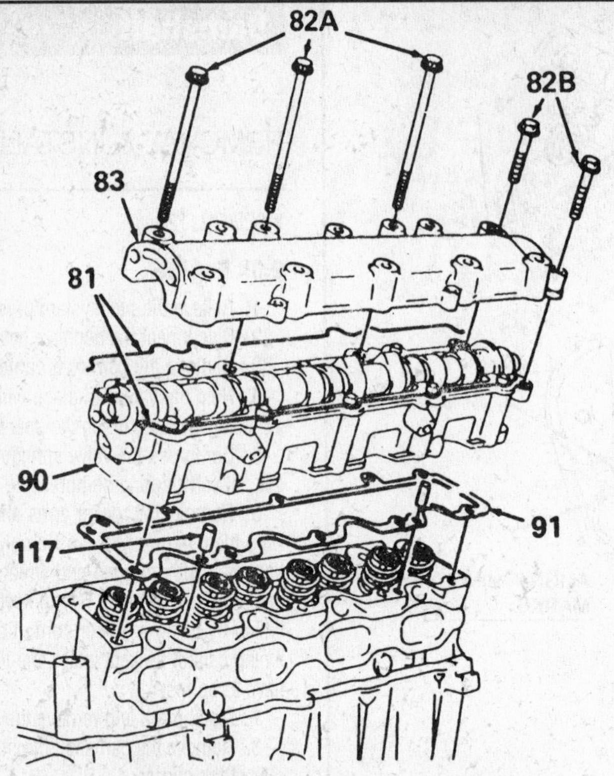

81. SEALS, CAMSHAFT HOUSING TO CAMSHAFT HOUSING COVER (EACH SEAL IS DIFFERENT)
82A. BOLT, CAMSHAFT HOUSING TO CYLINDER HEAD
82B. BOLT, CAMSHAFT HOUSING COVER TO CAMSHAFT HOUSING
83. COVER, CAMSHAFT
90. CAMSHAFT HOUSING (INTAKE SHOWN)
91. GASKET, CAMSHAFT HOUSING TO CYLINDER HEAD
117. DOWEL PIN (2)

FIG. 128. 2.3L Camshaft, Housing and Assembly

3. Remove 4 ignition coil and module assembly to camshaft housing bolts and remove assembly by pulling straight up. Use a special spark plug boot wire remover tool to remove connector assemblies, if they have stuck to the spark plugs.

4. Remove the idle speed power steering pressure switch connector.

5. Loosen 3 power steering pump pivot bolts and remove drive belt.

6. Disconnect the 2 rear power steering pump bracket to transaxle bolts.

7. Remove the front power steering pump bracket to cylinder block bolt.

8. Disconnect the power steering pump assembly and position aside.

9. Using the special tool, remove the power steering pump drive pulley from the intake camshaft.

10. Remove oil/air separator bolts and hoses. Leave the hoses attached to the separator, disconnect from the oil fill, chain housing and intake manifold. Remove as an assembly.

11. Remove vacuum line from fuel pressure regulator and disconnect the fuel injector harness connector.

12. Disconnect fuel line attaching clamp from bracket on top of intake camshaft housing.

13. Remove fuel rail to camshaft housing attaching bolts.

14. Remove the fuel rail from the cylinder head. Cover injector openings in cylinder head and cover injector nozzles. Leave fuel lines attached and position fuel rail aside.

15. Disconnect the timing chain and housing but do not remove from the engine.

16. Remove intake camshaft housing cover to camshaft housing attaching bolts.

17. Remove the intake camshaft housing to cylinder head attaching bolts. Use the reverse of the tightening sequence when loosening camshaft housing to cylinder head attaching bolts. Leave 2 bolts loosely in place to hold the camshaft housing while separating camshaft cover from housing.

18. Push the cover off the housing by threading 4 of the housing to head attaching bolts into the tapped holes in the cam housing cover. Tighten the bolts in evenly so the cover does not bind on the dowel pins.

19. Remove the 2 loosely installed camshaft housing to head bolts and remove the cover. Discard the gaskets.

20. Note the position of the chain sprocket dowel pin for reassembly. Remove the camshaft carefully; do not damage the camshaft oil seal.

21. Remove intake camshaft oil seal from camshaft and discard seal. This seal must be replaced any time the housing and cover are separated.

22. Remove the camshaft carrier from the cylinder head and remove the gasket.

To install:

23. Thoroughly clean the mating surfaces of the camshaft carrier and the cylinder head, bolts and bolt holes. Install a new gasket and place the housing on the head. Install 1 bolt loosely to hold in place.

24. Install the lifters into their bores. If the camshaft is being replaced, the lifters must also be replaced. Lubricate camshaft lobes, journals and lifters with camshaft and lifter prelube. The camshaft lobes and journals must be adequately lubricated or engine damage could occur upon start up.

25. Install the camshaft in the same position as when removed. The timing chain sprocket dowel pin should be straight up and align with the centerline of the lifter bores.

26. Install new camshaft housing to camshaft housing cover seals into cover; do not use sealer. Make sure the correct color seal is placed in each groove. Install the cover to the housing.

27. Apply thread locking compound to the camshaft housing and cover attaching bolt threads.

28. Install bolts and tighten to 11 ft. lbs. (15 Nm). Rotate the bolts, except the 2 rear bolts that hold the fuel pipe to the camshaft housing, an additional 75 degrees, in sequence. Tighten the excepted bolts to 16 ft. lbs. (15 Nm), then rotate an additional 25 degrees.

29. Install timing chain housing and timing chain.

30. Uncover fuel injectors and install new fuel injector O-ring seals lubricated with oil. Install the fuel rail.

31. Install the fuel line attaching clamp and retainer to bracket on top of the intake camshaft housing.

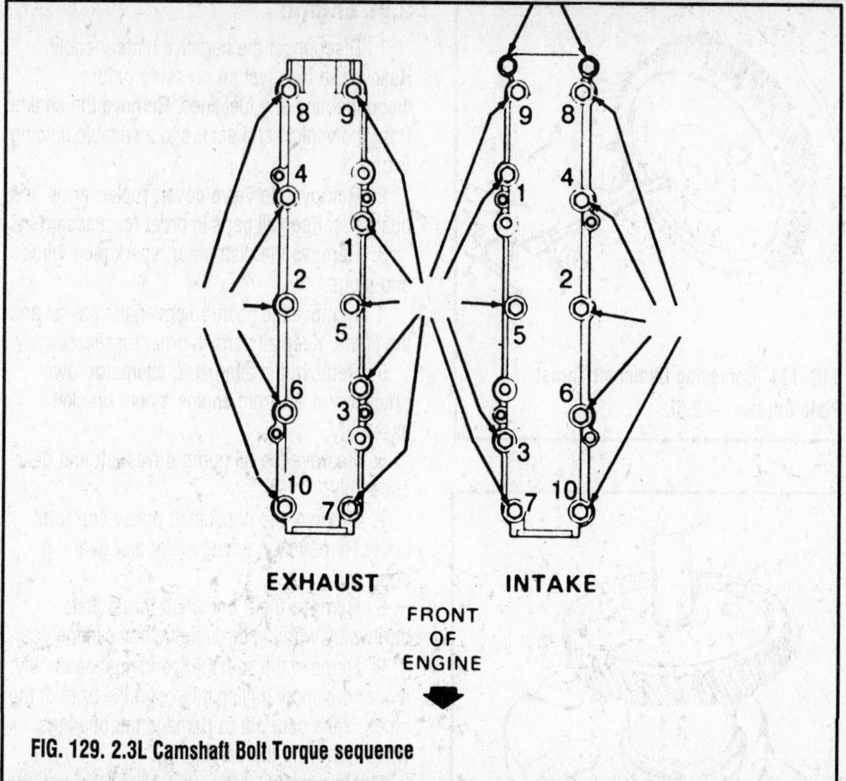

FIG. 129. 2.3L Camshaft Bolt Torque sequence

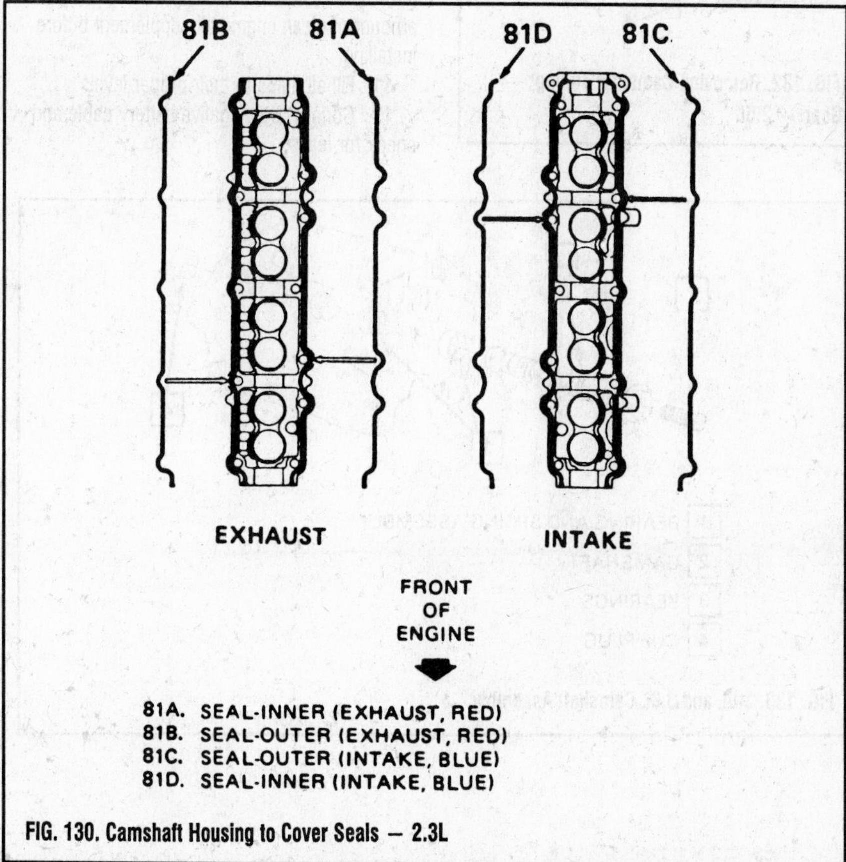

FIG. 130. Camshaft Housing to Cover Seals — 2.3L

32. Connect the vacuum line to the fuel pressure regulator.
33. Connect the fuel injectors harness connector.
34. Install the oil/air separator assembly.
35. Lubricate the inner sealing surface of the intake camshaft seal with oil and install the seal to the housing.
36. Install the power steering pump pulley onto the intake camshaft.
37. Install the power steering pump assembly and drive belt.
38. Connect the idle speed power steering pressure switch connector.
39. Clean any loose lubricant that is present on the ignition coil and module assembly to camshaft housing bolts. Apply Loctite® 592 or equivalent, onto the ignition coil and module assembly to camshaft housing bolts. Install the bolts and tighten to 13 ft. lbs. (18 Nm).
40. Connect the electrical connectors to ignition coil and module assembly.
41. Connect the negative battery cable and road test the vehicle. Check for leaks.

EXHAUST CAMSHAFT

➡ Any time the camshaft housing to cylinder head bolts are loosened or removed the camshaft housing to cylinder head gasket must be replaced.

1. Relieve the fuel system pressure. Disconnect the negative battery cable.
2. Label and disconnect the ignition coil and module assembly electrical connections.
3. Remove 4 ignition coil and module assembly to camshaft housing bolts and remove assembly by pulling straight up. Use a special tool to remove connector assemblies if they have stuck to the spark plugs.
4. Remove the idle speed power steering pressure switch connector.
5. Remove the transaxle fluid level indicator tube assembly from exhaust camshaft cover and position aside.
6. Remove exhaust camshaft cover and gasket.
7. Disconnect the timing chain and housing but do not remove from the engine.
8. Remove exhaust camshaft housing to cylinder head bolts. Use the reverse of the tightening procedure when loosening camshaft housing while separating camshaft cover from housing.
9. Push the cover off the housing by threading 4 of the housing to head attaching bolts into the tapped holes in the camshaft cover. Tighten the bolts in evenly so the cover does not bind on the dowel pins.

10. Remove the 2 loosely installed camshaft housing to cylinder head bolts and remove cover, discard gaskets.

11. Loosely reinstall 1 camshaft housing to cylinder head bolt to retain the housing during camshaft and lifter removal.

12. Note the position of the chain sprocket dowel pin for reassembly. Remove camshaft being careful not to damage the camshaft or journals.

13. Remove the camshaft carrier from the cylinder head and remove the gasket.

To install:

14. Thoroughly clean the mating surfaces of the camshaft carrier and the cylinder head, bolts and bolt holes. Install a new gasket and place the housing on the head. Install 1 bolt loosely to hold in place.

15. Install the lifters into their bores. If the camshaft is being replaced, the lifters must also be replaced. Lubricate camshaft lobes, journals and lifters with camshaft and lifter prelube. The camshaft lobes and journals must be adequately lubricated or engine damage could occur upon start up.

16. Install camshaft in same position as when removed. The timing chain sprocket dowel pin should be straight up and align with the centerline of the lifter bores.

17. Install new camshaft housing to camshaft housing cover seals into cover; do not use sealer. Make sure the correct color seal is placed in each groove. Install the cover to the housing.

18. Apply thread locking compound to the camshaft housing and cover attaching bolt threads.

19. Install bolts and tighten, in sequence, to 11 ft. lbs. (15 Nm). Then rotate the bolts an additional 75 degrees, in sequence.

20. Install timing chain housing and timing chain.

21. Install the transaxle fluid level indicator tube assembly to exhaust camshaft cover.

22. Connect the idle speed power steering pressure switch connector.

23. Clean any loose lubricant that is present on the ignition coil and module assembly to camshaft housing bolts. Apply Loctite® 592 or equivalent, onto the ignition coil and module assembly to camshaft housing bolts. Install the bolts and tighten to 13 ft. lbs. (18 Nm).

24. Connect the electrical connectors to ignition coil and module assembly.

25. Connect the negative battery cable and road test the vehicle. Check for leaks.

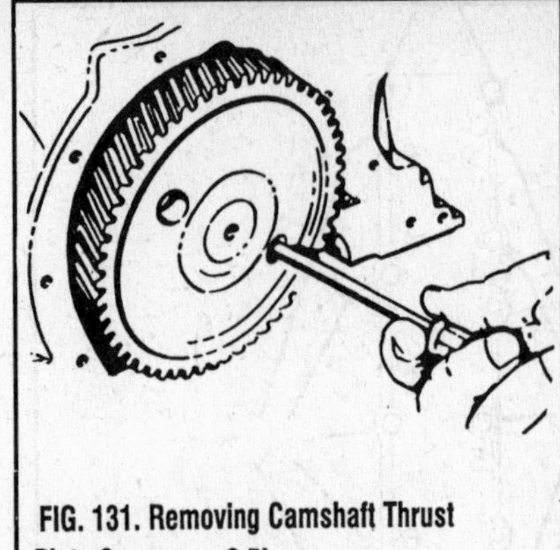

FIG. 131. Removing Camshaft Thrust Plate Screws – 2.5L

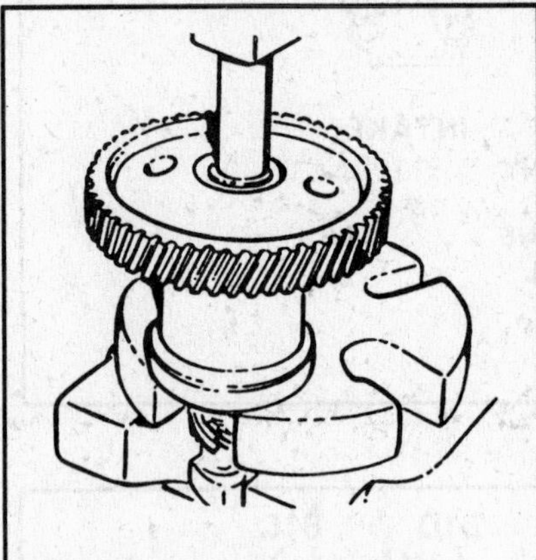

FIG. 132. Removing Camshaft Timing Gear – 2.5L

2.5L Engine

1. Disconnect the negative battery cable. Relieve the fuel system pressure before disconnecting any fuel lines. Remove the engine from the vehicle and secure to a suitable holding fixture.

2. Remove the valve cover, rocker arms and pushrods. Keep all parts in order for reassembly.

3. Remove the distributor, spark plug wires and plugs.

4. Remove the pushrod cover, the gasket and the lifters. Keep all parts in order for reassembly.

5. Remove the alternator, alternator lower bracket and the front engine mount bracket assembly.

6. Remove the oil pump driveshaft and gear assembly.

7. Remove the crankshaft pulley and front cover Remove the timing chain and gears, if equipped.

8. Remove the 2 camshaft thrust plate screws by working through the holes in the gear.

9. Remove the camshaft, and gear assembly, if gear driven by pulling it through the front of the block. Take care not to damage the bearings while removing the camshaft.

To install:

10. The installation is the reverse of the removal procedure. Coat all parts with a liberal amount of clean engine oil supplement before installing.

11. Fill all fluids to their proper levels.

12. Connect the negative battery cable and check for leaks.

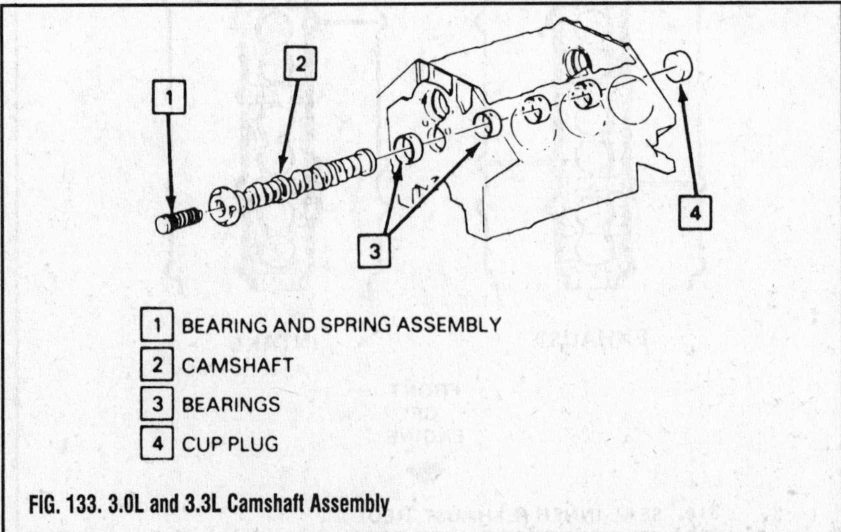

FIG. 133. 3.0L and 3.3L Camshaft Assembly

3.0L and 3.3L Engines

1. Disconnect the negative battery cable. Relieve the fuel system pressure before disconnecting any fuel lines. Remove the engine from the vehicle and secure to a suitable holding fixture.
2. Remove the intake manifold.
3. Remove the valve covers, rocker arm assemblies, pushrods and lifters. Keep all parts in order for reassembly.
4. Remove the crankshaft balancer from the crankshaft.
5. Remove the front cover.
6. Rotate the crankshaft to align the timing marks on the timing sprockets. Remove the camshaft sprocket and the timing chain.
7. Remove the camshaft retainer bolts and slide the camshaft forward out of the engine. Take care not to damage the bearings while removing the camshaft.

To install:

8. The installation is the reverse of the removal procedure. Coat all parts with a liberal amount of clean engine oil supplement before installing.
9. Fill all fluids to their proper levels.
10. Connect the negative battery cable and check for leaks.

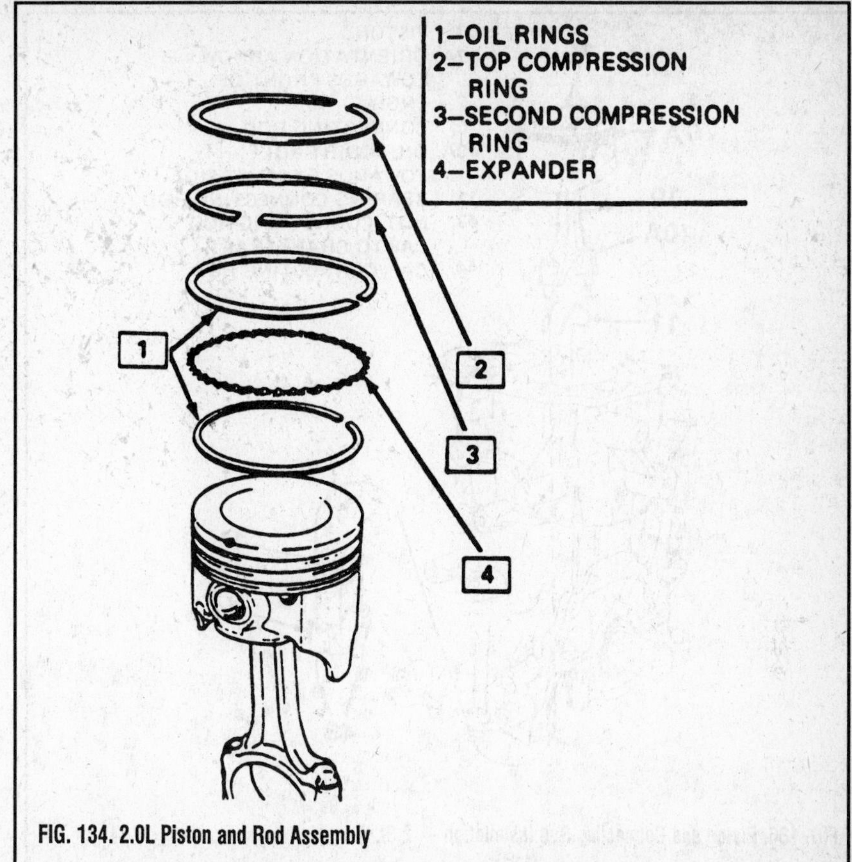

FIG. 134. 2.0L Piston and Rod Assembly

Pistons and Connecting Rods

REMOVAL

➧ SEE FIGS. 134–138

1. Disconnect the negative battery cable.
2. Remove the cylinder head and oil pan as previously described.
3. Mark the connecting rod and cap to ensure correct reassembly.
4. Remove the connecting rod bolts and cap.
5. Remove the piston and connecting rod assembly.

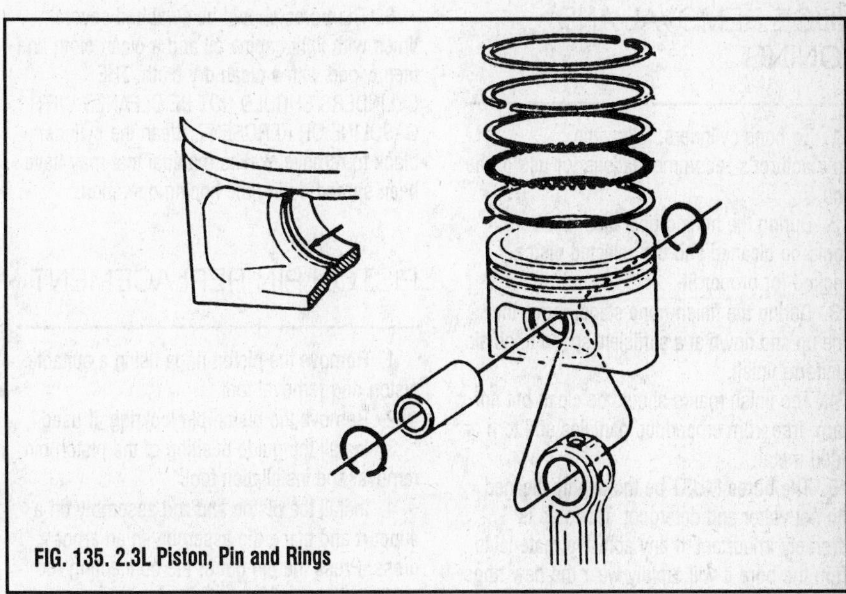
FIG. 135. 2.3L Piston, Pin and Rings

CLEANING AND INSPECTION

1. Inspect the piston for cracked ring lands, skirts or pin bosses.
2. Inspect for wavy or worn ring lands, scuffed or damaged skirts and for eroded areas at the top of the piston.
3. Replace the pistons if damaged or excessively worn.
4. Inspect the grooves for nicks or burrs that may interfere with the rings.
5. Measure the piston diameter and the cylinder bore diameter.
6. Subtract the piston diameter from the cylinder bore diameter to determine piston-to-bore clearance. Compare this with the recommended clearances.

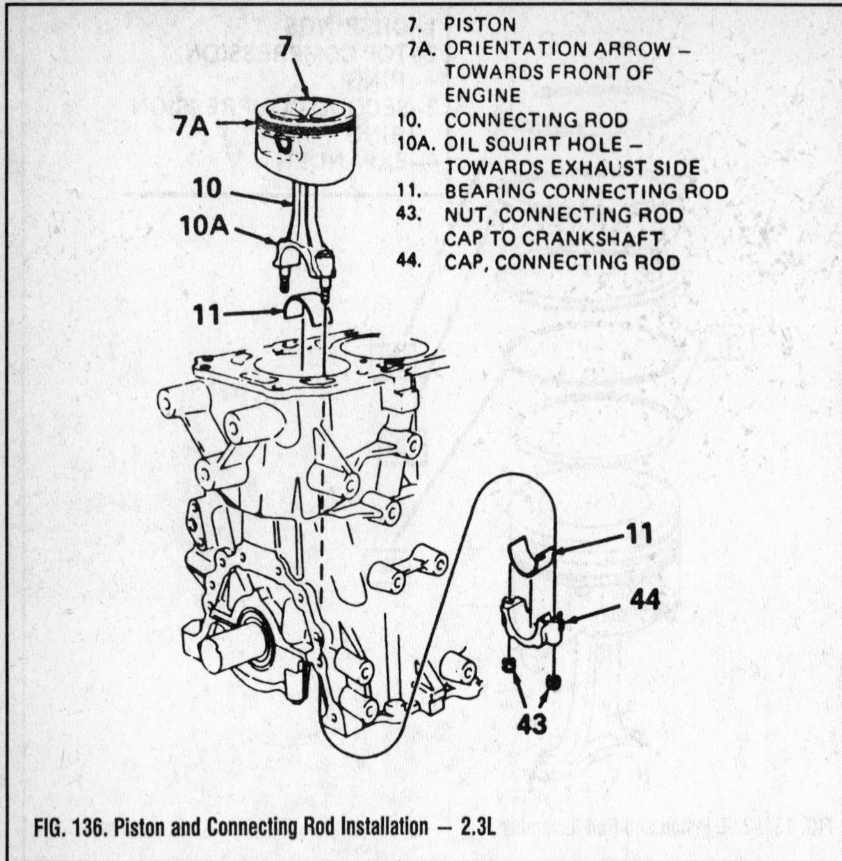

FIG. 136. Piston and Connecting Rod Installation – 2.3L

RIDGE REMOVAL AND HONING

1. To hone cylinders, follow the manufacturer's recommendations for use of the hone.
2. During the honing operation, the bore should be cleaned and the selected piston checked for proper fit.
3. During the finish-hone stage, move the hone up and down at a sufficient speed to obtain a uniform finish.
4. The finish marks should be clean but not sharp, free from empedded particles and torn or folded metal.
5. The bores MUST be thoroughly cleaned with hot water and detergent. This step is extremely important. If any abrasive material is left in the bore it will rapidly wear the new rings and the bores.
6. The bores should be swabbed several times with light engine oil and a clean cloth and then wiped with a clean dry cloth. THE CYLINDERS SHOULD NOT BE CLEANED WITH GASOLINE OR KEROSENE. Clean the cylinder block to remove excess material that may have been spread during the honing operation.

PISTON PIN REPLACEMENT

1. Remove the piston rings using a suitable piston ring removal tool.
2. Remove the piston pin lockring, if used.
3. Install the guide bushing of the piston pin removal and installation tool.
4. Install the piston and rod assembly on a support and place the assembly in an arbor press. Press the pin out of the connecting rod using the proper piston pin tool.
5. Assembly is the reverse of the removal procedure.

PISTON RING REPLACEMENT

1. Using a piston ring expander, install the lower oil control ring.
2. Install the upper oil control ring.
3. Making sure that the manufacturers marks are pointing upward, install the upper and lower compression rings.

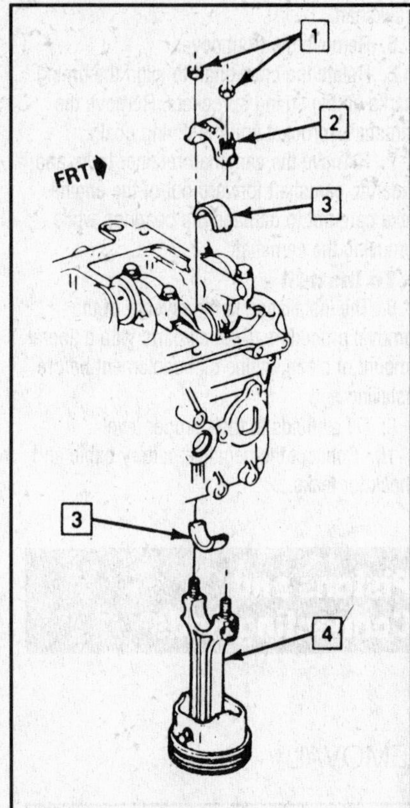

FIG. 137. Piston and Connecting Rod – 2.5L

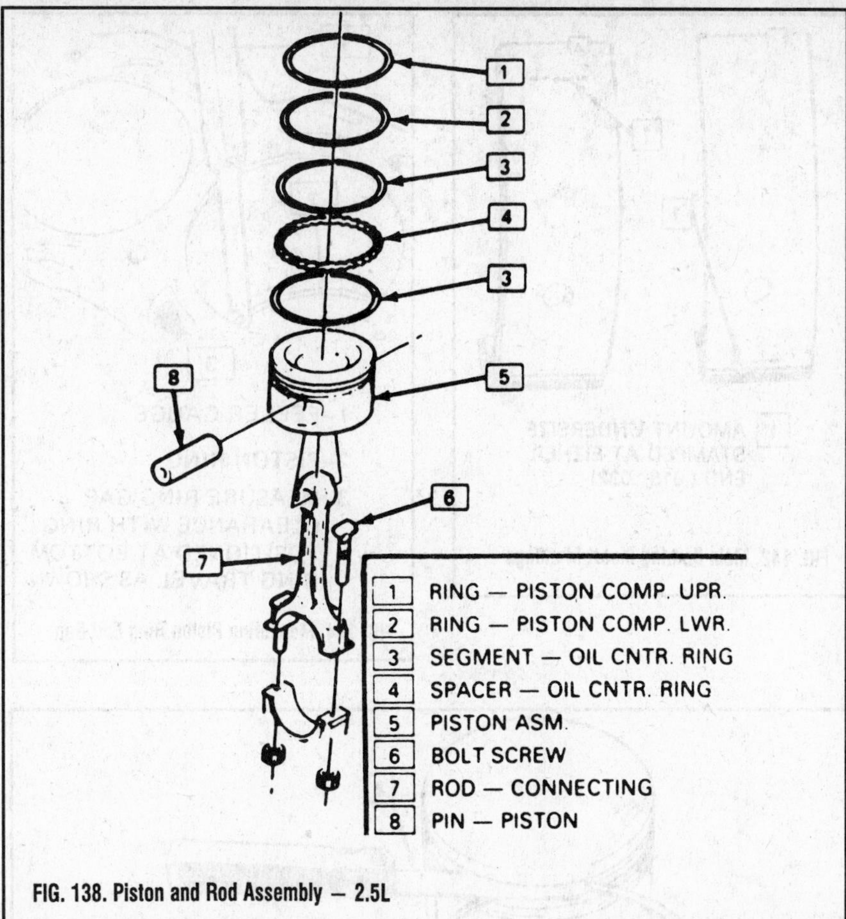

FIG. 138. Piston and Rod Assembly — 2.5L

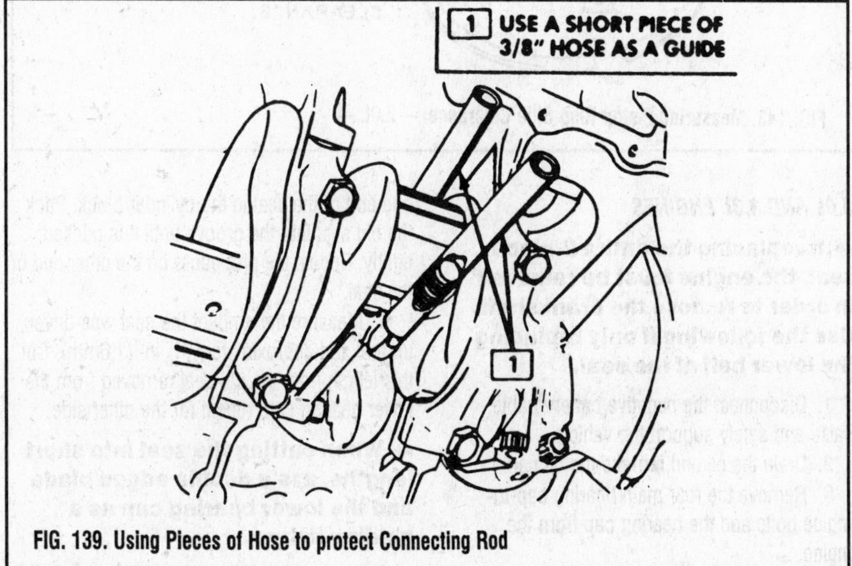

FIG. 139. Using Pieces of Hose to protect Connecting Rod

INSTALLATION

SEE FIGS. 139–147

1. Install the piston rings to the piston.
2. Turn the crankshaft to bottom dead center.
3. Lubricate the cylinder with engine oil.
4. Install the connecting rod bearing.
5. Using a ring compressor, install the piston and connecting rod assembly. Make sure that the ridges are toward the front of the engine.
6. Install the connecting rod cap and bolts and tighten to the specified torque.
7. Install the oil pan and cylinder head and connect the negative battery cable.

Rear Main Bearing Oil Seal

REMOVAL & INSTALLATION

2.0L AND 2.5L ENGINES

1. Disconnect the negative battery cable.
2. Remove the transaxle.
3. If equipped with a manual transaxle, remove the pressure plate and clutch disc.
4. Remove the flywheel-to-crankshaft bolts and the flywheel.
5. Using a medium prybar, pry out the old seal; be careful not to scratch the crankshaft surface.
6. Clean the block and crankshaft-to-seal mating surfaces.
7. Using the appropriate seal installation tool, install the new rear seal into the block. Lubricate the outside of the seal to aid installation and press the seal in evenly with the tool.
8. The installation is the reverse of the removal procedure.
9. Connect the negative battery cable and check for leaks.

2.3L ENGINE

1. Disconnect the negative battery cable.
2. Remove the transaxle.
3. If equipped with a manual transaxle, remove the pressure plate and clutch disc.
4. Remove the flywheel-to-crankshaft bolts and the flywheel.
5. Remove the oil pan-to-seal housing bolts and the block-to-seal housing bolts.
6. Remove the seal housing from the engine.
7. Place 2 blocks of equal thickness on a flat surface and position the seal housing on the 2 blocks. Remove the seal from the housing.

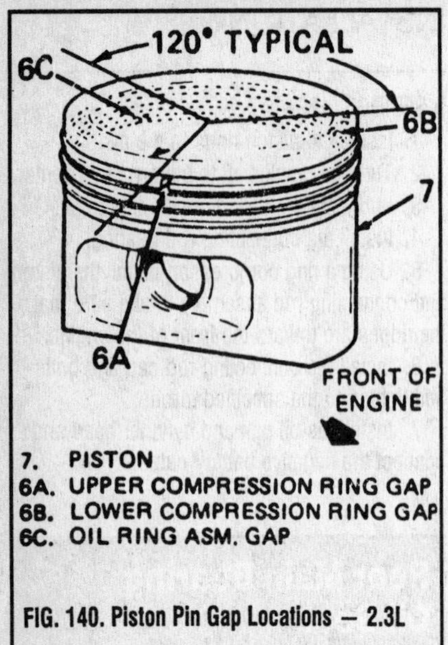

FIG. 140. Piston Pin Gap Locations — 2.3L

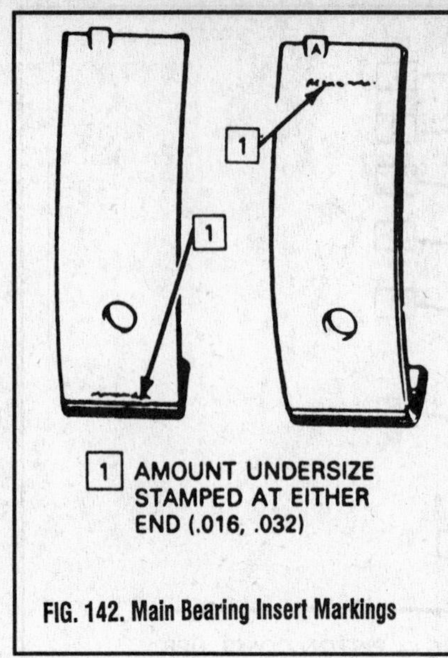

FIG. 142. Main Bearing Insert Markings

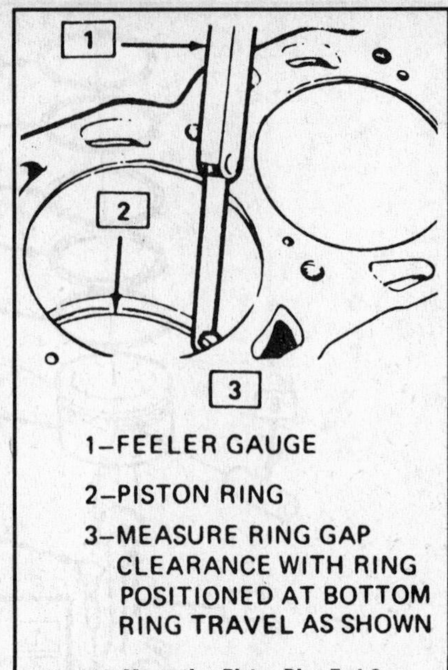

FIG. 144. Measuring Piston Ring End Gap

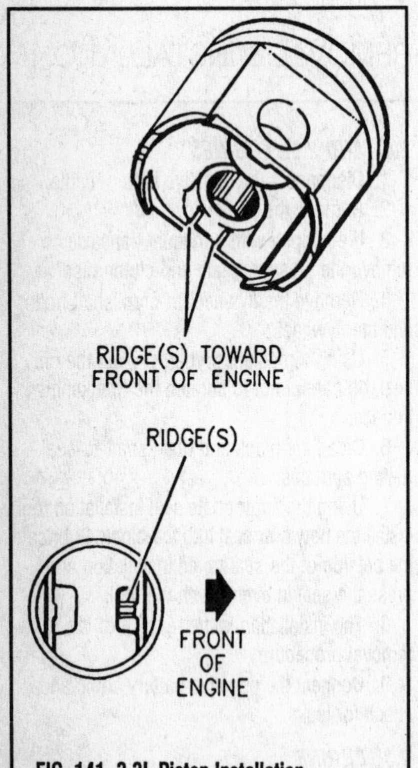

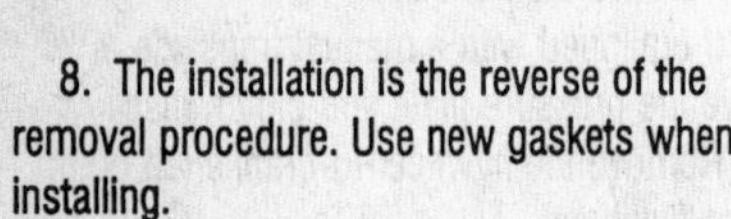

FIG. 141. 3.3L Piston Installation

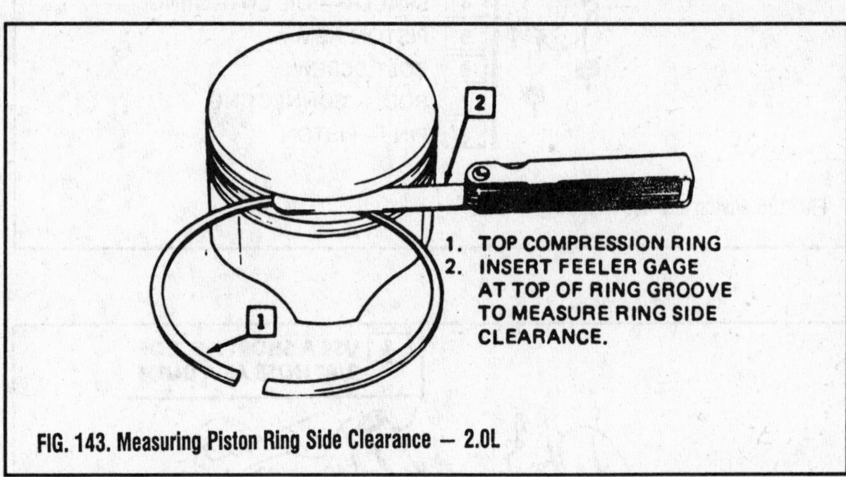

FIG. 143. Measuring Piston Ring Side Clearance — 2.0L

8. The installation is the reverse of the removal procedure. Use new gaskets when installing.

9. Connect the negative battery cable and for leaks.

3.0L AND 3.3L ENGINES

➡ **If replacing the entire 2-piece seal, the engine must be removed in order to remove the crankshaft. Use the following if only replacing the lower half of the seal.**

1. Disconnect the negative battery cable. Raise and safely support the vehicle.
2. Drain the oil and remove the oil pan.
3. Remove the rear main bearing cap-to-engine bolts and the bearing cap from the engine.
4. Remove the old seal from the bearing cap.

To Install:

5. Using a seal packing tool, insert it against one end of the seal in the cylinder block. Pack the old seal into the groove until it is packed tightly. Repeat the procedure on the other end of the seal.
6. Measure the amount the seal was driven up and add approximately $\frac{1}{16}$ in. (1.6mm). Cut this length from the old seal removed from the lower bearing cap, repeat for the other side.

➡ **When cutting the seal into short lengths, use a double edged blade and the lower bearing cap as a holding fixture.**

7. Using a seal packer guide, install it onto the cylinder block.
8. Using the packing tool, work the short

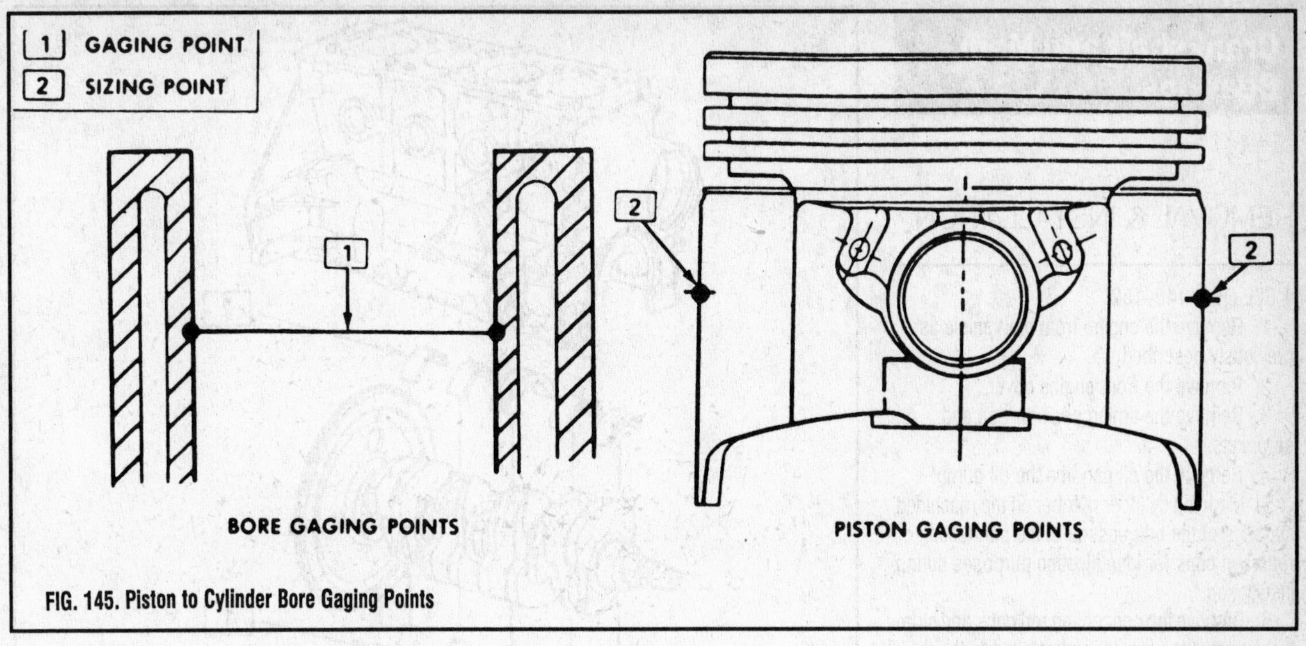

FIG. 145. Piston to Cylinder Bore Gaging Points

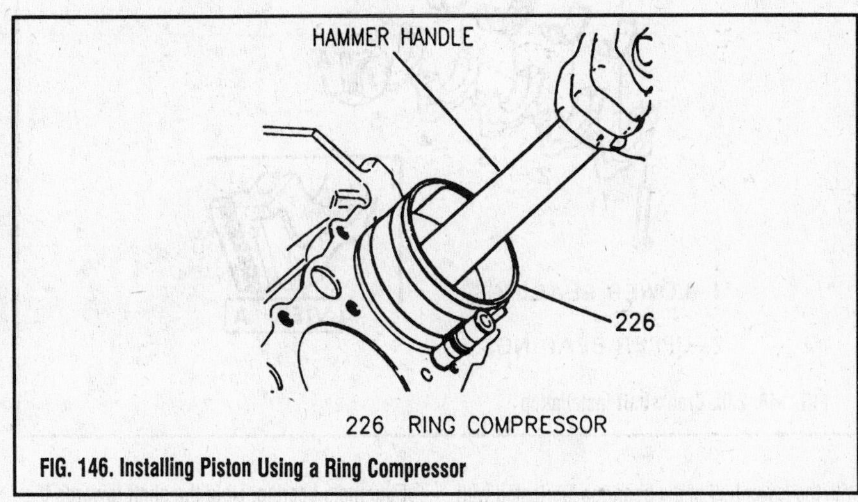

FIG. 146. Installing Piston Using a Ring Compressor

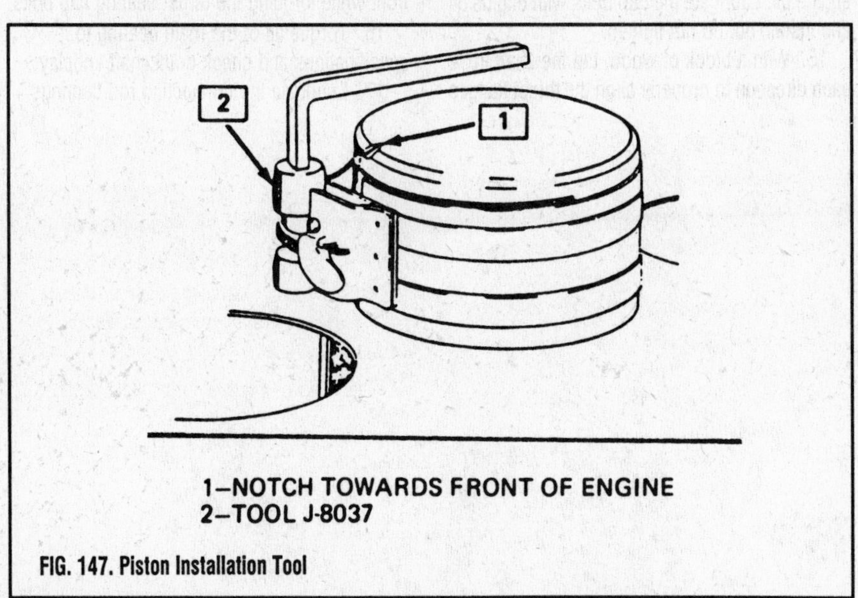

FIG. 147. Piston Installation Tool

pieces into the guide tool and pack into the cylinder block until the tool hits the built-in stop.

➡ It may help to use oil on the short seal pieces when packing into the block.

9. Repeat Steps 7 and 8 for the other side.
10. Remove the guide tool.
11. Install a new rope seal into the lower bearing cap.
12. Install the lower main bearing cap and tighten the main bearing cap bolts to 100 ft. lbs. (135 Nm) for 3.0L engine or 90 ft. lbs. (122 Nm) for 3.3L engine.
13. Install the oil pan.
14. Fill the crankcase with the proper engine oil.
15. Connect the negative battery cable and check for leaks.

Crankshaft and Main Bearings

REMOVAL & INSTALLATION

SEE FIGS. 148–152

1. Remove the engine from the vehicle as previously described.
2. Remove the front engine cover.
3. Remove the timing chain or belt and sprockets.
4. Remove the oil pan and the oil pump.
5. Mark the cylinder number on the machined surfaces of the bolt bosses of the connecting rods and caps for identification purposes during installation.
6. Remove the connecting rod caps and store them so that they may be reinstalled to their original position.
7. Remove all of the main bearing caps.
8. Note the position of the keyway in the crankshaft, so that it may be reinstalled to it's original position.
9. Lift the crankshaft away from the block.
10. Remove the rear main oil seal.

To Install:

11. Install sufficient oil pan bolts to the block to align with the connecting rod bolts. Use rubber bands between the bolts to hold the connecting rods in place.
12. Place the upper half of the main bearings in the block and lubricate them with clean engine oil.
13. Place the crankshaft keyway in the same position as removed and lower it into the block. The connecting rods should follow the crank pins into position as it is lowered.
14. Lubricate the thrust flanges with 10501609 lubricant or equivalent. Install caps with the lower half of the bearings lubricated with engine oil. Lubricate the cap bolts with engine oil and install, but do not tighten.
15. With a block of wood, tap the shaft in each direction to properly align the thrust flanges of the main bearing. Hold the shaft towards the front while torquing the thrust bearing cap bolts.
16. Torque all of the main bearing to specifications and check crankshaft endplay.
17. Lubricate the connecting rod bearings

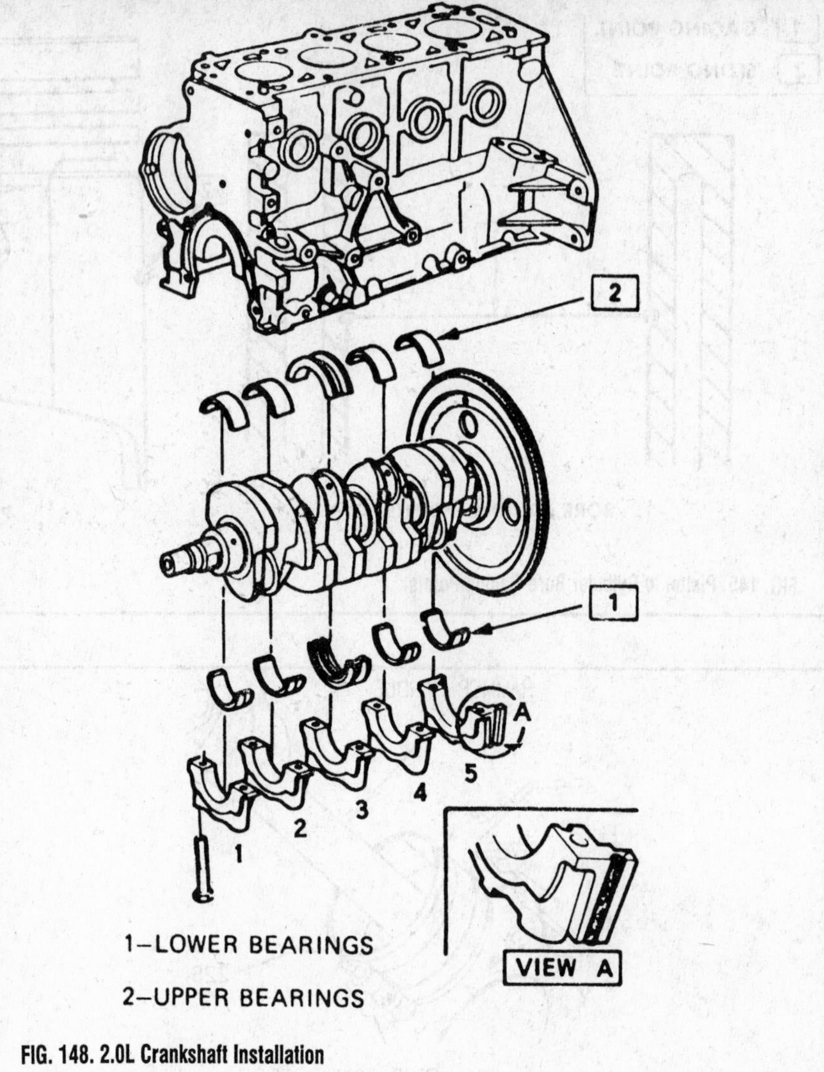

FIG. 148. 2.0L Crankshaft Installation

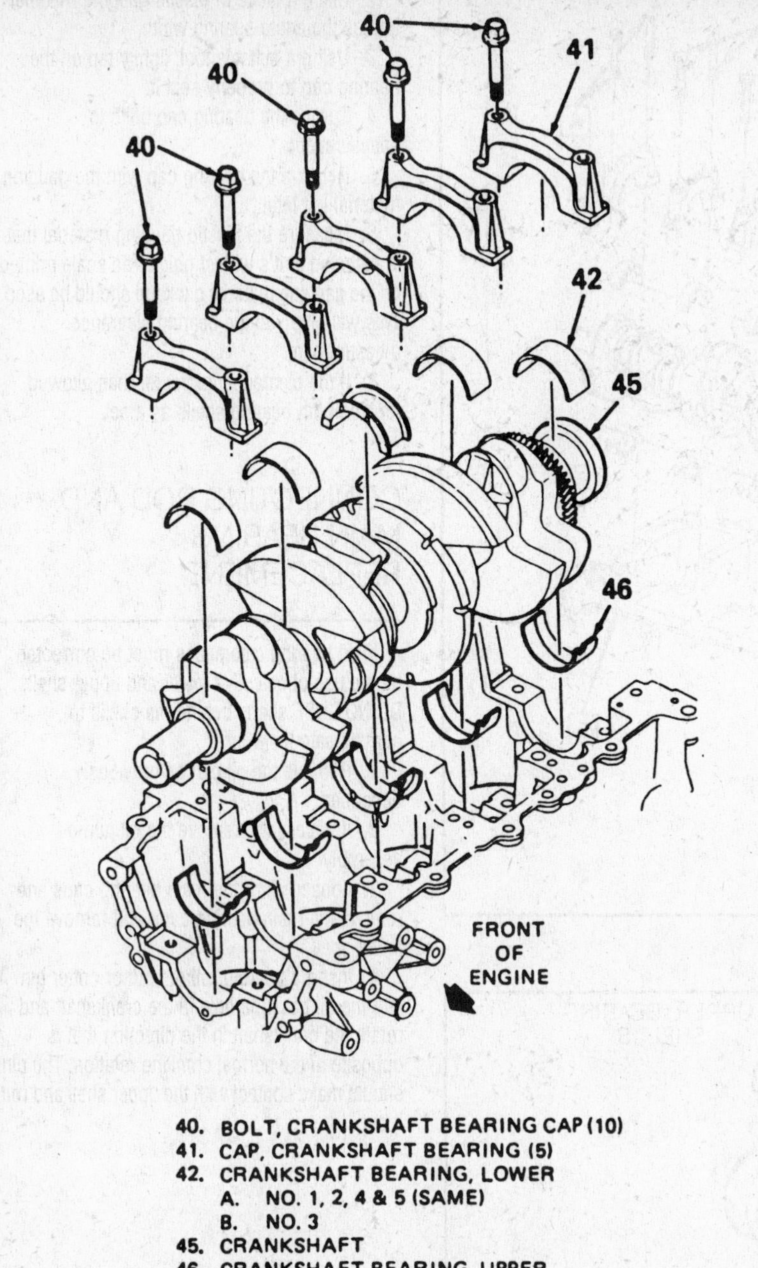

FIG. 149. 2.3L Crankshaft and Bearings

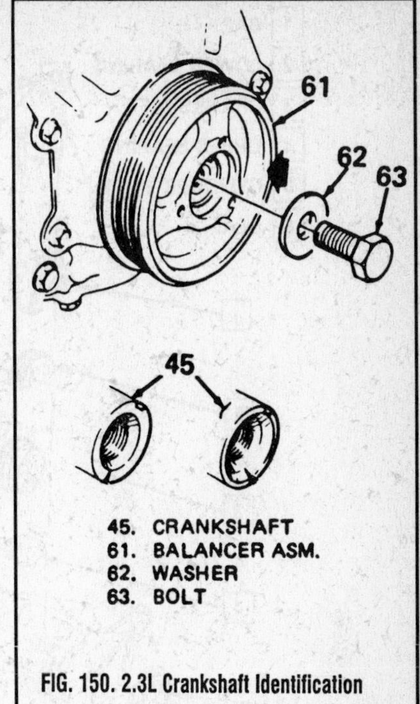

FIG. 150. 2.3L Crankshaft Identification

with clean oil. Install the connecting rod bearing caps to their original positions and tighten the nuts to specification.

18. Complete installation by reversing the removal steps.

CLEANING AND INSPECTION

1. Clean all oil passages in the block and crankshaft.

2. Using a dial indicator, check the crankshaft journal runout. Measure the journals with a micrometer to determine the correct size rod and main bearings to be used.

INSPECTING MAIN BEARING CLEARANCE

➧ SEE FIG. 153

1. Remove the bearing cap and wipe the oil from the crankshaft journal and the outer and inner bearing shell surfaces.

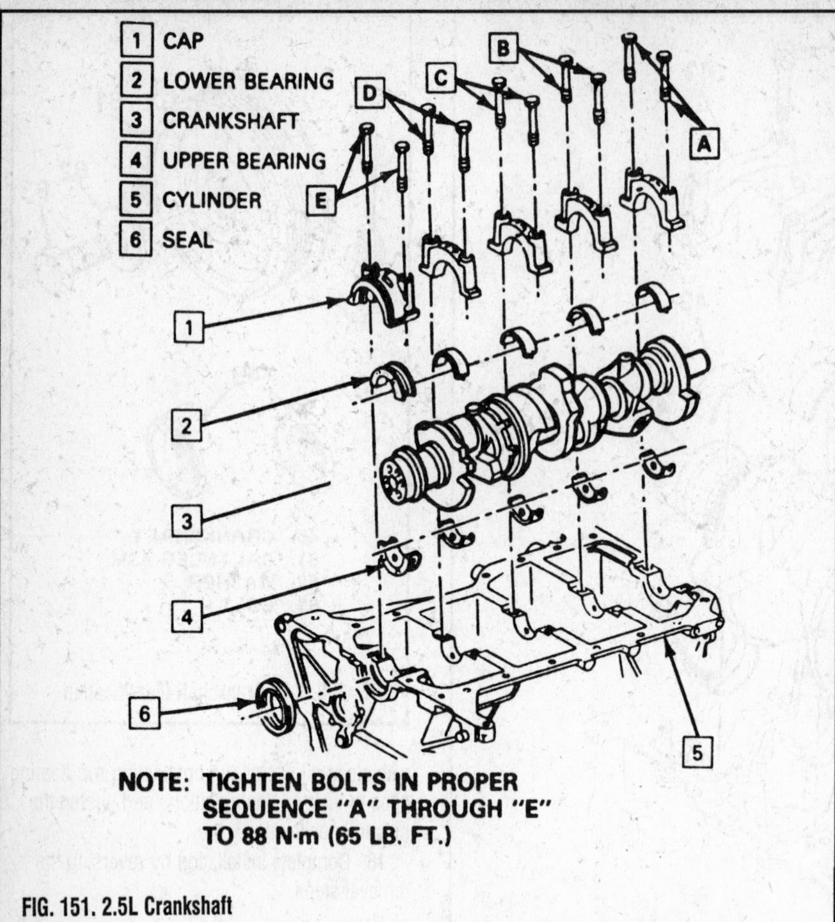

FIG. 151. 2.5L Crankshaft

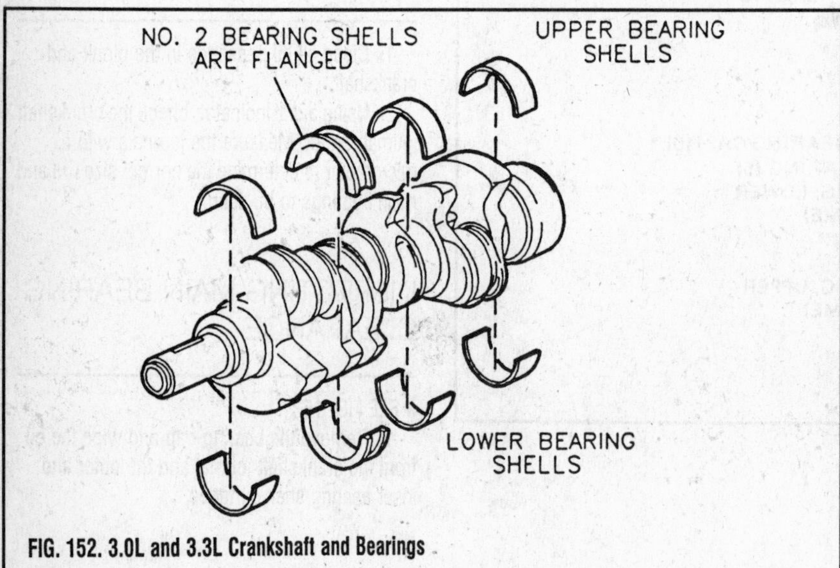

FIG. 152. 3.0L and 3.3L Crankshaft and Bearings

2. Place a piece of plastic gauging material across the entire bearing width.

3. Using a suitable tool, lightly tap on the bearing cap to properly seat it.

4. Torque the bearing cap bolts to specifications.

5. Remove the bearing cap with the gauging material left intact.

6. Measure the plastic gauging material that is flattened at it's widest point. The scale printed on the gauging material package should be used. This will give you the bearing clearance measurement.

7. If the clearance is greater than allowed, replace both bearing shells as a set.

CONNECTING ROD AND MAIN BEARING REPLACEMENT

Main bearing clearances must be corrected by the use of selective lower and upper shells. DO NOT USE shims behind the shells to compensate for wear.

1. Remove the oil pan as previously described.

2. If necessary, remove the oil pump assembly.

3. Loosen all of the main bearing caps and remove the main bearing caps and remove the lower shell.

4. Insert a bearing roll out pin or cotter pin into the oil passage hole in the crankshaft and rotate the crankshaft in the direction that is opposite of the normal cranking rotation. The pin should make contact with the upper shell and roll it out.

5. Inspect the main bearing journals for roughness and wear. Remove slight roughness with a fine grit polishing cloth saturated with engine oil.

6. If the journals are scored or ridged, the crankshaft must be replaced.

7. Thoroughly clean the crankshaft journals and bearing caps before installing new main bearings.

8. Apply special lubricant No. 1050169 or equivalent to the thrust flanges of the bearing shells.

9. Install a new upper shell on the crankshaft journal with the locating tang in the correct position and as in removal, rotate the shaft to turn it into place using a cotter pin or roll pin.

10. Install a new bearing shell to the bearing cap.

11. Install a new oil seal in the rear main bearing cap and block.

12. Lubricate the main bearings with engine oil and the thrust surface with special lubricant No. 1050169 or equivalent.

13. Lubricate the main bearing caps with engine oil and tighten the bolts to specifications.

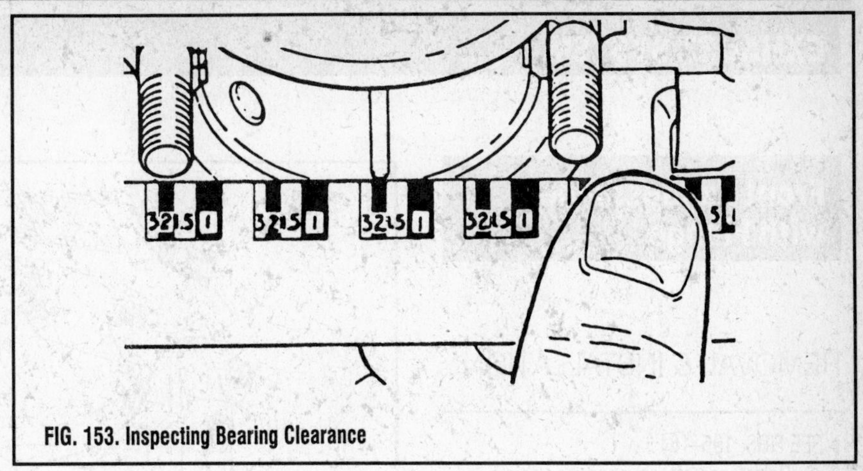

FIG. 153. Inspecting Bearing Clearance

Flywheel

REMOVAL & INSTALLATION

➧ SEE FIG. 154

1. Remove the transaxle assembly, refer to the transaxle section for this procedure.

2. Remove the splash shield, if so equipped.

3. If manual transaxle, remove the clutch and pressure plate.

4. Using special tool J38122 or equivalent, secure the crankshaft and remove the flywheel.

To Install:

5. Remove all thread adhesive from the bolts and from the holes before installation.

6. Apply locking type adhesive to all of the flywheel to crankshaft mounting bolts.

7. The remaining installation steps are the reverse of the removal procedure. Tighten the flywheel bolts in stages to the specified torque.

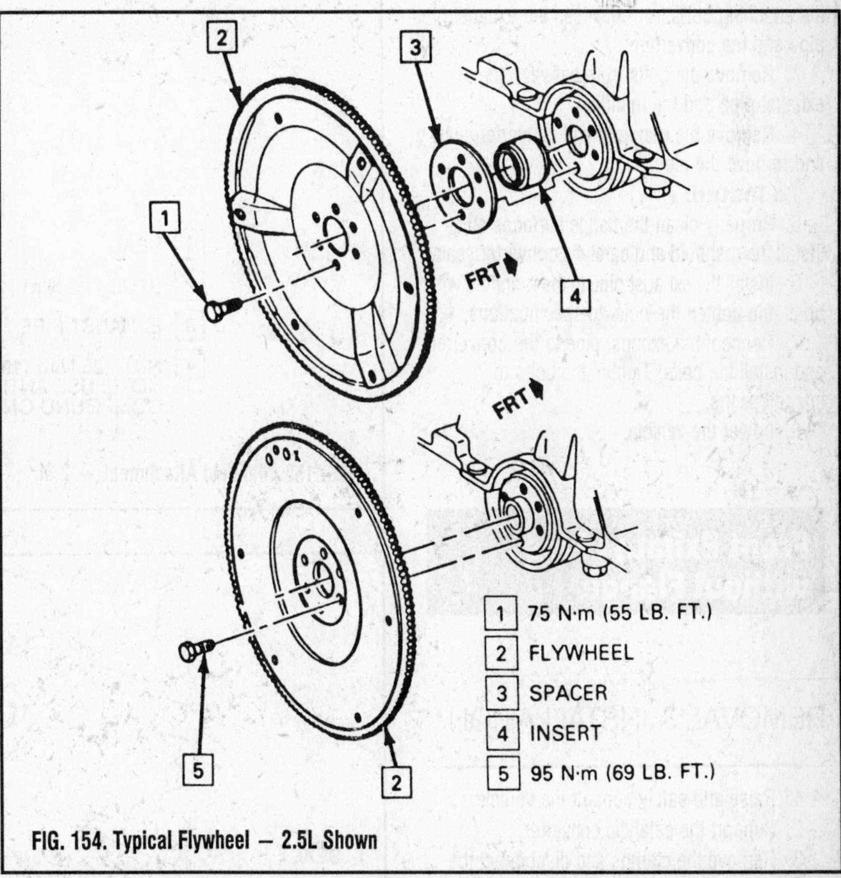

FIG. 154. Typical Flywheel — 2.5L Shown

EXHAUST SYSTEM

Front Exhaust Pipe with Flange

REMOVAL & INSTALLATION

➧ SEE FIGS. 155–161

1. Raise and safely support the vehicle.
2. Support the catalytic converter and remove the attaching bolts from between the exhaust pipe and the converter.
3. Remove the bolts from between the exhaust pipe and the manifold.
4. Remove the manifold and converter seals and remove the pipe.

To Install:

5. Properly clean the flange surfaces and install the manifold and catalytic converter seals.
6. Install the exhaust pipe to the manifold with bolts and tighten the bolts to specifications.
7. Connect the exhaust pipe to the converter and install the bolts. Tighten the bolts to specifications.
8. Lower the vehicle.

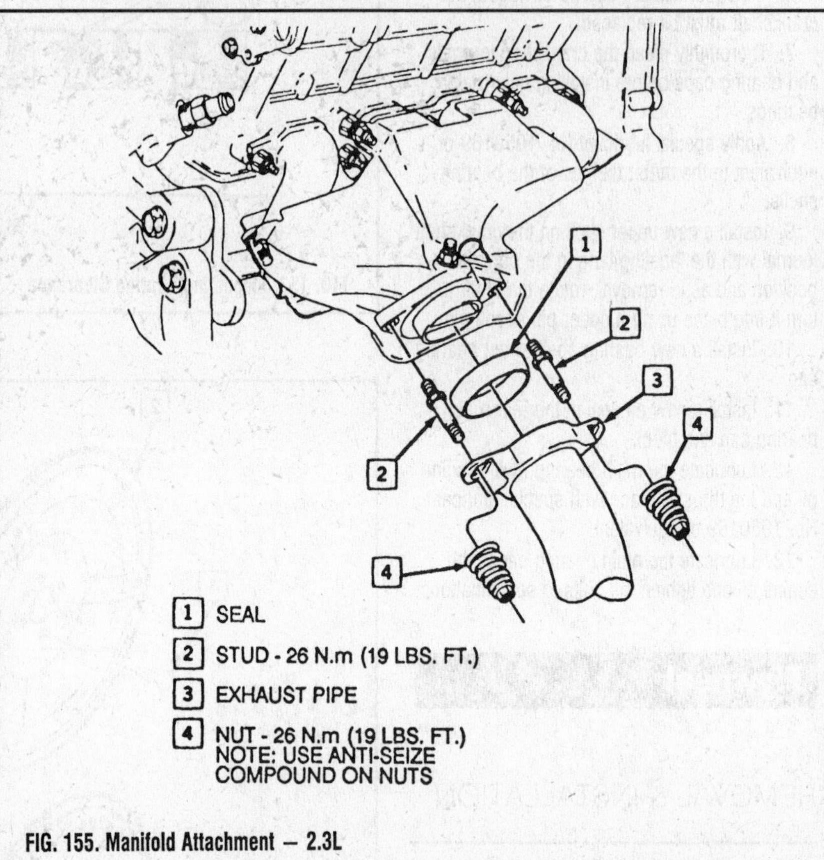

FIG. 155. Manifold Attachment — 2.3L

Front Exhaust Pipe without Flange

REMOVAL & INSTALLATION

1. Raise and safely support the vehicle.
2. Support the catalytic converter.
3. Remove the clamps and disconnect the exhaust pipe from the catalytic converter.
4. Disconnect the exhaust pipe from the manifold and remove the pipe.
5. Remove the manifold seal.

To Install:

6. Connect the exhaust pipe to the catalytic converter and install the clamp.
7. Install the manifold seal and connect the exhaust pipe to the manifold. Lower the vehicle.

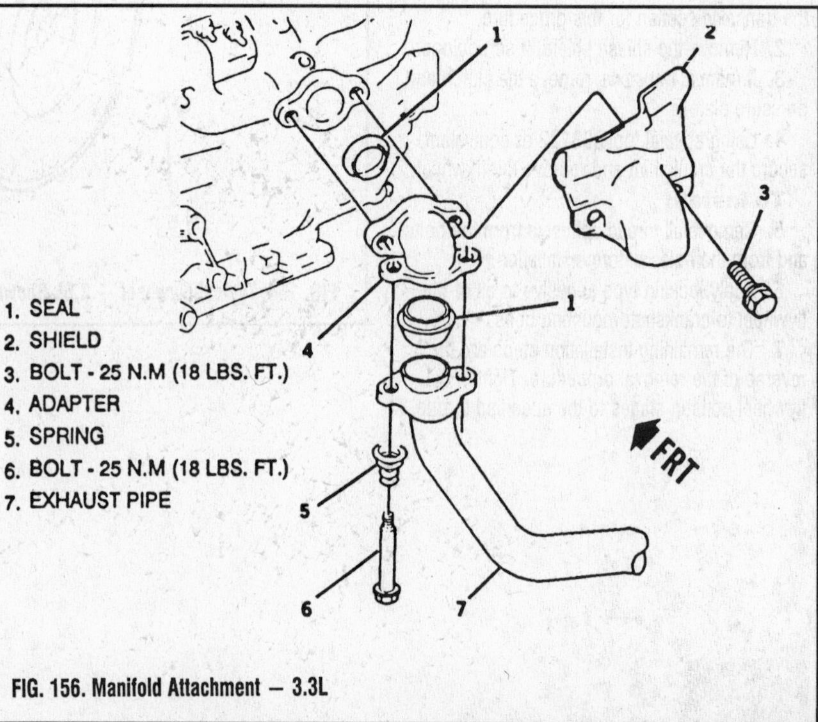

FIG. 156. Manifold Attachment — 3.3L

Exhaust Crossover Pipe

REMOVAL & INSTALLATION

3.3L Engine

1. Disconnect the negative battery cable.
2. Remove the air cleaner assembly.
3. Remove the engine cooling fan assembly.
4. Disconnect the front spark plug wires and place to the side.
5. Remove the exhaust crossover pipe attaching bolts.
6. Remove the front exhaust manifold heat shield.
7. Remove the front exhaust support bracket.
8. Loosen the exhaust manifold attaching bolts and position the manifold away from the engine for clearance reasons.
9. Remove the crossover pipe.

To Install:

10. Install the crossover pipe but do not install bolts yet.
11. Connect the exhaust manifold and tighten the bolts.
12. Install the crossover pipe bolts and tighten to specifications.
13. Install the exhaust manifold support bracket and heat shield.
14. Install the engine cooling fan assembly.
15. Install the air cleaner assembly and connect the negative battery cable.

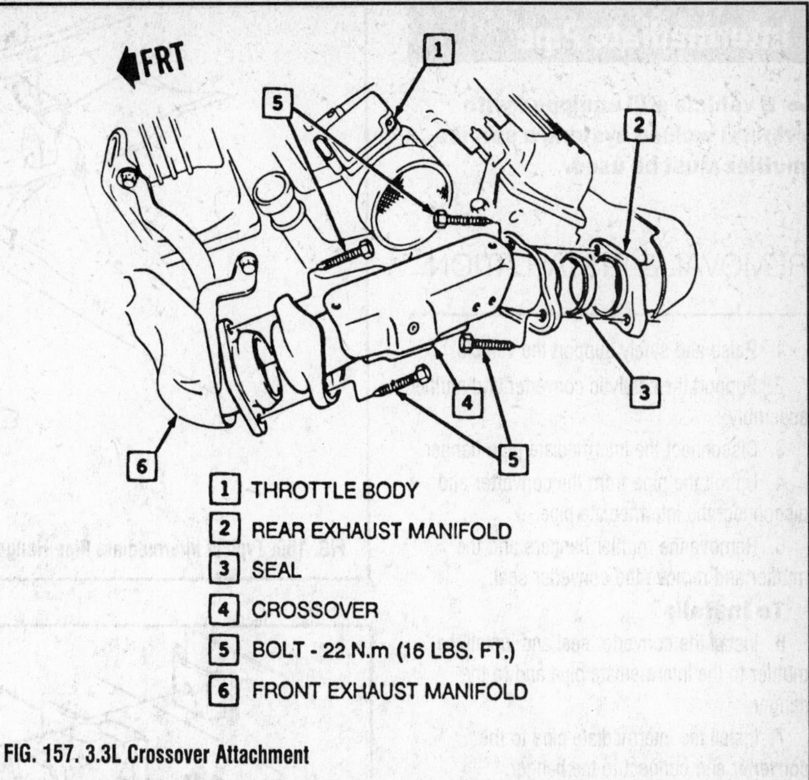

FIG. 157. 3.3L Crossover Attachment

Catalytic Converter

REMOVAL & INSTALLATION

1. Raise and safely support the vehicle.
2. Support the converter and remove the converter bolts or clamps.
3. Remove the converter and the converter seals.

To Install:

4. Clean all flange surfaces and install the converter seals.
5. Install the converter to the vehicle with the bolts or clamps and tighten the bolts to specifications.
6. Lower the vehicle.

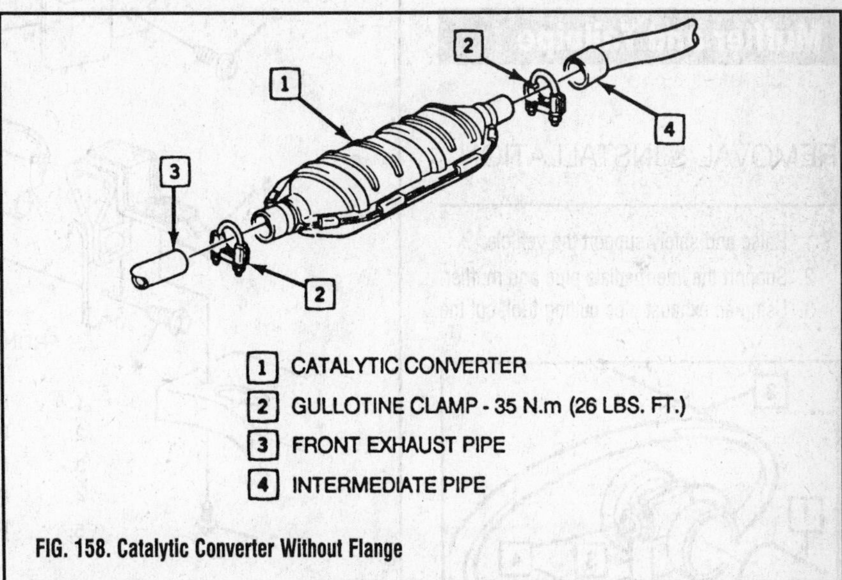

FIG. 158. Catalytic Converter Without Flange

Intermediate Pipe

➡ If vehicle still equipped with original welded system, a service muffler must be used.

REMOVAL & INSTALLATION

1. Raise and safely support the vehicle.
2. Support the catalytic converter and muffler assembly.
3. Disconnect the intermediate pipe hanger.
4. Unbolt the pipe from the converter and disconnect the intermediate pipe.
5. Remove the muffler hangers and the muffler and remove the converter seal.

To Install:

6. Install the converter seal and install the muffler to the intermediate pipe and to the hanger.
7. Install the intermediate pipe to the converter and connect to the hanger.
8. Lower the vehicle.

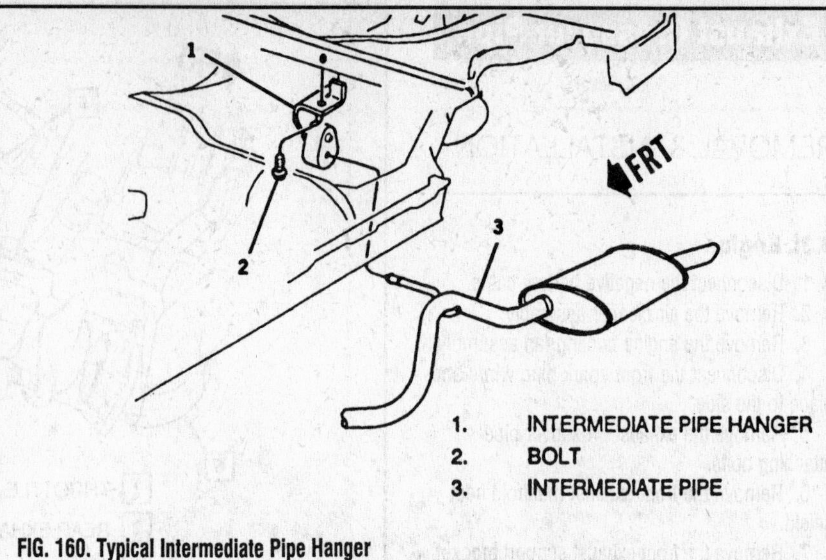

FIG. 160. Typical Intermediate Pipe Hanger

Muffler and Tailpipe

REMOVAL & INSTALLATION

1. Raise and safely support the vehicle.
2. Support the intermediate pipe and muffler.
3. Using an exhaust pipe cutting tool, cut the intermediate pipe as close to the weld as possible.
4. Remove the muffler hangers and the muffler.

To Install:

5. Connect the muffler to the intermediate pipe and install the hangers.
6. Install a U-Bolt type clamp and tighten. Lower the vehicle.

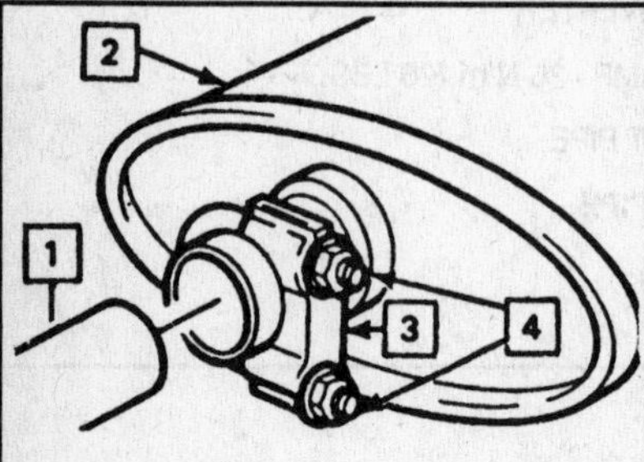

FIG. 161. Muffler Installation

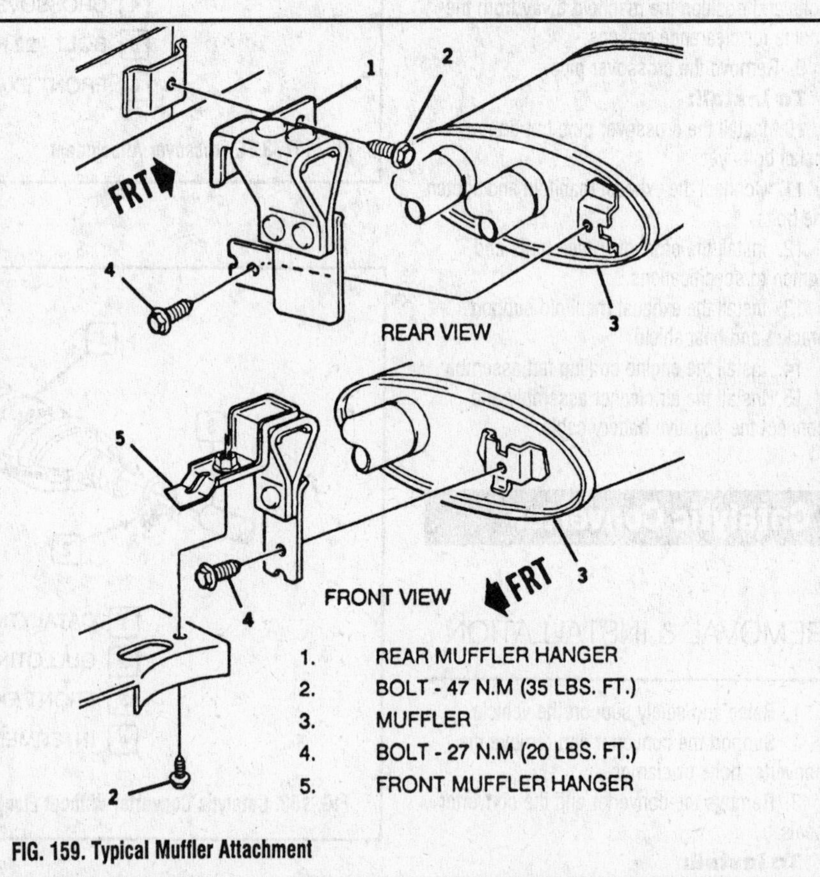

FIG. 159. Typical Muffler Attachment

Troubleshooting Basic Charging System Problems

Problem	Cause	Solution
Noisy alternator	• Loose mountings • Loose drive pulley • Worn bearings • Brush noise • Internal circuits shorted (High pitched whine)	• Tighten mounting bolts • Tighten pulley • Replace alternator • Replace alternator • Replace alternator
Squeal when starting engine or accelerating	• Glazed or loose belt	• Replace or adjust belt
Indicator light remains on or ammeter indicates discharge (engine running)	• Broken fan belt • Broken or disconnected wires • Internal alternator problems • Defective voltage regulator	• Install belt • Repair or connect wiring • Replace alternator • Replace voltage regulator
Car light bulbs continually burn out—battery needs water continually	• Alternator/regulator overcharging	• Replace voltage regulator/alternator
Car lights flare on acceleration	• Battery low • Internal alternator/regulator problems	• Charge or replace battery • Replace alternator/regulator
Low voltage output (alternator light flickers continually or ammeter needle wanders)	• Loose or worn belt • Dirty or corroded connections • Internal alternator/regulator problems	• Replace or adjust belt • Clean or replace connections • Replace alternator or regulator

Troubleshooting Basic Starting System Problems

Problem	Cause	Solution
Starter motor rotates engine slowly	• Battery charge low or battery defective • Defective circuit between battery and starter motor • Low load current • High load current	• Charge or replace battery • Clean and tighten, or replace cables • Bench-test starter motor. Inspect for worn brushes and weak brush springs. • Bench-test starter motor. Check engine for friction, drag or coolant in cylinders. Check ring gear-to-pinion gear clearance.
Starter motor will not rotate engine	• Battery charge low or battery defective • Faulty solenoid • Damage drive pinion gear or ring gear • Starter motor engagement weak • Starter motor rotates slowly with high load current • Engine seized	• Charge or replace battery • Check solenoid ground. Repair or replace as necessary. • Replace damaged gear(s) • Bench-test starter motor • Inspect drive yoke pull-down and point gap, check for worn end bushings, check ring gear clearance • Repair engine
Starter motor drive will not engage (solenoid known to be good)	• Defective contact point assembly • Inadequate contact point assembly ground • Defective hold-in coil	• Repair or replace contact point assembly • Repair connection at ground screw • Replace field winding assembly
Starter motor drive will not disengage	• Starter motor loose on flywheel housing • Worn drive end busing • Damaged ring gear teeth • Drive yoke return spring broken or missing	• Tighten mounting bolts • Replace bushing • Replace ring gear or driveplate • Replace spring
Starter motor drive disengages prematurely	• Weak drive assembly thrust spring • Hold-in coil defective	• Replace drive mechanism • Replace field winding assembly
Low load current	• Worn brushes • Weak brush springs	• Replace brushes • Replace springs

Troubleshooting Engine Mechanical Problems

Problem	Cause	Solution
External oil leaks	• Fuel pump gasket broken or improperly seated	• Replace gasket
	• Cylinder head cover RTV sealant broken or improperly seated	• Replace sealant; inspect cylinder head cover sealant flange and cylinder head sealant surface for distortion and cracks
	• Oil filler cap leaking or missing	• Replace cap
External oil leaks	• Oil filter gasket broken or improperly seated	• Replace oil filter
	• Oil pan side gasket broken, improperly seated or opening in RTV sealant	• Replace gasket or repair opening in sealant; inspect oil pan gasket flange for distortion
	• Oil pan front oil seal broken or improperly seated	• Replace seal; inspect timing case cover and oil pan seal flange for distortion
	• Oil pan rear oil seal broken or improperly seated	• Replace seal; inspect oil pan rear oil seal flange; inspect rear main bearing cap for cracks, plugged oil return channels, or distortion in seal groove
	• Timing case cover oil seal broken or improperly seated	• Replace seal
	• Excess oil pressure because of restricted PCV valve	• Replace PCV valve
	• Oil pan drain plug loose or has stripped threads	• Repair as necessary and tighten
	• Rear oil gallery plug loose	• Use appropriate sealant on gallery plug and tighten
	• Rear camshaft plug loose or improperly seated	• Seat camshaft plug or replace and seal, as necessary
	• Distributor base gasket damaged	• Replace gasket
Excessive oil consumption	• Oil level too high	• Drain oil to specified level
	• Oil with wrong viscosity being used	• Replace with specified oil
	• PCV valve stuck closed	• Replace PCV valve
	• Valve stem oil deflectors (or seals) are damaged, missing, or incorrect type	• Replace valve stem oil deflectors
	• Valve stems or valve guides worn	• Measure stem-to-guide clearance and repair as necessary
	• Poorly fitted or missing valve cover baffles	• Replace valve cover
	• Piston rings broken or missing	• Replace broken or missing rings
	• Scuffed piston	• Replace piston
	• Incorrect piston ring gap	• Measure ring gap, repair as necessary
	• Piston rings sticking or excessively loose in grooves	• Measure ring side clearance, repair as necessary
	• Compression rings installed upside down	• Repair as necessary
	• Cylinder walls worn, scored, or glazed	• Repair as necessary

Troubleshooting Engine Mechanical Problems (cont.)

Problem	Cause	Solution
	• Piston ring gaps not properly staggered	• Repair as necessary
	• Excessive main or connecting rod bearing clearance	• Measure bearing clearance, repair as necessary
No oil pressure	• Low oil level	• Add oil to correct level
	• Oil pressure gauge, warning lamp or sending unit inaccurate	• Replace oil pressure gauge or warning lamp
	• Oil pump malfunction	• Replace oil pump
	• Oil pressure relief valve sticking	• Remove and inspect oil pressure relief valve assembly
	• Oil passages on pressure side of pump obstructed	• Inspect oil passages for obstruction
	• Oil pickup screen or tube obstructed	• Inspect oil pickup for obstruction
	• Loose oil inlet tube	• Tighten or seal inlet tube
Low oil pressure	• Low oil level	• Add oil to correct level
	• Inaccurate gauge, warning lamp or sending unit	• Replace oil pressure gauge or warning lamp
	• Oil excessively thin because of dilution, poor quality, or improper grade	• Drain and refill crankcase with recommended oil
	• Excessive oil temperature	• Correct cause of overheating engine
	• Oil pressure relief spring weak or sticking	• Remove and inspect oil pressure relief valve assembly
	• Oil inlet tube and screen assembly has restriction or air leak	• Remove and inspect oil inlet tube and screen assembly. (Fill inlet tube with lacquer thinner to locate leaks.)
	• Excessive oil pump clearance	• Measure clearances
	• Excessive main, rod, or camshaft bearing clearance	• Measure bearing clearances, repair as necessary
High oil pressure	• Improper oil viscosity	• Drain and refill crankcase with correct viscosity oil
	• Oil pressure gauge or sending unit inaccurate	• Replace oil pressure gauge
	• Oil pressure relief valve sticking closed	• Remove and inspect oil pressure relief valve assembly
Main bearing noise	• Insufficient oil supply	• Inspect for low oil level and low oil pressure
	• Main bearing clearance excessive	• Measure main bearing clearance, repair as necessary
	• Bearing insert missing	• Replace missing insert
	• Crankshaft end play excessive	• Measure end play, repair as necessary
	• Improperly tightened main bearing cap bolts	• Tighten bolts with specified torque
	• Loose flywheel or drive plate	• Tighten flywheel or drive plate attaching bolts
	• Loose or damaged vibration damper	• Repair as necessary

Troubleshooting Engine Mechanical Problems (cont.)

Problem	Cause	Solution
Connecting rod bearing noise	• Insufficient oil supply	• Inspect for low oil level and low oil pressure
	• Carbon build-up on piston	• Remove carbon from piston crown
	• Bearing clearance excessive or bearing missing	• Measure clearance, repair as necessary
	• Crankshaft connecting rod journal out-of-round	• Measure journal dimensions, repair or replace as necessary
	• Misaligned connecting rod or cap	• Repair as necessary
	• Connecting rod bolts tightened improperly	• Tighten bolts with specified torque
Piston noise	• Piston-to-cylinder wall clearance excessive (scuffed piston)	• Measure clearance and examine piston
	• Cylinder walls excessively tapered or out-of-round	• Measure cylinder wall dimensions, rebore cylinder
	• Piston ring broken	• Replace all rings on piston
	• Loose or seized piston pin	• Measure piston-to-pin clearance, repair as necessary
	• Connecting rods misaligned	• Measure rod alignment, straighten or replace
	• Piston ring side clearance excessively loose or tight	• Measure ring side clearance, repair as necessary
	• Carbon build-up on piston is excessive	• Remove carbon from piston
Valve actuating component noise	• Insufficient oil supply	• Check for: (a) Low oil level (b) Low oil pressure (c) Plugged push rods (d) Wrong hydraulic tappets (e) Restricted oil gallery (f) Excessive tappet to bore clearance
	• Push rods worn or bent	• Replace worn or bent push rods
	• Rocker arms or pivots worn	• Replace worn rocker arms or pivots
	• Foreign objects or chips in hydraulic tappets	• Clean tappets
	• Excessive tappet leak-down	• Replace valve tappet
	• Tappet face worn	• Replace tappet; inspect corresponding cam lobe for wear
	• Broken or cocked valve springs	• Properly seat cocked springs; replace broken springs
	• Stem-to-guide clearance excessive	• Measure stem-to-guide clearance, repair as required
	• Valve bent	• Replace valve
	• Loose rocker arms	• Tighten bolts with specified torque
	• Valve seat runout excessive	• Regrind valve seat/valves
	• Missing valve lock	• Install valve lock
	• Push rod rubbing or contacting cylinder head	• Remove cylinder head and remove obstruction in head
	• Excessive engine oil (four-cylinder engine)	• Correct oil level

Troubleshooting the Cooling System

Problem	Cause	Solution
High temperature gauge indication—overheating	• Coolant level low	• Replenish coolant
	• Fan belt loose	• Adjust fan belt tension
	• Radiator hose(s) collapsed	• Replace hose(s)
	• Radiator airflow blocked	• Remove restriction (bug screen, fog lamps, etc.)
	• Faulty radiator cap	• Replace radiator cap
	• Ignition timing incorrect	• Adjust ignition timing
	• Idle speed low	• Adjust idle speed
	• Air trapped in cooling system	• Purge air
	• Heavy traffic driving	• Operate at fast idle in neutral intermittently to cool engine
	• Incorrect cooling system component(s) installed	• Install proper component(s)
	• Faulty thermostat	• Replace thermostat
	• Water pump shaft broken or impeller loose	• Replace water pump
	• Radiator tubes clogged	• Flush radiator
	• Cooling system clogged	• Flush system
	• Casting flash in cooling passages	• Repair or replace as necessary. Flash may be visible by removing cooling system components or removing core plugs.
	• Brakes dragging	• Repair brakes
	• Excessive engine friction	• Repair engine
	• Antifreeze concentration over 68%	• Lower antifreeze concentration percentage
	• Missing air seals	• Replace air seals
	• Faulty gauge or sending unit	• Repair or replace faulty component
	• Loss of coolant flow caused by leakage or foaming	• Repair or replace leaking component, replace coolant
	• Viscous fan drive failed	• Replace unit
Low temperature indication—undercooling	• Thermostat stuck open	• Replace thermostat
	• Faulty gauge or sending unit	• Repair or replace faulty component
Coolant loss—boilover	• Overfilled cooling system	• Reduce coolant level to proper specification
	• Quick shutdown after hard (hot) run	• Allow engine to run at fast idle prior to shutdown
	• Air in system resulting in occasional "burping" of coolant	• Purge system
	• Insufficient antifreeze allowing coolant boiling point to be too low	• Add antifreeze to raise boiling point
	• Antifreeze deteriorated because of age or contamination	• Replace coolant
	• Leaks due to loose hose clamps, loose nuts, bolts, drain plugs, faulty hoses, or defective radiator	• Pressure test system to locate source of leak(s) then repair as necessary

Troubleshooting the Cooling System (cont.)

Problem	Cause	Solution
Coolant loss—boilover	• Faulty head gasket • Cracked head, manifold, or block • Faulty radiator cap	• Replace head gasket • Replace as necessary • Replace cap
Coolant entry into crankcase or cylinder(s)	• Faulty head gasket • Crack in head, manifold or block	• Replace head gasket • Replace as necessary
Coolant recovery system inoperative	• Coolant level low • Leak in system • Pressure cap not tight or seal missing, or leaking • Pressure cap defective • Overflow tube clogged or leaking • Recovery bottle vent restricted	• Replenish coolant to FULL mark • Pressure test to isolate leak and repair as necessary • Repair as necessary • Replace cap • Repair as necessary • Remove restriction
Noise	• Fan contacting shroud • Loose water pump impeller • Glazed fan belt • Loose fan belt • Rough surface on drive pulley • Water pump bearing worn • Belt alignment	• Reposition shroud and inspect engine mounts • Replace pump • Apply silicone or replace belt • Adjust fan belt tension • Replace pulley • Remove belt to isolate. Replace pump. • Check pulley alignment. Repair as necessary.
No coolant flow through heater core	• Restricted return inlet in water pump • Heater hose collapsed or restricted • Restricted heater core • Restricted outlet in thermostat housing • Intake manifold bypass hole in cylinder head restricted • Faulty heater control valve • Intake manifold coolant passage restricted	• Remove restriction • Remove restriction or replace hose • Remove restriction or replace core • Remove flash or restriction • Remove restriction • Replace valve • Remove restriction or replace intake manifold

NOTE: *Immediately after shutdown, the engine enters a condition known as heat soak. This is caused by the cooling system being inoperative while engine temperature is still high. If coolant temperature rises above boiling point, expansion and pressure may push some coolant out of the radiator overflow tube. If this does not occur frequently it is considered normal.*

Troubleshooting the Serpentine Drive Belt

Problem	Cause	Solution
Tension sheeting fabric failure (woven fabric on outside circumference of belt has cracked or separated from body of belt)	• Grooved or backside idler pulley diameters are less than minimum recommended	• Replace pulley(s) not conforming to specification
	• Tension sheeting contacting (rubbing) stationary object	• Correct rubbing condition
	• Excessive heat causing woven fabric to age	• Replace belt
	• Tension sheeting splice has fractured	• Replace belt
Noise (objectional squeal, squeak, or rumble is heard or felt while drive belt is in operation)	• Belt slippage	• Adjust belt
	• Bearing noise	• Locate and repair
	• Belt misalignment	• Align belt/pulley(s)
	• Belt-to-pulley mismatch	• Install correct belt
	• Driven component inducing vibration	• Locate defective driven component and repair
	• System resonant frequency inducing vibration	• Vary belt tension within specifications. Replace belt.
Rib chunking (one or more ribs has separated from belt body)	• Foreign objects imbedded in pulley grooves	• Remove foreign objects from pulley grooves
	• Installation damage	• Replace belt
	• Drive loads in excess of design specifications	• Adjust belt tension
	• Insufficient internal belt adhesion	• Replace belt
Rib or belt wear (belt ribs contact bottom of pulley grooves)	• Pulley(s) misaligned	• Align pulley(s)
	• Mismatch of belt and pulley groove widths	• Replace belt
	• Abrasive environment	• Replace belt
	• Rusted pulley(s)	• Clean rust from pulley(s)
	• Sharp or jagged pulley groove tips	• Replace pulley
	• Rubber deteriorated	• Replace belt
Longitudinal belt cracking (cracks between two ribs)	• Belt has mistracked from pulley groove	• Replace belt
	• Pulley groove tip has worn away rubber-to-tensile member	• Replace belt
Belt slips	• Belt slipping because of insufficient tension	• Adjust tension
	• Belt or pulley subjected to substance (belt dressing, oil, ethylene glycol) that has reduced friction	• Replace belt and clean pulleys
	• Driven component bearing failure	• Replace faulty component bearing
	• Belt glazed and hardened from heat and excessive slippage	• Replace belt
"Groove jumping" (belt does not maintain correct position on pulley, or turns over and/or runs off pulleys)	• Insufficient belt tension	• Adjust belt tension
	• Pulley(s) not within design tolerance	• Replace pulley(s)
	• Foreign object(s) in grooves	• Remove foreign objects from grooves

Troubleshooting the Serpentine Drive Belt (cont.)

Problem	Cause	Solution
"Groove jumping" (belt does not maintain correct position on pulley, or turns over and/or runs off pulleys)	• Excessive belt speed • Pulley misalignment • Belt-to-pulley profile mismatched • Belt cordline is distorted	• Avoid excessive engine acceleration • Align pulley(s) • Install correct belt • Replace belt
Belt broken (Note: identify and correct problem before replacement belt is installed)	• Excessive tension • Tensile members damaged during belt installation • Belt turnover • Severe pulley misalignment • Bracket, pulley, or bearing failure	• Replace belt and adjust tension to specification • Replace belt • Replace belt • Align pulley(s) • Replace defective component and belt
Cord edge failure (tensile member exposed at edges of belt or separated from belt body)	• Excessive tension • Drive pulley misalignment • Belt contacting stationary object • Pulley irregularities • Improper pulley construction • Insufficient adhesion between tensile member and rubber matrix	• Adjust belt tension • Align pulley • Correct as necessary • Replace pulley • Replace pulley • Replace belt and adjust tension to specifications
Sporadic rib cracking (multiple cracks in belt ribs at random intervals)	• Ribbed pulley(s) diameter less than minimum specification • Backside bend flat pulley(s) diameter less than minimum • Excessive heat condition causing rubber to harden • Excessive belt thickness • Belt overcured • Excessive tension	• Replace pulley(s) • Replace pulley(s) • Correct heat condition as necessary • Replace belt • Replace belt • Adjust belt tension

ENGINE MECHANICAL SPECIFICATIONS

Component	U.S.	Metric
CYLINDER HEAD		
Surface Warpage		
ALL ENGINES	0.0-0.001 in.	0.0-0.025 mm
Valve		
Stem diameter		
2.0L Engine		
intake:	0.2753-0.2747 in.	6.992-6.978 mm
exhaust:	0.2760-0.2755 in.	7.012-6.998 mm
2.3L Engine		
intake:	0.2751-0.2745 in.	6.990-6.972 mm
exhaust:	0.2740-0.2747 in.	6.959-6.977 mm
2.5L Engine		
intake:	0.3130-0.3140 in.	7.960-7.980 mm
exhaust:	0.3120-0.3130 in.	7.920-7.960 mm
3.0L Engine		
intake:	0.3412-0.3401 in.	8.666-8.638 mm
exhaust:	0.3412-0.3405 in.	8.666-8.638 mm
Stem Clearance		
3.3L Engine		
intake	0.0015-0.0035 in.	0.038-0.089 mm
exhaust	0.0015-0.0032 in.	0.038-0.081 mm
Face angle		
2.0L	46 degrees	
2.3L	45 degrees	
2.5L	45 degrees	
3.0L	45 degrees	
3.3L	45 degrees	
Valve margin		
2.0L	0.025 in.	0.635 mm
2.3L	0.0098 in.	0.250 mm
2.5L	0.025 in.	0.640 mm
3.0L	0.025 in.	0.640 mm
3.3L	0.025 in.	0.635 mm
Stem-to-guide clearance		
2.0L		
intake:	0.0006-0.0020 in.	0.015-0.042 mm
exhaust:	0.0010-0.0024 in.	0.030-0.060 mm
2.3L		
intake:	0.0010-0.0027 in.	0.025-0.069 mm
exhaust:	0.0015-0.0032 in.	0.038-0.081 mm
2.5L		
intake:	0.0010-0.0026 in.	0.028-0.071 mm
exhaust:	0.0013-0.0041 in.	0.033-0.104 mm
3.0L		
intake:	0.0015-0.0035 in.	0.038-0.089 mm
exhaust:	0.0015-0.0035 in.	0.038-0.089 mm
3.3L		
intake:	0.0015-0.0032 in.	0.038-0.089 mm
exhaust:	0.0015-0.0035 in.	0.038-0.089 mm
Valve Spring		
Installed Height		
2.5L	1.68 in.	42.64 mm
3.3L	1.69-1.75 in.	42.93-44.45 mm
Valve seat		
Angle		
2.0L	45 degrees	
2.3L	45 degrees	
2.5L	46 degrees	
3.0L	45 degrees	
3.3L	45 degrees	

ENGINE MECHANICAL SPECIFICATIONS

Component	U.S.	Metric
Camshaft and Bearings		
Bearing clearance		
2.0L	0.0011-0.0035 in.	0.030-0.090 mm
2.3L	0.0019-0.0043 in.	0.050-0.110 mm
2.5L	0.0007-0.0027 in.	0.01778-0.0685 mm
3.0L		
No.1	0.0005-0.0025 in.	0.0127-0.0635 mm
2-4	0.0005-0.0035 in.	0.0127-0.0889 mm
3.3L	0.0005-0.0035 in.	0.013-0.089 mm

TORQUE SPECIFICATIONS

Component	U.S.	Metric
Camshaft Carrier and Cylinder Head Bolts		
2.0L	18 ft. lbs.	25 Nm
plus 3 turns of 60 degrees and 30-50 degrees after warm up		
Camshaft Pulley/Sprocket		
2.0L	20 ft. lbs.	27 Nm
2.3L	18 ft. lbs.	25 Nm
2.5L	89 in. lbs 10 Nm	
3.0L	31 ft. lbs.	42 Nm
3.3L	74 ft.lbs. +105 deg.	100 Nm +105 deg.
Cylinder Head		
2.3L		
1st step:	15 ft. lbs.	20 Nm
2nd step:	26 ft. lbs.	35 Nm
2.5L		
1st step:	18 ft. lbs.	25 Nm
2nd step:	26 ft. lbs.	35 Nm
3.0L		
1st step:	25 ft. lbs.	35 Nm
2nd step:	plus ¼ turn	
3.3L		
1st step:	35 ft. lbs.	47 Nm
2nd step:	plus 130 degree turn	
3rd step:	Center four bolts 30 deg.	
Connecting Rod		
2.0L	26 ft. lbs.	35 Nm
2.3L	18 ft. lbs.	25 Nm
2.5L	32 ft. lbs.	44 Nm
3.0L	45 ft. lbs.	61 Nm
3.3L	20 ft. lbs.	27 Nm
	plus 50 deg.	plus 50 deg.
Main Bearing Cap		
2.0L	44 ft. lbs.	60 Nm
2.5L	65 ft. lbs.	88 Nm
2.3L	15 ft. lbs.	20 Nm
3.0L	100 ft. lbs.	135 Nm
3.3L	20 ft. lbs.	27 Nm
CHECK	plus 50 deg.	plus 50 deg.
Crankshaft Dampener		
2.5L	162 ft. lbs.	220 Nm
Flywheel to Crankshaft		
2.0L	48 ft. lbs.	65 Nm
2.3L	22 ft. lbs.	30 Nm
2.5L		
MD9	55 ft. lbs.	75 Nm
MT2	69 ft. lbs.	93 Nm

TORQUE SPECIFICATIONS

Component	U.S.	Metric
3.0L	60 ft. lbs.	80 Nm
3.3L	11 ft. lbs. plus 50 deg.	15 Nm plus 50 deg.
Intake Manifold		
2.0L	16 ft. lbs.	22 Nm
2.3L	18 ft. lbs.	25 Nm
2.5L	25 ft. lbs.	34 Nm
3.0L	32 ft. lbs.	44 Nm
3.3L		
lower	88 in. lbs.	10 Nm
upper	22 ft. lbs.	30 Nm
Exhaust Manifold		
2.0L	16 ft. lbs.	22 Nm
2.3L	27 ft. lbs.	37 Nm
2.5L		
inner	37 ft. lbs.	50 Nm
outer	26 ft. lbs.	35 Nm
3.0L	37 ft. lbs.	50 Nm
3.3L	38 ft. lbs.	52 Nm
Exhaust Manifold-to-Pipe		
All engines	18-22 ft. lbs.	25-30 Nm
Spark Plug		
2.0L	17 ft. lbs.	22 Nm
2.3L	17 ft. lbs.	22 Nm
2.5L	17 ft. lbs.	22 Nm
3.0L	20 ft. lbs.	27 Nm
3.3L	12 ft. lbs.	16 Nm
Water Pump		
2.0L	18 ft. lbs.	24 Nm
2.3L	19 ft. lbs.	26 Nm
2.5L	25 ft. lbs.	34 Nm
3.0L	97 in. lbs.	11 Nm
3.3L	11 ft. lbs.	15 Nm
Water Pump Pulley		
All Engines	115 in. lbs.	13 Nm
Thermostat Housing		
2.3L	19 ft. lbs.	26 Nm
2.5L	20 ft. lbs.	27 Nm
3.0L	159 in. lbs.	18 Nm
3.3L	20 ft. lbs.	27 Nm
Front Cover		
2.3L	106 in. lbs.	12 Nm
2.5L	89 in. lbs.	10 Nm
3.0L	22 ft. lbs.	30 Nm
3.3L	22 ft. lbs.	30 Nm
Oil Pan		
2.0L	4 ft. lbs.	5 Nm
2.3L	17 ft. lbs.	24 Nm
2.5L	20 ft. lbs.	27 Nm
3.0L	88 in. lbs.	10 Nm
3.3L	124 in. lbs.	14 Nm

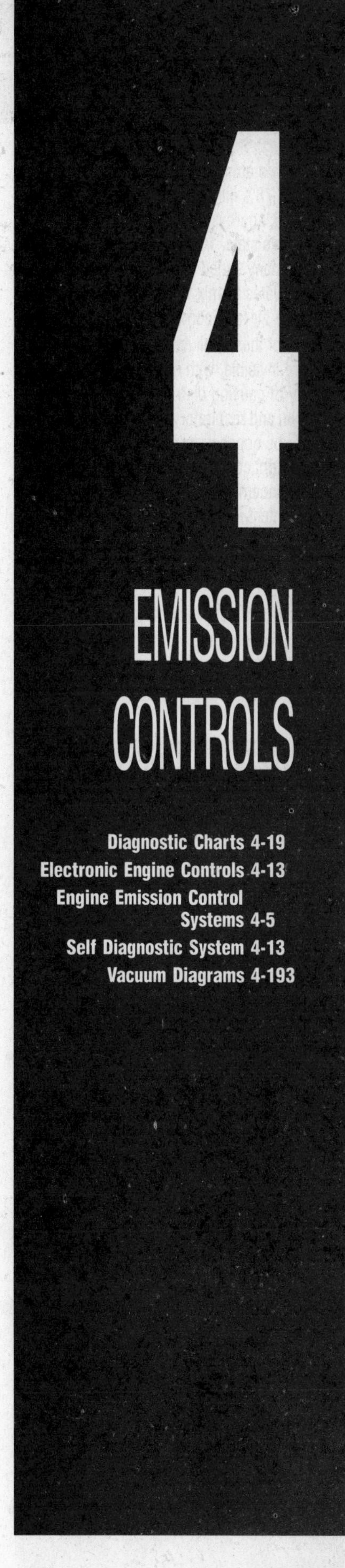

4 EMISSION CONTROLS

AIR POLLUTION

The earth's atmosphere, at or near sea level, consists of 78% nitrogen, 21% oxygen and 1% other gases, approximately. If it were possible to remain in this state, 100% clean air would result. However, many varied causes allow other gases and particulates to mix with the clean air, causing the air to become unclean or polluted.

Certain of these pollutants are visible while others are invisible, with each having the capability of causing distress to the eyes, ears, throat, skin and respiratory system. Should these pollutants be concentrated in a specific area and under the right conditions, death could result due to the displacement or chemical change of the oxygen content in the air. These pollutants can cause much damage to the environment and to the many man made objects that are exposed to the elements.

To better understand the causes of air pollution, the pollutants can be categorized into 3 separate types, natural, industrial and automotive.

Natural Pollutants

Natural pollution has been present on earth before man appeared and is still a factor to be considered when discussing air pollution, although it causes only a small percentage of the present overall pollution problem existing in our country. It is the direct result of decaying organic matter, wind born smoke and particulates from such natural events as plains and forest fires (ignited by heat or lightning), volcanic ash, sand and dust which can spread over a large area of the countryside.

Such a phenomenon of natural pollution has been recent volcanic eruptions, with the resulting plume of smoke, steam and volcanic ash blotting out the sun's rays as it spreads and rises higher into the atmosphere, where the upper air currents catch and carry the smoke and ash, while condensing the steam back into water vapor. As the water vapor, smoke and ash traveled on their journey, the smoke dissipates into the atmosphere while the ash and moisture settle back to earth in a trail hundred of miles long. In many cases, lives are lost and millions of dollars of property damage result, and ironically, man can only stand by and watch it happen.

Industrial Pollution

Industrial pollution is caused primarily by industrial processes, the burning of coal, oil and natural gas, which in turn produces smoke and fumes. Because the burning fuels contain much sulfur, the principal ingredients of smoke and fumes are sulfur dioxide (SO_2) and particulate matter. This type of pollutant occurs most severely during still, damp and cool weather, such as at night. Even in its less severe form, this pollutant is not confined to just cities. Because of air movements, the pollutants move for miles over the surrounding countryside, leaving in its path a barren and unhealthy environment for all living things.

Working with Federal, State and Local mandated rules, regulations and by carefully monitoring the emissions, industries have greatly reduced the amount of pollutant emitted from their industrial sources, striving to obtain an acceptable level. Because of the mandated industrial emission clean up, many land areas and streams in and around the cities that were formerly barren of vegetation and life, have now begun to move back in the direction of nature's intended balance.

Automotive Pollutants

The third major source of air pollution is the automotive emissions. The emissions from the internal combustion engine were not an appreciable problem years ago because of the small number of registered vehicles and the nation's small highway system. However, during the early 1950's, the trend of the American people was to move from the cities to the surrounding suburbs. This caused an immediate problem in the transportation areas because the majority of the suburbs were not afforded mass transit conveniences. This lack of transportation created an attractive market for the automobile manufacturers, which resulted in a dramatic increase in the number of vehicles produced and sold, along with a marked increase in highway construction between cities and the suburbs. Multi-vehicle families emerged with much emphasis placed on the individual vehicle per family member. As the increase in vehicle ownership and usage occurred, so did the pollutant levels in and around the cities, as the suburbanites drove daily to their businesses and employment in the city and its fringe area, returning at the end of the day to their homes in the suburbs.

It was noted that a fog and smoke type haze was being formed and at times, remained in suspension over the cities and did not quickly dissipate. At first this "smog", derived from the words "smoke" and "fog", was thought to result from industrial pollution but it was determined that the automobile emissions were largely to blame. It was discovered that as normal automobile emissions were exposed to sunlight for a period of time, complex chemical reactions would take place.

It was found the smog was a photo chemical layer and was developed when certain oxides of nitrogen (NOx) and unburned hydrocarbons (HC) from the automobile emissions were exposed to sunlight and was more severe when the smog would remain stagnant over an area in which a warm layer of air would settle over the top of a cooler air mass at ground level, trapping and holding the automobile emissions, instead of the emissions being dispersed and diluted through normal air flows. This type of air stagnation was given the name "Temperature Inversion".

Temperature Inversion

In normal weather situations, the surface air is warmed by the heat radiating from the earth's surface and the sun's rays and will rise upward, into the atmosphere, to be cooled through a convection type heat expands with the cooler upper air. As the warm air rises, the surface pollutants are carried upward and dissipated into the atmosphere.

When a temperature inversion occurs, we find the higher air is no longer cooler but warmer than the surface air, causing the cooler surface air to become trapped and unable to move. This warm air blanket can extend from above ground level to a few hundred or even a few thousand feet into the air. As the surface air is trapped, so are the pollutants, causing a severe smog condition. Should this stagnant air mass extend to a few thousand feet high, enough air movement with the inversion takes place to allow the smog layer to rise above ground level but the pollutants still cannot dissipate. This inversion can remain for days over an area, with only the smog level rising or lowering from ground level to a few hundred feet high. Meanwhile, the pollutant levels increases, causing eye irritation, respirator problems, reduced visibility, plant damage and in some cases, cancer type diseases.

This inversion phenomenon was first noted in the Los Angeles, California area. The city lies in a basin type of terrain and during certain weather conditions, a cold air mass is held in the basin while a warmer air mass covers it like a lid.

Because this type of condition was first documented as prevalent in the Los Angeles area, this type of smog was named Los Angeles Smog, although it occurs in other areas where a large concentration of automobiles are used and the air remains stagnant for any length of time.

Internal Combustion Engine Pollutants

Consider the internal combustion engine as a machine in which raw materials must be placed so a finished product comes out. As in any machine operation, a certain amount of wasted material is formed. When we relate this to the internal combustion engine, we find that by putting in air and fuel, we obtain power from this mixture during the combustion process to drive the vehicle. The by-product or waste of this power is, in part, heat and exhaust gases with which we must concern ourselves.

HEAT TRANSFER

The heat from the combustion process can rise to over 4000°F (2204°C). The dissipation of this heat is controlled by a ram air effect, the use of cooling fans to cause air flow and having a liquid coolant solution surrounding the combustion area and transferring the heat of combustion through the cylinder walls and into the coolant. The coolant is then directed to a thin-finned, multi-tubed radiator, from which the excess heat is transferred to the outside air by 1 or all of the 3 heat transfer methods, conduction, convection or radiation.

The cooling of the combustion area is an important part in the control of exhaust emissions. To understand the behavior of the combustion and transfer of its heat, consider the air/fuel charge. It is ignited and the flame front burns progressively across the combustion chamber until the burning charge reaches the cylinder walls. Some of the fuel in contact with the walls is not hot enough to burn, thereby snuffing out or Quenching the combustion process. This leaves unburned fuel in the combustion chamber. This unburned fuel is then forced out of the cylinder along with the exhaust gases and into the exhaust system.

Many attempts have been made to minimize the amount of unburned fuel in the combustion chambers due to the snuffing out or "Quenching", by increasing the coolant temperature and lessening the contact area of the coolant around the combustion area. Design limitations within the combustion chambers prevent the complete burning of the air/fuel charge, so a certain amount of the unburned fuel is still expelled into the exhaust system, regardless of modifications to the engine.

EXHAUST EMISSIONS

Composition Of The Exhaust Gases

The exhaust gases emitted into the atmosphere are a combination of burned and unburned fuel. To understand the exhaust emission and its composition review some basic chemistry.

When the air/fuel mixture is introduced into the engine, we are mixing air, composed of nitrogen (78%), oxygen (21%) and other gases (1%) with the fuel, which is 100% hydrocarbons (HC), in a semi-controlled ratio. As the combustion process is accomplished, power is produced to move the vehicle while the heat of combustion is transferred to the cooling system. The exhaust gases are then composed of nitrogen, a diatomic gas (N_2), the same as was introduced in the engine, carbon dioxide (CO2), the same gas that is used in beverage carbonation and water vapor (H_2O). The nitrogen (N_2), for the most part passes through the engine unchanged, while the oxygen (O_2) reacts (burns) with the hydrocarbons (HC) and produces the carbon dioxide (CO_2) and the water vapors (H_2O). If this chemical process would be the only process to take place, the exhaust emissions would be harmless. However, during the combustion process, other pollutants are formed and are considered dangerous. These pollutants are carbon monoxide (CO), hydrocarbons (HC), oxides of nitrogen (NOx) oxides of sulfur (SOx) and engine particulates.

Lead (Pb), is considered 1 of the particulates and is present in the exhaust gases whenever leaded fuels are used. Lead (Pb) does not dissipate easily. Levels can be high along roadways when it is emitted from vehicles and can pose a health threat. Since the increased usage of unleaded gasoline and the phasing out of leaded gasoline for fuel, this pollutant is gradually diminishing. While not considered a major threat lead is still considered a dangerous pollutant.

HYDROCARBONS

Hydrocarbons (HC) are essentially unburned fuel that have not been successfully burned during the combustion process or have escaped into the atmosphere through fuel evaporation. The main sources of incomplete combustion are rich air/fuel mixtures, low engine temperatures and improper spark timing. The main sources of hydrocarbon emission through fuel evaporation come from the vehicle's fuel tank and carburetor bowl.

To reduce combustion hydrocarbon emission, engine modifications were made to minimize dead space and surface area in the combustion chamber. In addition the air/fuel mixture was made more lean through improved carburetion, fuel injection and by the addition of external controls to aid in further combustion of the hydrocarbons outside the engine. Two such methods were the addition of an air injection system, to inject fresh air into the exhaust manifolds and the installation of a catalytic converter, a unit that is able to burn traces of hydrocarbons without affecting the internal combustion process or fuel economy.

To control hydrocarbon emissions through fuel evaporation, modifications were made to the fuel tank and carburetor bowl to allow storage of the fuel vapors during periods of engine shut-down, and at specific times during engine operation, to purge and burn these same vapors by blending them with the air/fuel mixture.

CARBON MONOXIDE

Carbon monoxide is formed when not enough oxygen is present during the combustion process to convert carbon (C) to carbon dioxide (CO_2). An increase in the carbon monoxide (CO) emission is normally accompanied by an increase in the hydrocarbon (HC) emission because of the lack of oxygen to completely burn all of the fuel mixture.

Carbon monoxide (CO) also increases the rate at which the photo chemical smog is formed by speeding up the conversion of nitric oxide (NO) to nitrogen dioxide (NO_2). To accomplish this, carbon monoxide (CO) combines with oxygen (O_2) and nitrogen dioxide (NO_2) to produce carbon dioxide (CO_2) and nitrogen dioxide (NO_2). ($CO + O_2 + NO = CO_2 + NO_2$).

The dangers of carbon monoxide, which is an odorless, colorless toxic gas are many. When carbon monoxide is inhaled into the lungs and passed into the blood stream, oxygen is replaced by the carbon monoxide in the red blood cells, causing a reduction in the amount of oxygen being supplied to the many parts of the body. This lack of oxygen causes headaches, lack of coordination, reduced mental alertness and should the carbon monoxide concentration be high enough, death could result.

NITROGEN

Normally, nitrogen is an inert gas. When heated to approximately 2500°F (1371°C) through the combustion process, this gas becomes active and causes an increase in the nitric oxide (NOx) emission.

Oxides of nitrogen (NOx) are composed of approximately 97–98% nitric oxide (NO2). Nitric oxide is a colorless gas but when it is passed into the atmosphere, it combines with oxygen and forms nitrogen dioxide (NO2). The nitrogen dioxide then combines with chemically active hydrocarbons (HC) and when in the presence of sunlight, causes the formation of photo chemical smog.

OZONE

To further complicate matters, some of the nitrogen dioxide (NO_2) is broken apart by the sunlight to form nitric oxide and oxygen. (NO_2 + sunlight = NO + O). This single atom of oxygen then combines with diatomic (meaning 2 atoms) oxygen (O_2) to form ozone (O_3). Ozone is 1 of the smells associated with smog. It has a pungent and offensive odor, irritates the eyes and lung tissues, affects the growth of plant life and causes rapid deterioration of rubber products. Ozone can be formed by sunlight as well as electrical discharge into the air.

The most common discharge area on the automobile engine is the secondary ignition electrical system, especially when inferior quality spark plug cables are used. As the surge of high voltage is routed through the secondary cable, the circuit builds up an electrical field around the wire, acting upon the oxygen in the surrounding air to form the ozone. The faint glow along the cable with the engine running that may be visible on a dark night, is called the "corona discharge." It is the result of the electrical field passing from a high along the cable, to a low in the surrounding air, which forms the ozone gas. The combination of corona and ozone has been a major cause of cable deterioration. Recently, different types and better quality insulating materials have lengthened the life of the electrical cables.

Although ozone at ground level can be harmful, ozone is beneficial to the earth's inhabitants. By having a concentrated ozone layer called the 'ozonosphere', between 10 and 20 miles (16–32km) up in the atmosphere much of the ultra violet radiation from the sun's rays are absorbed and screened. If this ozone layer were not present, much of the earth's surface would be burned, dried and unfit for human life.

There is much discussion concerning the ozone layer and its density. A feeling exists that this protective layer of ozone is slowly diminishing and corrective action must be directed to this problem. Much experimenting is presently being conducted to determine if a problem exists and if so, the short and long term effects of the problem and how it can be remedied.

OXIDES OF SULFUR

Oxides of sulfur (SOx) were initially ignored in the exhaust system emissions, since the sulfur content of gasoline as a fuel is less than $\frac{1}{10}$ of 1%. Because of this small amount, it was felt that it contributed very little to the overall pollution problem. However, because of the difficulty in solving the sulfur emissions in industrial pollutions and the introduction of catalytic converter to the automobile exhaust systems, a change was mandated. The automobile exhaust system, when equipped with a catalytic converter, changes the sulfur dioxide (SO_2) into the sulfur trioxide (SO_3).

When this combines with water vapors (H_2O), a sulfuric acid mist (H_2SO_4) is formed and is a very difficult pollutant to handle and is extremely corrosive. This sulfuric acid mist that is formed, is the same mist that rises from the vents of an automobile storage battery when an active chemical reaction takes place within the battery cells.

When a large concentration of vehicles equipped with catalytic converters are operating in an area, this acid mist will rise and be distributed over a large ground area causing land, plant, crop, paints and building damage.

PARTICULATE MATTER

A certain amount of particulate matter is present in the burning of any fuel, with carbon constituting the largest percentage of the particulates. In gasoline, the remaining percentage of particulates is the burned remains of the various other compounds used in its manufacture. When a gasoline engine is in good internal condition, the particulate emissions are low but as the engine wears internally, the particulate emissions increase. By visually inspecting the tail pipe emissions, a determination can be made as to where an engine defect may exist. An engine with light gray smoke emitting from the tail pipe normally indicates an increase in the oil consumption through burning due to internal engine wear. Black smoke would indicate a defective fuel delivery system, causing the engine to operate in a rich mode. Regardless of the color of the smoke, the internal part of the engine or the fuel delivery system should be repaired to a "like new" condition to prevent excess particulate emissions.

Diesel and turbine engines emit a darkened plume of smoke from the exhaust system because of the type of fuel used. Emission control regulations are mandated for this type of emission and more stringent measures are being used to prevent excess emission of the particulate matter. Electronic components are being introduced to control the injection of the fuel at precisely the proper time of piston travel, to achieve the optimum in fuel ignition and fuel usage. Other particulate after-burning components are being tested to achieve a cleaner particular emission.

Good grades of engine lubricating oils should be used, meeting the manufacturers specification. "Cut-rate" oils can contribute to the particulate emission problem because of their low "flash" or ignition temperature point. Such oils burn prematurely during the combustion process causing emissions of particulate matter.

The cooling system is an important factor in the reduction of particulate matter. With the cooling system operating at a temperature specified by the manufacturer, the optimum of combustion will occur. The cooling system must be maintained in the same manner as the engine oiling system, as each system is required to perform properly in order for the engine to operate efficiently for a long time.

Other Automobile Emission Sources

Before emission controls were mandated on the internal combustion engines, other sources of engine pollutants were discovered, along with the exhaust emission. It was determined the engine combustion exhaust produced 60% of the total emission pollutants, fuel evaporation from the fuel tank and carburetor vents produced 20%, with the another 20% being produced through the crankcase as a by-product of the combustion process.

CRANKCASE EMISSIONS

Crankcase emissions are made up of water, acids, unburned fuel, oil fumes and particulates. The emissions are classified as hydrocarbons (HC) and are formed by the small amount of unburned, compressed air/fuel mixture entering the crankcase from the combustion area during the compression and power strokes, between the cylinder walls and piston rings. The head of the compression and combustion help to form the remaining crankcase emissions.

Since the first engines, crankcase emissions were allowed to go into the air through a road draft tube, mounted on the lower side of the engine block. Fresh air came in through an open oil filler cap or breather. The air passed through the crankcase mixing with blow-by gases. The motion of the vehicle and the air blowing past the open end of the road draft tube caused a low pressure area at the end of the tube. Crankcase emissions were simply drawn out of the road draft tube into the air.

To control the crankcase emission, the road draft tube was deleted. A hose and/or tubing was routed from the crankcase to the intake manifold so the blow-by emission could be burned with the air/fuel mixture. However, it was found that intake manifold vacuum, used to draw the crankcase emissions into the manifold, would vary in strength at the wrong time and not allow the proper emission flow. A regulating type valve was needed to control the flow of air through the crankcase.

Testing, showed the removal of the blow-by gases from the crankcase as quickly as possible, was most important to the longevity of the engine. Should large accumulations of blow-by gases remain and condense, dilution of the engine oil would occur to form water, soots, resins, acids and lead salts, resulting in the formation of sludge and varnishes. This condensation of the blow-by gases occur more frequently on vehicles used in numerous starting and stopping conditions, excessive idling and when the engine is not allowed to attain normal operating temperature through short runs. The crankcase purge control or PCV system will be described in detail later in this section.

FUEL EVAPORATIVE EMISSIONS

Gasoline fuel is a major source of pollution, before and after it is burned in the automobile engine. From the time the fuel is refined, stored, pumped and transported, again stored until it is pumped into the fuel tank of the vehicle, the gasoline gives off unburned hydrocarbons (HC) into the atmosphere. Through redesigning of the storage areas and venting systems, the pollution factor has been diminished but not eliminated, from the refinery standpoint. However, the automobile still remained the primary source of vaporized, unburned hydrocarbon (HC) emissions.

Fuel pumped form an underground storage tank is cool but when exposed to a warner ambient temperature, will expand. Before controls were mandated, an owner would fill the fuel tank with fuel from an underground storage tank and park the vehicle for some time in warm area, such as a parking lot. As the fuel would warm, it would expand and should no provisions or area be provided for the expansion, the fuel would spill out the filler neck and onto the ground, causing hydrocarbon (HC) pollution and creating a severe fire hazard. To correct this condition, the vehicle manufacturers added overflow plumbing and/or gasoline tanks with built in expansion areas or domes.

However, this did not control the fuel vapor emission from the fuel tank and the carburetor bowl. It was determined that most of the fuel evaporation occurred when the vehicle was stationary and the engine not operating. Most vehicles carry 5–25 gallons (19–95 liters) of gasoline. Should a large concentration of vehicles be parked in one area, such as a large parking lot, excessive fuel vapor emissions would take place, increasing as the temperature increases.

To prevent the vapor emission from escaping into the atmosphere, the fuel system is designed to trap the fuel vapors while the vehicle is stationary, by sealing the fuel system from the atmosphere. A storage system is used to collect and hold the fuel vapors from the carburetor and the fuel tank when the engine is not operating. When the engine is started, the storage system is then purged of the fuel vapors, which are drawn into the engine and burned with the air/fuel mixture.

The components of the fuel evaporative system will be described in detail later in this section.

EMISSION CONTROLS

Crankcase Ventilation System

➧ SEE FIGS. 1–7

OPERATION

The Crankcase Ventilation system is used on all vehicles to evacuate the crankcase vapors. There are 2 types of ventilation systems: Crankcase Ventilation (CV) and Positive Crankcase Ventilation (PCV).

Both systems purge crankcase vapors and differ only in the use of fresh air, circulated through the crankcase, in the case of PCV systems. The CV system, used on the 2.3L engine, allows crankcase vapors to escape but does not introduce fresh air into the crankcase.

The PCV system, used on all other engines, circulates fresh air from the air cleaner or intake duct through the crankcase, where it mixes with blow-by gases and then passes through the Positive Crankcase Ventilation (PCV) valve or constant bleed orifice into the intake manifold.

When manifold vacuum is high, such as at idle, the orifice or valve restricts the flow of blow-by gases into the intake manifold. If abnormal operating conditions occur, the system will allow excessive blow-by gases to back flow through the hose into the air cleaner. These blow-by gases will then be mixed with the intake air in the air cleaner instead of the manifold. The air cleaner has a small filter attached to the inside wall that connects to the breather hose to trap impurities flowing in either direction.

A plugged PCV valve, orifice or hose may cause rough idle, stalling or slow idle speed, oil leaks, oil in the air cleaner or sludge in the engine. A leak could cause rough idle, stalling or high idle speed. The condition of the grommets in the valve cover will also affect system and engine performance.

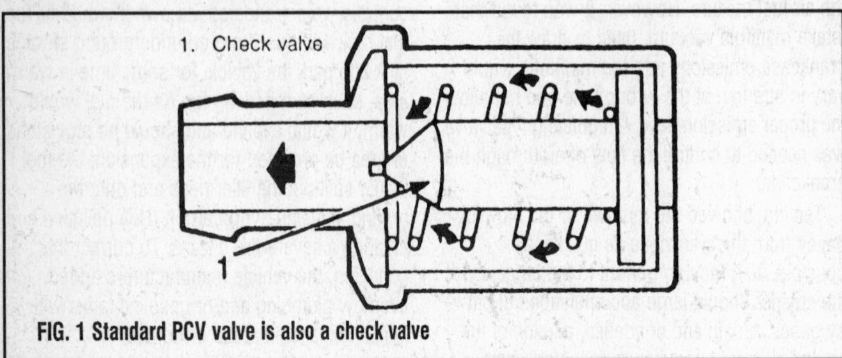

FIG. 1 Standard PCV valve is also a check valve

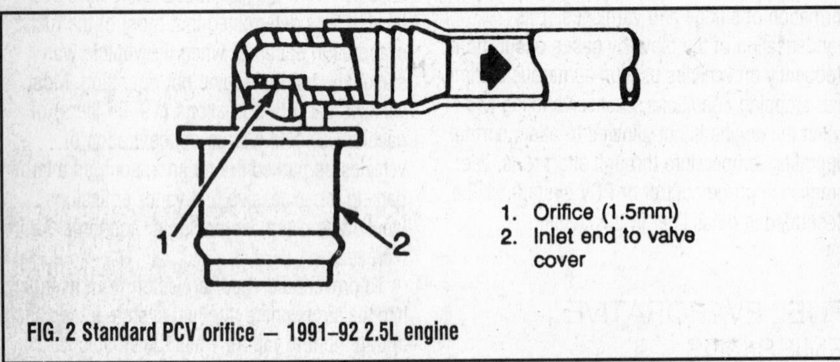

FIG. 2 Standard PCV orifice — 1991–92 2.5L engine

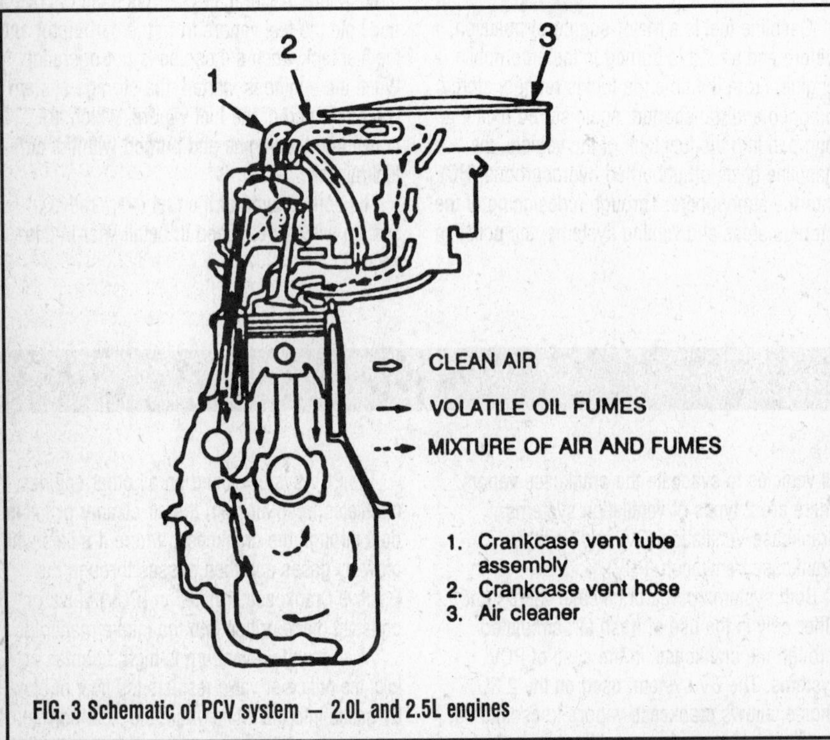

FIG. 3 Schematic of PCV system — 2.0L and 2.5L engines

SERVICE

PCV Valve

1. Remove the PCV valve from the rocker arm cover.
2. With the engine at normal operating temperature, run at idle.
3. Remove the PCV valve or orifice from the grommet in the valve cover and place thumb over the end to check if vacuum is present. If vacuum is not present, check for plugged hoses or manifold port. Repair or replace as necessary.
4. If the engine is equipped with a PCV valve, stop the engine and remove the valve. Shake and listen for the rattle of the check valve needle. If no rattle is heard, replace the valve.

PCV System

1. Check to make sure the engine has the correct PCV valve or bleed orifice.
2. Start the engine and bring to normal operating temperature.
3. Block off PCV system fresh air intake passage.
4. Remove the engine oil dipstick and install a vacuum gauge on the dipstick tube.
5. Run the engine at 1500 rpm for 30 seconds then read the vacuum gauge with the engine at 1500 rpm.
   - If vacuum is present, the PCV system is functioning properly.
   - If there is no vacuum, the engine may not be sealed and/or is drawing in outside air. Check the grommets and valve cover or oil pan gasket for leaks.
   - If the vacuum gauge registers a pressure or the vacuum gauge is pushed out of the dipstick tube, check for the correct PCV valve or bleed orifice, a plugged hose or excessive engine blow-by.

CV System

2.3L ENGINE

1. Check the CV system for proper flow by looking for oil sludging or leaks.
2. If noted, check the smaller nipple of the oil/air separator by blowing through it or inserting a 1.52mm plug gauge into the orifice inside the nipple.
3. If the orifice is plugged, replace the CV oil/air separator assembly.

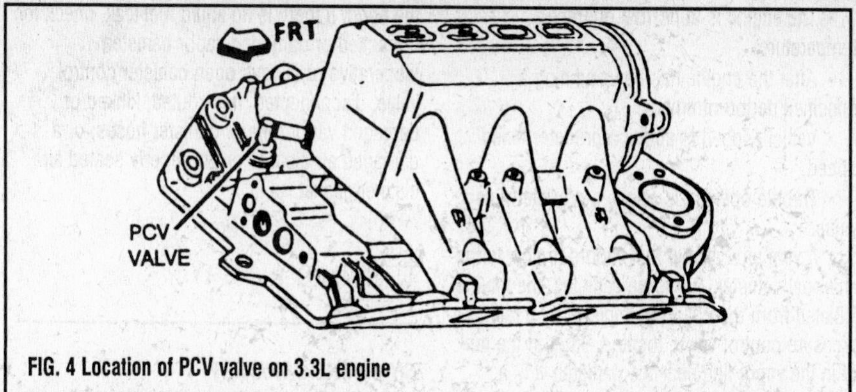

FIG. 4 Location of PCV valve on 3.3L engine

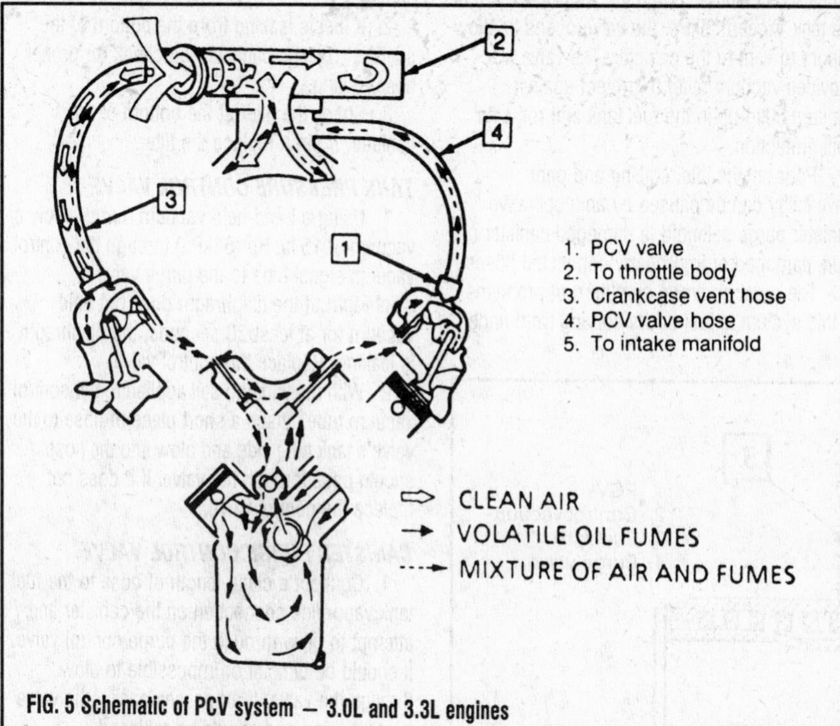

FIG. 5 Schematic of PCV system — 3.0L and 3.3L engines

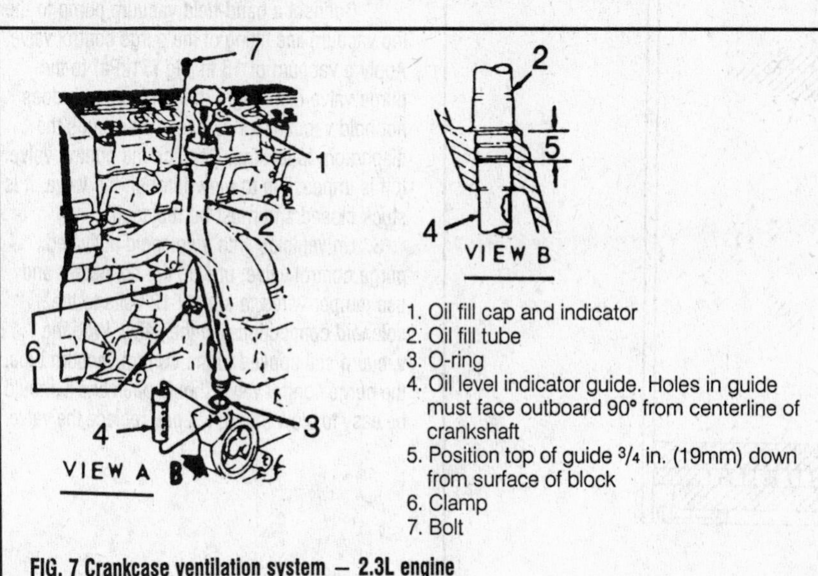

FIG. 7 Crankcase ventilation system — 2.3L engine

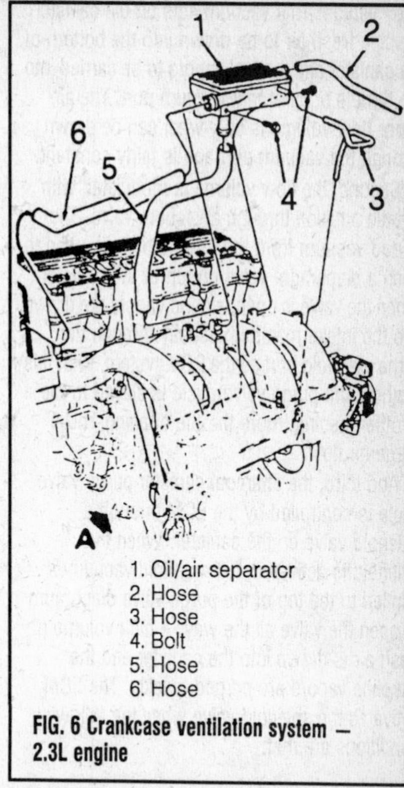

FIG. 6 Crankcase ventilation system — 2.3L engine

Fuel Evaporative Emission Control System

SEE FIGS. 8 AND 9

OPERATION

The Evaporative Emission Control System is designed to prevent fuel tank vapors from being emitted into the atmosphere. When the engine is not running, gasoline vapors from the tank are stored in a charcoal canister, mounted under the hood. The charcoal canister absorbs the gasoline vapors and stores them until certain engine conditions are met and the vapors can be purged and burned by the engine. In some vehicles with fuel injection, any liquid fuel entering the canister goes into a reservoir in the bottom of the canister to protect the integrity of the carbon element in the canister above. Three different methods are used to control the purge cycle of the charcoal canister.

First, the charcoal canister purge cycle is controlled by throttle position without the use of a valve on the canister. A vacuum line connects the canister to a ported vacuum source on the throttle body. When the throttle is at any position above idle, a vacuum is created in the throttle body venturi. That vacuum acts on the canister causing fresh air to be drawn into the bottom of the canister and the fuel vapors to be carried into the throttle body at that vacuum port. The air/vapor flow volume is only what can be drawn through the vacuum port and is fairly constant.

Second, the flow volume is modulated with throttle position through a vacuum valve. The ported vacuum from the throttle body is used to open a diaphragm valve on top of the canister. When the valve is open, air and vapors are drawn into the intake manifold, usually through the same manifold port as the PCV system. With this method, the purge valve cycle is slaved to the throttle opening; more throttle opening, more purge air flow.

And third, the charcoal canister purge valve cycle is controlled by the ECM through a solenoid valve on the canister. When the solenoid is activated, full manifold vacuum is applied to the top of the purge valve diaphragm to open the valve all the way. A high volume of fresh air is drawn into the canister and the gasoline vapors are purged quickly. The ECM activates the solenoid valve when the following conditions are met:

- The engine is at normal operating temperature.
- After the engine has been running a specified period of time.
- Vehicle speed is above a predetermined speed.
- Throttle opening is above a predetermined value.
- A vent pipe allows fuel vapors to flow to the charcoal canister. On some vehicles, the tank is isolated from the charcoal canister by a tank pressure control valve, located either in the tank or in the vapor line near the canister. It is a combination roll-over, integral pressure and vacuum relief valve. When the vapor pressure in the tank exceeds 5kPa, the valve opens to allow vapors to vent to the canister. The valve also provides vacuum relief to protect against vacuum build-up in the fuel tank and roll-over spill protection.
- Poor engine idle, stalling and poor driveability can be caused by an inoperative canister purge solenoid, a damaged canister or split, damaged or improperly connected hoses.
- The most common symptom of problems in this system is fuel odors coming from under the hood. If there is no liquid fuel leak, check for a cracked or damaged vapor canister, inoperative or always open canister control valve, disconnected, mis-routed, kinked or damaged vapor pipe or canister hoses; or a damaged air cleaner or improperly seated air cleaner gasket.

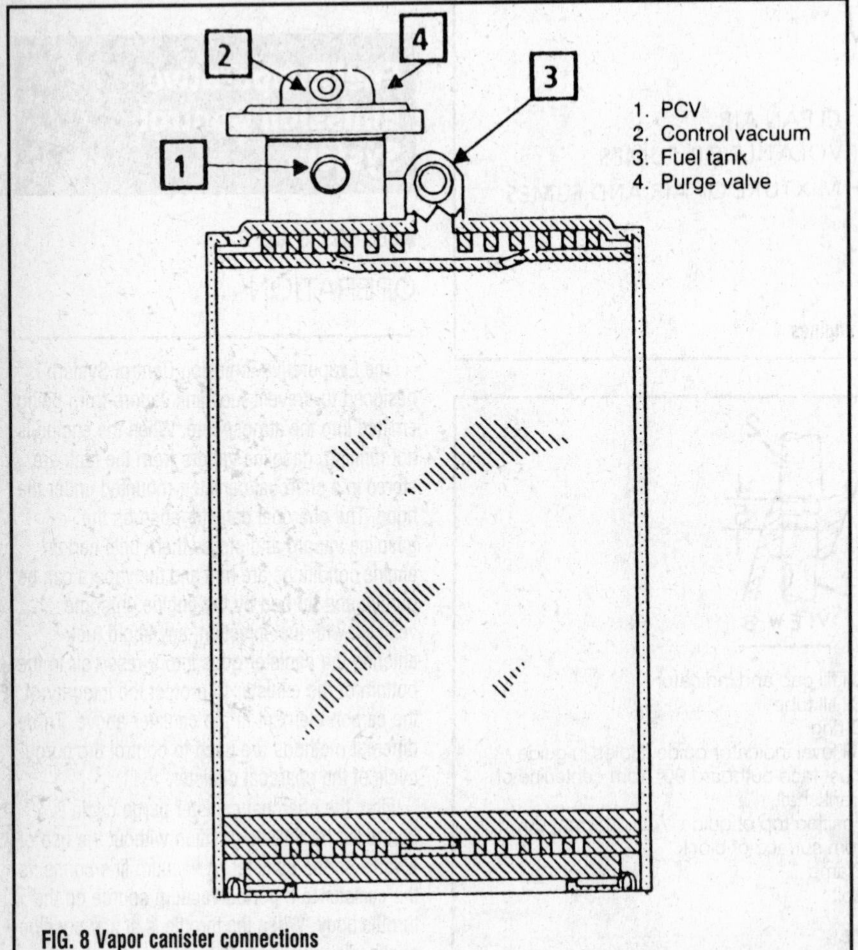

FIG. 8 Vapor canister connections

TESTING

CHARCOAL CANISTER

1. Visually check the canister for cracks or damage.
2. If fuel is leaking from the bottom of the canister, replace canister and check for proper hose routing.
3. Check the filter at the bottom of the canister. If dirty, replace the filter.

TANK PRESSURE CONTROL VALVE

1. Using a hand-held vacuum pump, apply a vacuum of 15 in. Hg (51kPa) through the control vacuum signal tube to the purge valve diaphragm. If the diaphragm does not hold vacuum for at least 20 seconds, the diaphragm is leaking. Replace the control valve.
2. With the vacuum still applied to the control vacuum tube, attach a short piece of hose to the valve's tank tube side and blow into the hose. Air should pass through the valve. If it does not, replace the control valve.

CANISTER PURGE CONTROL VALVE

1. Connect a clean length of hose to the fuel tank vapor line connection on the canister and attempt to blow through the purge control valve. It should be difficult or impossible to blow through the valve. If air passes easily, the valve is stuck open and should be replaced.
2. Connect a hand-held vacuum pump to the top vacuum line fitting of the purge control valve. Apply a vacuum of 15 in. Hg (51kPa) to the purge valve diaphragm. If the diaphragm does not hold vacuum for at least 20 seconds the diaphragm is leaking. Replace the control valve. If it is impossible to blow through the valve, it is stuck closed and must be replaced.
3. On vehicles with a solenoid activated purge control valve, unplug the connector and use jumper wires to supply 12 volts to the solenoid connections on the valve. With the vacuum still applied to the control vacuum tube, the purge control valve should open and it should be easy to blow through. If not, replace the valve.

REMOVAL & INSTALLATION

CHARCOAL CANISTER

1. Tag and disconnect the hoses from the canister.
2. Remove the charcoal canister retaining nut.
3. Remove the canister from the vehicle.
4. Installation is the reverse of the removal procedure. Torque the retainers to 25 inch lbs. (2.8 Nm). Refer to the Vehicle Emission Control Information label, located in the engine compartment, for proper routing of the vacuum hoses.

TANK PRESSURE CONTROL VALVE

1. Disconnect the hoses from the control valve.
2. Remove the mounting hardware.
3. Remove the control valve from the vehicle.
4. Installation is the reverse of the removal procedure. Refer to the Vehicle Emission Control Information label, located in the engine compartment, for proper routing of the vacuum hoses.

Exhaust Gas Recirculation System

➧ SEE FIGS. 10–16

OPERATION

➡ The 2.3L and 3.3L engines do not use an EGR valve.

The EGR system is used to reduce oxides of nitrogen (NOx) emission levels caused by high combustion chamber temperatures. This is accomplished by the use of an EGR valve which opens, under specific engine operating conditions, to admit a small amount of exhaust gas into the intake manifold, below the throttle plate. The exhaust gas mixes with the incoming air charge and displaces a portion of the oxygen in the air/fuel mixture entering the combustion chamber. The exhaust gas does not support combustion of the air/fuel mixture but it takes up volume, the net effect of which is to lower the temperature of the combustion process. This lower temperature also helps control detonation.

The EGR valve is a mounted on the intake manifold and has an opening into the exhaust manifold. The EGR valve is opened by ported vacuum and allows exhaust gases to flow into the intake manifold. If too much exhaust gas enters, combustion will not occur. Because of this, very little exhaust gas is allowed to pass through the valve. The EGR system will be activated once the engine reaches normal operating temperature and the EGR valve will open when engine operating conditions are above idle speed and below Wide Open Throttle (WOT). On California vehicles equipped with a Vehicle Speed Sensor (VSS), the EGR valve opens when the VSS signal is greater than 2 mph. The EGR system is deactivated on vehicles equipped with a Transmission Converter Clutch (TCC) when the TCC is engaged.

Too much EGR flow at idle, cruise, or during cold operation may result in the engine stalling after cold start, the engine stalling at idle after deceleration, vehicle surge during cruise and rough idle. If the EGR valve is always open, the vehicle may not idle. Too little or no EGR flow allows combustion temperatures to get too high which could result in spark knock (detonation), engine overheating and/or emission test failure.

The two types of EGR valves used on N body

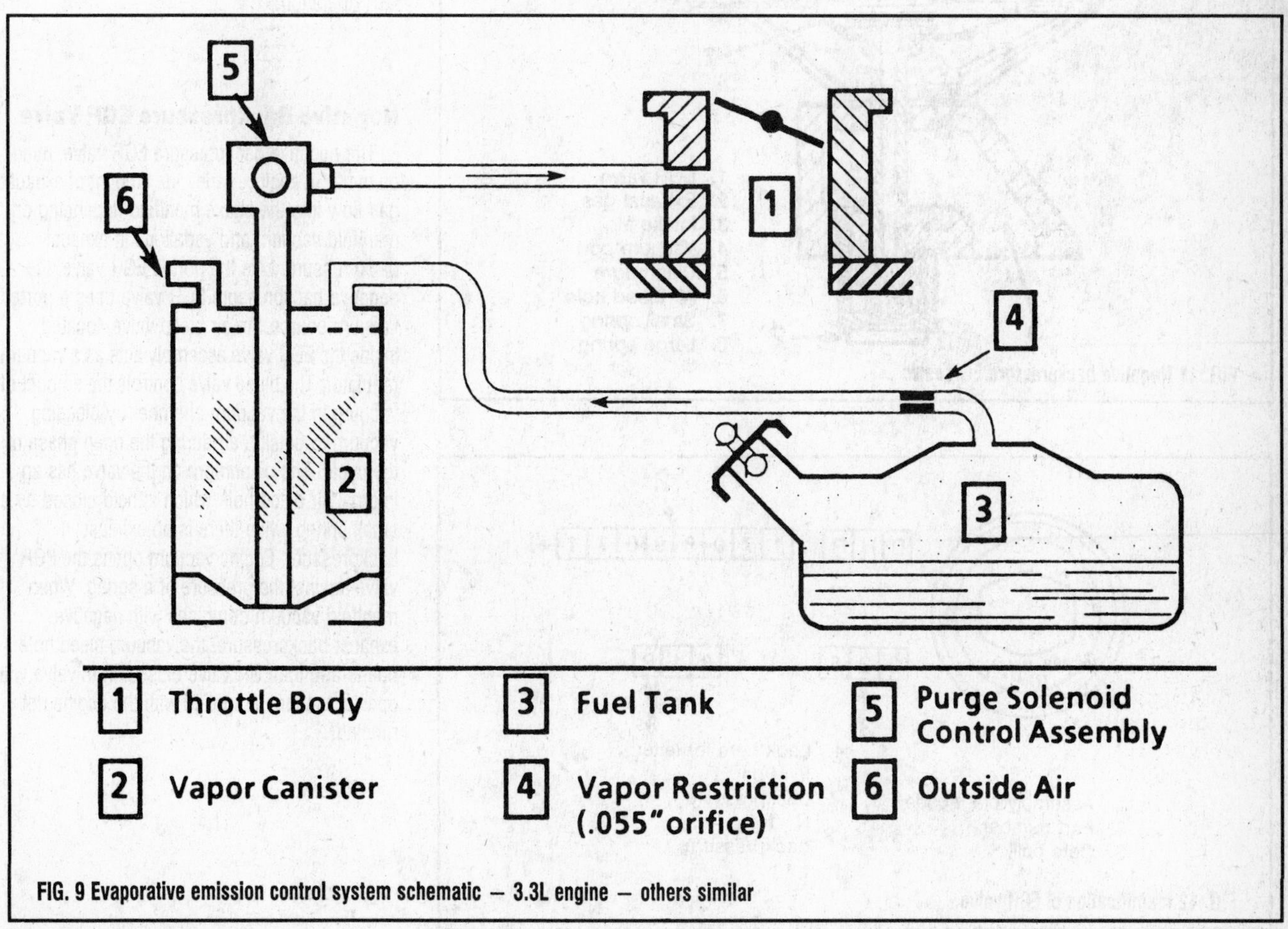

FIG. 9 Evaporative emission control system schematic — 3.3L engine — others similar

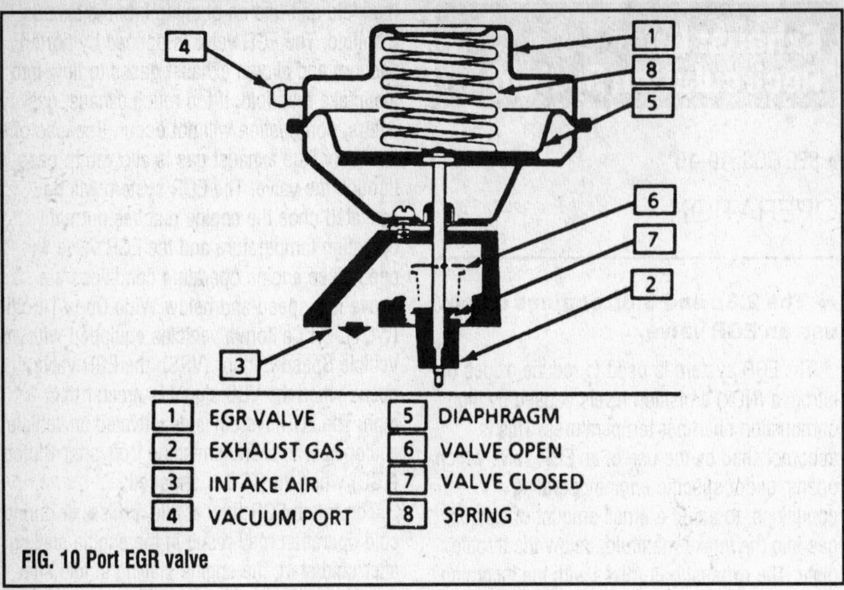

FIG. 10 Port EGR valve

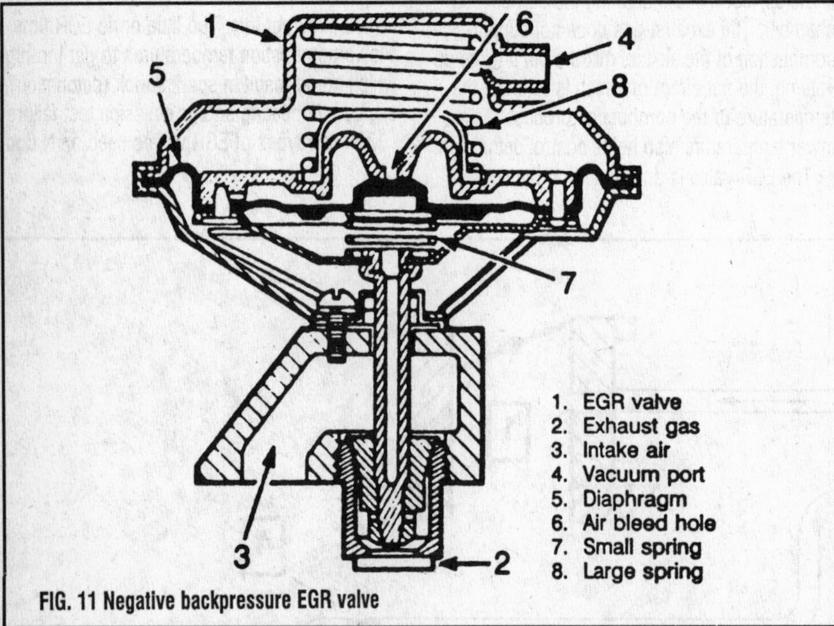

FIG. 11 Negative backpressure EGR valve

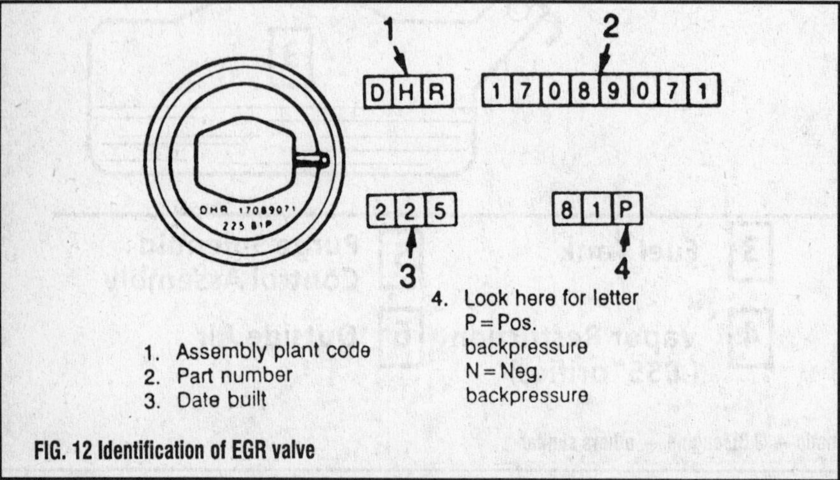

FIG. 12 Identification of EGR valve

vehicles are ported and negative backpressure and differ mainly in the way EGR flow is modulated.

Ported EGR Valve

The ported EGR valve takes its name from the fact that it uses a ported vacuum source to open the EGR valve and modulate the EGR flow. The ported vacuum source is a small opening just above the throttle blade in the throttle body. When the throttle begins to open the air passing through the venturi, creates a low pressure which draws on the EGR valve diaphragm causing it to open. As the throttle blade opens further, the ported vacuum increases and opens the valve further.

The ECM controls EGR operation through an EGR control solenoid. Ported vacuum must flow through the EGR control solenoid to open the EGR valve. The ECM uses information received from the Coolant Temperature Sensor (CTS), Throttle Position Sensor (TPS) and the Mass Air Flow (MAF) sensor to determine when to allow EGR operation. When certain parameters are met, such as engine at normal operating temperature and the engine speed is above idle, the ECM signals the solenoid to open, allowing EGR operation.

Negative Backpressure EGR Valve

The negative backpressure EGR valve, used on the 2.5L engine, varies the amount of exhaust gas flow into the intake manifold depending on manifold vacuum and variations in exhaust backpressure. Like the ported EGR valve, the negative backpressure EGR valve uses a ported vacuum source. An air bleed valve, located inside the EGR valve assembly acts as a vacuum regulator. The bleed valve controls the amount of vacuum in the vacuum chamber by bleeding vacuum to outside air during the open phase of the cycle. The diaphragm on the valve has an internal air bleed hole which is held closed by a small spring when there is no exhaust backpressure. Engine vacuum opens the EGR valve against the pressure of a spring. When manifold vacuum combines with negative exhaust backpressure, the vacuum bleed hole opens and the EGR valve closes. This valve will open if vacuum is applied with the engine not running.

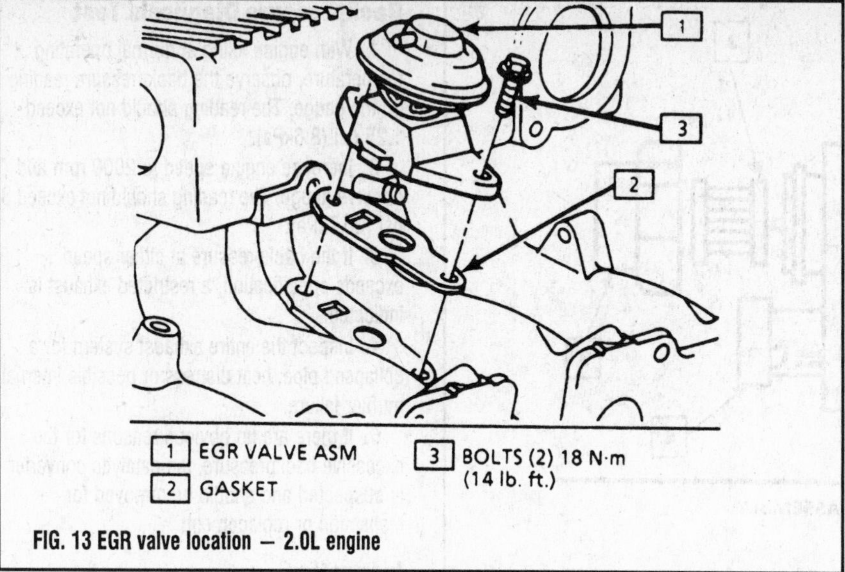

FIG. 13 EGR valve location — 2.0L engine

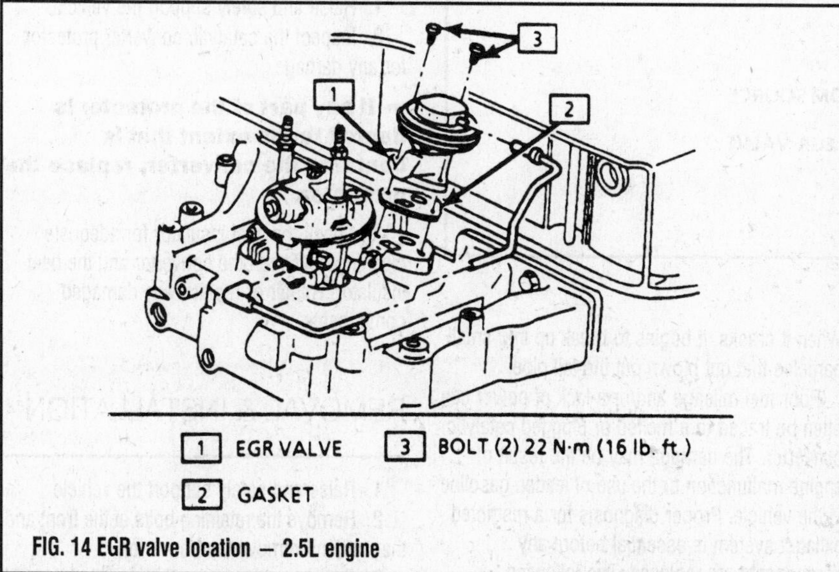

FIG. 14 EGR valve location — 2.5L engine

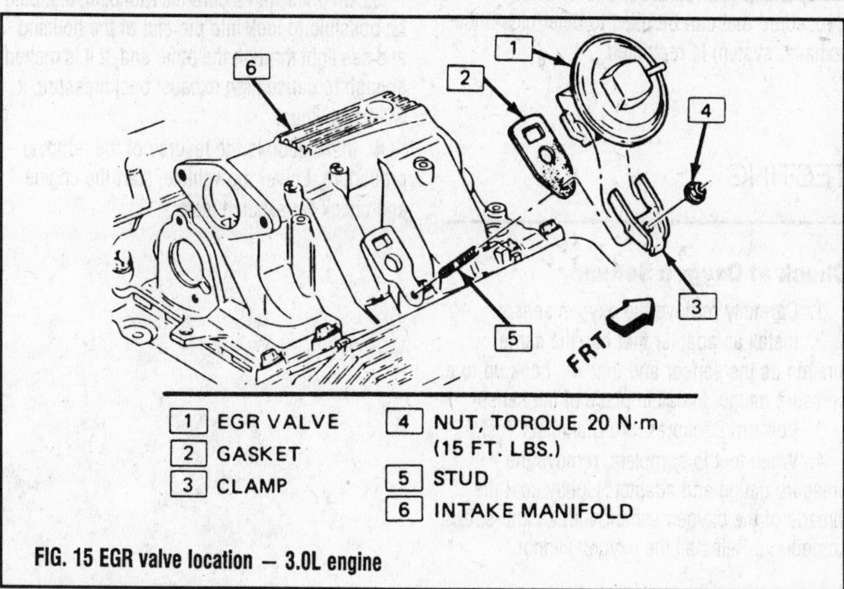

FIG. 15 EGR valve location — 3.0L engine

TESTING

1. Inspect all passages and moving parts for plugging, sticking and deposits.
2. Inspect the entire system (hoses, tubes, connections, etc.) for leakage. Replace any part that is leaking, hardened, cracked, or melted.
3. Run the engine to normal operating temperature, and allow the engine to idle for 2 minutes. Quickly accelerate the engine to 2,500 rpm. Visible movement of the EGR stem should occur indicating proper system function. If no movement occurs, check the vacuum source and hose.
4. To determine if gas is flowing through the system, connect a vacuum pump to the valve.
5. With the engine idling, slowly apply vacuum. Engine speed should start to decrease when applied vacuum reaches 3 in. Hg. The engine speed may drop quickly and could even stall; this indicated proper function.
6. If engine speed does not drop off, remove the EGR valve and check for plugged passages. If everything checks out, replace the valve.

REMOVAL & INSTALLATION

1. Disconnect the negative battery cable.
2. Remove the air cleaner assembly.
3. Tag and disconnect the necessary hoses and wiring to gain access to the EGR valve.
4. Remove the EGR valve retaining bolts.
5. Remove the EGR valve. Discard the gasket.
6. Buff the exhaust deposits from the mounting surface and around the valve using a wire wheel.
7. Remove deposits from the valve outlet.
8. Clean the mounting surfaces of the intake manifold and valve assembly.

To install:

9. Install a new EGR gasket.
10. Install the EGR valve to the manifold.
11. Install the retaining bolts and torque to 16 ft. lbs. (22 Nm).
12. Connect the wiring and hoses.
13. Install the air cleaner assembly.
14. Connect the negative battery cable.

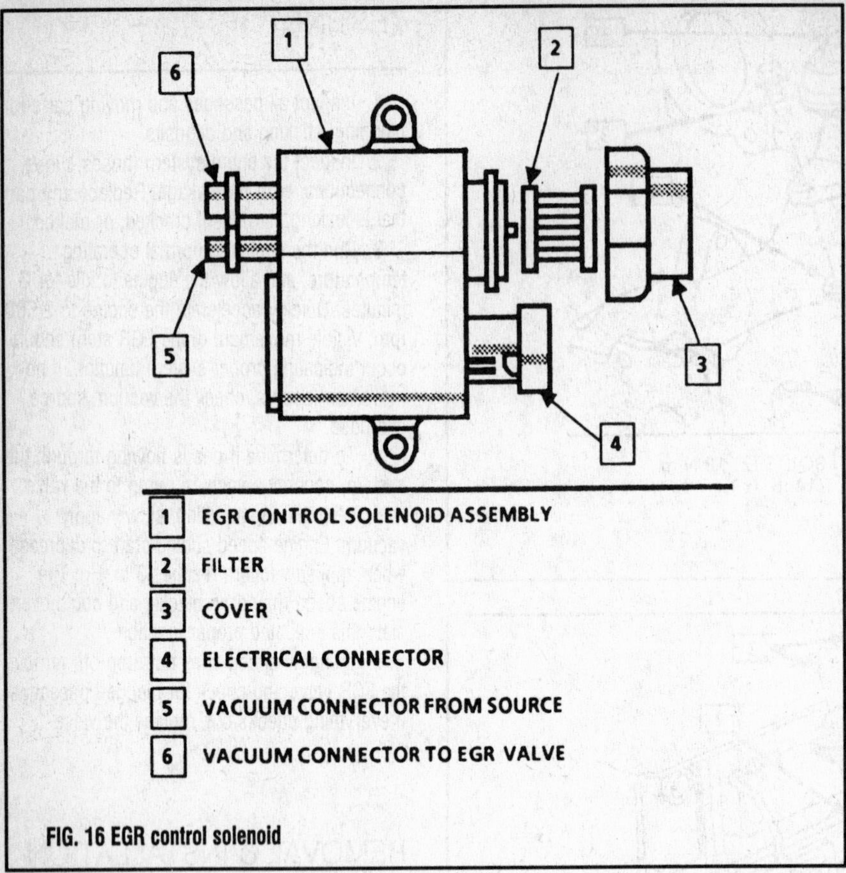

FIG. 16 EGR control solenoid

Catalytic Converter

OPERATION

The catalytic converter is mounted in the engine exhaust stream ahead of the muffler. Its function is to combine carbon monoxide (CO) and hydrocarbons (HC) with oxygen and break down nitrogen oxide (NOx) compounds. These gasses are converted to mostly CO_2 and water. It heats to operating temperature within about 1–2 minutes, depending on ambient temperature and driving conditions and will operate at temperatures up to about 1500°F. Inside the converter housing is a single or dual bed ceramic monolith, coated with various combinations of platinum, paladium and rhodium.

The catalytic converter is not serviceable. If tests and visual inspection show the converter to be damaged, it must be replaced. There are 2 types of failures: melting or fracturing. The most common failure is melting, resulting from unburned gasoline contacting the monolith, such as when a cylinder does not fire. Usually when the monolith melts, high backpressure results. When it cracks, it begins to break up into small particles that get blown out the tail pipe.

Poor fuel mileage and/or a lack of power can often be traced to a melted or plugged catalytic converter. The damage may be the result of engine malfunction or the use of leaded gasoline in the vehicle. Proper diagnosis for a restricted exhaust system is essential before any components are replaced. The following procedure that can be used to determine if the exhaust system is restricted.

TESTING

Check at Oxygen Sensor

1. Carefully remove the oxygen sensor.
2. Install an adapter that has the same threads as the sensor and that will hook up to a pressure gauge. Install in place of the sensor.
3. Perform Backpressure Diagnosis Test.
4. When test is complete, remove the pressure gauge and adapter. Lightly coat the threads of the oxygen sensor with an anti-seize compound. Reinstall the oxygen sensor.

Backpressure Diagnosis Test

1. With engine idling at normal operating temperature, observe the backpressure reading on the gauge. The reading should not exceed 1.25 psi (8.6kPa).
2. Increase engine speed to 2000 rpm and observe gauge. The reading should not exceed 3 psi (20.7kPa).
3. If the backpressure at either speed exceeds specification, a restricted exhaust is indicated.
4. Inspect the entire exhaust system for a collapsed pipe, heat distress or possible internal muffler failure.
5. If there are no obvious reasons for the excessive backpressure, the catalytic converter is suspected and should be removed for inspection or replacement.

Inspection

1. Raise and safely support the vehicle.
2. Inspect the catalytic converter protector for any damage.

➡ If any part of the protector is dented to the extent that is contacts the converter, replace the protector.

3. Check the heat insulator for adequate clearance between the converter and the heat insulator. Repair or replace any damaged components.

REMOVAL & INSTALLATION

1. Raise and safely support the vehicle.
2. Remove the retaining bolts at the front and the rear and remove the converter.
3. On units with a ceramic monolith, it should be possible to look into the end of the housing and see light through the other end. If it is melted enough to cause high exhaust backpressure, it will be obvious.
4. Installation is the reverse of the removal procedure. Lower the vehicle, start the engine and check for exhaust leaks.

ELECTRONIC ENGINE CONTROLS

Fuel System

➡ **For removal and installation procedures and additional information, please refer to Section 5.**

GENERAL INFORMATION

The basic function of the fuel metering system is to control the delivery of fuel to the meet all engine operating conditions. The fuel delivery system consists of the Throttle Body Injection (TBI) unit or fuel rail assembly with individual injectors and pressure regulator and throttle body assembly with Idle Air Control (IAC) valve and Throttle Position Sensor (TPS); the fuel pump, fuel pump relay, fuel tank, accelerator control, fuel lines, fuel filters and evaporative emission control system.

The fuel system is controlled by an Electronic Control Module (ECM) located in the passenger compartment. The ECM is the control center of the computer command control system processing information from various input sources to control certain engine functions. The ECM controls fuel delivery, ignition timing, electronic spark control, some emission control systems, engagement of the transmission converter clutch and downshift control or the manual transmission shift light. The ECM is also a valuable diagnostic tool in that it has the ability to store trouble codes which can by helpful in identifying malfunctioning systems. The ECM can also be used in conjunction with a SCAN tool to monitor values of engine sensors to see if they are within specification.

The ECM operates in 2 running mode conditions: open and closed loop. When the engine is cold and engine rpm is above a specified value, the ECM ignores any signal it may be receiving from the oxygen sensor and stays in open loop. The ECM will go into closed loop when the following conditions are met: the oxygen sensor is sending a fluctuating signal to the ECM (indicating that it is hot enough to operate properly and respond to changes in the oxygen content in the exhaust gas), the engine is at normal operating temperature and a specific amount of time has elapsed since engine start. When operating in closed loop, the ECM varies the injector on-time in order to maintain the ideal stoichiometric ratio of 14.7:1. This mixture ratio provides optimum fuel economy and engine performance as well as minimizing exhaust emissions.

Fuel Injection System

OPERATION

The fuel injection system uses a solenoid-operated fuel injector(s) mounted either on the throttle body (2.5L engine) or at the intake valve port of each cylinder (all other engines). The ECM controls the flow of fuel to the cylinders by varying the injector duty cycle or length of time the electrical solenoid is energized.

The TBI system used on the 2.5L (VIN U) uses model 700 fuel injector units. The model 700 unit consists of 2 major castings: the fuel meter assembly with pressure regulator and fuel injector, and the throttle body with the IAC valve and TPS.

MPFI systems deliver fuel to the intake port of each cylinder by a fuel injector which is controlled by the ECM.

Coolant Temperature Sensor

OPERATION

Most engine functions are affected by the coolant temperature. Determining whether the engine is hot or cold is largely dependent on the temperature of the coolant. An accurate temperature signal to the ECM is supplied by the coolant temperature sensor. The coolant temperature sensor is a thermistor mounted in the engine coolant stream. A thermistor is an electrical device that varies its resistance in relation to changes in temperature. Low coolant temperature produces a high resistance (100,000Ω at –40°F/–40°C) and high coolant temperature produces low resistance (70Ω at 266°F/130°C). The ECM supplies a signal of 5 volts to the coolant temperature sensor through a resistor in the ECM and measures the voltage. The voltage will be high when the engine is cold and low when the engine is hot.

Fuel Filter

OPERATION

The in-line fuel filter is a paper element filter designed to trap particles that may damage the fuel injection system. The filter element must be replaced periodically. The fuel system pressure must be relieved before opening the system to replace the filter.

Fuel Injector Assembly

➧ SEE FIGS. 17 AND 18

OPERATION

The fuel injector(s) are mounted on the fuel meter assembly or at the intake port of each cylinder. The fuel injector is a solenoid-operated device, controlled by the ECM. The ECM energizes the solenoid, which lifts a normally-closed ball valve off its seat. The fuel, which is under pressure, is injected in a conical spray pattern at the walls of the throttle body bore above the throttle valve. The amount of fuel sprayed is determined by the length of time the ECM energizes the injector solenoid, known as the pulse width.

The fuel which is not used by the injectors is cycled through the pressure regulator and back to the fuel tank; cycling the fuel helps prevent vapor lock.

Fuel Pressure Regulator

➧ SEE FIG. 19

OPERATION

The fuel pressure regulator keeps the fuel available to the injectors within a specified

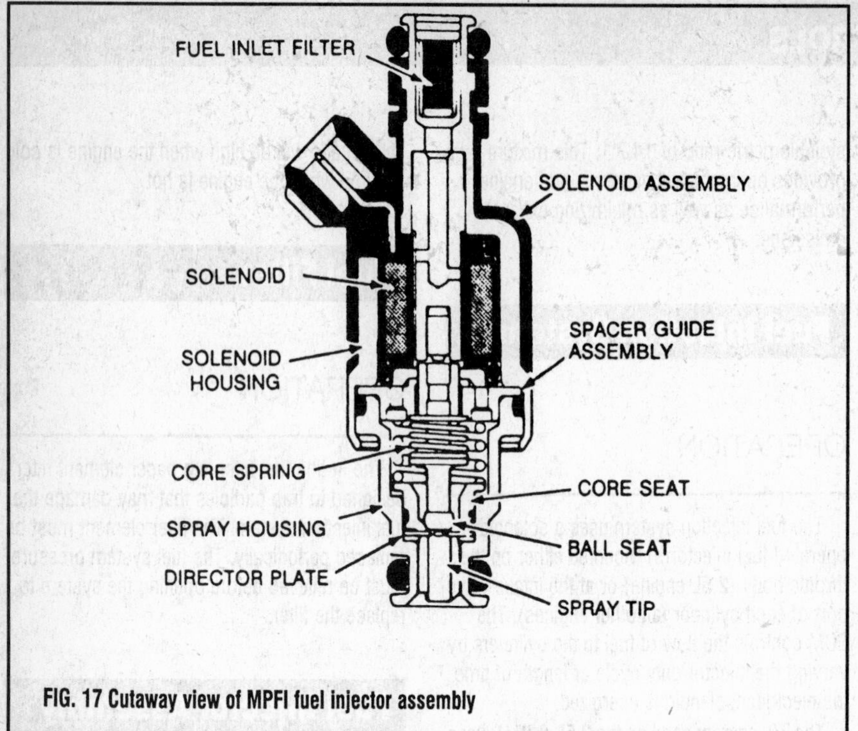

FIG. 17 Cutaway view of MPFI fuel injector assembly

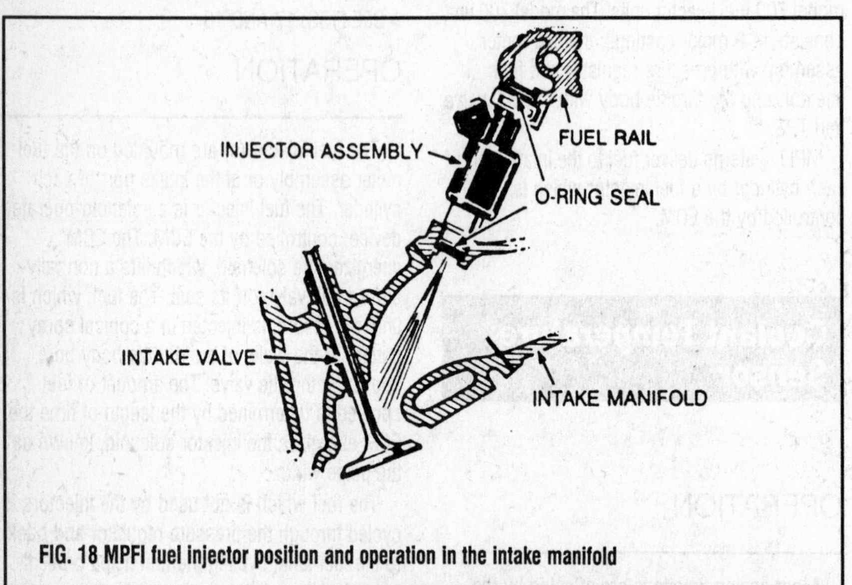

FIG. 18 MPFI fuel injector position and operation in the intake manifold

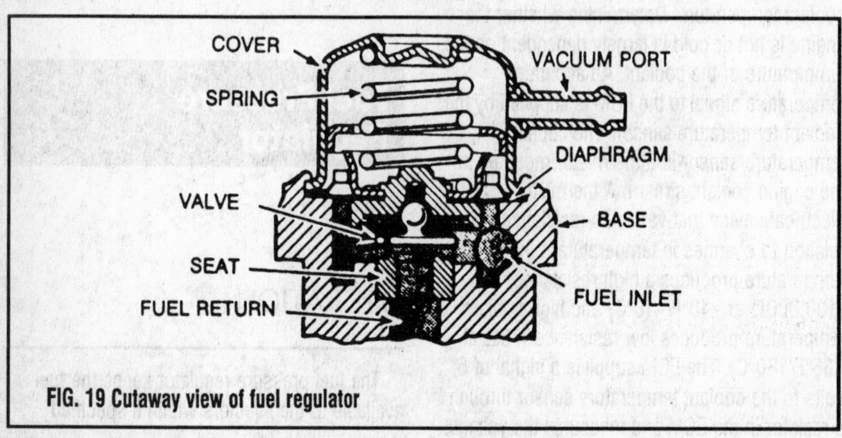

FIG. 19 Cutaway view of fuel regulator

pressure range. The pressure regulator is a diaphragm-operated relief valve with fuel pump pressure on one side and air cleaner pressure in vehicles equipped with TBI or intake manifold vacuum in others, acting on the other side. On some engines, the pressure regulator and fuel rail are serviced as an assembly, and the regulator cannot be removed from the fuel rail.

Idle Air Control (IAC) Valve

➧ SEE FIG. 20

OPERATION

Engine idle speeds are controlled by the ECM through the IAC valve mounted on the throttle body. The ECM sends voltage pulses to the IAC motor windings causing the IAC motor shaft and pintle to move **IN** or **OUT** a given distance (number of steps) for each pulse (called counts). The movement of the pintle controls the airflow around the throttle plate, which in turn, controls engine idle speed. Idle Air Control valve pintle position counts can be observed using a Scan tool. Zero (0) counts corresponds to a fully closed passage, while 140 counts or more correspond to full flow.

Idle speed can be categorized in 2 ways: actual (controlled) idle speed and minimum idle speed. Controlled idle speed is obtained by the ECM positioning the IAC valve pintle. Resulting idle speed is determined by total air flow (IAC/passage + PCV + throttle valve + calibrated vacuum leaks). Controlled idle speed is specified at normal operating conditions, which consists of engine coolant at normal operating temperature, air conditioning compressor **OFF**, manual transmission in neutral or automatic transmission in **D**.

Minimum idle air speed is set at the factory with a stop screw. This setting allows enough air flow by the throttle valves to cause the IAC valve pintle to be positioned a calibrated number of steps (counts) from the seat during normal controlled idle operation.

The idle speed is controlled by the ECM through the IAC valve. No adjustment is required during routine maintenance. Tampering with the minimum idle speed adjustment is highly discouraged and may result in premature failure of the IAC valve.

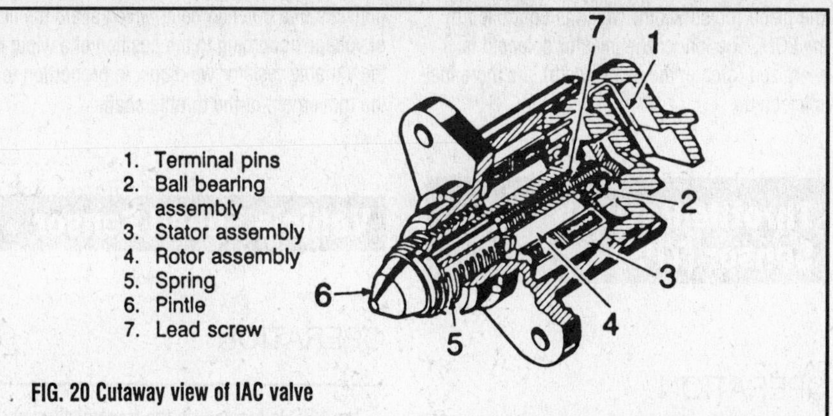

FIG. 20 Cutaway view of IAC valve

Manifold Absolute Pressure (MAP) Sensor

OPERATION

Except 3.0L (VIN L) and 3.3L (VIN N) Engines

The MAP sensor measures the changes in intake manifold pressure, which result from engine load and speed changes and converts this information to a voltage output. The MAP sensor reading is the opposite of a vacuum gauge reading: when manifold pressure is high, MAP sensor value is high and vacuum is low. A MAP sensor will produce a low output on engine coast down with a closed throttle while a wide open throttle will produce a high output. The high output is produced because the pressure inside the manifold is the same as outside the manifold, so 100% of the outside air pressure is measured.

The MAP sensor is also used to measure barometric pressure under certain conditions, which allows the ECM to automatically adjust for different altitudes.

The MAP sensor changes the 5 volt signal supplied by the ECM, which reads the change and uses the information to control fuel delivery and ignition timing.

Mass Air Flow (MAF) Sensor

OPERATION

3.0L (VIN L) and 3.3L (VIN N) Engines

The Mass Air Flow sensor, used on 3.0L (VIN L) and 3.3L (VIN N) engines, replaces the MAP sensor used on other engines. The MAF sensor is located in the incoming air stream and measures the amount of air that passes through the electrical grid. The MAF indicates air flow to the ECM as an electrical value. The ECM uses this information to determine the operating condition of the engine in order to determine fuel requirements. A large quantity of air passing through the MAF will be read by the ECM as acceleration condition and a small quantity as deceleration or idle.

Manifold Air Temperature (MAT)/ Intake Air Temperature Sensor(IAT)

OPERATION

The MAT/IAT sensor is a thermistor which supplies manifold air temperature information to the ECM. The MAT/IAT sensor produces high resistance (100,000Ω at –40°F/–40°C) at low temperatures and low resistance of 70Ω at 266°F (130°C) at high temperatures. The ECM supplies a 5 volt signal to the MAT sensor and measures MAT/IAT sensor output voltage. The voltage signal will be high when the air is cold and low when the air is hot.

Oxygen Sensor

OPERATION

The exhaust oxygen sensor or O_2 sensor, is mounted in the exhaust stream where it monitors oxygen content in the exhaust gas. The oxygen content in the exhaust is a measure of the air/fuel mixture going into the engine. The oxygen in the exhaust reacts with the oxygen sensor to produce a voltage which is read by the ECM. The voltage output is very low, ranging from 0.1 volt in a high oxygen-lean mixture condition to 0.9 volt in a low oxygen-rich mixture condition.

Precautions:

- Careful handling of the oxygen sensor is essential.
- The electrical pigtail and connector are permanently attached and should not be removed from the oxygen sensor.
- The in-line electrical connector and louvered end of the oxygen sensor must be kept free of grease, dirt and other contaminants.
- Avoid using cleaning solvents of any type on the oxygen sensor.
- Do not drop or roughly handle the oxygen sensor.
- The oxygen sensor may be difficult to remove if the engine temperature is below 120°F (48°C). Excessive force may damage the threads in the exhaust manifold or exhaust pipe.

Throttle Body Injection (TBI) Unit

OPERATION

The TBI unit is mounted on the intake manifold and contains the fuel injector(s), pressure regulator, IAC valve and fuel meter assembly. The fuel injector is/are solenoid-operated device, controlled by the ECM. The ECM energizes the solenoid, which lifts a normally closed ball valve off its seat. Fuel, under pressure, is injected in a conical spray pattern at the walls of the throttle body bore above the throttle valve. When the ECM de-energizes the solenoid, spring pressure closes the ball valve. The amount of fuel sprayed is determined by the length of time the injector is energized (pulse width) which is controlled by the ECM. The longer the injector solenoid is energized (greater the pulse width), the more fuel is injected.

Throttle Position Sensor (TPS)

OPERATION

The TPS is mounted to the throttle body, opposite the throttle lever and is connected to the throttle shaft. Its function is to sense the current throttle valve position and relay that information to the ECM. Throttle position information allows the ECM to generate the required injector control signals. The TPS consists of a potentiometer which alters the flow of voltage according to the position of a wiper on the variable resistor windings, in proportion to the movement of the throttle shaft.

Vehicle Speed Sensor

OPERATION

The VSS is located on the transmission and sends a pulsing voltage signal to the ECM which is converted to miles per hour. This sensor mainly controls the operation of the TCC system, shift light, cruise control and activation of the EGR system.

SELF-DIAGNOSTIC SYSTEMS

System Description

The Electronic Control Module (ECM) is required to maintain the exhaust emissions at acceptable levels. The module is a small, solid state computer which receives signals from many sources and sensors; it uses these data to make judgments about operating conditions and then control output signals to the fuel and emission systems to match the current requirements.

Inputs are received from many sources to form a complete picture of engine operating conditions. Some inputs are simply Yes or No messages, such as that from the Park/Neutral switch; the vehicle is either in gear or in Park/Neutral; there are no other choices. Other data is sent in quantitative input, such as engine RPM, coolant temperature and throttle position. The ECM is pre-programmed to recognize acceptable ranges or combinations of signals and control the outputs to control emissions while providing good driveability and economy. The ECM also monitors some output circuits, making sure that the components function as commanded. For proper engine operation, it is essential that all input and output components function properly and communicate properly with the ECM.

Since the control module is programmed to recognize the presence and value of electrical inputs, it will also note the lack of a signal or a radical change in values. It will, for example, react to the loss of signal from the vehicle speed sensor or note that engine coolant temperature has risen beyond acceptable (programmed) limits. Once a fault is recognized, a numeric code is assigned and held in memory. The dashboard warning lamp — CHECK ENGINE or SERVICE ENGINE SOON — will illuminate to advise the operator that the system has detected a fault.

More than one code may be stored. Although not every engine uses every code, possible codes range from 12 to 100. Additionally, the same code may carry different meanings relative to each engine or engine family.

In the event of an ECM failure, the system will default to a pre-programmed set of values. These are compromise values which allow the engine to operate, although possibly at reduced efficiency. This is variously known as the default, limp-in or back-up mode. Driveability is almost always affected when the ECM enters this mode.

Learning Ability

The ECM can compensate for minor variations within the fuel system through the block learn and fuel integrator systems. The fuel integrator monitors the oxygen sensor output voltage, adding or subtracting fuel to drive the mixture rich or lean as needed to reach the ideal air fuel ratio of 14.7:1. The integrator values may be read with a scan tool; the display will range from 0–255 and should center on 128 if the oxygen sensor is seeing a 14.7:1 mixture.

The temporary nature of the integrator's control is expanded by the block learn function. The name is derived from the fact that the entire engine operating range (load vs. rpm) is divided into 16 sections or blocks. Within each memory block is stored the correct fuel delivery value for that combination of load and engine speed. Once the operating range enters a certain block, that stored value controls the fuel delivery unless the integrator steps in to change it. If changes are made by the integrator, the new value is memorized and stored within the block. As the block learn makes the correction, the integrator correction will be reduced until the integrator returns to 128; the block learn then controls the fuel delivery with the new value.

The next time the engine operates within the block's range, the new value will be used. The block learn data can also be read by a scan tool; the range is the same as the integrator and should also center on 128. In this way, the systems can compensate for engine wear, small air or vacuum leaks or reduced combustion.

Any time the battery is disconnected, the block learn values are lost and must be relearned by the ECM. This loss of corrected values may be noticed as a significant change in driveability. To reteach the system, make certain the engine is fully warmed up. Drive the vehicle at part throttle using moderate acceleration and idle until normal performance is felt.

Dashboard Warning Lamp

The primary function of the dash warning lamp is to advise the operator and that a fault has been detected, and, in most cases, a code stored. Under normal conditions, the dash warning lamp will illuminate when the ignition is turned **ON**. Once the engine is started and running, the ECM will perform a system check and extinguish the warning lamp if no fault is found.

Additionally, the dash warning lamp can be used to retrieve stored codes after the system is placed in the Diagnostic Mode. Codes are transmitted as a series of flashes with short or long pauses. When the system is placed in the Field Service Mode, the dash lamp will indicate open loop or closed loop function to the technician.

Intermittents

If a fault occurs intermittently, such as a loose connector pin breaking contact as the vehicle hits a bump, the ECM will note the fault as it occurs and energize the dash warning lamp. If the problem self-corrects, as with the terminal pin again making contact, the dash lamp will extinguish after 10 seconds but a code will remain stored in the ECM memory.

When an unexpected code appears during diagnostics, it may have been set during an intermittent failure that self-corrected; the codes are still useful in diagnosis and should not be discounted.

Tools and Equipment

SCAN TOOLS

Although stored codes may be read with only the use of a small jumper wire, the use of a hand-held scan tool such as GM's TECH 1 or equivalent is recommended. There are many manufacturers of these tools; a purchaser must be certain that the tool is proper for the intended use. If you own a Scan type tool, it probably came with comprehensive instructions on proper use. Be sure to follow the instructions that came with your unit if they differ from what is given here; this is a general guide with useful information included.

The scan tool allows any stored codes to be read from the ECM memory. The tool also allows the operator to view the data being sent to the ECM while the engine is running. This ability has obvious diagnostic advantages; the use of the scan tool is frequently required by the diagnostic charts. Use of the scan tool provides additional data but does not eliminate the need for use of the charts. The scan tool makes collecting information easier; the data must be correctly interpreted by an operator familiar with the system.

An example of the usefulness of the scan tool may be seen in the case of a temperature sensor which has changed its electrical characteristics. The ECM is reacting to an apparently warmer engine (causing a driveability problem), but the sensor's voltage has not changed enough to set a fault code. Connecting the scan tool, the voltage signal being sent to the ECM may be viewed; comparison to either a chart of normal values or a known good vehicle reveals the problem quickly.

The ECM is capable of communicating with a scan tool in 3 modes:

Normal or Open Mode

This mode is not applicable to all engines. When engaged, certain engine data can be observed on the scanner without affecting engine operating characteristics. The number of items readable in this mode varies with engine family. Most scan tools are designed to change automatically to the ALDL mode if this mode is not available.

ALDL Mode

Also referred to as the 10K or SPECIAL mode, the scanner will present all readable data as available. Certain operating characteristics of the engine are changed or controlled when this mode is engaged. The closed loop timers are bypassed, the spark (EST) is advanced and the PARK/NEUTRAL restriction is bypassed. If applicable, the IAC controls the engine speed to 1000 rpm $\pm$ 50, and, on some engines, the canister purge solenoid is energized.

Factory Test

Sometimes referred to as BACK-UP mode, this level of communication is primarily used during vehicle assembly and testing. This mode will confirm that the default or limp-in system is working properly within the ECM. Other data obtainable in this mode has little use in diagnosis.

➡ **A scan tool that is known to display faulty data should not be used for diagnosis. Although the fault may be believed to be in only one area, it can possibly affect many other areas during diagnosis, leading to errors and incorrect repair.**

To properly read system values with a scan tool, the following conditions must be met. All normal values given in the charts will be based on these conditions:

- Engine running at idle, throttle closed
- Engine warm, upper radiator hose hot
- Vehicle in park or neutral
- System operating in closed loop
- All accessories **OFF**

ELECTRICAL TOOLS

The most commonly required electrical diagnostic tool is the Digital Multimeter, allowing voltage, ohmage (resistance) and amperage to be read by one instrument. The multimeter must be a high-impedance unit, with 10 megohms of impedance in the voltmeter. This type of meter will not place an additional load on the circuit it is testing; this is extremely important in low voltage circuits. The multimeter must be of high quality in all respects. It should be handled carefully and protected from impact or damage. Replace batteries frequently in the unit.

Other necessary tools include an unpowered test light, a quality tachometer with an inductive (clip-on) pick up, and the proper tools for releasing GM's Metri-Pack, Weather Pack and Micro-Pack terminals as necessary. The Micro-Pack connectors are used at the ECM connector. A vacuum pump/gauge may also be required for checking sensors, solenoids and valves.

Diagnosis and Testing

TROUBLESHOOTING

Diagnosis of a driveablility and/or emissions problems requires attention to detail and following the diagnostic procedures in the correct order. Resist the temptation to perform any repairs before performing the preliminary diagnostic steps. In many cases this will shorten diagnostic time and often cure the problem without electronic testing.

The proper troubleshooting procedure for these vehicles is as follows:

Visual/Physical Underhood Inspection

This is possibly the most critical step of diagnosis. A detailed examination of connectors, wiring and vacuum hoses can often lead to a repair without further diagnosis. Performance of this step relies on the skill of the technician performing it; a careful inspector will check the undersides of hoses as well as the integrity of hard-to-reach hoses blocked by the air cleaner or other component. Wiring should be checked carefully for any sign of strain, burning, crimping, or terminal pull-out from a connector. Checking connectors at components or in harnesses is required; usually, pushing them together will reveal a loose fit.

Diagnostic Circuit Check

This step is used to check that the on-board diagnostic system is working correctly. A system which is faulty or shorted may not yield correct codes when placed in the Diagnostic Mode. Performing this test confirms that the diagnostic system is not failed and is able to communicate through the dash warning lamp.

If the diagnostic system is not operating correctly, or if a problem exists without the dash warning lamp being lit, refer to the specific engine's A-Charts. These charts cover such conditions as Engine Cranks but Will Not Run or No Service Engine Soon Light.

Reading Codes and Use of Scan Tool

➧ SEE FIG. 21

Once the integrity of the system is confirmed, enter the Diagnostic Mode and read any stored codes. To enter the diagnostic mode:

1. Turn the ignition switch **OFF**. Locate the Assembly Line Diagnostic Link (ALDL), usually under the instrument panel. It may be within a plastic cover or housing labeled DIAGNOSTIC CONNECTOR. This link is used to communicate with the ECM.
2. The code(s) stored in memory may be read either through counting the flashes of the dashboard warning lamp or through the use of a hand-held scan tool. If using the scan tool, connect it correctly to the ALDL.
3. If reading codes via the dash warning lamp, use a small jumper wire to connect Terminal B to Terminal A of the ALDL. As the ALDL connector is viewed from the front, Terminal A is on the extreme right of the upper row; Terminal B is second from the right on the upper row.
4. After the terminals are connected, turn the ignition switch to the **ON** position but do not start the engine. The dash warning lamp should begin to flash Code 12. The code will display as one flash, a pause and two flashes. Code 12 is not a fault code. It is used as a system acknowledgement or handshake code; its presence indicates that the ECM can communicate as requested. Code 12 is used to begin every diagnostic sequence. Some vehicles also use Code 12 after all diagnostic codes have been sent.
5. After Code 12 has been transmitted 3 times, the fault codes, if any, will each be transmitted 3 times. The codes are stored and transmitted in numeric order from lowest to highest.

➡ The order of codes in the memory does not indicate the order of occurrence.

6. If there are no codes stored, but a driveability or emissions problem is evident, refer to the Symptoms and Intermittents Chart for the specific fuel system.
7. If one or more codes are stored, record them. At the end of the procedure, refer to the applicable Diagnostic Code chart.
8. If no fault codes are transmitted, connect the scan tool (if not already connected). Use the scan functions to view the values being sent to the ECM. Compare the actual values to the typical or normal values for the engine.
9. Switch the ignition **OFF** when finished with code retrieval or scan tool readings.

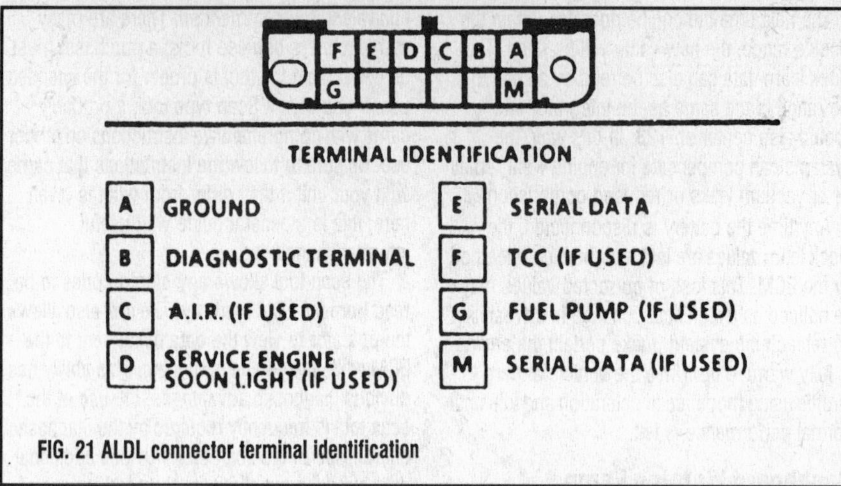

FIG. 21 ALDL connector terminal identification

Circuit/Component Diagnosis and Repair

Using the appropriate chart(s) based on the Diagnostic Circuit Check, the fault codes and the scan tool data will lead to diagnosis and checking of a particular circuit or component. It is important to note that the fault code indicates a fault or loss of signal in an ECM-controlled system, not necessarily in the specific component. Detailed procedures to isolate the problem are included in each code chart; these procedures must be followed accurately to insure timely and correct repair. Following the procedure will also insure that only truly faulty components are replaced.

DIAGNOSTIC MODE

The ECM may be placed into the diagnostic mode by turning the ignition switch from **OFF** to **ON**, then grounding ALDL Terminal B to Terminal A. When in the Diagnostic Mode, the ECM will:

- Display Code 12, indicating the system is operating correctly.
- Display any stored fault codes 3 times in succession.
- Energize all the relays controlled by the ECM except the fuel pump relay. This will allow the relays and circuits to be checked in the shop without recreating certain driving conditions.
- Move the IAC valve to its fully extended position, closing the idle air passage.

➡ Due to increased battery draw, do not allow the vehicle to remain in the Diagnostic Mode for more than 30 minutes. If longer periods are necessary, connect a battery charger.

FIELD SERVICE MODE

If ALDL terminal B is grounded to terminal A with the engine running, the system enters the Field Service Mode. In this mode, the dash warning lamp will indicate whether the system is operating in open loop or closed loop.

If working in open loop, the dash warning lamp will flash rapidly $2^1/_2$ times per second. In closed loop, the flash rate slows to once per second. Additionally, if the system is running lean in closed loop, the lamp will be off most of the cycle. A rich condition in closed loop will cause the lamp to remain lit for most of the 1 second cycle.

When operating in the Field Service Mode, additional codes cannot be stored by the ECM. The closed loop timer is bypassed in this mode.

CLEARING THE TROUBLE CODES

Stored fault codes may be erased from memory at any time by removing power from the ECM for at least 30 seconds. It may be necessary to clear stored codes during diagnosis to check for any recurrence during a test drive, but the stored codes must be written down when retrieved. The codes may still be required for subsequent troubleshooting. Whenever a repair is complete, the stored codes must be erased and the vehicle test driven to confirm correct operation and repair.

➡ **The ignition switch must be OFF any time power is disconnected or restored to the ECM. Severe damage may result if this precaution is not observed.**

Depending on the electrical distribution of the particular vehicle, power to the ECM may be disconnected by removing the ECM fuse in the fusebox, disconnecting the in-line fuse holder near the positive battery terminal or disconnecting the ECM power lead at the battery terminal. Disconnecting the negative battery cable to clear codes is not recommended as this will also clear other memory data in the vehicle such as radio presets or seat memory.

DIAGNOSTIC CHARTS

➡ **Following are charts that should help solve most emission-related problems. When checking the system, codes may appear that are not covered here; they are probably not emission-related. For additional information on those codes, etc. please refer to Chilton's Guide to Fuel Injection and Electronic Engine Controls – 1988-1990 General Motors Cars and Trucks (Book No. 7954) and/or Chilton's Guide to Fuel Injection and Electronic Engine Controls – 1990–1992 General Motors Cars**

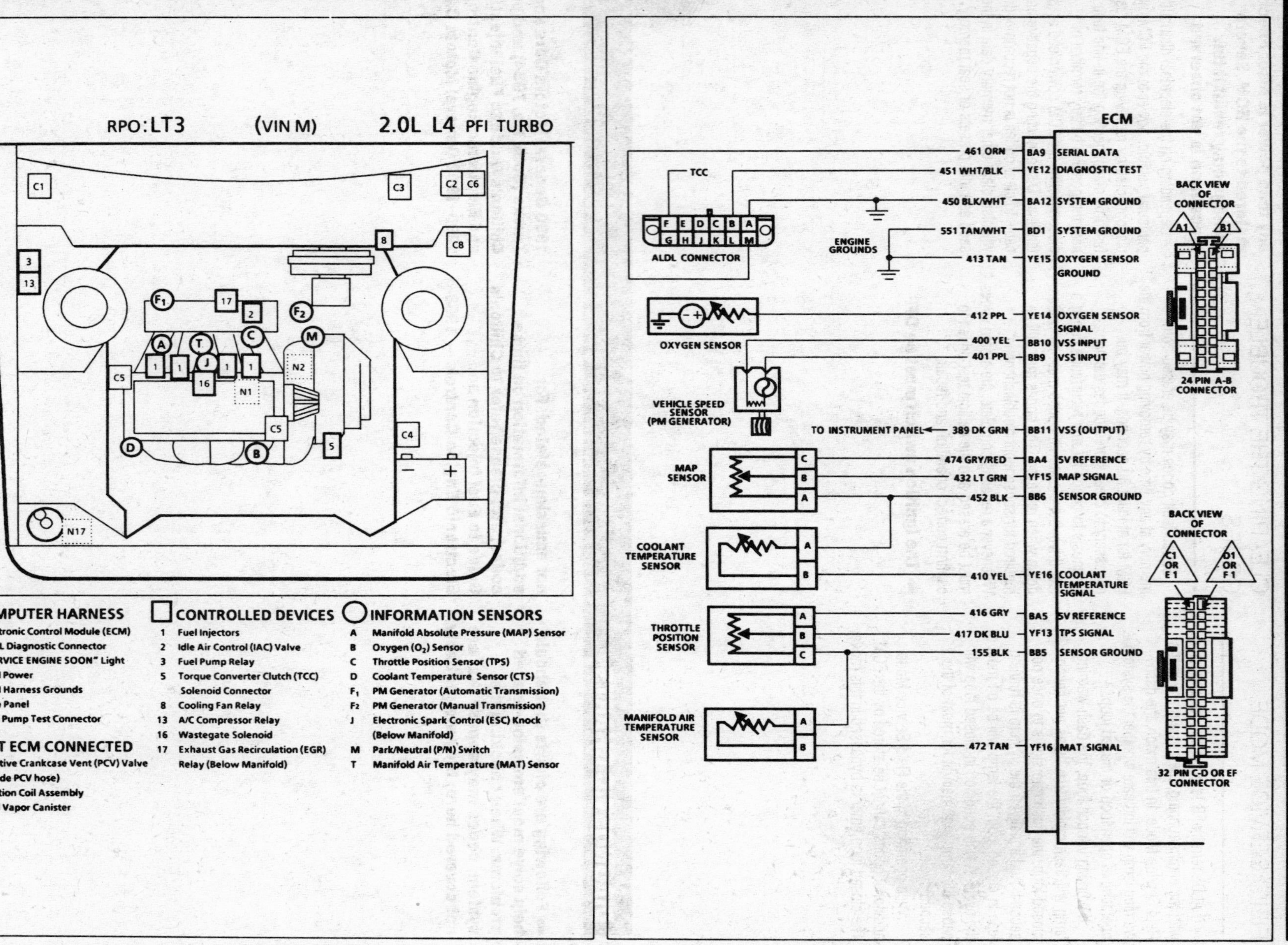
DIAGNOSTIC CHARTS — 2.0L ENGINE
RPO:LT3
(VIN M)
2.0L L4 PFI TURBO
COMPUTER HARNESS
C1 Electronic Control Module (ECM)
C2 ALDL Diagnostic Connector
C3 "SERVICE ENGINE SOON" Light
C4 ECM Power
C5 ECM Harness Grounds
C6 Fuse Panel
C8 Fuel Pump Test Connector
NOT ECM CONNECTED
N1 Positive Crankcase Vent (PCV) Valve (Inside PCV hose)
N2 Ignition Coil Assembly
N17 Fuel Vapor Canister
CONTROLLED DEVICES
1 Fuel Injectors
2 Idle Air Control (IAC) Valve
3 Fuel Pump Relay
5 Torque Converter Clutch (TCC) Solenoid Connector
8 Cooling Fan Relay
13 A/C Compressor Relay
16 Wastegate Solenoid
17 Exhaust Gas Recirculation (EGR) Relay (Below Manifold)
INFORMATION SENSORS
A Manifold Absolute Pressure (MAP) Sensor
B Oxygen (O2) Sensor
C Throttle Position Sensor (TPS)
D Coolant Temperature Sensor (CTS)
F1 PM Generator (Automatic Transmission)
F2 PM Generator (Manual Transmission)
J Electronic Spark Control (ESC) Knock (Below Manifold)
M Park/Neutral (P/N) Switch
T Manifold Air Temperature (MAT) Sensor
ECM
461 ORN BA9 SERIAL DATA
451 WHT/BLK YE12 DIAGNOSTIC TEST
450 BLK/WHT BA12 SYSTEM GROUND
551 TAN/WHT BD1 SYSTEM GROUND
413 TAN YE15 OXYGEN SENSOR GROUND
412 PPL YE14 OXYGEN SENSOR SIGNAL
400 YEL BB10 VSS INPUT
401 PPL BB9 VSS INPUT
TO INSTRUMENT PANEL 389 DK GRN BB11 VSS (OUTPUT)
474 GRY/RED BA4 5V REFERENCE
432 LT GRN YF15 MAP SIGNAL
452 BLK BB6 SENSOR GROUND
410 YEL YE16 COOLANT TEMPERATURE SIGNAL
416 GRY BA5 5V REFERENCE
417 DK BLU YF13 TPS SIGNAL
155 BLK BB5 SENSOR GROUND
472 TAN YF16 MAT SIGNAL
TCC
ALDL CONNECTOR
ENGINE GROUNDS
OXYGEN SENSOR
VEHICLE SPEED SENSOR (PM GENERATOR)
MAP SENSOR
COOLANT TEMPERATURE SENSOR
THROTTLE POSITION SENSOR
MANIFOLD AIR TEMPERATURE SENSOR
BACK VIEW OF CONNECTOR
A1
B1
24 PIN A-B CONNECTOR
BACK VIEW OF CONNECTOR
C1 OR E1
D1 OR F1
32 PIN C-D OR EF CONNECTOR

DIAGNOSTIC CHARTS — 2.0L ENGINE

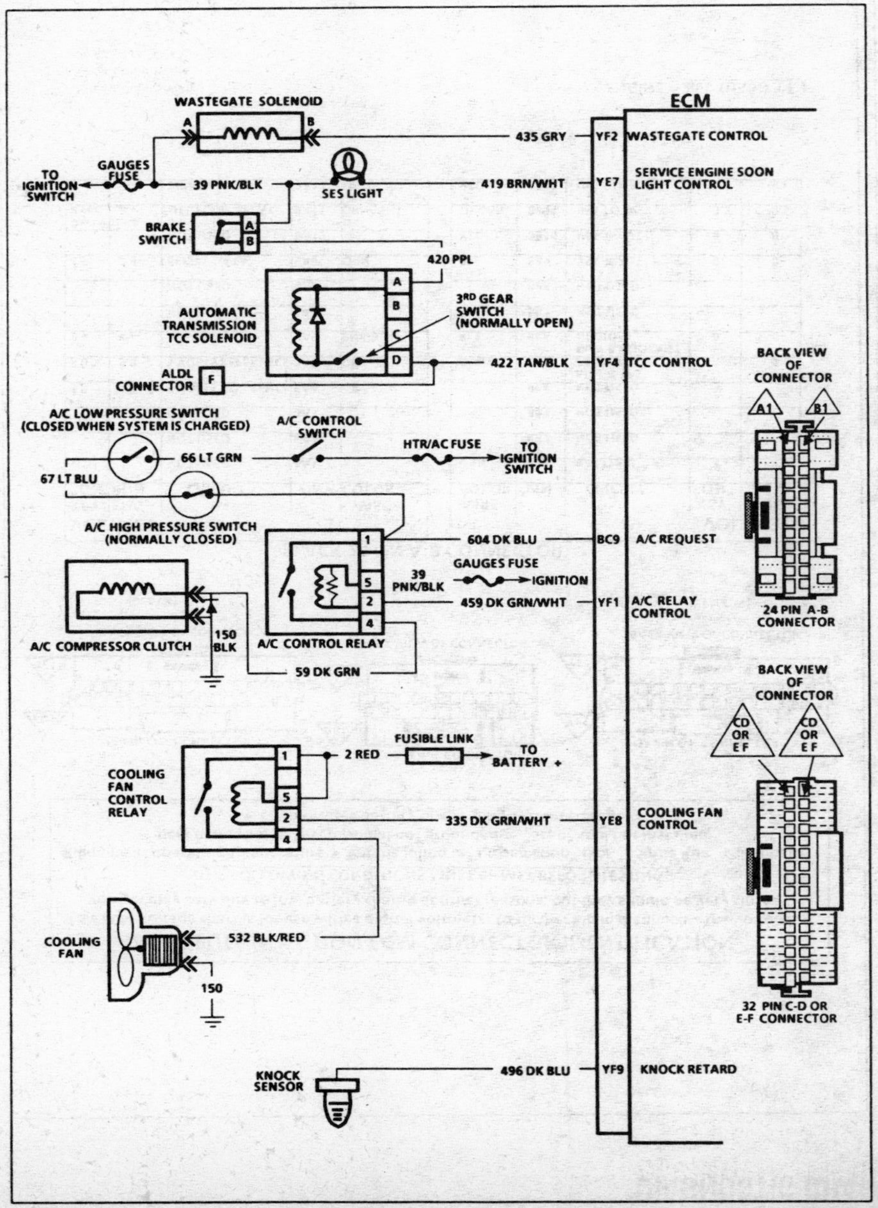

WASTEGATE SOLENOID
A
B
TO IGNITION SWITCH
GAUGES FUSE
39 PNK/BLK
SES LIGHT
BRAKE SWITCH
AUTOMATIC TRANSMISSION TCC SOLENOID
3RD GEAR SWITCH (NORMALLY OPEN)
420 PPL
ALDL CONNECTOR
A/C LOW PRESSURE SWITCH (CLOSED WHEN SYSTEM IS CHARGED)
A/C CONTROL SWITCH
66 LT GRN
67 LT BLU
HTR/AC FUSE
TO IGNITION SWITCH
A/C HIGH PRESSURE SWITCH (NORMALLY CLOSED)
GAUGES FUSE
39 PNK/BLK
IGNITION
A/C COMPRESSOR CLUTCH
150 BLK
A/C CONTROL RELAY
59 DK GRN
COOLING FAN CONTROL RELAY
2 RED
FUSIBLE LINK
TO BATTERY +
COOLING FAN
532 BLK/RED
150
KNOCK SENSOR

ECM
435 GRY — YF2 — WASTEGATE CONTROL
419 BRN/WHT — YE7 — SERVICE ENGINE SOON LIGHT CONTROL
422 TAN/BLK — YF4 — TCC CONTROL
604 DK BLU — BC9 — A/C REQUEST
459 DK GRN/WHT — YF1 — A/C RELAY CONTROL
335 DK GRN/WHT — YE8 — COOLING FAN CONTROL
496 DK BLU — YF9 — KNOCK RETARD

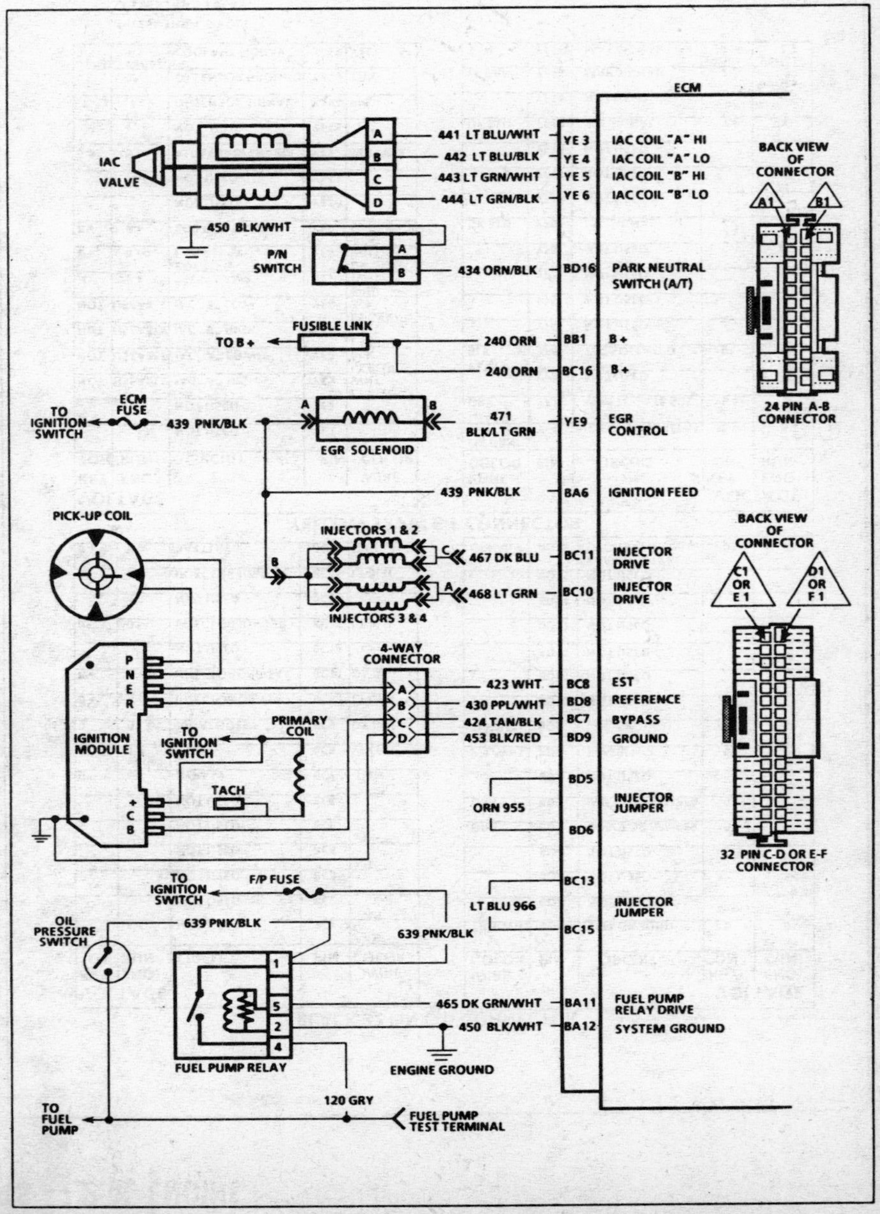

BACK VIEW OF CONNECTOR
A1
B1
24 PIN A-B CONNECTOR
BACK VIEW OF CONNECTOR
CD OR EF
CD OR EF
32 PIN C-D OR E-F CONNECTOR

IAC VALVE
450 BLK/WHT
P/N SWITCH
TO B +
FUSIBLE LINK
TO IGNITION SWITCH
ECM FUSE
439 PNK/BLK
EGR SOLENOID
PICK-UP COIL
INJECTORS 1 & 2
INJECTORS 3 & 4
4-WAY CONNECTOR
IGNITION MODULE
P N E R + C B
TO IGNITION SWITCH
PRIMARY COIL
TACH
TO IGNITION SWITCH
F/P FUSE
OIL PRESSURE SWITCH
639 PNK/BLK
FUEL PUMP RELAY
ENGINE GROUND
120 GRY
TO FUEL PUMP
FUEL PUMP TEST TERMINAL

ECM
441 LT BLU/WHT — YE 3 — IAC COIL "A" HI
442 LT BLU/BLK — YE 4 — IAC COIL "A" LO
443 LT GRN/WHT — YE 5 — IAC COIL "B" HI
444 LT GRN/BLK — YE 6 — IAC COIL "B" LO
434 ORN/BLK — BD16 — PARK NEUTRAL SWITCH (A/T)
240 ORN — BB1 — B +
240 ORN — BC16 — B +
471 BLK/LT GRN — YE9 — EGR CONTROL
439 PNK/BLK — BA6 — IGNITION FEED
467 DK BLU — BC11 — INJECTOR DRIVE
468 LT GRN — BC10 — INJECTOR DRIVE
423 WHT — BC8 — EST
430 PPL/WHT — BD8 — REFERENCE
424 TAN/BLK — BC7 — BYPASS
453 BLK/RED — BD9 — GROUND
ORN 955 — BD5, BD6 — INJECTOR JUMPER
LT BLU 966 — BC13, BC15 — INJECTOR JUMPER
639 PNK/BLK
465 DK GRN/WHT — BA11 — FUEL PUMP RELAY DRIVE
450 BLK/WHT — BA12 — SYSTEM GROUND

BACK VIEW OF CONNECTOR
A1
B1
24 PIN A-B CONNECTOR
BACK VIEW OF CONNECTOR
C1 OR E1
D1 OR F1
32 PIN C-D OR E-F CONNECTOR

DIAGNOSTIC CHARTS — 2.0L ENGINE

PORT FUEL INJECTION ECM CONNECTOR IDENTIFICATION

This ECM voltage chart is for use with a digital voltmeter to further aid in diagnosis. The voltages you get may vary due to low battery charge or other reasons, but they should be very close.

THE FOLLOWING CONDITIONS MUST BE MET BEFORE TESTING:

- Engine at operating temperature • Engine idling in "Closed Loop" (For "Engine Run" column) in park or neutral • Test terminal not grounded • "Scan" tool not installed
- B + indicates battery or charging system voltage

32 PIN C-D CONNECTOR
BD1
BC1
BACK VIEW OF CONNECTOR
(BLACK)

24 PIN A-B CONNECTOR
BB1
BA1
BACK VIEW OF CONNECTOR
(BLACK)

32 PIN E-F CONNECTOR
YF1
YE1
BACK VIEW OF CONNECTOR
(YELLOW)

BLACK 24 PIN A-B CONNECTOR

VOLTAGE KEY "ON"	VOLTAGE ENG. RUN	CIRCUIT	PIN	WIRE COLOR
		NOT USED	BA1	
		NOT USED	BA2	
		NOT USED	BA3	
5.0	5.0	5 VOLTS REFERENCE	BA4	GRY
5.0	5.0	5 VOLTS REFERENCE	BA5	GRY
B +	B +	IGN POWER	BA6	PNK/BLK
		NOT USED	BA7	
		NOT USED	BA8	
4.8	4.8	SERIAL DATA	BA9	ORN
		NOT USED	BA10	
B + 2 sec.	B +	FUEL PUMP RELAY	BA11	DK GRN/WHT
0	0	ECM GROUND	BA12	BLK/WHT

WIRE COLOR	PIN	CIRCUIT	VOLTAGE KEY "ON"	VOLTAGE ENG RUN
ORN	BB1	BATTERY	B +	B +
	BB2	NOT USED		
	BB3	NOT USED		
	BB4	NOT USED		
BLK/YEL	BB5	MAT & TPS GROUND	0	0
BLK	BB6	MAP & COOLANT GROUND	0	0
	BB7	NOT USED		
	BB8	NOT USED		
PPL	BB9	VSS INPUT	0	0
YEL	BB10	VSS INPUT	0	0
DKGRN	BB11	VSS TO I/P	3.8	9.5
RED	BB12	VSS OUTPUT	0	0

* Less than .5 Volt.
∇ Less than 1 Volt.
(1) A/C, Fan "OFF"

ENGINE 2.0L TURBO LT 3

BLACK 32 PIN C-D CONNECTOR

	VOLTAGE KEY "ON"	VOLTAGE ENG. RUN	CIRCUIT	PIN	WIRE COLOR
			NOT USED	BC1	
			NOT USED	BC2	
			NOT USED	BC3	
			NOT USED	BC4	
			NOT USED	BC5	
			NOT USED	BC6	
	0*	4.7	BYPASS	BC7	TAN
	0*	varies 1.2	EST	BC8	WHT
(1)	0	0	A/C REQUEST	BC9	DK BLU
	B +	B +	INJECTOR DRIVER	BC10	LT GRN
	B +	B +	INJECTOR DRIVER	BC11	DK BLU
			NOT USED	BC12	
	0*	0*	INJECTOR JUMPER	BC13	LT BLU
			NOT USED	BC14	
	0*	0*	INJECTOR JUMPER	BC15	LT BLU
	B +	B +	BATTERY	BC16	ORN

WIRE COLOR	PIN	CIRCUIT	VOLTAGE KEY "ON"	VOLTAGE ENG RUN
TAN/WHT	BD1	ECM GROUND	0	0
	BD2	NOT USED		
	BD3	NOT USED		
	BD4	NOT USED		
ORN	BD5	INJECTOR JUMPER	0*	0*
ORN	BD6	INJECTOR JUMPER	0*	0*
	BD7	NOT USED		
PPL/WHT	BD8	REFERENCE	0*	varies 1.0
BLK/RED	BD9	IGN. GROUND	0*	0*
	BD10	NOT USED		
	BD11	NOT USED		
	BD12	NOT USED		
	BD13	NOT USED		
	BD14	NOT USED		
	BD15	NOT USED		
ORN/BLK	BD16	PARK/NEUTRAL AUTO TRANS. ONLY	0*	0*

YELLOW 32 PIN E-F CONNECTOR

VOLTAGE KEY "ON"	VOLTAGE ENG. RUN	CIRCUIT	PIN	WIRE COLOR
		NOT USED	YE1	
		NOT USED	YE2	
NOT	USEABLE	IAC "A" HIGH	YE3	LT BLU/WHT
NOT	USEABLE	IAC "A" LOW	YE4	LT BLU/BLK
NOT	USEABLE	IAC "B" HIGH	YE5	LT GRN/WHT
NOT	USEABLE	IAC "B" LOW	YE6	LT GRN/BLK
.1	B +	"SES" LAMP	YE7	BRN/WHT
B +	B +	COOLING FAN RELAY	YE8	DK GRN/WHT
B +	B +	EGR CONTROL	YE9	BLK/LT GRN
		NOT USED	YE10	
		NOT USED	YE11	
5.0	5.0	ALDL DIAG. ENABLE	YE12	WHT/BLK
		NOT USED	YE13	
.1 - .3	varies .1 - .9	O^2 SENSOR SIGNAL	YE14	PPL
0*	0*	O^2 SENSOR GROUND	YE15	TAN
varies 1.5	varies 1.5	COOLANT SIGNAL	YE16	YEL

WIRE COLOR	PIN	CIRCUIT	VOLTAGE KEY "ON"	VOLTAGE ENG RUN	
DK GRN/WHT	YF1	A/C CONTROL RELAY	B +	B +	(1)
GRY	YF2	WASTE GATE SOL.	B +	.5	
	YF3	NOT USED			
TAN/BLK	YF4	TCC SOLENOID	0*	0*	
	YF5	NOT USED			
	YF6	NOT USED			
	YF7	NOT USED			
	YF8	NOT USED			
DK BLU	YF9	ESC SIGNAL	2.4	2.4	
	YF10	NOT USED			
	YF11	NOT USED			
	YF12	NOT USED			
DK BLU	YF13	TPS SIGNAL	.84	.84	
	YF14	NOT USED			
LT GRN	YF15	MAP SIGNAL	2.2	varies .8	
TAN	YF16	MAT SIGNAL	varies 2..4	varies 2.2	

* LESS THAN .5 VOLT
∇ LESS THAN 1 VOLT
(1) A/C, FAN OFF

DIAGNOSTIC CIRCUIT CHECK

The Diagnostic Circuit Check is an organized approach to identifying a problem created by an electronic engine control system malfunction. It must be the starting point for any driveability complaint diagnosis because it directs the service technician to the next logical step in diagnosing the complaint.

The "Scan" data listed in the table may be used for comparison after completing the diagnostic circuit check and finding the on-board diagnostics functioning properly with no trouble codes displayed. The "Typical Data Values" are an average of display values recorded from normally operating vehicles and are intended to represent what a normally functioning system would typically display.

A "SCAN" TOOL THAT DISPLAYS FAULTY DATA SHOULD NOT BE USED, AND THE PROBLEM SHOULD BE REPORTED TO THE MANUFACTURER. THE USE OF A FAULTY "SCAN" TOOL CAN RESULT IN MISDIAGNOSIS AND UNNECESSARY PARTS REPLACEMENT.

Only the parameters listed below are used in this manual for diagnosis. If a "Scan" tool reads other parameters, the values are not recommended by General Motors for use in diagnosis.
values and use of the "Scan" tool to diagnosis ECM inputs, refer to the applicable component diagnosis section in
If all values are within the range illustrated, refer to symptoms

"SCAN" TOOL DATA

Test Under Following Conditions: Idle, Upper Radiator Hose Hot, Closed Throttle, Park or Neutral, "Closed Loop", All Accessories "OFF"

"SCAN" Position	Units Displayed	Typical Data Value
Engine Speed	RPM	+ 50 RPM from desired rpm in drive (AUTO) ± 100 RPM from desired rpm in neutral (MANUAL)
Desired Idle	RPM	ECM idle command (varies with temperature)
Coolant Temperature	Degrees Celsius	85 - 105
MAT Temperature	Degrees Celsius	10 - 90 (varies with underhood temperature and sensor location)
MAP	kPa/Volts	1 - 2 Volts (varies with manifold and barometric pressures)
Baro	kPa/Volts	Varies with barometric pressure
Throttle Position	Volts	.4 - 1.25
Throttle Angle	0 - 100%	0
Oxygen Sensor	Millivolts	100 - 1000
Injector Pulse width	Milliseconds	.8 - 3.0
Spark Advance	Degrees	Varies
Fuel Integrator	Counts	110 - 145
Block Learn	Counts	118 - 138
Open/Closed Loop	Open/Closed	"Closed Loop" (may enter "Open Loop" with extended idle)
Knock Retard	Degrees	0
Knock Signal	Yes/No	No
Exhaust Recirculation	0 - 100%	0
Boost Pressure	kPa	0
Wastegate Duty Cycle	0 - 100%	100
Idle Air Control	Counts (Steps)	1 - 50
Park/Neutral Switch	P/N and R-D-L	Park/Neutral (P/N)
VSS	MPH/kPa	0
Torque Conv. Clutch	"ON"/"OFF"	"OFF"
Battery Voltage	Volts	13.5 - 14.5
A/C Request	Yes/No	No
A/C Clutch	"ON"/"OFF"	"OFF"
Cooling Fan Relay	"ON"/"OFF"	"OFF"

DIAGNOSTIC CIRCUIT CHECK

2.0L TURBO (VIN M) (PORT)

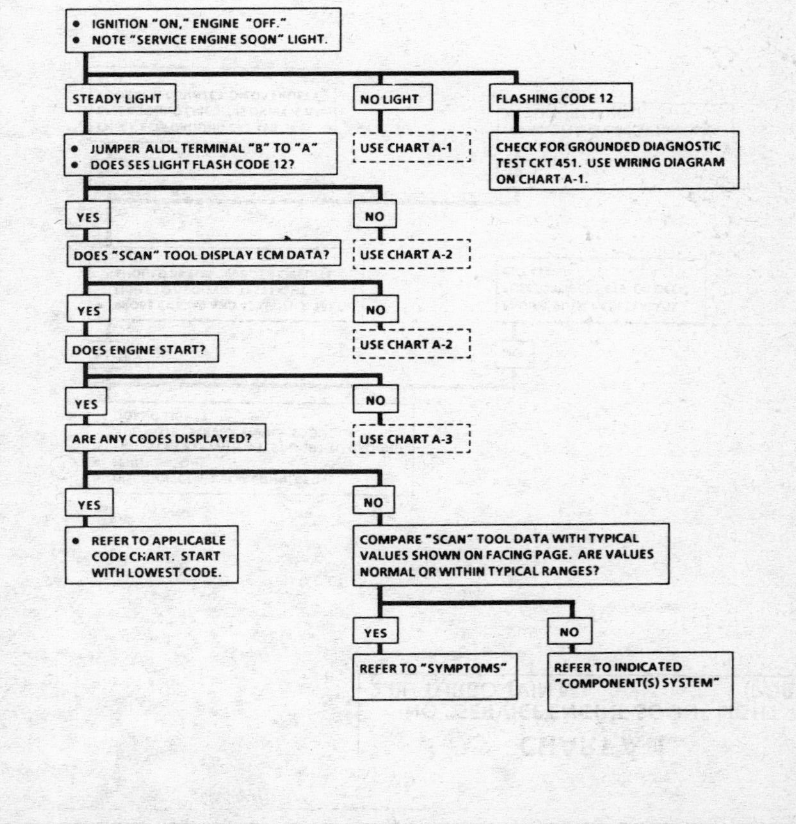

INSTRUMENT PANEL HARNESS CONNECTOR 15 PIN (FRONT VIEW)
ECM
TO B+ — FUSIBLE LINK — ECM POWER CONNECTOR — 240 ORN — BC16 — 240 ORN — BB1 — POWER FEEDS
TO IGNITION SWITCH — ECM FUSE — 439 PNK/BLK — BA6 — IGNITION FEED
GAUGES FUSE — SES LIGHT — C — 419 BRN/WHT — YE7
DIAGNOSTIC TEST TERMINAL — E — 451 WHT/BLK — YE12 — 5 VOLTS
ALDL CONNECTOR — M — 450 BLK/WHT — BA12 — GROUND
ENGINE GROUND
J — 461 ORN — BA9 — SERIAL DATA

CHART A-1

NO "SERVICE ENGINE SOON" LIGHT 2.0L TURBO (VIN M) (PORT)

Circuit Description:

There should always be a steady "Service Engine Soon" light when the ignition is "ON" and the engine is "OFF." Battery voltage is supplied directly to the light bulb. The electronic control module (ECM) controls the light and turns it "ON" by providing a ground path through CKT 419 to the ECM.

Test Description: Numbers below refer to circled numbers on the diagnostic chart.

1. Probing CKT 419 to ground creates an alternate ground. If the "Service Engine Soon" light illuminates, this verifies that the trouble is not in the lamp portion of the circuit.

Diagnostic Aids:

If engine runs OK, check the following:

- Faulty light bulb.
- CKT 419 open.
- Gage fuse blown. This will result in no oil or generator lights, seat belt reminder, etc.

If "Engine Cranks But Won't Run," use CHART A-3.

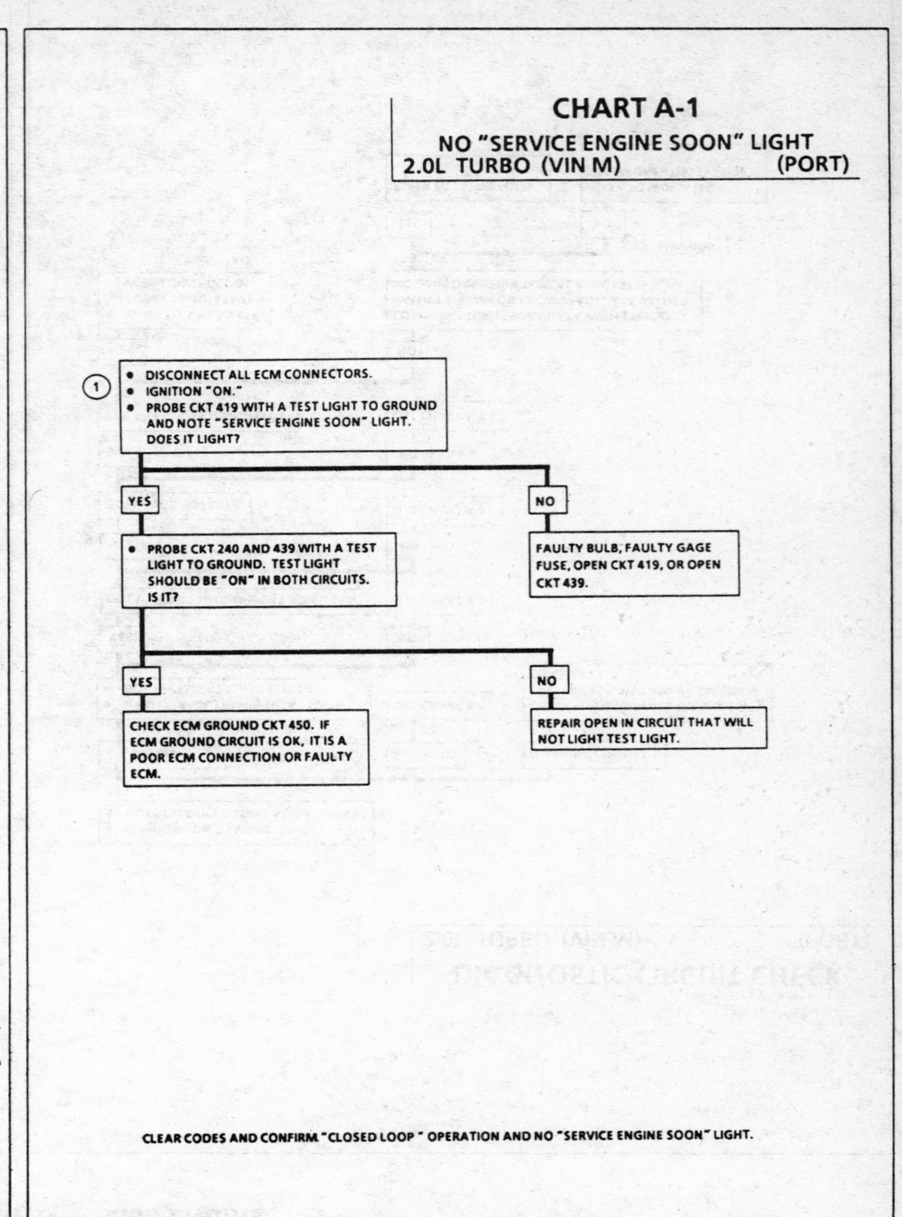

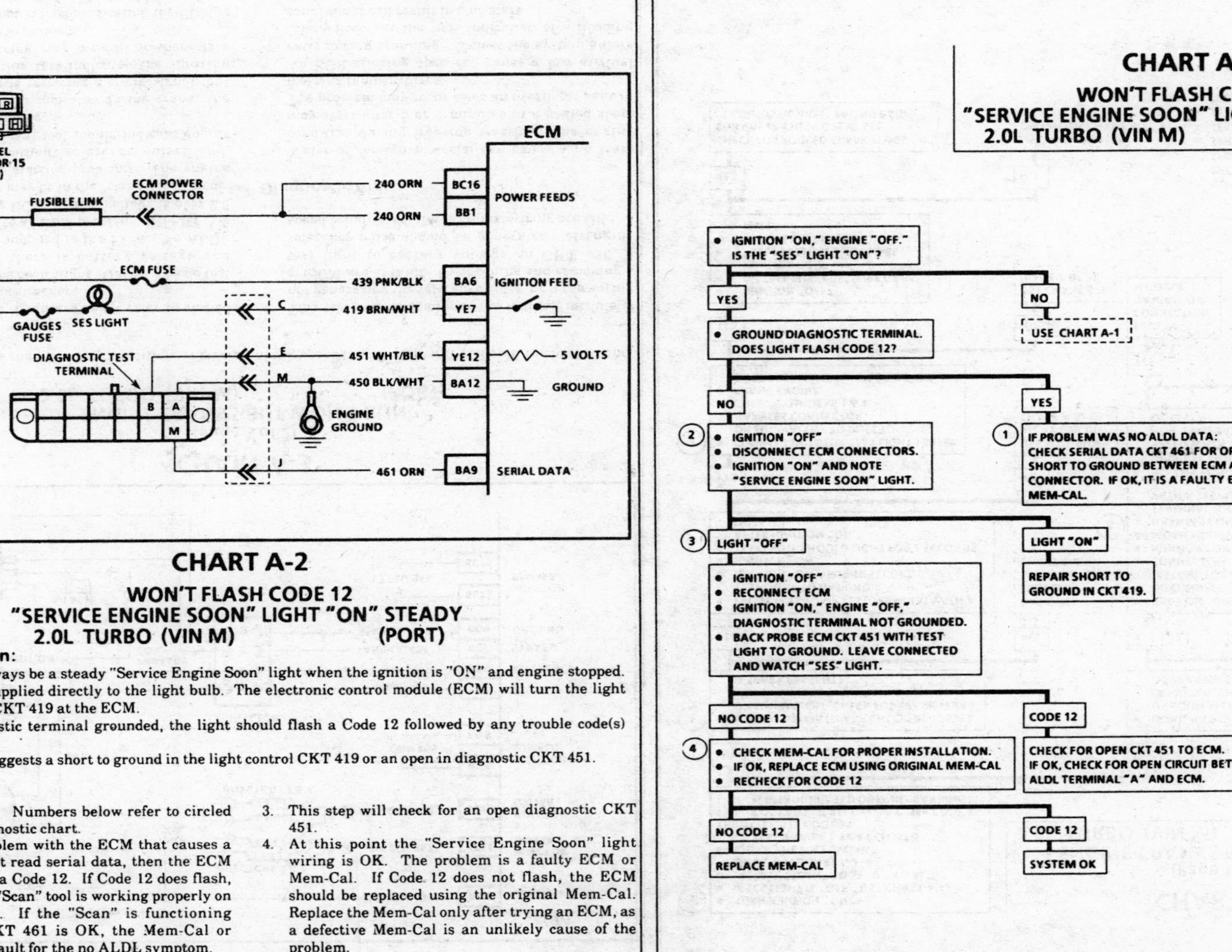

CHART A-2

WON'T FLASH CODE 12
"SERVICE ENGINE SOON" LIGHT "ON" STEADY
2.0L TURBO (VIN M) (PORT)

Circuit Description:

There should always be a steady "Service Engine Soon" light when the ignition is "ON" and engine stopped. Battery voltage is supplied directly to the light bulb. The electronic control module (ECM) will turn the light "ON" by grounding CKT 419 at the ECM.

With the diagnostic terminal grounded, the light should flash a Code 12 followed by any trouble code(s) stored in memory.

A steady light suggests a short to ground in the light control CKT 419 or an open in diagnostic CKT 451.

Test Description: Numbers below refer to circled numbers on the diagnostic chart.

1. If there is a problem with the ECM that causes a "Scan" tool to not read serial data, then the ECM should not flash a Code 12. If Code 12 does flash, be sure that the "Scan" tool is working properly on another vehicle. If the "Scan" is functioning properly and CKT 461 is OK, the Mem-Cal or ECM may be at fault for the no ALDL symptom.
2. If the light goes "OFF" when the ECM connector is disconnected, then CKT 419 is not shorted to ground.
3. This step will check for an open diagnostic CKT 451.
4. At this point the "Service Engine Soon" light wiring is OK. The problem is a faulty ECM or Mem-Cal. If Code 12 does not flash, the ECM should be replaced using the original Mem-Cal. Replace the Mem-Cal only after trying an ECM, as a defective Mem-Cal is an unlikely cause of the problem.

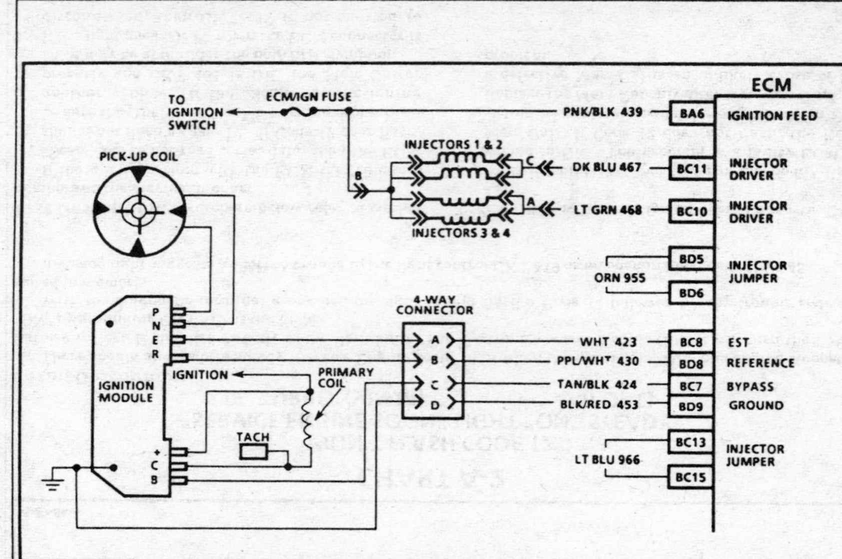

CHART A-3

(Page 1 of 2)

ENGINE CRANKS BUT WON'T RUN

2.0L TURBO (VIN M) (PORT)

Circuit Description:

Before using this chart, battery condition, engine cranking speed, and fuel quantity should be checked and verified as being OK.

Test Description: Numbers below refer to circled numbers on the diagnostic chart.

1. A "Service Engine Soon" light "ON" is a basic test to determine if there is battery voltage and ignition voltage supplied to the ECM. No ALDL data may be due to an ECM problem. CHART A-2 will diagnose the ECM. If TPS voltage is over 2.5 volts, the engine may be in the "clear flood" mode, which will cause starting problems. The engine will not start without reference pulses and, therefore, the "Scan" tool should indicate engine speed during cranking.
2. If engine speed was indicated during crank, the ignition module is receiving a crank signal, but "no spark" at this test indicates the ignition module is not triggering the coil or there is a secondary ignition problem.
3. The test light should flash, indicating the ECM is controlling the injectors. The brightness of the light is not important. However, the test light should be a J 34730 or equivalent.
4. This test will determine if the ignition module is not generating the reference pulse, or if the wiring or ECM are at fault. By touching and removing a test light to battery voltage on CKT 430, a reference pulse should be generated. If engine speed is indicated, the ECM and wiring are OK.

Diagnostic Aids:

- Water or foreign material can cause a no start condition during freezing weather. The engine may start after 5 or 6 minutes in a heated shop. The problem may recur after an overnight park in freezing temperatures.
- An EGR sticking open can cause a low air/fuel ratio during cranking. Unless the system enters "clear flood" at the first indication of a flooding condition it can result in a no start.
- Fuel pressure: Low fuel pressure can result in a very lean air/fuel ratio. See CHART A-7.

CHART A-3

(Page 1 of 2)

ENGINE CRANKS BUT WON'T RUN

2.0L TURBO (VIN M) (PORT)

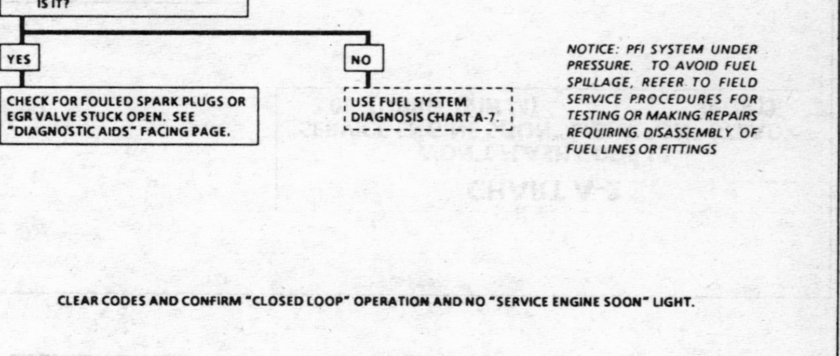

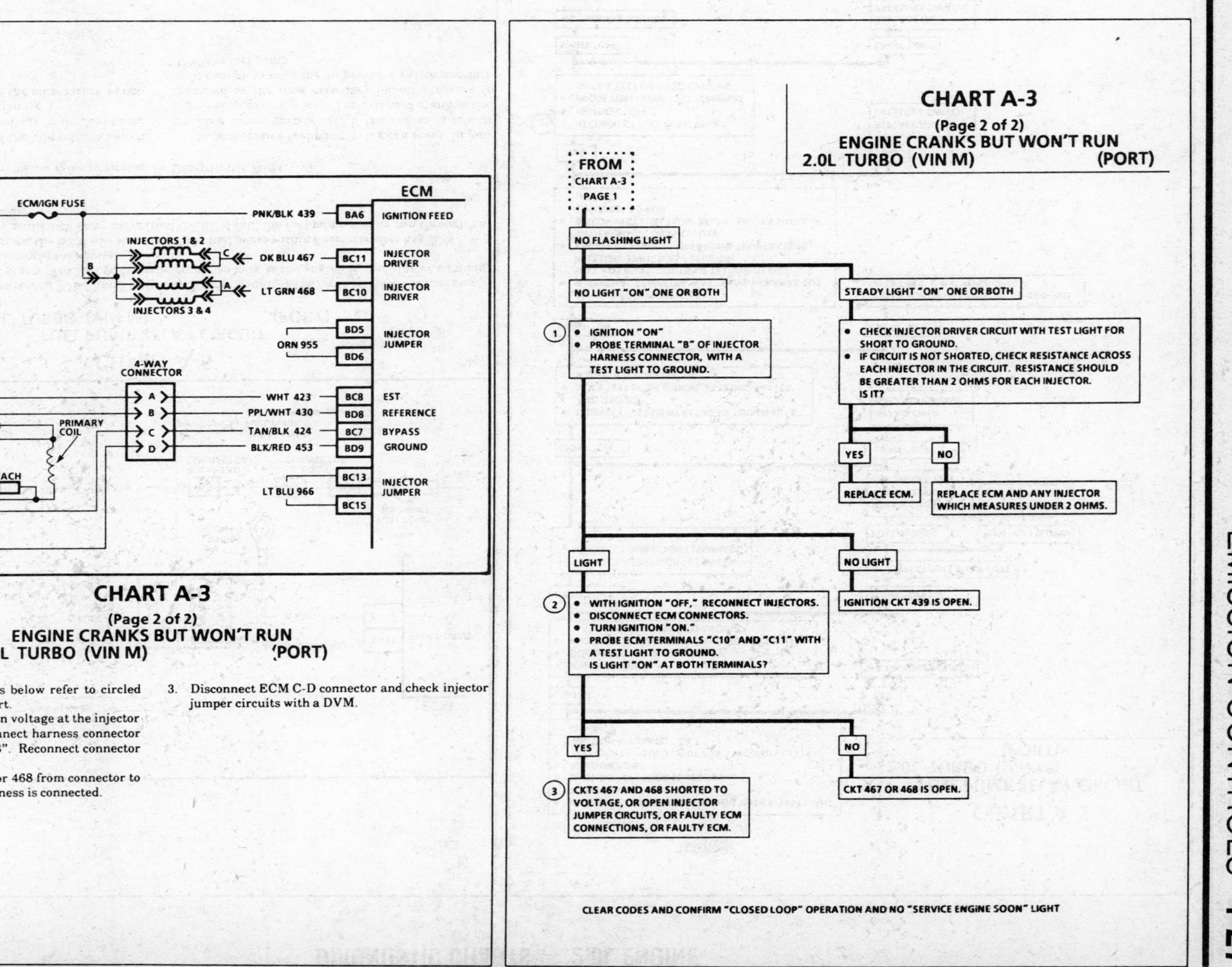

CHART A-3
(Page 2 of 2)
ENGINE CRANKS BUT WON'T RUN
2.0L TURBO (VIN M) (PORT)

Test Description: Numbers below refer to circled numbers on the diagnostic chart.

1. This step checks for ignition voltage at the injector harness connector. Disconnect harness connector before probing terminal "B". Reconnect connector after test.
2. Checks for open CKT 467 or 468 from connector to ECM. Be sure injector harness is connected.
3. Disconnect ECM C-D connector and check injector jumper circuits with a DVM.

TO IGNITION SWITCH
F/P FUSE
PNK/BLK 639
ECM
DK GRN/WHT 465
BA11
B+ RELAY DRIVE
BLK/WHT 450
BA12
FUEL PUMP RELAY
OIL PRESSURE SWITCH
ENGINE GROUND
FUEL PUMP (IN TANK)
GRY 120
BULKHEAD CONNECTOR
BODY CONNECTOR
150
UNDERHOOD FUEL PUMP TEST TERMINAL
FUEL PUMP RELAY HARNESS CONNECTOR

CHART A-5

FUEL PUMP RELAY CIRCUIT
2.0L TURBO (VIN M) (PORT)

Circuit Description:

When the ignition switch is turned "ON," the Electronic Control Module (ECM) will activate the fuel pump relay and run the in-tank fuel pump. The fuel pump will operate as long as the engine is cranking or running and the ECM is receiving ignition reference pulses.

If there are no reference pulses, the ECM will shut "OFF" the fuel pump within 2 seconds after key "ON."

Should the fuel pump relay or the 12V relay drive from the ECM fail, the fuel pump will be run through an oil pressure switch back-up circuit.

Test Description: Numbers below refer to circled numbers on the diagnostic chart.

1. This test will determine if the oil pressure switch is closing and supplying voltage to the fuel pump when the relay is not functioning.
2. This test will determine if the oil pressure switch is stuck open.

Diagnostic Aids:

An inoperative fuel pump relay can result in long cranking times, particularly if the engine is cold or engine oil pressure is low. The extended crank period is caused by the time necessary for oil pressure to build enough to close the oil pressure switch and turn "ON" the fuel pump.

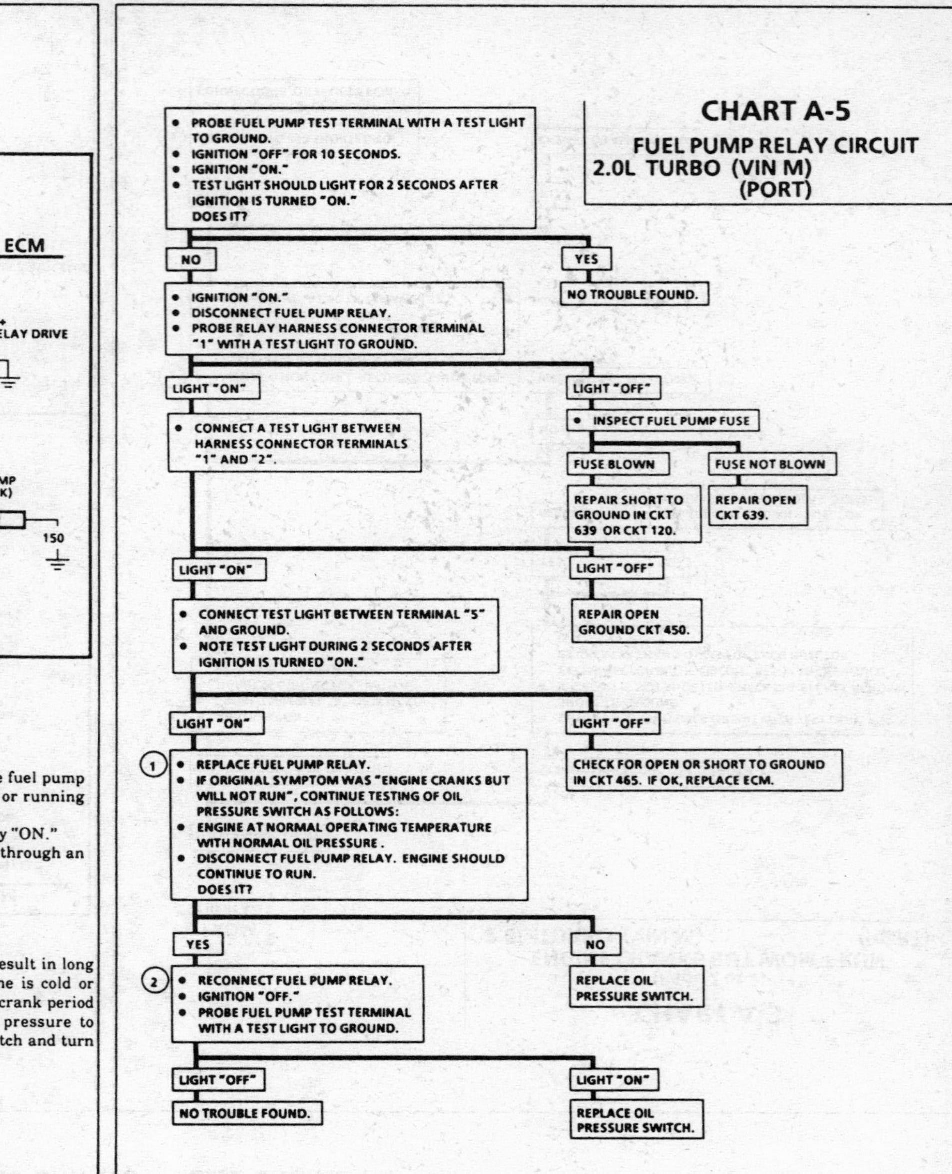

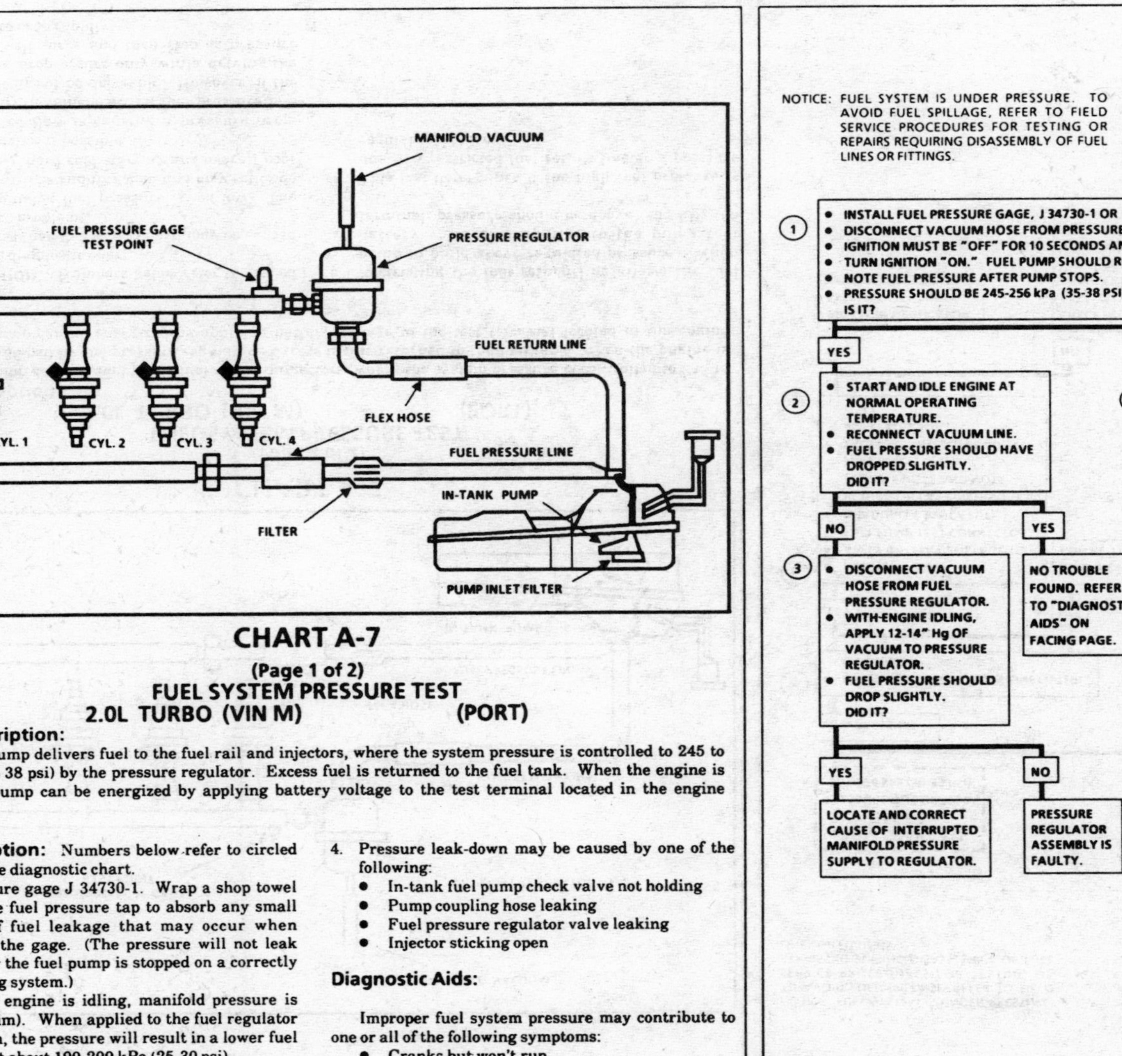

CHART A-7
(Page 1 of 2)
FUEL SYSTEM PRESSURE TEST
2.0L TURBO (VIN M) (PORT)

Circuit Description:

The fuel pump delivers fuel to the fuel rail and injectors, where the system pressure is controlled to 245 to 256 kPa (35 to 38 psi) by the pressure regulator. Excess fuel is returned to the fuel tank. When the engine is stopped, the pump can be energized by applying battery voltage to the test terminal located in the engine compartment.

Test Description: Numbers below refer to circled numbers on the diagnostic chart.

1. Use pressure gage J 34730-1. Wrap a shop towel around the fuel pressure tap to absorb any small amount of fuel leakage that may occur when installing the gage. (The pressure will not leak down after the fuel pump is stopped on a correctly functioning system.)
2. While the engine is idling, manifold pressure is low (vacuum). When applied to the fuel regulator diaphragm, the pressure will result in a lower fuel pressure at about 190-200 kPa (25-30 psi).
3. The application of vacuum to the pressure regulator should result in a fuel pressure drop.
4. Pressure leak-down may be caused by one of the following:
   - In-tank fuel pump check valve not holding
   - Pump coupling hose leaking
   - Fuel pressure regulator valve leaking
   - Injector sticking open

Diagnostic Aids:

Improper fuel system pressure may contribute to one or all of the following symptoms:

- Cranks but won't run
- Code 44 or 45
- Cutting out (May feel like ignition problem)
- Hesitation, loss of power or poor fuel economy

Refer to "Symptoms"

NOTICE: FUEL SYSTEM IS UNDER PRESSURE. TO AVOID FUEL SPILLAGE, REFER TO FIELD SERVICE PROCEDURES FOR TESTING OR REPAIRS REQUIRING DISASSEMBLY OF FUEL LINES OR FITTINGS.

CHART A-7
(Page 1 of 2)
FUEL SYSTEM PRESSURE TEST
2.0L TURBO (VIN M) (PORT)

(1)
- INSTALL FUEL PRESSURE GAGE, J 34730-1 OR EQUIVALENT.
- DISCONNECT VACUUM HOSE FROM PRESSURE REGULATOR.
- IGNITION MUST BE "OFF" FOR 10 SECONDS AND ENSURE THAT A/C IS "OFF."
- TURN IGNITION "ON." FUEL PUMP SHOULD RUN FOR ABOUT 2 SECONDS.
- NOTE FUEL PRESSURE AFTER PUMP STOPS.
- PRESSURE SHOULD BE 245-256 kPa (35-38 PSI) AND HOLDING STEADY.

IS IT?

YES →

(2)
- START AND IDLE ENGINE AT NORMAL OPERATING TEMPERATURE.
- RECONNECT VACUUM LINE.
- FUEL PRESSURE SHOULD HAVE DROPPED SLIGHTLY.

DID IT?

- YES → NO TROUBLE FOUND. REFER TO "DIAGNOSTIC AIDS" ON FACING PAGE.
- NO →

(3)
- DISCONNECT VACUUM HOSE FROM FUEL PRESSURE REGULATOR.
- WITH ENGINE IDLING, APPLY 12-14" Hg OF VACUUM TO PRESSURE REGULATOR.
- FUEL PRESSURE SHOULD DROP SLIGHTLY.

DID IT?

- YES → LOCATE AND CORRECT CAUSE OF INTERRUPTED MANIFOLD PRESSURE SUPPLY TO REGULATOR.
- NO → PRESSURE REGULATOR ASSEMBLY IS FAULTY.

NO →

- (4) PRESSURE WITHIN SPECIFICATION, BUT NOT HOLDING.
- PRESSURE OUT OF SPECIFICATION. → USE PAGE 2 OF THIS CHART.
- NO PRESSURE → USE CHART A-5.

(4) PRESSURE WITHIN SPECIFICATION, BUT NOT HOLDING:
- IGNITION "OFF."
- CONNECT FUSED JUMPER FROM BATTERY VOLTAGE TO FUEL PUMP TEST CONNECTOR IN ENGINE COMPARTMENT.
- GRADUALLY BLOCK FUEL <u>PRESSURE LINE</u> BY PINCHING FLEX HOSE.
- REMOVE JUMPER FROM TEST CONNECTOR WHILE CONTINUING TO BLOCK PRESSURE LINE.
- PRESSURE SHOULD HOLD.

DID IT?

- YES → CHECK FOR
  - LEAKING PUMP COUPLING HOSE
  - FAULTY IN-TANK PUMP.
- NO →
  - REPEAT ABOVE PROCEDURE WHILE BLOCKING FUEL <u>RETURN LINE</u> INSTEAD OF PRESSURE LINE BY PINCHING FLEX HOSE.
  - PRESSURE SHOULD HOLD.

  DID IT?

  - YES → PRESSURE REGULATOR ASSEMBLY IS FAULTY.
  - NO → LOCATE AND REPLACE LEAKING INJECTOR AND DRY SPARK PLUGS FROM FLOODED CYLINDERS.

CLEAR CODES AND CONFIRM "CLOSED LOOP" OPERATION AND NO "SERVICE ENGINE SOON" LIGHT.

MANIFOLD VACUUM
FUEL PRESSURE GAGE TEST POINT
PRESSURE REGULATOR
FUEL RETURN LINE
CYL. 1
CYL. 2
CYL. 3
CYL. 4
FLEX HOSE
FUEL PRESSURE LINE
IN-TANK PUMP
FILTER
PUMP INLET FILTER

CHART A-7

(Page 2 of 2)

FUEL SYSTEM PRESSURE TEST
2.0L TURBO (VIN M) (PORT)

Circuit Description:

The fuel pump delivers fuel to the fuel rail and injectors, where the system pressure is controlled to 245 to 256 kPa (35 to 36 psi) by the pressure regulator. Excess fuel is returned to the fuel tank. When the engine is stopped, the pump can be energized by applying battery voltage to the test terminal located in the engine compartment.

Test Description: Numbers below refer to circled numbers on the diagnostic chart.

5. Pressure less than 245 kPa (35 psi) may be caused by one of two problems.
   - The regulated fuel pressure is too low. The system will be running lean and may set Code 44. Also, hard cold starting and overall poor performance is possible.
   - Restricted flow is causing a pressure drop. Normally, a vehicle with a fuel pressure loss at idle will not be driveable. However, if the pressure drop occurs only while driving, the engine will surge and then stop as pressure begins to drop rapidly.
6. Restricting the fuel return line allows the fuel pump to build above regulated pressure. When battery voltage is applied to the pump test terminal, pressure should be above 450 kPa (65 psi).
7. This test determines if the high fuel pressure is due to a restricted fuel return line or a pressure regulator problem.

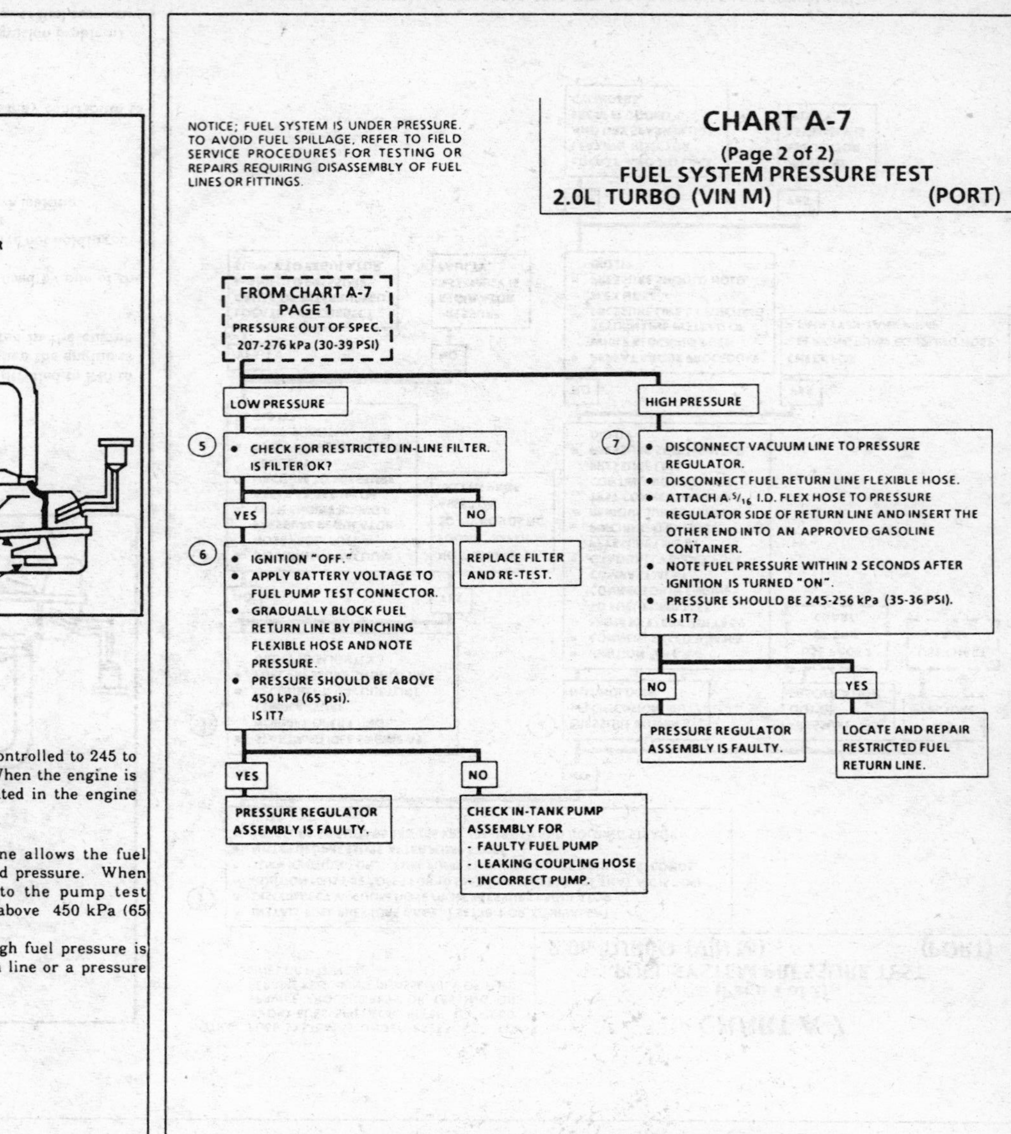

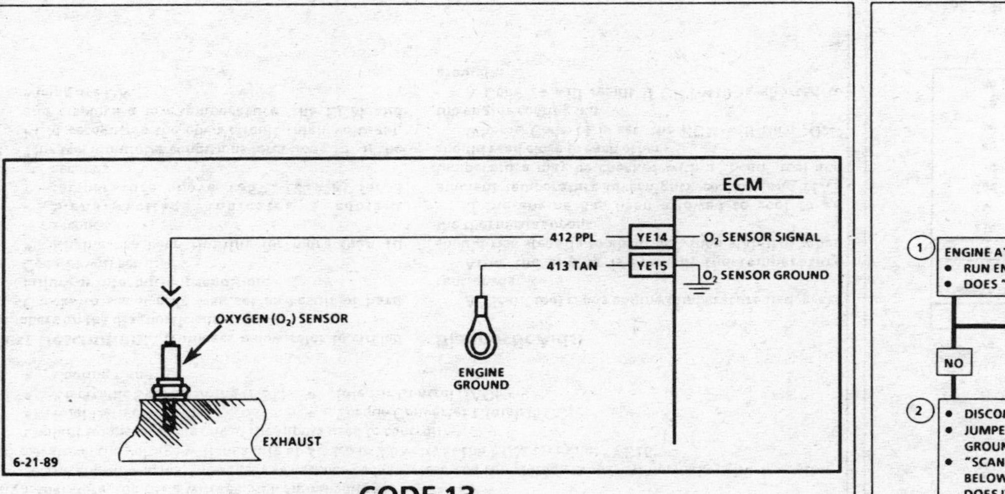

CODE 13

OXYGEN (O_2) SENSOR CIRCUIT
(OPEN CIRCUIT)
2.0L TURBO (VIN M)

Circuit Description:

The ECM supplies a voltage of about .45 volt between terminals "YE14" and "YE15". (If measured with a 10 megohm digital voltmeter, this may read as low as .32 volt.) The O_2 sensor varies the voltage within a range of about 1 volt if the exhaust is rich, down through about .10 volt if exhaust is lean.

The sensor is like an open circuit and produces no voltage when it is below 316°C (600°F). An open sensor circuit or cold sensor causes "Open Loop" operation.

Test Description: Numbers below refer to circled numbers on the diagnostic chart.

1. Code 13 will set:
   - Engine at normal operating temperature
   - O_2 signal voltage steady between .35 and .55 volt
   - Throttle position sensor signal above 6.5%
   - All conditions must be met for about 60 seconds.

   If the conditions for a Code 13 exist, the system will not go "Closed Loop."
2. This will determine if the sensor is at fault or the wiring or ECM is the cause of the Code 13.
3. In doing this test use only a high impedance digital volt ohm meter. This test checks the continuity of CKTs 412 and 413 because if CKT 413 is open, the ECM voltage on CKT 412 will be over .6 volt (600 mV).

Diagnostic Aids:

Normal "Scan" voltage varies between 100 mV to 999 mV (.1 and 1.0 volt) while in "Closed Loop." Code 13 will set in 3 seconds if all criteria have been met and the system will go "Open Loop."

Refer to "Intermittents"

CODE 13

OXYGEN (O_2) SENSOR CIRCUIT
(OPEN CIRCUIT)
2.0L TURBO (VIN M)

(1) ENGINE AT NORMAL OPERATING TEMPERATURE (ABOVE 80°C/176°F).
- RUN ENGINE ABOVE 1200 RPM FOR TWO MINUTES.
- DOES "SCAN" TOOL INDICATE "CLOSED LOOP"?

YES: CODE 13 IS INTERMITTENT. IF NO ADDITIONAL CODES WERE STORED, REFER TO "DIAGNOSTIC AIDS" ON FACING PAGE.

NO:

(2)
- DISCONNECT O_2 SENSOR.
- JUMPER HARNESS CKT 412 (ECM SIDE) TO GROUND.
- "SCAN" TOOL SHOULD DISPLAY O_2 VOLTAGE BELOW .2 VOLT (200 mV) WITH ENGINE RUNNING. DOES IT?

YES: FAULTY O_2 SENSOR CONNECTION OR SENSOR.

NO:

(3)
- REMOVE JUMPER.
- IGNITION "ON", ENGINE "OFF".
- CHECK VOLTAGE OF CKT 412 (ECM SIDE) AT O_2 SENSOR HARNESS CONNECTOR USING A DVM.

.3-.6 VOLT (300 - 600 mV): FAULTY ECM.

OVER .6 VOLT (600 mV): OPEN CKT 413 OR FAULTY CONNECTION OR FAULTY ECM.

LESS THAN .3 VOLT (300 mV): OPEN CKT 412 OR FAULTY ECM CONNECTION OR FAULTY ECM.

CLEAR CODES AND CONFIRM "CLOSED LOOP" OPERATION AND NO "SERVICE ENGINE SOON" LIGHT.

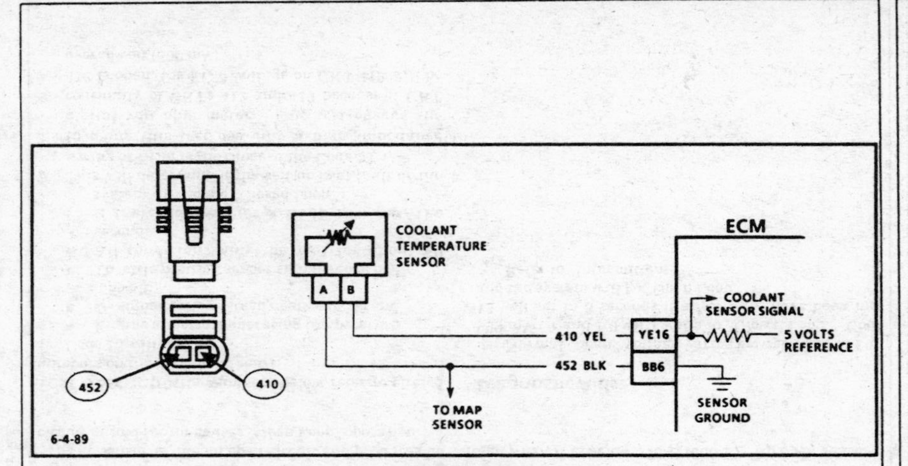

CODE 14

COOLANT TEMPERATURE SENSOR (CTS) CIRCUIT
(HIGH TEMPERATURE INDICATED)
2.0L TURBO (VIN M) (PORT)

Circuit Description:

The Coolant Temperature Sensor (CTS) uses a thermistor to control the signal voltage to the ECM. The ECM applies a voltage on CKT 410 to the sensor. When the engine is cold, the sensor (thermistor) resistance is high, therefore, the ECM will see high signal voltage.

As the engine warms, the sensor resistance becomes less and the voltage drops. At normal engine operating temperature, the voltage will measure about 1.5 to 2.0 volts at the ECM terminal "YE16".

Coolant temperature is one of the inputs used to control:

- Fuel Delivery
- Electronic Spark Timing (EST)
- Cooling Fan
- Torque Converter Clutch (TCC)
- Idle Air Control (IAC)

Test Description: Numbers below refer to circled numbers on the diagnostic chart.

1. Checks to see if code was set as result of hard failure or intermittent condition.
   Code 14 will set if:
   - Engine has been running for more than 10 seconds.
   - Signal voltage indicates a coolant temperature above 135°C (275°F) for 3 seconds.
2. This test simulates conditions for a Code 15. If the ECM recognizes the open circuit (high voltage), and displays a low temperature, the ECM and wiring are OK.

Diagnostic Aids:

A "Scan" tool reads engine temperature in degrees centigrade.

After the engine is started, the temperature should rise steadily to about 90°, then stabilize, when the thermostat opens.

If the engine has been allowed to cool to an ambient temperature (overnight), coolant and MAT temperature may be checked with a "Scan" tool and should read close to each other.

When a Code 14 is set, the ECM will turn "ON" the engine cooling fan.

A Code 14 will result if CKT 410 is shorted to ground.

CODE 14

COOLANT TEMPERATURE SENSOR (CTS) CIRCUIT
(HIGH TEMPERATURE INDICATED)
2.0L TURBO (VIN M) (PORT)

(1) DOES "SCAN" TOOL DISPLAY COOLANT TEMPERATURE OF 130°C OR HIGHER?

- YES → (2) • DISCONNECT SENSOR. "SCAN" TOOL SHOULD DISPLAY TEMPERATURE BELOW -30°C. DOES IT?
  - YES → REPLACE SENSOR.
  - NO → CKT 410 SHORTED TO GROUND, OR CKT 410 SHORTED TO SENSOR GROUND CIRCUIT OR FAULTY ECM.
- NO → CODE 14 IS INTERMITTENT. IF NO ADDITIONAL CODES WERE STORED, REFER TO "DIAGNOSTIC AIDS" ON FACING PAGE.

DIAGNOSTIC AID

COOLANT SENSOR
TEMPERATURE VS. RESISTANCE VALUES
(APPROXIMATE)

°F	°C	OHMS
210	100	185
160	70	450
100	38	1,800
70	20	3,400
40	4	7,500
20	-7	13,500
0	-18	25,000
-40	-40	100,700

CLEAR CODES AND CONFIRM "CLOSED LOOP" OPERATION AND NO "SERVICE ENGINE SOON" LIGHT.

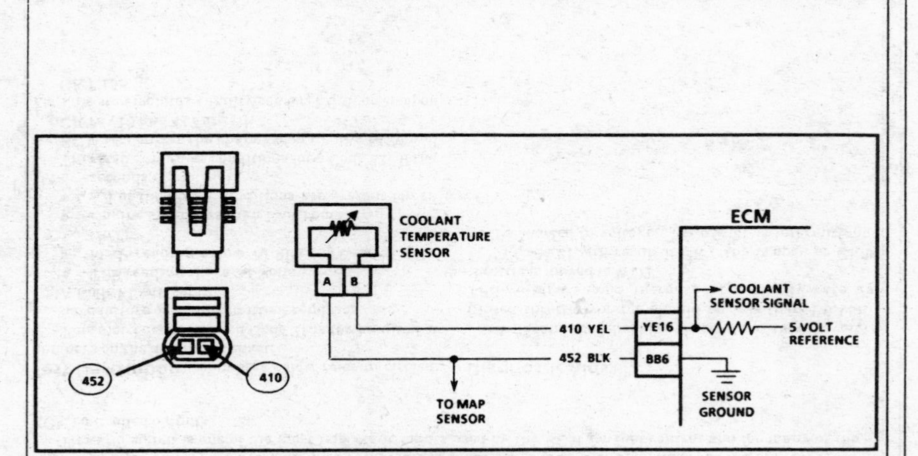

CODE 15

COOLANT TEMPERATURE SENSOR (CTS) CIRCUIT
(LOW TEMPERATURE INDICATED)
2.0L TURBO (VIN M) (PORT)

Circuit Description:

The Coolant Temperature Sensor (CTS) uses a thermistor to control the signal voltage to the ECM. The ECM applies a voltage on CKT 410 to the sensor. When the engine is cold, the sensor (thermistor) resistance is high, therefore, the ECM will see high signai voltage.

As the engine warms, the sensor resistance becomes less, and the voltage drops. At normal engine operating temperature, the voltage will measure about 1.5 volts to 2.0 volts at the ECM terminal "YE16".

Coolant temperature is one of the inputs used to control

- Fuel Delivery
- Electronic Spark Timing (EST)
- Cooling Fan
- Torque Converter Clutch (TCC)
- Idle Air Control (IAC)

Test Description: Numbers below refer to circled numbers on the diagnostic chart.

1. Checks to see if code was set as result of hard failure or intermittent condition.
   Code 15 will set if:
   - Engine has been running for more than 50 seconds.
   - Signal voltage indicates a coolant temperature below -30°C (-22°F).
2. This test simulates conditions for a Code 14. If the ECM recognizes the grounded circuit (low voltage) and displays a high temperature, the ECM and wiring are OK.
3. This test will determine if there is a wiring problem or a faulty ECM. If CKT 452 is open, there may also be a Code 21 stored.

Diagnostic Aids:

A "Scan" tool reads engine temperature in degrees centigrade.

After the engine is started, the temperature should rise steadily to about 90°C (194°F), then stabilize when the thermostat opens.

If the engine has been allowed to cool to an ambient temperature (overnight), coolant and MAT temperature may be checked with a "Scan" tool and should read close to each other.

When a Code 15 is set, the ECM will turn "ON" the engine cooling fan.

A Code 15 will result if CKTs 410 or 452 are open.

If Code 15 is intermittent,

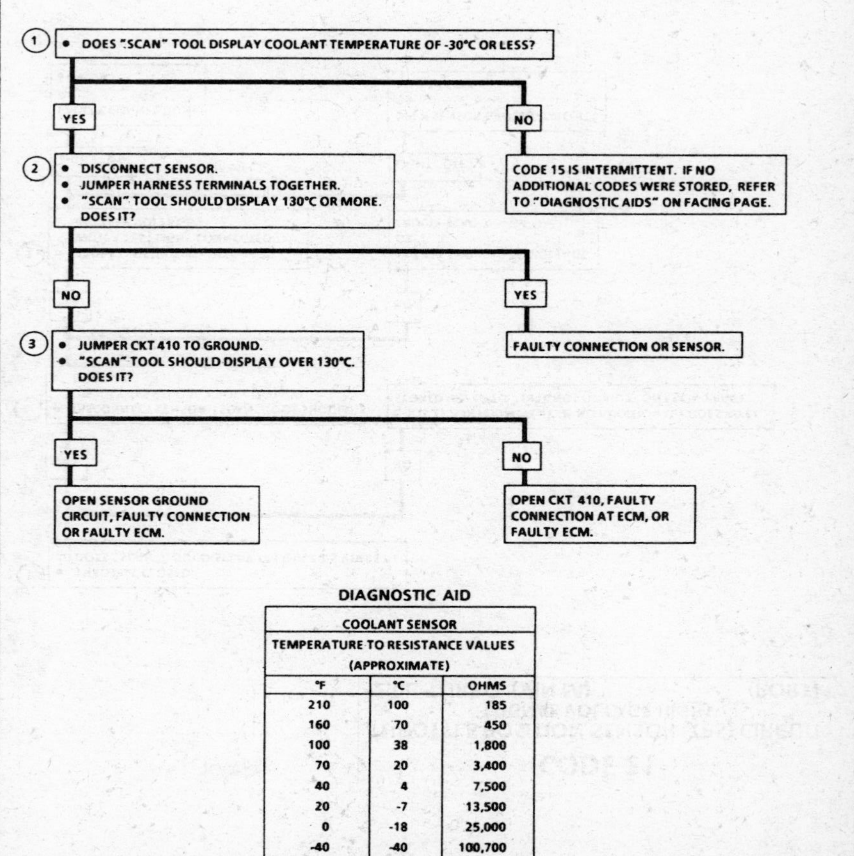

DIAGNOSTIC AID

COOLANT SENSOR
TEMPERATURE TO RESISTANCE VALUES
(APPROXIMATE)

°F	°C	OHMS
210	100	185
160	70	450
100	38	1,800
70	20	3,400
40	4	7,500
20	-7	13,500
0	-18	25,000
-40	-40	100,700

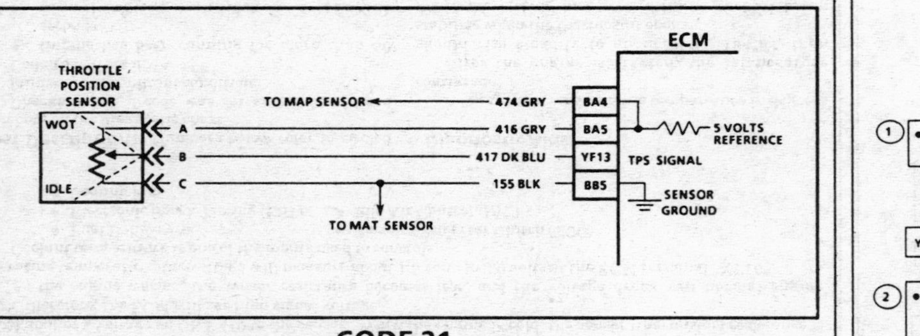

CODE 21

THROTTLE POSITION SENSOR (TPS) CIRCUIT
(SIGNAL VOLTAGE HIGH)

2.0L TURBO (VIN M) (PORT)

Circuit Description:

The Throttle Position Sensor (TPS) provides a voltage signal that changes relative to the throttle valve. Signal voltage will vary from less than 1.0 volt at idle to about 4.6 volts at wide open throttle (WOT).

The TPS signal is one of the most important inputs used by the ECM for fuel control and for many of the ECM controlled outputs.

Test Description: Numbers below refer to circled numbers on the diagnostic chart.

1. This step checks to see if Code 21 is the result of a hard failure or an intermittent condition.
   A Code 21 will set if:
   - TPS reading above 2.5 volts
   - MAP reading below 70 kPa (M/T) or 81 kPa (A/T)
   - Engine speed less than 1300 rpm
   - All of the above conditions are present for 10 seconds
2. This step simulates conditions for a Code 22. If the ECM recognizes the change of state, the ECM and CKTs 416 and 417 are OK.
3. This step isolates a faulty sensor, ECM, or an open CKT 155.

Diagnostic Aids:

A "Scan" tool displays throttle position in volts. Closed throttle voltage should be less than 1.0 volt. TPS voltage should increase at a steady rate as throttle is moved to WOT.

A Code 21 will result if CKT 155 is open or CKT 417 is shorted to voltage. If Code 21 is intermittent,

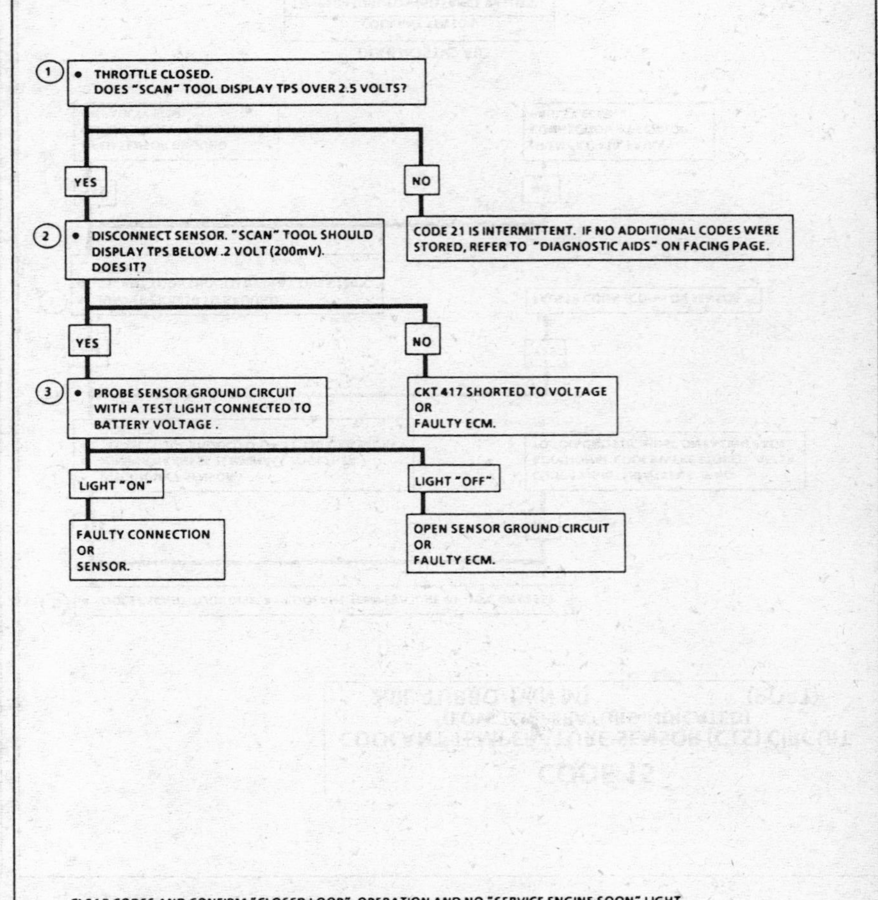

DIAGNOSTIC CHARTS — 2.0L ENGINE

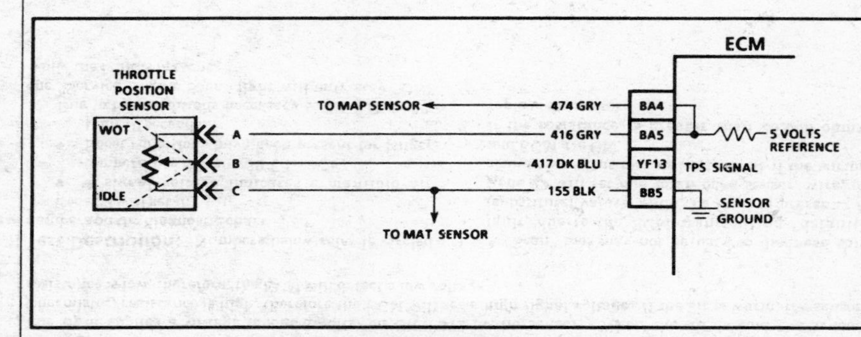

CODE 22

THROTTLE POSITION SENSOR (TPS) CIRCUIT (SIGNAL VOLTAGE LOW) 2.0L TURBO (VIN M) (PORT)

Circuit Description:

The Throttle Position Sensor (TPS) provides a voltage signal that changes relative to the throttle valve. Signal voltage will vary from less than 1.0 volt at idle to about 4.5 volts at wide open throttle (WOT).

The TPS signal is one of the most important inputs used by the ECM for fuel control and for many of the ECM controlled outputs.

Test Description: Numbers below refer to circled numbers on the diagnostic chart.

1. Code 22 will set if:
   - Engine is running
   - TPS signal voltage is less than .2 volt for 4 seconds
2. Simulates Code 21: (high voltage). If ECM recognizes the high signal voltage the ECM and wiring are OK.
3. With closed throttle, ignition "ON" or at idle, voltage at "YF13" should be .36-.44 volt. If not, replace the TPS.
4. Simulates a high signal voltage. Checks CKT 417 for an open.

Diagnostic Aids:

A "Scan" tool reads throttle position in volts. Voltage should increase at a steady rate as throttle is moved toward WOT.

Also some "Scan" tools will read throttle angle 0% = closed throttle, 100% = WOT.

An open or short to ground in CKTs 416 or 417 will result in a Code 22.

- Poor Connection or Damaged Harness. Inspect ECM harness connectors for backed out terminal "YF13", improper mating, broken locks, improperly formed or damaged terminals, poor terminal to wire connection, and damaged harness.
- Intermittent Test. If connections and harness check OK, monitor TPS voltage display while moving related connectors and wiring harness. If the failure is induced, the display will change. This may help to isolate the location of the malfunction.
- TPS Scaling. Observe TPS voltage display while depressing accelerator pedal with engine stopped and ignition "ON." Display should vary from closed throttle TPS voltage when throttle was closed, to over 4.5 volts (4500 mV) when throttle is held at wide open throttle position.

CODE 22

THROTTLE POSITION SENSOR (TPS) CIRCUIT (SIGNAL VOLTAGE LOW) 2.0L TURBO (VIN M) (PORT)

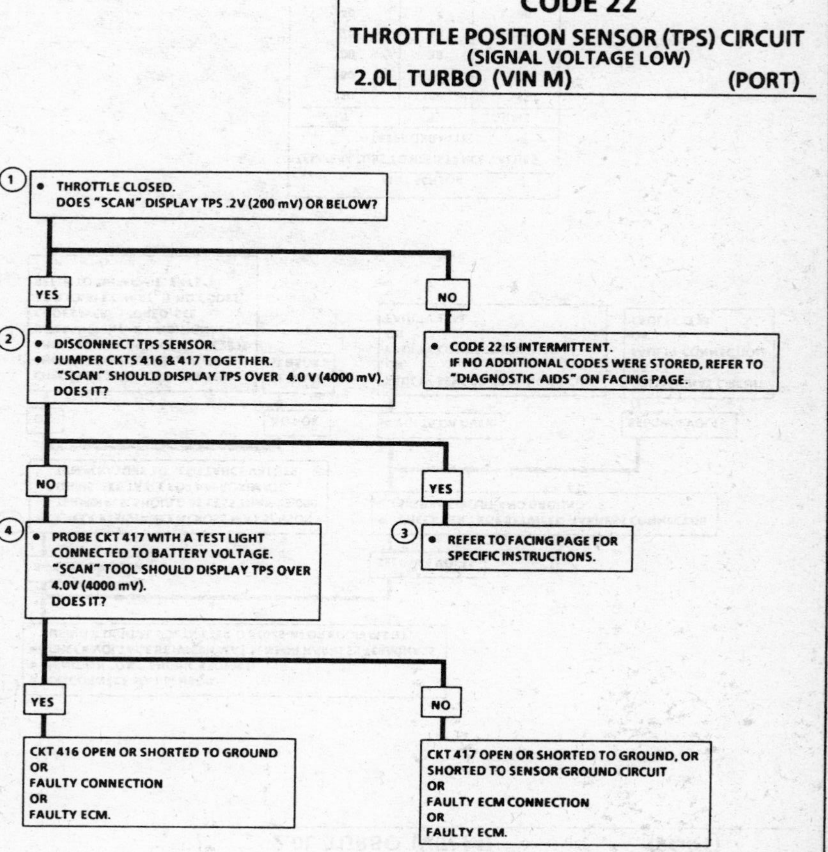

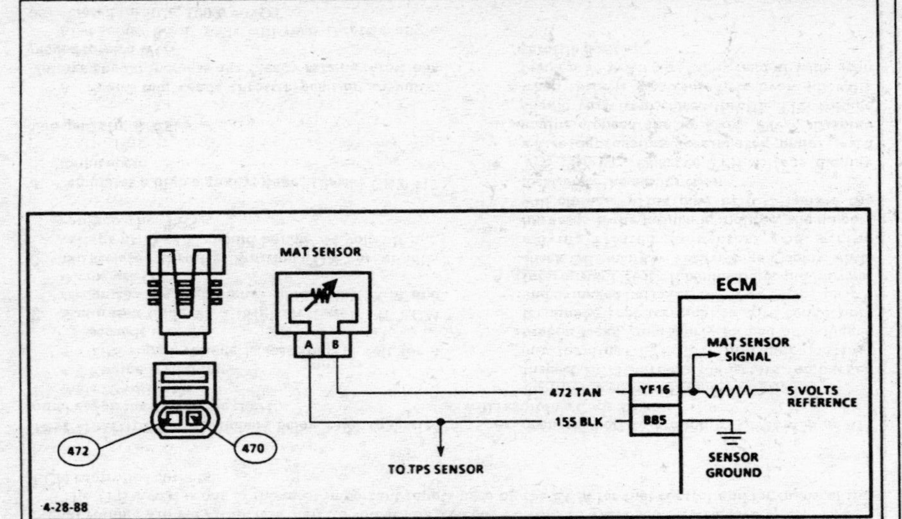

CODE 23

MANIFOLD AIR TEMPERATURE (MAT) SENSOR CIRCUIT
(LOW TEMPERATURE INDICATED)
2.0L TURBO (VIN M) (PORT)

Circuit Description:
The Manifold Air Temperature Sensor (MAT) uses a thermistor to control the signal voltage to the ECM. The ECM applies a voltage (about 5 volts) on CKT 472 to the sensor. When the air is cold the sensor (thermistor) resistance is high, therefore the ECM will see a high signal voltage. If the air is warm, the sensor resistance is low, therefore, the ECM will detect a low voltage.

Test Description: Numbers below refer to circled numbers on the diagnostic chart.

Code 23 will set if:

- A signal voltage indicates a manifold air temperature below −30°C (−22°F).
- Boost conditions have been present for longer than 10 seconds.

Due to the conditions necessary to set a Code 23, the "Service Engine Soon" light will only stay "ON" while the fault is present.

1. A "Scan" tool may not be used to diagnose this fault, due to the ECM transmitting "default" (substitute) values while the fault is present. A Code 23 will set due to an open sensor, wire, or connection. This test will determine if the wiring and ECM are OK.
2. If the resistance is greater than 25,000 ohms, replace the sensor.

CODE 23

MANIFOLD AIR TEMPERATURE (MAT) SENSOR CIRCUIT
(LOW TEMPERATURE INDICATED)
2.0L TURBO (VIN M) (PORT)

(1)
- DISCONNECT MAT SENSOR.
- IGNITION "ON," ENGINE STOPPED.
- CHECK VOLTAGE BETWEEN MAT SENSOR HARNESS TERMINALS USING A DIGITAL VOLTMETER (J 34029-A) OR EQUIVALENT.

4 VOLTS OR OVER

(2)
- CHECK RESISTANCE ACROSS MAT SENSOR TERMINALS. SHOULD BE LESS THAN 25,000 OHMS, SEE TABLE FOR APPROXIMATE TEMPERATURE TO RESISTANCE VALUES.

OK

CHECK FOR SIGNAL CIRCUIT BEING SHORTED TO VOLTAGE. IF NOT SHORTED TO VOLTAGE, CODE 23 IS INTERMITTENT. IF ADDITIONAL CODES WERE STORED, SEE APPLICABLE CHART. IF NO CODES, REFER TO "INTERMITTENTS"

NOT OK

REPLACE SENSOR

BELOW 4 VOLTS

- CHECK VOLTAGE BETWEEN HARNESS CONNECTOR SIGNAL CIRCUIT AND GROUND.

4 VOLTS OR OVER

FAULTY SENSOR GROUND CIRCUIT OR FAULTY CONNECTION(S) OR FAULTY ECM.

BELOW 4 VOLTS

OPEN SIGNAL CIRCUIT OR FAULTY CONNECTION OR FAULTY ECM.

MAT SENSOR		
TEMPERATURE TO RESISTANCE VALUES (APPROXIMATE)		
°F	°C	OHMS
210	100	185
160	70	450
100	38	1,800
70	20	3,400
40	4	7,500
20	-7	13,500
0	-18	25,000
-40	-40	100,700

CLEAR CODES AND CONFIRM "CLOSED LOOP" OPERATION AND NO "SERVICE ENGINE SOON" LIGHT.

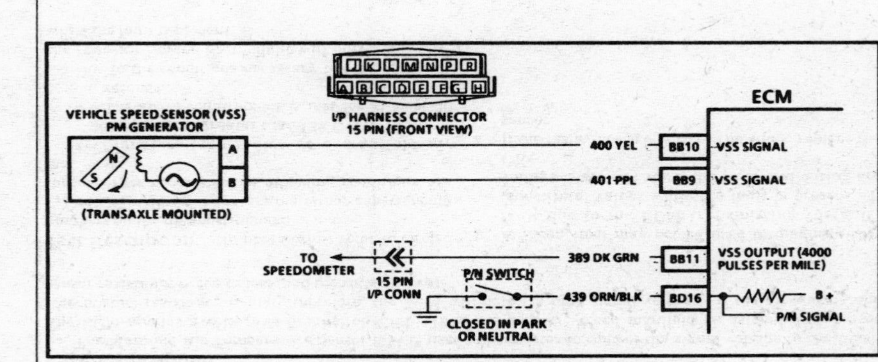

CODE 24

VEHICLE SPEED SENSOR (VSS) CIRCUIT 2.0L TURBO (VIN M) (PORT)

Circuit Description:

Vehicle speed information is provided to the ECM by the Vehicle Speed Sensor (VSS), which is a Permanent Magnet (PM) generator, located in the transaxle. The PM generator produces a pulsing voltage whenever vehicle speed is over 3 mph. The AC voltage level and the number of pulses increases with vehicle speed. The ECM then converts the pulsing voltage to mph which is used for calculations, and the mph can be displayed with a "Scan" tool.

The function of VSS buffer used in past model years has been incorporated into the ECM. The ECM then supplies the necessary signal for the instrument panel (4000 pulses per mile) for operating the speedometer and the odometer. If the vehicle is equipped with cruise control the ECM also provides a signal (2000 pulses per mile) to the cruise control module.

Test Description: Numbers below refer to circled numbers on the diagnostic chart.

1. Code 24 will set if vehicle speed equals 0 mph when:
   - Engine speed is between 1600 and 4400 rpm
   - TPS indicates closed throttle
   - Low load condition (low air flow)
   - Not in park or neutral
   - All conditions met for 5 seconds

   These conditions are met during a road load deceleration. Disregard Code 24 that sets when drive wheels are not turning.
   - The PM generator only produces a signal if drive wheels are turning greater than 3 mph.
2. Before replacing ECM, check Mem-Cal for proper application.

Diagnostic Aids:

"Scan" should indicate a vehicle speed whenever the drive wheels are turning greater than 3 mph.

A problem in CKT 381 or 389 will not affect the VSS input or the readings on a "Scan."

Check CKTs 400 and 401 to ensure that the connections are clean and tight and that the harness is routed correctly. Refer to "Intermittents" in Section "B".

(A/T) A faulty or misadjusted park/neutral switch can result in a false Code 24. Use a "Scan" and check for proper signal while in drive. Refer to CHART C-1A for P/N switch diagnosis check.

CODE 24

VEHICLE SPEED SENSOR (VSS) CIRCUIT 2.0L TURBO (VIN M) (PORT)

DISREGARD CODE 24 IF SET WHILE DRIVE WHEELS ARE NOT TURNING.

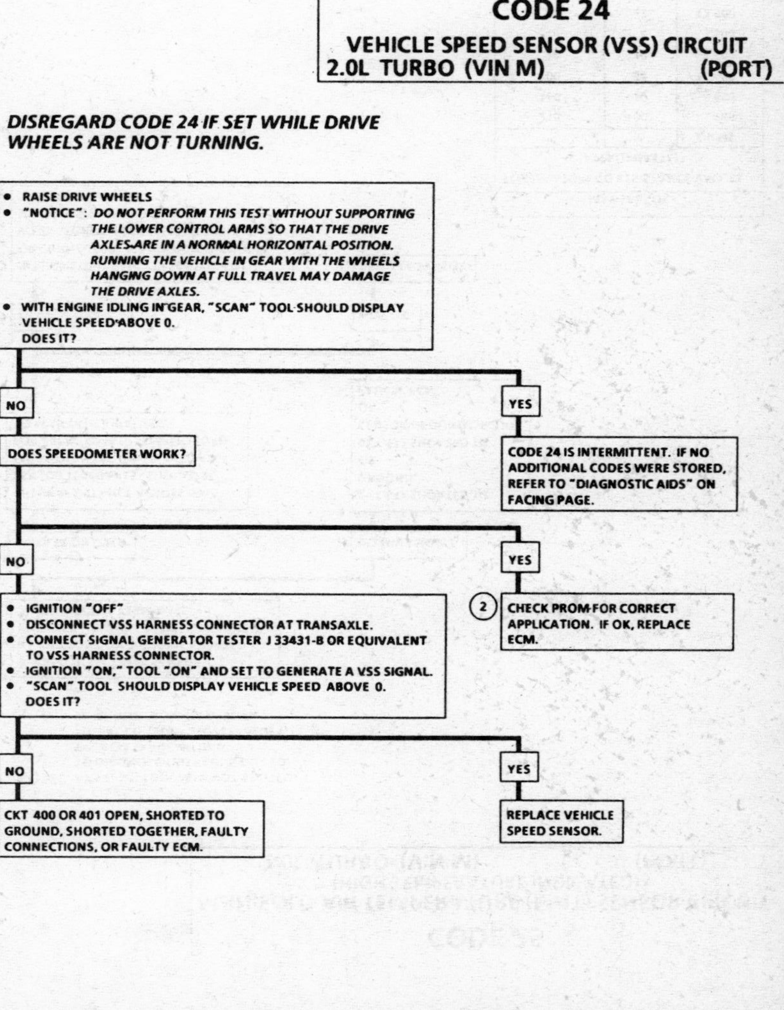

CLEAR CODES AND CONFIRM "CLOSED LOOP" OPERATION AND NO "SERVICE ENGINE SOON" LIGHT.

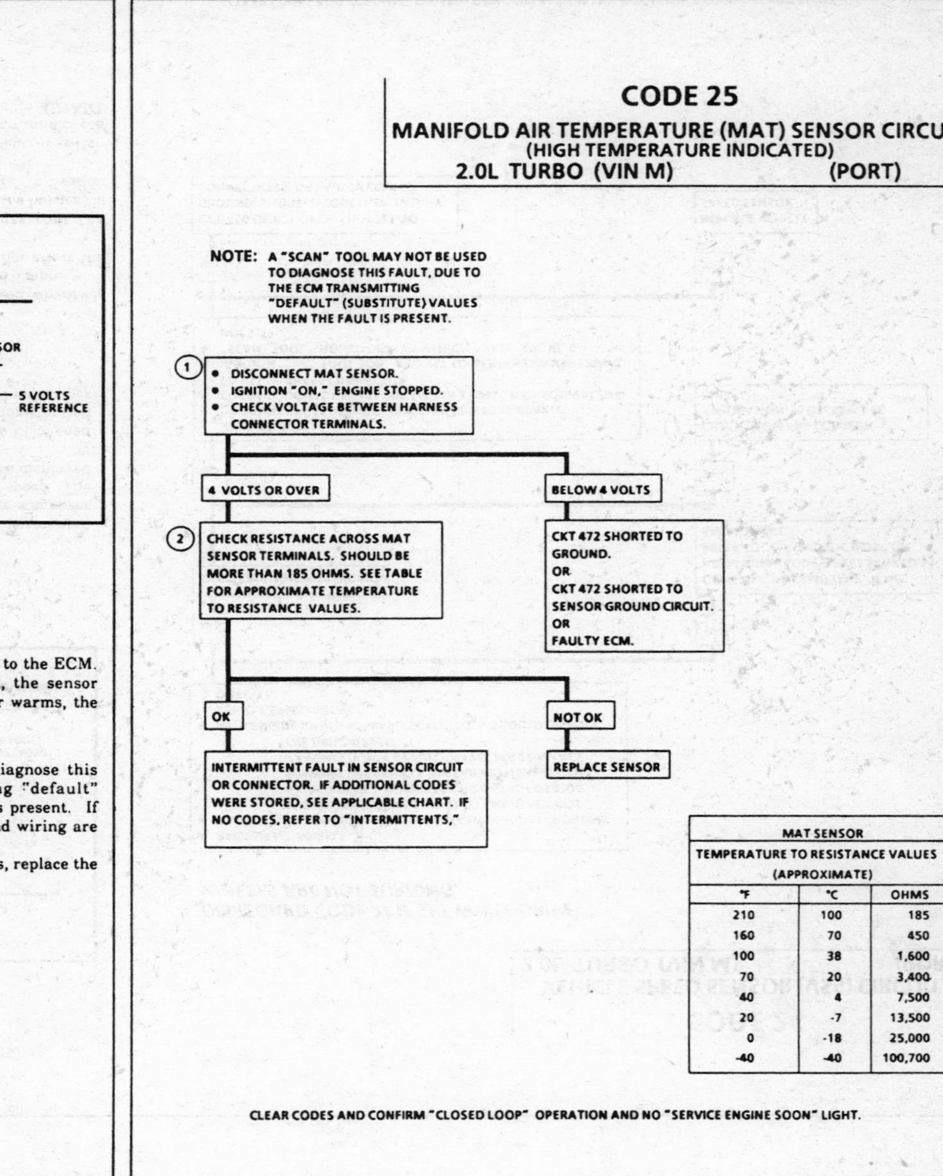

CODE 25

MANIFOLD AIR TEMPERATURE (MAT) SENSOR CIRCUIT
(HIGH TEMPERATURE INDICATED)
2.0L TURBO (VIN M) (PORT)

Circuit Description:

The Manifold Air Temperature Sensor (MAT) uses a thermistor to control the signal voltage to the ECM. The ECM applies a voltage (4-6 volts) on CKT 472 to the sensor. When manifold air is cold, the sensor (thermistor) resistance is high, therefore, the ECM will detect a high signal voltage. If the air warms, the sensor resistance becomes less, and the voltage drops.

Test Description: Numbers below refer to circled numbers on the diagnostic chart.

Code 25 will set if the engine is not experiencing turbocharger boost and the following conditions are met:

- Signal voltage indicates a manifold air temperature greater than 135°C (275°F).
- The above requirement is met for at least 30 seconds.

Due to the conditions necessary to set a Code 25, the "Service Engine Soon" light will only stay "ON" while the fault is present.

1. A "Scan" tool may not be used to diagnose this fault due to the ECM transmitting "default" (substitute) values while the fault is present. If voltage is above 4 volts, the ECM and wiring are OK.
2. If the resistance is less than 100 ohms, replace the sensor.

CODE 25

MANIFOLD AIR TEMPERATURE (MAT) SENSOR CIRCUIT
(HIGH TEMPERATURE INDICATED)
2.0L TURBO (VIN M) (PORT)

NOTE: A "SCAN" TOOL MAY NOT BE USED TO DIAGNOSE THIS FAULT, DUE TO THE ECM TRANSMITTING "DEFAULT" (SUBSTITUTE) VALUES WHEN THE FAULT IS PRESENT.

(1)
- DISCONNECT MAT SENSOR.
- IGNITION "ON," ENGINE STOPPED.
- CHECK VOLTAGE BETWEEN HARNESS CONNECTOR TERMINALS.

4 VOLTS OR OVER

(2) CHECK RESISTANCE ACROSS MAT SENSOR TERMINALS. SHOULD BE MORE THAN 185 OHMS. SEE TABLE FOR APPROXIMATE TEMPERATURE TO RESISTANCE VALUES.

OK

INTERMITTENT FAULT IN SENSOR CIRCUIT OR CONNECTOR. IF ADDITIONAL CODES WERE STORED, SEE APPLICABLE CHART. IF NO CODES, REFER TO "INTERMITTENTS,"

NOT OK

REPLACE SENSOR

BELOW 4 VOLTS

CKT 472 SHORTED TO GROUND.
OR
CKT 472 SHORTED TO SENSOR GROUND CIRCUIT.
OR
FAULTY ECM.

MAT SENSOR		
TEMPERATURE TO RESISTANCE VALUES (APPROXIMATE)		
°F	°C	OHMS
210	100	185
160	70	450
100	38	1,600
70	20	3,400
40	4	7,500
20	-7	13,500
0	-18	25,000
-40	-40	100,700

CLEAR CODES AND CONFIRM "CLOSED LOOP" OPERATION AND NO "SERVICE ENGINE SOON" LIGHT.

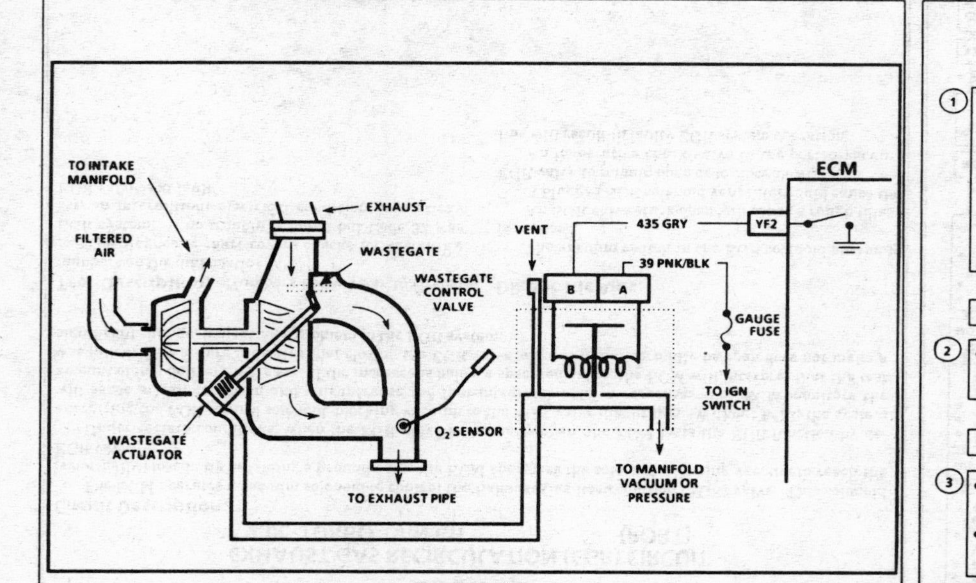

CODE 31

TURBO WASTEGATE OVERBOOST
2.0L TURBO (VIN M) (PORT)

Circuit Description:

On turbo charged engines, the exhaust gases pass from the exhaust manifold through the turbocharger, turning the turbine blades. The compressor side of the turbocharger also turns, pulling air through the air filter and pushing the air into the intake manifold, pressurizing the intake manifold.

The wastegate is normally closed, but opens to bypass exhaust gas to prevent an overboost condition. The wastegate will open when pressure is applied to the actuator, and is controlled by a wastegate control solenoid valve pulsed "ON" and "OFF" by the ECM. Under normal driving conditions, the control solenoid is energized all the time which closes "OFF" the manifold pressure to the wastegate actuator. This allows for a rapid increase in boost pressure. A boost increase will be detected by the MAP sensor, and the ECM will pulse the wastegate control valve. Manifold pressure will then be allowed to pass to the wastegate actuator, and the actuator will open the wastegate. This will prevent an overboost condition on heavy acceleration. As boost pressure decreases, the ECM closes the control valve and the wastegate actuator pressure bleeds "OFF" through the vent in the control valve. If an overboost does exist as indicated by the MAP sensor, the ECM will reduce fuel delivery to prevent damage to the engine.

Test Description: Numbers below refer to circled numbers on the diagnostic chart.

1. A Code 31 will set when the manifold pressure exceeds 143 kPa of boost for two seconds, and a Code 33 has not previously been set. Code 31 will set, but the "Service Engine Soon" light will stay "ON" only while the overboost exists. The light will stay "ON" for 10 seconds after the condition exists and then go "OUT."

   An overboost condition could be caused by
   - CKT 435 shorted to ground
   - A sticking wastegate actuator or wastegate
   - A control valve stuck in the closed position
   - A cut or pinched hose
   - A faulty ECM
   - An extremely dirty air filter

   With ignition shut "OFF," the control valve solenoid is open.
2. After the 103 kPa (15 psi) is applied to valve and then the pressure source is removed, the actuator should slowly move back and close the wastegate. If the pressure does not bleed "OFF," the vent in the control valve solenoid could be plugged.
3. With the ignition "ON" and the diagnostic terminal grounded, the control valve solenoid should be energized. This closes "OFF" the manifold to the wastegate actuator.
4. Checks the electrical control portion of the system. With key "ON" and engine not running, the solenoid should not be energized.

CODE 31

TURBO WASTEGATE OVERBOOST
2.0L TURBO (VIN M) (PORT)

(1)
- DISCONNECT HOSE BETWEEN INTAKE MANIFOLD AND WASTEGATE CONTROL VALVE SOLENOID.
- CONNECT RADIATOR PRESSURE TESTER TO CONTROL VALVE.
- APPLY PRESSURE AND OBSERVE WASTEGATE ACTUATOR.
- THE ACTUATOR SHOULD START TO MOVE AT 27 kPa (4 psi) AND REACH FULL TRAVEL AT 103 kPa (15 psi).
  DOES IT?

YES → (2)
- OBSERVE ACTUATOR AFTER PRESSURE IS APPLIED. DOES PRESSURE BLEED OFF THROUGH VENT IN WASTEGATE CONTROL VALVE SOLENOID?

  YES → (3)
  - TURN IGNITION KEY "ON" AND GROUND ALDL DIAGNOSTIC TERMINAL.
  - APPLY PRESSURE TO CONTROL VALVE SOLENOID.
    DOES ACTUATOR MOVE?

    YES → (4)
    - DISCONNECT SOLENOID ELECTRICAL CONNECTOR.
    - CONNECT TEST LIGHT BETWEEN HARNESS CONNECTOR TERMINALS.

      LIGHT "OFF" →
      - GROUND ALDL DIAGNOSTIC TERMINAL AND OBSERVE TEST LIGHT.

        LIGHT "OFF" →
        - CONNECT TEST LIGHT BETWEEN EACH HARNESS TERMINAL AND GROUND.

          LIGHT "ON"-ONE TERMINAL. → CHECK CKT 435 FOR OPEN. IF NOT OPEN, REPLACE.

          LIGHT "ON"-BOTH TERMINALS. → CHECK CKT 435 FOR SHORT TO VOLTAGE.

          NO LIGHT → REPAIR OPEN IN CKT 39 TO IGNITION.

        LIGHT "ON" → REPLACE CONTROL VALVE SOLENOID.

      LIGHT "ON" → CHECK CKT 435 FOR SHORT TO GROUND. IF IT IS NOT SHORTED, REPLACE ECM.

    NO → NO TROUBLE FOUND.

  NO → REPLACE CONTROL VALVE.

NO →
- REMOVE HOSE FROM WASTEGATE ACTUATOR SIDE OF CONTROL VALVE. APPLY PRESSURE TO HOSE AND OBSERVE ACTUATOR.

  DOESN'T MOVE →
  - CHECK ACTUATOR HOSE.

    OK →
    - DISCONNECT ACTUATOR LINKAGE AT WASTEGATE.
    - APPLY PRESSURE.
      DOES ACTUATOR MOVE?

      YES → WASTEGATE IS STICKING.

      NO → REPLACE ACTUATOR.

    NOT OK → REPLACE HOSE.

  MOVES → REPLACE WASTEGATE CONTROL VALVE SOLENOID.

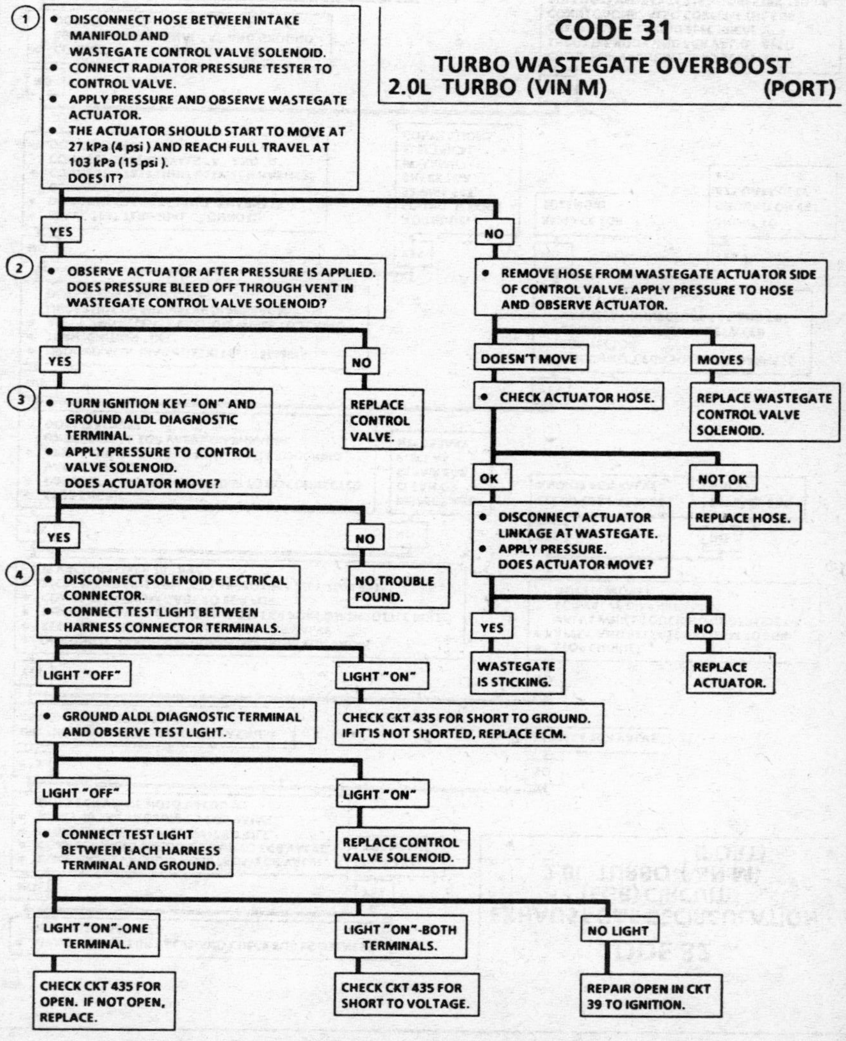

CLEAR CODES AND CONFIRM "CLOSED LOOP" OPERATION AND NO "SERVICE ENGINE SOON" LIGHT.

DIAGNOSTIC CHARTS — 2.0L ENGINE

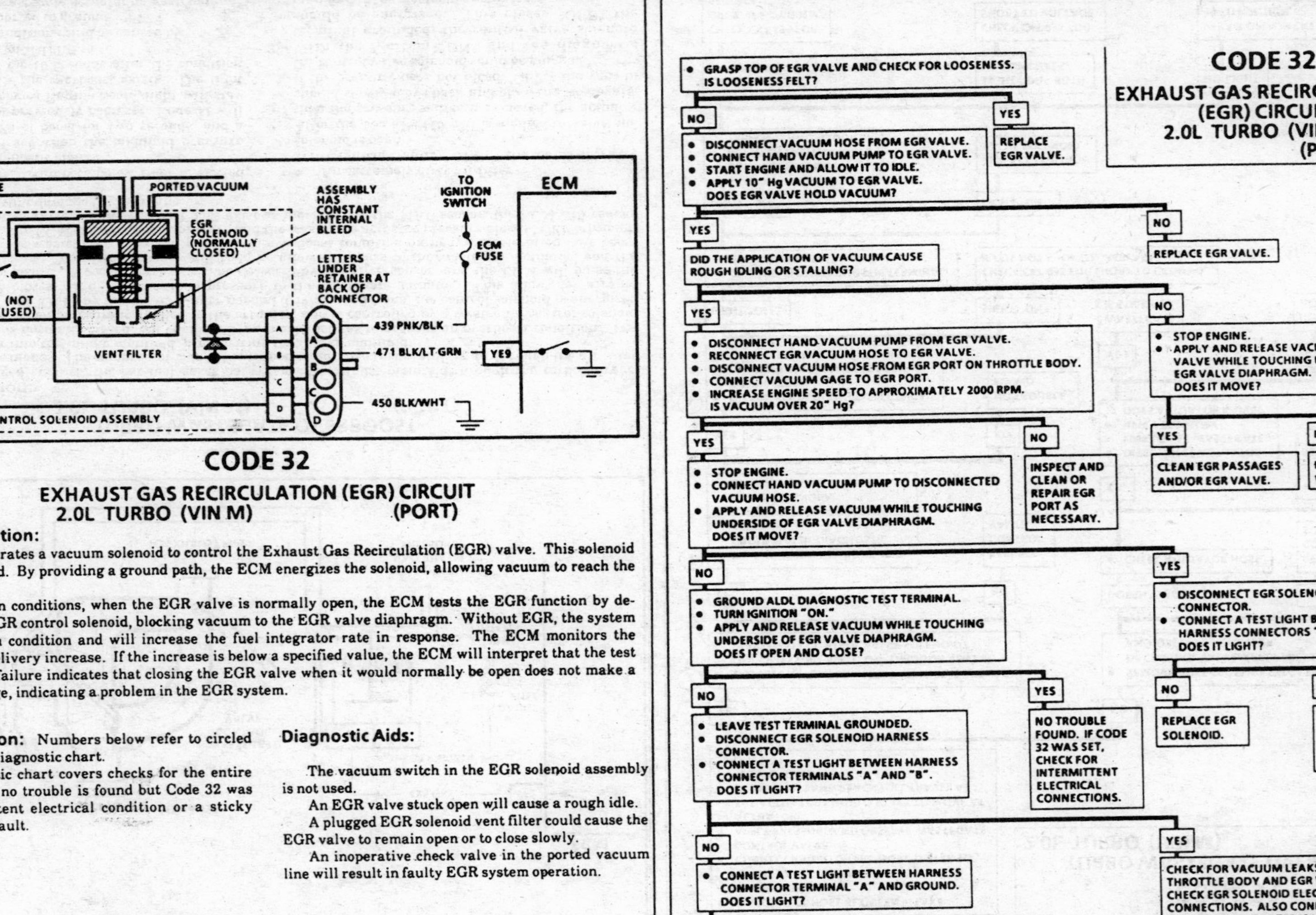

CODE 32

EXHAUST GAS RECIRCULATION (EGR) CIRCUIT 2.0L TURBO (VIN M) (PORT)

Circuit Description:

The ECM operates a vacuum solenoid to control the Exhaust Gas Recirculation (EGR) valve. This solenoid is normally closed. By providing a ground path, the ECM energizes the solenoid, allowing vacuum to reach the EGR valve.

Under certain conditions, when the EGR valve is normally open, the ECM tests the EGR function by de-energizing the EGR control solenoid, blocking vacuum to the EGR valve diaphragm. Without EGR, the system will sense a lean condition and will increase the fuel integrator rate in response. The ECM monitors the amount of fuel delivery increase. If the increase is below a specified value, the ECM will interpret that the test was failed. The failure indicates that closing the EGR valve when it would normally be open does not make a significant change, indicating a problem in the EGR system.

Test Description: Numbers below refer to circled numbers on the diagnostic chart.

The diagnostic chart covers checks for the entire EGR system. If no trouble is found but Code 32 was set, an intermittent electrical condition or a sticky EGR valve is at fault.

Diagnostic Aids:

The vacuum switch in the EGR solenoid assembly is not used.

An EGR valve stuck open will cause a rough idle.

A plugged EGR solenoid vent filter could cause the EGR valve to remain open or to close slowly.

An inoperative check valve in the ported vacuum line will result in faulty EGR system operation.

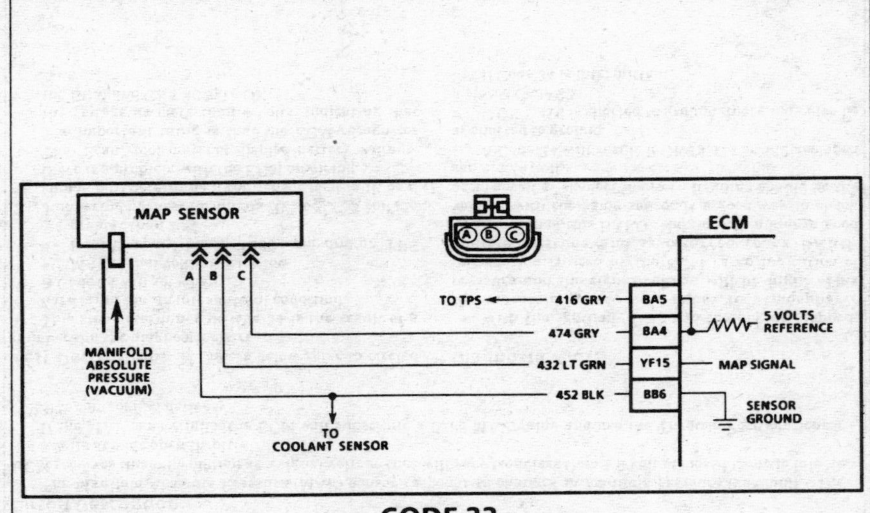

CODE 33

MANIFOLD ABSOLUTE PRESSURE (MAP) SENSOR CIRCUIT
(SIGNAL VOLTAGE HIGH - LOW VACUUM)
2.0L TURBO (VIN M) (PORT)

Circuit Description:

The Manifold Absolute Pressure (MAP) sensor responds to changes in manifold pressure (vacuum). The ECM receives this information as a signal voltage that will vary from about 1-1.5 volts at closed throttle idle, to 4-4.5 volts at wide open throttle (low vacuum or boost).

If the MAP sensor fails, the ECM will substitute a fixed MAP value and use the Throttle Position Sensor (TPS) to control fuel delivery.

Test Description: Numbers below refer to circled numbers on the diagnostic chart.

1. This step will determine if Code 33 is the result of a hard failure or an intermittent condition.
   A Code 33 will set if:
   - MAP signal voltage is too high (low vacuum)
   - TPS less than 2%
   - These conditions for a time longer than 5 seconds
2. This step simulates conditions for a Code 34. If the ECM recognizes the change, the ECM and CKTs 474 and 432 are OK. If CKT 452 is open, there may also be a stored Code 23.

Diagnostic Aids:

With the ignition "ON" and the engine stopped, the manifold pressure is equal to atmospheric pressure and the signal voltage will be high. This information is used by the ECM as an indication of vehicle altitude and is referred to as BARO. Comparison of this BARO reading with a known good vehicle with the same sensor is a good way to check accuracy of a "suspect" sensor. Reading should be the same ± .4 volt.

A Code 33 will result if CKT 452 is open, or if CKT 432 is shorted to voltage or to CKT 474.

If Code 33 is intermittent,

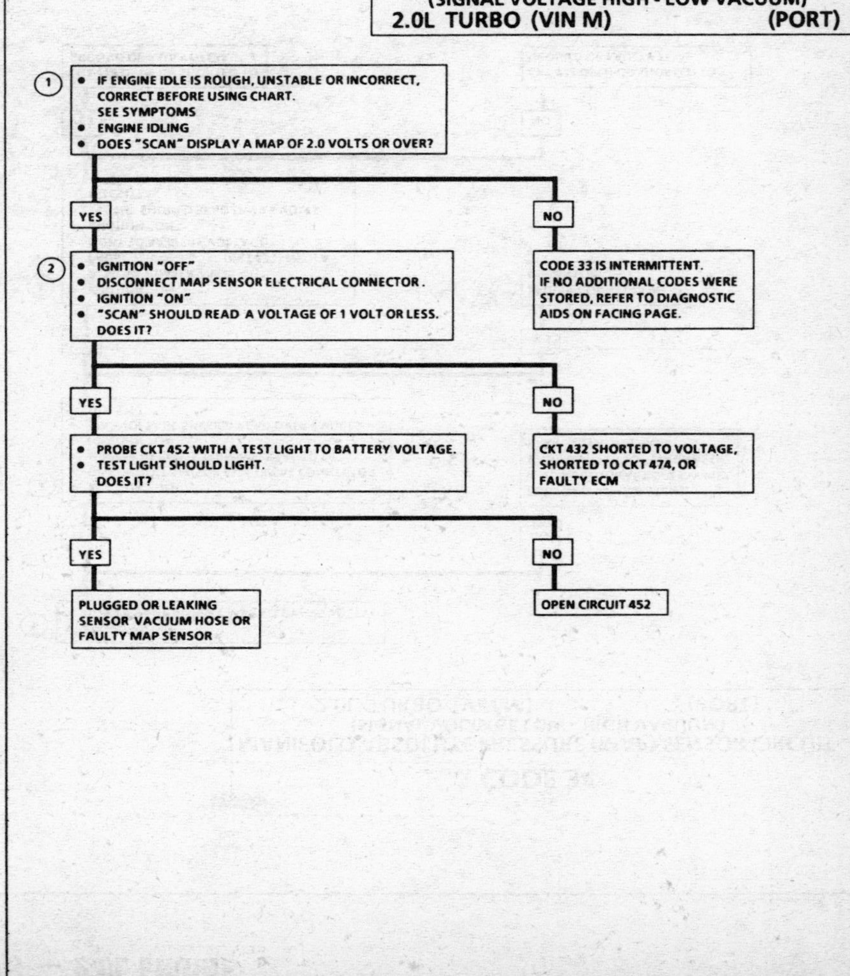

DIAGNOSTIC CHARTS — 2.0L ENGINE

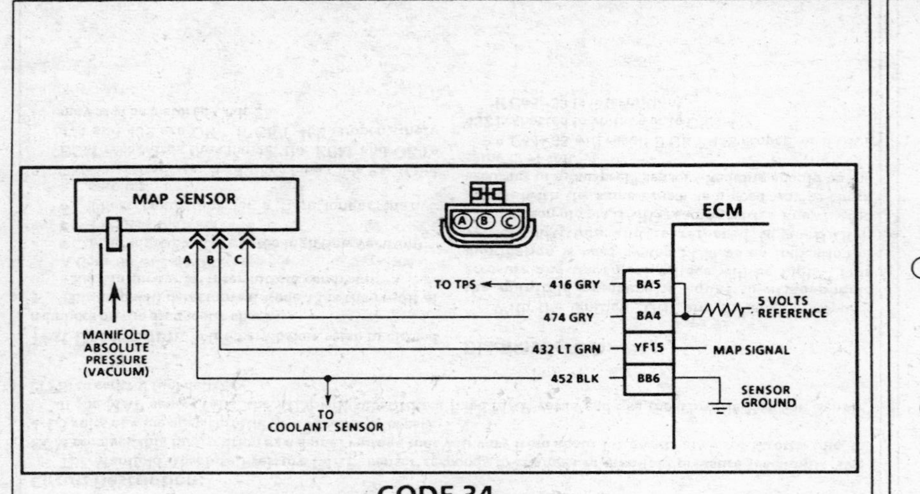

CODE 34

MANIFOLD ABSOLUTE PRESSURE (MAP) SENSOR CIRCUIT (SIGNAL VOLTAGE LOW - HIGH VACUUM) 2.0L TURBO (VIN M) (PORT)

Circuit Description:

The Manifold Absolute Pressure (MAP) sensor responds to changes in manifold pressure (vacuum). The ECM receives this information as a signal voltage that will vary from less than 1.0 volt at closed throttle idle, to 4-4.5 volts at wide open throttle.

If the MAP sensor fails, the ECM will substitute a fixed MAP value and use the Throttle Position Sensor (TPS) to control fuel delivery.

Test Description: Numbers below refer to circled numbers on the diagnostic chart.

1. This step determines if Code 34 is the result of a hard failure or an intermittent condition.
   A Code 34 will set when:
   - MAP signal voltage is too low
   - Engine speed below 1200 rpm and/or TPS greater than 20%
2. Jumpering harness terminals "B" to "C", 5 volts to signal, will determine if the sensor is at fault or if there is a problem with the ECM or wiring.
3. The "Scan" tool may not display battery voltage. The important thing is that the ECM recognizes the voltage as more than 4 volts, indicating that the ECM and CKT 432 are OK.

Diagnostic Aids:

With the ignition "ON" and the engine stopped, the manifold pressure is equal to atmospheric pressure and the signal voltage will be high. This information is used by the ECM as an indication of vehicle altitude and is referred to as BARO. Comparison of this BARO reading with a known good vehicle with the same sensor is a good way to check accuracy of a "suspect" sensor. Reading should be the same ± .4 volt.

A Code 34 will result if CKTs 474 or 432 are open or shorted to ground.

If CKT 416 is shorted to ground, there may also be a stored Code 22.

If Code 34 is intermittent,

CODE 34

MANIFOLD ABSOLUTE PRESSURE (MAP) SENSOR CIRCUIT (SIGNAL VOLTAGE LOW - HIGH VACUUM) 2.0L TURBO (VIN M) (PORT)

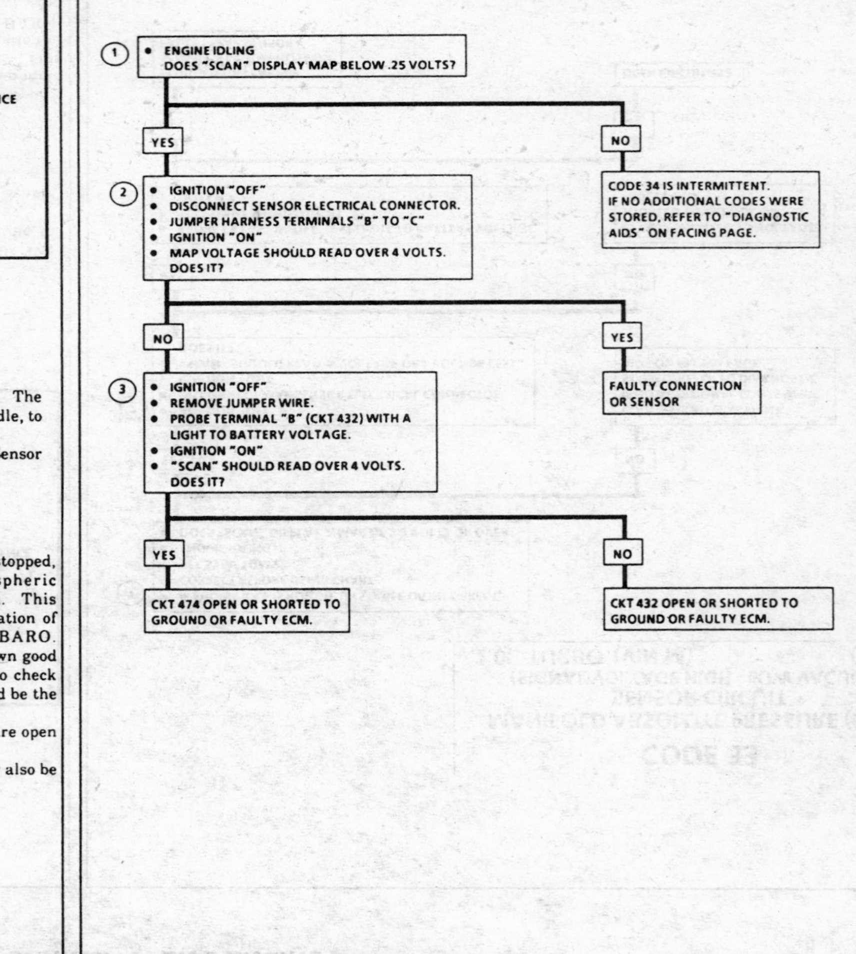

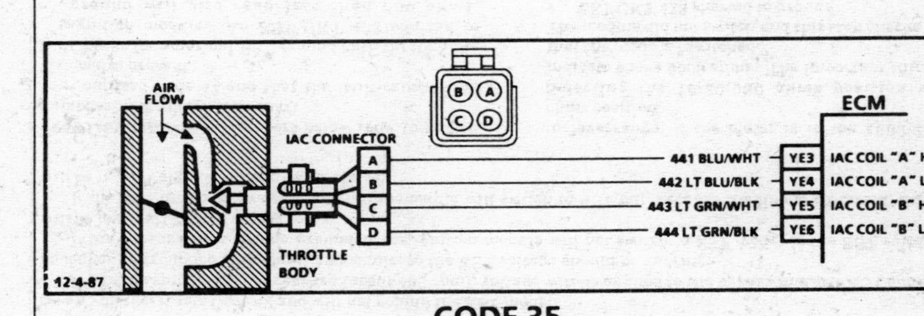

CODE 35
IDLE SPEED ERROR
2.0L TURBO (VIN M) (PORT)

Circuit Description:

The ECM controls engine idle speed with the IAC valve. To increase idle speed, the ECM retracts the IAC valve pintle away from its seat, allowing more air to bypass the throttle bore. To decrease idle speed, it extends the IAC valve pintle towards its seat, reducing bypass air flow. A "Scan" tool will read the ECM commands to the IAC valve in counts. Higher the counts indicate more air bypass (higher idle). The lower the counts indicate less air is allowed to bypass (lower idle). Code 35 will set when the closed throttle engine speed is 225 rpm above or below the desired (commanded) idle speed for 20 seconds. Review the general description of the IAC operation in section "C2".

Test Description: Numbers below refer to circled numbers on the diagnostic chart.

1. The Tech 1 rpm control mode is used to extend and retract the IAC valve. The valve should move smoothly within the specified range. If the idle speed is commanded (IAC extended) too low (below 700 rpm), the engine may stall. this may be normal and would not indicate a problem. Retracting the IAC beyond its controlled range (above 1500 rpm) will cause a delay before the rpm's start dropping. This too is normal.
2. This test uses the Tech 1 to command the IAC controlled idle speed. The ECM issues commands to obtain commended idle speed. the node lights each should flash red and green to indicate a good circuit as the ECM issues commands. While the sequence of color is not important if either light is "OFF" or does not flash red and green, check the circuits for faults, beginning with poor terminal contacts.

Diagnostic Aids:

A slow, unstable, or fast idle may be caused by a non--IAC system problem that cannot be overcome by the IAC valve. Out of control range IAC "Scan" tool counts will be above 60 if idle is too low, and zero counts if idle is too high. The following checks should be made to repair a non-IAC system problem:

- Vacuum Leak (High Idle)
  If idle is too high, stop the engine. Fully extend (low) IAC with tester. Start engine. If idle speed is above 800 rpm, locate and correct vacuum leak including PCV system. Also check for binding of throttle blade or linkage.
- System too lean (High Air/Fuel Ratio)
  The idle speed may be too high or too low. Engine speed may vary up and down and disconnecting the IAC valve does not help. Code 44 may be set. "Scan O_2 voltage will be less than 300 mV (.3 volts). Check for low regulated fuel pressure, water in the fuel or a restricted injector.
- System too rich (Low Air/Fuel Ratio)
  The idle speed will be too low. "Scan" tool IAC Counts will usually be above 80. System is obviously rich and may exhibit black smoke in exhaust.
  "Scan" tool O2 voltage will be fixed above 800 mV (.8 volt).
  Check for high fuel pressure, leaking or sticking injector. Silicone contaminated O2 "Scan" voltage will be slow to respond.
- Throttle Body
  Remove IAC valve and inspect bore for foreign material.
- IAC Valve Electrical Connections
  IAC valve connections should be carefully checked for proper contact.
- PCV Valve
  An incorrect or faulty PCV valve may result in an incorrect idle speed.
- Refer to "Rough, Unstable, Incorrect Idle or Stalling" in "Symptoms,"
- If intermittent poor driveability or idle symptoms are resolved by disconnecting the IAC, carefully recheck connections, valve terminal resistance, or replace IAC.

CODE 35
IDLE SPEED ERROR
2.0L TURBO (VIN M) (PORT)

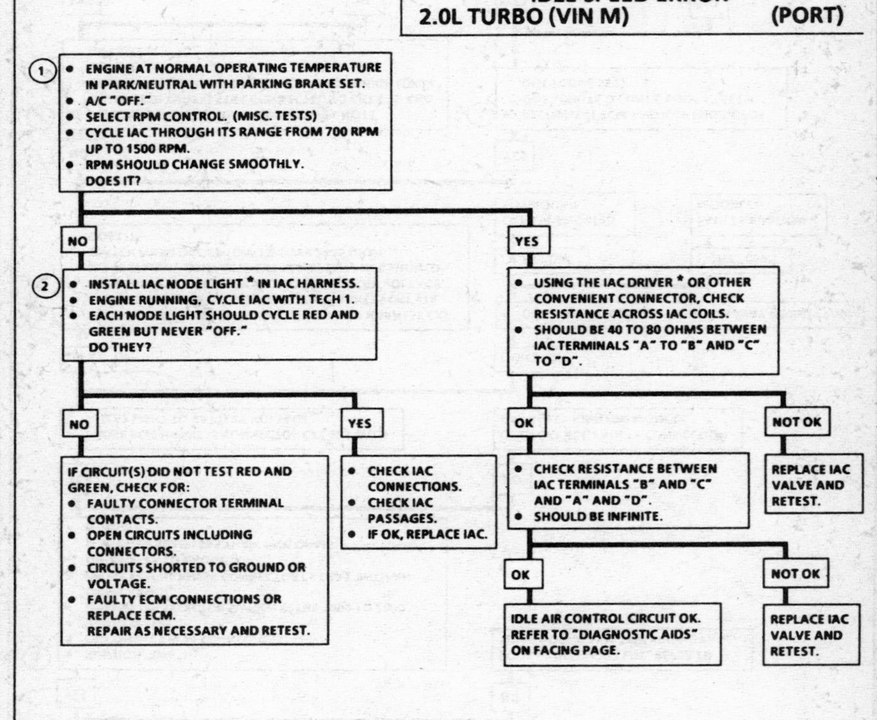

* IAC DRIVER AND NODE LIGHT REQUIRED KIT
222-L FROM: CONCEPT TECHNOLOGY, INC.
J 37027 FROM: KENT-MOORE, INC.

CLEAR CODES, CONFIRM "CLOSED LOOP" OPERATION, NO "SERVICE ENGINE SOON" LIGHT, PERFORM IAC RESET PROCEDURE PER APPLICABLE SERVICE MANUAL AND VERIFY CONTROLLED IDLE SPEED IS CORRECT.

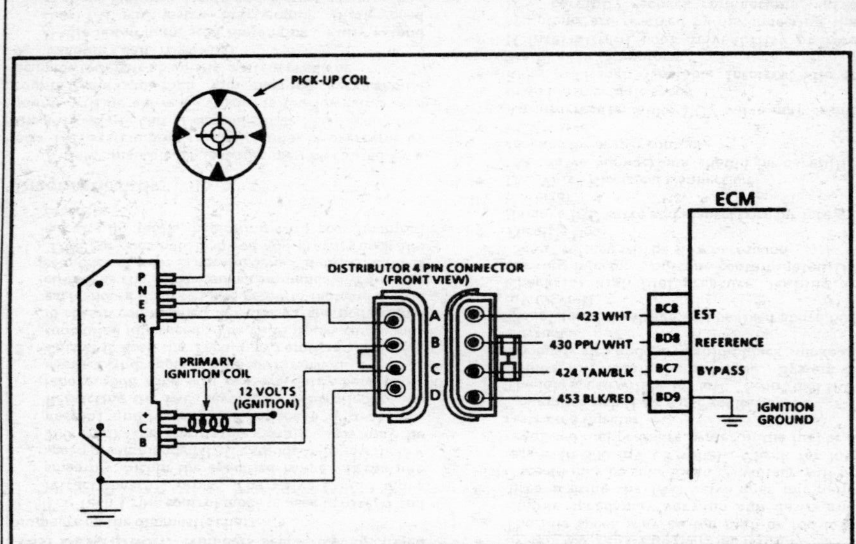

CODE 42

ELECTRONIC SPARK TIMING (EST) CIRCUIT
2.0L TURBO (VIN M) (PORT)

Circuit Description:

The ignition module sends a reference signal (CKT 430) to the ECM when the engine is cranking. While the engine speed is under 400 rpm, the ignition module will control ignition timing. When the engine speed exceeds 400 rpm, the ECM applies 5 volts to the bypass line (CKT 424) to switch the timing to ECM control (EST CKT 423).

When the system is running "ON" the ignition module, that is, no voltage on the bypass line, the ignition module grounds the EST signal. The ECM expects to see no voltage on the EST line during this condition. If it sees a voltage, it sets Code 42 and will not go into the EST mode.

When the rpm for EST is reached (about 400 rpm), voltage will be applied to the bypass line, the EST should no longer be grounded in the ignition module, so the EST voltage should be varying.

If the bypass line is open or grounded, the ignition module will not switch to EST mode, so the EST voltage will be low and Code 42 will be set.

If the EST line is grounded, the ignition module will switch to EST but, because the line is grounded, there will be no EST signal. A Code 42 will be set.

Test Description: Numbers below refer to circled numbers on the diagnostic chart.

1. Confirms Code 42 and that the fault causing the code is present.
2. Checks for a normal EST ground path through the ignition module. An EST CKT 423 shorted to ground will also read less than 500 ohms, however, this will be checked later.
3. As the test light voltage touches terminal "C7", the module should switch, causing the ohmmeter to "overrange" if the meter is in the 1000-2000 ohms position.
   Selecting the 10-20,000 ohms position will indicate above 5000 ohms. The important thing is that the module "switched."
4. The module did not switch and this step checks for
   - EST CKT 423 shorted to ground
   - Bypass CKT 424 open
   - Faulty ignition module connection or module
5. Confirms that Code 42 is a faulty ECM and not an intermittent in CKTs 423 or 424.

CODE 42

ELECTRONIC SPARK TIMING (EST) CIRCUIT
2.0L TURBO (VIN M) (PORT)

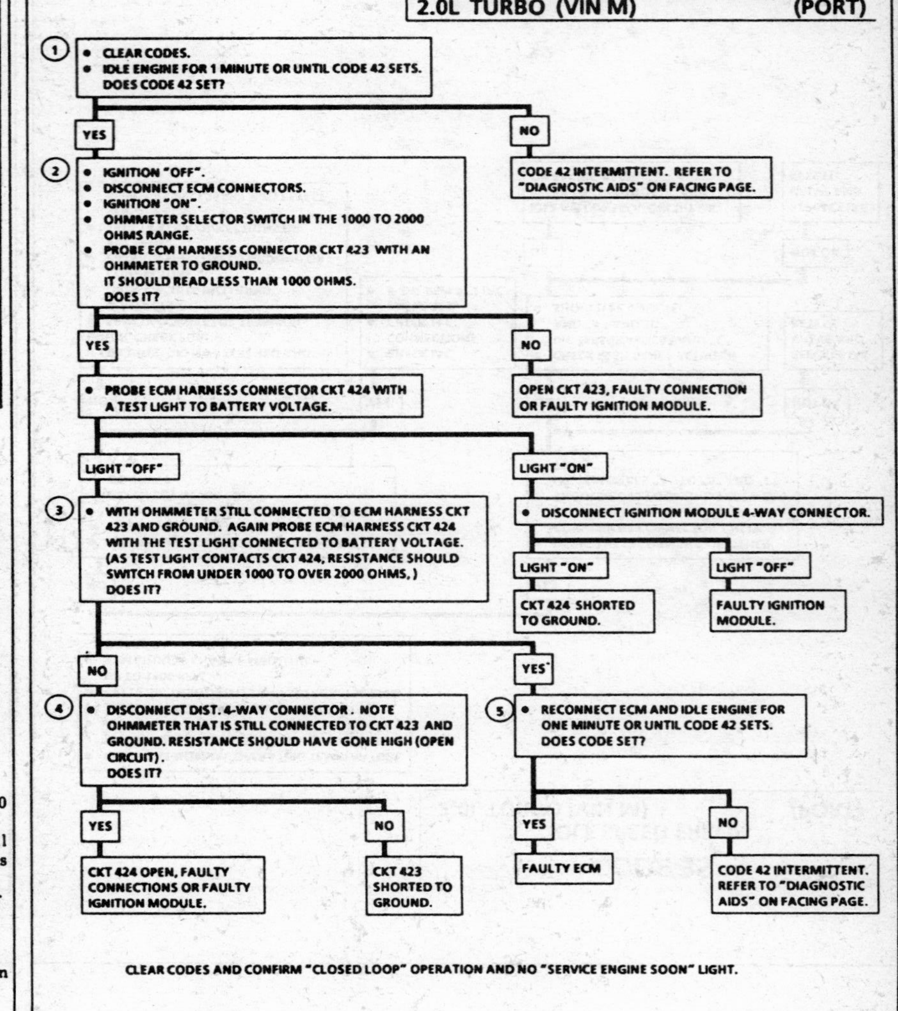

ECM
KNOCK SIGNAL TO MEM-CAL
5 VOLT REFERENCE
YF9
496 DK BLU
KNOCK SENSOR
10-26-87

CODE 43

ELECTRONIC SPARK CONTROL (ESC) CIRCUIT 2.0L TURBO (VIN M) (PORT)

Circuit Description:

The knock sensor is used to detect engine detonation and the ECM will retard the electronic spark timing based on the signal being received. The circuitry within the knock sensor causes the ECM 5 volts to be pulled down so that under a no knock condition, CKT 496 would measure about 2.5 volts. The knock sensor produces an A/C signal which rides on the 2.5 volts, DC voltage. The amplitude and signal frequency is dependent upon the knock level.

If CKT 496 becomes open or shorted to ground the voltage will either go above 3.5 volts or below 1.5 volts. If either of these conditions are met for about 5 seconds, a Code 43 will be stored.

Test Description: Numbers below refer to circled numbers on the diagnostic chart.

1. Code 43 will set when
   - Coolant temperature is over 90°C
   - MAT temperature is over 0°C
   - High engine load based on MAP and rpm
   - Voltage on CKT 496 goes above 3.5 volts or below 1.5 volts
   - All conditions present for 5 seconds

   If an audible knock is heard from the engine, repair the internal engine problem, as normally no knock should be detected at idle.
2. If tapping on the engine lift hook does not produce a knock signal, try tapping engine closer to sensor before proceeding.
3. The ECM has a 5 volts pull-up resistor, which should be present at the knock sensor terminal.
4. This test determines if the knock sensor is faulty or if the ESC portion of the Mem-Cal is faulty.

Diagnostic Aids:

Check CKT 496 for a potential open or short to ground. Also check for proper installation of Mem-Cal.

Refer to "Intermittents"

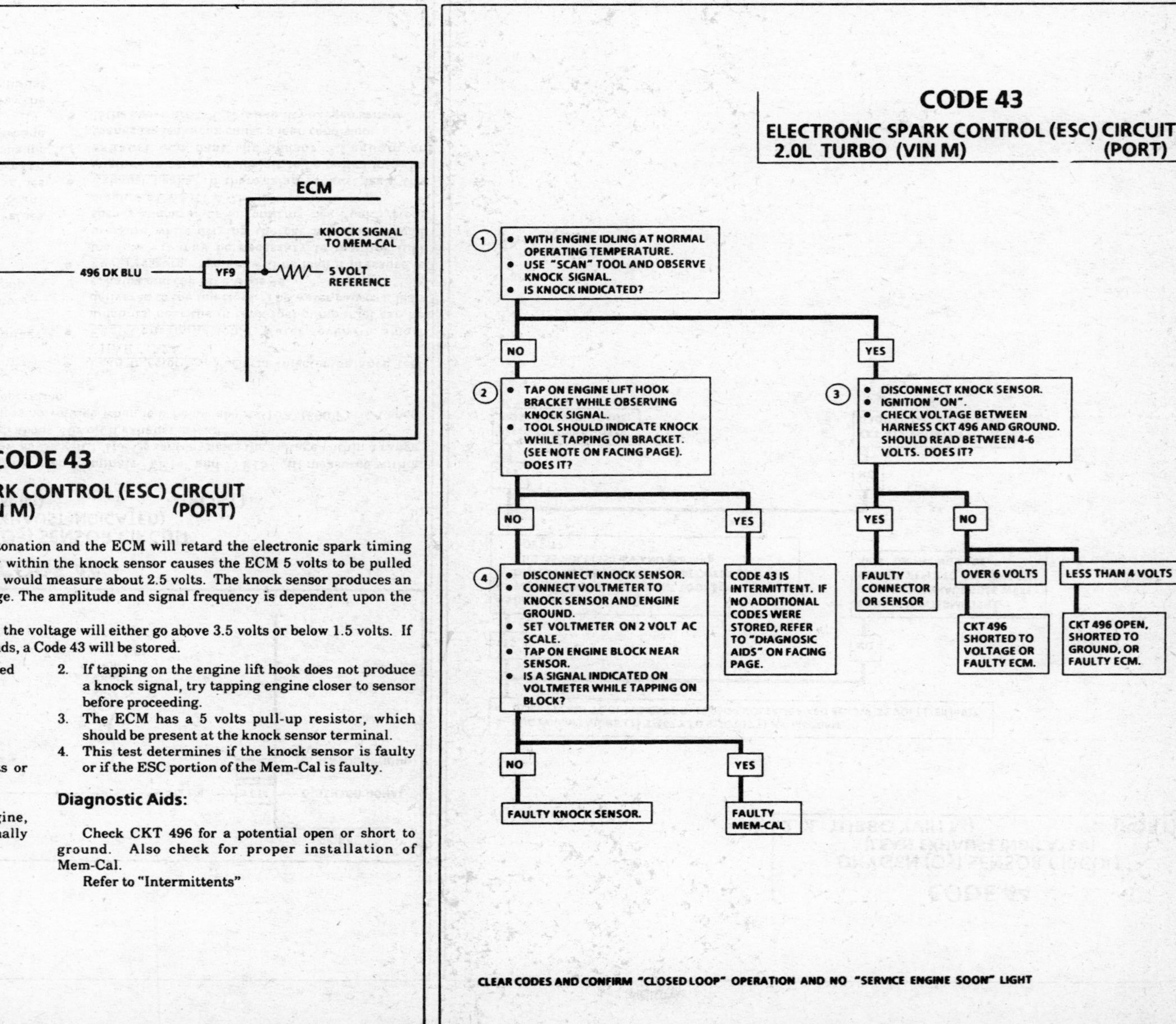

DIAGNOSTIC CHARTS — 2.0L ENGINE

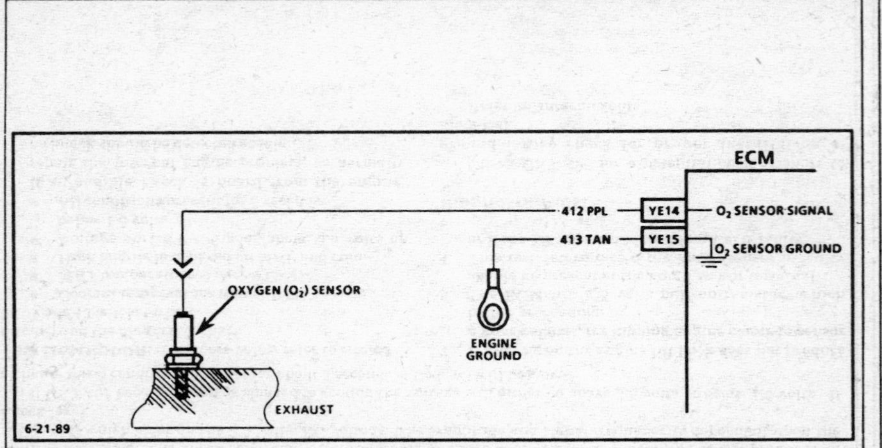

CODE 44

OXYGEN (O_2) SENSOR CIRCUIT
(LEAN EXHAUST INDICATED)
2.0L TURBO (VIN M) (PORT)

Circuit Description:

The ECM supplies a voltage of about .45 volt between terminals "YE14" and "YE15". (If measured with a 10 megohm digital voltmeter, this may read as low as .32 volt.) The O_2 sensor varies the voltage within a range of about 1 volt if the exhaust is rich, down through about .10 volt if exhaust is lean.

The sensor is like an open circuit and produces no voltage when it is below about 316°C (600°F). An open sensor circuit or cold sensor causes "Open Loop" operation.

Test Description: Numbers below refer to circled numbers on the diagnostic chart.

1. Code 44 is set when the O_2 sensor signal voltage on CKT 412:
   - Remains below .2 volt for 60 seconds or more
   - And the system is operating in "Closed Loop"

Diagnostic Aids:

Using the "Scan," observe the block learn values at different rpm and air flow conditions. The "Scan" also displays the block cells, so the block learn values can be checked in each of the cells to determine when the Code 44 may have been set. If the conditions for Code 44 exists, the block learn values will be around 150.

- O_2 Sensor Wire. Sensor pigtail may be mispositioned and contacting the exhaust manifold.
- Check for intermittent ground in wire between connector and sensor.
- Lean Injector(s). Perform injector balance test CHART C-2A.
- Fuel Contamination. Water, even in small amounts, near the in-tank fuel pump inlet can be delivered to the injectors. The water causes a lean exhaust and can set a Code 44.
- Fuel Pressure. System will be lean if pressure is too low. It may be necessary to monitor fuel pressure while driving the car at various road speeds and/or loads to confirm. See Fuel System diagnosis CHART A-7.
- Exhaust Leaks. If there is an exhaust leak, the engine can cause outside air to be pulled into the exhaust and past the sensor. Vacuum or crankcase leaks can cause a lean condition.
- If the above are OK, it is a faulty oxygen sensor.

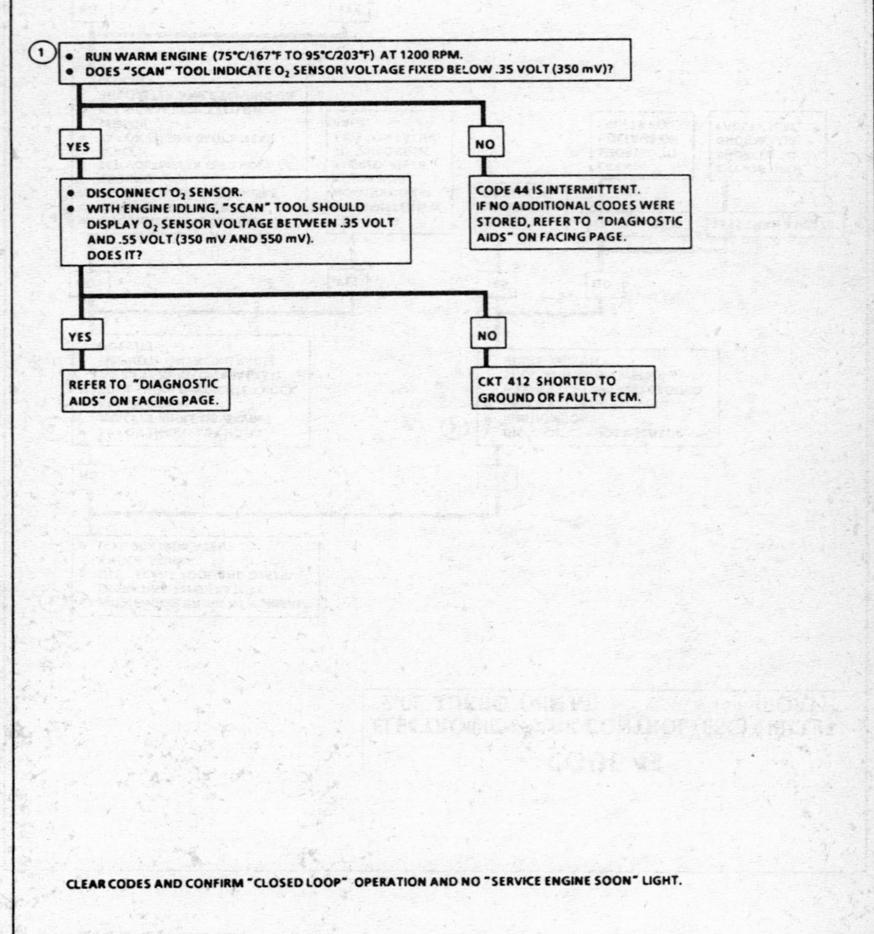

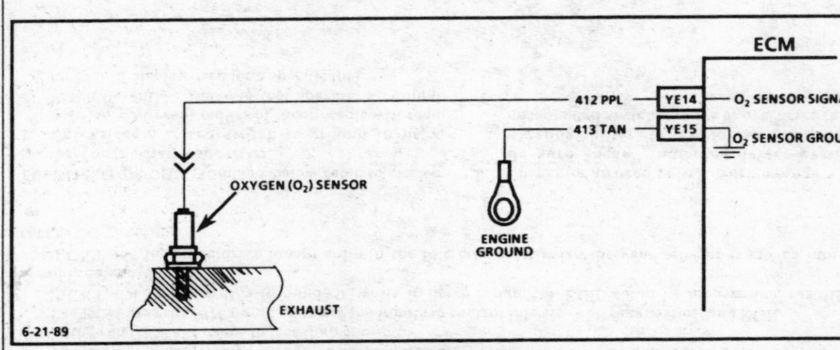

CODE 45

OXYGEN (O_2) SENSOR CIRCUIT
(RICH EXHAUST INDICATED)
2.0L TURBO (VIN M) (PORT)

Circuit Description:

The ECM supplies a voltage of about .45 volt between terminals "YE14" and "YE15". (If measured with a 10 megohm digital voltmeter, this may read as low as .32 volt.) The O_2 sensor varies the voltage within a range of about 1 volt if the exhaust is rich, down through about .10 volt if exhaust is lean.

The sensor is like an open circuit and produces no voltage when it is below about 316°C (600°F). An open sensor circuit or cold sensor causes "Open Loop" operation.

Test Description: Numbers below refer to circled numbers on the diagnostic chart.

1. Code 45 is set when the O_2 sensor voltage:
   - Remains above .75 volt for 50 seconds; and the system is in "Closed Loop"

Diagnostic Aids:

Using the "Scan," observe the block learn values at different rpm and air flow conditions. The "Scan" also displays the block cells, so the block learn values can be checked in each of the cells to determine when the Code 45 may have been set. If the conditions for Code 45 exists, the block learn values will be around 115.

- Fuel Pressure. System will go rich if pressure is too high. The ECM can compensate for some increase. However, if it gets too high, a Code 45 may be set. See Fuel System diagnosis CHART A-7.
- Rich Injector. Perform injector balance test CHART C-2A.
- Leaking Injector. See CHART A-7.
- Check for fuel contaminated oil.
- HEI Shielding. An open ignition ground CKT 453 may result in EMI, or induced electrical "noise." The ECM looks at this "noise" as reference pulses.

The additional pulses result in a higher than actual engine speed signal. The ECM then delivers too much fuel, causing system to go rich. Engine tachometer will also show higher than actual engine speed, which can help in diagnosing this problem.

- Canister purge. Check canister for fuel saturation. If full of fuel, check canister control and hoses. See "Canister Purge," Section "C3."
- MAP Sensor. An output that causes the ECM to sense a higher than normal manifold pressure can cause the system to go rich. Disconnecting the MAP sensor will allow the ECM to set a fixed value for the sensor. Substitute a different MAP sensor if the rich condition is gone while the sensor is disconnected.
- Check for leaking fuel pressure regulator diaphragm by checking vacuum line to regulator for fuel.
- TPS. An intermittent TPS output will cause the system to go rich, due to a false indication of the engine accelerating.
- EGR. An EGR staying open (especially at idle) will cause the O_2 sensor to indicate a rich exhaust, and this could result in a Code 45.

CODE 45

OXYGEN (O_2) SENSOR CIRCUIT
(RICH EXHAUST INDICATED)
2.0L. TURBO (VIN M) (PORT)

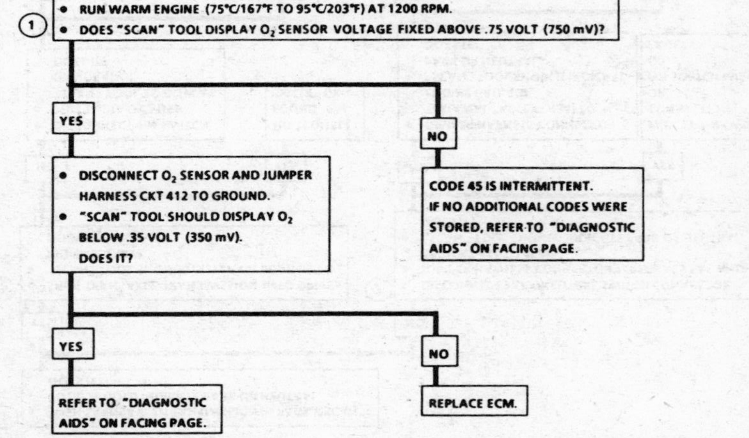

CODE 51

PROM ERROR
(FAULTY OR INCORRECT PROM)
2.0L TURBO (VIN M) (PORT)

CHECK THAT ALL PINS ARE FULLY INSERTED IN THE SOCKET AND THAT PROM IS PROPERLY SEATED. IF OK, REPLACE PROM, CLEAR MEMORY, AND RECHECK. IF CODE 51 REAPPEARS, REPLACE ECM.

CLEAR CODES AND CONFIRM "CLOSED LOOP" OPERATION AND NO "SERVICE ENGINE SOON" LIGHT.

HARNESS CONNECTOR
A B C D E F G
FRONT VIEW
ECM
PARK/NEUTRAL SWITCH
P/N SWITCH CONNECTOR
NEUTRAL START AND BACK-UP SWITCH TRANSAXLE MOUNTED
P R N D L
A ORN/BLK 434
B BLK/WHT 450
BD16
B+
P/N SIGNAL
CIRCUIT TO GROUND IN PARK AND NEUTRAL

CHART C-1A

PARK/NEUTRAL SWITCH DIAGNOSIS (AUTO TRANSAXLE ONLY) 2.0L TURBO (VIN M) (PORT)

Circuit Description:

The Park/Neutral switch contacts are a part of the neutral start switch they are closed to ground in park or neutral and open in drive ranges.

The ECM supplies voltage through a current limiting resistor to CKT 434 and senses a closed switch when the voltage on CKT 434 drops to less than one volt.

The ECM uses the P/N signal as one of the inputs to control idle air, VSS diagnostics, and EGR.

If CKT 434 indicates P/N (grounded), while in drive range, the EGR would be inoperative, resulting in possible detonation.

If CKT 434 indicates drive (open) a dip in the idle may exist when the gear selector is moved into drive range.

Test Description: Numbers below refer to circled numbers on the diagnostic chart.

1. Checks for a closed switch to ground in park position. Different makes of "Scan" tools will read P/N differently. Refer to tool operator's manual for type of display used for a specific tool.
2. Checks for an open switch in drive range.
3. Be sure "Scan" indicates drive, even whil wiggling shifter, to test for an intermittent o misadjusted switch in drive or overdrive range.

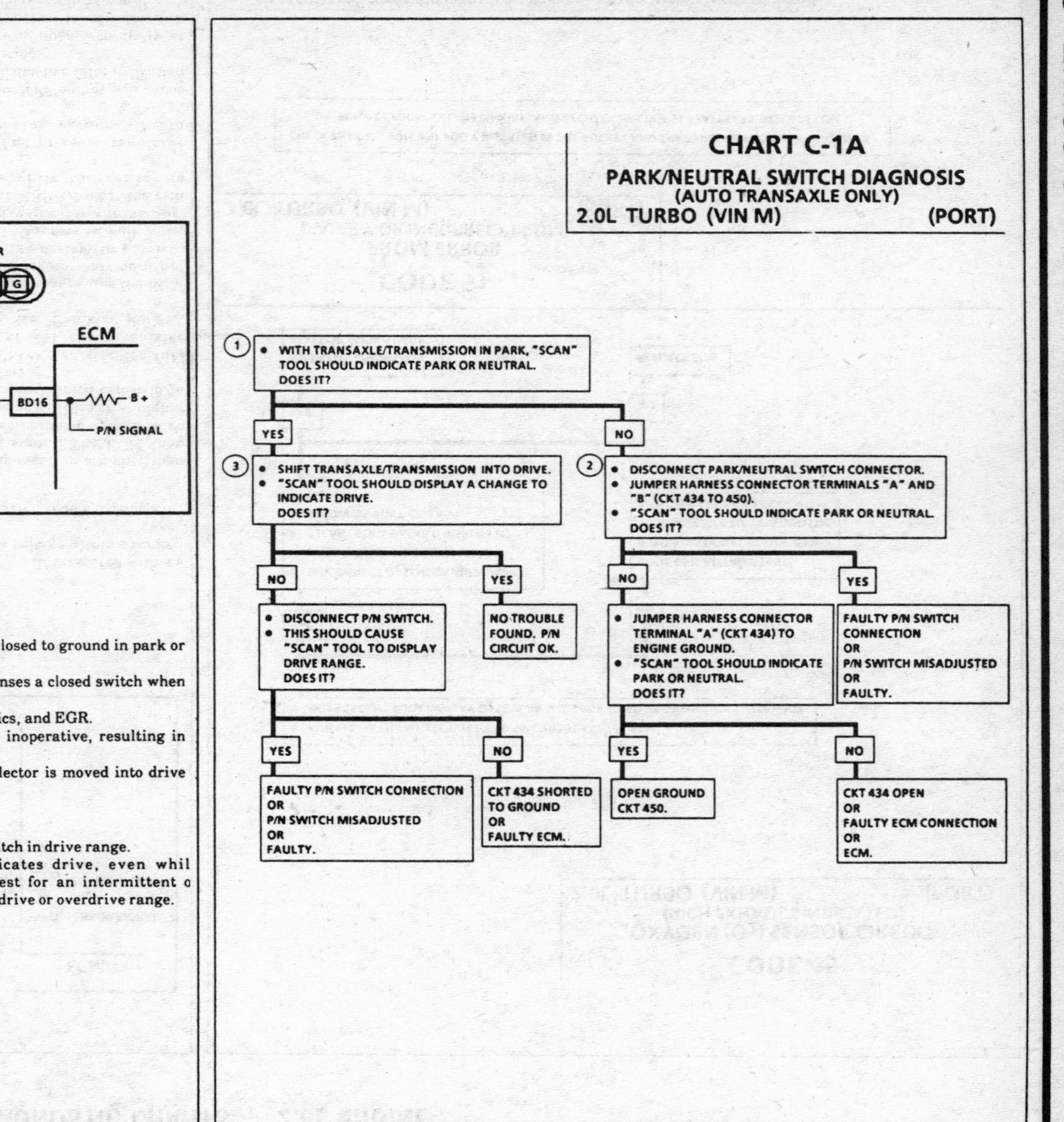

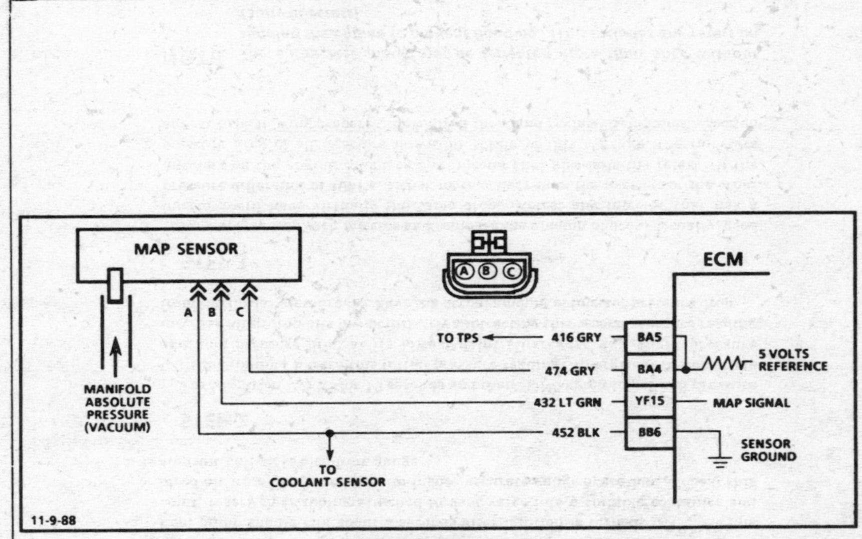

CHART C-1D

MANIFOLD ABSOLUTE PRESSURE (MAP) OUTPUT CHECK 2.0L TURBO (VIN M) (PORT)

Circuit Description:

The Manifold Absolute Pressure (MAP) sensor measures manifold pressure (vacuum) and sends that signal to the ECM. The MAP sensor is mainly used to calculate engine load, which is a fundamental input for spark and fuel calculations. The MAP sensor is also used to determine barometric pressure.

Test Description: Numbers below refer to circled numbers on the diagnostic chart.

1. Checks MAP sensor output voltage to the ECM. With the ignition "ON" and the engine stopped, the manifold pressure is equal to atmospheric pressure and the signal voltage will be high. This voltage, without engine running, represents a barometer reading to the ECM. Comparison of this BARO reading with a known good vehicle with the same sensor is a good way to check accuracy of a "suspect" sensor. Readings should be the same ± .4 volt.
2. Applying 34 kPa (10 inches Hg) vacuum to the MAP sensor should cause the voltage to be 1.2–2.3 volts less than the voltage at step 1. Upon applying vacuum to the sensor, the change in voltage should be instantaneous. A slow voltage change indicates a faulty sensor.
3. Check vacuum hose to sensor for leaking or restriction. Be sure no other vacuum devices are connected to the MAP hose.

CHART C-1D

MANIFOLD ABSOLUTE PRESSURE (MAP) OUTPUT CHECK 2.0L TURBO (VIN M) (PORT)

(1)
- IGNITION "ON", ENGINE "OFF."
- "SCAN" TOOL SHOULD INDICATE A VOLTAGE WITHIN THE VALUES SHOWN IN THE CHART BELOW. DOES IT?

NO → REPLACE SENSOR.

YES ↓

(2)
- DISCONNECT VACUUM HOSE AT MAP SENSOR AND PLUG HOSE.
- CONNECT A HAND VACUUM PUMP TO MAP SENSOR.
- START ENGINE.
- APPLY 34 kPa (10" Hg) OF VACUUM AND NOTE VOLTAGE CHANGE. VOLTAGE SHOULD BE 1.2 - 2.3 VOLTS LESS THAN STEP 1. IS IT?

NO → CHECK SENSOR CONNECTION. IF OK, REPLACE SENSOR.

YES ↓

(3) NO TROUBLE FOUND. CHECK SENSOR HOSE FOR LEAKAGE OR RESTRICTION. BE SURE THIS HOSE SUPPLIES VACUUM TO MAP SENSOR ONLY.

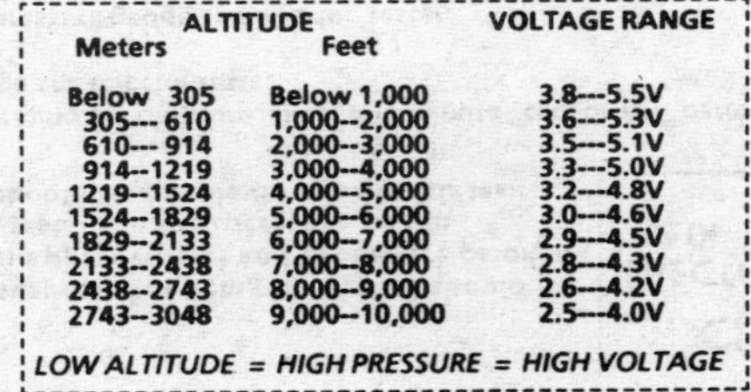

ALTITUDE Meters	ALTITUDE Feet	VOLTAGE RANGE
Below 305	Below 1,000	3.8—5.5V
305—610	1,000—2,000	3.6—5.3V
610—914	2,000—3,000	3.5—5.1V
914—1219	3,000—4,000	3.3—5.0V
1219—1524	4,000—5,000	3.2—4.8V
1524—1829	5,000—6,000	3.0—4.6V
1829—2133	6,000—7,000	2.9—4.5V
2133—2438	7,000—8,000	2.8—4.3V
2438—2743	8,000—9,000	2.6—4.2V
2743—3048	9,000—10,000	2.5—4.0V

LOW ALTITUDE = HIGH PRESSURE = HIGH VOLTAGE

CLEAR CODES AND CONFIRM "CLOSED LOOP" OPERATION AND NO "SERVICE ENGINE SOON" LIGHT.

CHART C-2A

INJECTOR BALANCE TEST

The injector balance tester is a tool used to turn the injector on for a precise amount of time, thus spraying a measured amount of fuel into the manifold. This causes a drop in fuel rail pressure that we can record and compare between each injector. All injectors should have the same amount of pressure drop (± 10 kpa). Any injector with a pressure drop that is 10 kpa (or more) greater or less than the average drop of the other injectors should be considered faulty and replaced.

STEP 1

Engine "cool down" period (10 minutes) is necessary to avoid irregular readings due to "Hot Soak" fuel boiling. With ignition "OFF" connect fuel gauge J 347301 or equivalent to fuel pressure tap. Wrap a shop towel around fitting while connecting gage to avoid fuel spillage.

Disconnect harness connectors at all injectors, and connect injector tester J 34730-3, or equivalent, to one injector. On Turbo equipped engines, use adaptor harness furnished with injector tester to energize injectors that are not accessible. Follow manufacturers instructions for use of adaptor harness. Ignition must be "OFF" at least 10 seconds to complete ECM shutdown cycle. Fuel pump should run about 2 seconds after ignition is turned "ON". At this point, insert clear tubing attached to vent valve into a suitable container and bleed air from gauge and hose to insure accurate gauge operation. Repeat this step until all air is bled from gauge.

STEP 2

Turn ignition "OFF" for 10 seconds and then "ON" again to get fuel pressure to its maximum. Record this initial pressure reading. Energize tester one time and note pressure drop at its lowest point (Disregard any slight pressure increase after drop hits low point). By subtracting this second pressure reading from the initial pressure, we have the actual amount of injector pressure drop.

STEP 3

Repeat step 2 on each injector and compare the amount of drop. Usually, good injectors will have virtually the same drop. Retest any injector that has a pressure difference of 10kPa, either more or less than the average of the other injectors on the engine. Replace any injector that also fails the retest. If the pressure drop of all injectors is within 10kPa of this average, the injectors appear to be flowing properly. Reconnect them and review "Symptoms", Section

NOTE: ***The entire test should not be repeated more than once without running the engine to prevent flooding. (This includes any retest on faulty injectors).***

CHART C-2A

INJECTOR BALANCE TEST 2.0L TURBO (VIN M) (PORT)

NOTE: **If injectors are suspected of being dirty, they should be cleaned using an approved tool and procedure prior to performing this test. The fuel pressure test in Chart A-7, should be completed prior to this test.**

Step 1. If engine is at operating temperature, allow a 10 minute "cool down" period then connect fuel pressure gauge and injector tester.

1. Ignition "OFF."
2. Connect fuel pressure gauge and injector tester.
3. Ignition "ON."
4. Bleed off air in gauge. Repeat until all air is bled from gauge.

Step 2. Run test:

1. Ignition "OFF" for 10 seconds.
2. Ignition "ON". Record gauge pressure. (Pressure must hold steady, if not see the Fuel System diagnosis, Chart A-7
3. Turn injector on, by depressing button on injector tester, and note pressure at the instant the gauge needle stops.

Step 3.

1. Repeat step 2 on all injectors and record pressure drop on each. Retest injectors that appear faulty (Any injectors that have a 10 kPa difference, either more or less, in pressure from the average). If no problem is found, review "Symptoms" Section

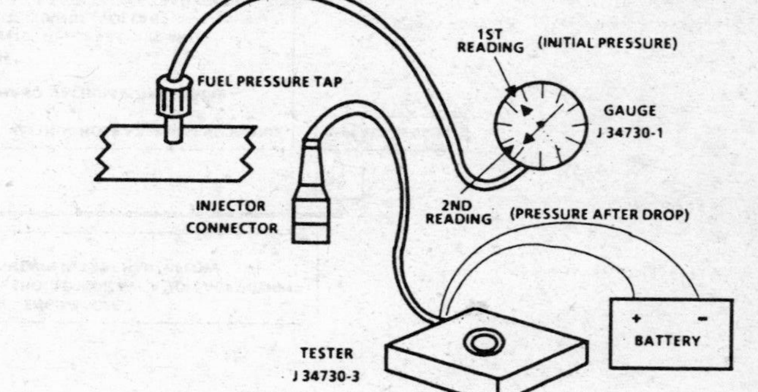

— EXAMPLE —

CYLINDER	1	2	3	4	5	6
1ST READING	225	225	225	225	225	225
2ND READING	100	100	100	90	100	115
AMOUNT OF DROP	125	125	125	135	125	110
	OK	OK	OK	FAULTY, RICH (TOO MUCH) (FUEL DROP)	OK	FAULTY, LEAN (TOO LITTLE) (FUEL DROP)

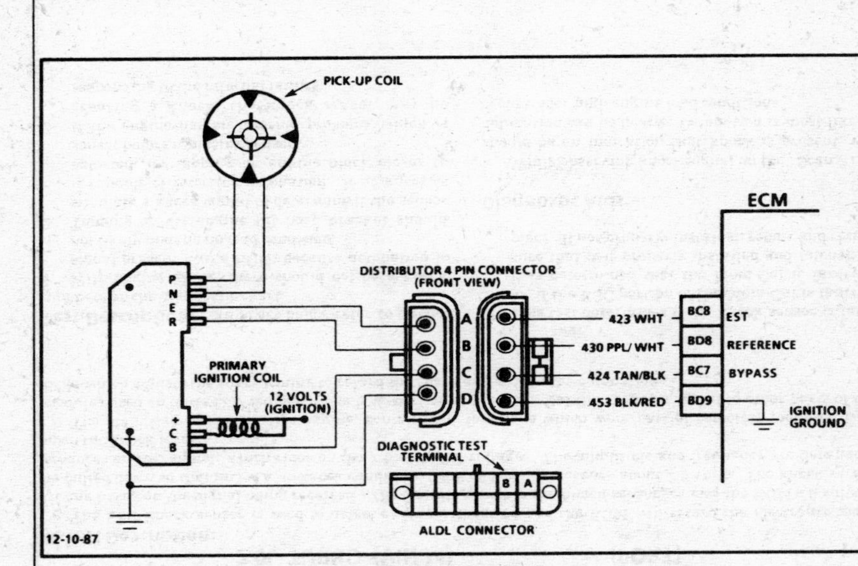

CHART C-4C

IGNITION SYSTEM CHECK (REMOTE COIL) 2.0L TURBO (VIN M) (PORT)

Test Description: Numbers below refer to circled numbers on the diagnostic chart.

1. Two wires are checked to ensure that an open is not present in a spark plug wire.

1A. If spark occurs with 4 terminal distributor connector disconnected, pick-up coil output is too low for EST operation.

2. A spark indicates the problem must be the distributor cap or rotor.

3. Normally, there should be battery voltage at the "C" and "+" terminals. Low voltage would indicate an open or a high resistance circuit from the distributor to the coil or ignition switch. If "C" terminal voltage was low, but "+" terminal voltage is 10 volts or more, circuit from "C" terminal to ignition coil or ignition coil primary winding is open.

4. Checks for a shorted module or grounded circuit from the ignition coil to the module. The distributor module should be turned "OFF". Normal voltage should be about 12 volts.

   If the module is turned "ON," the voltage would be low, but above 1 volt. This could cause the ignition coil to fail from excessive heat.

   With an open ignition coil primary winding, a small a mount of voltage will leak through the module from the "BATT" to the "tach" terminal.

5. Applying voltage (1.5 to 8 volts) to module terminal "P" should turn the module "ON" and the tachometer terminal voltage should drop to about 7-9 volts. This test will determine whether the module or coil is faulty or if the pick-up coil is not generating the proper signal to turn the module "ON." This test can be performed by using a DC battery with a rating of 1.5 to 8 volts. The use of the test light is mainly to allow the "P" terminal to be probed more easily.

   Some digital multi-meters can also be used to trigger the module by selecting ohms, usually the diode position. In this position the meter may have a voltage across its terminals which can be used to trigger the module. The voltage in the ohms position can be checked by using a second meter or by checking the manufacturer's specification of the tool being used.

6. This should turn "OFF" the module and cause a spark. If no spark occurs, the fault is most likely in the ignition coil because most module problems would have been found before this point in the procedure. A module tester (J 24642) could determine which is at fault.

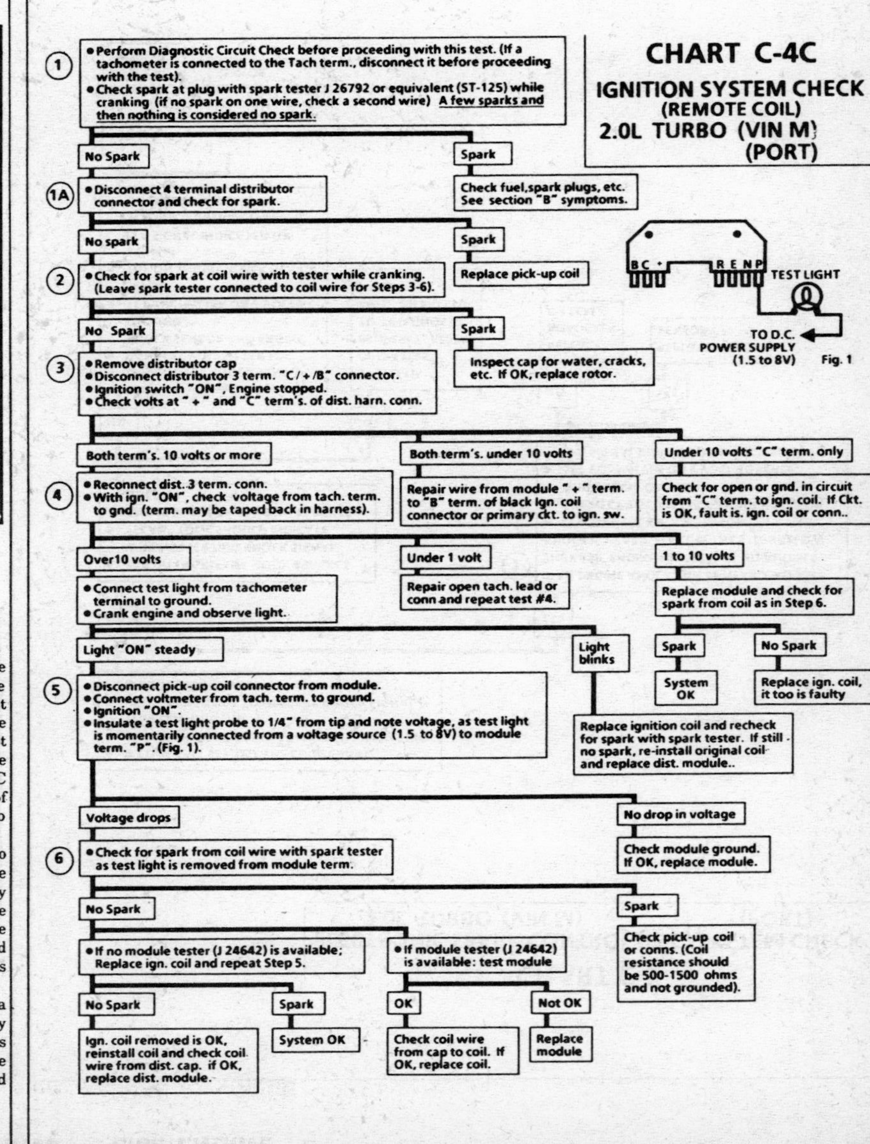

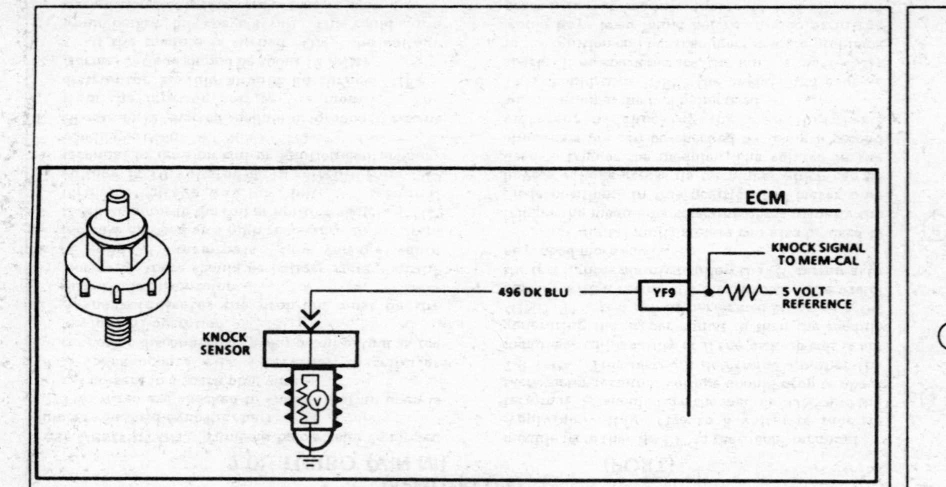

CHART C-5

ELECTRONIC SPARK CONTROL (ESC) SYSTEM CHECK 2.0L TURBO (VIN M) (PORT)

Circuit Description:

The ESC knock sensor is used to detect engine detonation and the ECM will retard the electronic spark timing based on the signal being received. The circuitry, within the knock sensor, causes the ECM's 5 volts to be pulled down so that under a no knock condition, CKT 496 would measure about 2.5 volts. The knock sensor produces an A/C signal, which rides on the 2.5 volts DC voltage. The amplitude and frequency are dependent upon the knock level.

The Mem-Cal, used with this engine, contains the functions which were part of remotely mounted ESC modules used on other GM vehicles. The ESC portion of the Mem-Cal then sends a signal to other parts of the ECM which adjusts the spark timing to retard the spark and reduce the detonation.

Test Description: Numbers below refer to circled numbers on the diagnostic chart.

1. With engine idling, there should not be a knock signal present at the ECM, because detonation is not likely under a no load condition.
2. Tapping on the engine lift hood bracket should simulate a knock signal to determine if the sensor is capable of detecting detonation. If no knock is detected, try tapping on engine block closer to sensor before replacing sensor.
3. If the engine has an internal problem, which is creating a knock, the knock sensor may be responding to the internal failure.
4. This test determines if the knock sensor is faulty, or, if the ESC portion of the Mem-Cal is faulty. If it is determined that the Mem-Cal is faulty, be sure that it is properly installed and latched into place. If not properly installed, repair and retest.

Diagnostic Aids:

While observing knock signal on the "Scan," there should be an indication that knock is present, when detonation can be heard. Detonation is most likely to occur under high engine load conditions.

CHART C-5

ELECTRONIC SPARK CONTROL (ESC) SYSTEM CHECK 2.0L TURBO (VIN M) (PORT)

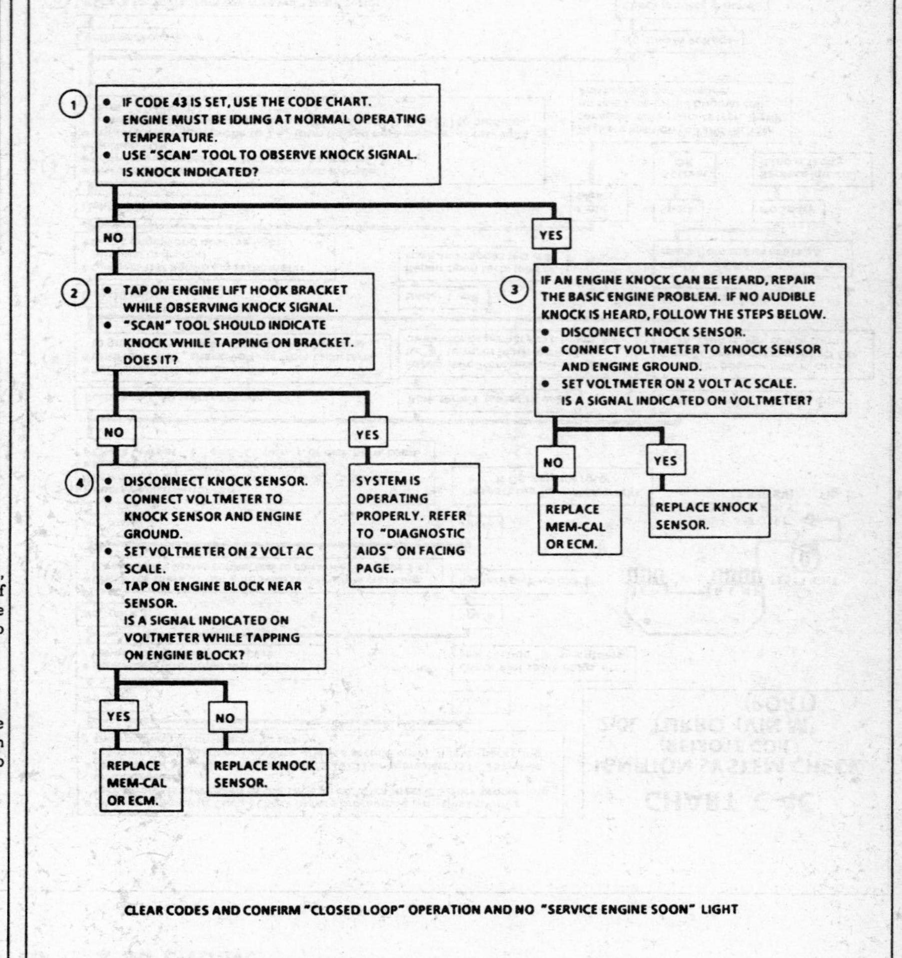

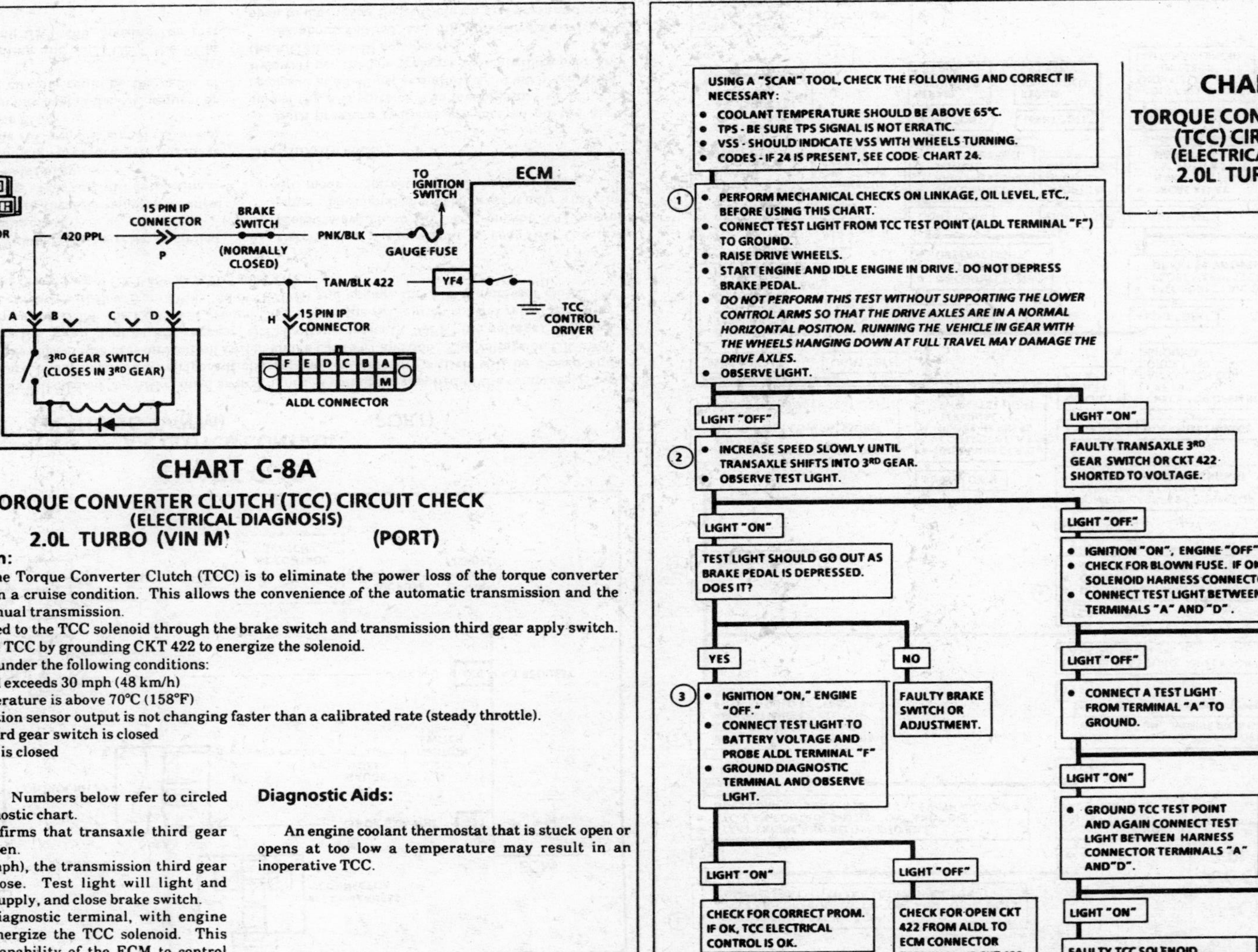

CHART C-8A

TORQUE CONVERTER CLUTCH (TCC) CIRCUIT CHECK
(ELECTRICAL DIAGNOSIS)
2.0L TURBO (VIN M) (PORT)

Circuit Description:

The purpose of the Torque Converter Clutch (TCC) is to eliminate the power loss of the torque converter when the vehicle is in a cruise condition. This allows the convenience of the automatic transmission and the fuel economy of a manual transmission.

Voltage is supplied to the TCC solenoid through the brake switch and transmission third gear apply switch. The ECM will engage TCC by grounding CKT 422 to energize the solenoid.

TCC will engage under the following conditions:

- Vehicle speed exceeds 30 mph (48 km/h)
- Engine temperature is above 70°C (158°F)
- Throttle position sensor output is not changing faster than a calibrated rate (steady throttle).
- Transaxle third gear switch is closed
- Brake switch is closed

Test Description: Numbers below refer to circled numbers on the diagnostic chart.

1. Light "OFF" confirms that transaxle third gear apply switch is open.
2. At 48 km/h (30 mph), the transmission third gear switch should close. Test light will light and confirm battery supply, and close brake switch.
3. Grounding the diagnostic terminal, with engine "OFF," should energize the TCC solenoid. This test checks the capability of the ECM to control the solenoid.

Diagnostic Aids:

An engine coolant thermostat that is stuck open or opens at too low a temperature may result in an inoperative TCC.

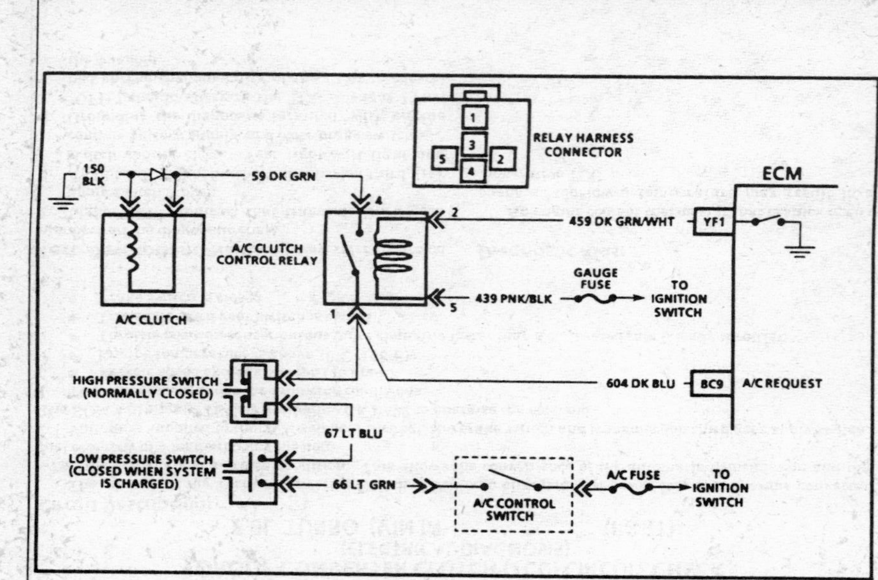

CHART C-10

A/C CLUTCH CONTROL 2.0L TURBO (VIN M) (PORT)

Circuit Description:

When an A/C mode is selected on the A/C control switch, ignition voltage is supplied to the compressor low pressure switch. If there is sufficient A/C refrigerant charge, the low pressure switch will be closed and complete the circuit to the closed high pressure cut-off switch and to CKTs 67 and 366. The voltage on CKT 366 to the ECM is shown by the "Scan" tool as A/C request "ON" (voltage present), "OFF" (no voltage). When a request for A/C is seen by the ECM, the ECM will ground CKT 459 of the A/C clutch control relay, the relay contact will close, and current will flow from CKT 366 to CKT 59 and engage the A/C compressor clutch. A "Scan" tool will show the grounding of CKT 459 as A/C clutch "ON."

Test Description: Numbers below refer to circled numbers on the diagnostic chart.

1. The ECM will energize the A/C relay only when the engine is running. This test will determine if the relay or CKT 459 is faulty.
2. The low pressure and high pressure switches must be closed so that the A/C request signal (12 volts) will be present at the ECM.
3. A short to ground in any part of the A/C request or A/C clutch control circuits could be the cause of the blown fuse.
4. With the engine idling and A/C "ON," the ECM should be grounding CKT 459, causing the test light to be "ON."
5. Determines if the signal is reaching the low pressure switch on CKT 66 from the A/C control panel. The signal should be present only when the A/C mode or defrost mode has been selected.

Diagnostic Aids:

Both pressure switches are located on the high side of the A/C system. The low pressure switch will be closed at 40-47 psi and allow A/C clutch operation. Below 37 psi, the low pressure switch will be open and the A/C clutch will not operate.

At about 430 psi, the high pressure switch will open to disengage the A/C clutch and prevent system damage.

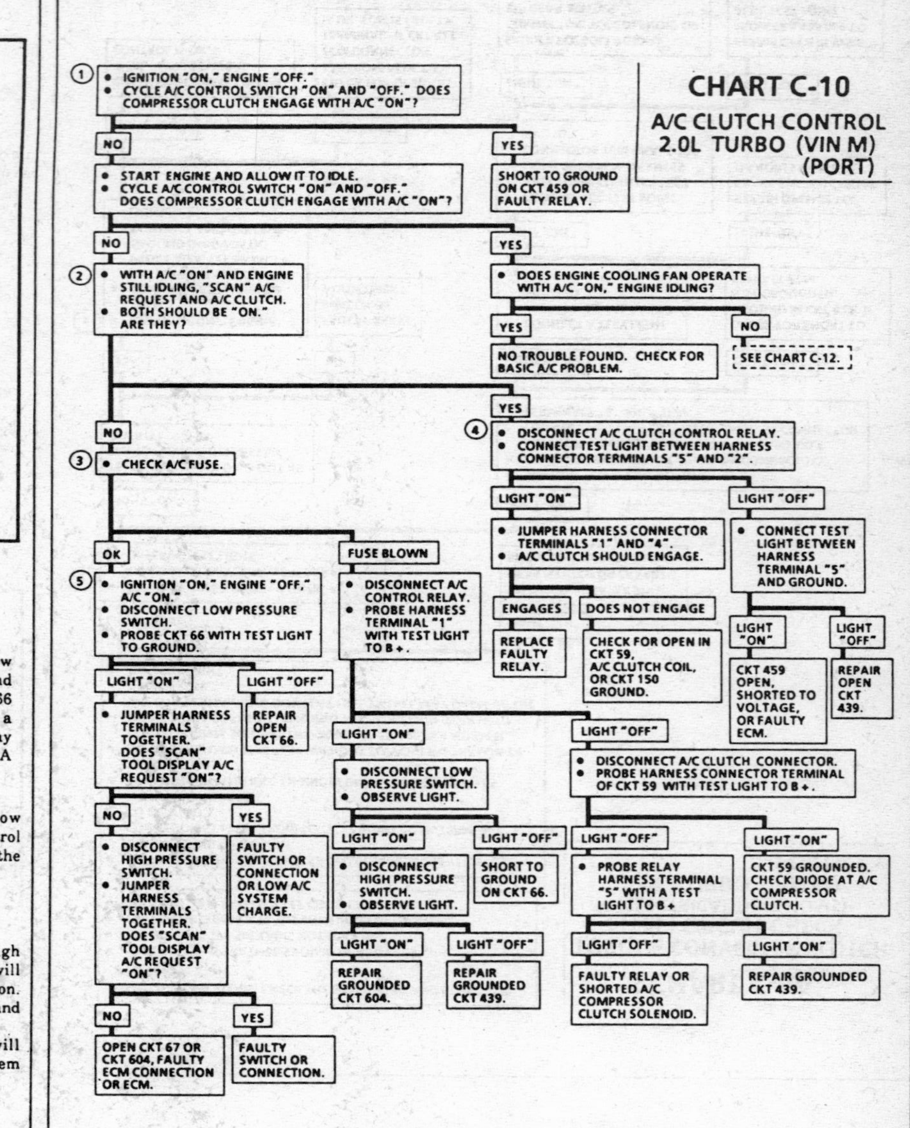

DIAGNOSTIC CHARTS — 2.3L ENGINE

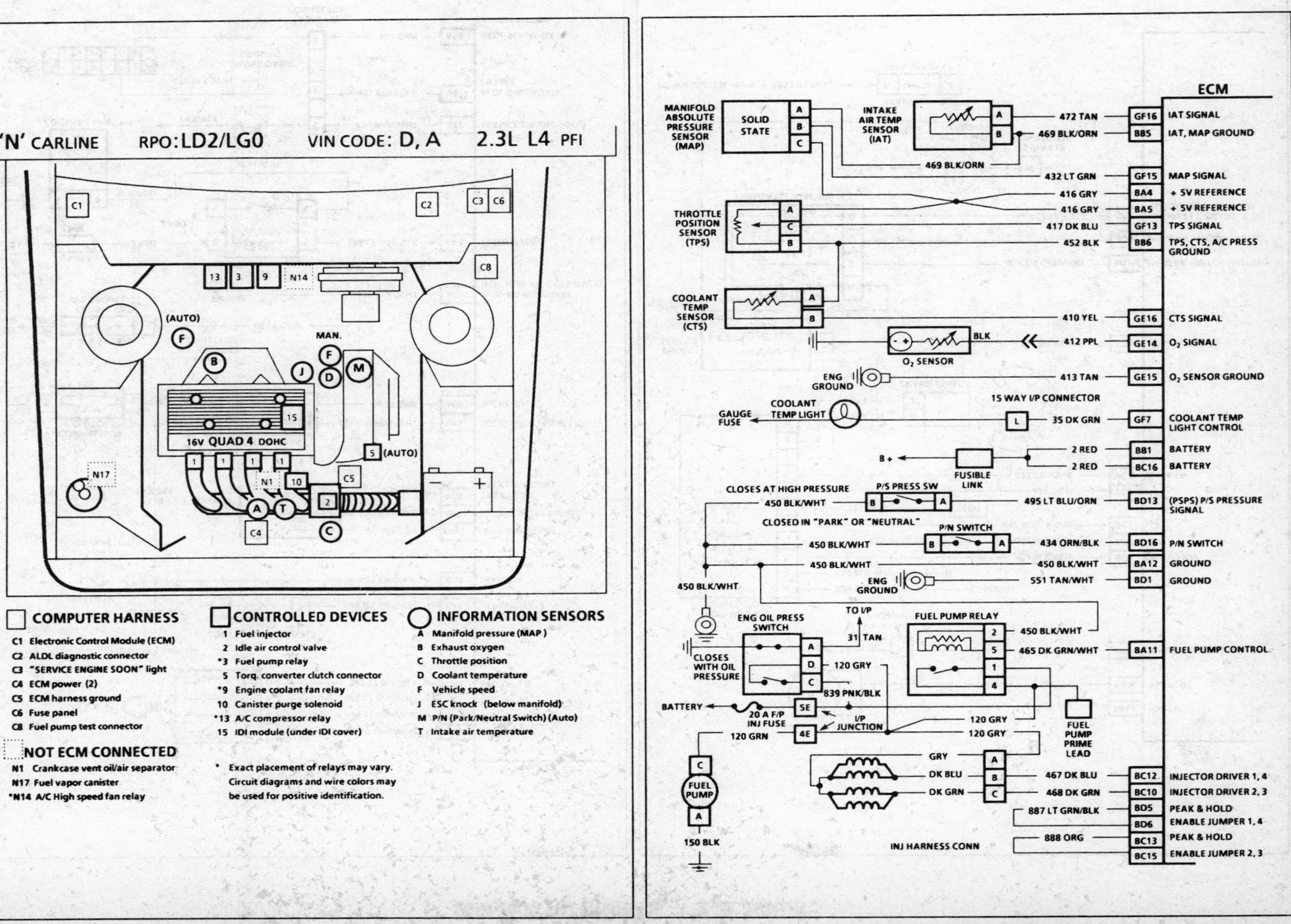

DIAGNOSTIC CHARTS — 2.3L ENGINE

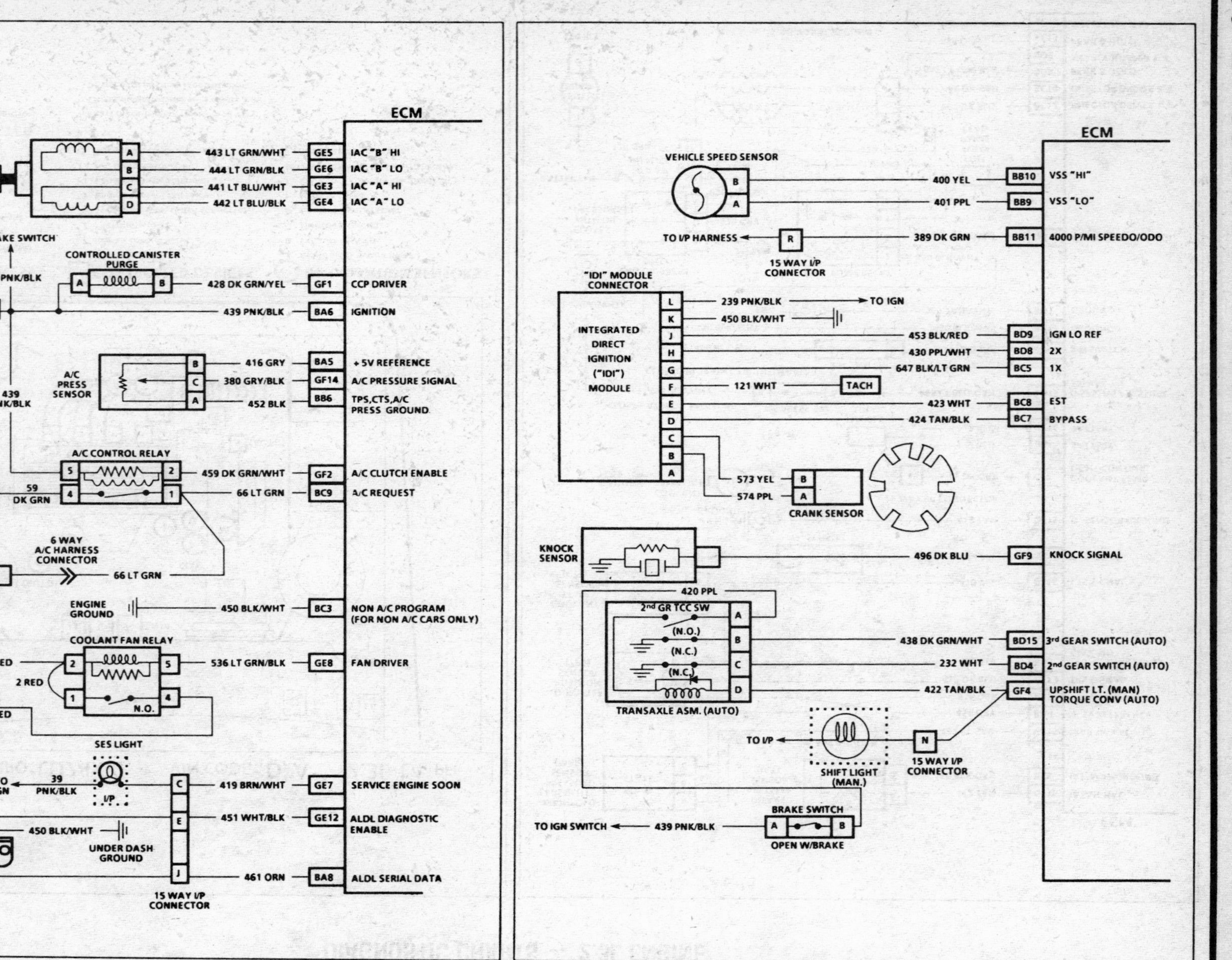

DIAGNOSTIC CHARTS — 2.3L ENGINE

PORT FUEL INJECTION ECM CONNECTOR IDENTIFICATION

This ECM voltage chart is for use with a digital voltmeter to further aid in diagnosis. The voltages you get may vary due to low battery charge or other reasons, but they should be very close. The "B+" symbol indicates a nominal system voltage of 12-14 V.

THE FOLLOWING CONDITIONS MUST BE MET BEFORE TESTING:

• Engine at operating temperature (upper rad. hose hot) • Engine idling in "Closed Loop" (For "Engine Run" column) in park or neutral • Test terminal not grounded • Tech 1 not installed

CONNECTOR (C1) 32 PIN C-D CONNECTOR — BD1, BC1 — BACK VIEW OF CONNECTOR (BLACK)

CONNECTOR (C2) 24 PIN A-B CONNECTOR — BB1, BA1 — BACK VIEW OF CONNECTOR (BLACK)

CONNECTOR (C3) 32 PIN E-F CONNECTOR — GF1, GE1 — BACK VIEW OF CONNECTOR (GREEN)

(NOTE: E, F CAVITY IDENTIFICATION IS VISIBLE ON CONNECTOR BODY WITH TERMINAL RETAINERS REMOVED.)

CONNECTOR 1 (C1)
BLACK 32 PIN C-D CONNECTOR

	VOLTAGE KEY ON	VOLTAGE ENG. RUN	CIRCUIT	PIN	WIRE COLOR
				BC1	
				BC2	
(5)	B+	B+	NON A/C PROG.	BC3	BLK/WHT
				BC4	
			1X SIGNAL	BC5	BLK/LT GRN
				BC6	
	0*	5.	IGNITION BYPASS	BC7	TAN/BLK
	0*	.2	IGNITION EST	BC8	WHT
	0*	ON B+ OFF 0*	A/C REQUEST	BC9	LT GRN
	B+	B+	INJ DRIVER 2 & 3	BC10	DK GRN
				BC11	
	B+	B+	INJ DRIVER 1 & 4	BC12	DK BLU
	0*	0*	PEAK & HOLD INJ JUMPER 2 & 3	BC13	ORG
				BC14	
	0*	0*	PEAK & HOLD INJ JUMPER 2 & 3	BC15	ORG
	B+	B+	BATTERY	BC16	RED

WIRE COLOR	PIN	CIRCUIT	VOLTAGE KEY ON	VOLTAGE ENG. RUN
TAN/WHT	BD1	ECM GROUND	0*	0*
	BD2			
	BD3			
WHT	BD4	2nd GEAR SW A/T	ON B+ OFF 0*	ON B+ OFF 0*
LT GRN/BLK	BD5	PEAK & HOLD INJ JUMPER 1 & 4	0*	0*
LT GRN/BLK	BD6	PEAK & HOLD INJ JUMPER 1 & 4	0*	0*
	BD7			
PPL/WHT	BD8	2X SIGNAL	0*	2.9
BLK/RED	BD9	IGN GROUND	0*	0*
	BD10			
	BD11			
	BD12			
LT BLU/ORN	BD13	P/S PRESS SIGNAL	B+	ON + OFF 0*
	BD14			
DK GRN/WHT	BD15	3rd GEAR SW A/T	ON 0* OFF B+	ON 0* OFF B+
ORN/BLK	BD16	P/N SWITCH A/T	ON 0* OFF B+	ON 0* OFF B+

NOTE: BC1-Black connector, cavity C1; GE1-Green connector, cavity E1, etc.

* Less than .5 volt.
(1) Varies from .60 to battery voltage depending on position of drive wheels.
(2) Varies.
(3) 12Volt first two seconds.
(4) Varies with temperature.
(5) Non A/C cars 0* volt. A/C cars should not have a wire in term. "BC3".

ENGINE - 2.3L / LD2/LGO
CARLINE - "N" Series

CONNECTOR 2 (C-2)
BLACK 24 PIN A-B CONNECTOR

	VOLTAGE KEY ON	VOLTAGE ENG. RUN	CIRCUIT	PIN	WIRE COLOR
				BA1	
				BA2	
				BA3	
	5.0	5.0	+5V REFERENCE	BA4	GRY
	5.0	5.0	+5V REFERENCE	BA5	GRY
	B+	B+	IGNITION FEED	BA6	PNK/BLK
				BA7	
(2)			SERIAL DATA/ALDL	BA8	ORN
				BA9	
				BA10	
(3)	0*	B+	FUEL PUMP	BA11	DK GRN/WHT
	0*	0*	ECM GROUND	BA12	BLK/WHT

WIRE COLOR	PIN	CIRCUIT	VOLTAGE KEY ON	VOLTAGE ENG. RUN
RED	BB1	BATTERY	B+	B+
	BB2			
	BB3			
	BB4			
BLK/ORN	BB5	IAT & MAP GND	0*	0*
BLK	BB6	A/C,CTS,TPS GND	0*	0*
	BB7			
	BB8			
PPL	BB9	MAG. VSS LOW	0*	0*
YEL	BB10	MAG. VSS HIGH	0*	0*
DK GRN	BB11	4000 P/MI SPEED	10.0	11.4
	BB12			

GREEN 32 PIN E-F CONNECTOR 3 (C-3)

	VOLTAGE KEY ON	VOLTAGE ENG. RUN	CIRCUIT	PIN	WIRE COLOR
				GE1	
				GE2	
	NOT USEABLE		IAC - A - HIGH	GE3	LT BLU/WHT
	NOT USEABLE		IAC - A - LOW	GE4	LT BLU/BLK
	NOT USEABLE		IAC - B - HIGH	GE5	LT GRN/WHT
	NOT USEABLE		IAC - B - LOW	GE6	LT GRN/BLK
	0*	B+	SES LIGHT	GE7	BRN/WHT
	B+	ON 0* OFF B+	CLG FAN RLY	GE8	LT GRN/BLK
				GE9	
				GE10	
				GE11	
	5.0	5.0	ALDL/DIAG TERM	GE12	WHT/BLK
				GE13	
(2)	.3-.5	.1-.9	O_2 SIGNAL	GE14	PPL
	0*	0*	O_2 GROUND	GE15	TAN
(2)	1.8	1.8	CLNT TEMP SIGNAL	GE16	YEL

WIRE COLOR	PIN	CIRCUIT	VOLTAGE KEY ON	VOLTAGE ENG. RUN	
DK GRN/YEL	GF1	CANISTER PURGE	B+	.3	
DK GRN/WHT	GF2	A/C CLUTCH RELAY	B+	OFF B+ ON 0✱	
	GF3				
TAN/BLK	GF4	TCC / SHIFT LT	0 / 12	0 / 12	
	GF5				
	GF6				
DK GRN	GF7	COOLANT TEMP LIGHT			
	GF8				
DK BLU	GF9	KNOCK SIGNAL	2.3	2.3	
	GF10				
	GF11				
	GF12				
DK BLU	GF13	TPS SIGNAL	.54	.54	
GRY/BLK	GF14	A/C PRESS SIGNAL			(2)
LT GRN	GF15	MAP SIGNAL	4.7	1.4	(2)
TAN	GF16	IAT SIGNAL	3.6	1.5	(2)

Note: BA1 = Black Connector, cavity A1, etc. GE1 - Green Connector, cavity E1, etc.

* Less than .5 volt.
1. Varies from .60 to battery voltage depending on position of drive wheels.
2. Varies.
3. B+ first two seconds.

ENGINE - 2.3L / LD2/LG0
CARLINE - "N" Series

DIAGNOSTIC CHARTS — 2.3L ENGINE

DIAGNOSTIC CIRCUIT CHECK

The Diagnostic Circuit Check is an organized approach to identifying a problem created by an electronic engine control system malfunction. It must be the starting point for any driveability complaint diagnosis, because it directs the service technician to the next logical step in diagnosing the complaint.

The Tech 1 data listed in the table may be used for comparison, after completing the diagnostic circuit check and finding the on-board diagnostics functioning properly and no trouble codes displayed. The "Typical Values" are an average of display values recorded from normally operating vehicles and are intended to represent what a normally functioning system would typically display.

A "SCAN" TOOL THAT DISPLAYS FAULTY DATA SHOULD NOT BE USED, AND THE PROBLEM SHOULD BE REPORTED TO THE MANUFACTURER. THE USE OF A FAULTY "SCAN" CAN RESULT IN MISDIAGNOSIS AND UNNECESSARY PARTS REPLACEMENT.

Only the parameters listed below are used in this manual for diagnosing. If a "Scan" reads other parameters, the values are not recommended by General Motors for use in diagnosing. For more description on the values and use of the "Scan" to diagnosis ECM inputs, If all values are within the range illustrated, refer to "Symptoms," Section

TECH 1 DATA

Idle / Upper Radiator Hose Hot / Closed Throttle / Park or Neutral / "Closed Loop" / Acc. "OFF"

"SCAN" Position	Units Displayed	Typical Data Value
Engine Speed	RPM	± 100 RPM from desired RPM (± 50 in drive)
Desired Idle	RPM	ECM idle command (varies with calibration. temp.)
Coolant Temp.	C° F°	85° – 115°C
IAT Temp.	C° F°	10° – 80°C (depends on underhood temp.)
MAP	kPa, V	1 – 3 Volts (depends on Vacuum & Baro pressure)
BARO	kPa, V	3–5 Volts (depends on altitude & Baro pressure)
Throttle Position	Volts	.400 – .900 (up to 5.0 at wide open throttle)
Throttle Angle	0 – 100%	0% (up to 100% at wide open throttle)
Oxygen Sensor	mV	1–1000 and varying
Injector Pulse Width	m Sec.	1 – 4 and varying
Spark Advance	# of Degrees	Varies
Eng. Speed	RPM	Varies
Fuel Integrator	Counts	Varies
Block Learn	Counts	58 – 198
Open/Closed Loop	Open/Closed	Closed Loop (may go open with extended idle)
Block Learn Cell	Cell Number	18 to 21 at idle (depends on Air Flow, RPM,P/N&A/C)
Knock Retard	Degrees of Retard	0
Knock Signal	Yes/No	No
BYP Line Volts	LOW/HI	HI
EST Command	Yes/No	Yes
Idle Air Control	Counts (steps)	5 – 60
Park Neutral Switch	Park Neutral and RDL	P - N -- (or -R-DL manual only)
VSS	MPH/KPH	0
Torque Conv. Cl (TCC)	On/Off	Off ("ON," with TCC commanded)
Battery Voltage	Volts	13.5 – 14.5
1X Ref Pulse	0 – 255 Counts	0 – 255 (Useable for Code 41)
2X Ref Pulse	Yes/No	Yes
A/C Request	Yes/No	No (yes, with A/C requested, ie: selector "ON")
A/C Clutch	On/Off	Off ("ON," with A/C commanded on)
A/C Clutch	On/Off	Off ("ON," with A/C commanded on)
A/C Pressure	psi/volts	0 – 450 psi (varying with high side pressure)
Power Steering	Normal/Hi Press.	Normal
Purge Duty Cycle	%	0–100%
Brake Switch (AT)	Yes/No	No or not avail.
Torque Conv Clutch	On/Off	Off
EGR 1 EGR 2	On/Off or N/A	Off
QDM A	LOW/HI	Low
QDM B	LOW/HI	Low
Fan LO Fan HI	On/Off	Off ("ON," with A/C "ON" or hot eng)
2nd Gear	Yes/No	No (yes, when in 2nd or 3rd gear)
3rd Gear	Yes/No	No (yes, when in 3rd gear) or yes (Man. Trans. only)
PROM ID	#	Production ECM/PROM ID (not useable)
Time From Start	min/sec	Varies (engine run time since start)

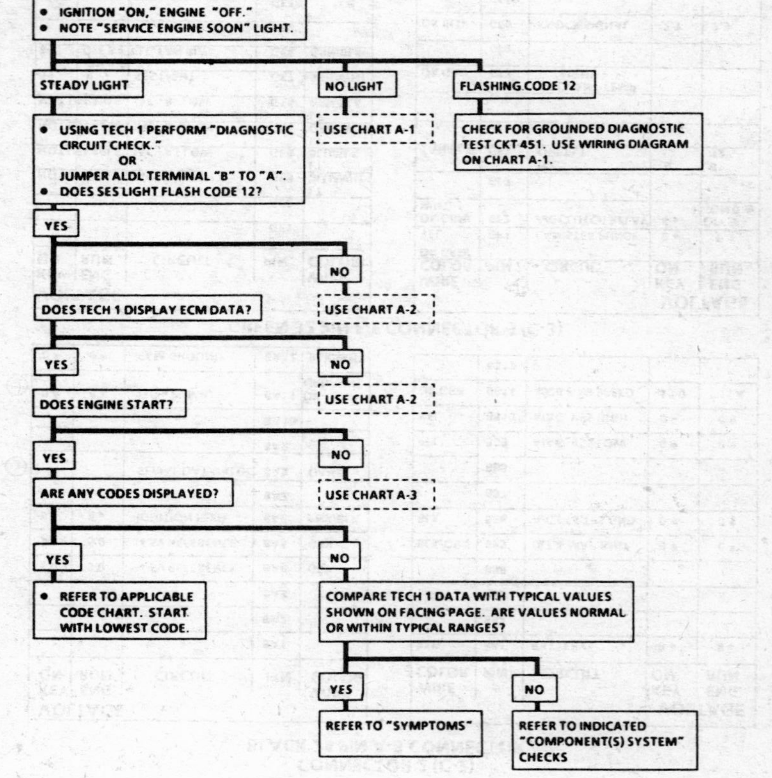

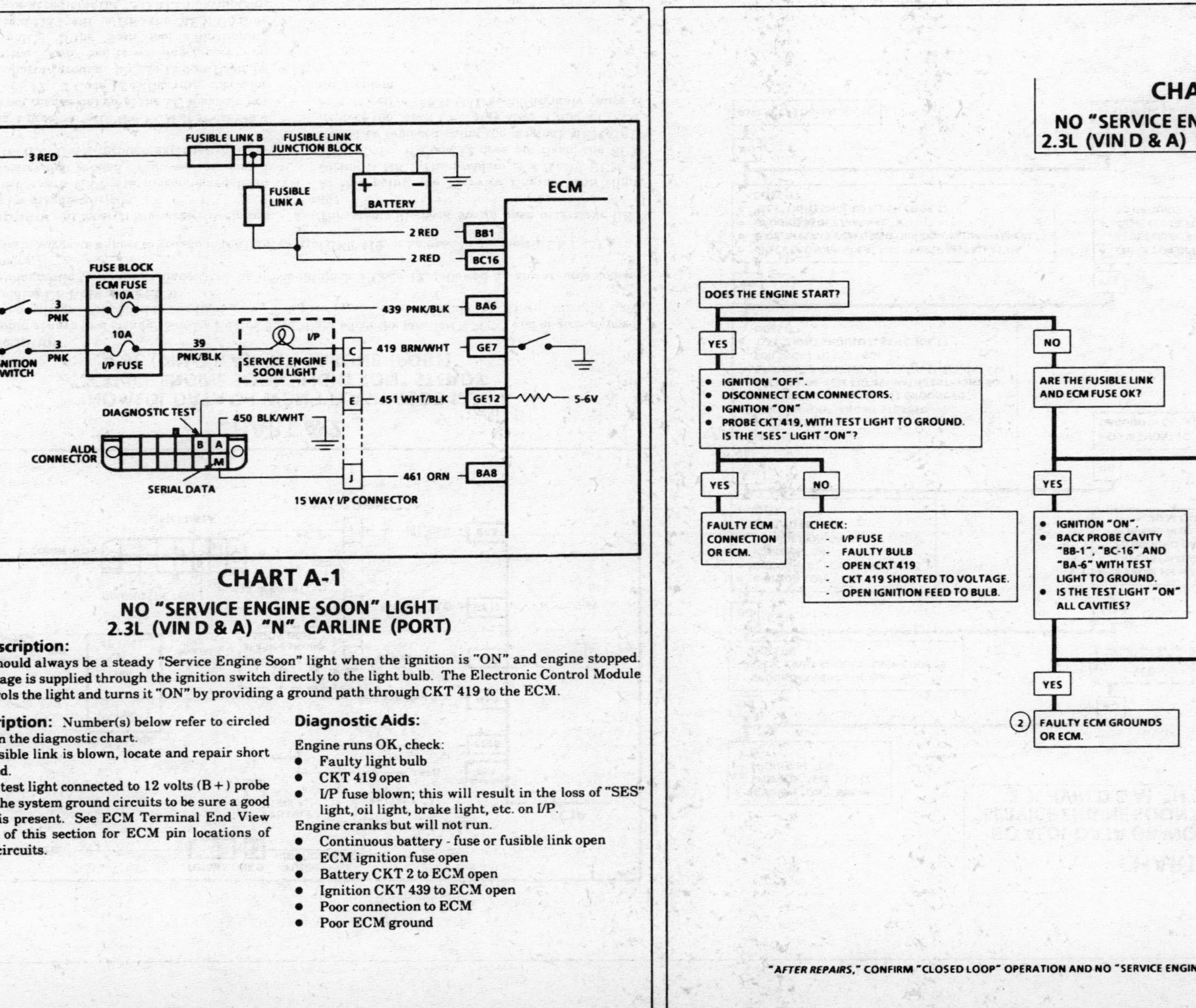

CHART A-1

NO "SERVICE ENGINE SOON" LIGHT
2.3L (VIN D & A) "N" CARLINE (PORT)

Circuit Description:

There should always be a steady "Service Engine Soon" light when the ignition is "ON" and engine stopped. Battery voltage is supplied through the ignition switch directly to the light bulb. The Electronic Control Module (ECM) controls the light and turns it "ON" by providing a ground path through CKT 419 to the ECM.

Test Description: Number(s) below refer to circled number(s) on the diagnostic chart.

1. If the fusible link is blown, locate and repair short to ground.
2. Using a test light connected to 12 volts (B+) probe each of the system ground circuits to be sure a good ground is present. See ECM Terminal End View in front of this section for ECM pin locations of ground circuits.

Diagnostic Aids:

Engine runs OK, check:

- Faulty light bulb
- CKT 419 open
- I/P fuse blown; this will result in the loss of "SES" light, oil light, brake light, etc. on I/P.

Engine cranks but will not run.

- Continuous battery - fuse or fusible link open
- ECM ignition fuse open
- Battery CKT 2 to ECM open
- Ignition CKT 439 to ECM open
- Poor connection to ECM
- Poor ECM ground

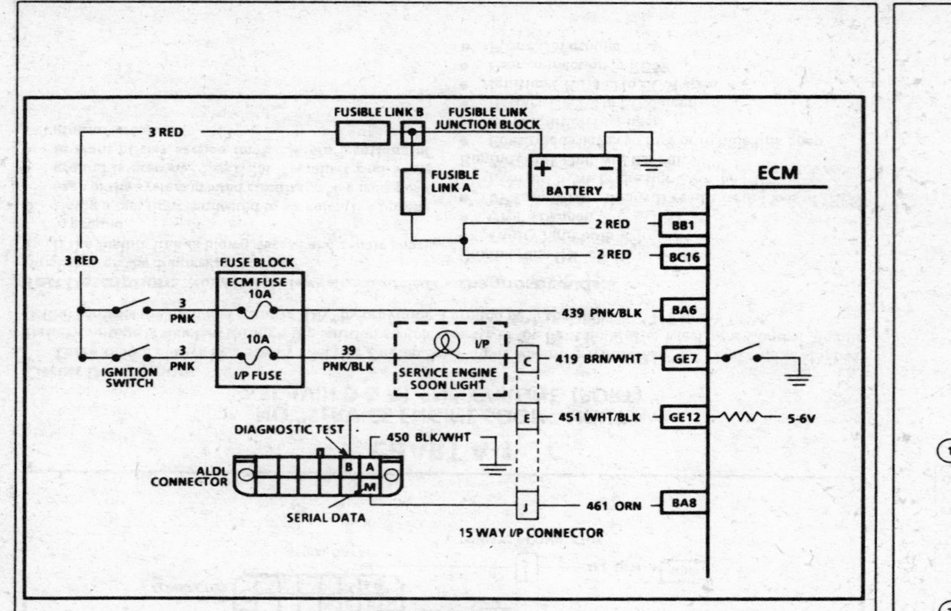

CHART A-2

NO ALDL DATA OR WON'T FLASH CODE 12 "SERVICE ENGINE SOON" LIGHT "ON" STEADY 2.3L (VIN D & A) "N" CARLINE (PORT)

Circuit Description:

There should always be a steady "Service Engine Soon" light when the ignition is "ON" and engine stopped. Battery ignition voltage is supplied to the light bulb. The Electronic Control Module (ECM) will turn the light "ON" by grounding CKT 419 at the ECM.

With the diagnostic terminal grounded, the light should flash a Code 12, followed by any trouble code(s) stored in memory.

A steady light suggests a short to ground in the light control CKT 419, or an open in diagnostic CKT 451.

Test Description: Number(s) below refer to circled number(s) on the diagnostic chart.

1. Light "OFF" with CKT 419 disconnected from ECM indicates that ground circuit was completed through the ECM, not through external short to ground.
2. If there is a problem with the ECM that causes a Tech 1 to not read serial data, the ECM should not flash a Code 12. If Code 12 is flashing, check for CKT 451 short to ground. If Code 12 does flash, be sure that the "Scan" tool is working properly on another vehicle. If the "Scan" tool is functioning properly and CKT 461 is OK, the MEM-CAL or ECM may be at fault for the "NO ALDL" symptom.
3. This step will check for an open diagnostic CKT 451.
4. At this point, the "Service Engine Soon" light wiring is OK. The problem is a faulty ECM or MEM-CAL. If Code 12 does not flash, the ECM should be replaced using the original MEM-CAL. Replace the MEM-CAL only after trying an ECM, as a defective MEM-CAL is an unlikely cause of the problem.

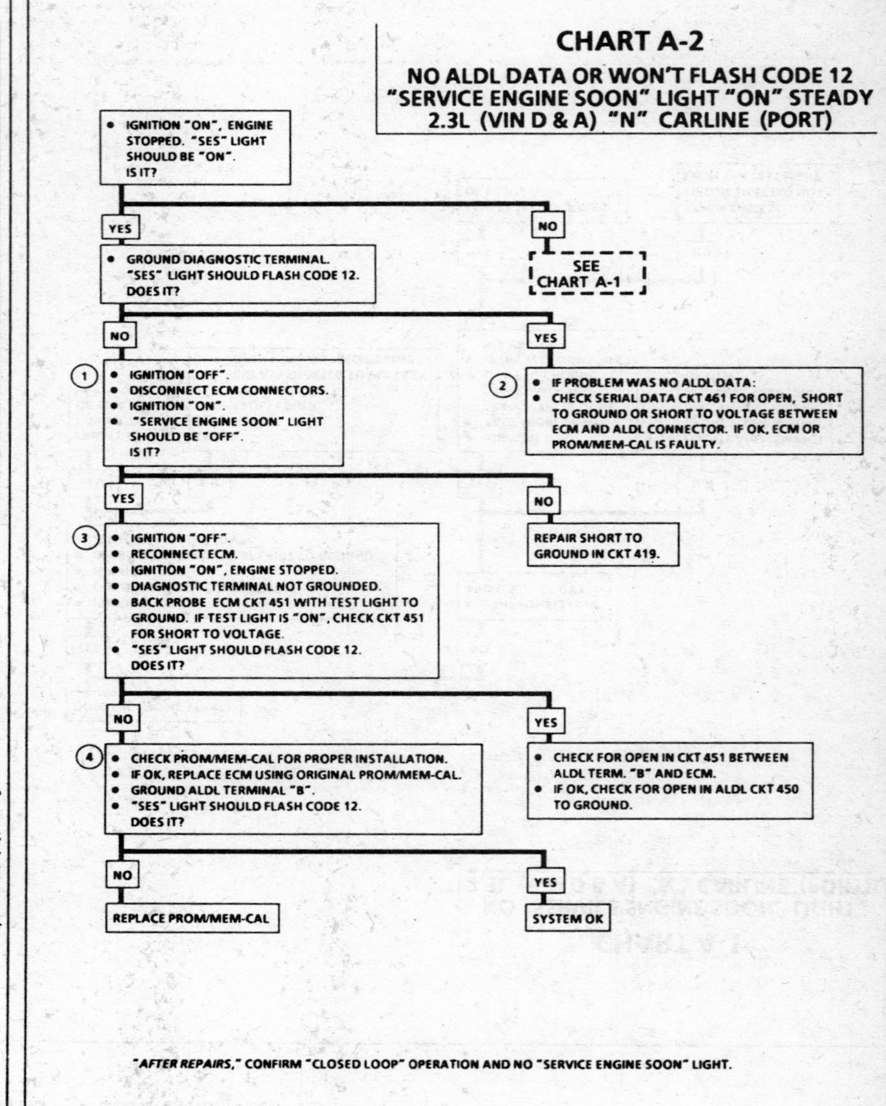

"AFTER REPAIRS," CONFIRM "CLOSED LOOP" OPERATION AND NO "SERVICE ENGINE SOON" LIGHT.

DIAGNOSTIC CHARTS — 2.3L ENGINE

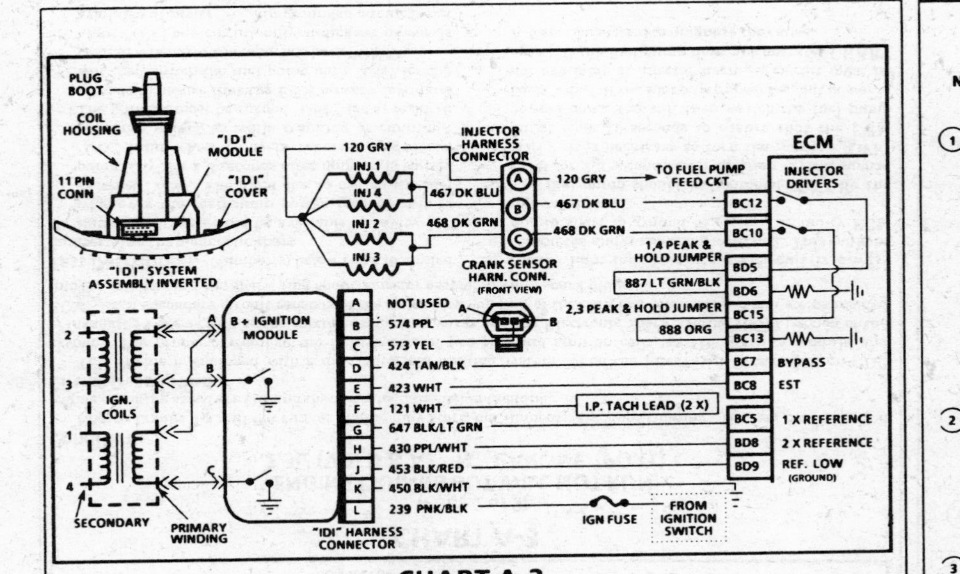

CHART A-3

(Page 1 of 3)

ENGINE CRANKS BUT WILL NOT RUN 2.3L (VIN D & A) "N" CARLINE (PORT)

Condition:

Engine cranks but will not run, or engine may start, but immediately stops running. Battery condition and engine cranking speed are OK and there is adequate fuel in the tank.

Circuit Description:

This engine is equipped with a distributorless ignition system called the Integrated Direct Ignition (IDI) system. The primary circuit of the IDI consists of two separate ignition coils, an IDI (ignition) module and crankshaft sensor as well as the related connecting wires and the Electronic Spark Timing (EST) portion of the ECM. Each secondary circuit consists of the secondary winding of the coil, two connecting metal strips molded into the coil housing, the spark plug boot/connector assemblies and spark plugs.

Test Description: Number(s) below refer to circled number(s) on the diagnostic chart.

1. This step verifies that "SES" light operation, on-board diagnostics, cranking rpm, TPS and coolant sensor signals are normal. A blinking test light verifies that the ECM is receiving the IDI reference signal and is attempting to activate the injectors.
2. This step checks injector harness and injectors for opens or shorts. Resistance should measure half that of one injector due to parallel circuit.
3. By installing spark plug jumper leads and testing for spark on two adjacent plug leads (do not use 2 & 3 as they are on same coil), each ignition coil's ability to produce at least 25,000 volts is verified.
4. Checks to see if fuel pump and relay are operating correctly (fuel pump only "ON" 2-3 seconds) and fuel pressure is within proper range.
5. If module can make the test light blink, the fault is coil harness or connections. If not, module or it's connections are faulty.
6. This step determines whether harness or injector is cause of incorrect resistance. Nominal injector resistance is 1.9 to 2.1 ohms at 60°C (140°F). Resistance will increase slightly at higher temperatures.

Diagnostic Aids:

Check For:

- TPS binding or sticking in Wide Open Throttle (WOT) position or intermittently shorted or open.
- Water or foreign material in fuel
- Low Compression (Timing chain failure)
- Verify that only resistor spark plugs are used

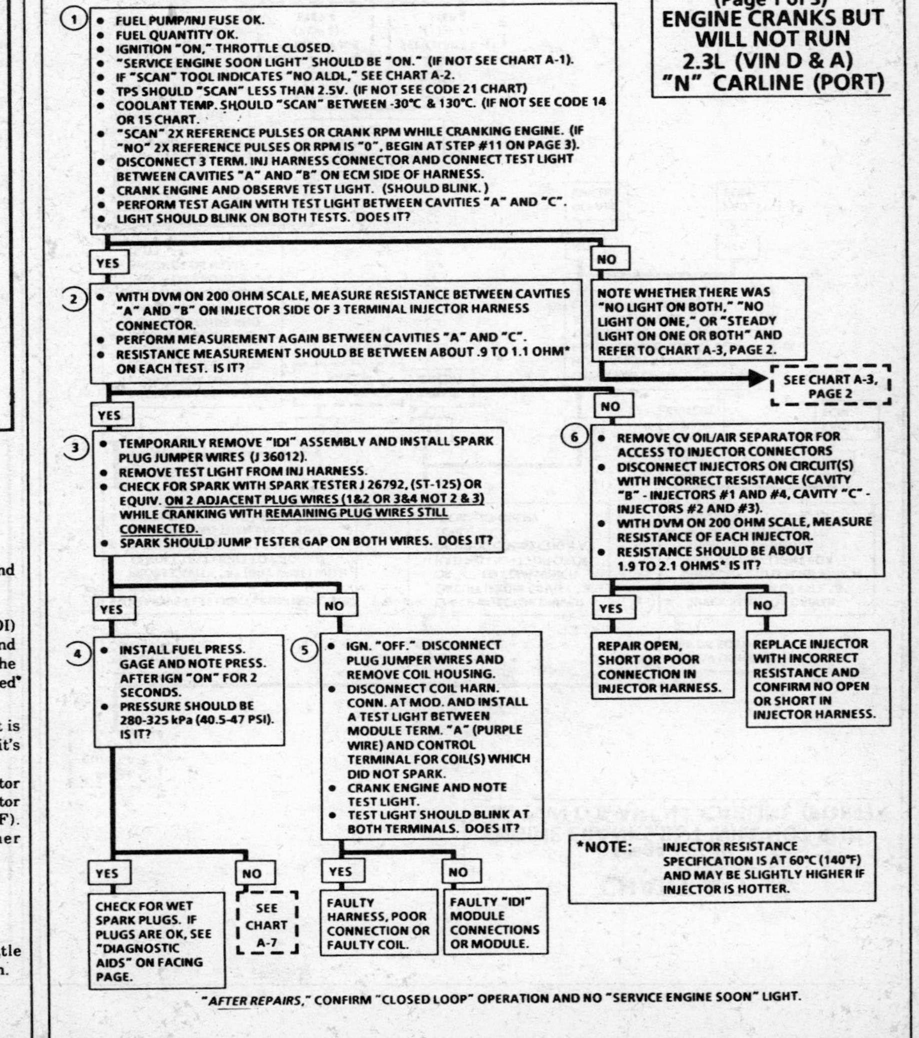

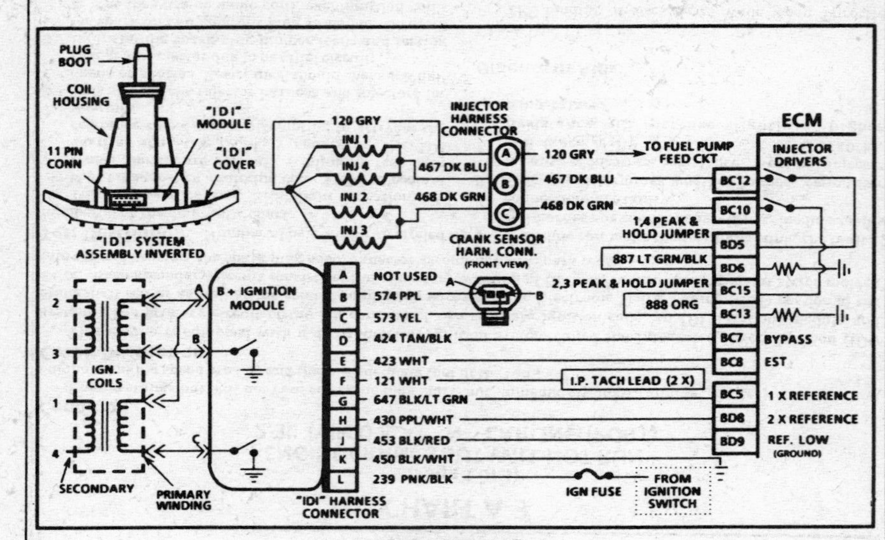

CHART A-3

(Page 2 of 3)

ENGINE CRANKS BUT WILL NOT RUN 2.3L (VIN D & A) "N" CARLINE (PORT)

Condition:

Engine cranks but will not run, or engine may start, but immediately stops running. Battery condition and engine cranking speed are OK and there is adequate fuel in the tank.

Circuit Description:

This engine is equipped with a distributorless ignition system called the Integrated Direct Ignition (IDI) system. The primary circuit of the IDI consists of two separate ignition coils, an IDI ignition module and crankshaft sensor as well as the related connecting wires and the Electronic Spark Timing (EST) portion of the ECM. Each secondary circuit consists of the secondary winding of the coil, two connecting metal strips molded into the coil housing, the spark plug boot/connector assemblies and spark plugs.

Test Description: Number(s) below refer to circled number(s) on the diagnostic chart.

7. Battery voltage should be available at cavity "A" whenever the fuel pump power feed circuit is switched "ON." The ECM should switch the fuel pump "ON" for 2-3 seconds after ignition is turned "ON" (and when ECM is receiving ignition reference pulses, as while cranking or running). The ignition must be turned "OFF" for at least 10 seconds to assure that the ECM powers down and will then switch the fuel pump back "ON" for 2-3 seconds when ignition is turned back "ON."
8. Light "ON" one circuit only indicates power is available at cavity "A", but grounded circuit is not being completed on the other circuit. This could be due to open circuit or ECM not switching the injector driver circuit to ground.
9. Steady light indicates ground circuit is always completed and is not being switched. This could be due to short to ground in circuit, or faulty ECM injector driver.
10. The fuel pump should be switched "ON" by the ECM for 2-3 seconds after ignition is first turned "ON." It is necessary to turn the ignition "OFF" for at least 10 seconds to assure that the ECM powers down and will then switch the fuel pump back "ON." If the fuel pump operates, but power is not available at injector harness, circuit must be open. If the fuel pump does not operate, CHART A-5 should be used to diagnose the cause.

CHART A-3

(Page 2 of 3)

ENGINE CRANKS BUT WILL NOT RUN 2.3L (VIN D & A) "N" CARLINE (PORT)

FROM CHART A-3 1 OF 3

NO LIGHT ON BOTH

(7)
- REMOVE TEST LIGHT FROM INJECTOR HARNESS.
- PROBE CAVITY "A" (GRY WIRE) WITH 12 VOLT TEST LIGHT TO GROUND.
- TURN IGNITION "OFF" FOR 10 SECONDS AND THEN BACK "ON"
- TEST LIGHT SHOULD BE "ON" FOR 2-3 SECONDS OR LONGER. IS IT?

YES: SEE CHART A-3, PAGE 3

NO:

(10)
- PROBE FUEL PUMP TEST CONNECTOR WITH TEST LIGHT CONNECTED TO GROUND.
- TURN IGNITION "OFF" FOR 10 SECONDS AND THEN BACK "ON".
- TEST LIGHT SHOULD BE "ON" FOR ABOUT 2 SECONDS OR MORE. IS IT?

YES: REPAIR OPEN OR GROUNDED CKT 120 BETWEEN FUEL PUMP POWER CIRCUIT AND INJECTORS.

NO:
- CHECK FUEL PUMP FUSE. IS FUSE OK?

YES: SEE CHART A-5 (1 OF 2) STEP 4

NO: SEE CHART A-5 (1 OF 2) STEP 2

NO LIGHT ON ONE

(8)
- CHECK INJECTOR DRIVER CIRCUIT (FROM CAVITY "B" OR "C" TO ECM) WHICH HAD NO LIGHT FOR OPEN OR POOR CONNECTION AT ECM.
- IS CIRCUIT OPEN?

YES: REPAIR CIRCUIT

NO: CHECK FOR OPEN IN PEAK AND HOLD JUMPER CIRCUITS OR POOR CONNECTION AT ECM TERMINALS. ARE CIRCUITS AND CONNECTIONS OK?

NO: REPAIR CIRCUIT

YES: FAULTY ECM

STEADY LIGHT ON ONE OR BOTH

(9)
- CHECK INJECTOR DRIVER CIRCUIT (FROM CAVITY "B" AND/OR "C" TO ECM) WHICH HAD STEADY LIGHT FOR SHORT TO GROUND.
- IS CIRCUIT SHORTED TO GROUND?

YES: REPAIR CIRCUIT

NO: FAULTY ECM

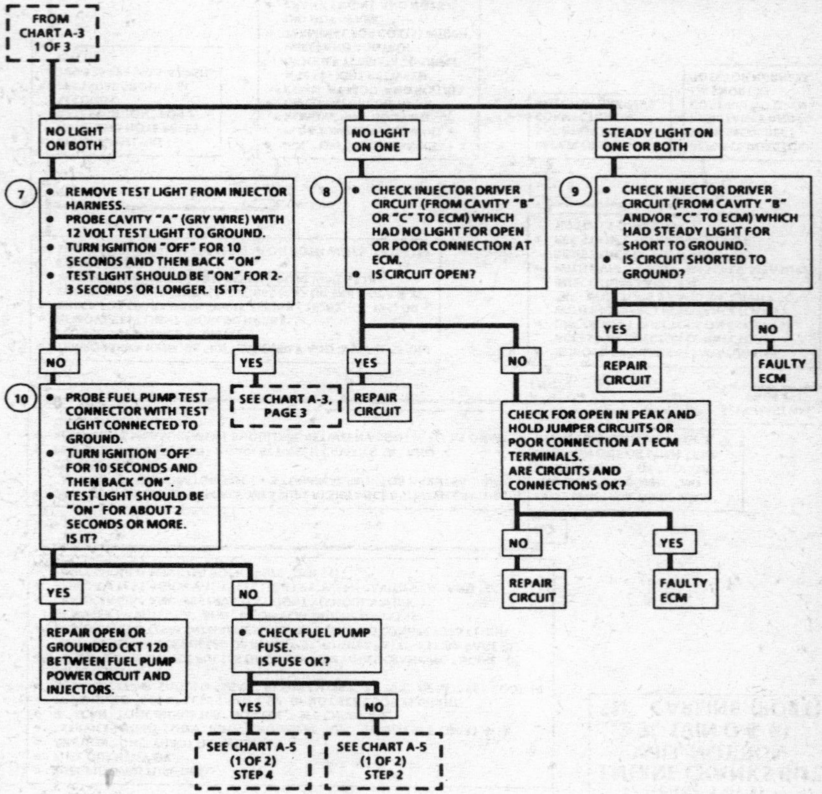

"AFTER REPAIRS," CONFIRM "CLOSED LOOP" OPERATION AND NO "SERVICE ENGINE SOON" LIGHT.

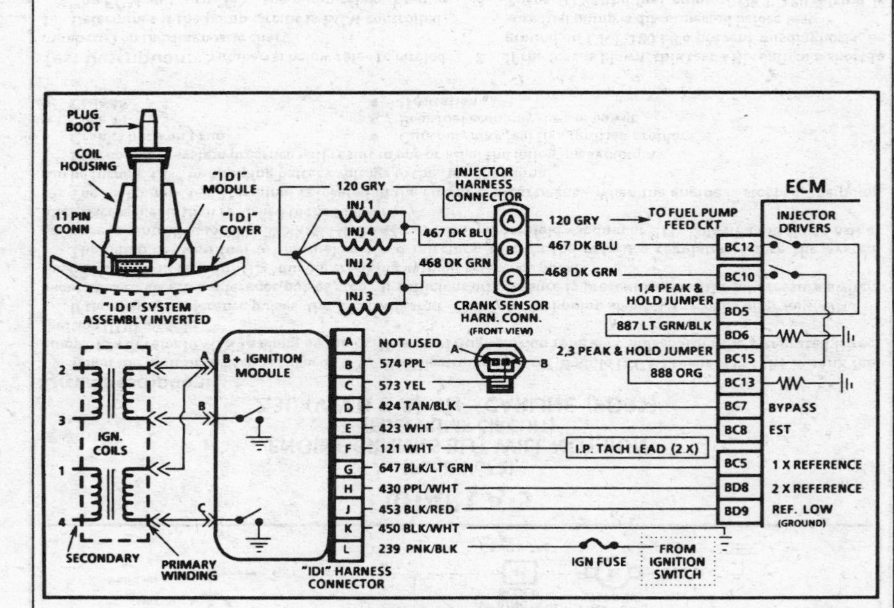

CHART A-3

(Page 3 of 3)

ENGINE CRANKS BUT WILL NOT RUN 2.3L (VIN D & A) "N" CARLINE (PORT)

Circuit Description:

The Integrated Direct Ignition (IDI) system uses a waste spark method of distribution. In this type of system, the ignition module triggers the #1-4 coil pair resulting in both #1 and #4 spark plugs firing at the same time. #1 cylinder is on the compression stroke at the same time #4 is on the exhaust stroke, resulting in a lower energy requirement to fire # 4 spark plug. This leaves the remainder of the high voltage to be used to fire #1 spark plug. On this application, the crank sensor is mounted to, and protrudes through the block to within approximately 0.050" of the crankshaft reluctor. Since the reluctor is a machined portion of the crankshaft and the sensor is mounted in a fixed position on the block, timing adjustments are not possible or necessary.

Test Description: Number(s) below refer to circled number(s) on the diagnostic chart.

11. Battery voltage should be available at terminal "L" of the IDI 11 pin connector, and terminal "K" should be a good ground.
12. The test light to 12 volts simulates a reference signal to the ECM which will result in an injector test light blink for every other touch of the test light, if CKT 430, the ECM and the injector driver circuit are all functioning properly.
13. The crankshaft sensor should output a voltage as the crankshaft turns. If no voltage is produced, the indication is a poor sensor connection or faulty sensor.
14. The crank sensors core is a magnet, therefore, it should be magnetized and the resistance should be within a range of 500 to 900 ohms.

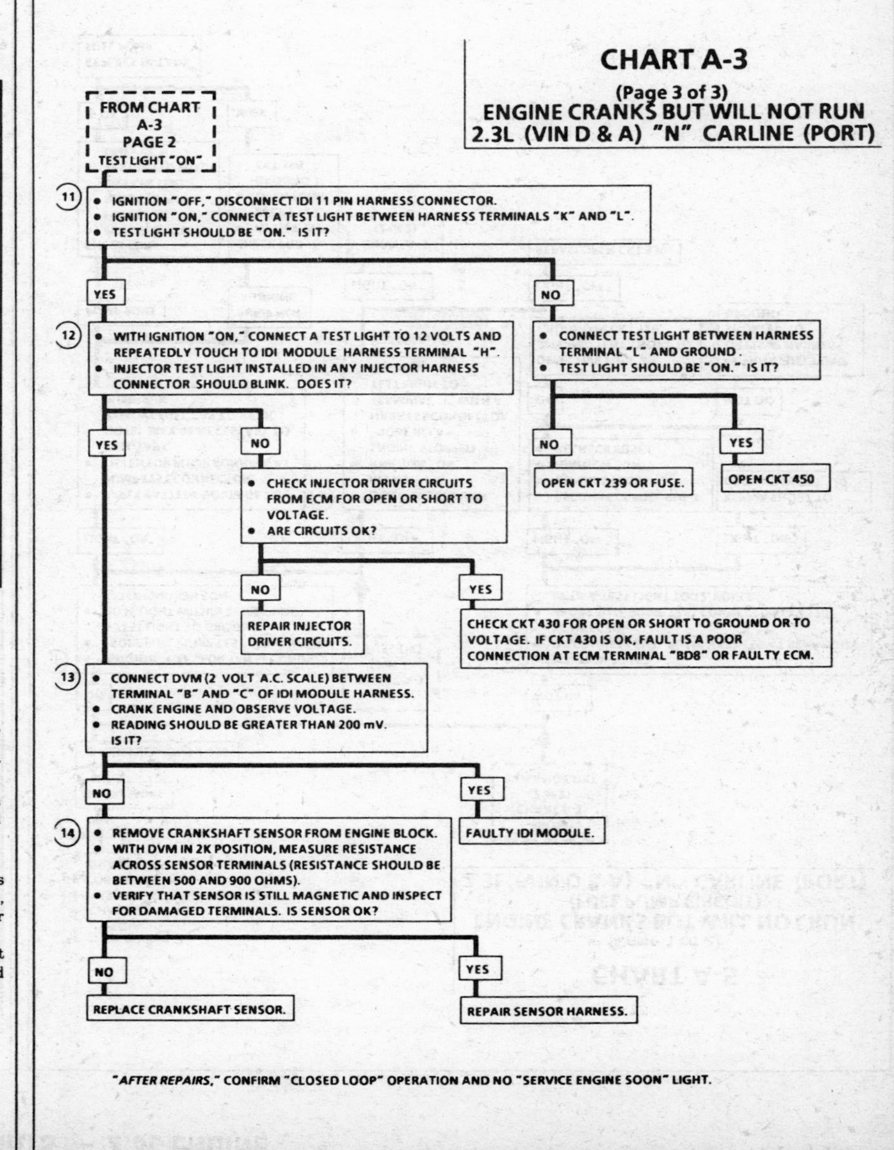

DIAGNOSTIC CHARTS — 2.3L ENGINE

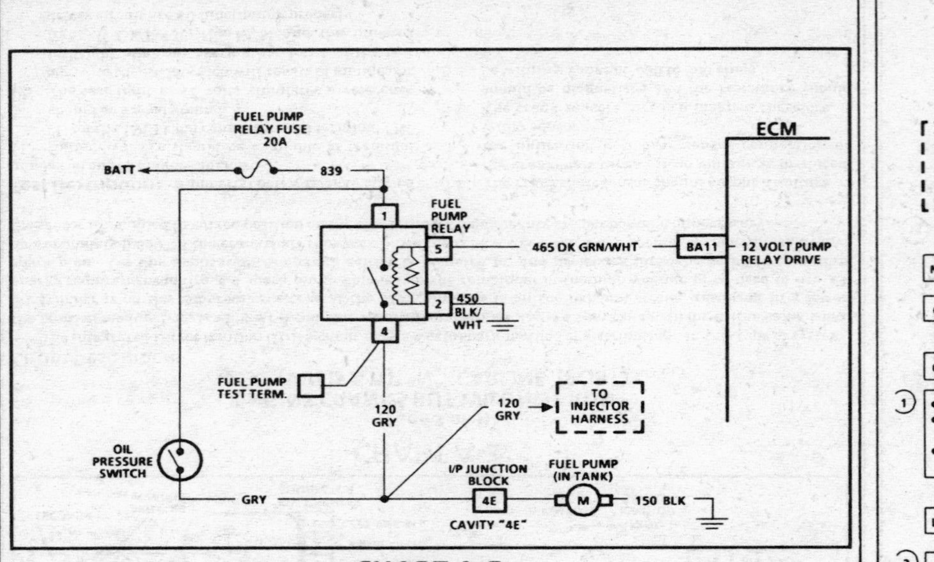

CHART A-5

(Page 1 of 2)

ENGINE CRANKS BUT WILL NOT RUN
(FUEL PUMP CIRCUIT)
2.3L (VIN D & A) "N" CARLINE (PORT)

Circuit Description:

When the ignition switch is turned "ON," the Electronic Control Module (ECM) turns "ON" the in-tank fuel pump. It will remain "ON" as long as the ECM is receiving ignition reference pulses from the Integrated Direct Ignition (IDI) module.

If there are no reference pulses, the ECM will shut "OFF" the fuel pump about 2-3 seconds after key "ON," or about 10 seconds after reference pulses stop. If sufficient oil pressure is present to close the oil pressure switch, the fuel pump will remain "ON" during cranking without reference pulses.

The pump delivers fuel to the fuel rail and injectors, then to the pressure regulator, where the system pressure is controlled to 280 - 325 kPa (40.5 - 47 psi) with no manifold vacuum or 211 - 304 kPa (30.5 - 44 psi) at idle. Excess fuel is then returned to the fuel tank.

The fuel pump "test" terminal is located in the engine compartment. When the engine is stopped, the pump can be turned "ON" by applying battery voltage to the "test" terminal.

Improper fuel system pressure will result in one or all of the following symptoms:

- Cranks but won't run
- Code 44
- Code 45
- Cuts out, may feel like ignition problem
- Poor fuel economy, loss of power
- Hesitation

Test Description: Number(s) below refer to circled number(s) on the diagnostic chart.

1. Determines if the pump circuit is ECM controlled. The ECM will turn "ON" the pump relay. Engine is not cranking or running so the ECM will turn "OFF" the relay within 2 seconds after ignition is turned "ON."
2. If the fuse is blown, this test will confirm a short to ground on CKT 120. To prevent misdiagnosis, be sure fuel pump is disconnected before test.
3. Turns "ON" the fuel pump if CKT 120 wiring is OK. If the pump runs, it is a basic fuel delivery problem which the following steps will locate.
4. Check for battery voltage at the pump relay.

CHART A-5

(Page 1 of 2)

ENGINE CRANKS BUT WILL NOT RUN
(FUEL PUMP CIRCUIT)
2.3L (VIN D & A) "N" CARLINE (PORT)

FROM CHART A-3 (2 of 3) OR FROM CHART A-7

NO PRESSURE

CHECK FUEL PUMP FUSE

FROM CHART A-3 (2 of 2) (FUSE NOT OK)

OK

(1)
- IGNITION "OFF" FOR TEN SECONDS.
- PROBE FUEL PUMP TEST TERM. WITH A TEST LIGHT TO GROUND.
- NOTE LIGHT WITHIN 2 SECONDS AFTER IGNITION "ON".

FROM CHART A-3 (2 of 2) (FUSE OK)

LIGHT "ON"

(3)
- APPLY BATTERY VOLTAGE TO PUMP TEST CONNECTOR.
- LISTEN FOR PUMP RUNNING AT FUEL TANK.

NOTE: MAY BE NECESSARY TO REMOVE FUEL CAP TO HEAR PUMP RUN.

PUMP RUNS

CHECK FOR:
- PLUGGED IN-LINE FILTER.
- PLUGGED PUMP INLET FILTER.
- RESTRICTED FUEL LINE.

IF OK

REPLACE IN-TANK FUEL PUMP.

PUMP NOT RUNNING

CHECK FOR:
- OPEN WIRE IN CKT 120.
- OPEN PUMP GROUND CKT 150.

IF OK

LIGHT "OFF"

(4)
- DISCONNECT PUMP RELAY.
- IGNITION "ON," ENGINE STOPPED
- PROBE RELAY HARNESS CONNECTOR TERMINAL "1" WITH A TEST LIGHT TO GROUND.

LIGHT "ON"

CHART A-5 (2 of 2)

NOT OK

(2)
- IGNITION "OFF".
- DISCONNECT FUEL PUMP HARNESS AT REAR BODY CONNECTOR.
- PROBE FUEL PUMP TEST CONNECTOR CKT 120, WITH A TEST LIGHT TO 12 VOLTS.

LIGHT "OFF"

- RECONNECT FUEL PUMP.
- REPLACE FUSE.
- IGNITION "ON".
- RECHECK FUSE.

OK

DEFECTIVE FUSE OR INTERMITTENT SHORT TO GROUND IN CKT 120.

NOT OK

IN-TANK FUEL PUMP OR PUMP HARNESS SHORTED TO GROUND.

LIGHT "ON"

REPAIR SHORT TO GROUND IN CKT 120.

LIGHT "OFF"

REPAIR OPEN CKT 839.

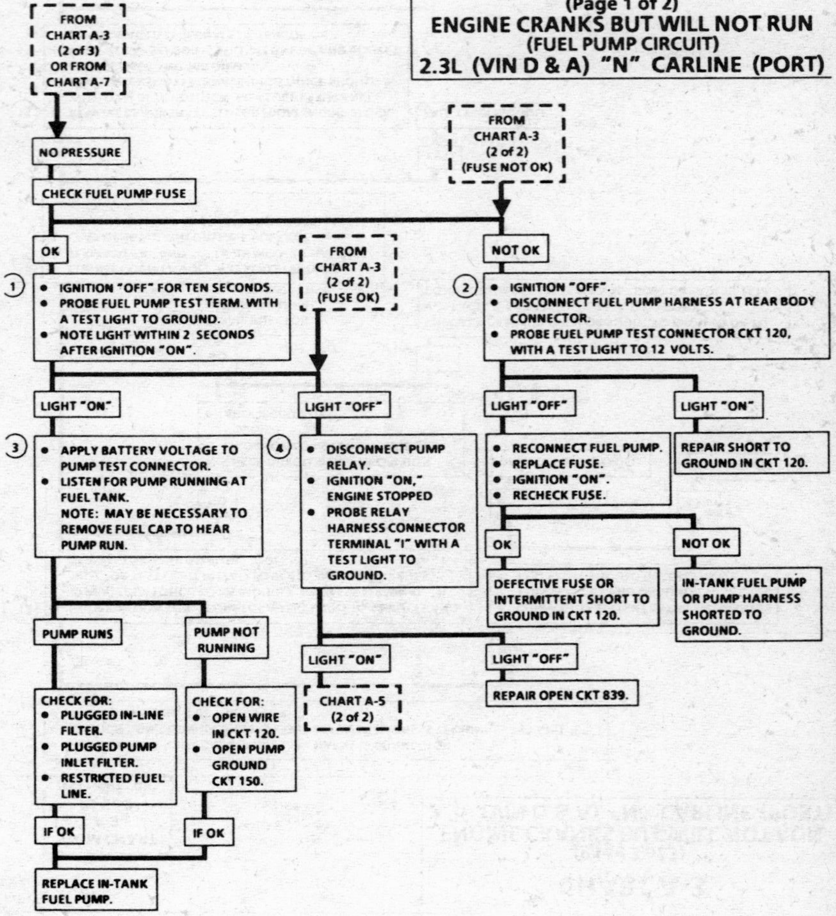

"AFTER REPAIRS," CONFIRM "CLOSED LOOP" OPERATION AND NO "SERVICE ENGINE SOON" LIGHT.

FUEL PUMP RELAY FUSE 20A
BATT
839
FUEL PUMP RELAY
1
5
2
4
465 DK GRN/WHT
BA11
12 VOLT PUMP RELAY DRIVE
ECM
450 BLK/WHT
FUEL PUMP TEST TERM.
120 GRY
120 GRY
TO INJECTOR HARNESS
OIL PRESSURE SWITCH
I/P JUNCTION BLOCK
4E
CAVITY "4E"
FUEL PUMP (IN TANK)
M
150 BLK
GRY

CHART A-5

(Page 2 of 2)

ENGINE CRANKS BUT WILL NOT RUN
(FUEL PUMP CIRCUIT)
2.3L (VIN D & A) "N" CARLINE (PORT)

Circuit Description:

When the ignition switch is turned "ON," the Electronic Control Module (ECM) turns "ON" the in-tank fuel pump. It will remain "ON" as long as the ECM is receiving ignition reference pulses from the Integrated Direct Ignition (IDI) module.

If there are no reference pulses, the ECM will shut "OFF" the fuel pump about 2-3 seconds after key "ON," or about 10 seconds after reference pulses stop. If sufficient oil pressure is present to close the oil pressure switch, the fuel pump will remain "ON" during cranking without reference pulses.

The pump delivers fuel to the fuel rail and injectors, then to the pressure regulator, where the system pressure is controlled to 280 - 325 kPa (40.5 - 47 psi) with no manifold vacuum or 211 - 304 kPa (30.5 - 44 psi) at idle. Excess fuel is then returned to the fuel tank.

The fuel pump "test" terminal is located in the engine compartment. When the engine is stopped, the pump can be turned "ON" by applying battery voltage to the "test" terminal.

Improper fuel system pressure will result in one or all of the following symptoms:

- Cranks but won't run
- Code 44
- Code 45
- Cuts out, may feel like ignition problem
- Poor fuel economy, loss of power
- Hesitation

Test Description: Number(s) below refer to circled number(s) on the diagnostic chart.

5. Check relay ground CKT 450.
6. Check for ECM control of relay through CKT 465.
7. The fuel pump voltage control circuit includes an engine oil pressure switch with a separate set of normally open contacts. The switch closes at about 28 kPa (4 psi) of oil pressure and provides a second battery feed path to the fuel pump. If the relay fails, the pump will continue to run using the battery feed supplied by the closed oil pressure switch.

   A failed pump relay will result in extended engine crank time, because of the time required to build enough oil pressure to close the oil pressure switch and turn "ON" the fuel pump. There may be instances when the relay has failed but the engine will not crank fast enough to build enough oil pressure to close the switch. This or a faulty oil pressure switch can result in "Engine Cranks But Will Not Run."
8. Check the oil pressure switch to be sure it provides battery feed to the fuel pump should the pump relay fail.

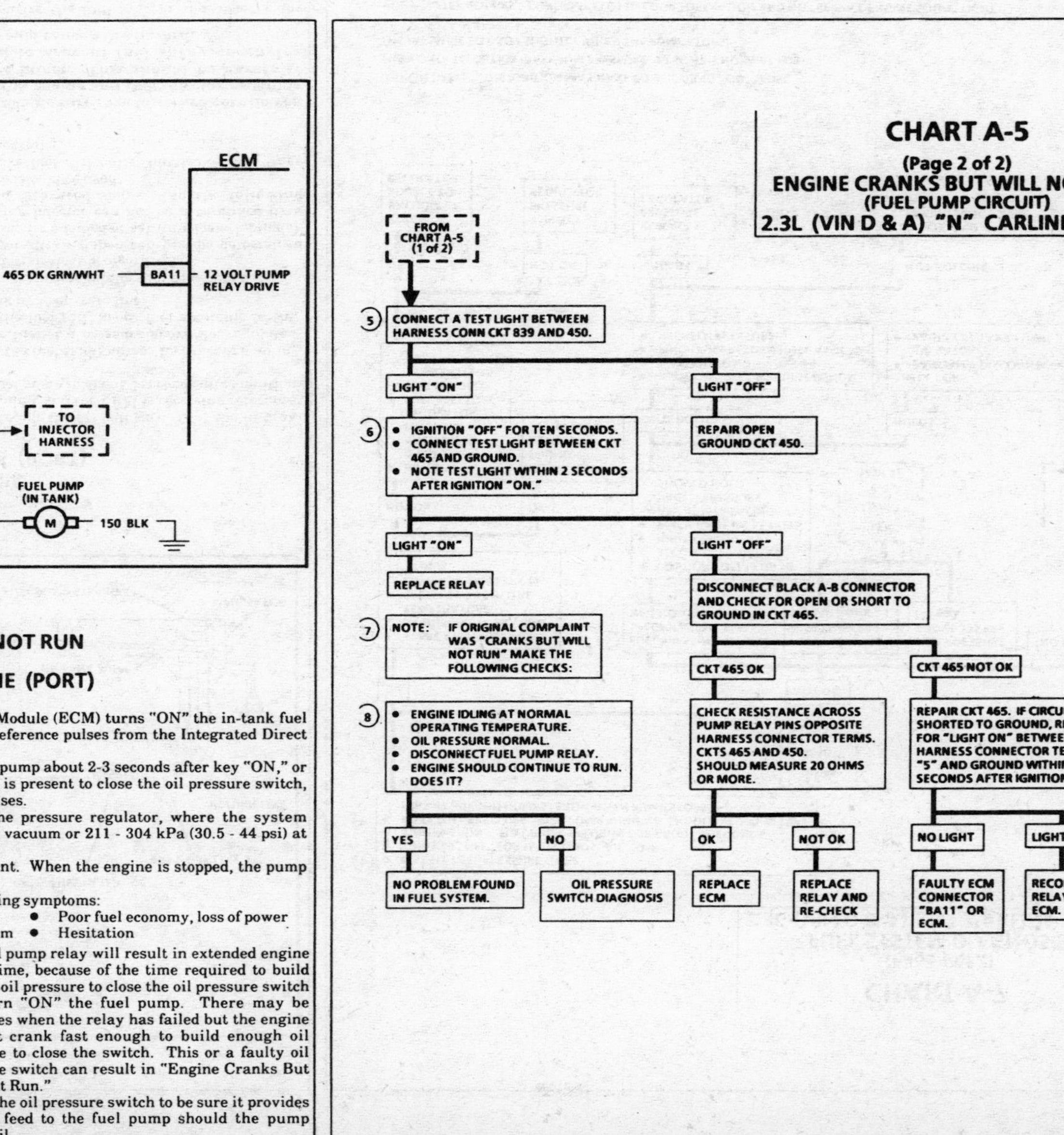

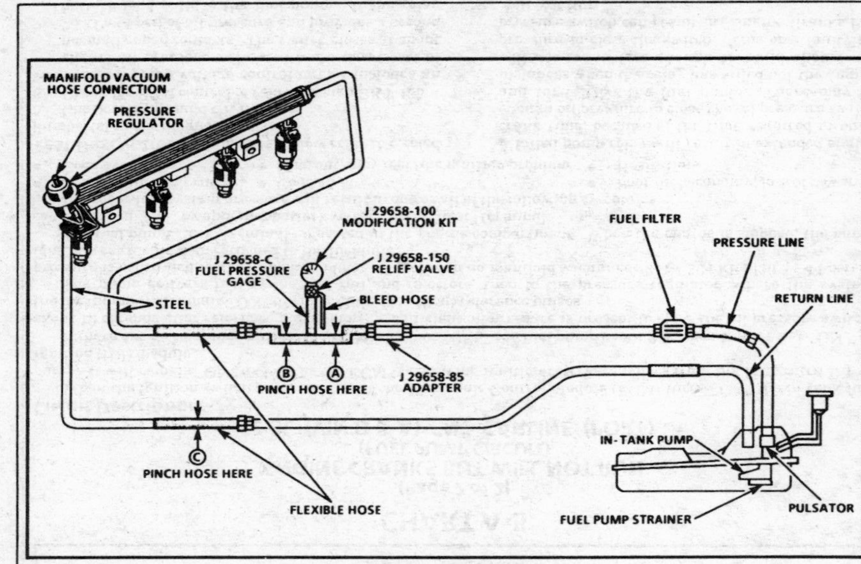

CHART A-7
(Page 1 of 3)
FUEL SYSTEM DIAGNOSIS
2.3L (VIN D & A) "N" CARLINE (PORT)

Circuit Description:

When the ignition switch is turned "ON," the Electronic Control Module (ECM) will turn "ON" the in-tank fuel pump. It will remain "ON" as long as the engine is cranking or running, and the ECM is receiving reference pulses. If there are no reference pulses, the ECM will shut "OFF" the fuel pump in about 2 seconds after ignition "ON" or 10 seconds after reference pulses stop.

An electric fuel pump, attached to the fuel sender assembly (inside the fuel tank) pumps fuel through an in-line filter to the fuel rail assembly. The pump is designed to provide fuel at a pressure above the regulated pressure needed by the injectors. A pressure regulator, attached to the fuel rail, keeps fuel available to the injectors at a regulated pressure. Unused fuel is returned to the fuel tank by a separate line.

Test Description: Number(s) below refer to circled number(s) on the diagnostic chart.

1. Install fuel pressure gage per instructions on Page 3 of 3. Ignition "ON" pump pressure should be 280-325 kPa (40.5-47 psi). This pressure is controlled by spring pressure within the regulator assembly.
2. When the engine is idling, the manifold pressure is low (high vacuum) and is applied to the fuel regulator diaphragm. This will offset the spring and result in a lower fuel pressure. This idle pressure will vary somewhat depending on barometric pressure, however, the pressure idling should be less indicating pressure regulator control.
3. Pressure that continues to fall quickly is caused by one of the following:
   - In-tank fuel pump check valve not holding
   - Partially disconnected pump pulsator
   - Fuel pressure regulator valve leaking
   - Injector(s) sticking open
4. An injector sticking open can best be determined by checking for a fouled or saturated spark plug(s). If a leaking injector can not be determined by a fouled or saturated spark plug the following procedure should be used.
   - Remove fuel rail bolts, but leave fuel lines connected.

CAUTION: Be sure injector(s) are not allowed to spray on engine and that injector retaining clips are intact. This should be carefully followed to prevent fuel spray on engine which would cause a fire hazard.

- Pressurize the fuel system and observe for injector(s) leaking.

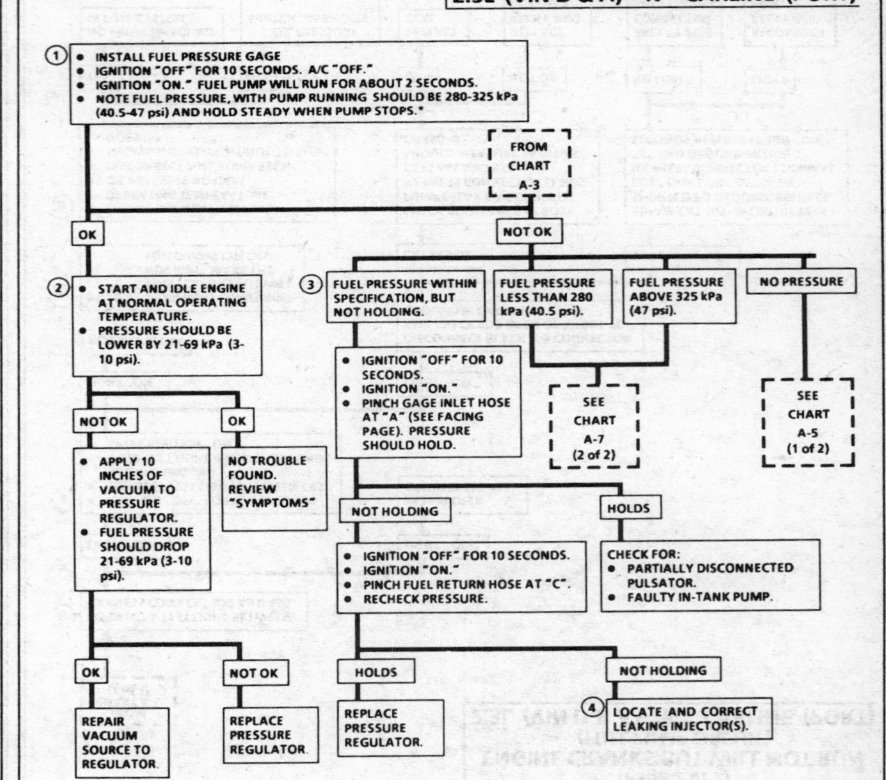

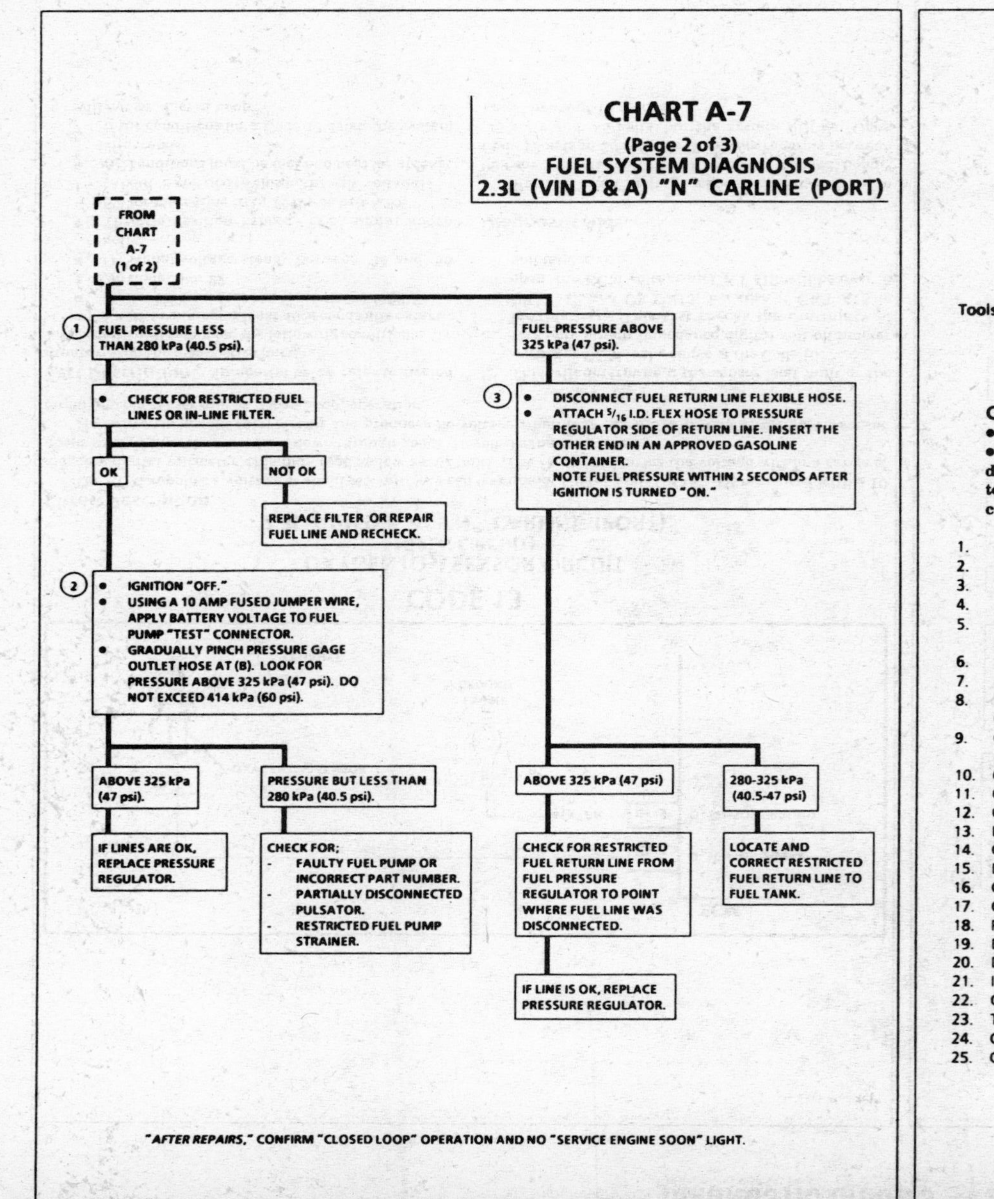

CHART A-7

(Page 3 of 3)
FUEL SYSTEM DIAGNOSIS
2.3L (VIN D & A) "N" CARLINE (PORT)

FUEL PRESSURE CHECK

Tools Required:
- J 29658-C - Fuel Pressure Gage
- J 29658-150 - Fuel Pressure Gage Relief Valve
- J29658-82 - O-ring Fuel Line Fitting Adapter
- J 29658-85 - Fuel Pressure Gage Adapter
- J 29658-100 - TBI Pressure Gage Modification Kit

CAUTION: To Reduce the Risk of Fire and Personal Injury:
- **It is necessary to relieve fuel system pressure before connecting a fuel pressure gage.**
- **After relieving system pressure, a small amount of fuel may be released when disconnecting the fuel lines. Cover fuel line fittings with a shop towel before disconnecting, to catch any fuel that may leak out. Place towel in approved container when disconnect is completed.**

1. Loosen fuel filler cap to relieve fuel tank pressure. (Do not tighten at this time.)
2. Raise vehicle.
3. Disconnect fuel pump electrical connector.
4. Lower vehicle.
5. Start and run engine until fuel supply remaining in fuel pipes is consumed. Engage starter for three seconds to assure relief of any remaining pressure.
6. Disconnect negative battery terminal.
7. Locate engine compartment fuel feed (pressure) line.
8. If not previously installed, connect Fuel Pressure Gage Relief Valve J 29658-150, on Fuel Pressure Gage J 29658-C.
9. Connect 414 kPa (60 psi) gage from TBI Pressure Gage Modification Kit J 29658-100 to Fuel Pressure Gage J 29658-C.
10. Connect Fuel Pressure Gage Adapter J 29658-85 to inlet side of pressure gage.
11. Connect O-ring fuel line fitting adapter J 29658-82 to outlet side of pressure gage.
12. Connect fuel pressure gage to fuel feed line.
13. Raise vehicle.
14. Connect fuel pump electrical connector.
15. Lower vehicle.
16. Connect negative battery terminal.
17. Check fuel pressure.
18. Place bleed hose into an approved container and open valve to bleed system pressure.
19. Disconnect negative battery cable.
20. Disconnect fuel pressure gage.
21. Inspect fuel feel line O-ring and replace if necessary.
22. Connect fuel feed line.
23. Tighten fuel filler cap.
24. Connect negative battery terminal.
25. Cycle ignition "ON" and "OFF" twice, waiting ten seconds between cycles, then check for fuel leaks.

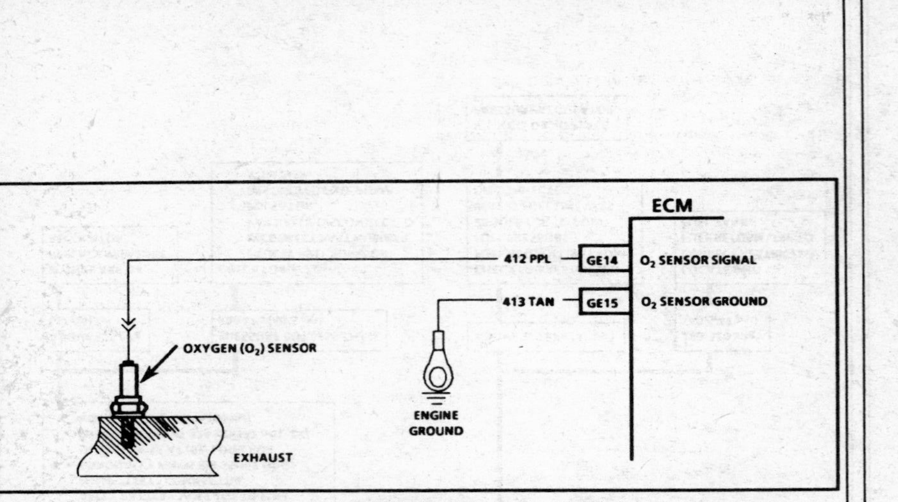

CODE 13

OXYGEN (O_2) SENSOR CIRCUIT (OPEN CIRCUIT) 2.3L (VIN D & A) "N" CARLINE (PORT)

Circuit Description:

The ECM supplies a voltage of about .45 volt between terminals "GE14" and "GE15". (If measured with a 10 megohm digital voltmeter, this may read as low as .32 volt). The O_2 sensor varies the voltage within a range of about 1 volt if the exhaust is rich, down through about .10 volt if exhaust is lean.

The sensor is like an open circuit and produces no voltage when it is below 315°C (600°F). An open sensor circuit or cold sensor causes "Open Loop" operation.

Test Description: Number(s) below refer to circled number(s) on the diagnostic chart.

1. Code 13 will set under the following conditions:
   - Engine running at least 40 seconds after start
   - Coolant temperature at least 42.5°C (108°F)
   - No Code 21 or 22
   - O_2 signal voltage steady between .34 and .55 volts.
   - Throttle Position Sensor (TPS) signal above 6% for more time than TPS was below 6%. (About .3 volt above closed throttle voltage)
   - All conditions must be met and held for at least 20 seconds.

   If the conditions for a Code 13 exist, the system will not go "Closed Loop."
2. This will determine if the sensor is at fault or the wiring or ECM is the cause of the Code 13.
3. Use only a high impedance digital volt ohmmeter for this test. This test checks the continuity of CKT 412 and CKT 413; because if CKT 413 is open, the ECM voltage on CKT 412 will be over .6 volt (600 mv).

Diagnostic Aids:

Normal "Scan" voltage varies between 100 mv to 999 mv (.1 volt to 1.0 volt) while in "Closed Loop." Code 13 sets in 20 seconds if voltage remains between .35 volts and .55 volts, but the system will go "Open Loop" in about 15 seconds.

CODE 13

OXYGEN (O_2) SENSOR CIRCUIT (OPEN CIRCUIT) 2.3L (VIN D & A) "N" CARLINE (PORT)

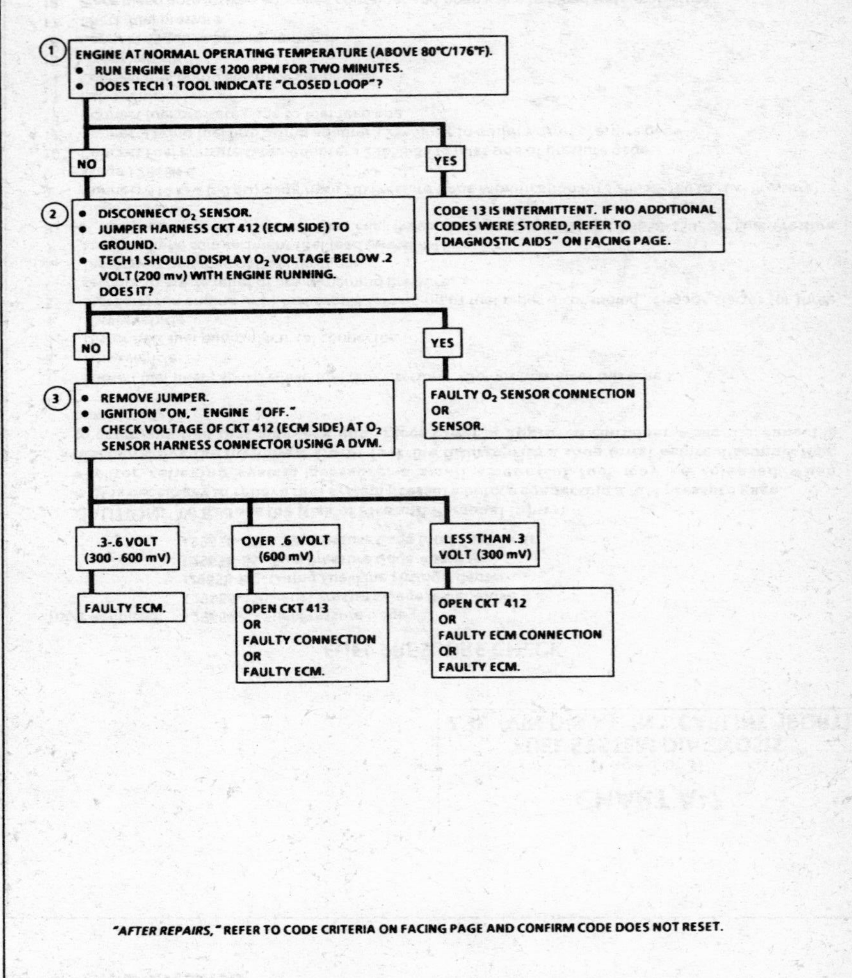

"AFTER REPAIRS," REFER TO CODE CRITERIA ON FACING PAGE AND CONFIRM CODE DOES NOT RESET.

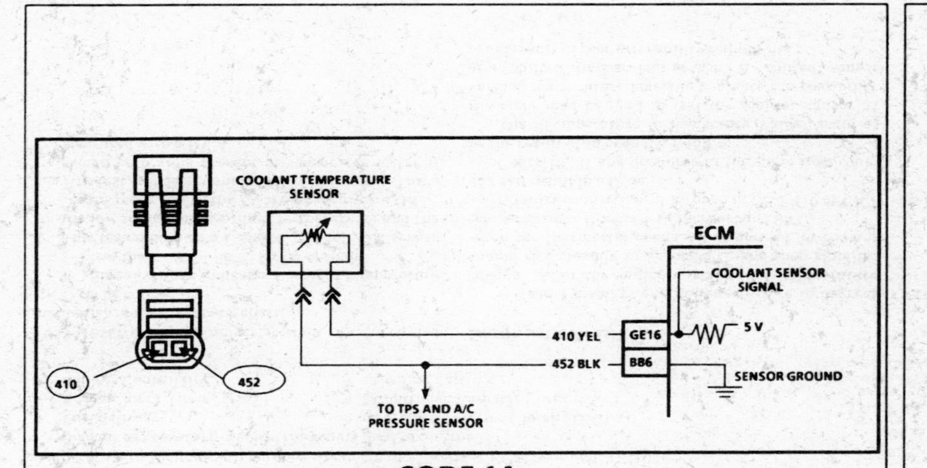

CODE 14

COOLANT TEMPERATURE SENSOR (CTS) CIRCUIT
(HIGH TEMPERATURE INDICATED)
2.3L (VIN D & A) "N" CARLINE (PORT)

Circuit Description:

The Coolant Temperature Sensor (CTS) uses a thermistor to control the signal voltage at the ECM. The ECM applies a voltage on CKT 410 to the sensor. When the engine is cold the sensor (thermistor) resistance is high, therefore ECM terminal "GE16" voltage will be high.

As the engine warms, the sensor resistance becomes less, and the voltage drops. At normal engine operating temperature, the voltage will measure about 1.5 to 2.0 volts at ECM terminal "GE16".

Coolant temperature is one of the inputs used to control:

- Fuel delivery
- Engine Spark Timing (EST)
- Idle Air Control (IAC)
- Torque Convertor Clutch (TCC)
- Controlled Canister Purge (CCP)
- Cooling Fan

Test Description: Number(s) below refer to circled number(s) on the diagnostic chart.

1. Code 14 will set if:
   - Signal voltage indicates a coolant temperature above 140°C (285°F).
   - Engine running longer than 128 seconds
2. This test will determine if CKT 410 is shorted to ground which will cause the conditions for Code 14.

Diagnostic Aids:

Check harness routing for a potential short to ground in CKT 410. A Tech 1 displays engine temperature in degrees celsius. After engine is started, the temperature should rise steadily to about 90°C, and then stabilize when thermostat opens. Refer to "Intermittents" in "Symptoms,"

Verify that engine is not overheating and has not been subjected to conditions which could create an overheating condition (i.e. overload, trailer towing, hilly terrain, heavy stop and go traffic, etc.). The "Temperature To Resistance Value" scale at the right may be used to test the coolant sensor at various temperature levels to evaluate the possibility of a "shifted" (mis-scaled) sensor. A "shifted" sensor could result in poor driveability complaints.

CODE 14

COOLANT TEMPERATURE SENSOR (CTS) CIRCUIT
(HIGH TEMPERATURE INDICATED)
2.3L (VIN D & A) "N" CARLINE (PORT)

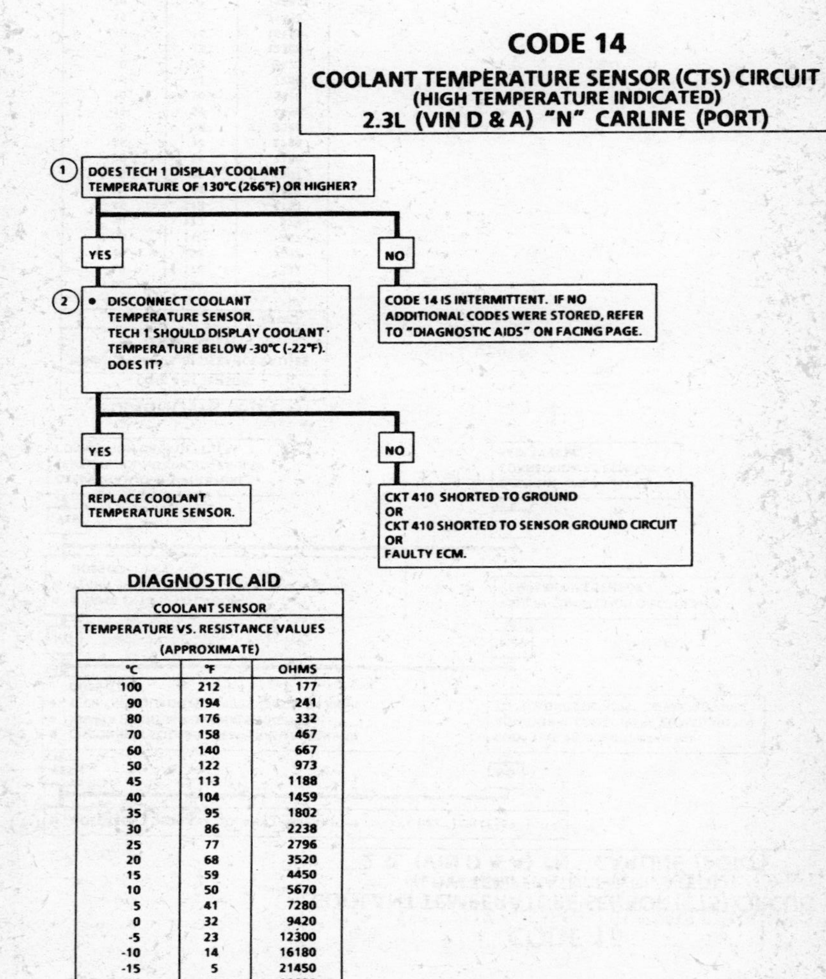

DIAGNOSTIC AID

COOLANT SENSOR
TEMPERATURE VS. RESISTANCE VALUES
(APPROXIMATE)

°C	°F	OHMS
100	212	177
90	194	241
80	176	332
70	158	467
60	140	667
50	122	973
45	113	1188
40	104	1459
35	95	1802
30	86	2238
25	77	2796
20	68	3520
15	59	4450
10	50	5670
5	41	7280
0	32	9420
-5	23	12300
-10	14	16180
-15	5	21450
-20	-4	28680
-30	-22	52700
-40	-40	100700

"AFTER REPAIRS," REFER TO CODE CRITERIA ON FACING PAGE AND CONFIRM CODE DOES NOT RESET.

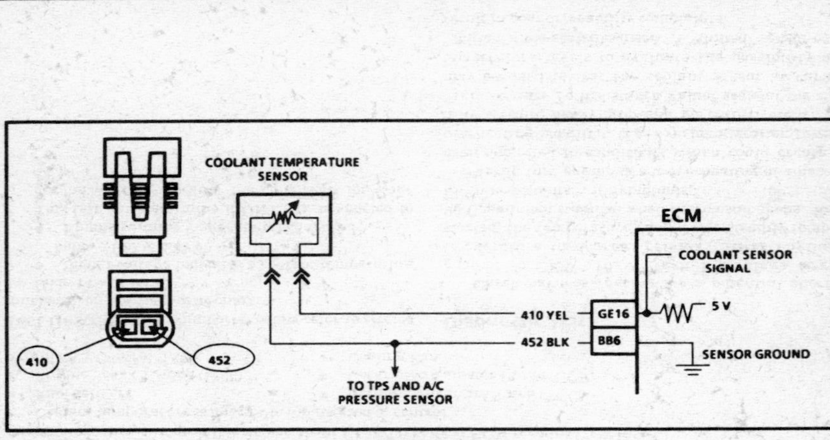

CODE 15

COOLANT TEMPERATURE SENSOR (CTS) CIRCUIT (LOW TEMPERATURE INDICATED) 2.3L (VIN D & A) "N" CARLINE (PORT)

Circuit Description:

The Coolant Temperature Sensor (CTS) uses a thermistor to control the signal voltage at the ECM. The ECM applies a voltage on CKT 410 to the sensor. When the engine is cold, the sensor (thermistor) resistance is high, therefore, ECM terminal "GE16" voltage will be high.

As the engine warms, the sensor resistance becomes less, and the voltage drops. At normal engine operating temperature the voltage will measure about 1.5 to 2.0 volts at ECM terminal "GE16".

Coolant temperature is one of the inputs used to control:

- Fuel delivery
- Engine Spark Timing (EST)
- Idle Air Control (IAC)
- Torque Convertor Clutch (TCC)
- Controlled Canister Purge (CCP)
- Cooling Fan

Test Description: Number(s) below refer to circled number(s) on the diagnostic chart.

1. Code 15 will set if:
   - Signal voltage indicates a coolant temperature less than -39°C (-38°F) for 60 seconds.
2. This test simulates a Code 14. If the ECM senses the low signal voltage (high temperature) and the "Scan" reads 130°C, the ECM and wiring are OK.
3. This test will determine if CKT 410 is open. There should be 5 volts present at sensor connector if measured with a DVM.

Diagnostic Aids:

A Tech 1 displays engine temperature in degrees celsius. After the engine is started the temperature should rise steadily to about 95°C, and then stabilize when the thermostat opens. It is normal for coolant temperature to fluctuate slightly around 95°C.

A faulty connection, or an open in CKT 410 or CKT 452 can result in a Code 15.

Codes 15, 21 and 66 stored at the same time could be the result of an open CKT 452.

The "Temperature to Resistance Value" scale at the right may be used to test the coolant sensor at various temperature levels to evaluate the possibility of a "shifted" (mis-scaled) sensor. A "shifted" sensor could result in poor driveability complaints.

CODE 15

COOLANT TEMPERATURE SENSOR (CTS) CIRCUIT (LOW TEMPERATURE INDICATED) 2.3L (VIN D & A) "N" CARLINE (PORT)

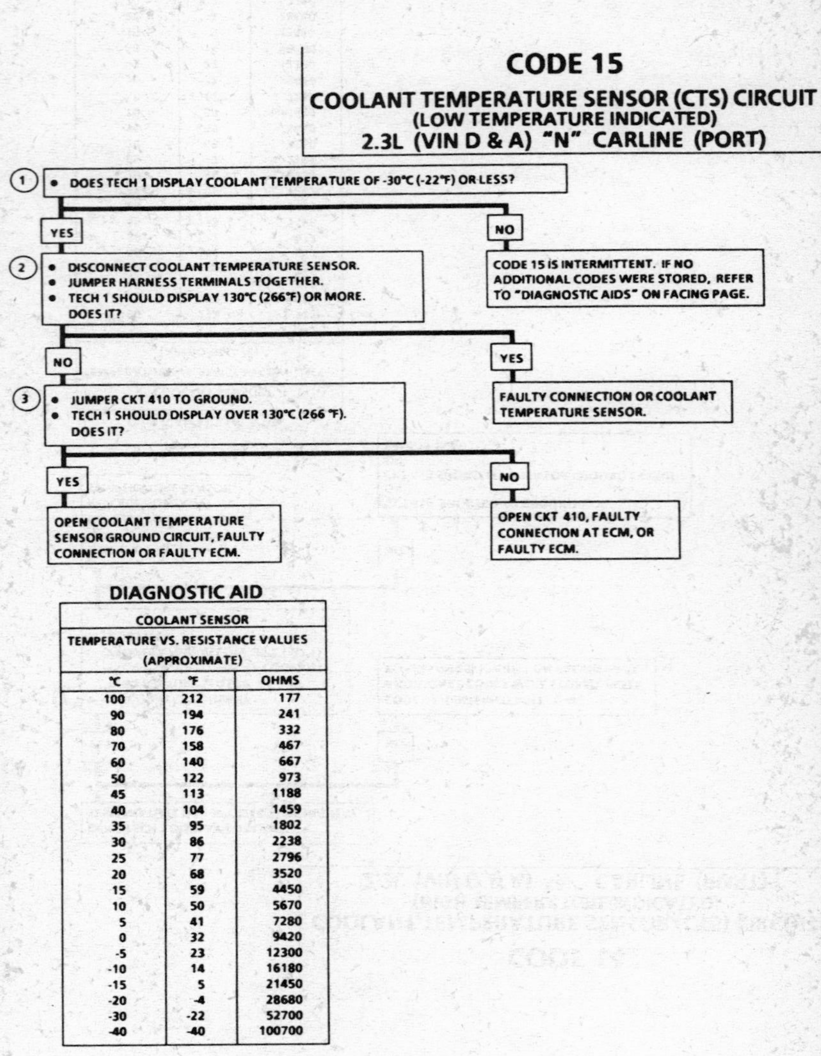

DIAGNOSTIC AID

COOLANT SENSOR
TEMPERATURE VS. RESISTANCE VALUES (APPROXIMATE)

°C	°F	OHMS
100	212	177
90	194	241
80	176	332
70	158	467
60	140	667
50	122	973
45	113	1188
40	104	1459
35	95	1802
30	86	2238
25	77	2796
20	68	3520
15	59	4450
10	50	5670
5	41	7280
0	32	9420
-5	23	12300
-10	14	16180
-15	5	21450
-20	-4	28680
-30	-22	52700
-40	-40	100700

"AFTER REPAIRS," REFER TO CODE CRITERIA ON FACING PAGE AND CONFIRM CODE DOES NOT RESET.

DIAGNOSTIC CHARTS — 2.3L ENGINE

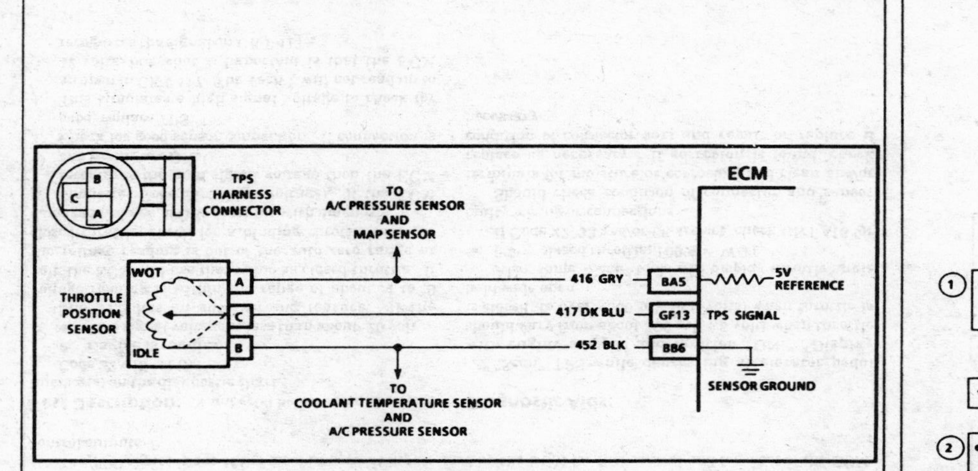

CODE 21

THROTTLE POSITION SENSOR (TPS) CIRCUIT
(SIGNAL VOLTAGE HIGH)
2.3L (VIN D & A) "N" CARLINE (PORT)

Circuit Description:

The Throttle Position Sensor (TPS) provides a voltage signal that changes relative to the throttle opening. Signal voltage will vary from about .5 volt at idle to about 4.9 volts at Wide Open Throttle (WOT).

The TPS signal is one of the most important inputs used by the ECM for fuel control and for most of the ECM control outputs.

Test Description: Number(s) below refer to circled number(s) on the diagnostic chart.

1. Code 21 will set if:
   - Engine is running
   - No Code 33 or 34
   - MAP less than 65 kPa
   - TPS signal voltage greater than approximately 4.0 volts (78%)
   - Above conditions exist for over 5 seconds.

   OR

   - TPS voltage greater than about 4.7 volts.

   With throttle closed the TPS should read less than .900 volt. If it doesn't, check for sticking TPS or throttle linkage. If OK, replace TPS.
2. With the TPS disconnected, the TPS voltage should go low if the ECM and wiring are OK.
3. Probing CKT 452 with a test light checks the TPS ground circuit because an open or very high resistance ground circuit will cause a Code 21.

Diagnostic Aids:

A Tech 1 displays throttle position in volts. It should display .400 volt to .900 volt with throttle closed and ignition "ON" or at idle. Voltage should increase at a steady rate as throttle is moved toward Wide Open Throttle (WOT).

Also some "Scan" tools will display throttle angle %, 0% = closed throttle 100% = WOT.

An open in CKT 452 will result in a Code 21.

Codes 15, 21 and 66 stored at the same time could be the result of an open CKT 452. "Scan" TPS while depressing accelerator pedal with engine stopped and ignition "ON." Display should vary from about .5 volt (500 mV) when throttle is closed, to over 4500 mV (4.5 volts) when throttle is held wide open.

Check condition of connector and sensor terminals for moisture or corrosion, and clean or replace as necessary. If corrosion is found, check condition of connector seal, repair and/or replace if necessary.

CODE 21

THROTTLE POSITION SENSOR (TPS) CIRCUIT
(SIGNAL VOLTAGE HIGH)
2.3L (VIN D & A) "N" CARLINE (PORT)

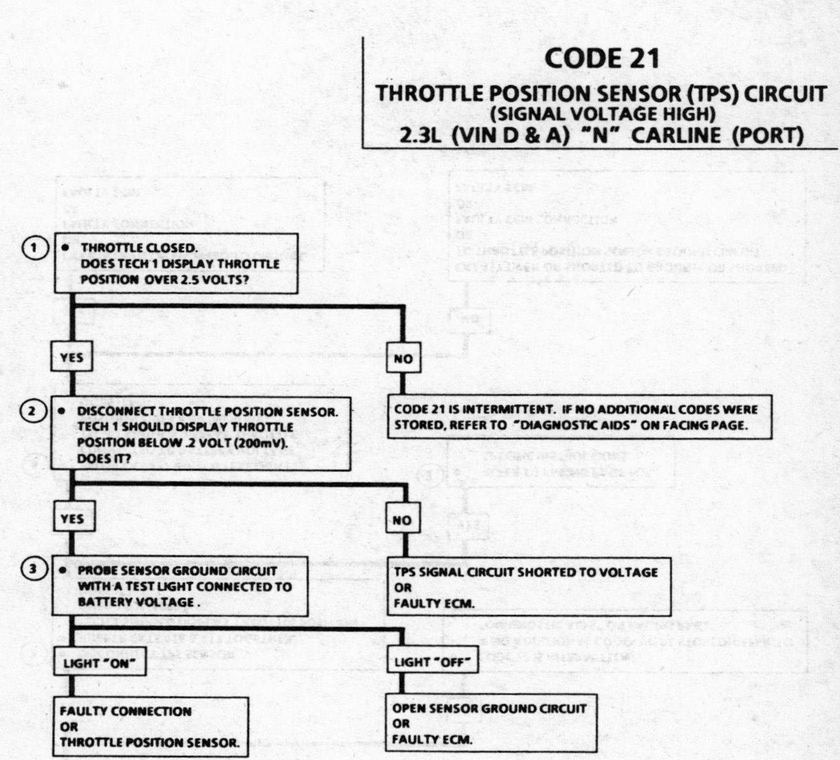

"AFTER REPAIRS," REFER TO CODE CRITERIA ON FACING PAGE AND CONFIRM CODE DOES NOT RESET.

TPS HARNESS CONNECTOR
TO A/C PRESSURE SENSOR AND MAP SENSOR
ECM
THROTTLE POSITION SENSOR
WOT
IDLE
A — 416 GRY — BA5 — 5V REFERENCE
C — 417 DK BLU — GF13 — TPS SIGNAL
B — 452 BLK — BB6 — SENSOR GROUND
TO COOLANT TEMPERATURE SENSOR AND A/C PRESSURE SENSOR

CODE 22

THROTTLE POSITION SENSOR (TPS) CIRCUIT
(SIGNAL VOLTAGE LOW)
2.3L (VIN D & A) "N" CARLINE (PORT)

Circuit Description:

The Throttle Position Sensor (TPS) provides a voltage signal that changes relative to the throttle opening. Signal voltage will vary from about .5 volt at idle to about 4.9 volts at Wide Open Throttle (WOT).

The TPS signal is one of the most important inputs used by the ECM for fuel control and for most of the ECM control outputs.

Test Description: Number(s) below refer to circled number(s) on the diagnostic chart.

1. Code 22 will set if:
   - Engine is running
   - TPS signal voltage is less than about .20 volt

   The TPS has an auto zeroing feature. If the voltage reading is within the range of about .4 to .9 volt, the ECM will use that value as closed throttle. If the voltage reading is out of the auto zero range at closed throttle, check for a binding throttle cable or damaged linkage, if OK, continue with diagnosis.
2. Simulates Code 21: (high voltage). If the ECM recognizes the high signal voltage then the ECM and wiring are OK.
3. Check for good sensor connection. If connection is good, replace TPS.
4. This simulates a high signal voltage to check for an open in CKT 417. The Tech 1 will not read up to 12 volts, but what is important is that the ECM recognizes the signal on CKT 417.

Diagnostic Aids:

"Scan" TPS while depressing accelerator pedal with engine stopped and ignition "ON." Display should vary from about 500 mV (.5 volt) when throttle is closed, to over 4500 mV (4.5 volts) when throttle is held wide open.

Also, some "Scan" tools will display throttle angle %: 0% = closed throttle; 100% = WOT.

If Code 22, 33 and/or 66 are set, check CKT 416 for faulty wiring or connections.

Should check condition of connector and sensor terminals for moisture or corrosion, and clean and/or replace as necessary. If corrosion is found, check condition of connector seal and repair or replace if necessary.

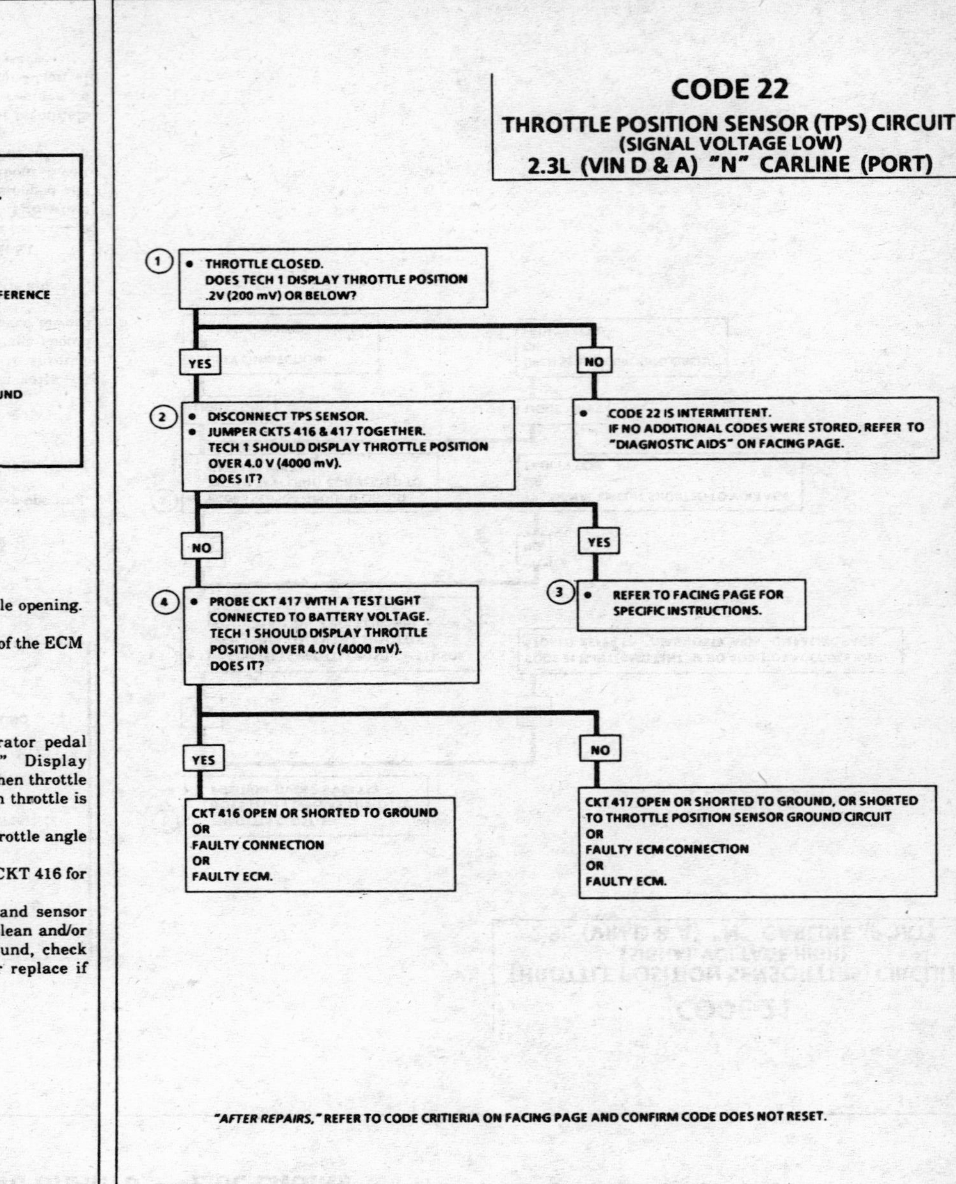

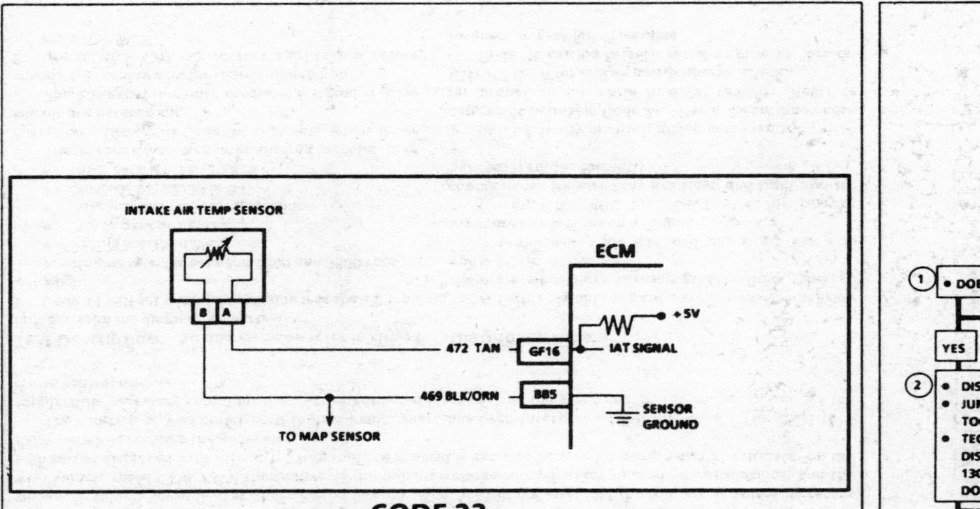

CODE 23

INTAKE AIR TEMPERATURE (IAT) SENSOR CIRCUIT
(LOW TEMPERATURE INDICATED)
2.3L (VIN D & A) "N" CARLINE (PORT)

Circuit Description:

The Intake Air Temperature (IAT) sensor uses a thermistor to control the signal voltage at the ECM. The ECM applies a voltage (about 5 volts) on CKT 472 to the sensor. When the air is cold the sensor (thermistor) resistance is high, therefore the ECM terminal "GF16" voltage will be high. If the air is warm the sensor resistance is low, therefore the ECM terminal "GF16" voltage will be low.

Test Description: Number(s) below refer to circled number(s) on the diagnostic chart.

1. Code 23 will set if:
   - A signal voltage indicates a intake air temperature below about -34°C (-29°F).
   - Time since engine start is 320 seconds or longer
   - Vehicle speed less than 15 mph
2. A Code 23 will set due to an open sensor, wire, or connection. This test will determine if the wiring and ECM are OK.
3. This will determine if the signal CKT 472 or the sensor ground CKT 469 is open.

Diagnostic Aids:

A Tech 1 displays temperature of the air entering the engine, which should be close to ambient air temperature when engine is cold, and rise as underhood temperature increases.

A faulty connection, or an open in CKT 472 or CKT 469 can result in a Code 23.

Codes 23 and 34 stored at the same time, could be the result of an open CKT 469. The "Temperature to Resistance Values" scale at the right may be used to test the IAT sensor at various temperature levels to evaluate the possibility of a "slewed" (mis-scaled) sensor. A "slewed" sensor could result in poor driveability complaints.

CODE 23

INTAKE AIR TEMPERATURE (IAT) SENSOR CIRCUIT
(LOW TEMPERATURE INDICATED)
2.3L (VIN D & A) "N" CARLINE (PORT)

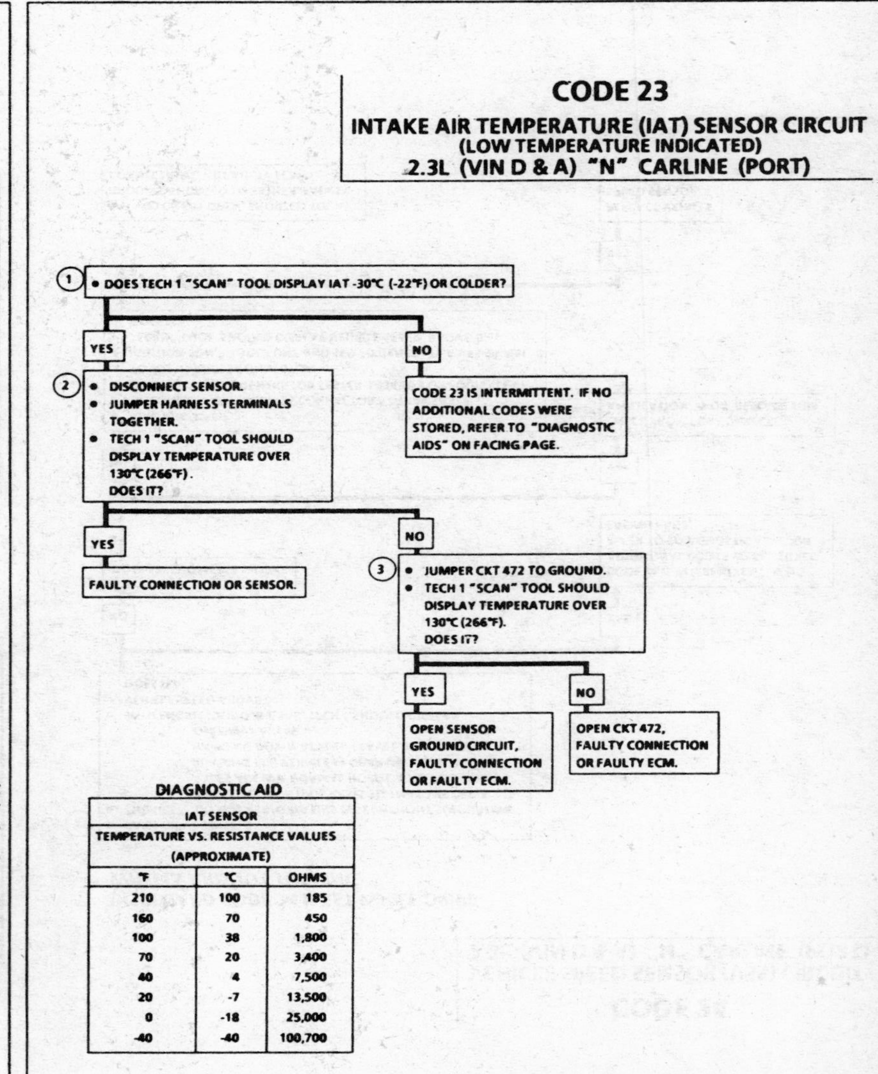

DIAGNOSTIC AID

IAT SENSOR		
TEMPERATURE VS. RESISTANCE VALUES (APPROXIMATE)		
°F	°C	OHMS
210	100	185
160	70	450
100	38	1,800
70	20	3,400
40	4	7,500
20	-7	13,500
0	-18	25,000
-40	-40	100,700

"AFTER REPAIRS," REFER TO CODE CRITERIA ON FACING PAGE AND CONFIRM CODE DOES NOT RESET.

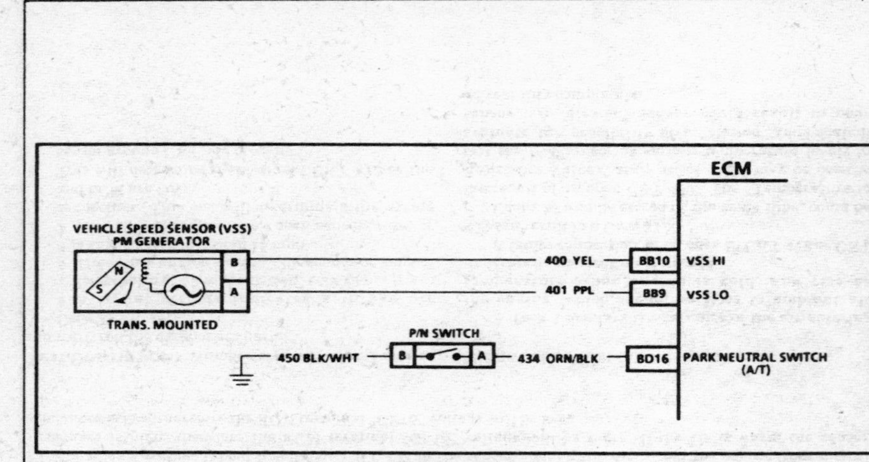

CODE 24

VEHICLE SPEED SENSOR (VSS) CIRCUIT 2.3L (VIN D & A) "N" CARLINE (PORT)

Circuit Description:

Vehicle speed information is provided to the ECM by the Vehicle Speed Sensor (VSS) which is a Permanent Magnet (PM) generator that is mounted in the transaxle. The PM generator produces a pulsing voltage whenever vehicle speed is over about 3 mph (5 kph). The AC voltage level and the number of pulses increases with vehicle speed. The ECM then converts the pulsing voltage to mph which is used for calculations, and the mph can be displayed with a Tech 1. Output of the generator can also be seen by using a digital voltmeter on the AC scale while rotating the generator.

The function of VSS buffer used in past model years has been incorporated into the ECM. The ECM then supplies the necessary signal for the instrument panel for operating the speedometer, the odometer, and for the cruise control module.

Test Description: Number(s) below refer to circled number(s) on the diagnostic chart.

1. Code 24 will set if vehicle speed is less than 2 mph when:
   - Engine speed is between 1500 and 3600 rpm
   - TPS is less than 2%
   - Not in park or neutral
   - All conditions met for 5 seconds
   - No Code 21, 22, 33 or 34
   - MAP between 12 - 30 kPa

   These conditions are met during a road load operation. Disregard Code 24 that sets when drive wheels are not turning.

   The PM generator only produces a signal if drive wheels are turning greater than 3 mph (5 kph).
2. Check MEM-CAL for correct application before replacing ECM.

Diagnostic Aids:

A Tech 1 should indicate a vehicle speed whenever the drive wheels are turning greater than 3 mph, (5 kph).

A problem in CKT 434 will not affect the VSS input or the readings on a "Scan."

Check CKT 400 and CKT 401 for proper connections. Be sure they are clean and tight and the harness is routed correctly.

(A/T) A faulty or misadjusted park/neutral switch can result in a false Code 24. Use a "Scan" and check for proper signal while in drive (3T40). Refer to CHART C-1A for P/N switch diagnosis check.

Code 24 can be falsely set if engine is "brake-torqued" in gear for 20 seconds.

CODE 24

VEHICLE SPEED SENSOR (VSS) CIRCUIT 2.3L (VIN D & A) "N" CARLINE (PORT)

DISREGARD CODE 24 IF SET WHILE DRIVE WHEELS ARE NOT TURNING.

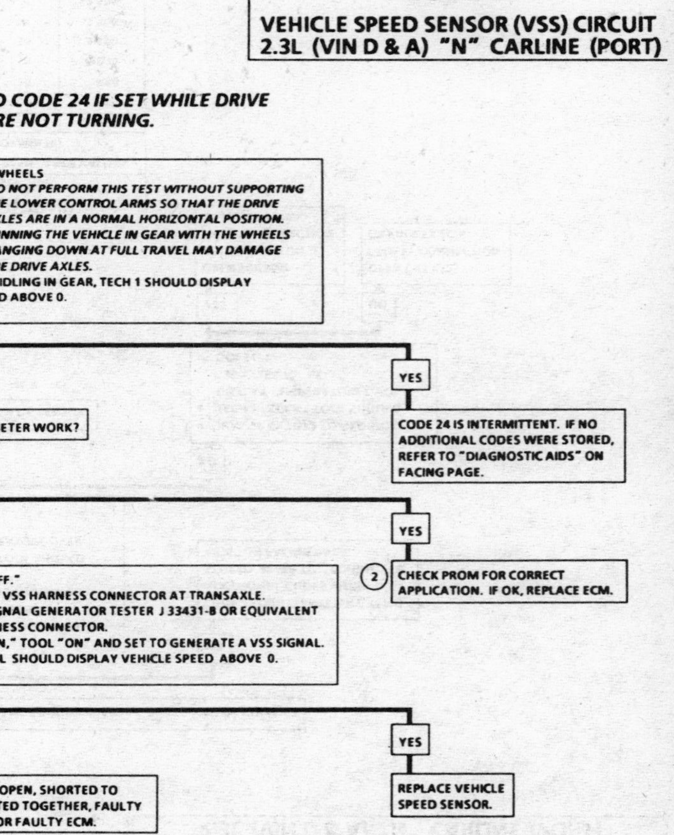

"AFTER REPAIRS," REFER TO CODE CRITERIA ON FACING PAGE AND CONFIRM CODE DOES NOT RESET.

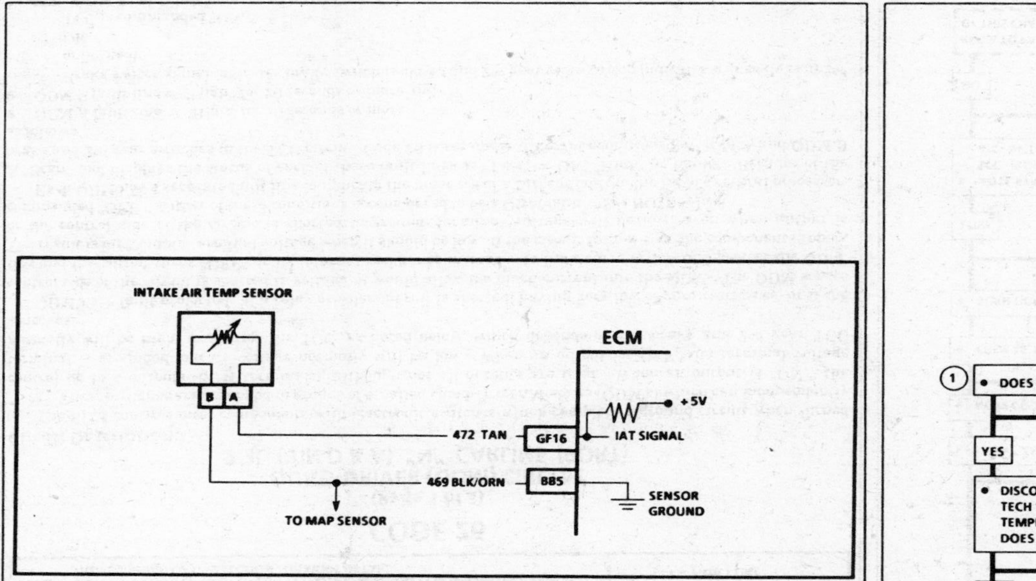

CODE 25

INTAKE AIR TEMPERATURE (IAT) SENSOR CIRCUIT
(HIGH TEMPERATURE INDICATED)
2.3L (VIN D & A) "N" CARLINE (PORT)

Circuit Description:

The Intake Air Temperature (IAT) sensor uses a thermistor to control the signal voltage to the ECM. The ECM applies a voltage (4-6 volts) on CKT 472 to the sensor. When intake air is cold, the sensor (thermistor) resistance is high, therefore, the ECM terminal "GF16" voltage is high. As the air warms, the sensor resistance becomes less, and the voltage drops. As the incoming air gets warmer, the sensor resistance decreases, causing ECM terminal "GF16" voltage to decrease.

Test Description: Number(s) below refer to circled number(s) on the diagnostic chart.

1. Code 25 will set if:
   - Signal voltage indicates a intake air temperature greater than about 159°C (318°F).
   - Vehicle speed is greater than 15 mph
   - Engine run time greater than 320 seconds.

Diagnostic Aids:

The "Temperature To Resistance Value" scale at the right may be used to test the IAT sensor at various temperature levels to evaluate the possibility of a "slewed" (mis-scaled) sensor. A "slewed" sensor could result in poor driveability complaints.

CODE 25

INTAKE AIR TEMPERATURE (IAT) SENSOR CIRCUIT
(HIGH TEMPERATURE INDICATED)
2.3L (VIN D & A) "N" CARLINE (PORT)

(1) • DOES TECH 1 "SCAN" TOOL DISPLAY IAT OF 145°C (293°F) OR HOTTER?

- YES → • DISCONNECT SENSOR. TECH 1 "SCAN" TOOL SHOULD DISPLAY TEMPERATURE BELOW -30°C (-22°F). DOES IT?
  - YES → REPLACE SENSOR.
  - NO → CKT 472 SHORTED TO GROUND, OR TO SENSOR GROUND, OR ECM IS FAULTY.
- NO → CODE 25 IS INTERMITTENT. IF NO ADDITIONAL CODES WERE STORED, REFER TO "DIAGNOSTIC AIDS" ON FACING PAGE.

DIAGNOSTIC AID

IAT SENSOR		
TEMPERATURE VS. RESISTANCE VALUES (APPROXIMATE)		
°F	°C	OHMS
210	100	185
160	70	450
100	38	1,800
70	20	3,400
40	4	7,500
20	-7	13,500
0	-18	25,000
-40	-40	100,700

"AFTER REPAIRS," REFER TO CODE CRITERIA ON FACING PAGE AND CONFIRM CODE DOES NOT RESET.

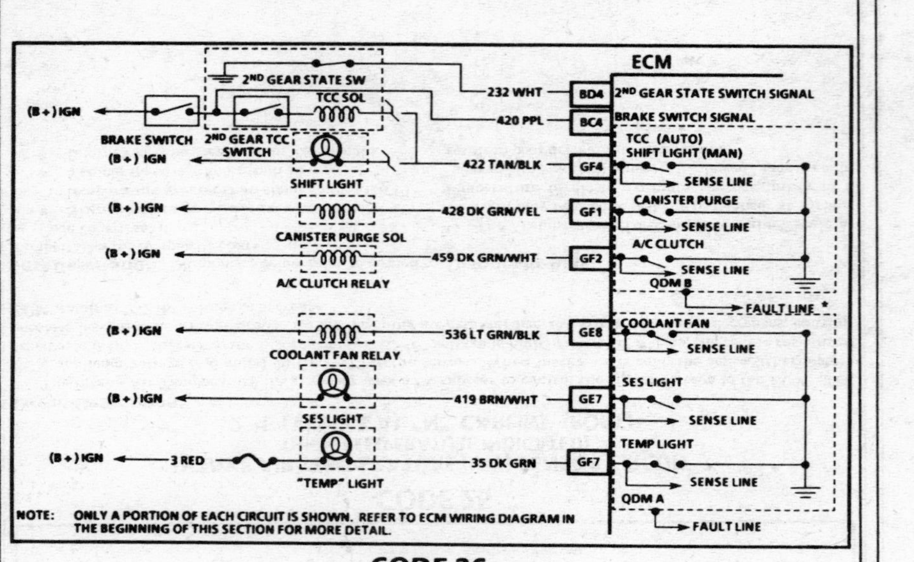

CODE 26

(Page 1 of 3)

QUAD-DRIVER (QDM) CIRCUIT
2.3L (VIN D & A) "N" CARLINE (PORT)

Circuit Description:

The ECM controls most components with electronic switches which complete a ground circuit when turned "ON." These switches are arranged in groups of 4, called Quad-Driver Modules (QDM's) which can independently control up to 4 outputs (ECM terminals), although not all outputs are used. When an output is "ON," the terminal is grounded and its voltage normally will be low. When an output is "OFF," its terminal voltage normally will be high, except for the TCC, as noted below, which depends on the brake and 2nd gear TCC switches.

QDM's are fault protected. If a relay or solenoid coil is shorted, having very low or zero resistance, or if the control side of the circuit is shorted to voltage, it would allow too much current into the QDM. The QDM senses this and the output turns "OFF" or its internal resistance increases to limit current flow and protect the QDM. The result is high output terminal voltage when it should be low. If the circuit from B+ or the component is open, or the control side of the circuit is shorted to ground, terminal voltage will be low, even when output is commanded "OFF." Either of these conditions is considered to be a QDM fault. *See **NOTE** below!

Each QDM has a separate fault line to indicate the presence of a current fault to the ECM's central processor. A "Scan" tool displays the status of each of these fault lines as "Low" = OK, "High" = Fault*. Because of the brake and 2nd gear switches in the TCC circuit, Code 26 is set under different conditions for QDM A and QDM B as follows:

- QDM A fault line = "High" for 20 seconds or more.
- QDM B fault line = "High" for 20 seconds or more and
  - Brake switch signal indicates brake switch is closed and 2nd gear state switch indicates transaxle is in 2nd or 3rd gear.

    OR
  - TCC is commanded "ON."

* **NOTE**: QDM B fault line on an automatic transaxle car will normally be "High" when the car is stopped. The ECM ignores the QDM B fault line except under conditions noted above.

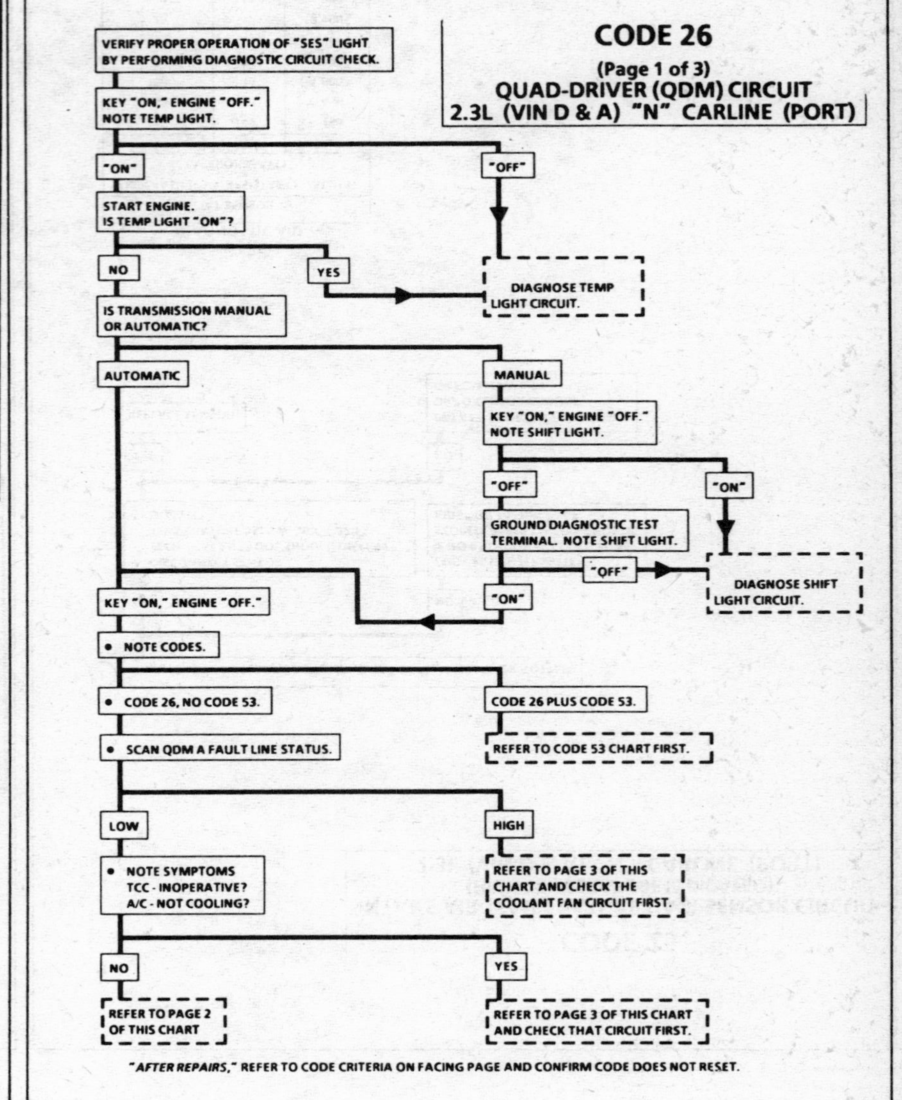

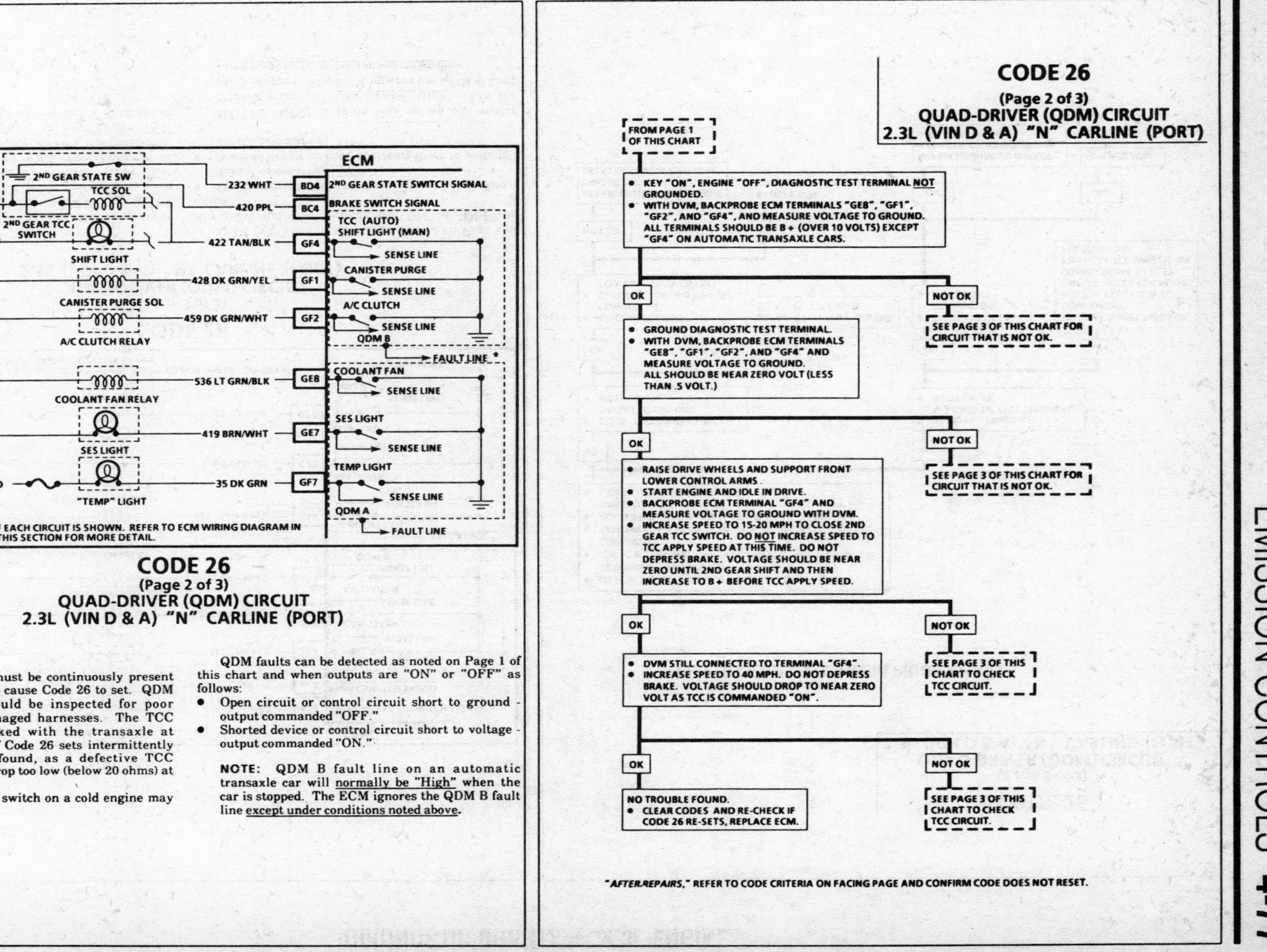

Diagnostic Aids:

Intermittent faults must be continuously present for at least 20 seconds to cause Code 26 to set. QDM controlled circuits should be inspected for poor terminal contact or damaged harnesses. The TCC circuit should be checked with the transaxle at operating temperature if Code 26 sets intermittently and no other cause is found, as a defective TCC solenoid resistance can drop too low (below 20 ohms) at high temperature.

A sticky second gear switch on a cold engine may cause Code 26.

QDM faults can be detected as noted on Page 1 of this chart and when outputs are "ON" or "OFF" as follows:

- Open circuit or control circuit short to ground - output commanded "OFF."
- Shorted device or control circuit short to voltage - output commanded "ON."

NOTE: QDM B fault line on an automatic transaxle car will normally be "High" when the car is stopped. The ECM ignores the QDM B fault line except under conditions noted above.

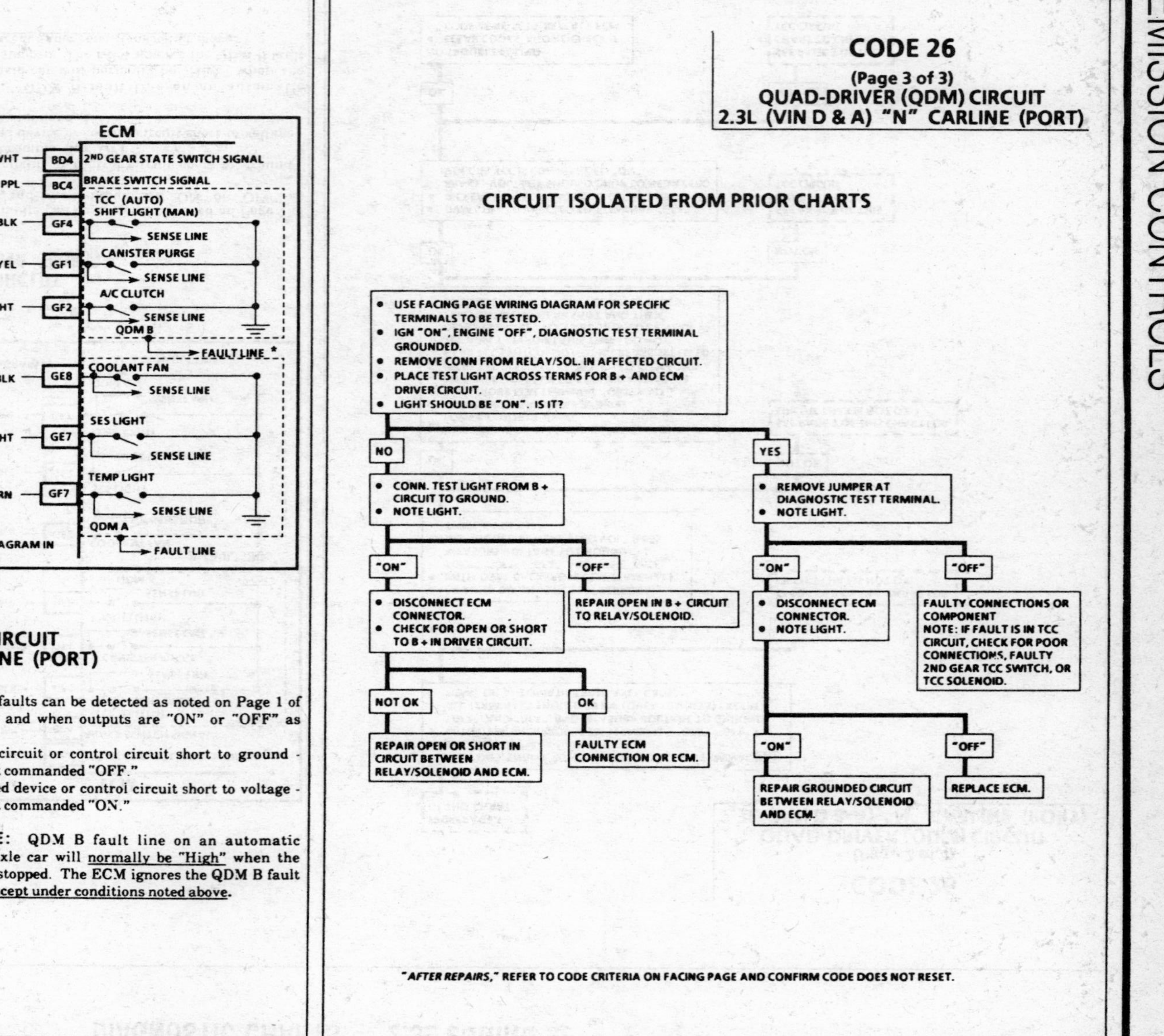

CODE 26

(Page 3 of 3)

QUAD-DRIVER (QDM) CIRCUIT
2.3L (VIN D & A) "N" CARLINE (PORT)

Diagnostic Aids:

Intermittent faults must be continuously present for at least 20 seconds to cause Code 26 to set. QDM controlled circuits should be inspected for poor terminal contact or damaged harnesses. The TCC circuit should be checked with the transaxle at operating temperature if Code 26 sets intermittently and no other cause is found, as a defective TCC solenoid resistance can drop too low (below 20 ohms) at high temperature.

QDM faults can be detected as noted on Page 1 of this chart and when outputs are "ON" or "OFF" as follows:

- Open circuit or control circuit short to ground - output commanded "OFF."
- Shorted device or control circuit short to voltage - output commanded "ON."

NOTE: QDM B fault line on an automatic transaxle car will normally be "High" when the car is stopped. The ECM ignores the QDM B fault line except under conditions noted above.

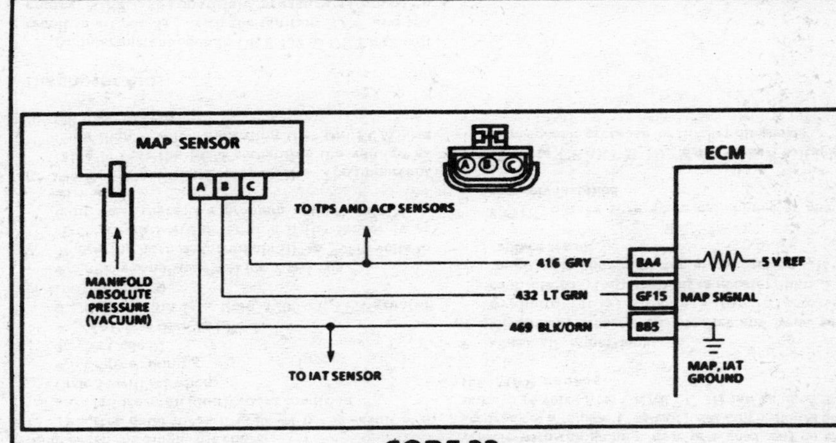

CODE 33

MANIFOLD ABSOLUTE PRESSURE (MAP) SENSOR CIRCUIT
(SIGNAL VOLTAGE HIGH - LOW VACUUM)
2.3L (VIN D & A) "N" CARLINE (PORT)

Circuit Description:

The Manifold Absolute Pressure (MAP) sensor responds to changes in manifold pressure (vacuum). The ECM receives this information as a signal voltage that will vary from about 1 to 1.5 volts at closed throttle (idle) to 4.5 - 4.8 volts at Wide Open Throttle (WOT) (low vacuum).

If the MAP sensor fails, the ECM will substitute a fixed MAP value and use the Throttle Position Sensor (TPS) to control fuel delivery.

Test Description: Number(s) below refer to circled number(s) on the diagnostic chart.

1. This step will determine if Code 33 is the result of a hard failure or an intermittent condition.
   Code 33 will set when:
   - MAP greater than 80 kPa
   - TPS less than 12%
   - VSS less than 1 mph
   - Code 21 or 22 not present
   - Above conditions met for 5 seconds
2. This step simulates conditions for a Code 34. If the ECM recognizes the change, the ECM and CKT 416 and CKT 432 are OK. If CKT 469 is open, there may also be a stored Code 23.

Diagnostic Aids:

With the ignition "ON" and the engine stopped, the manifold pressure is equal to atmospheric pressure and the signal voltage will be high. This information is used by the ECM as an indication of vehicle altitude. Comparison of this reading with a known good vehicle with the same sensor is a good way to check accuracy of a "suspect" sensor. Readings should be the same ± 4 volt.

A Code 33 will result if CKT 469 is open or if CKT 432 is shorted to voltage or to CKT 416.

If Code 33 is intermittent, refer to "Symptoms,"

- Check all connections.
- Disconnect sensor from bracket and twist sensor by hand (only) to check for intermittent connections. Output changes greater than .1 volt indicates a bad connector or connection. if OK, replace sensor.

NOTE: Make sure electrical connector remains securely fastened.

- Refer to CHART C-1D, MAP sensor voltage vs. atmospheric pressure for further diagnosis.

CODE 33

MANIFOLD ABSOLUTE PRESSURE (MAP) SENSOR CIRCUIT
(SIGNAL VOLTAGE HIGH - LOW VACUUM)
2.3L (VIN D & A) "N" CARLINE (PORT)

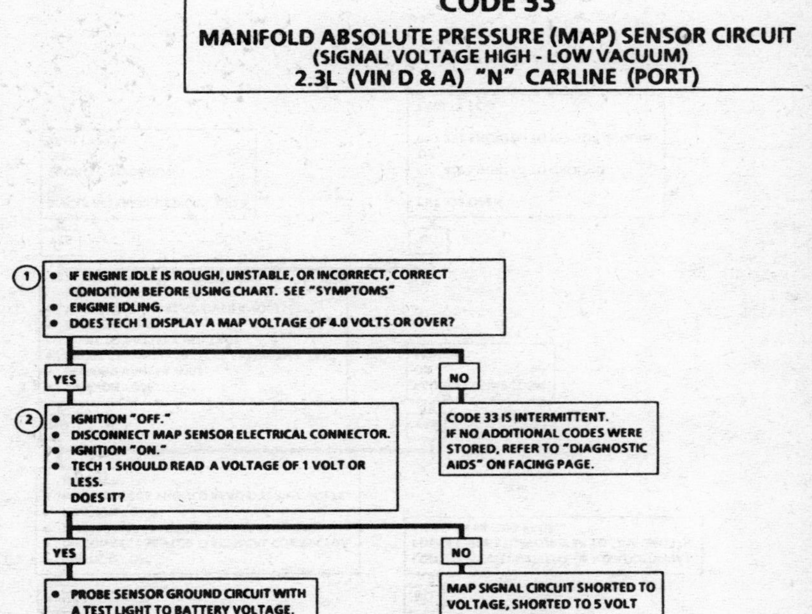

"AFTER REPAIRS," REFER TO CODE CRITERIA ON FACING PAGE AND CONFIRM CODE DOES NOT RESET.

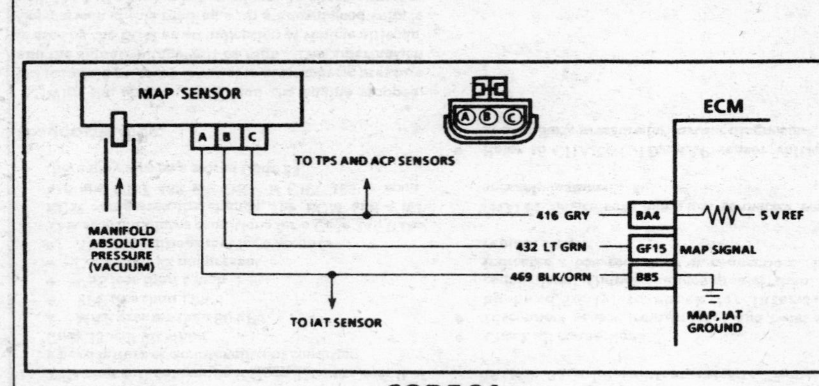

CODE 34

MANIFOLD ABSOLUTE PRESSURE (MAP) SENSOR CIRCUIT
(SIGNAL VOLTAGE LOW - HIGH VACUUM)
2.3L (VIN D & A) "N" CARLINE (PORT)

Circuit Description:

The Manifold Absolute Pressure (MAP) sensor responds to changes in manifold pressure (vacuum). The ECM receives this information as a signal voltage that will vary from about 1 to 1.5 volts at closed throttle (idle) to 4.5 - 4.8 volts at Wide Open Throttle (WOT) (low vacuum).

If the MAP sensor fails, the ECM will substitute a fixed MAP value and use the Throttle Position Sensor (TPS) to control fuel delivery.

Test Description: Numbers below refer to circled numbers on the diagnostic chart.

1. This step determines if Code 34 is the result of a hard failure or an intermittent condition.
   Code 34 will set when:
   - Engine running
   - No Code 21
   - MAP less than 14 kPa
   - Engine rpm less than 1200 or TPS greater than 15.2%
   - Above conditions met for .2 seconds
2. Jumpering harness terminals "B" to "C" (5 volts to signal circuit) will determine if the sensor is at fault, or if there is a problem with the ECM or wiring.
3. The Tech 1 may not display 5 volts. The important thing is that the ECM recognizes the voltage as more than 4 volts, indicating that the ECM and CKT 432 are OK.

Diagnostic Aids:

An intermittent open in CKT 432 or CKT 416 will result in a Code 34. With the ignition "ON" and the engine "OFF," the manifold pressure is equal to atmospheric pressure and the signal voltage will be high. This information is used by the ECM as an indication of vehicle altitude.

Comparison of this reading with a known good vehicle with the same sensor is a good way to check accuracy of a "suspect" sensor. Readings should be the same ± .4 volt. Also CHART C-1D can be used to test the MAP sensor.

- Check all connections
- Disconnect sensor from bracket and twist sensor by hand (only) to check for intermittent connections. Output changes greater than .1 volt indicates a bad connector or connection. If OK, replace sensor.

NOTE: Make sure electrical connector remains securely fastened.

- Refer to CHART C-1D, MAP sensor voltage vs. atmospheric pressure for further diagnosis.

CODE 34

MANIFOLD ABSOLUTE PRESSURE (MAP) SENSOR CIRCUIT
(SIGNAL VOLTAGE LOW - HIGH VACUUM)
2.3L (VIN D & A) "N" CARLINE (PORT)

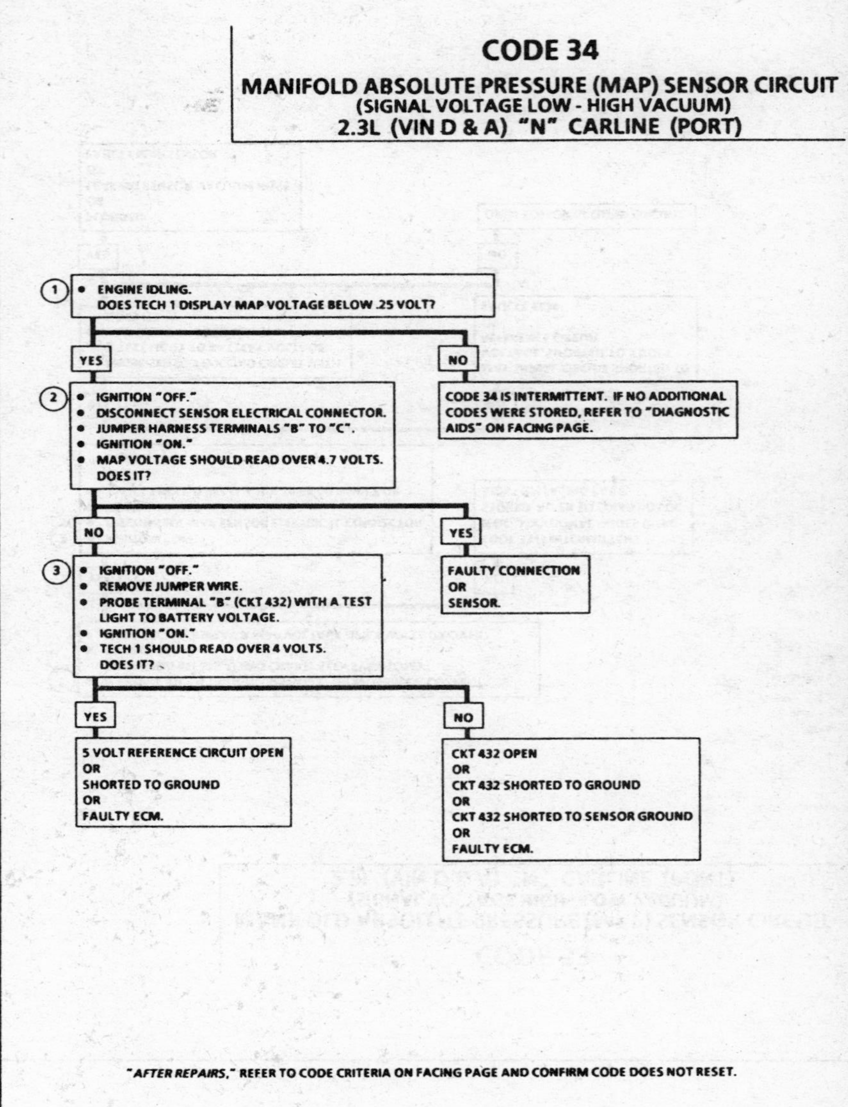

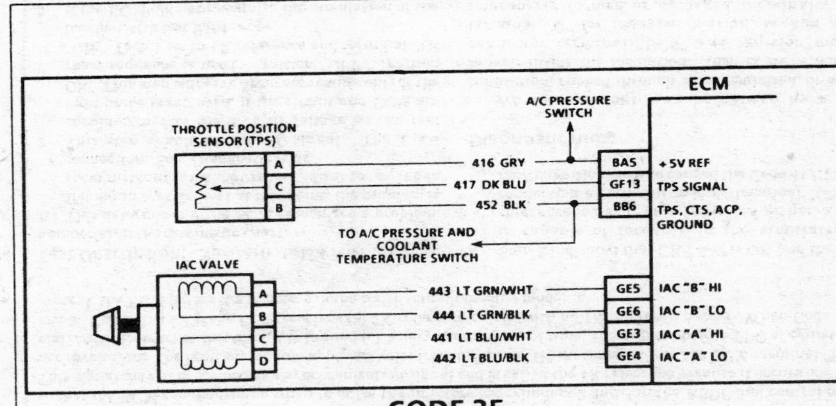

CODE 35

IDLE SPEED ERROR
2.3L (VIN D & A) "N" CARLINE (PORT)

Circuit Description:

The ECM controls idle speed to a calculated, "desired" rpm based on sensor inputs and actual engine rpm, determined by the time between successive 2X ignition reference pulses from the ignition module. The ECM uses 4 circuits to move an Idle Air Control (IAC) valve, which allows varying amounts of air flow into the intake manifold, controlling idle speed.

Code 35 sets when:

- Engine speed is at least 175 rpm more or less than "desired"
- TPS voltage indicates throttle is open less than 1%
- VSS indicates vehicle speed is less than 3 mph
- All above conditions are continuously met for 5 seconds or more
- IAC steps must be less than 10

Test Description: Number(s) below refer to circled number(s) on the diagnostic chart.

1. The Tech 1 is used to extend and retract the IAC valve. Valve movement is verified by an engine speed change. If no change in engine speed occurs, the valve can be retested when removed from the throttle body.
2. This step checks the quality of the IAC movement in Step 1. Between 700 rpm and about 1500 rpm, the engine speed should change smoothly with each flash of the tester light in both extend and retract. If the IAC valve is retracted beyond the control range (about 1500 rpm), it may take many flashes in the extend position before engine speed will begin to drop. This is normal on certain engines, fully extending IAC may cause engine stall. This may be normal.

   Step 1 verifies proper IAC valve operation while this step checks the IAC circuits. Each lamp on the node light should flash red and green while the IAC valve is cycled. While the sequence of color is not important if either light is "OFF" or does not flash red and green, check the circuits for faults, beginning with poor terminal contacts.

Diagnostic Aids:

Check for vacuum leaks, unconnected or brittle vacuum hoses, cuts, etc. Examine manifold and throttle body gaskets for proper seal. Check for cracked intake manifold. Check open, shorts, or poor connections to IAC valve in CKTs 441, 442, 443 and 444.

An open, short, or poor connection in CKTs 441, 442, 443, or 444 will result in improper idle control and may cause Code 35.

An IAC valve which is stopped and cannot respond to the ECM, a throttle stop screw which has been tampered with, or a damaged throttle body or linkage could cause Code 35. If no problem is found and Code resets, replace ECM.

CODE 35

IDLE SPEED ERROR
2.3L (VIN D & A) "N" CARLINE (PORT)

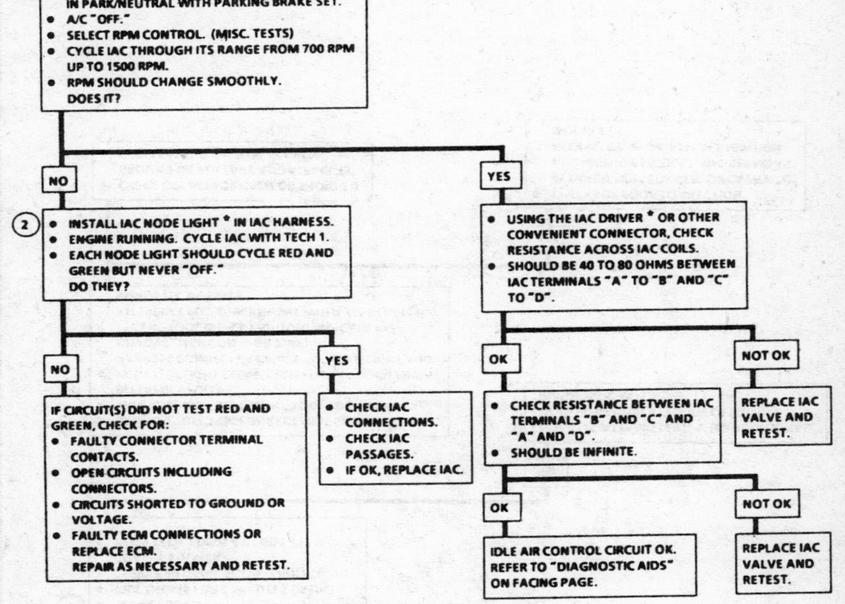

* IAC DRIVER AND NODE LIGHT REQUIRED KIT
222-L FROM: CONCEPT TECHNOLOGY, INC.
J 37027 FROM: KENT-MOORE, INC.

CLEAR CODES, CONFIRM "CLOSED LOOP" OPERATION, NO "SERVICE ENGINE SOON" LIGHT, PERFORM IAC RESET PROCEDURE PER APPLICABLE SERVICE MANUAL AND VERIFY CONTROLLED IDLE SPEED IS CORRECT.

"AFTER REPAIRS," **REFER TO CODE CRITERIA ON FACING PAGE AND CONFIRM CODE DOES NOT RESET.**

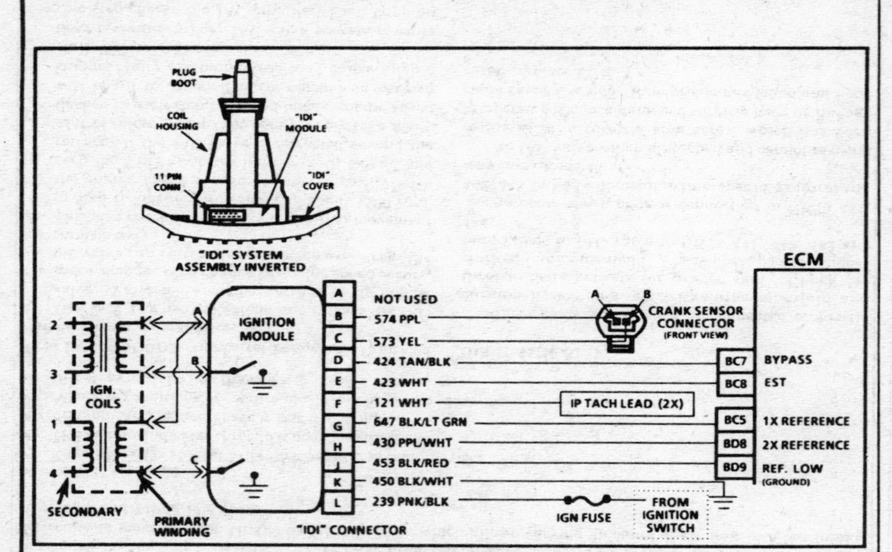

CODE 41

1X REFERENCE CIRCUIT
2.3L (VIN D & A) "N" CARLINE (PORT)

Circuit Description:

The ignition module sends a reference signal to the ECM once per revolution to indicate crankshaft position so that the ECM can determine when to pulse the injectors for cylinders 2 and 3 in the ASDF fuel control mode. This signal may be described as a synchronization signal and is called the 1X reference because it occurs one time per revolution. The ignition module applies 5 volts from terminal "G" through CKT 647 to ECM terminal "BC5" and in effect, switches this circuit to ground for a very short period of time, 125 degrees before TDC of cylinders 2 and 3. Code 41 is set if the ECM receives (8) 2X reference pulses with no 1X reference pulses. When Code 41 is present, the ECM pulses the injectors in the SSDF (simultaneous) mode.

Test Description: Number(s) below refer to circled number(s) on the diagnostic chart.

1. This determines if the ECM recognizes a problem. If it doesn't set Code 41 at this point, the problem is intermittent and could be due to a loose connection. See "Diagnostic Aids."
2. This step simulates the 1X signal. The ECM should recognize the drop in voltage as the test light probe is removed, if the circuit and ECM are OK. This step will give accurate results only if the chart sequence is used - ignition "OFF," ignition "ON," Tech 1 set to 1X reference and terminal "G" touched with test light probe.
3. If the ECM did not recognize the simulation of the 1X signal, CKT 647 may be open or shorted to ground or voltage. If CKT 647 is OK, the ECM is faulty.
4. Step 2 indicated that CKT 647 is OK and the ECM is capable of recognizing the simulated 1X reference pulse. This indicates either a poor connection at ignition module terminal "G" or a faulty ignition module caused the Code 41.

Diagnostic Aids:

An intermittent may be caused by a poor connection, rubbed through wire insulation, or a wire broken inside the insulation. Inspect ECM harness connector terminal "BC5" and ignition module terminal "G" for improper mating, broken locks, improperly formed or damaged terminals, poor terminal to wire connection and damaged harness.

CODE 41

1X REFERENCE CIRCUIT
2.3L (VIN D & A) "N" CARLINE (PORT)

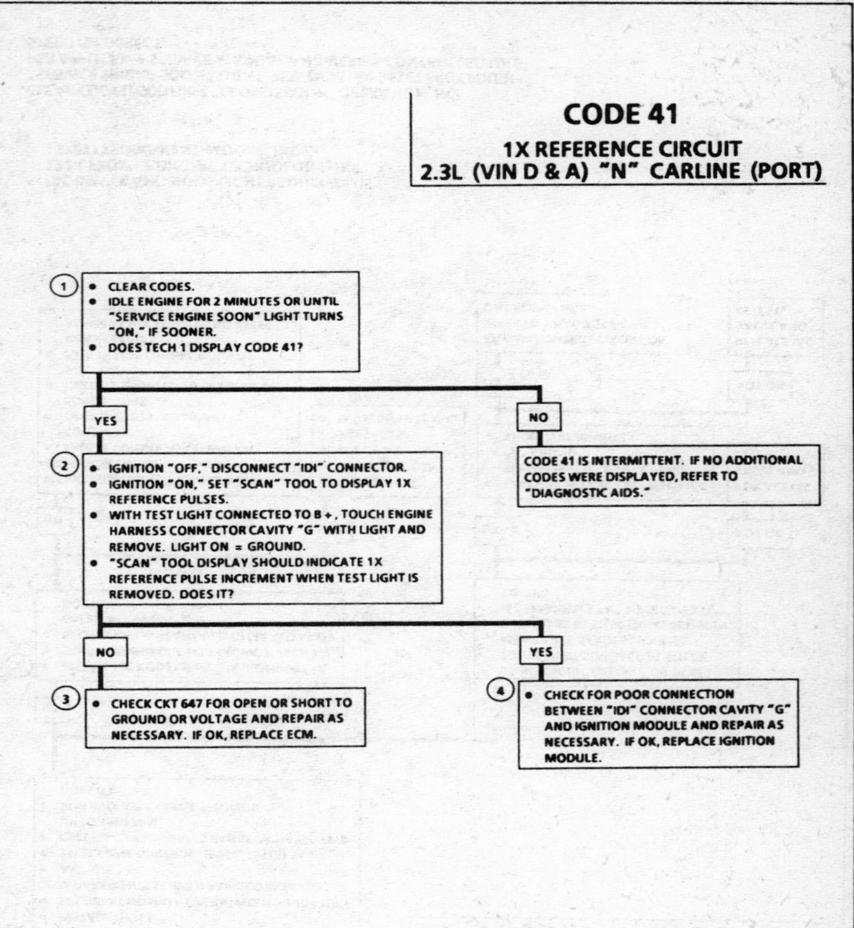

"AFTER REPAIRS," **REFER TO CODE CRITERIA ON FACING PAGE AND CONFIRM CODE DOES NOT RESET.**

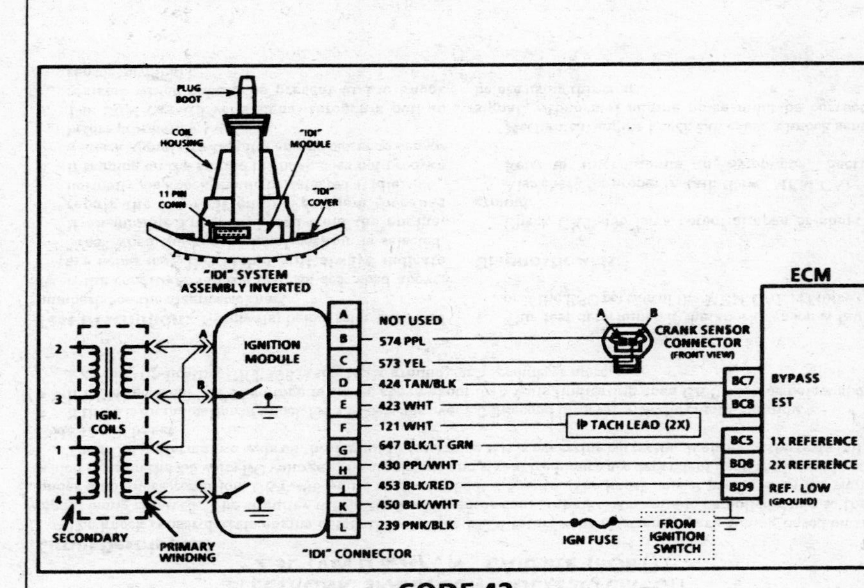

CODE 42

ELECTRONIC SPARK TIMING (EST) CIRCUIT 2.3L (VIN D & A) "N" CARLINE (PORT)

Circuit Description:

The ignition module sends a reference signal to the ECM when the engine is cranking or running. While the engine is under 700 rpm, the ignition module controls the ignition timing. When the engine speed exceeds 700 rpm, the ECM sends a 5 volts signal on the "bypass" CKT 424 to switch the timing to ECM control through the EST CKT 423. Engine will remain under EST control until rpm drops below 150.

An open or ground in the EST or "bypass" circuit will set a Code 42 and cause the engine to run on module or "bypass" timing. This will result in poor performance and poor fuel economy.

Test Description: Number(s) below refer to circled number(s) on the diagnostic chart.

1. Checks to see if ECM recognizes a problem. If it doesn't set Code 42 at this point, it is an intermittent problem and could be due to a loose connection.
2. With the ECM disconnected, the ohmmeter should be reading less than 500 ohms, which is the normal resistance of the ignition module. A higher resistance would indicate a fault in CKT 423, a poor ignition module connection or a faulty ignition module.
3. If the test light was "ON" when connected from 12 volts to ECM harness terminal "BC7", either CKT 423 is shorted to ground or the ignition module is faulty.
4. Checks to see if ignition module switches when the bypass circuit is energized by 12 volts through the test light.

   If the ignition module actually switches, the ohmmeter reading should shift to over 8000 ohms.
5. Disconnecting the ignition module should make the ohmmeter read as if it were monitoring an open circuit (infinite reading). If the ohmmeter has a reading other than infinite, CKT 423 is shorted to ground.

Diagnostic Aids:

An intermittent may be caused by a poor connection, rubbed through wire insulation, or a wire broken inside the insulation. Inspect ECM harness connectors for backed out terminals "BC7" or "BC8", improper mating, broken locks, improperly formed or damaged terminals, poor terminal to wire connection, and damaged harness.

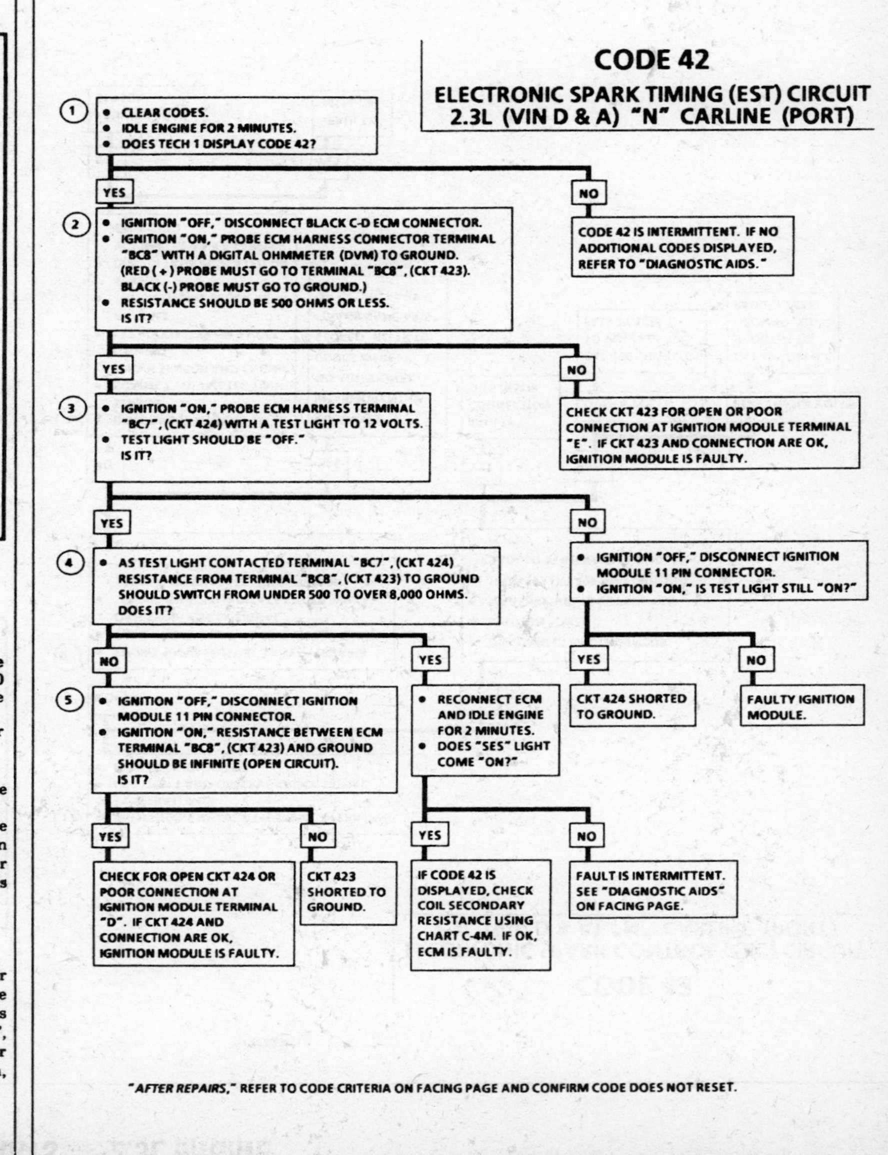

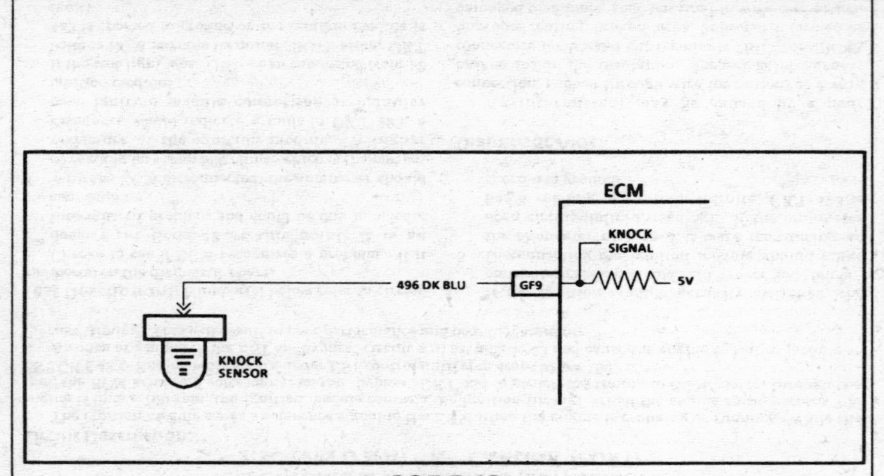

CODE 43

ELECTRONIC SPARK CONTROL (ESC) CIRCUIT 2.3L (VIN D & A) "N" CARLINE (PORT)

Circuit Description:

The knock sensor detects engine detonation and the ECM retards the electronic spark timing based on the signal being received. The circuitry within the knock sensor causes the ECM 5 volts to be pulled down so that, under a no knock condition, CKT 496 would measure about 2.5 volts. The knock sensor produces an AC signal which rides on the 2.5 volts DC voltage. The amplitude and signal frequency are dependent upon the knock level.

The ECM performs two tests on this circuit to determine if it is operating correctly. If either of the tests fail, a Code 43 will be set.

- If there is an indication of knock for 3.67 seconds over a 3.9 second interval with the engine running.
- If ECM terminal "GF9" voltage is either above about 3.75 volts (indicating open CKT 496), or below about 1.25 volts (indicating CKT 496 is shorted to ground) for 5 seconds or more.

Test Description: Number(s) below refer to circled number(s) on the diagnostic chart.

1. If the conditions for the test, as described above, are being met, the Tech 1 will always indicate "Yes" when the knock signal position is selected. If an audible knock is heard from the engine, repair the internal engine problem, because normally, no knock should be detected at idle.
2. If tapping on the engine lift hook does not produce a knock signal, try tapping engine closer to sensor before proceeding.
3. The ECM has a 5 volts signal through a pull-up resistor which should be present at the knock sensor terminal.
4. This test determines if the knock sensor is faulty or if the ESC portion of the MEM-CAL is faulty.

Diagnostic Aids:

Check CKT 496 for a potential open or short to ground.

Also check for proper installation of MEM-CAL.

Refer to "Intermittents" in "Symptoms," Section

Mechanical engine knock can cause a knock sensor signal. Abnormal engine noise must be corrected before using this chart.

CODE 43

ELECTRONIC SPARK CONTROL (ESC) CIRCUIT 2.3L (VIN D & A) "N" CARLINE (PORT)

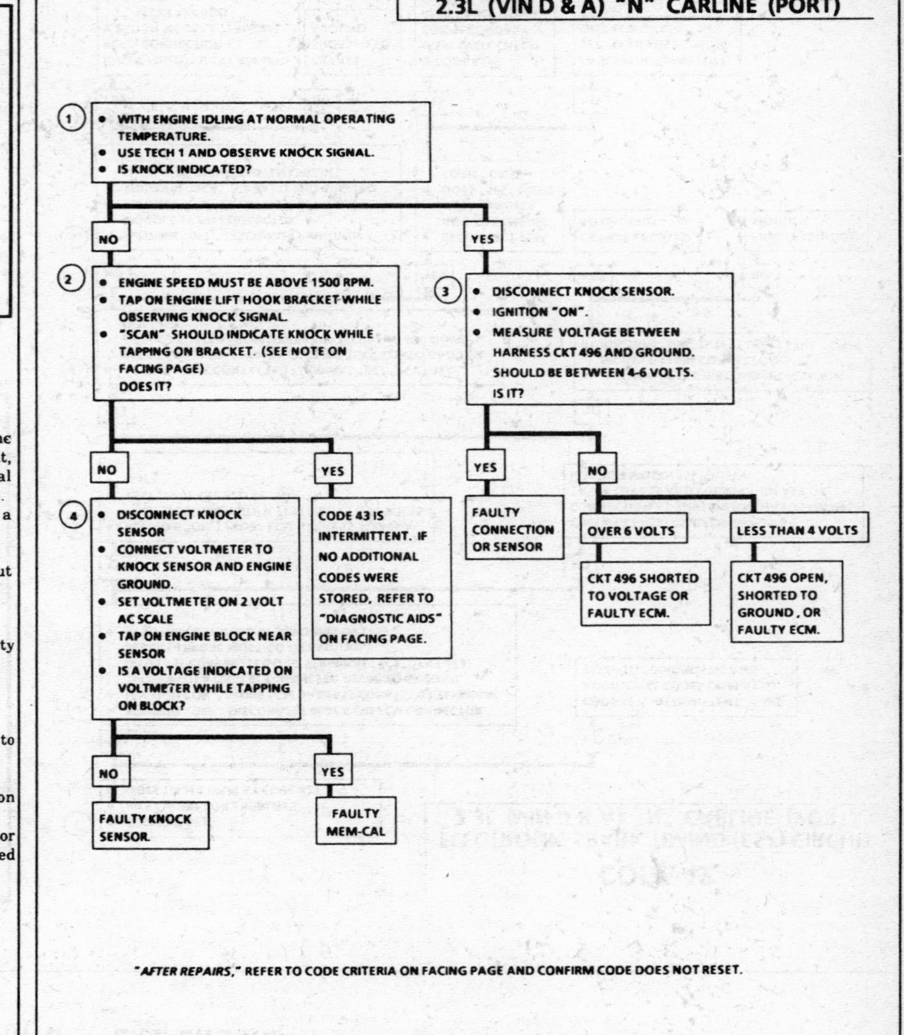

"AFTER REPAIRS," REFER TO CODE CRITERIA ON FACING PAGE AND CONFIRM CODE DOES NOT RESET.

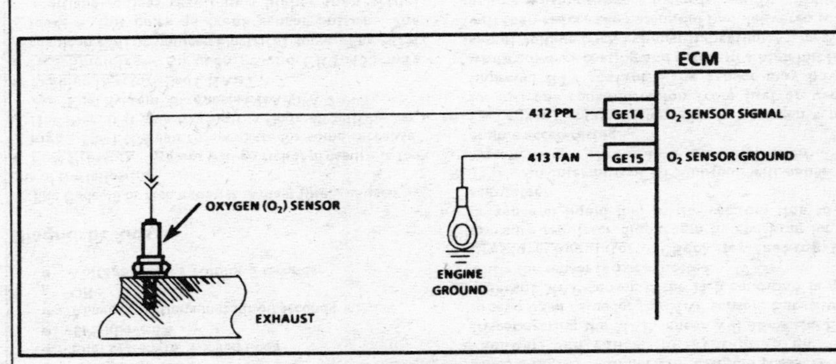

CODE 44

OXYGEN (O_2) SENSOR CIRCUIT
(LEAN EXHAUST INDICATED)
2.3L (VIN D & A) "N" CARLINE (PORT)

Circuit Description:

The ECM supplies a voltage of about .45 volt between terminals "GE14" and "GE15". (If measured with a 10 megohm digital voltmeter, this may read as low as .32 volt). The O_2 sensor varies the voltage within a range of about 1 volt if the exhaust is rich, down through about .10 volt if exhaust is lean.

The sensor is like an open circuit and produces no voltage when it is below 315°C (600°F). An open sensor circuit or cold sensor causes "Open Loop" operation.

Test Description: Number(s) below refer to the circled number(s) on the diagnostic chart.

1. Code 44 is set when the O_2 sensor signal voltage on CKT 412:
   - Remains below .3 volt for 50 seconds or more.
   - The system is operating in "Closed Loop."
   - No Code 33 or 34.
   - "Closed Loop" integrator active.
   - TPS above 5%.

Diagnostic Aids:

The Code 44 or lean exhaust is most likely caused by one of the following:

- Fuel Pressure - System will be lean if pressure is too low. It may be necessary to monitor fuel pressure while driving the car at various road speeds and/or loads to confirm. Refer to CHART A-7.
- MAP Sensor - An output that causes the ECM to sense a lower than normal manifold pressure (high vacuum) can cause the system to go lean. Disconnecting the MAP sensor will allow the ECM to substitute a fixed (default) value for the MAP sensor. If the rich condition is gone when the sensor is disconnected, substitute a known good sensor and recheck.
- Fuel Contamination - Water, even in small amounts, near the in-tank fuel pump inlet can be delivered to the injector. The water causes a lean exhaust and can set a Code 44.
- Sensor Harness - Sensor pigtail may be mispositioned and contacting the exhaust manifold.
- Engine Misfire - A cylinder misfire will result in unburned oxygen in the exhaust, which could cause Code 44. Refer to CHART C4-M and/or "Symptoms," Section "6E3-B".
- Cracked O_2 Sensor - A Cracked O_2 Sensor or poor ground at the sensor, could cause Code 44. Refer to "Symptoms," Section
- Plugged Fuel Filter - A plugged fuel filter can cause a lean condition, and can cause a Code 44 to set.

CODE 44

OXYGEN (O_2) SENSOR CIRCUIT
(LEAN EXHAUST INDICATED)
2.3L (VIN D & A) "N" CARLINE (PORT)

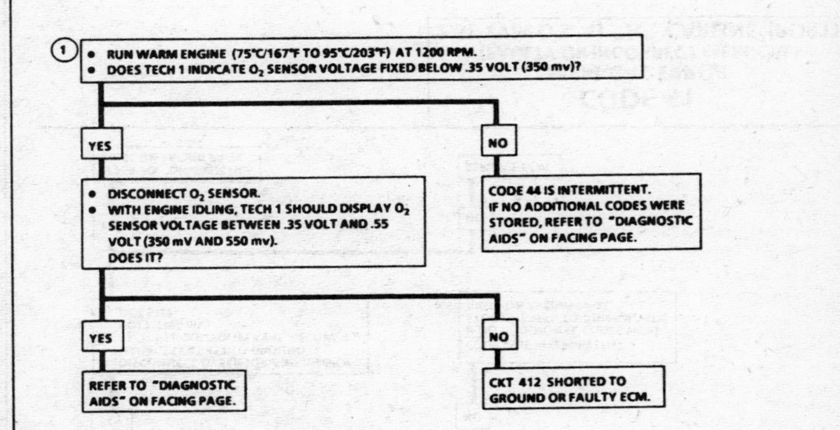

"AFTER REPAIRS," REFER TO CODE CRITERIA ON FACING PAGE AND CONFIRM CODE DOES NOT RESET.

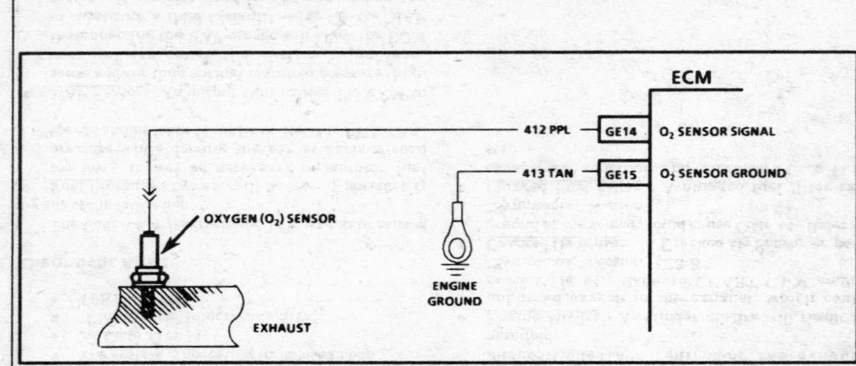

CODE 45

OXYGEN (O_2) SENSOR CIRCUIT (RICH EXHAUST INDICATED) 2.3L (VIN D & A) "N" CARLINE (PORT)

Circuit Description:

The ECM supplies a voltage of about .45 volt between terminals "GE14" and "GE15". (If measured with a 10 megohm digital voltmeter, this may read as low as .32 volt.) The O_2 sensor varies the voltage within a range of about 1 volt if the exhaust is rich, down through about .10 volt if exhaust is lean.

The sensor is like an open circuit and produces no voltage when it is below 315°C (600°F). An open sensor circuit or cold sensor causes "Open Loop" operation.

Test Description: Number(s) below refer to the circled number(s) on the diagnostic chart.

1. Code 45 is set when:
   - O_2 voltage is above .75 volt
   - No Code 33 or 34
   - Fuel system in "Closed Loop"
   - TPS above 5%
   - Above conditions met for 30 seconds
     OR
   - Voltage above 1 volt for 5 seconds

Diagnostic Aids:

The Code 45 or rich exhaust is most likely caused by one of the following:

- Fuel Pressure - System will go rich if pressure is too high. The ECM can compensate for some increase. However, if it gets too high, a Code 45 will be set. See "Fuel System" diagnosis CHART A-7.
- Leaking Injector - See CHART A-7.
- HEI Shielding - An open ground CKT 453 may result in EMI or induced electrical noise. The ECM looks at this noise as crank sensor pulses. The additional pulses result in a higher than actual engine speed signal. The ECM then delivers too much fuel causing system to go rich. Engine tachometer will also show higher than actual engine speed which can help in diagnosing this problem.
- Canister Purge - Check for fuel saturation. If full of fuel, check canister control and hoses.
- MAP Sensor - An output that causes the ECM to sense a higher than normal manifold pressure (low vacuum) can cause the system to go rich. Disconnecting the MAP sensor will allow the ECM to set a fixed value for the MAP sensor. Substitute a different MAP sensor if the rich condition is gone while the sensor is disconnected.
- Pressure Regulator - Check for leaking fuel pressure regulator diaphragm by checking for the presence of liquid fuel in the vacuum line to the regulator.
- TPS - An intermittent TPS output will cause the system to go rich due to a false indication of the engine accelerating.
- O_2 Sensor Contamination - Inspect oxygen sensor for silicone contamination from fuel or use of improper RTV sealant. The sensor may have a white powdery coating and result in a high but false signal voltage (rich exhaust indication). The ECM will then reduce the amount of fuel delivered to the engine causing a severe surge driveability problem.

CODE 45

OXYGEN (O_2) SENSOR CIRCUIT (RICH EXHAUST INDICATED) 2.3L (VIN D & A) "N" CARLINE (PORT)

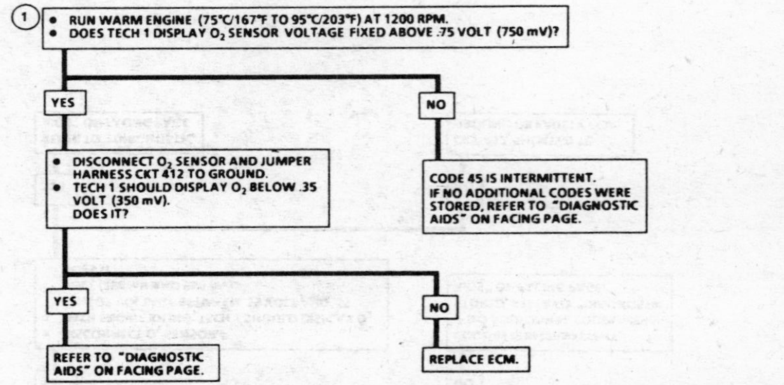

CODE 51

MEM-CAL ERROR (FAULTY OR INCORRECT MEM-CAL) 2.3L (VIN D & A) "N" CARLINE (PORT)

CHECK THAT ALL PINS ARE FULLY INSERTED IN THE SOCKET AND THAT MEM-CAL IS PROPERLY LATCHED. IF OK, REPLACE MEM-CAL, CLEAR MEMORY, AND RECHECK. IF CODE 51 REAPPEARS, REPLACE ECM.

NOTICE: TO PREVENT POSSIBLE ELECTROSTATIC DISCHARGE DAMAGE TO THE ECM OR MEM-CAL, DO NOT TOUCH THE COMPONENT LEADS, AND DO NOT REMOVE THE MEM CAL COVER OR THE INTEGRATED CIRCUIT FROM CARRIER.

"AFTER REPAIRS," REFER TO CODE CRITERIA ON FACING PAGE AND CONFIRM CODE DOES NOT RESET.

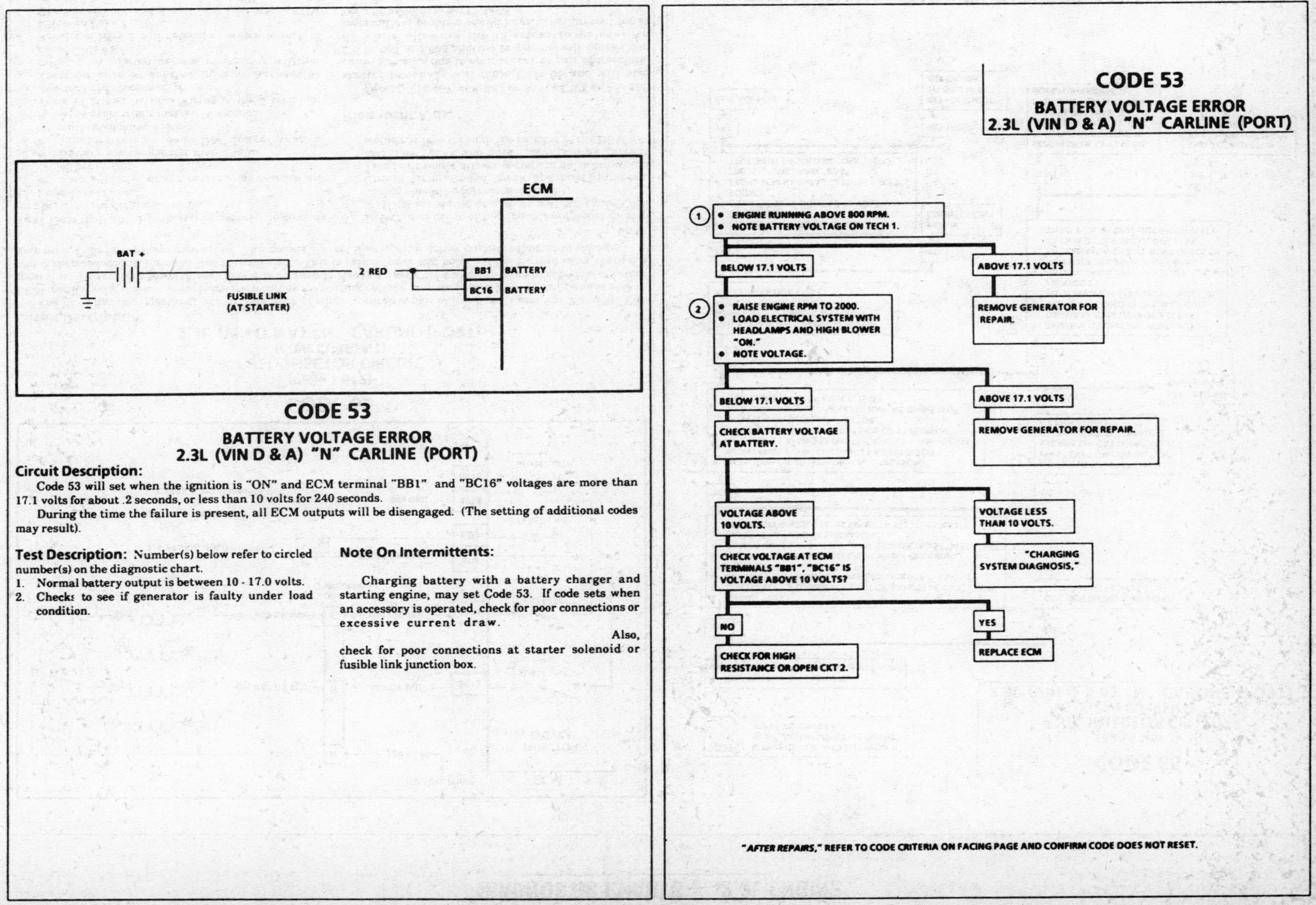

CODE 53

BATTERY VOLTAGE ERROR
2.3L (VIN D & A) "N" CARLINE (PORT)

Circuit Description:

Code 53 will set when the ignition is "ON" and ECM terminal "BB1" and "BC16" voltages are more than 17.1 volts for about .2 seconds, or less than 10 volts for 240 seconds.

During the time the failure is present, all ECM outputs will be disengaged. (The setting of additional codes may result).

Test Description: Number(s) below refer to circled number(s) on the diagnostic chart.

1. Normal battery output is between 10 - 17.0 volts.
2. Checks to see if generator is faulty under load condition.

Note On Intermittents:

Charging battery with a battery charger and starting engine, may set Code 53. If code sets when an accessory is operated, check for poor connections or excessive current draw.

Also, check for poor connections at starter solenoid or fusible link junction box.

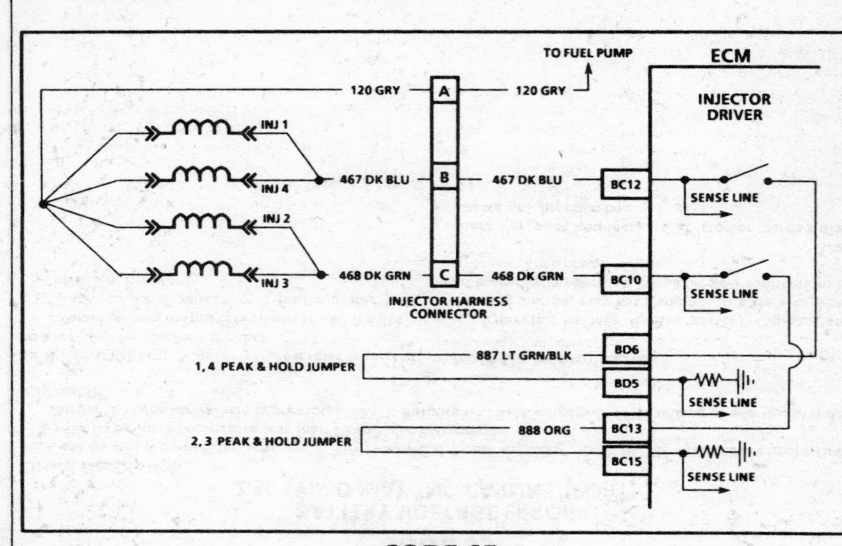

CODE 65

(Page 1 of 2)
FUEL INJECTOR CIRCUIT
(LOW CURRENT)
2.3L (VIN D & A) "N" CARLINE (PORT)

Circuit Description:

The ECM has two injector driver circuits, each of which controls a pair of injectors (1 and 4 or 2 and 3). The ECM monitors the current in each driver circuit by measuring voltage drop through a fixed resistor and is able to control it. The current through each driver is allowed to rise to a "peak" of 4 amps to quickly open the injectors and is then reduced to 1 amp to "hold" them open. This is called "peak and hold." If the current can't reach a 4 amp peak, Code 65 is set as noted below. This code is also set if an injector driver circuit is shorted to voltage.

Test Description: Number(s) below refer to circled number(s) on the diagnostic chart.

1. Code 65 sets when:
   - 4 amp injector driver current not reached on either circuit
   - Battery voltage greater than 9 volts.
   - Injectors commanded "ON" longer than a calibrated pulse width
   - Above conditions met for 10 seconds
2. Tests ECM and harness wiring to the 3 terminal injector harness connector.
3. Tests for open or shorted injector harness or injector. A shorted harness or injector will not cause Code 65.
4. Results of Step 2 will determine which branch to follow on Page 2.
5. Checks remainder of circuit from injectors to ECM as both harnesses were confirmed OK in Steps 2 and 3.
6. Determines cause of high resistance found in Step 3. (Low resistance or a short will not cause Code 65, but should be corrected if found.)
7. Checks for grounded "peak and hold" jumpers. This fault would allow injectors to pulse but would not allow "peak and hold" operation as current would not flow through the resistor in the ECM.

Diagnostic Aids:

Open CKTs 467, 468, 887 or 888 or CKT 467 or 468 shorted to voltage will cause Code 65 and will also cause a misfire due to an inoperative pair of injectors. CKTs 887 and 888 shorted to ground will cause Code 65 while allowing the injectors to pulse. An intermittent problem would have to be present for at least 20 seconds to set Code 65.

CODE 65

(Page 1 of 2)
FUEL INJECTOR CIRCUIT
(LOW CURRENT)
2.3L (VIN D & A) "N" CARLINE (PORT)

NOTE: IF ENGINE "CRANKS BUT WON'T RUN", DO NOT USE THIS CHART. REFER TO CHART A-3.

(1)
- IDLE ENGINE FOR 1 MINUTE.
- DOES TECH 1 INDICATE CODE 65?

NO → CODE IS INTERMITTENT REFER TO "DIAGNOSTIC AIDS."

YES ↓

(2)
- ENGINE "OFF".
- DISCONNECT 3 TERMINAL INJECTOR HARNESS CONNECTOR.
- CONNECT TEST LIGHT BETWEEN CAVITIES "A" AND "B", ECM SIDE.
- CHECK FOR BLINKING TEST LIGHT WHILE CRANKING.
- REPEAT CHECK WITH TEST LIGHT CONNECTED BETWEEN CAVITIES "A" AND "C", ECM SIDE.

TEST LIGHT SHOULD BLINK ON BOTH TESTS. DOES IT?

NO → (4) NOTE WHETHER TEST LIGHT WAS "OFF" ON ONE OR "ON" STEADY ON ONE IN PREVIOUS STEP AND REFER TO PAGE 2 OF THIS CHART. → SEE CODE 65 PAGE 2 OF 2.

YES ↓

(3)
- WITH DVM ON 200 OHM'S SCALE, MEASURE RESISTANCE BETWEEN CAVITIES A AND B (FOR INJECTORS 1,4) AND BETWEEN CAVITIES A AND C (FOR INJECTORS 2,3) ON INJECTOR SIDE OF 3 TERMINAL INJECTOR HARNESS CONNECTOR.

RESISTANCE SHOULD BE LESS THAN 1.5 OHMS (BUT NOT ZERO) ON EACH CHECK. IS IT?

NO → (6)
- REMOVE CRANKCASE VENTILATION OIL/AIR SEPARATOR FOR ACCESS.
- DISCONNECT INJECTORS IN CIRCUIT WITH HIGH (OR ZERO) RESISTANCE IN PREVIOUS STEP.
- WITH DVM ON 200 OHM SCALE, MEASURE RESISTANCE OF EACH INJECTOR (1,4 OR 2,3). RESISTANCE OF EACH INJECTOR SHOULD BE LESS THAN 3 OHMS (BUT NOT ZERO) IS IT?

  - YES → REPAIR OPEN CIRCUIT OR FAULTY CONNECTION IN INJECTOR HARNESS. (IF RESISTANCE WAS ZERO IN STEP 3, REPAIR SHORTED INJECTOR HARNESS).
  - NO → REPLACE INJECTOR WITH HIGH (OR ZERO) RESISTANCE.

YES ↓

(5) CHECK FOR POOR CONNECTIONS OR CRIMPS AT 3 TERMINAL INJECTOR HARNESS CONNECTOR. ARE CONNECTIONS OK?

NO → REPAIR CONNECTIONS

YES ↓

(7)
- DISCONNECT ECM BLACK C-D CONNECTOR.
- CONNECT TEST LIGHT TO 12 VOLT SOURCE.
- PROBE ECM HARNESS CAVITIES "BC13", "BC15", "BD5" AND "BD6".

TEST LIGHT SHOULD BE "OFF", IS IT?

- YES → REPLACE ECM.
- NO → REPAIR SHORT TO GND IN CKT 887 OR 888.

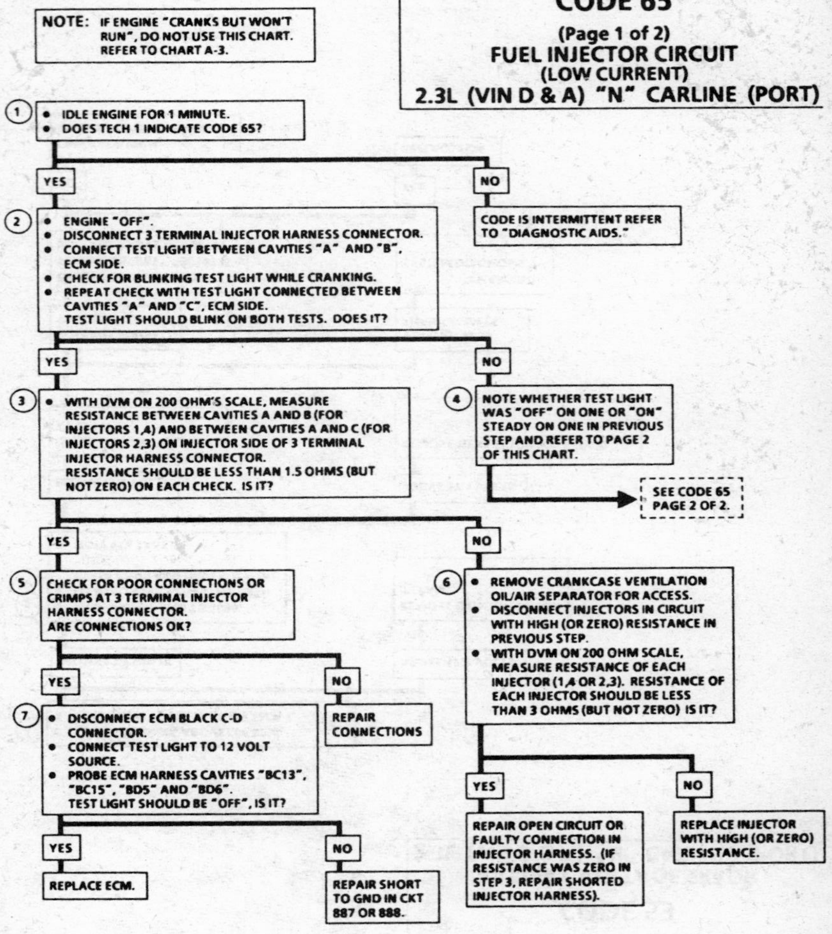

"AFTER REPAIRS," REFER TO CODE CRITERIA ON FACING PAGE AND CONFIRM CODE DOES NOT RESET.

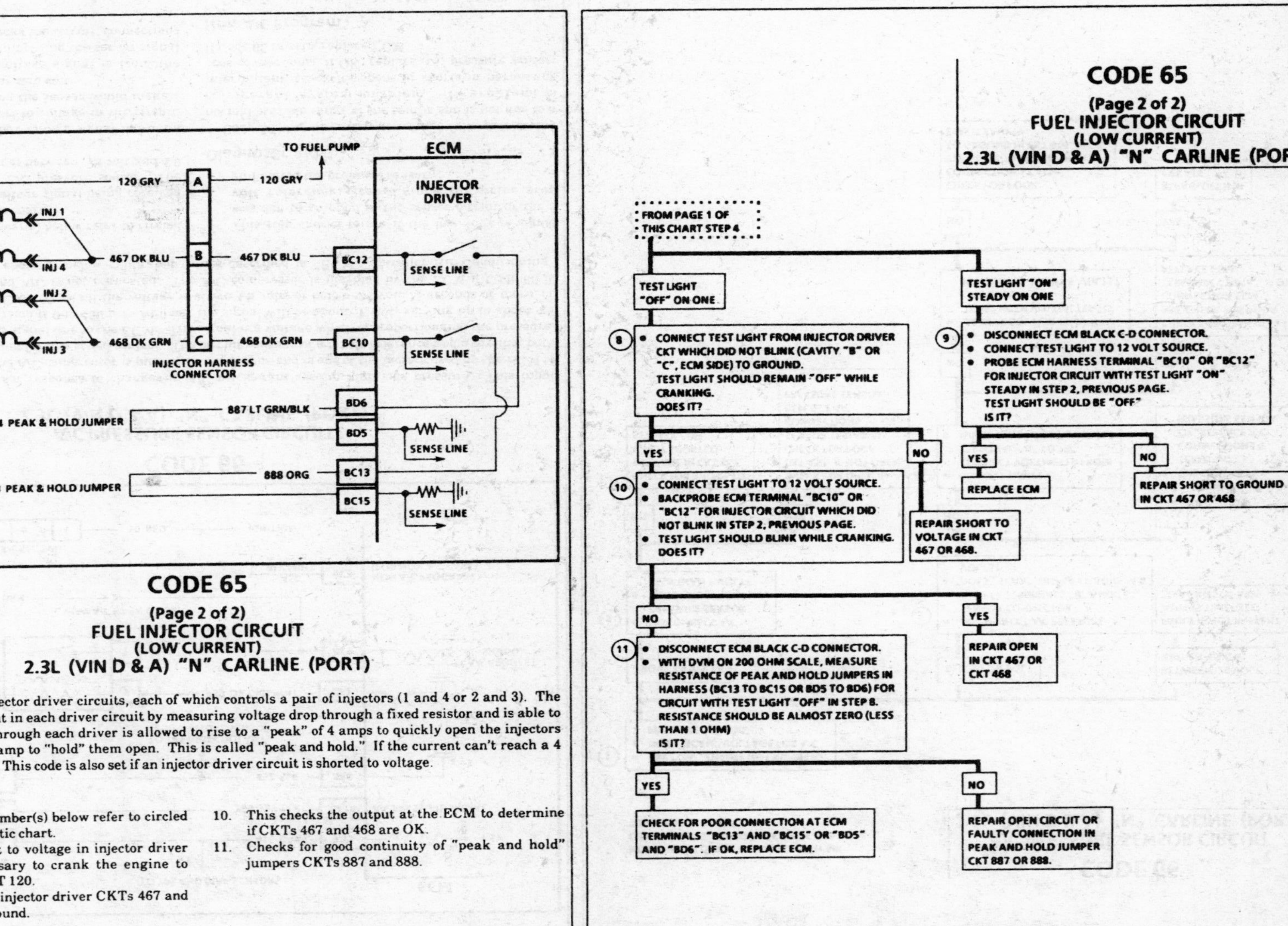

CODE 65

(Page 2 of 2)

FUEL INJECTOR CIRCUIT
(LOW CURRENT)
2.3L (VIN D & A) "N" CARLINE (PORT)

Circuit Description:

The ECM has two injector driver circuits, each of which controls a pair of injectors (1 and 4 or 2 and 3). The ECM monitors the current in each driver circuit by measuring voltage drop through a fixed resistor and is able to control it. The current through each driver is allowed to rise to a "peak" of 4 amps to quickly open the injectors and is then reduced to 1 amp to "hold" them open. This is called "peak and hold." If the current can't reach a 4 amp peak, Code 65 is set. This code is also set if an injector driver circuit is shorted to voltage.

Test Description: Number(s) below refer to circled number(s) on the diagnostic chart.

8. This checks for short to voltage in injector driver circuits. It is necessary to crank the engine to assure voltage to CKT 120.
9. Determines whether injector driver CKTs 467 and 468 are shorted to ground.
10. This checks the output at the ECM to determine if CKTs 467 and 468 are OK.
11. Checks for good continuity of "peak and hold" jumpers CKTs 887 and 888.

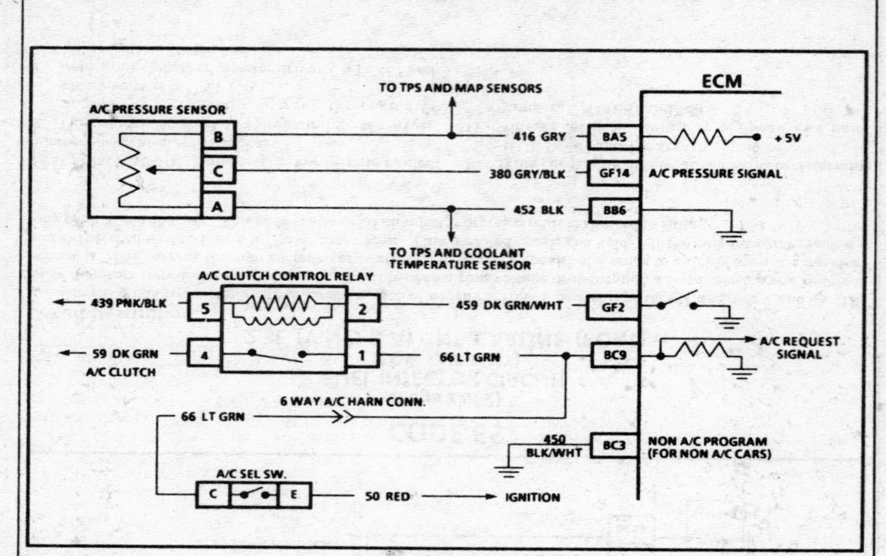

CODE 66

A/C PRESSURE SENSOR CIRCUIT 2.3L (VIN D & A) "N" CARLINE (PORT)

Circuit Description:

The A/C pressure sensor responds to changes in A/C refrigerant system high side pressure. This input indicates how much load the A/C compressor is putting on the engine and is one of the factors used by the ECM to determine IAC valve position for idle speed control. The circuit consists of a 5 volt reference and a ground, both provided by the ECM, and a signal line to the ECM. The signal is a voltage which is proportional to the pressure. The sensor's range of operation is 0 to 450 psi. At 0 psi, the signal will be about .1 volt, varying up to about 4.9 volts at 450 psi or above. Code 66 sets if the voltage is above 4.9 volts or below .28 volt 15 seconds or more, or voltage is above 4 volts and A/C is not requested. The A/C compressor is disabled by the ECM if Code 66 is present, or if pressure is above or below calibrated values described in "ECM Controller Air Conditioning"

Test Description: Number(s) below refer to circled number(s) on the diagnostic chart.

1. This step checks the voltage signal being received by the ECM from the A/C pressure sensor. The normal operating range is between .28 volt and 4.9 volts.
2. Checks to see if the high voltage signal is from a shorted sensor or a short to voltage in the circuit. Normally, disconnecting the sensor would make a normal circuit go to near zero volt.
3. Checks to see if low voltage signal is from the sensor or the circuit. Jumpering the sensor signal CKT 380 to 5 volts, checks the circuit, connections and ECM.
4. This step checks to see if the low voltage signal was due to an open in the sensor circuit or the 5 volt reference circuit since the prior step eliminated the pressure sensor.

Diagnostic Aids:

Code 66 sets when signal voltage falls outside the normal possible range of the sensor and is not due to a refrigerant system problem. If problem is intermittent, check for opens or shorts in harness or poor connections. If OK, replace A/C pressure sensor. If Code 66 re-sets, replace ECM.

Non-A/C Program

Code 66 will set on a Non-A/C car if CKT 450 to terminal "BC3" is open or shorted to B+.

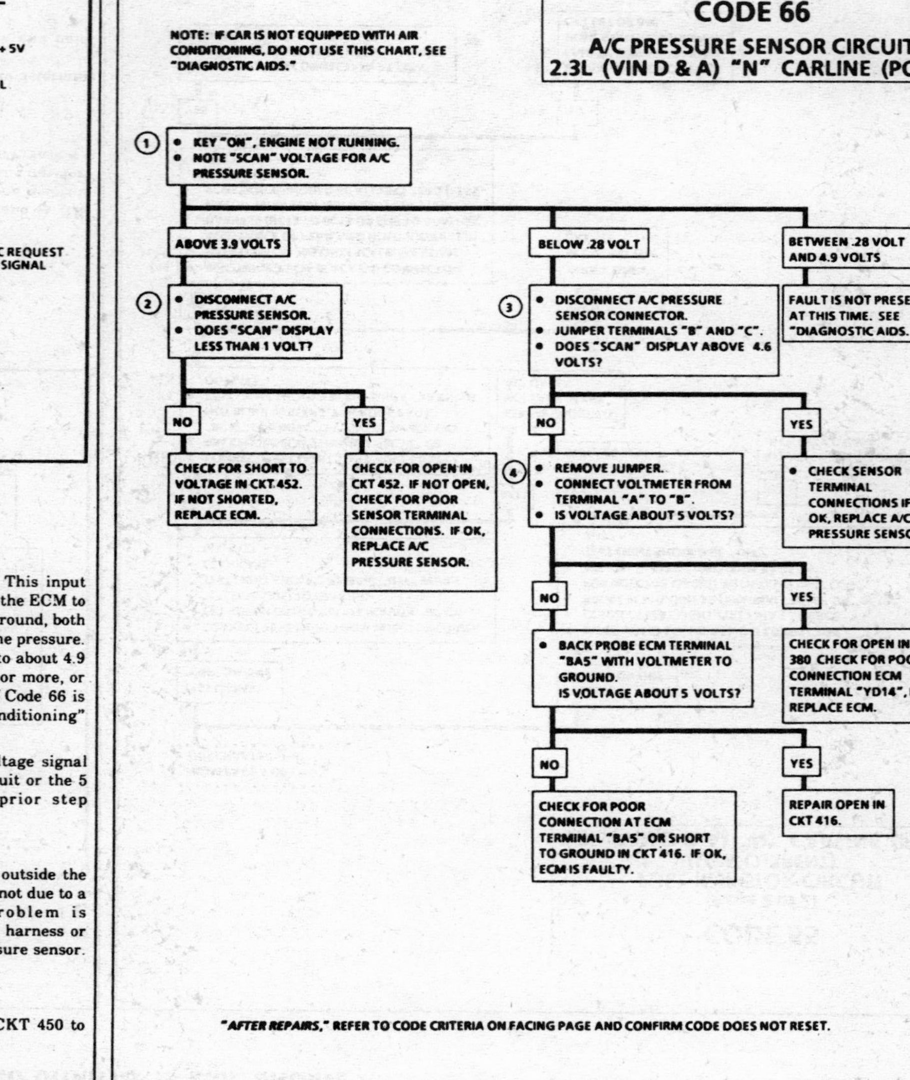

DIAGNOSTIC CHARTS — 2.3L ENGINE

ECM CONNECTOR "A"

PIN	PIN FUNCTION	CKT #	WIRE COLOR	COMPONENT CONNECTOR CAVITY	NORMAL VOLTAGES KEY "ON"	NORMAL VOLTAGES ENG RUN	CODES AFFECT	POSSIBLE SYMPTOMS FROM FAULTY CIRCUIT
BA1								
BA2								
BA3								
BA4	MAP, TPS 5 VOLT REFERENCE	416	GRY	MAP TERMINAL "C" TPS TERMINAL "A" BA4 SPLICE TO BA5	5V	5V	22 (10) 34 (10) 66 (10)	WITH BA4 AND BA5 OPEN OR SHORTED TO GROUND. STALLS, LACK OF PERFORMANCE.
BA5	MAP, TPS A/C PRESSURE SWITCH 5 VOLT REFERENCE	416	GRY	MAP TERMINAL "C" TPS TERMINAL "A" A/C PRESSURE TERMINAL "B"	5V	5V	22 (10) 34 (10) 66 (10)	WITH BA4 AND BA5 OPEN OR SHORTED TO GROUND. STALLS, LACK OF PERFORMANCE.
BA6	IGNITION FEED	439	PNK/BLK	15 WAY I/P TERMINAL "F" AND ECM 10 A FUSE	B +	B +		NO SES LIGHT, ENGINE CRANKS BUT WILL NOT START, NO DATA (8)
BA7								
BA8	SERIAL DATA	461	ORN	15 WAY I/P TERMINAL "J" AND ALDL TERMINAL "M"	2.5 (3)	2.5 (3)		NO SERIAL DATA "SCAN" TOOL WILL NOT WORK (10)
BA9								
BA10								
BA11	FUEL PUMP RELAY CONTROL	465	DK GRN/WHT	FUEL PUMP RELAY 5	0	B + (4)		LONG CRANKING TIME BEFORE ENGINE STARTS (8)
BA12	ECM GROUND	450	BLK/WHT	ENGINE BLOCK	0	0		

(1) Varies from .60 to battery voltage, depending on position of drive wheels.
(2) Battery voltage for first two seconds
(3) Varies
(4) Battery voltage when fuel pump is running
(5) Varies with temperature
(6) Reads battery voltage in gear
(7) Battery voltage when engine is cranking
(8) Open circuit
(9) Grounded circuit
(10) Open/Grounded circuit
(11) Less than 1 volt
* Less than .5 volt (500 mV)

ECM CONNECTOR "B"

PIN	PIN FUNCTION	CKT #	WIRE COLOR	COMPONENT CONNECTOR CAVITY	NORMAL VOLTAGES KEY "ON"	NORMAL VOLTAGES ENG RUN	CODES AFFECT	POSSIBLE SYMPTOMS FROM FAULTY CIRCUIT
BB1	BATTERY FEED	2	RED	FUSIBLE LINK AND B +	B +	B +		
BB2								
BB3								
BB4								
BB5	IAT, MAP GROUND	469	BLK/ORN	IAT TERMINAL "B" MAP TERMINAL "A"	0	0	23 (8) 33	STALLS AT IDLE. POOR PERFORMANCE.
BB6	TPS, CTS, A/C PRESS GROUND	452	BLK	TPS TERMINAL "B" CTS TERMINAL "A" A/C TERMINAL "A"	0	0	15 21 (8) 66	HESITATION ON ACCELERATION. LACK OF PERFORMANCE, EXHAUST ODOR
BB7								
BB8								
BB9	VEHICLE SPEED SENSOR (VSS) SIGNAL LOW	401	PPL	VEHICLE SPEED SENSOR (VSS) TERMINAL "A"	0	0	24 (10)	NO VSS SIGNAL INOPERATIVE SPEEDOMETER INOPERATIVE CRUISE CONTROL NO TCC
BB10	VEHICLE SPEED SENSOR (VSS) SIGNAL HIGH	400	YEL	VEHICLE SPEED SENSOR (VSS) TERMINAL "B"	(1) 0	(1) 0	24 (10)	NO VSS SIGNAL INOPERATIVE SPEEDOMETER INOPERATIVE CRUISE CONTROL NO TCC
BB11	ECM TO INSTRUMENT CLUSTER VSS	389	DK GRN	15 WAY I/P CLUSTER TERMINAL "R"	(1) 10.0	(1) 11.4		INOPERATIVE SPEEDOMETER/ODO
BB12								

(1) Varies from .60 to battery voltage, depending on position of drive wheels.
(2) Battery voltage for first two seconds
(3) Varies
(4) Battery voltage when fuel pump is running
(5) Varies with temperature
(6) Reads battery voltage in gear
(7) Battery voltage when engine is cranking
(8) Open circuit
(9) Grounded circuit
(10) Open/Grounded circuit
(11) Less than 1 volt
* Less than .5 volt (500 mV)

DIAGNOSTIC CHARTS — 2.3L ENGINE

ECM CONNECTOR "C"

PIN	PIN FUNCTION	CKT #	WIRE COLOR	COMPONENT CONNECTOR CAVITY	NORMAL VOLTAGES KEY "ON"	NORMAL VOLTAGES ENG RUN	CODES AFFECT	POSSIBLE SYMPTOMS FROM FAULTY CIRCUIT
BC1								
BC2								
BC3	NON A/C PROGRAM	450	BLK/WHT	GROUND	0	0		
BC4								
BC5	1X SIGNAL	647	BLK/LT GRN	IGNITION MODULE TERMINAL "G"		4.8 V	41 (10)	POOR PERFORMANCE
BC6								
BC7	IGNITION BYPASS	424	TAN/BLK	IGNITION MODULE TERMINAL "D"	0 *	5V	42 (10)	LACK OF POWER HUNTING IDLE, STALLING
BC8	ELECTRONIC SPARK TIMING (EST)	423	WHT	IGNITION MODULE TERMINAL "E"	0 *	0.2V	42 (10)	LACK OF POWER STALLS, SURGES
BC9	A/C REQUEST SIGNAL	66	LT GRN	A/C CONTROL RELAY TERMINAL "I"	0 * B +	0 * B +		INOPERATIVE A/C INCORRECT IDLE
BC10	INJECTOR DRIVER 2,3	468	DK GRN	INJ HARNESS CONNECTOR TERMINAL "C"	B +	B +	65 (10)	ROUGH IDLE, LACK OF PERFORMANCE, HARD TO START
BC11								
BC12	INJ DRIVER 1,4	467	DK BLU	INJ HARNESS CONNECTOR TERMINAL "B"	B +	B +	65 (10)	ROUGH IDLE, LACK OF PERFORMANCE, HARD TO START.
BC13	PEAK & HOLD INJ JUMPER 2,3	888	ORN	ECM TERMINAL "BC15"	0	0	65 (10)	ROUGH IDLE, LACK OF PERFORMANCE, HARD TO START.
BC14								
BC15	PEAK & HOLD INJ JUMPER 2,3	888	ORN	ECM TERMINAL "BC13"		0	65 (10)	ROUGH IDLE, LACK OF PERFORMANCE, HARD TO START
BC16	BATTERY FEED	2	RED	FUSIBLE LINK AND B +	B +	B +		

(1) Varies from .60 to battery voltage, depending on position of drive wheels.
(2) Battery voltage for first two seconds
(3) Varies
(4) Battery voltage when fuel pump is running
(5) Varies with temperature
(6) Reads battery voltage in gear
(7) Battery voltage when engine is cranking
(8) Open circuit
(9) Grounded circuit
(10) Open/Grounded circuit
(11) Less than 1 volt
* Less than .5 volt (500 mV)

ECM CONNECTOR "D"

PIN	PIN FUNCTION	CKT #	WIRE COLOR	COMPONENT CONNECTOR CAVITY	NORMAL VOLTAGES KEY "ON"	NORMAL VOLTAGES ENG RUN	CODES AFFECT	POSSIBLE SYMPTOMS FROM FAULTY CIRCUIT
BD1	ECM GROUND	551	TAN/WHT	ENGINE BLOCK	0	0		
BD2								
BD3								
BD4	2ND GEAR SWITCH A/T	232	WHT	TRANSAXLE ASM (AUTO) TERMINAL "C"	ON B + OFF 0	ON B + OFF 0		
BD5	PEAK AND HOLD INJ JUMPER 1 & 4	887	LT GRY/BLK	ECM TERMINAL "BD6"	0	0	65 (10)	ROUGH IDLE, LACK OF PERFORMANCE, HARD TO START.
BD6	PEAK AND HOLD INJ JUMPER 1 & 4	887	LT GRN/BLK	ECM TERMINAL "BD5"	0	0	65 (10)	ROUGH IDLE, LACK OF PERFORMANCE, HARD TO START.
BD7								
BD8	REFERENCE 2X SIGNAL	430	PPL/WHT	IGNITION MODULE TERMINAL "H"	0	2.9V		ENGINE CRANKS BUT WILL NOT START
BD9	REFERENCE IGNITION LOW	453	BLK/RED	IGNITION MODULE TERMINAL "J"	0*	0*		
BD10								
BD11								
BD12								
BD13	P/S PRESSURE SIGNAL	495	LT BLU/ORN	P/S PRESS SWITCH TERMINAL "A"	B +	ON B + OFF 0		
BD14								
BD15	3RD GEAR SWITCH A/T	438	DK GRN/WHT	TRANSAXLE ASM (AUTO) TERMINAL "B"	ON 0 OFF B +	ON 0 OFF B +		
BD16	PARK/NEUTRAL (P/N) SWITCH SIGNAL	434	ORN/BLK	PARK/NEUTRAL (P/N) SWITCH "A"	ON 0 OFF B +	ON 0 OFF B +		INCORRECT IDLE

(1) Varies from .60 to battery voltage, depending on position of drive wheels.
(2) Battery voltage for first two seconds
(3) Varies
(4) Battery voltage when fuel pump is running
(5) Varies with temperature
(6) Reads battery voltage in gear
(7) Battery voltage when engine is cranking
(8) Open circuit
(9) Grounded circuit
(10) Open/Grounded circuit
(11) Less than 1 volt
* Less than .5 volt (500 mV)

DIAGNOSTIC CHARTS — 2.3L ENGINE

ECM CONNECTOR "E"

PIN FUNCTION		CKT #	WIRE COLOR	COMPONENT CONNECTOR CAVITY	NORMAL VOLTAGES		CODES AFFECT	POSSIBLE SYMPTOMS FROM FAULTY CIRCUIT
					KEY "ON"	ENG RUN		
GE1								
GE2								
GE3	IAC COIL "A" HIGH	441	LT BLU/WHT	IAC VALVE "C"	0 OR B +	0 OR B +	35	INCORRECT IDLE SURGE
GE4	IAC COIL "A" LOW	442	LT BLU/BLK	IAC VALVE "D"	0 OR B +	0 OR B +	35	INCORRECT IDLE SURGE
GE5	IAC COIL "B" HIGH	443	LT GRN/WHT	IAC VALVE "A"	0 OR B +	0 OR B +	35	INCORRECT IDLE SURGE
GE6	IAC COIL "B" LOW	444	LT GRN/WHT	IAC VALVE "B"	0 OR B +	0 OR B +	35	INCORRECT IDLE SURGE
GE7	SERVICE ENGINE SOON LIGHT	419	BRN/WHT	I/P PRINTED CIRCUIT CONNECTOR "C"	0*	B +		NO SES LIGHT (8) SES LIGHT ON CONSTANTLY (9)
GE8	PRIMARY COOLING FAN (FAN 1) CONTROL RELAY	536	LT GRN/BLK	COOLANT FAN RELAY TERMINAL "5"	B +	ON 0 OFF B +		INOPERATIVE FAN 1 (8) FAN 1 RUNS ALL THE TIME (9)
GE9								
GE10								
GE11								
GE12	DIAGNOSTIC ENABLE TERMINAL	451	WHT/BLK	ALDL CONNECTOR "B"	5V (2)	5V (2)		SES LIGHT FLASHES ALL THE TIME (9) NO FIELD SERVICE MODE (8)
GE13								
GE14	OXYGEN (O_2) SENSOR SIGNAL	412	PPL	OXYGEN (O_2) SENSOR	.35 - .55	(3) .1 - .9	13 (8)	EXHAUST ODOR POOR PERFORMANCE
GE15	OXYGEN (O_2) SENSOR GROUND	413	TAN	ENGINE GROUND	0	0	13 (8)	EXHAUST ODOR POOR PERFORMANCE
GE16	COOLANT TEMP SENSOR SIGNAL	410	YEL	CTS "B"	1.8V (5)	1.8V (5)	14 (9) 15 (8)	LACK OF PERFORMANCE

(1) Varies from .60 to battery voltage, depending on position of drive wheels.
(2) Battery voltage for first two seconds
(3) Varies
(4) Battery voltage when fuel pump is running
(5) Varies with temperature
(6) Reads battery voltage in gear
(7) Battery voltage when engine is cranking
(8) Open circuit
(9) Grounded circuit
(10) Open/Grounded circuit
(11) Less than 1 volt
* Less than .5 volt (500 mV)

ECM CONNECTOR "F"

PIN FUNCTION		CKT #	WIRE COLOR	COMPONENT CONNECTOR CAVITY	NORMAL VOLTAGES		CODES AFFECT	POSSIBLE SYMPTOMS FROM FAULTY CIRCUIT
					KEY "ON"	ENG RUN		
GF1	CANISTER PURGE	428	DK GRN/YEL	CANISTER PURGE TERMINAL "B"	B +	.3		
GF2	A/C CLUTCH ENABLE	459	DK GRN/WHT	A/C CONTROL RELAY TERMINAL "2"	B +	OFF B + ON 0		A/C CLUTCH INOPERATIVE
GF3								
GF4	UPSHIFT LIGHT (MAN)	456	TAN/BLK	I/P CONNECTOR TERMINAL "N"				SHIFT LIGHT INOPERATIVE (8) SHIFT LIGHT "ON" (9)
GF4	TORQUE CONVERTER (AUTO)	422	TAN/BLK	TRANSAXLE CONNECTOR TERMINAL "D"	B +	OFF B + ON 0		TORQUE CONVERTER INOPERATIVE (8) TORQUE CONVERTER "ON" (9)
GF5								
GF6								
GF7	COOLANT TEMP LIGHT	35	DK GRN	15 WAY I/P CONNECTOR TERMINAL "L"	0*	B +	26 (8)	TEMP LIGHT OFF (8) TEMP LIGHT STAYS "ON" (9)
GF8								
GF9	ESC KNOCK SENSOR SIGNAL	496	DK BLU	KNOCK SENSOR	2.3V	2.3V	43 (10)	SPARK KNOCK
GF10								
GF11								
GF12								
GF13	TPS SIGNAL	417	DK BLU	TPS "C"	.54V	.54V	22 (10)	LACK OF PERFORMANCE
GF14	A/C PRESSURE SIGNAL	380	GRY/BLK	A/C PRESSURE SENSOR TERMINAL "C"	1.0V	1.0V	66 (10)	A/C CLUTCH INOPERATIVE
GF15	MAP SIGNAL	432	LT GRN	MAP SENSOR "B"	(2) 4.7V	(2) 1.4V	34 (10)	LACK OF PERFORMANCE ROUGH IDLE, SURGE
GF16	IAT SIGNAL	472	TAN	IAT SENSOR "A"	(3) 3.6V	(3) 1.5V	23 (8) 25 (9)	

(1) Varies from .60 to battery voltage, depending on position of drive wheels.
(2) Battery voltage for first two seconds
(3) Varies
(4) Battery voltage when fuel pump is running
(5) Varies with temperature
(6) Reads battery voltage in gear
(7) Battery voltage when engine is cranking
(8) Open circuit
(9) Grounded circuit
(10) Open/Grounded circuit
(11) Less than 1 volt
* Less than .5 volt (500 mV)

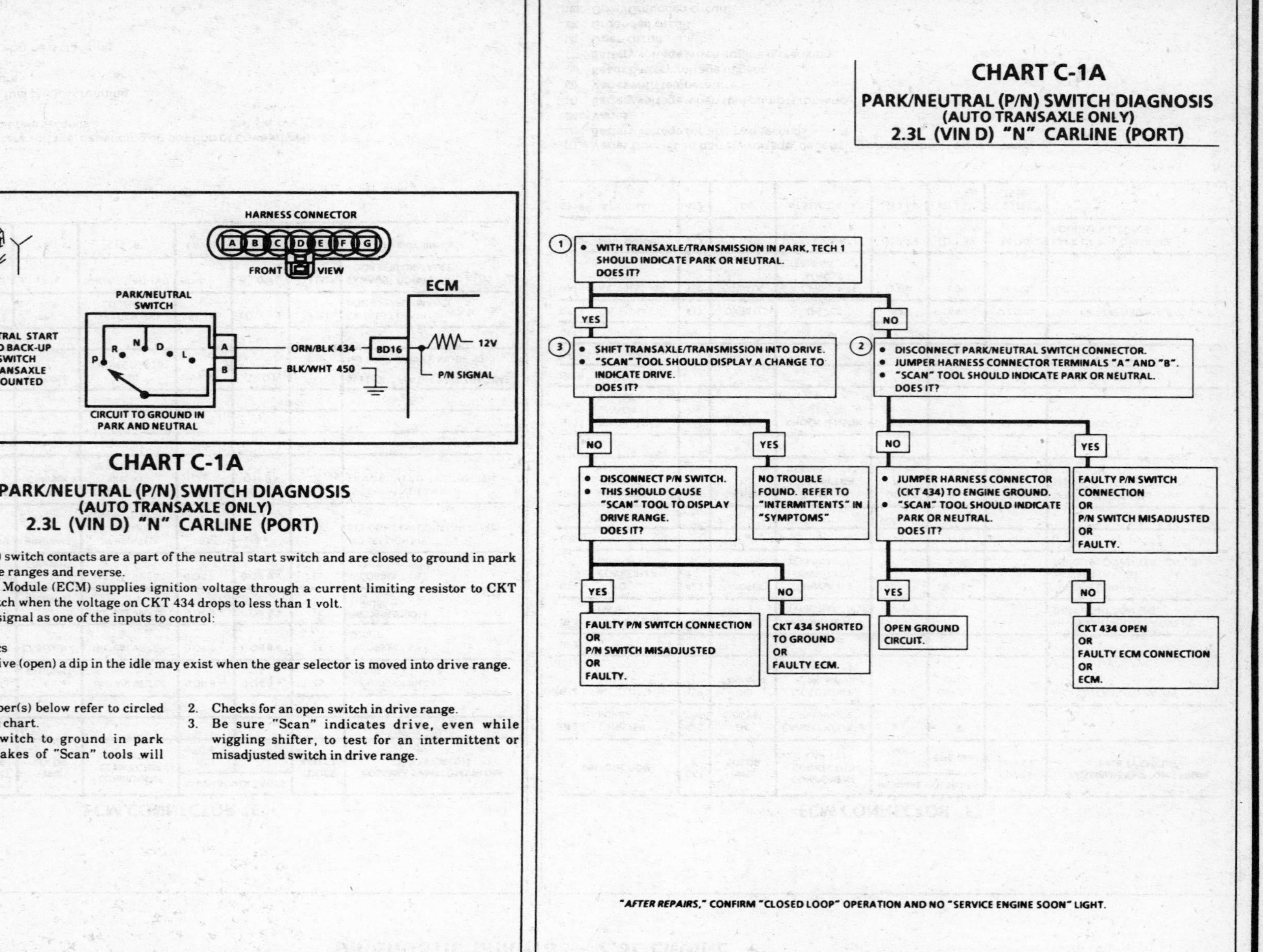

CHART C-1A

PARK/NEUTRAL (P/N) SWITCH DIAGNOSIS
(AUTO TRANSAXLE ONLY)
2.3L (VIN D) "N" CARLINE (PORT)

Circuit Description:

The Park/Neutral (P/N) switch contacts are a part of the neutral start switch and are closed to ground in park or neutral, and open in drive ranges and reverse.

The Electronic Control Module (ECM) supplies ignition voltage through a current limiting resistor to CKT 434 and senses a closed switch when the voltage on CKT 434 drops to less than 1 volt.

The ECM uses the P/N signal as one of the inputs to control:
Idle Air Control (IAC)
Code 24 VSS Diagnostics

If CKT 434 indicates drive (open) a dip in the idle may exist when the gear selector is moved into drive range.

Test Description: Number(s) below refer to circled number(s) on the diagnostic chart.

1. Checks for a closed switch to ground in park position. Different makes of "Scan" tools will display P/N differently.
2. Checks for an open switch in drive range.
3. Be sure "Scan" indicates drive, even while wiggling shifter, to test for an intermittent or misadjusted switch in drive range.

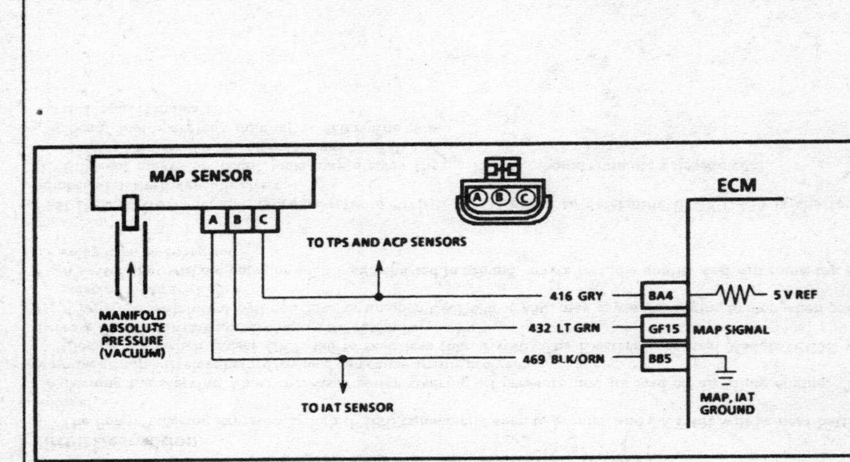

CHART C-1D

MANIFOLD ABSOLUTE PRESSURE (MAP) OUTPUT CHECK 2.3L (VIN D & A) "N" CARLINE (PORT)

Circuit Description:

The Manifold Absolute Pressure (MAP) sensor measures the changes in the intake manifold pressure which results from engine load (intake manifold vacuum) and rpm changes: and converts these into a voltage output. The ECM sends a 5 volt reference voltage to the MAP sensor. As the manifold pressure changed, the output voltage of the sensor also changes. By monitoring the sensor output voltage, the ECM knows the manifold pressure. A lower pressure (low voltage) output voltage will be about 1 - 2 volts at idle. While higher pressure (high voltage) output voltage will be about 4 - 4.8 at Wide Open Throttle (WOT). The MAP sensor is also used, under certain conditions, to measure barometric pressure, allowing the ECM to make adjustments for different altitudes. The ECM uses the map sensor to control fuel delivery and ignition timing.

Test Description: Number(s) below refer to circled number(s) on the diagnostic chart.

Important

- Be sure to use the same Diagnostic Test Equipment for all measurements.

1. When comparing Tech 1 readings to a known good vehicle, it is important to compare vehicles that use a MAP sensor having the same color insert or having the same "Hot Stamped" number. See figures on facing page.
2. Applying 34 kPa (10" Hg) vacuum to the MAP sensor should cause the voltage to change. Subtract second reading from the first. Voltage value should be greater than 1.5 volts. Upon applying vacuum to the sensor, the change in voltage should be instantaneous. A slow voltage change indicates a faulty sensor.
3. Check vacuum hose to sensor for leaking or restriction. Be sure no other vacuum devices are connected to the MAP hose.

   NOTICE: Make sure electrical connector remains securely fastened.

4. Disconnect sensor from bracket and twist sensor by hand (only) to check for intermittent connection. Output changes greater than .1 volt indicate a bad connector or connection. If OK, replace sensor.

CHART C-1D

MANIFOLD ABSOLUTE PRESSURE (MAP) OUTPUT CHECK 2.3L (VIN D & A) "N" CARLINE (PORT)

NOTE: THIS CHART ONLY APPLIES TO MAP SENSORS HAVING GREEN OR BLACK COLOR KEY INSERT (SEE BELOW).

(1)
- IGNITION "ON," ENGINE "OFF."
- TECH 1 SHOULD INDICATE A MAP SENSOR VOLTAGE.
- COMPARE THIS READING WITH THE READING OF A KNOWN GOOD VEHICLE. SEE FACING PAGE TEST DESCRIPTION, STEP 1.
- VOLTAGE READING SHOULD BE WITHIN, ± .4 VOLT.

IS IT?

YES → (2) / NO → REPLACE SENSOR.

(2)
- DISCONNECT AND PLUG VACUUM SOURCE TO MAP SENSOR.
- CONNECT A HAND VACUUM PUMP TO MAP SENSOR.
- START ENGINE.
- NOTE MAP SENSOR VOLTAGE.
- APPLY 34 kPa (10" Hg) OF VACUUM AND NOTE VOLTAGE CHANGE. SUBTRACT SECOND READING FROM THE FIRST. VOLTAGE VALUE SHOULD BE GREATER THAN 1.5 VOLTS.

IS IT?

YES → (3) NO TROUBLE FOUND. CHECK SENSOR VACUUM SOURCE FOR LEAKAGE OR RESTRICTION. BE SURE THIS SOURCE SUPPLIES VACUUM TO MAP SENSOR ONLY.

NO → (4) CHECK SENSOR CONNECTION. IF OK, REPLACE SENSOR.

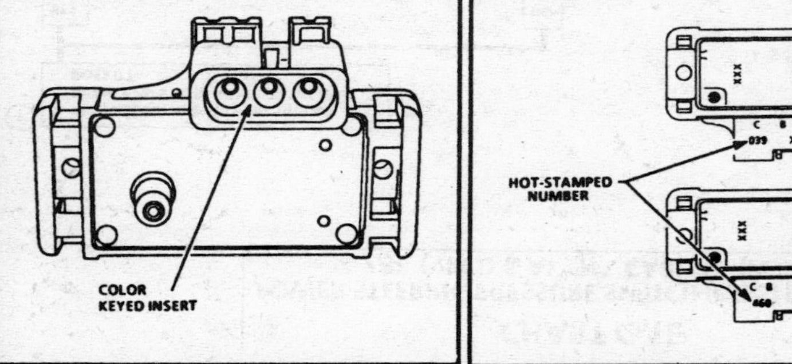

Figure 1 - Color Key Insert

Figure 2 - Hot-Stamped Number

"AFTER REPAIRS," CONFIRM "CLOSED LOOP" OPERATION AND NO "SERVICE ENGINE SOON" LIGHT.

POWER STEERING PRESSURE SWITCH (CLOSES WITH HIGH PRESSURE)
N.O.
A
B
495 LT BLU/ORN
450 BLK/WHT
ENGINE GROUND
BD13
ECM
12V
POWER STEERING PRESSURE SIGNAL
2-19-90
8S 4562-6E

CHART C-1E

POWER STEERING PRESSURE SWITCH (PSPS) DIAGNOSIS 2.3L (VIN D & A) "N" CARLINE (PORT)

Circuit Description:

The Power Steering Pressure Switch (PSPS) is normally open to ground, and CKT 495 will be near battery voltage.

Turning the steering wheel increases power steering oil pressure and its load on an idling engine. The pressure switch will close before the load can cause an idle problem.

Closing the switch causes CKT 495 to read less than 1 volt. The Electronic Control Module (ECM) will increase the idle air rate and disengage the A/C relay.

- A pressure switch that will not close, or an open CKT 495 or 450, may cause the engine to stop when power steering loads are high.
- A switch that will not open, or a CKT 495 shorted to ground, may affect idle quality and will cause the A/C relay to be de-energized.

Test Description: Number(s) below refer to circled number(s) on the diagnostic chart.

1. Different makes of "Scan" tools may display the state of this switch in different ways. Refer to "Scan" tool operator's manual to determine how this input is indicated.
2. Checks to determine if CKT 495 is shorted to ground.
3. This should simulate a closed switch.

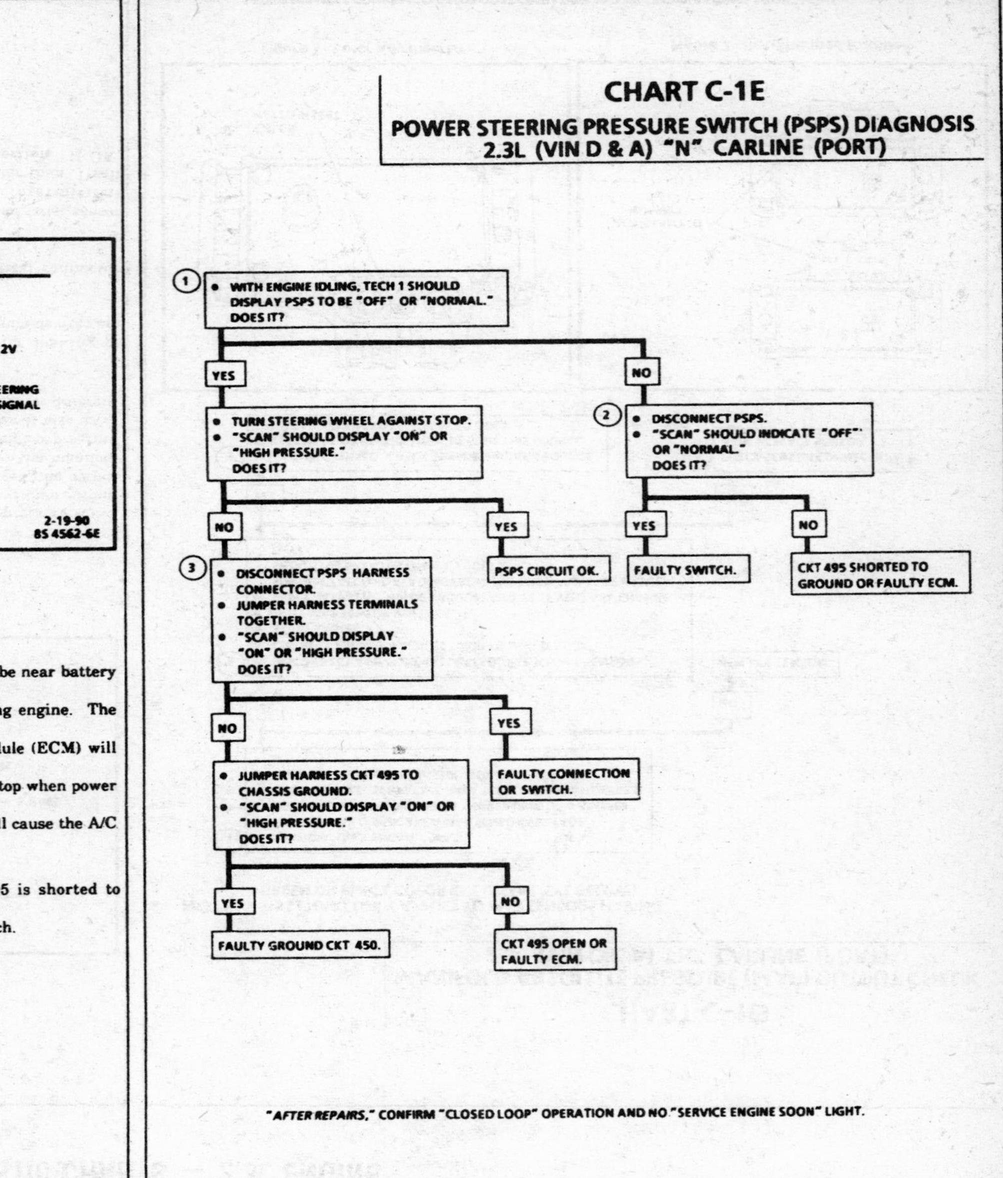

CHART C-2A

INJECTOR BALANCE TEST
2.3L (VIN D & A) "N" CARLINE (PORT)

The injector balance tester is a tool used to turn the injector on for a precise amount of time, thus spraying a measured amount of fuel into the manifold. This causes a drop in fuel rail pressure that we can record and compare between each injector. All injectors should have the same amount of pressure drop (± 10 kpa). Any injector with a pressure drop that is 10 kpa (or more) greater or less than the average drop of the other injectors should be considered faulty and replaced.

STEP 1

Engine "cool down" period (10 minutes) is necessary to avoid irregular readings due to "Hot Soak" fuel boiling. With ignition "OFF" connect fuel gauge J347301 or equivalent to fuel pressure tap. Wrap a shop towel around fitting while connecting gage to avoid fuel spillage.

Disconnect harness connectors at all injectors, and connect injector tester J-34730-3, or equivalent, to one injector. On Turbo equipped engines, use adaptor harness furnished with injector tester to energize injectors that are not accessible. Follow manufacturers instructions for use of adaptor harness. Ignition must be "OFF" at least 10 seconds to complete ECM shutdown cycle. Fuel pump should run about 2 seconds after ignition is turned "ON". At this point, insert clear tubing attached to vent valve into a suitable container and bleed air from gauge and hose to insure accurate gauge operation. Repeat this step until all air is bled from gauge.

STEP 2

Turn ignition "OFF" for 10 seconds and then "ON" again to get fuel pressure to its maximum. Record this initial pressure reading. Energize tester one time and note pressure drop at its lowest point (Disregard any slight pressure increase after drop hits low point.). By subtracting this second pressure reading from the initial pressure, we have the actual amount of injector pressure drop.

STEP 3

Repeat step 2 on each injector and compare the amount of drop. Usually, good injectors will have virtually the same drop. Retest any injector that has a pressure difference of 10kPa, either more or less than the average of the other injectors on the engine. Replace any injector that also fails the retest. If the pressure drop of all injectors is within 10kPa of this average, the injectors appear to be flowing properly. Reconnect them and review "Symptoms,"

NOTE: ***The entire test should <u>not</u> be repeated more than once without running the engine to prevent flooding. (This includes any retest on faulty injectors).***

CHART C-2A

INJECTOR BALANCE TEST
2.3L (VIN D & A) "N" CARLINE (PORT)

<u>NOTE</u>: If injectors are suspected of being dirty, they should be cleaned using an approved tool and procedure prior to performing this test. The fuel pressure test in CHART A-7, should be completed prior to this test.

Step 1. If engine is at operating temperature, allow a 10 minute "cool down" period then connect fuel pressure gauge and injector tester.

1. Ignition "OFF".
2. Connect fuel pressure gauge and injector tester.
3. Ignition "ON".
4. Bleed off air in gauge. Repeat until all air is bled from gauge.

Step 2. Run test:

1. Ignition "OFF" for 10 seconds.
2. Ignition "ON". Record gauge pressure. (Pressure must hold steady, if not see the Fuel System Diagnosis, CHART A-7
3. Turn injector "ON", by depressing button on injector tester, and note pressure at the instant the gauge needle stops.

Step 3.

1. Repeat step 2 on all injectors and record pressure drop on each. Retest injectors that appear faulty (any injectors that have a 10 kPa difference, either more or less, in pressure from the average). If no problem is found, review Symptoms

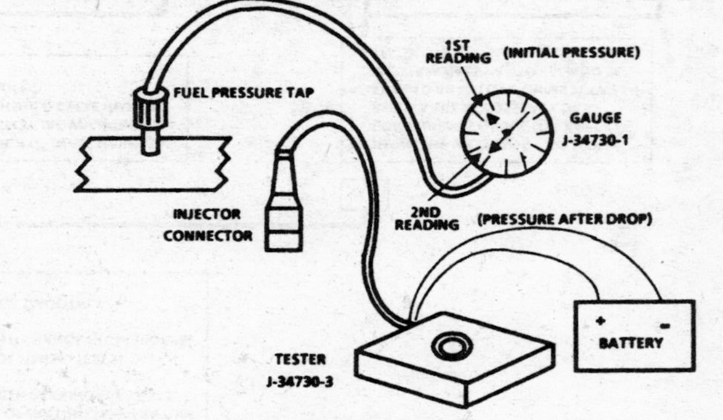

— EXAMPLE —

CYLINDER	1	2	3	4
1ST READING	225	225	225	225
2ND READING	100	115	100	85
AMOUNT OF DROP	125	110	125	140
	OK	FAULTY LEAN (TOO LITTLE) (FUEL DROP)	OK	FAULTY RICH (TOO MUCH) (FUEL DROP)

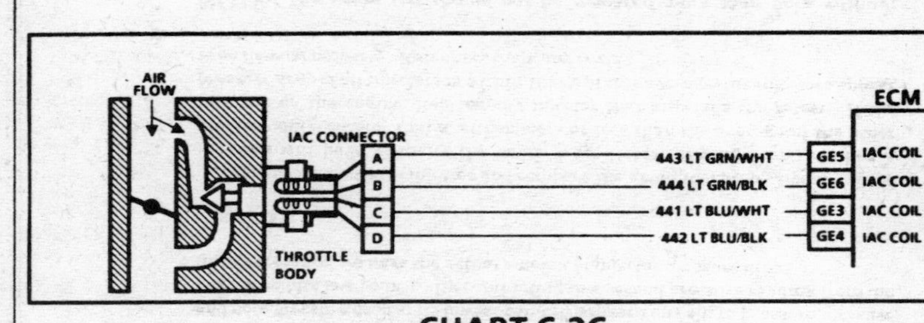

CHART C-2C

IDLE AIR CONTROL (IAC) VALVE CHECK 2.3L (VIN D & A) "N" CARLINE (PORT)

Circuit Description:

The ECM controls idle rpm with the IAC valve. To increase idle rpm, the ECM moves the IAC valve out, allowing more air to bypass the throttle plate. To decrease rpm, it moves the IAC valve in, reducing air flow bypassing the throttle plate. A Tech 1 will read the ECM commands to the IAC valve in counts. The higher the counts, the more air allowed (higher idle). The lower the counts, the less air allowed (lower idle).

Test Description: Number(s) below refer to circled number(s) on the diagnostic chart.

1. The Tech 1 is used to extend and retract the IAC valve. Valve movement is verified by an engine speed change. If no change in engine speed occurs, the valve can be retested when removed from the throttle body.
2. This step checks the quality of the IAC movement in Step 1. Between 700 rpm and about 1500 rpm, the engine speed should change smoothly with each flash of the tester light in both extend and retract. If the IAC valve is retracted beyond the control range (about 1500 rpm), it may take many flashes in the extend position before engine speed will begin to drop. This is normal on certain engines, fully extending IAC may cause engine stall. This may be normal.
   Step 1 verified proper IAC valve operation while this step checks IAC circuits. Each lamp on the node light should flash red and green while the IAC valve is cycled. While the sequence of color is not important if either light is "OFF" or does not flash red and green, check the circuits for faults, beginning with poor terminal contacts.

Diagnostic Aids:

A slow, unstable, or fast idle may be caused by a non-IAC system problem that cannot be overcome by the IAC valve. Out of control range IAC "Scan" tool counts will be above 60 if idle is too low, and zero counts if idle is too high. The following checks should be made to repair a non-IAC system problem.

- Vacuum Leak (High Idle) - If idle is too high, stop the engine. Fully extend (low) IAC with tester. Start engine. If Idle speed is above 800 rpm, locate and correct vacuum leak including PCV system. Also check for binding of throttle blade or linkage.
- System too lean (High Air/Fuel Ratio) - Idle speed may be too high or too low. Engine speed may vary up and down and disconnecting IAC does not help. Code 44 may be set. "Scan" O_2 voltage will be less than 300 mV (.3 volt.) Check for low regulated fuel pressure, water in the fuel or a restricted injector.
- System too rich (Low Air/Fuel Ratio) - The idle speed will be too low. "Scan" tool IAC counts will usually be above 80. System is obviously rich and may exhibit black smoke exhaust.
  "Scan" tool O_2 voltage will be fixed above 800 mV (.8 volt). Check for high fuel pressure, leaking or sticking injector. Silicone contaminated O_2 sensor will "Scan" an O_2 voltage slow to respond.
- Throttle Body - Remove IAC and inspect bore for foreign material.
- Refer to "Rough, Unstable, Incorrect Idle or Stalling" in "Symptoms," Section
- If intermittent poor driveability or idle symptoms are resolved by disconnecting the IAC, carefully recheck connections, valve terminal resistance, or replace IAC.

CHART C-2C

IDLE AIR CONTROL (IAC) VALVE CHECK 2.3L (VIN D & A) "N" CARLINE (PORT)

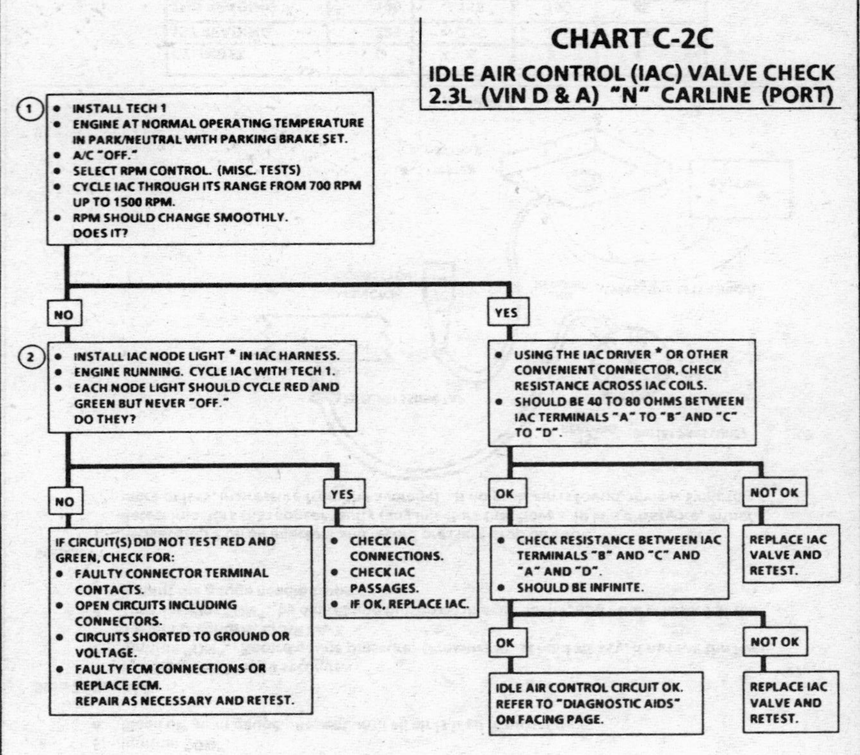

* IAC DRIVER AND NODE LIGHT REQUIRED KIT
222-L FROM: CONCEPT TECHNOLOGY, INC.
J 37027 FROM: KENT-MOORE, INC.

CLEAR CODES, CONFIRM "CLOSED LOOP" OPERATION, NO "SERVICE ENGINE SOON" LIGHT, PERFORM IAC RESET PROCEDURE PER APPLICABLE SERVICE MANUAL AND VERIFY CONTROLLED IDLE SPEED IS CORRECT.

"AFTER REPAIRS," CONFIRM "CLOSED LOOP" OPERATION AND NO "SERVICE ENGINE SOON" LIGHT.

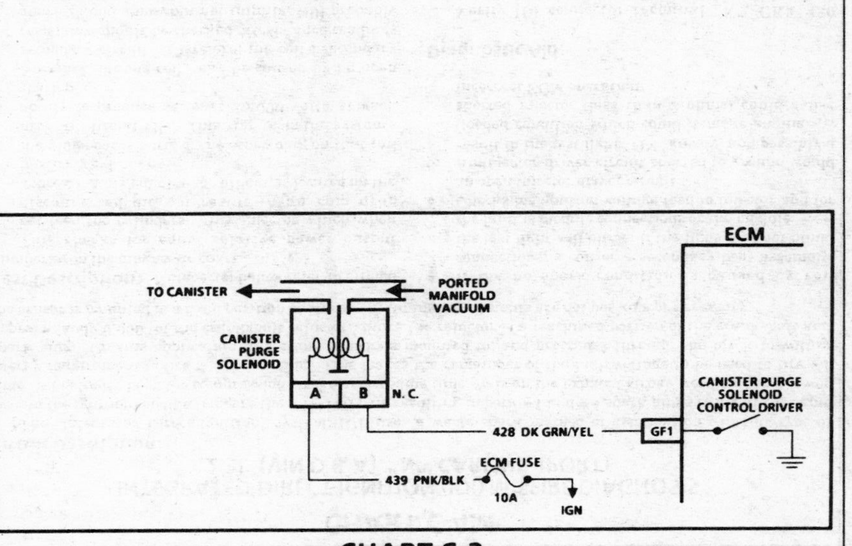

CHART C-3

CANISTER PURGE VALVE CHECK
2.3L (VIN D & A) "N" CARLINE (PORT)

Circuit Description:

Canister purge is controlled by a solenoid that allows manifold and/or ported vacuum to purge the canister when energized. The Electronic Control Module (ECM) supplies a ground to energize the solenoid (purge "ON"). The purge solenoid control by the ECM is pulse width modulated (turned "ON" and "OFF" several times a second). The duty cycle (pulse width) is determined by "Closed Loop" feed back from the O_2 sensor. The duty cycle is calculated by the ECM and the output commanded when the following conditions have been met:

- Engine run time after start more than 65 seconds
- Coolant temperature above 56°C

Also, if the diagnostic "test" terminal is grounded with the engine stopped, the purge solenoid is energized (purge "ON").

Test Description: Number(s) below refer to circled number(s) on the diagnostic chart.

1. Checks to see if the solenoid is opened or closed. The solenoid is normally de-energized in this step, so it should be closed.
2. Checks to determine if solenoid was open due to electrical circuit problem or defective solenoid.
3. Completes functional check by grounding "test" terminal. This should normally energize the solenoid opening the valve which should allow the vacuum to drop (purge "ON").

Diagnostic Aids:

Make a visual check of vacuum hose(s). Check throttle body for possible cracked, broken, or plugged vacuum block. Check engine for possible mechanical problem.

CHART C-3

CANISTER PURGE VALVE CHECK
2.3L (VIN D & A) "N" CARLINE (PORT)

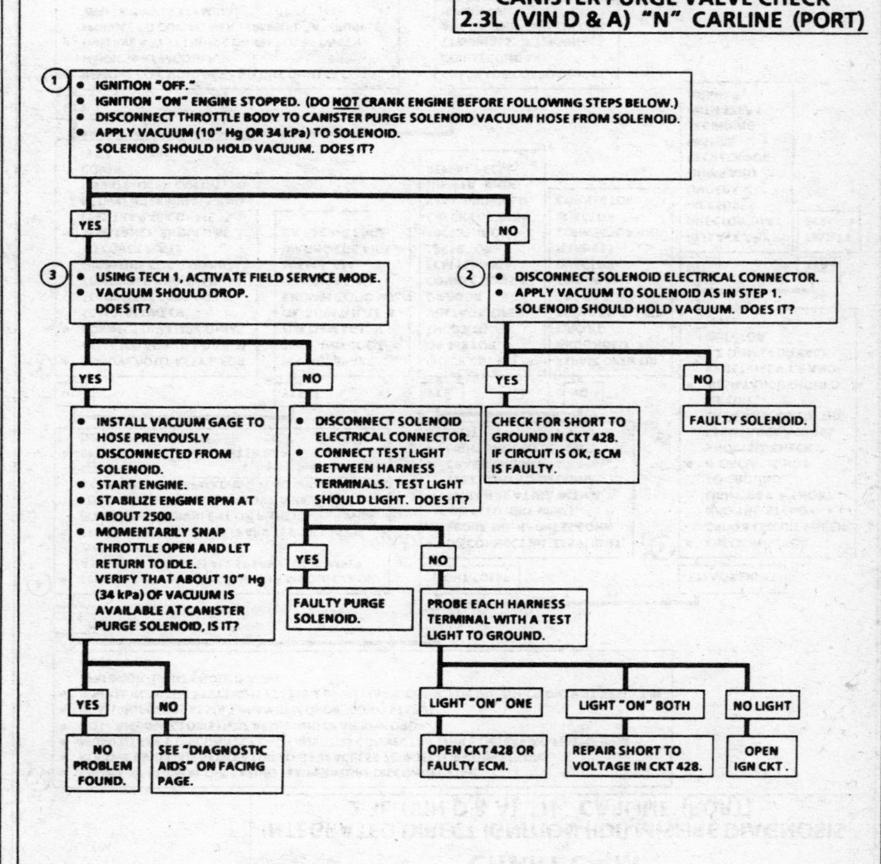

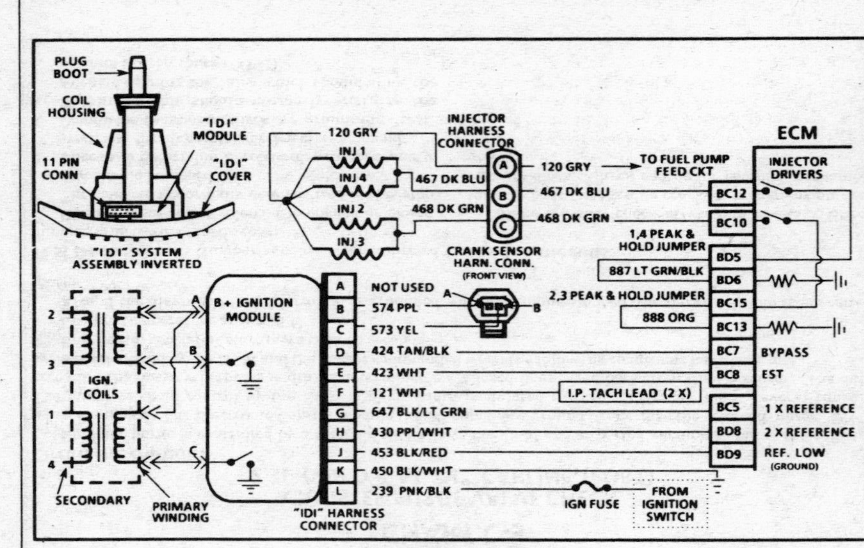

CHART C-4M

INTEGRATED DIRECT IGNITION (IDI) MISFIRE DIAGNOSIS 2.3L (VIN D & A) "N" CARLINE (PORT)

Circuit Description:

The "Integrated Direct Ignition" system (IDI) uses a waste spark method of distribution. In this type of system the ignition module triggers the #1-4 coil pair resulting in both #1 and #4 spark plugs firing at the same time. #1 cylinder is on the compression stroke at the same time #4 is on the exhaust stroke, resulting in a lower energy requirement to fire # 4 spark plug. This leaves the remainder of the high voltage to be used to fire #1 spark plug. On this application, the crank sensor is mounted to, and protrudes through the block to within approximately 0.050" of the crankshaft reluctor. Since the reluctor is a machined portion of the crankshaft and the sensor is mounted in a fixed position on the block, timing adjustments are not possible or necessary.

Test Description: Number(s) below refer to circled number(s) on the diagnostic chart.

1. This checks for equal relative power output between the cylinders. Any injector which when disconnected did not result in an rpm drop approximately equal to the others, is located on the misfiring cylinder.
2. If a plug boot is burned, the other plug on that coil may still fire at idle. This step tests the system's ability to produce at least 25,000 volts at each spark plug.
3. No spark, on one coil, may be caused by an open secondary circuit. Therefore, the coil's secondary resistance should be checked. Resistance readings above 20,000 ohms, but not infinite, will probably not cause a no start but may cause an engine miss under certain conditions.
4. If the no spark condition is caused by coil connections, a coil or a secondary boot assembly, the test light will blink. If the light does not blink, the fault is module connections or the module.
5. Checks for ignition voltage feed to injector and for an open injector driver circuit.
6. An injector driver circuit shorted to ground would result in the test light "ON" steady, and possibly a flooded condition which could damage engine. A shorted injector (less than 2 ohms) could cause incorrect ECM operation.

Diagnostic Aid:

Verify IDI connector terminal "K", CKT 450 resistance to ground is less than .5 ohm. A shorted or low resistance injector may cause a miss in the other injector in that pair (1 & 4 or 2 & 3).

CHART C-4M

INTEGRATED DIRECT IGNITION (IDI) MISFIRE DIAGNOSIS 2.3L (VIN D & A) "N" CARLINE (PORT)

(1)
- ENGINE AT NORMAL OPERATING TEMPERATURE DISCONNECT IAC.
- REMOVE CV OIL/AIR SEPARATOR TO GAIN ACCESS TO INJECTOR CONNECTORS.
- MOMENTARILY DISCONNECT EACH INJECTOR CONNECTOR WHILE OBSERVING ENGINE RPM.
- NOTE ANY INJECTOR(S) NOT RESULTING IN AN RPM DROP.
- (IF ALL INJECTORS RESULT IN AN RPM DROP, GO TO STEP 2).
- INSTALL INJECTOR TEST LIGHT J 34730-2 IN INJ. HARN. CONN. FOR INJ. WHICH DID NOT RESULT IN RPM DROP. LIGHT SHOULD BLINK.

DOES IT?

YES → (2)

(2)
- TEMPORARILY REMOVE IGNITION MODULE / COIL ASSEMBLY AND INSTALL SPARK PLUG JUMPER WIRES (J 36012)
- CHECK FOR SPARK WITH SPARK TESTER J 26792, (ST-125) OR EQUIVALENT ON PLUG JUMPER WIRE FOR CYLINDER(S) NOTED ABOVE WHILE CRANKING WITH REMAINING PLUG WIRES STILL CONNECTED.
- SPARK SHOULD JUMP TESTER GAP.

DOES IT?

NO → (3)

(3)
- REMOVE BOOT ASSYS. FOR AFFECTED COIL (1-4 OR 2-3)
- CONNECT DVM (20K OHMS SCALE) BETWEEN SECONDARY "IDI" COIL TERMINALS AND THEN FROM ONE COIL TERMINAL TO COVER PLATE.
- RESISTANCE SHOULD BE LESS THAN 10K OHMS BETWEEN TERMINALS AND INFINITE (OPEN CIRCUIT) TO COVER.

IS IT?

YES → (4)

(4)
- REMOVE COIL HOUSING AND DISCONNECT COIL HARNESS AT MODULE.
- OBSERVE A TEST LIGHT CONNECTED BETWEEN MODULE TO COIL POWER TERMINAL "A" (PURPLE WIRE) & DRIVER TERMINAL ("B" OR "C") FOR AFFECTED COIL, WHILE CRANKING ENGINE.
- SHOULD BLINK.

DOES IT?

NO → POOR CONNECTION OR FAULTY IDI MODULE.

YES → OPEN OR SHORTED COIL HARNESS, POOR COIL CONNECTION, FAULTY COIL OR BOOT ASSEMBLY.

(3) NO → CHECK FOR CORROSION AT COIL SECONDARY TERMINALS. IF TERMINALS ARE OK, THE IGNITION COIL IS FAULTY.

(2) YES → INSPECT SPARK PLUG AND BOOT FOR DAMAGE. IF OK, SUBSTITUTE A KNOWN GOOD INJ., IF ENGINE STILL MISSES, SEE DIAGNOSTIC AIDS ON FACING PAGE.

(1) NO → LIGHT "OFF" → (5)

(5)
- DISCONNECT INJ. TEST LIGHT.
- PROBE INJ. HARNESS CONN. IGN FEED (GRY WIRE) TERMINAL AT INJ. WITH A TEST LIGHT TO GROUND.
- CRANK ENGINE.
- LIGHT SHOULD BE "ON."

IS IT?

YES → CHECK CKT 467 OR 468 FOR SHORT TO VOLTAGE, OPEN OR POOR CONNECTIONS AT ECM TERMINAL "BC10" OR "BC12". IF OK, CHECK FOR OPEN PEAK AND HOLD JUMPER. IF OK, REPLACE ECM.

NO → REPAIR OPEN OR GROUNDED CIRCUIT BETWEEN CAVITY "A" OF 3 TERMINAL INJECTOR HARNESS CONNECTOR AND INJECTOR CONNECTOR.

(1) NO → STEADY LIGHT → (6)

(6)
- CHECK INJECTOR DRIVER CIRCUIT WHICH HAD THE STEADY LIGHT, FOR A SHORT TO GROUND.
- IF CIRCUIT IS NOT SHORTED, CHECK RESISTANCE ACROSS EACH INJECTOR IN THE CIRCUIT.
- RESISTANCE SHOULD BE BETWEEN 1.8 AND 2.2 OHMS FOR EACH INJECTOR.

IS IT?

NO → REPLACE ANY INJECTOR THAT MEASURES UNDER 1.8 OHMS AND RECHECK FOR MISFIRE BEGINNING WITH STEP 1 AGAIN.

YES → FAULTY ECM.

"AFTER REPAIRS," CONFIRM "CLOSED LOOP" OPERATION AND NO "SERVICE ENGINE SOON" LIGHT.

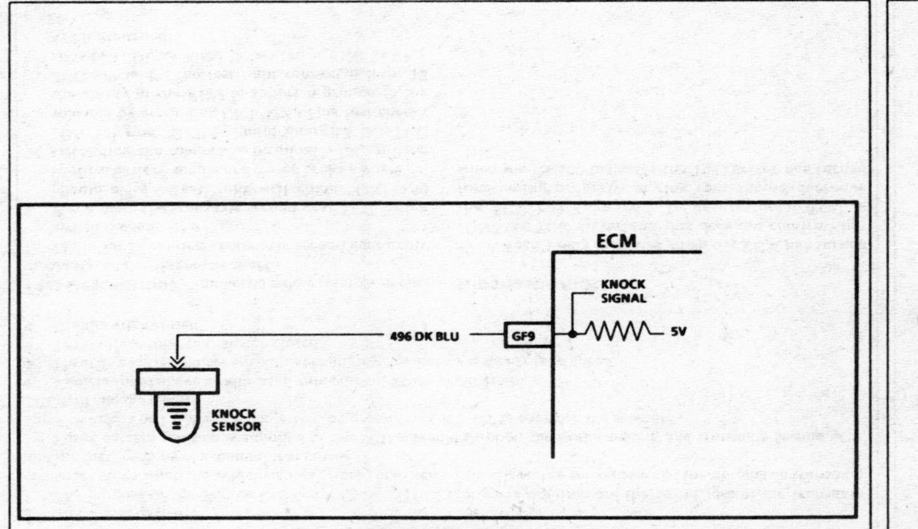

CHART C-5

ELECTRONIC SPARK CONTROL (ESC) SYSTEM CHECK 2.3L (VIN D & A) "N" CARLINE (PORT)

Circuit Description:

The knock sensor is used to detect engine detonation and the ECM will retard the electronic spark timing based on the signal being received. The circuitry within the knock sensor causes the ECM's 5 volts to be pulled down so that CKT 496 would measure about 2.5 volts. The knock sensor produces an AC signal which rides on the 2.5 volts DC voltage. The amplitude and frequency are dependent upon the knock level.

The MEM-CAL used with this engine contains the functions which were part of remotely mounted ESC modules used on other GM vehicles. The ESC portion of the MEM-CAL then sends a signal to other parts of the ECM which adjusts the spark timing to retard the spark and reduce the detonation.

Test Description: Number(s) below refer to circled number(s) on the diagnostic chart.

1. With engine idling, there should not be a knock signal present at the ECM because detonation is not likely under a no load condition.
2. Tapping on the engine lift hood bracket should simulate a knock signal to determine if the sensor is capable of detecting detonation. If no knock is detected, try tapping on engine block closer to sensor before replacing sensor.
3. If the engine has an internal problem which is creating a knock, the knock sensor may be responding to the internal failure.
4. This test determines if the knock sensor is faulty or if the ESC portion of the MEM-CAL is faulty. If it is determined that the MEM-CAL is faulty, be sure that is is properly installed and latched into place. If not properly installed, repair and retest.

Diagnostic Aids:

While observing knock signal on the Tech 1, there should be an indication that knock is present when detonation can be heard. Detonation is most likely to occur under high engine load conditions.

CHART C-5

ELECTRONIC SPARK CONTROL (ESC) SYSTEM CHECK 2.3L (VIN D & A) "N" CARLINE (PORT)

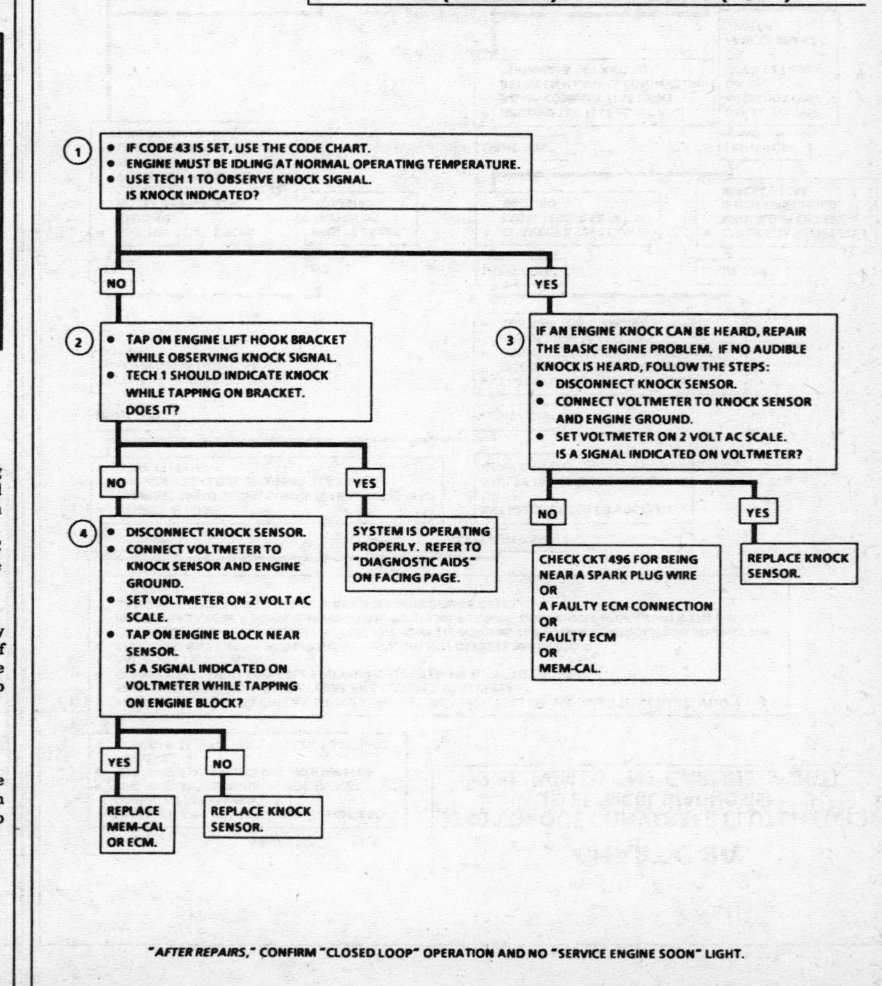

"AFTER REPAIRS," CONFIRM "CLOSED LOOP" OPERATION AND NO "SERVICE ENGINE SOON" LIGHT.

BRAKE SWITCH
IGN ← 439 PNK/BLK — A N.C B — 420 PPL
TCC SOLENOID IN TRANSAXLE ASSEMBLY
2nd GEAR TCC SWITCH (N.O.)
420 PPL
ECM
422 TAN/BLK — GF4
15 WAY I/P CONNECTOR
TCC CONTROL DRIVER
F E D C B A M
ALDL CONNECTOR

CHART C-8A
3T40 TORQUE CONVERTER CLUTCH (TCC)
(ELECTRICAL DIAGNOSIS)
2.3L (VIN D) "N" CARLINE (PORT)

Circuit Description:

The purpose of the Torque Converter Clutch (TCC) feature is to eliminate the power loss of the transaxle converter stage when the vehicle is in a cruise condition. This allows the convenience of the automatic transaxle and the fuel economy of a manual transaxle.

Fused battery ignition is supplied to the TCC solenoid through the brake switch, and transaxle second gear apply switch. The ECM will engage TCC by grounding CKT 422 to energize the solenoid.

TCC will engage when:

- Vehicle speed above a calibrated value (about 34 mph) (55 km/h).
- Throttle position sensor output not changing, indicating a steady road speed.
- Transaxle second gear switch closed.
- Brake switch closed.

Test Description: Number(s) below refer to circled number(s) on the diagnostic chart.

1. Light "OFF" confirms transaxle second gear apply switch is open.
2. By 25 mph, the transaxle second gear TCC switch should close. Test light will come "ON" and confirm battery supply and closed brake switch.
3. Grounding the diagnostic terminal with ignition "ON," engine "OFF," should energize the TCC solenoid by grounding CKT 422. This test checks the ability of the ECM to supply a ground to the TCC solenoid. The test light connected from 12 volts to ALDL terminal "F" will turn "ON" as CKT 422 is grounded.

Diagnostic Aids:

A Tech 1 only indicates when the ECM has turned "ON" the TCC driver and this does not confirm that the TCC has engaged. To determine if TCC is functioning properly, engine rpm should decrease when the "Scan" indicates the TCC driver has turned "ON."

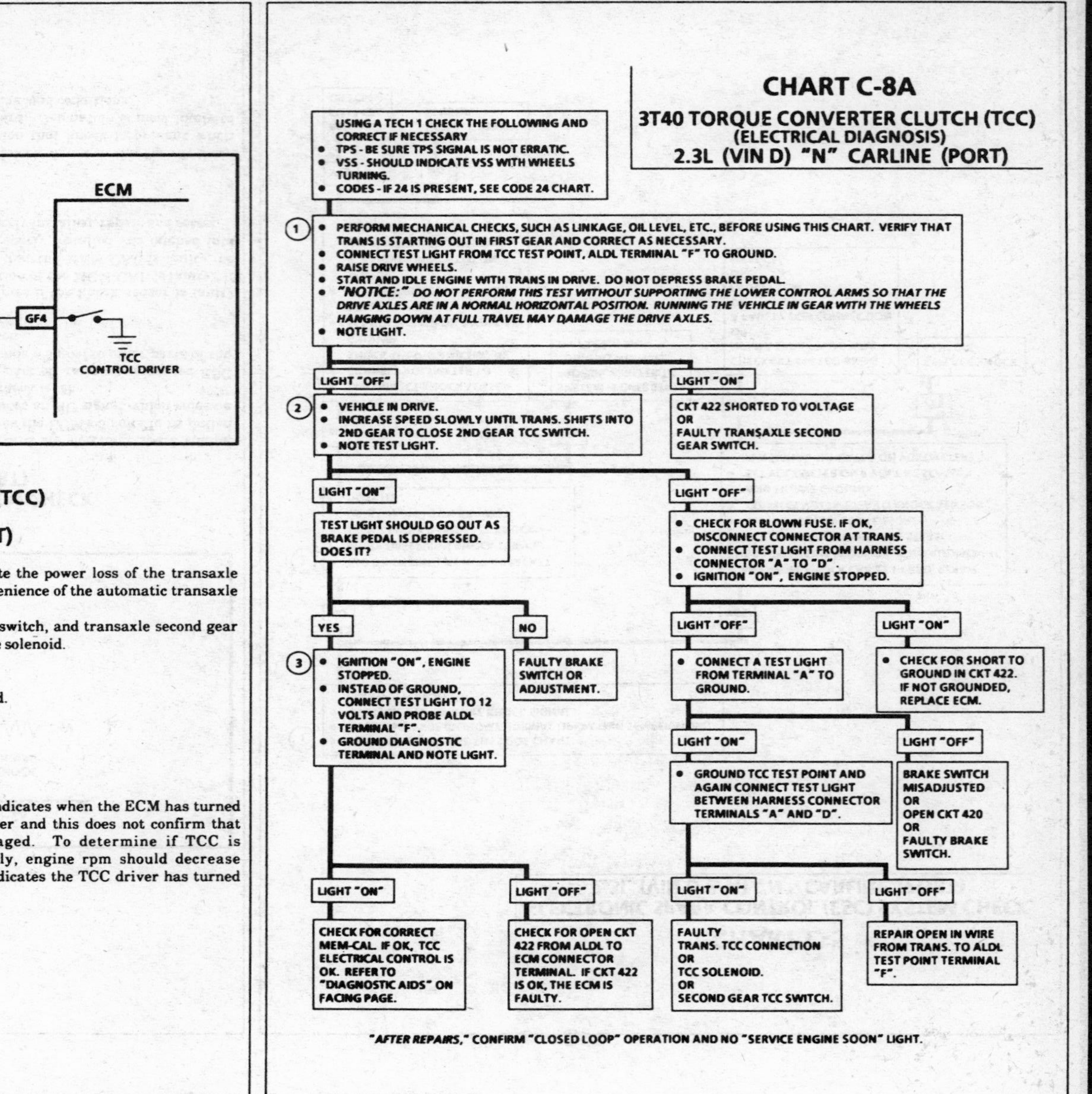

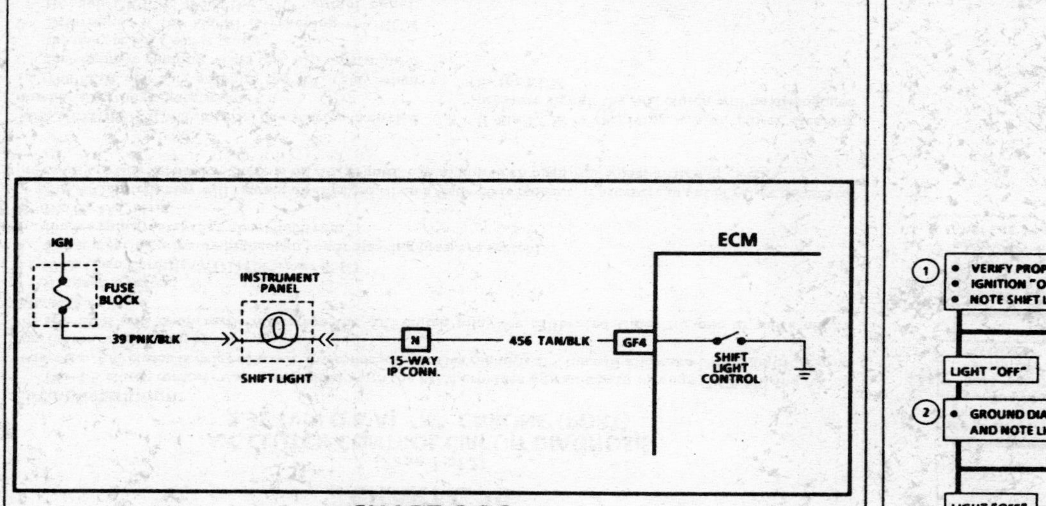

CHART C-8C

MANUAL TRANSAXLE (M/T) SHIFT LIGHT CHECK 2.3L (VIN A) "N" CARLINE (PORT)

Circuit Description:

The shift light indicates the best transaxle shift point for maximum fuel economy. The light is controlled by the ECM and is turned "ON" by grounding CKT 456.

The ECM uses inputs from various sensors to calculate when the shift light should be turned "ON" as follows:

- Coolant temperature must be above -10°C (14°F).
- ECM can determine the transaxle has been in a gear for at least 1.2 seconds, by comparison of vehicle speed (from VSS) with engine rpm.
- TPS is between minimum and maximum calibrated values for each gear.
- RPM is above a calibrated value for each gear (maximum 6500 rpm).

The light will be turned "ON" after a calibrated delay time which is dependent on last gear change or downshift, and will remain on for a maximum of 10 seconds.

Test Description: Number(s) below refer to circled number(s) on the diagnostic chart.

1. This should not turn "ON" the shift light. If the light is "ON," there is a short to ground in CKT 456 wiring or a fault in the ECM.
2. When the diagnostic terminal is grounded, the ECM should ground CKT 456 and the shift light should come "ON."
3. This checks the shift light circuit up to the ECM connector. If the shift light illuminates, then the ECM connector is faulty or the ECM does not have the ability to ground the circuit.

Diagnostic Aids:

Check for Code 24 (no VSS). Faulty thermostat or incorrect heat range. Incorrect or faulty MEM-CAL. A faulty or incorrect VSS may result in a shift light that does not operate.

CHART C-8C

MANUAL TRANSAXLE (M/T) SHIFT LIGHT CHECK 2.3L (VIN A) "N" CARLINE (PORT)

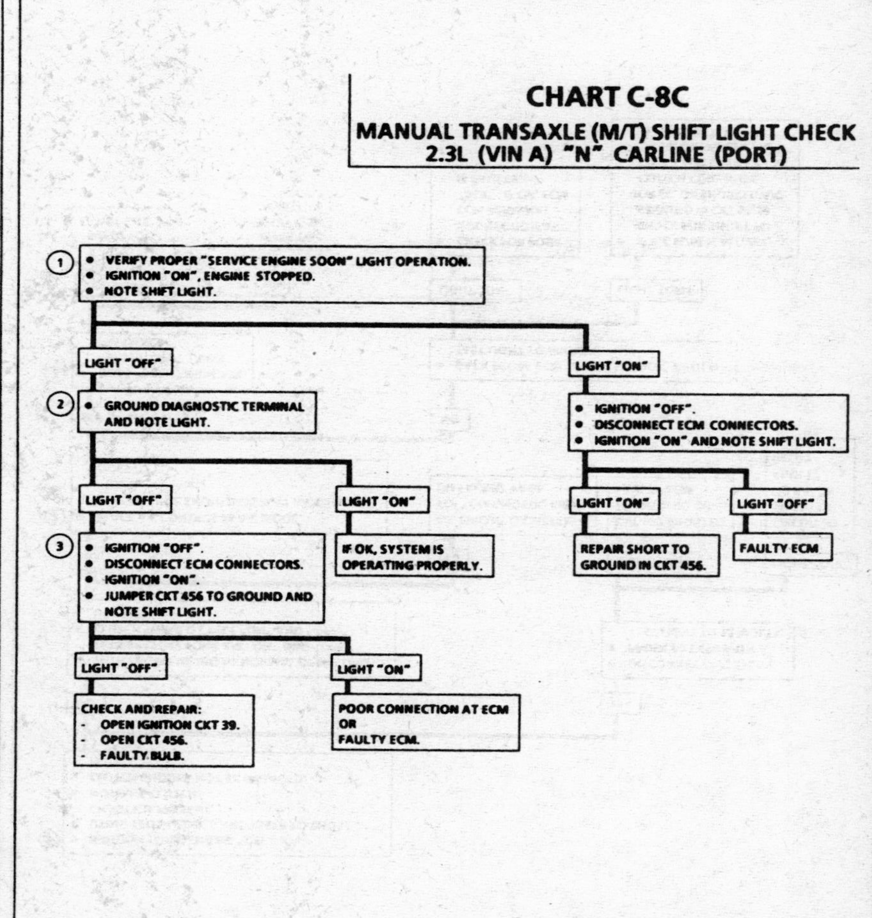

"AFTER REPAIRS," CONFIRM "CLOSED LOOP" OPERATION AND NO "SERVICE ENGINE SOON" LIGHT.

A/C PRESSURE SENSOR
TO TPS AND MAP SENSORS
ECM
416 GRY — BA5 — +5V
380 GRY/BLK — GF14 — A/C PRESSURE SIGNAL
452 BLK — BB6
TO TPS AND COOLANT TEMPERATURE SENSOR
A/C CLUTCH CONTROL RELAY
439 PNK/BLK
459 DK GRN/WHT — GF2
59 DK GRN A/C CLUTCH
66 LT GRN — BC9 — A/C REQUEST SIGNAL
6 WAY A/C HARN CONN.
66 LT GRN
450 BLK/WHT — BC3 — NON A/C PROGRAM (FOR NON A/C CARS)
A/C SEL SW.
50 RED — IGNITION

CHART C-10

(Page 1 of 2)

A/C CLUTCH CONTROL CIRCUIT DIAGNOSIS
2.3L (VIN D & A) "N" CARLINE (PORT)

Circuit Description:

The A/C clutch control relay is energized when the ECM provides a ground path through CKT 459 and A/C is requested. A/C clutch is delayed about .3 seconds after A/C is requested. This will allow the IAC to adjust engine rpm for the additional load.

The ECM will temporarily disengage the A/C clutch relay for calibrated times for one or more of the following:

- Hot engine restart
- Wide Open Throttle (WOT) (TPS over 90%)
- Power steering pressure high (open power steering pressure switch)
- Engine rpm greater than about 6000 rpm
- During IAC reset

The A/C clutch relay will remain disengaged when a Code 66 is present, if pressure is out of range described previously in this section, or there is no A/C request signal due to an open A/C select switch or circuit.

Test Description: Number(s) below refer to circled number(s) on the diagnostic chart.

1. The ECM will only energize the A/C relay when the engine is running. This test will determine if the relay or CKT 459 is faulty.
2. Determines if the signal is reaching the ECM through CKT 66 from the A/C control panel. Signal should only be present when an A/C mode or defrost mode has been selected.
3. If the ECM is receiving a high power steering pressure signal, the A/C clutch will be disengaged by the ECM.

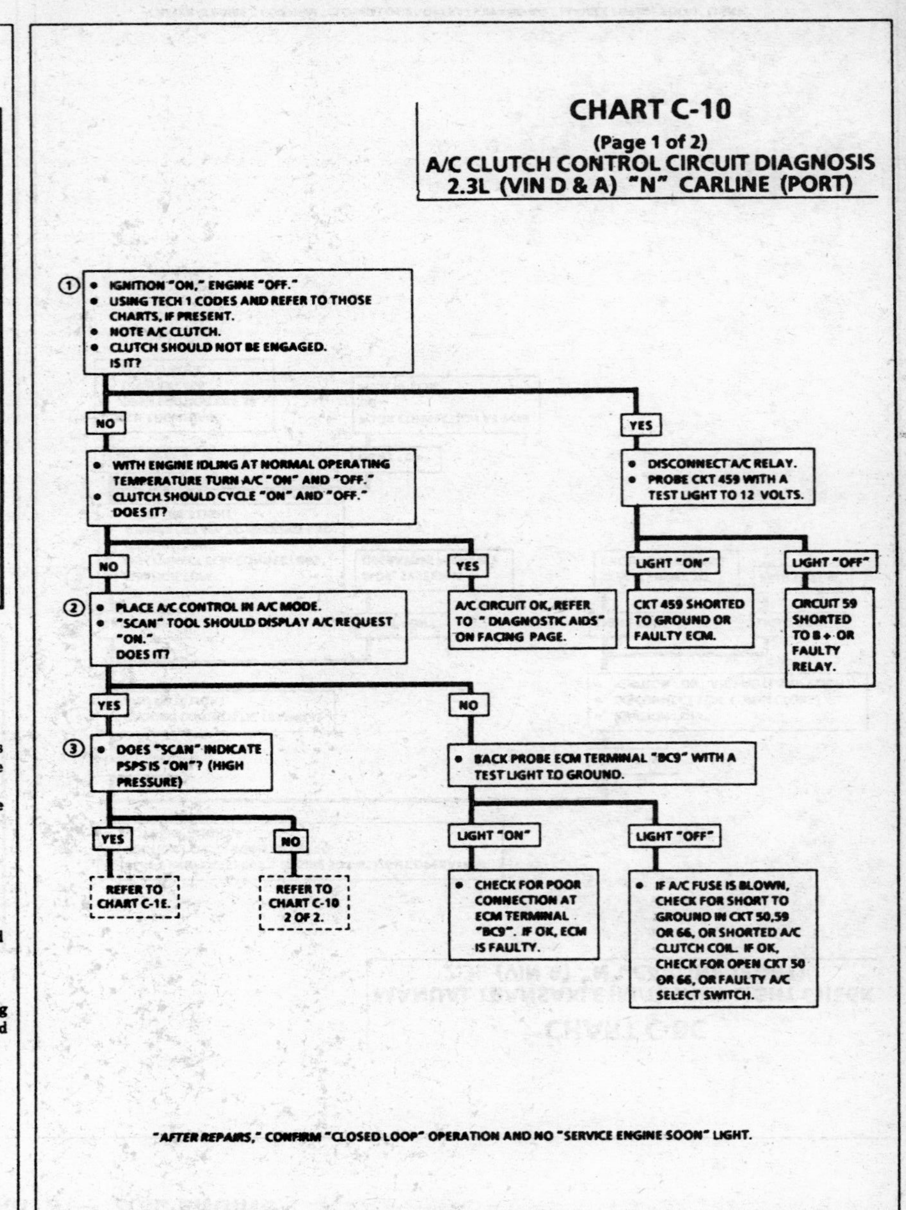

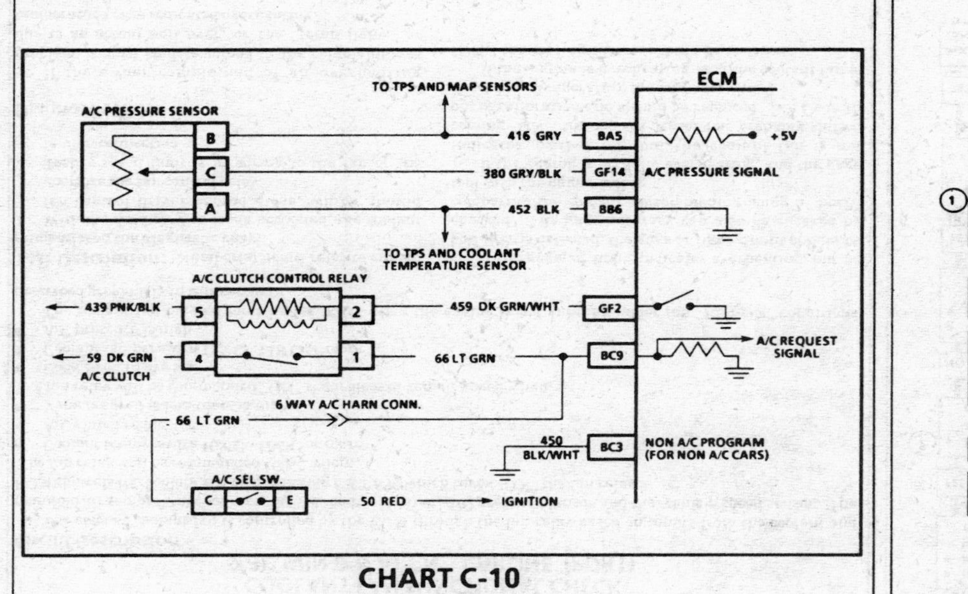

CHART C-10

(Page 2 of 2)

A/C CLUTCH CONTROL CIRCUIT DIAGNOSIS 2.3L (VIN D & A) "N" CARLINE (PORT)

Circuit Description:

The A/C clutch control relay is energized when the ECM provides a ground path through CKT 459 and A/C is requested. A/C clutch is delayed about .3 seconds after A/C is requested. This will allow the IAC to adjust engine rpm for the additional load.

The ECM will temporarily disengage the A/C clutch relay for calibrated times for one or more of the following:

- Hot engine restart
- Wide Open Throttle (WOT) (TPS over 90%)
- Power steering pressure high (open power steering pressure switch)
- Engine rpm greater than about 6000 rpm
- During IAC reset

The A/C clutch relay will remain disengaged when a Code 66 is present, if pressure is out of range as described previously in this section, or there is no A/C request signal due to an open A/C select switch or circuit.

Test Description: Numbers below refer to circled numbers on the diagnostic chart.

1. Determines if the pressure transducer is out of range causing the compressor clutch to be disengaged.
2. With the engine stopped and field service mode activated, the ECM should be grounding CKT 459, which should cause the test light to be "ON."

Diagnostic Aids:

If complaint is insufficient cooling, the problem may be caused by an inoperative cooling fan. See CHART C-12 for cooling fan diagnosis. operates correctly,

A/C pressure outside of a range of 43 to 428 psi will cause the compressor to be disabled by the ECM. Observe "Scan" A/C pressure for 2 minutes with engine idling and A/C "ON."

"Scan" pressure should be within 20 psi of actual. If not, check for a circuit problem using Code 66 chart or replace sensor.

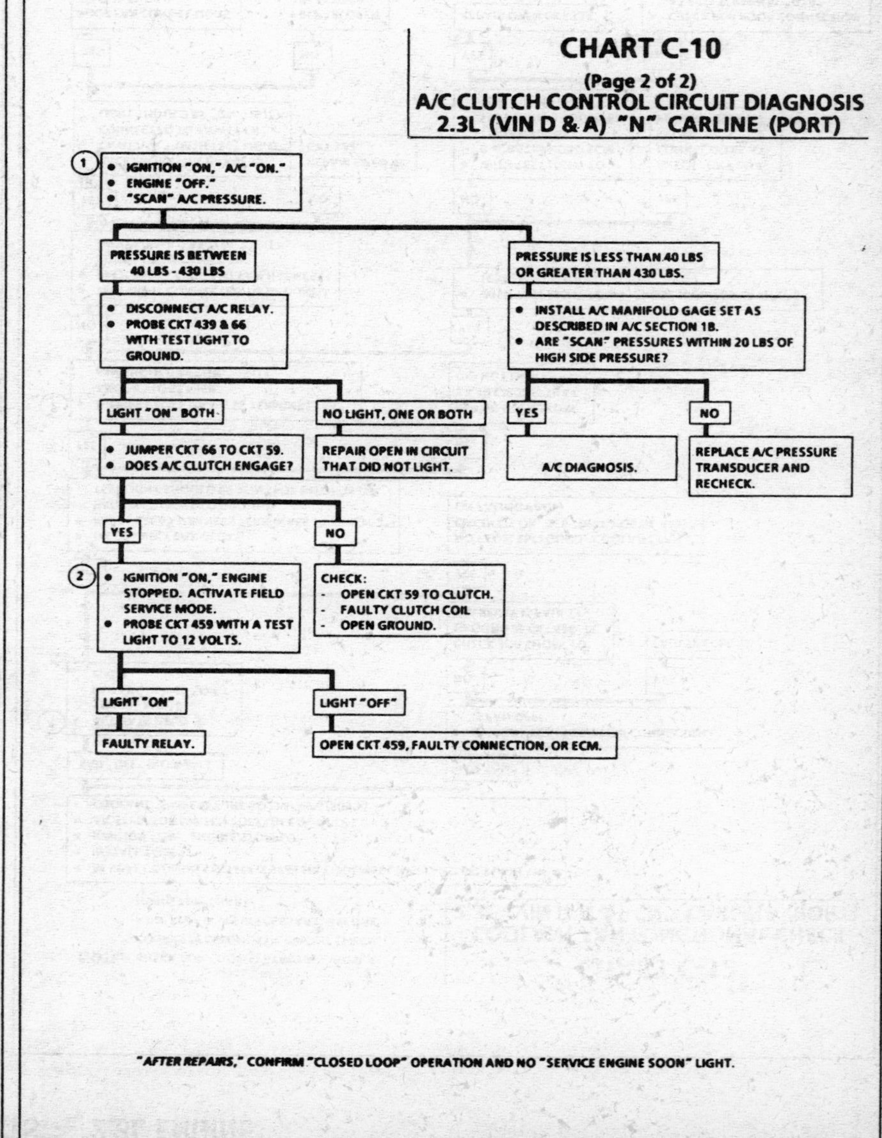

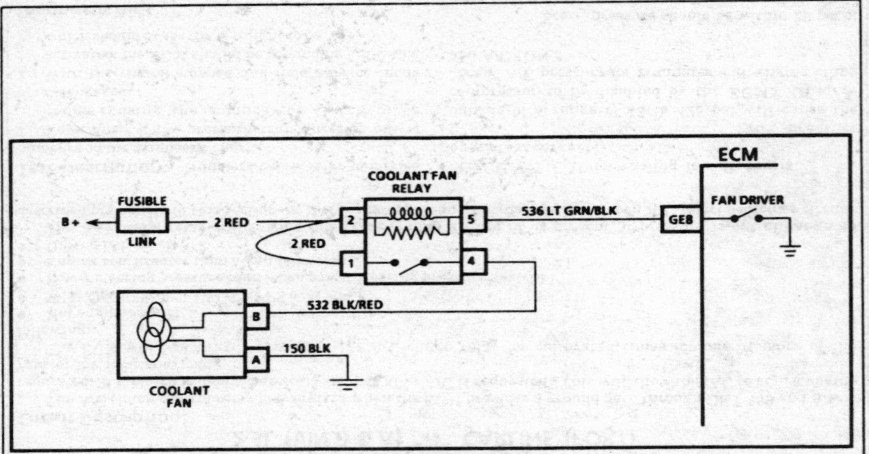

CHART C-12

COOLANT FAN FUNCTIONAL CHECK 2.3L (VIN D & A) "N" CARLINE (PORT)

Circuit Description:

The electric coolant fan is controlled by the ECM through the fan relay based on inputs from the coolant and manifold air temperature sensors, the A/C control switch, A/C pressure sensor and the vehicle speed sensor. The ECM controls the coolant fan by grounding CKT 536 which turns "ON" the fan relay.

The fan relay will be commanded "ON" when:

- Coolant temperature 103°C - 106°C or more
- A/C clutch requested
- Vehicle speed is less than 35 mph

The fan relay will be commanded "ON" regardless of vehicle speed when:

- Code 14 or 15 are set
- Coolant temperature 115°C - 118°C or more
- A/C pressure is high

The coolant fan may be commanded "ON" when the engine is not running under fan "Run-ON" conditions described previously in this section.

Test Description: Number(s) below refer to circled number(s) on the diagnostic chart.

1. With the field service mode activated, the coolant fan control driver should close, which should energize the fan control relay.
2. Test to see if fault is in wiring to the fan or the fan/fan connection.

Diagnostic Aids:

If the owner complained of an overheating problem, it must be determined if the complaint was due to an actual boil over, or the "temp light," or temperature gage indicated overheating.

If the gage, or light, indicates overheating, but no boil over is detected, the gage or light circuit should be checked. The gage accuracy can also be checked by comparing the coolant sensor reading using a "Scan" tool with the gage reading.

If the engine is actually overheating, and the gage indicates overheating, but the coolant fan is not coming "ON," the coolant sensor has probably shifted out of calibration and should be replaced. See Code 15 chart for a temperature to resistance chart.

If the engine is overheating, and the coolant fan is "ON," the cooling system should be checked.

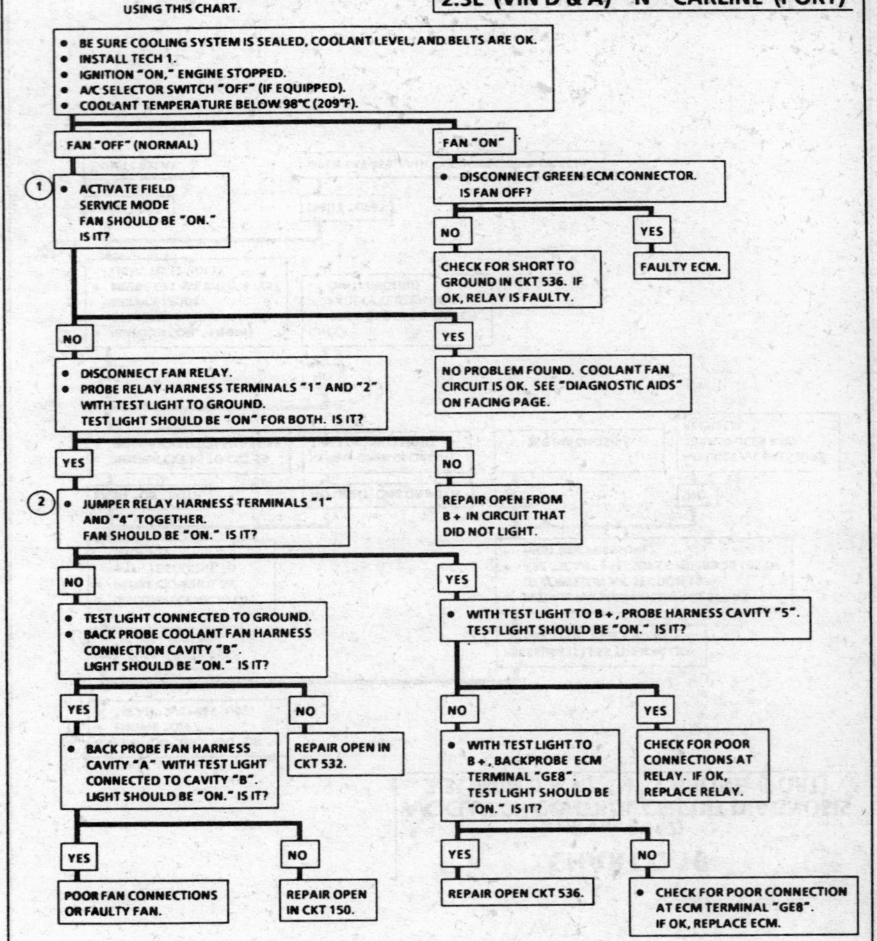

TO IGNITION SWITCH ← 3 RED — GAUGES FUSE — 39 PNK/BLK — "TEMP" LIGHT OR "CHECK GAUGES" WARNING LIGHT — 35 DK GRN — CHECK GAUGES BUFFER* SOLID STATE — 15 WAY I/P CONNECTOR L — GF7 — ECM

*WITH OPTION (U83) ON PONTIAC CARS ONLY.

CHART C-16

ECM CONTROLLED "WARNING" LIGHT CIRCUIT 2.3L (VIN D & A) "N" CARLINE (PORT)

Circuit Description:

The "Temp" light or optional "Check Gauges" light, is connected to battery voltage through the ignition switch. The ECM energizes the bulb by supplying a path to ground through "Quad-Driver" module #2.

Test Description: Number(s) below refer to circled number(s) on the diagnostic chart.

1. With the ignition "ON" and engine "OFF," the ECM should be grounding CKT 35.
2. While the engine is running, the "Temp" light or optional "Check Gauges" light should be turned "ON" by the ECM only when the coolant temperature is above 123°C (253°F). The "Temp" light or "Check Gauges" light should be turned "OFF" when the engine is running and the coolant temperature goes lower than 120°C (249°F).

Diagnostic Aids:

The coolant temperature sensor, in rare cases, may fail to indicate the correct engine coolant temperature without setting a malfunction code. This could result in turning "ON" the "Temp" light or optional "Check Gauges" light without having an overheating condition. It could also result in overheating without the "Temp/Check Gauges" light being turned "ON."

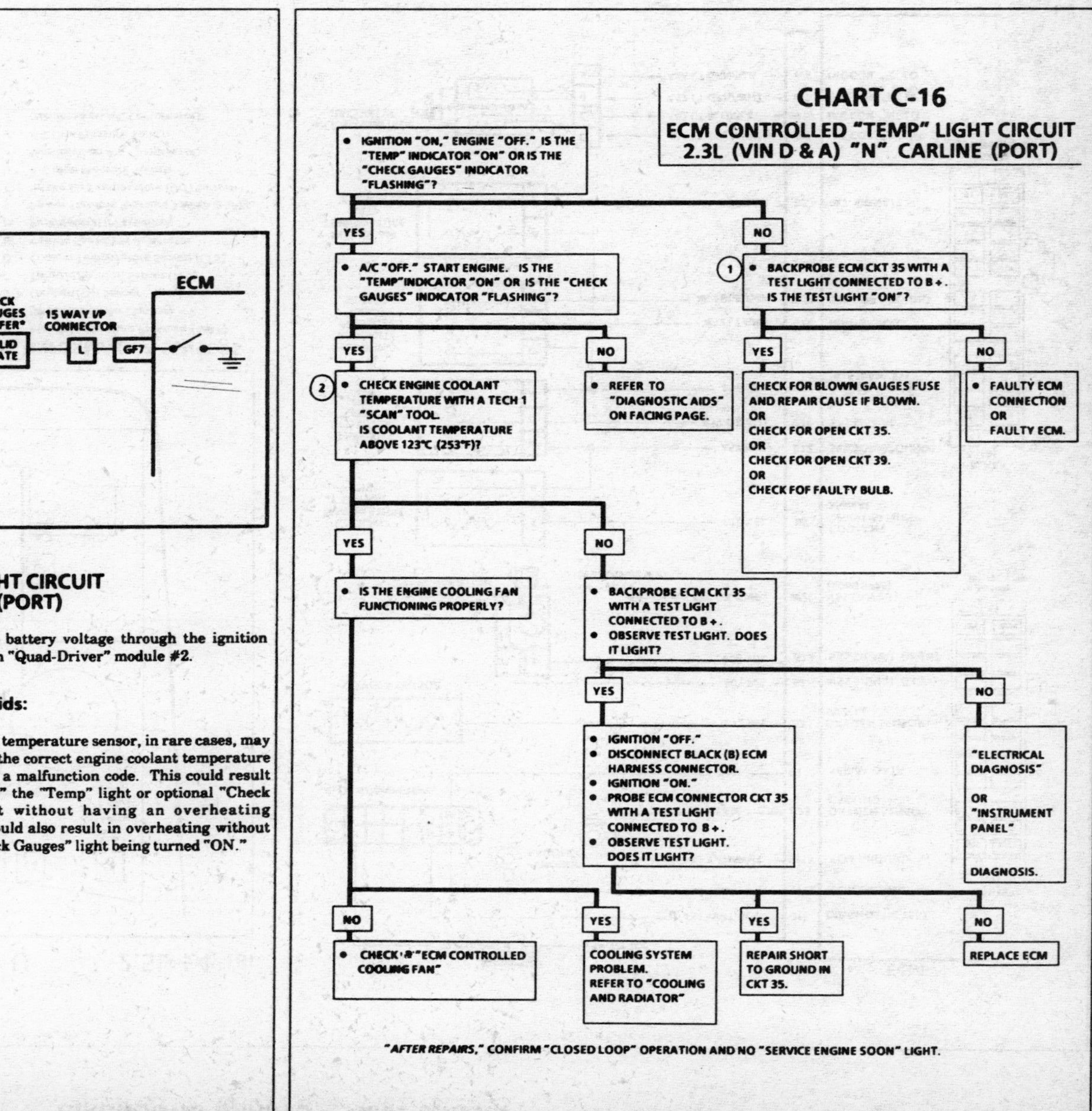

DIAGNOSTIC CHARTS — 2.5L ENGINE

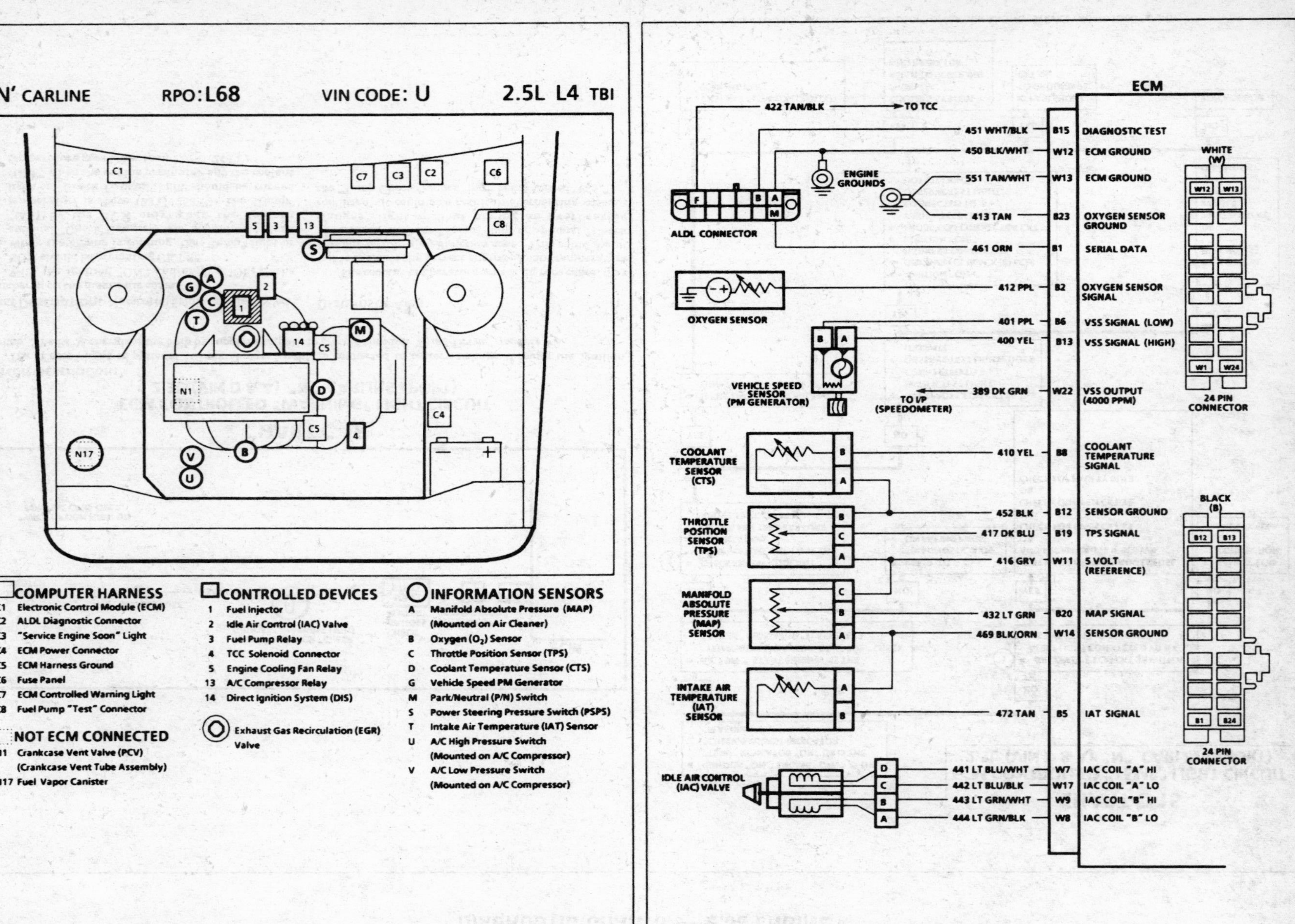

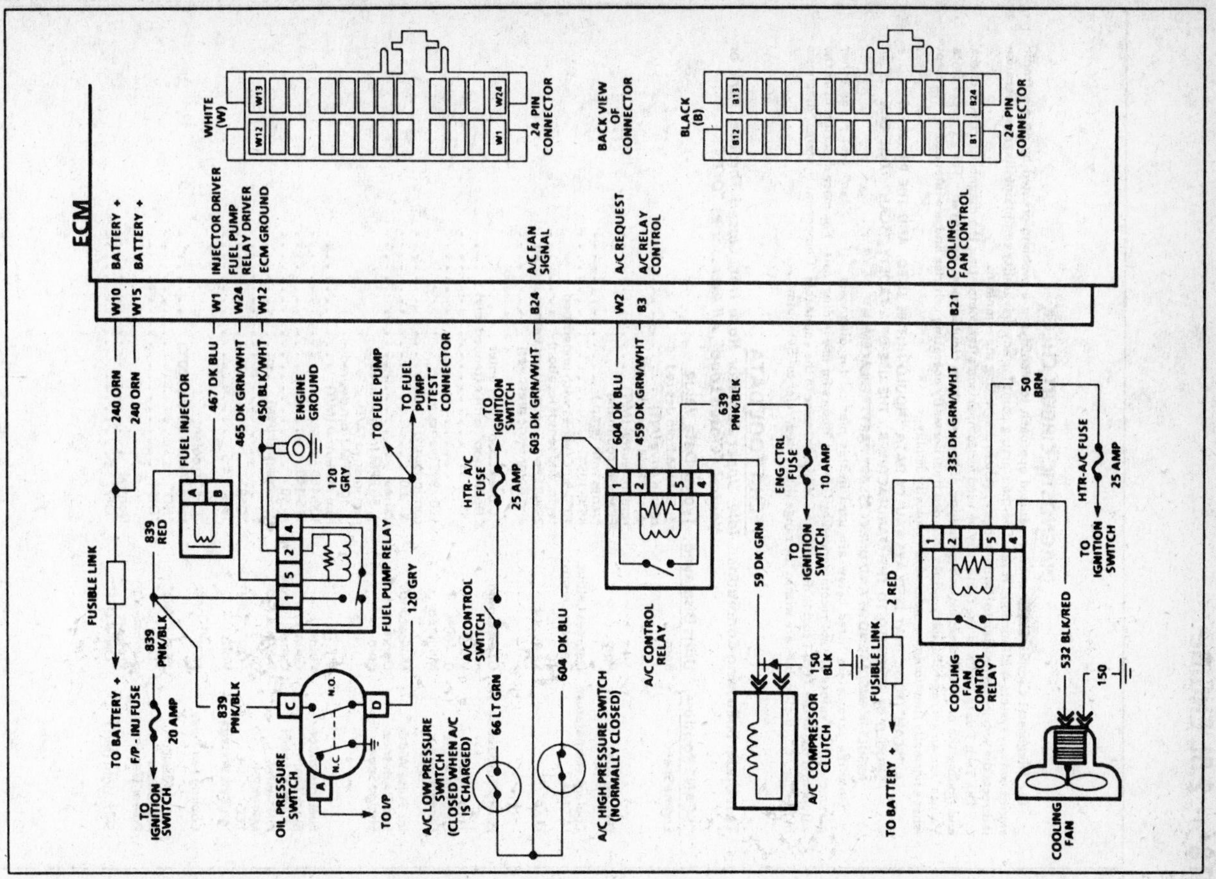

DIAGNOSTIC CHARTS — 2.5L ENGINE

ECM
450 BLK/WHT
P/N SWITCH
434 ORN/BLK — W18 PARK NEUTRAL SWITCH (A/T)
POWER STEERING PRESSURE SWITCH
450 BLK/WHT
495 LT BLU/ORN — W5 POWER STEERING PRESSURE SIGNAL
WHITE (W)
GAUGES FUSE
TO IGNITION SWITCH
10 AMP
39 PNK/BLK
"SES" LAMP
419 BRN/WHT — B22 SERVICE ENGINE SOON LIGHT CONTROL
SHIFT LIGHT (M/T ONLY)
39 PNK/BLK
ECM-RLYS FUSE
TO IGNITION SWITCH
10 AMP
439 PNK/BLK
456 TAN/BLK (M/T ONLY)
BRAKE SWITCH
420 PPL
3RD GEAR SWITCH
TORQUE CONVERTER CLUTCH (TCC) SOLENOID
24 PIN CONNECTOR
ALDL CONNECTOR
F
422 TAN/BLK — B7 TCC OR SHIFT LIGHT CONTROL
BACK VIEW OF CONNECTORS
BLACK (B)
COOLANT "TEMP" LIGHT OR "CHECK GAUGES" LIGHT (OPTIONAL)
GAUGES FUSE
TO IGNITION SWITCH
10 AMP
39 PNK/BLK
35 DK GRN — B18 COOLANT TEMPERATURE CONTROL
ECM-RLYS FUSE
TO IGNITION SWITCH
10 AMP
439 PNK/BLK — W16 IGNITION
TO IGNITION SWITCH
F4 BULKHEAD CONNECTOR
COIL ASSEMBLIES
B+
3 PNK
GROUND
450 BLK/WHT
ENGINE GROUND
CRANKSHAFT SENSOR
453 BLK/RED — B16 GROUND
430 PPL/WHT — B9 REFERENCE
424 TAN/BLK — W19 BYPASS
423 WHT — W6 EST
DIRECT IGNITION SYSTEM (DIS) MODULE
121 WHT
SECONDARY WINDING
PRIMARY WINDING
TO I/P FOR TACHOMETER
24 PIN CONNECTOR

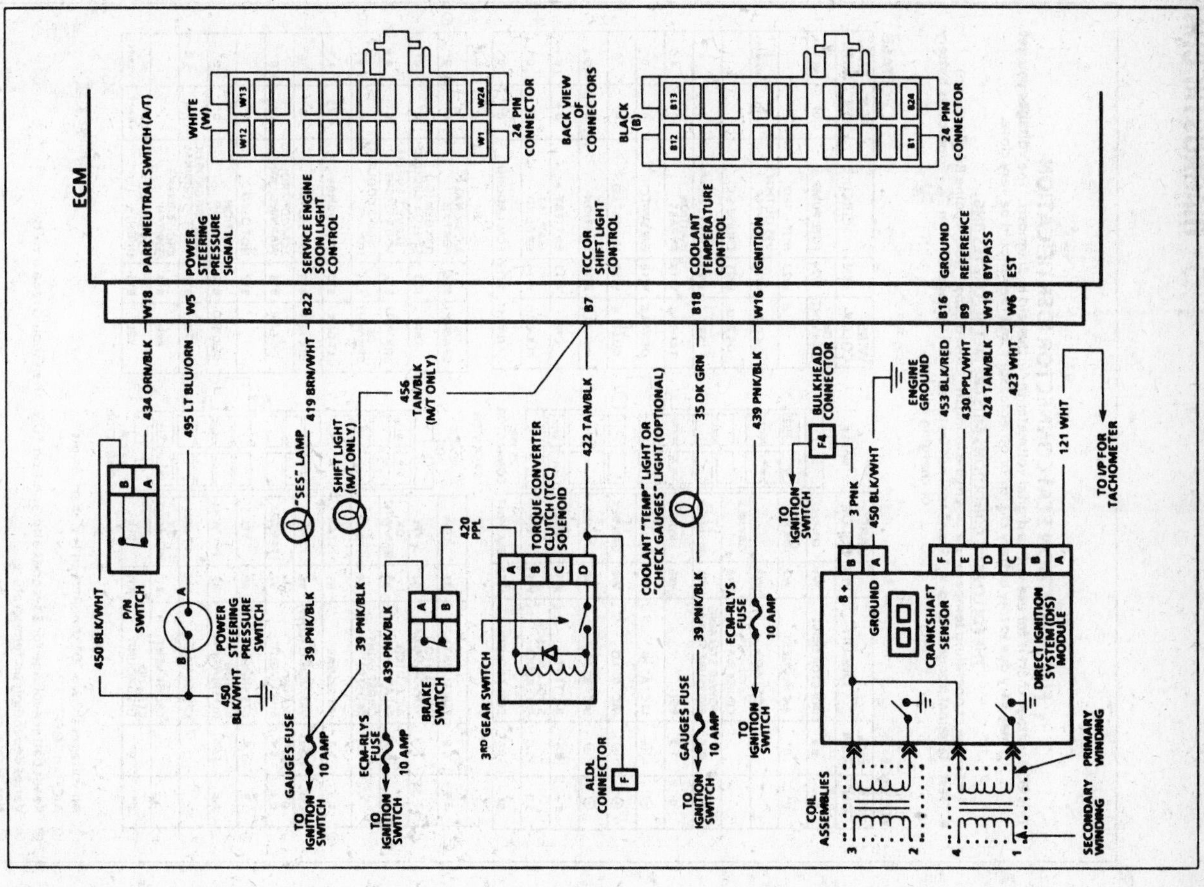

ECM
FUSIBLE LINK
TO BATTERY +
240 ORN — W10 BATTERY +
240 ORN — W15 BATTERY +
F/P - INJ FUSE
TO IGNITION SWITCH
20 AMP
839 PNK/BLK
839 RED
FUEL INJECTOR
467 DK BLU — W1 INJECTOR DRIVER
465 DK GRN/WHT — W24 FUEL PUMP RELAY DRIVER
450 BLK/WHT — W12 ECM GROUND
WHITE (W)
839 PNK/BLK
OIL PRESSURE SWITCH
N.C.
N.O.
ENGINE GROUND
120 GRY
TO I/P
FUEL PUMP RELAY
TO FUEL PUMP
120 GRY
TO FUEL PUMP "TEST" CONNECTOR
A/C LOW PRESSURE SWITCH (CLOSED WHEN A/C IS CHARGED)
A/C CONTROL SWITCH
HTR- A/C FUSE
TO IGNITION SWITCH
66 LT GRN
25 AMP
603 DK GRN/WHT — B24 A/C FAN SIGNAL
24 PIN CONNECTOR
604 DK BLU
A/C HIGH PRESSURE SWITCH (NORMALLY CLOSED)
604 DK BLU — W2 A/C REQUEST
BACK VIEW OF CONNECTOR
A/C CONTROL RELAY
459 DK GRN/WHT — B3 A/C RELAY CONTROL
639 PNK/BLK
BLACK (B)
59 DK GRN
A/C COMPRESSOR CLUTCH
150 BLK
ENG CTRL FUSE
TO IGNITION SWITCH
10 AMP
FUSIBLE LINK
TO BATTERY +
2 RED
COOLING FAN CONTROL RELAY
335 DK GRN/WHT — B21 COOLING FAN CONTROL
50 BRN
24 PIN CONNECTOR
COOLING FAN
532 BLK/RED
150
TO IGNITION SWITCH
HTR-A/C FUSE
25 AMP

FUEL INJECTION ECM CONNECTOR IDENTIFICATION

This ECM voltage chart is for use with a digital voltmeter to further aid in diagnosis. The voltages you get may vary due to low battery charge or other reasons, but they should be very close.

THE FOLLOWING CONDITIONS MUST BE MET BEFORE TESTING:

• Engine at operating temperature • Engine idling in "Closed Loop" (for "Engine Run" column) • "Test" terminal not grounded • "Scan" tool not installed • All voltages shown "B +" indicates battery or charging voltage.

WHITE (W) — 24 PIN CONNECTOR — BACK VIEW

	VOLTAGE KEY "ON"	VOLTAGE ENG. RUN	CIRCUIT	PIN	WIRE COLOR
	B+	B+	INJECTOR DRIVE	W1	DK BLU
①	0*	0*	A/C REQUEST	W2	DK BLU
			NOT USED	W3	
			CRUISE R/A	W4	GRY/BLK
	B+	B+	POWER STEERING PRESSURE SIGNAL	W5	LT BLU/ORN
	0	1.3	EST	W6	WHT
	④	④	IAC "A" HI	W7	LT BLU/WHT
	④	④	IAC "B" LO	W8	LT GRN/BLK
	④	④	IAC "B" HI	W9	LT GRN/WHT
	B+	B+	BATTERY +	W10	ORN
	5.0	5.0	5 VOLT SENSOR REFERENCE	W11	GRY
	0*	0*	ECM GROUND	W12	BLK/WHT

WIRE COLOR	PIN	CIRCUIT	VOLTAGE KEY "ON"	VOLTAGE ENG. RUN	
DK GRN/WHT	W24	FUEL PUMP	②	B+	
	W23	NOT USED			
DK GRN	W22	VSS OUTPUT 4000 PPM	VARIES	VARIES	
DK BLU	W21	CRUISE S/C			
GRY	W20	CRUISE ENABLE			
TAN/BLK	W19	IGNITION BYPASS	0*	4.5	
ORN/BLK	W18	P/N SWITCH	0*	0*	
LT BLU/BLK	W17	IAC "A" LO	④	④	
PNK/BLK	W16	IGNITION	B+	B+	
ORN	W15	BATTERY +	B+	B+	
BLK/ORN	W14	MAP, IAT GROUND	0*	0*	
TAN/WHT	W13	ECM GROUND	0*	0*	

BLACK (B) — 24 PIN CONNECTOR

	VOLTAGE KEY "ON"	VOLTAGE ENG. RUN	CIRCUIT	PIN	WIRE COLOR
	4.5	4.5	SERIAL DATA	B1	ORN
	.01-.55	.1-.9	OXYGEN (O_2) SENSOR SIGNAL	B2	PPL
①	B+	B+	A/C CLUTCH RELAY	B3	DK GRN/WHT
			CRUISE LIGHT (IF USED)	B4	WHT
③	1.3	1.3	IAT SIGNAL	B5	TAN
	VARIES	VARIES	VSS SIGNAL (LOW)	B6	PPL
	0* B+	0* B+	TCC OR SHIFT LIGHT	B7	TAN/BLK
③	1.9	1.9	CTS SIGNAL	B8	YEL
	4.6	3.05	IGNITION REFERENCE HI	B9	PPL/WHT
			CRUISE VAC	B10	LT GRN
			CRUISE VENT	B11	DK BLU/WHT
	0*	0*	CTS AND TPS GROUND	B12	BLK

WIRE COLOR	PIN	CIRCUIT	VOLTAGE KEY "ON"	VOLTAGE ENG. RUN	
DK GRN/WHT	B24	A/C SIGNAL FOR FAN	0*	0*	①
TAN	B23	OXYGEN (O_2) SENSOR GROUND	0*	0*	
BRN/WHT	B22	"SERVICE ENGINE SOON" LIGHT	0*	B+	
DK GRN/WHT	B21	ENGINE COOLING FAN	B+	B+	①
LT GRN	B20	MAP SIGNAL	4.75	1.1	
DK BLU	B19	TPS SIGNAL	.6	.6	
DK GRN	B18	ECM CONTROLLED WARNING LIGHT	0*	0*	
	B17	NOT USED			
BLK/RED	B16	IGNITION GROUND	0*	0*	
WHT/BLK	B15	ALDL DIAGNOSTIC "TEST" TERMINAL	5.0	5.0	
BRN	B14	CRUISE/BRAKE SWITCH			
YEL	B13	VSS SIGNAL (HIGH)	VARIES	VARIES	

ENGINE 2.5L

* All voltages shown "0" should read less than .5 volt.
① A/C, fan "OFF"
② Reads battery voltage for 2 seconds after ignition "ON" then should read 0 volts
③ Varies depending on temperature
④ Not usable

DIAGNOSTIC CIRCUIT CHECK

The Diagnostic Circuit Check is an organized approach to identifying a problem created by an electronic engine control system malfunction. It must be the starting point for any drivability complaint diagnosis because it directs the service technician to the next logical step in diagnosing the complaint.

The Tech 1 data listed in the table may be used for comparison after completing the diagnostic circuit check and finding the on-board diagnostics functioning properly with no trouble codes displayed. The "Typical Data Values" are an average of display values recorded from normally operating vehicles and are intended to represent what a normally functioning system would typically display.

A "SCAN" TOOL THAT DISPLAYS FAULTY DATA SHOULD NOT BE USED, AND THE PROBLEM SHOULD BE REPORTED TO THE MANUFACTURER. THE USE OF A FAULTY "SCAN" TOOL CAN RESULT IN MISDIAGNOSIS AND UNNECESSARY PARTS REPLACEMENT.

Only the parameters listed below are used in this manual for diagnosis. If a "Scan" tool reads other parameters, the values are not recommended by General Motors for use in diagnosis. For more description on the values and use of the Tech 1 tool to diagnosis ECM inputs, refer to the applicable "Component Systems" diagnosis in Section "C". If all values are within the range illustrated, refer to "Symptoms"

TECH 1 TOOL DATA

Test Under Following Conditions: ***Idle, Upper Radiator Hose Hot, Closed Throttle, Park or Neutral, "Closed Loop", All Accessories "OFF."***

"SCAN" Position	Units Displayed	Typical Data Value
Engine Speed	Rpm	± 50 RPM from desired rpm in drive (A/T) ± 100 RPM from desired rpm in neutral (M/T)
Desired Idle	Rpm	ECM idle command (varies with temp.)
Coolant Temperature	Degrees Celsius	85°C-105°C
IAT/MAT	Degrees Celsius	10°C-90°C (varies with underhood temp. and sensor location)
MAP	kPa/Volts	29-48 kPa/1-2 volts (varies with manifold and barometric pressures)
Open/Closed Loop	Open/Closed	"Closed Loop" (may enter "Open Loop" with extended idle)
Throt Position	Volts	.35 - 1.33
Throttle Angle	0 - 100%	0
Oxygen Sensor	Millivolts	100 - 999 (varies continuously)
Inj. Pulse Width	Milliseconds	.8 - 3.0
Spark Advance	Degrees	Varies
Engine Speed	Rpm	± 50 RPM from desired rpm in drive (A/T) ± 100 RPM from desired rpm in neutral (M/T)
Fuel Integrator	Counts	100-160
Block Learn	Counts	116-140
Idle Air Control	Counts (steps)	1 - 50
P/N Switch	P-N and R-D-L	Park/Neutral (P/N)
MPH/KPH	0-255	0
TCC	"ON"/"OFF"	"OFF"
Ign/Batt Voltage	Volts	13.5 - 14.5
Cooling Fan Relay	"ON"/"OFF"	"OFF" (coolant temperature below 100°C)
A/C Request	"YES"/"NO"	"NO"
A/C Clutch	"ON"/"OFF"	"OFF"
Power Steering	Normal/High Pressure	Normal
Shift Light (M/T)	"ON"/"OFF"	"OFF"

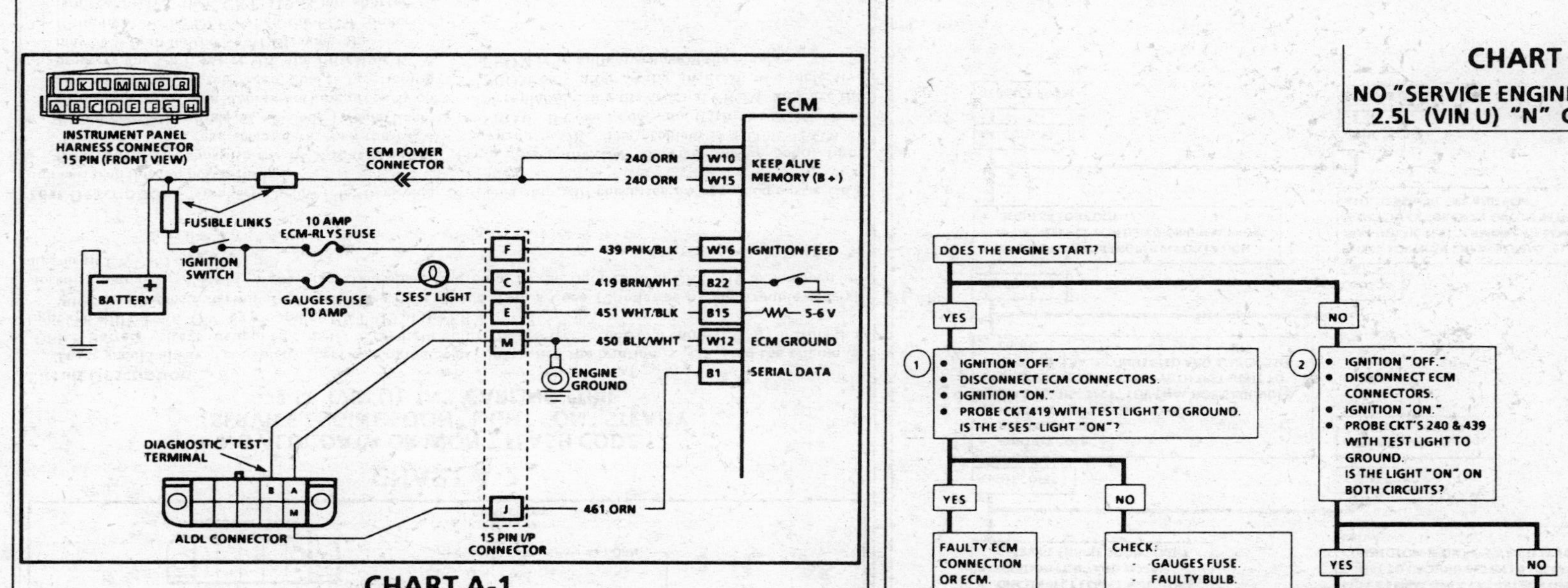

CHART A-1

NO "SERVICE ENGINE SOON" LIGHT 2.5L (VIN U) "N" CARLINE (TBI)

Circuit Description:

There should always be a steady "Service Engine Soon" ("SES") light when the ignition is "ON" and engine stopped. Battery voltage is supplied directly to the light bulb. The Electronic Control Module (ECM) controls the light and turns it "ON" by providing a ground path through CKT 419 to the ECM.

Test Description: Number(s) below refer to circled number(s) on the diagnostic chart.

1. This check determines if there is a fault in the "SES" light circuit or in the ECM.
2. If CKTs 240 and 439 have voltage, the ECM grounds or the ECM is faulty.
3. Using a test light connected to battery voltage, probe each of the system ground circuits to be sure a good ground is present. See ECM terminal end view in front of this section for the ECM terminal locations of ground circuits.

Diagnostic Aids:

If engine runs OK, check the following:

- Faulty light bulb.
- CKT 419 open.
- Gauges fuse blown. This will result in no oil or generator lights, seat belt reminder, etc.

If engine cranks but will not run, use CHART A-3.

CHART A-1

NO "SERVICE ENGINE SOON" LIGHT 2.5L (VIN U) "N" CARLINE (TBI)

DOES THE ENGINE START?

YES

(1)
- IGNITION "OFF."
- DISCONNECT ECM CONNECTORS.
- IGNITION "ON."
- PROBE CKT 419 WITH TEST LIGHT TO GROUND.

IS THE "SES" LIGHT "ON"?

YES: FAULTY ECM CONNECTION OR ECM.

NO: CHECK:
- GAUGES FUSE.
- FAULTY BULB.
- OPEN CKT 419.
- CKT 419 SHORTED TO VOLTAGE.
- OPEN IGNITION FEED TO BULB.

NO

(2)
- IGNITION "OFF."
- DISCONNECT ECM CONNECTORS.
- IGNITION "ON."
- PROBE CKT'S 240 & 439 WITH TEST LIGHT TO GROUND.

IS THE LIGHT "ON" ON BOTH CIRCUITS?

YES: (3) FAULTY ECM GROUNDS OR ECM.

NO: REPAIR OPEN IN CIRCUIT THAT DID NOT LIGHT THE TEST LIGHT. IF A FUSIBLE LINK OR FUSE WAS BLOWN, LOCATE AND CORRECT THE SHORT TO GROUND ON THAT CIRCUIT.

"AFTER REPAIRS," CONFIRM "CLOSED LOOP" OPERATION AND NO "SERVICE ENGINE SOON" LIGHT.

DIAGNOSTIC CHARTS — 2.5L ENGINE

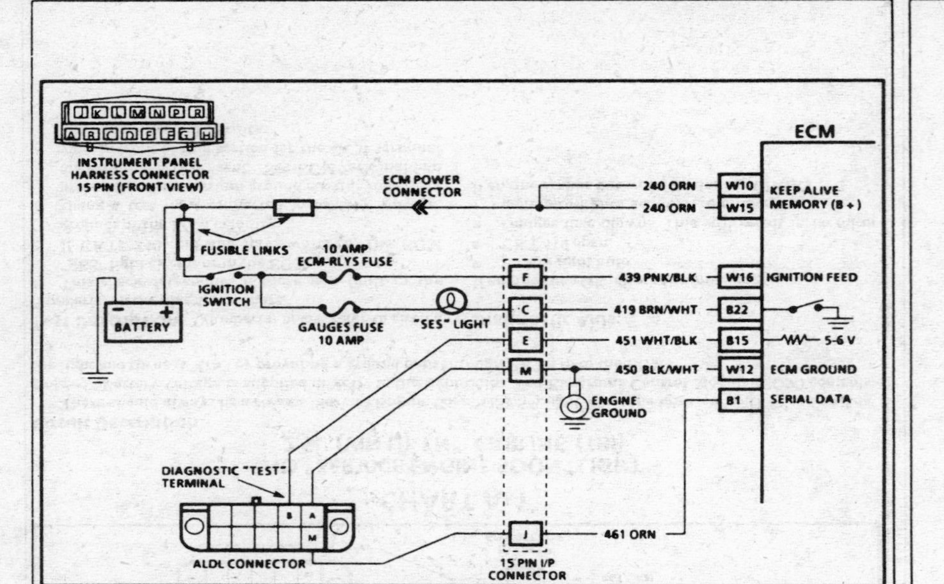

CHART A-2

NO ALDL DATA OR WON'T FLASH CODE 12 "SERVICE ENGINE SOON" LIGHT "ON" STEADY 2.5L (VIN U) "N" CARLINE (TBI)

Circuit Description:

There should always be a steady "Service Engine Soon" light when the ignition is "ON" and the engine is "OFF." Battery voltage is supplied directly to the light bulb. The electronic control module (ECM) controls the light and will turn it "ON" by grounding CKT 419 at the ECM.

With the diagnostic terminal grounded, the light should flash a Code 12 followed by any trouble code(s) stored in memory. A steady light suggests a short to ground in the light control CKT 419 or an open in diagnostic CKT 451.

Test Description: Number(s) below refer to circled number(s) on the diagnostic chart.

1. If there is a problem with the ECM that causes a "Scan" tool to not read serial data, then the ECM should not flash a Code 12. If Code 12 does flash, be sure that the "Scan" tool is working properly on another vehicle. If the "Scan" tool is functioning properly and CKT 461 is OK, the PROM or ECM may be at fault for the No ALDL symptom.
2. If the light turns "OFF" when the ECM connector is disconnected, then CKT 419 is not shorted to ground.
3. This step will check for an open diagnostic CKT 451.
4. At this point, the "Service Engine Soon" light wiring is OK. The problem is a faulty ECM or PROM. If Code 12 does not flash, the ECM should be replaced using the original PROM. Replace the PROM only after trying an ECM, as a defective PROM is an unlikely cause of the problem.

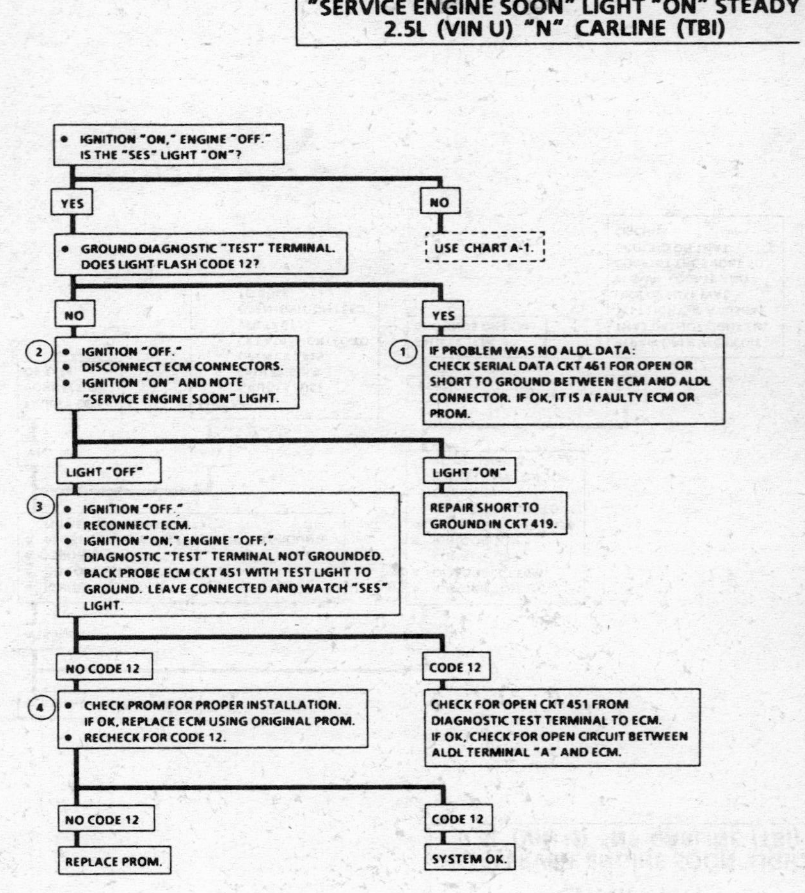

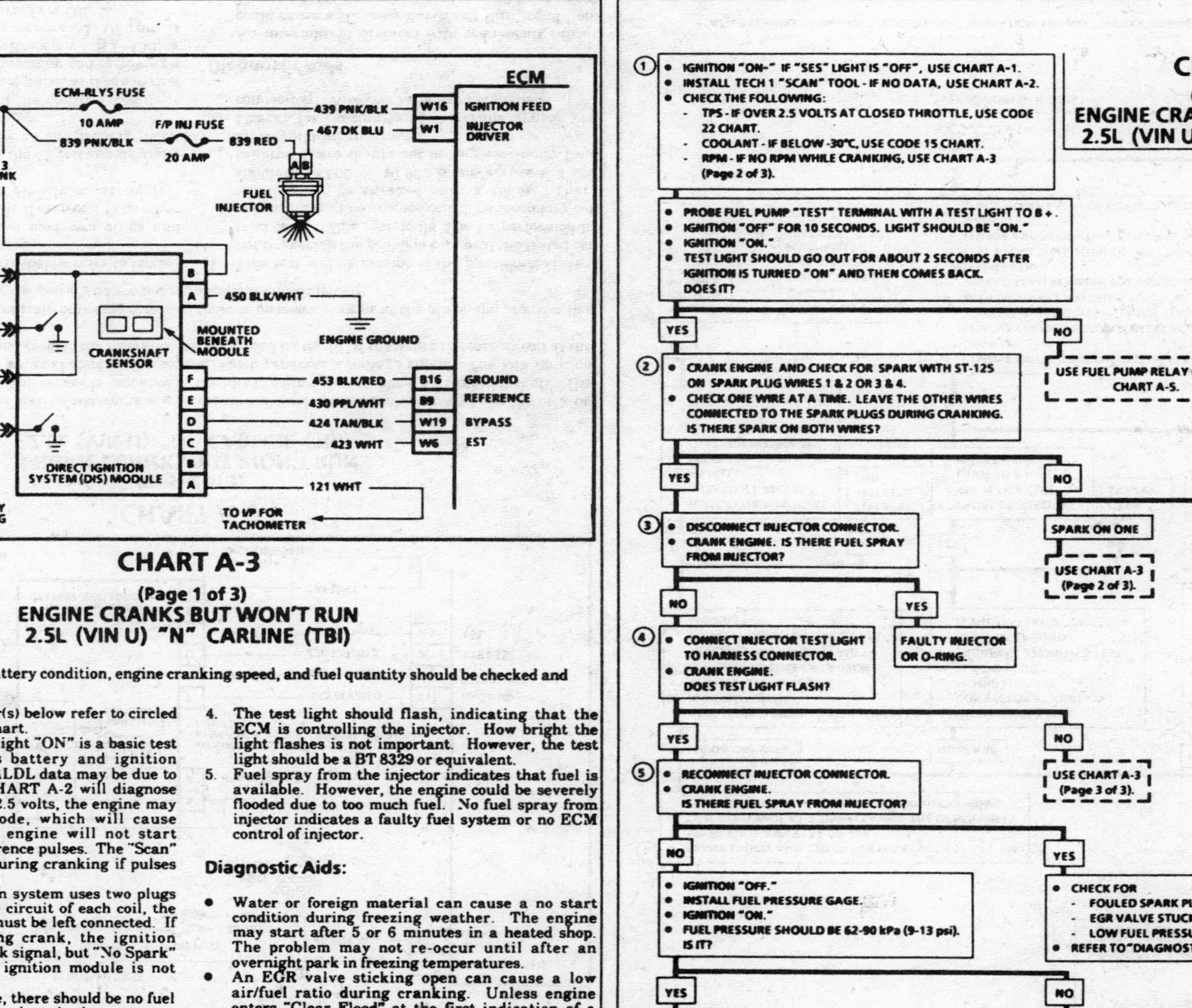

CHART A-3

(Page 1 of 3)

ENGINE CRANKS BUT WON'T RUN 2.5L (VIN U) "N" CARLINE (TBI)

Circuit Description:

Before using this chart, battery condition, engine cranking speed, and fuel quantity should be checked and verified as being OK.

Test Description: Number(s) below refer to circled number(s) on the diagnostic chart.

1. A "Service Engine Soon" light "ON" is a basic test to determine if there is battery and ignition voltage at the ECM. No ALDL data may be due to an ECM problem, and CHART A-2 will diagnose the ECM. If TPS is over 2.5 volts, the engine may be in the clear flood mode, which will cause starting problems. The engine will not start without crank sensor reference pulses. The "Scan" tool should display rpm during cranking if pulses are received at the ECM.
2. Because the direct ignition system uses two plugs and wires to complete the circuit of each coil, the opposite spark plug wire must be left connected. If rpm was indicated during crank, the ignition module is receiving a crank signal, but "No Spark" at this test indicates the ignition module is not triggering the coil.
3. While cranking the engine, there should be no fuel spray with the injector electrical connector disconnected. Replace the injector if it sprays fuel or drips.
4. The test light should flash, indicating that the ECM is controlling the injector. How bright the light flashes is not important. However, the test light should be a BT 8329 or equivalent.
5. Fuel spray from the injector indicates that fuel is available. However, the engine could be severely flooded due to too much fuel. No fuel spray from injector indicates a faulty fuel system or no ECM control of injector.

Diagnostic Aids:

- Water or foreign material can cause a no start condition during freezing weather. The engine may start after 5 or 6 minutes in a heated shop. The problem may not re-occur until after an overnight park in freezing temperatures.
- An EGR valve sticking open can cause a low air/fuel ratio during cranking. Unless engine enters "Clear Flood" at the first indication of a flooding condition, it can result in a no start.
- Fuel pressure: Low fuel pressure can result in a very lean air/fuel ratio. Use CHART A-7.

CHART A-3

(Page 1 of 3)

ENGINE CRANKS BUT WON'T RUN 2.5L (VIN U) "N" CARLINE (TBI)

(1)
- IGNITION "ON." IF "SES" LIGHT IS "OFF", USE CHART A-1.
- INSTALL TECH 1 "SCAN" TOOL - IF NO DATA, USE CHART A-2.
- CHECK THE FOLLOWING:
  - TPS - IF OVER 2.5 VOLTS AT CLOSED THROTTLE, USE CODE 22 CHART.
  - COOLANT - IF BELOW -30°C, USE CODE 15 CHART.
  - RPM - IF NO RPM WHILE CRANKING, USE CHART A-3 (Page 2 of 3).

- PROBE FUEL PUMP "TEST" TERMINAL WITH A TEST LIGHT TO B+.
- IGNITION "OFF" FOR 10 SECONDS. LIGHT SHOULD BE "ON."
- IGNITION "ON."
- TEST LIGHT SHOULD GO OUT FOR ABOUT 2 SECONDS AFTER IGNITION IS TURNED "ON" AND THEN COMES BACK. DOES IT?

NO: USE FUEL PUMP RELAY CIRCUIT CHART A-5.

YES:

(2)
- CRANK ENGINE AND CHECK FOR SPARK WITH ST-125 ON SPARK PLUG WIRES 1 & 2 OR 3 & 4.
- CHECK ONE WIRE AT A TIME. LEAVE THE OTHER WIRES CONNECTED TO THE SPARK PLUGS DURING CRANKING. IS THERE SPARK ON BOTH WIRES?

NO:
- SPARK ON ONE: USE CHART A-3 (Page 2 of 3).
- NO SPARK: REPLACE IGNITION MODULE.

YES:

(3)
- DISCONNECT INJECTOR CONNECTOR.
- CRANK ENGINE. IS THERE FUEL SPRAY FROM INJECTOR?

YES: FAULTY INJECTOR OR O-RING.

NO:

(4)
- CONNECT INJECTOR TEST LIGHT TO HARNESS CONNECTOR.
- CRANK ENGINE. DOES TEST LIGHT FLASH?

NO: USE CHART A-3 (Page 3 of 3).

YES:

(5)
- RECONNECT INJECTOR CONNECTOR.
- CRANK ENGINE. IS THERE FUEL SPRAY FROM INJECTOR?

YES:
- CHECK FOR
  - FOULED SPARK PLUGS
  - EGR VALVE STUCK OPEN
  - LOW FUEL PRESSURE, USE CHART A-7
- REFER TO "DIAGNOSTIC AIDS" ON FACING PAGE.

NO:
- IGNITION "OFF."
- INSTALL FUEL PRESSURE GAGE.
- IGNITION "ON."
- FUEL PRESSURE SHOULD BE 62-90 kPa (9-13 psi). IS IT?

NO: USE FUEL SYSTEM DIAGNOSIS CHART A-7.

YES: REPLACE INJECTOR.

"AFTER REPAIRS," CONFIRM "CLOSED LOOP" OPERATION AND NO "SERVICE ENGINE SOON" LIGHT.

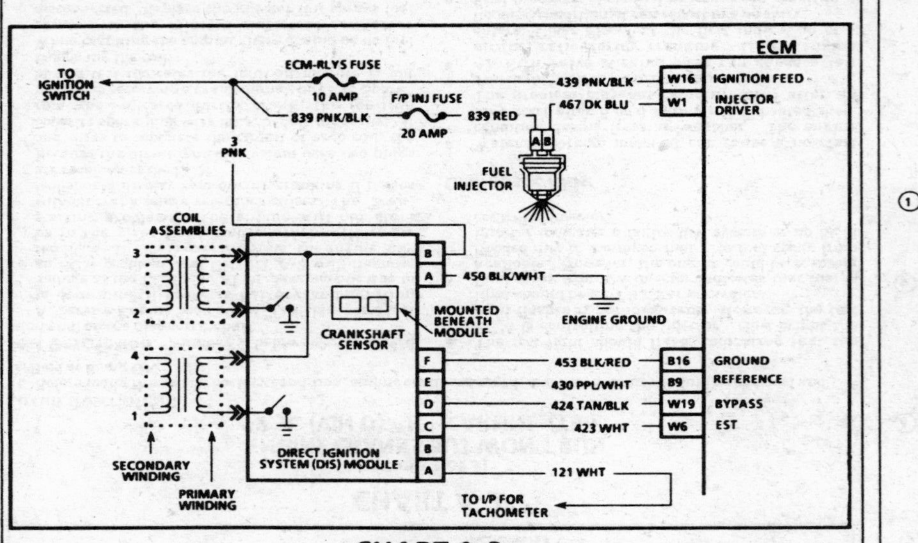

CHART A-3

(Page 2 of 3)

ENGINE CRANKS BUT WON'T RUN
2.5L (VIN U) "N" CARLINE (TBI)

Circuit Description:

A magnetic crank sensor is used to determine engine crankshaft position, much the same way as the pick-up coil did in HEI type systems. The sensor is mounted in the block, near a slotted wheel on the crankshaft. The rotation of the wheel creates a flux change in the sensor, which produces a voltage signal. The DIS ignition module processes this signal and creates the reference pulses needed by the ECM to trigger the correct coil at the correct time.

If the "Scan" tool did not indicate cranking rpm, and there is no spark present at the plugs, the problem lies in the direct ignition system or the power and ground supplies to the module.

Test Description: Number(s) below refer to circled number(s) on the diagnostic chart.

1. The direct ignition system uses two plugs and wires to complete the circuit of each coil. The other spark plug wire in the circuit must be left connected to create a spark.
2. This test will determine if the 12 volt supply and a good ground is available at the DIS ignition module.
3. This test will determine if the ignition module is not generating the reference pulse, or if the wiring or ECM are at fault. By touching and removing a test light to battery voltage on CKT 430, a reference pulse should be generated. If rpm is indicated, the ECM and wiring are OK.
4. This test will determine if the ignition module is not triggering the problem coil, or if the tested coil is at fault. This test could also be performed by substituting a known good coil. The secondary coil winding can be checked with a DVM. There should be 5,000 to 10,000 ohms across the coil towers. There should not be any continuity from either coil tower to ground.
5. Checks for continuity of the crank sensor and connections. Also checks sensor magnetism.

Diagnostic Aids:

An intermittent problem with crankshaft sensor could cause a "Cranks But Won't Run" condition. Therefore, the crankshaft sensor must be replaced first. If the "Cranks But Won't Run" condition persists, then replace the DIS module.

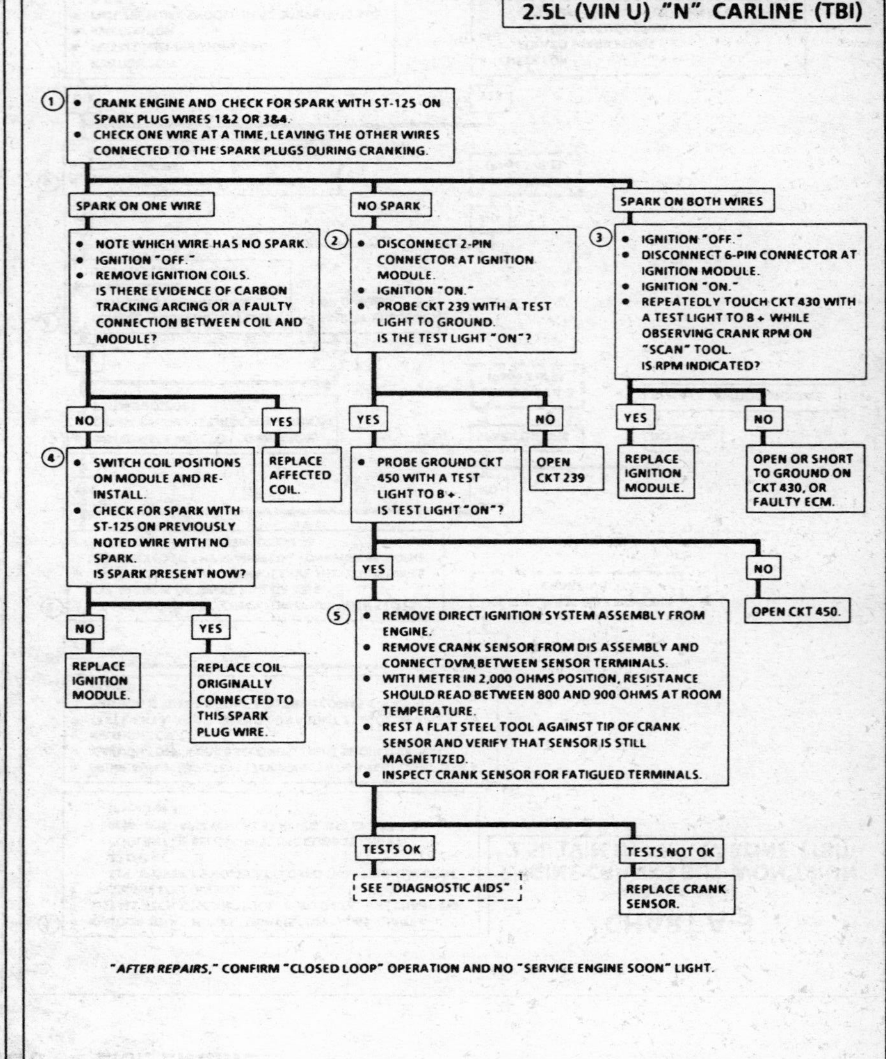

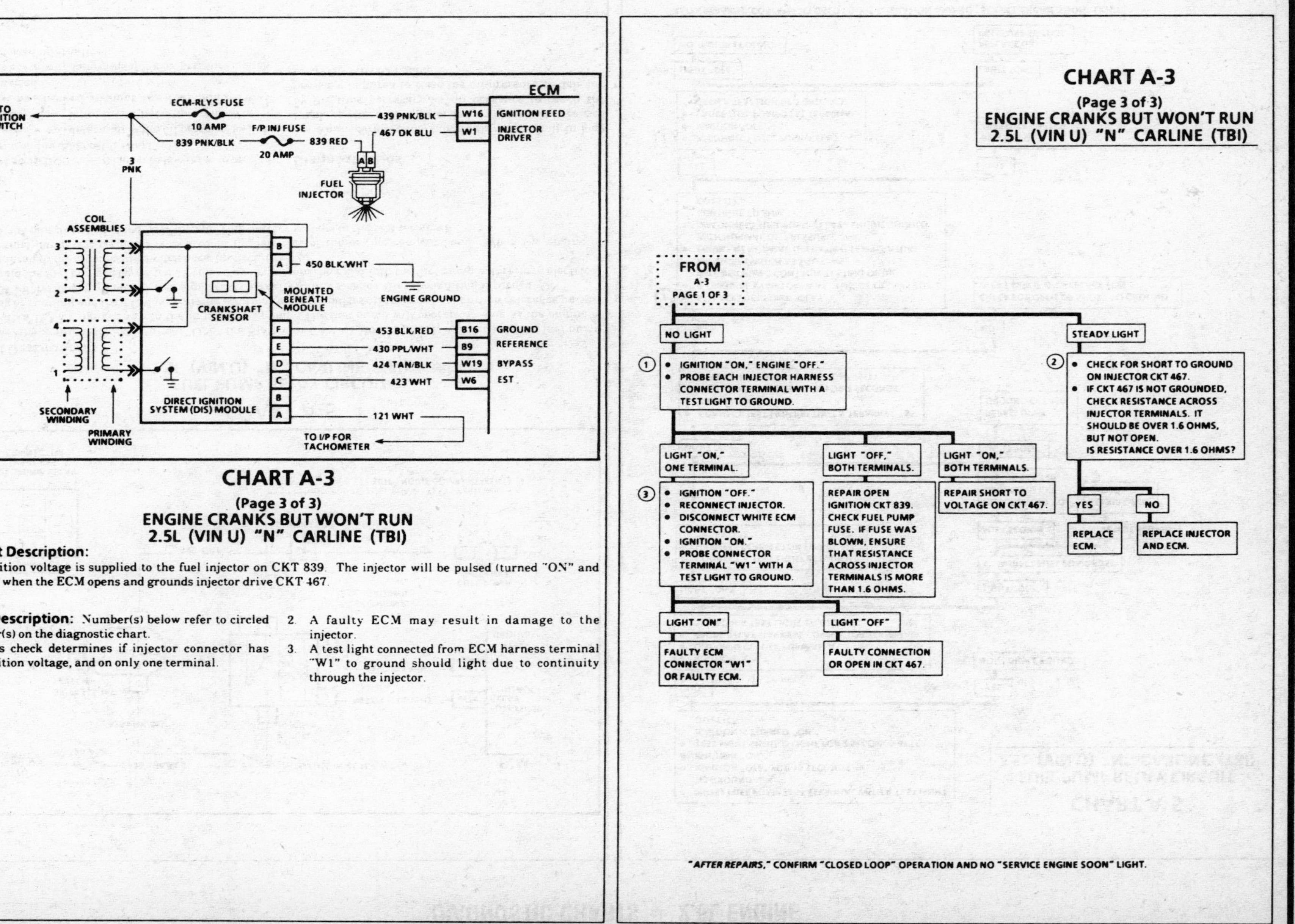

CHART A-3

(Page 3 of 3)

ENGINE CRANKS BUT WON'T RUN 2.5L (VIN U) "N" CARLINE (TBI)

Circuit Description:

Ignition voltage is supplied to the fuel injector on CKT 839. The injector will be pulsed (turned "ON" and "OFF") when the ECM opens and grounds injector drive CKT 467.

Test Description: Number(s) below refer to circled number(s) on the diagnostic chart.

1. This check determines if injector connector has ignition voltage, and on only one terminal.
2. A faulty ECM may result in damage to the injector.
3. A test light connected from ECM harness terminal "W1" to ground should light due to continuity through the injector.

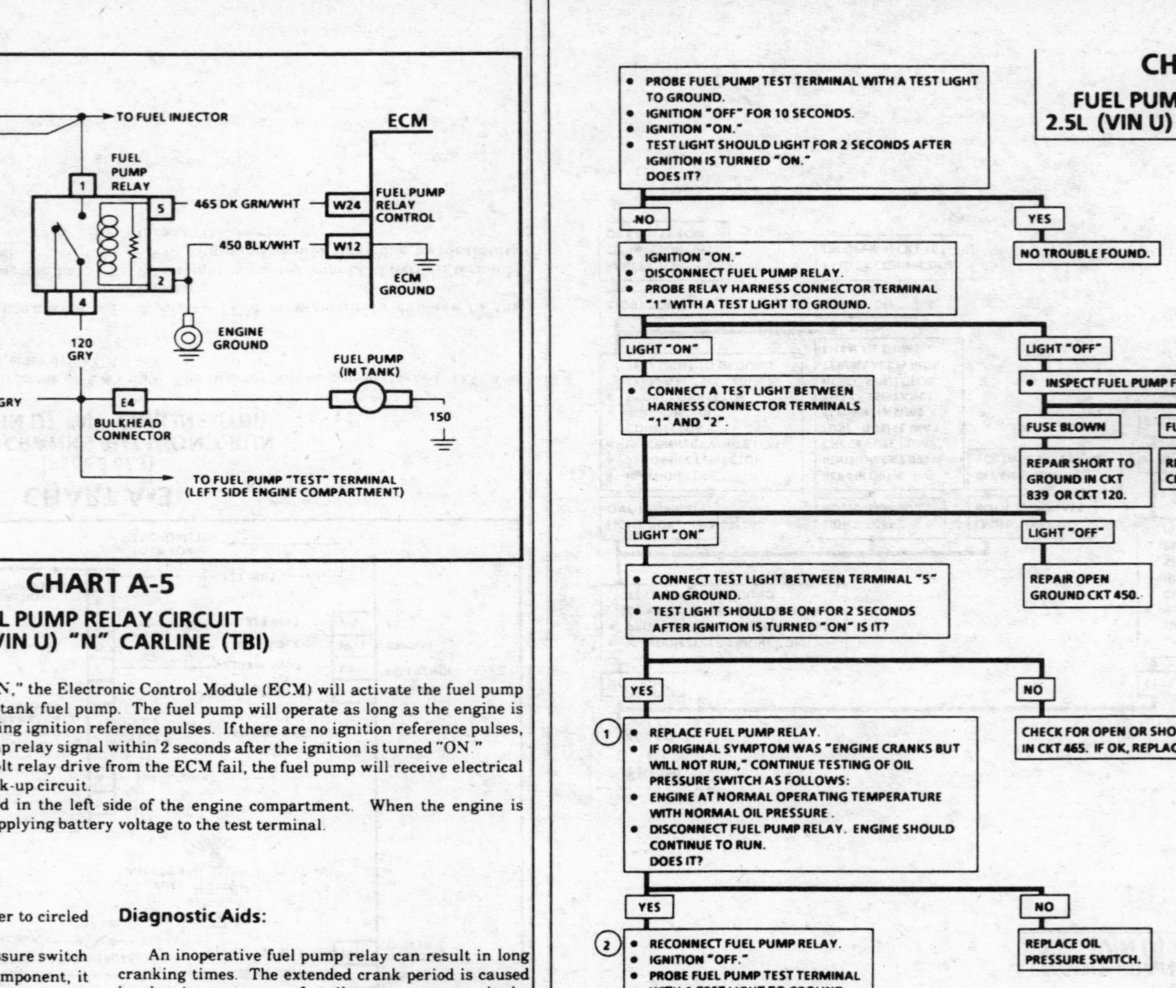

CHART A-5

FUEL PUMP RELAY CIRCUIT
2.5L (VIN U) "N" CARLINE (TBI)

Circuit Description:

When the ignition switch is turned "ON," the Electronic Control Module (ECM) will activate the fuel pump relay with a 12 volt signal and run the in-tank fuel pump. The fuel pump will operate as long as the engine is cranking or running and the ECM is receiving ignition reference pulses. If there are no ignition reference pulses, the ECM will no longer supply the fuel pump relay signal within 2 seconds after the ignition is turned "ON."

Should the fuel pump relay or the 12 volt relay drive from the ECM fail, the fuel pump will receive electrical current through the oil pressure switch back-up circuit.

The fuel pump test terminal is located in the left side of the engine compartment. When the engine is stopped, the pump can be turned "ON" by applying battery voltage to the test terminal.

Test Description: Number(s) below refer to circled number(s) on the diagnostic chart.

1. This check will determine if the oil pressure switch is faulty also. Since it is a back-up component, it must be checked without the fuel pump relay connected.
2. This check will determine if the oil pressure switch is shorted internally.

Diagnostic Aids:

An inoperative fuel pump relay can result in long cranking times. The extended crank period is caused by the time necessary for oil pressure to reach the pressure required to close the oil pressure switch and turn "ON" the fuel pump.

CHART A-5

FUEL PUMP RELAY CIRCUIT
2.5L (VIN U) "N" CARLINE (TBI)

- PROBE FUEL PUMP TEST TERMINAL WITH A TEST LIGHT TO GROUND.
- IGNITION "OFF" FOR 10 SECONDS.
- IGNITION "ON."
- TEST LIGHT SHOULD LIGHT FOR 2 SECONDS AFTER IGNITION IS TURNED "ON."

DOES IT?

YES: NO TROUBLE FOUND.

NO:

- IGNITION "ON."
- DISCONNECT FUEL PUMP RELAY.
- PROBE RELAY HARNESS CONNECTOR TERMINAL "1" WITH A TEST LIGHT TO GROUND.

LIGHT "OFF":

- INSPECT FUEL PUMP FUSE

FUSE BLOWN: REPAIR SHORT TO GROUND IN CKT 839 OR CKT 120.

FUSE NOT BLOWN: REPAIR OPEN CKT 839.

LIGHT "ON":

- CONNECT A TEST LIGHT BETWEEN HARNESS CONNECTOR TERMINALS "1" AND "2".

LIGHT "OFF": REPAIR OPEN GROUND CKT 450.

LIGHT "ON":

- CONNECT TEST LIGHT BETWEEN TERMINAL "5" AND GROUND.
- TEST LIGHT SHOULD BE ON FOR 2 SECONDS AFTER IGNITION IS TURNED "ON" IS IT?

NO: CHECK FOR OPEN OR SHORT TO GROUND IN CKT 465. IF OK, REPLACE ECM.

YES:

(1)
- REPLACE FUEL PUMP RELAY.
- IF ORIGINAL SYMPTOM WAS "ENGINE CRANKS BUT WILL NOT RUN," CONTINUE TESTING OF OIL PRESSURE SWITCH AS FOLLOWS:
- ENGINE AT NORMAL OPERATING TEMPERATURE WITH NORMAL OIL PRESSURE.
- DISCONNECT FUEL PUMP RELAY. ENGINE SHOULD CONTINUE TO RUN.

DOES IT?

NO: REPLACE OIL PRESSURE SWITCH.

YES:

(2)
- RECONNECT FUEL PUMP RELAY.
- IGNITION "OFF."
- PROBE FUEL PUMP TEST TERMINAL WITH A TEST LIGHT TO GROUND.

LIGHT "OFF": NO TROUBLE FOUND.

LIGHT "ON": REPLACE OIL PRESSURE SWITCH.

"AFTER REPAIRS," CONFIRM "CLOSED LOOP" OPERATION AND NO "SERVICE ENGINE SOON" LIGHT.

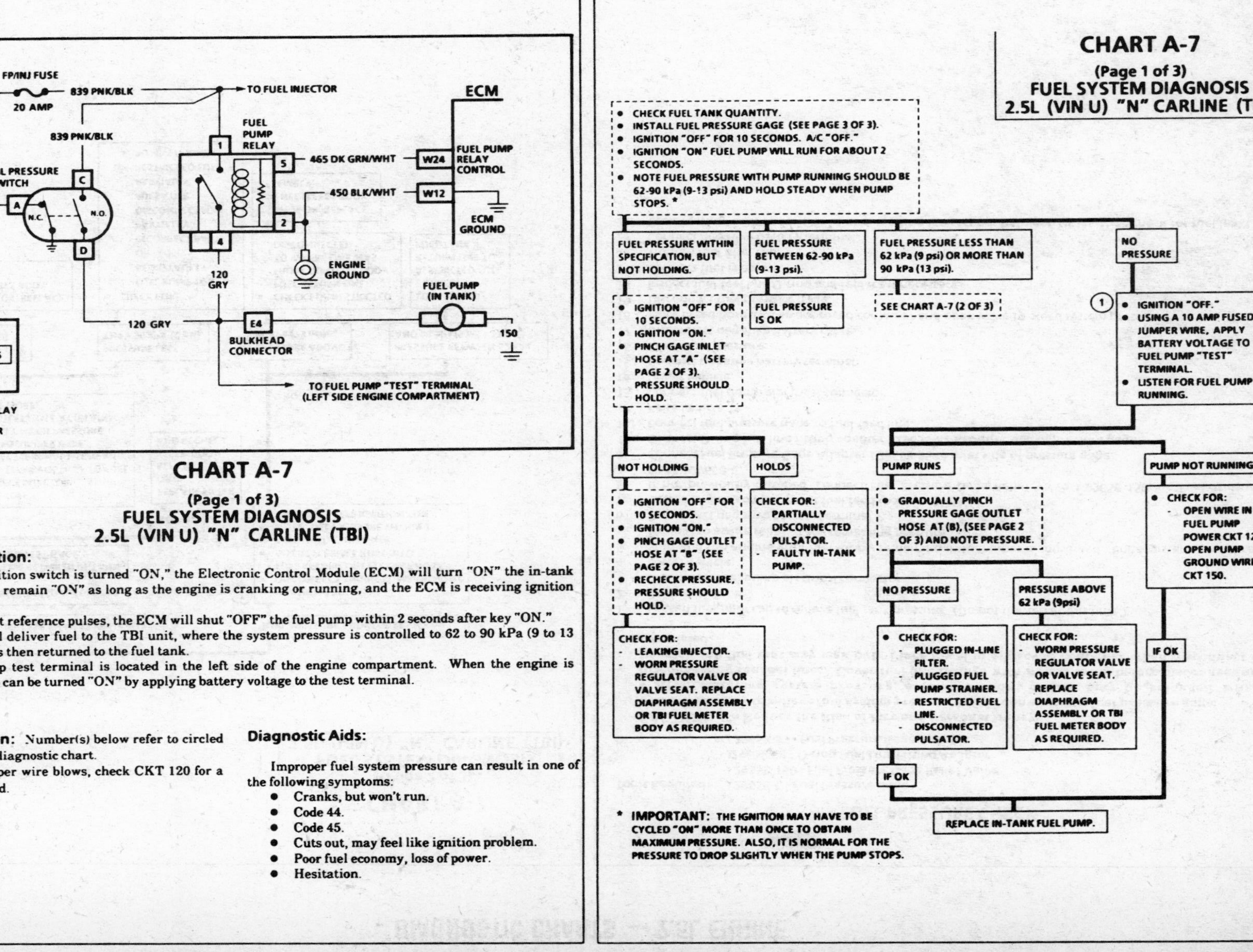

CHART A-7

(Page 1 of 3)

FUEL SYSTEM DIAGNOSIS

2.5L (VIN U) "N" CARLINE (TBI)

Circuit Description:

When the ignition switch is turned "ON," the Electronic Control Module (ECM) will turn "ON" the in-tank fuel pump. It will remain "ON" as long as the engine is cranking or running, and the ECM is receiving ignition reference pulses.

If there are not reference pulses, the ECM will shut "OFF" the fuel pump within 2 seconds after key "ON."

The pump will deliver fuel to the TBI unit, where the system pressure is controlled to 62 to 90 kPa (9 to 13 psi). Excess fuel is then returned to the fuel tank.

The fuel pump test terminal is located in the left side of the engine compartment. When the engine is stopped, the pump can be turned "ON" by applying battery voltage to the test terminal.

Test Description: Number(s) below refer to circled number(s) on the diagnostic chart.

1. If fuse in jumper wire blows, check CKT 120 for a short to ground.

Diagnostic Aids:

Improper fuel system pressure can result in one of the following symptoms:

- Cranks, but won't run.
- Code 44.
- Code 45.
- Cuts out, may feel like ignition problem.
- Poor fuel economy, loss of power.
- Hesitation.

CHART A-7

(Page 1 of 3)

FUEL SYSTEM DIAGNOSIS

2.5L (VIN U) "N" CARLINE (TBI)

* **IMPORTANT:** THE IGNITION MAY HAVE TO BE CYCLED "ON" MORE THAN ONCE TO OBTAIN MAXIMUM PRESSURE. ALSO, IT IS NORMAL FOR THE PRESSURE TO DROP SLIGHTLY WHEN THE PUMP STOPS.

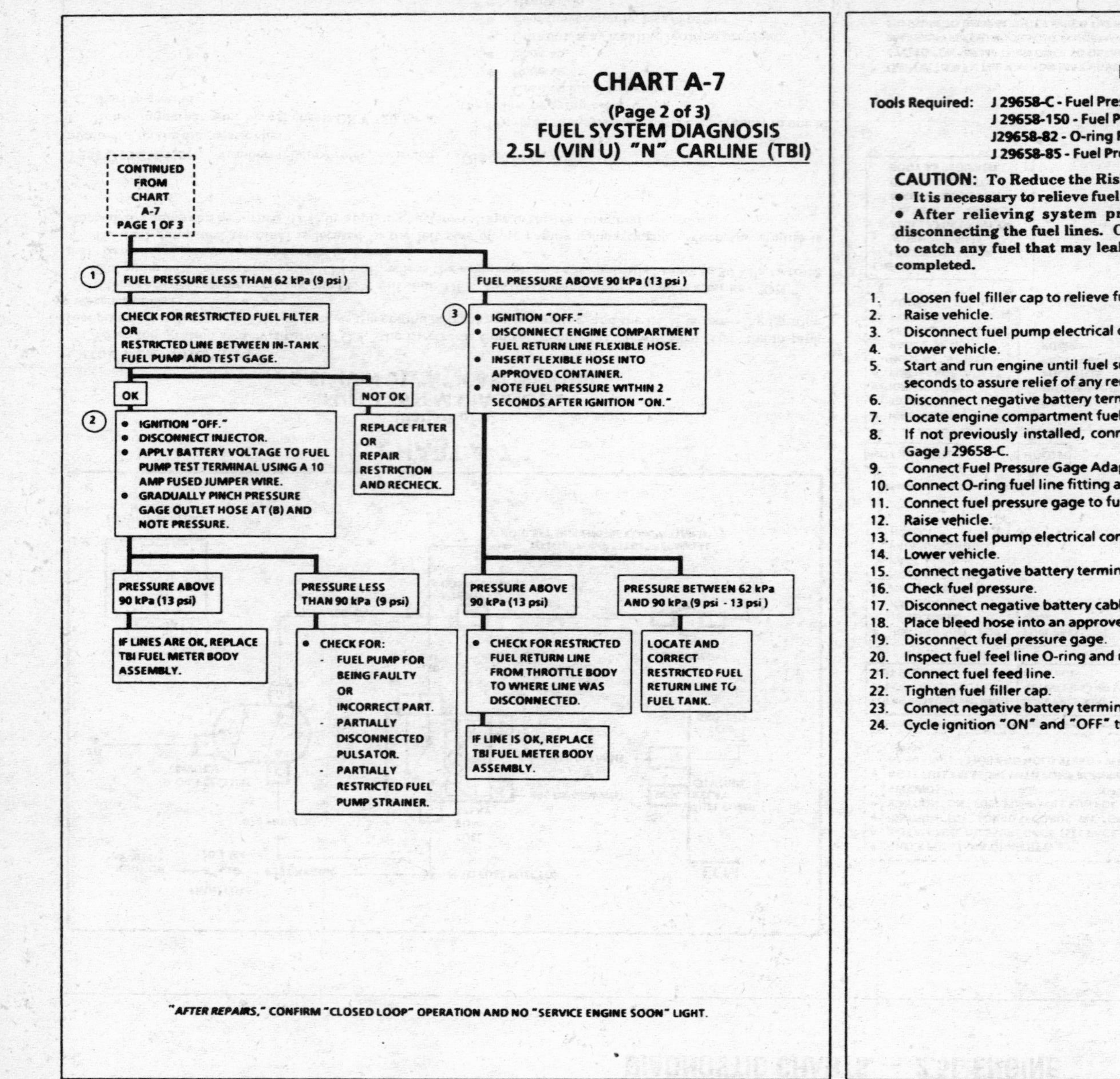

FUEL PRESSURE CHECK

Tools Required:
J 29658-C - Fuel Pressure Gage
J 29658-150 - Fuel Pressure Gage Relief Valve
J29658-82 - O-ring Fuel Line Fitting Adapter
J 29658-85 - Fuel Pressure Gage Adapter

CAUTION: To Reduce the Risk of Fire and Personal Injury:
- **It is necessary to relieve fuel system pressure before connecting a fuel pressure gage.**
- **After relieving system pressure, a small amount of fuel may be released when disconnecting the fuel lines. Cover fuel line fittings with a shop towel before disconnecting, to catch any fuel that may leak out. Place towel in approved container when disconnect is completed.**

1. Loosen fuel filler cap to relieve fuel tank pressure. (Do not tighten at this time.)
2. Raise vehicle.
3. Disconnect fuel pump electrical connector.
4. Lower vehicle.
5. Start and run engine until fuel supply remaining in fuel pipes is consumed. Engage starter for three seconds to assure relief of any remaining pressure.
6. Disconnect negative battery terminal.
7. Locate engine compartment fuel feed (pressure) line.
8. If not previously installed, connect Fuel Pressure Gage Relief Valve J 29658-150, on Fuel Pressure Gage J 29658-C.
9. Connect Fuel Pressure Gage Adapter J 29658-85 to inlet side of pressure gage.
10. Connect O-ring fuel line fitting adapter J 29658-82 to outlet side of pressure gage.
11. Connect fuel pressure gage to fuel feed line.
12. Raise vehicle.
13. Connect fuel pump electrical connector.
14. Lower vehicle.
15. Connect negative battery terminal.
16. Check fuel pressure.
17. Disconnect negative battery cable.
18. Place bleed hose into an approved container and open valve to bleed system pressure.
19. Disconnect fuel pressure gage.
20. Inspect fuel feel line O-ring and replace if necessary.
21. Connect fuel feed line.
22. Tighten fuel filler cap.
23. Connect negative battery terminal.
24. Cycle ignition "ON" and "OFF" twice, waiting ten seconds between cycles, then check for fuel leaks.

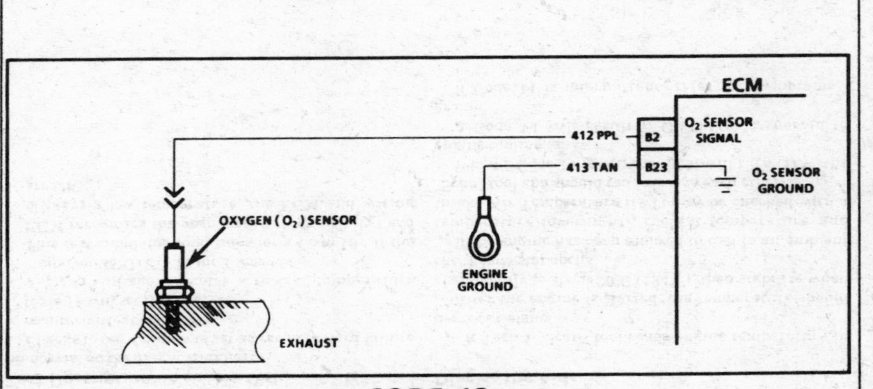

CODE 13

OXYGEN (O_2) SENSOR CIRCUIT (OPEN CIRCUIT) 2.5L (VIN U) "N" CARLINE (TBI)

Circuit Description:

The ECM supplies a voltage of about .45 volt between terminals "B2" and "B23". (If measured with a 10 megohm digital voltmeter, this may read as low as .32 volt).

When the O_2 sensor reaches operating temperature, it varies this voltage from about .1 volt (exhaust is lean) to about .9 volt (exhaust is rich).

The sensor is like an open circuit and produces no voltage when it is below 316°C (600°F). An open sensor circuit or cold sensor causes "Open Loop" operation.

Test Description: Number(s) below refer to circled number(s) on the diagnostic chart.

1. Code 13 will set under the following conditions:
   - Engine at normal operating temperature.
   - At least 40 seconds have elapsed since engine start-up.
   - O_2 signal voltage is steady between .35 and .55 volt.
   - Throttle angle is above 6%.
   - All above conditions are met for about 4 seconds.

   If the conditions for a Code 13 exist, the system will not operate in "Closed Loop."
2. This test determines if the O_2 sensor is the problem or if the ECM and wiring are at fault.
3. In doing this test, use only a 10 megohm digital voltmeter. This test checks the continuity of CKTs 412 and 413. If CKT 413 is open, the ECM voltage on CKT 412 will be over .6 volt (600 mV).

Diagnostic Aids:

Normal "Scan" tool O_2 sensor voltage varies between 100 mV to 999 mV (.1 and 1.0 volt) while in "Closed Loop." Code 13 sets in one minute if sensor signal voltage remains between .35 and .55 volt, but the system will go to "Open Loop" in about 15 seconds.

Verify a clean, tight ground connection for CKT 413. Open CKT(s) 412 or 413 will result in a Code 13. If Code 13 is intermittent, refer to "Symptoms,"

CODE 13

OXYGEN (O_2) SENSOR CIRCUIT (OPEN CIRCUIT) 2.5L (VIN U) "N" CARLINE (TBI)

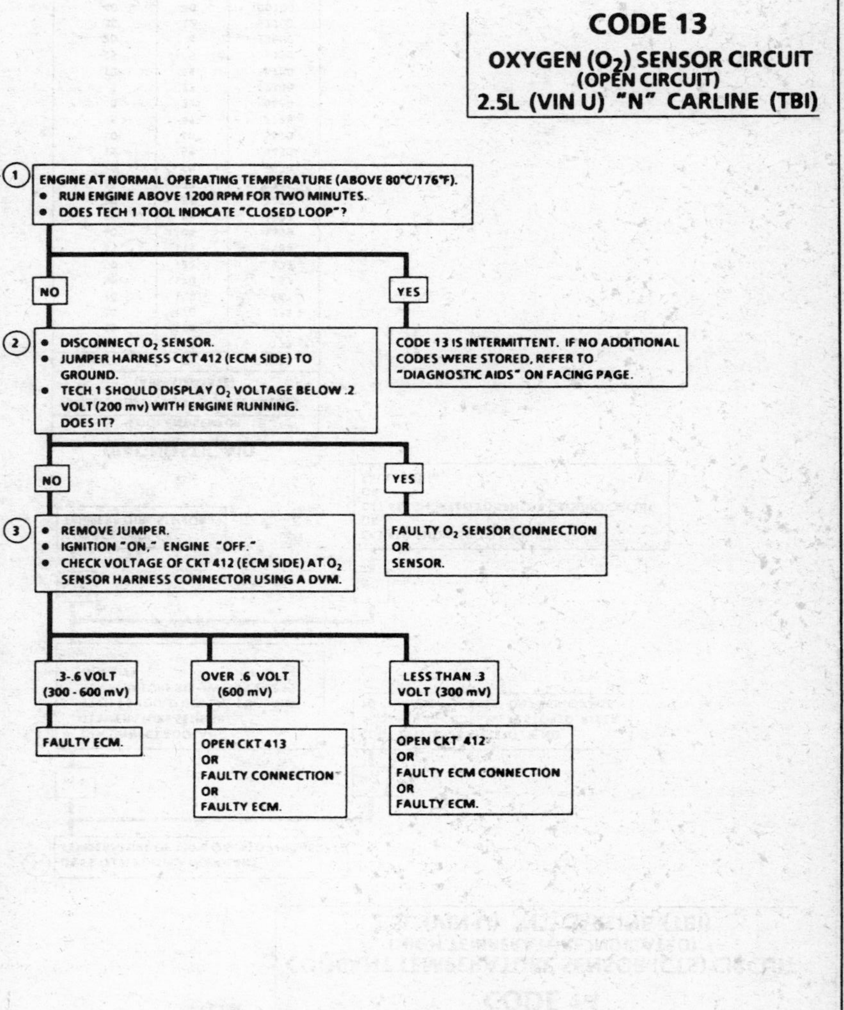

"AFTER REPAIRS," REFER TO CODE CRITERIA ON FACING PAGE AND CONFIRM CODE DOES NOT RESET.

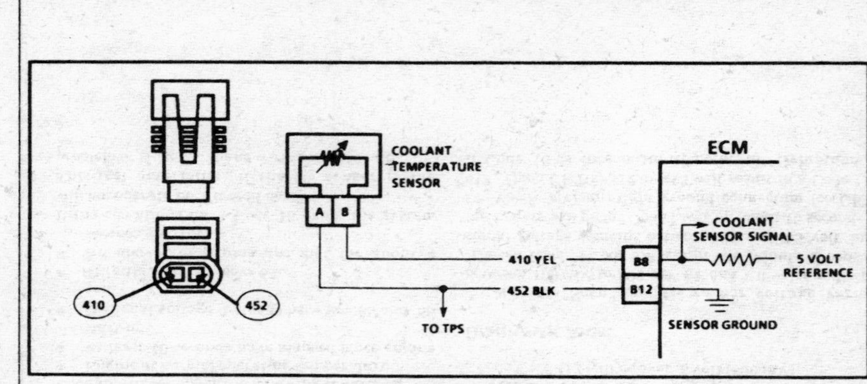

CODE 14

COOLANT TEMPERATURE SENSOR (CTS) CIRCUIT
(HIGH TEMPERATURE INDICATED)
2.5L (VIN U) "N" CARLINE (TBI)

Circuit Description:

The Coolant Temperature Sensor (CTS) uses a thermistor to control the signal voltage to the ECM. The ECM applies a reference voltage on CKT 410 to the sensor. When the engine is cold, the sensor (thermistor) resistance is high. The ECM will then sense a high signal voltage.

As the engine warms up, the sensor resistance decreases and the voltage drops. At normal engine operating temperature, the voltage will measure about 1.5 to 2.0 volts at ECM terminal "B8".

Coolant temperature is one of the inputs used to control the following:

- Fuel Delivery.
- Electronic Spark Timing (EST).
- Cooling Fan.
- Torque Converter Clutch (TCC).
- Idle Air Control (IAC).

Test Description: Number(s) below refer to circled number(s) on the diagnostic chart.

1. Checks to see if code was set as result of hard failure or intermittent condition.
   Code 14 will set if:
   - Signal voltage indicates a coolant temperature above 135°C (275°F) for 3 seconds.
2. This test simulates conditions for a Code 15. If the ECM recognizes the open circuit (high voltage) and displays a low temperature, the ECM and wiring are OK.

Diagnostic Aids:

A Tech 1 "Scan" tool reads engine temperature in degrees Celsius.

After the engine is started, the temperature should rise steadily to about 90°C (194°F), then stabilize when the thermostat opens.

If the engine has been allowed to cool to an ambient temperature (overnight), coolant temperature and Intake Air Temperature (IAT) may be checked with a "Scan" tool and should read close to each other.

When a Code 14 is set, the ECM will turn "ON" the engine cooling fan.

A Code 14 will result if CKT 410 is shorted to ground.

If Code 14 is intermittent, refer to "Symptoms."

CODE 14

COOLANT TEMPERATURE SENSOR (CTS) CIRCUIT
(HIGH TEMPERATURE INDICATED)
2.5L (VIN U) "N" CARLINE (TBI)

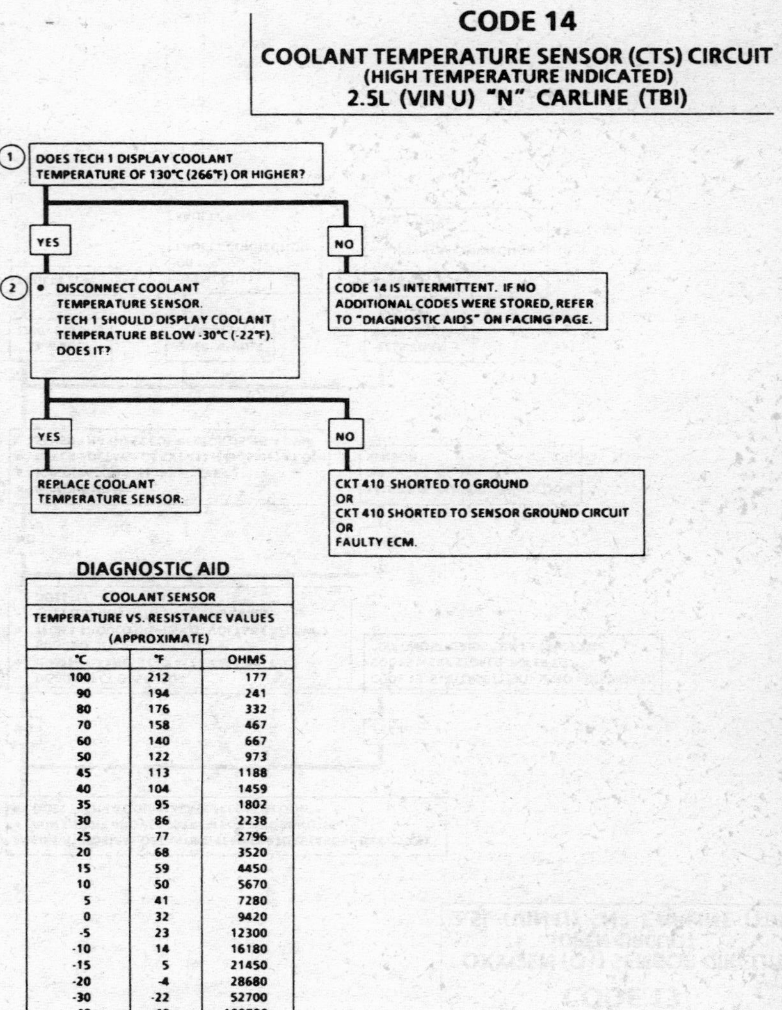

DIAGNOSTIC AID

COOLANT SENSOR
TEMPERATURE VS. RESISTANCE VALUES
(APPROXIMATE)

°C	°F	OHMS
100	212	177
90	194	241
80	176	332
70	158	467
60	140	667
50	122	973
45	113	1188
40	104	1459
35	95	1802
30	86	2238
25	77	2796
20	68	3520
15	59	4450
10	50	5670
5	41	7280
0	32	9420
-5	23	12300
-10	14	16180
-15	5	21450
-20	-4	28680
-30	-22	52700
-40	-40	100700

"AFTER REPAIRS," REFER TO CODE CRITERIA ON FACING PAGE AND CONFIRM CODE DOES NOT RESET.

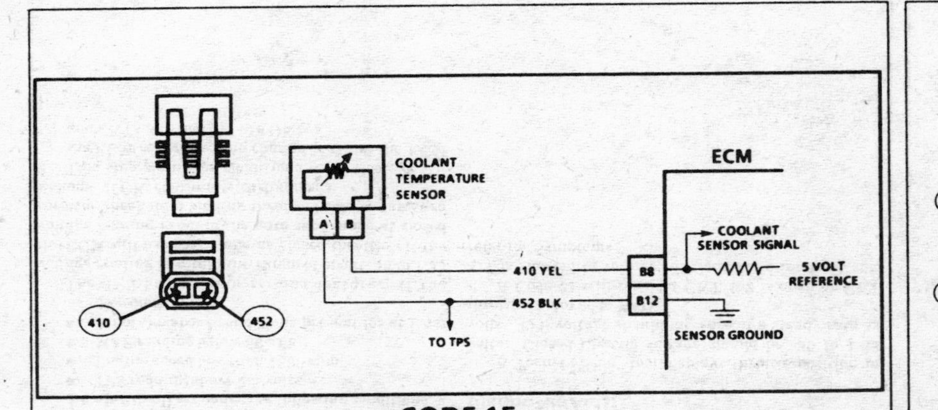

CODE 15

COOLANT TEMPERATURE SENSOR (CTS) CIRCUIT
(LOW TEMPERATURE INDICATED)
2.5L (VIN U) "N" CARLINE (TBI)

Circuit Description:

The Coolant Temperature Sensor (CTS) uses a thermistor to control the signal voltage to the ECM. The ECM applies a reference voltage on CKT 410 to the sensor. When the engine is cold, the sensor (thermistor) resistance is high. The ECM will then sense a high signal voltage.

As the engine warms up, the sensor resistance decreases and the voltage drops. At normal engine operating temperature, the voltage will measure about 1.5 to 2.0 volts at ECM terminal "B8".

Coolant temperature is one of the inputs used to control the following:

- Fuel Delivery
- Electronic Spark Timing (EST).
- Cooling Fan.
- Torque Convertor Clutch (TCC).
- Idle Air Control (IAC).

Test Description: Number(s) below refer to circled number(s) on the diagnostic chart.

1. Checks to see if code was set as result of hard failure or intermittent condition.
   Code 15 will set if:
   - Signal voltage indicates a coolant temperature below -30°C (-22°F) for 60 seconds.
2. This test simulates conditions for a Code 14. If the ECM recognizes the grounded circuit (low voltage) and displays a high temperature, the ECM and wiring are OK.
3. This test will determine if there is a wiring problem or a faulty ECM. If CKT 452 is open, there may also be a Code 21 stored.

Diagnostic Aids:

A Tech 1 "Scan" tool reads engine temperature in degrees Celsius. After the engine is started, the temperature should rise steadily to about 90°C (194°F), then stabilize when the thermostat opens.

If the engine has been allowed to cool to an ambient temperature (overnight), coolant temperature and Intake Air Temperature (IAT) may be checked with a "Scan" tool and should read close to each other.

When a Code 15 is set, the ECM will turn "ON" the engine cooling fan.

A Code 15 will result if CKTs 410 or 452 are open.

If Code 15 is intermittent, refer to "Symptoms,"

CODE 15

COOLANT TEMPERATURE SENSOR (CTS) CIRCUIT
(LOW TEMPERATURE INDICATED)
2.5L (VIN U) "N" CARLINE (TBI)

(1)
- DOES TECH 1 DISPLAY COOLANT TEMPERATURE OF -30°C (-22°F) OR LESS?

NO → CODE 15 IS INTERMITTENT. IF NO ADDITIONAL CODES WERE STORED, REFER TO "DIAGNOSTIC AIDS" ON FACING PAGE.

YES ↓

(2)
- DISCONNECT COOLANT TEMPERATURE SENSOR.
- JUMPER HARNESS TERMINALS TOGETHER.
- TECH 1 SHOULD DISPLAY 130°C (266°F) OR MORE. DOES IT?

YES → FAULTY CONNECTION OR COOLANT TEMPERATURE SENSOR.

NO ↓

(3)
- JUMPER CKT 410 TO GROUND.
- TECH 1 SHOULD DISPLAY OVER 130°C (266 °F). DOES IT?

YES → OPEN COOLANT TEMPERATURE SENSOR GROUND CIRCUIT, FAULTY CONNECTION OR FAULTY ECM.

NO → OPEN CKT 410, FAULTY CONNECTION AT ECM, OR FAULTY ECM.

DIAGNOSTIC AID

COOLANT SENSOR
TEMPERATURE VS. RESISTANCE VALUES
(APPROXIMATE)

°C	°F	OHMS
100	212	177
90	194	241
80	176	332
70	158	467
60	140	667
50	122	973
45	113	1188
40	104	1459
35	95	1802
30	86	2238
25	77	2796
20	68	3520
15	59	4450
10	50	5670
5	41	7280
0	32	9420
-5	23	12300
-10	14	16180
-15	5	21450
-20	-4	28680
-30	-22	52700
-40	-40	100700

"AFTER REPAIRS," REFER TO CODE CRITERIA ON FACING PAGE AND CONFIRM CODE DOES NOT RESET.

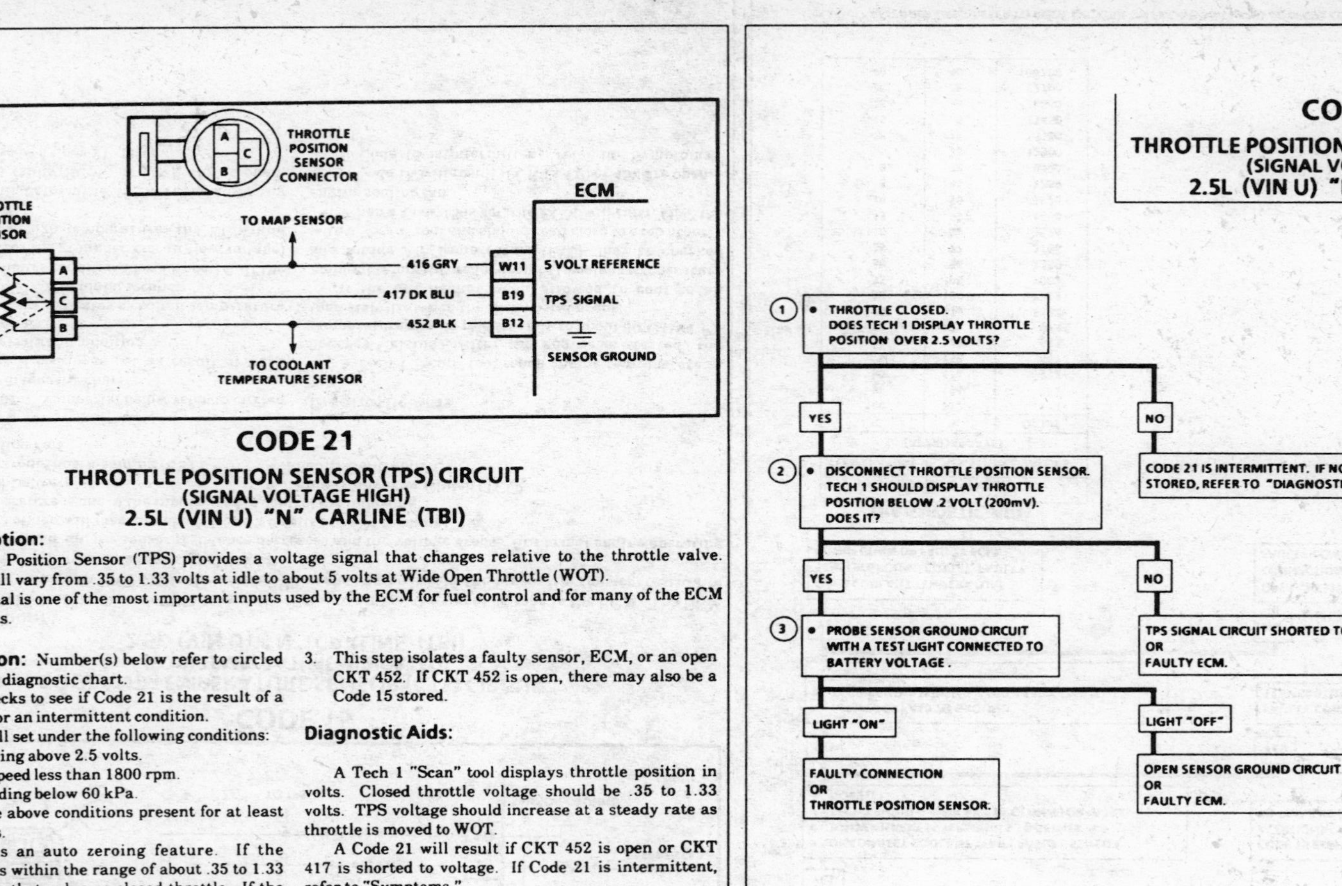

CODE 21

THROTTLE POSITION SENSOR (TPS) CIRCUIT
(SIGNAL VOLTAGE HIGH)
2.5L (VIN U) "N" CARLINE (TBI)

Circuit Description:

The Throttle Position Sensor (TPS) provides a voltage signal that changes relative to the throttle valve. Signal voltage will vary from .35 to 1.33 volts at idle to about 5 volts at Wide Open Throttle (WOT).

The TPS signal is one of the most important inputs used by the ECM for fuel control and for many of the ECM controlled outputs.

Test Description: Number(s) below refer to circled number(s) on the diagnostic chart.

1. This step checks to see if Code 21 is the result of a hard failure or an intermittent condition.
   A Code 21 will set under the following conditions:
   - TPS reading above 2.5 volts.
   - Engine speed less than 1800 rpm.
   - MAP reading below 60 kPa.
   - All of the above conditions present for at least 2 seconds.

   The TPS has an auto zeroing feature. If the voltage reading is within the range of about .35 to 1.33 the ECM will use that value as closed throttle. If the voltage reading is out of the auto zero range at closed throttle, check for a binding throttle cable or damaged linkage. If OK, continue with diagnosis.
2. This step simulates conditions for a Code 22. If the ECM recognizes the change of state, the ECM and CKTs 416 and 417 are OK.
3. This step isolates a faulty sensor, ECM, or an open CKT 452. If CKT 452 is open, there may also be a Code 15 stored.

Diagnostic Aids:

A Tech 1 "Scan" tool displays throttle position in volts. Closed throttle voltage should be .35 to 1.33 volts. TPS voltage should increase at a steady rate as throttle is moved to WOT.

A Code 21 will result if CKT 452 is open or CKT 417 is shorted to voltage. If Code 21 is intermittent, refer to "Symptoms,"

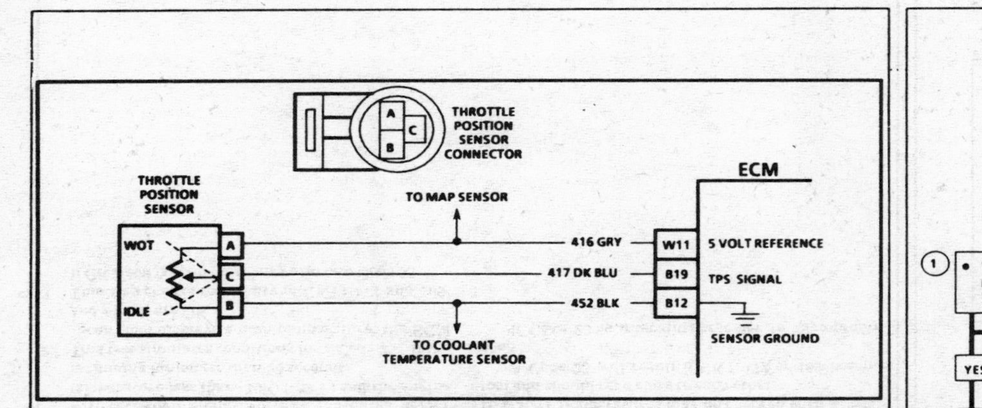

CODE 22

THROTTLE POSITION SENSOR (TPS) CIRCUIT (SIGNAL VOLTAGE LOW) 2.5L (VIN U) "N" CARLINE (TBI)

Circuit Description:

The Throttle Position Sensor (TPS) provides a voltage signal that changes, relative to the throttle valve. Signal voltage will vary from .35 to 1.33 volts at idle to about 4.5 volts at Wide Open Throttle (WOT).

The TPS signal is one of the most important inputs used by the ECM for fuel control and for many of the ECM controlled outputs.

Test Description: Number(s) below refer to circled number(s) on the diagnostic chart.

1. Code 22 will set if:
   - Engine is running.
   - TPS signal voltage is less than .20 volt.

   The TPS has an auto zeroing feature. If the voltage reading is within the range of about .35 to 1.33 volts, the ECM will use that value as closed throttle. If the voltage reading is out of the auto zero range at closed throttle, check for a binding throttle cable or damaged linkage, if OK, continue with diagnosis.
2. Simulates Code 21: (high voltage). If the ECM recognizes the high signal voltage then the ECM and wiring are OK.
3. Check for good sensor connection. If connection is good, replace TPS.
4. This simulates a high signal voltage to check for an open in CKT 417. The "Scan" tool will not read up to 12 volts. but what is important is that the ECM recognizes the signal on CKT 417.

Diagnostic Aids:

A Tech 1 "Scan" tool reads throttle position in volts. With ignition "ON" or at idle TPS signal voltage should read from about .35 to 1.33 volts with the throttle closed and increase at a steady rate as throttle is moved toward WOT.

An open or short to ground in CKT 416 or CKT 417 will result in a Code 22.

If Code is intermittent, refer to "Intermittents" in "Symptoms,"

CODE 22

THROTTLE POSITION SENSOR (TPS) CIRCUIT (SIGNAL VOLTAGE LOW) 2.5L (VIN U) "N" CARLINE (TBI)

(1)
- THROTTLE CLOSED.
  DOES TECH 1 DISPLAY THROTTLE POSITION .2V (200 mV) OR BELOW?

NO:
- CODE 22 IS INTERMITTENT.
  IF NO ADDITIONAL CODES WERE STORED, REFER TO "DIAGNOSTIC AIDS" ON FACING PAGE.

YES:

(2)
- DISCONNECT TPS SENSOR.
- JUMPER CKTS 416 & 417 TOGETHER.
  TECH 1 SHOULD DISPLAY THROTTLE POSITION OVER 4.0 V (4000 mV).
  DOES IT?

YES:

(3)
- REFER TO FACING PAGE FOR SPECIFIC INSTRUCTIONS.

NO:

(4)
- PROBE CKT 417 WITH A TEST LIGHT CONNECTED TO BATTERY VOLTAGE.
  TECH 1 SHOULD DISPLAY THROTTLE POSITION OVER 4.0V (4000 mV).
  DOES IT?

YES:
CKT 416 OPEN OR SHORTED TO GROUND
OR
FAULTY CONNECTION
OR
FAULTY ECM.

NO:
CKT 417 OPEN OR SHORTED TO GROUND, OR SHORTED TO THROTTLE POSITION SENSOR GROUND CIRCUIT
OR
FAULTY ECM CONNECTION
OR
FAULTY ECM.

"AFTER REPAIRS," REFER TO CODE CRITERIA ON FACING PAGE AND CONFIRM CODE DOES NOT RESET.

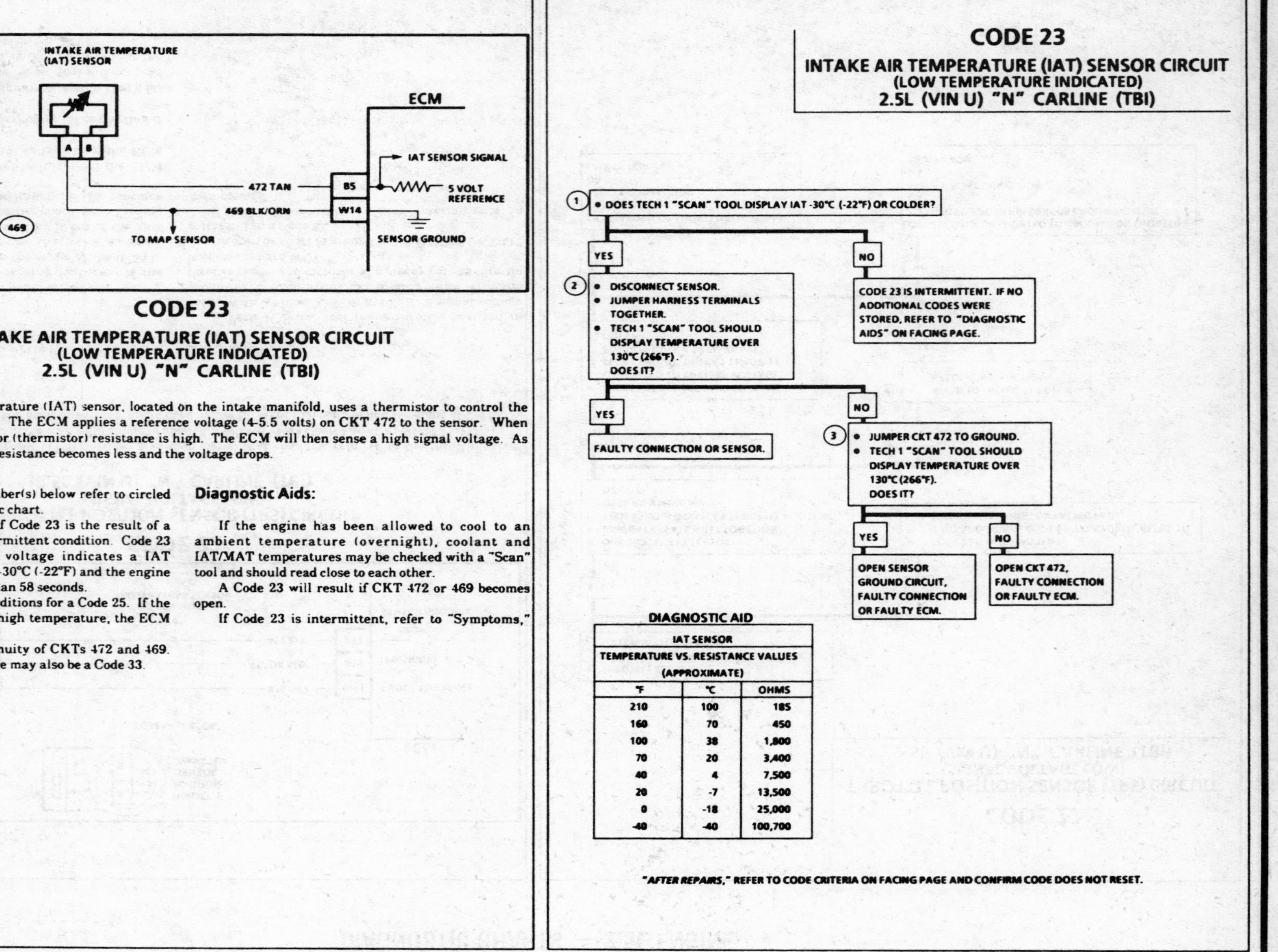

CODE 23

INTAKE AIR TEMPERATURE (IAT) SENSOR CIRCUIT
(LOW TEMPERATURE INDICATED)
2.5L (VIN U) "N" CARLINE (TBI)

Circuit Description:

The Intake Air Temperature (IAT) sensor, located on the intake manifold, uses a thermistor to control the signal voltage to the ECM. The ECM applies a reference voltage (4-5.5 volts) on CKT 472 to the sensor. When intake air is cold, the sensor (thermistor) resistance is high. The ECM will then sense a high signal voltage. As the air warms, the sensor resistance becomes less and the voltage drops.

Test Description: Number(s) below refer to circled number(s) on the diagnostic chart.

1. This step determines if Code 23 is the result of a hard failure or an intermittent condition. Code 23 will set when signal voltage indicates a IAT temperature less than -30°C (-22°F) and the engine is running for longer than 58 seconds.
2. This test simulates conditions for a Code 25. If the "Scan" tool displays a high temperature, the ECM and wiring are OK.
3. This step checks continuity of CKTs 472 and 469. If CKT 469 is open there may also be a Code 33.

Diagnostic Aids:

If the engine has been allowed to cool to an ambient temperature (overnight), coolant and IAT/MAT temperatures may be checked with a "Scan" tool and should read close to each other.

A Code 23 will result if CKT 472 or 469 becomes open.

If Code 23 is intermittent, refer to "Symptoms,"

CODE 23

INTAKE AIR TEMPERATURE (IAT) SENSOR CIRCUIT
(LOW TEMPERATURE INDICATED)
2.5L (VIN U) "N" CARLINE (TBI)

DIAGNOSTIC AID

IAT SENSOR
TEMPERATURE VS. RESISTANCE VALUES
(APPROXIMATE)

°F	°C	OHMS
210	100	185
160	70	450
100	38	1,800
70	20	3,400
40	4	7,500
20	-7	13,500
0	-18	25,000
-40	-40	100,700

"AFTER REPAIRS," REFER TO CODE CRITERIA ON FACING PAGE AND CONFIRM CODE DOES NOT RESET.

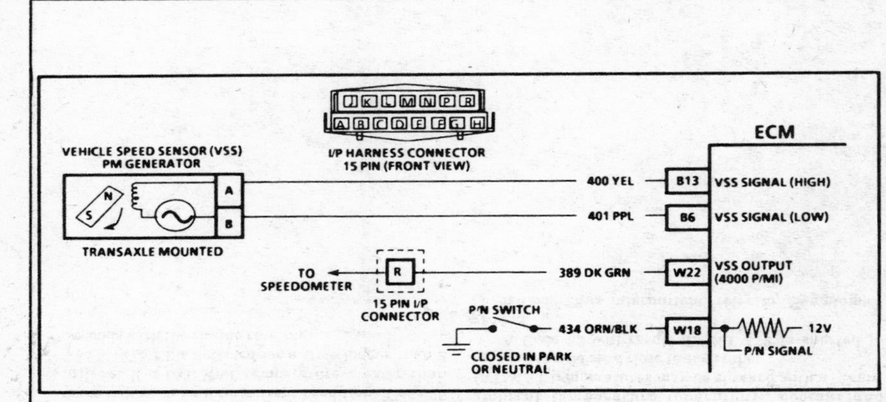

CODE 24

VEHICLE SPEED SENSOR (VSS) CIRCUIT 2.5L (VIN U) "N" CARLINE (TBI)

Circuit Description:

Vehicle speed information is provided to the ECM by the Vehicle Speed Sensor (VSS). It is a Permanent Magnet (PM) generator and is mounted in the transmission. The PM generator produces a pulsing voltage whenever vehicle speed is over about 3 mph. The A/C voltage level and the number of pulses increases with vehicle speed. The ECM converts the pulsing voltage to miles per hour. This data is used for calculations and can be displayed on a Tech 1 "Scan" tool.

The function of VSS buffer used in past model years has been incorporated into the ECM. The ECM supplies the necessary signal for the instrument panel (4000 pulses per mile) for operating the speedometer and the odometer.

Test Description: Number(s) below refer to circled number(s) on the diagnostic chart.

Code 24 will set if vehicle speed equals 0 mph when:

- Engine speed is between 1500 and 4400 rpm.
- TPS is less than 2%.
- Low load condition (low MAP voltage, high manifold vacuum).
- Transmission not in park or neutral.
- All above conditions are met for 4 seconds.

These conditions are met during a road load deceleration.

Disregard a Code 24 that sets when the drive wheels are not turning. This can be caused by a faulty park/neutral switch circuit.

The PM generator only produces a signal if the drive wheels are turning greater than 3 mph.

Diagnostic Aids:

A "Scan" tool should indicate a vehicle speed whenever the drive wheels are turning greater than 3 mph.

A problem in CKT 389 will not affect the VSS input or the readings on a "Scan" tool.

Check CKTs 400 and 401 for proper connections to be sure they are clean and tight and the harness is routed correctly. Refer to intermittents in "Symptoms,"

(A/T) - A faulty or misadjusted park/neutral switch can result in a false Code 24. Use a "Scan" tool and check for the proper signal while in a drive range. Refer to CHART C-1A for the P/N switch check.

CODE 24

VEHICLE SPEED SENSOR (VSS) CIRCUIT 2.5L (VIN U) "N" CARLINE (TBI)

DISREGARD CODE 24 IF SET WHILE DRIVE WHEELS ARE NOT TURNING.

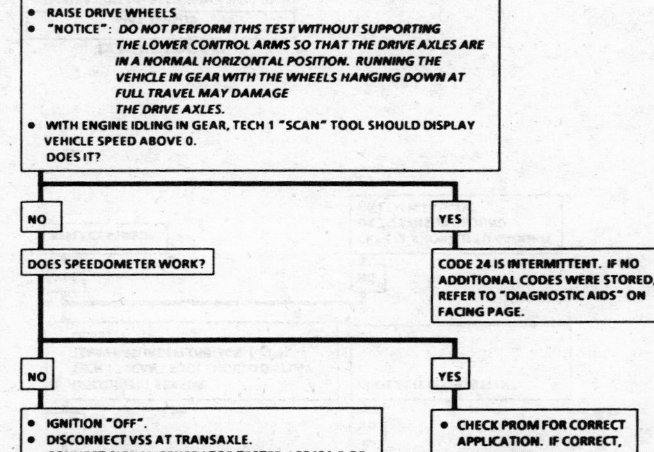

"AFTER REPAIRS," **REFER TO CODE CRITERIA ON FACING PAGE AND CONFIRM CODE DOES NOT RESET.**

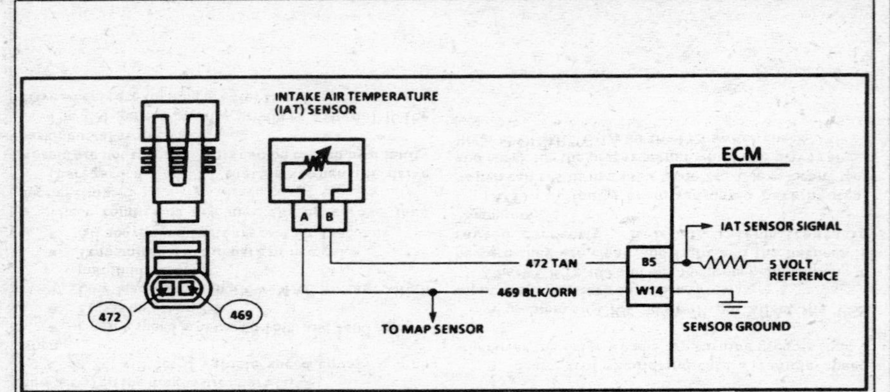

CODE 25

INTAKE AIR TEMPERATURE (IAT) SENSOR CIRCUIT (HIGH TEMPERATURE INDICATED) 2.5L (VIN U) "N" CARLINE (TBI)

Circuit Description:

The Intake Air Temperature (IAT) sensor, located on the intake manifold, uses a thermistor to control the signal voltage to the ECM. The ECM applies a reference voltage (4-5.5 volts) on CKT 472 to the sensor. When intake air is cold, the sensor (thermistor) resistance is high. Therefore, the ECM will see a high signal voltage. As the air warms, the sensor resistance becomes less and the voltage drops.

Test Description: Number(s) below refer to circled number(s) on the diagnostic chart.

1. This check determines if Code 25 is the result of a hard failure or an intermittent condition. Code 25 will set if a IAT/MAT temperature greater than 135°C (275°F) is detected for a time longer than 2 seconds with the engine running

Diagnostic Aids:

If the engine has been allowed to cool to an ambient temperature (overnight), coolant and IAT/MAT temperatures may be checked with a "Scan" tool and should read close to each other.

A Code 25 will result if CKT 472 is shorted to ground.

If Code 25 is intermittent, refer to "Symptoms,"

CODE 25

INTAKE AIR TEMPERATURE (IAT) SENSOR CIRCUIT (HIGH TEMPERATURE INDICATED) 2.5L (VIN U) "N" CARLINE (TBI)

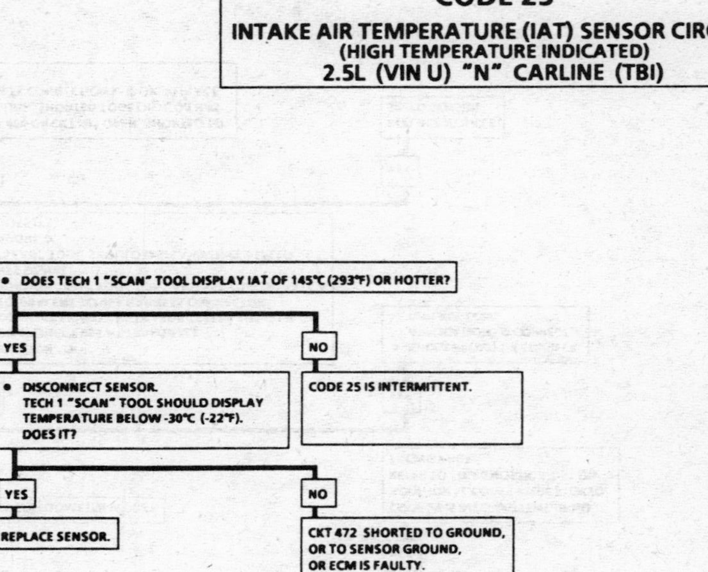

DIAGNOSTIC AID

IAT SENSOR		
TEMPERATURE VS. RESISTANCE VALUES (APPROXIMATE)		
°F	°C	OHMS
210	100	185
160	70	450
100	38	1,800
70	20	3,400
40	4	7,500
20	-7	13,500
0	-18	25,000
-40	-40	100,700

AFTER REPAIRS," REFER TO CODE CRITERIA ON FACING PAGE AND CONFIRM CODE DOES NOT RESET.

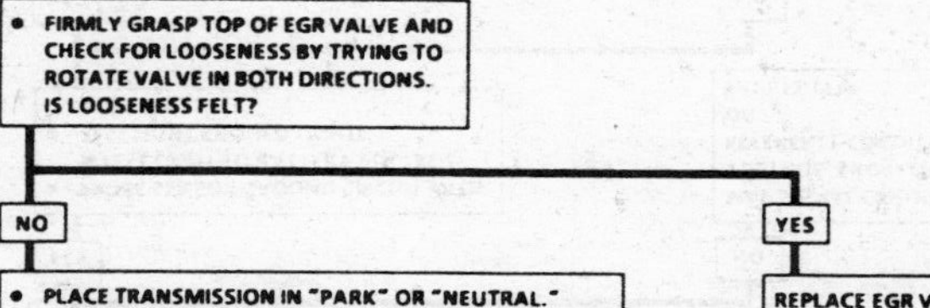

CODE 32

EXHAUST GAS RECIRCULATION (EGR) SYSTEM FAILURE
2.5L (VIN U) "N" CARLINE (TBI)

Circuit Description:

A properly operating EGR system will directly affect the air/fuel requirements of the engine. Since the exhaust gas introduced into the air/fuel mixture is an inert gas (contains very little or no oxygen), less fuel is required to maintain a correct air/fuel ratio. If the EGR system were to become inoperative, the inert exhaust gas would be replaced with air and the air/fuel mixture would be leaner. The ECM would compensate for the lean condition by adding fuel, resulting in higher block learn values.

The engine control system operates within two block learn cells, a closed throttle cell, and an open throttle cell. Since EGR is not used at idle, the closed throttle cell would not be affected by EGR system operation. The open throttle cell is affected by EGR operation and, when the EGR system is operating properly, the block learn values in both cells should be close to being the same. If the EGR system was inoperative, the block learn value in the open throttle cell would change (become higher) to compensate for the resulting lean system, but the block learn value in the closed throttle cell would not change.

This change or difference in block learn values is used to monitor EGR system performance. When the change becomes too great, a Code 32 is set.

Diagnostic Aids:

The Code 32 chart is a functional check of the EGR system. If the EGR system works properly, but a Code 32 has been set, check other items that could result in high block learn values in the open throttle cell, but not in the closed throttle cell.

CHECK:

EGR Passages
Restricted or blocked.

MAP Sensor
A MAP sensor may shift in calibration enough to affect fuel delivery. Use CHART C-1D, "Manifold Absolute Pressure (MAP) Output Check."

CODE 32

EXHAUST GAS RECIRCULATION (EGR) SYSTEM FAILURE
2.5L (VIN U) "N" CARLINE (TBI)

IF CODES 21, 22, 33, OR 34 ARE PRESENT, REPAIR CAUSES FOR THOSE CODES BEFORE USING THIS CHART.

- FIRMLY GRASP TOP OF EGR VALVE AND CHECK FOR LOOSENESS BY TRYING TO ROTATE VALVE IN BOTH DIRECTIONS. IS LOOSENESS FELT?

YES: REPLACE EGR VALVE ASSEMBLY.

NO:

- PLACE TRANSMISSION IN "PARK" OR "NEUTRAL."
- RUN WARM ENGINE AT IDLE. ENGINE TEMPERATURE MUST BE ABOVE 90°C (195°F).
- PUSH ON UNDERSIDE OF EGR VALVE DIAPHRAGM. ENGINE SPEED SHOULD DROP. DOES IT?

NO: CLEAN EGR VALVE OR PASSAGES. REPLACE VALVE IF NECESSARY.

YES:

- CHECK FOR MOVEMENT OF EGR VALVE DIAPHRAGM AS ENGINE SPEED IS INCREASED FROM IDLE TO 2000 RPM. DOES DIAPHRAGM MOVE?

YES: REFER TO "DIAGNOSTIC AIDS" ON FACING PAGE.

NO:

- CHECK VACUUM AT EGR VALVE AS ENGINE SPEED IS INCREASED FROM IDLE TO 2000 RPM.

VACUUM IS UNDER 20 kPa (6 in. Hg/15 cm Hg): CHECK VACUUM HOSES FOR RESTRICTIONS, LEAKS AND CONNECTIONS.

VACUUM IS OVER 20 kPa (6 in. Hg/15 cm Hg): REPLACE EGR VALVE.

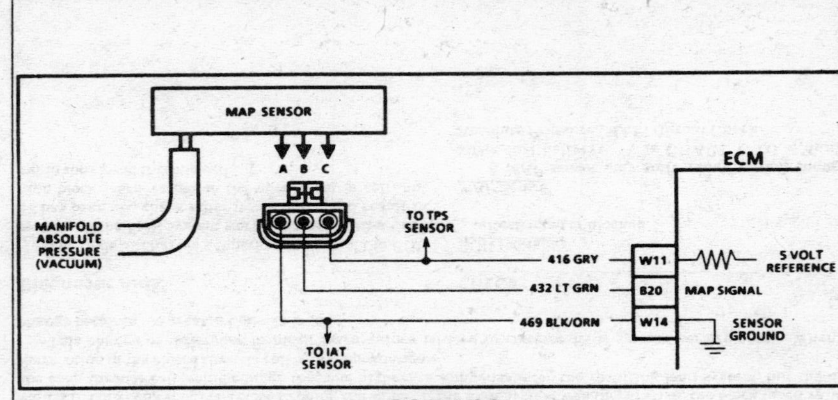

CODE 33

MANIFOLD ABSOLUTE PRESSURE (MAP) SENSOR CIRCUIT
(SIGNAL VOLTAGE HIGH - LOW VACUUM)
2.5L (VIN U) "N" CARLINE (TBI)

Circuit Description:

The Manifold Absolute Pressure (MAP) sensor responds to changes in manifold pressure (vacuum). The ECM receives this information as a signal voltage that will vary from about 1 to 1.5 volts, at closed throttle idle, to 4-4.5 volts at wide open throttle (low vacuum).

If the MAP sensor fails, the ECM will substitute a fixed MAP value and use the Throttle Position Sensor (TPS) to control fuel delivery.

Test Description: Number(s) below refer to circled number(s) on the diagnostic chart.

1. This step will determine if Code 33 is the result of a hard failure or an intermittent condition.
   A Code 33 will set under the following conditions:
   - MAP signal voltage is too high (low vacuum).
   - TPS less than 2%.
   - These conditions exist longer than 5 seconds.
2. This step simulates conditions for a Code 34. If the ECM recognizes the change, the ECM and CKTs 416 and 432 are OK. If CKT 469 is open, there may also be a stored Code 23.

Diagnostic Aids:

With the ignition "ON" and the engine stopped, the manifold pressure is equal to atmospheric pressure and the signal voltage will be high. This information is used by the ECM as and indication of vehicle altitude. Comparison of this reading with a known good vehicle with the same sensor is a good way to check accuracy of a "suspect" sensor. Readings should be the same ± .4 volt.

A Code 33 will result if CKT 469 is open or if CKT 432 is shorted to voltage or to CKT 416.

If Code 33 is intermittent refer to "Intermittents" in "Symptoms,"

- Check all connections.
- Disconnect sensor from bracket and twist sensor (**by hand only**) to check for intermittent connections. Output changes greater than .1 volt indicates a faulty connector or connection. If OK, replace sensor.

NOTE: Make sure electrical connector remains securely fastened.

- Refer to CHART C-1D, MAP sensor voltage vs. atmospheric pressure for further diagnosis.

CODE 33

MANIFOLD ABSOLUTE PRESSURE (MAP) SENSOR CIRCUIT
(SIGNAL VOLTAGE HIGH - LOW VACUUM)
2.5L (VIN U) "N" CARLINE (TBI)

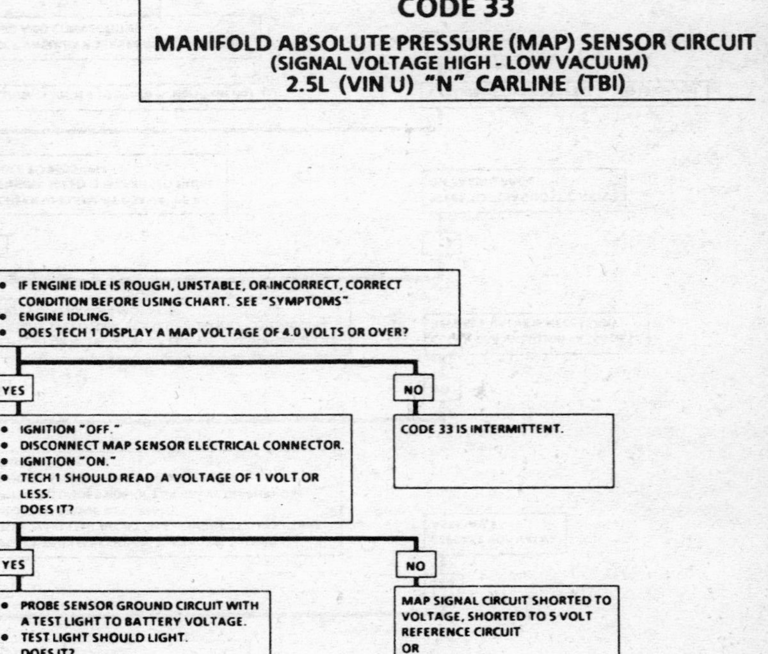

"*AFTER REPAIRS*," REFER TO CODE CRITERIA ON FACING PAGE AND CONFIRM CODE DOES NOT RESET.

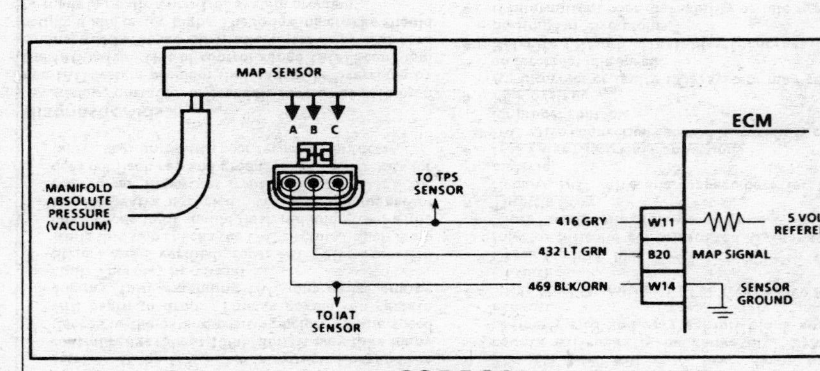

CODE 34

MANIFOLD ABSOLUTE PRESSURE (MAP) SENSOR CIRCUIT
(SIGNAL VOLTAGE LOW - HIGH VACUUM)
2.5L (VIN U) "N" CARLINE (TBI)

Circuit Description:

The Manifold Absolute Pressure (MAP) sensor responds to changes in manifold pressure (vacuum). The ECM receives this information as a signal voltage that will vary from about 1 to 1.5 volts at closed throttle (idle) to 4 - 4.5 volts at wide open throttle (low vacuum).

If the MAP sensor fails, the ECM will substitute a fixed MAP value and use the Throttle Position Sensor (TPS) to control fuel delivery.

Test Description: Number(s) below refer to circled number(s) on the diagnostic chart.

1. This step determines if Code 34 is the result of a hard failure or an intermittent condition. A Code 34 will set under the following conditions:
   - Code 21 is not detected.
   - MAP signal voltage is too low.
   - Engine speed is less than 1200 rpm.
   - Engine speed is greater than 1200 rpm and throttle angle is greater than 20%.
   - All conditions above have been present for a period of time greater than .02 second.
2. Jumpering harness terminals "B" to "C" (5 volts to signal circuit) will determine if the sensor is at fault, or if there is a problem with the ECM or wiring.
3. The "Scan" tool may not display 5 volts. The important thing is that the ECM recognizes the voltage as more than 4 volts, indicating that the ECM and CKT 432 are OK.

Diagnostic Aids:

An intermittent open in CKT 432 or CKT 416 will result in a Code 34. If CKT 416 is open or shorted to ground, there may also be a stored Code 22. With the ignition "ON" and the engine "OFF," the manifold pressure is equal to atmospheric pressure and the signal voltage will be high. This information is used by the ECM as an indication of vehicle altitude.

Comparison of this reading with a known good vehicle with the same sensor is a good way to check accuracy of a "suspect" sensor. Reading s should be the same ± .4 volts. Also CHART C-1D can be used to test the MAP sensor. Refer to "Intermittents," in "Symptoms,"

- Check all connections.
- Disconnect sensor from bracket and twist sensor (**by hand only**) to check for intermittent connections. Output changes greater than .1 volt indicates a faulty connector or connection. If OK, replace sensor.

NOTE: Make sure electrical connector remains securely fastened.

- Refer to CHART C-1D, MAP sensor voltage vs. atmospheric pressure for further diagnosis.

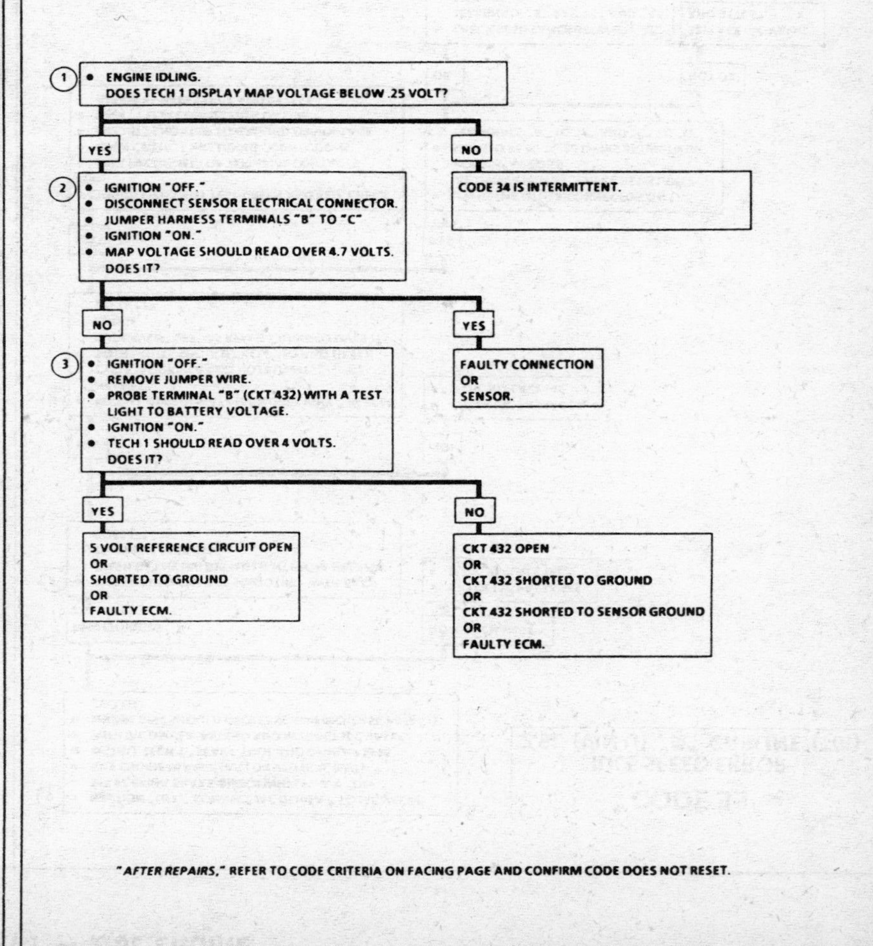

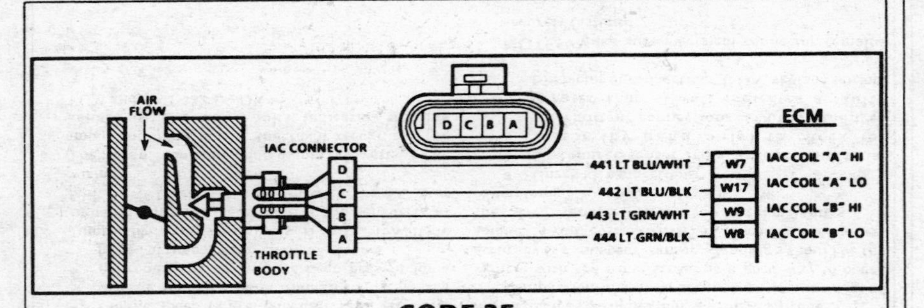

CODE 35

IDLE SPEED ERROR
2.5L (VIN U) "N" CARLINE (TBI)

Circuit Description:

The ECM controls engine idle speed with the IAC valve. To increase idle speed, the ECM retracts the IAC valve pintle away from its seat, allowing more air to bypass the throttle bore. To decrease idle speed, it extends the IAC valve pintle towards its seat, reducing bypass air flow. A Tech 1 "Scan" tool will read the ECM commands to the IAC valve in counts. Higher the counts indicate more air bypass (higher idle). The lower the counts indicate less air is allowed to bypass (lower idle). Code 35 will be set when the closed throttle speed is 100 rpm above or below the desired idle speed for 25 seconds. Review general description in "Component Systems,"

Test Description: Number(s) below refer to circled number(s) on the diagnostic chart.

1. The IAC tester is used to extend and retract the IAC valve. Valve movement is verified by an engine speed change. If no change in engine speed occurs, the valve can be retested when removed from the throttle body.
2. This step checks the quality of the IAC movement in Step 1. Between 700 rpm and about 1500 rpm, the engine speed should change smoothly with each flash of the tester light in both extend and retract. If the IAC valve is retracted beyond the control range (about 1500 rpm), it may take many flashes in the extend position before engine speed will begin to drop. This is normal on certain engines, fully extending IAC may cause engine stall. This may be normal.
3. Steps 1 and 2 verified proper IAC valve operation while this stop checks the IAC circuits. Each lamp on the node light should flash red and green while the IAC valve is cycled. While the sequence of color is not important if either light is "OFF" or does not flash red and green, check the circuits for faults, beginning with poor terminal contacts.

Diagnostic Aids:

A slow, unstable, or fast idle may be caused by a non-IAC system problem that cannot be overcome by the IAC valve. Out of control range IAC "Scan" tool counts will be above 60 if idle is too low, and zero counts if idle is too high. The following checks should be made to repair a non-IAC system problem:

- Vacuum Leak (High Idle)
  If idle is too high, stop the engine. Fully extend (low) IAC with tester. Start engine. If idle speed is above 800 rpm, locate and correct vacuum leak including PCV system. Also check for binding of throttle blade or linkage.
- System too lean (High Air/Fuel Ratio)
  The idle speed may be too high or too low. Engine speed may vary up and down and disconnecting the IAC valve does not help. Code 44 may be set. "Scan" O_2 voltage will be less than 300 mV (.3 volt). Check for low regulated fuel pressure, water in fuel, or a restricted injector.
- System too rich (Low Air/Fuel Ratio)
  The idle speed will be too low. "Scan" tool IAC counts will usually be above 80. System is obviously rich and may exhibit black smoke in exhaust.
  "Scan" tool O_2 voltage will be fixed above 800 mV (.8 volt).
  Check for high fuel pressure, leaking or sticking injector. Silicone contaminated O_2 sensor will "Scan" an O_2 voltage slow to respond.
- Throttle Body
  Remove IAC valve and inspect bore for foreign material.
- IAC Valve Electrical Connections
  IAC valve connections should be carefully checked for proper contact.
- PCV System
  An incorrect or faulty PCV system may result in an incorrect idle speed.
- Refer to "Rough, Unstable, Incorrect Idle or Stalling" in "Symptoms,"
- If intermittent poor driveability or idle symptoms are resolved by disconnecting the IAC, carefully recheck connections, valve terminal resistance, or replace IAC.

CODE 35

IDLE SPEED ERROR
2.5L (VIN U) "N" CARLINE (TBI)

(1)
- IGNITION "OFF," CONNECT IAC DRIVER * TO IAC VALVE.
- SET PARKING BRAKE, BLOCK WHEELS, A/C "OFF."
- IDLE ENGINE IN PARK (A/T) OR NEUTRAL (M/T).
- INSTALL TECH 1 "SCAN" TOOL AND DISPLAY RPM.
- WITH IAC DRIVER, EXTEND AND RETRACT IAC VALVE.
- ENGINE RPM SHOULD DECREASE AND INCREASE AS IAC IS CYCLED.

RPM CHANGES

(2)
- RPM SHOULD CHANGE SMOOTHLY WITH EACH FLASH OF THE IAC DRIVER LIGHT FROM 700 RPM TO ABOUT 1500 RPM.
  DOES IT?

YES

(3)
- INSTALL APPROPRIATE IAC NODE LIGHT * IN ECM HARNESS.
- CYCLE IAC DRIVER AND NOTE LIGHTS.
- BOTH LIGHTS SHOULD CYCLE RED AND GREEN BUT NEVER "OFF" AS RPM IS CHANGED OVER ITS RANGE.
  DO THEY?

NO

IF CIRCUIT(S) DID NOT TEST GREEN AND RED, CHECK FOR:
- FAULTY CONNECTOR TERMINAL CONTACTS.
- OPEN CIRCUITS INCLUDING CONNECTIONS.
- CIRCUITS SHORTED TO GROUND OR VOLTAGE.
- FAULTY ECM CONNECTION OR ECM.

REPAIR AS NECESSARY AND RETEST.

YES

- USING THE OTHER CONNECTOR ON THE IAC DRIVER PIGTAIL, CHECK RESISTANCE ACROSS IAC COILS.
- SHOULD BE 40 TO 80 OHMS BETWEEN IAC TERMINALS "A" TO "B" AND "C" TO "D".

OK

- CHECK RESISTANCE BETWEEN IAC TERMINALS "B" AND "C" AND "A" AND "D".
- SHOULD BE INFINITE.

OK

IDLE AIR CONTROL VALVE AND CIRCUIT OK. REFER TO "DIAGNOSTIC AIDS" ON FACING PAGE.

NOT OK

REPLACE IAC VALVE AND RETEST.

NOT OK

REPLACE IAC VALVE AND RETEST.

NO (step 2)

- CHECK IAC PASSAGES.
- IF OK, REPLACE IAC.

NO RPM CHANGE (step 1)

- CHECK IAC PASSAGES.
- IF OK, REPLACE IAC.

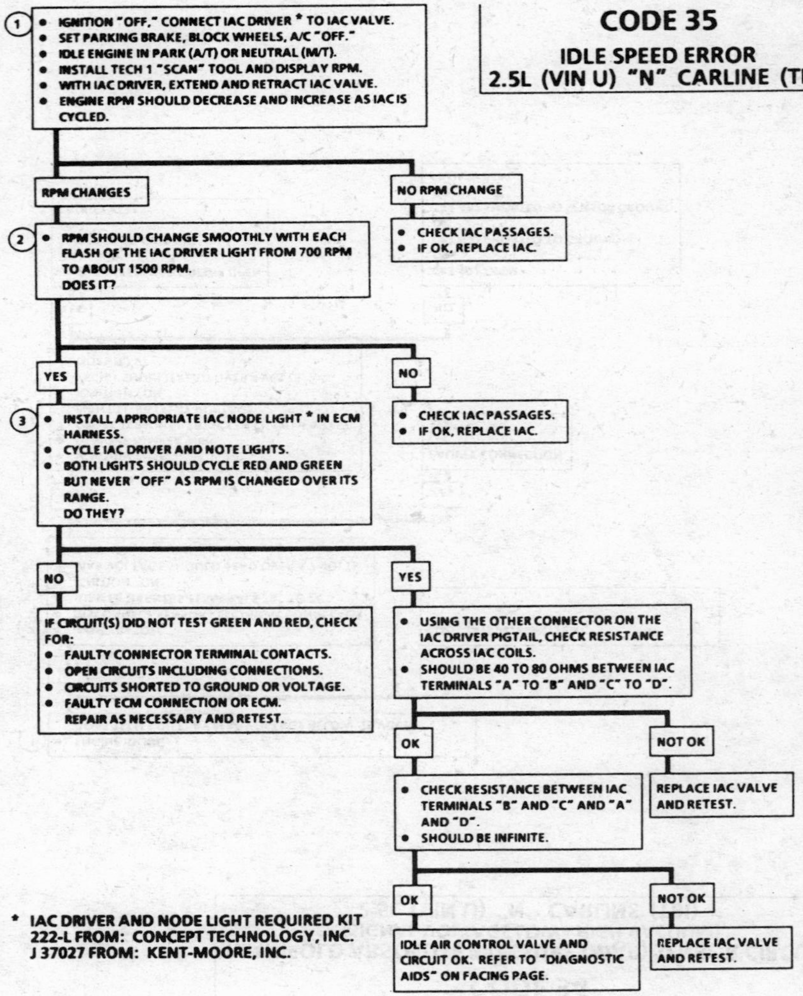

* IAC DRIVER AND NODE LIGHT REQUIRED KIT
222-L FROM: CONCEPT TECHNOLOGY, INC.
J 37027 FROM: KENT-MOORE, INC.

"AFTER REPAIRS," REFER TO CODE CRITERIA ON FACING PAGE AND CONFIRM CODE DOES NOT RESET.

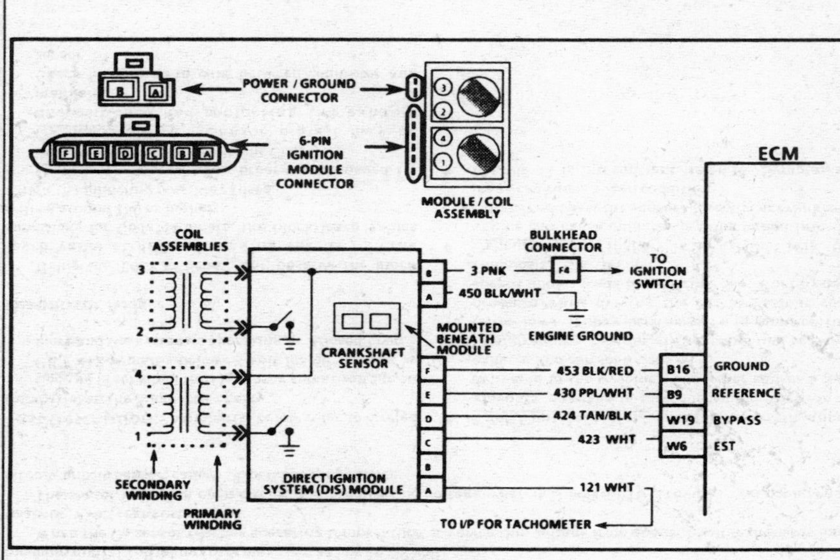

CODE 42

ELECTRONIC SPARK TIMING (EST) CIRCUIT 2.5L (VIN U) "N" CARLINE (TBI)

Circuit Description:

The DIS module sends a reference signal to the ECM when the engine is cranking. While the engine speed is under 400 rpm, the DIS module controls the ignition timing. When the system is running on the ignition module (no voltage on the bypass line), the ignition module grounds the EST signal. The ECM expects to sense no voltage on the EST line during this condition. If it senses a voltage, it sets Code 42 and will not enter the EST mode.

When the engine speed exceeds 400 rpm, the ECM applies 5 volts to the bypass line to switch the timing to ECM control (EST). If the bypass line is open or grounded, once the rpm for EST control is reached, the ignition module will not switch to EST mode. This results in low EST voltage and the setting of Code 42. If the EST line is grounded, the ignition module will switch to EST, but because the line is grounded, there will be no EST signal. A Code 42 will be set.

Test Description: Number(s) below refer to circled number(s) on the diagnostic chart.

1. Code 42 means the ECM has sensed an open or short to ground in the EST or bypass circuits. This test confirms Code 42 and that the fault causing the code is present.
2. Checks for a normal EST ground path through the ignition module. An EST CKT 423, shorted to ground, will also read less than 500 ohms, but this will be checked later.
3. As the test light voltage contacts CKT 424, the module should switch, causing the ohmmeter to "overrange" if the meter is in the 1000-2000 ohms position. Selecting the 10 - 20,000 ohms position will indicate a reading above 5000 ohms. The important thing is that the module "switched."
4. The module did not switch and this step checks for
   - EST CKT 423 shorted to ground.
   - Bypass CKT 424 open.
   - Faulty ignition module connection or module.
5. Confirms that Code 42 is a faulty ECM and not an intermittent in CKT(s) 423 or 424.

Diagnostic Aids:

The "Scan" tool does not have any ability to help diagnose a Code 42 problem.

If Code 42 is intermittent, refer to "Symptoms,"

CODE 42

ELECTRONIC SPARK TIMING (EST) CIRCUIT 2.5L (VIN U) "N" CARLINE (TBI)

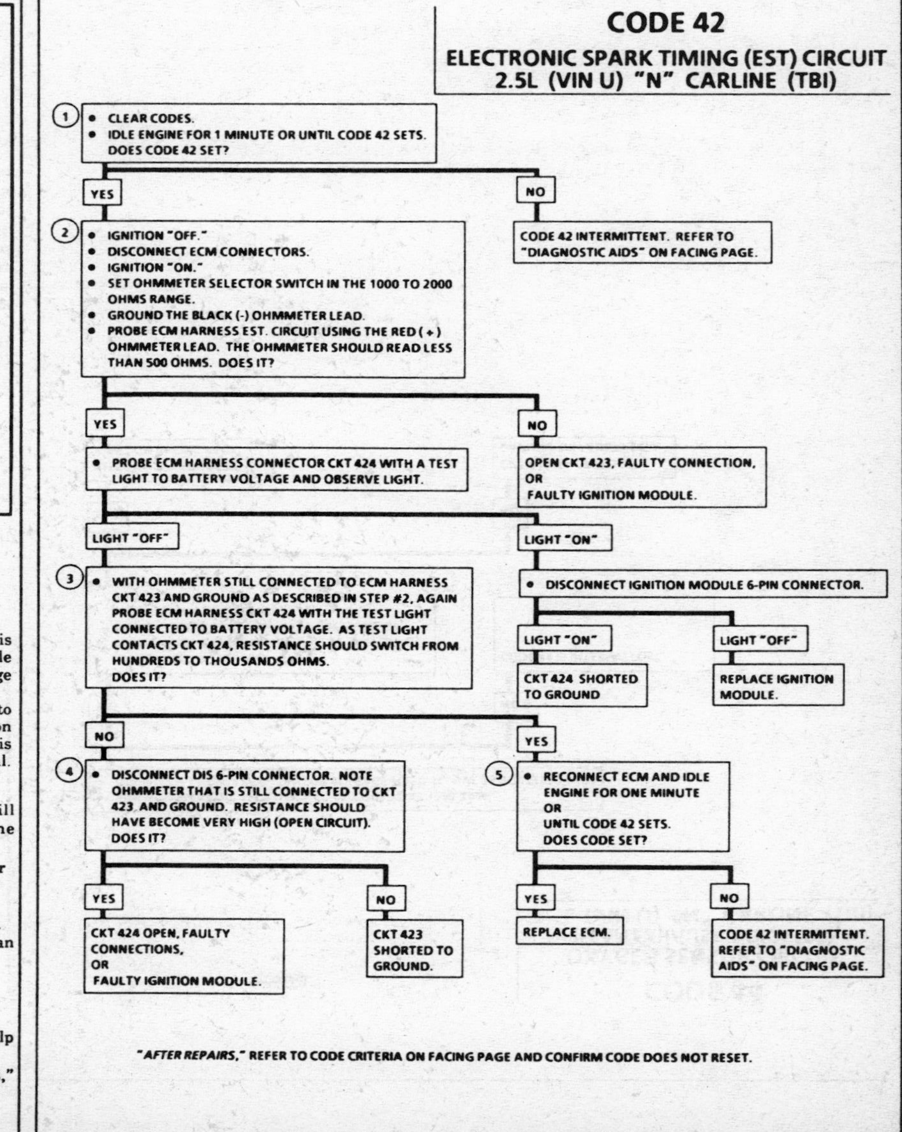

"AFTER REPAIRS," REFER TO CODE CRITERIA ON FACING PAGE AND CONFIRM CODE DOES NOT RESET.

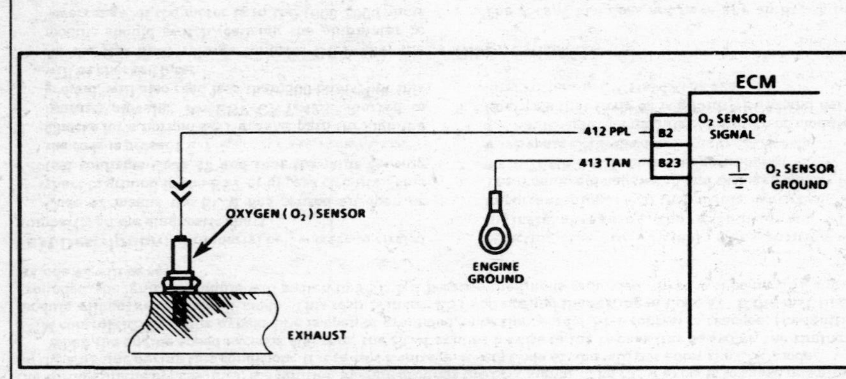

CODE 44

OXYGEN SENSOR CIRCUIT
(LEAN EXHAUST INDICATED)
2.5L (VIN U) "N" CARLINE (TBI)

Circuit Description:

The ECM supplies a voltage of about .45 volt between terminals "B2" and "B23" (If measured with a 10 megohm digital voltmeter, this may read as low as .32 volt).

When the O_2 sensor reaches operating temperature, it varies this voltage from about .1 volt (exhaust is lean) to about .9 volt (exhaust is rich).

The sensor is like an open circuit and produces no voltage when it is below 316°C (600°F). An open sensor circuit, or cold sensor, causes "Open Loop" operation.

Test Description: Number(s) below refer to circled number(s) on the diagnostic chart.

1. Code 44 is set when the O_2 sensor signal voltage on CKT 412 remains below .2 volt for 60 seconds or more and the system is operating in "Closed Loop."

Diagnostic Aids:

Using the Tech 1 "Scan" tool, observe the block learn value at different engine speeds. If the conditions for Code 44 exists, the block learn values will be around 150 or higher.

Check the following possible causes:

- O_2 Sensor. A cracked or otherwise damaged O_2 sensor may set an intermittent Code 44.
- O_2 Sensor Wire. Sensor pigtail may be mispositioned and contacting the exhaust manifold. Check for ground in wire between connector and sensor.
- Fuel Contamination. Water, even in small amounts, near the in-tank fuel pump inlet can be delivered to the injector. The water causes a lean exhaust and can set a Code 44.
- Fuel Pressure. System will be lean if fuel pressure is too low. It may be necessary to monitor fuel pressure while driving the car at various road speeds and/or loads to confirm. See "Fuel System Diagnosis," CHART A-7.
- Exhaust Leaks. If there is an exhaust leak, the engine can cause outside air to be pulled into the exhaust and past the sensor. Vacuum or crankcase leaks can cause a lean condition.
- If Code 44 is intermittent, refer to "Symptoms,"

CODE 44

OXYGEN SENSOR CIRCUIT
(LEAN EXHAUST INDICATED)
2.5L (VIN U) "N" CARLINE (TBI)

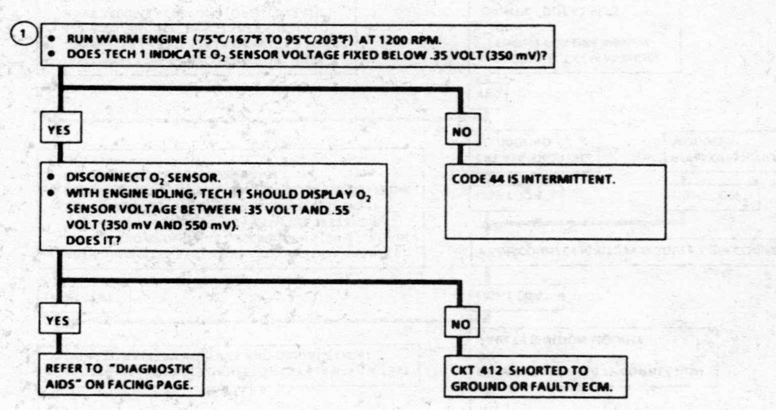

"AFTER REPAIRS," REFER TO CODE CRITERIA ON FACING PAGE AND CONFIRM CODE DOES NOT RESET.

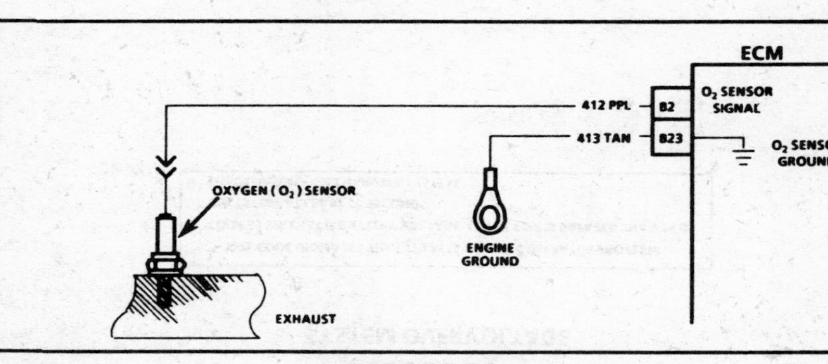

CODE 45

OXYGEN SENSOR CIRCUIT
(RICH EXHAUST INDICATED)
2.5L (VIN U) "N" CARLINE (TBI)

Circuit Description:

The ECM supplies a voltage of about .45 volt between terminals "B2" and "B23". (If measured with a 10 megohm digital voltmeter, this may read as low as .32 volt).

When the O_2 sensor reaches operating temperature, it varies this voltage from about .1 volt (exhaust is lean) to about .9 volt (exhaust is rich).

The sensor is like an open circuit and produces no voltage when it is below 316° C (600°F). An open sensor circuit or cold sensor causes "Open Loop" operation.

Test Description: Number(s) below refer to circled number(s) on the diagnostic chart.

1. Code 45 is set when the O_2 sensor signal voltage on CKT 412 remains above 750 mV under the following conditions:
   - 50 seconds or more at idle.
   - System is operating in "Closed Loop."
   - Engine run time after start is 1 minute or more.
   - Throttle angle is between 3% and 45%.

Diagnostic Aids:

Code 45 or rich exhaust is most likely caused by one of the following:

- Fuel Pressure. System will go rich, if pressure is too high. The ECM can compensate for some increase. However, if it gets too high, a Code 45 will be set. See "Fuel System Diagnosis," CHART A-7.
- Leaking Injector. See CHART A-7.
- HEI Shielding. An open ground CKT 453 may result in EMI, or induced electrical "noise." The ECM looks at this "noise" as reference pulses. The additional pulses result in a higher than actual engine speed signal. The ECM then delivers too much fuel causing the system to go rich. The engine tachometer will also show higher than actual engine speed, which can help in diagnosing this problem.
- Canister Purge. Check for fuel saturation. If full of fuel, check canister control and hoses. See "Canister Purge," "Evaporative Emission Control System (EECS),"
- MAP Sensor. An output that causes the ECM to sense a higher than normal manifold pressure (low vacuum) can cause the system to go rich. Disconnecting the MAP sensor will allow the ECM to set a fixed value for the MAP sensor. Substitute a different MAP sensor if the rich condition is gone, while the sensor is disconnected.
- TPS. An intermittent TPS output will cause the system to operate richly due to a false indication of the engine accelerating.
- O_2 Sensor Contamination. Inspect oxygen sensor for silicone contamination from fuel, or use of improper RTV sealant. The sensor may have a white, powdery coating and result in a high but false signal voltage (rich exhaust indication). The ECM will then reduce the amount of fuel delivered to the engine causing a severe surge driveability problem.
- EGR Valve. EGR sticking open at idle is usually accompanied by a rough idle and/or stall condition. If Code 45 is intermittent, refer to "Symptoms,"
- Engine Oil Contamination. Fuel fouled engine oil could cause the O_2 sensor to sense a rich air/fuel mixture and set a Code 45.

CODE 45

OXYGEN SENSOR CIRCUIT
(RICH EXHAUST INDICATED)
2.5L (VIN U) "N" CARLINE (TBI)

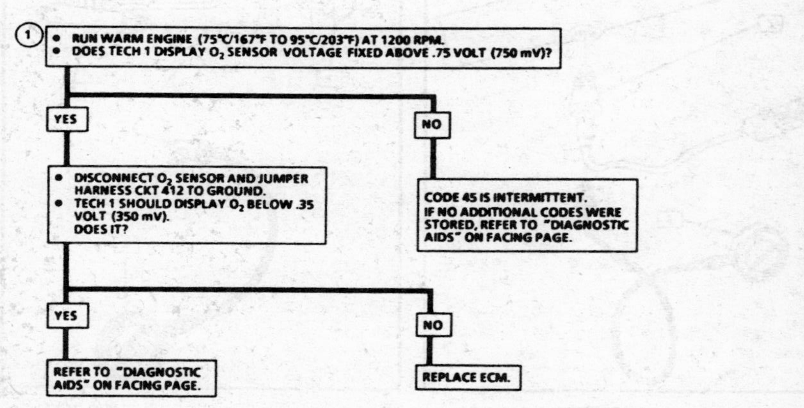

"AFTER REPAIRS," REFER TO CODE CRITERIA ON FACING PAGE AND CONFIRM CODE DOES NOT RESET.

CODE 51
PROM ERROR
(FAULTY OR INCORRECT PROM)
2.5L (VIN U) "N" CARLINE (TBI)

CODE 51
PROM ERROR
(FAULTY OR INCORRECT PROM)

CHECK THAT ALL PINS ARE FULLY INSERTED IN THE SOCKET AND THAT PROM IS PROPERLY SEATED. IF OK, REPLACE PROM, CLEAR MEMORY, AND RECHECK. IF CODE 51 REAPPEARS, REPLACE ECM.

"AFTER REPAIRS," CONFIRM "CLOSED LOOP" OPERATION AND NO "SERVICE ENGINE SOON" LIGHT.

CODE 53
SYSTEM OVERVOLTAGE

THIS CODE INDICATES THAT THERE IS A BASIC GENERATOR PROBLEM.

- CODE 53 WILL SET IF BATTERY VOLTAGE AT THE ECM IS GREATER THAN 16.9 VOLTS FOR AT LEAST 50 SECONDS.
- CHECK AND REPAIR CHARGING SYSTEM.

"AFTER REPAIRS," CONFIRM "CLOSED LOOP" OPERATION AND NO "SERVICE ENGINE SOON" LIGHT.

CHART B-1
RESTRICTED EXHAUST SYSTEM CHECK
ALL ENGINES

Proper diagnosis for a restricted exhaust system is essential before any components are replaced. Either of the following procedures may be used for diagnosis, depending upon engine or tool used:

CHECK AT A. I. R. PIPE:

1. Remove the rubber hose at the exhaust manifold A.I.R. pipe check valve. Remove check valve.
2. Connect a fuel pump pressure gauge to a hose and nipple from a Propane Enrichment Device (J 26911) (see illustration).
3. Insert the nipple into the exhaust manifold A.I.R. pipe.

OR

CHECK AT O_2 SENSOR:

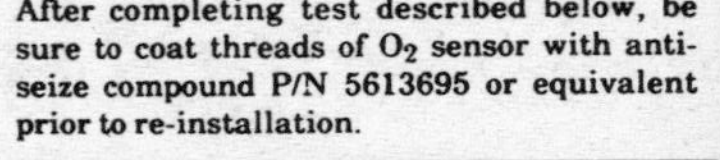

1. Carefully remove O_2 sensor.
2. Install Borroughs exhaust backpressure tester (BT 8515 or BT 8603) or equivalent in place of O_2 sensor (see illustration).
3. After completing test described below, be sure to coat threads of O_2 sensor with anti-seize compound P/N 5613695 or equivalent prior to re-installation.

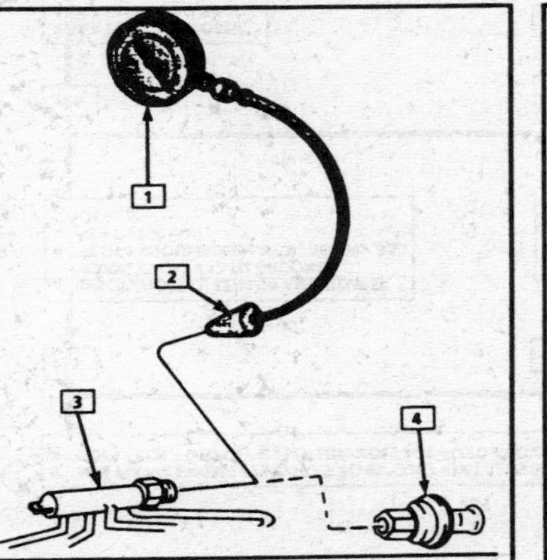

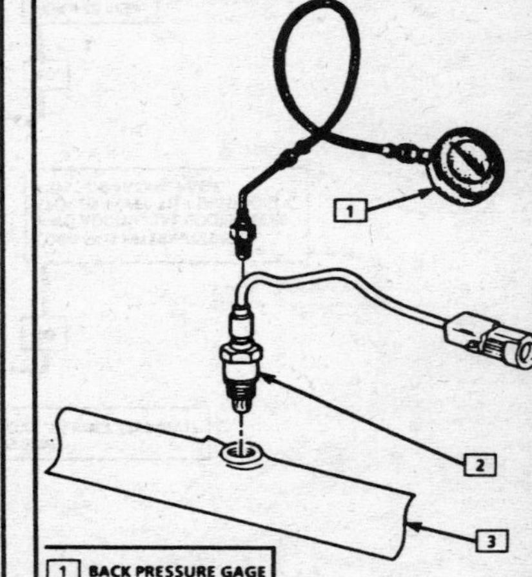

DIAGNOSIS:

1. With the engine idling at normal operating temperature, observe the exhaust system backpressure reading on the gage. Reading should not exceed 8.6 kPa (1.25 psi).
2. Increase engine speed to 2000 rpm and observe gage. Reading should not exceed 20.7 kPa (3 psi).
3. If the backpressure at either speed exceeds specification, a restricted exhaust system is indicated.
4. Inspect the entire exhaust system for a collapsed pipe, heat distress, or possible internal muffler failure.
5. If there are no obvious reasons for the excessive backpressure, the catalytic converter is suspected to be restricted and should be replaced using current recommended procedures.

DIAGNOSTIC CHARTS — 2.5L ENGINE

WHITE (W) 24 PIN ECM CONNECTOR

PIN FUNCTION	CKT #	WIRE COLOR	COMPONENT/ CONNECTOR CAVITY	NORMAL VOLTAGE KEY "ON"*	NORMAL VOLTAGE ENG RUN**	CODES AFFECT.	POSSIBLE SYMPTOMS FROM FAULTY CIRCUIT
W1 INJECTOR DRIVER	467	DK BLU	FUEL INJECTOR "B"	B +	B +		(5) CRANKS, BUT WON'T RUN
W2 A/C REQUEST	604	DK GRN/WHT	A/C RELAY "1" A/C HIGH PRESSURE SWITCH "B"	0*	0*		(3) NO A/C COOLING, A/C CLUTCH INOPERATIVE. (4) NO A/C COOLING, A/C CLUTCH INOPERATIVE, BLOWN A/C FUSE
W4 CRUISE R/A	87	GRY/BLK					REFER TO ELECTRICAL DIAGNOSIS (SECTION 8A)
W5 POWER STEERING SIGNAL	495	LT BLU/ORN	POWER STEERING PRESSURE SWITCH "A"	B +	B +		(3) UNSTABLE IDLE WITH STEERING WHEEL CRAMPED
W6 EST	423	WHT	"DIS" MODULE "C"	0*	1.3V	42 (5)	(5) STUMBLES, UNSTABLE IDLE
W7 IAC "A" HI	441	LT BLU/WHT	IAC VALVE "D"	NOT USABLE	NOT USABLE	35 (5)	(5) UNSTABLE, INCORRECT IDLE
W8 IAC "B" LO	444	LT GRN/BLK	IAC VALVE "A"	NOT USABLE	NOT USABLE	35 (5)	(5) UNSTABLE, INCORRECT IDLE
W9 IAC "B" HI	443	LT GRN/WHT	IAC VALVE "B"	NOT USABLE	NOT USABLE	35 (5)	(5) UNSTABLE, INCORRECT IDLE
W10 ECM MEMORY (B +)	240	ORN	BATTERY + FEED	B +	B +		(3) NO EFFECT. IF W15 IS ALSO OPEN, NO START (4) NO START. BLOWN FUSIBLE LINK.
W11 5 VOLT REF, TPS & MAP	416	GRY	TPS "A" MAP "C"	5.0V	5.0V	22 (5) 34 (5)	(5) STUMBLES, HESITATES, STRONG EXHAUST ODOR; TECH 1 INDICATES FUEL INTEGRATOR REMOVING FUEL. (LOW COUNTS)
W12 ECM GROUND, FUEL PUMP RELAY GROUND	450	BLK/WHT	ENGINE GROUND ALDL "A" FUEL PUMP RELAY "2"	0*	0*		(3) NO EFFECT. IF W13 IS ALSO OPEN, NO START.
W13 ECM GROUND	551	TAN/WHT	ENGINE GROUND	0*	0*		(3) NO EFFECT. IF W12 IS ALSO OPEN, NO START.

NOTICE: The voltages you get may vary due to low battery charge or other reasons, but they should be very close.

* All voltages shown 0* should read less than .5 volt.
** All voltages shown are typical with engine at Idle, Closed Throttle, Normal Operating Temperature, Park or Neutral and "Closed Loop." All accessories "OFF."
(1) Changes with IAC valve activity (when moving throttle slightly up and down).
(2) Varies
(3) Open circuit
(4) Grounded circuit
(5) Open or grounded circuit
(6) Reads B + for 2 seconds after ignition "ON," then should read 0 volts.

WHITE (W) 24 PIN ECM CONNECTOR

PIN FUNCTION	CKT #	WIRE COLOR	COMPONENT/ CONNECTOR CAVITY	NORMAL VOLTAGE KEY "ON"*	NORMAL VOLTAGE ENG RUN**	CODES AFFECT.	POSSIBLE SYMPTOMS FROM FAULTY CIRCUIT
W14 MAP, IAT SENSOR GROUND	469	BLK/ORN	MAP "A" IAT "A"	0*	0*	33 (3)	(3) POOR PERFORMANCE, STRONG EXHAUST ODOR
W15 ECM MEMORY (B +)	240	ORN	BATTERY + FEED	B +	B +		(3) NO EFFECT. IF W10 IS ALSO OPEN, NO START. (4) NO START, BLOWN FUSIBLE LINK.
W16 IGNITION FEED	439	PNK/BLK	ECM - RLYS FUSE	B +	B +		(3) NO START (4) NO START, BLOWN ECM - RLYS FUSE.
W17 IAC "A" LO	442	LT BLU/BLK	IAC VALVE "C"	NOT USABLE	NOT USABLE	35 (5)	(5) UNSTABLE, INCORRECT IDLE
W18 PARK/NEUTRAL (P/N) SWITCH	434	ORN/BLK	P/N SWITCH "A"	0* P-N B + R-DL	0* P-N B + R-DL		(5) INCORRECT IDLE
W19 IGNITION BYPASS	424	TAN/BLK	"DIS" MODULE "D"	0*	4.7V	42 (5)	(5) POOR PERFORMANCE
W20 CRUISE ENABLE	397	GRY					REFER TO ELECTRICAL DIAGNOSIS
W21 CRUISE S/C	84	DK BLU					REFER TO ELECTRICAL DIAGNOSIS
W22 VSS OUTPUT	389	DK GRN					REFER TO ELECTRICAL DIAGNOSIS
W24 FUEL PUMP RELAY DRIVE	465	DK GRN/WHT	FUEL PUMP RELAY "5"	(6)	B +		(5) LONG CRANKING TIME UNTIL ENGINE STARTS

NOTICE: The voltages you get may vary due to low battery charge or other reasons, but they should be very close.

* All voltages shown 0* should read less than .5 volt.
** All voltages shown are typical with engine at Idle, Closed Throttle, Normal Operating Temperature, Park or Neutral and "Closed Loop." All accessories "OFF."
(1) Changes with IAC valve activity (when moving throttle slightly up and down).
(2) Varies
(3) Open circuit
(4) Grounded circuit
(5) Open or grounded circuit
(6) Reads B + for 2 seconds after ignition "ON," then should read 0 volts.

DIAGNOSTIC CHARTS — 2.5L ENGINE

BLACK (B) 24 PIN ECM CONNECTOR

PIN FUNCTION	CKT #	WIRE COLOR	COMPONENT CONNECTOR CAVITY	NORMAL VOLTAGE		CODES AFFECT	POSSIBLE SYMPTOMS FROM FAULTY CIRCUIT
				KEY "ON"	ENG RUN**		
B1 SERIAL DATA	461	ORN	ALDL "M"	4.5V	4.0V		(5) NO TECH 1 DATA
B2 OXYGEN (O_2) SENSOR SIGNAL	412	PPL	O_2 SENSOR	.01-.55V	.1-.9V	13 (3) 44 (4)	(5) OPEN LOOP, EXHAUST ODOR
B3 A/C COMPRESSOR RELAY	459	DK GRN/WHT	A/C COMPRESSOR RELAY "2"	B + (A)	B + (A)		(3) A/C CLUTCH INOPERATIVE (4) BLOWN ECM - RLYS FUSE, A/C CLUTCH INOPERATIVE
B4 CRUISE LIGHT (IF USED)	85	WHT					REFER TO ELECTRICAL DIAGNOSIS (SECTION 8A)
B5 IAT SIGNAL	472	TAN	AT SENSOR "B"	1.3V (B)	1.3V (B)	23 (3) 25 (4)	(3) POSSIBLE EXHAUST ODOR. TECH 1 INDICATES -38°C (4) TECH 1 INDICATES 179°C
B6 VSS SIGNAL (LOW)	401	PPL	PM GENERATOR "3"	VARIES	VARIES	24 (3)	(5) POOR FUEL ECONOMY, TCC DISENGAGED AT ALL TIMES, SPEEDOMETER INOPERATIVE. REFER TO ELECTRICAL DIAGNOSIS (SECTION 8A)
B7 TCC CONTROL (A/T) OR SHIFT LIGHT (M/T)	422 (A/T) 456 (M/T)	TAN/BLK	TCC SOLENOID "D" (A/T) 15-PIN I/P CONNECTOR "H" (A/T) "N" (M/T)	0* (A/T) B + (M/T)	0* (A/T) B + (M/T)		(3) (A/T) POOR FUEL ECONOMY, TCC DOES NOT ENGAGE. TECH 1 INDICATES TCC "ON." (M/T) SHIFT LIGHT INOPERATIVE (4) (A/T) TCC ENGAGES TOO SOON IN 3RD GEAR, LUGS ENGINE AT HIGHWAY SPEEDS. (M/T) SHIFT LIGHT "ON" AT ALL TIMES.
B8 COOLANT TEMPERATURE SIGNAL (CTS)	410	YEL	CTS "B"	1.9V (B)	1.9V (B)	14 (4) 15 (3)	(3) INCORRECT IDLE, COOLING FAN RUNS AT ALL TIMES, TECH 1 INDICATES -39°C (4) SAME AS OPEN EXCEPT TECH 1 INDICATES 151°C.
B9 IGNITION REFERENCE HI	430	PPL/WHT	"DIS" MODULE "E"	4.6V	3.1V		(5) NO START
B10 CRUISE (VAC)	402	LT GRN					REFER TO ELECTRICAL DIAGNOSIS
B11 CRUISE (VENT)	403	DK BLU/WHT					REFER TO ELECTRICAL DIAGNOSIS

NOTICE: The voltages you get may vary due to low battery charge or other reasons, but they should be very close.

* All voltages shown 0* should read less than .5 volt.
** All voltages shown are typical with engine at Idle, Closed Throttle, Normal Operating Temperature, Park or Neutral and "Closed Loop." All accessories "OFF."
(A) A/C select switch "OFF"
(B) Varies depending on temperature
(1) Changes with IAC valve activity (when moving throttle slightly up and down).
(2) Varies
(3) Open circuit
(4) Grounded circuit
(5) Open or grounded circuit

BLACK (B) 24 PIN ECM CONNECTOR

PIN FUNCTION	CKT #	WIRE COLOR	COMPONENT CONNECTOR CAVITY	NORMAL VOLTAGE		CODES AFFECT	POSSIBLE SYMPTOMS FROM FAULTY CIRCUIT
				KEY "ON"	ENG RUN**		
B12 CTS & TPS GROUND	452	BLK	CTS "A" TPS "B"	0*	0*	15 (3) 21 (3)	(3) INCORRECT IDLE, HESITATION WITH TECH 1, TPS INDICATES 5V. CTS INDICATES -39°C.
B13 VSS SIGNAL (HIGH)	400	YEL	PM GENERATOR "A"	VARIES	VARIES	24 (3)	(5) POOR FUEL ECONOMY, TCC INOPERATIVE.
B14 CRUISE BRAKE SWITCH	86	BRN					REFER TO ELECTRICAL DIAGNOSIS
B15 DIAGNOSTIC TEST	451	WHT/BLK	ALDL "B"	5.0V	5.0V		(4) FIELD SERVICE MODE ACTIVE. "SES" LIGHT FLASHES RICH/LEAN
B16 IGNITION GROUND	453	BLK/RED	"DIS" MODULE "F"	0*	0*		(5) NO EFFECT
B18 COOLANT "TEMP" LIGHT OR "CHECK GAUGES" LIGHT (OPTIONAL)	35	DK GRN	18-PIN CLUSTER CONNECTOR #1 "C8"	0*	B +		(4) COOLANT "TEMP" LIGHT "ON" OR OPTIONAL "CHECK GAUGES" LIGHT "FLASHES" AT ALL TIMES. REFER TO ELECTRICAL DIAGNOSIS
B19 TPS SIGNAL	417	DK BLU	TPS "C"	6V	6V IDLE	22 (5)	(5) POOR PERFORMANCE, BACKFIRE, HESITATION
B20 MAP SIGNAL	432	LT GRN	MAP SENSOR "B"	4.75V (A)	1.1V (A)	34 (5)	(5) INCORRECT IDLE, CHUGGLE. POOR PERFORMANCE
B21 COOLING FAN RELAY	335	DK GRN/WHT	COOLING FAN RELAY "2"	B + (A)	B + (A)		(3) POSSIBLE OVERHEATING, SPARK KNOCK (4) COOLING FAN RUNS AT ALL TIMES
B22 "SERVICE ENGINE SOON" LIGHT	419	BRN/WHT	15 PIN I/P CONNECTOR "C"	0*	B +		(4) "SES" LIGHT "ON" AT ALL TIMES
B23 OXYGEN (O_2) SENSOR GROUND	413	TAN	ENGINE GROUND	0*	0*	13 (3)	(3) OPEN LOOP, TECH 1 INDICATES (O_2) SENSOR VOLTAGE FIXED AT 400-500 mv
B24 A/C SIGNAL FOR COOLING FAN	603	DK GRN/WHT	A/C LOW PRESSURE SWITCH "B" A/C HIGH PRESSURE SWITCH "B"	0*	0*		(3) POOR A/C PERFORMANCE (4) NO A/C, A/C COMPRESSOR CLUTCH INOPERATIVE

NOTICE: The voltages you get may vary due to low battery charge or other reasons, but they should be very close.

* All voltages shown 0* should read less than .5 volt.
** All voltages shown are typical with engine at Idle, Closed Throttle, Normal Operating Temperature, Park or Neutral and "Closed Loop." All accessories "OFF."
(A) A/C select switch "OFF"
(B) Varies depending on temperature
(1) Changes with IAC valve activity (when moving throttle slightly up and down).
(2) Varies
(3) Open circuit
(4) Grounded circuit
(5) Open or grounded circuit

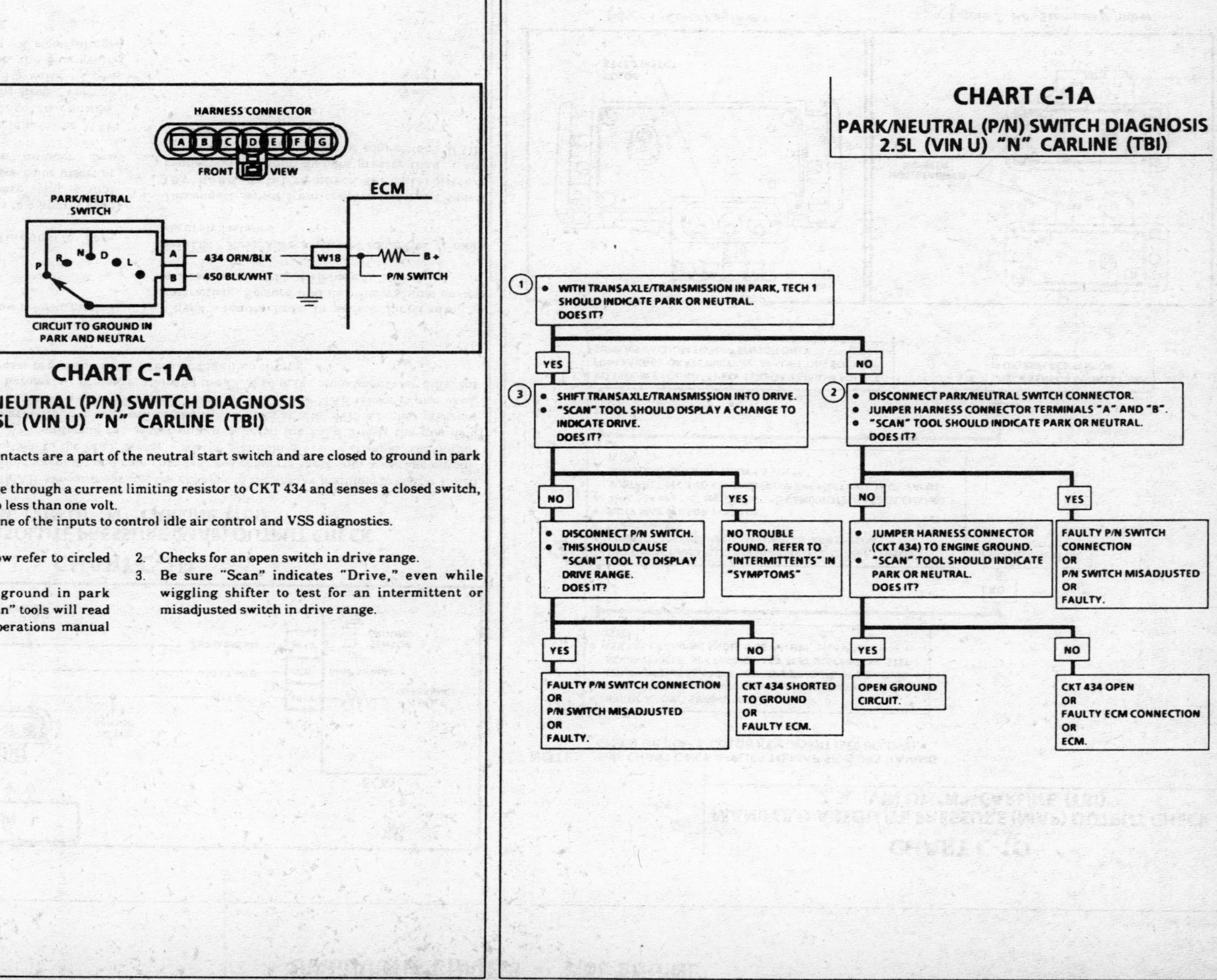

CHART C-1A

PARK/NEUTRAL (P/N) SWITCH DIAGNOSIS 2.5L (VIN U) "N" CARLINE (TBI)

Circuit Description:

The Park/Neutral (P/N) switch contacts are a part of the neutral start switch and are closed to ground in park or neutral, and open in drive ranges.

The ECM supplies ignition voltage through a current limiting resistor to CKT 434 and senses a closed switch, when the voltage on CKT 434 drops to less than one volt.

The ECM uses the P/N signal as one of the inputs to control idle air control and VSS diagnostics.

Test Description: Number(s) below refer to circled number(s) on the diagnostic chart.

1. Checks for a closed switch to ground in park position. Different makes of "Scan" tools will read P/N differently. Refer to tool operations manual for type of display used.
2. Checks for an open switch in drive range.
3. Be sure "Scan" indicates "Drive," even while wiggling shifter to test for an intermittent or misadjusted switch in drive range.

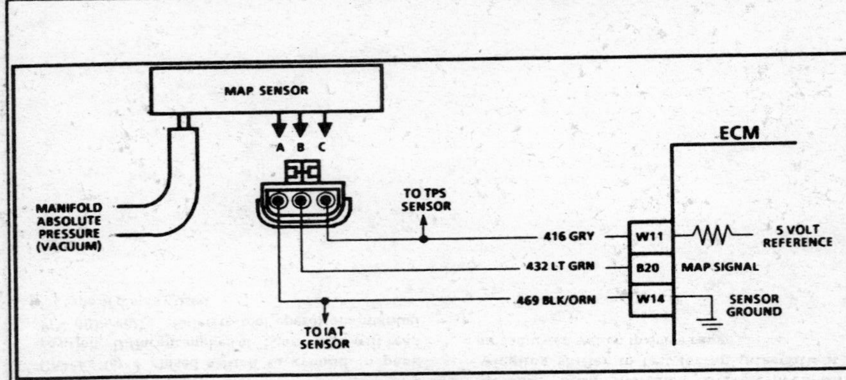

CHART C-1D

MANIFOLD ABSOLUTE PRESSURE (MAP) OUTPUT CHECK 2.5L (VIN U) "N" CARLINE (TBI)

Circuit Description:

The Manifold Absolute Pressure (MAP) sensor measures the changes in the intake manifold pressure which result from engine load (intake manifold vacuum) and rpm changes; and converts these into a voltage output. The ECM sends a 5 volt reference voltage to the MAP sensor. As the manifold pressure changes, the output voltage of the sensor also changes. By monitoring the sensor output voltage, the ECM knows the manifold pressure. A lower pressure (low voltage) output voltage will be about 1 - 2 volts at idle. While higher pressure (high voltage) output voltage will be about 4 - 4.8 at Wide Open Throttle (WOT). the MAP sensor is also used, under certain conditions, to measure barometric pressure, allowing the ECM to make adjustments for different altitudes. The ECM used the MAP sensor to control fuel delivery and ignition timing.

Test Description: Number(s) below refer to circled number(s) on the diagnostic chart.

Important

- Be sure to use the same Diagnostic Test Equipment for all measurements.

1. When comparing Tech 1 readings to a known good vehicle, it is important to compare vehicles that use a MAP sensor having the same color insert or having the same "Hot Stamped" number. See figures on facing page.
2. Applying 34 kPa (10 in. Hg) vacuum to the MAP sensor should cause the voltage to change. Subtract second reading from the first. Voltage value should be greater than 1.5 volts. Upon applying vacuum to the sensor, the change in voltage should be instantaneous. A slow voltage change indicates a faulty sensor.
3. Check vacuum hose to sensor for leading or restriction. Be sure that no other vacuum devices are connected to the MAP hose.

NOTE: Make sure electrical connector remains securely fastened.

4. Disconnect sensor from bracket and twist sensor **(by hand only)** to check for intermittent connection. Output changes greater than .1 volt indicate a faulty connector or connection. If OK, replace sensor.

CHART C-1D

MANIFOLD ABSOLUTE PRESSURE (MAP) OUTPUT CHECK 2.5L (VIN U) "N" CARLINE (TBI)

NOTE: THIS CHART ONLY APPLIES TO MAP SENSORS HAVING GREEN OR BLACK COLOR KEY INSERT (SEE BELOW).

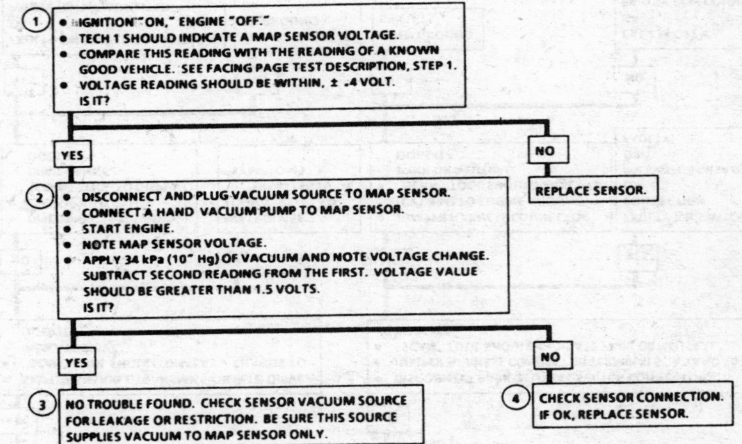

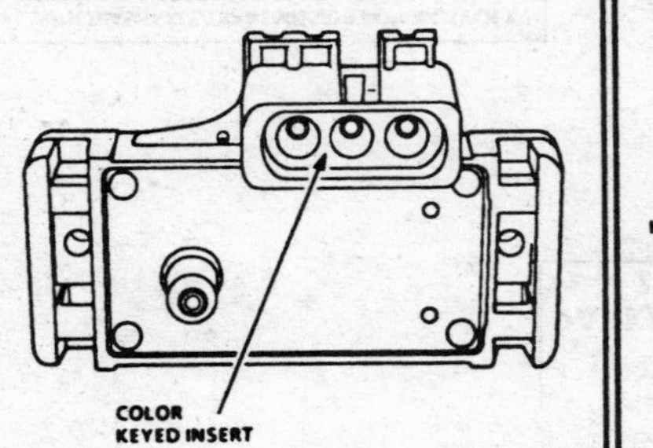

Figure 1 - Color Key Insert

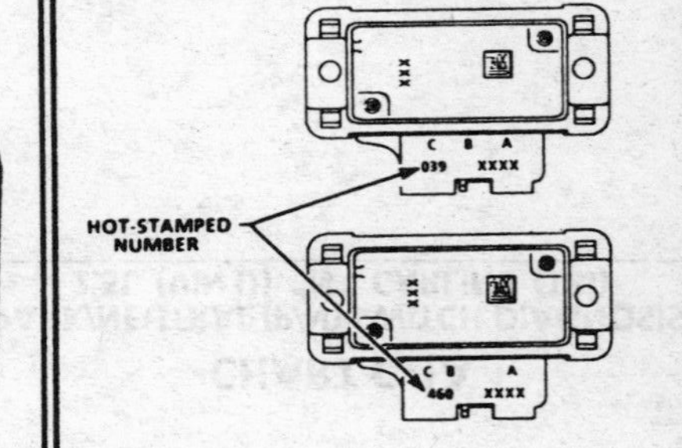

Figure 2 - Hot-Stamped Number

"AFTER REPAIRS," CONFIRM "CLOSED LOOP" OPERATION AND NO "SERVICE ENGINE SOON" LIGHT.

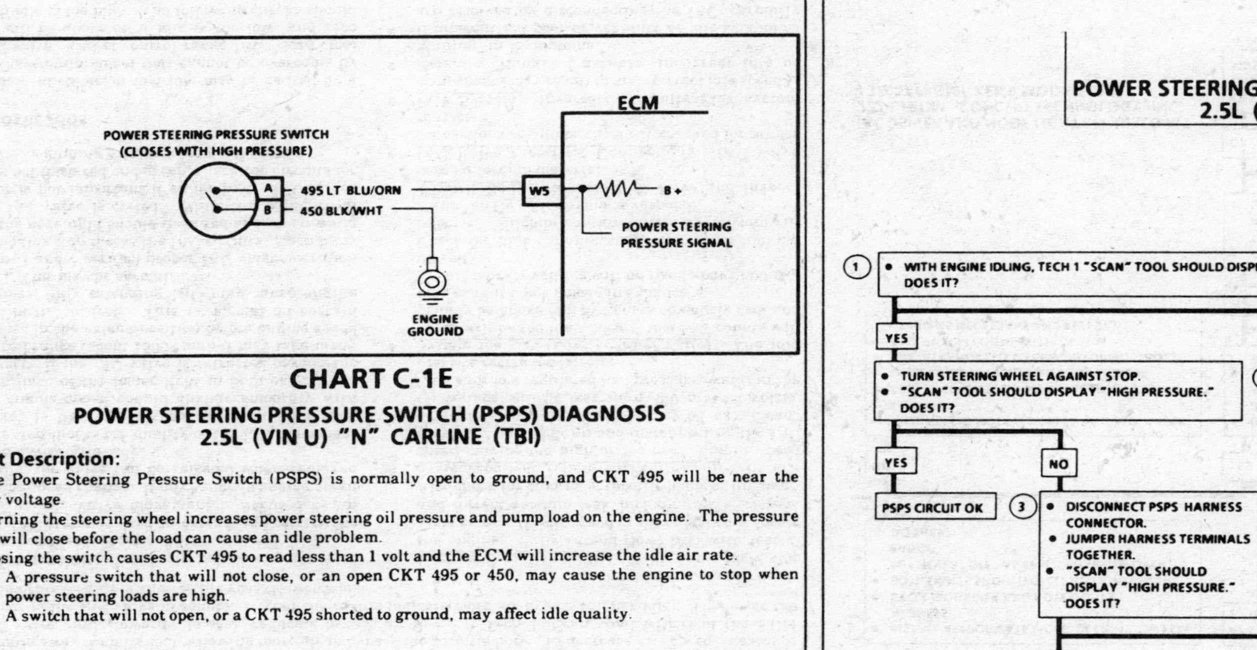

CHART C-1E

POWER STEERING PRESSURE SWITCH (PSPS) DIAGNOSIS 2.5L (VIN U) "N" CARLINE (TBI)

Circuit Description:

The Power Steering Pressure Switch (PSPS) is normally open to ground, and CKT 495 will be near the battery voltage.

Turning the steering wheel increases power steering oil pressure and pump load on the engine. The pressure switch will close before the load can cause an idle problem.

Closing the switch causes CKT 495 to read less than 1 volt and the ECM will increase the idle air rate.

- A pressure switch that will not close, or an open CKT 495 or 450, may cause the engine to stop when power steering loads are high.
- A switch that will not open, or a CKT 495 shorted to ground, may affect idle quality.

Test Description: Number(s) below refer to circled number(s) on the diagnostic chart.

1. Different makes of "Scan" tools may display the state of this switch in different ways. Refer to "Scan" tool user's manual to determine how this input is indicated.
2. Checks to determine if CKT 495 is shorted to ground.
3. This should simulate a closed switch.

CHART C-1E

POWER STEERING PRESSURE SWITCH (PSPS) DIAGNOSIS 2.5L (VIN U) "N" CARLINE (TBI)

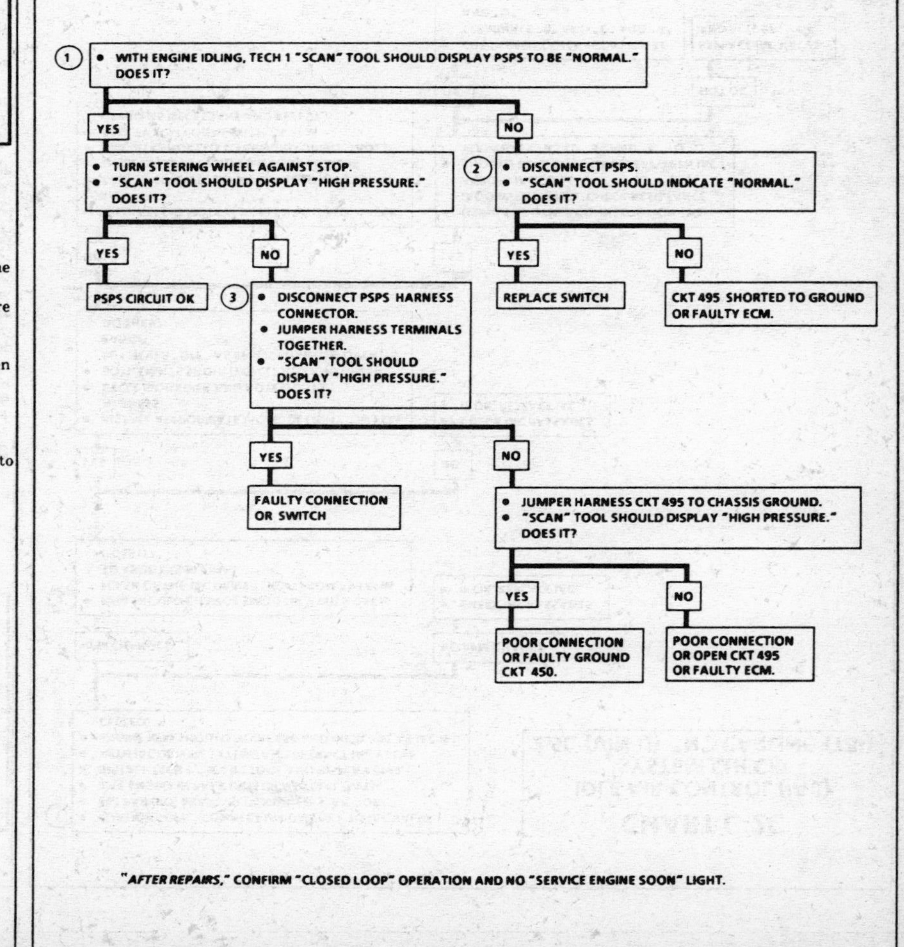

"*AFTER REPAIRS*," CONFIRM "CLOSED LOOP" OPERATION AND NO "SERVICE ENGINE SOON" LIGHT.

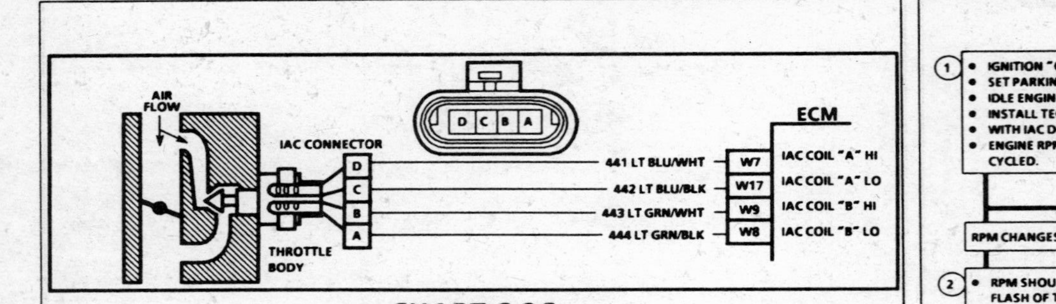

CHART C-2C

IDLE AIR CONTROL (IAC) SYSTEM CHECK 2.5L (VIN U) "N" CARLINE (TBI)

Circuit Description:

The ECM controls engine idle speed with the IAC valve. To increase idle speed, the ECM retracts the IAC valve pintle away from its seat, allowing more air to bypass the throttle bore. To decrease idle speed, it extends the IAC valve pintle towards its seat, reducing bypass air flow. A Tech 1 "Scan" tool will read the ECM commands to the IAC valve in counts. Higher the counts indicate more air bypass (higher idle). The lower the counts indicate less air is allowed to bypass (lower idle).

Test Description: Number(s) below refer to circled number(s) on the diagnostic chart.

1. The IAC tester is used to extend and retract the IAC valve. Valve movement is verified by an engine speed change. If no change in engine speed occurs, the valve can be retested when removed from the throttle body.
2. This step checks the quality of the IAC movement in step 1. Between 700 rpm and about 1500 rpm, the engine speed should change smoothly with each flash of the tester light in both extend and retract. If the IAC valve is retracted beyond the control range (about 1500 rpm), it may take many flashes in the extend position before engine speed will begin to drop. This is normal on certain engines, fully extending IAC may cause engine stall. This may be normal.
3. Steps 1 and 2 verified proper IAC valve operation while this step checks the IAC circuits. Each lamp on the node light should flash red and green while the IAC valve is cycled. While the sequence of color is not important if either light is "OFF" or does not flash red and green, check the circuits for faults, beginning with poor terminal contacts.

Diagnostic Aids:

A slow, unstable, or fast idle may be caused by a non-IAC system problem that cannot be overcome by the IAC valve. Out of control range IAC "Scan" tool counts will be above 60 if idle is too low, and zero counts if idle is too high. The following checks should be made to repair a non-IAC system problem:

- Vacuum Leak (High Idle) - If idle is too high, stop the engine. Fully extend (low) IAC with tester. Start engine. If idle speed is above 800 rpm, locate and correct vacuum leak including PCV system. Also check for binding of throttle blade or linkage.
- System too lean (High Air/Fuel Ratio) - The idle speed may be too high or too low. Engine speed may vary up and down and disconnecting the IAC valve does not help. Code 44 may be set. "Scan" O_2 voltage will be less than 300 mV (.3 volts). Check for low regulated fuel pressure, water in the fuel or a restricted injector.
- System too rich (Low Air/Fuel Ratio) - The idle speed will be too low. "Scan" tool IAC counts will usually be above 80. System is obviously rich and may exhibit black smoke in exhaust.
  "Scan" tool O_2 voltage will be fixed above 800 mV (.8 volt).
  Check for high fuel pressure, leaking or sticking injector. Silicone contaminated O_2 sensor will "Scan" an O_2 voltage slow to respond.
- Throttle Body - Remove IAC valve and inspect bore for foreign material.
- IAC Valve Electrical Connections - IAC valve connections should be carefully checked for proper contact.
- PCV System - Incorrect or faulty PCV system components may result in an incorrect idle speed.
- Refer to "Rough, Unstable, Incorrect Idle or Stalling" in "Symptoms,"
- If intermittent poor driveability or idle symptoms are resolved by disconnecting the IAC, carefully recheck connections, valve terminal resistance, or replace IAC.

CHART C-2C

IDLE AIR CONTROL (IAC) SYSTEM CHECK 2.5L (VIN U) "N" CARLINE (TBI)

(1)
- IGNITION "OFF," CONNECT IAC DRIVER * TO IAC VALVE.
- SET PARKING BRAKE, BLOCK WHEELS, A/C "OFF."
- IDLE ENGINE IN PARK (A/T) OR NEUTRAL (M/T).
- INSTALL TECH 1 "SCAN" TOOL AND DISPLAY RPM.
- WITH IAC DRIVER, EXTEND AND RETRACT IAC VALVE.
- ENGINE RPM SHOULD DECREASE AND INCREASE AS IAC IS CYCLED.

NO RPM CHANGE →
- CHECK IAC PASSAGES.
- IF OK, REPLACE IAC.

RPM CHANGES →

(2)
- RPM SHOULD CHANGE SMOOTHLY WITH EACH FLASH OF THE IAC DRIVER LIGHT FROM 700 RPM TO ABOUT 1500 RPM.
DOES IT?

NO →
- CHECK IAC PASSAGES.
- IF OK, REPLACE IAC.

YES →

(3)
- INSTALL APPROPRIATE IAC NODE LIGHT * IN ECM HARNESS.
- CYCLE IAC DRIVER AND NOTE LIGHTS.
- BOTH LIGHTS SHOULD CYCLE RED AND GREEN BUT NEVER "OFF" AS RPM IS CHANGED OVER ITS RANGE.
DO THEY?

NO →

IF CIRCUIT(S) DID NOT TEST GREEN AND RED, CHECK FOR:
- FAULTY CONNECTOR TERMINAL CONTACTS.
- OPEN CIRCUITS INCLUDING CONNECTIONS.
- CIRCUITS SHORTED TO GROUND OR VOLTAGE.
- FAULTY ECM CONNECTION OR ECM.
REPAIR AS NECESSARY AND RETEST.

YES →
- USING THE OTHER CONNECTOR ON THE IAC DRIVER PIGTAIL, CHECK RESISTANCE ACROSS IAC COILS.
- SHOULD BE 40 TO 80 OHMS BETWEEN IAC TERMINALS "A" TO "B" AND "C" TO "D".

NOT OK → REPLACE IAC VALVE AND RETEST.

OK →
- CHECK RESISTANCE BETWEEN IAC TERMINALS "B" AND "C" AND "A" AND "D".
- SHOULD BE INFINITE.

NOT OK → REPLACE IAC VALVE AND RETEST.

OK → IDLE AIR CONTROL VALVE AND CIRCUIT OK. REFER TO "DIAGNOSTIC AIDS" ON FACING PAGE.

* IAC DRIVER AND NODE LIGHT REQUIRED KIT
222-L FROM: CONCEPT TECHNOLOGY, INC.
J 37027 FROM: KENT-MOORE, INC.

"AFTER REPAIRS," CONFIRM "CLOSED LOOP" OPERATION AND NO "SERVICE ENGINE SOON" LIGHT.

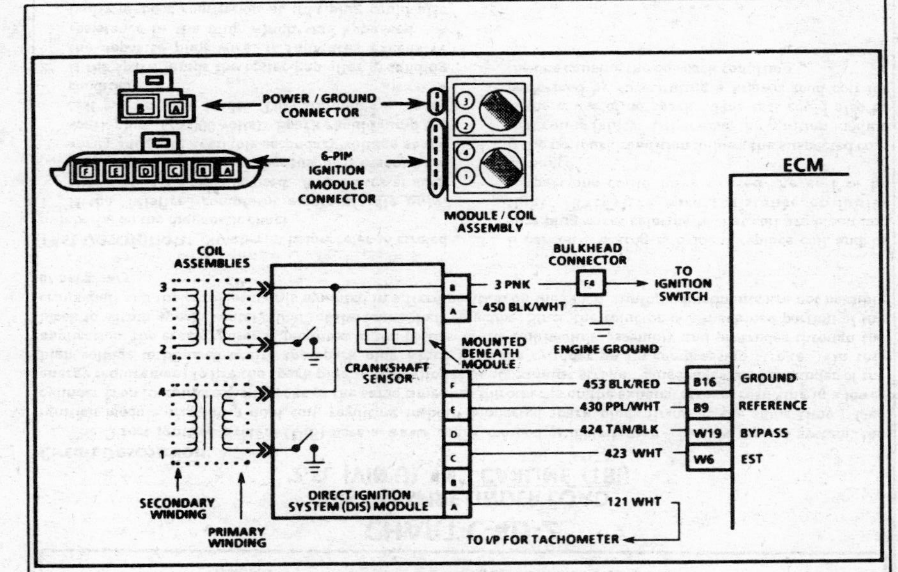

CHART C-4D-1

"DIS" MISFIRE AT IDLE 2.5L (VIN U) "N" CARLINE (TBI)

Circuit Description:

The Direct Ignition System (DIS) uses a waste spark method of distribution. In this type of system, the ignition module triggers a dual coil, resulting in both connected spark plugs firing at the same time. One cylinder is on its compression stroke at the same time that the other is on the exhaust stroke, resulting in a lower energy requirement to fire the spark plug in the cylinder on its exhaust stroke. This leaves the remainder of the high voltage to be used to fire the spark plug which is in the cylinder on its compression stroke. On this application, the crank sensor is mounted to the bottom of the coil/module assembly and protrudes through the block to within approximately .050" of the crankshaft reluctor. Since the reluctor is a machined portion of the crankshaft and the crankshaft sensor is mounted in a fixed position on the block, timing adjustments are not possible or necessary.

Test Description: Number(s) below refer to circled number(s) on the diagnostic chart.

1. If the "Misfire" complaint exists under load only, CHART C-4D-2 must be used. Engine rpm should drop approximately equally on all plug leads.
2. A spark tester such as a ST-125 must be used because it is essential to verify adequate available secondary voltage at the spark plug. (25,000 volts.)
3. If the spark jumps the test gap after grounding the opposite plug wire, it indicates excessive resistance in the plug which was bypassed. A faulty or poor connection at that plug could also result in the miss condition. Also check for carbon deposits inside the spark plug boot.
4. If carbon tracking is evident, replace coil and be sure plug wires relating to that coil are clean and tight. Excessive wire resistance or faulty connections could have caused the coil to be damaged.
5. If the no spark condition follows the suspected coil, that coil is faulty. Otherwise, the ignition module is the cause of no spark. This test could also be performed by substituting a known good coil for the one causing the no spark condition.

CHART C-4D-1

"DIS" MISFIRE AT IDLE 2.5L (VIN U) "N" CARLINE (TBI)

(1)
- IGNITION "ON" - IF SES LIGHT IS "OFF", USE CHART A-1.
- INSTALL TECH 1 "SCAN" TOOL - IF NO DATA, USE CHART A-2.
- CHECK THE FOLLOWING:
  - TPS - IF OVER 2.5 VOLTS AT CLOSED THROTTLE, SEE CODE 22 CHART.
  - COOLANT - IF BELOW -30°C, USE CODE 15 CHART.
  - IS RPM INDICATED WHILE CRANKING?

YES → (2)
- USING A ST-125, J 26792 OR EQUIVALENT, CHECK FOR SPARK WHILE CRANKING (CHECK TWO WIRES). IS SPARK PRESENT?

NO → BASIC HEI PROBLEM. REFER TO CHART C-4.

YES →
- PROBE FUEL PUMP TEST TERMINAL WITH A TEST LIGHT TO GROUND.
- IGNITION "OFF" FOR 10 SECONDS.
- TURN IGNITION "ON."
- TEST LIGHT SHOULD LIGHT FOR 2 SECONDS AFTER IGNITION IS TURNED "ON." DOES IT?

NO → SEE FUEL PUMP RELAY CIRCUIT CHART A-5

YES → (3)
- DISCONNECT INJECTOR CONNECTOR.
- CRANK ENGINE.
- IS THERE FUEL SPRAY FROM INJECTOR?

YES → FAULTY INJECTOR OR O-RING

NO → (4)
- CONNECT INJECTOR TEST LIGHT TO HARNESS CONNECTOR.
- CRANK ENGINE.
- DOES TEST LIGHT BLINK?

NO → SEE CHART A-3 PAGE 2 OF 2.

YES → (5)
- RECONNECT INJECTOR CONNECTOR.
- CRANK ENGINE.
- IS THERE FUEL SPRAY FROM INJECTOR?

YES →
- CHECK FOR: FOULED SPARK PLUGS. EGR VALVE STUCK OPEN. LOW FUEL PRESSURE (CHART A-7). DIAGNOSTIC AIDS FACING PAGE.

NO →
- IGNITION "OFF".
- INSTALL FUEL PRESSURE GAGE.
- IGNITION "ON".
- FUEL PRESSURE SHOULD BE 62-90 kPa (9-13 psi). IS IT?

YES → FAULTY INJECTOR

NO → SEE FUEL SYSTEM DIAGNOSIS CHART A-7.

(1) NO →
- USING A ST-125 (SPARK CHECKER), J 26792 OR EQUIVALENT, CHECK FOR SPARK WHILE CRANKING (CHECK TWO WIRES). IS SPARK PRESENT?

NO → CHECK FOR BATT. VOLTAGE TO IGNITION SYSTEM. IF OK, THERE IS A BASIC HEI PROBLEM. REFER TO CHART C-4C.

YES → (6)
- IGNITION "OFF."
- DISCONNECT DISTRIBUTOR 4-PIN CONNECTOR.
- IGNITION "ON."
- MOMENTARILY TOUCH HARNESS CONNECTOR TERMINAL (CKT 430) WITH A TEST LIGHT TO B+.
- "SCAN" SHOULD INDICATE RPM WHEN TEST IS PERFORMED. DOES IT?

YES → FAULTY CONNECTION OR IGNITION MODULE.

NO → CKT 430 OPEN, SHORTED TO GROUND OR FAULTY ECM.

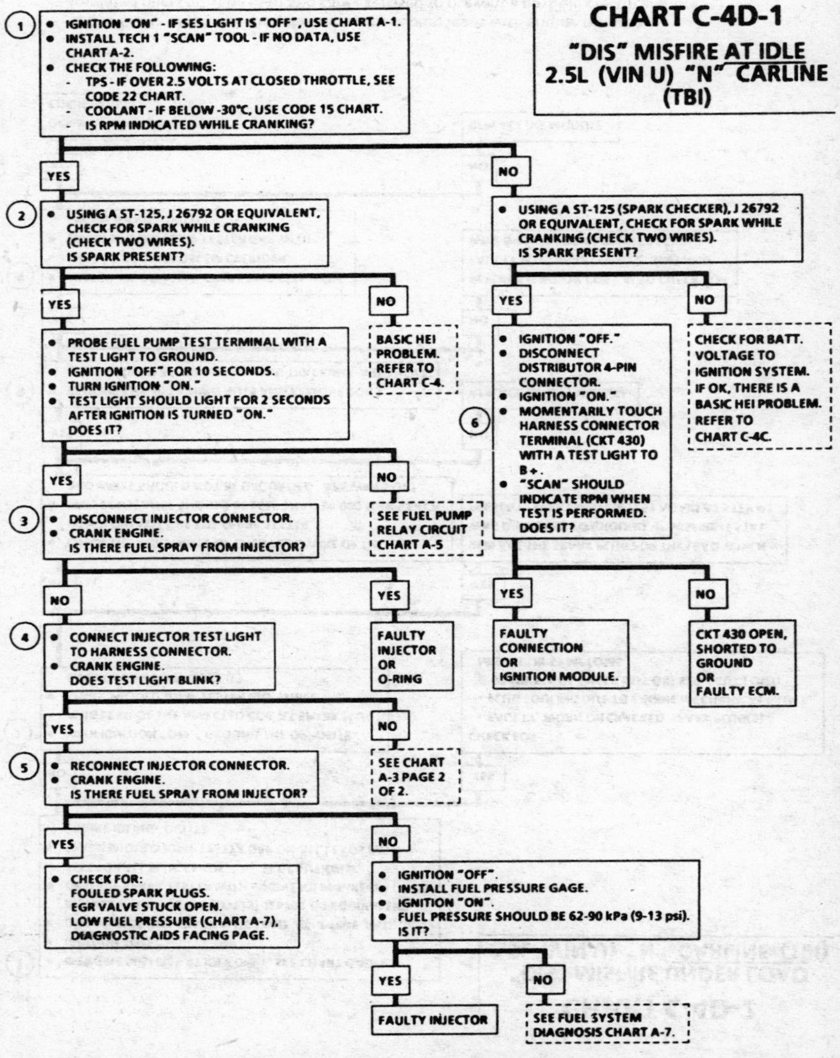

"AFTER REPAIRS," CONFIRM "CLOSED LOOP" OPERATION AND NO "SERVICE ENGINE SOON" LIGHT.

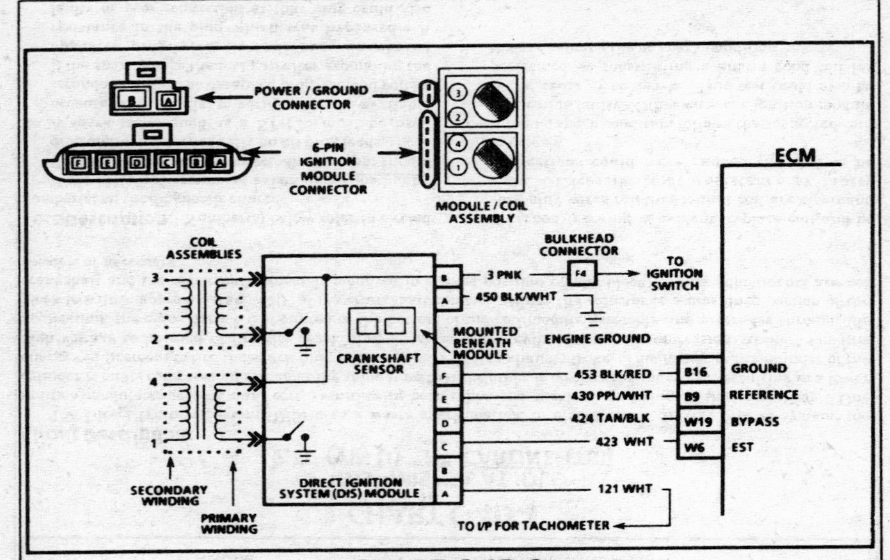

CHART C-4D-2

"DIS" MISFIRE UNDER LOAD
2.5L (VIN U) "N" CARLINE (TBI)

Circuit Description:

The Direct Ignition System (DIS) uses a waste spark method of distribution. In this type of system, the ignition module triggers a dual coil, resulting in both connected spark plugs firing at the same time. One cylinder is on its compression stroke at the same time that the other is on the exhaust stroke, resulting in a lower energy requirement to fire the spark plug in the cylinder on its exhaust stroke. This leaves the remainder of the high voltage to be used to fire the spark plug which is in the cylinder on its compression stroke. On this application, the crank sensor is mounted to the bottom of the coil/module assembly and protrudes through the block to within approximately .050" of the crankshaft reluctor. Since the reluctor is a machined portion of the crankshaft and the crank sensor is mounted in a fixed position on the block, timing adjustments are not possible or necessary.

Test Description: Number(s) below refer to circled number(s) on the diagnostic chart.

1. If the "Misfire" complaint exists at idle only, CHART C-4D-1 must be used. A spark tester such as a ST-125 must be used because it is essential to verify adequate available secondary voltage at the spark plug. (25,000 volts). Spark should jump the test gap on all 4 leads. This simulates a "load" condition.
2. If the spark jumps the tester gap after grounding the opposite plug wire, it indicates excessive resistance in the plug which was bypassed. A faulty or poor connection at that plug could also result in the miss condition. Also check for carbon deposits inside the spark plug boot.
3. If carbon tracking is evident replace coil and be sure plug wires relating to that coil are clean and tight. Excessive wire resistance or faulty connections could have caused the coil to be damaged.
4. If the no spark condition follows the suspected coil, that coil is faulty. Otherwise, the ignition module is the cause of no spark. This test could also be performed by substituting a known good coil for the one causing the no spark condition.

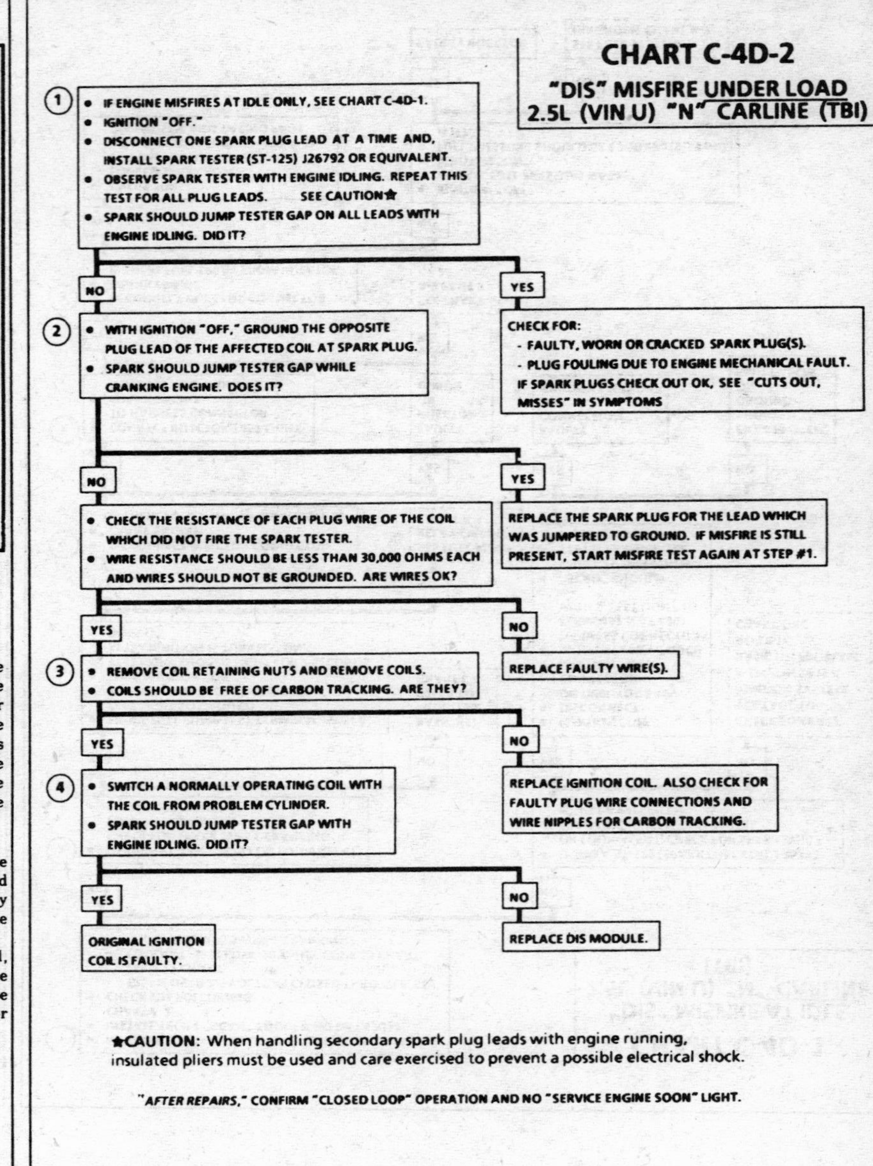

★**CAUTION:** When handling secondary spark plug leads with engine running, insulated pliers must be used and care exercised to prevent a possible electrical shock.

"AFTER REPAIRS," CONFIRM "CLOSED LOOP" OPERATION AND NO "SERVICE ENGINE SOON" LIGHT.

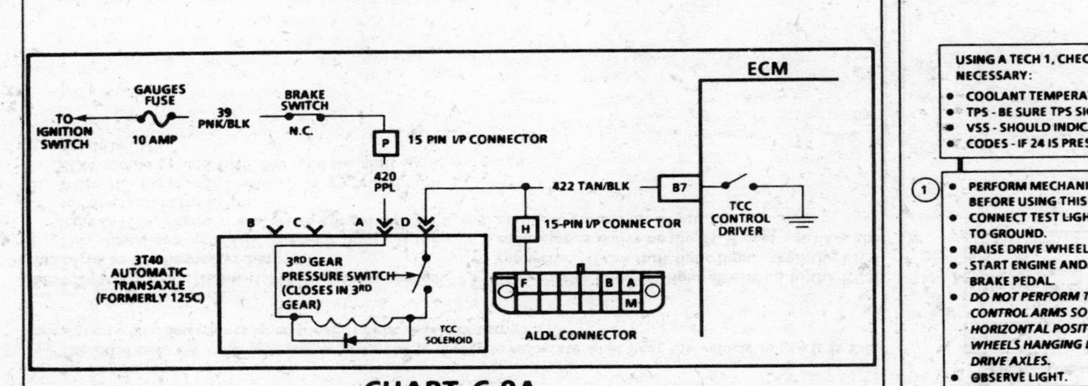

CHART C-8A

TORQUE CONVERTER CLUTCH (TCC) (ELECTRICAL DIAGNOSIS) 2.5L (VIN U) "N" CARLINE (TBI)

Circuit Description:

The purpose of the Torque Converter Clutch (TCC) is to eliminate the power loss of the torque converter when the vehicle is in a cruise condition. This allows the convenience of the automatic transaxle and the fuel economy of a manual transaxle.

Voltage is supplied to the TCC solenoid through the brake switch and transaxle third gear apply switch. The ECM will engage TCC by grounding CKT 422 to energize the solenoid.

The TCC will engage under the following conditions:

- Vehicle speed exceeds 56 km/h (35 mph) with A/C "OFF," or above 70 km/h (44 mph) with A/C "ON."
- Engine coolant temperature exceeds 70°C (158°F).
- Throttle position is not changing faster than a calibrated rate (steady throttle).
- Transaxle third gear switch is closed.
- Brake switch is closed.

Test Description: Number(s) below refer to circled number(s) on the diagnostic chart.

1. Light "OFF" confirms transaxle third gear apply switch is open.
2. At approximately 48 km/h (30 mph), the transaxle third gear switch should close. This depends on throttle position. The minimum speed at which the third gear switch will close is approximately 34 km/h (21 mph). The test light should turn "ON" and confirm ignition voltage in the circuit and a closed brake switch.
3. Grounding the diagnostic terminal with the ignition "ON" and the engine "OFF," should light the test light. This test checks the capability of the ECM to control the solenoid.

Diagnostic Aids:

An engine coolant thermostat that is stuck open or opens at too low a temperature may result in an inoperative TCC.

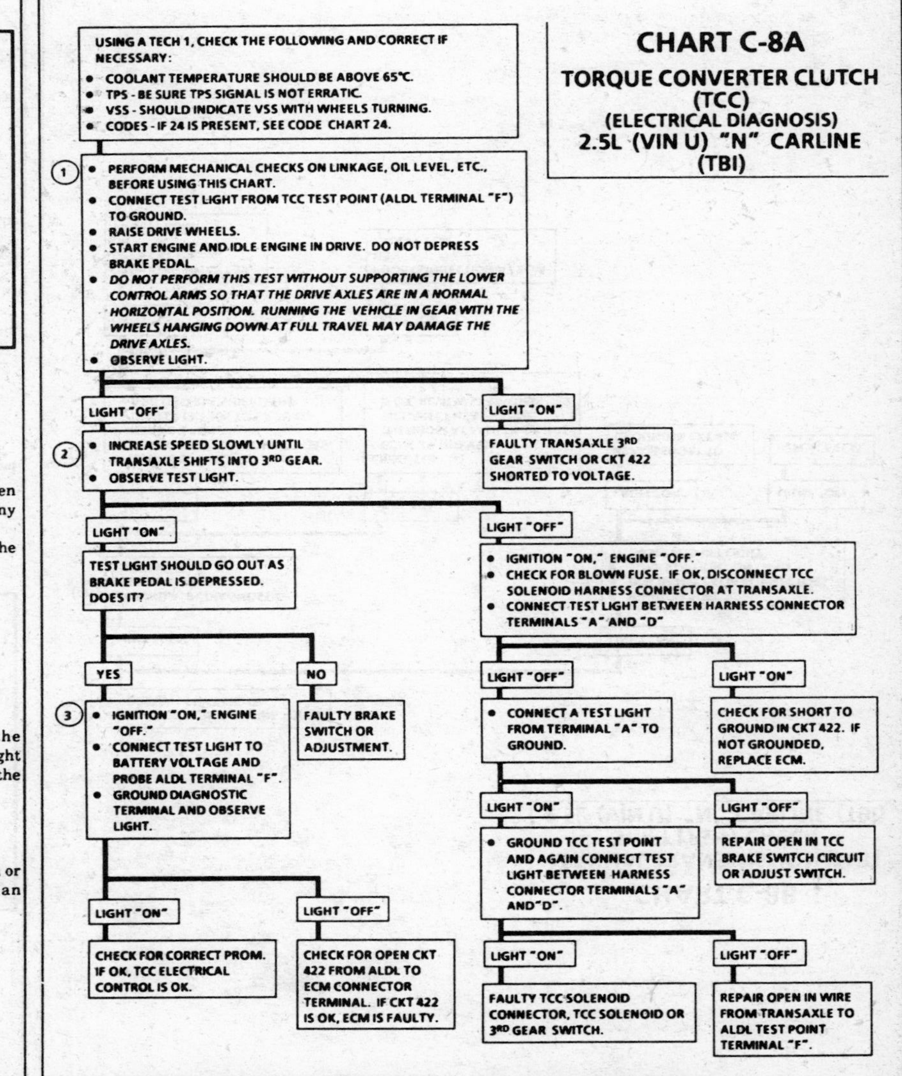

TO IGNITION SWITCH
GAUGES FUSE
10 AMP
39 PNK/BLK
INSTRUMENT PANEL
N
15 PIN I/P CONNECTOR
455 TAN/BLK
B7
ECM
SHIFT LIGHT CONTROL
J K L M N P R
A B C D E F G H
I/P HARNESS CONNECTOR 15 WAY (FRONT VIEW)

CHART C-8B

MANUAL TRANSMISSION (M/T) SHIFT LIGHT CHECK 2.5L (VIN U) "N" CARLINE (TBI)

Circuit Description:

The shift light indicates the best transmission shift point for maximum fuel efficiency. The light is controlled by the ECM and is turned "ON" by grounding CKT 456.

The ECM uses information from the following inputs to control the shift light:

- Coolant temperature.
- Throttle position.
- Vehicle speed.
- Engine speed.

The ECM uses the measured engine and vehicle speeds to calculate what gear the vehicle is in. It is this calculation which determines when the shift light should be turned "ON."

Test Description: Number(s) below refer to circled number(s) on the diagnostic chart.

1. This should not turn "ON" the shift light. If the light is "ON," there is a short to ground in CKT 456 or a fault in the ECM.
2. When the diagnostic terminal is grounded, the ECM should ground CKT 456, and the shift light should be "ON."
3. This checks the shift light circuit up to the ECM connector. If the shift light lights, then the ECM connector is faulty or the ECM does not have the ability to ground the circuit.

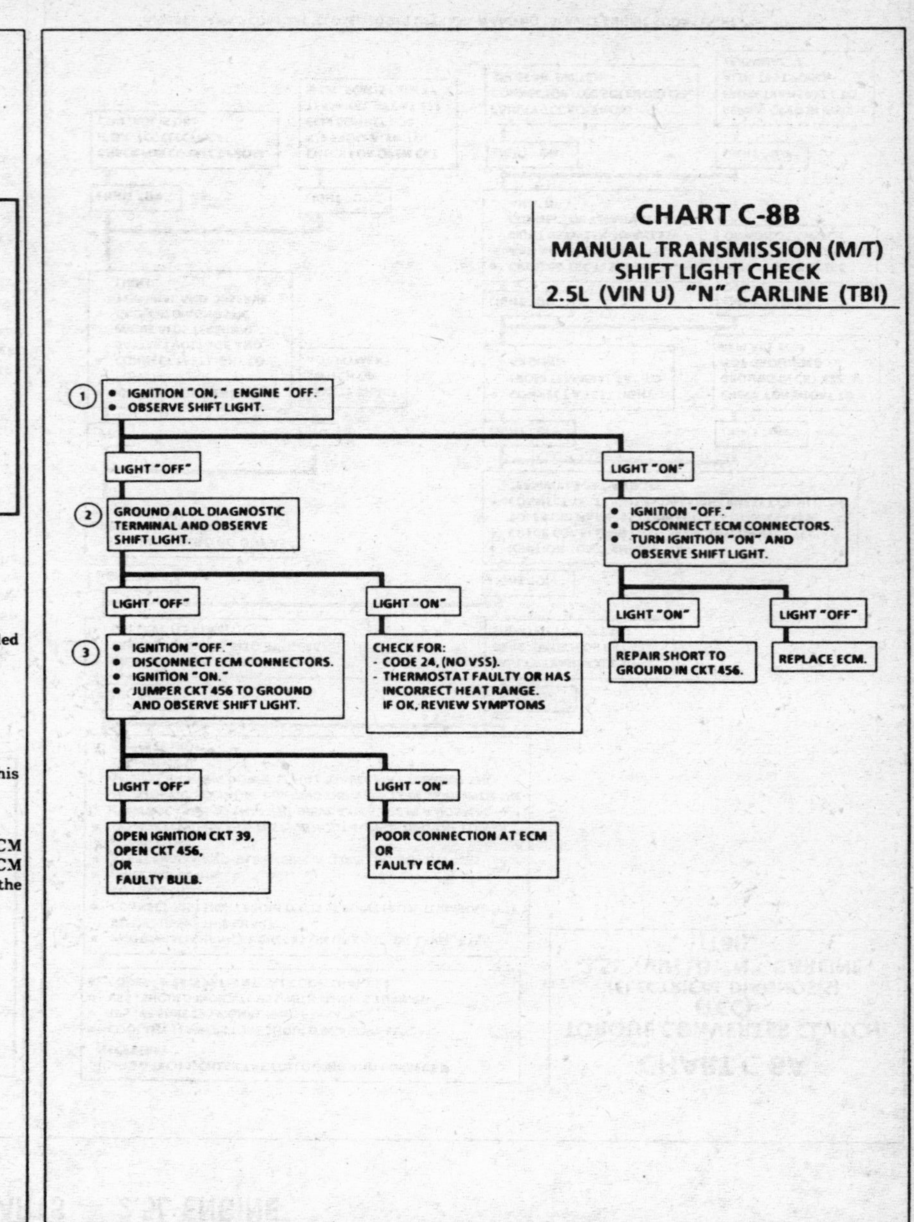

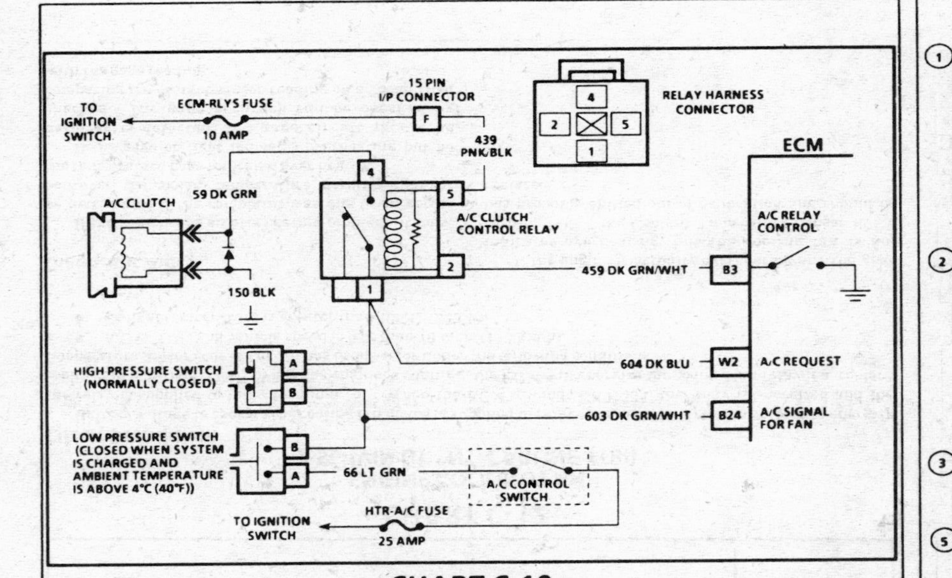

CHART C-10

A/C CLUTCH CONTROL
2.5L (VIN U) "N" CARLINE (TBI)

Circuit Description:

When an A/C mode is selected on the A/C control switch, ignition voltage is supplied to the compressor low pressure switch. If there is sufficient A/C refrigerant pressure, the low pressure switch will be closed and complete the circuit to the closed high pressure cut-off switch and to CKT 604. The voltage on CKT 604 to the ECM is shown by the "Scan" tool as A/C request "YES" (voltage present) or "NO" (no voltage). When a request for A/C is sensed by the ECM, the ECM will ground CKT 459 of the A/C clutch control relay, the relay contact will close, and current will flow from CKT 604 to CKT 59 to engage the A/C compressor clutch. A "Scan" tool will show the grounding of CKT 459 as A/C clutch "ON." If voltage is sensed by the ECM on CKT 603, the cooling fan will be turned "ON."

Test Description: Numbers below refer to circled numbers on the diagnostic chart.

1. The ECM will energize the A/C relay only when the engine is running. This test will determine if the relay or CKT 459 is faulty.
2. The low pressure and high pressure switches must be closed so that the A/C request signal (12 volts) will be present at the ECM.
3. A short to ground in any part of the A/C request or A/C clutch control circuits could be the cause of the blown fuse.
4. With the engine idling and A/C "ON," the ECM should be grounding CKT 459, causing the test light to be "ON."
5. Determines if the signal is reaching the low pressure switch on CKT 66 from the A/C control panel. The signal should be present only when the A/C mode or defrost mode has been selected.

Diagnostic Aids:

If complaint was insufficient cooling, the problem may be caused by an inoperative cooling fan or A/C low pressure switch. The engine cooling fan should turn "ON" when A/C pressure exceeds a value to close the low pressure switch, which causes the ECM to energize the cooling fan relay. See CHART C-12 for cooling fan diagnosis. If fan operates correctly, see A/C Diagnosis

CHART C-10

A/C CLUTCH CONTROL
2.5L (VIN U) "N" CARLINE (TBI)

(1)
- IGNITION "ON," ENGINE "OFF."
- CYCLE A/C CONTROL SWITCH "ON" AND "OFF." DOES COMPRESSOR CLUTCH ENGAGE WITH A/C "ON"?

YES — SHORT TO GROUND ON CKT 459 OR FAULTY RELAY.

NO
- START ENGINE AND ALLOW IT TO IDLE.
- CYCLE A/C CONTROL SWITCH "ON" AND "OFF." DOES COMPRESSOR CLUTCH ENGAGE WITH A/C "ON"?

YES
- DOES ENGINE COOLING FAN OPERATE WITH A/C "ON," ENGINE IDLING?
  - YES — NO TROUBLE FOUND. CHECK FOR BASIC A/C PROBLEM.
  - NO — CHECK FOR OPEN CKT 603 OR FAULTY ECM CONNECTION AT TERMINAL "B24". IF OK, USE CHART C-12.

NO

(2)
- WITH A/C "ON" AND ENGINE STILL IDLING, "SCAN" A/C REQUEST AND A/C CLUTCH.
- SHOULD BE "YES" AND "ON" RESPECTIVELY. ARE THEY?

YES

(4)
- DISCONNECT A/C CLUTCH CONTROL RELAY.
- CONNECT TEST LIGHT BETWEEN HARNESS CONNECTOR TERMINALS "2" AND "5".

LIGHT "ON"
- JUMPER HARNESS CONNECTOR TERMINALS "4" AND "5".
- A/C CLUTCH SHOULD ENGAGE.
  - ENGAGES — REPLACE FAULTY RELAY.
  - DOES NOT ENGAGE — CHECK FOR OPEN IN CKT 59, A/C CLUTCH COIL, OR CKT 150 GROUND.

LIGHT "OFF"
- CONNECT TEST LIGHT BETWEEN HARNESS TERMINAL "5" AND GROUND.
  - LIGHT "ON" — CKT 459 OPEN, SHORTED TO VOLTAGE, OR FAULTY ECM.
  - LIGHT "OFF" — REPAIR OPEN CKT 439.

NO

(3)
- CHECK HTR-A/C FUSE.

OK

(5)
- IGNITION "ON," ENGINE "OFF," A/C "ON."
- DISCONNECT LOW PRESSURE SWITCH.
- PROBE CKT 66 WITH TEST LIGHT TO GROUND.

LIGHT "ON"
- JUMPER HARNESS TERMINALS TOGETHER. DOES "SCAN" TOOL DISPLAY A/C REQUEST "YES"?
  - YES — FAULTY SWITCH OR CONNECTION OR LOW A/C SYSTEM CHARGE.
  - NO
    - DISCONNECT HIGH PRESSURE SWITCH.
    - JUMPER HARNESS TERMINALS TOGETHER. DOES "SCAN" TOOL DISPLAY A/C REQUEST "YES"?
      - YES — FAULTY SWITCH OR CONNECTION.
      - NO — OPEN CKT 603 OR CKT 604, FAULTY ECM CONNECTION OR ECM.

LIGHT "OFF" — REPAIR OPEN CKT 66.

FUSE BLOWN
- DISCONNECT A/C CONTROL RELAY.
- PROBE HARNESS CONNECTOR TERMINAL "1" WITH TEST LIGHT TO B+.

LIGHT "ON"
- DISCONNECT LOW PRESSURE SWITCH.
- OBSERVE LIGHT.
  - LIGHT "OFF" — SHORT TO GROUND ON CKT 66.
  - LIGHT "ON"
    - DISCONNECT HIGH PRESSURE SWITCH.
    - OBSERVE LIGHT.
      - LIGHT "ON" — REPAIR SHORT TO GROUND ON CKT 604.
      - LIGHT "OFF" — SHORT TO GROUND ON CKT 603.

LIGHT "OFF"
- DISCONNECT A/C CLUTCH CONNECTOR.
- PROBE HARNESS CONNECTOR TERMINAL OF CKT 59 WITH TEST LIGHT TO B+.
  - LIGHT "ON" — CKT 59 GROUNDED CHECK DIODE AT A/C COMPRESSOR CLUTCH.
  - LIGHT "OFF"
    - PROBE RELAY HARNESS TERMINAL "5" WITH A TEST LIGHT TO B+.
      - LIGHT "OFF" — FAULTY RELAY OR SHORTED A/C COMPRESSOR CLUTCH SOLENOID.
      - LIGHT "ON" — REPAIR GROUNDED CKT 439.

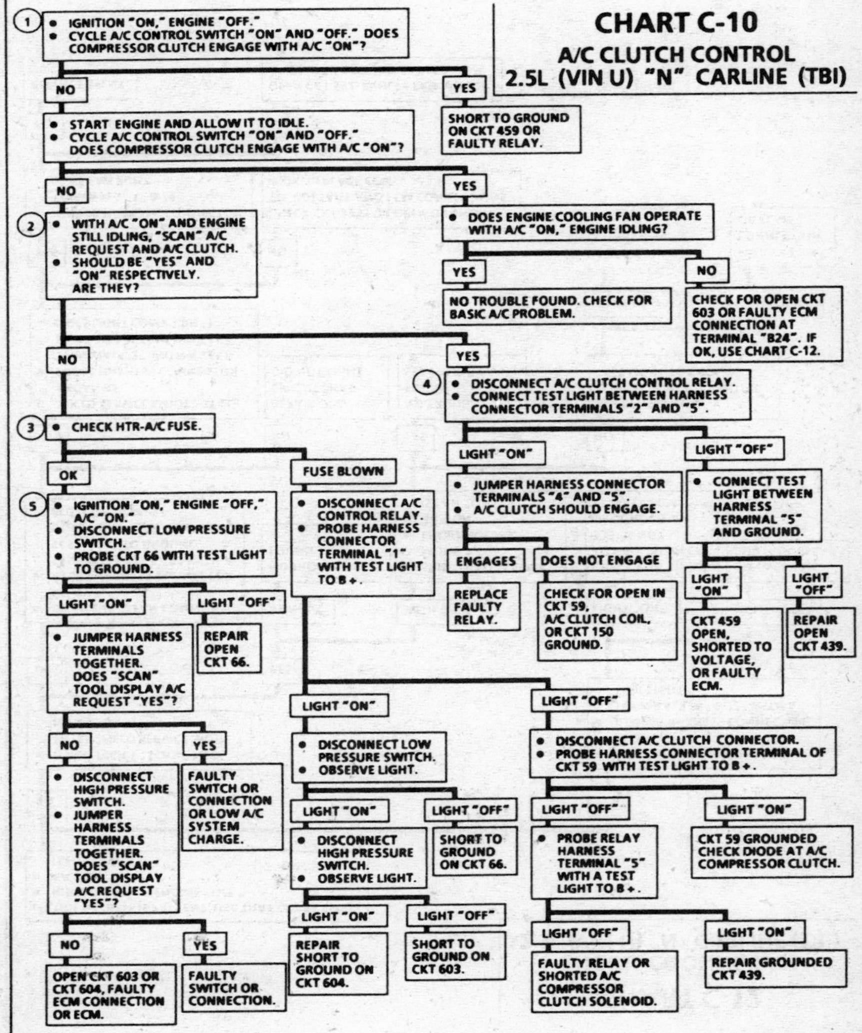

FAN CONTROL RELAY HARNESS CONNECTOR
TO A/C PRESSURE SWITCHES
603 DK GRN/WHT — B24 — A/C SIGNAL FOR FAN
ECM
TO IGNITION SWITCH
HTR-A/C FUSE 25 AMP
FUSIBLE LINK
TO B+ — 2 RED
50 BRN
COOLING FAN CONTROL RELAY
COOLING FAN RELAY CONTROL
335 DK GRN/WHT — B21
COOLING FAN
532 BLK/RED
TO COOLANT TEMPERATURE SENSOR (CTS) — 410 YEL — B8 — COOLANT TEMPERATURE SIGNAL
150 BLK

CHART C-12

ENGINE COOLING FAN
2.5L (VIN U) "N" CARLINE (TBI)

Circuit Description:

Battery voltage to operate the cooling fan motor is supplied to relay terminal "1". Ignition voltage to energize the relay is supplied to relay terminal "5". When the ECM grounds CKT 335, the relay is energized and the cooling fan is turned "ON." When the engine is running, the ECM will energize the cooling fan relay if a coolant temperature sensor code (14 or 15) has been set, or under the following conditions:

- A/C is "ON" and vehicle speed is less than 70 mph (113 km/h).
- Coolant temperature is greater than 106°C (223°F).

Diagnostic Aids:

If the vehicle has an overheating problem, it must be determined if the complaint was due to an actual boil over, the coolant temperature warning light, or the temperature gage indicated over heating.

If the gage or light indicates overheating but no boilover is detected, the gage circuit should be checked. The gage accuracy can be checked by comparing the coolant sensor reading on a "Scan" tool with the gage reading.

If the engine is actually overheating and the gage indicates overheating, but the cooling fan is not turning "ON," the Coolant Tmperature Sensor (CTS) has probably shifted out of calibration and should be replaced.

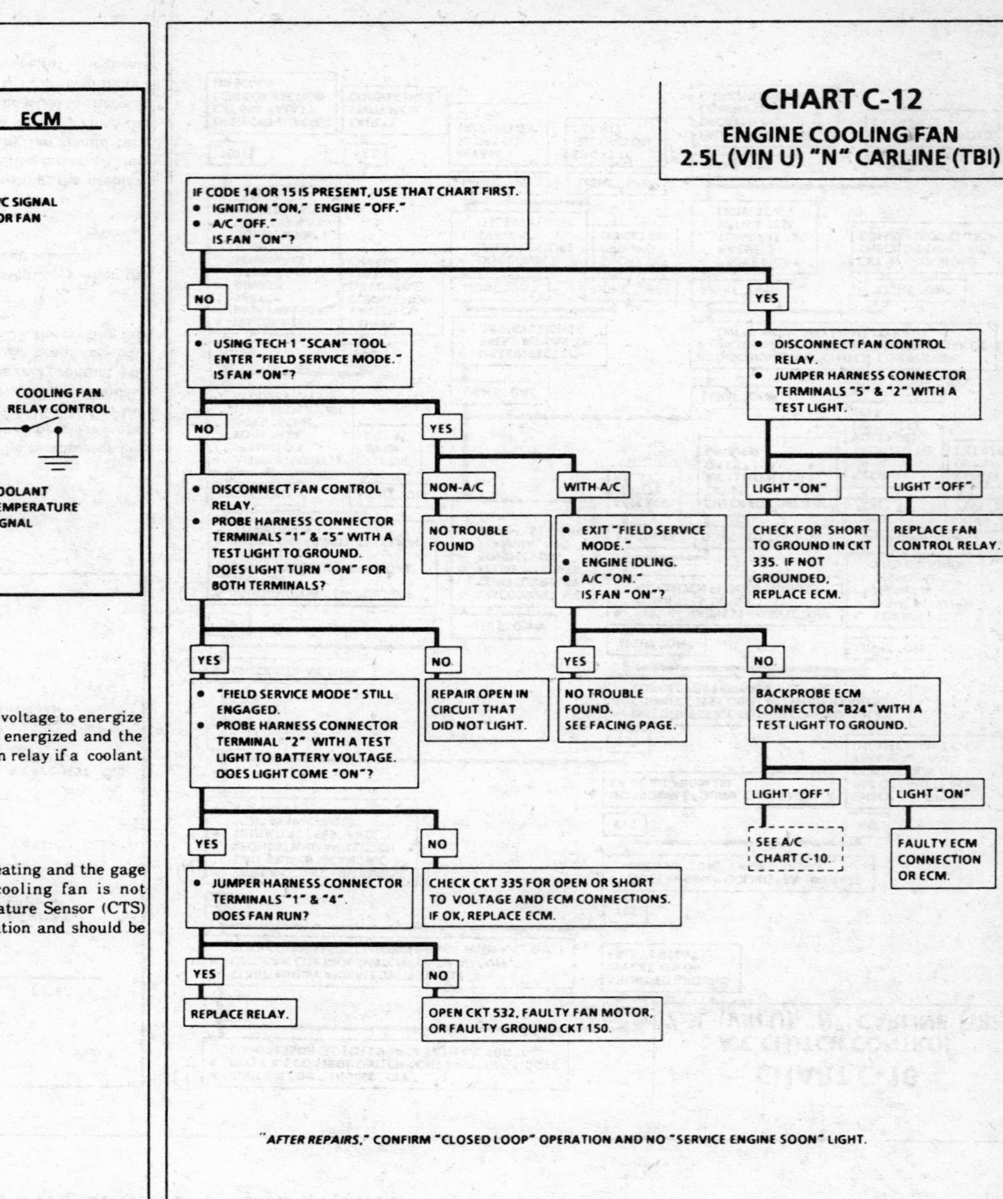

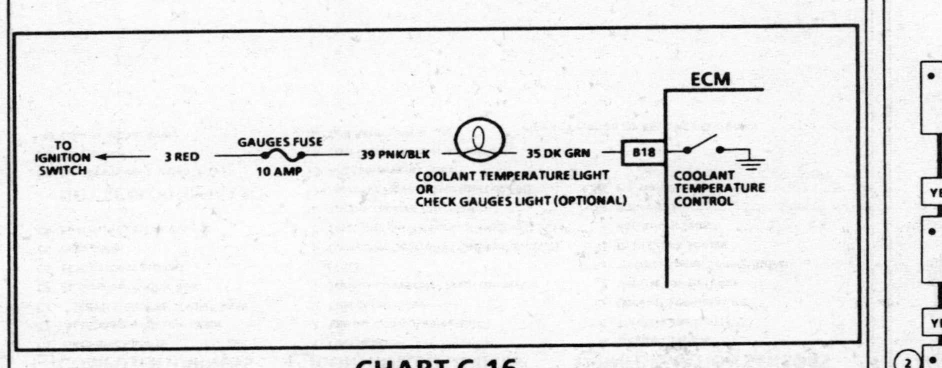

CHART C-16

ECM CONTROLLED WARNING LIGHT CIRCUIT 2.5L (VIN U) "N" CARLINE (TBI)

Circuit Description:

The "TEMP" light or optional "CHECK GAUGES" light, is connected to battery voltage through the ignition switch. The ECM energizes the bulb by supplying a path to ground through quad-driver module #2.

Test Description: Numbers below refer to circled numbers on the diagnostic chart.

1. With the ignition "ON" and engine "OFF," the ECM should be grounding CKT 35.
2. While the engine is running, the "TEMP" light or optional "CHECK GAUGES" light should be turned "ON" by the ECM only when the coolant temperature is above 123°C (253°F). The "TEMP" light or "Check Gauges" light should be turned "OFF" when the engine is running and the coolant temperature goes lower than 120°C (249°F).

Diagnostic Aids:

The coolant temperature sensor, in rare cases, may fail to indicate the correct engine coolant temperature without setting a malfunction code. This could result in turning "ON" the "TEMP" light or optional "CHECK GAUGES" light without having an overheating condition. It could also result in overheating without the "TEMP"/"CHECK GAUGES" warning light light being turned "ON."

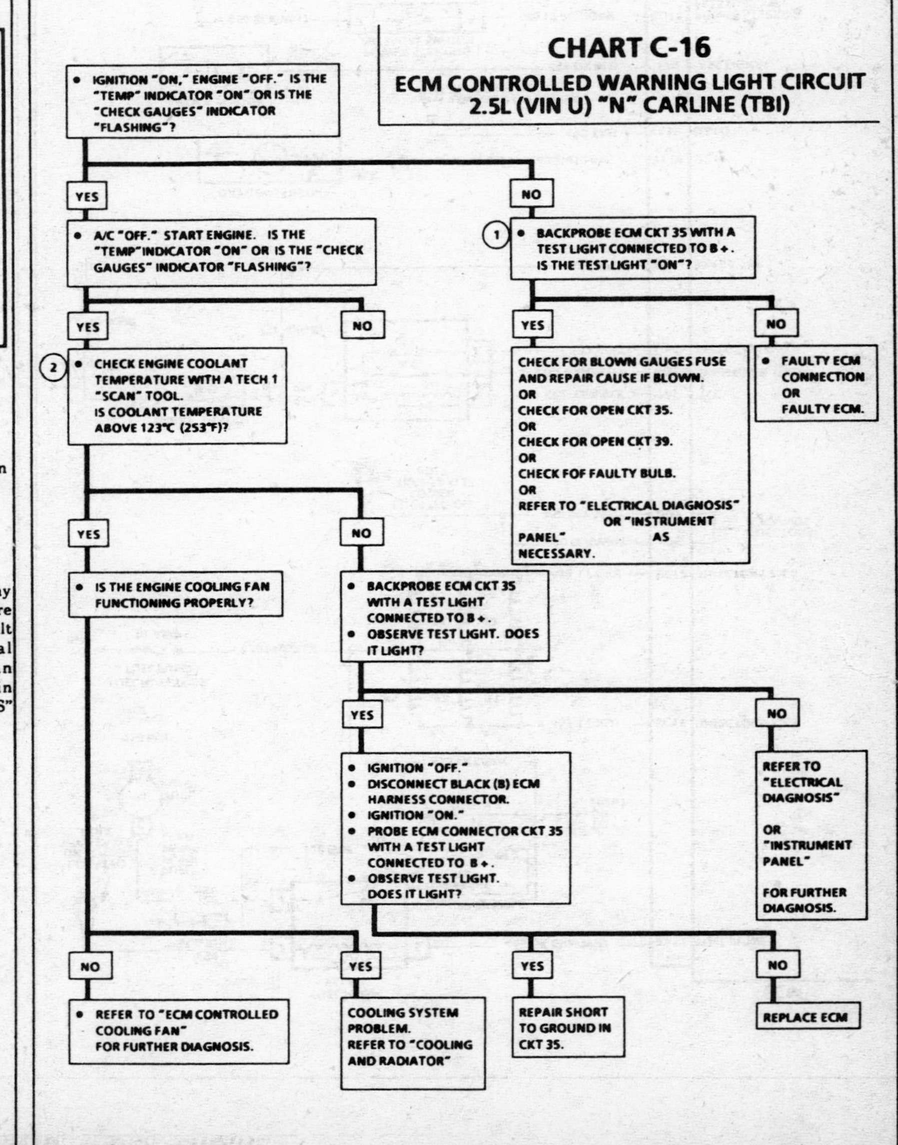

DIAGNOSTIC CHARTS — 3.3L ENGINE

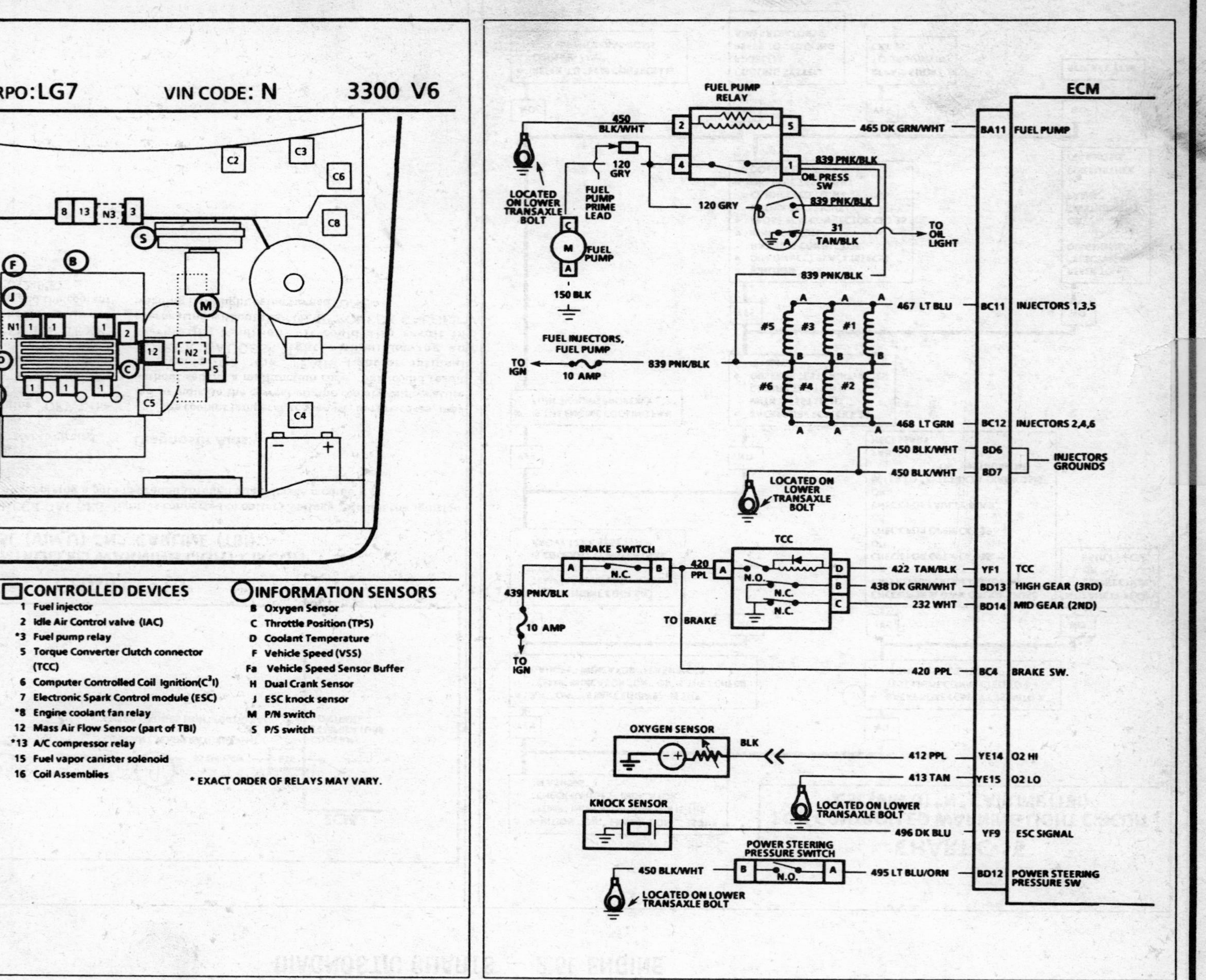

DIAGNOSTIC CHARTS — 3.3L ENGINE

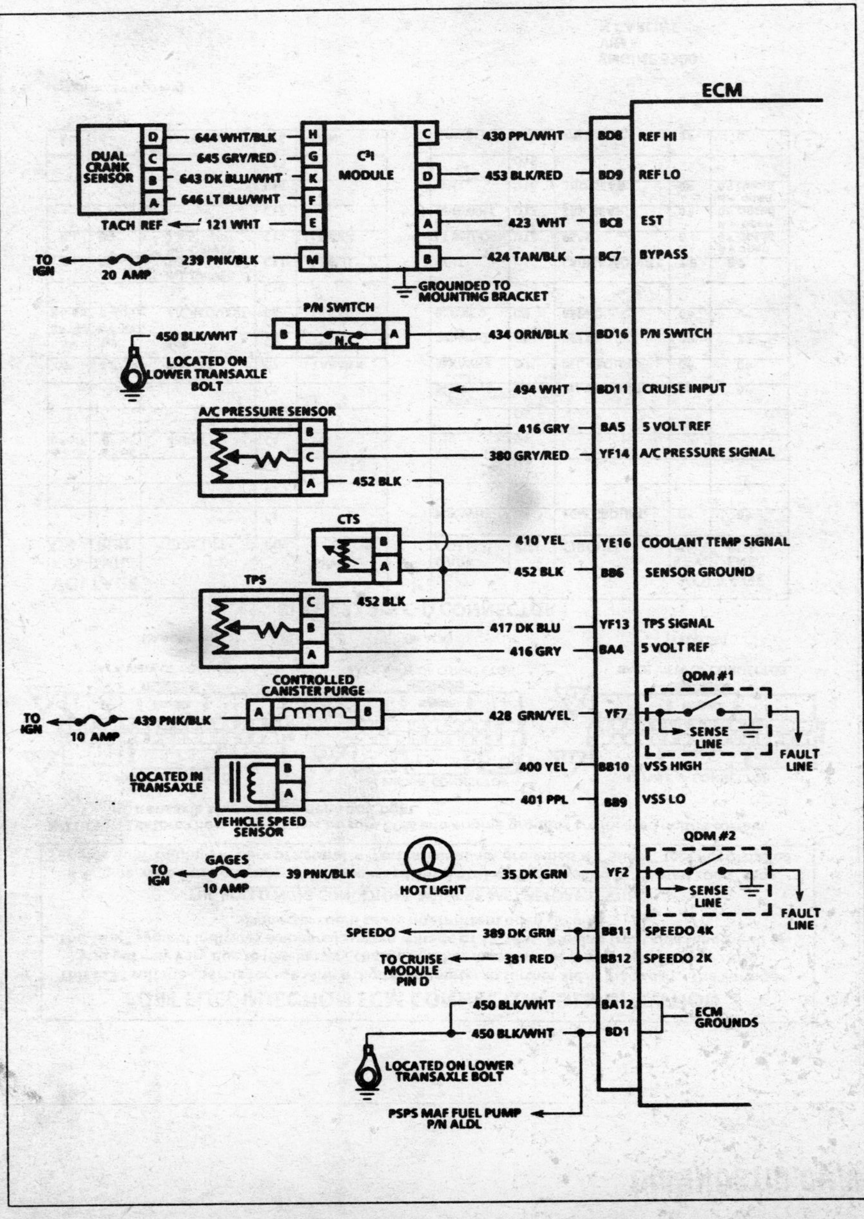

Wire	ECM Terminal	Function
430 PPL/WHT	BD8	REF HI
453 BLK/RED	BD9	REF LO
423 WHT	BC8	EST
424 TAN/BLK	BC7	BYPASS
434 ORN/BLK	BD16	P/N SWITCH
494 WHT	BD11	CRUISE INPUT
416 GRY	BA5	5 VOLT REF
380 GRY/RED	YF14	A/C PRESSURE SIGNAL
410 YEL	YE16	COOLANT TEMP SIGNAL
452 BLK	BB6	SENSOR GROUND
417 DK BLU	YF13	TPS SIGNAL
416 GRY	BA4	5 VOLT REF
428 GRN/YEL	YF7	QDM #1
400 YEL	BB10	VSS HIGH
401 PPL	BB9	VSS LO
35 DK GRN	YF2	QDM #2
389 DK GRN	BB11	SPEEDO 4K
381 RED	BB12	SPEEDO 2K
450 BLK/WHT	BA12	ECM GROUNDS
450 BLK/WHT	BD1	ECM GROUNDS

DUAL CRANK SENSOR (D, C, B, A): 644 WHT/BLK, 645 GRY/RED, 643 DK BLU/WHT, 646 LT BLU/WHT

C³I MODULE (H, G, K, F, E, M; C, D, A, B)

TACH REF ← 121 WHT

TO IGN ← 20 AMP — 239 PNK/BLK

GROUNDED TO MOUNTING BRACKET

P/N SWITCH (B, N.C, A) — 450 BLK/WHT — LOCATED ON LOWER TRANSAXLE BOLT

A/C PRESSURE SENSOR (B, C, A) — 452 BLK

CTS (B, A)

TPS (C, B, A) — 452 BLK

CONTROLLED CANISTER PURGE (A, B) — 439 PNK/BLK — 10 AMP — TO IGN

QDM #1 — SENSE LINE — FAULT LINE

LOCATED IN TRANSAXLE — VEHICLE SPEED SENSOR (B, A)

TO IGN — GAGES 10 AMP — 39 PNK/BLK — HOT LIGHT

QDM #2 — SENSE LINE — FAULT LINE

SPEEDO ← 389 DK GRN

TO CRUISE MODULE PIN D ← 381 RED

LOCATED ON LOWER TRANSAXLE BOLT

PSPS MAF FUEL PUMP P/N ALDL

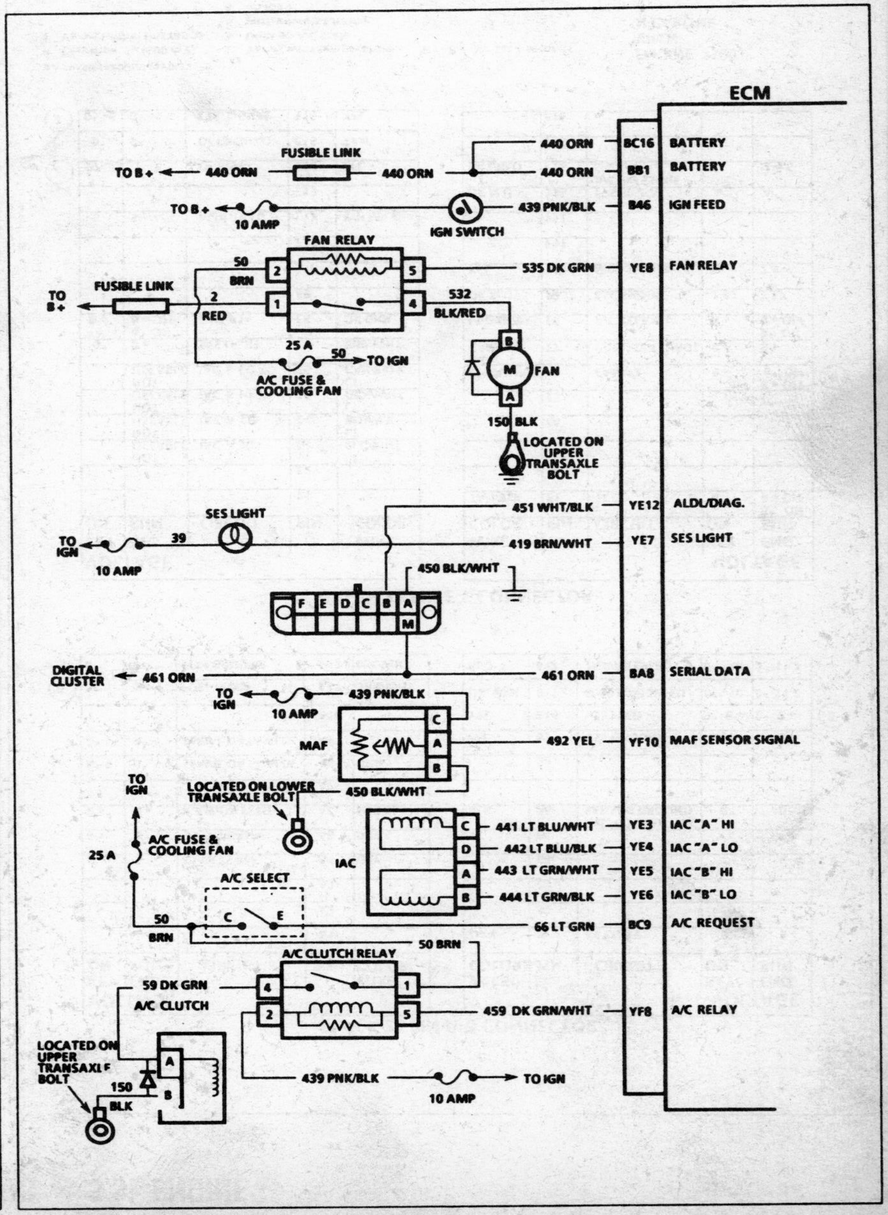

Wire	ECM Terminal	Function
440 ORN	BC16	BATTERY
440 ORN	BB1	BATTERY
439 PNK/BLK	B46	IGN FEED
535 DK GRN	YE8	FAN RELAY
451 WHT/BLK	YE12	ALDL/DIAG.
419 BRN/WHT	YE7	SES LIGHT
461 ORN	BA8	SERIAL DATA
492 YEL	YF10	MAF SENSOR SIGNAL
441 LT BLU/WHT	YE3	IAC "A" HI
442 LT BLU/BLK	YE4	IAC "A" LO
443 LT GRN/WHT	YE5	IAC "B" HI
444 LT GRN/BLK	YE6	IAC "B" LO
66 LT GRN	BC9	A/C REQUEST
459 DK GRN/WHT	YF8	A/C RELAY

TO B+ ← 440 ORN — FUSIBLE LINK — 440 ORN

TO B+ ← 10 AMP — IGN SWITCH

FAN RELAY (2, 1, 5, 4) — 50 BRN — 2 RED — 532 BLK/RED

TO B+ — FUSIBLE LINK

25 A — 50 — TO IGN — A/C FUSE & COOLING FAN

FAN (B, M, A) — 150 BLK — LOCATED ON UPPER TRANSAXLE BOLT

TO IGN ← 10 AMP — 39 — SES LIGHT

450 BLK/WHT

ALDL connector (F, E, D, C, B, A, M)

DIGITAL CLUSTER ← 461 ORN

TO IGN ← 10 AMP — 439 PNK/BLK

MAF (C, A, B) — 450 BLK/WHT — LOCATED ON LOWER TRANSAXLE BOLT

TO IGN — 25 A — A/C FUSE & COOLING FAN

IAC (C, D, A, B)

A/C SELECT (C, E) — 50 BRN

50 BRN

A/C CLUTCH RELAY (4, 2, 1, 5) — 59 DK GRN — A/C CLUTCH

LOCATED ON UPPER TRANSAXLE BOLT — 150 BLK

439 PNK/BLK — 10 AMP — TO IGN

DIAGNOSTIC CHARTS — 3.3L ENGINE

PORT FUEL INJECTION ECM CONNECTOR IDENTIFICATION

This ECM voltage chart is for use with a digital voltmeter to further aid in diagnosis. The voltages you get may vary due to low battery charge or other reasons, but they should be very close. The "B+" symbol indicates a nominal system voltage of 12-14 V. Probing front side (end view) of connector could cause intermittent open circuits.

THE FOLLOWING CONDITIONS MUST BE MET BEFORE TESTING:

• Engine at operating temperature (upper rad. hose hot) • Engine idling in "Closed Loop" (For "Engine Run" column) in park or neutral • Test terminal not grounded • "SCAN" tool not installed

NOTICE: Before checking voltages be sure ECM and engine grounds are located on the correct transaxle stud and are clean and tight.

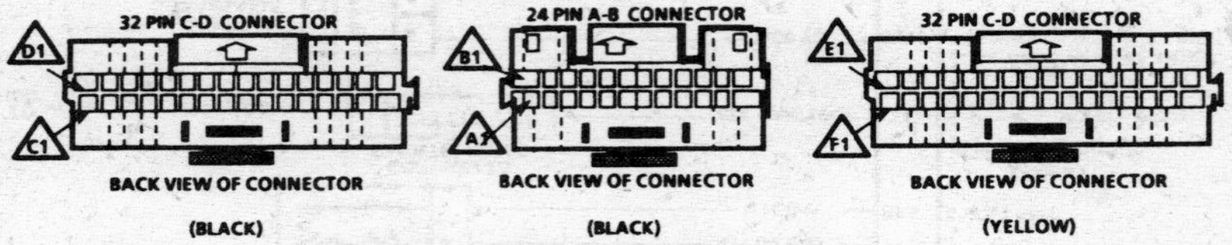

32 PIN C-D CONNECTOR (D1, C1) — BACK VIEW OF CONNECTOR (BLACK)

24 PIN A-B CONNECTOR (B1, A1) — BACK VIEW OF CONNECTOR (BLACK)

32 PIN C-D CONNECTOR (E1, F1) — BACK VIEW OF CONNECTOR (YELLOW)

BLACK 32 PIN C-D CONNECTOR

VOLTAGE KEY ON	VOLTAGE ENG. RUN	CIRCUIT	PIN	WIRE COLOR
			C1	
			C2	
			C3	
B+on 0*off	B+on 0* off	BRAKE	C4	PPL
			C5	
			C6	
0*	4.8	IGNITION BYPASS	C7	TAN/BLK
0*	1-2	EST	C8	WHT
0* off B+on	0* off B+on	A/C REQUEST	C9	LT GRN
			C10	
B+	B+	INJ. DRIVER 1,3,5	C11	LT BLU
B+	B+	INJ. DRIVER 2,4,6	C12	LT GRN
			C13	
			C14	
			C15	
B+	B+	BATTERY	C16	ORN

WIRE COLOR	PIN	CIRCUIT	VOLTAGE KEY ON	VOLTAGE ENG. RUN	Note
BLK/WHT	D1	ECM GROUND	0*	0*	
	D2				
	D3				
	D4				
	D5				
BLK/WHT	D6	INJ. GROUND	0*	0*	
BLK/WHT	D7	INJ. GROUND	0*	0*	
PPL/WHT	D8	REF HI	0*	3.6	
BLK/RED	D9	REF LO	0*	0*	
	D10				
WHT	D11	CRUISE MODULE	7.8	8.7	
LT BLU/ORN	D12	PSPS	B+	B+open 0* closed	
DK GRN/WHT	D13	3RD GEAR	0*	B+ open 0* closed	1
WHT	D14	2ND GEAR	0*	B+ open 0* closed	1
	D15				
ORN/BLK	D16	P/N SWITCH	0*	0	2

* Less than .5V (500 mV).

ENGINE 3300
VIN N
N CARLINE

BLACK 24 PIN A-B CONNECTOR

Note	VOLTAGE KEY ON	VOLTAGE ENG. RUN	CIRCUIT	PIN	WIRE COLOR
				A1	
				A2	
				A3	
	5	5	5 VOLTS REF	A4	GRY
	5	5	5 VOLTS REF	A5	GRY
	B+	B+	IGNITION FEED	A6	PNK/BLK
				A7	
	0*-5	0*-5	SERIAL DATA/ALDL	A8	ORN
	0*-5	0*-5	SERIAL DATA/ALDL	A9	
				A10	
5	0*	B+	FUEL PUMP	A11	DK GRN/WHT
	0*	0*	ECM GROUND	A12	BLK/WHT

WIRE COLOR	PIN	CIRCUIT	VOLTAGE KEY ON	VOLTAGE ENG. RUN	Note
ORN	B1	BATTERY	B+	B+	
	B2				
	B3				
	B4				
	B5				
BLK	B6	TPS, COOLANT A/C SENSOR GROUND	0*	0*	
	B7				
	B8				
PPL	B9	VSS GROUND	0*	0*	
YEL	B10	VSS FEED	0*-B+	0*-B+	3
DK. GRN	B11	4000 P/MI SPEED	0*-10	0*-11.2	
RED	B12	2K P/MI SPEED	0*-10	0*-11.2	

GREEN 32 PIN E-F CONNECTOR

Note	VOLTAGE KEY ON	VOLTAGE ENG. RUN	CIRCUIT	PIN	WIRE COLOR
				E1	
				E2	
		NOT USEABLE	IAC A HI	E3	LT BLU/WHT
		NOT USEABLE	IAC A LO	E4	LT BLU/BLK
		NOT USEABLE	IAC B HI	E5	LT GRN/WHT
		NOT USEABLE	IAC B LO	E6	LT GRN/BKLK
	0*	B+	SES LIGHT	E7	BRN/WHT
	B+	0* ON B+OFF	FAN #1	E8	DK GRN
				E9	
				E10	
				E11	
	5	5	ALDL/DIAG	E12	WHT/BLK
				E13	
2	.07-.36	.1-.9	O² HIGH	E14	PPL
	0*	0*	O² GROUND	E15	TAN
2	0*-.5	0*-.5	CTS SIGNAL	E16	YEL

WIRE COLOR	PIN	CIRCUIT	VOLTAGE KEY ON	VOLTAGE ENG. RUN	Note
TAN/BLK	F1	TCC	0*	0* ON B+OFF	
	F2				
	F3				
	F4				
	F5				
LT GRN/BLK	F6	FAN #2	B+	B+OFF 0* ON	4
DK GRN/YEL	F7	CANISTER PURGE	B+	B+	
LT GRN/BK	F8	A/C RELAY	B+	0* ON B+OFF	
DK BLU	F9	ESC SIGNAL	2.37	2.37	
YEL	F10	MAF SIGNAL	2	2.4	
	F11				
	F12				
DK BLU	F13	TPS SIGNAL	.4	.4	
GRY/RED	F14	A/C PRESSURE SIGNAL	1	2-4.5	
	F15				
	F16				

**. VARIES AROUND 10 VOLTS.
* Less than .5v (500 mV).
1 Varies within this range
2. Varies with temperature.
3. DVM on A/C scale with wheels turning
4. on road
5. B+ for 1st 2 seconds

ENGINE 3300
VIN N
N CARLINE

DIAGNOSTIC CIRCUIT CHECK

The Diagnostic Circuit Check must be the starting point for any driveability complaint diagnosis. Before using this you should perform a careful visual/physical check of the ECM and engine grounds for being clean and tight, and on the correct studs

The diagnostic circuit check is an organized approach to identifying a problem created by an electronic engine control system malfunction because it directs the service technician to the next logical step in diagnosing the complaint.

If after completing the diagnostic circuit check and finding the on-board diagnostics functioning properly and no trouble codes displayed, a comparison of "Typical Scan Values," for the appropriate engine, may be used for comparison. The "Typical Values" are an average of display values recorded from normally operating vehicles and are intended to represent what a normally functioning system would display.

A "SCAN" TOOL THAT DISPLAYS FAULTY DATA SHOULD NOT BE USED, AND THE PROBLEM SHOULD BE REPORTED TO THE MANUFACTURER. THE USE OF A FAULTY "SCAN" CAN RESULT IN MISDIAGNOSIS AND UNNECESSARY PARTS REPLACEMENT.

Only the parameters listed below are used in this manual for diagnosis. If a "Scan" reads other parameters, the values are not recommended by General Motors for use in diagnosis. For more description on the values and use of the "Scan" to diagnose ECM inputs, refer to the applicable diagnosis section If all values are within the range illustrated, refer to "Symptoms" Section

TYPICAL "Scan" DATA VALUES

Idle / Upper Radiator Hose Hot / Closed Throttle / Park or Neutral / Closed Loop / Acc. off

"SCAN" Position	Units Displayed	Typical Data Value
Engine Speed	RPM	900 - 1000 P/N
Desired Idle	RPM	675 - 750 In Drive
Coolant Temp.	C° F°	85°C - 105°C (185°F - 221°F)
Throttle Position	Volts	.33 - .46 V
LV8 (Eng. Load)	Number	60 - 50
O_2 Sensor	mV	100-900 mV
Inj. Pulse Width	m Sec	4.0-5.0 mSec (varies)
O_2 Cross counts	# number	0-20
Air Fuel Ratio	Ratio	14.7
Rich/Lean	Lean/Rich	Lean - Rich
Spark Advance	Degrees	20° varies
Mass Air Flow (MAF)	Gram Per Second (Gm/Sec)	4 - 7 varies
Fuel Integrator	Counts	110 - 138
Block Learn	Counts	110 - 138
Open/Closed Loop	Open/Closed	Closed Loop
Block Learn Cell	Cell Number	Cell number varies with engine RPM and Mass Air Flow
Knock Retard	Degrees of Retard	0°
Knock Signal	Yes/No	No (Yes, if detonation is present)
Idle Air Control (IAC)	Counts (Steps)	10 - 30
P/N Switch	P/N and RDL	P/N
Vehicle Speed (VSS)	MPH	0(mph)
Torque Converter Clutch (TCC)	On/Off	Off
Battery Voltage	Volts	13.8 volts (varies)
Purge Duty Cycle	%	15%
IAC Learned	Yes/No	Yes
Air Fuel Learned	Yes/No	Yes
A/C Pressure	Volts/PSI	.2 - 4.5V/139-399 PSI (varies with Pressure)
A/C Request	Off/On	Off/On
A/C Clutch	Off/On	Off/On
Brake Switch	Yes/No	No (Yes with pedal depressed)
Cruise Engaged	Yes/No	No
Power Steering (PSPS)	Normal/High	Normal
Fan 1/Fan 2	Off/On	Off (On if temperature is above 100°C (212°F)
QDM1	High/Low	Low
QDM2	High/Low	Low (High if A/C head pressure's high)
QDM3	High/Low	Low (High with brake pedal depressed)
2nd Gear	Off/On	Off
3rd/4th Gear	Off/On	Off
Prom ID	Number	Internal ID only
Time From Start	Min/Sec	Start when engine is running and varies

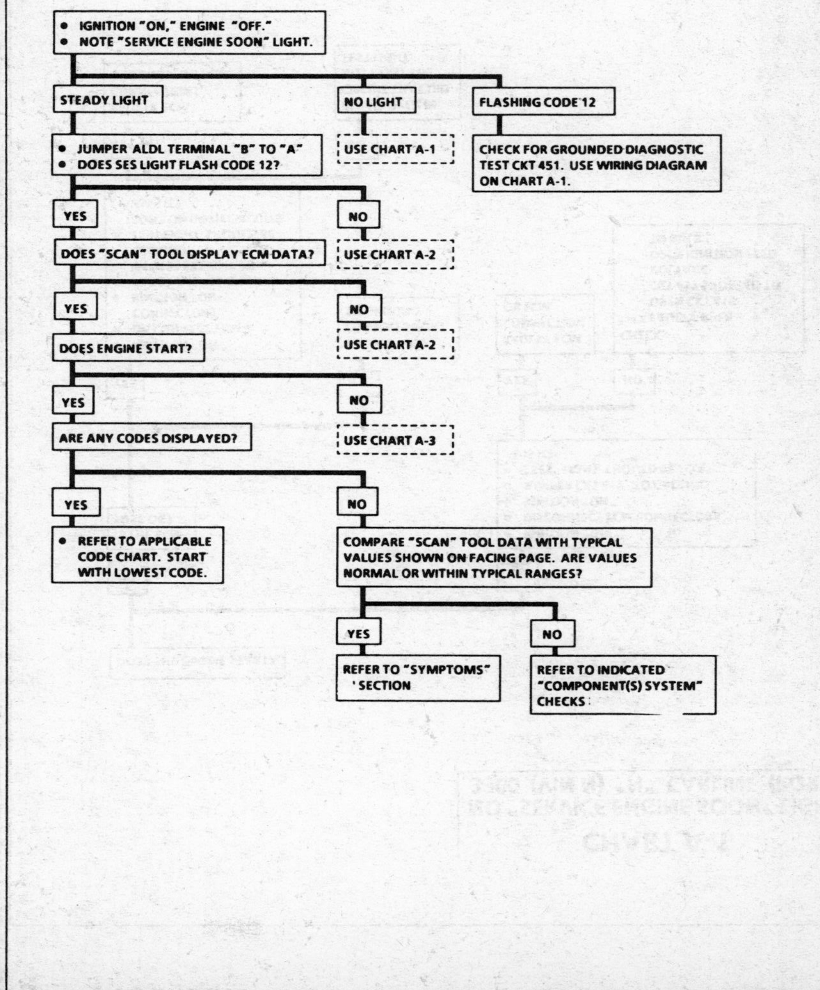

BATTERY JUNCTION BOX
FUSIBLE LINK
ECM
ORN 440 — BC16
ORN 440 — BB1 — BATTERY FEED
Battery
TO B+
IGN SWITCH
PNK/BLK 439 — BA6 — IGN FEED
10 AMP
GAGE FUSE
SES LIGHT
TO IGN SWITCH
10 AMP
BRN/WHT 419 — YE7 — QDM
WHT/BLK 451 — YE12 — 3-6 V
450 BLK/WHT
ALDL CONNECTOR
B A M
ORN 461 — BA8 — SERIAL DATA
TO DIS
10-6-87

CHART A-1

NO "SERVICE ENGINE SOON" LIGHT
3300 (VIN N) "N" CARLINE (PORT)

Circuit Description:

There should always be a steady "Service Engine Soon" light when the ignition is "ON" and engine stopped. Battery is supplied directly to the light bulb. The Electronic Control Module (ECM) will control the light and turn it "ON" by providing a ground path through CKT 419 to the ECM.

Test Description: Numbers below refer to circled numbers on the diagnostic chart.

1. "Service Engine Soon" light should be "ON."
2. Using a test light connected to 12 volts, probe each of the system ground circuits to be sure a good ground is present. See ECM terminal end view in front of this section for ECM pin locations of ground circuits.

Diagnostic Aids:

Engine runs OK, check:
- Gage fuse
- Faulty light bulb
- CKT 419 open

Engine cranks, but will not run:
- Continuous battery - fuse or fusible link open
- ECM ignition fuse open
- Ignition CKT 439 to ECM open
- Poor connection to ECM

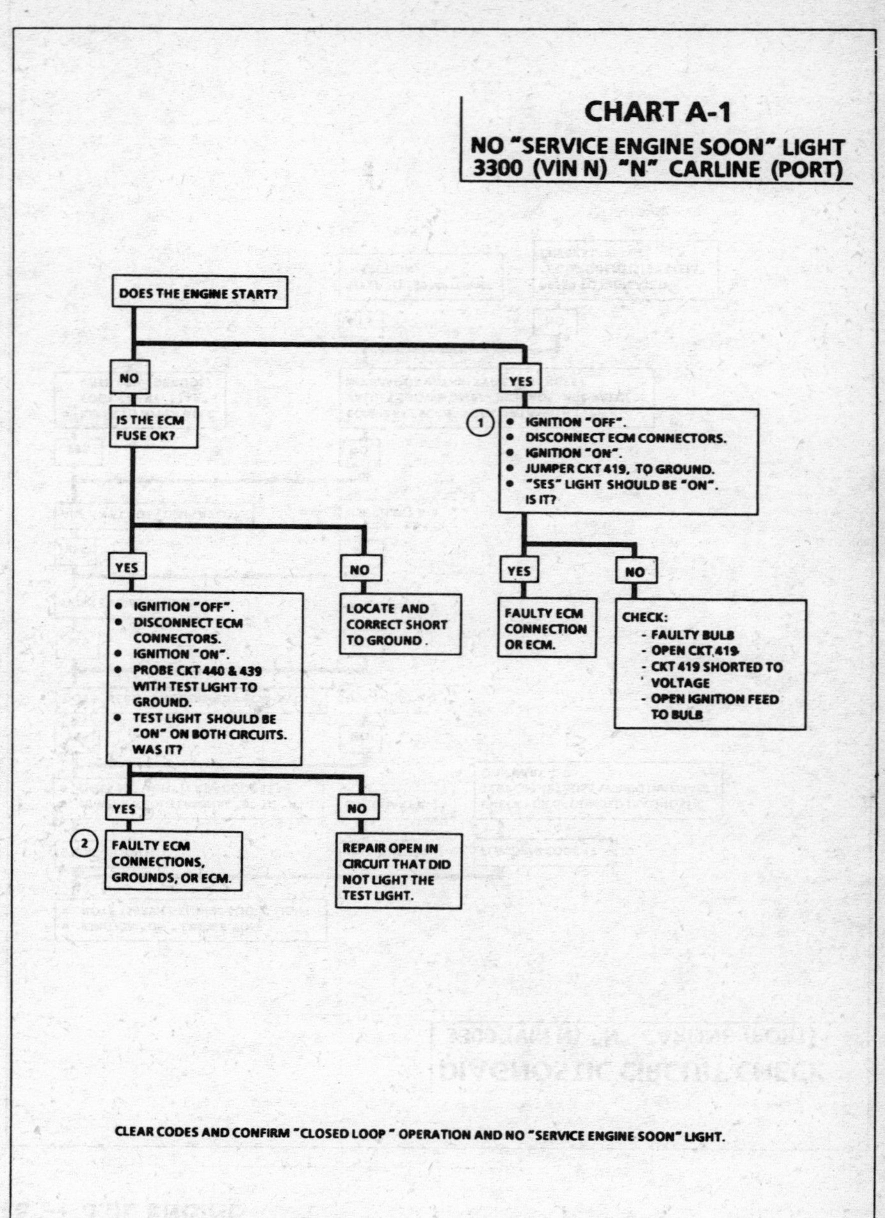

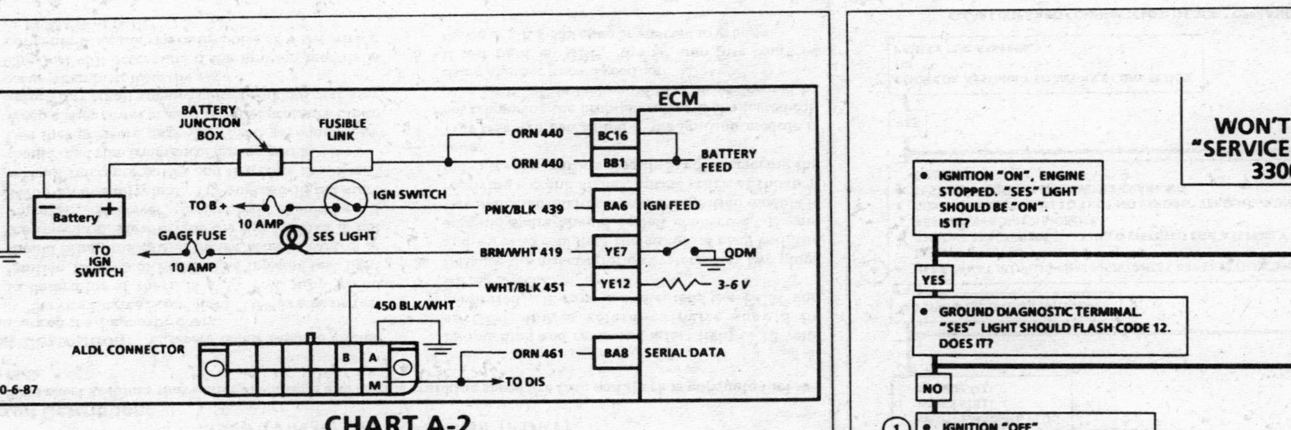

CHART A-2

WON'T FLASH CODE 12 - NO SERIAL DATA "SERVICE ENGINE SOON" LIGHT "ON" STEADY 3300 (VIN N) "N" CARLINE (PORT)

Circuit Description:

There should always be a steady "Service Engine Soon" light when the ignition is "ON" and engine not running. Ignition is supplied directly to the light bulb. The Electronic Control Module (ECM) will turn the light "ON" by grounding CKT 419 at the ECM.

With the diagnostic terminal grounded, the light should flash a Code 12, followed by any trouble code(s) stored in memory.

A steady light suggests a short to ground in the light control CKT 419 or an open in diagnostic CKT 451 or an open in the 450 circuit.

Test Description: Numbers below refer to circled numbers on the diagnostic chart.

1. If the light goes "OFF" when the ECM connector is disconnected, then CKT 419 is not shorted to ground.
2. If there is a problem with the ECM that causes a "Scan" tool to not read serial data, then the ECM should not flash a Code 12. If Code 12 does flash, be sure that the "Scan" tool is working properly on another vehicle. If the "Scan" is functioning properly and CKT 461 is OK, the Mem-Cal or ECM may be at fault for the NO ALDL symptom.
3. This step will check for an open diagnostic CKT 451.
4. At this point, the "Service Engine Soon" light wiring is OK. The problem is a faulty ECM or Mem-Cal. If Code 12 does not flash, the ECM should be replaced using the original Mem-Cal. Replace the Mem-Cal only after trying an ECM, as a defective Mem-Cal is an unlikely cause of the problem.

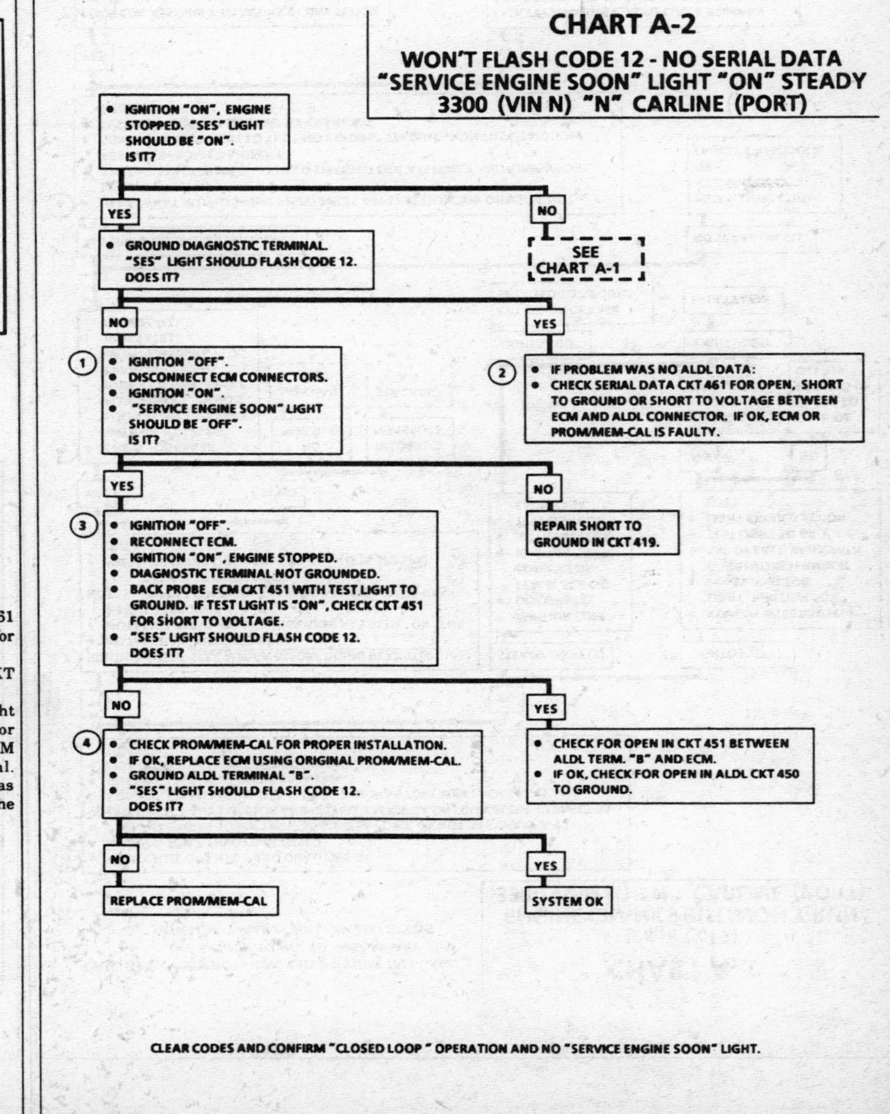

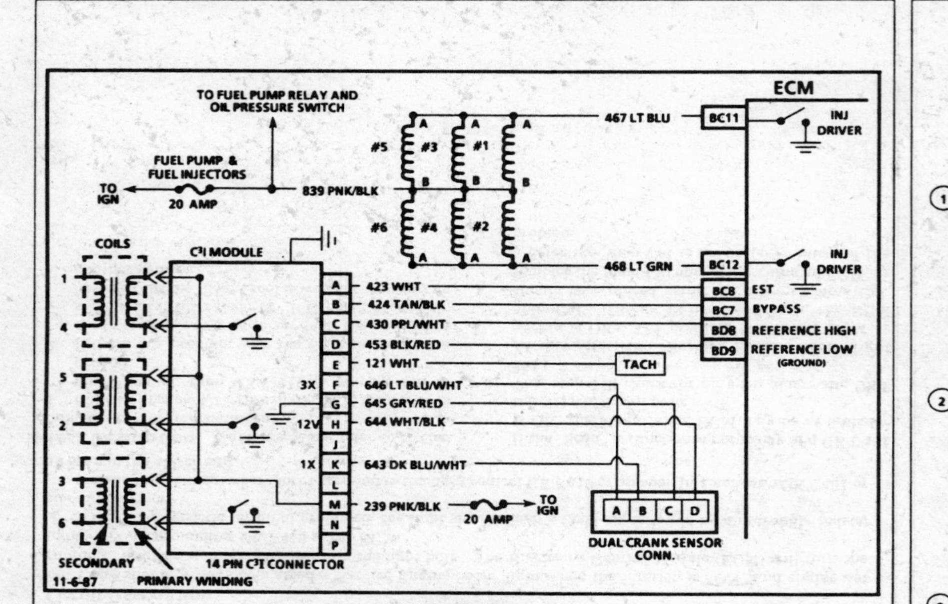

CHART A-3

(Page 1 of 2)

ENGINE CRANKS BUT WON'T RUN
3300 (VIN N) "N" CARLINE (PORT)

Circuit Description:

This chart assumes that battery condition and engine cranking speed are OK, and there is adequate fuel in the tank.

Test Description: Numbers below refer to circled numbers on the diagnostic chart.

1. A "Service Engine Soon" light "ON" is a basic test to determine if there is a 12 volt supply and ignition 12 volts to ECM. The injector test light should blink, indicating the ECM is in control of the injectors. How bright the light blinks is not important. However, the test light should be a J 34730-2A or equivalent. The engine will not start without reference pulses and therefore the "Scan" should read rpm (reference) during crank.
2. Use fuel pressure gage J 34730-1 or equivalent. Wrap a shop towel around the fuel pressure tap to absorb any small amount of fuel leakage that may occur when installing the gage.
   This test will determine if the ignition module is not generating the reference pulse or if the wiring or ECM are at fault. By touching and removing a test light to 12 volts on CKT 430, a reference pulse should be generated. If rpm is indicated, the ECM and wiring are OK.
3. Because the direct ignition system uses two plugs and wires to complete the circuit of each coil, the opposite spark should be left connected. If rpm was indicated during crank, the ignition module is receiving a crank signal, but no spark at this test indicates the ignition module is not triggering the coils.
4. This test will determine if the ignition module is not triggering the problem coil or if the tested coil is at fault. This test could also be performed by using another known good coil.
5. If test light is "OFF," the 20 amp fuse could be blown or CKT 839 open or shorted to ground.

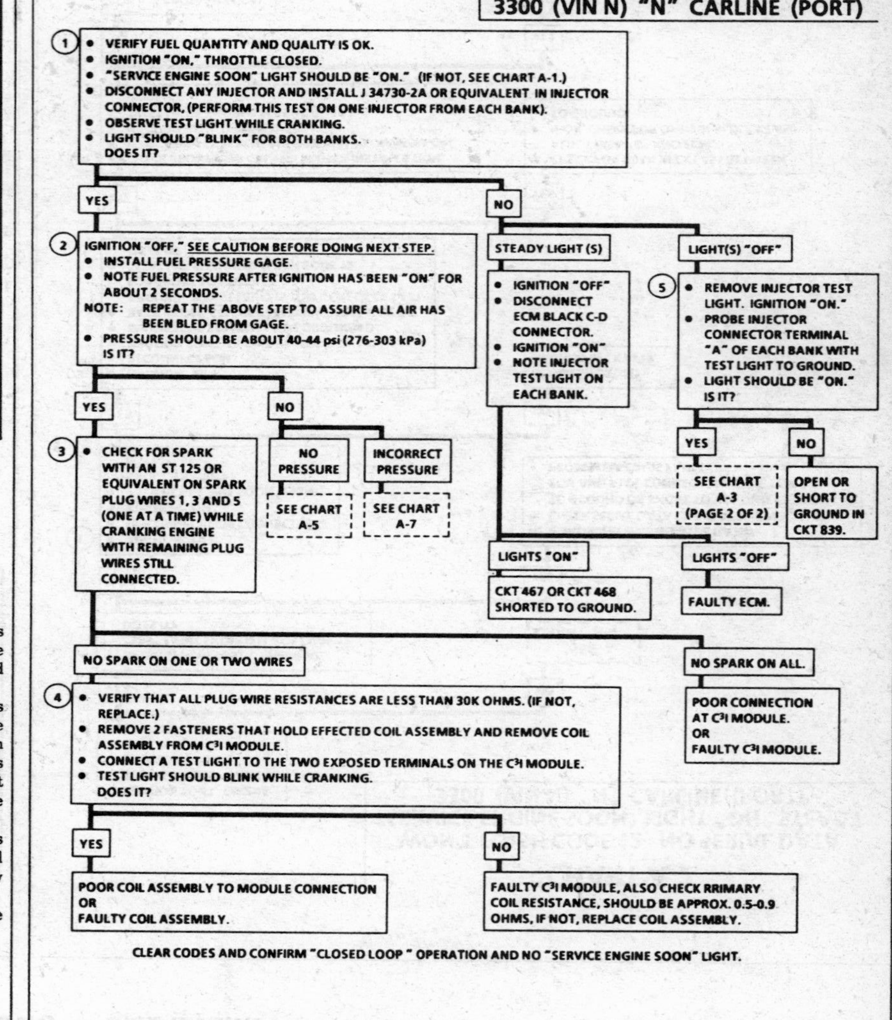

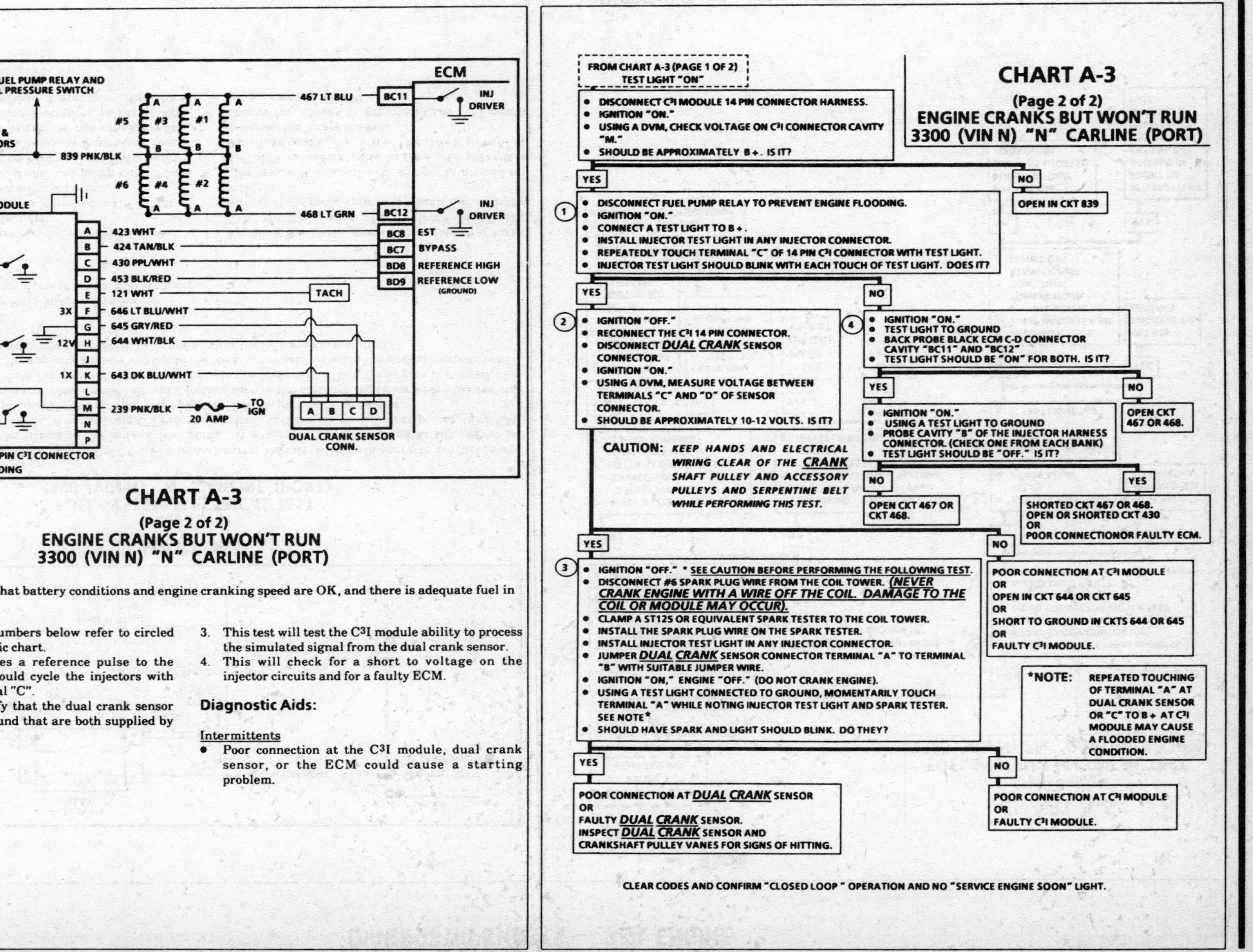

CHART A-3

(Page 2 of 2)

ENGINE CRANKS BUT WON'T RUN
3300 (VIN N) "N" CARLINE (PORT)

Circuit Description:

This chart assumes that battery conditions and engine cranking speed are OK, and there is adequate fuel in the tank.

Test Description: Numbers below refer to circled numbers on the diagnostic chart.

1. This check simulates a reference pulse to the ECM. The ECM should cycle the injectors with each touch of terminal "C".
2. The check is to verify that the dual crank sensor has power and a ground that are both supplied by the C3I module.
3. This test will test the C3I module ability to process the simulated signal from the dual crank sensor.
4. This will check for a short to voltage on the injector circuits and for a faulty ECM.

Diagnostic Aids:

Intermittents

- Poor connection at the C3I module, dual crank sensor, or the ECM could cause a starting problem.

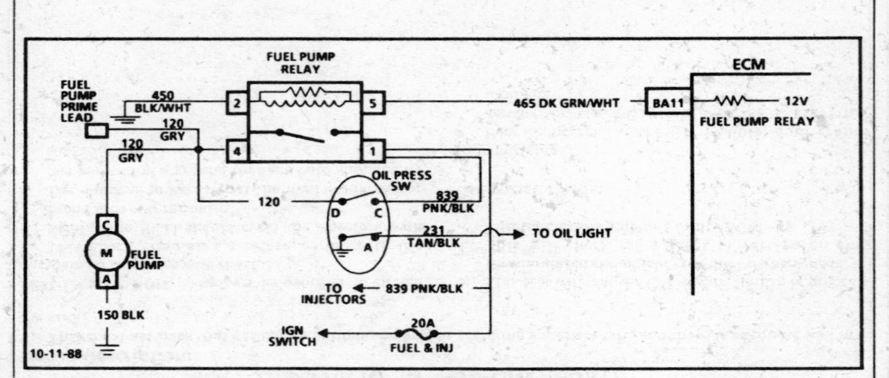

CHART A-5

(Page 1 of 2)

FUEL SYSTEM ELECTRICAL TEST
3300 (VIN N) "N" CARLINE (PORT)

Circuit Description:

When the ignition switch is turned "ON," the Electronic Control Module (ECM) will energize the fuel pump relay which completes the circuit to the in-tank fuel pump. It will remain "ON" as long as the engine is cranking or running and the ECM is receiving C3I reference pulses. If there are no reference pulses, the ECM will de-energize the fuel pump relay within 2 seconds after key "ON" or the engine is stopped.

The fuel pump will deliver fuel to the fuel rail and injectors, then to the pressure regulator where the system pressure is controlled. Excess fuel pressure is bypassed back to the fuel tank. When the engine is stopped, the pump can be turned "ON" by applying battery voltage to the "test" terminal located in the engine compartment.

Improper fuel system pressure may contribute to one or all of the following symptoms:

- Cranks but won't run
- Code 44 or 45
- Cuts out, may feel like ignition problem
- Hesitation, loss of power or poor fuel economy

Test Description: Numbers below refer to circled numbers on the diagnostic chart.

1. If the fuse is blown, a short to ground in CKTs 120, 839, or the fuel pump itself is the cause.
2. This step determines if the fuel pump circuit is being controlled by the ECM. The ECM should energize the fuel pump relay and turn the fuel pump "ON." If the engine is not cranking or running, the ECM should de-energize the relay and/or fuel pump within 2 seconds after the ignition is turned "ON."
3. Applying B+ to the pump prime connector turns "ON" the fuel pump. This validates CKT 120 wiring. If the pump runs, it is a basic fuel delivery problem.
4. This test will determine if a short to ground on CKT 120 caused the fuse to blow. To prevent a mis-diagnosis, be sure the fuel pump is disconnected before the test.
5. Checks for a short to ground in the fuel pump relay harness CKT 839.

CHART A-5

(Page 1 of 2)

FUEL SYSTEM ELECTRICAL TEST
3300 (VIN N) "N" CARLINE (PORT)

FROM CHART A-3 PAGE 1 NO PRESSURE

(1)
- INSPECT FUEL PUMP FUSE.
- IS FUSE OK?

YES → (2)
- PROBE FUEL PUMP TEST CONNECTOR WITH A TEST LIGHT TO GROUND.
- IGNITION "OFF" FOR 10 SECONDS.
- NOTE LIGHT, WITHIN 2 SECONDS, AFTER IGNITION IS TURNED "ON".
- WAS TEST LIGHT "ON"?

TEST POINT FROM SECTION "B" → (2)

(2) YES → (3)
- APPLY BATTERY VOLTAGE TO PUMP PRIME CONNECTOR.
- LISTEN AT FUEL TANK FOR PUMP RUNNING.
- IS PUMP RUNNING?

(3) YES → CHECK FOR;
- PLUGGED IN-LINE FILTER.
- PLUGGED PUMP INLET FILTER
- RESTRICTED FUEL LINE.

(3) NO → CHECK FOR;
- OPEN CKT 120
- OPEN PUMP GROUND CKT.

IF ALL CHECK OUT OK, REPLACE IN-TANK FUEL PUMP.

(2) NO →
- DISCONNECT FUEL PUMP RELAY.
- IGN. "ON", ENGINE STOPPED.
- PROBE RELAY HARN. TERMINAL "1" WITH TEST LIGHT TO GROUND.
- IS TEST LIGHT "ON"?

YES → SEE PAGE 2 OF THIS CHART

NO → OPEN CKT 839

(1) NO → (4)
- DISCONNECT FUEL PUMP HARNESS AT REAR BODY CONNECTOR.
- IGNITION "OFF", PROBE FUEL PUMP PRIME CONNECTOR WITH A TEST LIGHT TO 12 VOLTS.
- IS TEST LIGHT "ON"?

(4) YES → CKT 120 OR 490 SHORTED TO GROUND.

(4) NO → (5)
- REMOVE FUEL PUMP RELAY.
- PROBE RELAY CONNECTOR TERMINAL "1" WITH TEST LIGHT TO 12 VOLTS.
- IS TEST LIGHT "ON"?

(5) YES → CKT 839 SHORTED TO GROUND.

(5) NO →
- RECONNECT FUEL PUMP HARNESS AND INSTALL NEW FUSE.
- TURN IGNITION "ON" THEN RECHECK FUSE.
- IS FUSE OK?

NO → IN TANK FUEL PUMP OR PUMP HARNESS SHORTED TO GROUND.

YES → INTERMITTENT SHORT TO GROUND IN CKT 120, CKT 839, OR FUEL PUMP RELAY, OR FAULTY FUSE.

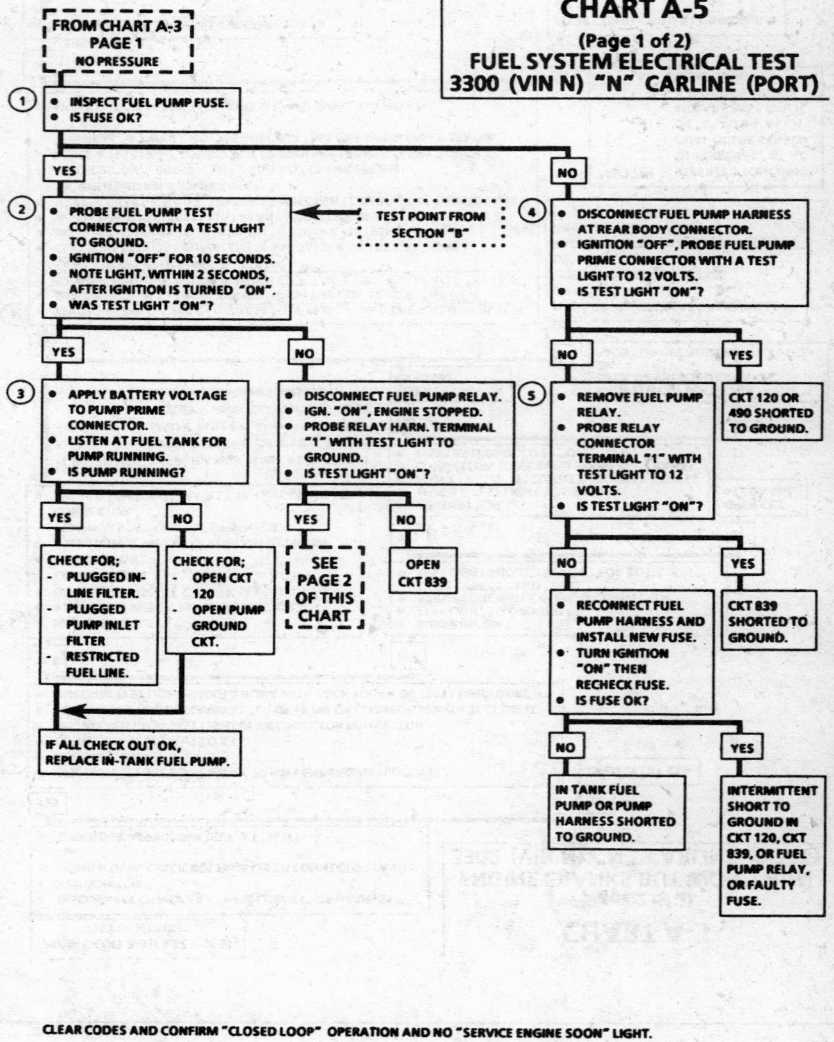

CLEAR CODES AND CONFIRM "CLOSED LOOP" OPERATION AND NO "SERVICE ENGINE SOON" LIGHT.

FUEL PUMP PRIME LEAD
FUEL PUMP RELAY
ECM
450 BLK/WHT
120 GRY
120 GRY
465 DK GRN/WHT
BA11
12V
FUEL PUMP RELAY
OIL PRESS SW
120
839 PNK/BLK
231 TAN/BLK
TO OIL LIGHT
FUEL PUMP
TO INJECTORS
839 PNK/BLK
150 BLK
IGN SWITCH
20A
FUEL & INJ
10-11-88

CHART A-5
(Page 2 of 2)
FUEL SYSTEM ELECTRICAL TEST
3300 (VIN N) "N" CARLINE (PORT)

Circuit Description:

When the ignition switch is turned "ON," the Electronic Control Module (ECM) will energize the fuel pump relay which completes the circuit to the in-tank fuel pump. It will remain "ON" as long as the engine is cranking or running and the ECM is receiving C3I reference pulses. If there are no reference pulses, the ECM will de-energize the fuel pump relay within 2 seconds after key "ON" or the engine is stopped.

Test Description: Numbers below refer to circled numbers on the diagnostic chart.

6. Checks for open in the fuel pump relay ground CKT 450.
7. Determines if the ECM is in control of the fuel pump relay through CKT 465 (terminal "A").
8. The fuel pump control circuit includes an engine oil pressure switch with a separate set of normally open contacts. The switch closes at about (4 lbs) 28 kPa of oil pressure and provides a second ignition feed path to the fuel pump. If the relay fails, the pump will run using the ignition feed supplied by the closed oil pressure switch.

This step checks the oil pressure switch to be sure it provides ignition feed to the fuel pump should the pump relay fail. A failed pump relay will result in extended engine crank time because of the time required to build enough oil pressure to close the oil pressure switch and turn "ON" the fuel pump. There may be instances when the relay has failed but the engine will not crank fast enough to build enough oil pressure to close the switch. This or a faulty oil pressure switch can result in "Engine Cranks But Won't Run."

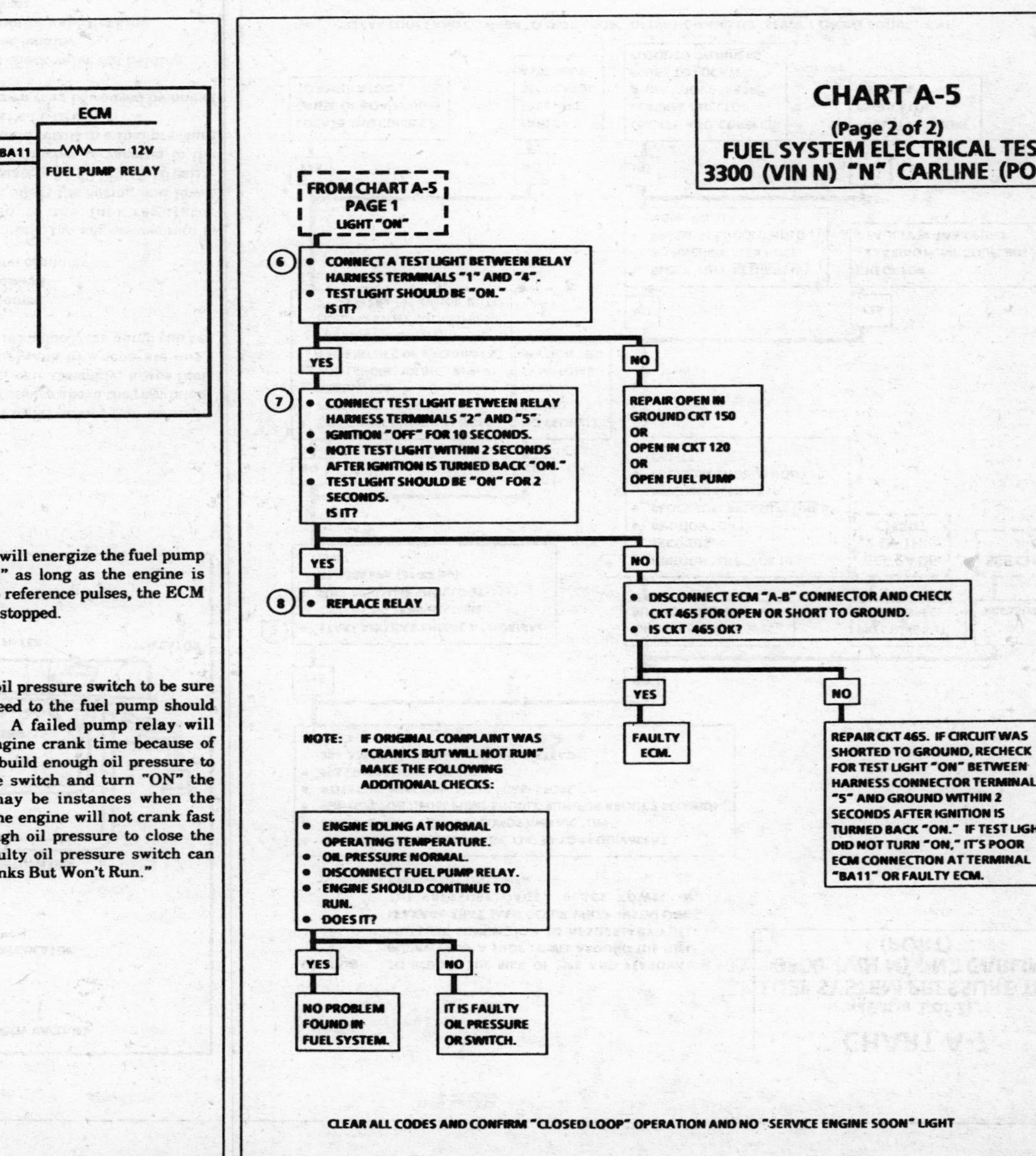

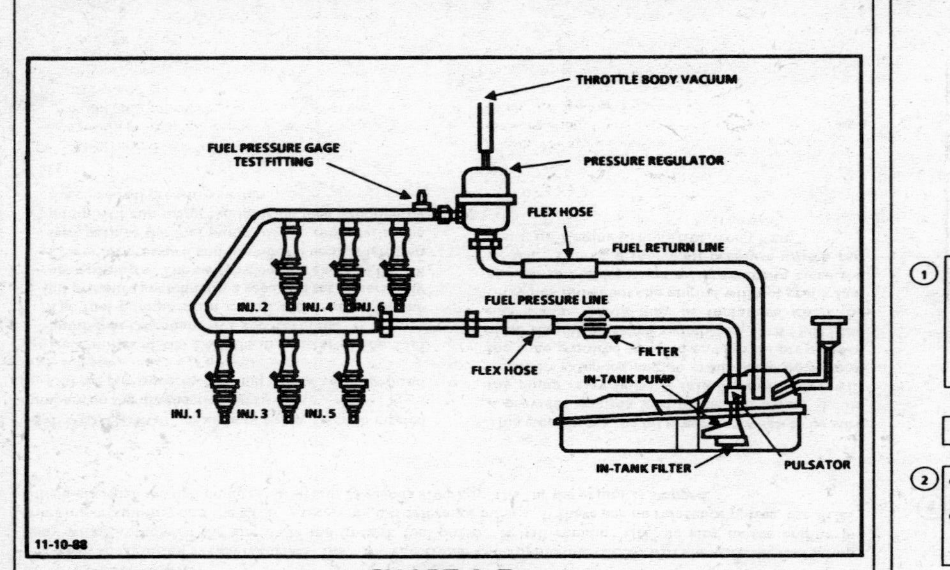

CHART A-7

(Page 1 of 2)

FUEL SYSTEM PRESSURE TEST

3300 (VIN N) "N" CARLINE (PORT)

Circuit Description:

An electric fuel pump, attached to the fuel level meter assembly (inside the fuel tank) pumps fuel through an in-line filter to the fuel rail assembly. The pump is designed to provide fuel at a pressure above the regulated pressure needed by the injectors. A pressure regulator, an integral part of the fuel rail assembly, keeps fuel available to the injectors at a regulated pressure. Unused fuel is returned to the fuel tank by a separate line. The fuel pump test terminal is located in the engine compartment. When the engine is stopped, the pump can be turned "ON" by applying battery voltage to the test terminal.

Improper fuel system pressure may contribute to one or all of the following symptoms:

- Cranks but won't run
- Code 44 or 45
- Cuts out, may feel like ignition problem
- Hesitation, loss of power or poor fuel economy

Test Description: Numbers below refer to circled numbers on the diagnostic chart.

1. Use pressure gage J-34730-1. Wrap a shop towel around the fuel pressure tap to absorb any small amount of fuel leakage that may occur when installing the gage.
   When ignition "ON", engine off, fuel pressure should be 284-325 kPa (41-47 psi). This pressure is controlled by spring pressure and throttle body vacuum within the pressure regulator assembly. Pressure should not leak down after the fuel pump is shut "OFF."
2. When the engine is idling, the engine vacuum is high and is applied to the fuel regulator diaphragm. This will offset the spring and lower fuel pressure approximately 21-69 kPa (3-10 psi)..
3. The application of 12-14 inches of vacuum to the pressure regulator should result in a fuel pressure drop of at least 21-69 kPa (3-10 psi).
4. Pressure that leaks down may be caused by one of the following:
   - In-tank fuel pump check valve not holding.
   - Pump coupling hose leaking.
   - Fuel pressure regulator valve leaking.
   - Injector sticking open.

CHART A-7

(Page 1 of 2)

FUEL SYSTEM PRESSURE TEST

3300 (VIN N) "N" CARLINE (PORT)

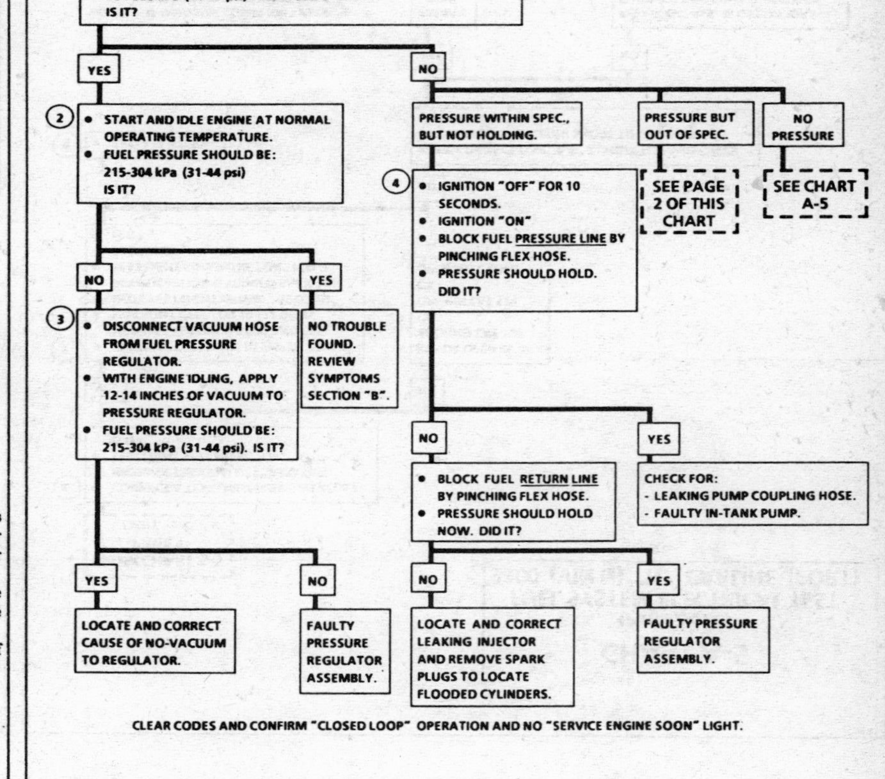

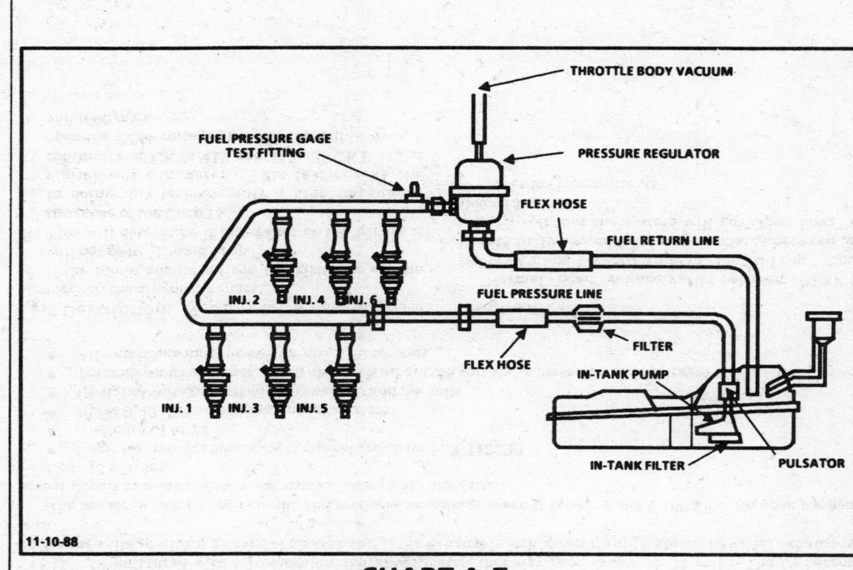

CHART A-7

(Page 2 of 2)

FUEL SYSTEM PRESSURE TEST

3300 (VIN N) "N" CARLINE (PORT)

Circuit Description:

The fuel pump will deliver fuel to the fuel rail and injectors, then to the pressure regulator, where the system pressure is controlled. Excess fuel pressure is bypassed back to the fuel tank. When the engine is stopped, the pump can be turned "ON" by applying battery voltage to the test terminal located in the engine compartment.

Improper fuel system pressure may contribute to one or all of the following symptoms:

- Cranks but won't run
- Code 44 or 45
- Cuts out, may feel like ignition problem
- Hesitation, loss of power, or poor fuel economy

Test Description: Numbers below refer to circled numbers on the diagnostic chart.

5. Pressure but less than specifications falls into two areas:
   - Regulated pressure but less than specifications; the amount of fuel to injectors is OK, but pressure is too low. The system will be lean running and may set Code 44. Also, possible hard starting cold and overall poor performance.
   - Restricted flow causing pressure drop; Normally, a vehicle with a fuel pressure of less than 165 kPa (24 psi) at idle will not be driveable. However, if the pressure drop occurs only while driving, the engine will normally surge then stop as pressure begins to drop rapidly.
6. Restricting the fuel return line allows the fuel pressure to build above regulated pressure. With battery voltage applied to the pump test terminal, pressure should rise above 325 kPa (47 psi) as the return line is slowly pinched off.

NOTICE: Do Not allow pressure to exceed 414 kPa (60 psi), as damage to the regulator may result.

7. This test determines if the high fuel pressure is due to a restricted fuel return line or a pressure regulator problem.

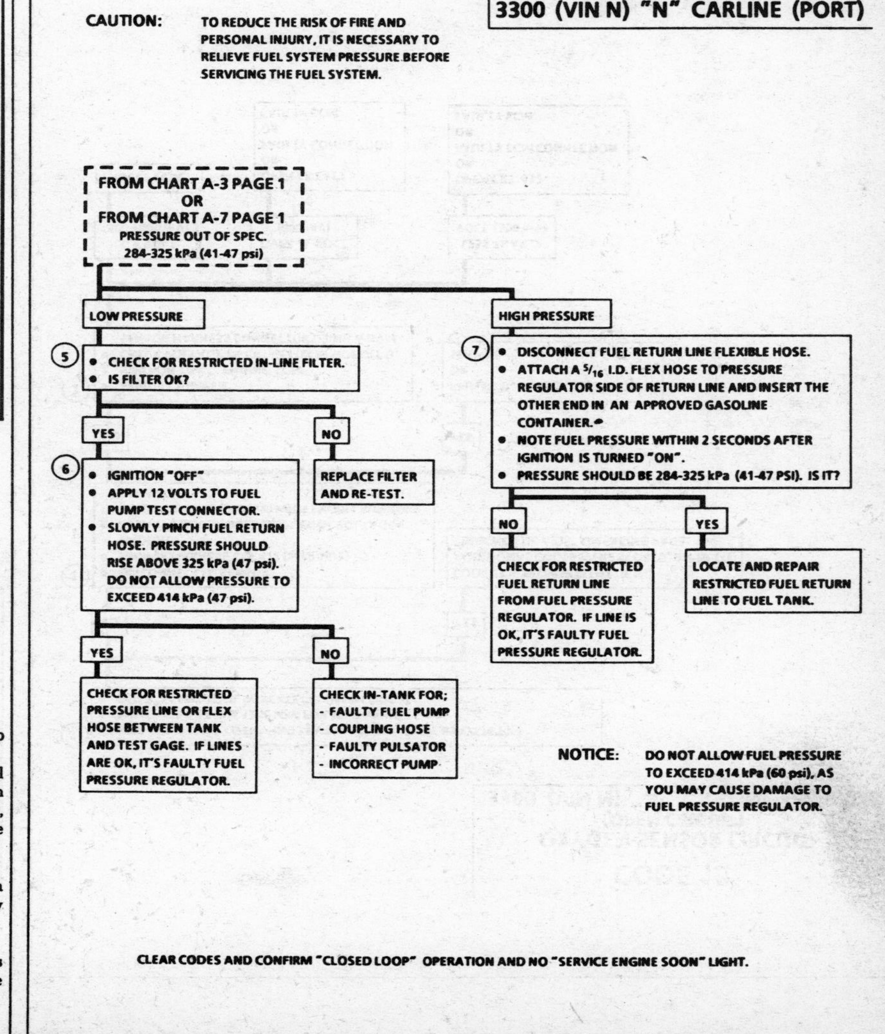

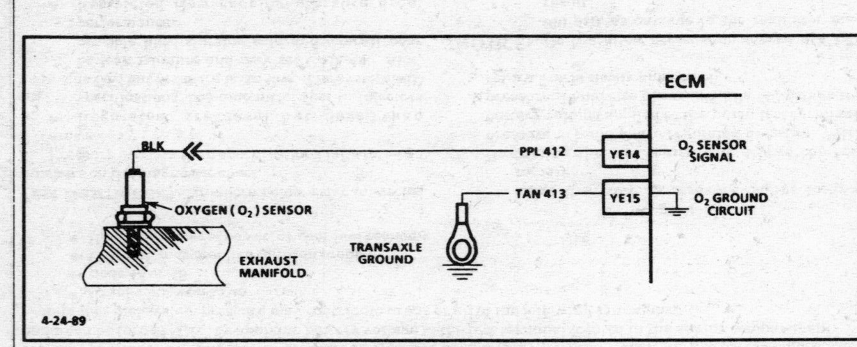

CODE 13

OXYGEN SENSOR CIRCUIT (OPEN CIRCUIT) 3300 (VIN N) "N" CARLINE (PORT)

Circuit Description:

The Electronic Control Module (ECM) supplies a voltage of about .45 volt between terminals "YE14" and "YE15". (If measured with a 10 megohm digital voltmeter, this may read as low as .32 volt.) The O_2 sensor varies the voltage within a range of about 1 volt if the exhaust is rich, down through about .10 volt if exhaust is lean.

The sensor is like an open circuit and produces no voltage when it is below 360°C (600°F). An open oxygen sensor circuit or cold oxygen sensor causes "Open Loop" operation.

Code 13 will set:

- Engine at normal operating temperature above 50°C (122°F)
- No Codes 21 or 22
- At least 40 seconds engine time after start
- O_2 signal voltage is steady between .30 and .55 volts
- Throttle position sensor signal above 4% (about .58 volt above closed throttle voltage)
- All conditions must be met for about 30 seconds

Test Description: Numbers below refer to circled numbers on the diagnostic chart.

1. If the conditions for a Code 13 exists, the system will not go to "Closed Loop."
2. This will determine if the sensor or the wiring is the cause of the Code 13.
3. In doing this test use only a high impedance digital volt ohmmeter. This test checks the continuity of CKTs 412 and 413. If CKT 413 is open the ECM voltage on CKT 412 will be over .6 volt (600 mV).

Diagnostic Aids:

Normal "Scan" voltage varies between 100mV to 999 mV (.1 and 1.0 volt) while in "Closed Loop." Code 13 sets in 30 seconds if voltage remains between .30 and .55 volt, but the system will go "Open Loop" in about 15 seconds.

Refer to "Intermittents"

CODE 13

OXYGEN SENSOR CIRCUIT (OPEN CIRCUIT) 3300 (VIN N) "N" CARLINE (PORT)

(1) ENGINE AT NORMAL OPERATING TEMPERATURE (ABOVE 80°C/176°F).
- RUN ENGINE ABOVE 1200 RPM FOR TWO MINUTES.
- DOES "SCAN" TOOL INDICATE "CLOSED LOOP"?

YES → CODE 13 IS INTERMITTENT. IF NO ADDITIONAL CODES WERE STORED, REFER TO "DIAGNOSTIC AIDS" ON FACING PAGE.

NO → (2)
- DISCONNECT O_2 SENSOR.
- JUMPER HARNESS CKT 412 (ECM SIDE) TO GROUND.
- "SCAN" TOOL SHOULD DISPLAY O_2 VOLTAGE BELOW .2 VOLT (200 mV) WITH ENGINE RUNNING. DOES IT?

YES → FAULTY O_2 SENSOR CONNECTION OR SENSOR.

NO → (3)
- REMOVE JUMPER.
- IGNITION "ON", ENGINE "OFF".
- CHECK VOLTAGE OF CKT 412 (ECM SIDE) AT O_2 SENSOR HARNESS CONNECTOR USING A DVM.

.3-.6 VOLT (300 - 600 mV) → FAULTY ECM.

OVER .6 VOLT (600 mV) → OPEN CKT 413 OR FAULTY CONNECTION OR FAULTY ECM.

LESS THAN .3 VOLT (300 mV) → OPEN CKT 412 OR FAULTY ECM CONNECTION OR FAULTY ECM.

CLEAR CODES AND CONFIRM "CLOSED LOOP" OPERATION AND NO "SERVICE ENGINE SOON" LIGHT.

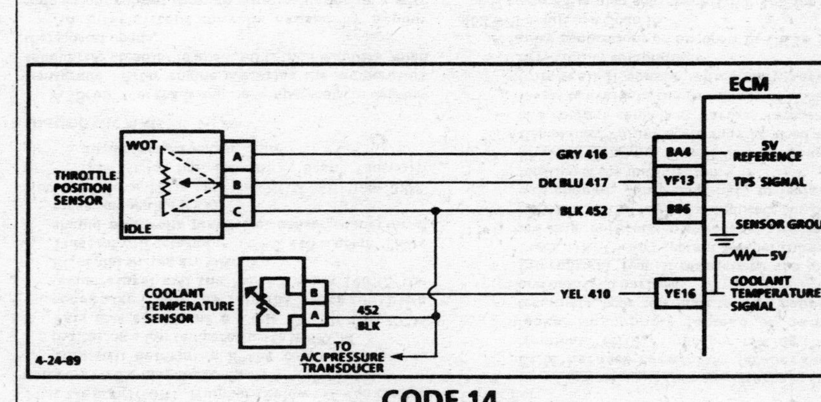

CODE 14

COOLANT TEMPERATURE SENSOR CIRCUIT
(HIGH TEMPERATURE INDICATED)
3300 (VIN N) "N" CARLINE (PORT)

Circuit Description:

The coolant temperature sensor uses a thermistor to control the signal voltage to the ECM. The ECM applies a voltage on CKT 410 to the sensor. When the engine is cold the sensor (thermistor) resistance is high, therefore, the ECM will see high signal voltage.

As the engine warms, the sensor resistance becomes less, and the voltage drops. At normal engine operating temperature (85°C to 95°C), the voltage will measure about 1.5 to 2.0 volts.

Code 14 will set if:

- Engine run time is 10 seconds or more.
- Signal voltage indicates a coolant temperature above 147°C (296°F) for .4 seconds.

Test Description: Numbers below refer to circled numbers on the diagnostic chart.

1. This will determine if the coolant sensor is indicating a high temperature to the ECM.
2. This test will determine if CKT 410 is shorted to ground which will cause the conditions for Code 14.

   If Code 14 is set, the ECM will use a default coolant temperature value of 49°C (120°F) for fuel control. "Scan" tool will read actual value - not default value.

Diagnostic Aids:

"Scan" tool displays engine temperature in degrees centigrade. After engine is started, the temperature should rise steadily to about 90°C then stabilize when thermostat opens.

An intermittent may be caused by a poor connection, rubbed through wire insulation, or a wire broken inside the insulation.

Check For:

- Poor Connection or Damaged Harness Inspect ECM harness connectors for backed out terminal "YE16", improper mating, broken locks, improperly formed or damaged terminals, poor terminal to wire connection, and damaged harness.
- Intermittent Test If connections and harness check OK, "Scan" coolant temperature while moving related connectors and wiring harness. If the failure is induced, the "coolant temperature" display will change.. This may help to isolate the location of the malfunction.
- Shifted Sensor The "Temperature To Resistance Value" scale may be used to test the coolant sensor at various temperature levels to evaluate the possibility of a "shifted" (mis-scaled) sensor, which may result in driveability complaints.

CODE 14

COOLANT TEMPERATURE SENSOR CIRCUIT
(HIGH TEMPERATURE INDICATED)
3300 (VIN N) "N" CARLINE (PORT)

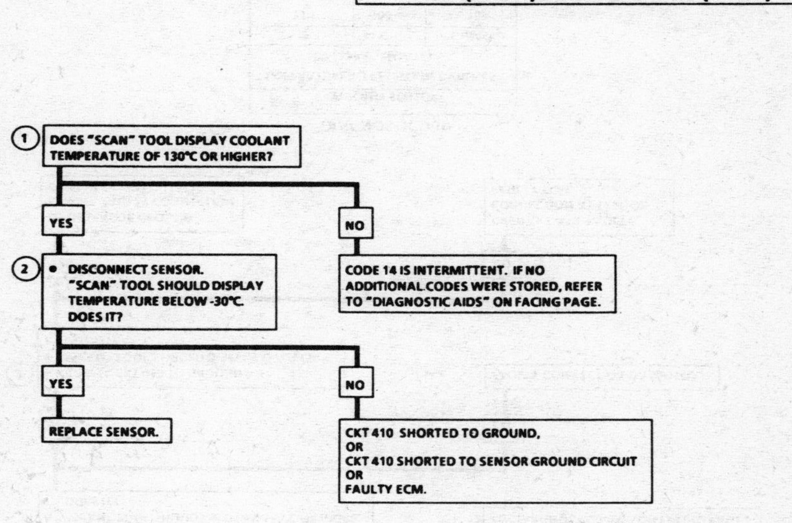

DIAGNOSTIC AID

COOLANT SENSOR		
TEMPERATURE VS. RESISTANCE VALUES (APPROXIMATE)		
°F	°C	OHMS
210	100	185
160	70	450
100	38	1,800
70	20	3,400
40	4	7,500
20	-7	13,500
0	-18	25,000
-40	-40	100,700

CLEAR CODES AND CONFIRM "CLOSED LOOP" OPERATION AND NO "SERVICE ENGINE SOON" LIGHT.

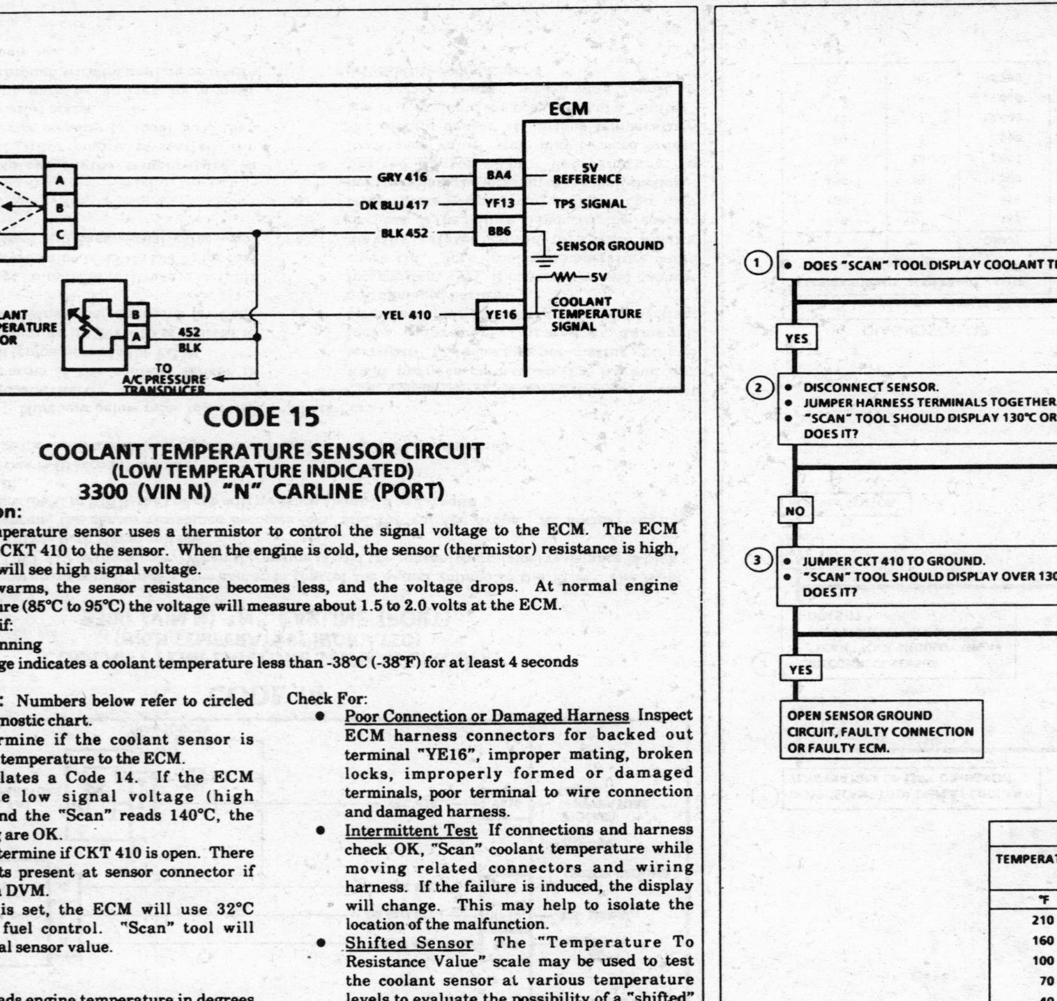

CODE 15

COOLANT TEMPERATURE SENSOR CIRCUIT (LOW TEMPERATURE INDICATED) 3300 (VIN N) "N" CARLINE (PORT)

Circuit Description:

The coolant temperature sensor uses a thermistor to control the signal voltage to the ECM. The ECM applies a voltage on CKT 410 to the sensor. When the engine is cold, the sensor (thermistor) resistance is high, therefore, the ECM will see high signal voltage.

As the engine warms, the sensor resistance becomes less, and the voltage drops. At normal engine operating temperature (85°C to 95°C) the voltage will measure about 1.5 to 2.0 volts at the ECM.

Code 15 will set if:

- Engine is running
- Signal voltage indicates a coolant temperature less than -38°C (-38°F) for at least 4 seconds

Test Description: Numbers below refer to circled numbers on the diagnostic chart.

1. This will determine if the coolant sensor is indicating a low temperature to the ECM.
2. This test simulates a Code 14. If the ECM recognizes the low signal voltage (high temperature) and the "Scan" reads 140°C, the ECM and wiring are OK.
3. This test will determine if CKT 410 is open. There should be 5 volts present at sensor connector if measured with a DVM.

Note: If Code 15 is set, the ECM will use 32°C (120°F) for fuel control. "Scan" tool will display actual sensor value.

Diagnostic Aids:

A "Scan" tool reads engine temperature in degrees centigrade. After engine is started the temperature should rise steadily to about 90°C then stabilize when thermostat opens.

An intermittent may be caused by a poor connection, rubbed through wire insulation or a wire broken inside the insulation.

Check For:

- Poor Connection or Damaged Harness Inspect ECM harness connectors for backed out terminal "YE16", improper mating, broken locks, improperly formed or damaged terminals, poor terminal to wire connection and damaged harness.
- Intermittent Test If connections and harness check OK, "Scan" coolant temperature while moving related connectors and wiring harness. If the failure is induced, the display will change. This may help to isolate the location of the malfunction.
- Shifted Sensor The "Temperature To Resistance Value" scale may be used to test the coolant sensor at various temperature levels to evaluate the possibility of a "shifted" (mis-scaled) sensor which may result in driveability complaints.

A faulty connection, or an open in CKTs 410 or 452 will result in a Code 15.

If Code 23 is also set, check CKT 452 for faulty wiring or connections. Check terminals at sensor for good contact. Refer to "Intermittents" in Section "B".

CODE 15

COOLANT TEMPERATURE SENSOR CIRCUIT (LOW TEMPERATURE INDICATED) 3300 (VIN N) "N" CARLINE (PORT)

(1) • DOES "SCAN" TOOL DISPLAY COOLANT TEMPERATURE OF -30°C OR LESS?

- YES → (2)
- NO → CODE 15 IS INTERMITTENT. IF NO ADDITIONAL CODES WERE STORED, REFER TO "DIAGNOSTIC AIDS" ON FACING PAGE.

(2)
- DISCONNECT SENSOR.
- JUMPER HARNESS TERMINALS TOGETHER.
- "SCAN" TOOL SHOULD DISPLAY 130°C OR MORE. DOES IT?

- NO → (3)
- YES → FAULTY CONNECTION OR SENSOR.

(3)
- JUMPER CKT 410 TO GROUND.
- "SCAN" TOOL SHOULD DISPLAY OVER 130°C. DOES IT?

- YES → OPEN SENSOR GROUND CIRCUIT, FAULTY CONNECTION OR FAULTY ECM.
- NO → OPEN CKT 410, FAULTY CONNECTION AT ECM, OR FAULTY ECM.

DIAGNOSTIC AID

COOLANT SENSOR TEMPERATURE TO RESISTANCE VALUES (APPROXIMATE)		
°F	°C	OHMS
210	100	185
160	70	450
100	38	1,800
70	20	3,400
40	4	7,500
20	-7	13,500
0	-18	25,000
-40	-40	100,700

CLEAR CODES AND CONFIRM "CLOSED LOOP" OPERATION AND NO "SERVICE ENGINE SOON" LIGHT.

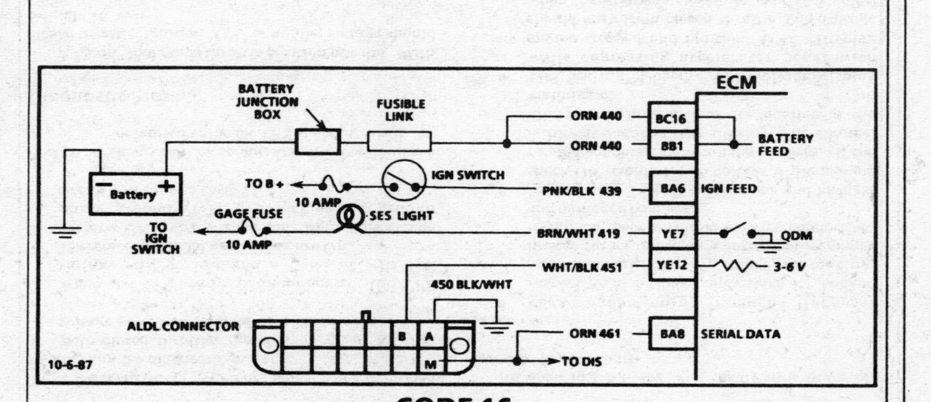

CODE 16

SYSTEM VOLTAGE HIGH 3300 (VIN N) "N" CARLINE (PORT)

Circuit Description:

The ECM monitors battery or system voltage on CKT 440 to terminals "BC16" and "BB1". If the ECM detects voltage above 16 volts for more than 10 seconds, it will turn the SES light "ON" and set Code 16 in memory.

Test Description: Numbers below refer to circled numbers on the diagnostic chart.

1. Test generator output to determine proper operation of the voltage regulator. Run engine at moderate speed and measure voltage across the battery. If over 16 volts, repair generator

Diagnostic Aids:

An intermittent may be caused by a poor connection, rubbed through insulation, a wire broken inside the insulation or poor ECM grounds.

Check For:

- Poor Connection or Damaged Harness Inspect ECM harness connectors for backed out terminal "BC16" or "BB1", improper mating, broken locks, improperly formed or damaged terminals, poor terminal to wire connection and damaged harness.
- Intermittent Test If connections and harness checks OK, monitor battery voltage display while moving related connectors. If the failure is induced, the battery voltage will abruptly change. This may help to isolate the location of the malfunction. An engine stall while manipulating the harness indicates that the ECM has lost voltage at terminal "BC16" or "BB1". Check for loose connectors in CKT 440.

NOTE: Charging battery with a battery charger and starting the engine may set a Code 16.

IMPORTANT: If ECM grounds and battery grounds are located on the same stud at transaxle, this could cause intermittent or improper sensor data to ECM.

CODE 16

SYSTEM VOLTAGE HIGH 3300 (VIN N) "N" CARLINE (PORT)

- INSTALL "SCAN" TOOL
- START ENGINE, WITH ENGINE RUNNING ABOVE 800 RPM.
- "SCAN" BATTERY VOLTAGE.

ABOVE 16 VOLTS

(1)
- INSTALL DVM ACROSS BATTERY.
- RUN ENGINE ABOVE 800 RPM.
- DOES DVM SHOW BATTERY VOLTAGE ABOVE 16 VOLTS.

NO

REPLACE ECM

YES

- REMOVE GENERATOR FOR REPAIR

BELOW 16 VOLTS

- LOAD ELECTRICAL SYSTEM WITH HEADLAMPS AND HIGH A/C BLOWER
- RAISE ENGINE RPM TO 2000
- NOTE BATTERY VOLTAGE ON "SCAN" TOOL

ABOVE 16 VOLTS

- REMOVE GENERATOR FOR REPAIR

BELOW 16 VOLTS

- FAULT IS NOT PRESENT
- REFER TO "DIAGNOSTIC AIDS" ON FACING PAGE.

WHEN ALL DIAGNOSIS AND REPAIRS ARE COMPLETED, CLEAR CODES AND VERIFY OPERATION

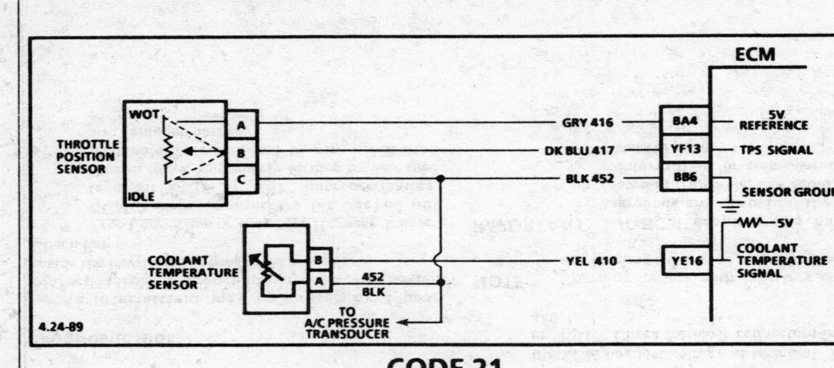

CODE 21

THROTTLE POSITION SENSOR (TPS) CIRCUIT
(SIGNAL VOLTAGE HIGH)
3300 (VIN N) "N" CARLINE (PORT)

Circuit Description:

The Throttle Position Sensor (TPS) provides a voltage signal that changes relative to throttle blade angle. Signal voltage will vary from about .4 at idle to about 5 volts at wide open throttle.

The TPS signal is one of the most important inputs used by the ECM for fuel control and for most of the ECM control outputs.

Code 21 will set if:

- TPS voltage is greater than 4.9 volts at any time or
- Engine is running and air flow is less than 15 gm/sec
- RPM is greater than 600
- TPS signal voltage is greater than 1.5 volts (30%)
- Code 34 not present
- All conditions met for 5 seconds.

Test Description: Numbers below refer to circled numbers on the diagnostic chart.

1. With closed throttle, ignition "ON," or at idle, voltage at "YF13" should be .33-.46 volt.
2. When the TPS sensor is disconnected, the TPS voltage will go low and a Code 22 will set. Therefore, the ECM and wiring are OK.
3. Probing CKT 452 with a test light checks the sensor ground CKT. A faulty sensor ground circuit will cause a Code 21.

NOTE: If a Code 21 is set, the ECM will use a defaulted value for TPS of about .5 volt.

Diagnostic Aids:

A "Scan" tool reads throttle position in volts. With closed throttle, ignition "ON" or at idle, voltage should be .33-.46 volt.

Also some "Scan" tools will read throttle angle 0% = closed throttle 100% = WOT.

An open in CKT 452 will result in a Code 21. Refer to "Intermittents"

Check For:

- Poor Connection or Damaged Harness Inspect ECM harness connectors for backed out terminal "YF13", improper mating, broken locks, improperly formed or damaged terminals, poor terminal to wire connection, and damaged harness.
- Intermittent Test If connections and harness check OK, monitor TPS voltage while moving related connectors and wiring harness. If the failure is induced, the display will change. This may help to isolate the location of the malfunction.
- TPS Scaling Observe TPS voltage display while depressing accelerator pedal with engine stopped and ignition "ON." Display should vary from closed throttle TPS voltage when throttle was closed, to over (4.5 volts) 4500 mV when throttle is held at wide open throttle position.

CODE 21

THROTTLE POSITION SENSOR (TPS) CIRCUIT
(SIGNAL VOLTAGE HIGH)
3300 (VIN N) "N" CARLINE (PORT)

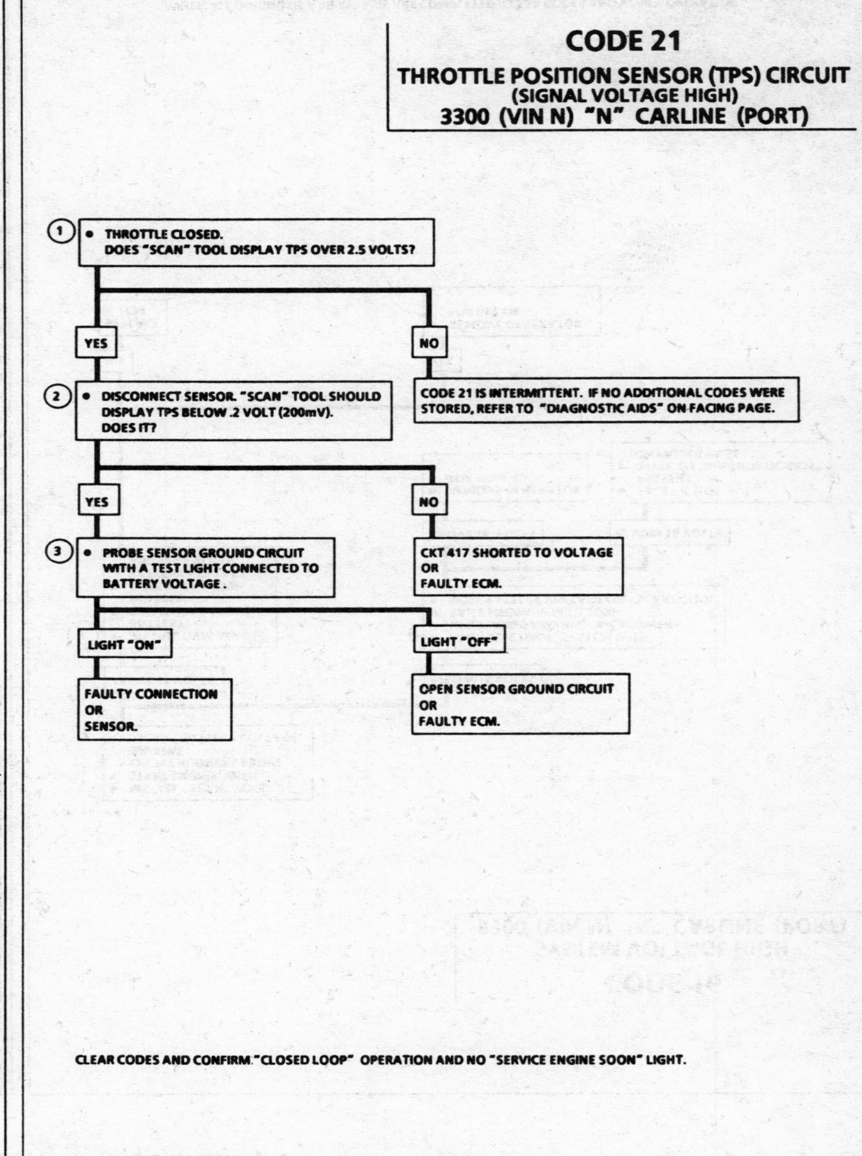

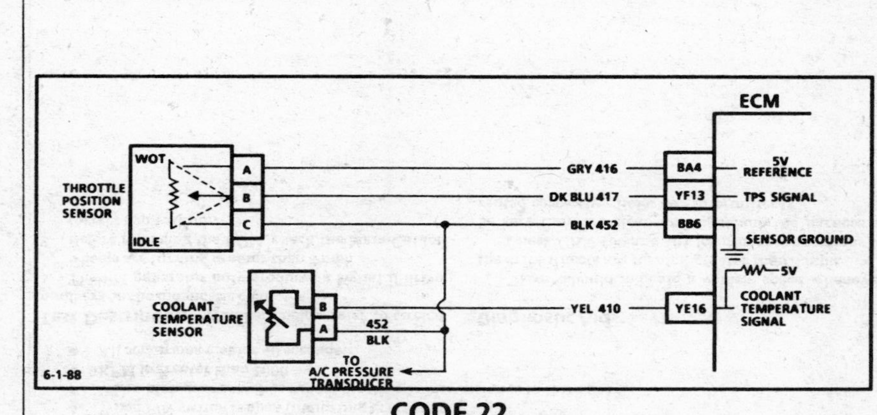

CODE 22

THROTTLE POSITION SENSOR (TPS) CIRCUIT
(SIGNAL VOLTAGE LOW)
3300 (VIN N) "N" CARLINE (PORT)

Circuit Description:

The Throttle Position Sensor (TPS) provides a voltage signal that changes relative to throttle blade angle. Signal voltage will vary from about .4 at idle to about 5 volts at wide open throttle.

The TPS signal is one of the most important inputs used by the ECM for fuel control and for most of the ECM control outputs.

Code 22 will set if:

- The ignition key is "ON"
- TPS signal voltage is less than .24 volt for 4 seconds

Test Description: Numbers below refer to circled numbers on the diagnostic chart.

1. With closed throttle, ignition "ON" or at idle voltage at "YD13" should be .33-.46 volt.
2. Simulates Code 21: (high voltage) If ECM recognizes the high signal voltage the ECM and wiring are OK.
3. With closed throttle, ignition "ON" or at idle, voltage at "YF13" should be .33-.46 volt. If not, check adjustment.
4. Simulates a high signal voltage. Checks CKT 417 for an open.

Diagnostic Aids:

A "Scan" tool reads throttle position in volts. Voltage should increase at a steady rate as throttle is moved toward WOT.

Also some "Scan" tools will read throttle angle 0% = closed throttle 100% = WOT.

An open or short to ground in CKTs 416 or 417 will result in a Code 22.

Check For:

- Poor Connection or Damaged Harness Inspect ECM harness connectors for backed out terminal "YF13", improper mating, broken locks, improperly formed or damaged terminals, poor terminal to wire connection, and damaged harness.
- Intermittent Test If connections and harness check OK, monitor TPS voltage display while moving related connectors and wiring harness. If the failure is induced, the display will change. This may help to isolate the location of the malfunction.
- TPS Scaling Observe TPS voltage display while depressing accelerator pedal with engine stopped and ignition "ON." Display should vary from closed throttle TPS voltage when throttle was closed, to approximately 4.5 volts (4500 mV) when throttle is held at wide open throttle position.

CODE 22

THROTTLE POSITION SENSOR (TPS) CIRCUIT
(SIGNAL VOLTAGE LOW)
3300 (VIN N) "N" CARLINE (PORT)

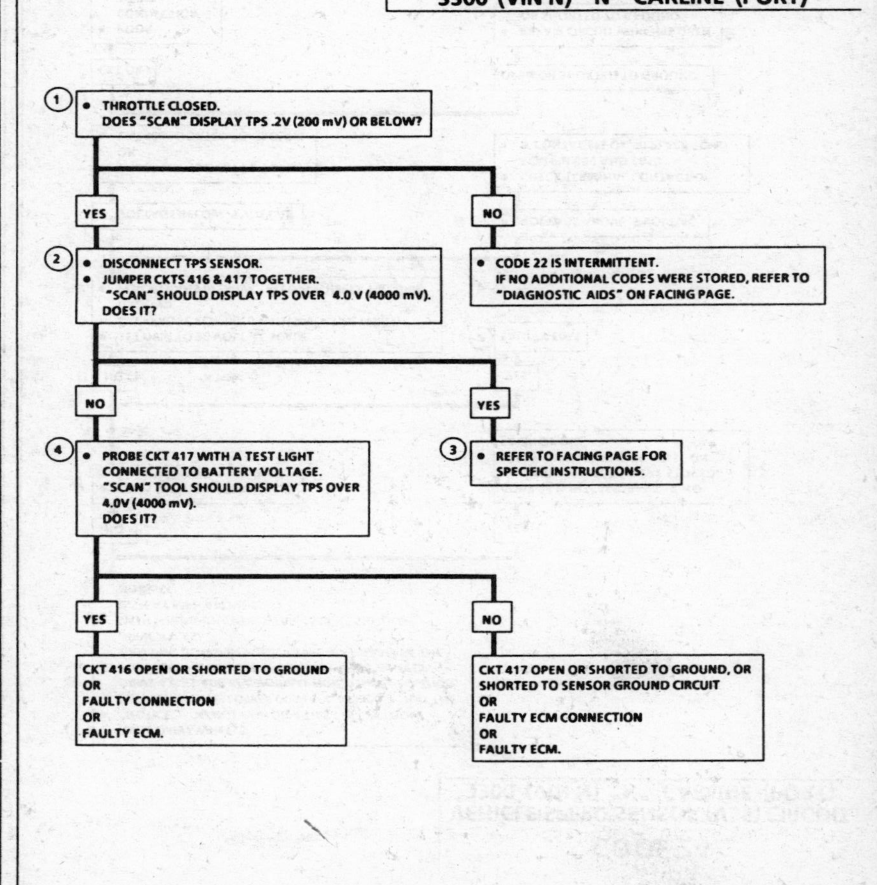

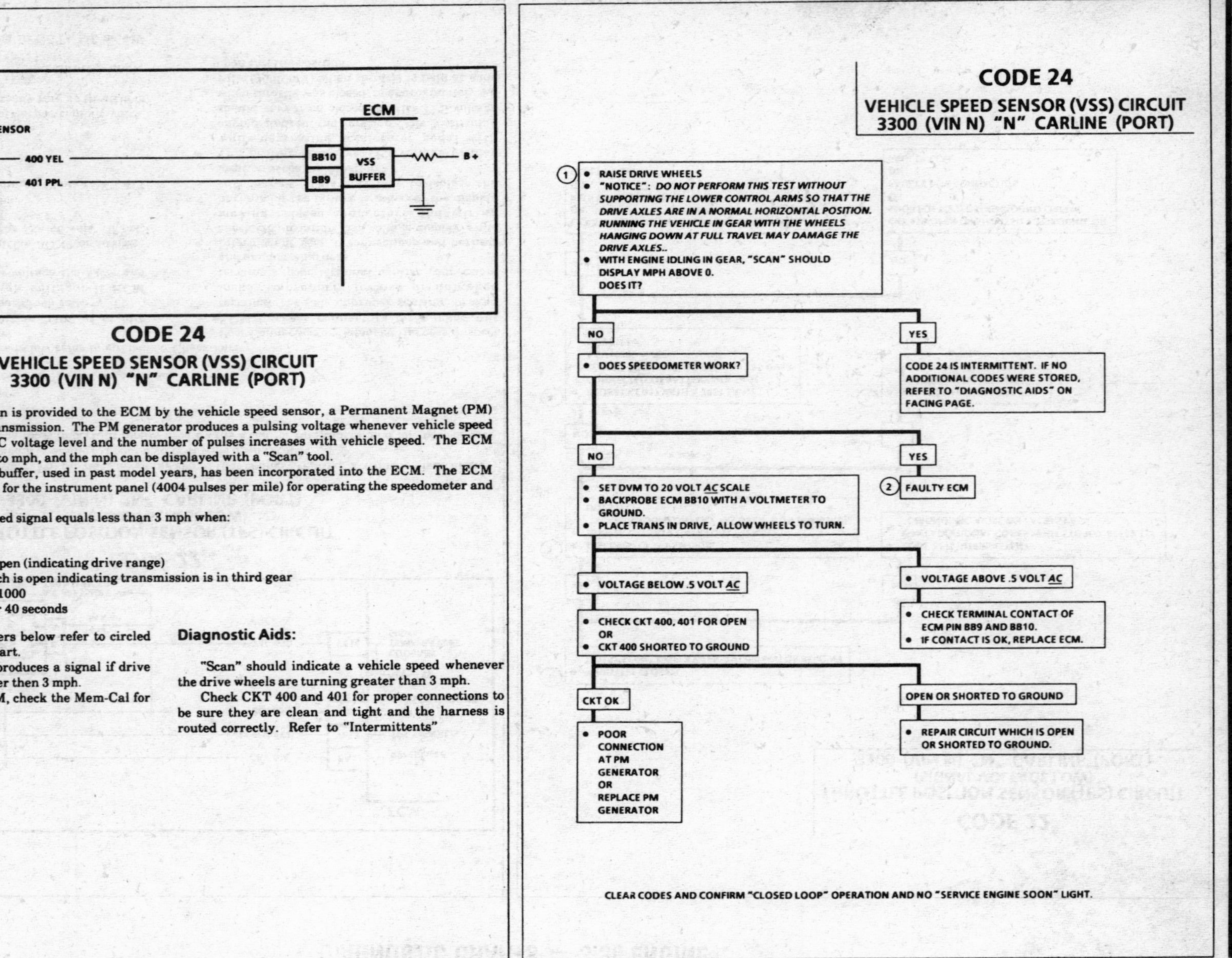

CODE 24

VEHICLE SPEED SENSOR (VSS) CIRCUIT 3300 (VIN N) "N" CARLINE (PORT)

Circuit Description:

Vehicle speed information is provided to the ECM by the vehicle speed sensor, a Permanent Magnet (PM) generator mounted in the transmission. The PM generator produces a pulsing voltage whenever vehicle speed is over about 3 mph. The A/C voltage level and the number of pulses increases with vehicle speed. The ECM converts the pulsing voltage to mph, and the mph can be displayed with a "Scan" tool.

The function of the VSS buffer, used in past model years, has been incorporated into the ECM. The ECM supplies the necessary signal for the instrument panel (4004 pulses per mile) for operating the speedometer and the odometer.

Code 24 will set if vehicle speed signal equals less than 3 mph when:

- Engine is running
- No Code 28 or 31
- When P/N switch is open (indicating drive range)
- When high gear switch is open indicating transmission is in third gear
- RPM is greater than 1000
- All conditions met for 40 seconds

Test Description: Numbers below refer to circled numbers on the diagnostic chart.

1. The PM generator only produces a signal if drive wheels are turning greater then 3 mph.
2. Before replacing the ECM, check the Mem-Cal for correct application.

Diagnostic Aids:

"Scan" should indicate a vehicle speed whenever the drive wheels are turning greater than 3 mph.

Check CKT 400 and 401 for proper connections to be sure they are clean and tight and the harness is routed correctly. Refer to "Intermittents"

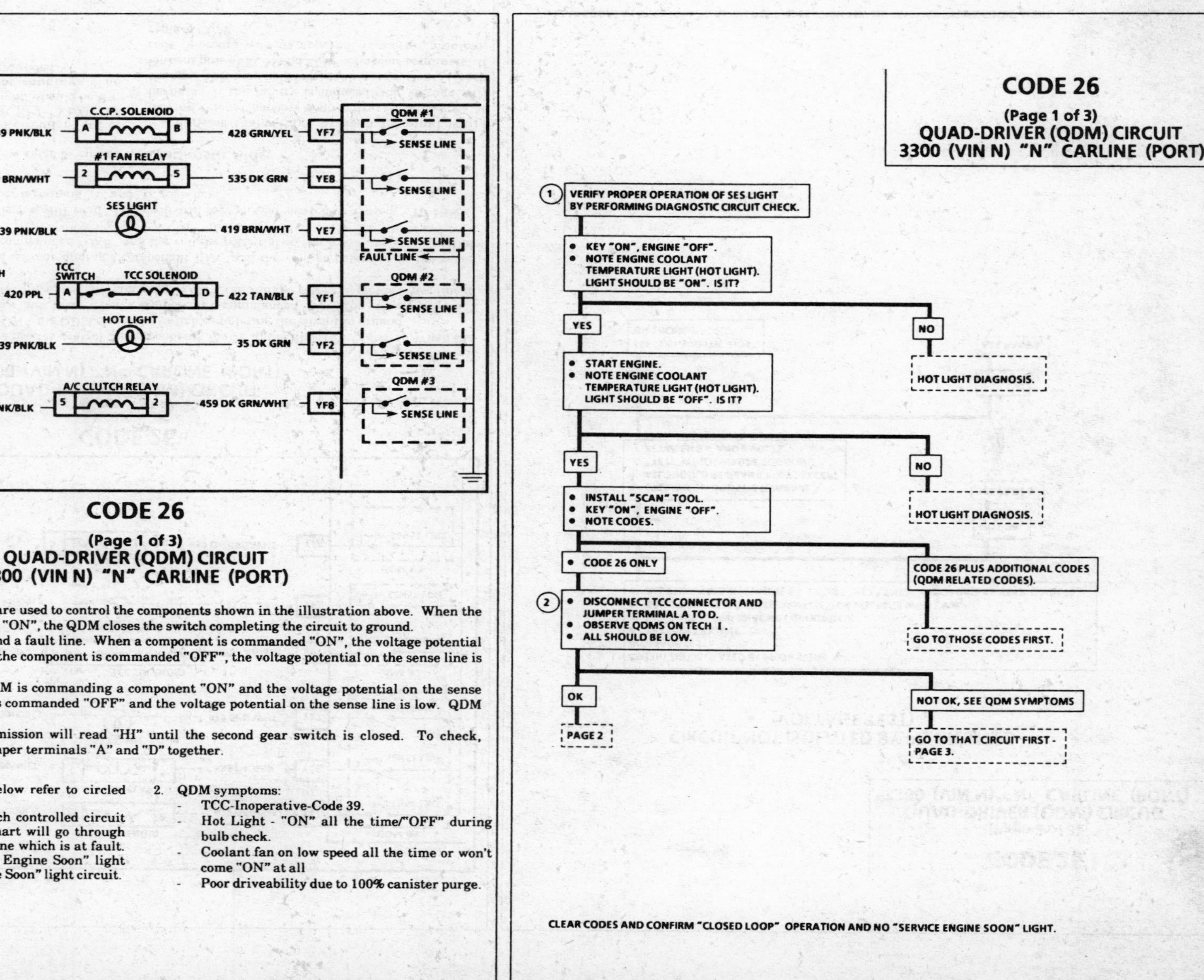

CODE 26

(Page 1 of 3)
QUAD-DRIVER (QDM) CIRCUIT
3300 (VIN N) "N" CARLINE (PORT)

Circuit Description:

Quad-driver Modules (QDM) are used to control the components shown in the illustration above. When the ECM is commanding a component "ON", the QDM closes the switch completing the circuit to ground.

Each QDM has a sense line and a fault line. When a component is commanded "ON", the voltage potential on the sense line is low and when the component is commanded "OFF", the voltage potential on the sense line is high.

Code 26 will set when the ECM is commanding a component "ON" and the voltage potential on the sense line is high, or if the component is commanded "OFF" and the voltage potential on the sense line is low. QDM number 3 will **not** set a code 26.

Vehicles with a 125C Transmission will read "HI" until the second gear switch is closed. To check, disconnect TCC connector and jumper terminals "A" and "D" together.

Test Description: Numbers below refer to circled numbers on the diagnostic chart.

1. The ECM does not know which controlled circuit caused the Code 26 so this chart will go through each of the circuits to determine which is at fault. This test checks the "Service Engine Soon" light driver and the "Service Engine Soon" light circuit.
2. QDM symptoms:
   - TCC-Inoperative-Code 39.
   - Hot Light - "ON" all the time/"OFF" during bulb check.
   - Coolant fan on low speed all the time or won't come "ON" at all
   - Poor driveability due to 100% canister purge.

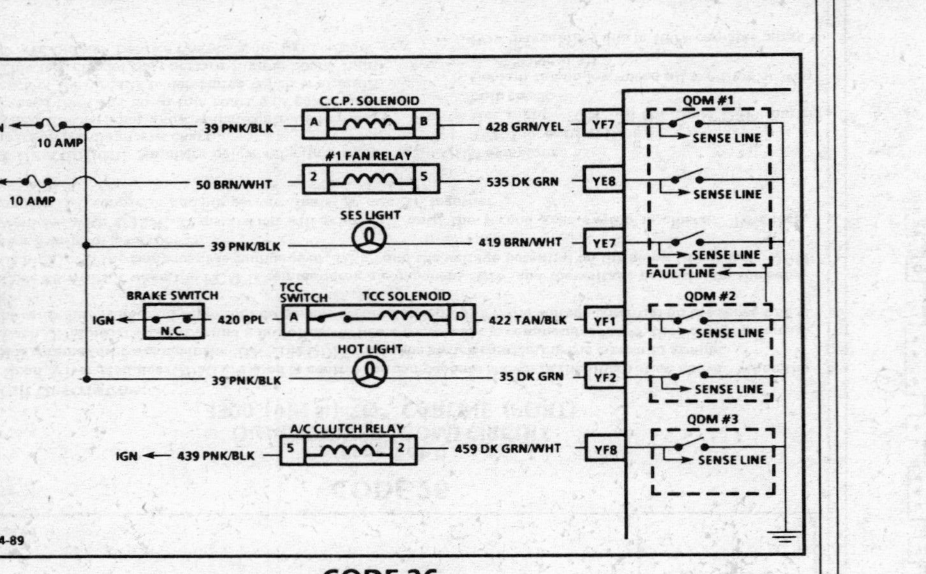

CODE 26

(Page 2 of 3)
QUAD-DRIVER (QDM) CIRCUIT
3300 (VIN N) "N" CARLINE (PORT)

Circuit Description:

Quad-driver Modules (QDM) are used to control the components shown in the illustration above. When the ECM is commanding a component "ON", the QDM closes the switch completing the circuit to ground.

Each QDM has a sense line and a fault line. When a component is commanded "ON", the voltage potential on the sense line is low and when the component is commanded "OFF", the voltage potential on the sense line is high.

Code 26 will set when the ECM is commanding a component "ON" and the voltage potential on the sense line is high, or if the component is commanded "OFF" and the voltage potential on the sense line is low. QDM number 3 will **not** set a code 26.

Vehicles with a 125C Transmission will read "HI" until the second gear switch is closed. To check, disconnect TCC connector and jumper terminals "A" and "D" together.

Test Description: Numbers below refer to circled numbers on the diagnostic chart.

3. This test will determine which circuit is out of specifications. All circuits *EXCEPT* "YE7", the SES light and "YF2", the "hot light" should be B+ when key is "ON", engine not running. The diagnostic test terminal is not grounded.

Diagnostic Aids:

Monitor the voltage at each terminal while moving related harness connectors, including ECM harness. If the failure is induced, the voltage will change. This may help locate the intermittent. Check for bent pins at ECM and ECM connector terminals. If code re-occurs with no apparent connector problem, replace ECM.

CODE 26

(Page 2 of 3)
QUAD-DRIVER (QDM) CIRCUIT
3300 (VIN N) "N" CARLINE (PORT)

CIRCUIT NOT ISOLATED BY PRIOR STEPS (VOLTAGE TEST)

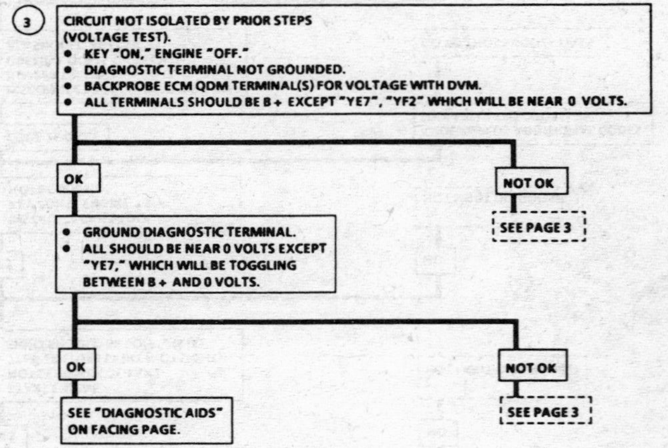

CLEAR CODES AND CONFIRM "CLOSED LOOP" OPERATION AND NO "SERVICE ENGINE SOON" LIGHT.

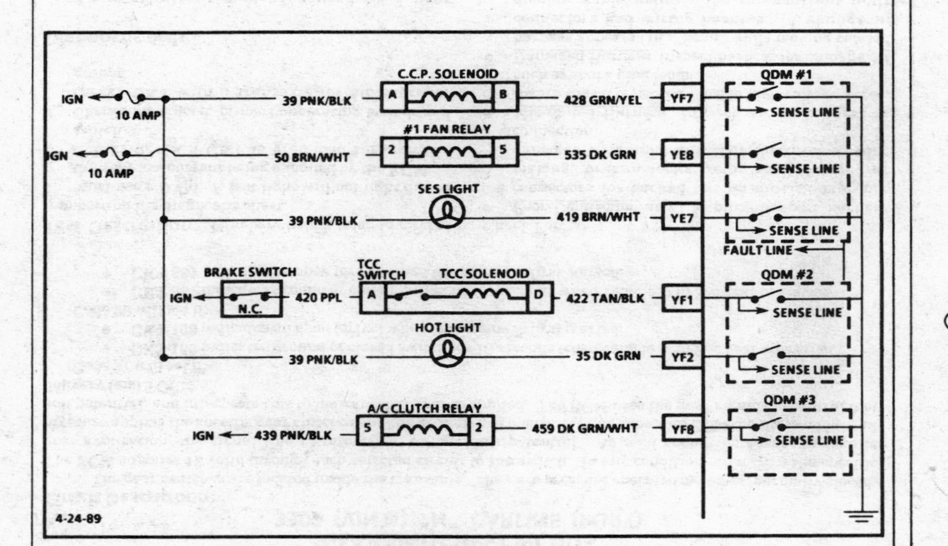

CODE 26

(Page 3 of 3)

QUAD-DRIVER (QDM) CIRCUIT
3300 (VIN N) "N" CARLINE (PORT)

Circuit Description:

Quad-driver Modules (QDM) are used to control the components shown in the illustration above. When the ECM is commanding a component "ON", the QDM closes the switch completing the circuit to ground.

Each QDM has a sense line and a fault line. When a component is commanded "ON", the voltage potential on the sense line is low and when the component is commanded "OFF", the voltage potential on the sense line is high.

Code 26 will set when the ECM is commanding a component "ON" and the voltage potential on the sense line is high, or if the component is commanded "OFF" and the voltage potential on the sense line is low. QDM number 3 will **not** set a code 26.

Vehicles with a 125C Transmission will read "HI" until the second gear switch is closed. To check, disconnect TCC connector and jumper terminals "A" and "D" together.

Test Description: Numbers below refer to circled numbers on the diagnostic chart.

4. This test will determine if the problem is the circuit or the component. As the factory installed ECM is protected with an internal fuse, it is highly unlikely that the ECM needs to be replaced.

CODE 26

(Page 3 of 3)

QUAD-DRIVER (QDM) CIRCUIT
3300 (VIN N) "N" CARLINE (PORT)

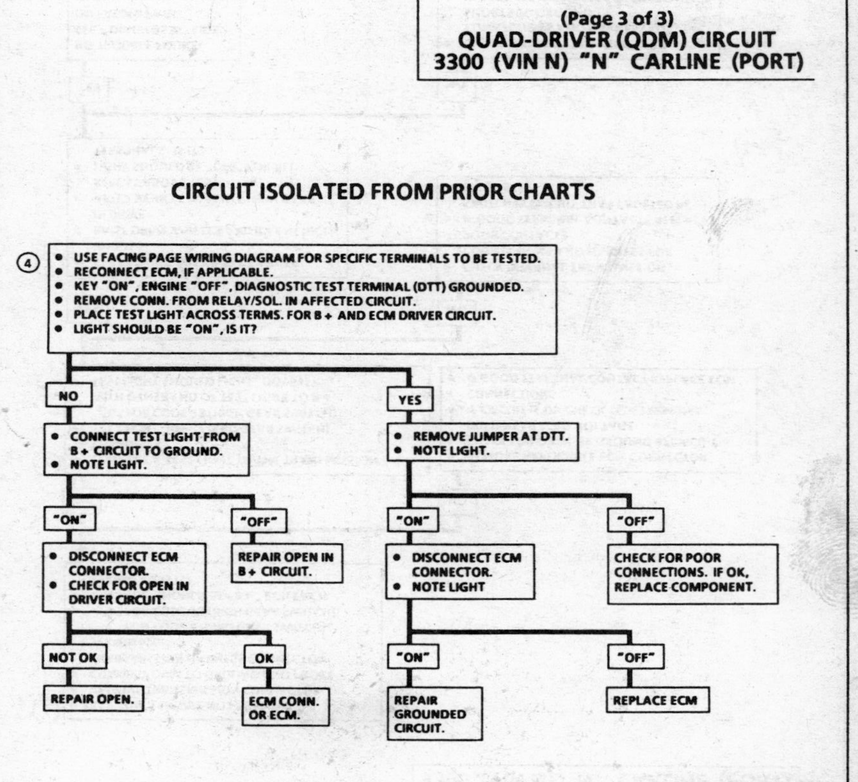

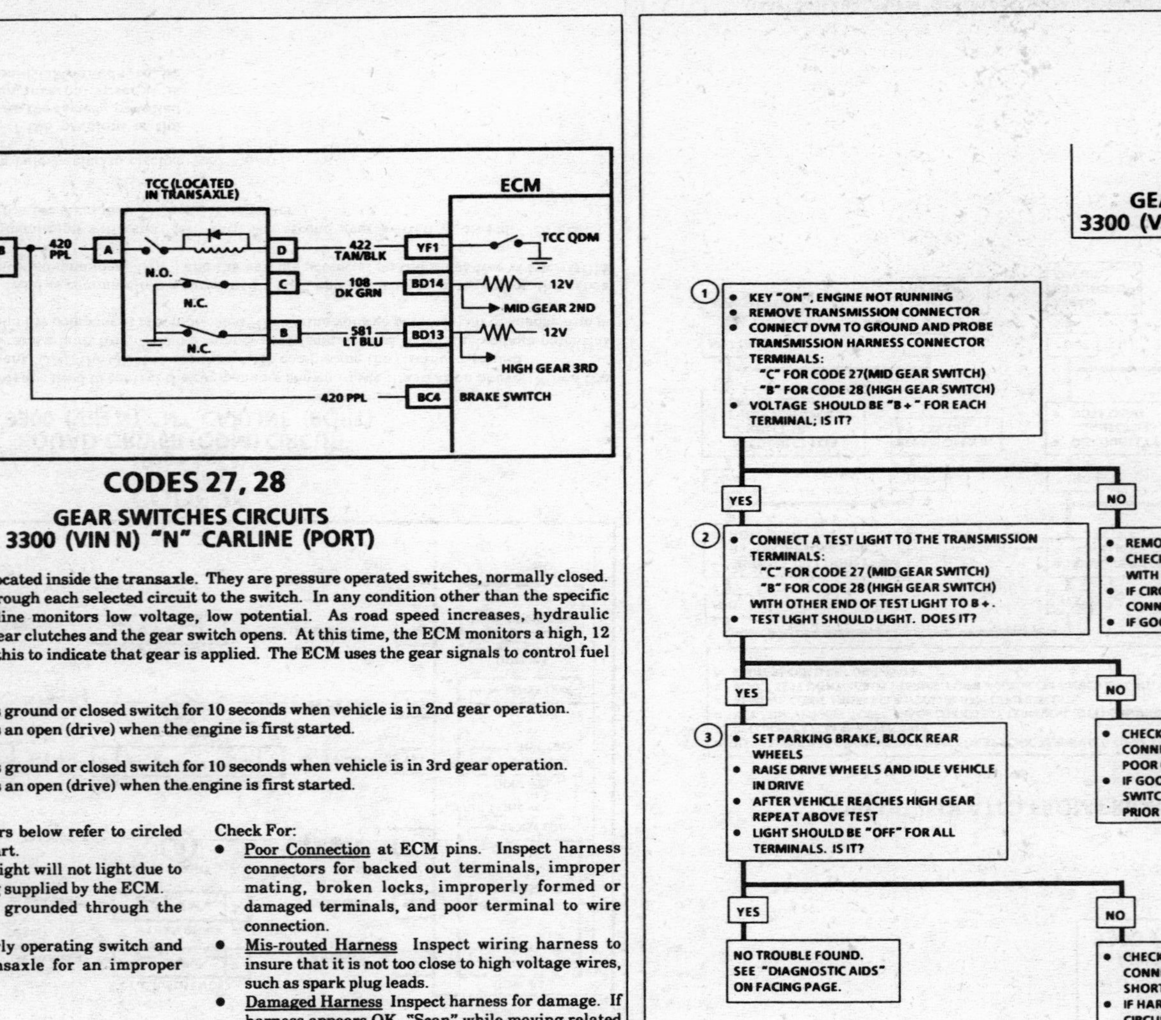

CODES 27, 28

GEAR SWITCHES CIRCUITS
3300 (VIN N) "N" CARLINE (PORT)

Circuit Description:

The gear switches are located inside the transaxle. They are pressure operated switches, normally closed. The ECM supplies 12 volts through each selected circuit to the switch. In any condition other than the specific gear application, the signal line monitors low voltage, low potential. As road speed increases, hydraulic pressure applies the specific gear clutches and the gear switch opens. At this time, the ECM monitors a high, 12 volt potential, and interprets this to indicate that gear is applied. The ECM uses the gear signals to control fuel delivery (and TCC).

Code 27 will set if:

- CKT 108 indicates ground or closed switch for 10 seconds when vehicle is in 2nd gear operation.
- CKT 108 indicates an open (drive) when the engine is first started.

Code 28 will set if:

- CKT 581 indicates ground or closed switch for 10 seconds when vehicle is in 3rd gear operation.
- CKT 581 indicates an open (drive) when the engine is first started.

Test Description: Numbers below refer to circled numbers on the diagnostic chart.

1. Must use a DVM. A test light will not light due to the very low current being supplied by the ECM.
2. Checks to see if CKT is grounded through the switch.
3. Checks for a good, properly operating switch and checks CKT within transaxle for an improper ground.

Diagnostic Aids:

An intermittent may be caused by a poor connection, mis-routed harness, rubbed through wire insulation, or a wire broken inside the insulation.

Check For:

- Poor Connection at ECM pins. Inspect harness connectors for backed out terminals, improper mating, broken locks, improperly formed or damaged terminals, and poor terminal to wire connection.
- Mis-routed Harness Inspect wiring harness to insure that it is not too close to high voltage wires, such as spark plug leads.
- Damaged Harness Inspect harness for damage. If harness appears OK, "Scan" while moving related connectors and wiring harness. A change in display would indicate the intermittent fault location.

CODES 27, 28

GEAR SWITCHES CIRCUITS
3300 (VIN N) "N" CARLINE (PORT)

(1)
- KEY "ON", ENGINE NOT RUNNING
- REMOVE TRANSMISSION CONNECTOR
- CONNECT DVM TO GROUND AND PROBE TRANSMISSION HARNESS CONNECTOR TERMINALS:
  "C" FOR CODE 27(MID GEAR SWITCH)
  "B" FOR CODE 28 (HIGH GEAR SWITCH)
- VOLTAGE SHOULD BE "B+" FOR EACH TERMINAL; IS IT?

YES → (2)

NO:
- REMOVE APPLICABLE ECM CONNECTOR
- CHECK FOR OPEN OR GROUND IN CIRCUIT WITH NEAR ZERO VOLTAGE
- IF CIRCUIT IS OK CHECK ECM TERMINAL CONNECTIONS
- IF GOOD TERMINAL CONTACT REPLACE ECM

(2)
- CONNECT A TEST LIGHT TO THE TRANSMISSION TERMINALS:
  "C" FOR CODE 27 (MID GEAR SWITCH)
  "B" FOR CODE 28 (HIGH GEAR SWITCH)
  WITH OTHER END OF TEST LIGHT TO B+.
- TEST LIGHT SHOULD LIGHT. DOES IT?

YES → (3)

NO:
- CHECK INTERNAL TRANSMISSION CONNECTIONS AND HARNESS FOR POOR CONTACTS
- IF GOOD TERMINAL CONTACTS REPLACE SWITCH IN CIRCUIT THAT FAULTED IN PRIOR STEP

(3)
- SET PARKING BRAKE, BLOCK REAR WHEELS
- RAISE DRIVE WHEELS AND IDLE VEHICLE IN DRIVE
- AFTER VEHICLE REACHES HIGH GEAR REPEAT ABOVE TEST
- LIGHT SHOULD BE "OFF" FOR ALL TERMINALS. IS IT?

YES:
NO TROUBLE FOUND.
SEE "DIAGNOSTIC AIDS" ON FACING PAGE.

NO:
- CHECK INTERNAL TRANSMISSION CONNECTIONS AND HARNESS FOR SHORTS TO GROUND
- IF HARNESS IS OK REPLACE SWITCH IN CIRCUIT THAT FAULTED IN PRIOR STEP

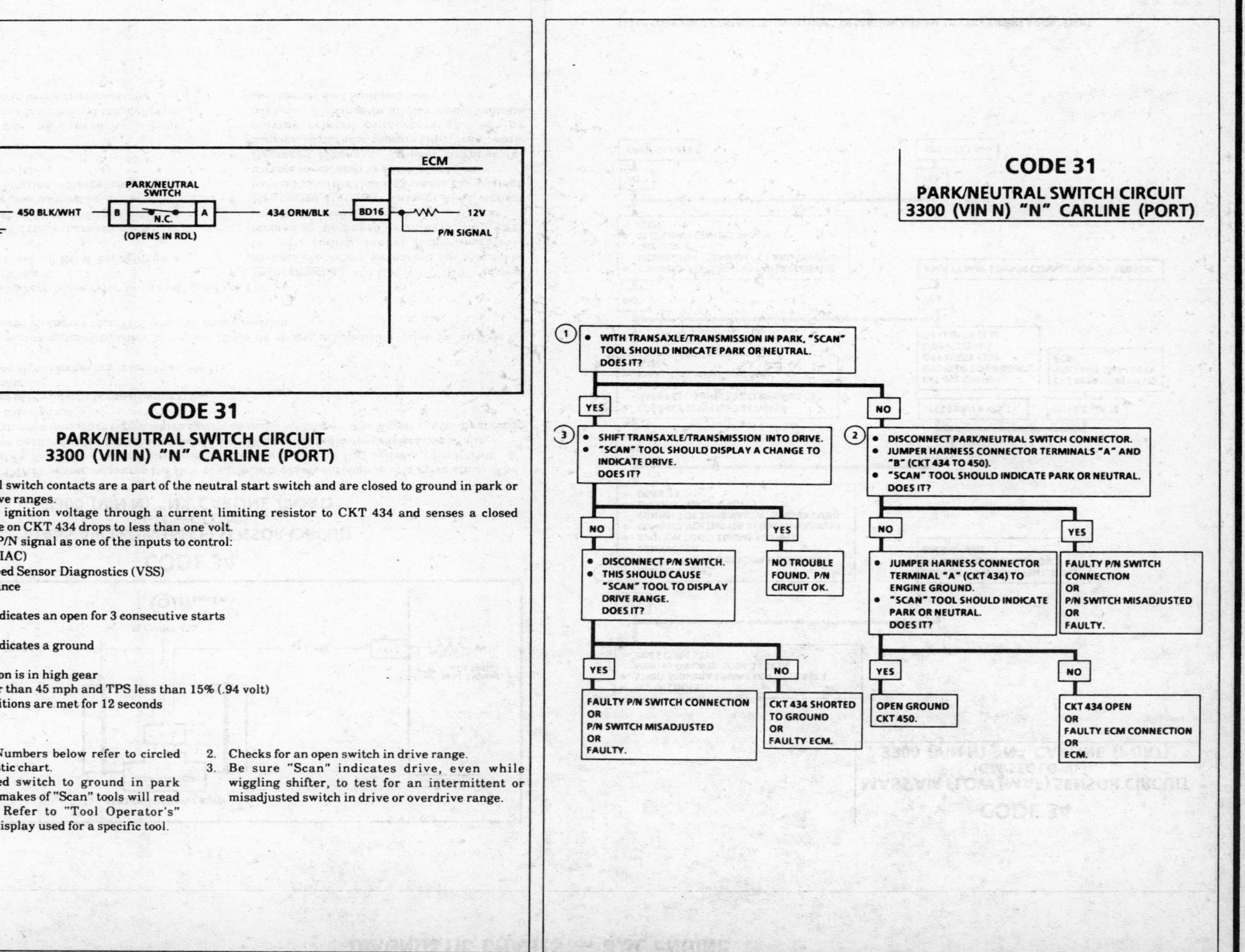

CODE 31

PARK/NEUTRAL SWITCH CIRCUIT
3300 (VIN N) "N" CARLINE (PORT)

Circuit Description:

The park/neutral switch contacts are a part of the neutral start switch and are closed to ground in park or neutral and open in drive ranges.

The ECM supplies ignition voltage through a current limiting resistor to CKT 434 and senses a closed switch when the voltage on CKT 434 drops to less than one volt.

The ECM uses the P/N signal as one of the inputs to control:

- Idle Speed (IAC)
- Vehicle Speed Sensor Diagnostics (VSS)
- Spark Advance

Code 31 will set if:

- CKT 434 indicates an open for 3 consecutive starts

Or if:

- CKT 434 indicates a ground
- No Code 38
- Transmission is in high gear
- VSS greater than 45 mph and TPS less than 15% (.94 volt)
- Above conditions are met for 12 seconds

Test Description: Numbers below refer to circled numbers on the diagnostic chart.

1. Checks for a closed switch to ground in park position. Different makes of "Scan" tools will read P/N differently. Refer to "Tool Operator's" manual for type of display used for a specific tool.
2. Checks for an open switch in drive range.
3. Be sure "Scan" indicates drive, even while wiggling shifter, to test for an intermittent or misadjusted switch in drive or overdrive range.

PART OF THROTTLE BODY
MAF SENSOR
C B A
ECM
10A ECM FUSE
TO IGN
439 PNK/BLK
BLK/WHT 450
ON TRANSAXLE
492 YEL
YF10
MAF SIGNAL VOLTAGE
5V
2-5-88

CODE 34

MASS AIR FLOW (MAF) SENSOR CIRCUIT
(GM/SEC LOW)
3300 (VIN N) "N" CARLINE (PORT)

Circuit Description:

The Mass Air Flow (MAF) sensor measures the flow of air which passes through it in a given time. The ECM uses this information to monitor the operating condition of the engine for fuel delivery calculations. A large quantity of air movement indicates acceleration, while a small quantity indicates deceleration or idle.

The MAF sensor produces a frequency signal which cannot be easily measured. The sensor can be diagnosed using the procedures on this chart.

Code 34 will set when of the following conditions exists:

- Engine running
- If MAF sensor signal frequency is less than 960 Hz

NOTE: If the MAF sensor signal frequency is too low (Code 34 is set), a substitute value for airflow is calculated based on engine rpm, TPS, and IAC motor position.

Test Description: Numbers below refer to circled numbers on the diagnostic chart.

1. This step checks to see if ECM recognizes a problem.
2. A voltage reading at sensor harness connector terminal "A" of less than 4 or over 6 volts indicates a fault in CKT 492 or poor connection.
3. Verifies that both ignition voltage and a good ground circuit are available.

Diagnostic Aids:

An intermittent may be caused by a poor connection, mis-routed harness, rubbed through wire insulation, or a wire broken inside the insulation.

Check For:

- Poor connection at ECM pin "YD10". Inspect harness connectors for backed out terminals, improper mating, broken locks, improperly formed or damaged terminals, and poor terminal to wire connection.
- Mis-routed Harness Inspect MAF sensor harness to insure that it is not too close to high voltage wires, such as spark plug leads.
- Damaged Harness Inspect harness for damage. If harness appears OK, "Scan" while moving related connectors and wiring harness. A change in display would indicate the intermittent fault location.

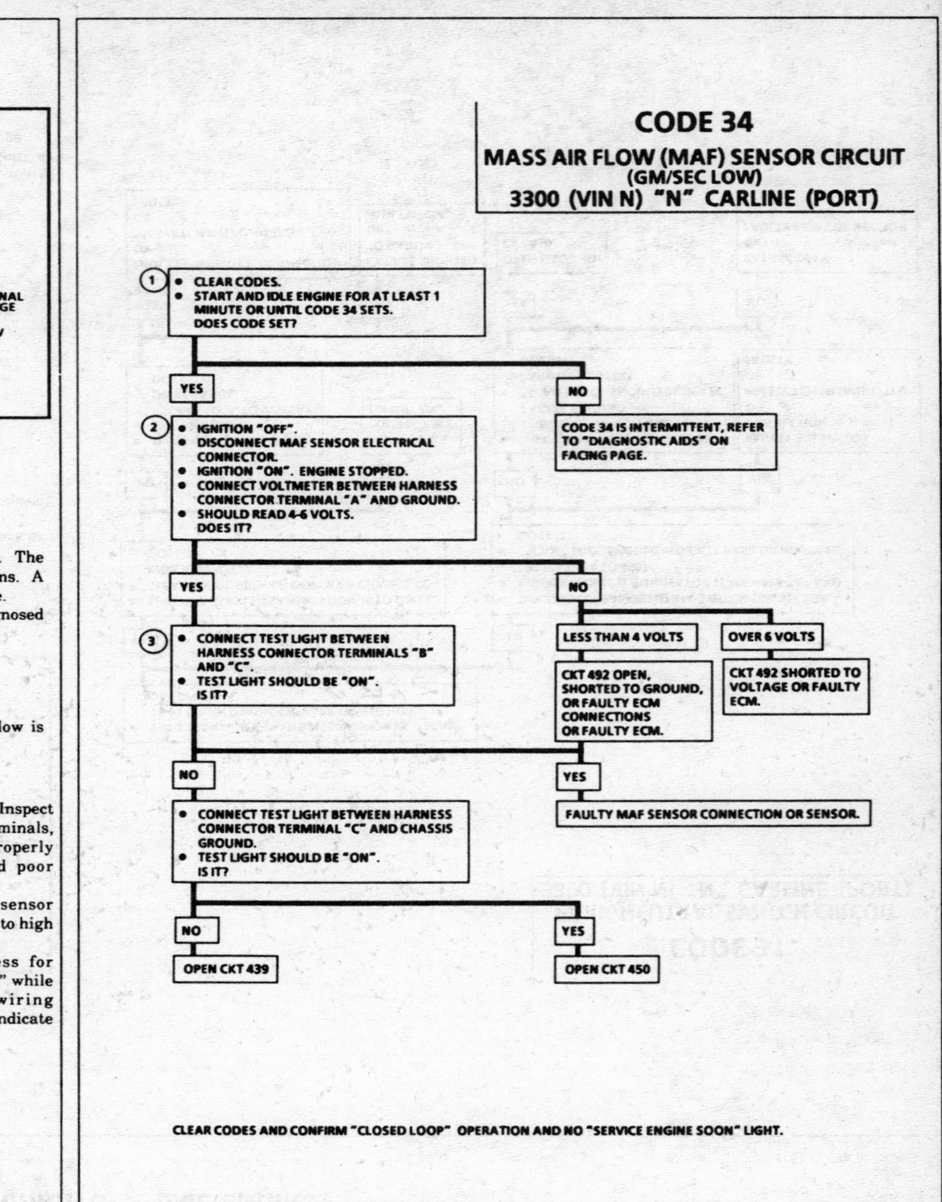

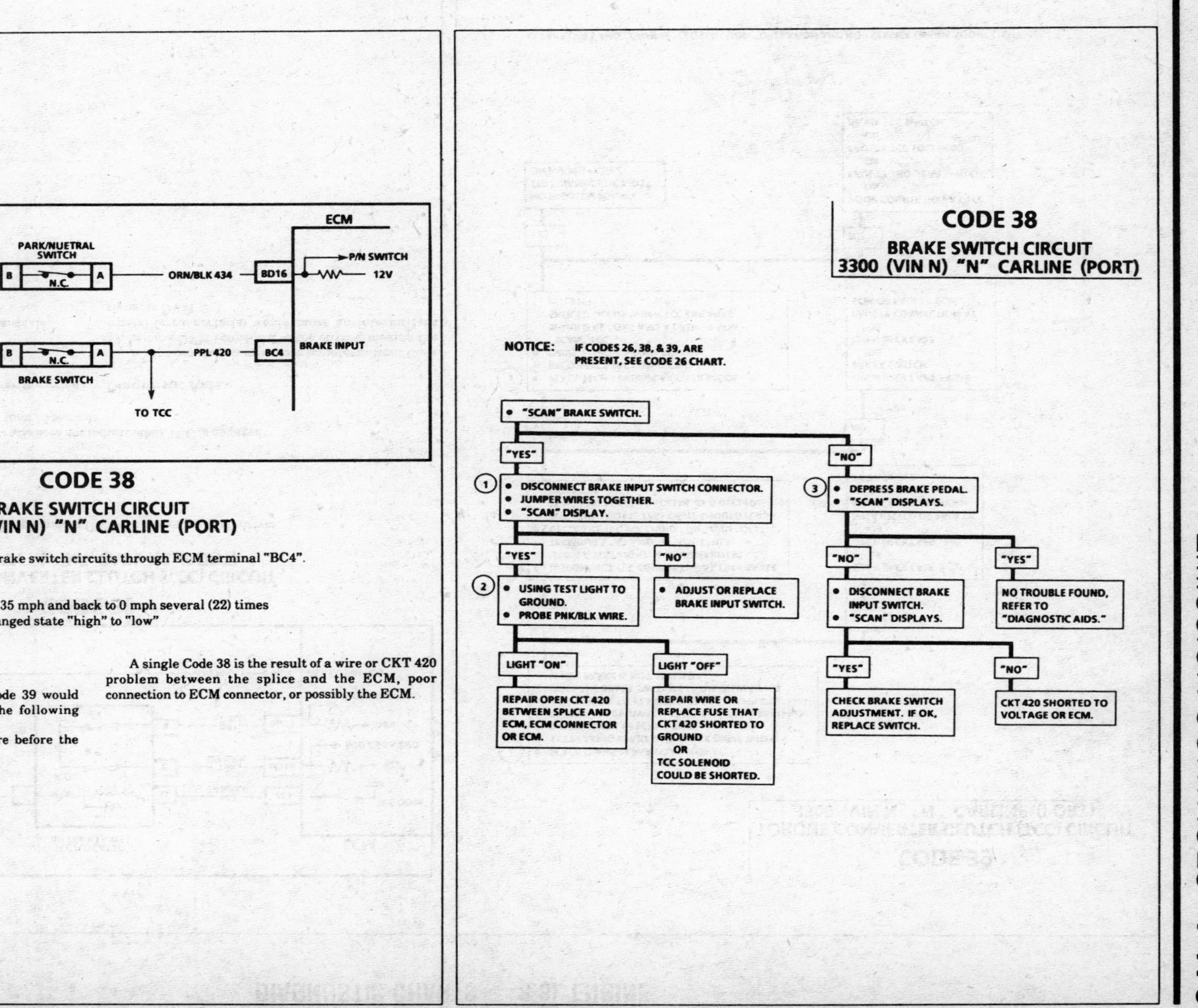

CODE 38

BRAKE SWITCH CIRCUIT
3300 (VIN N) "N" CARLINE (PORT)

Circuit Description:

The ECM monitors the status of the brake switch circuits through ECM terminal "BC4". Code 38 will set if:

- No Code 24 is present
- Vehicle speed has been above 35 mph and back to 0 mph several (22) times
- Status of CKT 420 has not changed state "high" to "low"

Diagnostic Aids:

A Code 38 in combination with a Code 39 would mean a problem with one or more of the following components.

Fuse, CKT 439, brake switch or wire before the splice.

A single Code 38 is the result of a wire or CKT 420 problem between the splice and the ECM, poor connection to ECM connector, or possibly the ECM.

DIAGNOSTIC CHARTS — 3.3L ENGINE

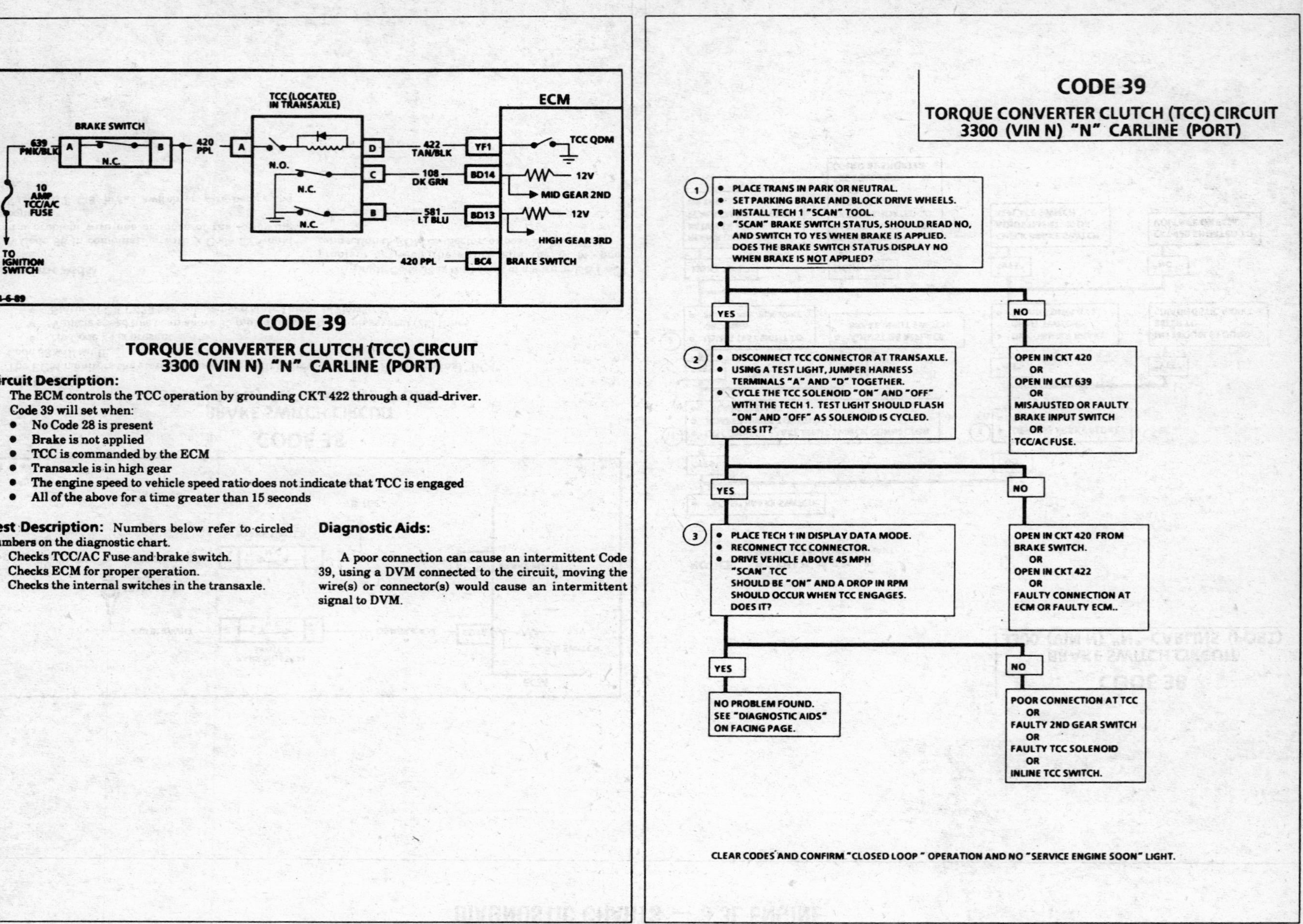

CODE 39

TORQUE CONVERTER CLUTCH (TCC) CIRCUIT 3300 (VIN N) "N" CARLINE (PORT)

Circuit Description:

The ECM controls the TCC operation by grounding CKT 422 through a quad-driver. Code 39 will set when:

- No Code 28 is present
- Brake is not applied
- TCC is commanded by the ECM
- Transaxle is in high gear
- The engine speed to vehicle speed ratio does not indicate that TCC is engaged
- All of the above for a time greater than 15 seconds

Test Description: Numbers below refer to circled numbers on the diagnostic chart.

1. Checks TCC/AC Fuse and brake switch.
2. Checks ECM for proper operation.
3. Checks the internal switches in the transaxle.

Diagnostic Aids:

A poor connection can cause an intermittent Code 39, using a DVM connected to the circuit, moving the wire(s) or connector(s) would cause an intermittent signal to DVM.

CODE 39

TORQUE CONVERTER CLUTCH (TCC) CIRCUIT 3300 (VIN N) "N" CARLINE (PORT)

(1)
- PLACE TRANS IN PARK OR NEUTRAL.
- SET PARKING BRAKE AND BLOCK DRIVE WHEELS.
- INSTALL TECH 1 "SCAN" TOOL.
- "SCAN" BRAKE SWITCH STATUS, SHOULD READ NO, AND SWITCH TO YES WHEN BRAKE IS APPLIED. DOES THE BRAKE SWITCH STATUS DISPLAY NO WHEN BRAKE IS NOT APPLIED?

NO: OPEN IN CKT 420 OR OPEN IN CKT 639 OR MISAJUSTED OR FAULTY BRAKE INPUT SWITCH OR TCC/AC FUSE.

YES:

(2)
- DISCONNECT TCC CONNECTOR AT TRANSAXLE.
- USING A TEST LIGHT, JUMPER HARNESS TERMINALS "A" AND "D" TOGETHER.
- CYCLE THE TCC SOLENOID "ON" AND "OFF" WITH THE TECH 1. TEST LIGHT SHOULD FLASH "ON" AND "OFF" AS SOLENOID IS CYCLED. DOES IT?

NO: OPEN IN CKT 420 FROM BRAKE SWITCH. OR OPEN IN CKT 422 OR FAULTY CONNECTION AT ECM OR FAULTY ECM..

YES:

(3)
- PLACE TECH 1 IN DISPLAY DATA MODE.
- RECONNECT TCC CONNECTOR.
- DRIVE VEHICLE ABOVE 45 MPH "SCAN" TCC SHOULD BE "ON" AND A DROP IN RPM SHOULD OCCUR WHEN TCC ENGAGES. DOES IT?

YES: NO PROBLEM FOUND. SEE "DIAGNOSTIC AIDS" ON FACING PAGE.

NO: POOR CONNECTION AT TCC OR FAULTY 2ND GEAR SWITCH OR FAULTY TCC SOLENOID OR INLINE TCC SWITCH.

CLEAR CODES AND CONFIRM "CLOSED LOOP" OPERATION AND NO "SERVICE ENGINE SOON" LIGHT.

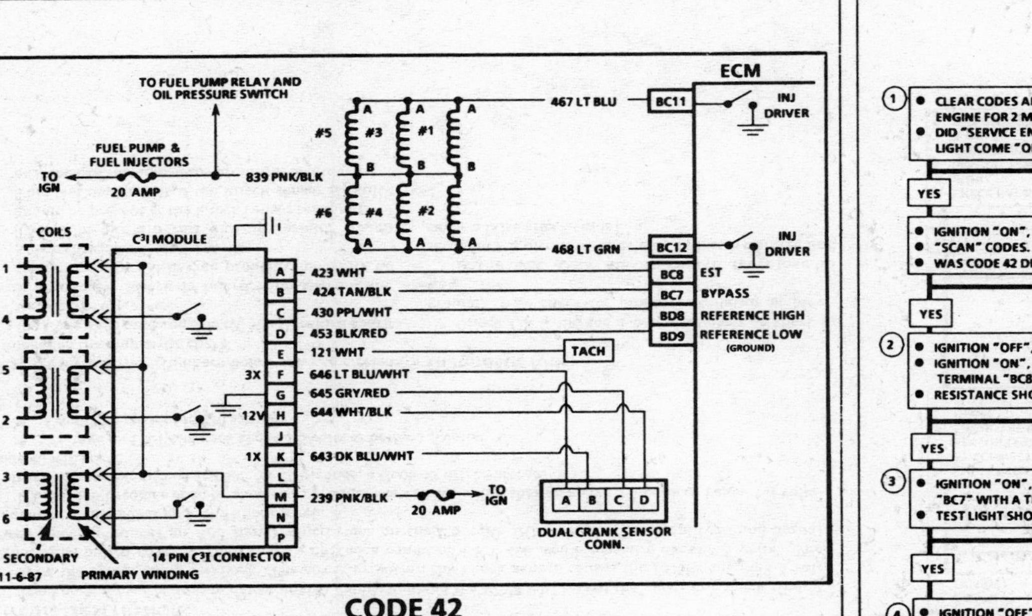

CODE 42

ELECTRONIC SPARK TIMING (EST) CIRCUIT 3300 (VIN N) "N" CARLINE (PORT)

Circuit Description:

The C3I module sends a reference signal to the ECM when the engine is cranking. Under 400 rpm, the C3I module controls ignition timing. When the engine speed exceeds 400 rpm, the ECM sends a 5 volt signal on the bypass CKT 424 to switch timing to ECM control. If an open or ground occurs while engine is running in EST mode, the engine will stall and set a Code 42. If circuit 424 is open or grounded while engine is cranking, the engine will start and remain in backup.

To set a Code 42 the following conditions must be met:

- Engine speed greater than 600 rpm with no EST pulse for 200 mS (open or grounded CKT 423), or
- ECM commanding bypass mode (open or grounded CKT 424)

Test Description: Numbers below refer to circled numbers on the diagnostic chart.

1. Checks to see if ECM recognizes a problem. If it does not set Code 42, it is an intermittent problem and could be due to a loose connection.
2. With the ECM disconnected, the ohmmeter should be reading less than 200 ohms, which is the normal resistance of the EST circuit through the C3I module. A higher resistance would indicate a fault in CKT 423, a poor C3I module connection, or a faulty C3I module.
3. If test light was "ON" when connected from 12 volts to ECM harness terminal "BC7" either CKT 424 is shorted to ground or the C3I module is faulty.
4. Checks to see if C3I module switches when the bypass circuit is energized by 12 volts through the test light. If the C3I module actually switches, the ohmmeter reading should shift to over 6,000 ohms.
5. Disconnecting the ignition module should make the ohmmeter read as if it were monitoring an open circuit (infinite reading). Otherwise, CKT 423 is shorted to ground.

Diagnostic Aids:

An intermittent may be caused by a poor connection, rubbed through wire insulation, or a wire broken inside the insulation. Check For:

- Poor Connection or Damaged Harness Inspect ECM harness connectors for backed out terminals "BC7" or "BC8", improper mating, broken locks, improperly formed or damaged terminals, poor terminal to wire connection, and damaged harness.
- Intermittent Test If connections and harness check OK, a digital voltmeter connected from affected terminal to ground while moving related connectors and wiring harness. If the failure is induced, the voltage reading will change.

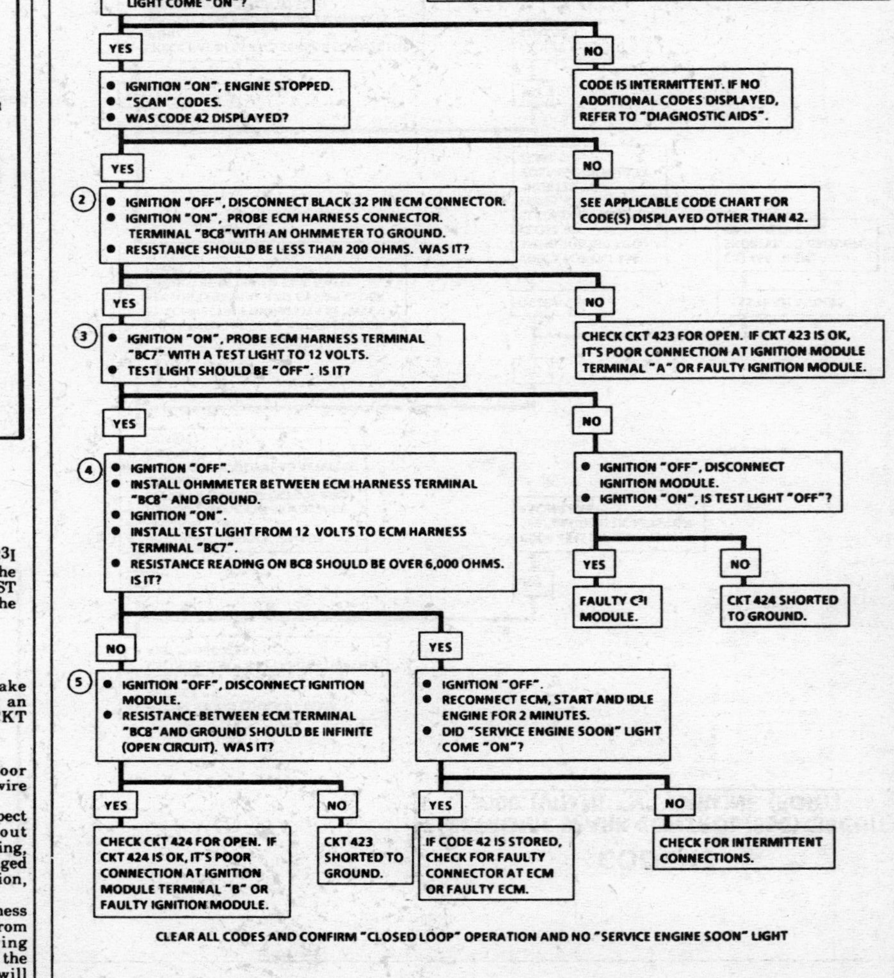

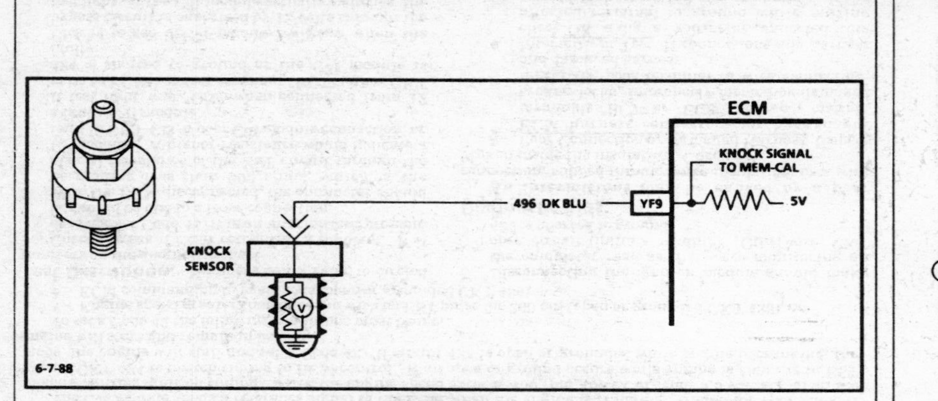

CODE 43

ELECTRONIC SPARK CONTROL (ESC) CIRCUIT 3300 (VIN N) "N" CARLINE (PORT)

Circuit Description:

The knock sensor is used to detect engine detonation and the ECM will retard the electronic spark timing based on the signal being received. The circuitry within the knock sensor causes the ECM's supplied 5 volt signal to be pulled down, so that under a no knock condition CKT 496 would measure about 2.5 volts. The knock sensor produces an A/C signal which rides on the 2.5 volts DC voltage. The amplitude and signal frequency is dependent upon the knock level.

If CKT 496 becomes open or shorted to ground, the voltage will either go above 3.5 volts or below 1.5 volts. If either of these conditions are met for 20 seconds, a Code 43 will be stored.

Code 43 will set if:

- Voltage on CKT 496 goes above 3.5 volts or below 1.5 volts
- Condition present for 20 seconds

Test Description: Numbers below refer to circled numbers on the diagnostic chart.

1. If a Code 43 is detected, the ECM will retard spark timing by 10 degrees.
   If an audible knock is heard from the engine, repair the internal engine problem, normally no knock should be detected at idle.
2. The ECM has a 5 volt pull-up resistor which should be present at the knock sensor terminal.
3. This test determines if the knock sensor is faulty or if the ESC portion of the Mem-Cal is faulty.

Diagnostic Aids:

Check CKT 496 for a potential open or short to ground. Also check for proper installation of Mem-Cal.

If the ESC CKT 496 is routed too close to secondary ignition wires it may induce a voltage and cause a false knock signal.

CODE 43

ELECTRONIC SPARK CONTROL (ESC) CIRCUIT 3300 (VIN N) "N" CARLINE (PORT)

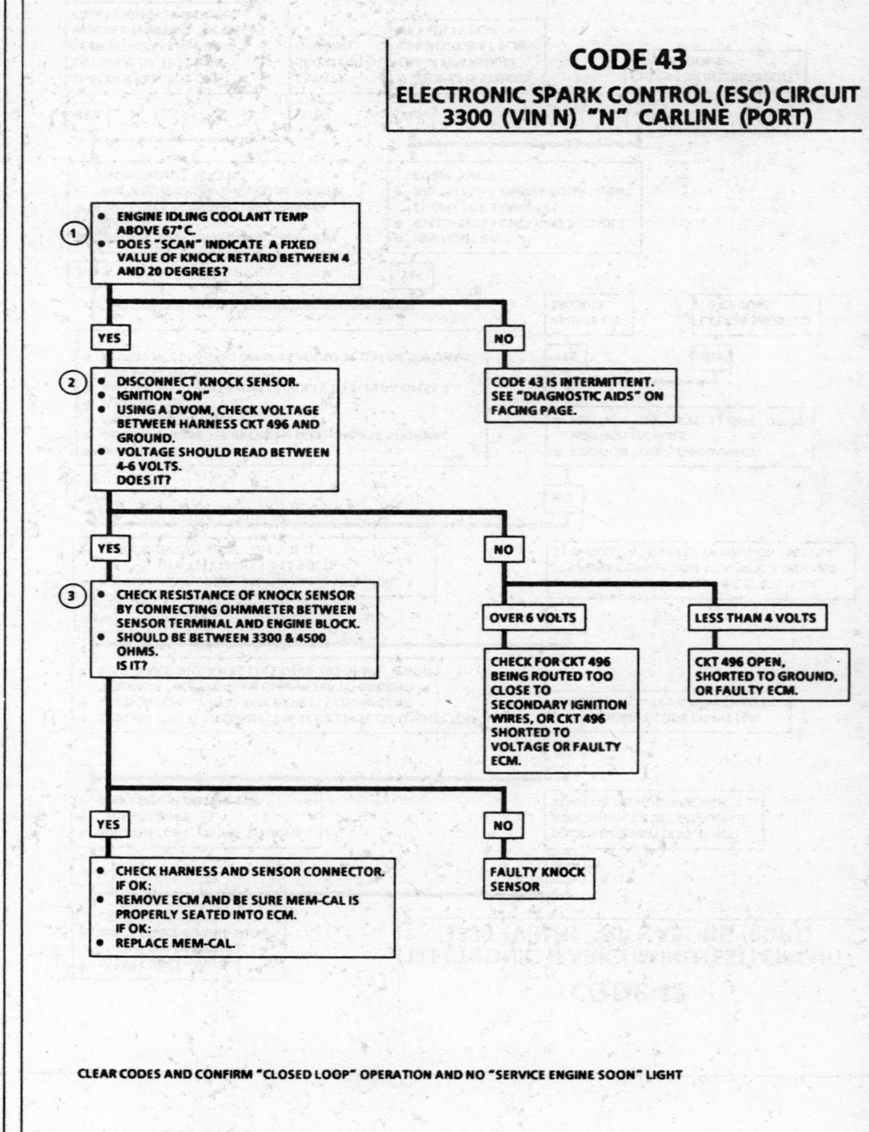

CLEAR CODES AND CONFIRM "CLOSED LOOP" OPERATION AND NO "SERVICE ENGINE SOON" LIGHT

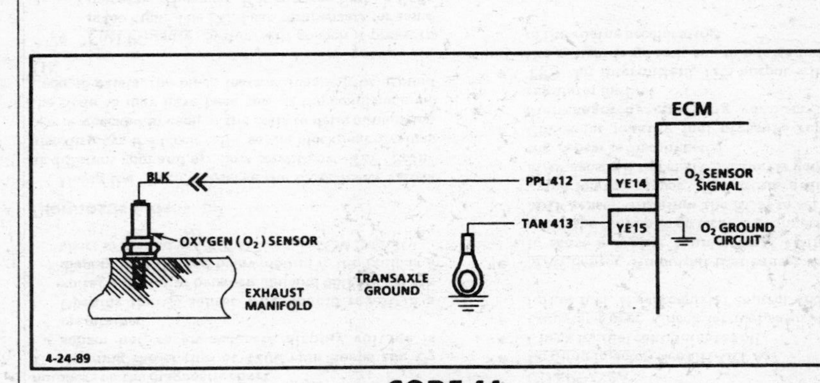

CODE 44

OXYGEN SENSOR CIRCUIT (LEAN EXHAUST INDICATED) 3300 (VIN N) "N" CARLINE (PORT)

Circuit Description:

The ECM supplies a voltage of about .45 volt (450 mV) between terminals "YE14" and "YE15". (If measured with a 10 megohm digital voltmeter, this may read as low as .32 volt.) The O_2 sensor varies the voltage within a range of about 1 volt, (1000 mV) if the exhaust is rich, down through about .10 volt (100 mV) if exhaust is lean.

The sensor is like an open circuit and produces no voltage when it is below about 360°C (600°F). An open sensor circuit or cold sensor causes "Open Loop" operation.

Code 44 is set when the O_2 sensor signal voltage on CKT 412

- Remains below 301 mV for up to 4.5 minutes
- The system is operating in "Closed Loop"

Test Description: Numbers below refer to circled numbers on the diagnostic chart.

1. Running the engine at 1000 rpm keeps the O_2 sensor hot, so an accurate display voltage is maintained.
   Opening the O_2 sensor wire should result in a voltage display of between 350 and 550 mV. If the display is still fixed below 350 mV, the fault is a short to ground in CKT 412 or the ECM is faulty.

Diagnostic Aids:

Using the "Scan," observe the block learn values at different rpm and air flow conditions. The "Scan" also displays the block cells, so the block learn values can be checked in each of the cells to determine when the Code 44 may have been set. If the conditions for Code 44 exists, the block learn values will be around 150.

- O_2 Sensor Wire Sensor pigtail may be mispositioned and contacting the exhaust manifold.
- Check for intermittent ground in wire between connector and sensor.
- MAF Sensor A Mass Air Flow (MAF) sensor output that causes the ECM to sense a lower than normal air flow will cause the system to go lean. Disconnect the MAF sensor and if the lean condition is gone, replace the MAF sensor.
- Lean Injector(s) Perform injector balance test CHART C-2A.
- Fuel Contamination Water, even in small amounts, near the in-tank fuel pump inlet can be delivered to the injectors. The water causes a lean exhaust and can set a Code 44.
- Fuel Pressure System will be lean if pressure is too low. It may be necessary to monitor fuel pressure while driving the car at various road speeds and/or loads to confirm. See "Fuel System Diagnosis," CHART A-7.
- Exhaust Leaks If there is an exhaust leak, the engine can cause outside air to be pulled into the exhaust and past the sensor.
- If the above are OK, it is a faulty oxygen sensor.
- Vacuum or crankcase leaks can cause a lean condition.

CODE 44

OXYGEN SENSOR CIRCUIT (LEAN EXHAUST INDICATED) 3300 (VIN N) "N" CARLINE (PORT)

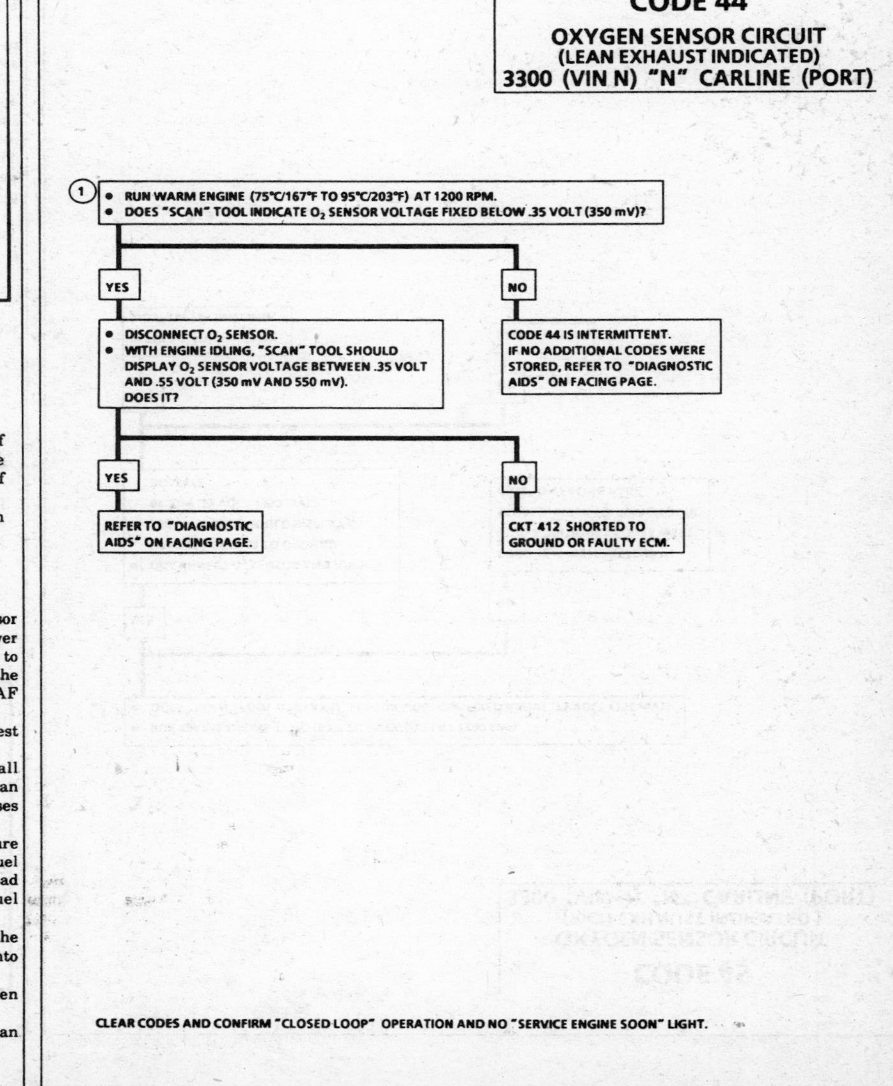

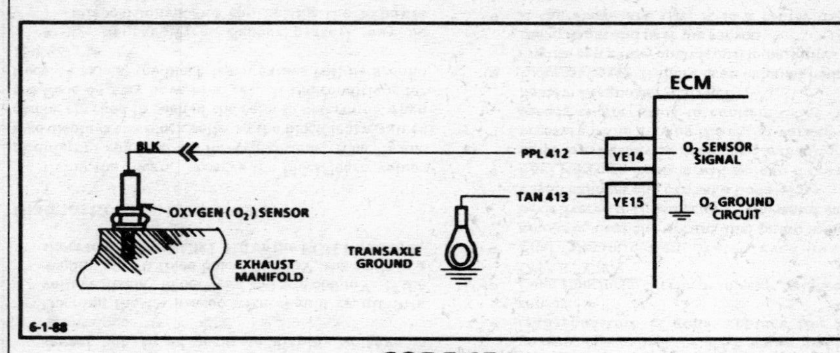

CODE 45

OXYGEN SENSOR CIRCUIT (RICH EXHAUST INDICATED) 3300 (VIN N) "N" CARLINE (PORT)

Circuit Description:

The ECM supplies a voltage of about .45 volt (450 mV) between terminals "YE14" and "YE15". (If measured with a 10 megohm digital voltmeter, this may read as low as .32 volt.) The O_2 sensor varies the voltage within a range of about 1 volt (1000 mV) if the exhaust is rich, down through about .10 volt (100 mV) if exhaust is lean.

The sensor is like an open circuit and produces no voltage when it is below about 360°C (600°F). An open sensor circuit or cold sensor causes "Open Loop" operation.

Code 45 is set when the O_2 sensor signal voltage or CKT 412:

- Remains above .75 volt for 2 minutes and in "Closed Loop"
- Throttle angle between .52 and 1.1 volts
- Engine time after start is 1 minute or more
- No Code 21 or Code 22

Test Description: Numbers below refer to circled numbers on the diagnostic chart.

1. Running the engine at 1200 rpm keeps the O_2 sensor hot, so an accurate display voltage is maintained.
   Opening the O_2 sensor wire should result in a voltage display of between 350 and 550 mV. If the display is still fixed below 350 mV, the fault is a short to ground in CKT 412 or the ECM is faulty.

Diagnostic Aids:

Using the "Scan," observe the block learn values at different rpm and air flow conditions. The "Scan" also displays the block cells, so the block learn values can be checked in each of the cells to determine when the Code 45 may have been set. If the conditions for Code 45 exists, the block learn values will be around 115.

- Fuel Pressure System will go rich if pressure is too high. The ECM can compensate for some increase. However, if it gets too high, a Code 45 may be set. See "Fuel System Diagnosis," CHART A-7.
- Rich Injector Perform injector balance test CHART C-2A.
- Leaking Injector See CHART A-7.
- Check for fuel contaminated oil.
- Canister Purge Check for fuel saturation. If full of fuel, check canister control and hoses.
- MAF Sensor An output that causes the ECM to sense a higher than normal airflow can cause the system to go rich. Disconnecting the MAF sensor will allow the ECM to set a fixed value for the sensor. Substitute a different MAF sensor if the rich condition is gone while the sensor is disconnected.
- Check for leaking fuel pressure regulator diaphragm by checking vacuum line to regulator for fuel.
- TPS An intermittent TPS output will cause the system to go rich due to a false indication of the engine accelerating.

CODE 45

OXYGEN SENSOR CIRCUIT (RICH EXHAUST INDICATED) 3300 (VIN N) "N" CARLINE (PORT)

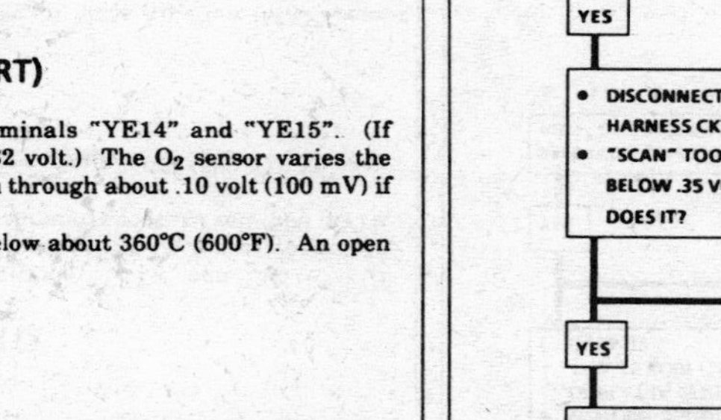

(1)
- RUN WARM ENGINE (75°C/167°F TO 95°C/203°F) AT 1200 RPM.
- DOES "SCAN" TOOL DISPLAY O_2 SENSOR VOLTAGE FIXED ABOVE .75 VOLT (750 mV)?

YES:
- DISCONNECT O_2 SENSOR AND JUMPER HARNESS CKT 412 TO GROUND.
- "SCAN" TOOL SHOULD DISPLAY O_2 BELOW .35 VOLT (350 mV).

DOES IT?

YES: REFER TO "DIAGNOSTIC AIDS" ON FACING PAGE.

NO: REPLACE ECM.

NO: CODE 45 IS INTERMITTENT. IF NO ADDITIONAL CODES WERE STORED, REFER TO "DIAGNOSTIC AIDS" ON FACING PAGE.

CLEAR CODES AND CONFIRM "CLOSED LOOP" OPERATION AND NO "SERVICE ENGINE SOON" LIGHT.

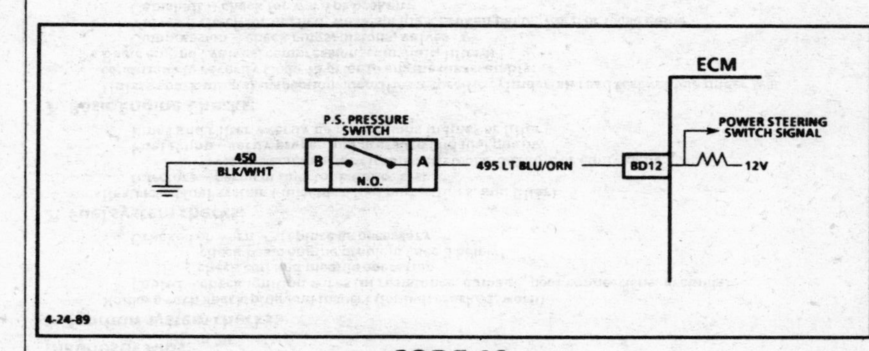

CODE 46

POWER STEERING PRESSURE SWITCH (PSPS) CIRCUIT 3300 (VIN N) "N" CARLINE (PORT)

Circuit Description:

The power steering pressure switch is incorporated as an ECM discrete input signal representing the parasitic load placed on the engine during high power steering demand periods, such as parking. This load may cause the engine to stall under high power steering pump pressure conditions, therefore, the ECM compensates by automatically increasing the engine idle speed, via IAC whenever the switch closes and a low voltage is monitored at ECM terminal "BD12". This low voltage indicates a high pressure within the power steering system resulting from high demand. The ECM turns the current "OFF" to the A/C compressor relay so the A/C clutch is disengaged to further reduce engine load.

To set a Code 46, the following conditions must be met:

- Closed power steering switch. "LO" (low voltage potential)
- Vehicle speed is greater than 40 mph
- Both conditions existing for a time greater than 15 seconds

Test Description: Numbers below refer to circled numbers on the diagnostic chart.

1. Tests for normally open power steering switch.
2. This step determines whether the fault is in the switch or the circuit. A jumpered switch connector should normally indicate "HI" if the circuit is complete. If so, the power steering pressure switch or connection is faulty.
3. If the display switches to "HI" when CKT 495 is grounded, the fault is an open in CKT 450.

Diagnostic Aids:

An intermittent may be caused by a poor connection, rubbed through wire insulation or a wire broken inside the insulation.

Check For:

- Poor Connection or Damaged Harness Inspect ECM harness connectors for backed out terminal "BD12", improper mating, broken locks, improperly formed or damaged terminals, poor terminal to wire connection, and damaged harness.
- Intermittent Test If connections and harness check OK, monitor power steering pressure switch display while moving related connectors and wiring harness. If the failure is induced, the power steering pressure switch display will abruptly change. This may help to isolate the location of the malfunction.

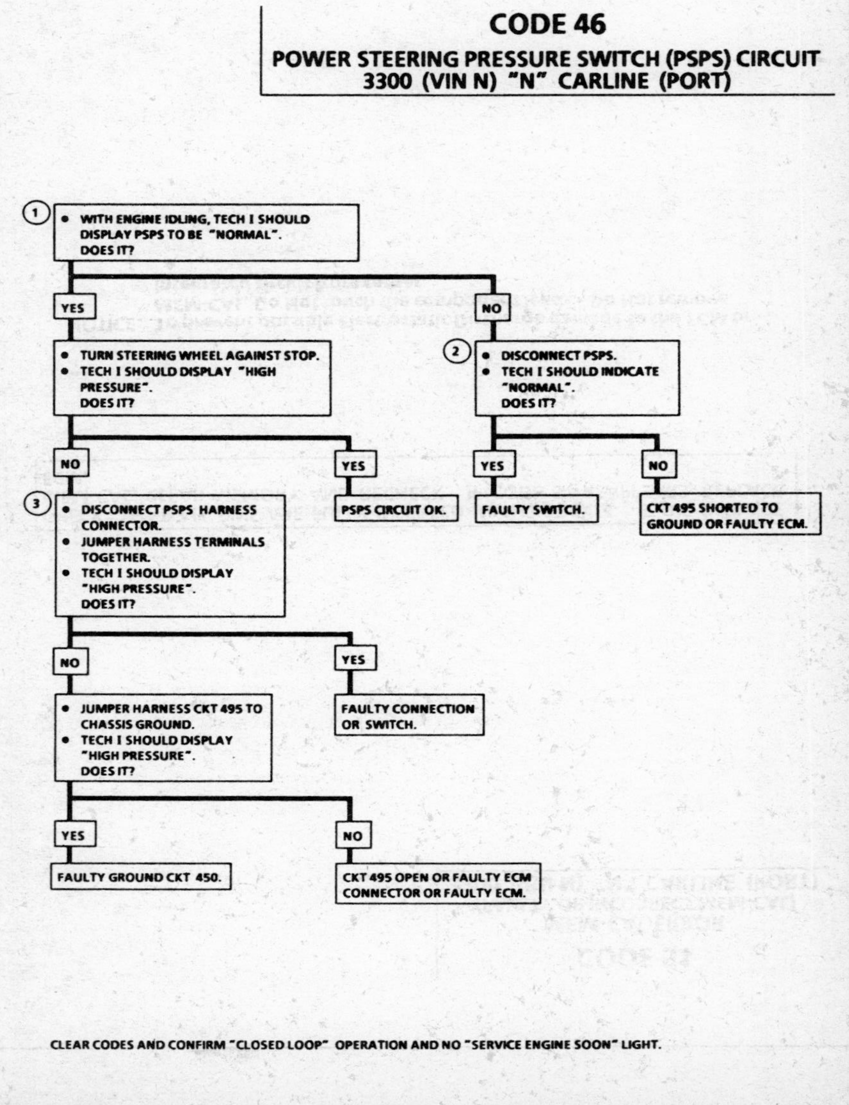

DIAGNOSTIC CHARTS — 3.3L ENGINE

CODE 48

MISFIRE DIAGNOSIS
3300 (VIN N) "N" CARLINE (PORT)

If multiple codes are set, go to the lowest code first.
Repairing for a Code 13, 44, or 45 may correct Code 48.

Test Description:

Code 48 will set if the following:

- TPS is between .58 and 1.02 volts.
- Rpm is between 1500 and 2500.
- Mph is between 50 and 60.
- O_2 cross counts greater than 30.
- All of the above for 30 seconds.

O_2 Sensor Test:

Code 48 could be set if the O_2 sensor is degraded and cannot travel over the full rich to lean voltage range. This narrowed range could allow O_2 cross counts to be above the value necessary to set the code.

- WITH "SCAN" TOOL INSTALLED, VERIFY ENGINE IS AT NORMAL OPERATING TEMPERATURE AND IN "CLOSED LOOP".

- ENGINE IDLING IN PARK.
- SELECT O_2 SENSOR POSITION ON "SCAN".
- RAPIDLY FLASH THE THROTTLE FROM IDLE TO NEAR WIDE OPEN THROTTLE AND BACK WHILE OBSERVING O_2 VOLTAGE.
- REPEAT IF NECESSARY TO CONFIRM VOLTAGE RANGE, AND "CLOSED LOOP".

VOLTAGE EXCEEDS 250-750 mV RANGE. → O_2 SENSOR OK, SEE "DIAGNOSTIC AIDS".

VOLTAGE REMAINS WITHIN 250-750 mV RANGE. → REPLACE O_2 SENSOR.

Diagnostic Aids:

1. Ignition system checks:

Remove each spark plug and inspect (fouled, cracked, worn)
Fouled -- check ignition wires (hi resistance, damage, poor connections, grounds)
check coil and module operation
check basic engine problem (see 3 below)
Cracked or worn -- replace as necessary

2. Fuel system checks:

Restricted fuel system (injectors, fuel pump, lines, and filter)
Injectors -- perform injector balance test
verify each injector circuit with tool J-34730-2 or equivalent
Fuel Pump --verify proper fuel pressure and fuel quality
Lines and Filter --verify no restrictions in lines or filter

3. Basic Engine Checks:

Unless spark plug(s) inspection identifies a specific cylinder(s), road test vehicle under test conditions to reverify Code 48 prior to engine disassembly.
Basic engine (valves, compression, camshaft, lifters)
Compression -- check rings, pistons, valves
Valves -- check for burned, weak springs, broken parts, worn or loose guide
Camshaft -- check for worn or broken
Lifters -- check for worn, broken
For additional items see Section "B" under "Rough Unstable Idle", "Hard Start", or "Hesitation, Sag, or Stumble".

CODE 51

MEM-CAL ERROR
(FAULTY OR INCORRECT MEM-CAL)
3300 (VIN N) "N" CARLINE (PORT)

CHECK THAT ALL PINS ARE FULLY INSERTED IN THE SOCKET. IF OK, REPLACE MEM-CAL, CLEAR MEMORY AND RECHECK. IF CODE 51 REAPPEARS, REPLACE ECM.

NOTICE: To prevent possible Electrostatic Discharge damage to the ECM or MEM-CAL, Do Not touch the component leads. Do Not remove integrated circuit from carrier.

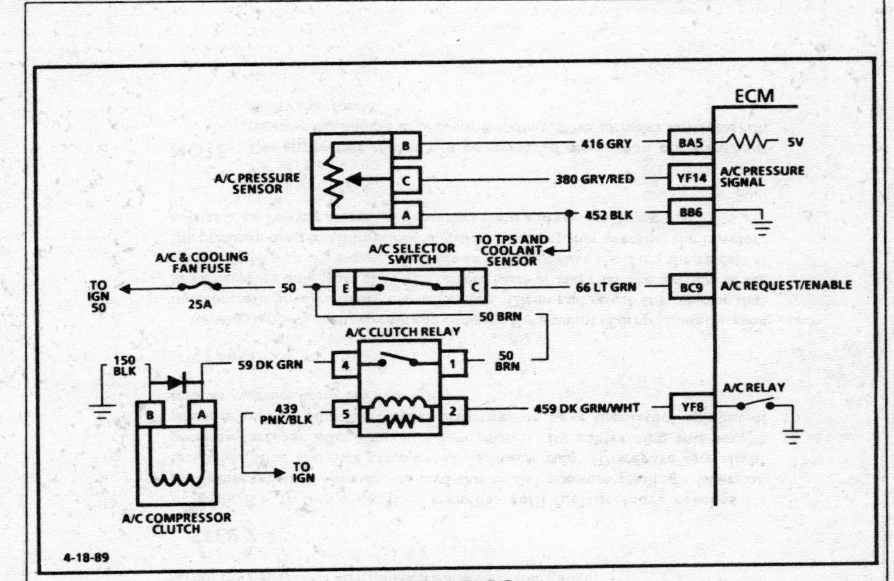

CODE 66

A/C PRESSURE SENSOR CIRCUIT 3300 (VIN N) "N" CARLINE (PORT)

Circuit Description:

The A/C pressure sensor responds to changes in A/C refrigerant system high side pressure. This input indicates how much load the A/C compressor is putting on the engine and is one of the factors used by the ECM to determine IAC valve position for idle speed control. The circuit consists of a 5 volts reference and a ground, both provided by the ECM, and a signal line to the ECM. The signal is a voltage which is proportional to the pressure. The sensor's range of operation is 165 to 399 psi. At 165 psi or less, the signal will be about .5 volt, varying up to about 4.5 volts at 399 psi or above. Code 66 sets if the voltage falls outside of calibrated minimum and less than .1 volt or more than 4.9 volts for 25 seconds, while the A/C is requested on. The A/C compressor is disabled by the ECM if Code 66 is present.

Test Description: Numbers below refer to circled numbers on the diagnostic chart.

1. This step checks the voltage signal being received by the ECM from the A/C pressure sensor. The normal operating range is between .5 volt and 4.5 volts.
2. Checks to see if the high voltage signal is from a shorted sensor or a short to voltage in the circuit. Normally, disconnecting the sensor would make a normal circuit go to near zero volts.
3. Checks to see if low voltage signal is from the sensor or the circuit. Jumpering the sensor signal CKT 380 to 5 volts, checks the circuit, connections, and ECM.
4. This step checks to see if the low voltage signal was due to an open in the sensor circuit or the 5 volts reference circuit since the prior step eliminated the pressure switch.

Diagnostic Aids:

Code 66 sets when signal voltage falls outside the normal possible range of the sensor and is not due to a refrigerant system problem. If problem is intermittent, check for opens or shorts in harness or poor connections. If OK, replace A/C pressure sensor. If Code 66 re-sets, replace ECM.

CODE 66

A/C PRESSURE SENSOR CIRCUIT 3300 (VIN N) "N" CARLINE (PORT)

NOTE: IF CAR IS NOT EQUIPPED WITH AIR CONDITIONING, DO NOT USE THIS CHART, SEE "DIAGNOSTIC AIDS".

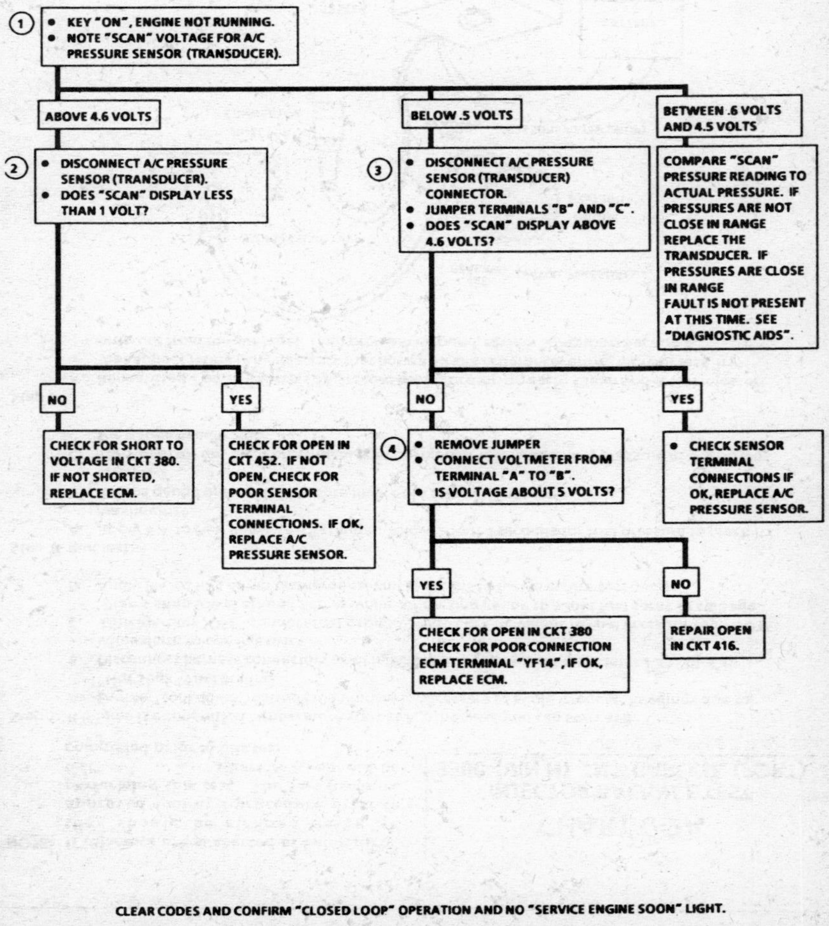

(1)
- KEY "ON", ENGINE NOT RUNNING.
- NOTE "SCAN" VOLTAGE FOR A/C PRESSURE SENSOR (TRANSDUCER).

ABOVE 4.6 VOLTS

(2)
- DISCONNECT A/C PRESSURE SENSOR (TRANSDUCER).
- DOES "SCAN" DISPLAY LESS THAN 1 VOLT?

- NO: CHECK FOR SHORT TO VOLTAGE IN CKT 380. IF NOT SHORTED, REPLACE ECM.
- YES: CHECK FOR OPEN IN CKT 452. IF NOT OPEN, CHECK FOR POOR SENSOR TERMINAL CONNECTIONS. IF OK, REPLACE A/C PRESSURE SENSOR.

BELOW .5 VOLTS

(3)
- DISCONNECT A/C PRESSURE SENSOR (TRANSDUCER) CONNECTOR.
- JUMPER TERMINALS "B" AND "C".
- DOES "SCAN" DISPLAY ABOVE 4.6 VOLTS?

- NO:

  (4)
  - REMOVE JUMPER
  - CONNECT VOLTMETER FROM TERMINAL "A" TO "B".
  - IS VOLTAGE ABOUT 5 VOLTS?

  - YES: CHECK FOR OPEN IN CKT 380. CHECK FOR POOR CONNECTION ECM TERMINAL "YF14". IF OK, REPLACE ECM.
  - NO: REPAIR OPEN IN CKT 416.
- YES:
  - CHECK SENSOR TERMINAL CONNECTIONS IF OK, REPLACE A/C PRESSURE SENSOR.

BETWEEN .6 VOLTS AND 4.5 VOLTS

COMPARE "SCAN" PRESSURE READING TO ACTUAL PRESSURE. IF PRESSURES ARE NOT CLOSE IN RANGE REPLACE THE TRANSDUCER. IF PRESSURES ARE CLOSE IN RANGE FAULT IS NOT PRESENT AT THIS TIME. SEE "DIAGNOSTIC AIDS".

CLEAR CODES AND CONFIRM "CLOSED LOOP" OPERATION AND NO "SERVICE ENGINE SOON" LIGHT.

CHART C-2A

INJECTOR BALANCE TEST

The injector balance tester is a tool used to turn the injector on for a precise amount of time, thus spraying a measured amount of fuel into the manifold. This causes a drop in fuel rail pressure that we can record and compare between each injector. All injectors should have the same amount of pressure drop (± 10 kPa). Any injector with a pressure drop that is 10 kPa (or more) greater than the average drop of the other injectors should be considered faulty and replaced. Any injector with a pressure drop of less than 10 kPa from the average drop of the other injectors should be cleaned and retested.

STEP 1

Engine "cool down" period (10 minutes) is necessary to avoid irregular readings due to "Hot Soak" fuel boiling.
Disconnect harness connectors at all injectors, and connect injector tester J 34730-3, or equivalent, to one injector. With ignition "OFF" connect fuel gauge J 347301 or equivalent to fuel pressure tap. Wrap a shop towel around fitting while connecting gage to avoid fuel spillage. At this point, insert clear tubing attached to vent valve into a suitable container and bleed air from gauge and hose to insure accurate gauge operation, by applying B+ to fuel pump test terminal. Repeat this step until all air is bled from gauge.

STEP 2

Apply B+ to fuel pump test terminal until fuel pressure reaches its maximum, about 3 seconds. Record this initial pressure reading. Energize tester one time and note pressure at its lowest point (Disregard any slight pressure increase after drop hits low point.). By subtracting this second pressure reading from the initial pressure, we have the actual amount of injector pressure drop. See note below.

STEP 3

Repeat step 2 on each injector and compare the amount of drop. Usually, good injectors will have virtually the same drop. Clean and retest any injector that has a pressure difference of 10 kPa, either more or less than the average of the other injectors on the engine. Replace any injector that also fails the retest. If the pressure drop of all injectors is within 10kPa of this average, the injectors appear to be flowing properly. Reconnect them and review "Symptoms,"

NOTE: ***The entire test should <u>not</u> be repeated more than once without running the engine to prevent flooding. (This includes any retest on faulty injectors).***

CHART C-2A

INJECTOR BALANCE TEST
3300 (VIN N) "N" CARLINE (PORT)

<u>NOTE:</u> **If injectors are suspected of being dirty, they should be cleaned using an approved tool and procedure prior to performing this test. The fuel pressure test Chart A-7, should be completed prior to this test.**

Step 1. If engine is at operation temperature start at A, otherwise you can start at B
- A. Engine "cool down" period (10 minutes) is necessary to avoid Irregular Readings due to "Hot Soak" Fuel Boiling.
- B. Disconnect harness connectors at all injectors and connect injector tester J-34730-3, or equivalent, to one injector.
- C. With ignition "OFF" connect fuel gauge J-347301 or equivalent to Fuel Pressure Tap. NOTE: Wrap a shop towel around fitting while connecting gauge to avoid fuel spray or spillage.
- D. Apply B + to fuel pump test terminal and bleed off to fuel pressure test gauge.

Step 2. Run test:
- A. Apply B + to Fuel Pump Test Terminal. Allow about 3 seconds for fuel pressure to reach its maximum.
- B. Record gauge pressure. (Pressure must hold steady, if not see Chart A-7
- C. Turn injector on, by depressing button on injector tester, and note pressure at the instant the gauge needle stops.

Step 3.
- A. Repeat step 2 on all injectors and record pressure drop on each. Clean and retest injectors that appear faulty (Any injectors that have a 10 kPa difference, either more or less, in pressure from the average). If no problem is found, review Symptoms Section B.

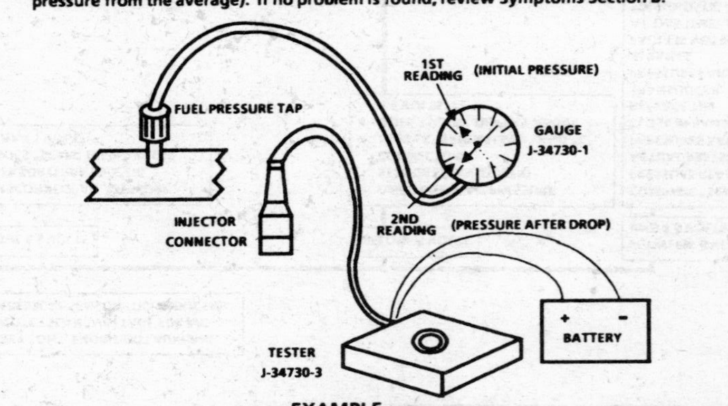

— EXAMPLE —

CYLINDER	1	2	3	4	5	6
1ST READING	225	225	225	225	225	225
2ND READING	100	100	100	90	100	115
AMOUNT OF DROP	125	125	125	135	125	110
	OK	OK	OK	FAULTY, RICH (TOO MUCH) (FUEL DROP)	OK	FAULTY, LEAN (TOO LITTLE) (FUEL DROP)

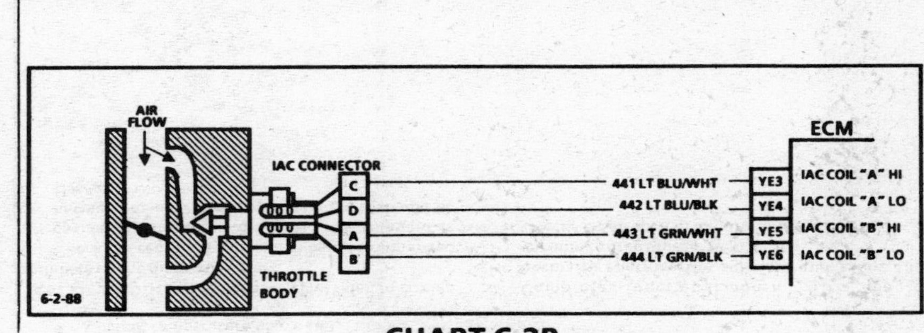

CHART C-2B

IDLE AIR CONTROL (IAC) VALVE CHECK 3300 (VIN N) "N" CARLINE (PORT)

Circuit Description:

The ECM controls idle rpm with the IAC valve. To increase idle rpm, the ECM retracts the IAC pintle, allowing more air to bypass the throttle plate. To decrease rpm, it extends the IAC pintle valve, reducing air flow through the IAC valve port in the throttle body. A "Scan" tool will read the ECM commands to the IAC valve in counts. The higher the counts, the more air allowed (higher idle). The lower the counts, the less air allowed (lower idle). The ECM learns a new IAC position every time the ignition is cycled and in "Closed Loop" with the transmission in drive. This is to control engine speed at different idle conditions.

Test Description: Numbers below refer to circled numbers on the diagnostic chart.

1. The Tech I is used to extend and retract the IAC valve. Valve movement is verified by an engine speed change.
2. This test checks all wires, connectors, and the ECM.
3. This test checks for shorted or open IAC valve coils.

Diagnostic Aids:

A slow, unstable idle may be caused by a system problem that cannot be overcome by the IAC. "Scan" counts will be above 60 counts, if idle speed is too low. If idle speed is too high, IAC counts will be "0".

- System lean (High Air/Fuel Ratio)
  Idle speed may be too high or too low. Engine speed may vary up and down, disconnecting IAC does not help. May set Code 44.
  "Scan" and/or voltmeter will read an oxygen sensor output less than 300 mV (.3 volt). Check for low regulated fuel pressure or water in fuel. A lean exhaust, with an oxygen sensor output fixed above 800 mV (.8 volt indicating rich exhaust to ECM), will be a contaminated sensor, usually silicone. This may also set Code 45.
- System rich (Low Air/Fuel Ratio)
  Idle speed too low. "Scan" counts usually above 80. System obviously rich and may exhibit black smoke exhaust.
  "Scan" tool and/or voltmeter will read an oxygen sensor signal fixed above 800 mV (.8 volt).
  Check:
  - High fuel pressure
  - Injector leaking or sticking
- Throttle Body - Remove IAC and inspect bore for foreign material or evidence of IAC pintle dragging the bore.
- Refer to "Rough, Unstable, Incorrect Idle or Stalling" in "Symptoms"

CHART C-2B

IDLE AIR CONTROL (IAC) VALVE CHECK 3300 (VIN N) "N" CARLINE (PORT)

(1)
- ENGINE AT NORMAL OPERATING TEMPERATURE IN PARK/NEUTRAL WITH PARKING BRAKE SET.
- INSTALL TECH 1.
- SELECT RPM CONTROL (MISC. TESTS).
- CYCLE IAC THROUGH ITS RANGE FROM 700 RPM UP TO 1500 RPM.
- RPM SHOULD CHANGE SMOOTHLY. DOES IT?

NO →

(2)
- DISCONNECT IAC MOTOR CONNECTOR.
- INSTALL IAC NODE LIGHT J 37027 OR EQUIVALENT IN IAC HARNESS.
- ENGINE RUNNING. CYCLE IAC WITH TECH 1.
- EACH NODE LIGHT SHOULD CYCLE RED AND GREEN BUT NEVER "OFF." DO THEY?

NO → IF CIRCUIT (S) 441, 442, 443, OR 444 DID NOT TEST RED AND GREEN, CHECK FOR:
- FAULTY CONNECTOR TERMINAL CONTACTS.
- OPEN CIRCUITS INCLUDING CONNECTORS.
- CIRCUITS SHORTED TO GROUND OR VOLTAGE.

ARE CKT'S OK?

YES →
- FAULTY ECM CONNECTIONS OR REPLACE ECM.

REPAIR AS NECESSARY AND RETEST.

NO → REPAIR CKT AND RETEST.

YES →
- CHECK IAC CONNECTIONS.
- CHECK IAC PASSAGES.
- IF OK, REPLACE IAC.

YES →

(3)
- DISCONNECT IAC MOTOR HARNESS.
- INSTALL IAC MOTOR TESTER J 37027 OR EQUIVALENT.

USING THE OTHER CONNECTOR ON THE IAC TESTER PIGTAIL, CHECK RESISTANCE ACROSS IAC COILS. SHOULD BE 40 TO 80 OHMS BETWEEN IAC TERMINALS "A" TO "B" AND "C" TO "D".

OK → CHECK RESISTANCE BETWEEN IAC TERMINALS "B" AND "C" AND "A" AND "D". SHOULD BE INFINITE.

OK → IDLE AIR CONTROL CIRCUIT OK. REFER TO "DIAGNOSTIC AIDS" ON FACING PAGE.

NOT OK → REPLACE IAC VALVE AND RETEST.

NOT OK → REPLACE IAC VALVE AND RETEST.

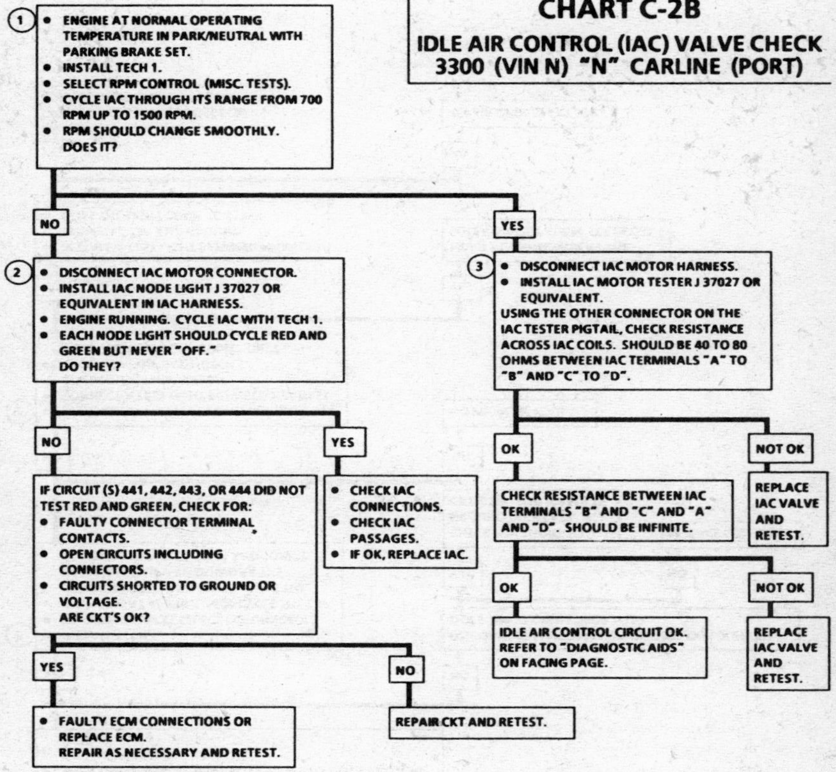

CLEAR CODES, CONFIRM "CLOSED LOOP" OPERATION, NO "SERVICE ENGINE SOON" LIGHT, PERFORM IAC RESET PROCEDURE PER APPLICABLE SERVICE MANUAL AND VERIFY CONTROLLED IDLE SPEED IS CORRECT.

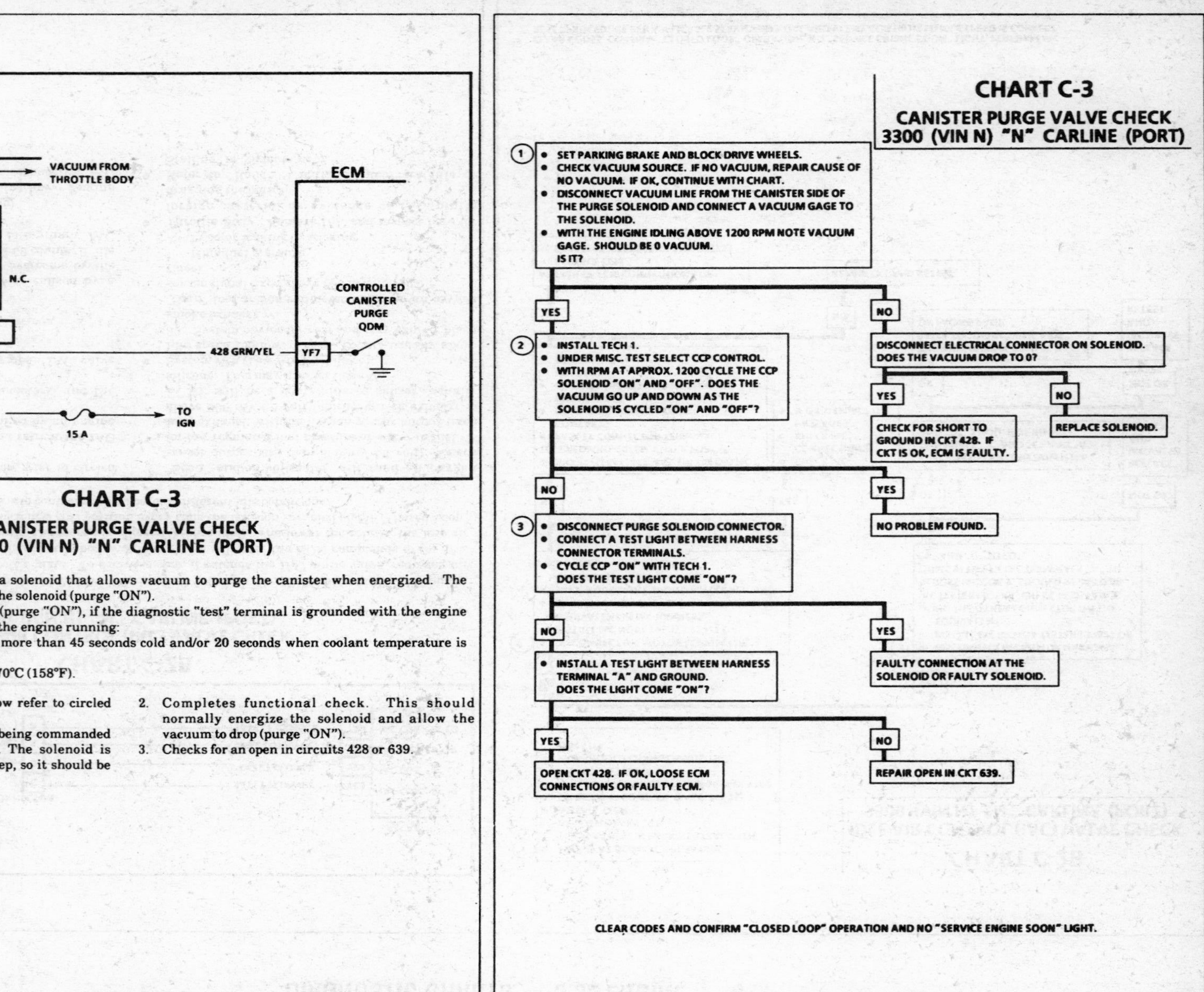

CHART C-3

CANISTER PURGE VALVE CHECK 3300 (VIN N) "N" CARLINE (PORT)

Circuit Description:

Canister purge is controlled by a solenoid that allows vacuum to purge the canister when energized. The ECM supplies a ground to energize the solenoid (purge "ON").

The purge solenoid is energized (purge "ON"), if the diagnostic "test" terminal is grounded with the engine stopped or the following is met with the engine running:

- Engine run time after start more than 45 seconds cold and/or 20 seconds when coolant temperature is greater than 85°C (185°F).
- Coolant temperature above 70°C (158°F).

Test Description: Numbers below refer to circled numbers on the diagnostic chart.

1. Checks to see if the solenoid is being commanded opened or closed by the ECM. The solenoid is normally de-energized in this step, so it should be closed.
2. Completes functional check. This should normally energize the solenoid and allow the vacuum to drop (purge "ON").
3. Checks for an open in circuits 428 or 639.

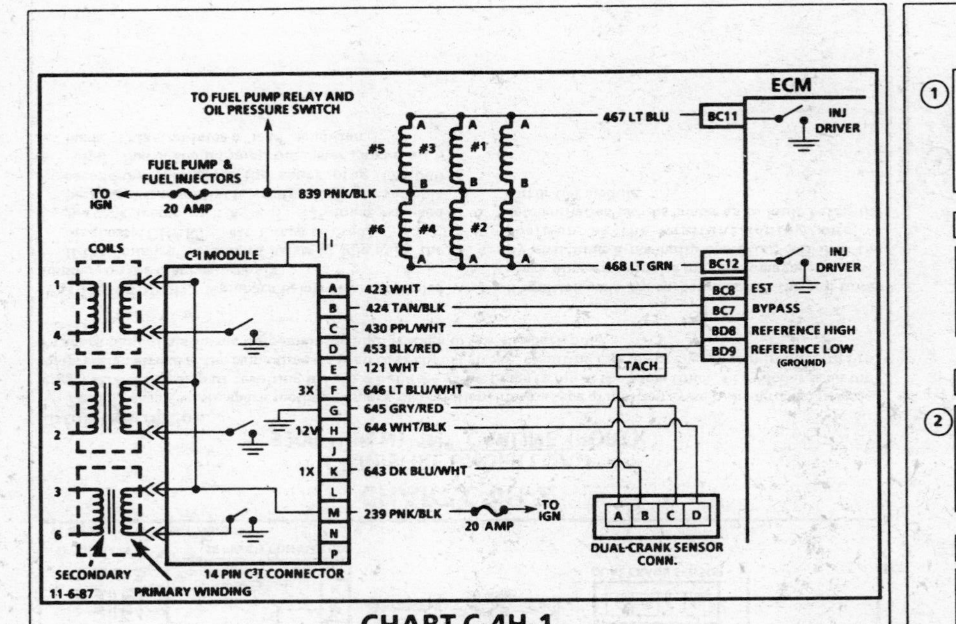

CHART C-4H-1

C3I MISFIRE AT IDLE
3300 (VIN N) (PORT)

Circuit Description:

The C3I uses a waste spark method of spark distribution. In this type of ignition system the ignition module triggers the #1/4 coil pair resulting in both #1 and #4 spark plugs firing at the same time. #1 cylinder is on the compression stroke at the same time #4 is on the exhaust stroke, resulting in a lower energy requirement to fire #4 spark plug. This leaves the remaining high voltage to fire #1 spark plug.

Test Description: Numbers below refer to circled numbers on the diagnostic chart.

1. If the "misfire" complaint exists under load only, the diagnostic CHART C-4H-2 must be used. Engine rpm should drop approximately equally on all plug leads.
2. A spark tester such as a ST-125 must be used because it is essential to verify adequate available secondary voltage at the spark plug. (25,000 volts). Secondary voltage of at least (25,000 volts) must be present to jump the gap of a ST-125.
3. If ignition coils are carbon tracked, the coil tower spark plug wire nipples may be damaged.
4. By checking the secondary resistance, a coil with an open secondary may be located.
5. By switching a normally operating coil into the position of the malfunctioning one, a determination can be made as to fault being the coil or C3I module.

CHART C-4H-1

C3I MISFIRE AT IDLE
3300 (VIN N) "N" CARLINE (PORT)

(1)
- IF ENGINE MISFIRES AT IDLE ONLY, SEE CHART C-4H-1.
- ENGINE IDLING AT NORMAL OPERATING TEMPERATURE, DISCONNECT IAC.
- MOMENTARILY DISCONNECT EACH INJECTOR CONNECTOR, WHILE OBSERVING ENGINE RPM.
- ALL INJECTOR(S) SHOULD RESULT IN AN RPM DROP. DOES IT?

YES: CHECK FOR;
- FAULTY, WORN OR CRACKED SPARK PLUG(S)
- PLUG FOULING DUE TO ENGINE MECHANICAL FAULT.

IF SPARK PLUGS CHECK OUT OK, SEE "CUTS OUT, MISSES" IN "SYMPTOMS"

NO:
- IGNITION "OFF," INSTALL INJECTOR TESTER J 3470-2 OR EQUIVALENT ON INJECTOR CONNECTOR WHICH DID NOT RESULT IN AN RPM DROP.
- LIGHT SHOULD "BLINK" WHILE CRANKING ENGINE. DID IT?

NO: SEE CHART A-3 SECTION "A"

YES:

(2)
- IGNITION "OFF," INSTALL SPARK TESTER (ST-125) J 26792 OR EQUIVALENT ON PLUG LEAD(S) WHICH DID NOT RESULT IN RPM DROP (1,3,5 AT PLUG AND 2,4,6 AT COIL).
- SPARK SHOULD JUMP TESTER GAP WHILE CRANKING ENGINE. DOES IT?

YES: REPLACE THE SPARK PLUG FOR THE LEAD WHICH WAS CONNECTED TO SPARK TESTER (ST-125) J 26792 OR EQUIVALENT. IS MISFIRE STILL PRESENT? START MISFIRE TEST AGAIN AT STEP #1.

NO:
- CHECK THE RESISTANCE OF PLUG WIRE WHICH DID NOT FIRE THE SPARK TESTER.
- WIRE RESISTANCE SHOULD BE LESS THAN 30,000 OHMS AND SHOULD NOT BE GROUNDED. ARE WIRES OK?

NO: REPLACE FAULTY WIRE (S)

YES:

(3)
- REMOVE COIL FROM MODULE
- INSPECT COILS, PLUG WIRES AND PLUG WIRE NIPPLES. THEY SHOULD BE FREE OF CARBON TRACKING. ARE THEY?

NO: REPLACE FAULTY COMPONENT.

YES:
- CHECK SECONDARY COIL RESISTANCE. SHOULD BE 5-8K OHMS RESISTANCE. IS IT?

NO: REPLACE COIL

YES:

(4)
- INSTALL A KNOWN GOOD COIL.
- SPARK SHOULD JUMP TESTER GAP AT PROBLEM CYLINDER WITH ENGINE IDLING. DID IT?

YES: ORIGINAL IGNITION COIL IS FAULTY

NO: FAULTY C3I MODULE

CLEAR CODES AND CONFIRM "CLOSED LOOP" OPERATION AND NO "SERVICE ENGINE SOON" LIGHT.

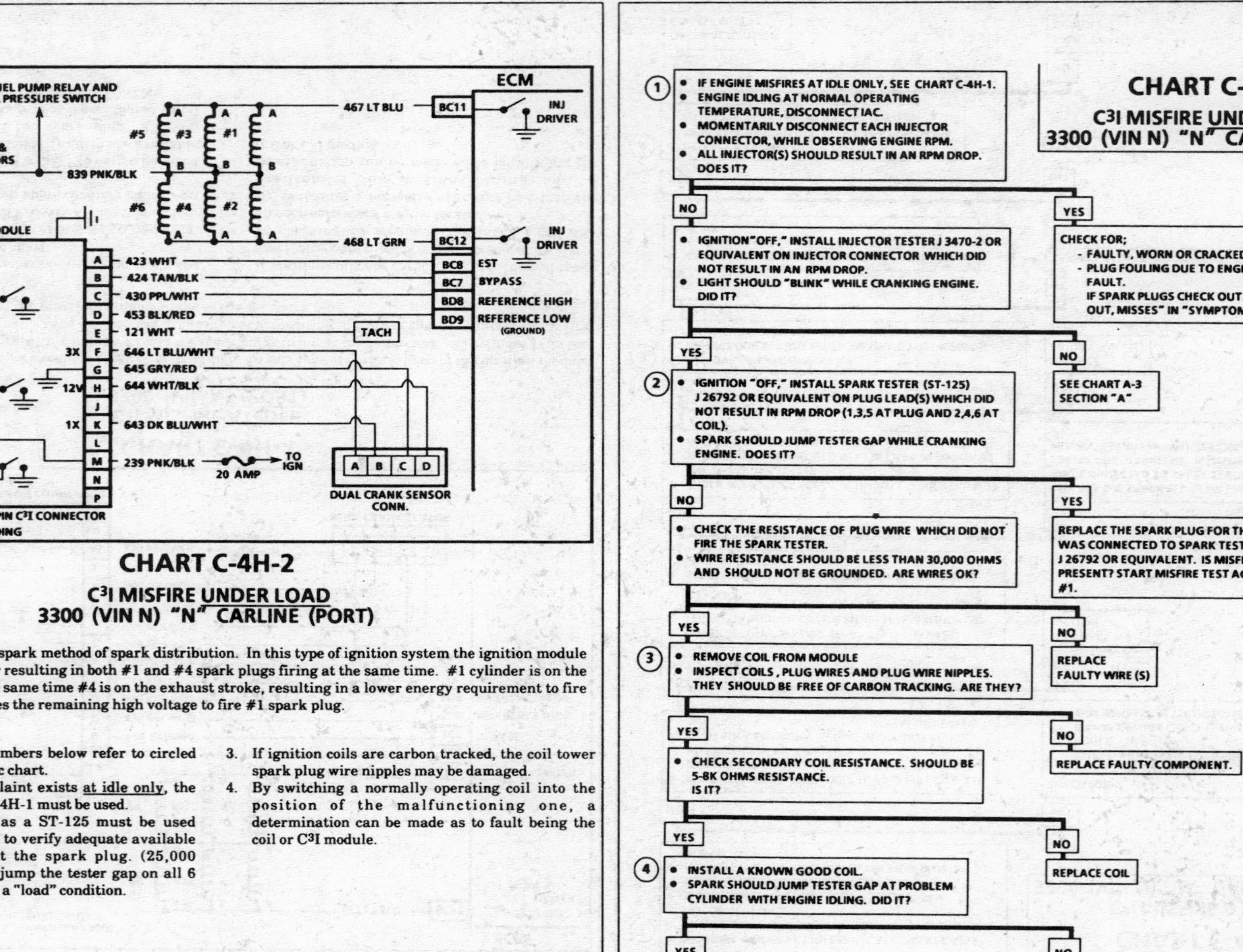

CHART C-4H-2

C³I MISFIRE UNDER LOAD
3300 (VIN N) "N" CARLINE (PORT)

Circuit Description:

The C³I uses a waste spark method of spark distribution. In this type of ignition system the ignition module triggers the #1/4 coil pair resulting in both #1 and #4 spark plugs firing at the same time. #1 cylinder is on the compression stroke at the same time #4 is on the exhaust stroke, resulting in a lower energy requirement to fire #4 spark plug. This leaves the remaining high voltage to fire #1 spark plug.

Test Description: Numbers below refer to circled numbers on the diagnostic chart.

1. If the "misfire" complaint exists at idle only, the diagnostic CHART C-4H-1 must be used.
2. A spark tester such as a ST-125 must be used because it is essential to verify adequate available secondary voltage at the spark plug. (25,000 volts). Spark should jump the tester gap on all 6 leads. This simulates a "load" condition.
3. If ignition coils are carbon tracked, the coil tower spark plug wire nipples may be damaged.
4. By switching a normally operating coil into the position of the malfunctioning one, a determination can be made as to fault being the coil or C³I module.

CHART C-4H-2

C³I MISFIRE UNDER LOAD
3300 (VIN N) "N" CARLINE (PORT)

(1)
- IF ENGINE MISFIRES AT IDLE ONLY, SEE CHART C-4H-1.
- ENGINE IDLING AT NORMAL OPERATING TEMPERATURE, DISCONNECT IAC.
- MOMENTARILY DISCONNECT EACH INJECTOR CONNECTOR, WHILE OBSERVING ENGINE RPM.
- ALL INJECTOR(S) SHOULD RESULT IN AN RPM DROP. DOES IT?

YES: CHECK FOR;
- FAULTY, WORN OR CRACKED SPARK PLUG(S)
- PLUG FOULING DUE TO ENGINE MECHANICAL FAULT.

IF SPARK PLUGS CHECK OUT OK, SEE "CUTS OUT, MISSES" IN "SYMPTOMS"

NO:
- IGNITION "OFF," INSTALL INJECTOR TESTER J 3470-2 OR EQUIVALENT ON INJECTOR CONNECTOR WHICH DID NOT RESULT IN AN RPM DROP.
- LIGHT SHOULD "BLINK" WHILE CRANKING ENGINE. DID IT?

NO: SEE CHART A-3 SECTION "A"

YES:

(2)
- IGNITION "OFF," INSTALL SPARK TESTER (ST-125) J 26792 OR EQUIVALENT ON PLUG LEAD(S) WHICH DID NOT RESULT IN RPM DROP (1,3,5 AT PLUG AND 2,4,6 AT COIL).
- SPARK SHOULD JUMP TESTER GAP WHILE CRANKING ENGINE. DOES IT?

YES: REPLACE THE SPARK PLUG FOR THE LEAD WHICH WAS CONNECTED TO SPARK TESTER (ST-125) J 26792 OR EQUIVALENT. IS MISFIRE STILL PRESENT? START MISFIRE TEST AGAIN AT STEP #1.

NO:
- CHECK THE RESISTANCE OF PLUG WIRE WHICH DID NOT FIRE THE SPARK TESTER.
- WIRE RESISTANCE SHOULD BE LESS THAN 30,000 OHMS AND SHOULD NOT BE GROUNDED. ARE WIRES OK?

NO: REPLACE FAULTY WIRE (S)

YES:

(3)
- REMOVE COIL FROM MODULE
- INSPECT COILS, PLUG WIRES AND PLUG WIRE NIPPLES. THEY SHOULD BE FREE OF CARBON TRACKING. ARE THEY?

NO: REPLACE FAULTY COMPONENT.

YES:
- CHECK SECONDARY COIL RESISTANCE. SHOULD BE 5-8K OHMS RESISTANCE. IS IT?

NO: REPLACE COIL

YES:

(4)
- INSTALL A KNOWN GOOD COIL.
- SPARK SHOULD JUMP TESTER GAP AT PROBLEM CYLINDER WITH ENGINE IDLING. DID IT?

YES: ORIGINAL IGNITION COIL IS FAULTY

NO: FAULTY C³I MODULE

CLEAR CODES AND CONFIRM "CLOSED LOOP" OPERATION AND NO "SERVICE ENGINE SOON" LIGHT.

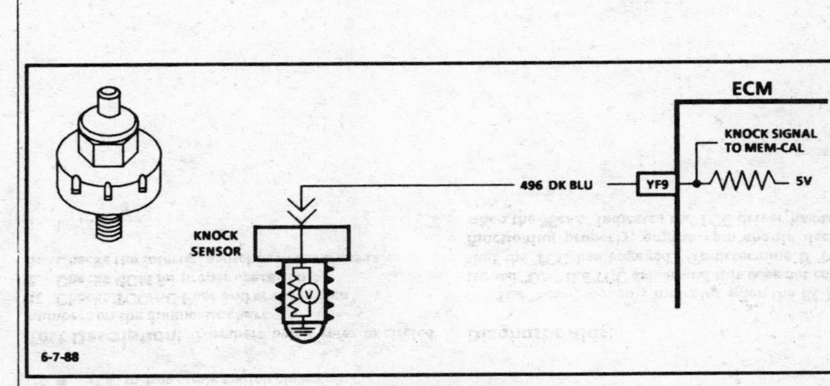

CHART C-5

ELECTRONIC SPARK CONTROL (ESC) SYSTEM CHECK 3300 (VIN N) "N" CARLINE (PORT)

Circuit Description:

The knock sensor is used to detect engine detonation and the ECM will retard the electronic spark timing based on the signal being received. The circuitry within the knock sensor causes the ECM's supplied 5 volt signal to be pulled down so that under a no knock condition, CKT 496 would measure about 2.5 volts. The knock sensor produces an A/C signal which rides on the 2.5 volts DC voltage. The amplitude and frequency are dependent upon the knock level.

The Mem-Cal used with this engine contains the functions which were part of the remotely mounted ESC modules used on other GM vehicles. The ESC portion of the Mem-Cal then sends a signal to other parts of the ECM which adjusts the spark timing to retard the spark and reduce the detonation.

Test Description: Numbers below refer to circled numbers on the diagnostic chart.

1. With engine idling, there should not be a knock signal present at the ECM because detonation is not likely under a no load condition.
2. Tapping on the engine lift hook should simulate a knock signal to determine if the sensor is capable of detecting detonation. If no knock is detected, try tapping on engine block closer to sensor before replacing sensor.
3. If the engine has an internal problem which is creating a knock, the knock sensor may be responding to the internal failure.
4. This test determines if the knock sensor is faulty or if the ESC portion of the Mem-Cal is faulty. If it is determined that the Mem-Cal is faulty, be sure that it is properly installed and latched into place. If not properly installed, repair and retest.

Diagnostic Aids:

While observing knock signal on the "Scan," there should be an indication that knock is present when detonation can be heard. Detonation is most likely to occur under high engine load conditions.

If the ESC CKT 496 is routed too close to secondary ignition wires it may induce a voltage and cause a false knock signal.

CHART C-5

ELECTRONIC SPARK CONTROL (ESC) SYSTEM CHECK 3300 (VIN N) "N" CARLINE (PORT)

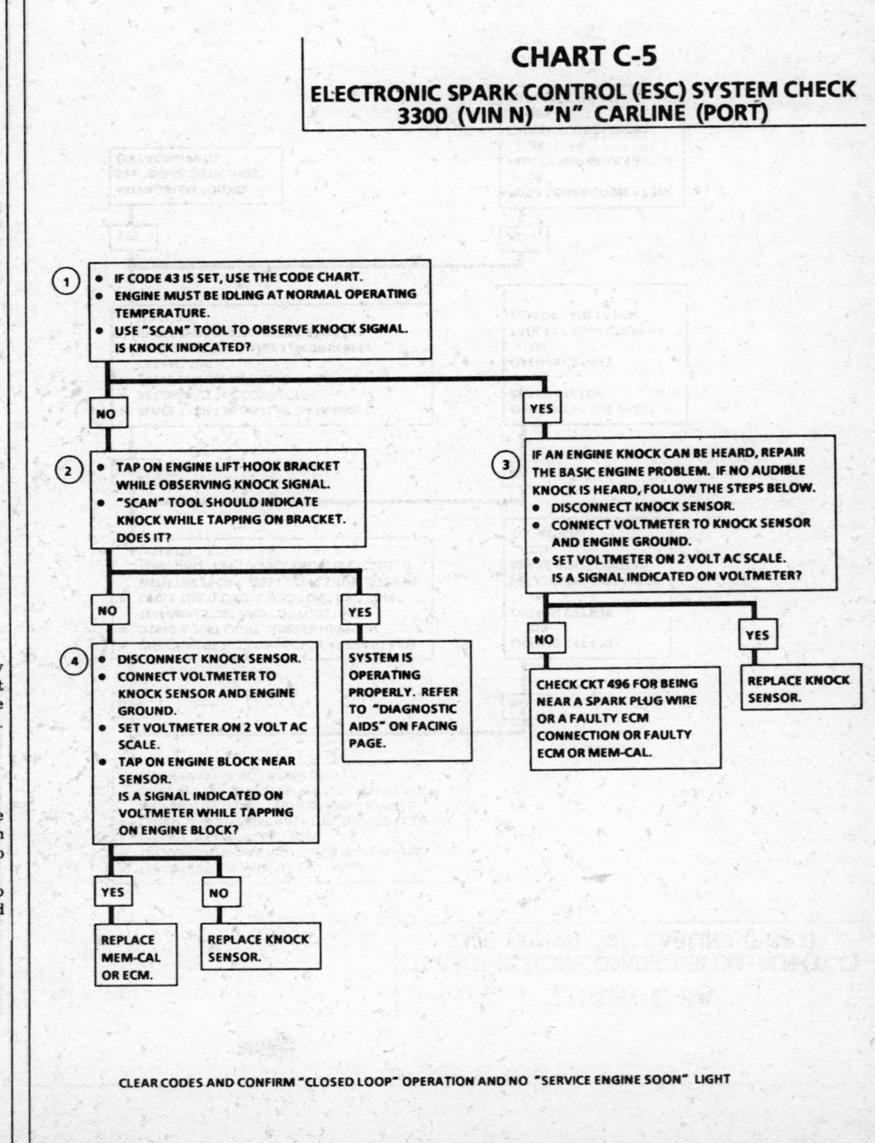

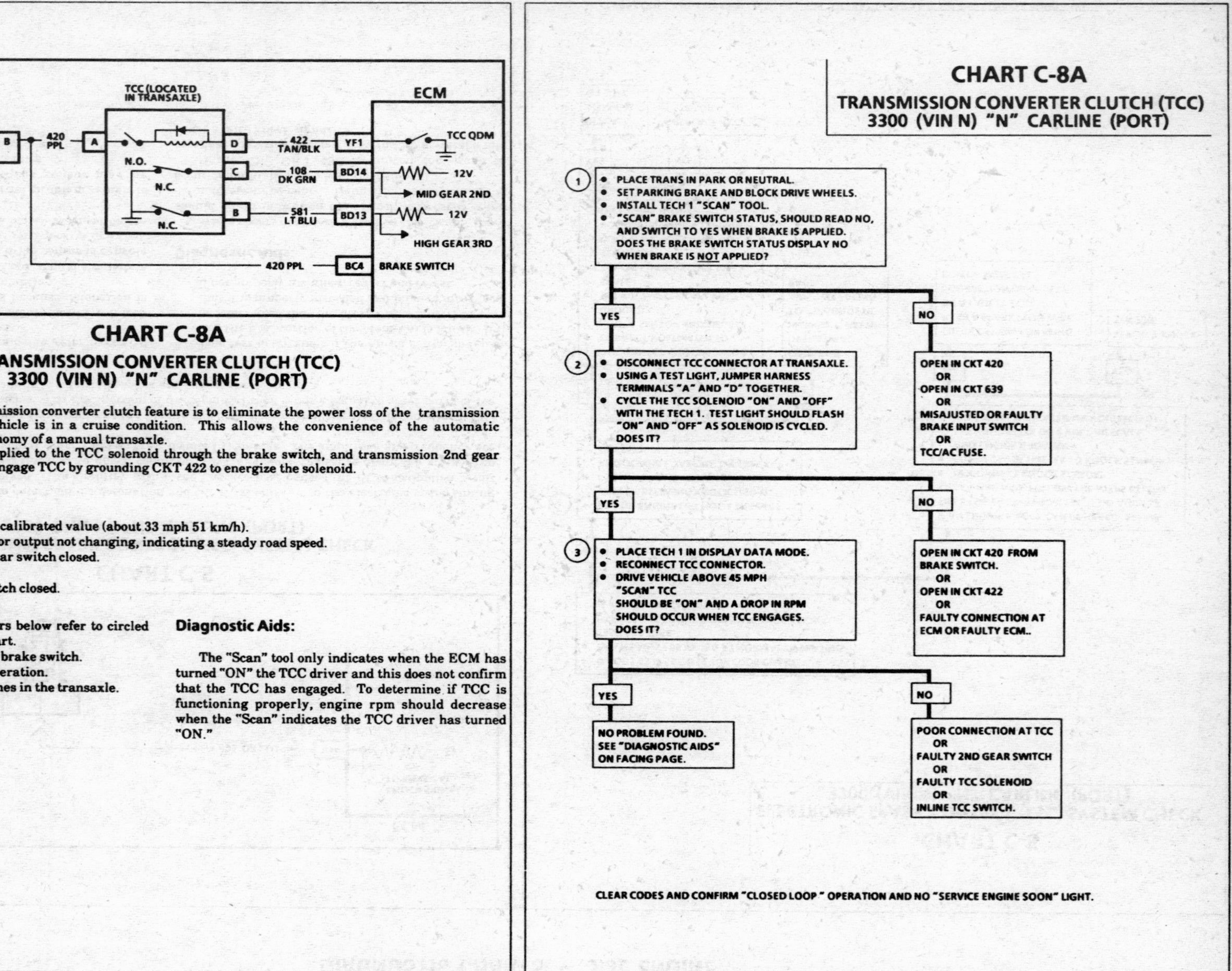

CHART C-8A

TRANSMISSION CONVERTER CLUTCH (TCC)
3300 (VIN N) "N" CARLINE (PORT)

Circuit Description:

The purpose of the transmission converter clutch feature is to eliminate the power loss of the transmission converter stage when the vehicle is in a cruise condition. This allows the convenience of the automatic transmission and the fuel economy of a manual transaxle.
Fused battery ignition is supplied to the TCC solenoid through the brake switch, and transmission 2nd gear apply switch. The ECM will engage TCC by grounding CKT 422 to energize the solenoid.

TCC will engage when:
- Engine warmed up.
- Vehicle speed above a calibrated value (about 33 mph 51 km/h).
- Throttle position sensor output not changing, indicating a steady road speed.
- Transmission third gear switch closed.
- Brake switch closed.
- TCC in-line apply switch closed.

Test Description: Numbers below refer to circled numbers on the diagnostic chart.
1. Checks TCC/AC Fuse and brake switch.
2. Checks ECM for proper operation.
3. Checks the internal switches in the transaxle.

Diagnostic Aids:

The "Scan" tool only indicates when the ECM has turned "ON" the TCC driver and this does not confirm that the TCC has engaged. To determine if TCC is functioning properly, engine rpm should decrease when the "Scan" indicates the TCC driver has turned "ON."

A/C PRESSURE
B C A
TO IGN
25 A
A/C FUSE & COOLING FAN
450 BLK/WHT
POWER STEERING PRESSURE SWITCH
B N.O. A
416 GRY — BA5 — 5 VOLT REF
380 GRY/RED — YF14 — A/C PRESSURE SIGNAL
452 BLK — BB6 — SENSOR GROUND
495 LT BLU/ORN — BD12 — POWER STEERING PRESSURE SWITCH
A/C SELECT
C E
50 BRN
50 BRN
66 LT GRN — BC9 — A/C REQUEST
A/C CLUTCH RELAY
59 DK GRN
A/C CLUTCH
4 5 1 2
459 DK GRN/WHT — YF8 — A/C RELAY QDM
439 PNK/BLK
10 AMP
TO IGN
150 BLK

CHART C-10

A/C CLUTCH CONTROL CIRCUIT DIAGNOSIS 3300 (VIN N) "N" CARLINE (PORT)

Circuit Description:

The A/C clutch control relay is energized when the ECM provides a ground path through CKT 459 and A/C is requested. A/C clutch is delayed about .3 seconds after A/C is requested. This will allow the IAC to adjust engine rpm for the additional load.

The ECM will temporarily disengage the A/C clutch relay for a calibrated time for one or more of the following:

- Hot engine restart
- Wide open throttle (TPS over 90%).
- Power steering pressure high (open power steering pressure switch).
- Engine rpm greater than about 6000 rpm.
- During IAC reset.

The A/C clutch relay will remain disengaged when a Code 66 is present or there is no A/C request signal due to an open A/C select switch or low pressure signal.

Test Description: Numbers below refer to circled numbers on the diagnostic chart.

1. The ECM will only energize the A/C relay when the engine is running. This test will determine if the relay or CKT 459 or ECM is faulty.
2. Determines if the signal is reaching the ECM through CKTs 50 and 66 from the A/C control panel. Signal should only be present when the A/C mode or defrost mode has been selected.
3. A short to ground in any part of the A/C request (CKTs 50 and 66). CKT 66 to the relay, CKT 59 to the A/C clutch, or the A/C clutch, could be the cause of a blown fuse.
4. If the ECM is receiving a high power steering pressure signal, the A/C clutch will be disengaged by the ECM.
5. With the engine idling and A/C "ON," the ECM should be grounding CKT 459, which should cause the test light to be "ON."

Diagnostic Aids:

If complaint is insufficient cooling, the problem may be caused by an inoperative cooling fan. See CHART C-12 for cooling fan diagnosis.

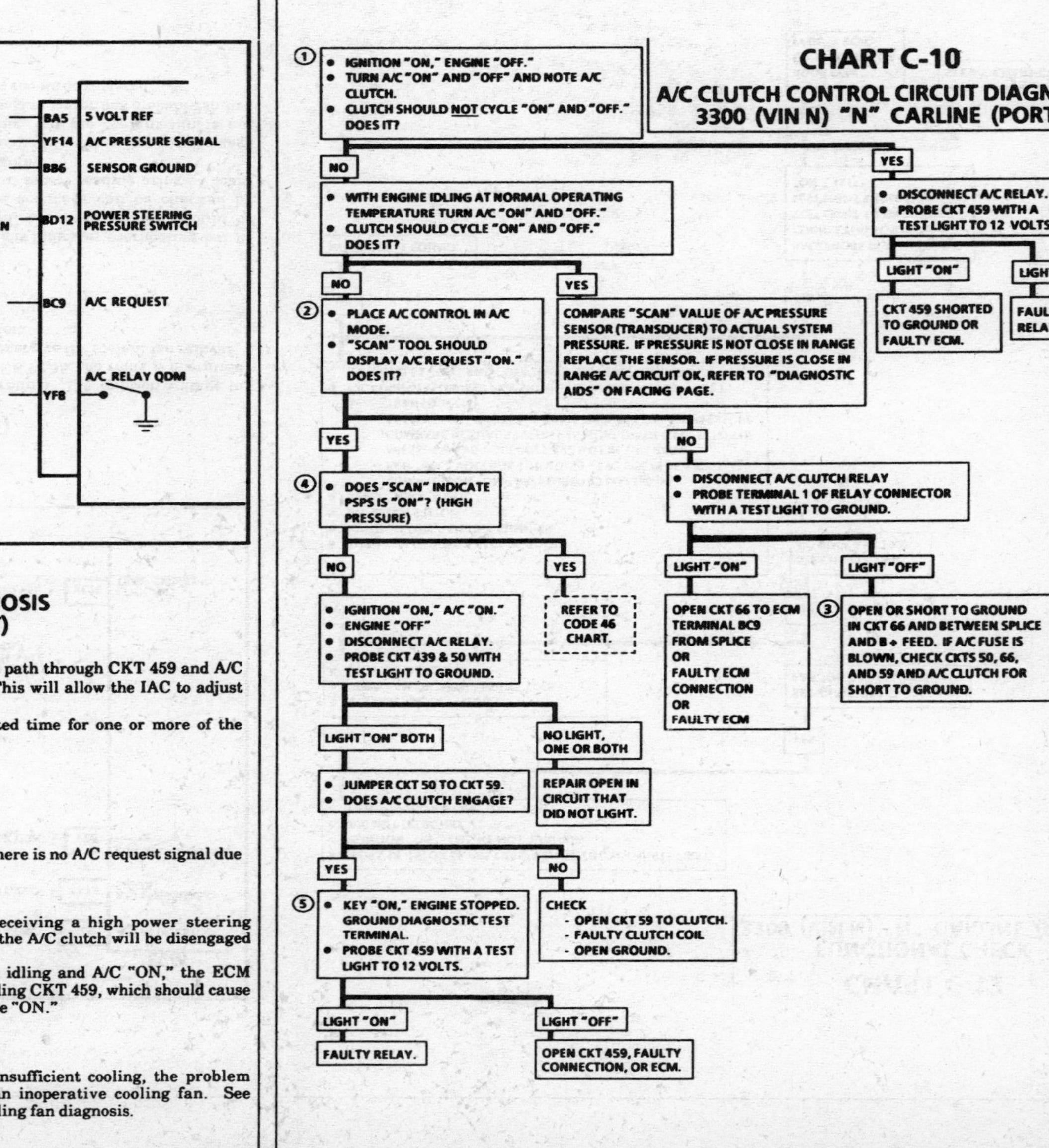

TO A/C SELECT SWITCH ← 66 LT GRN — BC9 A/C REQUEST
TO A/C PRESSURE TRANSDUCER ← 380 GRY/RED — YF14 A/C PRESSURE SIGNAL
FAN RELAY
50 BRN — 2 — 5 — 535 DK GRN — YE8 FAN RELAY QDM
TO B+ ← FUSIBLE LINK — 2 RED — 1 — 4 — 532 BLK/RED
25 A → TO IGN
A/C FUSE & COOLING FAN
B M A FAN
150 BLK LOCATED ON TRANSAXLE BOLT
TO COOLANT TEMP SENSOR ← 410 YEL — YE16 COOLANT TEMP SIGNAL
ECM
5-2-88

CHART C-12

FUNCTIONAL CHECK
3300 (VIN N) "N" CARLINE (PORT)

Circuit Description:

Battery voltage to operate the coolant fan motor is supplied to relay terminal "1". Ignition voltage to energize the relay is supplied to relay terminal "2". When the ECM grounds CKT 535, the relay is energized and the coolant fan is turned "ON." When the engine is running, the ECM will energize the coolant fan relay if:

- Code 14 or 15 is present or when one or all of the following conditions exists:
  - A/C pressure is above 170 psi.
  - Coolant temperature is greater than 100C° (212°F).

Test Description: Numbers below refer to circled numbers on the diagnostic chart.

1. Fan should be on as using the Tech I to on turn the QDM provides a ground path for current to flow through the relay coil.
2. The fan should be running if the A/C pressure is above 170 psi as the ECM monitors B+ at terminal BC9 when A/C is requested.

If the gage or light indicates overheating but no boilover is detected, the gage circuit should be checked. The gage accuracy can be checked by comparing the coolant sensor reading using a "Scan" tool with the gage reading.

If the engine is actually overheating and the gage indicates overheating, but the coolant fan is not turning "ON," the coolant sensor has probably shifted out of calibration and should be replaced.

Diagnostic Aids:

If the vehicle has an overheating problem, it must be determined if the complaint was due to an actual boilover, the coolant temperature warning light, or the temperature gage indicated over heating.

CHART C-12

FUNCTIONAL CHECK
3300 (VIN N) "N" CARLINE (PORT)

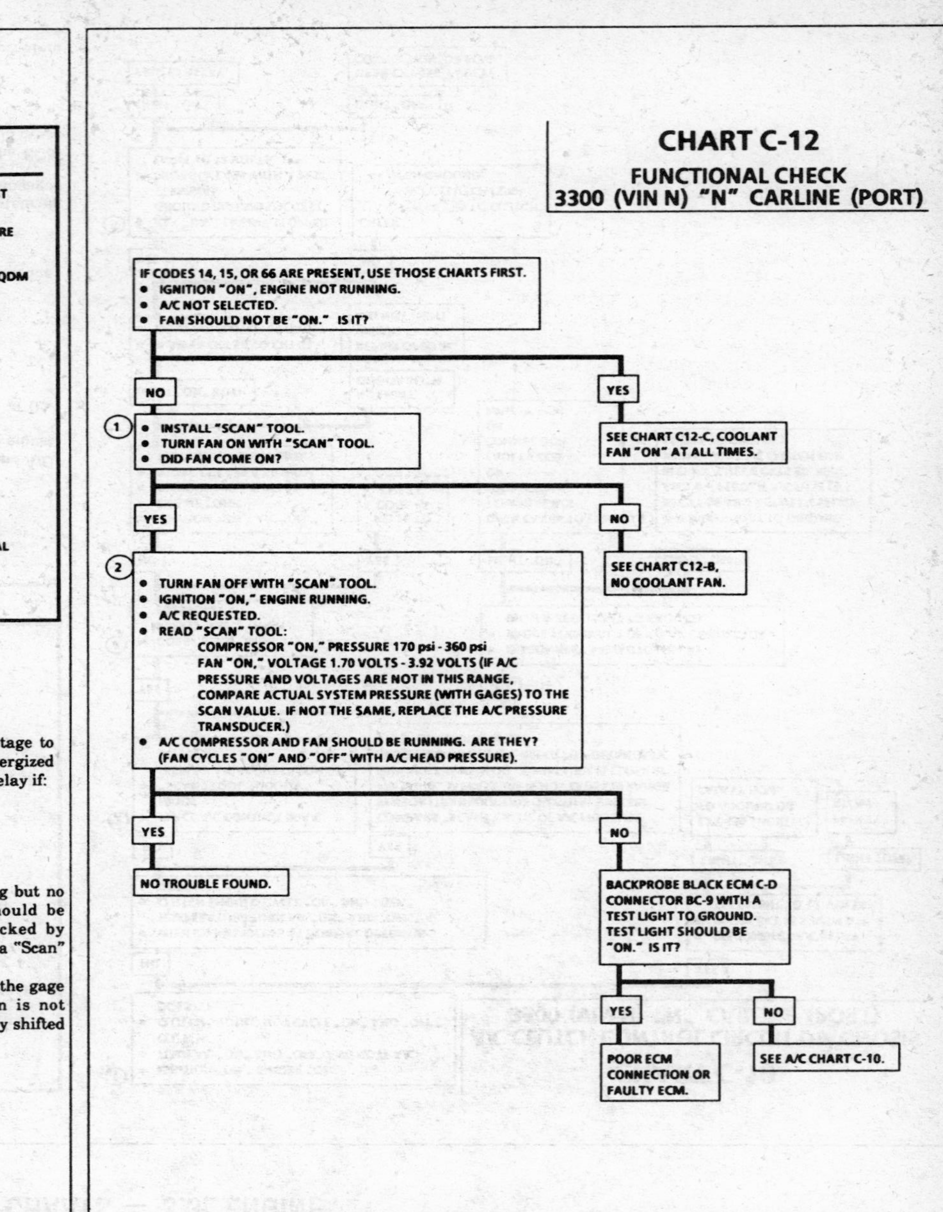

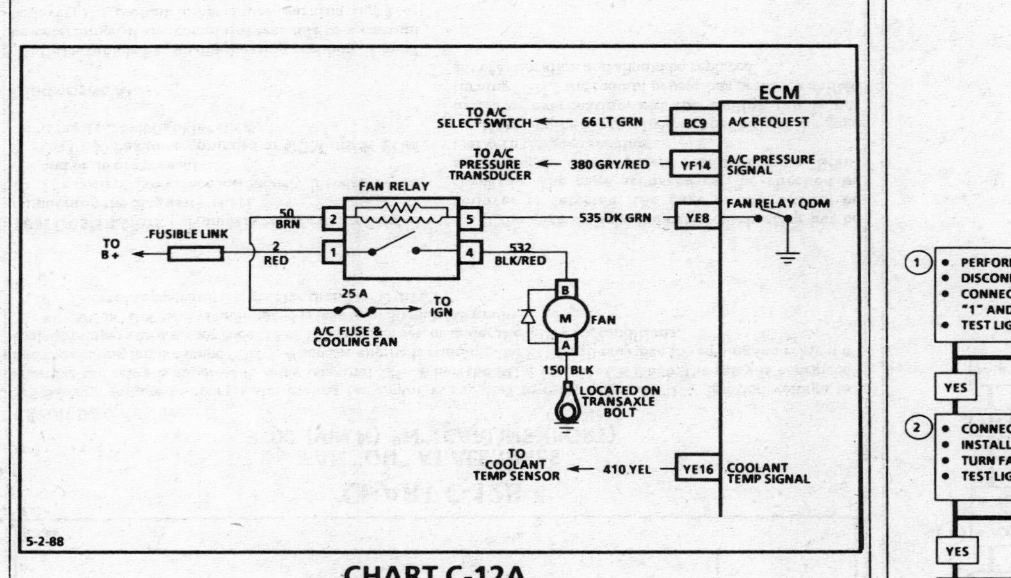

CHART C-12A

NO COOLANT FAN
3300 (VIN N) "N" CARLINE (PORT)

Circuit Description:

Battery voltage to operate the cooling fan motor is supplied to relay terminal "1". Ignition voltage to energize the relay is supplied to relay terminal "2". When the ECM grounds CKT 535, the relay is energized and the cooling fan is turned "ON." When the engine is running, the ECM will energize the cooling fan relay if a coolant temperature sensor code (14 or 15) has been set, or under the following conditions:

- A/C is "ON" and vehicle speed is less than 30 mph (48 km/h).
- Coolant temperature is greater than 100°C (212°F).

Test Description: Numbers below refer to circled numbers on the diagnostic chart.

1. Terminal 2 should be B+ when the ignition is turned "ON." Terminal 1 is connected directly to B+.
2. Test light should be "ON" as using the Tech I to turn the QDM "ON" allows current to flow to ground.

If the gage or light indicates overheating but no boilover is detected, the gage circuit should be checked. The gage accuracy can be checked by comparing the coolant sensor reading using a "Scan" tool with the gage reading.

If the engine is actually overheating and the gage indicates overheating, but the cooling fan is not turning "ON," the coolant sensor has probably shifted out of calibration and should be replaced.

Diagnostic Aids

If the vehicle has an overheating problem, it must be determined if the complaint was due to an actual boilover, the coolant temperature warning light, or the temperature gage indicated overheating.

CHART C-12A

NO COOLANT FAN
3300 (VIN N) "N" CARLINE (PORT)

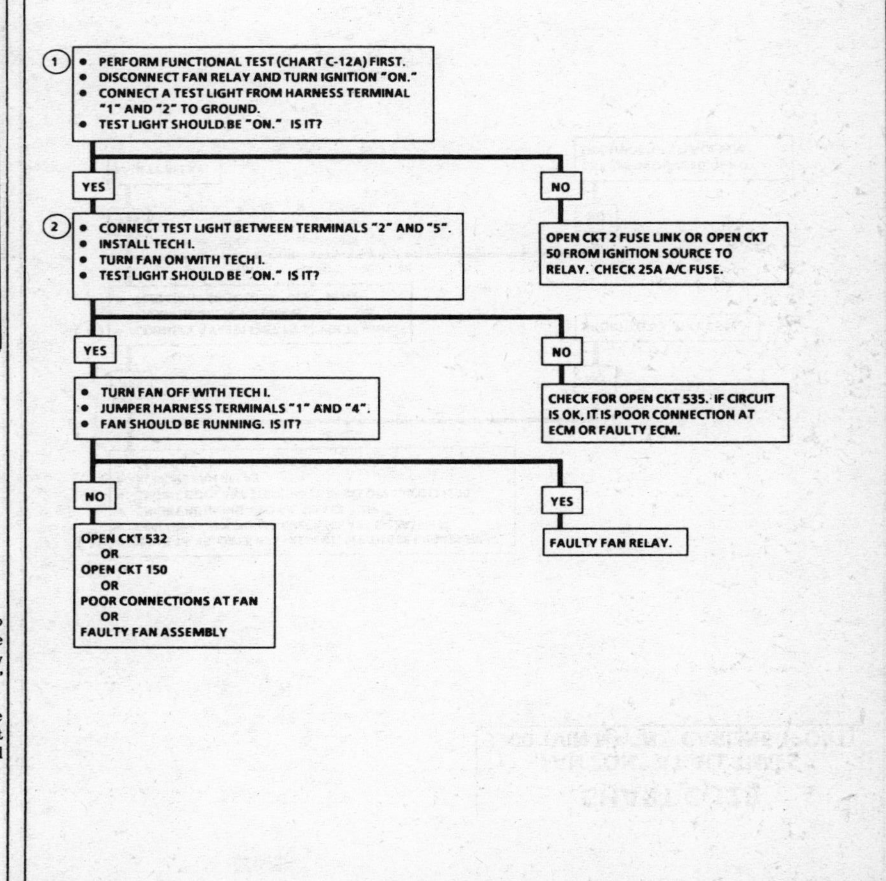

ECM
TO A/C SELECT SWITCH ← 66 LT GRN — BC9 A/C REQUEST
TO A/C PRESSURE TRANSDUCER ← 380 GRY/RED — YF14 A/C PRESSURE SIGNAL
FAN RELAY
535 DK GRN — YE8 FAN RELAY QDM
TO B+ ← FUSIBLE LINK 50 BRN 2 RED
532 BLK/RED
25 A → TO IGN
A/C FUSE & COOLING FAN
M FAN
150 BLK
LOCATED ON TRANSAXLE BOLT
TO COOLANT TEMP SENSOR ← 410 YEL — YE16 COOLANT TEMP SIGNAL
6-3-88

CHART C-12B

FAN "ON" AT ALL TIMES
3300 (VIN N) "N" CARLINE (PORT)

Circuit Description:

Battery voltage to operate the cooling fan motor is supplied to relay terminal "1". Ignition voltage to energize the relay is supplied to relay terminal "2". When the ECM grounds CKT 535, the relay is energized and the cooling fan is turned "ON." When the engine is running, the ECM will energize the cooling fan relay if a coolant temperature sensor code (14 or 15) has been set, or under the following conditions:

- A/C is "ON" and vehicle speed is less than 30 mph (48 km/h).
- Coolant temperature is greater than 100°C (212°F).

Test Description: Numbers below refer to circled numbers on the diagnostic chart.

1. The coolant fan runs continuously if codes 14, 15 and/or 66 are present.
2. CKT 535 has to be grounded or QDM inside ECM is faulty if test light is "ON."

Diagnostic Aids:

If the vehicle has an overheating problem, it must be determined if the complaint was due to an actual boilover, the coolant temperature warning light, or the temperature gage indicated overheating.

If the gage or light indicates overheating but no boilover is detected, the gage circuit should be checked. The gage accuracy can be checked by comparing the coolant sensor reading using a "Scan" tool with the gage reading.

If the engine is actually overheating and the gage indicates overheating, but the cooling fan is not turning "ON," the coolant sensor has probably shifted out of calibration and should be replaced.

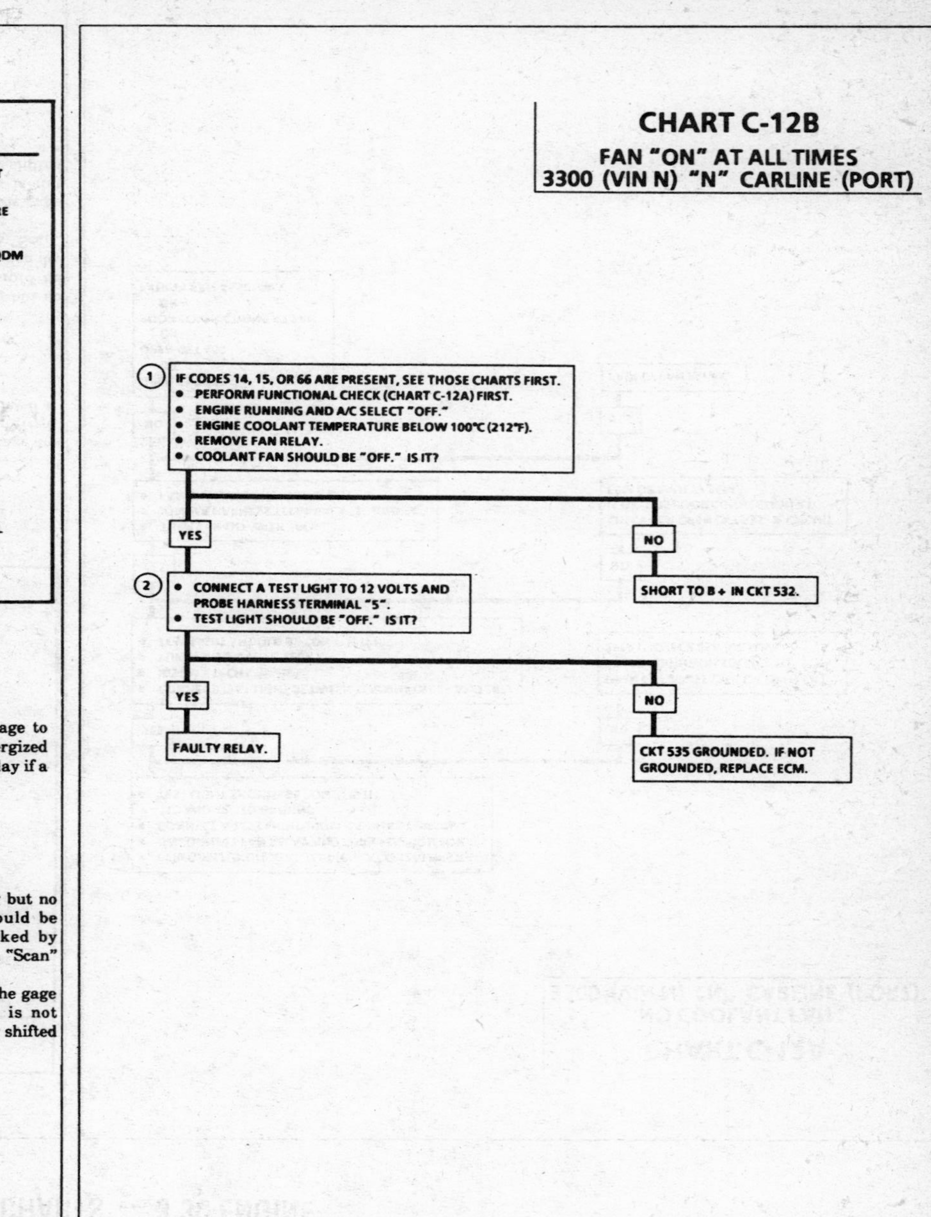

VEHICLE EMISSION CONTROL INFORMATION (VECI) LABELS

➡ Following is an assortment of representative Vehicle Emission Control Information labels. It is by no means a complete collection; only what was available at the time of publication was printed here. Always follow the VECI label information on your vehicle. The VECI label is found in the engine compartment and can be affixed to the radiator support, air cleaner housing or the underside of the hood.

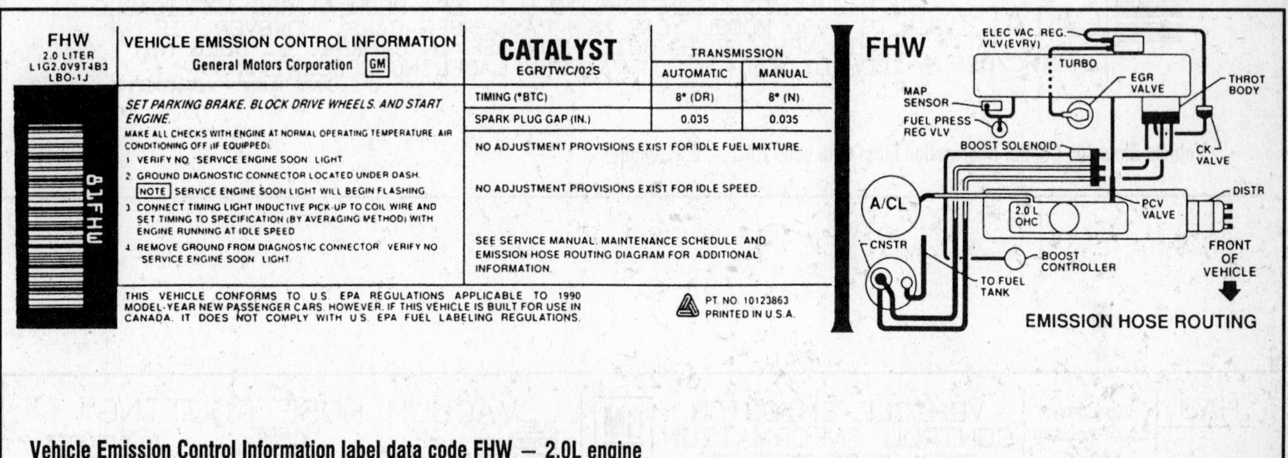

Vehicle Emission Control Information label data code FHW — 2.0L engine

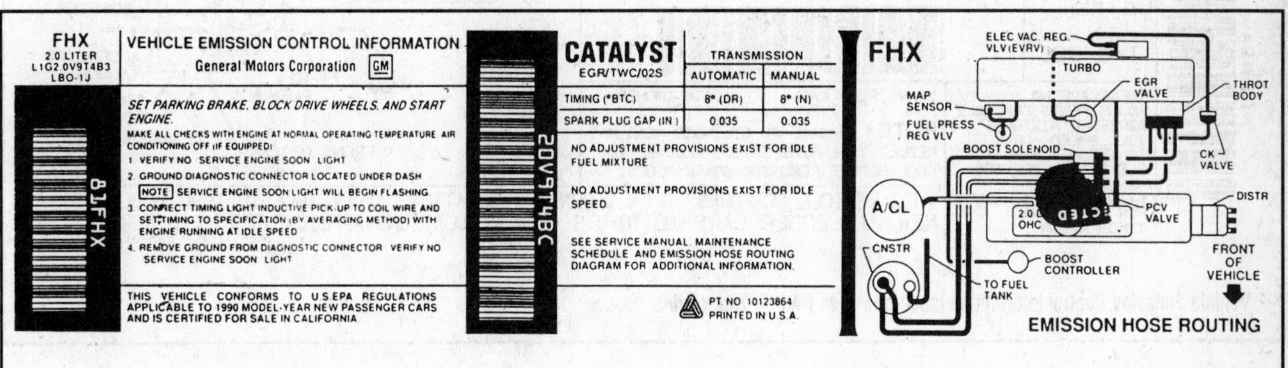

Vehicle Emission Control Information label data code FHX — 2.0L engine

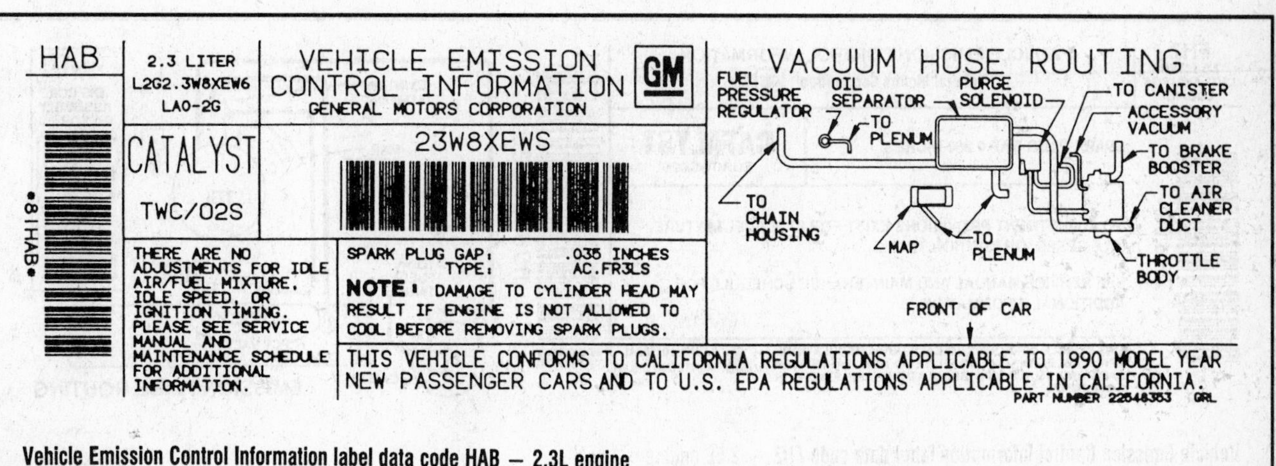

Vehicle Emission Control Information label data code HAB — 2.3L engine

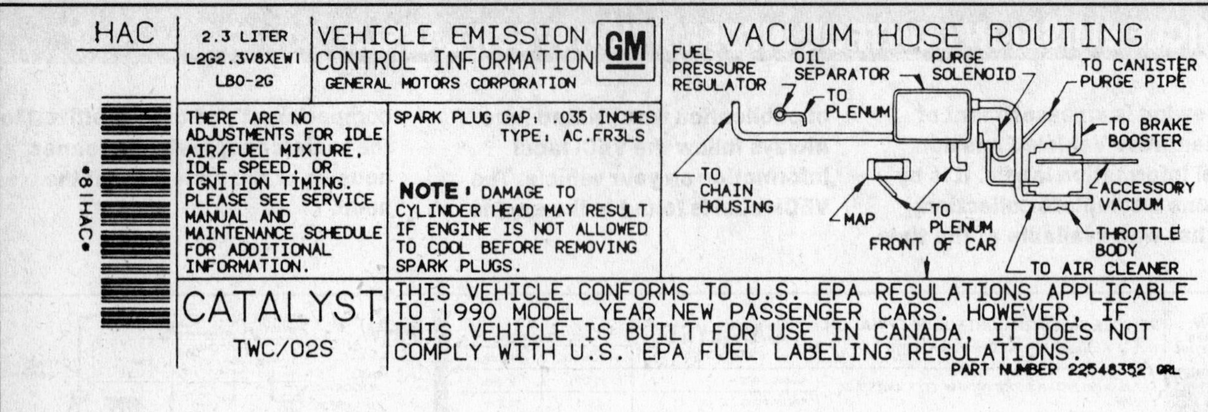

Vehicle Emission Control Information label data code HAC — 2.3L engine

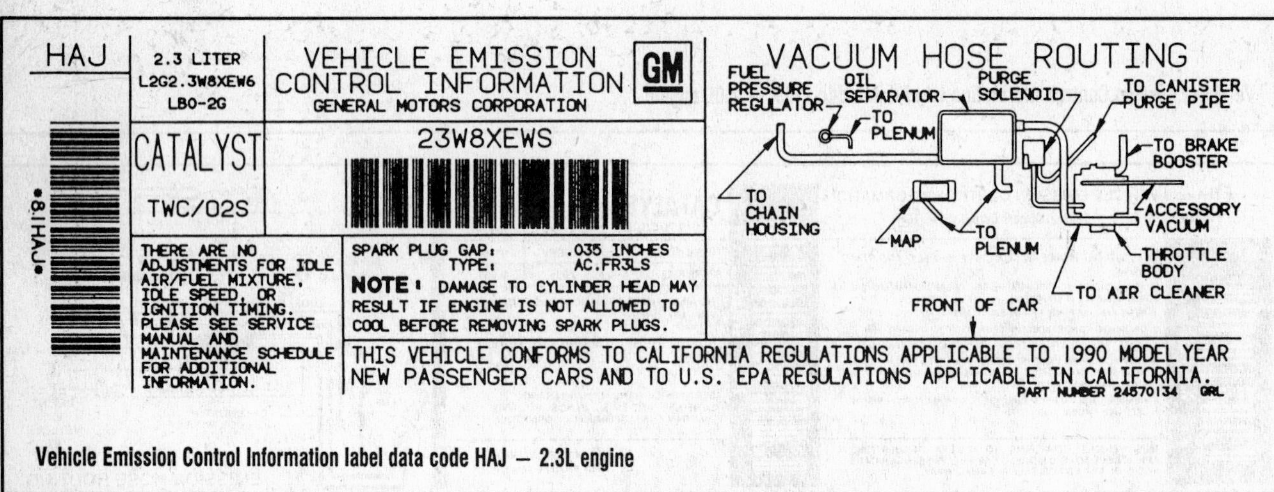

Vehicle Emission Control Information label data code HAJ — 2.3L engine

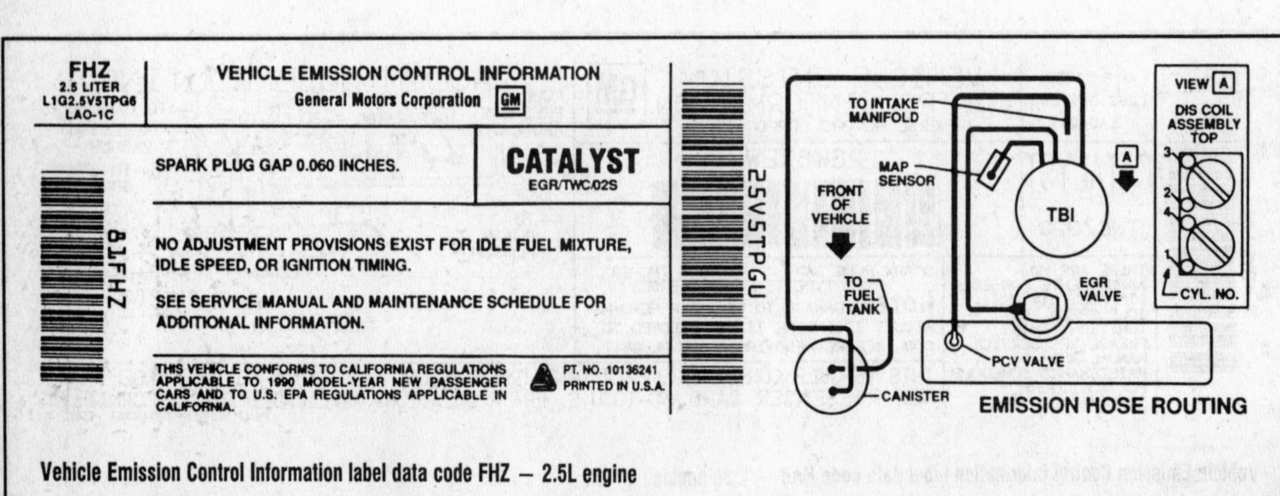

Vehicle Emission Control Information label data code FHZ — 2.5L engine

water at 50°F (15°C). The resistance across the terminals should approximately 5600Ω. Check Code 14 or 15 engine chart for specific resistance on vehicle being serviced. If not within specifications, replace the sensor.

4. Apply some pipe tape to the threaded sensor and install the sensor.

5. Fill the cooling system if any coolant was removed. Reconnect the sensor connector and the negative battery cable.

Torque Converter Clutch Solenoid

REMOVAL & INSTALLATION

1. Remove the negative battery cable. Raise and support the vehicle safely.

2. Drain the transmission fluid into a suitable drain pan. Remove the transmission pan.

3. Remove the TCC solenoid retaining screws and then remove the electrical connector, solenoid and check ball.

4. Clean and inspect all parts. Replace defective parts as necessary.

To install:

5. Install the check ball, TCC solenoid and electrical connector. Install the solenoid retaining screws and torque them to 10 ft. lbs. (14 Nm).

6. Install the transmission pan with a new gasket and torque the pan retaining bolts to 10 ft. lbs. (14 Nm).

7. Lower the vehicle and refill the transmission with the proper amount of the automatic transmission fluid.

Throttle Position Sensor

REMOVAL & INSTALLATION

The TPS is not adjustable and is not supplied with attaching screw retainers. Since these TPS configurations can be mounted interchangeably, be sure to order the correct one for your engine with the identical part number of the one being replaced. Refer to Fig. 1 if desired.

1. Disconnect the negative battery cable. Remove the air cleaner assembly along with the necessary duct work.

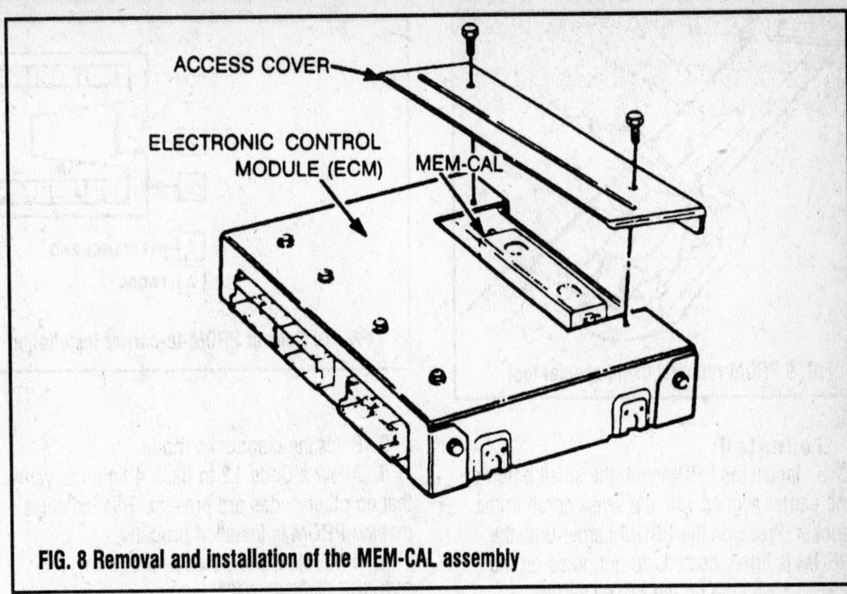

FIG. 8 Removal and installation of the MEM-CAL assembly

2. Remove the TPS attaching screws. If the TPS is riveted to the throttle body, it will be necessary to drill out the rivets.

3. Remove the TPS from the throttle body assembly.

➡ **The throttle position sensor is an electrical component and should not be immersed in any type of liquid solvent or cleaner, as damage may result.**

4. With the throttle valve closed, install the TPS onto the throttle shaft. Rotate the TPS counterclockwise to align the mounting holes. Install the retaining screws or rivets. Torque the retaining screws to 18 inch lbs. (2.0 Nm).

5. Install the air cleaner assembly and connect the negative battery cable.

MEM-CAL

REMOVAL & INSTALLATION

➧ SEE FIG. 8

1. Remove the ECM.

2. Remove the Mem-Cal access panel.

3. Using 2 fingers, push both retaining clips back away from the MEM-Cal. At the same time, grasp it at both ends and lift it out of the socket. Do not remove the cover of the Mem-Cal. Use of an unapproved Mem-Cal removal procedures may cause damage to the Mem-Cal or the socket.

To install:

4. Install the new Mem-Cal by pressing only the ends of the Mem-Cal. Small notches in the Mem-Cal must be aligned with the small notches in the Mem-Cal socket.

5. Press on the ends of the Mem-Cal until the retaining clips snap into the ends of the Mem-Cal. Do not press on the middle of the Mem-Cal, only on the ends.

6. Install the Mem-Cal access cover and reinstall the ECM.

PROM

REMOVAL & INSTALLATION

➧ SEE FIGS. 9 AND 10

1. Remove the ECM.

2. Remove the PROM access panel.

3. Using the rocker type PROM removal tool, engage 1 end of the PROM carrier with the hook end of the tool. Press on the vertical bar end of the tool and rock the engaged end of the PROM carrier up as far as possible.

4. Engage the opposite end of the PROM carrier in the same manner and rock this end up as far as possible.

5. Repeat this process until the PROM carrier and PROM are free of the PROM socket. The PROM carrier with PROM in it should lift off of the PROM socket easily.

6. The PROM carrier should only be removed by using the special PROM removal tool. Other methods could cause damage to the PROM or PROM socket.

7. Before installing a new PROM, be sure the new PROM part number is the same as the old one or the as the updated number per a service bulletin.

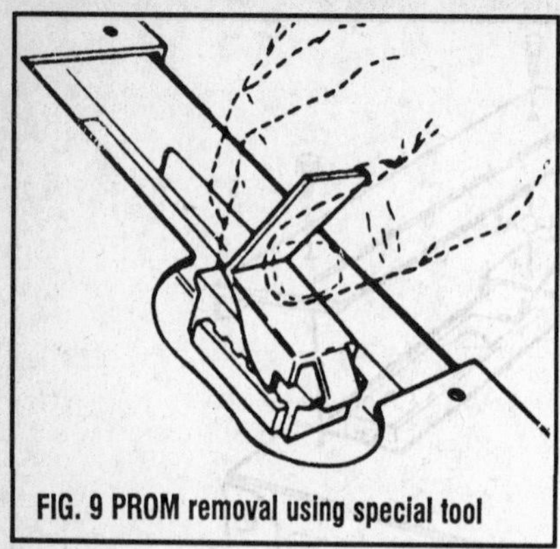
FIG. 9 PROM removal using special tool

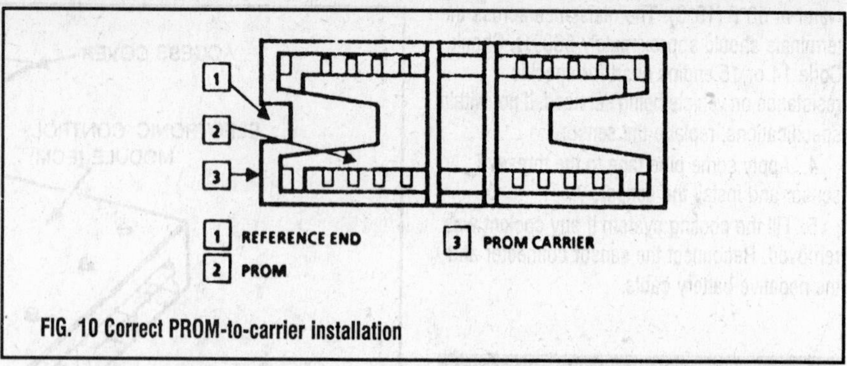

FIG. 10 Correct PROM-to-carrier installation

To install:

8. Install the PROM with the small notch of the carrier aligned with the small notch in the socket. Press on the PROM carrier until the PROM is firmly seated, do not press on the PROM itself only on the PROM carrier.

9. Install the PROM access cover and reinstall the ECM.

FUNCTIONAL CHECK

1. Turn the ignition switch to the **ON** position.
2. Enter the diagnostic mode.
3. Allow a Code 12 to flash 4 times to verify that no other codes are present. This indicates that the PROM is installed properly.
4. If trouble Code 51 occurs or if the SERVICE ENGINE SOON light in on constantly with no codes, the PROM is not fully seated, installed backwards, has bent pins or is defective.
5. If not fully seated press down firmly on the PROM carrier.
6. If installed backwards, replace the PROM.

➡ Any time the PROM is installed backwards and the ignition switch is turned ON, the PROM is destroyed.

7. If the pins are bent, remove the PROM straighten the pins and reinstall the PROM. If the bent pins break or crack during straightening, discard the PROM and replace with a new PROM.

➡ To prevent possible electrostatic discharge damage to the PROM or Cal-Pak, do not touch the component leads and do not remove the integrated circuit from the carrier.

MULTI-PORT FUEL INJECTION SYSTEM (2.0L, 2.3L, 3.0L AND 3.3L ENGINES)

System Description

The Multi-Port Fuel Injection (MPI) system is controlled by an Electronic Control Module (ECM) which monitors engine operations and generates output signals to provide the correct air/fuel mixture, ignition timing and engine idle speed control. Input to the control unit is provided by an oxygen sensor, coolant temperature sensor, detonation (knock) sensor on some engines, hot film Mass Air Flow (MAF) sensor or Manifold Absolute Pressure (MAP) sensor and Throttle Position Sensor (TPS). The ECM also receives information concerning engine rpm, vehicle speed, transaxle selector position, power steering and air conditioning.

The injectors are located, one at each intake port, rather than the single injector found on the throttle body system. The injectors are mounted on a fuel rail and are activated by a signal from the Electronic Control Module (ECM). The injector is a solenoid-operated valve which remains open depending on the width of the electronic pulses (length of the signal) from the ECM; the longer the open time, the more fuel is injected. In this manner, the air/fuel mixture can be precisely controlled for maximum performance with minimum emissions. On all multi-port fuel injection systems, except the 2.3L engine, the ECM fires all of the injectors at once.

The system of 2.3L engines is slightly different in that the injectors are paired by companion cylinders and are fired in pairs. This system is called Alternating Synchronous Double Fire (ASDF) fuel injection and is similar in operation to the other injection systems except that each pair of cylinders fires once per crankshaft revolution. That means cylinders 1 and 4, and 2 and 3 fire once per crankshaft revolution. In this way, a cylinder's injector fires on the intake stroke and exhaust stroke. Firing the injector on the exhaust stroke (when the intake valve is closed) helps provide better fuel vaporization.

Fuel is pumped from the tank by a high pressure fuel pump, located inside the fuel tank. It is a positive displacement roller vane pump. The impeller serves as a vapor separator and pre-charges the high pressure assembly. A pressure regulator maintains 28–36 psi (193–248kpa) — 28–50 psi (193–345kpa) on turbocharged engines — in the fuel line to the injectors and the excess fuel is fed back to the tank. A fuel accumulator is used to dampen the hydraulic line hammer in the system created when all injectors open simultaneously.

The MAP sensor, used on all except the 3.0L and 3.3L engines, measures the changes in intake manifold pressure, which result from engine load and speed changes and converts this information to a voltage output. The MAP sensor reading is the opposite of a vacuum gauge reading: when manifold pressure is high, MAP sensor value is high and vacuum is low. A MAP sensor will produce a low output on engine coast down with a closed throttle while a wide open throttle will produce a high output. The high output is produced because the pressure inside the manifold is the same as outside the manifold, so 100 percent of the outside air pressure is measured.

The MAP sensor is also used to measure barometric pressure under certain conditions, which allows the ECM to automatically adjust for different altitudes.

The MAP sensor changes the 5 volt signal supplied by the ECM, which reads the change and uses the information to control fuel delivery and ignition timing.

The Mass Air Flow (MAF) Sensor used on 3.0L and 3.3L engines, measures the mass of air that is drawn into the engine. It is located just ahead of the throttle in the intake system and consists of a heated grid which measures the mass of air, rather than just the volume. A resistor is used to measure the temperature of the film at 75° above ambient temperature. As the ambient (outside) air temperature rises and the rate of air flowing through the grid increases (indicating the throttle opening), more energy is required to maintain the heated grid at the higher temperature. The ECM calculates the difference in energy required to maintain the grid temperature in order to determine the mass of the incoming air. The control unit uses this information to determine the duration of fuel injection pulse, timing and EGR.

The throttle body incorporates an Idle Air Control (IAC) that provides for a bypass channel through which air can flow. It consists of an orifice and pintle which is controlled by the ECM through a step motor. The IAC provides air flow for idle and allows additional air during cold start until the engine reaches operating temperature. As the engine temperature rises, the opening through which air passes is slowly closed.

The Throttle Position Sensor (TPS) provides the control unit with information on throttle position, in order to determine injector pulse width and hence correct mixture. The TPS is connected to the throttle shaft on the throttle body and consists of as potentiometer with on end connected to a 5 volt source from the ECM and the other to ground. A third wire is connected to the ECM to measure the voltage output from the TPS which changes as the throttle valve angle is changed (accelerator pedal moves). At the closed throttle position, the output is low (approximately 0.4 volts); as the throttle valve opens, the output increases to a maximum 5 volts at Wide Open Throttle (WOT). The TPS can be misadjusted open, shorted, or loose and if it is out of adjustment, the idle quality or WOT performance may be poor. A loose TPS can cause intermittent bursts of fuel from the injectors and an unstable idle because the ECM thinks the throttle is moving. This should cause a trouble code to be set. Once a trouble code is set, the ECM will use a preset value for TPS and some vehicle performance may return. A small amount of engine coolant is routed through the throttle assembly to prevent freezing inside the throttle bore during cold operation.

Service Precautions

When working around any part of the fuel system, take precautionary steps to prevent fire and/or explosion:

- Disconnect negative terminal from battery (except when testing with battery voltage is required).
- When ever possible, use a flashlight instead of a drop light.
- Keep all open flame and smoking material out of the area.
- Use a shop cloth or similar to catch fuel when opening a fuel system.
- Relieve fuel system pressure before servicing.
- Use eye protection.
- Always keep a dry chemical (class B) fire extinguisher near the area.

Relieving Fuel System Pressure

WITH FUEL RAIL TEST FITTING

1. Disconnect the negative battery cable.
2. Loosen the fuel filler cap to relieve fuel tank vapor pressure.
3. Connect a fuel pressure gauge with valve to the fuel pressure relief connection at the fuel rail.
4. Wrap a shop towel around the fittings while connecting the tool to prevent fuel spillage.
5. Install a bleed hose into an approved container and open the valve to bleed the system pressure.
6. Install the fuel filler cap.

WITHOUT FUEL RAIL TEST FITTING

1. Remove the fuel filler cap to relieve fuel tank vapor pressure.
2. From under the vehicle, disconnect the fuel pump electrical connector. It should be the only connector coming from the fuel tank.
3. Start the engine and run until the engine stalls. Engage the starter an additional 3 seconds to assure complete relief.
4. Install the fuel filler cap.
5. Disconnect the negative battery cable and continue with fuel system work.

Electric Fuel Pump

➧ SEE FIG. 1

FUEL PRESSURE CHECK

1. Connect pressure gauge J-34730-1, or equivalent, to fuel pressure test point on the fuel rail. Wrap a rag around the pressure tap to absorb any leakage that may occur when installing the gauge.
2. Turn the ignition **ON**. The fuel pump pressure should read as follows:
   - 2.0L engine — 35–38 psi (245–256 kPa)
   - 2.3L engine — 41–47 psi (280–325 kPa)
   - 1985–86 3.0L engine — 37–43 psi (255–298 kPa)
   - 1987–88 3.0L engine — 41–47 psi (280–325 kPa)
   - 3.3L engine — 41–47 psi (280–325 kPa)
3. Start the engine and allow it to idle. The fuel pressure should drop no more than 3–10 psi (21–69kpa).

➡ The idle pressure will vary somewhat depending on barometric pressure. Check for a drop in pressure indicating regulator control, rather than specific values.

4. On turbocharged vehicles, use a low pressure air pump to apply air pressure to the regulator to simulate turbocharger boost pressure. Boost pressure should increase fuel pressure 1 psi (7kpa) for every lb. of boost. Again, look for changes rather than specific pressures. The maximum fuel pressure should not exceed 46 psi (317kpa).
5. If the fuel pressure drops, check the operation of the check valve, the pump coupling connection, fuel pressure regulator valve and the injectors. A restricted fuel line or filter may also cause a pressure drip. To check the fuel pump output, restrict the fuel return line and run 12 volts to the pump. The fuel pressure should rise to approximately 75 psi (517kpa) with the return line restricted.
6. Before attempting to remove or service any fuel system component, it is necessary to relieve the fuel system pressure.

REMOVAL & INSTALLATION

1. Disconnect the negative battery cable.
2. Relieve the fuel system pressure.
3. Raise and safely support the vehicle with jackstands.
4. Safely drain and remove the fuel tank assembly as outlined in the "Fuel tank" removal procedures in this Section.
5. Turn the fuel pump cam lock ring counterclockwise and lift the assembly out of the tank.
6. Remove the fuel pump from the level sensor unit as follows:
   a. Pull the pump up into the attaching hose or pulsator while pulling outward away from the bottom support.
   b. Take care to prevent damage to the rubber insulator and strainer during removal.
   c. When the pump assembly is clear of the bottom support, pull the pump out of the rubber connector for removal.

To install:

7. Replace any attaching hoses or rubber sound insulator that show signs of deterioration.
8. Push the fuel pump into the attaching hoses and install the pump/sensor assembly into the tank. Always use a new O-ring seal. Be careful not to fold over or twist the strainer when installing the sensor unit. Also, make sure the strainer does not block full travel of the float arm.
9. Install the cam lock and turn clockwise to lock.
10. Install the fuel tank as outlined in this Section.
11. Fill the tank with four gallons of gas and check for fuel leaks.

Throttle Body

➧ SEE FIGS. 11–13

REMOVAL & INSTALLATION

CAUTION

When draining the coolant, keep in mind that cats and dogs are attracted by the ethylene glycol antifreeze, and are quite likely to drink any that is left in an uncovered container or in puddles on the ground. This will prove fatal in sufficient quantity. Always drain the coolant into a sealable container. Coolant should be reused unless it is contaminated or several years old.

2.3L Engine

1. Disconnect the negative battery cable. Drain the top half of the engine coolant into a suitable drain pan.
2. Remove the air inlet duct. Disconnect the idle air control valve and throttle position sensor connectors.
3. Remove and mark all necessary vacuum lines. Remove and plug the 2 coolant hoses.
4. Remove the throttle, T.V. and cruise control cables. Remove the power steering pump brace.
5. Remove the throttle body retaining bolts and then remove the throttle body assembly. Discard the flange gasket.
6. Installation is the reverse order of the removal procedure. Torque the retaining bolts to 20 ft. lbs. (27 Nm).
7. Connect the negative battery cable. Refill the cooling system.

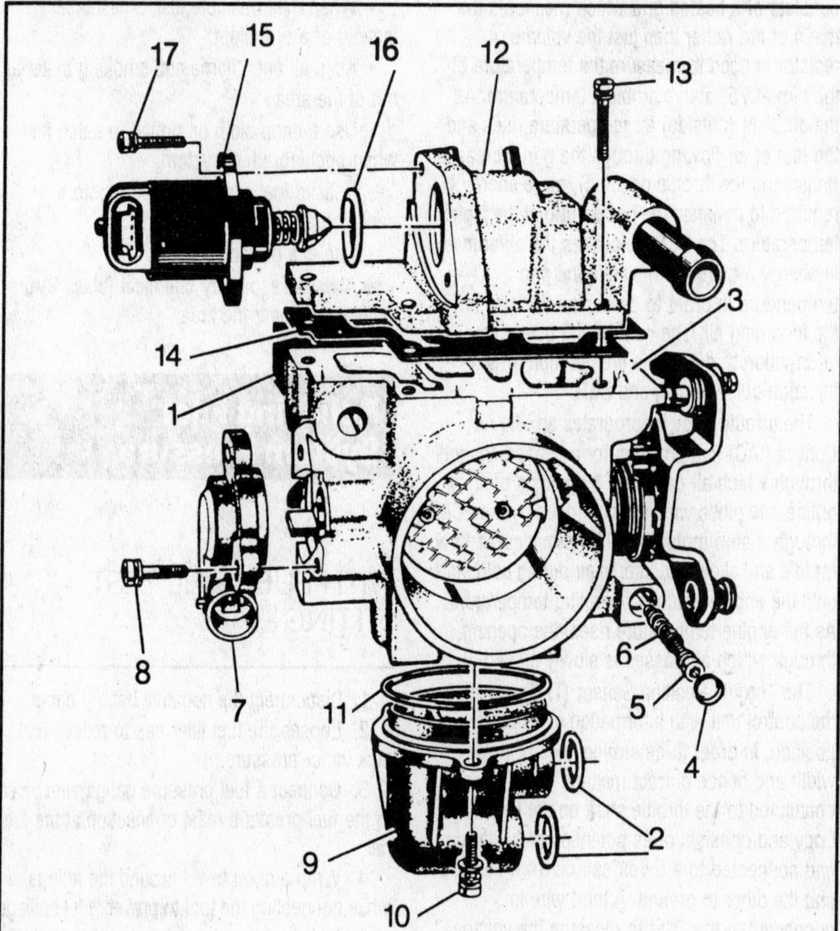

1. Flange gasket
2. Coolant line O-ring
3. Throttle body assembly
4. Idle stop crew plug
5. Idle stop screw assembly
6. Idle stop screw assembly spring
7. Throttle Position Sensor (TPS)
8. TPS attaching screw
9. Coolant passage cover
10. Coolant passage cover attaching screw
11. Coolant cover-to-throttle body O-ring
12. Idle air/vacuum signal housing assembly
13. Idle air/vacuum signal housing assembly screw
14. Idle air/vacuum signal housing assembly gasket
15. Idle Air Control (IAC) valve assembly
16. IAC valve O-ring
17. Idle air control valve attaching screw

FIG. 11 Throttle body assembly — 2.3L engine

Except 2.3L Engine

1. Disconnect the negative battery cable.
2. Partially drain the cooling system to allow the coolant hoses at the throttle body to be removed.
3. Remove the air inlet duct at the throttle body and crankcase vent pipe at the valve cover grommet.
4. Disconnect the TPS and IAC valve electrical connectors.
5. Disconnect the vacuum harness connector from the throttle body.
6. Disconnect the throttle, TV (transmission control) and cruise control cables.
7. Disconnect the coolant hoses from the throttle body.
8. Remove the throttle body attaching bolts.
9. Remove the throttle body assembly and flange gasket. Discard the gasket.

To install:

➡ **Use care in the cleaning of old gasket material from machined aluminum surfaces. Sharp tools may cause damage to sealing surfaces.**

10. Install the throttle body assembly with a new flange gasket. Install the throttle body attaching bolts. Tighten to 18–20 ft. lbs. (24–27 Nm).
11. Connect the coolant hoses to the throttle body.
12. Connect the throttle, TV and cruise cables.

➡ **Ensure that the throttle and cruise control linkage does not hold the throttle open.**

13. Connect the vacuum harness connector to the throttle body.
14. Connect the TPS and IAC valve electrical connectors.
15. Connect the air inlet duct to the throttle body and crankcase vent pipe to the valve cover grommet.
16. Refill the radiator.
17. Connect the negative battery cable.
18. With the ignition switch in the **OFF** position, ensure that the movement of the accelerator is free.

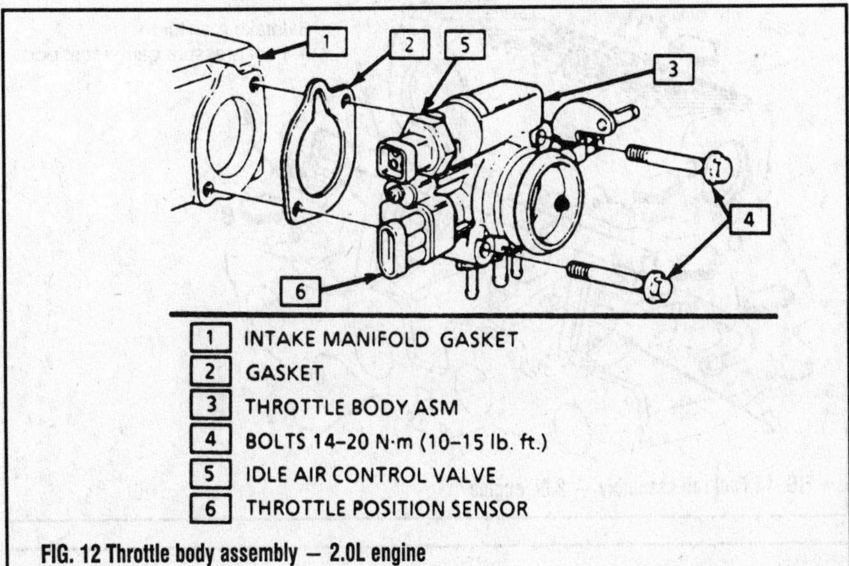

FIG. 12 Throttle body assembly — 2.0L engine

Fuel Rail Assembly

➧ SEE FIGS. 14–17

When servicing the fuel rail assembly, be careful to prevent dirt and other contaminants from entering the fuel passages. Fittings should be capped and holes plugged during servicing. At any time the fuel system is opened for service, the O-ring seals and retainers used with related components should be replaced.

Before removing the fuel rail, the fuel rail assembly may be cleaned with a spray type cleaner, GM–30A or equivalent, following package instructions. Do not immerse fuel rails in liquid cleaning solvent. Be sure to always use new O-rings and seals when reinstalling the fuel rail assemblies.

There is an 8-digit number stamped on the under side of the fuel rail assembly on 4 cylinder engines and on the left hand fuel rail on dual rail

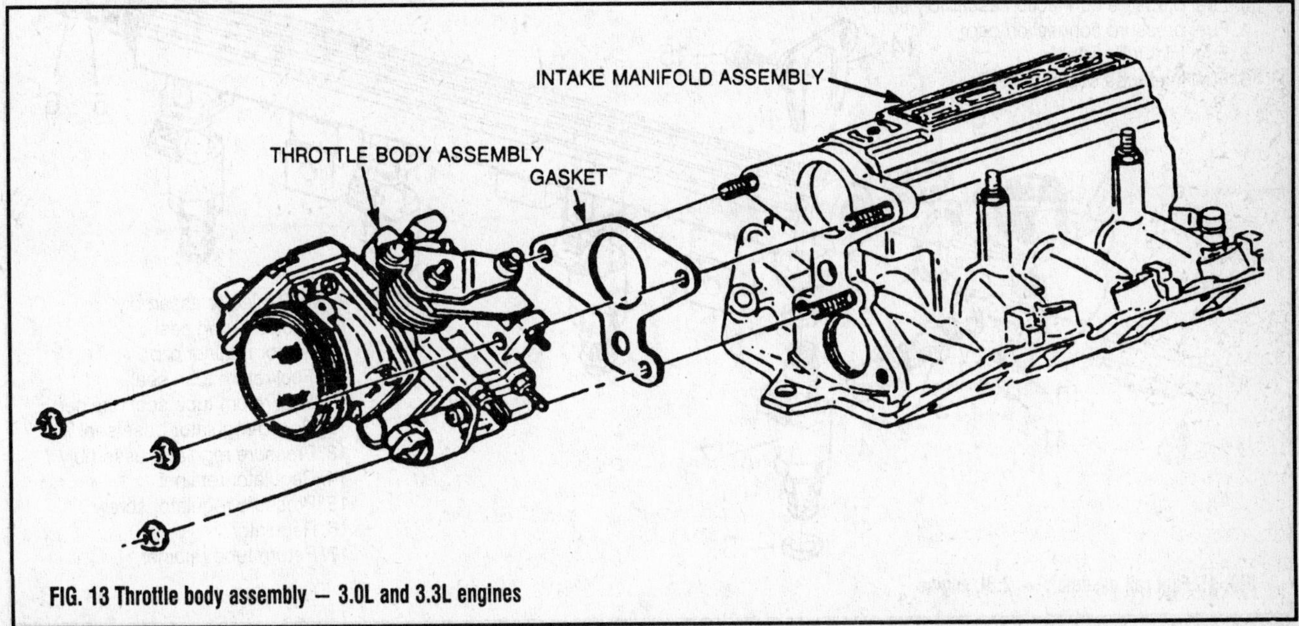

FIG. 13 Throttle body assembly — 3.0L and 3.3L engines

assemblies (fueling even cylinders No. 2, 4, 6). Refer to this number if servicing or part replacement is required.

REMOVAL & INSTALLATION

2.0L Engine

1. Relieve fuel system pressure. Disconnect the negative battery cable.
2. Remove the air intake ducts and/or passages in order to gain access to the fuel rail.
3. Disconnect the fuel line from the fuel rail.
4. Carefully, disconnect the fuel injector electrical connectors. Lay the harness aside.
5. Remove the pressure regulator assembly, as required to ease removal of the fuel rail.
6. Remove the fuel rail mounting hardware.
7. Carefully remove the fuel injectors from the intake manifold.
8. Remove the fuel rail from the vehicle.
9. Discard the fuel injector O-rings.

To install:

10. Install new fuel injector O-rings. Lubricate with a light coating of engine oil.
11. Carefully, install the fuel injectors to the intake manifold.
12. Install the fuel rail attaching hardware.
13. If removed, install the pressure regulator.
14. Connect the fuel injector electrical connectors.
15. Connect the fuel line to the fuel rail.
16. Install the air intake ducts and/or passages.
17. Connect the negative battery cable.
18. Turn the ignition key to the **ON** position. Check for fuel leaks.
19. Start the engine and allow to idle. Recheck for leaks.

2.3L Engine

1. Relieve fuel system pressure. Disconnect the negative battery cable.
2. Remove the crankcase ventilation oil/air separator and the canister purge solenoid.
3. Disconnect the fuel feed line and return line from the fuel rail assembly, be sure to use a backup wrench on the inlet fitting to prevent turning.
4. Remove the vacuum line at the pressure regulator. Remove the fuel rail assembly retaining bolts.
5. Push in the wire connector clip, while pulling the connector away from the injector.
6. Remove the fuel rail assembly and cover all openings with masking tape to prevent dirt entry.

➡ **If any injectors become separated from the fuel rail and remain in the intake manifold, both O-ring seals and injector retaining clip must be replaced. Use care in removing the fuel rail assembly, to prevent damage to the injector**

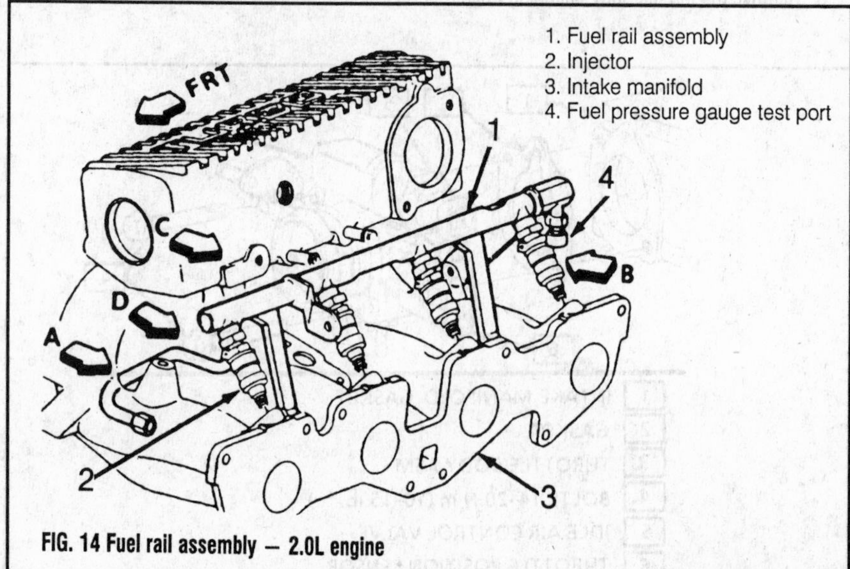

FIG. 14 Fuel rail assembly — 2.0L engine

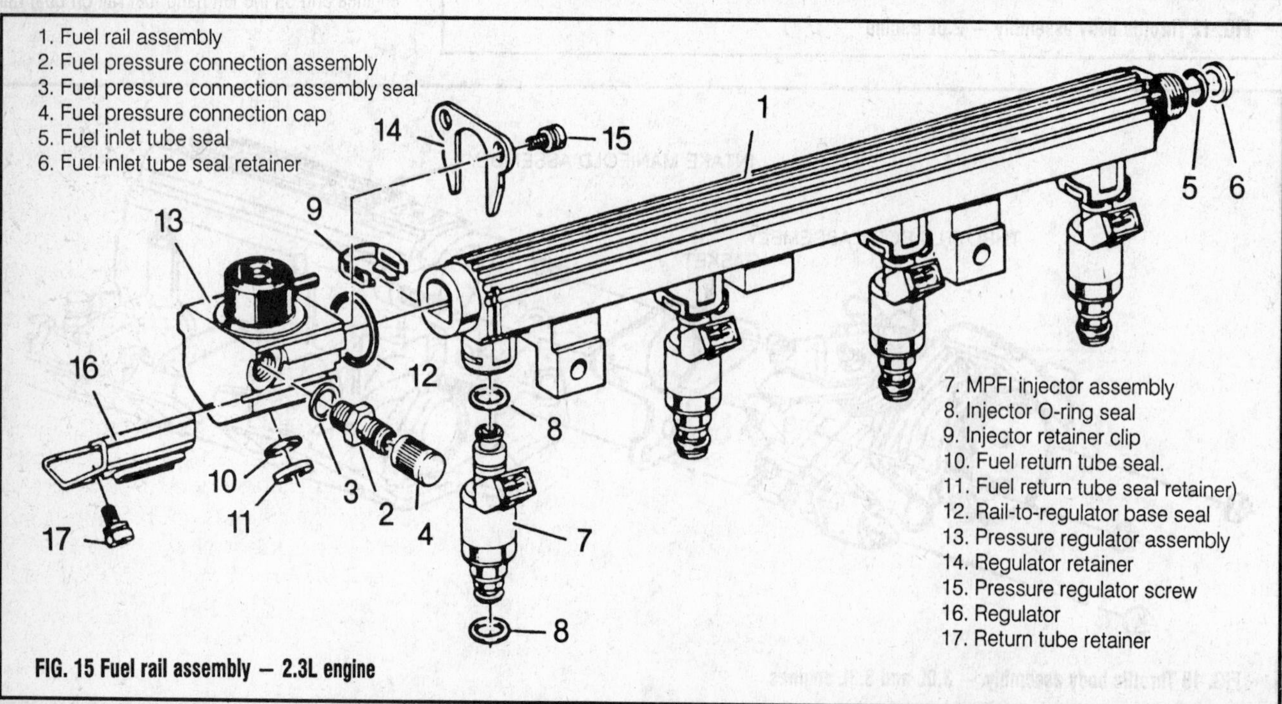

FIG. 15 Fuel rail assembly — 2.3L engine

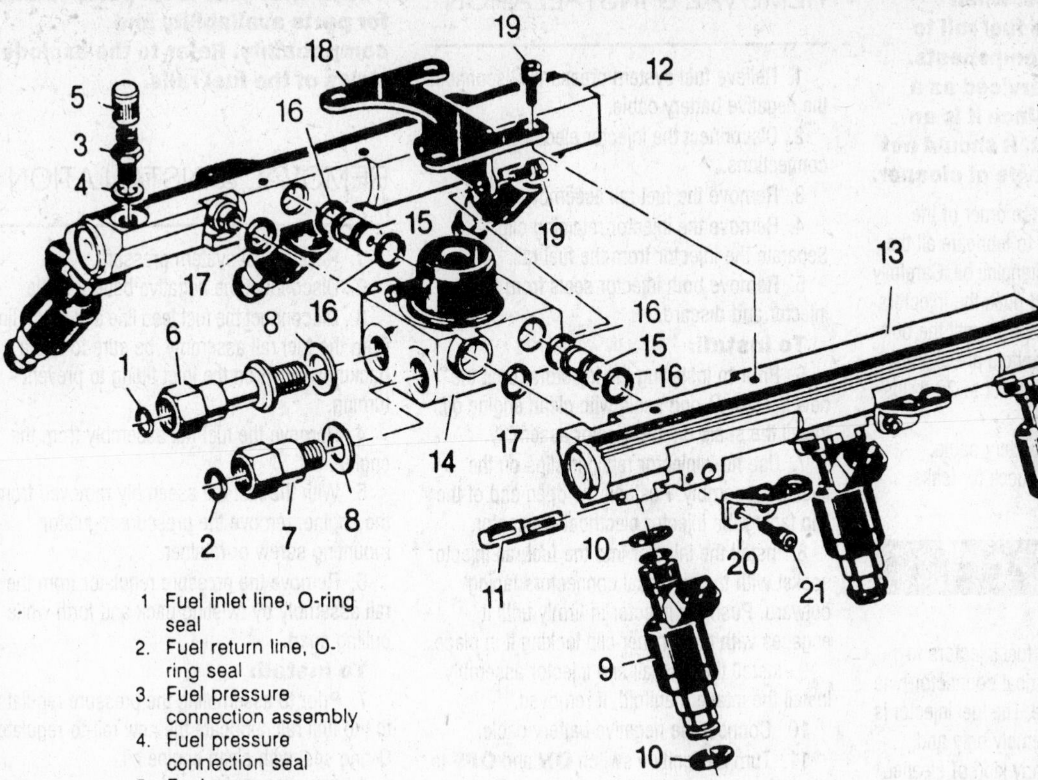

1. Fuel inlet line, O-ring seal
2. Fuel return line, O-ring seal
3. Fuel pressure connection assembly
4. Fuel pressure connection seal
5. Fuel pressure connection cap
6. Fitting fuel inlet
8. Fuel fitting gasket
9. MPFI injector assembly
10. Injector O-ring seal
11. Retainer
12. Fuel rail and plug assembly (left)
13. Fuel rail and plug assembly (Right)
14. Pressure regulator assembly
15. Base ball-to-rail connector
16. O-ring seal
17. Fuel return O-ring seal
18. Pressure regulator mounting bracket
19. Screw
20. Fuel rail mounting bracket
21. Bracket mounting screw

FIG. 16 Fuel rail assembly — V6 engine

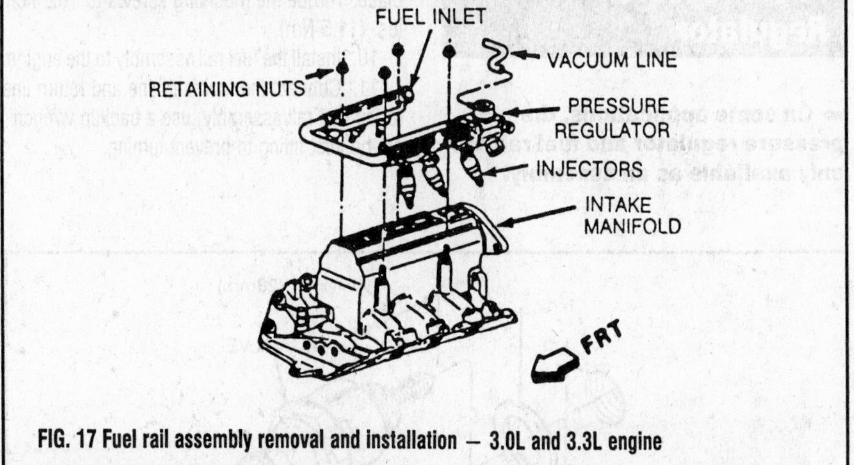

FIG. 17 Fuel rail assembly removal and installation — 3.0L and 3.3L engine

electrical connector terminals and the injector spray tips. When removed, support the fuel rail to avoid damaging its components. The fuel injector is serviced as a complete unit only. Since it is an electrical component, it should not be immersed in any type of cleaner.

7. Be sure to lubricate all the O-rings and seals with clean engine oil. Carefully push the injectors into the cylinder head intake ports until the bolt holes on the fuel rail and manifold are aligned.

8. The remainder of the installation is the reverse order of the removal procedure.

9. Apply a coating of tread locking compound on the treads of the fittings. Torque the fuel rail retaining bolts to 19 ft. lbs. (26 Nm), the fuel feed line nut to 22 ft. lbs. (30 Nm) and the fuel pipe fittings to 20 ft. lbs. (26 Nm).

10. Energize the fuel pump and check for leaks.

3.0L and 3.3L Engines

1. Disconnect the negative battery cable. Relieve fuel system pressure.

2. Remove the intake manifold plenum.

3. Disconnect the fuel feed line and return line from the fuel rail assembly, be sure to use a backup wrench on the inlet fitting to prevent turning.

4. Remove the vacuum line at the pressure regulator. Remove the fuel rail assembly retaining bolts.

5. Push in the wire connector clip, while pulling the connector away from the injector.

6. Remove the fuel rail assembly and cover all openings with masking tape to prevent dirt entry.

➡ If any injectors become separated from the fuel rail and remain in the intake manifold, both O-ring seals and injector retaining clip must be replaced. Use care in removing the fuel rail assembly, to prevent damage to the injector electrical connector terminals and

the injector spray tips. When removed, support the fuel rail to avoid damaging its components. The fuel injector is serviced as a complete unit only. Since it is an electrical component, it should not be immersed in any type of cleaner.

7. Installation is the reverse order of the removal procedure. Be sure to lubricate all the O-rings and seals with clean engine oil. Carefully tilt the fuel rail assembly and push the injectors into the cylinder head intake ports until the bolt holes on the fuel rail and manifold are aligned. Tighten the fuel rail attaching bolts to 20 ft. lbs. (27 Nm).

8. Connect the negative battery cable. Energize the fuel pump and check for leaks.

Fuel Injectors

➧ SEE FIG. 18

Use care in removing the fuel injectors to prevent damage to the electrical connector pins on the injector and the nozzle. The fuel injector is serviced as a complete assembly only and should not be immersed in any kind of cleaner. Support the fuel rail to avoid damaging other components while removing the injector. Be sure to note that different injectors are calibrated for different flow rates. When ordering new fuel injectors, be sure to order the identical part number that is inscribed on the bottom of the old injector.

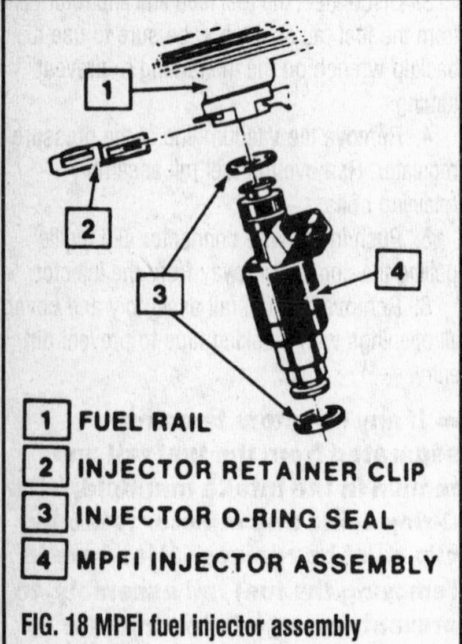

FIG. 18 MPFI fuel injector assembly

REMOVAL & INSTALLATION

1. Relieve fuel system pressure. Disconnect the negative battery cable.
2. Disconnect the injector electrical connections.
3. Remove the fuel rail assembly.
4. Remove the injector retaining clip. Separate the injector from the fuel rail.
5. Remove both injector seals from the injector and discard.

To install:

6. Prior to installing the injectors, coat the new injector O-ring seals with clean engine oil. Install the seals on the injector assembly.
7. Use new injector retainer clips on the injector assembly. Position the open end of the clip facing the injector electrical connector.
8. Install the injector into the fuel rail injector socket with the electrical connectors facing outward. Push the injector in firmly until it engages with the retainer clip locking it in place.
9. Install the fuel rail and injector assembly. Install the intake manifold, if removed.
10. Connect the negative battery cable.
11. Turn the ignition switch **ON** and **OFF** to allow fuel pressure back into system. Check for leaks.

Fuel Pressure Regulator

➡ On some applications, the pressure regulator and fuel rail are only available as an assembly. Check with your local parts retailer for parts availability and compatibility. Refer to the exploded views of the fuel rails.

REMOVAL & INSTALLATION

1. Relieve fuel system pressure.
2. Disconnect the negative battery cable.
3. Disconnect the fuel feed line and return line from the fuel rail assembly, be sure to use a backup wrench on the inlet fitting to prevent turning.
4. Remove the fuel rail assembly from the engine.
5. With the fuel rail assembly removed from the engine, remove the pressure regulator mounting screw or retainer.
6. Remove the pressure regulator from the rail assembly by twisting back and forth while pulling apart.

To install:

7. Prior to assembling the pressure regulator to the fuel rail, lubricate the new rail-to-regulator O-ring seal with clean engine oil.
8. Place the O-ring on the pressure regulator and install the pressure regulator to the fuel rail.
9. Install the retainer or coat the regulator mounting screws with an approved tread locking compound and secure the pressure regulator in place. Torque the mounting screws to 102 inch lbs. (11.5 Nm).
10. Install the fuel rail assembly to the engine.
11. Connect the fuel feed line and return line to the fuel rail assembly, use a backup wrench on the inlet fitting to prevent turning.

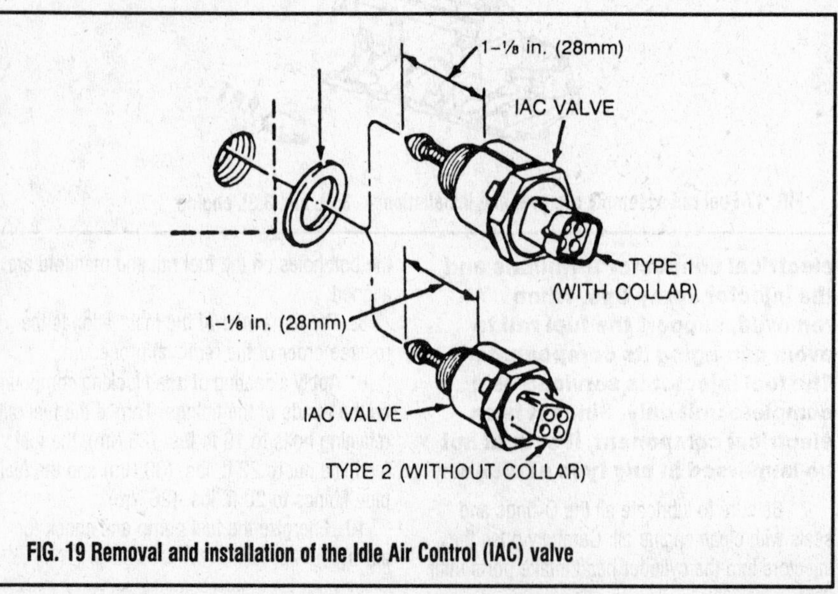

FIG. 19 Removal and installation of the Idle Air Control (IAC) valve

12. Connect the negative battery cable.
13. Turn the ignition switch **ON** and **OFF** to allow fuel pressure back into system. Check for leaks.

Idle Air Control Valve

➧ SEE FIG. 19

REMOVAL & INSTALLATION

1. Disconnect the negative battery cable.
2. Disconnect electrical connector from idle air control valve.
3. Remove the screws retaining the idle air control valve. Remove the idle air control valve from mounting position.

To install:

4. Prior to installing the idle air control valve, measure the distance the valve plunger is extended. Measurement should be made from the edge of the valves mounting flange to the end of the cone. The distance should not exceed 1$^{1}/_{8}$ in. (28mm), or damage to the valve may occur when installed. If measuring distance is greater than specified above, press on the valve firmly to retract it, using a slight side to side motion to help it retract easier.
5. Use a new gasket and install the idle air control valve in mounting position.
6. Install the retaining screws. Torque the retaining screws to 27 inch lbs. (3 Nm). Connect the electrical connector.
7. The idle may be unstable for up to 7 minutes upon restarting while the ECM resets the IAC valve pintle to the correct position.

Coolant Temperature Sensor

The coolant temperature sensor is located on the intake manifold water jacket or near (or on) the thermostat housing. It may be necessary to drain some of the coolant from the coolant system.

REMOVAL & INSTALLATION

✲✲ CAUTION

When draining the coolant, keep in mind that cats and dogs are attracted by the ethylene glycol antifreeze, and are quite likely to drink any that is left in an uncovered container or in puddles on the ground. This will prove fatal in sufficient quantity. Always drain the coolant into a sealable container. Coolant should be reused unless it is contaminated or several years old.

1. Disconnect the negative battery cable and disconnect the electrical connector at the sensor.
2. Remove the threaded temperature sensor from the engine.
3. Check the sensor with the tip immersed in water at 50°F (15°C). The resistance across the terminals should approximately 5600Ω. Check Code 14 or 15 engine chart for specific resistance on vehicle being serviced. If not within specifications, replace the sensor.
4. Apply some pipe tape to the threaded sensor and install the sensor.
5. Fill the cooling system if any coolant was removed. Reconnect the sensor connector and the negative battery cable.

Throttle Position Sensor

➧ SEE FIG. 20

REMOVAL & INSTALLATION

1. Disconnect the electrical connector from the sensor. Refer to the throttle body exploded views for location of the TPS.
2. Remove the attaching screws, lock washers and retainers.
3. Remove the throttle position sensor. If necessary, remove the screw holding the actuator to the end of the throttle shaft.
4. With the throttle valve in the normal closed idle position, install the throttle position sensor on the throttle body assembly, making sure the sensor pickup lever is located above the tang on the throttle actuator lever.
5. Install the retainers, screws and lock washers using a thread locking compound. Tighten to 18 inch lbs. (2 Nm).

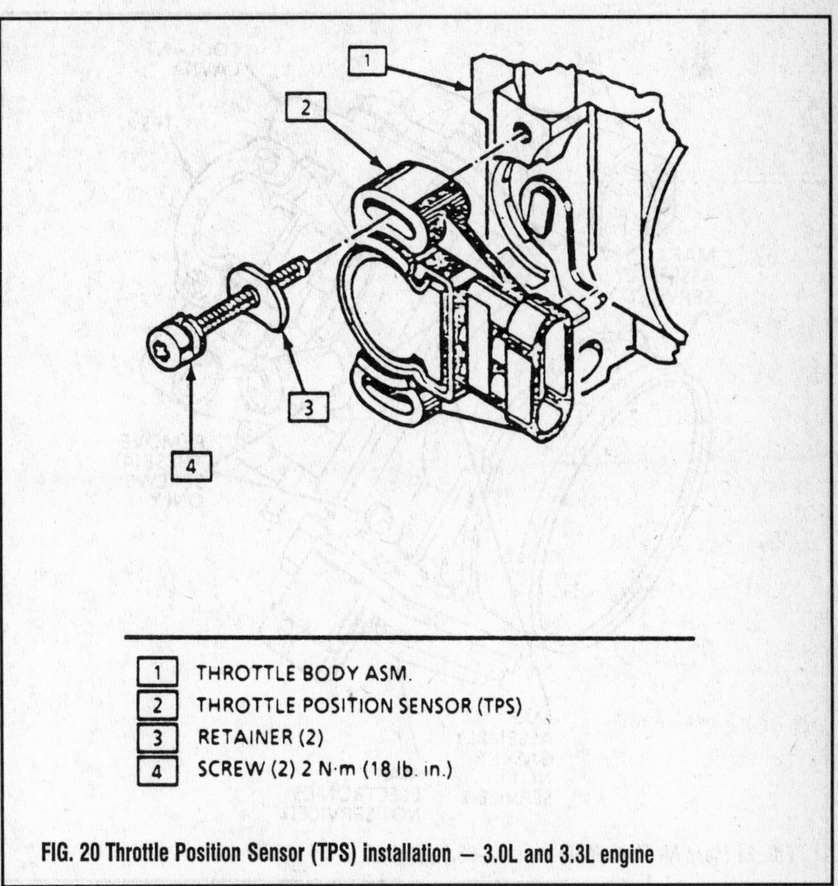

FIG. 20 Throttle Position Sensor (TPS) installation — 3.0L and 3.3L engine

ADJUSTMENT

3.0L and 3.3L Engines

1. Connect SCAN tool and view throttle position
2. With the ignition in the **ON** position and the throttle closed, adjust the position of the throttle sensor to obtain a reading of 0.50–0.59 volts for a 3.0L engine and 0.38–0.42 volts for a 3.3L engine.
3. Tighten the screws to 18 inch lbs. (2.0 Nm).
4. Recheck reading.

TPS Output Check Test

WITH SCAN TOOL

1. Use a suitable scan tool to read the TPS voltage.
2. With the ignition switch **ON** and the engine **OFF**, the TPS voltage should be less, than 1.25 volts.
3. If the voltage reading is higher than specified, replace the throttle position sensor.

WITHOUT SCAN TOOL

1. Disconnect the TPS harness from the TPS.
2. Using suitable jumper wires, connect a digital voltmeter to terminals A and B on the TPS.
3. With the ignition **ON** and the engine running, the TPS voltage should be 0.450–1.25 volts at base idle to approximately 4.5 volts at wide open throttle.
4. If the reading on the TPS is out of specification, replace it.
5. Turn ignition **OFF**, remove jumper wires, then reconnect harness to throttle position switch.

Mass Air Flow Sensor

REMOVAL & INSTALLATION

➧ SEE FIG. 21

1. Disconnect the negative battery cable.
2. Disconnect the electrical connector to the MAF sensor.
3. Remove the air cleaner and duct assembly. Remove the sensor retaining clamps and remove the sensor.
4. Installation is the reverse order of the removal procedure.

Torque Converter Clutch Solenoid

REMOVAL & INSTALLATION

1. Remove the negative battery cable. Raise and support the vehicle safely.
2. Drain the transmission fluid into a suitable drain pan. Remove the transmission pan.
3. Remove the TCC solenoid retaining screws and then remove the electrical connector, solenoid and check ball.
4. Clean and inspect all parts. Replace defective parts as necessary.

To install:

5. Install the check ball, TCC solenoid and electrical connector. Install the solenoid retaining screws and torque them to 10 ft. lbs. (14 Nm).
6. Install the transmission pan with a new gasket and torque the pan retaining bolts to 10 ft. lbs. (14 Nm).
7. Lower the vehicle and refill the transmission with the proper amount of the automatic transmission fluid.

MEM-CAL

REMOVAL & INSTALLATION

➧ SEE FIG. 8

1. Remove the ECM.
2. Remove the Mem-Cal access panel.
3. Using 2 fingers, push both retaining clips back away from the Mem-Cal. At the same time, grasp it at both ends and lift it out of the socket. Do not remove the cover of the Mem-Cal. Use of an unapproved Mem-Cal removal procedures may cause damage to the Mem-Cal or the socket.

To install:

4. Install the new Mem-Cal by pressing only the ends of the Mem-Cal. Small notches in the Mem-Cal must be aligned with the small notches in the Mem-Cal socket.
5. Press on the ends of the Mem-Cal until the retaining clips snap into the ends of the Mem-Cal. Do not press on the middle of the Mem-Cal, only on the ends.
6. Install the Mem-Cal access cover and reinstall the ECM.

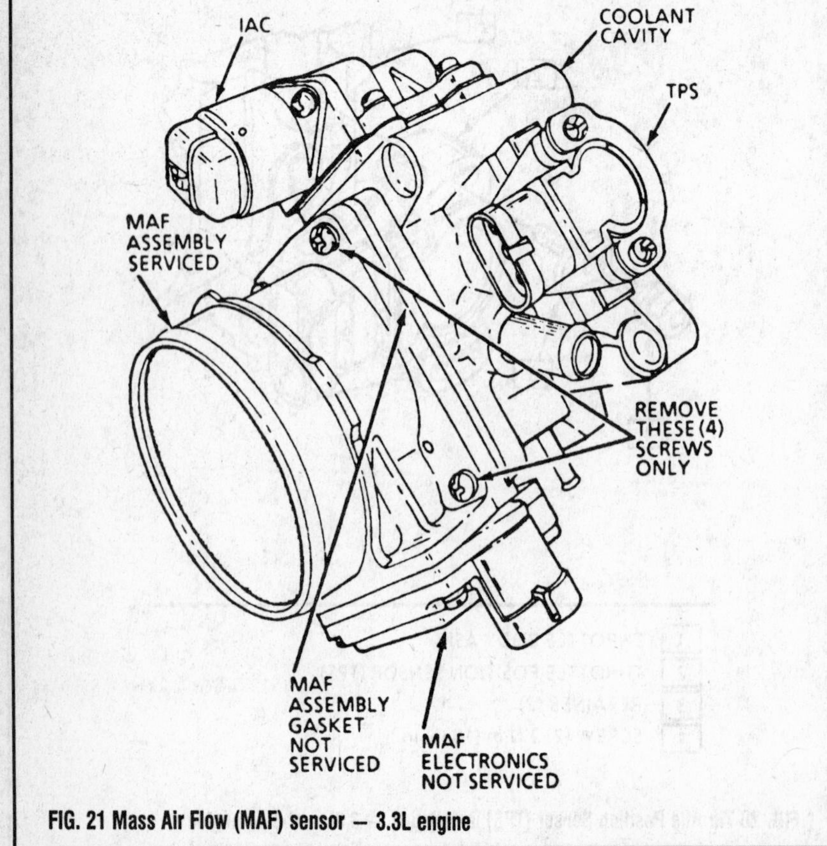

FIG. 21 Mass Air Flow (MAF) sensor — 3.3L engine

PROM

REMOVAL & INSTALLATION

➧ SEE FIGS. 9 AND 10

1. Remove the ECM.
2. Remove the PROM access panel.
3. Using the rocker type PROM removal tool, engage 1 end of the PROM carrier with the hook end of the tool. Press on the vertical bar end of the tool and rock the engaged end of the PROM carrier up as far as possible.
4. Engage the opposite end of the PROM carrier in the same manner and rock this end up as far as possible.
5. Repeat this process until the PROM carrier and PROM are free of the PROM socket. The PROM carrier with PROM in it should lift off of the PROM socket easily.
6. The PROM carrier should only be removed by using the special PROM removal tool. Other methods could cause damage to the PROM or PROM socket.
7. Before installing a new PROM, be sure the new PROM part number is the same as the old one or the as the updated number per a service bulletin.

To install:

8. Install the PROM with the small notch of the carrier aligned with the small notch in the socket. Press on the PROM carrier until the PROM is firmly seated, do not press on the PROM itself only on the PROM carrier.
9. Install the PROM access cover and reinstall the ECM.

FUNCTIONAL CHECK

1. Turn the ignition switch to the **ON** position.
2. Enter the diagnostic mode.
3. Allow a Code 12 to flash 4 times to verify that no other codes are present. This indicates that the PROM is installed properly.
4. If trouble Code 51 occurs or if the SERVICE ENGINE SOON light in on constantly with no codes, the PROM is not fully seated, installed backwards, has bent pins or is defective.
5. If not fully seated press down firmly on the PROM carrier.
6. If installed backwards, replace the PROM.

➡ Any time the PROM is installed backwards and the ignition switch is turned ON, the PROM is destroyed.

7. If the pins are bent, remove the PROM straighten the pins and reinstall the PROM. If the bent pins break or crack during straightening, discard the PROM and replace with a new PROM.

➡ To prevent possible electrostatic discharge damage to the PROM or Cal-Pak, do not touch the component leads and do not remove the integrated circuit from the carrier.

FUEL TANK

DRAINING

1. Disconnect the negative battery cable.

⁂ CAUTION

To reduce the risk of fire and personal injury, always keep a dry chemical (Class B) fire extinguisher near the work area.

2. Remove the fuel cap.
3. Raise the vehicle and support with jackstands.
4. Disconnect the filler vent hose from the tank.
5. Use a hand operated pump approved for gasoline to drain as much fuel as possible through the filler vent hose.
6. Reconnect the filler vent hose and tighten the clamp.
7. Install any removed lines, hoses and cap. Connect the negative battery cable.

REMOVAL & INSTALLATION

1. Disconnect the negative battery cable.
2. Drain the fuel tank.
3. Remove the fuel filler door assembly and disconnect the screw retaining the filler pipe-to-body bracket.
4. Raise the vehicle and support with jackstands.
5. Disconnect the tank level sender lead connector.
6. Support the tank with a transmission jack or equivalent. Remove the two tank retaining straps.
7. Lower the tank far enough to disconnect the ground lead and fuel hoses from the pump assembly.
8. Remove the tank from the vehicle slowly to ensure all connections and hoses have been disconnected.
9. Remove the fuel pump/level sender assembly using a locking cam tool J-24187 or equivalent.

To install:

10. Using a new fuel pump O-ring gasket, install the pump/sender assembly into the tank.

⁂ CAUTION

Do not twist the strainer when installing the pump/sender assembly. Make sure the strainer does not block the full travel of the float arm.

11. Place the tank on the jack.
12. Position the tank sound insulators in their original positions and raise the tank far enough to connect the electrical and hose connectors.
13. Raise the tank to the proper position and loosely install the retaining straps. Make sure the tank is in the proper position before tightening the retaining straps.
14. Torque the straps to 26 ft. lbs. (35 Nm).
15. Connect the grounding strap and negative battery cable.
16. With the engine OFF, turn the ignition key to the ON position and check for fuel leaks at the tank.

TORQUE SPECIFICATIONS

Component	U.S.	Metric
Coolant temperature sensor	22 ft. lbs.	30 Nm
Fuel feed line nut	22 ft. lbs.	30 Nm
Fuel line fittings	20 ft. lbs.	26 Nm
Fuel meter assembly attaching screws	2.5L 53 inch lbs.	6 Nm
Fuel pressure regulator retaining screws		
2.5L engine	22 inch lbs.	2.5 Nm
Except 2.5L engine	.102 inch lbs.	11.5 Nm
Fuel rail retaining bolts	19 ft. lbs.	26 Nm
Fuel tank straps	26 ft. lbs.	35 Nm
Idle air control valve retaining screw	27 inch lbs.	3 Nm
Injector retaining screw	27 inch lbs.	3 Nm
Throttle body retaining screws		
2.0L engine	10–15 ft. lbs.	14–20 Nm
2.3L engine	20 ft. lbs.	27 Nm
2.5L engine	18 ft. lbs.	24 Nm
3.0L engine	11 ft. lbs.	15 Nm
3.3L engine	21 ft. lbs.	28 Nm
TCC solenoid retaining screws	10 ft. lbs.	14 Nm
TPS retaining screws	18 inch lbs.	2 Nm

6 CHASSIS ELECTRICAL

UNDERSTANDING AND TROUBLESHOOTING ELECTRICAL SYSTEMS

The following section outlines basic diagnosis techniques for dealing with computerized automotive control systems. Along with a general explanation of the various types of test equipment available to aid in servicing modern electronic automotive systems, basic repair techniques for wiring harnesses and connectors is given. Read the basic information before attempting any repairs or testing on any computerized system, to provide the background of information necessary to avoid the most common and obvious mistakes that can cost both time and money. Although the replacement and testing procedures are simple in themselves, the systems are not, and unless one has a thorough understanding of all components and their function within a particular computerized control system, the logical test sequence these systems demand cannot be followed. Minor malfunctions can make a big difference, so it is important to know how each component affects the operation of the overall electronic system to find the ultimate cause of a problem without replacing good components unnecessarily. It is not enough to use the correct test equipment; the test equipment must be used correctly.

SAFETY PRECAUTIONS

CAUTION

Whenever working on or around any computer based microprocessor control system, always observe these general precautions to prevent the possibility of personal injury or damage to electronic components.

- Never install or remove battery cables with the key ON or the engine running. Jumper cables should be connected with the key OFF to avoid power surges that can damage electronic control units. Engines equipped with computer controlled systems should avoid both giving and getting jump starts due to the possibility of serious damage to components from arcing in the engine compartment when connections are made with the ignition ON.
- Always remove the battery cables before charging the battery. Never use a high output charger on an installed battery or attempt to use any type of "hot shot" (24 volt) starting aid.
- Exercise care when inserting test probes into connectors to insure good connections without damaging the connector or spreading the pins. Always probe connectors from the rear (wire) side, NOT the pin side, to avoid accidental shorting of terminals during test procedures.
- Never remove or attach wiring harness connectors with the ignition switch ON, especially to an electronic control unit.
- Do not drop any components during service procedures and never apply 12 volts directly to any component (like a solenoid or relay) unless instructed specifically to do so. Some component electrical windings are designed to safely handle only 4 or 5 volts and can be destroyed in seconds if 12 volts are applied directly to the connector.
- Remove the electronic control unit if the vehicle is to be placed in an environment where temperatures exceed approximately 176°F (80°C), such as a paint spray booth or when arc or gas welding near the control unit location in the vehicle.

ORGANIZED TROUBLESHOOTING

When diagnosing a specific problem, organized troubleshooting is a must. The complexity of a modern automobile demands that you approach any problem in a logical, organized manner. There are certain troubleshooting techniques that are standard:

1. Establish when the problem occurs. Does the problem appear only under certain conditions? Were there any noises, odors, or other unusual symptoms?
2. Isolate the problem area. To do this, make some simple tests and observations; then eliminate the systems that are working properly. Check for obvious problems such as broken wires, dirty connections or split or disconnected vacuum hoses. Always check the obvious before assuming something complicated is the cause.
3. Test for problems systematically to determine the cause once the problem area is isolated. Are all the components functioning properly? Is there power going to electrical switches and motors? Is there vacuum at vacuum switches and/or actuators? Is there a mechanical problem such as bent linkage or loose mounting screws? Doing careful, systematic checks will often turn up most causes on the first inspection without wasting time checking components that have little or no relationship to the problem.
4. Test all repairs after the work is done to make sure that the problem is fixed. Some causes can be traced to more than one component, so a careful verification of repair work is important to pick up additional malfunctions that may cause a problem to reappear or a different problem to arise. A blown fuse, for example, is a simple problem that may require more than another fuse to repair. If you don't look for a problem that caused a fuse to blow, for example, a shorted wire may go undetected.

Experience has shown that most problems tend to be the result of a fairly simple and obvious cause, such as loose or corroded connectors or air leaks in the intake system; making careful inspection of components during testing essential to quick and accurate troubleshooting. Special, hand held computerized testers designed specifically for diagnosing the system are available from a variety of aftermarket sources, as well as from the vehicle manufacturer, but care should be taken that any test equipment being used is designed to diagnose that particular computer controlled system accurately without damaging the control unit (ECM) or components being tested.

TEST EQUIPMENT

➡ **Pinpointing the exact cause of trouble in an electrical system can sometimes only be accomplished by the use of special test equipment. The following describes commonly used test equipments and explains how to put them to best use in diagnosis. The manufacturer's instructions booklet provided with the tester should also be read and clearly understood before attempting any test procedures.**

JUMPER WIRES

Jumper wires are simple, yet extremely

valuable, pieces of test equipment. Jumper wires are merely wires that are used to bypass sections of a circuit. The simplest type of jumper wire is merely a length of multi-strand wire with an alligator clip at each end. Jumper wires are usually fabricated from lengths of standard automotive wire and whatever type of connector (alligator clip, spade connector or pin connector) that is required for the particular vehicle being tested. The well equipped tool box will have several different styles of jumper wires in several different lengths. Some jumper wires are made with three or more terminals coming from a common splice for special purpose testing. In cramped, hard-to-reach areas it is advisable to have insulated boots over the jumper wire terminals in order to prevent accidental grounding, sparks, and possible fire, especially when testing fuel system components.

Jumper wires are used primarily to locate open electrical circuits, on either the ground (-) side of the circuit or on the hot (+) side. If an electrical component fails to operate, connect the jumper wire between the component and a good ground. If the component operates only with the jumper installed, the ground circuit is open. If the ground circuit is good, but the component does not operate, the circuit between the power feed and component is open. You can sometimes connect the jumper wire directly from the battery to the hot terminal of the component, but first make sure the component uses 12 volts in operation. Some electrical components, such as fuel injectors, are designed to operate on about 4 volts and running 12 volts directly to the injector terminals can burn out the wiring. By inserting an in-line fuseholder between a set of test leads, a fused jumper wire can be used for bypassing open circuits. Use a 5 amp fuse to provide protection against voltage spikes. When in doubt, use a voltmeter to check the voltage input to the component and measure how much voltage is being applied normally. By moving the jumper wire successively back from the lamp toward the power source, you can isolate the area of the circuit where the open is located. When the component stops functioning, or the power is cut off, the open is in the segment of wire between the jumper and the point previously tested.

- Never use jumpers made from wire that is of lighter gauge than used in the circuit under test. If the jumper wire is of too small gauge, it may overheat and possibly melt.
- Never use jumpers to bypass high resistance loads in a circuit. Bypassing resistances, in effect, creates a short circuit which may, in turn, cause damage and fire.
- Never use a jumper for anything other than temporary bypassing of components in a circuit.

TEST LIGHT (12-VOLTS)

The 12 volt test light is used to check circuits and components while electrical current is flowing through them. It is used for voltage and ground tests. Twelve volt test lights come in different styles but all have three main parts; a ground clip, a probe, and a light. The most commonly used 12 volt test lights have pick-type probes. To use a 12 volt test light, connect the ground clip to a good ground and probe wherever necessary with the pick. The pick should be sharp so that it can penetrate wire insulation to make contact with the wire, without making a large hole in the insulation. The wrap-around light is handy in hard to reach areas or where it is difficult to support a wire to push a probe pick into it. To use the wrap around light, hook the wire to probed with the hook and pull the trigger. A small pick will be forced through the wire insulation into the wire core.

➡ Do not use a test light to probe electronic ignition spark plug or coil wires. Never use a pick-type test light to probe wiring on computer controlled systems unless specifically instructed to do so. Any wire insulation that is pierced by the test light probe should be taped and sealed with silicone after testing.

Similar to jumper wires, the 12 volt test light can used to isolate opens in circuits. However, where the jumper wire is used to bypass the open circuit and operate the load, the 12 volt test light is used to locate the presence of voltage in the circuit. If the test light glows, you know that there is power up to that point; if the 12 volt test light does not glow when its probe is inserted into the wire or connector, you know that there is an open circuit (no power). Move the test light in successive steps back toward the power source until the light in the handle does glow. When it does glow, the open is between the probe and point previously probed.

➡ The test light does not detect that 12 volts (or any particular amount of voltage) is present; it only detects that some voltage is present. It is advisable before using the test light to touch its terminals across the battery posts to make sure the light is operating properly.

SELF-POWERED TEST LIGHT

The self-powered test light usually contains a 1.5 volt penlight battery. One type of self-powered test light is similar in design to the 12 volt test light. This type has both the battery and the light in the handle and pick-type probe tip. The second type has the light toward the open tip, so that the light illuminates the contact point. The self-powered test light is dual purpose piece of test equipment. It can be used to test for either open or short circuits when power is isolated from the circuit (continuity test). A powered test light should not be used on any computer controlled system or component unless specifically instructed to do so. Many engine sensors can be destroyed by even this small amount of voltage applied directly to the terminals.

Open Circuit Testing

To use the self-powered test light to check for open circuits, first isolate the circuit from the vehicle's 12 volt power source by disconnecting the battery or wiring harness connector. Connect the test light ground clip to a good ground and probe sections of the circuit sequentially with the test light. (start from either end of the circuit). If the light is out, the open is between the probe and the circuit ground. If the light is on, the open is between the probe and end of the circuit toward the power source.

Short Circuit Testing

By isolating the circuit both from power and from ground, and using a self-powered test light, you can check for shorts to ground in the circuit. Isolate the circuit from power and ground. Connect the test light ground clip to a good ground and probe any easy-to-reach test point in the circuit. If the light comes on, there is a short somewhere in the circuit. To isolate the short, probe a test point at either end of the isolated circuit (the light should be on). Leave the test light probe connected and open connectors, switches, remove parts, etc., sequentially, until the light goes out. When the light goes out, the short is between the last circuit component opened and the previous circuit opened.

➡ The 1.5 volt battery in the test light does not provide much current. A weak battery may not provide enough power to illuminate the test light even when a complete circuit is made (especially if there are high resistances in the circuit). Always make sure that the test battery is strong. To check the battery, briefly touch the ground clip to the probe; if the light glows brightly the battery is strong enough for testing. Never use a self-powered test light to perform checks for opens or shorts when power is applied to the electrical system under test. The 12 volt vehicle power will quickly burn out the 1.5 volt light bulb in the test light.

VOLTMETER

A voltmeter is used to measure voltage at any point in a circuit, or to measure the voltage drop across any part of a circuit. It can also be used to check continuity in a wire or circuit by indicating current flow from one end to the other. Voltmeters usually have various scales on the meter dial and a selector switch to allow the selection of different voltages. The voltmeter has a positive and a negative lead. To avoid damage to the meter, always connect the negative lead to the negative (–) side of circuit (to ground or nearest the ground side of the circuit) and connect the positive lead to the positive (+) side of the circuit (to the power source or the nearest power source). Note that the negative voltmeter lead will always be black and that the positive voltmeter will always be some color other than black (usually red). Depending on how the voltmeter is connected into the circuit, it has several uses.

A voltmeter can be connected either in parallel or in series with a circuit and it has a very high resistance to current flow. When connected in parallel, only a small amount of current will flow through the voltmeter current path; the rest will flow through the normal circuit current path and the circuit will work normally. When the voltmeter is connected in series with a circuit, only a small amount of current can flow through the circuit. The circuit will not work properly, but the voltmeter reading will show if the circuit is complete or not.

Available Voltage

Set the voltmeter selector switch to the 20V position and connect the meter negative lead to the negative post of the battery. Connect the positive meter lead to the positive post of the battery and turn the ignition switch ON to provide a load. Read the voltage on the meter or digital display. A well charged battery should register over 12 volts. If the meter reads below 11.5 volts, the battery power may be insufficient to operate the electrical system properly. This test determines voltage available from the battery and should be the first step in any electrical trouble diagnosis procedure. Many electrical problems, especially on computer controlled systems, can be caused by a low state of charge in the battery. Excessive corrosion at the battery cable terminals can cause a poor contact that will prevent proper charging and full battery current flow.

Normal battery voltage is 12 volts when fully charged. When the battery is supplying current to one or more circuits it is said to be "under load". When everything is off the electrical system is under a "no-load" condition. A fully charged battery may show about 12.5 volts at no load; will drop to 12 volts under medium load; and will drop even lower under heavy load. If the battery is partially discharged the voltage decrease under heavy load may be excessive, even though the battery shows 12 volts or more at no load. When allowed to discharge further, the battery's available voltage under load will decrease more severely. For this reason, it is important that the battery be fully charged during all testing procedures to avoid errors in diagnosis and incorrect test results.

Voltage Drop

When current flows through a resistance, the voltage beyond the resistance is reduced (the larger the current, the greater the reduction in voltage). When no current is flowing, there is no voltage drop because there is no current flow. All points in the circuit which are connected to the power source are at the same voltage as the power source. The total voltage drop always equals the total source voltage. In a long circuit with many connectors, a series of small, unwanted voltage drops due to corrosion at the connectors can add up to a total loss of voltage which impairs the operation of the normal loads in the circuit.

Indirect Computation of Voltage Drops

1. Set the voltmeter selector switch to the 20 volt position.
2. Connect the meter negative lead to a good ground.
3. Probe all resistances in the circuit with the positive meter lead.
4. Operate the circuit in all modes and observe the voltage readings.

Direct Measurement of Voltage Drops

1. Set the voltmeter switch to the 20 volt position.
2. Connect the voltmeter negative lead to the ground side of the resistance load to be measured.
3. Connect the positive lead to the positive side of the resistance or load to be measured.
4. Read the voltage drop directly on the 20 volt scale.

Too high a voltage indicates too high a resistance. If, for example, a blower motor runs too slowly, you can determine if there is too high a resistance in the resistor pack. By taking voltage drop readings in all parts of the circuit, you can isolate the problem. Too low a voltage drop indicates too low a resistance. If, for example, a blower motor runs too fast in the MED and/or LOW position, the problem can be isolated in the resistor pack by taking voltage drop readings in all parts of the circuit to locate a possibly shorted resistor. The maximum allowable voltage drop under load is critical, especially if there is more than one high resistance problem in a circuit because all voltage drops are cumulative. A small drop is normal due to the resistance of the conductors.

High Resistance Testing

1. Set the voltmeter selector switch to the 4 volt position.
2. Connect the voltmeter positive lead to the positive post of the battery.
3. Turn on the headlights and heater blower to provide a load.
4. Probe various points in the circuit with the negative voltmeter lead.
5. Read the voltage drop on the 4 volt scale. Some average maximum allowable voltage drops are:

FUSE PANEL: 7 volts
IGNITION SWITCH: 5 volts
HEADLIGHT SWITCH: 7 volts
IGNITION COIL (+): 5 volts
ANY OTHER LOAD: 1.3 volts

➡ Voltage drops are all measured while a load is operating; without current flow, there will be no voltage drop.

OHMMETER

The ohmmeter is designed to read resistance in ohms (Ω) in a circuit or component. Although there are several different styles of ohmmeters, all will usually have a selector switch which permits the measurement of different ranges of resistance (usually the selector switch allows the multiplication of the meter reading by 10, 100, 1,000, and 10,000). A calibration knob allows the meter to be set at zero for accurate measurement. Since all ohmmeters are powered by an internal battery (usually 9 volts), the ohmmeter can be used as a self-powered test light. When the ohmmeter is connected, current from the ohmmeter flows through the circuit or component being tested. Since the ohmmeter's internal resistance and voltage are known values, the amount of current flow through the meter depends on the resistance of the circuit or component being tested.

The ohmmeter can be used to perform continuity test for opens or shorts (either by observation of the meter needle or as a self-powered test light), and to read actual resistance in a circuit. It should be noted that the ohmmeter is used to check the resistance of a component or wire while there is no voltage applied to the circuit. Current flow from an outside voltage source (such as the vehicle battery) can damage the ohmmeter, so the circuit or component should be isolated from the vehicle electrical system before any testing is done. Since the ohmmeter uses its own voltage source, either lead can be connected to any test point.

➡ When checking diodes or other solid state components, the

ohmmeter leads can only be connected one way in order to measure current flow in a single direction. Make sure the positive (+) and negative (-) terminal connections are as described in the test procedures to verify the one-way diode operation.

In using the meter for making continuity checks, do not be concerned with the actual resistance readings. Zero resistance, or any resistance readings, indicate continuity in the circuit. Infinite resistance indicates an open in the circuit. A high resistance reading where there should be none indicates a problem in the circuit. Checks for short circuits are made in the same manner as checks for open circuits except that the circuit must be isolated from both power and normal ground. Infinite resistance indicates no continuity to ground, while zero resistance indicates a dead short to ground.

Resistance Measurement

The batteries in an ohmmeter will weaken with age and temperature, so the ohmmeter must be calibrated or "zeroed" before taking measurements. To zero the meter, place the selector switch in its lowest range and touch the two ohmmeter leads together. Turn the calibration knob until the meter needle is exactly on zero.

➡ **All analog (needle) type ohmmeters must be zeroed before use, but some digital ohmmeter models are automatically calibrated when the switch is turned on. Self-calibrating digital ohmmeters do not have an adjusting knob, but its a good idea to check for a zero readout before use by touching the leads together. All computer controlled systems require the use of a digital ohmmeter with at least 10MΩ (megohms) impedance for testing. Before any test procedures are attempted, make sure the ohmmeter used is compatible with the electrical system or damage to the on-board computer could result.**

To measure resistance, first isolate the circuit from the vehicle power source by disconnecting the battery cables or the harness connector. Make sure the key is OFF when disconnecting any components or the battery. Where necessary, also isolate at least one side of the circuit to be checked to avoid reading parallel resistances. Parallel circuit resistances will always give a lower reading than the actual resistance of either of the branches. When measuring the resistance of parallel circuits, the total resistance will always be lower than the smallest resistance in the circuit. Connect the meter leads to both sides of the circuit (wire or component) and read the actual measured ohms on the meter scale. Make sure the selector switch is set to the proper ohm scale for the circuit being tested to avoid misreading the ohmmeter test value.

✱✱ WARNING

Never use an ohmmeter with power applied to the circuit. Like the self-powered test light, the ohmmeter is designed to operate on its own power supply. The normal 12 volt automotive electrical system current could damage the meter!

AMMETER

An ammeter measures the amount of current flowing through a circuit in units called amperes or amps. Amperes are units of electron flow which indicate how fast the electrons are flowing through the circuit. Since Ohms Law dictates that current flow in a circuit is equal to the circuit voltage divided by the total circuit resistance, increasing voltage also increases the current level (amps). Likewise, any decrease in resistance will increase the amount of amps in a circuit. At normal operating voltage, most circuits have a characteristic amount of amperes, called "current draw" which can be measured using an ammeter. By referring to a specified current draw rating, measuring the amperes, and comparing the two values, one can determine what is happening within the circuit to aid in diagnosis. An open circuit, for example, will not allow any current to flow so the ammeter reading will be zero. More current flows through a heavily loaded circuit or when the charging system is operating.

An ammeter is always connected in series with the circuit being tested. All of the current that normally flows through the circuit must also flow through the ammeter; if there is any other path for the current to follow, the ammeter reading will not be accurate. The ammeter itself has very little resistance to current flow and therefore will not affect the circuit, but it will measure current draw only when the circuit is closed and electricity is flowing. Excessive current draw can blow fuses and drain the battery, while a reduced current draw can cause motors to run slowly, lights to dim and other components to not operate properly. The ammeter can help diagnose these conditions by locating the cause of the high or low reading.

MULTI-METER

Different combinations of test meters can be built into a single unit designed for specific tests. Some of the more common combination test devices are known as Volt/Amp testers, Tach/Dwell meters, or Digital Multimeters. The Volt/Amp tester is used for charging system, starting system or battery tests and consists of a voltmeter, an ammeter and a variable resistance carbon pile. The voltmeter will usually have at least two ranges for use with 6, 12 and 24 volt systems. The ammeter also has more than one range for testing various levels of battery loads and starter current draw and the carbon pile can be adjusted to offer different amounts of resistance. The Volt/Amp tester has heavy leads to carry large amounts of current and many later models have an inductive ammeter pickup that clamps around the wire to simplify test connections. On some models, the ammeter also has a zero-center scale to allow testing of charging and starting systems without switching leads or polarity. A digital multimeter is a voltmeter, ammeter and ohmmeter combined in an instrument which gives a digital readout. These are often used when testing solid state circuits because of their high input impedance (usually 10 megohms or more).

The tach/dwell meter combines a tachometer and a dwell (cam angle) meter and is a specialized kind of voltmeter. The tachometer scale is marked to show engine speed in rpm and the dwell scale is marked to show degrees of distributor shaft rotation. In most electronic ignition systems, dwell is determined by the control unit, but the dwell meter can also be used to check the duty cycle (operation) of some electronic engine control systems. Some tach/dwell meters are powered by an internal battery, while others take their power from the car battery in use. The battery powered testers usually require calibration much like an ohmmeter before testing.

SPECIAL TEST EQUIPMENT

A variety of diagnostic tools are available to help troubleshoot and repair computerized engine control systems. The most sophisticated of these devices are the console type engine analyzers that usually occupy a garage service bay, but there are several types of aftermarket electronic testers available that will allow quick circuit tests of the engine control system by plugging directly into a special connector located in the engine compartment or under the dashboard. Several tool and equipment manufacturers offer simple, hand held testers that measure various circuit voltage levels on command to check all system components for proper operation. Although these testers usually cost about $300–500, consider that the average computer control unit (or ECM) can cost just as much and the money saved by not replacing perfectly good sensors or components in an attempt to correct a problem could justify the purchase price of a special diagnostic tester the first time it's used.

These computerized testers can allow quick and easy test measurements while the engine is operating or while the car is being driven. In addition, the on-board computer memory can be read to access any stored trouble codes; in effect allowing the computer to tell you where it hurts and aid trouble diagnosis by pinpointing exactly which circuit or component is malfunctioning. In the same manner, repairs can be tested to make sure the problem has been corrected. The biggest advantage these special testers have is their relatively easy hookups that minimize or eliminate the chances of making the wrong connections and getting false voltage readings or damaging the computer accidentally.

➡ It should be remembered that these testers check voltage levels in circuits; they don't detect mechanical problems or failed components if the circuit voltage falls within the preprogrammed limits stored in the tester PROM unit. Also, most of the hand held testers are designed to work only on one or two systems made by a specific manufacturer.

A variety of aftermarket testers are available to help diagnose different computerized control systems. Owatonna Tool Company (OTC), for example, markets a device called the OTC Monitor which plugs directly into the assembly line diagnostic link (ALDL). The OTC tester makes diagnosis a simple matter of pressing the correct buttons and, by changing the internal PROM or inserting a different diagnosis cartridge, it will work on any model from full size to subcompact, over a wide range of years. An adapter is supplied with the tester to allow connection to all types of ALDL links, regardless of the number of pin terminals used. By inserting an updated PROM into the OTC tester, it can be easily updated to diagnose any new modifications of computerized control systems.

WIRING HARNESSES

The average automobile contains about ½ mile of wiring, with hundreds of individual connections. To protect the many wires from damage and to keep them from becoming a confusing tangle, they are organized into bundles, enclosed in plastic or taped together and called wire harnesses. Different wiring harnesses serve different parts of the vehicle. Individual wires are color coded to help trace them through a harness where sections are hidden from view.

A loose or corroded connection or a replacement wire that is too small for the circuit will add extra resistance and an additional voltage drop to the circuit. A ten percent voltage drop can result in slow or erratic motor operation, for example, even though the circuit is complete. Automotive wiring or circuit conductors can be in any one of three forms:

1. Single strand wire
2. Multi-strand wire
3. Printed circuitry

Single strand wire has a solid metal core and is usually used inside such components as alternators, motors, relays and other devices. Multi-strand wire has a core made of many small strands of wire twisted together into a single conductor. Most of the wiring in an automotive electrical system is made up of multi-strand wire, either as a single conductor or grouped together in a harness. All wiring is color coded on the insulator, either as a solid color or as a colored wire with an identification stripe. A printed circuit is a thin film of copper or other conductor that is printed on an insulator backing. Occasionally, a printed circuit is sandwiched between two sheets of plastic for more protection and flexibility. A complete printed circuit, consisting of conductors, insulating material and connectors for lamps or other components is called a printed circuit board. Printed circuitry is used in place of individual wires or harnesses in places where space is limited, such as behind instrument panels.

WIRE GAUGE

Since computer controlled automotive electrical systems are very sensitive to changes in resistance, the selection of properly sized wires is critical when systems are repaired. The wire gauge number is an expression of the cross section area of the conductor. The most common system for expressing wire size is the American Wire Gauge (AWG) system.

Wire cross section area is measured in circular mils. A mil is $^1/_{1000}$ in. (0.001 in. [0.0254mm]); a circular mil is the area of a circle one mil in diameter. For example, a conductor ¼ in. (6mm) in diameter is 0.250 in. or 250 mils. The circular mil cross section area of the wire is 250 squared (250^2)or 62,500 circular mils. Imported car models usually use metric wire gauge designations, which is simply the cross section area of the conductor in square millimeters (mm^2).

Gauge numbers are assigned to conductors of various cross section areas. As gauge number increases, area decreases and the conductor becomes smaller. A 5 gauge conductor is smaller than a 1 gauge conductor and a 10 gauge is smaller than a 5 gauge. As the cross section area of a conductor decreases, resistance increases and so does the gauge number. A conductor with a higher gauge number will carry less current than a conductor with a lower gauge number.

➡ Gauge wire size refers to the size of the conductor, not the size of the complete wire. It is possible to have two wires of the same gauge with different diameters because one may have thicker insulation than the other.

12 volt automotive electrical systems generally use 10, 12, 14, 16 and 18 gauge wire. Main power distribution circuits and larger accessories usually use 10 and 12 gauge wire. Battery cables are usually 4 or 6 gauge, although 1 and 2 gauge wires are occasionally used. Wire length must also be considered when making repairs to a circuit. As conductor length increases, so does resistance. An 18 gauge wire, for example, can carry a 10 amp load for 10 feet without excessive voltage drop; however if a 15 foot wire is required for the same 10 amp load, it must be a 16 gauge wire.

An electrical schematic shows the electrical current paths when a circuit is operating properly. It is essential to understand how a circuit works before trying to figure out why it does not. Schematics break the entire electrical system down into individual circuits and show only one particular circuit. In a schematic, no attempt is made to represent wiring and components as they physically appear on the vehicle; switches and other components are shown as simply as possible. Face views of harness connectors show the cavity or terminal locations in all multi-pin connectors to help locate test points.

If you need to backprobe a connector while it is on the component, the order of the terminals must be mentally reversed. The wire color code can help in this situation, as well as a keyway, lock tab or other reference mark.

WIRING REPAIR

Soldering is a quick, efficient method of joining metals permanently. Everyone who has the occasion to make wiring repairs should know how to solder. Electrical connections that are soldered are far less likely to come apart and will conduct electricity much better than connections that are only "pig-tailed" together. The most popular (and preferred) method of soldering is with an electrical soldering gun. Soldering irons are available in many sizes and wattage ratings. Irons with higher wattage ratings deliver higher temperatures and recover lost heat faster. A small soldering iron rated for no more than 50 watts is recommended, especially on electrical systems where excess heat can damage the components being soldered.

There are three ingredients necessary for successful soldering; proper flux, good solder and sufficient heat. A soldering flux is necessary to clean the metal of tarnish, prepare it for soldering and to enable the solder to spread into tiny crevices. When soldering, always use a resin flux or resin core solder which is non-corrosive and will not attract moisture once the job is finished. Other types of flux (acid core) will leave a residue that will attract moisture and cause the wires to corrode. Tin is a unique metal with a low melting point. In a molten state, it dissolves and alloys easily with many metals. Solder is made by mixing tin with lead. The most common proportions are 40/60, 50/50 and 60/40, with the percentage of tin listed first. Low priced solders usually contain less tin, making them very difficult for a beginner to use because more heat is required to melt the solder. A common solder is 40/60 which is well suited for all-around general use, but 60/40 melts easier, has more tin for a better joint and is preferred for electrical work.

SOLDERING TECHNIQUES

Successful soldering requires that the metals to be joined be heated to a temperature that will melt the solder, usually 360–460°F (182–238°C). Contrary to popular belief, the purpose of the soldering iron is not to melt the solder itself, but to heat the parts being soldered to a temperature high enough to melt the solder when it is touched to the work. Melting flux-cored solder on the soldering iron will usually destroy the effectiveness of the flux.

➡ **Soldering tips are made of copper for good heat conductivity, but must be "tinned" regularly for quick transference of heat to the project and to prevent the solder from sticking to the iron. To "tin" the iron, simply heat it and touch the flux-cored solder to the tip; the solder will flow over the hot tip. Wipe the excess off with a clean rag, but be careful as the iron will be hot.**

After some use, the tip may become pitted. If so, simply dress the tip smooth with a smooth file and "tin" the tip again. An old saying holds that "metals well cleaned are half soldered." Flux-cored solder will remove oxides but rust, bits of insulation and oil or grease must be removed with a wire brush or emery cloth. For maximum strength in soldered parts, the joint must start off clean and tight. Weak joints will result in gaps too wide for the solder to bridge.

If a separate soldering flux is used, it should be brushed or swabbed on only those areas that are to be soldered. Most solders contain a core of flux and separate fluxing is unnecessary. Hold the work to be soldered firmly. It is best to solder on a wooden board, because a metal vise will only rob the piece to be soldered of heat and make it difficult to melt the solder. Hold the soldering tip with the broadest face against the work to be soldered. Apply solder under the tip close to the work, using enough solder to give a heavy film between the iron and the piece being soldered, while moving slowly and making sure the solder melts properly. Keep the work level or the solder will run to the lowest part and favor the thicker parts, because these require more heat to melt the solder. If the soldering tip overheats (the solder coating on the face of the tip burns up), it should be retinned. Once the soldering is completed, let the soldered joint stand until cool. Tape and seal all soldered wire splices after the repair has cooled.

WIRE HARNESS AND CONNECTORS

The on-board computer (ECM) wire harness electrically connects the control unit to the various solenoids, switches and sensors used by the control system. Most connectors in the engine compartment or otherwise exposed to the elements are protected against moisture and dirt which could create oxidation and deposits on the terminals. This protection is important because of the very low voltage and current levels used by the computer and sensors. All connectors have a lock which secures the male and female terminals together, with a secondary lock holding the seal and terminal into the connector. Both terminal locks must be released when disconnecting ECM connectors.

These special connectors are weather-proof and all repairs require the use of a special terminal and the tool required to service it. This tool is used to remove the pin and sleeve terminals. If removal is attempted with an ordinary pick, there is a good chance that the terminal will be bent or deformed. Unlike standard blade type terminals, these terminals cannot be straightened once they are bent. Make certain that the connectors are properly seated and all of the sealing rings in place when connecting leads. On some models, a hinge-type flap provides a backup or secondary locking feature for the terminals. Most secondary locks are used to improve the connector reliability by retaining the terminals if the small terminal lock tangs are not positioned properly.

Molded-on connectors require complete replacement of the connection. This means splicing a new connector assembly into the harness. All splices in on-board computer systems should be soldered to insure proper contact. Use care when probing the connections or replacing terminals in them as it is possible to short between opposite terminals. If this happens to the wrong terminal pair, it is possible to damage certain components. Always use jumper wires between connectors for circuit checking and never probe through weatherproof seals.

Open circuits are often difficult to locate by sight because corrosion or terminal misalignment are hidden by the connectors. Merely wiggling a connector on a sensor or in the wiring harness may correct the open circuit condition. This should always be considered when an open circuit or a failed sensor is indicated. Intermittent problems may also be caused by oxidized or loose connections. When using a circuit tester for diagnosis, always probe connections from the wire side. Be careful not to damage sealed connectors with test probes.

All wiring harnesses should be replaced with identical parts, using the same gauge wire and connectors. When signal wires are spliced into a harness, use wire with high temperature insulation only. With the low voltage and current levels found in the system, it is important that the best possible connection at all wire splices be made by soldering the splices together. It is seldom necessary to replace a complete harness. If replacement is necessary, pay close attention to insure proper harness routing. Secure the harness with suitable plastic wire clamps to prevent vibrations from causing the harness to wear in spots or contact any hot components.

➡ **Weatherproof connectors cannot be replaced with standard connectors. Instructions are provided with replacement connector and terminal packages. Some wire harnesses have mounting indicators (usually pieces of colored tape) to mark where the harness is to be secured.**

In making wiring repairs, it's important that you always replace damaged wires with wires that are the same gauge as the wire being replaced. The heavier the wire, the smaller the gauge number. Wires are color-coded to aid in identification and whenever possible the same color coded wire should be used for replacement. A wire stripping and crimping tool is necessary to install solderless terminal connectors. Test all crimps by pulling on the wires; it should not be possible to pull the wires out of a good crimp.

Wires which are open, exposed or otherwise damaged are repaired by simple splicing. Where possible, if the wiring harness is accessible and the damaged place in the wire can be located, it is best to open the harness and check for all possible damage. In an inaccessible harness, the wire must be bypassed with a new insert, usually taped to the outside of the old harness.

When replacing fusible links, be sure to use fusible link wire, NOT ordinary automotive wire. Make sure the fusible segment is of the same gauge and construction as the one being replaced and double the stripped end when crimping the terminal connector for a good contact. The melted (open) fusible link segment of the wiring harness should be cut off as close to the harness as possible, then a new segment spliced in as described. In the case of a damaged fusible link that feeds two harness wires, the harness connections should be replaced with two fusible link wires so that each circuit will have its own separate protection.

➡ Most of the problems caused in the wiring harness are due to bad ground connections. Always check all vehicle ground connections for corrosion or looseness before performing any power feed checks to eliminate the chance of a bad ground affecting the circuit.

REPAIRING HARD SHELL CONNECTORS

Unlike molded connectors, the terminal contacts in hard shell connectors can be replaced. Weatherproof hard-shell connectors with the leads molded into the shell have non-replaceable terminal ends. Replacement usually involves the use of a special terminal removal tool that depress the locking tangs (barbs) on the connector terminal and allow the connector to be removed from the rear of the shell. The connector shell should be replaced if it shows any evidence of burning, melting, cracks, or breaks. Replace individual terminals that are burnt, corroded, distorted or loose.

➡ The insulation crimp must be tight to prevent the insulation from sliding back on the wire when the wire is pulled. The insulation must be visibly compressed under the crimp tabs, and the ends of the crimp should be turned in for a firm grip on the insulation.

The wire crimp must be made with all wire strands inside the crimp. The terminal must be fully compressed on the wire strands with the ends of the crimp tabs turned in to make a firm grip on the wire. Check all connections with an ohmmeter to insure a good contact. There should be no measurable resistance between the wire and the terminal when connected.

HEATER

General Information

The heater and air conditioning systems are controlled manually. The manual system controls air temperature through a cable-actuated lever and air flow through a vacuum switching valve and vacuum actuators.

The heating system provides heating, ventilation and defrosting for the windshield and side windows. The heater core is a heat exchanger supplied with coolant from the engine cooling system. Temperature is controlled by the temperature valve which moves an air door that directs air flow through the heater core for more heat or bypasses the heater core for less heat.

Vacuum actuators control the mode doors which direct air flow to the outlet ducts. The mode selector on the control panel directs engine vacuum to the actuators. The position of the mode doors determines whether air flows from the floor, panel, defrost or panel and defrost ducts (bi-level mode).

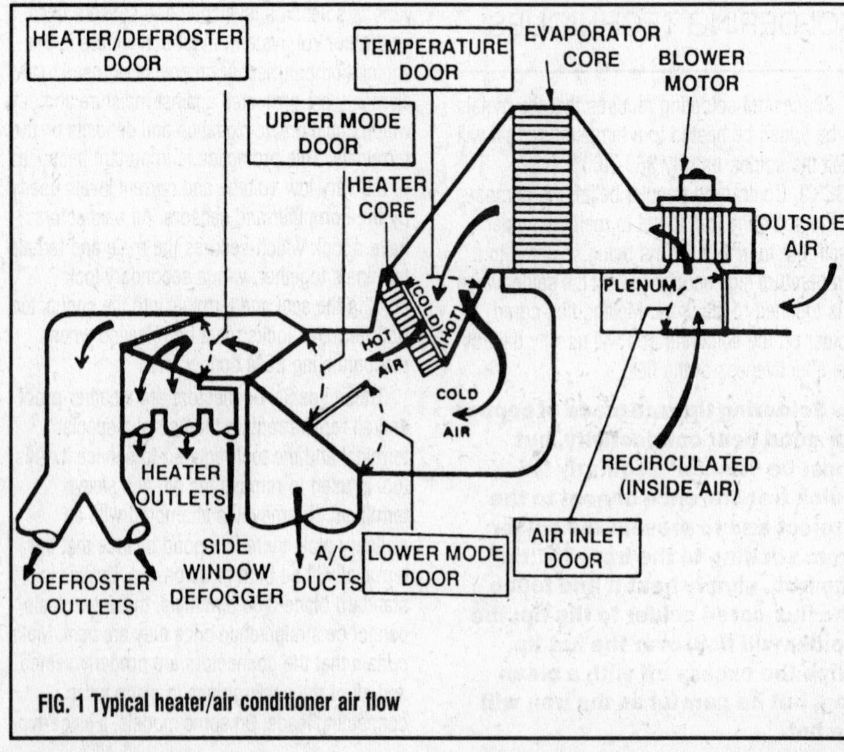

FIG. 1 Typical heater/air conditioner air flow

Blower Motor

REMOVAL & INSTALLATION

➧ SEE FIG. 2

1. Disconnect negative battery cable.
2. Remove the serpentine belt and/or the power steering pressure hose, as required.
3. Disconnect the connector to the blower motor and remove the cooling tube.
4. Remove the attaching screws and remove the blower from the case.
5. If necessary, remove the fan from the blower motor.
6. The installation is the reverse of the removal procedure.
7. Connect the negative battery cable and check the blower motor for proper operation.

Heater Core

REMOVAL & INSTALLATION

➧ SEE FIG. 3

1. Disconnect the negative battery cable.
2. Drain the engine coolant into a clean container for reuse.
3. Raise and safely support the vehicle.
4. Remove the rear lateral transaxle strut mount, if necessary.
5. Remove the drain tube and disconnect the heater hoses from the core tubes. Lower the vehicle.
6. Remove the sound insulators, console extensions and/or steering column filler, as required.
7. Remove the floor or console outlet ductwork and hoses.
8. Remove the heater core cover.
9. Remove the heater core mounting clamps and remove the heater core.

To install:

10. Install the heater core and clamps.
11. Install the heater core cover.
12. Install the outlet hoses and ducts.
13. Install the sound insulators, console extensions and/or steering column filler.
14. Raise and safely support the vehicle. Install the drain tube and connect the heater hoses to the core tubes.
15. Install the rear lateral transaxle strut mount, if removed. Lower the vehicle.
16. Connect the negative battery cable.

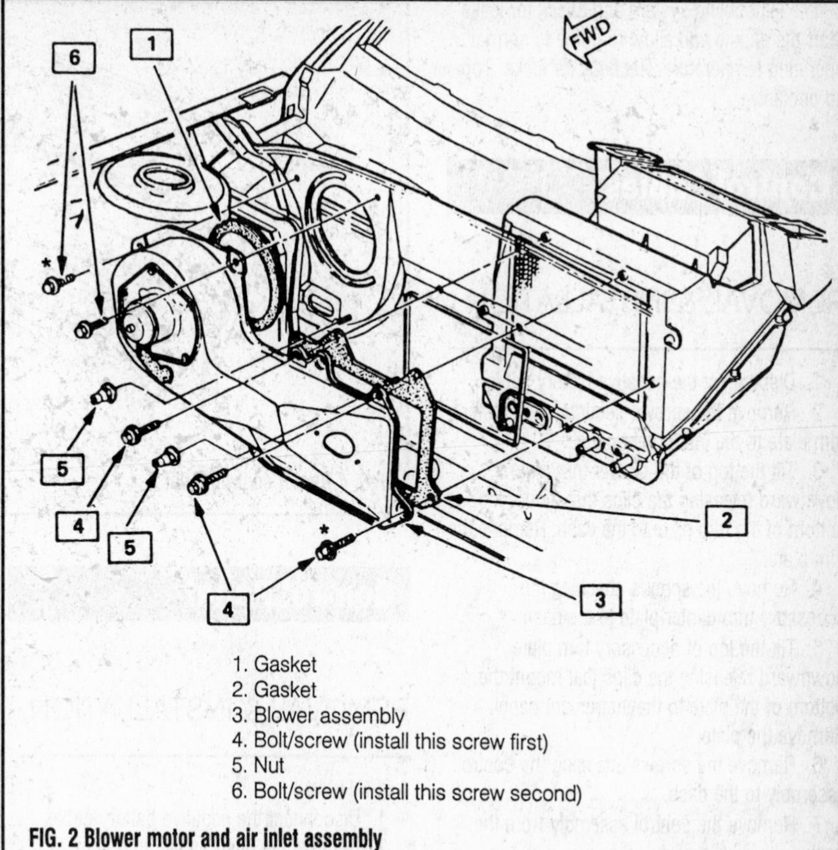

1. Gasket
2. Gasket
3. Blower assembly
4. Bolt/screw (install this screw first)
5. Nut
6. Bolt/screw (install this screw second)

FIG. 2 Blower motor and air inlet assembly

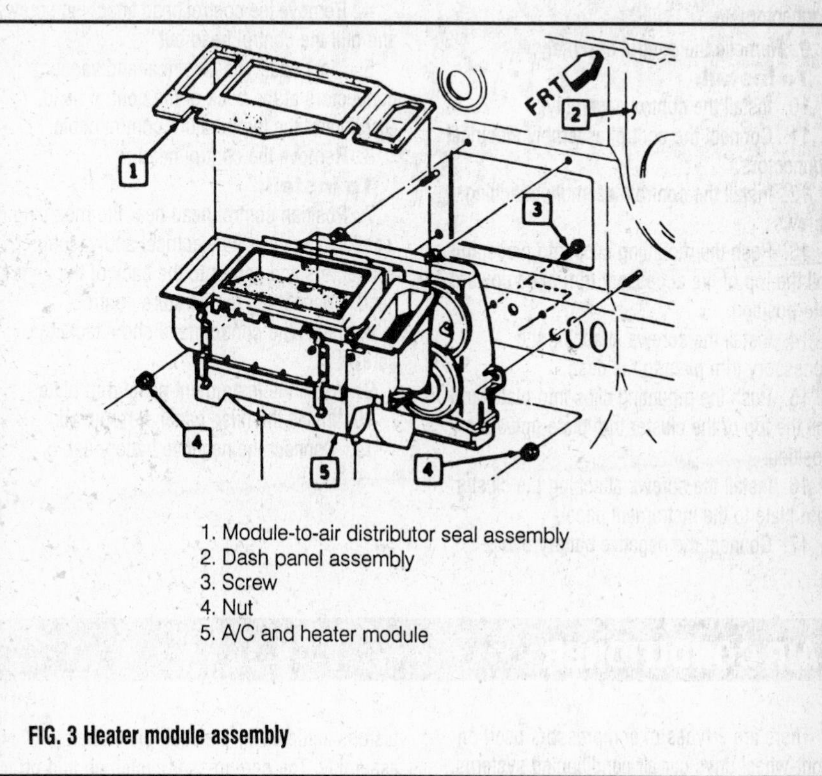

1. Module-to-air distributor seal assembly
2. Dash panel assembly
3. Screw
4. Nut
5. A/C and heater module

FIG. 3 Heater module assembly

17. Fill cooling system and check for leaks. Start the engine and allow to come to normal operating temperature. Recheck for leaks. Top-up coolant.

Control Cables

REMOVAL & INSTALLATION

1. Disconnect the negative battery cable.
2. Remove the screws securing the cluster trim plate to the instrument panel.
3. Tilt the top of the cluster trim plate downward releasing the clips that mount the bottom of the trim plate to the dash. Remove the trim plate.
4. Remove the screws attaching the accessory trim center plate to the dash.
5. Tilt the top of accessory trim plate downward releasing the clips that mount the bottom of the plate to the instrument panel. Remove the plate.
6. Remove the screws attaching the control assembly to the dash.
7. Remove the control assembly from the dash.
8. Disconnect the control assembly electrical connectors.
9. Remove the control assembly.

To install:

10. Install the control assembly.
11. Connect the control assembly electrical connectors.
12. Install the control assembly attaching screws.
13. Push the mounting clips into place and roll the top of the accessory trim plate upward into position.
14. Install the screws attaching the accessory trim plate to the dash.
15. Push the mounting clips into place and roll the top of the cluster trim plate upward into position.
16. Install the screws attaching the cluster trim plate to the instrument panel.
17. Connect the negative battery cable.

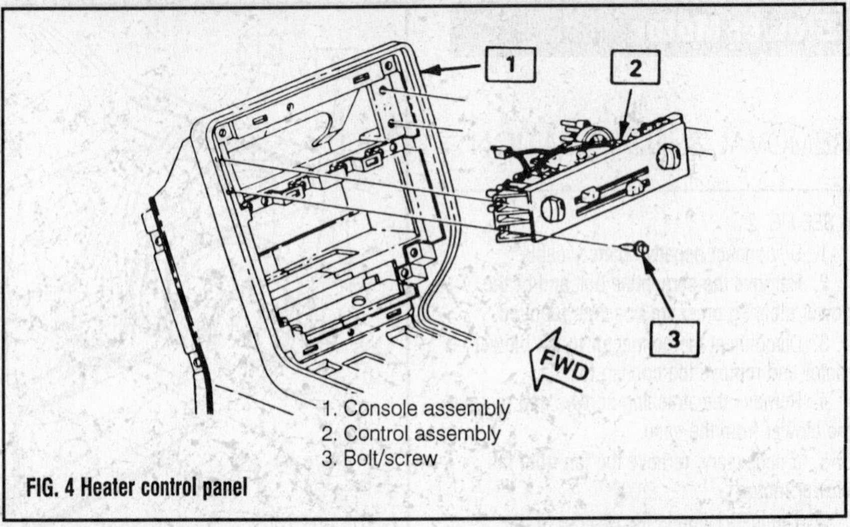

FIG. 4 Heater control panel

Control Panel

REMOVAL & INSTALLATION

➧ SEE FIG. 4

1. Disconnect the negative battery cable.
2. Remove the hush panel, as required.
3. Remove the instrument panel trim plate.
4. Remove the control head attaching screws and pull the control head out.
5. Disconnect the electrical and vacuum connectors at the back of the control head. Disconnect the temperature control cable.
6. Remove the control head.

To install:

7. Position control head near the mounting location. Connect the electrical and vacuum connectors and cables to the back of the control head. Connect the temperature control.
8. Install the control head and attaching screws.
9. Install the instrument panel trim plate.
10. Install the hush panel, if removed.
11. Connect the negative battery cable.

Blower Switch

REMOVAL & INSTALLATION

1. Disconnect the negative battery cable.
2. Remove the console forward trim plate by gently prying it out of its retainer clips or by removing the trim plate attaching screws.
3. Remove the heater/air conditioner control assembly screws and pull the control assembly away from the instrument panel.
4. Remove the blower switch knob.
5. Disconnect the electrical connector.
6. Remove the blower switch attaching screws and blower switch.

To install:

7. Install the blower switch and attaching screws.
8. Connect the blower switch electrical connector.
9. Reposition the control assembly and install the attaching screws.
10. Install the forward console trim plate by aligning the tabs and gently push until it snaps into place or by installing the attaching screws.
11. Connect the negative battery cable.

AIR CONDITIONER

There are 2 types of compressors used on front-wheel drive car air conditioning systems. The HR-6 compressor, used on Cycling Clutch Orifice Tube (CCOT) systems, is a 6 cylinder axial compressor consisting of 3 double-ended pistons actuated by a swash plate shaft assembly. The compressor cycles on and off according to system demands. The compressor driveshaft is driven by the serpentine belt when the electro-magnetic clutch is engaged.

The V-5 compressor, used on Variable Displacement Orifice Tube (VDOT) systems, is designed to meet the demands of the air conditioning system without cycling. The compressor employs a variable angle wobble plate controlling the displacement of 5 axially oriented cylinders. Displacement is controlled by a bellows actuated control valve located in the rear head of the compressor. The electromagnetic compressor clutch connects the compressor shaft to the serpentine drive belt when the coil is energized.

➡ **R-12 refrigerant is a chlorofluorocarbon which, when released into the atmosphere, can contribute to the depletion of the ozone layer in the upper atmosphere. Ozone filters out harmful radiation from the sun. It is essential that every effort be made to avoid discharging the refrigerant system to the atmosphere. When discharging the system, use an approved R-12 Recovery/Recycling machine that meets SAE standards. Follow the operating instructions provided with the approved equipment exactly to properly discharge the system.**

Cooling Fan

TESTING

1. Check fuse or circuit breaker for power to cooling fan motor.
2. Remove connector(s) at cooling fan motor(s). Connect jumper wire and apply battery voltage to the positive terminal of the cooling fan motor.
3. Using an ohmmeter, check for continuity in cooling fan motor.

➡ **Remove the cooling fan connector at the fan motor before performing continuity checks. Perform continuity check of the motor windings only. The cooling fan control circuit is connected electrically to the ECM through the cooling fan relay center. Ohmmeter battery voltage must not be applied to the ECM.**

4. Ensure proper continuity of cooling fan motor ground circuit at chassis ground connector.

REMOVAL & INSTALLATION

Except 2.3L Engine

➧ SEE FIGS. 5 AND 6

1. Disconnect the negative battery cable.
2. Disconnect the wiring harness from the motor and fan frame.
3. Fan guard and hose support, as required.
4. Remove the fan assembly from the radiator support.

To install:

5. Install the fan assembly on the radiator support.
6. If removed, install the fan guard and hose support.
7. Connect the wiring harness to the motor and fan frame.
8. Connect the negative battery cable.

2.3L Engine

➧ SEE FIG. 7

1. Disconnect the negative battery cable.
2. Remove the air cleaner-to-throttle body duct.
3. Disconnect the electrical connectors from the Throttle Position Sensor (TPS), Idle Air

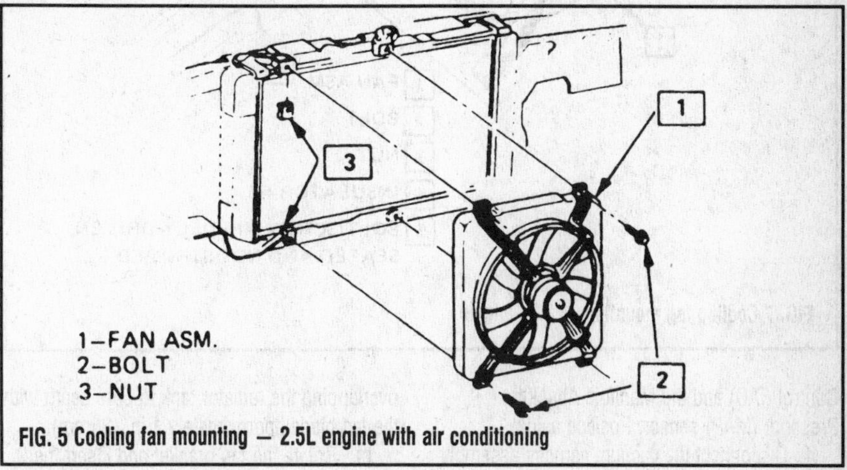

FIG. 5 Cooling fan mounting — 2.5L engine with air conditioning

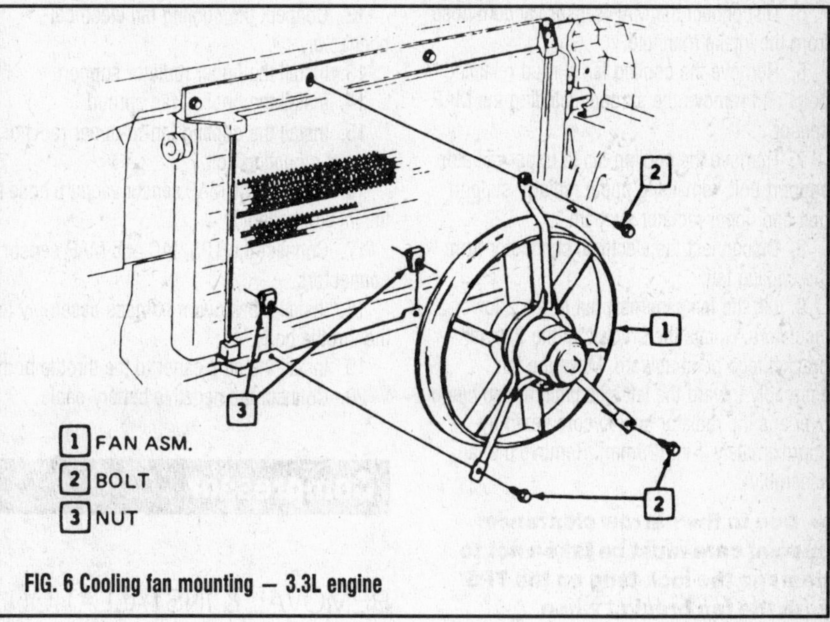

FIG. 6 Cooling fan mounting — 3.3L engine

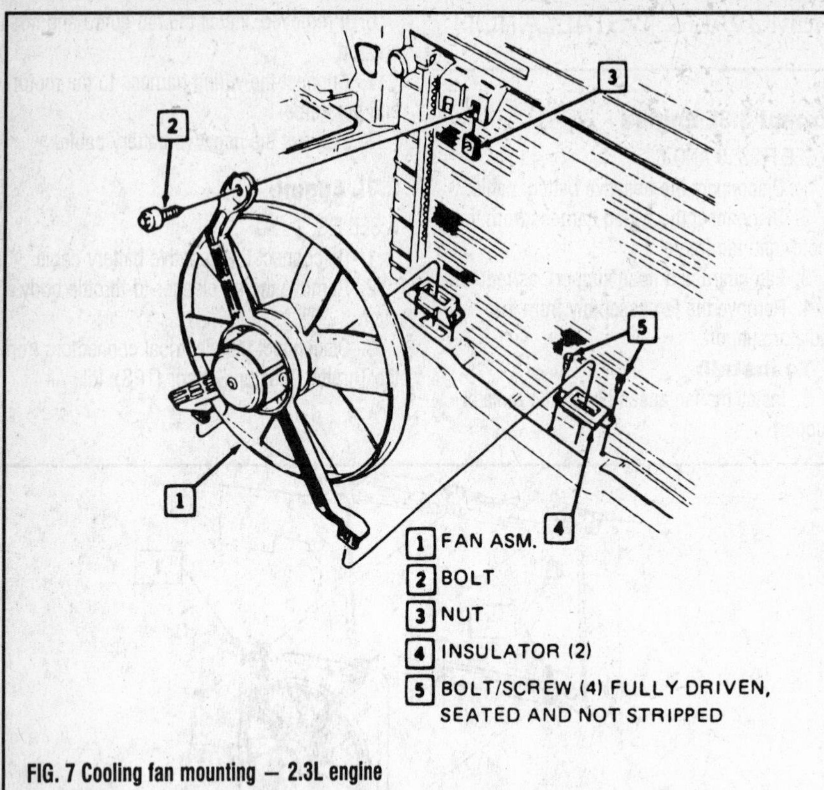

FIG. 7 Cooling fan mounting — 2.3L engine

Control (IAC) and the Manifold Absolute Pressure (MAP) sensor. Position aside.

4. Disconnect the vacuum harness assembly from the throttle body and position aside.
5. Disconnect the MAP sensor vacuum hose from the intake manifold.
6. Remove the cooling fan shroud retaining bolts and remove the shroud including the MAP sensor.
7. Remove the cooling fan to upper radiator support bolt, remaining upper radiator support bolt and upper radiator support.
8. Disconnect the electrical connector from the cooling fan.
9. Lift the fan assembly out of the 2 lower insulators. Rotate the bracket so the 2 lower bracket legs point upward. Move the fan assembly toward the left side until the fan blade overlaps the radiator tank to core seam by approximately 1 in. (25mm). Remove the fan assembly.

➡ Due to the narrow clearance, special care must be taken not to damage the lock tang on the TPS with the fan bracket when removing and installing the fan assembly.

To install:

10. Rotate the fan assembly so the 2 lower legs face upward. Install the fan assembly down between the throttle body and the radiator while overlapping the radiator tank to core seam with the fan blade approximately 1 in. (25mm).
11. Rotate the fan bracket and insert the 2 lower legs into the insulators.
12. Connect the cooling fan electrical connector.
13. Install the upper radiator support.
14. Install the cooling fan shroud.
15. Install the cooling fan-to-upper radiator support mounting bolt.
16. Connect the MAP sensor vacuum hose to the intake manifold.
17. Connect the TPS, IAC and MAP sensor connectors.
18. Install the vacuum harness assembly to the throttle body.
19. Install the air cleaner to the throttle body.
20. Connect the negative battery cable.

Compressor

REMOVAL & INSTALLATION

➧ SEE FIGS. 8–10

➡ Please refer to Section 1 for important instructions pertaining to discharging, evacuating and recharging the system.

1. Disconnect the negative battery cable.
2. Properly discharge the air conditioning system.
3. If equipped with the 2.3L engine, when removing the compressor for the first time only, perform the following:
   a. Remove the oil filter.
   b. Using a 7mm socket, remove the stud in the back of the compressor.
   c. Discard the stud.
   d. Install the oil filter.
4. If equipped with the 2.0L or 3.3L engine, remove the serpentine belt.
5. If equipped with the 3.3L engine, install a suitable engine support fixture.
6. Raise and safely support the vehicle.
7. Remove the right side splash shield.
8. If equipped with the 3.3L engine, remove the lower support bracket. Lower the vehicle.
9. If equipped with the 2.3L or 2.5L engine, remove the serpentine belt.
10. Disconnect the compressor electrical connector.
11. Remove the refrigerant line assembly from the back of the compressor. Discard the O-rings.

➡ Cap the refrigerant lines when opening the system to prevent the entry of dirt and moisture and the loss of refrigerant lubricant.

12. Remove the compressor attaching bolts.
13. Remove the compressor.
14. Drain and measure the refrigerant oil from the compressor. Discard the old oil.

To install:

15. If the compressor is to be replaced, drain the oil from the new compressor and discard. Add new refrigerant oil equivalent to the amount drained from the old compressor.
16. Install the compressor and attaching bolts.
17. Install new O-rings to the compressor refrigerant lines. Lubricate with refrigerant oil.
18. Install the refrigerant line assembly to the back of the compressor.
19. Connect the compressor electrical connector.
20. If equipped with the 2.3L or 2.5L engine, install the serpentine belt.
21. If equipped with the 3.3L engine, raise and safely support the vehicle. Install the lower support bracket.
22. Install the right side splash shield.
23. Lower the vehicle.
24. If equipped with the 3.3L engine, remove the engine support fixture.
25. If equipped with the 2.0L or 3.3L engine, install the serpentine belt.

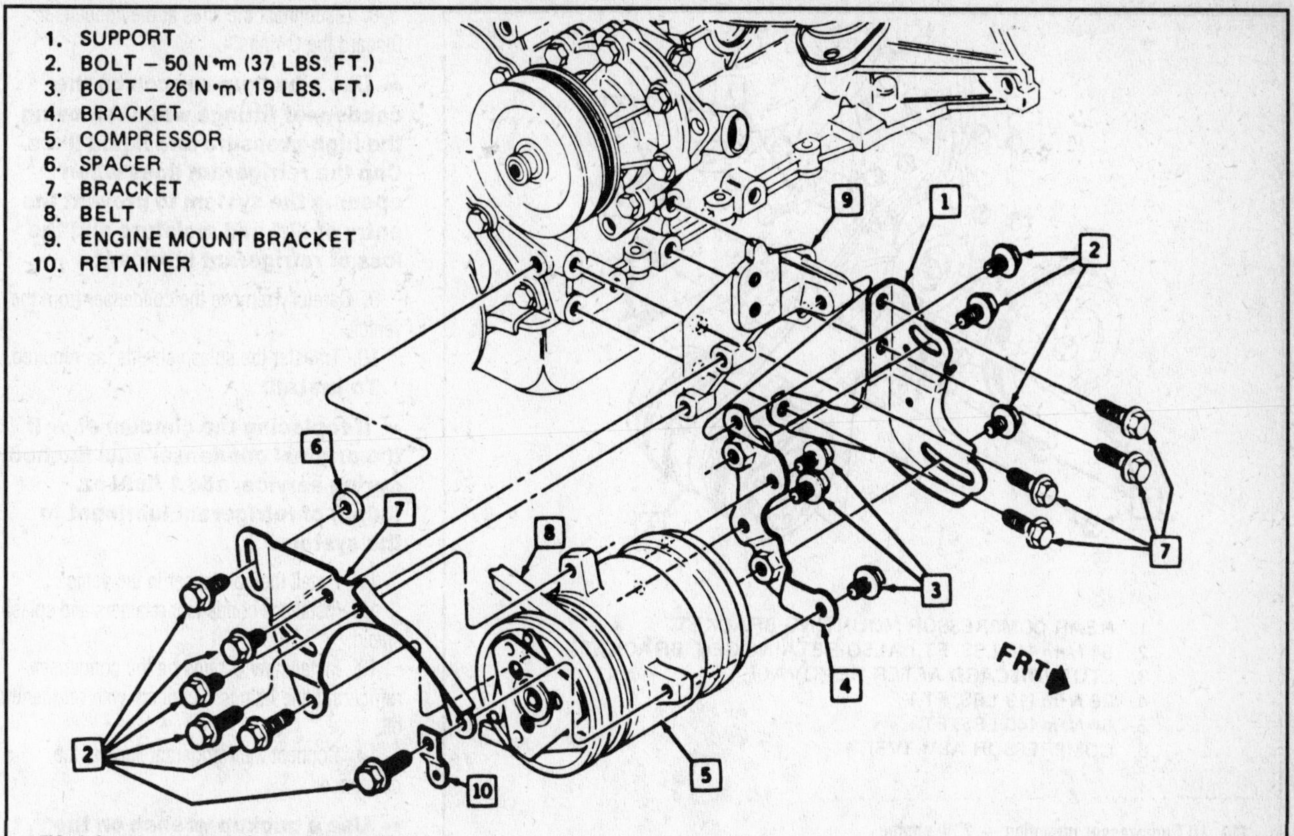

1. SUPPORT
2. BOLT – 50 N•m (37 LBS. FT.)
3. BOLT – 26 N•m (19 LBS. FT.)
4. BRACKET
5. COMPRESSOR
6. SPACER
7. BRACKET
8. BELT
9. ENGINE MOUNT BRACKET
10. RETAINER
FRT

FIG. 8 Compressor mounting – 2.5L engine

1 BOLT – 50 N•m (37 LBS. FT.)
2 NUT – 50 N•m (37 LBS. FT.)
3 BOLT – 25 N•m (17 LBS. FT.)
4 BRACKET – A/C COMPRESSOR
5 STUD – 12 N•m (9 LBS. FT.)
6 A/C COMPRESSOR

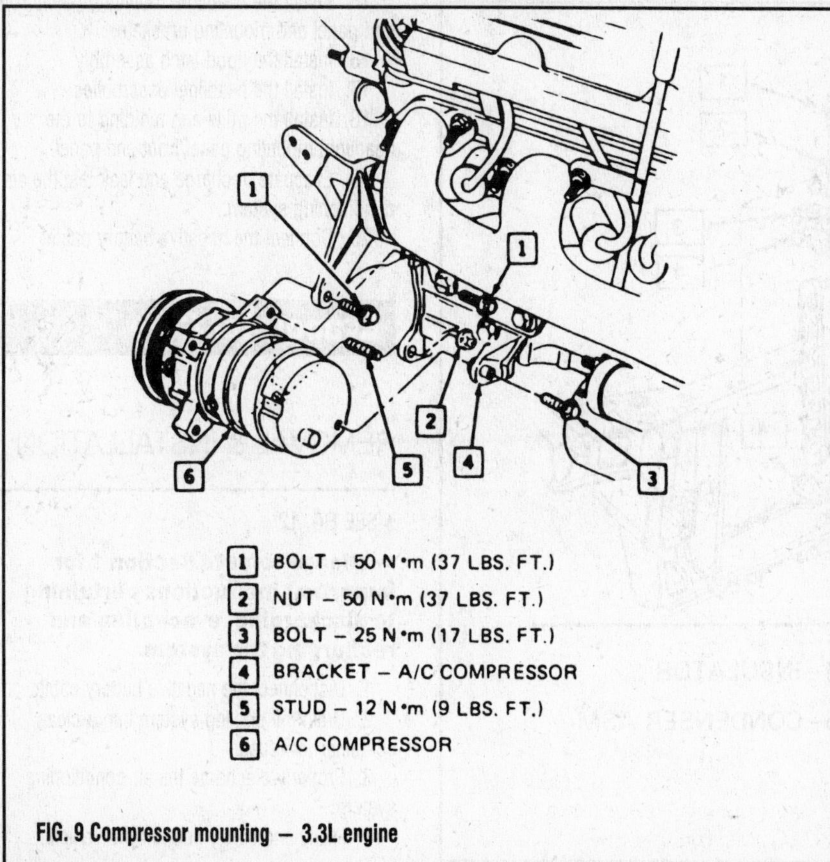

FIG. 9 Compressor mounting – 3.3L engine

26. Evacuate, recharge and leak test the air conditioning system.
27. Connect the negative battery cable.

Condenser

REMOVAL & INSTALLATION

➧ SEE FIG. 11

➡ Please refer to Section 1 for important instructions pertaining to discharging, evacuating and recharging the system.

1. Disconnect the negative battery cable.
2. Properly discharge the air conditioning system.
3. Remove the grille and molding.
4. Remove the headlights.
5. Remove the headlight mounting panel/front end panel and mounting brackets.
6. Remove the hood latch assembly. Scribe a mark on the radiator support for use during reinstallation.
7. Remove the condenser retainers and splash shields.

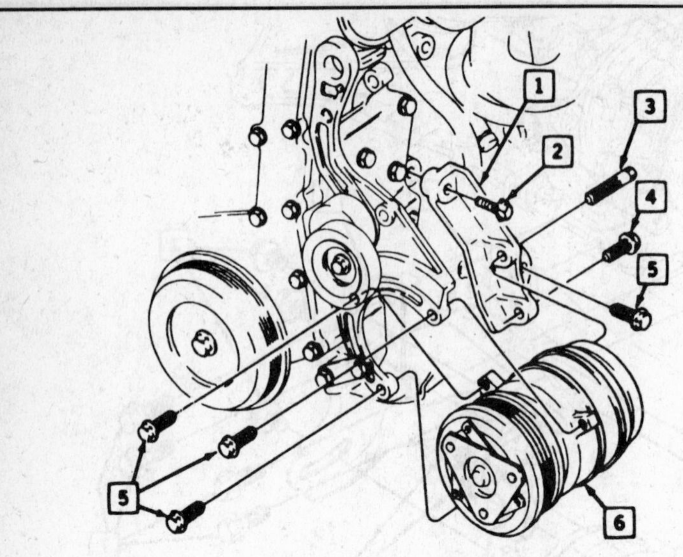

1. REAR COMPRESSOR MOUNTING BRACKET
2. 54 N•m (40 LBS. FT.) ALSO RETAINS GEN. BRACKET
3. STUD (DISCARD AFTER REMOVAL)
4. 26 N•m (19 LBS. FT.)
5. 54 N•m (40 LBS. FT.)
6. COMPRESSOR ASM. (V5)

FIG. 10 Compressor mounting — 2.3L engine

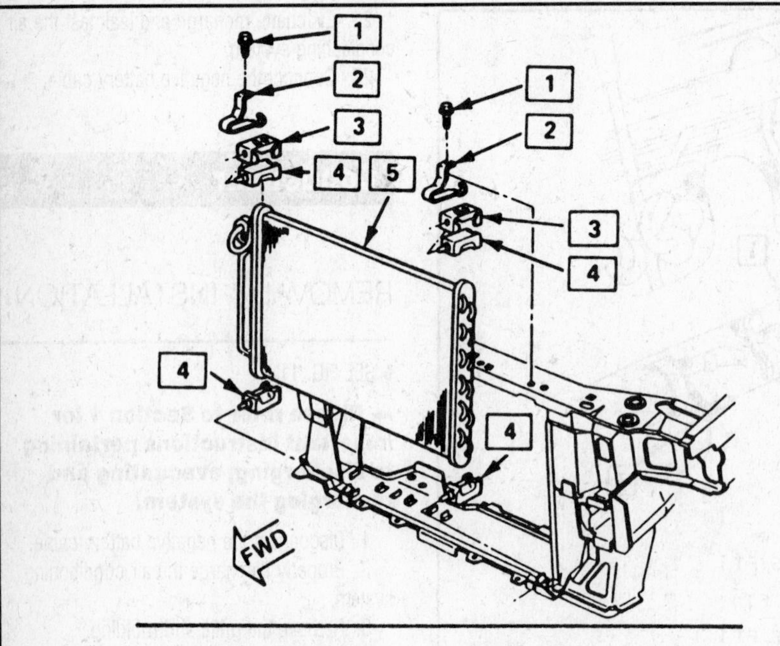

1 - BOLT/SCREW
2 - BRACKET
3 - RETAINER
4 - INSULATOR
5 - CONDENSER ASM.

FIG. 11 Condenser mounting

8. Disconnect the lines at the condenser. Discard the O-rings.

➡ **Use a backup wrench on the condenser fittings when removing the high-pressure and liquid lines. Cap the refrigerant lines when opening the system to prevent the entry of dirt and moisture and the loss of refrigerant lubricant.**

9. Carefully remove the condenser from the vehicle.
10. Transfer the splash shields, as required.

To install:

➡ **If replacing the condenser or if the original condenser was flushed during service, add 1 fluid oz. (30ml) of refrigerant lubricant to the system.**

11. Install the condenser in the vehicle.
12. Install the condenser retainers and splash shield.
13. Install new O-rings on the condenser refrigerant line fittings. Lubricate with refrigerant oil.
14. Connect the refrigerant lines at the condenser.

➡ **Use a backup wrench on the condenser fittings when tightening lines.**

15. Install the headlight mounting panel/front end panel and mounting brackets.
16. Install the hood latch assembly.
17. Install the headlight assemblies.
18. Install the grille and molding to the headlight mounting panel/front end panel.
19. Evacuate, recharge and leak test the air conditioning system.
20. Connect the negative battery cable.

Evaporator Core

REMOVAL & INSTALLATION

➧ SEE FIG. 12

➡ **Please refer to Section 1 for important instructions pertaining to discharging, evacuating and recharging the system.**

1. Disconnect the negative battery cable.
2. Drain the cooling system into a clean container for reuse.
3. Properly discharge the air conditioning system.
4. Raise and safely support the vehicle.

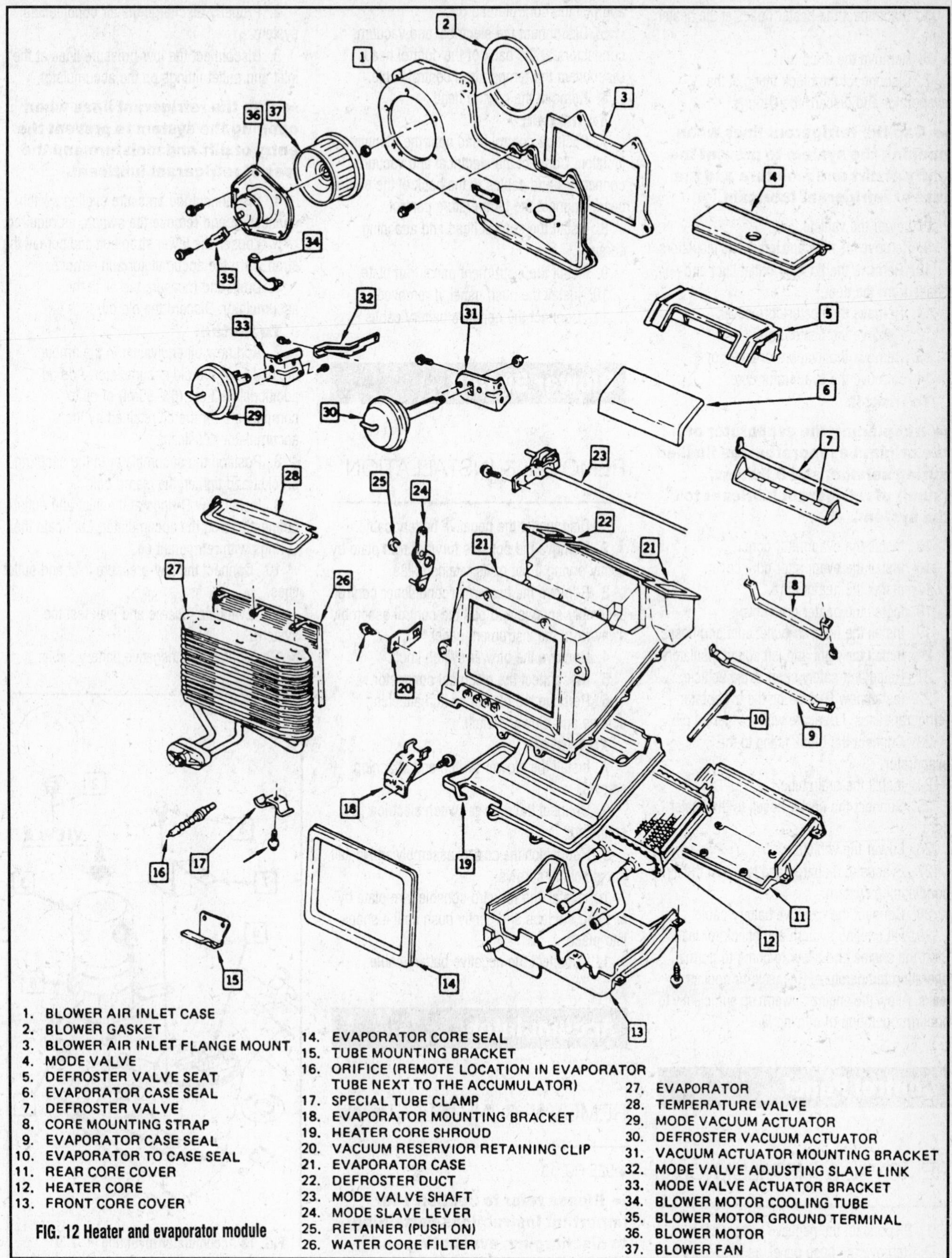

1. BLOWER AIR INLET CASE
2. BLOWER GASKET
3. BLOWER AIR INLET FLANGE MOUNT
4. MODE VALVE
5. DEFROSTER VALVE SEAT
6. EVAPORATOR CASE SEAL
7. DEFROSTER VALVE
8. CORE MOUNTING STRAP
9. EVAPORATOR CASE SEAL
10. EVAPORATOR TO CASE SEAL
11. REAR CORE COVER
12. HEATER CORE
13. FRONT CORE COVER
14. EVAPORATOR CORE SEAL
15. TUBE MOUNTING BRACKET
16. ORIFICE (REMOTE LOCATION IN EVAPORATOR TUBE NEXT TO THE ACCUMULATOR)
17. SPECIAL TUBE CLAMP
18. EVAPORATOR MOUNTING BRACKET
19. HEATER CORE SHROUD
20. VACUUM RESERVIOR RETAINING CLIP
21. EVAPORATOR CASE
22. DEFROSTER DUCT
23. MODE VALVE SHAFT
24. MODE SLAVE LEVER
25. RETAINER (PUSH ON)
26. WATER CORE FILTER
27. EVAPORATOR
28. TEMPERATURE VALVE
29. MODE VACUUM ACTUATOR
30. DEFROSTER VACUUM ACTUATOR
31. VACUUM ACTUATOR MOUNTING BRACKET
32. MODE VALVE ADJUSTING SLAVE LINK
33. MODE VALVE ACTUATOR BRACKET
34. BLOWER MOTOR COOLING TUBE
35. BLOWER MOTOR GROUND TERMINAL
36. BLOWER MOTOR
37. BLOWER FAN

FIG. 12 Heater and evaporator module

5. Disconnect the heater hoses at the heater core.
6. Remove the drain tube.
7. Disconnect the block fitting at the evaporator and discard the O-rings.

➡ **Cap the refrigerant lines when opening the system to prevent the entry of dirt and moisture and the loss of refrigerant lubricant.**

8. Lower the vehicle.
9. Remove the right and left sound insulators.
10. Remove the floor air outlet duct and hoses from the duct.
11. Remove the heater core cover.
12. Remove the heater core.
13. Remove the evaporator core cover.
14. Remove the evaporator core.

To install:

➡ **If replacing the evaporator or if the original evaporator was flushed during service, add 3 fluid oz. (90ml) of refrigerant lubricant to the system.**

15. Install the evaporator core.
16. Install the evaporator core cover.
17. Install the heater core.
18. Install the heater core cover.
19. Install the floor air outlet duct and hoses.
20. Install the right and left sound insulators.
21. Raise and safely support the vehicle.
22. Install new O-rings on the evaporator refrigerant lines. Lubricate with refrigerant oil.
23. Connect the block fitting to the evaporator.
24. Install the drain tube.
25. Connect the heater hoses to the heater core.
26. Lower the vehicle.
27. Evacuate, recharge and leak test the air conditioning system.
28. Connect the negative battery cable.
29. Fill cooling system and check for leaks. Start the engine and allow to come to normal operating temperature. Recheck for coolant leaks. Allow the engine to warm up sufficiently to confirm operation of cooling fan.

Control Panel

REMOVAL & INSTALLATION

1. Disconnect the negative battery cable.
2. Remove the hush panel, as required.
3. Remove the instrument panel trim plate.
4. Remove the control head attaching screws and pull the control head out.
5. Disconnect the electrical and vacuum connectors at the back of the control head. Disconnect the temperature control cable.
6. Remove the control head.

To install:

7. Position control head near the mounting location. Connect the electrical and vacuum connectors and cables to the back of the control head. Connect the temperature control.
8. Install the control head and attaching screws.
9. Install the instrument panel trim plate.
10. Install the hush panel, if removed.
11. Connect the negative battery cable.

Blower Switch

REMOVAL & INSTALLATION

1. Disconnect the negative battery cable.
2. Remove the console forward trim plate by gently prying it out of its retainer clips.
3. Remove the heater/air conditioner control assembly screws and pull the control assembly away from the instrument panel.
4. Remove the blower switch knob.
5. Disconnect the electrical connector.
6. Remove the blower switch attaching screws and blower switch.

To install:

7. Install the blower switch and attaching screws.
8. Connect the blower switch electrical connector.
9. Reposition the control assembly and install the attaching screws.
10. Install the forward console trim plate by aligning the tabs and gently push until it snaps into place.
11. Connect the negative battery cable.

Accumulator

REMOVAL & INSTALLATION

➧ SEE FIG. 13

➡ **Please refer to Section 1 for important instructions pertaining to discharging, evacuating and recharging the system.**

1. Disconnect the negative battery cable.
2. Properly discharge the air conditioning system.
3. Disconnect the low-pressure lines at the inlet and outlet fittings on the accumulator.

➡ **Cap the refrigerant lines when opening the system to prevent the entry of dirt and moisture and the loss of refrigerant lubricant.**

4. Disconnect the pressure cycling switch connection and remove the switch, as required.
5. Loosen the lower strap bolt and spread the strap. Turn the accumulator and remove.
6. Drain and measure the oil in the accumulator. Discard the old oil.

To install:

7. Add new oil equivalent to the amount drained from the old accumulator. Add an additional 2–3 oz. (60–90ml) of oil to compensate for the oil retained by the accumulator dessicant.
8. Position the accumulator in the securing bracket and tighten the clamp bolt.
9. Install new O-rings at the inlet and outlet connections on the accumulator. Lubricate the O-rings with refrigerant oil.
10. Connect the low-pressure inlet and outlet lines.
11. Evacuate, charge and leak test the system.
12. Connect the negative battery cable.

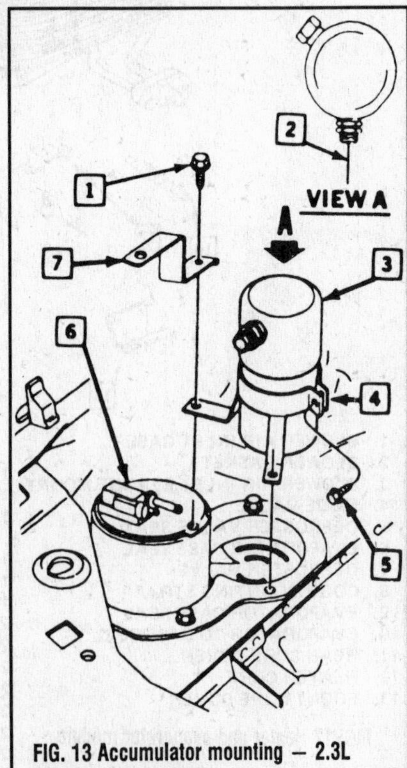

FIG. 13 Accumulator mounting — 2.3L shown, others similar

Refrigerant Lines

REMOVAL & INSTALLATION

➡ **Please refer to Section 1 for important instructions pertaining to discharging, evacuating and recharging the system.**

1. Disconnect the negative battery cable.
2. Properly discharge the air conditioning system.
3. Disconnect the refrigerant line connectors, using a backup wrench as required.
4. Remove refrigerant line support or routing brackets, as required.
5. Remove refrigerant line.

To install:

6. Position new refrigerant line in place, leaving protective caps installed until ready to connect.
7. Install new O-rings on refrigerant line connector fittings. Lubricate with refrigerant oil.
8. Connect refrigerant line, using a backup wrench, as required.
9. Install refrigerant line support or routing brackets, as required.
10. Evacuate, recharge and leak test the system.
11. Connect the negative battery cable.

Vacuum Motors

REMOVAL & INSTALLATION

➧ SEE FIG. 14

1. Remove the vacuum lines from the actuator.
2. Disconnect the linkage from the actuator.
3. Remove the hardware attaching the actuator.
4. Remove the actuator.

To install:

5. Install the actuator and attaching hardware.
6. Connect the linkage to the actuator.
7. Connect the vacuum lines to the actuator.
8. Test system to confirm proper functioning of the actuator.

Control Cables

REMOVAL & INSTALLATION

➧ SEE FIG. 15

1. Disconnect the negative battery cable.
2. Remove the screws securing the cluster trim plate to the instrument panel.
3. Tilt the top of the cluster trim plate downward releasing the clips that mount the bottom of the trim plate to the dash. Remove the trim plate.
4. Remove the screws attaching the accessory trim center plate to the dash.
5. Tilt the top of accessory trim plate downward releasing the clips that mount the bottom of the plate to the instrument panel. Remove the plate.
6. Remove the screws attaching the control assembly to the dash.
7. Remove the control assembly from the dash.
8. Disconnect the control assembly electrical connectors.
9. Remove the control assembly.

To install:

10. Install the control assembly.
11. Connect the control assembly electrical connectors.
12. Install the control assembly attaching screws.
13. Push the mounting clips into place and roll the top of the accessory trim plate upward into position.
14. Install the screws attaching the accessory trim plate to the dash.
15. Push the mounting clips into place and roll the top of the cluster trim plate upward into position.
16. Install the screws attaching the cluster trim plate to the instrument panel.
17. Connect the negative battery cable.

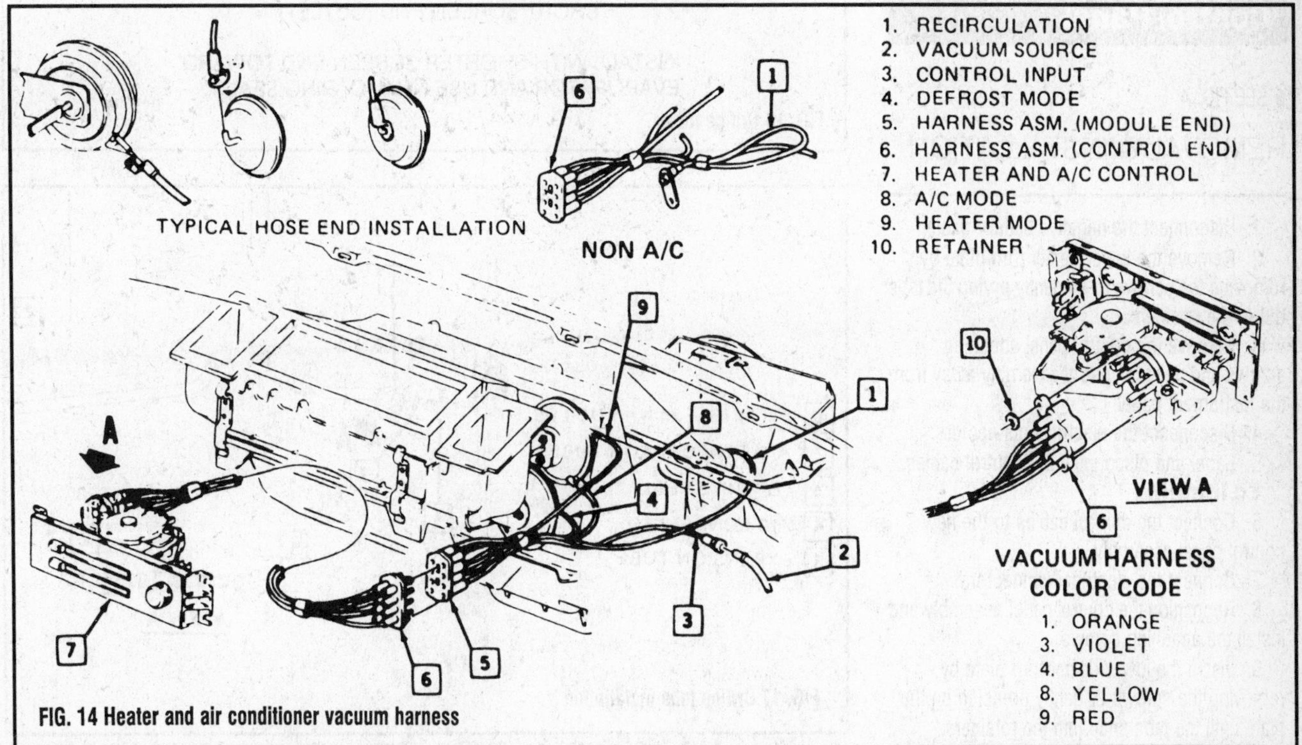

FIG. 14 Heater and air conditioner vacuum harness

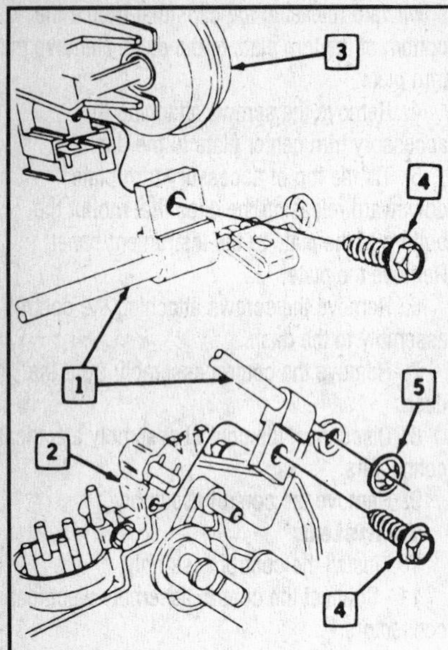

FIG. 15 Temperature control cable repair

Heater/Air Conditioner Control Panel

➧ SEE FIG. 4

REMOVAL & INSTALLATION

1. Disconnect the negative battery cable.
2. Remove the lower center trim plate by removing the screws or by gently prying the tabs out of the retainers.
3. Remove the control panel attaching screws and pull the control assembly away from the instrument panel.
4. Disconnect the electrical connectors.
5. Label and disconnect the control cables.

To install:

6. Connect the control cables to the new control panel assembly.
7. Connect the electrical connectors.
8. Reposition the control panel assembly and install the attaching screws.
9. Install the lower center trim plate by removing the screws or gently pressing on the plate until the tabs snap into the retainers.
10. Connect the negative battery cable.

Orifice Tube

REMOVAL & INSTALLATION

➧ SEE FIGS. 16 AND 17

➡ **Please refer to Section 1 for important instructions pertaining to discharging, evacuating and recharging the system.**

1. Properly discharge the air conditioning system.
2. Loosen the fitting at the liquid line outlet on the condenser or evaporator inlet pipe and disconnect. Discard the O-ring.

➡ **Use a backup wrench on the condenser outlet fitting when loosening the lines.**

3. If equipped with the 2.0L (VIN K) engine, remove the expansion tube by performing the following:
   a. Loosen the nut and separate the front evaporator tube from the rear evaporator tube near the compressor to gain access to the expansion tube.
   b. Carefully remove the tube with needle-nose pliers or special tool J-26549D.
   c. Inspect the tube for contamination or metal cuttings.
4. Carefully, remove the fixed orifice tube from the tube fitting in the evaporator inlet line.
5. In the event that the restricted or plugged orifice tube is difficult to remove, perform the following:
   a. Remove as much of the impacted residue as possible.
   b. Using a hair dryer, epoxy drier or equivalent, carefully apply heat approximately 1/4 in. (6mm) from the dimples on the inlet pipe. Do not overheat the pipe.

➡ **If the system has a pressure switch near the orifice tube, it should be removed prior to heating the pipe to avoid damage to the switch.**

   c. While applying heat, use special tool J

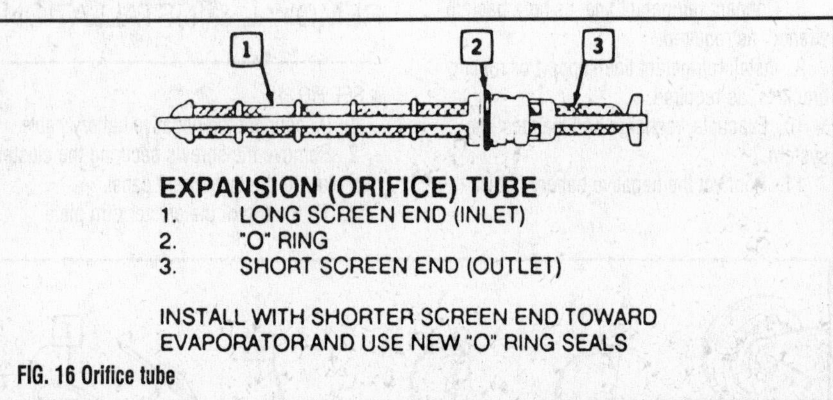

FIG. 16 Orifice tube

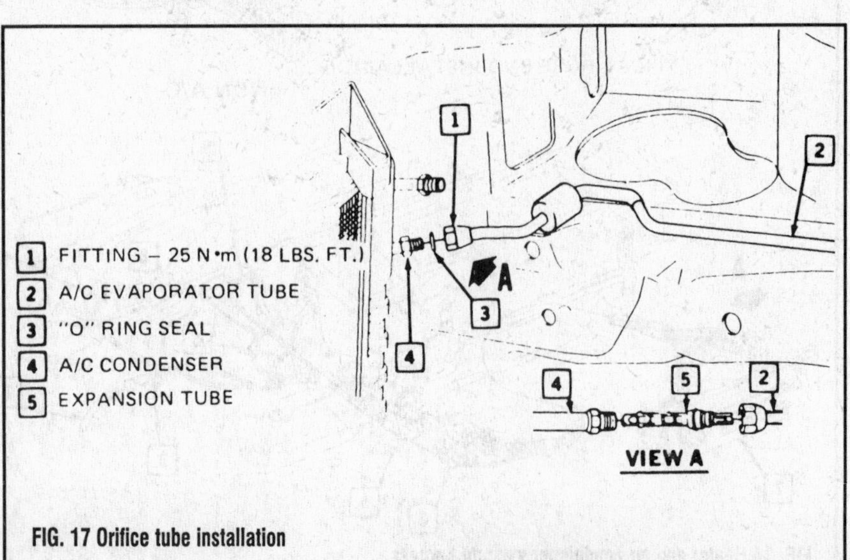

FIG. 17 Orifice tube installation

26549-C or equivalent to grip the orifice tube. Use a turning motion along with a push-pull motion to loosen the impacted orifice tube and remove it.

6. Swab the inside of the evaporator inlet pipe with R-11 to remove any remaining residue.

7. Add 1 oz. of 525 viscosity refrigerant oil to the system.

8. Lubricate the new O-ring and orifice tube with refrigerant oil and insert into the inlet pipe.

➡ **Ensure that the new orifice tube is inserted in the inlet tube with the smaller screen end first.**

9. Connect the evaporator inlet pipe with the condenser outlet fitting.

➡ **Use a backup wrench on the condenser outlet fitting when tightening the lines.**

10. Evacuate, recharge and leak test the system.

CRUISE CONTROL

Electric Brake Release Switch and Clutch Release Switch

REMOVAL & INSTALLATION

➧ SEE FIGS. 18 AND 19

1. At the brake switch, remove either the 2 electrical connectors or the electrical connector and the vacuum hose.
2. Remove the switch from the retainer.
3. Remove the tubular retainer from the brake pedal mounting bracket.

To Install:

4. Install the tubular retainer to the brake pedal mounting bracket.
5. Press the brake pedal and install the release switch into the retainer until fully seated in the clips.
6. Connect the wiring and/or vacuum lines. Adjust the switch.

ADJUSTMENT

1. Depress the brake pedal and check that the release switch is fully seated in the clips.
2. Slowly pull the brake pedal back to the at-rest position; the switch and valve assembly will move within the clips to the adjusted position.
3. Measure pedal travel and check switch engagement. The electric brake release switch contacts must open at $\frac{1}{8}$–$\frac{1}{2}$ in. (3–13mm) of pedal travel when measured at the centerline of the pedal pad. The brake lights should illuminate after another $\frac{1}{16}$ in. (1.6mm) of travel. The vacuum release should engage at $\frac{5}{8}$–1 in. (16–25mm) of pedal travel.

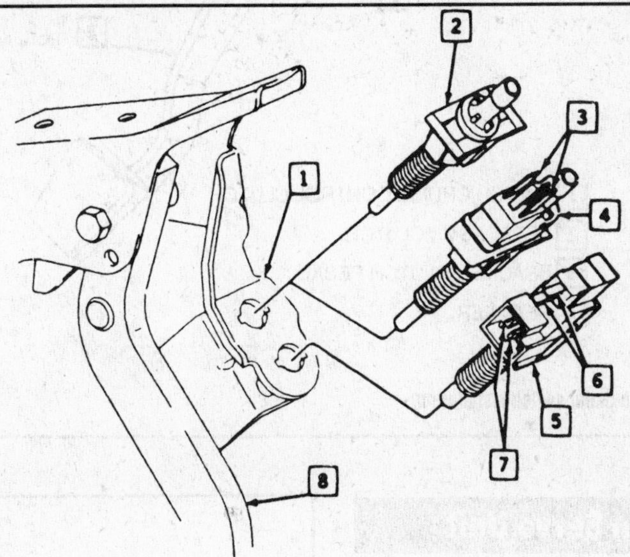

1 BRAKE PEDAL MOUNTING BRACKET
2 CRUISE CONTROL RELEASE VALVE (VACUUM) (MANUAL TRANSAXLE ONLY)
3 TORQUE CONVERTER CLUTCH TERMINALS
4 TCC AND CRUISE CONTROL RELEASE SWITCH/ VALVE (AUTOMATIC TRANSAXLE ONLY)
5 STOPLAMP SWITCH
6 CRUISE CONTROL RELEASE SWITCH TERMINALS
7 STOP LAMP SWITCH TERMINALS
8 BRAKE PEDAL ASM

FIG. 18 Brake pedal switch installation

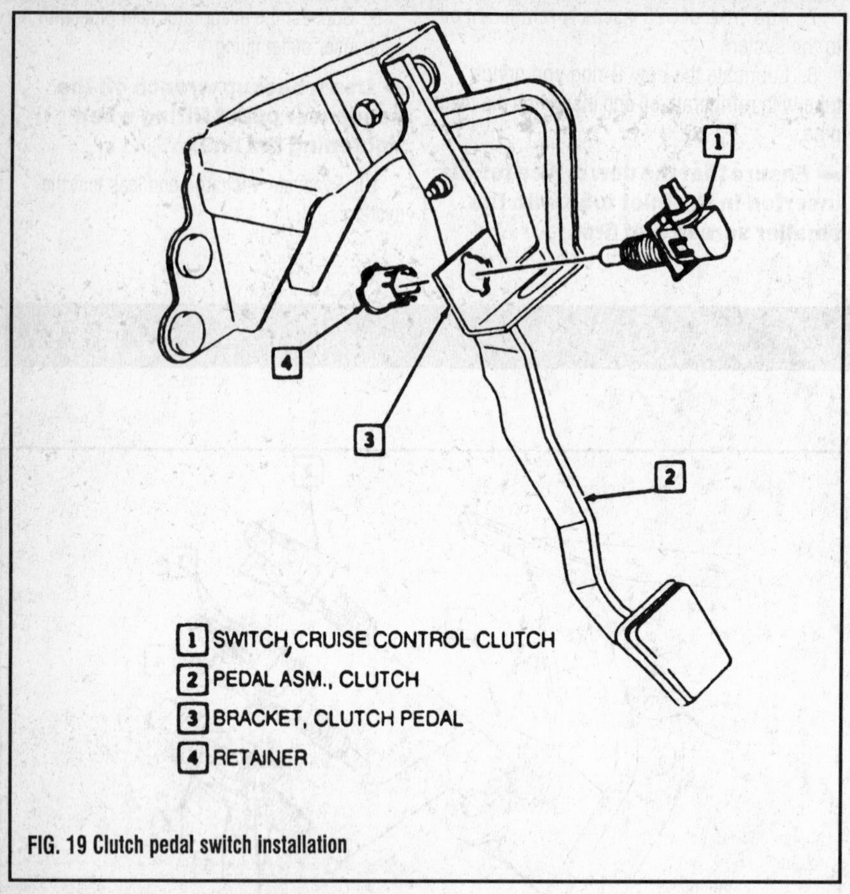

FIG. 19 Clutch pedal switch installation

Vacuum Servo Unit

REMOVAL & INSTALLATION

➧ SEE FIG. 20

1. Disconnect the electrical connector and vacuum hoses at the servo.
2. Disconnect the actuating chain, cable or rod from the servo.
3. Remove the screws holding the vacuum servo and solenoid unit to the bracket and remove the unit.

To Install:

4. Connect the large diameter brake release vacuum line to the servo unit. Connect the vacuum hose from the vacuum control valve to the servo unit.
5. Connect the actuating chain, rod or cable to the servo.
6. Install the servo unit to the bracket; tighten the screws to 12 inch lbs. (1.4 Nm).
7. Install the electrical connector to the servo.
8. Adjust the cable, rod or chain.

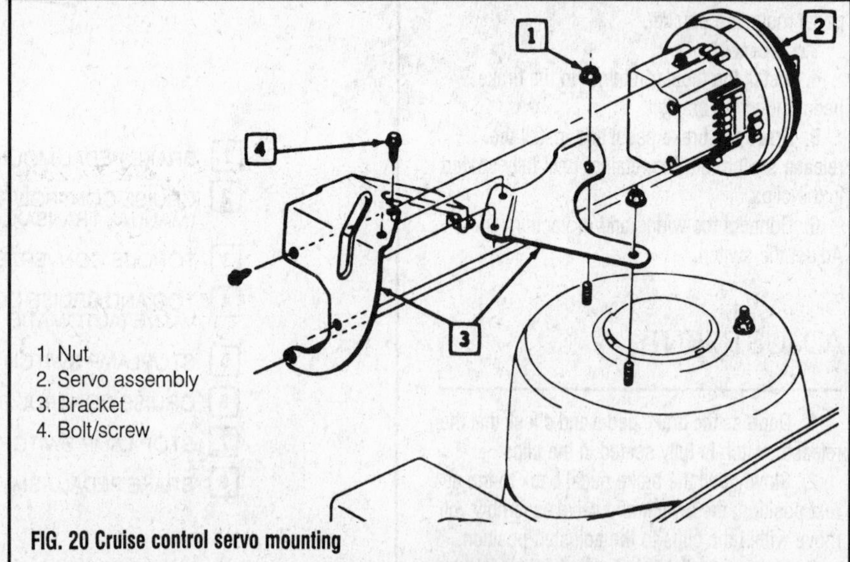

FIG. 20 Cruise control servo mounting

VACUUM SYSTEM LINKAGE ADJUSTMENT

➡ Do not stretch cables to make pins fit or holes align. This will prevent the engine from returning to idle.

Cable Type

1. Check that the cable is properly installed and that the throttle is closed to the idle position.
2. Pull the servo end of the cable toward the linkage bracket of the servo. Place the servo connector in one of the 6 holes in the bracket which allows the least amount of slack and does not move the throttle linkage.
3. Install the retainer clip. Check that the throttle linkage is still in the idle position.

Multi-Function Lever With Set/Coast and Resume/Accel

REMOVAL & INSTALLATION

1. Disconnect the negative battery terminal.
2. Disconnect cruise control switch connector at the base of steering column. it may be necessary to remove an under dash panel or trim piece for access.
3. Make sure lever is in **CENTER** or **OFF** position.
4. Pull lever straight out of retaining clip within the steering column.
5. Attach mechanic's wire or similar to the connector; gently pull the harness through the column, leaving the pull wire in place.

To install:

6. Place the transmission selector in **LOW** or **1**. Attach the mechanic's wire to the

connector. Gently pull the harness into place, checking that the harness is completely clear of any moving or movable components such as tilt-column, telescoping column, brake pedal linkage, etc.

7. Position the lever and push it squarely into the retainer until it snaps in place.

8. Remove the mechanics' wire and connect the cruise control harness connector.

9. Reinstall any panels or insulation which were removed for access.

10. Connect the negative battery terminal.

Set/Coast and Resume/Accel Switches On Wheel

REMOVAL & INSTALLATION

1. Disconnect the negative battery cable.
2. Remove the horn pad.
3. Remove the retainer and nut.
4. Remove the steering wheel.
5. Disconnect the electrical connectors.
6. Remove the horn switch if necessary.

To install:

7. Install the horn switch if necessary. Connect the electrical connectors.
8. Install the steering wheel; tighten the nut to 30 ft. lbs. (41 Nm).
9. Install the retainer and clip.
10. Install the horn pad.
11. Connect the negative battery cable.

Speed Sensor

REMOVAL & INSTALLATION

Optical Type With Buffer

1. Disconnect the negative battery cable.
2. To gain access to the sensor and buffer behind the speedometer, the instrument cluster must be partially removed. When doing so, disconnect the harness connector at the rear of the cluster; if the cluster is pulled too far outward with the harness attached, both may be damaged.
3. Disconnect the amplifier connector.
4. Remove the speed sensor attaching screw and remove the sensor through the opening in the base of the instrument panel.

To install:

5. Route the sensor wire connector and harness through the opening in the base of the instrument panel.
6. Install the sensor on its bracket and install the retaining screw.
7. Connect the amplifier connector.
8. Reinstall the instrument cluster and connect the electrical harness.
9. Connect the negative battery cable.

Permanent Magnet Type

1. Disconnect the wiring harness from the speed sensor. If the sensor also contains the speedometer cable, remove the cable.
2. Remove the retainer clip.
3. Carefully lift the sensor out of the transmission.
4. Remove the O-ring.

To install:

5. Lubricate a new O-ring with appropriate transmission fluid and install the ring on the sensor.
6. Install the sensor and secure the retaining clip.
7. Connect the speedometer cable if it was removed; connect the wiring harness. Make certain the harness is routed clear of moving or hot components.

Vacuum Reservoir

REMOVAL & INSTALLATION

Disconnect the vacuum line, remove the retaining screws and remove the reservoir. When reinstalling, tighten the retaining screws to 53 inch lbs. (6 Nm).

ENTERTAINMENT SYSTEMS

Radio Receiver/ Amplifier/Tape Player

REMOVAL & INSTALLATION

Console Mounted

➡ **If equipped with a compact disc player, removal and installation procedures are the same as for the radio.**

1. Disconnect the negative battery cable.
2. Remove the console bezel.
3. Remove the screws that attach the radio to the console.
4. Pull the radio out, disconnect the connectors, ground cable and antenna and remove the radio.
5. The installation is the reverse of the removal procedure.
6. Connect the negative battery cable and check the radio for proper operation.

Dash Mounted

1. Disconnect the negative battery cable.
2. Remove the instrument panel extension bezel.
3. Remove the radio bracket.
4. Remove the screws that attach the radio to the instrument panel.
5. Pull the radio out, disconnect the connectors, ground cable and antenna and remove the radio.
6. The installation is the reverse of the removal procedure.
7. Connect the negative battery cable and check the radio for proper operation.

Speakers

REMOVAL & INSTALLATION

Front Speakers

➧ SEE FIG. 21

1. Remove the speaker/defroster grille from the instrument panel.
2. Remove the speaker attaching screws.
3. Lift the speaker and disconnect the electrical connectors.
4. Remove the speaker.

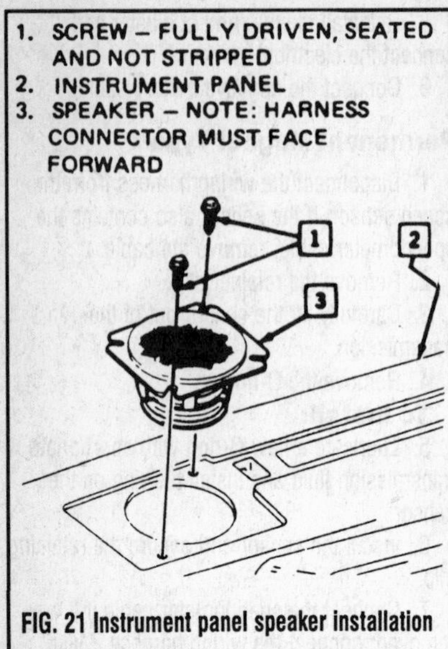

FIG. 21 Instrument panel speaker installation

To install:

5. Connect the speaker electrical connector.
6. Place the speaker into position and install the attaching screws.
7. Install the speaker/defroster grille to the instrument panel.

Rear Speakers

➧ SEE FIGS. 22 AND 23

1. Remove the rear seat cushion by removing the bolts from the bracket at the front of the seat.
2. Grasp the seat cushion and lift up and outward.
3. Remove the cushion from the vehicle.
4. Remove the anchor bolts from the bottom of the seatback securing the rear seat retainers and center seat safety belts.
5. Grasp the bottom of the seatback and swing upward to disengage the offsets on the back upper frame bar from the hangers; lift the seatback upward to remove.
6. If equipped with 4 doors, remove the upper rear quarter interior trim panels by performing the following:
   a. Disconnect the tabs on the trim pale from the slots in the body by grasping the trim panel and pulling toward the front of the car.
   b. Remove the trim panel by rotating inboard.
7. If equipped with 4 doors, remove the lower rear quarter interior trim panels by performing the following:
   a. Remove the 2 attaching screws.
   b. Remove the trim panel by grasping the panel and pulling inboard to disengage the tabs from the retainers.
8. If equipped with 2 doors, remove the lower rear quarter interior trim panels by performing the following:
   a. Remove the carpet retainer by

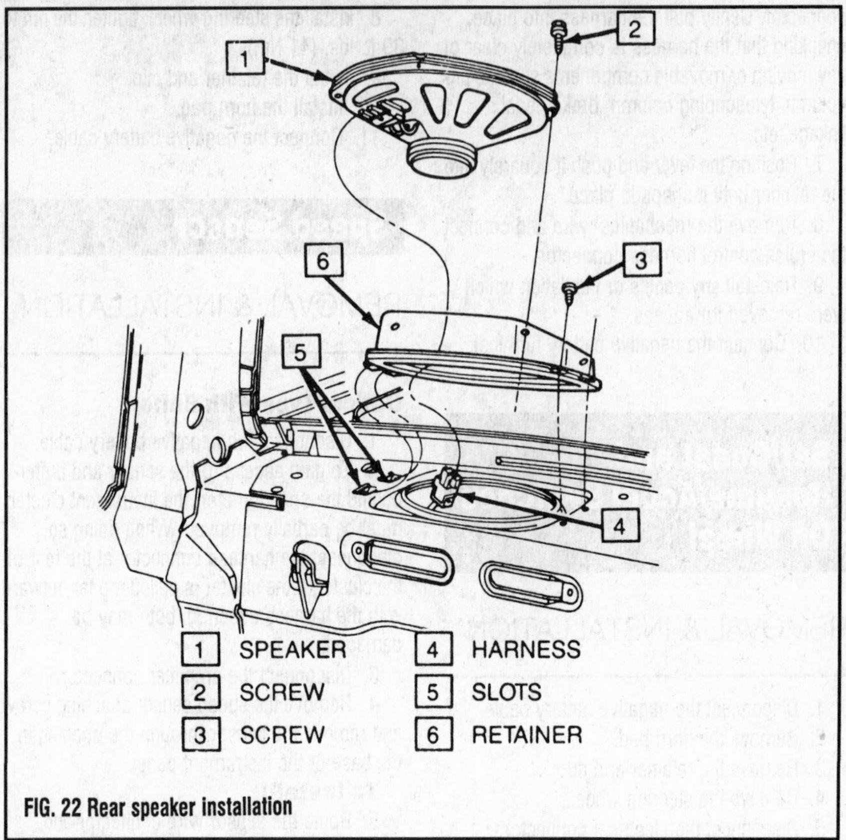

FIG. 22 Rear speaker installation

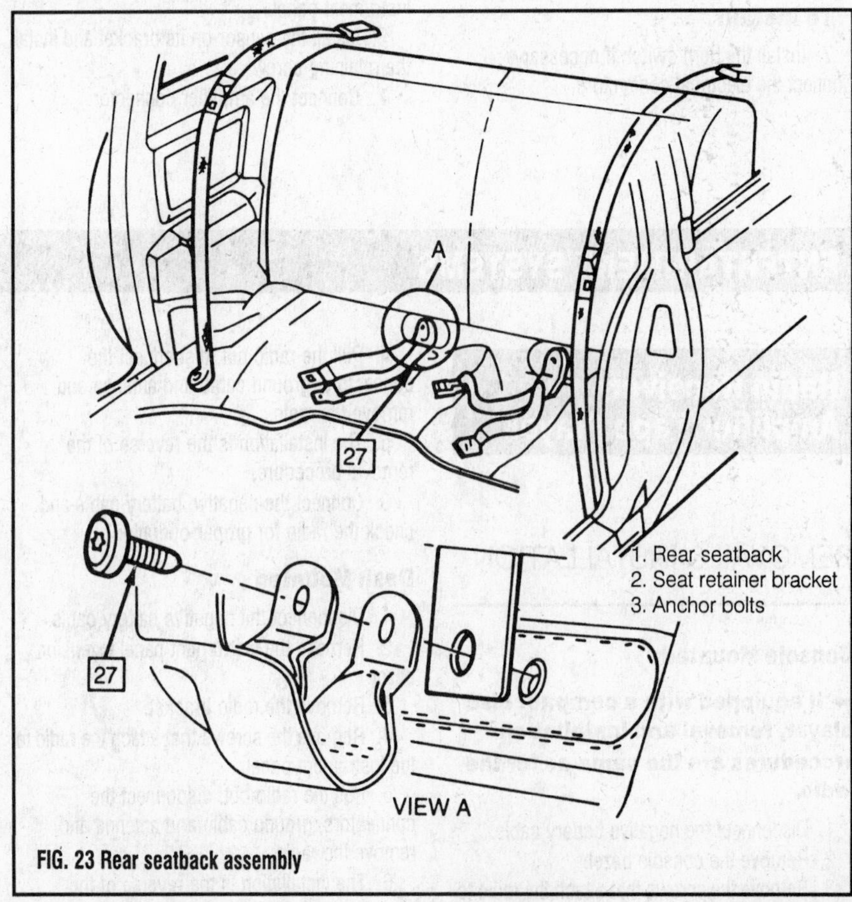

FIG. 23 Rear seatback assembly

removing the screws and lifting up on the carpet retainer.

b. Remove the upper windshield molding by grasping the molding and pulling down to disengage the molding from the clips.

c. Remove the trim panel attaching screws.

d. Remove the trim panel by grasping the panel and pulling inboard.

9. Remove the center high-mount stop light by removing the screws, lifting the light and disconnecting the electrical connector.

10. Remove the rear seat back-to-window panel by sliding the panel out from under the remaining quarter trim.

11. Disconnect the speaker harness.

12. Remove the speaker attaching screws.

13. Remove the speaker assembly by lifting and sliding the assembly out of the slots.

14. Remove the speaker from the retainer by removing the screws.

To install:

15. Install the speaker to the retainer and install the attaching screws.

16. Install the speaker assembly by inserting the tabs into the slots.

17. Install the speaker retainer assembly attaching screws.

18. Connect the speaker electrical connectors.

19. Install the rear seat-to-back window trim panel by sliding the panel under the quarter trim.

20. Install the center high-mount stop light by connecting the electrical connector, positioning the assembly and installing the attaching screws.

21. If equipped with 2 doors, install the lower rear quarter interior trim panels by performing the following:

a. Align the fasteners to the retainers in the body and pushing outboard on the panel.

b. Install the 2 attaching screws.

c. Install the upper windshield molding by starting at the top rear of the body lock pillar and engaging the tabs on the molding clips in the body.

d. Install the carpet retainer.

22. If equipped with 4 doors, install the lower upper rear quarter interior trim panels by performing the following:

a. Align the tabs to the retainers and press the trim panel until the tabs are fully engaged to the retainers.

b. Install the attaching screws.

23. If equipped with 4 doors, install the upper rear quarter interior trim panels by aligning the tabs in the slots, and pushing rearward and rotating outboard.

24. Install the rear seat back by aligning the seat back and engaging the upper retaining hook. An audible snap will be heard to indicate proper engagement.

25. Install the safety belt anchors on the top of the seat retainer brackets. Install the attaching bolts and tighten to 28 ft. lbs. (38 Nm).

26. Install the rear seat by aligning to the proper position. Install the attaching bolts and tighten to 13 ft. lbs. (18 Nm).

WINDSHIELD WIPERS AND WASHERS

Windshield Wiper Blade and Arm Assembly

REMOVAL & INSTALLATION

➧ SEE FIG. 24

1. Turn the ignition switch to the **ON** position. Turn the windshield wiper switch to the **ON** position.

2. When the wiper arms have reaches the center of the windshield, turn the ignition switch to the **OFF** position.

3. Place a piece of masking tape on the windshield under each wiper arm and mark the position of the wiper arm.

4. Lift the wiper arm from the windshield and pull the retaining latch.

5. Remove the wiper arm from the transmission shaft.

To install:

6. Align the wiper arm with the marks made before removal and slide the wiper arm onto the transmission shaft.

7. Push the retaining latch in and allow the wiper arm to return to the windshield. Make sure the marks are still in alignment.

8. Remove the masking tape.

Windshield Wiper Motor

REMOVAL & INSTALLATION

➧ SEE FIG. 25

1. Disconnect the negative battery cable.

2. Remove the wiper arm assembly(s) and cowl cover, if necessary.

3. Remove the wiper arm drive link from the crank arm.

4. Disconnect the connectors from the motor.

5. Remove the wiper motor attaching bolts.

6. Remove the wiper motor and crank arm by guiding the assembly through the access hole in the upper shroud panel.

To install:

7. Guide the wiper motor and crank arm assembly through the access hole and into position.

8. Install the wiper motor attaching bolts.

9. Connect the wiper motor electrical connector.

10. Install the wiper arm drive link to the crank arm.

11. If removed, install the wiper arm assembly(s) and cowl cover.

12. Connect the negative battery cable.

Wiper Linkage

REMOVAL & INSTALLATION

1. Remove the wiper arms.

2. Remove the wiper motor.

3. Remove the bolts attaching the left and right side transmission assemblies.

4. Remove the wiper linkage.

To install:

5. Install the wiper linkage.

6. Install the bolts attaching the left and right side transmission assemblies.

7. Install the wiper motor.

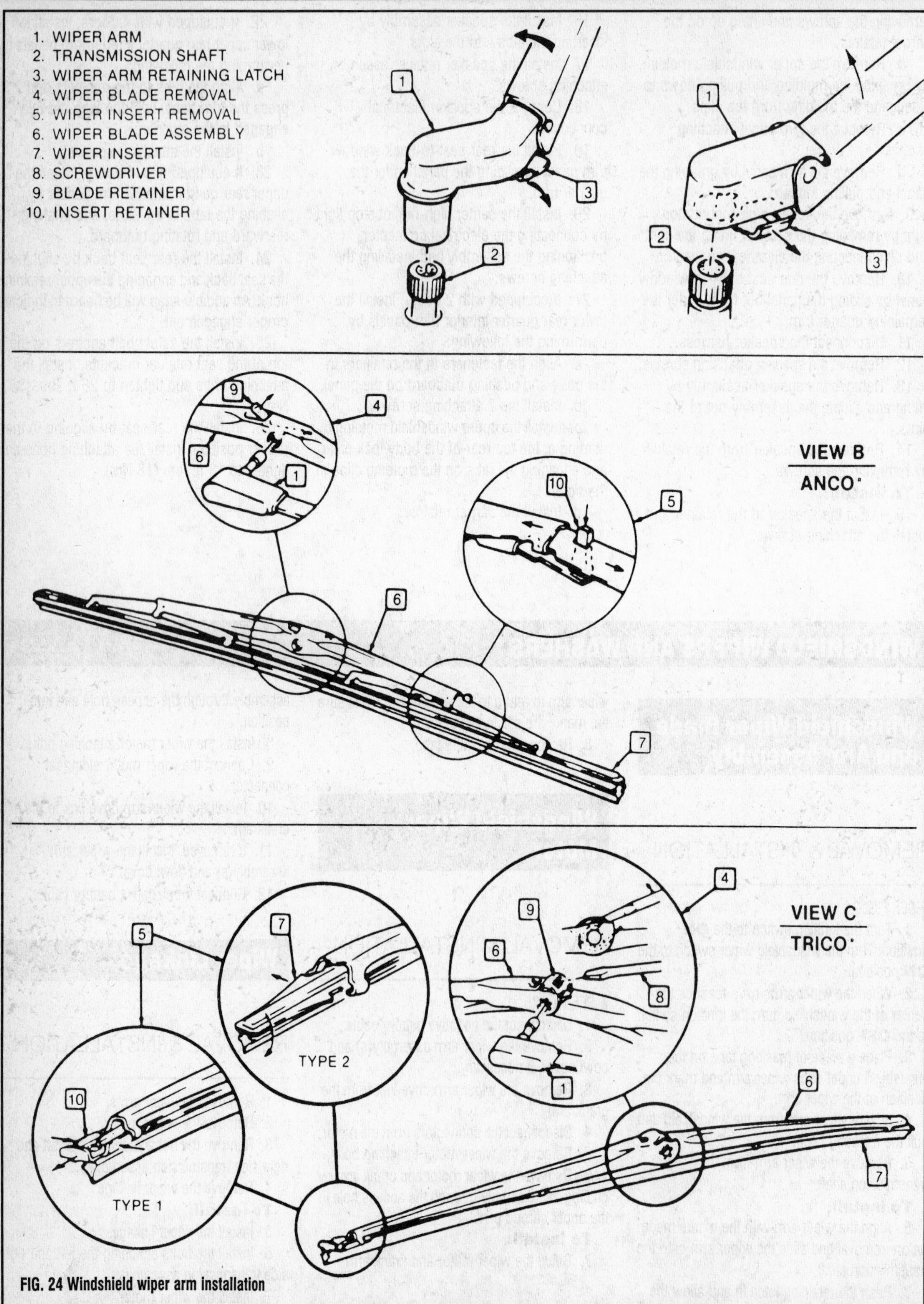

FIG. 24 Windshield wiper arm installation

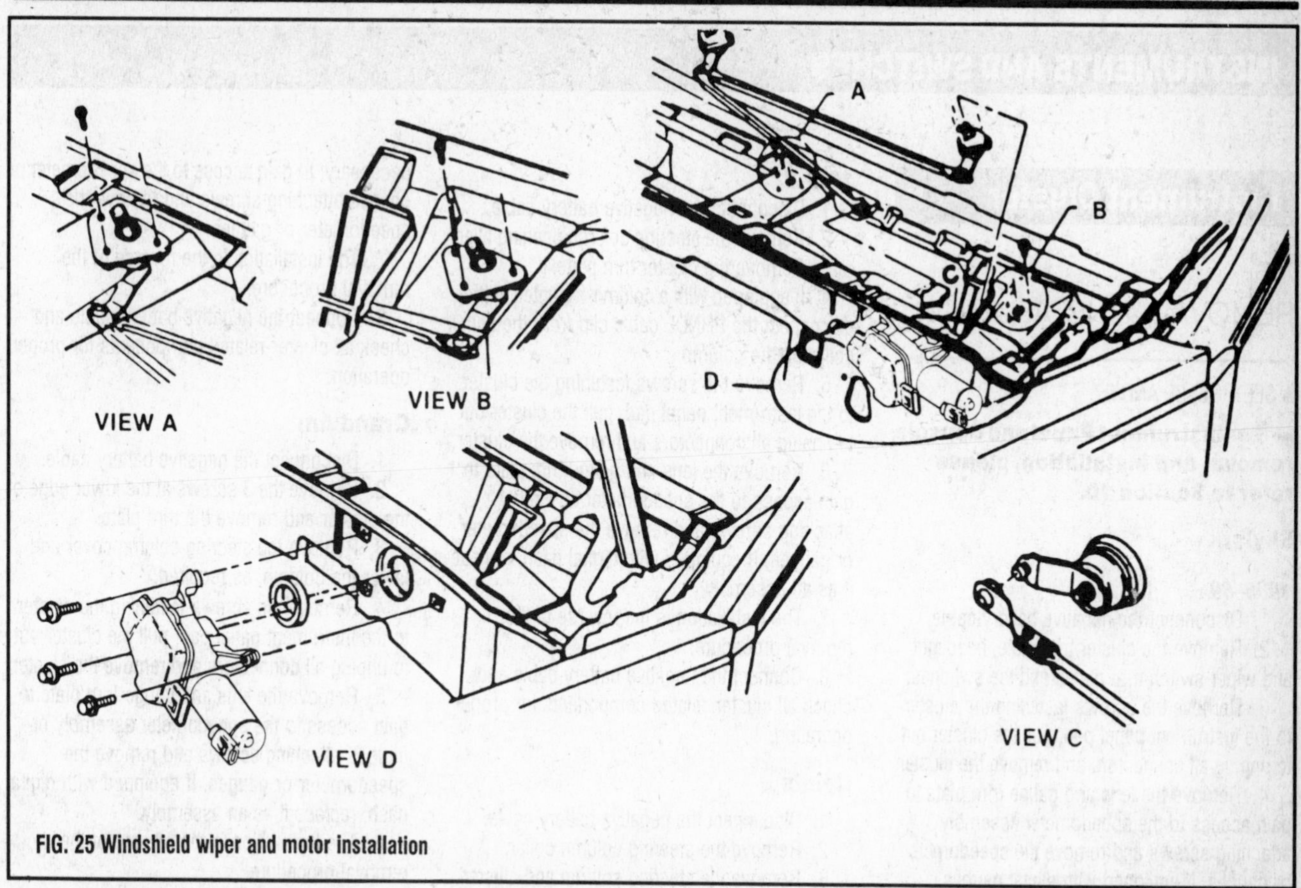

FIG. 25 Windshield wiper and motor installation

8. Install the wiper arms.

Windshield Washer Fluid Reservoir

REMOVAL & INSTALLATION

1. Disconnect the electrical connectors and washer hose from the reservoir.
2. Remove the reservoir attaching bolts.
3. Remove the reservoir from the vehicle

To install:

4. Install the vehicle in its mounting location.
5. Install the attaching bolts.
6. Connect the washer hose and electrical connectors.

Windshield Washer Pump Motor

REMOVAL & INSTALLATION

1. Remove the washer solvent from the reservoir.
2. Remove the brace.
3. Remove the reservoir bolts.
4. Disconnect the electrical connectors and washer hose.
5. Remove the washer pump from the reservoir.

To install:

6. Install the washer pump motor to the reservoir.

➡ **Make sure the new washer pump is pushed all the way into the reservoir gasket.**

7. Connect the electrical connectors and washer hose.
8. Install the reservoir attaching screws.
9. Install the brace.
10. Refill the reservoir with washer solvent.

INSTRUMENTS AND SWITCHES

Instrument Cluster

REMOVAL & INSTALLATION

➧ SEE FIGS. 26 AND 27

➡ **For Instrument Panel and Console removal and installation, please refer to Section 10.**

Skylark

1985–89

1. Disconnect the negative battery cable.
2. Remove the cluster trim plate, headlight and wiper switch trim plates and the switches.
3. Remove the screws fastening the cluster to the instrument panel pad, pull the cluster out to unplug all connectors and remove the cluster.
4. Remove the lens and gauge trim plate to gain access to the speedometer assembly attaching screws and remove the speedometer or gauges. If equipped with digital gauges, replace them as an assembly.
5. The installation is the reverse of the removal procedure.
6. Connect the negative battery cable and check all cluster-related components for proper operation.

1990–92

1. Disconnect the negative battery cable.
2. Remove the steering column opening filler.
3. Remove the cluster trim plate.
4. If equipped with a column-mounted shifter, disconnect the PRNDL cable clip from the shift collar on the column.
5. Remove the screws fastening the cluster to the instrument panel pad, pull the cluster out to unplug all connectors and remove the cluster.
6. Remove the lens and gauge trim plate to gain access to the speedometer assembly attaching screws and remove the speedometer or gauges. If equipped with digital dash, replace it as an assembly.
7. The installation is the reverse of the removal procedure.
8. Connect the negative battery cable and check all cluster-related components for proper operation.

Calais

1. Disconnect the negative battery cable.
2. Remove the steering column collar.
3. Remove the steering column and cluster trim plates.
4. Lower the steering column.
5. Remove the screws fastening the cluster to the instrument panel pad, pull the cluster out to unplug all connectors and remove the cluster.
6. Remove the lens and applique, if necessary, to gain access to the speedometer or gauges attaching screws and remove the speedometer or gauges.
7. The installation is the reverse of the removal procedure.
8. Connect the negative battery cable and check all cluster-related components for proper operation.

Grand Am

1. Disconnect the negative battery cable.
2. Remove the 3 screws at the lower edge of the cluster and remove the trim plate.
3. Remove the steering column cover and lower the column, as required.
4. Remove the screws fastening the cluster to the instrument panel pad, pull the cluster out to unplug all connectors and remove the cluster.
5. Remove the lens and gauge trim plate to gain access to the speedometer assembly or gauges attaching screws and remove the speedometer or gauges. If equipped with digital dash, replace it as an assembly.
6. The installation is the reverse of the removal procedure.
7. Connect the negative battery cable and check all cluster-related components for proper operation.

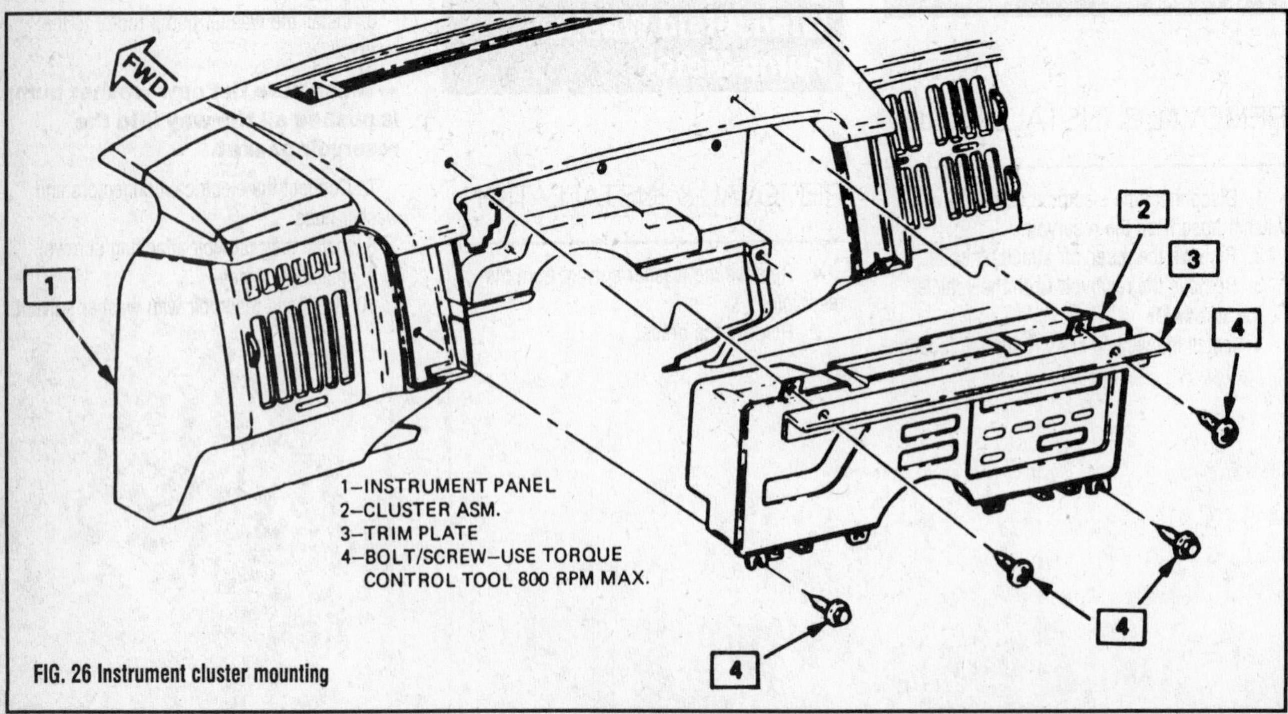

FIG. 26 Instrument cluster mounting

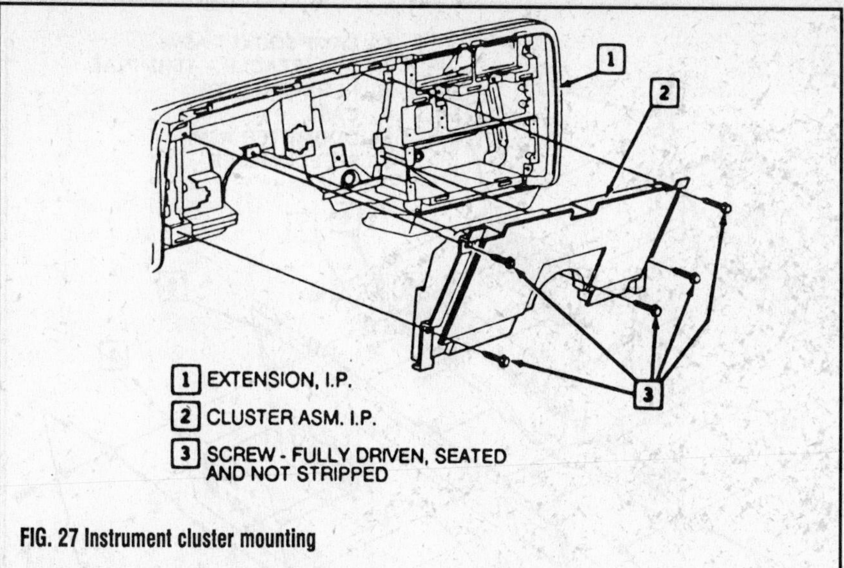

FIG. 27 Instrument cluster mounting

Speedometer

REMOVAL & INSTALLATION

➡ **If equipped with electronic instrumentation, the speedometer cannot be replaced separately; the entire instrument cluster must be replaced.**

Standard Cluster

1. Remove the instrument cluster.
2. Remove the screws from the cluster lens.
3. Remove the cluster lens.
4. Carefully, lift the speedometer facing.
5. Unplug the odometer motor leads.

To install:

6. Plug the odometer motor leads.
7. Install the speedometer facing.
8. Install the cluster lens.
9. Install the cluster lens attaching screws.
10. Install the instrument cluster.

Speedometer Cable

REMOVAL & INSTALLATION

➧ SEE FIG. 28

➡ **Only vehicles equipped with standard gauge clusters have mechanically driven speedometers. Electronic gauges use a vehicle speed sensor to drive the speedometer.**

1. Remove the instrument cluster far enough to reach behind and disconnect the speedometer cable from the back of the cluster.
2. Remove the left side sound insulator panel.
3. Push the speedometer cable grommet through the fire wall.
4. Observe the routing of the speedometer cable from the firewall up to the instrument cluster. If possible, tape a length of wire or string to the cable to aid installation of the new cable. Feed the cable down and through the hole in firewall.
5. Disconnect the speedometer cable from the transxle by removing the bolt attaching the cable to the drive assembly on the transaxle.
6. Remove the speedometer cable.

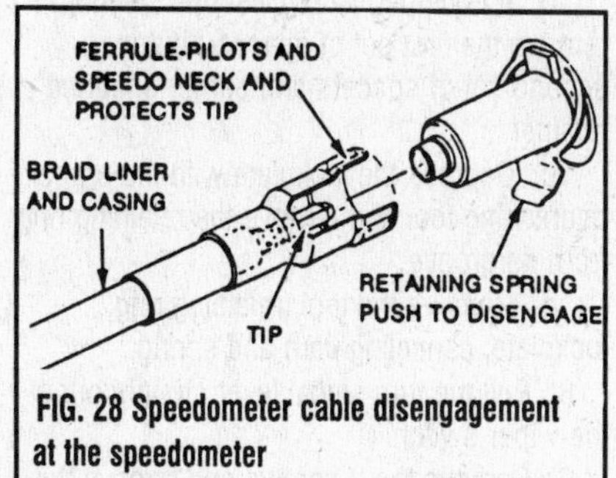

FIG. 28 Speedometer cable disengagement at the speedometer

To install:

7. Attach the length of wire or string to the new speedometer cable and pull through the firewall and up behind the instrument panel.
8. Connect the speedometer cable to the speedometer drive assembly on the transaxle. Install the attaching bolt.
9. Connect the speedometer cable to the speedometer.
10. Install the instrument cluster.
11. Make sure the speedometer cable is routed freely and has not kinks or sharp bends.
12. Install the grommet in the firewall.
13. Install the left side sound insulator panel.

Printed Circuit Board

REMOVAL & INSTALLATION

➧ SEE FIG. 29

1. Remove the instrument panel.
2. Remove the screws from the cluster lens.
3. Carefully, lift up on the lens and trim plate.
4. Remove the foam gasket from the trip odometer reset.
5. Remove the screws from the fuel gauge, speedometer and odometer.
6. Disconnect the fuel gauge.
7. Remove the speedometer and odometer.
8. Disconnect the odometer connector from the circuit board.
9. Remove the circuit board from inside the case.

To install:

10. Install the circuit board inside the case.
11. Connect the odometer connector to the circuit board.
12. Install the speedometer and odometer.
13. Connect the fuel gauge electrical connector.
14. Install the screws to the fuel gauge, speedometer and odometer.
15. Install the foam gasket on the trip odometer reset.
16. Install the trim plate and lens.
17. Install the screws through the lens and trim plate into the case.
18. Install the instrument cluster.

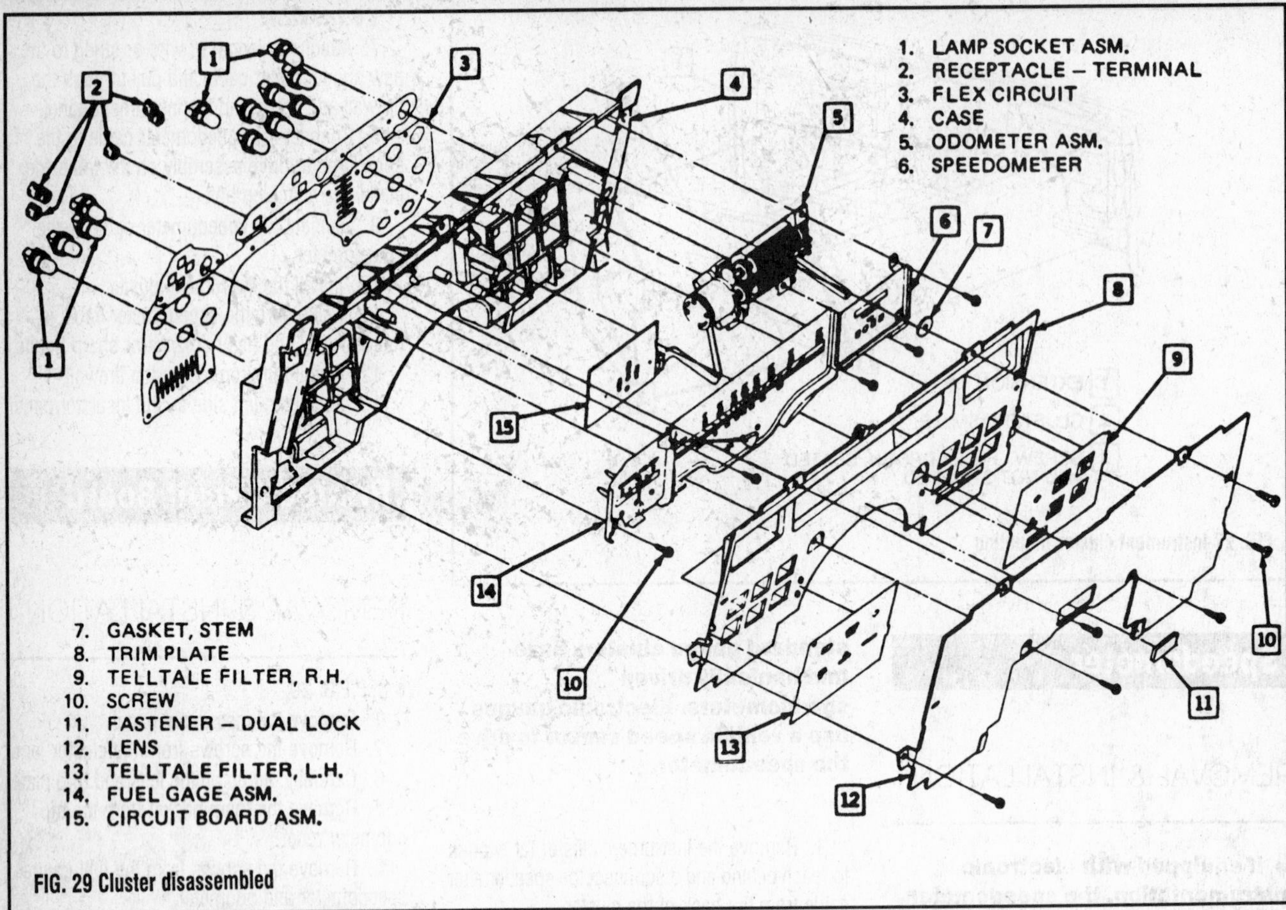

FIG. 29 Cluster disassembled

Windshield Wiper Switch

REMOVAL & INSTALLATION

Except Skylark

1. Disconnect the negative battery cable.
2. Remove the cluster trim, instrument panel trim or wiper switch trim screws, as required.
3. Remove the wiper switch attaching screws.
4. Pull the switch out, unplug the connectors and remove the switch assembly.
5. The installation is the reverse of the removal procedure.
6. Connect the negative battery cable and check the wipers and washers for proper operation.

Skylark

1. Disconnect the negative battery cable.
2. Remove the lower instrument panel sound insulator, trim pad and steering column trim collar.
3. Straighten the steering wheel so the tires are pointing straight ahead.
4. Remove the steering wheel.
5. Remove the plastic wire protector from under the steering column.
6. Disconnect the turn signal switch, wiper switch and cruise control connectors, if equipped.
7. To disassemble the top of the column:
   a. Remove the shaft lock cover.
   b. If equipped with telescope steering, remove the first set of spacers, bumper, second set of spacers and carrier snapring retainer.
   c. Depress the lockplate with the proper depressing tool and remove the retaining ring from its groove.
   d. Remove the tool, retaining ring, lockplate, canceling cam and spring.
8. Pull the turn signal lever straight out of the wiper switch.
9. Remove the 3 screws and remove the turn signal switch and actuator lever.
10. Remove the ignition key light.
11. Place the key in the **RUN** position and use a thin suitable tool to remove the buzzer switch.
12. Remove the key lock cylinder attaching screw and remove the lock cylinder.
13. Remove the 3 housing cover screws and remove the housing cover assembly.
14. Remove the wiper switch pivot pin and remove the switch.

To install:

15. Run the wiring through the opening and down the steering column, position the switch and install the wiper switch pivot pin.
16. Install the housing cover assembly, making sure the dimmer switch actuator is properly aligned.
17. Install the key lock cylinder and place in the **RUN** position. Install the buzzer switch and key light.
18. Install the turn signal switch and lever.
19. To assemble the top end of the column:
   a. Install the spring, canceling cam, lockplate and retaining ring on the steering shaft.
   b. Depress the plate with the depressing tool and install the ring securely in the groove. Remove the tool slowly.

c. If equipped with telescopic steering, install the carrier snapring retainer, lower set of spacers, bumper and upper set of spacers.

d. Install the shaft lock cover.

20. Connect the turn signal switch, wiper switch and cruise control connectors. Install the wire protector.

21. Install and steering wheel.

22. Install the steering column trim collar, lower instrument panel trim pad and sound insulator.

23. Connect the negative battery cable and check the key lock cylinder, wiper and washer, cruise control, turn signal switch and dimmer switch for proper operation.

Headlight Switch

REMOVAL & INSTALLATION

1. Disconnect the negative battery cable.

2. Remove the cluster trim, instrument panel trim or headlight switch trim screws, as required.

3. Remove the headlight switch attaching screws.

4. Pull the switch out, unplug the connectors and remove the switch assembly.

5. The installation is the reverse of the removal procedure.

6. Connect the negative battery cable and check the headlight switch for proper operation.

LIGHTING

Headlights

REMOVAL & INSTALLATION

➧ SEE FIGS. 30-32

Sealed Beam

1. Remove the headlight bezel attaching screws.

➡ To avoid turning the vertical or horizontal aiming screws, refer to the illustration before removing the headlight retainer.

2. Remove the headlight retainer attaching screws.

3. Pull the headlight out and, carefully, disconnect the electrical connector.

To install:

4. Connect the electrical connector to the new headlamp.

5. Place the headlamp into the socket.

6. Install the retainer and attaching screws.

7. Turn the headlight switch on to confirm headlight operation.

8. Install the headlight bezel and attaching screws.

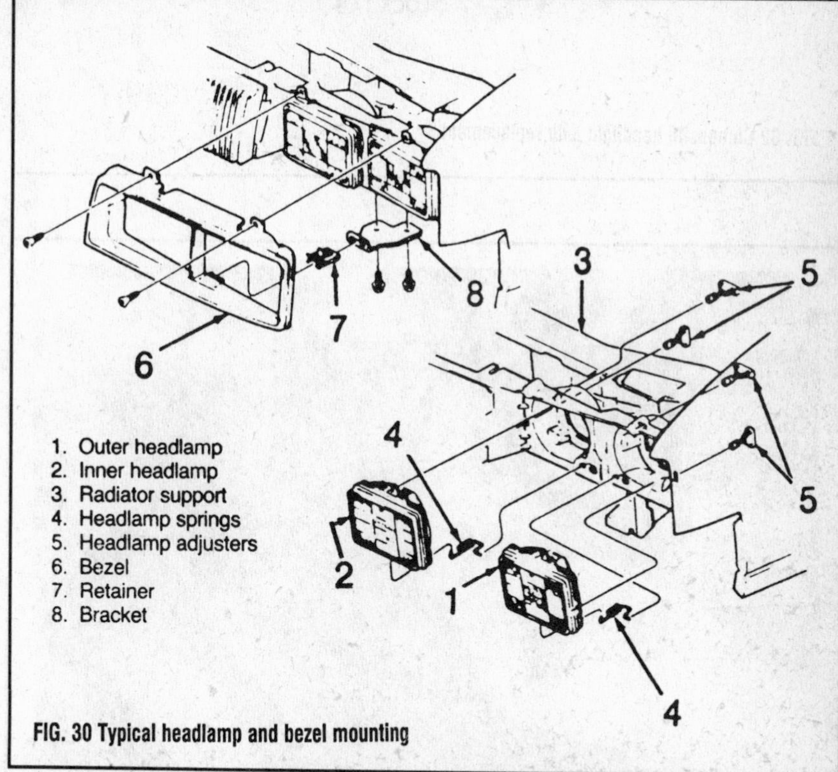

FIG. 30 Typical headlamp and bezel mounting

Composite

⁂ CAUTION

Halogen bulbs contain gas under pressure. Improper handling of the bulb could cause it to shatter into flying glass fragments. To avoid possible personal injury, follow the safety precautions listed below.

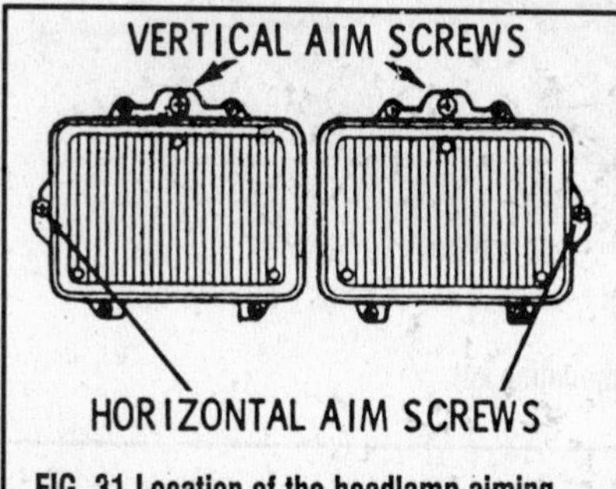

FIG. 31 Location of the headlamp aiming screws

- Turn off the headlight switch and allow the bulb to cool before attempting to change.
- Always wear eye protection when changing a halogen bulb.
- Handle the bulb only by its base. Avoid touching the glass.
- Do not drop or scratch the bulb.
- Keep dirt and moisture off the bulb.
- Place the used bulb in the new bulb's carton and dispose of it properly.

1. Raise the hood and locate the bulb mounting location at the rear of the composite headlamp body.

2. Grasp the plastic base, press in and turn

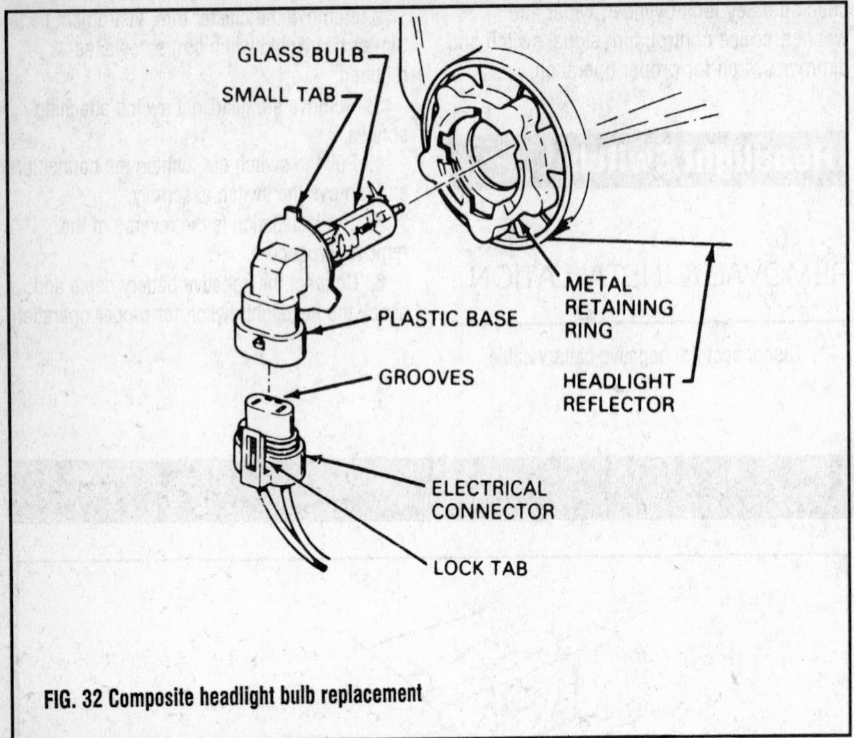

FIG. 32 Composite headlight bulb replacement

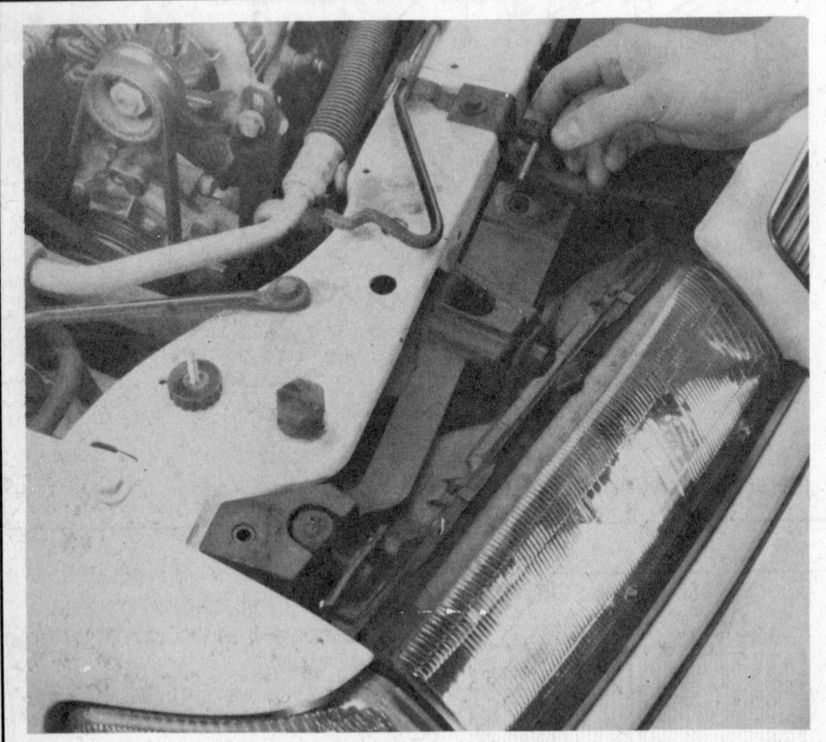
FIG. 32A Removing composite headlight assembly mounting nut

the base 1/4 turn counterclockwise and remove from the metal retaining ring by gently pulling back and away from the headlight.

3. Remove the electrical connector from the bulb by raising the lock tab and pulling the connector down and away from the bulb's plastic base.

4. Install the electrical connector on the new bulb's plastic base making sure that the lock tab is in place.

5. Install the bulb by inserting the smallest tab located on top of the plastic base into the corresponding notch in the metal retaining ring. Turn clockwise 1/4 turn until it stops. The small plastic tab should be at the top of the metal ring.

AIMING

The headlights must be aimed properly to get the right amount of light on the road and out of the eyes of oncoming motorists. With halogen sealed beam and composite headlights, proper aiming is even more important as the increased range and power of these lights can make even slight variations from the recommended settings hazardous to approaching traffic. Accordingly, aiming of the headlights should be performed by a qualified service technician using the proper aiming equipment.

The headlights are aimed by turning the vertical or horizontal aiming screws. The vehicle should be at its normal weight with the spare tire stowed in the trunk, normal fluid levels and the fuel tank at least half full. Tires should be uniformly inflated to the proper pressure. If the car normally carries an unusual load in the trunk or tows a trailer, these loads should be on the car when the headlamps are aimed.

Signal and Marker Lights

REMOVAL & INSTALLATION

Front Turn Signal and Parking Lights

1. Remove the socket from the lamp housing by turning counterclockwise.

2. Remove the lamp from the socket by pressing in and turning counterclockwise.

FIG. 32B Removing composite headlight assembly

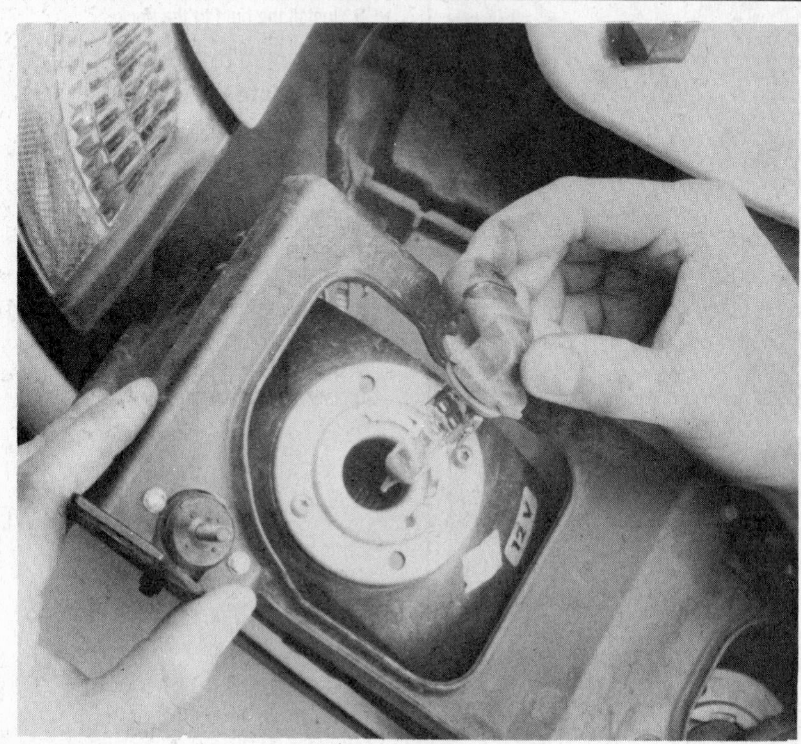

FIG. 32C Removing halogen bulb from composite headlight assembly

To install:

3. Install the replacement lamp into the socket, matching the directional alignment pins on the base of the bulb with the complementary slots in the socket. This will assure that the proper filament is energized at the right time; i.e.: the turn signal filament and not the parking lamp filament is energized when the turn signal is turned on.
4. Push the lamp into the socket and turn clockwise.
5. Install the socket to the lamp housing by turning clockwise.
6. Check operation of the parking lamp and turn signal.

Front Side Marker Lights

1. Remove the side marker housing attaching screws.
2. Remove the housing far enough to remove the socket from the housing by turning 45 degrees counterclockwise.
3. Remove the bulb and socket from the housing.
4. Remove the bulb.

To install:

5. Install the bulb into the socket.
6. Install the socket to the lamp housing.
7. Secure the socket to the lamp housing by turning 45 degrees clockwise.
8. Install the side marker housing and attaching screws.

Rear Side Marker, Turn, Stop, Parking and Back-Up Lights

1. Open the trunk.
2. Remove the nuts from the rear trim.
3. Remove the housing cover nuts.
4. Remove the lamp socket by turning counterclockwise.
5. Remove the lamp from the socket by pressing in and turning counterclockwise.

To install:

6. Install the lamp to the socket and pressing in and turning clockwise.
7. Install the socket and turn clockwise.
8. Install the housing cover nuts.
9. Install the rear trim.
10. Check operation of the rear lights.

High-Mount Brake Light

1. Remove the 2 lens screws.
2. Remove the lens.
3. Remove the bulb from the socket.

To install:

4. Install the bulb to the socket.
5. Install the lens.
6. Install the 2 lens screws.
7. Check operation of the light.

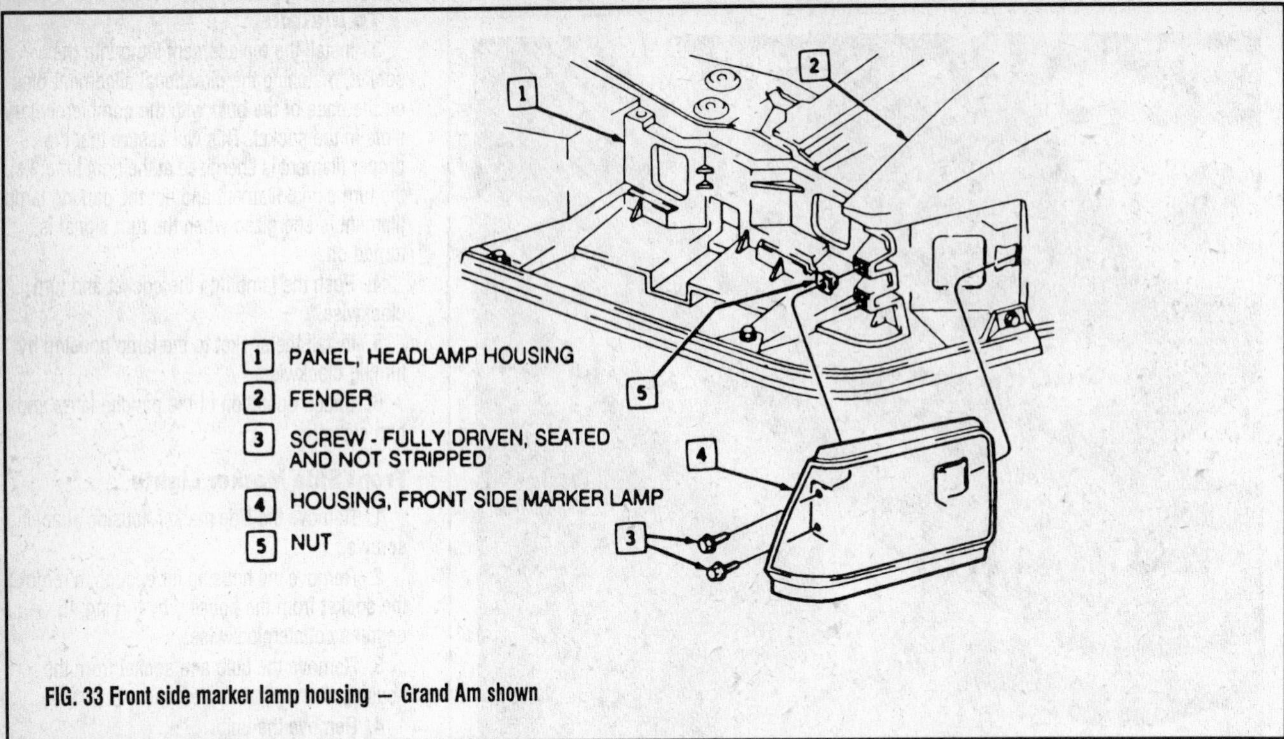

FIG. 33 Front side marker lamp housing — Grand Am shown

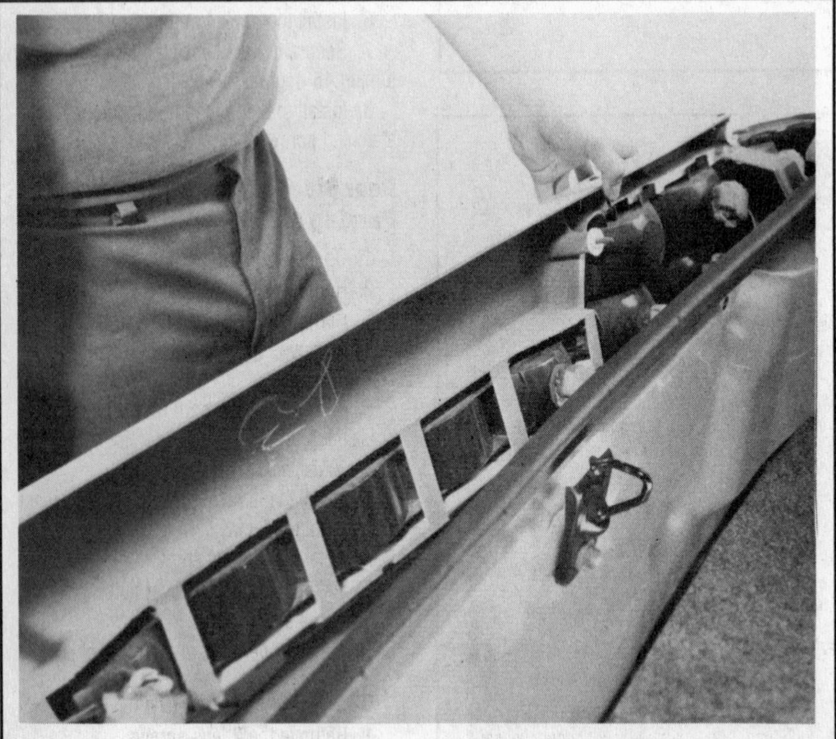

FIG. 33A Removing rear fascia with rear light assembly—Grand Am shown

Dome Light

1. Carefully, pry the lens from the housing.
2. Remove the bulb.

To install:

3. Install the bulb to the socket.
4. Install the lens.

License Plate Lights

1. Remove the 2 screws from the lamp assembly.
2. Carefully, pull the assembly down.
3. Remove the bulb from the socket by turning counterclockwise.

To install:

4. Install the bulb to the socket by pressing in and turning clockwise.
5. Reposition the lamp assembly.
6. Install the mounting screws.

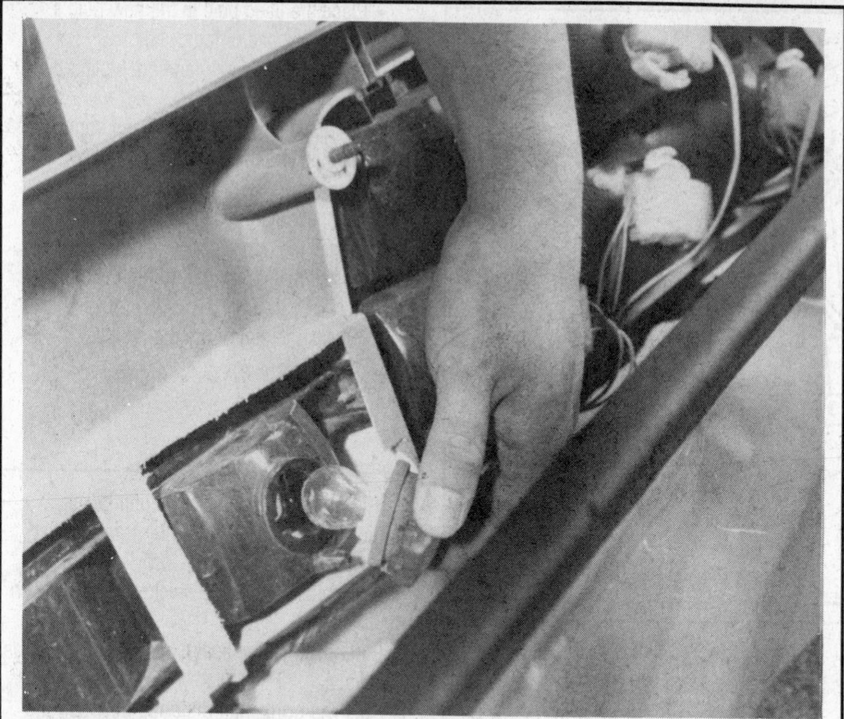

FIG. 33B Removing rear light socket for bulb replacement

Fog Lights

REMOVAL & INSTALLATION

**** CAUTION**

Halogen bulbs contain gas under pressure. Improper handling of the bulb could cause it to shatter into flying glass fragments. To avoid possible personal injury, follow the safety precautions listed below.

- Turn off the headlight switch and allow the bulb to cool before attempting to change.
- Always wear eye protection when changing a halogen bulb.
- Handle the bulb only by its base. Avoid touching the glass.
- Do not drop or scratch the bulb.
- Keep dirt and moisture off the bulb.

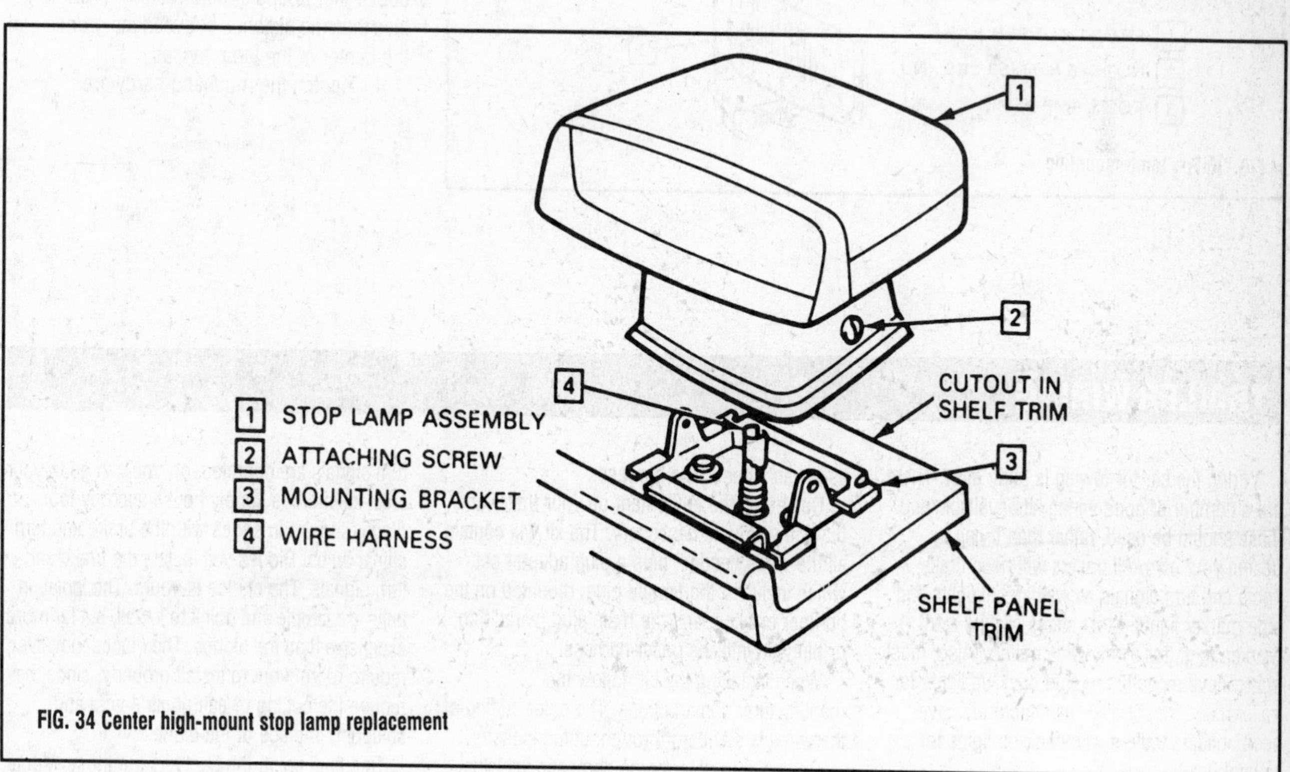

FIG. 34 Center high-mount stop lamp replacement

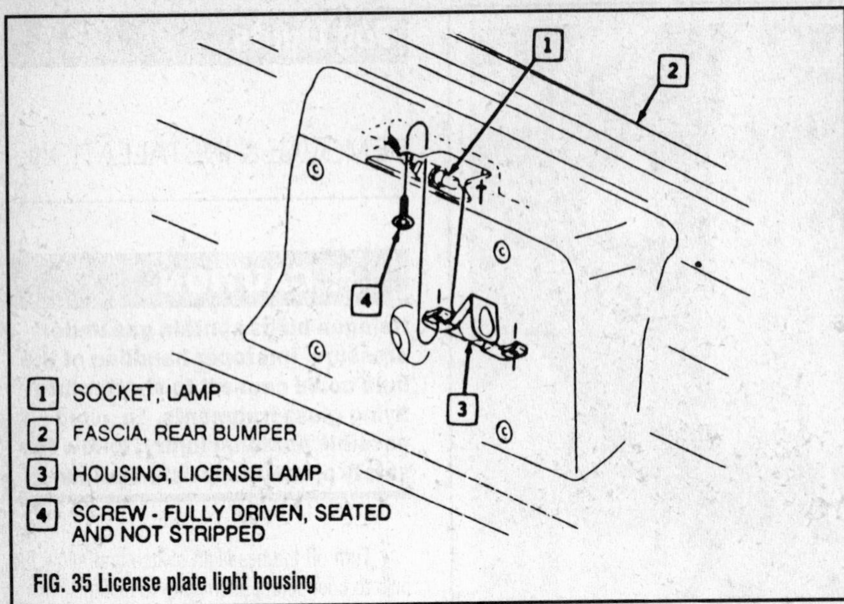

FIG. 35 License plate light housing

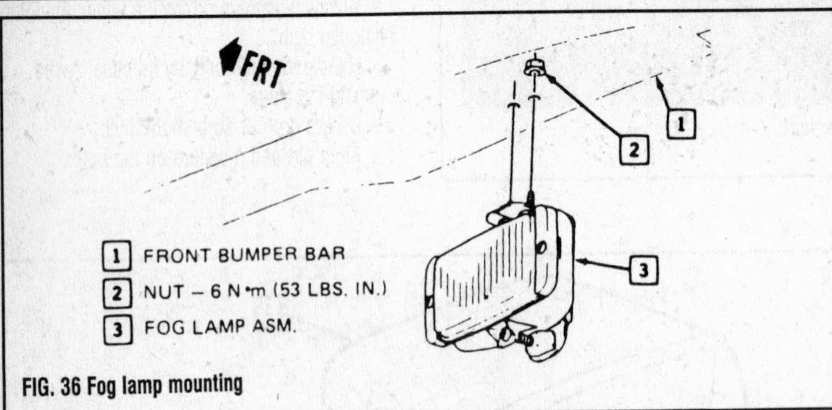

FIG. 36 Fog lamp mounting

- Place the used bulb in the new bulb's carton and dispose of it properly.

1. Remove the screw and nut behind the assembly
2. Remove the upper screw and spring.
3. Disconnect the electrical connector.

To install:

4. Connect the electrical connector.
5. Install the upper screw and spring.
6. Install the screw and spring behind the assembly
7. Check the aim of the fog lamps.

AIMING

1. Park the car on level ground facing, perpendicular to, and about 25 ft. from a flat wall.
2. Remove any stone shields and switch on the fog lights.
3. Loosen the mounting hardware and aim as follows:
    a. The horizontal distance between the light beams on the wall should be the same as between the lights themselves.
    b. The vertical height of the light beams above the ground should be 4 in. (102mm) less than the distance between the ground and the center of the lamp lenses.
4. Tighten the mounting hardware.

TRAILER WIRING

Wiring the car for towing is fairly easy. There are a number of good wiring kits available and these should be used, rather than trying to design your own. All trailers will need brake lights and turn signals as well as tail lights and side marker lights. Most states require extra marker lights for overly wide trailers. Also, most states have recently required back-up lights for trailers, and most trailer manufacturers have been building trailers with back-up lights for several years.

Additionally, some Class I, most Class II and just about all Class III trailers will have electric brakes.

Add to this number an accessories wire, to operate trailer internal equipment or to charge the trailer's battery, and you can have as many as seven wires in the harness.

Determine the equipment on your trailer and buy the wiring kit necessary. The kit will contain all the wires needed, plus a plug adapter set which included the female plug, mounted on the bumper or hitch, and the male plug, wired into, or plugged into the trailer harness.

When installing the kit, follow the manufacturer's instructions. The color coding of the wires is standard throughout the industry.

One point to note: some domestic vehicles, and most imported vehicles, have separate turn signals. On most domestic vehicles, the brake lights and rear turn signals operate with the same bulb. For those vehicles with separate turn signals, you can purchase an isolation unit so that the brake lights won't blink whenever the turn signals are operated, or, you can go to your local electronics supply house and buy four diodes to wire in series with the brake and turn signal bulbs. Diodes will isolate the brake and turn signals. The choice is yours. The isolation units are simple and quick to install, but far more expensive than the diodes. The diodes, however, require more work to install properly, since they require the cutting of each bulb's wire and soldering in place of the diode.

One final point, the best kits are those with a spring loaded cover on the vehicle mounted socket. This cover prevents dirt and moisture from corroding the terminals. Never let the vehicle socket hang loosely; always mount it securely to the bumper or hitch.

CIRCUIT PROTECTION

Fuses

REPLACEMENT

SEE FIGS. 37 AND 38

1. Locate the fuse for the circuit in question.
2. Check the fuse by removing it and observing the fuse element. If it is broken, replace the fuse. If the fuse blows again, check the circuit for a short to ground or faulty device in the circuit protected by the fuse.
3. Continuity can also be checked with the fuse installed in the fuse block with the use of a test light connected across the 2 test points on the end of the fuse. If the test light lights, replace the fuse. Check the circuit for a short to ground or faulty device in the circuit protected by the fuse.

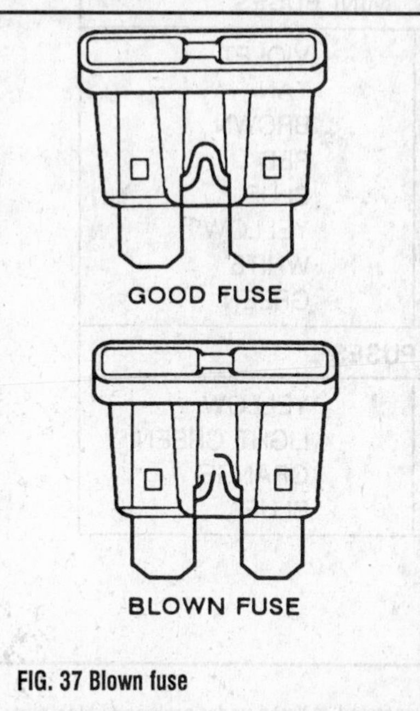

FIG. 37 Blown fuse

Fusible Links

Like fuses, fusible links are one-time circuit protectors. They are usually installed to protect circuits between the battery and the fuse panel. When a fusible link burns out, it generally creates a great deal of smoke which is intended partially to get your attention. Since the device in the circuit it protects could be destroyed if the problem is not rectified, the problem in the circuit must be diagnosed and corrected before replacing the fusible link.

REPLACEMENT

1. Disconnect the negative battery cable.
2. Locate the burned out link.
3. Strip away all the melted harness insulation.
4. Cut the burned link ends from the circuit wire.
5. Strip the circuit wire back approximately 1/2 in. (13mm) to allow soldering of the new link.
6. Using fusible link about 10 in. (254mm) long and 4 gauges smaller than the wire in the circuit to be protected, solder a new link into the circuit.

➡ Use only resin core solder. Do not use acid core solder as corrosion could result. Do not connect the fusible link in any other manner than soldering.

7. Tape the soldered ends securely using electrical tape.
8. After taping the wire, tape the harness, leaving an exposed loop of wire approximately 5 in. (127mm) in length.
9. Connect the negative battery cable.

Circuit Breakers

REPLACEMENT

Circuit breakers differ from fuses in that they are reusable. Circuit breakers open when the

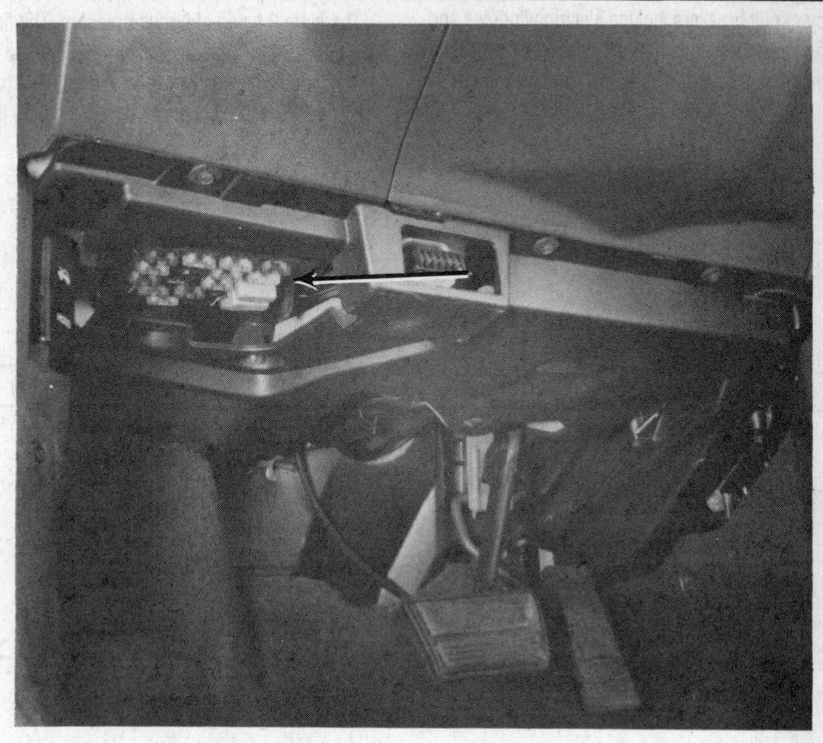

FIG. 37A Fuse panel location—Grand Am shown

CURRENT RATING AMPERES	COLOR
AUTO-FUSES, MINI FUSES	
3	VIOLET
5	TAN
7.5	BROWN
10	RED
15	BLUE
20	YELLOW
25	WHITE
30	GREEN
MAXI FUSES	
20	YELLOW
30	LIGHT GREEN
40	ORANGE
60	BLUE

FIG. 38 Fuse rating and color

flow of current exceeds specified value and will close after a few seconds when current flow returns to normal. Some of the circuits protected by circuit breakers include electric windows and power accessories. Circuits breakers are used in these applications due to the fact that they must operated at times under prolonged high current flow due to demand even though there is not malfunction in the circuit.

There are 2 types of circuit breakers. The first type opens when high current flow is detected. A few seconds after the excessive current flow has been removed, the circuit breaker will close. If the high current flow is experienced again, the circuit will open again.

The second type is referred to as the Positive Temperature Coefficient (PTC) circuit breaker. When excessive current flow passes through the PTC circuit breaker, the circuit is not opened but its resistance increases. As the device heats ups with the increase in current flow, the resistance increases to the point where the circuit is effectively open. Unlike other circuit breakers, the PTC circuit breaker will not reset until the circuit is opened, removing voltage from the terminals. Once the voltage is removed, the circuit breaker will re-close within a few seconds.

Replace the circuit breaker by unplugging the old one and plugging in the new one. Confirm proper circuit operation.

Flashers

REPLACEMENT

The hazard flasher is located forward of the console on all N-Body vehicles. The turn signal flasher is located behind the instrument panel, on the left side of the steering column bracket. Replace the flasher by unplugging the old one and plugging in the new one. Confirm proper flasher operation.

FUSIBLE LINK CHART

Fusible Link	Capacity (amps)	Circuit
Link A	0.5	Electronic Control Module
Link B	2	Alternator/Ignition Switch/Fuse Panel
Link C	1	Blower Relay, Fuse Panel
Link D	1	Lighting circuits
Link E	2/3	Alternator
Link F	2/3	Coolant Fan Relay

LIGHT BULB CHART

LAMP USAGE & QUANTITY	TRADE NO.	POWER RATING
Exterior:		
Back-up 2	1156	32
Front-Park-Turn 2	2057	2 & 32
Front-Park-Turn (GT) 2	2057NA	1.5 & 24
Park Only 2	194NA	32
Headlamp		
Low 2	4652	50 & 60 W
Headlamp, High Beam (Halogen) 2	H4651	50 & 60 W
Headlamp-Low Beam 2	9006	55 W
Headlamp-High Beam 2	9005	65 W
Composite 2	9004	45 & 65 W
License 2	194	2
Side Marker, Front 2	194	2
Side Marker, Rear 2	194	2
Tail-Stop-Turn 2	2057	2 & 32
Turn Only-Rear 2	1156	32
Center High-Mount Stop		
Package Shelf 1	1156	32
Luggage Carrier 1	577	21
Interior:		
Ashtray 1	194	2
Courtesy Light 2	194	2
Dome Light (Single Reading Lt.) 2	562	12
Dome Light (Dual Reading Lt.) 2	906	6
I.P. Compartment 1	194	2
Heater and A/C Control 2	37	0.5
Park/Neutral 1	161	1
Standard Cluster:		
Panel Illumination 2	168	3
Panel Illumination 1	194	2
Odometer 1	168	3
PRNDL/Cover 1	168	3
Turn Signal 2	74	0.7
High Beam 1	74	0.7
Charge 1	194	2
Brake 1	74	0.7
Service Engine Soon 1	194	2
Up-Shift 1	194	2
Temp 1	194	2
Fasten Belts 1	194	2
Low Coolant 1	194	2
Fuel Gauge 1	168	3
Odometer 1	168	3
Oil 1	74	0.7
Gauge Cluster:		
Panel Illumination 4	161	1
Panel Illumination 2	168	3
Panel Illumination 2	194	2
Panel Illumination 1	25082841	2
PRNDL/Cover 1	168	3
Turn Signal 2	25085641	0.7
High Beam 1	25085641	0.7
Charge 1	194	2
Battery 1	168	3
Brake 1	74	0.7
Service Engine Soon 1	194	2
Up-Shift 1	25085641	2
Temp 1	194	2
Fasten Belts 1	194	2
Low Coolant 1	194	2
Fuel Gauge 1	161	1
Odometer 1	168	3
Oil 1	74	0.7
Anti-Lock 1	74	0.7

FUSE AND CIRCUIT BREAKER APPLICATION CHART

NOTE: The following list is meant only as a guide. Be sure to refer to your owner's manual, fuse panel, circuit breaker or fusible link itself when replacing circuit protectors to confirm the proper amperage for your vehicle.

FUSE	RATING (AMPS)	CIRCUITRY
Tail lts.	20	Interior lights dimming, exterior lights
Ctsy lts.	20	Interior lights, power antenna, automatic seat belts, warnings and alarms
Radio	10	Cruise control, radio
Clk-cig	20	Cig. ltr., horns, power door locks, I/P compartment light
Driver Information Center		
Stop haz	20	Exterior lts.
Wiper	25	Wiper, washer
Radio	10	Radio
Ignition	20	Multi-port fuel injection
Inst. lts.	5	Interior lts dimming, headlights: fog lts.
F/P-inj	20	Multi-port fuel injection, throttle body injection
Turn, back-up	20	Back-up lts., exterior lts., warnings and alarms
Gauges	10	Throttle body injection, multi-port injection, starter and charging system, brake warning system, rear defogger, warnings and alarms, instrument panel, driver information system, interior lights, automatic safety belts, remoteless key entry
ECM-relays	10	Multi-port fuel injection, throttle body injection, starter and charging system, air conditioning: compressor controls, cruise control, instrument panel, vehicle speed sensor, EVO steering, ABS brake lamp
Heater, A/C	25	Coolant fan, heater, air conditioner, luggage compartment lid release, daytime running lts.
Power widow	30	Power windows (circuit breaker)
Power accy.	30	Rear defogger, power seats, power door locks, remote keyless entry (circuit breaker)

Troubleshooting Basic Turn Signal and Flasher Problems

Most problems in the turn signals or flasher system can be reduced to defective flashers or bulbs, which are easily replaced. Occasionally, problems in the turn signals are traced to the switch in the steering column, which will require professional service.

F = Front R = Rear ● = Lights off o = Lights on

Problem		Solution
Turn signals light, but do not flash	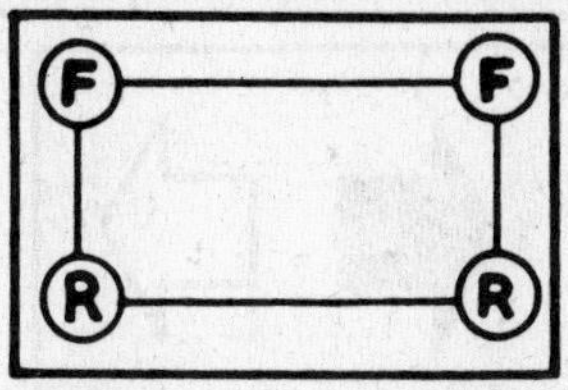 F F / R R	• Replace the flasher
No turn signals light on either side	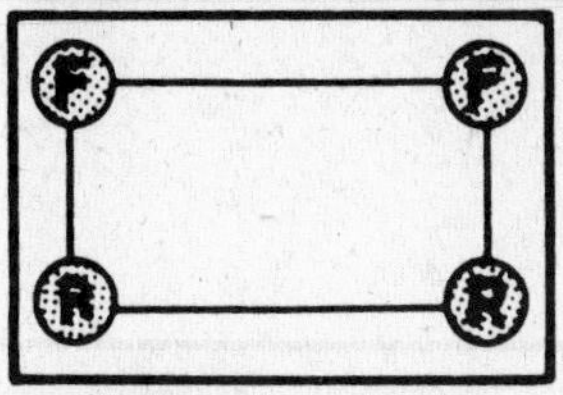 F F / R R	• Check the fuse. Replace if defective. • Check the flasher by substitution • Check for open circuit, short circuit or poor ground
Both turn signals on one side don't work	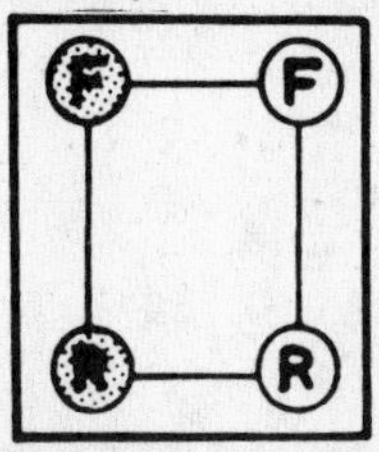 F F / R R	• Check for bad bulbs • Check for bad ground in both housings
One turn signal light on one side doesn't work	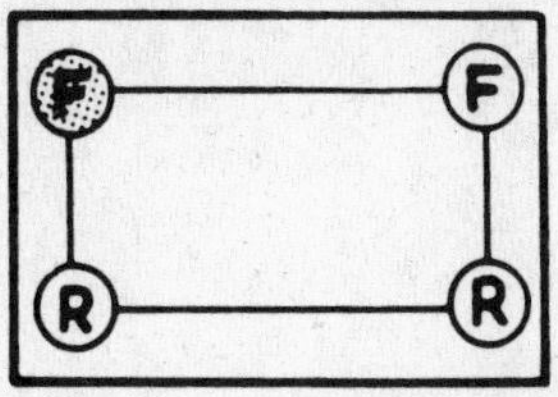 F F / R R	• Check and/or replace bulb • Check for corrosion in socket. Clean contacts. • Check for poor ground at socket
Turn signal flashes too fast or too slow	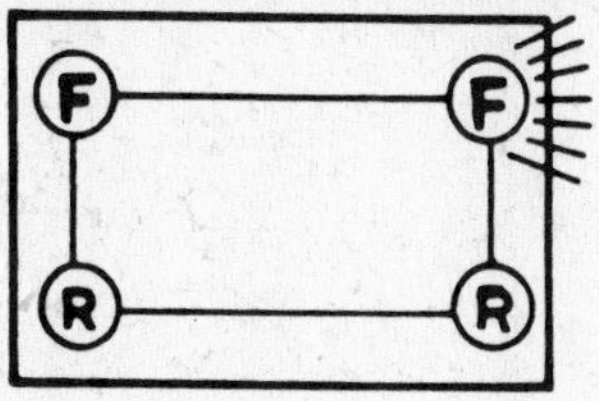 F F / R R	• Check any bulb on the side flashing too fast. A heavy-duty bulb is probably installed in place of a regular bulb. • Check the bulb flashing too slow. A standard bulb was probably installed in place of a heavy-duty bulb. • Check for loose connections or corrosion at the bulb socket
Indicator lights don't work in either direction		• Check if the turn signals are working • Check the dash indicator lights • Check the flasher by substitution

Troubleshooting Basic Turn Signal and Flasher Problems

Most problems in the turn signals or flasher system can be reduced to defective flashers or bulbs, which are easily replaced. Occasionally, problems in the turn signals are traced to the switch in the steering column, which will require professional service.

F = Front R = Rear • = Lights off o = Lights on

Problem		Solution
One indicator light doesn't light		• On systems with 1 dash indicator: See if the lights work on the same side. Often the filaments have been reversed in systems combining stoplights with taillights and turn signals. Check the flasher by substitution • On systems with 2 indicators: Check the bulbs on the same side Check the indicator light bulb Check the flasher by substitution

Troubleshooting Basic Lighting Problems

Problem	Cause	Solution
Lights		
One or more lights don't work, but others do	• Defective bulb(s) • Blown fuse(s) • Dirty fuse clips or light sockets • Poor ground circuit	• Replace bulb(s) • Replace fuse(s) • Clean connections • Run ground wire from light socket housing to car frame
Lights burn out quickly	• Incorrect voltage regulator setting or defective regulator • Poor battery/alternator connections	• Replace voltage regulator • Check battery/alternator connections
Lights go dim	• Low/discharged battery • Alternator not charging • Corroded sockets or connections • Low voltage output	• Check battery • Check drive belt tension; repair or replace alternator • Clean bulb and socket contacts and connections • Replace voltage regulator
Lights flicker	• Loose connection • Poor ground • Circuit breaker operating (short circuit)	• Tighten all connections • Run ground wire from light housing to car frame • Check connections and look for bare wires
Lights "flare"—Some flare is normal on acceleration—if excessive, see "Lights Burn Out Quickly"	• High voltage setting	• Replace voltage regulator
Lights glare—approaching drivers are blinded	• Lights adjusted too high • Rear springs or shocks sagging • Rear tires soft	• Have headlights aimed • Check rear springs/shocks • Check/correct rear tire pressure
Turn Signals		
Turn signals don't work in either direction	• Blown fuse • Defective flasher • Loose connection	• Replace fuse • Replace flasher • Check/tighten all connections
Right (or left) turn signal only won't work	• Bulb burned out • Right (or left) indicator bulb burned out • Short circuit	• Replace bulb • Check/replace indicator bulb • Check/repair wiring
Flasher rate too slow or too fast	• Incorrect wattage bulb • Incorrect flasher	• Flasher bulb • Replace flasher (use a variable load flasher if you pull a trailer)
Indicator lights do not flash (burn steadily)	• Burned out bulb • Defective flasher	• Replace bulb • Replace flasher
Indicator lights do not light at all	• Burned out indicator bulb • Defective flasher	• Replace indicator bulb • Replace flasher

Troubleshooting Basic Dash Gauge Problems

Problem	Cause	Solution
Coolant Temperature Gauge		
Gauge reads erratically or not at all	• Loose or dirty connections • Defective sending unit	• Clean/tighten connections • Bi-metal gauge: remove the wire from the sending unit. Ground the wire for an instant. If the gauge registers, replace the sending unit.
	• Defective gauge	• Magnetic gauge: disconnect the wire at the sending unit. With ignition ON gauge should register COLD. Ground the wire; gauge should register HOT.
Ammeter Gauge—Turn Headlights ON (do not start engine). Note reaction		
Ammeter shows charge	• Connections reversed on gauge	• Reinstall connections
Ammeter shows discharge	• Ammeter is OK	• Nothing
Ammeter does not move	• Loose connections or faulty wiring • Defective gauge	• Check/correct wiring • Replace gauge
Oil Pressure Gauge		
Gauge does not register or is inaccurate	• On mechanical gauge, Bourdon tube may be bent or kinked	• Check tube for kinks or bends preventing oil from reaching the gauge
	• Low oil pressure	• Remove sending unit. Idle the engine briefly. If no oil flows from sending unit hole, problem is in engine.
	• Defective gauge	• Remove the wire from the sending unit and ground it for an instant with the ignition ON. A good gauge will go to the top of the scale.
	• Defective wiring	• Check the wiring to the gauge. If it's OK and the gauge doesn't register when grounded, replace the gauge.
	• Defective sending unit	• If the wiring is OK and the gauge functions when grounded, replace the sending unit
All Gauges		
All gauges do not operate	• Blown fuse • Defective instrument regulator	• Replace fuse • Replace instrument voltage regulator
All gauges read low or erratically	• Defective or dirty instrument voltage regulator	• Clean contacts or replace
All gauges pegged	• Loss of ground between instrument voltage regulator and car • Defective instrument regulator	• Check ground • Replace regulator

Troubleshooting Basic Dash Gauge Problems

Problem	Cause	Solution
Warning Lights		
Light(s) do not come on when ignition is ON, but engine is not started	• Defective bulb • Defective wire • Defective sending unit	• Replace bulb • Check wire from light to sending unit • Disconnect the wire from the sending unit and ground it. Replace the sending unit if the light comes on with the ignition ON.
Light comes on with engine running	• Problem in individual system • Defective sending unit	• Check system • Check sending unit (see above)

Troubleshooting the Heater

Problem	Cause	Solution
Blower motor will not turn at any speed	• Blown fuse • Loose connection • Defective ground • Faulty switch • Faulty motor • Faulty resistor	• Replace fuse • Inspect and tighten • Clean and tighten • Replace switch • Replace motor • Replace resistor
Blower motor turns at one speed only	• Faulty switch • Faulty resistor	• Replace switch • Replace resistor
Blower motor turns but does not circulate air	• Intake blocked • Fan not secured to the motor shaft	• Clean intake • Tighten security
Heater will not heat	• Coolant does not reach proper temperature • Heater core blocked internally • Heater core air-bound • Blend-air door not in proper position	• Check and replace thermostat if necessary • Flush or replace core if necessary • Purge air from core • Adjust cable
Heater will not defrost	• Control cable adjustment incorrect • Defroster hose damaged	• Adjust control cable • Replace defroster hose

Troubleshooting Basic Windshield Wiper Problems

Problem	Cause	Solution
Electric Wipers		
Wipers do not operate— Wiper motor heats up or hums	• Internal motor defect • Bent or damaged linkage • Arms improperly installed on linking pivots	• Replace motor • Repair or replace linkage • Position linkage in park and reinstall wiper arms
Electric Wipers		
Wipers do not operate— No current to motor	• Fuse or circuit breaker blown • Loose, open or broken wiring • Defective switch • Defective or corroded terminals • No ground circuit for motor or switch	• Replace fuse or circuit breaker • Repair wiring and connections • Replace switch • Replace or clean terminals • Repair ground circuits
Wipers do not operate— Motor runs	• Linkage disconnected or broken	• Connect wiper linkage or replace broken linkage
Vacuum Wipers		
Wipers do not operate	• Control switch or cable inoperative • Loss of engine vacuum to wiper motor (broken hoses, low engine vacuum, defective vacuum/fuel pump) • Linkage broken or disconnected • Defective wiper motor	• Repair or replace switch or cable • Check vacuum lines, engine vacuum and fuel pump • Repair linkage • Replace wiper motor
Wipers stop on engine acceleration	• Leaking vacuum hoses • Dry windshield • Oversize wiper blades • Defective vacuum/fuel pump	• Repair or replace hoses • Wet windshield with washers • Replace with proper size wiper blades • Replace pump

TORQUE SPECIFICATIONS

Component	U.S.	Metric
Compressor mounting bolt-2.5L engine	37 ft. lbs.	50 Nm
Compressor mounting bolt-2.5L engine	19 ft. lbs.	26 Nm
Compressor mounting bolt-3.3L engine	37 ft. lbs.	50 Nm
Compressor mounting nut-3.3L engine	37 ft. lbs.	50 Nm
Compressor mounting bolt-3.3L engine	17 ft. lbs.	25 Nm
Compressor mounting stud-3.3L engine	9 ft. lbs.	12 Nm
Compressor mounting bolt-2.3L engine	40 ft. lbs.	54 Nm
Compressor mounting bolt-2.3L engine	19 ft. lbs.	26 Nm
Compressor mounting bolt-2.3L engine	40 ft. lbs.	54 Nm
Cruise control vacuum servo attaching screws	12 inch lbs.	1.4 Nm
Evaporator line fitting	18 ft. lbs.	25 Nm
Rear seat attaching bolts	13 ft. lbs.	18 Nm
Seat belt anchors	28 ft. lbs.	38 Nm
Steering wheel nut	30 ft. lbs.	41 Nm
Vacuum reservoir	53 inch lbs.	6 Nm

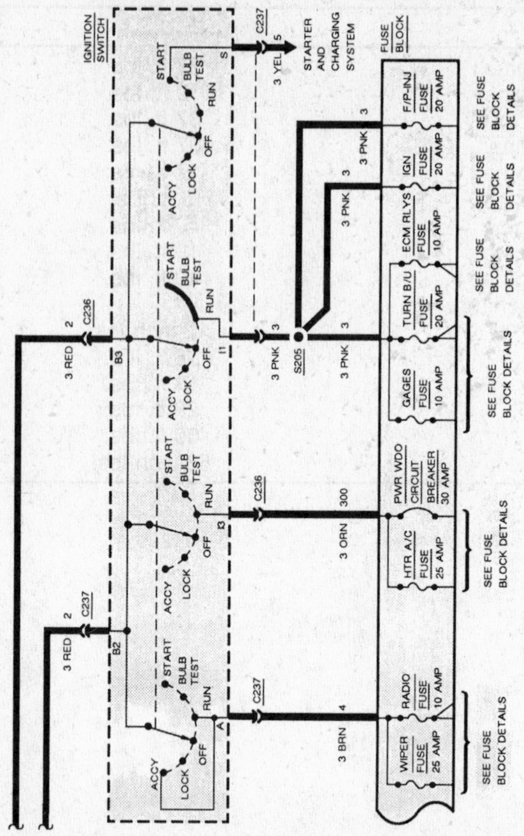

Somerset and Skylark — Power distribution — 2.3L engine

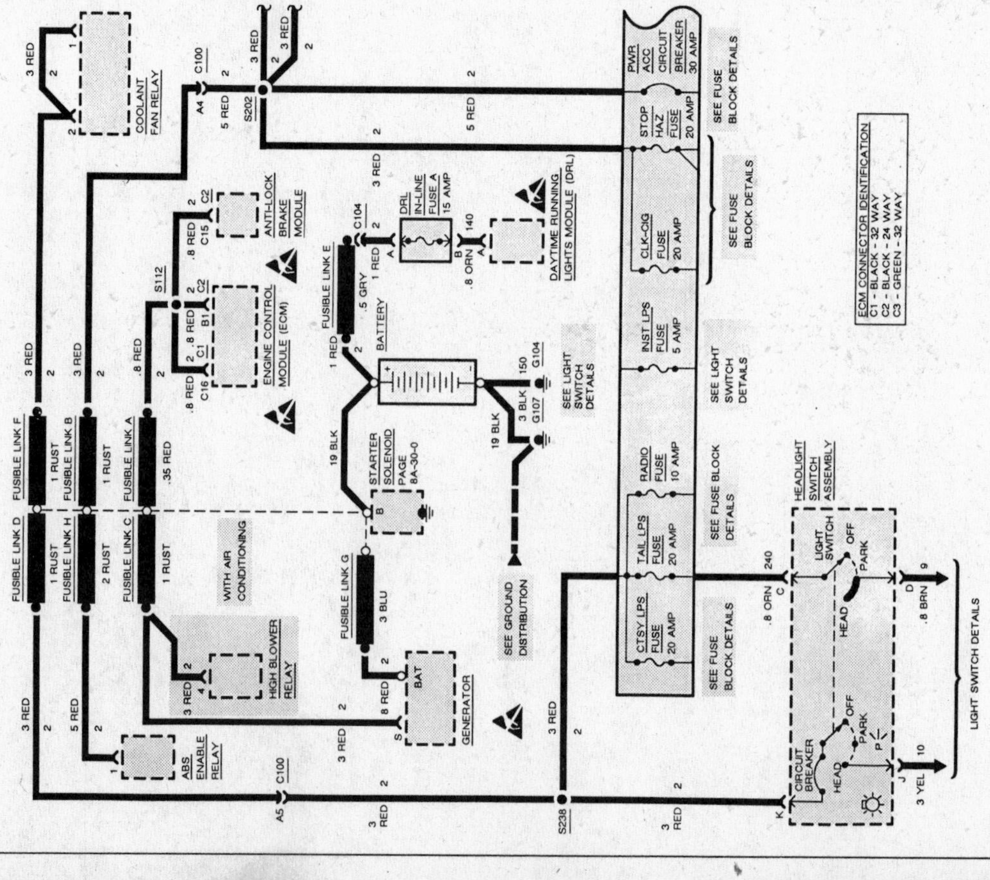

Somerset and Skylark — Power distribution — 2.3L engine

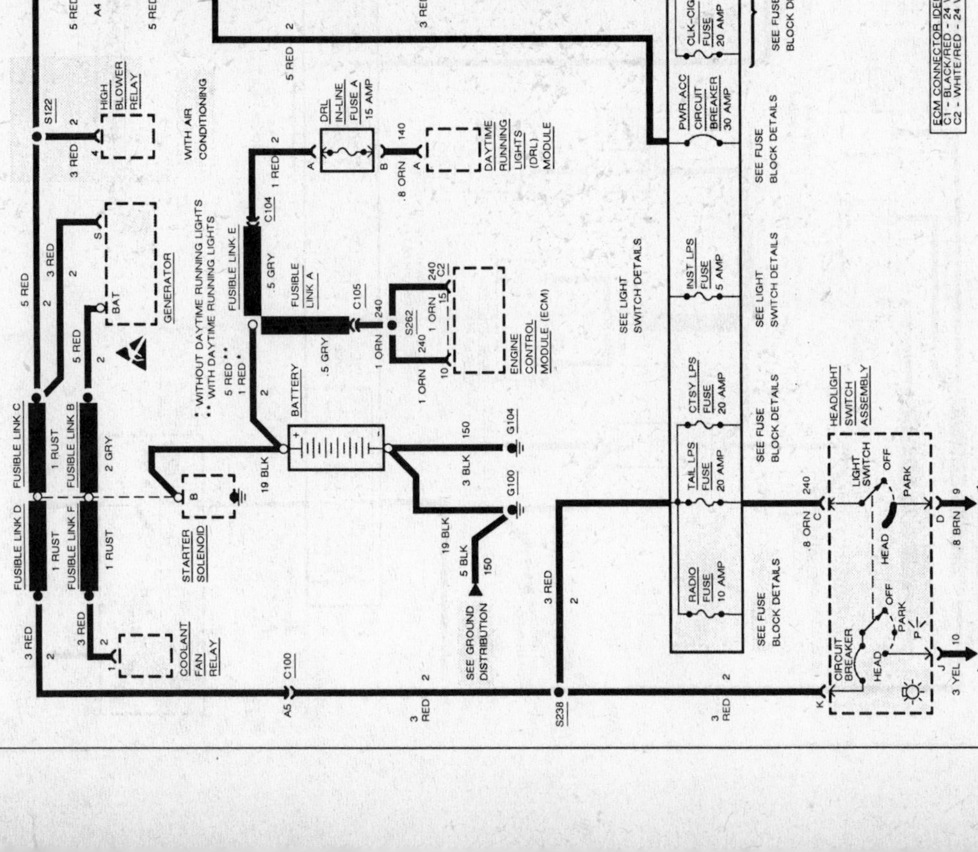

Somerset and Skylark — Power distribution — 2.5L engine

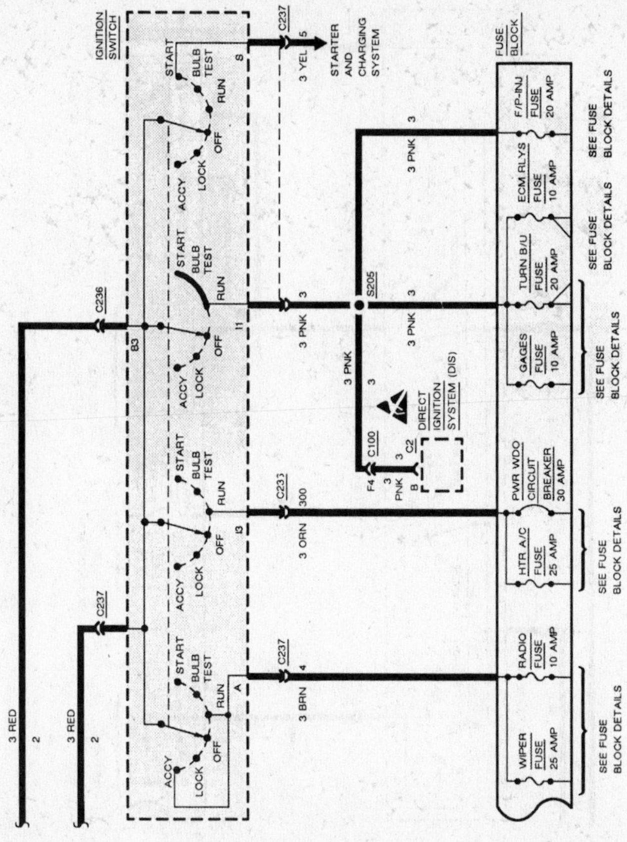

Somerset and Skylark — Power distribution — 2.5L engine

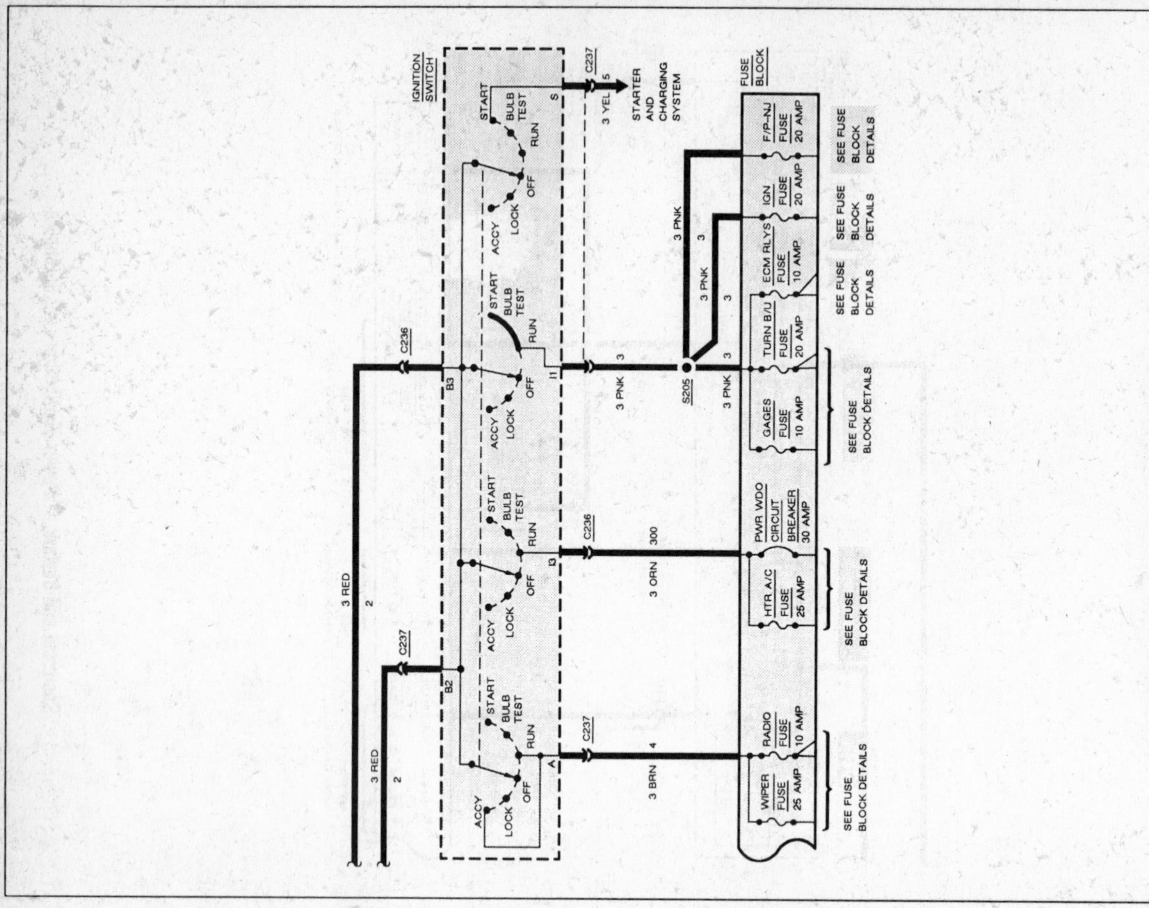

Somerset and Skylark — Power distribution — 3.3L engine

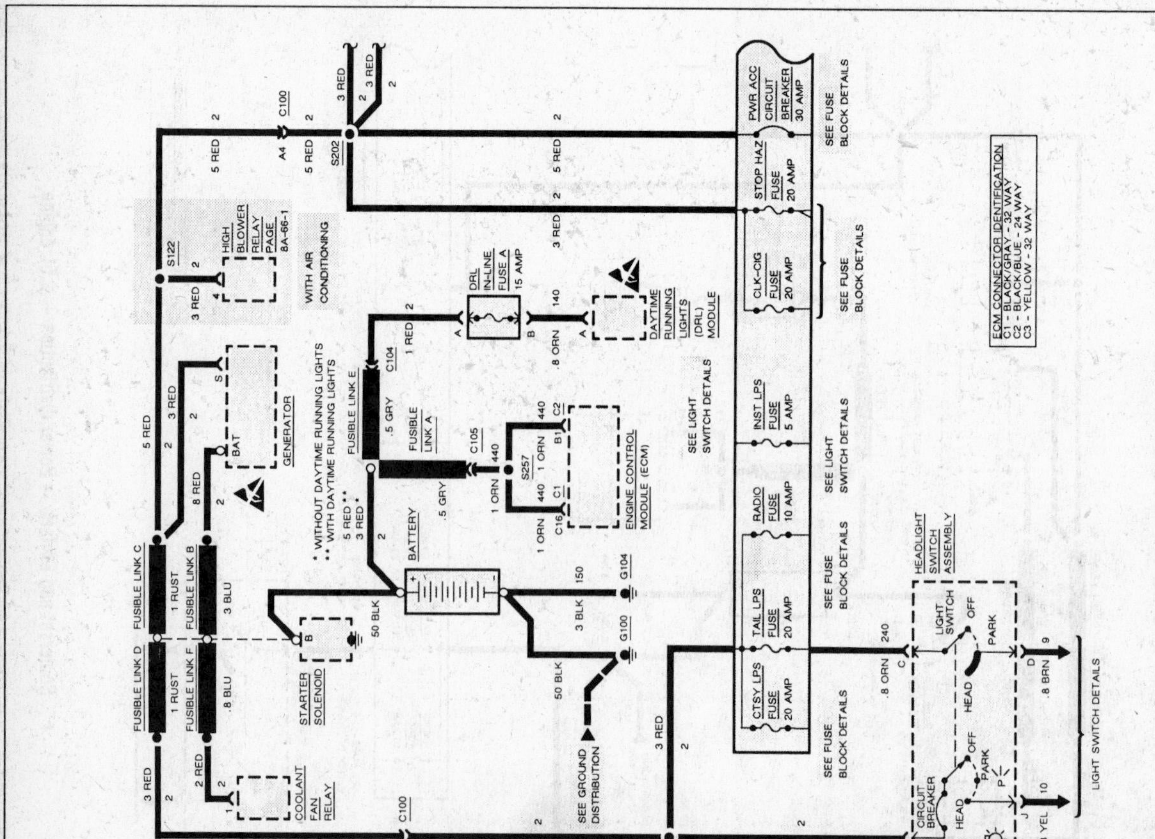

Somerset and Skylark — Power distribution — 3.3L engine

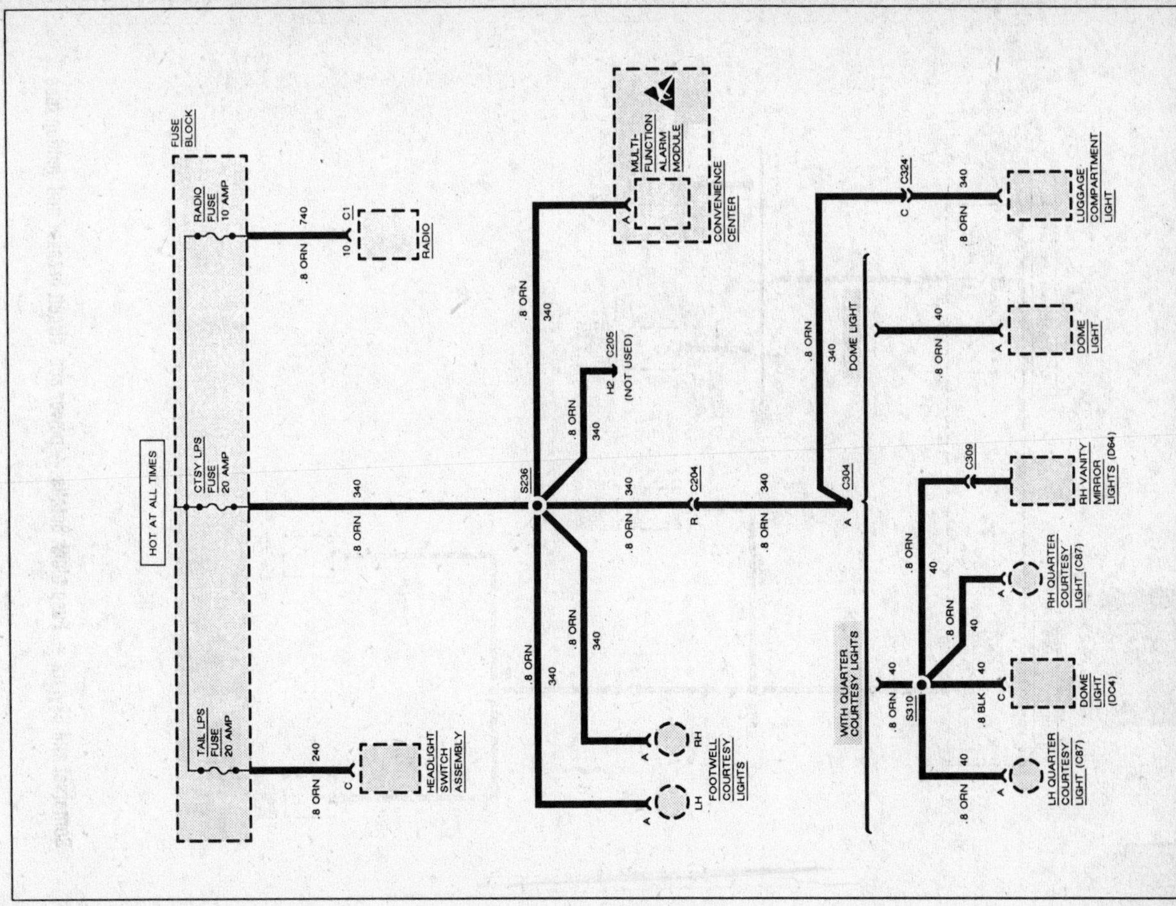

Somerset and Skylark — Fuse block details — courtesy lights fuse, radio fuse and tail lights fuse

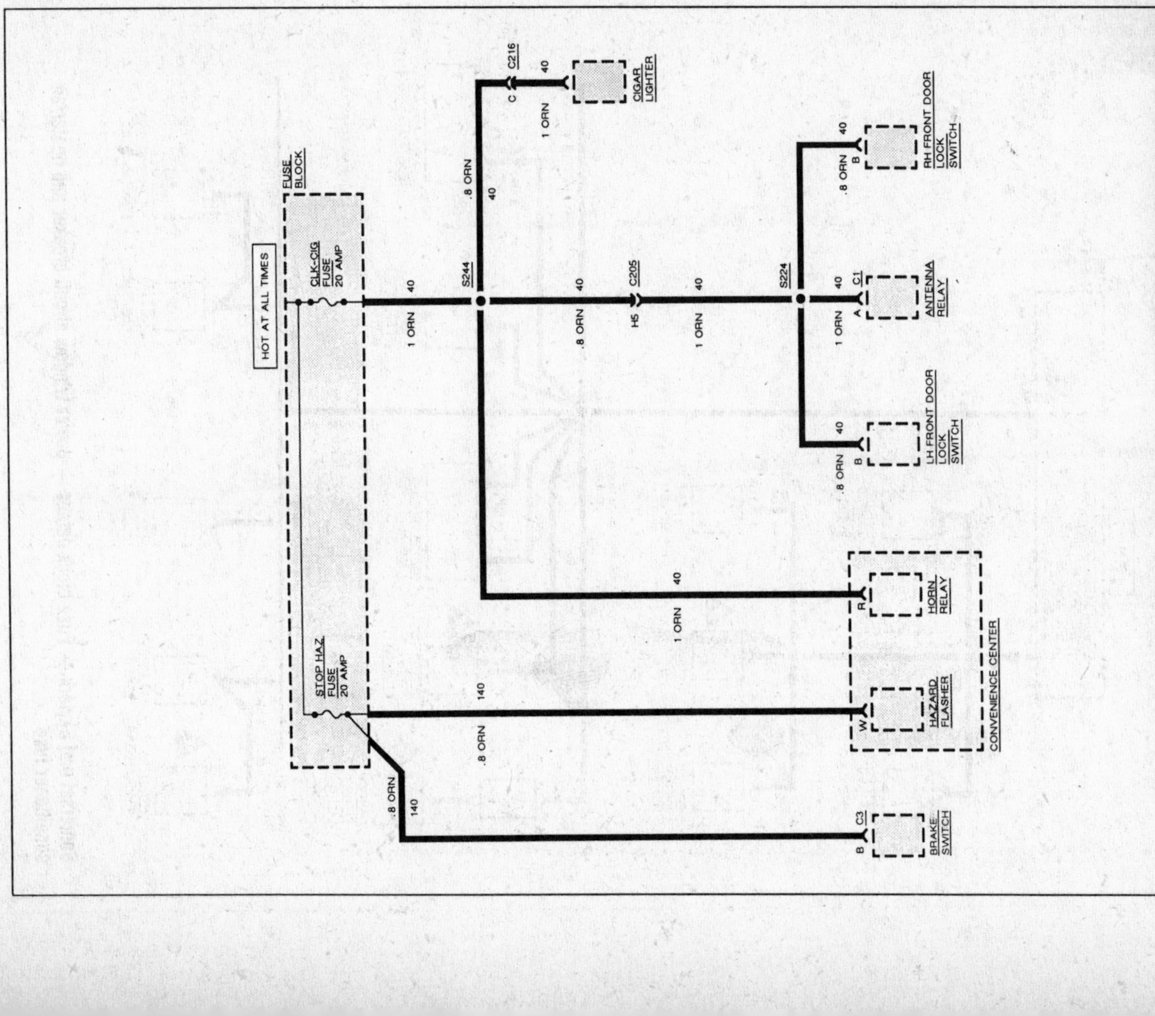

Somerset and Skylark — Fuse block details — stop/hazard fuse and clock/cig. fuse

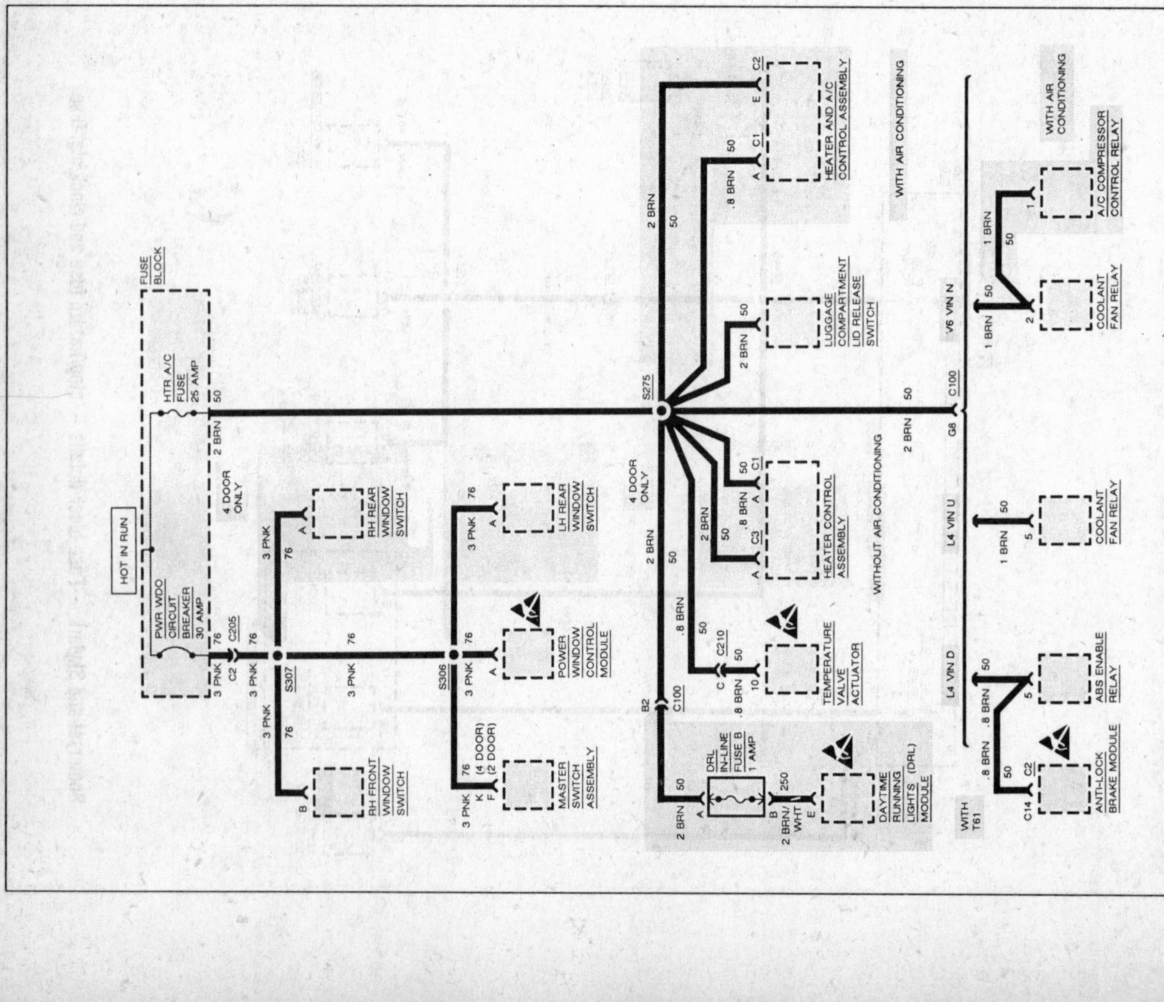

Somerset and Skylark — Fuse block details — power acc. circuit breaker and ignition fuse

Somerset and Skylark — Fuse block details — power window circuit breaker and heater/air conditioner fuse

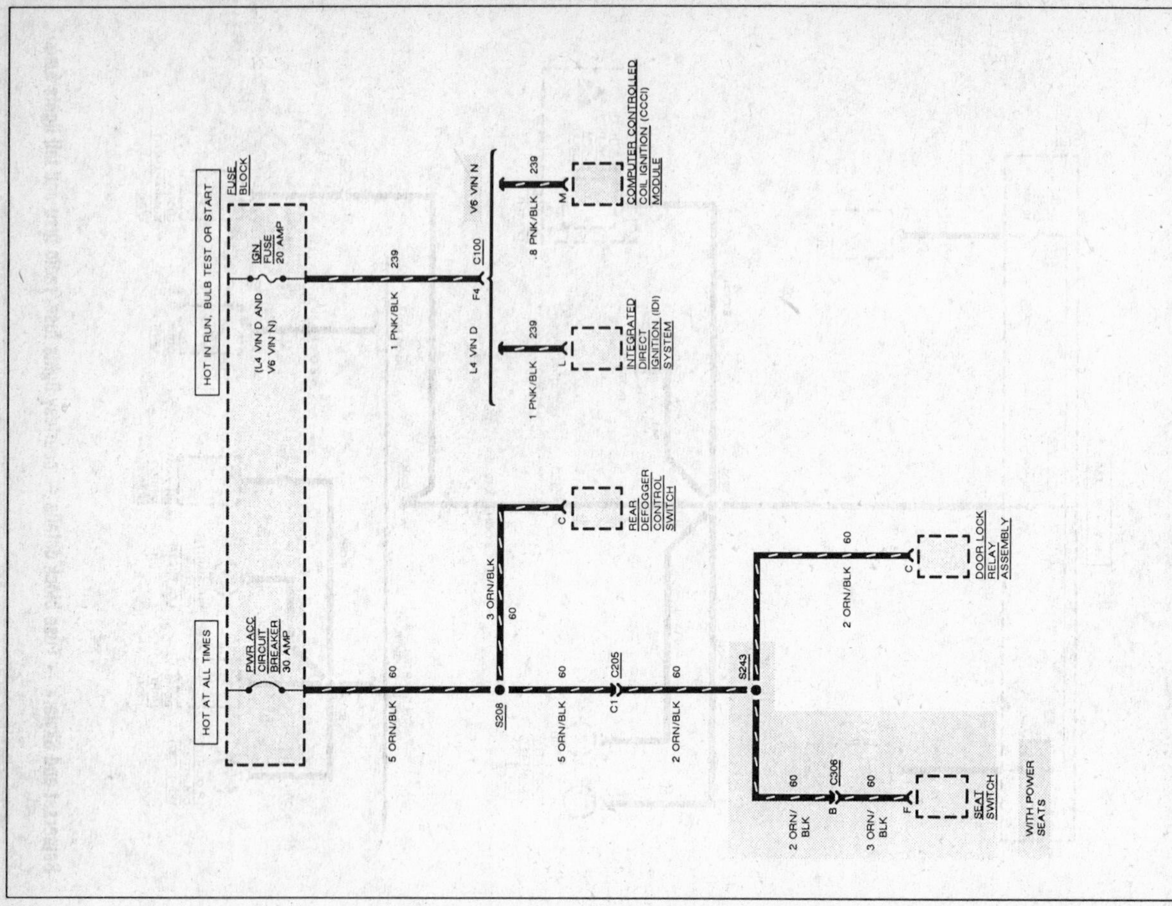

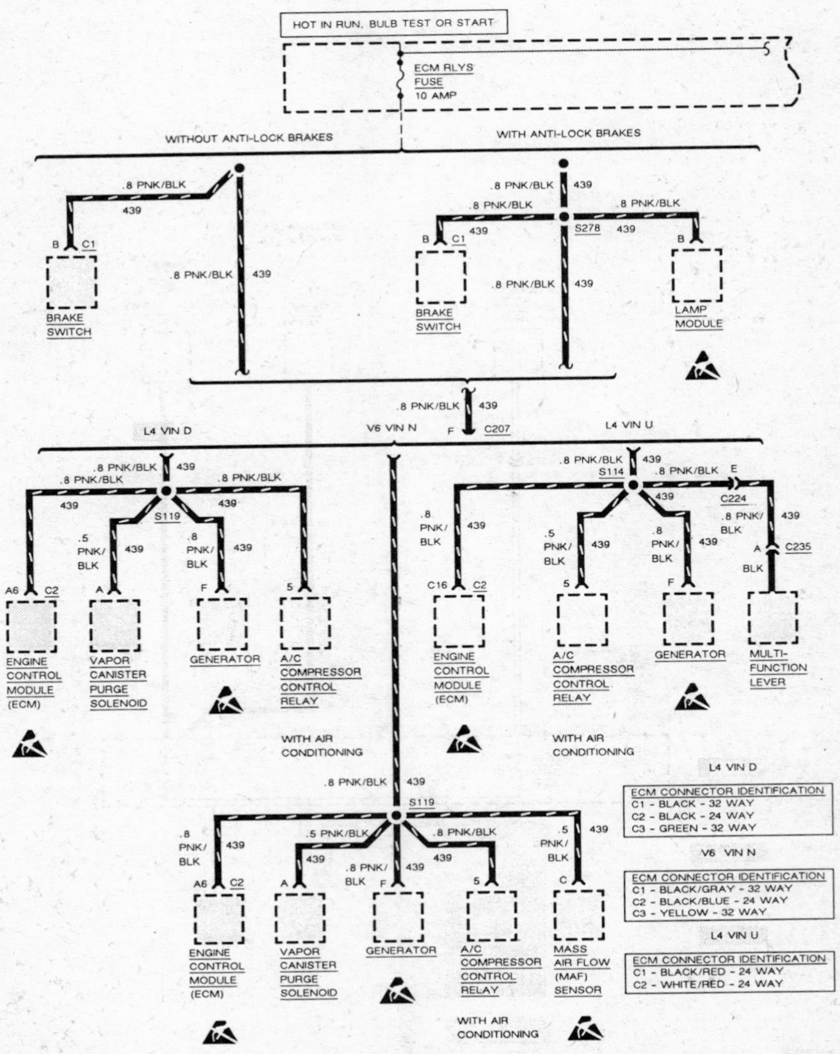

HOT IN RUN, BULB TEST OR START

ECM RLYS FUSE 10 AMP

WITHOUT ANTI-LOCK BRAKES

.8 PNK/BLK 439

B C1 BRAKE SWITCH

WITH ANTI-LOCK BRAKES

.8 PNK/BLK 439

S278

B C1 BRAKE SWITCH

B LAMP MODULE

.8 PNK/BLK 439 F C207

L4 VIN D

S119

A6 C2 ENGINE CONTROL MODULE (ECM)

A VAPOR CANISTER PURGE SOLENOID

F GENERATOR

5 A/C COMPRESSOR CONTROL RELAY

WITH AIR CONDITIONING

L4 VIN U

S114

C16 C2 ENGINE CONTROL MODULE (ECM)

5 A/C COMPRESSOR CONTROL RELAY

F GENERATOR

E C224 A C235 BLK MULTI-FUNCTION LEVER

WITH AIR CONDITIONING

V6 VIN N

S119

A6 C2 ENGINE CONTROL MODULE (ECM)

A VAPOR CANISTER PURGE SOLENOID

F GENERATOR

5 A/C COMPRESSOR CONTROL RELAY

C MASS AIR FLOW (MAF) SENSOR

WITH AIR CONDITIONING

L4 VIN D

ECM CONNECTOR IDENTIFICATION
C1 - BLACK - 32 WAY
C2 - BLACK - 24 WAY
C3 - GREEN - 32 WAY

V6 VIN N

ECM CONNECTOR IDENTIFICATION
C1 - BLACK/GRAY - 32 WAY
C2 - BLACK/BLUE - 24 WAY
C3 - YELLOW - 32 WAY

L4 VIN U

ECM CONNECTOR IDENTIFICATION
C1 - BLACK/RED - 24 WAY
C2 - WHITE/RED - 24 WAY

Somerset and Skylark — Fuse block details — ECM rlys fuse, turn/backup fuse and gauges fuse

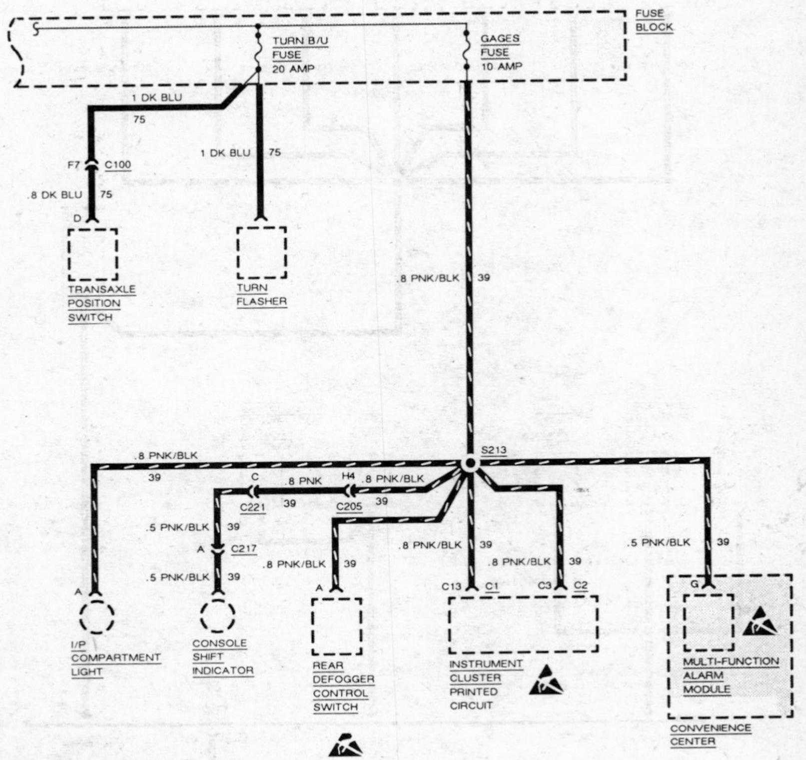

FUSE BLOCK

TURN B/U FUSE 20 AMP

GAGES FUSE 10 AMP

1 DK BLU 75

F7 C100 .8 DK BLU 75

D TRANSAXLE POSITION SWITCH

TURN FLASHER

.8 PNK/BLK 39

S213

A I/P COMPARTMENT LIGHT

C C221 .8 PNK 39

A C217 .5 PNK/BLK 39

CONSOLE SHIFT INDICATOR

H4 C205 .8 PNK/BLK 39

A REAR DEFOGGER CONTROL SWITCH

C13 C1 C3 C2 INSTRUMENT CLUSTER PRINTED CIRCUIT

.5 PNK/BLK 39

G MULTI-FUNCTION ALARM MODULE

CONVENIENCE CENTER

Somerset and Skylark — Fuse block details — ECM rlys fuse, turn/backup fuse and gauges fuse

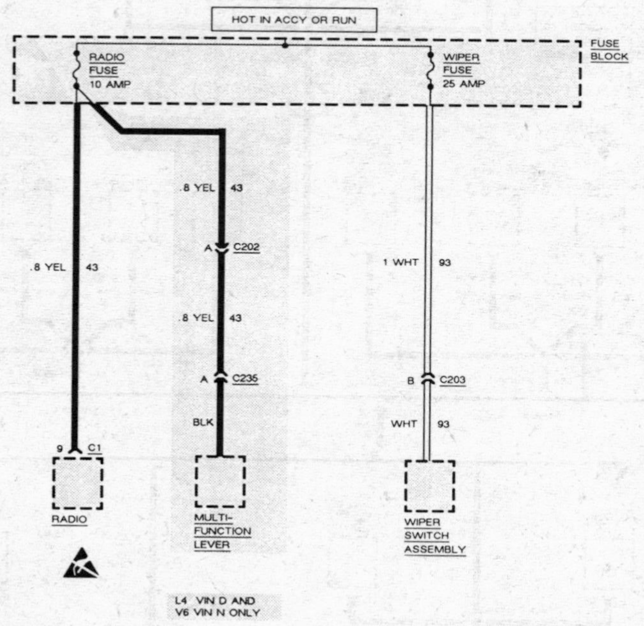

HOT IN ACCY OR RUN
FUSE BLOCK
RADIO FUSE 10 AMP
WIPER FUSE 25 AMP
.8 YEL 43
.8 YEL 43
A C202
.8 YEL 43
A C235
BLK
9 C1
RADIO
MULTI-FUNCTION LEVER
L4 VIN D AND V6 VIN N ONLY
1 WHT 93
B C203
WHT 93
WIPER SWITCH ASSEMBLY

Somerset and Skylark — Fuse block details — radio fuse and wiper fuse

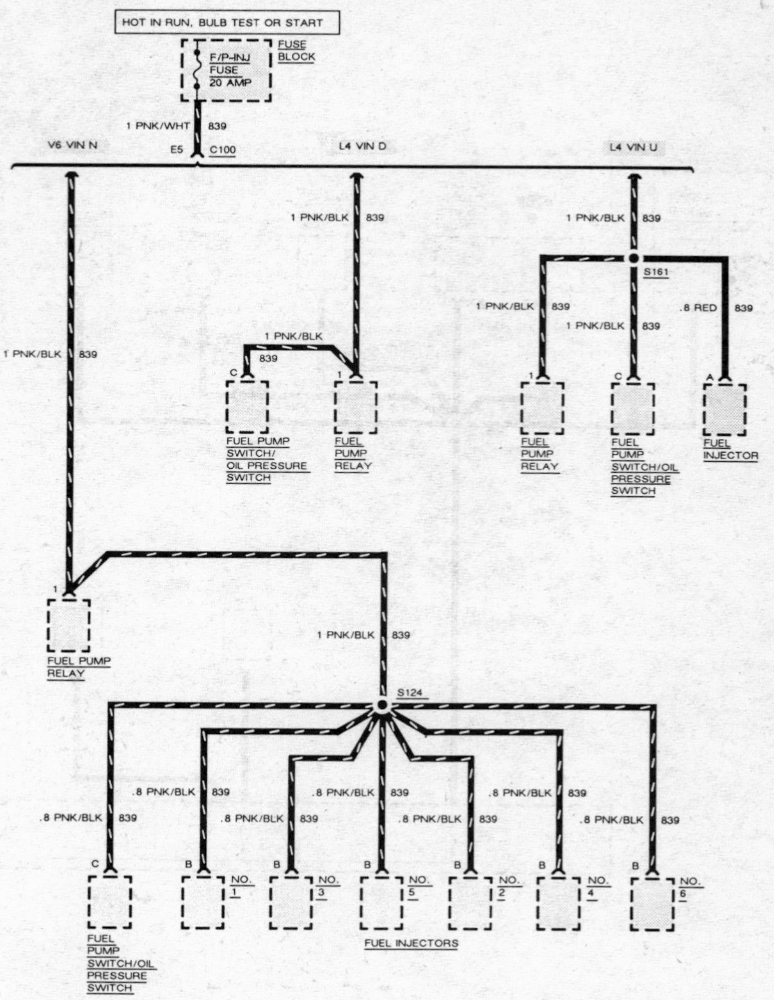

HOT IN RUN, BULB TEST OR START
F/P-INJ FUSE 20 AMP
FUSE BLOCK
1 PNK/WHT 839
E5 C100
V6 VIN N
L4 VIN D
L4 VIN U
1 PNK/BLK 839
1 PNK/BLK 839
S161
1 PNK/BLK 839
1 PNK/BLK 839
.8 RED 839
1 PNK/BLK 839
1 PNK/BLK 839
C FUEL PUMP SWITCH/OIL PRESSURE SWITCH
1 FUEL PUMP RELAY
1 FUEL PUMP RELAY
C FUEL PUMP SWITCH/OIL PRESSURE SWITCH
A FUEL INJECTOR
1 FUEL PUMP RELAY
1 PNK/BLK 839
S124
.8 PNK/BLK 839
.8 PNK/BLK 839
.8 PNK/BLK 839
.8 PNK/BLK 839
.8 PNK/BLK 839
.8 PNK/BLK 839
.8 PNK/BLK 839
C FUEL PUMP SWITCH/OIL PRESSURE SWITCH
B NO. 1
B NO. 3
B NO. 5
B NO. 2
B NO. 4
B NO. 6
FUEL INJECTORS

Somerset and Skylark — Fuse block details — f/p-inj. fuse

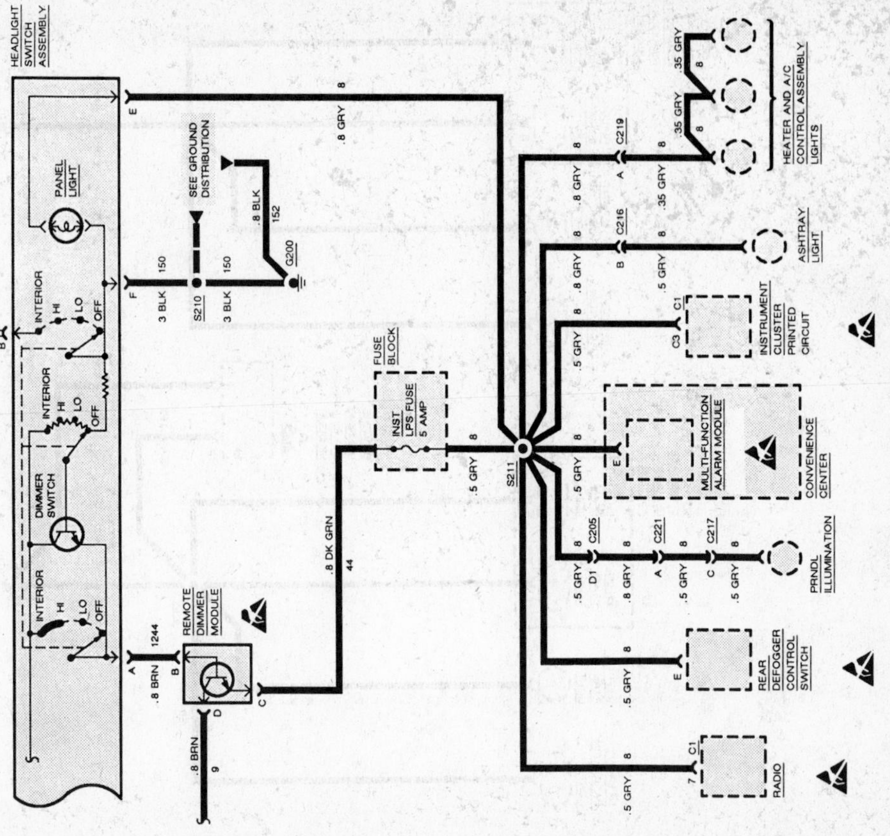

Somerset and Skylark — Light switch details

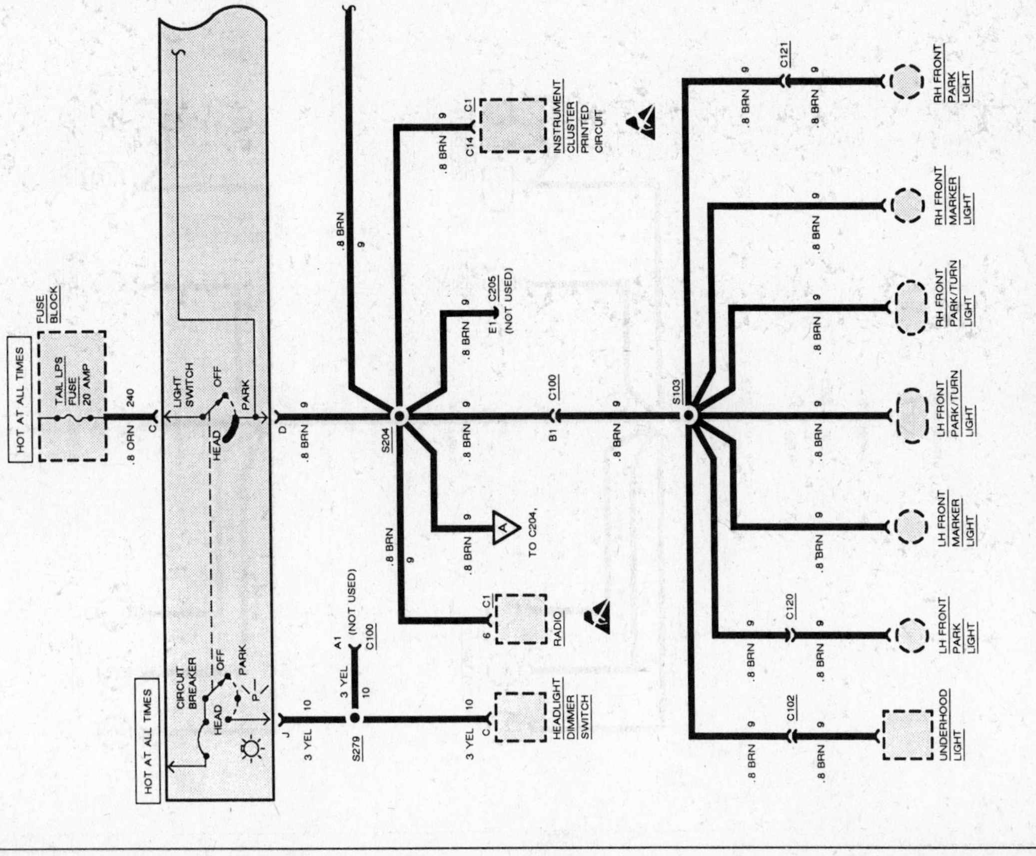

Somerset and Skylark — Light switch details

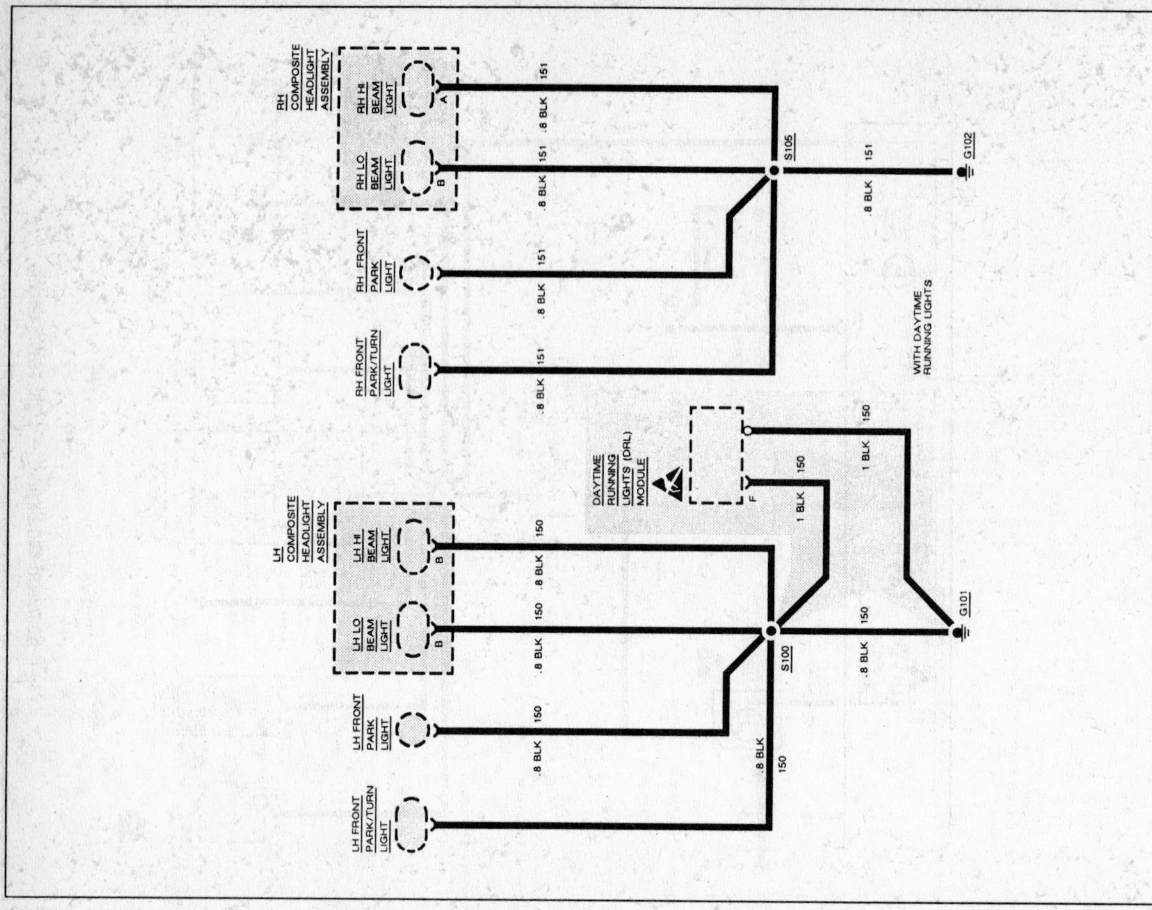

Somerset and Skylark – Ground distribution – front lights ground

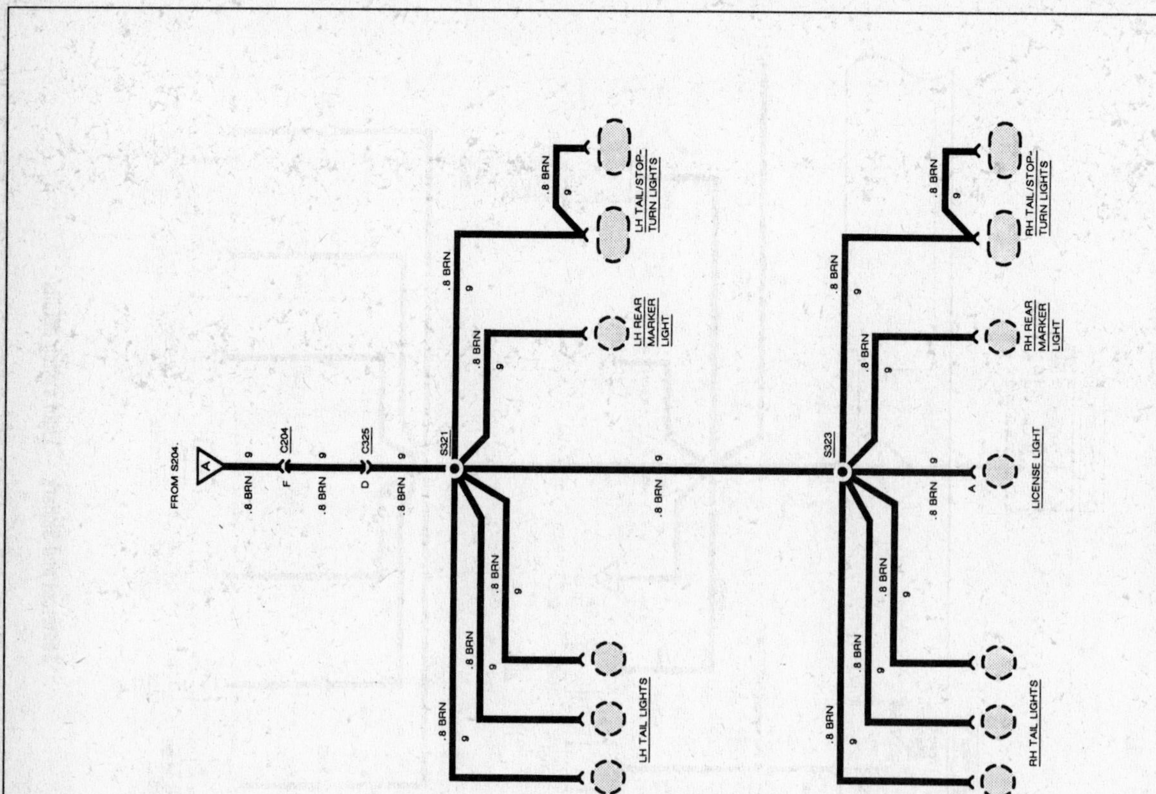

Somerset and Skylark – Light switch details

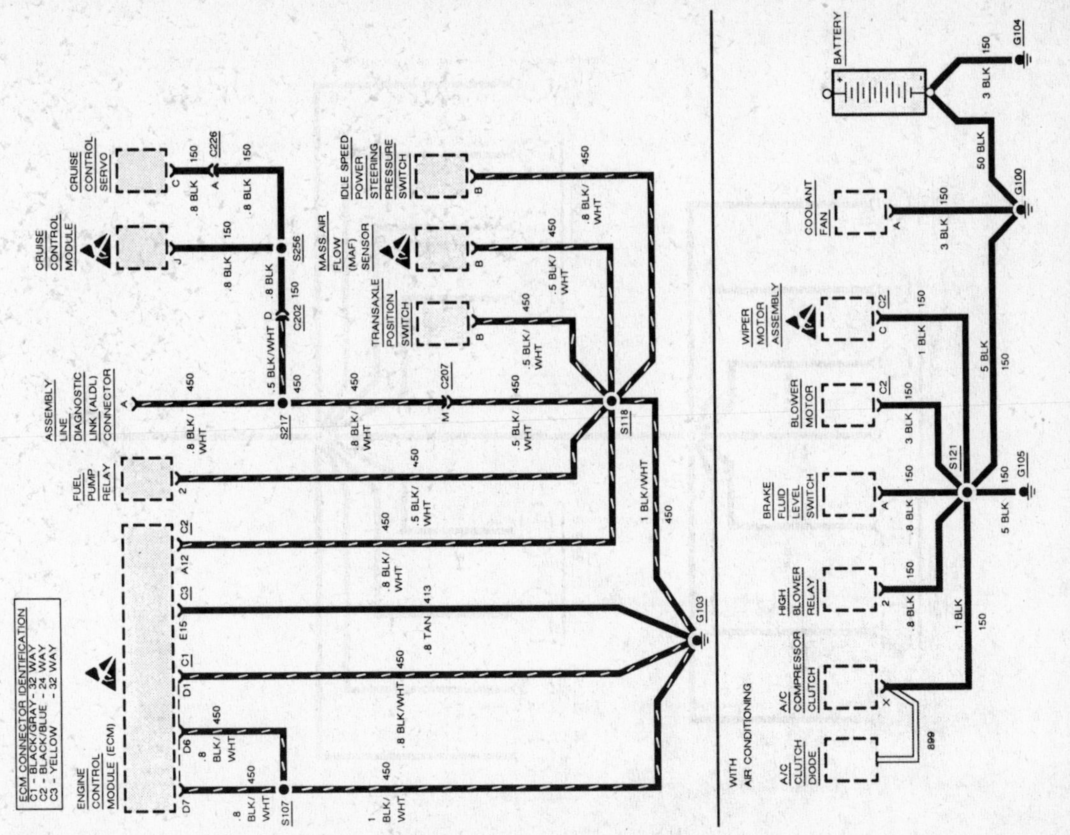

ECM CONNECTOR IDENTIFICATION
C1 - BLACK/RED - 24 WAY
C2 - WHITE/RED - 24 WAY

HIGH BLOWER RELAY
BLOWER MOTOR
BLOWER MOTOR
COOLANT FAN
WIPER MOTOR ASSEMBLY
WITH AIR CONDITIONING
A/C COMPRESSOR CLUTCH
A/C CLUTCH DIODE
CRUISE CONTROL SERVO
BRAKE FLUID LEVEL SWITCH
WITH AIR CONDITIONING
WITHOUT AIR CONDITIONING
S131
DIRECT IGNITION SYSTEM (DIS)
TRANSAXLE POSITION SWITCH
FUEL PUMP RELAY
ASSEMBLY LINE DIAGNOSTIC LINK (ALDL) CONNECTOR
IDLE SPEED POWER STEERING PRESSURE SWITCH
ENGINE CONTROL MODULE (ECM)
BATTERY
S129
G106
G103
G104
G100
G105

Somerset and Skylark – Ground distribution – 2.5L engine

ECM CONNECTOR IDENTIFICATION
C1 - BLACK/GRAY - 32 WAY
C2 - BLACK/BLUE - 24 WAY
C3 - YELLOW - 32 WAY

ENGINE CONTROL MODULE (ECM)
FUEL PUMP RELAY
ASSEMBLY LINE DIAGNOSTIC LINK (ALDL) CONNECTOR
CRUISE CONTROL MODULE
CRUISE CONTROL SERVO
C226
S107
S217
C202
S256
MASS AIR FLOW (MAF) SENSOR
TRANSAXLE POSITION SWITCH
IDLE SPEED POWER STEERING PRESSURE SWITCH
C207
S118
G103
WITH AIR CONDITIONING
A/C CLUTCH DIODE
A/C COMPRESSOR CLUTCH
HIGH BLOWER RELAY
BRAKE FLUID LEVEL SWITCH
BLOWER MOTOR
WIPER MOTOR ASSEMBLY
COOLANT FAN
BATTERY
S121
G105
G100
G104

Somerset and Skylark – Ground distribution – 3.3L engine

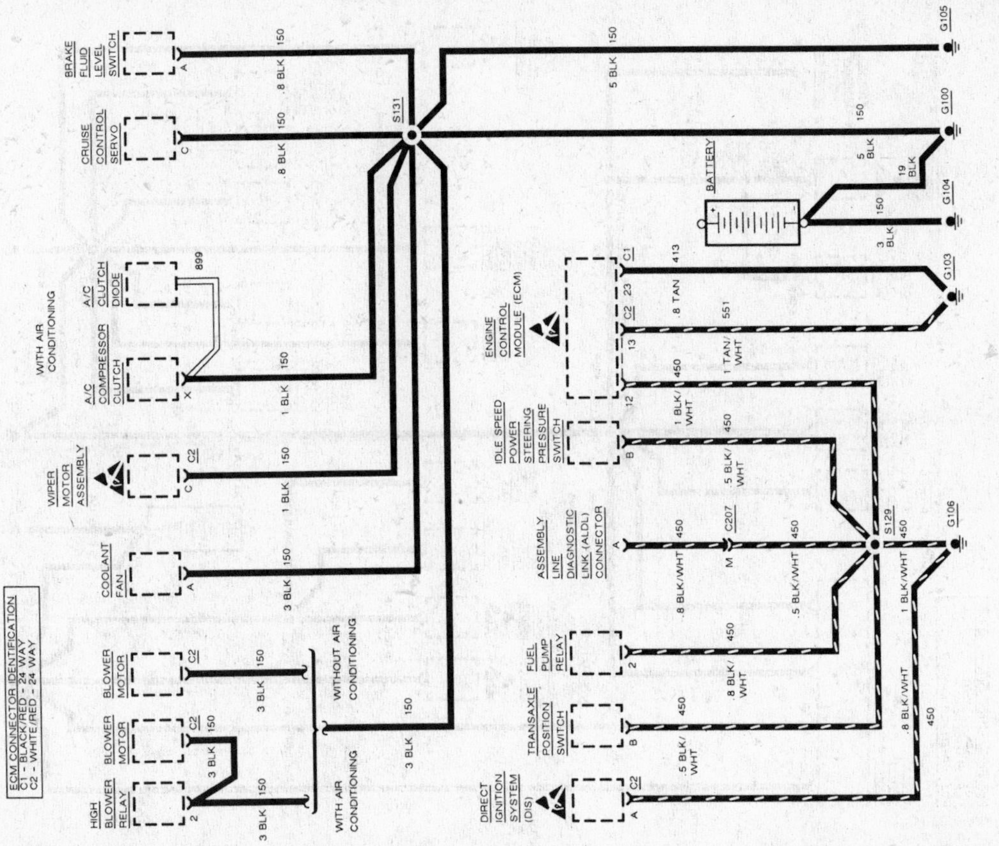

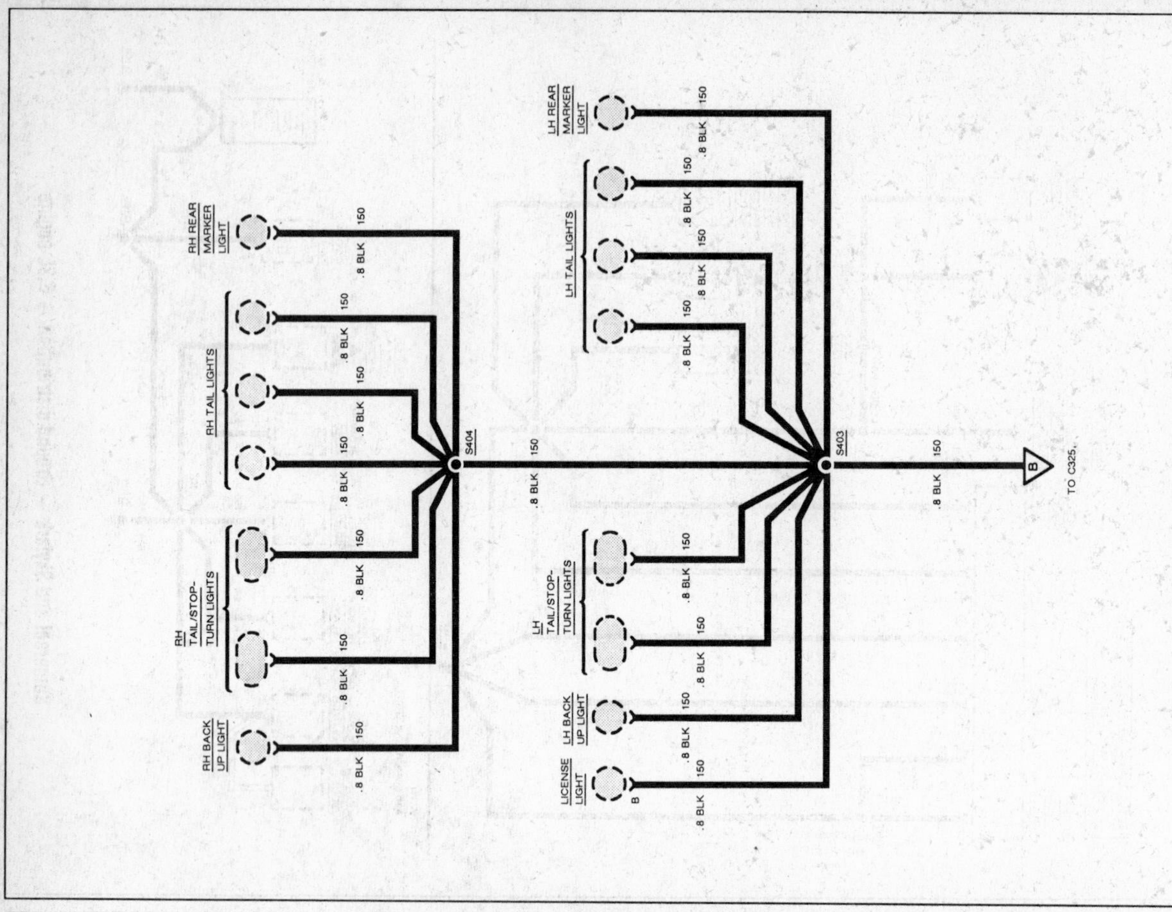

Somerset and Skylark — Ground distribution — rear lights

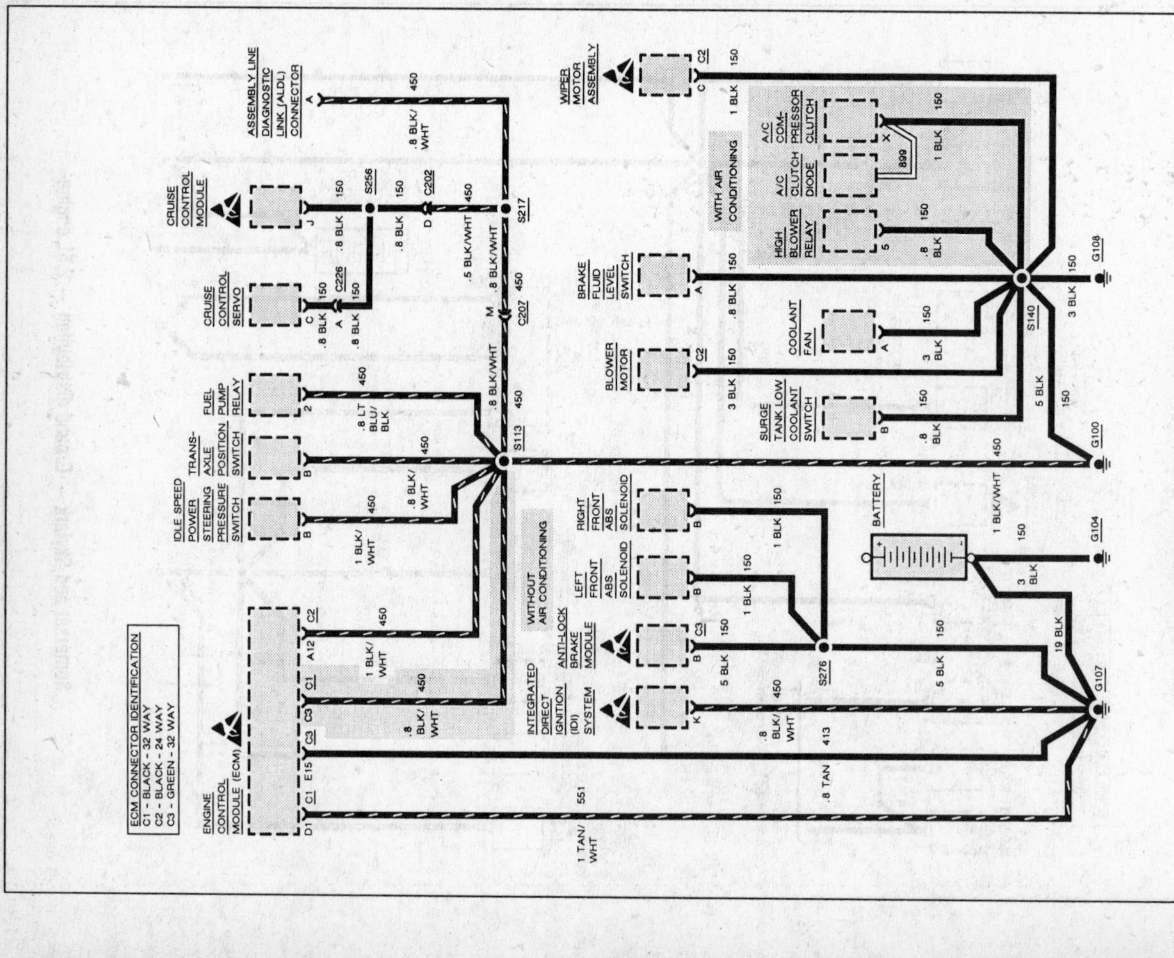

Somerset and Skylark — Ground distribution — 2.3L engine

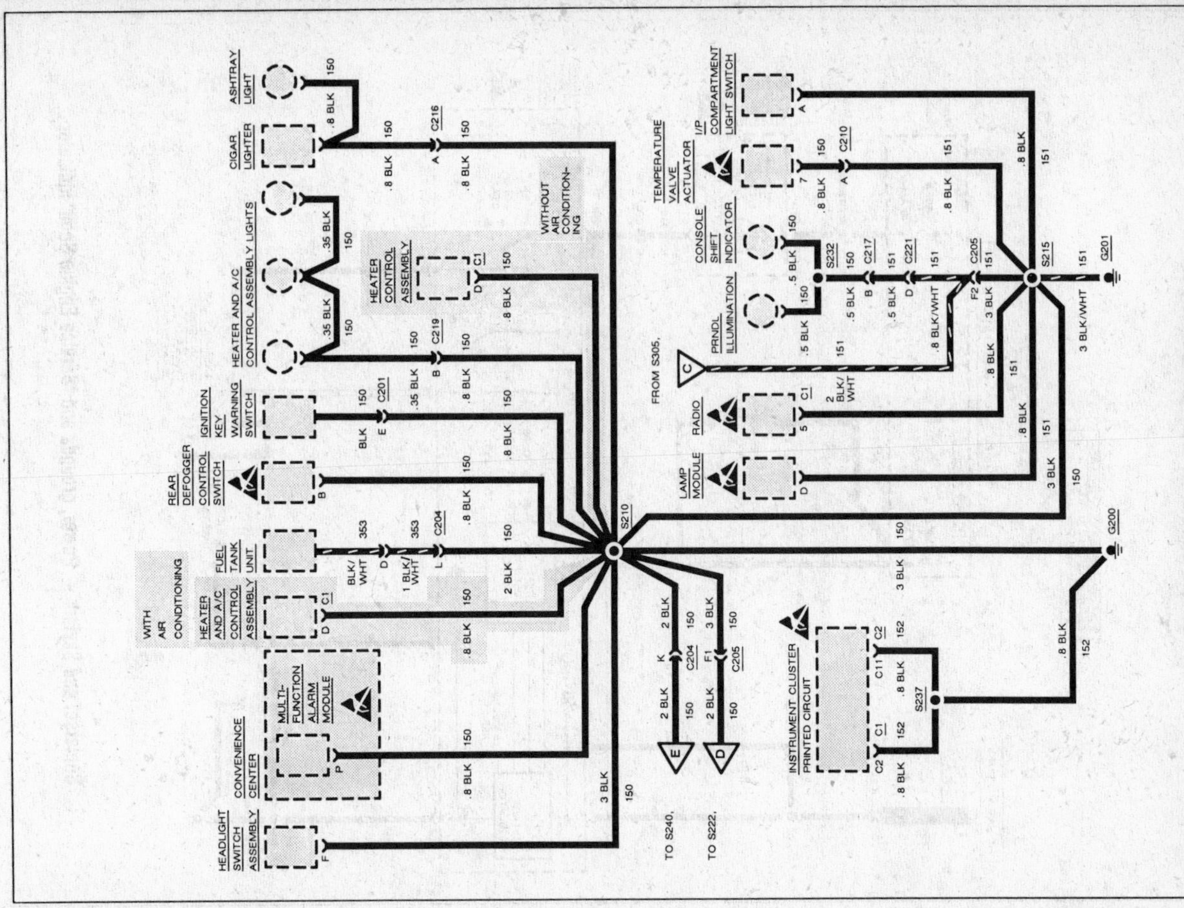

Somerset and Skylark — Ground distribution

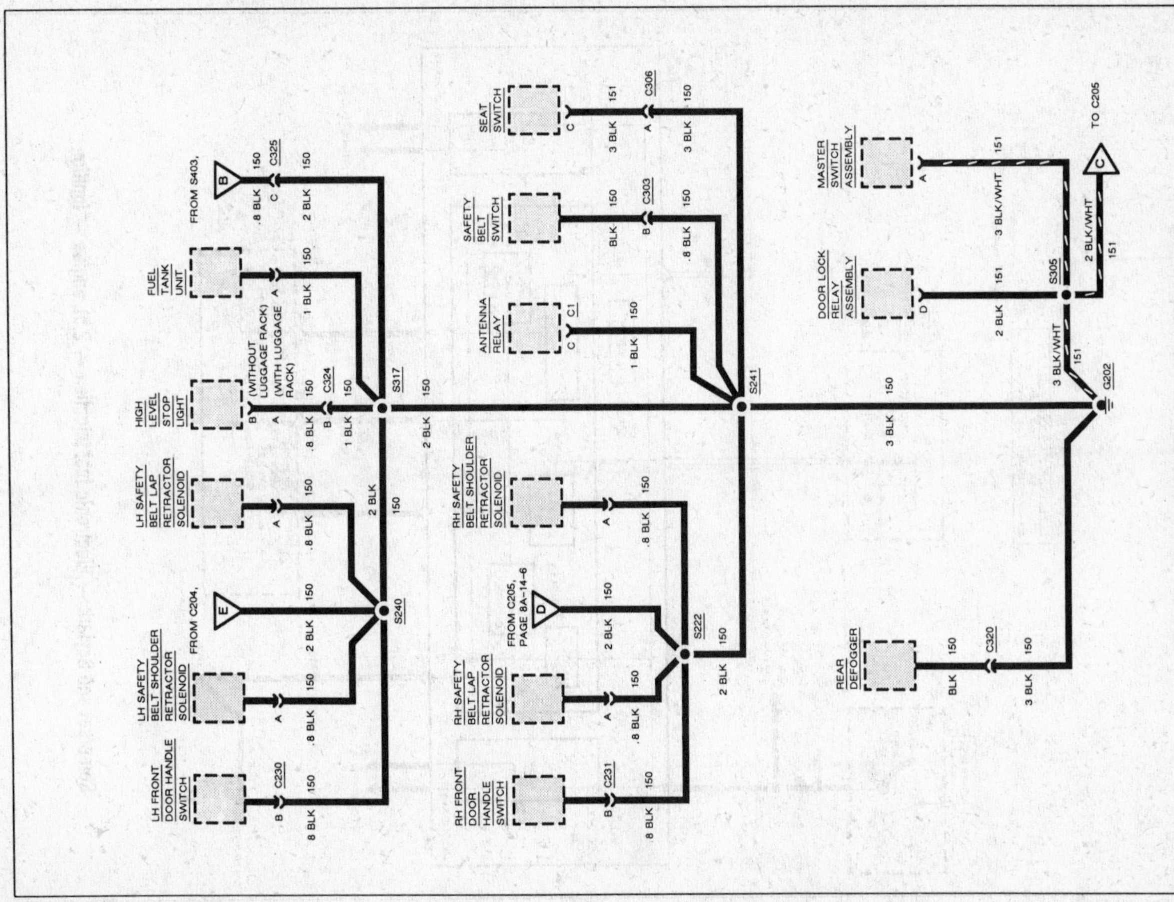

Somerset and Skylark — Ground distribution

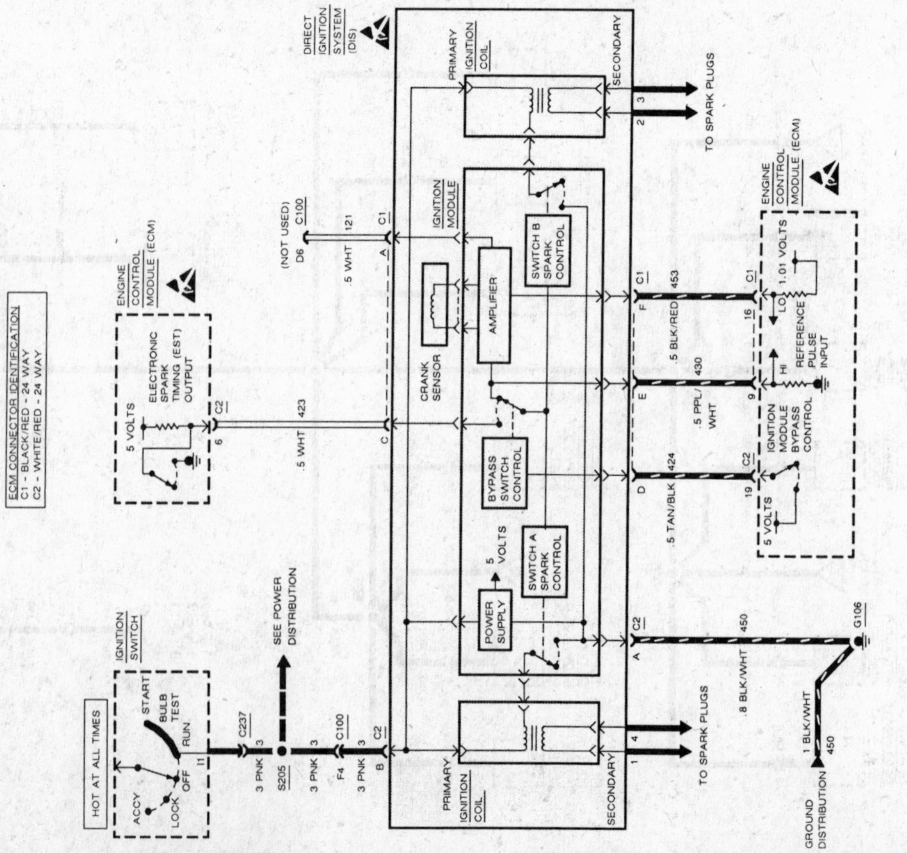

ECM CONNECTOR IDENTIFICATION
C1 - BLACK/RED - 24 WAY
C2 - WHITE/RED - 24 WAY

HOT AT ALL TIMES
IGNITION SWITCH
ACCY
LOCK
OFF
RUN
START
BULB TEST
I1
C237
3 PNK 3
S205
SEE POWER DISTRIBUTION
3 PNK 3
F4 C100
3 PNK 3
B C2

ENGINE CONTROL MODULE (ECM)
5 VOLTS
ELECTRONIC SPARK TIMING (EST) OUTPUT
6 C2
.5 WHT 423
C

(NOT USED)
D6 C100
.5 WHT 121
A C1

DIRECT IGNITION SYSTEM (DIS)

PRIMARY
IGNITION COIL
SECONDARY
POWER SUPPLY
5 VOLTS
SWITCH A SPARK CONTROL
BYPASS SWITCH CONTROL
CRANK SENSOR
AMPLIFIER
IGNITION MODULE
SWITCH B SPARK CONTROL
PRIMARY
IGNITION COIL
SECONDARY

1 4
TO SPARK PLUGS
A C2
.8 BLK/WHT 450
GROUND DISTRIBUTION
1 BLK/WHT
450
G106

D
.5 TAN/BLK 424
E
.5 PPL/WHT 430
F C1
.5 BLK/RED 453

2 3
TO SPARK PLUGS

19 C2
9
16 C1
5 VOLTS
IGNITION MODULE BYPASS CONTROL
HI
LO
REFERENCE PULSE INPUT
1.01 VOLTS
ENGINE CONTROL MODULE (ECM)

Somerset and Skylark — Electronic fuel injection — 2.5L engine — ignition

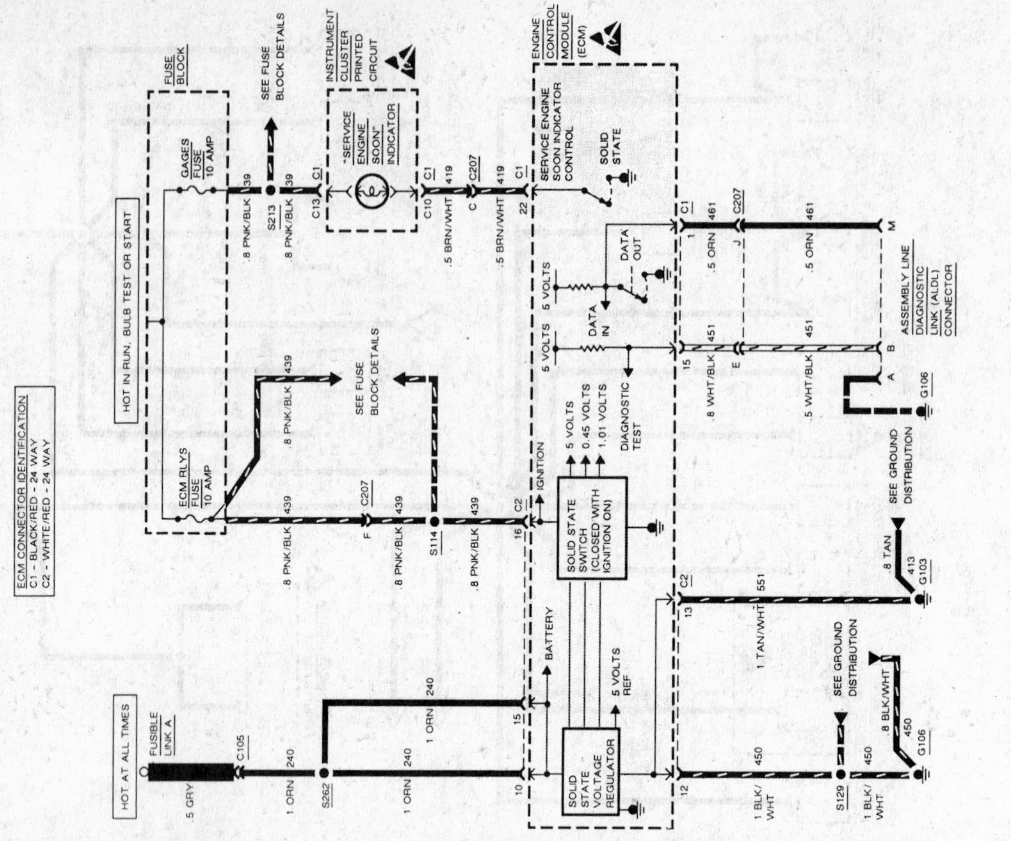

ECM CONNECTOR IDENTIFICATION
C1 - BLACK/RED - 24 WAY
C2 - WHITE/RED - 24 WAY

HOT AT ALL TIMES
FUSIBLE LINK A
.5 GRY
C105
1 ORN 240
S262
1 ORN 240
1 ORN 240

HOT IN RUN, BULB TEST OR START
FUSE BLOCK
ECM RLYS FUSE 10 AMP
GAGES FUSE 10 AMP
.8 PNK/BLK 439
.8 PNK/BLK 439
SEE FUSE BLOCK DETAILS
F C207
.8 PNK/BLK 439
S114
.8 PNK/BLK 439

.8 PNK/BLK 39
S213
SEE FUSE BLOCK DETAILS
.8 PNK/BLK 39
C13 C1
"SERVICE ENGINE SOON" INDICATOR
INSTRUMENT CLUSTER PRINTED CIRCUIT
C10 C1
.5 BRN/WHT 419
C C207
.5 BRN/WHT 419
22 C1

10
15
16 C2
BATTERY
IGNITION
SOLID STATE VOLTAGE REGULATOR
5 VOLTS REF
SOLID STATE SWITCH (CLOSED WITH IGNITION ON)
5 VOLTS
0.45 VOLTS
1.01 VOLTS
DIAGNOSTIC TEST
5 VOLTS
5 VOLTS
DATA IN
DATA OUT
SERVICE ENGINE SOON INDICATOR CONTROL
SOLID STATE
ENGINE CONTROL MODULE (ECM)

12
1 BLK/WHT 450
S129
SEE GROUND DISTRIBUTION
1 BLK/WHT 450
.8 BLK/WHT
450
G106

13 C2
1 TAN/WHT 551
.8 TAN
413
G103
SEE GROUND DISTRIBUTION

15
.8 WHT/BLK 451
E
.5 WHT/BLK 451
1 C1
.5 ORN 461
J C207
.5 ORN 461
A B M
G106
ASSEMBLY LINE DIAGNOSTIC LINK (ALDL) CONNECTOR

Somerset and Skylark — Power, grounds and "Service Engine Soon" indicator

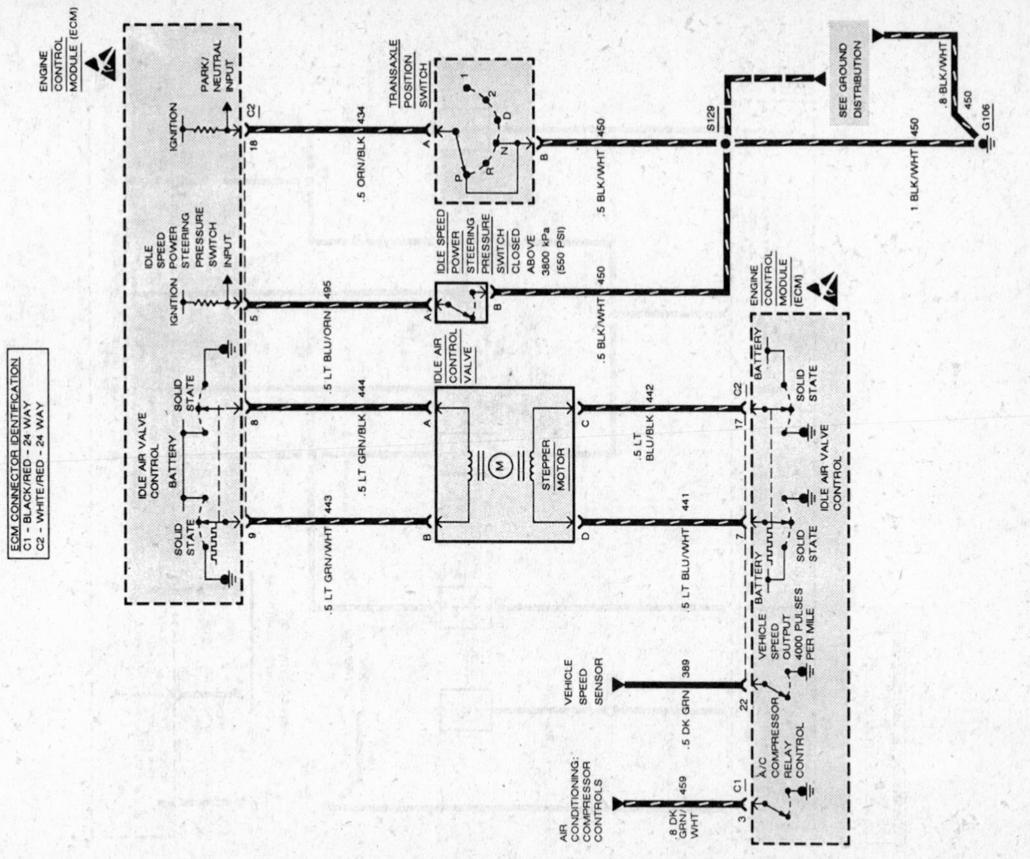

HOT IN RUN, BULB TEST OR START

F/P-INJ FUSE 20 AMP

FUSE BLOCK

ECM CONNECTOR IDENTIFICATION
C1 - BLACK/RED - 24 WAY
C2 - WHITE/RED - 24 WAY

1 PNK/WHT 839

E5 C100

IGNITION

SOLID STATE

FUEL PUMP RELAY CONTROL

ENGINE CONTROL MODULE (ECM)

24 C2

.8 DK GRN/WHT 465

1 PNK/BLK 839

S161

.8 RED 839

1 PNK/BLK 839

1 PNK/BLK 839

FUEL PUMP RELAY

FUEL PUMP SWITCH/OIL PRESSURE SWITCH CLOSED ABOVE 41.7 kPa (6.05 PSI)

FUEL INJECTOR

1 GRY 120

1 GRY 120

S160

FUEL PUMP PRIME CONNECTOR

1 GRY 120

.8 DK BLU 467

1 C2

FUEL INJECTOR CONTROL SOLID STATE

ENGINE CONTROL MODULE (ECM)

NOTE: JUMPERING FUEL PUMP PRIME CONNECTOR TO BATTERY VOLTAGE WILL OPERATE FUEL PUMP.

.8 BLK/WHT 450

1 GRY 120

E4 C100

1 GRY 120

J C204

1 GRY 120

S129

SEE GROUND DISTRIBUTION

FUEL PUMP

FUEL TANK UNIT

1 BLK/WHT 450

.8 BLK/WHT 450

SEE GROUND DISTRIBUTION

G106

G202

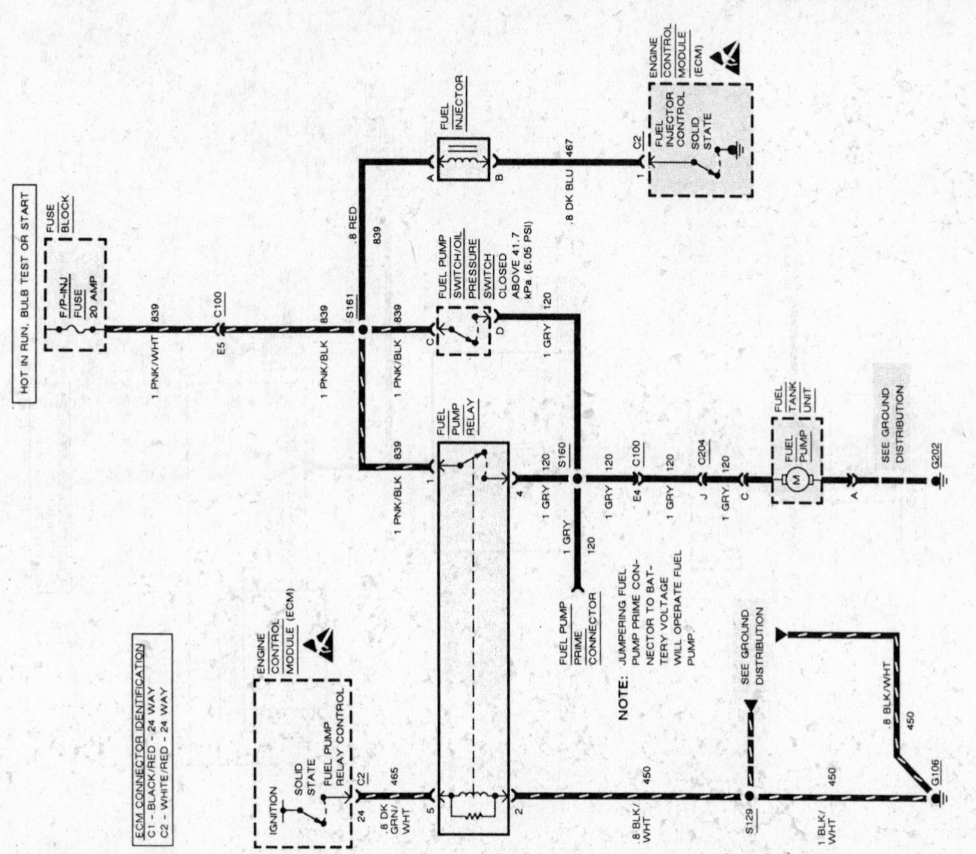

Somerset and Skylark — Electronic fuel injection — 2.5L engine — fuel injector and fuel control

ECM CONNECTOR IDENTIFICATION
C1 - BLACK/RED - 24 WAY
C2 - WHITE/RED - 24 WAY

ENGINE CONTROL MODULE (ECM)

IDLE AIR VALVE CONTROL

SOLID STATE

BATTERY

SOLID STATE

IGNITION

IDLE SPEED POWER STEERING PRESSURE SWITCH INPUT

IGNITION

PARK/NEUTRAL INPUT

9 8 5 18 C2

.5 LT GRN/WHT 443

.5 LT GRN/BLK 444

.5 LT BLU/ORN 495

.5 ORN/BLK 434

TRANSAXLE POSITION SWITCH

IDLE AIR CONTROL VALVE

STEPPER MOTOR

IDLE SPEED POWER STEERING PRESSURE SWITCH CLOSED ABOVE 3800 kPa (550 PSI)

AIR CONDITIONING: COMPRESSOR CONTROLS

VEHICLE SPEED SENSOR

.5 BLK/WHT 450

.5 BLK/WHT 450

.5 LT BLU/BLK 442

.8 DK GRN/WHT 459

.5 DK GRN 389

.5 LT BLU/WHT 441

S129

3 C1

22

7

17 C2

A/C COMPRESSOR RELAY CONTROL

VEHICLE SPEED OUTPUT 4000 PULSES PER MILE

BATTERY

SOLID STATE

IDLE AIR VALVE CONTROL

BATTERY

SOLID STATE

ENGINE CONTROL MODULE (ECM)

SEE GROUND DISTRIBUTION

1 BLK/WHT 450

.8 BLK/WHT 450

G106

Somerset and Skylark — Vehicle data sensors and idle air control

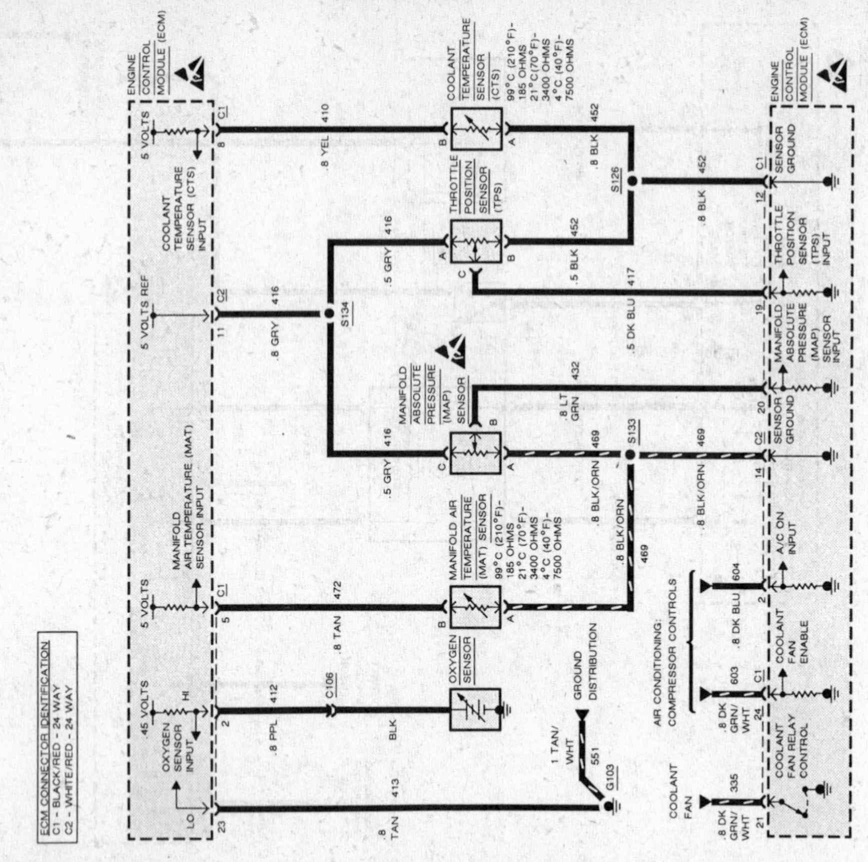

Somerset and Skylark — Engine data sensors

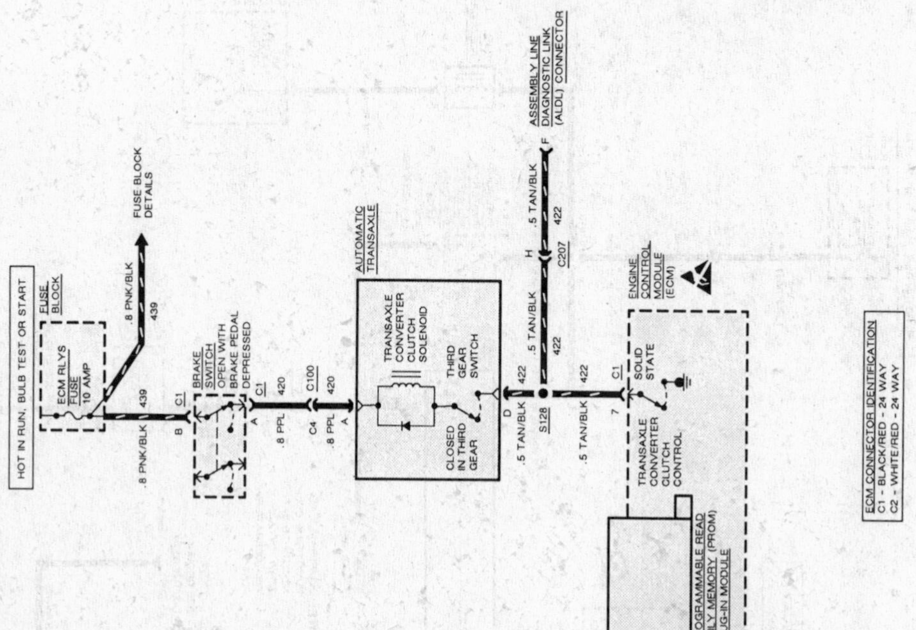

Somerset and Skylark — Electronic fuel injection — 2.5L engine — transaxle converter clutch

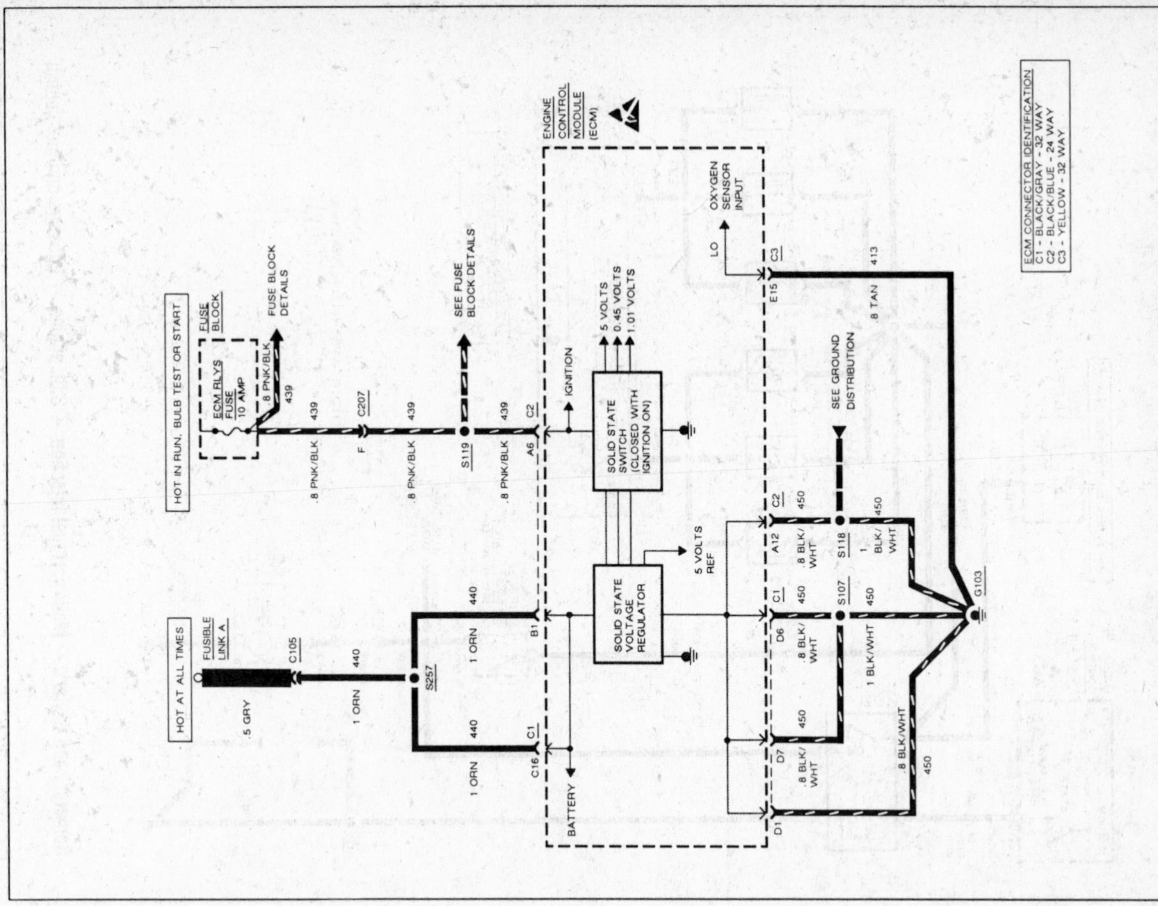

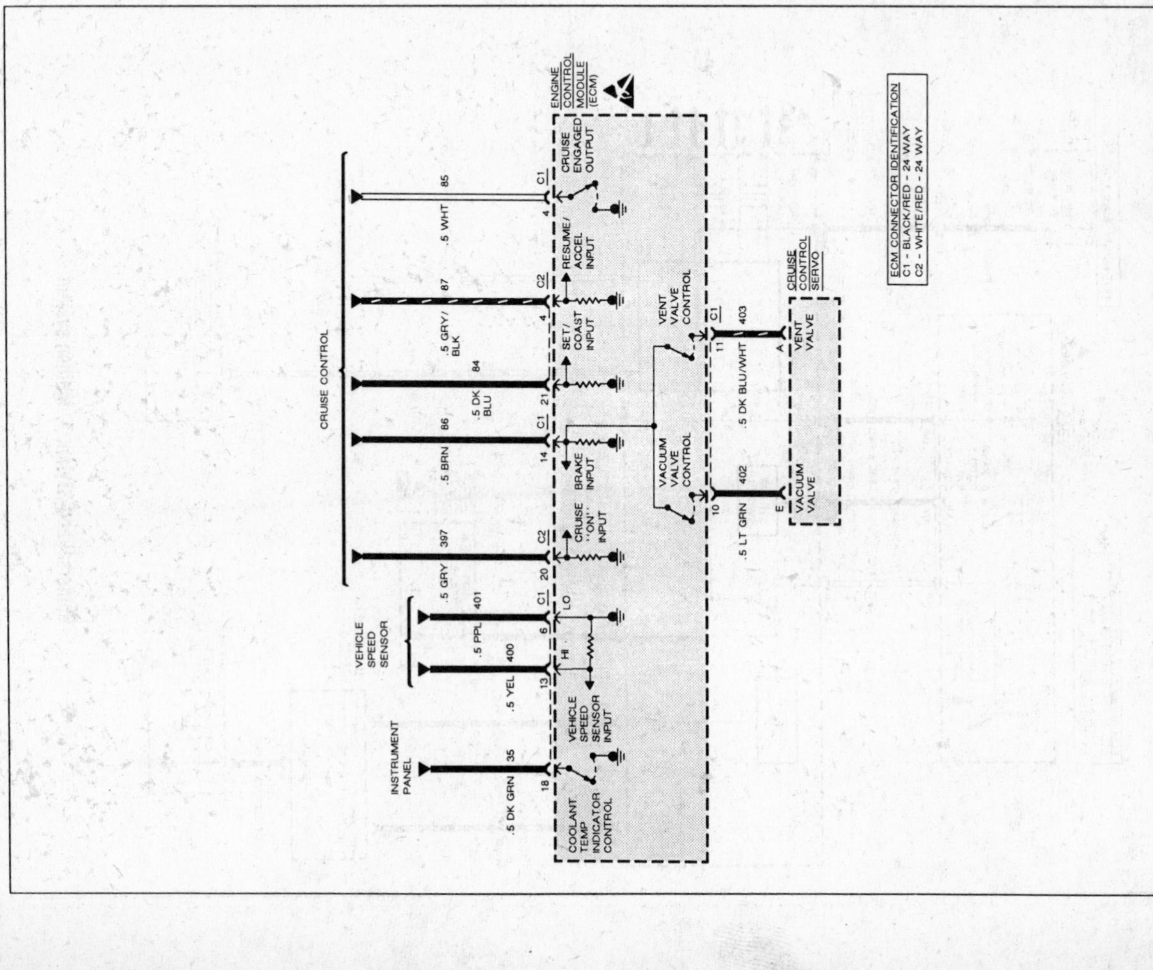

Somerset and Skylark — Electronic fuel injection — 2.5L engine — vehicle data sensors

Somerset and Skylark — Multi-port fuel injection — 3.3L engine — power and grounds

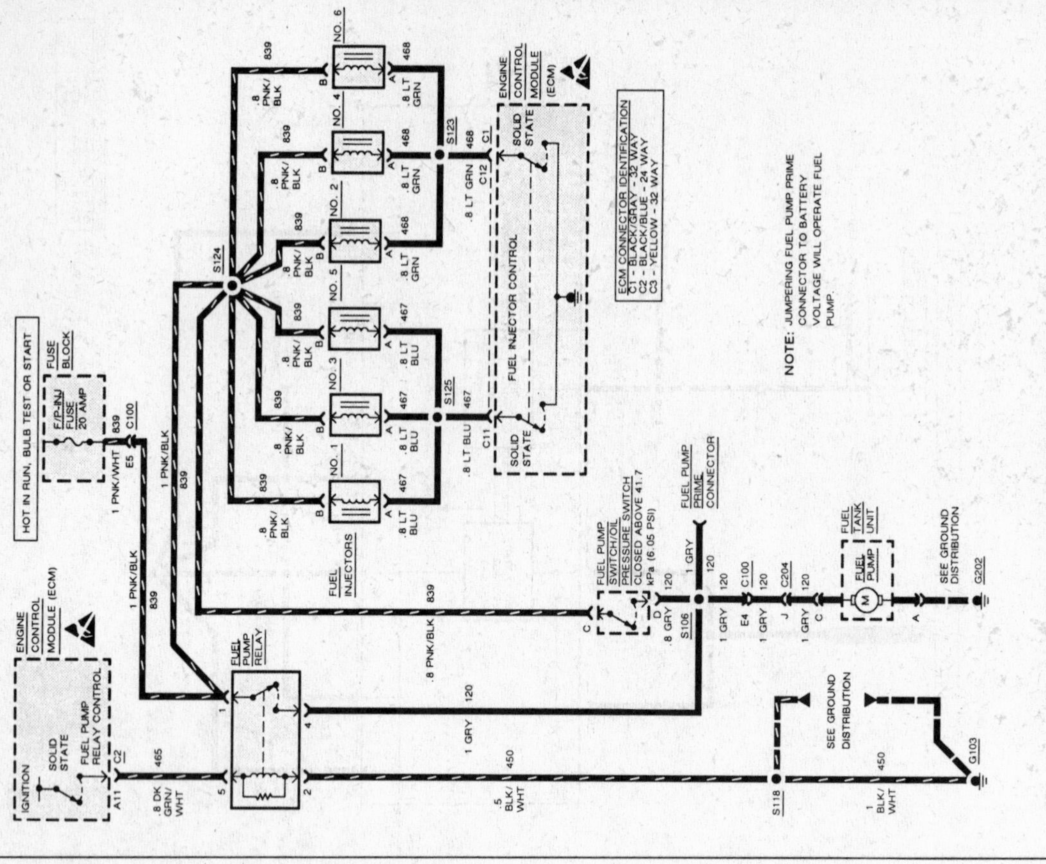

ECM CONNECTOR IDENTIFICATION
C1 - BLACK/GRAY - 32 WAY
C2 - BLACK/BLUE - 24 WAY
C3 - YELLOW - 32 WAY

NOTE: JUMPERING FUEL PUMP PRIME CONNECTOR TO BATTERY VOLTAGE WILL OPERATE FUEL PUMP

Somerset and Skylark — Multi-port fuel injection — 3.3L engine — injectors and fuel control

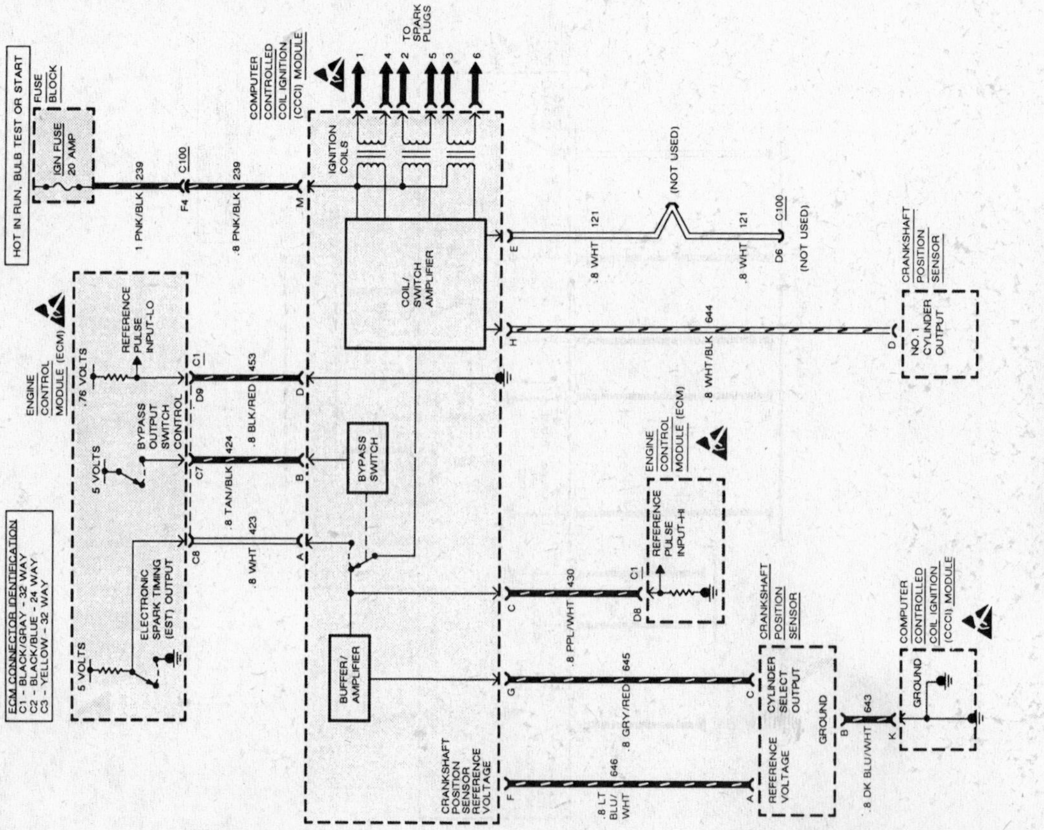

ECM CONNECTOR IDENTIFICATION
C1 - BLACK/GRAY - 32 WAY
C2 - BLACK/BLUE - 24 WAY
C3 - YELLOW - 32 WAY

Somerset and Skylark — Ignition system

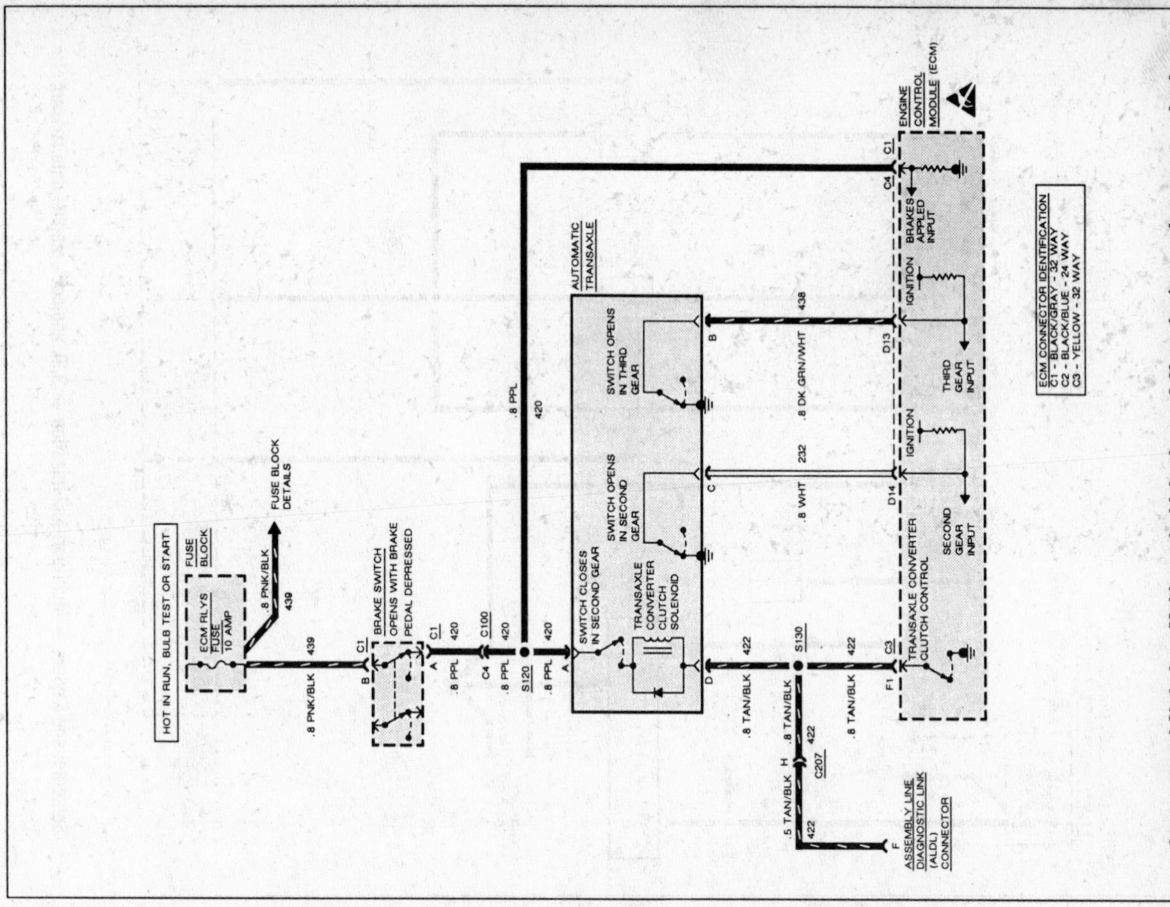

HOT IN RUN, BULB TEST OR START

FUSE BLOCK

GAGES FUSE 10 AMP

.8 PNK/BLK 39

SEE FUSE BLOCK DETAILS

S213

INSTRUMENT CLUSTER PRINTED CIRCUIT

.8 PNK/BLK 39

C13 C1

INDICATORS

"SERVICE ENGINE SOON" INDICATOR

C10 C1

ECM CONNECTOR IDENTIFICATION
C1 - BLACK/GRAY - 32 WAY
C2 - BLACK/BLUE - 24 WAY
C3 - YELLOW - 32 WAY

VEHICLE SPEED SENSOR

COOLANT FAN

AIR CONDITIONING: COMPRESSOR CONTROLS

VEHICLE SPEED SENSOR

.5 BRN/WHT 419

C C207

ENGINE CONTROL MODULE (ECM)

.5 DK GRN 389 | .8 DK GRN 535 | .8 LT GRN 66 | .8 DK GRN/WHT 459 | .5 YEL 400 | .5 PPL 401 | .5 BRN/WHT 419

B11 C2 | E8 C3 | C9 C1 | F8 C3 | B10 | B9 C2 | E7 C3

VEHICLE SPEED OUTPUT 4000 PULSES PER MILE

COOLANT FAN RELAY CONTROL

A/C ON INPUT

A/C COMPRESSOR CONTROL RELAY CONTROL

VEHICLE SPEED SENSOR INPUT

HI LO

SERVICE ENGINE SOON INDICATOR CONTROL

5 VOLTS

5 VOLTS

DATA IN

DATA OUT

DIAGNOSTIC TEST

5 VOLTS

DETONATION SENSOR INPUT

E12 C3 .8 WHT/BLK 451

E

A8 C2 .5 ORN 461

J C207

F9 C3 .8 DK BLU 496

.5 WHT/BLK 451

.5 ORN 461

SEE GROUND DISTRIBUTION

G103

A B M

ASSEMBLY LINE DIAGNOSTIC LINK (ALDL) CONNECTOR

DETONATION SENSOR

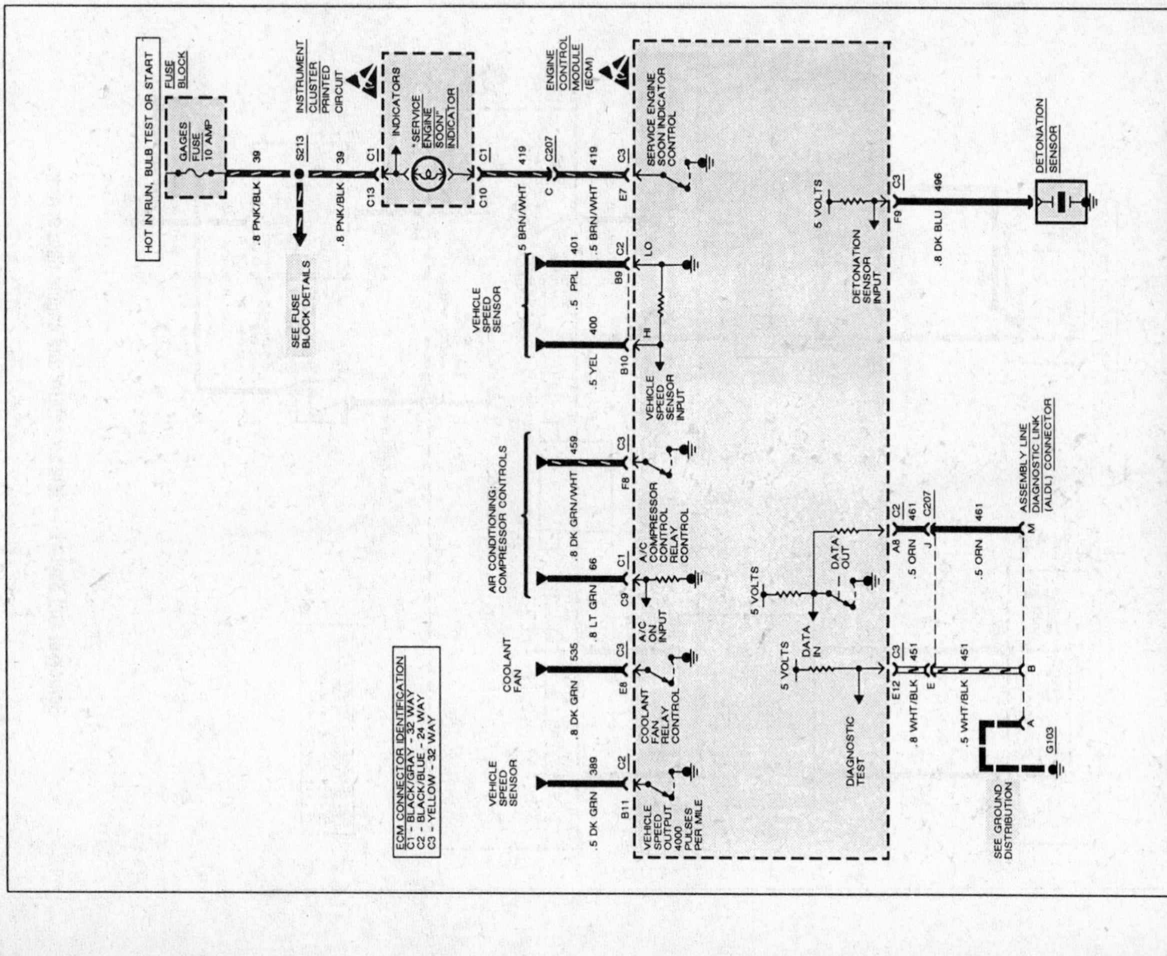

Somerset and Skylark — "Service Engine Soon" indicator and engine data sensors

HOT IN RUN, BULB TEST OR START

FUSE BLOCK

ECM RLYS FUSE 10 AMP

.8 PNK/BLK 439

FUSE BLOCK DETAILS

.8 PNK/BLK 439

B C1

BRAKE SWITCH OPENS WITH BRAKE PEDAL DEPRESSED

A C1

.8 PPL 420

C4 C100

.8 PPL 420

S120

.8 PPL 420

.8 PPL 420

A

SWITCH CLOSES IN SECOND GEAR

AUTOMATIC TRANSAXLE

TRANSAXLE CONVERTER CLUTCH SOLENOID

SWITCH OPENS IN SECOND GEAR

SWITCH OPENS IN THIRD GEAR

D C B

.8 TAN/BLK 422

.5 TAN/BLK H .8 TAN/BLK

422 C207 422

S130

.8 WHT 232

.8 DK GRN/WHT 438

.8 TAN/BLK 422

F

ASSEMBLY LINE DIAGNOSTIC LINK (ALDL) CONNECTOR

F1 C3

D14

D13

C4 C1

TRANSAXLE CONVERTER CLUTCH CONTROL

IGNITION

SECOND GEAR INPUT

IGNITION

THIRD GEAR INPUT

BRAKES APPLIED INPUT

ENGINE CONTROL MODULE (ECM)

ECM CONNECTOR IDENTIFICATION
C1 - BLACK/GRAY - 32 WAY
C2 - BLACK/BLUE - 24 WAY
C3 - YELLOW - 32 WAY

Somerset and Skylark — Multi-port fuel injection — 3.3L engine/transaxle converter clutch

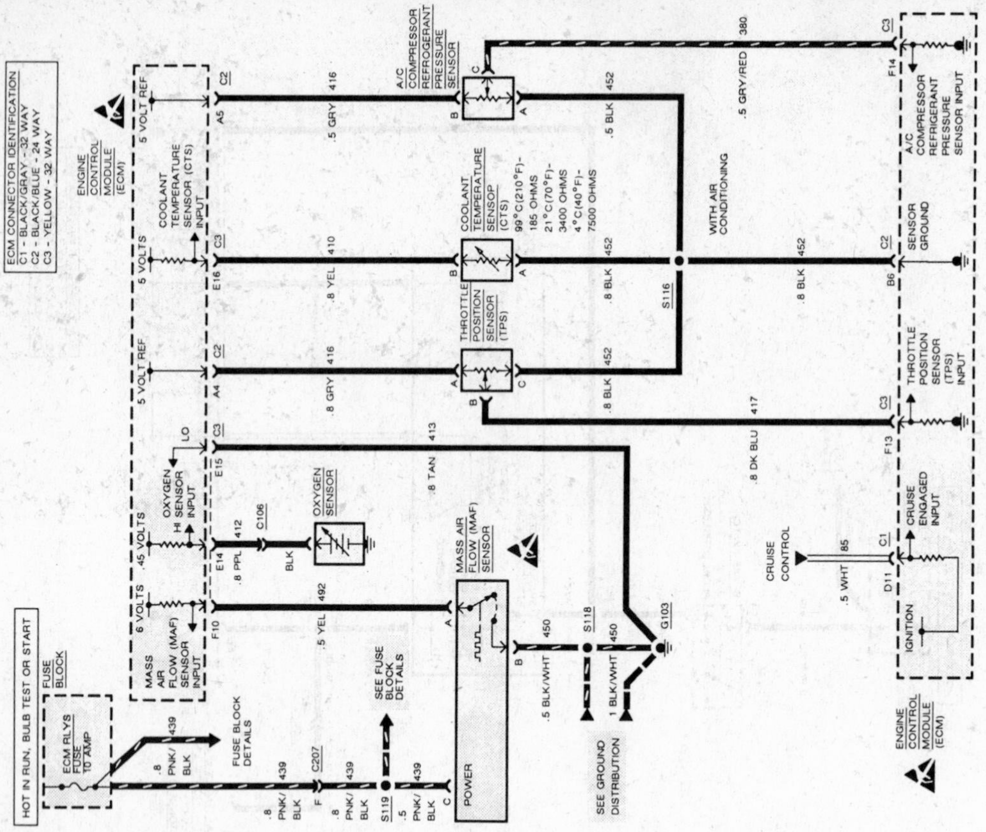

Somerset and Skylark — Multi-port fuel injection — 3.3L engine — engine data sensors

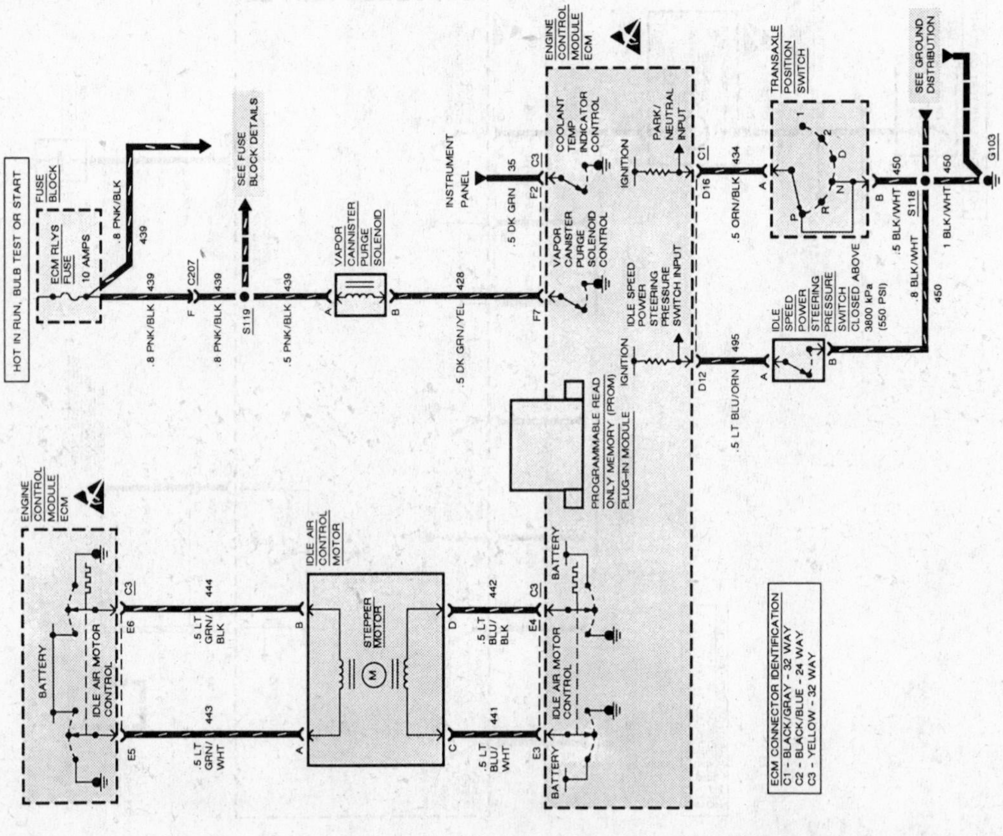

Somerset and Skylark — Idle air control and engine data sensors

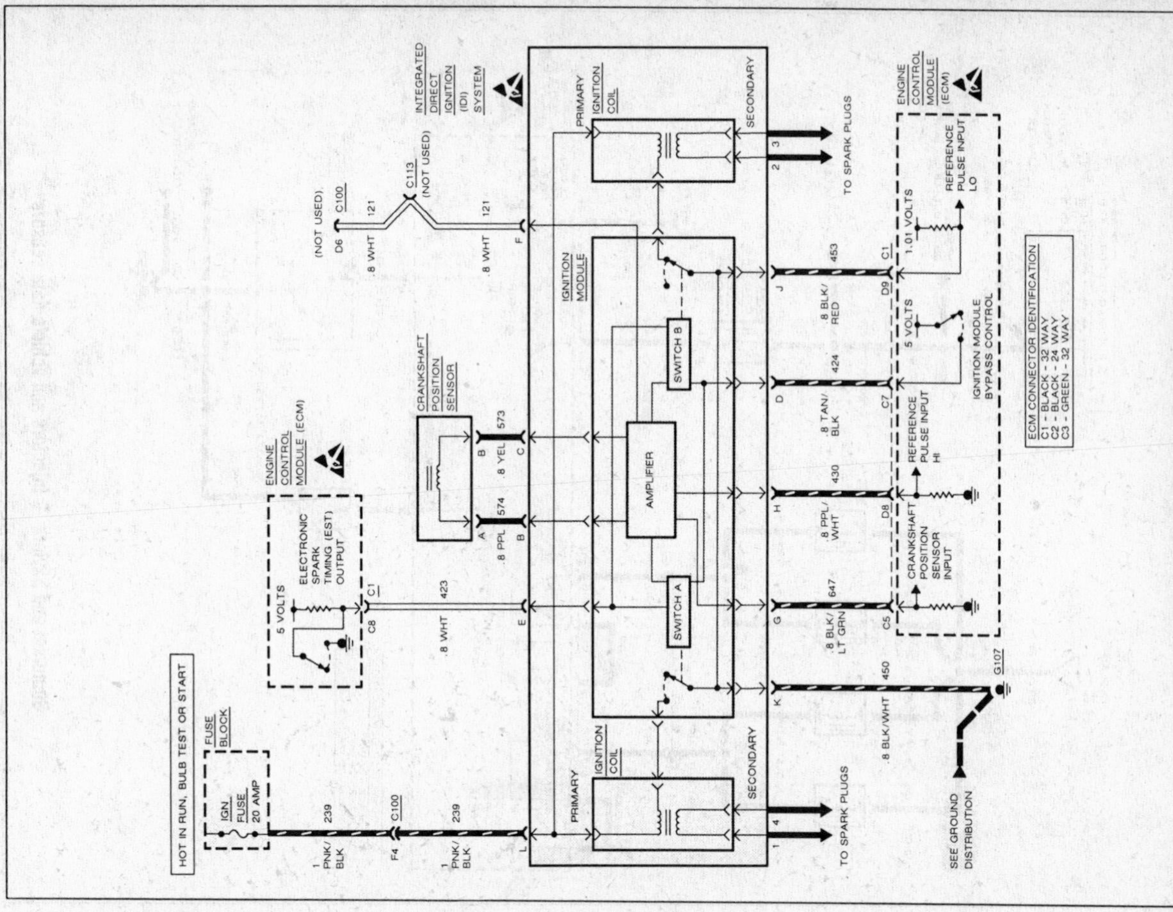

ECM CONNECTOR IDENTIFICATION
C1 - BLACK - 32 WAY
C2 - BLACK - 24 WAY
C3 - GREEN - 32 WAY

Somerset and Skylark — Ignition system

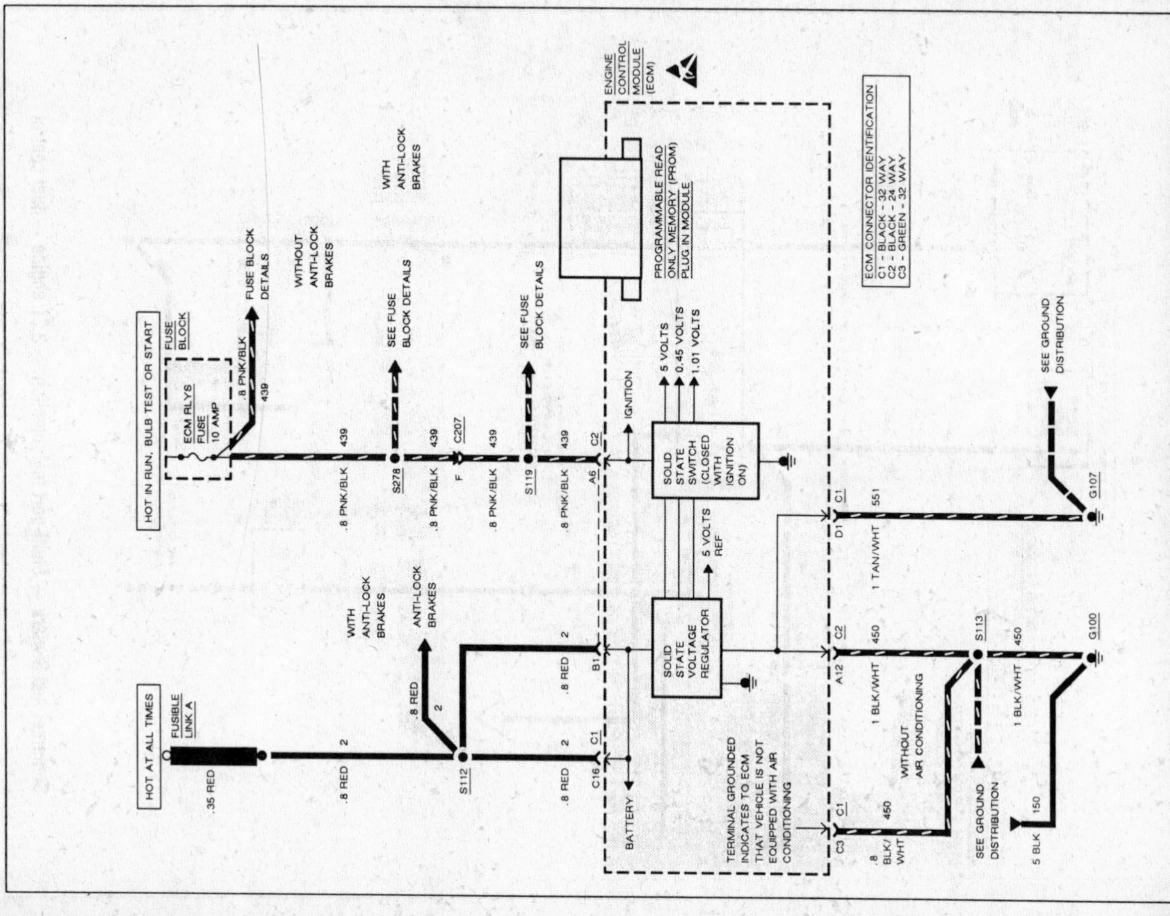

ECM CONNECTOR IDENTIFICATION
C1 - BLACK - 32 WAY
C2 - BLACK - 24 WAY
C3 - GREEN - 32 WAY

Somerset and Skylark — Multi-port fuel injection — 3.3L engine — power and grounds

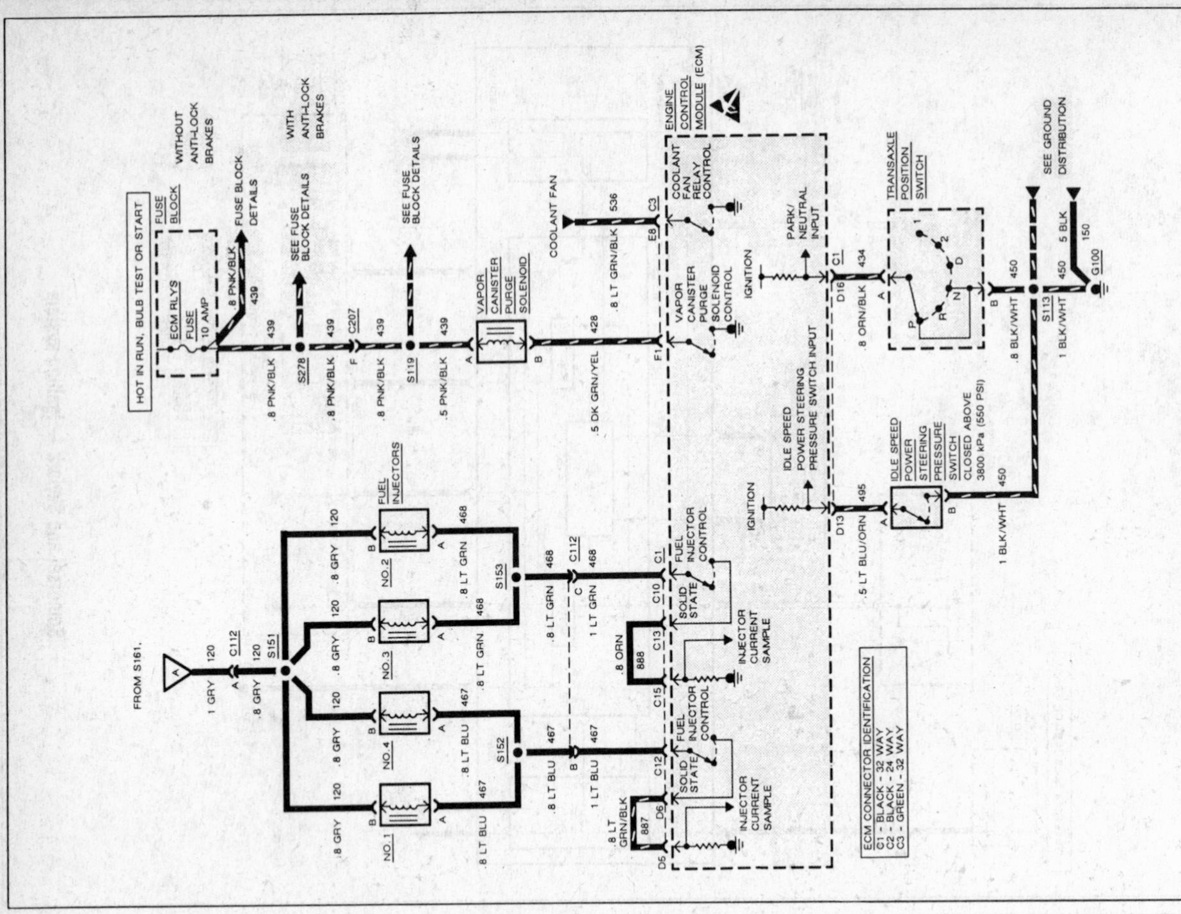

Somerset and Skylark — Injectors and vehicle data sensors

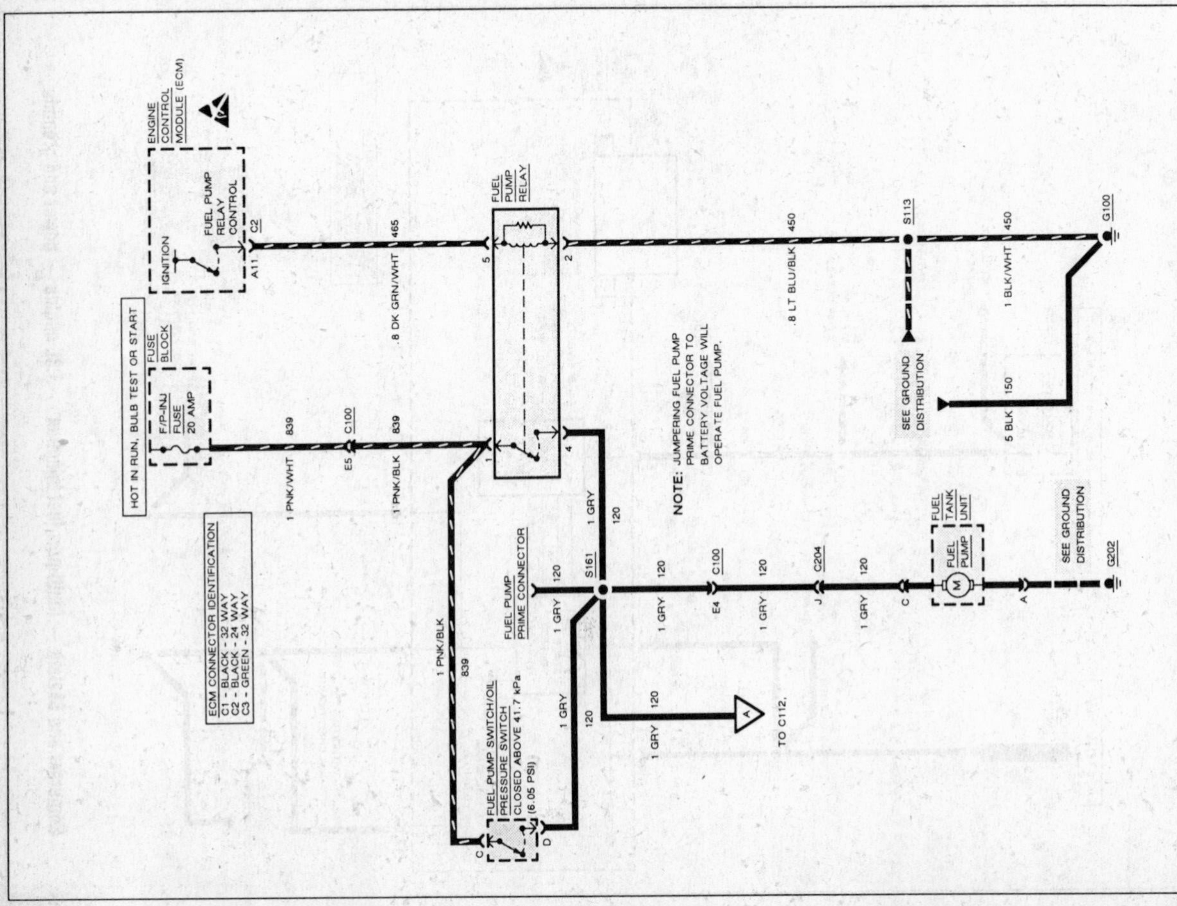

Somerset and Skylark — Multi-port fuel injection — 3.3L engine — fuel control

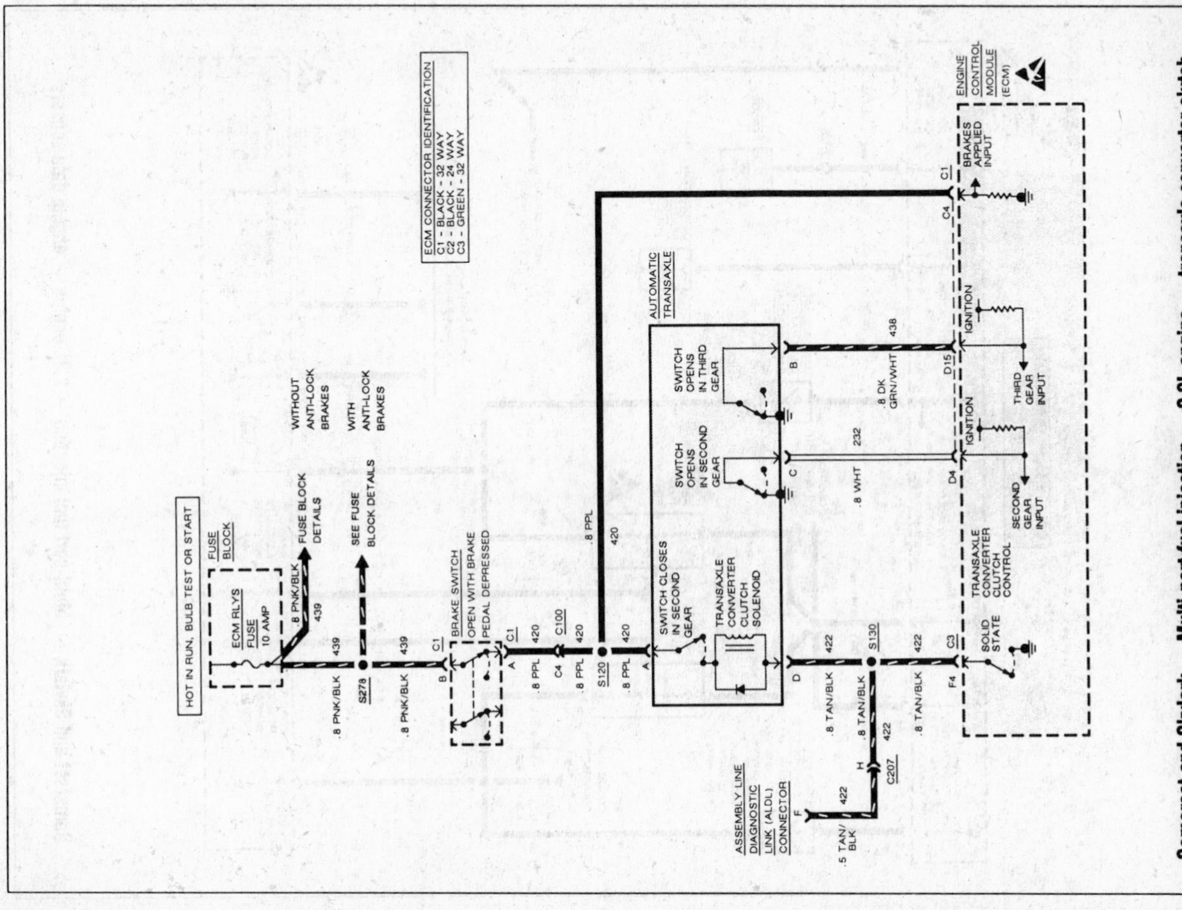

ECM CONNECTOR IDENTIFICATION
C1 - BLACK - 32 WAY
C2 - BLACK - 24 WAY
C3 - GREEN - 32 WAY

Somerset and Skylark — Multi-port fuel injection — 2.3L engine — transaxle converter clutch

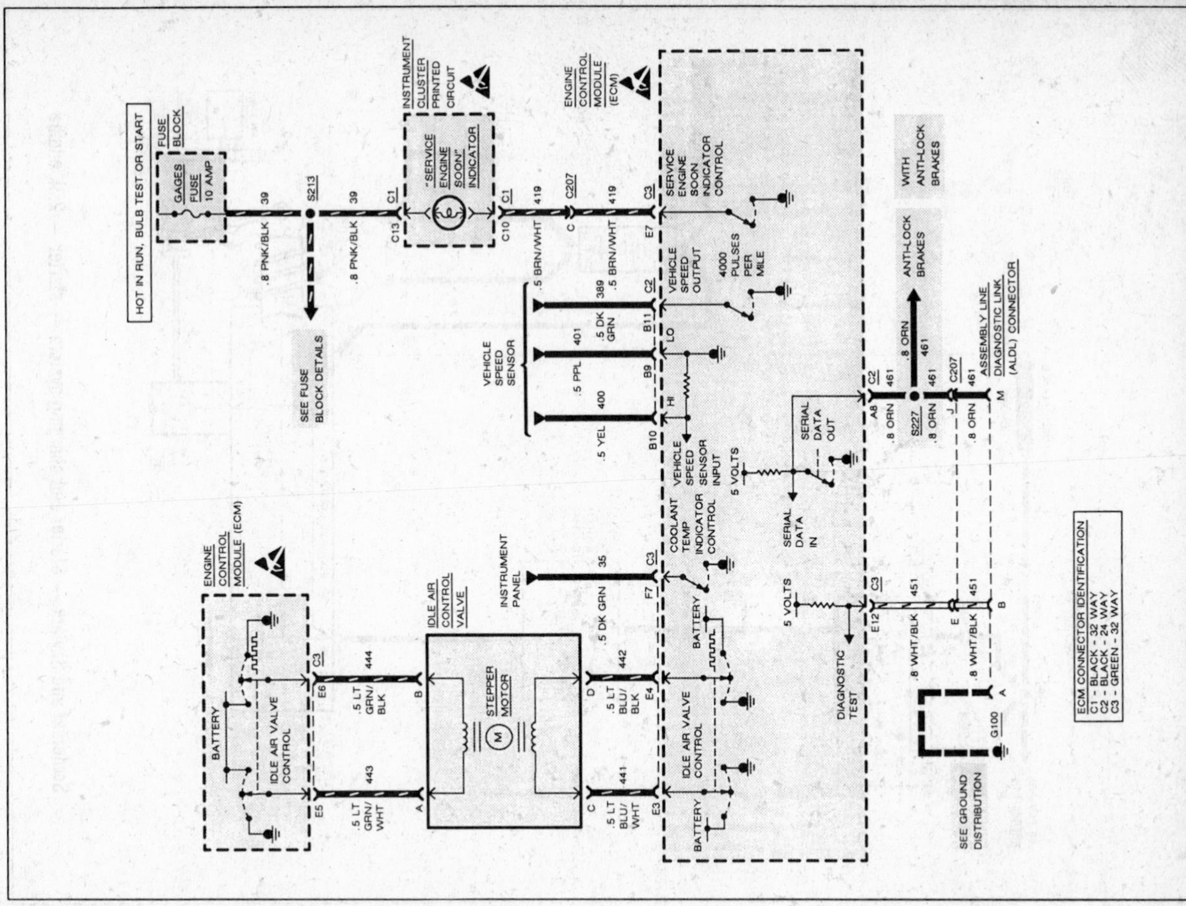

ECM CONNECTOR IDENTIFICATION
C1 - BLACK - 32 WAY
C2 - BLACK - 24 WAY
C3 - GREEN - 32 WAY

Somerset and Skylark — Idle air control, "Service Engine Soon" indicator and engine data sensors

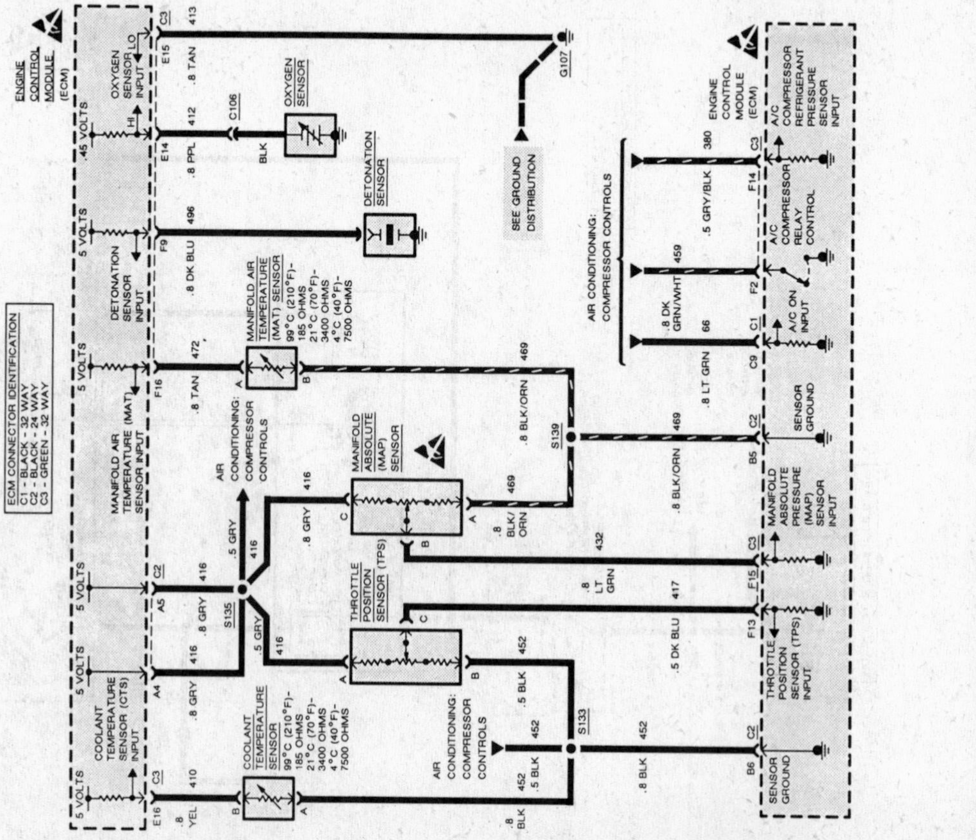

ECM CONNECTOR IDENTIFICATION
C1 - BLACK - 32 WAY
C2 - BLACK - 24 WAY
C3 - GREEN - 32 WAY

Somerset and Skylark — Multi-port fuel injection — 2.3L engine — engine date sensors

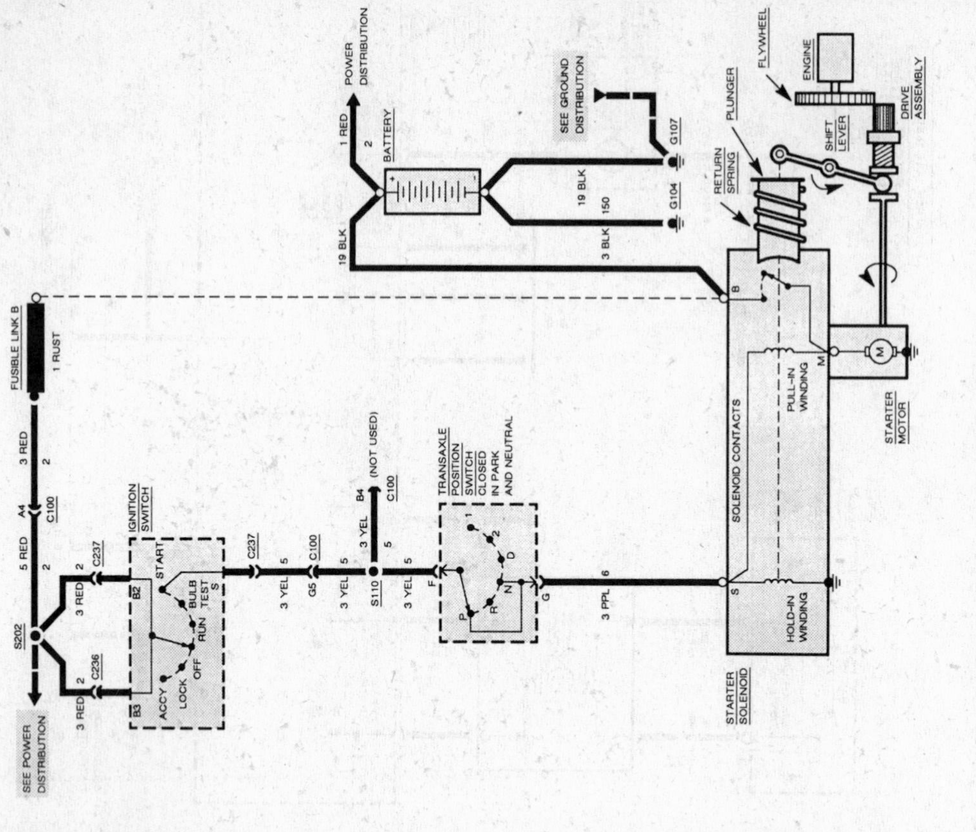

Somerset and Skylark — Starter and charging system — starter — 2.3L engine

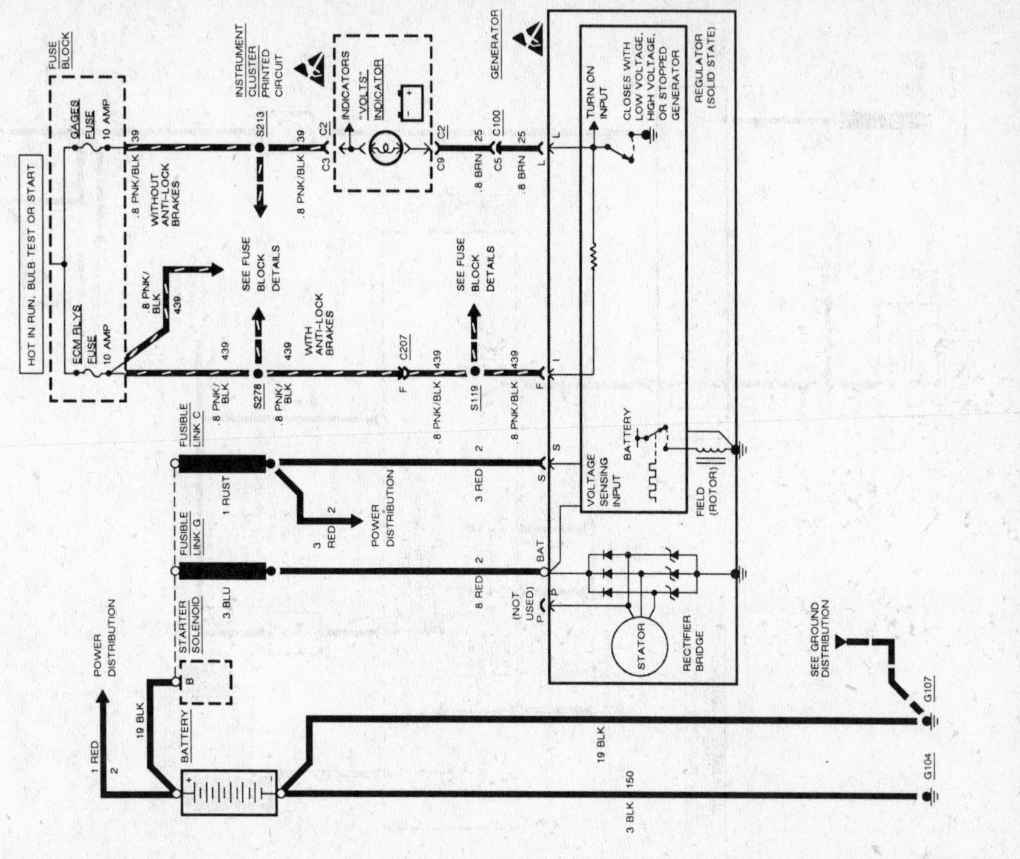

Somerset and Skylark — Starter — 2.5L and 3.3L engines

Somerset and Skylark — Starter and charging system — charging system — 2.3L engine

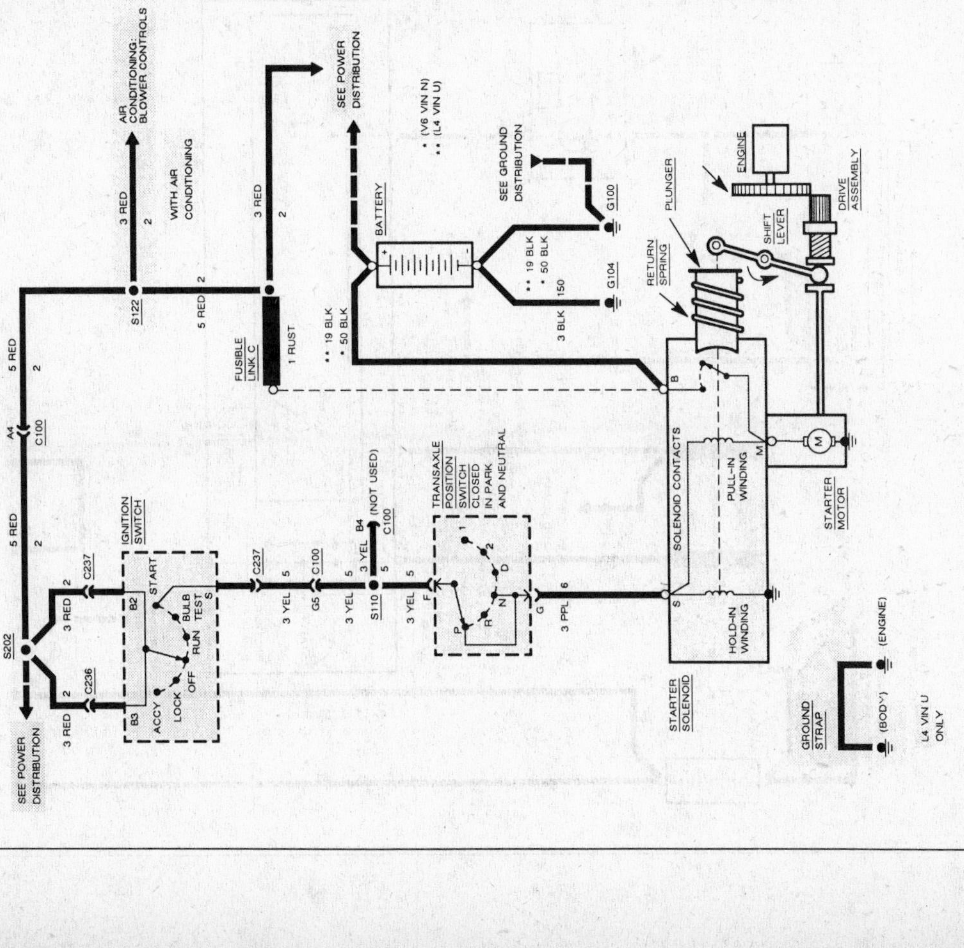

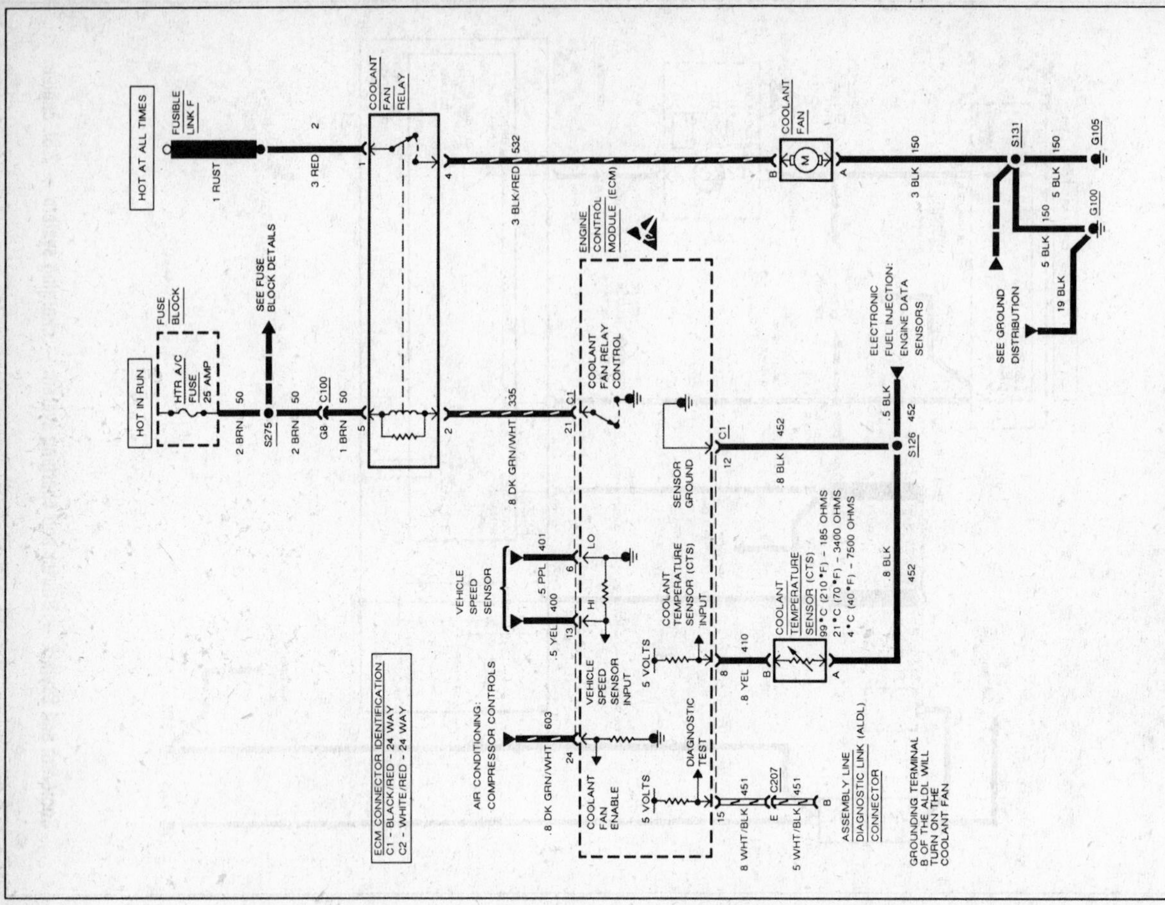

* WITHOUT DAYTIME RUNNING LIGHTS
** WITH DAYTIME RUNNING LIGHTS
** 5 RED
* 1 RED (L4 VIN U)
* 3 RED (V6 VIN N)
POWER DISTRIBUTION
2
50 BLK (V6 VIN N)
19 BLK (L4 VIN U)
BATTERY
B
STARTER SOLENOID
2 GRY (L4 VIN U)
3 BLU (V6 VIN N)
FUSIBLE LINK B
1 RUST
FUSIBLE LINK C
5
RED 2
POWER DISTRIBUTION
3 RED 2
5 RED 2 (L4 VIN U)
8 RED 2 (V6 VIN N)
HOT IN RUN, BULB TEST OR START
ECM RLYS FUSE 10 AMP
GAGES FUSE 10 AMP
FUSE BLOCK
.8 PNK/BLK
439
SEE FUSE BLOCK DETAILS
.8 PNK/BLK 39
S213
.8 PNK/BLK 39
INSTRUMENT CLUSTER PRINTED CIRCUIT
.8 PNK/BLK 439
F C207
C3 C2
INDICATORS "VOLTS" INDICATOR
C9 C2
.8 BRN 25
C5 C100
.8 BRN 25
.8 PNK/BLK 439
S114 (L4 VIN U)
S119 (V6 VIN N)
SEE FUSE BLOCK DETAILS
.8 PNK/BLK 439
GENERATOR
(NOT USED)
P
BAT
S
F
L
P
S
I
L
19 BLK (L4 VIN U)
50 BLK (V6 VIN N)
3 BLK 150
STATOR
RECTIFIER BRIDGE
VOLTAGE SENSING INPUT
BATTERY
FIELD (ROTOR)
TURN ON INPUT
CLOSES WITH LOW VOLTAGE, HIGH VOLTAGE, OR STOPPED GENERATOR
REGULATOR (SOLID STATE)
SEE GROUND DISTRIBUTION
GROUND STRAP
L4 VIN U ONLY
G104
G100
(ENGINE)
(BODY)

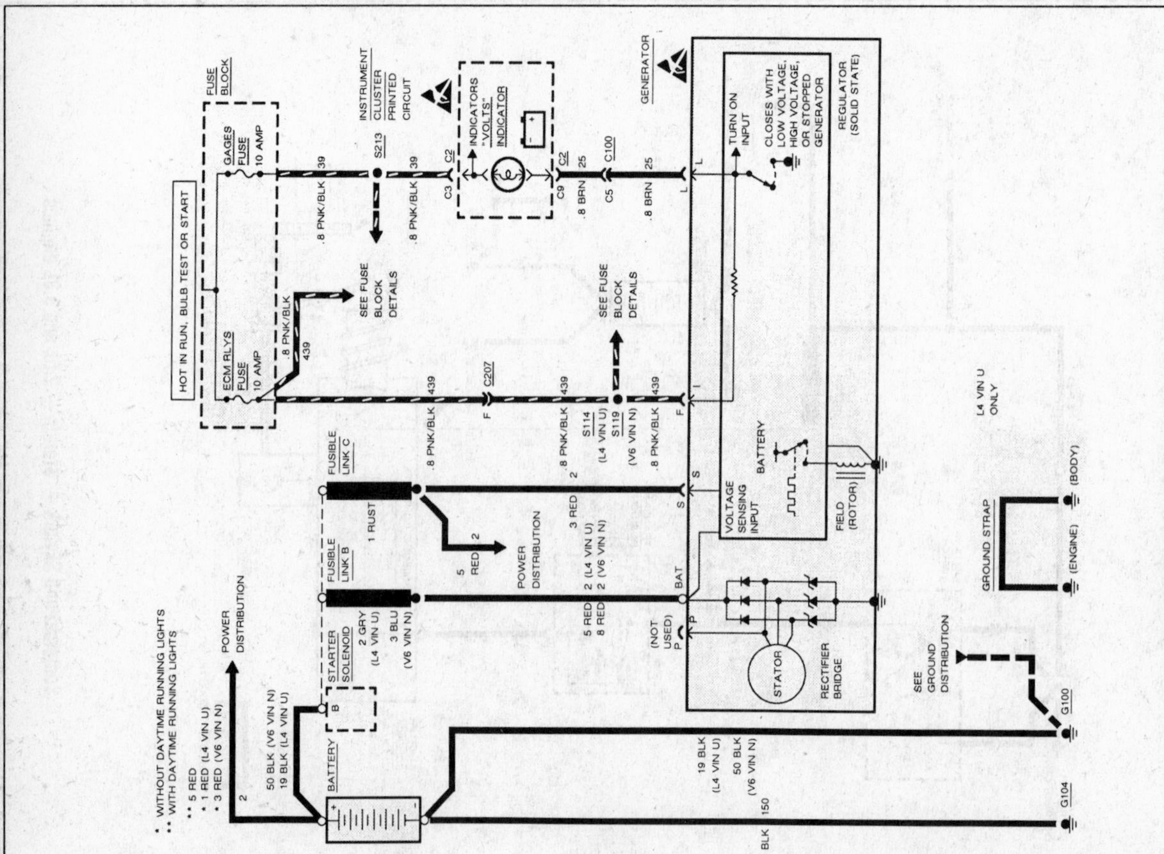

Somerset and Skylark – Charging system – 2.5L and 3.3L engines

HOT IN RUN
HTR A/C FUSE 25 AMP
FUSE BLOCK
HOT AT ALL TIMES
FUSIBLE LINK F
1 RUST
2 BRN 50
S275
SEE FUSE BLOCK DETAILS
2 BRN 50
G8 C100
1 BRN 50
3 RED 2
5
1
COOLANT FAN RELAY
2
4
ECM CONNECTOR IDENTIFICATION
C1 - BLACK/RED - 24 WAY
C2 - WHITE/RED - 24 WAY
AIR CONDITIONING: COMPRESSOR CONTROLS
VEHICLE SPEED SENSOR
.8 DK GRN/WHT 335
3 BLK/RED 532
.8 DK GRN/WHT 603
.5 PPL 401
.5 YEL 400
24
13
6
21 C1
COOLANT FAN ENABLE
VEHICLE SPEED SENSOR INPUT
HI
LO
COOLANT FAN RELAY CONTROL
ENGINE CONTROL MODULE (ECM)
5 VOLTS
5 VOLTS
DIAGNOSTIC TEST
COOLANT TEMPERATURE SENSOR (CTS) INPUT
SENSOR GROUND
15
8
12 C1
8 WHT/BLK 451
.8 YEL 410
E C207
5 WHT/BLK 451
B
B
COOLANT TEMPERATURE SENSOR (CTS)
99°C (210°F) - 185 OHMS
21°C (70°F) - 3400 OHMS
4°C (40°F) - 7500 OHMS
A
.8 BLK 452
ASSEMBLY LINE DIAGNOSTIC LINK (ALDL) CONNECTOR
.8 BLK
452
S126 452
.5 BLK
ELECTRONIC FUEL INJECTION: ENGINE DATA SENSORS
GROUNDING TERMINAL B OF THE ALDL WILL TURN ON THE COOLANT FAN
B
COOLANT FAN
M
A
3 BLK 150
SEE GROUND DISTRIBUTION
S131
5 BLK 150
19 BLK
5 BLK 150
G100
G105

Somerset and Skylark – Coolant fan – 2.5L engine

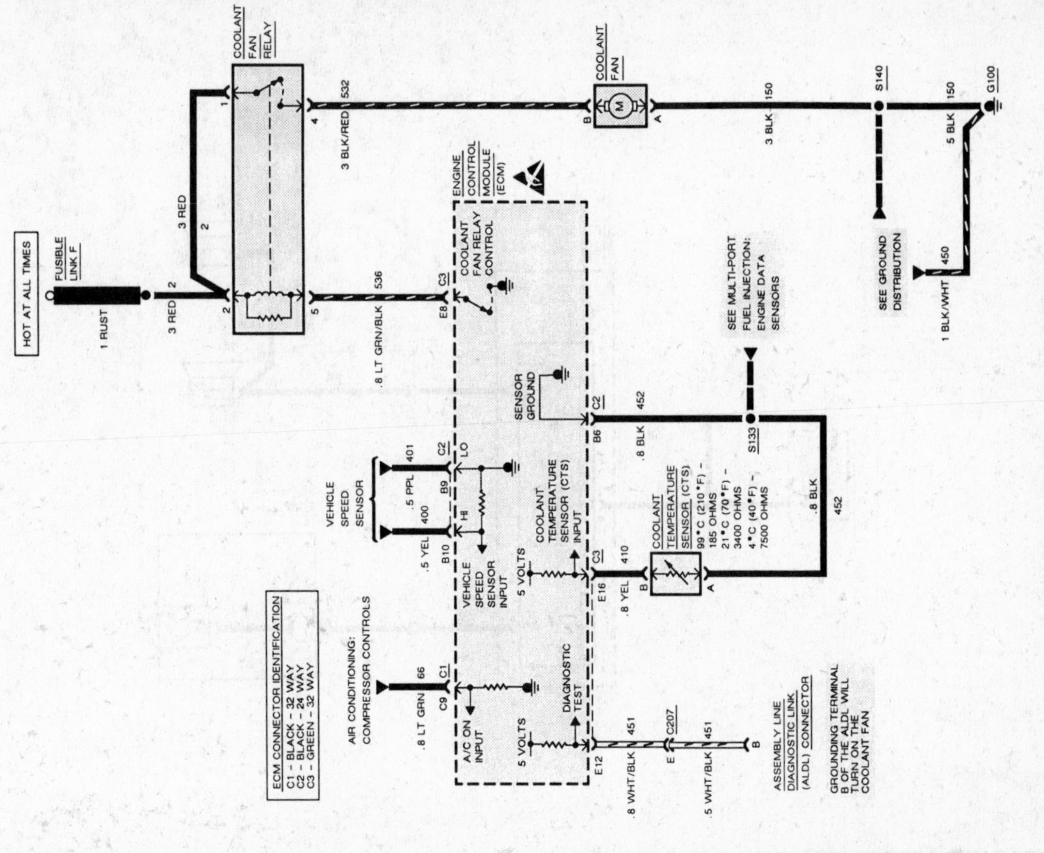

HOT IN RUN
FUSE BLOCK
HTR A/C FUSE 25 AMP
2 BRN 50
S275
SEE FUSE BLOCK DETAILS
2 BRN 50
G8 C100
1 BRN 50
AIR CONDITIONING: COMPRESSOR CONTROLS
1 BRN 50
HOT AT ALL TIMES
FUSIBLE LINK F
.8 BLU
2 RED 2
COOLANT FAN RELAY
ECM CONNECTOR IDENTIFICATION
C1 - BLACK/GRAY - 32 WAY
C2 - BLACK/BLUE - 24 WAY
C3 - YELLOW - 32 WAY
.8 DK GRN 535
3 BLK/RED 532
AIR CONDITIONING: COMPRESSOR CONTROLS
VEHICLE SPEED SENSOR
.8 LT GRN 66
.5 YEL 400
.5 PPL 401
C9 C1
B10 B9 C2
E8 C3
A/C ON INPUT
VEHICLE SPEED SENSOR INPUT
HI LO
COOLANT FAN RELAY CONTROL
ENGINE CONTROL MODULE (ECM)
COOLANT FAN
5 VOLTS
DIAGNOSTIC TEST
5 VOLTS
COOLANT TEMPERATURE SENSOR (CTS) INPUT
SENSOR GROUND
E12
E16 C3
B6 C2
.8 WHT/BLK 451
.8 YEL 410
.8 BLK 452
E C207
.5 WHT/BLK 451
COOLANT TEMPERATURE SENSOR (CTS)
99°C (210°F) - 185 OHMS
21°C (70°F) - 3400 OHMS
4°C (40°F) - 7500 OHMS
3 BLK 150
ASSEMBLY LINE DIAGNOSTIC LINK (ALDL) CONNECTOR
GROUNDING TERMINAL B OF THE ALDL WILL TURN ON THE COOLANT FAN
.8 BLK 452
S116
SEE MULTI-PORT FUEL INJECTION: ENGINE DATA SENSORS
SEE GROUND DISTRIBUTION
G100

Somerset and Skylark — Coolant fan — 3.3L engine

HOT AT ALL TIMES
FUSIBLE LINK F
1 RUST
3 RED 2
3 RED 2
COOLANT FAN RELAY
ECM CONNECTOR IDENTIFICATION
C1 - BLACK - 32 WAY
C2 - BLACK - 24 WAY
C3 - GREEN - 32 WAY
VEHICLE SPEED SENSOR
AIR CONDITIONING: COMPRESSOR CONTROLS
.8 LT GRN/BLK 536
3 BLK/RED 532
.8 LT GRN 66
.5 YEL 400
.5 PPL 401
C9 C1
B10 B9 C2
E8 C3
A/C ON INPUT
VEHICLE SPEED SENSOR INPUT
HI LO
COOLANT FAN RELAY CONTROL
ENGINE CONTROL MODULE (ECM)
5 VOLTS
DIAGNOSTIC TEST
5 VOLTS
COOLANT TEMPERATURE SENSOR (CTS) INPUT
SENSOR GROUND
COOLANT FAN
E12
E16 C3
B6 C2
.8 WHT/BLK 451
.8 YEL 410
.8 BLK 452
E C207
.5 WHT/BLK 451
COOLANT TEMPERATURE SENSOR (CTS)
99°C (210°F) - 185 OHMS
21°C (70°F) - 3400 OHMS
4°C (40°F) - 7500 OHMS
S133
SEE MULTI-PORT FUEL INJECTION: ENGINE DATA SENSORS
3 BLK 150
ASSEMBLY LINE DIAGNOSTIC LINK (ALDL) CONNECTOR
GROUNDING TERMINAL B OF THE ALDL WILL TURN ON THE COOLANT FAN
.8 BLK 452
SEE GROUND DISTRIBUTION
S140
1 BLK/WHT 450
5 BLK 150
G100

Somerset and Skylark — Coolant fan — 2.3L engine

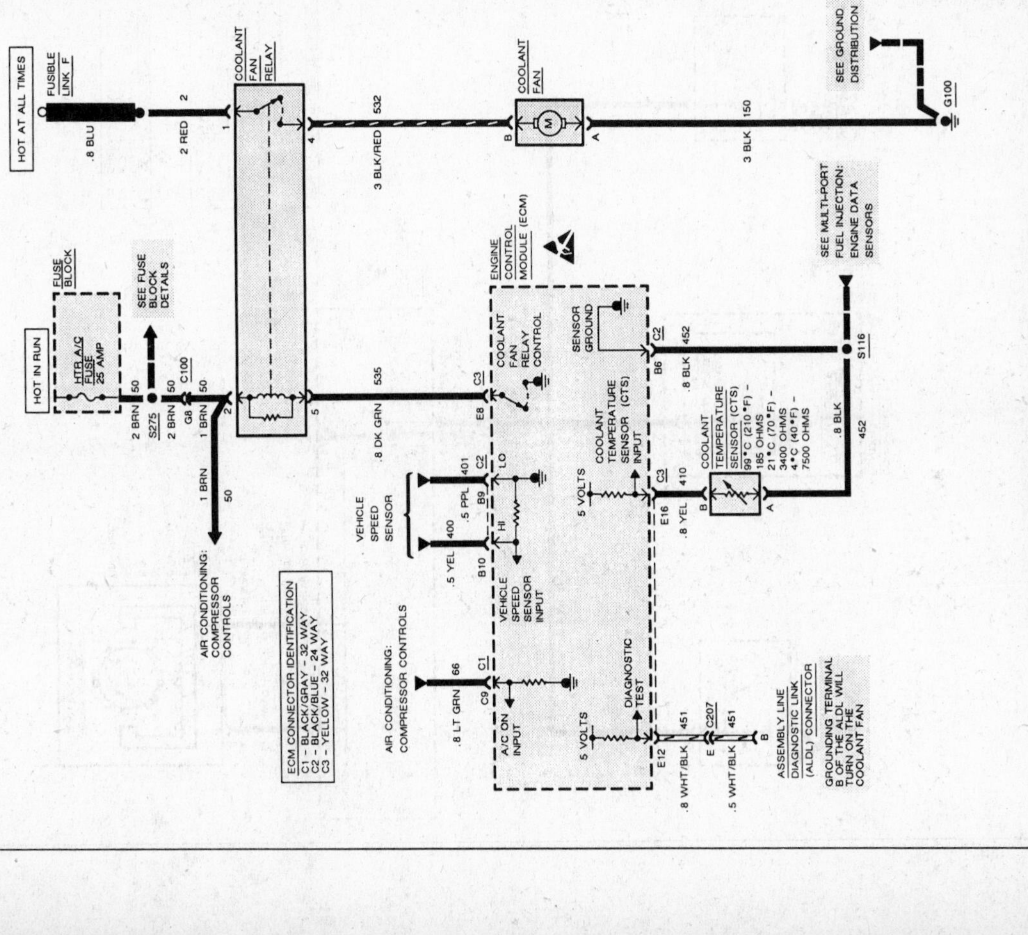

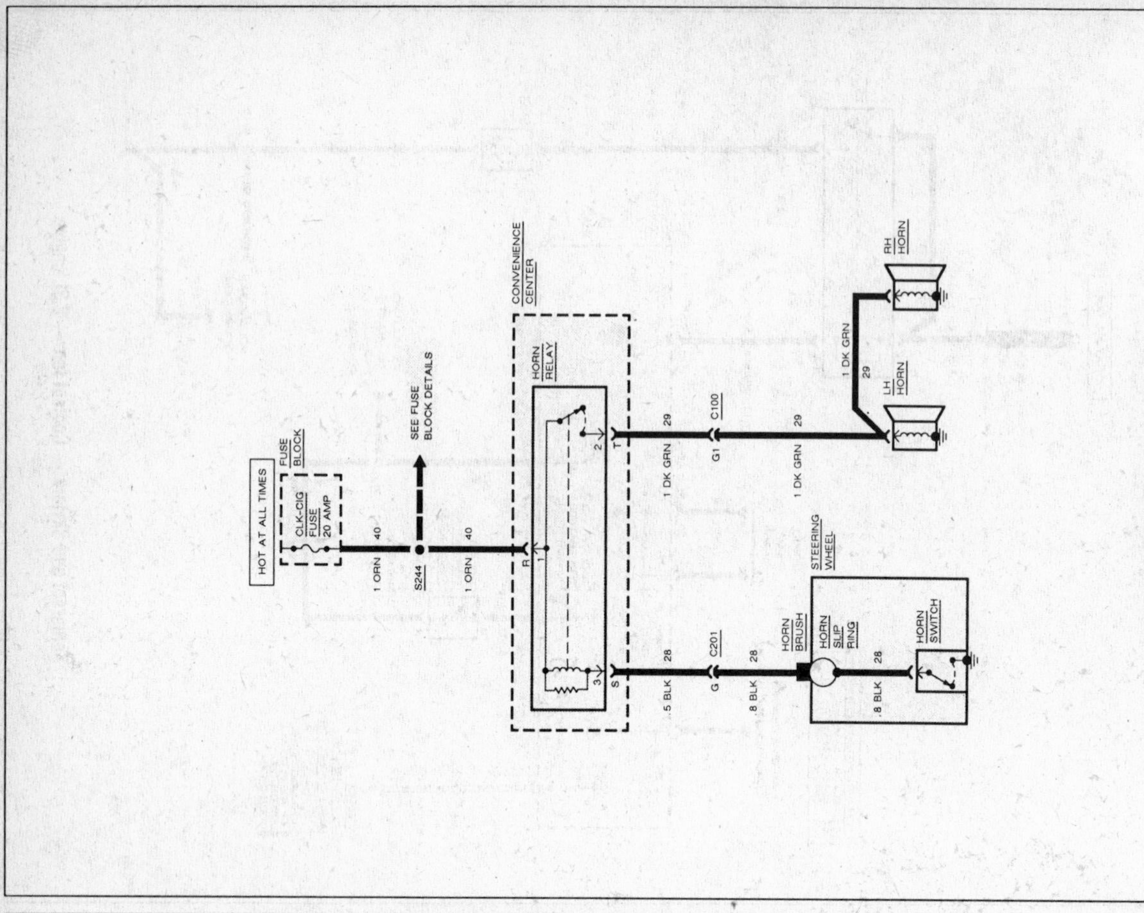

V6 VIN N AND
L4 VIN D

CRUISE CONTROL MODULE

5 VOLTS

VEHICLE SPEED INPUT

D

.35 DK GRN 389

C C202

CONVENIENCE CENTER

MULTI-FUNCTION ALARM MODULE

IGNITION

VEHICLE SPEED INPUT

N

.5 DK GRN 389

INSTRUMENT CLUSTER PRINTED CIRCUIT

IGNITION

VEHICLE SPEED INPUT

C5 C1

.5 DK GRN 389

.5 DK GRN 389

S220

.5 DK GRN 389

R C207

.5 DK GRN 389

22 C2 (L4 VIN U)

B11 C2 (V6 VIN N, L4 VIN D)

VEHICLE SPEED OUTPUT

4000 PULSES PER MILE

ENGINE CONTROL MODULE (ECM)

VEHICLE SPEED SENSOR INPUT

HI LO

B10 13

B9 C2 (V6 VIN N, L4 VIN D)

6 C1 (L4 VIN U)

.5 YEL 400 .5 PPL 401

A B

B A

(L4 VIN U)
(V6 VIN N, L4 VIN D)

VEHICLE SPEED SENSOR (PERMANENT MAGNET GENERATOR) 4000 PULSES PER MILE

ROTOR DRIVEN BY GEAR IN TRANSAXLE

L4 VIN U

ECM CONNECTOR IDENTIFICATION
C1 - BLACK/RED - 24 WAY
C2 - WHITE/RED - 24 WAY

V6 VIN N

ECM CONNECTOR IDENTIFICATION
C1 - BLACK/GRAY 32 WAY
C2 - BLACK/BLUE - 24 WAY
C3 - YELLOW - 32 WAY

L4 VIN D

ECM CONNECTOR IDENTIFICATION
C1 - BLACK - 32 WAY
C2 - BLACK - 24 WAY
C3 - GREEN - 32 WAY

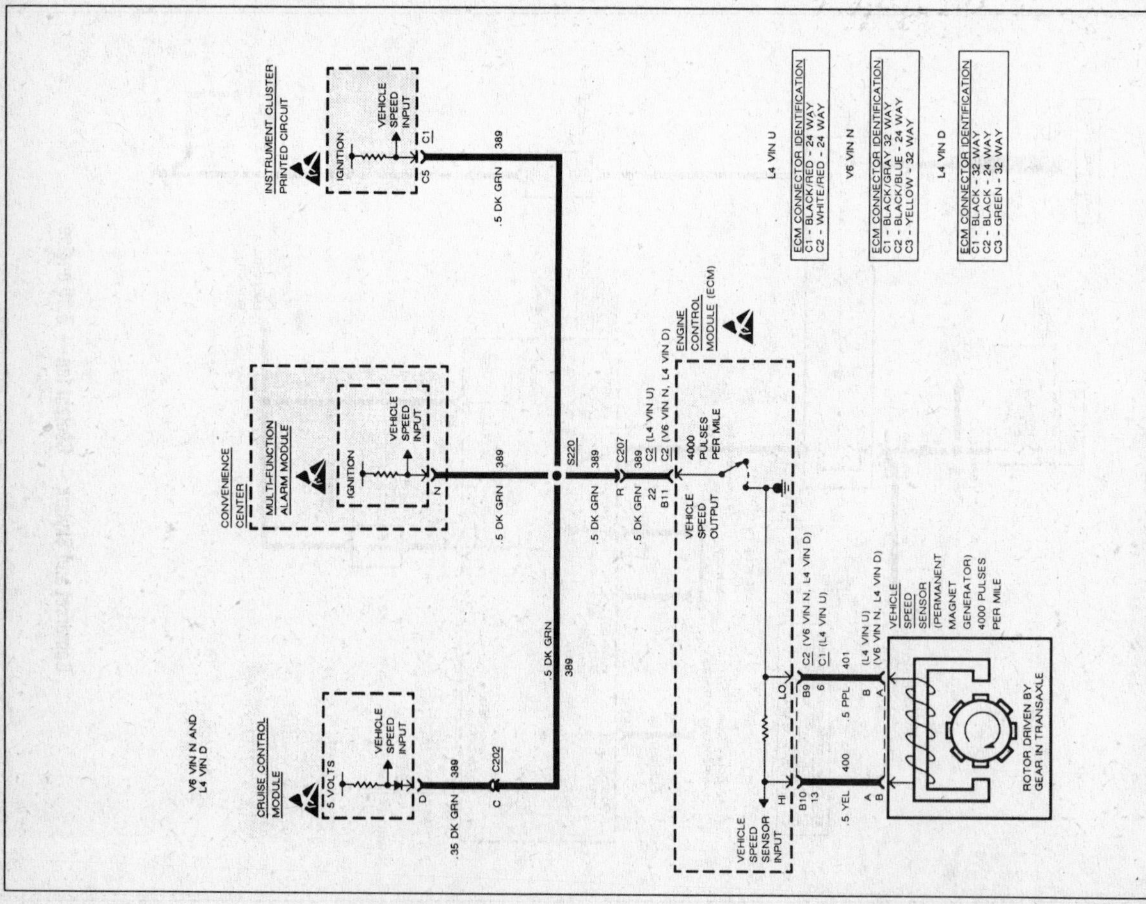

Somerset and Skylark — Vehicle speed sensor — permanent magnet generator

HOT AT ALL TIMES

CLK-CIG FUSE 20 AMP

FUSE BLOCK

1 ORN 40

S244

SEE FUSE BLOCK DETAILS

1 ORN 40

R

1

CONVENIENCE CENTER

HORN RELAY

3 2

S T

.5 BLK 28

1 DK GRN 29

G C201

G1 C100

.8 BLK 28

1 DK GRN 29

HORN BRUSH

HORN SLIP RING

STEERING WHEEL

.8 BLK 28

HORN SWITCH

1 DK GRN 29

LH HORN

RH HORN

Somerset and Skylark — Horns

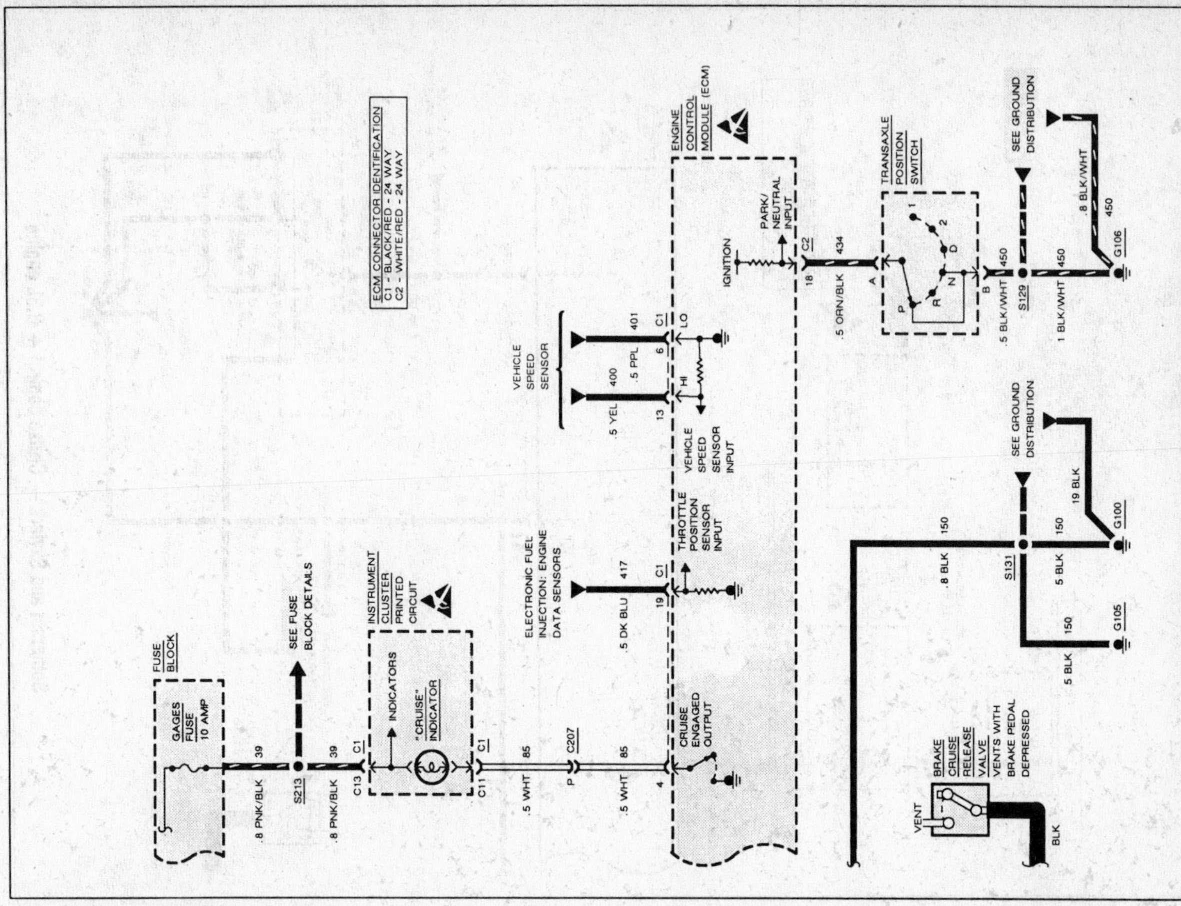

HOT IN RUN, BULB TEST OR START

ECM CONNECTOR IDENTIFICATION
C1 - BLACK/RED - 24 WAY
C2 - WHITE/RED - 24 WAY

Somerset and Skylark — Cruise control — 2.5L engine

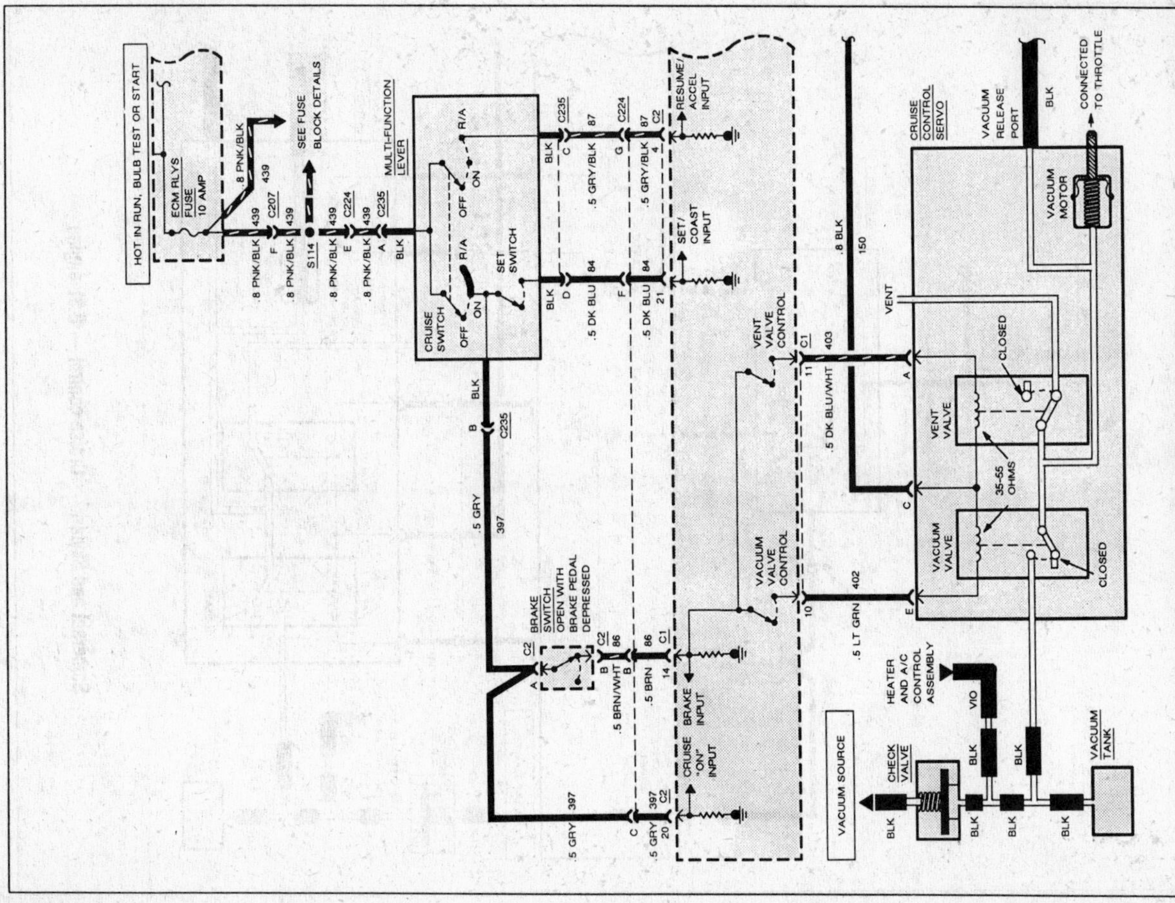

Somerset and Skylark — Cruise control — 2.5L engine

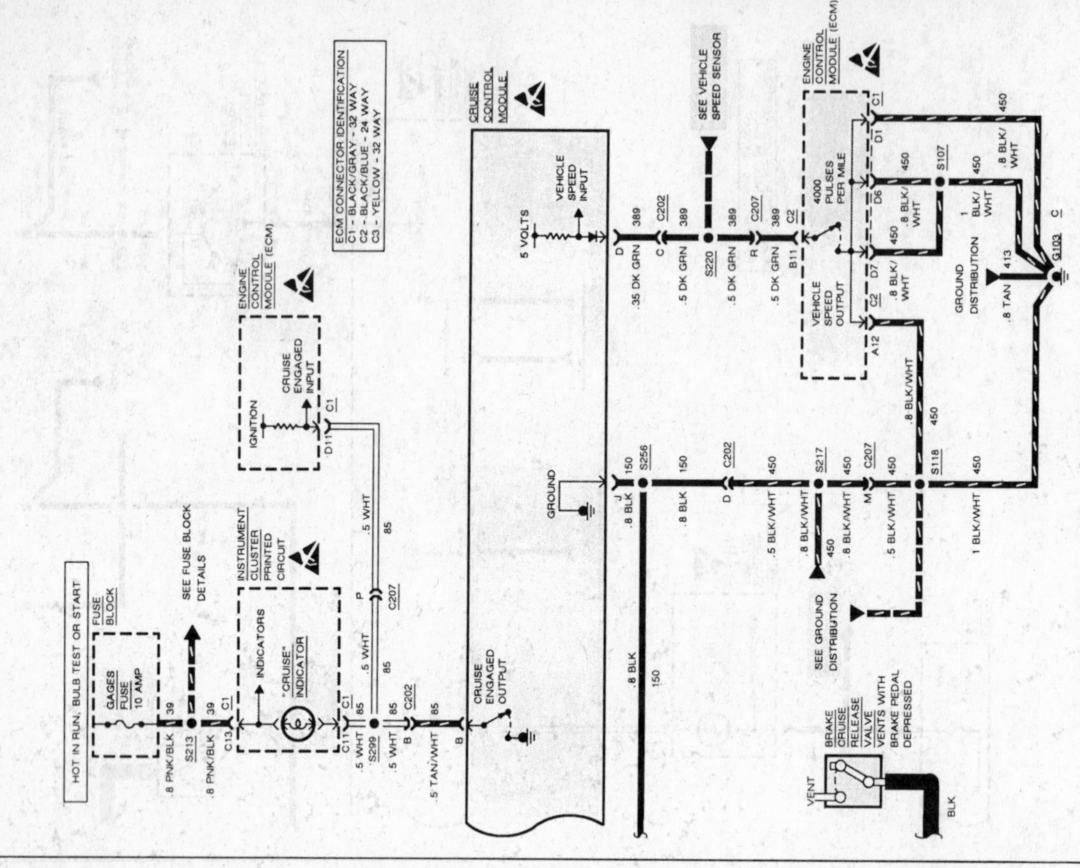

Somerset and Skylark – Cruise control – 3.3L engine

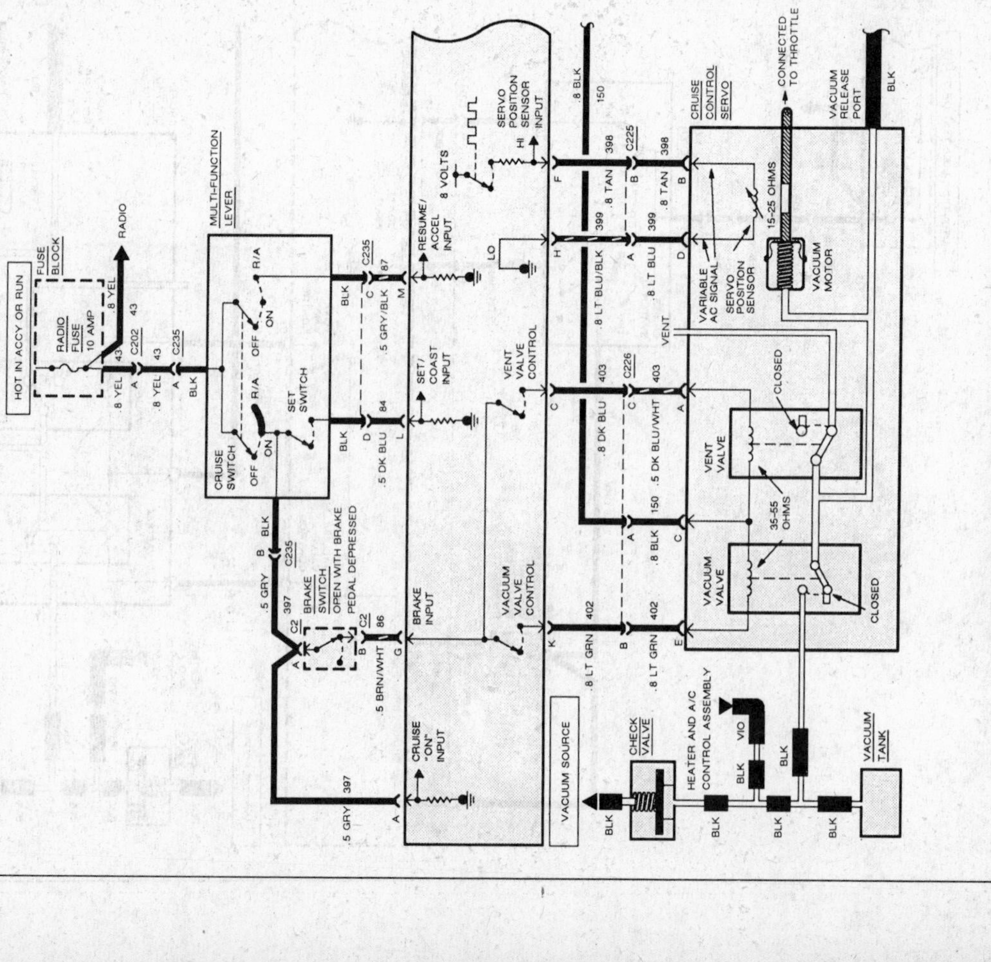

Somerset and Skylark – Cruise control – 3.3L engine

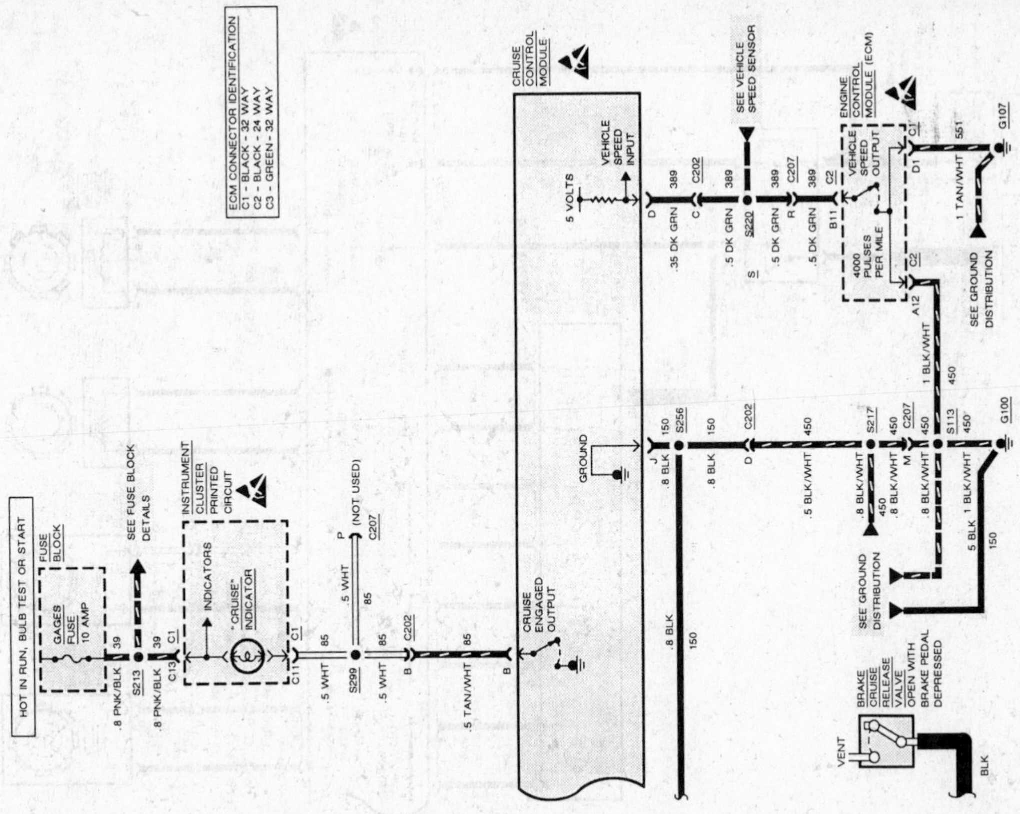

ECM CONNECTOR IDENTIFICATION
C1 - BLACK - 32 WAY
C2 - BLACK - 24 WAY
C3 - GREEN - 32 WAY

Somerset and Skylark — Cruise control — 2.3L engine

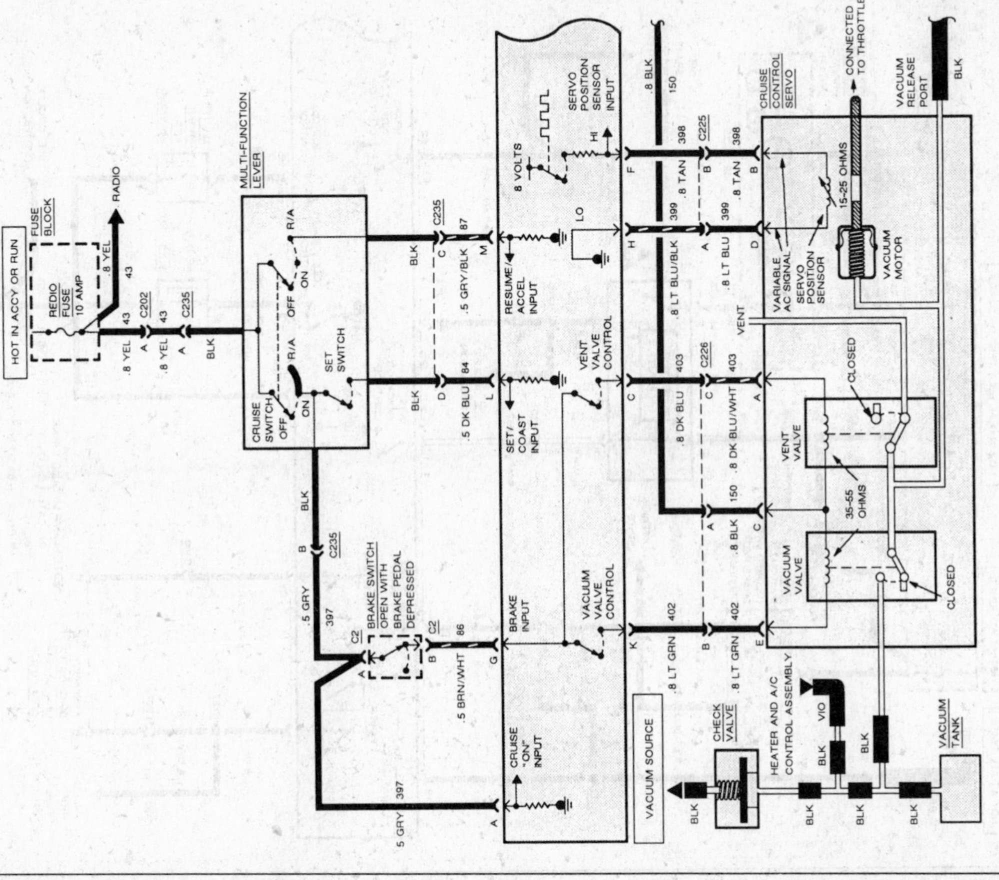

Somerset and Skylark — Cruise control — 2.3L engine

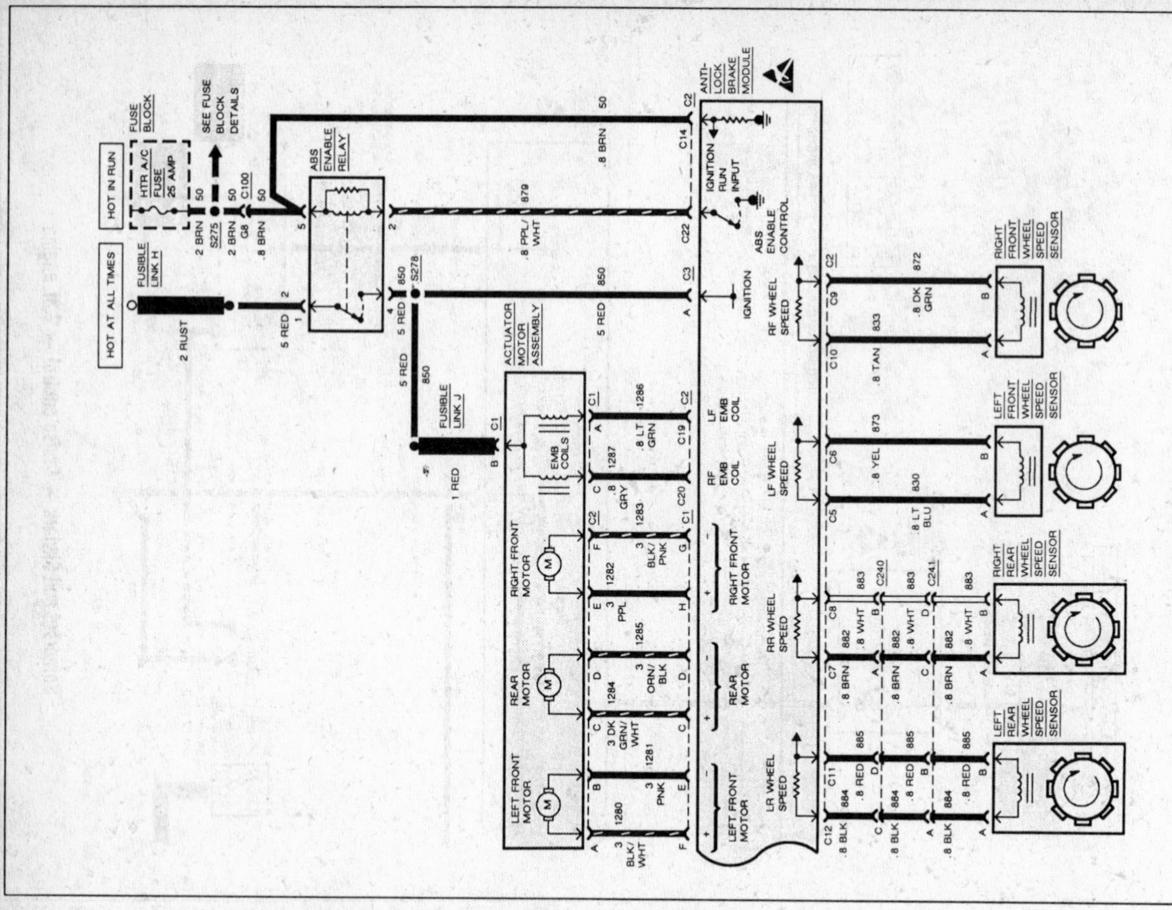

Somerset and Skylark — Anti-lock brakes

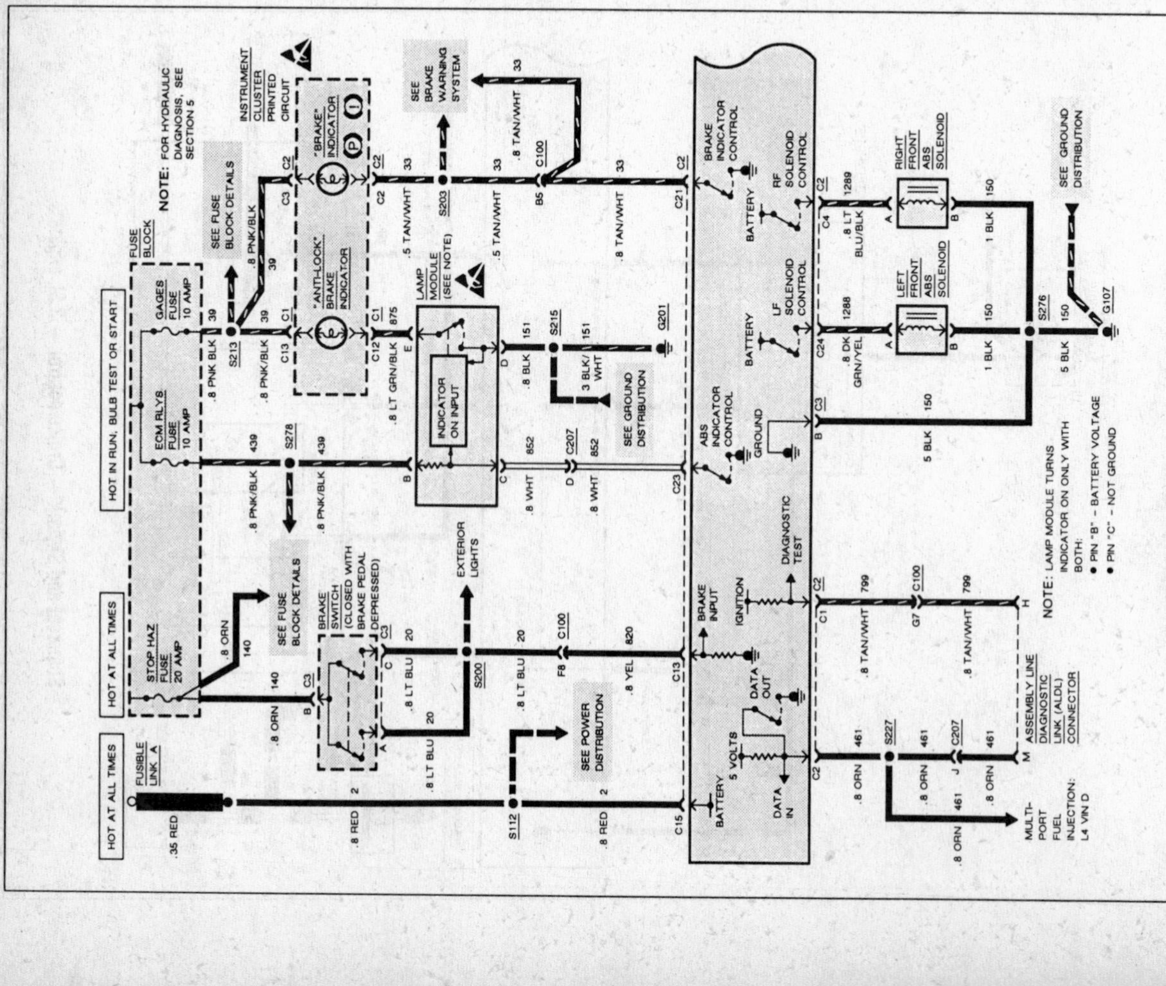

Somerset and Skylark — Anti-lock brakes

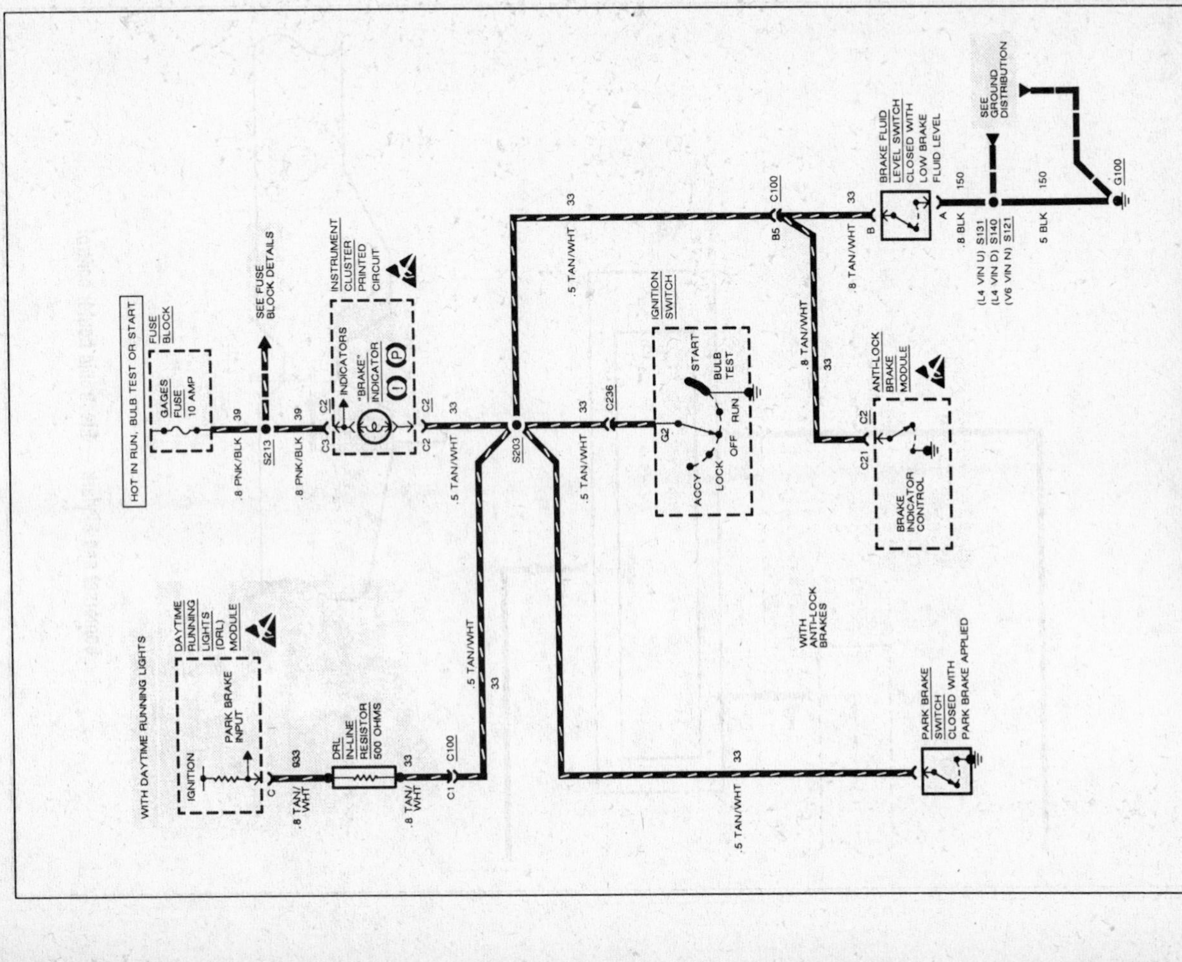

WITH DAYTIME RUNNING LIGHTS
IGNITION
PARK BRAKE INPUT
DAYTIME RUNNING LIGHTS (DRL) MODULE
.8 TAN/WHT 933
DRL IN-LINE RESISTOR 500 OHMS
.8 TAN/WHT 33
C1 C100
.5 TAN/WHT 33
HOT IN RUN, BULB TEST OR START
GAGES FUSE 10 AMP
FUSE BLOCK
.8 PNK/BLK 39
S213
SEE FUSE BLOCK DETAILS
.8 PNK/BLK 39
C3 C2
INDICATORS
"BRAKE" INDICATOR
INSTRUMENT CLUSTER PRINTED CIRCUIT
C2 C2
.5 TAN/WHT 33
S203
.5 TAN/WHT 33
C236
IGNITION SWITCH
G2
ACCY LOCK OFF RUN START BULB TEST
.5 TAN/WHT 33
WITH ANTI-LOCK BRAKES
.5 TAN/WHT 33
B5 C100
.8 TAN/WHT 33
C21 C2
BRAKE INDICATOR CONTROL
ANTI-LOCK BRAKE MODULE
.8 TAN/WHT 33
B
BRAKE FLUID LEVEL SWITCH CLOSED WITH LOW BRAKE FLUID LEVEL
A
.8 BLK 150
(L4 VIN U) S131
(L4 VIN D) S140
(V6 VIN N) S121
SEE GROUND DISTRIBUTION
5 BLK 150
G100
PARK BRAKE SWITCH CLOSED WITH PARK BRAKE APPLIED

Somerset and Skylark — Brake warning system

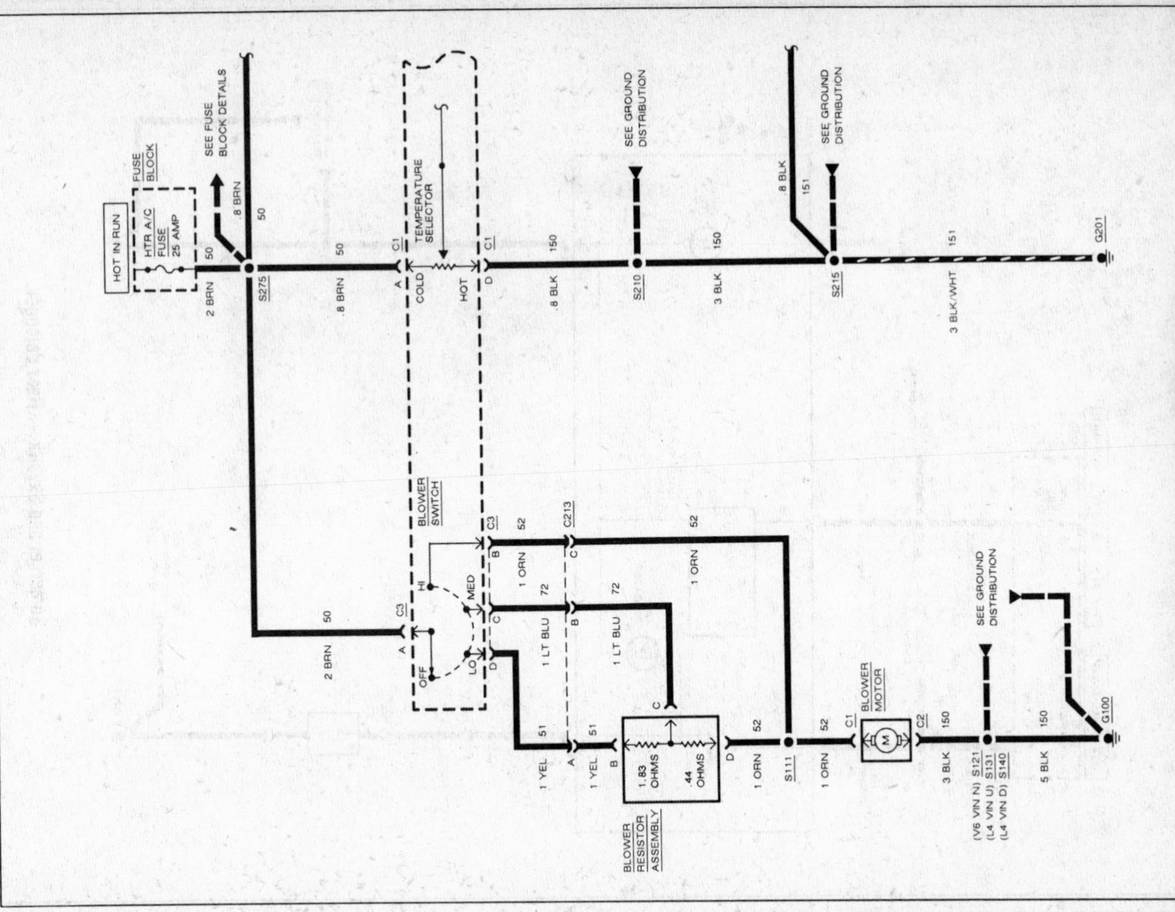

HOT IN RUN
HTR A/C FUSE 25 AMP
FUSE BLOCK
2 BRN 50
SEE FUSE BLOCK DETAILS
.8 BRN
S275 50
2 BRN 50
.8 BRN 50
A C3
OFF HI LO MED
BLOWER SWITCH
D C B C3
A C1
COLD
TEMPERATURE SELECTOR
HOT
D C1
1 ORN 52
1 YEL 51
1 LT BLU 72
A B C C213
1 YEL 51
1 LT BLU 72
B
BLOWER RESISTOR ASSEMBLY
1.83 OHMS
.44 OHMS
C
1 ORN 52
D
1 ORN 52
S111
1 ORN 52
C1
BLOWER MOTOR
C2
3 BLK 150
(V6 VIN N) S121
(L4 VIN U) S131
(L4 VIN D) S140
SEE GROUND DISTRIBUTION
5 BLK 150
G100
.8 BLK 150
S210
SEE GROUND DISTRIBUTION
3 BLK 150
.8 BLK
151
S215
SEE GROUND DISTRIBUTION
3 BLK/WHT 151
G201

Somerset and Skylark — Electronic heater control

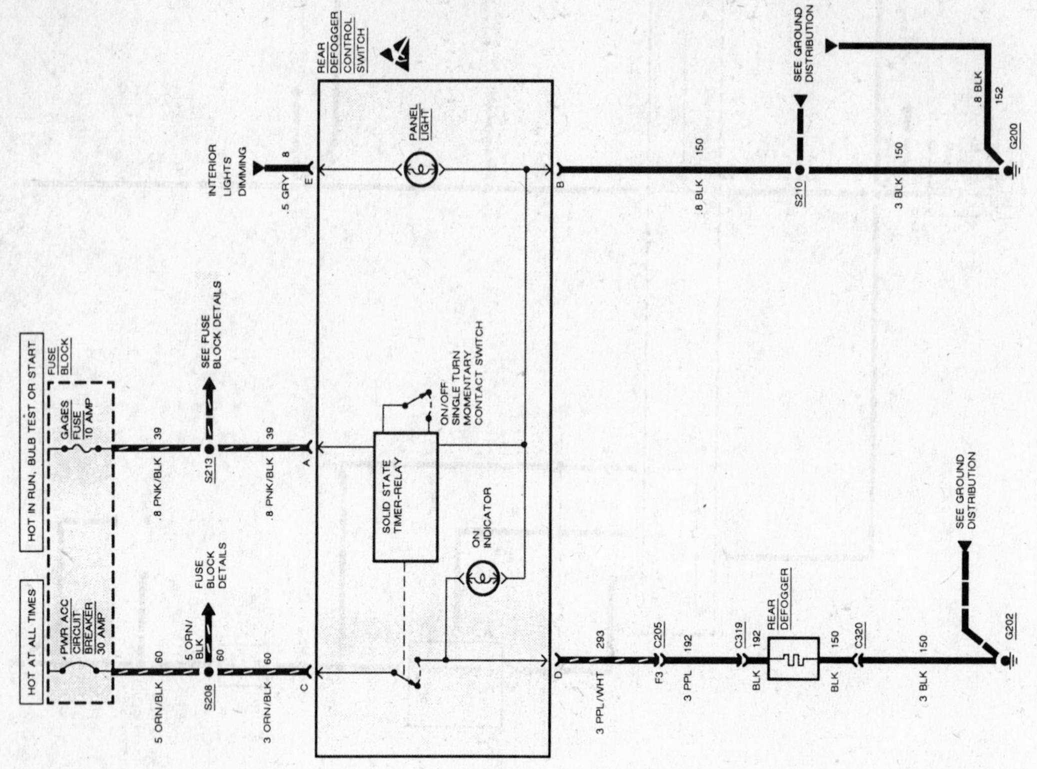

Somerset and Skylark — Rear defogger

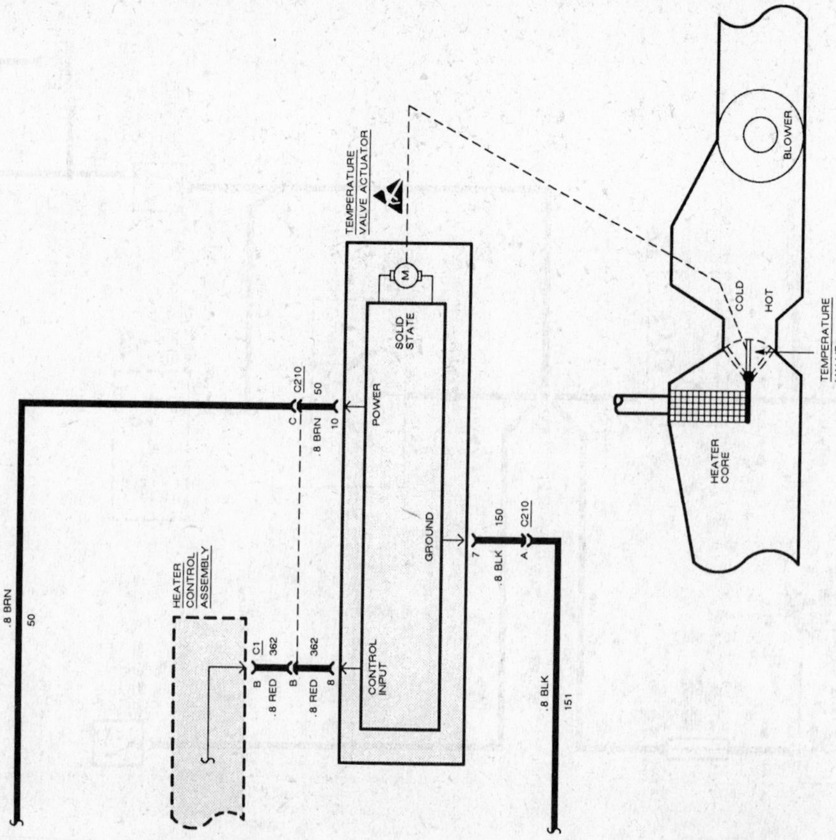

Somerset and Skylark — Electronic heater control

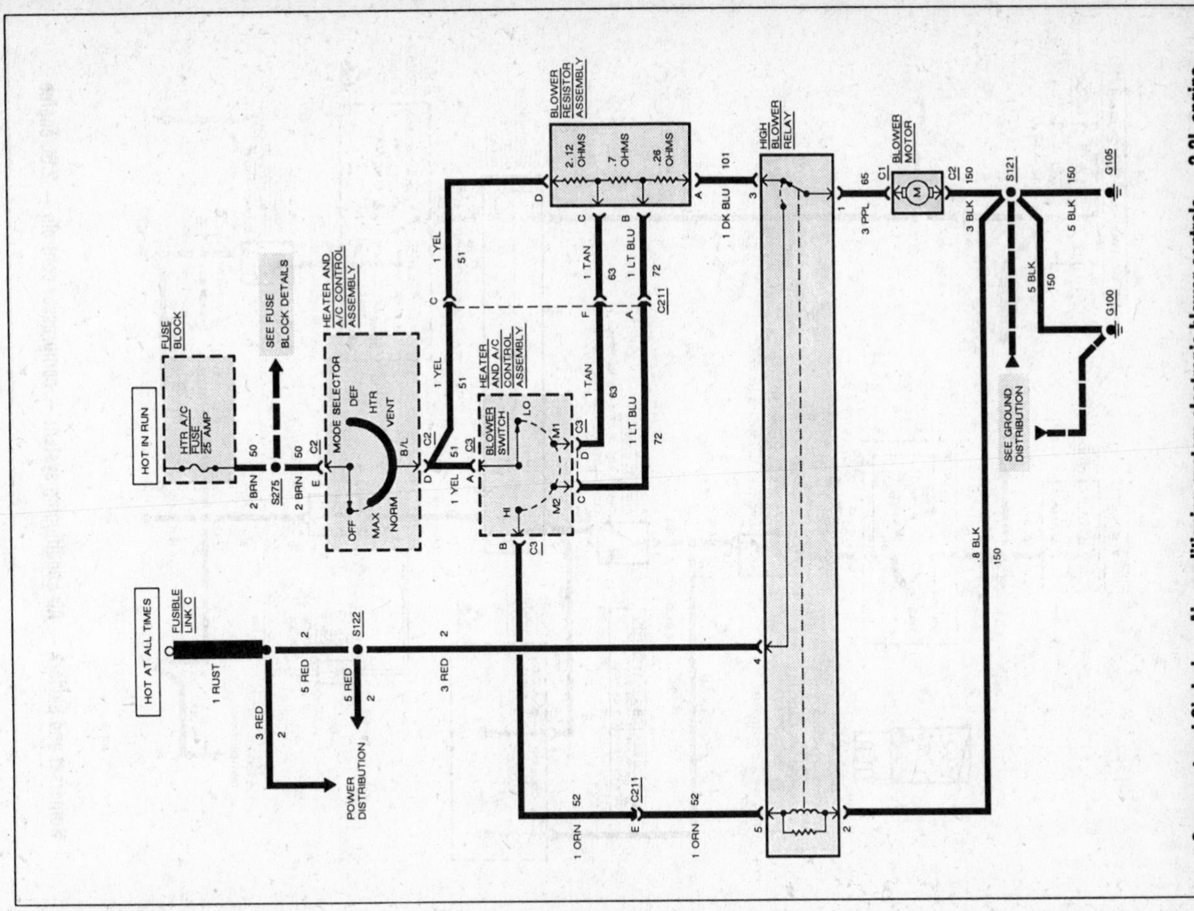

Somerset and Skylark — Air conditioning system electronic blower controls — 3.3L engine

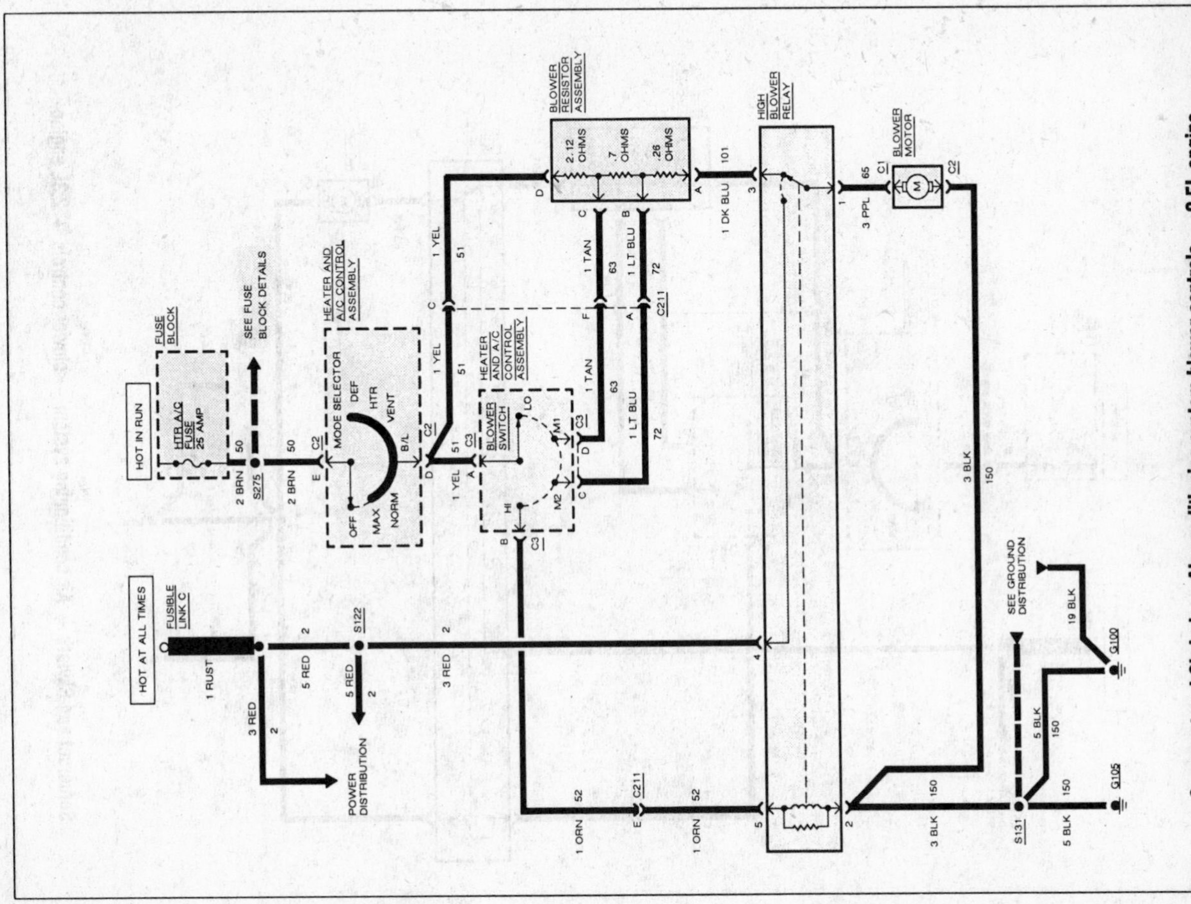

Somerset and Skylark — Air conditioning system blower controls — 2.5L engine

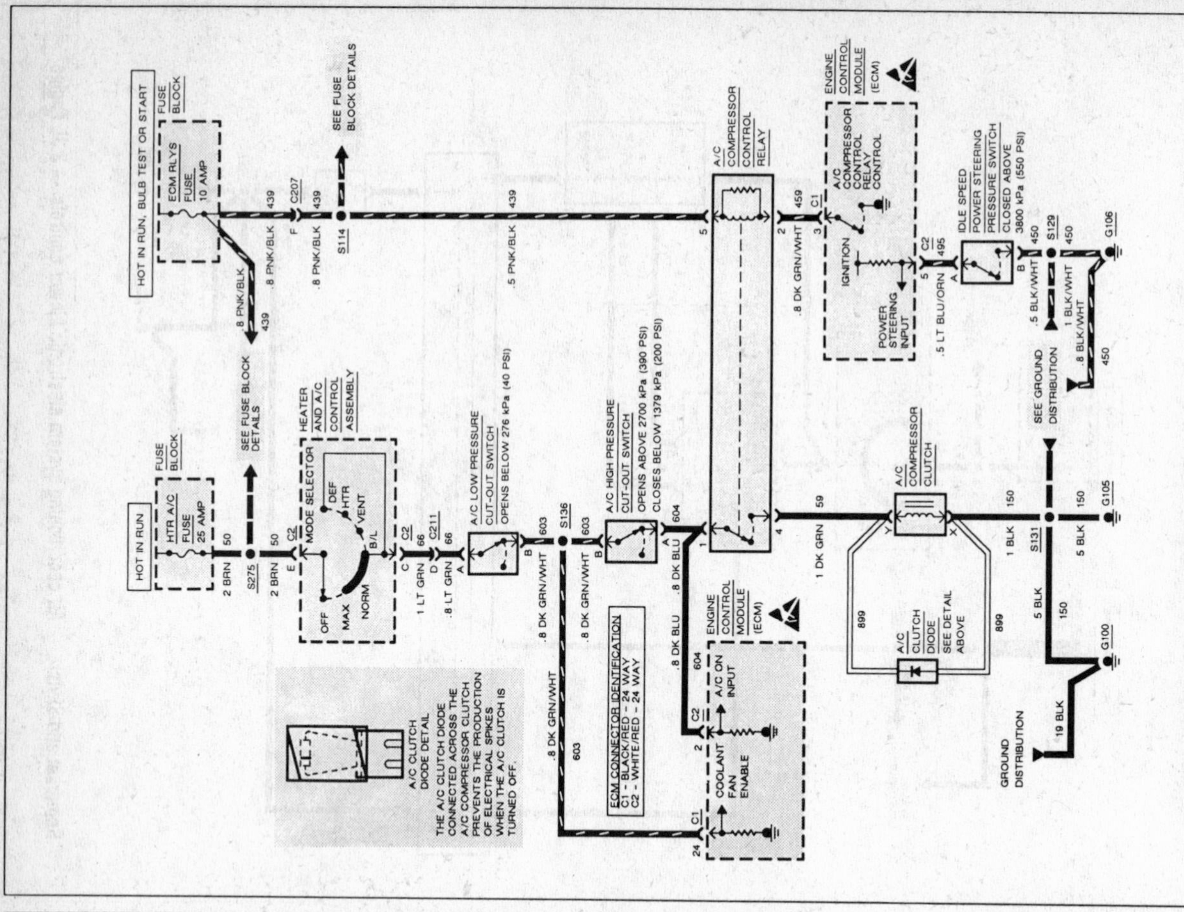

Somerset and Skylark — Air conditioning system — compressor controls — 2.5L engine

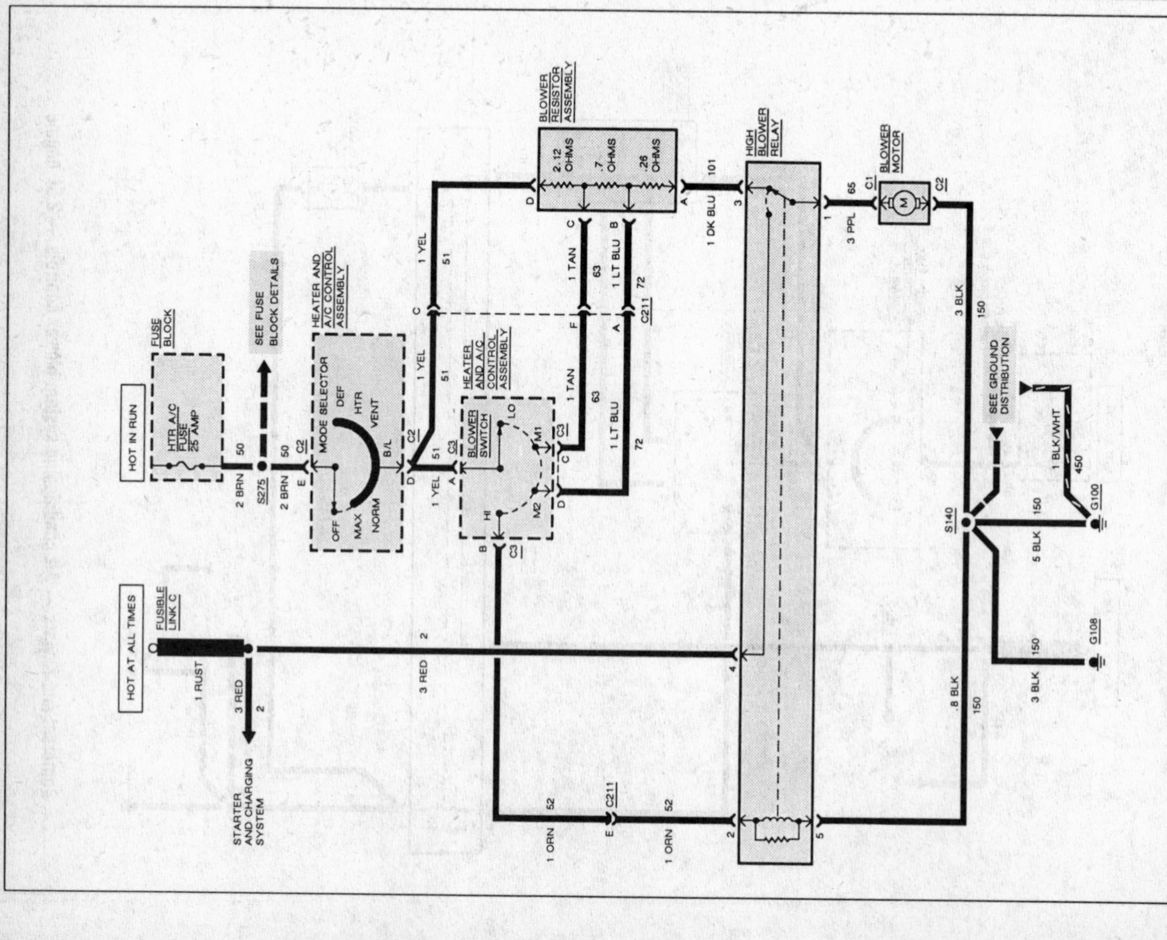

Somerset and Skylark — Air conditioning system — blower controls — 2.3L engine

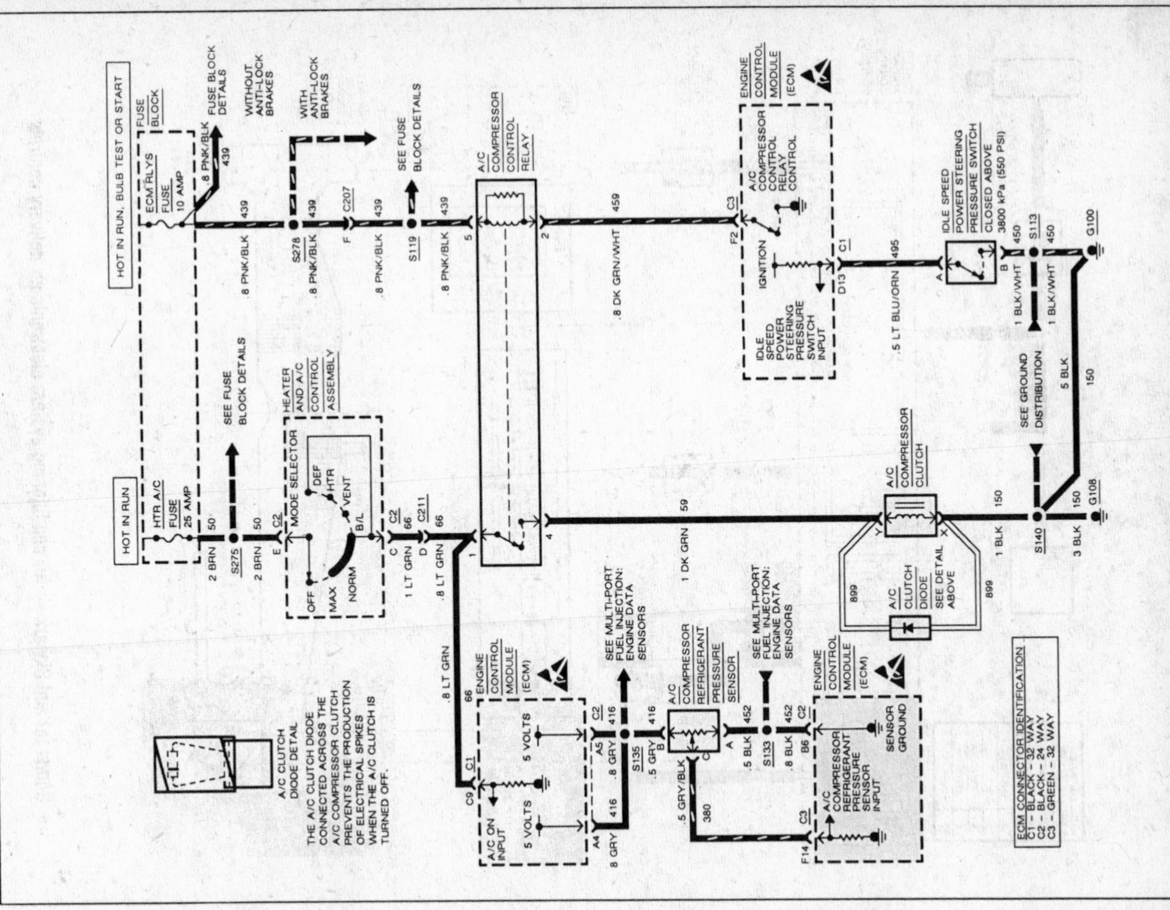

Somerset and Skylark — Air conditioning system compressor controls — 2.3L engine

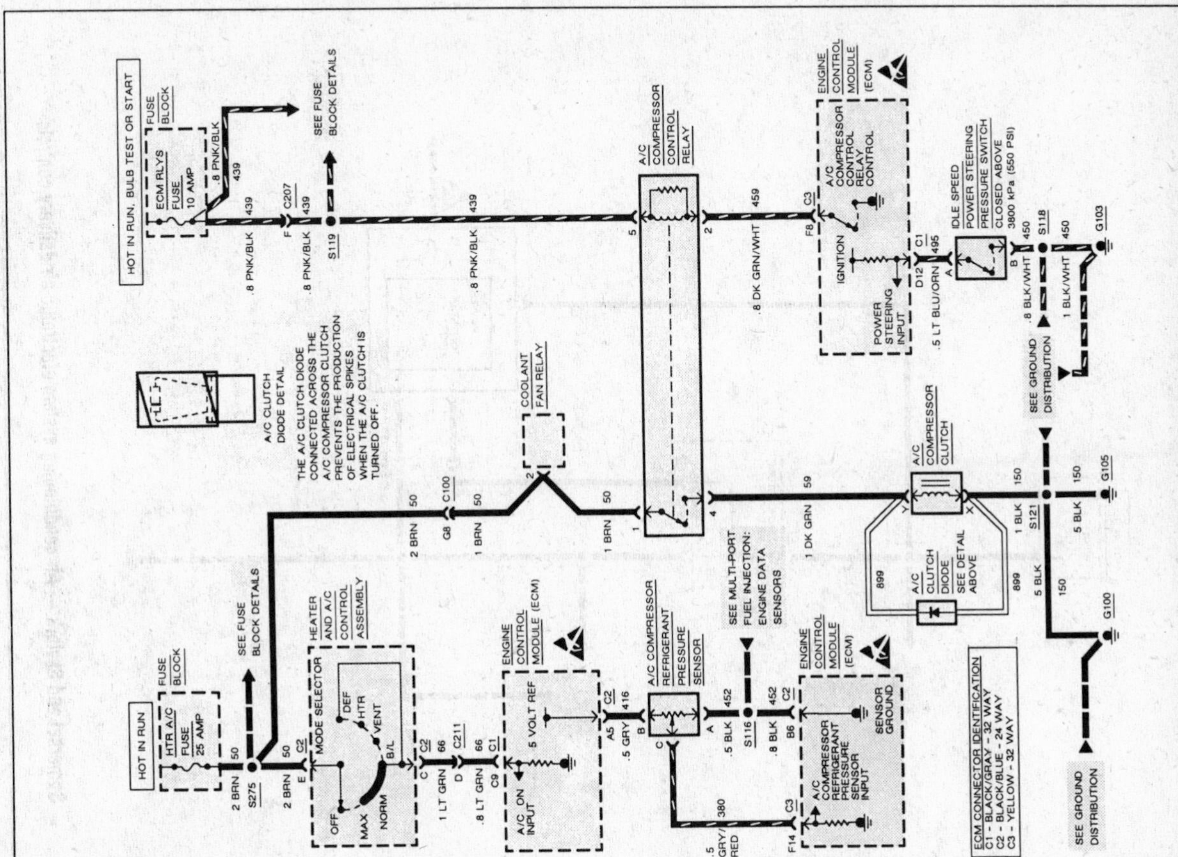

Somerset and Skylark — Air conditioning system electronic compressor controls — 3.3L engine

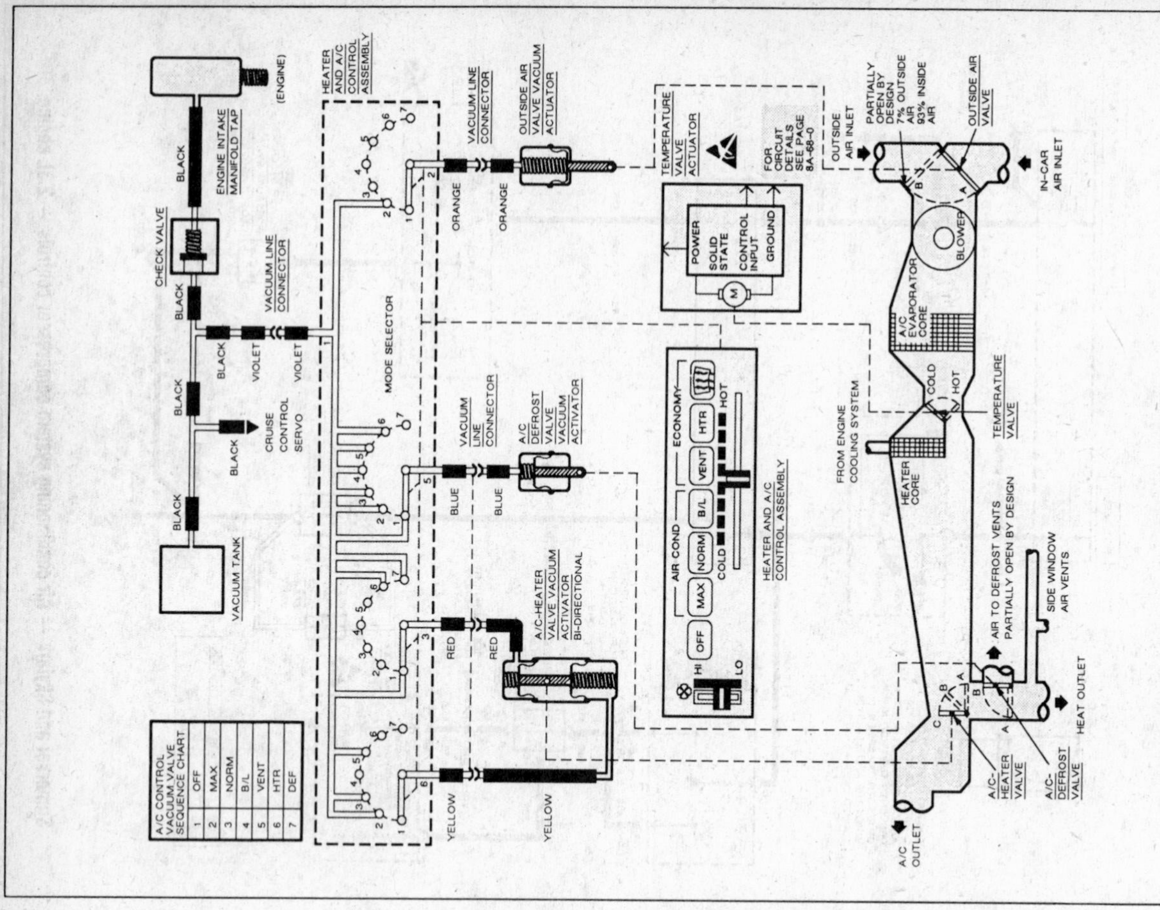

Somerset and Skylark — Air conditioning system electronic air delivery controls

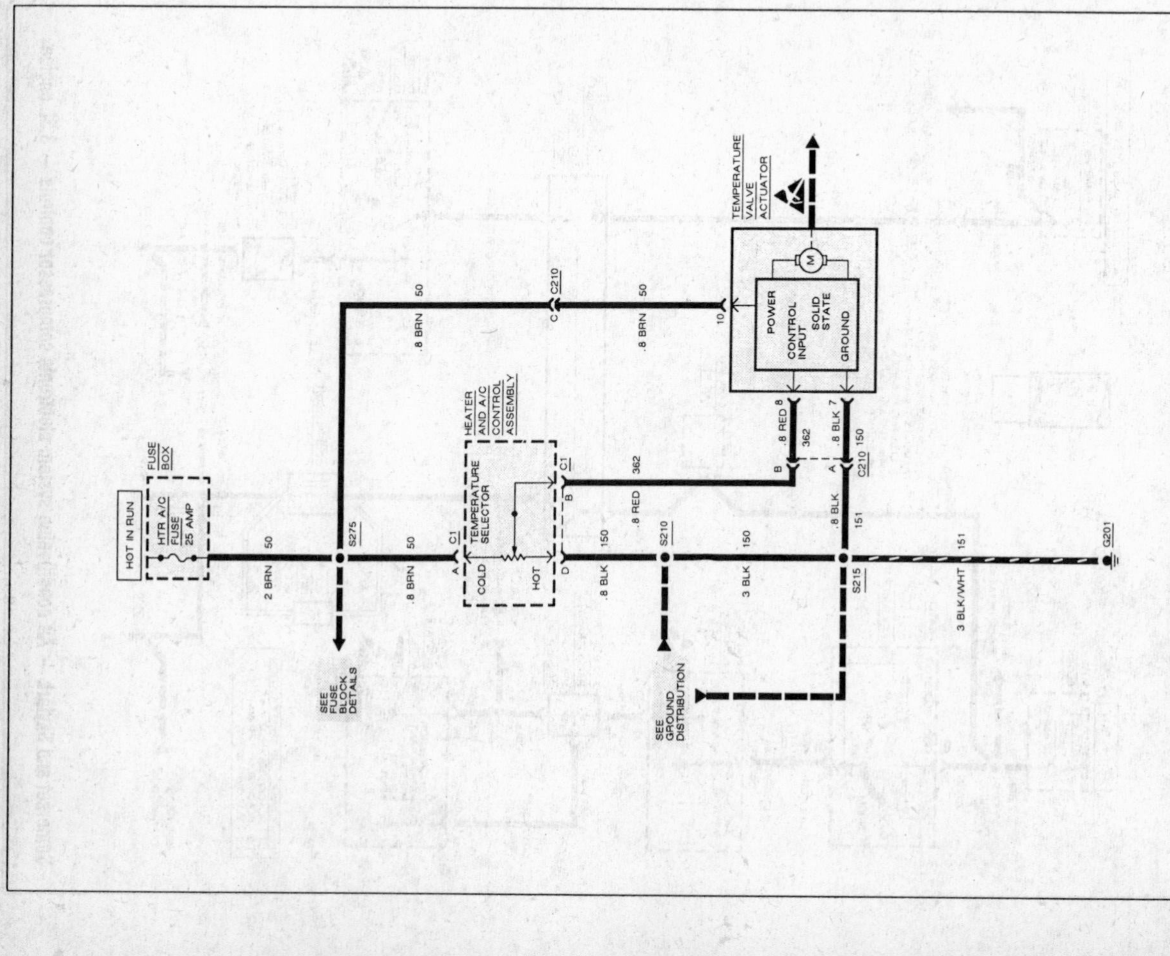

A/C CONTROL VACUUM VALVE SEQUENCE CHART

1	OFF
2	MAX
3	NORM
4	B/L
5	VENT
6	HTR
7	DEF

Somerset and Skylark — Air conditioning system electronic air delivery controls

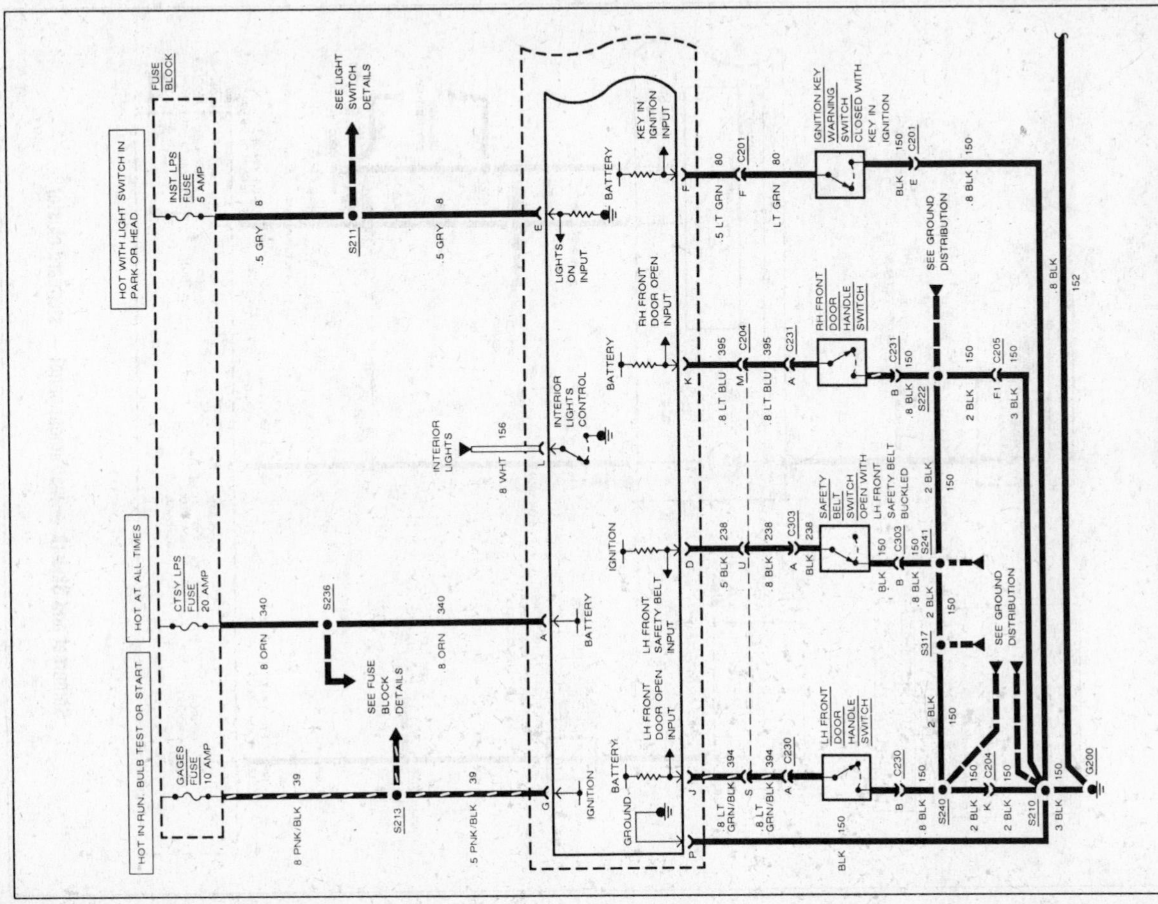

HOT IN RUN, BULB TEST OR START
HOT AT ALL TIMES
HOT WITH LIGHT SWITCH IN PARK OR HEAD
GAGES FUSE 10 AMP
CTSY LPS FUSE 20 AMP
INST LPS FUSE 5 AMP
FUSE BLOCK
8 PNK/BLK 39
8 ORN 340
.5 GRY 8
S236
SEE FUSE BLOCK DETAILS
S213
S211
SEE LIGHT SWITCH DETAILS
.5 PNK/BLK 39
.8 ORN 340
.5 GRY 8
INTERIOR LIGHTS
8 WHT 156
G A L E
IGNITION
BATTERY
INTERIOR LIGHTS CONTROL
LIGHTS ON INPUT
BATTERY
GROUND
LH FRONT DOOR OPEN INPUT
IGNITION
LH FRONT SAFETY BELT INPUT
BATTERY
RH FRONT DOOR OPEN INPUT
BATTERY
KEY IN IGNITION INPUT
P J D K F
.8 LT GRN/BLK 394
S
.8 LT GRN/BLK 394
A C230
.5 BLK 238
U
.8 BLK 238
A C303
BLK 238
.8 LT BLU 395
M C204
.8 LT BLU 395
A C231
.5 LT GRN 80
F C201
LT GRN 80
LH FRONT DOOR HANDLE SWITCH
SAFETY BELT SWITCH OPEN WITH LH FRONT SAFETY BELT BUCKLED
RH FRONT DOOR HANDLE SWITCH
IGNITION KEY WARNING SWITCH CLOSED WITH KEY IN IGNITION
BLK 150
B C230
.8 BLK 150
S240
2 BLK 150
S317
2 BLK 150
BLK 150
B C303
.8 BLK 150
S241
2 BLK 150
B C231
.8 BLK 150
S222
SEE GROUND DISTRIBUTION
BLK 150
E C201
2 BLK 150
K C204
2 BLK 150
SEE GROUND DISTRIBUTION
2 BLK 150
F1 C205
3 BLK 150
.8 BLK 150
S210
3 BLK 150
.8 BLK 152
G200

Somerset and Skylark – Warnings and alarms – chime

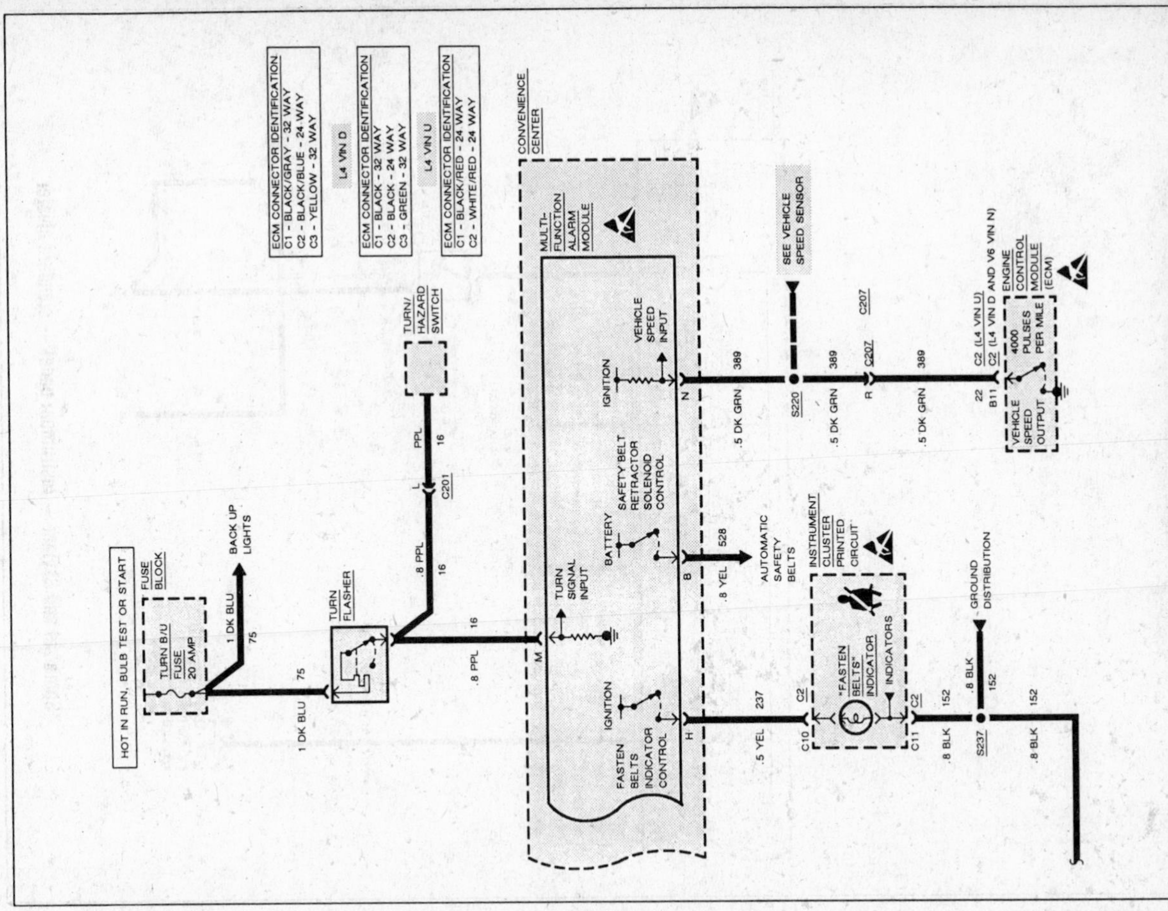

HOT IN RUN, BULB TEST OR START
TURN B/U FUSE 20 AMP
FUSE BLOCK
1 DK BLU 75
BACK UP LIGHTS
1 DK BLU 75
TURN FLASHER
.8 PPL 16
L
PPL 16
C201
TURN/ HAZARD SWITCH
.8 PPL 16

ECM CONNECTOR IDENTIFICATION
C1 - BLACK/GRAY - 32 WAY
C2 - BLACK/BLUE - 24 WAY
C3 - YELLOW - 32 WAY

L4 VIN D

ECM CONNECTOR IDENTIFICATION
C1 - BLACK - 32 WAY
C2 - BLACK - 24 WAY
C3 - GREEN - 32 WAY

L4 VIN U

ECM CONNECTOR IDENTIFICATION
C1 - BLACK/RED - 24 WAY
C2 - WHITE/RED - 24 WAY

CONVENIENCE CENTER
M
TURN SIGNAL INPUT
MULTI-FUNCTION ALARM MODULE
IGNITION
FASTEN BELTS INDICATOR CONTROL
BATTERY
SAFETY BELT RETRACTOR SOLENOID CONTROL
IGNITION
VEHICLE SPEED INPUT
H B N
.8 YEL 528
AUTOMATIC SAFETY BELTS
.5 YEL 237
.5 DK GRN 389
C10 C2
INSTRUMENT CLUSTER PRINTED CIRCUIT
"FASTEN BELTS" INDICATOR
INDICATORS
S220
SEE VEHICLE SPEED SENSOR
.5 DK GRN 389
R C207
C207
C11 C2
.5 DK GRN 389
.8 BLK 152
S237
.8 BLK 152
GROUND DISTRIBUTION
.8 BLK 152
22 C2 (L4 VIN U)
B11 C2 (L4 VIN D AND V6 VIN N)
VEHICLE SPEED OUTPUT
4000 PULSES PER MILE
ENGINE CONTROL MODULE (ECM)

Somerset and Skylark – Warnings and alarms – chime

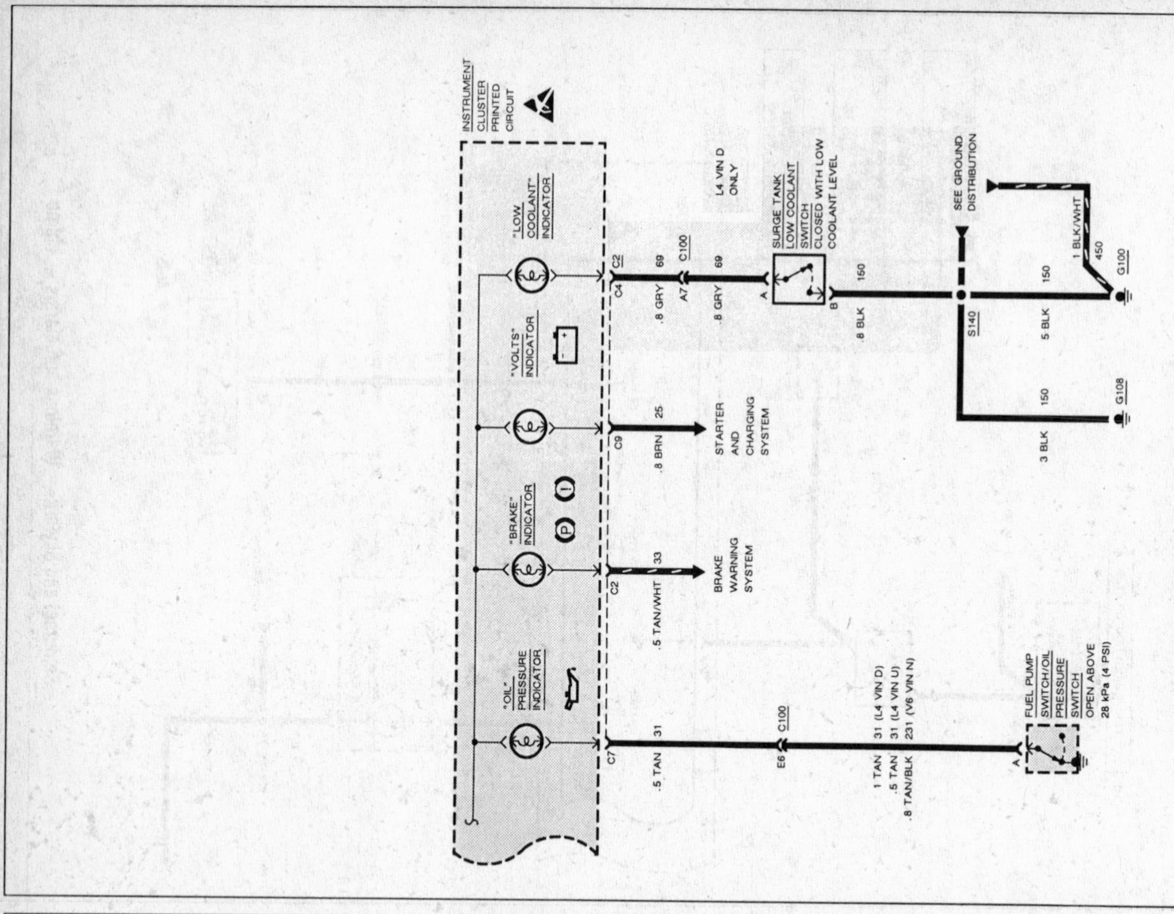

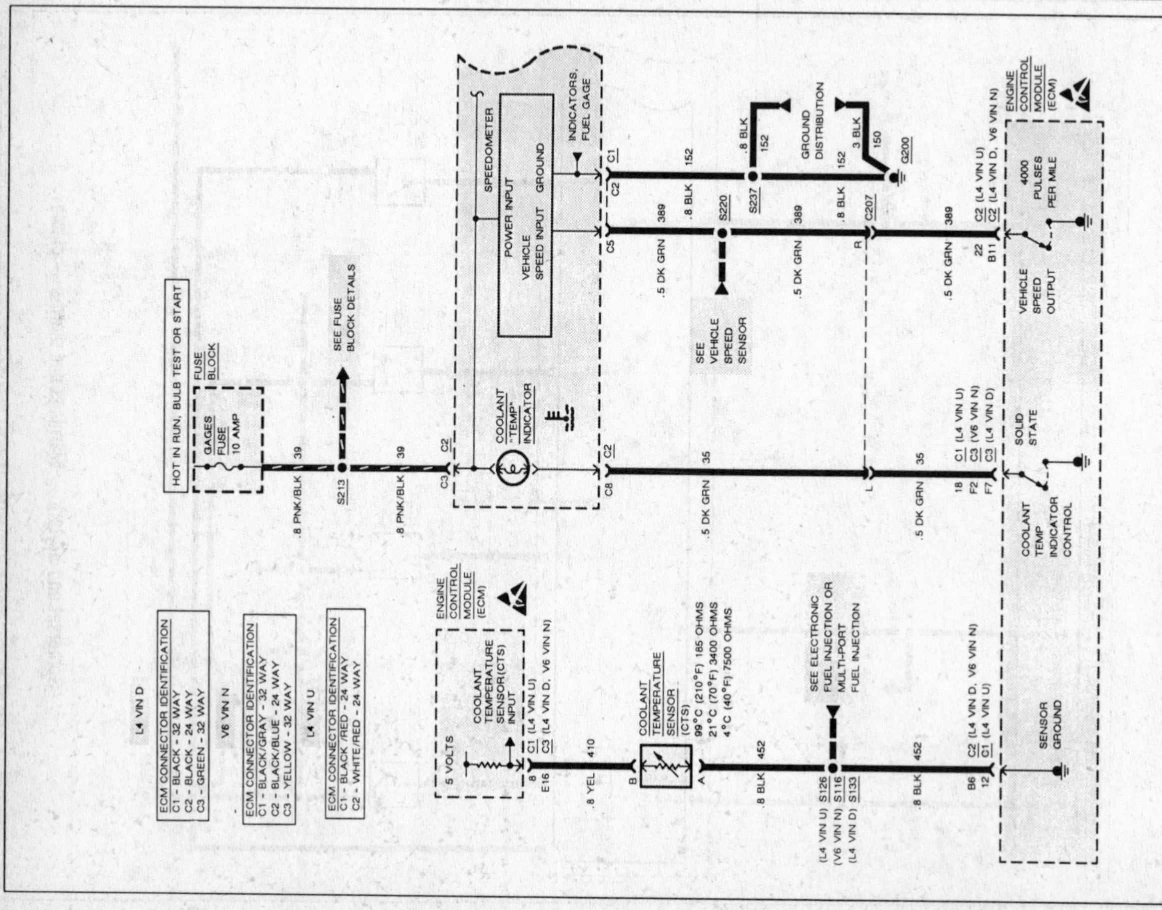

L4 VIN D

ECM CONNECTOR IDENTIFICATION
C1 - BLACK - 32 WAY
C2 - BLACK - 24 WAY
C3 - GREEN - 32 WAY

V6 VIN N

ECM CONNECTOR IDENTIFICATION
C1 - BLACK/GRAY - 32 WAY
C2 - BLACK/BLUE - 24 WAY
C3 - YELLOW - 32 WAY

L4 VIN U

ECM CONNECTOR IDENTIFICATION
C1 - BLACK /RED - 24 WAY
C2 - WHITE/RED - 24 WAY

HOT IN RUN, BULB TEST OR START
GAGES FUSE 10 AMP
FUSE BLOCK
.8 PNK/BLK 39
S213
SEE FUSE BLOCK DETAILS
.8 PNK/BLK 39
C3 C2

5 VOLTS
COOLANT TEMPERATURE SENSOR(CTS) INPUT
ENGINE CONTROL MODULE (ECM)
8 C1 (L4 VIN U)
E16 C3 (L4 VIN D, V6 VIN N)
.8 YEL 410
B
COOLANT TEMPERATURE SENSOR (CTS)
99°C (210°F) 185 OHMS
21°C (70°F) 3400 OHMS
4°C (40°F) 7500 OHMS
A
.8 BLK 452
(L4 VIN U) S126
(V6 VIN N) S116
(L4 VIN D) S133
SEE ELECTRONIC FUEL INJECTION OR MULTI-PORT FUEL INJECTION
.8 BLK 452
B6 C2 (L4 VIN D, V6 VIN N)
12 C1 (L4 VIN U)
SENSOR GROUND

COOLANT "TEMP" INDICATOR
SPEEDOMETER
POWER INPUT
VEHICLE SPEED INPUT
GROUND
INDICATORS, FUEL GAGE
C8 C2
.5 DK GRN 35
L
.5 DK GRN 35
18 C1 (L4 VIN U)
F2 C3 (V6 VIN N)
F7 C3 (L4 VIN D)
COOLANT TEMP INDICATOR CONTROL
SOLID STATE

C5
.5 DK GRN 389
SEE VEHICLE SPEED SENSOR
S220
.5 DK GRN 389
R
C207
.5 DK GRN 389
22 C2 (L4 VIN U)
B11 C2 (L4 VIN D, V6 VIN N)
VEHICLE SPEED OUTPUT
4000 PULSES PER MILE
ENGINE CONTROL MODULE (ECM)

C2 C1
.8 BLK 152
S237
.8 BLK 152
GROUND DISTRIBUTION
.8 BLK 152
3 BLK 150
G200

Somerset and Skylark — Instrument panel — standard cluster

INSTRUMENT CLUSTER PRINTED CIRCUIT
"OIL" PRESSURE INDICATOR
"BRAKE" INDICATOR
"VOLTS" INDICATOR
"LOW COOLANT" INDICATOR

C7
.5 TAN 31
E6 C100
1 TAN 31 (L4 VIN D)
.5 TAN 31 (L4 VIN U)
.8 TAN/BLK 231 (V6 VIN N)
A
FUEL PUMP SWITCH/OIL PRESSURE SWITCH
OPEN ABOVE 28 kPa (4 PSI)

C2
.5 TAN/WHT 33
BRAKE WARNING SYSTEM

C9
.8 BRN 25
STARTER AND CHARGING SYSTEM

C4 C2
.8 GRY 69
A7 C100
.8 GRY 69
L4 VIN D ONLY
A
SURGE TANK LOW COOLANT SWITCH
CLOSED WITH LOW COOLANT LEVEL
B
.8 BLK 150
S140
SEE GROUND DISTRIBUTION
3 BLK 150
G108
5 BLK 150
1 BLK/WHT 450
G100

Somerset and Skylark — Instrument panel — standard cluster

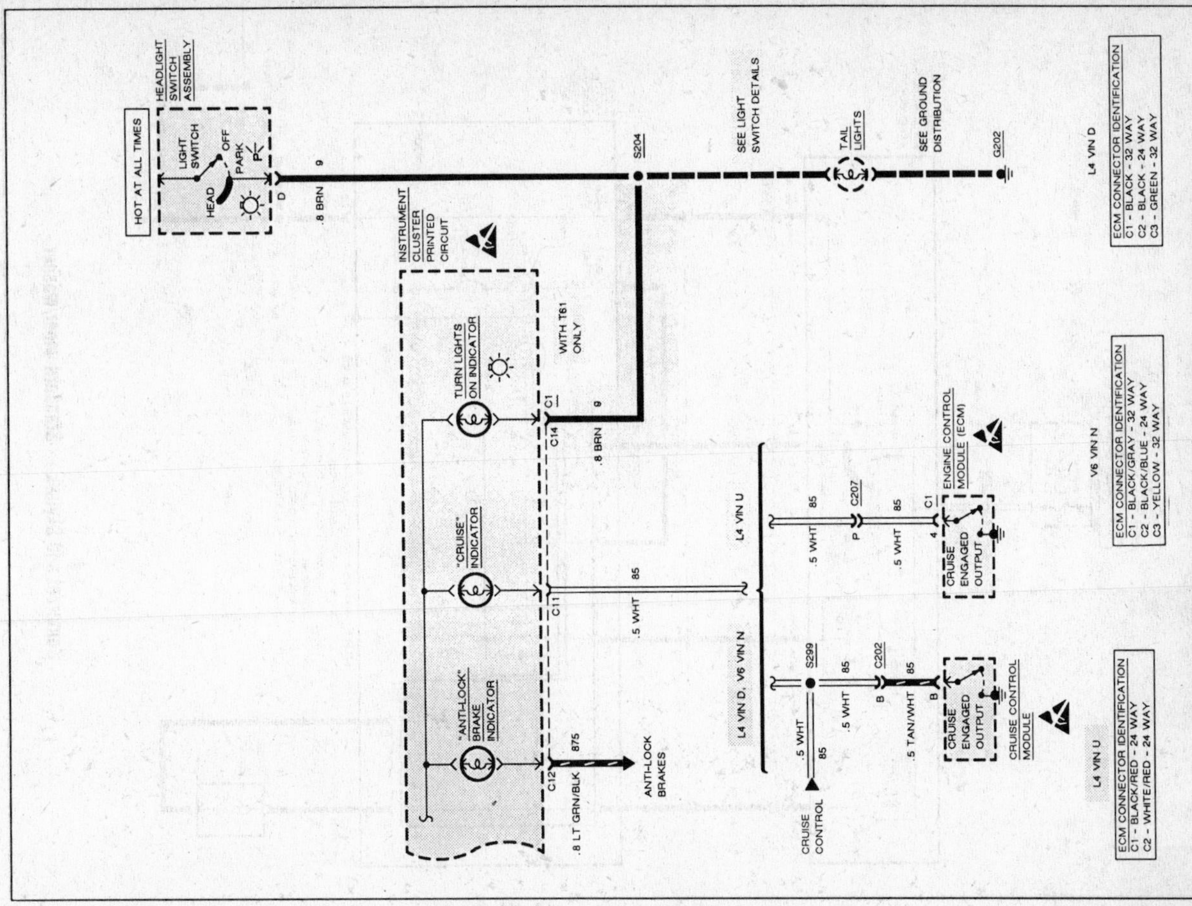

Somerset and Skylark — Instrument panel — standard cluster

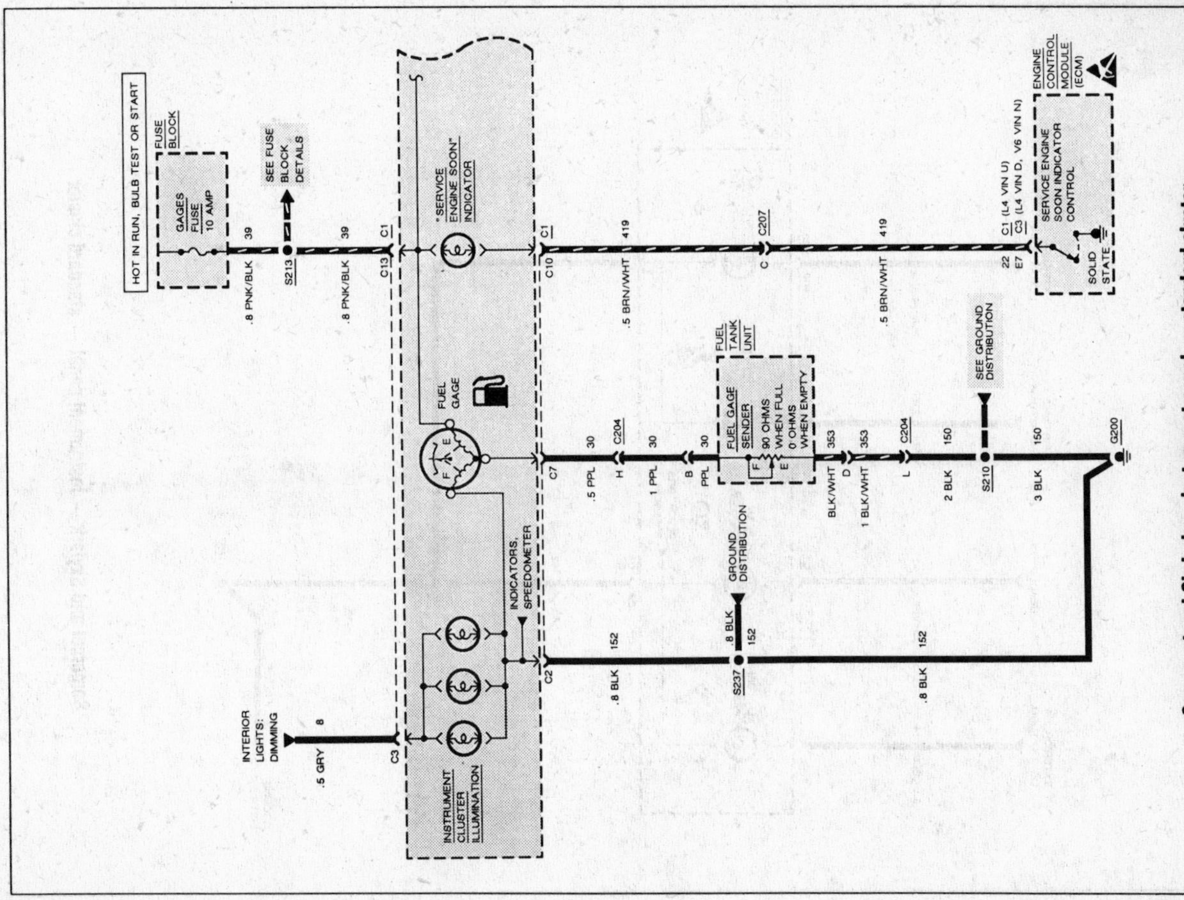

Somerset and Skylark — Instrument panel — standard cluster

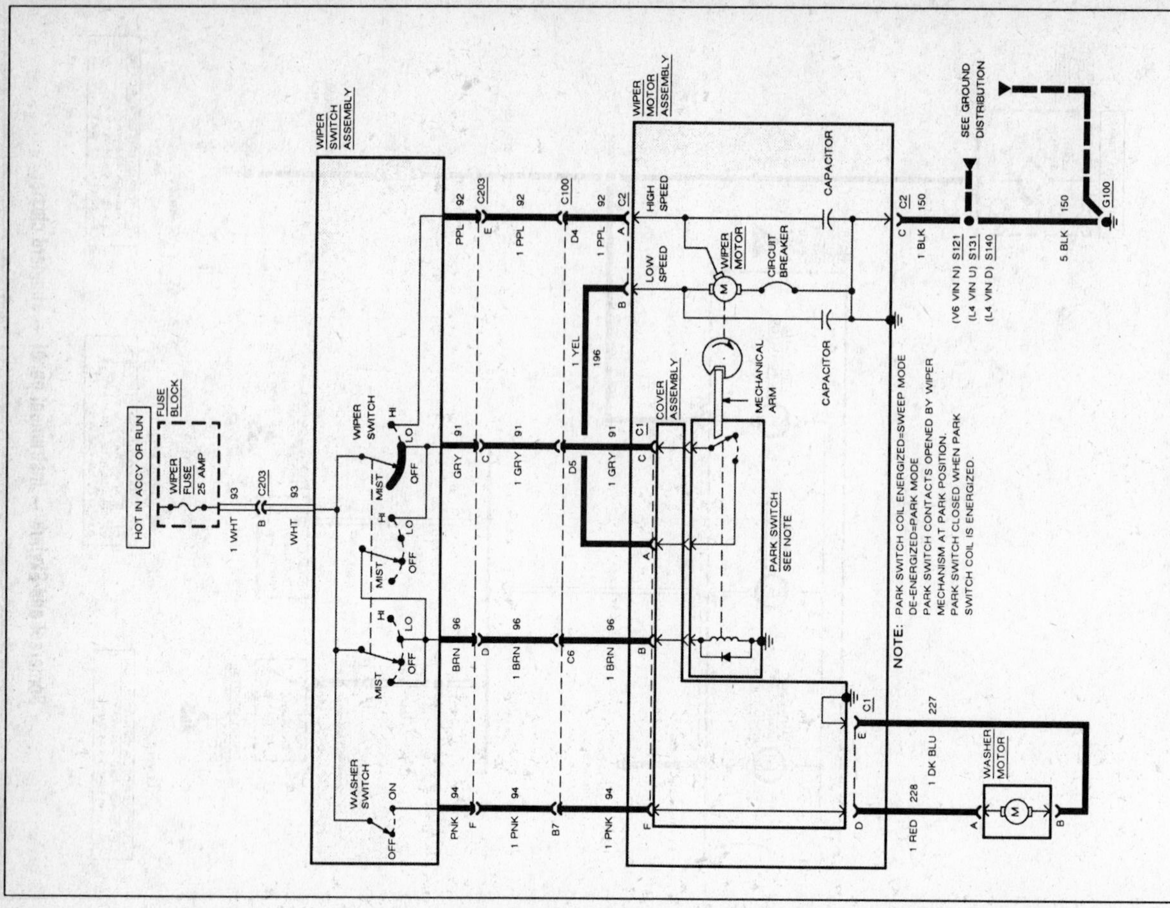

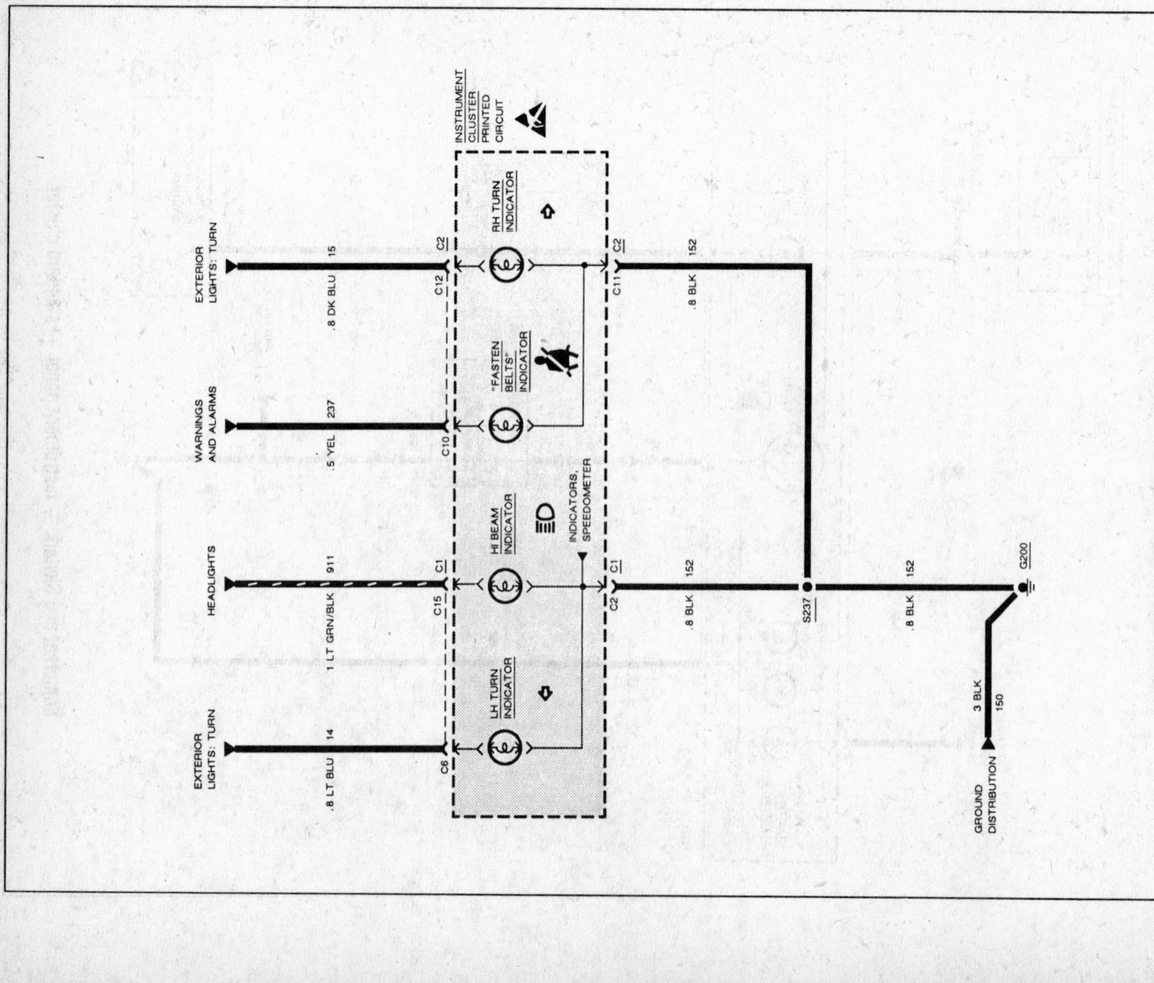

Somerset and Skylark — Instrument panel — standard cluster

NOTE: PARK SWITCH COIL ENERGIZED=SWEEP MODE
DE-ENERGIZED=PARK MODE
PARK SWITCH CONTACTS OPENED BY WIPER MECHANISM AT PARK POSITION.
PARK SWITCH CLOSED WHEN PARK SWITCH COIL IS ENERGIZED.

Somerset and Skylark — Standard wiper/washer

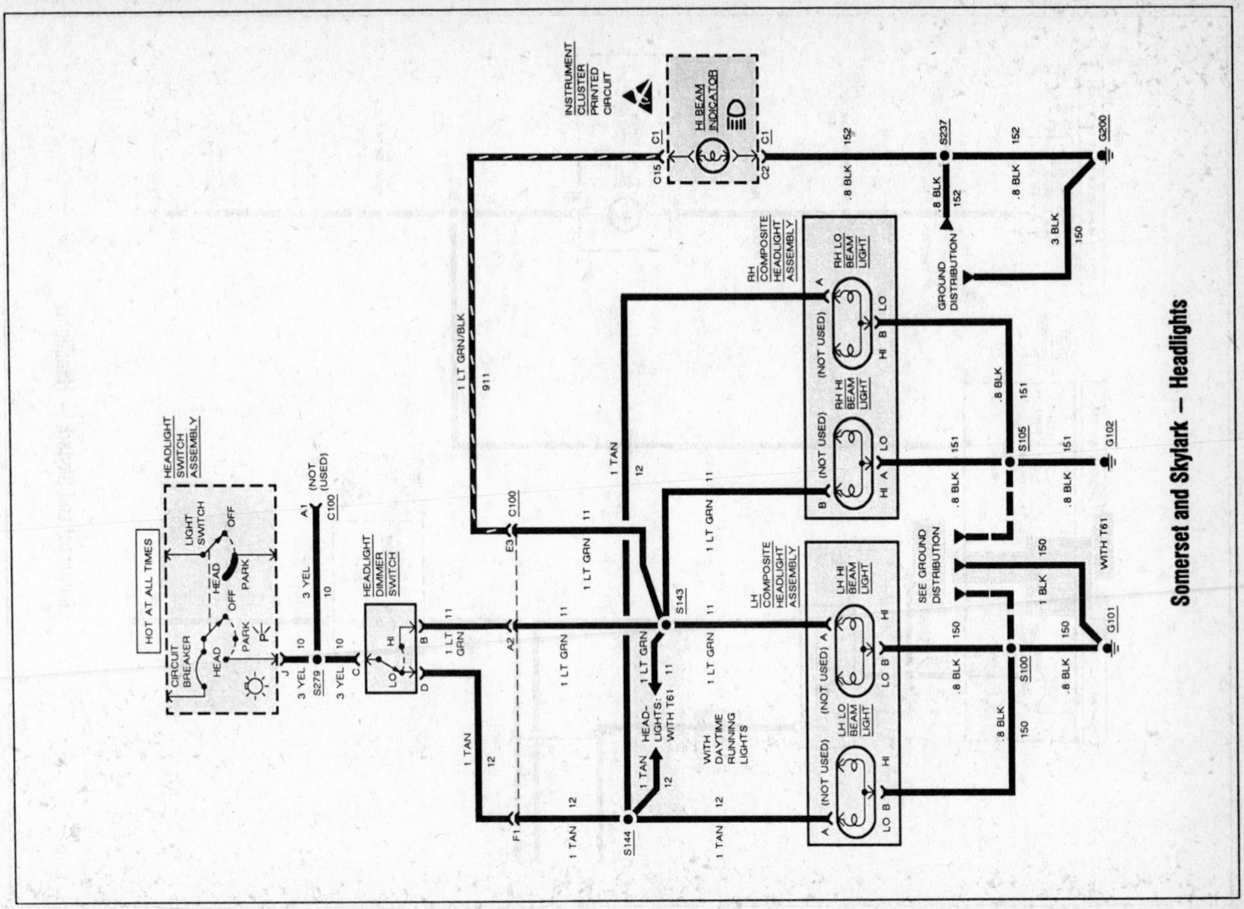

NOTE:
PARK SWITCH COIL ENERGIZED = SWEEP MODE
DE-ENERGIZED = PARK MODE
PARK SWITCH CONTACTS OPENED BY WIPER
MECHANISM AT PARK POSITION.
PARK SWITCH CLOSED WHEN PARK SWITCH COIL
IS ENERGIZED.

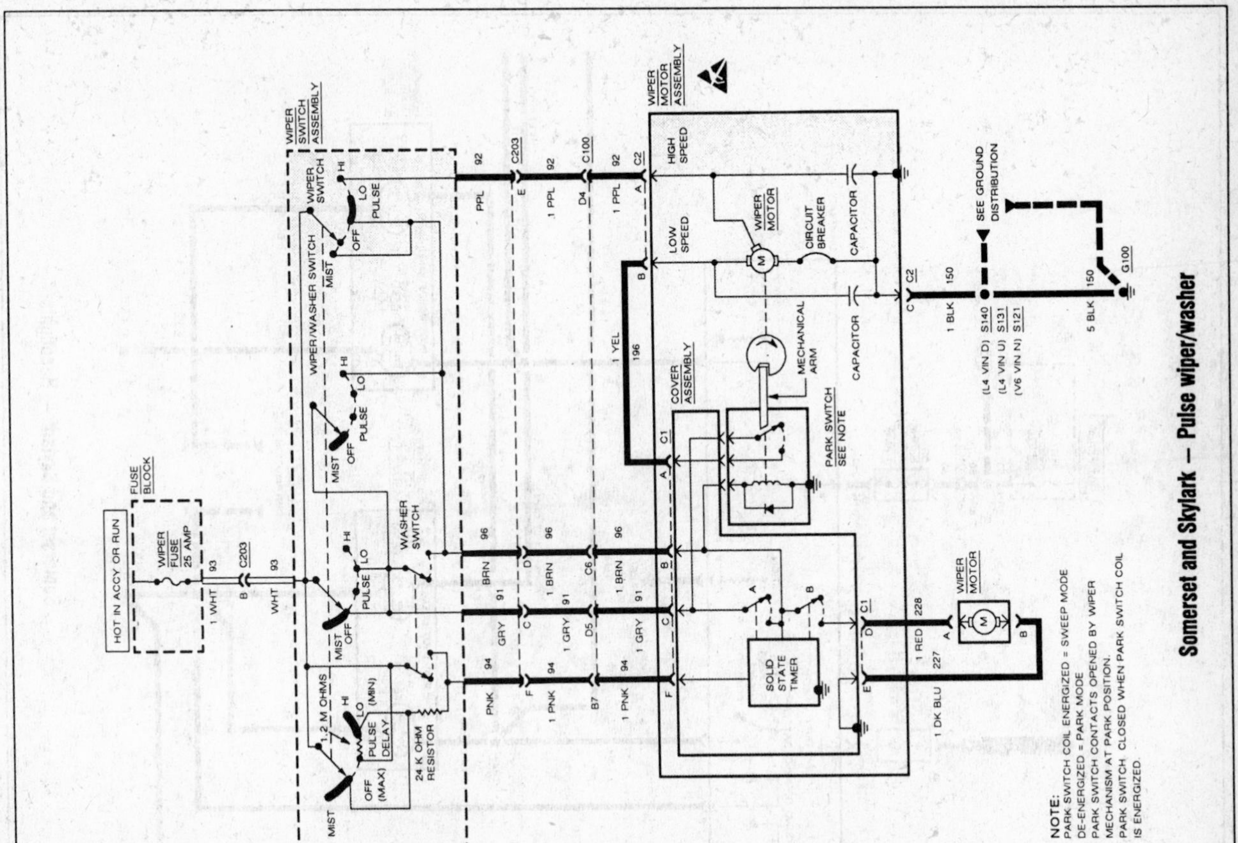

Somerset and Skylark — Pulse wiper/washer

Somerset and Skylark — Headlights

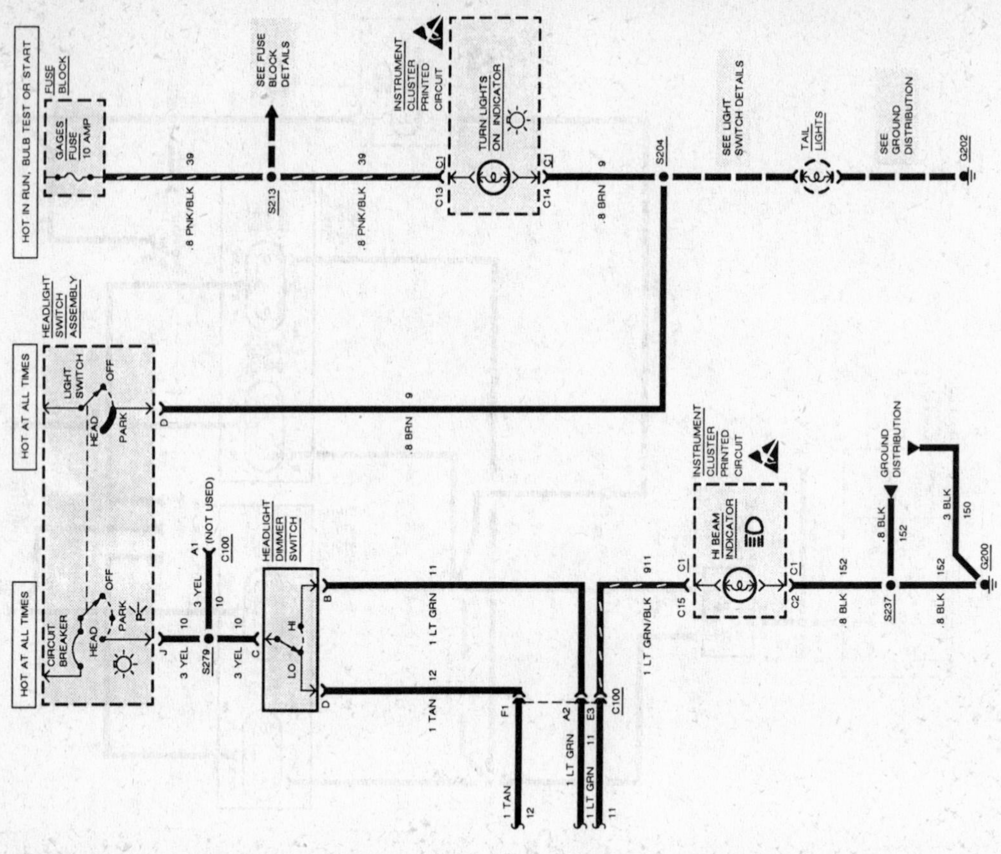

Somerset and Skylark — Headlights

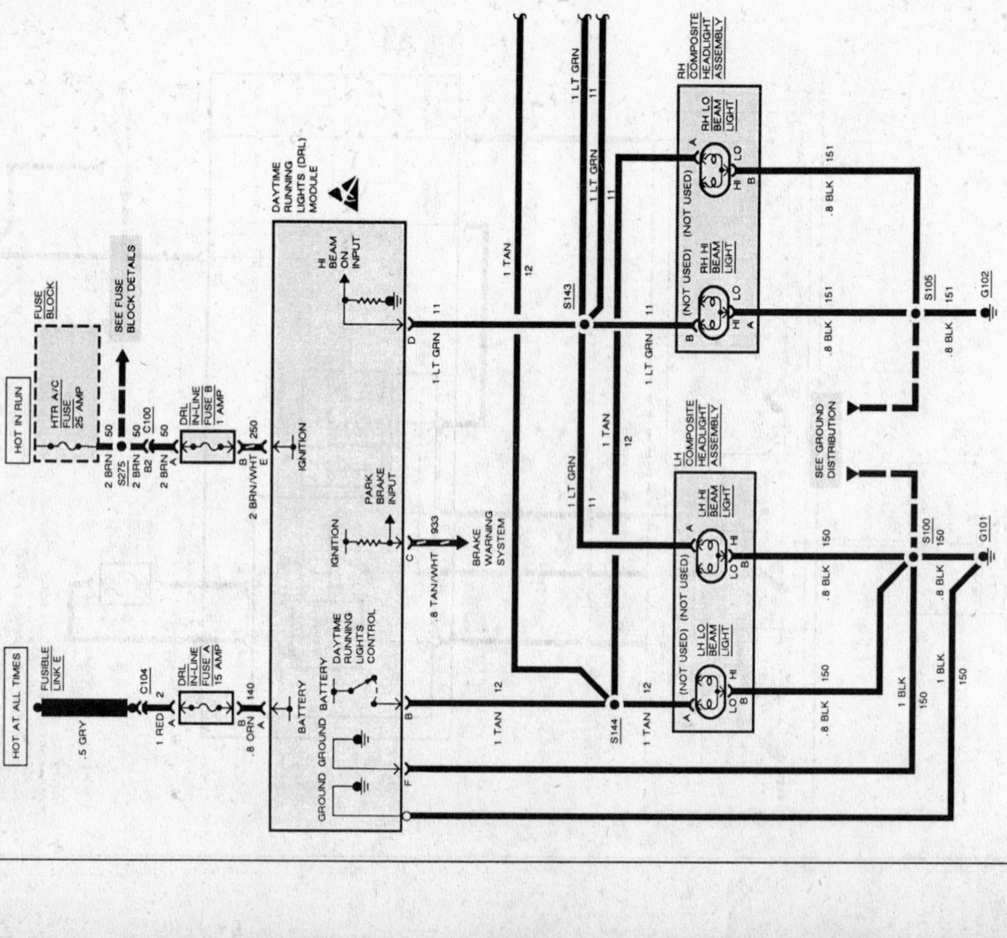

Somerset and Skylark — Headlights

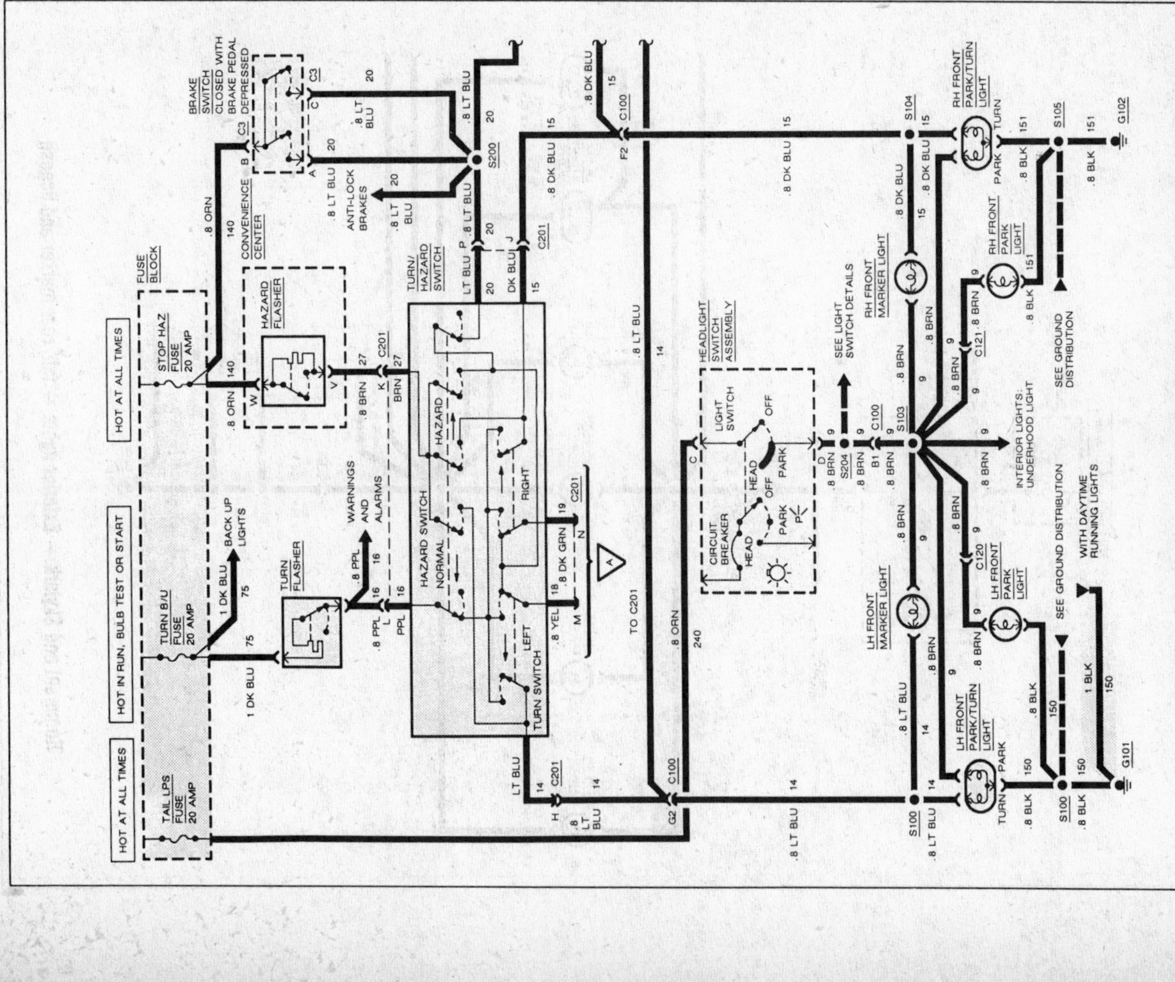

Somerset and Skylark – Exterior lights – hazard, front marker, park, turn and stop

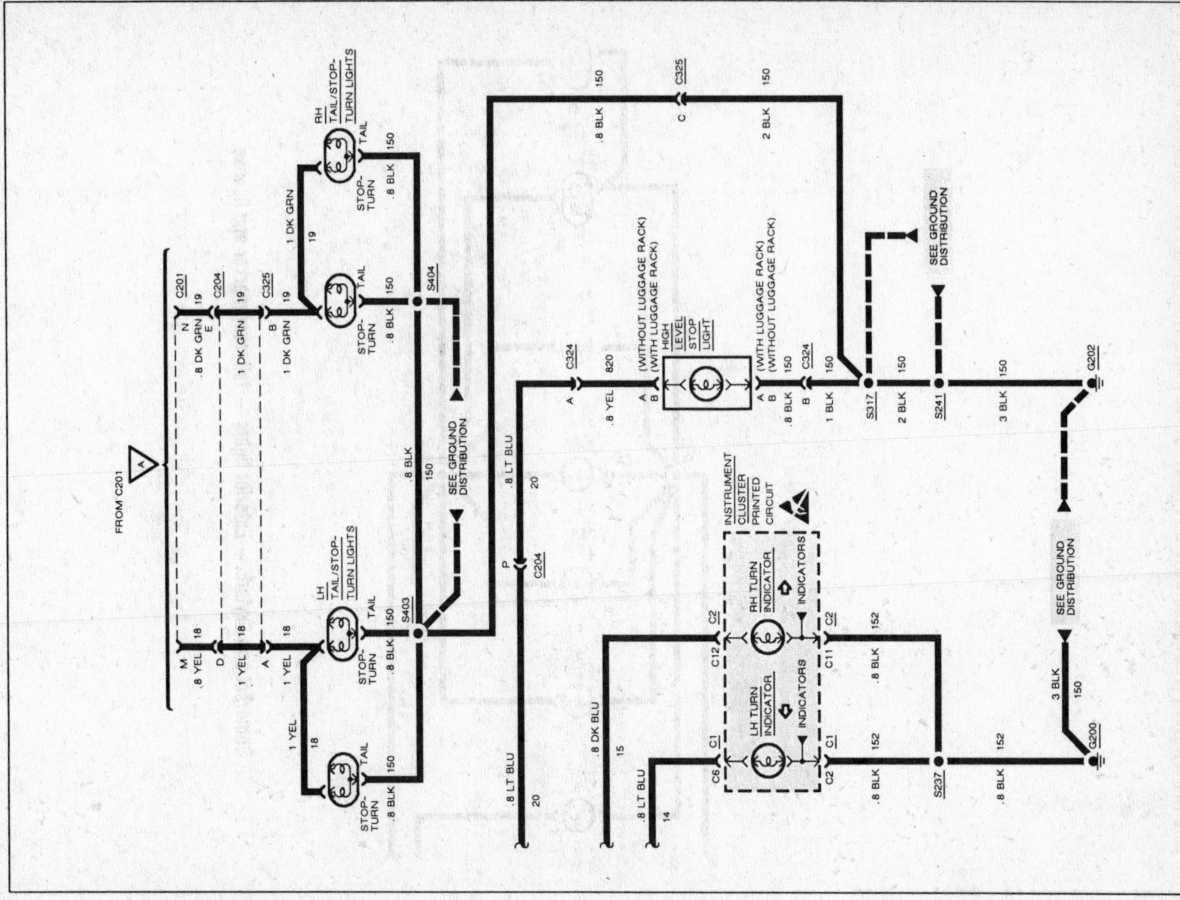

Somerset and Skylark – Exterior lights – hazard, front marker, park, turn and stop

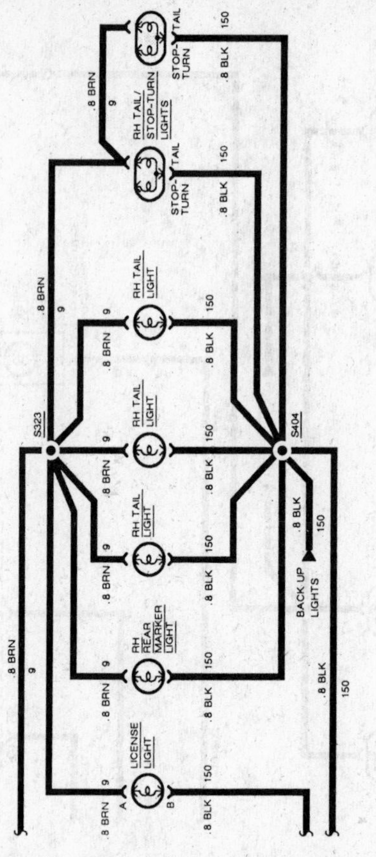

Somerset and Skylark — Exterior lights — tail, rear marker and license

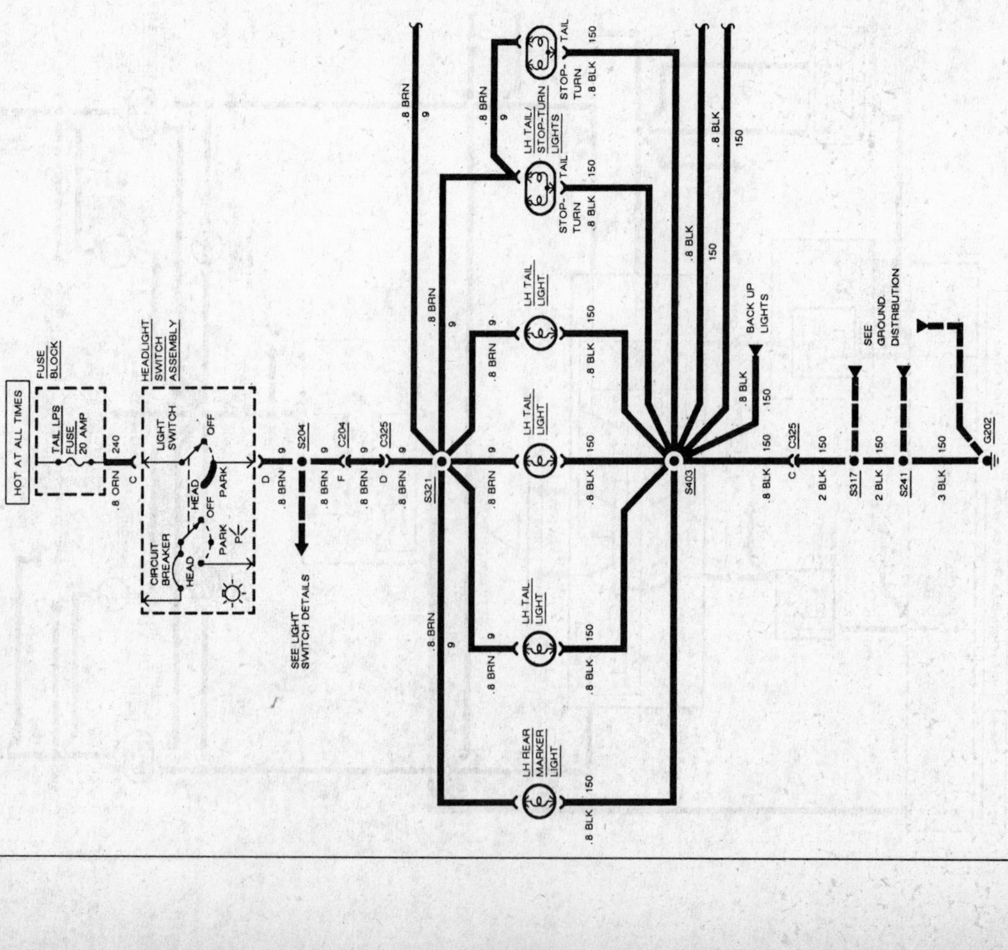

Somerset and Skylark — Exterior lights — tail, rear marker and license

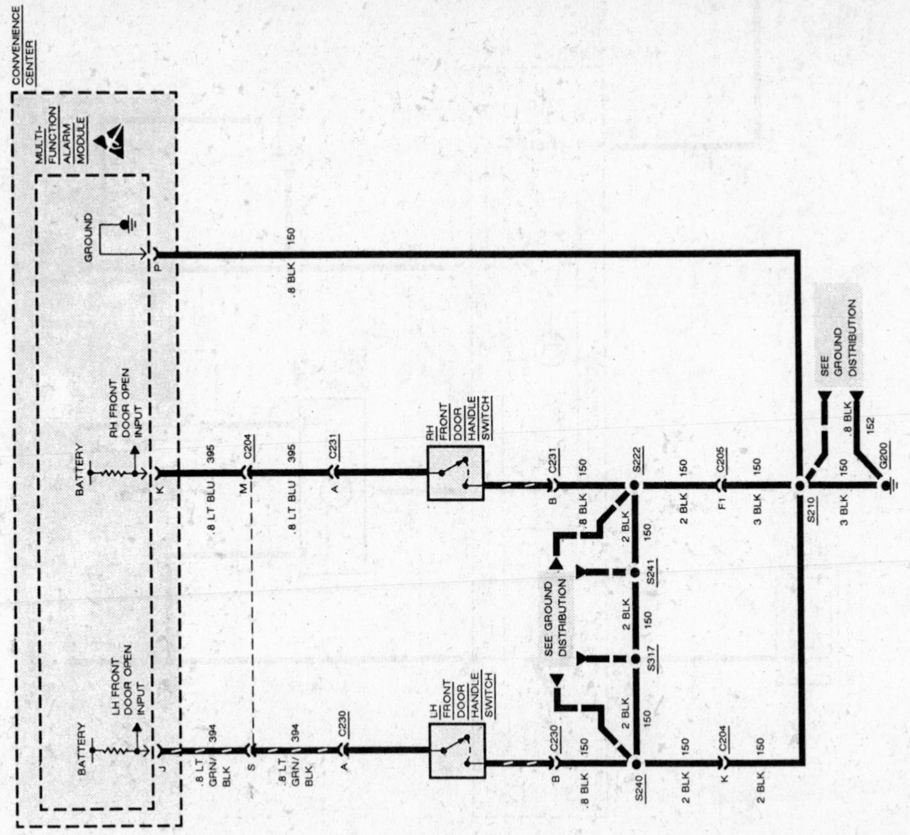

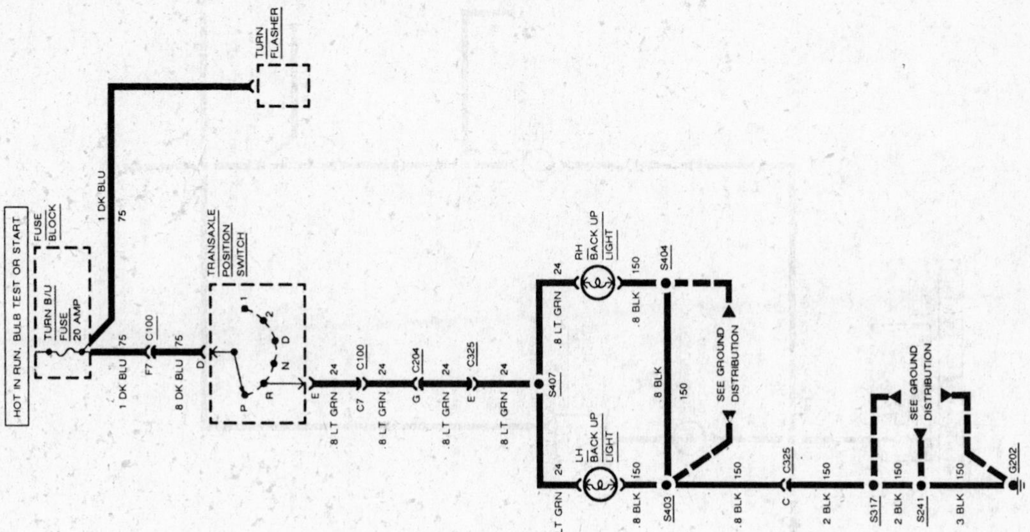

Somerset and Skylark — Back-up lights

Somerset and Skylark — Interior lights — illuminated entry

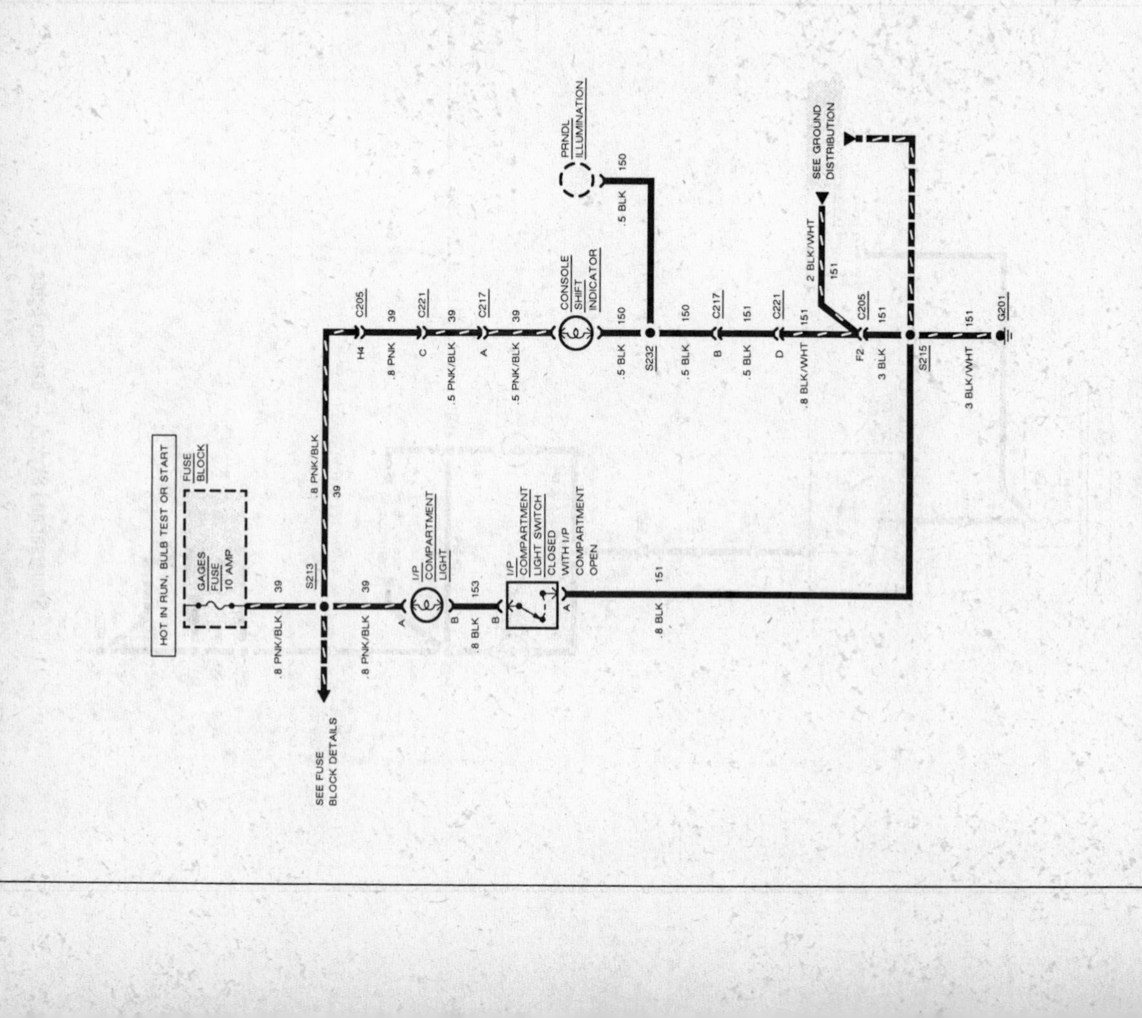

Somerset and Skylark — Interior lights — instrument panel compartment and console shift indicator

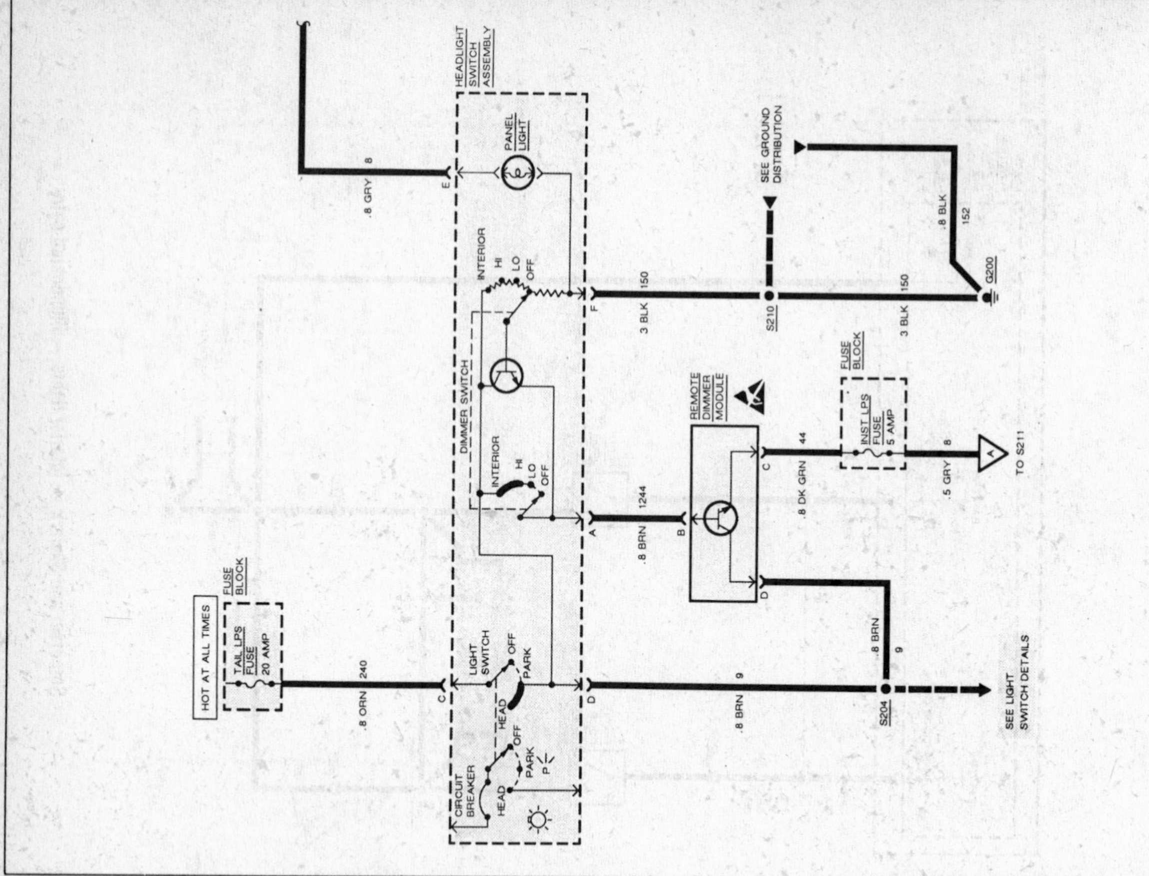

Somerset and Skylark — Interior lights dimming

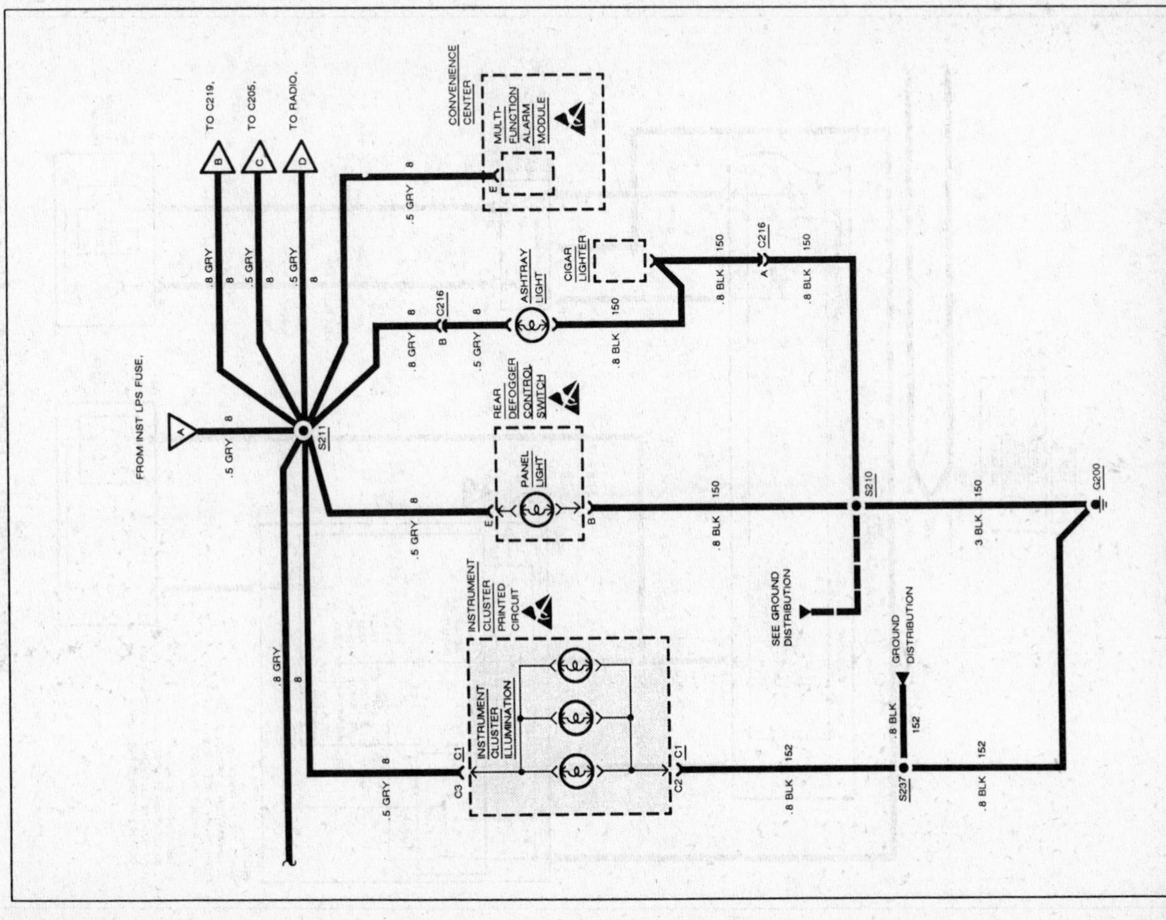

Somerset and Skylark — Interior lights dimming

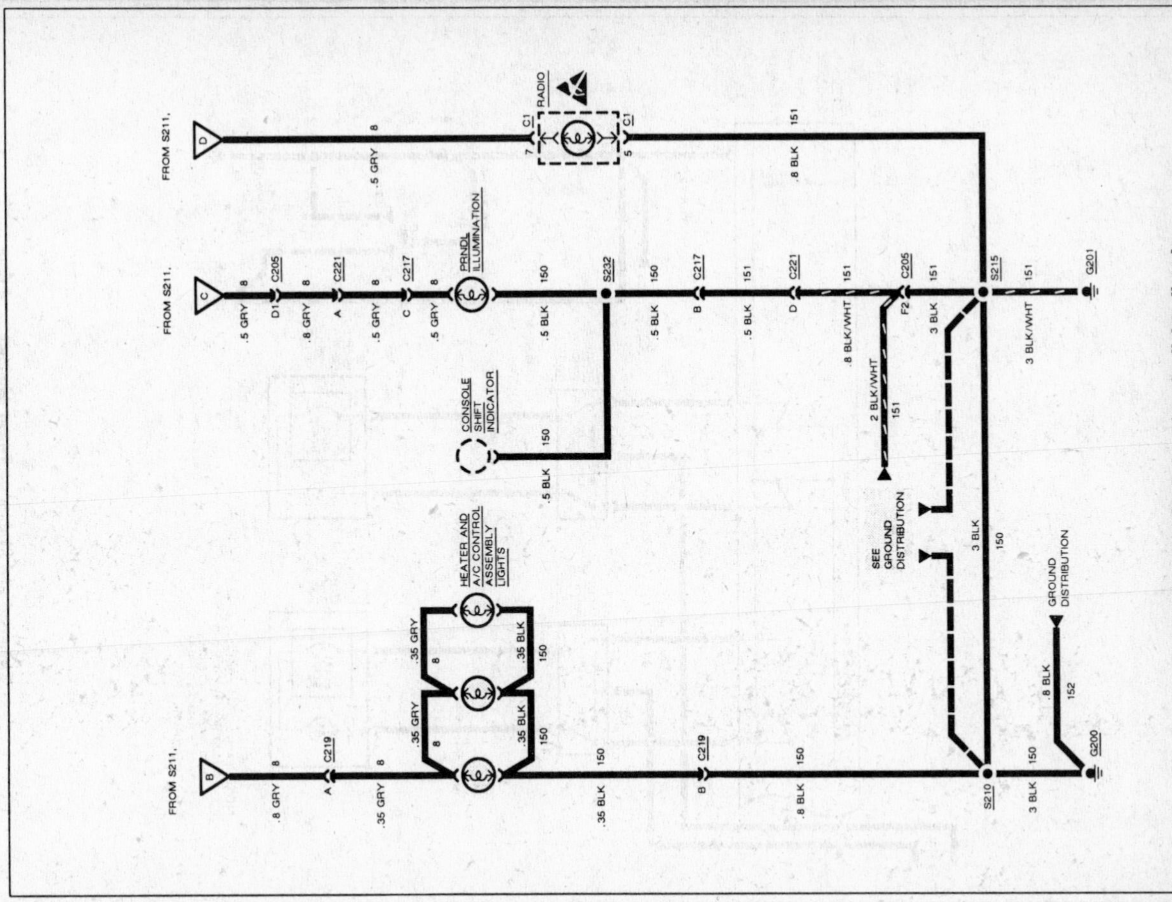

Somerset and Skylark — Interior lights dimming

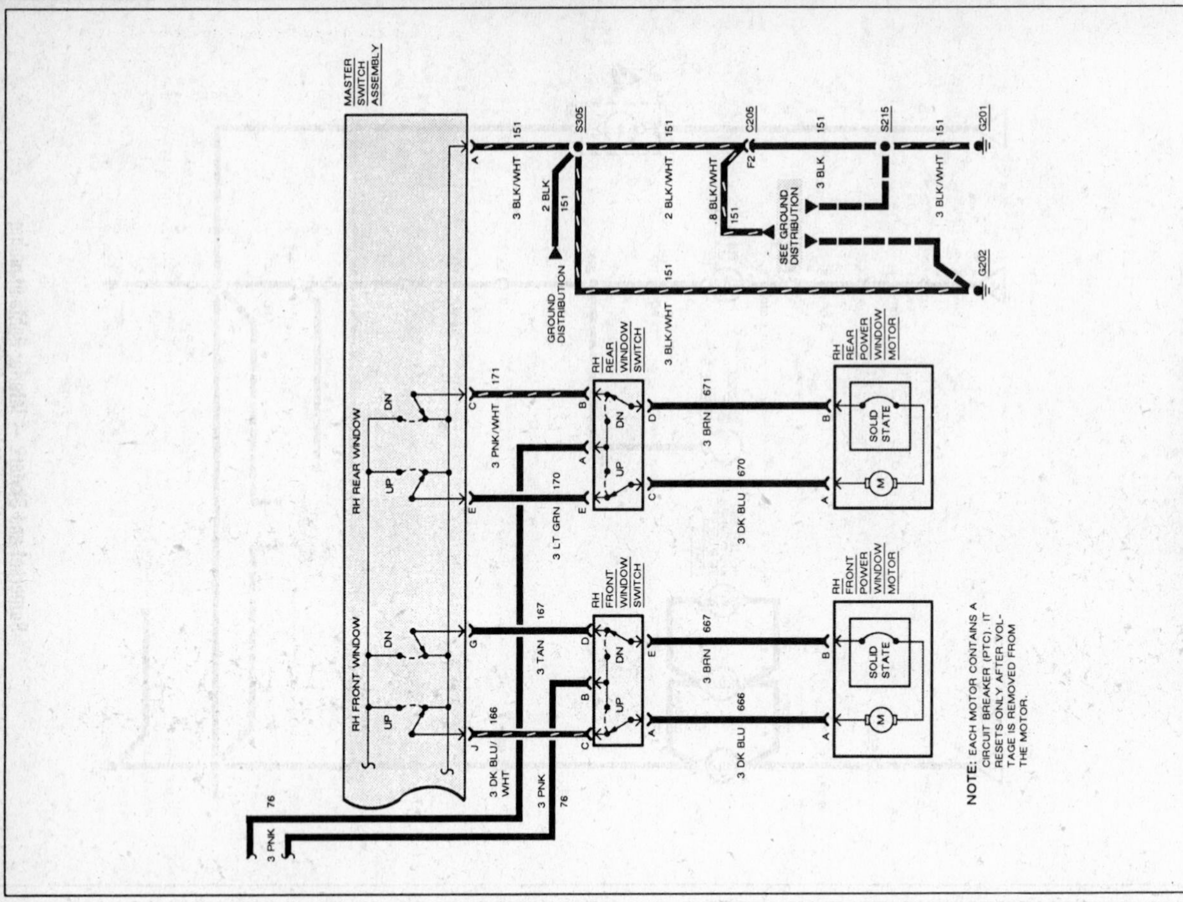

NOTE:
WHEN THE LH FRONT WINDOW DOWN SWITCH IS PRESSED FOR MORE THAN .3 SECONDS, THE RELAY WILL ENERGIZE AND WILL STAY SO UNTIL:
1) THE MOTOR STALLS,
2) 30 SECONDS ELAPSE, OR
3) EITHER THE LH FRONT WINDOW UP OR DOWN SWITCH IS PRESSED.

Somerset and Skylark – Power windows – 4 door

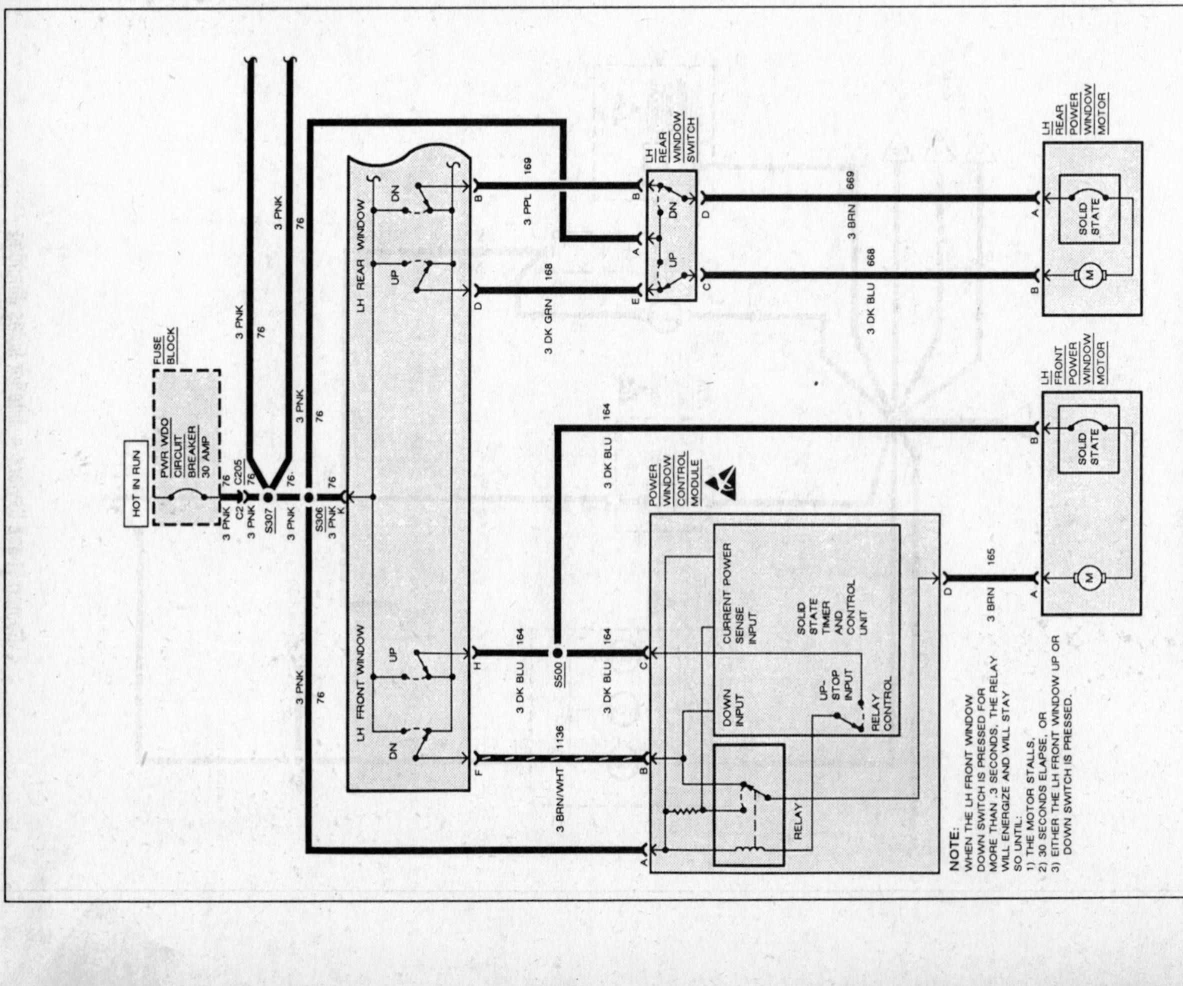

NOTE: EACH MOTOR CONTAINS A CIRCUIT BREAKER (PTC). IT RESETS ONLY AFTER VOLTAGE IS REMOVED FROM THE MOTOR.

Somerset and Skylark – Power windows – 4 door

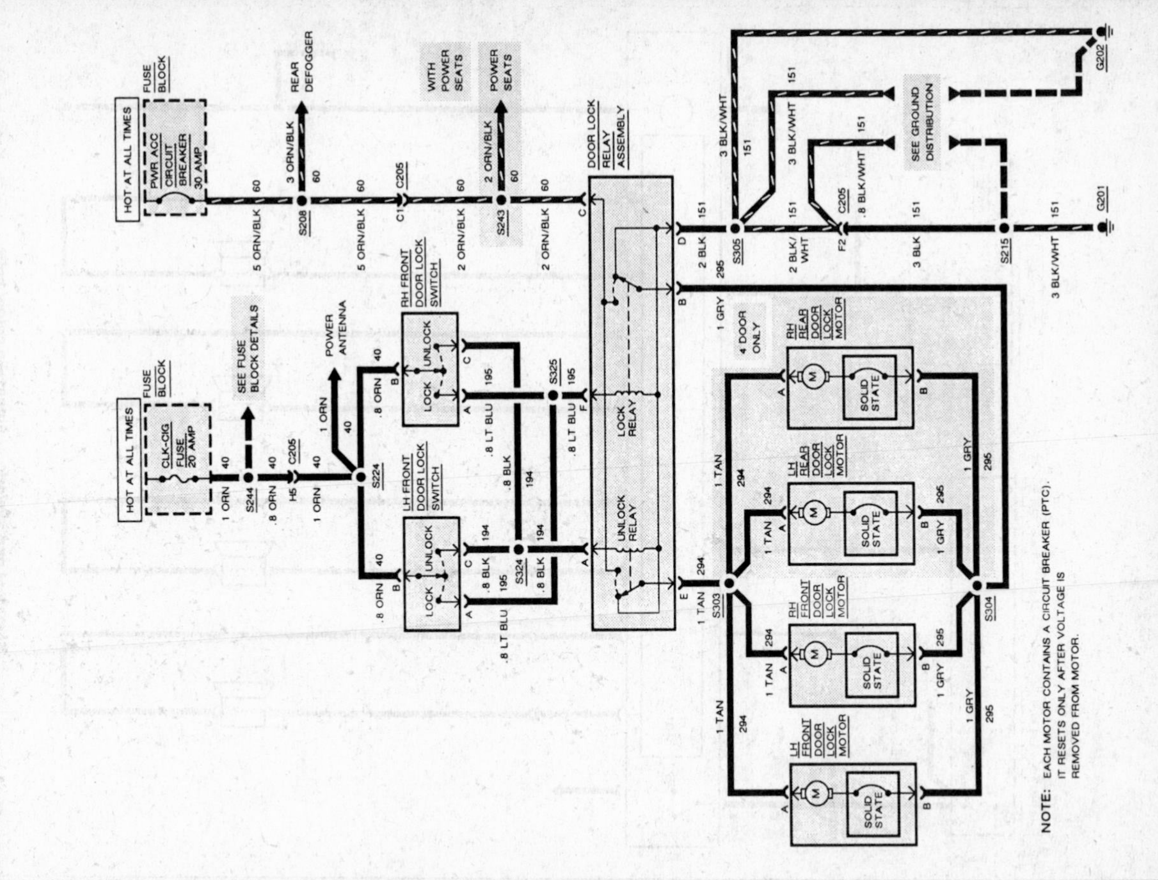
HOT AT ALL TIMES
CLK-CIG FUSE 20 AMP
FUSE BLOCK
SEE FUSE BLOCK DETAILS
POWER ANTENNA
HOT AT ALL TIMES
PWR ACC CIRCUIT BREAKER 30 AMP
FUSE BLOCK
REAR DEFOGGER
WITH POWER SEATS
POWER SEATS
LH FRONT DOOR LOCK SWITCH
RH FRONT DOOR LOCK SWITCH
DOOR LOCK RELAY ASSEMBLY
UNLOCK RELAY
LOCK RELAY
SEE GROUND DISTRIBUTION
4 DOOR ONLY
LH FRONT DOOR LOCK MOTOR
RH FRONT DOOR LOCK MOTOR
LH REAR DOOR LOCK MOTOR
RH REAR DOOR LOCK MOTOR
SOLID STATE
NOTE: EACH MOTOR CONTAINS A CIRCUIT BREAKER (PTC). IT RESETS ONLY AFTER VOLTAGE IS REMOVED FROM MOTOR.

Somerset and Skylark — Power door locks

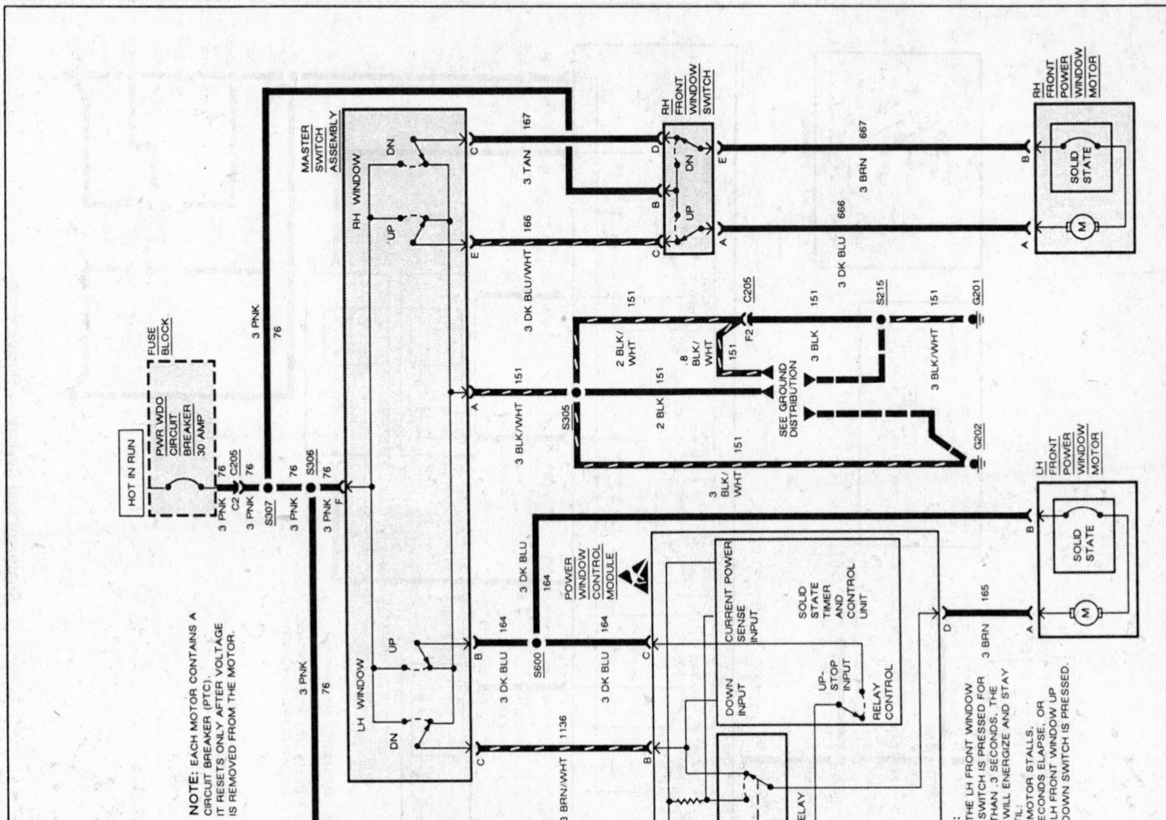
NOTE: EACH MOTOR CONTAINS A CIRCUIT BREAKER (PTC). IT RESETS ONLY AFTER VOLTAGE IS REMOVED FROM THE MOTOR.
HOT IN RUN
PWR WDO CIRCUIT BREAKER 30 AMP
FUSE BLOCK
MASTER SWITCH ASSEMBLY
LH WINDOW
RH WINDOW
RH FRONT WINDOW SWITCH
SEE GROUND DISTRIBUTION
POWER WINDOW CONTROL MODULE
CURRENT POWER SENSE INPUT
DOWN INPUT
SOLID STATE TIMER AND CONTROL UNIT
UP-STOP INPUT
RELAY CONTROL
RELAY
LH FRONT POWER WINDOW MOTOR
RH FRONT POWER WINDOW MOTOR
SOLID STATE
NOTE: WHEN THE LH FRONT WINDOW DOWN SWITCH IS PRESSED FOR MORE THAN .3 SECONDS, THE RELAY WILL ENERGIZE AND STAY SO UNTIL:
1) THE MOTOR STALLS,
2) 30 SECONDS ELAPSE, OR
3) THE LH FRONT WINDOW UP OR DOWN SWITCH IS PRESSED.

Somerset and Skylark — Power windows — 2 door

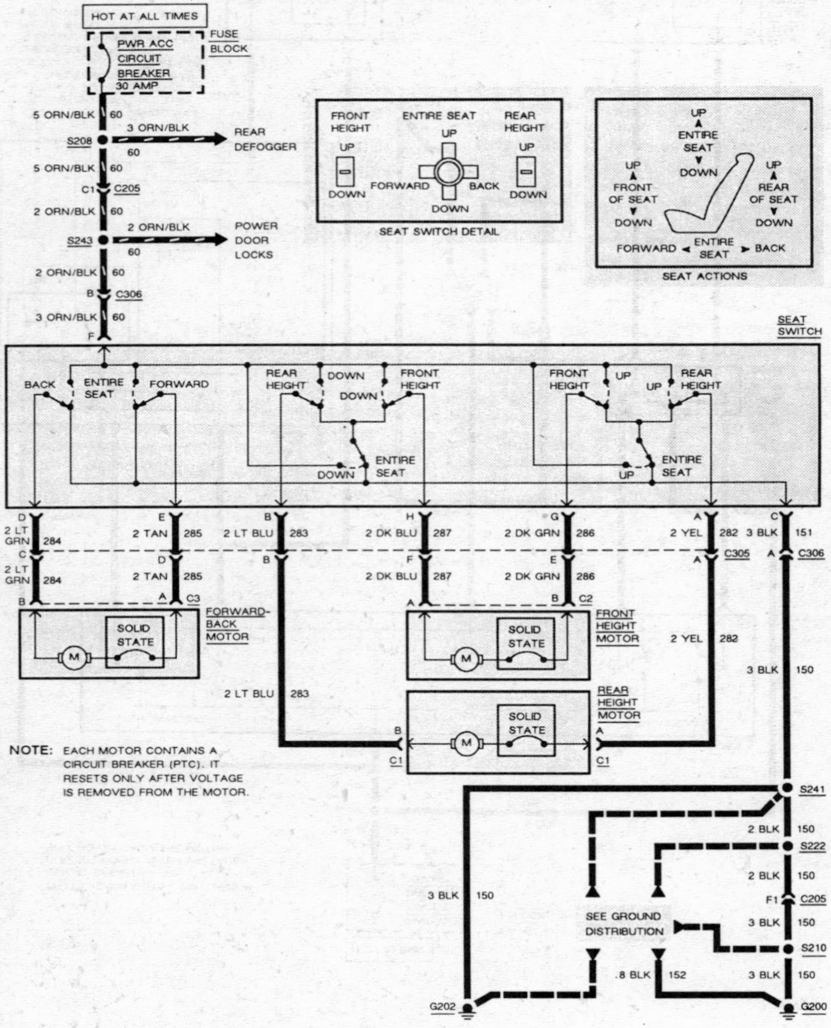

Somerset and Skylark — Power seats

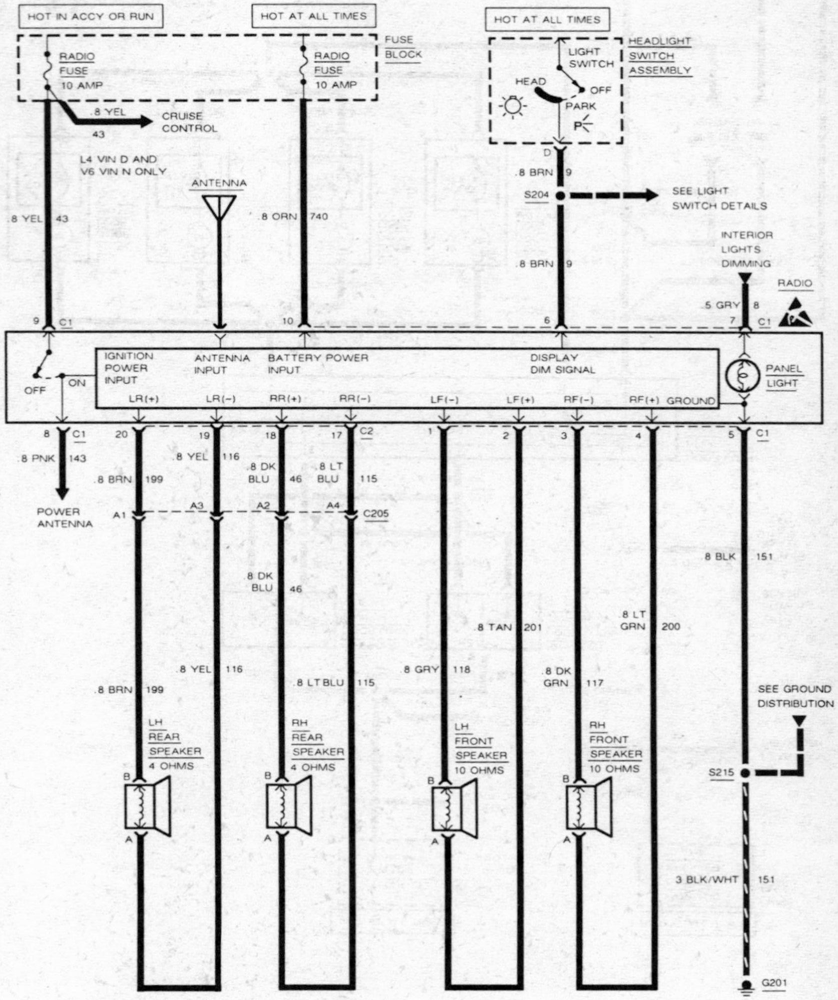

Somerset and Skylark — Automatic safety belts

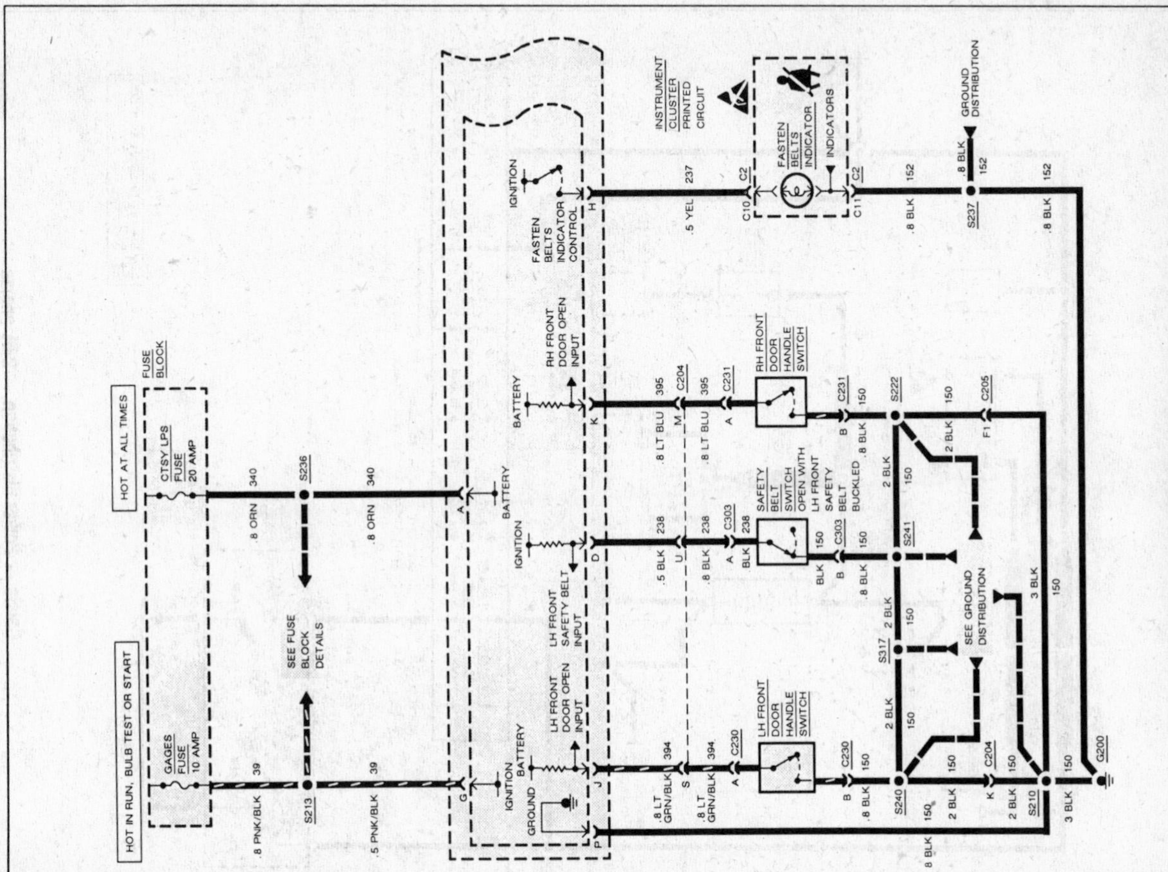

L4 VIN U

ECM CONNECTOR IDENTIFICATION
C1 - BLACK/RED - 24 WAY
C2 - WHITE/RED - 24 WAY

V6 VIN N

ECM CONNECTOR IDENTIFICATION
C1 - BLACK/GRAY - 32 WAY
C2 - BLACK/BLUE - 24 WAY
C3 - YELLOW - 32 WAY

L4 VIN D

ECM CONNECTOR IDENTIFICATION
C1 - BLACK - 32 WAY
C2 - BLACK - 24 WAY
C3 - GREEN - 32 WAY

Somerset and Skylark — Automatic safety belts

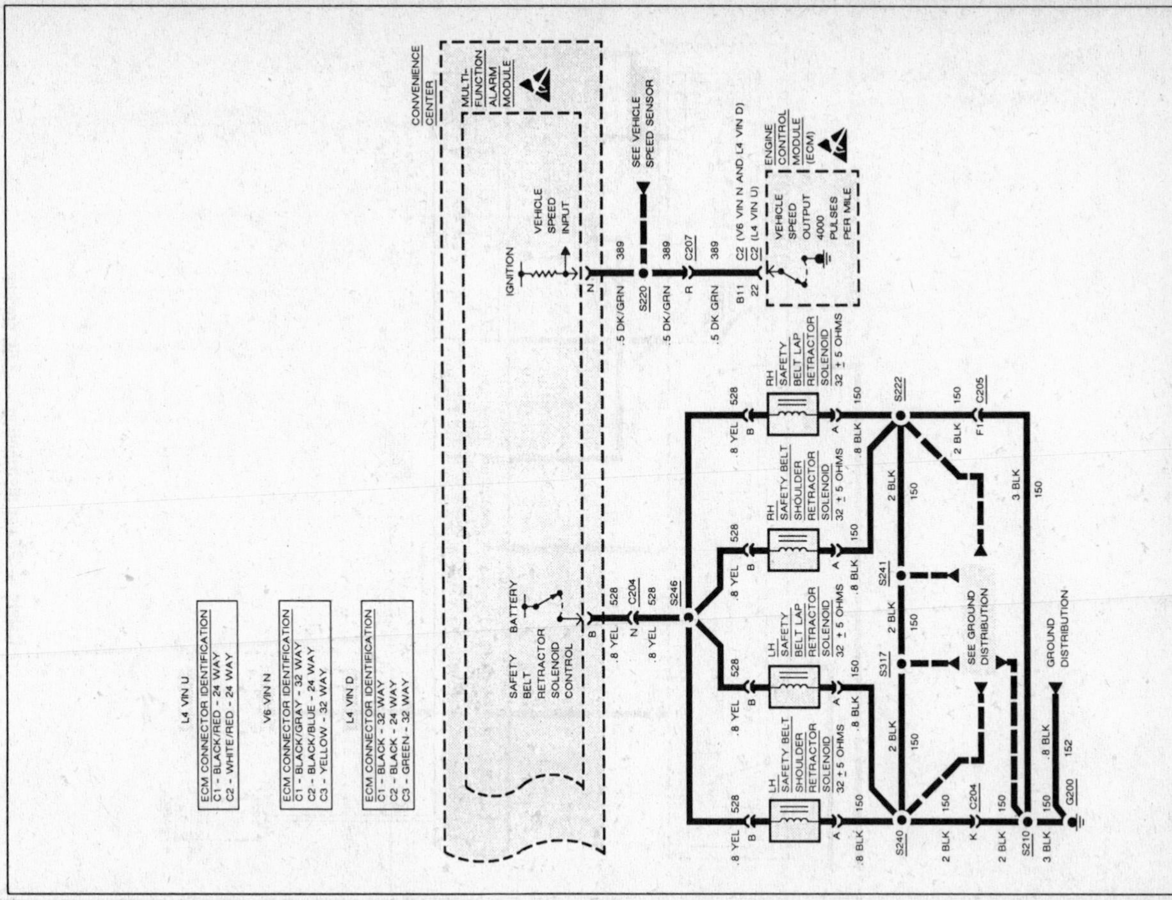

Somerset and Skylark — Radio

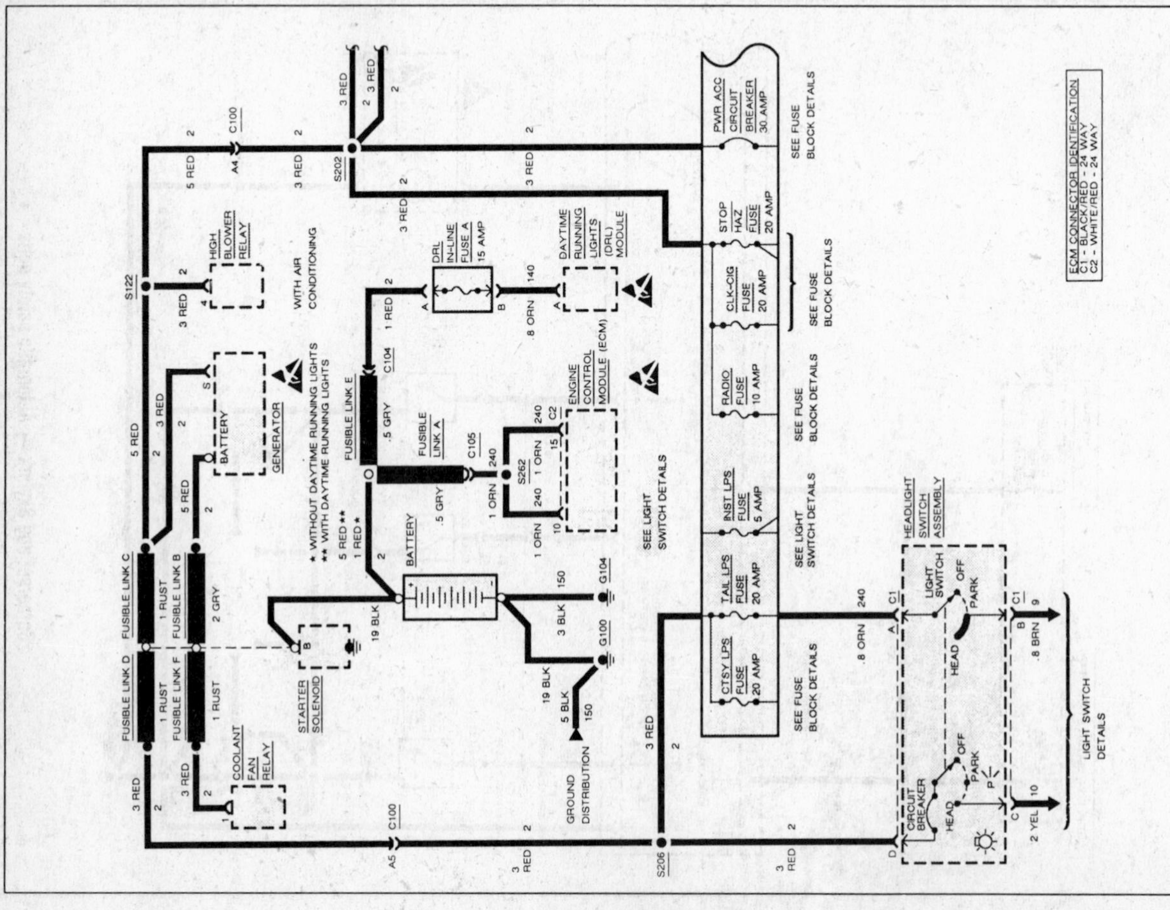

Calais — Power distribution — 2.5L engine

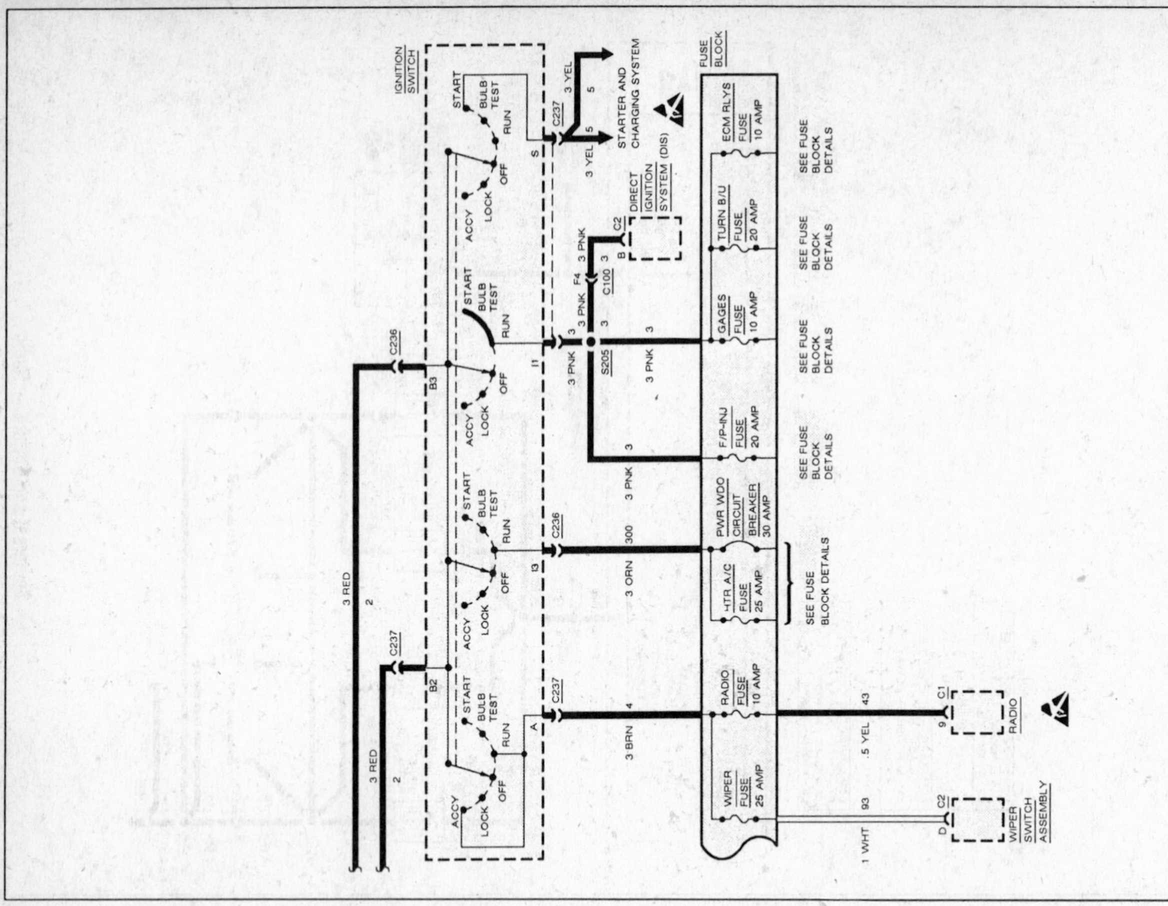

Calais — Power distribution — 2.5L engine

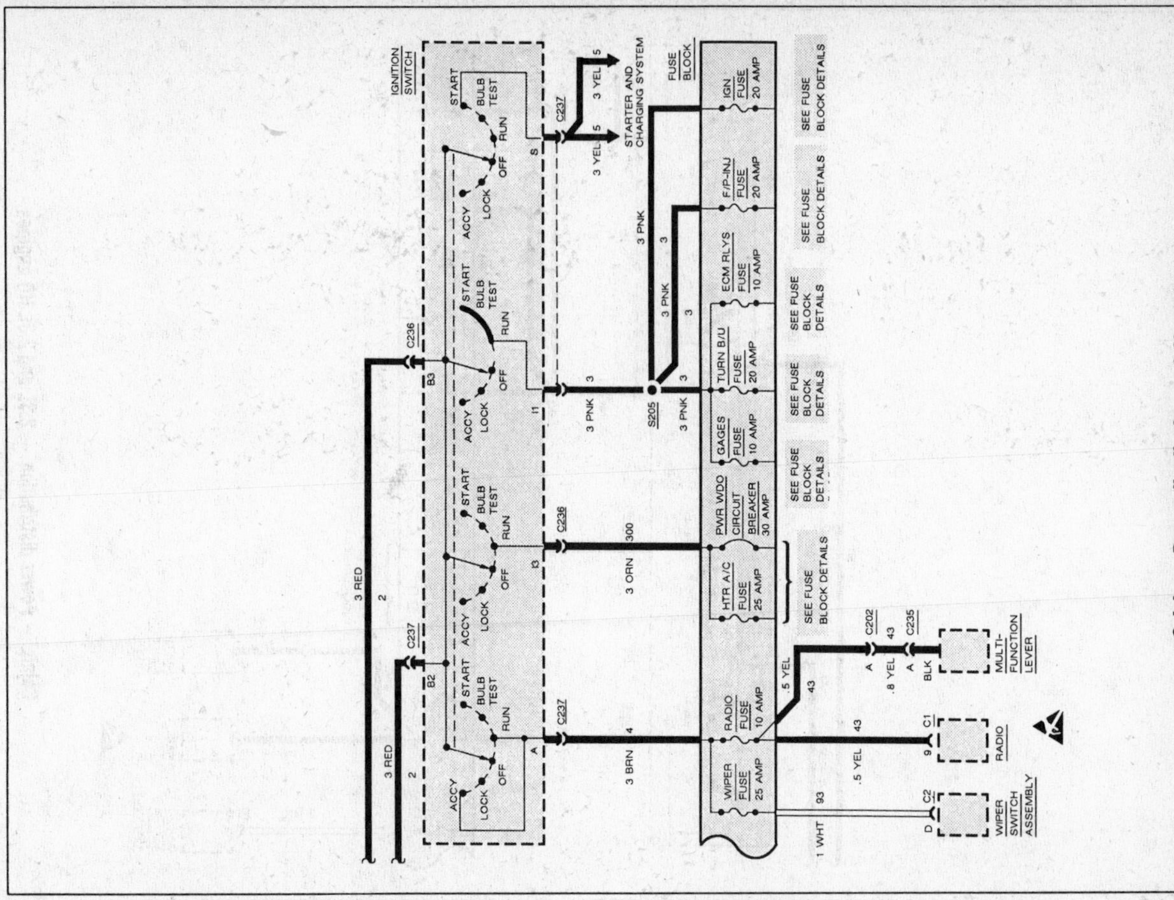

ECM CONNECTOR IDENTIFICATION
C1 - BLACK/GRAY - 32 WAY
C2 - BLACK/BLUE - 24 WAY
C3 - YELLOW - 32 WAY

Calais — Power distribution — 3.3L engine

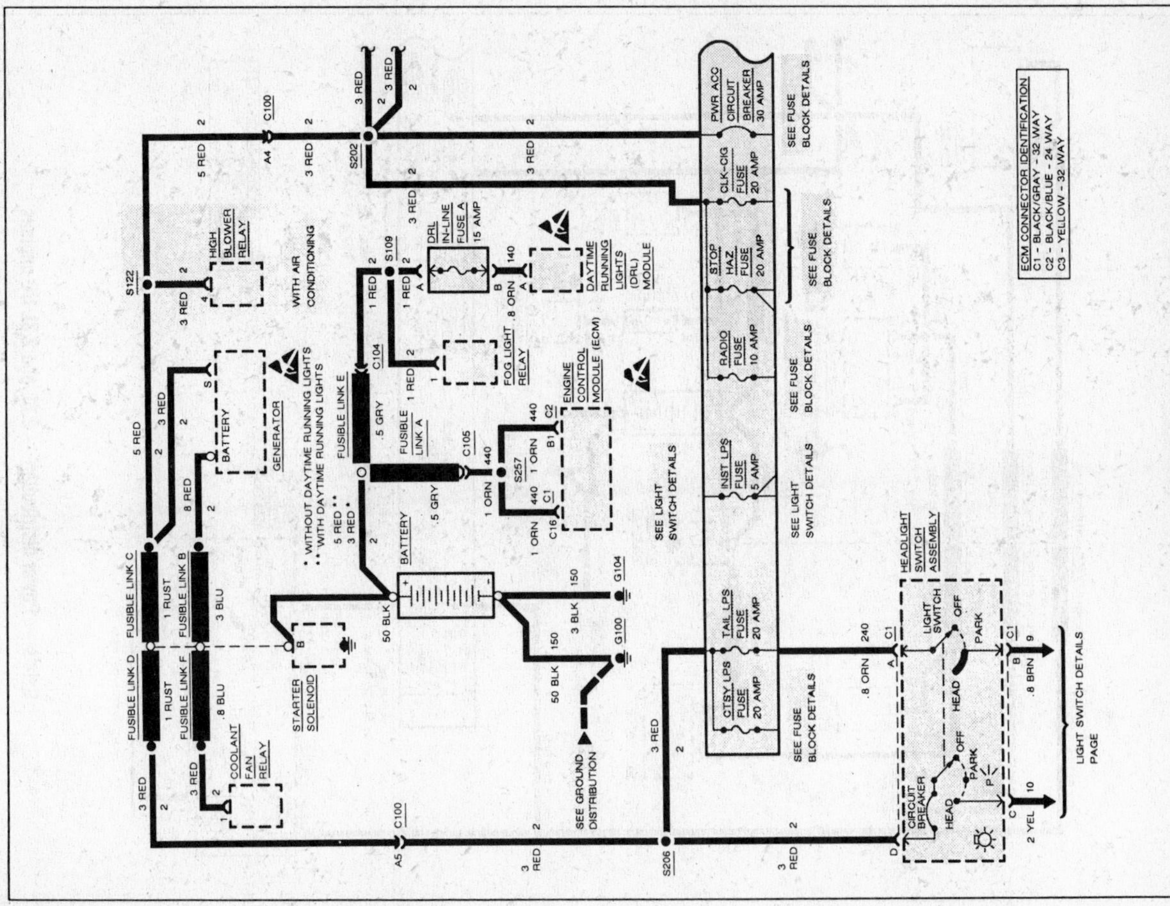

Calais — Power distribution — 3.3L engine

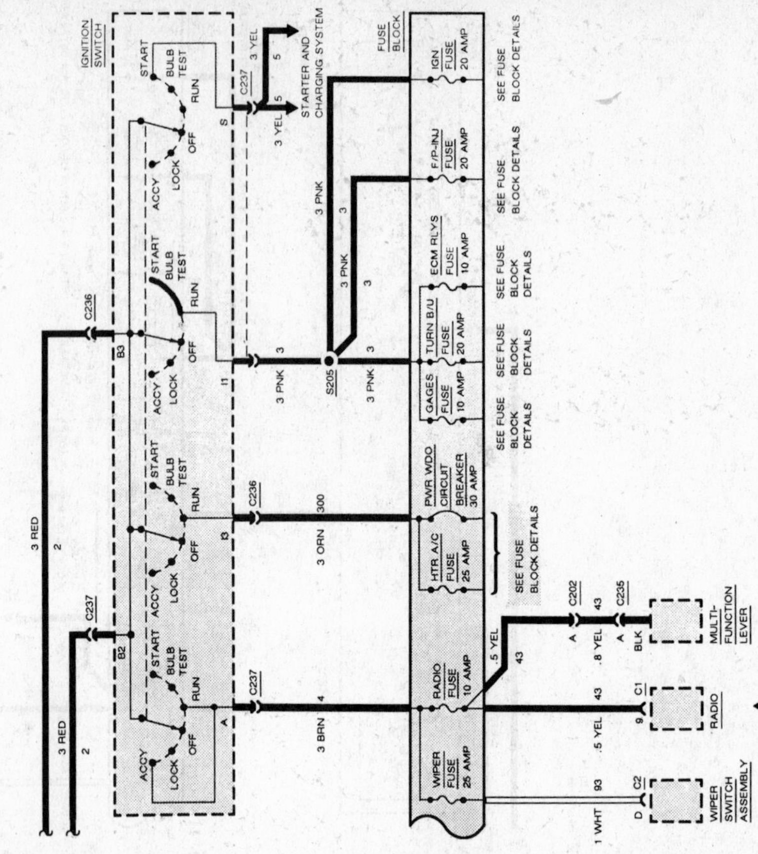

Calais — Power distribution — 2.3L and 2.3L HO engines

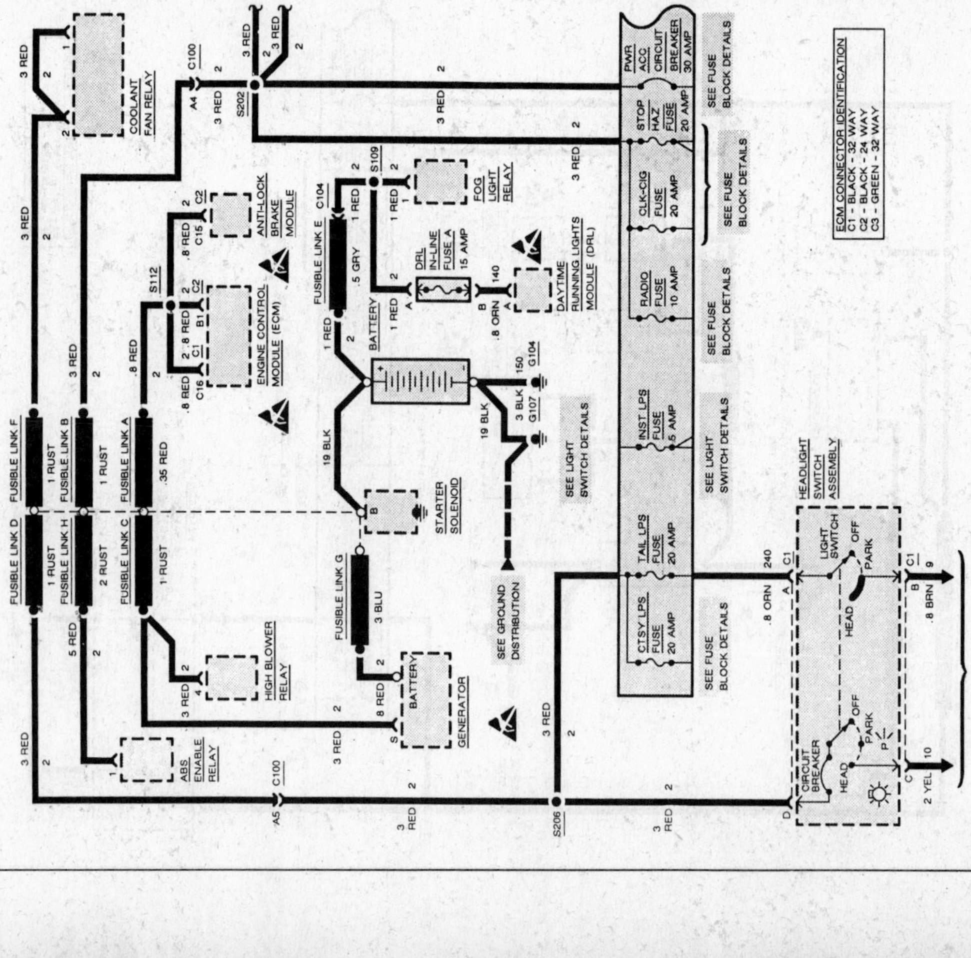

Calais — Power distribution — 2.3L and 2.3L HO engines

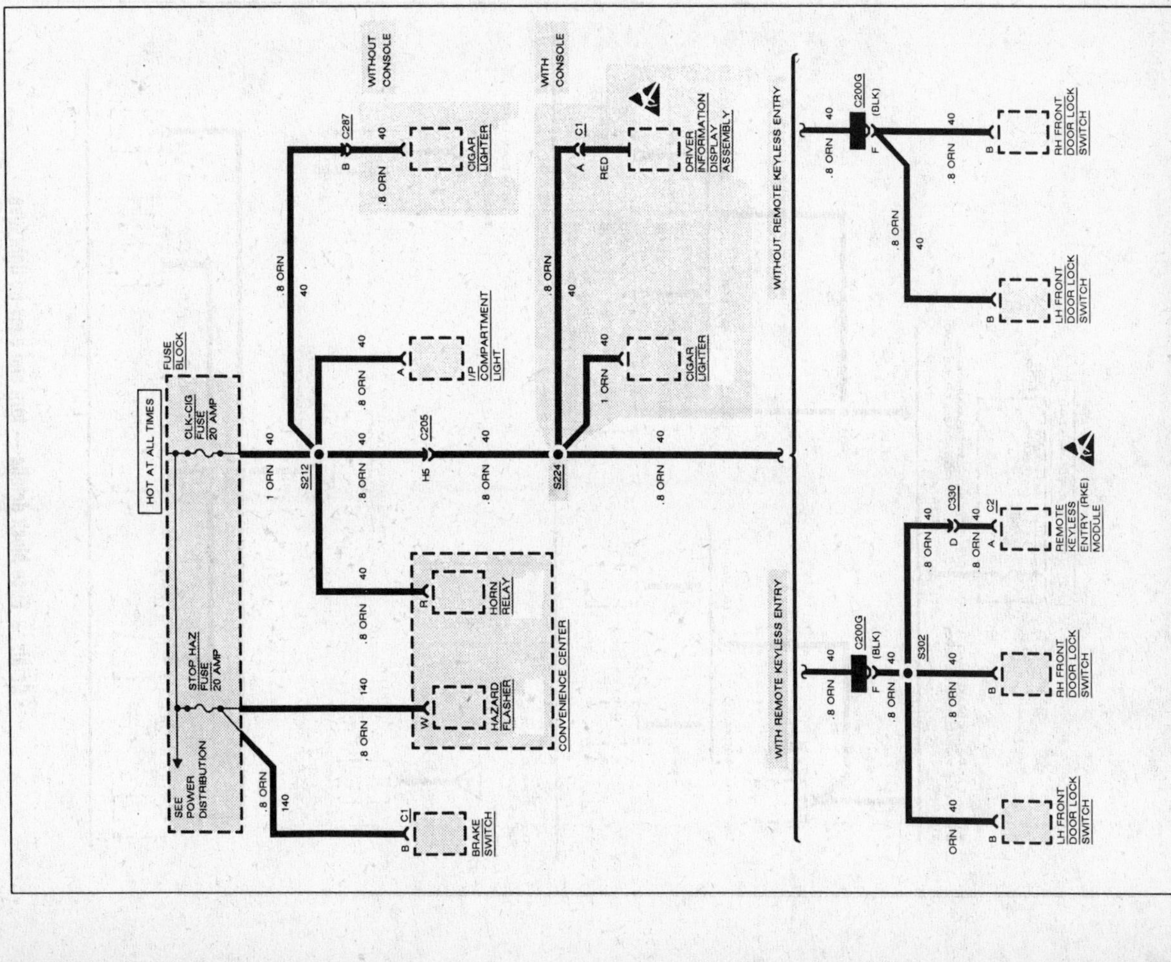

Calais — Fuse block details — stop, hazard fuse and clock, cig. fuse

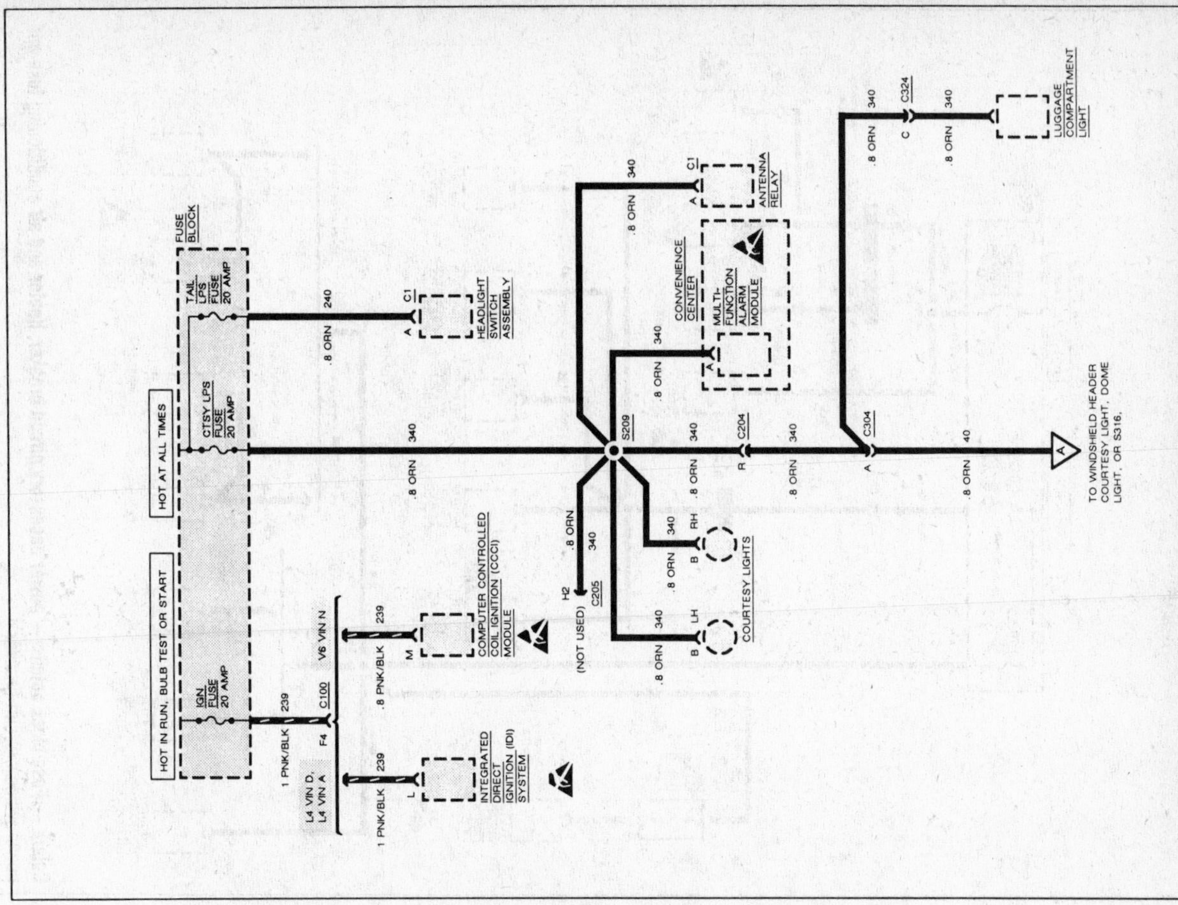

Calais — Fuse block details — ignition fuse, courtesy light fuse and tail light fuse

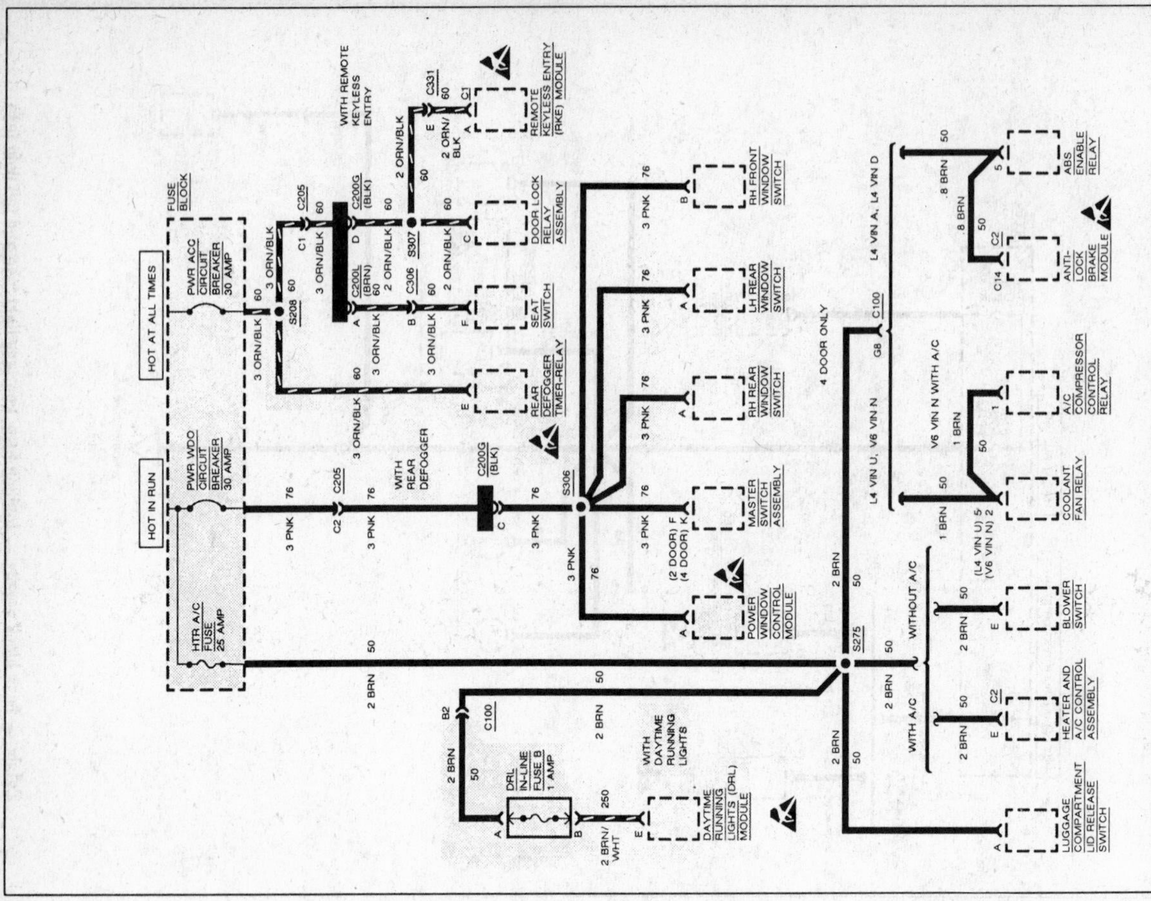

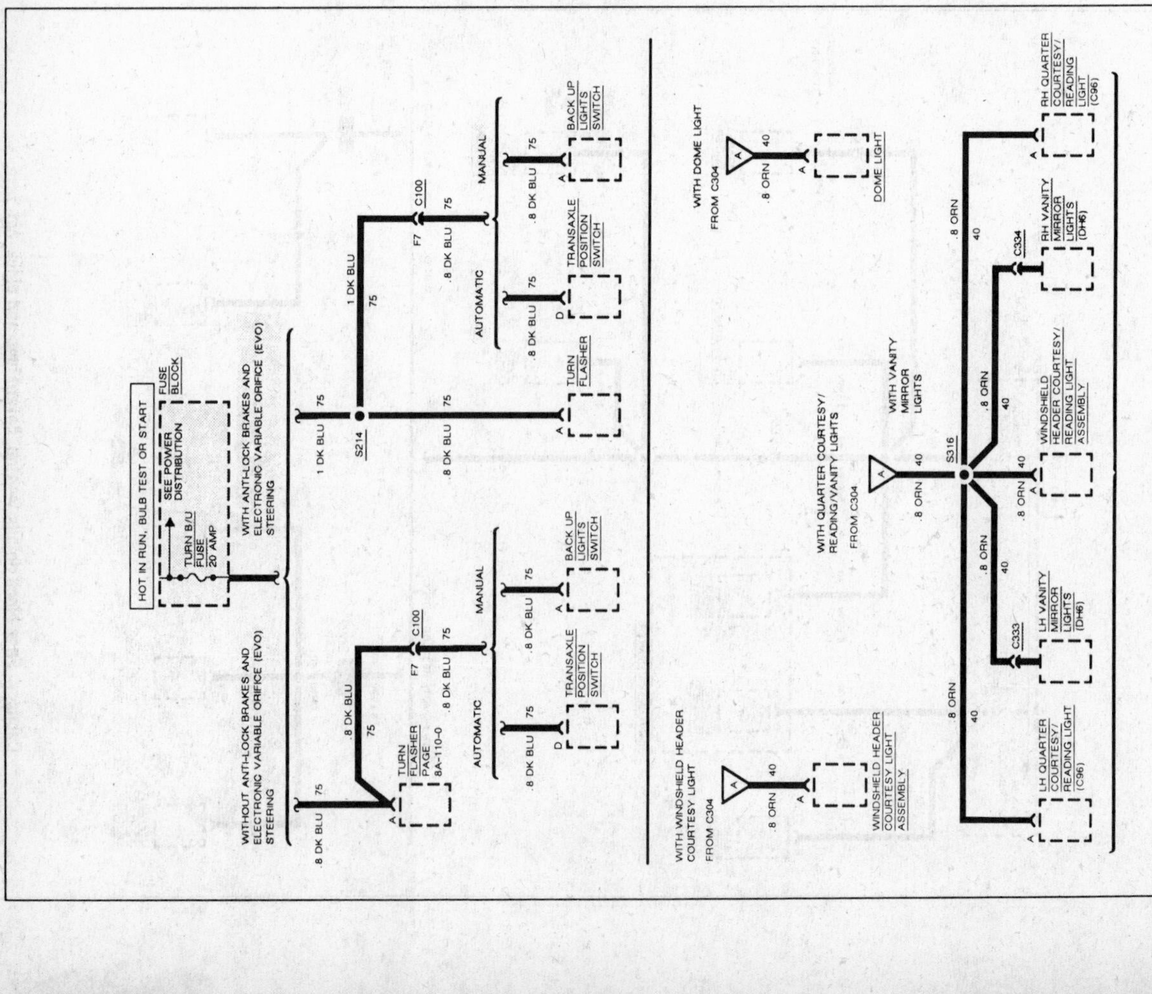

HOT IN RUN, BULB TEST OR START

TURN B/U FUSE 20 AMP — SEE POWER DISTRIBUTION — FUSE BLOCK

WITHOUT ANTI-LOCK BRAKES AND ELECTRONIC VARIABLE ORIFICE (EVO) STEERING

WITH ANTI-LOCK BRAKES AND ELECTRONIC VARIABLE ORIFICE (EVO) STEERING

TURN FLASHER PAGE 8A-110-0

AUTOMATIC — TRANSAXLE POSITION SWITCH

MANUAL — BACK UP LIGHTS SWITCH

TURN FLASHER

WITH WINDSHIELD HEADER COURTESY LIGHT FROM C304

WINDSHIELD HEADER COURTESY LIGHT ASSEMBLY

WITH DOME LIGHT FROM C304

DOME LIGHT

WITH QUARTER COURTESY/ READING/VANITY LIGHTS FROM C304

WITH VANITY MIRROR LIGHTS

LH QUARTER COURTESY/ READING LIGHT (C96)

LH VANITY MIRROR LIGHTS (DH6)

WINDSHIELD HEADER COURTESY/ READING LIGHT ASSEMBLY

RH VANITY MIRROR LIGHTS (DH6)

RH QUARTER COURTESY/ READING LIGHT (C96)

Calais — Fuse block details — turn and back-up light fuse

HOT IN RUN

HOT AT ALL TIMES

HTR A/C FUSE 25 AMP

PWR WDO CIRCUIT BREAKER 30 AMP

PWR ACC CIRCUIT BREAKER 30 AMP

FUSE BLOCK

WITH REAR DEFOGGER

WITH REMOTE KEYLESS ENTRY

REAR DEFOGGER TIMER-RELAY

SEAT SWITCH

DOOR LOCK RELAY ASSEMBLY

REMOTE KEYLESS ENTRY (RKE) MODULE

DRL IN-LINE FUSE B 1 AMP

WITH DAYTIME RUNNING LIGHTS

DAYTIME RUNNING LIGHTS (DRL) MODULE

POWER WINDOW CONTROL MODULE

MASTER SWITCH ASSEMBLY

RH REAR WINDOW SWITCH

LH REAR WINDOW SWITCH

RH FRONT WINDOW SWITCH

4 DOOR ONLY

WITH A/C — WITHOUT A/C

L4 VIN U, V6 VIN N — L4 VIN A, L4 VIN D — V6 VIN N WITH A/C

LUGGAGE COMPARTMENT LID RELEASE SWITCH

HEATER AND A/C CONTROL ASSEMBLY

BLOWER SWITCH

COOLANT FAN RELAY

A/C COMPRESSOR CONTROL RELAY

ANTI-LOCK BRAKE MODULE

ABS ENABLE RELAY

Calais — Fuse block details — power accessory circuit breaker, heater and air conditioning fuse and power window circuit breaker

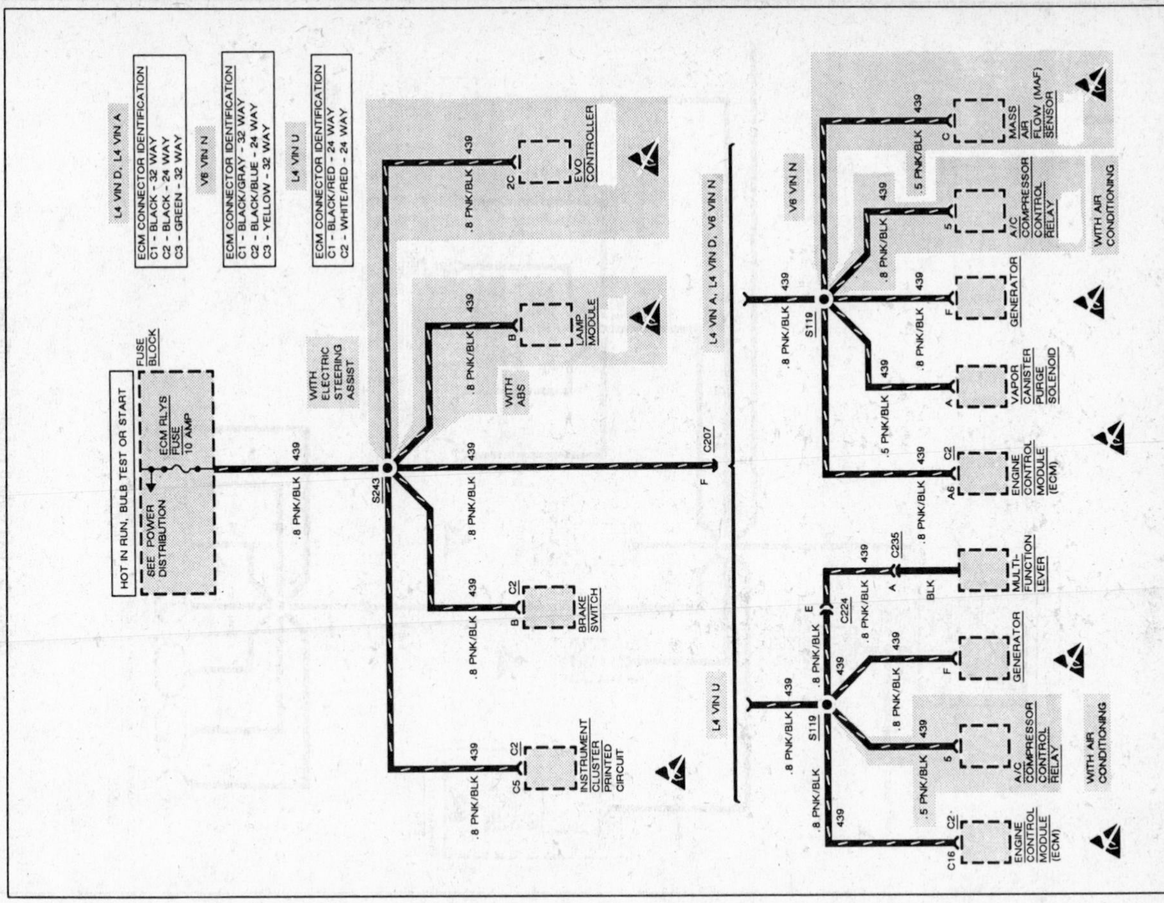

L4 VIN D, L4 VIN A

ECM CONNECTOR IDENTIFICATION
C1 - BLACK - 32 WAY
C2 - BLACK - 24 WAY
C3 - GREEN - 32 WAY

V6 VIN N

ECM CONNECTOR IDENTIFICATION
C1 - BLACK/GRAY - 32 WAY
C2 - BLACK/BLUE - 24 WAY
C3 - YELLOW - 32 WAY

L4 VIN U

ECM CONNECTOR IDENTIFICATION
C1 - BLACK/RED - 24 WAY
C2 - WHITE/RED - 24 WAY

Calais — Fuse block details — f/p-inj. fuse

Calais — Fuse block details — ECM rlys fuse

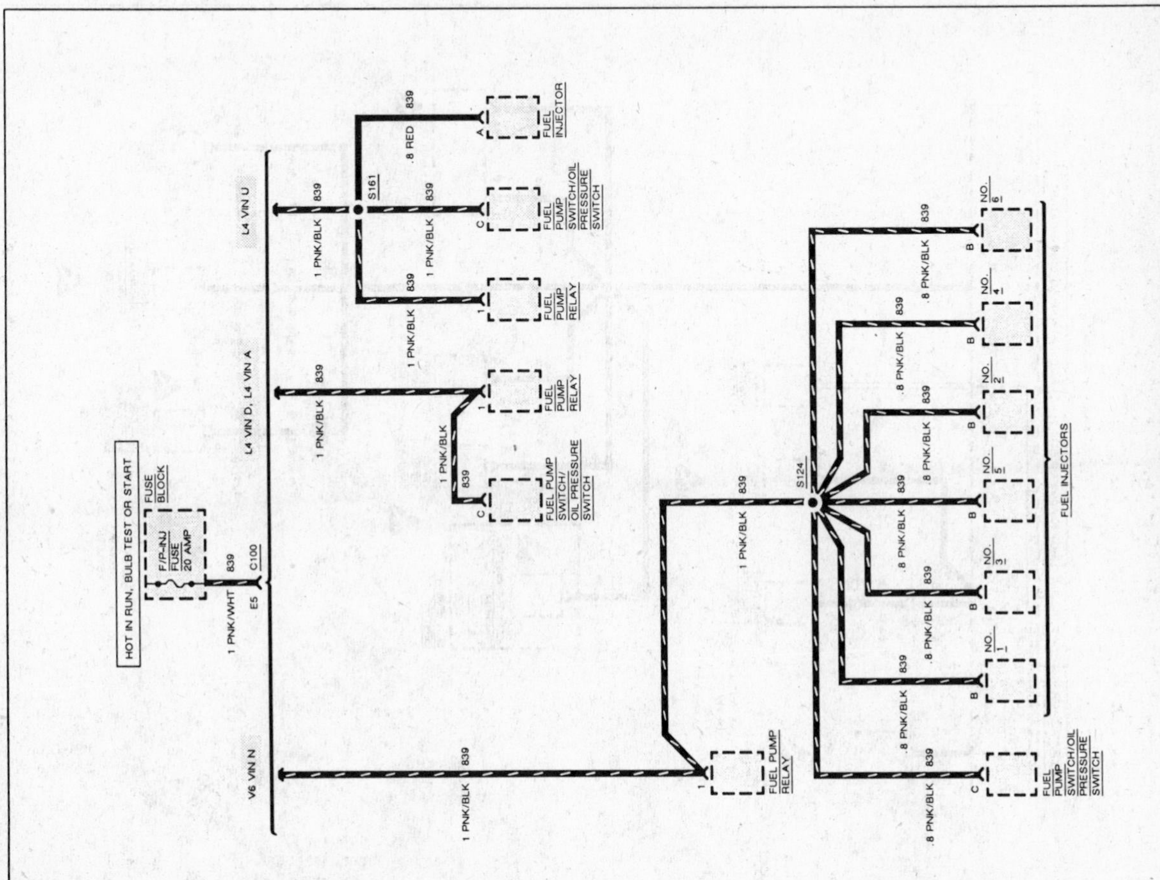

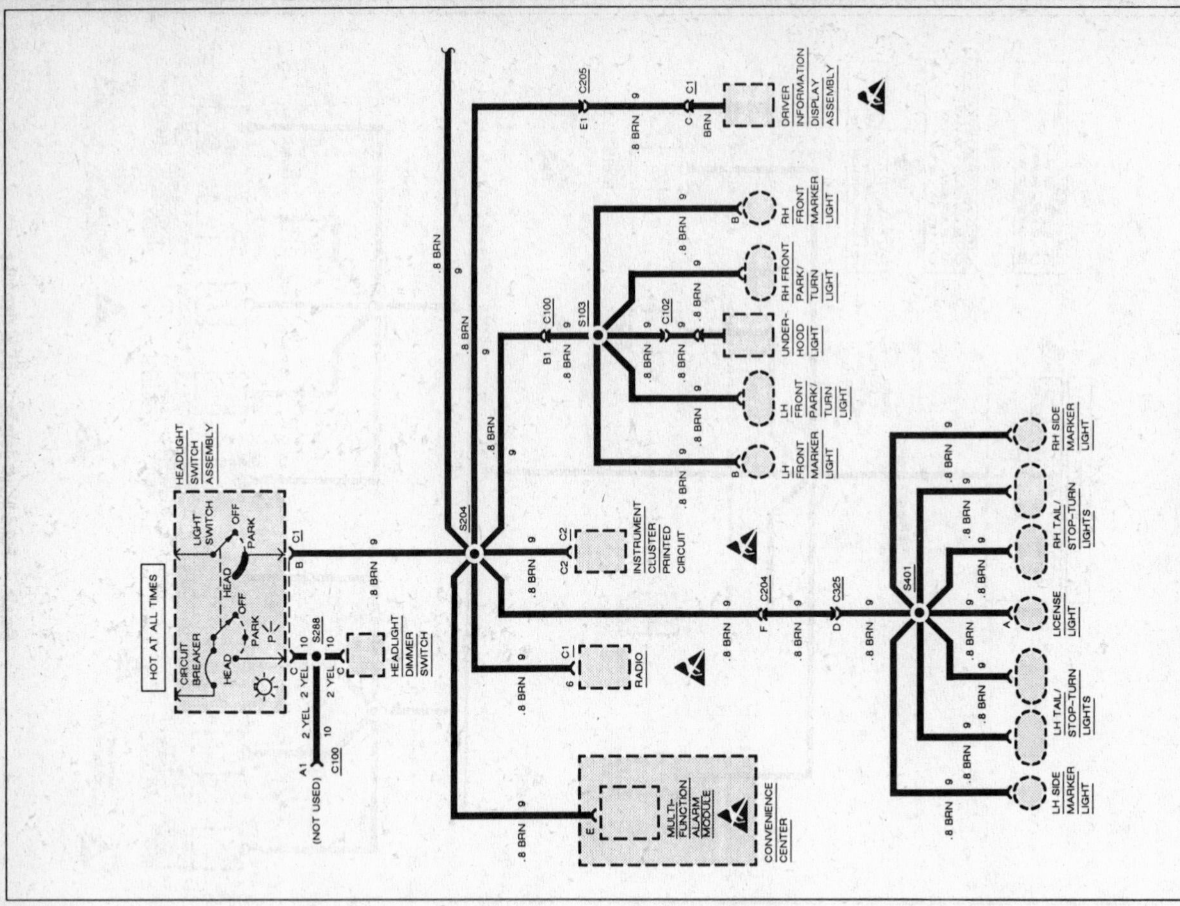
HOT AT ALL TIMES
CIRCUIT BREAKER
LIGHT SWITCH
HEAD
OFF
PARK
HEADLIGHT SWITCH ASSEMBLY
C1
S288
2 YEL
10
HEADLIGHT DIMMER SWITCH
A1
C100
(NOT USED)
.8 BRN
9
S204
INSTRUMENT CLUSTER PRINTED CIRCUIT
C2
RADIO
MULTI-FUNCTION ALARM MODULE
CONVENIENCE CENTER
C204
C325
S401
B1
S103
C102
C205
LH FRONT MARKER LIGHT
LH FRONT PARK/TURN LIGHT
UNDER-HOOD LIGHT
RH FRONT PARK/TURN LIGHT
RH FRONT MARKER LIGHT
BRN
DRIVER INFORMATION DISPLAY ASSEMBLY
LH SIDE MARKER LIGHT
LH TAIL/STOP-TURN LIGHTS
LICENSE LIGHT
RH TAIL/STOP-TURN LIGHTS
RH SIDE MARKER LIGHT

Calais — Light switch details — with fog lights

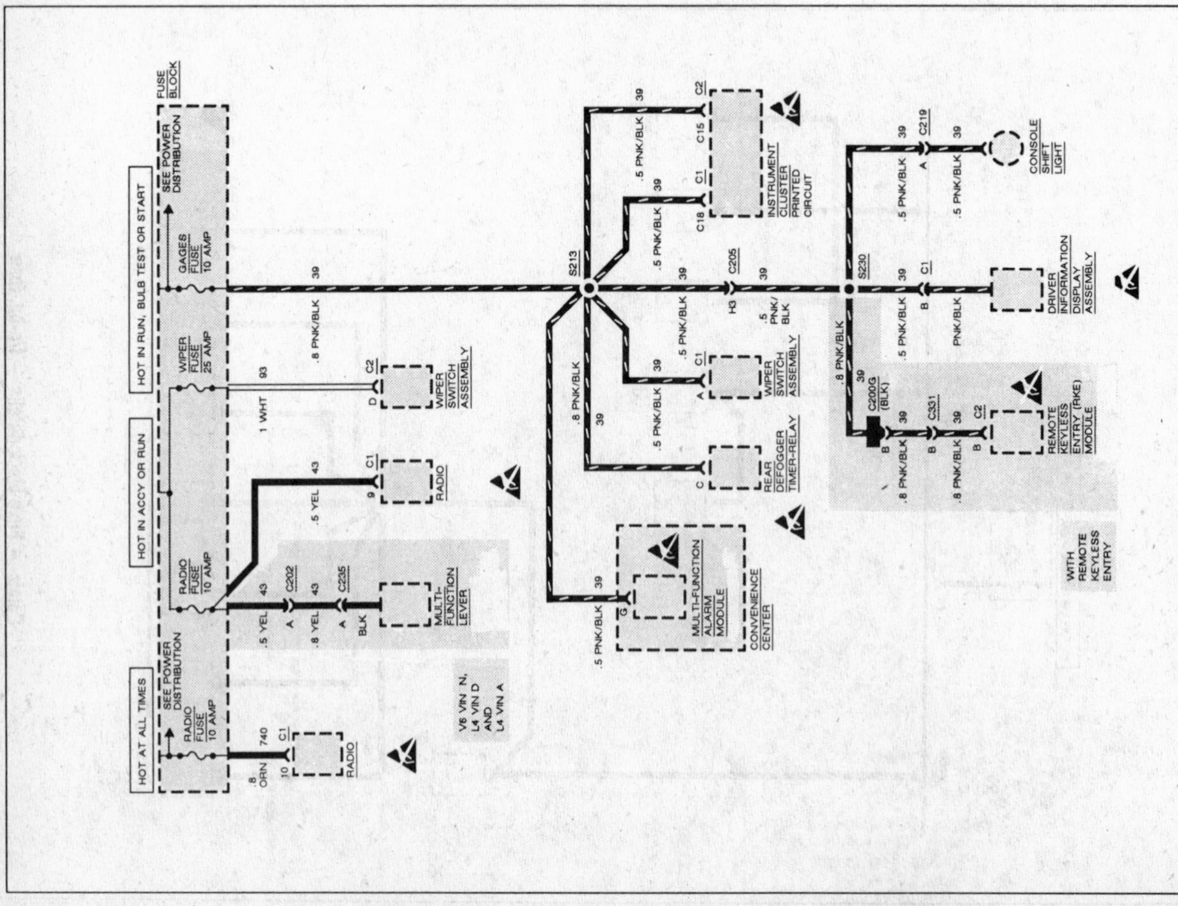
HOT AT ALL TIMES
SEE POWER DISTRIBUTION
RADIO FUSE 10 AMP
HOT IN ACCY OR RUN
HOT IN RUN, BULB TEST OR START
WIPER FUSE 25 AMP
GAGES FUSE 10 AMP
FUSE BLOCK
.8 ORN
740
C1
RADIO
V6 VIN N, L4 VIN D AND L4 VIN A
.5 YEL
.8 YEL
43
C202
C235
BLK
MULTI-FUNCTION LEVER
1 WHT
93
C2
WIPER SWITCH ASSEMBLY
.8 PNK/BLK
.5 PNK/BLK
39
S213
REAR DEFOGGER TIMER-RELAY
MULTI-FUNCTION ALARM MODULE
CONVENIENCE CENTER
C18
C15
INSTRUMENT CLUSTER PRINTED CIRCUIT
C205
H3
S230
C200G (BLK)
C331
REMOTE KEYLESS ENTRY (RKE) MODULE
WITH REMOTE KEYLESS ENTRY
C219
CONSOLE SHIFT LIGHT
DRIVER INFORMATION DISPLAY ASSEMBLY

Calais — Fuse block details — radio fuse, wiper fuse and gauges fuse

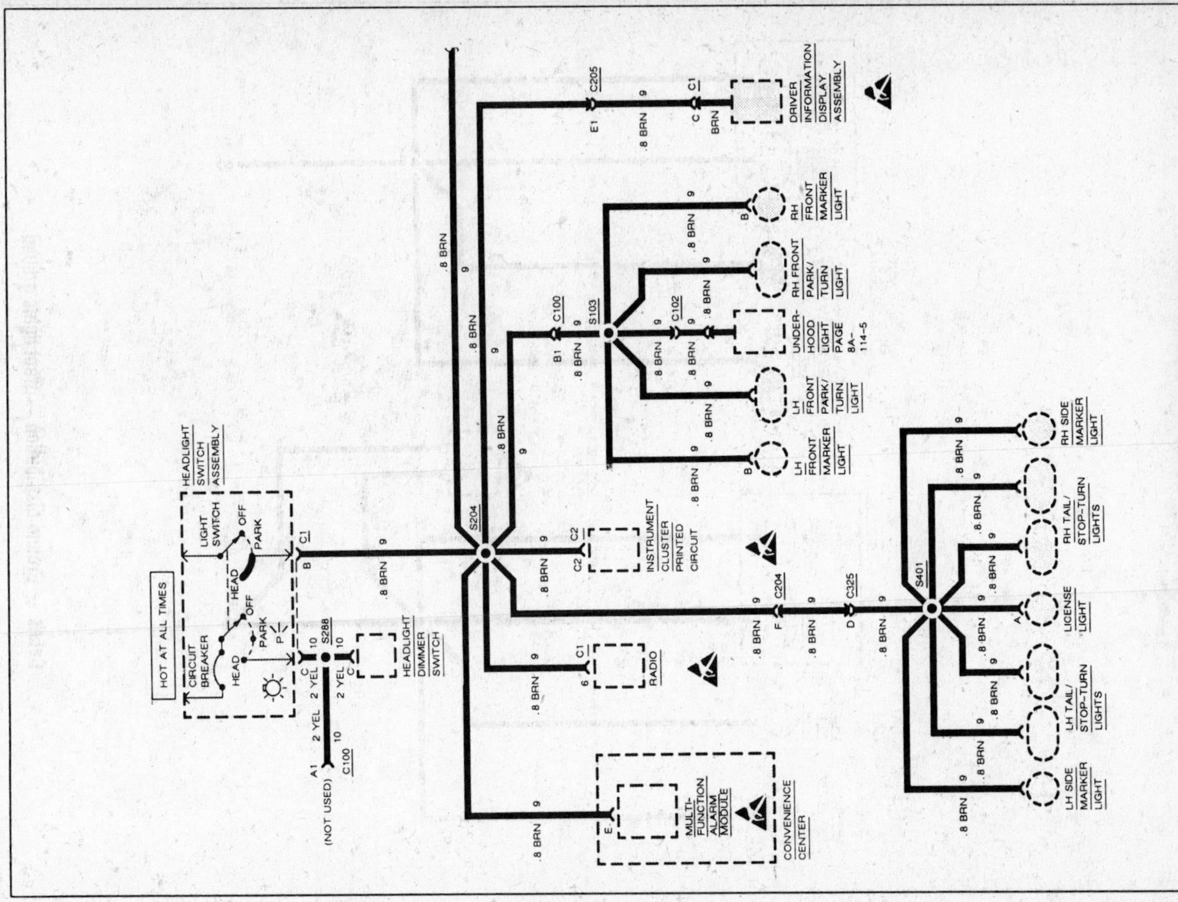

Calais — Light switch details — with fog lights

Calais — Light switch details — without fog lights

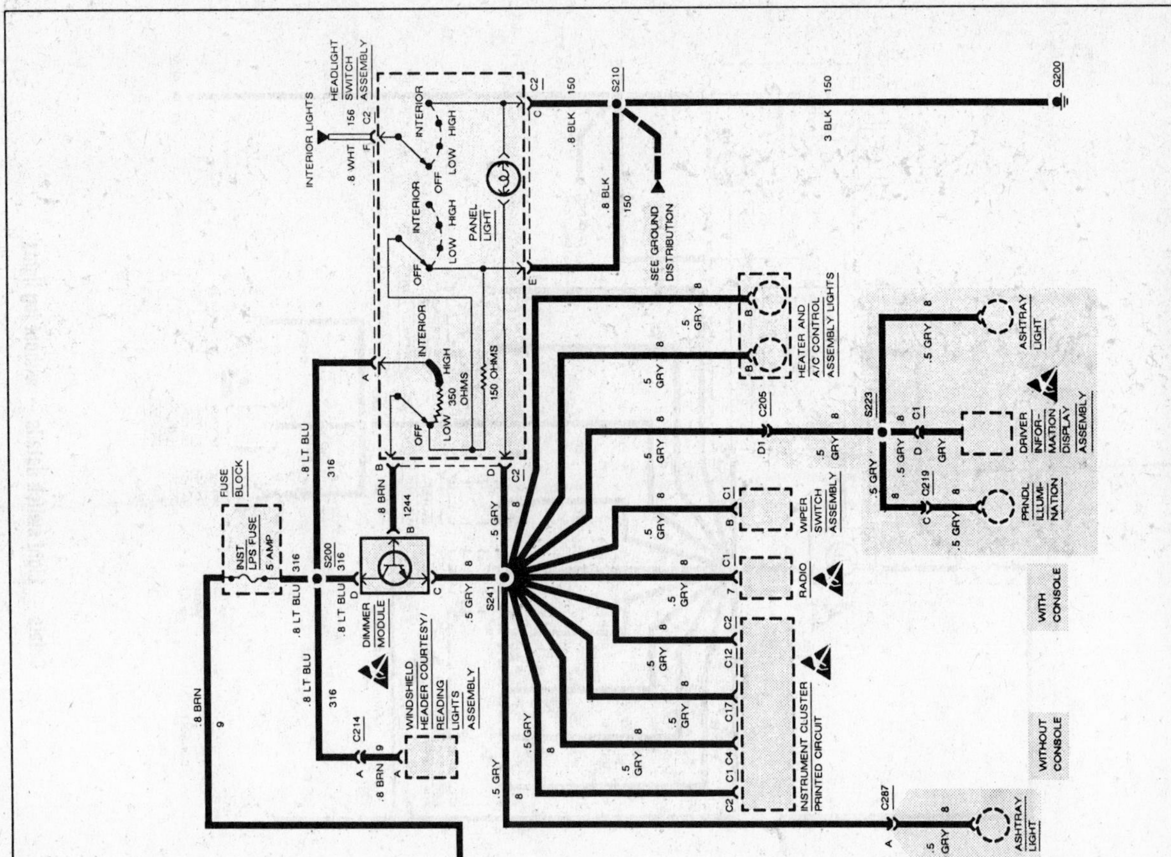

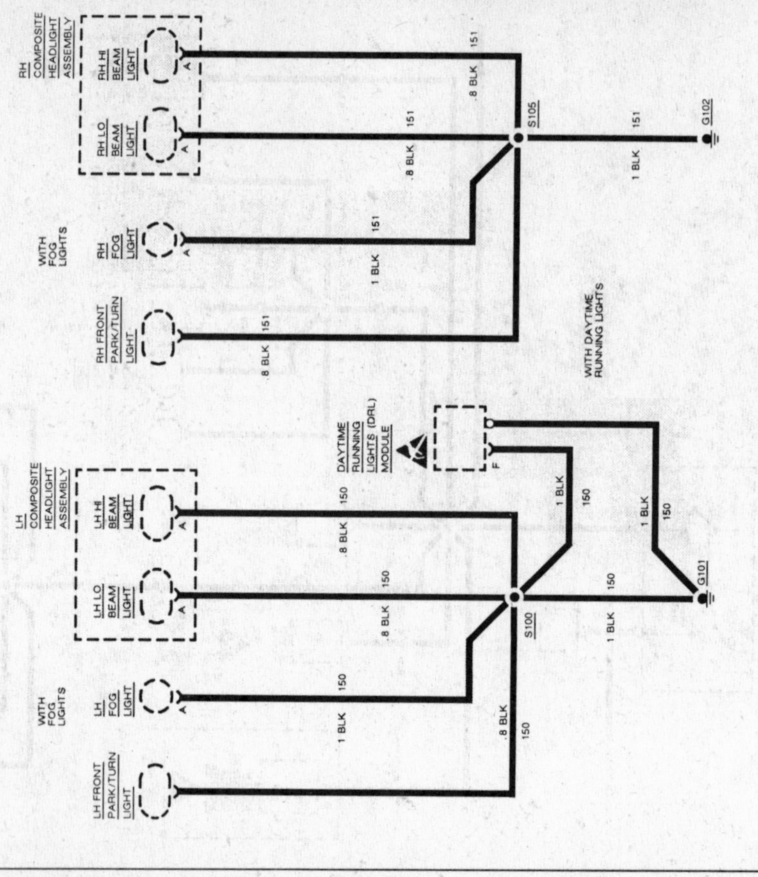

Calais — Ground distribution — front lights ground

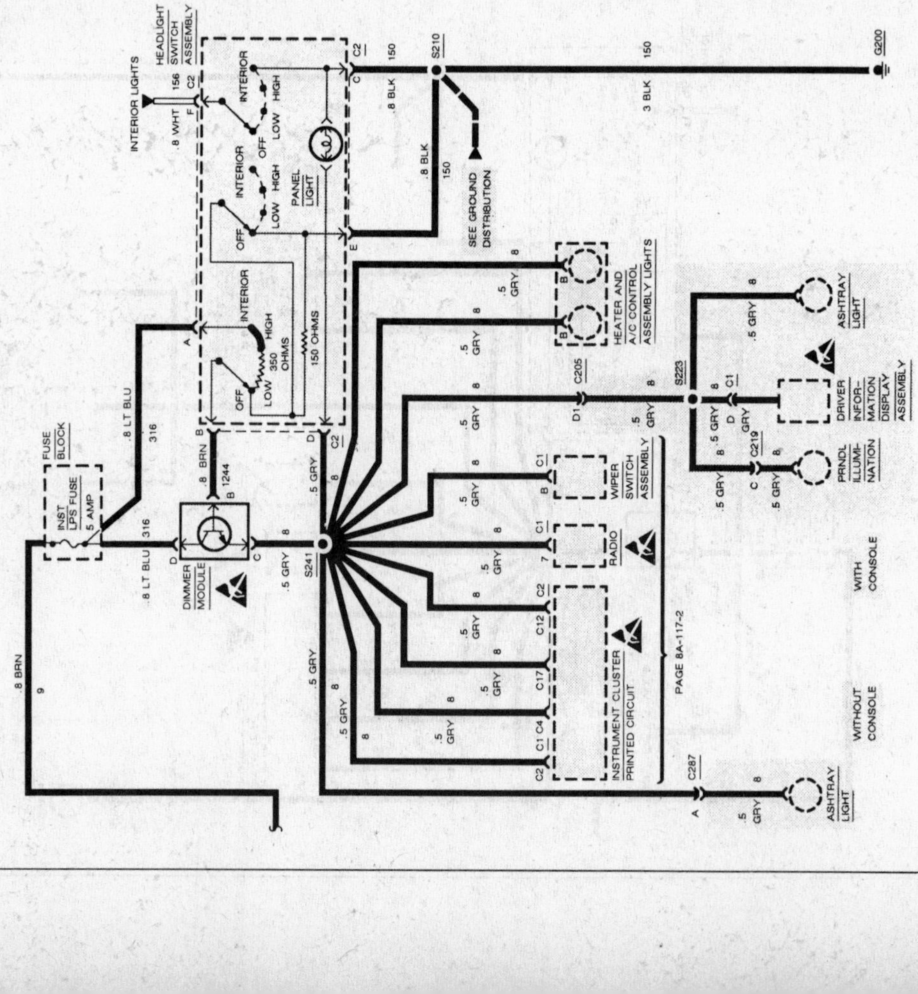

Calais — Light switch details — without fog lights

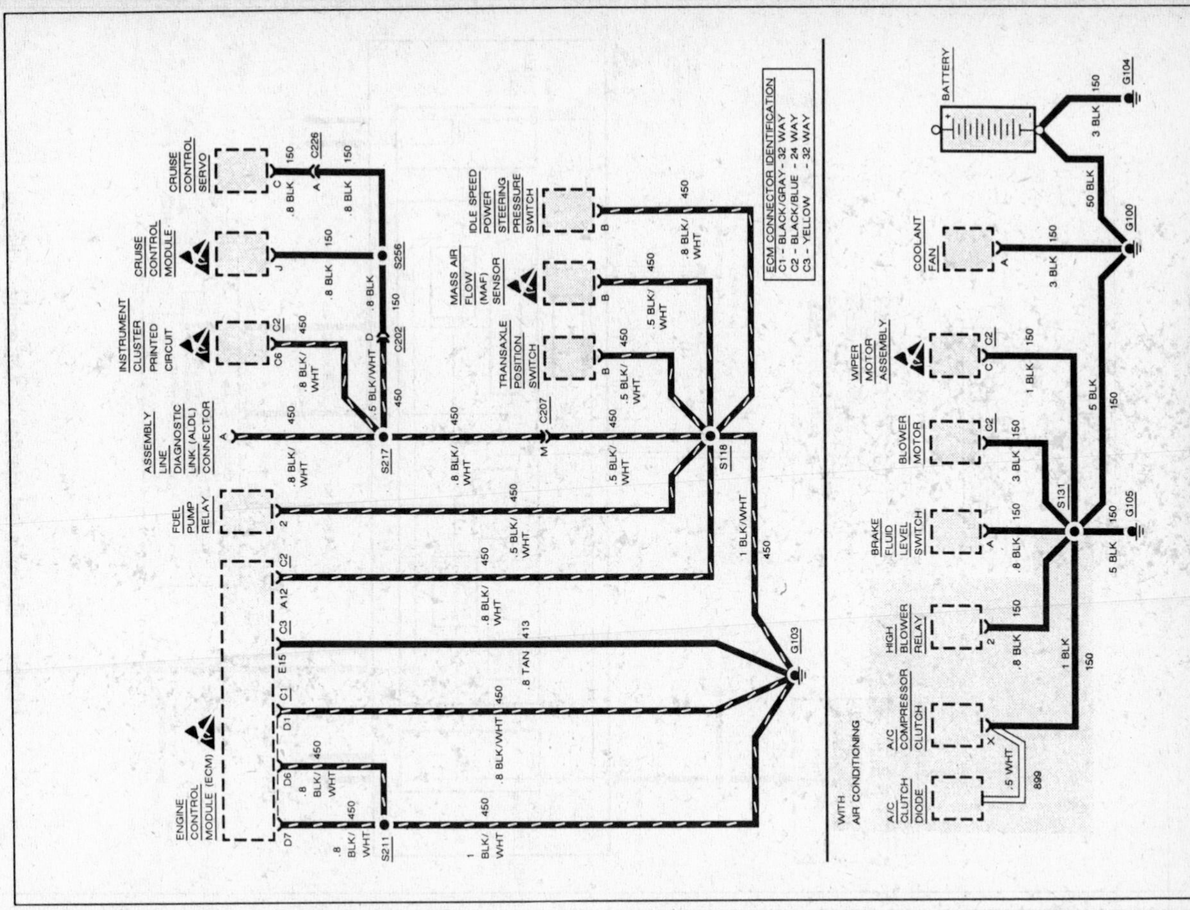

ENGINE CONTROL MODULE (ECM)
FUEL PUMP RELAY
ASSEMBLY LINE DIAGNOSTIC LINK (ALDL) CONNECTOR
INSTRUMENT CLUSTER PRINTED CIRCUIT
CRUISE CONTROL MODULE
CRUISE CONTROL SERVO
TRANSAXLE POSITION SWITCH
MASS AIR FLOW (MAF) SENSOR
IDLE SPEED POWER STEERING PRESSURE SWITCH

ECM CONNECTOR IDENTIFICATION
C1 - BLACK/GRAY - 32 WAY
C2 - BLACK/BLUE - 24 WAY
C3 - YELLOW - 32 WAY

WITH AIR CONDITIONING
A/C CLUTCH DIODE
A/C COMPRESSOR CLUTCH
HIGH BLOWER RELAY
BRAKE FLUID LEVEL SWITCH
BLOWER MOTOR
WIPER MOTOR ASSEMBLY
COOLANT FAN
BATTERY

Calais – Ground distribution – 3.3L engine

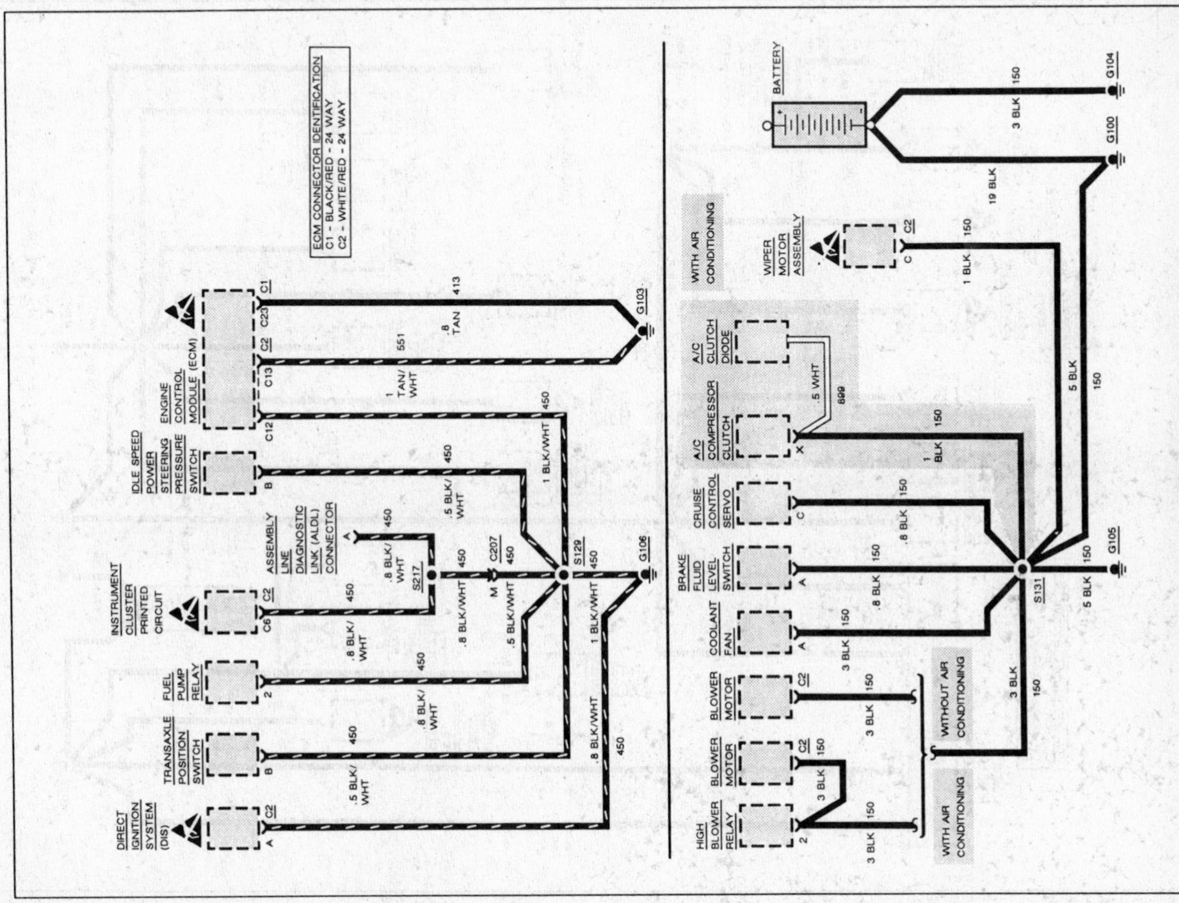

DIRECT IGNITION SYSTEM (DIS)
TRANSAXLE POSITION SWITCH
FUEL PUMP RELAY
INSTRUMENT CLUSTER PRINTED CIRCUIT
ASSEMBLY LINE DIAGNOSTIC LINK (ALDL) CONNECTOR
IDLE SPEED POWER STEERING PRESSURE SWITCH
ENGINE CONTROL MODULE (ECM)

ECM CONNECTOR IDENTIFICATION
C1 - BLACK/RED - 24 WAY
C2 - WHITE/RED - 24 WAY

HIGH BLOWER RELAY
BLOWER MOTOR
BLOWER MOTOR
COOLANT FAN
BRAKE FLUID LEVEL SWITCH
CRUISE CONTROL SERVO
A/C COMPRESSOR CLUTCH
A/C CLUTCH DIODE
WIPER MOTOR ASSEMBLY
WITH AIR CONDITIONING
WITHOUT AIR CONDITIONING
BATTERY

Calais – Ground distribution – 2.5L engine

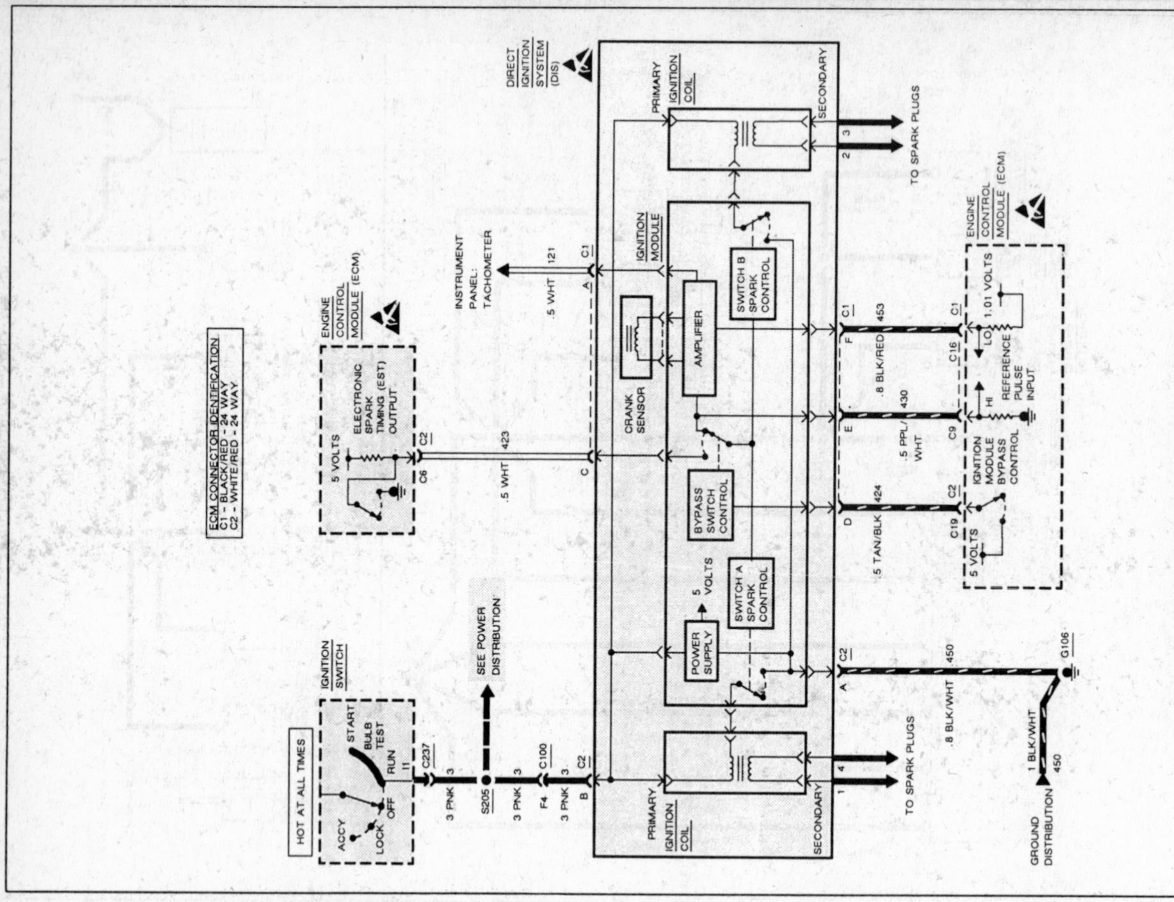

Calais — Electronic fuel injection — 2.5L engine — ignition

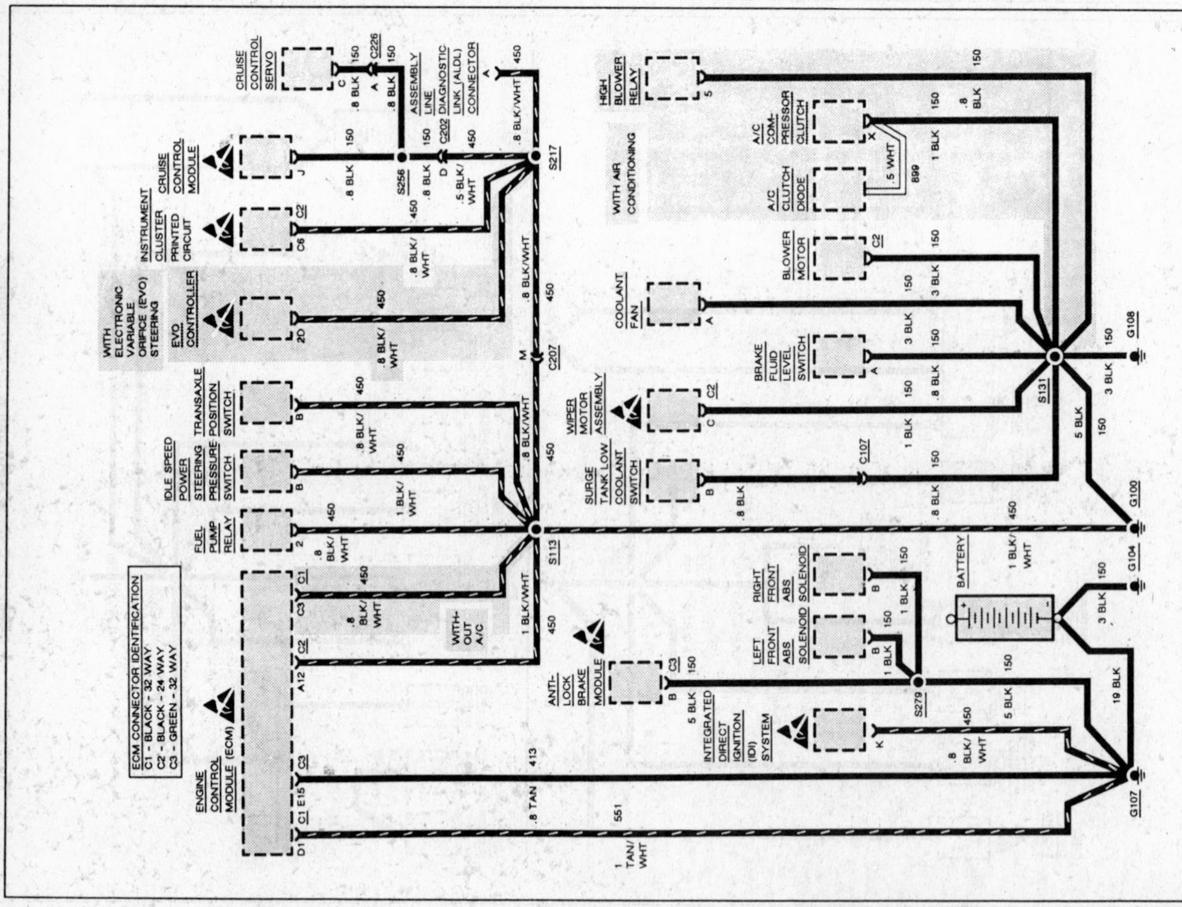

Calais — Ground distribution — 2.3L and 2.3L HO engines

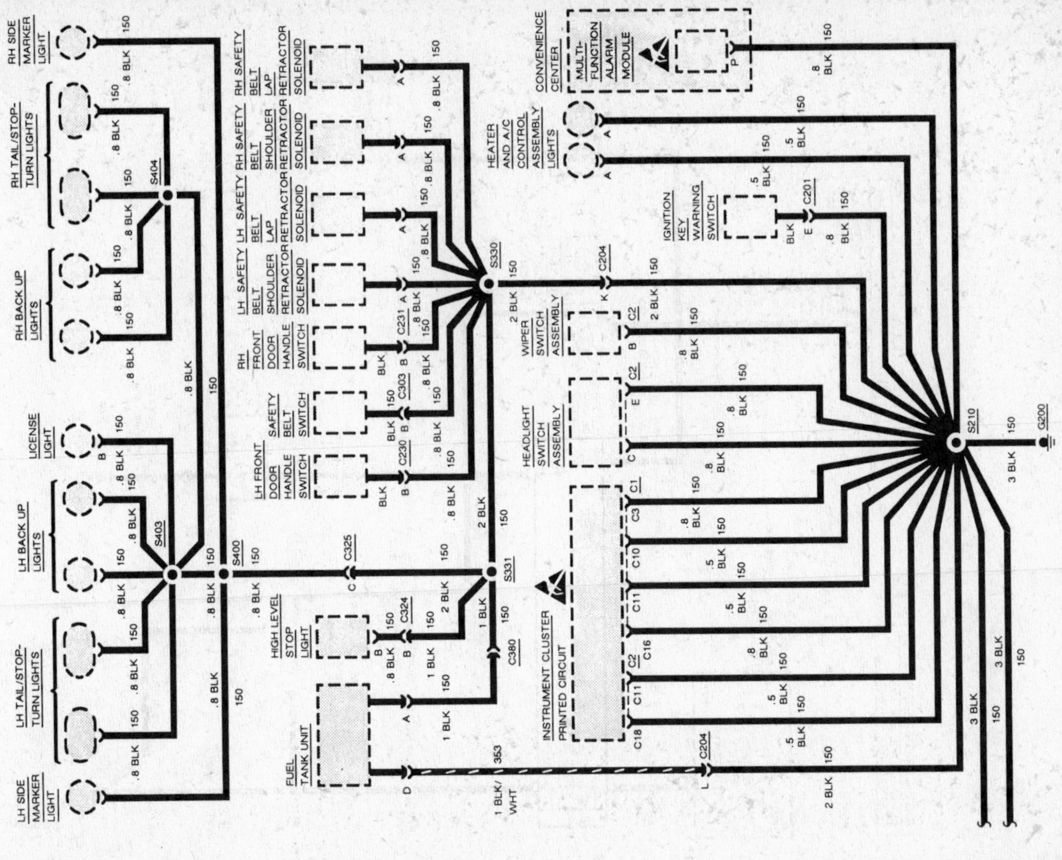

Calais — Ground distribution

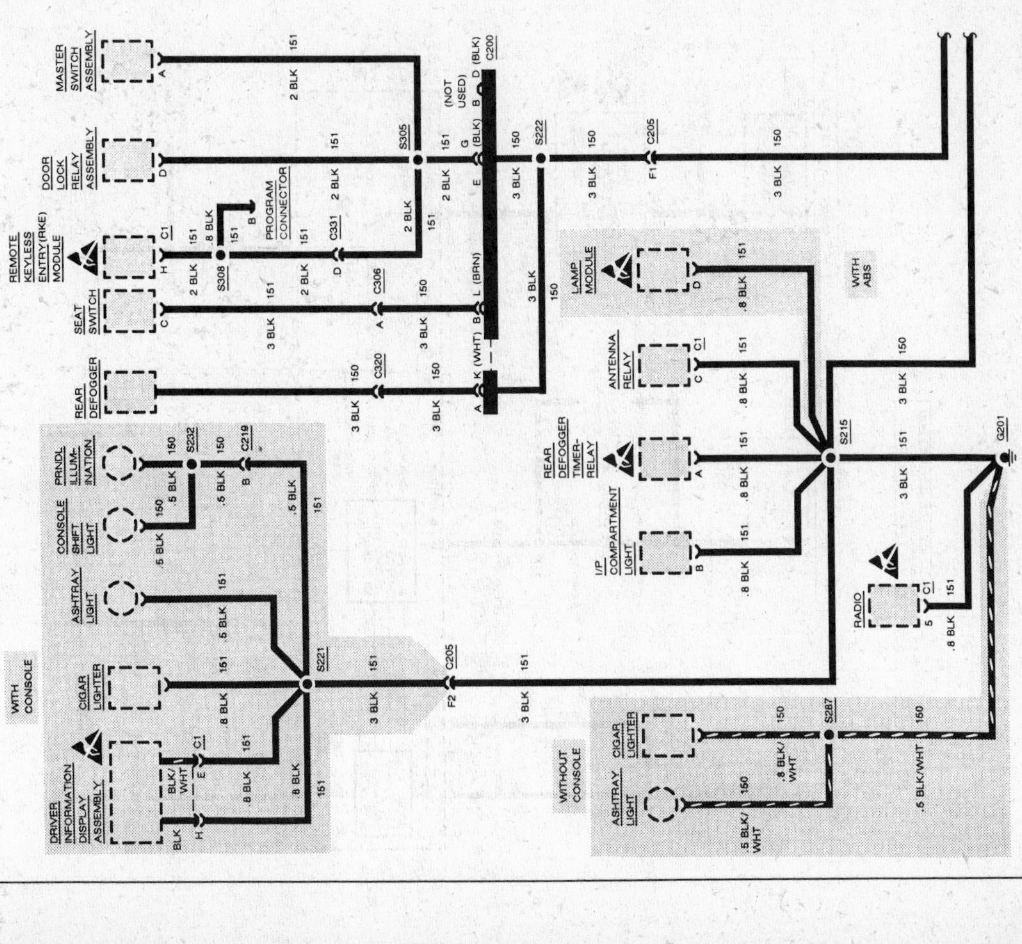

Calais — Ground distribution

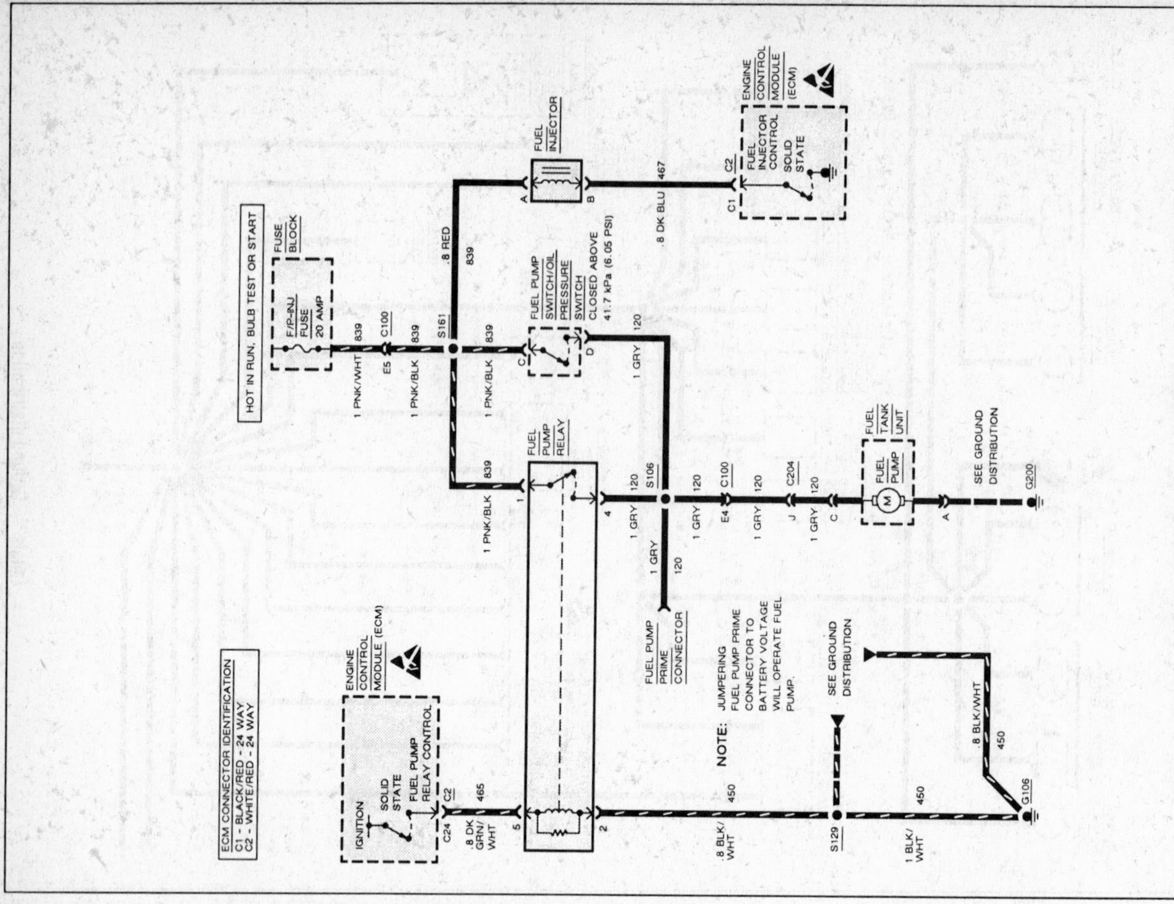

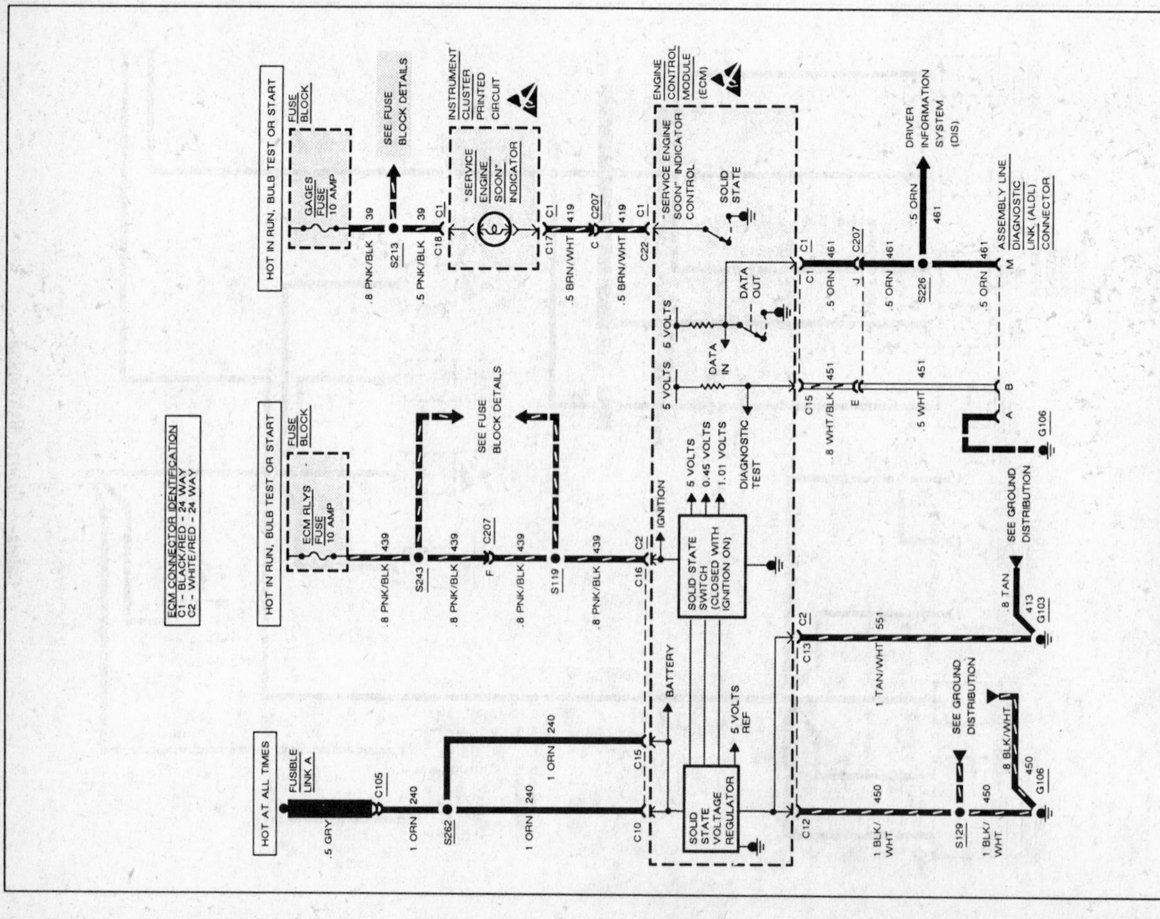

Calais — Power, grounds and "Service Engine Soon" indicator

NOTE: JUMPERING FUEL PUMP PRIME CONNECTOR TO BATTERY VOLTAGE WILL OPERATE FUEL PUMP.

Calais — Electronic fuel injection — 2.5L engine — fuel injector and fuel control

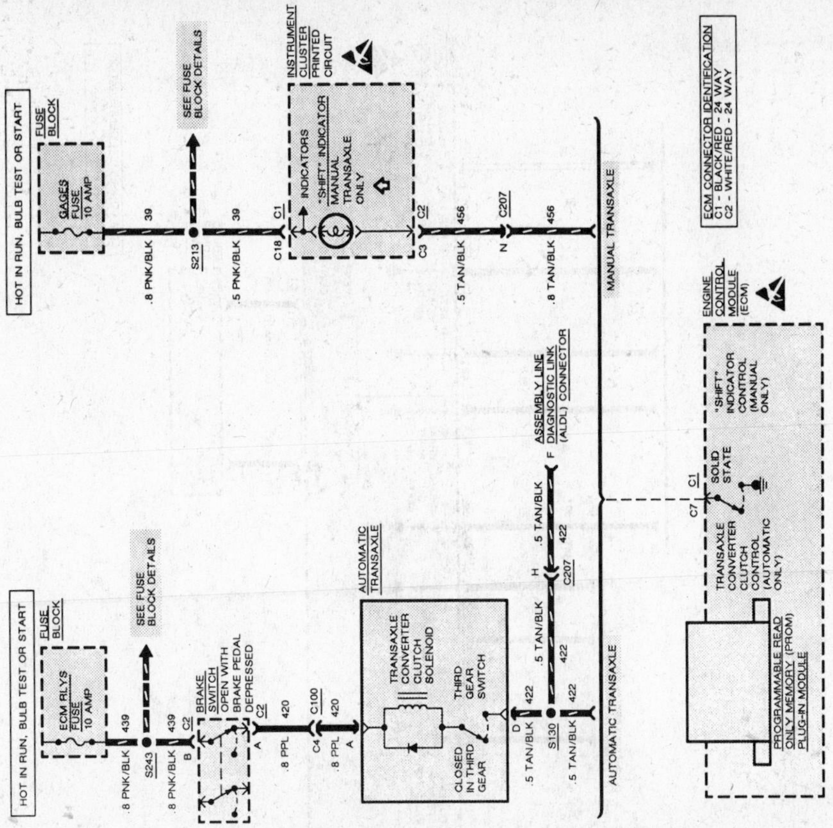

Calais — Electronic fuel injection — 2.5L engine — transaxle converter clutch/shift indicator

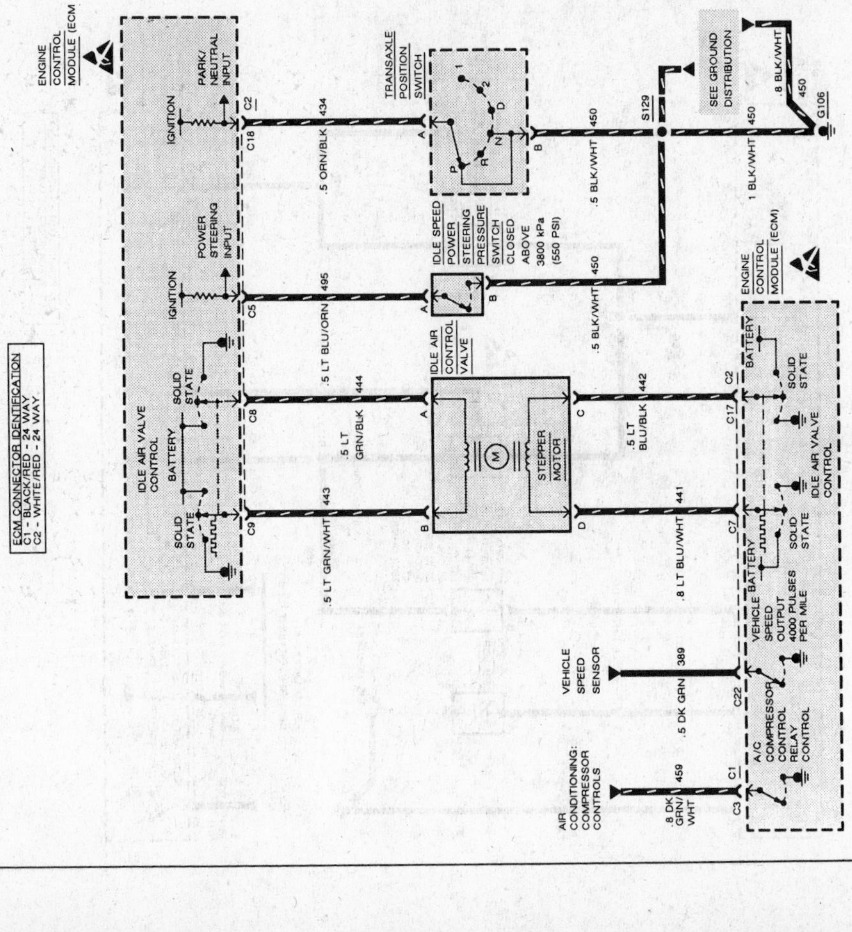

Calais — Vehicle data sensors and idle air control

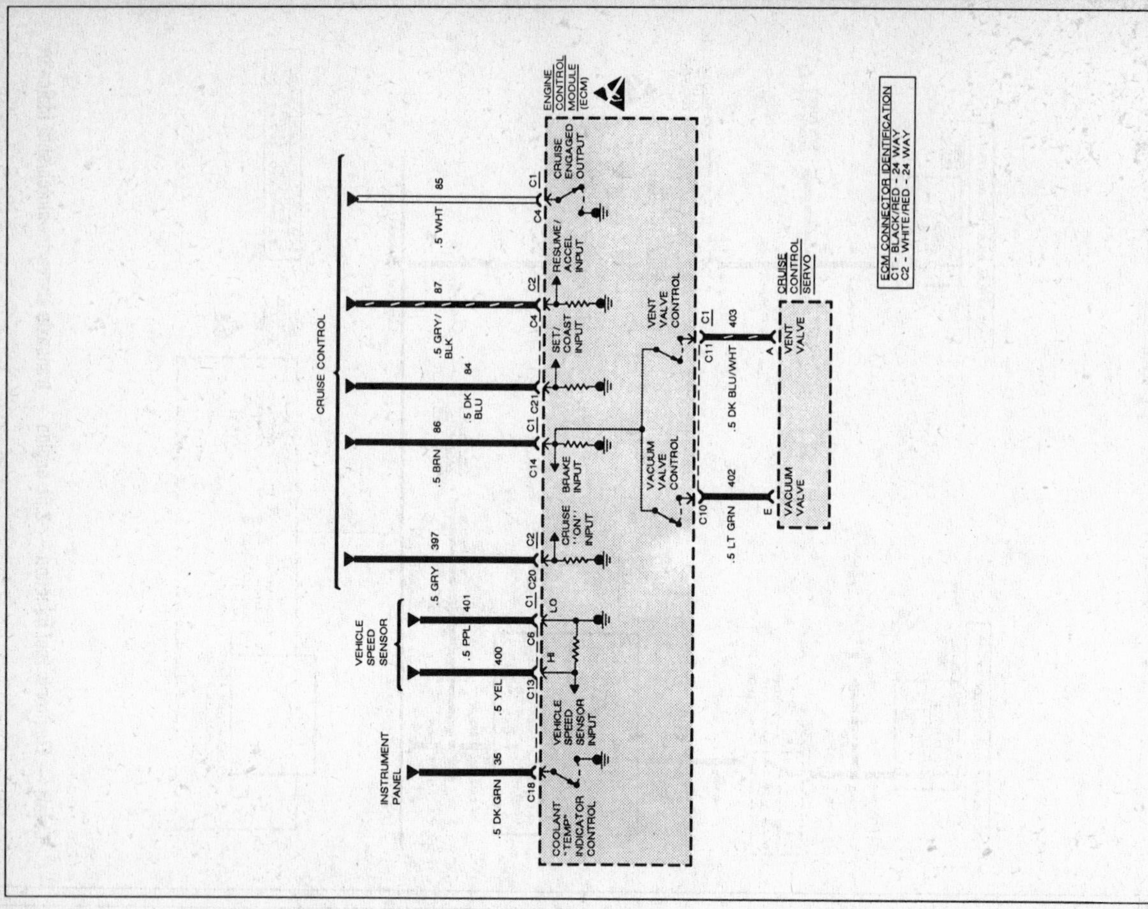

Calais — Electronic fuel injection — 2.5L engine — vehicle data sensors

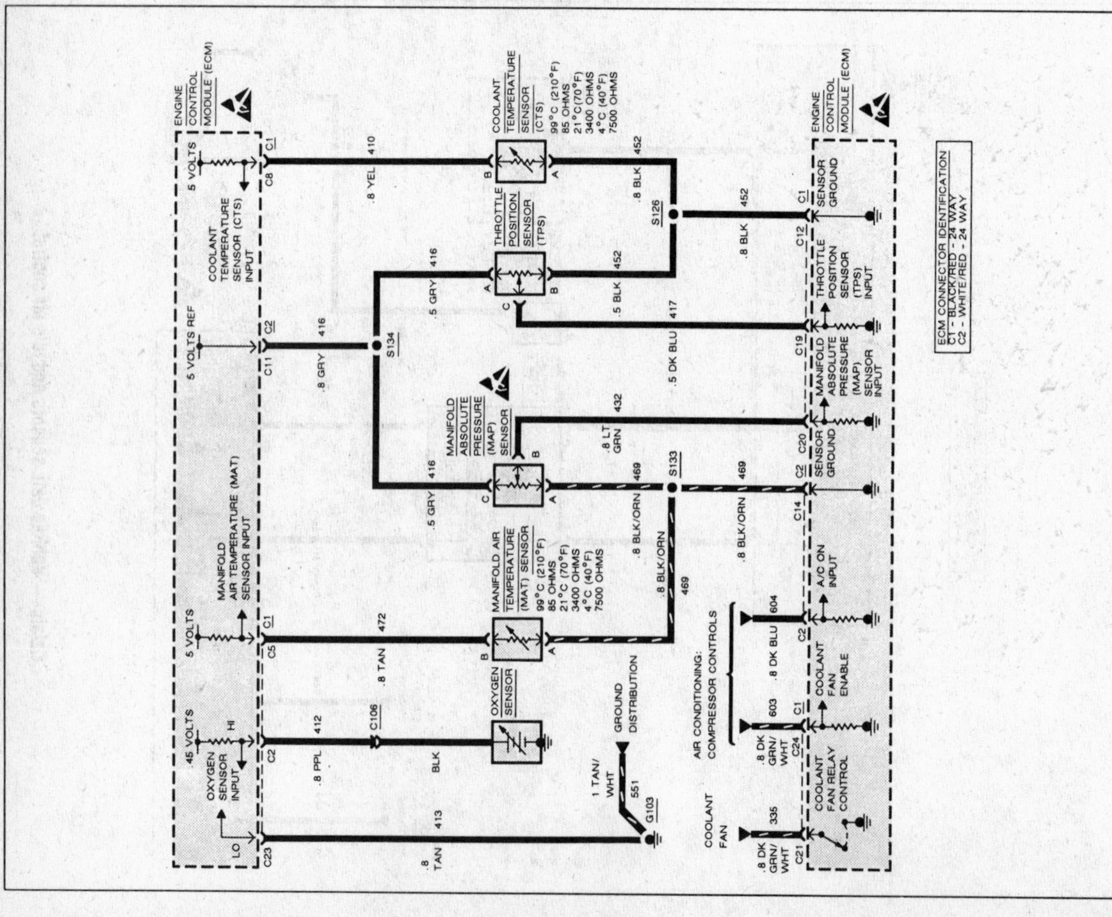

Calais — Engine data sensors

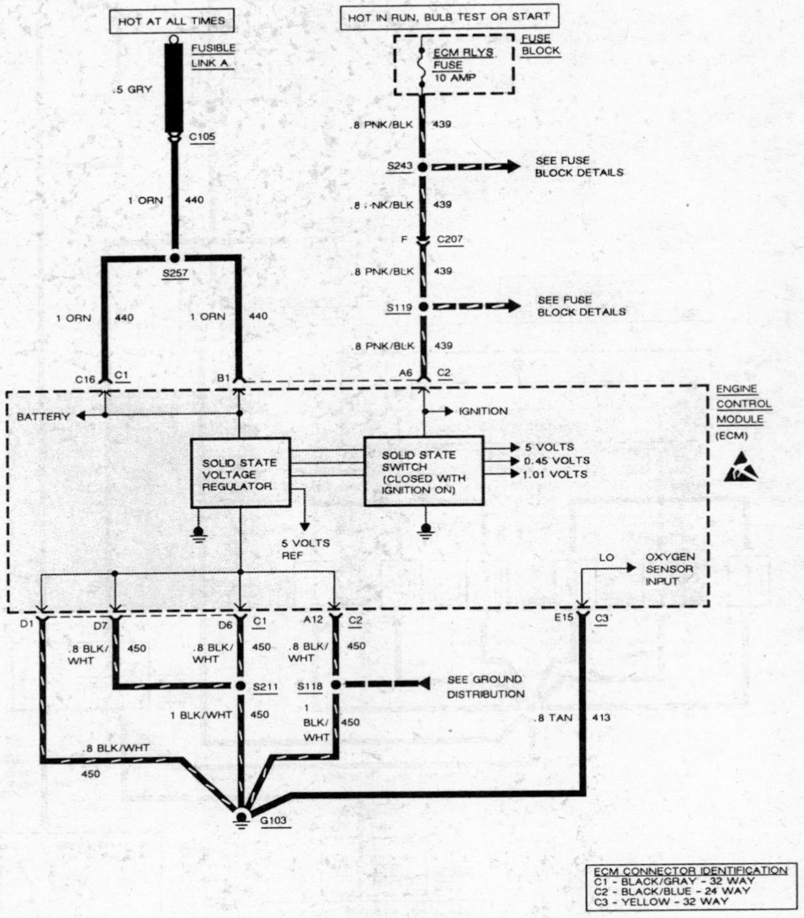

Calais — Multi-port fuel injection — 3.3L engine — power and grounds

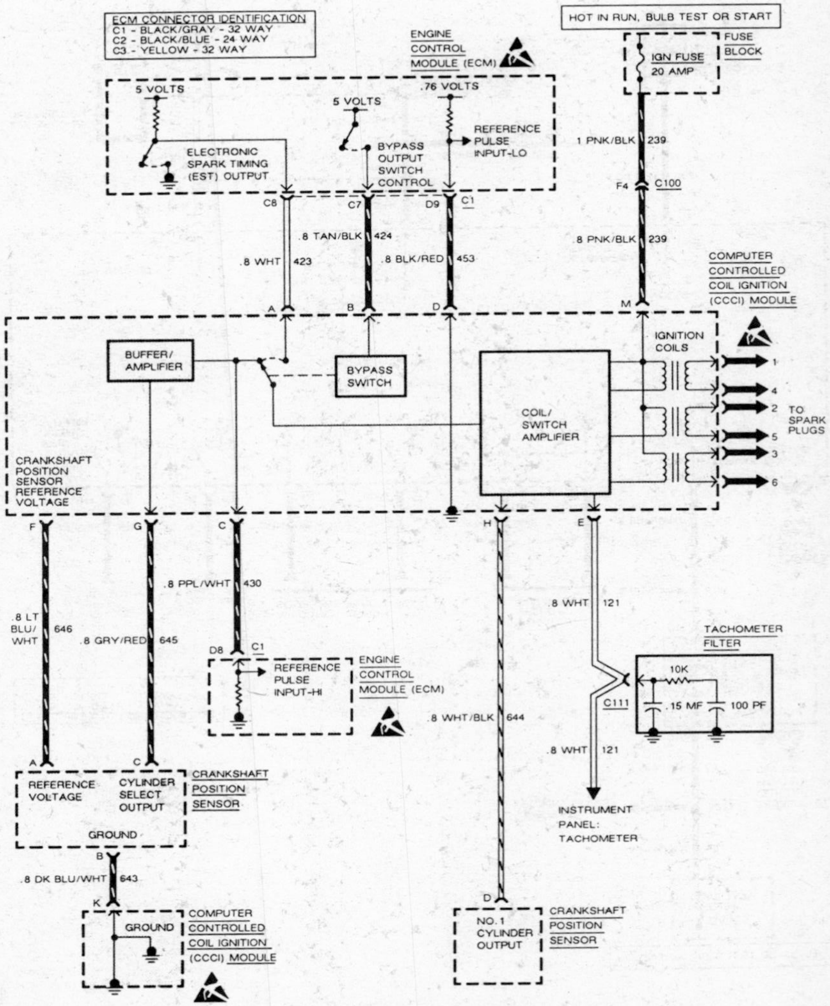

Calais — Ignition

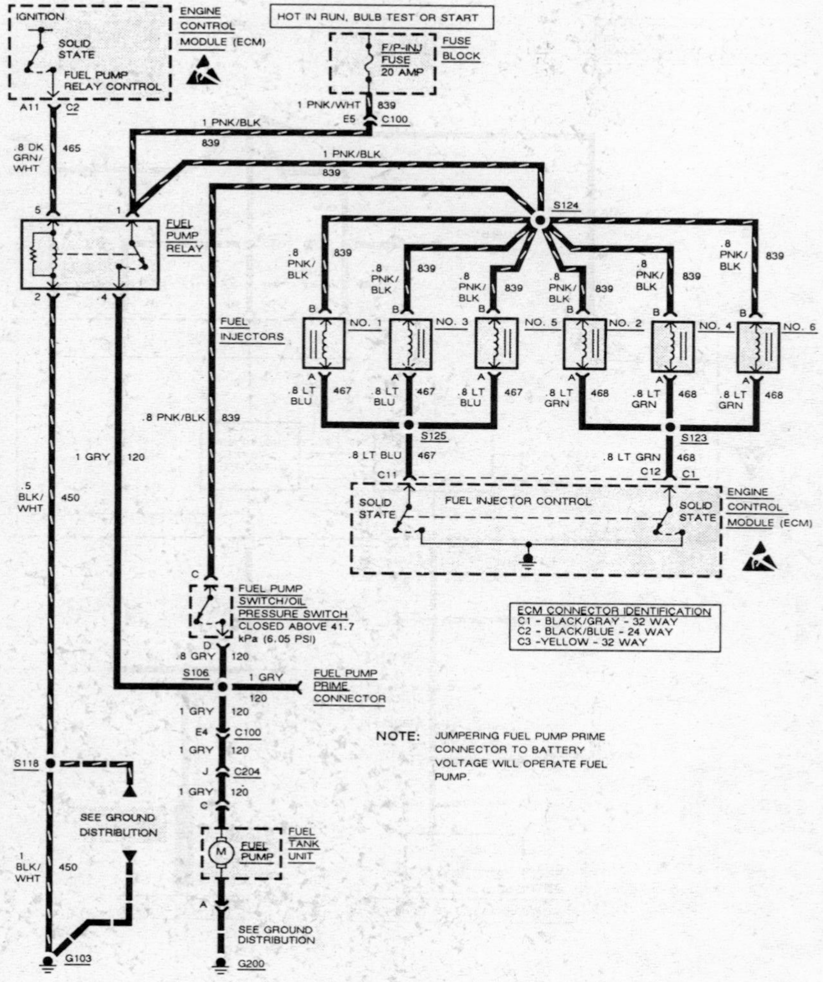

Calais – Multi-port fuel injection – 3.3L engine – injectors and fuel control

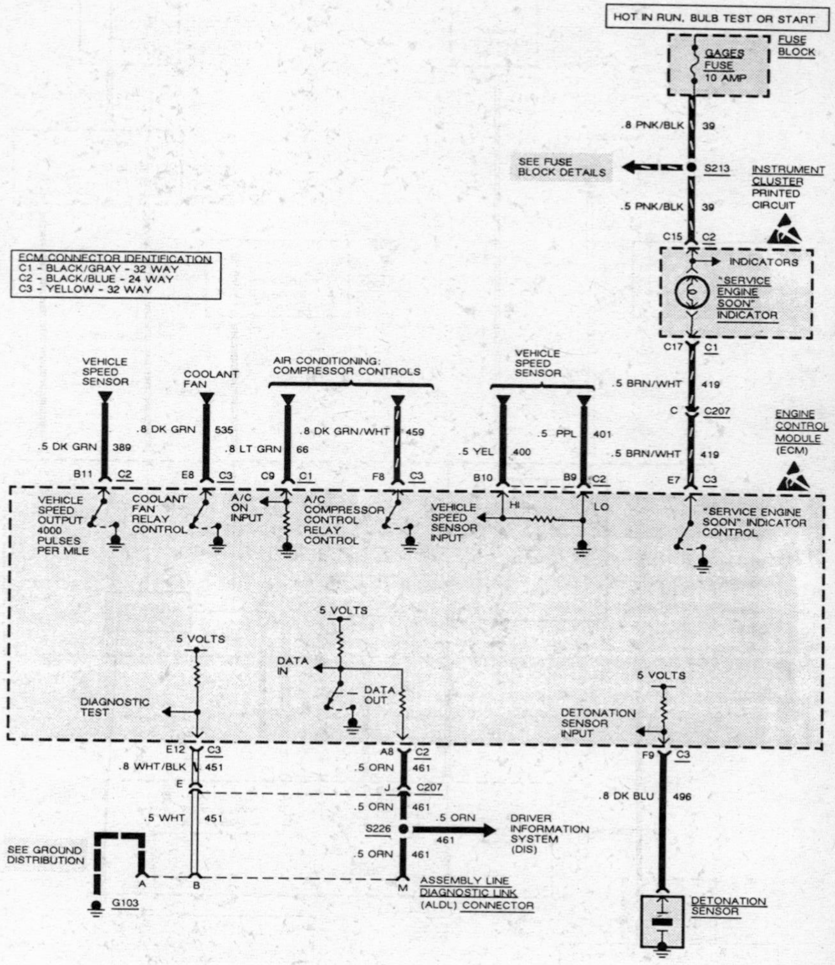

Calais – "Service Engine Soon" indicator and engine data sensors

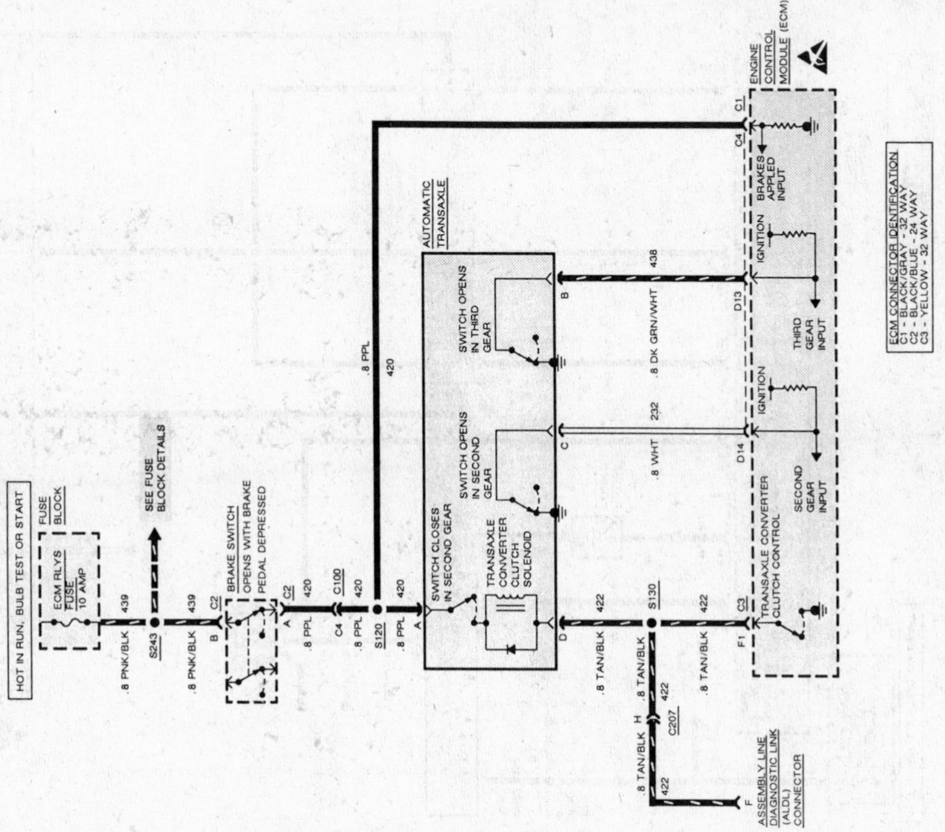

HOT IN RUN, BULB TEST OR START
FUSE BLOCK
ECM RLYS FUSE 10 AMP
.8 PNK/BLK 439
S243
SEE FUSE BLOCK DETAILS
.8 PNK/BLK 439
B C2
BRAKE SWITCH OPENS WITH BRAKE PEDAL DEPRESSED
A C2
.8 PPL 420
C4 C100
.8 PPL 420
S120
.8 PPL 420
.8 PPL 420
A
AUTOMATIC TRANSAXLE
SWITCH CLOSES IN SECOND GEAR
TRANSAXLE CONVERTER CLUTCH SOLENOID
SWITCH OPENS IN SECOND GEAR
SWITCH OPENS IN THIRD GEAR
D C B
.8 TAN/BLK 422
.8 TAN/BLK H .8 TAN/BLK
422 C207 422
S130
.8 WHT 232
.8 DK GRN/WHT 438
.8 TAN/BLK 422
F
ASSEMBLY LINE DIAGNOSTIC LINK (ALDL) CONNECTOR
F1 C3 D14 D13 C4 C1
TRANSAXLE CONVERTER CLUTCH CONTROL
IGNITION
SECOND GEAR INPUT
IGNITION
THIRD GEAR INPUT
BRAKES APPLIED INPUT
ENGINE CONTROL MODULE (ECM)

ECM CONNECTOR IDENTIFICATION
C1 - BLACK/GRAY - 32 WAY
C2 - BLACK/BLUE - 24 WAY
C3 - YELLOW - 32 WAY

Calais — Multi-port fuel injection — 3.3L engine — transaxle converter clutch

ENGINE CONTROL MODULE (ECM)
BATTERY
IDLE AIR MOTOR CONTROL
E5 E6 C3
.5 LT GRN/WHT 443
.5 LT GRN/BLK 444
A B
IDLE AIR CONTROL MOTOR
STEPPER MOTOR
M
C D
.5 LT BLU/WHT 441
.5 LT BLU/BLK 442
E3 E4 C3
BATTERY
IDLE AIR MOTOR CONTROL
BATTERY
PROGRAMMABLE READ ONLY MEMORY (PROM) PLUG-IN MODULE

HOT IN RUN, BULB TEST OR START
FUSE BLOCK
ECM RLYS FUSE 10 AMPS
.8 PNK/BLK 439
S243
SEE FUSE BLOCK DETAILS
.8 PNK/BLK 439
F C207
.8 PNK/BLK 439
S119
SEE FUSE BLOCK DETAILS
.5 PNK/BLK 439
A
VAPOR CANISTER PURGE SOLENOID
B
.5 DK GRN/YEL 428
INSTRUMENT PANEL: GAGES
.5 DK GRN 35
F7 F2 C3
VAPOR CANISTER PURGE SOLENOID CONTROL
COOLANT "TEMP" INDICATOR CONTROL
ENGINE CONTROL MODULE (ECM)
IGNITION
POWER STEERING INPUT
IGNITION
PARK/ NEUTRAL INPUT
D12 D16 C1
.5 LT BLU/ORN 495
.5 ORN/BLK 434
A A
IDLE SPEED POWER STEERING PRESSURE SWITCH CLOSED ABOVE 3800 kPa (550 PSI)
B
TRANSAXLE POSITION SWITCH
P R N D 2 1
B
.5 BLK/WHT 450
.8 BLK/WHT S118
450
SEE GROUND DISTRIBUTION
1 BLK/WHT 450
G103

ECM CONNECTOR IDENTIFICATION
C1 - BLACK/GRAY - 32 WAY
C2 - BLACK/BLUE - 24 WAY
C3 - YELLOW - 32 WAY

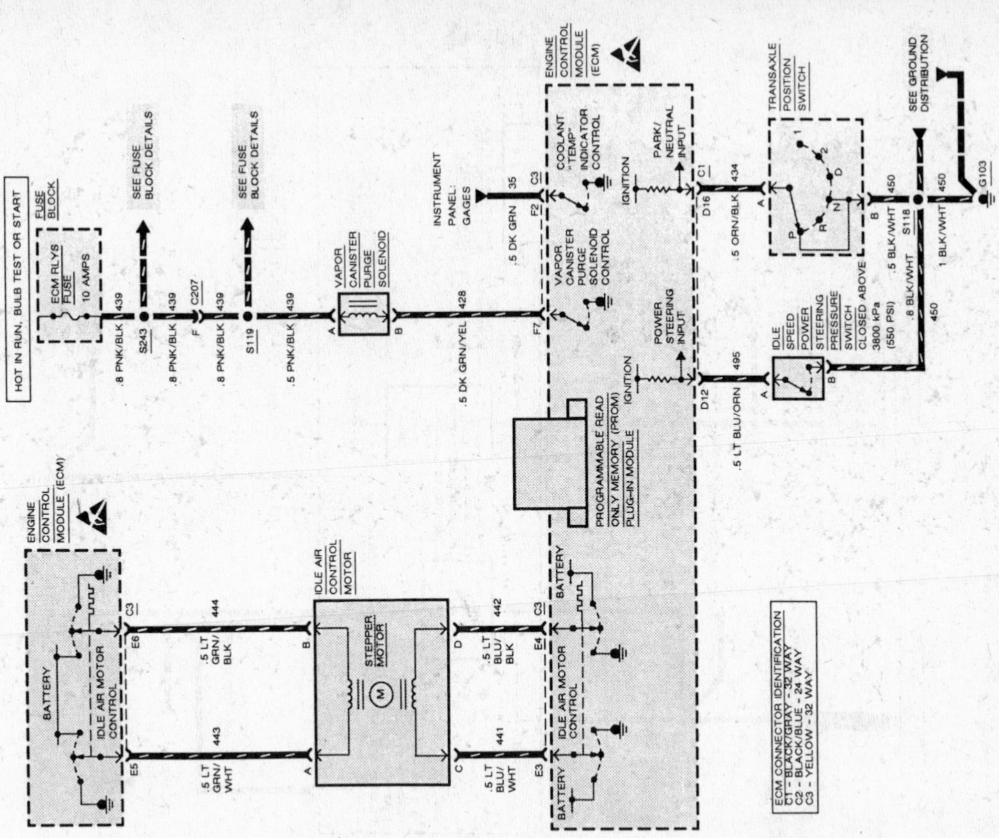

Calais — Idle air control and engine data sensors

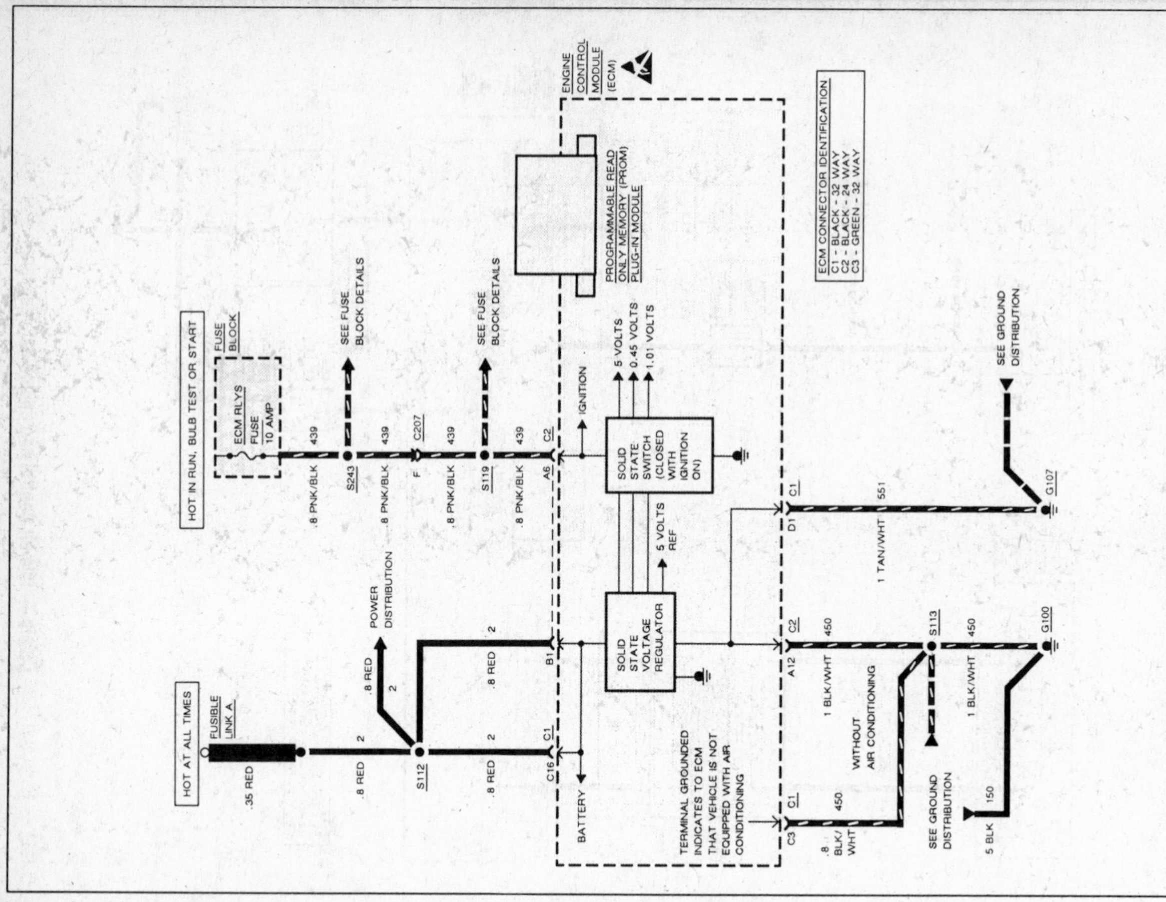

Calais — Multi-port fuel injection — 2.3L and 2.3L HO engines — power and grounds

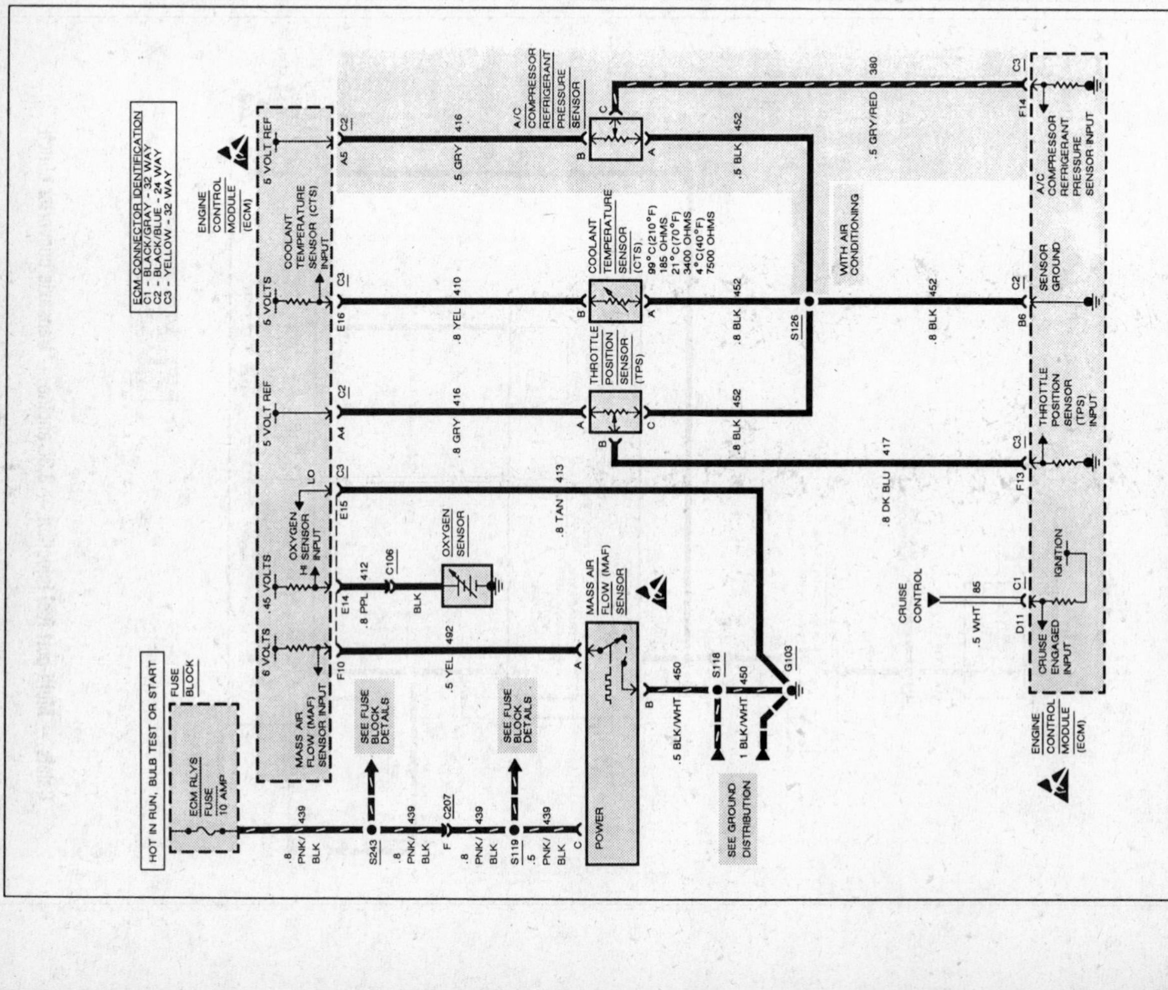

Calais — Multi-port fuel injection — 3.3L engine — engine data sensors

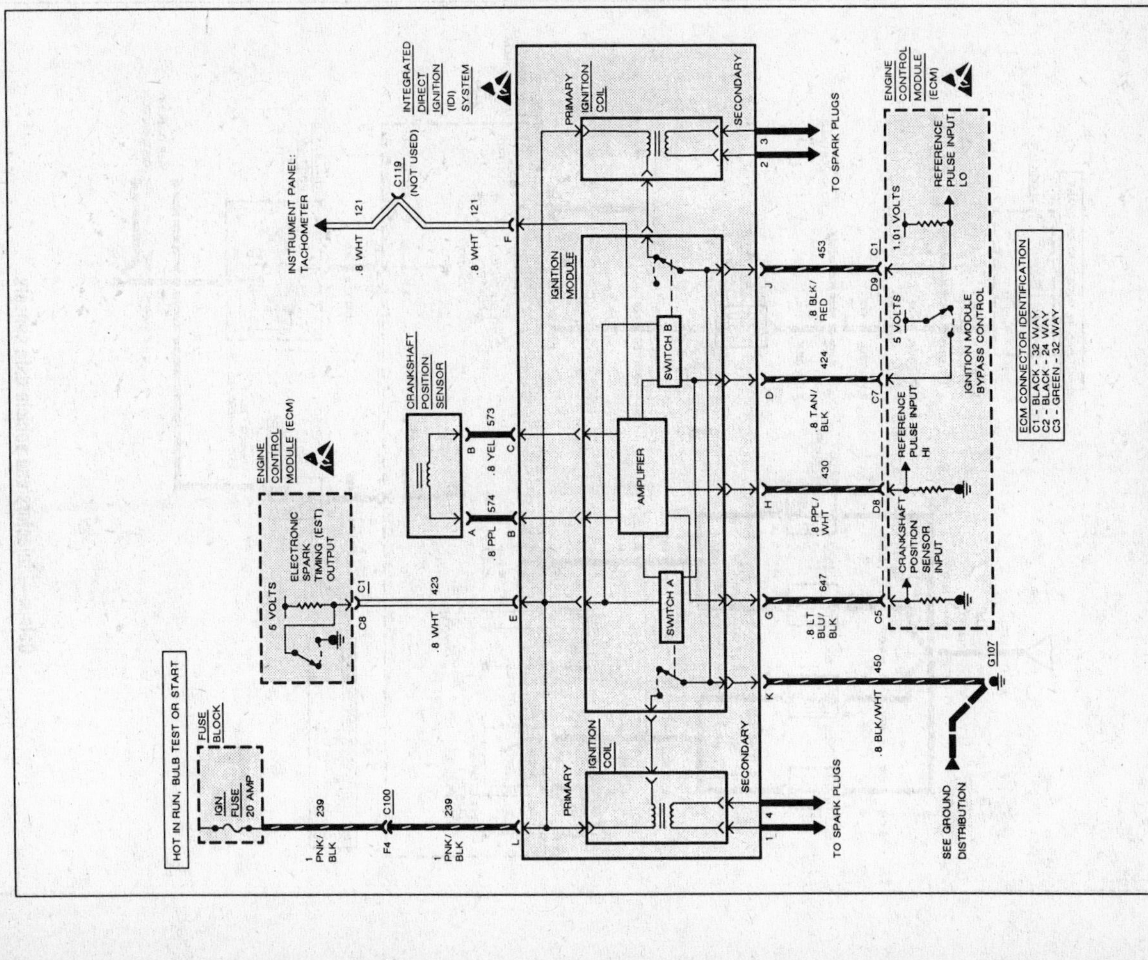

HOT IN RUN, BULB TEST OR START
FUSE BLOCK
IGN FUSE 20 AMP
1 PNK/BLK 239
F4 C100
1 PNK/BLK 239
ENGINE CONTROL MODULE (ECM)
5 VOLTS
ELECTRONIC SPARK TIMING (EST) OUTPUT
C8 C1
.8 WHT 423
CRANKSHAFT POSITION SENSOR
A B
.8 PPL 574 .8 YEL 573
INSTRUMENT PANEL: TACHOMETER
.8 WHT 121
C119 (NOT USED)
.8 WHT 121
INTEGRATED DIRECT IGNITION (IDI) SYSTEM
L E B C F
PRIMARY
IGNITION COIL
IGNITION MODULE
AMPLIFIER
SWITCH A
SWITCH B
PRIMARY
IGNITION COIL
SECONDARY
SECONDARY
1 4 K G H D J 2 3
TO SPARK PLUGS
.8 LT BLU/BLK 647
.8 PPL/WHT 430
.8 TAN/BLK 424
.8 BLK/RED 453
TO SPARK PLUGS
.8 BLK/WHT 450
C5 D8 C7 D9 C1
CRANKSHAFT POSITION SENSOR INPUT
REFERENCE PULSE INPUT HI
5 VOLTS
1.01 VOLTS
REFERENCE PULSE INPUT LO
IGNITION MODULE BYPASS CONTROL
ENGINE CONTROL MODULE (ECM)
SEE GROUND DISTRIBUTION
G107

ECM CONNECTOR IDENTIFICATION
C1 - BLACK - 32 WAY
C2 - BLACK - 24 WAY
C3 - GREEN - 32 WAY

Calais – Ignition

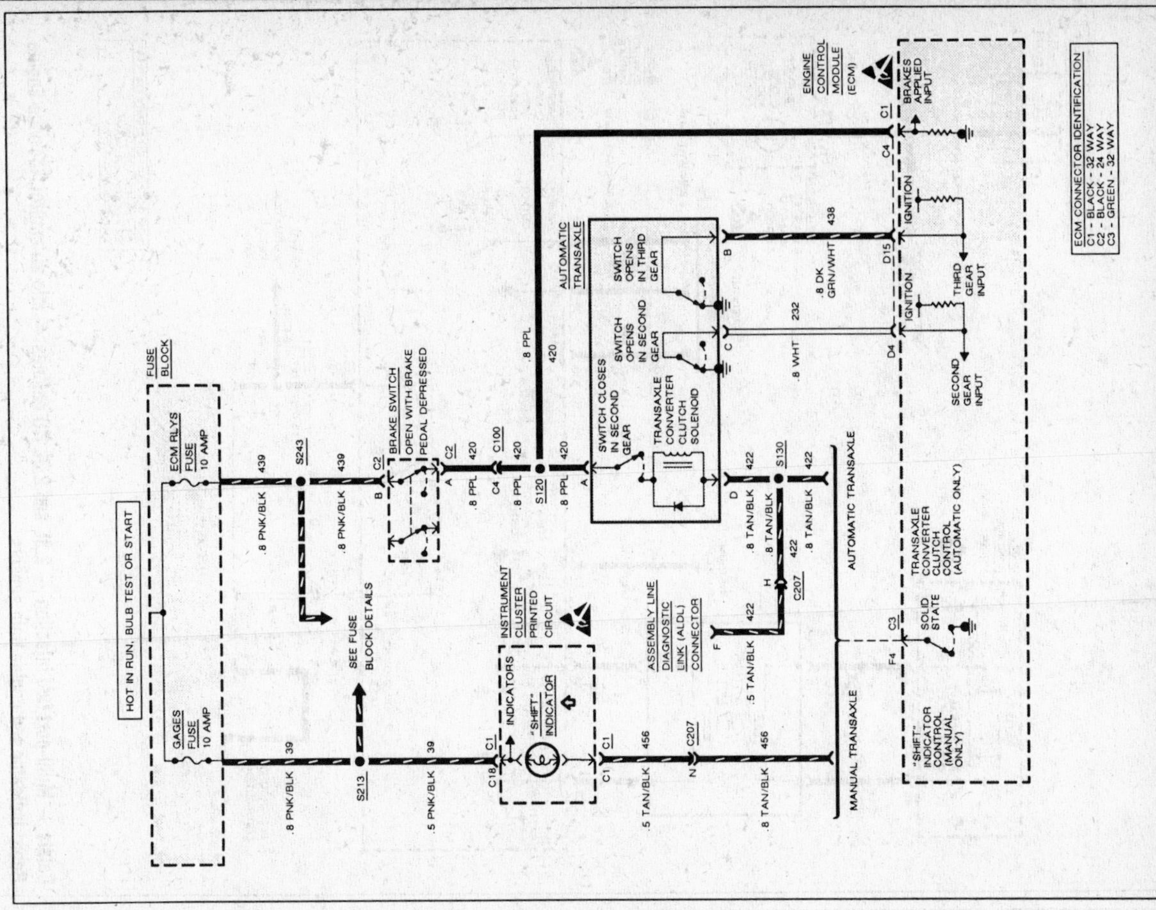

HOT IN RUN, BULB TEST OR START
FUSE BLOCK
GAGES FUSE 10 AMP
ECM RLYS FUSE 10 AMP
.8 PNK/BLK 39
.8 PNK/BLK 439
S243
S213
SEE FUSE BLOCK DETAILS
.8 PNK/BLK 439
B C2
BRAKE SWITCH
OPEN WITH BRAKE PEDAL DEPRESSED
.5 PNK/BLK 39
A C2
.8 PPL 420
C4 C100
.8 PPL 420
S120
.8 PPL 420
.8 PPL 420
C18 C1
INDICATORS
"SHIFT" INDICATOR
INSTRUMENT CLUSTER PRINTED CIRCUIT
C1 C1
A
AUTOMATIC TRANSAXLE
SWITCH CLOSES IN SECOND GEAR
TRANSAXLE CONVERTER CLUTCH SOLENOID
SWITCH OPENS IN SECOND GEAR
SWITCH OPENS IN THIRD GEAR
.5 TAN/BLK 456
N C207
ASSEMBLY LINE DIAGNOSTIC LINK (ALDL) CONNECTOR
F
.5 TAN/BLK 422
D
.8 TAN/BLK 422
.8 TAN/BLK
H S130
C207 422
.8 TAN/BLK 422
.8 TAN/BLK 456
C B
.8 WHT 232
.8 DK GRN/WHT 438
MANUAL TRANSAXLE
AUTOMATIC TRANSAXLE
ENGINE CONTROL MODULE (ECM)
F4 C3 D4 D15 C4 C1
"SHIFT" INDICATOR CONTROL (MANUAL ONLY)
SOLID STATE
TRANSAXLE CONVERTER CLUTCH CONTROL (AUTOMATIC ONLY)
IGNITION
IGNITION
BRAKES APPLIED INPUT
SECOND GEAR INPUT
THIRD GEAR INPUT

ECM CONNECTOR IDENTIFICATION
C1 - BLACK - 32 WAY
C2 - BLACK - 24 WAY
C3 - GREEN - 32 WAY

Calais – Multi-port fuel injection – 2.3L and 2.3L HO engines – transaxle converter clutch/shift indicator

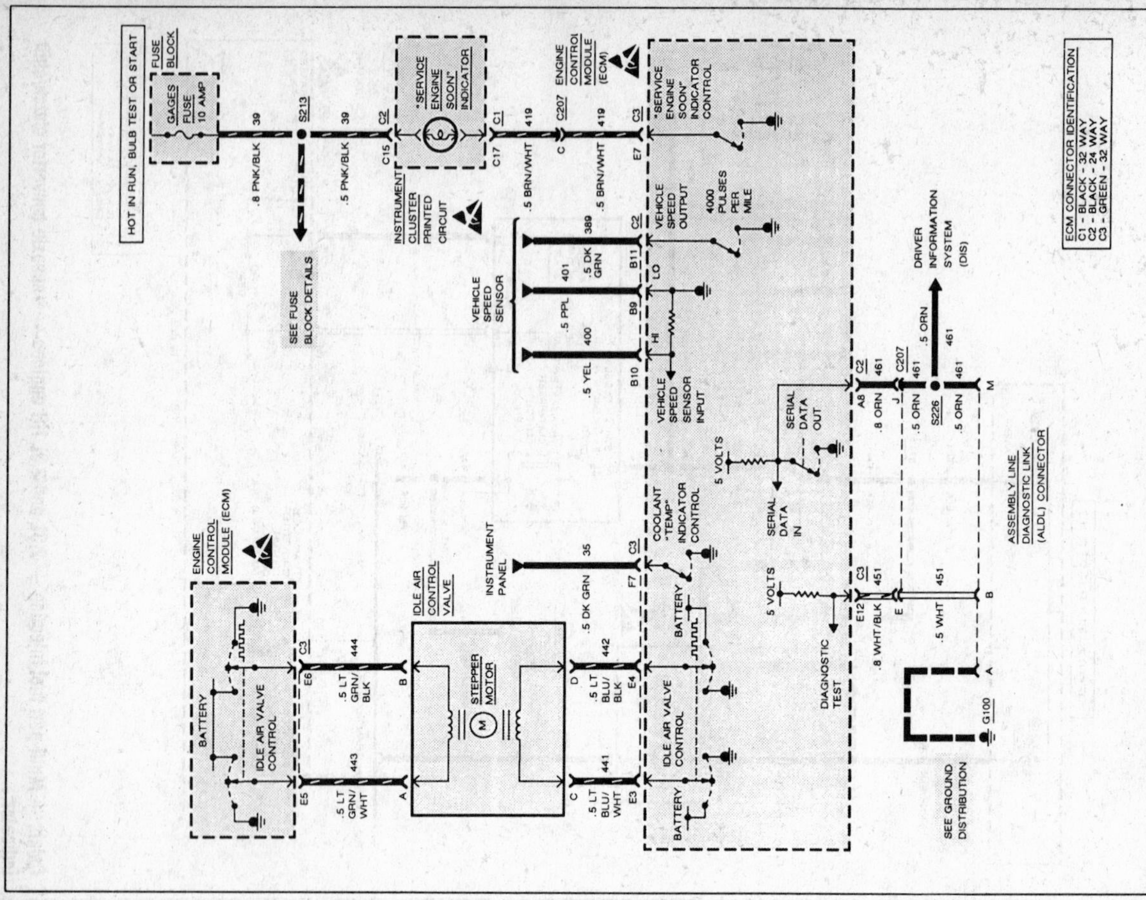

ECM CONNECTOR IDENTIFICATION
C1 - BLACK - 32 WAY
C2 - BLACK - 24 WAY
C3 - GREEN - 32 WAY

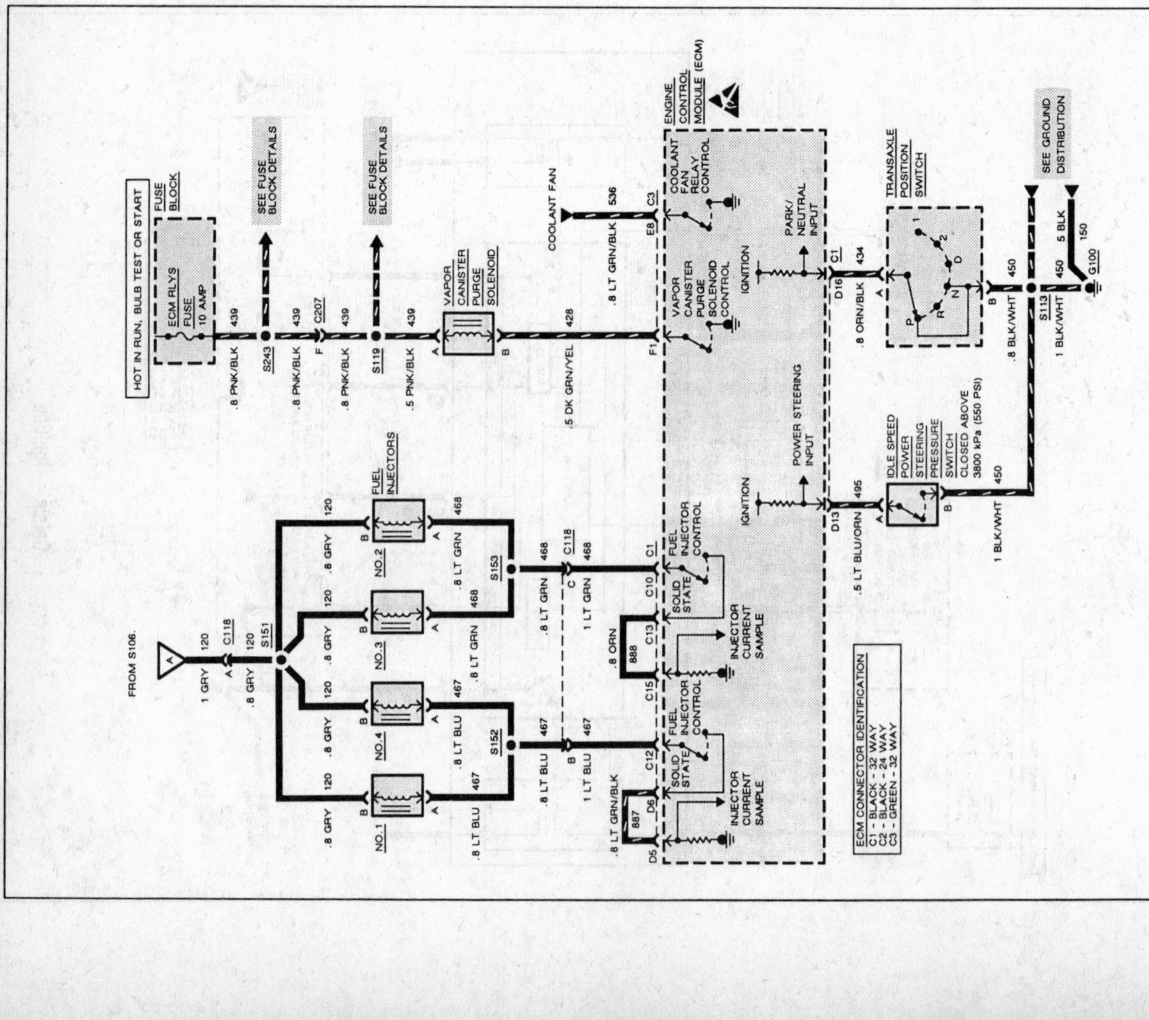

Calais — Injectors and vehicle data sensors

ECM CONNECTOR IDENTIFICATION
C1 - BLACK - 32 WAY
C2 - BLACK - 24 WAY
C3 - GREEN - 32 WAY

Calais — Multi-port fuel injection — 2.3L and 2.3L HO engines — idle air control, "Service Engine Soon" indicator and engine data sensors

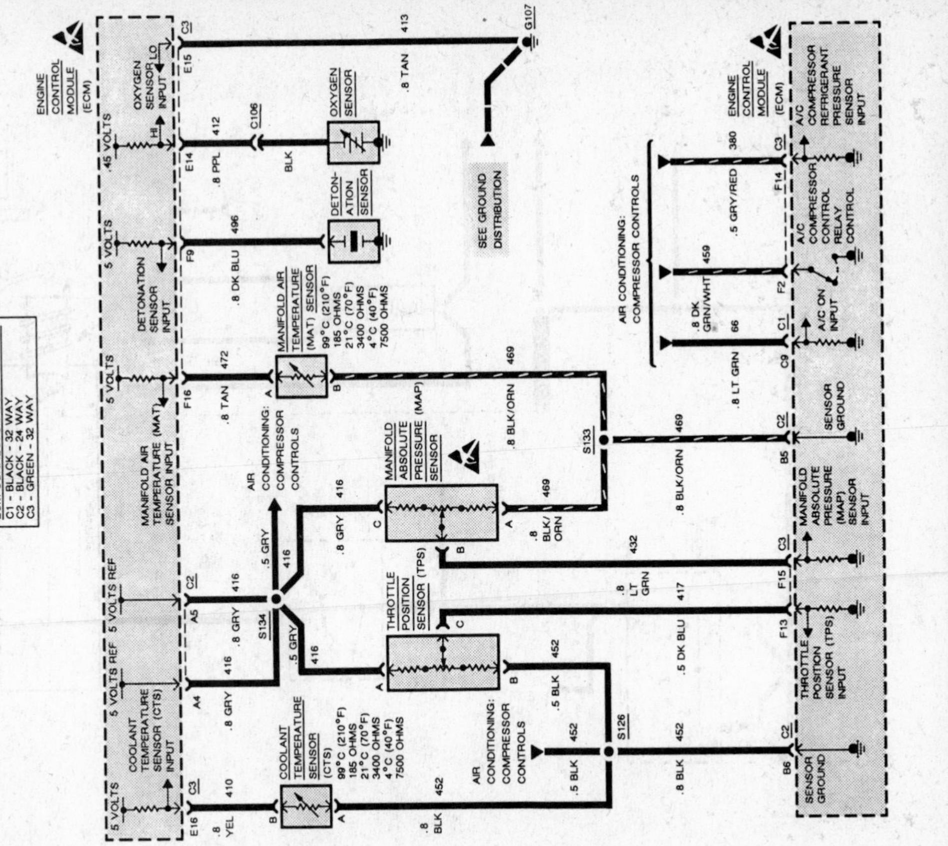

Calais — Fuel control

Calais — Multi-port fuel injection — 2.3L and 2.3L HO engines — engine data sensors

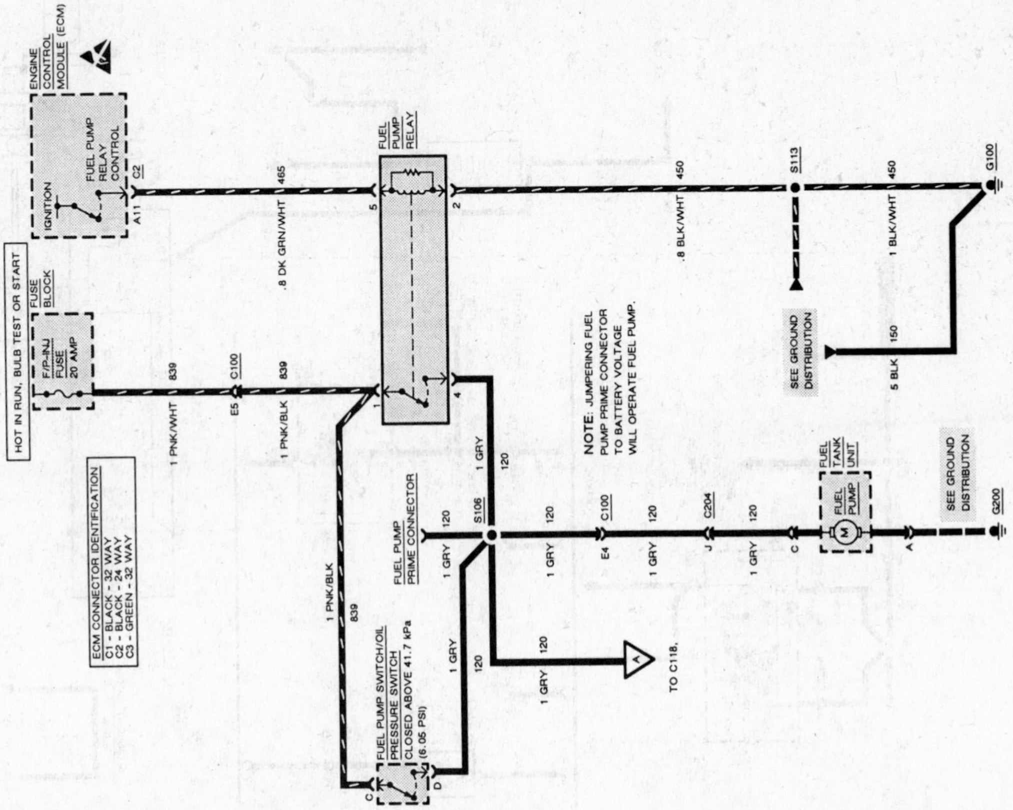

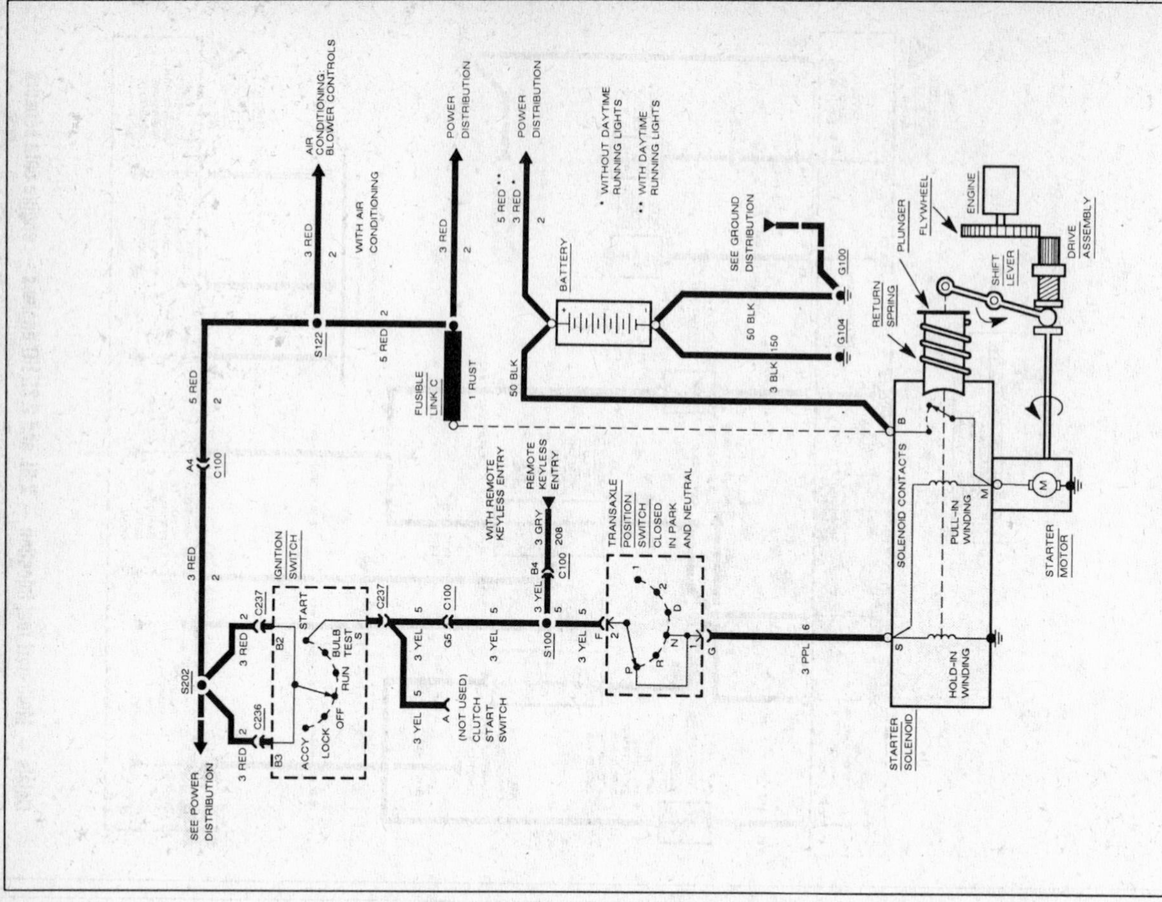

SEE POWER DISTRIBUTION
S202
3 RED 2
A4 C100
5 RED 2
S122
5 RED 2
FUSIBLE LINK C
1 RUST
3 RED 2
C236
3 RED 2
C237
3 RED 2
3 RED 2
B3
B2
IGNITION SWITCH
ACCY
LOCK
OFF
RUN
BULB TEST
START
S
C237
AIR CONDITIONING: BLOWER CONTROLS
WITH AIR CONDITIONING
CHARGING SYSTEM, POWER DISTRIBUTION
* WITHOUT DAYTIME RUNNING LIGHTS
** WITH DAYTIME RUNNING LIGHTS
POWER DISTRIBUTION
5 RED 2 **
1 RED 2 *
3 YEL 5
3 YEL 5
MANUAL
AUTOMATIC
3 YEL 5
3 YEL 5
G5 C100
(NOT USED)
3 YEL 5
A
(NOT USED)
CLUTCH START SWITCH
3 YEL 5
G5 C100
3 YEL 5
S110
3 YEL B4
5 C100
3 GRY
208
WITH REMOTE KEYLESS ENTRY
REMOTE KEYLESS ENTRY
3 YEL 5
A
CLUTCH START SWITCH CLOSED WITH CLUTCH PEDAL DEPRESSED
B
3 PPL 6
G4 C100
3 PPL 6
F
2
P
1
R
N
D
2
1
G
TRANSAXLE POSITION SWITCH CLOSED IN PARK AND NEUTRAL
3 PPL 6
19 BLK
BATTERY
GROUND DISTRIBUTION
19 BLK
3 BLK 150
5 BLK 150
G104
G100
STARTER SOLENOID
S
SOLENOID CONTACTS
B
HOLD-IN WINDING
PULL-IN WINDING
M
RETURN SPRING
PLUNGER
FLYWHEEL
ENGINE
SHIFT LEVER
STARTER MOTOR
DRIVE ASSEMBLY
GROUND STRAP 6 BLK
(ENGINE)
(BODY)

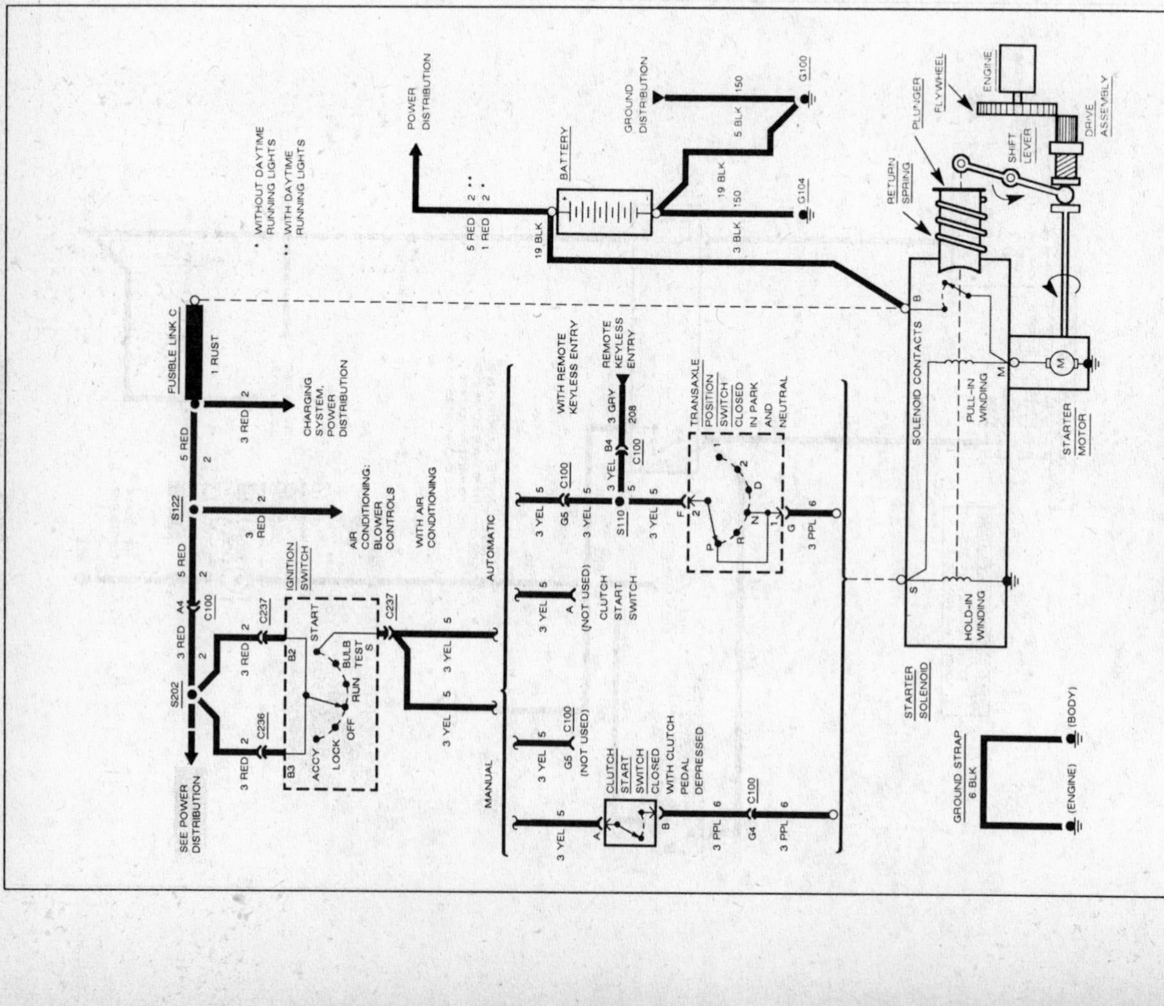

Calais — Starter and charging system — 2.5L engine

SEE POWER DISTRIBUTION
S202
3 RED 2
A4 C100
5 RED 2
3 RED 2
C236
3 RED 2
C237
B3
B2
IGNITION SWITCH
ACCY
LOCK
OFF
RUN
BULB TEST
START
S
S122
3 RED 2
AIR CONDITIONING: BLOWER CONTROLS
WITH AIR CONDITIONING
5 RED 2
C237
3 YEL 5
3 YEL 5
A
(NOT USED) CLUTCH START SWITCH
G5 C100
FUSIBLE LINK C
1 RUST
3 RED 2
POWER DISTRIBUTION
3 YEL 5
WITH REMOTE KEYLESS ENTRY
50 BLK
5 RED **
3 RED *
2
POWER DISTRIBUTION
S100
3 YEL B4
3 GRY
REMOTE KEYLESS ENTRY
5 C100 208
3 YEL 5
BATTERY
F
2
P
1
R
N
D
2
1
G
TRANSAXLE POSITION SWITCH CLOSED IN PARK AND NEUTRAL
* WITHOUT DAYTIME RUNNING LIGHTS
** WITH DAYTIME RUNNING LIGHTS
SEE GROUND DISTRIBUTION
50 BLK
3 BLK 150
3 PPL 6
G104
G100
STARTER SOLENOID
S
SOLENOID CONTACTS
B
HOLD-IN WINDING
PULL-IN WINDING
M
RETURN SPRING
PLUNGER
FLYWHEEL
ENGINE
SHIFT LEVER
STARTER MOTOR
DRIVE ASSEMBLY

Calais — Starter — 3.3L engine

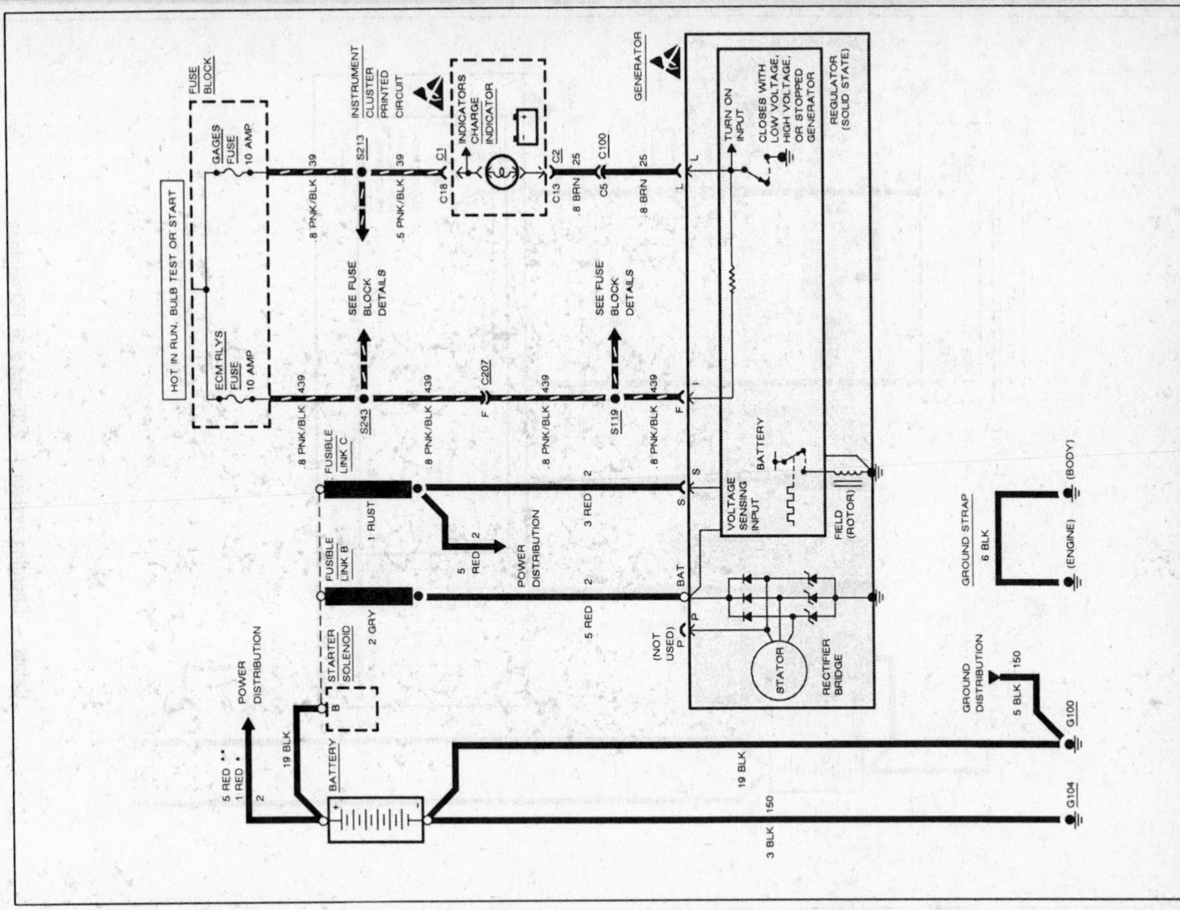

Calais — Charging system — 2.5L engine

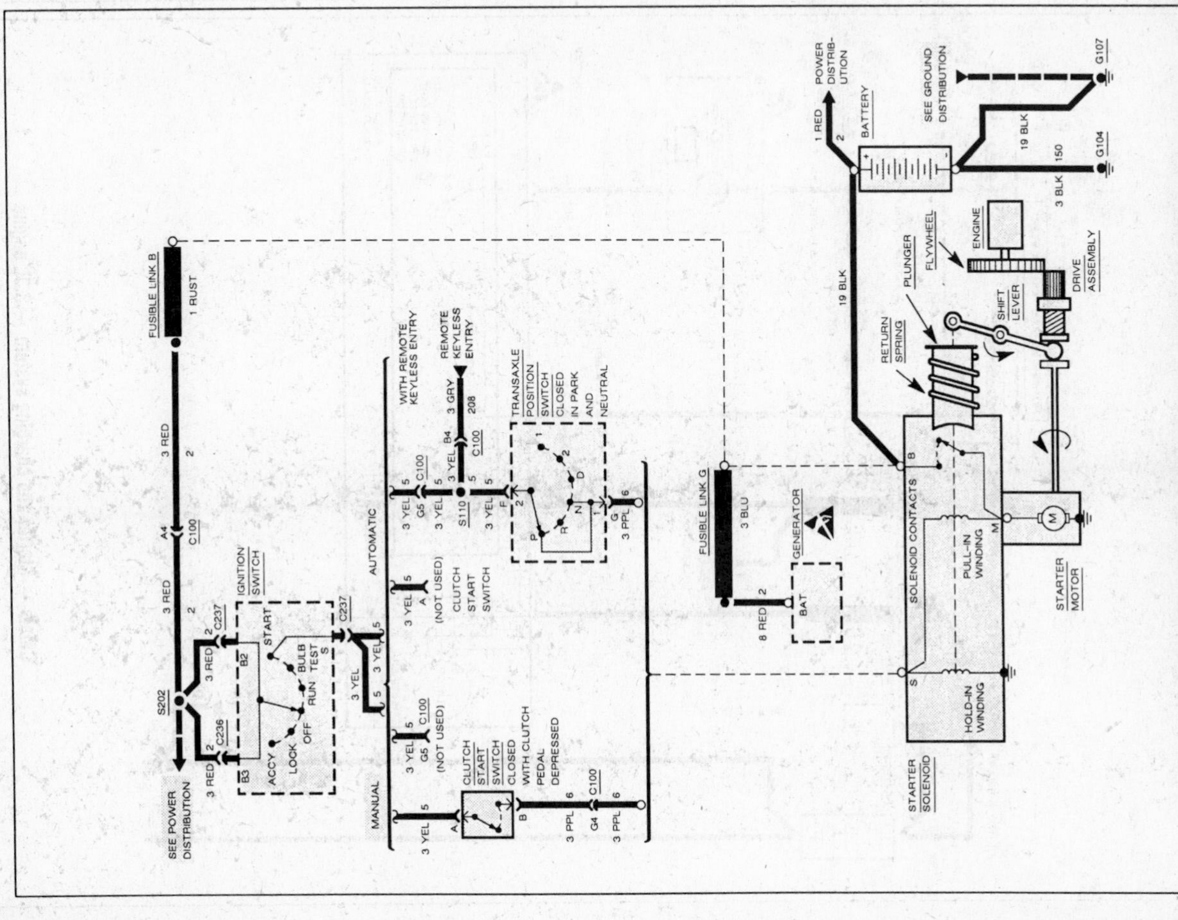

Calais — Starter and charging system — Starter — 2.3L and 2.3L HO engines

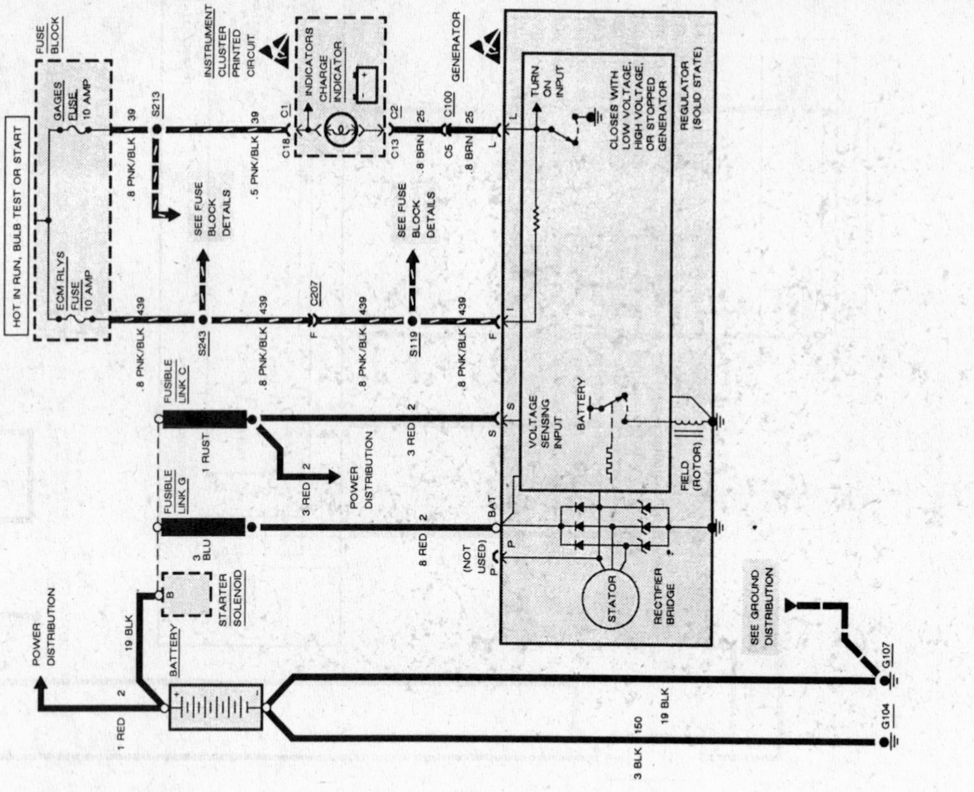

Calais — Charging system — 2.3L and 2.3L HO engines

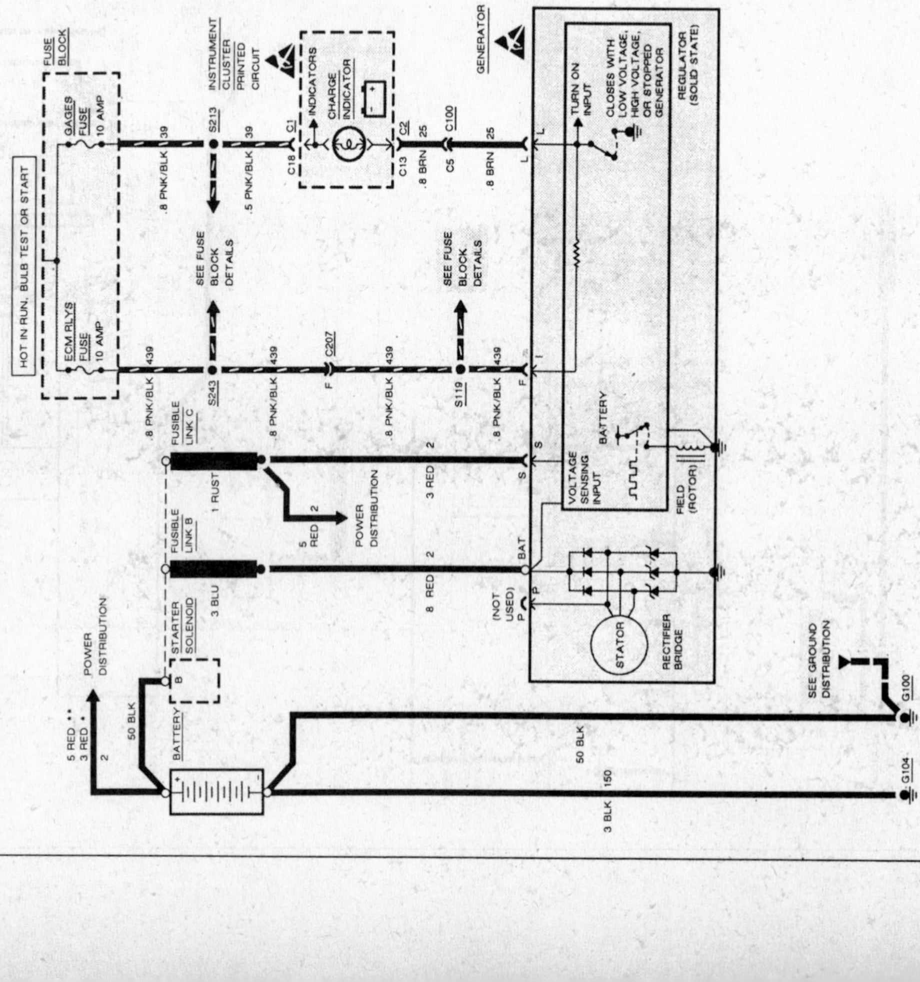

Calais — Starter and charging system — 3.3L engine

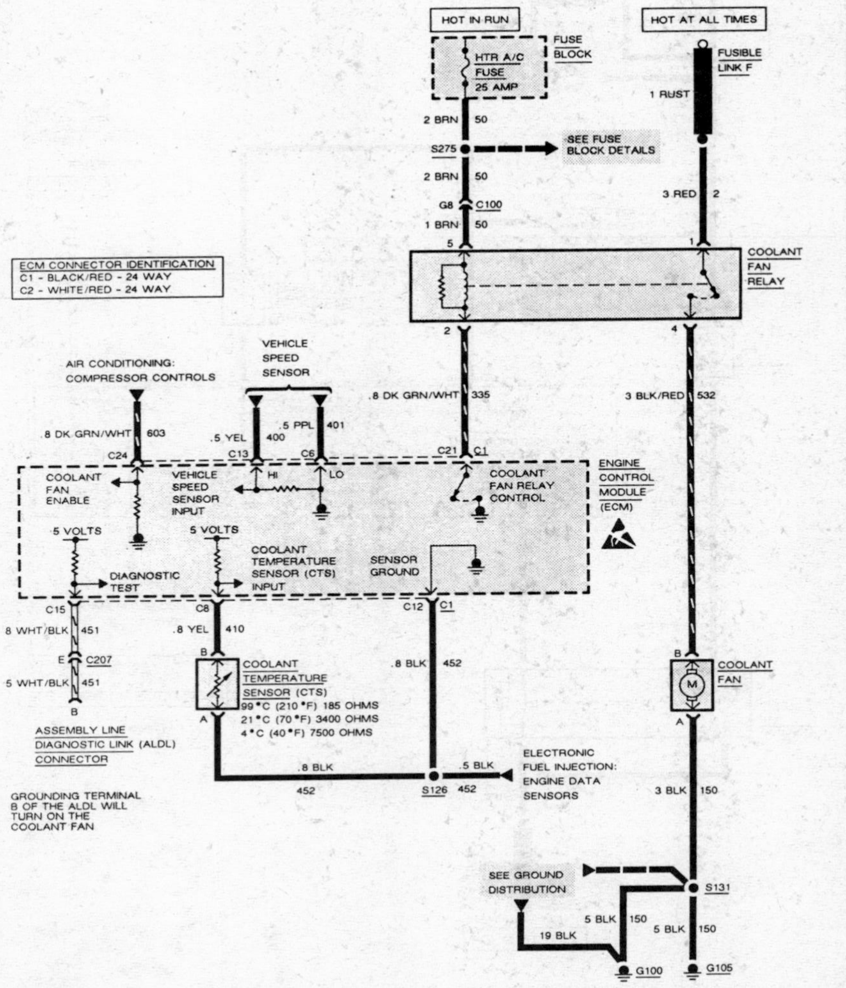

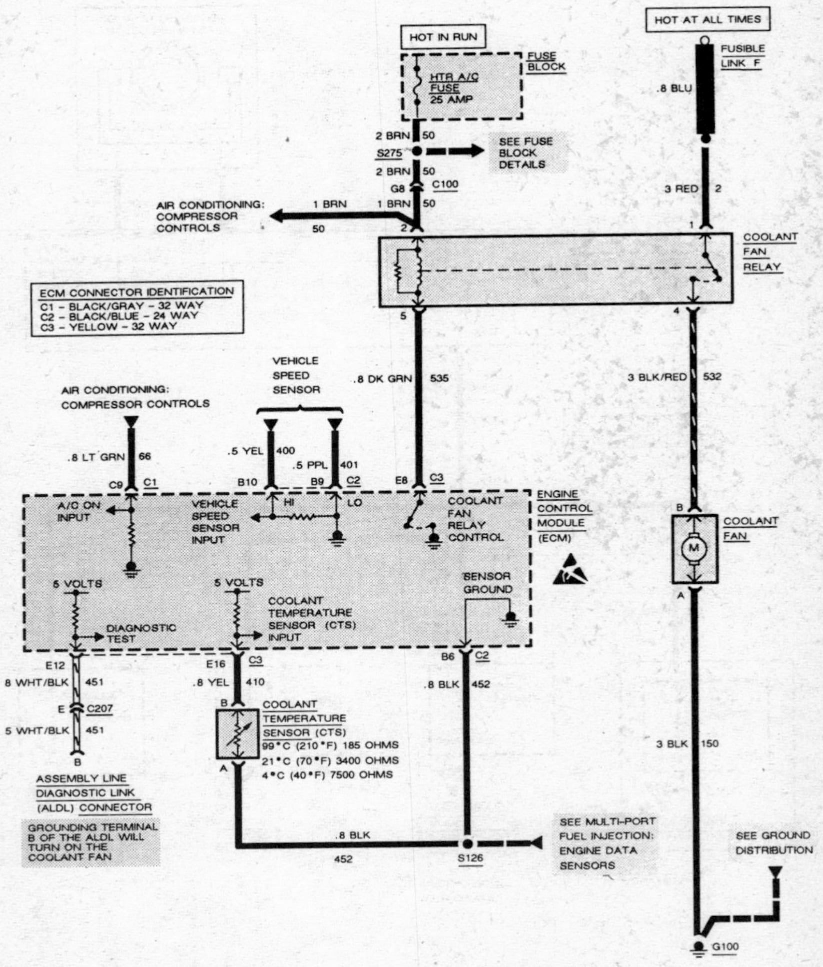

Calais — Coolant fan — 3.3L engine

Calais — Coolant fan — 2.5L engine

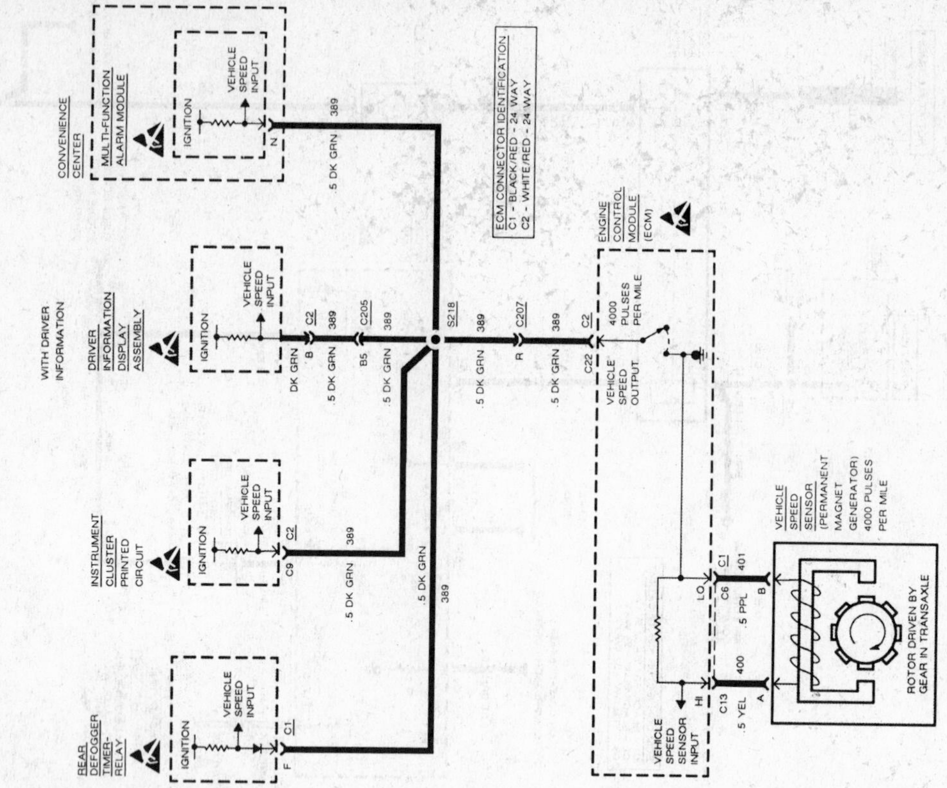

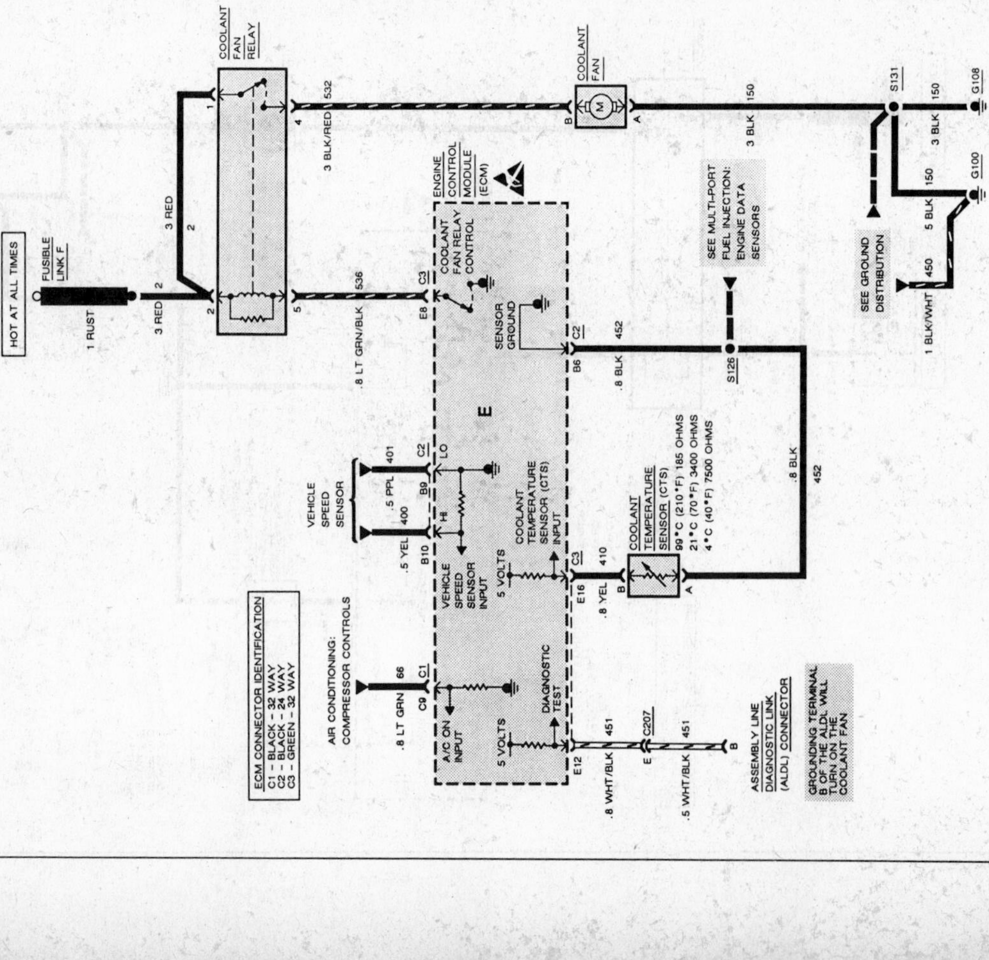

Calais — Coolant fan — 2.3L and 2.3L HO engines

HOT AT ALL TIMES
FUSIBLE LINK F
1 RUST
3 RED 2
3 RED
2
COOLANT FAN RELAY
2 1 5 4
ECM CONNECTOR IDENTIFICATION
C1 - BLACK - 32 WAY
C2 - BLACK - 24 WAY
C3 - GREEN - 32 WAY
AIR CONDITIONING: COMPRESSOR CONTROLS
.8 LT GRN 66
C9 C1
VEHICLE SPEED SENSOR
.5 YEL 400
.5 PPL 401
B10 B9 C2
.8 LT GRN/BLK 536
E8 C3
3 BLK/RED 532
A/C ON INPUT
VEHICLE SPEED SENSOR INPUT
HI LO
COOLANT FAN RELAY CONTROL
ENGINE CONTROL MODULE (ECM)
E
5 VOLTS
5 VOLTS
DIAGNOSTIC TEST
COOLANT TEMPERATURE SENSOR (CTS) INPUT
SENSOR GROUND
E12
E16 C3
B6 C2
.8 WHT/BLK 451
.8 YEL 410
.8 BLK 452
E C207
.5 WHT/BLK 451
B
COOLANT TEMPERATURE SENSOR (CTS)
99°C (210°F) 185 OHMS
21°C (70°F) 3400 OHMS
4°C (40°F) 7500 OHMS
B A
COOLANT FAN
M
B A
S126
SEE MULTI-PORT FUEL INJECTION: ENGINE DATA SENSORS
3 BLK 150
ASSEMBLY LINE DIAGNOSTIC LINK (ALDL) CONNECTOR
GROUNDING TERMINAL B OF THE ALDL WILL TURN ON THE COOLANT FAN
.8 BLK
452
SEE GROUND DISTRIBUTION
S131
1 BLK/WHT 450
5 BLK 150
3 BLK 150
G100
G108

Calais — Vehicle speed sensor — permanent magnet generator — 2.5L engine

WITH DRIVER INFORMATION
REAR DEFOGGER TIMER-RELAY
INSTRUMENT CLUSTER PRINTED CIRCUIT
DRIVER INFORMATION DISPLAY ASSEMBLY
CONVENIENCE CENTER
MULTI-FUNCTION ALARM MODULE
IGNITION
VEHICLE SPEED INPUT
F C1
C9 C2
DK GRN
B C2
N
.5 DK GRN 389
B5 C205
.5 DK GRN 389
.5 DK GRN
389
S218
R C207
ECM CONNECTOR IDENTIFICATION
C1 - BLACK/RED - 24 WAY
C2 - WHITE/RED - 24 WAY
C22 C2
VEHICLE SPEED OUTPUT
4000 PULSES PER MILE
ENGINE CONTROL MODULE (ECM)
VEHICLE SPEED SENSOR INPUT
HI LO
C13 C6 C1
.5 YEL 400
.5 PPL 401
A B
VEHICLE SPEED SENSOR (PERMANENT MAGNET GENERATOR) 4000 PULSES PER MILE
ROTOR DRIVEN BY GEAR IN TRANSAXLE

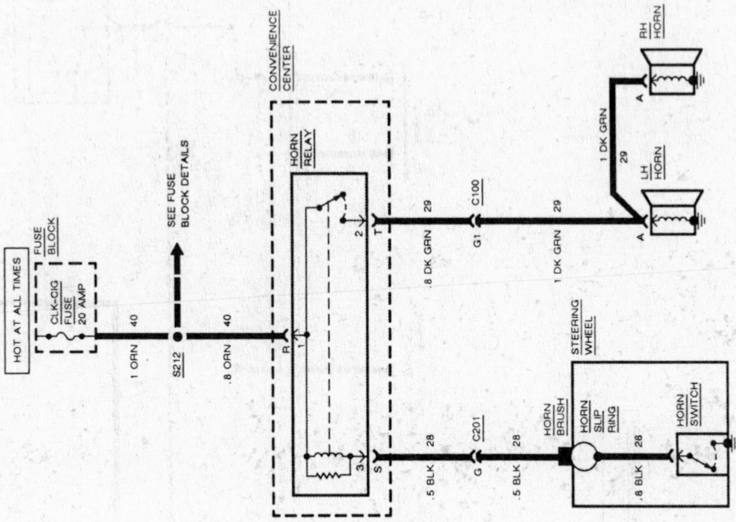

EVO CONTROLLER
WITH ELECTRONIC VARIABLE ORIFICE (EVO) STEERING
5 VOLTS
VEHICLE SPEED INPUT
2A
WITH DRIVER INFORMATION
CONVENIENCE CENTER
CRUISE CONTROL MODULE
INSTRUMENT CLUSTER PRINTED CIRCUIT
DRIVER INFORMATION DISPLAY ASSEMBLY
REAR DEFOGGER TIMER-RELAY
MULTI-FUNCTION ALARM MODULE
5 VOLTS
IGNITION
VEHICLE SPEED INPUT
D
C9 C2
DK GRN
B C2
F C1
N
.35 DK GRN 389
.5 DK GRN 389
.5 DK GRN 389
.5 DK GRN 389
.5 DK GRN 389
.5 DK GRN 389
C C202
B5 C205
.5 DK GRN 389
S218
R C207
B11 C2
ENGINE CONTROL MODULE (ECM)
VEHICLE SPEED OUTPUT
4000 PULSES PER MILE
VEHICLE SPEED SENSOR INPUT
HI
LO
B10
B9 C2
.5 YEL 400
.5 PPL 401
B
A
VEHICLE SPEED SENSOR (PERMANENT MAGNET GENERATOR) 4000 PULSES PER MILE
ROTOR DRIVEN BY GEAR IN TRANSAXLE

V6 VIN N

ECM CONNECTOR IDENTIFICATION
C1 - BLACK/GRAY - 32 WAY
C2 - BLACK/BLUE - 24 WAY
C3 - YELLOW - 32 WAY

L4 VIN A AND L4 VIN D

ECM CONNECTOR IDENTIFICATION
C1 - BLACK - 32 WAY
C2 - BLACK - 24 WAY
C3 - GREEN - 32 WAY

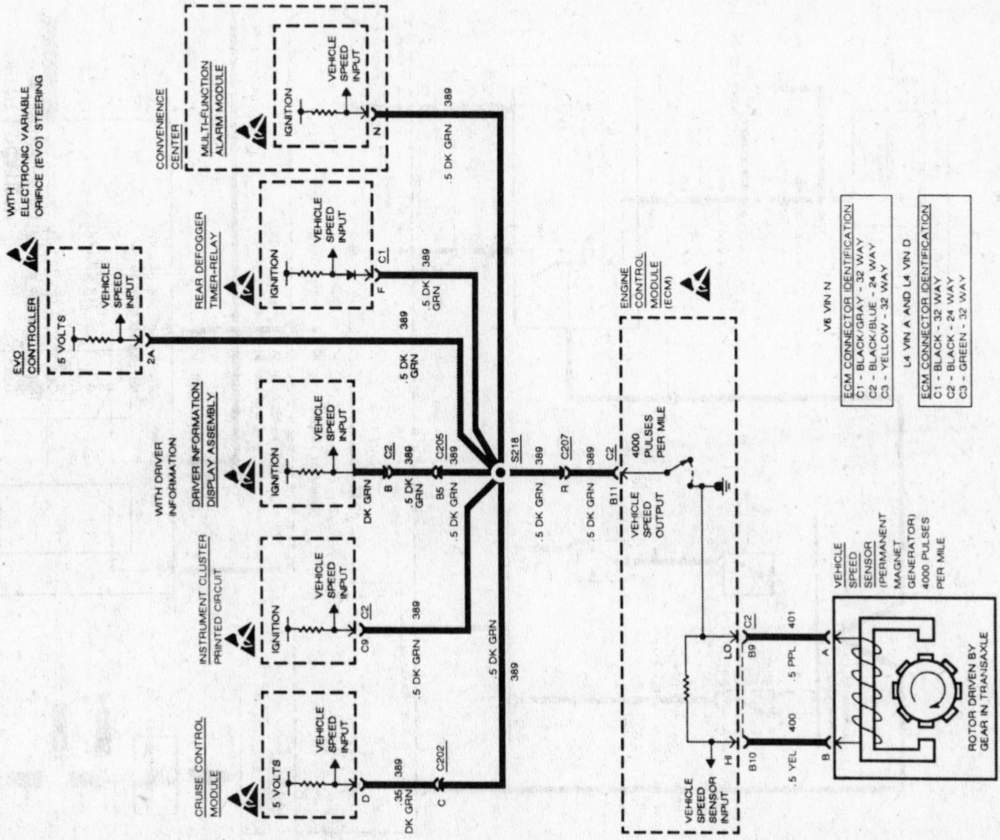

Calais — 3.3L, 2.3L and 2.3L HO engines

HOT AT ALL TIMES
CLK-CIG FUSE 20 AMP
FUSE BLOCK
1 ORN 40
S212
SEE FUSE BLOCK DETAILS
.8 ORN 40
R
1
CONVENIENCE CENTER
HORN RELAY
3
2
S
T
.5 BLK 28
G C201
.5 BLK 28
.8 DK GRN 29
G1 C100
1 DK GRN 29
HORN BRUSH
HORN SLIP RING
STEERING WHEEL
.8 BLK 28
HORN SWITCH
1 DK GRN 29
A
LH HORN
A
RH HORN

Calais — Horns

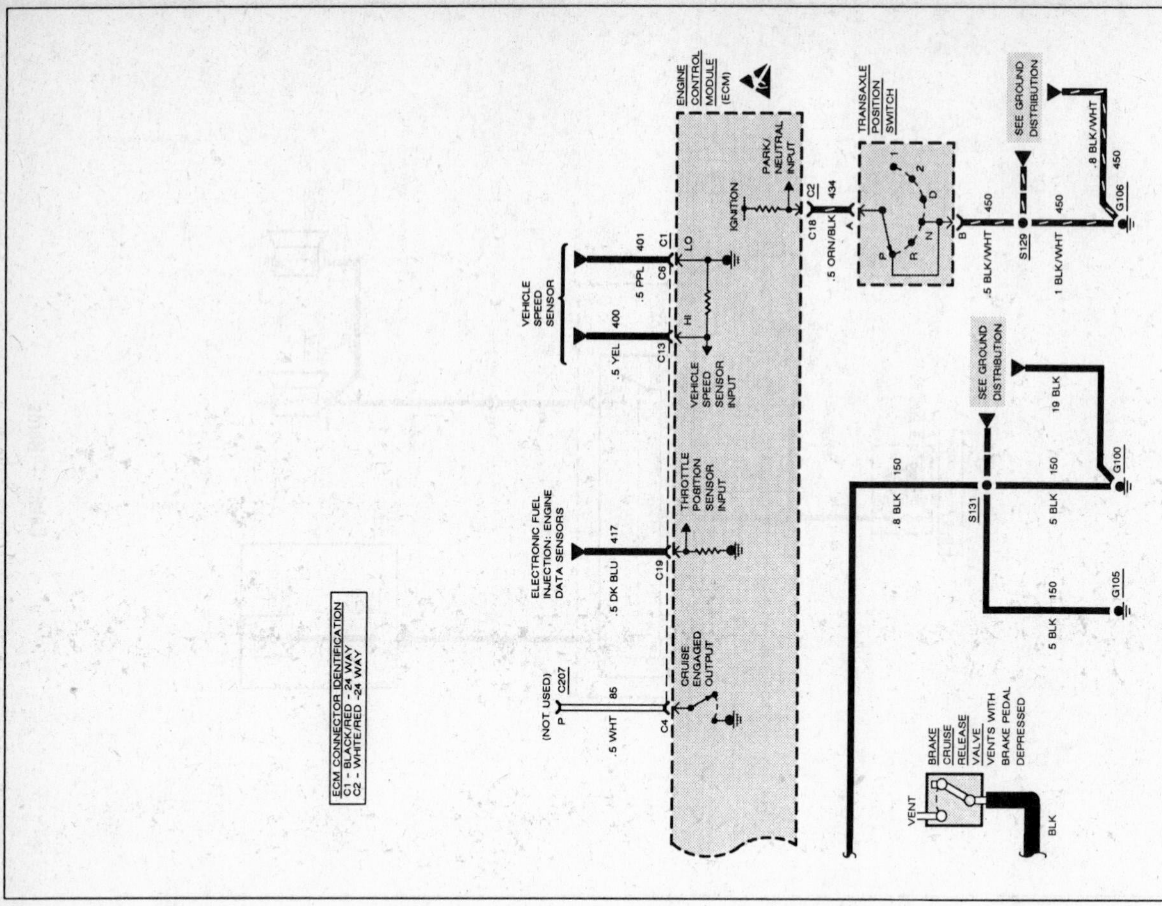

Calais — Cruise control — 2.5L engine

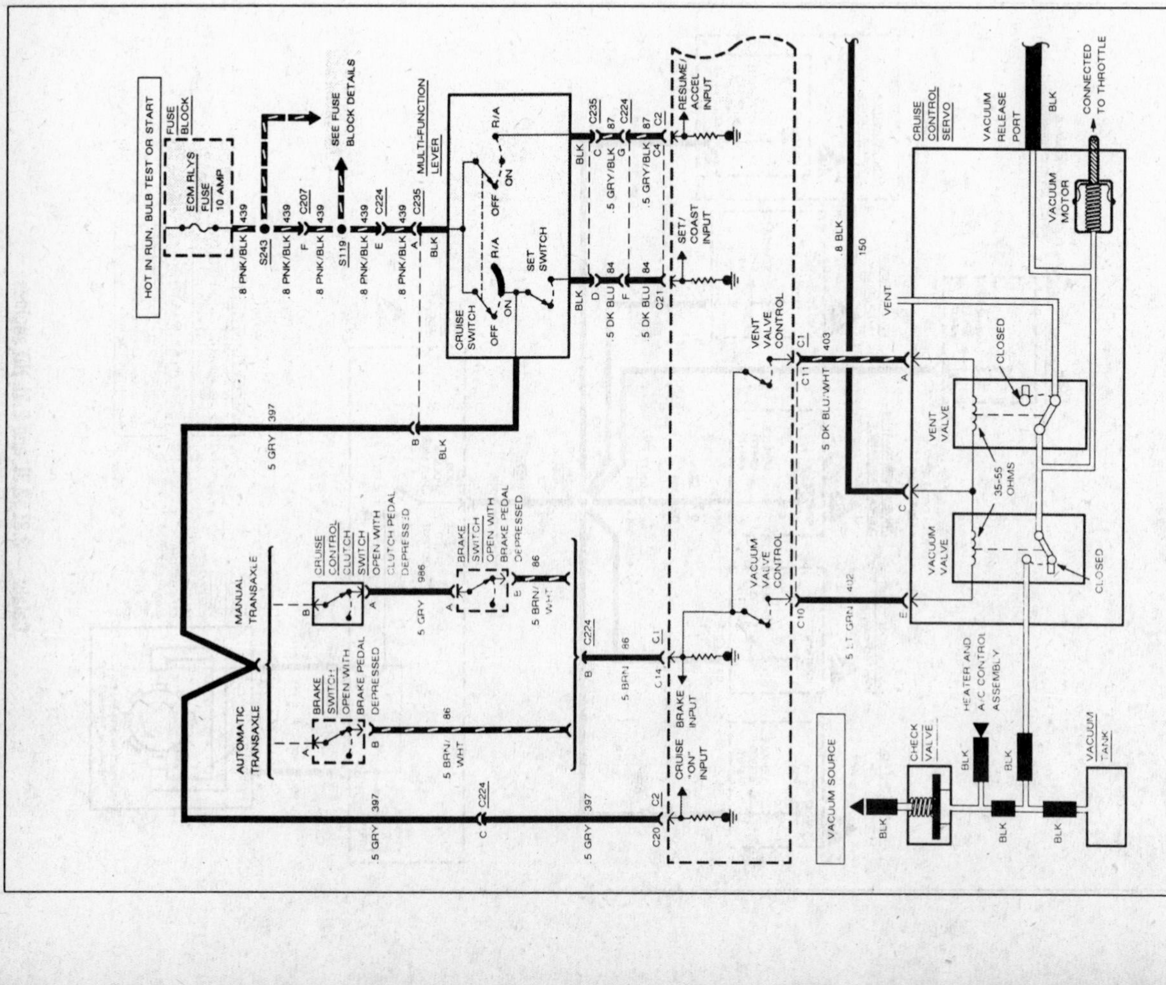

Calais — Cruise control — 2.5L engine

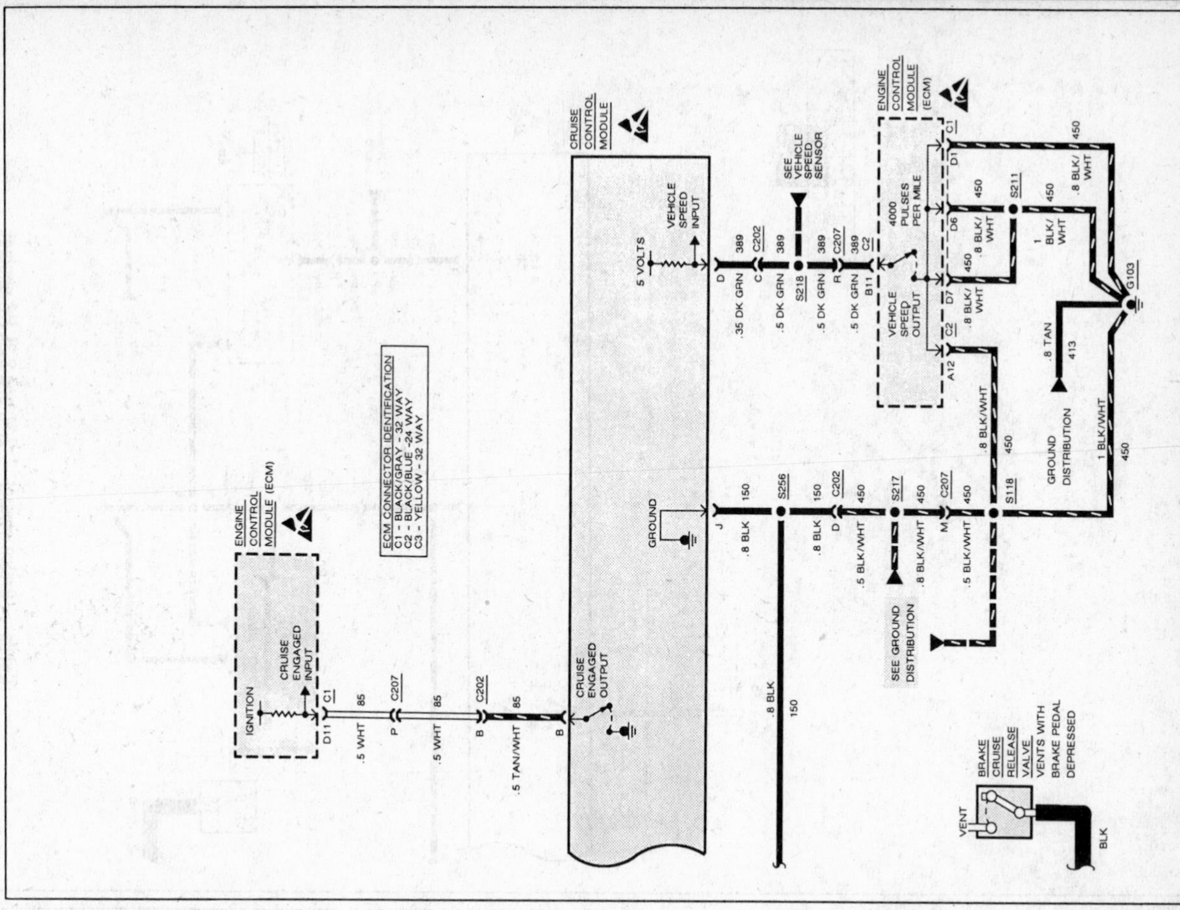

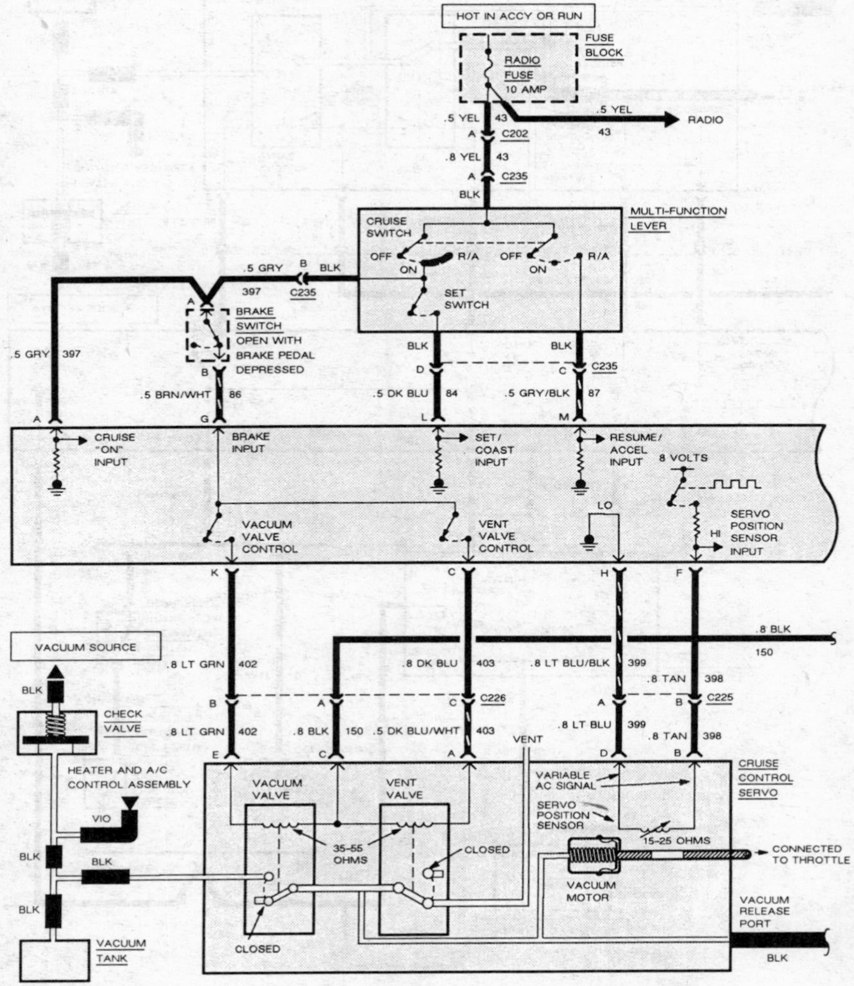

Calais — Cruise control — 3.3L engine

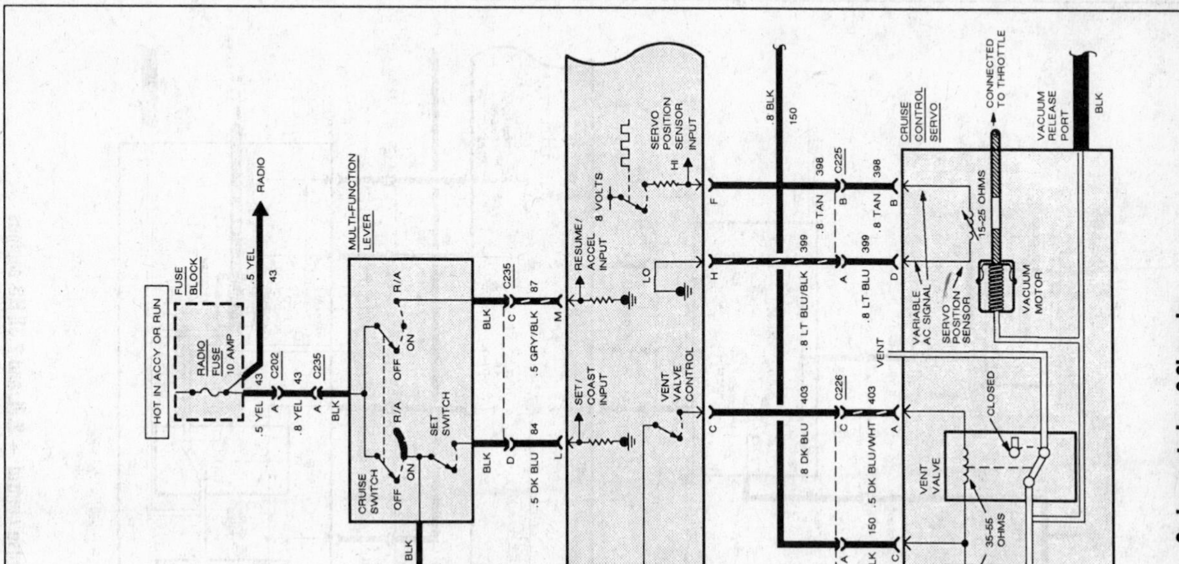

Calais — Cruise control — 3.3L engine

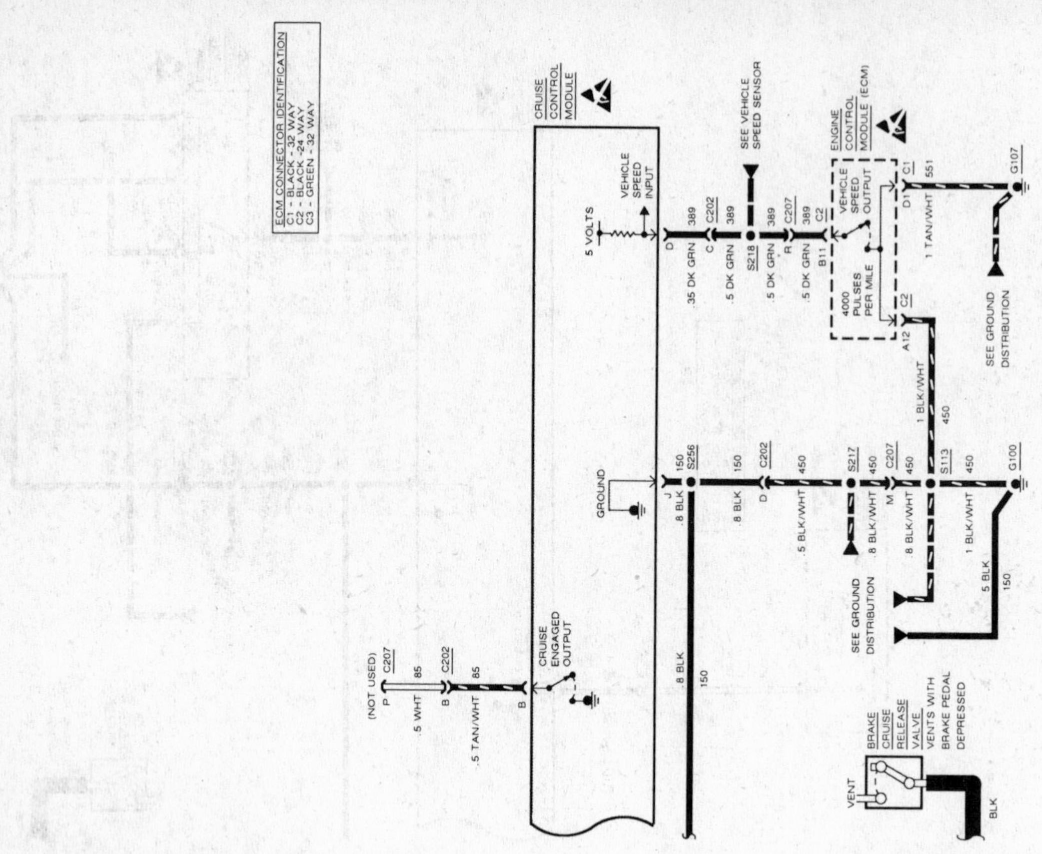

MANUAL TRANSAXLE
AUTOMATIC TRANSAXLE
CRUISE CONTROL CLUTCH SWITCH OPEN WITH CLUTCH PEDAL DEPRESSED
BRAKE SWITCH OPEN WITH BRAKE PEDAL DEPRESSED
.5 GRY 397
.5 GRY 986
.5 BRN/WHT 86
HOT IN ACCY OR RUN
FUSE BLOCK
RADIO FUSE 10 AMP
.5 YEL 43
RADIO
.5 YEL 43 C202
.8 YEL 43 C235
BLK
MULTI-FUNCTION LEVER
CRUISE SWITCH OFF ON R/A
OFF ON R/A
SET SWITCH
.5 DK BLU 84
.5 GRY/BLK 87
CRUISE "ON" INPUT
BRAKE INPUT
SET/ COAST INPUT
RESUME/ ACCEL INPUT
8 VOLTS
VACUUM VALVE CONTROL
VENT VALVE CONTROL
LO
HI
SERVO POSITION SENSOR INPUT
VACUUM SOURCE
.8 LT GRN 402
.8 DK BLU 403
.8 LT BLU/BLK 399
.8 TAN 398
.8 BLK 150
C226
C225
CHECK VALVE
.8 BLK 150
.8 DK/BLU/WHT 403
.8 LT BLU 399
VENT
HEATER AND A/C CONTROL ASSEMBLY
VIO
BLK
VACUUM VALVE
VENT VALVE
35-55 OHMS
CLOSED
VARIABLE AC SIGNAL
SERVO POSITION SENSOR
15-25 OHMS
CRUISE CONTROL SERVO
CONNECTED TO THROTTLE
VACUUM MOTOR
VACUUM RELEASE PORT
VACUUM TANK

Calais — Cruise control — 2.3L and 2.3L HO engines

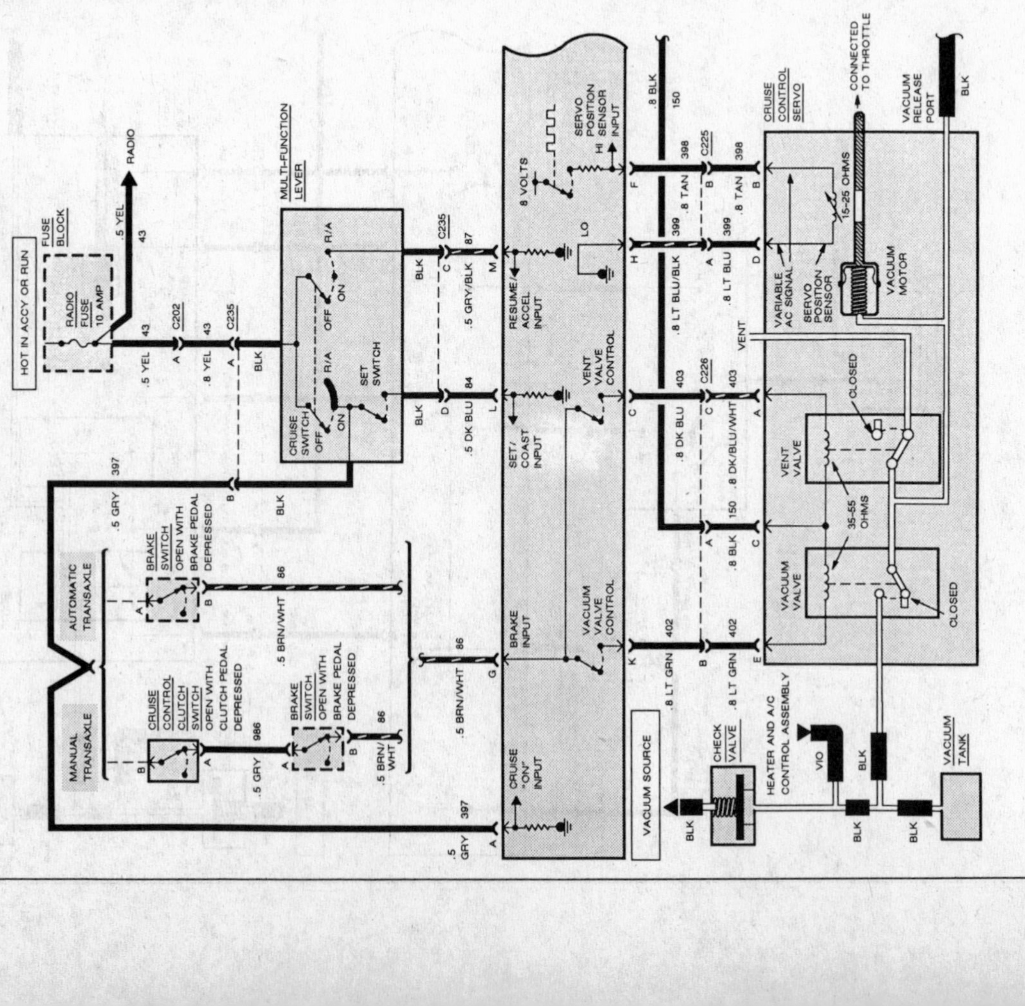

ECM CONNECTOR IDENTIFICATION
C1 - BLACK - 32 WAY
C2 - BLACK -24 WAY
C3 - GREEN - 32 WAY

(NOT USED)
P C207
.5 WHT 85
B C202
.5 TAN/WHT 85
CRUISE ENGAGED OUTPUT
CRUISE CONTROL MODULE
GROUND
5 VOLTS
VEHICLE SPEED INPUT
.8 BLK 150
.8 BLK 150 S256
.35 DK GRN 389
C202
.5 DK GRN 389
S218
SEE VEHICLE SPEED SENSOR
D C202
.5 DK GRN 389
R C207
.5 BLK/WHT 450
.5 DK GRN 389
B11 C2
SEE GROUND DISTRIBUTION
S217
.8 BLK/WHT 450
M C207
4000 PULSES PER MILE
VEHICLE SPEED OUTPUT
ENGINE CONTROL MODULE (ECM)
VENT
BRAKE CRUISE RELEASE VALVE
VENTS WITH BRAKE PEDAL DEPRESSED
.8 BLK/WHT 450
A12 C2
D1 C1
1 BLK/WHT
S113 450
1 TAN/WHT 551
1 BLK/WHT 450
.5 BLK 150
G100
SEE GROUND DISTRIBUTION
G107

Calais — Cruise control — 2.3L and 2.3L HO engines

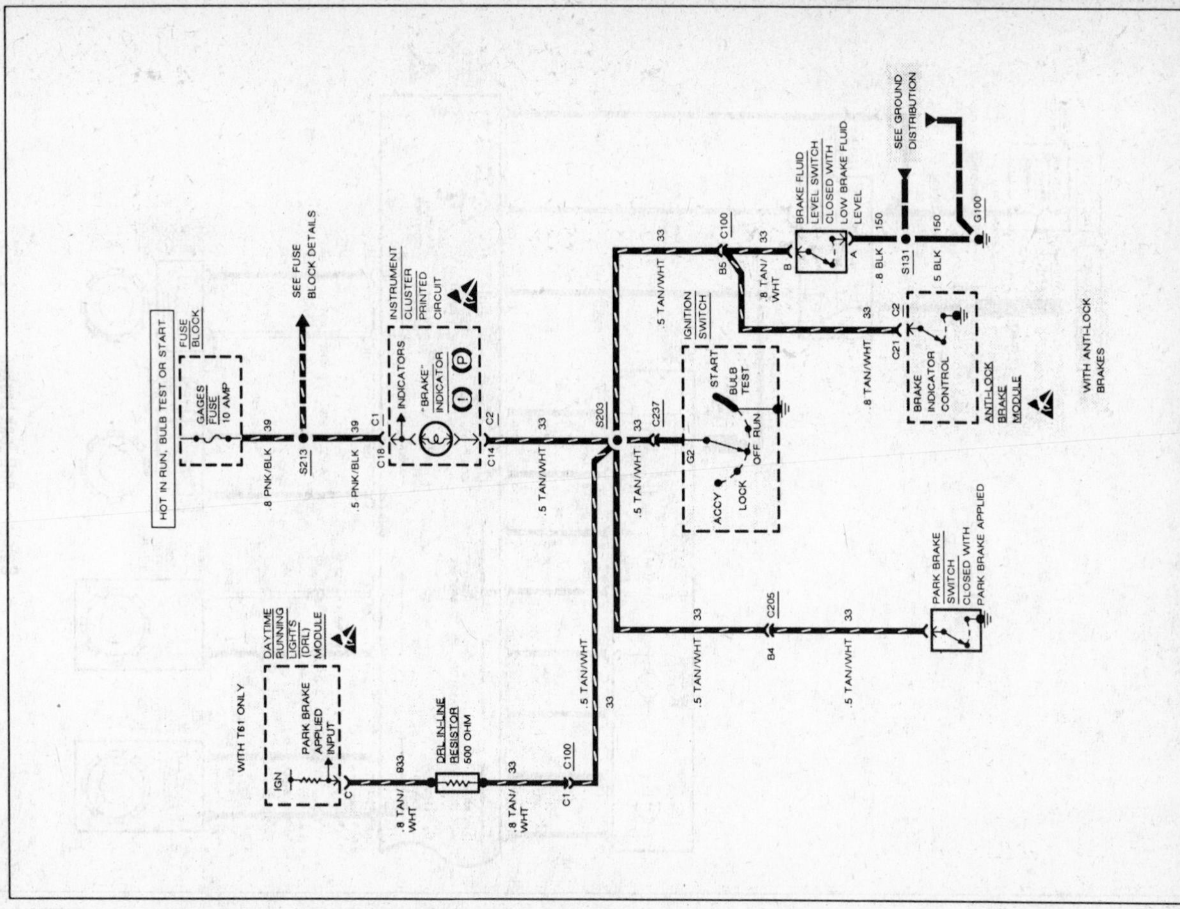

HOT IN RUN, BULB TEST OR START
GAGES FUSE 10 AMP
FUSE BLOCK
.8 PNK/BLK 39
S213
SEE FUSE BLOCK DETAILS
.5 PNK/BLK 39
WITH T61 ONLY
IGNITION
PARK BRAKE APPLIED INPUT
DAYTIME RUNNING LIGHTS (DRL) MODULE
C18 C1
INDICATORS
"BRAKE" INDICATOR
INSTRUMENT CLUSTER PRINTED CIRCUIT
C14 C2
BATTERY
KEYLESS ENTRY ENABLE INPUT
REMOTE KEYLESS ENTRY (RKE) MODULE
G C1
3 GRY 208
C C331
3 GRY 208
A C200G
3 GRY 208
C3 C205
3 GRY 208
B4 C100
.8 TAN WHT 933
DRL IN-LINE RESISTOR 500 OHM
.8 TAN WHT 33
C1 C100
.5 TAN/WHT 33
.5 TAN/WHT 33
S203
.5 TAN/WHT B5 .8 TAN/WHT
.8 TAN/WHT 33
33 C100 33
S279
.5 TAN/WHT 33
C237
.8 TAN/WHT 33
G2
IGNITION SWITCH
ACCY
LOCK
OFF RUN
START
BULB TEST
.8 TAN/WHT 33
.5 TAN/WHT 33
B4 C205
C21 C2
BRAKE INDICATOR CONTROL
ANTI-LOCK BRAKE MODULE
B
BRAKE FLUID LEVEL SWITCH CLOSED WITH LOW BRAKE FLUID LEVEL
A
.8 BLK 150
S131
SEE GROUND DISTRIBUTION
.5 BLK 150
G100
.5 TAN/WHT 33
PARK BRAKE SWITCH CLOSED WITH PARK BRAKE APPLIED
WITH ANTI-LOCK BRAKES

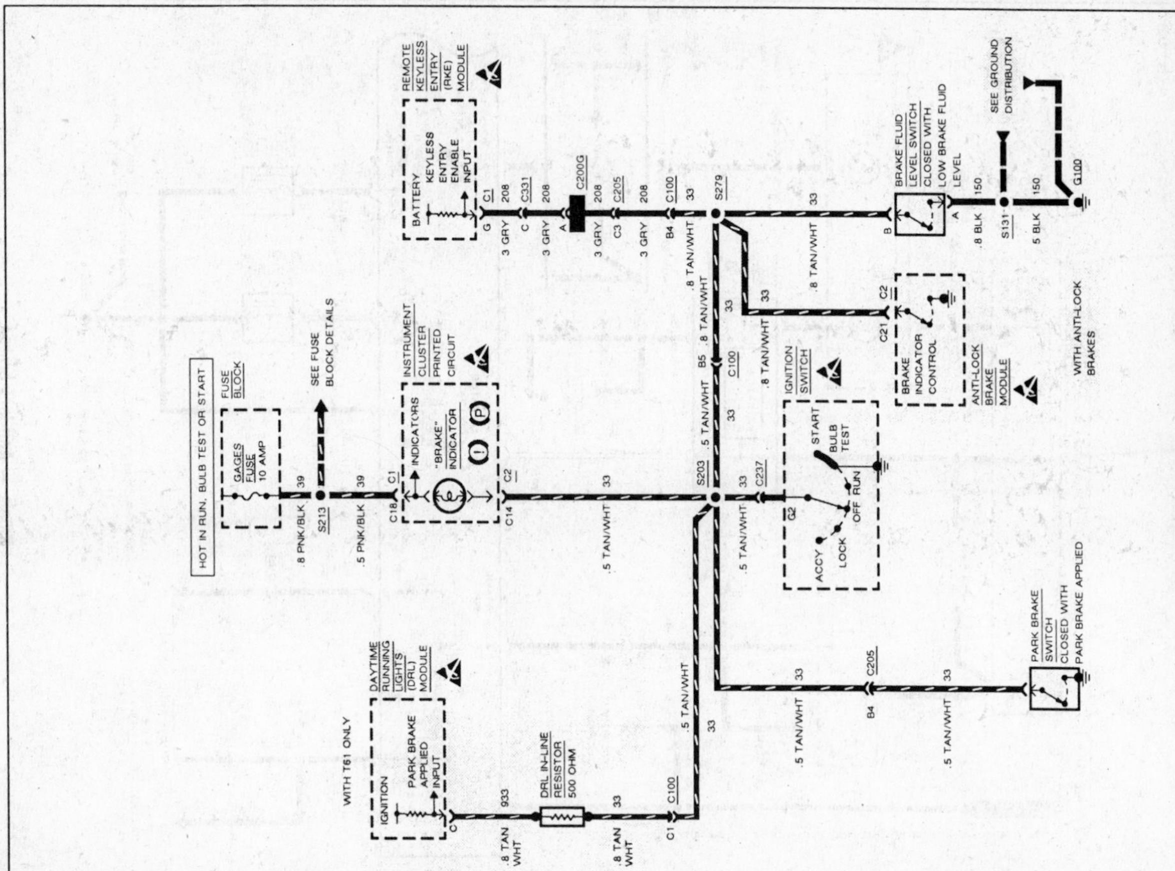

Calais — Brake warning system — manual transaxle

HOT IN RUN, BULB TEST OR START
GAGES FUSE 10 AMP
FUSE BLOCK
.8 PNK/BLK 39
S213
SEE FUSE BLOCK DETAILS
.5 PNK/BLK 39
WITH T61 ONLY
IGN
PARK BRAKE APPLIED INPUT
DAYTIME RUNNING LIGHTS (DRL) MODULE
C18 C1
INDICATORS
"BRAKE" INDICATOR
INSTRUMENT CLUSTER PRINTED CIRCUIT
C14 C2
.8 TAN/ WHT 933
DRL IN-LINE RESISTOR 500 OHM
.8 TAN/ WHT 33
C1 C100
.5 TAN/WHT 33
.5 TAN/WHT 33
S203
.5 TAN/WHT 33
C237
G2
IGNITION SWITCH
ACCY
LOCK
OFF RUN
START
BULB TEST
.5 TAN/WHT 33
.5 TAN/WHT 33
B5 C100
.8 TAN/ WHT 33
B4 C205
B
BRAKE FLUID LEVEL SWITCH CLOSED WITH LOW BRAKE FLUID LEVEL
A
.5 TAN/WHT 33
.8 TAN/WHT 33
.8 BLK 150
C21 C2
S131
SEE GROUND DISTRIBUTION
BRAKE INDICATOR CONTROL
.5 BLK 150
PARK BRAKE SWITCH CLOSED WITH PARK BRAKE APPLIED
G100
ANTI-LOCK BRAKE MODULE
WITH ANTI-LOCK BRAKES

Calais — Automatic transaxle

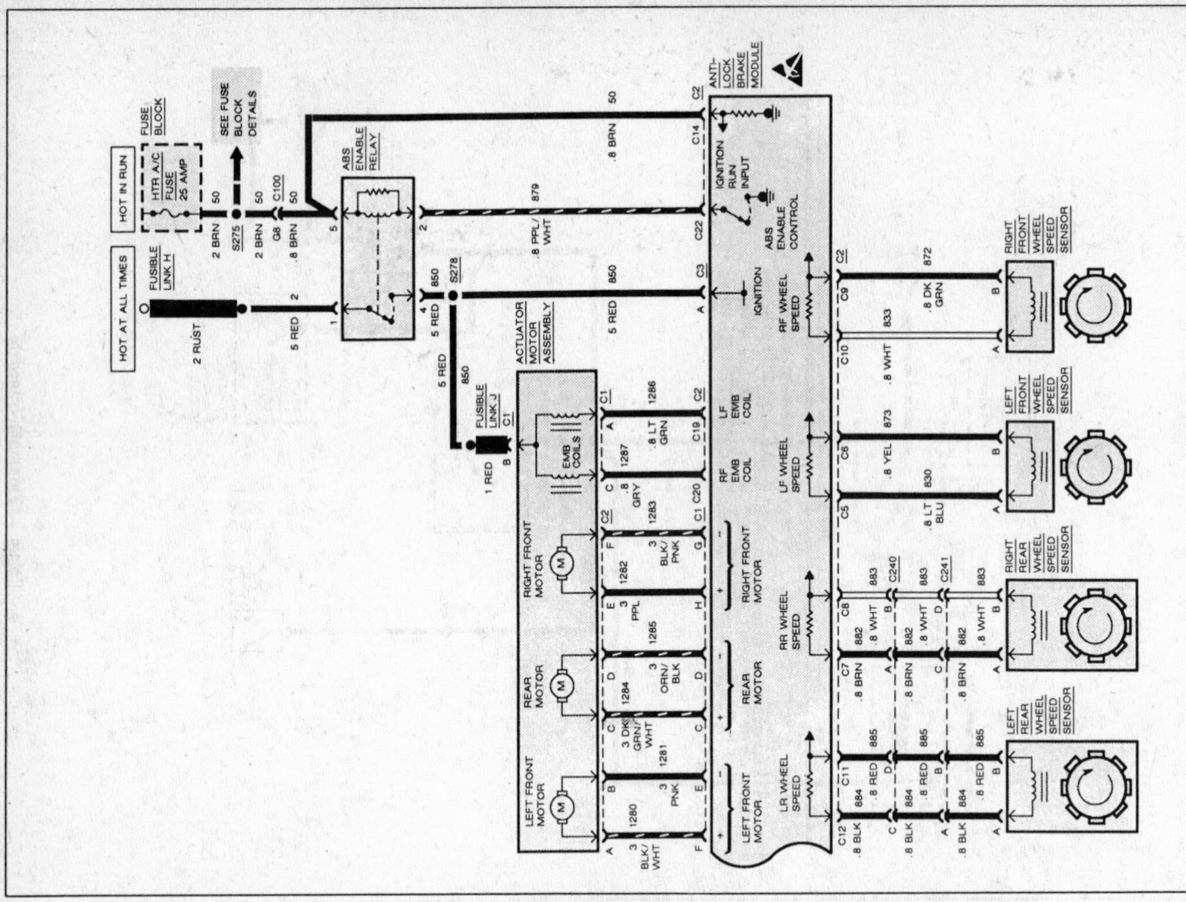

Calais – Anti-lock brakes

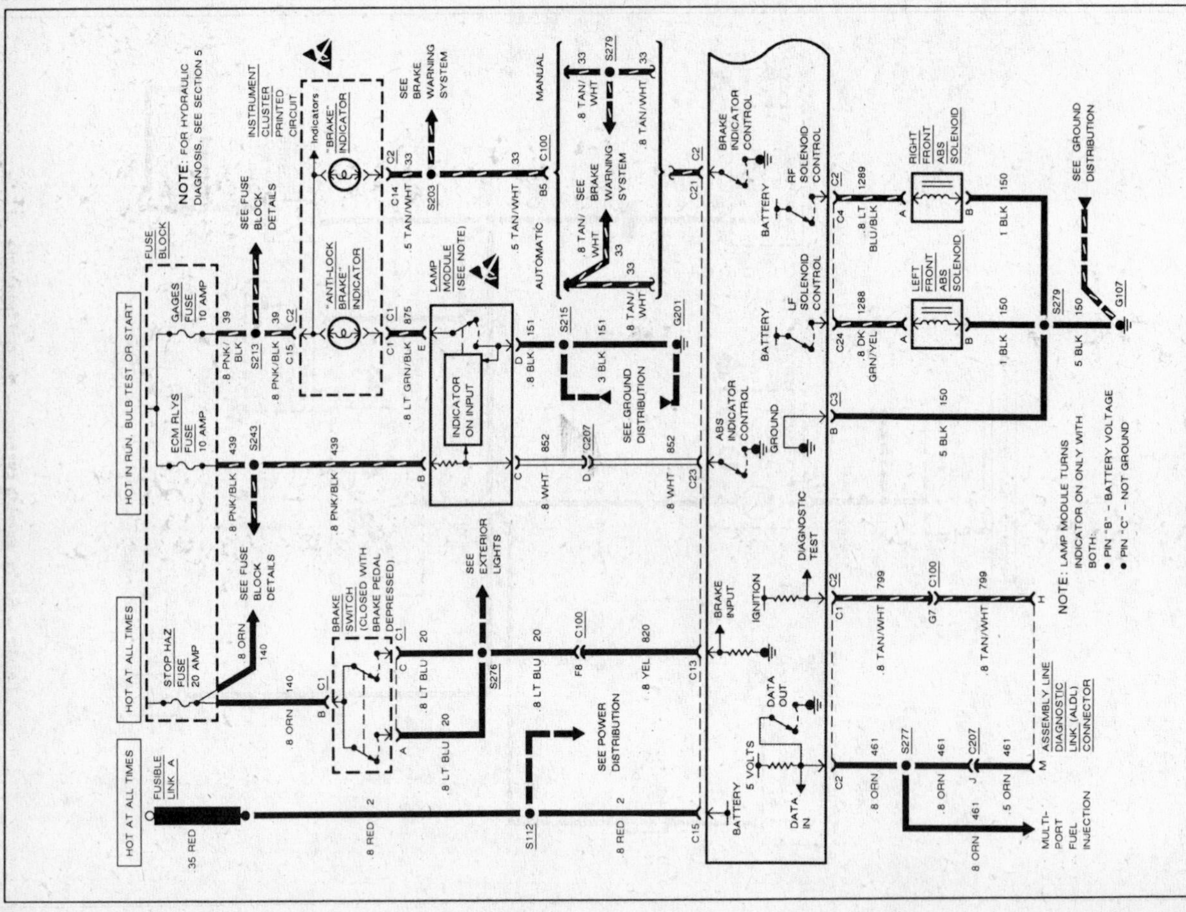

Calais – Anti-lock brakes

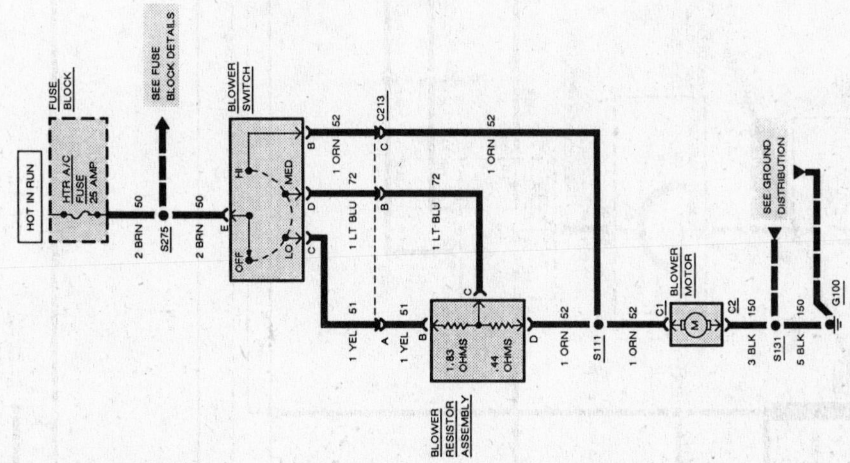

ECM CONNECTOR IDENTIFICATION
C1 - BLACK - 32 WAY
C2 - BLACK - 24 WAY
C3 - GREEN - 32 WAY

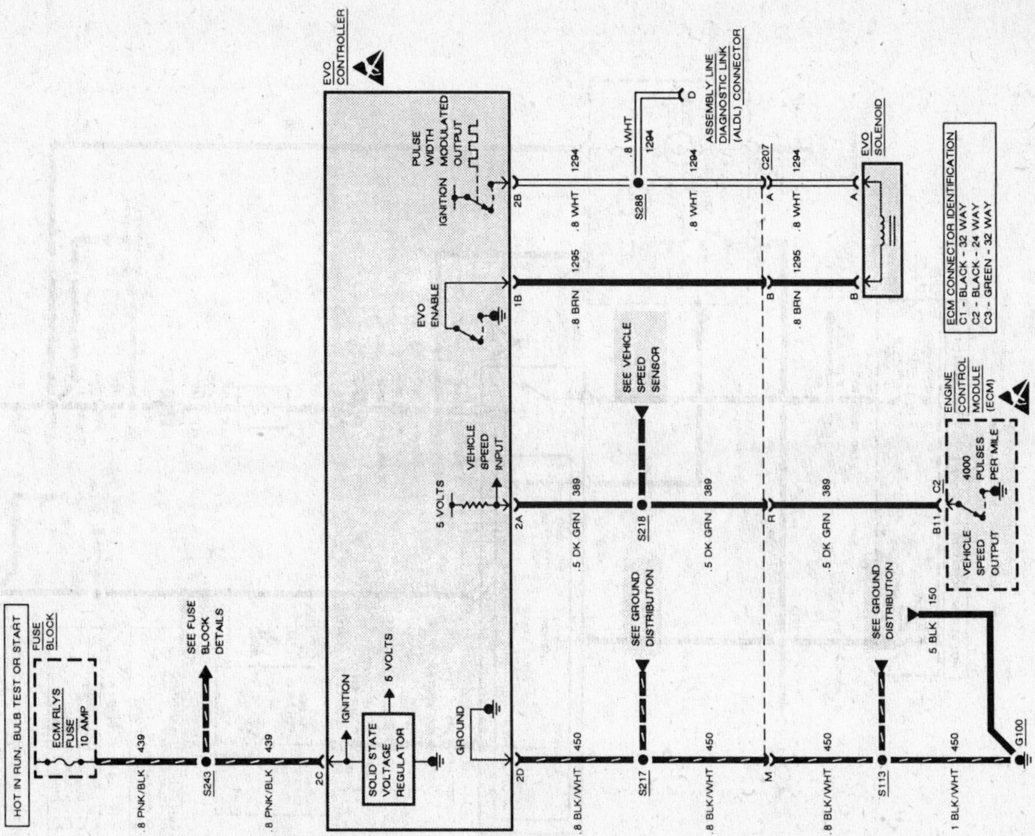

Calais — Electronic Variable Orifice (EVO) steering

Calais — Heater

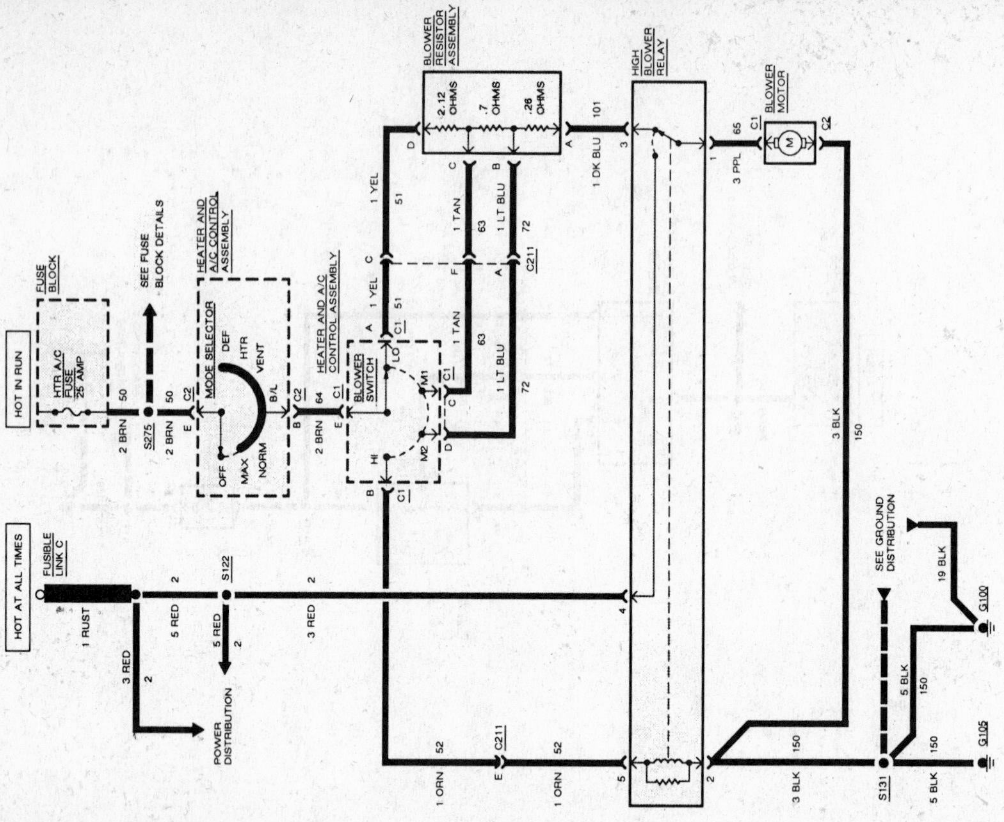

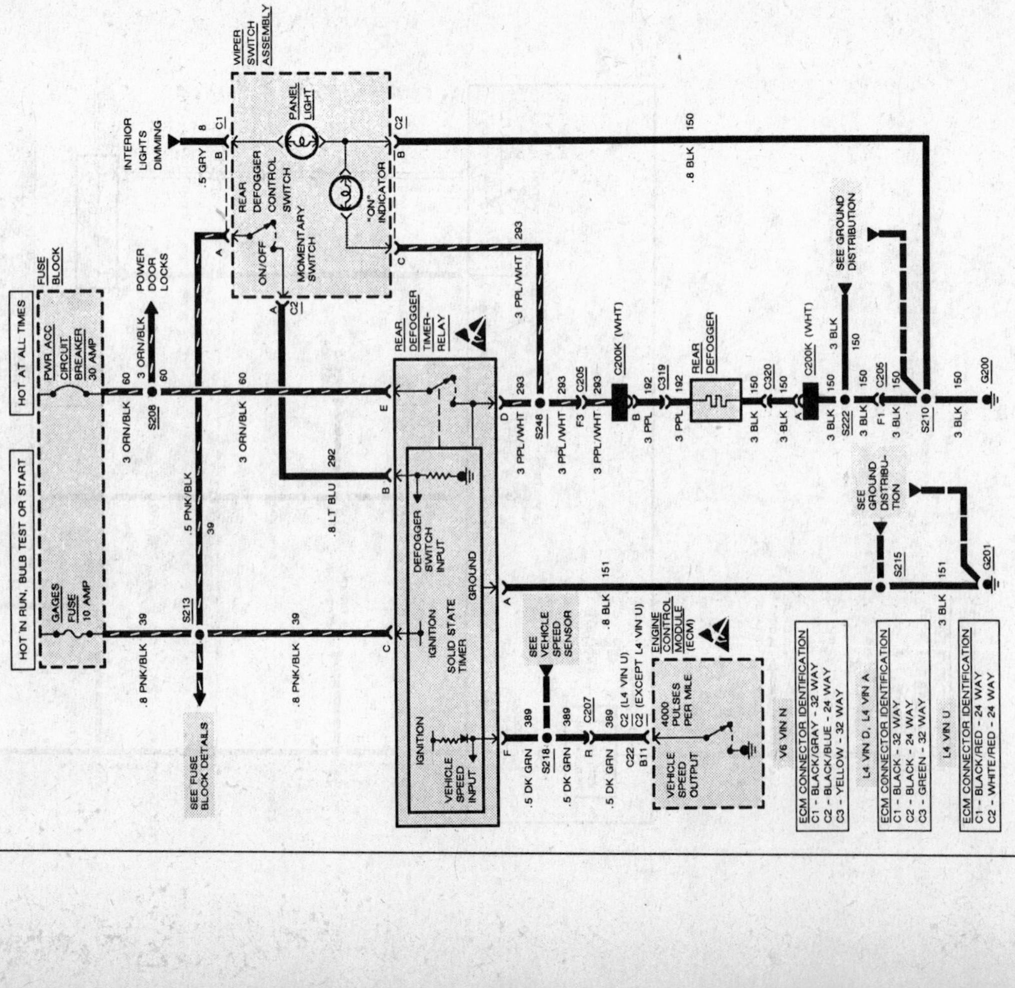

Calais – Rear defogger

Calais – Air conditioning – blower controls – 2.5L engine

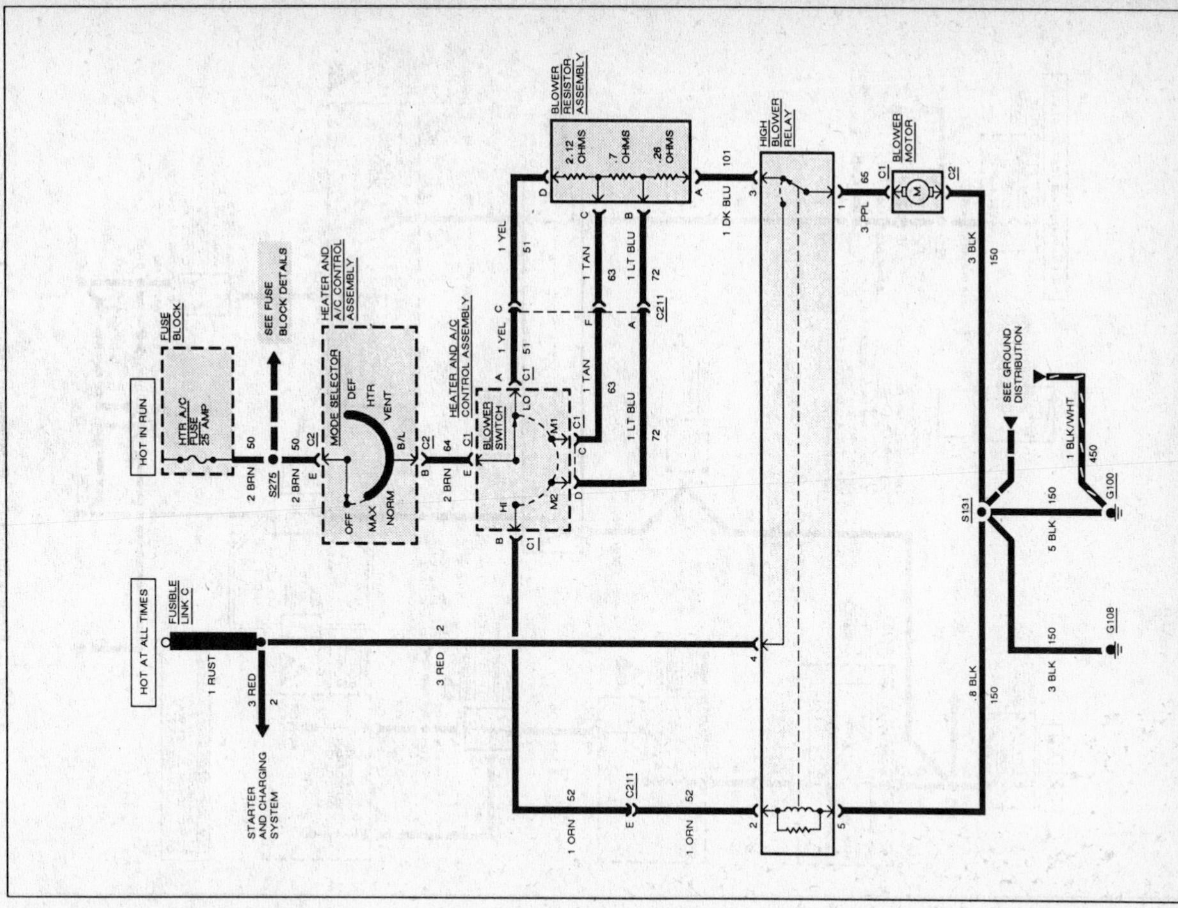

Calais — Air conditioning — blower controls — 2.3L and 2.3L HO engines

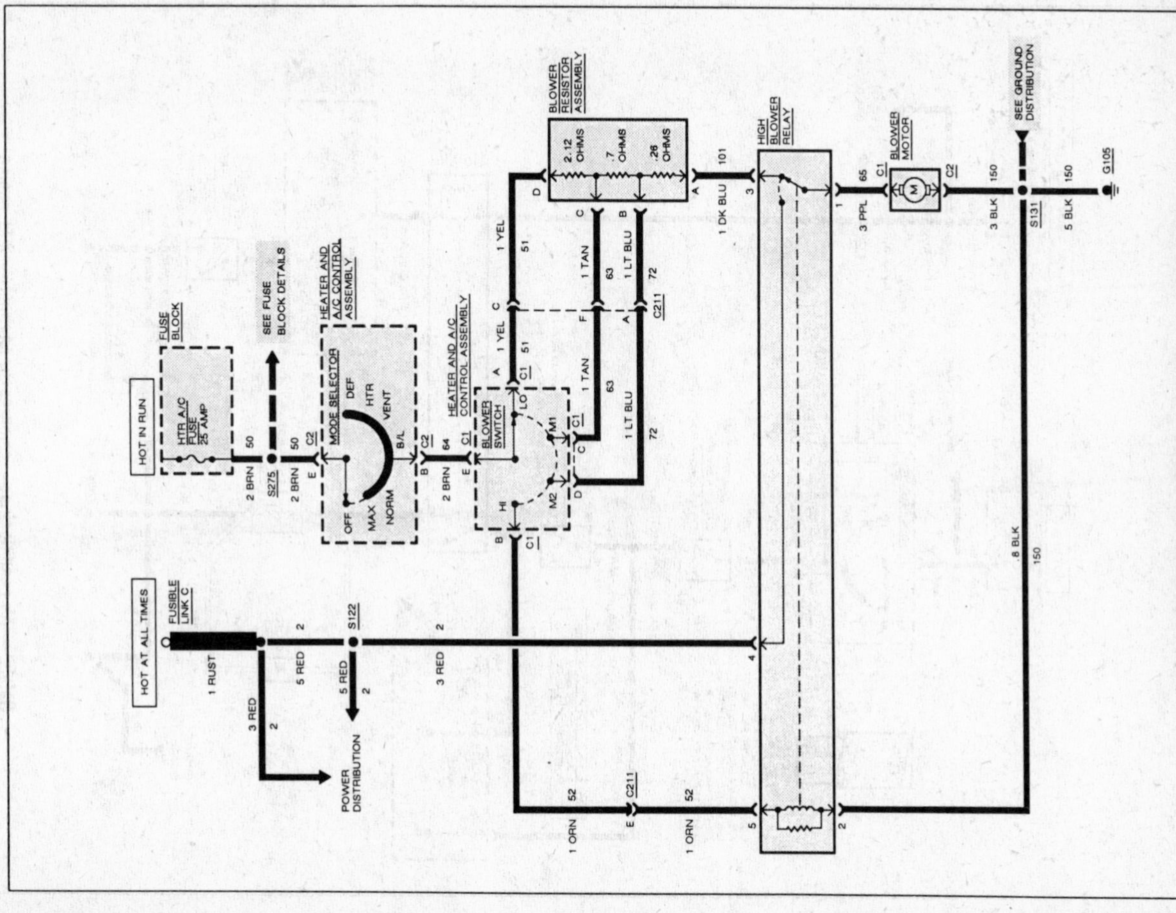

Calais — Air conditioning — blower controls — 3.3L engine

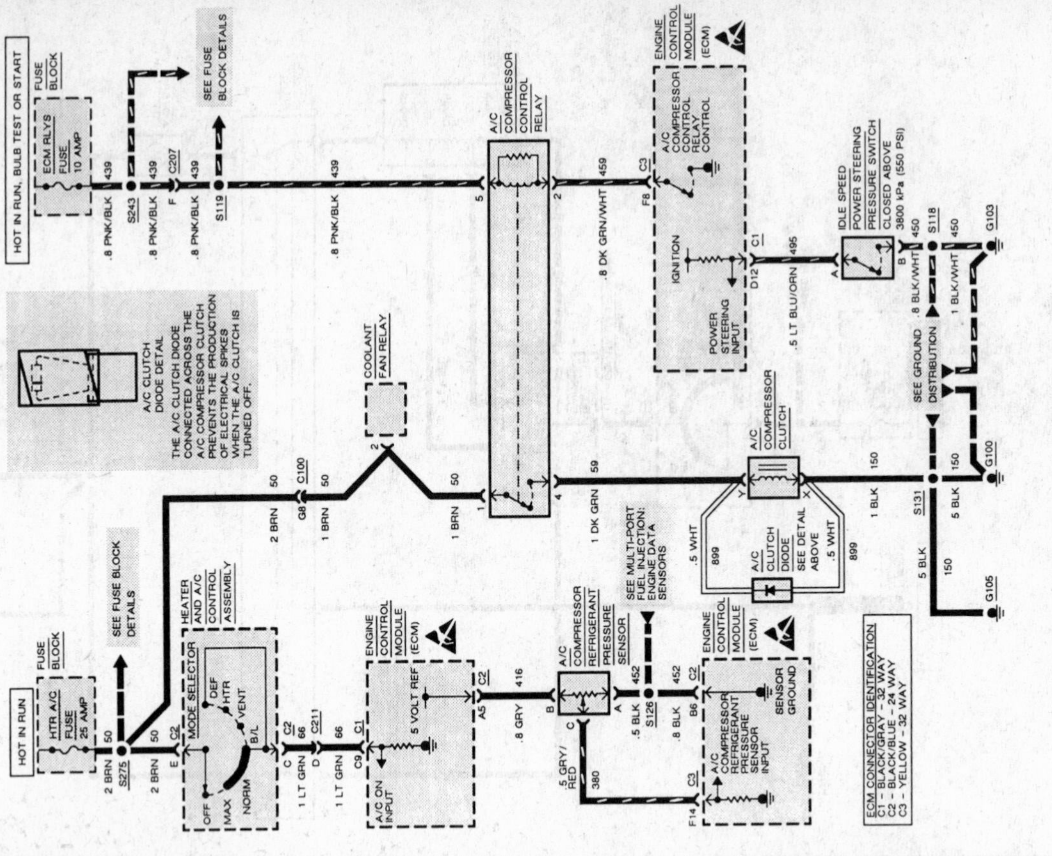

HOT IN RUN
HTR A/C FUSE 25 AMP
FUSE BLOCK
2 BRN 50
S275
SEE FUSE BLOCK DETAILS
2 BRN 50
E C2
MODE SELECTOR
OFF
MAX
NORM
DEF
HTR
VENT
B/L
HEATER AND A/C CONTROL ASSEMBLY
C C2
1 LT GRN 66
D C211
.8 LT GRN 66
A
A/C LOW PRESSURE CUT-OUT SWITCH
OPENS BELOW 55 kPa (8 PSI)
B
.8 DK GRN/WHT 603
S138
.8 DK GRN/WHT
603
.8 DK GRN/WHT 603
B
A/C HIGH PRESSURE CUT-OUT SWITCH
OPENS ABOVE 2827 kPa (410 PSI)
CLOSES BELOW 1379 kPa (200 PSI)
A
.8 DK BLU
.8 DK BLU 604
ECM CONNECTOR IDENTIFICATION
C1 - BLACK/RED - 24 WAY
C2 - WHITE/RED - 24 WAY
C24 C1
C2 C2 604
COOLANT FAN ENABLE
A/C ON INPUT
ENGINE CONTROL MODULE (ECM)

A/C CLUTCH DIODE DETAIL
THE A/C CLUTCH DIODE CONNECTED ACROSS THE A/C COMPRESSOR CLUTCH PREVENTS THE PRODUCTION OF ELECTRICAL SPIKES WHEN THE A/C CLUTCH IS TURNED OFF.

HOT IN RUN, BULB TEST OR START
ECM RLYS FUSE 10 AMP
FUSE BLOCK
.8 PNK/BLK 439
S243
.8 PNK/BLK 439
F C207
.8 PNK/BLK 439
S119
SEE FUSE BLOCK DETAILS
.5 PNK/BLK 439
1
5
A/C COMPRESSOR CONTROL RELAY
4
2
.8 DK GRN/WHT 459
C3 C1
IGNITION
A/C COMPRESSOR CONTROL RELAY CONTROL
ENGINE CONTROL MODULE (ECM)
POWER STEERING INPUT
C5 C2
.5 LT BLU/ORN 495
A
IDLE SPEED POWER STEERING PRESSURE SWITCH
CLOSED ABOVE 3800 kPa (550 PSI)
B
1 DK GRN 59
.5 WHT
899
Y
A/C CLUTCH DIODE
SEE DETAIL ABOVE
A/C COMPRESSOR CLUTCH
X
.5 WHT
899
1 BLK 150
GROUND DISTRIBUTION
5 BLK
S131
SEE GROUND DISTRIBUTION
.5 BLK/WHT 450
S129
1 BLK/WHT 450
.8 BLK/WHT
450
19 BLK
150
5 BLK 150
G100
G105
G106

Calais — Air conditioning — compressor controls — 2.5L engine

HOT IN RUN
HTR A/C FUSE 25 AMP
FUSE BLOCK
2 BRN 50
S275
SEE FUSE BLOCK DETAILS
2 BRN 50
E C2
MODE SELECTOR
OFF
MAX
NORM
DEF
HTR
VENT
B/L
HEATER AND A/C CONTROL ASSEMBLY
C C2
1 LT GRN 66
D C211
1 LT GRN 66
C9 C1
A/C ON INPUT
5 VOLT REF
ENGINE CONTROL MODULE (ECM)
A5 C2
.8 GRY 416
B
A/C COMPRESSOR REFRIGERANT PRESSURE SENSOR
.5 GRY/RED
C
380
A
.5 BLK 452
S126
SEE MULTI-PORT FUEL INJECTION: ENGINE DATA SENSORS
.8 BLK 452
F14 C3
B6 C2
A/C COMPRESSOR REFRIGERANT PRESSURE SENSOR INPUT
SENSOR GROUND
ENGINE CONTROL MODULE (ECM)
ECM CONNECTOR IDENTIFICATION
C1 - BLACK/GRAY - 32 WAY
C2 - BLACK/BLUE - 24 WAY
C3 - YELLOW - 32 WAY

2 BRN 50
G8 C100
1 BRN 50
2
COOLANT FAN RELAY
1 BRN 50
1

A/C CLUTCH DIODE DETAIL
THE A/C CLUTCH DIODE CONNECTED ACROSS THE A/C COMPRESSOR CLUTCH PREVENTS THE PRODUCTION OF ELECTRICAL SPIKES WHEN THE A/C CLUTCH IS TURNED OFF.

HOT IN RUN, BULB TEST OR START
ECM RLYS FUSE 10 AMP
FUSE BLOCK
.8 PNK/BLK 439
S243
.8 PNK/BLK 439
F C207
.8 PNK/BLK 439
S119
SEE FUSE BLOCK DETAILS
.8 PNK/BLK 439
5
A/C COMPRESSOR CONTROL RELAY
4
2
.8 DK GRN/WHT 459
F8 C3
IGNITION
A/C COMPRESSOR CONTROL RELAY CONTROL
ENGINE CONTROL MODULE (ECM)
POWER STEERING INPUT
D12 C1
.5 LT BLU/ORN 495
A
IDLE SPEED POWER STEERING PRESSURE SWITCH
CLOSED ABOVE 3800 kPa (550 PSI)
B
1 DK GRN 59
.5 WHT
899
Y
A/C CLUTCH DIODE
SEE DETAIL ABOVE
A/C COMPRESSOR CLUTCH
X
.5 WHT
899
1 BLK 150
5 BLK
S131
SEE GROUND DISTRIBUTION
.8 BLK/WHT 450
S118
1 BLK/WHT 450
150
5 BLK 150
G105
G100
G103

Calais — Air conditioning — compressor controls — 3.3L engine

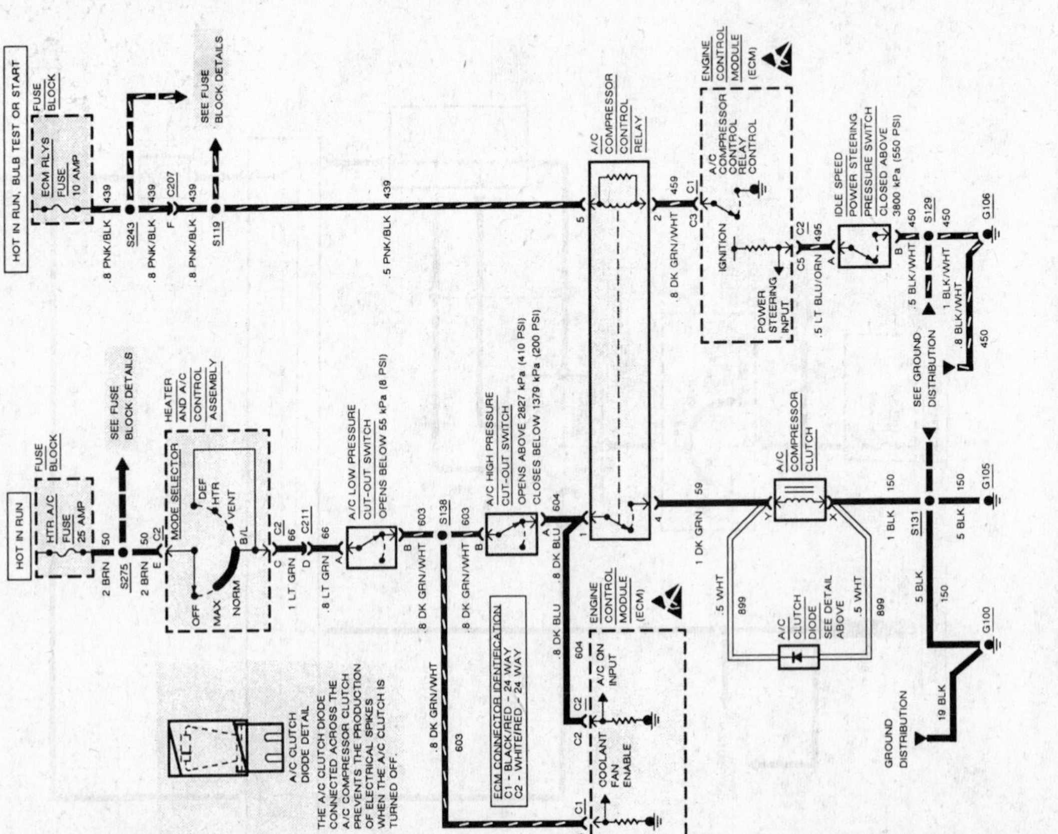

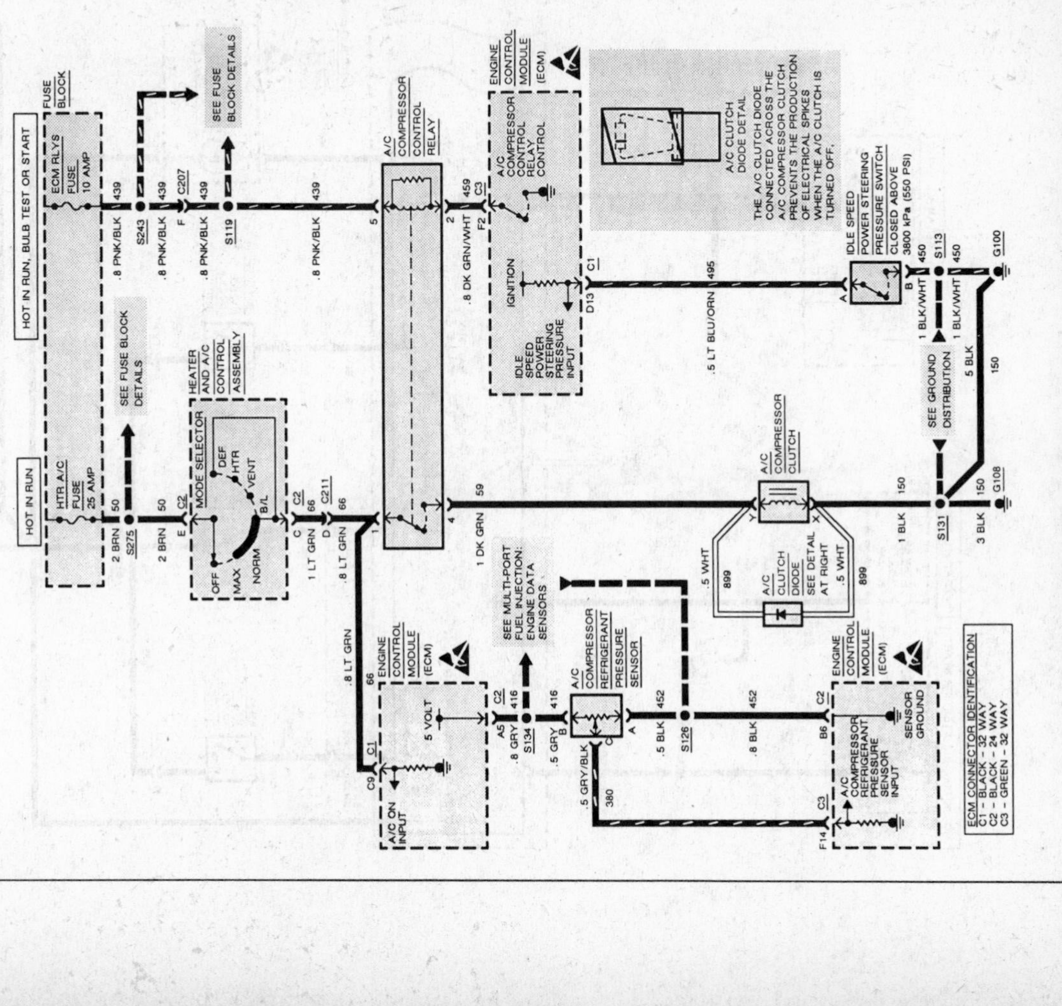

HOT IN RUN
HOT IN RUN, BULB TEST OR START
HTR A/C FUSE 25 AMP
ECM RLYS FUSE 10 AMP
FUSE BLOCK
2 BRN 50
S275
SEE FUSE BLOCK DETAILS
.8 PNK/BLK 439
S243
2 BRN 50
E C2
.8 PNK/BLK 439
F C207
.8 PNK/BLK 439
S119
SEE FUSE BLOCK DETAILS
MODE SELECTOR
OFF MAX NORM B/L VENT HTR DEF
HEATER AND A/C CONTROL ASSEMBLY
C C2
1 LT GRN 66
D C211
.8 LT GRN 66
.8 PNK/BLK 439
.8 LT GRN
C9 C1 66
A/C ON INPUT
5 VOLT
ENGINE CONTROL MODULE (ECM)
A/C COMPRESSOR CONTROL RELAY
1 DK GRN 59
.8 DK GRN/WHT 459
F2 C3
IDLE SPEED POWER STEERING PRESSURE INPUT
IGNITION
A/C COMPRESSOR CONTROL RELAY CONTROL
ENGINE CONTROL MODULE (ECM)
A5 C2
.8 GRY 416
S134
SEE MULTI-PORT FUEL INJECTION: ENGINE DATA SENSORS
.5 GRY 416
.5 GRY/BLK 380
A/C COMPRESSOR REFRIGERANT PRESSURE SENSOR
.5 BLK 452
S126
D13 C1
A/C CLUTCH DIODE DETAIL
THE A/C CLUTCH DIODE CONNECTED ACROSS THE A/C COMPRESSOR CLUTCH PREVENTS THE PRODUCTION OF ELECTRICAL SPIKES WHEN THE A/C CLUTCH IS TURNED OFF.
.5 LT BLU/ORN 495
.5 WHT 899
A/C CLUTCH DIODE SEE DETAIL AT RIGHT
A/C COMPRESSOR CLUTCH
.8 BLK 452
F14 C3
B6 C2
A/C COMPRESSOR REFRIGERANT PRESSURE SENSOR INPUT
SENSOR GROUND
ENGINE CONTROL MODULE (ECM)
IDLE SPEED POWER STEERING PRESSURE SWITCH CLOSED ABOVE 3800 kPa (550 PSI)
1 BLK 150
S131
SEE GROUND DISTRIBUTION
1 BLK/WHT 450
S113
1 BLK/WHT 450
5 BLK
3 BLK 150
G108
150
G100

ECM CONNECTOR IDENTIFICATION
C1 - BLACK - 32 WAY
C2 - BLACK - 24 WAY
C3 - GREEN - 32 WAY

Calais — Air conditioning — compressor controls — 2.3L and 2.3L HO engines

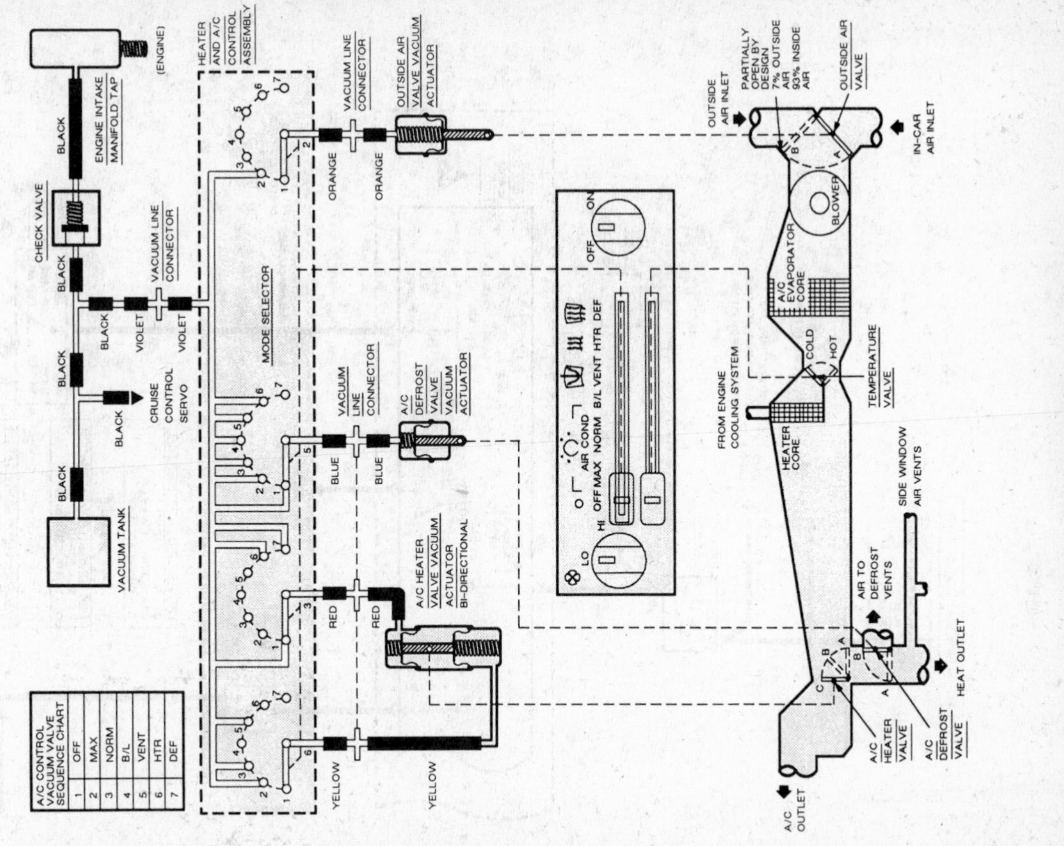

A/C CONTROL VACUUM VALVE SEQUENCE CHART

1	OFF
2	MAX
3	NORM
4	B/L
5	VENT
6	HTR
7	DEF

VACUUM TANK
BLACK
CRUISE CONTROL SERVO
VIOLET
VACUUM LINE CONNECTOR
CHECK VALVE
ENGINE INTAKE MANIFOLD TAP
(ENGINE)
HEATER AND A/C CONTROL ASSEMBLY
MODE SELECTOR
YELLOW
RED
BLUE
ORANGE
VACUUM LINE CONNECTOR
A/C HEATER VALVE VACUUM ACTUATOR BI-DIRECTIONAL
A/C DEFROST VALVE VACUUM ACTUATOR
OUTSIDE AIR VALVE VACUUM ACTUATOR
LO HI OFF MAX NORM B/L VENT HTR DEF AIR COND OFF ON
FROM ENGINE COOLING SYSTEM
OUTSIDE AIR INLET
PARTIALLY OPEN BY DESIGN 7% OUTSIDE AIR 93% INSIDE AIR
A/C OUTLET
HEATER CORE
COLD
HOT
A/C EVAPORATOR CORE
BLOWER
OUTSIDE AIR VALVE
A/C HEATER VALVE
AIR TO DEFROST VENTS
SIDE WINDOW AIR VENTS
TEMPERATURE VALVE
IN-CAR AIR INLET
A/C DEFROST VALVE
HEAT OUTLET

Calais — Air conditioning — air delivery

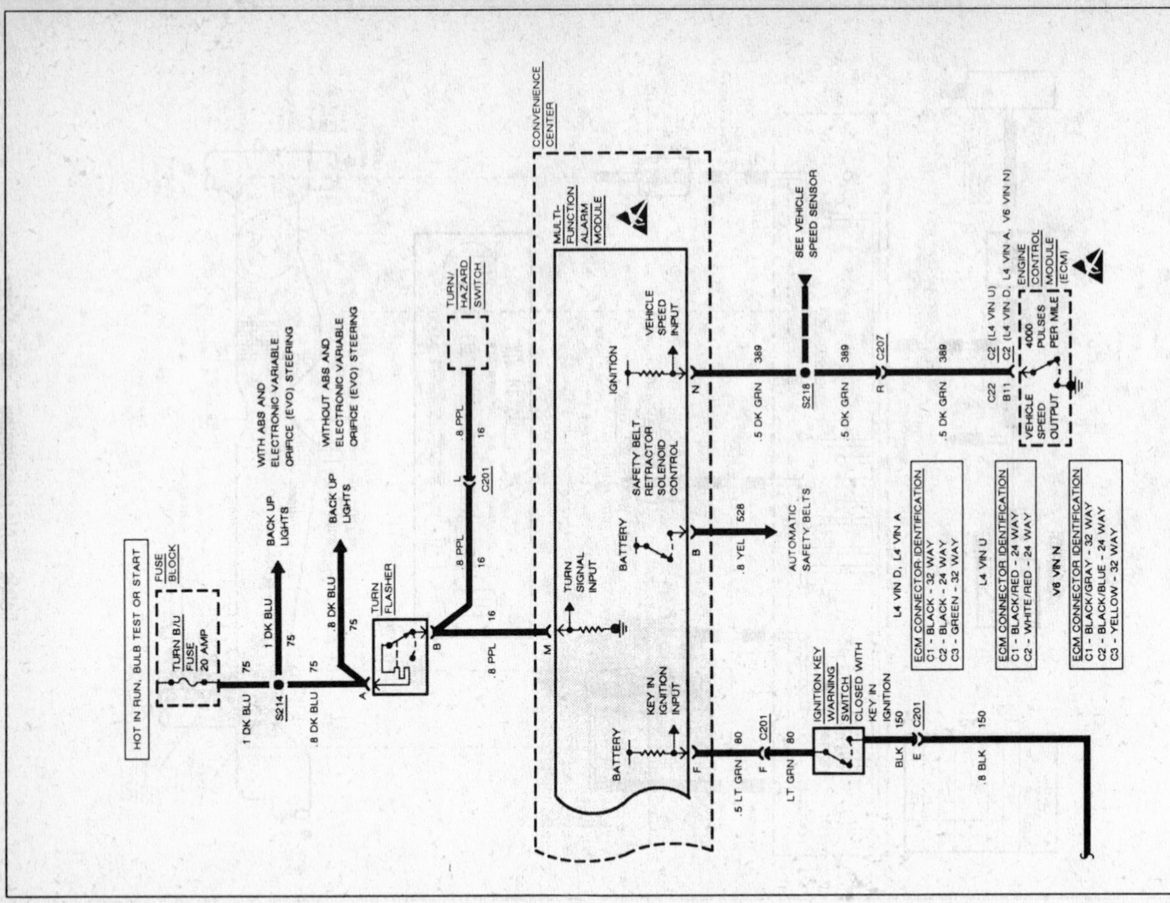

ECM CONNECTOR IDENTIFICATION (L4 VIN D, L4 VIN A)
C1 - BLACK - 32 WAY
C2 - BLACK - 24 WAY
C3 - GREEN - 32 WAY

ECM CONNECTOR IDENTIFICATION (L4 VIN U)
C1 - BLACK/RED - 24 WAY
C2 - WHITE/RED - 24 WAY

ECM CONNECTOR IDENTIFICATION (V6 VIN N)
C1 - BLACK/GRAY - 32 WAY
C2 - BLACK/BLUE - 24 WAY
C3 - YELLOW - 32 WAY

Calais — Warnings and alarms — chime

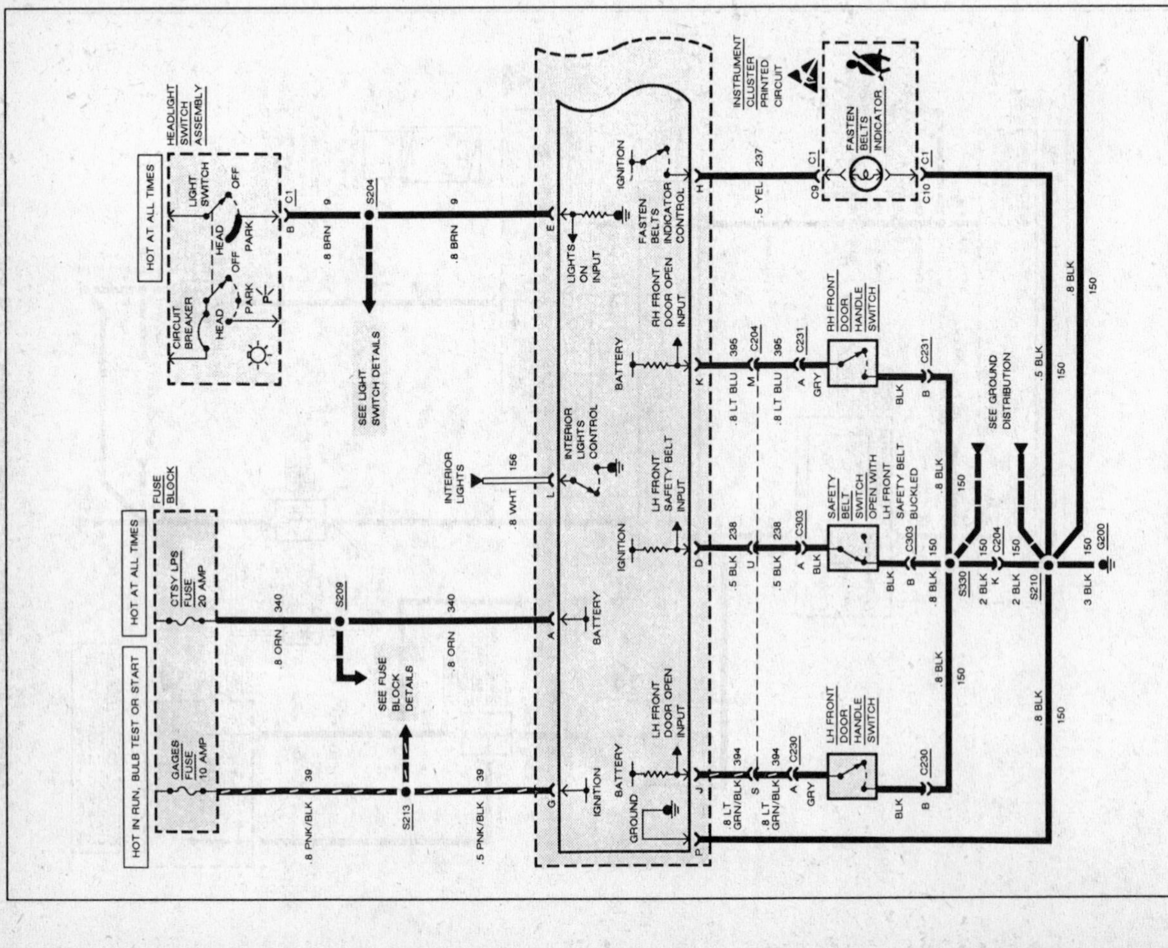

Calais — Warnings and alarms — chime

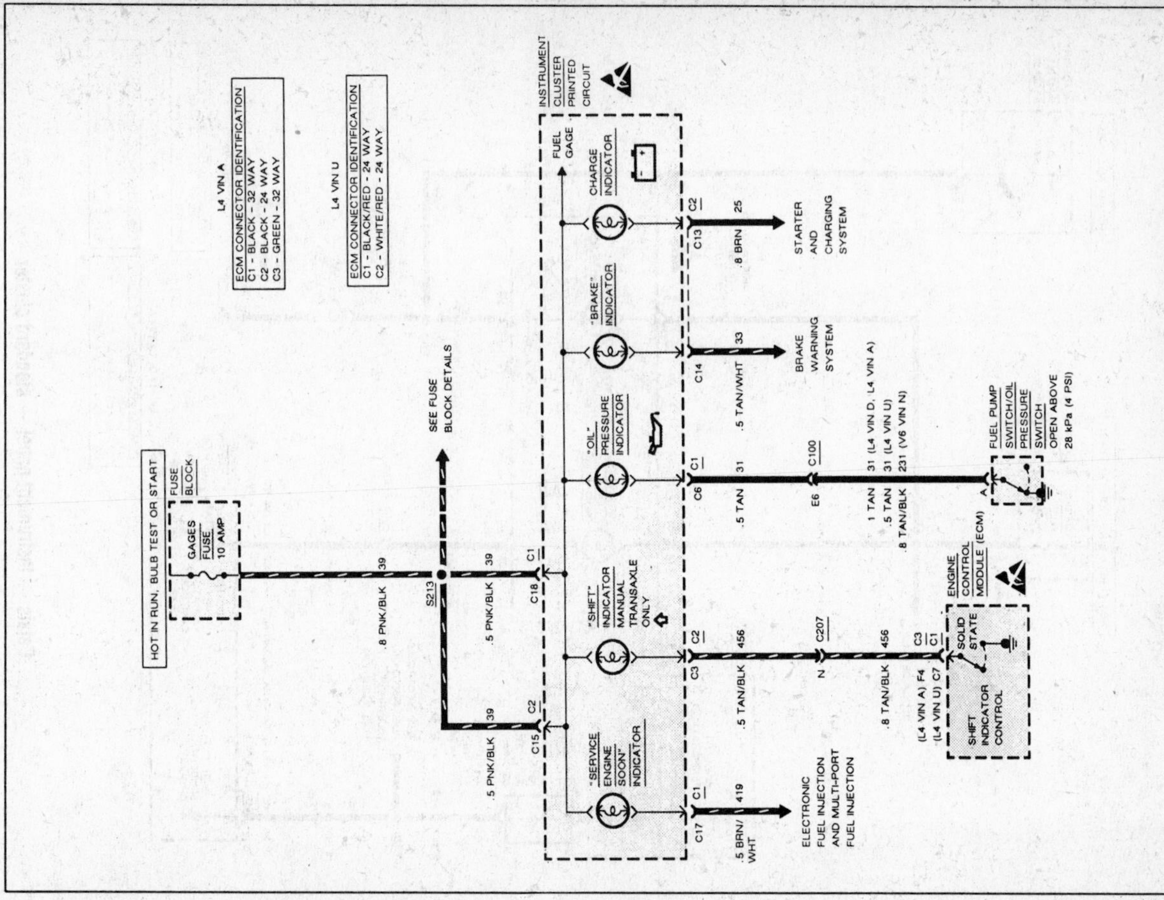

HOT IN RUN, BULB TEST OR START
GAGES FUSE 10 AMP
FUSE BLOCK
.8 PNK/BLK 39
S213
SEE FUSE BLOCK DETAILS
.5 PNK/BLK 39
C15
INTERIOR LIGHTS DIMMING
HEADLIGHTS
EXTERIOR LIGHTS: TURN
WARNINGS AND ALARMS: CHIME
.5 GRY 8 C17
.5 GRY 8 C12
.5 GRY 8 C4 C2
.5 GRY 8 C2
1 LT GRN/BLK 911 C13
.8 LT BLU 14 C14
.8 DK BLU 15 C12
.5 YEL 237 C9 C1
INSTRUMENT CLUSTER PRINTED CIRCUIT
INDICATORS
FUEL GAGE
(1 BULB)
(2 BULBS)
(4 BULBS)
(2 BULBS)
CLUSTER ILLUMINATION
HI BEAM INDICATOR
LH TURN INDICATOR
RH TURN INDICATOR
FASTEN BELTS INDICATOR
C16 C18 C11 C2 C16 C3 C11 C10 C1
.5 PPL 30
DRIVER INFORMATION SYSTEM
WITH DRIVER INFORMATION SYSTEM
.5 PPL 30
H C204
1 PPL 30
B
FUEL GAGE SENDER
90 OHMS WHEN FULL
0 OHMS WHEN EMPTY
FUEL TANK UNIT
D
1 BLK/WHT 353
L C204
.5 BLK 150
.5 BLK 150
.8 BLK 150
.8 BLK 150
.5 BLK 150
.5 BLK 150
2 BLK 150
S210
3 BLK 150
G200
SEE GROUND DISTRIBUTION

Calais — Instrument panel — standard cluster

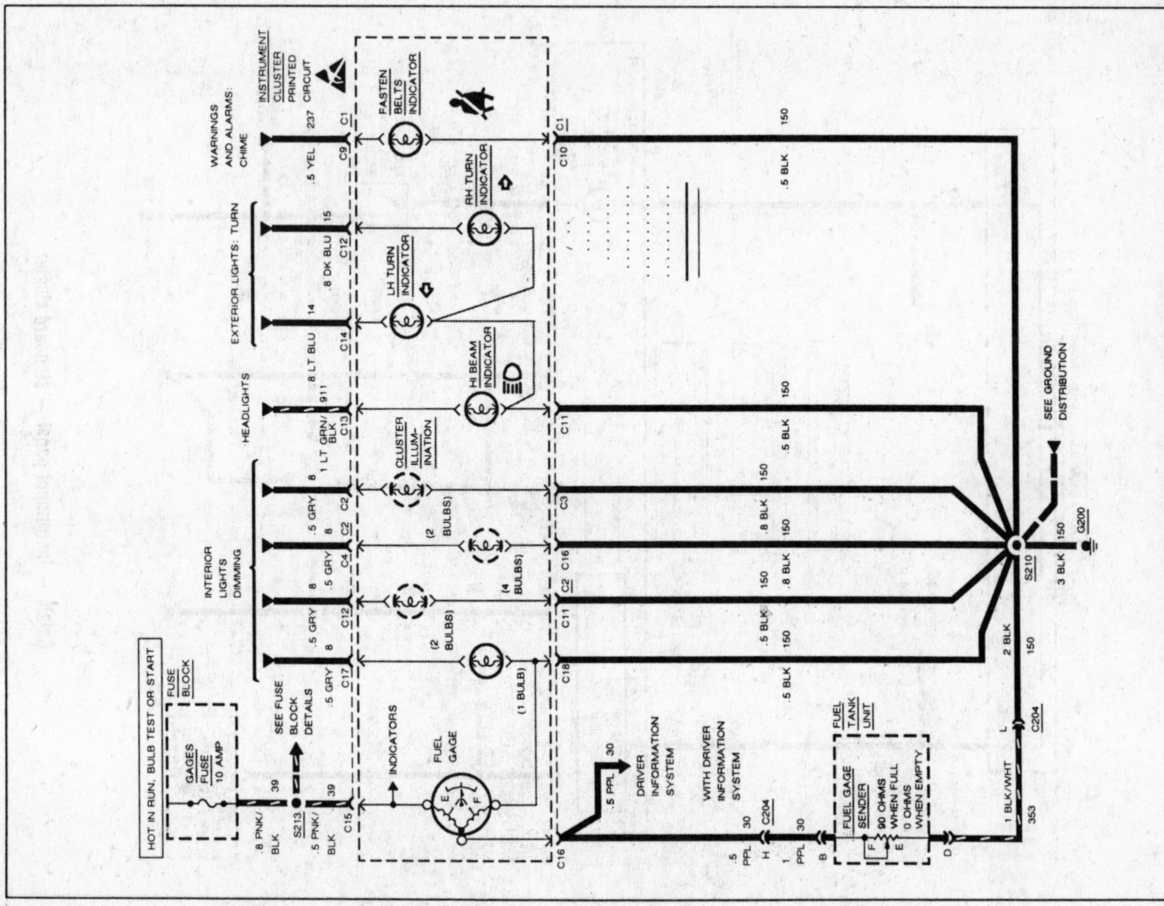

HOT IN RUN, BULB TEST OR START
GAGES FUSE 10 AMP
FUSE BLOCK
L4 VIN A
ECM CONNECTOR IDENTIFICATION
C1 - BLACK - 32 WAY
C2 - BLACK - 24 WAY
C3 - GREEN - 32 WAY
L4 VIN U
ECM CONNECTOR IDENTIFICATION
C1 - BLACK/RED - 24 WAY
C2 - WHITE/RED - 24 WAY
.8 PNK/BLK 39
S213
SEE FUSE BLOCK DETAILS
.5 PNK/BLK 39
.5 PNK/BLK 39
C15 C2
C18 C1
FUEL GAGE
INSTRUMENT CLUSTER PRINTED CIRCUIT
"SERVICE ENGINE SOON" INDICATOR
"SHIFT" INDICATOR MANUAL TRANSAXLE ONLY
"OIL" PRESSURE INDICATOR
"BRAKE" INDICATOR
CHARGE INDICATOR
C17 C1
C3 C2
C6 C1
C14
C13 C2
.5 BRN/WHT 419
.5 TAN/BLK 456
.5 TAN 31
.5 TAN/WHT 33
.8 BRN 25
ELECTRONIC FUEL INJECTION AND MULTI-PORT FUEL INJECTION
N C207
E6 C100
BRAKE WARNING SYSTEM
STARTER AND CHARGING SYSTEM
1 TAN 31 (L4 VIN D, L4 VIN A)
.5 TAN 31 (L4 VIN U)
.8 TAN/BLK 231 (V6 VIN N)
.8 TAN/BLK 456
(L4 VIN A) F4 C3
(L4 VIN U) C7 C1
SHIFT INDICATOR CONTROL
SOLID STATE
ENGINE CONTROL MODULE (ECM)
A
FUEL PUMP SWITCH/OIL PRESSURE SWITCH
OPEN ABOVE 28 kPa (4 PSI)

Calais — Instrument panel — standard cluster

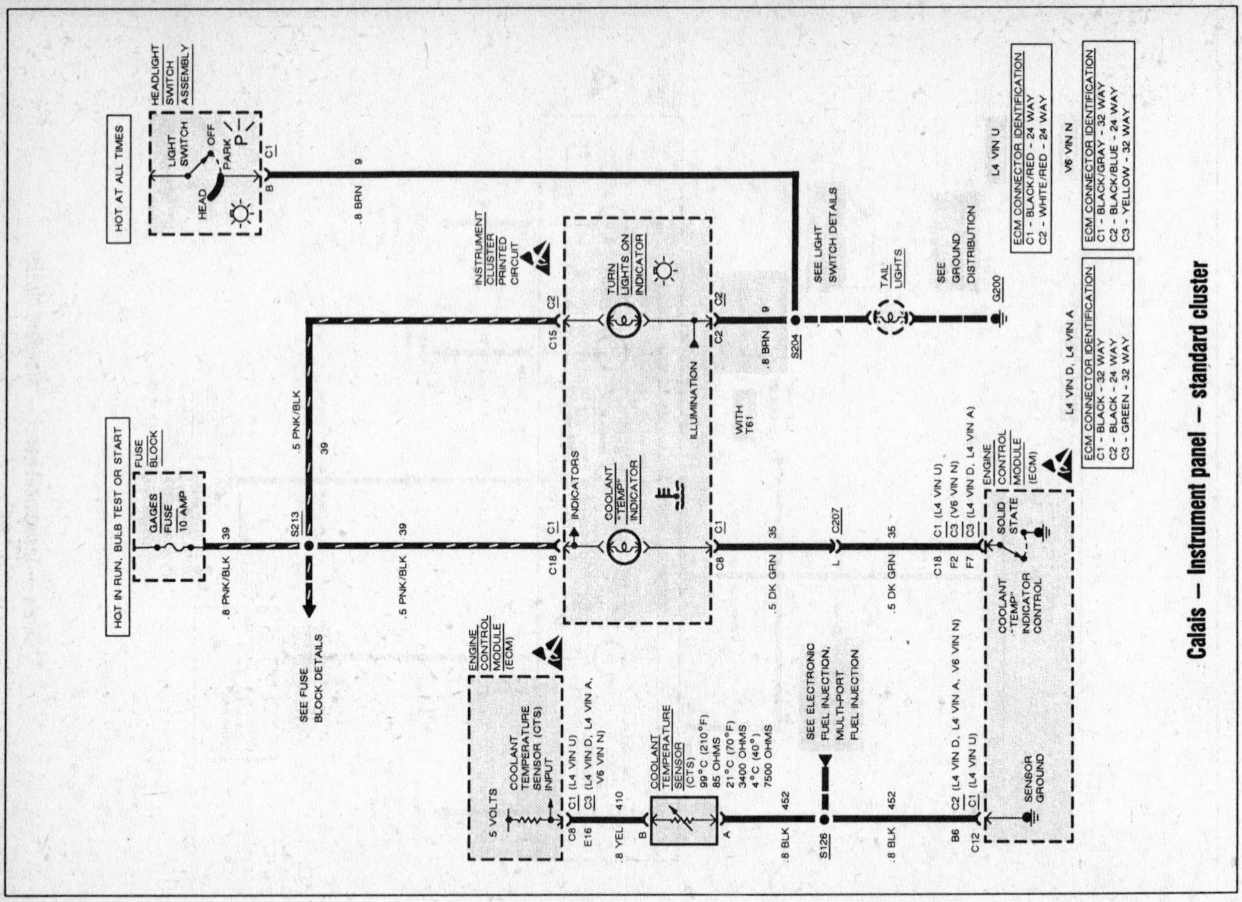

L4 VIN U

ECM CONNECTOR IDENTIFICATION
C1 - BLACK/RED - 24 WAY
C2 - WHITE/RED - 24 WAY

V6 VIN N

ECM CONNECTOR IDENTIFICATION
C1 - BLACK/GRAY - 24 WAY
C2 - BLACK/BLUE - 24 WAY
C3 - YELLOW - 32 WAY

L4 VIN D, L4 VIN A

ECM CONNECTOR IDENTIFICATION
C1 - BLACK - 32 WAY
C2 - BLACK - 24 WAY
C3 - GREEN - 32 WAY

Calais – Instrument panel – standard cluster

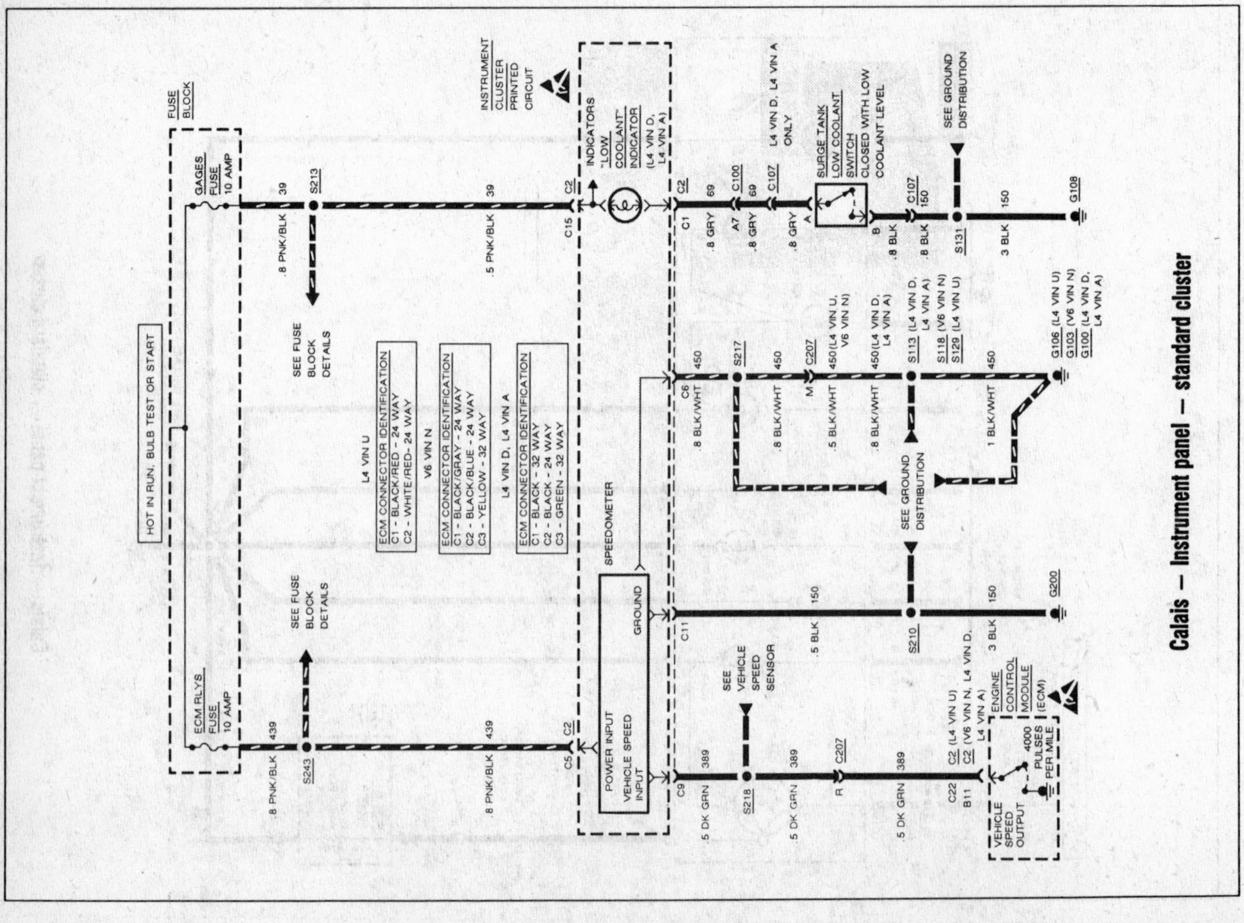

L4 VIN U

ECM CONNECTOR IDENTIFICATION
C1 - BLACK/RED - 24 WAY
C2 - WHITE/RED - 24 WAY

L4 VIN D, L4 VIN A

ECM CONNECTOR IDENTIFICATION
C1 - BLACK - 32 WAY
C2 - BLACK - 24 WAY
C3 - GREEN - 32 WAY

V6 VIN N

ECM CONNECTOR IDENTIFICATION
C1 - BLACK/GRAY - 32 WAY
C2 - BLACK/BLUE - 24 WAY
C3 - YELLOW - 32 WAY

Calais – Instrument panel – standard cluster

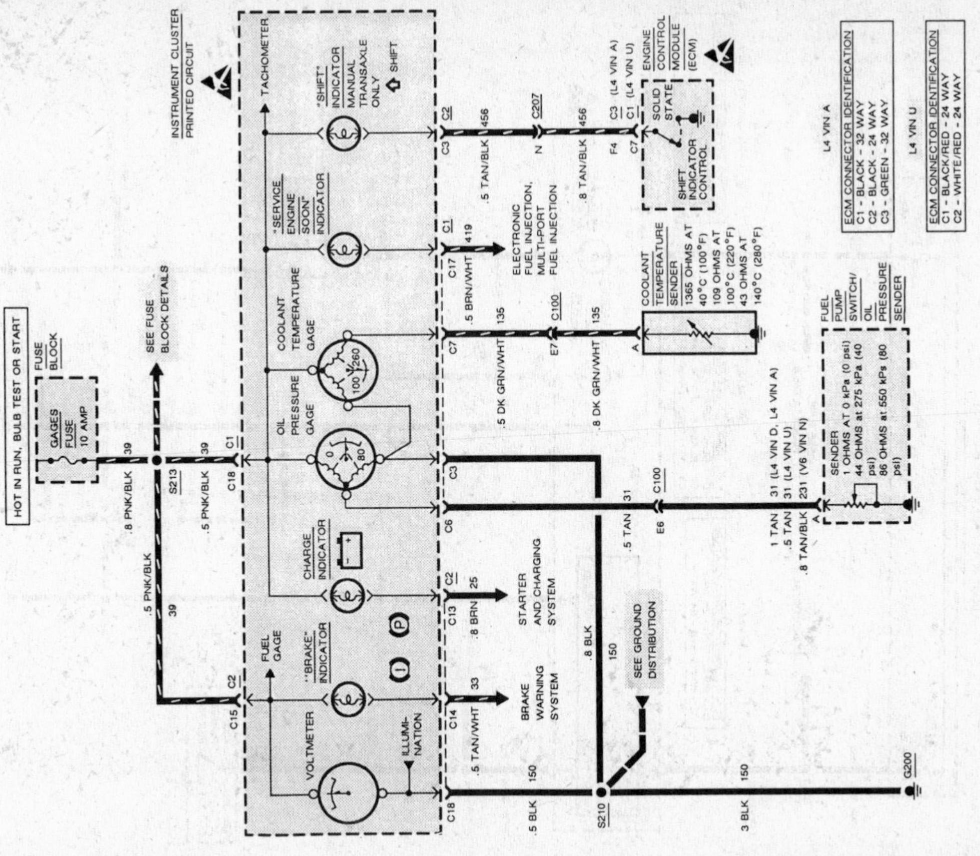

HOT IN RUN, BULB TEST OR START
GAGES FUSE 10 AMP
FUSE BLOCK
.8 PNK/BLK 39
S213
SEE FUSE BLOCK DETAILS
.5 PNK/BLK 39
INTERIOR LIGHTS DIMMING
HEADLIGHTS
EXTERIOR LIGHTS: TURN
WARNINGS AND ALARMS: CHIME
INSTRUMENT CLUSTER PRINTED CIRCUIT
.5 GRY 8
.5 GRY 8
.5 GRY 8
.5 GRY 8
1 LT GRN/BLK 911
.8 LT BLU 14
.8 DK BLU 15
.5 YEL 237
C15 C17 C12 C4 C2 C2 C13 C14 C12 C9 C1
VOLTMETER
FUEL GAGE
(1 BULB)
(2 BULBS)
(4 BULBS)
(2 BULBS)
CLUSTER ILLUMINATION
HI BEAM INDICATOR
LH TURN INDICATOR
RH TURN INDICATOR
FASTEN BELTS INDICATOR
TACHOMETER
VOLTMETER
C16 C18 C11 C2 C16 C3 C11 C10 C1
.5 PPL 30
DRIVER INFORMATION SYSTEM (DIS)
.5 PPL 30
WITH DRIVER INFORMATION SYSTEM
H C204
1 PPL 30
B
FUEL GAGE SENDER
90 OHMS WHEN FULL
0 OHMS WHEN EMPTY
FUEL TANK UNIT
D
1 BLK/WHT 353
L C204
2 BLK 150
.5 BLK 150
.5 BLK 150
.8 BLK 150
.8 BLK 150
.5 BLK 150
.5 BLK 150
S210
SEE GROUND DISTRIBUTION
3 BLK 150
G200

Calais — Instrument panel — gauges and cluster

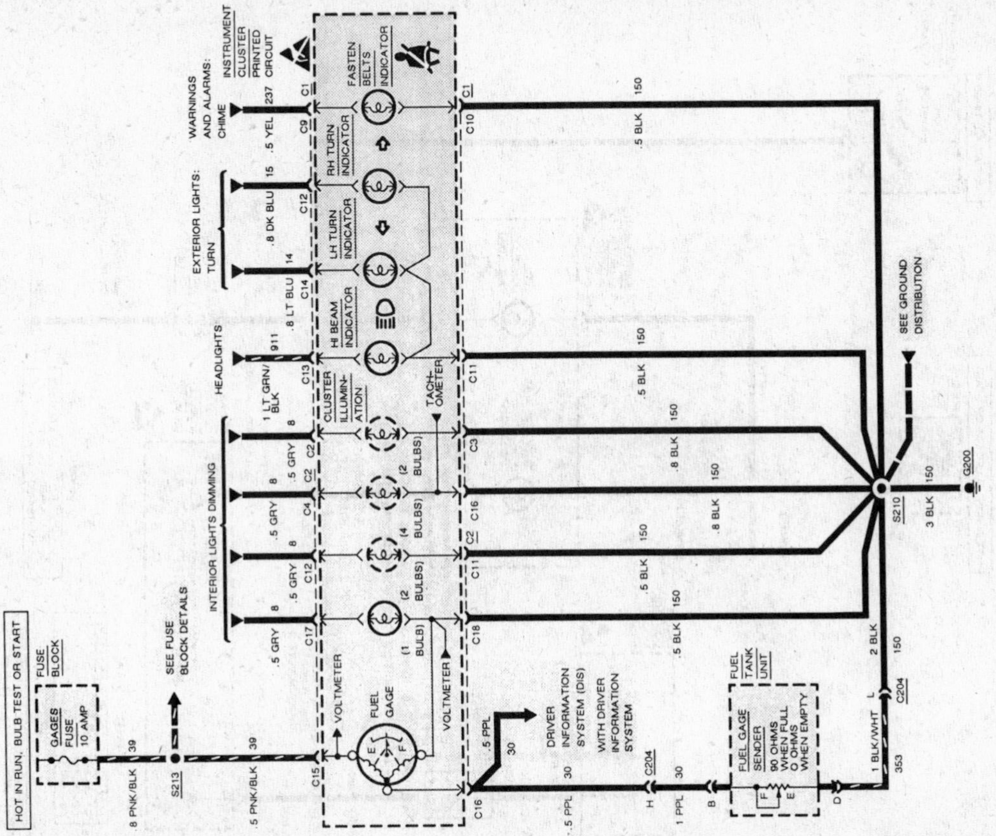

HOT IN RUN, BULB TEST OR START
GAGES FUSE 10 AMP
FUSE BLOCK
.8 PNK/BLK 39
.5 PNK/BLK 39
S213
SEE FUSE BLOCK DETAILS
.5 PNK/BLK 39
INSTRUMENT CLUSTER PRINTED CIRCUIT
C15 C2
C18 C1
FUEL GAGE
TACHOMETER
VOLTMETER
"BRAKE" INDICATOR
CHARGE INDICATOR
OIL PRESSURE GAGE
COOLANT TEMPERATURE GAGE
"SERVICE ENGINE SOON" INDICATOR
"SHIFT" INDICATOR MANUAL TRANSAXLE ONLY
SHIFT
ILLUMINATION
C18 C14 C13 C2 C6 C3 C7 C17 C1 C3 C2
.5 TAN/WHT 33
.8 BRN 25
.5 BRN/WHT 419
.5 TAN/BLK 456
BRAKE WARNING SYSTEM
STARTER AND CHARGING SYSTEM
.5 DK GRN/WHT 135
ELECTRONIC FUEL INJECTION, MULTI-PORT FUEL INJECTION
.5 BLK 150
N C207
E7 C100
.8 BLK
.8 DK GRN/WHT 135
.8 TAN/BLK 456
S210
150
.5 TAN 31
F4 C3 (L4 VIN A)
C7 C1 (L4 VIN U)
SEE GROUND DISTRIBUTION
E6 C100
A
COOLANT TEMPERATURE SENDER
1365 OHMS AT 40°C (100°F)
109 OHMS AT 100°C (220°F)
43 OHMS AT 140°C (280°F)
SOLID STATE
SHIFT INDICATOR CONTROL
ENGINE CONTROL MODULE (ECM)
3 BLK 150
1 TAN 31 (L4 VIN D, L4 VIN A)
.5 TAN 31 (L4 VIN U)
.8 TAN/BLK 231 (V6 VIN N)
A
SENDER
1 OHMS AT 0 kPa (0 psi)
44 OHMS at 275 kPa (40 psi)
86 OHMS at 550 kPa (80 psi)
FUEL PUMP SWITCH/ OIL PRESSURE SENDER
G200

L4 VIN A

ECM CONNECTOR IDENTIFICATION
C1 - BLACK - 32 WAY
C2 - BLACK - 24 WAY
C3 - GREEN - 32 WAY

L4 VIN U

ECM CONNECTOR IDENTIFICATION
C1 - BLACK/RED - 24 WAY
C2 - WHITE/RED - 24 WAY

Calais — Instrument panel — gauges and cluster

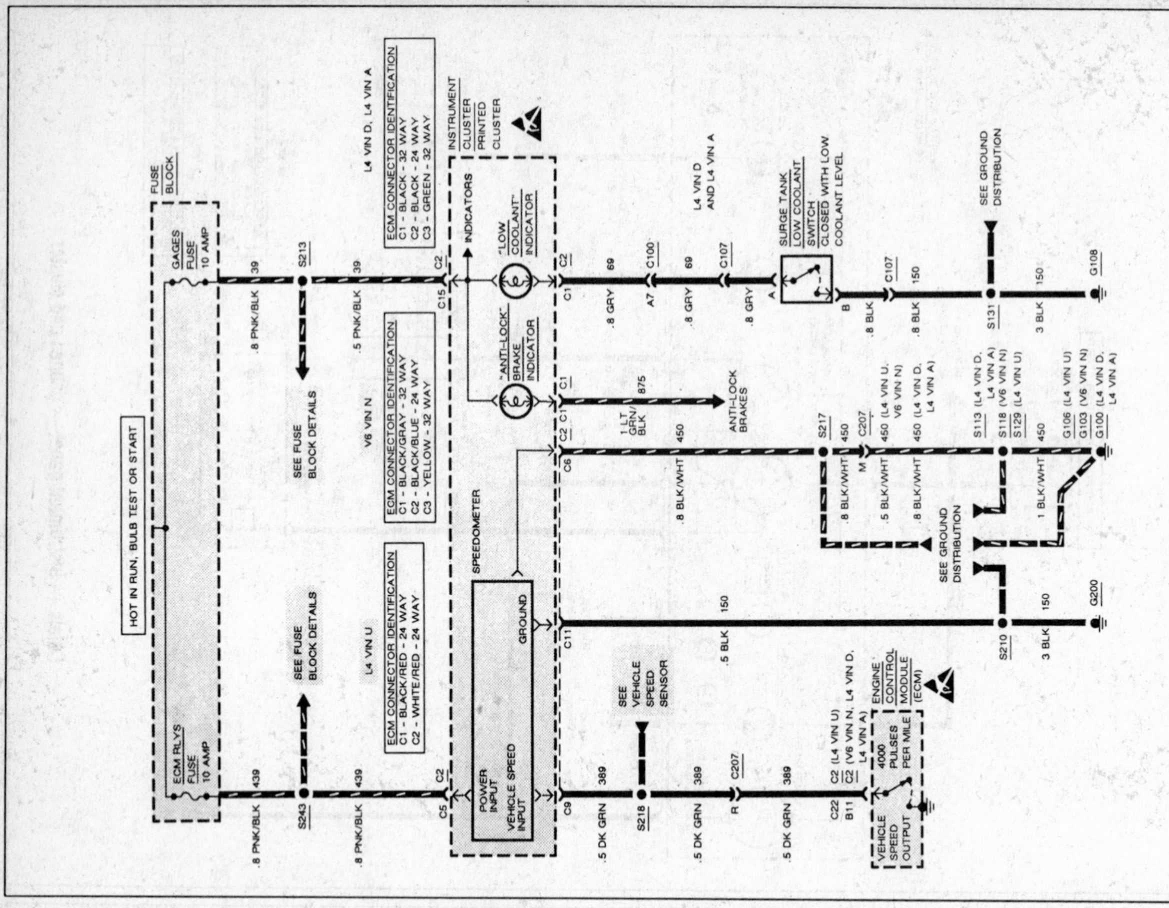

Calais — Instrument panel — gauges and cluster

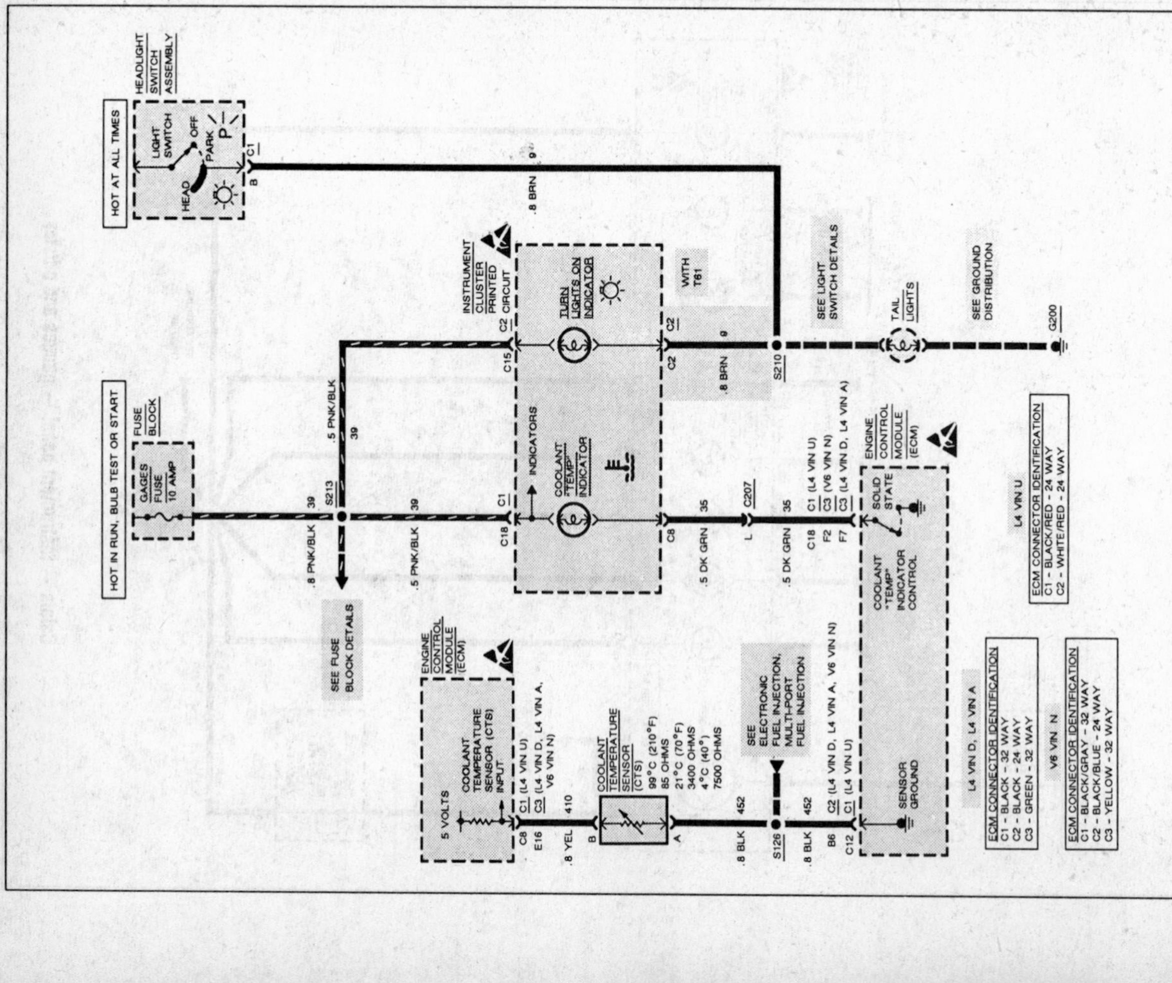

Calais — Instrument panel — gauges and cluster

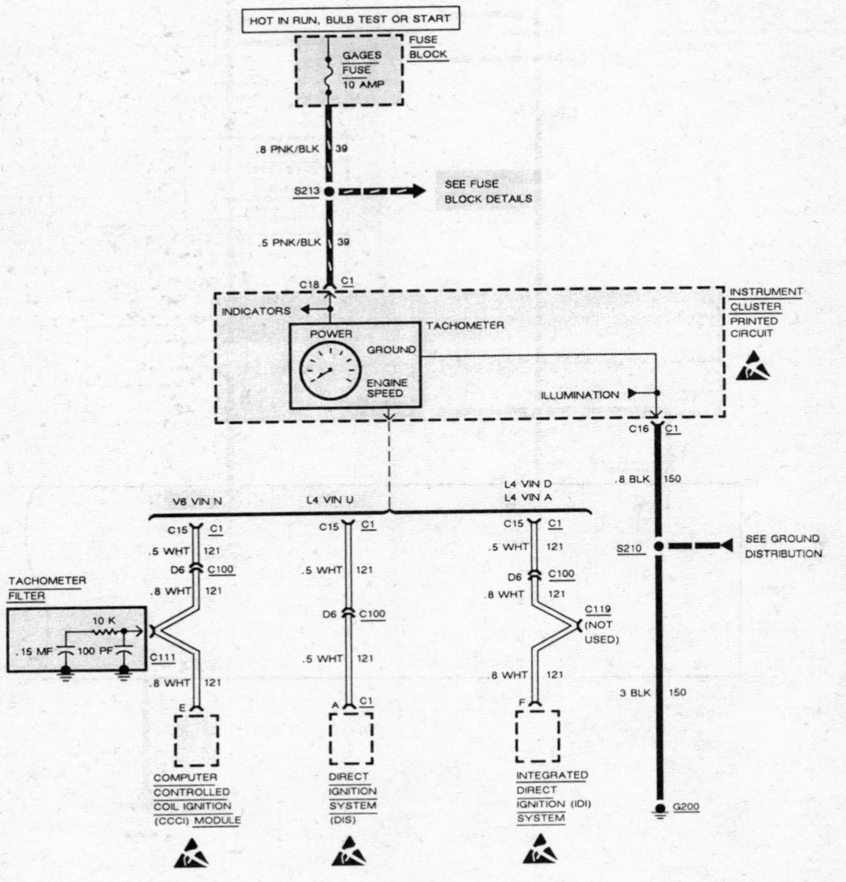

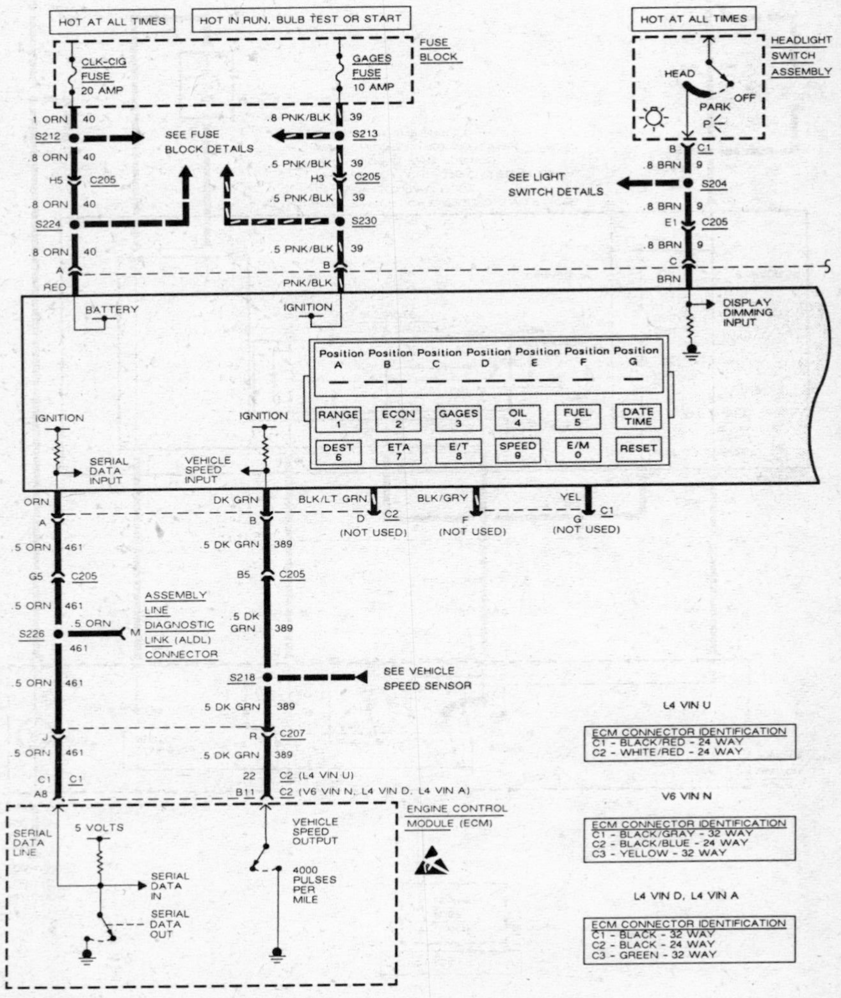

Calais — Driver information system

Calais — Instrument panel — gauges and cluster

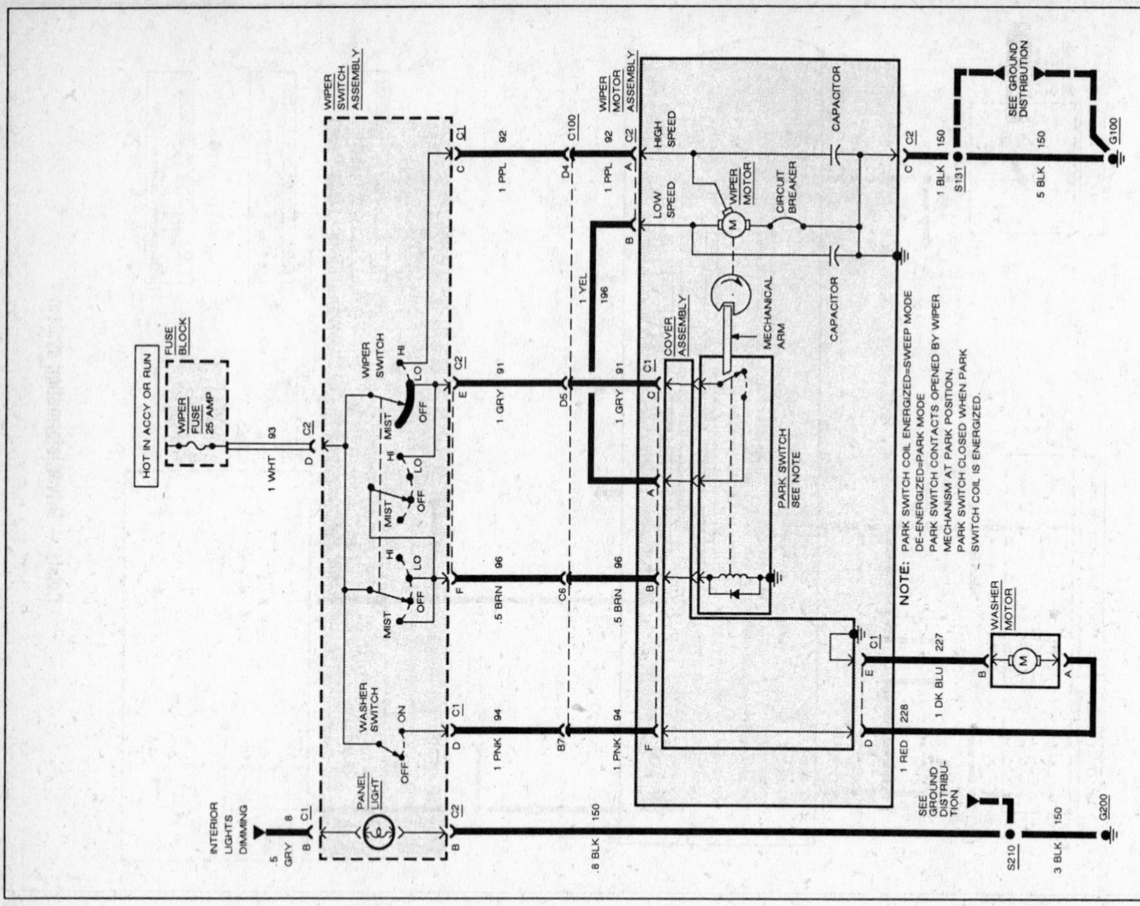

Calais — Wiper/washer — standard

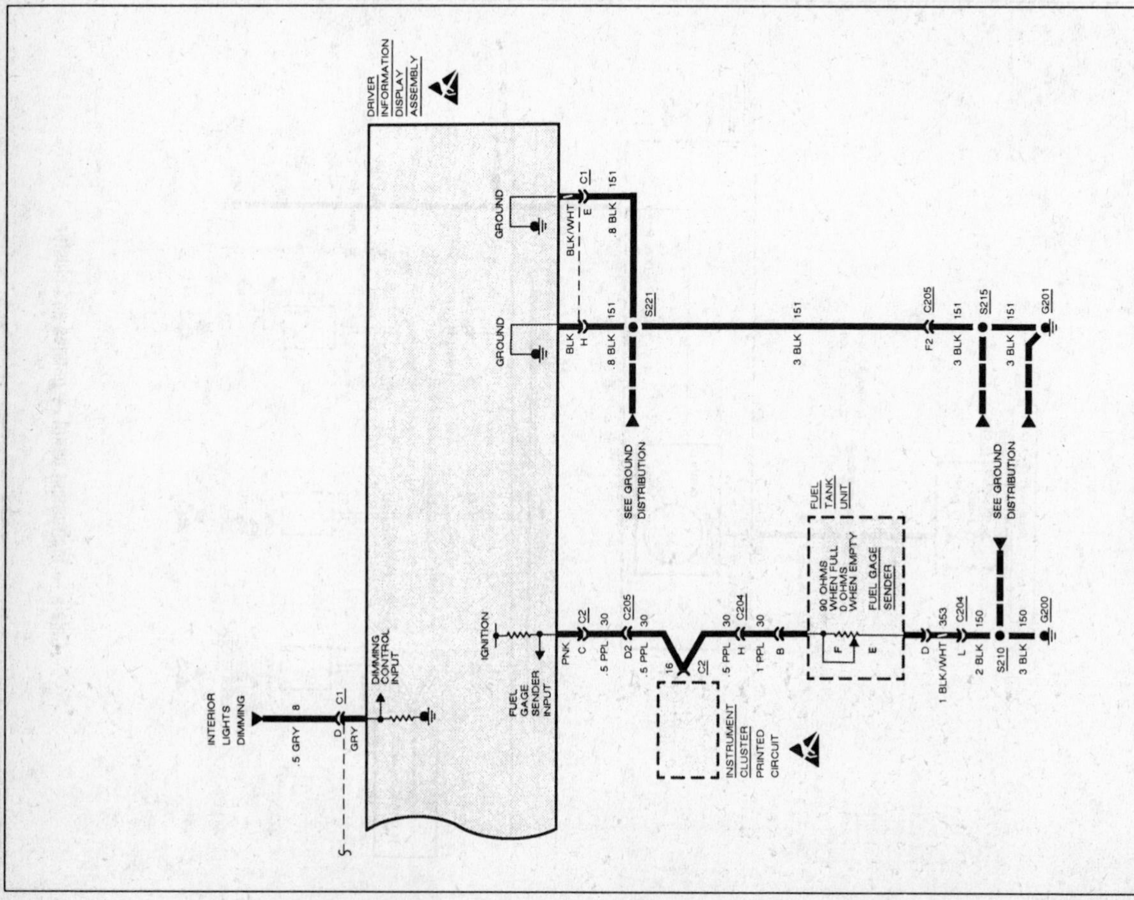

Calais — Driver information system

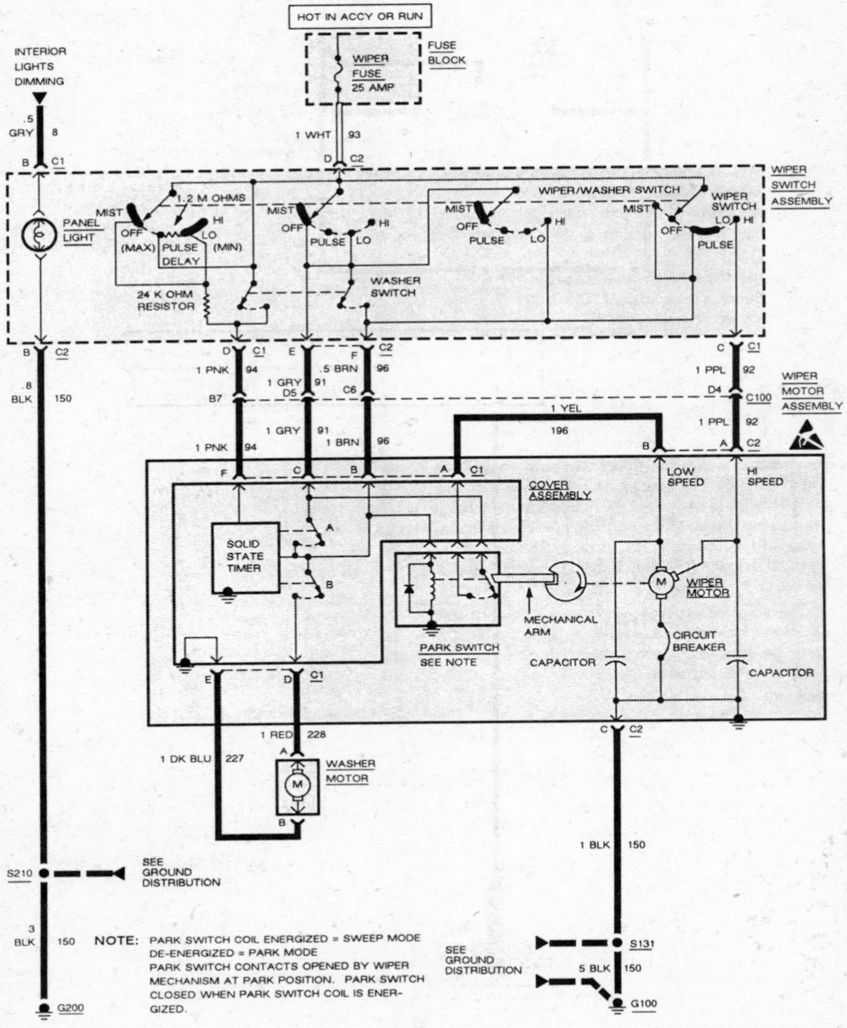

Calais — Wiper/washer — pulse

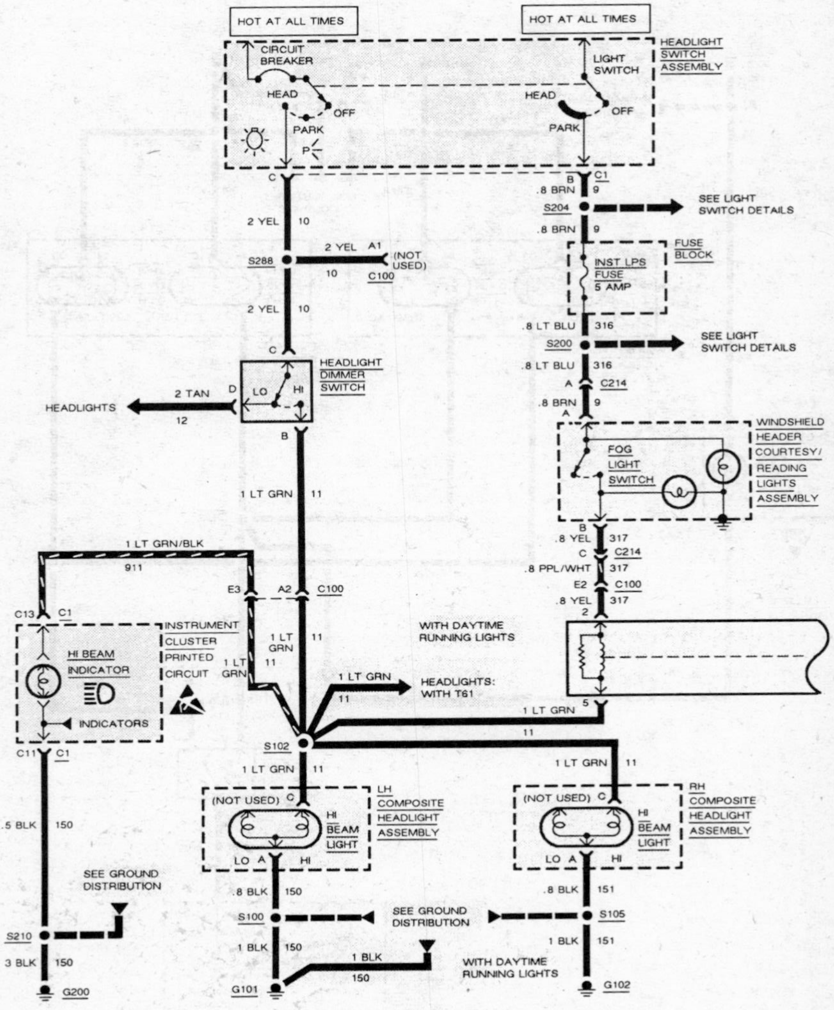

Calais — Headlights and fog lights

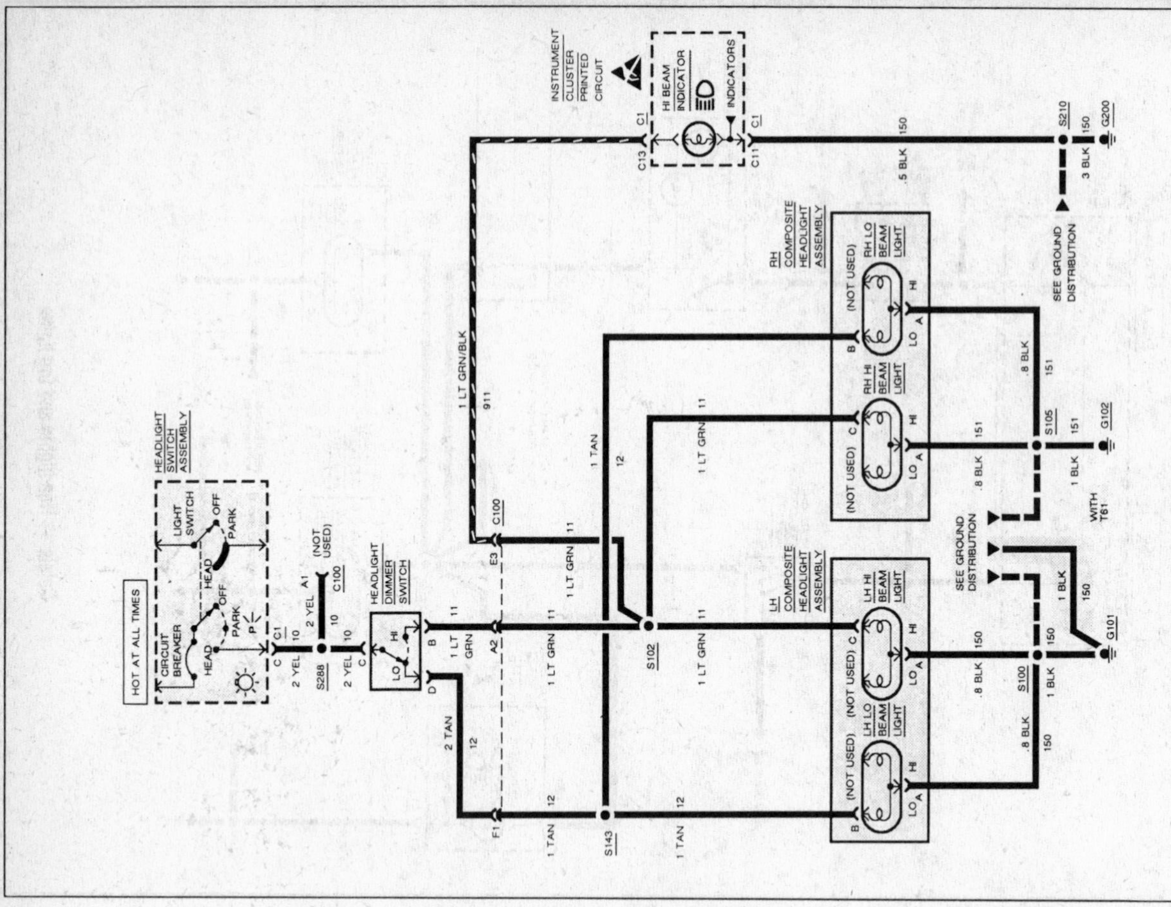

Calais — Headlights

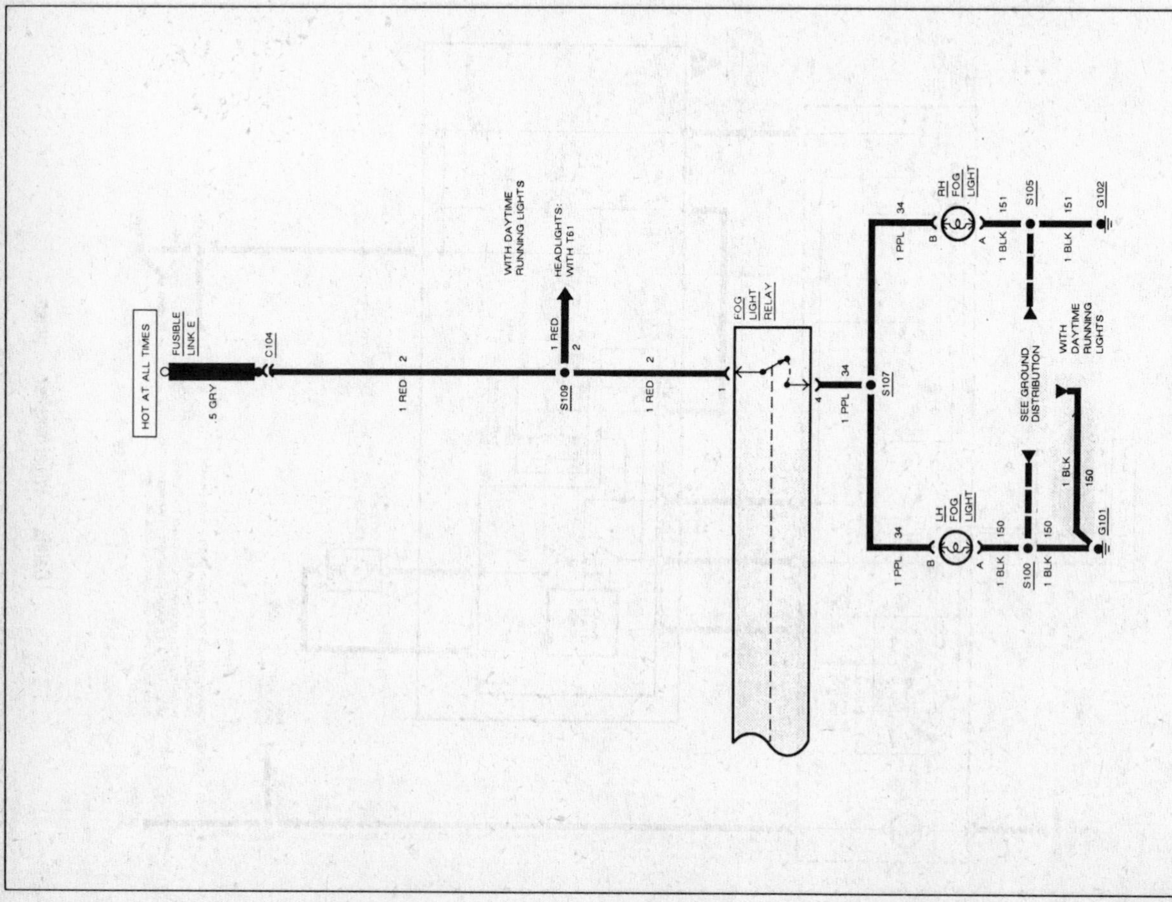

Calais — Headlights and fog lights

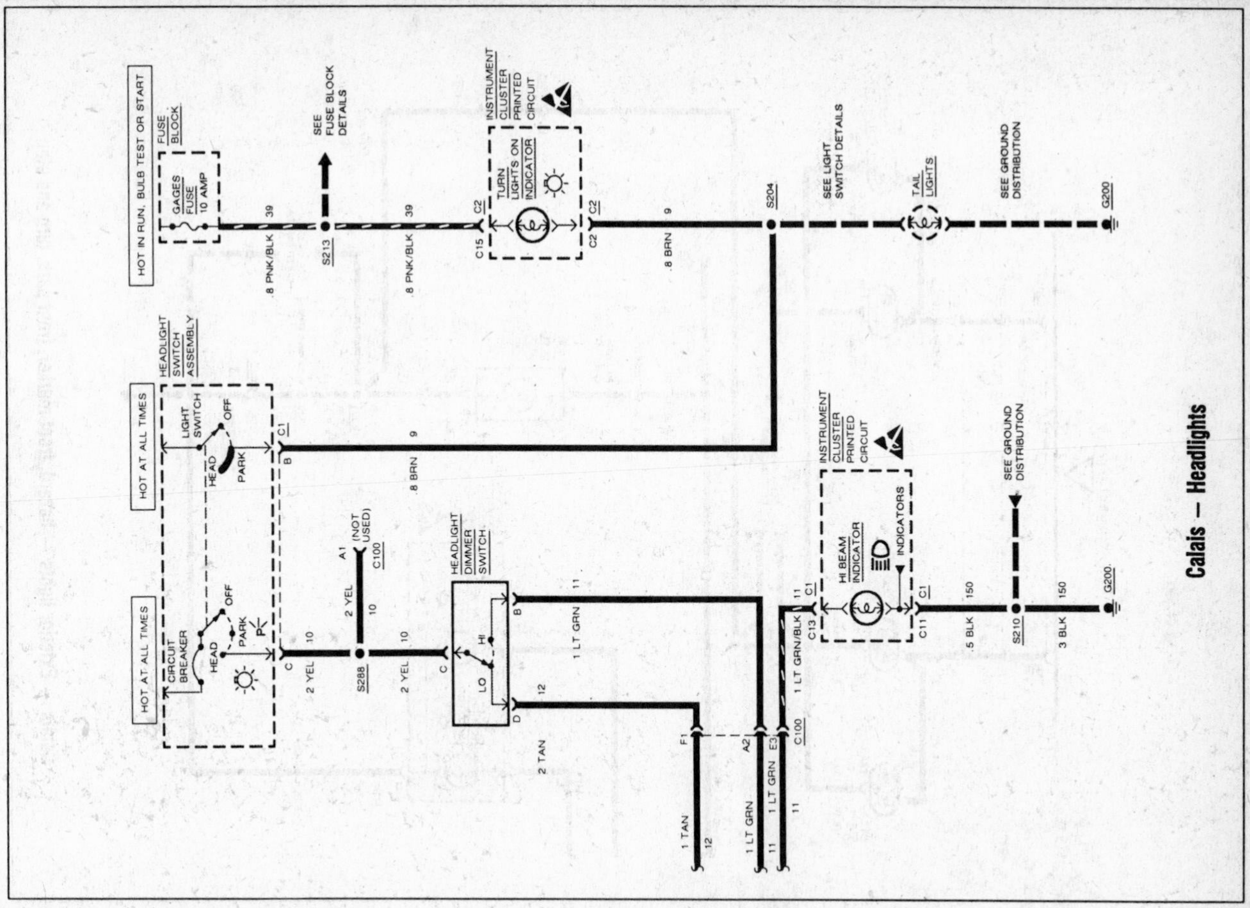

HOT AT ALL TIMES
FUSIBLE LINK E
.5 GRY
C104
1 RED 2
S109
1 RED 2
1 RED 2
POWER DISTRIBUTION
L4 VIN D
L4 VIN A
AND V6 VIN N
DRL IN-LINE FUSE A 15 AMP
A
B
.8 ORN 140
HOT IN RUN
HTR A/C FUSE 25 AMP
FUSE BLOCK
2 BRN 50
S275
SEE FUSE BLOCK DETAILS
2 BRN 50
B2 C100
2 BRN 50
DRL IN-LINE FUSE B 1 AMP
2 BRN/WHT 250
E
DAYTIME RUNNING LIGHTS (DRL) MODULE
BATTERY
IGNITION
GROUND GROUND BATTERY
DAYTIME RUNNING LIGHTS CONTROL
IGNITION
PARK BRAKE INPUT
HI BEAM ON INPUT
F B C D
.8 TAN/WHT 933
BRAKE WARNING SYSTEM
1 TAN 12
1 TAN
12 WITH FOG LIGHTS
HEADLIGHTS: WITH FOG LIGHTS
1 LT GRN 11
S102
1 LT GRN 11
S143
1 TAN 12
1 TAN 12
(NOT USED)
(NOT USED)
LH LO BEAM LIGHT
LH HI BEAM LIGHT
LH COMPOSITE HEADLIGHT ASSEMBLY
(NOT USED) (NOT USED)
RH HI BEAM LIGHT
RH LO BEAM LIGHT
RH COMPOSITE HEADLIGHT ASSEMBLY
.8 BLK 150
.8 BLK 150
.8 BLK 151
.8 BLK 151
SEE GROUND DISTRIBUTION
S100
1 BLK 150
1 BLK 150
1 BLK 150
G101
S105
1 BLK 151
G102

Calais – Headlights

HOT AT ALL TIMES
CIRCUIT BREAKER
HEAD
OFF
PARK
HOT AT ALL TIMES
LIGHT SWITCH
HEAD
OFF
PARK
HEADLIGHT SWITCH ASSEMBLY
C B C1
2 YEL 10
S288
2 YEL 10
A1 (NOT USED)
C100
2 YEL 10
.8 BRN 9
HEADLIGHT DIMMER SWITCH
LO HI
D B
2 TAN 12
1 LT GRN 11
1 TAN 12
F1
1 LT GRN 11
A2
1 LT GRN 11
E3
C100
1 LT GRN/BLK 11
C13 C1
HI BEAM INDICATOR
INDICATORS
INSTRUMENT CLUSTER PRINTED CIRCUIT
C11 C1
.5 BLK 150
S210
SEE GROUND DISTRIBUTION
3 BLK 150
G200
HOT IN RUN, BULB TEST OR START
GAGES FUSE 10 AMP
FUSE BLOCK
.8 PNK/BLK 39
S213
SEE FUSE BLOCK DETAILS
.8 PNK/BLK 39
C15 C2
TURN LIGHTS ON INDICATOR
INSTRUMENT CLUSTER PRINTED CIRCUIT
C2 C2
.8 BRN 9
S204
SEE LIGHT SWITCH DETAILS
TAIL LIGHTS
SEE GROUND DISTRIBUTION
G200

Calais – Headlights

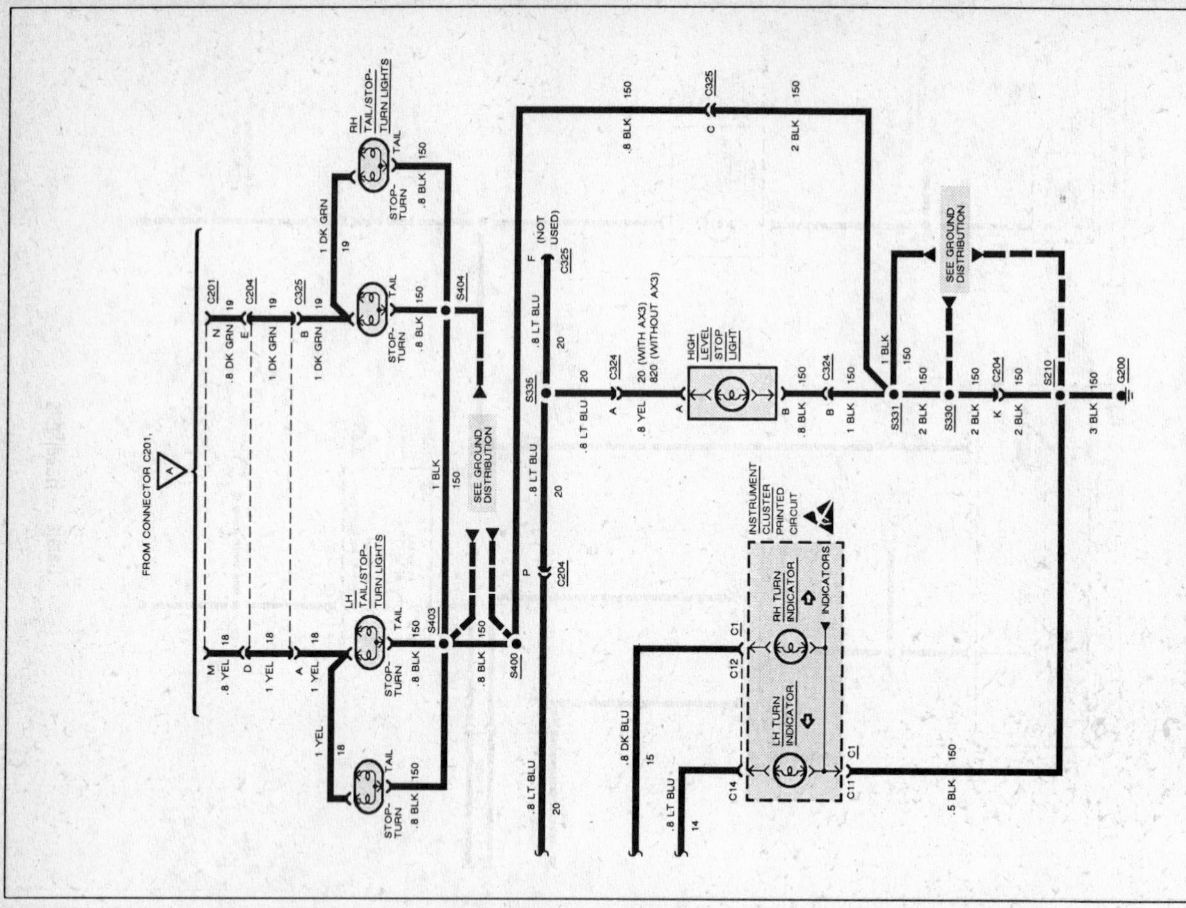

Calais — Exterior lights — hazard, front marker, front park, turn and stop

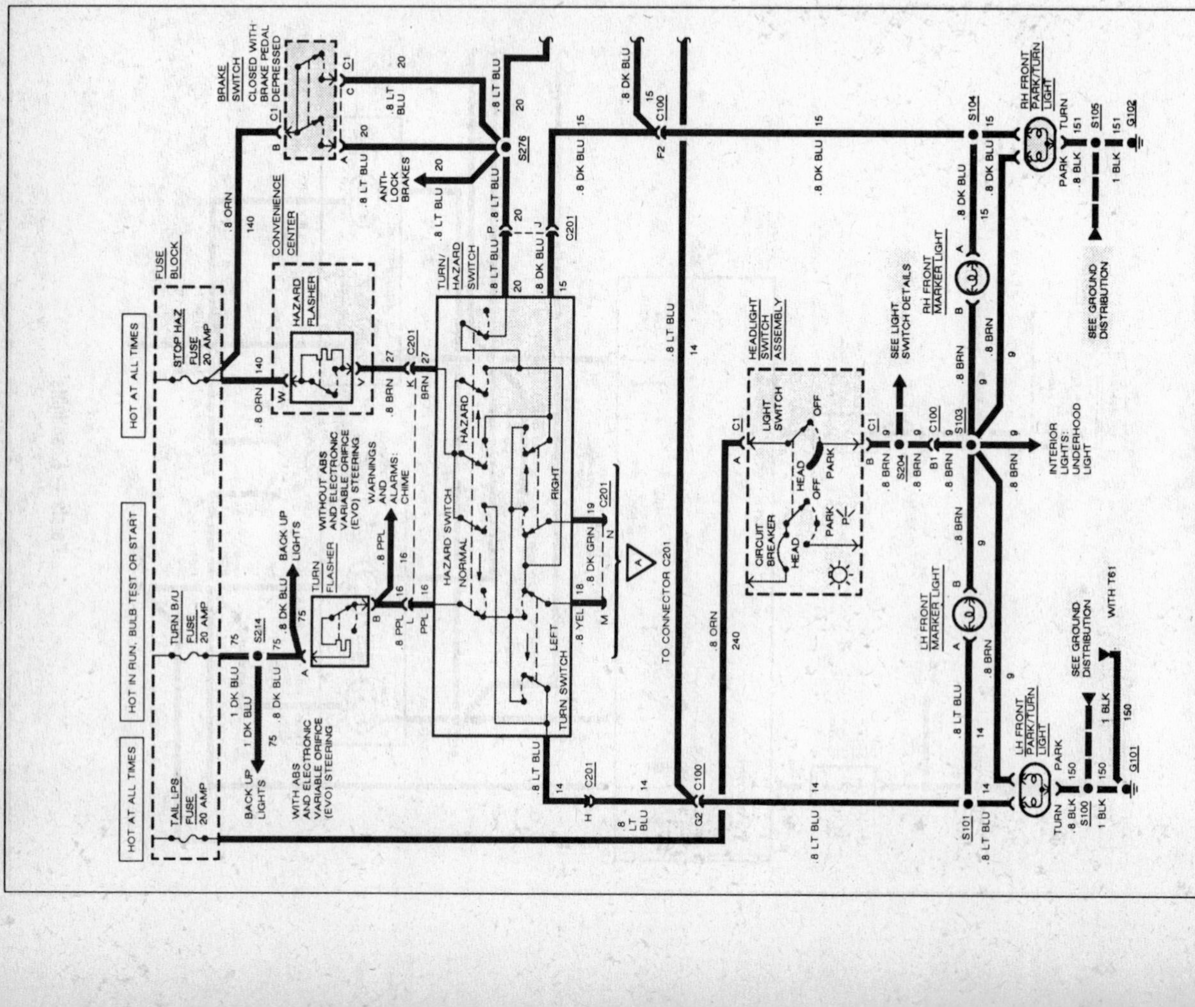

Calais — Exterior lights — hazard, front marker, front park, turn and stop

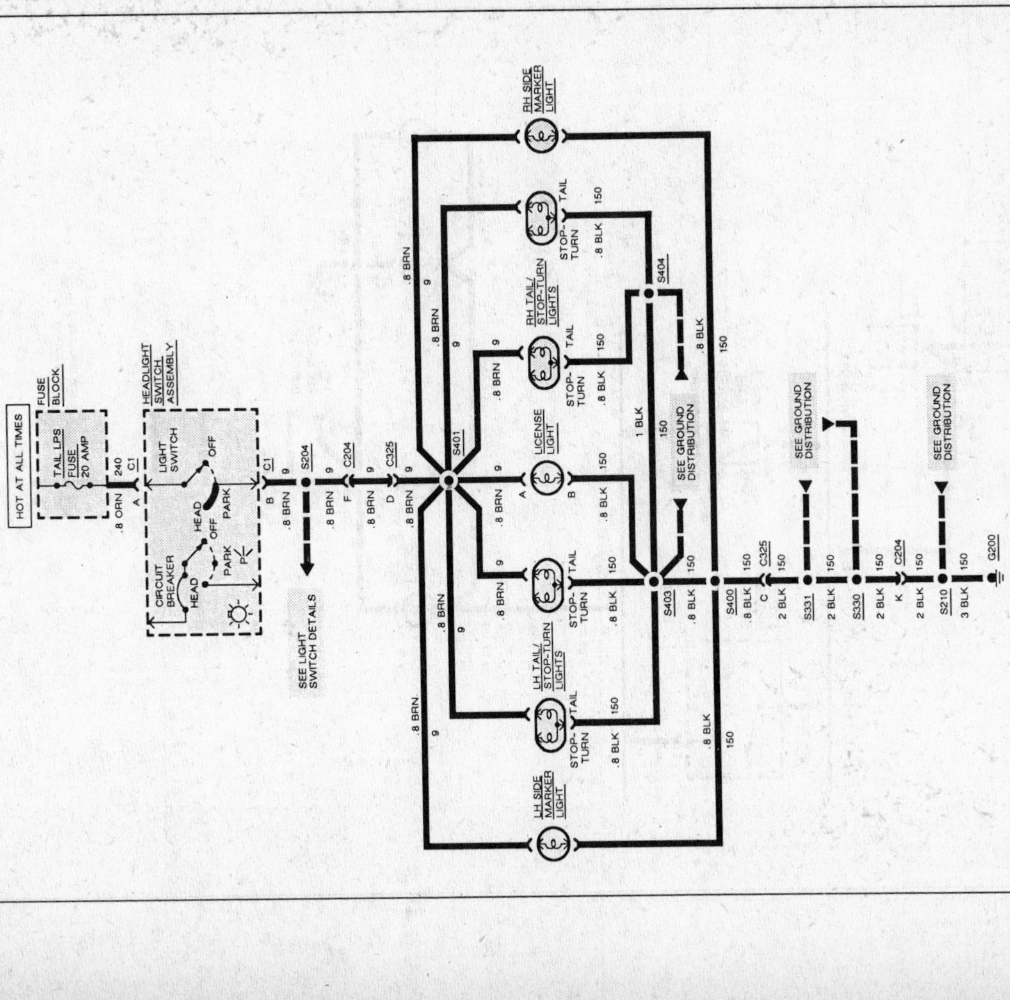

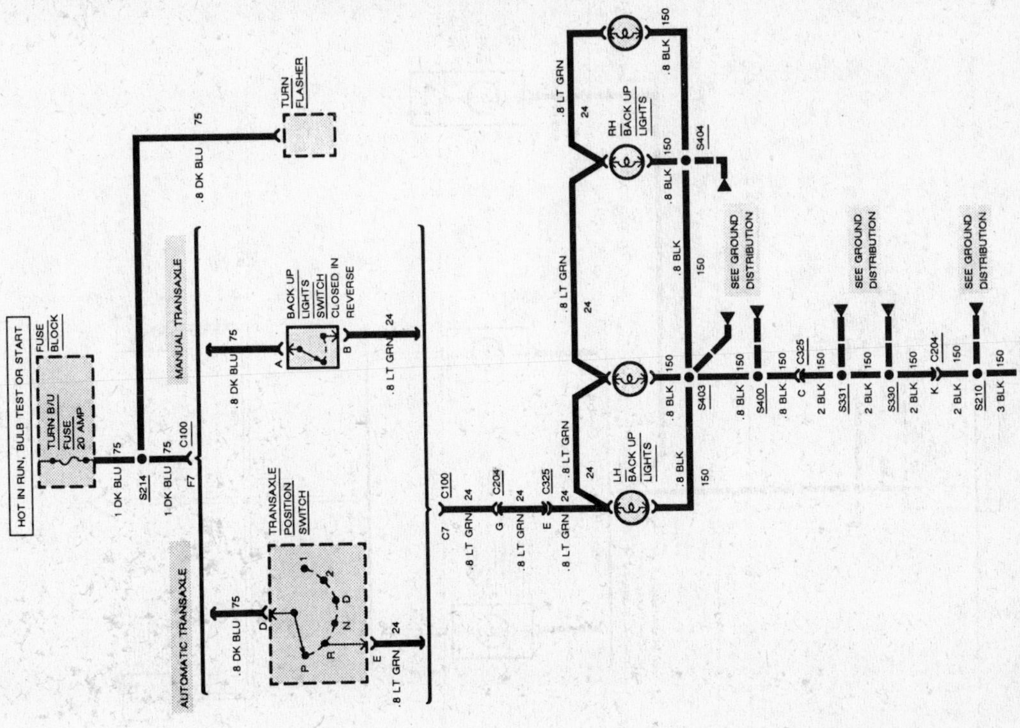

Calais — Back-up lights with ABS and Electronic Variable Orifice (EVO) steering

Calais — Exterior lights — tail, side marker and license

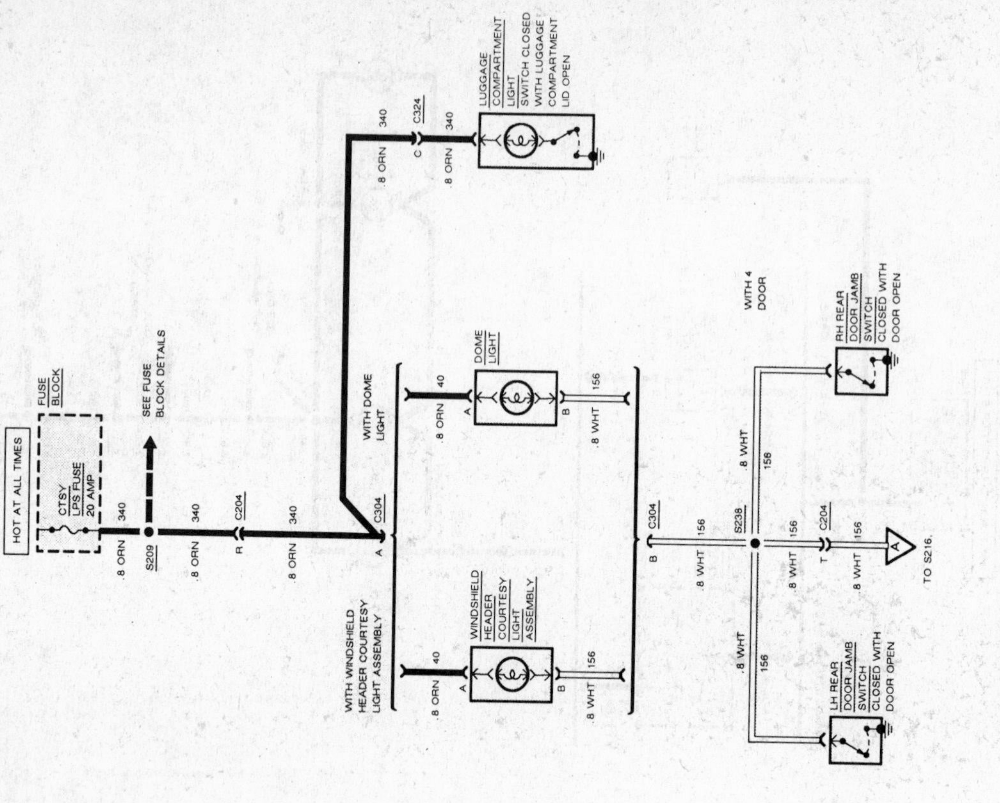

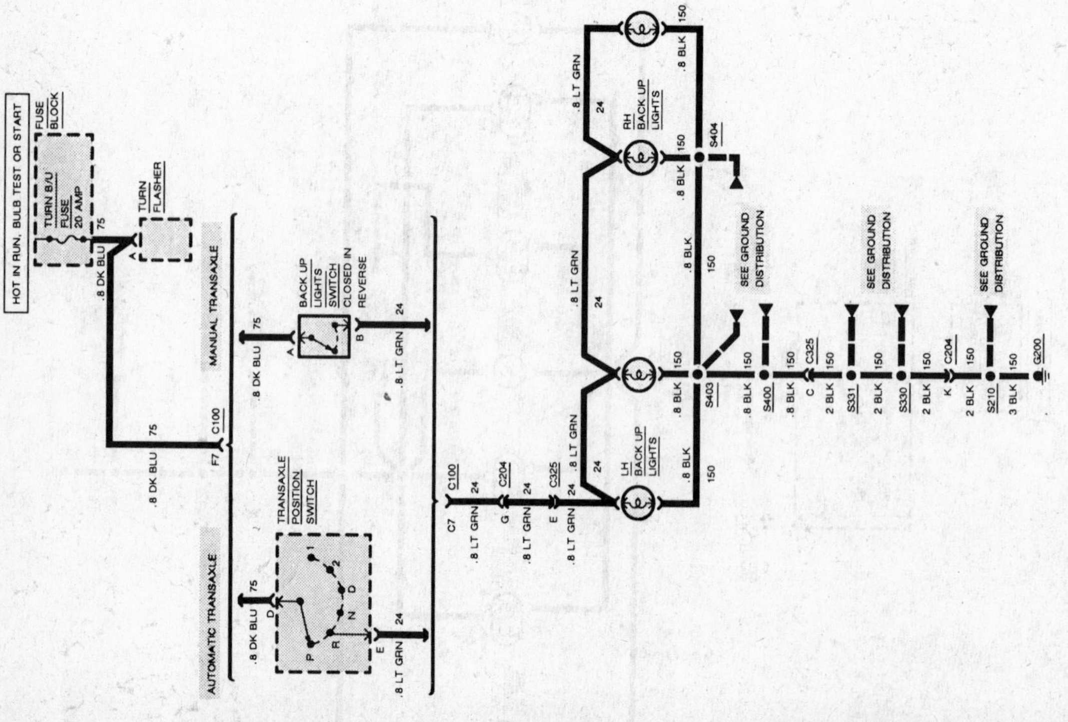

Calais — Back-up lights with ABS and Electronic Variable Orifice (EVO) steering

Calais — Interior lights — dome, luggage compartment and courtesy lights

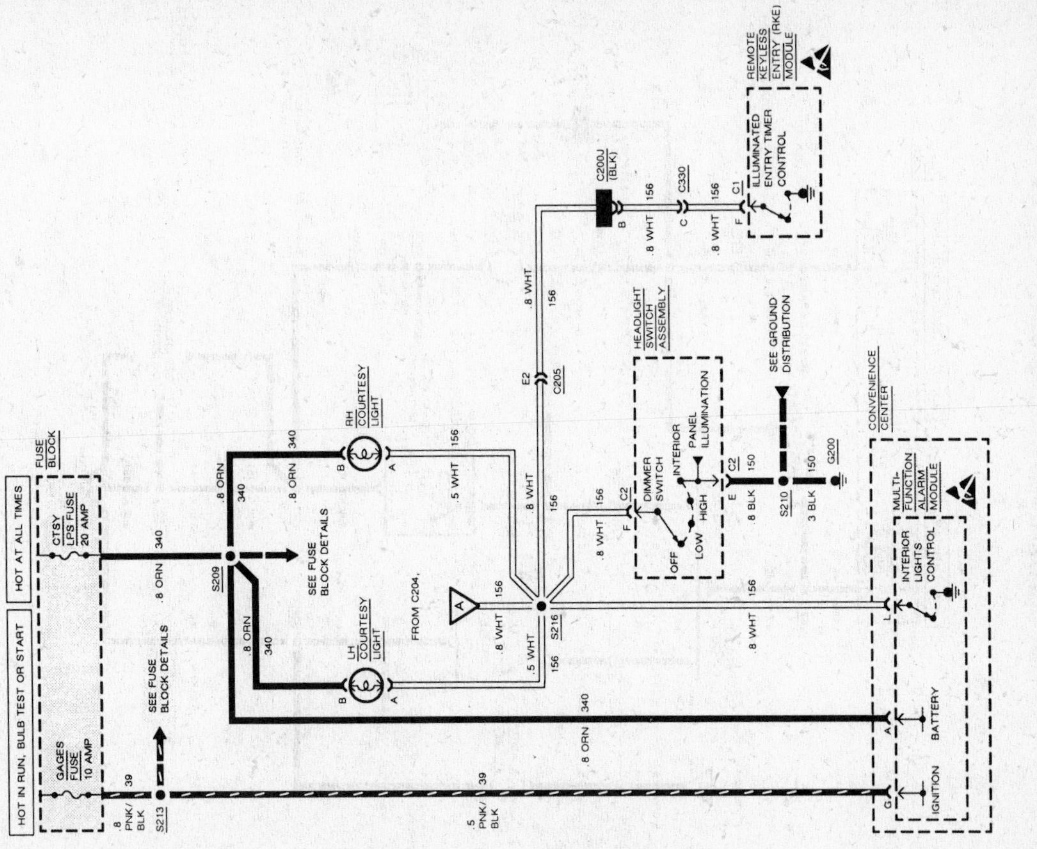

Calais — Interior lights — courtesy and illuminated entry

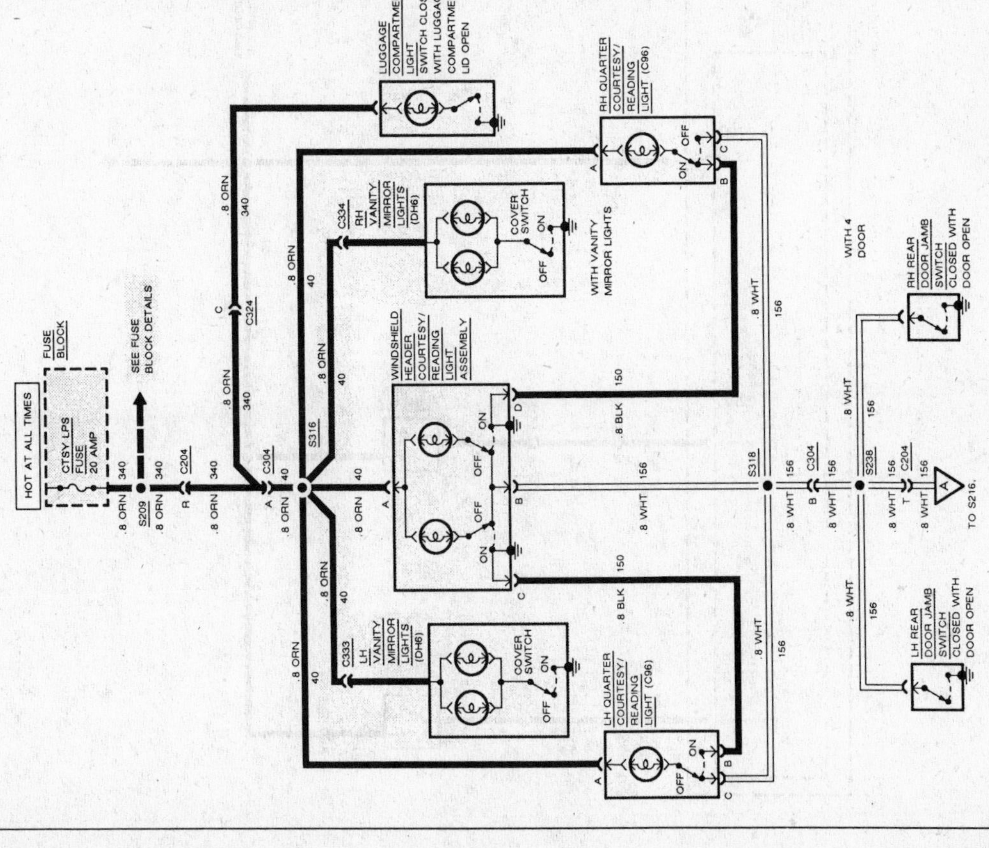

Calais — Interior lights — courtesy, reading, vanity luggage compartment

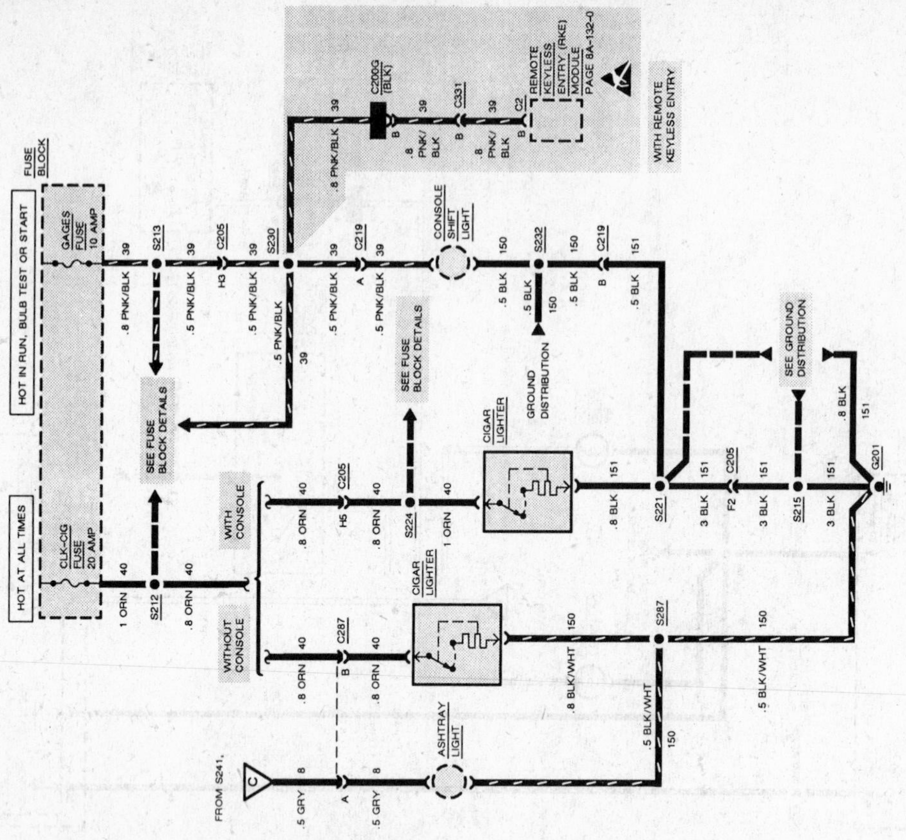

Calais — Interior lights — illuminated entry

Calais — Interior lights — cigar lighter, ashtray and console shift

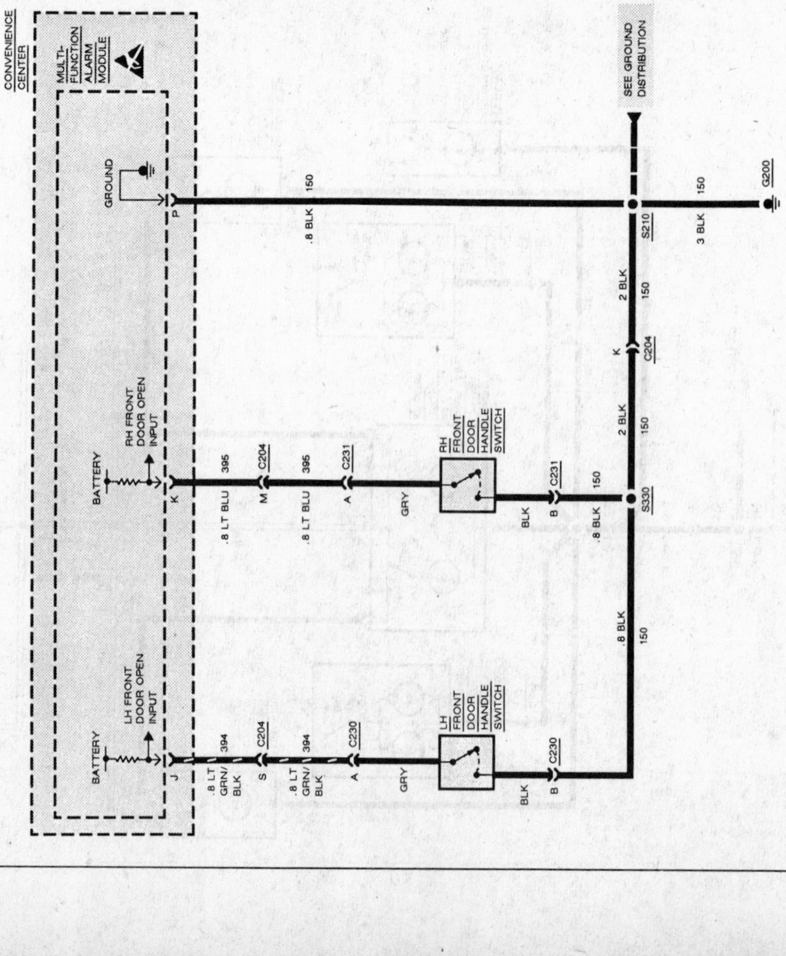

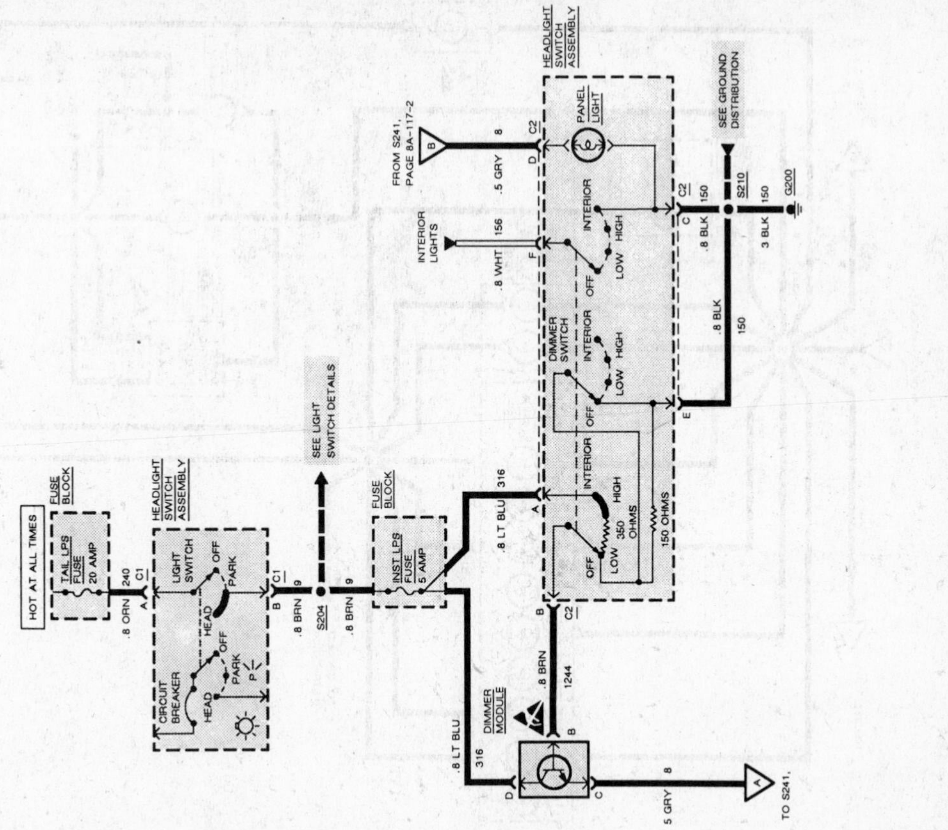

HOT AT ALL TIMES
FUSE BLOCK
CLK-CIG FUSE 20 AMP
1 ORN 40
S212
SEE FUSE BLOCK DETAILS
.8 ORN 40
A
I/P COMPARTMENT LIGHT SWITCH CLOSED WITH I/P COMPARTMENT OPEN
B
.8 BLK 151
S215
SEE GROUND DISTRIBUTION
3 BLK 151
G201

HOT AT ALL TIMES
HEADLIGHT SWITCH ASSEMBLY
LIGHT SWITCH
HEAD
OFF
PARK
P
B C1
.8 BRN 9
S204
SEE LIGHT SWITCH DETAILS
.8 BRN 9
B1 C100
.8 BRN 9
S103
SEE LIGHT SWITCH DETAILS
.8 BRN 9
C102
.8 BRN 9
UNDERHOOD LIGHT (U26) SWITCH CLOSED WITH HOOD OPEN
.8 BLK 150
G109

Calais — Interior lights — instrument panel compartment and underhood light

HOT AT ALL TIMES
FUSE BLOCK
TAIL LPS FUSE 20 AMP
.8 ORN 240
A C1
HEADLIGHT SWITCH ASSEMBLY
CIRCUIT BREAKER
LIGHT SWITCH
HEAD
OFF
PARK
P
B C1
.8 BRN 9
S204
SEE LIGHT SWITCH DETAILS
.8 BRN 9
FUSE BLOCK
INST LPS FUSE 5 AMP
.8 LT BLU 316
DIMMER MODULE
D
B
C
.8 BRN 1244
.8 LT BLU 316
FROM S241, PAGE 8A-117-2
INTERIOR LIGHTS
.8 WHT 156
.5 GRY 8
B C2
A F D C2
HEADLIGHT SWITCH ASSEMBLY
DIMMER SWITCH
OFF
INTERIOR
LOW
350 OHMS
HIGH
150 OHMS
PANEL LIGHT
E C C2
.8 BLK 150
.8 BLK 150
S210
SEE GROUND DISTRIBUTION
3 BLK 150
G200
5 GRY 8
TO S241,

Calais — Interior lights — dimming — without fog lights

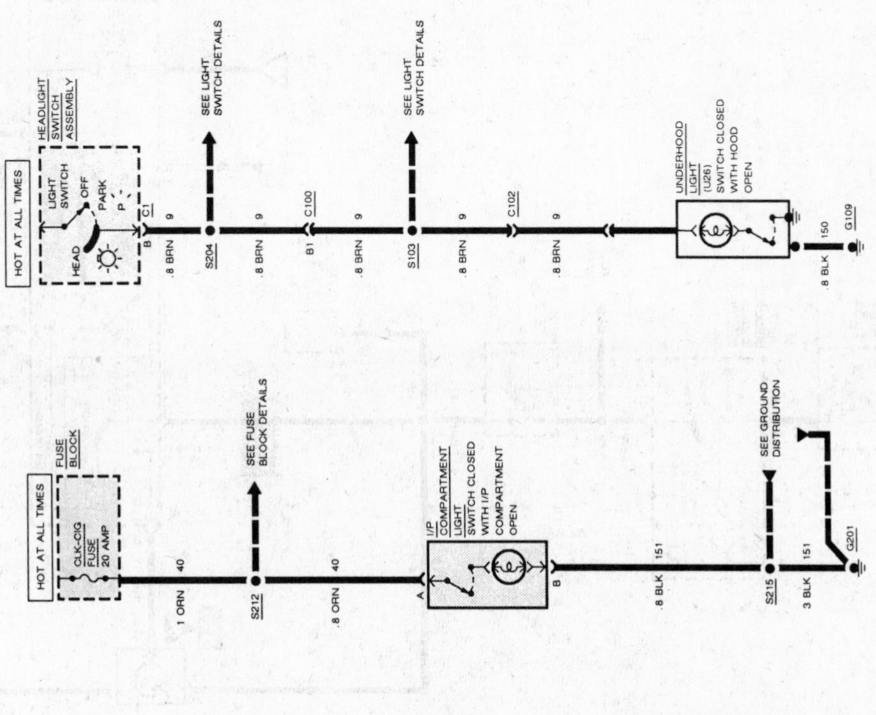

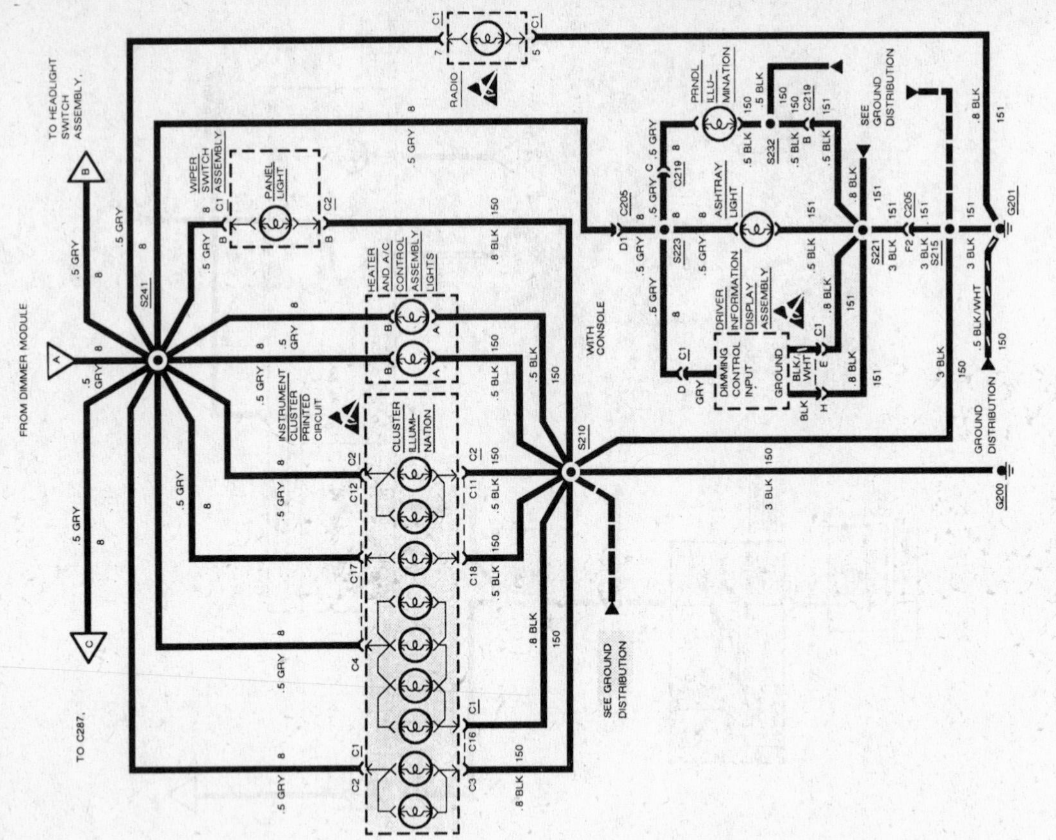

Calais – Interior lights – dimming

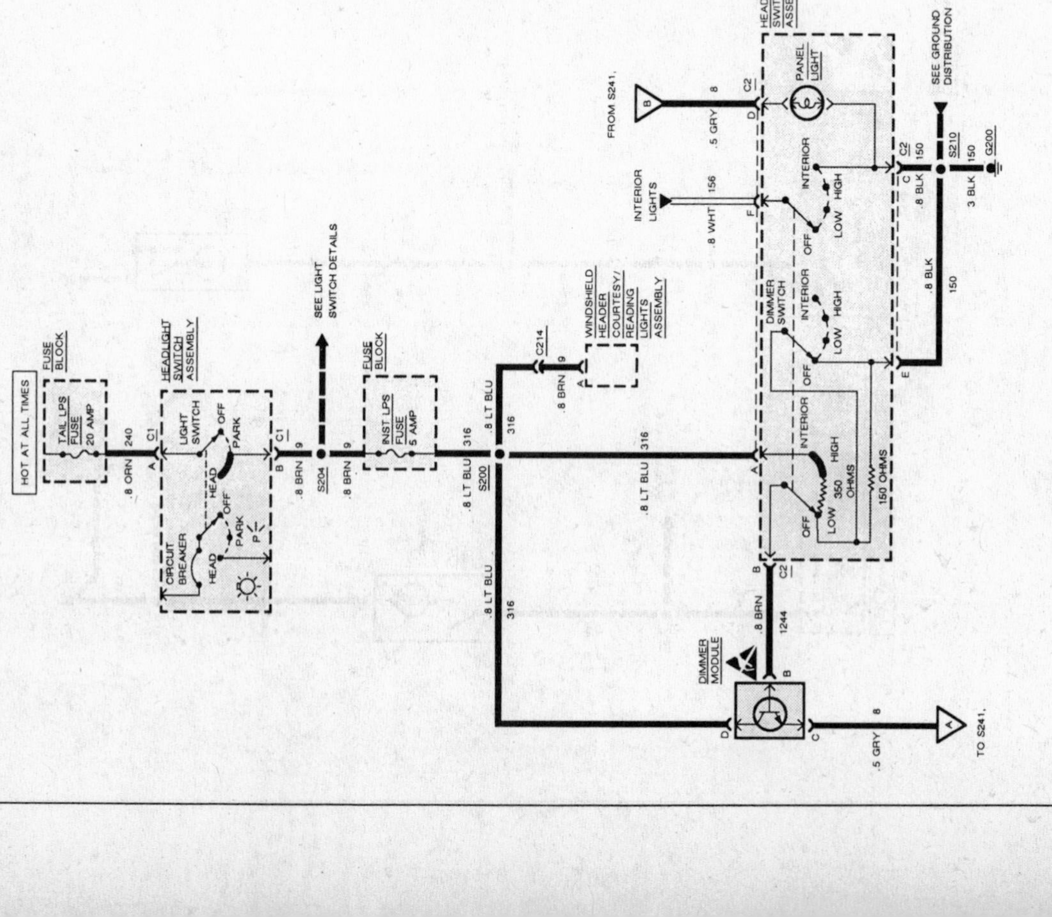

Calais – Interior lights – dimming – with fog lights

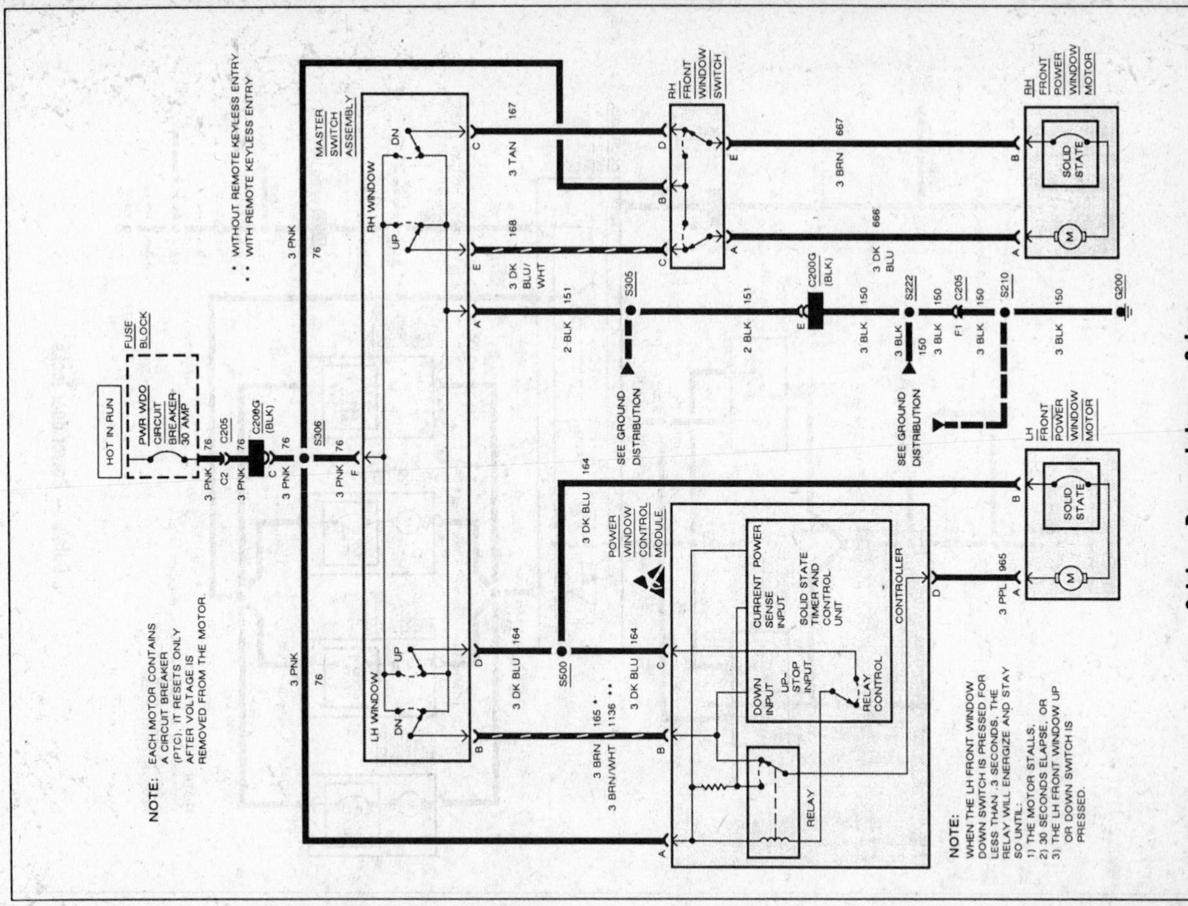
HOT IN RUN
PWR WDO CIRCUIT BREAKER 30 AMP
FUSE BLOCK
C205
C200G (BLK)
S306
MASTER SWITCH ASSEMBLY
RH WINDOW
LH WINDOW
UP
DN
RH FRONT WINDOW SWITCH
RH FRONT POWER WINDOW MOTOR
LH FRONT POWER WINDOW MOTOR
SOLID STATE
POWER WINDOW CONTROL MODULE
CURRENT POWER SENSE INPUT
SOLID STATE TIMER AND CONTROL UNIT
DOWN INPUT
UP-STOP INPUT
RELAY CONTROL
RELAY
CONTROLLER
S500
S305
S222
S210
G200
SEE GROUND DISTRIBUTION
* WITHOUT REMOTE KEYLESS ENTRY
** WITH REMOTE KEYLESS ENTRY
NOTE: EACH MOTOR CONTAINS A CIRCUIT BREAKER (PTC). IT RESETS ONLY AFTER VOLTAGE IS REMOVED FROM THE MOTOR.
NOTE: WHEN THE LH FRONT WINDOW DOWN SWITCH IS PRESSED FOR LESS THAN .3 SECONDS, THE RELAY WILL ENERGIZE AND STAY SO UNTIL: 1) THE MOTOR STALLS, 2) 30 SECONDS ELAPSE, OR 3) THE LH FRONT WINDOW UP OR DOWN SWITCH IS PRESSED.

Calais — Power windows — 2 door

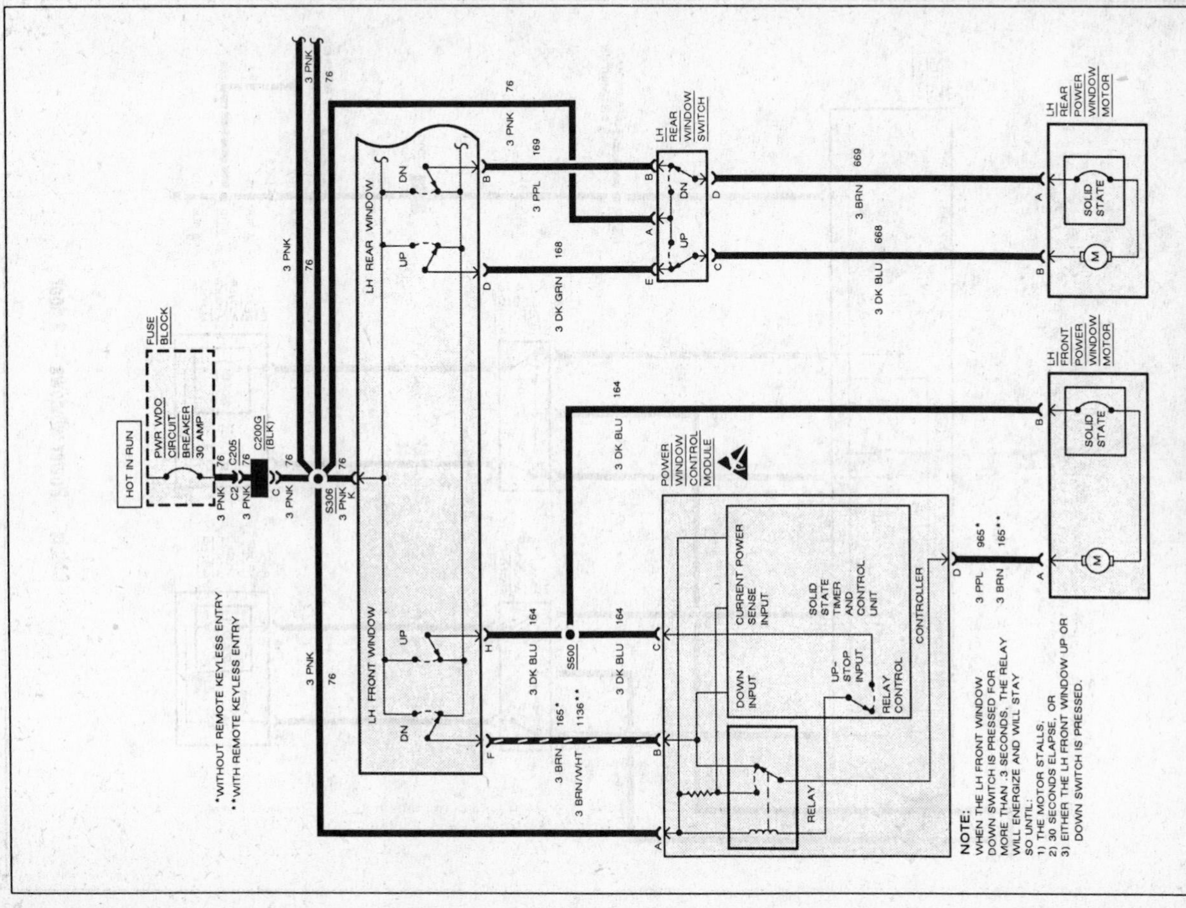
HOT IN RUN
PWR WDO CIRCUIT BREAKER 30 AMP
FUSE BLOCK
C205
C200G (BLK)
S306
LH REAR WINDOW
LH FRONT WINDOW
UP
DN
LH REAR WINDOW SWITCH
LH REAR POWER WINDOW MOTOR
LH FRONT POWER WINDOW MOTOR
SOLID STATE
POWER WINDOW CONTROL MODULE
CURRENT POWER SENSE INPUT
SOLID STATE TIMER AND CONTROL UNIT
DOWN INPUT
UP-STOP INPUT
RELAY CONTROL
RELAY
CONTROLLER
S500
*WITHOUT REMOTE KEYLESS ENTRY
**WITH REMOTE KEYLESS ENTRY
NOTE: WHEN THE LH FRONT WINDOW DOWN SWITCH IS PRESSED FOR MORE THAN .3 SECONDS, THE RELAY WILL ENERGIZE AND WILL STAY SO UNTIL: 1) THE MOTOR STALLS, 2) 30 SECONDS ELAPSE, OR 3) EITHER THE LH FRONT WINDOW UP OR DOWN SWITCH IS PRESSED.

Calais — Power windows — 4 door

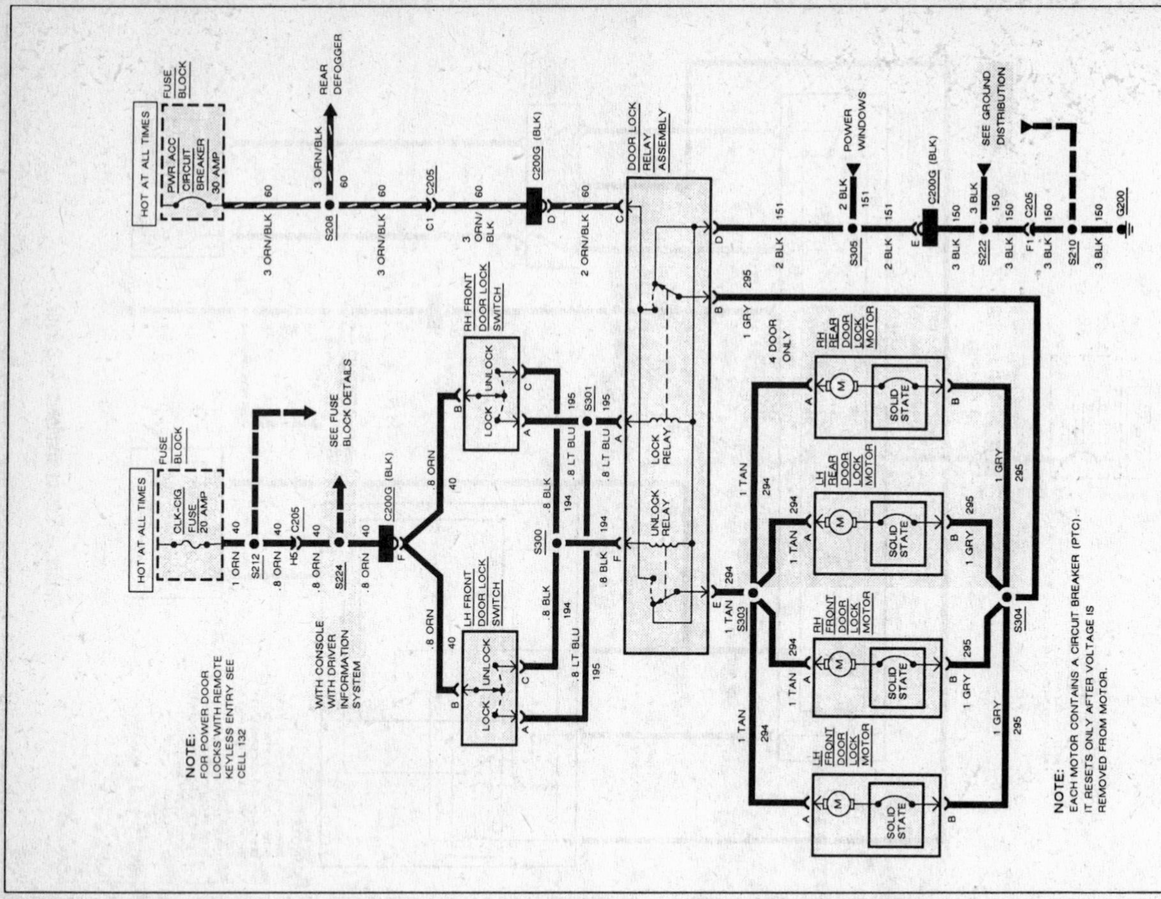

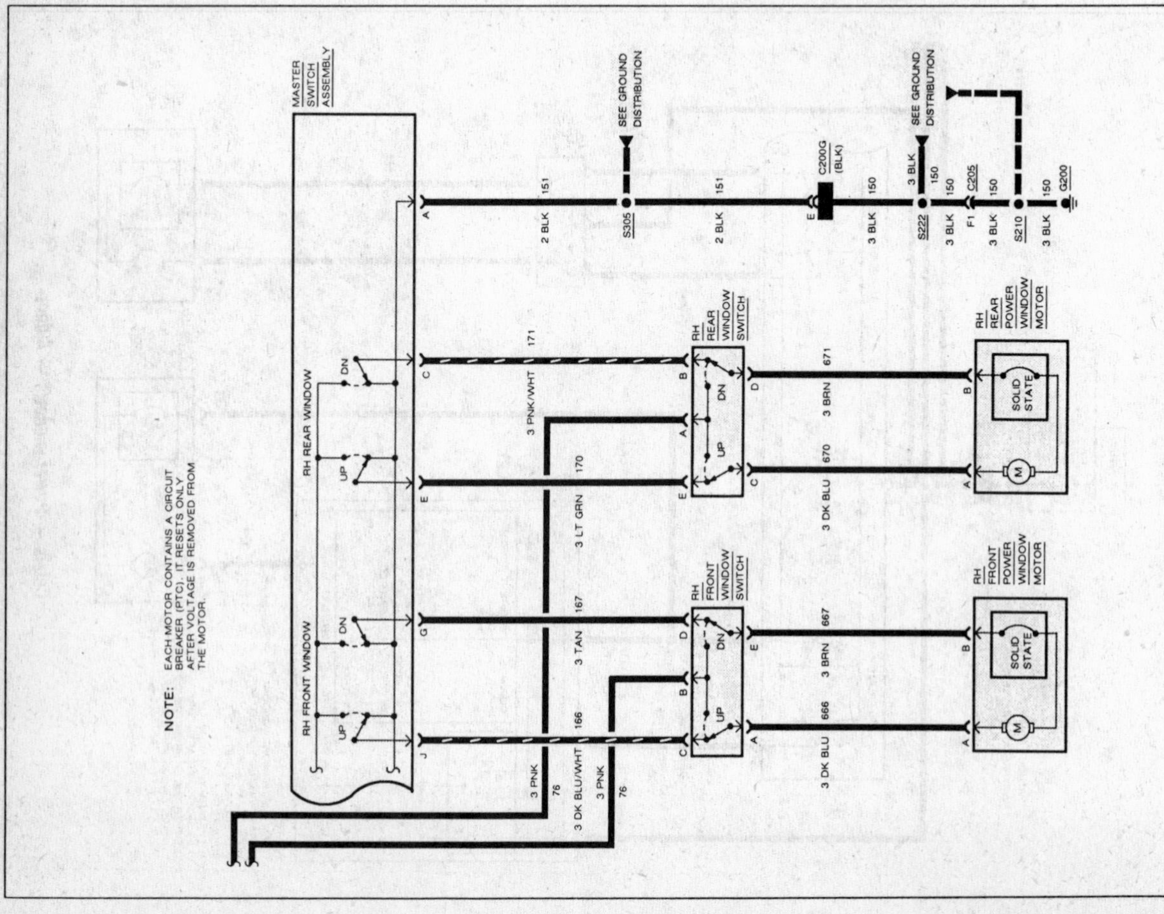

Calais — Power windows — 2 door

Calais — Power door locks

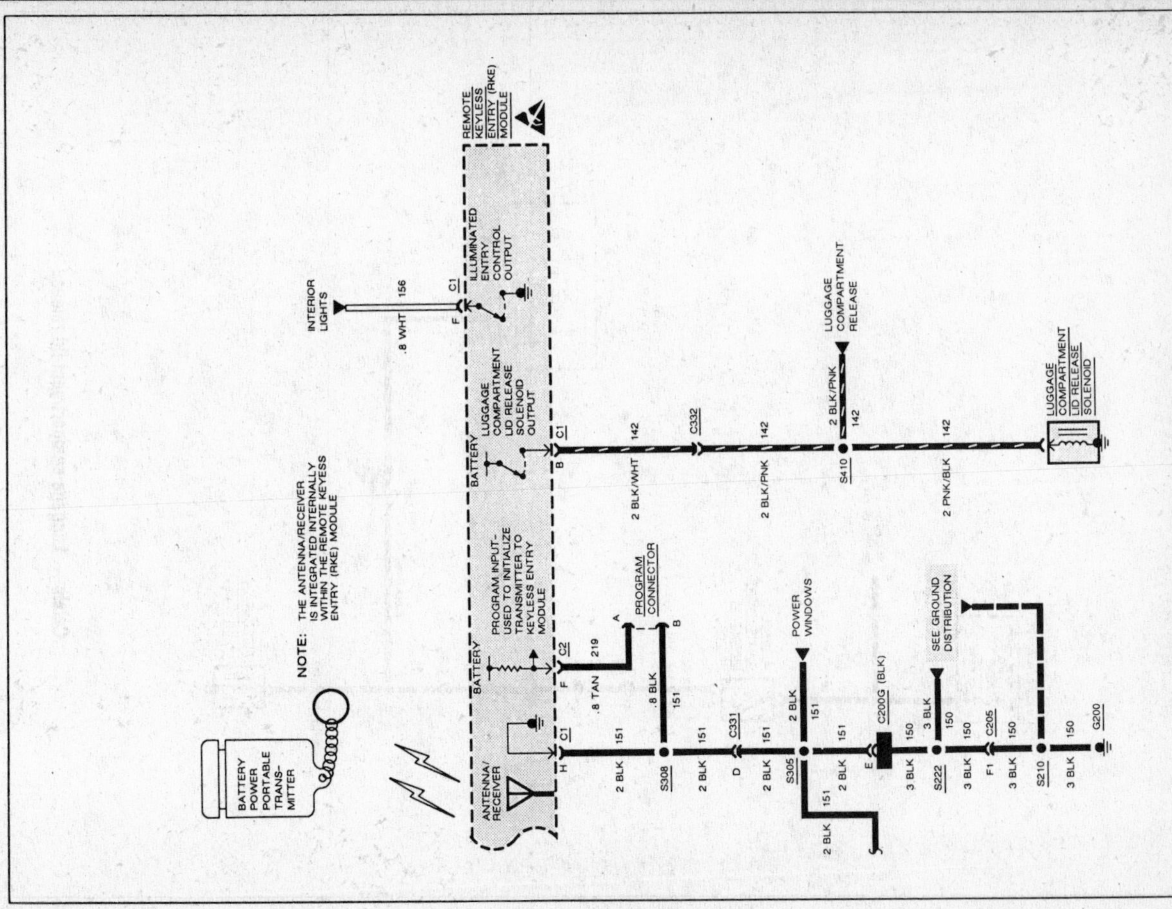

NOTE: THE ANTENNA/RECEIVER IS INTEGRATED INTERNALLY WITHIN THE REMOTE KEYESS ENTRY (RKE) MODULE

Calais — Remote keyless entry

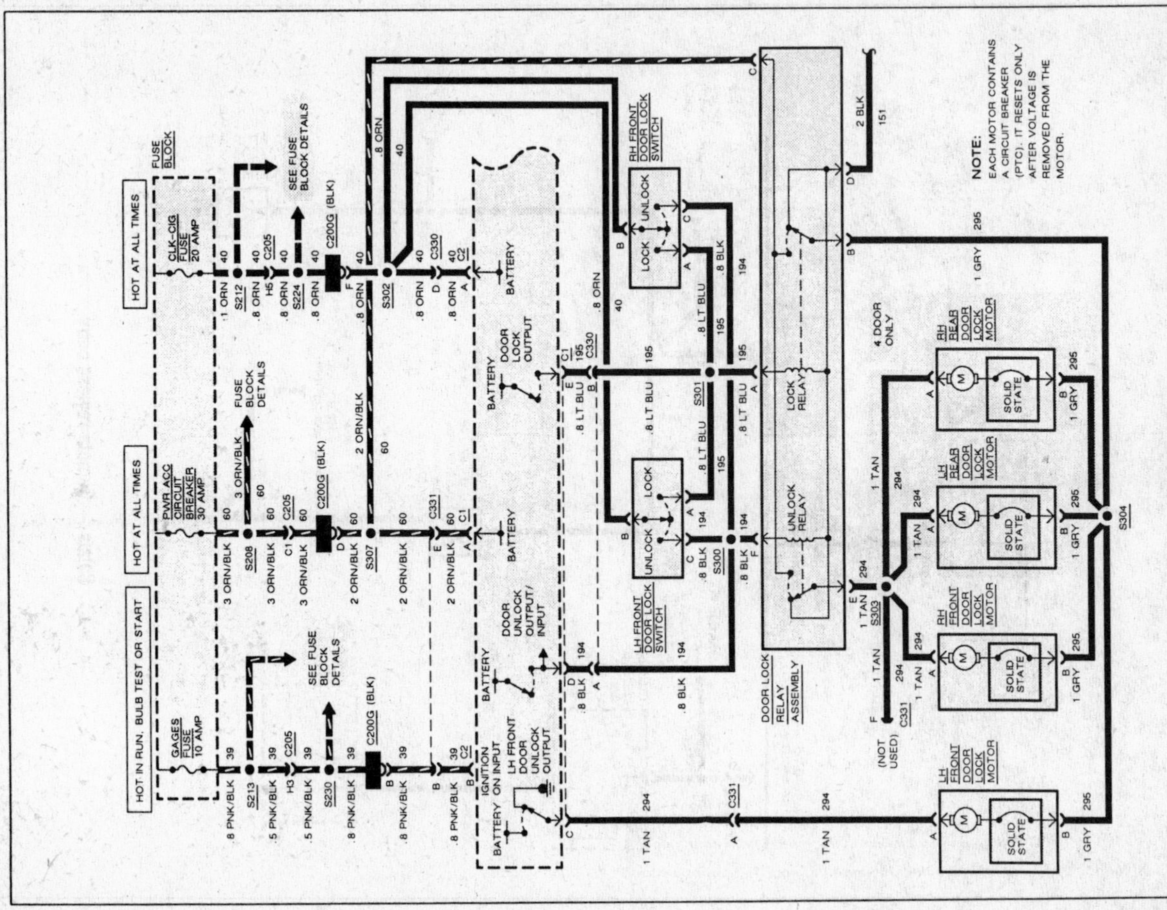

NOTE: EACH MOTOR CONTAINS A CIRCUIT BREAKER (PTC). IT RESETS ONLY AFTER VOLTAGE IS REMOVED FROM THE MOTOR.

Calais — Remote keyless entry

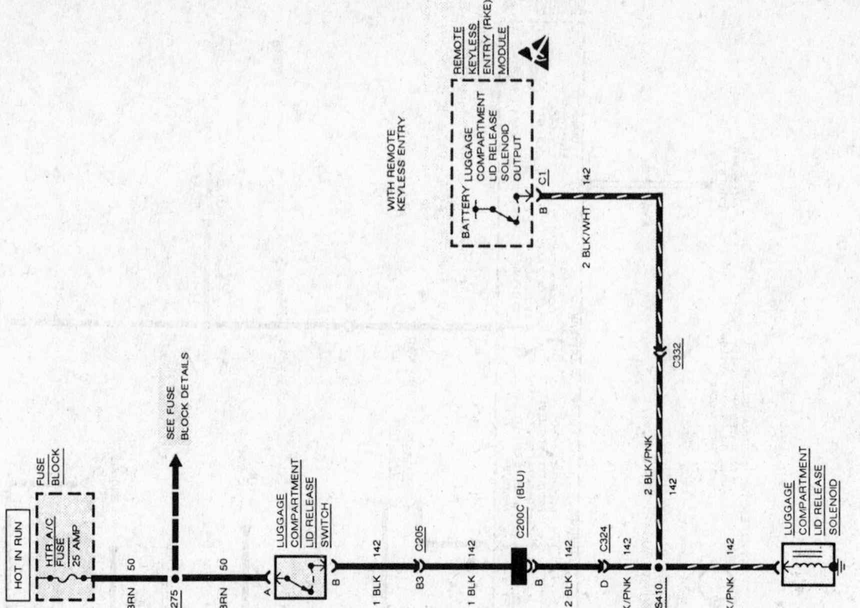

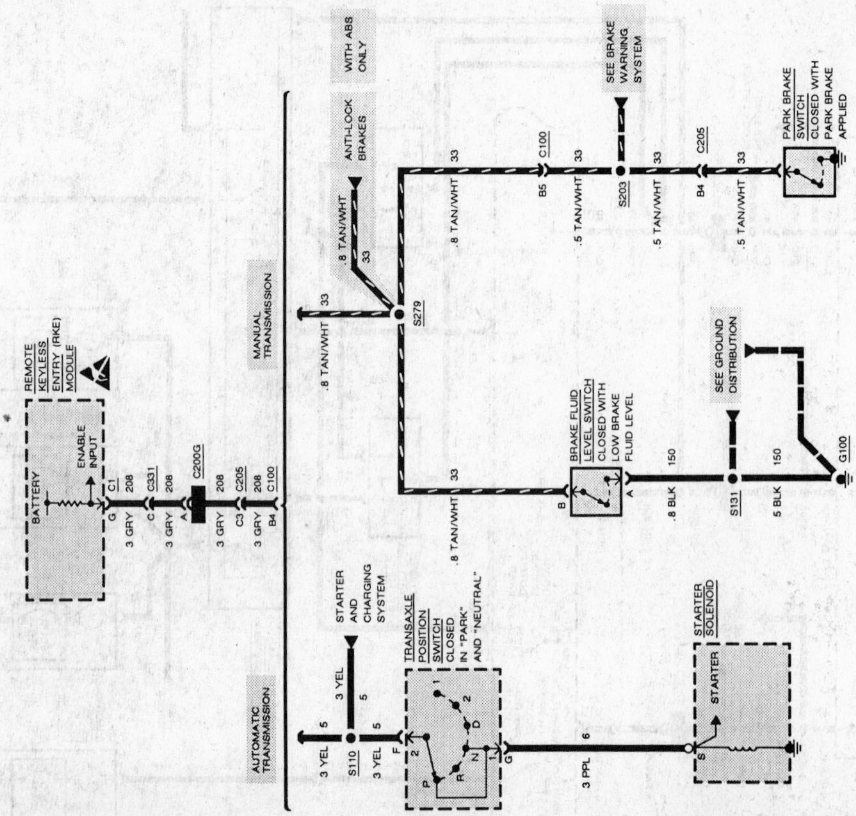

Calais — Remote keyless entry

Calais — Luggage compartment lid release

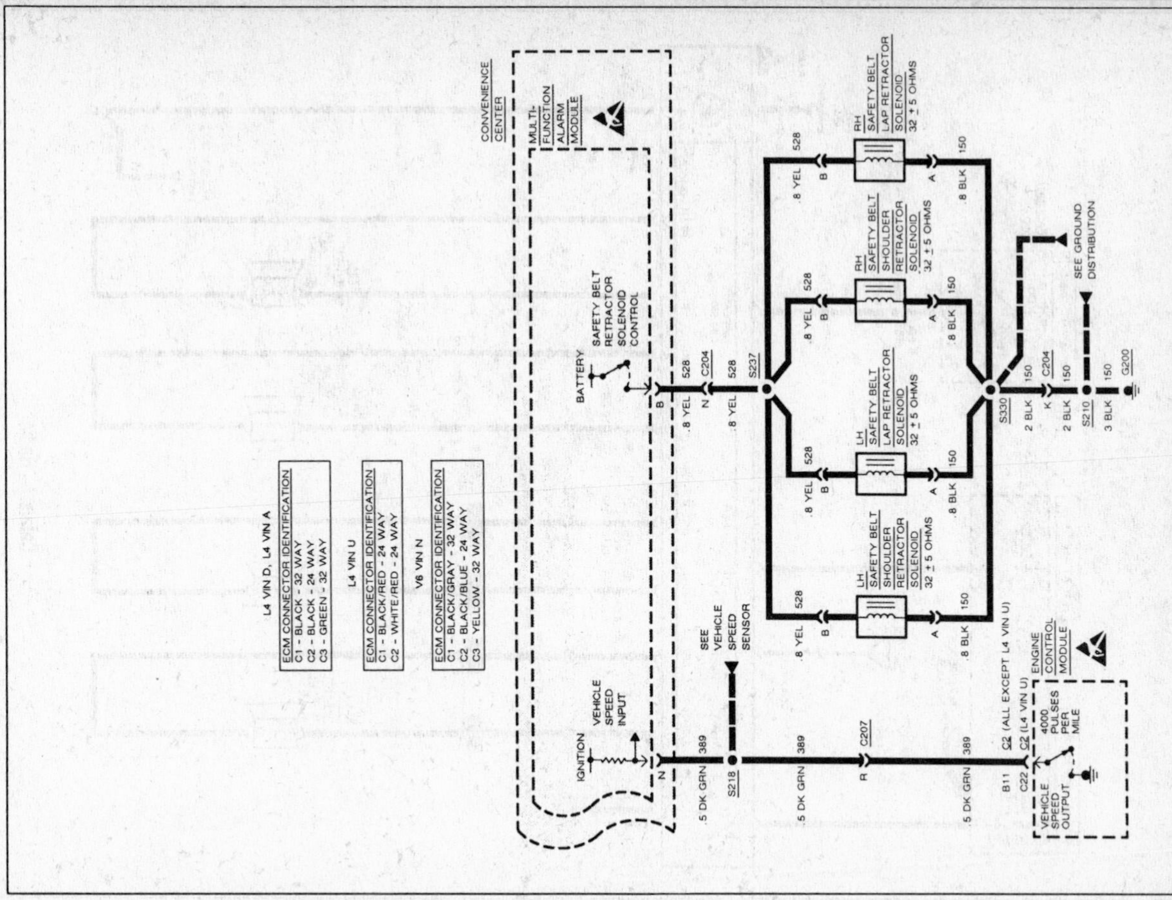

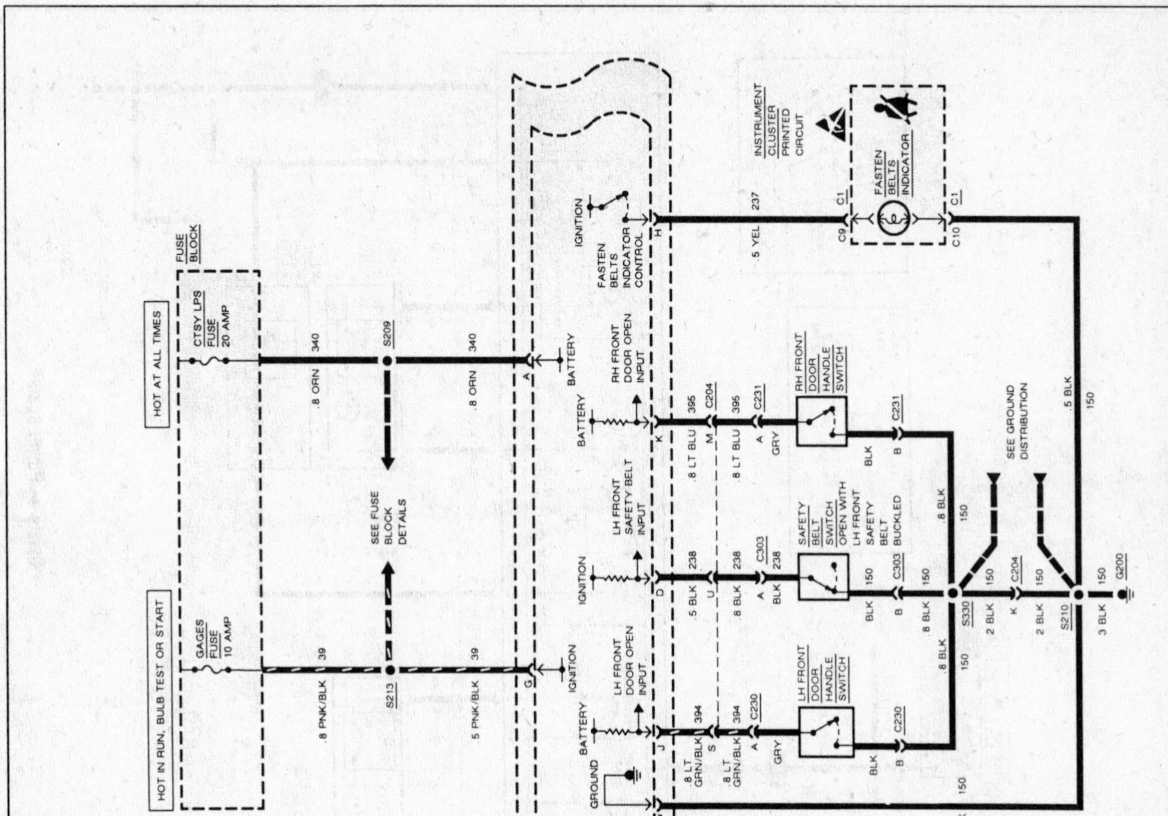

HOT IN RUN, BULB TEST OR START
HOT AT ALL TIMES
FUSE BLOCK
GAGES FUSE 10 AMP
CTSY LPS FUSE 20 AMP
.8 PNK/BLK 39
.8 ORN 340
S213
SEE FUSE BLOCK DETAILS
S209
.5 PNK/BLK 39
.8 ORN 340
G
A
IGNITION
BATTERY
GROUND
BATTERY
LH FRONT DOOR OPEN INPUT
IGNITION
LH FRONT SAFETY BELT INPUT
BATTERY
RH FRONT DOOR OPEN INPUT
IGNITION
FASTEN BELTS INDICATOR CONTROL
P J D K H
.8 LT GRN/BLK 394
S
.8 LT GRN/BLK 394
A C230
GRY
.5 BLK 238
U
.8 BLK 238
A C303
BLK 238
.8 LT BLU 395
M C204
.8 LT BLU 395
A C231
GRY
.5 YEL 237
INSTRUMENT CLUSTER PRINTED CIRCUIT
LH FRONT DOOR HANDLE SWITCH
SAFETY BELT SWITCH OPEN WITH LH FRONT SAFETY BELT BUCKLED
RH FRONT DOOR HANDLE SWITCH
C9 C1
FASTEN BELTS INDICATOR
BLK
B C230
BLK 150
B C303
BLK
B C231
8 BLK 150
.8 BLK
.8 BLK
.8 BLK 150
150
S330
150
C10 C1
2 BLK 150
K C204
SEE GROUND DISTRIBUTION
2 BLK 150
S210
.5 BLK
150
3 BLK 150
G200

Calais — Automatic safety belts

L4 VIN D, L4 VIN A

ECM CONNECTOR IDENTIFICATION
C1 - BLACK - 32 WAY
C2 - BLACK - 24 WAY
C3 - GREEN - 32 WAY

L4 VIN U

ECM CONNECTOR IDENTIFICATION
C1 - BLACK/RED - 24 WAY
C2 - WHITE/RED - 24 WAY

V6 VIN N

ECM CONNECTOR IDENTIFICATION
C1 - BLACK/GRAY - 32 WAY
C2 - BLACK/BLUE - 24 WAY
C3 - YELLOW - 32 WAY

CONVENIENCE CENTER
MULTI-FUNCTION ALARM MODULE
IGNITION
VEHICLE SPEED INPUT
BATTERY
SAFETY BELT RETRACTOR SOLENOID CONTROL
N
B
.5 DK GRN 389
SEE VEHICLE SPEED SENSOR
S218
.5 DK GRN 389
R C207
.5 DK GRN 389
B11 C2 (ALL EXCEPT L4 VIN U)
C22 C2 (L4 VIN U)
VEHICLE SPEED OUTPUT
4000 PULSES PER MILE
ENGINE CONTROL MODULE
.8 YEL 528
N C204
.8 YEL 528
S237
.8 YEL 528
B
LH SAFETY BELT SHOULDER RETRACTOR SOLENOID 32 ± 5 OHMS
LH SAFETY BELT LAP RETRACTOR SOLENOID 32 ± 5 OHMS
RH SAFETY BELT SHOULDER RETRACTOR SOLENOID 32 ± 5 OHMS
RH SAFETY BELT LAP RETRACTOR SOLENOID 32 ± 5 OHMS
A
.8 BLK 150
S330
2 BLK 150
K C204
2 BLK 150
S210
SEE GROUND DISTRIBUTION
3 BLK 150
G200

Calais — Automatic safety belts

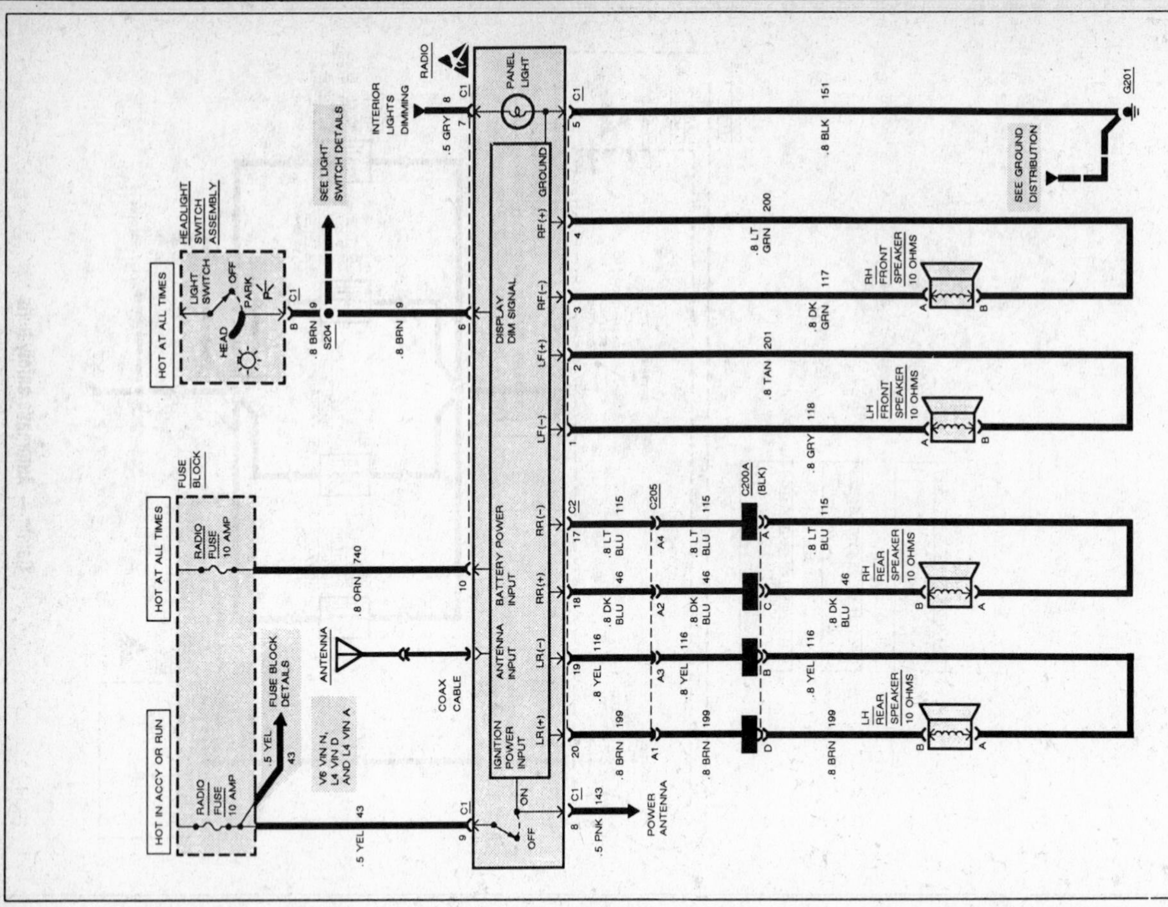

Calais — Radio

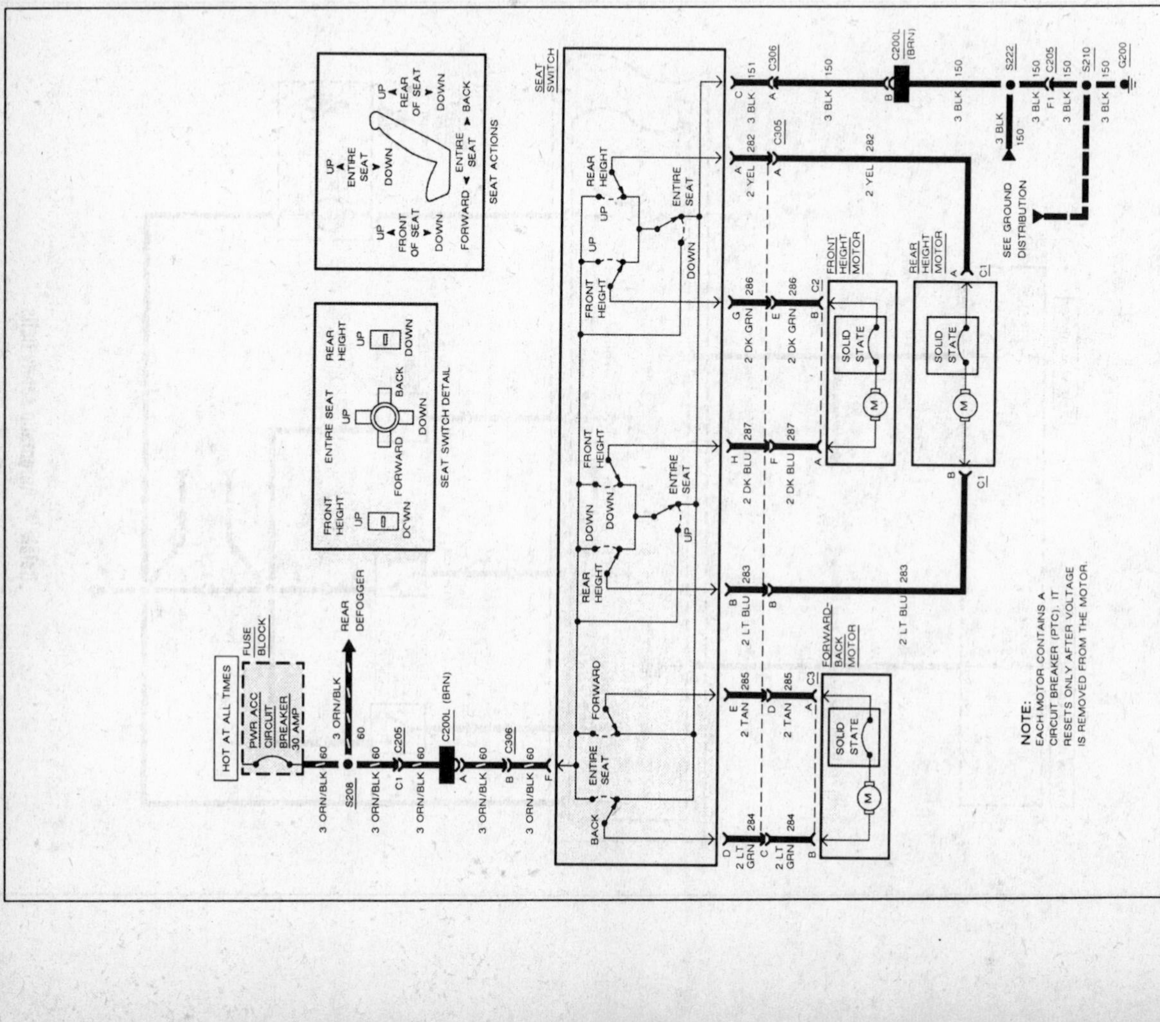

Calais — Power seats

NOTE:
EACH MOTOR CONTAINS A CIRCUIT BREAKER (PTC). IT RESETS ONLY AFTER VOLTAGE IS REMOVED FROM THE MOTOR.

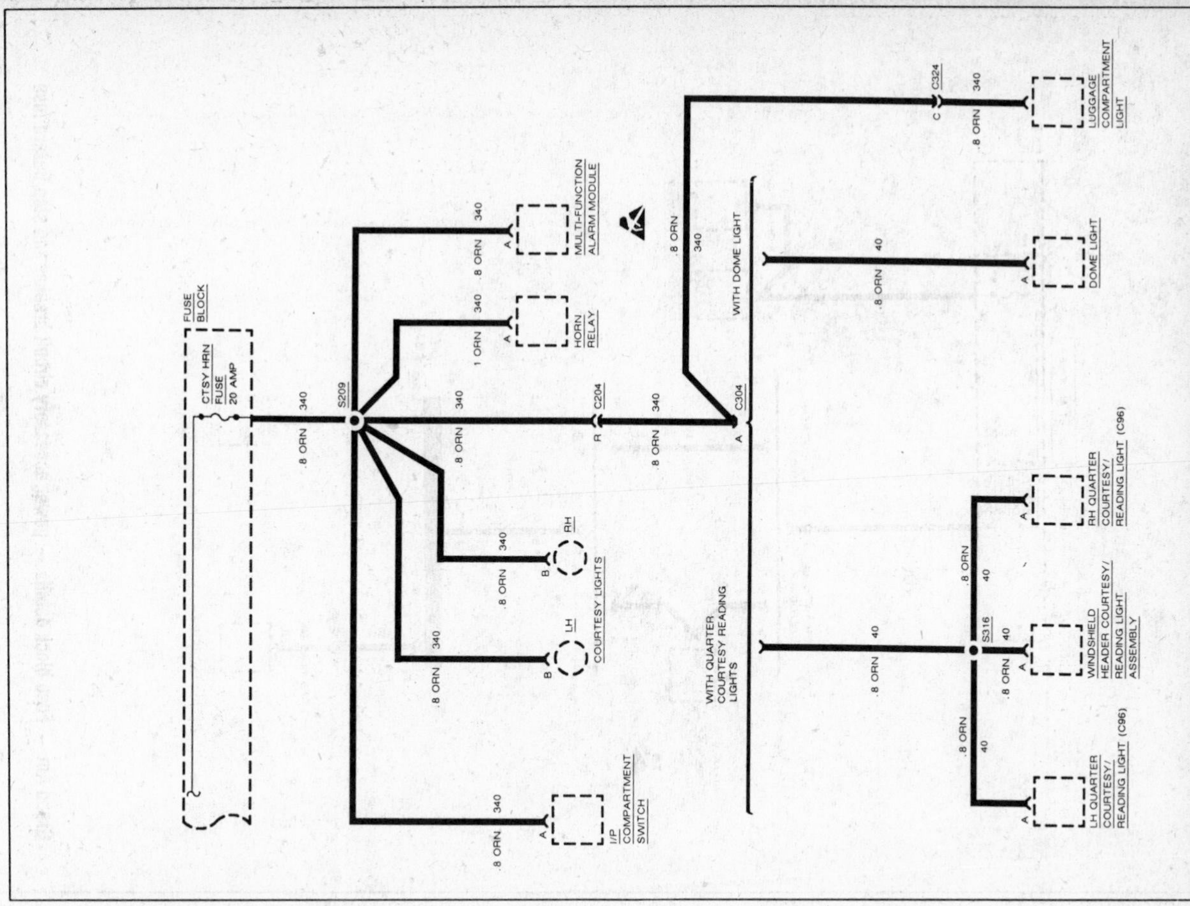

Grand Am — Fuse block details — tail light fuse, cig/clock fuse and courtesy/horn fuse

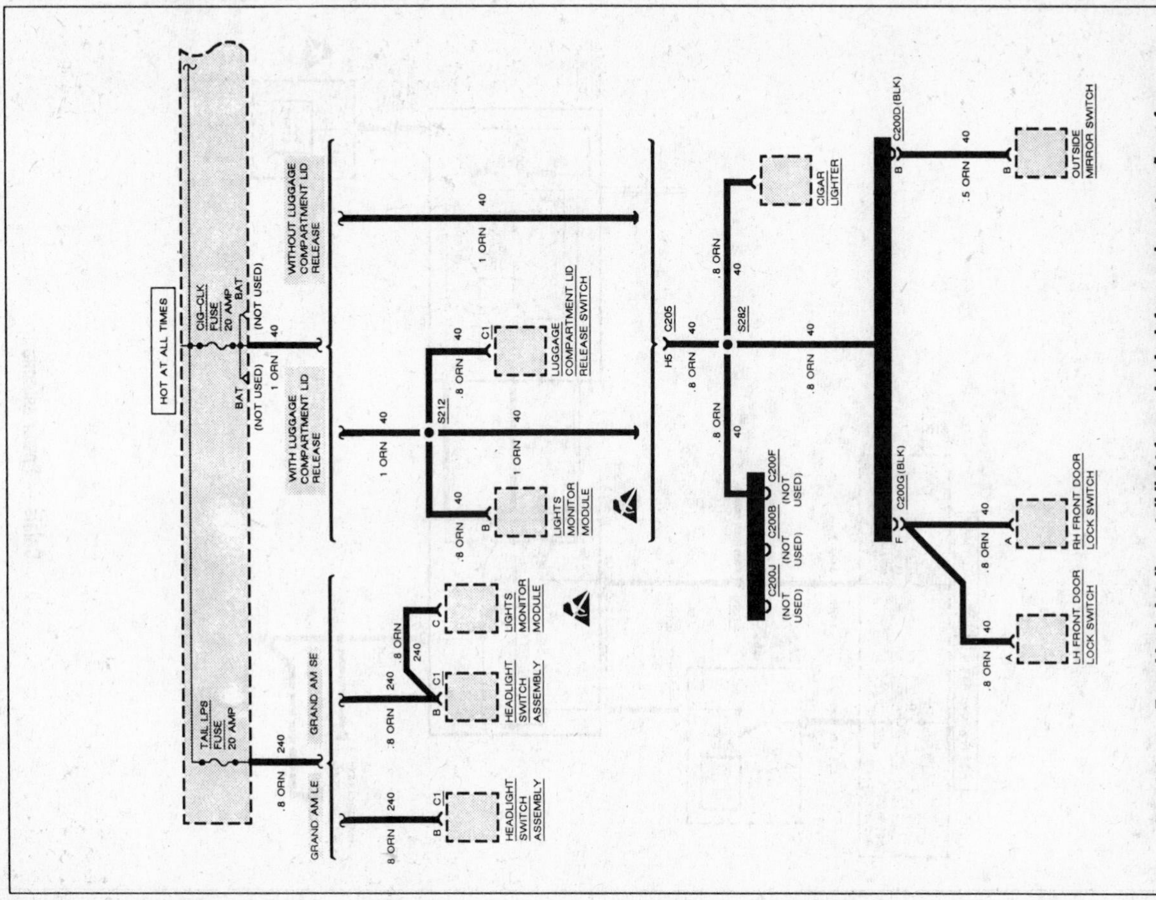

Grand Am — Fuse block details — tail light fuse, cig/clock fuse and courtesy/horn fuse

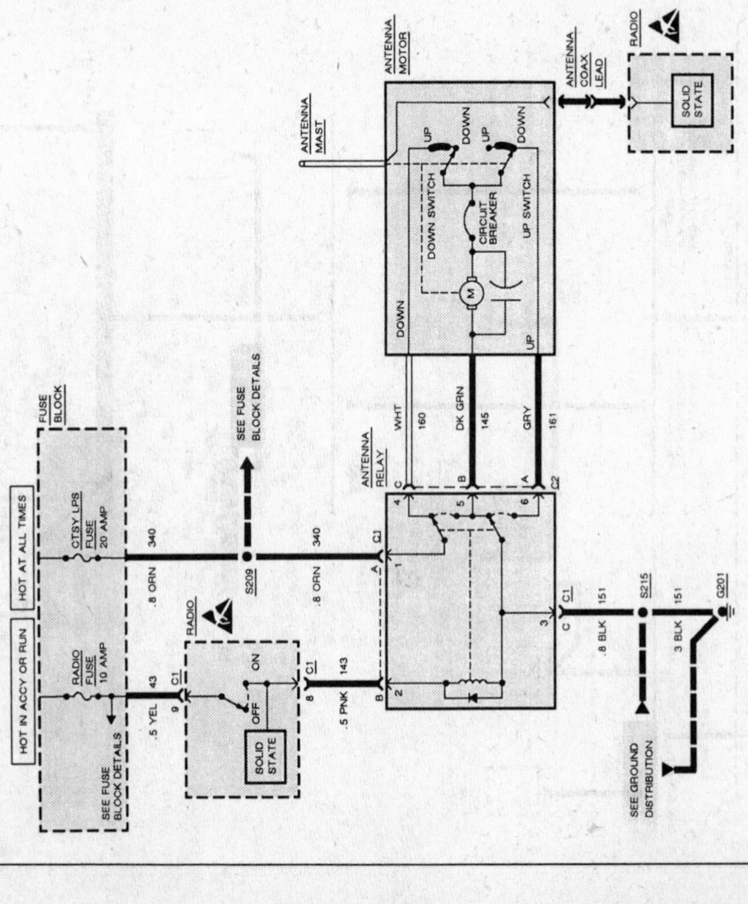

Calais — Power antenna

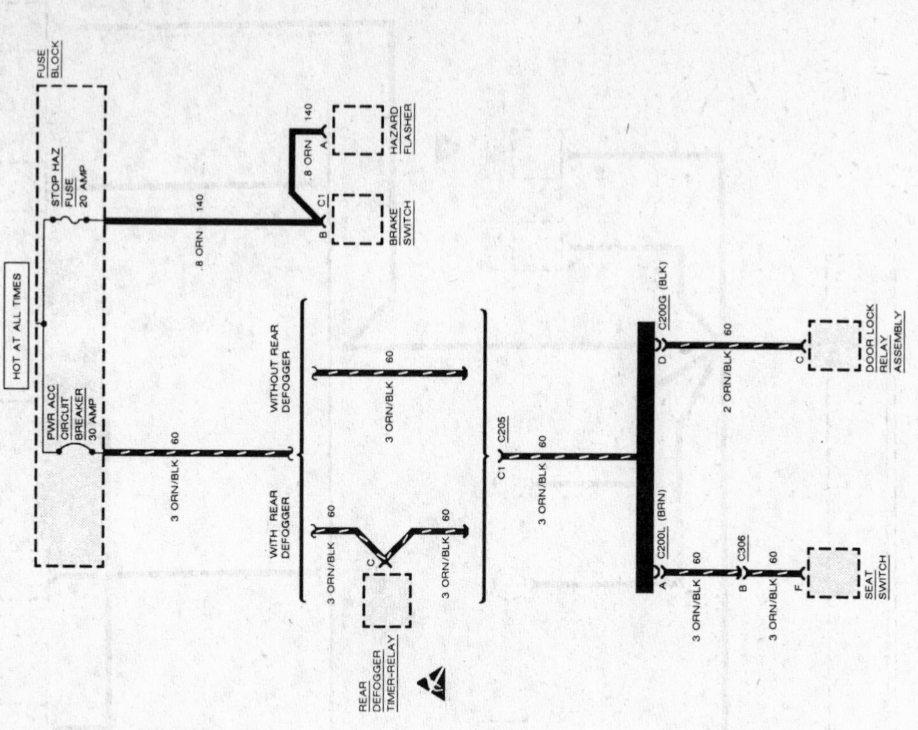

Grand Am — Fuse block details — power accessory circuit breaker and stop/hazard fuse

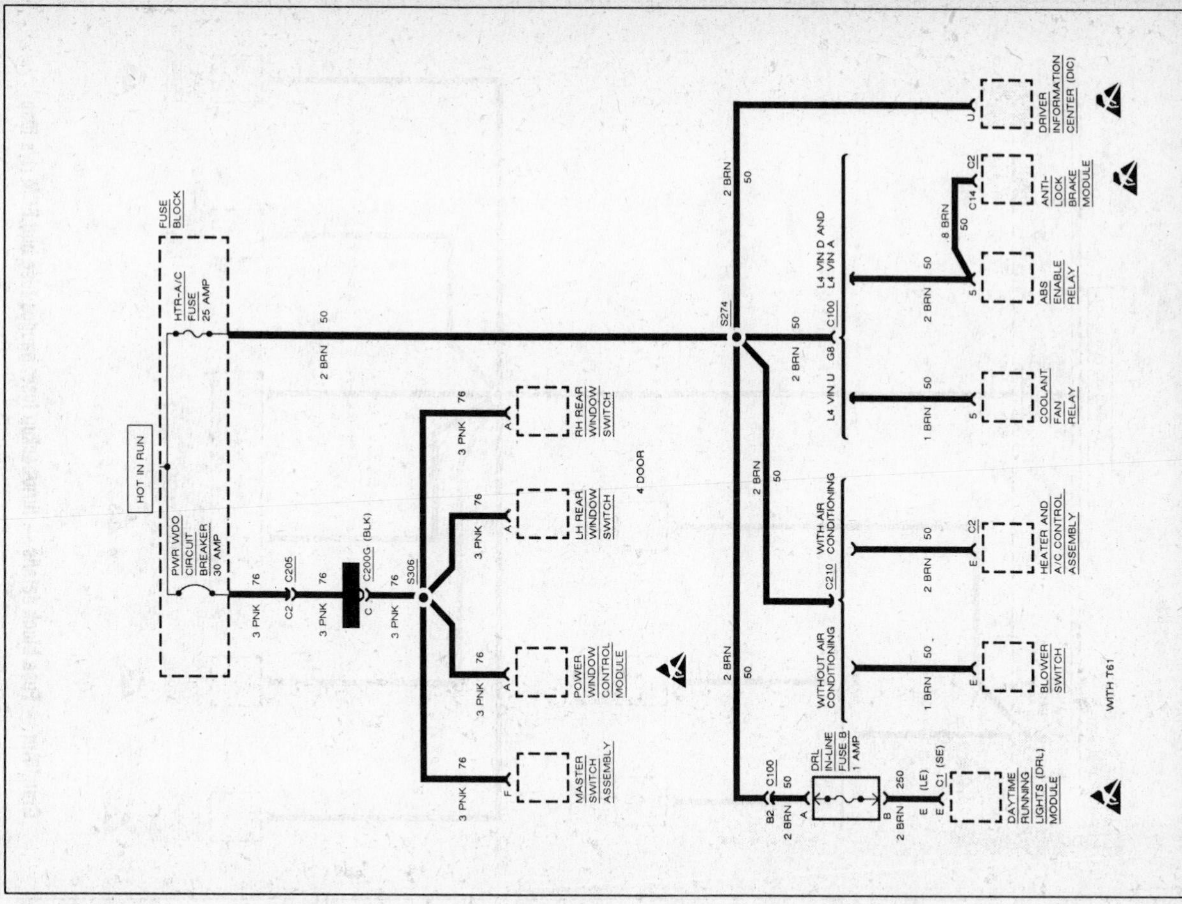

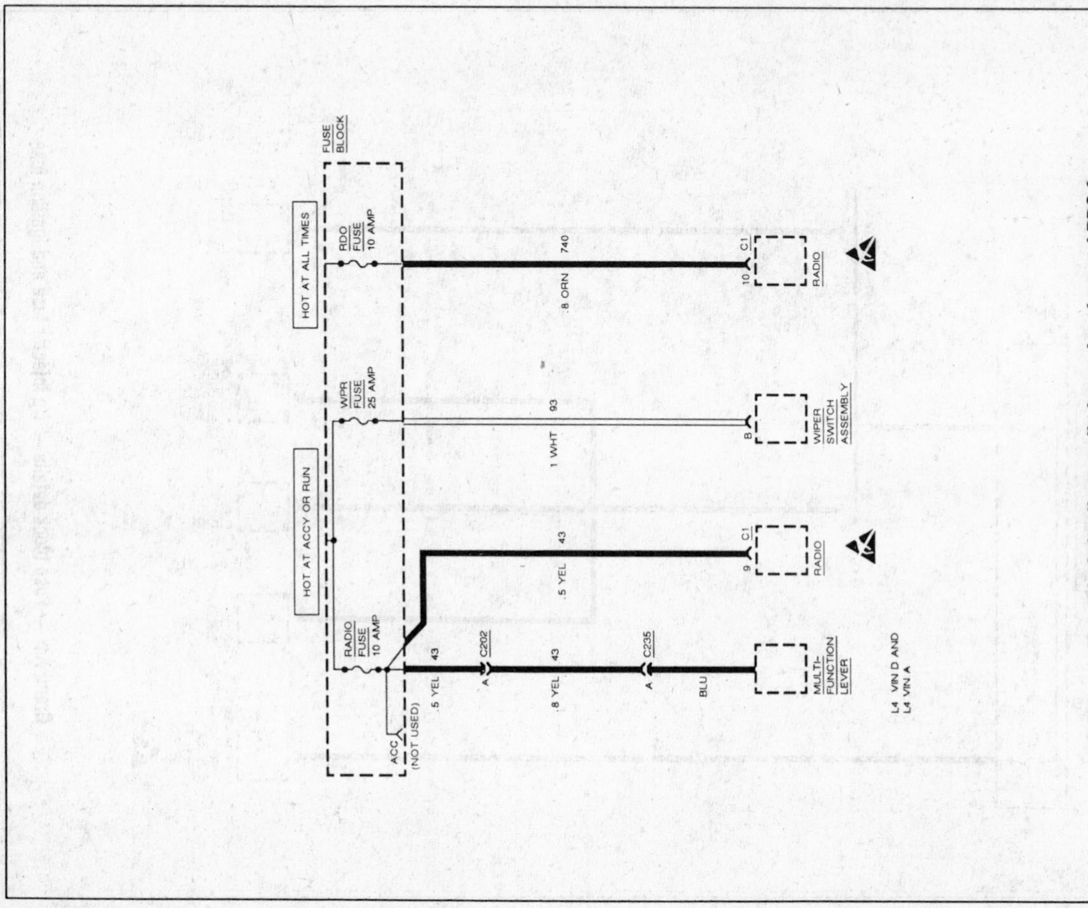

HOT AT ACCY OR RUN
HOT AT ALL TIMES
FUSE BLOCK
RADIO FUSE 10 AMP
WPR FUSE 25 AMP
RDO FUSE 10 AMP
ACC (NOT USED)
.5 YEL 43
A C202
.8 YEL 43
A C235
BLU
.5 YEL 43
1 WHT 93
.8 ORN 740
9 C1
B
10 C1
MULTI-FUNCTION LEVER
RADIO
WIPER SWITCH ASSEMBLY
RADIO
L4 VIN D AND L4 VIN A

Grand Am — Fuse block details — radio fuse, wiper fuse and RDO fuse

HOT IN RUN
FUSE BLOCK
PWR WDO CIRCUIT BREAKER 30 AMP
HTR-A/C FUSE 25 AMP
3 PNK 76
C2 C205
3 PNK 76
C C200G (BLK)
3 PNK 76
S306
3 PNK 76
2 BRN 50
F
A
MASTER SWITCH ASSEMBLY
POWER WINDOW CONTROL MODULE
LH REAR WINDOW SWITCH
RH REAR WINDOW SWITCH
4 DOOR
S274
2 BRN 50
B2 C100
2 BRN 50
A
DRL IN-LINE FUSE B 1 AMP
B
2 BRN 250
E (LE)
E C1 (SE)
WITHOUT AIR CONDITIONING
C210
WITH AIR CONDITIONING
L4 VIN U
G8 C100
L4 VIN D AND L4 VIN A
1 BRN 50
8 BRN 50
E
E C2
5
C14 C2
U
DAYTIME RUNNING LIGHTS (DRL) MODULE
BLOWER SWITCH
HEATER AND A/C CONTROL ASSEMBLY
COOLANT FAN RELAY
ABS ENABLE RELAY
ANTI-LOCK BRAKE MODULE
DRIVER INFORMATION CENTER (DIC)
WITH T61

Grand Am — Fuse block details — power window circuit breaker and heater/air conditioner fuse

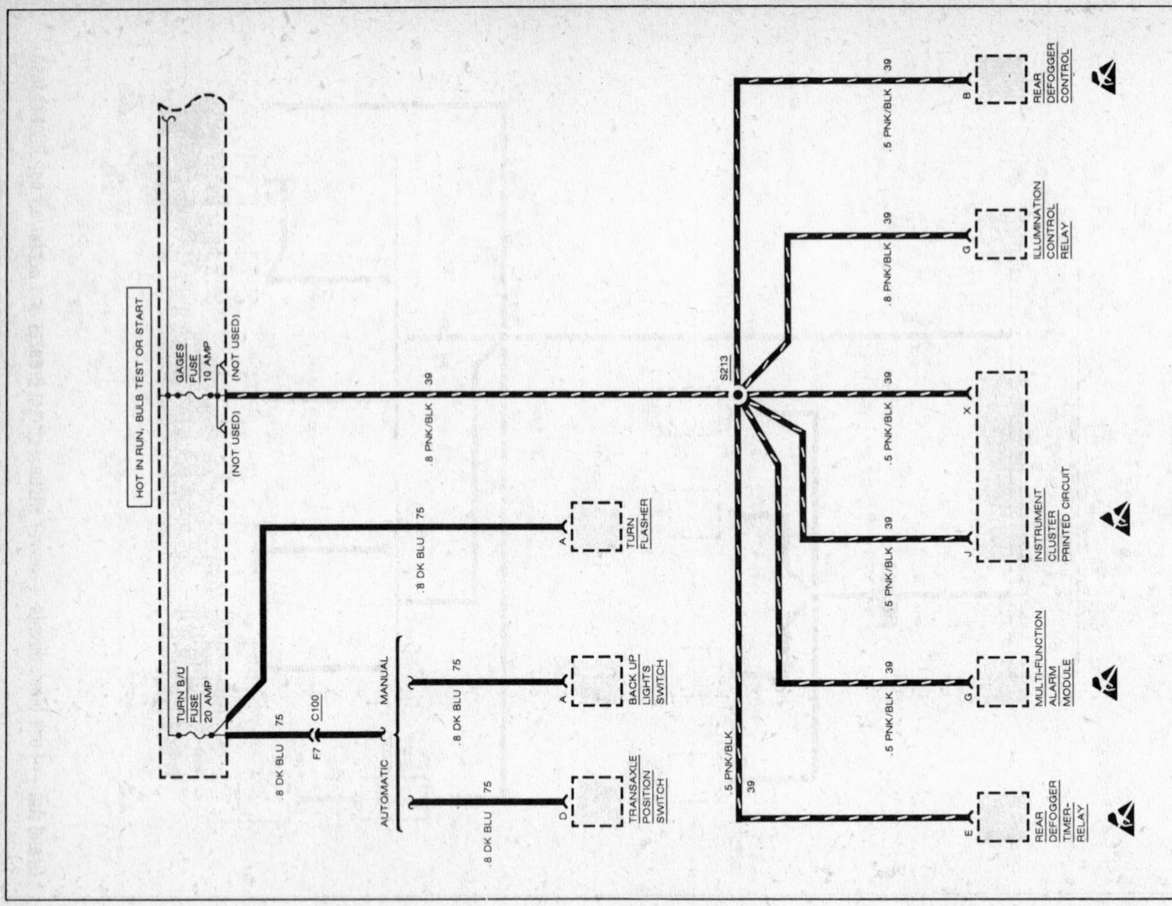

HOT IN RUN, BULB TEST OR START
FUSE BLOCK
IGN FUSE 20 AMP (L4 VIN D, L4 VIN A)
F/P-INJ FUSE 20 AMP
1 PNK/WHT 839
L4 VIN U E5 C100 L 4 VIN D AND L4 VIN A
1 PNK/BLK 239
F4 C100
1 PNK/BLK 839
S161
1 PNK/BLK 239 .8 RED 839 1 PNK/BLK 839 1 PNK/BLK 839 1 PNK/BLK 839
1 PNK/BLK 839
L INTEGRATED DIRECT IGNITION (IDI) SYSTEM
A FUEL INJECTOR
1 FUEL PUMP RELAY
C FUEL PUMP SWITCH/OIL PRESSURE SWITCH
1 FUEL PUMP RELAY
C FUEL PUMP SWITCH/OIL PRESSURE SWITCH

Grand Am — Fuse block details — f/p injector fuse and ignition fuse

HOT IN RUN, BULB TEST OR START
TURN B/U FUSE 20 AMP
GAGES FUSE 10 AMP
(NOT USED) (NOT USED)
.8 DK BLU 75
F7 C100
AUTOMATIC MANUAL
.8 DK BLU 75 .8 DK BLU 75 .8 DK BLU 75
.8 PNK/BLK 39
D TRANSAXLE POSITION SWITCH
A BACK UP LIGHTS SWITCH
A TURN FLASHER
S213
.5 PNK/BLK 39
.5 PNK/BLK 39 .5 PNK/BLK 39 .5 PNK/BLK 39 .8 PNK/BLK 39 .5 PNK/BLK 39
E REAR DEFOGGER TIMER-RELAY
G MULTI-FUNCTION ALARM MODULE
J X INSTRUMENT CLUSTER PRINTED CIRCUIT
G ILLUMINATION CONTROL RELAY
B REAR DEFOGGER CONTROL

Grand Am — Fuse block details — turn/backup fuse, gauges fuse and ECM rlys fuse

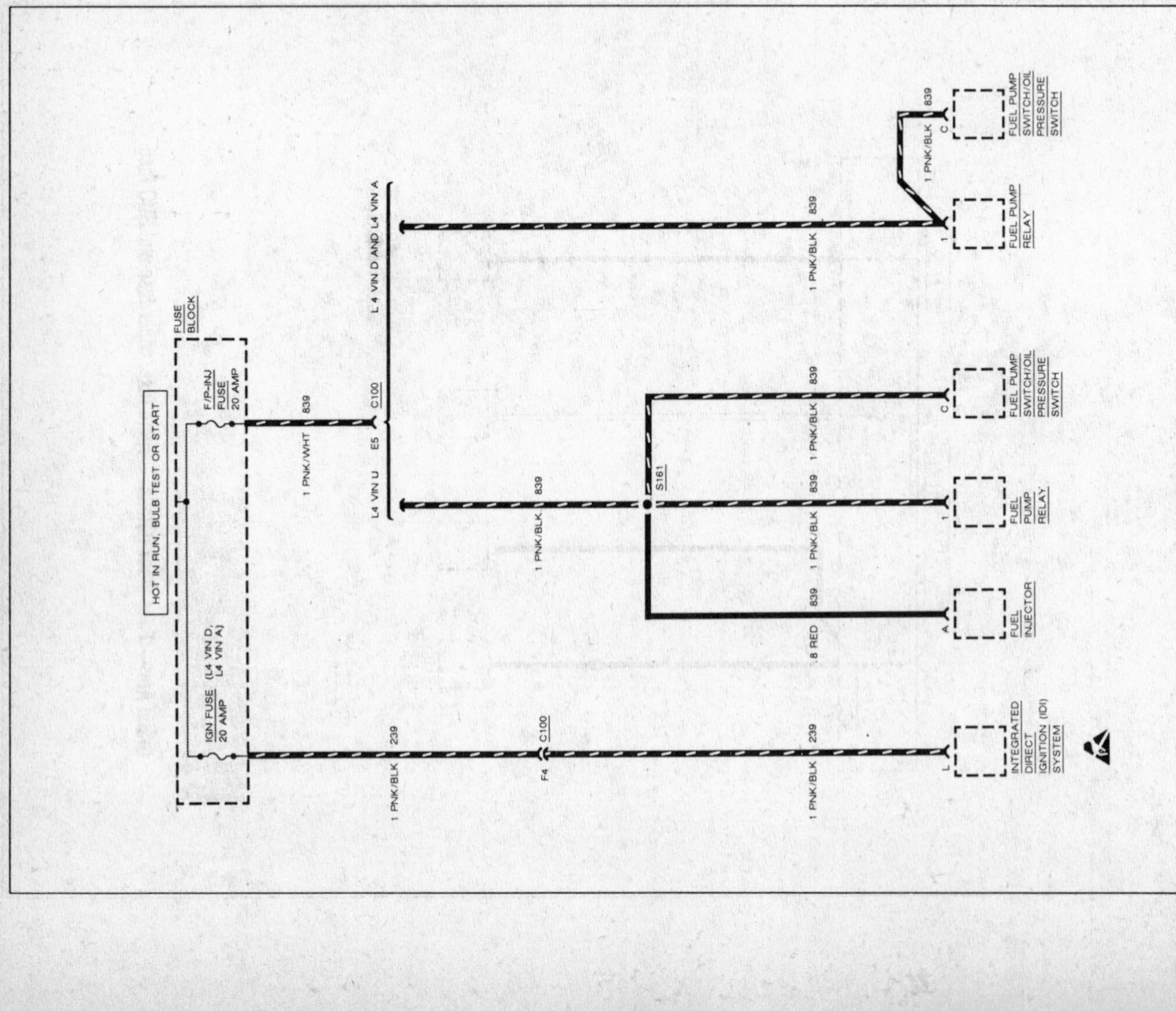

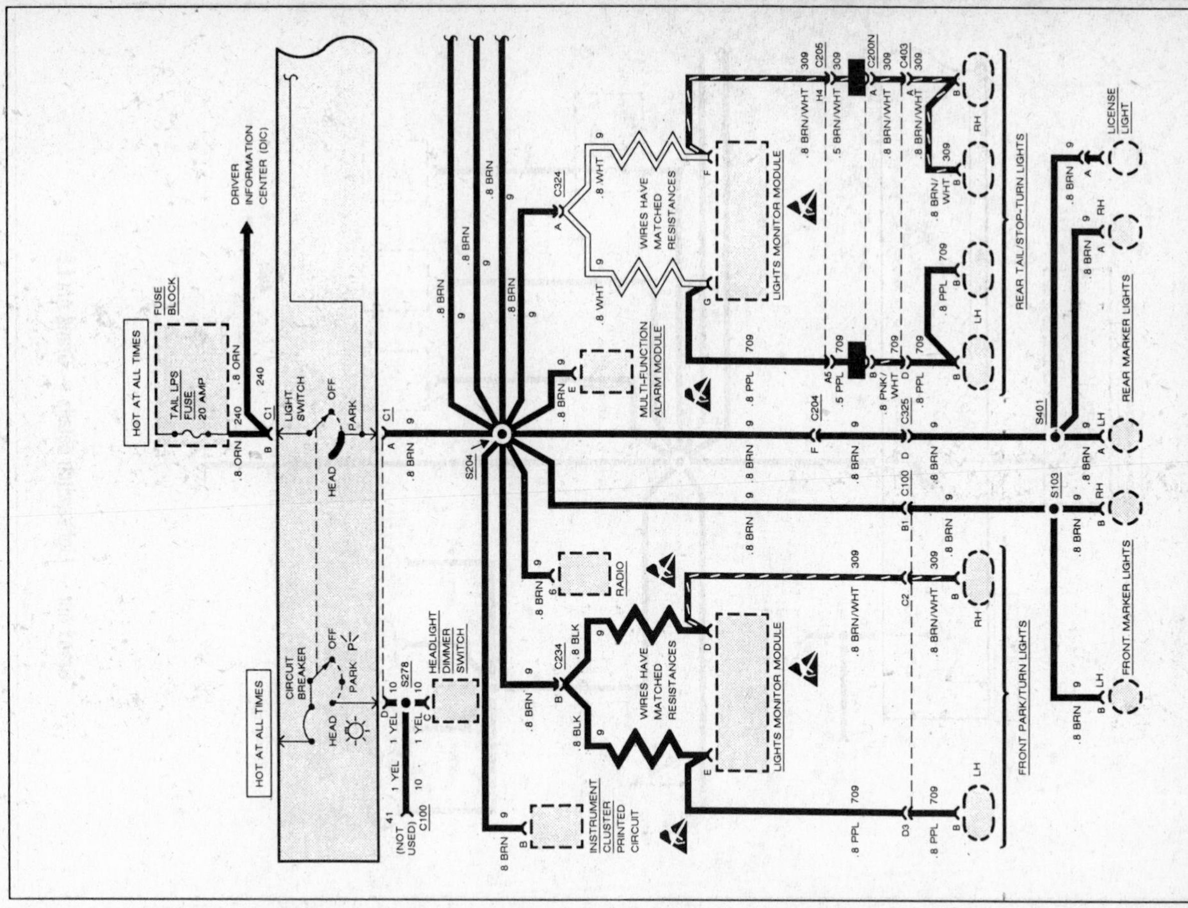

L4 VIN U ECM CONNECTOR IDENTIFICATION
C1 - BLACK/RED - 24 WAY
C2 - WHITE/RED - 24 WAY

L4 VIN D AND L4 VIN A ECM CONNECTOR IDENTIFICATION
C1 - BLACK - 32 WAY
C2 - BLACK - 24 WAY
C3 - GREEN - 32 WAY

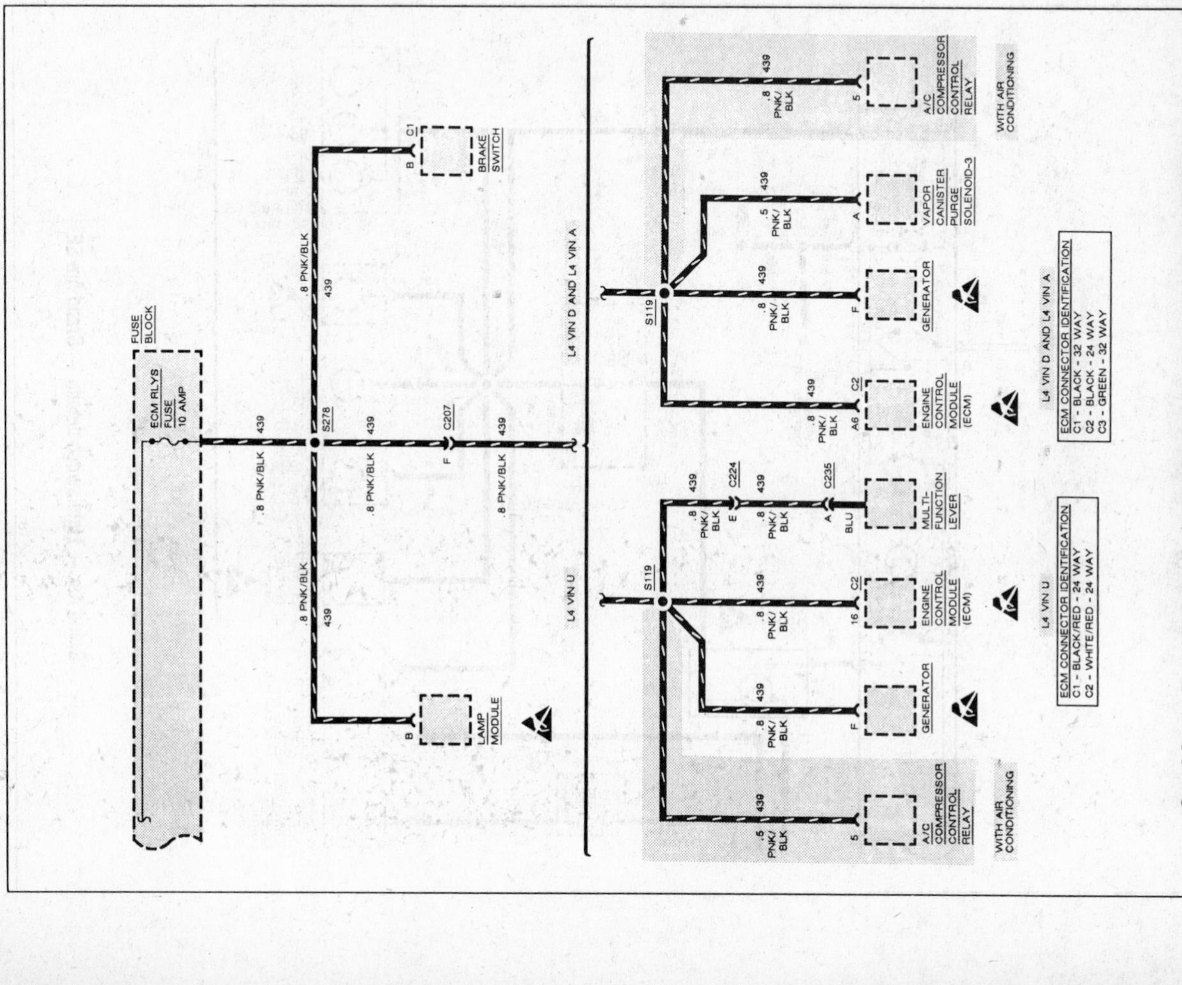

Grand Am — Fuse block details — turn/backup fuse, gauges fuse and ECM rlys fuse

Grand Am — Light switch details — Grand Am SE

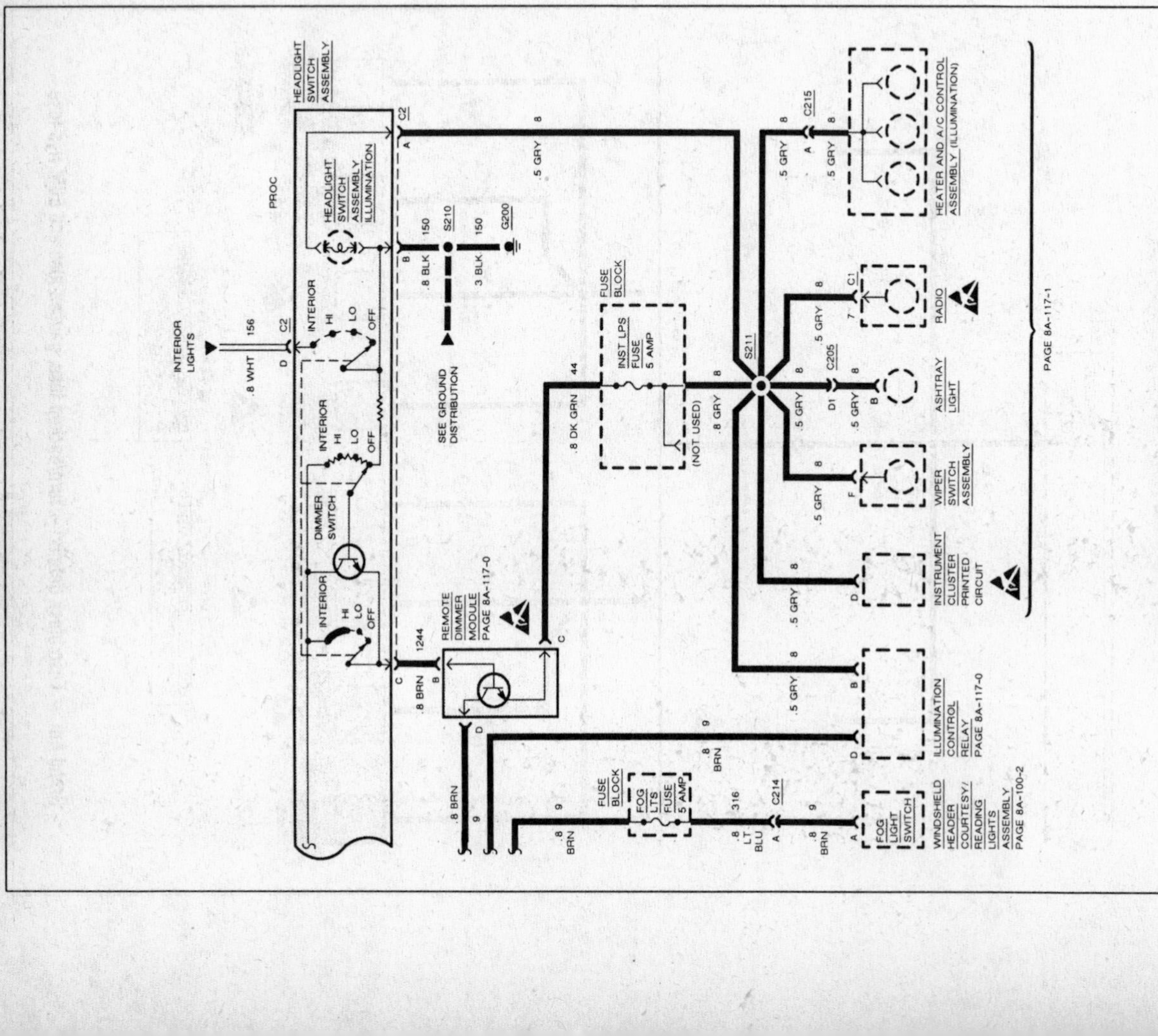

Grand Am — Light switch details — Grand Am LE

Grand Am — Light switch details — Grand Am SE

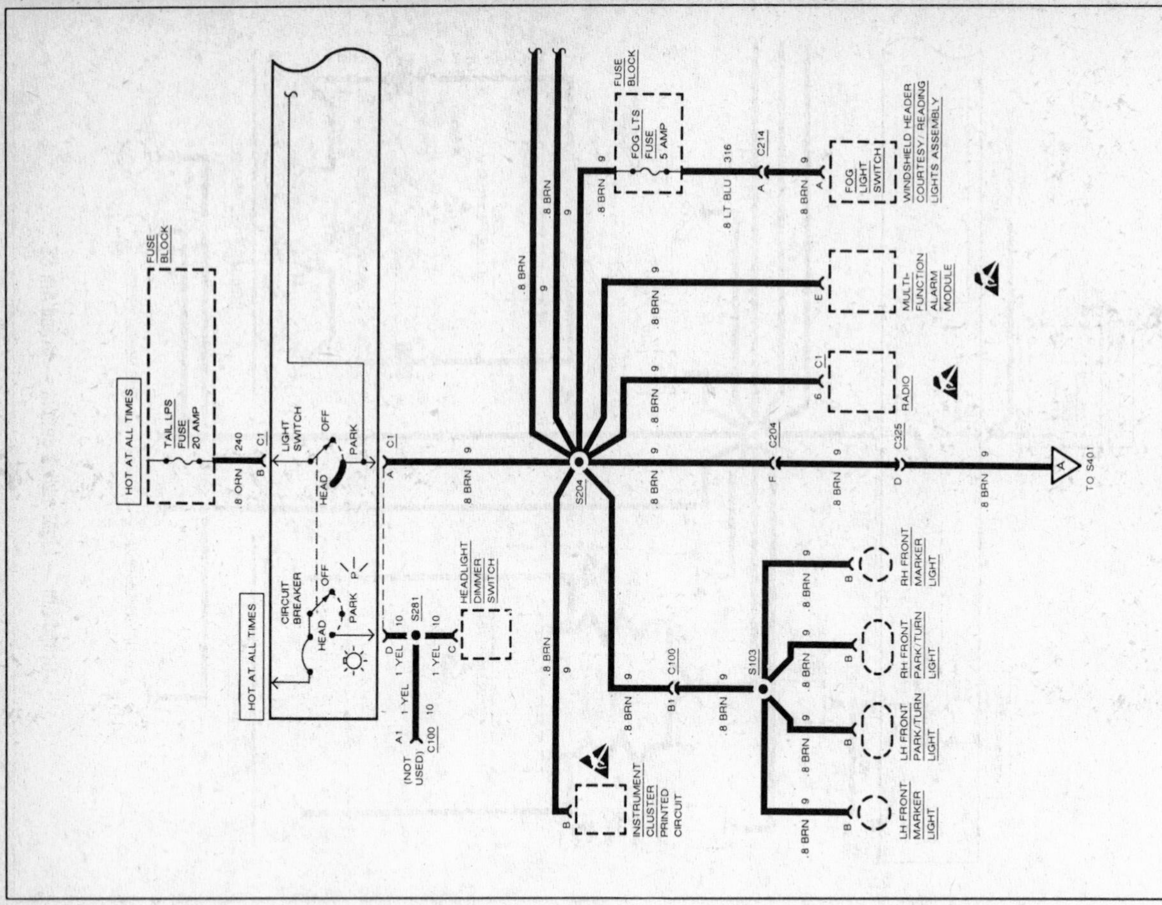

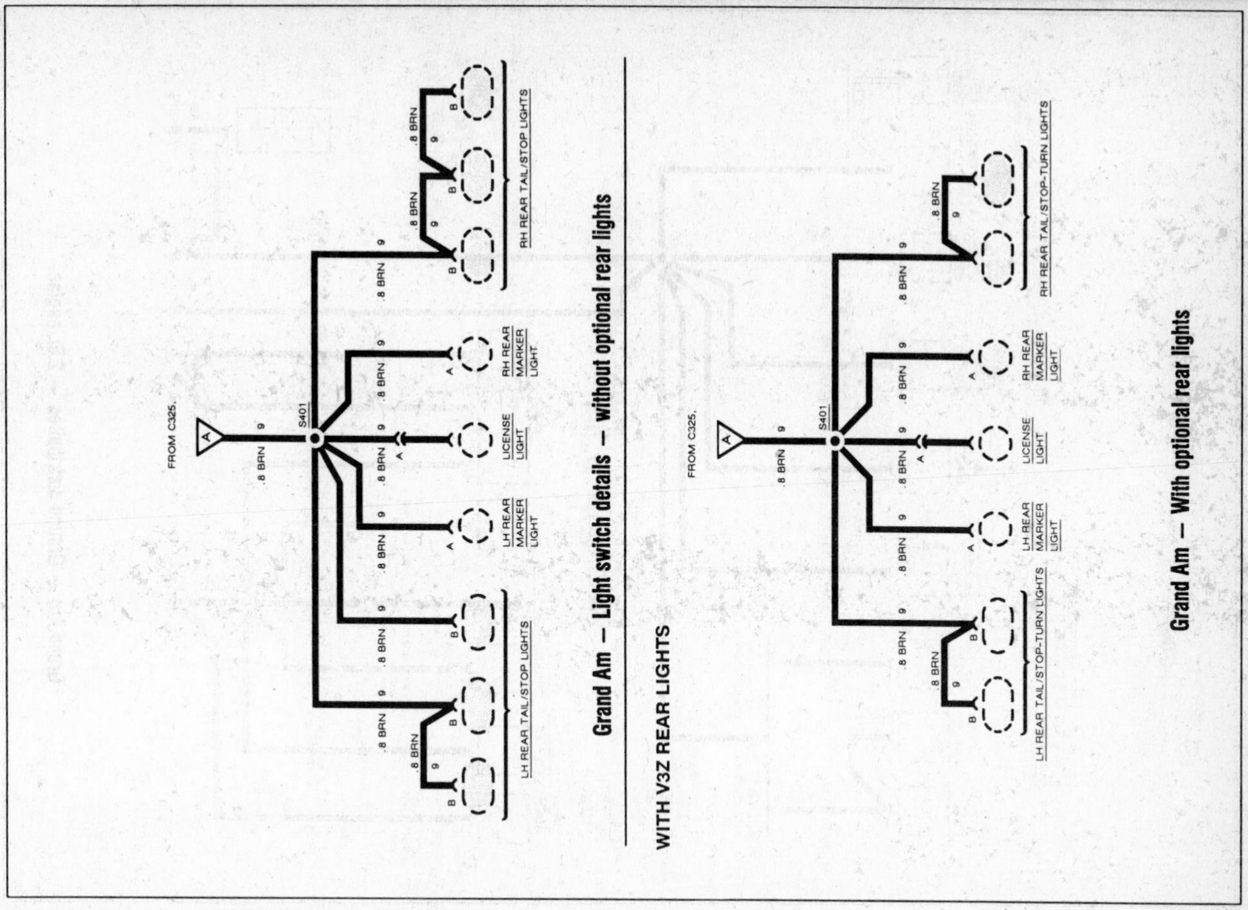

INTERIOR LIGHTS
.8 WHT 156
D C2
HEADLIGHT SWITCH ASSEMBLY
INTERIOR HI LO OFF
DIMMER SWITCH
INTERIOR HI LO OFF
INTERIOR HI LO OFF
HEADLIGHT SWITCH ASSEMBLY ILLUMINATION
C B A C2
.8 BRN 1244
.8 BLK 150
SEE GROUND DISTRIBUTION
S210
3 BLK 150
G200
B REMOTE DIMMER MODULE
.8 BRN 9 D
C
.8 DK GRN 44
.5 GRY 8
.8 BRN 9
FUSE BLOCK
INST LPS FUSE 5 AMP
(NOT USED)
.8 GRY 8
S211
.5 GRY 8
D1 C205
.5 GRY 8
.5 GRY 8
.5 GRY 8
.5 GRY 8
.5 GRY 8
.5 GRY 8
A C215
.5 GRY 8
D B ILLUMINATION CONTROL RELAY
F WIPER SWITCH ASSEMBLY
7 C1 RADIO
B ASHTRAY LIGHT
D INSTRUMENT CLUSTER PRINTED CIRCUIT
HEATER AND A/C CONTROL ASSEMBLY (ILLUMINATION)

Grand Am – Light switch details – Grand Am LE

FROM C325.
A
.8 BRN 9
S401
.8 BRN 9
.8 BRN 9
.8 BRN 9
.8 BRN 9
.8 BRN 9
.8 BRN 9
.8 BRN 9
.8 BRN 9
.8 BRN 9
B B B A A A B B B
LH REAR TAIL/STOP LIGHTS
LH REAR MARKER LIGHT
LICENSE LIGHT
RH REAR MARKER LIGHT
RH REAR TAIL/STOP LIGHTS

Grand Am – Light switch details – without optional rear lights

WITH V3Z REAR LIGHTS

FROM C325.
A
.8 BRN 9
S401
.8 BRN 9
.8 BRN 9
.8 BRN 9
.8 BRN 9
.8 BRN 9
.8 BRN 9
.8 BRN 9
B B A A A
LH REAR TAIL/STOP-TURN LIGHTS
LH REAR MARKER LIGHT
LICENSE LIGHT
RH REAR MARKER LIGHT
RH REAR TAIL/STOP-TURN LIGHTS

Grand Am – With optional rear lights

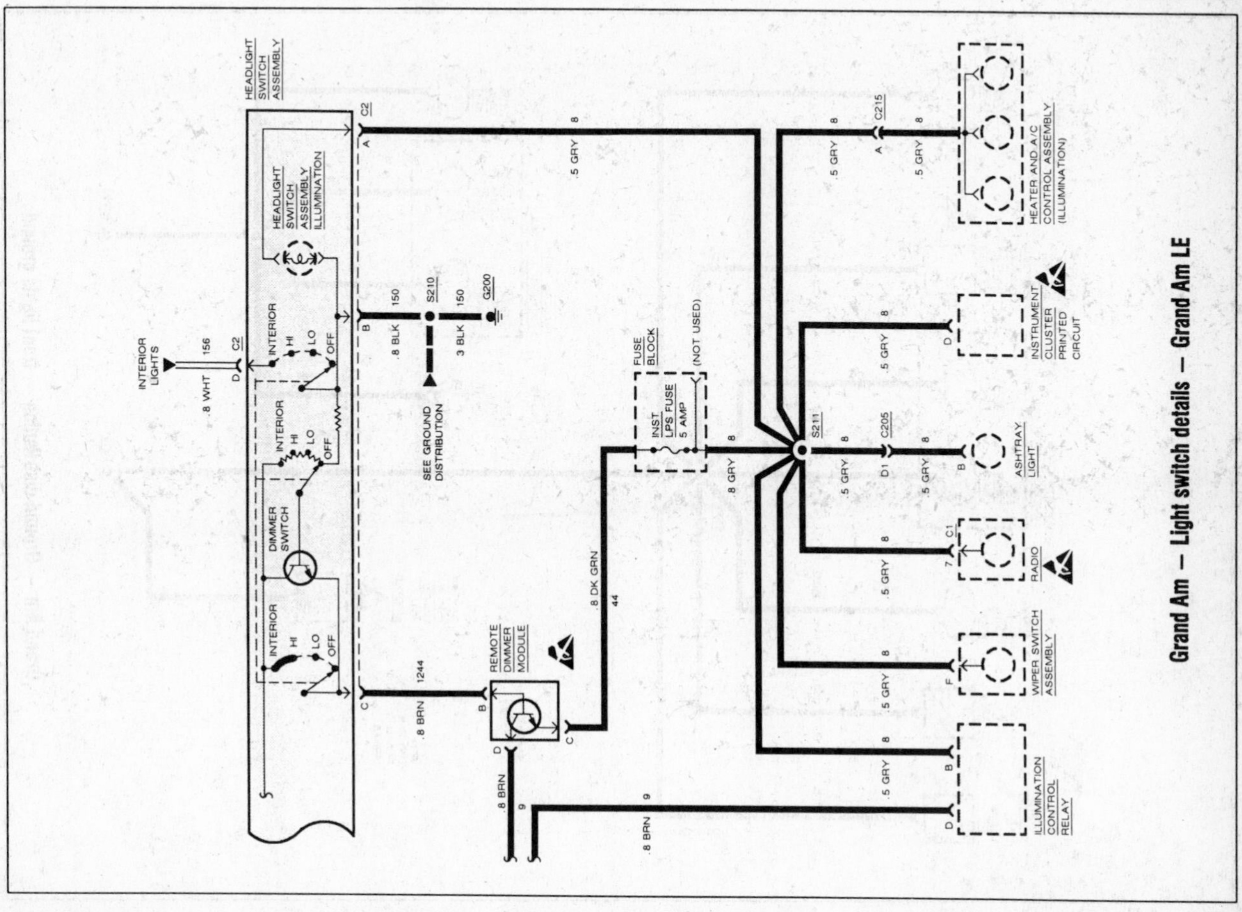

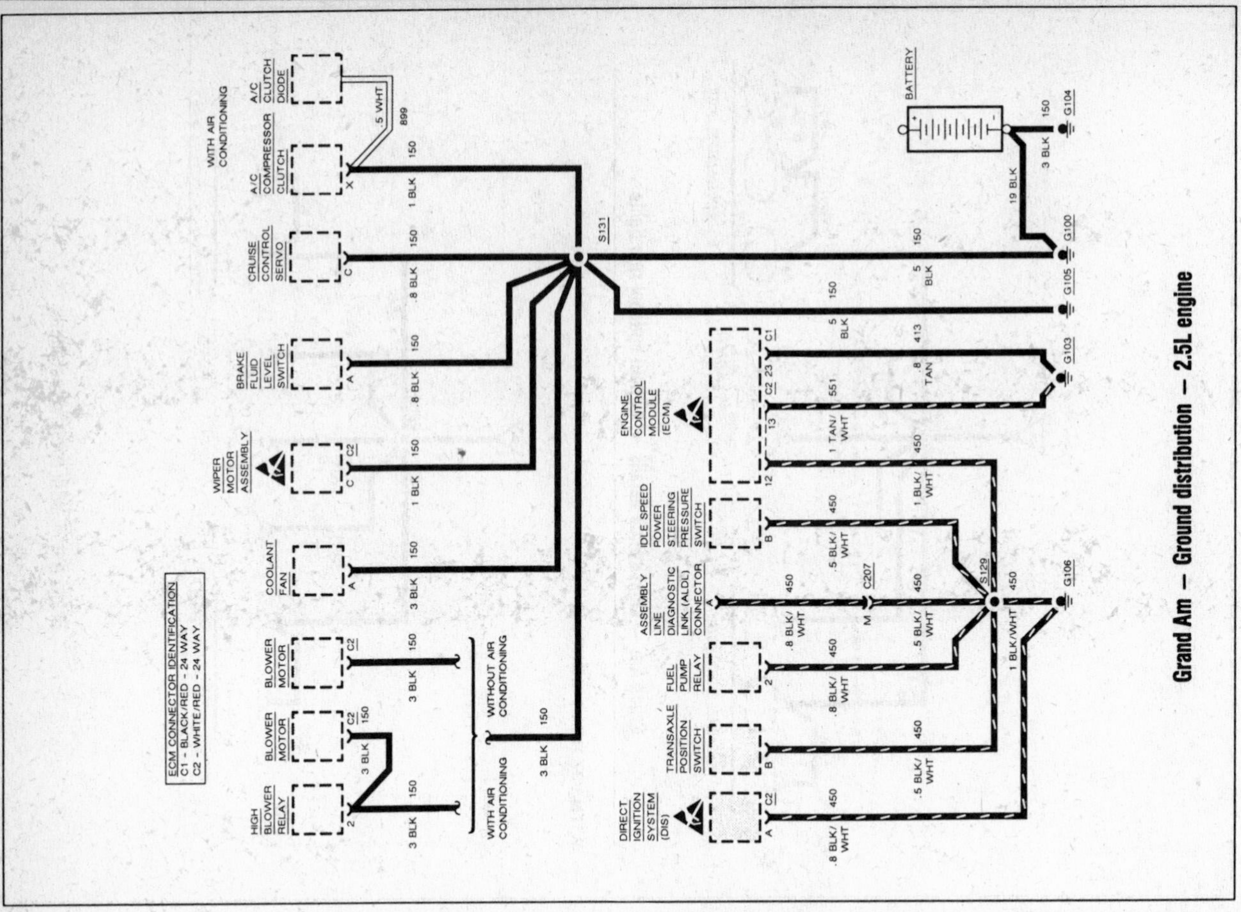

Grand Am — Ground distribution — 2.5L engine

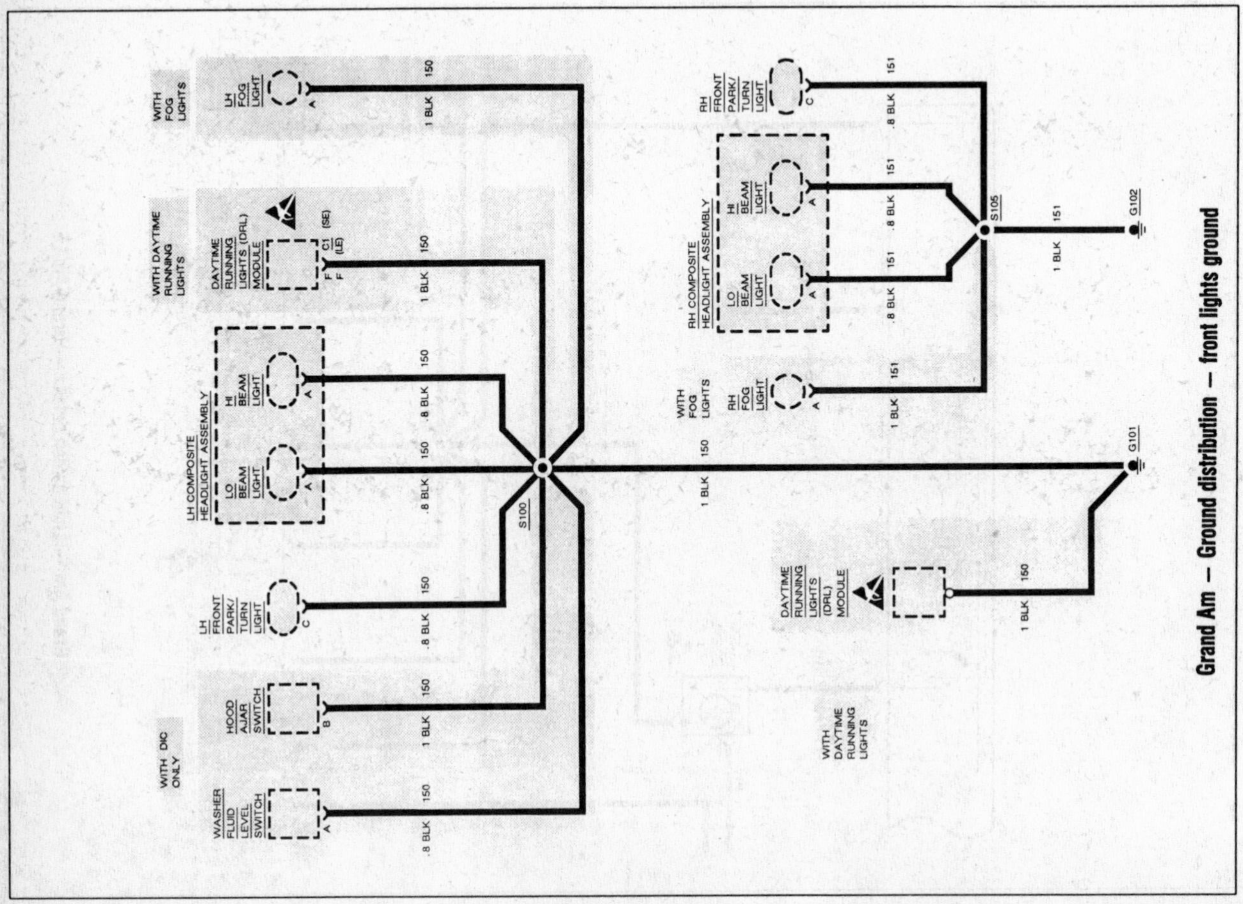

Grand Am — Ground distribution — front lights ground

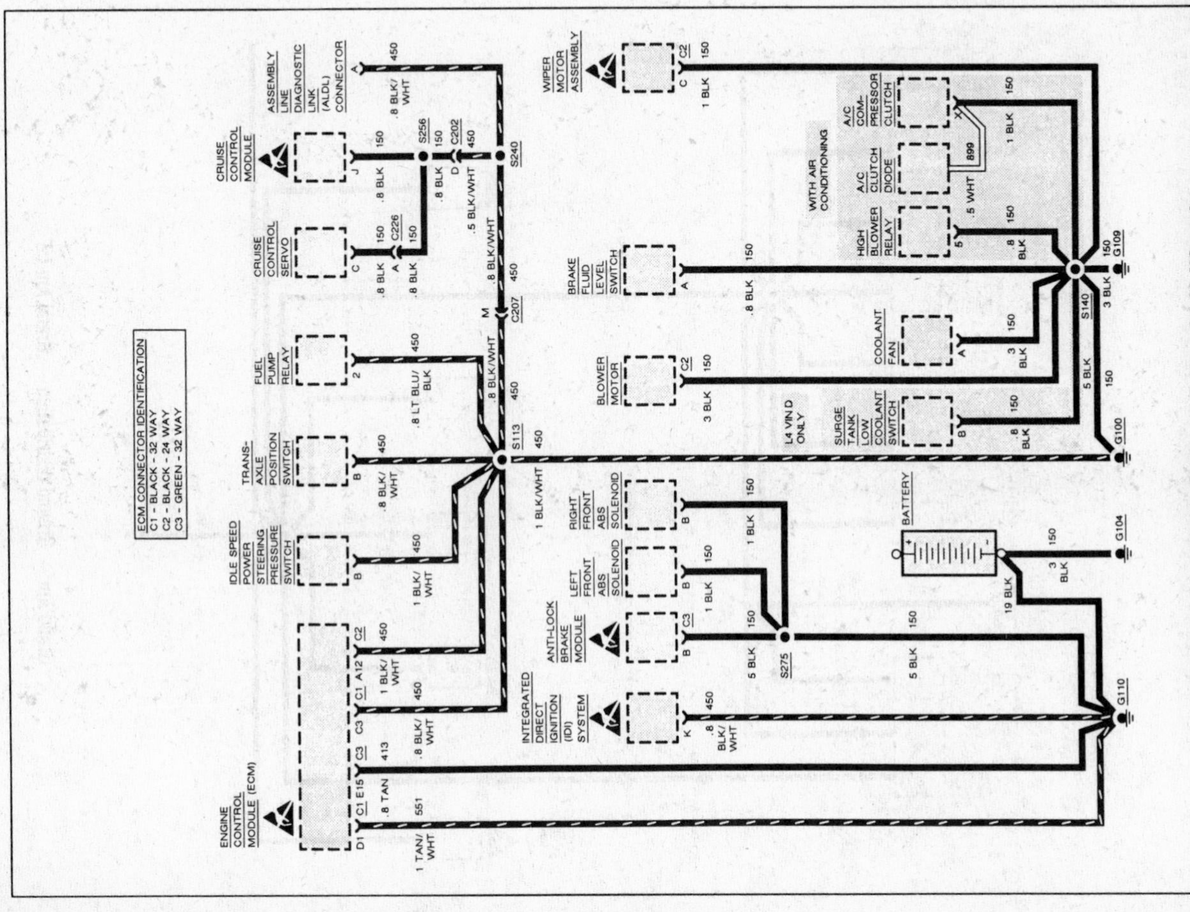

ECM CONNECTOR IDENTIFICATION
C1 - BLACK - 32 WAY
C2 - BLACK - 24 WAY
C3 - GREEN - 32 WAY

Grand Am — Ground distribution — 2.3L and 2.3L HO engines

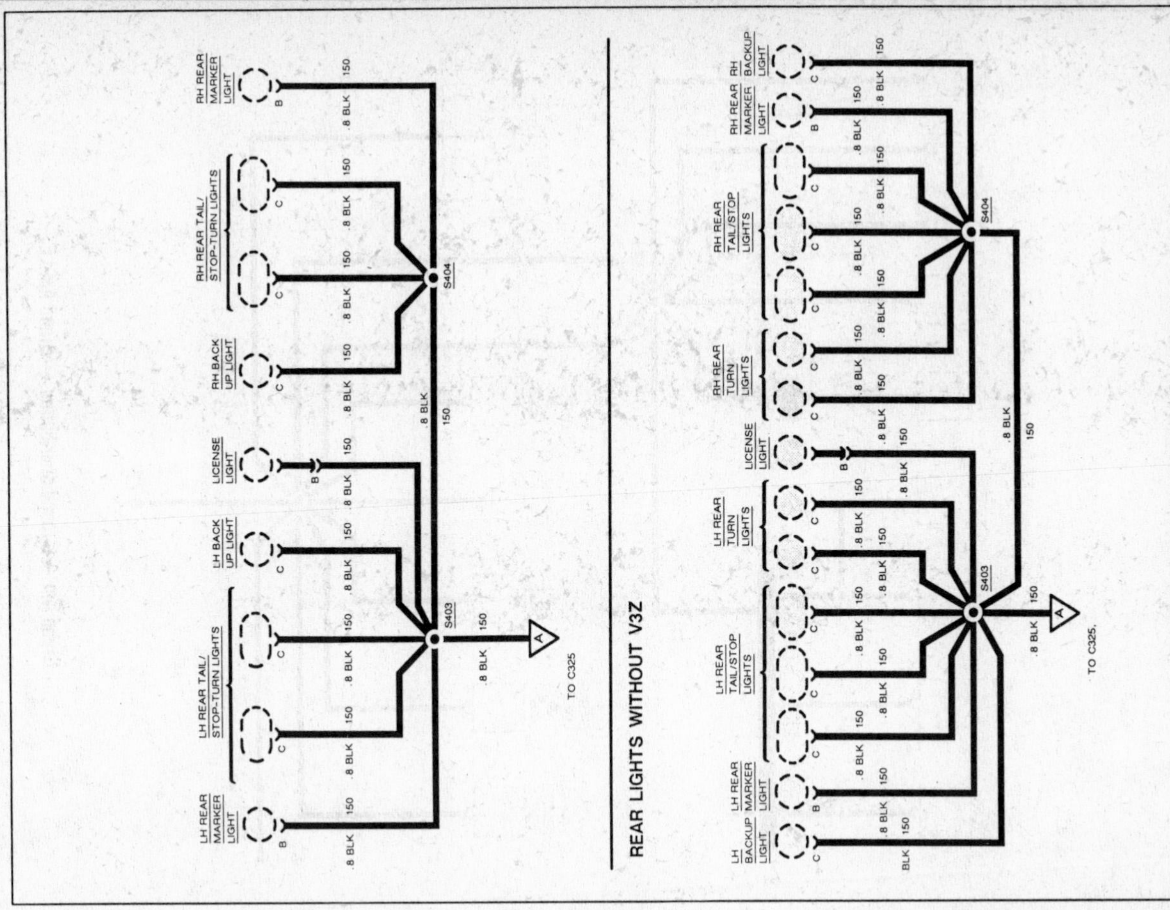

REAR LIGHTS WITHOUT V3Z

Grand Am — Ground distribution — Grand Am LE

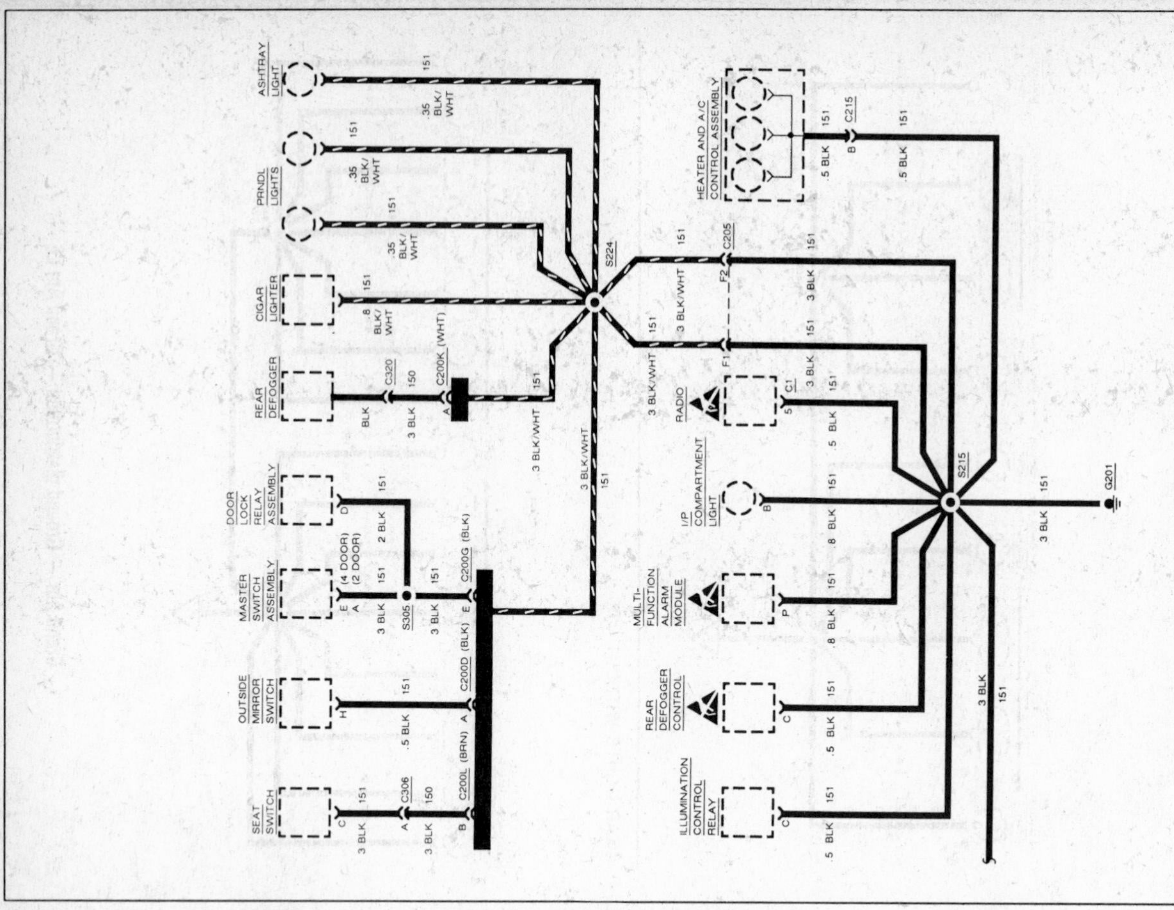

Grand Am – Ground distribution – Grand Am LE

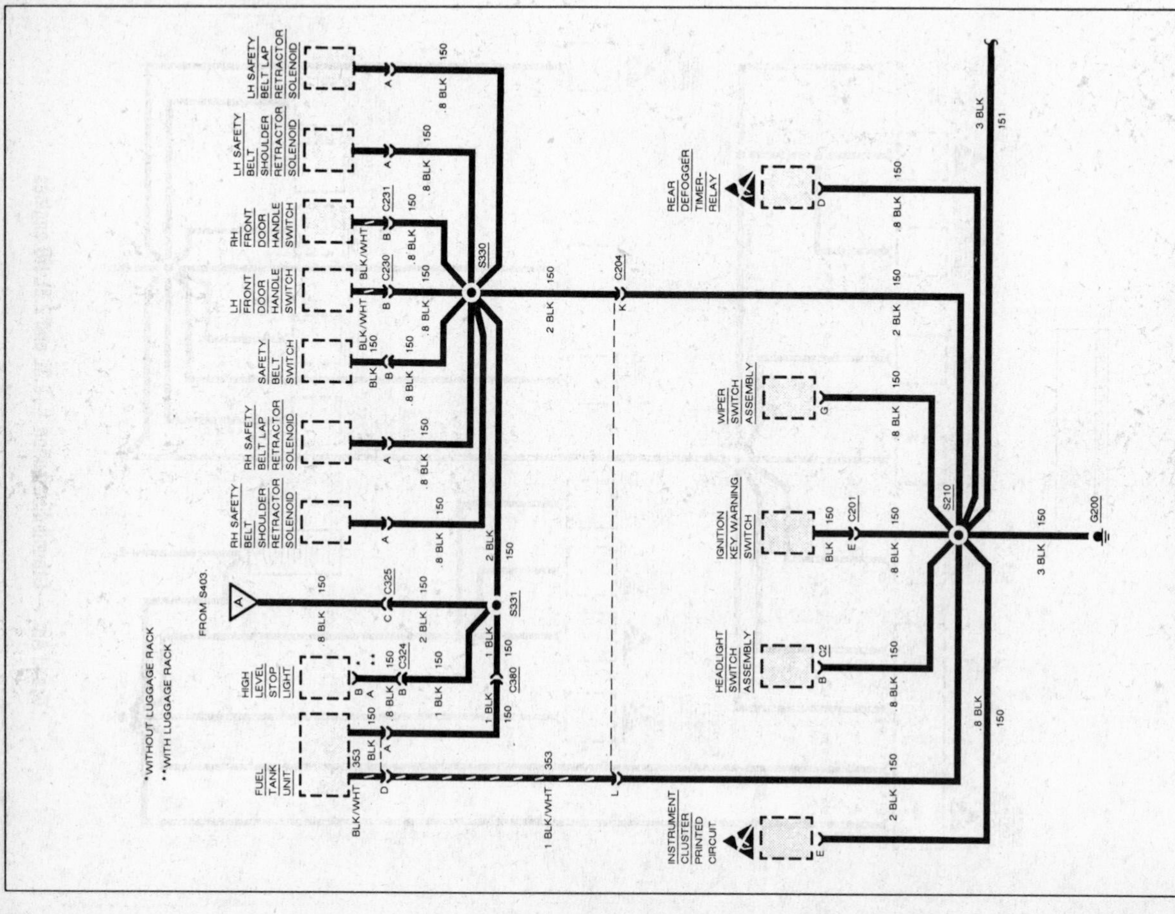

Grand Am – Ground distribution – Grand Am LE

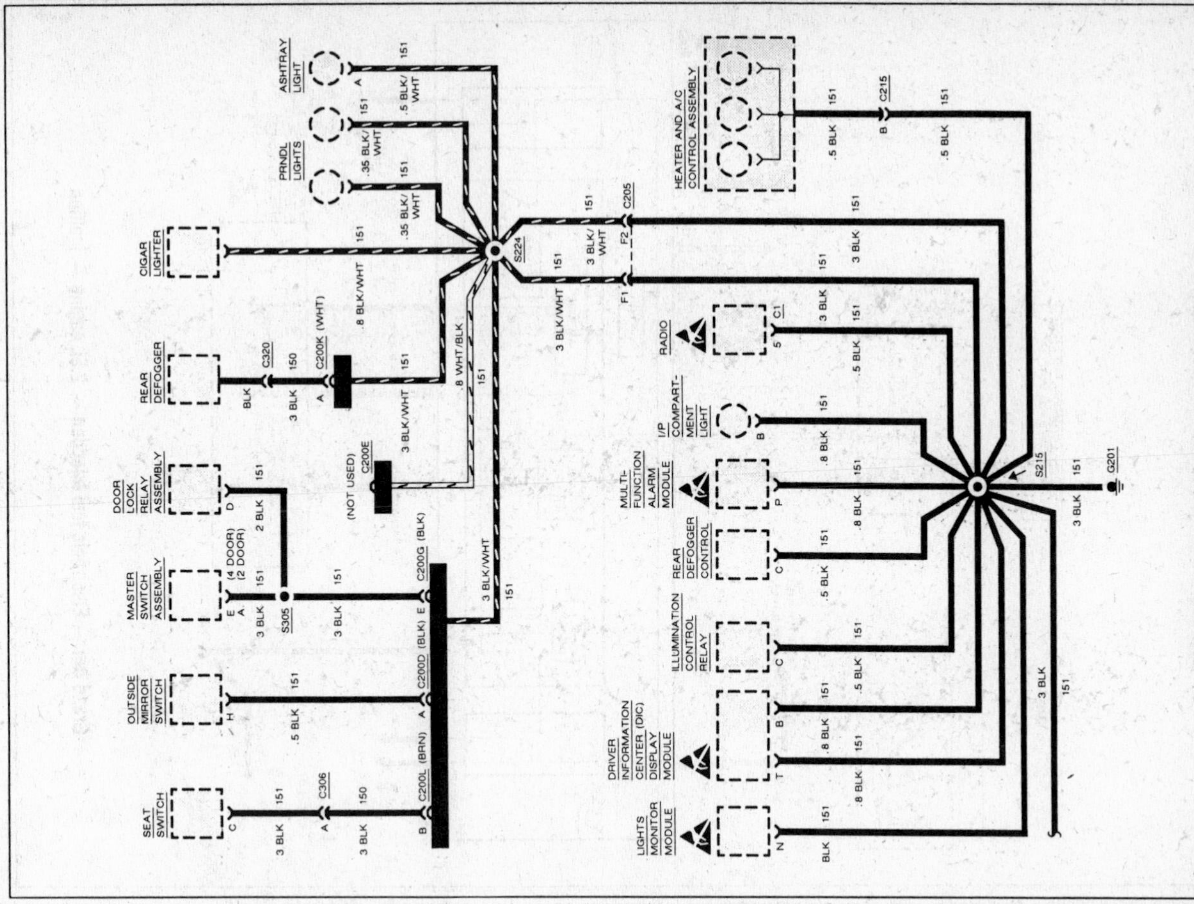

Grand Am — Ground distribution — Grand Am SE

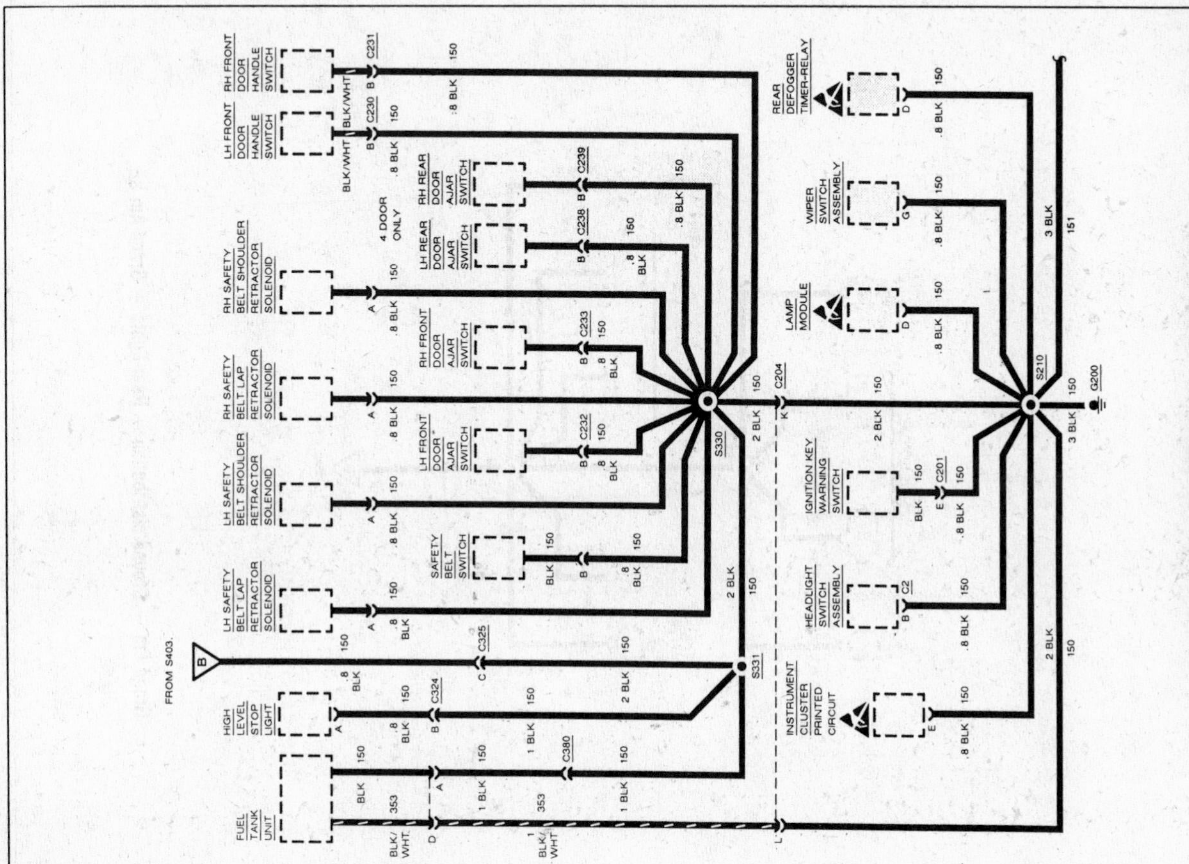

Grand Am — Ground distribution — Grand Am SE

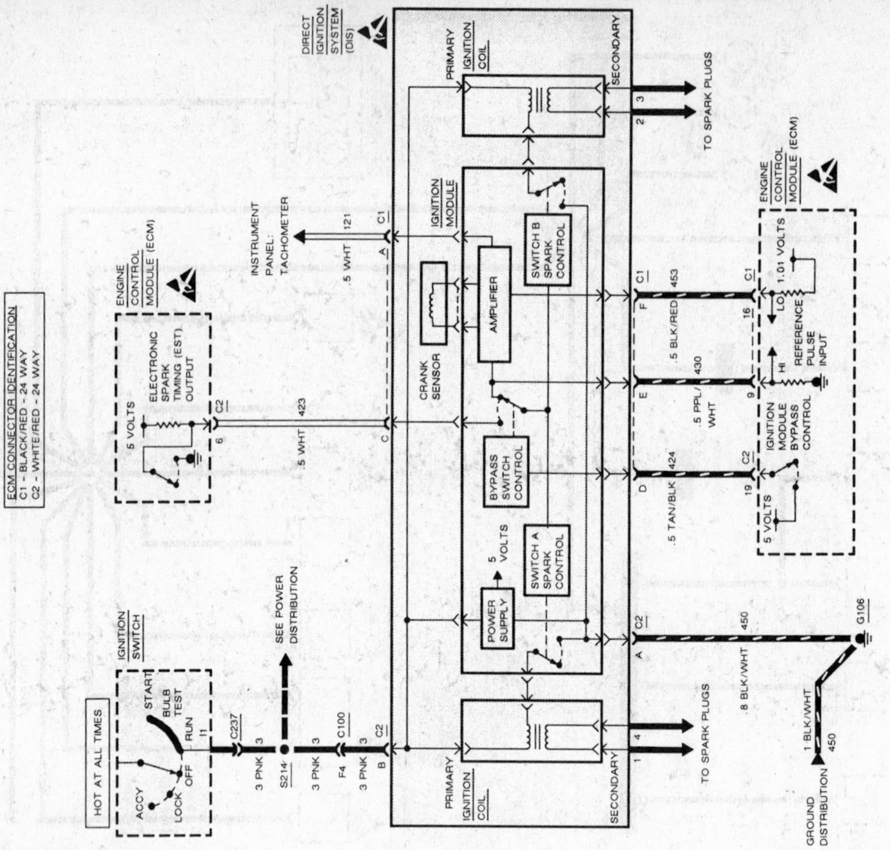

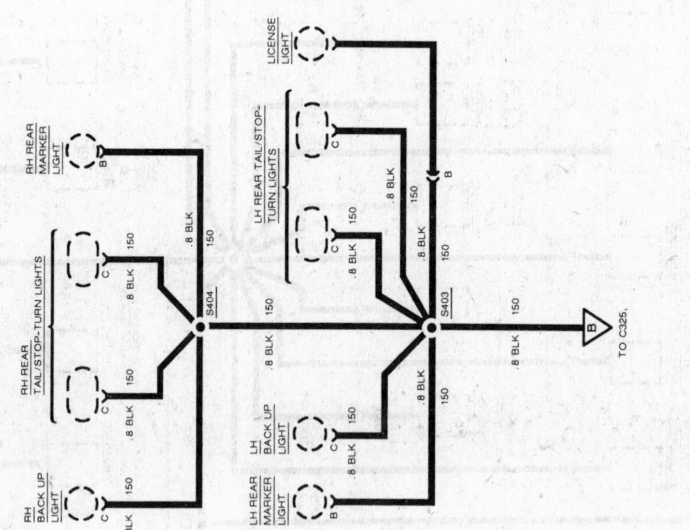

Grand Am — Ground distribution — Rear lights — Grand Am SE

Grand Am — Electronic fuel injection — 2.5L engine — ignition

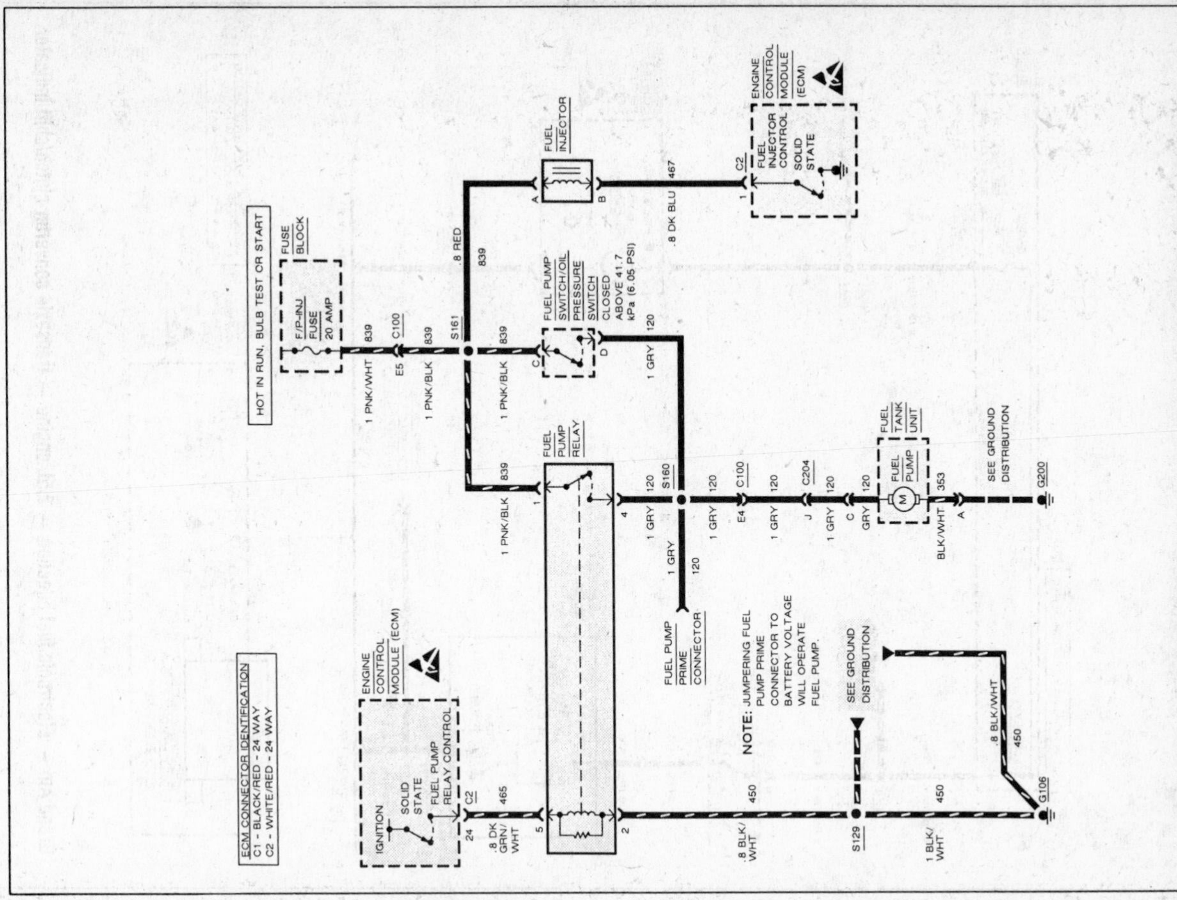

ECM CONNECTOR IDENTIFICATION
C1 - BLACK/RED - 24 WAY
C2 - WHITE/RED - 24 WAY

HOT AT ALL TIMES

HOT IN RUN, BULB TEST OR START

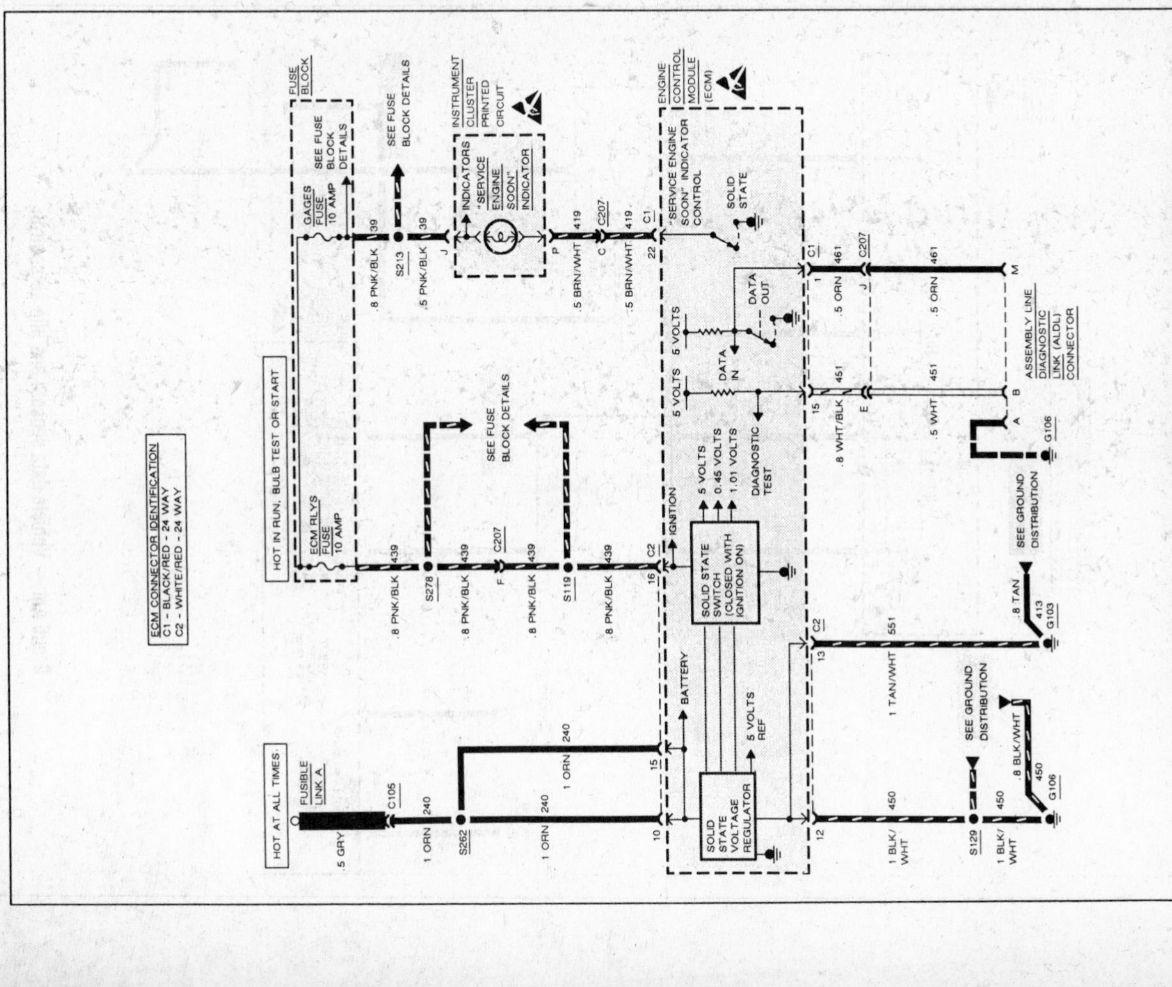

Grand Am — Power, grounds and "Service Engine Soon" indicator

ECM CONNECTOR IDENTIFICATION
C1 - BLACK/RED - 24 WAY
C2 - WHITE/RED - 24 WAY

HOT IN RUN, BULB TEST OR START

NOTE: JUMPERING FUEL PUMP PRIME CONNECTOR TO BATTERY VOLTAGE WILL OPERATE FUEL PUMP.

Grand Am — Electronic fuel injection — 2.5L engine — fuel injector and fuel control

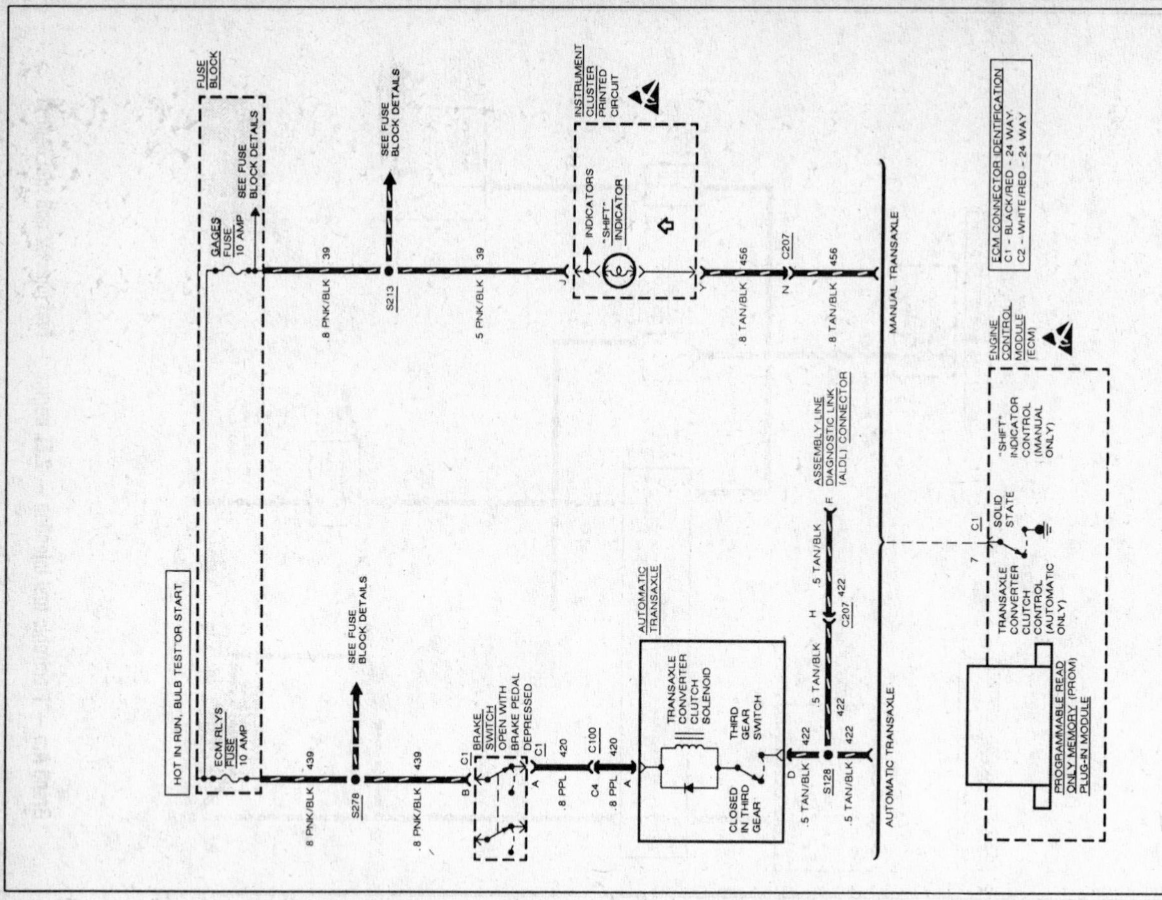

Grand Am — Electronic fuel injection — 2.5L engine — transaxle converter clutch/shift indicator

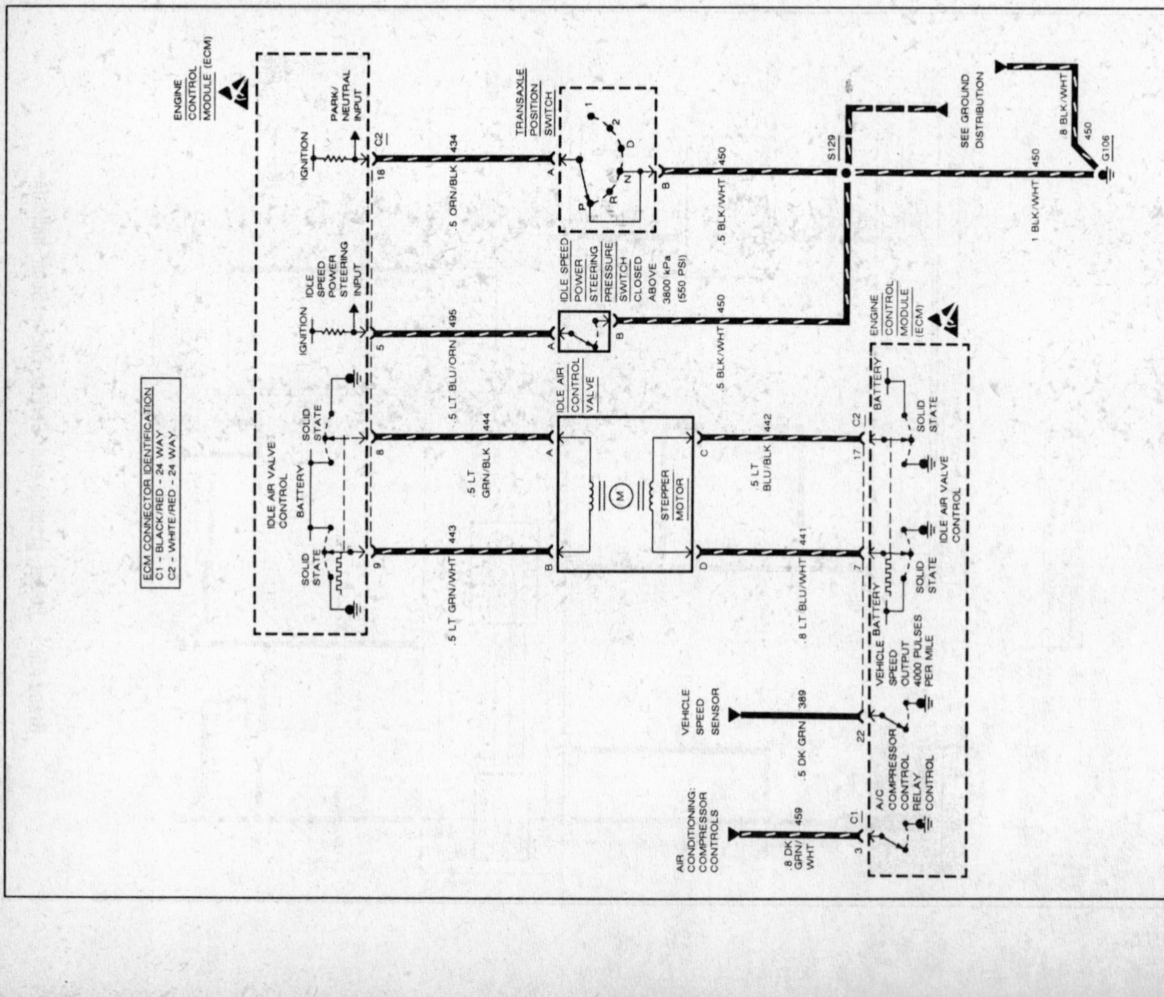

Grand Am — Vehicle data sensors and idle air control

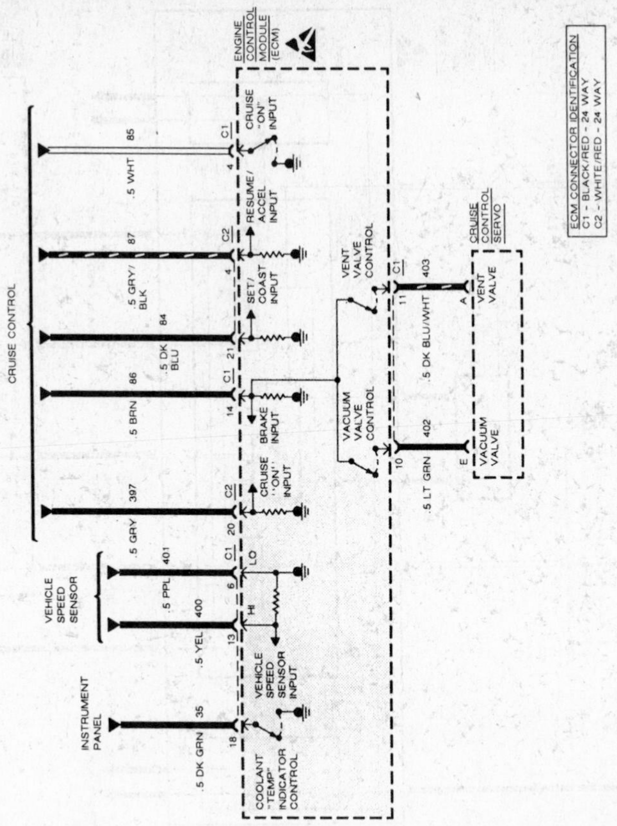

ECM CONNECTOR IDENTIFICATION
C1 - BLACK/RED - 24 WAY
C2 - WHITE/RED - 24 WAY

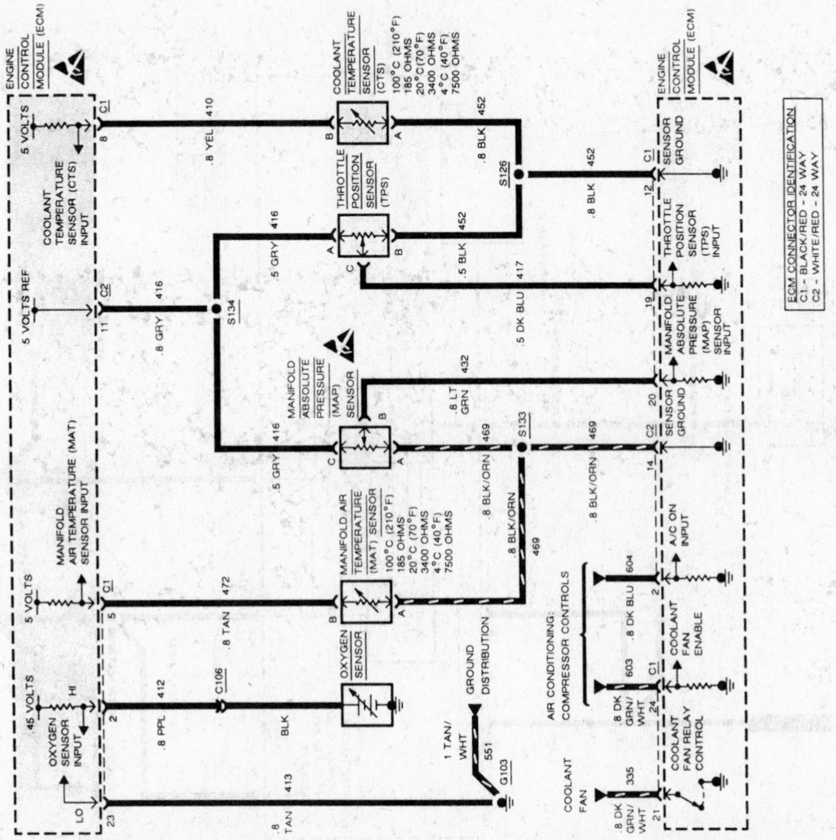

Grand Am — Engine data sensors

ECM CONNECTOR IDENTIFICATION
C1 - BLACK/RED - 24 WAY
C2 - WHITE/RED - 24 WAY

Grand Am — Electronic fuel injection — 2.5L engine vehicle data sensors

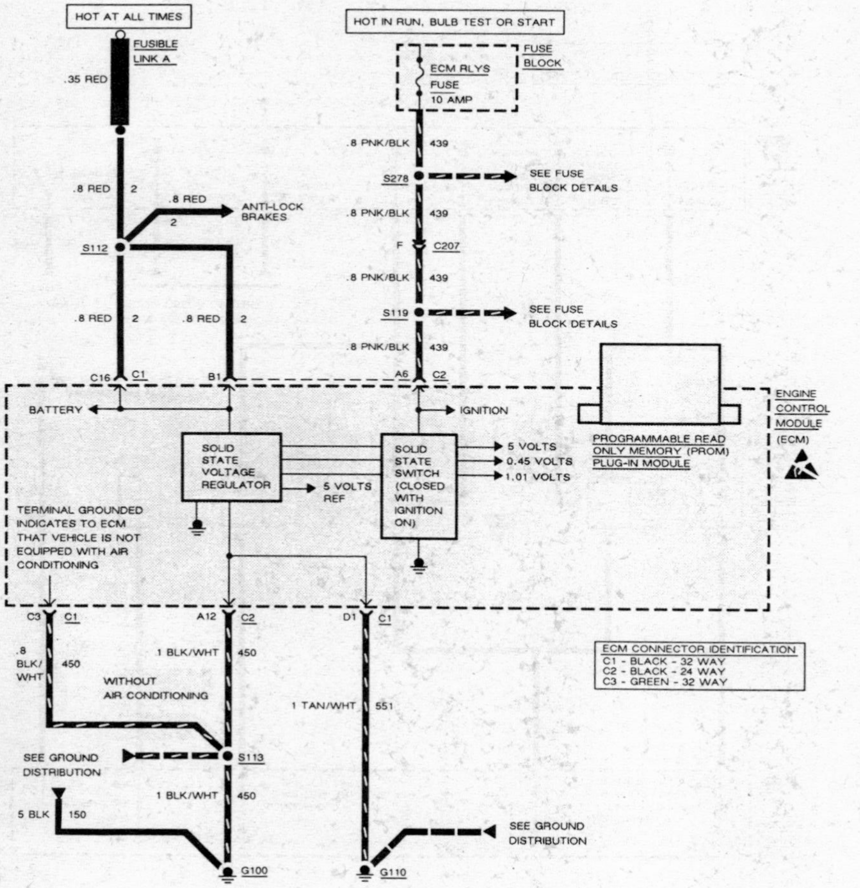

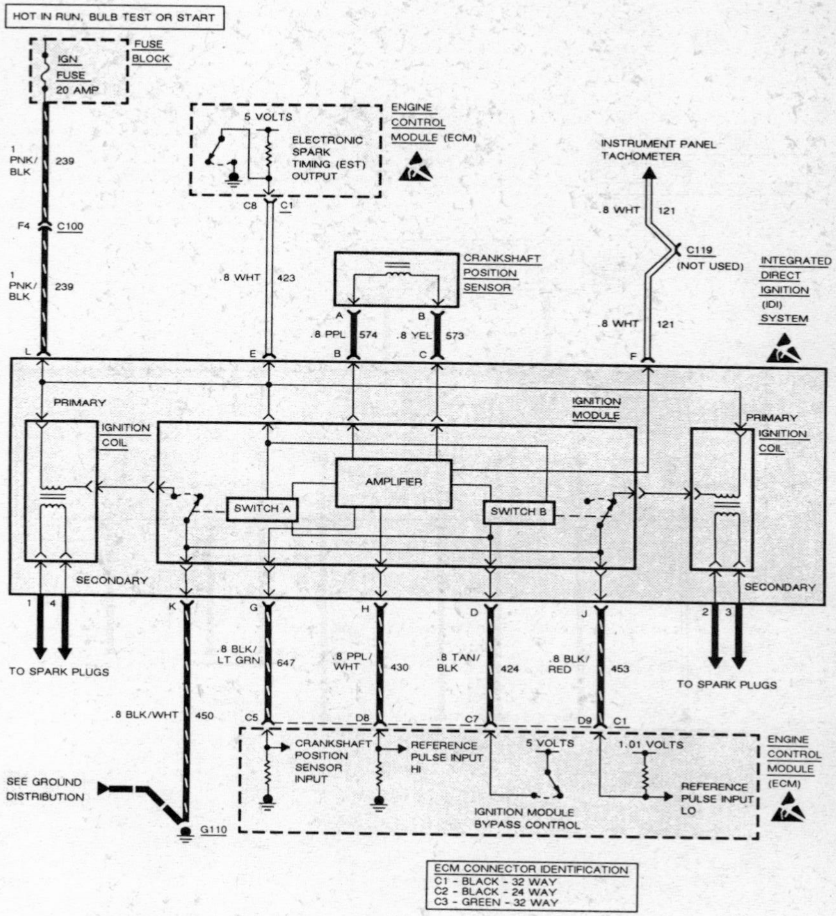

Grand Am — Ignition

Grand Am — Multi-port fuel injection — 2.3L and 2.3L HO engines — power and grounds

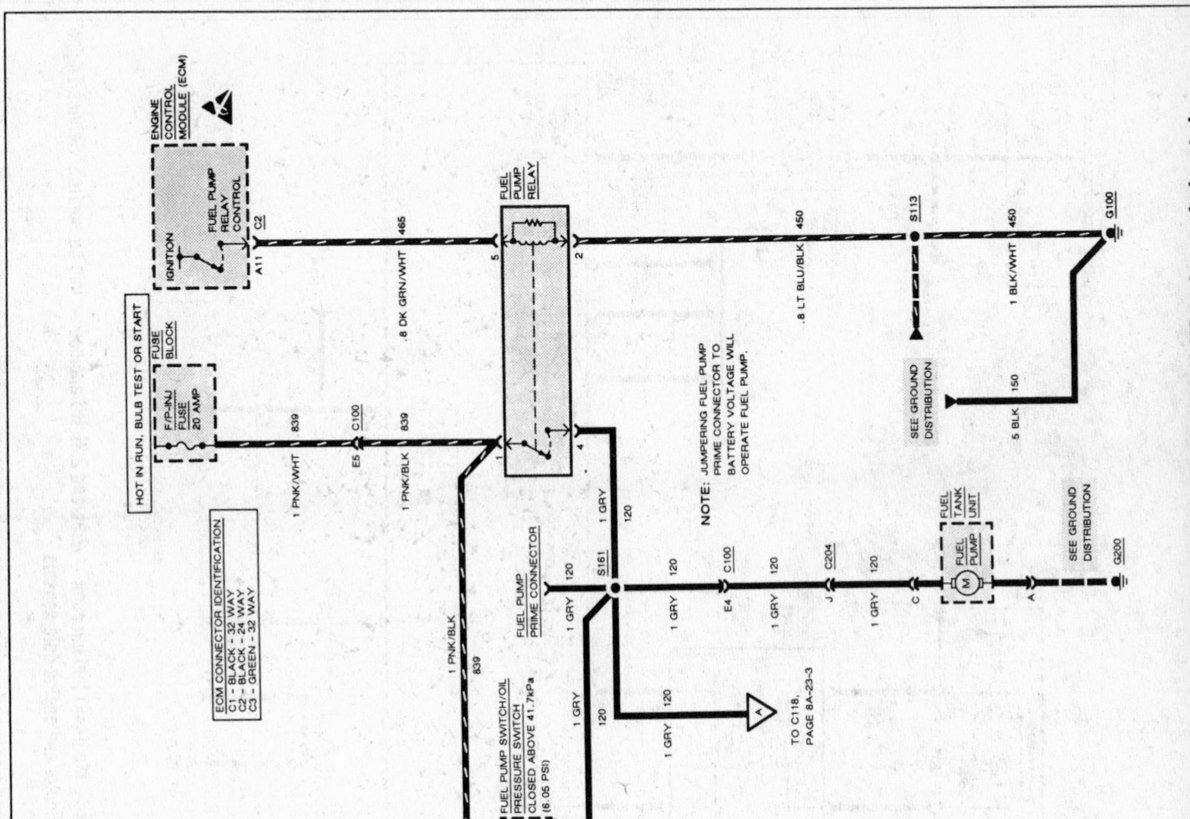
HOT IN RUN, BULB TEST OR START
F/P-INJ FUSE 20 AMP
FUSE BLOCK
ENGINE CONTROL MODULE (ECM)
IGNITION
FUEL PUMP RELAY CONTROL
ECM CONNECTOR IDENTIFICATION
C1 - BLACK - 32 WAY
C2 - BLACK - 24 WAY
C3 - GREEN - 32 WAY
FUEL PUMP RELAY
NOTE: JUMPERING FUEL PUMP PRIME CONNECTOR TO BATTERY VOLTAGE WILL OPERATE FUEL PUMP.
FUEL PUMP PRIME CONNECTOR
FUEL PUMP SWITCH/OIL PRESSURE SWITCH CLOSED ABOVE 41.7kPa (6.05 PSI)
TO C118, PAGE 8A-23-3
FUEL TANK UNIT
FUEL PUMP
SEE GROUND DISTRIBUTION
.8 DK GRN/WHT 465
.8 LT BLU/BLK 450
1 BLK/WHT 450
5 BLK 150
1 PNK/WHT 839
1 PNK/BLK 839
1 GRY 120
S161
S113
G100
G200
C100
C204

Grand Am — Multi-port fuel injection — 2.3L and 2.3L HO engines — fuel control

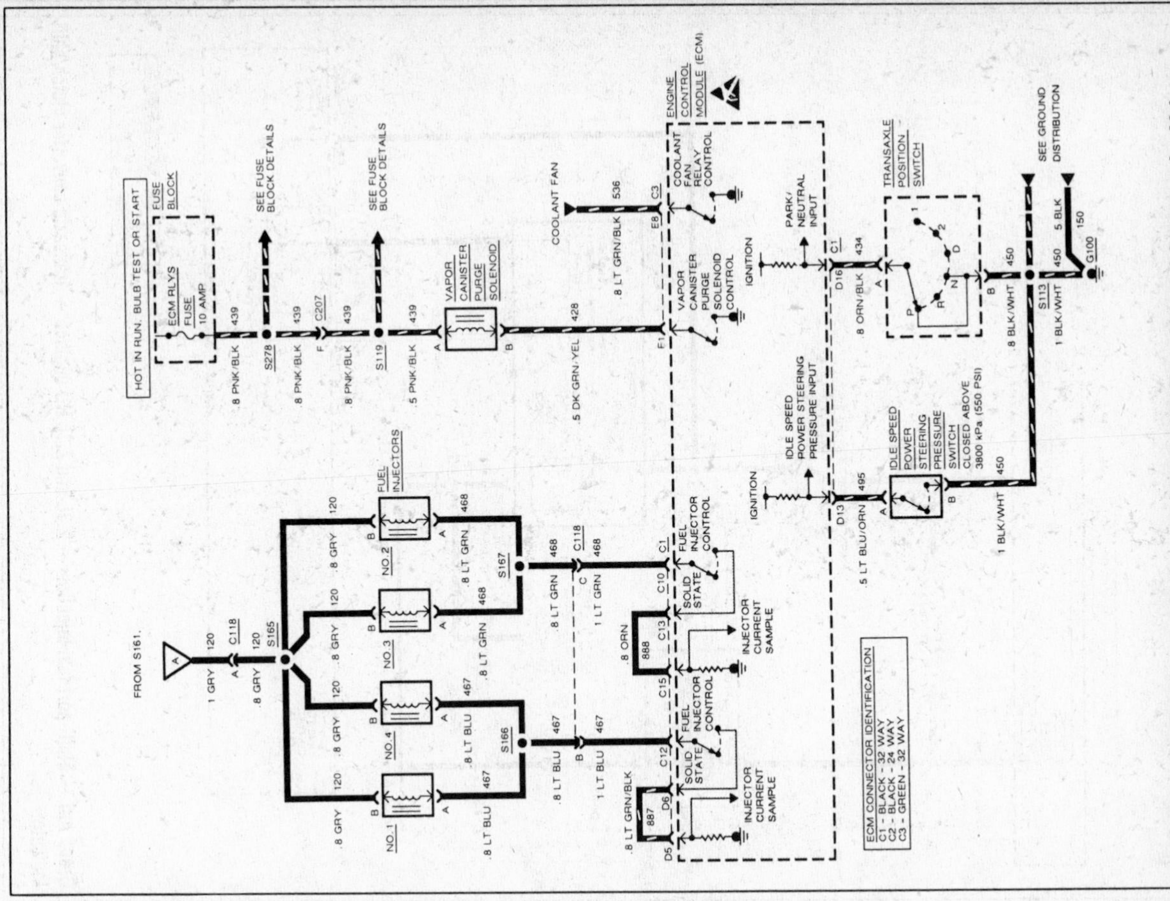
HOT IN RUN, BULB TEST OR START
ECM RLYS FUSE 10 AMP
FUSE BLOCK
SEE FUSE BLOCK DETAILS
FROM S161
FUEL INJECTORS
NO.1
NO.2
NO.3
NO.4
VAPOR CANISTER PURGE SOLENOID
COOLANT FAN
ENGINE CONTROL MODULE (ECM)
SOLID STATE
FUEL INJECTOR CONTROL
INJECTOR CURRENT SAMPLE
VAPOR CANISTER PURGE SOLENOID CONTROL
COOLANT FAN RELAY CONTROL
IGNITION
PARK/NEUTRAL INPUT
IDLE SPEED POWER STEERING PRESSURE INPUT
IDLE SPEED POWER STEERING PRESSURE SWITCH CLOSED ABOVE 3800 kPa (550 PSI)
TRANSAXLE POSITION SWITCH
SEE GROUND DISTRIBUTION
ECM CONNECTOR IDENTIFICATION
C1 - BLACK - 32 WAY
C2 - BLACK - 24 WAY
C3 - GREEN - 32 WAY
.8 PNK/BLK 439
.5 PNK/BLK 439
.5 DK GRN/YEL 428
.8 LT GRN/BLK 536
.8 LT GRN 468
.8 LT BLU 467
.8 GRY 120
.8 ORN 888
.8 LT GRN/BLK 887
.5 LT BLU/ORN 495
.8 ORN/BLK 434
.8 BLK/WHT 450
1 BLK/WHT 450
5 BLK 150
S278
S119
S165
S166
S167
S113
G100
C207
C118

Grand Am — Multi-port fuel injection — 2.3L and 2.3L HO engines — injectors and vehicle data sensors

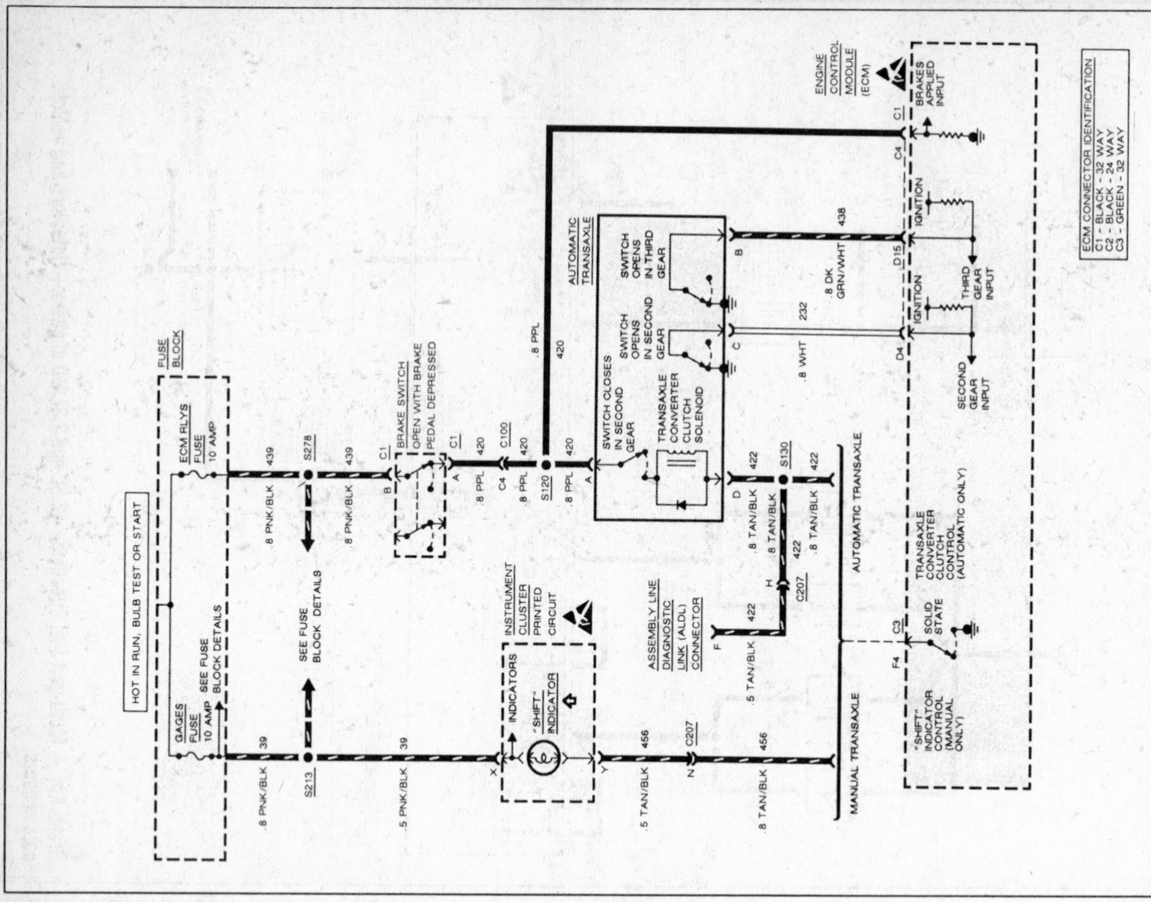

HOT IN RUN, BULB TEST OR START

FUSE BLOCK

GAGES FUSE 10 AMP

SEE FUSE BLOCK DETAILS

ENGINE CONTROL MODULE (ECM)

BATTERY

IDLE AIR VALVE CONTROL

E5 E6 C3

.5 LT GRN/WHT 443

.5 LT GRN/BLK 444

.8 PNK/BLK 39

S213

.5 PNK/BLK 39

IDLE AIR CONTROL VALVE

STEPPER MOTOR

INSTRUMENT CLUSTER PRINTED CIRCUIT

INDICATORS "SERVICE ENGINE SOON" INDICATOR

INSTRUMENT PANEL

VEHICLE SPEED SENSOR

.5 BRN/WHT 419

C207

.5 LT BLU/WHT 441

.5 LT BLU/BLK 442

.5 DK GRN 35

.5 YEL 400

.5 PPL 401

.5 DK GRN 389

E3 E4 F7 C3 B10 B9 B11 C2 E7 C3

BATTERY

IDLE AIR VALVE CONTROL

COOLANT "TEMP" INDICATOR CONTROL

VEHICLE SPEED SENSOR INPUT

HI LO

VEHICLE SPEED OUTPUT

4000 PULSES PER MILE

"SERVICE ENGINE SOON" INDICATOR CONTROL

5 VOLTS

SERIAL DATA IN

SERIAL DATA OUT

DIAGNOSTIC TEST

E12 C3

A8 C2

.8 WHT/BLK 451

.8 ORN 461

S277

.8 ORN 461

ANTI-LOCK BRAKES

C207

.5 WHT/BLK 451

.5 ORN 461

SEE GROUND DISTRIBUTION

G100

ASSEMBLY LINE DIAGNOSTIC LINK (ALDL) CONNECTOR

ECM CONNECTOR IDENTIFICATION
C1 - BLACK - 32 WAY
C2 - BLACK - 24 WAY
C3 - GREEN - 32 WAY

Grand Am — Multi-port fuel injection — 2.3L and 2.3L HO engines — idle air control, "Service Engine Soon" indicator and engine data sensors

HOT IN RUN, BULB TEST OR START

FUSE BLOCK

GAGES FUSE 10 AMP

SEE FUSE BLOCK DETAILS

ECM RLYS FUSE 10 AMP

.8 PNK/BLK 39

.8 PNK/BLK 439

S213

SEE FUSE BLOCK DETAILS

S278

.8 PNK/BLK 439

.5 PNK/BLK 39

C1

BRAKE SWITCH OPEN WITH BRAKE PEDAL DEPRESSED

C1

.8 PPL 420

C100

.8 PPL 420

S120

.8 PPL 420

INDICATORS "SHIFT" INDICATOR

INSTRUMENT CLUSTER PRINTED CIRCUIT

AUTOMATIC TRANSAXLE

SWITCH CLOSES IN SECOND GEAR

SWITCH OPENS IN SECOND GEAR

SWITCH OPENS IN THIRD GEAR

TRANSAXLE CONVERTER CLUTCH SOLENOID

.5 TAN/BLK 456

C207

ASSEMBLY LINE DIAGNOSTIC LINK (ALDL) CONNECTOR

.5 TAN/BLK 422

.8 TAN/BLK 422

.8 TAN/BLK

C207 422

S130

.8 TAN/BLK 422

.8 TAN/BLK 456

.8 WHT 232

.8 DK GRN/WHT 438

MANUAL TRANSAXLE

AUTOMATIC TRANSAXLE

ENGINE CONTROL MODULE (ECM)

F4 C3

D4 D15 C4 C1

"SHIFT" INDICATOR CONTROL (MANUAL ONLY)

SOLID STATE

TRANSAXLE CONVERTER CLUTCH CONTROL (AUTOMATIC ONLY)

IGNITION

IGNITION

SECOND GEAR INPUT

THIRD GEAR INPUT

BRAKES APPLIED INPUT

ECM CONNECTOR IDENTIFICATION
C1 - BLACK - 32 WAY
C2 - BLACK - 24 WAY
C3 - GREEN - 32 WAY

Grand Am — Multi-port fuel injection — 2.3L and 2.3L HO engines — transaxle converter clutch/shift indicator

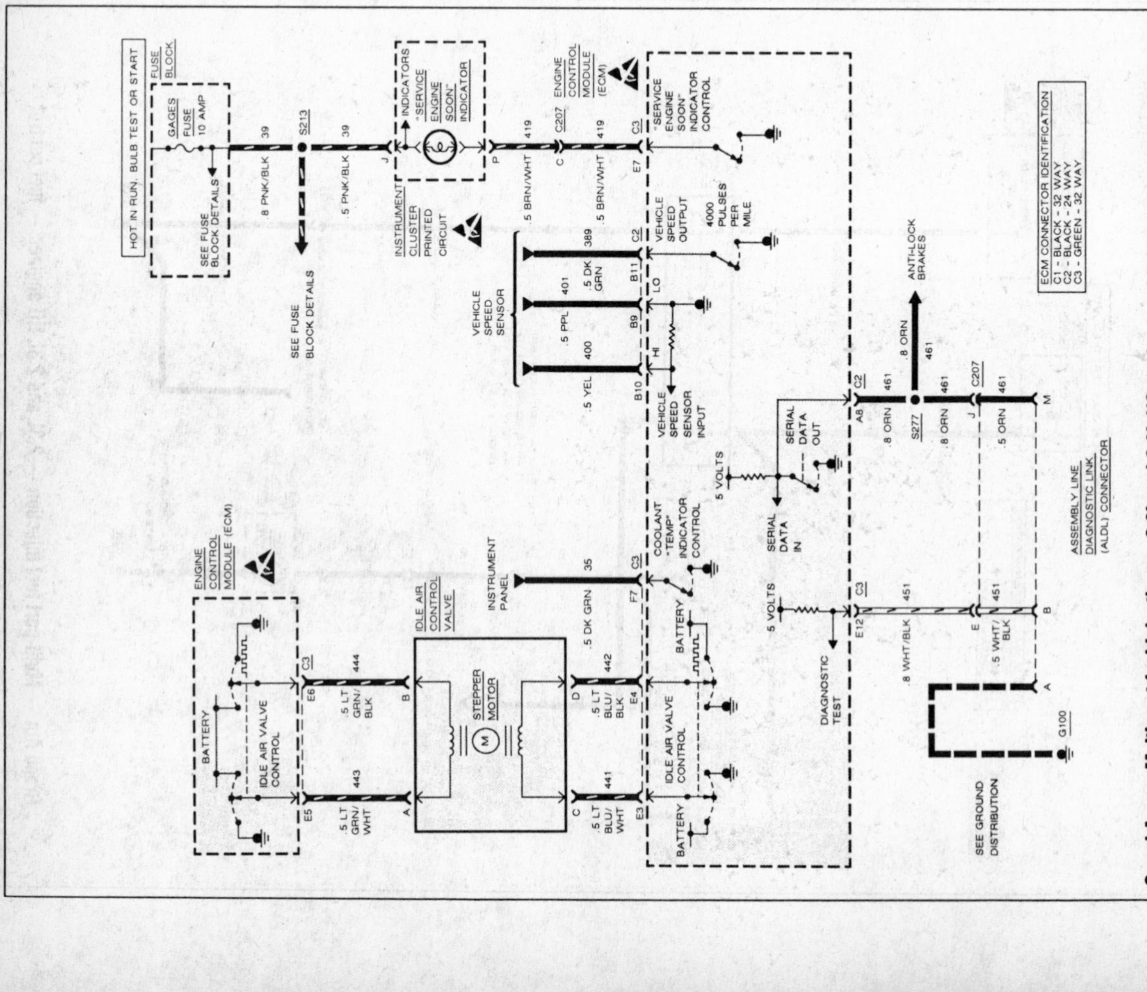

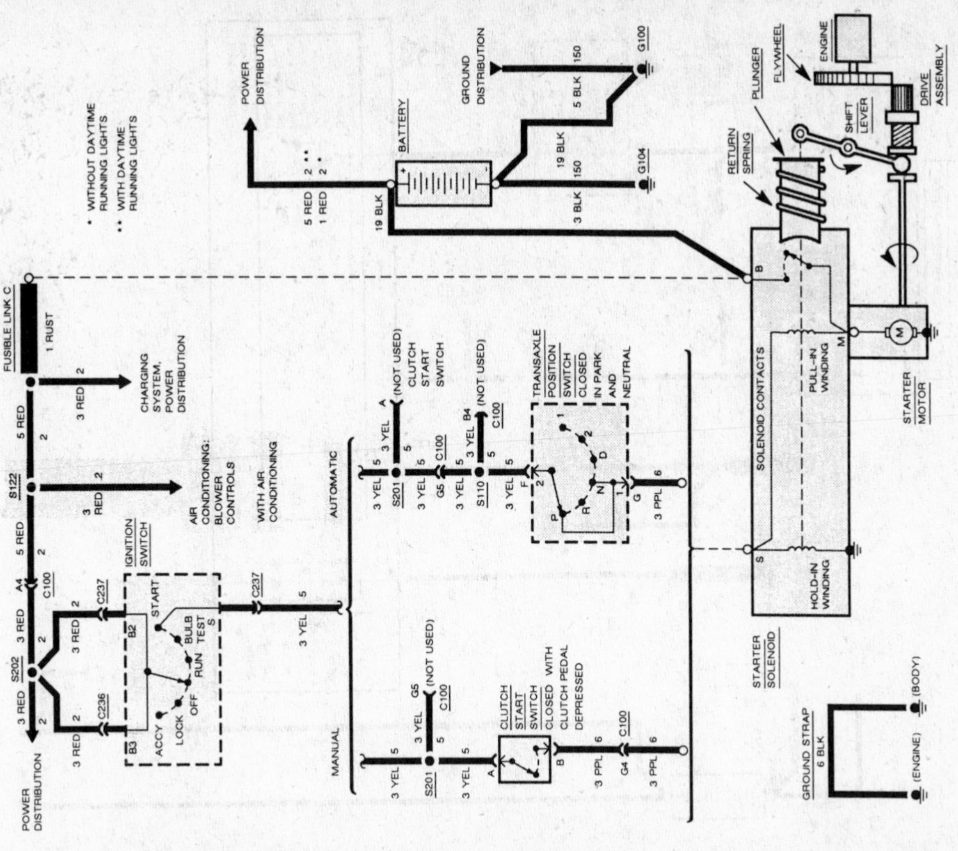

ECM CONNECTOR IDENTIFICATION
C1 - BLACK - 32 WAY
C2 - BLACK - 24 WAY
C3 - GREEN - 32 WAY

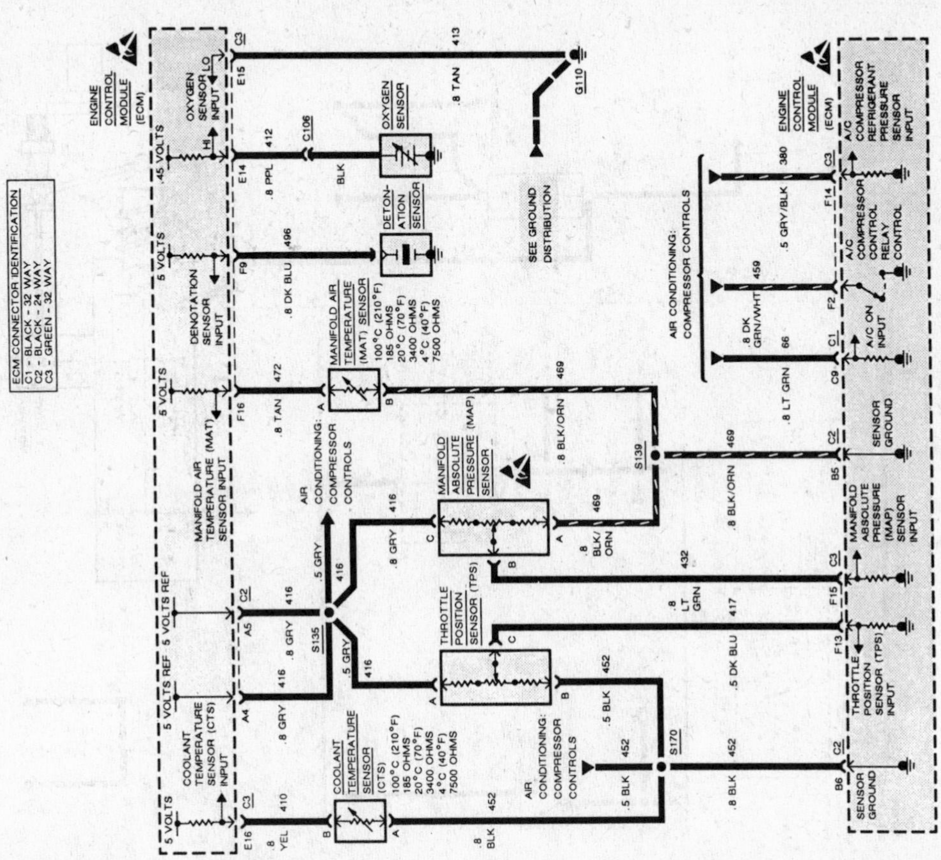

Grand Am — Multi-port fuel injection — 2.3L and 2.3L HO engines — engine data sensors

* WITHOUT DAYTIME RUNNING LIGHTS
** WITH DAYTIME RUNNING LIGHTS

Grand Am — Starter and charging system — starter — 2.5L engine

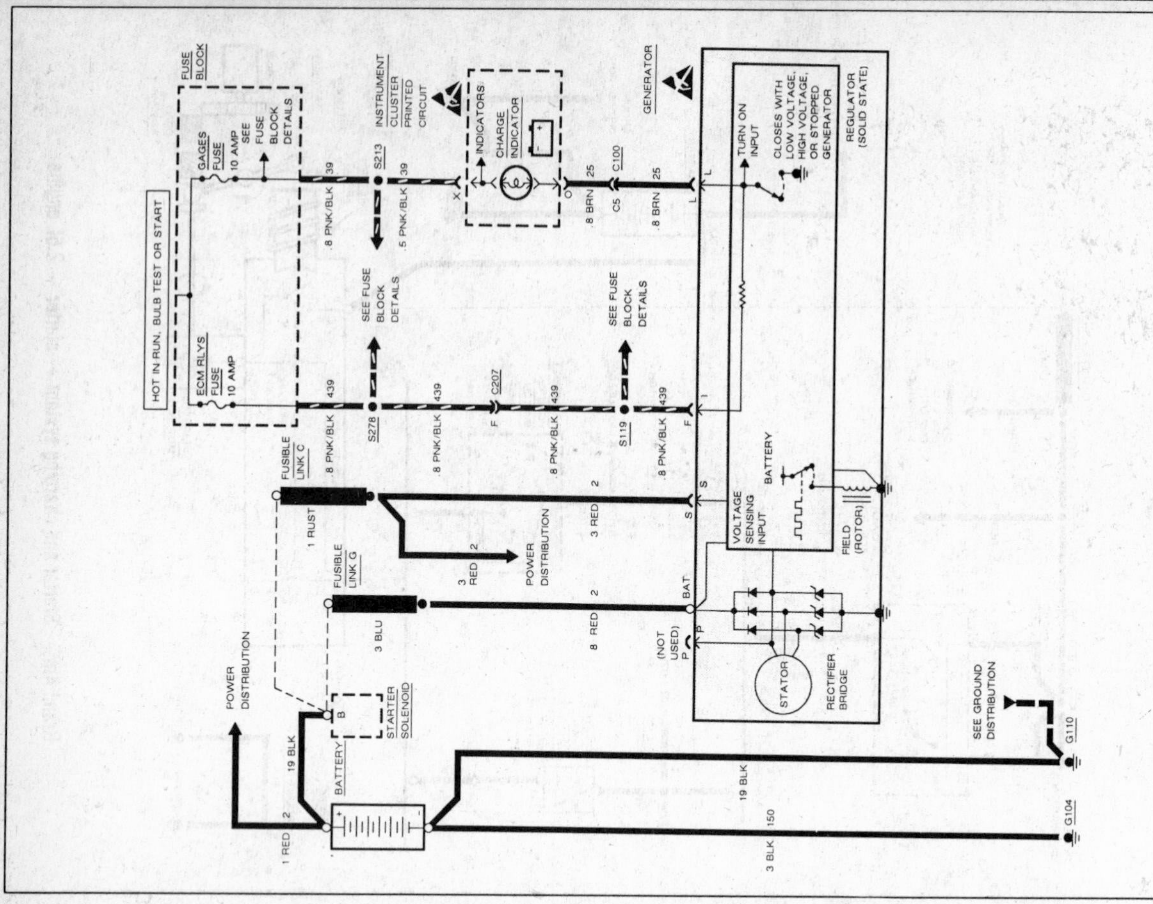

Grand Am — Starter and charging system — starter — 2.3L and 2.3L HO engines

Grand Am — Starter and charging system — charging — 2.3L and 2.3L HO engines

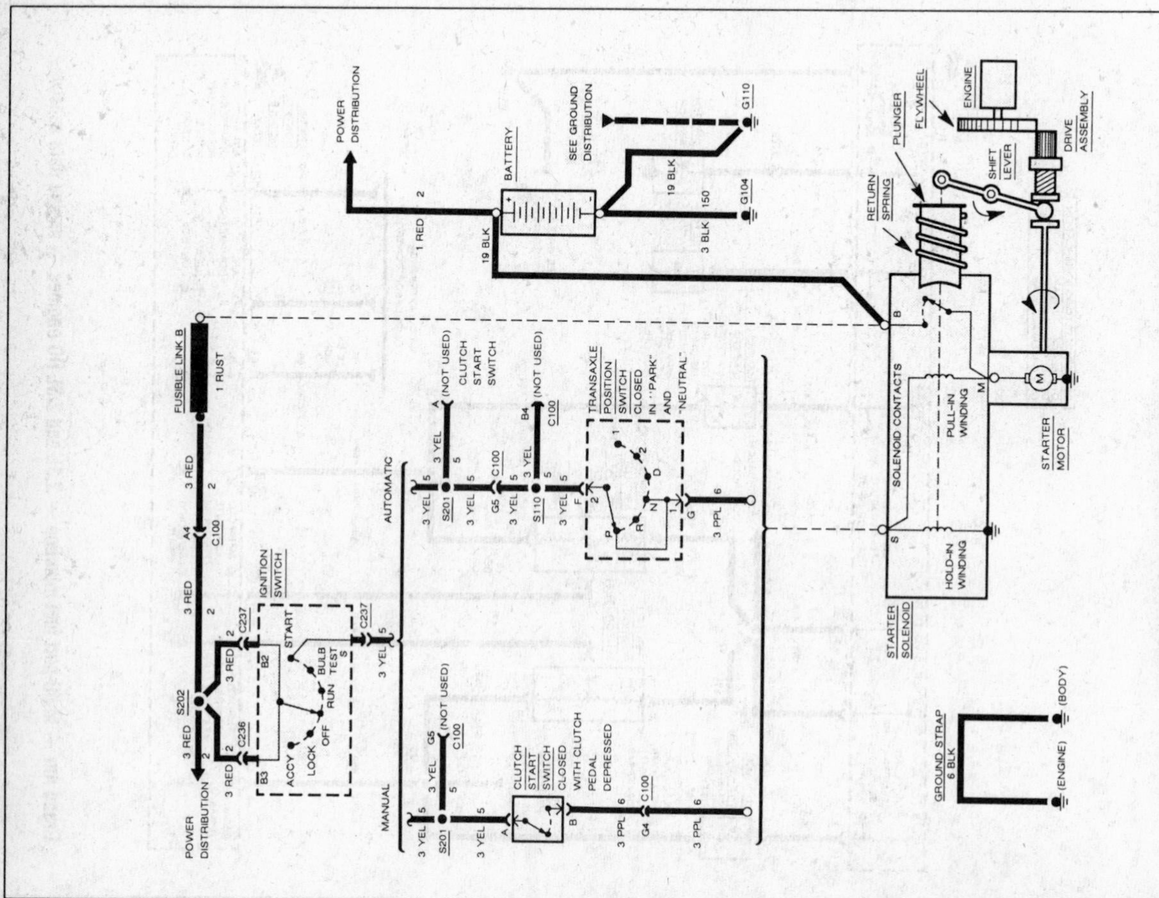

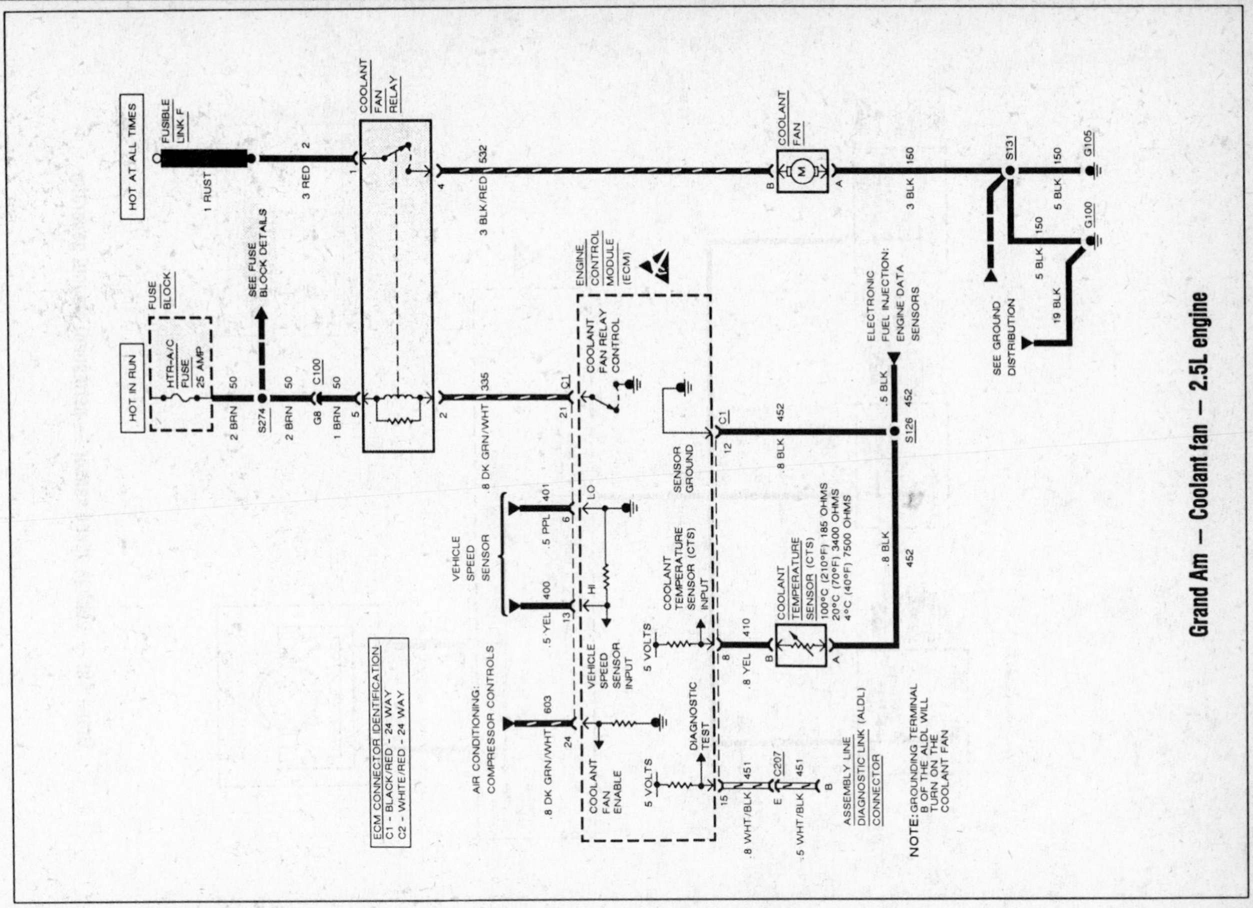

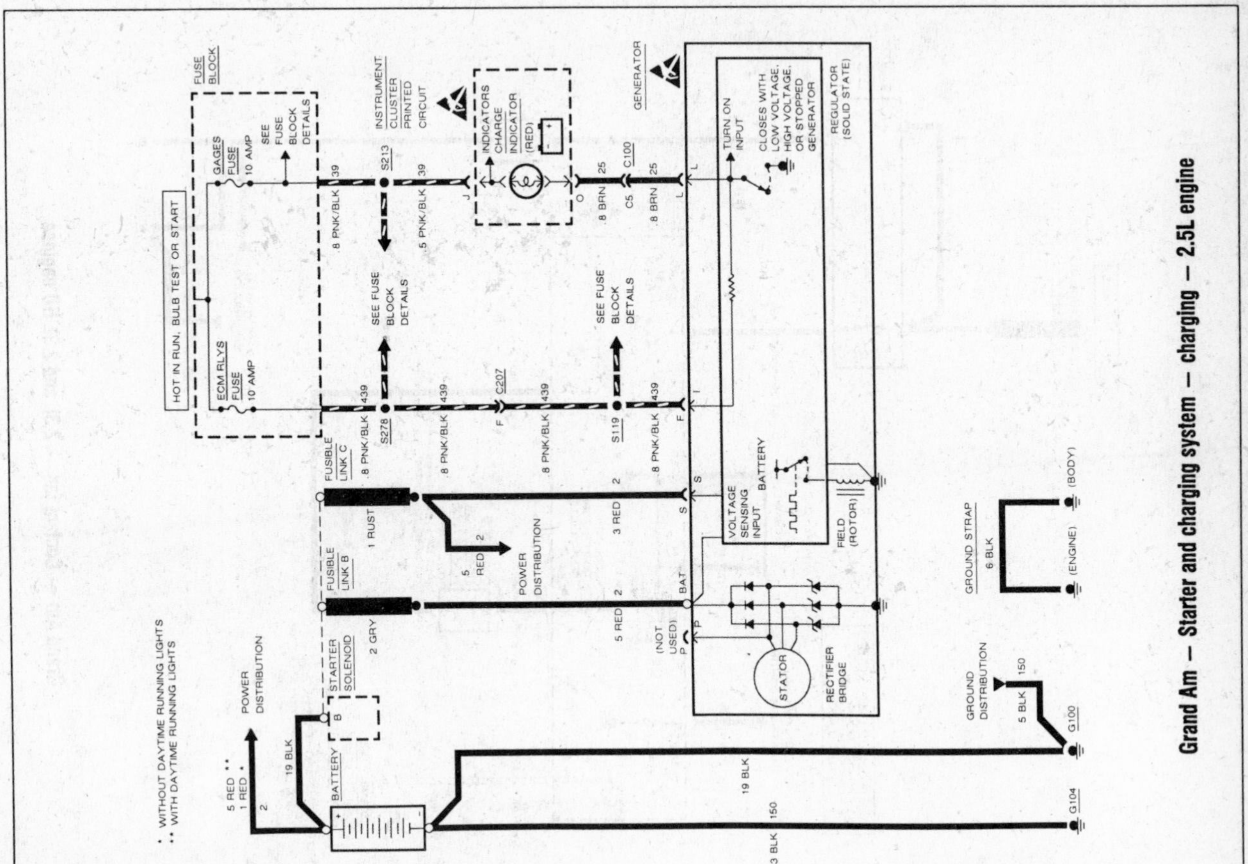

Grand Am — Starter and charging system — charging — 2.5L engine

NOTE: GROUNDING TERMINAL B OF THE ALDL WILL TURN ON THE COOLANT FAN

Grand Am — Coolant fan — 2.5L engine

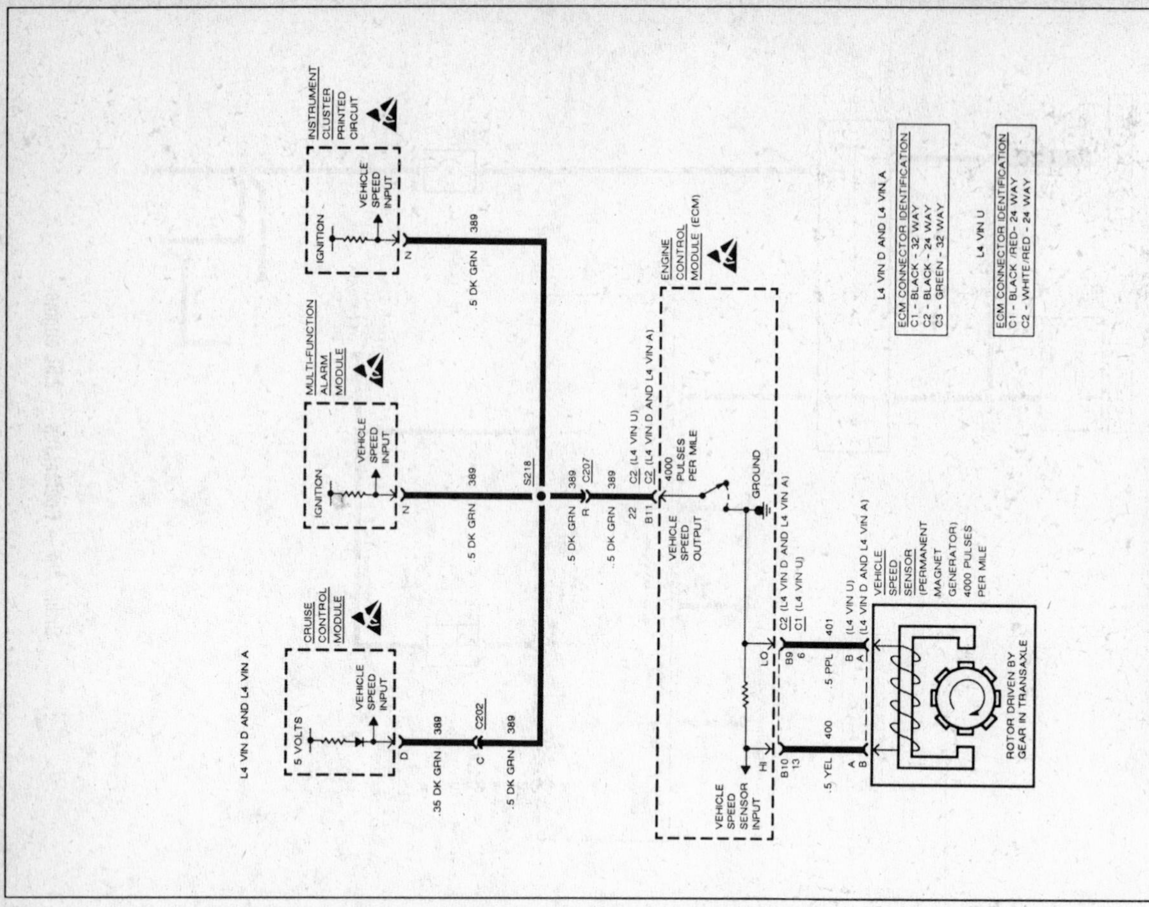

HOT AT ALL TIMES
FUSIBLE LINK F
1 RUST
3 RED 2
3 RED 2
COOLANT FAN RELAY
ECM CONNECTOR IDENTIFICATION
C1 - BLACK - 32 WAY
C2 - BLACK - 24 WAY
C3 - GREEN - 32 WAY
AIR CONDITIONING: COMPRESSOR CONTROLS
VEHICLE SPEED SENSOR
.8 LT GRN/BLK 536
3 BLK/RED 532
.8 LT GRN 66
.5 YEL 400
.5 PPL 401
C9 C1
B10
B9 C2
E8 C3
A/C ON INPUT
VEHICLE SPEED SENSOR INPUT
HI
LO
COOLANT FAN RELAY CONTROL
ENGINE CONTROL MODULE (ECM)
5 VOLTS
5 VOLTS
SENSOR GROUND
COOLANT TEMPERATURE SENSOR (CTS) INPUT
DIAGNOSTIC TEST
E12
E16 C3
B6 C2
.8 WHT/BLK 451
.8 YEL 410
.8 BLK 452
E C207
.5 WHT/BLK 451
COOLANT TEMPERATURE SENSOR (CTS)
100°C (210°F) 185 OHMS
20°C (70°F) 3400 OHMS
4°C (40°F) 7500 OHMS
COOLANT FAN
S170
SEE MULTI-PORT FUEL INJECTION: ENGINE DATA SENSORS
3 BLK 150
ASSEMBLY LINE DIAGNOSTIC LINK (ALDL) CONNECTOR
NOTE: GROUNDING TERMINAL B OF THE ALDL WILL TURN ON THE COOLANT FAN
.8 BLK
452
SEE GROUND DISTRIBUTION
S140
1 BLK/WHT 450
5 BLK 150
3 BLK 150
G100
G109

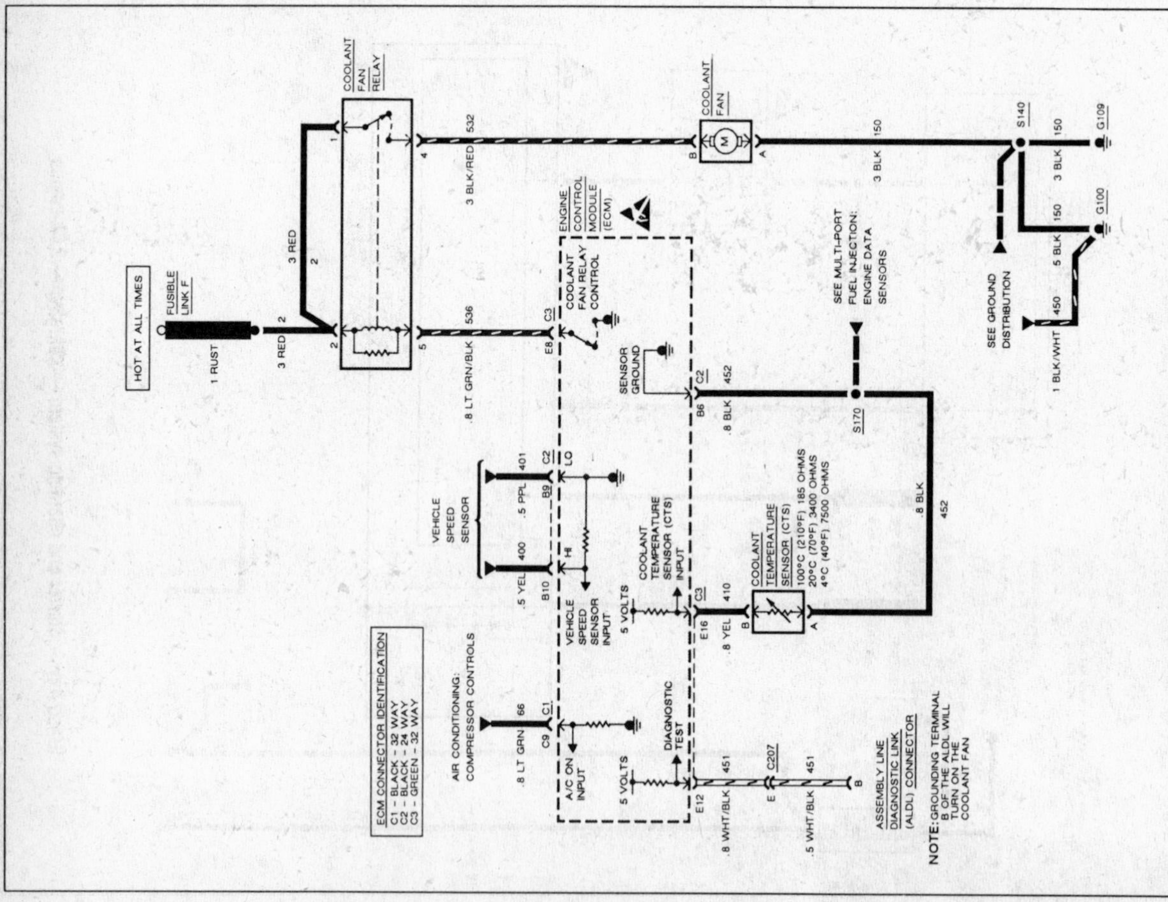

Grand Am — Coolant fan — 2.3L and 2.3L HO engines

L4 VIN D AND L4 VIN A
5 VOLTS
VEHICLE SPEED INPUT
CRUISE CONTROL MODULE
IGNITION
VEHICLE SPEED INPUT
MULTI-FUNCTION ALARM MODULE
IGNITION
VEHICLE SPEED INPUT
INSTRUMENT CLUSTER PRINTED CIRCUIT
D
N
N
.35 DK GRN 389
C C202
.5 DK GRN 389
.5 DK GRN 389
.5 DK GRN 389
S218
.5 DK GRN 389
R C207
.5 DK GRN 389
22 C2 (L4 VIN U)
B11 C2 (L4 VIN D AND L4 VIN A)
VEHICLE SPEED OUTPUT
4000 PULSES PER MILE
ENGINE CONTROL MODULE (ECM)
VEHICLE SPEED SENSOR INPUT
GROUND
HI
LO
B10 13
B9 6
C2 (L4 VIN D AND L4 VIN A)
C1 (L4 VIN U)
.5 YEL 400
.5 PPL 401
A B
B A
(L4 VIN U)
(L4 VIN D AND L4 VIN A)
VEHICLE SPEED SENSOR (PERMANENT MAGNET GENERATOR) 4000 PULSES PER MILE
ROTOR DRIVEN BY GEAR IN TRANSAXLE

L4 VIN D AND L4 VIN A
ECM CONNECTOR IDENTIFICATION
C1 - BLACK - 32 WAY
C2 - BLACK - 24 WAY
C3 - GREEN - 32 WAY

L4 VIN U
ECM CONNECTOR IDENTIFICATION
C1 - BLACK /RED- 24 WAY
C2 - WHITE/RED - 24 WAY

Grand Am — Vehicle speed sensor — permanent magnet generator

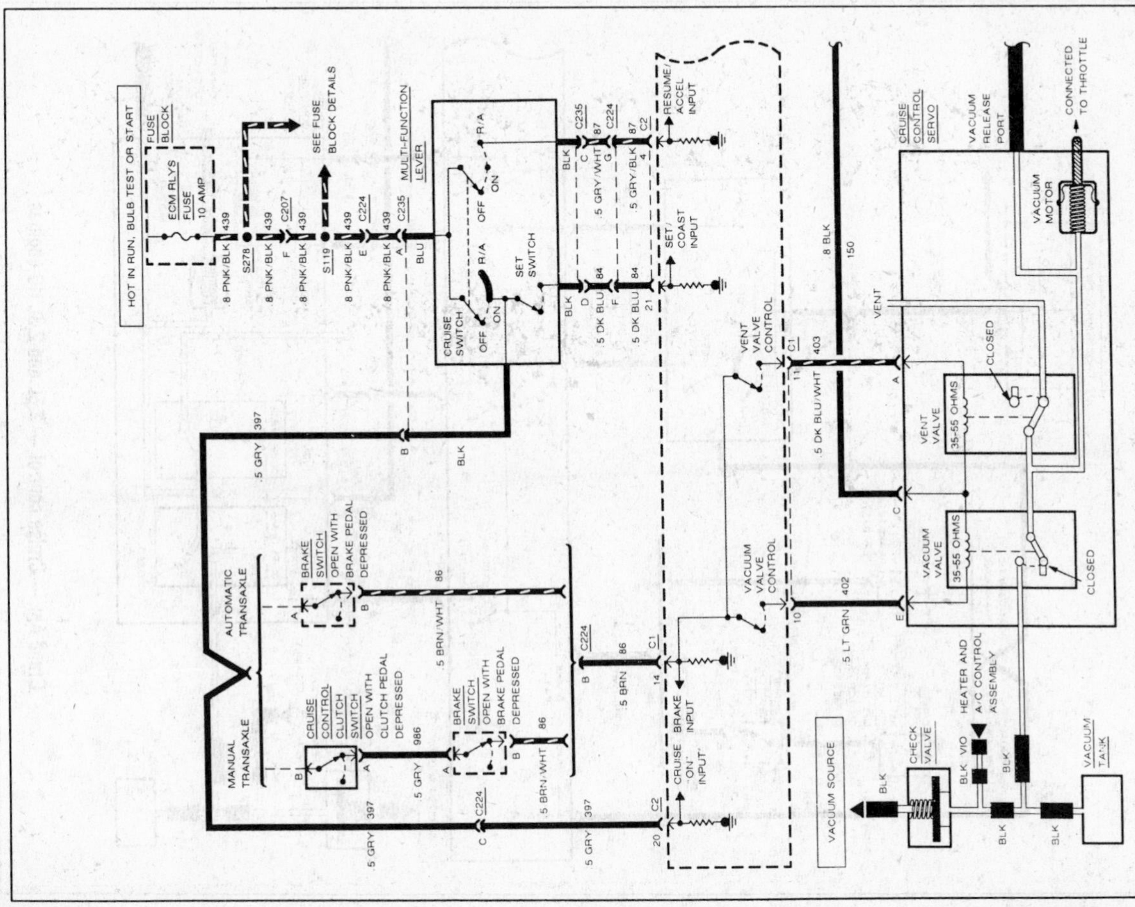

Grand Am — Cruise control — 2.5L engine

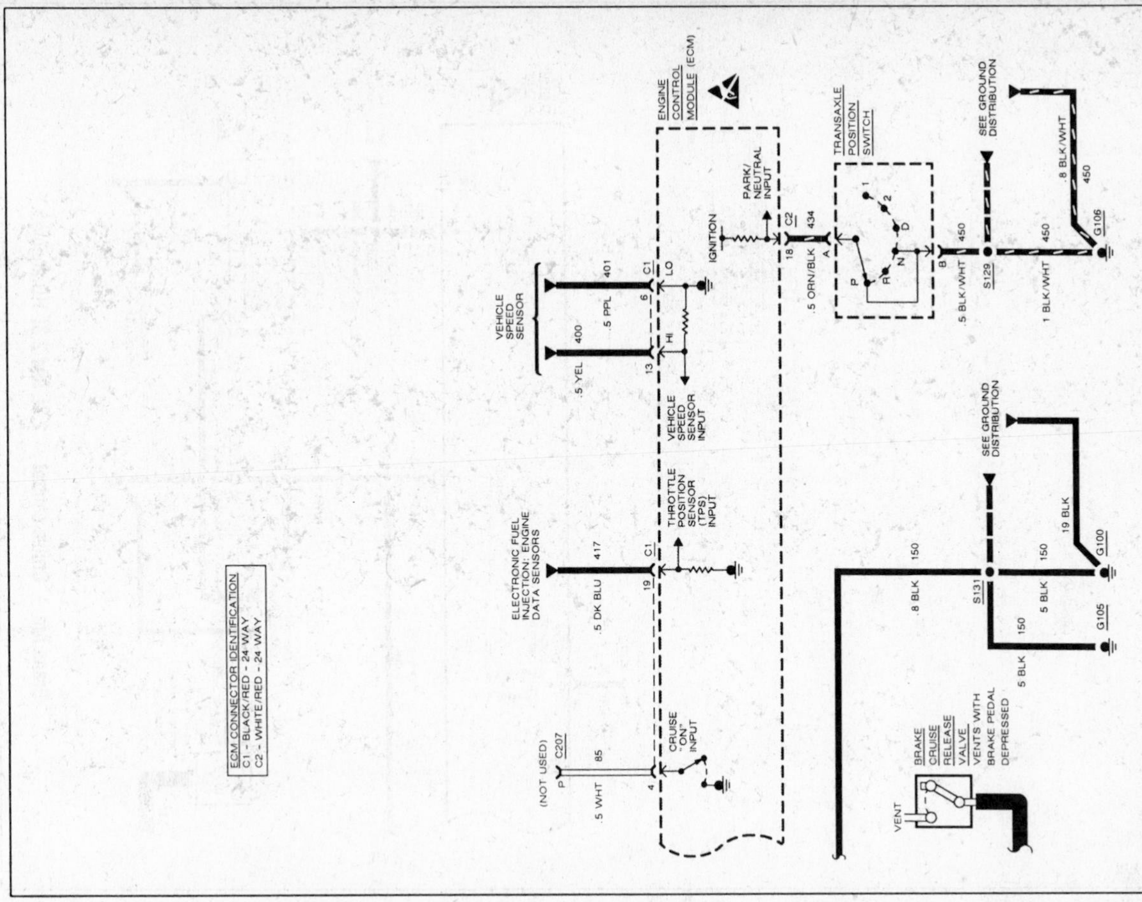

Grand Am — Cruise control — 2.5L engine

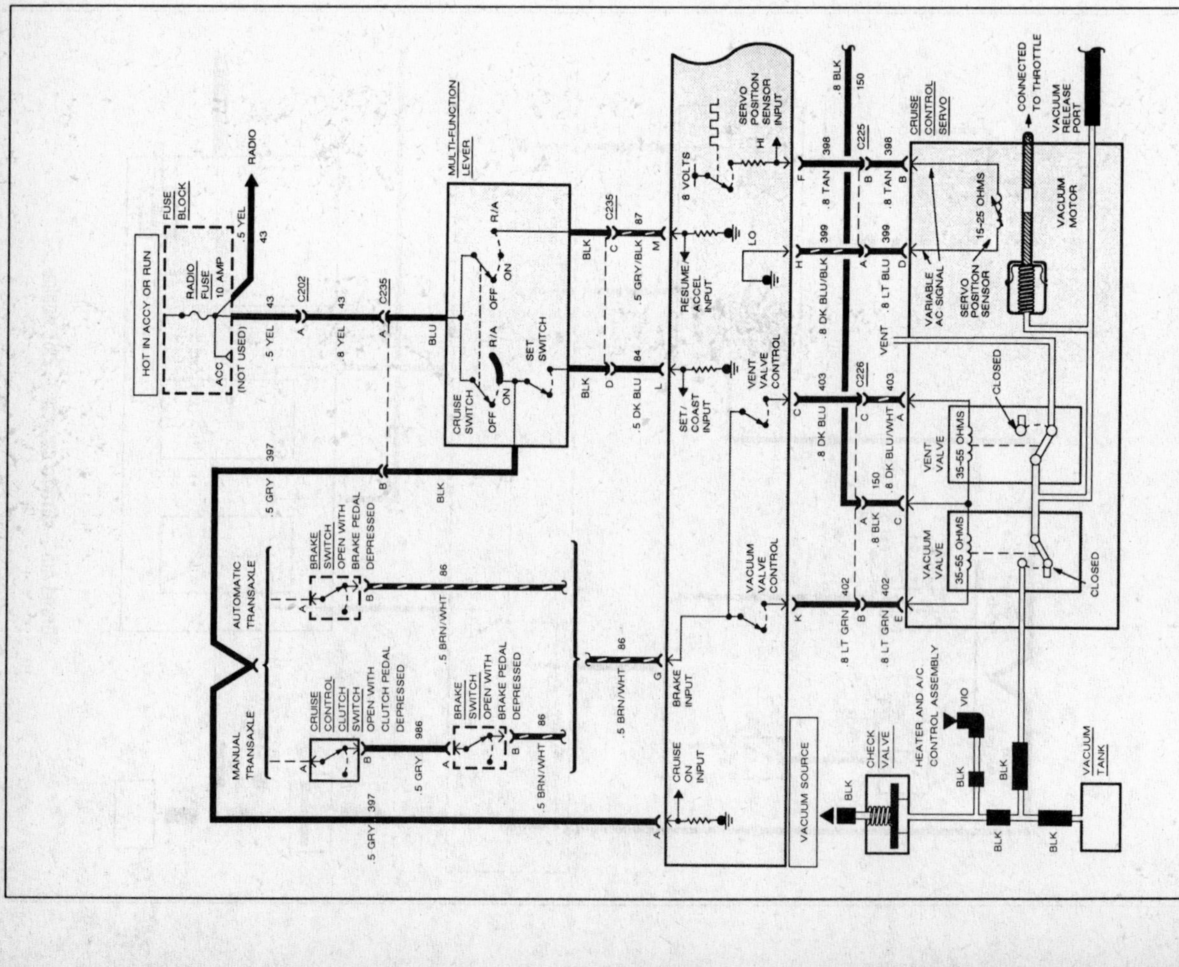

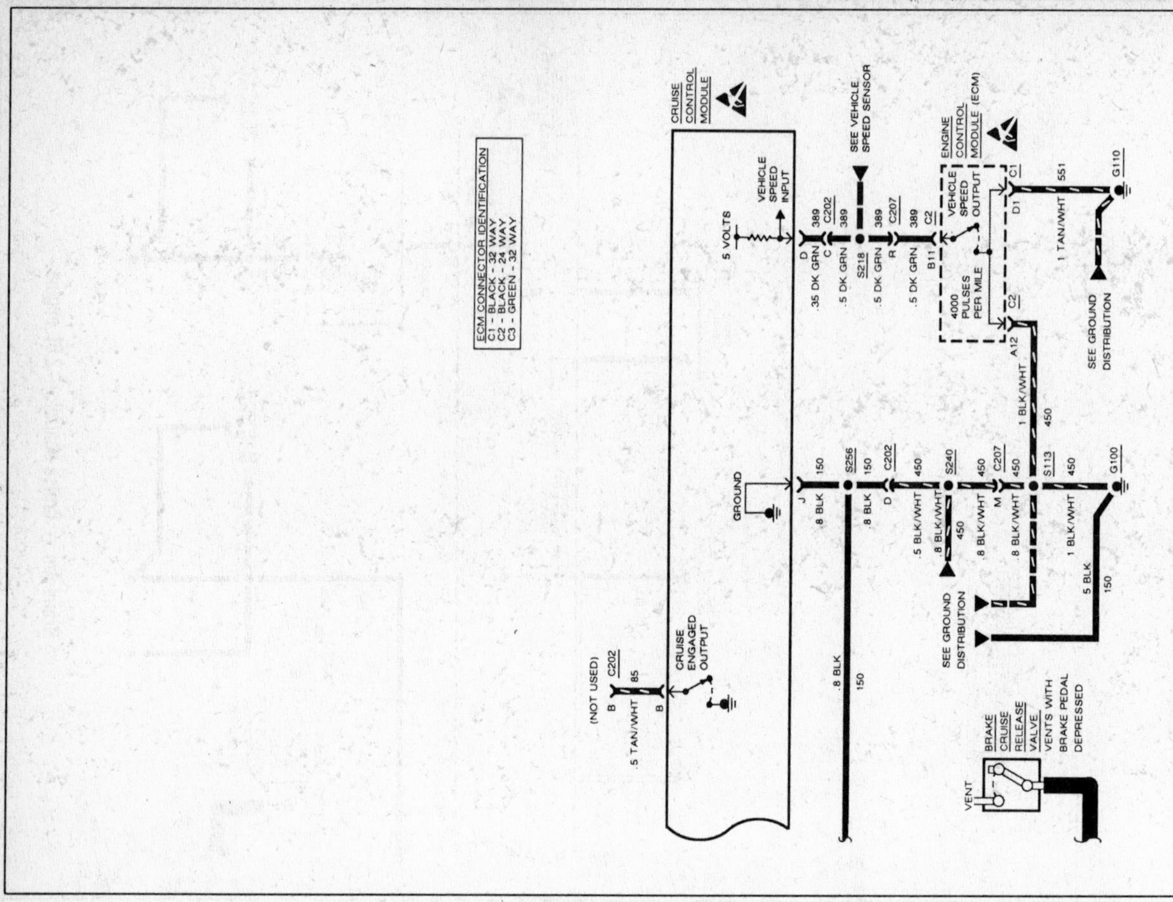

ECM CONNECTOR IDENTIFICATION
C1 - BLACK - 32 WAY
C2 - BLACK - 24 WAY
C3 - GREEN - 32 WAY

Grand Am — Cruise control — 2.3L and 2.3L HO engines

Grand Am — Cruise control — 2.3L and 2.3L HO engines

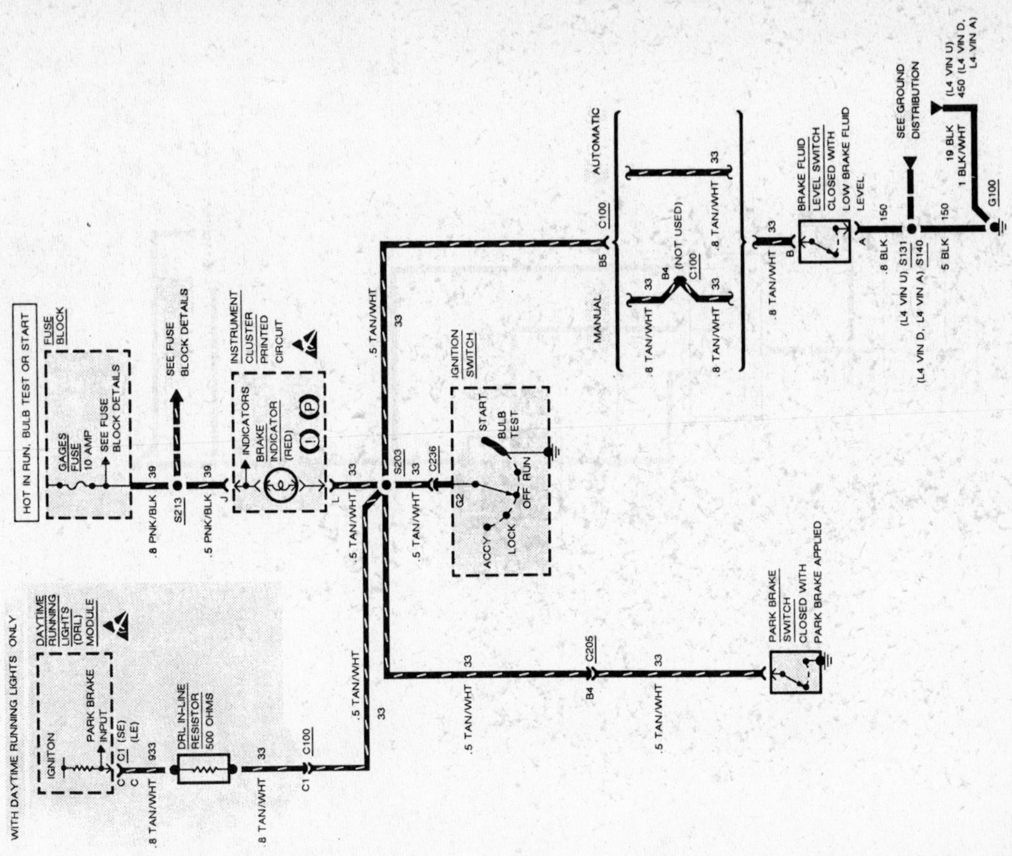

Grand Am — Brake warning system — without anti-lock brakes

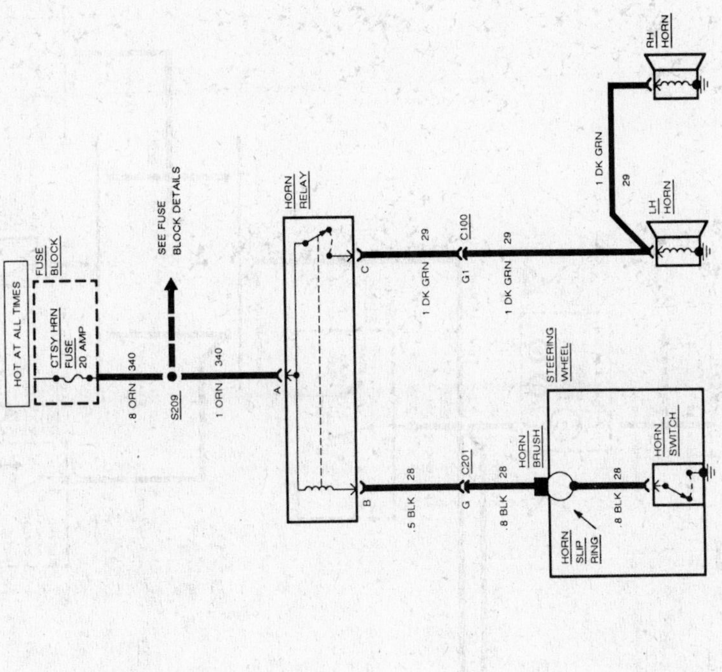

Grand Am — Horns

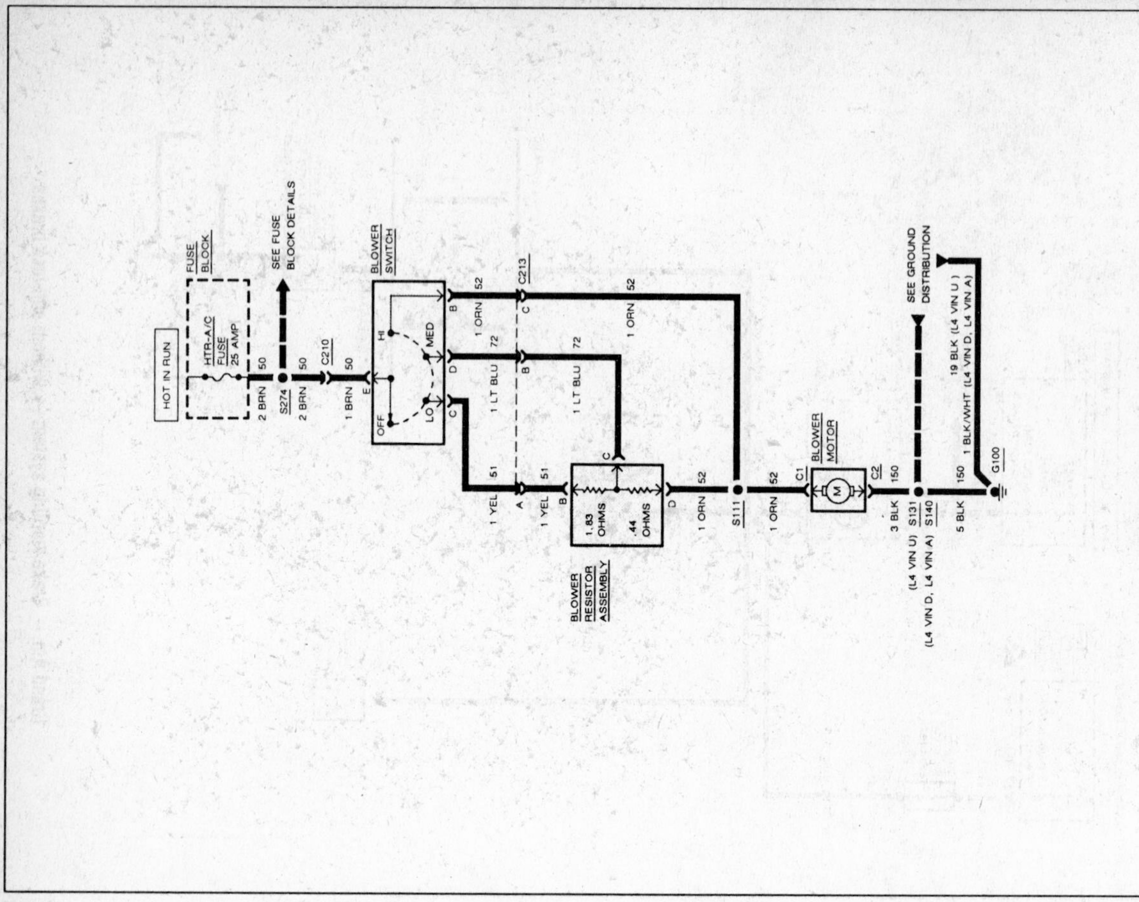

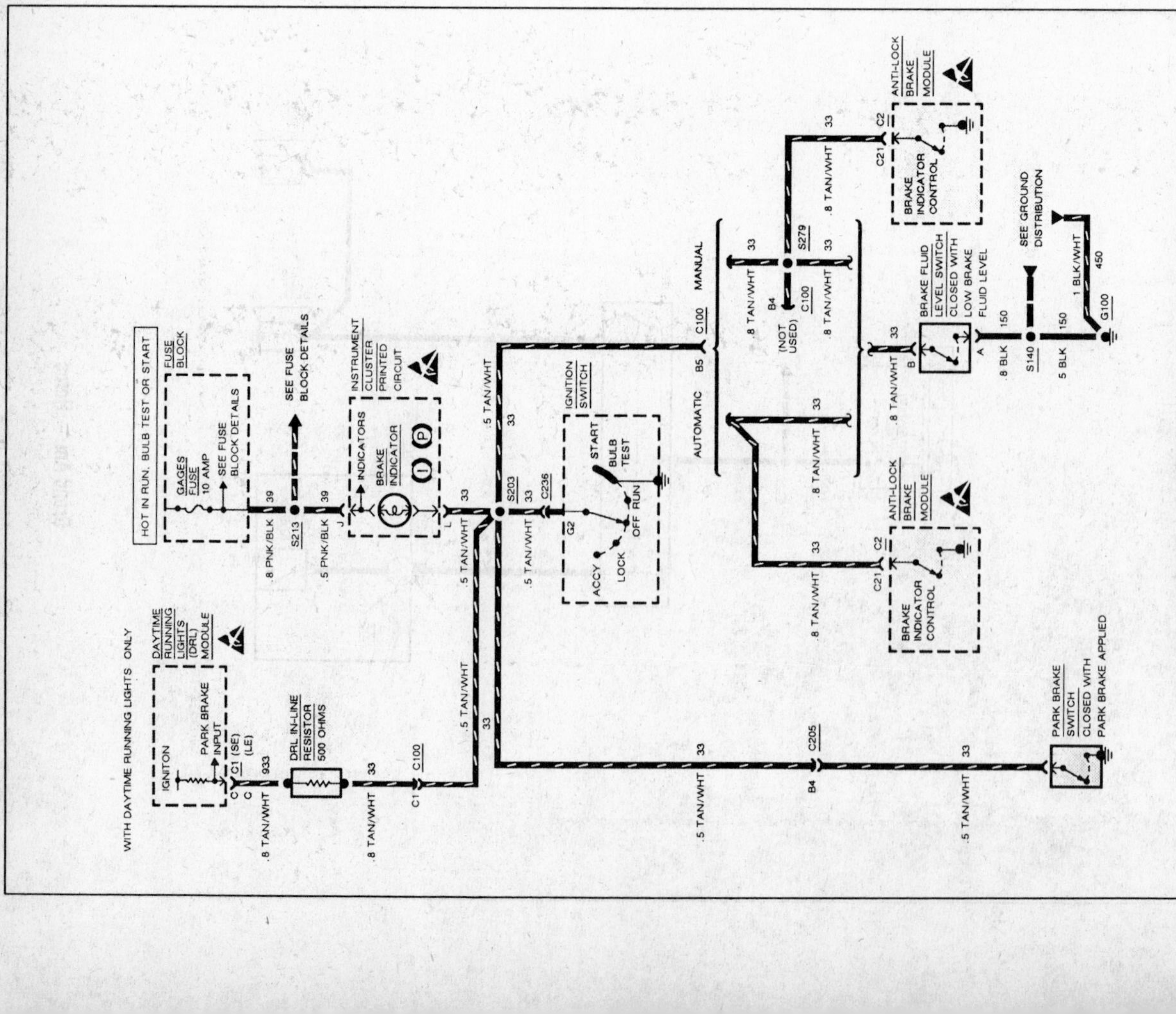

Grand Am — Brake warning system — with anti-lock brakes

Grand Am — Heater

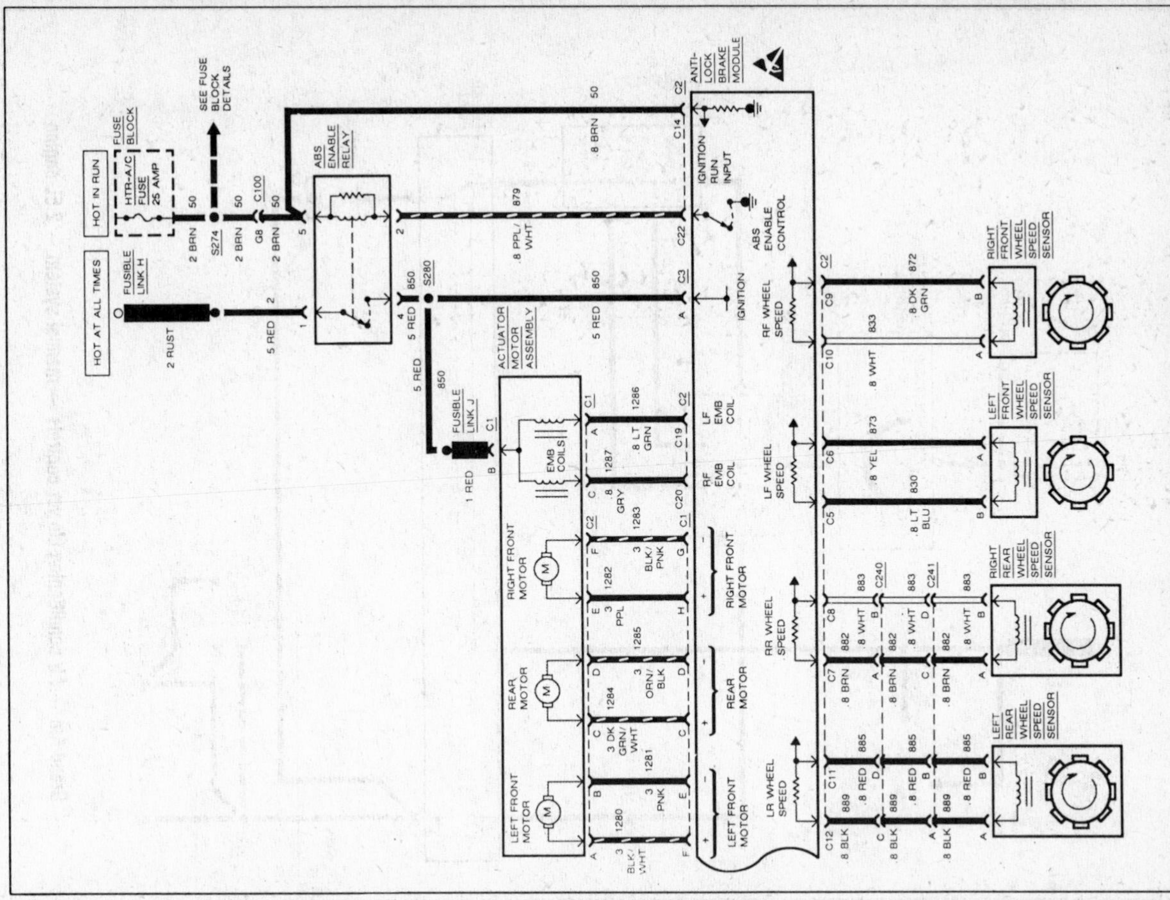

Grand Am — Anti-lock brakes

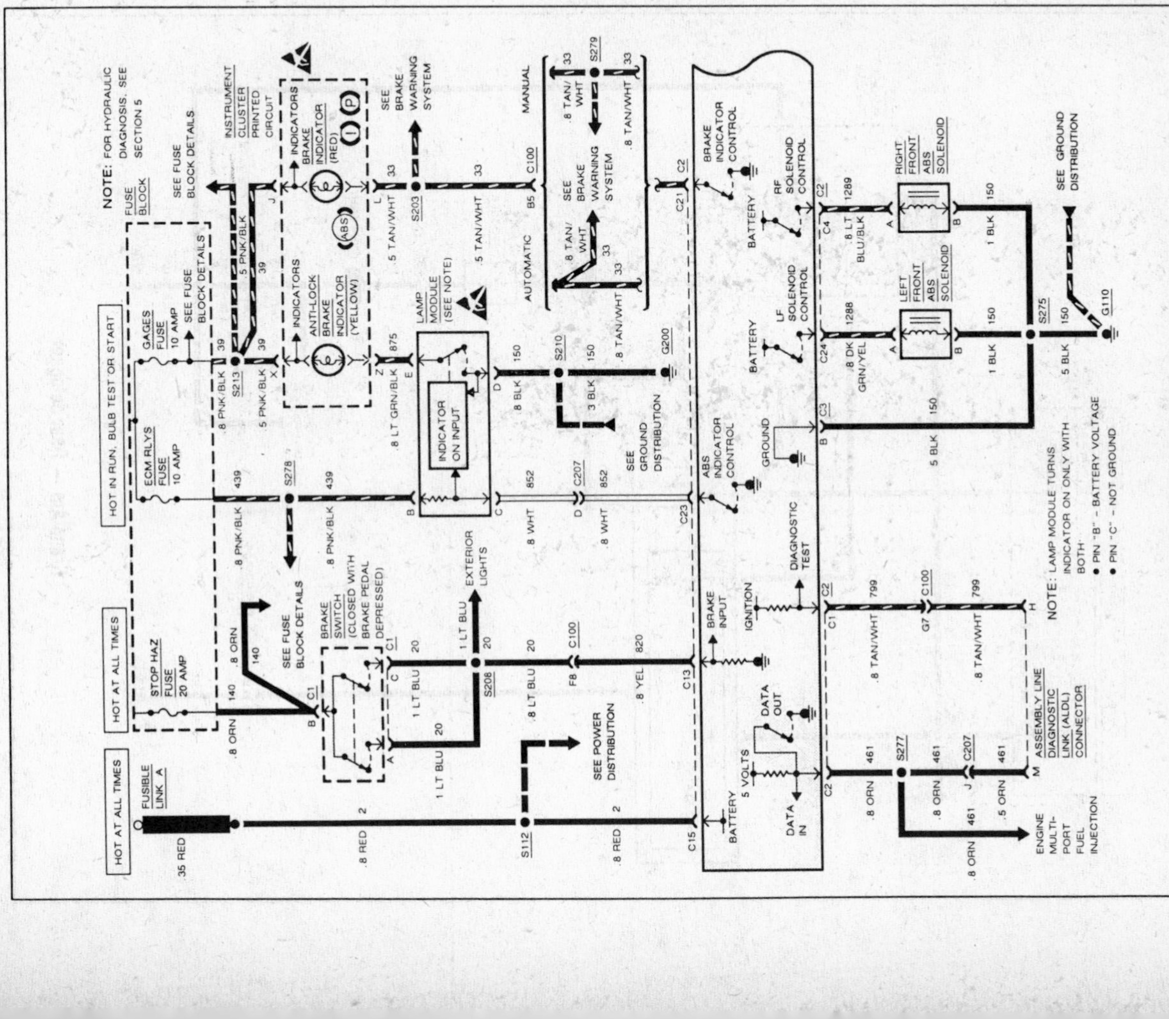

Grand Am — Anti-lock brakes

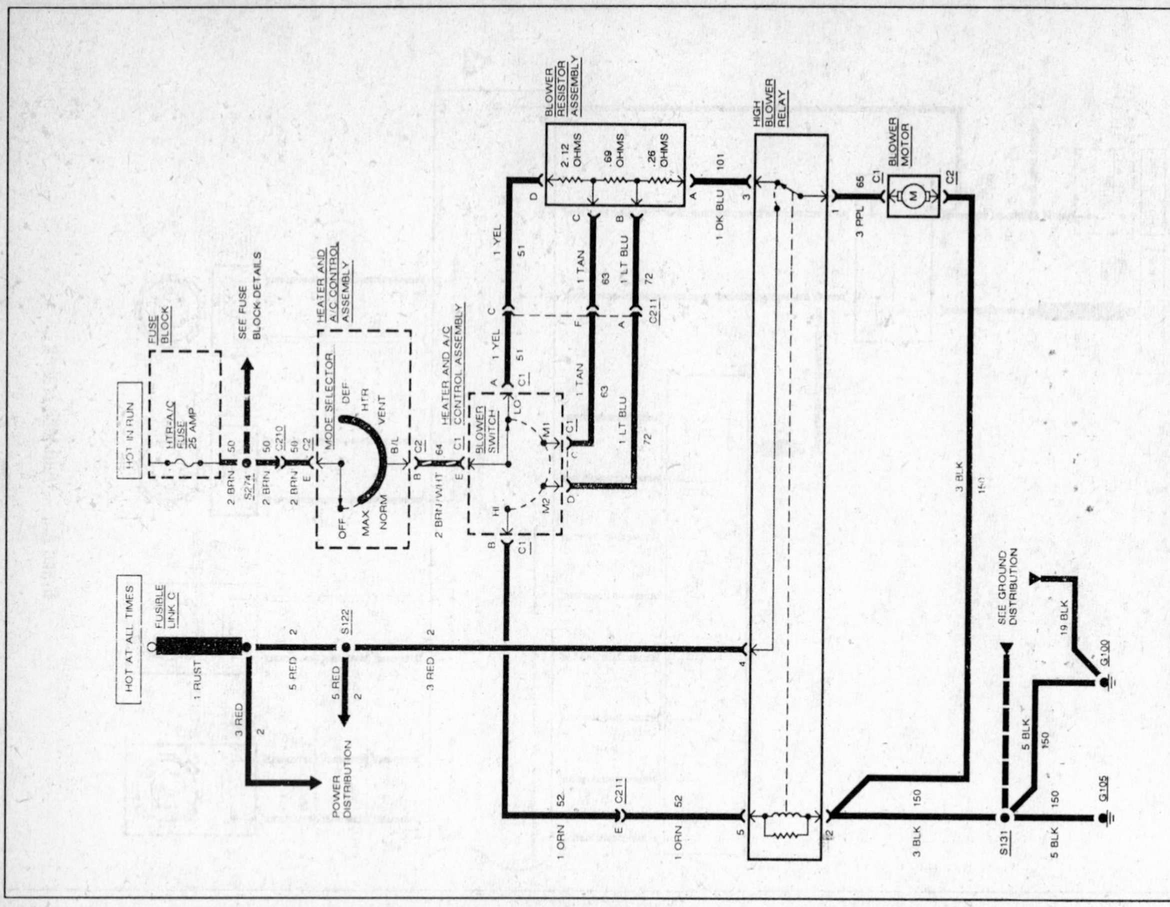

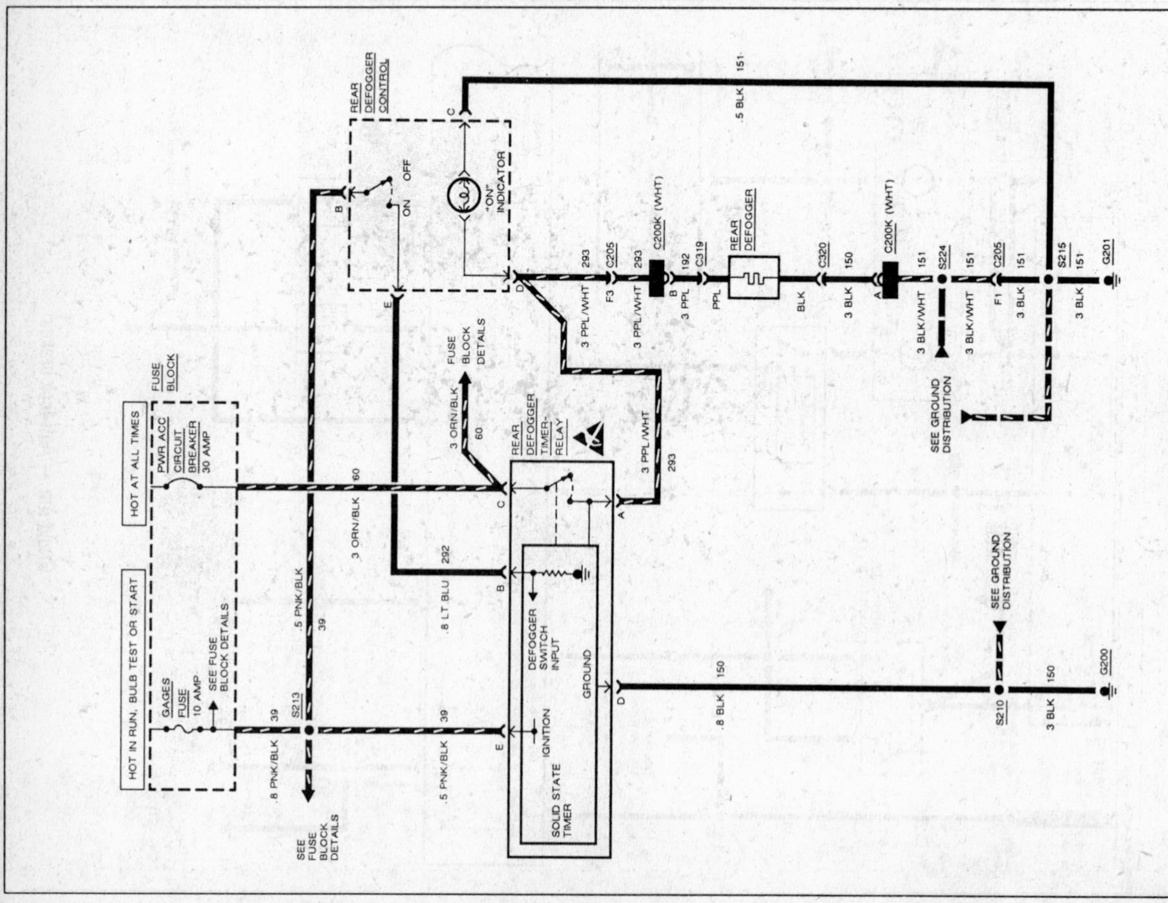

HOT IN RUN, BULB TEST OR START
HOT AT ALL TIMES
GAGES FUSE 10 AMP
SEE FUSE BLOCK DETAILS
PWR ACC CIRCUIT BREAKER 30 AMP
FUSE BLOCK
.8 PNK/BLK 39
S213
.5 PNK/BLK 39
SEE FUSE BLOCK DETAILS
3 ORN/BLK 60
REAR DEFOGGER CONTROL
ON OFF
"ON" INDICATOR
.5 PNK/BLK 39
.8 LT BLU 292
3 ORN/BLK 60
FUSE BLOCK DETAILS
SOLID STATE TIMER
IGNITION
DEFOGGER SWITCH INPUT
GROUND
REAR DEFOGGER TIMER-RELAY
3 PPL/WHT 293
F3 C205
3 PPL/WHT 293
C200K (WHT)
3 PPL 192
C319
PPL
REAR DEFOGGER
BLK
C320
3 BLK 150
C200K (WHT)
3 BLK/WHT 151
SEE GROUND DISTRIBUTION
S224
3 BLK/WHT 151
F1 C205
3 BLK 151
S215
3 BLK 151
G201
.5 BLK 151
.8 BLK 150
S210
SEE GROUND DISTRIBUTION
3 BLK 150
G200

Grand Am — Rear defogger

HOT AT ALL TIMES
FUSIBLE LINK C
1 RUST
3 RED 2
POWER DISTRIBUTION
5 RED 2
S122
3 RED 2
HOT IN RUN
HTR-A/C FUSE 25 AMP
FUSE BLOCK
2 BRN 50
S274
SEE FUSE BLOCK DETAILS
C210
C2
MODE SELECTOR
OFF DEF MAX HTR NORM VENT B/L
HEATER AND A/C CONTROL ASSEMBLY
2 BRN/WHT 64
HEATER AND A/C CONTROL ASSEMBLY
BLOWER SWITCH
HI LO M1 M2
1 YEL 51
1 TAN 63
1 LT BLU 72
C211
BLOWER RESISTOR ASSEMBLY
2.12 OHMS
.69 OHMS
.26 OHMS
1 ORN 52
1 DK BLU 101
HIGH BLOWER RELAY
3 PPL 65
BLOWER MOTOR
3 BLK 150
S131
SEE GROUND DISTRIBUTION
5 BLK 150
19 BLK
G105
G100

Grand Am — Air conditioning blower controls — manual system — 2.5L engine

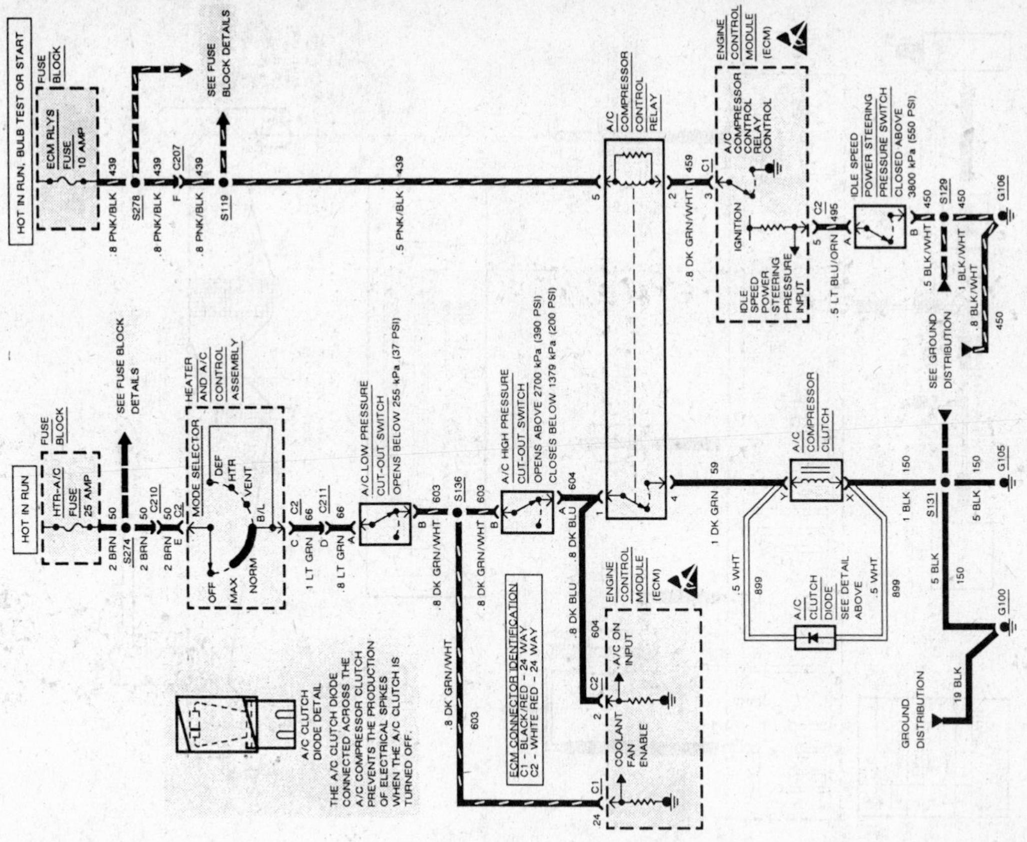

Grand Am — Air conditioning compressor controls — manual system — 2.5L engine

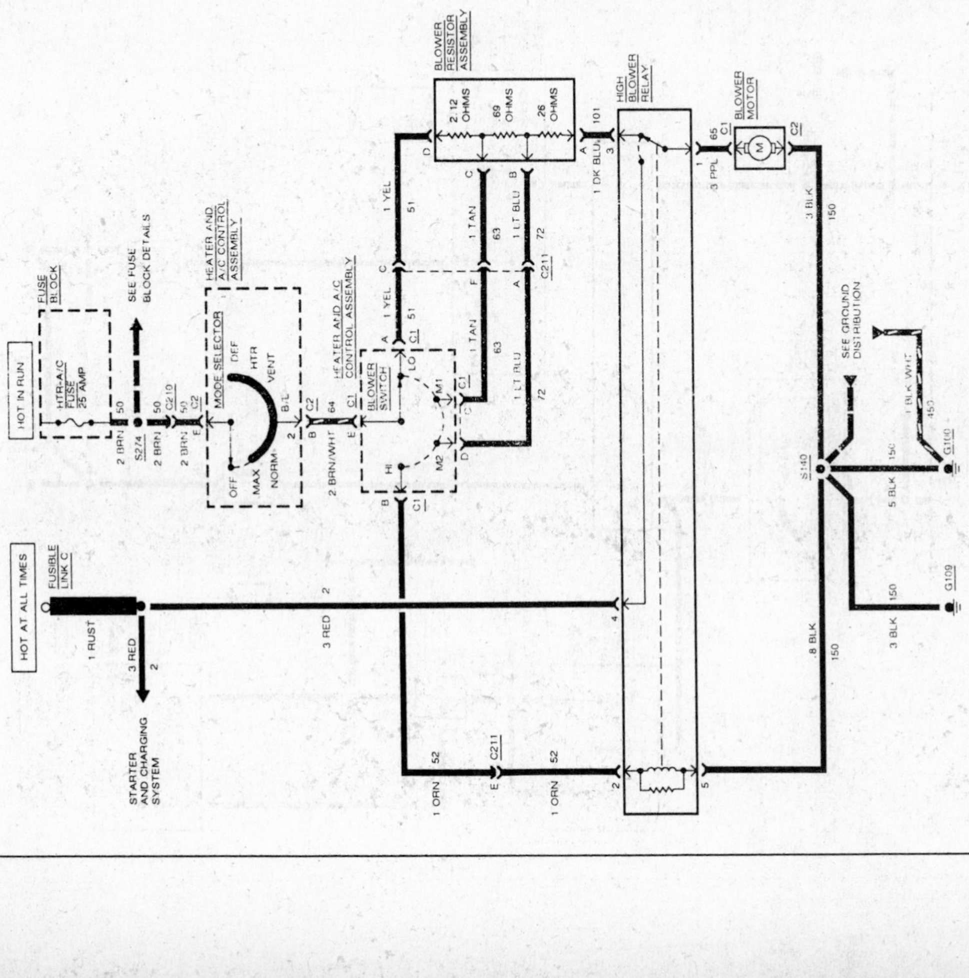

Grand Am — Air conditioning blower controls — manual system — 2.3L and 2.3L HO engines

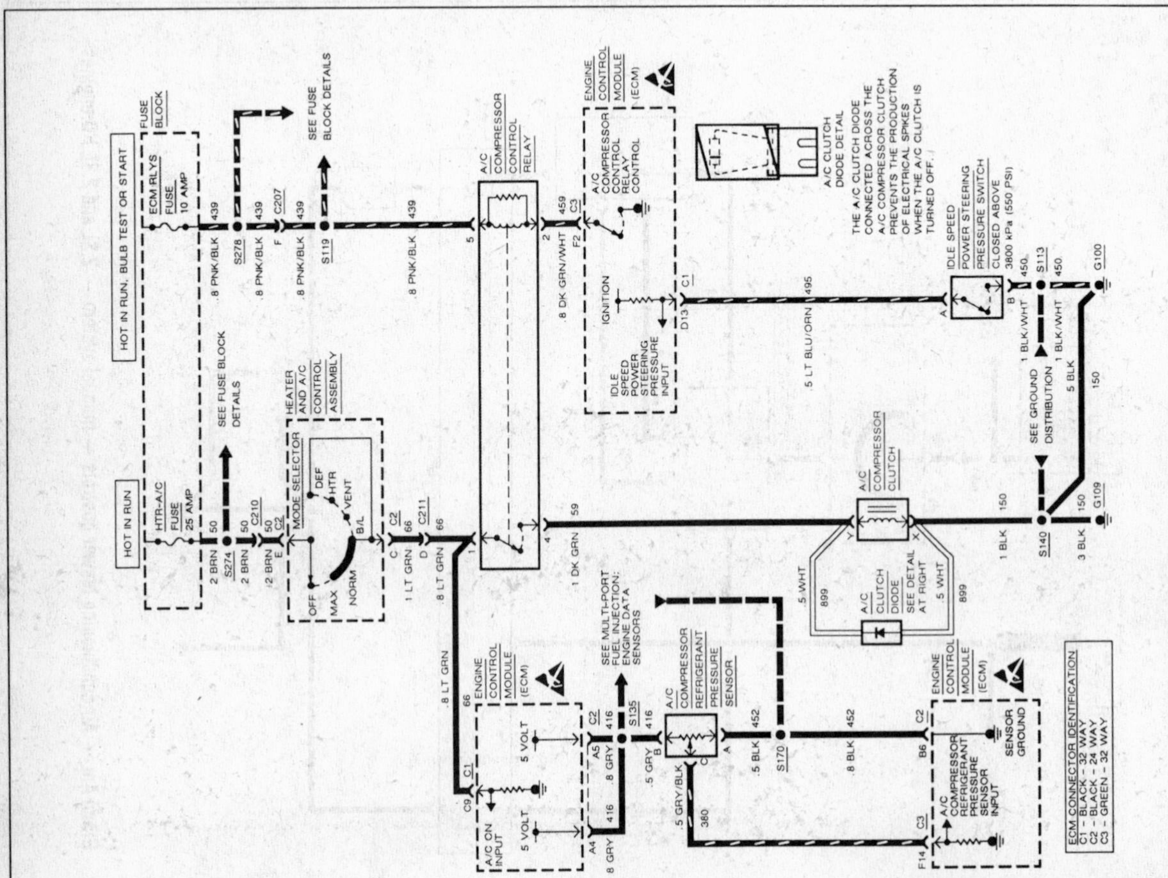

A/C CLUTCH DIODE DETAIL

THE A/C CLUTCH DIODE CONNECTED ACROSS THE A/C COMPRESSOR CLUTCH PREVENTS THE PRODUCTION OF ELECTRICAL SPIKES WHEN THE A/C CLUTCH IS TURNED OFF.

ECM CONNECTOR IDENTIFICATION
C1 - BLACK - 32 WAY
C2 - BLACK - 24 WAY
C3 - GREEN - 32 WAY

Grand Am — Air conditioning compressor controls — manual system — 2.3L and 2.3L HO engines

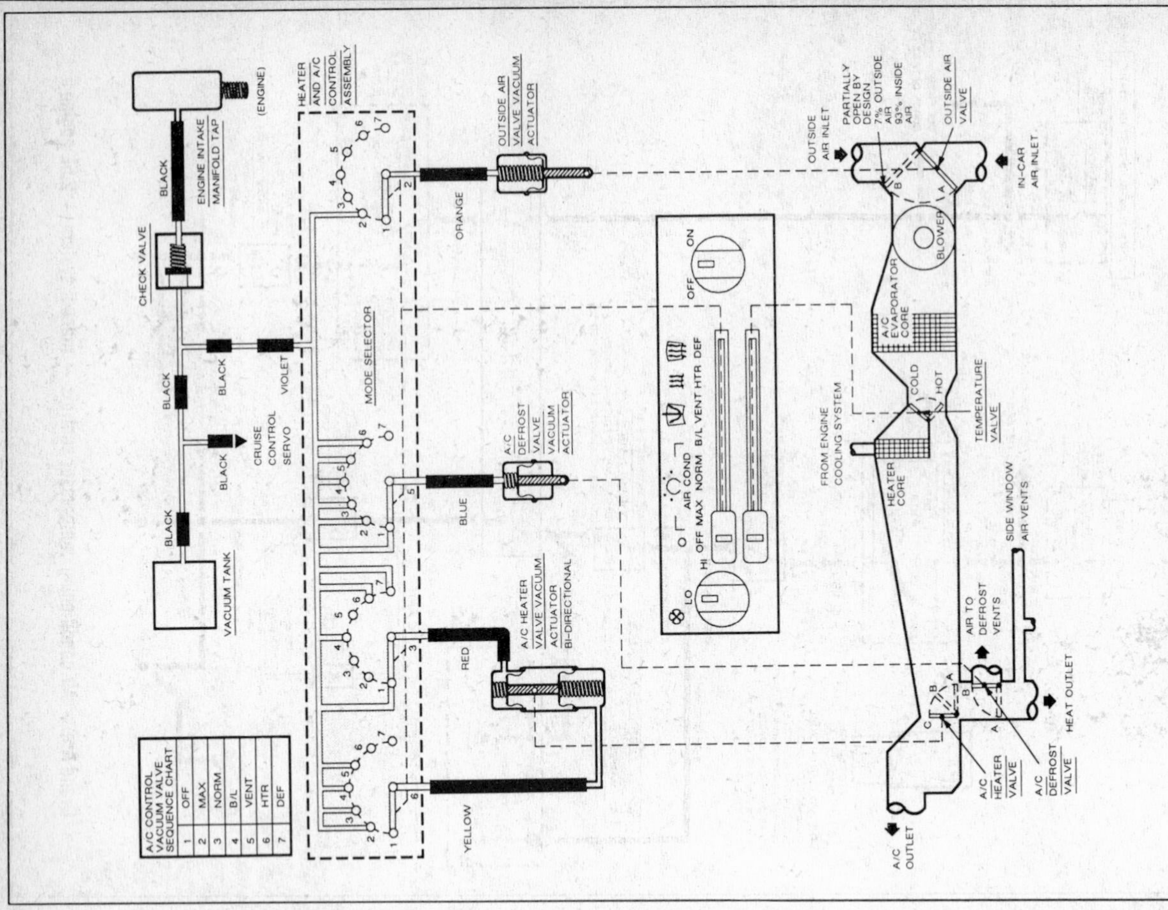

A/C CONTROL VACUUM VALVE SEQUENCE CHART	
1	OFF
2	MAX
3	NORM
4	B/L
5	VENT
6	HTR
7	DEF

Grand Am — Air conditioning air delivery — manual

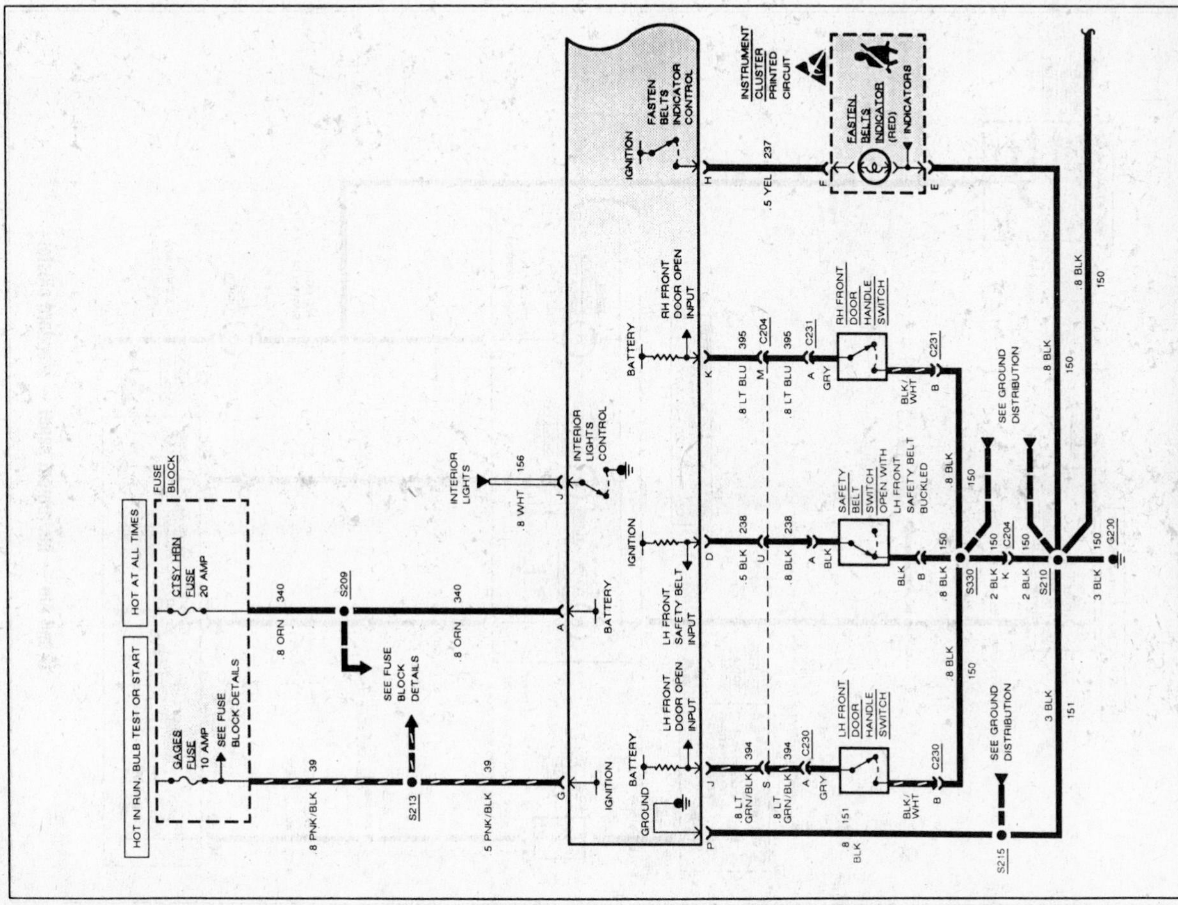

HOT IN RUN, BULB TEST OR START
HOT AT ALL TIMES
FUSE BLOCK
GAGES FUSE 10 AMP
SEE FUSE BLOCK DETAILS
CTSY HRN FUSE 20 AMP
.8 ORN 340
.8 PNK/BLK 39
S209
S213
SEE FUSE BLOCK DETAILS
.8 ORN 340
5 PNK/BLK 39
INTERIOR LIGHTS
.8 WHT 156
G A J
IGNITION
BATTERY
INTERIOR LIGHTS CONTROL
GROUND
BATTERY
LH FRONT DOOR OPEN INPUT
IGNITION
LH FRONT SAFETY BELT INPUT
BATTERY
RH FRONT DOOR OPEN INPUT
IGNITION
FASTEN BELTS INDICATOR CONTROL
P J D K H
.8 LT GRN/BLK 394
S
.8 LT GRN/BLK 394
A C230
GRY
.5 BLK 238
U
.8 BLK 238
A
BLK
.8 LT BLU 395
M C204
.8 LT BLU 395
A C231
GRY
.5 YEL 237
INSTRUMENT CLUSTER PRINTED CIRCUIT
F
FASTEN BELTS INDICATOR (RED)
INDICATORS
E
.8 BLK 151
LH FRONT DOOR HANDLE SWITCH
SAFETY BELT SWITCH OPEN WITH LH FRONT SAFETY BELT BUCKLED
RH FRONT DOOR HANDLE SWITCH
BLK/WHT
B C230
BLK
B
.8 BLK 150
BLK/WHT
B C231
.8 BLK 150
.8 BLK 150
S330
150
2 BLK 150
K C204
2 BLK 150
S215
SEE GROUND DISTRIBUTION
SEE GROUND DISTRIBUTION
S210
3 BLK 151
.8 BLK 150
.8 BLK 150
3 BLK 150
G230

Grand Am — Warnings and alarms — chime

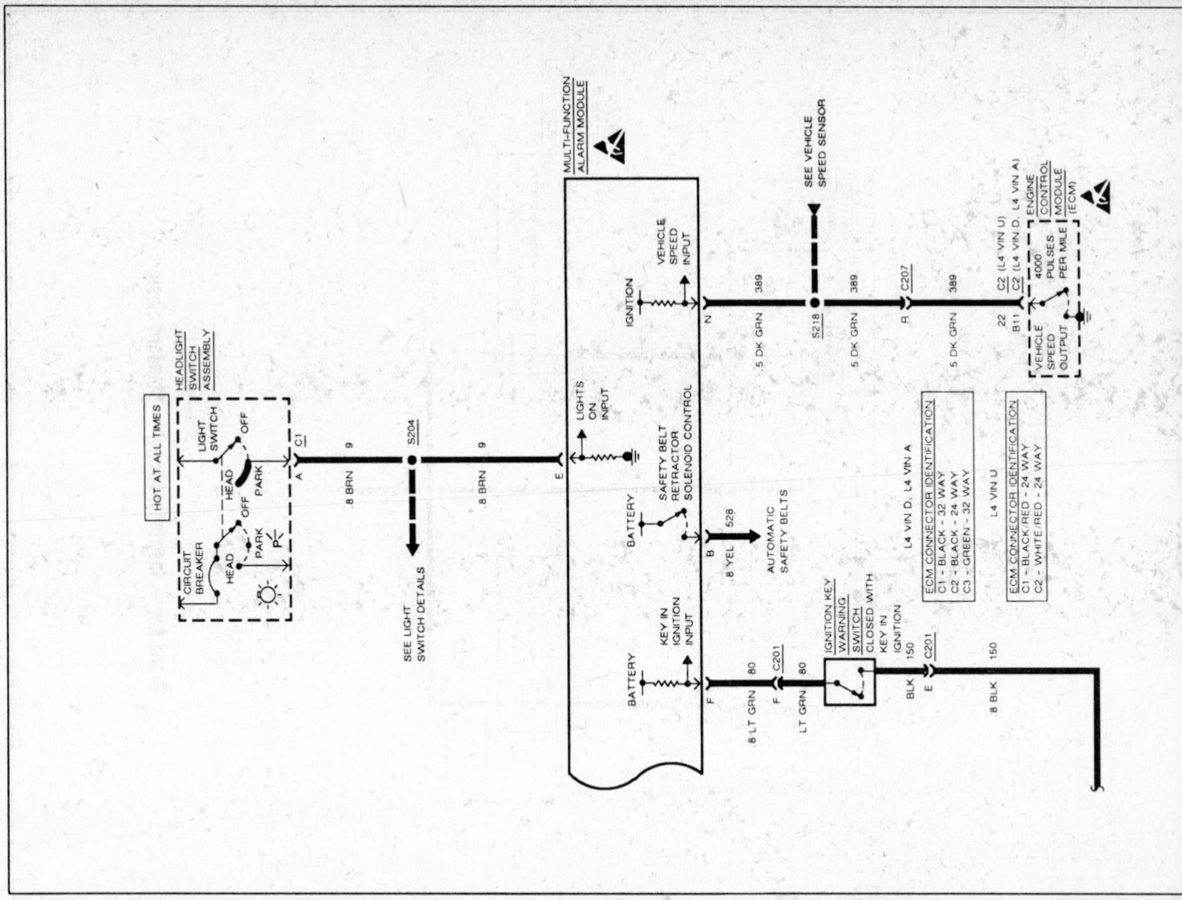

HOT AT ALL TIMES
CIRCUIT BREAKER
LIGHT SWITCH
HEADLIGHT SWITCH ASSEMBLY
HEAD OFF PARK
HEAD OFF PARK
A C1
.8 BRN 9
SEE LIGHT SWITCH DETAILS
S204
.8 BRN 9
E
LIGHTS ON INPUT
MULTI-FUNCTION ALARM MODULE
BATTERY
KEY IN IGNITION INPUT
BATTERY
SAFETY BELT RETRACTOR SOLENOID CONTROL
IGNITION
VEHICLE SPEED INPUT
F B N
.8 LT GRN 80
F C201
LT GRN 80
.8 YEL 528
AUTOMATIC SAFETY BELTS
.5 DK GRN 389
S218
SEE VEHICLE SPEED SENSOR
IGNITION KEY WARNING SWITCH CLOSED WITH KEY IN IGNITION
BLK 150
E C201
.8 BLK 150
5 DK GRN 389
R C207
5 DK GRN 389
L4 VIN D, L4 VIN A

ECM CONNECTOR IDENTIFICATION
C1 - BLACK - 32 WAY
C2 - BLACK - 24 WAY
C3 - GREEN - 32 WAY

L4 VIN U

ECM CONNECTOR IDENTIFICATION
C1 - BLACK/RED - 24 WAY
C2 - WHITE/RED - 24 WAY

22 C2 (L4 VIN U)
B11 C2 (L4 VIN D, L4 VIN A)
VEHICLE SPEED OUTPUT
4000 PULSES PER MILE
ENGINE CONTROL MODULE (ECM)

Grand Am — Warnings and alarms — chime

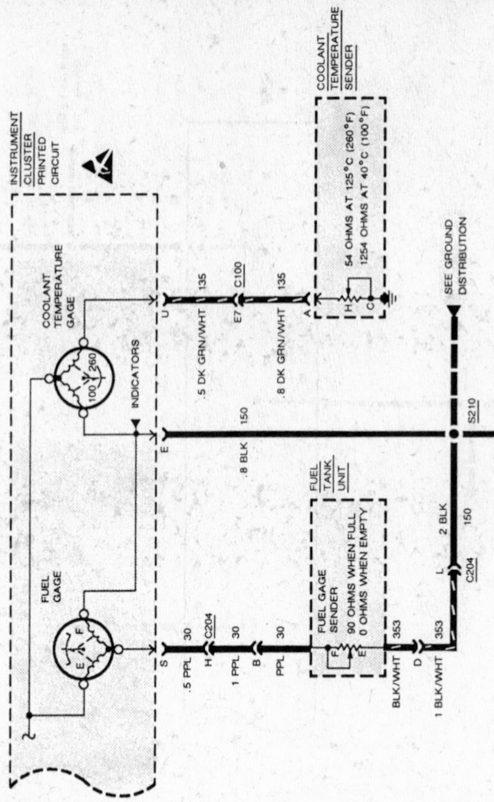

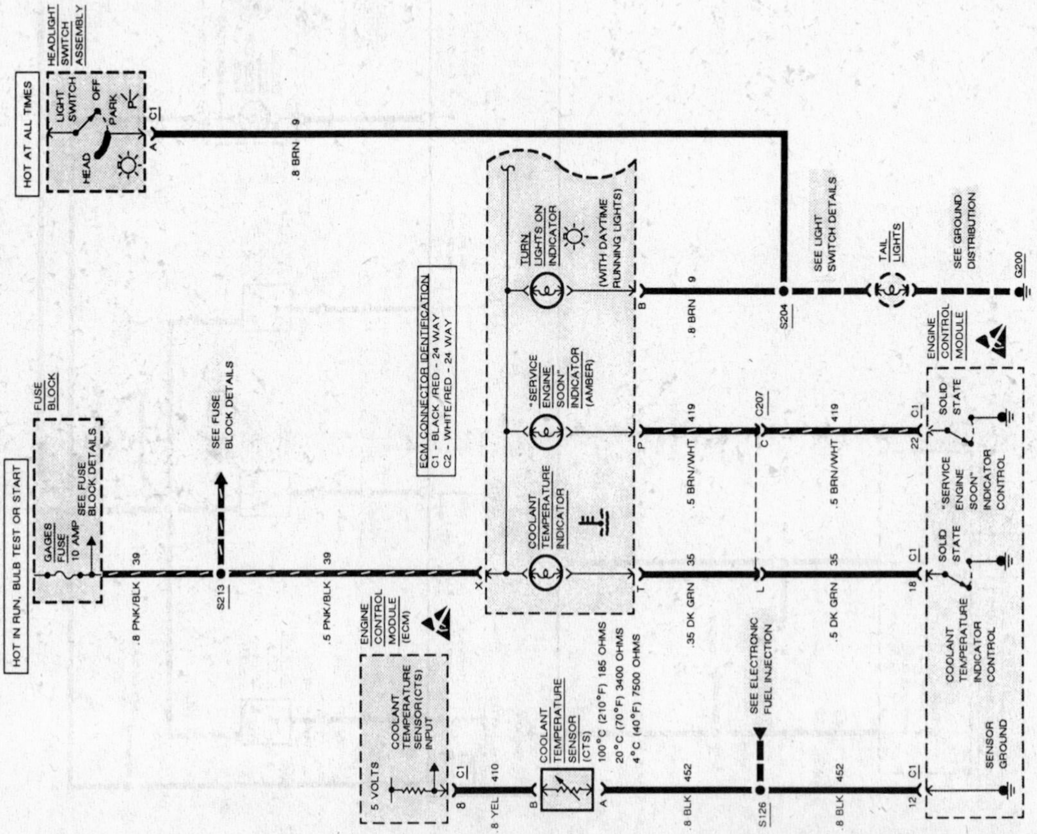

HOT IN RUN, BULB TEST OR START
FUSE BLOCK
GAGES FUSE 10 AMP
SEE FUSE BLOCK DETAILS
.8 PNK/BLK 39
S213
SEE FUSE BLOCK DETAILS
.5 PNK/BLK 39
HOT AT ALL TIMES
HEADLIGHT SWITCH ASSEMBLY
LIGHT SWITCH
HEAD
OFF
PARK
A C1
.8 BRN 9
5 VOLTS
COOLANT TEMPERATURE SENSOR(CTS) INPUT
ENGINE CONTROL MODULE (ECM)
8 C1
.8 YEL 410
B
COOLANT TEMPERATURE SENSOR (CTS)
100°C (210°F) 185 OHMS
20°C (70°F) 3400 OHMS
4°C (40°F) 7500 OHMS
A
ECM CONNECTOR IDENTIFICATION
C1 - BLACK /RED - 24 WAY
C2 - WHITE/RED - 24 WAY
X
COOLANT TEMPERATURE INDICATOR
"SERVICE ENGINE SOON" INDICATOR (AMBER)
TURN LIGHTS ON INDICATOR
(WITH DAYTIME RUNNING LIGHTS)
T P B
.8 BLK 452
.35 DK GRN 35
.5 BRN/WHT 419
.8 BRN 9
S126
SEE ELECTRONIC FUEL INJECTION
L C207 C
S204
SEE LIGHT SWITCH DETAILS
.8 BLK 452
.5 DK GRN 35
.5 BRN/WHT 419
TAIL LIGHTS
12 C1
18 C1
22 C1
SENSOR GROUND
COOLANT TEMPERATURE INDICATOR CONTROL
SOLID STATE
"SERVICE ENGINE SOON" INDICATOR CONTROL
SOLID STATE
ENGINE CONTROL MODULE
SEE GROUND DISTRIBUTION
G200

Grand Am — Instrument panel — standard cluster

INSTRUMENT CLUSTER PRINTED CIRCUIT
FUEL GAGE
COOLANT TEMPERATURE GAGE
E F
100 260
INDICATORS
S E U
.5 PPL 30
H C204
1 PPL 30
B
PPL 30
.8 BLK 150
.5 DK GRN/WHT 135
E7 C100
.8 DK GRN/WHT 135
A
FUEL GAGE SENDER
90 OHMS WHEN FULL
0 OHMS WHEN EMPTY
FUEL TANK UNIT
COOLANT TEMPERATURE SENDER
54 OHMS AT 125°C (260°F)
1254 OHMS AT 40°C (100°F)
H C
BLK/WHT 353
D
1 BLK/WHT 353
L 2 BLK
C204 150
S210
SEE GROUND DISTRIBUTION
3 BLK 150
G200

Grand Am — Instrument panel — standard cluster

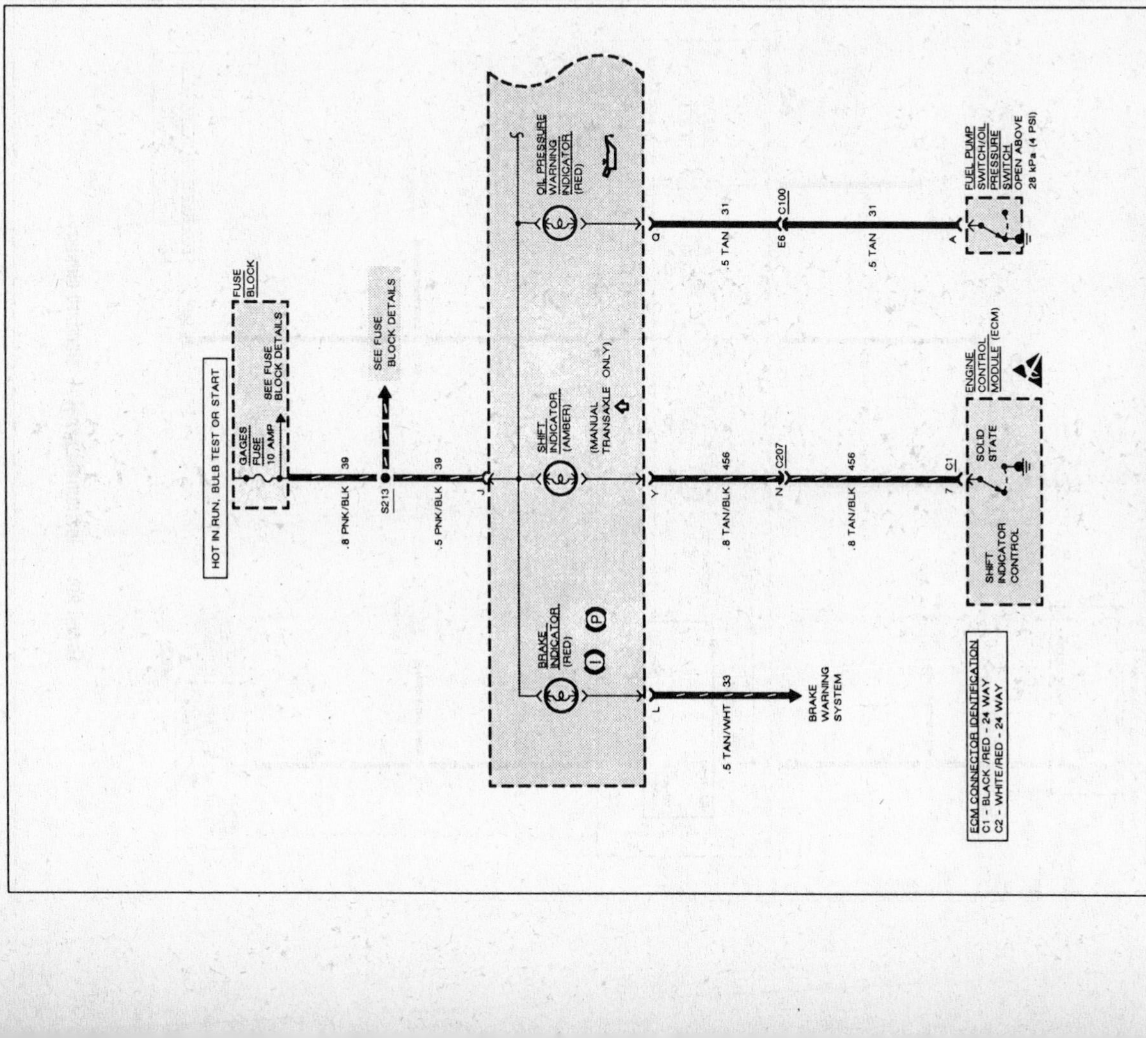

Grand Am — Instrument panel — standard cluster

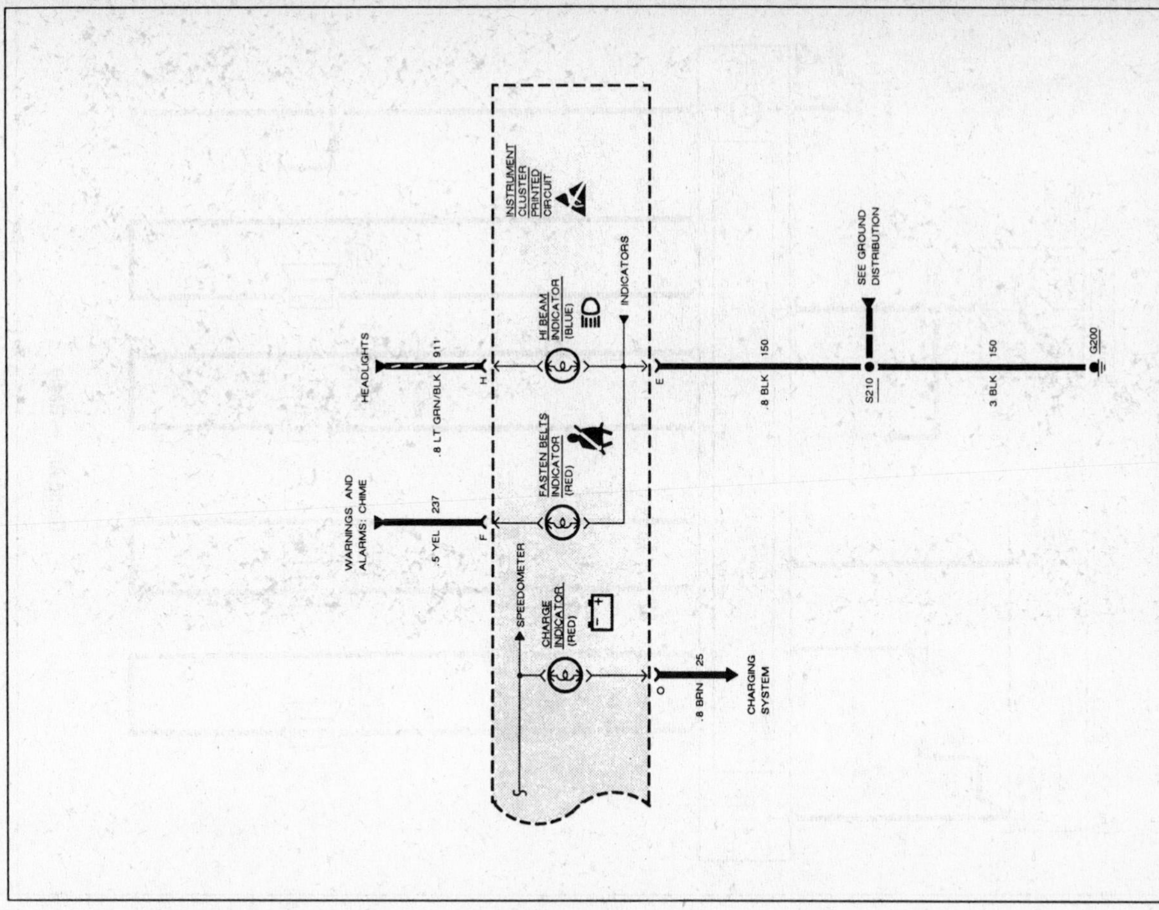

Grand Am — Instrument panel — standard cluster

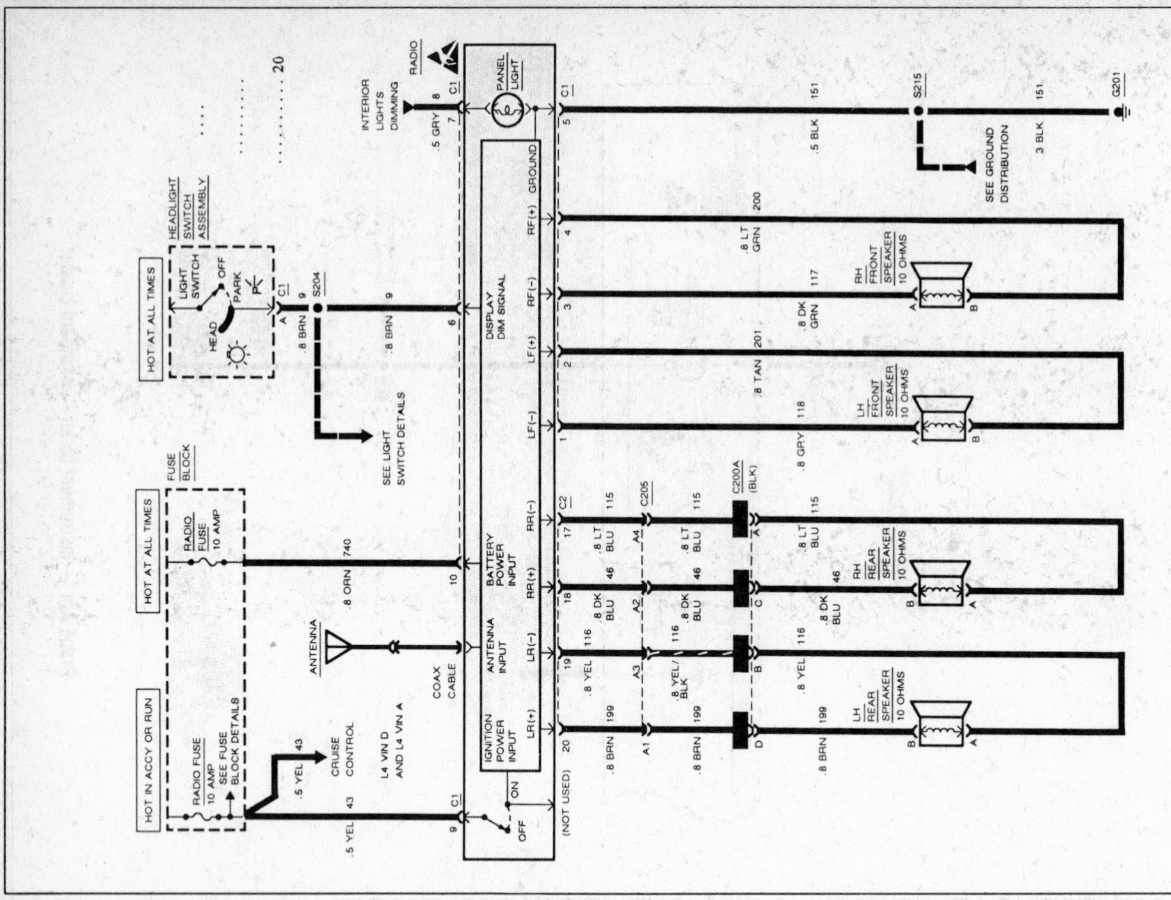

Grand Am — Radio

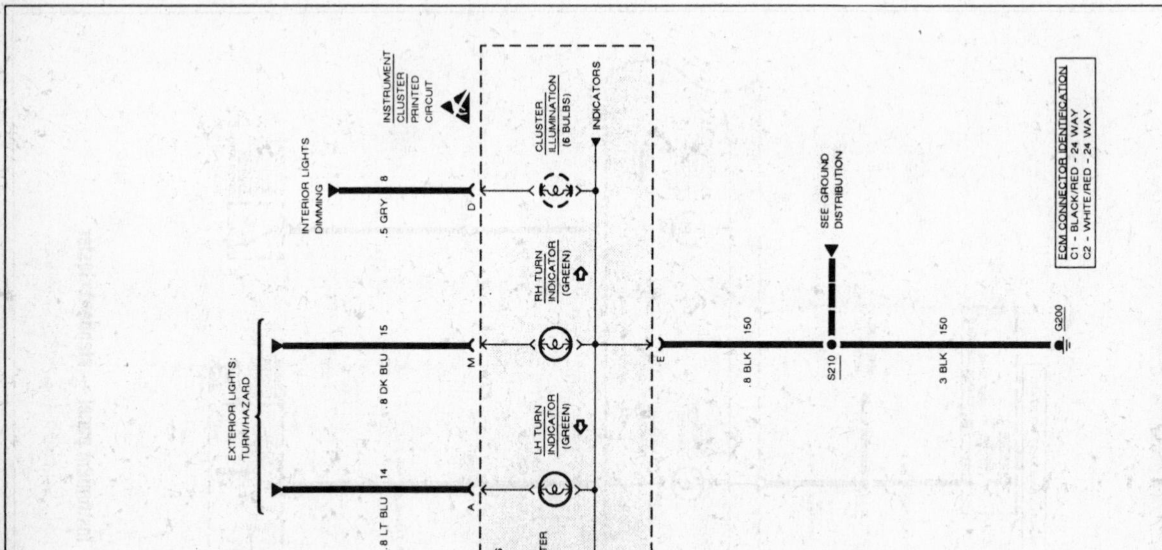

Grand Am — Instrument panel — standard cluster

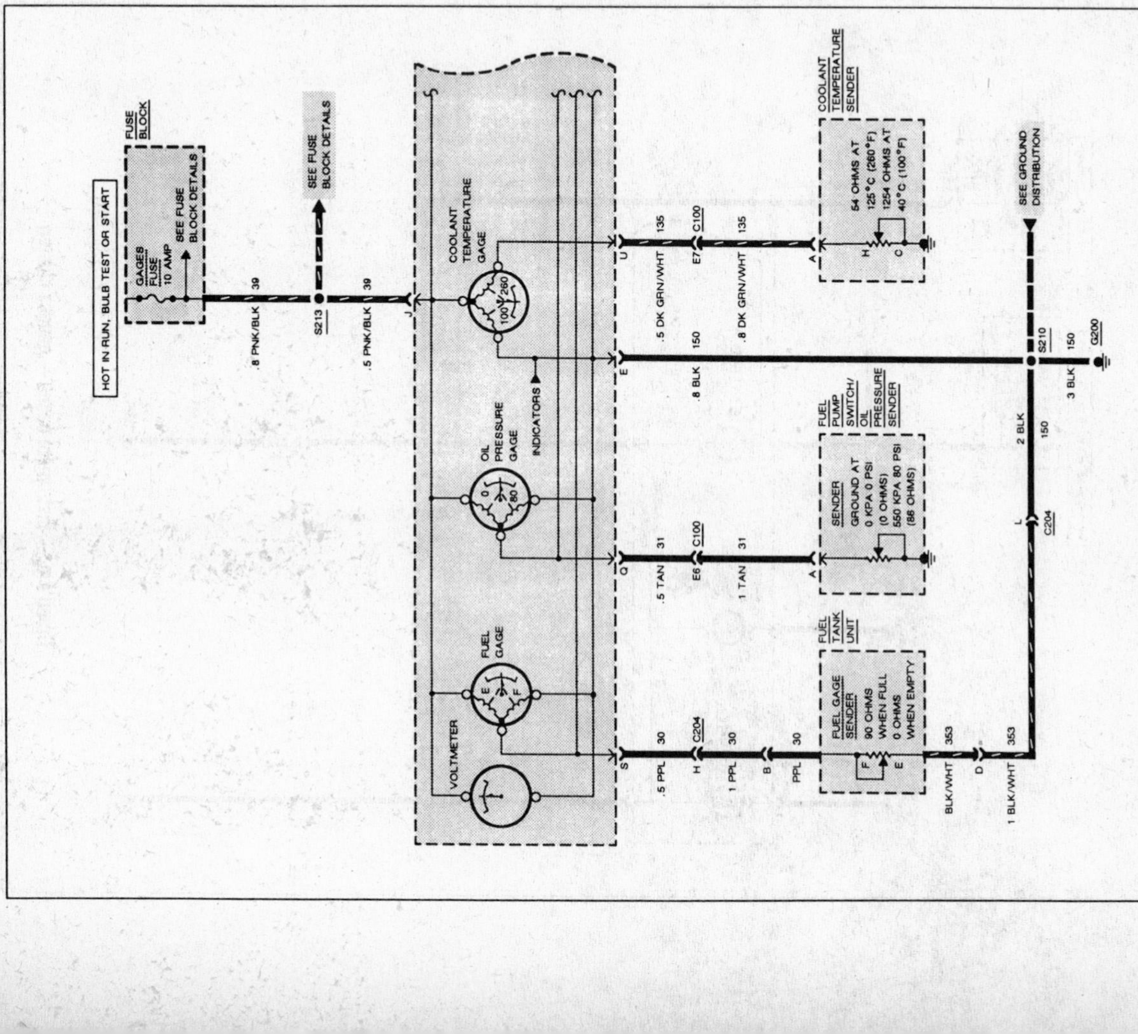

HOT IN RUN, BULB TEST OR START

FUSE BLOCK
GAGES FUSE 10 AMP
SEE FUSE BLOCK DETAILS

.8 PNK/BLK 39
S213
SEE FUSE BLOCK DETAILS
.5 PNK/BLK 39
J

VOLTMETER
FUEL GAGE
E F
OIL PRESSURE GAGE
0 80
INDICATORS
COOLANT TEMPERATURE GAGE
100 260

S Q E U

.5 PPL 30
H C204
1 PPL 30
B
PPL 30

FUEL GAGE SENDER
90 OHMS WHEN FULL
0 OHMS WHEN EMPTY
F E
FUEL TANK UNIT

BLK/WHT 353
D
1 BLK/WHT 353

.5 TAN 31
E6 C100
1 TAN 31
A

SENDER
GROUND AT 0 KPA 0 PSI (0 OHMS)
550 KPA 80 PSI (86 OHMS)
FUEL PUMP SWITCH/ OIL PRESSURE SENDER

.8 BLK 150

.5 DK GRN/WHT 135
E7 C100
.8 DK GRN/WHT 135
A

54 OHMS AT 125°C (260°F)
1254 OHMS AT 40°C (100°F)
H C
COOLANT TEMPERATURE SENDER

L
C204
2 BLK
150
S210
SEE GROUND DISTRIBUTION
3 BLK 150
G200

Grand Am — Instrument panel — gauges cluster

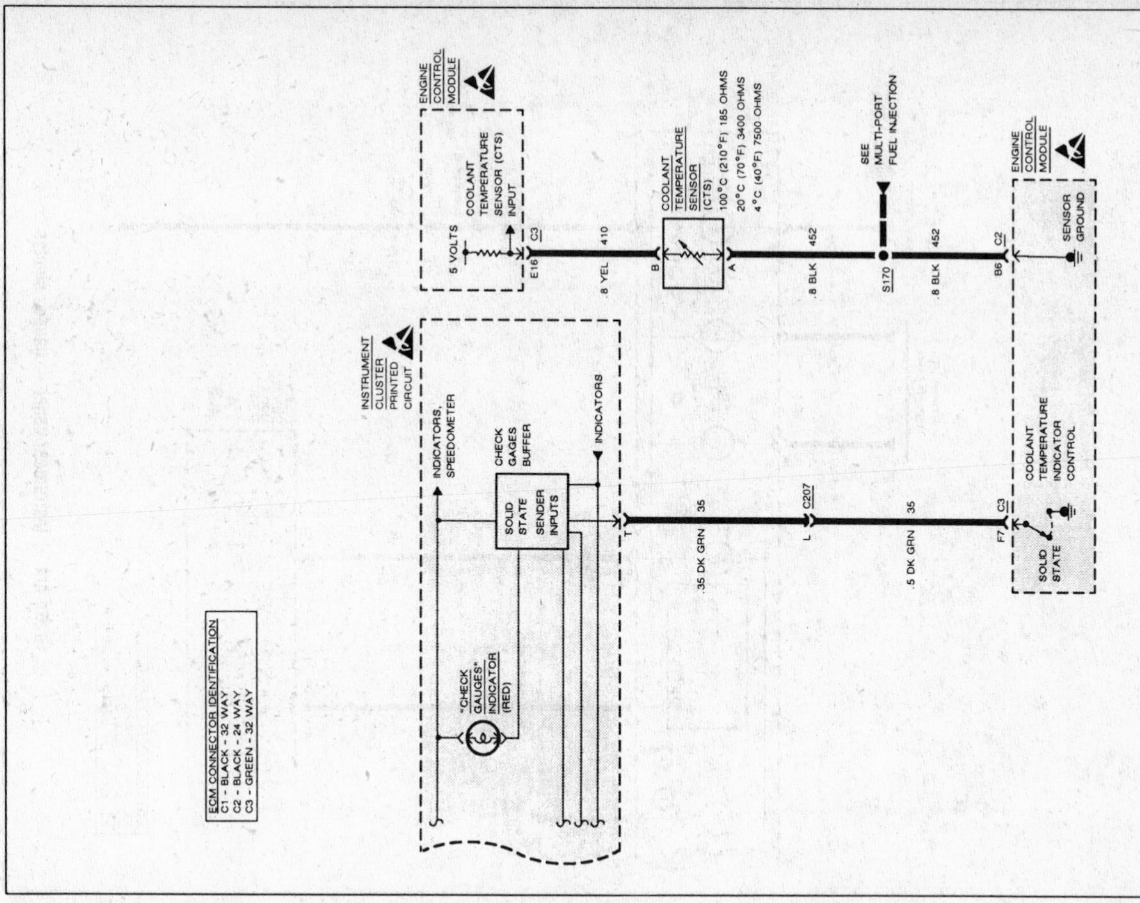

ECM CONNECTOR IDENTIFICATION
C1 - BLACK - 32 WAY
C2 - BLACK - 24 WAY
C3 - GREEN - 32 WAY

INSTRUMENT CLUSTER PRINTED CIRCUIT

INDICATORS, SPEEDOMETER
"CHECK GAUGES" INDICATOR (RED)
SOLID STATE SENDER INPUTS
CHECK GAGES BUFFER
INDICATORS

T
.35 DK GRN 35
L C207
.5 DK GRN 35
F7 C3

SOLID STATE
COOLANT TEMPERATURE INDICATOR CONTROL

ENGINE CONTROL MODULE
5 VOLTS
COOLANT TEMPERATURE SENSOR (CTS) INPUT
E16 C3
.8 YEL 410
B
COOLANT TEMPERATURE SENSOR (CTS)
100°C (210°F) 185 OHMS
20°C (70°F) 3400 OHMS
4°C (40°F) 7500 OHMS
A
.8 BLK 452
S170
SEE MULTI-PORT FUEL INJECTION
.8 BLK 452
B6 C2

ENGINE CONTROL MODULE
SENSOR GROUND

Grand Am — Instrument panel — gauges cluster

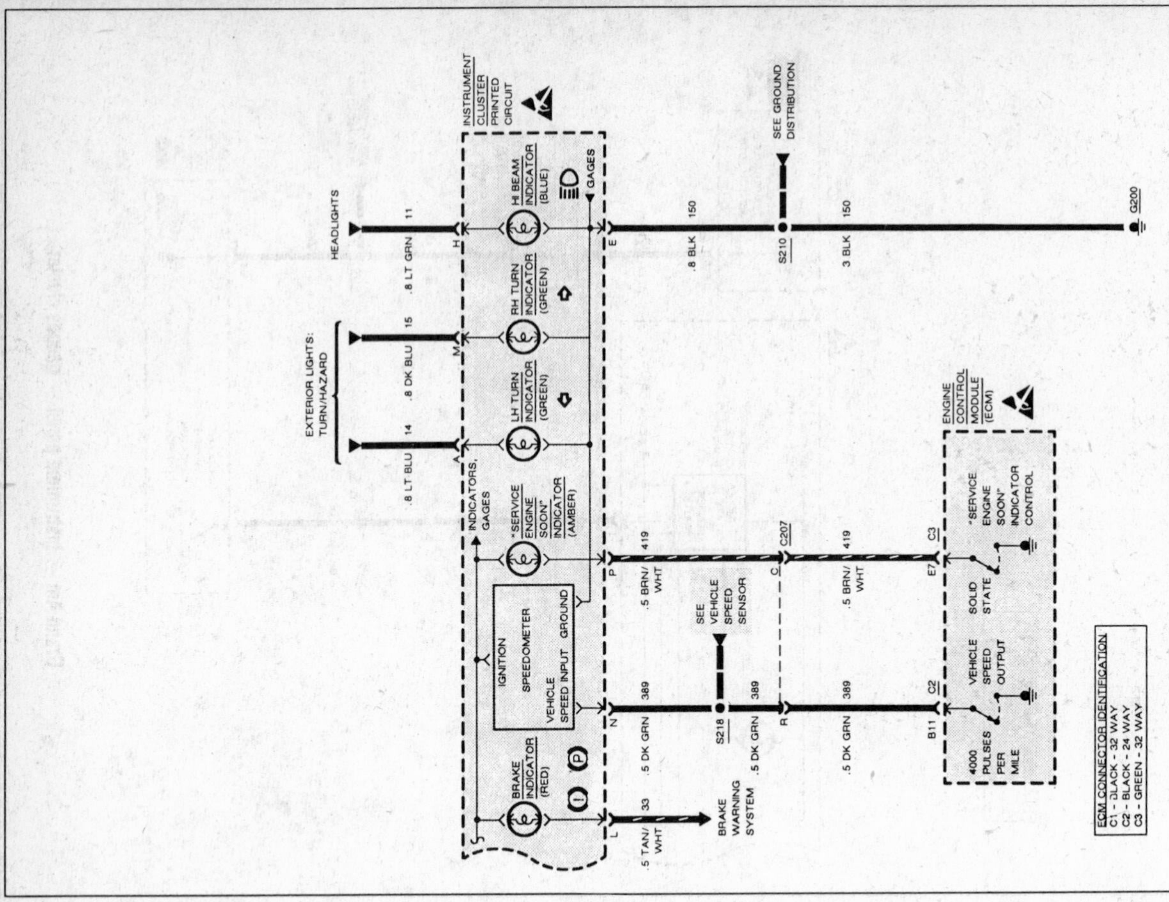

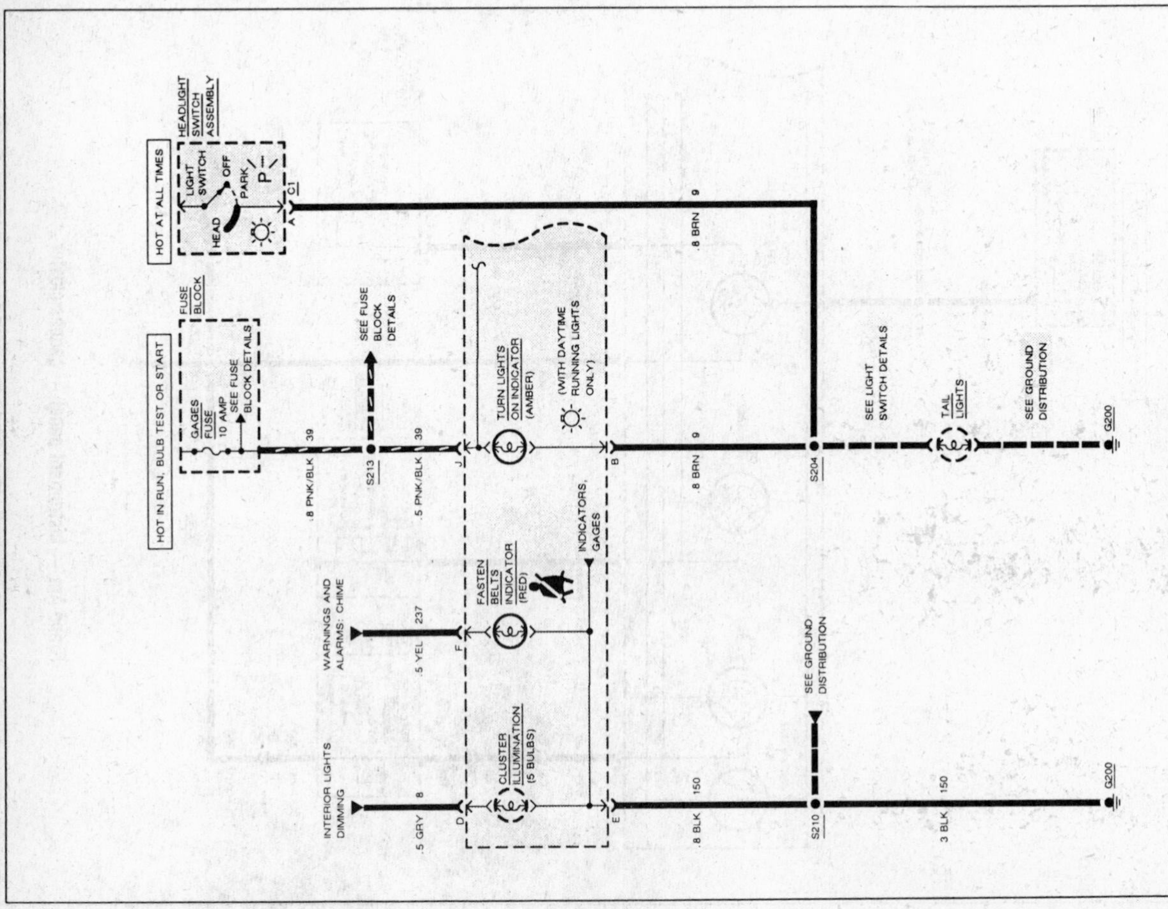

HOT IN RUN, BULB TEST OR START
GAGES FUSE 10 AMP
SEE FUSE BLOCK DETAILS
FUSE BLOCK
HOT AT ALL TIMES
LIGHT SWITCH
HEAD
OFF
PARK
HEADLIGHT SWITCH ASSEMBLY
A C1
.8 PNK/BLK 39
INTERIOR LIGHTS DIMMING
WARNINGS AND ALARMS: CHIME
S213
SEE FUSE BLOCK DETAILS
.5 GRY 8
.5 YEL 237
.5 PNK/BLK 39
D
F
J
CLUSTER ILLUMINATION (5 BULBS)
FASTEN BELTS INDICATOR (RED)
TURN LIGHTS ON INDICATOR (AMBER)
(WITH DAYTIME RUNNING LIGHTS ONLY)
INDICATORS, GAGES
E
B
.8 BLK 150
.8 BRN 9
.8 BRN 9
S210
SEE GROUND DISTRIBUTION
S204
SEE LIGHT SWITCH DETAILS
3 BLK 150
TAIL LIGHTS
SEE GROUND DISTRIBUTION
G200
G200

Grand Am – Instrument panel – gauges cluster

EXTERIOR LIGHTS: TURN/HAZARD
HEADLIGHTS
.8 LT BLU 14
.8 DK BLU 15
.8 LT GRN 11
A
M
H
INDICATORS, GAGES
INSTRUMENT CLUSTER PRINTED CIRCUIT
BRAKE INDICATOR (RED)
IGNITION
SPEEDOMETER
VEHICLE SPEED INPUT GROUND
"SERVICE ENGINE SOON" INDICATOR (AMBER)
LH TURN INDICATOR (GREEN)
RH TURN INDICATOR (GREEN)
HI BEAM INDICATOR (BLUE)
GAGES
L
N
P
E
.5 TAN/WHT 33
.5 DK GRN 389
.5 BRN/WHT 419
.8 BLK 150
BRAKE WARNING SYSTEM
S218
SEE VEHICLE SPEED SENSOR
.5 DK GRN 389
R
C
C207
S210
SEE GROUND DISTRIBUTION
.5 DK GRN 389
.5 BRN/WHT 419
3 BLK 150
B11 C2
E7 C3
4000 PULSES PER MILE
VEHICLE SPEED OUTPUT
SOLID STATE
"SERVICE ENGINE SOON" INDICATOR CONTROL
ENGINE CONTROL MODULE (ECM)

ECM CONNECTOR IDENTIFICATION
C1 - BLACK - 32 WAY
C2 - BLACK - 24 WAY
C3 - GREEN - 32 WAY

G200

Grand Am – Instrument panel – gauges cluster

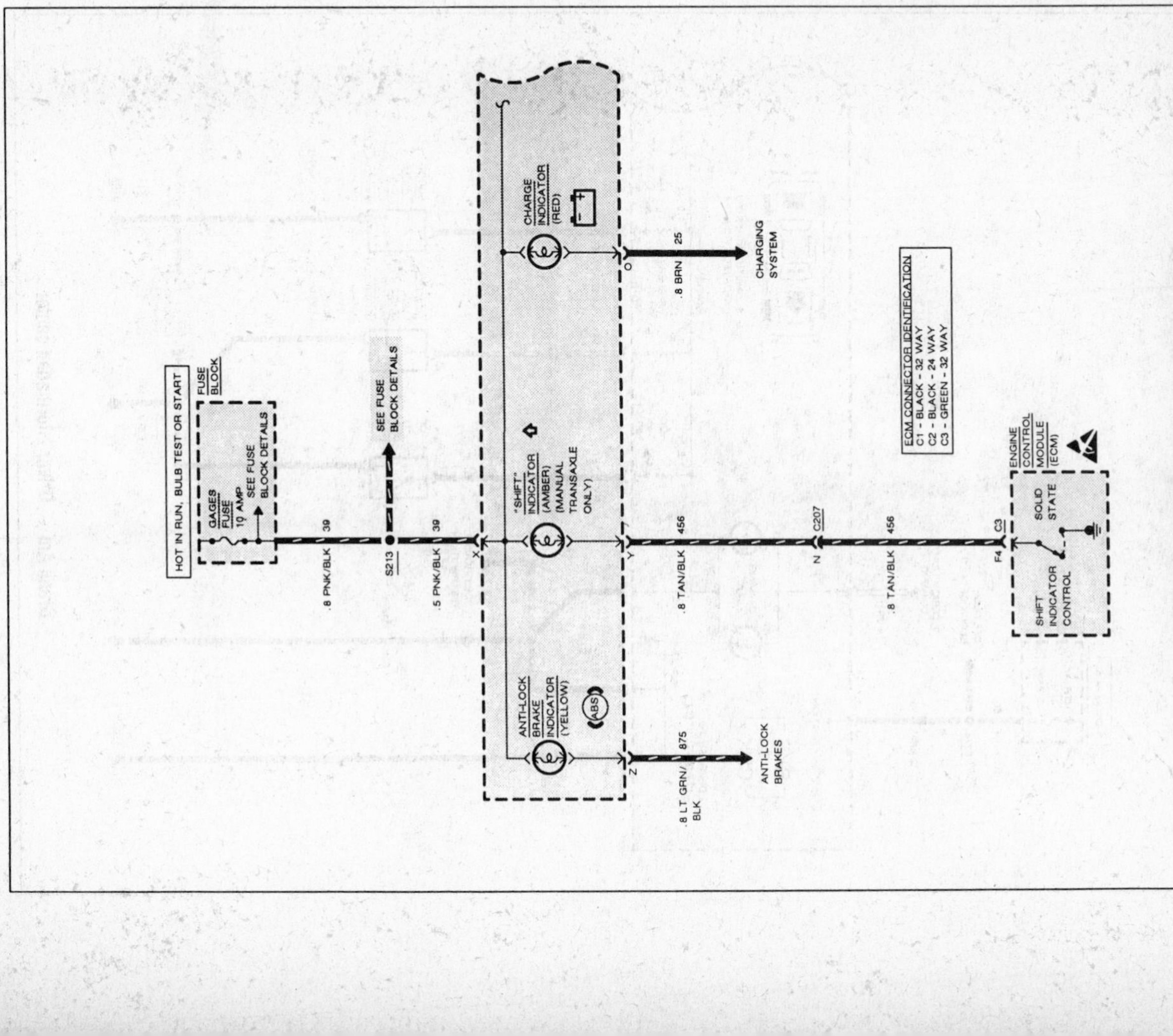

Grand Am — Instrument panel — gauges cluster

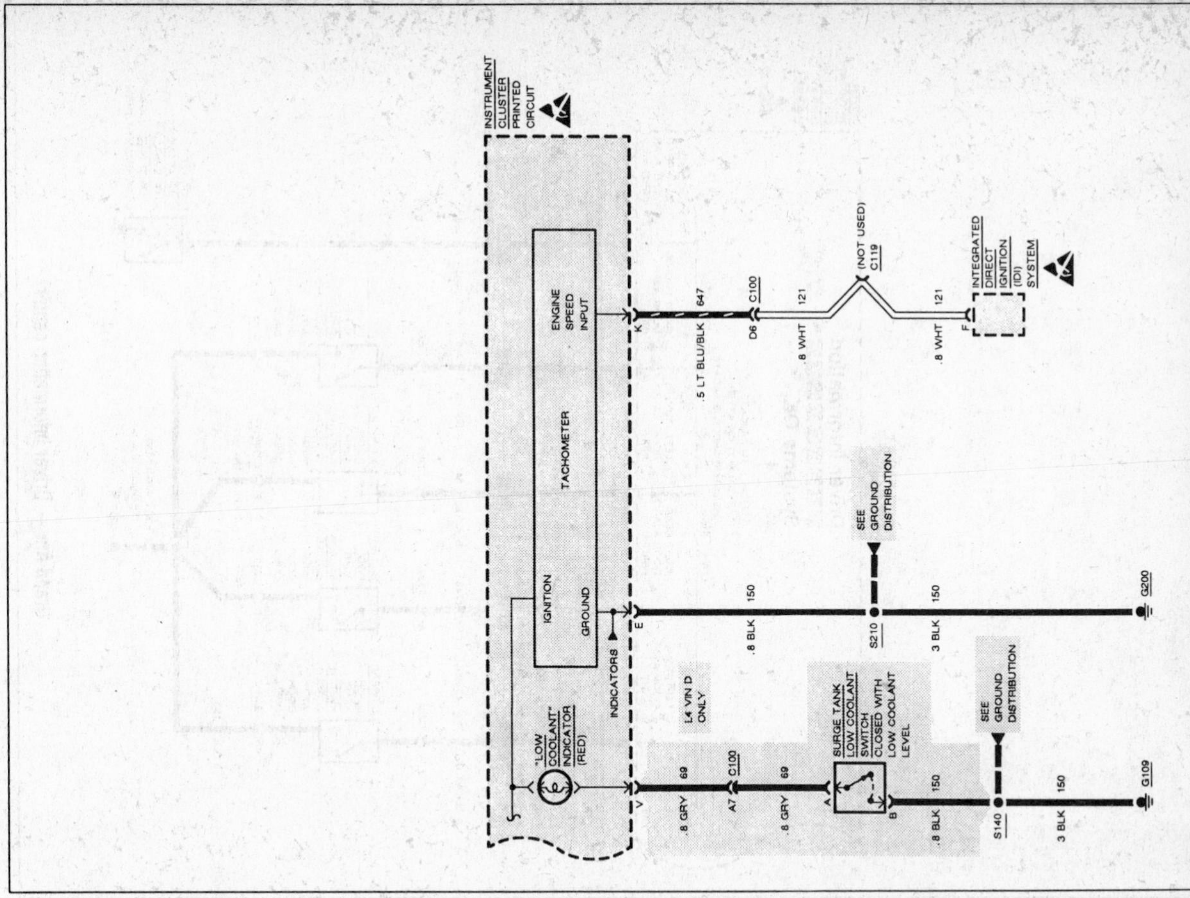

Grand Am — Instrument panel — gauges cluster

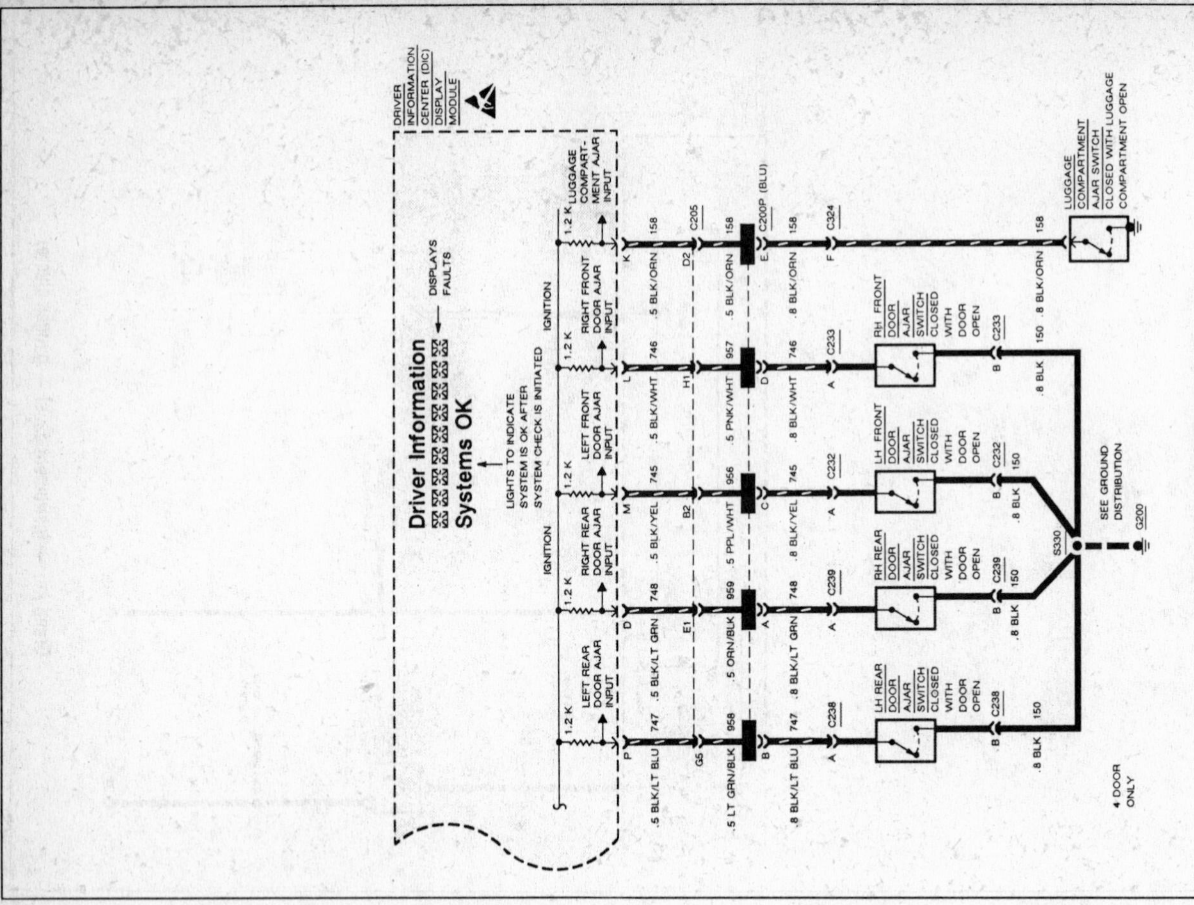

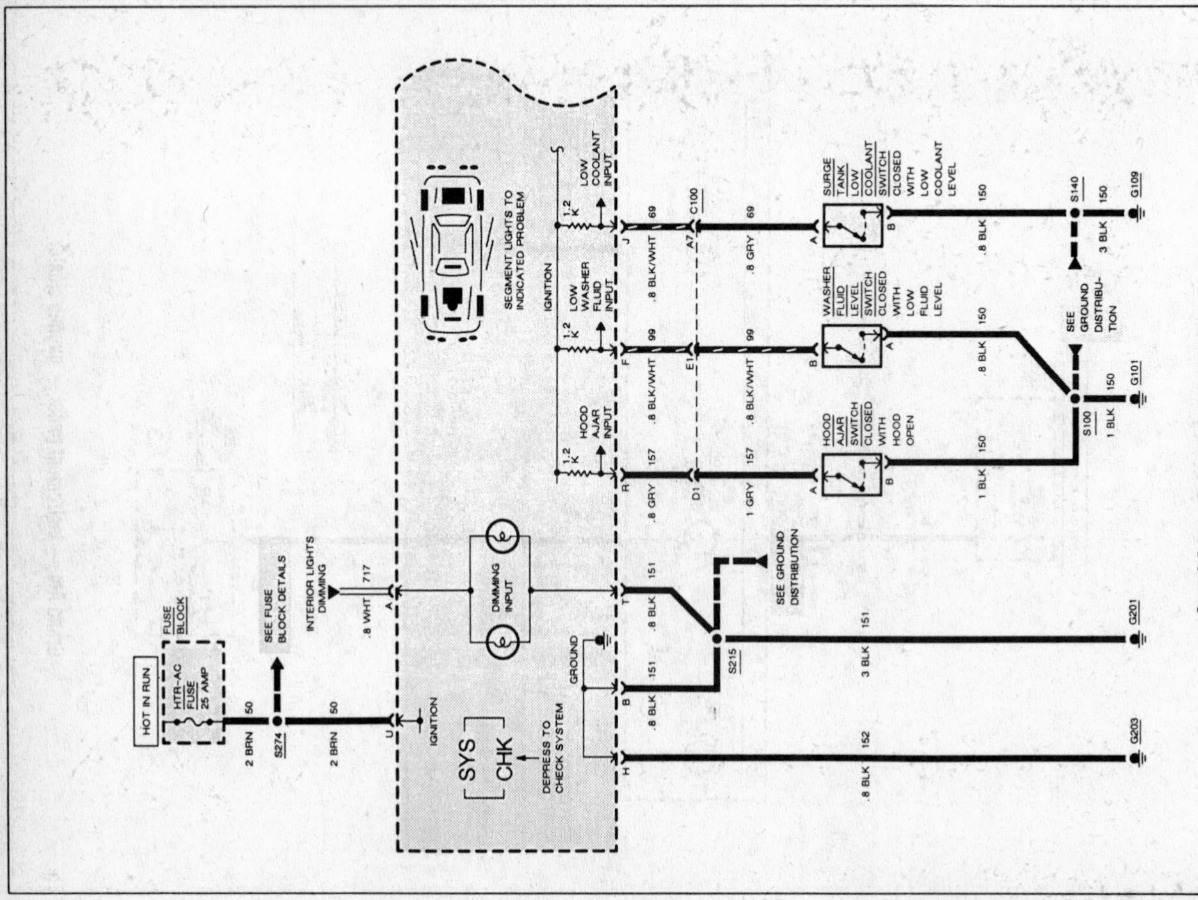

HOT IN RUN
FUSE BLOCK
HTR-AC FUSE 25 AMP
2 BRN 50
S274
SEE FUSE BLOCK DETAILS
2 BRN 50
INTERIOR LIGHTS DIMMING
.8 WHT 717
U A
IGNITION
SYS CHK
DEPRESS TO CHECK SYSTEM
DIMMING INPUT
SEGMENT LIGHTS TO INDICATED PROBLEM
GROUND
IGNITION
1.2 K HOOD AJAR INPUT
1.2 K LOW WASHER FLUID INPUT
1.2 K LOW COOLANT INPUT
H B T R F J
.8 BLK 151 .8 BLK 151 .8 GRY 157 .8 BLK/WHT 99 .8 BLK/WHT 69
D1 E1 A7 C100
S215
1 GRY 157 .8 BLK/WHT 99 .8 GRY 69
SEE GROUND DISTRIBUTION
A HOOD AJAR SWITCH CLOSED WITH HOOD OPEN B
B WASHER FLUID LEVEL SWITCH CLOSED WITH LOW FLUID LEVEL A
A SURGE TANK LOW COOLANT SWITCH CLOSED WITH LOW COOLANT LEVEL B
.8 BLK 152
3 BLK 151
1 BLK 150 .8 BLK 150 .8 BLK 150
S100 SEE GROUND DISTRIBUTION S140
1 BLK 150 3 BLK 150
G203 G201 G101 G109

Grand Am — Driver information center

Driver Information
Systems OK
DISPLAYS FAULTS
LIGHTS TO INDICATE SYSTEM IS OK AFTER SYSTEM CHECK IS INITIATED
DRIVER INFORMATION CENTER (DIC) DISPLAY MODULE
IGNITION IGNITION
1.2 K LEFT REAR DOOR AJAR INPUT
1.2 K RIGHT REAR DOOR AJAR INPUT
1.2 K LEFT FRONT DOOR AJAR INPUT
1.2 K RIGHT FRONT DOOR AJAR INPUT
1.2 K LUGGAGE COMPARTMENT AJAR INPUT
P D M L K
.5 BLK/LT BLU 747 .5 BLK/LT GRN 748 .5 BLK/YEL 745 .5 BLK/WHT 746 .5 BLK/ORN 158
G5 E1 B2 H1 D2 C205
.5 LT GRN/BLK 958 .5 ORN/BLK 959 .5 PPL/WHT 956 .5 PNK/WHT 957 .5 BLK/ORN 158
B A C D E C200P (BLU)
.8 BLK/LT BLU 747 .8 BLK/LT GRN 748 .8 BLK/YEL 745 .8 BLK/WHT 746 .8 BLK/ORN 158
A C238 A C239 A C232 A C233 F C324
LH REAR DOOR AJAR SWITCH CLOSED WITH DOOR OPEN
RH REAR DOOR AJAR SWITCH CLOSED WITH DOOR OPEN
LH FRONT DOOR AJAR SWITCH CLOSED WITH DOOR OPEN
RH FRONT DOOR AJAR SWITCH CLOSED WITH DOOR OPEN
B C238 B C239 B C232 B C233
.8 BLK 150 .8 BLK 150 .8 BLK 150 .8 BLK 150 .8 BLK/ORN 158
S330
SEE GROUND DISTRIBUTION
G200
4 DOOR ONLY
LUGGAGE COMPARTMENT AJAR SWITCH CLOSED WITH LUGGAGE COMPARTMENT OPEN

Grand Am — Driver information center

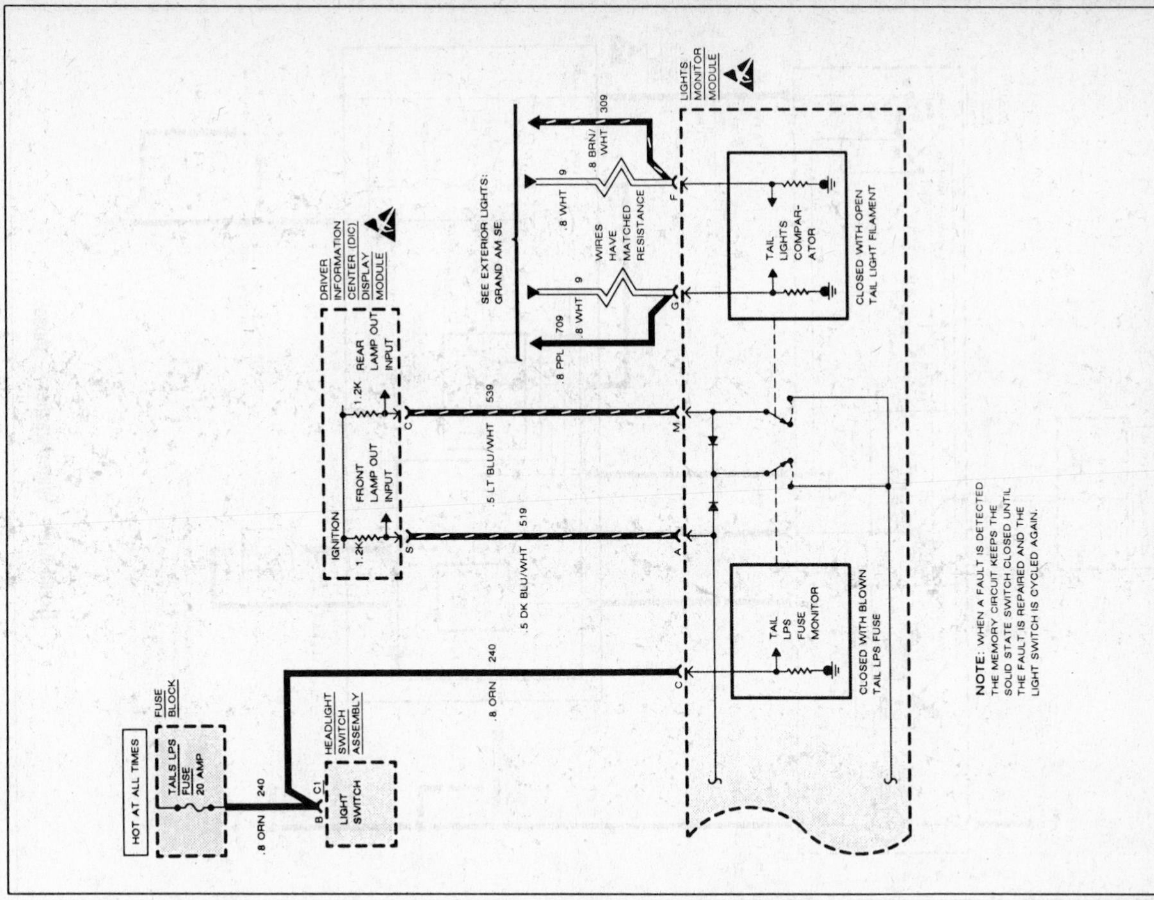

HOT AT ALL TIMES
FUSE BLOCK
CIG-CLK FUSE 20 AMP
SEE FUSE BLOCK DETAILS
1 ORN 40
S212
SEE FUSE BLOCK DETAILS
.8 ORN 40
SEE HEADLIGHTS: GRAND AM SE
SEE EXTERIOR LIGHTS: GRAND AM SE
1 YEL/BLK 712
.8 BLK 12
.8 TAN 12
1 TAN/WHT 312
1 DK GRN/WHT 711
.8 DK GRN 11
.8 LT GRN 11
1 LT GRN/BLK 311
.8 PPL 709
.8 BLK 9
.8 BLK 9
.8 BRN/WHT 309
WIRES HAVE MATCHED RESIST-ANCE
WIRES HAVE MATCHED RESIST-ANCE
WIRES HAVE MATCHED RESIST-ANCE
B J H L K E D
BATTERY
LOW BEAM COMPAR-ATOR
CLOSED WITH OPEN LOW BEAM FILAMENT
HIGH BEAM COMPAR-ATOR
CLOSED WITH OPEN HIGH BEAM FILAMENT
PARK LIGHTS COMPAR-ATOR
CLOSED WITH OPEN PARK LIGHT FILAMENT
N
8 BLK 151
S215
SEE GROUND DISTRIBUTION
3 BLK 151
G201

Grand Am — Driver information center

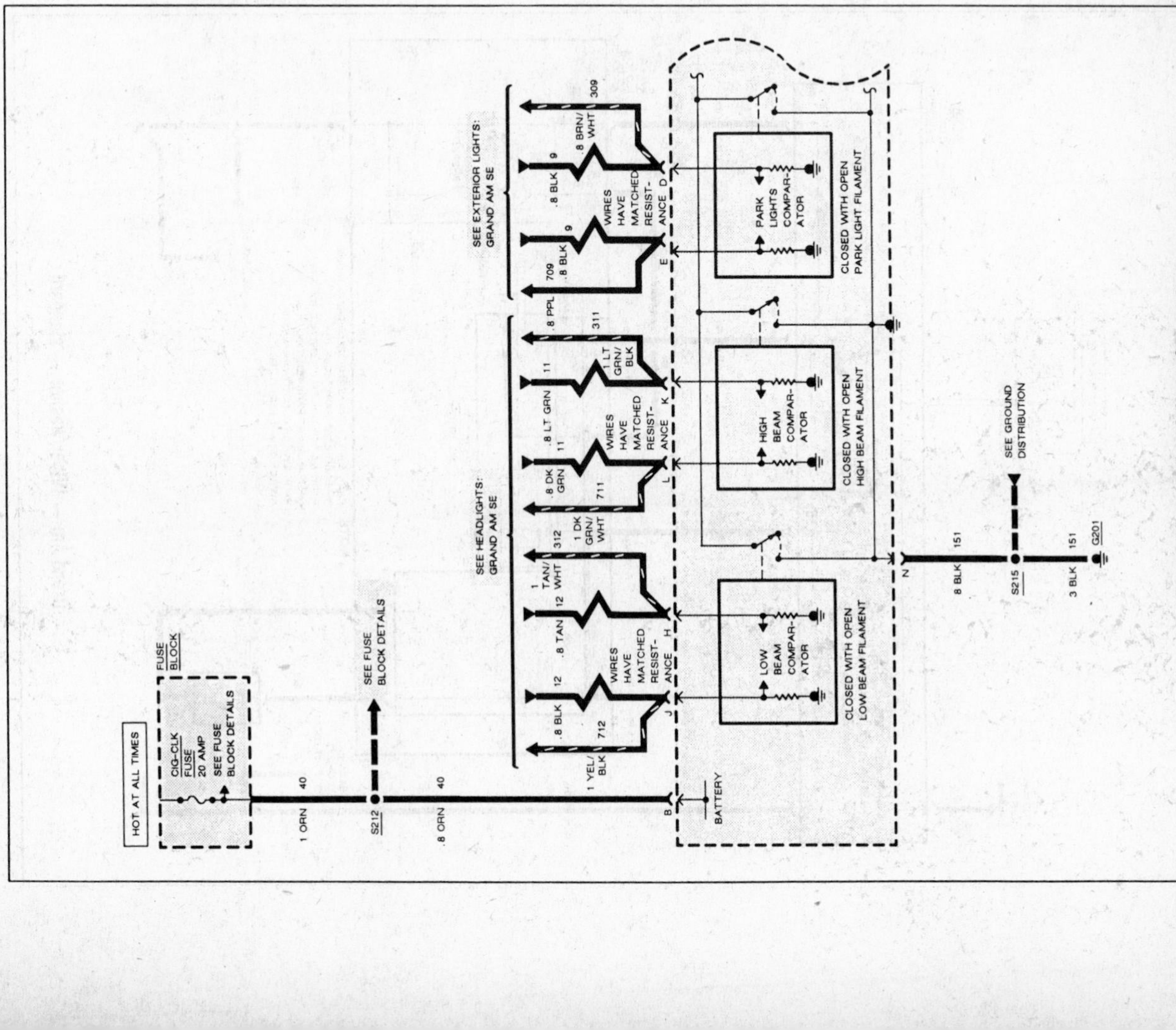

HOT AT ALL TIMES
FUSE BLOCK
TAILS LPS FUSE 20 AMP
.8 ORN 240
B C1
LIGHT SWITCH
HEADLIGHT SWITCH ASSEMBLY
IGNITION
1.2K
FRONT LAMP OUT INPUT
1.2K
REAR LAMP OUT INPUT
DRIVER INFORMATION CENTER (DIC) DISPLAY MODULE
S C
.8 ORN 240
.5 DK BLU/WHT 519
.5 LT BLU/WHT 539
SEE EXTERIOR LIGHTS: GRAND AM SE
.8 PPL 709
.8 WHT 9
.8 WHT 9
.8 BRN/WHT 309
WIRES HAVE MATCHED RESISTANCE
C A M G F
LIGHTS MONITOR MODULE
TAIL LPS FUSE MONITOR
CLOSED WITH BLOWN TAIL LPS FUSE
TAIL LIGHTS COMPAR-ATOR
CLOSED WITH OPEN TAIL LIGHT FILAMENT

NOTE: WHEN A FAULT IS DETECTED THE MEMORY CIRCUIT KEEPS THE SOLID STATE SWITCH CLOSED UNTIL THE FAULT IS REPAIRED AND THE LIGHT SWITCH IS CYCLED AGAIN.

Grand Am — Driver information center

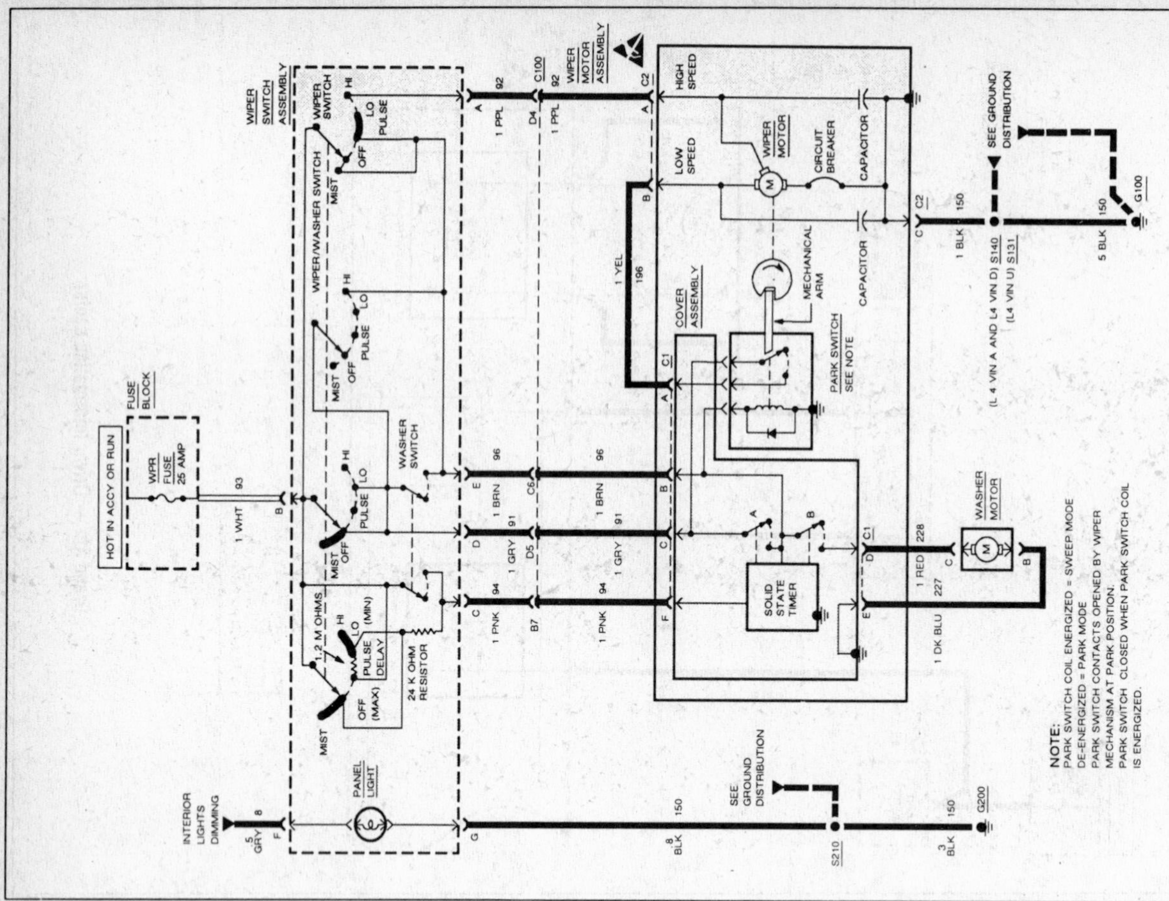
HOT IN ACCY OR RUN
FUSE BLOCK
WPR FUSE 25 AMP
WIPER SWITCH ASSEMBLY
WIPER/WASHER SWITCH
WASHER SWITCH
24 K OHM RESISTOR
1.2 M OHMS
PANEL LIGHT
INTERIOR LIGHTS DIMMING
SOLID STATE TIMER
WIPER MOTOR ASSEMBLY
COVER ASSEMBLY
MECHANICAL ARM
PARK SWITCH SEE NOTE
CIRCUIT BREAKER
CAPACITOR
HIGH SPEED
LOW SPEED
WASHER MOTOR
SEE GROUND DISTRIBUTION
NOTE:
PARK SWITCH COIL ENERGIZED = SWEEP MODE
DE-ENERGIZED = PARK MODE
PARK SWITCH CONTACTS OPENED BY WIPER MECHANISM AT PARK POSITION.
PARK SWITCH CLOSED WHEN PARK SWITCH COIL IS ENERGIZED.

Grand Am — Wiper/washer — pulse

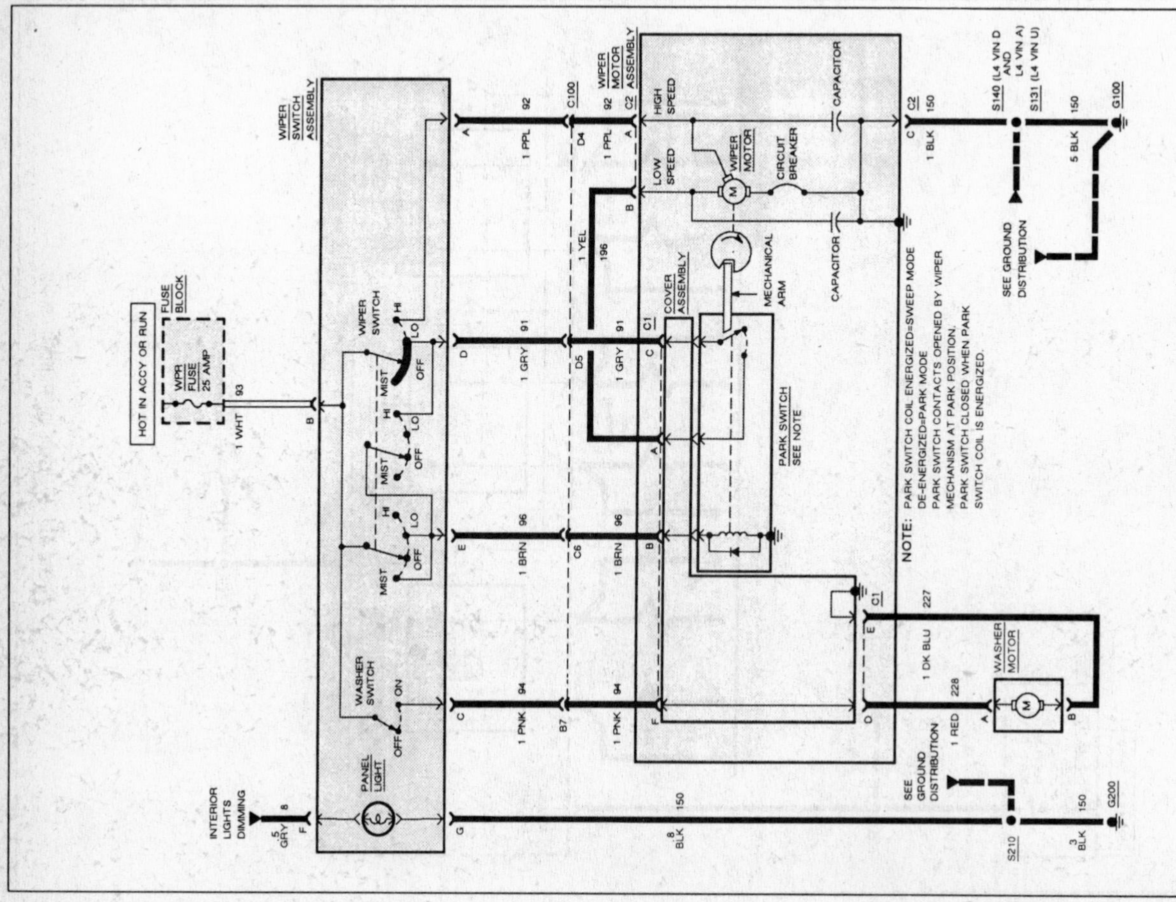
HOT IN ACCY OR RUN
FUSE BLOCK
WPR FUSE 25 AMP
WIPER SWITCH ASSEMBLY
WIPER SWITCH
WASHER SWITCH
PANEL LIGHT
INTERIOR LIGHTS DIMMING
WIPER MOTOR ASSEMBLY
COVER ASSEMBLY
MECHANICAL ARM
PARK SWITCH SEE NOTE
CIRCUIT BREAKER
CAPACITOR
HIGH SPEED
LOW SPEED
WASHER MOTOR
SEE GROUND DISTRIBUTION
NOTE: PARK SWITCH COIL ENERGIZED=SWEEP MODE
DE-ENERGIZED=PARK MODE
PARK SWITCH CONTACTS OPENED BY WIPER MECHANISM AT PARK POSITION.
PARK SWITCH CLOSED WHEN PARK SWITCH COIL IS ENERGIZED.

Grand Am — Wiper/washer — standard

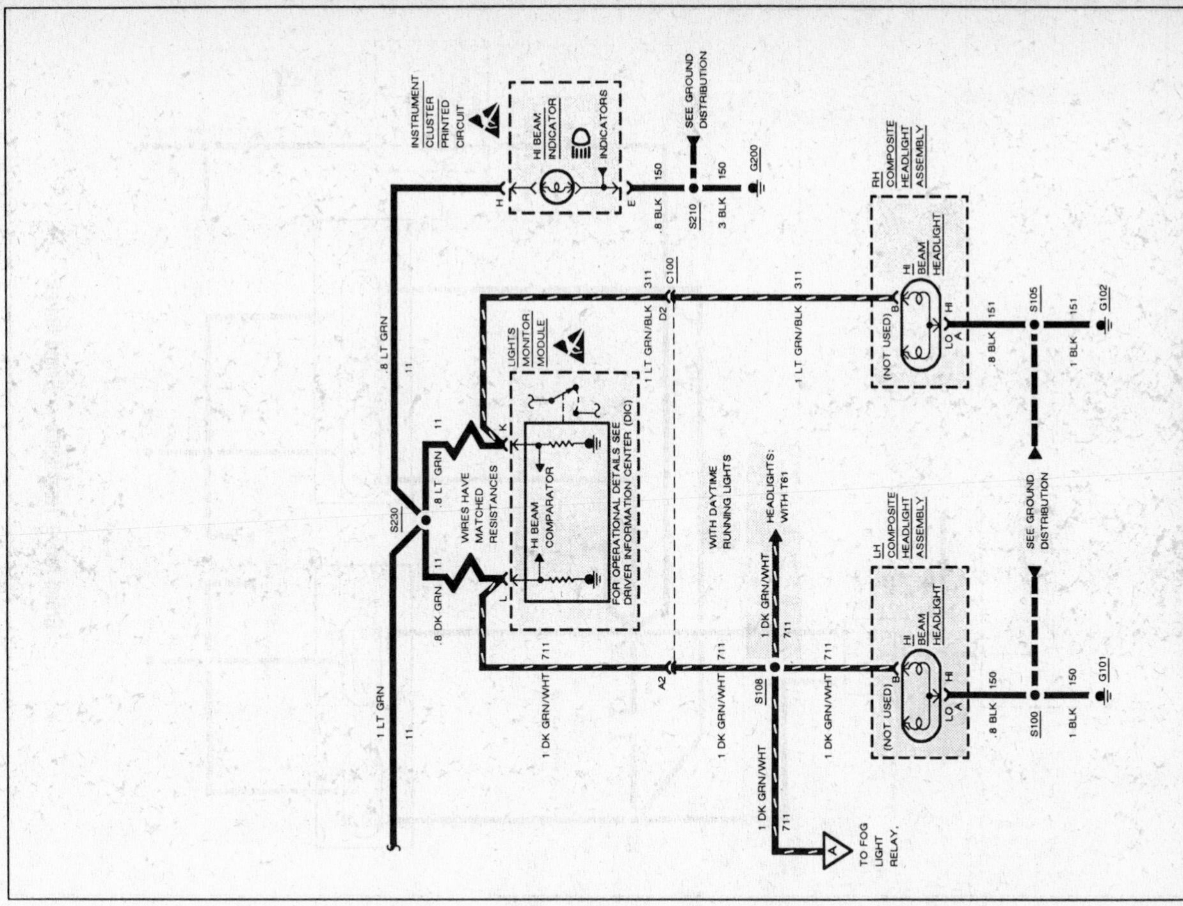

Grand Am — Headlights — Grand Am SE

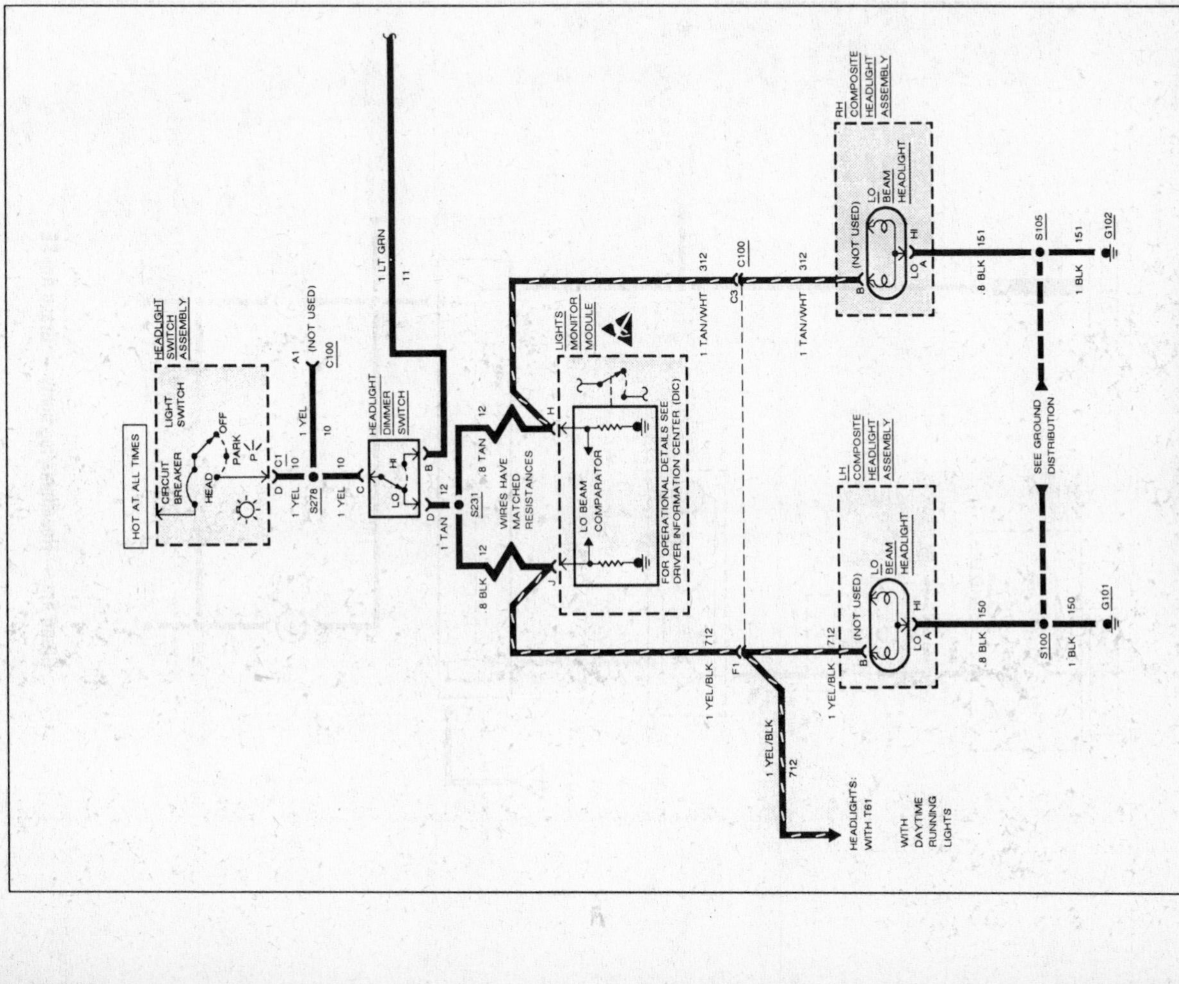

Grand Am — Headlights — Grand Am SE

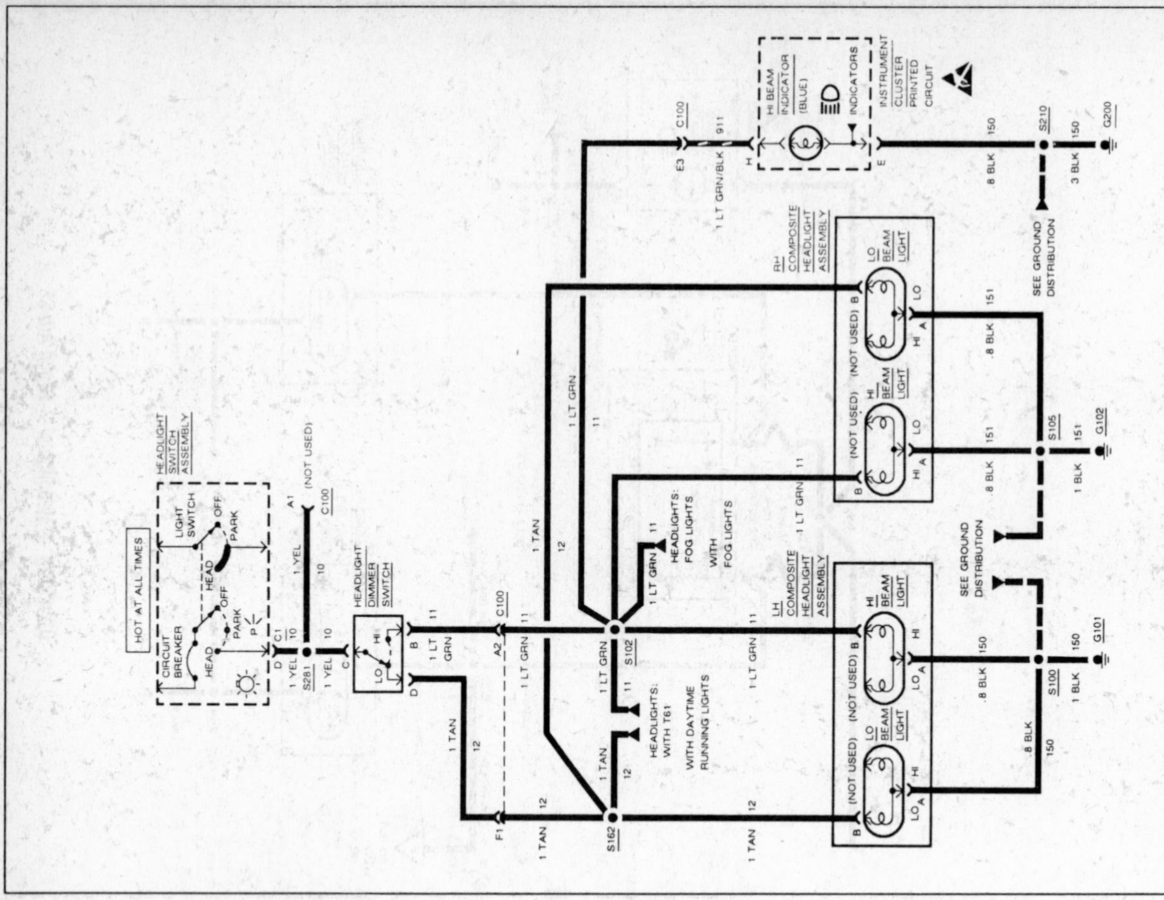

Grand Am — Headlights — Grand Am LE

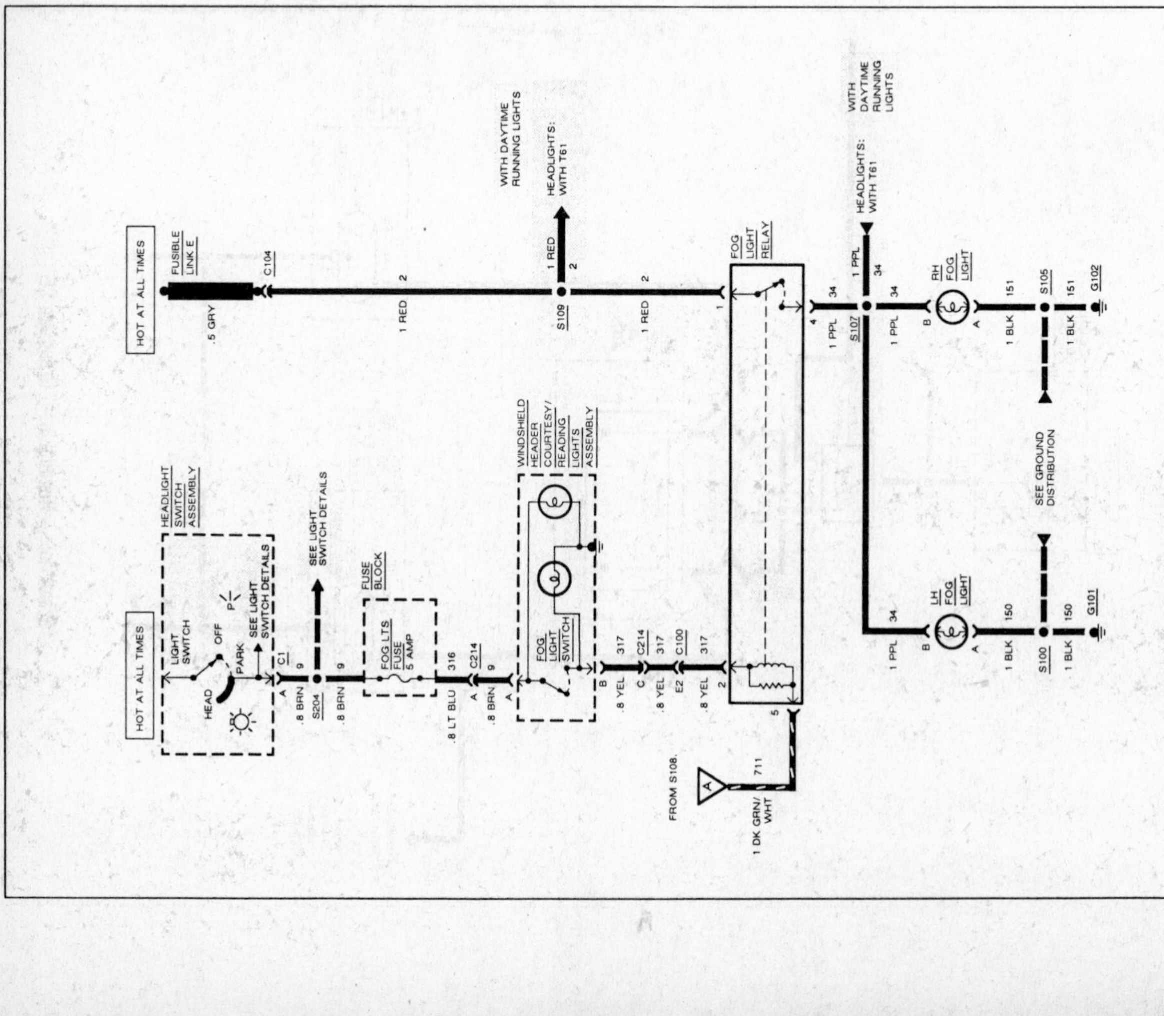

Grand Am — Headlights/fog lights — Grand Am SE

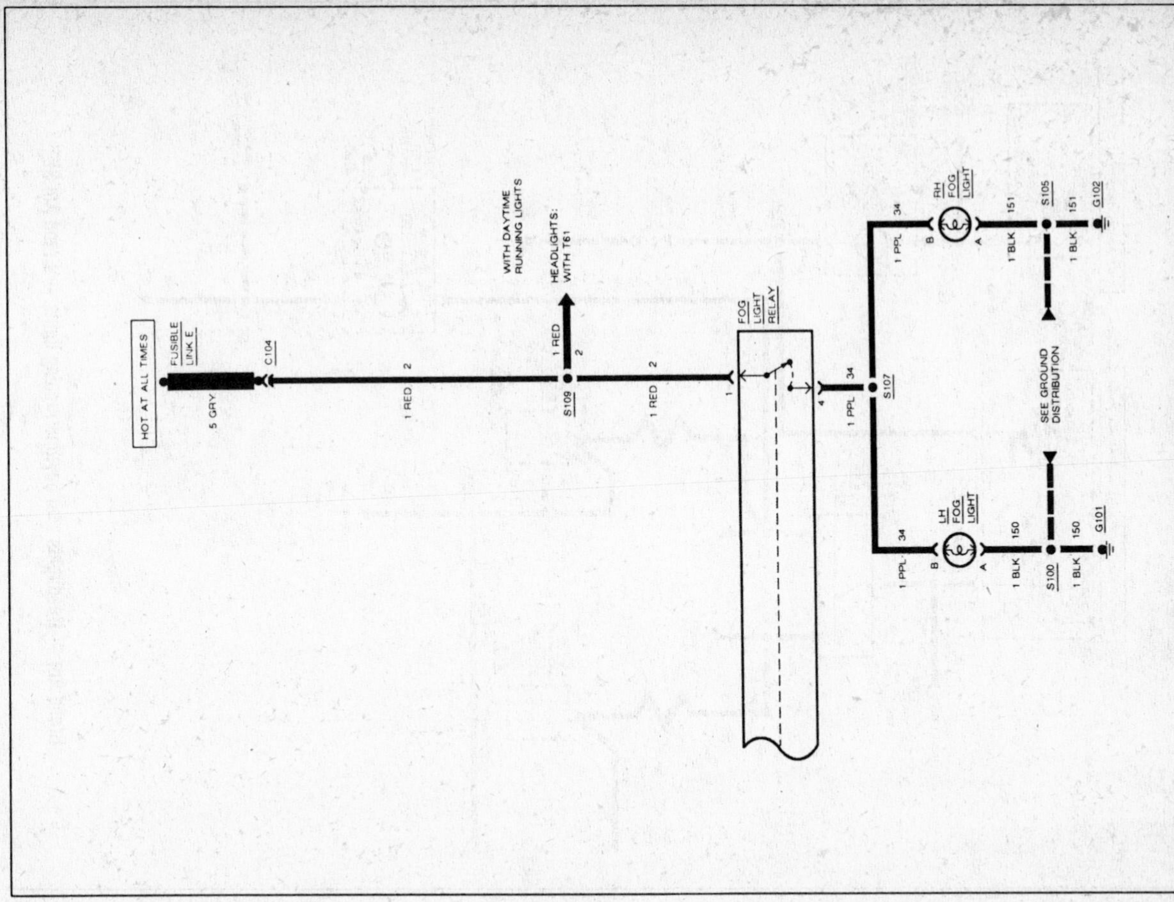

Grand Am — Headlights/fog lights — Grand Am LE

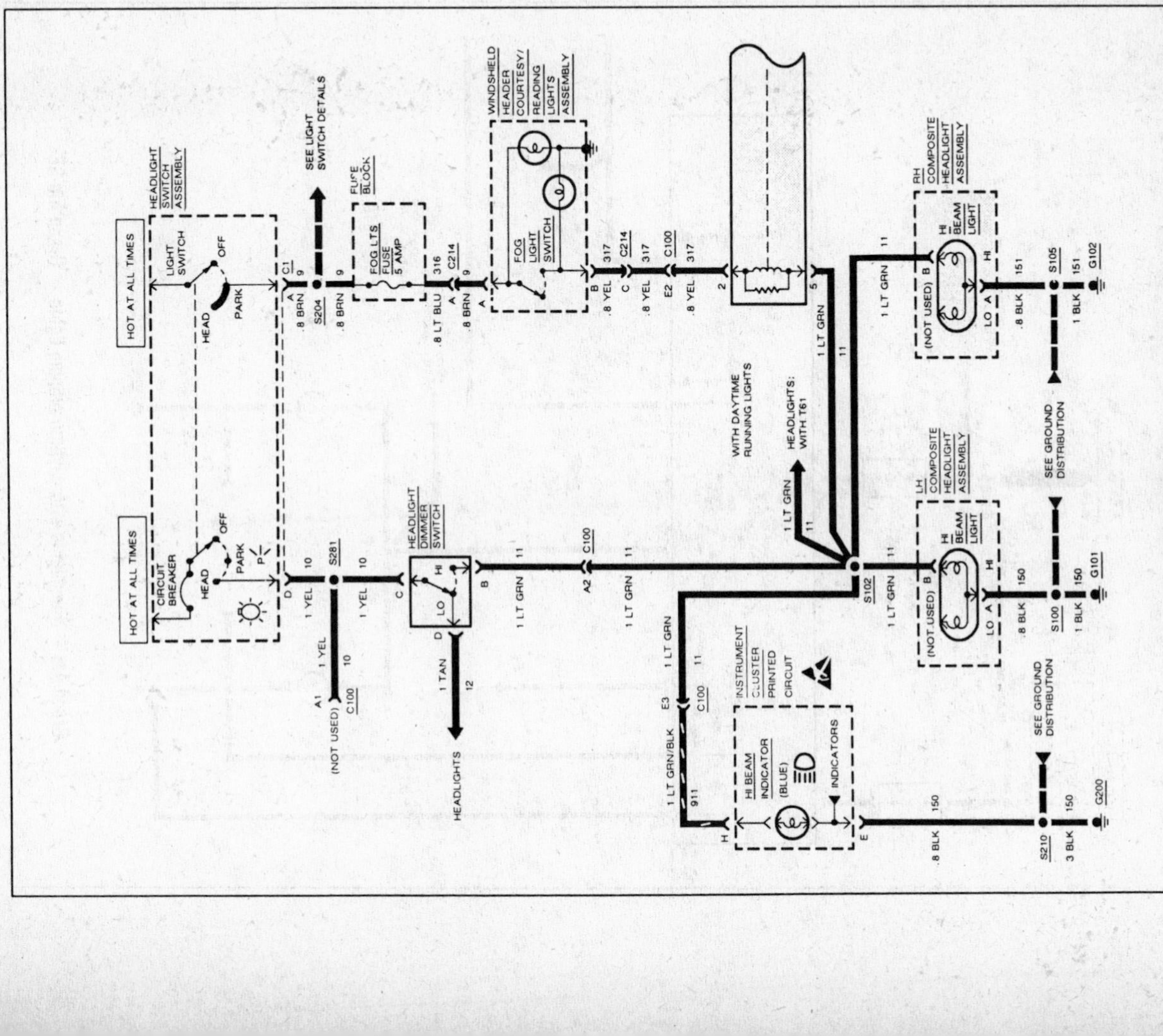

Grand Am — Headlights/fog lights — Grand Am LE

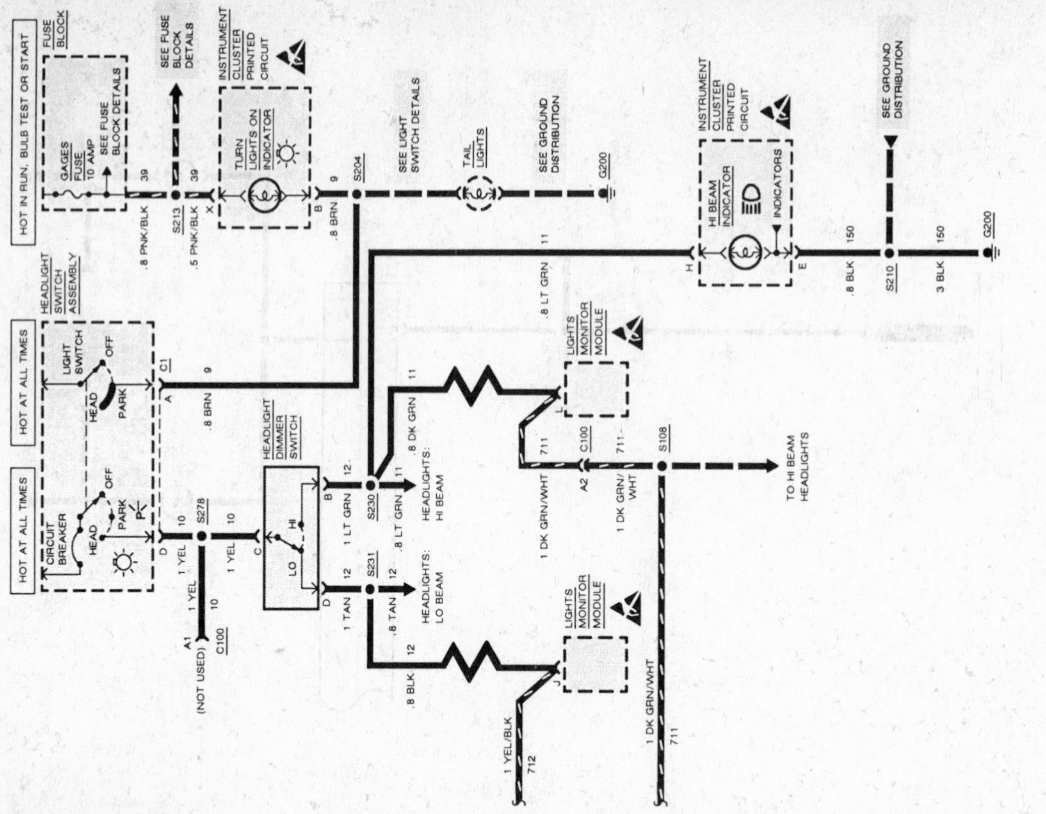

Grand Am — Headlights with daytime running lights — Grand Am SE

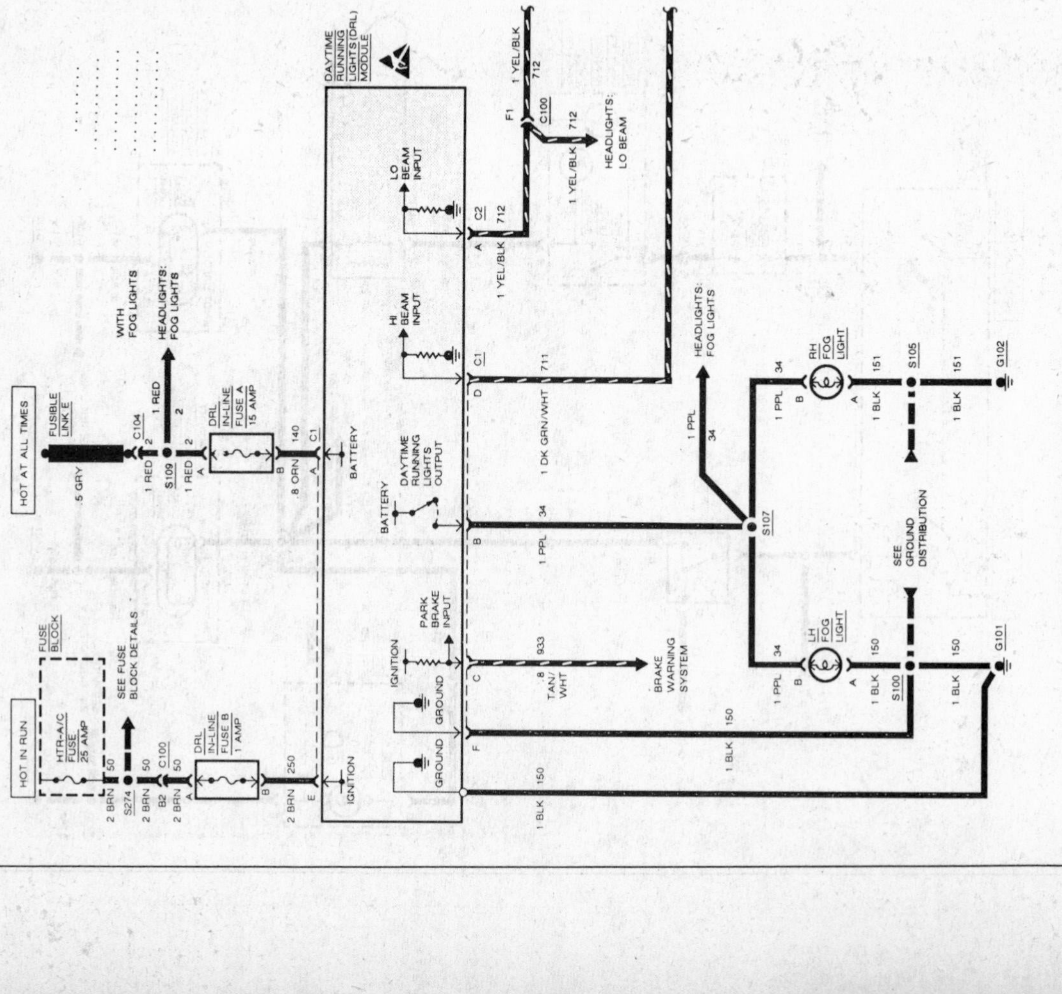

Grand Am — Headlights with daytime running lights — Grand Am SE

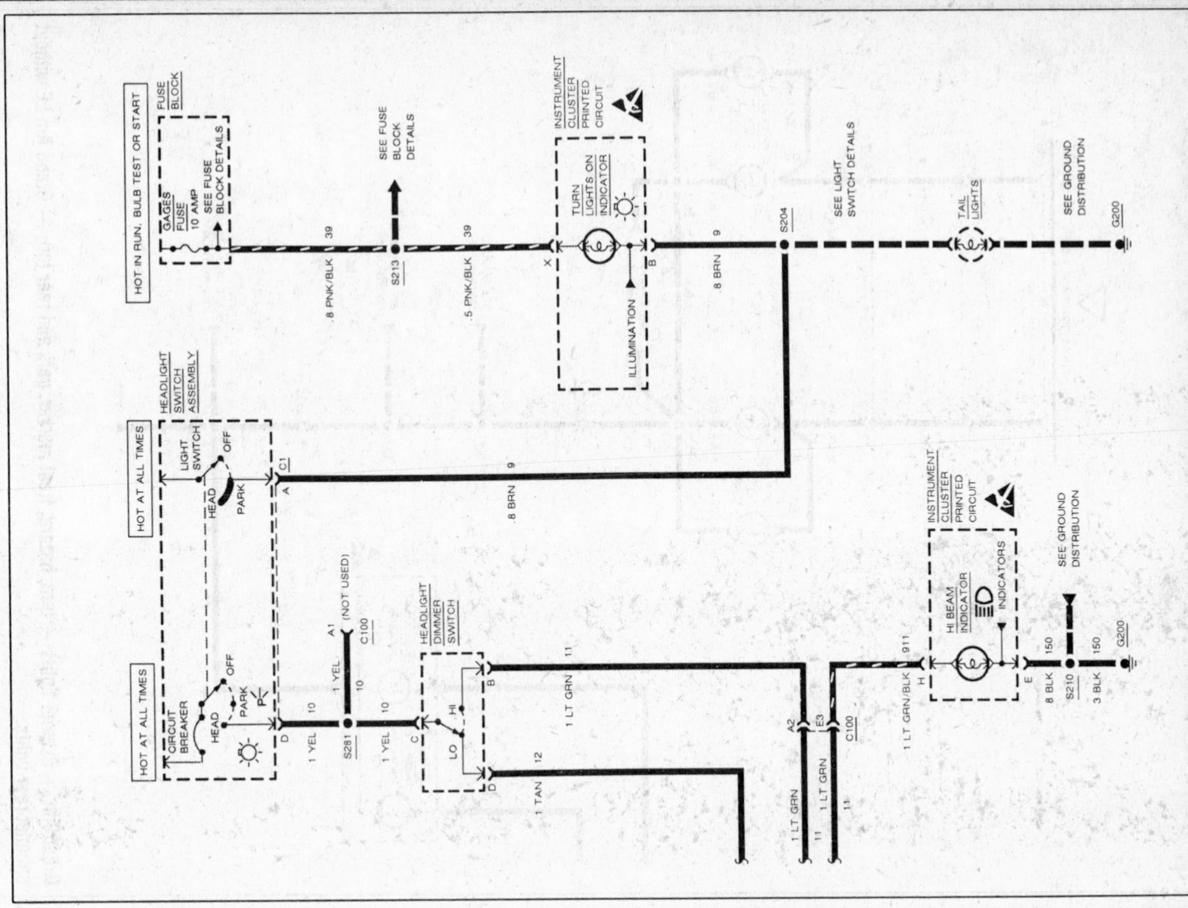

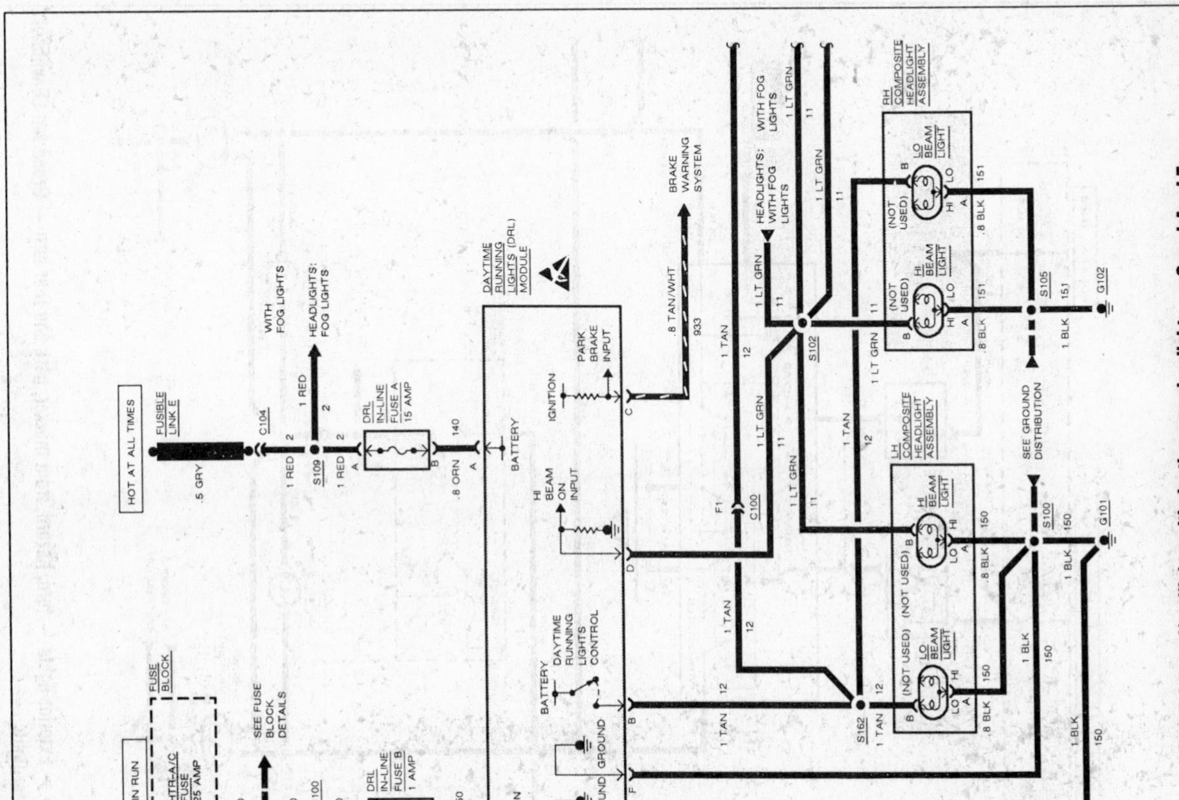

HOT IN RUN
HTR-A/C FUSE 25 AMP
FUSE BLOCK
2 BRN 50
S274
SEE FUSE BLOCK DETAILS
2 BRN 50
B2 C100
2 BRN 50
DRL IN-LINE FUSE B 1 AMP
2 BRN 250
HOT AT ALL TIMES
FUSIBLE LINK E
.5 GRY
C104
1 RED 2
WITH FOG LIGHTS
1 RED
S109
HEADLIGHTS: FOG LIGHTS
1 RED 2
DRL IN-LINE FUSE A 15 AMP
.8 ORN 140
IGNITION
BATTERY
DAYTIME RUNNING LIGHTS (DRL) MODULE
BATTERY
DAYTIME RUNNING LIGHTS CONTROL
GROUND GROUND
HI BEAM ON INPUT
IGNITION
PARK BRAKE INPUT
.8 TAN/WHT
933
BRAKE WARNING SYSTEM
1 TAN 12
1 TAN
F1
C100
1 TAN 12
1 LT GRN 11
HEADLIGHTS: WITH FOG LIGHTS
WITH FOG LIGHTS
1 LT GRN 11
S102
S162
1 TAN 12
(NOT USED) (NOT USED)
LO BEAM LIGHT
HI BEAM LIGHT
LH COMPOSITE HEADLIGHT ASSEMBLY
(NOT USED)
HI BEAM LIGHT
LO BEAM LIGHT
RH COMPOSITE HEADLIGHT ASSEMBLY
.8 BLK 150
.8 BLK 151
1 BLK 150
S100
SEE GROUND DISTRIBUTION
S105
1 BLK 151
G101
G102

Grand Am — Headlights with daytime running lights — Grand Am LE

HOT AT ALL TIMES
CIRCUIT BREAKER
HEAD PARK OFF
HOT AT ALL TIMES
LIGHT SWITCH
HEAD PARK OFF
HEADLIGHT SWITCH ASSEMBLY
C1
1 YEL 10
S281
1 YEL 10
A1 (NOT USED)
C100
HEADLIGHT DIMMER SWITCH
LO HI
1 TAN 12
1 LT GRN 11
.8 BRN 9
HOT IN RUN, BULB TEST OR START
GAGES FUSE 10 AMP
SEE FUSE BLOCK DETAILS
FUSE BLOCK
.8 PNK/BLK 39
S213
SEE FUSE BLOCK DETAILS
.5 PNK/BLK 39
TURN LIGHTS ON INDICATOR
ILLUMINATION
INSTRUMENT CLUSTER PRINTED CIRCUIT
.8 BRN 9
S204
SEE LIGHT SWITCH DETAILS
TAIL LIGHTS
SEE GROUND DISTRIBUTION
G200
1 LT GRN 11
A2
E3
C100
1 LT GRN/BLK 911
HI BEAM INDICATOR
INDICATORS
INSTRUMENT CLUSTER PRINTED CIRCUIT
8 BLK 150
S210
SEE GROUND DISTRIBUTION
3 BLK 150
G200

Grand Am — Headlights with daytime running lights — Grand Am LE

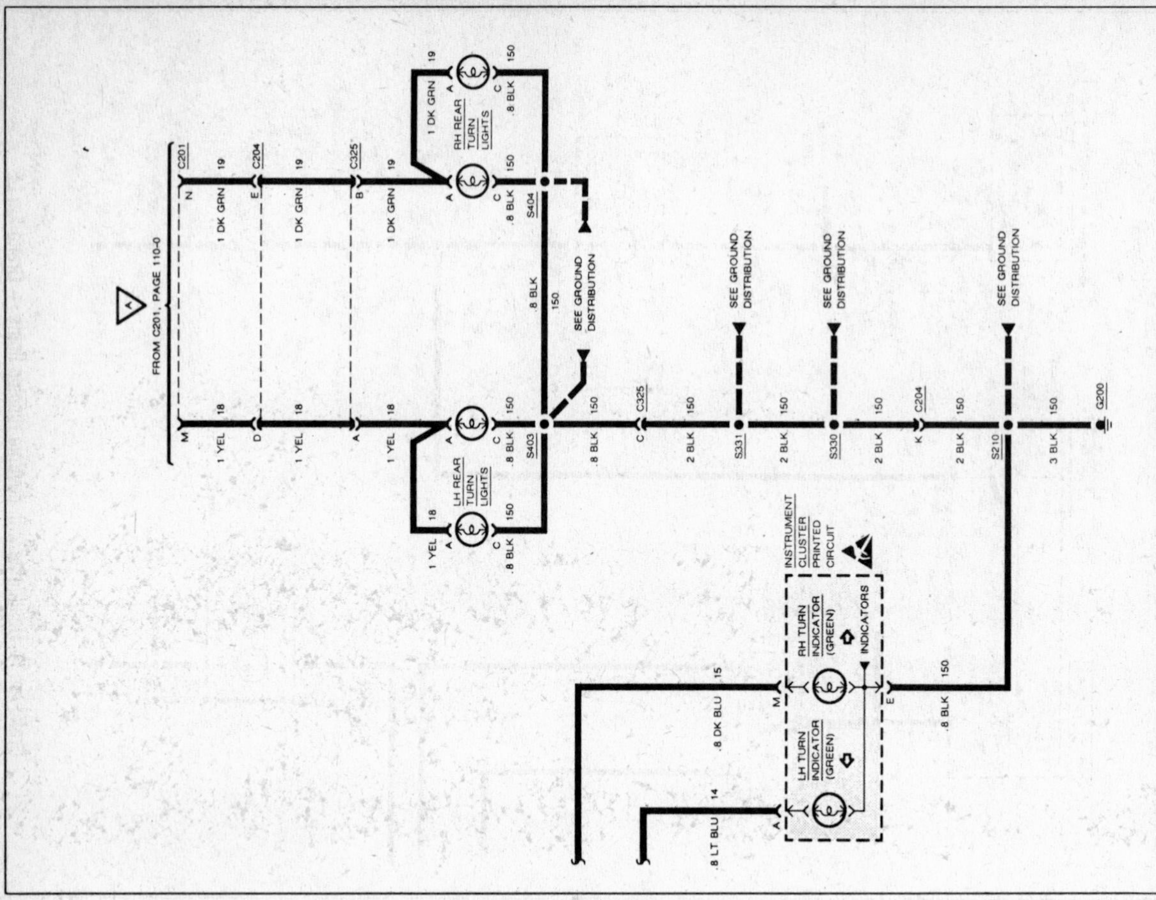

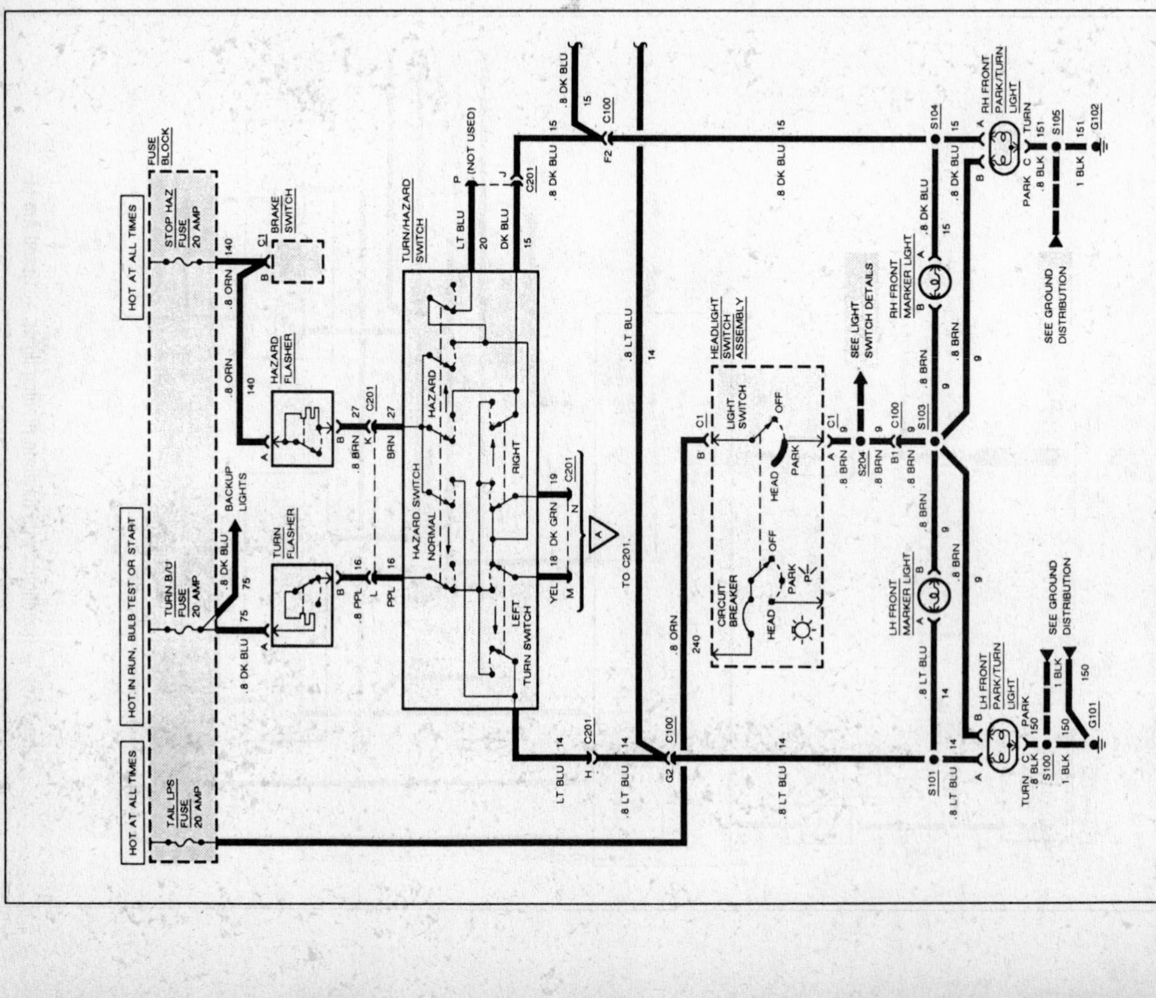

HOT AT ALL TIMES
HOT IN RUN, BULB TEST OR START
HOT AT ALL TIMES
FUSE BLOCK
TAIL LPS FUSE 20 AMP
TURN B/U FUSE 20 AMP
STOP HAZ FUSE 20 AMP
.8 DK BLU 75
.8 DK BLU 75
BACKUP LIGHTS
.8 ORN 140
.8 ORN 140
TURN FLASHER
HAZARD FLASHER
C1 BRAKE SWITCH
.8 PPL 16
.8 BRN 27
C201
PPL 16
BRN 27
TURN/HAZARD SWITCH
HAZARD SWITCH
NORMAL
HAZARD
LEFT
RIGHT
TURN SWITCH
LT BLU 20
(NOT USED)
DK BLU 15
C201
YEL 18
DK GRN 19
C201
TO C201.
LT BLU 14
C201
.8 LT BLU 14
.8 DK BLU 15
.8 DK BLU 15
C100
.8 LT BLU 14
C100
.8 ORN 240
C1
CIRCUIT BREAKER
HEAD
OFF
PARK
LIGHT SWITCH
HEAD
OFF
PARK
HEADLIGHT SWITCH ASSEMBLY
.8 LT BLU 14
.8 DK BLU 15
C1
.8 BRN 9
S204
SEE LIGHT SWITCH DETAILS
.8 BRN 9
C100
.8 BRN 9
S103
LH FRONT MARKER LIGHT
RH FRONT MARKER LIGHT
S101
.8 LT BLU 14
.8 BRN 9
.8 BRN 9
.8 DK BLU 15
S104
.8 LT BLU 14
.8 BRN 9
.8 BRN 9
.8 DK BLU 15
LH FRONT PARK/TURN LIGHT
RH FRONT PARK/TURN LIGHT
TURN
PARK
.8 BLK 150
S100
1 BLK 150
1 BLK
SEE GROUND DISTRIBUTION
G101
PARK
TURN
.8 BLK 151
SEE GROUND DISTRIBUTION
S105
1 BLK 151
G102

Grand Am — Exterior lights — turn, hazard, front marker, park and rear turn — Grand Am LE without optional rear lights

FROM C201, PAGE 110-0
C201
1 YEL 18
1 DK GRN 19
C204
1 YEL 18
1 DK GRN 19
C325
1 YEL 18
1 DK GRN 19
1 YEL 18
1 DK GRN 19
LH REAR TURN LIGHTS
RH REAR TURN LIGHTS
.8 BLK 150
.8 BLK 150
.8 BLK 150
.8 BLK 150
S403
.8 BLK 150
S404
SEE GROUND DISTRIBUTION
.8 BLK 150
C325
2 BLK 150
.8 LT BLU 14
.8 DK BLU 15
S331
SEE GROUND DISTRIBUTION
2 BLK 150
LH TURN INDICATOR (GREEN)
RH TURN INDICATOR (GREEN)
INDICATORS
INSTRUMENT CLUSTER PRINTED CIRCUIT
S330
SEE GROUND DISTRIBUTION
2 BLK 150
C204
.8 BLK 150
2 BLK 150
S210
SEE GROUND DISTRIBUTION
3 BLK 150
G200

Grand Am — Exterior lights — turn, hazard, front marker, park and rear turn — Grand Am LE without optional rear lights

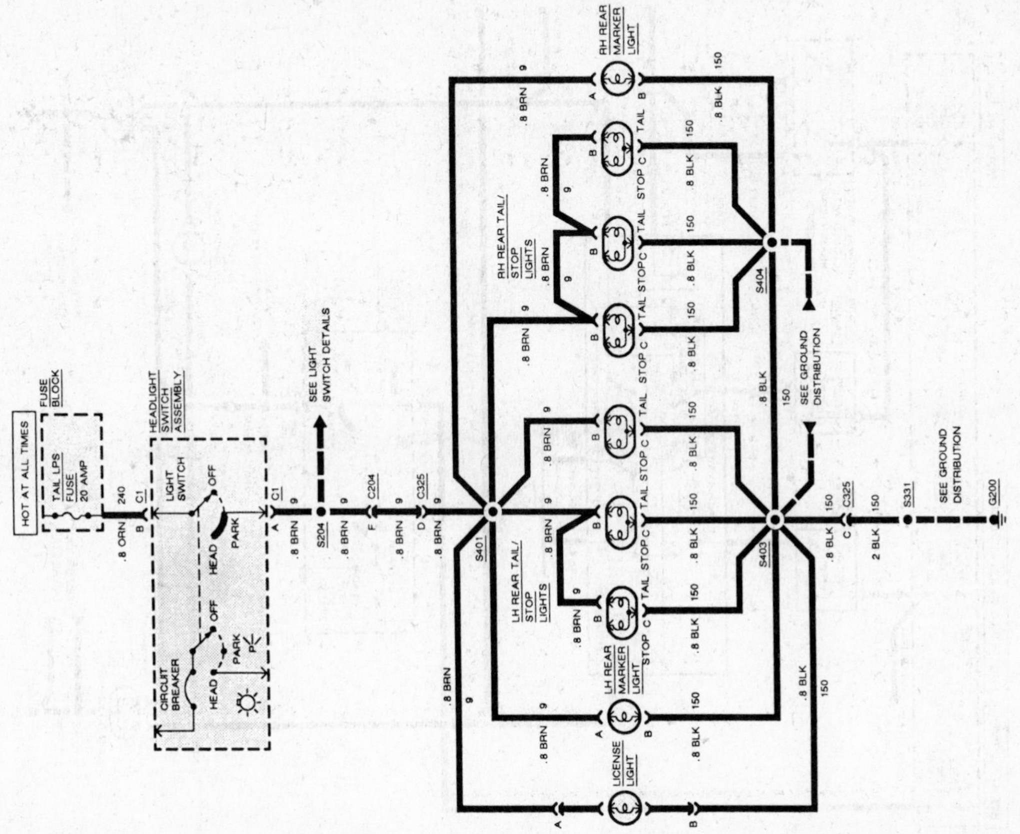

HOT AT ALL TIMES
FUSE BLOCK
TAIL LPS FUSE 20 AMP
.8 ORN 240
B C1
HEADLIGHT SWITCH ASSEMBLY
CIRCUIT BREAKER
LIGHT SWITCH
HEAD OFF HEAD OFF
PARK PARK
A C1
.8 BRN 9
S204
SEE LIGHT SWITCH DETAILS
.8 BRN 9
F C204
.8 BRN 9
D C325
.8 BRN 9
S401
LH REAR TAIL/ STOP LIGHTS
RH REAR TAIL/ STOP LIGHTS
LICENSE LIGHT
LH REAR MARKER LIGHT
RH REAR MARKER LIGHT
STOP C TAIL
.8 BLK 150
S403
S404
SEE GROUND DISTRIBUTION
C C325
2 BLK 150
S331
SEE GROUND DISTRIBUTION
G200

Grand Am — Exterior lights — tail, rear marker and license — Grand Am LE without optional rear lights

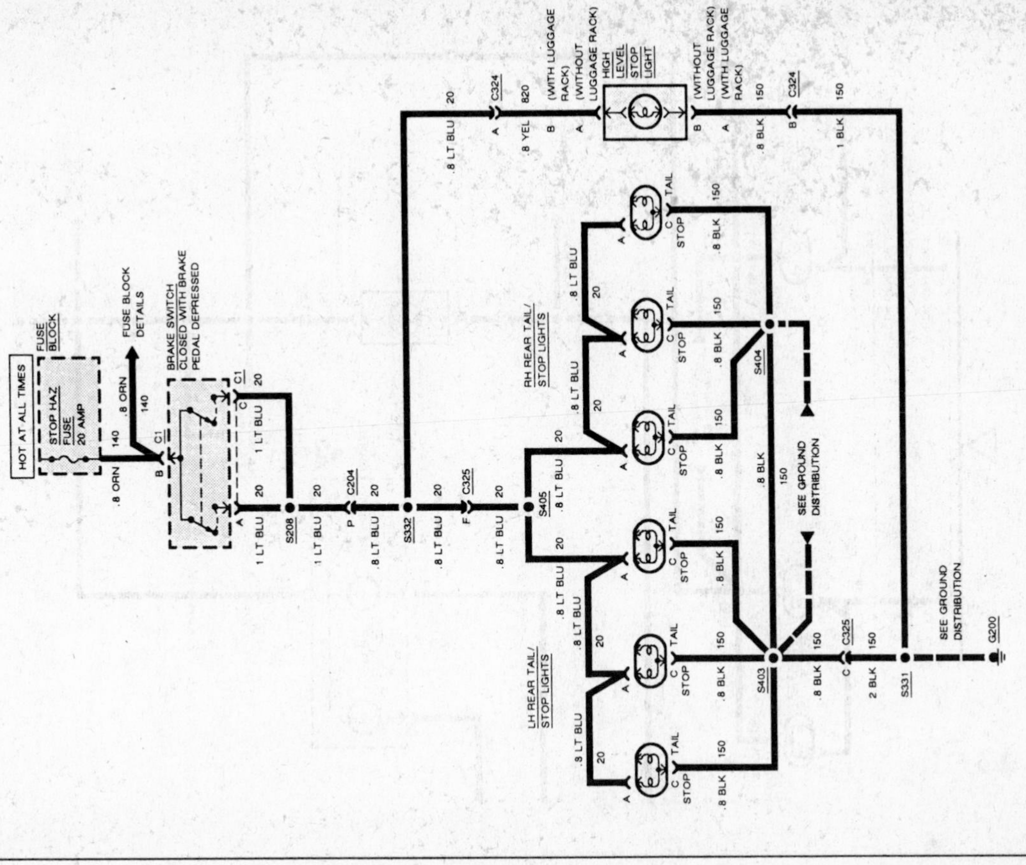

HOT AT ALL TIMES
FUSE BLOCK
STOP HAZ FUSE 20 AMP
.8 ORN 140
FUSE BLOCK DETAILS
B C1
BRAKE SWITCH CLOSED WITH BRAKE PEDAL DEPRESSED
A C C1
1 LT BLU 20
S208
P C204
.8 LT BLU 20
S332
F C325
S405
LH REAR TAIL/ STOP LIGHTS
RH REAR TAIL/ STOP LIGHTS
A C324
.8 YEL 820
B (WITH LUGGAGE RACK)
A (WITHOUT LUGGAGE RACK)
HIGH LEVEL STOP LIGHT
B (WITHOUT LUGGAGE RACK)
A (WITH LUGGAGE RACK)
.8 BLK 150
B C324
1 BLK 150
S403
S404
SEE GROUND DISTRIBUTION
C C325
2 BLK 150
S331
SEE GROUND DISTRIBUTION
G200

Grand Am — Exterior lights — stop — Grand Am LE without optional rear lights

Grand Am — Exterior lights — turn, hazard, front marker, park and stop — Grand Am LE with optional rear lights

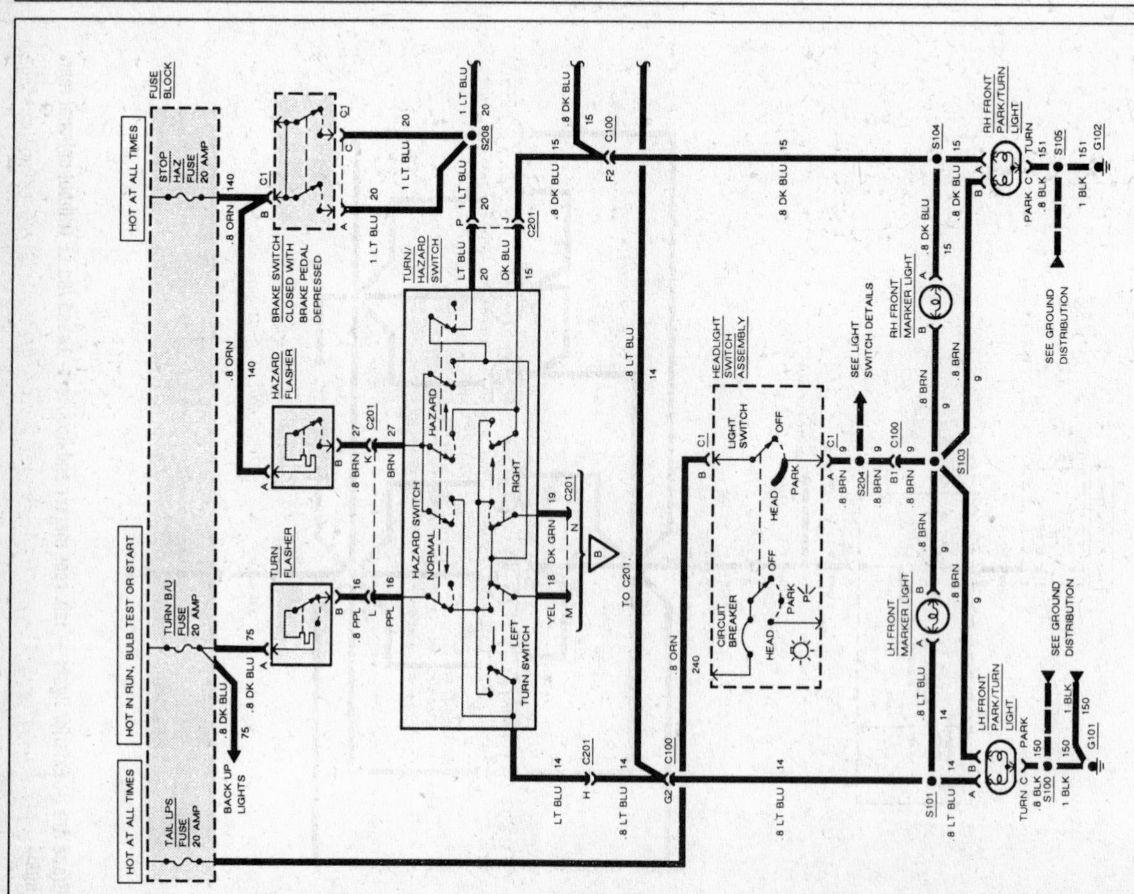

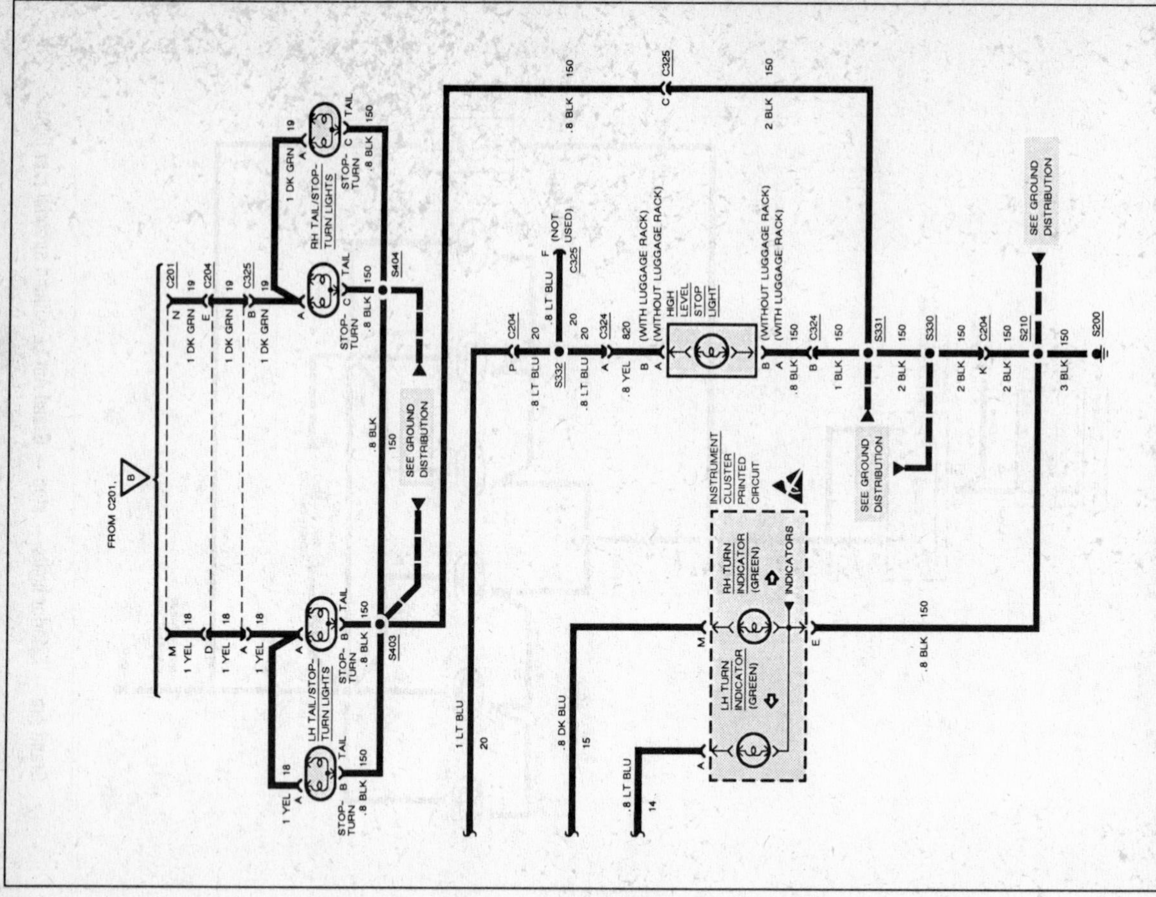

Grand Am — Exterior lights — turn, hazard, front marker, park and stop — Grand Am LE with optional rear lights

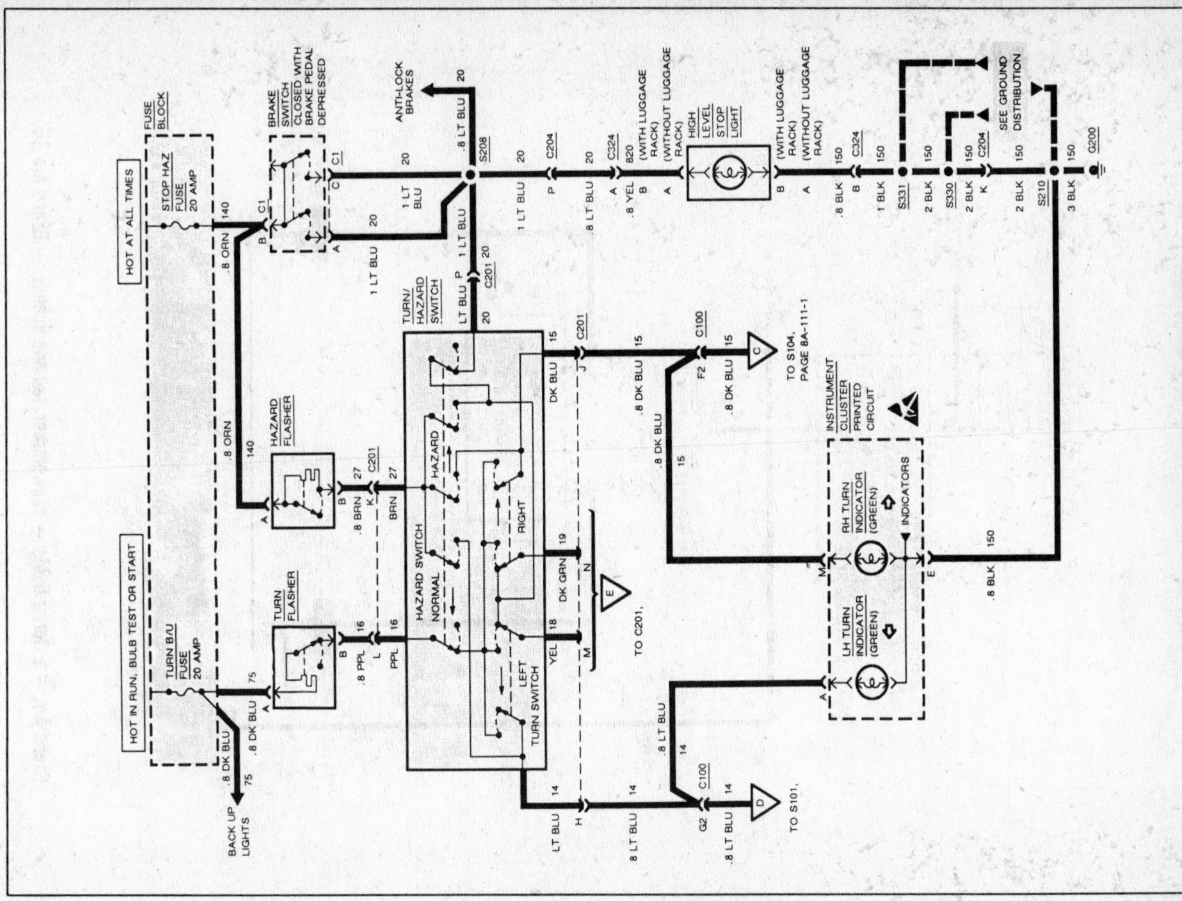

Grand Am — Exterior lights — Grand Am SE

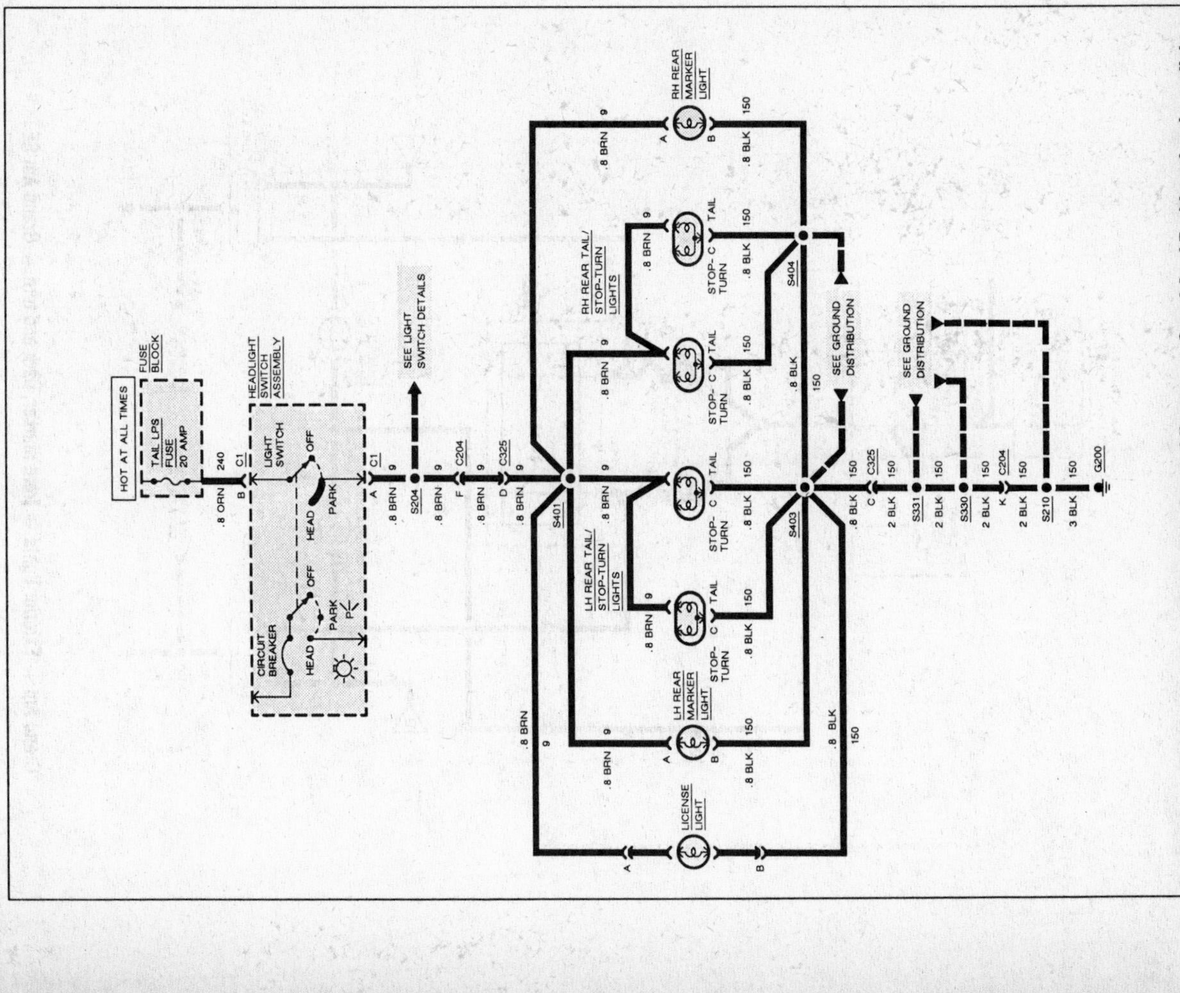

Grand Am — Exterior lights — tail, rear marker and license — Grand Am LE with optional rear lights

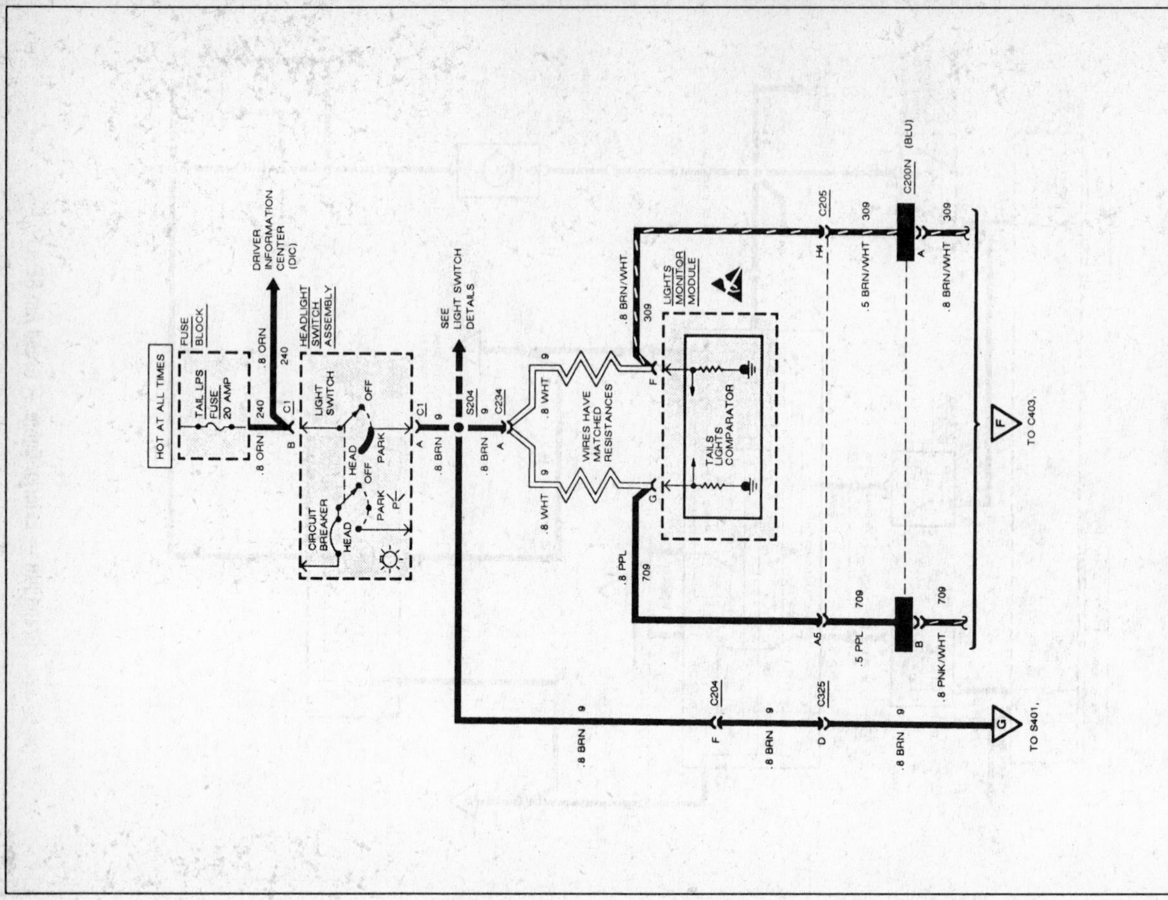

Grand Am — Exterior lights — rear marker, tail and license — Grand Am SE

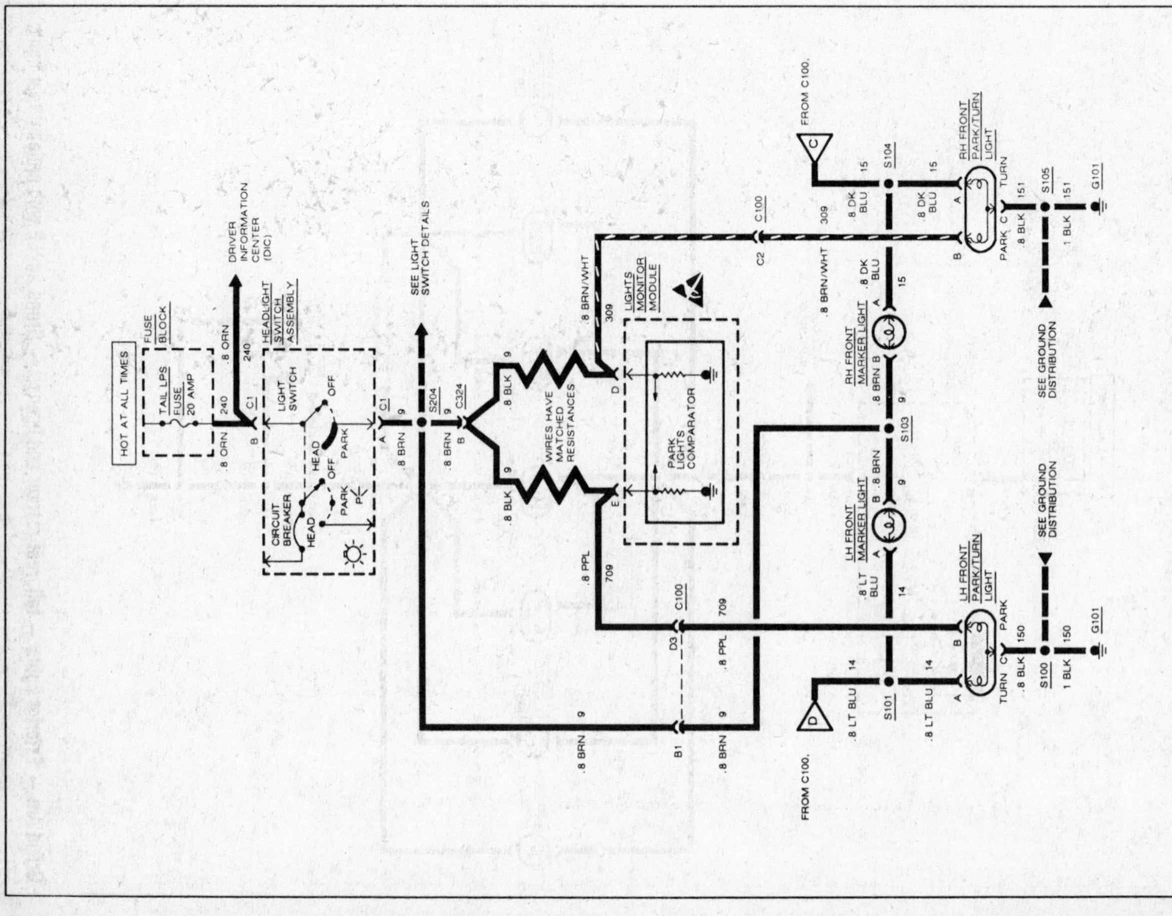

Grand Am — Exterior lights — front marker, park and turn — Grand Am SE

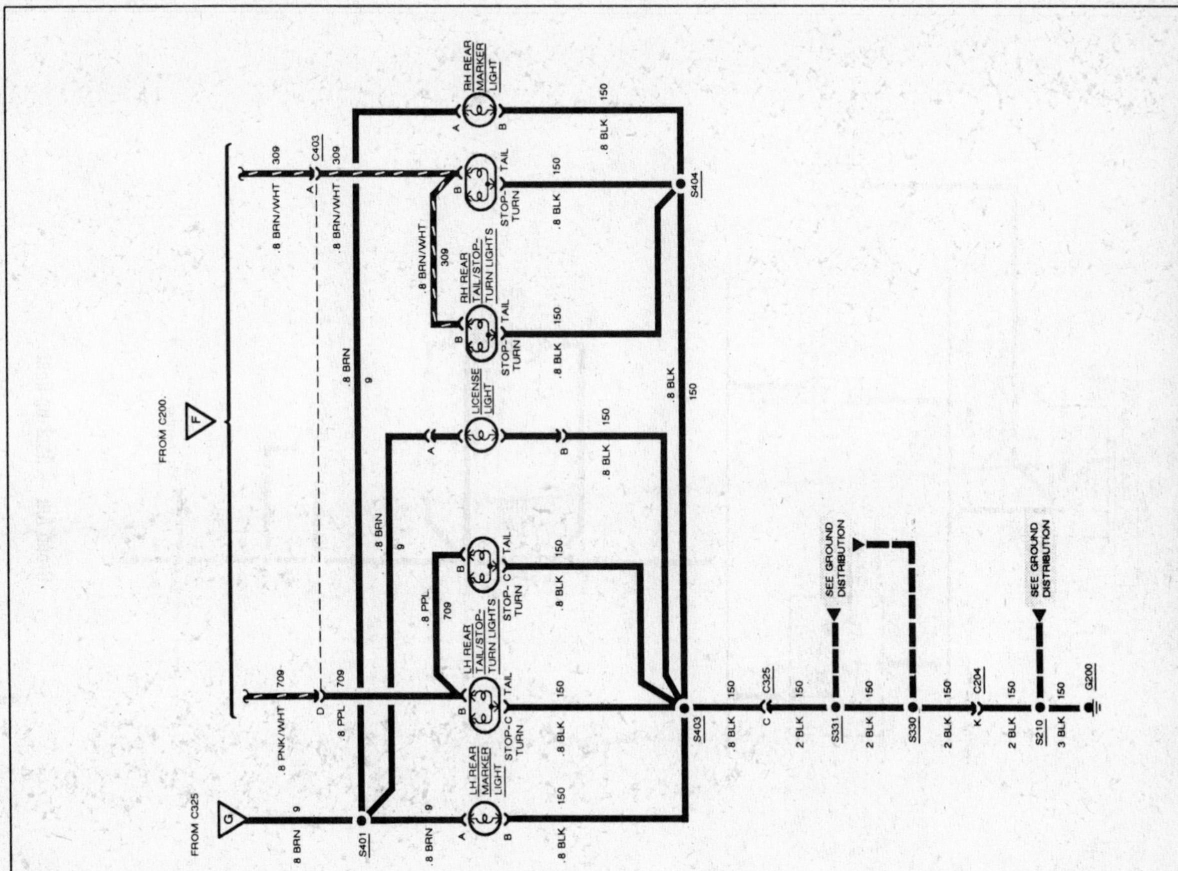

Grand Am — Exterior lights — rear marker, tail and license — Grand Am SE

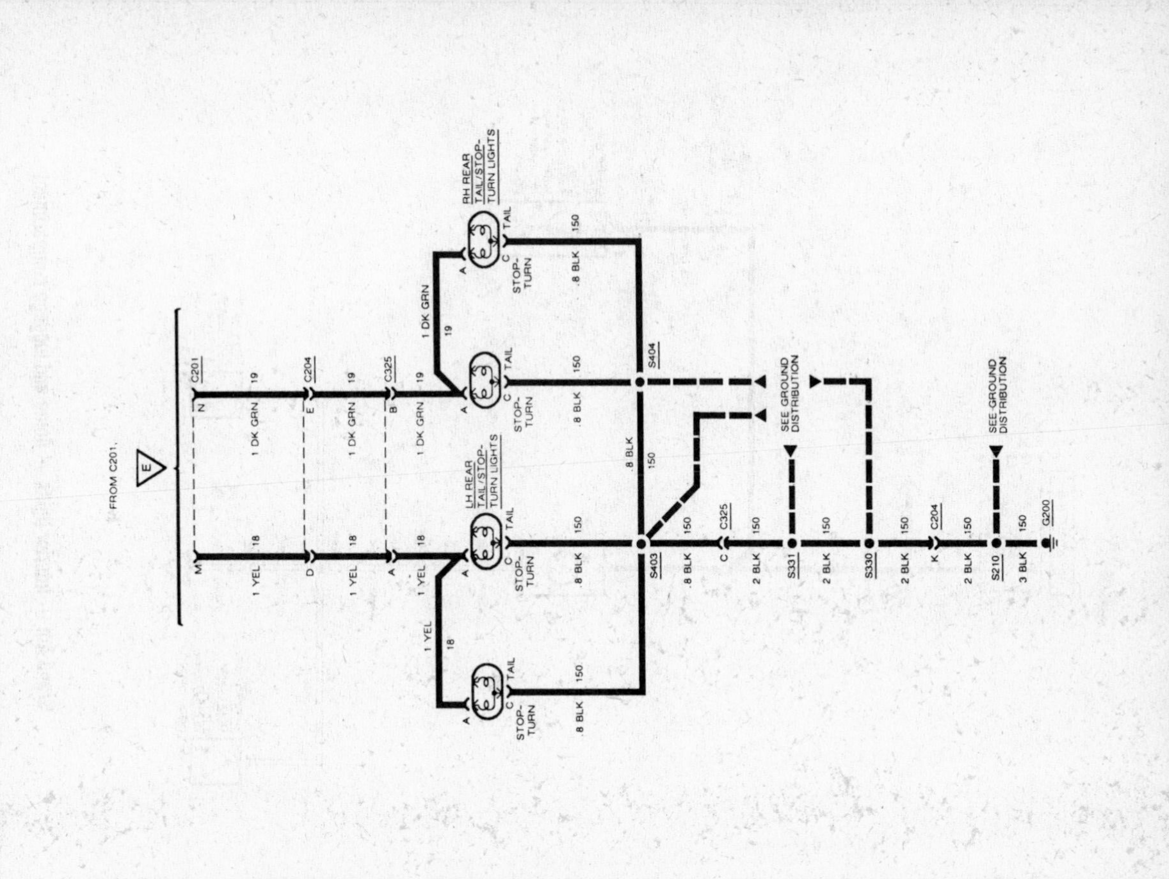

Grand Am — Exterior lights — stop, hazard and turn — Grand Am SE

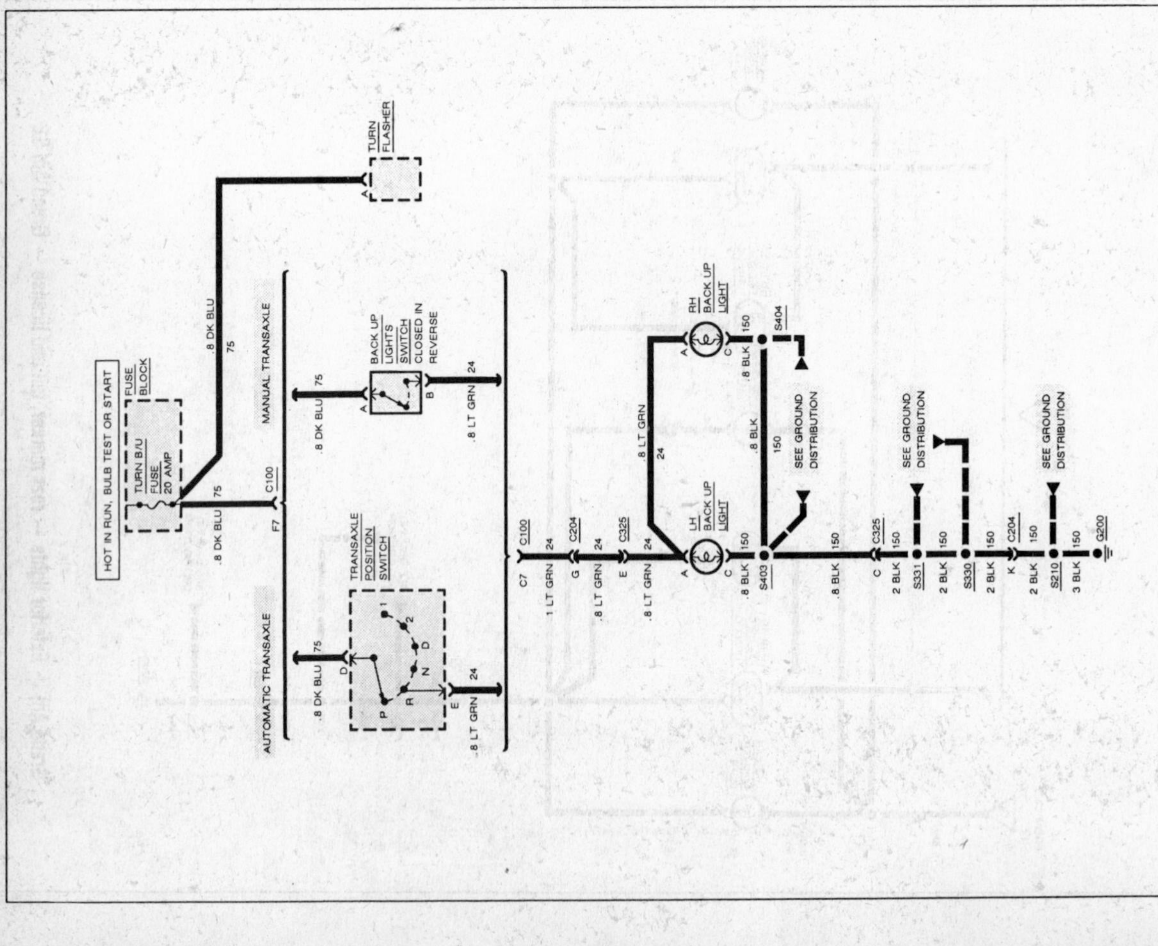

Grand Am — Back-up lights

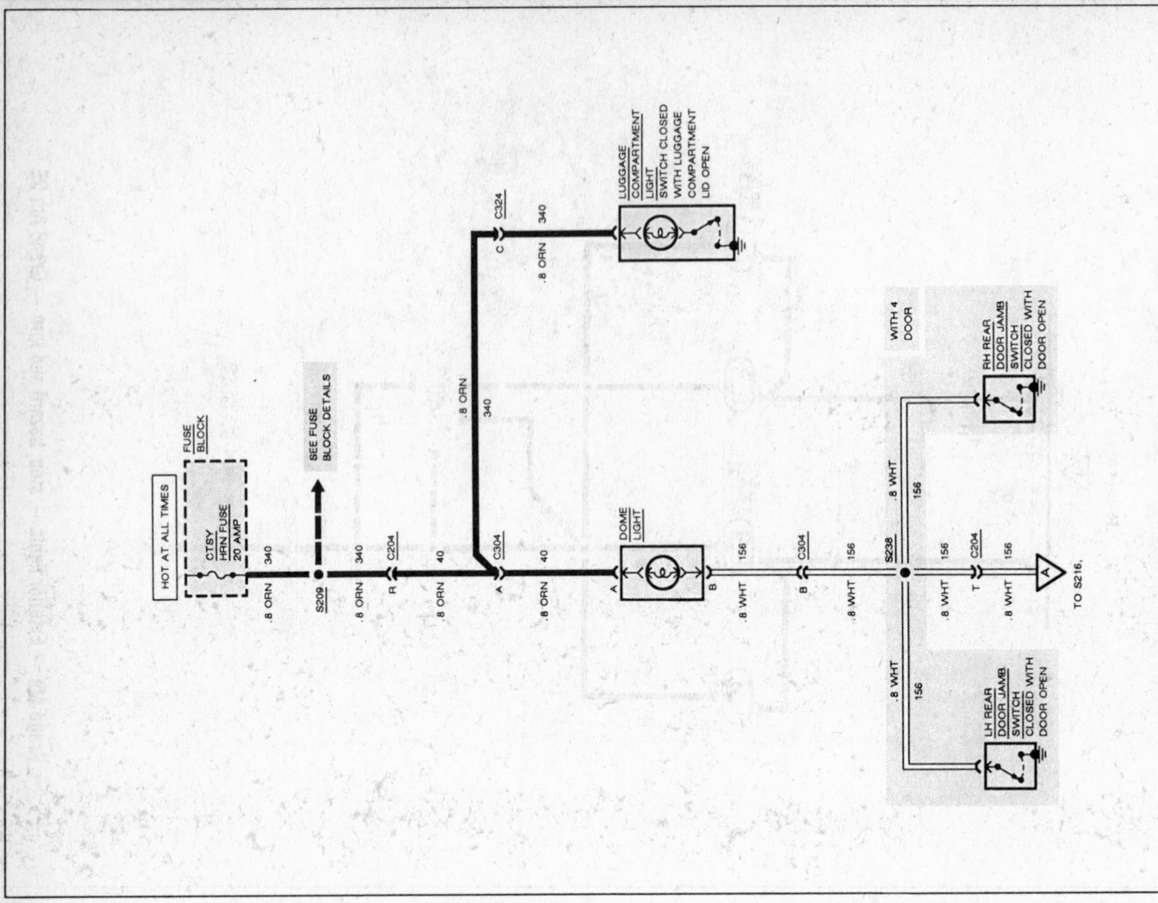

Grand Am — Interior lights — dome and luggage compartment

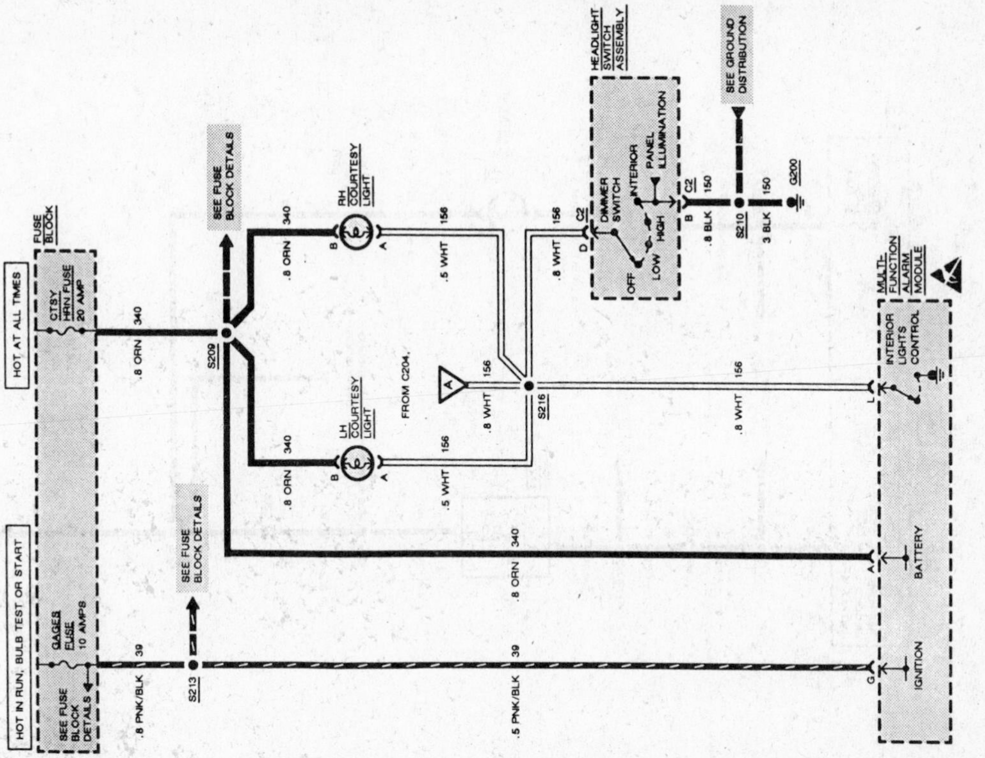

Grand Am — Interior lights — courtesy, reading and luggage compartment

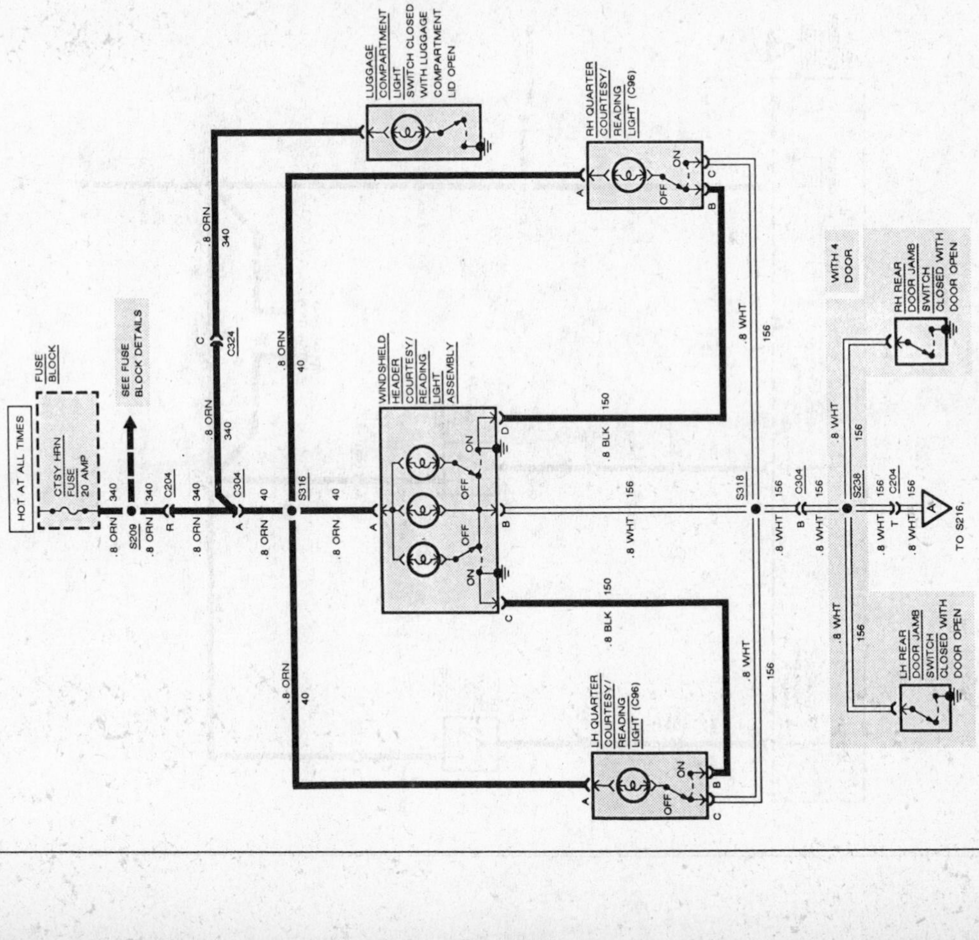

Grand Am — Interior lights — courtesy

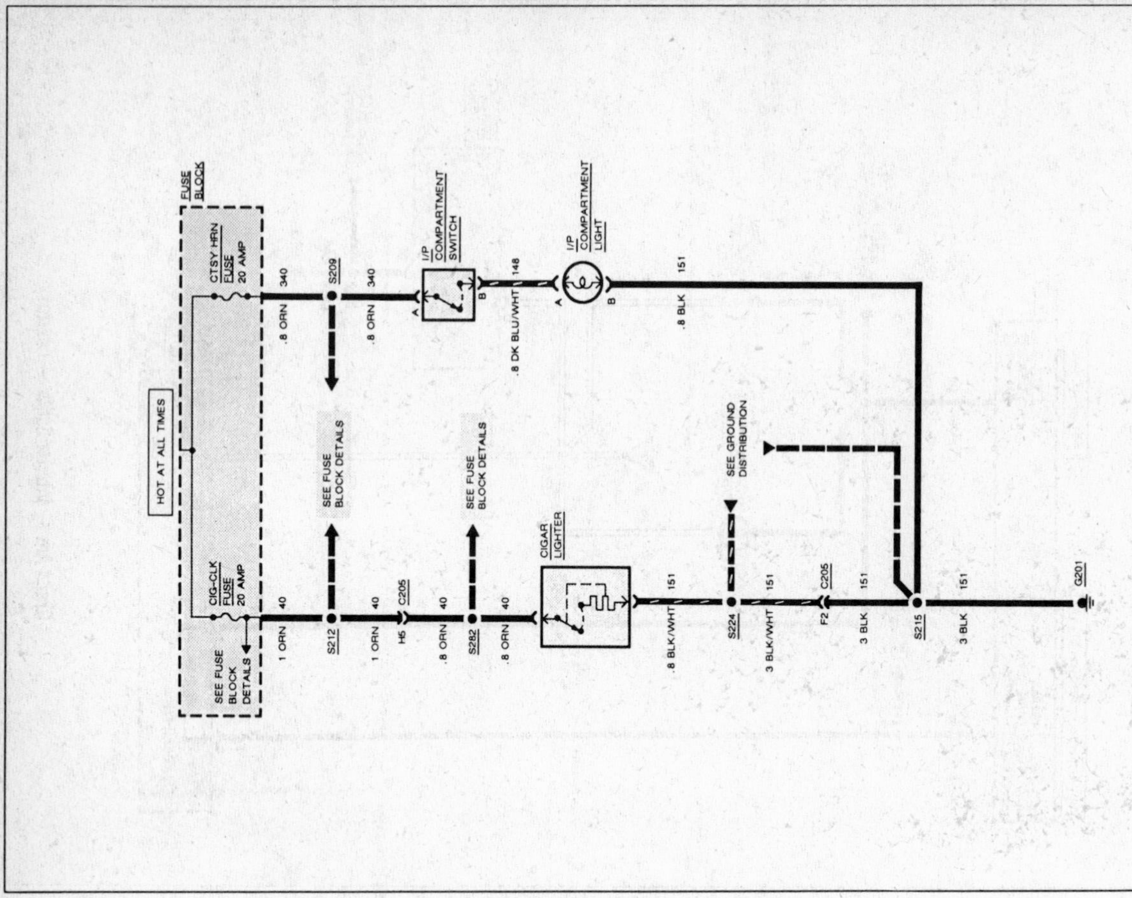

Grand Am — Interior lights — cigar lighter and instrument panel compartment

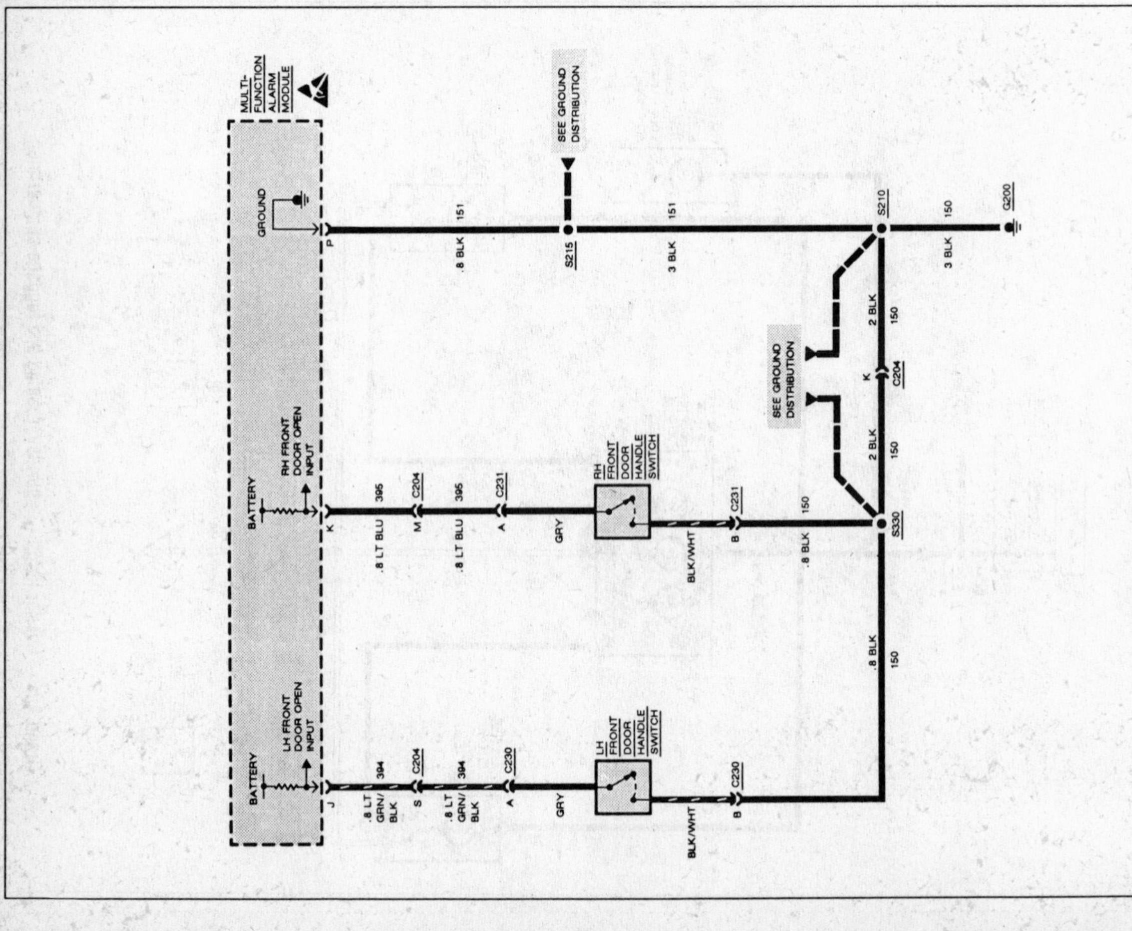

Grand Am — Interior lights — illuminated entry

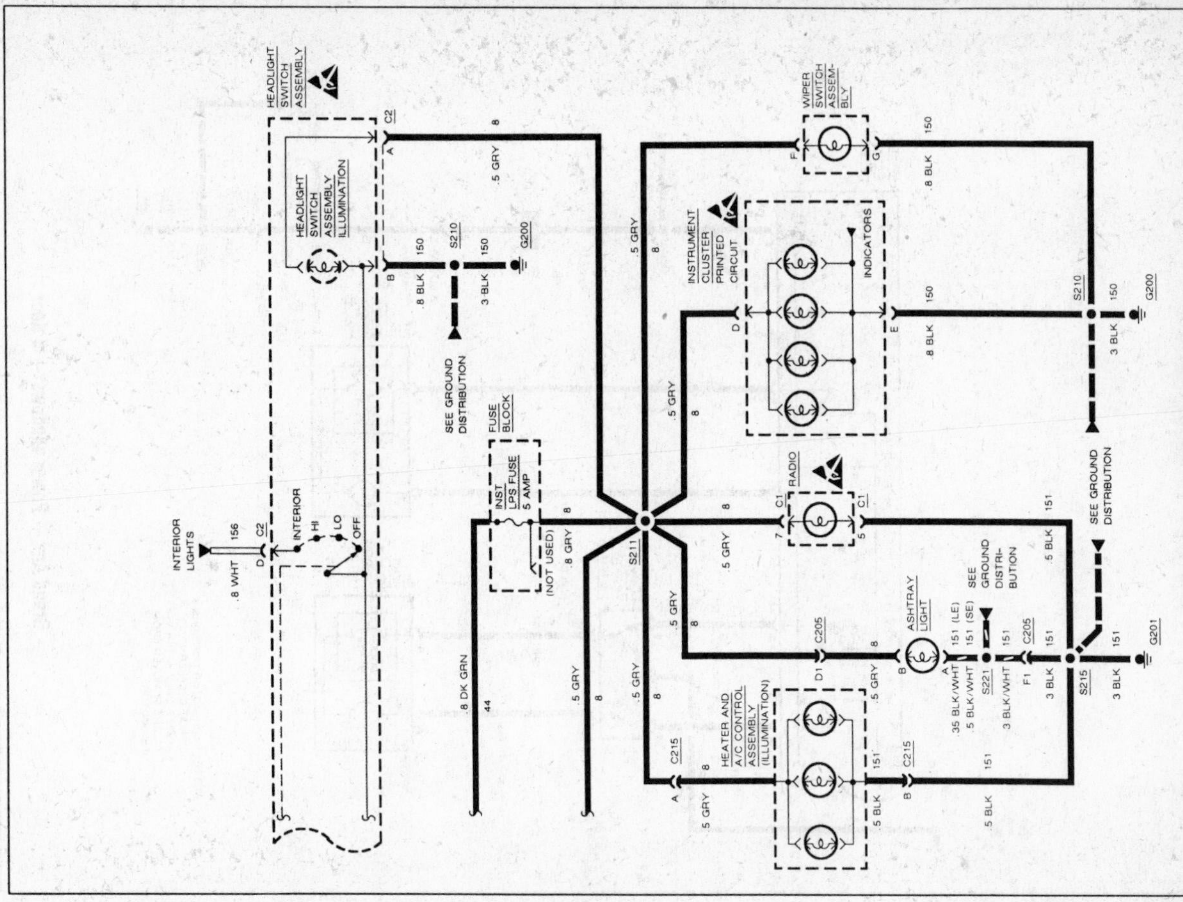

Grand Am — Interior lights dimming

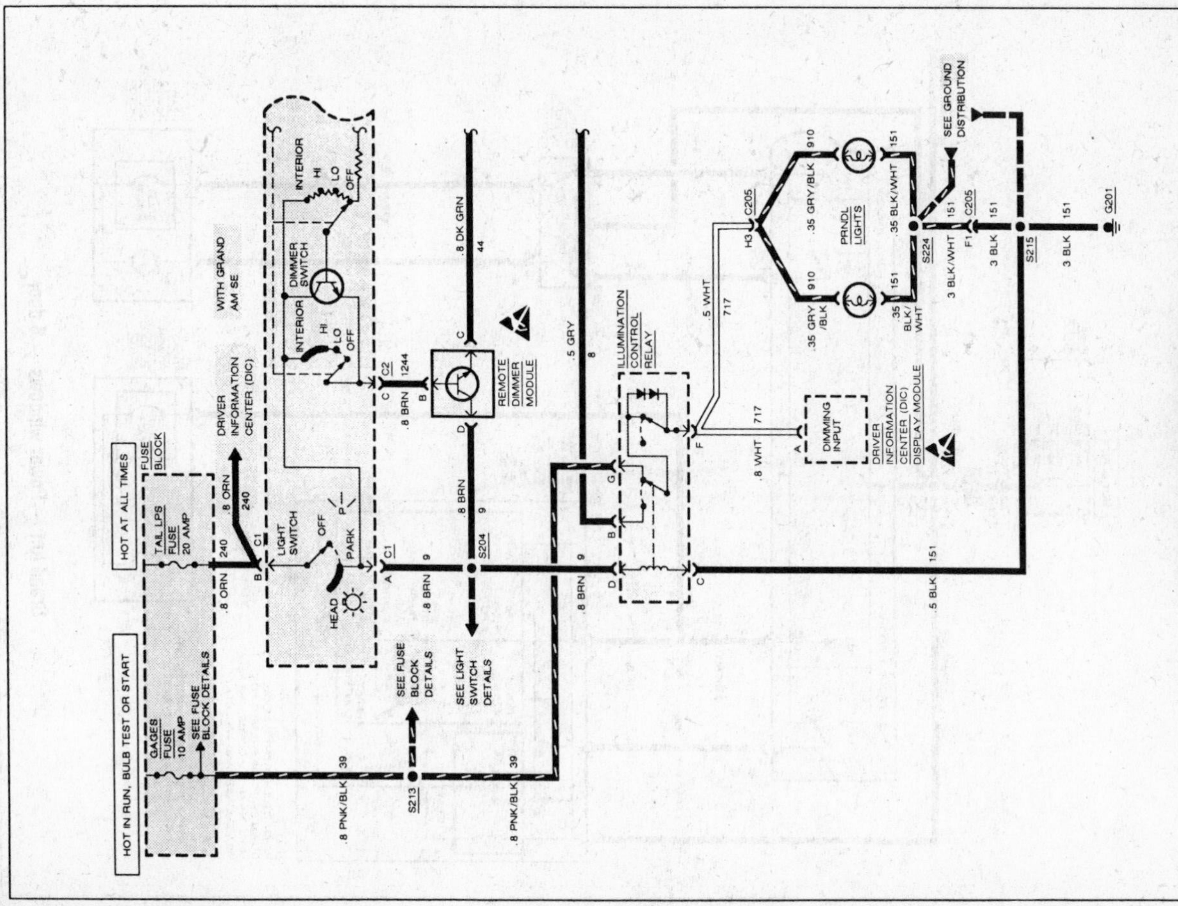

Grand Am — Interior lights dimming

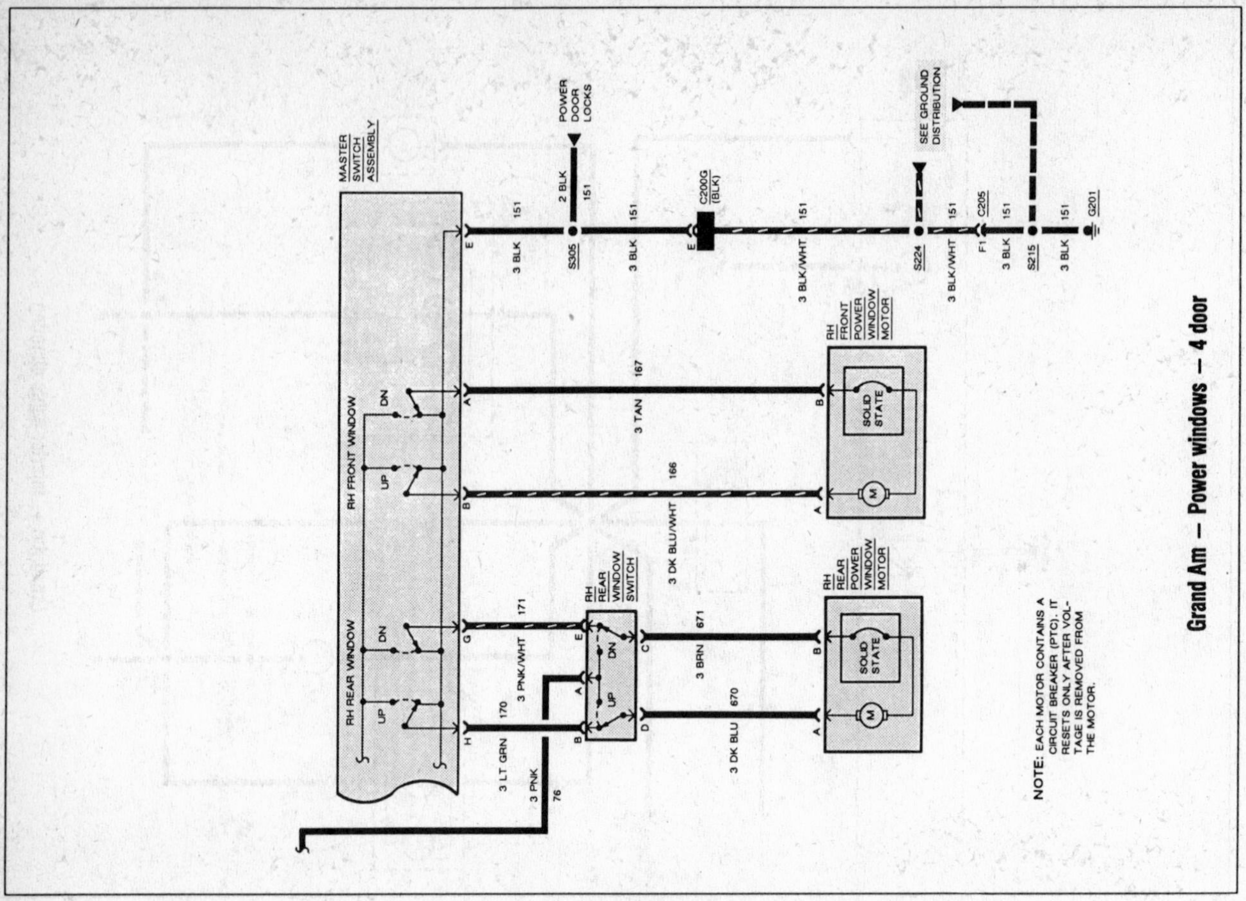

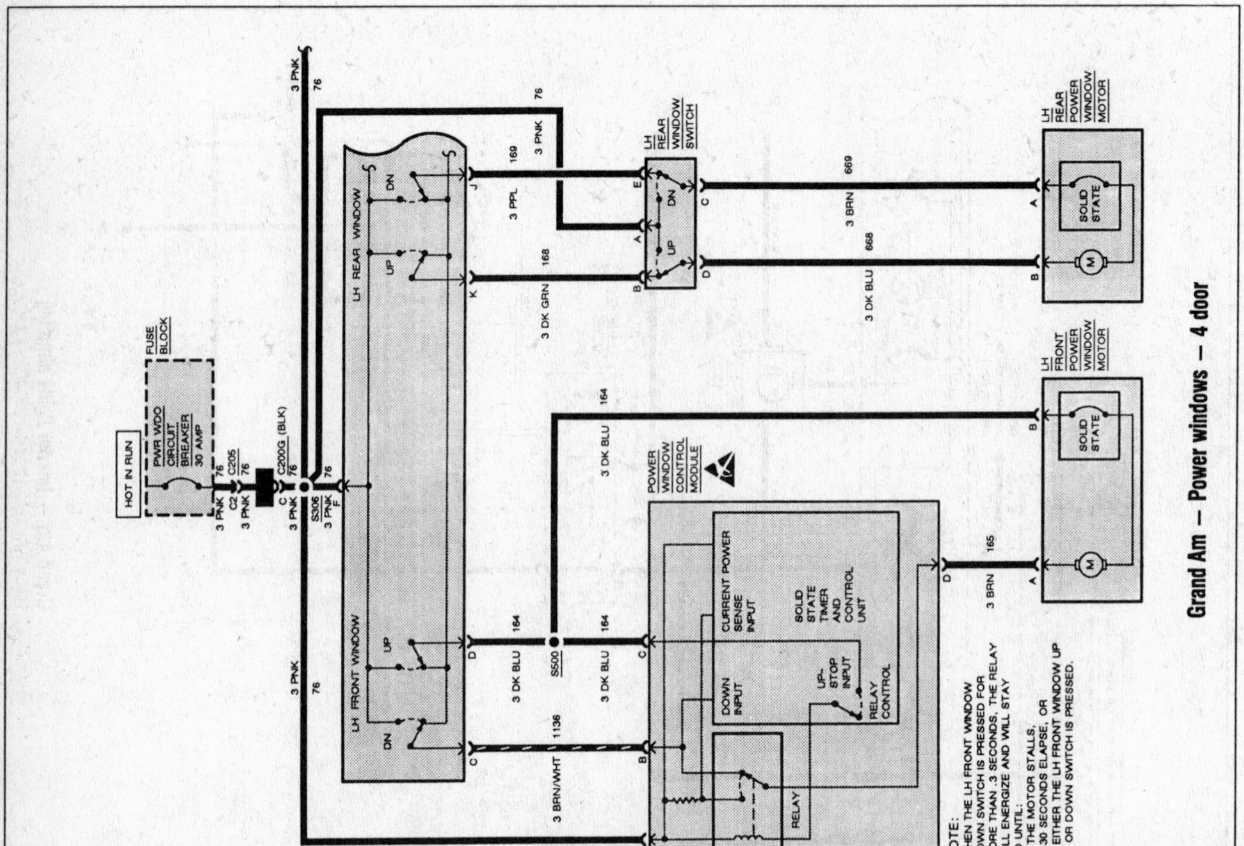

HOT IN RUN
FUSE BLOCK
PWR WDO CIRCUIT BREAKER 30 AMP
3 PNK 76
C2 C205
3 PNK 76
C C200G (BLK)
3 PNK 76
S306
3 PNK F 76
3 PNK 76
LH FRONT WINDOW
DN UP
LH REAR WINDOW
UP DN
C D K J
3 DK BLU 164
3 BRN/WHT 1136
S500
3 DK BLU 164
3 DK BLU 164
3 DK GRN 168
3 PPL 169
3 PNK 76
A B C
POWER WINDOW CONTROL MODULE
DOWN INPUT
CURRENT POWER SENSE INPUT
RELAY
SOLID STATE TIMER AND CONTROL UNIT
UP-STOP INPUT
RELAY CONTROL
B A E
UP DN
LH REAR WINDOW SWITCH
D C
3 DK BLU 668
3 BRN 669
D
3 BRN 165
A B
SOLID STATE
LH FRONT POWER WINDOW MOTOR
B A
SOLID STATE
LH REAR POWER WINDOW MOTOR

NOTE:
WHEN THE LH FRONT WINDOW DOWN SWITCH IS PRESSED FOR MORE THAN .3 SECONDS, THE RELAY WILL ENERGIZE AND WILL STAY SO UNTIL:
1) THE MOTOR STALLS,
2) 30 SECONDS ELAPSE, OR
3) EITHER THE LH FRONT WINDOW UP OR DOWN SWITCH IS PRESSED.

Grand Am — Power windows — 4 door

MASTER SWITCH ASSEMBLY
RH REAR WINDOW
UP DN
RH FRONT WINDOW
UP DN
H G B A E
3 LT GRN 170
3 PNK/WHT 171
3 PNK 76
B A E
UP DN
RH REAR WINDOW SWITCH
D C
3 DK BLU 670
3 BRN 671
3 DK BLU/WHT 166
3 TAN 167
A B
SOLID STATE
RH REAR POWER WINDOW MOTOR
A B
SOLID STATE
RH FRONT POWER WINDOW MOTOR
3 BLK 151
S305
2 BLK 151
POWER DOOR LOCKS
3 BLK 151
E C200G (BLK)
3 BLK/WHT 151
S224
SEE GROUND DISTRIBUTION
3 BLK/WHT 151
F1 C205
3 BLK 151
S215
3 BLK 151
G201

NOTE: EACH MOTOR CONTAINS A CIRCUIT BREAKER (PTC). IT RESETS ONLY AFTER VOLTAGE IS REMOVED FROM THE MOTOR.

Grand Am — Power windows — 4 door

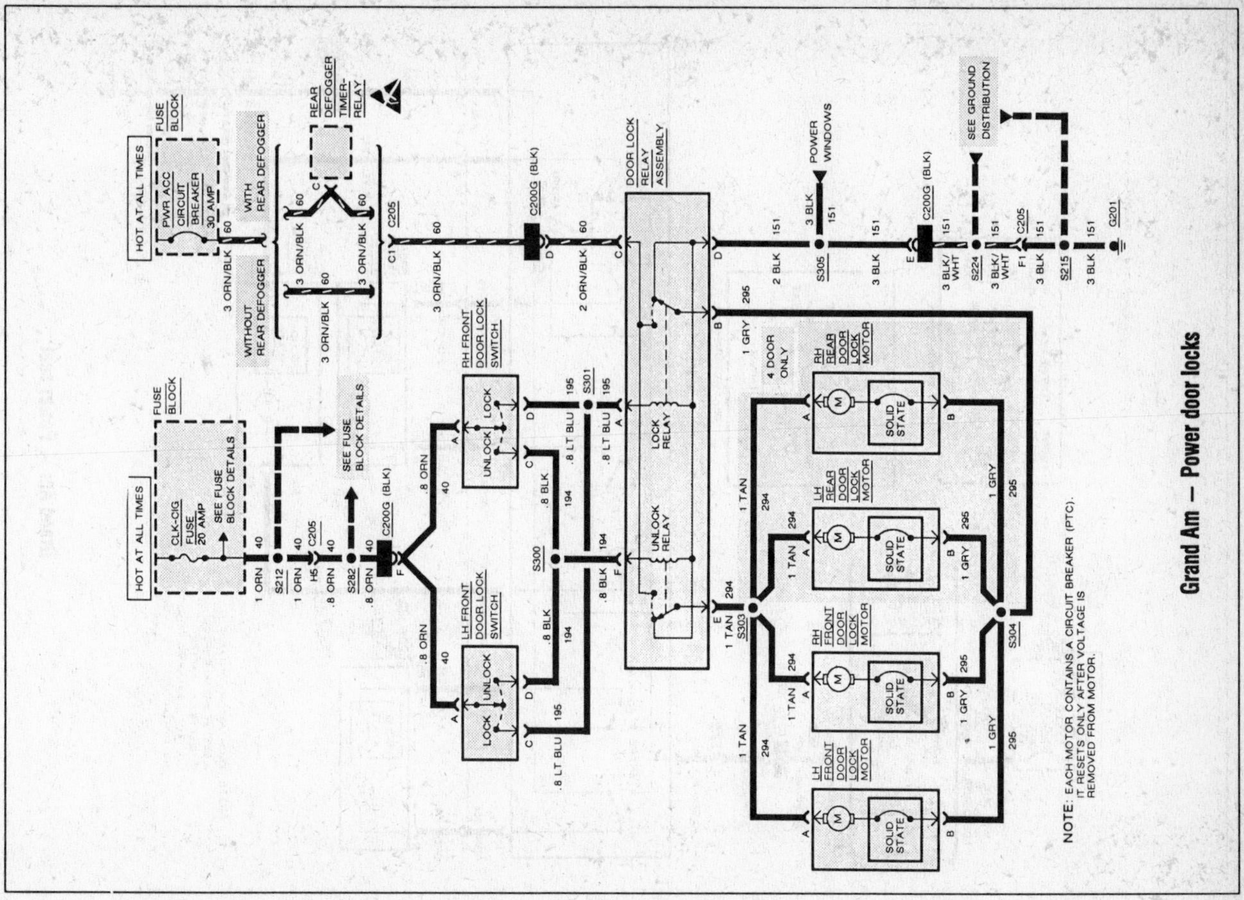

NOTE: EACH MOTOR CONTAINS A CIRCUIT BREAKER (PTC). IT RESETS ONLY AFTER VOLTAGE IS REMOVED FROM THE MOTOR.

NOTE:
WHEN THE LH FRONT WINDOW DOWN SWITCH IS PRESSED FOR MORE THAN .3 SECONDS, THE RELAY WILL ENERGIZE AND STAY SO UNTIL:
1) THE MOTOR STALLS,
2) 30 SECONDS ELAPSE, OR
3) THE LH FRONT WINDOW UP OR DOWN SWITCH IS PRESSED.

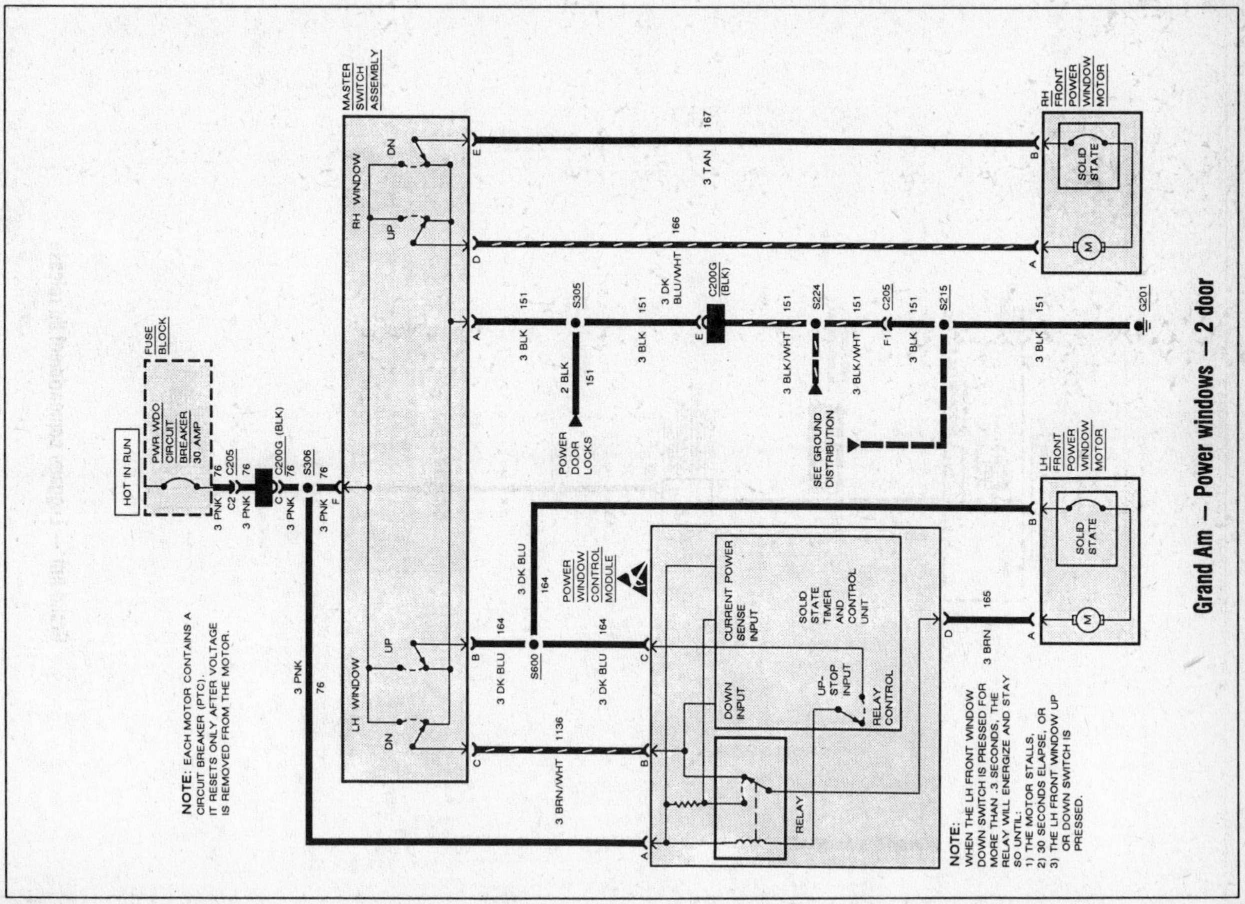

Grand Am — Power windows — 2 door

NOTE: EACH MOTOR CONTAINS A CIRCUIT BREAKER (PTC). IT RESETS ONLY AFTER VOLTAGE IS REMOVED FROM MOTOR.

Grand Am — Power door locks

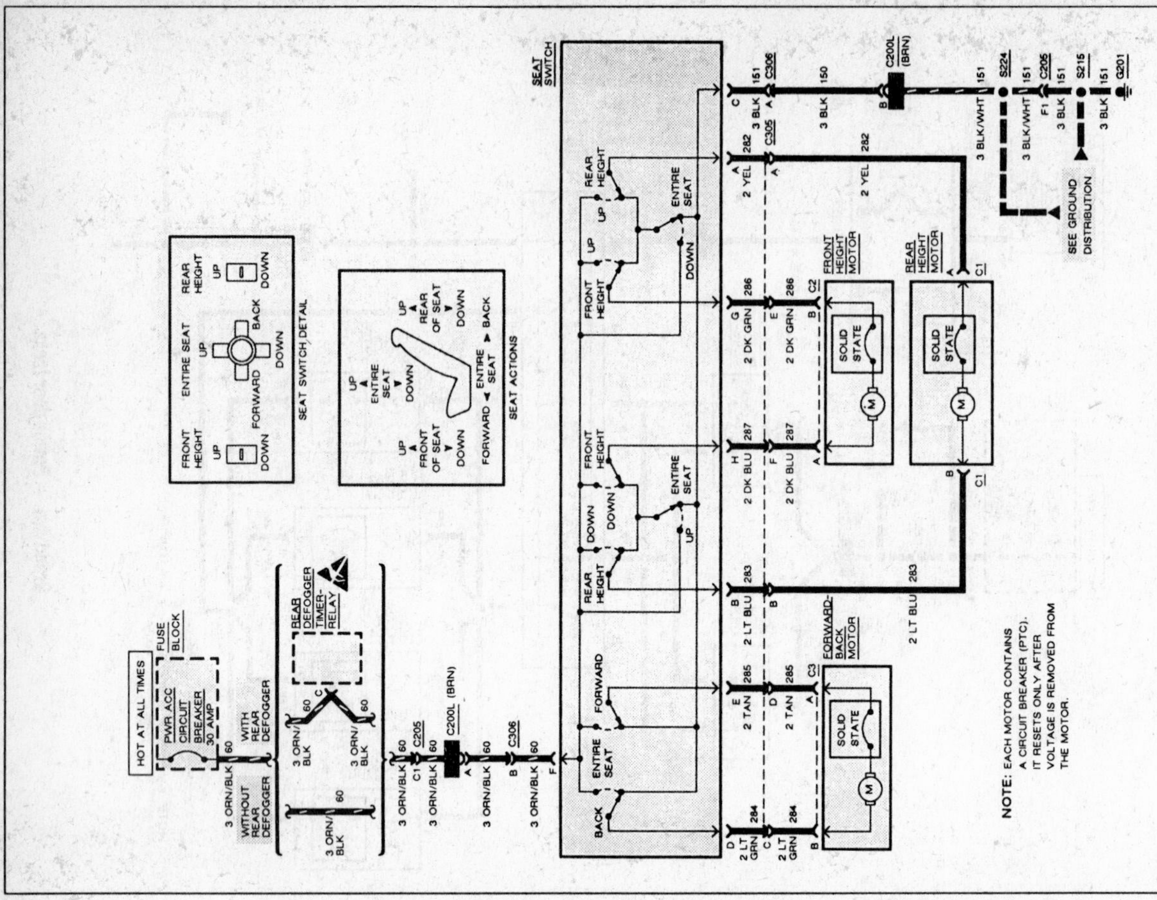

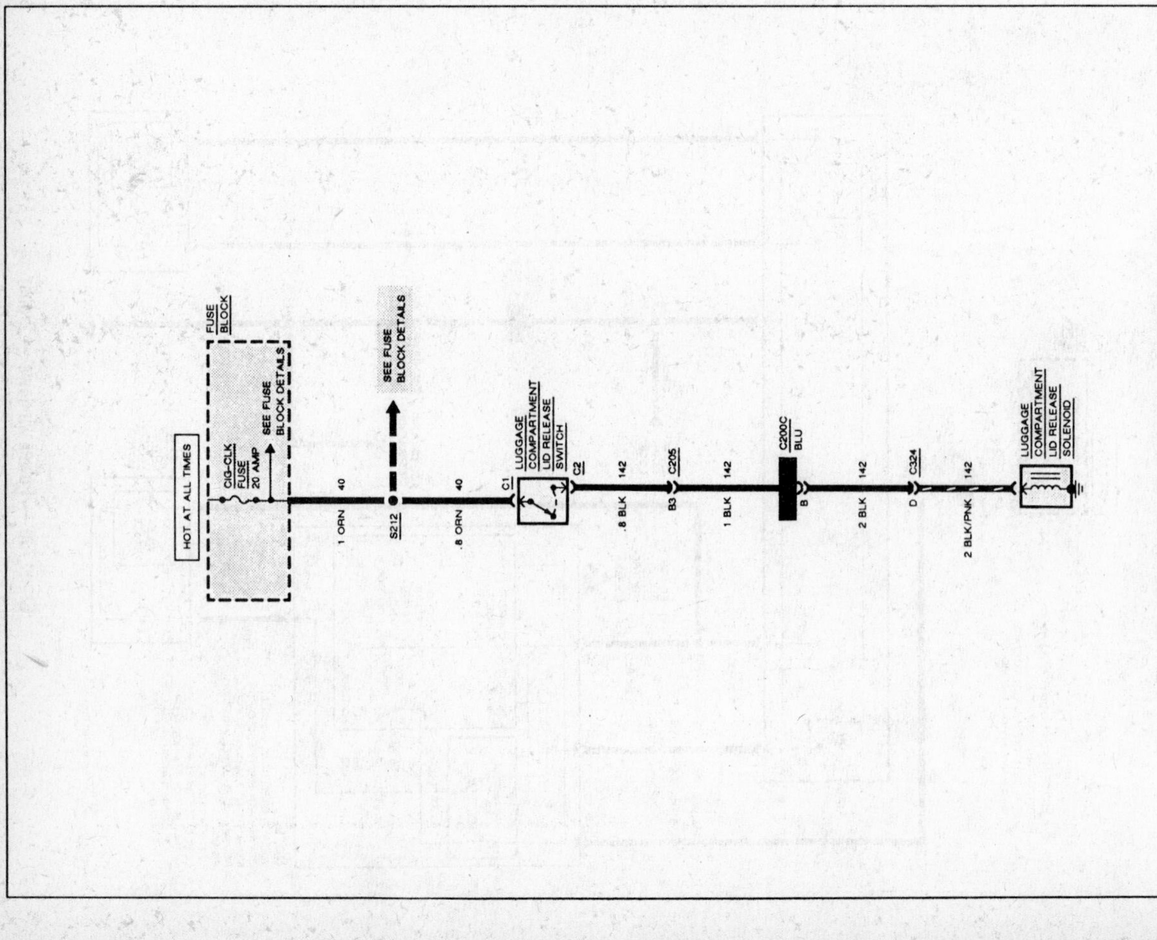

Grand Am — Luggage compartment lid release

NOTE: EACH MOTOR CONTAINS A CIRCUIT BREAKER (PTC). IT RESETS ONLY AFTER VOLTAGE IS REMOVED FROM THE MOTOR.

Grand Am — Power seat

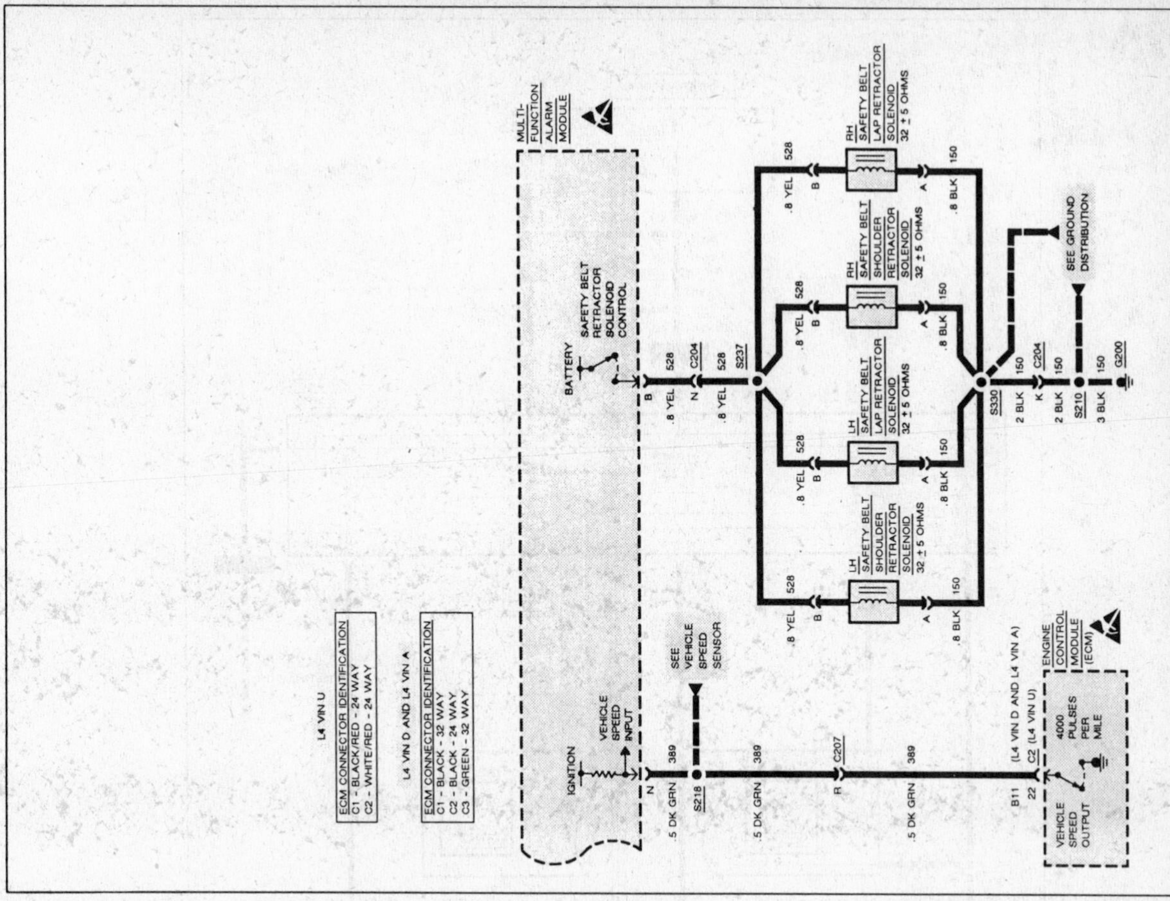

Grand Am — Automatic safety belts

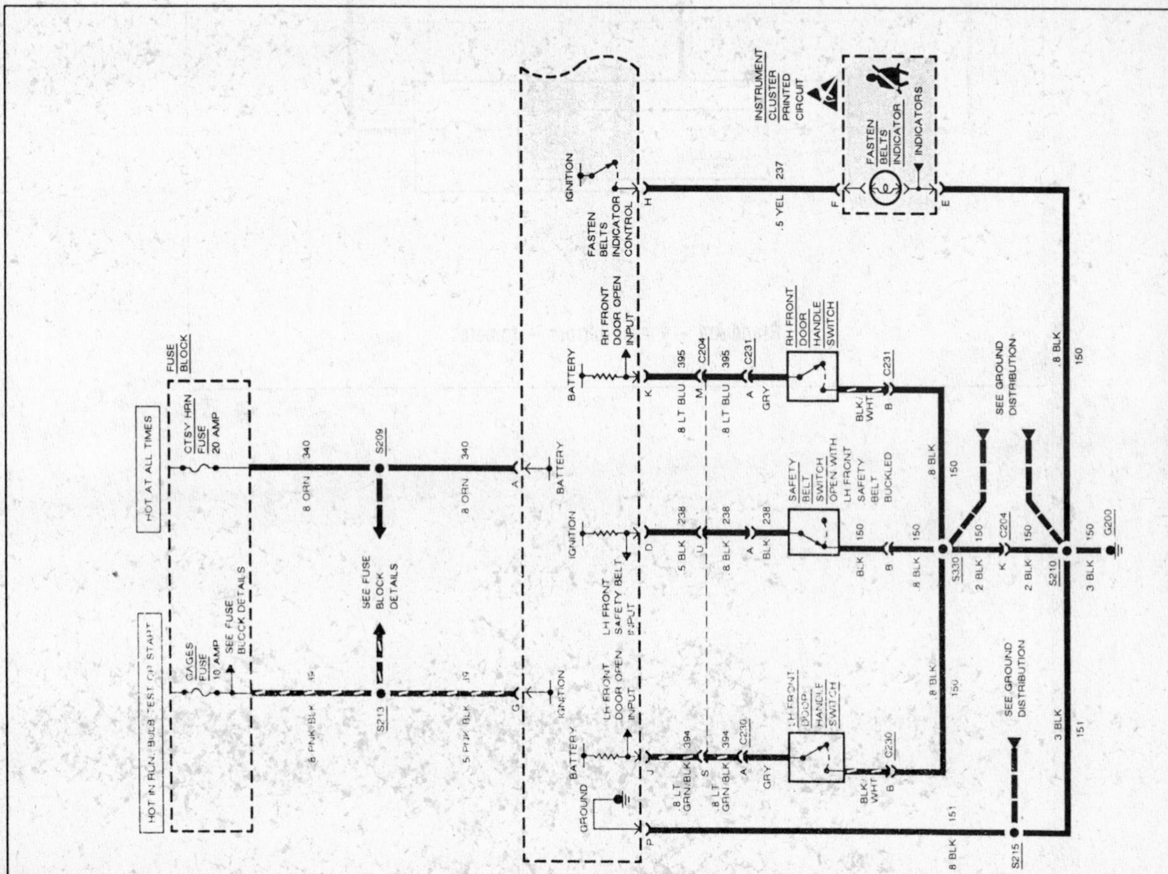

Grand Am — Automatic safety belts

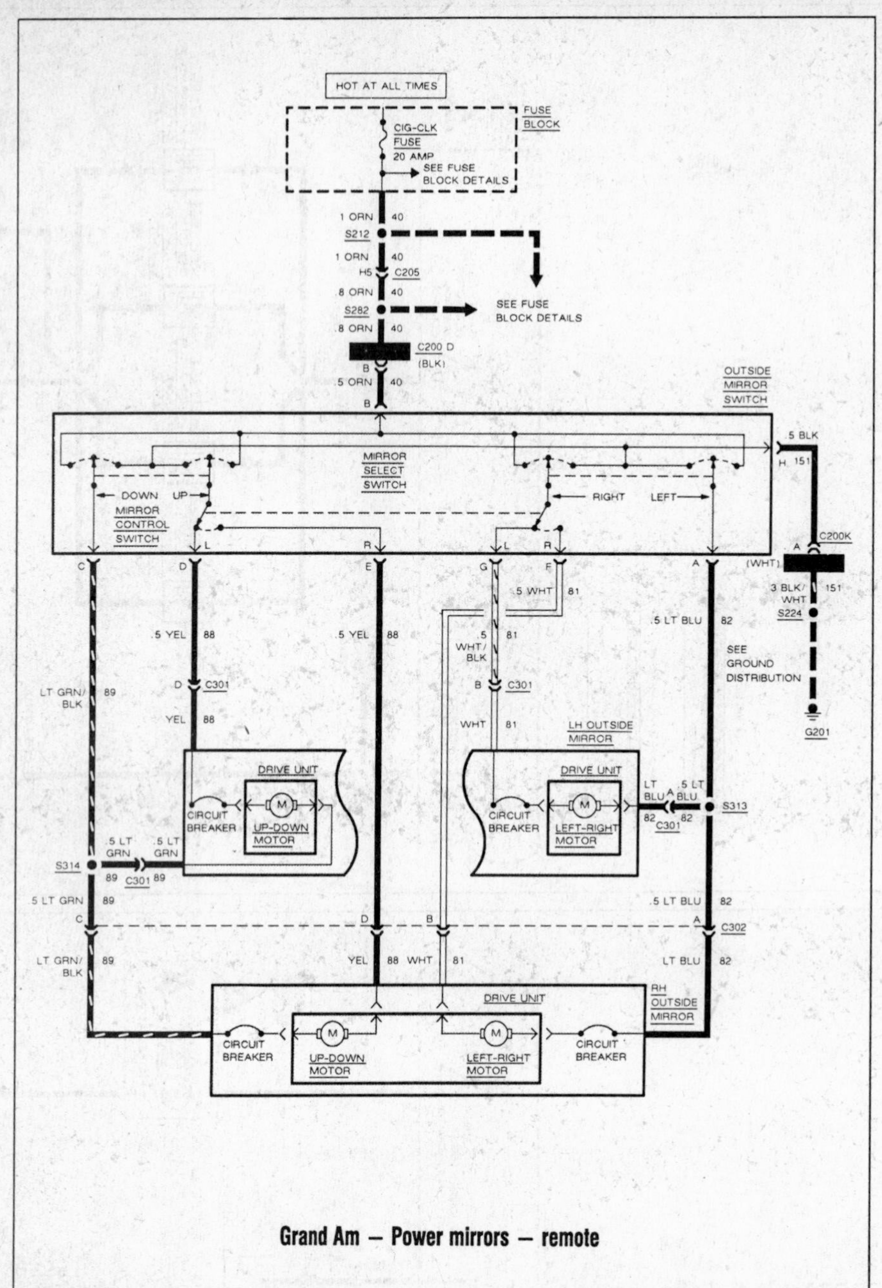

Grand Am — Power mirrors — remote

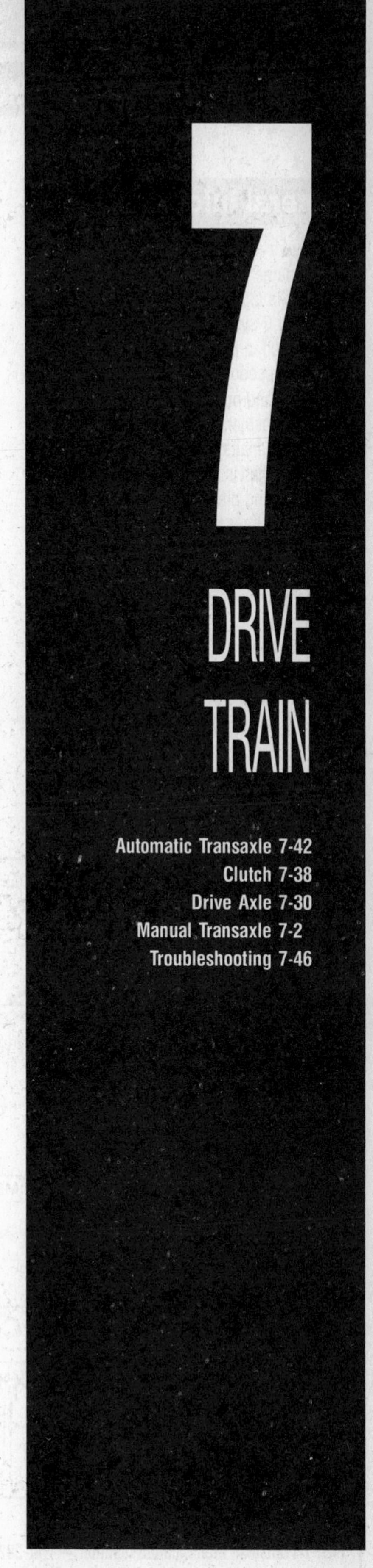
7
DRIVE
TRAIN
Automatic Transaxle 7-42
Clutch 7-38
Drive Axle 7-30
Manual Transaxle 7-2
Troubleshooting 7-46

HM-282/5TM40 5-SPEED MANUAL TRANSAXLE

General Information

The Hydra-matic Muncie 282 (HM–282) transaxle name was changed to the 5TM40 in 1990. This is a 5 speed unit with gearing that provides for 5 synchronized forward speeds, a reverse speed, a final drive with differential output and speedometer drive.

The input and output gear clusters are nested very close together, requiring extremely tight tolerances of shafts, gears and synchronizers.

The input shaft is supported by a roller bearing in the clutch and differential housing and a ball bearing in the transaxle case.

The output shaft is supported by a roller bearing in the clutch and differential housing and a combination ball-and-roller bearing in the transaxle case.

The differential case is supported by opposed tapered roller bearings which are under preload.

The speed gears are supported by roller bearings. A bushing supports the reverse idler gear.

Identification

➧ SEE FIGS. 1 AND 2

The transaxle identification stamp is located at the center top of the case. The transaxle identification tag is located on the left side near the left side cover.

Metric Fasteners

The metric fastener dimensions are very close to the dimensions of the familiar inch system fasteners and, for this reason, replacement fasteners must have the same measurement and strength as those removed.

Do not attempt to interchange metric fasteners with standard fasteners. Mismatched or incorrect fasteners can result in damage to the transaxle unit through malfunctions, breakage or possible personal injury.

Care should be taken to re-use the fasteners in the same locations as removed.

Backup Light Switch

REMOVAL & INSTALLATION

➧ SEE FIG. 3

1. Disconnect the negative battery cable.
2. Disconnect the back-up light connector.
3. Remove the back-up light switch assembly.

To install:

4. Install the back-up light switch assembly using a suitable pipe sealant compound. Tighten to 24 ft. lbs. (33 Nm).
5. Connect the back-up light switch connector.
6. Connect the negative battery cable.

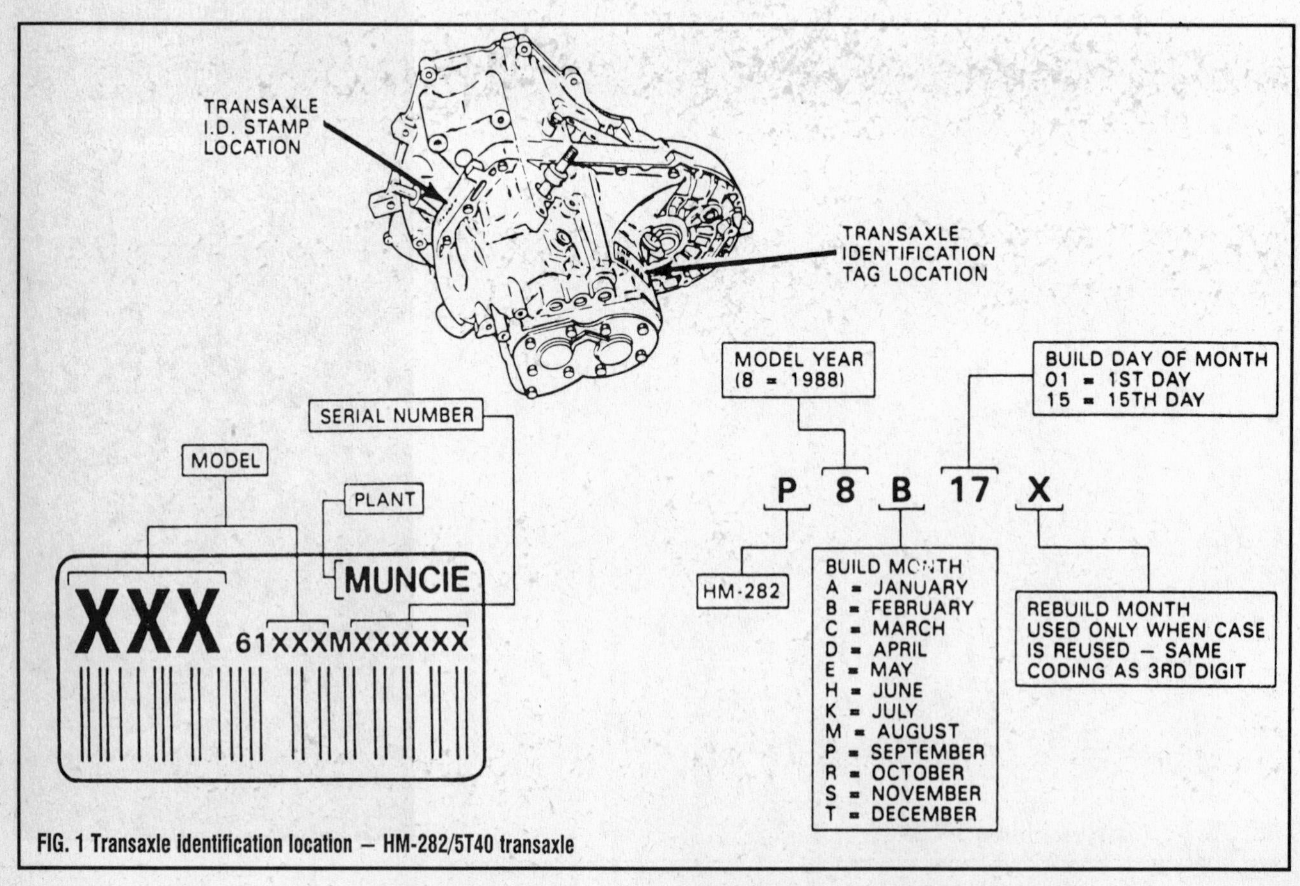

FIG. 1 Transaxle identification location — HM-282/5T40 transaxle

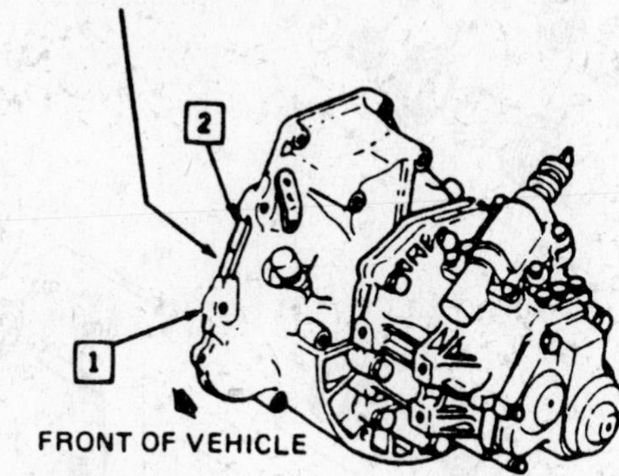

FIG. 2 Transaxle identification location — Isuzu transaxle

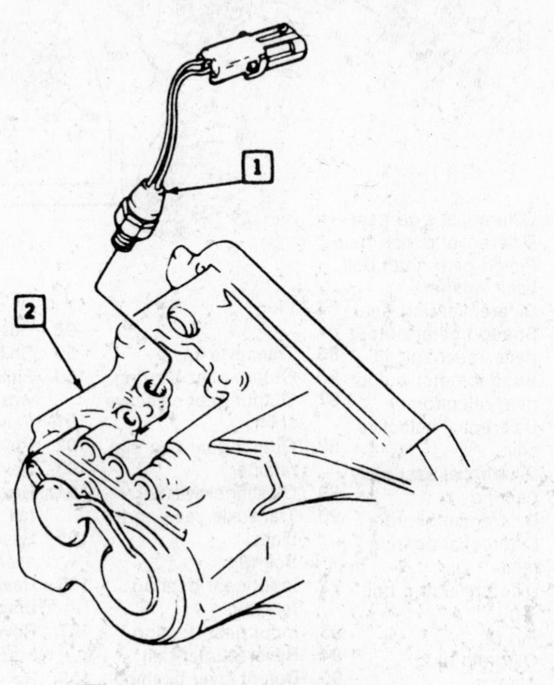

FIG. 3 Back-up light switch installation — HM-282/5T40 transaxle

Transaxle

REMOVAL & INSTALLATION

1. Disconnect the negative battery cable.
2. Install the engine support fixture tool J–28467 or equivalent. Raise the engine enough to take pressure off the motor mounts.
3. Remove the left sound panel.
4. Remove the clutch master cylinder pushrod from the clutch pedal.
5. Remove the air cleaner and air intake duct assembly.
6. Remove the clutch slave cylinder from the transaxle support bracket and lay aside.
7. Remove the transaxle mount through bolt.
8. Raise and safely support the vehicle.
9. Remove the exhaust crossover bolts at the right manifold.
10. Lower the vehicle.
11. Remove the left exhaust manifold.
12. Remove the transaxle mount bracket.
13. Disconnect the shift cables.
14. Remove the upper transaxle-to-engine bolts.
15. Raise the vehicle and support the safely.
16. Remove the left wheel assembly.
17. Remove the left front inner splash shield.
18. Remove the transaxle strut and bracket.
19. Drain the transaxle.
20. Remove the clutch housing cover bolts.
21. Disconnect the speedometer cable.
22. Disconnect the stabilizer bar at the left suspension support and control arm.
23. Disconnect the ball joint from the steering knuckle.
24. Remove the left suspension support attaching bolts and remove the support and control arm as an assembly.
25. Disconnect the driveshafts at the transaxle and remove the left driveshaft from the transaxle. Support the right driveshaft.
26. Attach the transaxle case to a jack.
27. Remove the remaining transaxle-to-engine bolts.
28. Remove the transaxle by sliding toward the drive side away from the engine. Carefully lower the jack, guiding the right driveshaft out of the transaxle.

To Install:

29. When installing the transaxle, guide the right driveshaft into its bore as the transaxle is being raised. The right driveshaft can not be readily installed after the transaxle is connected to the engine.
30. Install the transaxle-to-engine mounting bolts and tighten to specifications.

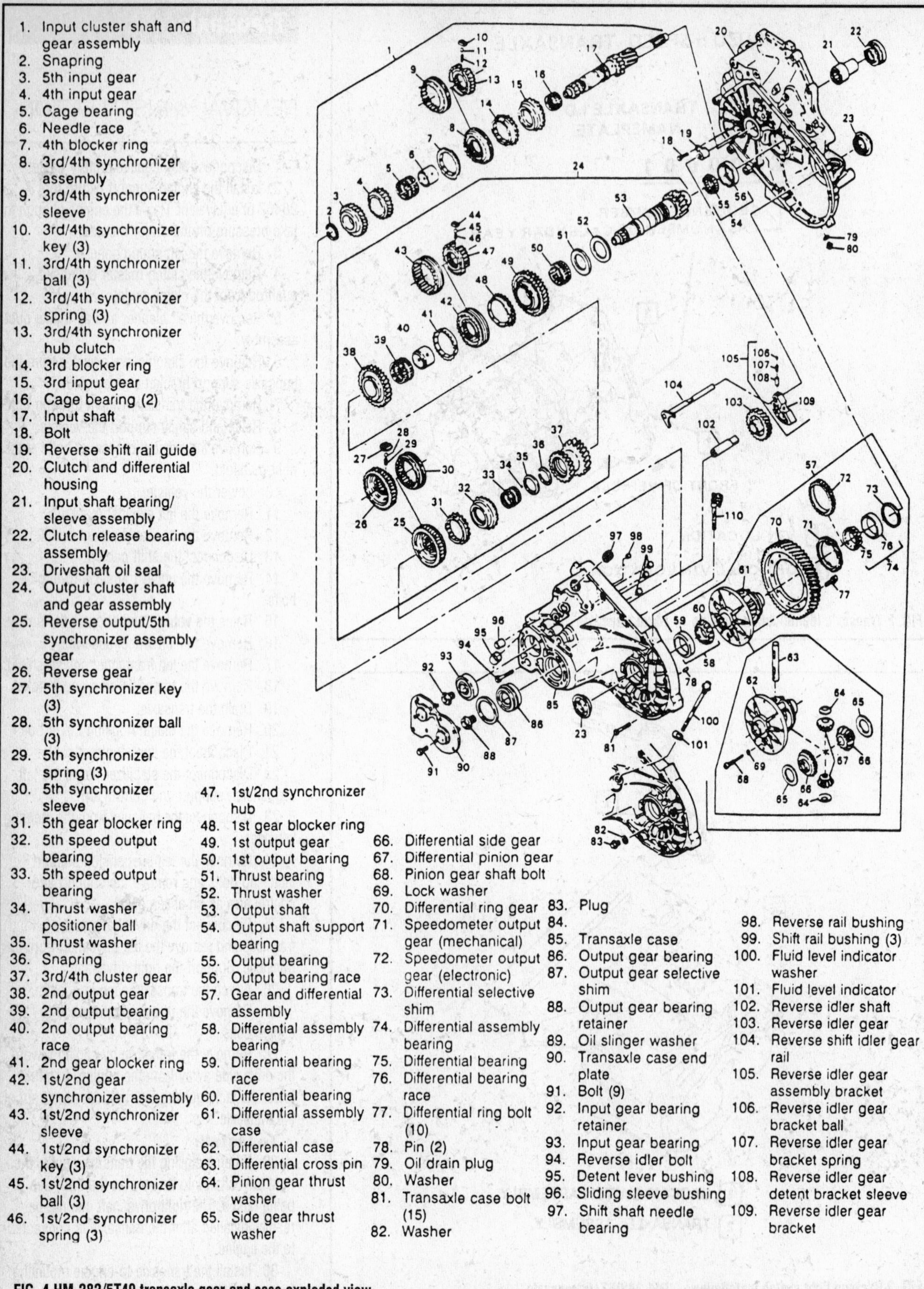

FIG. 4 HM-282/5T40 transaxle gear and case exploded view

1. Selector pin retainer
2. Selector lever retainer
3. Selector lever pilot pin
4. Bolt (2)
5. Selector lever
6. Shift shaft collar
7. Spring pin
8. Shift lever
9. Washer
10. Nut
11. Selector lever retainer
12. Selector lever pivot pin
13. Bolt (2)
14. Selector lever
15. Shift shaft collar
16. Shift lever
17. Washer
18. Nut
19. Spring pin
20. Snapring
21. Shift shaft cover
22. Bolt
23. 5th detent outer spring seat
24. Spring
25. 5th detent inner spring seat
26. Detent assembly lever
27. Detent pin retainer
28. Detent lever
29. Detent lever pin
30. Detent lever spacer
31. Detent lever roller
32. Detent pin retainer
33. Detent roller (4)
34. Reverse lever
35. Detent lever rollers pin (2)
36. Shift shaft
37. 3rd/4th bias spring
38. Shift lever
39. Roll pin
40. Bolt (3)
41. Flat washer (3)
42. Spacer (3)
43. Shift interlock plate
44. Outer clutch fork bushing
45. Clutch fork seal
46. Clutch fork shaft
47. Breather assembly
48. Reverse shift rail bushing
49. Interlock pin (2)
50. Detent holder
51. Detent spring (4)
52. Detent ball (4)
53. Speedometer signal assembly
54. Spring pin
55. Detent holder cover
56. Bolt (2)
57. Shift rail bushings (3)
58. Inner clutch fork bushing
59. Output bearing race retainer
60. Bolt (2)
61. Reverse shift assembly rail 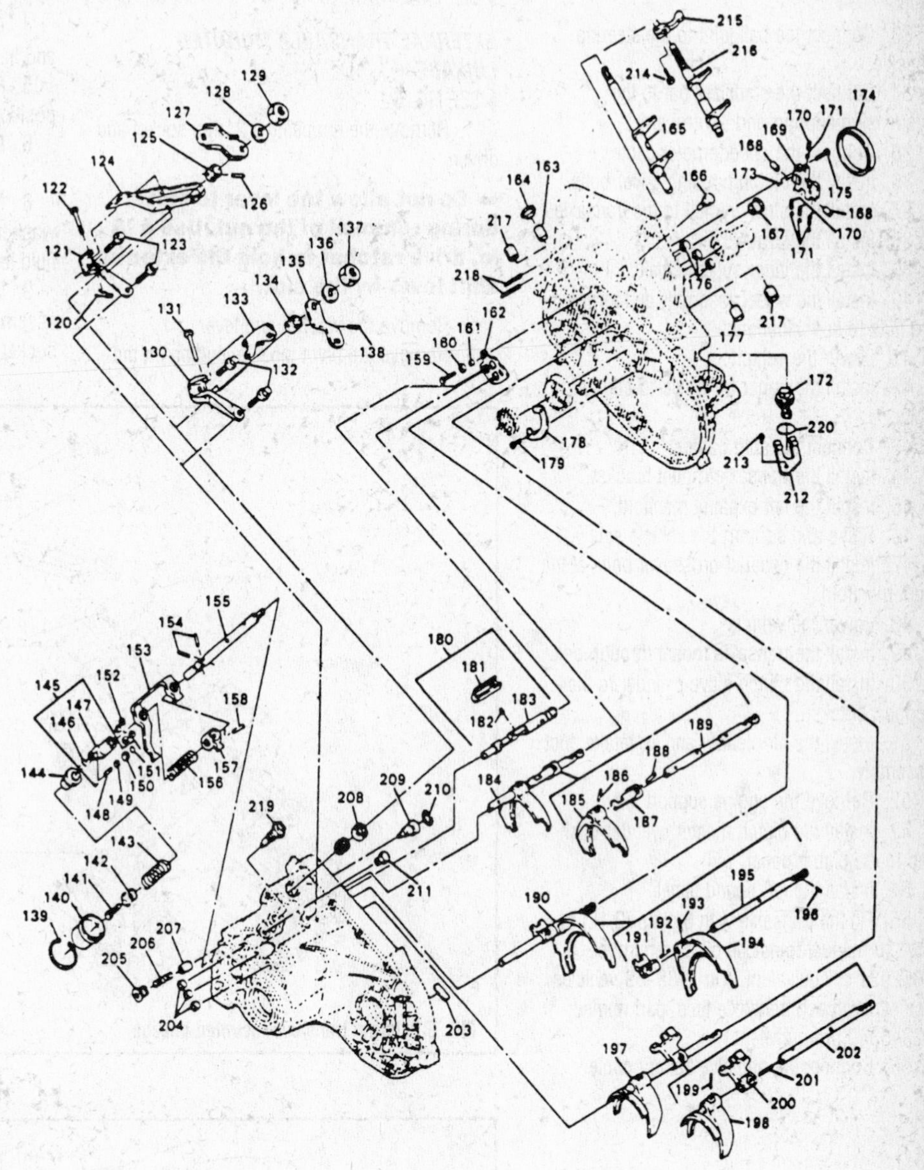
62. 5th/reverse shift gate
63. Gear disengage roller
64. Reverse shift shaft
65. 3rd/4th shift assembly rail
66. 3rd/4th shift shift fork
67. Fork retainer pin
68. 3rd/4th select lever
69. Lever retainer pin
70. 3rd/4th shift shaft
71. 1st/2nd shift assembly rail
72. 1st/2nd select lever
73. Lever retainer pin
74. Fork retainer pin
75. 1st/2nd shift fork
76. 1st/2nd shift shaft
77. Lock pin
78. 5th shift assembly rail
79. 5th shift fork
80. Fork retainer pin
81. 5th shift lever
82. Lever retainer pin
83. 5th shift shaft
84. Chip collector magnet
85. Shift rail plug (3)
86. Bolt
87. Sliding sleeve spring
88. Sliding sleeve
89. Shift shaft seal
90. Plug
91. Snapring
92. Stud
93. Speedometer signal assembly retainer
94. Bolt

FIG. 5 HM-282/5T40 transaxle shift mechanism exploded view

31. Install the left driveshaft into its bore at the transaxle and seat both driveshafts at the transaxle.
32. Install the suspension support-to-body bolts.
33. Connect the ball joint to the steering knuckle.
34. Connect the stabilizer bar to the suspension support and control arm.
35. Connect the speedometer cable.
36. Install the clutch housing cover bolts.
37. Install the strut bracket to the transaxle.
38. Install the strut.
39. Install the inner splash shield.
40. Install the wheel assembly and torque the lug nuts to specifications.
41. Lower the vehicle.
42. Install the upper transaxle-to-engine bolts.
43. Connect the shift cables.
44. Install the transaxle mount bracket.
45. Install the left exhaust manifold.
46. Raise and support the vehicle safely.
47. Install the exhaust crossover bolts at the right manifold.
48. Lower the vehicle.
49. Install the transaxle mount through bolt.
50. Install the clutch slave cylinder to the support bracket.
51. Install the air cleaner and air intake duct assembly.
52. Remove the engine support fixture.
52. Install the clutch master cylinder push rod to the clutch pedal.
54. Install the left sound panel.
55. Fill the transaxle with 5 pints (2.1L) of 5W–30 manual transaxle oil, part number 1052931 or equivalent. (On 1988–89 vehicles, use syncromesh transaxle fluid, part number 12345349 or equivalent.)
56. Connect the negative battery cable.

OVERHAUL

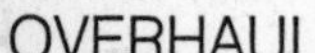

Before Disassembly

Cleanliness is an important factor in the overhaul of the transaxle. Before attempting any disassembly operation, the exterior of the transaxle should be thoroughly cleaned to prevent the possibility of dirt entering the transaxle internal mechanism. During inspection and reassembly, all parts should be thoroughly cleaned with cleaning fluid and then air dried. Wiping cloths or rags should not be used to dry parts. All oil passages should be blown out and checked to make sure that they are not obstructed. Small passages should be checked with tag wire. All parts should be inspected to determine which parts are to be replaced.

Transaxle Disassembly

➧ SEE FIGS. 4 AND 5

EXTERNAL TRANSAXLE MOUNTED LINKAGE

➧ SEE FIG. 6

1. Remove the nut using a 21mm socket and driver.

➡ Do not allow the lever to move during removal of the nut. Use a $^3/_8$ in. drive ratchet to hold the external shift lever by the slot.

2. Remove the washer and lever.
3. Remove the pivot pin. Depending on the type of linkage, this pin may be removed by using a hammer and punch to drive it out of the bracket (replace with part number 14091786) or removing a retaining clip and sliding the pin out of the bracket, which may be reused.
4. Remove the pivot using a $^3/_{16}$ in. punch and hammer.
5. Remove the pin and collar. Note the position of the slot in the collar for installation.
6. Remove the bolts.
7. Remove the bracket.
8. Remove the fluid level indicator and washer. A wrench may be needed to loosen the fluid level indicator.
9. Remove the electronic speedometer signal assembly, retainer and bolt using a 10mm socket and driver.

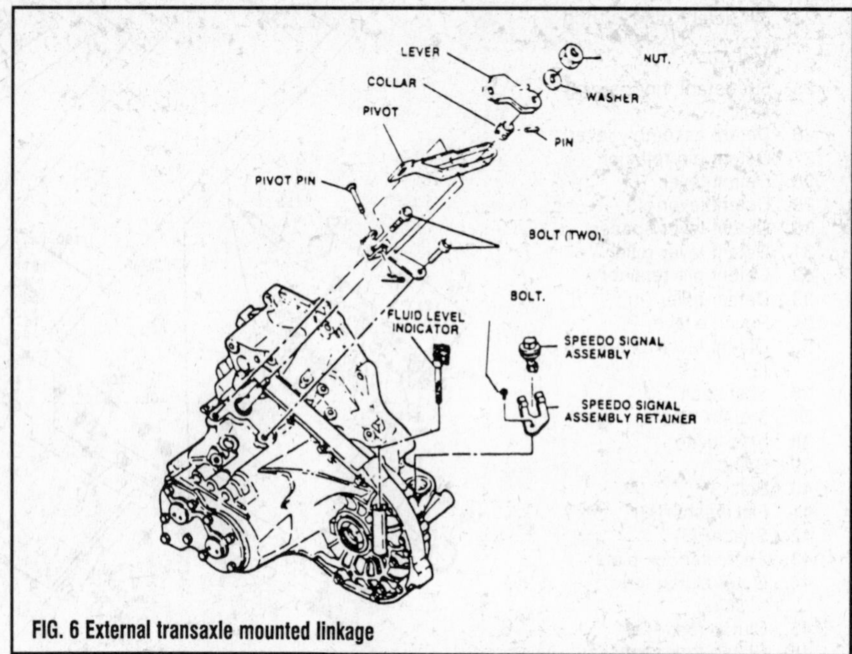

FIG. 6 External transaxle mounted linkage

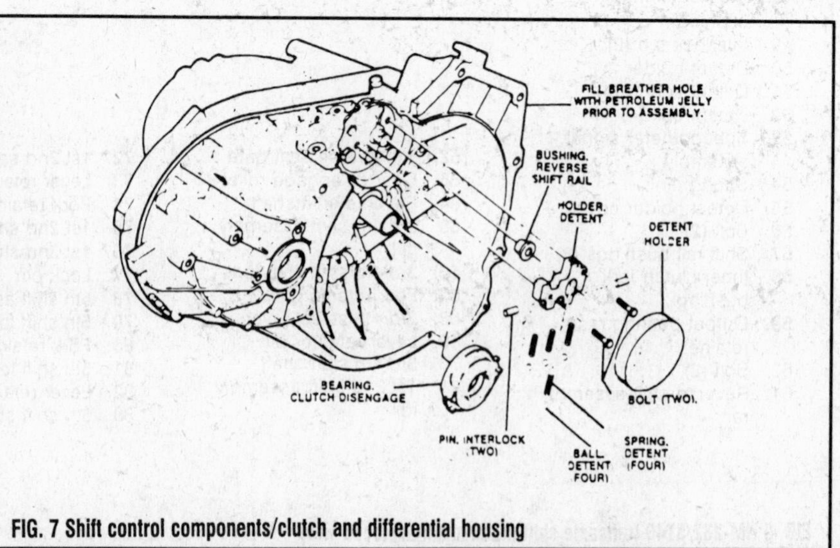

FIG. 7 Shift control components/clutch and differential housing

SHIFT RAIL DETENT/CLUTCH AND DIFFERENTIAL HOUSING

➧ SEE FIG. 7

1. Remove the bearing.
2. Remove the detent holder cover. Puncture the cover in the middle and pry off. Discard this part and replace it with part number 14082039.
3. Remove the bolts and interlock plate (early transaxles). If the detent holder is not 18mm thick, interlock plate kit must be used.
4. Remove the holder, detent, springs and interlock pins.
5. Remove the balls and detent.
6. Remove the bushing by prying loose (2 small pry bars in the slots). Two Allen wrenches work well to pry this bushing.

SHIFT SHAFT DETENT/TRANSAXLE HOUSING

➧ SEE FIG. 8

1. Remove the snapring.
2. Remove the cover using a soft faced hammer.
3. Remove screw and outer spring seat using a 5mm bit and driver.
4. Remove the 5th/reverse bias spring and inner spring seat.

TRANSAXLE CASE AND CLUTCH HOUSING

➧ SEE FIG. 9

1. Remove the bolts using a 13mm socket and driver.
2. Remove the clutch housing using a soft faced hammer. Remove the Loctite®518 anaerobic sealer with either a liquid gasket remover or J–28410 or equivalent, scraper.
3. Remove the differential gear assembly. Support the transaxle case on a workbench top, being careful to support it properly.
4. Remove the magnet.
5. Remove the bearing. Note the position of the bearing cage for installation.

SHIFT SHAFT COMPONENTS

➧ SEE FIGS. 10–15

1. Remove the pin using a size $^{3}/_{16}$ in. punch and hammer.

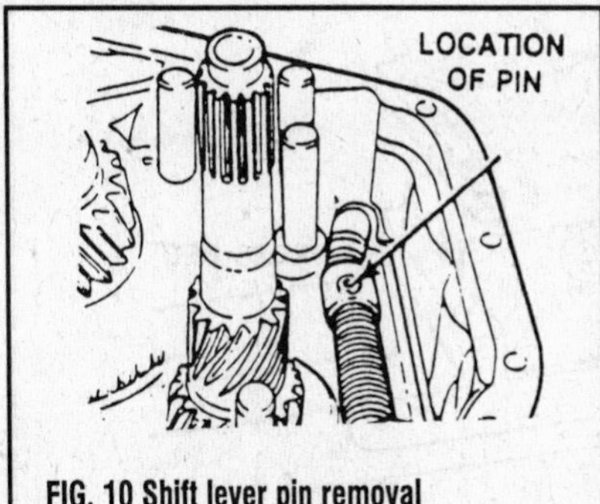

FIG. 10 Shift lever pin removal

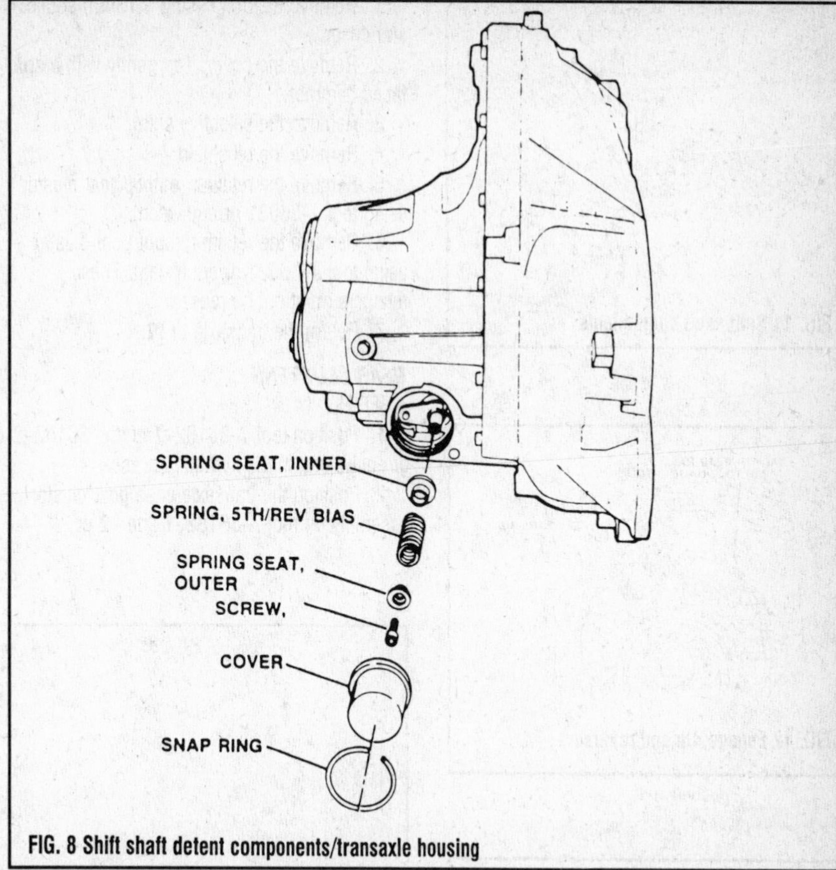

FIG. 8 Shift shaft detent components/transaxle housing

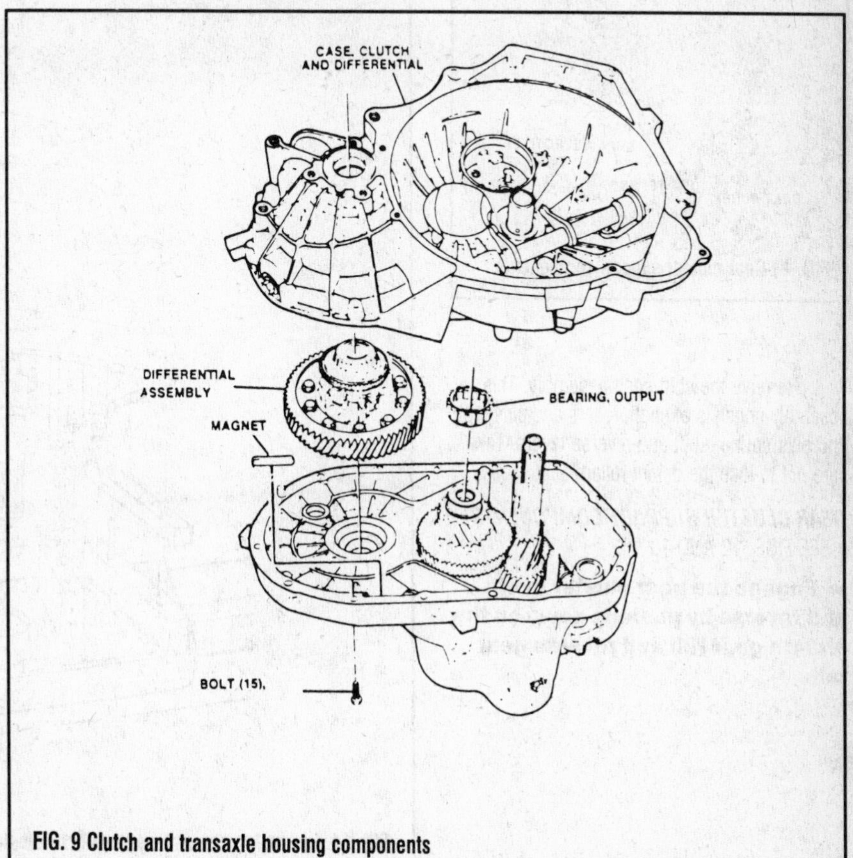

FIG. 9 Clutch and transaxle housing components

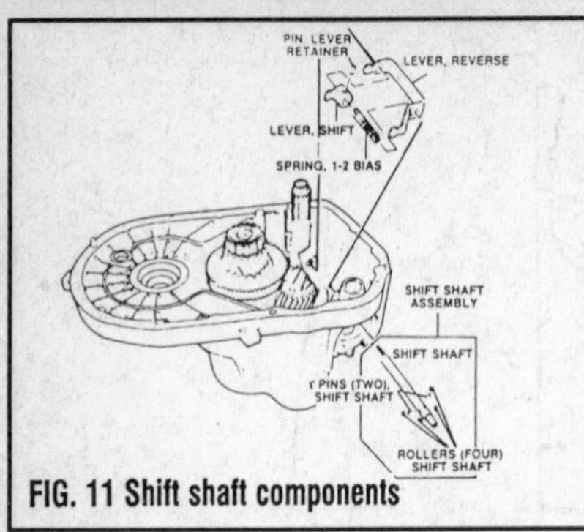

FIG. 11 Shift shaft components

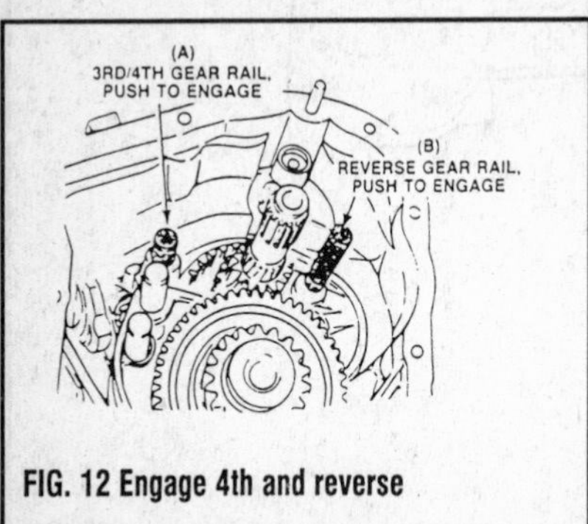

FIG. 12 Engage 4th and reverse

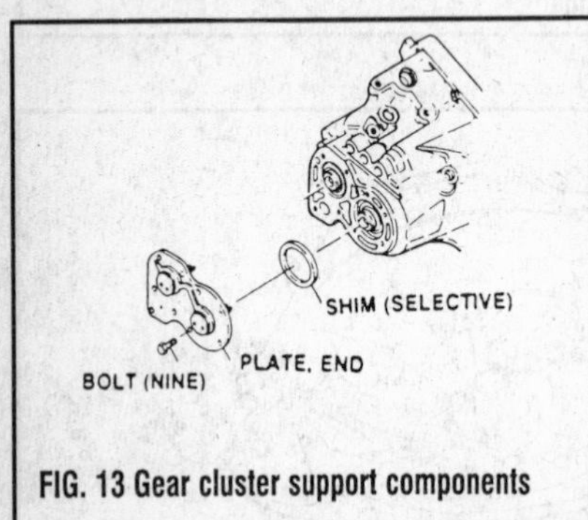

FIG. 13 Gear cluster support components

2. Remove the shift shaft assembly. This assembly consists of shaft, rollers and pins, 1st/2nd bias spring, shift and reverse levers. Take care not to lose the detent rollers.

GEAR CLUSTER SUPPORT COMPONENTS

➧ SEE FIGS. 12 AND 13

➡ **Engage the gear cluster in 4th and reverse by pushing down on the 3rd/4th gear rail and reverse gear rail.**

1. Remove the bolts using a 13mm socket and driver.
2. Remove the cover. Tap gently with a soft faced hammer.
3. Remove the selective shim.
4. Remove the oil shield.
5. Remove the retainer, output gear cluster using tool J-36031 or equivalent.
6. Remove the retainer, input gear cluster using tool J-36031 or equivalent. These retainers must not be reused.
7. Return the transaxle to **N**.

GEAR CLUSTERS

➧ SEE FIG. 14

1. Position tool J-36182-1 and J-36182-2 or equivalent, in the hydraulic press.
2. Position the transaxle case/gear cluster assembly on tool J-36182-1 and -2 or equivalent. Align the shift rail and shaft pilots to the fixture.
3. Position tool J-36185 or equivalent, on the shaft support bearings and pilots. Using a hydraulic press, separate the shaft and gear clusters from the transaxle case.
4. After this operation, the input and output shaft bearings should be discarded. Remove the gear clusters from the pallets, as an entire assembly.

GEAR CLUSTERS AND SHIFT RAILS

➧ SEE FIG. 15

➡ **This should be done on a workbench after taking the gear clusters off the pallet.**

1. Remove the 1/2 shift rail assembly and lock pin.
2. Remove the 3/4 rail assembly.

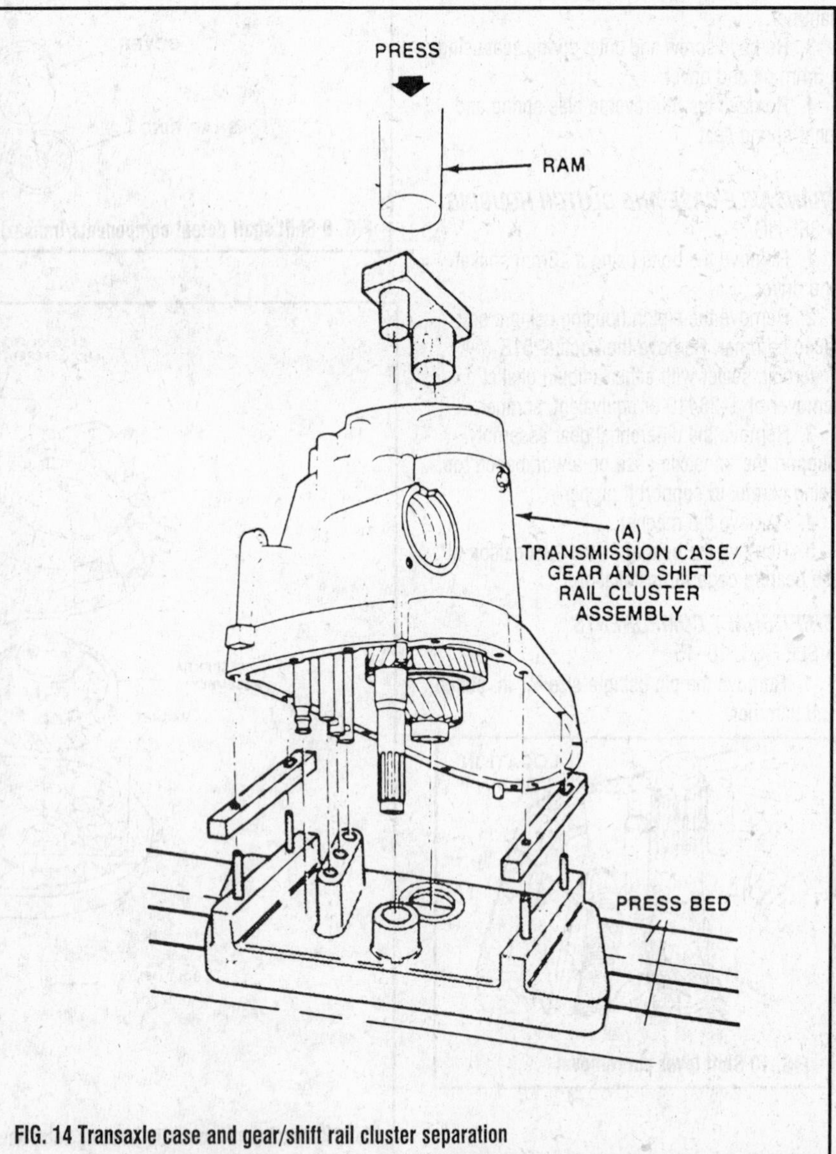

FIG. 14 Transaxle case and gear/shift rail cluster separation

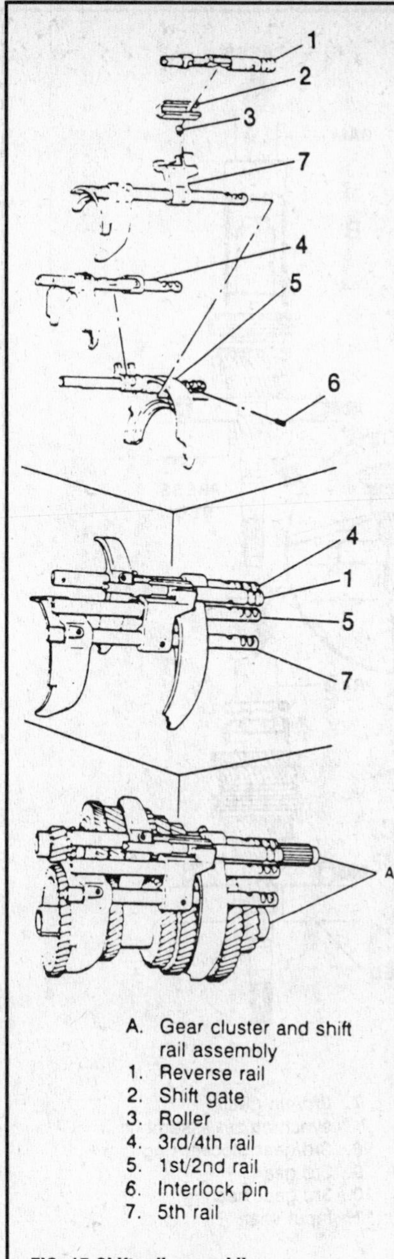

A. Gear cluster and shift rail assembly
1. Reverse rail
2. Shift gate
3. Roller
4. 3rd/4th rail
5. 1st/2nd rail
6. Interlock pin
7. 5th rail

FIG. 15 Shift rail assemblies

3. Remove the 5th rail assembly.
4. Remove the reverse rail assembly, consisting of the shift gate and disengage roller.

➡ **Be careful not to lose both the lock pin and the gear disengage roller, as they are small parts.**

Unit Disassembly and Assembly

➡ **The following components will require heating prior to installation during assembly procedures. A suggested heating oven is a toaster oven (used as a kitchen appliance). Heat the races, gear assembly and speedometer gear (electronic) for 7-10 minutes at 250°F (120°C). Heat the speedometer gear (mechanical) in hot tap water for 5 minutes. Heat the gear cluster for a minimum of 20 minutes at 250°F (120°C).**

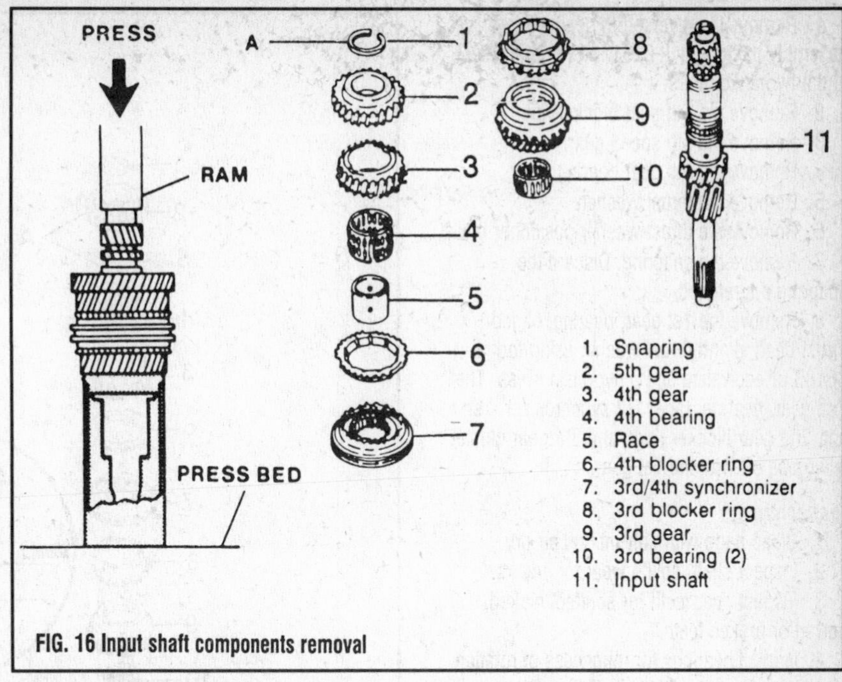

1. Snapring
2. 5th gear
3. 4th gear
4. 4th bearing
5. Race
6. 4th blocker ring
7. 3rd/4th synchronizer
8. 3rd blocker ring
9. 3rd gear
10. 3rd bearing (2)
11. Input shaft

FIG. 16 Input shaft components removal

INPUT SHAFT

Disassembly

➧ SEE FIG. 16

➡ **Identify blocker ring for 3rd gear and blocker ring for 4th gear. Do not mix.**

1. Remove the snapring and discard, if stretched.
2. Remove the gear, bearing, race, blocker ring, synchronizer assembly and gear using tool J-36183, J-36184 or equivalent and a hydraulic press.
3. Remove the 3rd gear bearing.

Inspection

1. Clean parts with solvent and air dry.
2. Inspect shaft, spline wear for cracks.
3. Inspect gear teeth for scuffed, nicked, burred or broken teeth.
4. Inspect bearings for roughness of rotation, burred or pitted condition.
5. Inspect bearing races for scoring, wear or overheating.
6. Inspect snaprings for nicks, distortion or wear.
7. Inspect synchronizers assembly for wear.

Assembly

➧ SEE FIG. 17

1. Install the 3rd gear bearing, 3rd gear (cone up) and blocker ring.

➡ **When pressing the 3rd/4th synchronizer assembly, start press operation, stop before tangs engage. Lift and rotate the 3rd gear into the synchronizer tangs. Continue to press until seated. Be sure all shavings are removed.**

2. Install the 3/4 synchronizer, using tool J–22912–01, J–36183, J–36184 or equivalent and a hydraulic press. Tool J–22828 presses 4th gear bearing race on very well. The small outer diameter groove of the sleeve toward the 3rd gear and small end of the hub facing 4th.
3. Install the bearing race and bearing using gloves to handle the hot race. Check the temperature with Tempilstick® or thermometer.
4. Install the 4th gear blocker ring.
5. Install the 4th gear with the cone down.
6. Install the 5th gear (flat side down) using tool J–36183, J–36184 or equivalent and a hydraulic press.
7. Install the snapring.

OUTPUT SHAFT

Disassembly

➧ SEE FIG. 18

➡ **Identify the blocker ring for 5th gear, blocker ring for 2nd gear and blocker ring for 1st gear. Do not mix.**

1. Remove the reverse/5th gear synchronizer assembly using tool J–22912–01 or equivalent and a hydraulic press.
2. Remove the 5th gear blocker ring.
3. Remove the 5th speed gear.
4. Remove the 5th gear bearing.
5. Remove the thrust washer.
6. Remove the thrust washer positioner ball.
7. Remove the snapring. Discard the snapring if stretched.
8. Remove the 1st gear, bearing, caged thrust bearing and thrust washer using tool J–36183 or equivalent and a hydraulic press. The 2nd gear, bearing, race, 1/2 synchronizer, 1st and 2nd gear blocker rings and 3/4 gear cluster will press off with the 1st gear.

Inspection

1. Clean parts with solvent and air dry.
2. Inspect shaft, spline wear for cracks.
3. Inspect gear teeth for scuffed, nicked, burred or broken teeth.
4. Inspect bearings for roughness of rotation, burred or pitted condition.
5. Inspect bearing races for scoring, wear or overheating.
6. Inspect snaprings for nicks, distortion or wear.
7. Inspect synchronizers assembly for wear.

Assembly

➧ SEE FIG. 19

➡ The 2nd gear bearing race requires heating 250°F (120°C) in oven, minimum of 7–10 minutes. The 3/4 gear cluster requires heating 250°F (120°C) in oven, minimum of 20 minutes. Lubricate all components as assembly progresses.

1. Install thrust washer with the chamfer down.
2. Install the thrust bearing with the needles down.
3. Install the 1st gear bearing.
4. Install the 1st gear with the cone up.
5. Install the 1st gear blocker ring.
6. Install the 1/2 synchronizer using tool J–36183, J–36184 or equivalent and a hydraulic press. Use tool J–22828 or equivalent, to do this. The small outer diameter groove on the sleeve (and small end of the hub) toward the 1st gear.

➡ When pressing the 1/2 synchronizer assembly, start press operation, stop before tangs engage. Lift and rotate the 1st gear and 1st gear blocker ring, to engage the blocker ring tangs. Continue to press until seated. Be sure all the shavings are removed.

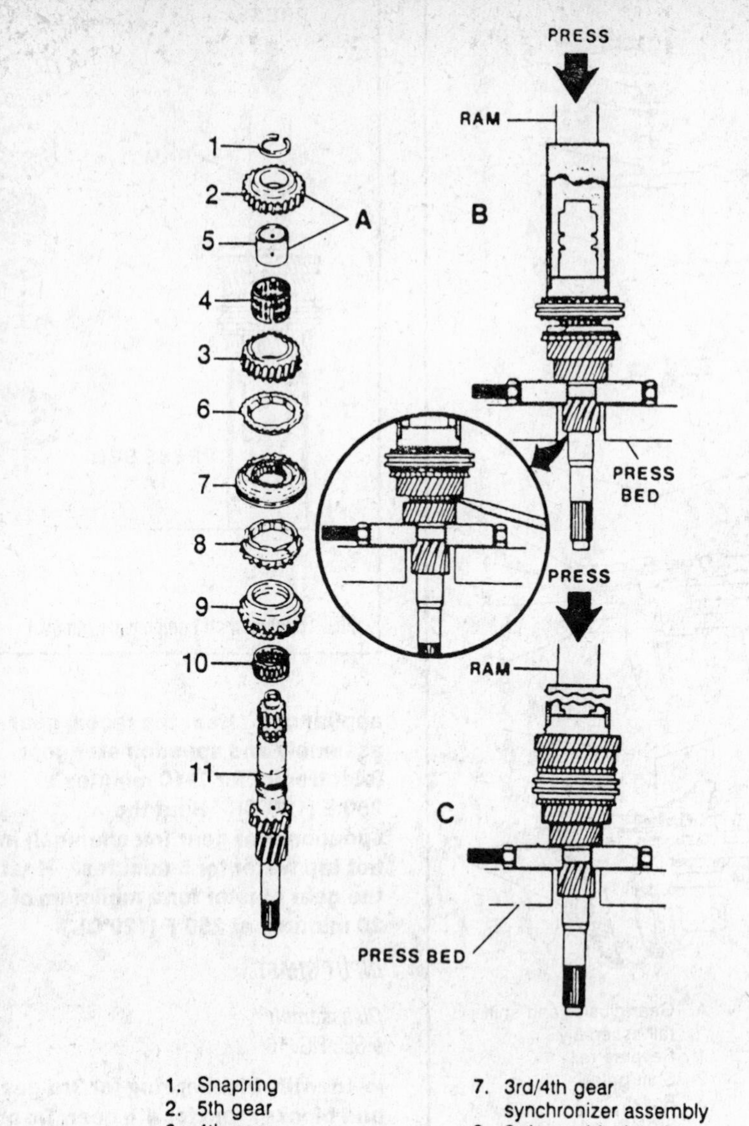

FIG. 17 Input shaft components installation

7. Install the 2nd gear bearing race (be careful handling the hot bearing race), 2nd gear bearing and 2nd gear (cone down).
8. Install the 3rd/4th gear cluster (be careful when handling hot cluster gear) using tool J–36183 or equivalent and a hydraulic press. The large outer diameter gear down.
9. Install the snapring, thrust washer positioning ball (retain with petroleum jelly) and slotted thrust washer. Align the inner diameter slot with the ball.
10. Install the 5th gear bearing and the 5th gear with the cone up.
11. Install the 5th gear blocker ring.
12. Install the reverse/5th gear synchronizer assembly using tool J–36183, J–36184 or equivalent and hydraulic press.

➡ When pressing the reverse/5th synchronizer, start press operation, stop before tangs engage. Lift and rotate the 5th gear and 5th gear blocker ring (thrust washer must stay down), engaging tangs. Continue to press until seated. Be sure all shavings are removed.

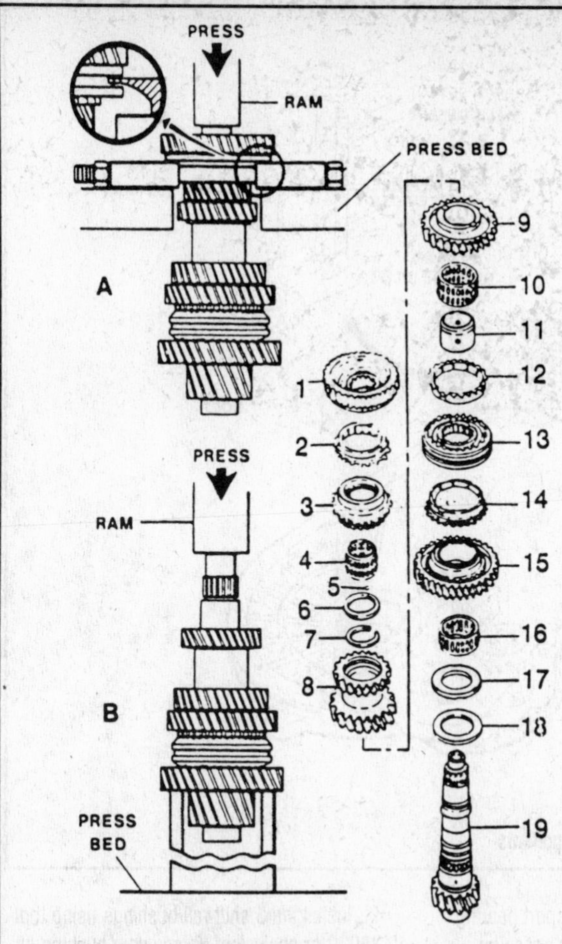

1. Reverse/5th gear synchronizer
2. 5th gear blocker ring
3. 5th speed gear
4. 5th gear bearing
5. Thrust washer positioner ball
6. Thrust washer
7. Snapring
8. 3rd/4th cluster gear
9. 2nd speed gear
10. 2nd gear bearing
11. 2nd gear bearing race
12. 2nd gear blocker ring
13. 1st/2nd gear synchronizer assembly
14. 1st gear blocker ring
15. 1st speed gear
16. 1st gear bearing
17. Thrust bearing
18. Thrust washer
19. Output shaft

FIG. 18 Output shaft components removal

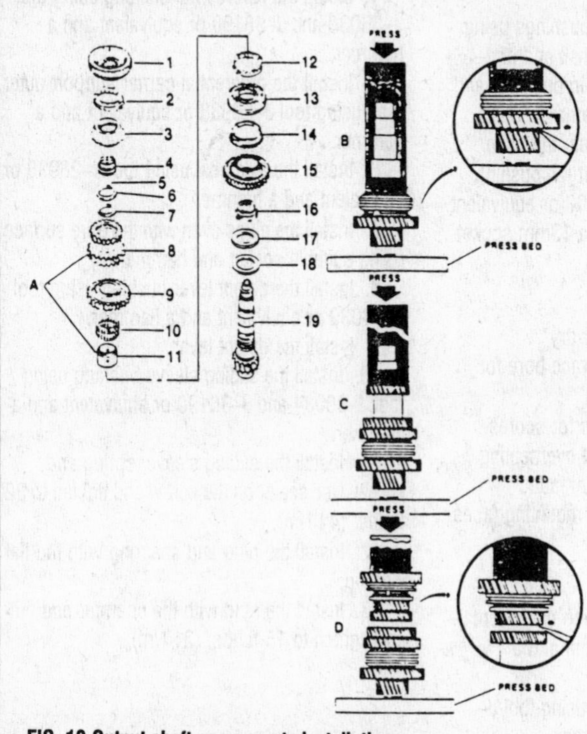

1. Reverse/5th gear synchronizer
2. 5th gear blocker ring
3. 5th speed gear
4. 5th gear bearing
5. Thrust washer positioner ball
6. Thrust washer
7. Snapring
8. 3rd/4th cluster gear
9. 2nd speed gear
10. 2nd gear bearing
11. 2nd gear bearing race
12. 2nd gear blocker ring
13. 1st/2nd gear synchronizer assembly
14. 1st gear blocker ring
15. 1st speed gear
16. 1st gear bearing
17. Thrust bearing
18. Thrust washer
19. Output shaft

FIG. 19 Output shaft components installation

REVERSE IDLER GEAR

Disassembly

➧ SEE FIG. 20

1. Remove the bolt using a 13mm socket and driver.
2. Remove the shift rail, gear, shaft and bracket.
3. Remove the shift rail, detent ball and spring.

Inspection

1. Clean parts with solvent and air dry.
2. Inspect gear teeth for scuffed, nicked, burred or broken teeth.
3. Inspect bushings for roughness, burred, scores or overheating.
4. Inspect shaft for scoring, wear or overheating.

Assembly

1. Lubricate all components as assembly progresses.
2. Assemble spring and ball in bracket.
3. Install the shaft in the bracket assembly.
4. Install the gear on the shaft with the slot on the gear toward the threaded hole in the shaft.
5. Install the reverse idler gear assembly.
6. Install sealer to the bolt threads and install the bolt. Torque to 16 ft. lbs. (21 Nm).

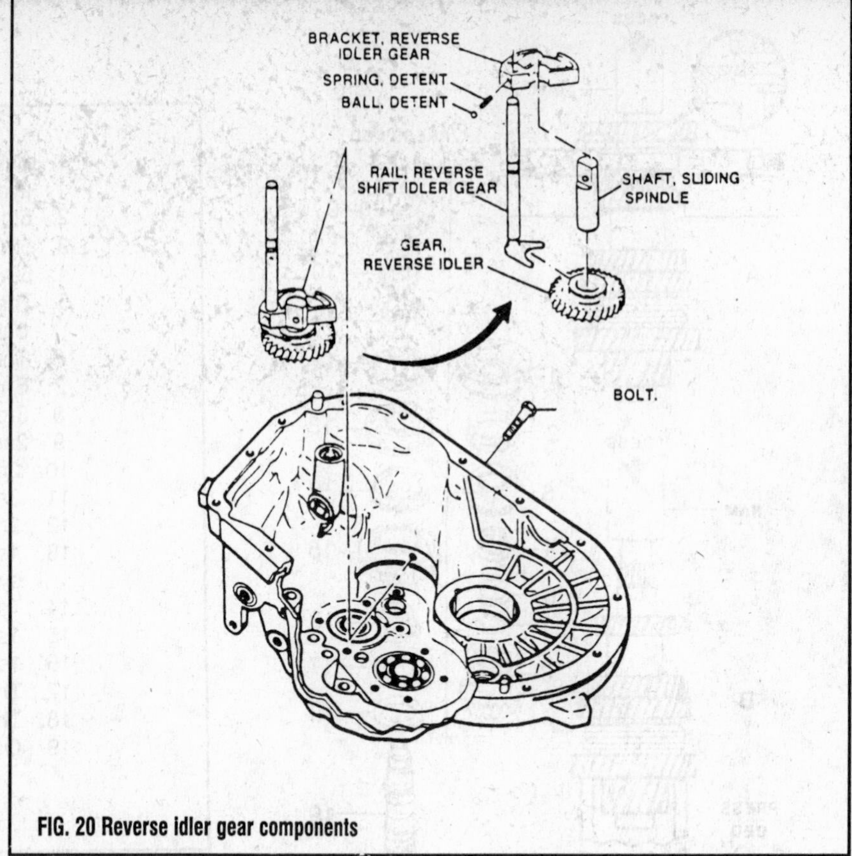

FIG. 20 Reverse idler gear components

TRANSAXLE CASE

Disassembly

➧ SEE FIG. 21

➡ Remove the bearings and bushings only if there is evidence of damage or a mating part is being replaced.

1. Remove the snapring.
2. Remove the plug.
3. Remove the sliding sleeve screw, sliding sleeve spring and sliding sleeve.
4. Remove the sliding sleeve bushing using tool J-36034 and J-36190 or equivalent and a hammer.
5. Remove the detent lever.
6. Remove the bushing shift detent lever using tool J-36039 and J-36190 or equivalent and a hammer.
7. Remove the shift shaft seal using a small suitable tool.
8. Remove the bearing shift shaft using tool J-36027 and J-36190 or equivalent and a hammer.
9. Remove the axle seal using a punch and hammer.
10. Remove the differential case support outer race using tool J-36181 and J-8092 or equivalent and a hammer.
11. Remove the shift rails plugs using a punch and a hammer.
12. Remove the input shaft support bearing. Remember that these bearings are not to be reused.
13. Remove the output shaft support bearing using a hammer.
14. Remove the 3 shift rail bushings using tool J-36029 or equivalent, (small end of J-36029-2 or equivalent adapter in bushing) and J-36190 or equivalent and a hammer. Make sure the tool is positioned to clear the case.
15. Remove the reverse shift rail bushing using tool J-36032 and J-23907 or equivalent.
16. Remove the stud using a 13mm socket and driver.

Inspection

1. Clean with solvent and air dry.
2. Inspect the case bearing race bore for wear, scratches or grooves.
3. Inspect the case bushings for scores, burrs, roundness or evidence of overheating.
4. Inspect case for cracks, threaded openings for damaged threads, mounting faces for nicks, burrs or scratches.

Assembly

1. Install the shift shaft bearing using tool J-36189 and J-36190 or equivalent and a hammer.
2. Install the shift shaft seal using tool J-35823 or equivalent and a hammer.
3. Install the 3 shift rail bushings using tool J-36029 or equivalent, (place new bushing on -2 adapter and retain between the -1 and -2 tool parts) and J-36190 or equivalent and a hammer.
4. Install the reverse rail bushing using tool J-36030 and J-36190 or equivalent and a hammer.
5. Install the differential carrier support outer race using tool J-26938 or equivalent and a hammer.
6. Install the axle seal using tool J-26938 or equivalent and a hammer.
7. Install the plugs even with the bore surface using suitable socket and hammer.
8. Install the detent lever bushing using tool J-36039 or equivalent and a hammer.
9. Install the detent lever.
10. Install the sliding sleeve bushing using tool J-36034 and J-36190 or equivalent and a hammer.
11. Install the sliding sleeve, spring and screw. Use sealer on the screw and tighten to 32 ft. lbs. (44 Nm).
12. Install the plug and snapring with the flat side up.
13. Install the stud with the chamfer end out and tighten to 15 ft. lbs. (21 Nm).

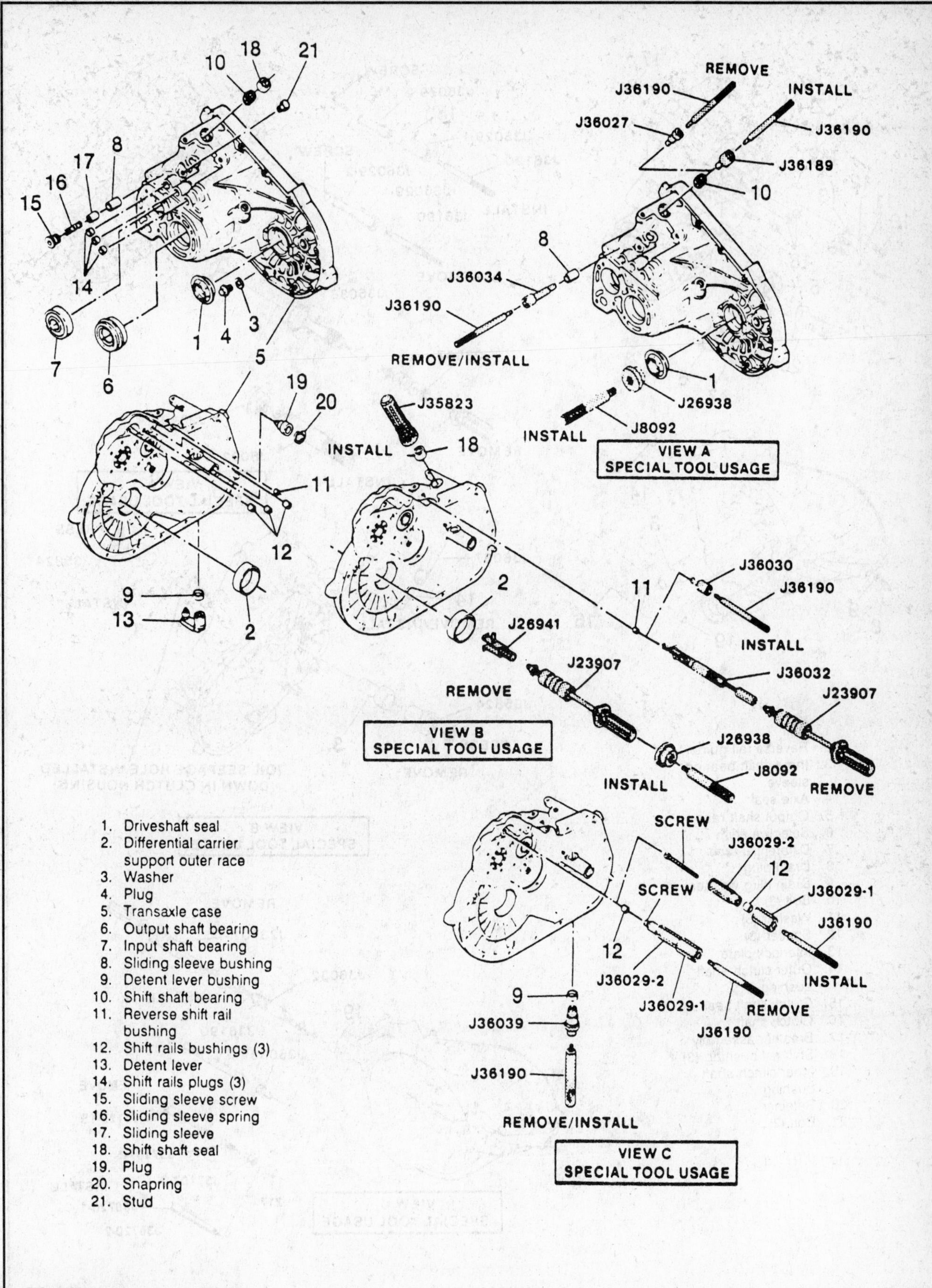

1. Driveshaft seal
2. Differential carrier support outer race
3. Washer
4. Plug
5. Transaxle case
6. Output shaft bearing
7. Input shaft bearing
8. Sliding sleeve bushing
9. Detent lever bushing
10. Shift shaft bearing
11. Reverse shift rail bushing
12. Shift rails bushings (3)
13. Detent lever
14. Shift rails plugs (3)
15. Sliding sleeve screw
16. Sliding sleeve spring
17. Sliding sleeve
18. Shift shaft seal
19. Plug
20. Snapring
21. Stud

FIG. 21 Transaxle case components

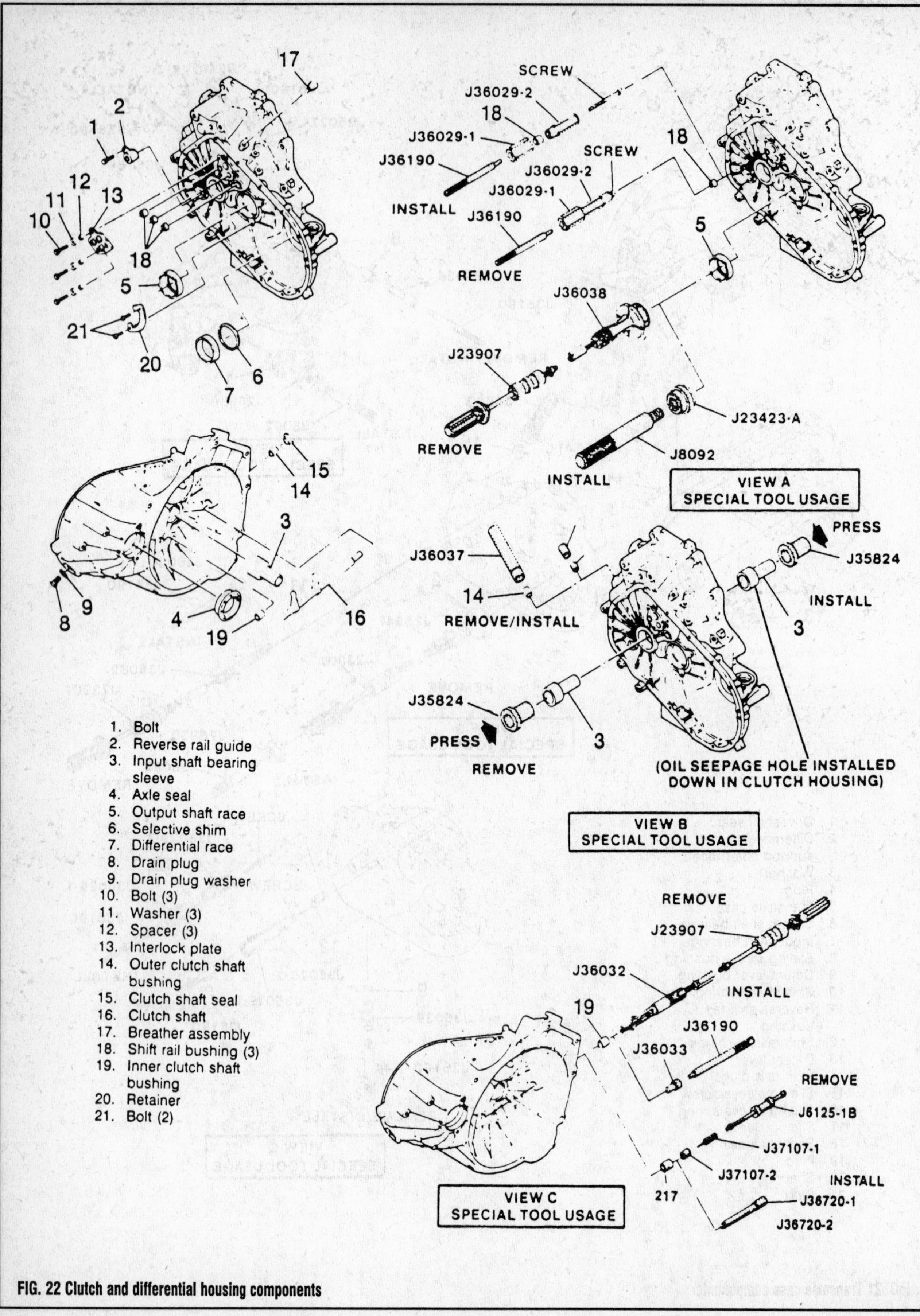

FIG. 22 Clutch and differential housing components

CLUTCH AND DIFFERENTIAL HOUSING

Disassembly

➧ SEE FIG. 22

1. Remove the bolts and retainer using a 10mm socket and driver.
2. Remove the output shaft race using tool J-36038 and J-23907 or equivalent and a hammer.
3. Remove the bolts, washers, spacer and plate using a 10mm socket and driver.
4. Remove the reverse rail guide bolt and guide. This may be difficult to remove. Use a 10mm socket and driver.
5. Remove the axle seal using a punch and hammer.
6. Remove the differential race and shim using tool J-36181 and J-8092 or equivalent and a hammer.
7. Remove the clutch shaft seal using small pry bar.
8. Remove the outer clutch shaft upper bushing using tool J-36037 or equivalent and a hammer.
9. Remove the clutch shaft.
10. Remove the inner clutch shaft bushing using tool J-36032 and J-23907 or equivalent.
11. Remove the input shaft bearing sleeve assembly using tool J-35824 or equivalent and a hydraulic press.
12. Remove the shift rail bushings using tool J-36029 or equivalent, (small end of -2 adapter in bushing) and hammer.
13. Remove the drain plug and washer using a 15mm socket and hammer.
14. Remove the breather assembly. Pry with a suitable tool.

Inspection

1. Clean with solvent and air dry.
2. Inspect the housing bearing race bore for wear, scratches or grooves.
3. Inspect the housing bushings for scores, burrs, roundness or evidence of overheating.
4. Inspect housing for cracks, threaded openings for damaged threads, mounting faces for nicks, burrs or scratches.

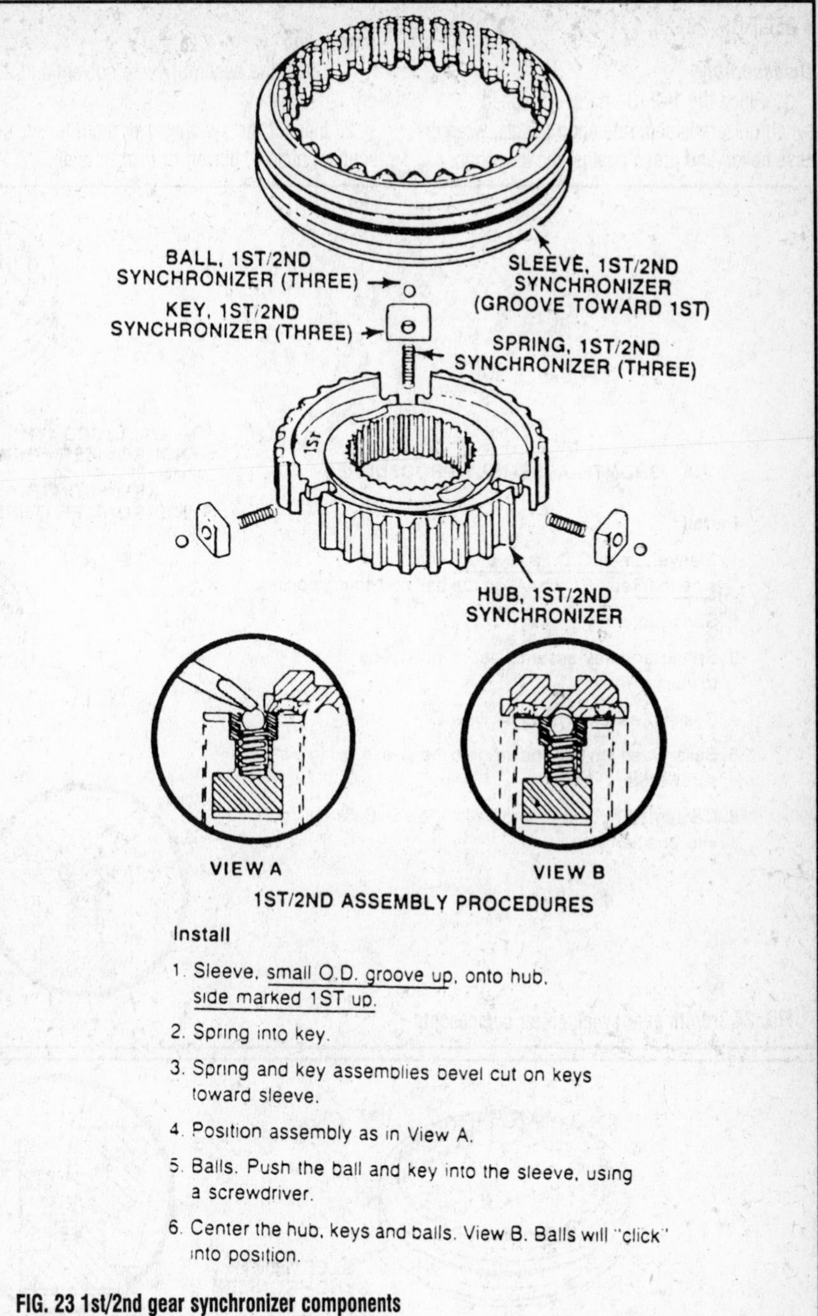

FIG. 23 1st/2nd gear synchronizer components

Assembly

➡ Do not install the differential bearing race and axle seal or shim. Installation will be after differential bearing selective shimming.

1. Install the drain plug and new washer and tighten to 18 ft. lbs. (24 Nm).
2. Install the shift rail bushings using tool J-36029 or equivalent, (place the new bushings on -2 adapter and retain between the -1 and -2 tool parts) and J-36190 or equivalent and a hammer. Bushings must not protrude into the case side of the clutch housing.
3. Install the input shaft bearing sleeve (oil seepage hole installed down in the clutch housing) using tool J-35824 or equivalent and a hydraulic press.
4. Install the inner clutch shaft bushing using tool J-36033 and J-36190 or equivalent and a hammer.
5. Install the clutch shaft.
6. Install the outer clutch shaft upper bushing using tool J-36037 or equivalent and a hammer.
7. Install the clutch shaft seal using a suitable socket and hammer.
8. Install the reverse rail guide using hammer. Short side in the bore and tighten bolt to 15 ft. lbs. (21 Nm).
9. Install the output shaft race using tool J-23423-A and J-8092 or equivalent and a hammer. Be sure to use side A of the driver. Align the race cutouts with the slots in the case.
10. Install the retainer and bolts and tighten to 15 ft. lbs. (21 Nm). Use Loctite® 242 on the bolt.
11. Install the interlock plate, spacers, washers and bolts. Use Loctite® 242 and torque bolts to 15 ft. lbs. (21 Nm).
12. Install the breather assembly using a hammer.

SYNCHRONIZERS

➧ SEE FIGS. 23–26

Disassembly

1. Place the 1–2, 3–4 and 5th speed synchronizers in separate shop towels, wrap the assemblies and press against the inner hub.

2. Mark the sleeve and hub for installation.

Inspection

1. Clean the assembly with solvent and air dry.

2. Inspect the synchronizer teeth for wear, scuffed, nicked, burred or broken teeth.

3. Inspect the synchronizer keys for wear or distortion.

4. Inspect the synchronizer balls and springs for distortion, cracks or wear.

3RD/4TH ASSEMBLY PROCEDURES

Install

1. Sleeve, small O.D. groove up, onto hub, side marked 3RD up. Align the ball and spring pockets.
2. Spring into key.
3. Spring and key assemblies, stepped side of keys toward sleeve.
4. Position assemblys as in View C.
5. Balls. Push the ball and key into the sleeve, using a small screwdriver.
6. Center the hub, keys and balls. View D. Balls will "click" into position.

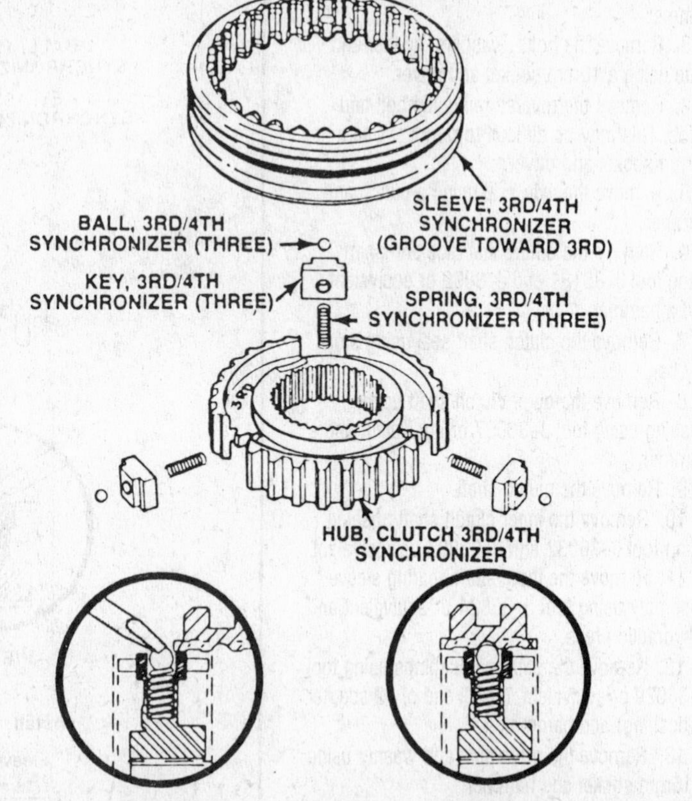

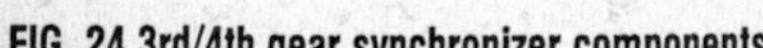

FIG. 24 3rd/4th gear synchronizer components

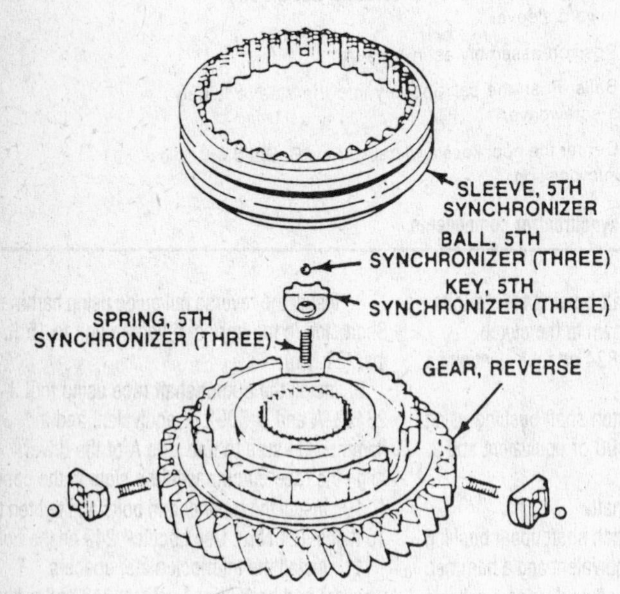

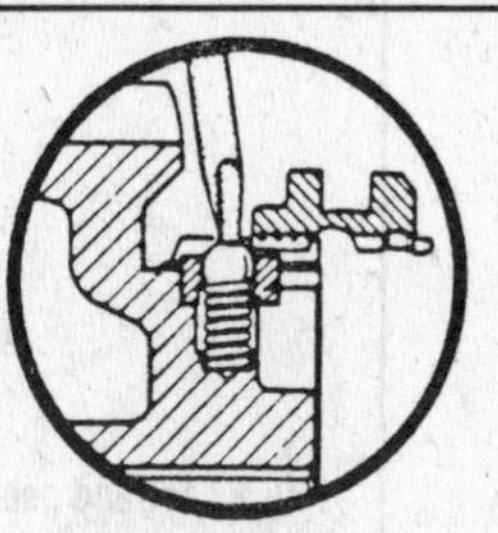

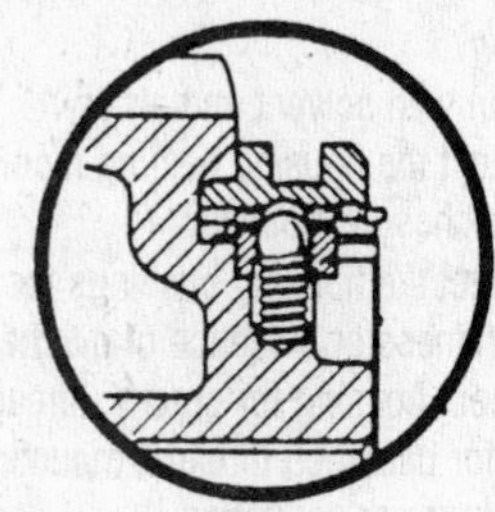

5TH ASSEMBLY PROCEDURES

Install

1. Spring into key.
2. Spring and key assemblies, teeth on keys out into slots on gear.
3. Sleeve, teeth up. Align the ball and spring pockets.
4. Position assembly as in View E.
5. Balls. Push the ball and key into the sleeve, using a small screwdriver.
6. Center the sleeve, keys and balls. View F. Balls will "click" into position.

FIG. 25 5th gear synchronizer components

1. Reverse shift assembly rail
2. 5th/reverse shift gate
3. Gear disengage roller
4. Reverse shift shaft
5. 3rd/4th shift assembly rail
6. 3rd/4th shift shaft fork
7. Fork retainer pin
8. 3rd/4th select lever
9. Lever retainer pin
10. 3rd/4th shift shaft
11. 1st/2nd shift assembly rail
12. 1st/2nd shift lever
13. Lever retainer pin
14. Fork retainer pin
15. 1st/2nd shift fork
16. 1st/2nd shift shaft
17. Lock pin
18. 5th shift assembly rail
19. 5th shift fork
20. Fork retainer pin
21. 5th shift lever
22. Lever retainer pin
23. 5th shift shaft

FIG. 26 Shift rail and fork assemblies

Assembly

1. Install the 1st/2nd gear synchronizer assembly.
2. Install the 3rd/4th gear synchronizer assembly.
3. Install the 5th gear synchronizer assembly.

DIFFERENTIAL AND RING GEAR

➧ SEE FIG. 27

Removal

1. Remove the differential carrier assembly bolts using a 15mm socket and driver.
2. Remove the differential ring gear.
3. Remove the differential bearings using tool J–22888 or equivalent, J–22888–35 or equivalent and J–2241–11 or equivalent or J–23598 or equivalent.
4. Remove the speedometer gear using a prybar. Do not reuse; the removal will destroy the gear.
5. Remove the differential cross pin locking bolt and washer.
6. Remove the differential cross pin.
7. Remove the differential pinion gear and washer, differential side gear and side gear thrust washer. Identify the parts for same installation.

Inspection

1. Clean the parts with a solvent and air dry.

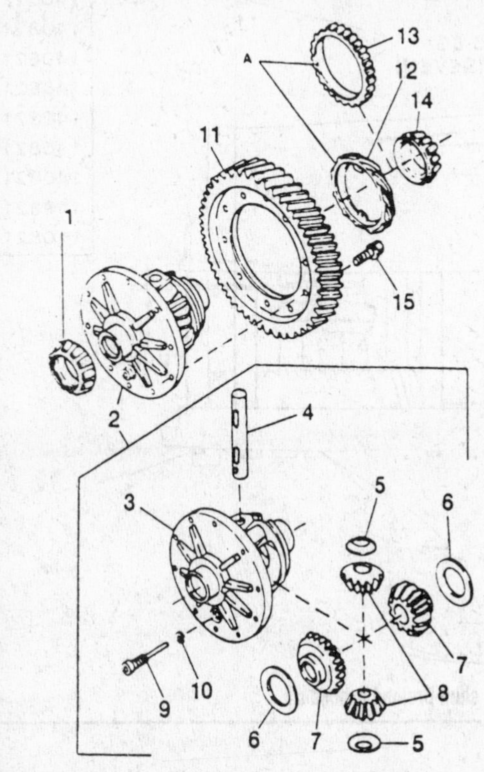

1. Differential bearing
2. Differential assembly carrier
3. Differential carrier
4. Differential cross pin
5. Pinion gear thrust washer
6. Side gear thrust washer
7. Differential side gear
8. Differential pinion gear
9. Screw
10. Lock washer
11. Differential ring gear
12. Speedometer gear (mechanical)
13. Speedometer gear (electronic)
14. Differential bearing
15. Bolt (10)

FIG. 27 Differential and ring gear components

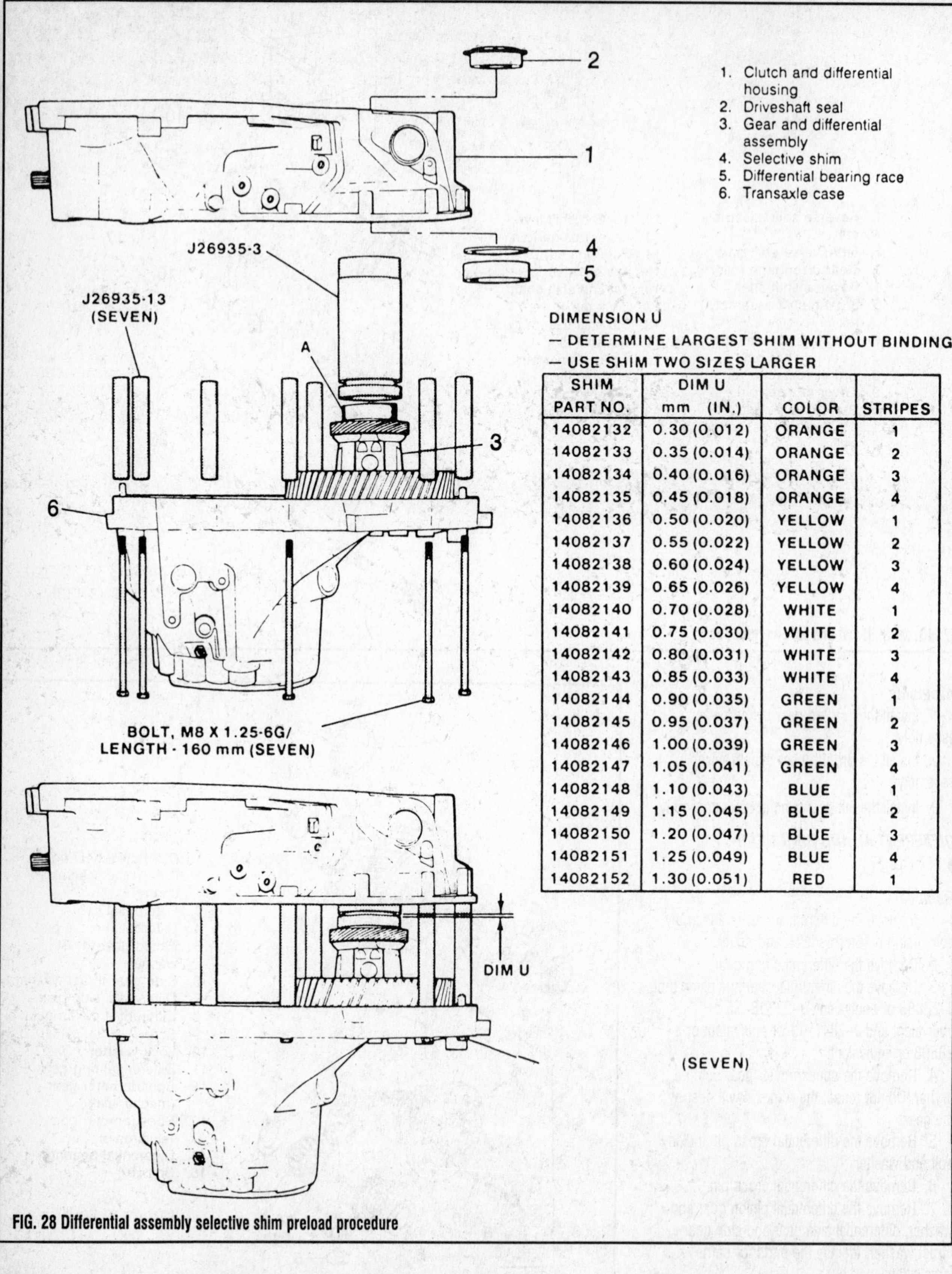

SHIM PART NO.	DIM U mm (IN.)	COLOR	STRIPES
14082132	0.30 (0.012)	ORANGE	1
14082133	0.35 (0.014)	ORANGE	2
14082134	0.40 (0.016)	ORANGE	3
14082135	0.45 (0.018)	ORANGE	4
14082136	0.50 (0.020)	YELLOW	1
14082137	0.55 (0.022)	YELLOW	2
14082138	0.60 (0.024)	YELLOW	3
14082139	0.65 (0.026)	YELLOW	4
14082140	0.70 (0.028)	WHITE	1
14082141	0.75 (0.030)	WHITE	2
14082142	0.80 (0.031)	WHITE	3
14082143	0.85 (0.033)	WHITE	4
14082144	0.90 (0.035)	GREEN	1
14082145	0.95 (0.037)	GREEN	2
14082146	1.00 (0.039)	GREEN	3
14082147	1.05 (0.041)	GREEN	4
14082148	1.10 (0.043)	BLUE	1
14082149	1.15 (0.045)	BLUE	2
14082150	1.20 (0.047)	BLUE	3
14082151	1.25 (0.049)	BLUE	4
14082152	1.30 (0.051)	RED	1

FIG. 28 Differential assembly selective shim preload procedure

2. Inspect the gears for scuffed, nicked, burred or broken teeth.

3. Inspect the carrier for distortion, bores out of round or scoring.

4. Inspect the bearings for roughness of rotation, burred or pitted condition.

5. Inspect the thrust washers for wear, scuffed, nicked or burred condition.

Installation

➡ Heat the mechanical configuration nylon speedometer drive gear in hot tap water for 5 minutes prior to installation. Heat the electronic configuration steel speedometer drive gear in an oven at 250°F (120°C) for 7-10 minutes prior to installation. Do not reuse bolts.

1. Install the speedometer gear and allow to cool.

2. Install the differential bearings using tool J-22919 or equivalent and a hydraulic press.

3. Install the differential side gear and side gear thrust washer and differential pinion gear and pinion gear side thrust washer.

4. Install the differential cross pin.

5. Install the differential cross locking bolt and washer. Torque to 84 inch lbs. (9 Nm).

6. Install the differential ring gear with the identification chamfer to the carrier.

7. Install new bolts and torque to 61 ft. lbs. (83 Nm).

DIFFERENTIAL ASSEMBLY SELECTIVE SHIM PRELOAD PROCEDURE

➧ SEE FIG. 28

1. Install tool J-26935 or equivalent, to the clutch housing and transaxle housing.

2. Measure the largest shim possible on tool J-26935-3; use the shim 2 sizes larger.

3. Install the selective shim.

4. Install the differential bearing race using tool J-26938 or equivalent and J-8092 or equivalent and a hammer.

5. Install the driveshaft seal using tool J-8092 or equivalent and a hammer.

Transaxle Assembly

➧ SEE FIGS 29-40

GEAR/SHIFT RAIL ASSEMBLIES AND SUPPORT COMPONENT

1. Position the gear cluster/shift rail assembly on tool J-36182-1 or equivalent. Align the shift rail and shaft pilots to the fixture.

2. Install the transaxle case. Align the bearing bores in the case with the shaft pilots.

3. Install the new output shaft bearing using tool J-35824 or equivalent and a hydraulic press.

4. Install the new input shaft bearing using tool J-35824 or equivalent and a hydraulic press. Push the rails to engage and hold the transaxle in 4th and reverse gear. The bearings must be seated.

5. Install the new input and output retainers using tool J-36031 or equivalent and torque to 50 ft. lbs. (70 Nm). Return the transaxle to **N**.

SHIFT SHAFT

1. Assemble the pins and rollers on the shift shaft. Retain with petroleum jelly.

2. Install the shift shaft assembly. Tap in with a light hammer and align the hole in the shaft with the hole in the shift lever.

3. Install the lever retainer pin using a $^3/_{16}$ in. punch and a hammer. Install pin till it is even with the surface of the shift lever.

CLUTCH AND DIFFERENTIAL HOUSING

1. Apply sealant, part number 1052942 or equivalent, to the outside of the bolt hole pattern of the gear case flange.

2. Install the differential.

3. Install the output bearing noting the position of the cage. The small inner diameter of the bearing cage is toward the clutch housing.

4. Install the magnet.

5. Install the clutch housing.

6. Install the bolts and torque to 15 ft. lbs. (21 Nm).

OUTPUT SHAFT SUPPORT BEARING SELECTIVE SHIM PROCEDURE

➡ Be sure that the output bearing is seated in the bore by tapping the bearing into the case. Be sure that the bearing retainer is properly torqued. Selected shim can be 0.001 in. (0.03mm) above, or 0.004 in. (0.12mm) below the end plate mounting surface.

1. Using tool J-26900-19 metric dial depth gauge or equivalent, measure the distance between the end plate mounting surface and the outer race of the output shaft bearing.

2. Select the proper shim.

TRANSAXLE CASE END PLATE

1. Apply sealant, part number 1052942 or equivalent, to the outside of the end plate bolt hole pattern of the case.

2. Install the selective shim.

3. Install the oil shield.

4. Install the end cover plate.

5. Install the bolts and torque to 15 ft. lbs. (21 Nm).

SHIFT RAIL DETENT/CLUTCH AND DIFFERENTIAL HOUSING

1. Position the shift rails to expose the interlock notches in the **N** position.

2. Position the reverse shift rail to allow the detent ball to sit in the notch and on the reverse bushing.

3. Install the reverse bushing using a suitable socket.

4. Install the detent balls. Place them in the notched areas of the shift rails. Retain the ball positions with petroleum jelly.

5. Assemble the interlock pins and springs into the bores in the detent holder.

6. Install the detent holder and spring assembly. Position the detent balls over the springs using a small suitable tool. After all the detent balls are positioned over the springs, pry the reverse shift rail up to allow its detent ball to enter the spring pocket.

7. Position the detent holder using a pry to align the bolt holes with the threads.

8. Install the bolts and torque to 84 inch lbs. (9 Nm).

9. Install the protective cover by tapping with a hammer until seated in the bore.

10. Install the bearing. Apply high temperature grease to the inside of the bore.

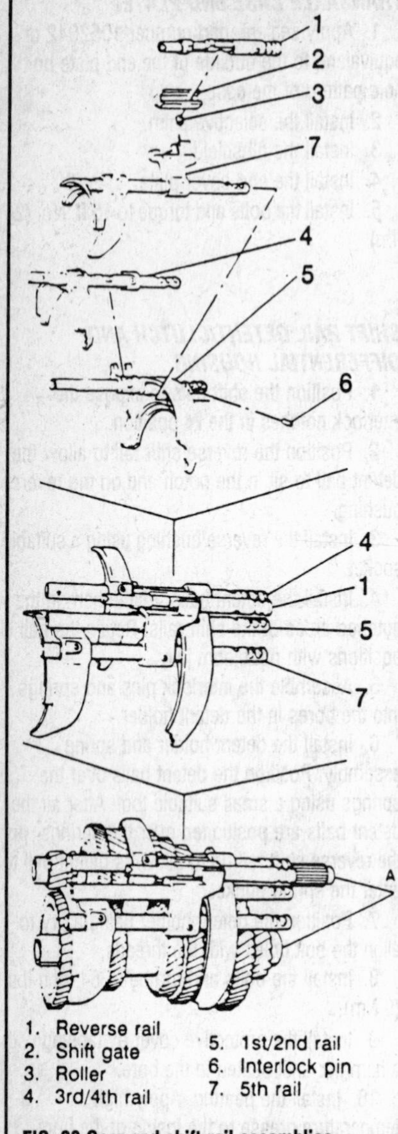

FIG. 29 Gear and shift rail assemblies

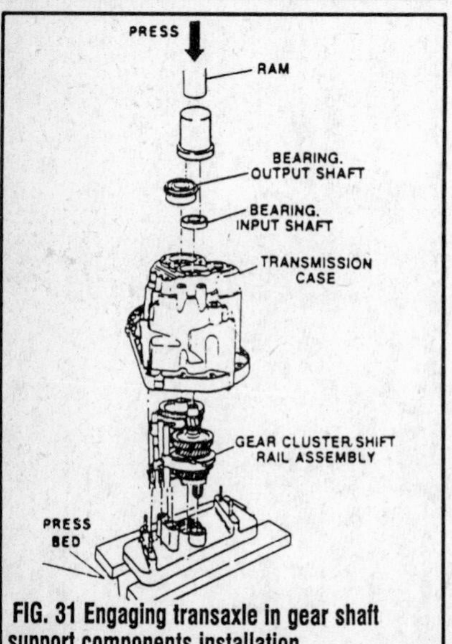

FIG. 31 Engaging transaxle in gear shaft support components installation

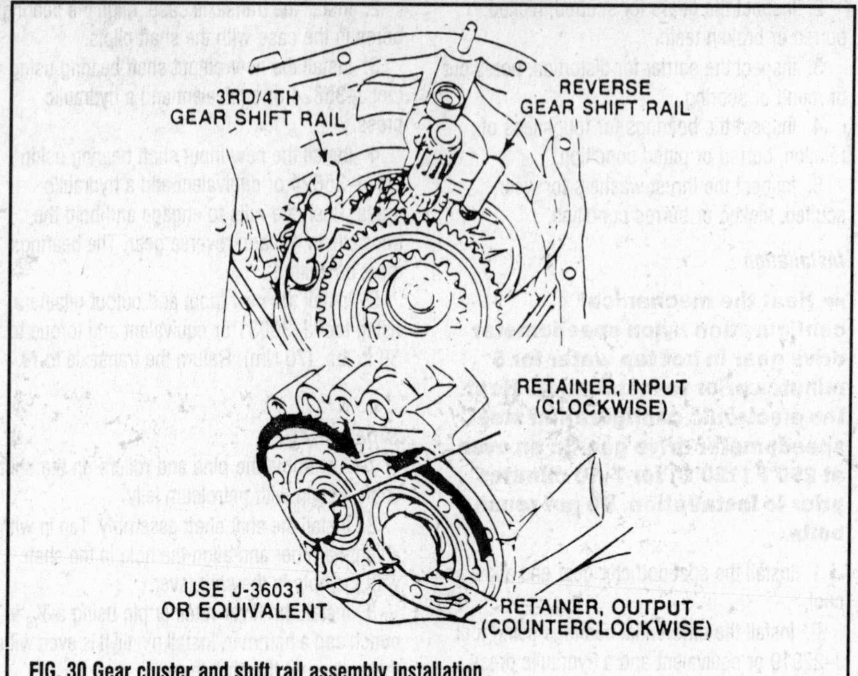

FIG. 30 Gear cluster and shift rail assembly installation

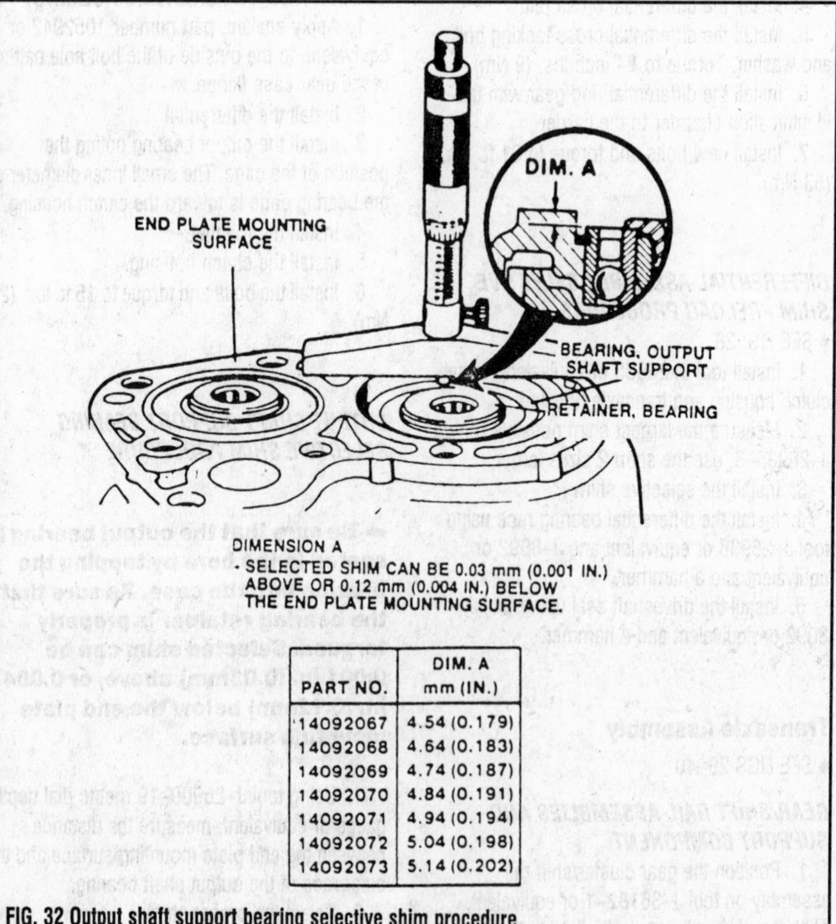

PART NO.	DIM. A mm (IN.)
14092067	4.54 (0.179)
14092068	4.64 (0.183)
14092069	4.74 (0.187)
14092070	4.84 (0.191)
14092071	4.94 (0.194)
14092072	5.04 (0.198)
14092073	5.14 (0.202)

FIG. 32 Output shaft support bearing selective shim procedure

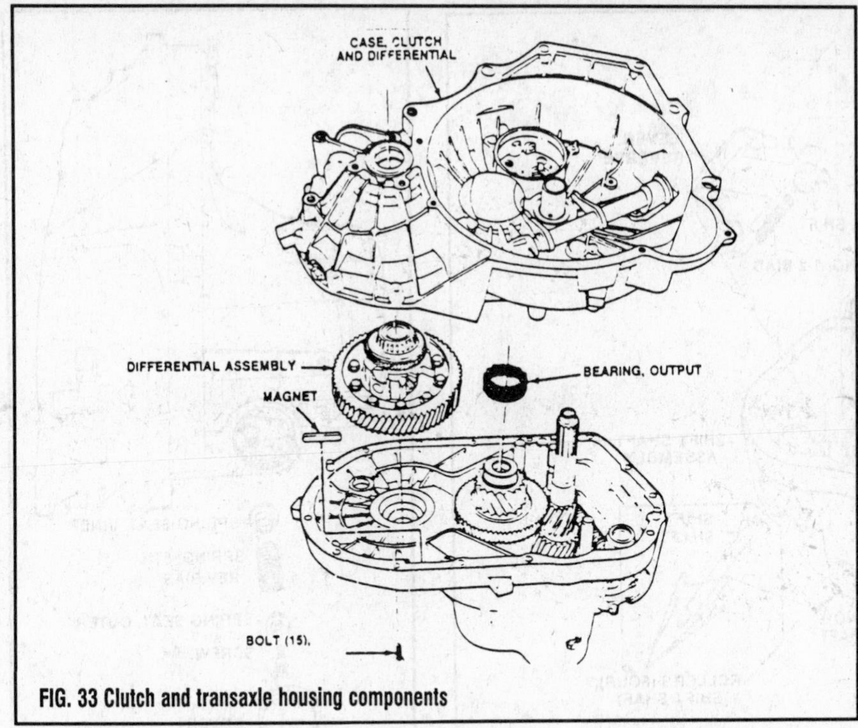

FIG. 33 Clutch and transaxle housing components

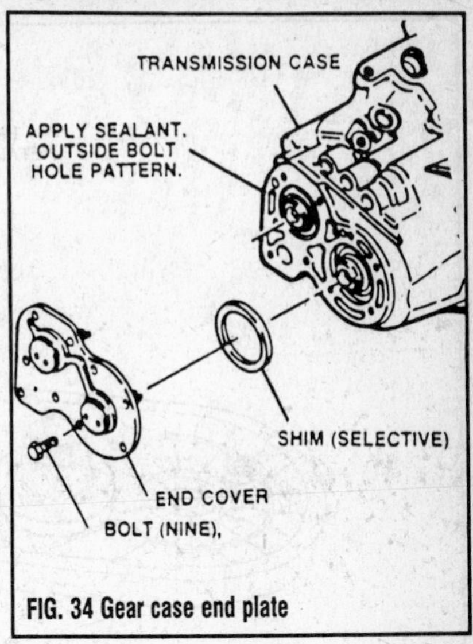

FIG. 34 Gear case end plate

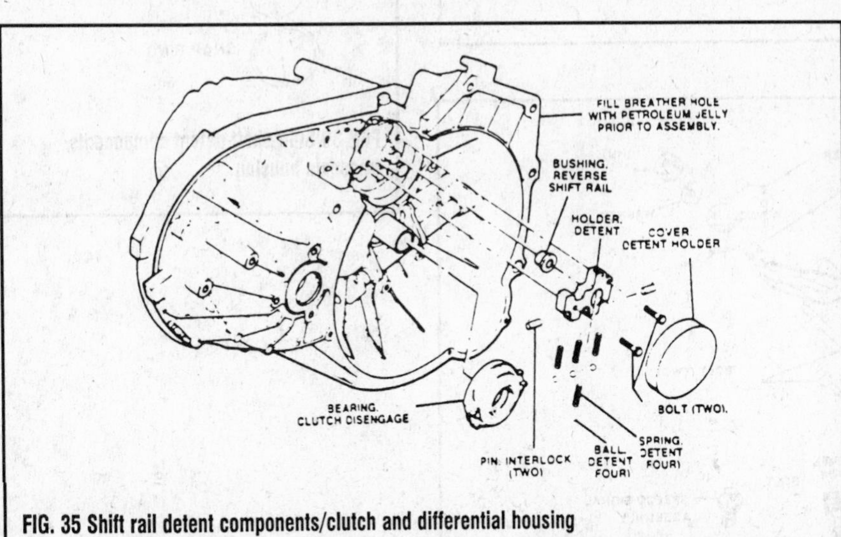

FIG. 35 Shift rail detent components/clutch and differential housing

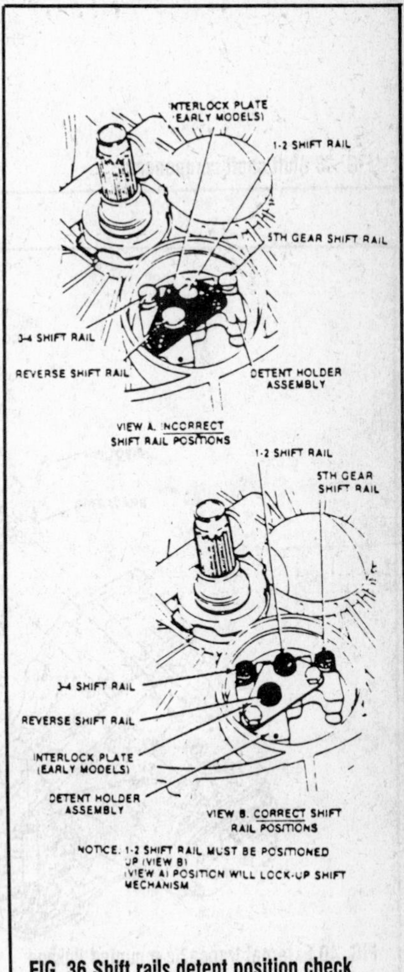

FIG. 36 Shift rails detent position check

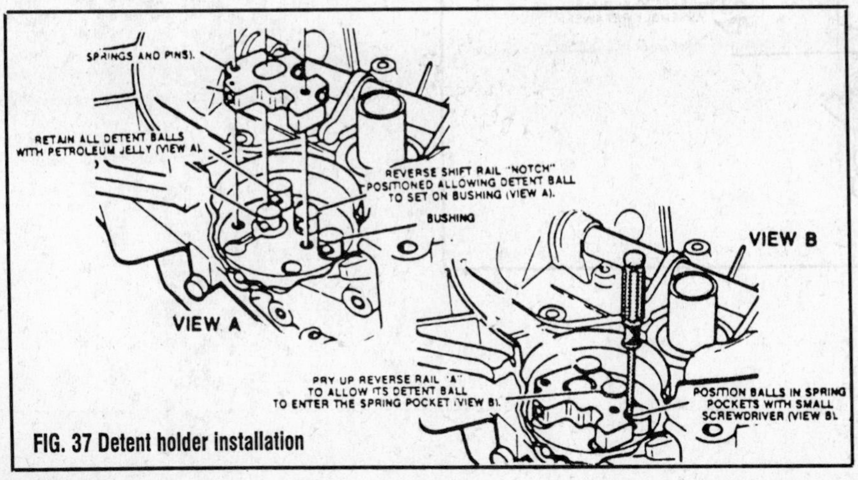

FIG. 37 Detent holder installation

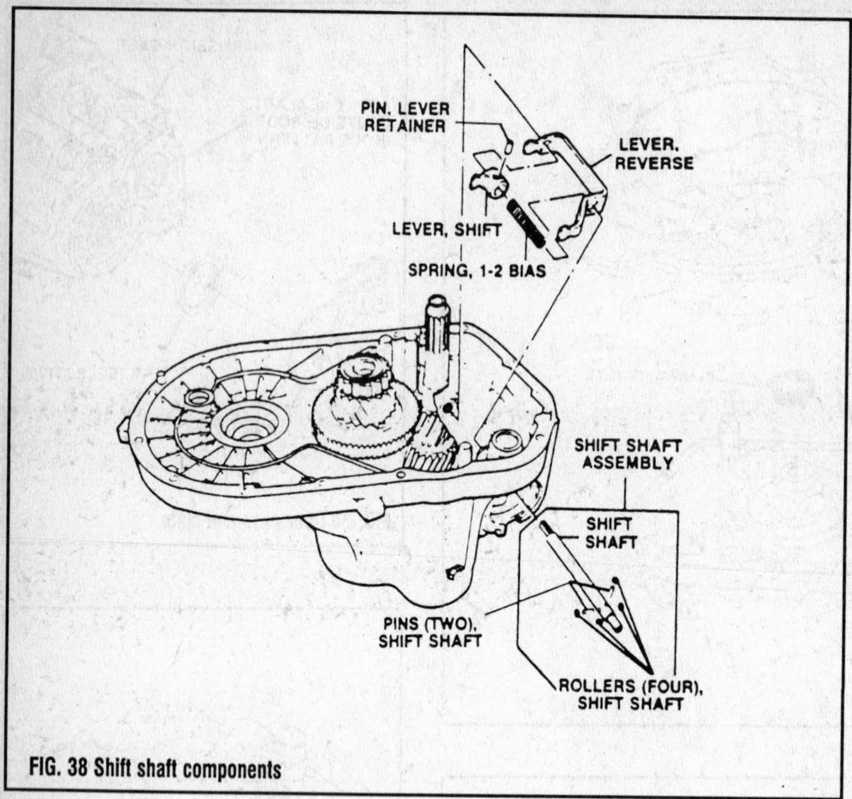

FIG. 38 Shift shaft components

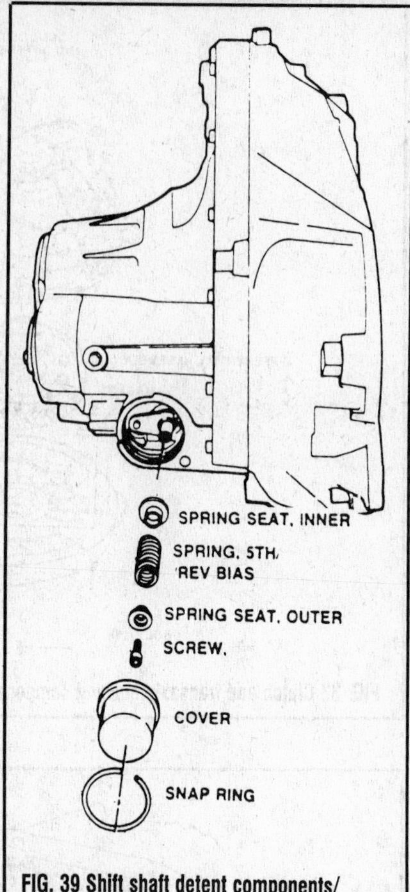

FIG. 39 Shift shaft detent components/ transaxle housing

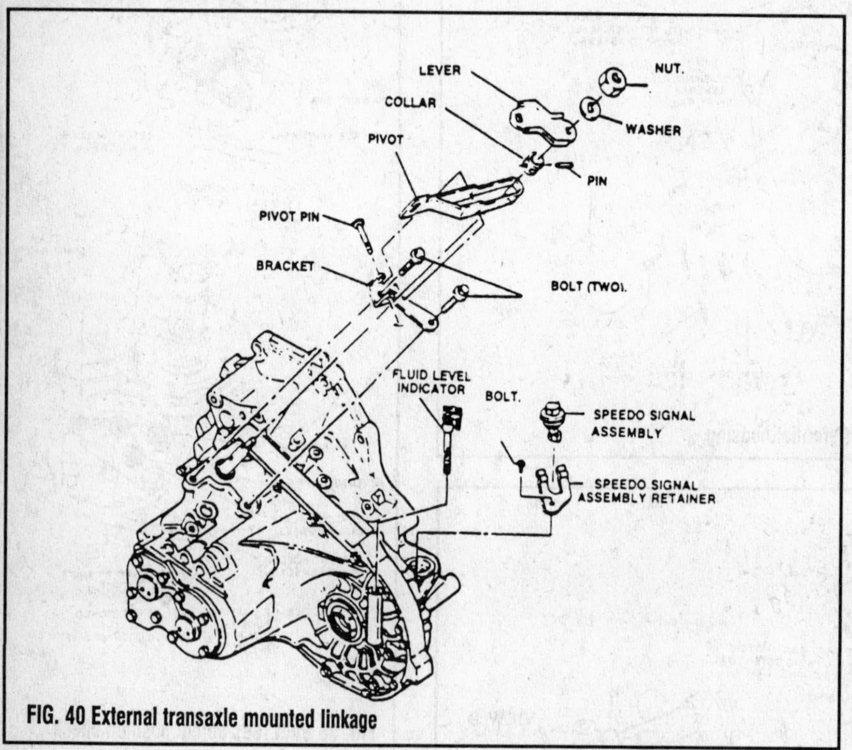

FIG. 40 External transaxle mounted linkage

SHIFT SHAFT DETENT/TRANSAXLE HOUSING

1. Install the inner spring seat.
2. Install the 5th/reverse bias spring.
3. Install the outer spring seat.
4. Install the spring screw and torque to 84 inch lbs. (9 Nm). Use a small amount of thread sealant, part number 11052624 or equivalent, tc the screw.
5. Install the protective cover using a hammer. Position to below the snapring groove.
6. Install the snapring.

EXTERNAL TRANSAXLE MOUNTED LINKAGE

1. Install the bracket.
2. Install the bolts and torque to 17 ft. lbs. (23 Nm).
3. Install the collar and pin using a punch and a hammer.
4. Install the pivot.
5. Install a new pin.
6. Install the lever.
7. Install the washer and nut. Torque to 61 ft. lbs. (83 Nm). Do not allow the lever to move during installation of the nut.
8. Install the fluid level indicator and a new washer.
9. Install the electronic speedometer sensor assembly, retainer and bolt. Torque to 84 inch lbs. (9 Nm).

ISUZU 5-SPEED MANUAL TRANSAXLE

Identification

The identification number is stamped into a tag mounted on the shift quadrant box on the left side.

Capacities

To fill a dry transaxle on N-body, add 5 pints (2.1L) of 5W–30 manual transaxle oil, part number 1052931 or equivalent. On 1988–92 vehicles, use syncromesh transaxle fluid, part number 12345349 or equivalent.

Adjustments

SHIFT LINKAGE

➧ SEE FIG. 47

The shift linkage procedure shown in the

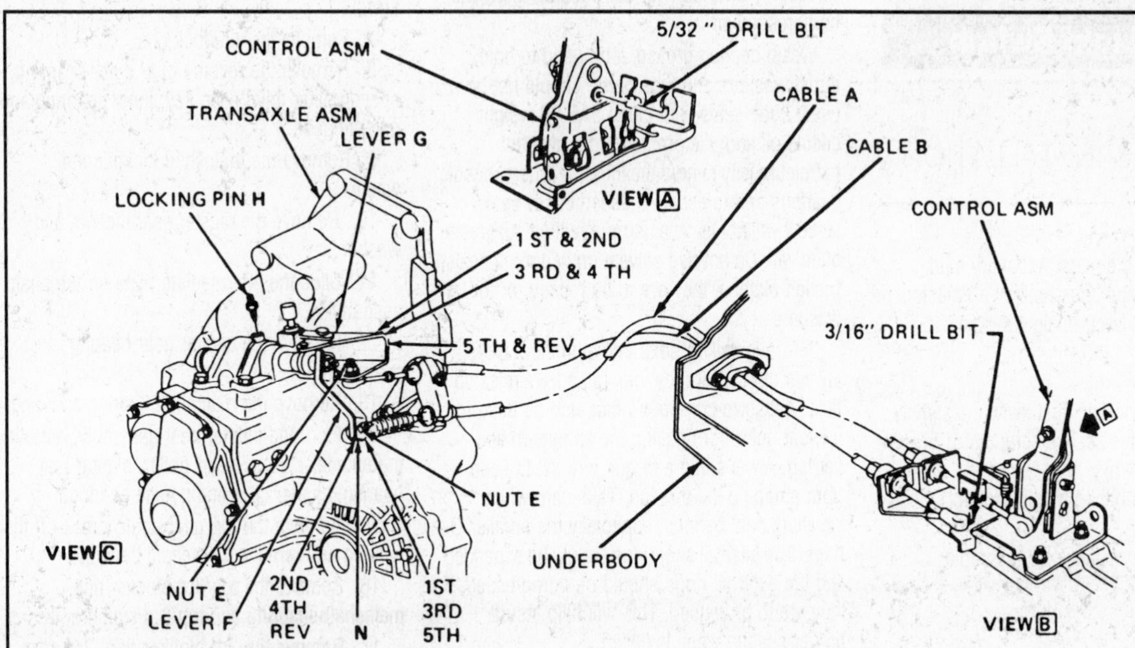

1. Disconnect negative cable at battery.
2. Shift transaxle into third gear. Remove lock pin (H) and reinstall with tapered end down. This will lock transaxle in third gear.
3. Loosen shift cable attaching nuts (E) at transaxle levers (G) and (F).
4. Remove console trim plate and slide shifter boot up shifter handle. Remove console.
5. Install a 5/32" or No. 22 drill bit into alignment hole at side of shifter assembly, as shown in View A.
6. Align the hole in the select lever (View B) with the slot in the shifter plate and install a 3/16" drill bit.
7. Tighten nuts E at levers G and F. Remove drill bits from alignments holes at the shifter. Remove lockpin (H) and reinstall with tapered end up.
8. Install console, shifter boot and trim plate.
9. Connect negative cable at battery.
10. Road test vehicle to check for a good neutral gate feel during shifting. It may be necessary to fine tune the adjustment after testing.

FIG. 47 Manual shift linkage adjustment — Isuzu transaxle

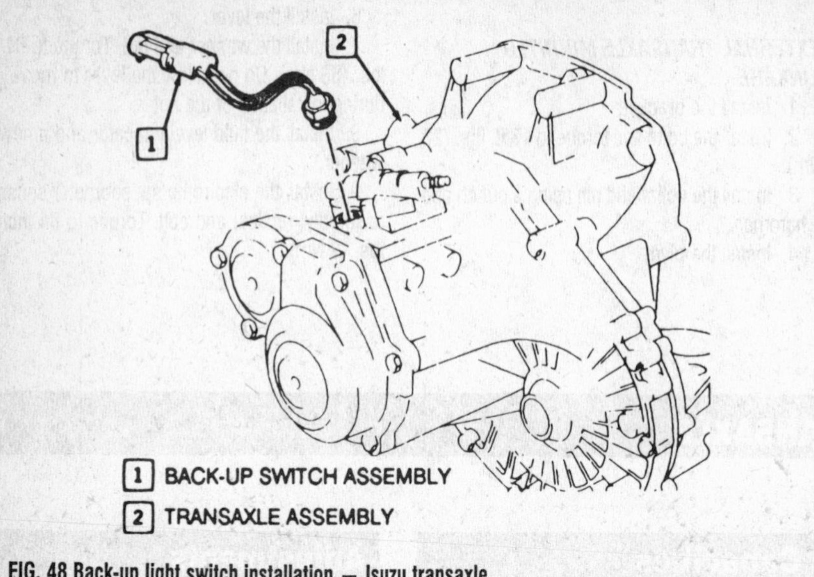

FIG. 48 Back-up light switch installation — Isuzu transaxle

illustration is for 1985–87 vehicles equipped with an Isuzu 5 speed transaxle. No adjustment procedure is provided from 1988–92.

Backup Light Switch

REMOVAL & INSTALLATION

➧ SEE FIG. 48

1. Disconnect the negative battery cable.
2. Disconnect the back-up light connector.
3. Remove the back-up light switch assembly.

To install:

4. Install the back-up light switch assembly using a suitable pipe sealant compound. Tighten to 24 ft. lbs. (33 Nm).
5. Connect the back-up light switch connector.
6. Connect the negative battery cable.

Overhaul

BEFORE DISASSEMBLY

Cleanliness is an important factor in the overhaul of the manual transmission. Before opening up this unit, the entire outside of the transmission assembly should be cleaned, preferably with a high pressure washer such as a car wash spray unit. Dirt entering the transmission internal parts will negate all the time and effort spent on the overhaul. During inspection and reassembly all parts should be thoroughly cleaned with solvent then dried with compressed air.

Wheel bearing grease, long used to hold thrust washers and lube parts, should not be used. Lube seals with clean SAE 30 weight engine oil and use ordinary unmedicated petroleum jelly to hold the thrust washers, needle bearings and to ease the assembly of seals, since it will not leave a harmful residue as grease often will. Do not use solvent on neoprene seals, friction plates if they are to be reused, or thrust washers.

Before installing bolts into aluminum parts, always dip the threads into clean transmission fluid. Antiseize compound can also be used to prevent bolts from galling the aluminum and seizing. Always use a torque wrench to keep from stripping the threads. Take care when installing new O-rings, especially the smaller O-rings. The internal snaprings should be expanded and the external rings should be compressed, if they are to be reused. This will help insure proper seating when installed.

MAJOR COMPONENT DISASSEMBLY

➧ SEE FIGS. 49–51

1. Remove the shift quadrant box, shift block and withdraw the lever.
2. Remove the front cover retainer, oil seal and Belleville spring.
3. Remove the front bearing snapring.
4. Remove the speedometer driven gear and backup light switch.
5. Remove the rear housing and oil seal.
6. Remove the mainshaft, cluster gear and top gear shaft assemblies.

MAINSHAFT, CLUSTER GEAR AND TOP GEAR SHAFT DISASSEMBLY

➧ SEE FIG. 52

1. Remove the reverse idler gear thrust washers and idler gear.
2. Remove the reverse idler shaft retaining bolt, lock plate and shaft.
3. Remove the detent plate, spring and ball.
4. Remove the reverse shift rod and arm.
5. Remove the top/3rd and low/2nd shift rod by driving out the pins.
6. Remove the top/3rd and low/2nd shift arms.
7. Remove the interlock pin.
8. Remove the reverse gear outer snapring, speedometer drive gear, key, inner snapring and reverse gear.
9. Remove the mainshaft locknut and washer.
10. Remove the cluster gear locknut and washer.
11. Slide the intermediate plate off the shaft assemblies.
12. Remove the cluster gear bearing snapring.
13. Remove the mainshaft bearing snapring.
14. From the cluster gear assembly, remove the counter reverse gear, collar, cluster rear bearing, cluster gear and needle bearings.
15. Remove the top gear shaft, press off the bearing and remove the needle bearings.
16. Remove the top/3rd blocker ring, mainshaft snapring and top/3rd synchronizer.
17. Remove the 3rd blocker ring, 3rd gear and needle bearings.
18. Remove the mainshaft bearing, thrust washer, low gear, needle bearings and collar.
19. Remove the outer low/2nd blocker ring, low/2nd synchronizer, inner low/2nd blocker ring, 2nd gear, needle bearings and mainshaft.

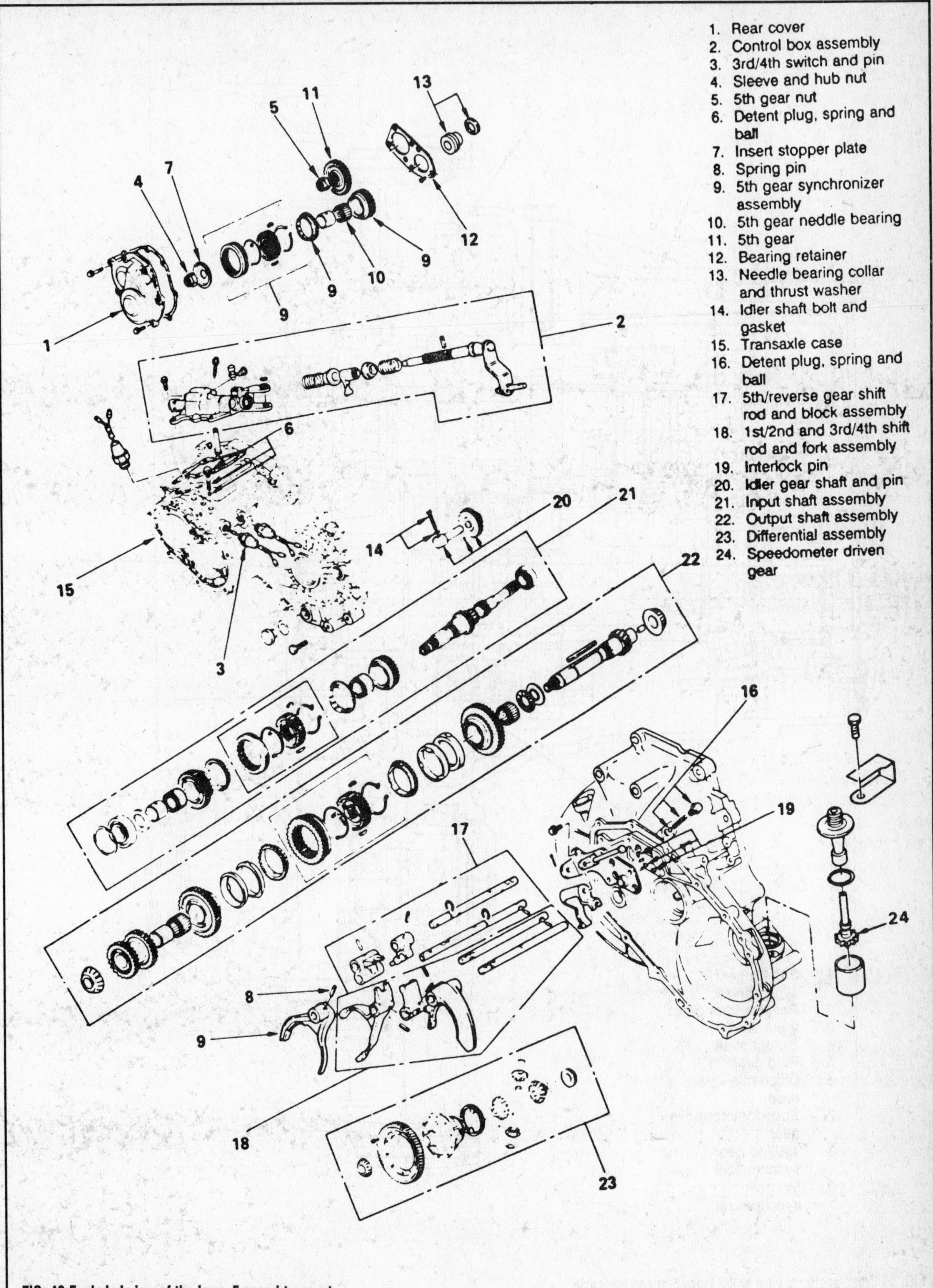

FIG. 49 Exploded view of the Isuzu 5 speed transaxle

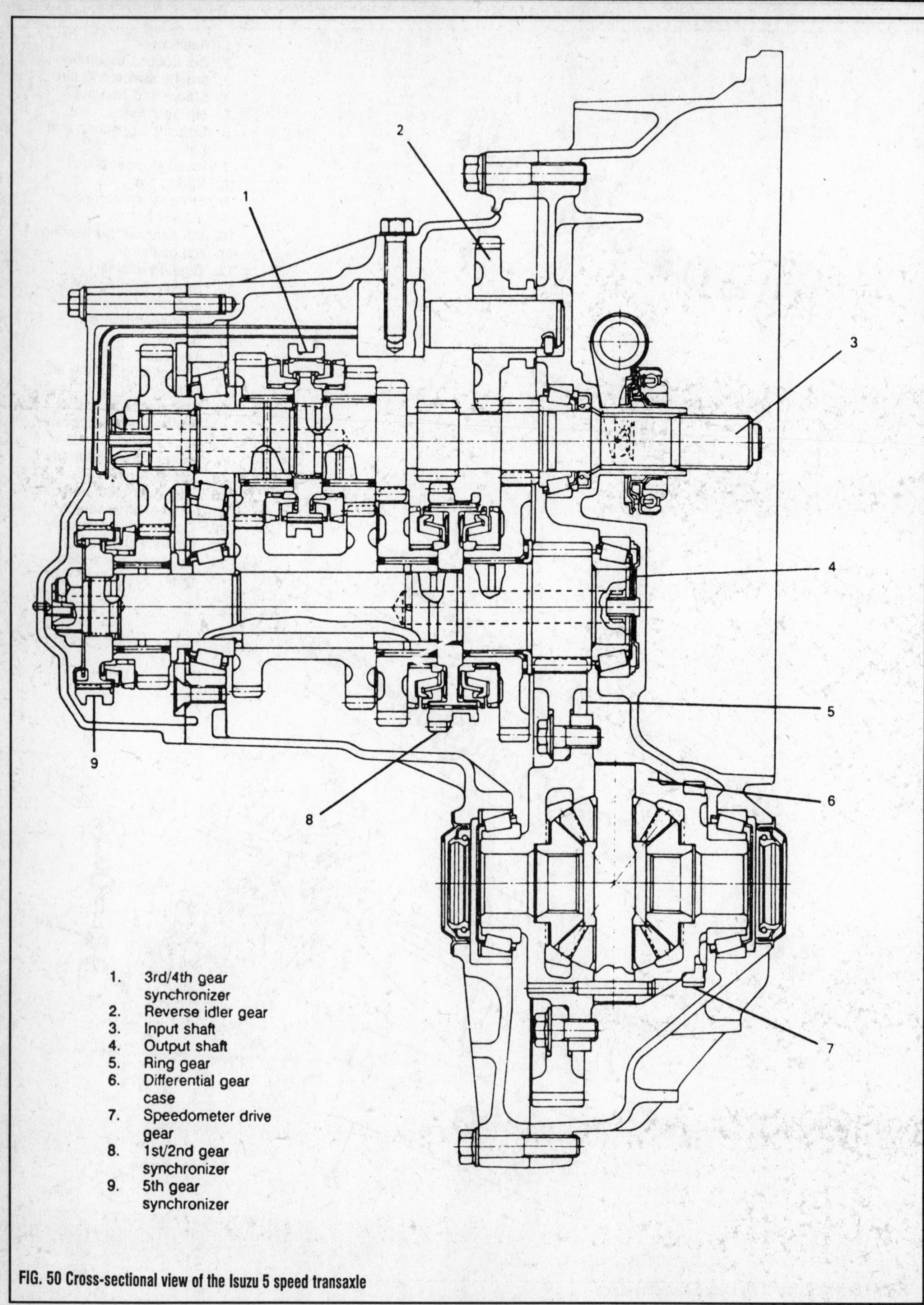

FIG. 50 Cross-sectional view of the Isuzu 5 speed transaxle

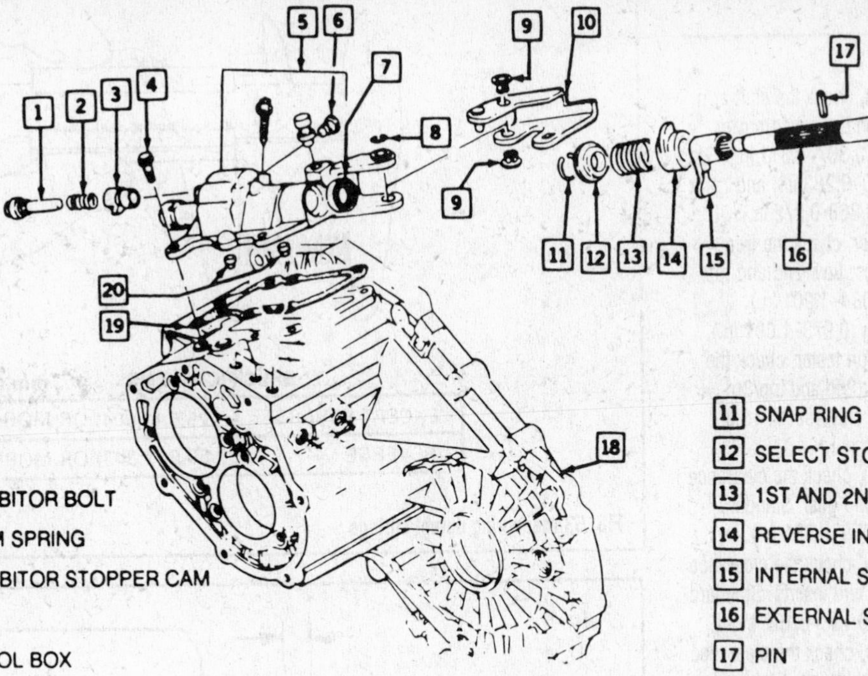

1 REVERSE INHIBITOR BOLT
2 STOPPER CAM SPRING
3 REVERSE INHIBITOR STOPPER CAM
4 BOLT
5 SHIFT CONTROL BOX
6 BOLT
7 OIL SEAL
8 SNAP RING
9 SELECT LEVER BUSHING
10 EXTERNAL SELECT LEVER
11 SNAP RING
12 SELECT STOP SPRING SEAT
13 1ST AND 2ND SELECT STOP RING
14 REVERSE INHIBITOR STOPPER
15 INTERNAL SHIFT LEVER
16 EXTERNAL SHIFT LEVER
17 PIN
18 TRANSAXLE ASSEMBLY
19 GASKET
20 PIN

FIG. 51 Shift control box — Isuzu 5 speed transaxle

1. Rear bearing
2. 3rd/4th gear
3. Collar
4. Neddle bearing
5. 2nd gear
6. Inner 2nd gear ring
7. Outer 2nd gear ring
8. Blocker ring 2nd gear
9. Synchronizer sleeve
10. Spring
11. Synchronizer hub
12. Insert
13. Spring
14. Blocker ring/1st gear
15. Outer 1st gear ring
16. Inner 1st gear ring
17. 1st gear
18. Needle bearing
19. Thrust bearing
20. Thrust washer
21. Key
22. Output shaft
23. Front bearing
24. 1st/2nd gear synchronizer assemblv

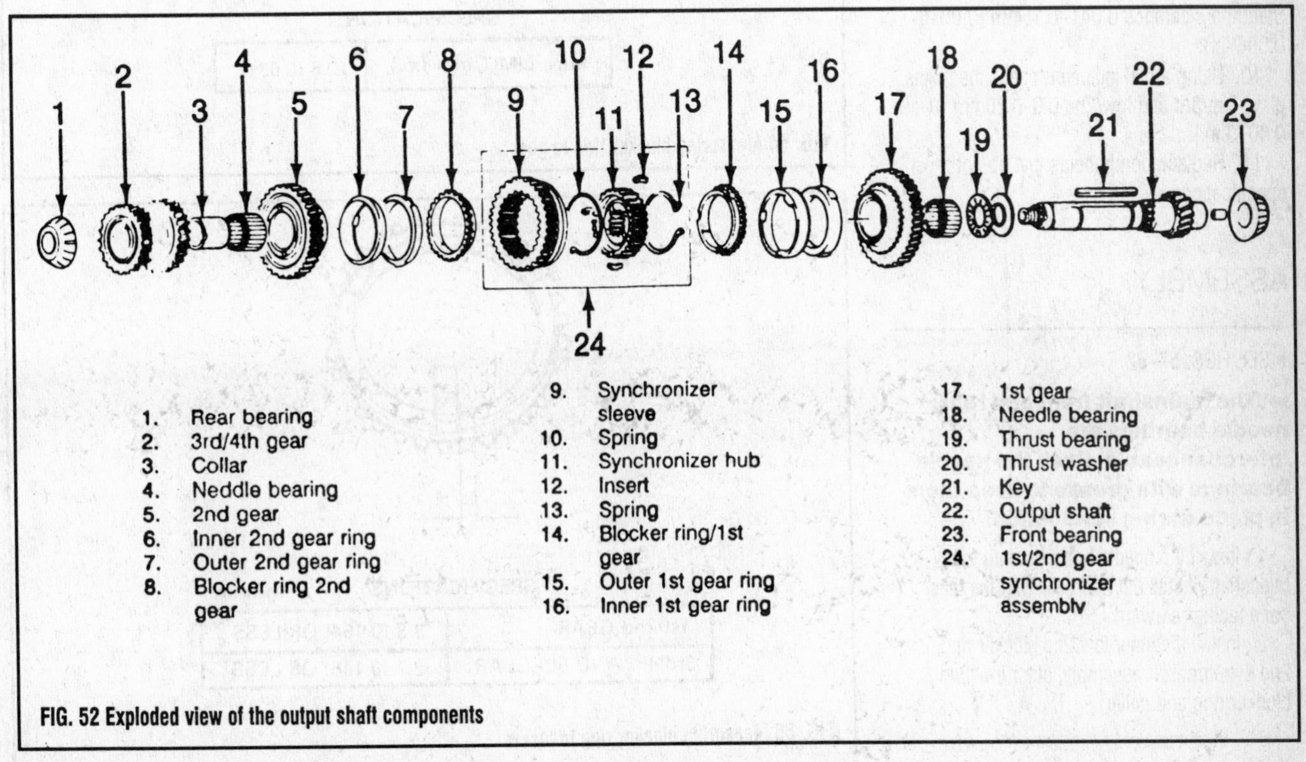

FIG. 52 Exploded view of the output shaft components

INSPECTION

➧ SEE FIGS. 53–56

1. Using a micrometer, check the shift arm thickness where it rides on the synchronizer. Low/2nd = 7.8–7.9mm (0.307–0.311 in.), 3rd/4th = 7.1–7.2mm (0.280–0.283 in.) and reverse = 6.8–6.9mm (0.268-0.272 in.).
2. Using a inside caliper, check the free length of the detent springs. Low/2nd and top/3rd = 27.5–30.5mm (1.084–1.201 in.). Reverse = 24.7–27.7mm (0.973–1.091 in.).
3. Using a spring tension tester, check the detent spring tension. Low/2nd and top/3rd = 8.8–9.3 lbs. (4.0–4.2 kg). Reverse = 13.9–14.8 lbs. (6.3–6.7 kg).
4. Using a feeler gauge, check the clearance between the blocker ring and gear. Standard clearance 1.5–0.8mm (0.059–0.031 in.).
5. Using a feeler gauge, check the clearance between the blocker rings and inserts. Standard clearance 3.51–4.00mm (0.138–0.157 in.).
6. Using a feeler gauge, check the clearance between the clutch hub and inserts. Standard clearance 0.01–0.3mm (0.0004–0.012 in.).
7. Using a dial indicator and holding fixture, check the mainshaft run-out. Limit 0.03mm (0.001 in.).
8. Using an inside T-gauge, check the gear inside diameter. Low/rev gear 45.0–45.1mm (1.772–1.776 in.). 2nd/3rd gear 41.0–41.1mm (1.614–1.618 in.).
9. Using a micrometer, check the clearance between the bushing and idler gear shaft. Standard clearance 0.041–0.15mm (0.0016–0.006 in.).
10. Using a dial indicator, check the spline play. Top/3rd and low/2nd 0.0–0.20mm (0–0.0079 in.).
11. Replace components that do not meet specifications.

ASSEMBLY

➧ SEE FIGS. 57–62

➡ The mainshaft front and rear needle bearings are interchangeable. Pack the needle bearings with grease to keep them in place during installation.

1. Install the needle bearings onto the mainshaft. Install the 2nd gear with the taper cone facing rearward.
2. Install the inner low/2nd blocker ring, low/2nd synchronizer assembly, outer low/2nd blocker ring and collar.

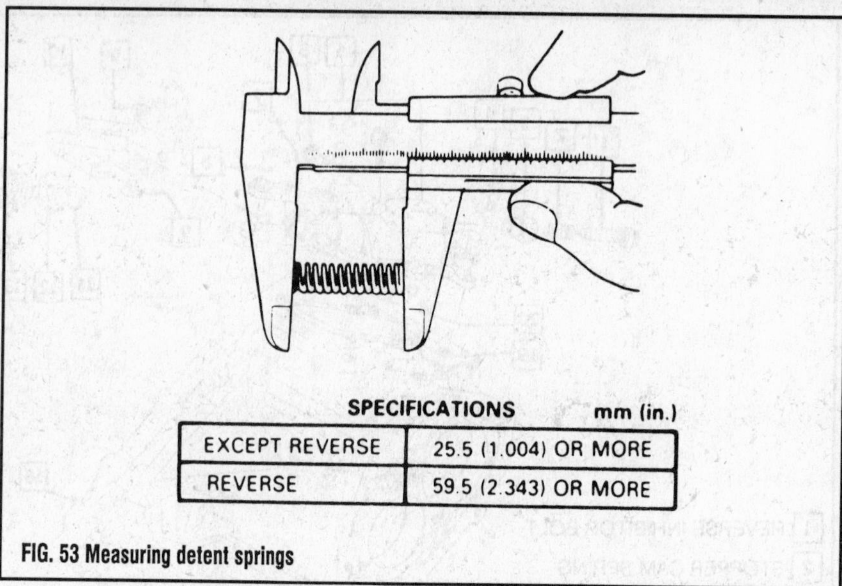

SPECIFICATIONS	mm (in.)
EXCEPT REVERSE	25.5 (1.004) OR MORE
REVERSE	59.5 (2.343) OR MORE

FIG. 53 Measuring detent springs

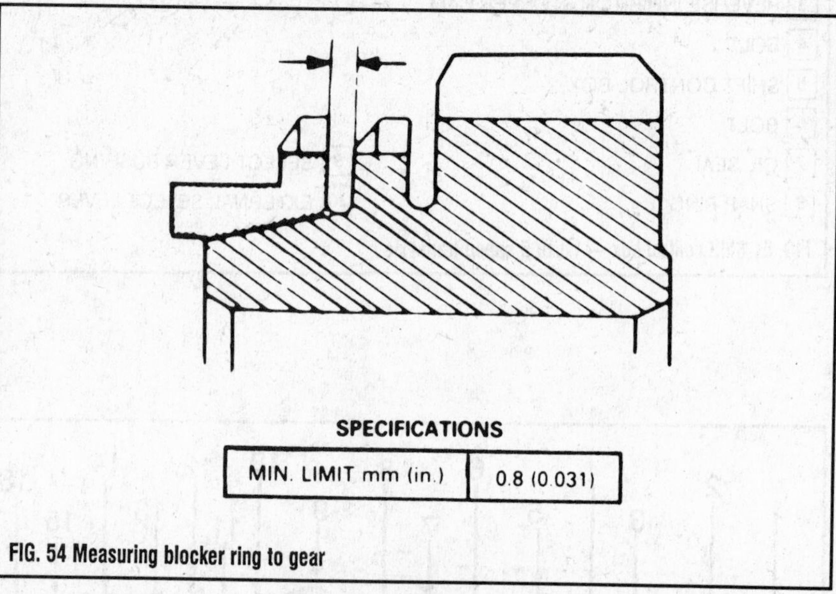

SPECIFICATIONS	
MIN. LIMIT mm (in.)	0.8 (0.031)

FIG. 54 Measuring blocker ring to gear

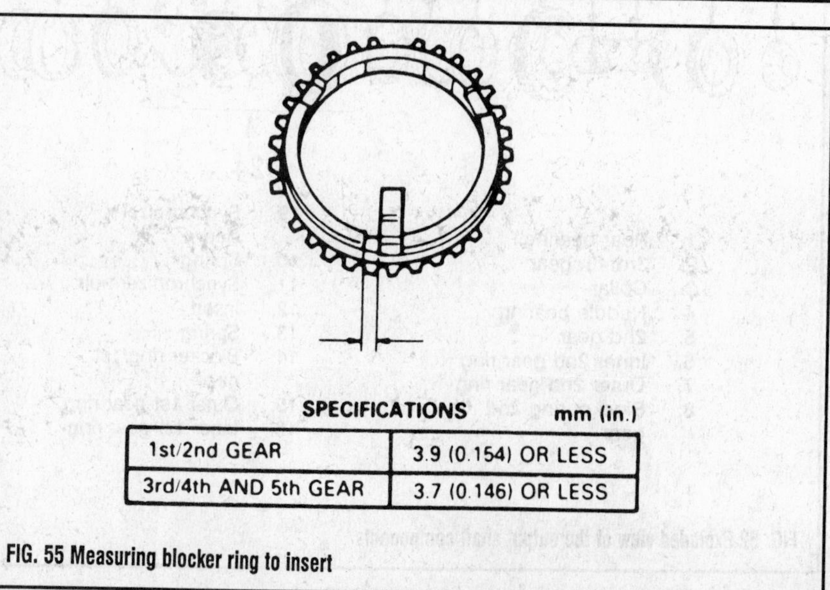

SPECIFICATIONS	mm (in.)
1st/2nd GEAR	3.9 (0.154) OR LESS
3rd/4th AND 5th GEAR	3.7 (0.146) OR LESS

FIG. 55 Measuring blocker ring to insert

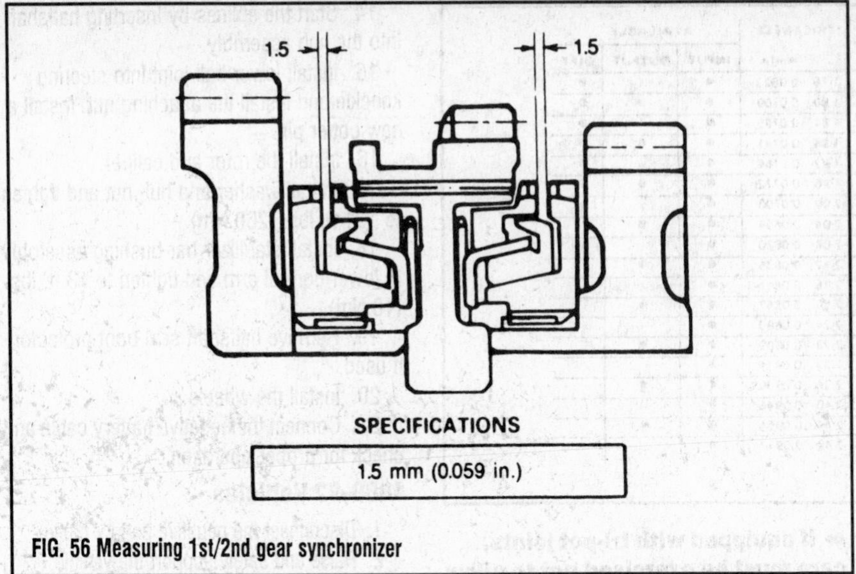

FIG. 56 Measuring 1st/2nd gear synchronizer

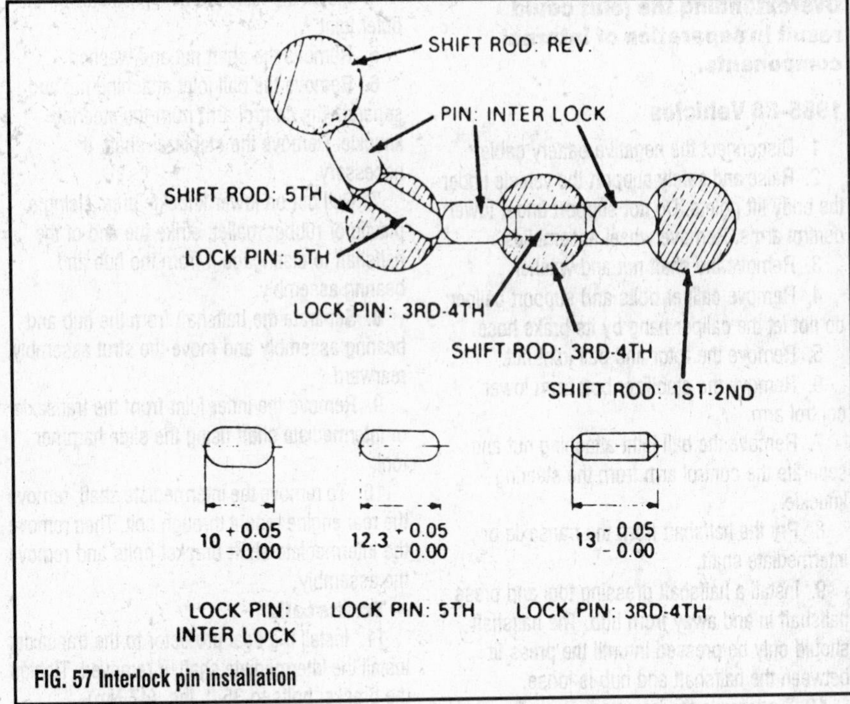

FIG. 57 Interlock pin installation

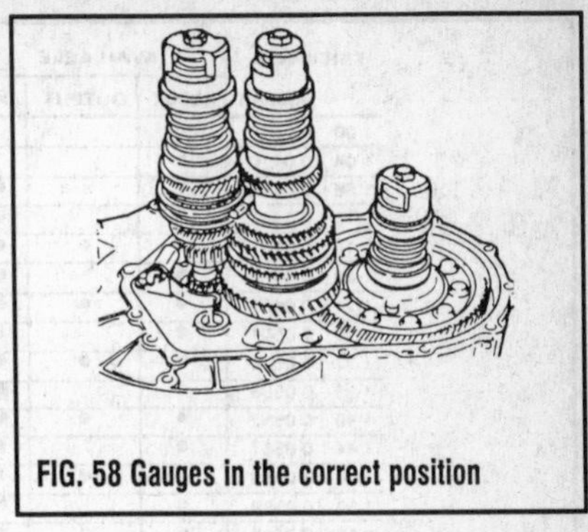
FIG. 58 Gauges in the correct position

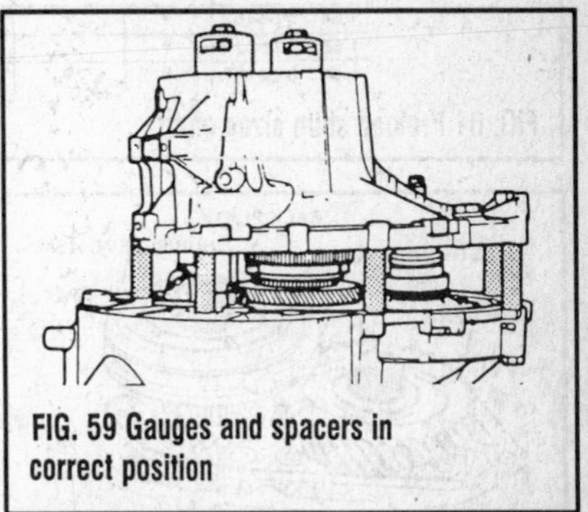
FIG. 59 Gauges and spacers in correct position

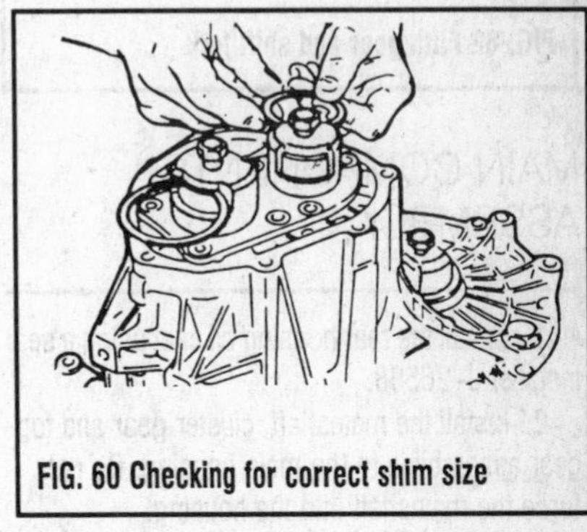
FIG. 60 Checking for correct shim size

3. Install the needle bearing onto the mainshaft and low gear with the taper cone facing forwards.

4. Install the thrust washer with the oil groove facing forward. Press on the mainshaft bearing.

5. Install the needle bearings, 3rd gear, top/3rd blocker ring and top/3rd synchronizer assembly.

6. Install the mainshaft snapring and measure clearance with a feeler gauge. Selective snaprings can be purchased to adjust clearance. Standard clearance is 0.0–0.05mm (0.0–0.0019 in.).

7. Install the top/3rd blocker ring and needle bearings.

8. Using a press install the top shaft bearing so that the snapring groove faces forward. Install the cluster gear rear bearing so the ring groove is facing rearward.

9. Install the needle bearings and intermediate plate.

10. Install the mainshaft bearing snapring.

11. Install the cluster gear bearing snapring.

12. Install the cluster gear collar, reverse counter gear, washer and locknut. Torque the locknut to 72–87 ft. lbs. (100–120 Nm).

13. Install the mainshaft lock washer and nut Torque to 87–101 ft. lbs. (120–140 Nm).

14. Install the reverse gear, snapring, key, speedometer drive gear and snapring.

15. Install the reverse idler shaft, lock plate and bolt. Torque to 30 ft. lbs. (34 Nm).

16. Install the interlock pin, top/3rd shift arm, low/2nd shift arm and bolt. Torque the bolt to 16 ft. lbs. (22 Nm).

17. Install the reverse shift arm, reverse shift rod, detent ball, detent spring and spring plate.

18. Install the reverse idler gear thrust washer with the flange is fitted to the stopper in the intermediate plate. Also, install the idler gear so that the undercut teeth are turned outward.

19. Install the reverse idler gear and outer thrust washer.

THICKNESS mm	(in.)	AVAILABLE INPUT	AVAILABLE OUTPUT	AVAILABLE DIFF	THICKNESS mm	(in.)	AVAILABLE INPUT	AVAILABLE OUTPUT	AVAILABLE DIFF
1.00	0.0394	•			1.76	0.0693	•		•
1.04	0.0410	•			1.80	0.0709	•	•	•
1.08	0.0426	•		•	1.84	0.0725	•		•
1.12	0.0441	•		•	1.88	0.0741	•	•	•
1.16	0.0457	•	•	•	1.92	0.0756	•		•
1.20	0.0473	•		•	1.96	0.0772	•	•	•
1.24	0.0489	•	•	•	2.00	0.0788	•		•
1.28	0.0504	•		•	2.04	0.0804	•	•	
1.32	0.0520	•	•	•	2.08	0.0820	•		
1.36	0.0536	•		•	2.12	0.0835	•	•	
1.40	0.0552	•	•	•	2.16	0.0851	•		
1.44	0.0567	•		•	2.20	0.0867	•	•	
1.48	0.0583	•	•	•	2.24	0.0883	•		
1.52	0.0599	•		•	2.28	0.0899	•	•	
1.56	0.0615	•	•	•	2.32	0.0914	•		
1.60	0.0630	•		•	2.36	0.0930	•	•	
1.64	0.0646	•	•	•	2.40	0.0946	•		
1.68	0.0662	•		•	2.44	0.0951	•	•	
1.72	0.0678	•	•	•	2.48	0.0977	•		

FIG. 61 Preload shim sizes chart

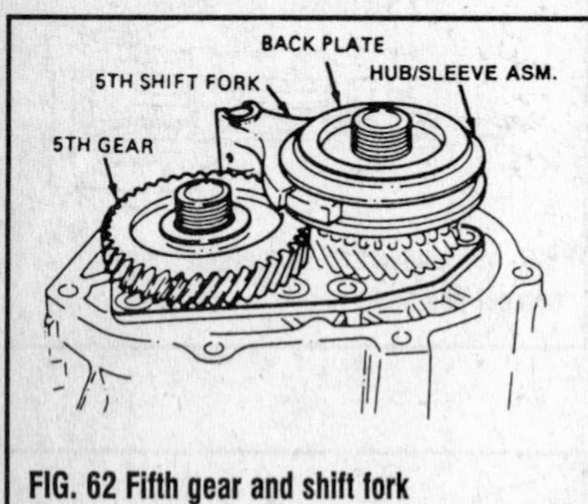

FIG. 62 Fifth gear and shift fork

MAIN COMPONENTS ASSEMBLY

1. Install the rear housing oil seal using a seal installer J–26508.
2. Install the mainshaft, cluster gear and top gear assemblies to the main housing. Do not force the mainshaft into the housing.
3. Install the rear housing and torque the bolts to 30 ft. lbs. (42 Nm).
4. Install the backup light switch, speedometer driven gear and mainshaft front bearing snapring.
5. Install the Belleville spring, front cover oil seal, front cover and torque the bolts to 16 ft. lbs. (22 Nm).
6. Install the clutch fork, shift block and quadrant box assemblies. Make sure the shift lever is fitted into the support properly.

Halfshafts

REMOVAL & INSTALLATION

➧ SEE FIGS. 63–68

➡ If equipped with tri-pot joints, care must be exercised not to allow joints to become overextended. Overextending the joint could result in separation of internal components.

1985–88 Vehicles

1. Disconnect the negative battery cable.
2. Raise and safely support the vehicle under the body lift points. Do not support under lower control arms. Remove wheel assemblies.
3. Remove the shaft nut and washer.
4. Remove caliper bolts and support caliper; do not let the caliper hang by its brake hose.
5. Remove the rotor and ball joint nut.
6. Remove the stabilizer bolt from lower control arm.
7. Remove the ball joint attaching nut and separate the control arm from the steering knuckle.
8. Pry the halfshaft from the transaxle or intermediate shaft.
9. Install a halfshaft pressing tool and press halfshaft in and away from hub. The halfshaft should only be pressed in until the press fit between the halfshaft and hub is loose.
10. To remove the intermediate shaft:
    a. Remove the detonation sensor.
    b. Remove the power steering pump brace.
    c. Remove the intermediate shaft bracket bolts and remove the assembly.

To install:

11. Install the intermediate shaft, if removed. Tighten the bracket bolts to 35 ft. lbs. (47 Nm).
12. Install the halfshaft seal boot protectors on all tri-pot inner joints with silicone boots.
13. Start splines of halfshaft into transaxle and push halfshaft until it snaps into place.
14. Start the splines by inserting halfshaft into the hub assembly.
15. Install lower ball joint into steering knuckle and install the attaching nut. Install a new cotter pin.
16. Install the rotor and caliper.
17. Install washer and hub nut and tighten to 191 ft. lbs. (260 Nm).
18. Install stabilizer bar bushing assembly to lower control arm and tighten to 13 ft. lbs. (18 Nm).
19. Remove halfshaft seal boot protector, if used.
20. Install the wheels.
21. Connect the negative battery cable and check for proper operation.

1989–92 Vehicles

1. Disconnect the negative battery cable.
2. Raise and safely support the vehicle.
3. Remove the wheels.
4. Install the halfshaft seal protector on the outer joint.
5. Remove the shaft nut and washer.
6. Remove the ball joint attaching nut and separate the control arm from the steering knuckle. Remove the stabilizer shaft, if necessary.
7. Pull out on lower knuckle area. Using a plastic or rubber mallet, strike the end of the halfshaft to disengage it from the hub and bearing assembly.
8. Separate the halfshaft from the hub and bearing assembly and move the strut assembly rearward.
9. Remove the inner joint from the transaxle or intermediate shaft using the slide hammer tool.
10. To remove the intermediate shaft, remove the rear engine mount through bolt. Then remove the intermediate shaft bracket bolts and remove the assembly.

To install:

11. Install the seal protector to the transaxle. Install the intermediate shaft, if removed. Tighten the bracket bolts to 35 ft. lbs. (47 Nm).
12. Drive the halfshaft into the transaxle or intermediate shaft by placing a suitable tool into the groove on the joint housing and tapping until seated. Be careful not to damage the axle seal or spring. Verify that the axle is seated by grasping the inner joint housing and pulling outboard.
13. Install the axle to the hub and bearing assembly.
14. Install the washer and nut and tighten to 185 ft. lbs. (260 Nm).
15. Install the ball joint to the steering knuckle. Install the stabilizer shaft, if removed.
16. Remove the seal protectors.
17. Install the wheels.
18. Connect the negative battery cable and check for proper operation.

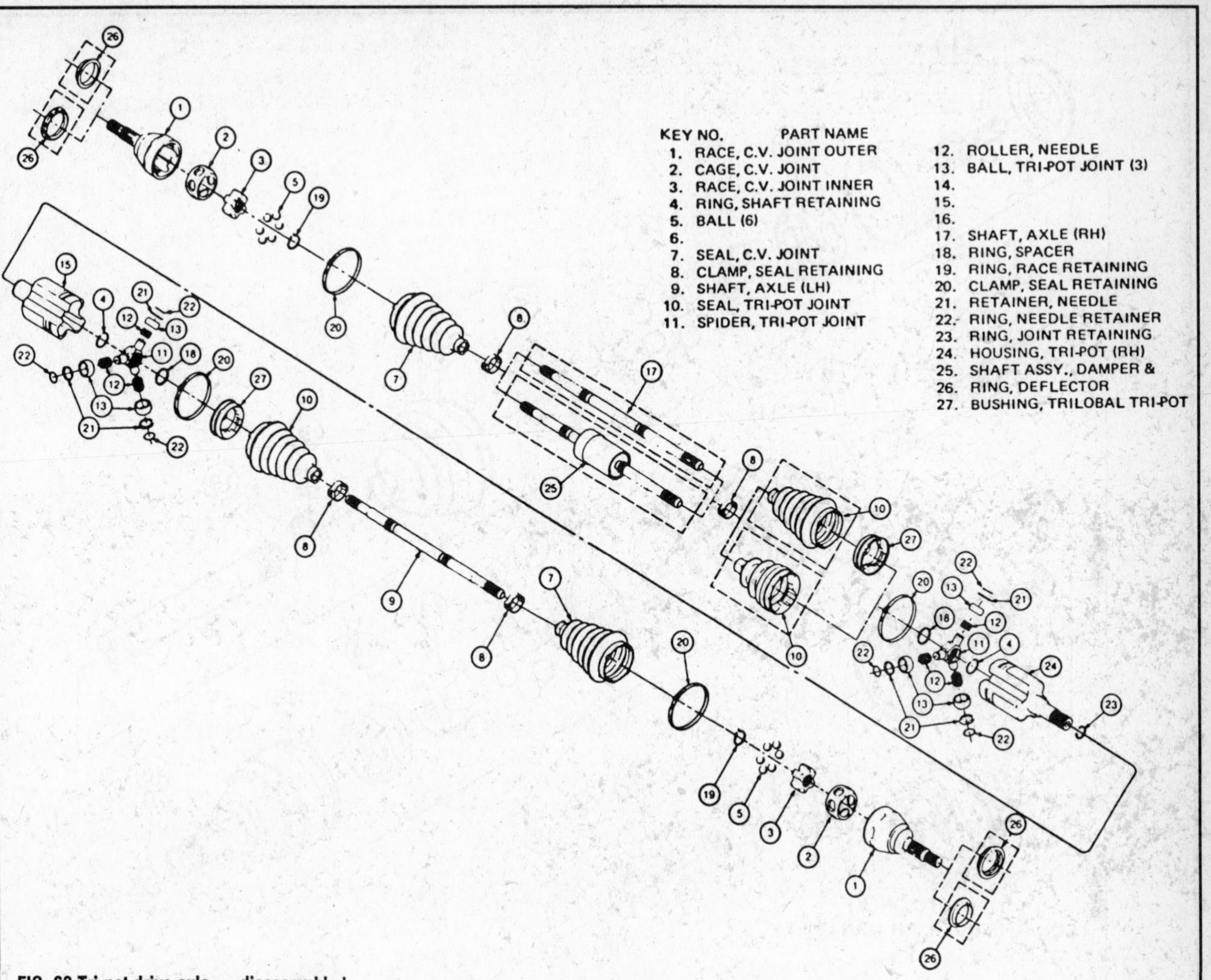

KEY NO. PART NAME
1. RACE, C.V. JOINT OUTER
2. CAGE, C.V. JOINT
3. RACE, C.V. JOINT INNER
4. RING, SHAFT RETAINING
5. BALL (6)
6.
7. SEAL, C.V. JOINT
8. CLAMP, SEAL RETAINING
9. SHAFT, AXLE (LH)
10. SEAL, TRI-POT JOINT
11. SPIDER, TRI-POT JOINT
12. ROLLER, NEEDLE
13. BALL, TRI-POT JOINT (3)
14.
15.
16.
17. SHAFT, AXLE (RH)
18. RING, SPACER
19. RING, RACE RETAINING
20. CLAMP, SEAL RETAINING
21. RETAINER, NEEDLE
22. RING, NEEDLE RETAINER
23. RING, JOINT RETAINING
24. HOUSING, TRI-POT (RH)
25. SHAFT ASSY., DAMPER &
26. RING, DEFLECTOR
27. BUSHING, TRILOBAL TRI-POT

FIG. 63 Tri-pot drive axle — disassembled

1 RIGHT DRIVE AXLE
2 LEFT DRIVE AXLE
3 J 28468 OR J 33008
4 J 29794
5 J 2619-01
FRT

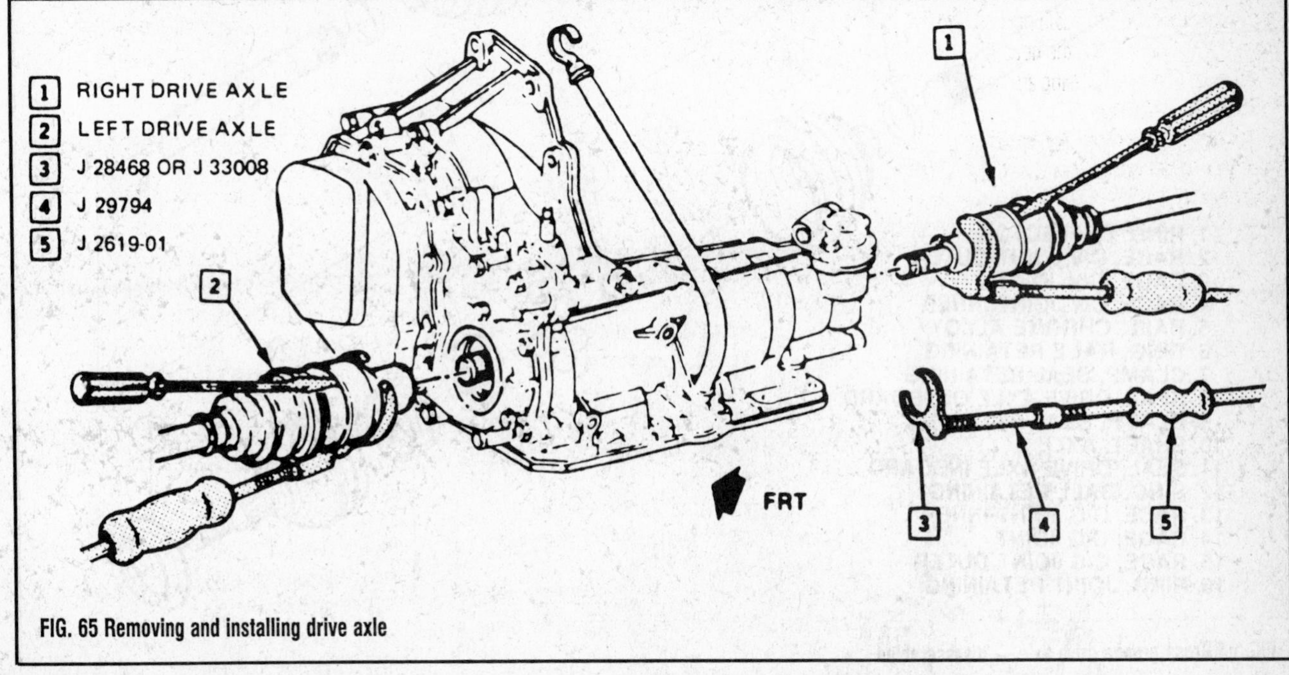

FIG. 65 Removing and installing drive axle

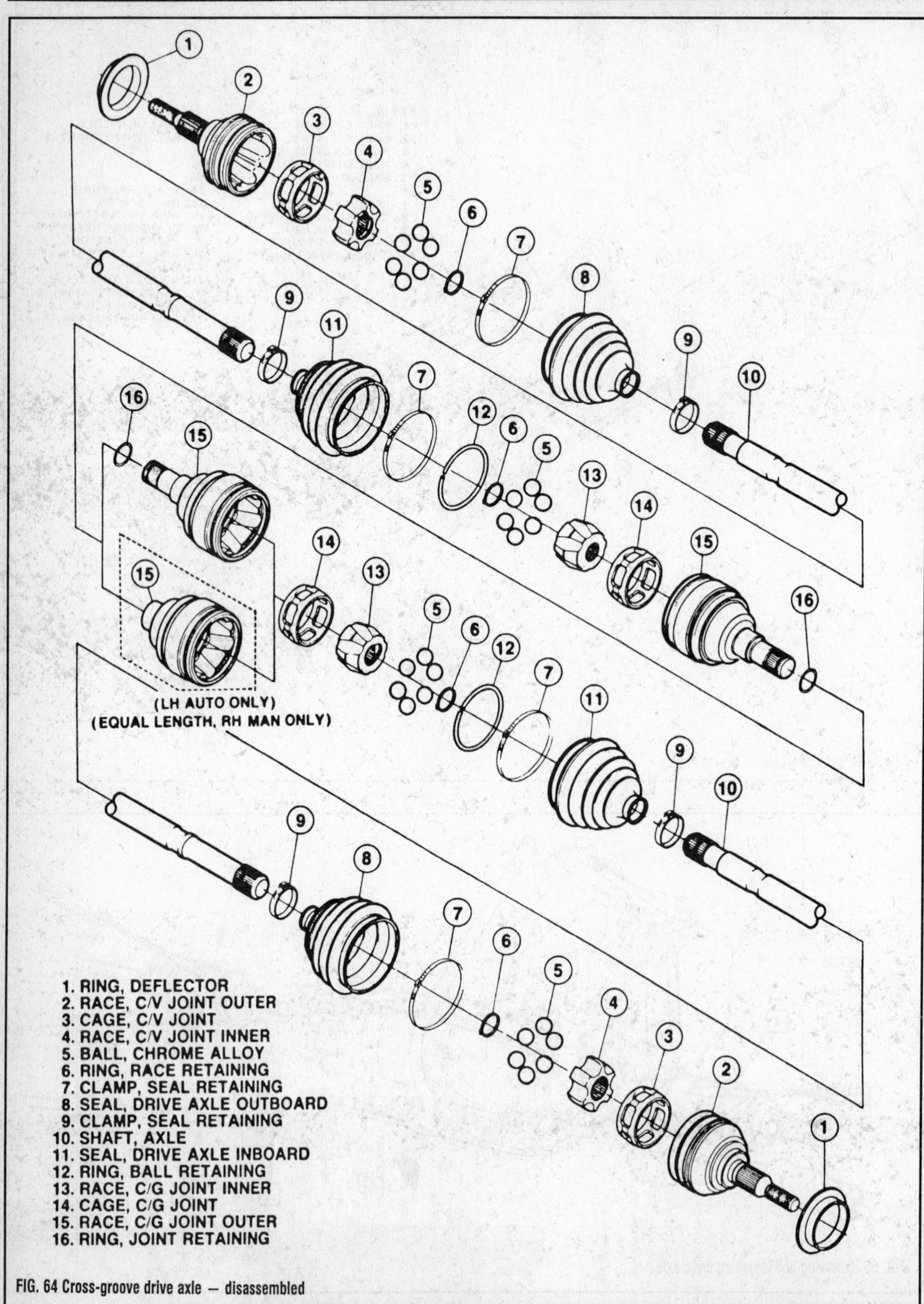

FIG. 64 Cross-groove drive axle — disassembled

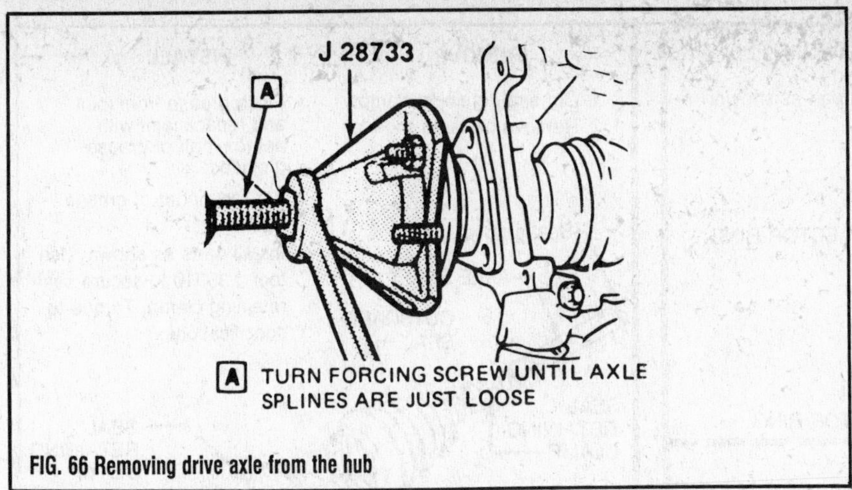

FIG. 66 Removing drive axle from the hub

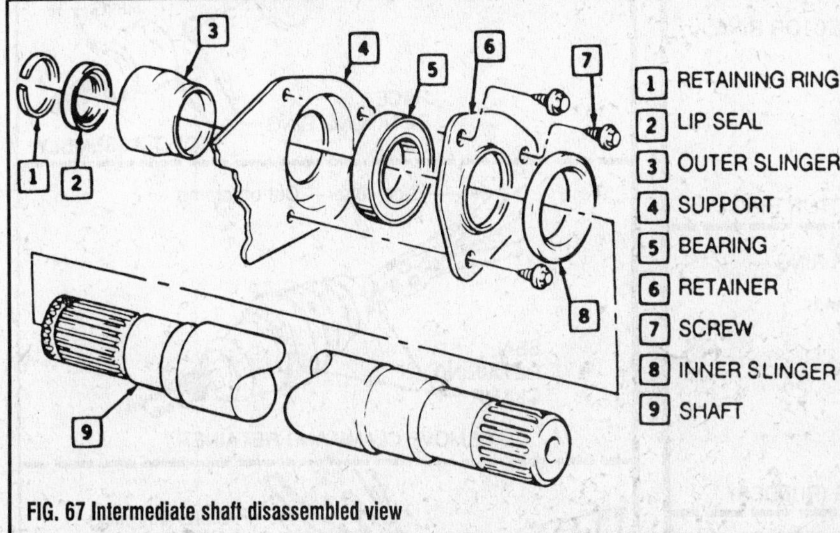

FIG. 67 Intermediate shaft disassembled view

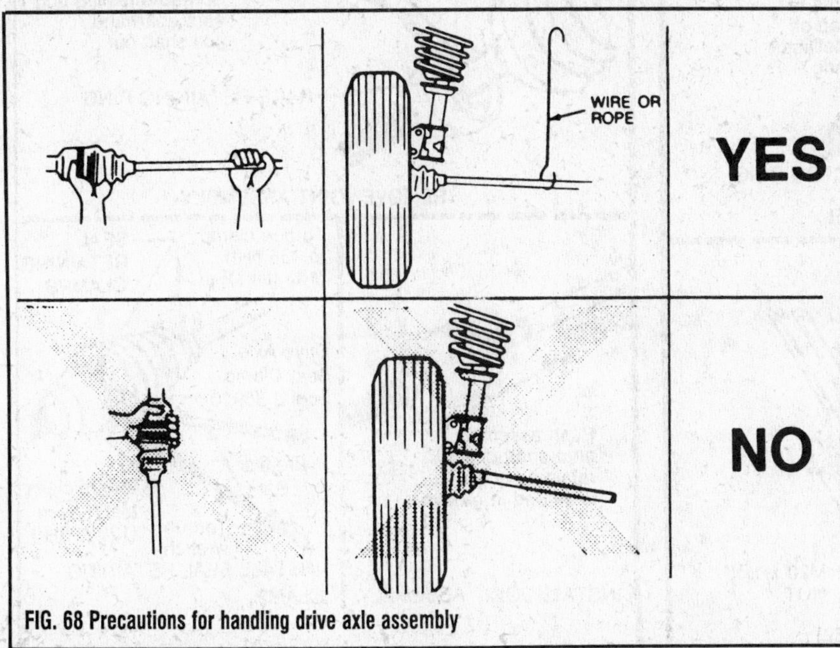

FIG. 68 Precautions for handling drive axle assembly

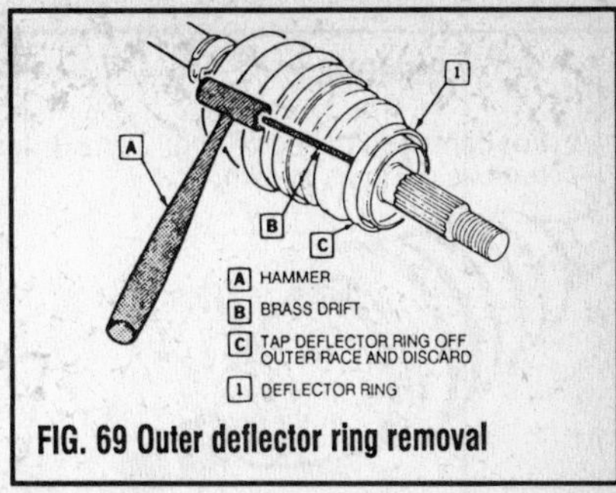

FIG. 69 Outer deflector ring removal

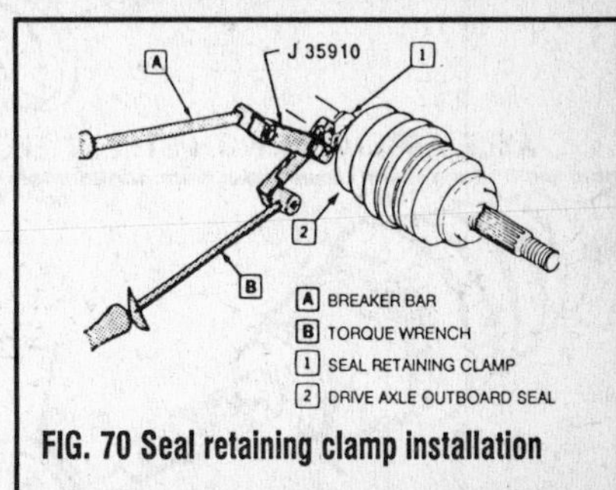

FIG. 70 Seal retaining clamp installation

CV-Boot

REMOVAL & INSTALLATION

➧ SEE FIGS. 69 AND 70

1. Disconnect the negative battery cable. Raise and safely support the vehicle. Remove the halfshaft assembly.
2. Remove the steel deflector ring by using brass drift to tap it off. If rubber ring is used, slide it off.
3. Cut the seal's retaining clamps and lift the boot up to gain access to retaining ring.
4. Remove the snapring and remove the joint from the shaft.
5. Slide the boot off shaft.

To install:

6. Clean the splines of the shaft and the CV-joint.
7. Install the clamp and boot onto the shaft. Fill the boot with amount of grease specified in the package.
8. Install the joint to the shaft and install a new retaining ring.
9. Crimp the outer clamp securely in the groove.
10. Install the steel deflector ring or rubber ring.
11. Install the halfshaft assembly.
12. Connect the negative battery cable and check for proper operation.

CV-Joint Overhaul

➧ SEE FIGS. 71-74

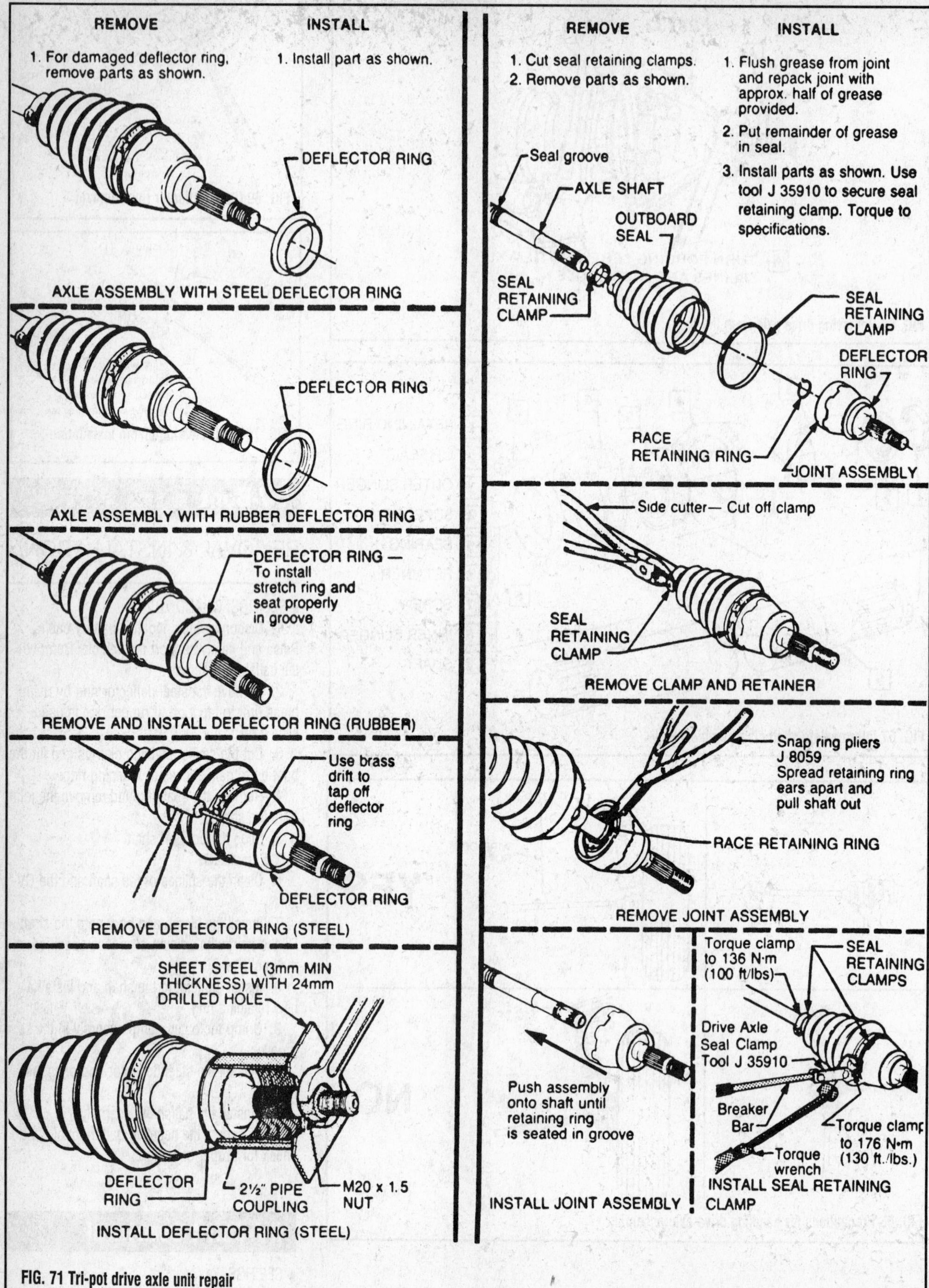

FIG. 71 Tri-pot drive axle unit repair

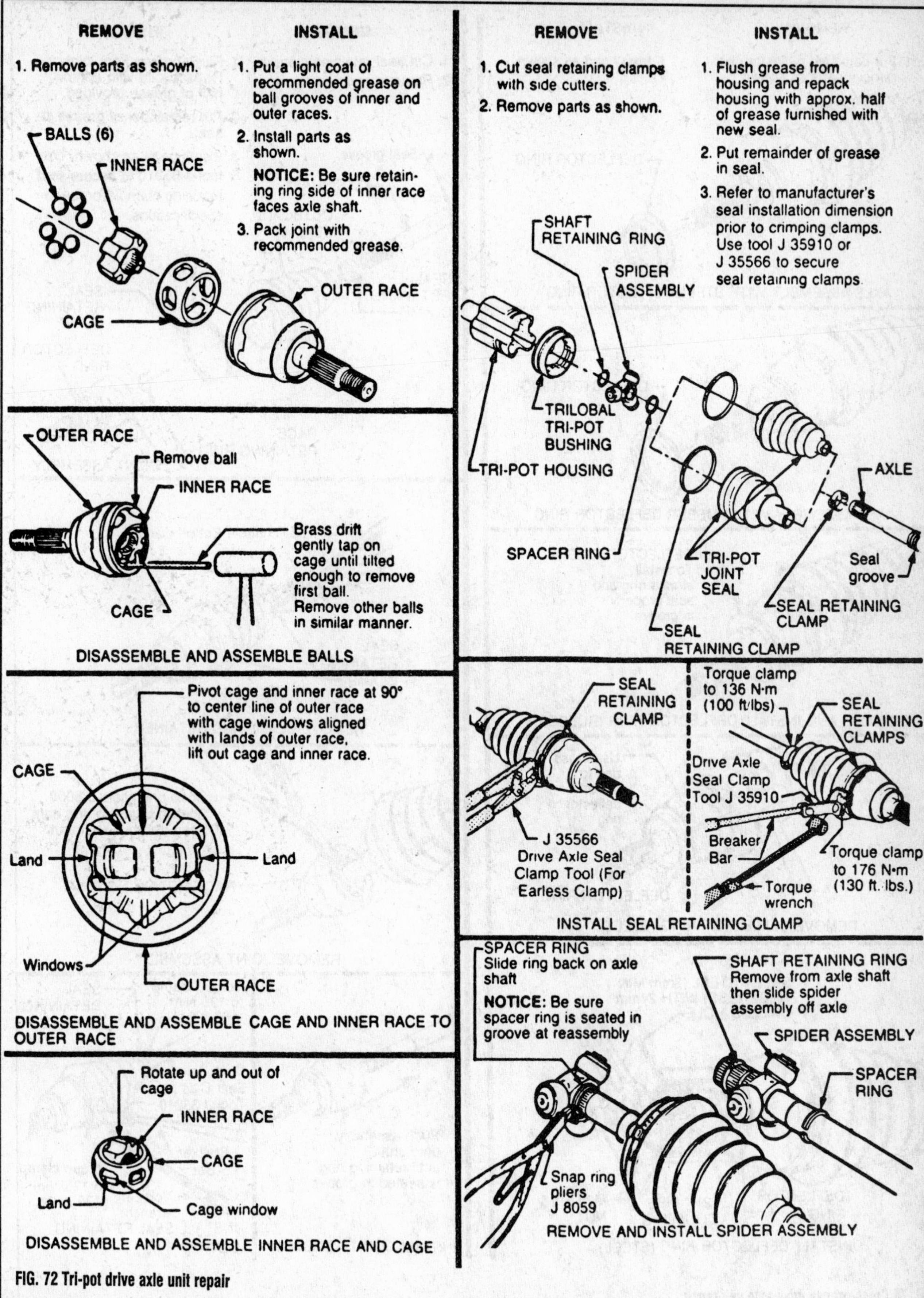

FIG. 72 Tri-pot drive axle unit repair

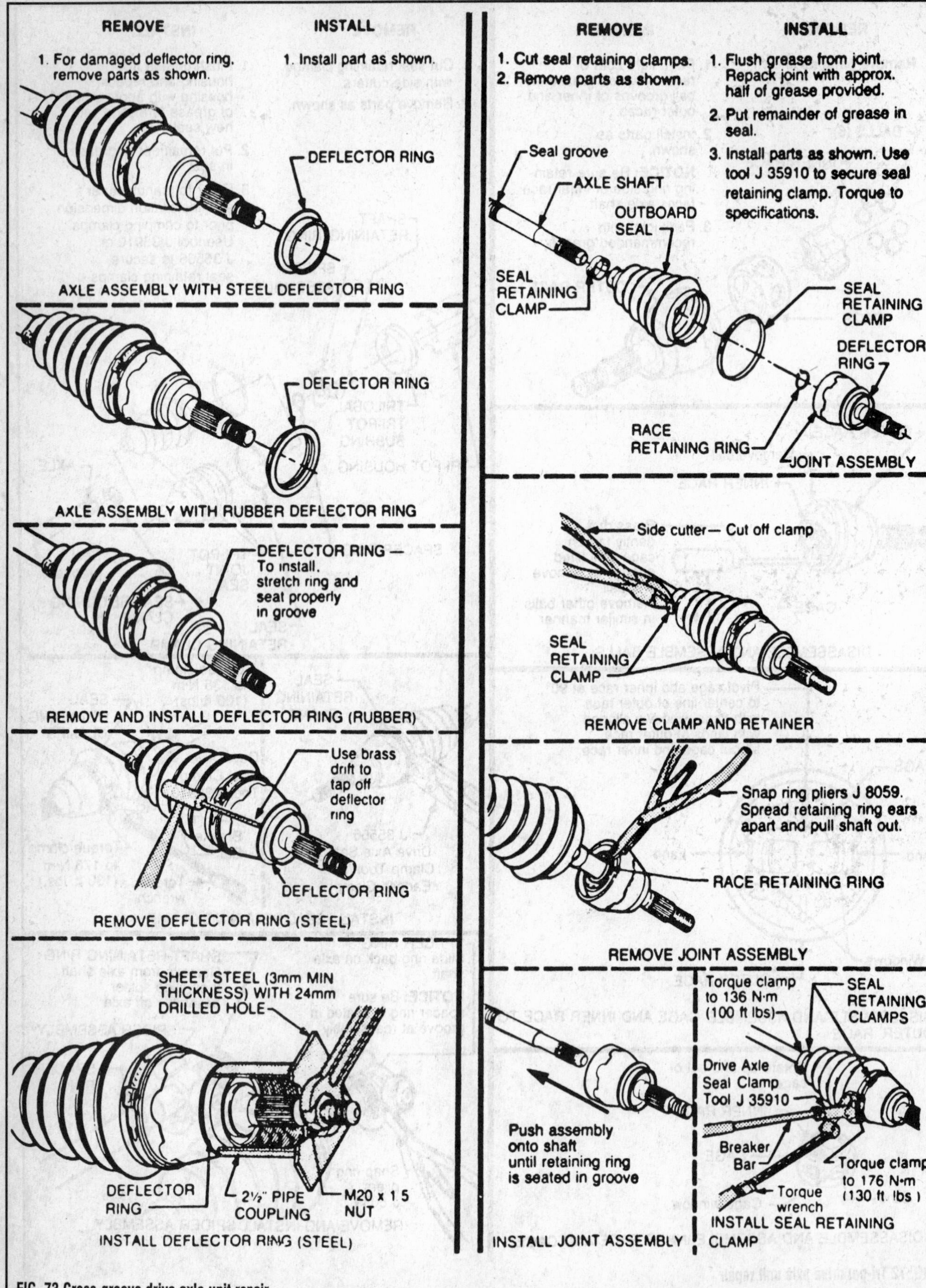

FIG. 73 Cross-groove drive axle unit repair

REMOVE

1. Remove parts as shown.

INSTALL

1. Put a light coat of recommended grease on ball grooves of inner and outer races.
2. Install parts as shown.

NOTICE: Be sure retaining ring side of inner race faces axle shaft.

3. Pack joint with recommended grease.

BALLS (6)

INNER RACE

OUTER RACE

CAGE

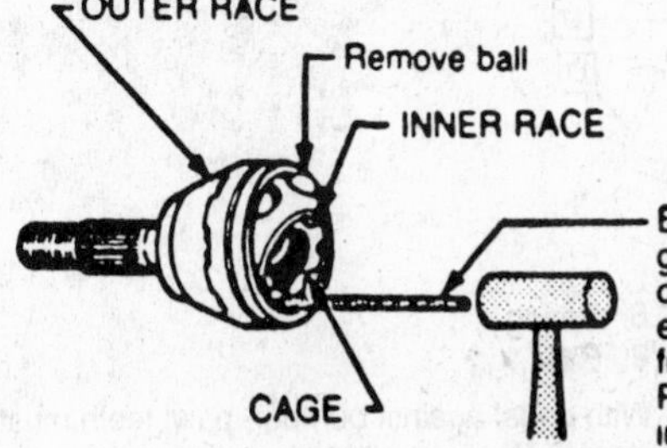

DISASSEMBLE AND ASSEMBLE BALLS

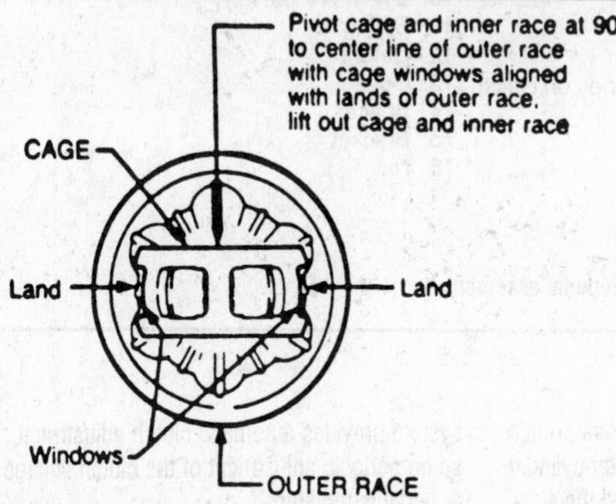

DISASSEMBLE AND ASSEMBLE CAGE AND INNER RACE TO OUTER RACE

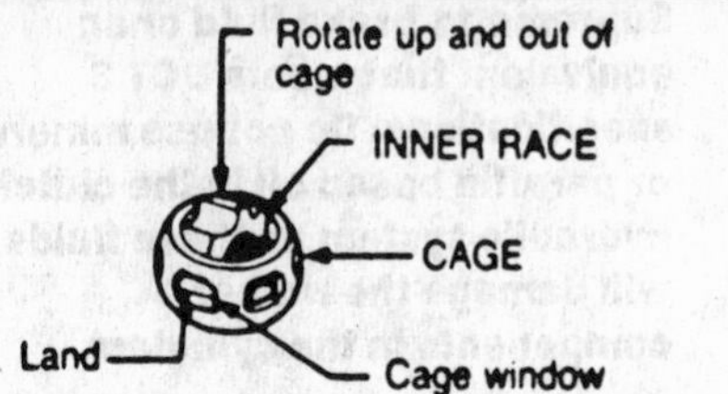

DISASSEMBLE AND ASSEMBLE INNER RACE AND CAGE

REMOVE

1. Cut seal retaining clamps.
2. Remove parts as shown.

INSTALL

1. Flush grease from joint. Repack joint with approx. half of grease provided.
2. Put remainder of grease in seal.
3. Install parts as shown. Use tool J 35910 to secure seal retaining clamp. Torque to specifications.

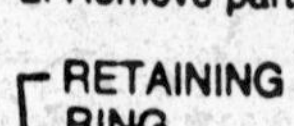

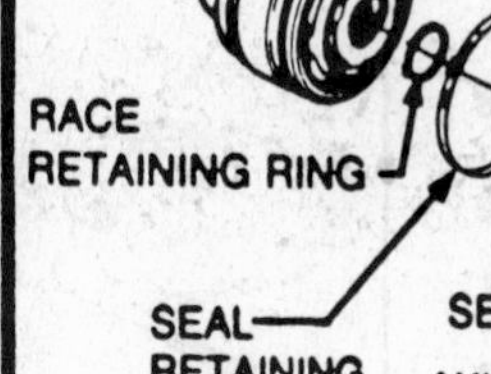

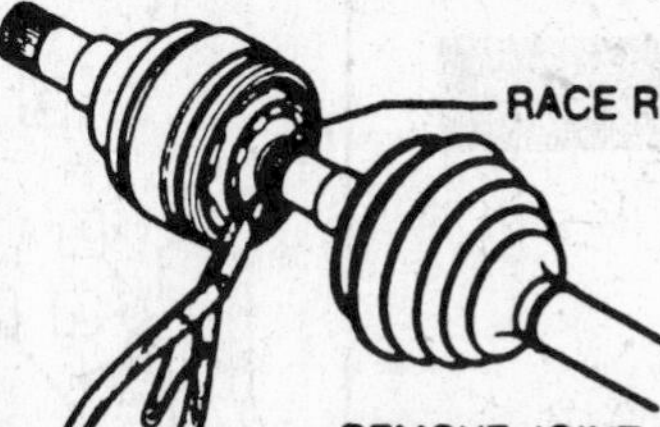

REMOVE JOINT ASSEMBLY

INSTALL JOINT ASSEMBLY

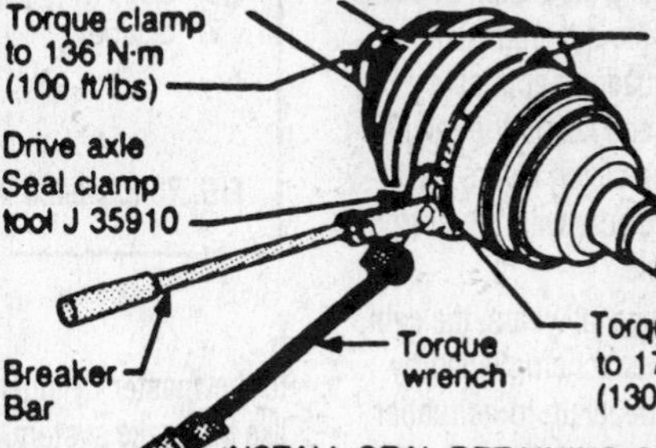

INSTALL SEAL RETAINING CLAMP

5. CLEAN AND FLUSH INNER JOINT

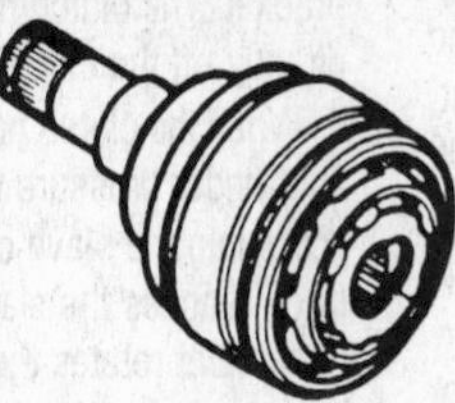

1. Push inner race and cage to bottom of housing to displace grease.
2. Thoroughly wipe all excess grease from joint.
3. Repack joint with recommended grease.

NOTICE: The cross-groove joint design uses precision grinding and selected dimensional component fits for proper assembly and operation. Due to its complexity, it is not recommended that the joint be disassembled for service.

FIG. 74 Cross-groove drive axle unit repair

CLUTCH

**** CAUTION**

The clutch driven disc contains asbestos, which has been determined to be a cancer causing agent. Never clean clutch surfaces with compressed air! Avoid inhaling any dust from any clutch surface! When cleaning clutch surfaces, use a commercially available brake cleaning fluid.

Adjustments

SEE FIG. 75

CLUTCH CABLE

The adjusting mechanism is mounted to the clutch pedal and bracket assembly. The cable is a fixed length and cannot be lengthened or shortened; however, the position of the cable can be changed by adjusting the position of the quadrant in relation to the clutch pedal. This mechanism makes adjustments in the quadrant position which changes the effective cable length. This is done by lifting the clutch pedal to disengage the pawl from the quadrant. The spring in the hub of the quadrant applies a tension load to the cable and keeps the release bearing in contact with the clutch levers. This results in a balanced condition, with the correct tension applied to the cable.

As the clutch friction material wears, the cable must be lengthened. This is accomplished by simply pulling the clutch pedal up to its rubber bumper. This action forces the pawl against its stop and rotates it out of mesh with the quadrant teeth, allowing the cable to play out until the quadrant spring load is balanced against the load applied by the release bearing. This adjustment procedure is required approximately every 5000 miles.

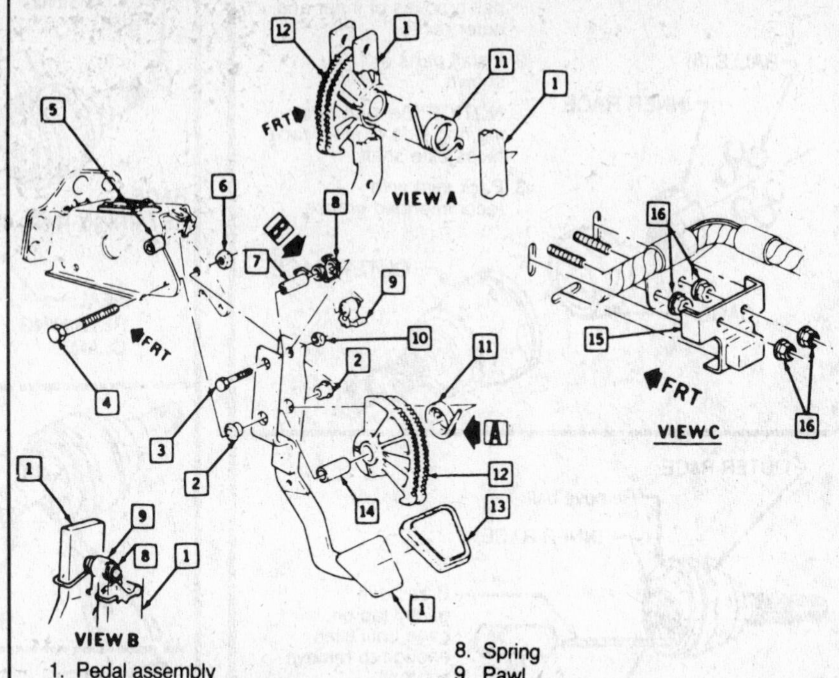

FIG. 75 Exploded view of the clutch pedal assembly

HYDRAULIC CLUTCH

The hydraulic clutch release system consists of a clutch master cylinder with an integral or remote reservoir and a slave cylinder connected to the master cylinder by a hydraulic line, much like the brake system. The clutch master cylinder is mounted to the front of the dash and the slave cylinder is mounted to the transaxle support bracket. The clutch master cylinder is operated directly off the clutch pedal by the pushrod.

When the clutch pedal is depressed, hydraulic fluid under pressure from the master cylinder flows into the slave cylinder. As the hydraulic force reaches the slave cylinder, the pushrod movement rotates the clutch fork which forces the release bearing into the clutch diaphragm and disengages the clutch. The hydraulic clutch system provides automatic clutch adjustment, so no periodic adjustment of the clutch linkage or pedal is required.

➡ When adding fluid to the clutch master cylinder, use Delco Supreme 11 brake fluid or an equivalent that meets DOT 3 specifications. Do not use mineral or paraffin based oil in the clutch hydraulic system as these fluids will damage the rubber components in the cylinders.

Clutch Cable

REMOVAL & INSTALLATION

SEE FIGS. 75–77

1. Support the clutch pedal upward against the bumper stop to release the pawl from the quadrant.
2. Disconnect the end of the cable from the clutch release lever at the transaxle. Be careful to prevent the cable from snapping toward the rear of the car. The quadrant in the adjusting mechanism can be damaged by allowing the cable to snap back.
3. Disconnect the clutch cable from the quadrant. Lift the locking pawl away from the quadrant, then slide the cable out on the right side of the quadrant.
4. From the engine side of the cowl, disconnect the 2 upper nuts holding the cable retainer to the upper studs. Disconnect the cable from the bracket mounted to the transaxle and remove the cable.
5. Inspect the clutch cable from signs of fraying, kinks, worn ends or excessive cable friction. Replace the cable if any of these problems are noted.

To install:

6. Place the gasket into position on the 2 upper studs, then position the cable with the retaining flange against the bracket.
7. Attach the end of the cable to the quadrant, being sure to route the cable underneath the pawl. Attach the 2 upper nuts to the retainer mounting studs and tighten.
8. Attach the cable to the bracket mounted to the transaxle.
9. Support the clutch pedal upward against the bumper to release the pawl from the quadrant. Attach the outer end of the cable to the clutch release lever.

➡ Be sure NOT to yank on the cable, since overloading the cable could damage the quadrant.

10. Check clutch operation and adjust by lifting the clutch pedal up to allow the mechanism to adjust the cable length. Depress the pedal slowly several times to set the pawl into mesh with the quadrant teeth.

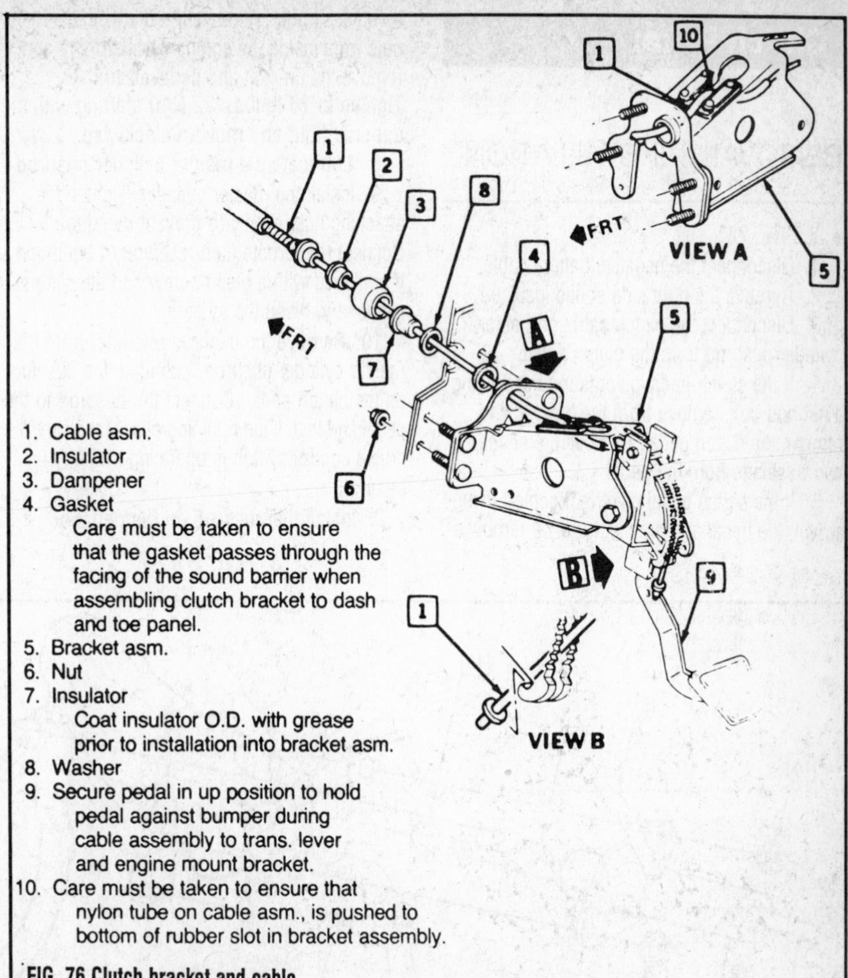

FIG. 76 Clutch bracket and cable

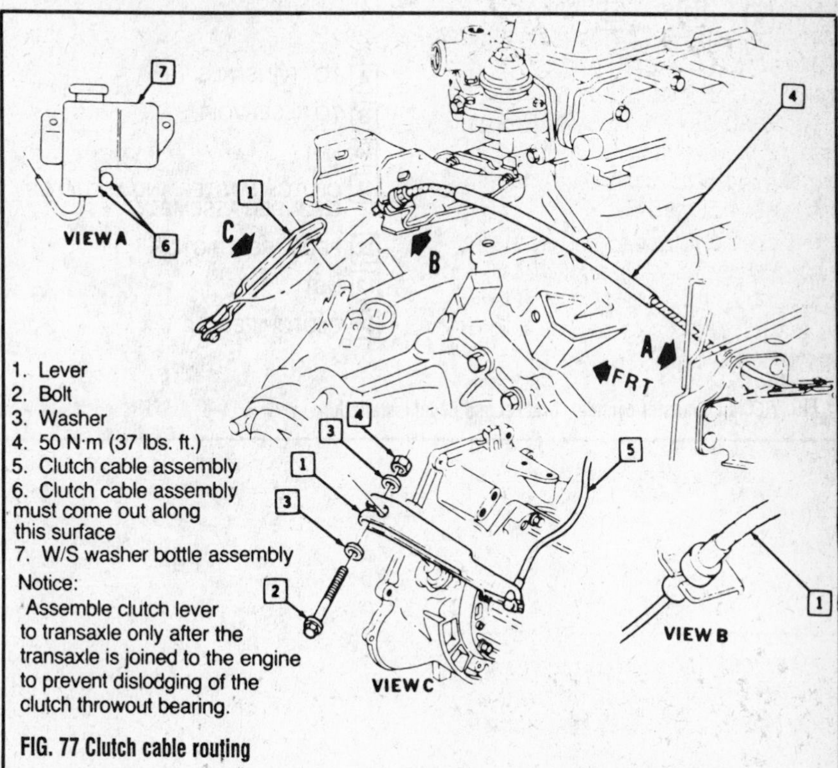

FIG. 77 Clutch cable routing

Clutch Pedal

REMOVAL & INSTALLATION

➧ SEE FIG. 78

1. Disconnect the negative battery cable.
2. Remove the right side sound insulator.
3. Disconnect the clutch cable or master cylinder pushrod from the clutch pedal.
4. If the clutch pedal pivot is mounted using a nut and bolt, remove from the bracket and remove the clutch pedal. Remove the spaces and bushings from the pedal.
5. If the clutch pedal pivot is mounted using a rivet, the pedal and bracket must be removed as an assembly. Remove the bracket attaching nuts from inside the engine compartment and remove the bracket and pedal assembly. Tighten to 16 ft. lbs. (22 Nm) starting with the upper left nut and moving clockwise.
8. Lubricate the master cylinder pushrod
9. Install the master cylinder. Tighten the attaching nuts evenly to prevent damage. Connect the remote fluid reservoir, if equipped. If equipped with a bleed screw and bleeding is necessary, bleed the system.
10. Remove the pushrod restrictor from the master cylinder pushrod. Lubricate the bushing on the clutch pedal. Connect the pushrod to the pedal and install the retaining clip. Make sure the cruise control switch is operating properly. busing
9. Install the pushrod on the pedal or connect the cable. If equipped with cruise control, check the switch adjustment at the clutch pedal bracket.
10. Install the right side sound insulator.
11. Connect the negative battery cable.

To install:

6. If mounted with a nut and bolt, perform the following;
   a. Install the spacer and bushings on the pedal. Lubricate the bushings before installing on the pedal.
   b. Position the clutch pedal to the mounting bracket and install the pivot bolt and retaining nut. Tighten to 23 ft. lbs. (31 Nm).
7. If rivet mounted, install the bracket and pedal assembly. Install the attaching nuts.

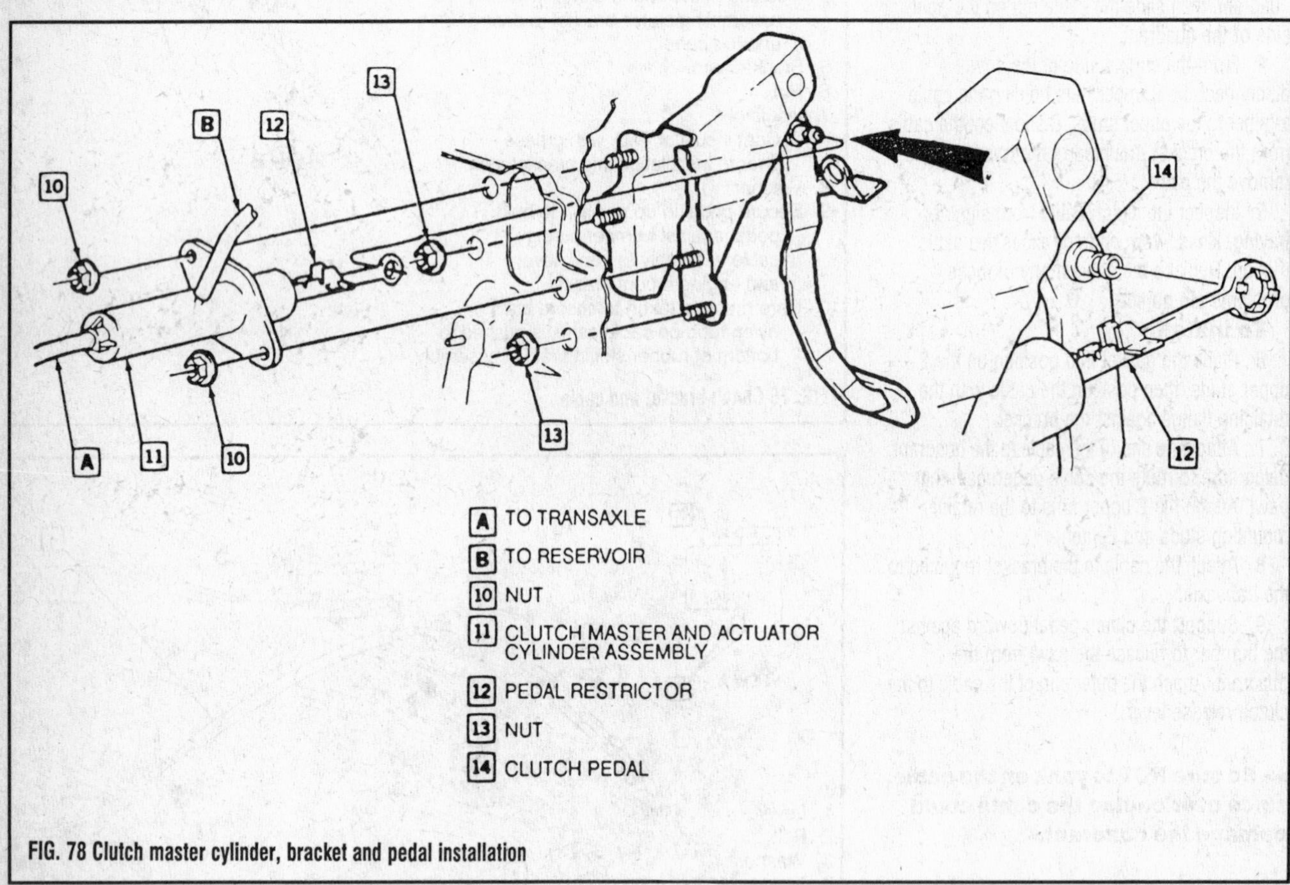

FIG. 78 Clutch master cylinder, bracket and pedal installation

Drive Disc and Pressure Plate

REMOVAL & INSTALLATION

▶ SEE FIG. 79

1. Disconnect the negative battery cable. Remove the transaxle.
2. Matchmark the clutch/pressure plate cover and flywheel, if reinstalling old parts. Insert a clutch plate alignment tool into the clutch disc hub.
3. Loosen the flywheel to pressure plate bolts gradually and evenly to avoid warpage.
4. Remove the pressure plate/clutch assembly from the flywheel.
5. Sand the flywheel or replace it, if scored, cracked or heat damaged.
6. Sparingly apply anti-seize compound to the input shaft and clutch disc splines. Install a new release bearing.

To install:

7. Using a clutch disc alignment tool, tighten the pressure plate bolts to center the disc.
8. Tighten the pressure plate/clutch assembly mounting bolts to the flywheel gradually and evenly to 20–25 ft. lbs. (27–34 Nm).
9. Install the transaxle.
10. Connect the negative battery cable and check the clutch and reverse lights for proper operation.

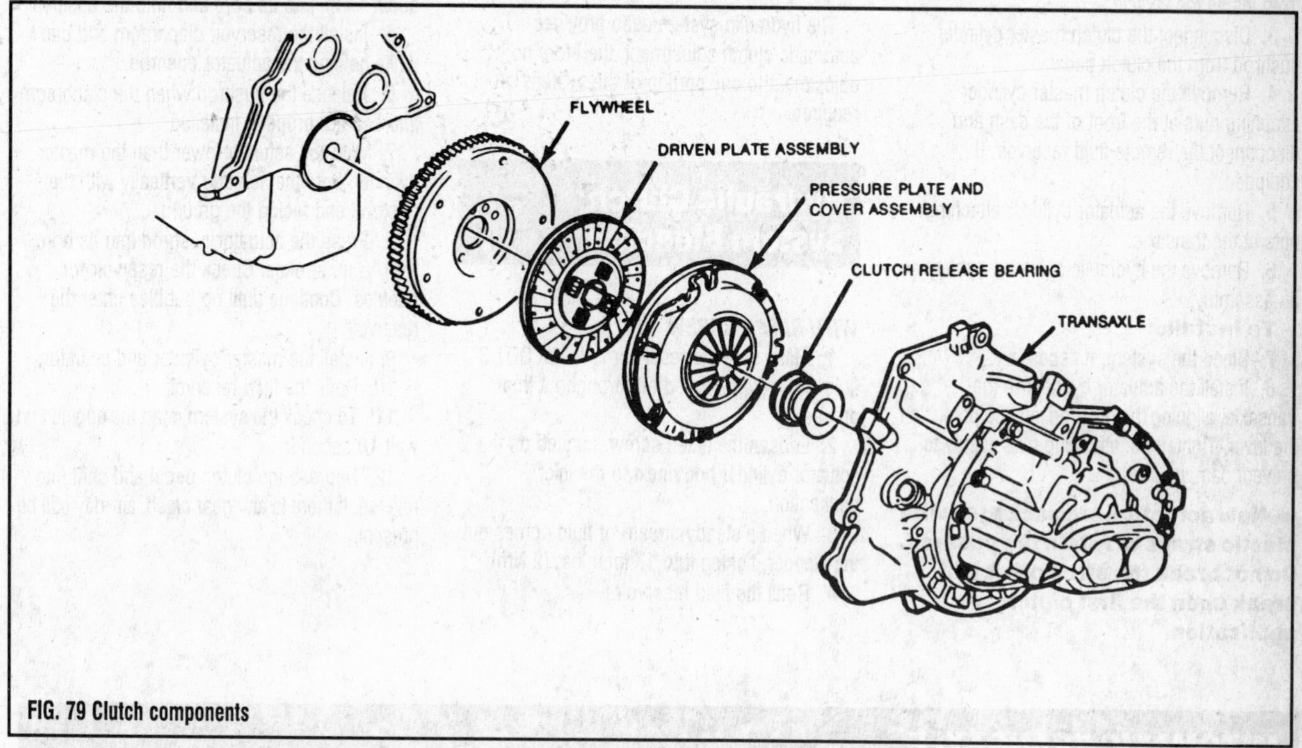

FIG. 79 Clutch components

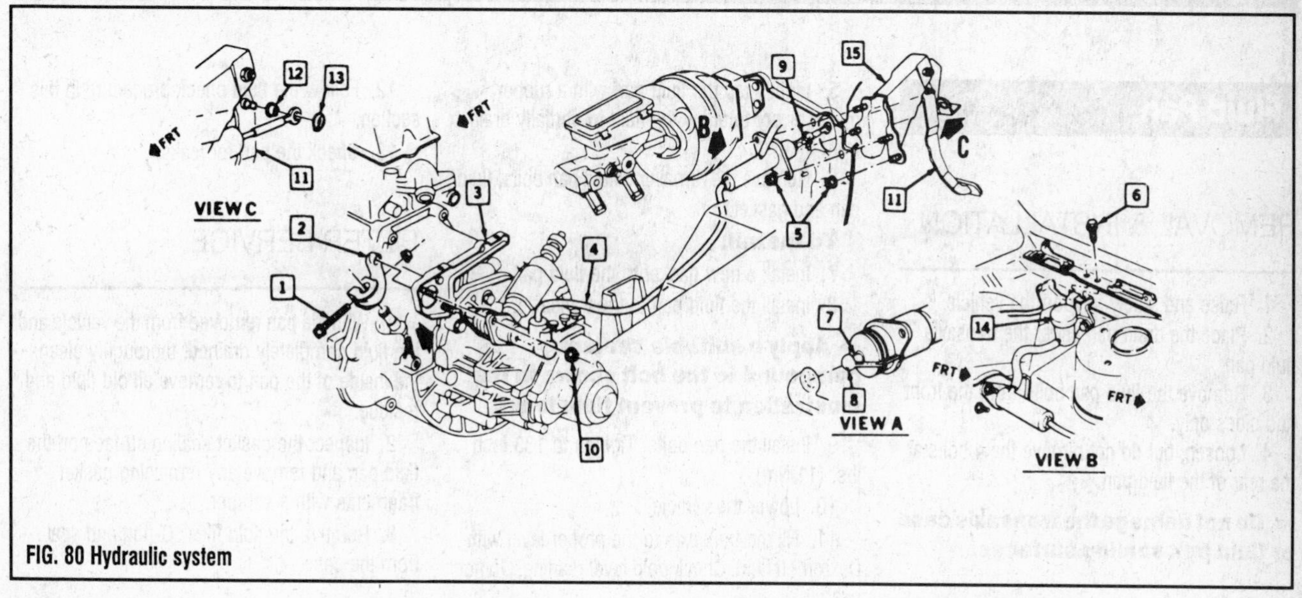

FIG. 80 Hydraulic system

Clutch Master and Slave Cylinders

REMOVAL & INSTALLATION

➧ SEE FIG. 80

1. Disconnect the negative battery cable.
2. Remove the steering column opening filler from inside the vehicle.
3. Disconnect the clutch master cylinder pushrod from the clutch pedal.
4. Remove the clutch master cylinder attaching nuts at the front of the dash and disconnect the remote fluid reservoir, if equipped.
5. Remove the actuator cylinder attaching nuts at the transaxle.
6. Remove the hydraulic actuating system as an assembly.

To install:

7. Bleed the system, if necessary.
8. Install the actuator cylinder to the transaxle, aligning the pushrod into the pocket on the lever. Tighten the attaching nuts evenly to prevent damage.

➡ New actuators are packaged with plastic straps to retain the pushrod. Do not break the strap off; it will break upon the first clutch application.

➡ When adjusting the cruise control switch, do not use a force of more than 20 lbs. to pull the pedal up, or damage to the master cylinder pushrod retaining ring could result.

11. Install the steering column opening filler from inside the vehicle.
12. Push the clutch pedal down a few times. This will break the plastic straps on the actuator.
13. Connect the negative battery cable and check for proper operation.

Adjustment

The hydraulic system used provides automatic clutch adjustment, therefore no adjustment to any portion of the system is required.

Hydraulic Clutch System Bleeding

WITH BLEED SCREW

1. Make sure the reservoir is full of DOT 3 fluid and is kept topped off throughout this procedure.
2. Loosen the bleed screw, located on the actuator cylinder body next to the inlet connection.
3. When a steady stream of fluid comes out the bleeder, tighten it to 17 inch lbs. (2 Nm).
4. Refill the fluid reservoir.
5. To check the system, start the engine and wait 10 seconds.
6. Depress the clutch pedal and shift into Reverse. If there is any gear clash, air may still be present.

WITHOUT BLEED SCREW

1. Remove the actuator cylinder from the transaxle.
2. Loosen the master cylinder attaching nuts to the ends of the studs.
3. Remove the reservoir cap and diaphragm.
4. Depress the actuator cylinder pushrod about 3/4 in. into its bore and hold the position.
5. Install the reservoir diaphragm and cap while holding the actuator pushrod.
6. Release the pushrod when the diaphragm and cap are properly installed.
7. With the actuator lower than the master cylinder, hold the actuator vertically with the pushrod end facing the ground.
8. Press the actuator pushrod into its bore with 1/2 in. strokes. Check the reservoir for bubbles. Continue until no bubbles enter the reservoir.
9. Install the master cylinder and actuator.
10. Refill the fluid reservoir.
11. To check the system, start the engine and wait 10 seconds.
12. Depress the clutch pedal and shift into reverse. If there is any gear clash, air may still be present.

AUTOMATIC TRANSAXLE

Fluid Pan

REMOVAL & INSTALLATION

1. Raise and safely support the vehicle.
2. Place the drain pan under the transaxle fluid pan.
3. Remove the fluid pan bolts from the front and sides only.
4. Loosen, but do not remove the 4 bolts at the rear of the fluid pan.

➡ Do not damage the transaxle case or fluid pan sealing surfaces.

5. Lightly tap the fluid pan with a rubber mallet or pry to allow the fluid to partially drain from the pan.
6. Remove the remaining fluid pan bolts, fluid pan and gasket.

To install:

7. Install a new gasket to the fluid pan.
8. Install the fluid pan to the transaxle.

➡ Apply a suitable sealant compound to the bolt shown in the illustration to prevent fluid leaks.

9. Install the pan bolts. Tighten to 133 inch lbs. (11 Nm).
10. Lower the vehicle.
11. Fill the transaxle to the proper level with Dexron® II fluid. Check cold level reading. Do not overfill.
12. Follow the fluid check procedure in this section.
13. Check the pan for leaks.

FILTER SERVICE

1. With the pan removed from the vehicle and the fluid completely drained, thoroughly clean the inside of the pan to remove all old fluid and residue.
2. Inspect the gasket sealing surface on the fluid pan and remove any remaining gasket fragments with a scraper.
3. Remove the fluid filter, O-ring and seal from the case.

To install:

4. Apply a small amount of Transjel to the new seal and install the seal.
5. Install a new filter O-ring and filter.
6. Install the new gasket to the pan.

Adjustments

TV CABLE ADJUSTMENT

➧ SEE FIGS. 81 AND 82

Except 2.3L Engine

1. Disconnect the negative battery cable.
2. Depress and hold the adjustment tap at the TV cable adjuster.
3. Release the throttle lever by hand to its full travel position. On the 2.5L engine press, the accelerator pedal to the full travel position.
4. The slider must move toward the lever when the lever is rotated to the full travel position or when the accelerator pedal is pressed to the full travel position on the 2.5L engine.
5. Inspect the cable for freedom of movement. The cable may appear to function properly with the engine stopped and cold. Recheck the cable after the engine is warm.
6. Road test the vehicle and check for proper shifting.

2.3L Engine

1. Disconnect the negative battery cable.
2. Rotate the TV cable adjuster body at the transaxle 90 degrees and pull the cable conduit out until the slider mechanism contacts the stop.
3. Rotate the adjuster body back to the original position.
4. Using a torque wrench, rotate the TV cable adjuster until 75 inch lbs. (9 Nm) is reached.
5. Road test the vehicle and check for proper shifting.

SHIFT CABLE ADJUSTMENT

➧ SEE FIG. 83

1. Place the selector in the **N** detent.
2. Raise the locking tab on the cable adjuster.
3. Place the shift control assembly on the transaxle in the neutral position.
4. Push the locking tab back into position.

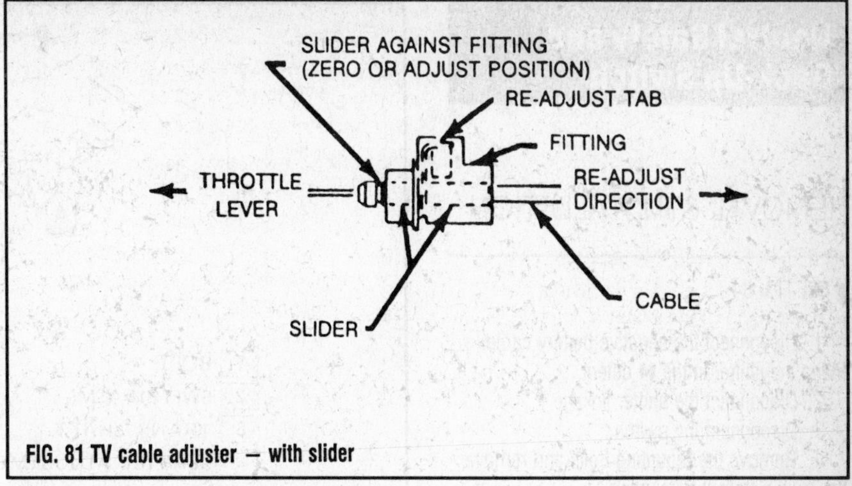

FIG. 81 TV cable adjuster — with slider

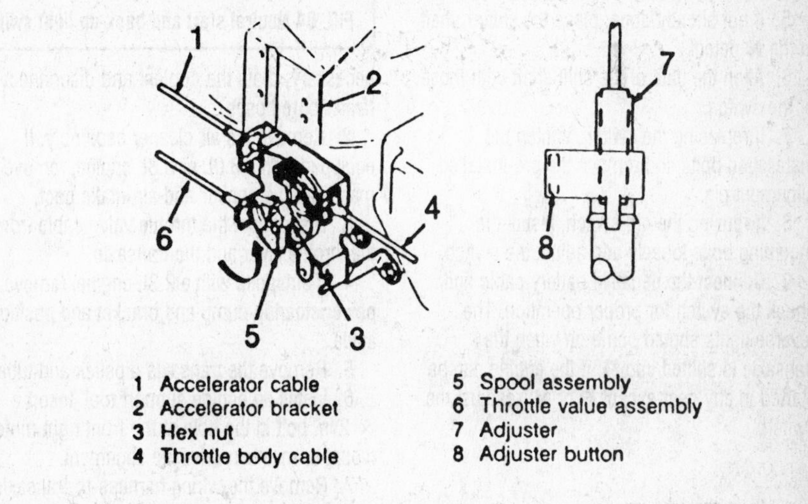

FIG. 82 TV cable adjuster — without slider

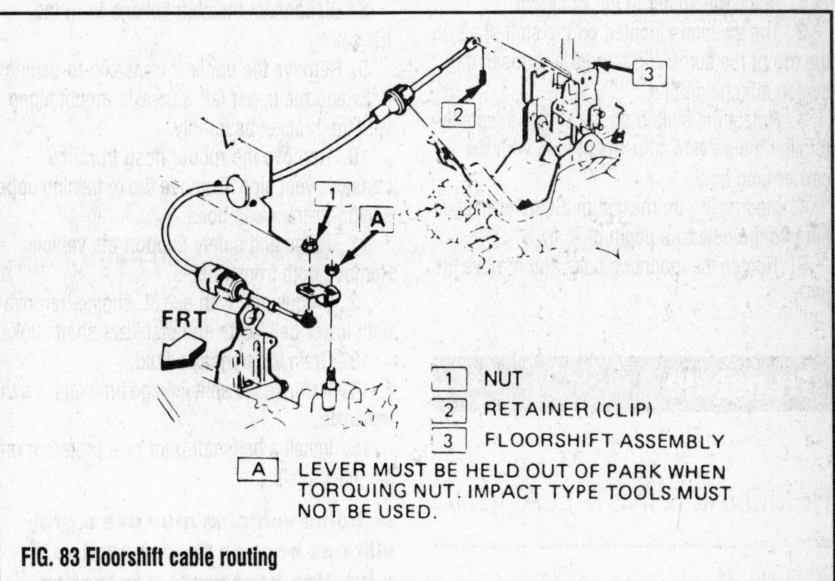

FIG. 83 Floorshift cable routing

Neutral Safety and Back-Up Switch

REMOVAL & INSTALLATION

➧ SEE FIG. 84

1. Disconnect the negative battery cable. Place the shifter in the **N** detent.
2. Disconnect the shifter linkage.
3. Disconnect the switch.
4. Remove the mounting bolts and remove the switch from the transaxle.

To install:

5. If not already done, place the shifter shaft in the **N** detent.
6. Align the flats of the shift shaft with those of the switch.
7. If replacing the switch, tighten the installation bolts and remove the pre-installed alignment pin.
8. If reusing the old switch, install the mounting bolts loosely and adjust the switch.
9. Connect the negative battery cable and check the switch for proper operation. The reverse lights should come on when the transaxle is shifted into **R**. If the engine can be started in any gear except **P** or **N**, readjust the switch.

ADJUSTMENT

1. Place the shifter in the **N** detent.
2. The switch is located on the shift shaft on the top of the automatic transaxle. Loosen the switch attaching bolts.
3. Rotate the switch on the shifter assembly to align the service adjustment hole with the carrier tang hole.
4. Insert a $\frac{3}{32}$ in. maximum diameter gauge pin into the hole to a depth of $\frac{5}{8}$ in.
5. Tighten the mounting bolts and remove the pin.

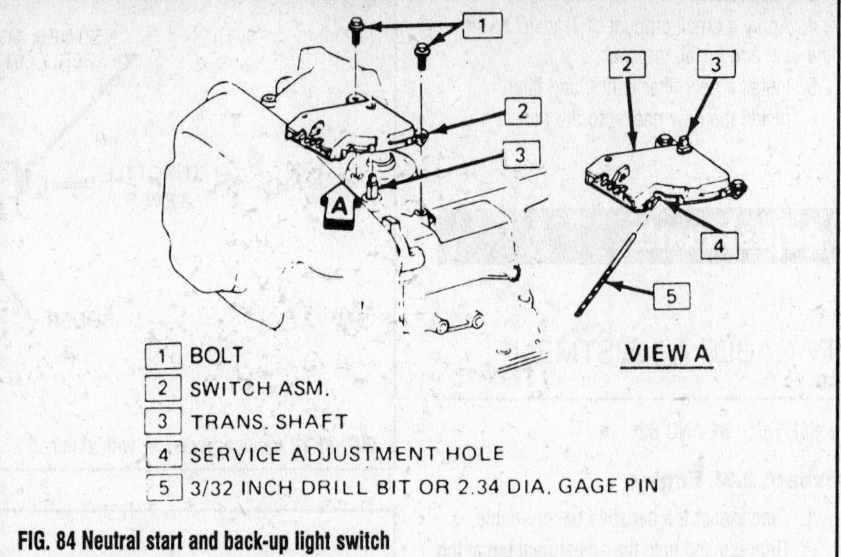

FIG. 84 Neutral start and back-up light switch

Transaxle

REMOVAL & INSTALLATION

➧ SEE FIG. 85

1. Disconnect the negative battery cable. If necessary, drain the coolant and disconnect the heater core hoses.
2. Remove the air cleaner assembly. If equipped with a 3.0L or 3.3L engine, remove the mass air flow sensor and air intake duct.
3. Disconnect the throttle valve cable from the throttle lever and the transaxle.
4. If equipped with a 2.3L engine, remove the power steering pump and bracket and position it aside.
5. Remove the transaxle dipstick and tube.
6. Install an engine support tool. Insert a $\frac{1}{4} \times 2$ in. bolt in the hole at the front right motor mount to maintain driveline alignment.
7. Remove the wiring harness-to-transaxle nut. Disconnect the wiring connectors from the speed sensor, TCC connector, neutral safety switch and reverse light switch.
8. Disconnect the shift linkage from the transaxle.
9. Remove the upper 2 transaxle-to-engine bolts and the upper left transaxle mount along with the bracket assembly.
10. Remove the rubber hose from the transaxle vent pipe. Remove the remaining upper engine-to-transaxle bolts.
11. Raise and safely support the vehicle. Remove both front wheels.
12. If equipped with a 2.3L engine, remove both lower ball joints and stabilizer shafts links.
13. Drain the transaxle fluid.
14. Remove the shift linkage bracket from the transaxle.
15. Install a halfshaft boot seal protector on the inner seals.

➡ Some vehicles may use a gray silicone boot on the inboard axle joint. Use boot protector tool on these boots. All other boots are made from a black thermo-plastic material and do not require the use of a boot seal protector.

16. Remove both ball joint-to-control arm nuts and separate the ball joints from the control arms.
17. Remove both halfshafts and support them with a cord or wire.
18. Remove the transaxle mounting strut.
19. Remove the left stabilizer bar link pin bolt, left frame bushing clamp nuts and left frame support assembly.
20. Remove the torque converter cover. Matchmark the flexplate and torque converter for installation purposes. Remove the torque converter-to-flexplate bolts.
21. Disconnect and plug the transaxle oil cooler lines.
22. Remove the transaxle-to-engine support bracket and install the transaxle removal jack.
23. Remove the remaining transaxle-to-engine attaching bolts and the transaxle from the vehicle.

To install:

24. Securely mount the transaxle on the jack.
25. Apply a small amount of grease on the torque converter hub and seat in the oil pump.
26. Position the transaxle in the vehicle and install the lower engine to transaxle bolts.
27. Install the transaxle to engine support bracket. Once the transaxle is securely held in place, remove the jack. Connect the cooler lines.
28. Install the torque converter bolts and tighten to specification.
29. Install the torque converter cover.
30. Install the left frame support assembly.
31. Install the left stabilizer shaft frame busing nuts and link pin bolt.

32. Install the transaxle mounting strut.

33. Install the halfshafts. Install the ball joints.

34. Install the shift linkage bracket to the transaxle.

35. Install the wheels and lower the vehicle.

36. Install the upper transaxle to engine bolts.

37. Install the left side transaxle mount.

38. Connect the shift linkage to the transaxle.

39. Connect the wiring connectors to their switches on the transaxle.

40. Remove the 1/4 × 2 in. bolt that was placed in the hole at the front right motor mount to maintain driveline alignment. Remove an engine support tool.

41. Replace the O-ring, lubricate it and install the dipstick tube and dipstick.

42. Install the TV cable and rubber vent tube.

43. Install the air cleaner assembly and air tubes.

44. Connect the heater hoses, if disconnected.

45. Fill all fluids to their proper levels. Adjust cables as required.

46. Connect the negative battery cable and check the transaxle for proper operation and leaks.

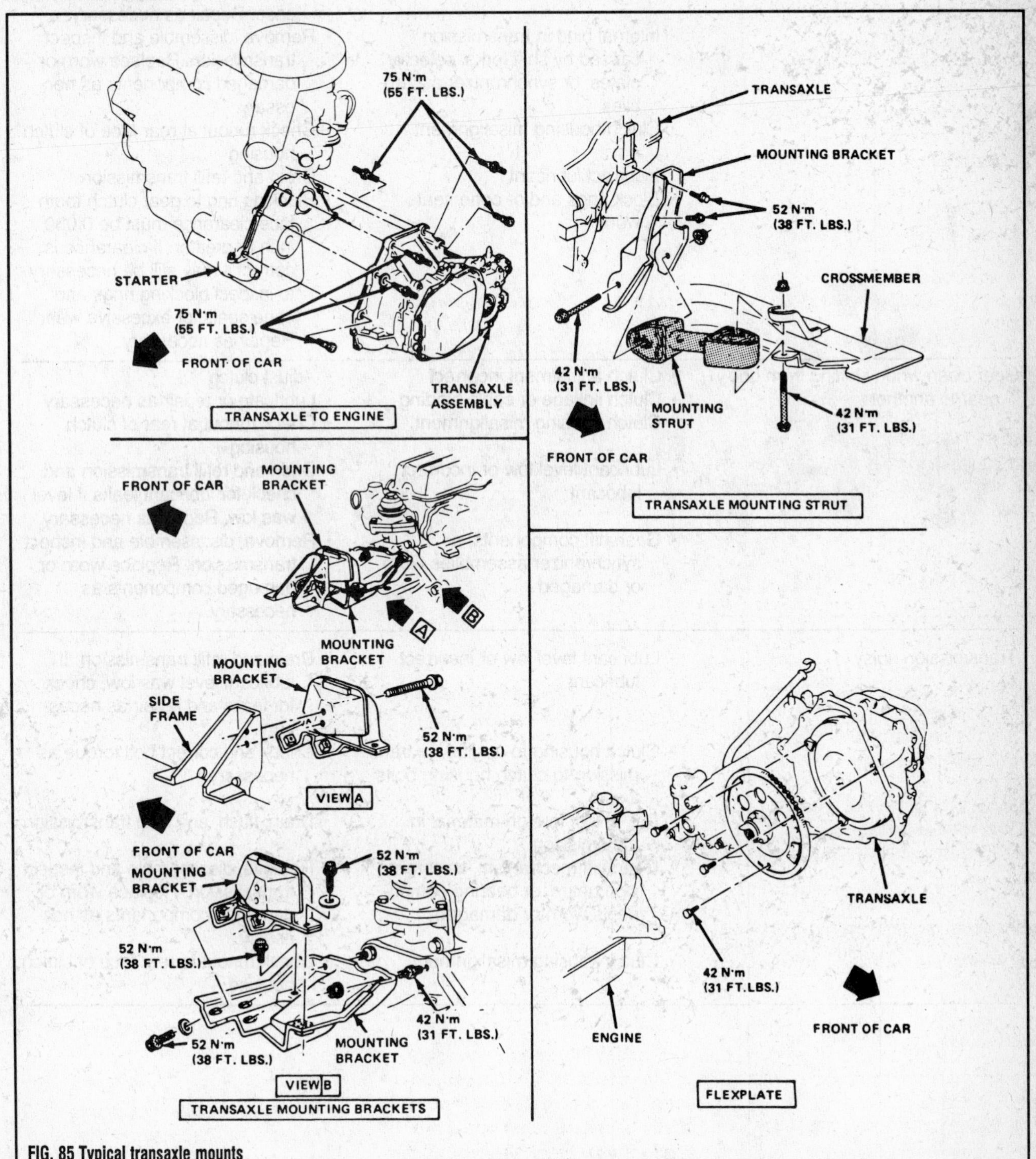

FIG. 85 Typical transaxle mounts

Troubleshooting the Manual Transmission

Problem	Cause	Solution
Transmission shifts hard	• Clutch adjustment incorrect	• Adjust clutch
	• Clutch linkage or cable binding	• Lubricate or repair as necessary
	• Shift rail binding	• Check for mispositioned selector arm roll pin, loose cover bolts, worn shift rail bores, worn shift rail, distorted oil seal, or extension housing not aligned with case. Repair as necessary.
	• Internal bind in transmission caused by shift forks, selector plates, or synchronizer assemblies	• Remove, dissemble and inspect transmission. Replace worn or damaged components as necessary.
	• Clutch housing misalignment	• Check runout at rear face of clutch housing
	• Incorrect lubricant	• Drain and refill transmission
	• Block rings and/or cone seats worn	• Blocking ring to gear clutch tooth face clearance must be 0.030 inch or greater. If clearance is correct it may still be necessary to inspect blocking rings and cone seats for excessive wear. Repair as necessary.
Gear clash when shifting from one gear to another	• Clutch adjustment incorrect	• Adjust clutch
	• Clutch linkage or cable binding	• Lubricate or repair as necessary
	• Clutch housing misalignment	• Check runout at rear of clutch housing
	• Lubricant level low or incorrect lubricant	• Drain and refill transmission and check for lubricant leaks if level was low. Repair as necessary.
	• Gearshift components, or synchronizer assemblies worn or damaged	• Remove, disassemble and inspect transmission. Replace worn or damaged components as necessary.
Transmission noisy	• Lubricant level low or incorrect lubricant	• Drain and refill transmission. If lubricant level was low, check for leaks and repair as necessary.
	• Clutch housing-to-engine, or transmission-to-clutch housing bolts loose	• Check and correct bolt torque as necessary
	• Dirt, chips, foreign material in transmission	• Drain, flush, and refill transmission
	• Gearshift mechanism, transmission gears, or bearing components worn or damaged	• Remove, disassemble and inspect transmission. Replace worn or damaged components as necessary.
	• Clutch housing misalignment	• Check runout at rear face of clutch housing

Troubleshooting the Manual Transmission

Problem	Cause	Solution
Jumps out of gear	• Clutch housing misalignment	• Check runout at rear face of clutch housing
	• Gearshift lever loose	• Check lever for worn fork. Tighten loose attaching bolts.
	• Offset lever nylon insert worn or lever attaching nut loose	• Remove gearshift lever and check for loose offset lever nut or worn insert. Repair or replace as necessary.
	• Gearshift mechanism, shift forks, selector plates, interlock plate, selector arm, shift rail, detent plugs, springs or shift cover worn or damaged	• Remove, disassemble and inspect transmission cover assembly. Replace worn or damaged components as necessary.
	• Clutch shaft or roller bearings worn or damaged	• Replace clutch shaft or roller bearings as necessary
Jumps out of gear (cont.)	• Gear teeth worn or tapered, synchronizer assemblies worn or damaged, excessive end play caused by worn thrust washers or output shaft gears	• Remove, disassemble, and inspect transmission. Replace worn or damaged components as necessary.
	• Pilot bushing worn	• Replace pilot bushing
Will not shift into one gear	• Gearshift selector plates, interlock plate, or selector arm, worn, damaged, or incorrectly assembled	• Remove, disassemble, and inspect transmission cover assembly. Repair or replace components as necessary.
	• Shift rail detent plunger worn, spring broken, or plug loose	• Tighten plug or replace worn or damaged components as necessary
	• Gearshift lever worn or damaged	• Replace gearshift lever
	• Synchronizer sleeves or hubs, damaged or worn	• Remove, disassemble and inspect transmission. Replace worn or damaged components.
Locked in one gear—cannot be shifted out	• Shift rail(s) worn or broken, shifter fork bent, setscrew loose, center detent plug missing or worn	• Inspect and replace worn or damaged parts
	• Broken gear teeth on countershaft gear, clutch shaft, or reverse idler gear	• Inspect and replace damaged part
	Gearshift lever broken or worn, shift mechanism in cover incorrectly assembled or broken, worn damaged gear train components	• Disassemble transmission. Replace damaged parts or assemble correctly.

Troubleshooting Basic Clutch Problems

Problem	Cause
Excessive clutch noise	Throwout bearing noises are more audible at the lower end of pedal travel. The usual causes are: · Riding the clutch · Too little pedal free-play · Lack of bearing lubrication A bad clutch shaft pilot bearing will make a high pitched squeal, when the clutch is disengaged and the transmission is in gear or within the first 2″ of pedal travel. The bearing must be replaced. Noise from the clutch linkage is a clicking or snapping that can be heard or felt as the pedal is moved completely up or down. This usually requires lubrication. Transmitted engine noises are amplified by the clutch housing and heard in the passenger compartment. They are usually the result of insufficient pedal free-play and can be changed by manipulating the clutch pedal.
Clutch slips (the car does not move as it should when the clutch is engaged)	This is usually most noticeable when pulling away from a standing start. A severe test is to start the engine, apply the brakes, shift into high gear and SLOWLY release the clutch pedal. A healthy clutch will stall the engine. If it slips it may be due to: · A worn pressure plate or clutch plate · Oil soaked clutch plate · Insufficient pedal free-play
Clutch drags or fails to release	The clutch disc and some transmission gears spin briefly after clutch disengagement. Under normal conditions in average temperatures, 3 seconds is maximum spin-time. Failure to release properly can be caused by: · Too light transmission lubricant or low lubricant level · Improperly adjusted clutch linkage
Low clutch life	Low clutch life is usually a result of poor driving habits or heavy duty use. Riding the clutch, pulling heavy loads, holding the car on a grade with the clutch instead of the brakes and rapid clutch engagement all contribute to low clutch life.

Troubleshooting Basic Automatic Transmission Problems

Problem	Cause	Solution
Fluid leakage	· Defective pan gasket	· Replace gasket or tighten pan bolts
	· Loose filler tube	· Tighten tube nut
	· Loose extension housing to transmission case	· Tighten bolts
	· Converter housing area leakage	· Have transmission checked professionally
Fluid flows out the oil filler tube	· High fluid level	· Check and correct fluid level
	· Breather vent clogged	· Open breather vent
	· Clogged oil filter or screen	· Replace filter or clean screen (change fluid also)
	· Internal fluid leakage	· Have transmission checked professionally

Troubleshooting Basic Automatic Transmission Problems

Problem	Cause	Solution
Transmission overheats (this is usually accompanied by a strong burned odor to the fluid)	• Low fluid level • Fluid cooler lines clogged • Heavy pulling or hauling with insufficient cooling • Faulty oil pump, internal slippage	• Check and correct fluid level • Drain and refill transmission. If this doesn't cure the problem, have cooler lines cleared or replaced. • Install a transmission oil cooler • Have transmission checked professionally
Buzzing or whining noise	• Low fluid level • Defective torque converter, scored gears	• Check and correct fluid level • Have transmission checked professionally
No forward or reverse gears or slippage in one or more gears	• Low fluid level • Defective vacuum or linkage controls, internal clutch or band failure	• Check and correct fluid level • Have unit checked professionally
Delayed or erratic shift	• Low fluid level • Broken vacuum lines • Internal malfunction	• Check and correct fluid level • Repair or replace lines • Have transmission checked professionally

Lockup Torque Converter Service Diagnosis

Problem	Cause	Solution
No lockup	• Faulty oil pump • Sticking governor valve • Valve body malfunction (a) Stuck switch valve (b) Stuck lockup valve (c) Stuck fail-safe valve • Failed locking clutch • Leaking turbine hub seal • Faulty input shaft or seal ring	• Replace oil pump • Repair or replace as necessary • Repair or replace valve body or its internal components as necessary • Replace torque converter • Replace torque converter • Repair or replace as necessary
Will not unlock	• Sticking governor valve • Valve body malfunction (a) Stuck switch valve (b) Stuck lockup valve (c) Stuck fail-safe valve	• Repair or replace as necessary • Repair or replace valve body or its internal components as necessary
Stays locked up at too low a speed in direct	• Sticking governor valve • Valve body malfunction (a) Stuck switch valve (b) Stuck lockup valve (c) Stuck fail-safe valve	• Repair or replace as necessary • Repair or replace valve body or its internal components as necessary
Locks up or drags in low or second	• Faulty oil pump • Valve body malfunction (a) Stuck switch valve (b) Stuck fail-safe valve	• Replace oil pump • Repair or replace valve body or its internal components as necessary

Lockup Torque Converter Service Diagnosis

Problem	Cause	Solution
Sluggish or stalls in reverse	• Faulty oil pump • Plugged cooler, cooler lines or fittings • Valve body malfunction (a) Stuck switch valve (b) Faulty input shaft or seal ring	• Replace oil pump as necessary • Flush or replace cooler and flush lines and fittings • Repair or replace valve body or its internal components as necessary
Loud chatter during lockup engagement (cold)	• Faulty torque converter • Failed locking clutch • Leaking turbine hub seal	• Replace torque converter • Replace torque converter • Replace torque converter
Vibration or shudder during lockup engagement	• Faulty oil pump • Valve body malfunction • Faulty torque converter • Engine needs tune-up	• Repair or replace oil pump as necessary • Repair or replace valve body or its internal components as necessary • Replace torque converter • Tune engine
Vibration after lockup engagement	• Faulty torque converter • Exhaust system strikes underbody • Engine needs tune-up • Throttle linkage misadjusted	• Replace torque converter • Align exhaust system • Tune engine • Adjust throttle linkage
Vibration when revved in neutral Overheating: oil blows out of dip stick tube or pump seal	• Torque converter out of balance • Plugged cooler, cooler lines or fittings • Stuck switch valve	• Replace torque converter • Flush or replace cooler and flush lines and fittings • Repair switch valve in valve body or replace valve body
Shudder after lockup engagement	• Faulty oil pump • Plugged cooler, cooler lines or fittings • Valve body malfunction • Faulty torque converter • Fail locking clutch • Exhaust system strikes underbody • Engine needs tune-up • Throttle linkage misadjusted	• Replace oil pump • Flush or replace cooler and flush lines and fittings • Repair or replace valve body or its internal components as necessary • Replace torque converter • Replace torque converter • Align exhaust system • Tune engine • Adjust throttle linkage

Transmission Fluid Indications

The appearance and odor of the transmission fluid can give valuable clues to the overall condition of the transmission. Always note the appearance of the fluid when you check the fluid level or change the fluid. Rub a small amount of fluid between your fingers to feel for grit and smell the fluid on the dipstick.

If the fluid appears:	It indicates:
Clear and red colored	• Normal operation
Discolored (extremely dark red or brownish) or smells burned	• Band or clutch pack failure, usually caused by an overheated transmission. Hauling very heavy loads with insufficient power or failure to change the fluid, often result in overheating. Do not confuse this appearance with newer fluids that have a darker red color and a strong odor (though not a burned odor).
Foamy or aerated (light in color and full of bubbles)	• The level is too high (gear train is churning oil) • An internal air leak (air is mixing with the fluid). Have the transmission checked professionally.
Solid residue in the fluid	• Defective bands, clutch pack or bearings. Bits of band material or metal abrasives are clinging to the dipstick. Have the transmission checked professionally.
Varnish coating on the dipstick	• The transmission fluid is overheating

TORQUE SPECIFICATIONS

Component	U.S.	Metric
	HM-282/5TM40 TRANSAXLE	
Back-up switch assembly-to-transaxle	24 ft. lbs.	33 Nm
Front transaxle strut-to-body bolt	40 ft. lbs.	54 Nm
Front transaxle strut-to-transaxle	50 ft. lbs.	68 Nm
Rear transaxle mount-to-body	23 ft. lbs.	30 Nm
Rear mount bracket-to-mount	38 ft. lbs.	52 Nm
Rear mount bracket-to-transaxle	40 ft. lbs.	54 Nm
Shift cable grommet-to-shroud	18 inch lbs.	2 Nm
Shift control-to-floor	18 ft. lbs.	24 Nm
Shift linkage retainer-to-transaxle case	17 ft. lbs.	23 Nm
Shift shaft-to-lever nut	61 ft. lbs.	83 Nm
Speedometer/vehicle speed sensor housing-to-transaxle	84 inch lbs.	9 Nm
Transaxle shift cable bracket-to-cables	18 ft. lbs.	25 Nm
Transaxle shift lever-to-cable stud	18 ft. lbs.	25 Nm
Transaxle-to-engine stud/bolt	55 ft. lbs.	75 Nm
Transaxle-to-engine nut	55 ft. lbs.	75 Nm
Transaxle-to engine stud	106 inch lbs.	12 Nm
Transaxle mount-to-transaxle	37 ft. lbs.	50 Nm

TORQUE SPECIFICATIONS

Component	U.S.	Metric
ISUZU TRANSAXLE		
Actuator cylinder support to transaxle	37 ft. lbs.	54 Nm
Back-up switch assembly-to-transaxle	24 ft. lbs.	33 Nm
Clutch housing cover-to-transaxle	115 inch lbs.	13 Nm
Front transaxle strut-to-body bolt	40 ft. lbs.	54 Nm
Front transaxle strut-to-transaxle	50 ft. lbs.	68 Nm
Rear transaxle mount-to-body	23 ft. lbs.	30 Nm
Rear mount bracket-to-mount	88 ft. lbs.	120 Nm
Rear mount bracket-to-transaxle	40 ft. lbs.	54 Nm
Shift cable grommet-to-shroud	18 inch lbs.	2 Nm
Shift control-to-floor	18 ft. lbs.	24 Nm
Shift control box-to-transaxle	13 ft. lbs.	17 Nm
Shift linkage retainer-to-transaxle case	17 ft. lbs.	23 Nm
Shift retainer-to-transaxle case	90 inch lbs.	10 Nm
Speedometer/vehicle speed sensor housing-to-transaxle	84 inch lbs.	9 Nm
Transaxle shift cable bracket-to-cables	19 ft. lbs.	27 Nm
Transaxle shift lever-to-cable stud	18 ft. lbs.	25 Nm
Transaxle-to-engine bolts and studs	55 ft. lbs.	75 Nm
DRIVE AXLE		
Ball joint-to-steering knuckle nut	41–50 ft. lbs.	55–65 Nm
Drive shaft nut	185 ft. lbs.	260 Nm
Intermediate drive shaft support bolt	35 ft. lbs.	47 Nm
Intermediate shaft retainer-to-support screws	106 inch lbs.	12 Nm
CLUTCH		
Upper clutch pedal bolt	44 inch lbs.	5 Nm
Lower clutch pedal bolt	26 ft. lbs.	35 Nm
Actuator cylinder bleed screw	17 ft. lbs.	2 Nm
Clutch release lever bolt	37 ft. lbs.	50 Nm
Clutch start switch nut	53 inch lbs.	6 Nm
Clutch master cylinder and clutch pedal bracket nut	16 ft. lbs.	21 Nm
Clutch actuator cylinder nut	16 ft. lbs.	21 Nm
Fluid reservoir bolt	80 inch lbs.	9 Nm
Clutch cover-to-flywheel bolt:		
2.0L engine	22 ft. lbs.	30 Nm
2.3L engine	15 ft. lbs. + 30°	20 Nm + 30°
2.5L engine	22 ft. lbs.	30 Nm
AUTOMATIC TRANSAXLE		
Cooler pipes at transaxle case	16 ft. lbs.	22 Nm
Cooler pipes at radiator	20 ft. lbs.	27 Nm
Converter shield	10 ft. lbs.	13 Nm
Flywheel-to-torque converter	46 ft. lbs.	62 Nm
Neutral start switch-to-case	22 ft. lbs.	30 Nm
Starter mounting bolts	32 ft. lbs.	43 Nm
Transaxle mount bolts	22 ft. lbs.	30 Nm
Transaxle-to-engine mount bolts	55 ft. lbs.	75 Nm
TV cable-to-case bolts	90 inch lbs.	10 Nm
Oil pan-to-case	133 inch lbs.	11 Nm

8

SUSPENSION AND STEERING

WHEELS

Front and Rear Wheels

REMOVAL & INSTALLATION

➧ SEE FIG. 1

1. Remove the wheel cover.
2. Loosen, but do not remove the lug nut.
3. Raise and safely support the vehicle so the tire is clear of the ground.
4. Remove the lug nuts.
5. Remove the wheel.

To install:

6. Install the wheel.
7. Install the lug nuts and tighten in a star pattern.
8. Lower the vehicle.
9. Tighten the lug nuts in a star pattern to 100 ft. lbs. (140 Nm).
10. Install the wheel cover.

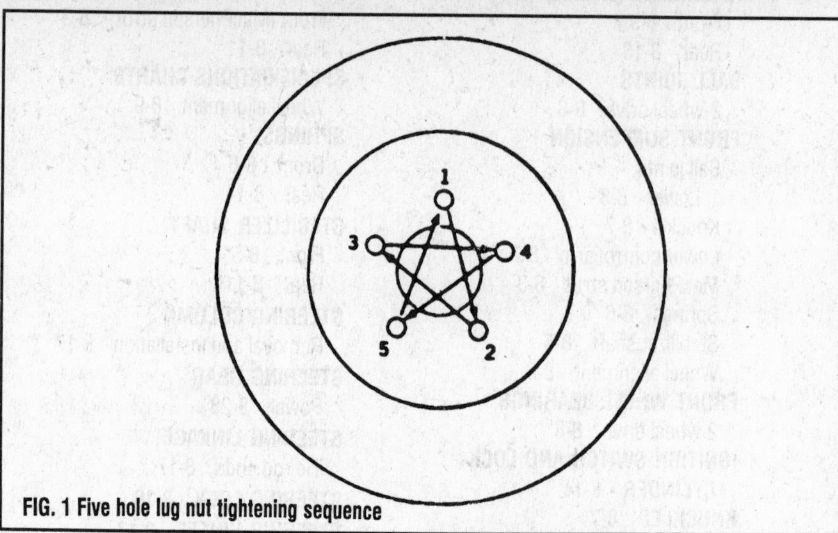

FIG. 1 Five hole lug nut tightening sequence

INSPECTION

1. Inspect the wheels for dents, excess corrosion and build-up of dried mud, especially on the inside surface of the wheel.
2. Inspect the tires for uneven wear, tread separation and cracks in the sidewalls due to dry rotting or curb damage.
3. Inspect the tire valve for leaking and proper sealing in the wheel assembly.
4. Take corrective action or replace as necessary.

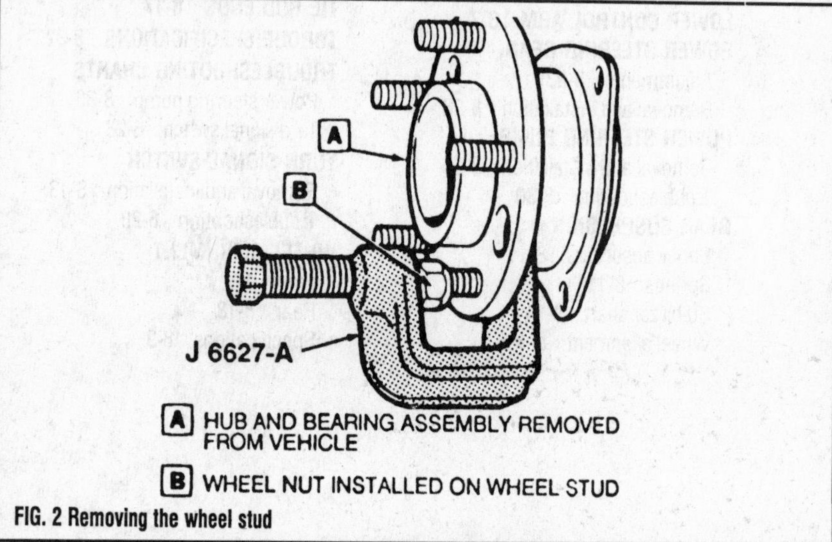

FIG. 2 Removing the wheel stud

Wheel Lug Studs

REPLACEMENT

➧ SEE FIGS. 2 AND 3

Front Wheels

1. Remove the tire and wheel assembly.
2. Remove the wheel stud using a wheel stud removal tool.

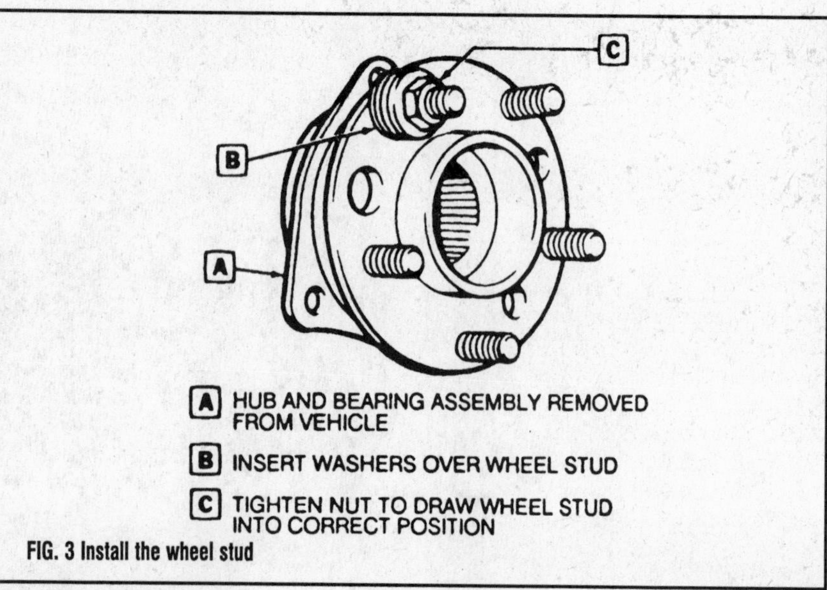

FIG. 3 Install the wheel stud

To install:

5. Insert the new stud from the rear of the hub.
6. Install 4 flat washers onto the stud.
7. Install the wheel nut with the flat side toward the washers.
8. Tighten the nut until the stud head is properly seated in the hub flange.
9. Remove the nut and washers.
10. Install the tire and wheel assembly.

Rear Wheels

1. Remove the tire and wheel assembly.
2. Remove the brake drum.
3. Remove the wheel stud using a wheel stud removal tool.

To install:

4. Insert the new stud from the rear of the hub.
5. Install 4 flat washers onto the stud.
6. Install the wheel nut with the flat side toward the washers.
7. Tighten the nut until the stud head is properly seated in the hub flange.
8. Remove the nut and washers.
9. Install the brake drum.
10. Install the tire and wheel assembly.

FRONT SUSPENSION

The front suspension on all N-Body models is a MacPherson strut design. This combination strut and shock absorber adapts to front wheel drive. The lower control arm pivots from the engine cradle, which has isolation mounts to the body and conventional rubber bushings for the lower control arm pivots. The upper end of the strut is isolated by a rubber mount which contains a nonserviceable bearing for wheel turning.

The lower end of the wheel steering knuckle pivots on a ball stud for wheel turning. The ball stud is retained in the lower control arm and the steering knuckle clamps to the stud portion.

All front suspension fasteners are an important attaching part in that it could affect the performance of vital parts and systems and/or could result in major repair expense. They must be replaced with one of the same part number or with an equivalent part if replacement becomes necessary. Do not use a replacement part of lesser quality or substitute design. Never attempt to heat, quench or straighten any front suspension part. If bent or damaged, the part should be replaced.

MacPherson Strut

REMOVAL & INSTALLATION

➧ SEE FIGS. 4–6

➡ **Before removing front suspension components, their positions should be marked so they may assembled correctly. Scribe the knuckle along the lower outboard strut radius (A), the strut flange on the inboard side along the curve of the knuckle (B) and make a chisel mark across the strut/knuckle interface (C). When reassembling, carefully match the marks to the components.**

1. Remove the three nuts attaching the top of the strut assembly to the body.
2. Raise the car and support it safely.
3. Place jackstands under the frame.
4. Lower the car slightly so that the weight rests on the jackstands and not on the control arms.
5. Remove the front tire.

CAUTION

Whenever working near the drive axles, take care to prevent the inner Tri-Pot joints from being overextended. Overextension of the joint could result in separation of internal components which could go undetected and result in failure of the joint.

6. Some vehicles may use a silicone (gray) boot on the inboard axle joint. Use boot protector J-33162 or equivalent on these boots. All other boots are made from a thermoplastic material (black) and do not require the use of a boot seal protector.
7. Disconnect the brake line bracket from the strut assembly.
8. Remove the strut to steering knuckle bolts.
9. Remove the strut assembly from the vehicle. Care should be taken to avoid chipping or cracking the spring coating when handling the front suspension coil spring assembly.
10. Installation is the reverse of removal.

OVERHAUL

➧ SEE FIG. 7

Lower Ball Joint

INSPECTION

1. Raise and safely support the vehicle on jackstands. Allow the suspension to hang freely.
2. Grasp the tire at the top and bottom and move the top of the tire in and out.
3. Observe for any horizontal movement of the steering knuckle relative to the front lower control arm. If any movement is detected, replace the ball joint.
4. If the ball stud is disconnected from the steering knuckle and any looseness is detected, or if the ball stud can be twisted in its socket using finger pressure, replace the ball joint.

REMOVAL & INSTALLATION

➧ SEE FIG. 8

1. Raise and safely support the vehicle.
2. Place jackstands under the frame.
3. Lower the car slightly so the weight rests on the jackstands and not the control arm.
4. Remove the front tire.
5. If a silicone (gray) boot is used on the inboard axle joint, install boot seal protector J-33162 or equivalent. If a thermoplastic (black) boot is used, no protector is necessary.
6. Remove the cotter pin from the ball joint castellated nut.

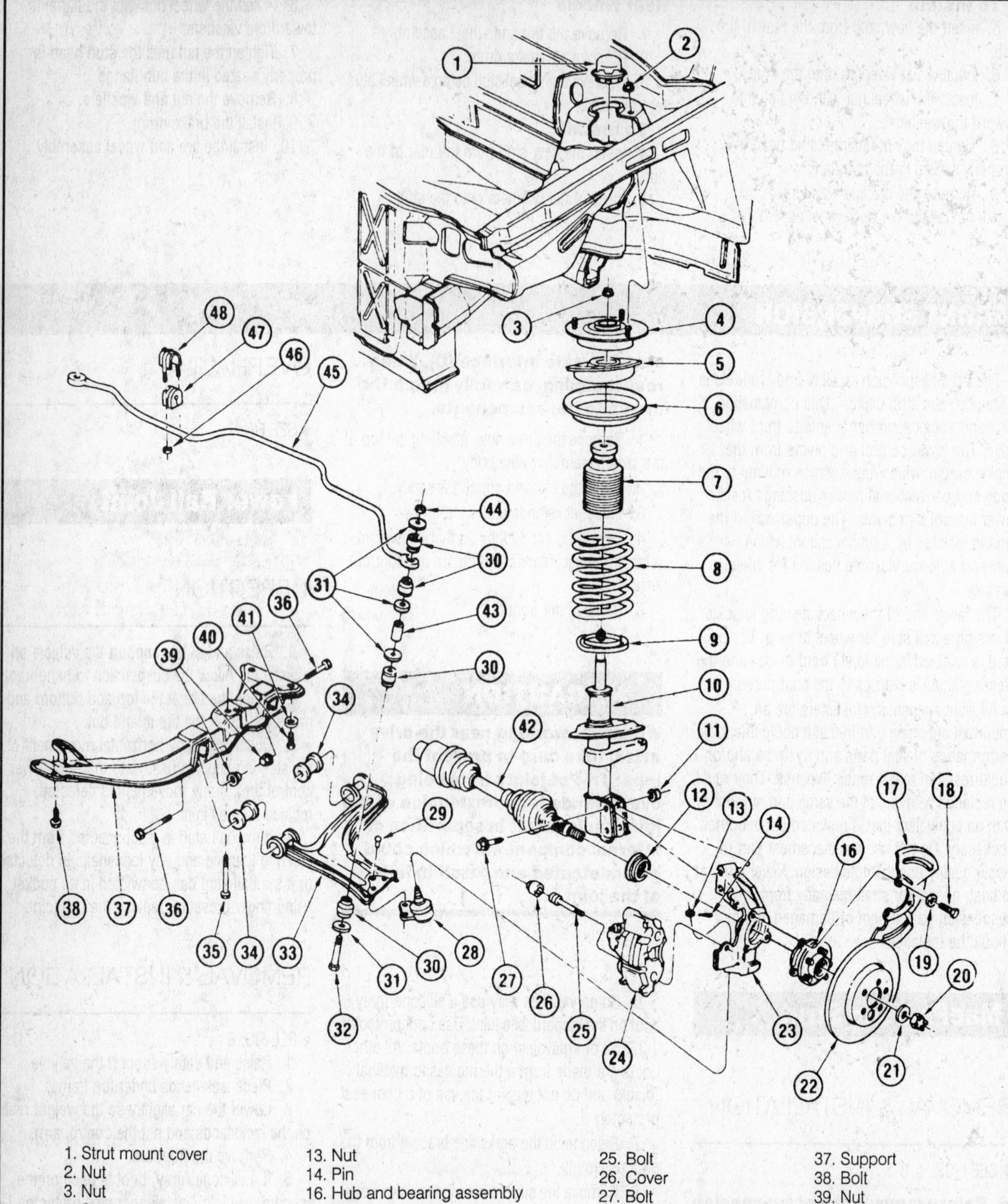

1. Strut mount cover
2. Nut
3. Nut
4. Strut mount
5. Spring seat
6. Spring upper insulator
7. Bumper
8. Spring
9. Spring lower insulator
10. Strut
11. Nut
12. Wheel bearing seal
13. Nut
14. Pin
16. Hub and bearing assembly
17. Disc brake splash shield
18. Bolt
19. Washer
20. Drive shaft nut
21. Washer
22. Rotor
23. Steering knuckle
24. Disc brake caliper
25. Bolt
26. Cover
27. Bolt
28. Lower ball joint
29. Rivet
30. Insulator
31. Washer
32. Bolt
33. Lower control arm
34. Bushing
35. Bolt
36. Bolt
37. Support
38. Bolt
39. Nut
40. Bolt
41. Washer
42. Drive shaft
43. Spacer
44. Nut
45. Stabilizer shaft
46. Nut
47. Insulator
48. Clamp

FIG. 4 Front suspension assembly

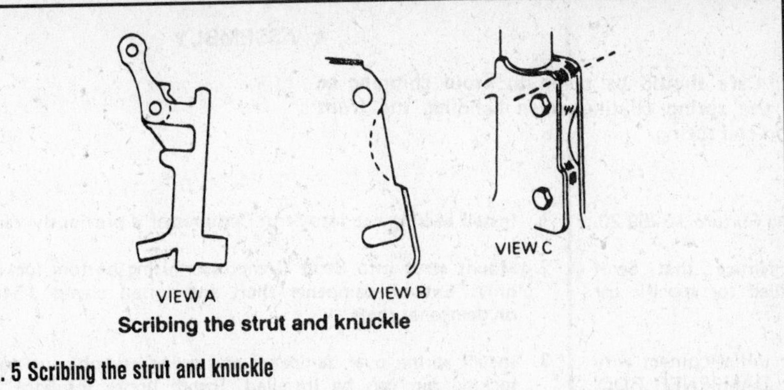

FIG. 5 Scribing the strut and knuckle

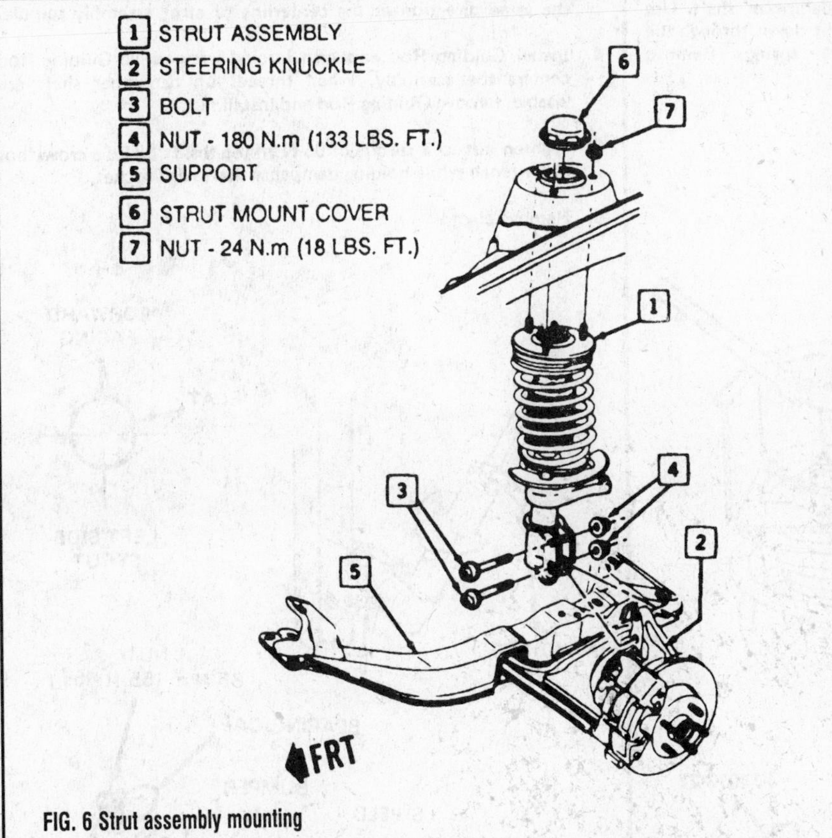

FIG. 6 Strut assembly mounting

7. Remove the castellated nut and disconnect the ball joint from the steering knuckle using ball joint separator J-34505 or equivalent.

8. Drill out the three rivets retaining the ball joint.

➡ Be careful not to damage the drive axle boot when drilling out the ball joint rivets.

9. Loosen the stabilizer shaft bushing assembly nut.

10. Remove the ball joint from the control arm.

To install:

11. Install the ball joint to the control arm.

12. Tighten the stabilizer shaft bushing assembly nut to 15 ft. lbs. (20 Nm).

13. Install the 3 ball joint attaching bolts and tighten to 50 ft. lbs. (68 Nm).

14. Connect the ball joint to the steering knuckle. Install the castellated nut and tighten to 41–50 ft. lbs. (55–65 Nm).

15. Install the cotter pin to the ball joint castellated nut.

16. If installed, remove the boot protector.

17. Install the front tire.

18. Raise the vehicle and remove the jackstands.

19. Lower the vehicle.

➡ The front end alignment should be checked and adjusted whenever the strut assemblies are removed.

Stabilizer Shaft and Bushings

REMOVAL & INSTALLATION

➧ SEE FIG. 9

1. Raise and safely support the vehicle with jackstands, allowing the front suspension to hang freely.

2. Remove the front tire.

3. Disconnect the stabilizer shaft from the control arms.

4. Disconnect the stabilizer shaft from the suspension support assemblies.

5. Loosen the front bolts and remove the rear and center bolts from the support assemblies to lower them enough to remove the stabilizer shaft.

6. Remove the stabilizer shaft and bushings.

To install:

7. Install the stabilizer shaft with bushings and insulators.

8. Raise the front suspension assemblies and install the center and rear bolts. Loosely assembly all components while ensuring that the stabilizer shaft is centered side-to-side.

9. Install the shaft to front suspension support assemblies and loosely install the insulators and clamps.

10. Install the stabilizer shaft to control arms and loosely install the bolts.

11. Tighten the suspension support bolts as follows and in sequence:

- First—center bolts to 66 ft. lbs. (90 Nm)
- Second—front bolts to 65 ft. lbs. (88 Nm)
- Third—rear bolts to 65 ft. lbs. (88 Nm)
- Stabilizer shaft to support assembly nuts to 16 ft. lbs. (22 Nm)
- Stabilizer shaft to control arm nuts to 13 ft. lbs. (17 Nm).

12. Install the wheels.

13. Lower the vehicle.

NOTICE: Care should be taken to avoid chipping or cracking the spring coating when handling the front suspension coil spring.

DISASSEMBLY

1. Mount Strut Compressor J-34013 in Holding Fixture J-3289-20.
2. Mount strut into Strut Compressor. Notice that Strut Compressor has strut mounting holes drilled for specific car lines.
3. Compress strut approx. ½ its height after initial contact with top cap. NEVER BOTTOM SPRING OR DAMPENER ROD.
4. Remove the nut from the strut dampener shaft and place the J-34013-27 Guiding Rod on top of the dampener shaft. Use this rod to guide the dampener shaft straight down through the bearing cap while decompressing the spring. Remove components.
5. Perform services as required.

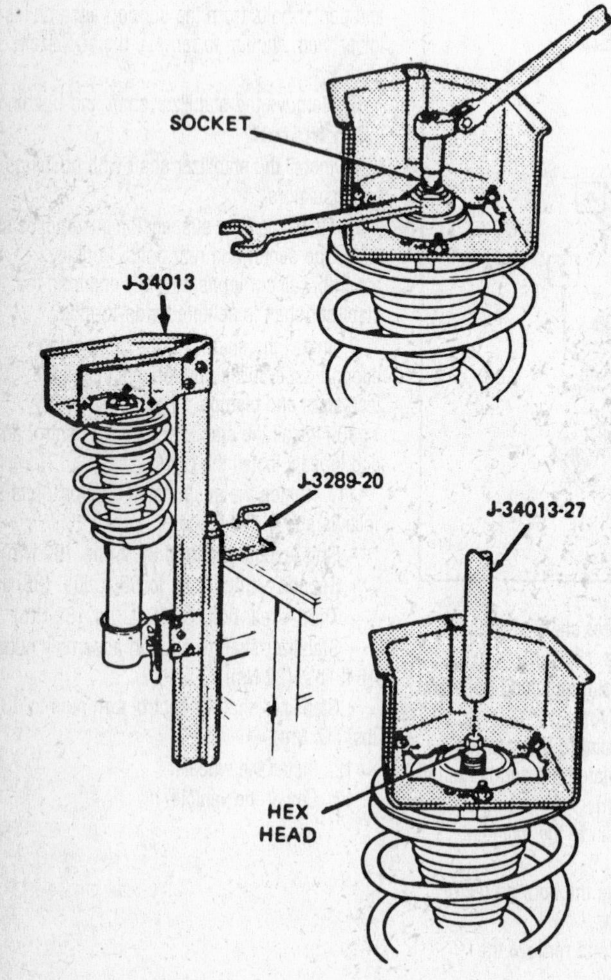

ASSEMBLY

1. Install bearing cap into Strut Compressor if previously removed.
2. Mount strut into Strut Compressor using bottom locking pin only. Extend dampener shaft and install clamp J-34013-20 on dampener shaft.
3. Install spring over dampener and swing assembly up so upper locking pin can be installed. Install upper insulator, shield, bumper, and upper spring seat. Be sure flat on upper spring seat is facing in proper direction. The spring seat flat should be facing the same direction as the centerline of strut assembly spindle.
4. Install Guiding Rod and turn forcing screw while Guiding Rod centers the assembly. When threads on dampener shaft are visable, remove Guiding Rod and install nut.
5. Tighten nut to a torque of 85 N•m (65 lbs. ft.). Use a crowsfoot line wrench while holding dampener shaft with socket.
6. Remove clamp.

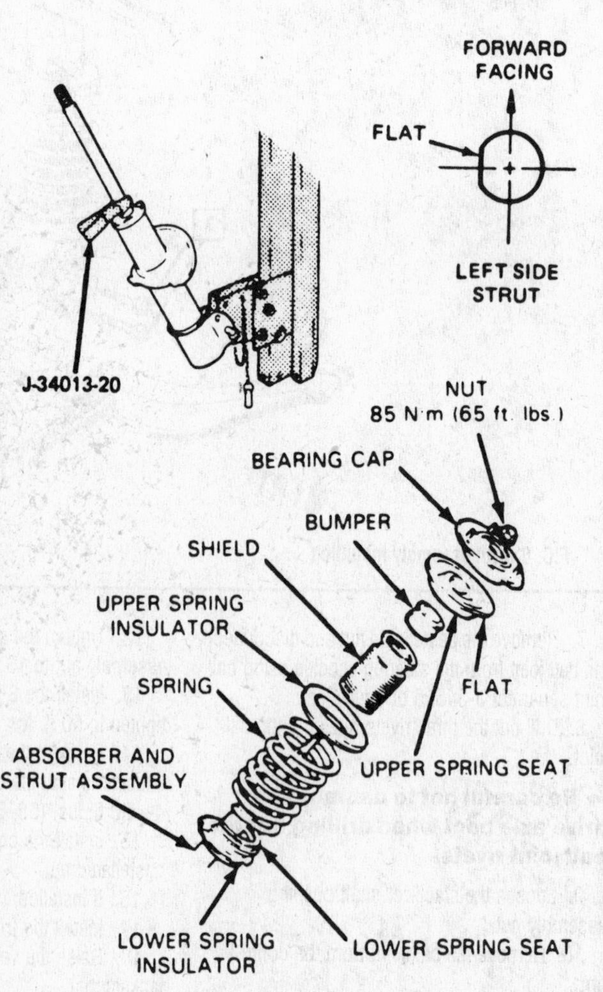

FIG. 7 Strut assembly overhaul

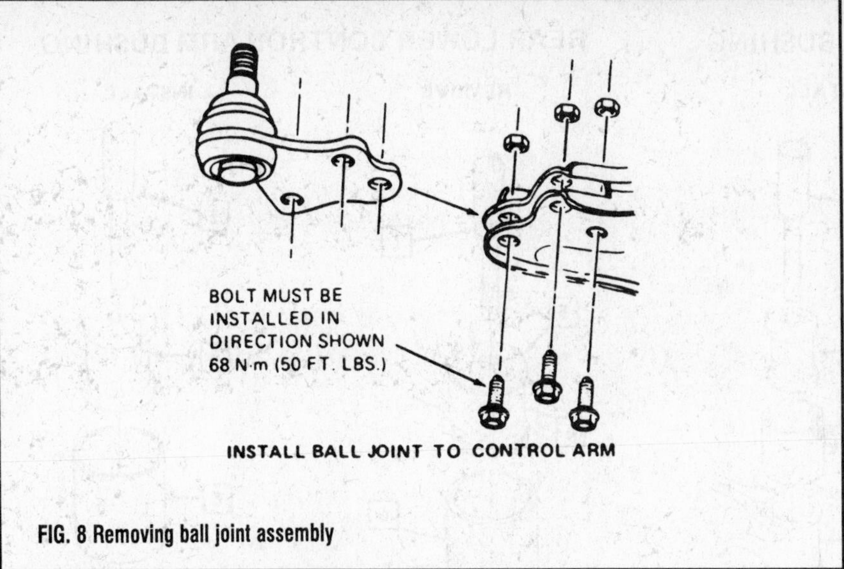

FIG. 8 Removing ball joint assembly

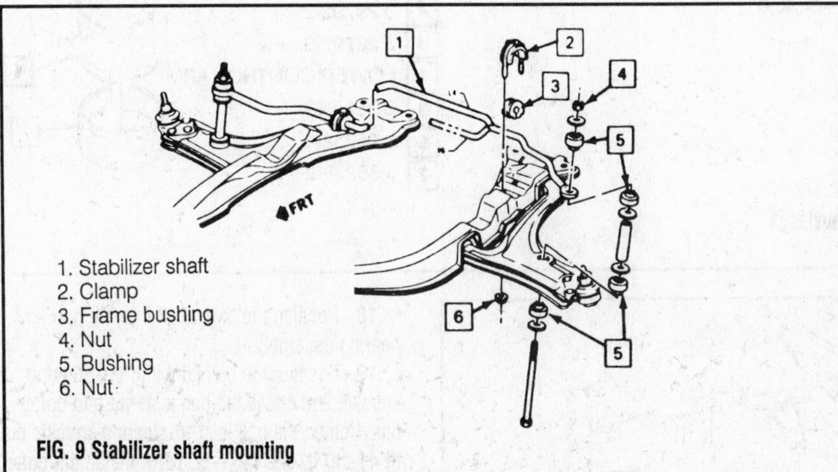

FIG. 9 Stabilizer shaft mounting

Lower Control Arm

REMOVAL & INSTALLATION

➧ SEE FIG. 10

1. Raise and safely support the vehicle on jackstands. Place the jackstands under the frame so that the suspension hangs freely.
2. Remove the tire.
3. Disconnect the stabilizer shaft from the control arm and/or support assembly.
4. Disconnect the ball joint from the steering knuckle using separator tool J-29330 or equivalent. See "Ball Joint Removal."
5. To remove the support assembly with the control arm attached, remove the bolts mounting the support assembly to the car. To remove the control arm only, remove the control arm to support assembly bolts.
6. Installation is the reverse of the removal procedure. Tighten the ball joint castellated nut to 45 ft.lbs. (60 Nm).
7. If the support assembly was removed, tighten the rear bolts first to 65 ft.lbs. (88 Nm); the center bolts second to 66 ft.lb. (90 Nm); and the front bolts last to 65 ft.lb. (88 Nm). Tighten the control arm pivot bolts to 60 ft.lb. (85 Nm) with the weight of the car on the control arm.

CONTROL ARM BUSHING REPLACEMENT

➧ SEE FIG. 11

1. Remove the lower control arm.
2. Install bushing removal tool.
3. Coat the threads of the tool with extreme pressure lubricant.
4. Remove the lower control arm bushings.

To install:

5. Install the bushing installation tools.
6. Coat the outer case of the bushing with a light coating of a suitable lubricant.
7. Install the lower control arm bushings.
8. Install the lower control arm.

Steering Knuckle

REMOVAL & INSTALLATION

1. Raise and safely support the vehicle.
2. Remove the front wheels.

➡ When drive axles are disconnected, care must be taken to avoid over-extending Tri-pot joints which could result in separation of internal joint components and possible joint failure. Also, the use of CV-joint boot protectors is recommended.

3. Install outer boot protector.
4. Insert a drift punch through the rotor cooling vanes to lock the rotor in place and remove the hub nut. Clean the drive axle threads of all dirt and grease.
5. Remove the drive shaft nut and washer.
6. Disengage the axle from the hub and bearing.
7. Disconnect the ball joint from the steering knuckle.
8. Move the axle shaft inward.
9. Remove the caliper bolts and caliper. Support the caliper using a length of wire. Do not allow the caliper to hang by the brake hose unsupported.
10. Remove the rotor.
11. Remove the hub and bearing assembly bolts. Remove the hub and bearing assembly from the knuckle.
12. Remove the strut-to-steering knuckle bolts. Remove the steering knuckle.

To install:

13. Install the steering knuckle into the strut and install the steering knuckle-to-strut assembly bolts. Tighten to 133 ft. lbs. (180 Nm).
14. Install the hub and assembly onto the knuckle and install the hub and bearing assembly bolts. Tighten to 70 ft. lbs. (95 Nm).
15. Install a new hub and bearing seal.
16. Install the rotor.
17. Install the caliper and caliper bolts. Tighten to 38 ft. lbs. (51 Nm).

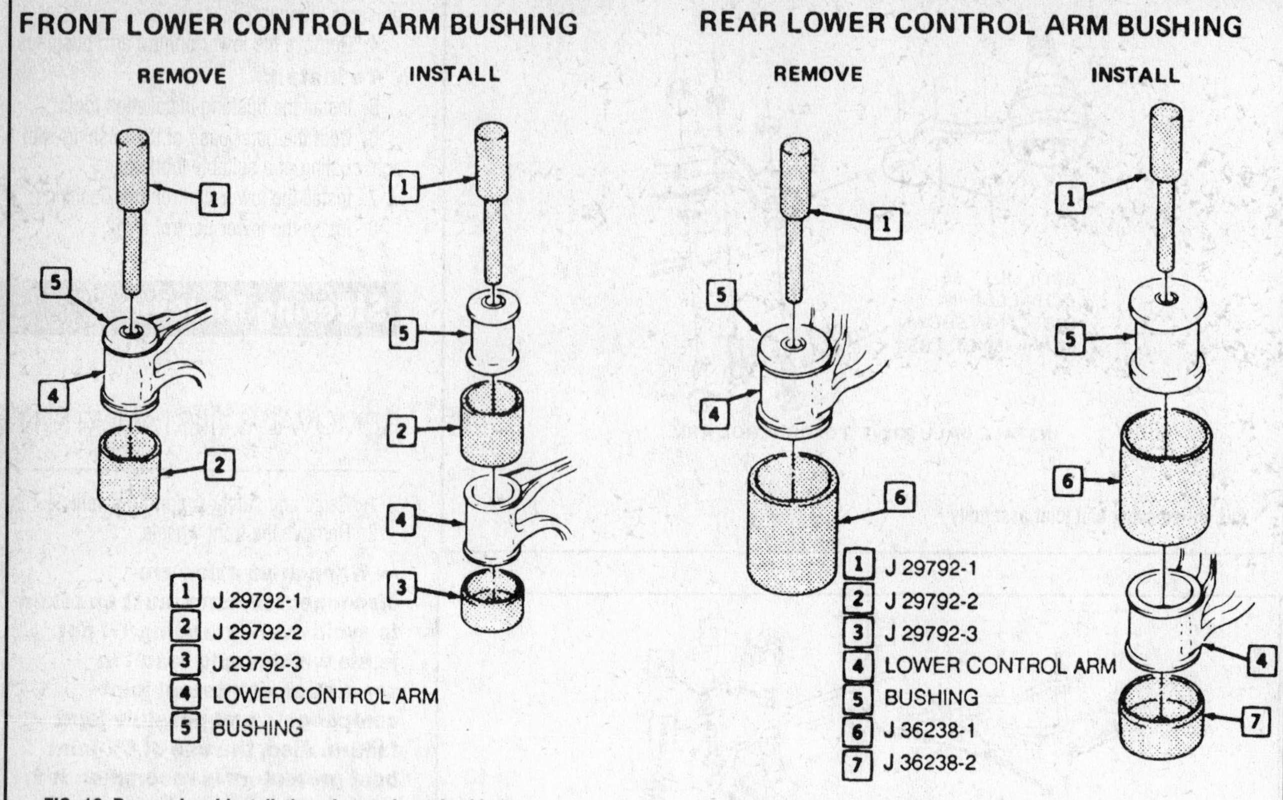

FRONT LOWER CONTROL ARM BUSHING

REMOVE INSTALL

1 J 29792-1
2 J 29792-2
3 J 29792-3
4 LOWER CONTROL ARM
5 BUSHING

REAR LOWER CONTROL ARM BUSHING

REMOVE INSTALL

1 J 29792-1
2 J 29792-2
3 J 29792-3
4 LOWER CONTROL ARM
5 BUSHING
6 J 36238-1
7 J 36238-2

FIG. 10 Removal and installation of control arm bushings

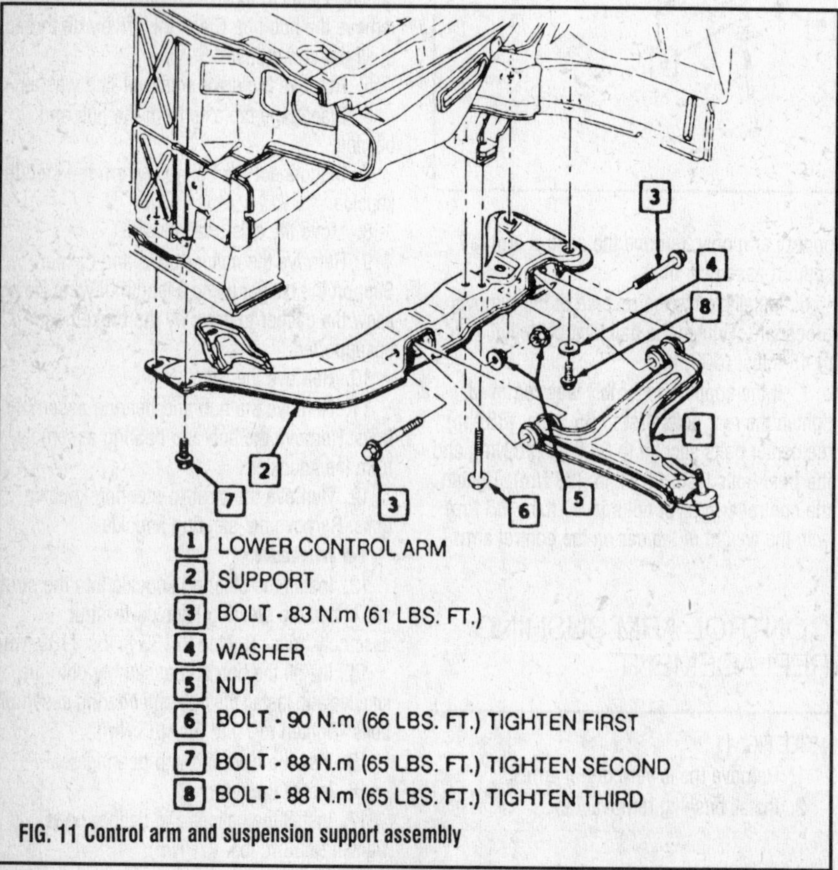

FIG. 11 Control arm and suspension support assembly

18. Position the axle shaft into the hub and bearing assembly.
19. Position the ball joint into the steering knuckle and install the ball joint nut and cotter pin. Tighten the ball joint-to-steering knuckle nut to 41–50 ft. lbs. (55–65 Nm). Install the cotter pin.
20. Insert the drift through the rotor.
21. Install the washer and new drive shaft nut loosely on the drive shaft. Tighten the nut as much as possible until the axle starts to turn.
22. Remove the boot protectors.
23. Install the wheels.
24. Lower the vehicle.
25. Tighten the drive shaft nut, using a torque wrench to 180 ft. lbs. (260 Nm).

Front Hub and Bearing Assembly

REMOVAL & INSTALLATION

➧ SEE FIG. 12

➡ This procedure requires the use of a number of special tools.

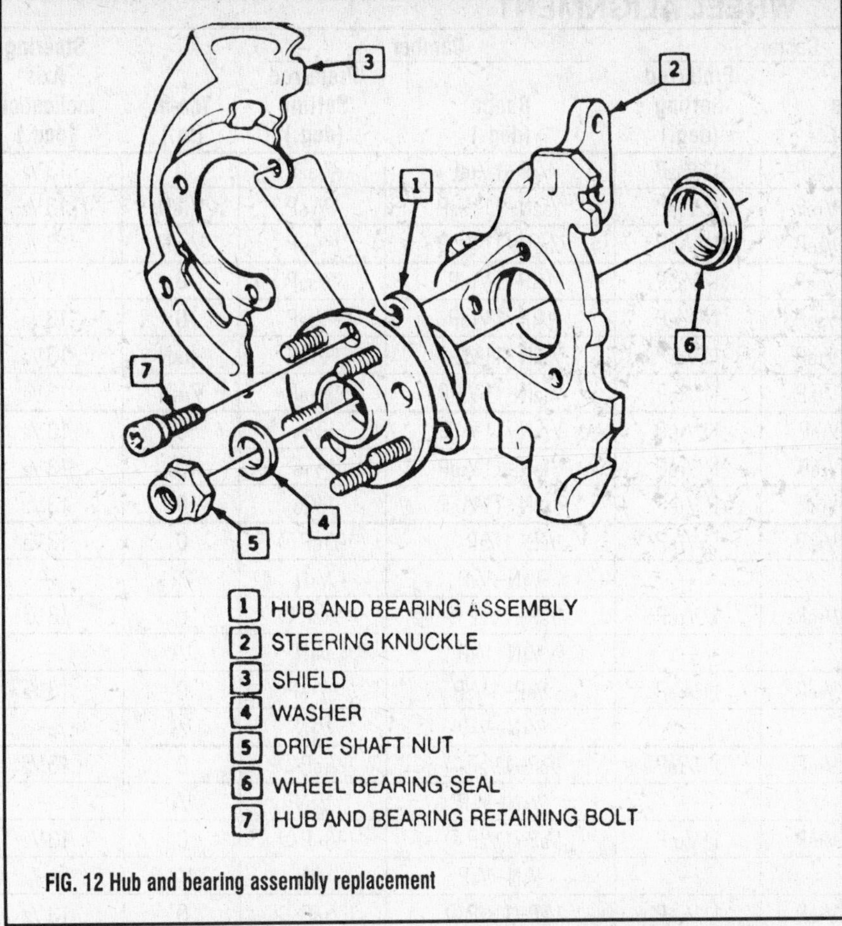

FIG. 12 Hub and bearing assembly replacement

1. Raise and safely support the vehicle with jackstands. Place the jackstands under the frame so that the front suspension hangs freely.
2. Remove the front tire.
3. If a silicone (gray) boot is used on the inboard axle joint, place boot seal protector J-33162 or equivalent. If a thermoplastic (black) boot is used, no seal protector is necessary.
4. Insert a drift punch through the rotor cooling vanes to lock the rotor in place and remove the hub nut. Clean the drive axle threads of all dirt and grease.
5. Remove the brake caliper mounting bolts and remove the caliper from the spindle assembly. Support the caliper with string or wire. Do not allow it to hang by the brake hose.
6. Remove the brake rotor.
7. Attach tool J-28733 or equivalent and separate the hub and drive axle.
8. Remove the three hub and bearing retaining bolts, shield, hub and bearing assembly and O-ring.

➡ **The hub and bearing are replaced as an assembly**

9. Using a punch, tap the seal toward the engine. When the seal is removed from the steering knuckle, cut it off the drive axle using wire cutters. The factory seal is installed from the engine side of the steering knuckle, but the service replacement is installed from the wheel side of the steering knuckle.
10. Install the new hub and bearing seal in the steering knuckle using a suitable hub seal installer tool.
11. The remainder of the installation is in reverse order of removal. Lubricate the hub and bearing seal with grease and install a new O-ring around the hub and bearing assembly. Tighten the hub and bearing bolts to 70 ft.lbs. (95 Nm). Tighten the hub nut to 180 ft.lb. (260 Nm).

Front End Alignment

Front alignment refers to the angular relationship between the front wheels, the front suspension attaching parts and the ground. Camber is the tilting of the front wheels from the vertical when viewed from the front of the car. When the wheels tilt outward at the top, the camber is said to be positive (+); when the wheels tilt inward at the top, the camber is said to be negative (–). The amount of tilt is measured in degrees from the vertical and this measurement is called camber angle.

Toe-in is the turning in of the front wheels. The actual amount of toe-in is normally only a fraction of one degree. The purpose of the toe-in specification is to insure parallel rolling of the front wheels. Excessive toe-in or toe-out may increase tire wear. Toe-in also serves to offset the small deflections of the wheel support system which occur when the car is rolling forward. In other words, even when the wheels are set to toe-in slightly when the car is standing still, they tend to roll parallel on the road when the car is moving.

Toe setting is the only adjustment normally required. However, in special circumstances such as damage due to road hazard, collision, etc., camber adjustment may be required. To perform a camber adjustment, the bottom hole in the strut mounting must be slotted. Caster is not adjustable.

WHEEL ALIGNMENT

Year	Model	Caster Range (deg.)	Caster Preferred Setting (deg.)	Camber Range (deg.)	Camber Preferred Setting (deg.)	Toe-in (in.)	Steering Axis Inclination (deg.)
1985	Somerset	1P–3P	2P	1/2N–1/2P	0	0	NA
	Calais	11/16P–2 11/16P	1 11/16P	7/32N–1 13/32P	13/16P	1/16N	13 1/2
	Grand Am	11/16P–2 11/16P	1 11/16P	7/32N–1 13/32P	13/16P	1/16N	13 1/2

WHEEL ALIGNMENT

			Caster		Camber			Steering Axis
Year	Model		Range (deg.)	Preferred Setting (deg.)	Range (deg.)	Preferred Setting (deg.)	Toe-in (in.)	Inclination (deg.)
1986	Somerset		$\frac{23}{34}$P–$2\frac{23}{32}$P	$1\frac{23}{32}$P	$\frac{1}{4}$P–$1\frac{7}{16}$P	$\frac{27}{32}$P	0	$13\frac{1}{2}$
	Calais		$\frac{11}{16}$P–$2\frac{11}{16}$P	$1\frac{11}{16}$P	$\frac{7}{32}$N–$1\frac{13}{32}$P	$\frac{13}{16}$P	$\frac{1}{16}$N	$13\frac{1}{2}$
	Grand Am		$\frac{11}{16}$P–$2\frac{11}{16}$P	$1\frac{11}{16}$P	$\frac{7}{32}$N–$1\frac{13}{32}$P	$\frac{13}{16}$P	$\frac{1}{16}$N	$13\frac{1}{2}$
1987	Skylark		$\frac{23}{34}$P–$2\frac{23}{32}$P	$1\frac{23}{32}$P	$\frac{1}{4}$P–$1\frac{7}{16}$P	$\frac{27}{32}$P	0	$13\frac{1}{2}$
	Somerset		$\frac{23}{34}$P–$2\frac{23}{32}$P	$1\frac{23}{32}$P	$\frac{1}{4}$P–$1\frac{7}{16}$P	$\frac{27}{32}$P	0	$13\frac{1}{2}$
	Calais		$\frac{11}{16}$P–$2\frac{11}{16}$P	$1\frac{11}{16}$P	$\frac{7}{32}$N–$1\frac{13}{32}$P	$\frac{13}{16}$P	$\frac{1}{16}$N	$13\frac{1}{2}$
	Grand Am		$\frac{11}{16}$P–$2\frac{11}{16}$P	$1\frac{11}{16}$P	$\frac{7}{32}$N–$1\frac{13}{32}$P	$\frac{13}{16}$P	$\frac{1}{16}$N	$13\frac{1}{2}$
1988	Skylark		$\frac{13}{16}$N–$4\frac{3}{16}$P	$1\frac{11}{16}$P	$\frac{3}{16}$N–$1\frac{13}{16}$P	$\frac{13}{16}$	0	$13\frac{1}{2}$
	Calais		$\frac{13}{16}$N–$4\frac{3}{16}$P	$1\frac{11}{16}$P	$\frac{3}{16}$N–$1\frac{13}{16}$P	$\frac{13}{16}$	0	$13\frac{1}{2}$
	Grand Am		$\frac{13}{16}$N–$4\frac{3}{16}$P	$1\frac{11}{16}$P	$\frac{3}{16}$N–$1\frac{13}{16}$P	$\frac{13}{16}$	0	$13\frac{1}{2}$
1989	Calais	front	$\frac{11}{16}$P–$2\frac{11}{16}$P	$1\frac{11}{16}$P	$\frac{1}{8}$P–$1\frac{1}{2}$P ②	$\frac{13}{16}$P ①	0	$13\frac{1}{2}$
		rear	—	—	$\frac{3}{4}$N–$\frac{1}{4}$P	$\frac{1}{4}$N	$\frac{1}{4}$	—
	Grand Am	front	$\frac{11}{16}$P–$2\frac{11}{16}$P	$1\frac{11}{16}$P	$\frac{1}{8}$P–$1\frac{1}{2}$P ②	$\frac{13}{16}$P ①	0	$13\frac{1}{2}$
		rear	—	—	$\frac{3}{4}$N–$\frac{1}{4}$P	$\frac{1}{4}$N	$\frac{1}{4}$	—
	Skylark	front	$\frac{11}{16}$P–$2\frac{11}{16}$P	$1\frac{11}{16}$P	$\frac{1}{8}$P–$1\frac{1}{2}$P	$\frac{13}{16}$P	0	$13\frac{1}{2}$
		rear	—	—	$\frac{3}{4}$N–$\frac{1}{4}$P	$\frac{1}{4}$N	$\frac{1}{4}$	—
1990	Calais	front	$\frac{11}{16}$P–$2\frac{11}{16}$P	$1\frac{11}{16}$P	$\frac{1}{8}$P–$1\frac{1}{2}$P ②	$\frac{13}{16}$P ①	0	$13\frac{1}{2}$
		rear	—	—	$\frac{3}{4}$N–$\frac{1}{4}$P	$\frac{1}{4}$N	$\frac{1}{4}$	—
	Grand Am	front	$\frac{11}{16}$P–$2\frac{11}{16}$P	$1\frac{11}{16}$P	$\frac{1}{8}$P–$1\frac{1}{2}$P ②	$\frac{13}{16}$P ①	0	$13\frac{1}{2}$
		rear	—	—	$\frac{3}{4}$N–$\frac{1}{4}$P	$\frac{1}{4}$N	$\frac{1}{4}$	—
	Skylark	front	$\frac{11}{16}$P–$2\frac{11}{16}$P	$1\frac{11}{16}$P	$\frac{1}{8}$P–$1\frac{1}{2}$P ②	$\frac{13}{16}$P ①	0	$13\frac{1}{2}$
		rear	—	—	$\frac{3}{4}$N–$\frac{1}{4}$P	$\frac{1}{4}$N	$\frac{1}{4}$	—
1991	Calais	front	$\frac{11}{16}$P–$2\frac{11}{16}$P	$1\frac{11}{16}$P	$\frac{11}{16}$N–$1\frac{1}{16}$P	0	0	$13\frac{1}{2}$
		rear	—	—	$\frac{13}{16}$N–$\frac{5}{16}$P	$\frac{1}{4}$N	$\frac{1}{8}$	—
	Grand Am	front	$\frac{11}{16}$P–$2\frac{11}{16}$P	$1\frac{11}{16}$P	$\frac{1}{16}$N–$\frac{11}{16}$P	0	0	$13\frac{1}{2}$
		rear	—	—	$\frac{13}{16}$N–$\frac{5}{16}$P	$\frac{1}{4}$N	$\frac{1}{8}$	—
	Skylark	front	$\frac{11}{16}$P–$2\frac{11}{16}$P	$1\frac{11}{16}$P	$\frac{11}{16}$N–$1\frac{1}{16}$P	0	0	$13\frac{1}{2}$
		rear	—	—	$\frac{3}{4}$N–$\frac{1}{4}$P	$\frac{1}{4}$N	$\frac{1}{8}$	—
1992	Achieva	front	$\frac{11}{16}$P–$2\frac{11}{16}$P	$1\frac{11}{16}$P	$\frac{11}{16}$N–$1\frac{1}{16}$P	0	0	—
		rear	—	—	$\frac{13}{16}$N–$\frac{5}{16}$P	$\frac{1}{4}$N	$\frac{1}{8}$	—
	Grand Am	front	$\frac{11}{16}$P–$2\frac{11}{16}$P	$1\frac{11}{16}$P	$\frac{11}{16}$N–$1\frac{1}{16}$P	0	0	—
		rear	—	—	$\frac{13}{16}$N–$\frac{5}{16}$P	$\frac{1}{4}$N	$\frac{1}{8}$	—
	Skylark	front	$\frac{11}{16}$P–$2\frac{11}{16}$P	$1\frac{11}{16}$P	$\frac{11}{16}$N–$1\frac{1}{16}$P	0	0	$13\frac{1}{2}$
		rear	—	—	$\frac{3}{4}$N–$\frac{1}{2}$P	$\frac{1}{4}$N	$\frac{1}{8}$	—

N—Negative
P—Positive
① with 16 in. wheels: 0
② with 16 in. wheels: $\frac{11}{16}$N–$1\frac{1}{16}$P

REAR SUSPENSION

Coil Springs and Insulators

REMOVAL & INSTALLATION

➧ SEE FIG. 13

❊❊ CAUTION

The coil springs are under tension. To avoid personal injury, support the vehicle with jackstands under the body and allow the rear suspension to hang freely. Then, support the rear axle assembly with a floor jack. When the axle bolts have been removed, lower the jack to relax the spring tension

1. Raise and safely support the vehicle. Remove the rear wheels.
2. Using the proper equipment, support the weight of the rear axle. Disconnect the brake lines from the rear axle.
3. Remove the bolts that attach the shock to the lower mounting bracket.
4. Lower the axle and remove the coil spring from the vehicle.

To install:

➡ Prior to installing the coil springs, install the insulators in their seats using an adhesive to hold them in place.

5. Install the springs and insulators in their seats and raise the axle assembly into position. Ensure the end of the upper coil on the spring is positioned in the spring seat and within $^{9}/_{16}$ in. (15 mm) of the spring stop.
6. Connect the shock absorbers to the rear axle, but do not tighten the bolts to specification. The final tightening must take place with the vehicle at the proper trim height with the wheels on the ground.
7. Connect the brake lines to the body. Tighten the brake line bracket screws to 8 ft. lbs. (11 Nm).
8. Install the rear wheels.
9. Remove the floor jack and jackstands.
10. Lower the vehicle.
11. With all 4 wheels on the ground, tighten the rear axle attaching bolts to 35 ft. lbs. (47 Nm)

Shock Absorber

REMOVAL & INSTALLATION

➧ SEE FIG. 13

1. Disconnect the negative battery cable.
2. Open the deck lid and remove the trim cover.
3. Remove the upper shock attaching nut. Remove 1 shock at a time if removing both.
4. Raise and safely support the vehicle.
5. Remove the lower mounting bolt.
6. Remove the shock from the vehicle.

To install:

7. Connect the shock absorbers at the lower attachment and install the attaching bolt.
8. Lower the vehicle enough to guide the shock absorber upper stud through the body opening and install the upper shock absorber attaching nut loosely. Tighten the lower shock absorber mounting bolt to 35 ft. lbs. (47 Nm).
9. Remove the axle support and lower the vehicle. Tighten the shock absorber upper nut to 21 ft. lbs. (29 Nm).
10. Replace the rear trim cover.

Control Arm Bushing

REMOVAL & INSTALLATION

➧ SEE FIG. 14

1. Raise and safely support the vehicle.
2. Remove the rear wheels.
3. Replace 1 bushing at a time. If the right side bushing is being replaced, disconnect the brake lines from the body. If the left busing is being removed, disconnect the brake line bracket from the body and parking brake cable from the hook guide on the body.
4. Remove the nut, bolt and washer from the control arm and bracket attachment and rotate the control arm downward.
5. Remove the bushing by performing the following:
   a. Install tool J-29376-1 receiver on the control arm over the bushing and tighten the attaching nuts until the tool is securely in place.
   b. Install tool J-21474-19 bolt through plate J-29376-7 and install into J-29376-1 receiver.
   c. Place tool J-29376-6 remover into position on the bushing and install nut J-21474-18 onto J-21474-19 bolt.
   d. Remove the bushing from the control arm by turning the bolt.

To install:

6. Install the bushing by performing the following:
   a. Install tool J-29376-1 receiver onto the control arm
   b. Install tool J-21474-19 bolt through plate J-29376-7 and install into J-29376-1 receiver.
   c. Install bushing onto bolt and position into housing. Align bushing installer arrow with the arrow onto the receiver for proper indexing of the bushing.
   d. Install nut J-21474-18 onto bolt J-21474-19.
   e. Press the bushing into the control arm by turning the bolt. When the bushing is in proper position, the end flange will be flush against the face of the control arm.
7. Raise the control arm into position and install the bolt, washer and nut. Do not tighten to specification at this time.
8. Connect the brake line bracket to the frame. Tighten to 8 ft. lbs. (11 Nm).
9. If the left side was disconnected, reconnect the brake cables to the bracket and reinstall the brake cable to the hook. Adjust the parking brake cable as necessary.
10. Install the rear wheels.
11. Lower the vehicle.
12. With the vehicle at proper trim height, tighten the control arm bushing bolts to 68 ft. lbs. (93 Nm).

Stabilizer Bar

REMOVAL & INSTALLATION

➧ SEE FIG. 13

1. Raise the vehicle and support it safely with jackstands.

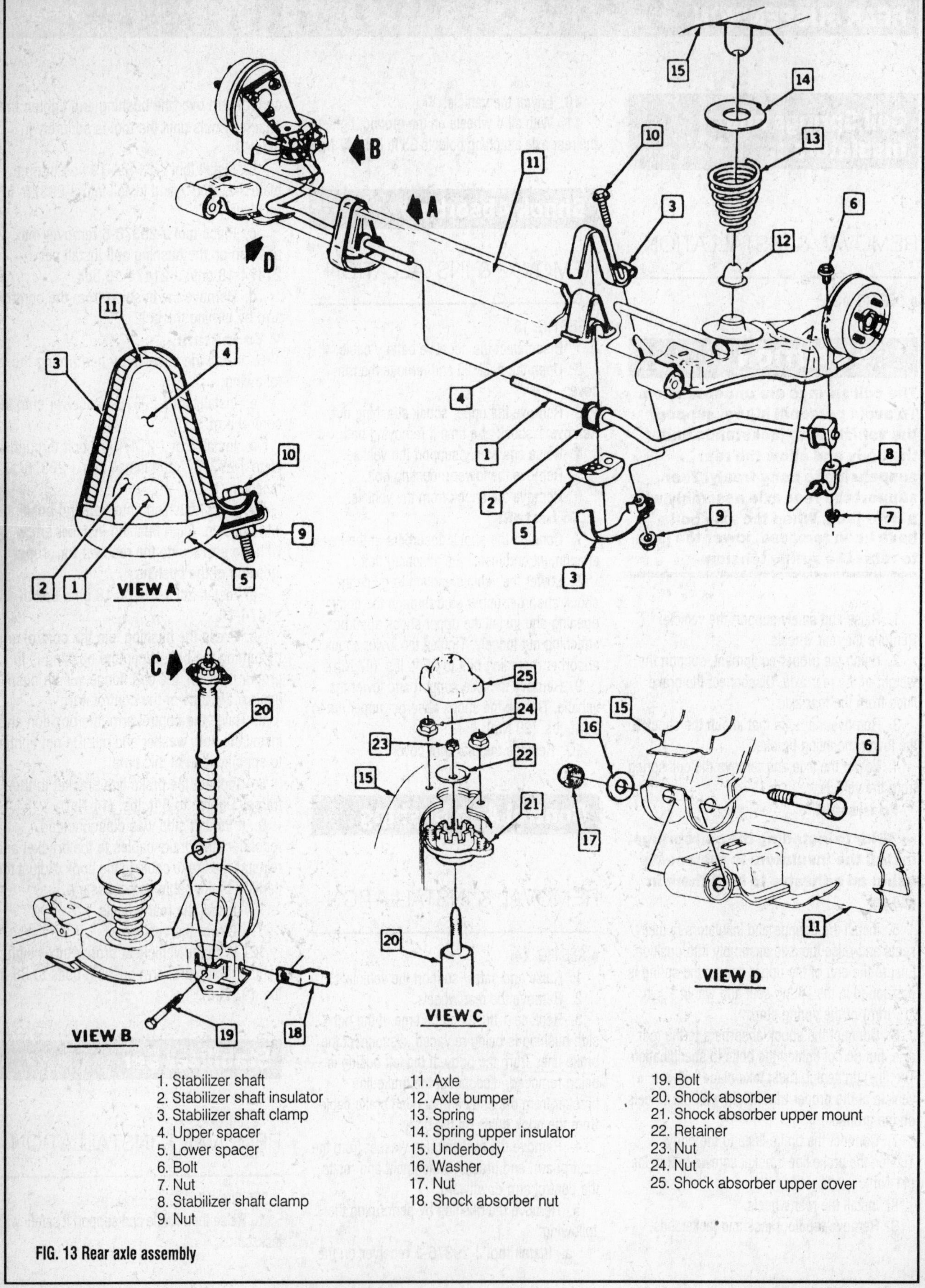

FIG. 13 Rear axle assembly

2. Remove the nuts and bolts at both the axle and control arm attachments and remove the bracket, insulator and stabilizer bar.

To install:

3. Install the U-bolts, upper clamp, spacer and insulator in the trailing axle. Position the stabilizer bar in the insulators and loosely install the lower clamp and nuts.

4. Attach the end of the stabilizer bar to the control arms and torque all nuts to 15 ft.lb. (20 Nm).

5. Tighten the axle attaching nut, then lower the vehicle.

Rear End Alignment

Rear wheel alignment is not adjustable. If a check of the rear alignment is determined to be out of specification, check for bent or broken rear suspension parts.

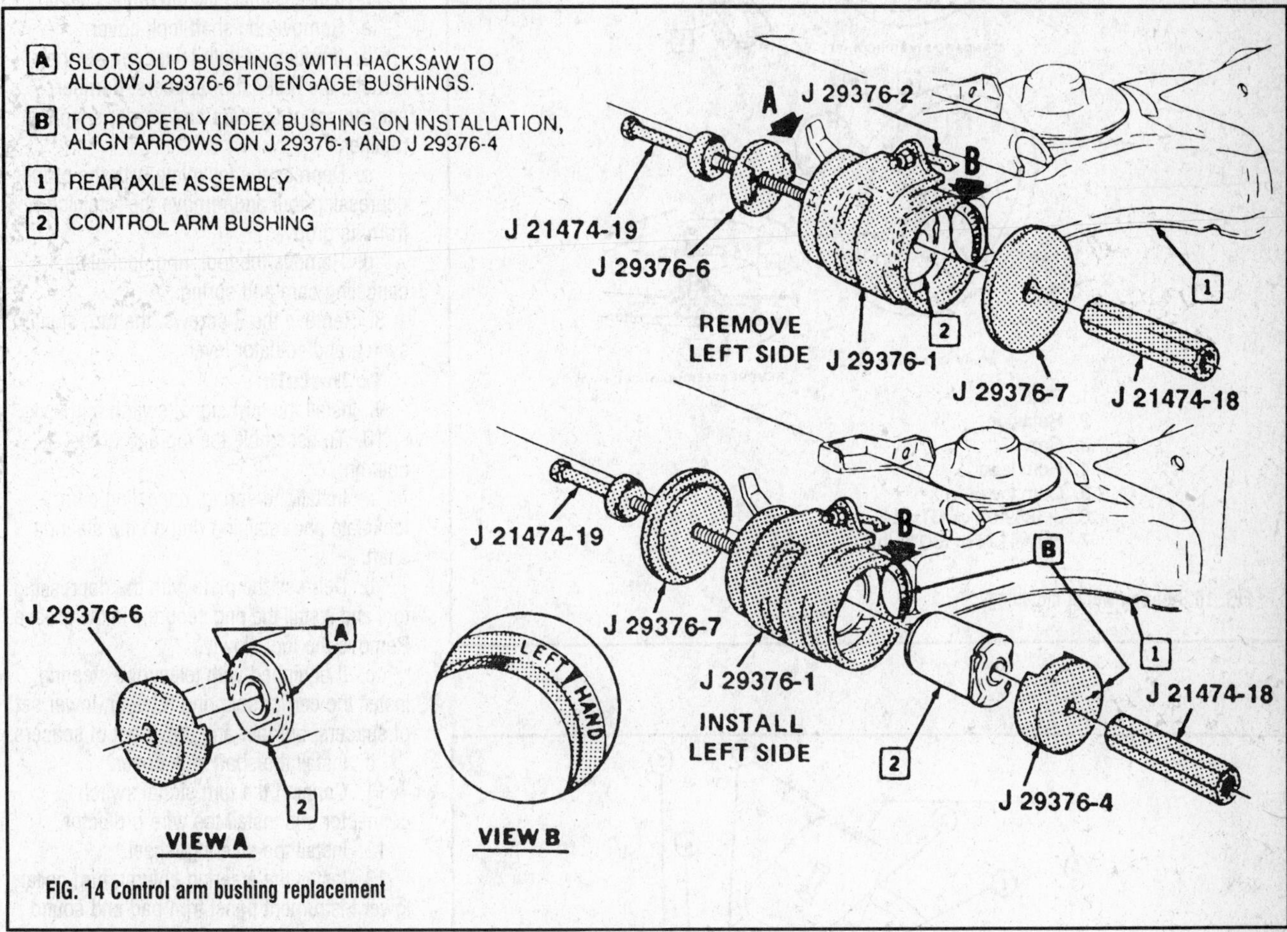

FIG. 14 Control arm bushing replacement

STEERING

Steering Wheel

REMOVAL & INSTALLATION

➧ SEE FIGS. 15 AND 16

1. Disconnect the negative battery cable.

2. Remove the 2 screws that retain the steering pad.

3. Disconnect the horn lead and remove the horn pad.

4. Remove the retainer, nut and dampener, if equipped.

5. Matchmark the steering wheel to the shaft and remove the steering wheel from the vehicle.

6. The installation is the reverse of the removal procedure. Tighten the attaching nut to 30 ft. lbs. (41 Nm).

Turn Signal Switch

REMOVAL & INSTALLATION

➧ SEE FIGS. 17-19

1. Disconnect the negative battery cable.

2. Remove the lower instrument panel sound insulator, trim pad and steering column trim collar.

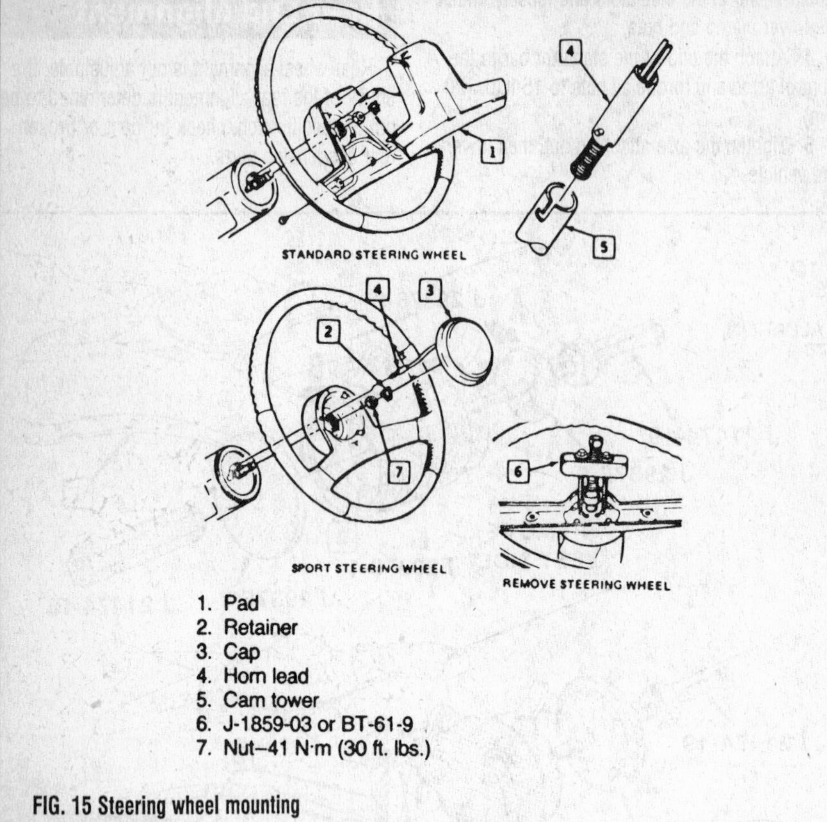

1. Pad
2. Retainer
3. Cap
4. Horn lead
5. Cam tower
6. J-1859-03 or BT-61-9
7. Nut–41 N·m (30 ft. lbs.)

FIG. 15 Steering wheel mounting

1. Steering wheel nut 41 N·m (30 ft. lbs.)
2. Steering wheel nut retainer
3. Telescoping adjuster lever
4. Steering shaft lock knob bolt
5. Steering shaft lock knob bolt positioning screw (2)
6. Steering wheel pad
7. Horn contact spring
8. Horn lead
9. Fully driven, seated and not stripped

FIG. 16 Tilt-wheel mounting

3. Straighten the steering wheel so the tires are pointing straight ahead.
4. Remove the steering wheel.
5. Remove the plastic wire protector from under the steering column.
6. Disconnect the turn signal switch connector at the bottom of the column.
7. To disassemble the top of the column:
   a. Remove the shaft lock cover.
   b. If equipped with telescope steering, remove the first set of spacers, bumper, second set of spacers and carrier snapring retainer.
   c. Depress the lockplate with the proper depressing tool and remove the retaining ring from its groove.
   d. Remove the tool, ring, lockplate, canceling cam and spring.
8. Remove the 3 screws, the turn signal switch and actuator lever.

To install:

9. Install the turn signal switch and lever.
10. To assemble the top end of the column:
    a. Install the spring, canceling cam, lockplate and retaining ring on the steering shaft.
    b. Depress the plate with the depressing tool and install the ring securely in the groove. Remove the tool slowly.
    c. If equipped with telescope steering, install the carrier snapring retainer, lower set of spacers, bumper and upper set of spacers.
    d. Install the shaft lock cover.
11. Connect the turn signal switch connector and install the wire protector.
12. Install the steering wheel.
13. Install the steering column trim collar, lower instrument panel trim pad and sound insulator.
14. Connect the negative battery cable and check the turn signal switch for proper operation.

Ignition Switch

REMOVAL & INSTALLATION

➧ SEE FIGS. 17–21

1. Disconnect the negative battery cable.
2. Remove the left instrument panel insulator.
3. Remove the left instrument panel trim pad and the steering column trim collar.
4. Remove the steering column upper support bracket bolts and remove the support bracket.

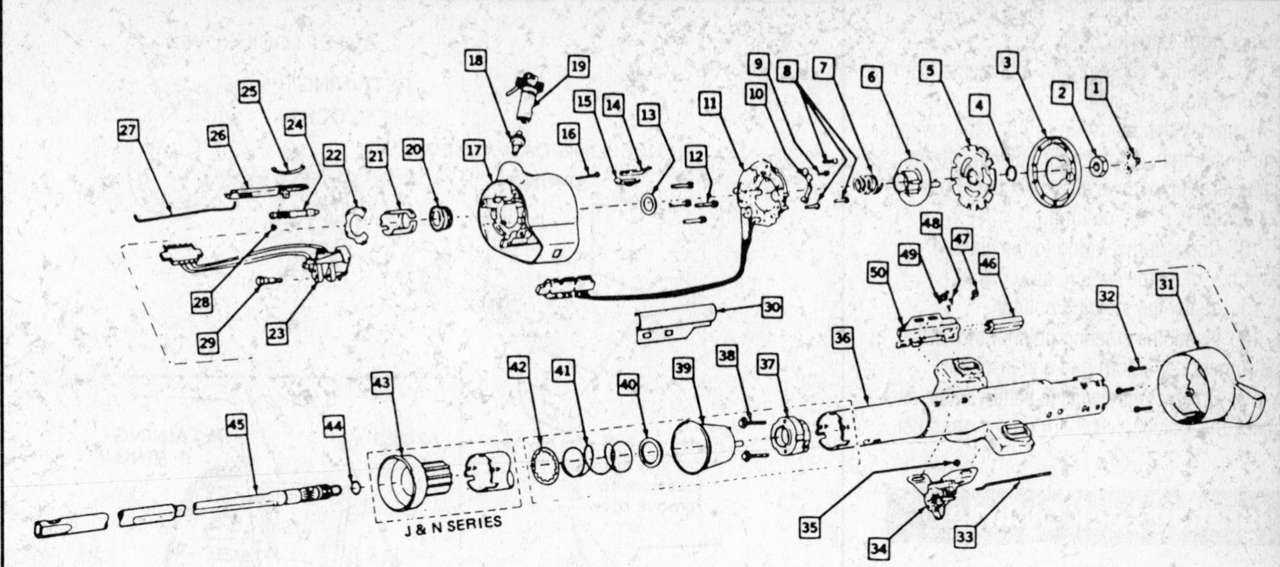

1. Retainer
2. Hexagon jam nut
3. Shaft lock cover
4. Retaining ring
5. Steering shaft lock
6. Turn signal canceling cam assembly
7. Upper bearing spring
8. Binding head cross recess screw
9. Round washer head screw
10. Switch actuator arm assembly
11. Turn signal switch assembly
12. Hex washer head tapping screw
13. Thrust washer
14. Buzzer switch assembly
15. Buzzer switch retaining clip
16. Lock retaining screw
17. Steering column housing
18. Switch actuator sector
19. Steering column lock cylinder set
20. Bearing assembly
21. Bearing retaining bushing
22. Upper bearing retainer
23. Pivot and switch assembly (windshield wiper switch)
24. Lock bolt
25. Rack preload spring
26. Switch actuator rack
27. Switch actuator rod
28. Spring thrust washer
29. Switch actuator pivot pin
30. Wiring protector
31. Floor shift bowl
32. Binding head cross recess screw
33. Dimmer switch actuator rod
34. Dimmer switch assembly
35. Hexagon nut
36. Steering column jacket assembly
37. Adapter and bearing assembly
38. Hex washer head tapping screw
39. Bearing retainer
40. Lower bearing seat
41. Lower bearing spring
42. Lower spring retainer
43. Steering column jacket bushing
44. Retaining ring
45. Steering shaft assembly
46. Ignition switch housing assembly
47. Washer head screw
48. Pan head screw
49. Dimmer and ignition switch mounting stud
50. Ignition switch assembly

FIG. 17 Park lock standard steering column for automatic floor shift shown — others similar

5. Lower the steering column and support it safely.

6. Disconnect the wiring from the ignition switch.

7. Remove the ignition switch-to-steering column screws. Remove the ignition switch from the steering column.

To install:

8. Before installing, place the slider in the proper position (switch viewed with the terminals pointing up), according to the steering column and accessories:

a. Standard column with key release—extreme left detent.

b. Standard column with PARK/LOCK—1 detent from extreme left.

c. All other standard columns—2 detents from extreme left.

d. Tilt column with key release—extreme right detent.

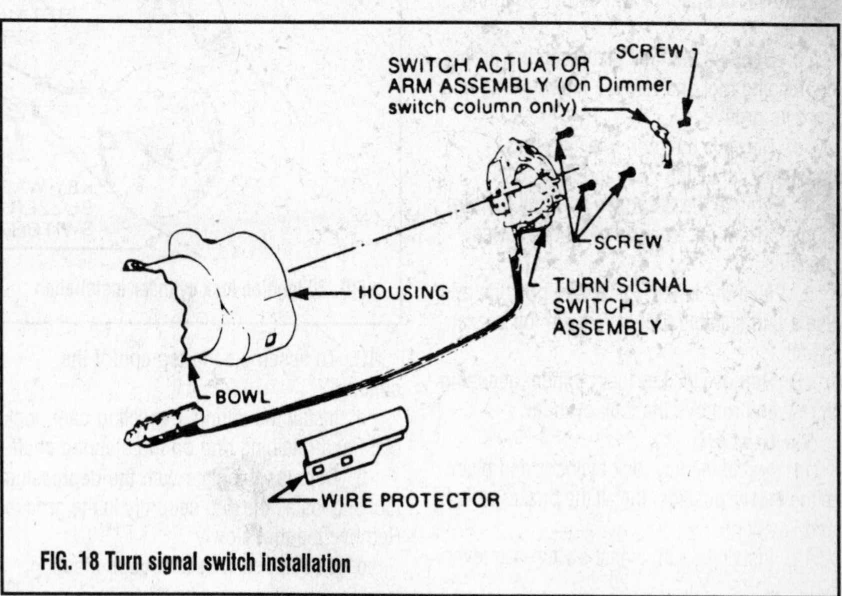

FIG. 18 Turn signal switch installation

e. Tilt column with PARK/LOCK—1 detent from extreme right.

f. All other tilt columns—2 detents from extreme right.

9. Install the activating rod into the switch and install the switch to the column. Do not use oversized screws as they could impair the collapsibility of the column.

10. Connect the wiring to the ignition switch. Adjust the switch, as required.

11. Install the steering column.

12. Install the steering column trim collar, instrument panel trim pad and insulator.

13. Connect the negative battery cable and check the ignition switch for proper operation.

Ignition Lock Cylinder

REMOVAL & INSTALLATION

➧ SEE FIGS. 17–20

1. Disconnect the negative battery cable.
2. Remove the lower instrument panel sound insulator, trim pad and steering column trim collar.
3. Straighten the steering wheel so the tires are pointing straight ahead.
4. Remove the steering wheel.
5. Remove the plastic wire protector from under the steering column.
6. Disconnect the turn signal switch.
7. To disassemble the top of the column:

a. Remove the shaft lock cover.

b. If equipped with telescope steering, remove the first set of spacers, bumper, second set of spacers and carrier snapring retainer.

c. Depress the lock plate with the proper depressing tool and remove the retaining ring from its groove.

d. Remove the tool, retaining ring, lockplate, canceling cam and spring.

8. Remove the 3 screws and pull the turn signal switch out from its mount as far as possible.
9. Place the key in the **RUN** position and use a thin suitable tool to remove the buzzer switch.
10. Remove the key lock cylinder attaching screw and remove the lock cylinder.

To install:

11. Install the key lock cylinder and place in the **RUN** position. Install the buzzer switch and key light.
12. Install the turn signal switch and lever.

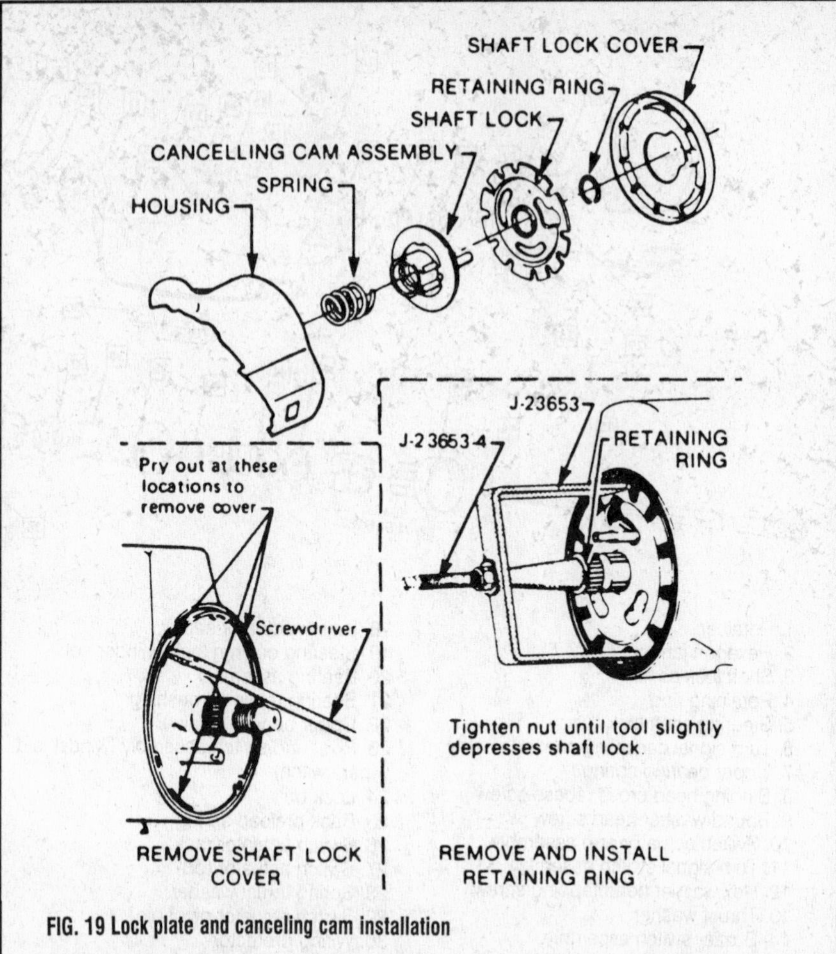

FIG. 19 Lock plate and canceling cam installation

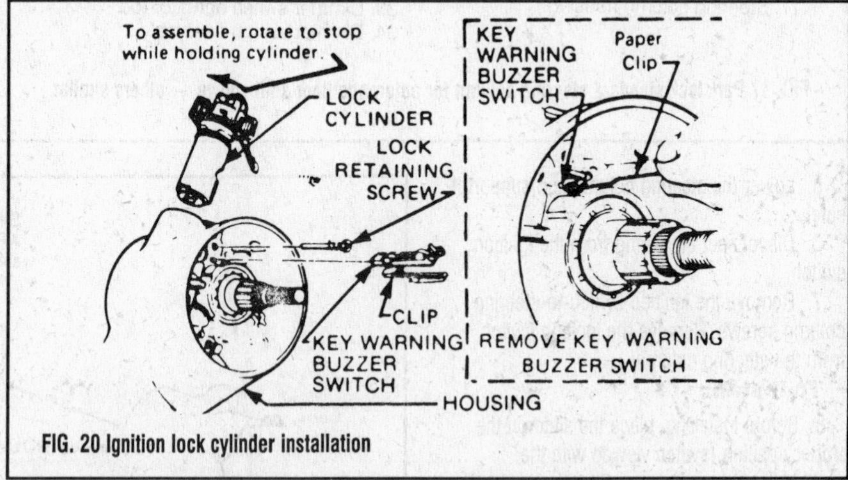

FIG. 20 Ignition lock cylinder installation

13. To assemble the top end of the column:

a. Install the spring, canceling cam, lock plate and retaining ring on the steering shaft.

b. Depress the plate with the depressing tool and install the ring securely in the groove. Remove the tool slowly.

c. If equipped with telescope steering, install the carrier snapring retainer, lower set of spacers, bumper and upper set of spacers.

d. Install the shaft lock cover.

14. Connect the turn signal switch connector. Install the wire protector.
15. Install the steering wheel.
16. Install the steering column trim collar, lower instrument panel trim pad and sound insulator.

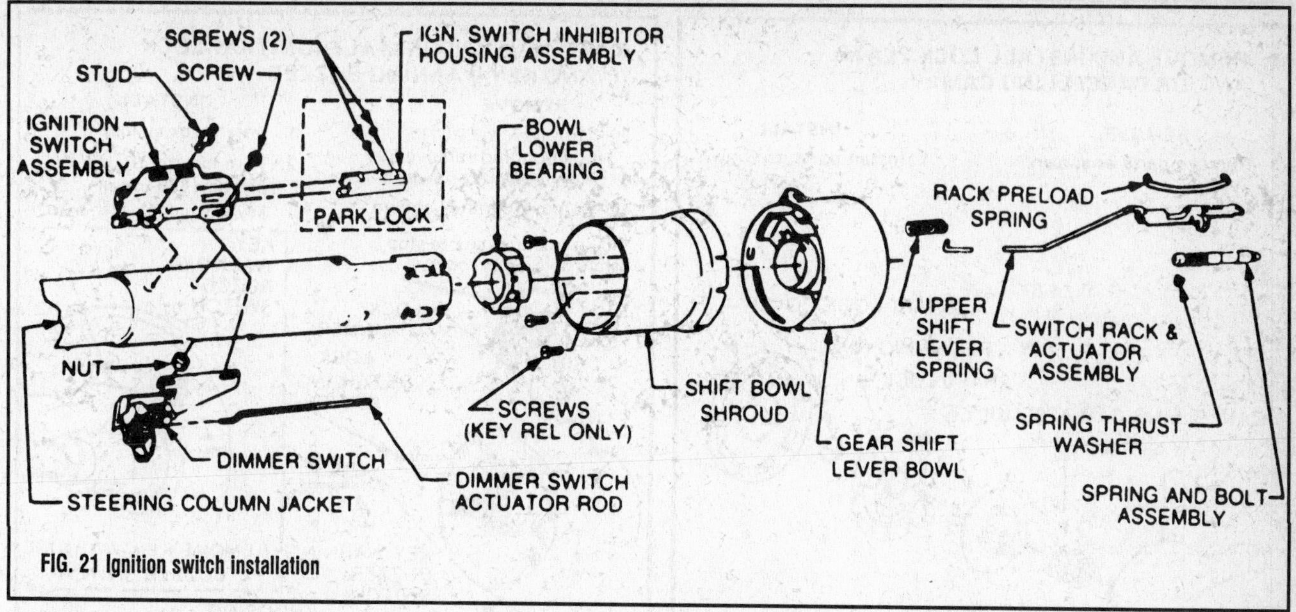

FIG. 21 Ignition switch installation

17. Connect the negative battery cable and check the key lock cylinder and turn signal switch for proper operation.

Steering Column

REMOVAL & INSTALLATION

➧ SEE FIG. 17

1. Disconnect the negative battery cable.
2. If column repairs are to be made, remove the steering wheel.
3. Remove the steering column-to-intermediate shaft coupling pinch bolt. Remove the safety strap and bolt, if equipped.
4. Remove the steering column trim shrouds and column covers.
5. Disconnect all wiring harness connectors. If equipped with column shift, disconnect the shift indicator cable. Remove the dust boot mounting screws and steering column-to-dash bracket bolts.
6. Lower the column to clear the mounting bracket and carefully remove from the vehicle.

To install:

7. Carefully, install the steering column into the vehicle.
8. If equipped with column shift, connect the shift indicator cable.
9. Connect the electrical harness connectors.
10. Install the column bracket bolts.
11. Install the flange and upper steering coupling upper pinch bolt. Tighten the column bracket support bolts to 22 ft. lbs. (30 Nm) and the upper pinch bolt to 30 ft. lbs. (41 Nm).
12. Adjust the shift indicator, if equipped.
13. If removed, install the steering wheel.
14. If removed, install the steering wheel pad.
15. Connect the negative battery cable.

DISASSEMBLY

➧ SEE FIGS. 22–26

Steering Linkage

REMOVAL & INSTALLATION

➧ SEE FIG. 27

Tie Rod Ends

INNER TIE ROD

1. Disconnect the negative battery cable. Remove the rack and pinion gear from the vehicle.
2. Remove the lock plate from the inner tie rod bolts.
3. If removing both tie rods, remove both bolts, the bolt support plate and 1 of the tie rod assemblies. Reinstall the removed tie rod's bolt to keep inner parts of the rack aligned. Remove the remaining tie rod.
4. If only removing 1 tie rod, slide the assembly out from between the support plate and the center housing cover washer.

To install:

5. Install the center housing cover washer fitted into the rack and pinion boot.
6. Install the inner tie rod bolts through the holes in the bolt support plate, inner pivot bushing, center housing cover washer, rack housing and into the threaded holes.
7. Tighten the bolts to 65 ft. lbs. (90 Nm).
8. Install a new lock plate with its notches over the bolt flats.
9. Install the rack and pinion gear.
10. Fill the power steering pump with fluid and bleed the system.
11. Connect the negative battery cable and check the rack for proper operation and leaks.

OUTER TIE ROD

1. Disconnect the negative battery cable.
2. Remove the cotter pin and the nut from the tie rod ball stud at the steering knuckle.
3. Loosen the pinch bolts.
4. Using the proper tools, separate the tie rod taper from the steering knuckle.
5. Remove the tie rod from the adjuster.
6. The installation is the reverse of the removal procedure.
7. Perform a front end alignment.

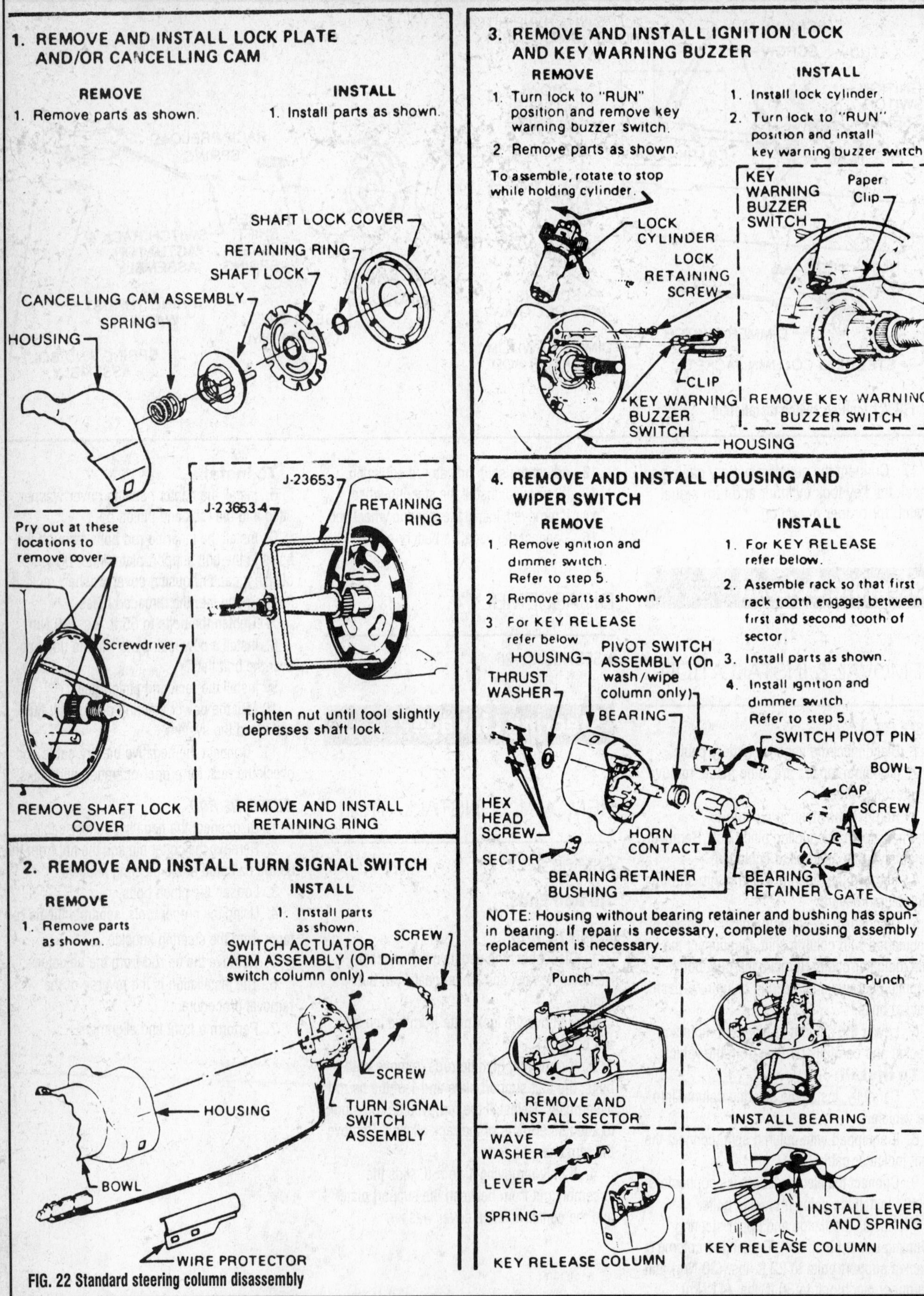

FIG. 22 Standard steering column disassembly

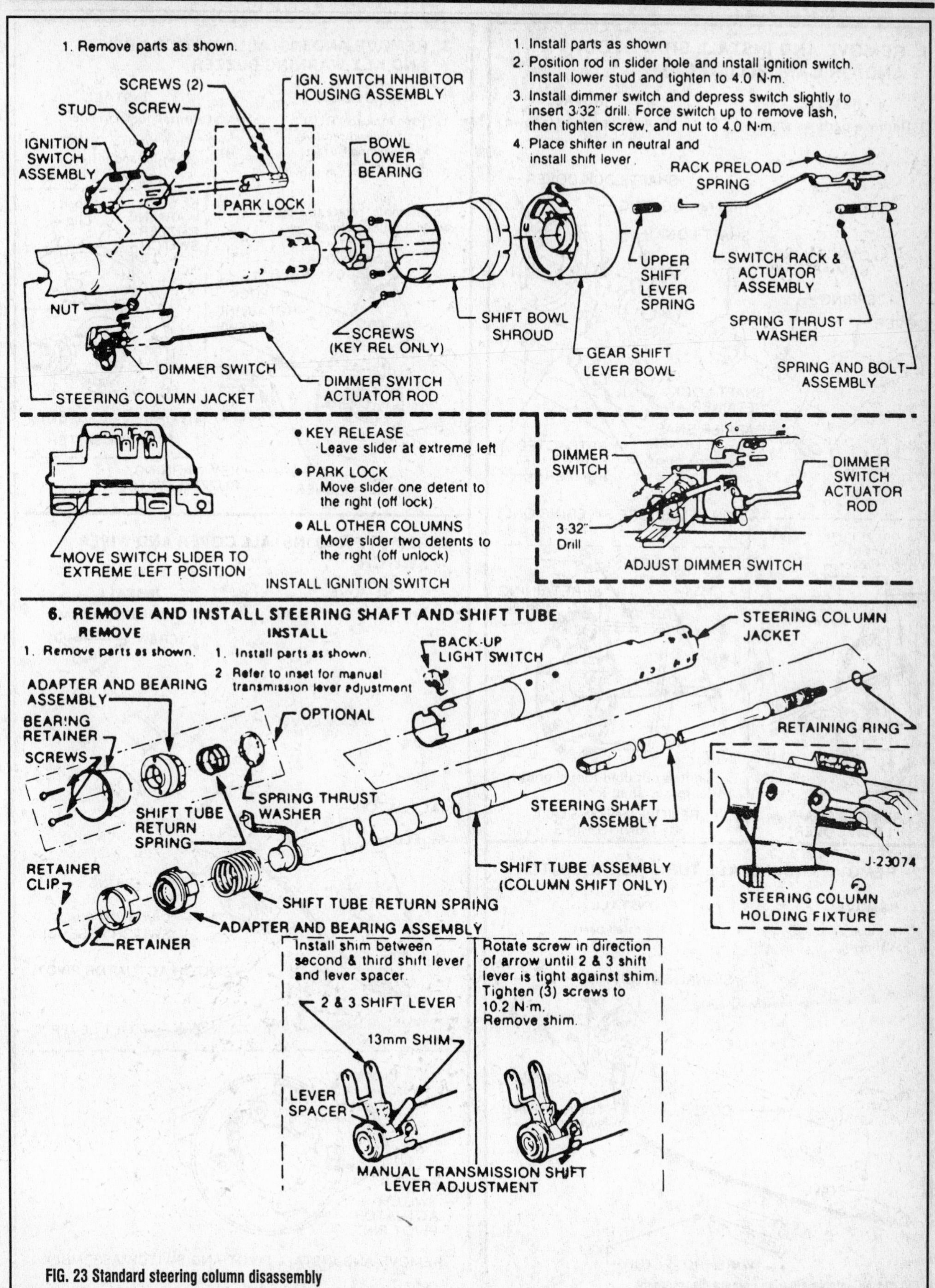

FIG. 23 Standard steering column disassembly

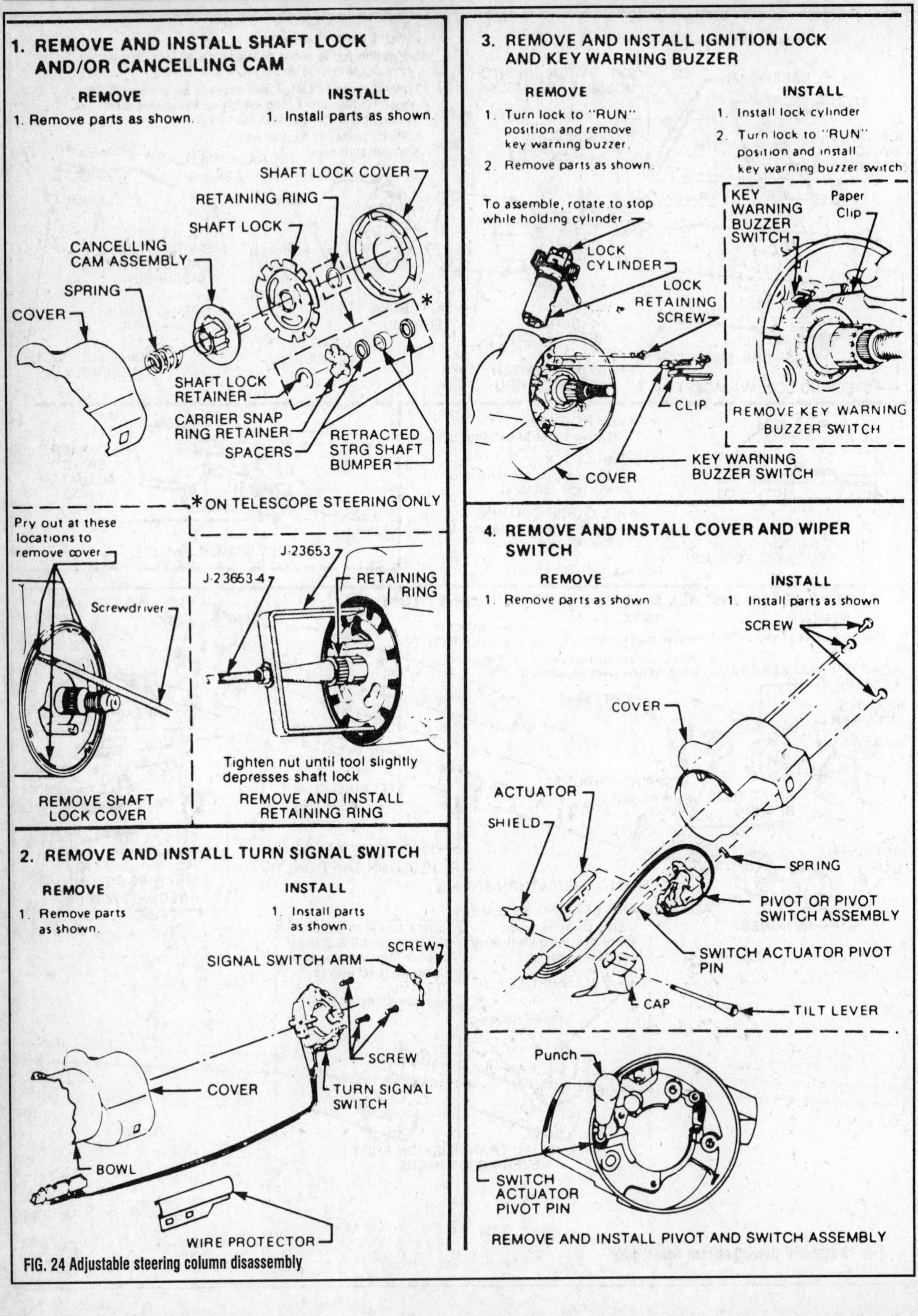

1. REMOVE AND INSTALL SHAFT LOCK AND/OR CANCELLING CAM
REMOVE
1. Remove parts as shown.
INSTALL
1. Install parts as shown.
SHAFT LOCK COVER
RETAINING RING
SHAFT LOCK
CANCELLING CAM ASSEMBLY
SPRING
COVER
*
SHAFT LOCK RETAINER
CARRIER SNAP RING RETAINER
SPACERS
RETRACTED STRG SHAFT BUMPER
*ON TELESCOPE STEERING ONLY
Pry out at these locations to remove cover
Screwdriver
REMOVE SHAFT LOCK COVER
J-23653
J-23653-4
RETAINING RING
Tighten nut until tool slightly depresses shaft lock
REMOVE AND INSTALL RETAINING RING
2. REMOVE AND INSTALL TURN SIGNAL SWITCH
REMOVE
1. Remove parts as shown.
INSTALL
1. Install parts as shown
SCREW
SIGNAL SWITCH ARM
SCREW
COVER
TURN SIGNAL SWITCH
BOWL
WIRE PROTECTOR
3. REMOVE AND INSTALL IGNITION LOCK AND KEY WARNING BUZZER
REMOVE
1. Turn lock to "RUN" position and remove key warning buzzer.
2. Remove parts as shown.
INSTALL
1. Install lock cylinder
2. Turn lock to "RUN" position and install key warning buzzer switch.
To assemble, rotate to stop while holding cylinder
LOCK CYLINDER
LOCK RETAINING SCREW
CLIP
COVER
KEY WARNING BUZZER SWITCH
KEY WARNING BUZZER SWITCH
Paper Clip
REMOVE KEY WARNING BUZZER SWITCH
4. REMOVE AND INSTALL COVER AND WIPER SWITCH
REMOVE
1. Remove parts as shown
INSTALL
1. Install parts as shown
SCREW
COVER
ACTUATOR
SHIELD
SPRING
PIVOT OR PIVOT SWITCH ASSEMBLY
SWITCH ACTUATOR PIVOT PIN
CAP
TILT LEVER
Punch
SWITCH ACTUATOR PIVOT PIN
REMOVE AND INSTALL PIVOT AND SWITCH ASSEMBLY

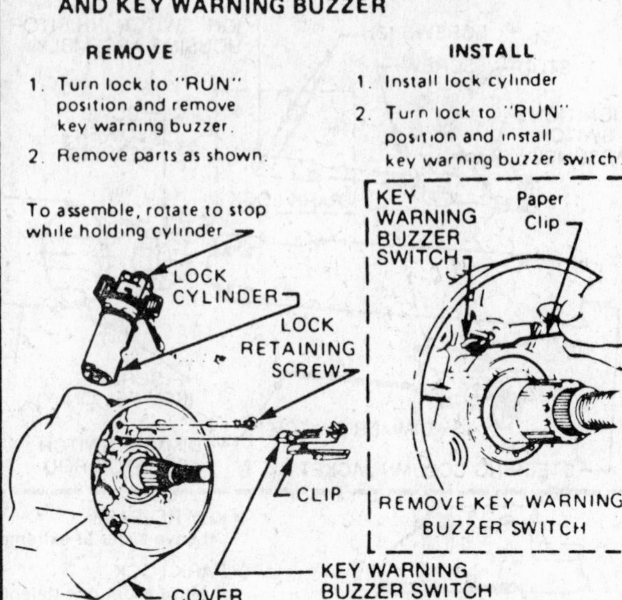

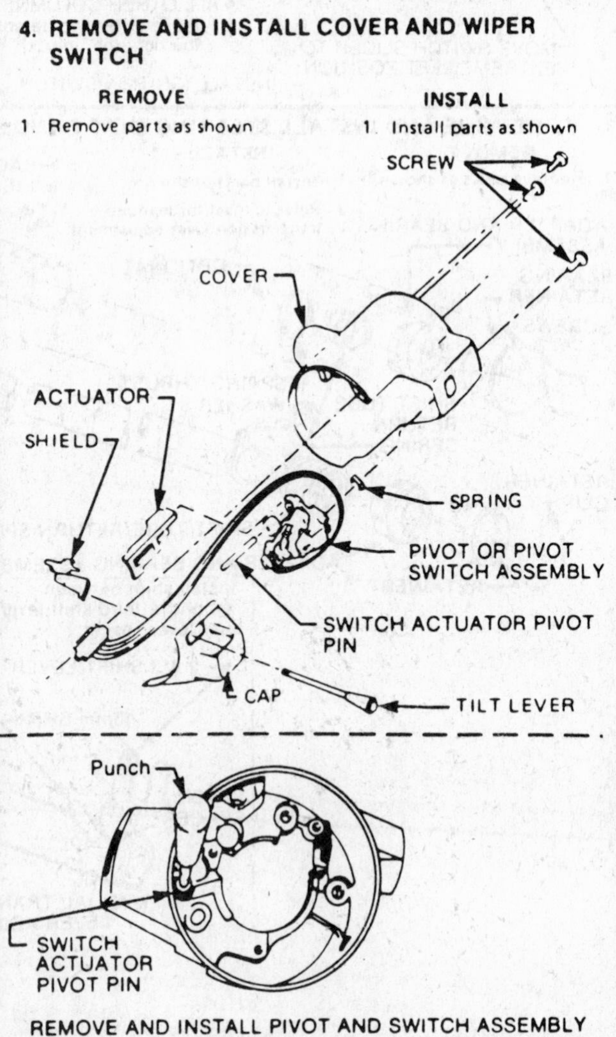

FIG. 24 Adjustable steering column disassembly

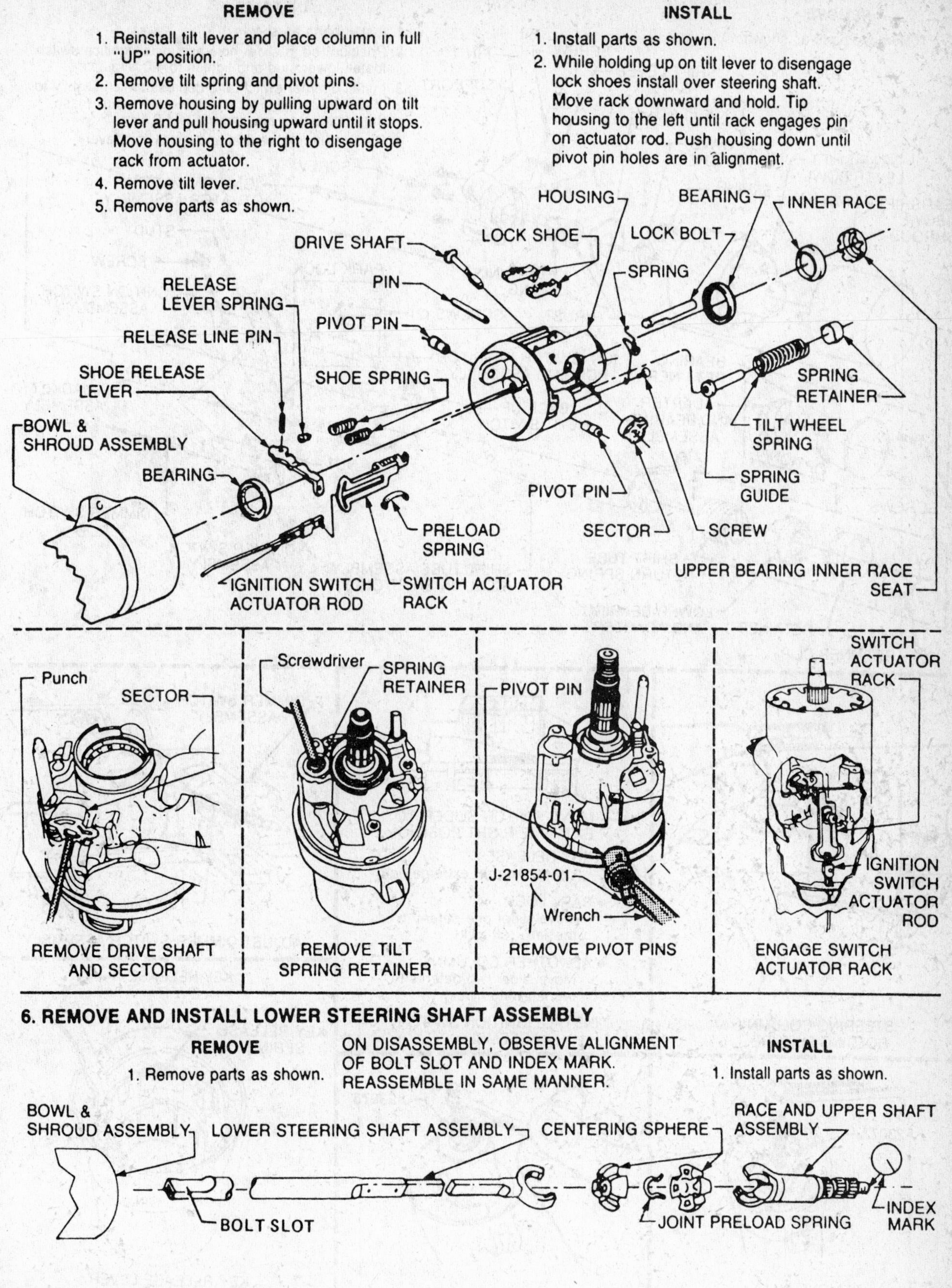

FIG. 25 Adjustable steering column disassembly

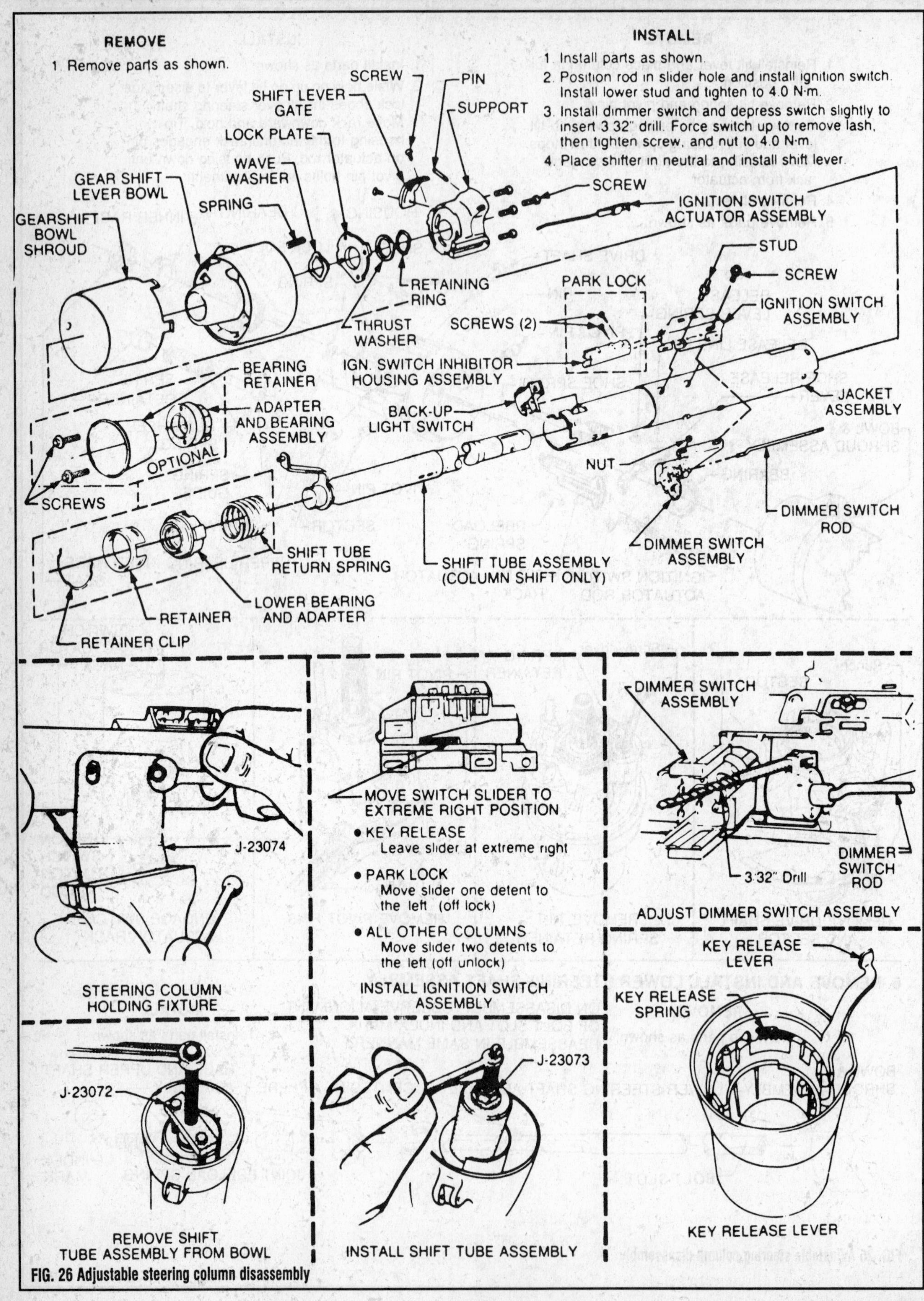

FIG. 26 Adjustable steering column disassembly

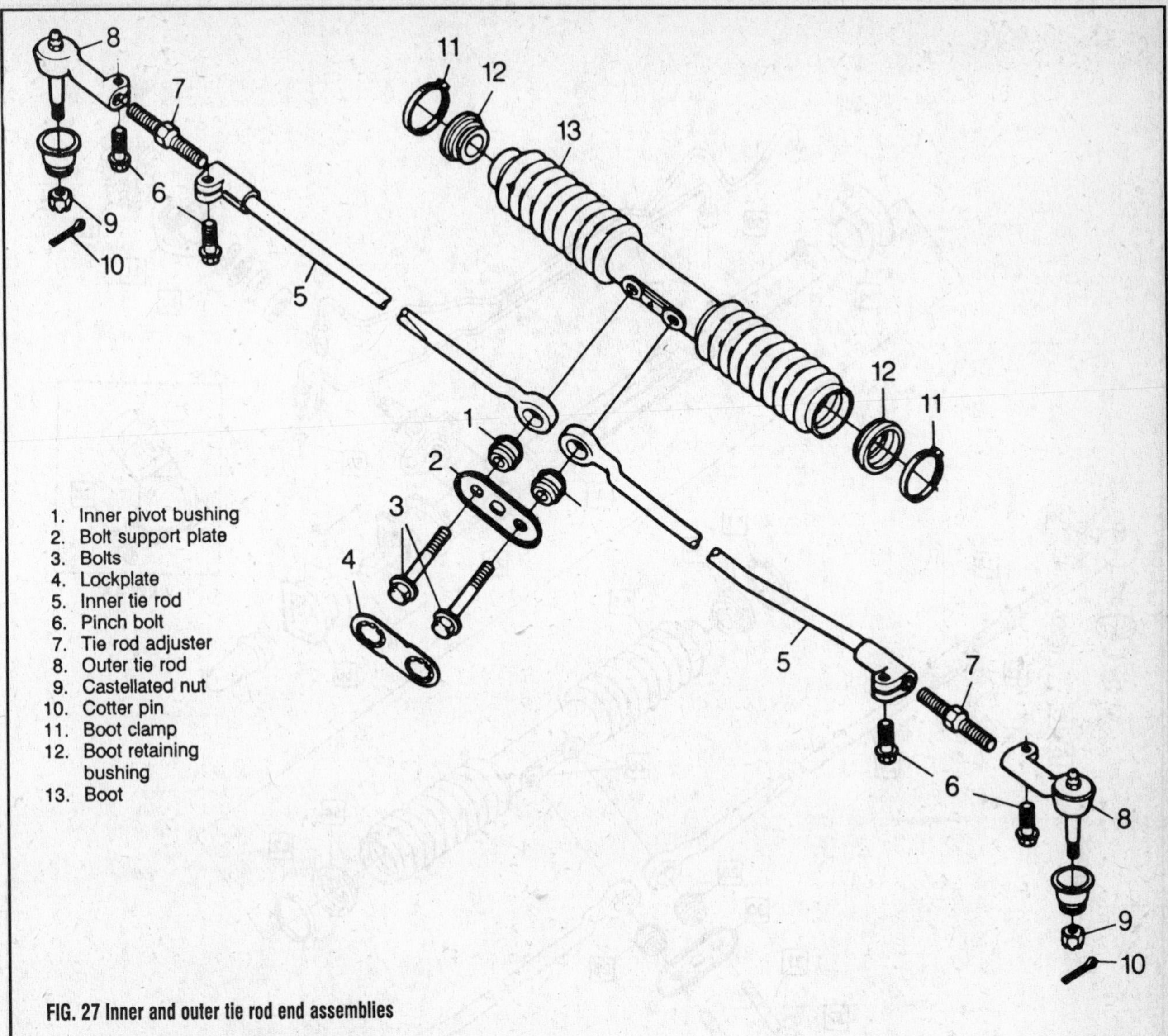

FIG. 27 Inner and outer tie rod end assemblies

Power Rack and Pinion Steering Gear

ADJUSTMENT

RACK BEARING PRELOAD

1. Center the steering wheel. Raise and safely support the vehicle.
2. Loosen the locknut and turn the adjuster plug clockwise until it bottoms in the housing. Then back off about 1/8 turn and tighten the locknut while holding the position of the adjuster plug.
3. Check the steering for ability to return to center after the adjustment has been completed.

REMOVAL & INSTALLATION

➧ SEE FIGS. 28 AND 29

1. Disconnect the negative battery cable. Remove the left side sound insulator.
2. Disconnect the upper pinch bolt on the steering coupling assembly.
3. Disconnect the clamp nuts.
4. Raise and safely support the vehicle. Remove both front wheel assemblies.
5. Remove the clamp nut and the fluid line retainer.
6. Remove the tie rod end-to-steering knuckle cotter pin and castle nut. Using a puller tool, disconnect the tie rod ends from the steering knuckles.
7. Lower the vehicle.
8. Disconnect and plug the fluid lines from the power steering rack.
9. Remove the mounting clamps. Move the steering rack forward and remove the lower pinch bolt on the coupling assembly.
10. Disconnect the coupling from the steering rack.
11. Remove the rack and pinion assembly with the dash seal through the left wheel opening.

To install:

12. If the studs were removed with the mounting clamps, reinstall the studs into the cowl. If the stud is being reused, use Loctite® to secure the threads.

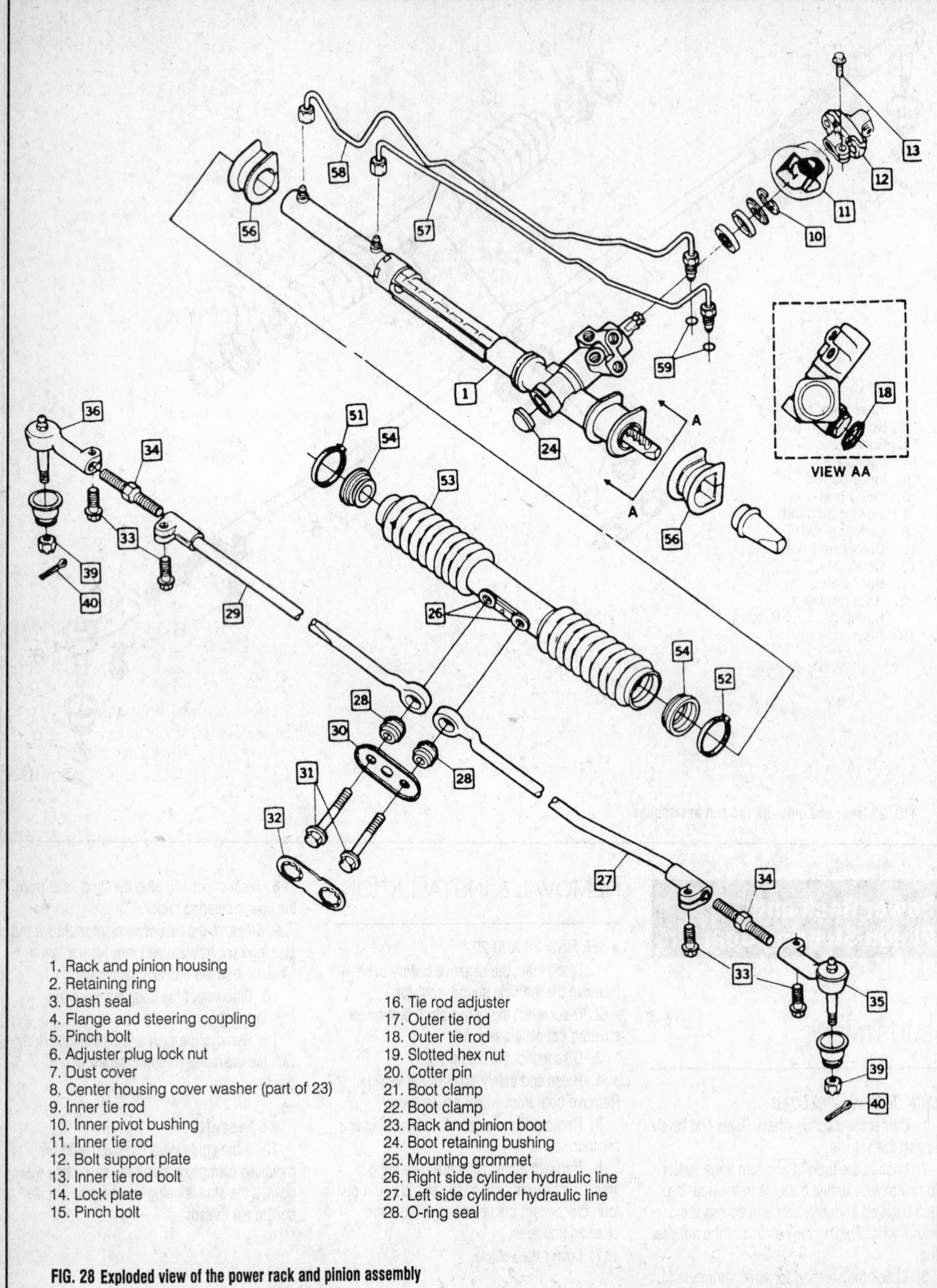

FIG. 28 Exploded view of the power rack and pinion assembly

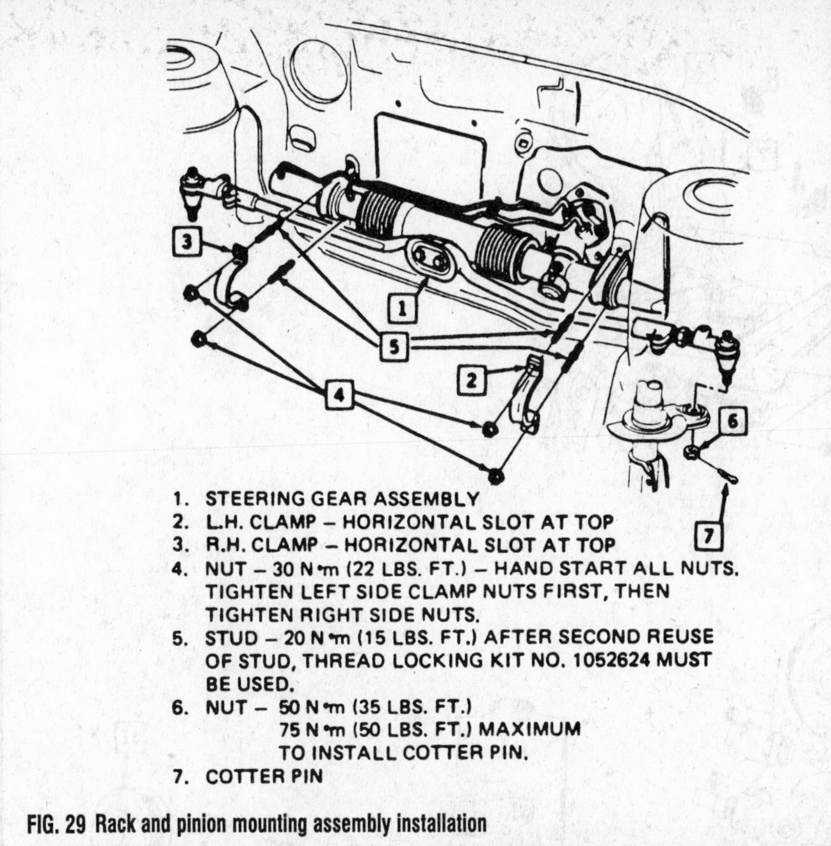

FIG. 29 Rack and pinion mounting assembly installation

13. Slide the rack and pinion assembly through the left side wheel housing opening and secure the dash seal.
14. Move the assembly forward and install the coupling.
15. Install the lower pinch bolt and tighten to 29 ft. lbs. (40 Nm).
16. Connect the fluid lines.
17. Install the clamp nuts. Tighten the left side clamp first, then tighten the right side. Raise and safely support the vehicle.
18. Connect the tie rod ends to the steering knuckle, tighten the nut to 35 ft. lbs. (47 Nm) and install a new cotter pin. Install the wheels.
19. Install the line retainer and lower the vehicle.
20. Install the upper pinch bolt on the coupling assembly. Tighten to 29 ft. lbs. (40 Nm).
21. Install the sound insulator.
22. Fill the power steering pump with fluid and bleed the system.
23. Connect the negative battery cable and check the rack for proper operation and leaks.
24. Check and adjust front end alignment, as required.

Power Steering Pump

REMOVAL & INSTALLATION

2.3L ENGINE

➧ SEE FIG. 30

1. Disconnect the negative battery cable.
2. Disconnect the pressure and return lines from the pump.
3. Remove the rear bracket to pump bolts.
4. Remove the drive belt and position aside.
5. Remove the rear bracket to transaxle bolts.
6. Remove the front bracket to engine bolt.
7. Remove the pump and bracket as an assembly.
8. Transfer pulley and bracket, as necessary.
9. The installation is the reverse of the removal procedure.
10. Fill the power steering pump with fluid and bleed the system.
11. Connect the negative battery cable and check the pump for proper operation and leaks.

2.5L ENGINE

➧ SEE FIG. 31

1. Disconnect the negative battery cable.
2. Remove the drive belt.
3. Disconnect and plug the pressure tubes from the power steering pump.
4. Remove the front adjustment bracket-to-rear adjustment bracket bolt.
5. Remove the front adjustment bracket-to-engine bolt and spacer.
6. Remove the pump with the front adjustment bracket.
7. If installing a new pump, transfer the pulley and front adjustment bracket to the new pump.

To install:

8. The installation is the reverse of the removal procedure.
9. Adjust the drive belt tension.
10. Fill the power steering pump with fluid and bleed the system.
11. Connect the negative battery cable and check the pump for proper operation and leaks.

2.0L, 3.0L AND 3.3L ENGINES

➧ SEE FIG. 32

1. Disconnect the negative battery cable.
2. Remove the serpentine drive belt.
3. Remove the power steering pump-to-engine bolts.
4. Pull the pump forward and disconnect the pressure tubes.
5. Remove the pump and transfer the pulley, as necessary.
6. The installation is the reverse of the removal procedure.
7. Adjust the drive belt tension.
8. Fill the power steering pump with fluid and bleed the system.
9. Connect the negative battery cable and check the pump for proper operation and leaks.

Belt Adjustment

➡ Serpentine belt driven power steering pumps do not require adjustment. If the belt is stretched beyond usable limits, replace it.

1. Place the appropriate gauge on the belt and measure the tension. The specifications are:
   - 2.3L engine, new and used belt—110 lbs.
   - 2.5L and 3.0L engine, used belt—100 lbs; new belt—180 lbs.
2. If the tension is not at specifications, loosen the mounting bolts and move the pump or turn the adjustment stud.
3. Tighten the mounting bolts while holding the adjusted position of the pump.
4. Run the engine for 2 minutes and recheck the tension.

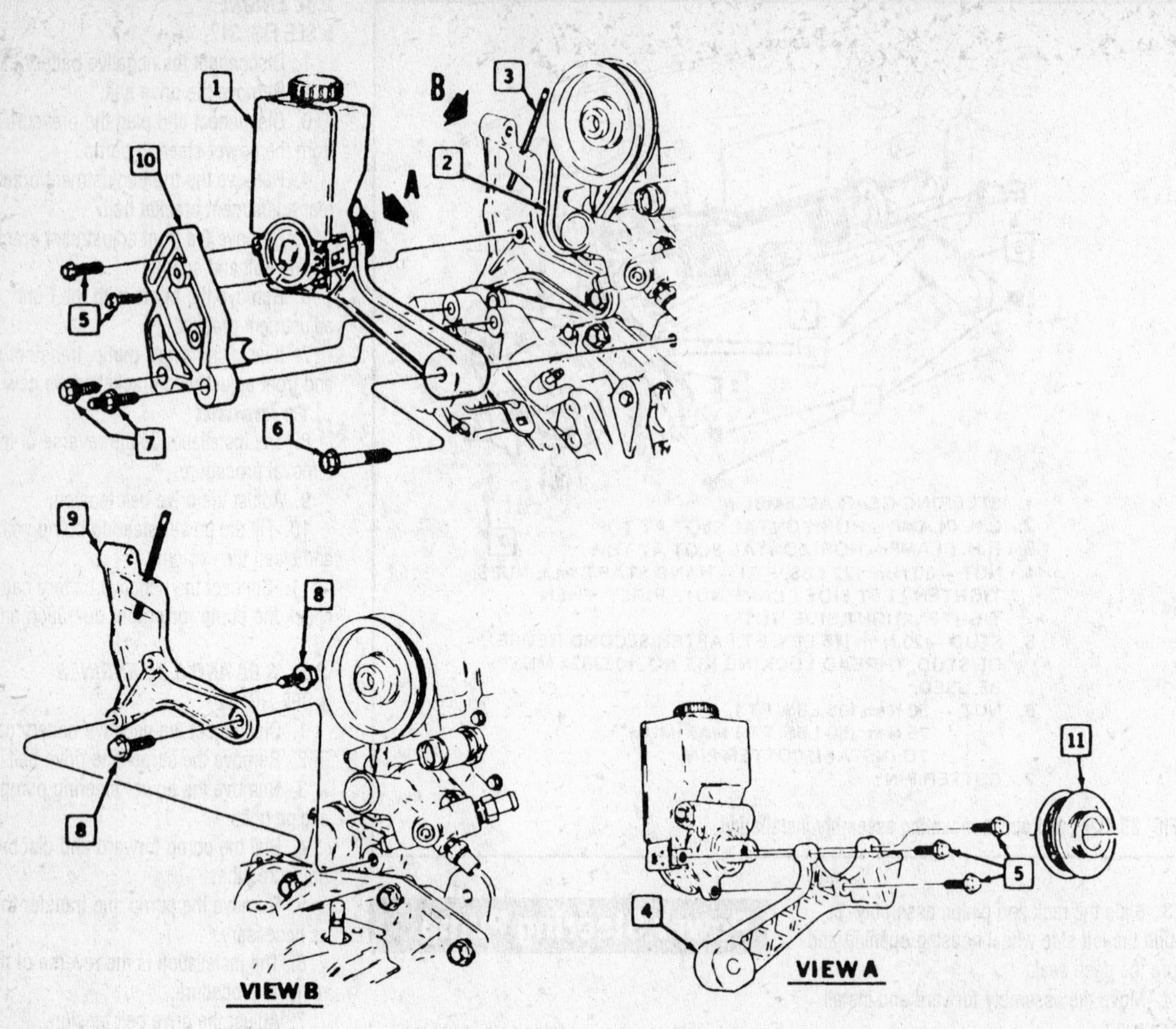

1. Power steering pump
2. Drive belt
3. Adjustment screw
4. Front bracket
5. Bolt
6. Bolt
7. Bolt/stud
8. Bolt
9. Rear support
10. Front support
11. Pulley — Note: when tensioning belt, tighten rear bracket adjustment belt first, then the bolt just below it. Tighten bolt 6 last.

FIG. 30 Power steering pump installation — 2.3L engine

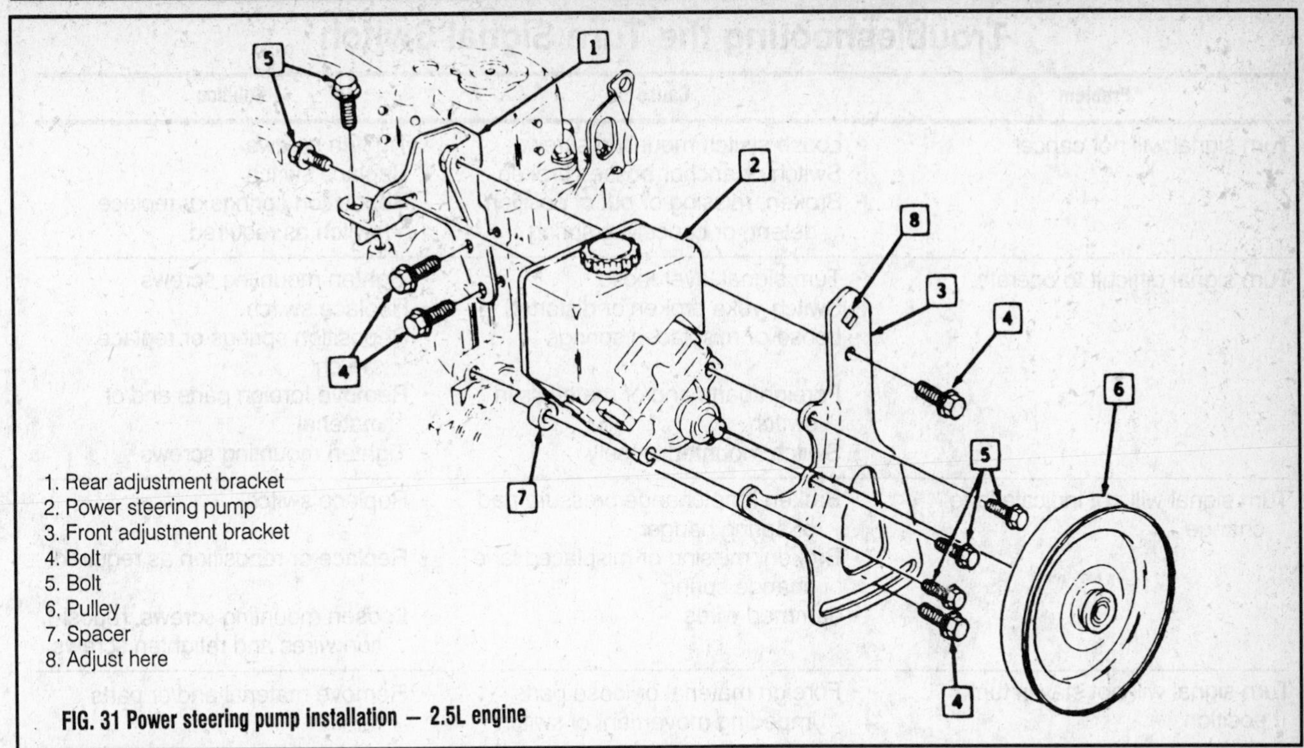

FIG. 31 Power steering pump installation — 2.5L engine

System Bleeding

1. Raise the vehicle so the wheels are off the ground. Turn the wheels all the way to the left. Add power steering fluid to the **COLD** or **FULL COLD** mark on the fluid level indicator.
2. Start the engine and check the fluid level at fast idle. Add fluid, if necessary to bring the level up to the mark.
3. Bleed air from the system by turning the wheels from side-to-side without hitting the stops. Keep the fluid level at the **COLD** or **FULL COLD** mark. Fluid with air in it has a tan appearance.
4. Return the wheels to the center position and continue running the engine for 2–3 minutes.
5. Lower the vehicle and road test to check steering function and recheck the fluid level with the system at its normal operating temperature. Fluid should be at the **HOT** mark when finished.

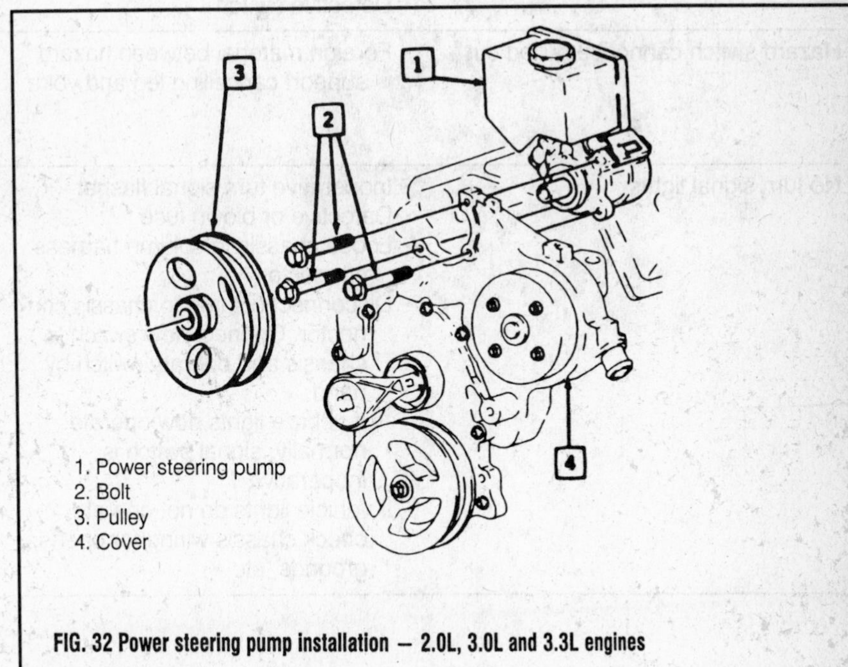

FIG. 32 Power steering pump installation — 2.0L, 3.0L and 3.3L engines

Troubleshooting the Turn Signal Switch

Problem	Cause	Solution
Turn signal will not cancel	• Loose switch mounting screws • Switch or anchor bosses broken • Broken, missing or out of position detent, or cancelling spring	• Tighten screws • Replace switch • Reposition springs or replace switch as required
Turn signal difficult to operate	• Turn signal lever loose • Switch yoke broken or distorted • Loose or misplaced springs • Foreign parts and/or materials in switch • Switch mounted loosely	• Tighten mounting screws • Replace switch • Reposition springs or replace switch • Remove foreign parts and/or material • Tighten mounting screws
Turn signal will not indicate lane change	• Broken lane change pressure pad or spring hanger • Broken, missing or misplaced lane change spring • Jammed wires	• Replace switch • Replace or reposition as required • Loosen mounting screws, reposition wires and retighten screws
Turn signal will not stay in turn position	• Foreign material or loose parts impeding movement of switch yoke • Defective switch	• Remove material and/or parts • Replace switch
Hazard switch cannot be pulled out	• Foreign material between hazard support cancelling leg and yoke	• Remove foreign material. No foreign material impeding function of hazard switch—replace turn signal switch.
No turn signal lights	• Inoperative turn signal flasher • Defective or blown fuse • Loose chassis to column harness connector • Disconnect column to chassis connector. Connect new switch to chassis and operate switch by hand. If vehicle lights now operate normally, signal switch is inoperative • If vehicle lights do not operate, check chassis wiring for opens, grounds, etc.	• Replace turn signal flasher • Replace fuse • Connect securely • Replace signal switch • Repair chassis wiring as required

Troubleshooting the Turn Signal Switch (cont.)

Problem	Cause	Solution
Instrument panel turn indicator lights on but not flashing	• Burned out or damaged front or rear turn signal bulb	• Replace bulb
	• If vehicle lights do not operate, check light sockets for high resistance connections, the chassis wiring for opens, grounds, etc.	• Repair chassis wiring as required
	• Inoperative flasher	• Replace flasher
	• Loose chassis to column harness connection	• Connect securely
	• Inoperative turn signal switch	• Replace turn signal switch
	• To determine if turn signal switch is defective, substitute new switch into circuit and operate switch by hand. If the vehicle's lights operate normally, signal switch is inoperative.	• Replace turn signal switch
Stop light not on when turn indicated	• Loose column to chassis connection	• Connect securely
	• Disconnect column to chassis connector. Connect new switch into system without removing old.	• Replace signal switch
Stop light not on when turn indicated (cont.)	Operate switch by hand. If brake lights work with switch in the turn position, signal switch is defective.	
	• If brake lights do not work, check connector to stop light sockets for grounds, opens, etc.	• Repair connector to stop light circuits using service manual as guide
Turn indicator panel lights not flashing	• Burned out bulbs	• Replace bulbs
	• High resistance to ground at bulb socket	• Replace socket
	• Opens, ground in wiring harness from front turn signal bulb socket to indicator lights	• Locate and repair as required
Turn signal lights flash very slowly	• High resistance ground at light sockets	• Repair high resistance grounds at light sockets
	• Incorrect capacity turn signal flasher or bulb	• Replace turn signal flasher or bulb
	• If flashing rate is still extremely slow, check chassis wiring harness from the connector to light sockets for high resistance	• Locate and repair as required
	• Loose chassis to column harness connection	• Connect securely
	• Disconnect column to chassis connector. Connect new switch into system without removing old. Operate switch by hand. If flashing occurs at normal rate, the signal switch is defective.	• Replace turn signal switch

Troubleshooting the Power Steering Pump

Problem	Cause	Solution
Chirp noise in steering pump	• Loose belt	• Adjust belt tension to specification
Belt squeal (particularly noticeable at full wheel travel and stand still parking)	• Loose belt	• Adjust belt tension to specification
Growl noise in steering pump	• Excessive back pressure in hoses or steering gear caused by restriction	• Locate restriction and correct. Replace part if necessary.
Growl noise in steering pump (particularly noticeable at stand still parking)	• Scored pressure plates, thrust plate or rotor • Extreme wear of cam ring	• Replace parts and flush system • Replace parts
Groan noise in steering pump	• Low oil level • Air in the oil. Poor pressure hose connection.	• Fill reservoir to proper level • Tighten connector to specified torque. Bleed system by operating steering from right to left—full turn.
Rattle noise in steering pump	• Vanes not installed properly • Vanes sticking in rotor slots	• Install properly • Free up by removing burrs, varnish, or dirt
Swish noise in steering pump	• Defective flow control valve	• Replace part
Whine noise in steering pump	• Pump shaft bearing scored	• Replace housing and shaft. Flush system.
Hard steering or lack of assist	• Loose pump belt • Low oil level in reservoir **NOTE:** Low oil level will also result in excessive pump noise	• Adjust belt tension to specification • Fill to proper level. If excessively low, check all lines and joints for evidence of external leakage. Tighten loose connectors.
	• Steering gear to column misalignment • Lower coupling flange rubbing against steering gear adjuster plug • Tires not properly inflated	• Align steering column • Loosen pinch bolt and assemble properly • Inflate to recommended pressure
Foaming milky power steering fluid, low fluid level and possible low pressure	• Air in the fluid, and loss of fluid due to internal pump leakage causing overflow	• Check for leaks and correct. Bleed system. Extremely cold temperatures will cause system aeriation should the oil level be low. If oil level is correct and pump still foams, remove pump from vehicle and separate reservoir from body. Check welsh plug and body for cracks. If plug is loose or body is cracked, replace body.

Troubleshooting the Power Steering Pump (cont.)

Problem	Cause	Solution
Low pump pressure	• Flow control valve stuck or inoperative • Pressure plate not flat against cam ring	• Remove burrs or dirt or replace. Flush system. • Correct
Momentary increase in effort when turning wheel fast to right or left	• Low oil level in pump • Pump belt slipping • High internal leakage	• Add power steering fluid as required • Tighten or replace belt • Check pump pressure. (See pressure test)
Steering wheel surges or jerks when turning with engine running especially during parking	• Low oil level • Loose pump belt • Steering linkage hitting engine oil pan at full turn • Insufficient pump pressure	• Fill as required • Adjust tension to specification • Correct clearance • Check pump pressure. (See pressure test). Replace flow control valve if defective.
Steering wheel surges or jerks when turning with engine running especially during parking (cont.)	• Sticking flow control valve	• Inspect for varnish or damage, replace if necessary
Excessive wheel kickback or loose steering	• Air in system	• Add oil to pump reservoir and bleed by operating steering. Check hose connectors for proper torque and adjust as required.
Low pump pressure	• Extreme wear of cam ring • Scored pressure plate, thrust plate, or rotor • Vanes not installed properly • Vanes sticking in rotor slots • Cracked or broken thrust or pressure plate	• Replace parts. Flush system. • Replace parts. Flush system. • Install properly • Freeup by removing burrs, varnish, or dirt • Replace part

TORQUE SPECIFICATIONS

Component	U.S.	Metric
Ball joint assembly attaching bolts	50 ft. lbs	68 Nm
Ball joint-to-steering knuckle castellated nut	41–50 ft. lbs	55–65 Nm
Brake lines	8 ft. lbs	11 Nm
Caliper attaching bolts	38 ft. lbs	51 Nm
Drive axle stub shaft bolt	180 ft. lbs	260 Nm
Hub and bearing assembly attaching bolts	70 ft. lbs	95 Nm
Inner tie rod attaching bolts	65 ft. lbs	90 Nm
Lower control arm attaching bolts	65–66 ft. lbs	88–90 Nm
Lug nuts	100 ft. lbs	140 Nm
Rack assembly clamp bolt	22 ft. lbs	30 Nm
Rear axle attaching bolts	35 ft. lbs	47 Nm
Rear axle control arm bushing attaching bolt	68 ft. lbs	93 Nm
Shock absorber lower attaching bolt	35 ft. lbs	47 Nm
Shock absorber upper attaching bolt	21 ft. lbs	29 Nm
Stabilizer shaft bushing assembly nut	15 ft. lbs	20 Nm
Stabilizer shaft suspension support bolts	65–66 ft. lbs	88–90 Nm
Stabilizer shaft-to-support assembly nuts	16 ft. lbs	22 Nm
Stabilizer shaft-to control arm nuts	13 ft. lbs	17 Nm
Steering knuckle-to-strut bolts	133 ft. lbs	180 Nm
Steering wheel attaching bolt	30 ft. lbs	41 Nm
Steering column bracket support bolts	22 ft. lbs	30 Nm
Steering column upper pinch bolt	29–30 ft. lbs	40–41 Nm
Steering column lower pinch bolt	29 ft. lbs	40 Nm
Strut-to-strut tower nut	18 ft. lbs	24 Nm
Strut bearing cap retainer nut	65 ft. lbs	85 Nm
Tie rod end-to-steering knuckle nut	35–50 ft. lbs	47–75 Nm
Tie rod stud	15 ft. lbs	20 Nm

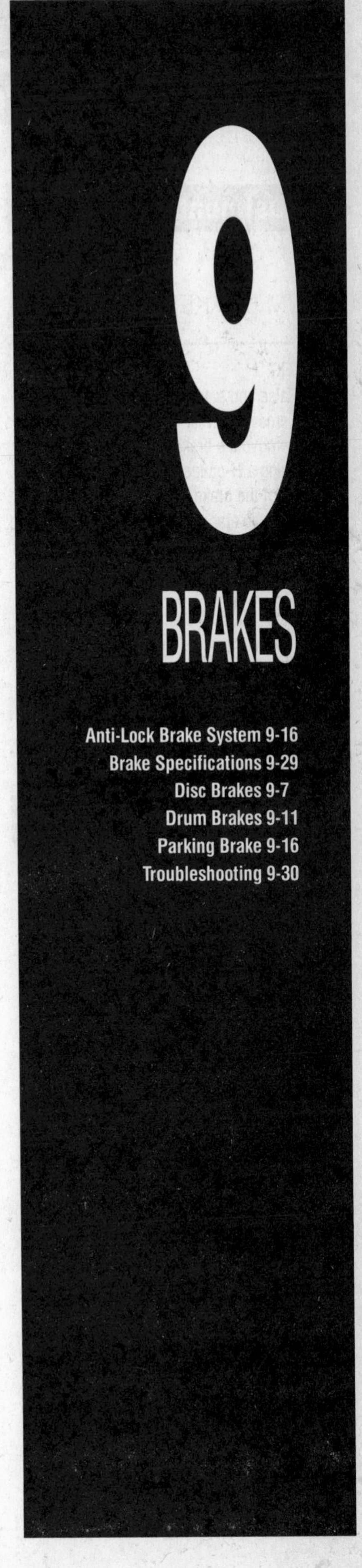

9 BRAKES

BRAKE OPERATING SYSTEM

Adjustments

DRUM BRAKES

➧ SEE FIG. 1

1. Raise and safely support the vehicle.
2. Remove the rear wheels.
3. Remove the brake drum.
4. Using a H-gauge, measure the inside diameter of the brake drum
5. Turn the star wheel to adjust the shoe and lining diameter to be 0.030 in. (0.76mm) less than the inside diameter of the drum for each wheel.
6. Install the drums and wheels.
7. Tighten the wheel nuts.
8. Make several alternate forward and reverse stops applying firm force to the brake pedal. Repeat this procedure until ample pedal reserve is built up.

Brake Light Switch

REMOVAL & INSTALLATION

➧ SEE FIG. 2

1. Disconnect the negative battery cable.
2. Remove the left sound insulator.
3. Disconnect the wiring from the switch.
4. Pull the switch out of the retainer in the bracket.

To install:

5. Install the retainer in the bracket, at the underside of the bracket.
6. Depress the brake pedal and insert the switch into the retainer until the switch seats. Allow the pedal to return.
7. Connect the connector.
8. To adjust the switch, pull the pedal up against the switch until no more clicks are heard. The switch will automatically move up in the retainer providing adjustment. Repeat a few times to ensure that the switch is properly adjusted.
9. Connect the negative battery cable and check the switch for proper operation.

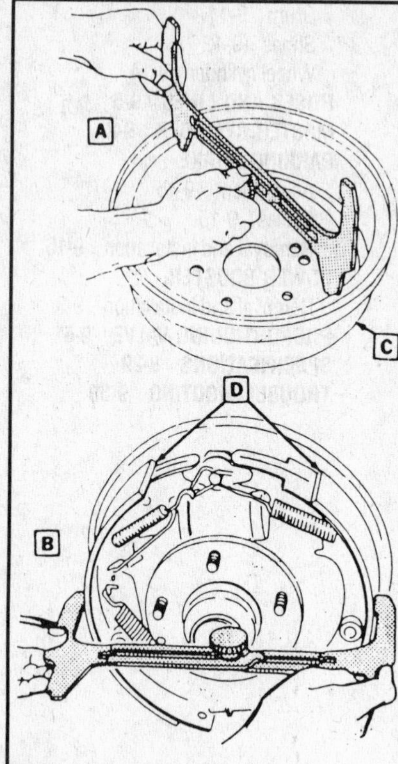

FIG. 1 Adjusting rear brakes

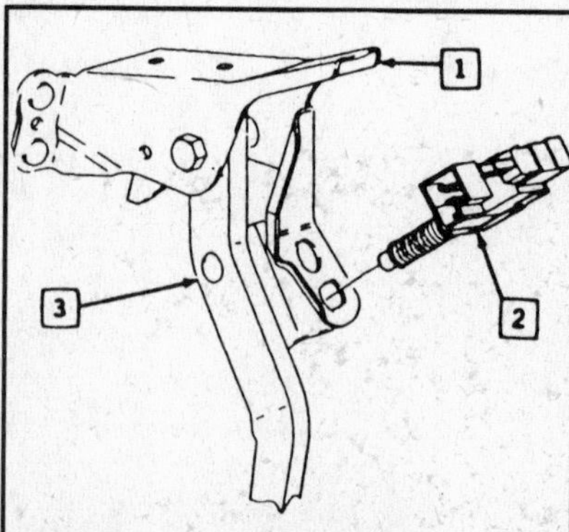

FIG. 2 Brake light switch installation

Brake Pedal

REMOVAL & INSTALLATION

➧ SEE FIG. 3

1. Remove the left side sound insulator.
2. Remove the brake pedal bracket.
3. Disconnect the pushrod from the brake pedal.
4. Remove the pivot bolt and bushing.
5. Remove the brake pedal.

To install:

6. Install the brake pedal.
7. Install the brake pedal bushing and pivot bolt. Tighten to 25 ft. lbs. (34 Nm).
8. Install the brake pedal bracket.
9. Install the left side sound insulator.

Master Cylinder

REMOVAL & INSTALLATION

➧ SEE FIG. 4

Except Anti-Lock Brakes

1. Disconnect the negative battery cable. Unplug the fluid level sensor connector.
2. Disconnect and plug the brake lines from the master cylinder.
3. Remove the nuts attaching the master cylinder to the power booster.
4. Remove the master cylinder from the mounting studs.
5. Remove the retaining roll pins and remove the fluid reservoir from the cylinder, if necessary.

To install:

6. Replace the reservoir O-rings and bench bleed the master cylinder.
7. Install to the booster and install the nuts.
8. Install the brake lines to the master cylinder.
9. Fill the reservoir with brake fluid.
10. Connect the negative battery cable and check the brakes for proper operation.

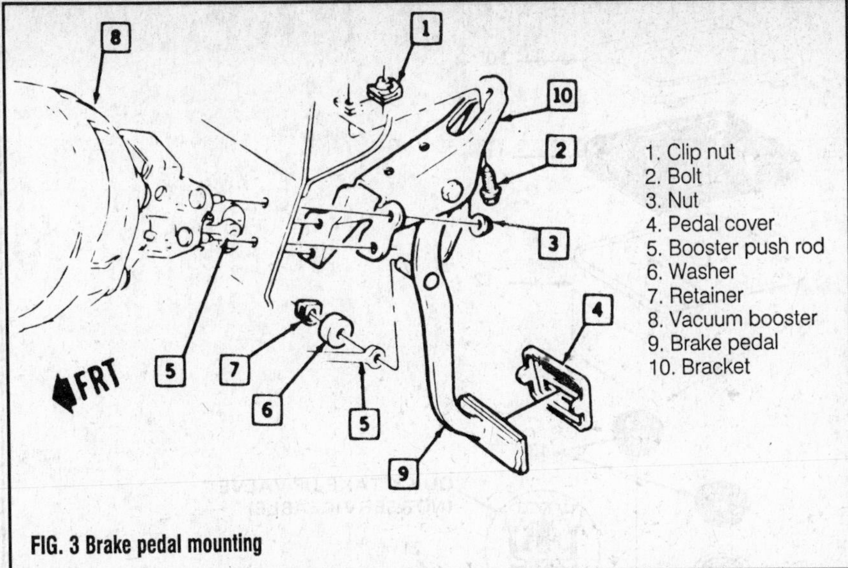

FIG. 3 Brake pedal mounting

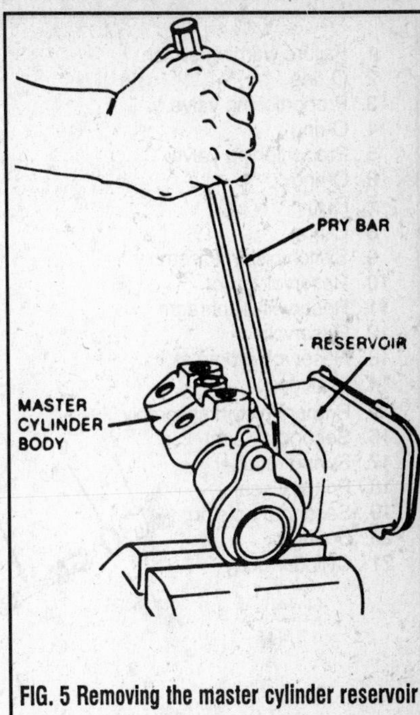

FIG. 5 Removing the master cylinder reservoir

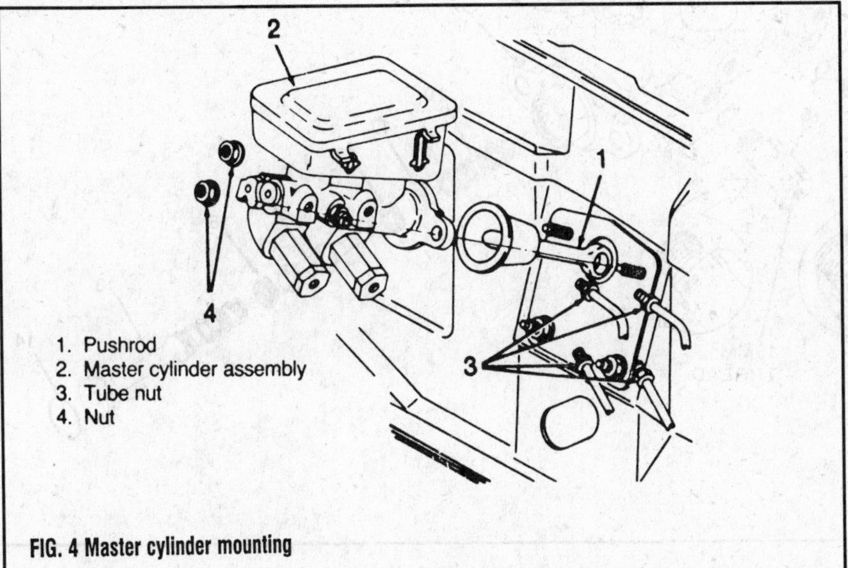
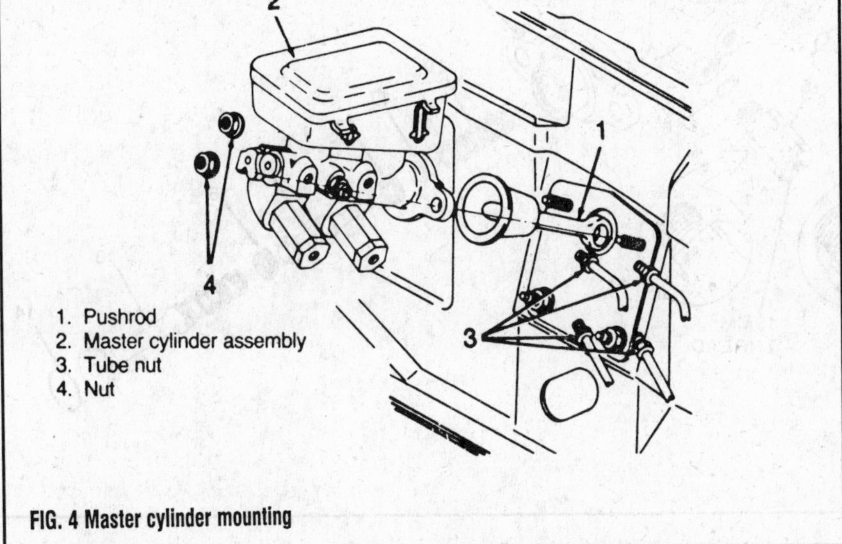

FIG. 4 Master cylinder mounting

OVERHAUL

➧ SEE FIGS. 4–7

1. Remove the master cylinder from the car.
2. Empty any remaining brake fluid from the reservoir.
3. Secure the master cylinder in a soft-jawed vise by clamping it on the mounting flange.
4. Using a small prybar, carefully lever the reservoir from the master cylinder body.
5. Remove the lockring while depressing the primary piston with a suitable blunt drift.
6. Use compressed air applied at the rear outlet to force out the pistons, retainer and spring.
7. Wash all parts in denatured alcohol and inspect for wear, scoring or other defects. Replace any parts found to be suspect. If any defect is found in the master cylinder bore, the entire cylinder must be replaced.

➡ The master cylinder cannot be honed and no abrasives are to be used in the bore.

8. Assemble the master cylinder components in reverse order of disassembly. Lubricate all parts and seals with clean brake fluid. Install the reservoir by pushing in with a rocking motion.
9. Bench bleeding the master cylinder reduces the possibility of getting air into the lines when the unit is installed. Connect two short pieces of brake line to the outlet fittings, then bend them until the free end is below the fluid level in the master cylinder reservoirs.
10. Fill the reservoirs with fresh brake fluid, then slowly pump the piston with a suitable blunt drift until no more air bubbles appear in the reservoirs.
11. Disconnect the two short lines, top up the brake fluid level and install the reservoir cap.
12. Install the master cylinder on the car. Attach the lines, but do not tighten them. Force out any air that might have been trapped at the connection by slowly depressing the brake pedal, then tighten the lines before releasing the pedal. Bleed the brake system as described below.

Power Brake Booster

REMOVAL & INSTALLATION

➧ SEE FIGS. 8–10

1. Disconnect the negative battery cable.
2. Disconnect the vacuum hose(s) from the booster.
3. Remove the master cylinder.
4. From inside of the vehicle, remove the booster pushrod from the brake pedal.
5. Remove the nuts that attach the booster to the dash panel and remove it from the vehicle.
6. Transfer the necessary parts to the new booster.
7. The installation is the reverse of the removal procedure.
8. Bleed the brake system, connect the negative battery cable and check the brakes for proper operation.

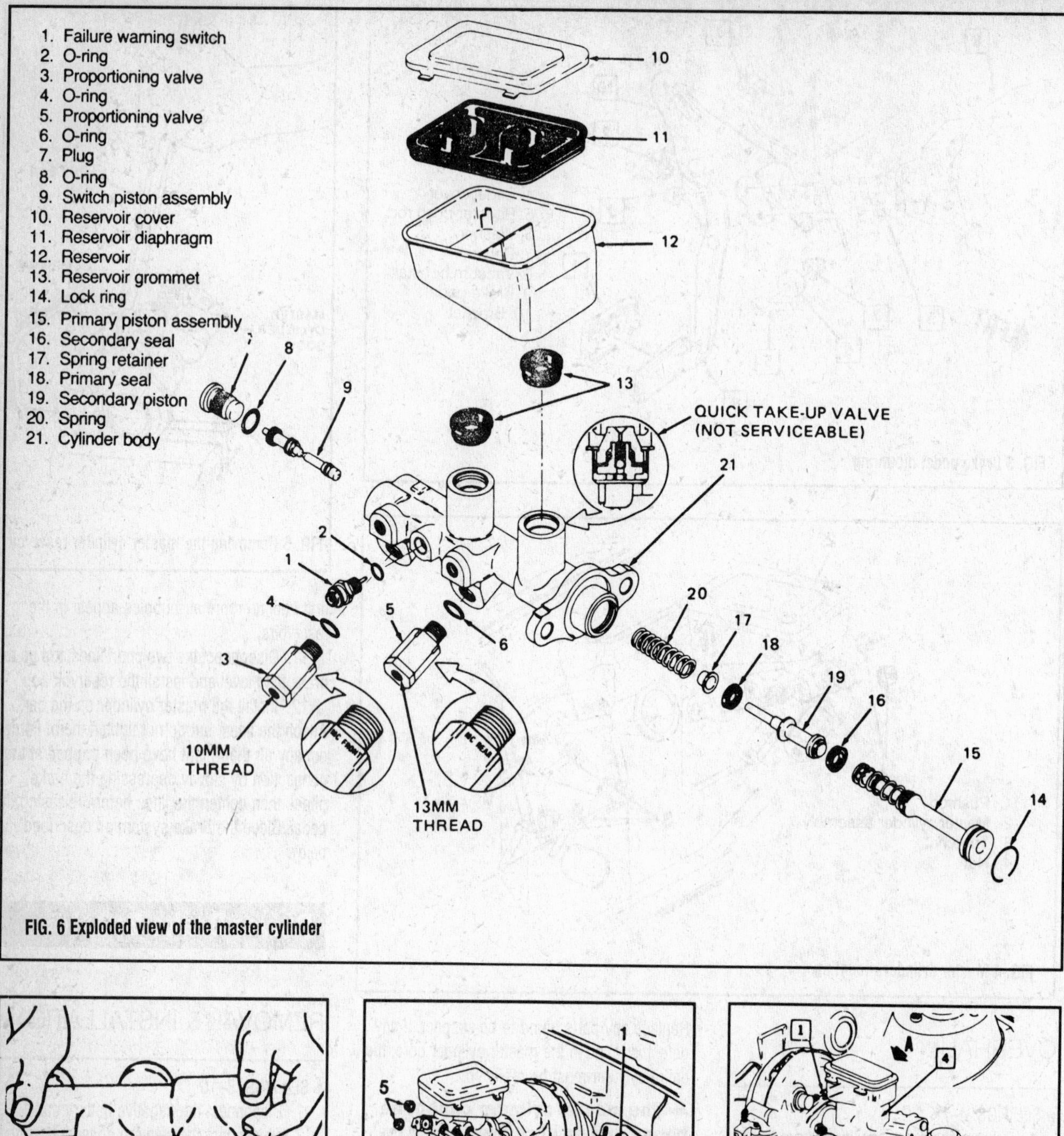

1. Failure warning switch
2. O-ring
3. Proportioning valve
4. O-ring
5. Proportioning valve
6. O-ring
7. Plug
8. O-ring
9. Switch piston assembly
10. Reservoir cover
11. Reservoir diaphragm
12. Reservoir
13. Reservoir grommet
14. Lock ring
15. Primary piston assembly
16. Secondary seal
17. Spring retainer
18. Primary seal
19. Secondary piston
20. Spring
21. Cylinder body
QUICK TAKE-UP VALVE
(NOT SERVICEABLE)
10MM
THREAD
13MM
THREAD

FIG. 6 Exploded view of the master cylinder

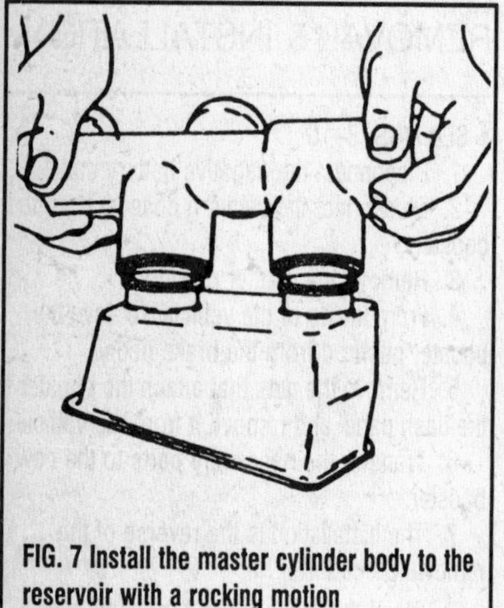

FIG. 7 Install the master cylinder body to the reservoir with a rocking motion

1. Pushrod
2. Master cylinder
3. Brake booster
4. Nut
5. Nut

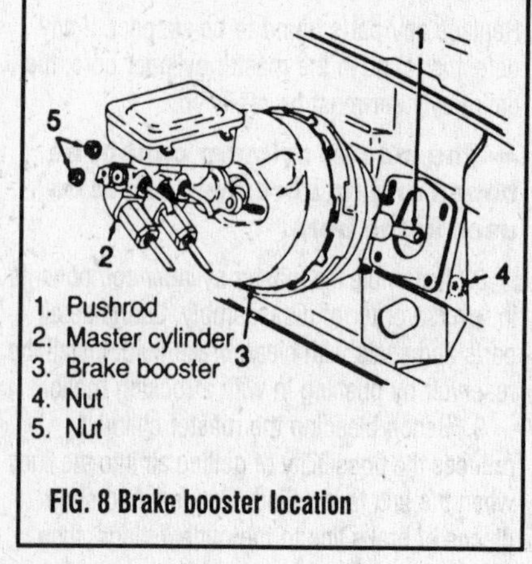

FIG. 8 Brake booster location

FRT
FRT
VIEW A
1. Hose
2. Filter
3. Support
4. Master cylinder
5. Vacuum booster

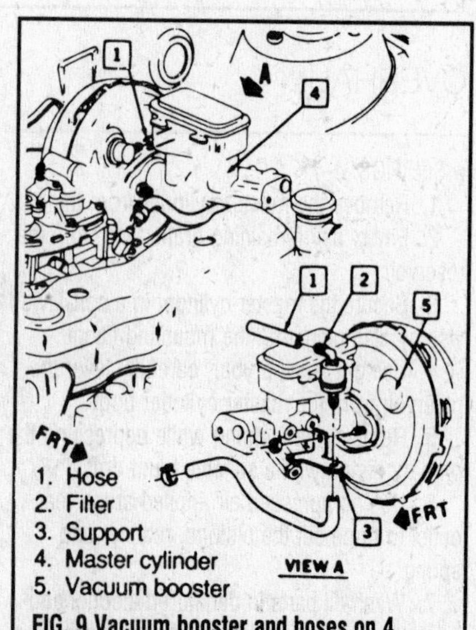

FIG. 9 Vacuum booster and hoses on 4 cylinder engine

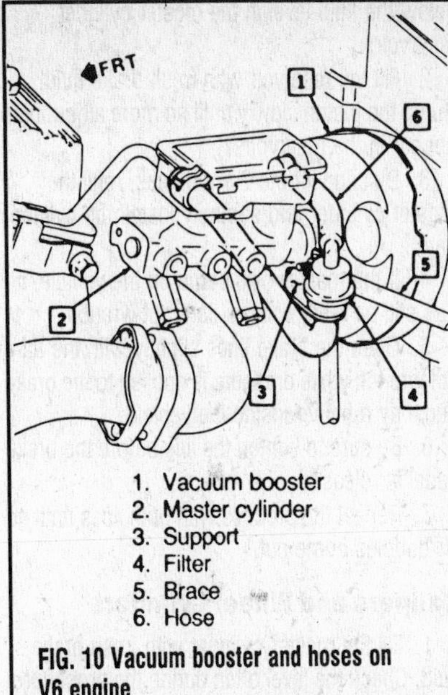

FIG. 10 Vacuum booster and hoses on V6 engine

Proportioning Valve

REMOVAL & INSTALLATION

➧ SEE FIG. 6

1. Disconnect the negative battery cable.
2. Remove the retaining roll pins and remove the fluid reservoir from the cylinder, if necessary.
3. Remove the proportioner valve cap assemblies.
4. Remove the O-rings.
5. Remove the springs.
6. Carefully remove the proportioner valve pistons.
7. Remove the seals from the pistons.

To install:

8. Thoroughly clean and dry all parts.
9. Lubricate the new piston seals with the silicone grease included in the repair kit or brake assembly fluid. Install to the pistons with the seal lips facing upward toward the cap assembly.
10. Lubricate the stem of the pistons and install to their bores.
11. Install the springs.
12. Lubricate and install the new O-rings in their grooves in the cap assemblies.
13. Install the caps to the master cylinder and tighten to 20 ft. lbs. (27 Nm).
14. Install the reservoir, if replaced.
15. Fill the reservoir with brake fluid.
16. Connect the negative battery cable and check the brakes for proper operation.

Brake Hoses and Pipes

REMOVAL & INSTALLATION

1. If brake line fittings are corroded, apply a coating of penetrating oil and allow to stand before disconnecting the brake lines.
2. Use a brake line wrench to loosen the brake hose or pipe.
3. Remove the support brackets.
4. Note the location of the brake pipe before removal.
5. Remove the brake pipe or hose.

To install:

6. Install the new hose or pipe, observing the location of original installation.
7. Install the support brackets.
8. Ensure the pipes or hoses are clear of rotating parts and will not chafe on suspension parts.
9. Tighten the brake hose or pipe using a brake line wrench. Do not overtighten.
10. Properly bleed the brake hydraulic system.
11. Test drive the vehicle.

BRAKE PIPE FLARING

➧ SEE FIGS. 11–13

Precautions:

Always use double walled steel brake pipe.

Carefully route and retain replacement pipes.

Always use the correct fasteners and mount in the original location.

Use only double lap flaring tools. The use of single lap flaring tools produces a flare which may not withstand system pressure.

1. Obtain the recommended pipe and steel fitting nut of the correct size. Use the outside diameter of the pipe to specify size.
2. Cut the pipe to the appropriate length with a pipe cutter. Do not force the cutter. Correct length of pipe is determined by measuring the old pipe using a string and adding approximately $^1/_8$ in. (3mm) for each flare.
3. Make sure the fittings are installed before starting the flare.
4. Chamfer the inside and outside diameter of the pipe with the de-buring tool.
5. Remove all traces of lubricant from the brake pipe and flaring tool.
6. Clamp the flaring tool body in a vise.
7. Select the correct size collet and forming mandrel for the pipe size used.
8. Insert the proper forming mandrel into the tool body. While holding forming mandrel in place with your finger, thread in the forcing screw until it makes contact and begins to move the forming mandrel. When contact is made, turn the forcing screw back 1 complete turn.
9. Slide the clamping nut over the brake pipe and insert the prepared brake pipe into the correct collet. Leave approximately 0.750 in. (19mm) of tubing extending out of the collet. Insert the assembly into the tool body. The brake pipe end must contact the face of the forming mandrel.
10. Tighten the clamping nut into the tool body very tight or the pipe may push out.
11. Wrench tighten the forcing screw in until it bottoms. Do not over-tighten the forcing screw or the flare may become over-sized.
12. Back the clamping nut out of the toll body and disassemble the clamping the clamping nut and collet assembly. The flare is now ready for use.
13. Bend the pipe assembly to match the old pipe. Clearance of 0.750 in. (19mm) must be maintained to all moving or vibrating parts.

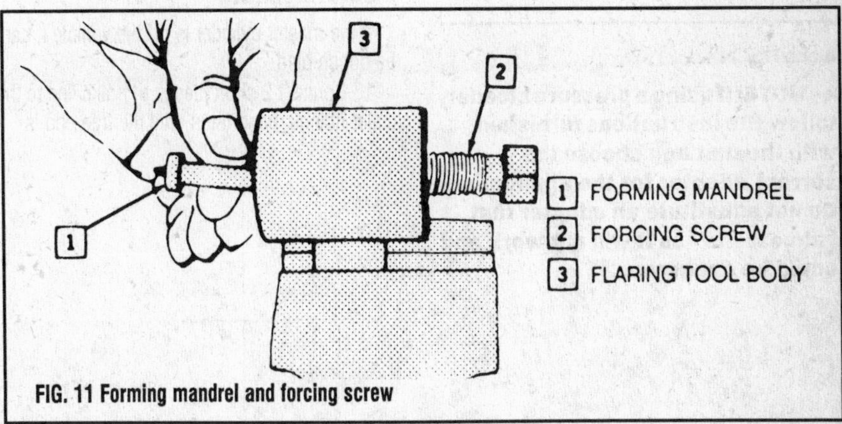

FIG. 11 Forming mandrel and forcing screw

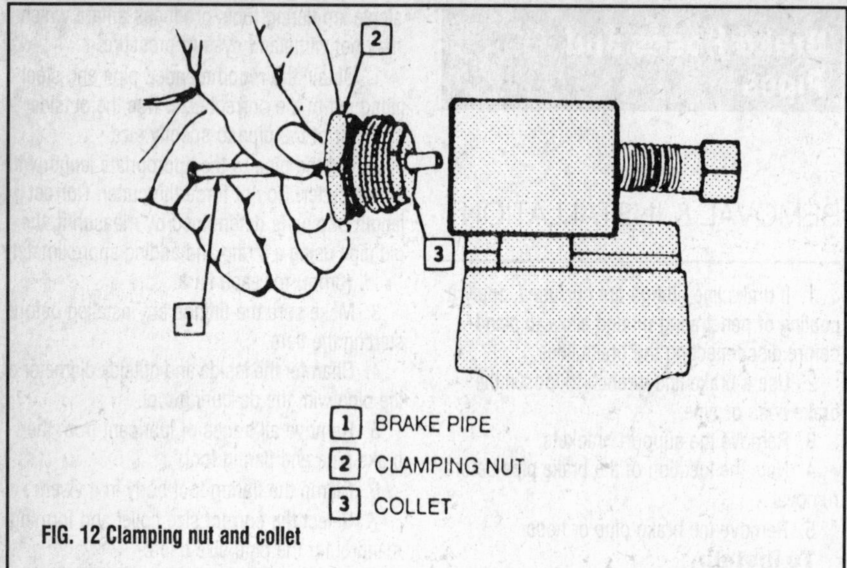

FIG. 12 Clamping nut and collet

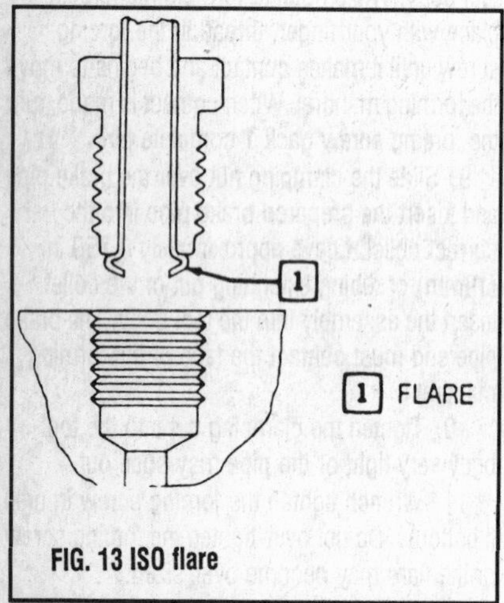

FIG. 13 ISO flare

Bleeding

EXCEPT ANTI-LOCK BRAKES

➧ SEE FIG. 14

➡ **NOTE: If using a pressure bleeder, follow the instructions furnished with the unit and choose the correct adaptor for the application. Do not substitute an adapter that "almost fits" as it will not work and could be dangerous.**

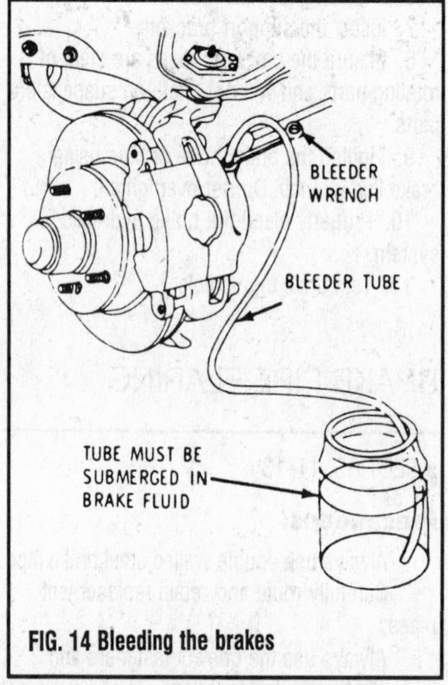

FIG. 14 Bleeding the brakes

Master Cylinder

If the master cylinder is off the vehicle it can be bench bled.

1. Connect 2 short pieces of brake line to the outlet fittings, bend them until the free end is below the fluid level in the master cylinder reservoirs.
2. Fill the reservoir with fresh brake fluid. Pump the piston slowly until no more air bubbles appear in the reservoirs.
3. Disconnect the 2 short lines, refill the master cylinder and securely install the cylinder caps.
4. If the master cylinder is on the vehicle, it can still be bled, using a flare nut wrench.
5. Open the brake lines slightly with the flare nut wrench while pressure is applied to the brake pedal by a helper inside the vehicle.
6. Be sure to tighten the line before the brake pedal is released.
7. Repeat the process with both lines until no air bubbles come out.

Calipers and Wheel Cylinders

1. Fill the master cylinder with fresh brake fluid. Check the level often during the procedure.
2. Starting with the right rear wheel, remove the protective cap from the bleeder, if equipped, and place where it will not be lost. Clean the bleed screw.

✲✲ CAUTION

When bleeding the brakes, keep face away from the brake area. Spewing fluid may cause facial and/or visual damage. Do not allow brake fluid to spill on the car's finish; it will remove the paint.

3. If the system is empty, the most efficient way to get fluid down to the wheel is to loosen the bleeder about 1/2–3/4 turn, place a finger firmly over the bleeder and have a helper pump the brakes slowly until fluid comes out the bleeder. Once fluid is at the bleeder, close it before the pedal is released inside the vehicle.

➡ **NOTE: If the pedal is pumped rapidly, the fluid will churn and create small air bubbles, which are almost impossible to remove from the system. These air bubbles will eventually congregate and a spongy pedal will result.**

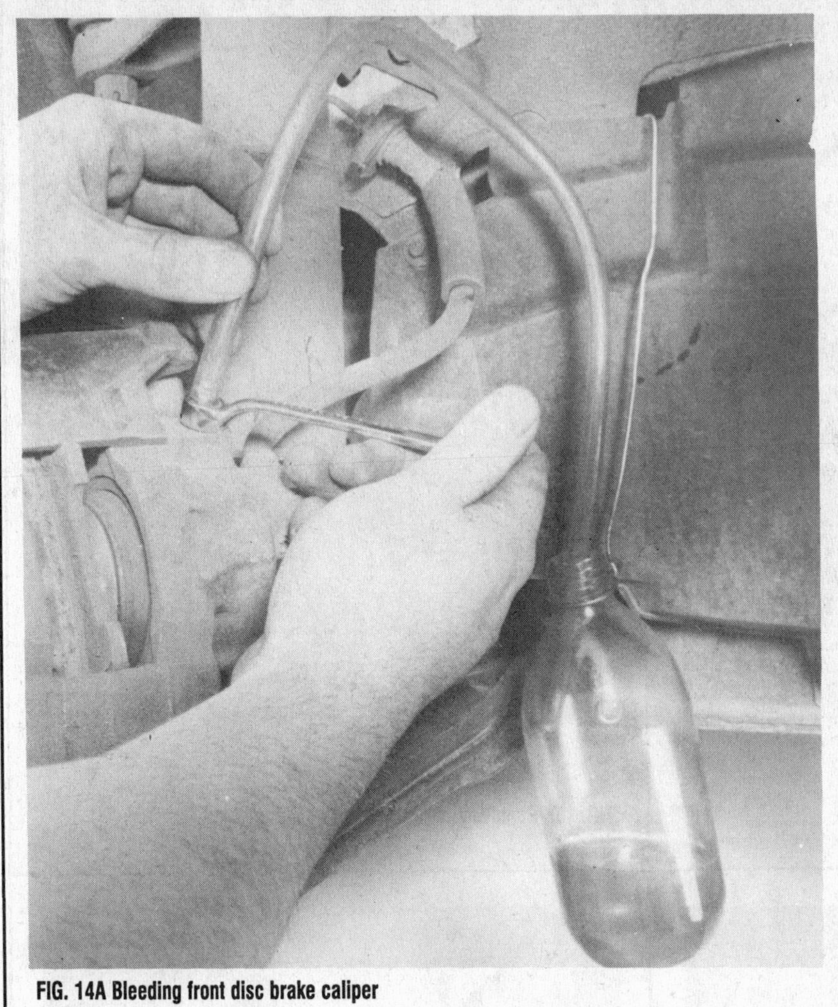

FIG. 14A Bleeding front disc brake caliper

4. Once fluid has been pumped to the caliper or wheel cylinder, open the bleed screw again, have the helper press the brake pedal to the floor, lock the bleeder and have the helper slowly release the pedal. Wait 15 seconds and repeat the procedure (including the 15 second wait) until no more air comes out of the bleeder upon application of the brake pedal. Remember to close the bleeder before the pedal is released inside the vehicle each time the bleeder is opened. If not, air will be induced into the system.

5. If a helper is not available, connect a small hose to the bleeder, place the end in a container of brake fluid and proceed to pump the pedal from inside the vehicle until no more air comes out the bleeder. The hose will prevent air from entering the system.

6. Repeat the procedure on remaining wheel cylinders in order:

a. left front
b. left rear
c. right front

7. Hydraulic brake systems must be totally flushed if the fluid becomes contaminated with water, dirt or other corrosive chemicals. To flush, bleed the entire system until all fluid has been replaced with the correct type of new fluid.

8. Install the bleeder cap(s), if equipped, on the bleeder to keep dirt out. Always road test the vehicle after brake work of any kind is done.

FRONT DISC BRAKES

✱✱ CAUTION

Brake shoes contain asbestos, which has been determined to be a cancer causing agent. Never clean the brake surfaces with compressed air! Avoid inhaling any dust from any brake surface! When cleaning brake surfaces, use a commercially available brake cleaning fluid.

Brake Pads

REMOVAL & INSTALLATION

➧ SEE FIGS. 15–20

1. Remove some of the fluid from the master cylinder. Raise and safely support the vehicle.
2. Remove the tire and wheel assembly.
3. Bottom the piston in its bore for clearance.
4. Remove the caliper mounting bolt and sleeve assemblies.
5. Lift the caliper off of the rotor.
6. Remove the pads from the caliper.

To install:

7. Use a large C-clamp to compress the piston back into the caliper bore.
8. Install the pads and anti-rattle clip to the caliper. Adjust the bent-over tabs for a tight fit.
9. Position the caliper over the rotor so the caliper engages the adaptor correctly. Lubricate and install the sleeves and bolts. Tighten to 38 ft. lbs. (51 Nm).
10. Install the tire and wheel assembly.
11. Fill the master cylinder and check the brakes for proper operation.

FIG. 15A Inspecting front disc brake linings

FIG. 15B Removing front disc brake caliper mounting bolts

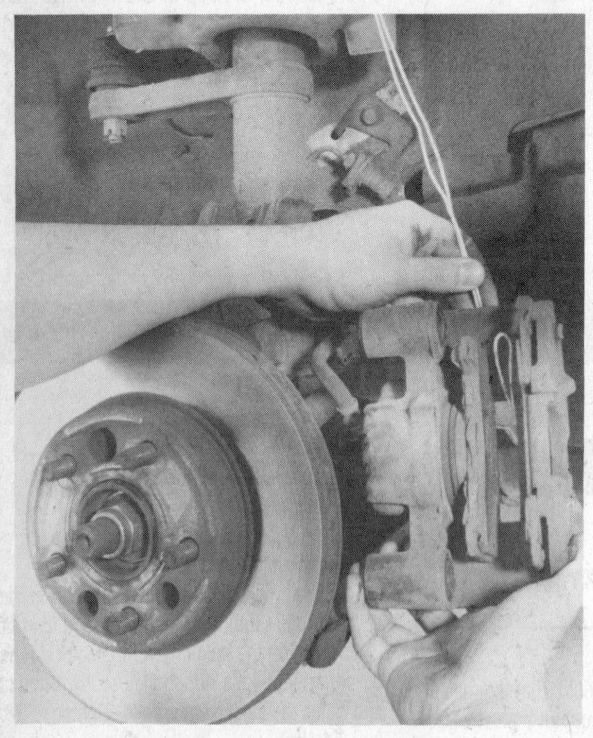

FIG. 15C Supporting front disc brake caliper after removal—hydraulic line connected

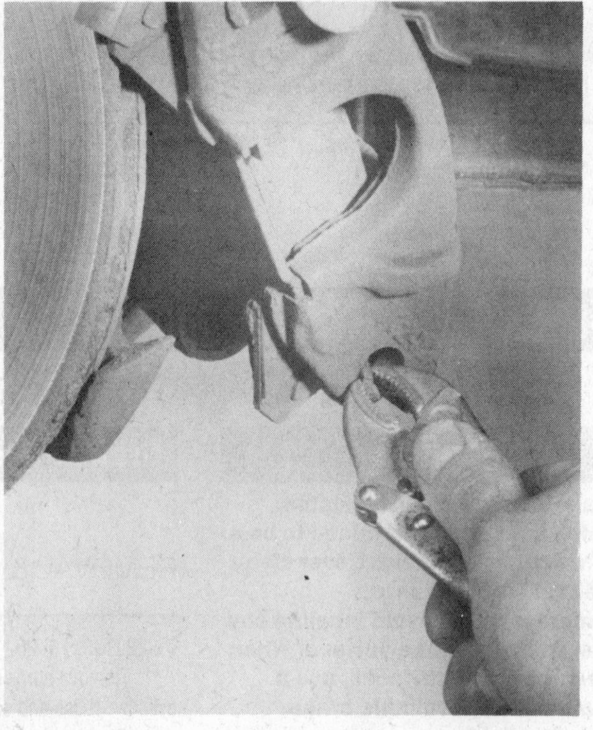

FIG. 15D Removing front disc brake pad from caliper

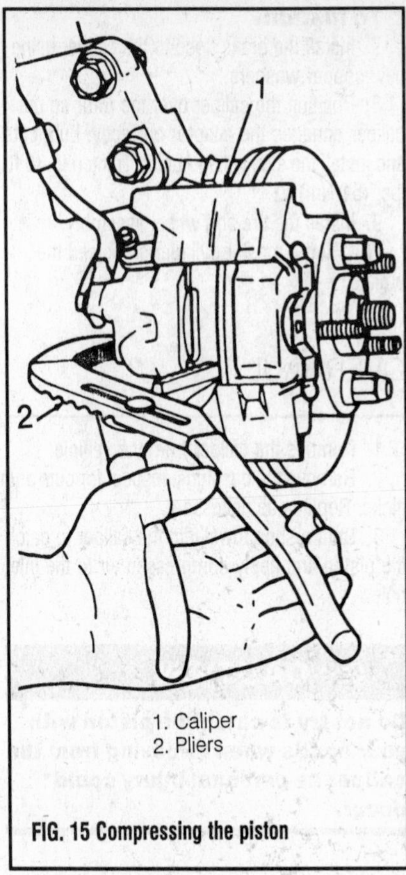

FIG. 15 Compressing the piston

FIG. 15E Compressing caliper piston into bore prior to installation of new disc brake pads

INSPECTION

1. Inspect the brake linings approximately every 6,000 miles or whenever the wheels are removed.

2. Check both ends of the pad for uneven wear.

3. Check the lining thickness on the inner shoe to make sure it is wearing evenly.

➡ **Some inboard shoes have a thermal lining against the shoe, molded integrally with the lining. Do not confuse this lining with uneven inboard-outboard lining wear.**

4. Whenever the thickness of the lining is worn to the wear indicator, replace the pads on both sides.

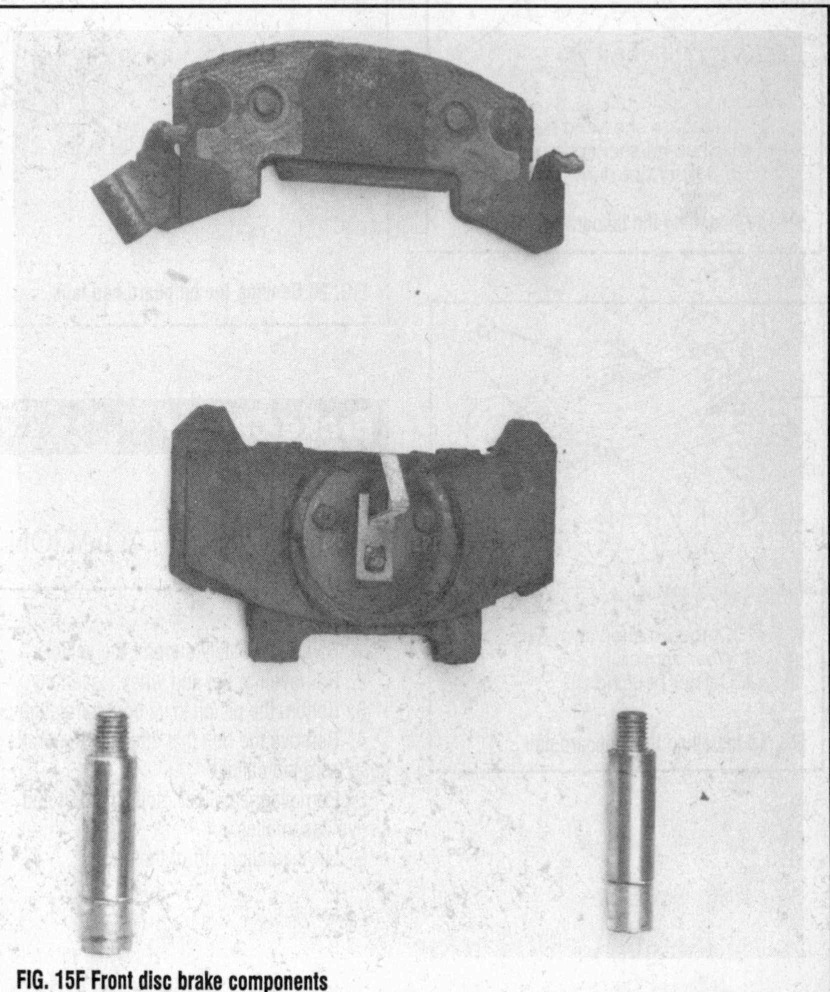
FIG. 15F Front disc brake components

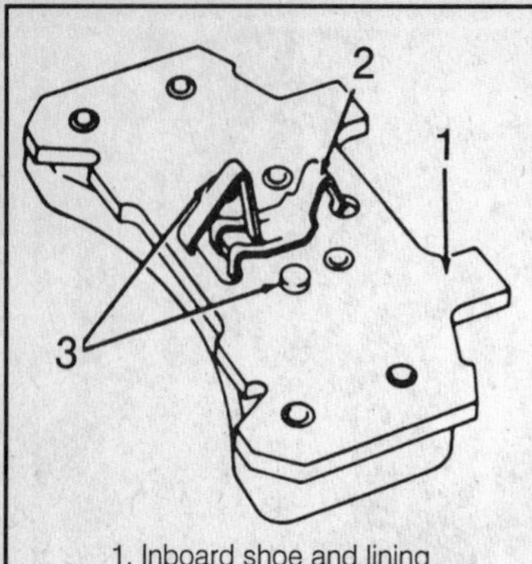

1. Inboard shoe and lining
2. Shoe retainer spring
3. Retention lug

FIG. 16 Inboard pad and retainer

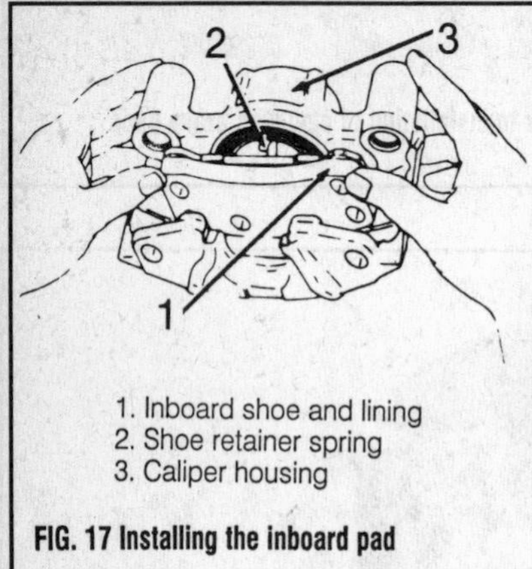

1. Inboard shoe and lining
2. Shoe retainer spring
3. Caliper housing

FIG. 17 Installing the inboard pad

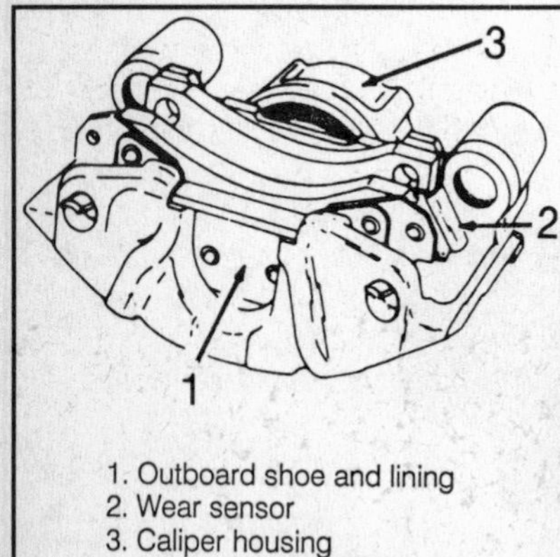

1. Outboard shoe and lining
2. Wear sensor
3. Caliper housing

FIG. 18 Installing the outboard pad

SILICONE GREASE

2 3 4 1

1. Mounting sleeve
2. Sleeve
3. Bushing
4. Caliper housing

FIG. 19 Lubrication points

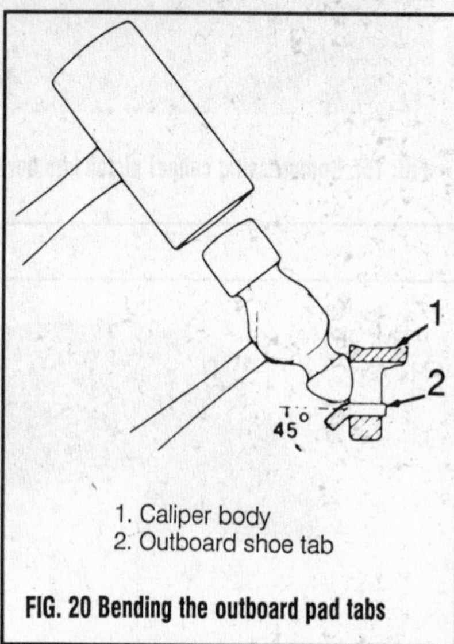

1. Caliper body
2. Outboard shoe tab

FIG. 20 Bending the outboard pad tabs

Brake Caliper

REMOVAL & INSTALLATION

➧ SEE FIG. 21

1. Raise and safely support the vehicle.
2. Remove the tire and wheel assembly.
3. Bottom the piston in its bore for clearance.
4. Remove the bolt that attaches the brake hose from the caliper.
5. Remove the caliper mounting bolt and sleeve assemblies.
6. Lift the caliper off of the rotor.

To install:

7. Install the brake hose to the caliper using new copper washers.
8. Position the caliper over the rotor so the caliper engages the adaptor correctly. Lubricate and install the sleeves and bolts. Tighten to 38 ft. lbs. (51 Nm).
9. Install the tire and wheel assembly.
10. Fill the master cylinder and bleed the brakes.

OVERHAUL

1. Remove the caliper from the vehicle.
2. Remove the bushings. Inspect for cuts and nicks. Replace as necessary.
3. Stuff a shop towel into the caliper to catch the piston and apply compressed air to the inlet hole.

**** CAUTION**

Do not try to catch the piston with your hands when removing from the caliper as personal injury could occur.

4. Inspect the piston for scoring, nicks, corrosion and worn chrome plating. Replace as necessary.
5. Remove the boot from the caliper housing bore.
6. Remove the piston seal from the groove with a small wooden or plastic tool.
7. Inspect the housing bore and seal groove for scoring, nicks, corrosion and wear. Crocus cloth can be used to polish out light corrosion.
8. Remove the bleeder valve and bleeder valve cap.

To install:

9. Install the bleeder valve and bleeder valve cap into the caliper.
10. Lubricate all rubber parts with clean brake fluid.
11. Install the piston seal into the caliper seal groove. Make sure it is not twisted.
12. Install the boot onto the piston.
13. Carefully, install the piston and boot into the caliper bore and push to the bottom of the bore.
14. Lubricate the bevelled end of the bushings with silicone grease. Pinch the bushing and install the bevelled end first. Push the bushing through the housing mounting bore.
15. Install the caliper assembly.

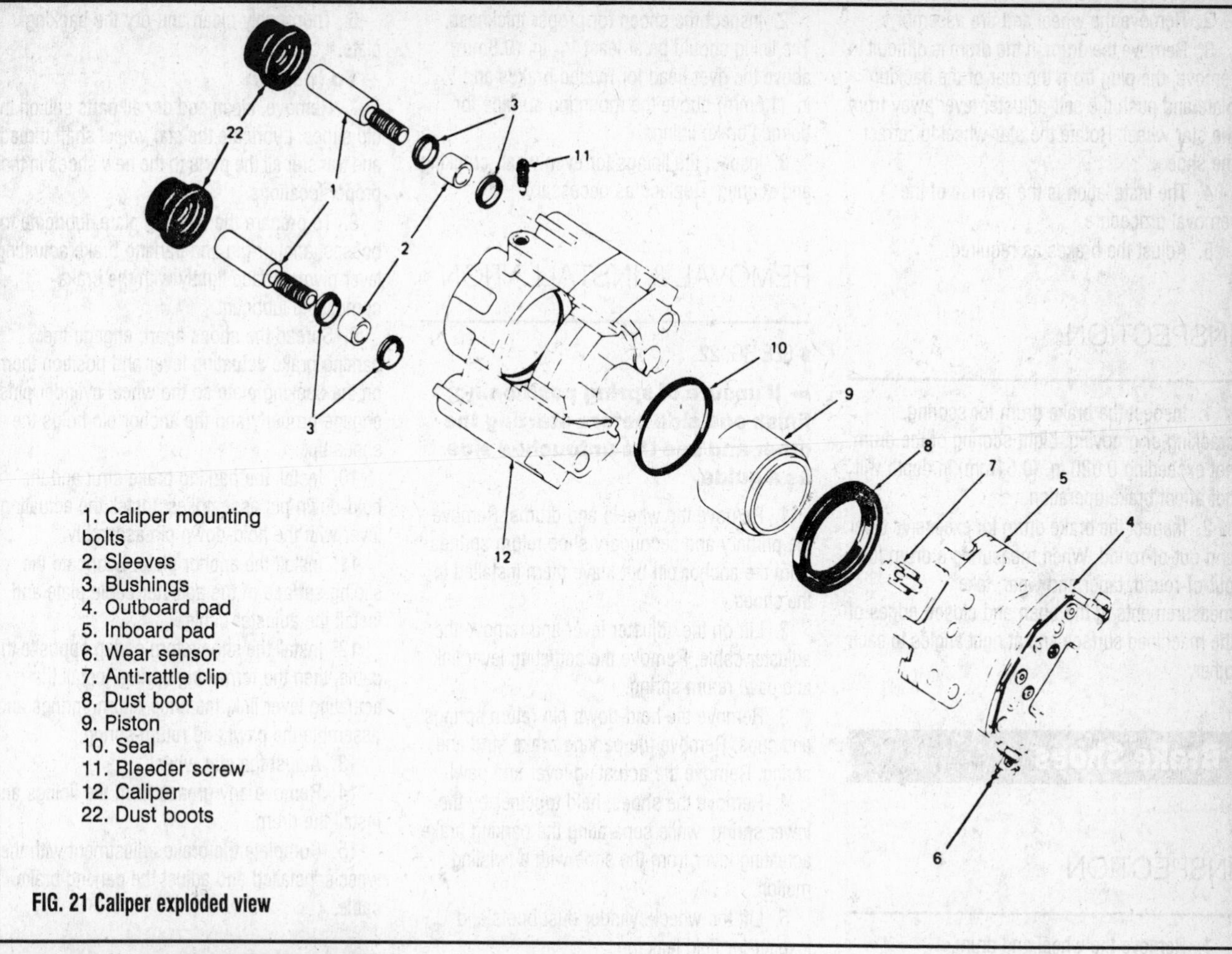

FIG. 21 Caliper exploded view

Brake Rotor

REMOVAL & INSTALLATION

1. Raise and safely support the vehicle. Remove the tire and wheel assembly.
2. Remove the caliper and brake pads.
3. Remove the rotor from the hub.
4. The installation is the reverse of the removal procedure.

INSPECTION

Thickness Variation

1. Measure the thickness at 4 points on the rotor. Make all measure measurements at the same distance in from the edge of the rotor.
2. If the variation from lowest to highest reading is greater than 0.0005 in. (0.013mm), the rotor should be resurfaced or replaced.

Lateral Runout

1. Remove the caliper and install 2 lug nuts to hold the rotor in position.
2. Secure a dial indicator to the steering knuckle so the indicator stylus contacts the rotor at about 1 in. (25mm) from the outer edge of the rotor.
3. Zero the dial indicator.
4. Move the rotor 1 complete revolution and observe the total indicated runout.
5. If the runout exceeds 0.0031 in. (0.08mm), resurface or replace the rotor.

REAR DRUM BRAKES

CAUTION

Brake shoes contain asbestos, which has been determined to be a cancer causing agent. Never clean the brake surfaces with compressed air! Avoid inhaling any dust from any brake surface! When cleaning brake surfaces, use a commercially available brake cleaning fluid.

Brake Drums

REMOVAL & INSTALLATION

1. Raise and safely support the vehicle.

2. Remove the wheel and tire assembly.

3. Remove the drum. If the drum is difficult to remove, the plug from the rear of the backing plate and push the self-adjuster lever away from the star wheel. Rotate the star wheel to retract the shoes.

4. The installation is the reverse of the removal procedure.

5. Adjust the brakes as required.

INSPECTION

1. Inspect the brake drum for scoring, cracking or grooving. Light scoring of the drum not exceeding 0.020 in. (0.51mm) in depth will not affect brake operation.

2. Inspect the brake drum for excessive taper and out-of-round. When measuring a drum for out-of-round, taper and wear, take measurements at the open and closed edges of the machined surface and at right angles to each other.

Brake Shoes

INSPECTION

1. Remove the wheel and drum.

2. Inspect the shoes for proper thickness. The lining should be at least $\frac{1}{32}$ in. (0.8mm) above the rivet head for riveted brakes and $\frac{1}{16}$ in. (1.6mm) above the mounting surface for bonded brake linings.

3. Inspect the linings for even wear, cracking and scoring. Replace as necessary.

REMOVAL & INSTALLATION

➧ SEE FIG. 22

➡ If unsure of spring positioning, finish one side before starting the other and use the untouched side as a guide.

1. Remove the wheels and drums. Remove the primary and secondary shoe return springs from the anchor pin but leave them installed in the shoes.

2. Lift on the adjuster lever and remove the adjuster cable. Remove the actuating lever link and pawl return spring.

3. Remove the hold-down pin return springs and cups. Remove the parking brake strut and spring. Remove the actuating lever and pawl.

4. Remove the shoes, held together by the lower spring, while separating the parking brake actuating lever from the shoe with a twisting motion.

5. Lift the wheel cylinder dust boots and inspect for fluid leakage.

6. Thoroughly clean and dry the backing plate.

To install:

7. Remove, clean and dry all parts still on the old shoes. Lubricate the star wheel shaft threads and transfer all the parts to the new shoes in their proper locations.

8. To prepare the backing plate, lubricate the bosses, anchor pin and parking brake actuating lever pivot surface lightly with the brake-compatible lubricant.

9. Spread the shoes apart, engage the parking brake actuating lever and position them on the backing plate so the wheel cylinder pins engage properly and the anchor pin holds the shoes up.

10. Install the parking brake strut and the hold-down pin assemblies. Install the actuating lever with the hold-down pin assembly.

11. Install the anchor plate. Lubricate the sliding surface of the adjuster cable plate and install the adjuster cable.

12. Install the shoe return spring opposite the cable, then the remaining spring. Install the actuating lever link, the shoe return springs and assemble the pawl and return spring.

13. Adjust the star wheel.

14. Remove any grease from the linings and install the drum.

15. Complete the brake adjustment with the wheels installed and adjust the parking brake cable.

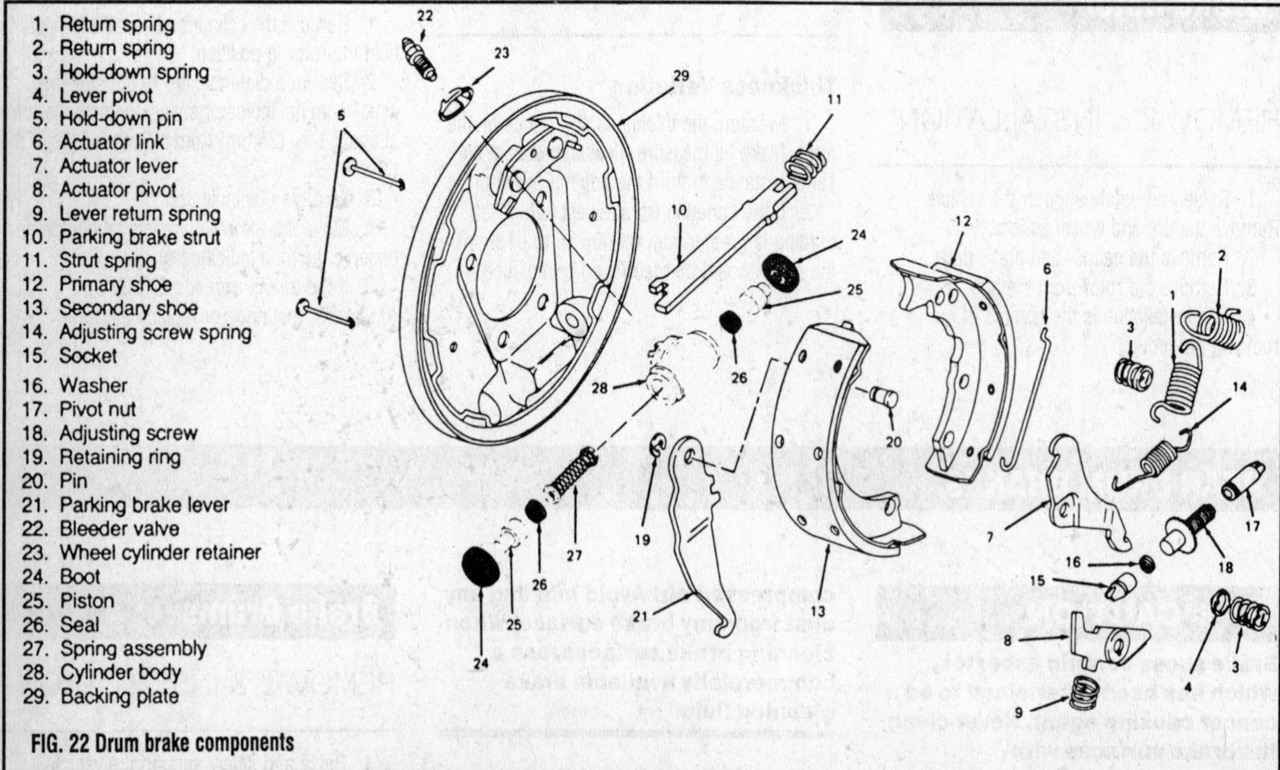

FIG. 22 Drum brake components

FIG. 22A Removing rear brake shoes

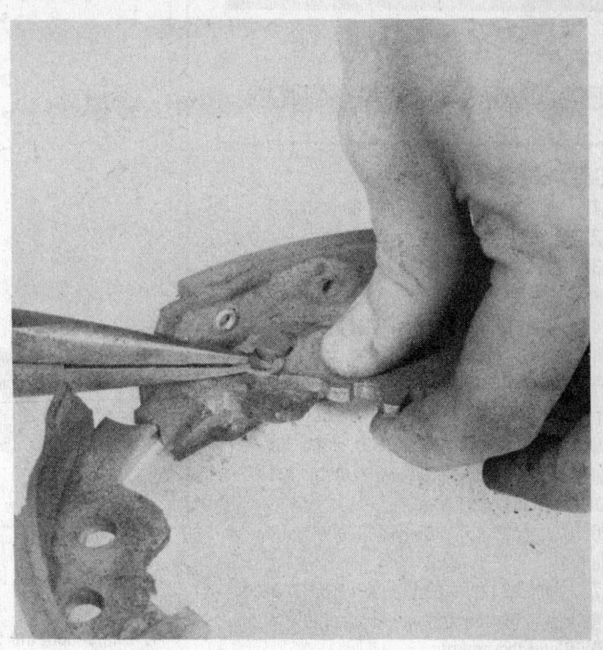

FIG. 22B Removing parking brake actuator lever pin circlip

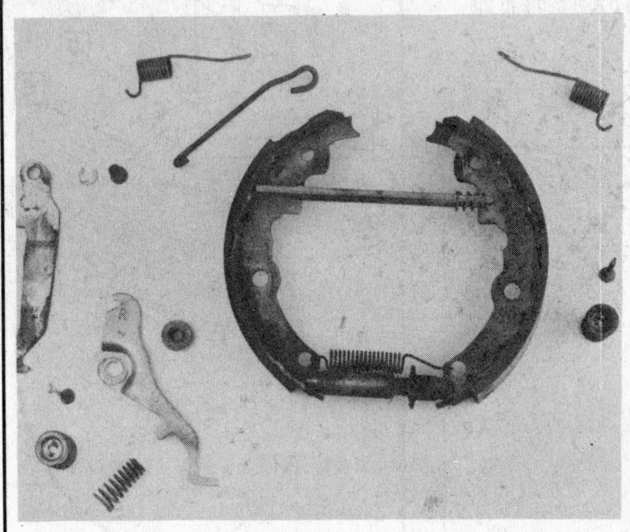

FIG. 22C Rear brake assembly components

FIG. 22D Applying grease to brake shoe mounting bosses on backing plate prior to installation of brake shoes

Wheel Cylinders

REMOVAL & INSTALLATION

➧ SEE FIGS. 23–25

1. Raise and safely support the vehicle.
2. Remove the wheel, drum and brake shoes.
3. Remove and plug the brake line from the wheel cylinder.
4. Remove the wheel cylinder bolts and remove the cylinder from the backing plate.

To install:

5. Apply a very thin coating of silicone sealer to the cylinder mounting surface, install the cylinder to the backing plate and install the attaching bolts.
6. Connect the brake line to the wheel cylinder.
7. Install all brake parts that were removed.
8. Install the tire and wheel assembly.
9. Bleed the brakes.

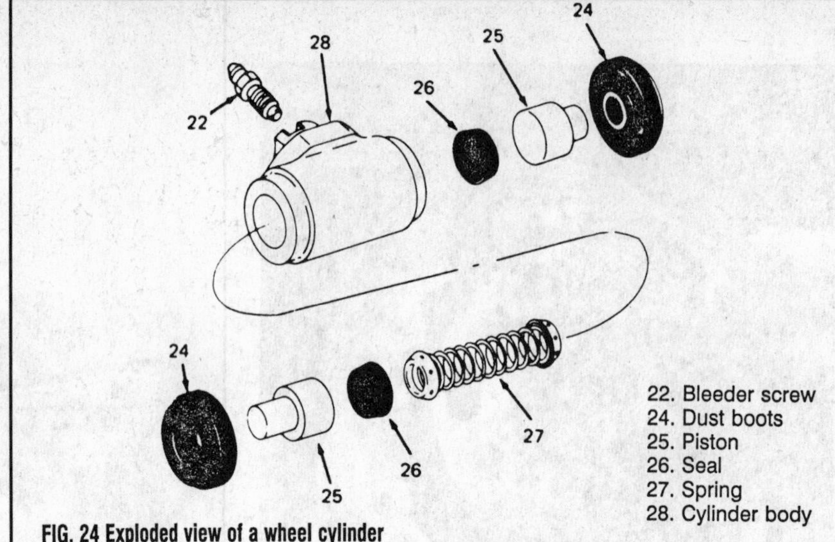

FIG. 24 Exploded view of a wheel cylinder

Brake Backing Plate

REMOVAL & INSTALLATION

1. Raise and safely support the vehicle. Remove the rear wheel(s).
2. Remove the brake components.
3. Disconnect the inlet tube and nut from the wheel cylinder.
4. Disconnect the parking brake cable from the backing plate.
5. Remove the hub and bearing assembly bolts.
6. Remove the backing plate.

To install:

7. Install the backing plate to the axle assembly.
8. Install the hub and bearing assembly bolts.
9. Connect the parking brake cable to the backing plate.
10. Connect the inlet tube and nut to the wheel cylinder. Tight to 12 ft. lbs. (17 Nm).
11. Install the brake system components. Check the brake adjustment.
12. Bleed the brake system.
13. Install the rear wheel(s).
14. Lower the vehicle.
15. Adjust the parking brake.

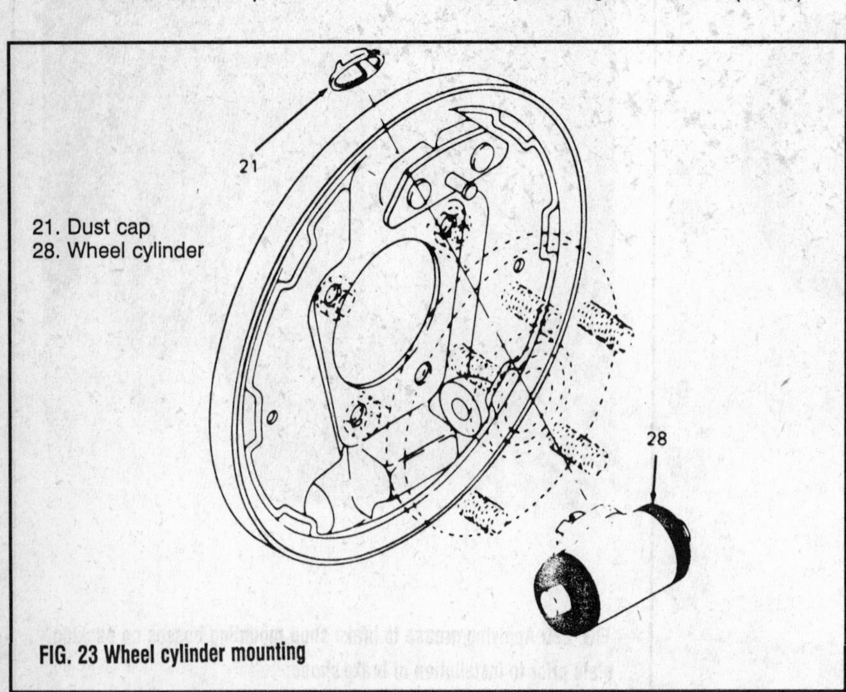

FIG. 23 Wheel cylinder mounting

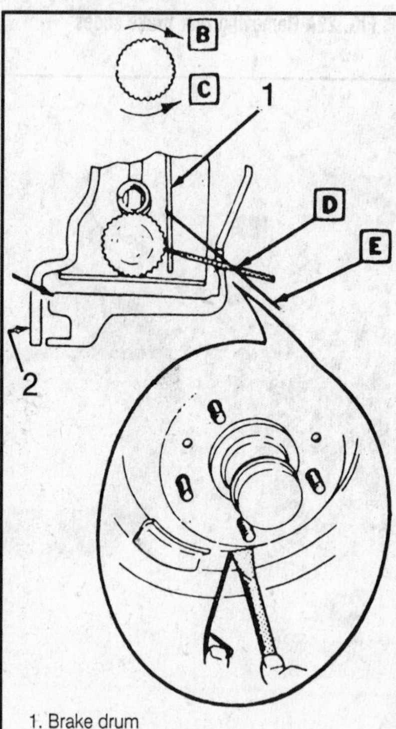

FIG. 25 Backing-off rear brake adjusting screw

PARKING BRAKE

Cables

REMOVAL & INSTALLATION

➧ SEE FIG. 26

FRONT CABLE

1. Disconnect the negative battery cable. Raise and safely support the vehicle.
2. Loosen or remove the equalizer nut. Lower the vehicle.
3. Remove the console.
4. Disconnect the parking brake cable from the lever.
5. Remove the nut that secures the front cable to the floor pan.
6. Loosen the catalytic converter shield and the parking brake cable from the body.
7. Remove the cable from the equalizer, guide and underbody clips.
8. The installation is the reverse of the removal procedure.
9. Adjust the cable.
10. Connect the negative battery cable and check the parking brakes for proper operation.

REAR CABLES

1. Disconnect the negative battery cable. Raise and safely support the vehicle.
2. Loosen or remove the equalizer nut.
3. Remove the wheel(s) and drum(s).
4. Insert a suitable tool between the brake shoe and the top part of the brake adjuster bracket. Push the bracket to the front and release the top adjuster bracket rod.
5. Remove the hold-down spring, actuator lever and lever return spring.
6. Remove the adjuster spring.
7. Remove the top rear brake shoe return spring.
8. Disconnect the parking brake cable from the actuating lever.
9. Pull the cable through the backing plate while depressing the retaining tangs.
10. On the right side, remove the cable end button from the connector.
11. Remove the conduit fitting from the axle bracket while depressing the retaining tangs.

To install:

12. Install the conduit fitting into the axle bracket, securing the retaining tangs.
13. Install the cable end button to the connector, if working on the right side.
14. Click the cable assembly into the backing plate.
15. Connect the cable to the actuating lever.
16. Assemble the rear brake components.
17. Install the drum(s) and wheel(s).
18. Adjust the rear brakes and parking brake cable.
19. Connect the negative battery cable and check the parking brakes for proper operation.

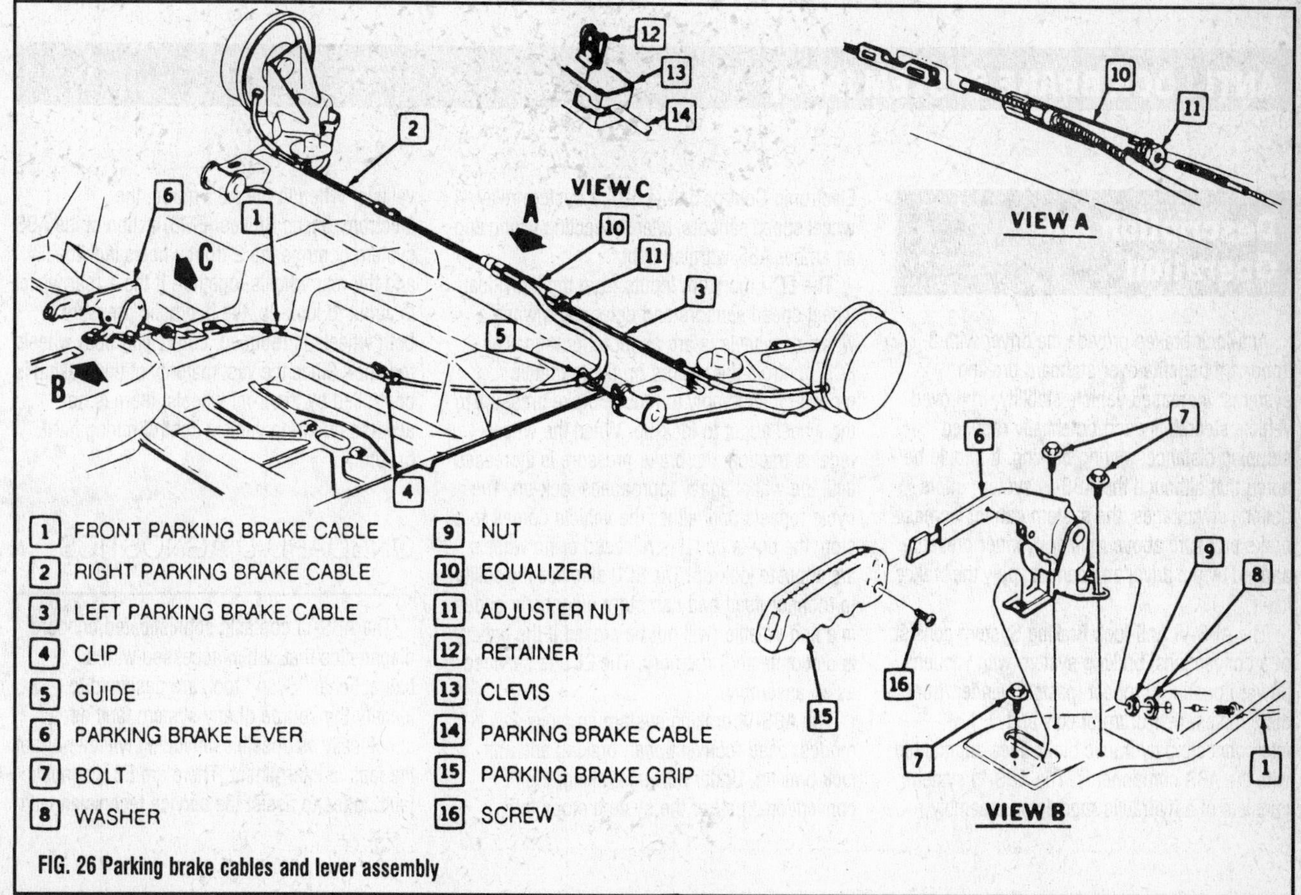

FIG. 26 Parking brake cables and lever assembly

ADJUSTMENT

1. Adjust the rear brake shoes.
2. Depress the parking brake pedal exactly 3 ratchet clicks.
3. Raise and safely support the vehicle.
4. Check that the equalizer nut groove is liberally lubricated with chassis lube. Tighten the adjusting nut until the right rear wheel can just be turned to the rear with both hands but is locked when forward rotation is attempted.
5. With the mechanism totally disengaged, both rear wheels should turn freely in either direction with no brake drag. Do not adjust the parking brake so tightly as to cause brake drag.

Parking Brake Lever

REMOVAL & INSTALLATION

1. Raise and safely support the vehicle.
2. Loosen the cable adjustment to allow the cable to be disconnected from the lever.
3. Remove the console.
4. Disconnect the parking brake cable from the lever assembly.
5. Disconnect the electrical connector.
6. Remove the bolts securing the lever to the floor pan.
7. Install the parking brake lever and attaching bolts. Tighten to 18 ft. lbs. (25 Nm).
8. Connect the parking brake cable to the lever assembly. Tighten the parking brake cable-to-lever assembly nut to 21 ft. lbs. (28 Nm).
9. Install the console.
10. Adjust the parking brake cable.
11. Lower the vehicle.

ANTI-LOCK BRAKE SYSTEM (ABS)

Description and Operation

Anti-lock brakes provide the driver with 3 important benefits over standard braking systems: increased vehicle stability, improved vehicle steerability and potentially reduced stopping distances during braking. It should be noted that although the ABS-VI system offers definite advantages, the system cannot increase brake pressure above master cylinder pressure applied by the driver and cannot apply the brakes itself.

The ABS-VI Anti-lock Braking System consist of a conventional braking system with vacuum power booster, compact master cylinder, front disc brakes, rear drum brakes and interconnecting hydraulic brake lines augmented with the ABS components. The ABS-VI system consists of a hydraulic modulator assembly, Electronic Control Unit (ECU), a system relay, 4 wheel speed sensors, interconnecting wiring and an amber ABS warning light.

The ECU monitors inputs from the individual wheel speed sensors and determines when a wheel or wheels is/are about to lock-up. The ECU controls the motors on the hydraulic modulator assembly to reduce brake pressure to the wheel about to lock-up. When the wheel regains traction, the brake pressure is increased until the wheel again approaches lock-up. The cycle repeats until either the vehicle comes to a stop, the brake pedal is released or no wheels are about to lock-up. The ECU also has the ability to monitor itself and can store diagnostic codes in a non-volatile (will not be erased if the battery is disconnected) memory. The ECU is serviced as an assembly.

The ABS-VI braking system employs 2 modes: base (conventional) braking and anti-lock braking. Under normal braking, the conventional part of the system stops the vehicle. When in the ABS mode, the Electromagnetic Brakes (EMB) action of the ABS system controls the 2 front wheels individually and the rear wheels together. If the 1 rear wheel is about to lock-up, the hydraulic pressure to both wheels is reduced, controlling both wheels together. Since the vast majority of the braking is controlled by the front wheels, there is no adverse effect on vehicle control during hard braking.

ONBOARD DIAGNOSTICS

The ABS-VI contains sophisticated onboard diagnostics that, when accessed with a bidirectional "Scan" tool, are designed to identify the source of any system fault as specifically as possible, including whether or not the fault is intermittent. There are 58 diagnostic fault codes to assist the service technician with diagnosis. The last diagnostic fault code to occur is specifically identified, and specific ABS data is stored at the time of this fault, also, the first five codes set. Additionally, using a bidirectional "Scan" tool, each input and output can be monitored, thus enabling fault confirmation and repair verification. Manual control of components and automated functional tests are also available when using a GM approved "Scan" tool. Details of many of these functions are contained in the following sections.

ENHANCED DIAGNOSTICS

Enhanced Diagnostic Information, found in the CODE HISTORY function of the bidirectional "Scan" tool, is designed to provide the service technician with specific fault occurrence information. For each of the first five (5) and the very last diagnostic fault codes stored, data is stored to identify the specific fault code number, the number of failure occurrences, and the number of drive cycles since the failure first and last occurred (a drive cycle occurs when the ignition is turned "ON" and the vehicle is driven faster than 10 mph). However, if a fault is present, the drive cycle counter will increment by turning the ignition "ON" and "OFF". These first five (5) diagnostic fault codes are also stored in the order of occurrence. The order in which the first 5 faults occurred can be useful in determining if a previous fault is linked to the most recent faults, such as an intermittent wheel speed sensor which later becomes completely open.

During difficult diagnosis situations, this information can be used to identify fault occurrence trends. Does the fault occur more frequently now than it did during the last time when it only failed 1 out of 35 drive cycles? Did the fault only occur once over a large number of drive cycles, indication an unusual condition present when the fault occurred? Does the fault occur infrequently over a large number of drive cycles, indication special diagnosis techniques may be required to identify the source of the fault?

If a fault occurred 1 out of 20 drive cycles, the fault is intermittent and has not reoccurred for 19 drive cycles. This fault may be difficult or impossible to duplicate and may have been caused by a severe vehicle impact (large pot hole, speed bump at high speed, etc.) that momentarily opened an electrical connector or caused unusual vehicle suspension movement. Problem resolution is unlikely, and the problem may never reoccur (check diagnostic aids proved for that code). If the fault occurred 3 out of 15 drive cycles, the odds of finding the cause are still not good, but you know how often it occurs and you can determine whether or not the fault is becoming more frequent based on an additional or past occurrences visit if the source of the problem can not or could not be found. If the fault occurred 10 out of 20 drive cycles, the odds of finding the cause are very good, as the fault may be easily reproduced.

By using the additional fault data, you can also determine if a failure is randomly intermittent or if it has not reoccurred for long periods of time due to weather changes or a repair prior to this visit. Say a diagnostic fault code occurred 10 of 20 drive cycles but has not reoccurred for 10 drive cycles. This means the failure occurred 10 of 10 drive cycles but has not reoccurred since. A significant environmental change or a repair occurred 10 drive cycles ago. A repair may not be necessary if a recent repair can be confirmed. If no repair was made, the service can focus on diagnosis techniques used to locate difficult to recreate problems.

DIAGNOSTIC PROCESS

When servicing the ABS-VI, the following steps should be followed in order. Failure to follow these steps may result in the loss of important diagnostic data and may lead to difficult and time consuming diagnosis procedures.

1. Using a bidirectional "Scan" tool, read all current and history diagnostic codes. Be certain to note which codes are current diagnostic code failures. DO NOT CLEAR CODES unless directed to do so.

2. Using a bidirectional "Scan" tool, read the CODE HISTORY data. Note the diagnostic fault codes stored and their frequency of failure. Specifically note the last failure that occurred and the conditions present when this failure occurred. This "last failure" should be the starting point for diagnosis and repair.

3. Perform a vehicle preliminary diagnosis inspection. This should include:

a. Inspection of the compact master cylinder for proper brake fluid level.

b. Inspection of the ABS hydraulic modulator for any leaks or wiring damage.

c. Inspection of brake components at all four (4) wheels. Verify no drag exists. Also verify proper brake apply operation.

d. Inspection for worn or damaged wheel bearings that allow a wheel to "wobble."

e. Inspection of the wheel speed sensors and their wiring. Verify correct air gap range, solid sensor attachment, undamaged sensor toothed ring, and undamaged wiring, especially at vehicle attachment points.

f. Verify proper outer CV joint alignment and operation.

g. Verify tires meet legal tread depth requirements.

4. If no codes are present, or mechanical component failure codes are present, perform the automated modulator test using the Tech 1 or T-100 to isolate the cause of the problem. If the failure is intermittent and not reproducible, test drive the vehicle while using the automatic snapshot feature of the bidirectional "Scan" tool.

Perform normal acceleration, stopping, and turning maneuvers. If this does not reproduce the failure, perform an ABS stop, on a low coefficient surface such as gravel, from approximately 30 - 50 mph while triggering on any ABS code. If the failure is still not reproducible, use the enhanced diagnostic information found in CODE HISTORY to determine whether or not this failure should be further diagnosed.

5. Once all system failures have been corrected, clear the ABS codes.

The Tech 1 and T-100, when plugged into the ALDL connector, becomes part of the vehicle's electronic system. The Tech 1 and T-100 can also perform the following functions on components linked by the Serial Data Link (SDL):

- Display ABS data
- Display and clear ABS trouble codes
- Control ABS components
- Perform extensive ABS diagnosis
- Provide diagnostic testing for "Intermittent" ABS conditions.

Each test mode has specific diagnosis capabilities which depend upon various keystrokes. In general, five (5) keys control sequencing: "YES," "NO," "EXIT," "UP" arrow and "DOWN" arrow. The F0 through F9 keys select operating modes, perform functions within an operating mode, or enter trouble code or model year designations.

In general, the Tech 1 has five (5) test modes for diagnosing the anti-lock brake system. The five (5) test modes are as follows:

MODE F0: DATA LIST - In this test mode, the Tech 1 continuously monitors wheel speed data, brake switch status and other inputs and outputs.

MODE F1: CODE HISTORY - In this mode, fault code history data is displayed. This data includes how many ignition cycles since the fault code occurred, along with other ABS information. The first five (5) and last fault codes set are included in the ABS history data.

MODE F2: TROUBLE CODES - In this test mode, trouble codes stored by the

ABS SYMPTOM AND TROUBLE CODE TABLE

CHART	SYMPTOM
A	ABS (Amber) Warning Light "ON" Constantly, No Codes Stored
B	ABS (Amber) Warning Light "ON" Intermittently, No Codes Stored
TROUBLE CODE	**DESCRIPTION**
A011	ABS Warning Light Circuit Open or Shorted to Ground
A013	ABS Warning Light Circuit Shorted to Battery
A014	Enable Relay Contacts Or Fuse Open
A015	Enable Relay Contacts Shorted to Battery
A016	Enable Relay Coil Circuit Open
A017	Enable Relay Coil Circuit Shorted to Ground
A018	Enable Relay Coil Circuit Shorted to Battery
A021	Left Front Wheel Speed = 0 (1 of 2)
A022	Right Front Wheel Speed = 0 (1 of 2)
A023	Left Rear Wheel Speed = 0 (1 of 2)
A024	Right Rear Wheel Speed = 0 (1 of 2)
A025	Left Front Excessive Wheel Speed Variation (1 of 2)
A026	Right Front Excessive Wheel Speed Variation (1 of 2)
A027	Left Rear Excessive Wheel Speed Variation (1 of 2)
A028	Right Rear Excessive Wheel Speed Variation (1 of 2)
A031	Two Wheel Speeds = 0 (1 of 2) (Non-Tubular Rear Axle)
A031	Two Wheel Speeds = 0 (1 of 2) (Tubular Rear Axle)
A036	Low System Voltage
A037	High System Voltage
A038	Left Front EMB Will Not Hold Motor
A041	Right Front EMB Will Not Hold Motor
A042	Rear Axle ESB Will Not Hold Motor
A044	Left Front Channel Will Not Move
A045	Right Front Channel Will Not Move
A046	Rear Axle Channel Will Not Move
A047	Left Front Motor Free Spins
A048	Right Front Motor Free Spins
A051	Rear Axle Motor Free Spins
A052	Left Front Channel in Release Too Long
A053	Right Front Channel In Release Too Long
A054	Rear Axle Channel in Release Too Long
A055	Motor Driver Fault Detected
A056	Left Front Motor Circuit Open
A057	Left Front Motor Circuit Shorted to Ground
A058	Left Front Motor Circuit Shorted to Battery or Motor Shorted
A061	Right Front Motor Circuit Open
A062	Right Front Motor Circuit Shorted to Ground
A063	Right Front Motor Circuit Shorted to Battery or Motor Shorted

FIG. 27 ABS-VI trouble codes

ABS SYMPTOM AND TROUBLE CODE TABLE

TROUBLE CODE	DESCRIPTION
A064	Rear Axle Motor Circuit Open
A065	Rear Axle Motor Circuit Shorted to Ground
A066	Rear Axle Motor Circuit Shorted to Battery or Motor Shorted
A067	Left Front EMB Circuit Open or Shorted to Ground
A068	Left Front EMB Circuit Shorted to Battery or EMB Shorted
A071	Right Front EMB Circuit Open or Shorted to Ground
A072	Right Front EMB Circuit Shorted to Battery or EMB Shorted
A076	Left Front Solenoid Circuit Shorted to Battery or Open
A077	Left Front Solenoid Circuit Shorted to Ground or Driver Open
A078	Right Front Solenoid Circuit Shorted to Battery or Open
A081	Right Front Solenoid Circuit Shorted to Ground or Driver Open
A082	Calibration Memory Failure
A086	Red Brake Warning Light Activated by ABS
A087	Red Brake Warning Light Circuit Open
A088	Red Brake Warning Light Circuit Shorted to Battery
A091	Open Brake Switch Contacts During Deceleration
A092	Open Brake Switch Contacts When ABS Was Required
A093	Code 91 or 92 Set in Current or Previous Ignition Cycle
A094	Brake Switch Contacts Always Closed
A095	Brake Switch Circuit Open
A096	Brake Lights Circuit Open

FIG. 28 ABS-VI trouble codes

EBCM, both current ignition cycle and history, may be displayed or cleared.

MODE F3: ABS SNAPSHOT - In this test mode, the Tech 1 captures ABS data before and after a fault occurrence or a forced manual trigger.

MODE F4: ABS TESTS - In this test mode, the Tech 1 performs hydraulic modulator functional tests to assist in problem isolation during troubleshooting. Included here is manual control of the motors which is used prior to bleeding the brake system.

Press F7 to covert from English to metric.

DISPLAYING CODES

Diagnostic fault codes can only be read through the use of a bidirectional "Scan" tool. There are no provisions for "Flash Code" diagnostics.

CLEARING CODES

The trouble codes in EBCM memory are erased in one of two ways:

1. Tech 1 "Clear Codes" selection.
2. Ignition cycle default.

These two methods are detailed below. Be sure to verify proper system operation and absence of codes when clearing procedure is completed.

The EBCM will not permit code clearing until all of the codes have been displayed. Also, codes cannot be cleared by unplugging the EBCM, disconnecting the battery cables, or turning the ignition "OFF" (except on an ignition cycle default).

Tech 1 "Clear Codes" Method

Select F2 for trouble codes. After codes have been viewed completely, Tech 1 will ask, "CLEAR ABS CODES"; ANSWER "yes." Tech 1 will then read, "DISPLAY CODE HIST. DATA"? "LOST" IF CODES CLEARED. "NO" TO CLEAR CODES. Answer "NO" and codes will be cleared.

Ignition Cycle Default

If no diagnostic fault code occurs for 100 drive cycles (a drive cycle occurs when the ignition is turned "ON" and the vehicle is driven faster than 10 mph), any existing fault codes are cleared from the EBCM memory.

INTERMITTENT FAILURES

As with most electronic systems, intermittent failures may be difficult to accurately diagnose. The following is a method to try to isolate an intermittent failure especially wheel speed circuitry failures.

If an ABS fault occurs, the "ABS" warning light indicator will be "ON" during the ignition cycle in which the fault was detected. If it is an intermittent problem which seems to have corrected itself ("ABS" warning light "OFF"), a history trouble code will be stored. Also stored

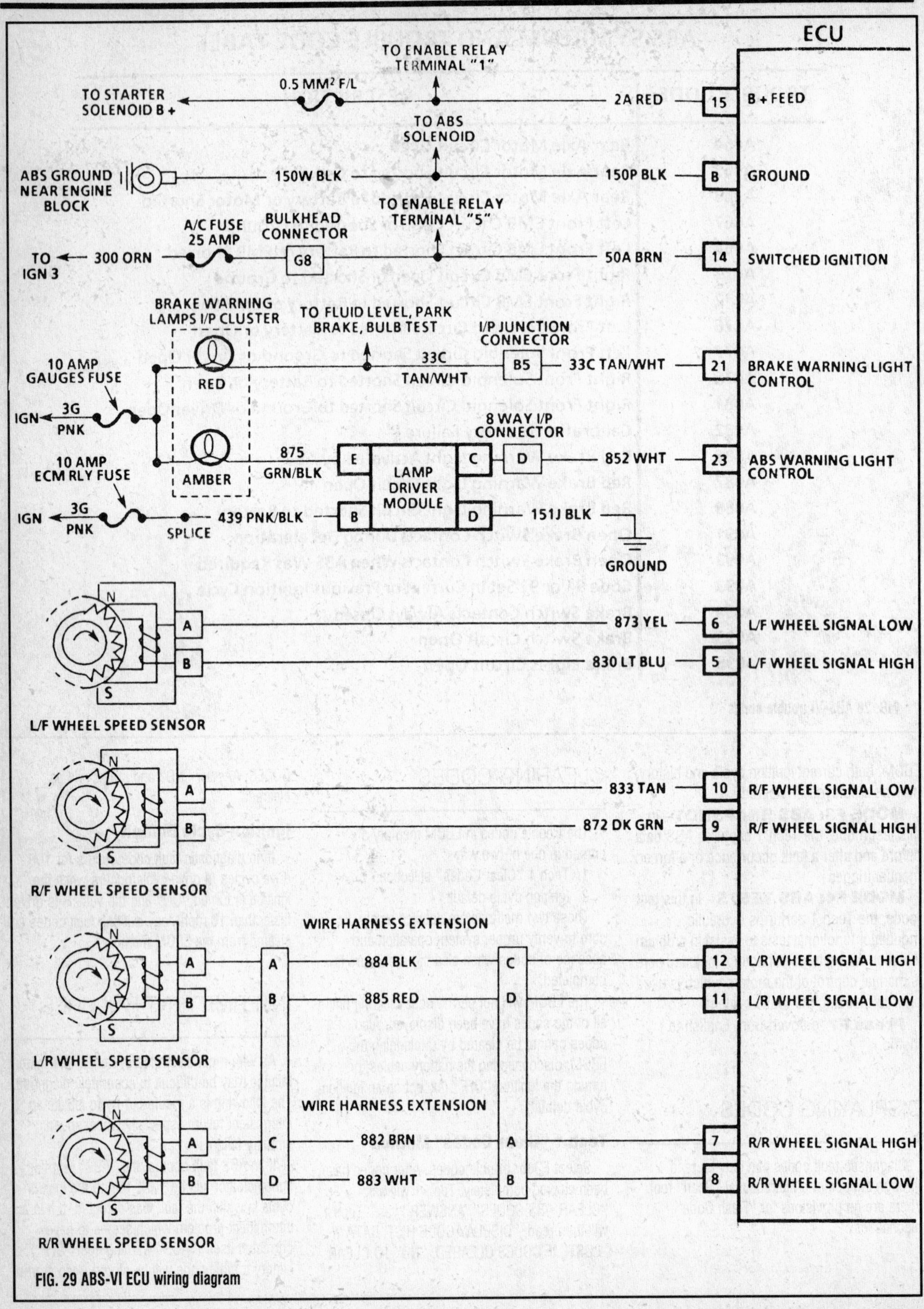

FIG. 29 ABS-VI ECU wiring diagram

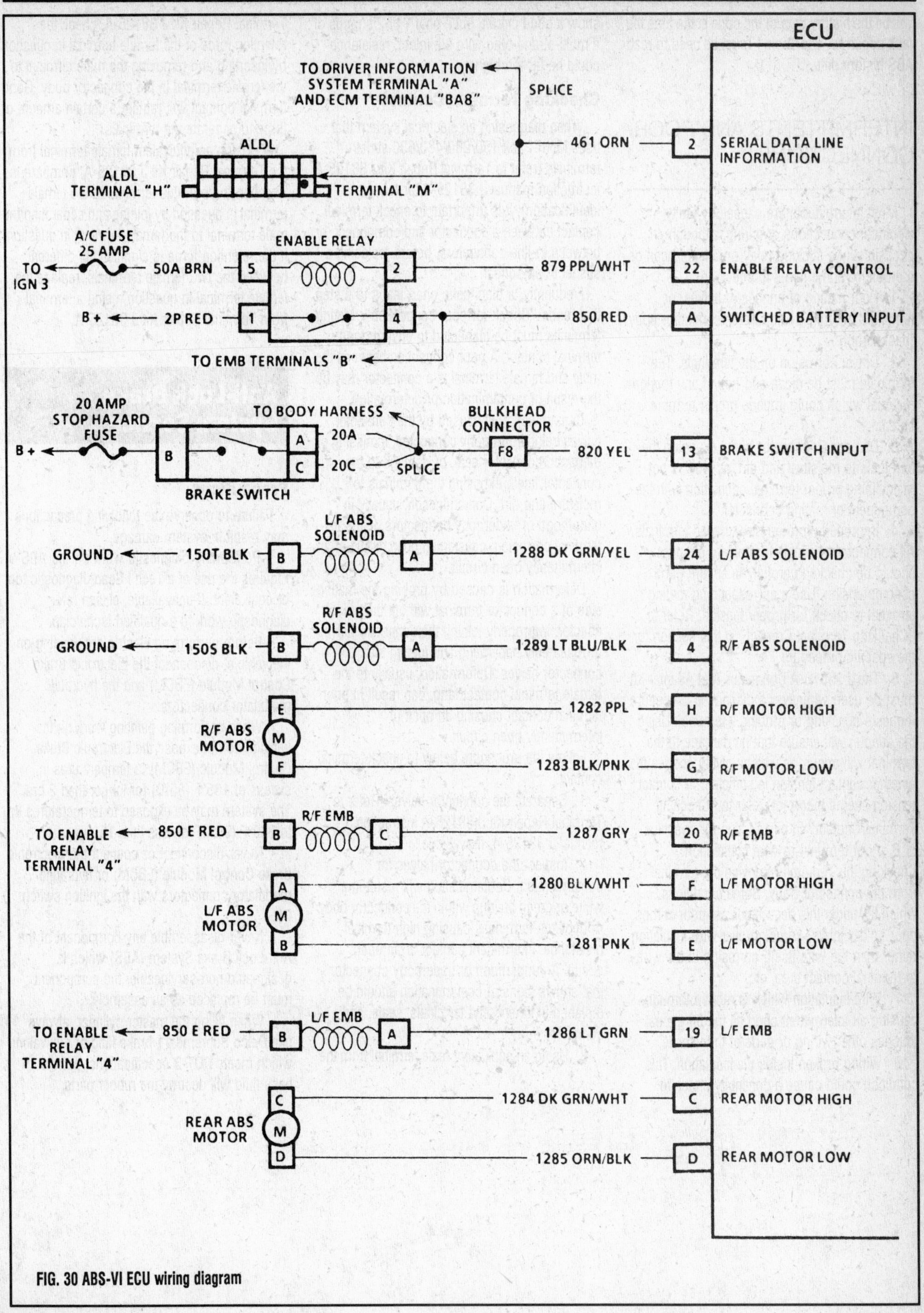

FIG. 30 ABS-VI ECU wiring diagram

will be the history data of the code at the time the fault occurred. The Tech 1 must be used to read ABS history data.

INTERMITTENTS AND POOR CONNECTIONS

Most intermittents are caused by faulty electrical connections or wiring, although occasionally a sticking relay or solenoid can be a problem. Some items to check are:

1. Poor mating of connector halves, or terminals not fully seated in the connector body (backed out).
2. Dirt or corrosion on the terminals. The terminals must be clean and free of any foreign material which could impede proper terminal contact.
3. Damaged connector body, exposing the terminals to moisture and dirt, as well as not maintaining proper terminal orientation with the component or mating connector.
4. Improperly formed or damaged terminals. All connector terminals in problem circuits should be checked carefully to ensure good contact tension. Use a corresponding mating terminal to check for proper tension. Refer to "Checking Terminal Contact" in this section for the specific procedure.
5. The J 35616-A Connector Test Adapter Kit must be used whenever a diagnostic procedure requests checking or probing a terminal. Using the adapter will ensure that no damage to the terminal will occur, as well as giving an idea of whether contact tension is sufficient. If contact tension seems incorrect, refer to "Checking Terminal Contact" in this section for specifics.
6. Poor terminal-to-wire connection. Checking this requires removing the terminal from the connector body. Some conditions which fall under this description are poor crimps, poor solder joints, crimping over wire insulation rather than the wire itself, corrosion in the wire-to-terminal contact area, etc.
7. Wire insulation which is rubbed through, causing an intermittent short as the bare area touches other wiring or parts of the vehicle.
8. Wiring broken inside the insulation. This condition could cause a continuity check to show a good circuit, but if only 1 or 2 strands of a multi-strand-type wire are intact, resistance could be far too high.

Checking Terminal Contact

When diagnosing an electrical system that uses Metri-Pack 150/280/480/630 series terminals (refer to Terminal Repair Kit J 38125-A instruction manual J 38125-4 for terminal identification), it is important to check terminal contact between a connector and component, or between in-line connectors, before replacing a suspect component.

Frequently, a diagnostic chart leads to a step that reads "Check for poor connection". Mating terminals must be inspected to ensure good terminal contact. A poor connection between the male and female terminal at a connector may be the result of contamination or deformation.

Contamination is caused by the connector halves being improperly connected, a missing or damaged connector seal, or damage to the connector itself, exposing the terminals to moisture and dirt. Contamination, usually in underhood or underbody connectors, leads to terminal corrosion, causing an open circuit or an intermittently open circuit.

Deformation is caused by probing the mating side of a connector terminal without the proper adapter, improperly joining the connector halves or repeatedly separating and joining the connector halves. Deformation, usually to the female terminal contact tang, can result in poor terminal contact causing an open or intermittently open circuit.

Follow the procedure below to check terminal contact.

1. Separate the connector halves. Refer to Terminal Repair Kit J 38125-A instruction manual J 38125-4, if available.
2. Inspect the connector halves for contamination. Contamination will result in a white or green buildup within the connector body or between terminals, causing high terminal resistance, intermittent contact or an open circuit. An underhood or underbody connector that shows signs of contamination should be replaced in its entirety: terminals, seals, and connector body.
3. Using an equivalent male terminal from the Terminal Repair Kit J 38125-A, check the retention force of the female terminal in question by inserting and removing the male terminal to the female terminal in the connector body. Good terminal contact will require a certain amount of force to separate the terminals.
4. Using an equivalent female terminal from the Terminal Repair Kit J 38125-A, compare the retention force of this terminal to the female terminal in question by joining and separating the male terminal to the female terminal in question. If the retention force is significantly different between the two female terminals, replace the female terminal in question, using a terminal from Terminal Repair Kit J 38125-A.

Anti-Lock Brake System Service

Precautions

Failure to observe the following precautions may result in system damage.

- Performing diagnostic work on the ABS-VI requires the use of a Tech I Scan diagnostic tool or equivalent. If unavailable, please refer diagnostic work to a qualified technician.
- Before performing electric arc welding on the vehicle, disconnect the Electronic Brake Control Module (EBCM) and the hydraulic modulator connectors.
- When performing painting work on the vehicle, do not expose the Electronic Brake Control Module (EBCM) to temperatures in excess of 185°F (85°C) for longer than 2 hrs. The system may be exposed to temperatures up to 200°F (95°C) for less than 15 min.
- Never disconnect or connect the Electronic Brake Control Module (EBCM) or hydraulic modulator connectors with the ignition switch ON.
- Never disassemble any component of the Anti-Lock Brake System (ABS) which is designated non-serviceable; the component must be replaced as an assembly.
- When filling the master cylinder, always use Delco Supreme 11 brake fluid or equivalent, which meets DOT-3 specifications; petroleum base fluid will destroy the rubber parts.

ECU 24 PIN WORLD CONNECTOR

PIN	CIRCUIT NO.	COLOR	CIRCUIT
1	OPEN		NOT USED
2	461	ORN	SERIAL DATA LINE
3	OPEN		NOT USED
4	1289	LT BLU/BLK	R/F ABS SOLENOID
5	830	LT BLU	L/F WHEEL SIGNAL HIGH
6	873	YEL	L/F WHEEL SIGNAL LOW
7	882	BRN	R/R WHEEL SIGNAL HIGH
8	883	WHT	R/R WHEEL SIGNAL LOW
9	872	DK GRN	R/F WHEEL SIGNAL HIGH
10	833	TAN	R/F WHEEL SIGNAL LOW
11	885	RED	L/R WHEEL SIGNAL LOW
12	884	BLK	L/R WHEEL SIGNAL HIGH
13	820	YEL	BRAKE SWITCH INPUT
14	50A	BRN	SWITCH IGNITION
15	2A	RED	B + FEED
16	OPEN		NOT USED
17	OPEN		NOT USED
18	VENT TUBE	BLK	VENT TUBE
19	1286	LT GRN	L/F EMB
20	1287	GRY	R/F EMB
21	33C	TAN/WHT	BRAKE TELLTALE
22	879	PPL/WHT	ENABLE RELAY CONTROL
23	852	WHT	ABS WARNING LIGHT CONTROL
24	1288	DK GRN/YEL	L/F ABS SOLENOID

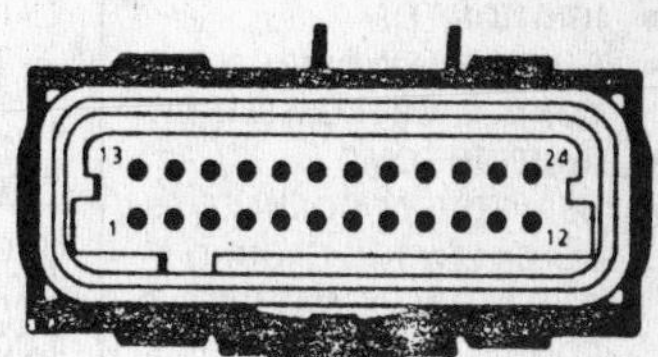

FIG. 31 ABS-VI ECU connector view

2 WAY ECU CONNECTOR

PIN	CIRCUIT No.	COLOR	CIRCUIT
A	850	RED	SWITCHED BATTERY INPUT
B	150P	BLK	GROUND

6 WAY ECU CONNECTOR

PIN	CIRCUIT No.	COLOR	CIRCUIT
C	1284	DK GRN/WHT	REAR MOTOR HIGH
D	1285	ORN/BLK	REAR MOTOR LOW
E	1281	PNK	L/F MOTOR LOW
F	1280	BLK/WHT	L/F MOTOR HIGH
G	1283	BLK/PNK	R/F MOTOR LOW
H	1282	PPL	R/F MOTOR HIGH

FIG. 32 ABS-VI ECU connector view

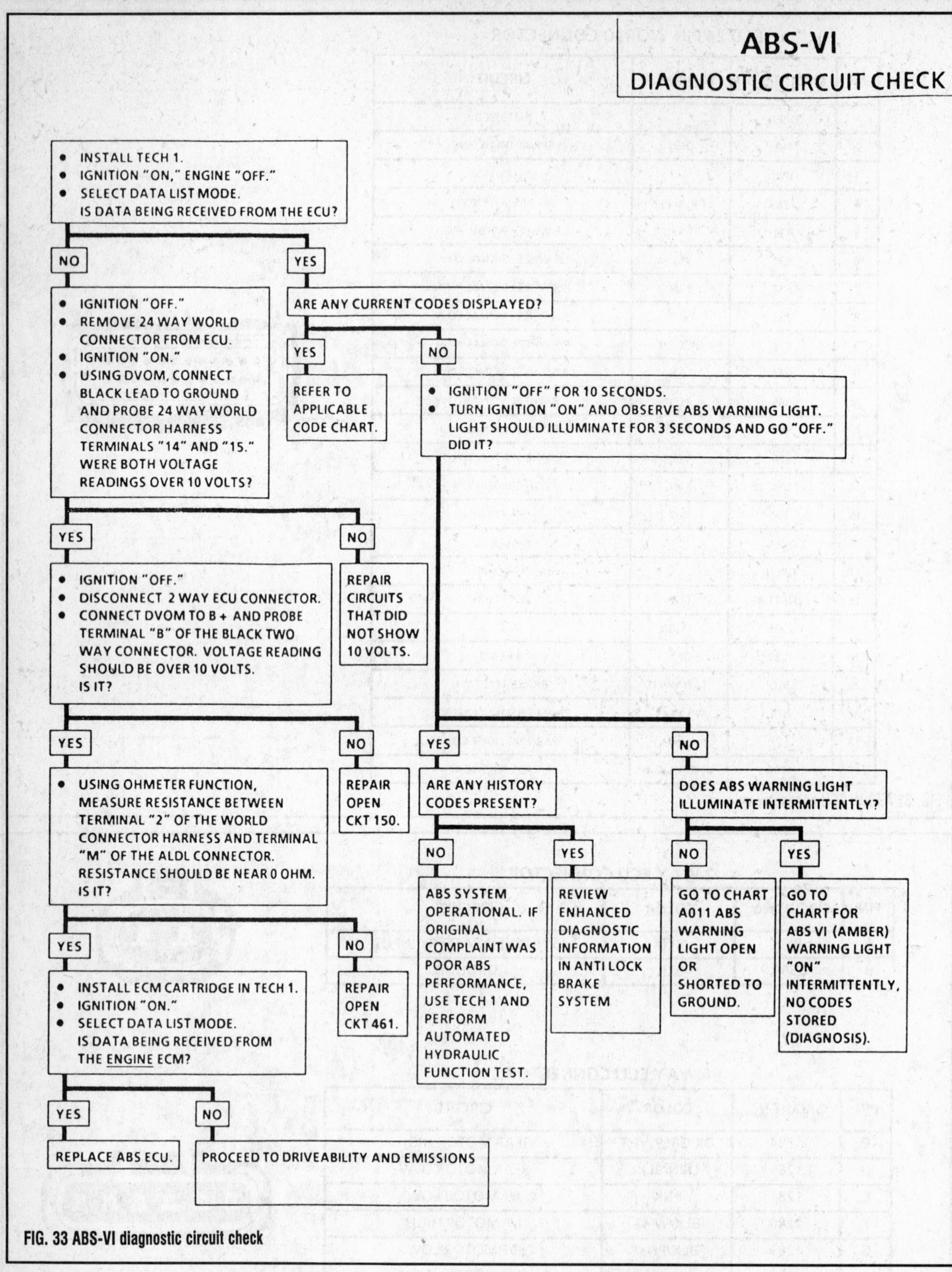

FIG. 33 ABS-VI diagnostic circuit check

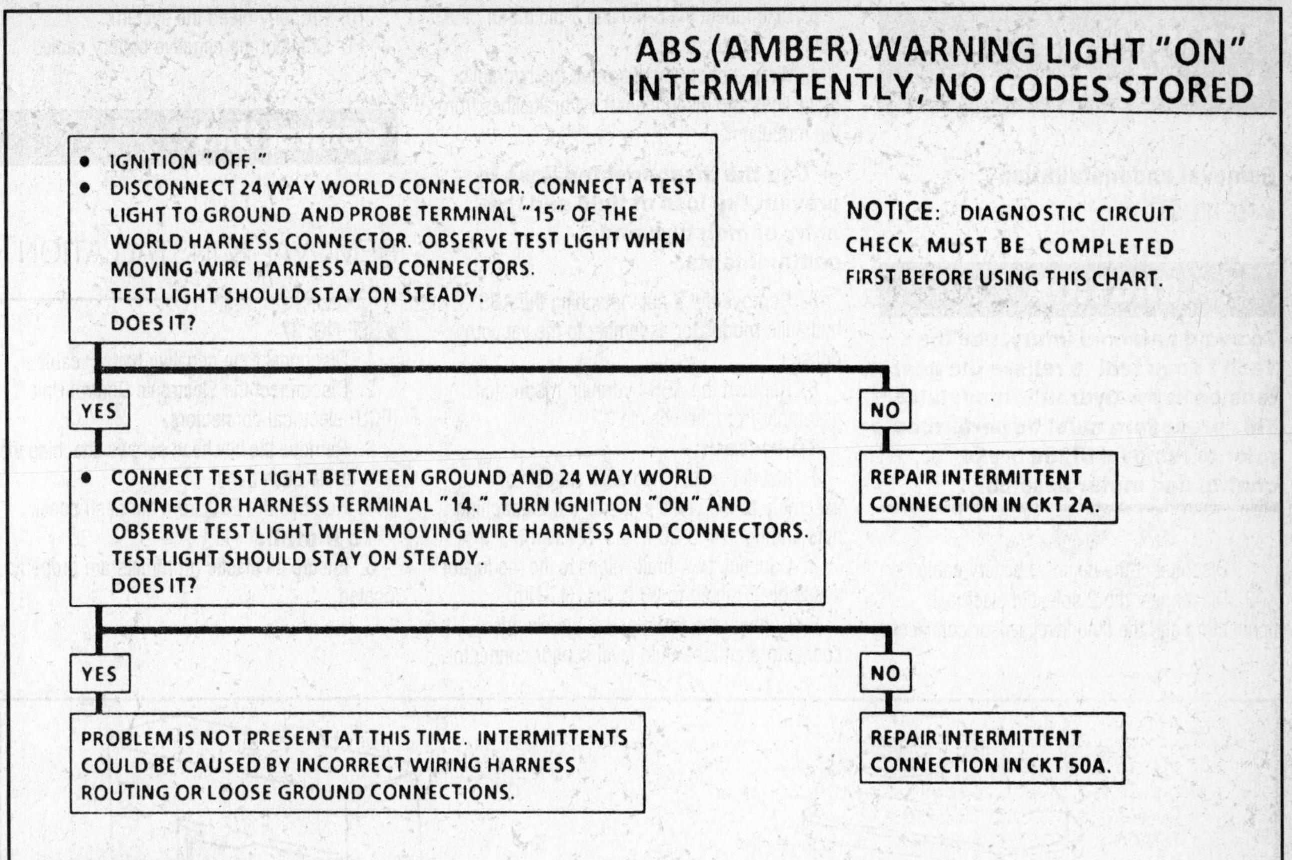

ABS (AMBER) WARNING LIGHT "ON" INTERMITTENTLY, NO CODES STORED

NOTICE: DIAGNOSTIC CIRCUIT CHECK MUST BE COMPLETED FIRST BEFORE USING THIS CHART.

- IGNITION "OFF."
- DISCONNECT 24 WAY WORLD CONNECTOR. CONNECT A TEST LIGHT TO GROUND AND PROBE TERMINAL "15" OF THE WORLD HARNESS CONNECTOR. OBSERVE TEST LIGHT WHEN MOVING WIRE HARNESS AND CONNECTORS. TEST LIGHT SHOULD STAY ON STEADY. DOES IT?

NO → REPAIR INTERMITTENT CONNECTION IN CKT 2A.

YES →

- CONNECT TEST LIGHT BETWEEN GROUND AND 24 WAY WORLD CONNECTOR HARNESS TERMINAL "14." TURN IGNITION "ON" AND OBSERVE TEST LIGHT WHEN MOVING WIRE HARNESS AND CONNECTORS. TEST LIGHT SHOULD STAY ON STEADY. DOES IT?

YES → PROBLEM IS NOT PRESENT AT THIS TIME. INTERMITTENTS COULD BE CAUSED BY INCORRECT WIRING HARNESS ROUTING OR LOOSE GROUND CONNECTIONS.

NO → REPAIR INTERMITTENT CONNECTION IN CKT 50A.

FIG. 34 ABS-VI diagnosis

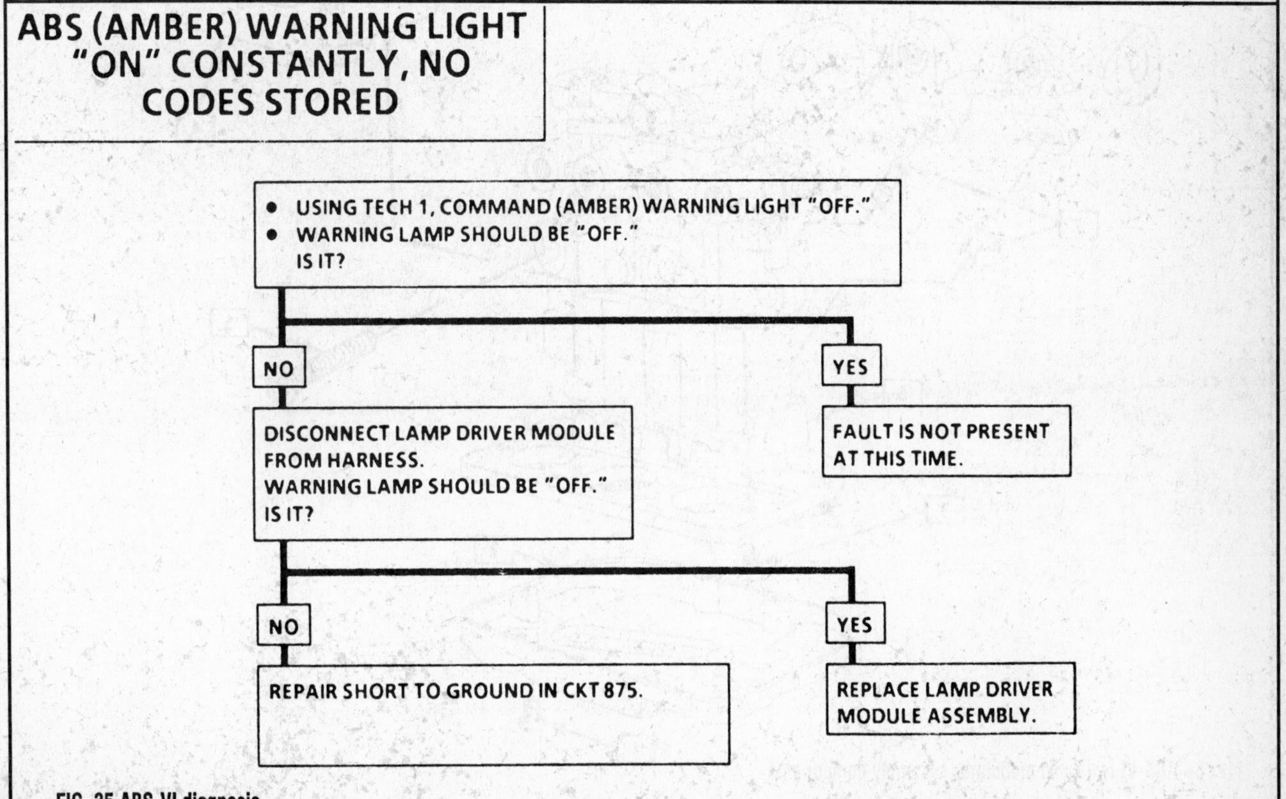

ABS (AMBER) WARNING LIGHT "ON" CONSTANTLY, NO CODES STORED

- USING TECH 1, COMMAND (AMBER) WARNING LIGHT "OFF."
- WARNING LAMP SHOULD BE "OFF." IS IT?

YES → FAULT IS NOT PRESENT AT THIS TIME.

NO → DISCONNECT LAMP DRIVER MODULE FROM HARNESS. WARNING LAMP SHOULD BE "OFF." IS IT?

NO → REPAIR SHORT TO GROUND IN CKT 875.

YES → REPLACE LAMP DRIVER MODULE ASSEMBLY.

FIG. 35 ABS-VI diagnosis

ABS Hydraulic Modulator Assembly

Removal and Installation

➧ SEE FIG. 36

✲✲ CAUTION

To avoid personal injury, use the Tech I Scan tool to relieve the gear tension in the hydraulic modulator. This procedure must be performed prior to removal of the brake control and motor assembly.

1. Disconnect the negative battery cable.
2. Disconnect the 2 solenoid electrical connectors and the fluid level sensor connector.
3. Disconnect the 6-pin and 3-pin motor pack electrical connectors.
4. Wrap a shop towel around the hydraulic brake lines and disconnect the 4 brake lines from the modulator.

➡ Cap the disconnected lines to prevent the loss of fluid and the entry of moisture and contaminants.

5. Remove the 2 nuts attaching the ABS hydraulic modulator assembly to the vacuum booster.
6. Remove the ABS hydraulic modulator assembly from the vehicle.

To install:

7. Install the ABS hydraulic modulator assembly to the vehicle. Install the 2 attaching nuts and tighten to 20 ft. lbs. (27 Nm).
8. Connect the 4 brake pipes to the modulator assembly. Tighten to 13 ft. lbs. (17 Nm).
9. Connect the 6-pin and 3-pin electrical connectors and the fluid level sensor connector.
10. Properly bleed the system.
11. Connect the negative battery cable.

Control Unit

REMOVAL & INSTALLATION

➧ SEE FIG. 37

1. Disconnect the negative battery cable.
2. Disconnect the Electronic Control Unit (ECU) electrical connectors.
3. Remove the hex head screws attaching the ECU to the dash panel
4. Remove the ECU from the dash panel.

To install:

5. Ensure all plastic grommets are properly located.

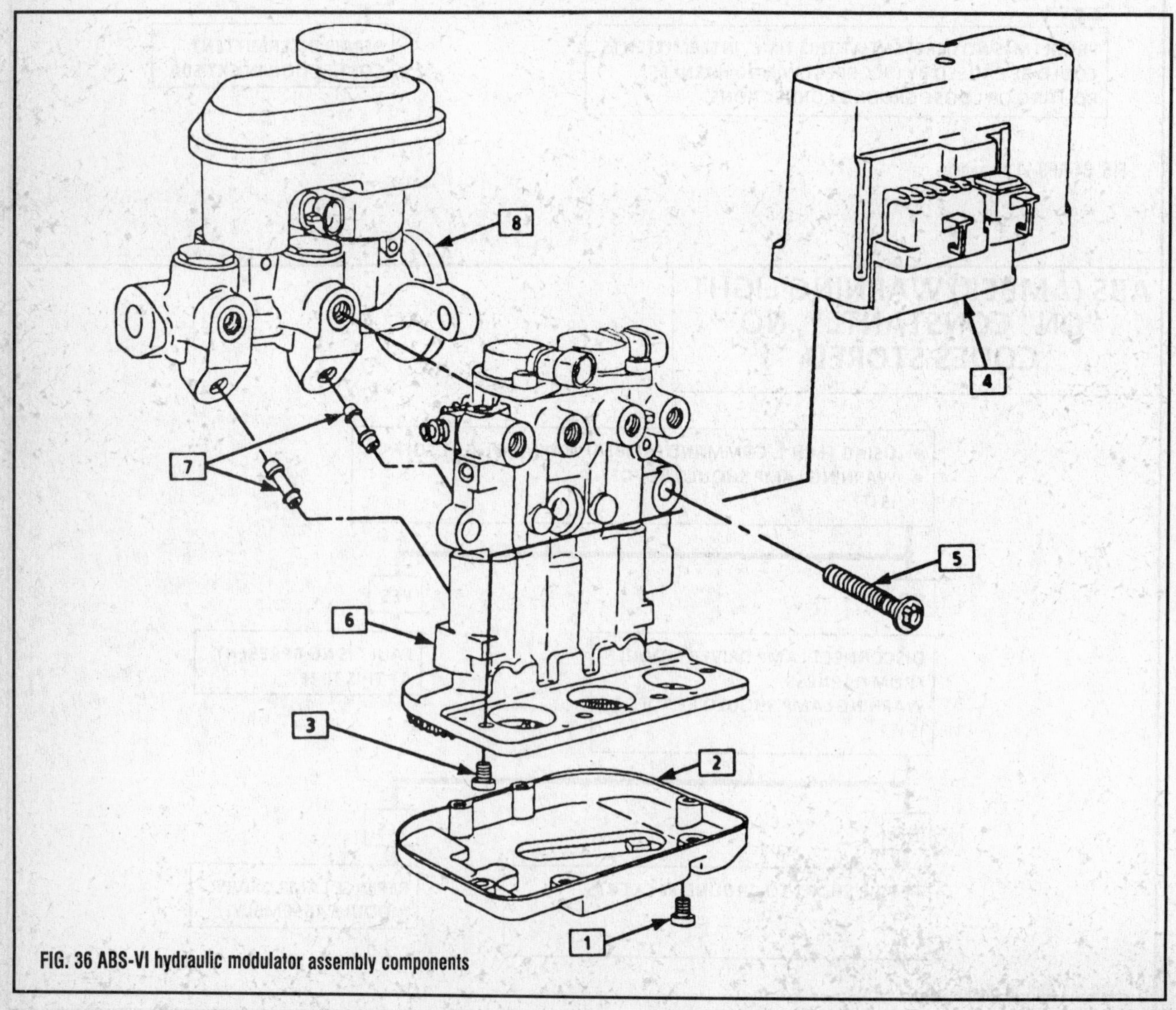

FIG. 36 ABS-VI hydraulic modulator assembly components

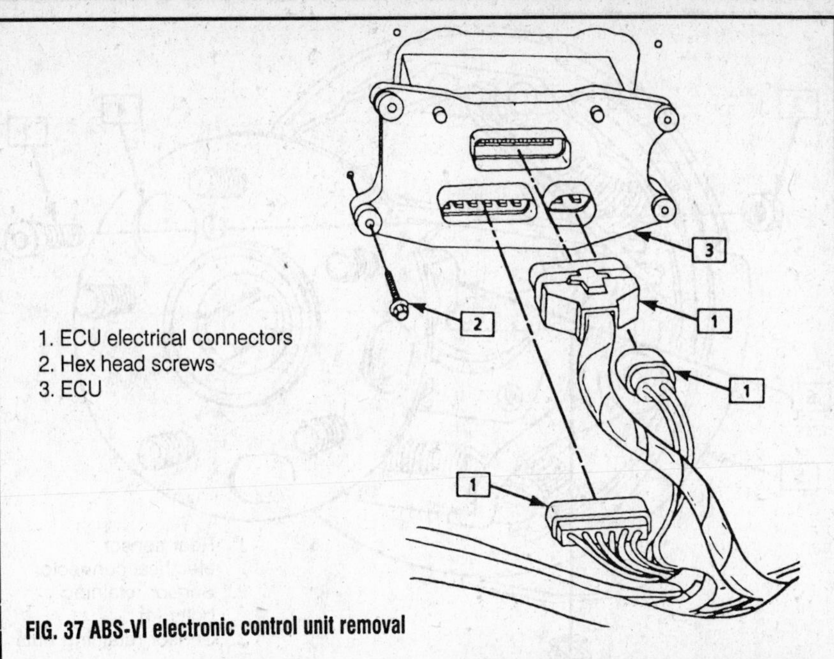

FIG. 37 ABS-VI electronic control unit removal

6. Install the ECU to the dash panel, aligning screw holes.
7. Install the hex head screws attaching the ECU.
8. Connect the ECU electrical connectors.
9. Connect the negative battery cable.

Speed Sensors

REMOVAL & INSTALLATION

➧ SEE FIGS. 38 AND 39

Front Wheel Speed Sensor

1. Disconnect the negative battery cable.
2. Raise and safely support the vehicle.
3. Disconnect the front sensor electrical connector.
4. Remove the Torx® bolt.
5. Remove the front wheel speed sensor.

To install:

6. Install the front wheel speed sensor on the mounting bracket.

➡ Ensure the front wheel speed sensor is properly aligned and lays flat against the bracket bosses.

7. Install the Torx® bolt. Tighten to 106 inch lbs. (12 Nm).
8. Connect the front sensor electrical connector.
9. Lower the vehicle.
10. Connect the negative battery cable.

Rear Wheel Bearing And Speed Sensor Assembly

➡ The rear integral wheel bearing and sensor assembly must be replaced as a unit.

1. Disconnect the negative battery cable.
2. Raise and safely support the vehicle.
3. Remove the rear wheel.
4. Remove the brake drum.
5. Disconnect the rear sensor electrical connector.
6. Remove the bolts and nuts attaching the

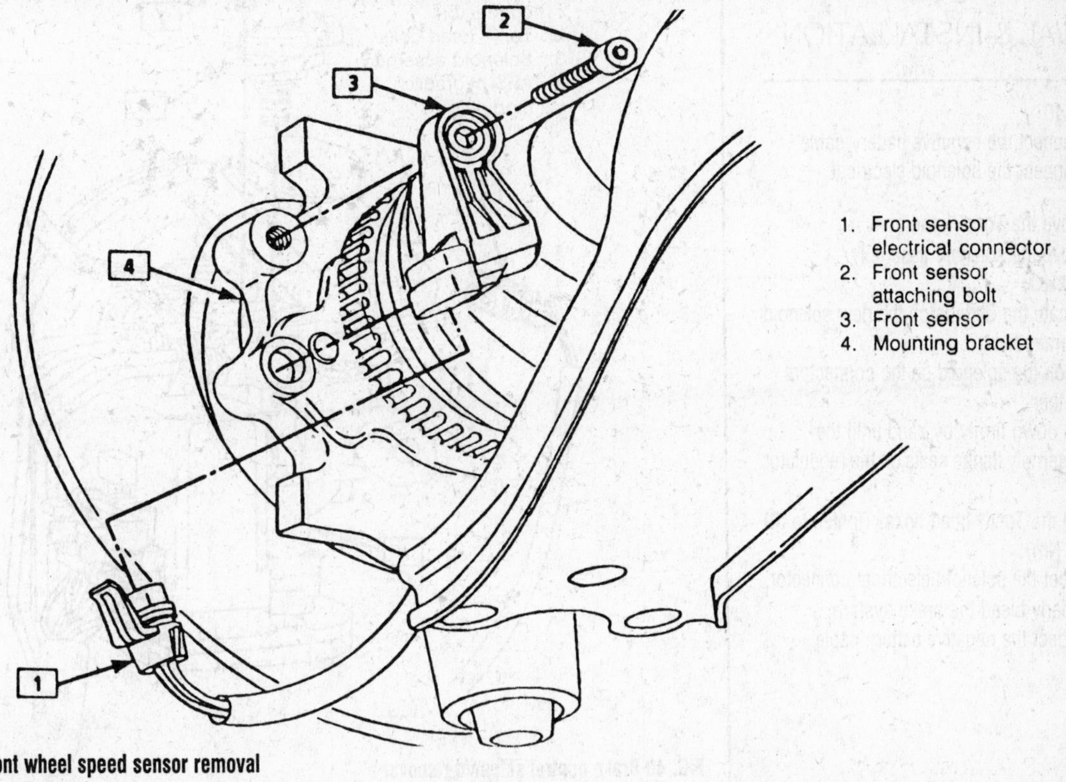

1. Front sensor electrical connector
2. Front sensor attaching bolt
3. Front sensor
4. Mounting bracket

FIG. 38 Front wheel speed sensor removal

rear wheel bearing and speed sensor assembly to the backing plate.

➡ **With the rear wheel bearing and speed sensor attaching bolts and nuts removed, the drum brake assembly is supported only by the brake line connection. To avoid bending or damage to the brake line, do not bump or exert force on the assembly.**

7. Remove the rear wheel bearing and speed sensor assembly.

To install:

8. Install the rear wheel bearing and speed sensor assembly by aligning the bolt hoses in the wheel bearing and speed sensor assembly, drum brake assembly and rear suspension bracket. Install the attaching bolts and nuts. Tighten to 37 ft. lbs. (50 Nm).
9. Connect the rear speed sensor electrical connector.
10. Install the brake drum.
11. Install the rear wheel.
12. Lower the vehicle.
13. Connect the negative battery cable.

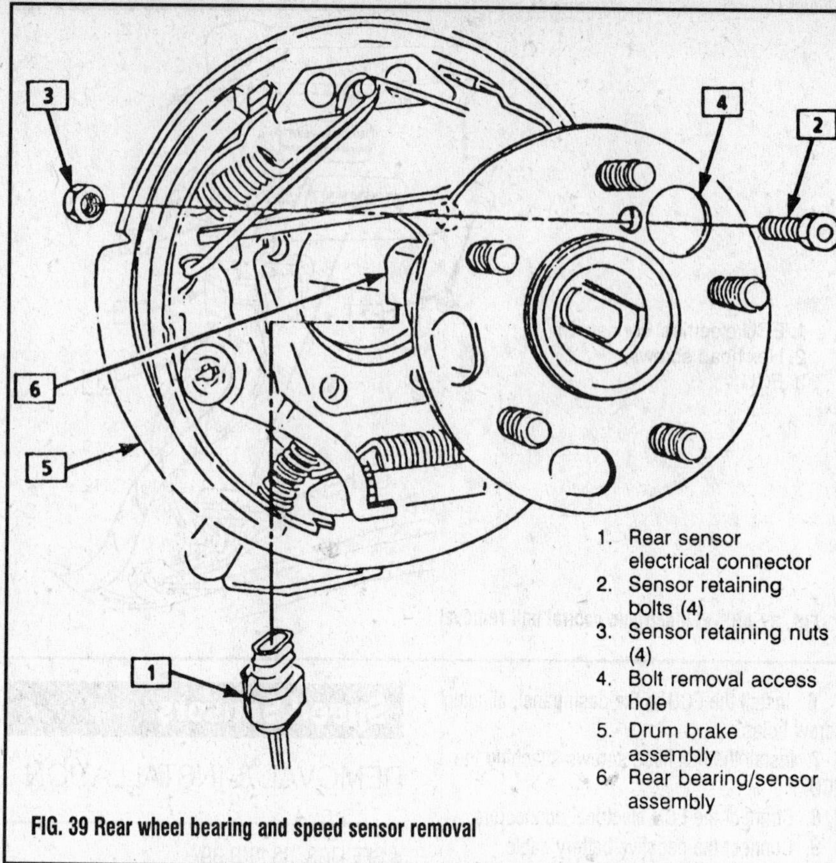

FIG. 39 Rear wheel bearing and speed sensor removal

Brake Control Solenoid Assembly

REMOVAL & INSTALLATION

➧ SEE FIG. 40

1. Disconnect the negative battery cable.
2. Disconnect the solenoid electrical connector.
3. Remove the Torx® head bolts.
4. Remove the solenoid assembly.

To install:

5. Lubricate the O-rings on the new solenoid with clean brake fluid.
6. Position the solenoid so the connectors face each other.
7. Press down firmly by hand until the solenoid assembly flange seats on the modulator assembly.
8. Install the Torx® head bolts. Tighten to 39 inch lbs. (5 Nm).
9. Connect the solenoid electrical connector.
10. Properly bleed the brake system.
11. Connect the negative battery cable.

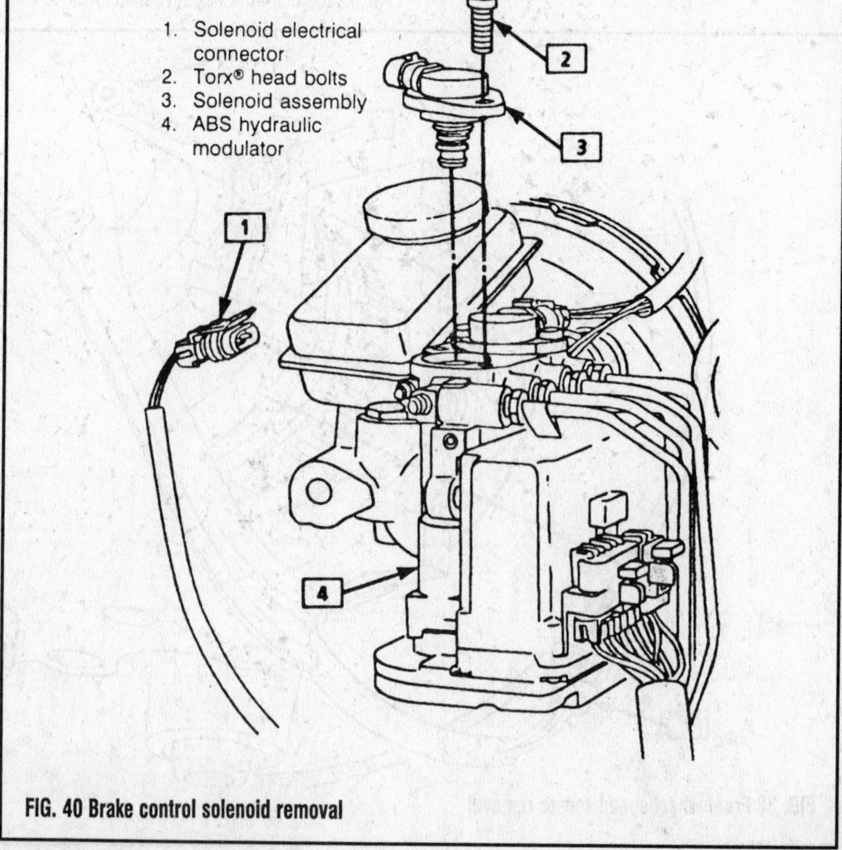

FIG. 40 Brake control solenoid removal

Filling and Bleeding

BRAKE CONTROL ASSEMBLY

➡ **Only use brake fluid from a sealed container which meets DOT 3 specifications.**

1. Clean the area around the master cylinder cap.
2. Check fluid level in master cylinder reservoir and top-up, as necessary. Check fluid level frequently during bleeding procedure.
3. Attach a bleeder hose to the rear bleeder valve on the brake control assembly. Slowly open the bleeder valve.
4. Depress the brake pedal slowly until fluid begins to flow.
5. Close the valve and release the brake pedal.
6. Repeat for the front bleeder valve on the brake control assembly.

➡ **When fluid flows from both bleeder valves, the brake control assembly is sufficiently full of fluid. However, it may not be completely purged of air. Bleed the individual wheel calipers/cylinders and return to the control assembly to purge the remaining air.**

WHEEL CALIPERS/ CYLINDERS

➡ **Prior to bleeding the rear brakes, the rear displacement cylinder must be returned to the top-most position. This can be accomplished using the Tech I Scan tool or T-100 (CAMS), by entering the manual control function and applying the rear motor.**

If a Tech I or T-100 are unavailable, bleed the front brakes. Ensure the pedal is firm. Carefully drive the vehicle to a speed above 4 mph to cause the ABS system to initialize. This will return the rear displacement cylinder to the top-most position.

1. Clean the area around the master cylinder cap.
2. Check fluid level in master cylinder reservoir and top-up, as necessary. Check fluid level frequently during bleeding procedure.
3. Raise and safely support the vehicle.
4. Attach a bleeder hose to the bleeder valve of the right rear wheel and submerge the opposite hose in a clean container partially filled with brake fluid.
5. Open the bleeder valve.
6. Slowly depress the brake pedal.
7. Close the bleeder valve and release the brake pedal.
8. Wait 5 seconds.
9. Repeat Steps 5–8 until the pedal begins to feel firm and no air bubbles appear in the bleeder hose.
10. Repeat Steps 5–9, until the pedal is firm and no air bubbles appear in the brake hose, for the remaining wheels in the following order:
    a. left rear
    b. right front
    c. left front.
11. Lower the vehicle.

BRAKE SPECIFICATIONS

All measurements in inches unless noted

Year	Model	Master Cylinder Bore	Brake Disc Original Thickness	Brake Disc Minimum Thickness	Brake Disc Maximum Runout	Brake Drum Diameter Original Inside Diameter	Brake Drum Diameter Max. Wear Limit	Brake Drum Diameter Maximum Machine Diameter	Minimum Lining Thickness Front	Minimum Lining Thickness Rear
1985	All	0.875	0.885	0.830	0.004	7.879	7.929	7.899	0.030	0.030
1986	All	0.875	0.885	0.830	0.004	7.879	7.929	7.899	0.030	0.030
1987	All	0.875	0.885	0.830	0.004	7.879	7.929	7.899	0.030	0.030
1988	All	①	0.885	0.830	0.004	7.879	7.929	7.899	② 0.060	② 0.060
1989	All	0.874	0.885	0.830	0.004	7.879	7.929	7.899	② 0.060	② 0.060
1990	All	0.874	0.885	0.830	0.004	7.879	7.929	7.899	② 0.060	② 0.060
1991	All	0.874	0.806	0.786	0.003	7.879	7.929	7.899	② 0.060	② 0.060
1992	All	0.874	0.806	0.786	0.003	7.879	7.929	7.899	② 0.060	② 0.060

① 0.874 in. or 0.937
② Measured above the rivet head

Troubleshooting the Brake System

Problem	Cause	Solution
Low brake pedal (excessive pedal travel required for braking action.)	• Excessive clearance between rear linings and drums caused by inoperative automatic adjusters	• Make 10 to 15 alternate forward and reverse brake stops to adjust brakes. If brake pedal does not come up, repair or replace adjuster parts as necessary.
	• Worn rear brakelining	• Inspect and replace lining if worn beyond minimum thickness specification
	• Bent, distorted brakeshoes, front or rear	• Replace brakeshoes in axle sets
	• Air in hydraulic system	• Remove air from system. Refer to Brake Bleeding.
Low brake pedal (pedal may go to floor with steady pressure applied.)	• Fluid leak in hydraulic system	• Fill master cylinder to fill line; have helper apply brakes and check calipers, wheel cylinders, differential valve tubes, hoses and fittings for leaks. Repair or replace as necessary.
	• Air in hydraulic system	• Remove air from system. Refer to Brake Bleeding.
	• Incorrect or non-recommended brake fluid (fluid evaporates at below normal temp).	• Flush hydraulic system with clean brake fluid. Refill with correct-type fluid.
	• Master cylinder piston seals worn, or master cylinder bore is scored, worn or corroded	• Repair or replace master cylinder
Low brake pedal (pedal goes to floor on first application—o.k. on subsequent applications.)	• Disc brake pads sticking on abutment surfaces of anchor plate. Caused by a build-up of dirt, rust, or corrosion on abutment surfaces	• Clean abutment surfaces
Fading brake pedal (pedal height decreases with steady pressure applied.)	• Fluid leak in hydraulic system	• Fill master cylinder reservoirs to fill mark, have helper apply brakes, check calipers, wheel cylinders, differential valve, tubes, hoses, and fittings for fluid leaks. Repair or replace parts as necessary.
	• Master cylinder piston seals worn, or master cylinder bore is scored, worn or corroded	• Repair or replace master cylinder
Spongy brake pedal (pedal has abnormally soft, springy, spongy feel when depressed.)	• Air in hydraulic system	• Remove air from system. Refer to Brake Bleeding.
	• Brakeshoes bent or distorted	• Replace brakeshoes
	• Brakelining not yet seated with drums and rotors	• Burnish brakes
	• Rear drum brakes not properly adjusted	• Adjust brakes

Troubleshooting the Brake System (cont.)

Problem	Cause	Solution
Decreasing brake pedal travel (pedal travel required for braking action decreases and may be accompanied by a hard pedal.)	• Caliper or wheel cylinder pistons sticking or seized • Master cylinder compensator ports blocked (preventing fluid return to reservoirs) or pistons sticking or seized in master cylinder bore • Power brake unit binding internally	• Repair or replace the calipers, or wheel cylinders • Repair or replace the master cylinder • Test unit according to the following procedure: (a) Shift transmission into neutral and start engine (b) Increase engine speed to 1500 rpm, close throttle and fully depress brake pedal (c) Slow release brake pedal and stop engine (d) Have helper remove vacuum check valve and hose from power unit. Observe for backward movement of brake pedal. (e) If the pedal moves backward, the power unit has an internal bind—replace power unit
Grabbing brakes (severe reaction to brake pedal pressure.)	• Brakelining(s) contaminated by grease or brake fluid • Parking brake cables incorrectly adjusted or seized • Incorrect brakelining or lining loose on brakeshoes • Caliper anchor plate bolts loose • Rear brakeshoes binding on support plate ledges • Incorrect or missing power brake reaction disc • Rear brake support plates loose	• Determine and correct cause of contamination and replace brakeshoes in axle sets • Adjust cables. Replace seized cables. • Replace brakeshoes in axle sets • Tighten bolts • Clean and lubricate ledges. Replace support plate(s) if ledges are deeply grooved. Do not attempt to smooth ledges by grinding. • Install correct disc • Tighten mounting bolts
Chatter or shudder when brakes are applied (pedal pulsation and roughness may also occur.)	• Brakeshoes distorted, bent, contaminated, or worn • Caliper anchor plate or support plate loose • Excessive thickness variation of rotor(s)	• Replace brakeshoes in axle sets • Tighten mounting bolts • Refinish or replace rotors in axle sets
Noisy brakes (squealing, clicking, scraping sound when brakes are applied.)	• Bent, broken, distorted brakeshoes • Excessive rust on outer edge of rotor braking surface	• Replace brakeshoes in axle sets • Remove rust

Troubleshooting the Brake System (cont.)

Problem	Cause	Solution
Hard brake pedal (excessive pedal pressure required to stop vehicle. May be accompanied by brake fade.)	• Loose or leaking power brake unit vacuum hose	• Tighten connections or replace leaking hose
	• Incorrect or poor quality brake-lining	• Replace with lining in axle sets
	• Bent, broken, distorted brakeshoes	• Replace brakeshoes
	• Calipers binding or dragging on mounting pins. Rear brakeshoes dragging on support plate.	• Replace mounting pins and bushings. Clean rust or burrs from rear brake support plate ledges and lubricate ledges with molydisulfide grease. **NOTE:** If ledges are deeply grooved or scored, do not attempt to sand or grind them smooth—replace support plate.
	• Caliper, wheel cylinder, or master cylinder pistons sticking or seized	• Repair or replace parts as necessary
	• Power brake unit vacuum check valve malfunction	• Test valve according to the following procedure: (a) Start engine, increase engine speed to 1500 rpm, close throttle and immediately stop engine (b) Wait at least 90 seconds then depress brake pedal (c) If brakes are not vacuum assisted for 2 or more applications, check valve is faulty
	• Power brake unit has internal bind	• Test unit according to the following procedure: (a) With engine stopped, apply brakes several times to exhaust all vacuum in system (b) Shift transmission into neutral, depress brake pedal and start engine (c) If pedal height decreases with foot pressure and less pressure is required to hold pedal in applied position, power unit vacuum system is operating normally. Test power unit. If power unit exhibits a bind condition, replace the power unit.

Troubleshooting the Brake System (cont.)

Problem	Cause	Solution
Hard brake pedal (excessive pedal pressure required to stop vehicle. May be accompanied by brake fade.)	• Master cylinder compensator ports (at bottom of reservoirs) blocked by dirt, scale, rust, or have small burrs (blocked ports prevent fluid return to reservoirs).	• Repair or replace master cylinder **CAUTION:** Do not attempt to clean blocked ports with wire, pencils, or similar implements. Use compressed air only.
	• Brake hoses, tubes, fittings clogged or restricted	• Use compressed air to check or unclog parts. Replace any damaged parts.
	• Brake fluid contaminated with improper fluids (motor oil, transmission fluid, causing rubber components to swell and stick in bores	• Replace all rubber components, combination valve and hoses. Flush entire brake system with DOT 3 brake fluid or equivalent.
	• Low engine vacuum	• Adjust or repair engine
Dragging brakes (slow or incomplete release of brakes)	• Brake pedal binding at pivot	• Loosen and lubricate
	• Power brake unit has internal bind	• Inspect for internal bind. Replace unit if internal bind exists.
	• Parking brake cables incorrrectly adjusted or seized	• Adjust cables. Replace seized cables.
	• Rear brakeshoe return springs weak or broken	• Replace return springs. Replace brakeshoe if necessary in axle sets.
	• Automatic adjusters malfunctioning	• Repair or replace adjuster parts as required
	• Caliper, wheel cylinder or master cylinder pistons sticking or seized	• Repair or replace parts as necessary
	• Master cylinder compensating ports blocked (fluid does not return to reservoirs).	• Use compressed air to clear ports. Do not use wire, pencils, or similar objects to open blocked ports.
Vehicle moves to one side when brakes are applied	• Incorrect front tire pressure	• Inflate to recommended cold (reduced load) inflation pressure
	• Worn or damaged wheel bearings	• Replace worn or damaged bearings
	• Brakelining on one side contaminated	• Determine and correct cause of contamination and replace brakelining in axle sets
	• Brakeshoes on one side bent, distorted, or lining loose on shoe	• Replace brakeshoes in axle sets
	• Support plate bent or loose on one side	• Tighten or replace support plate
	• Brakelining not yet seated with drums or rotors	• Burnish brakelining
	• Caliper anchor plate loose on one side	• Tighten anchor plate bolts
	• Caliper piston sticking or seized	• Repair or replace caliper
	• Brakelinings water soaked	• Drive vehicle with brakes lightly applied to dry linings
	• Loose suspension component attaching or mounting bolts	• Tighten suspension bolts. Replace worn suspension components.
	• Brake combination valve failure	• Replace combination valve

Troubleshooting the Brake System (cont.)

Problem	Cause	Solution
Noisy brakes (squealing, clicking, scraping sound when brakes are applied.) (cont.)	• Brakelining worn out—shoes contacting drum of rotor	• Replace brakeshoes and lining in axle sets. Refinish or replace drums or rotors.
	• Broken or loose holdown or return springs	• Replace parts as necessary
	• Rough or dry drum brake support plate ledges	• Lubricate support plate ledges
	• Cracked, grooved, or scored rotor(s) or drum(s)	• Replace rotor(s) or drum(s). Replace brakeshoes and lining in axle sets if necessary.
	• Incorrect brakelining and/or shoes (front or rear).	• Install specified shoe and lining assemblies
Pulsating brake pedal	• Out of round drums or excessive lateral runout in disc brake rotor(s)	• Refinish or replace drums, re-index rotors or replace

TORQUE SPECIFICATIONS

Component	U.S.	Metric
ABS hydraulic modulator assembly attaching nuts	20 ft. lbs.	27 Nm
Booster to pedal bracket	15 ft. lbs.	21 Nm
Brake control solenoid assembly attaching screws	39 inch lbs.	5 Nm
Brake lines to hydraulic modulator	13 ft. lbs.	17 Nm
Brake pedal bushing and pivot bolt	25 ft. lbs.	34 Nm
Caliper attaching bolts	38 ft. lbs.	51 Nm
Master cylinder to booster	20 ft. lbs.	27 Nm
Parking brake cable-to-lever assembly nut	21 ft. lbs.	28 Nm
Parking brake lever attaching bolts	18 ft. lbs.	25 Nm
Proportioner valve caps	20 ft. lbs.	27 Nm
Rear wheel bearing and speed sensor assembly	37 ft. lbs.	50 Nm
Wheel cylinder inlet tube	12 ft. lbs.	17 Nm
Wheel speed sensor attaching screws	106 inch lbs.	12 Nm

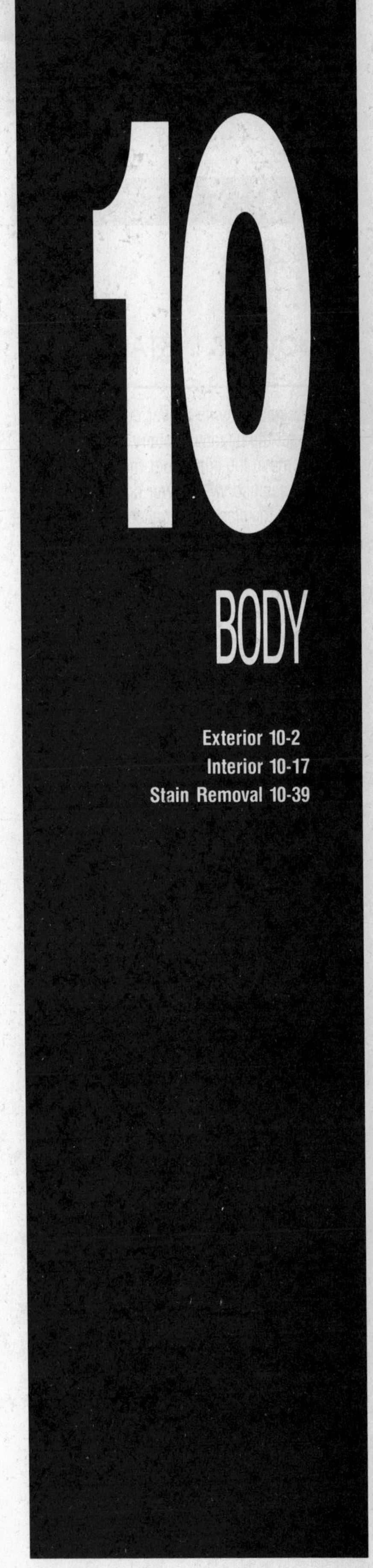

10

BODY

EXTERIOR

Doors

➧ SEE FIGS. 1–4

REMOVAL & INSTALLATION

1. If equipped with power door components, disconnect the negative battery cable.
2. Remove the inner door trim panel.
3. If equipped with power door components, disconnect the electrical connectors and remove the harness.
4. Using a suitable tool mark the location of the door hinges in relation to the door and remove the door detent bolt.
5. With an assistant supporting the door, remove the hinge to door bolts and remove the door from the vehicle.

To install:

6. With the aid of an assistant, reposition the door and install the hinge to door bolts. Torque the bolts to 18 ft. lbs. (24 Nm).
7. If so equipped, install the electrical harness and connect the electrical connectors to the power door components.
8. Install the inner door trim panel and install the door detent bolt.
9. Connect the negative battery cable.

ADJUSTMENT

1. Adjust the door so that the door to body and lock to striker align properly.
2. The hinge to door bolts may need to be loosened to adjust the alignment properly.

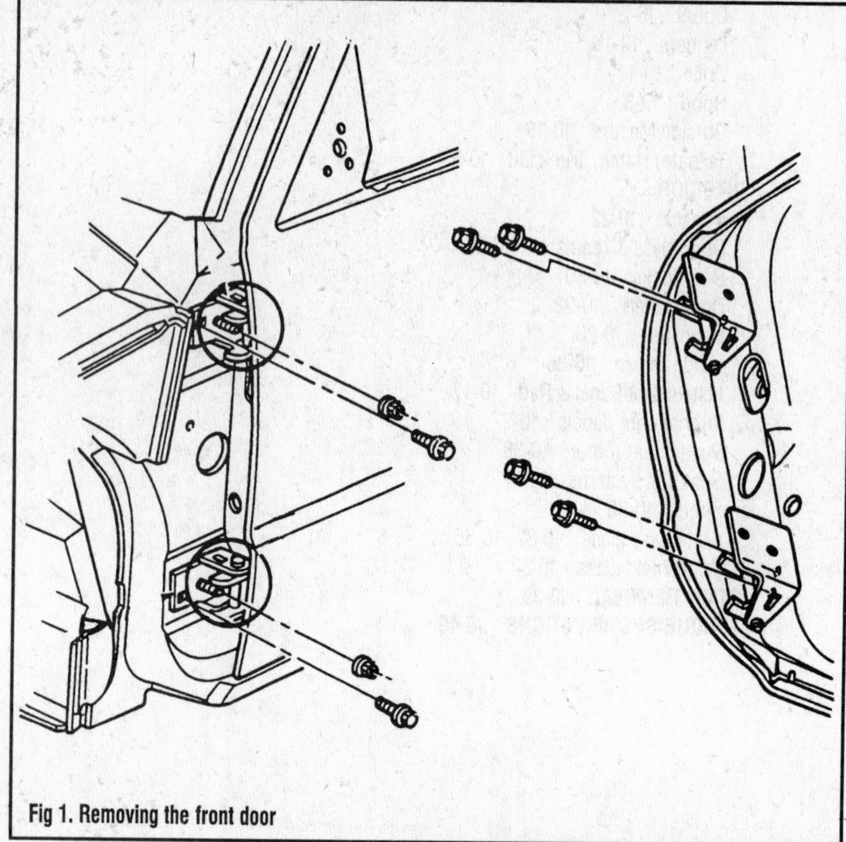

Fig 1. Removing the front door

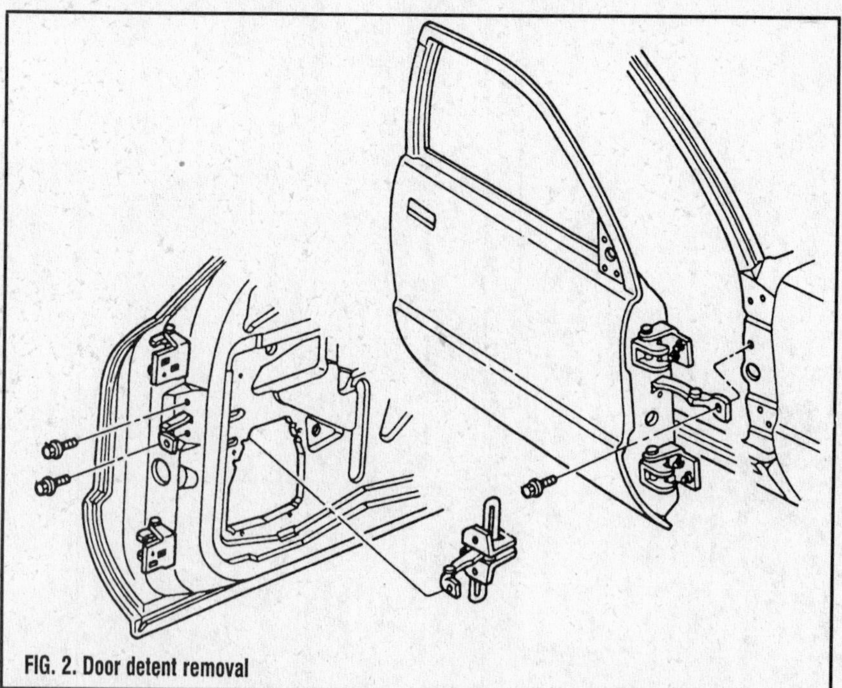

FIG. 2. Door detent removal

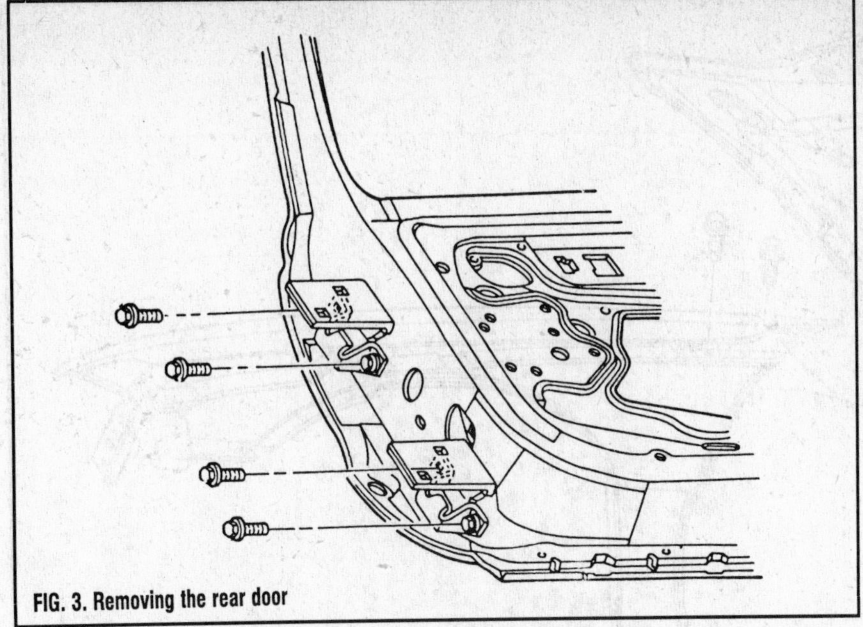
FIG. 3. Removing the rear door

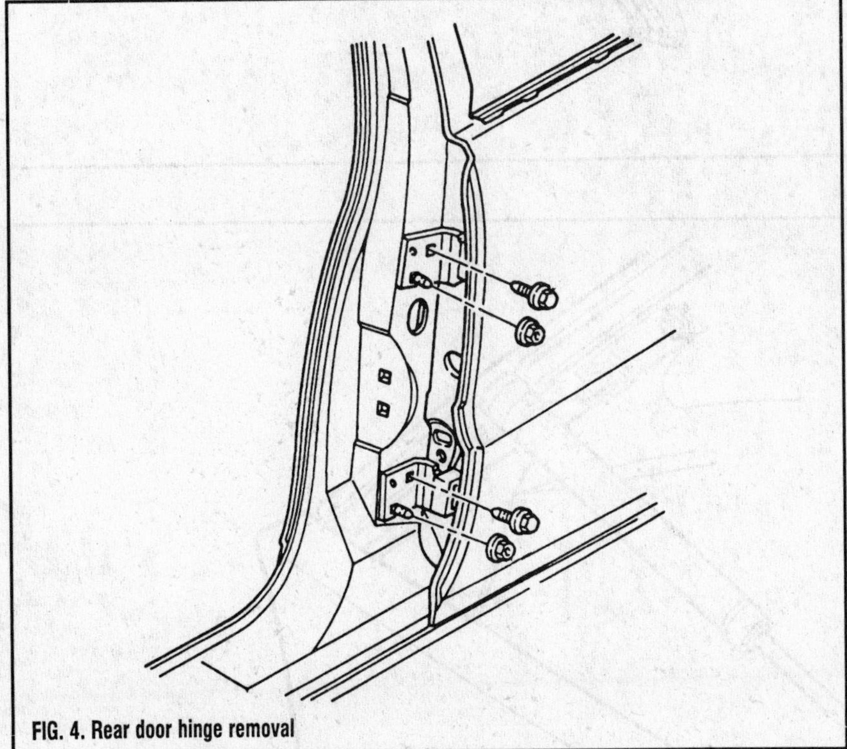
FIG. 4. Rear door hinge removal

Hood

SEE FIGS. 5–6

REMOVAL & INSTALLATION

1. Raise the hood and remove the engine compartment lamp.
2. Using a suitable tool, mark the position of the hinges in relation to the hood.
3. Disconnect the hood assist rod strut, if equipped.
4. With an assistant supporting the hood, remove the bolts attaching the hinge to the hood and remove the hood from the vehicle.

To install:

5. With the aid of an assistant align the hood to the hinges and install the retaining bolts.
6. Check alignment marks and tighten the bolts to 20 ft. lbs. (27 Nm).
7. Connect the hood assist rod strut, if equipped and connect the engine compartment lamp.

ALIGNMENT

Rear Corners

1. Loosen the lower hinge to hood attaching bolts.
2. Add or remove shims under the hinge to adjust as needed.
3. Tighten the hinge to hood bolts to 20 ft. lbs. (27 Nm).

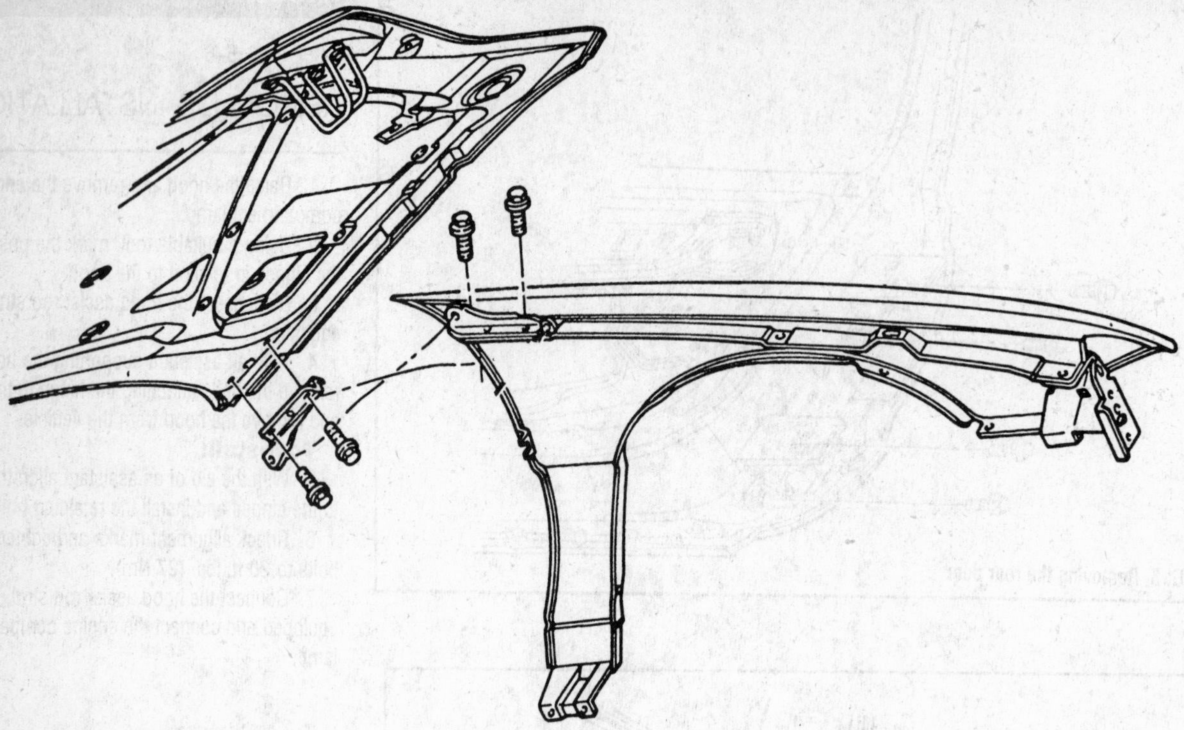

FIG. 5. Hood removal and installation

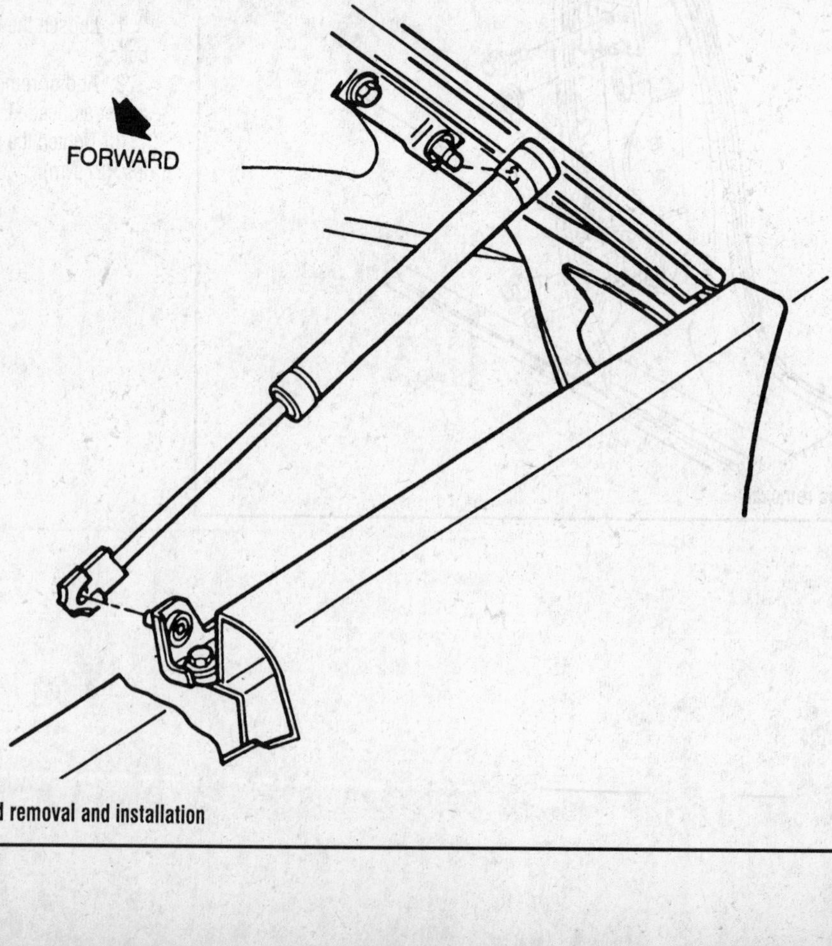

FIG. 6. Hood open assist rod removal and installation

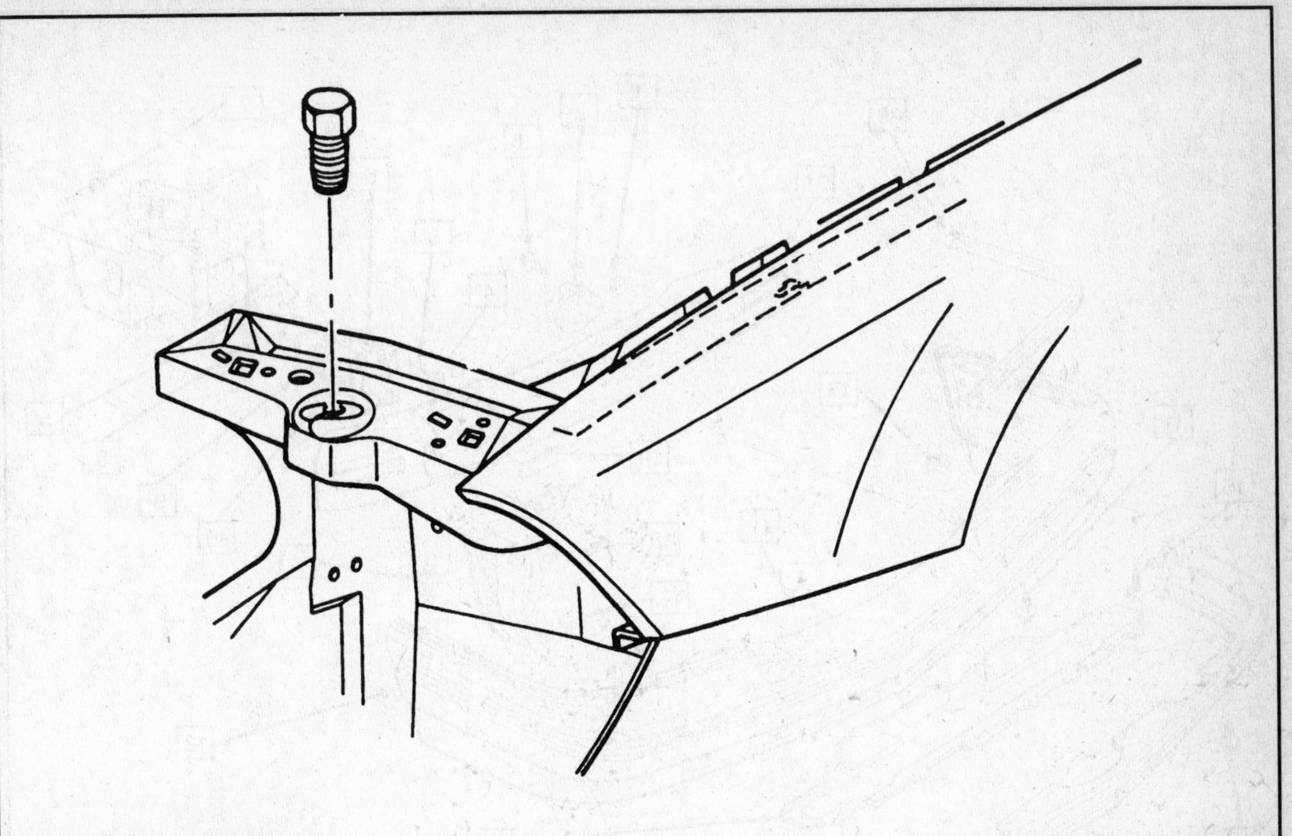

FIG. 7. Hood bumper adjustment

Front Corners

➧ SEE FIG. 7

1. Close hood completely and determine how much adjustment is required.
2. Open the hood and raise or lower the adjustable hood bumpers as needed.
3. Close hood completely and inspect, repeat if needed.

Fore and Aft

1. Loosen the hinge to fender attaching bolts.
2. Reposition the hinge assembly as needed and tighten bolts.
3. If needed, repeat on opposite side of the hood.

Trunk Lid

➧ SEE FIG. 8

REMOVAL & INSTALLATION

1. Open trunk and disconnect all electrical connectors attached to electrical components connected to the trunk lid.
2. If so equipped, disconnect the lock out solenoid.
3. Tie a string to the wire harness and pull it out of the trunk lid.

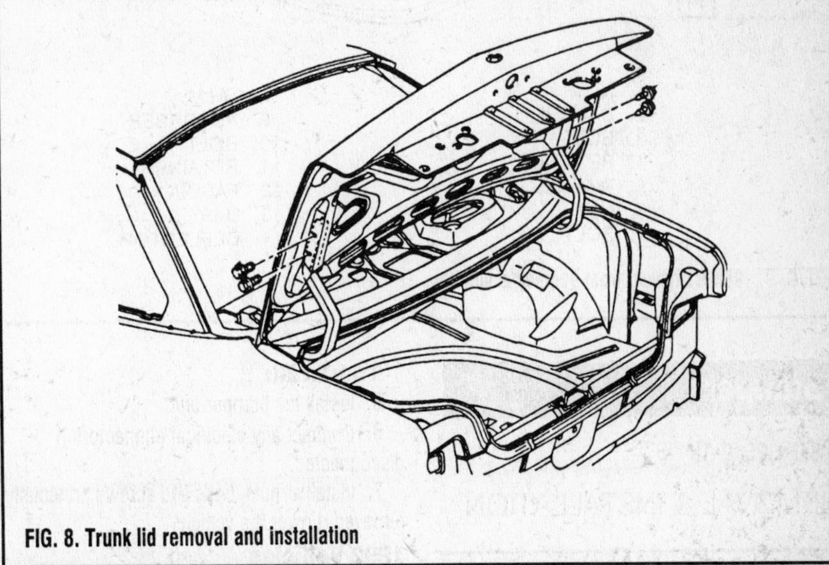

FIG. 8. Trunk lid removal and installation

4. While an assistant supports the lid, remove the lid to hinge bolts and remove the lid.

To install:

5. With the aid of an assistant, reposition the trunk lid to the hinges and install the bolts.
6. Adjust the hood as needed and tighten retaining bolts to 18 ft. lbs. (24 Nm).
7. Feed string attached to electrical harness through lid and pull wire harness through lid.
8. Connect electrical connectors and lock out solenoid connector if so equipped.

ALIGNMENT

1. Loosen the lid to hinge bolts.
2. Align trunk lid as needed and tighten bolts.

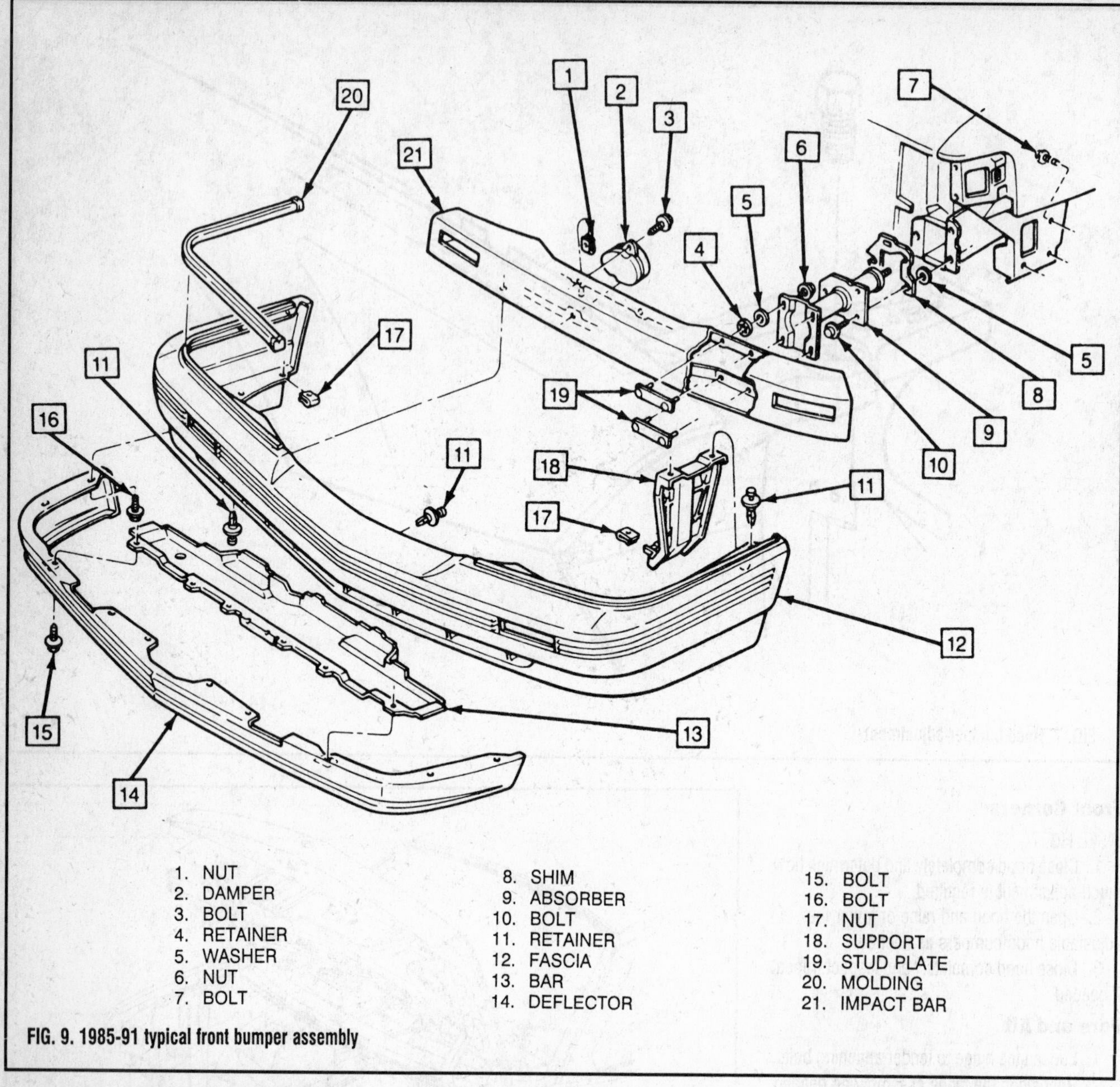

FIG. 9. 1985-91 typical front bumper assembly

Bumpers

SEE FIGS. 9–15

REMOVAL & INSTALLATION

Front

1985-91 Vehicles

1. Raise and safely support the vehicle.
2. Remove the nuts, bolts and screws attaching the front fascia to the fender.
3. Remove the park/turn signal bulb connectors if necessary.
4. Remove the bolts attaching the bumper bar and energy absorber assembly and remove the bumper assembly.

To install:

5. Install the bumper unit.
6. Connect any electrical connectors if disconnected.
7. Install all nuts, bolts and screws previously removed. Lower the vehicle.

1992 Vehicles

1. Remove the right and left wheel housing.
2. Remove the right and left fascia to fender bolts. On the 1992 GRAND AM, remove the parking lamp assemblies.
3. Remove the fascia retainers and remove the fascia from the impact bar.
4. Remove the impact bar bolts and remove the front impact bar from the vehicle.

To install:

5. Install the front impact bar to the vehicle and tighten the bolts to 22 ft. lbs. (30 Nm). Install the parking lamp assemblies on the 1992 GRAND AM.
6. Install the energy absorber to the impact bar and connect with nine 3/16 in. rivets.
7. Install the front fascia to the energy absorber and install the retainers and bolts.
8. Install the right and left wheel housings.

Rear Bumpers

1985-91 Vehicles

1. Remove the fascia attaching screws and bolts.
2. From inside the trunk, remove the bumper attaching nuts and washers.
3. Remove the bumper assembly from the vehicle.

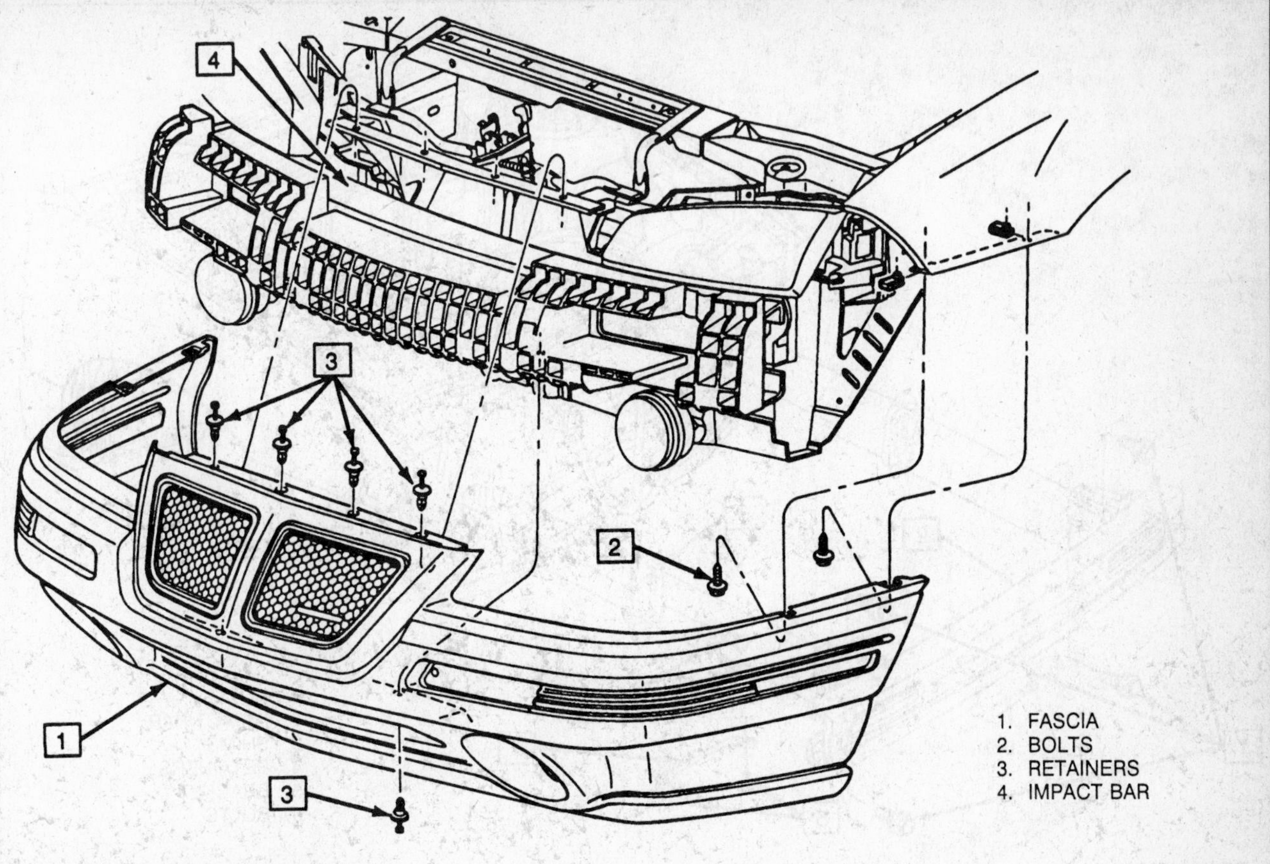

FIG. 10. 1992 Grand Am front bumper fascia

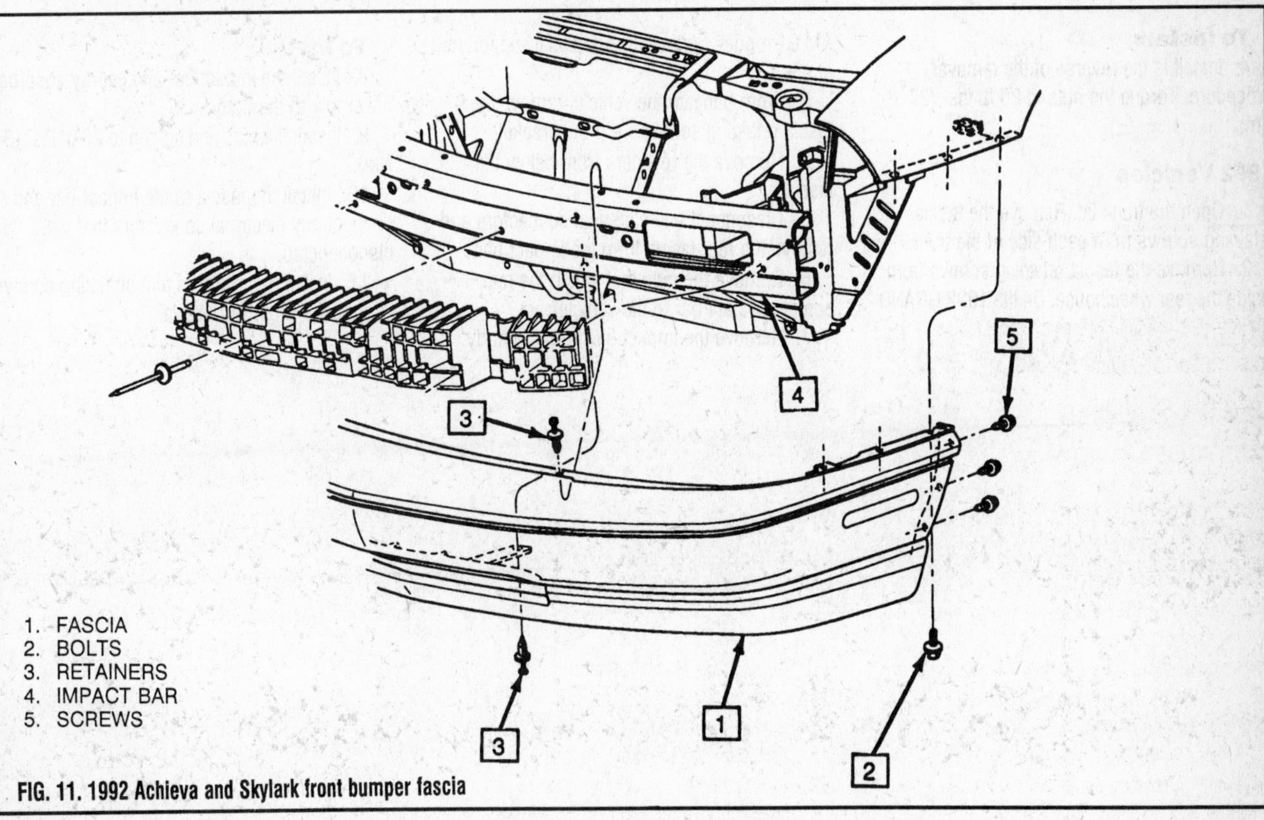

FIG. 11. 1992 Achieva and Skylark front bumper fascia

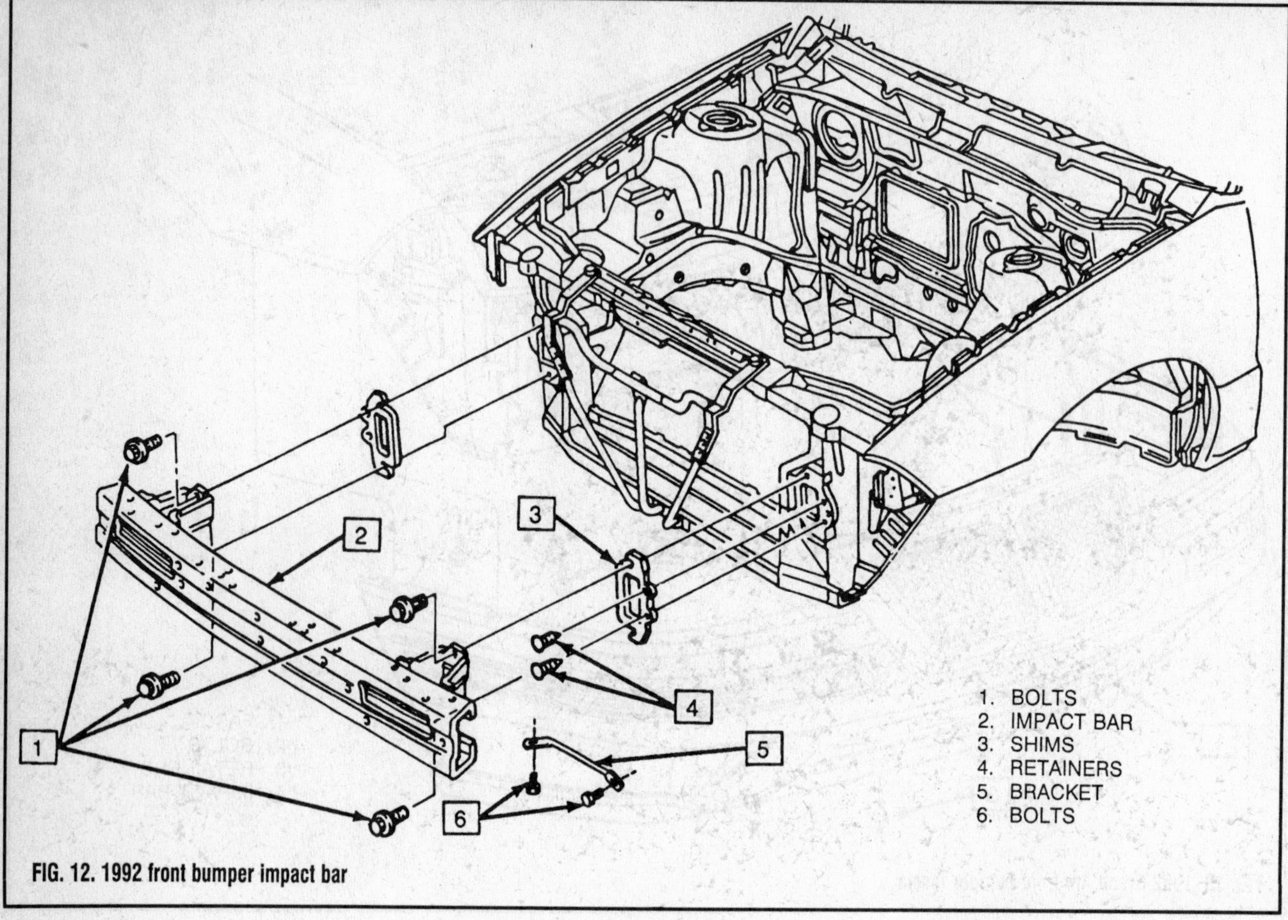

FIG. 12. 1992 front bumper impact bar

To install:

4. Install is the reverse of the removal procedure. Torque the nuts to 20 ft. lbs. (27 Nm).

1992 Vehicles

1. Open the trunk lid. Remove the fascia retaining screws from each side of the trunk.
2. Remove the fascia retaining screws from inside the rear wheelhouse. On the 1992 GRAND AM GT model, remove the additional support and screw.
3. From beneath the vehicle, remove the 4 fascia retaining screws from the bracket.
4. Remove the retainers from below the fascia.
5. Disconnect any electrical connectors and remove the rear fascia from the impact bar.
6. Remove the nuts that attach the rear bumper impact bar to the vehicle.
7. Remove the impact bar from the body.

To install:

8. Install the impact bar and energy absorber assembly to the body.
9. Install the nuts and tighten to 26 ft. lbs. (35 Nm).
10. Install the fascia to the impact bar and connect any electrical connectors that were disconnected.
11. Install the retainers and attaching screws in opposite order of removal.

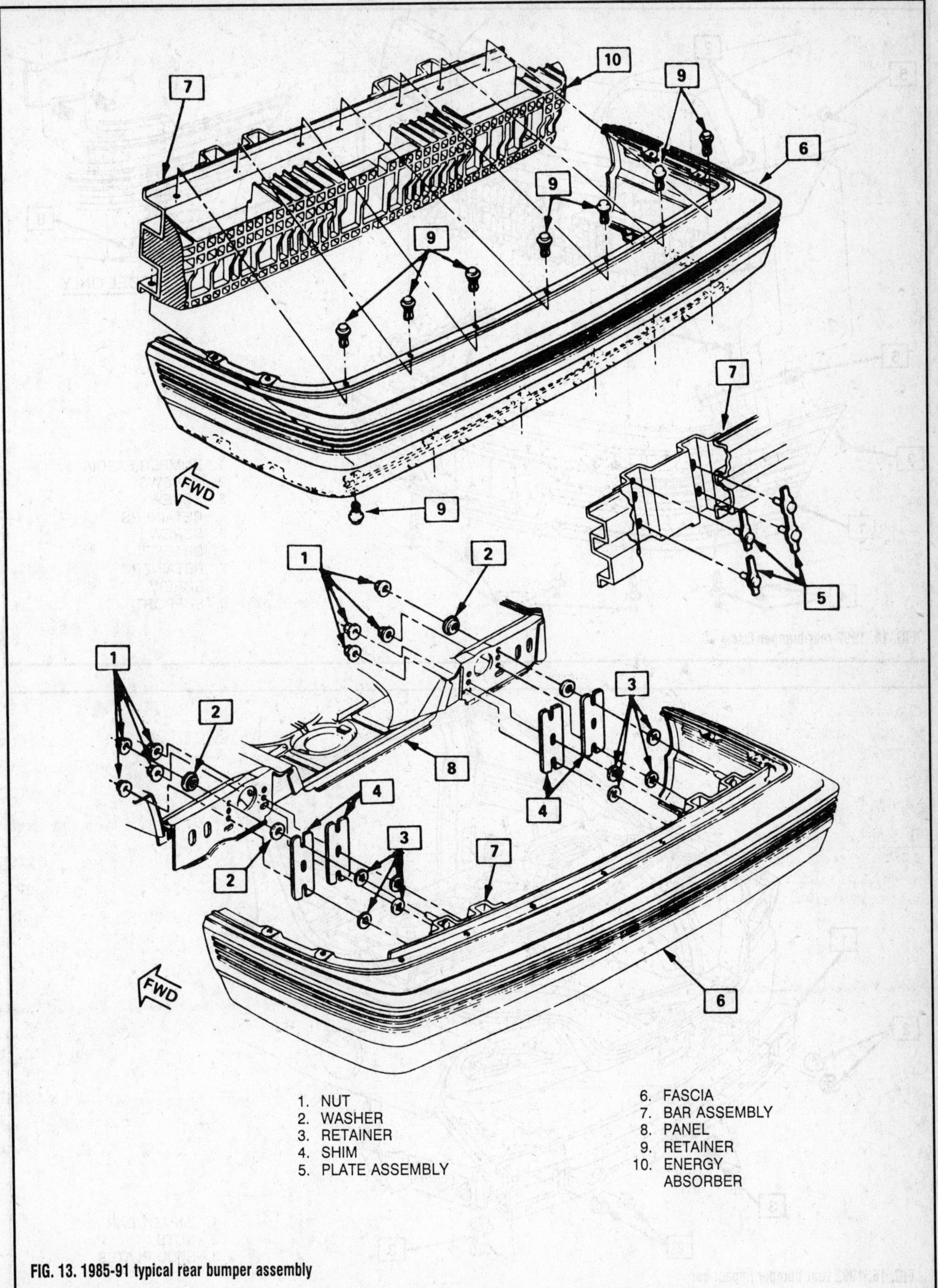

FIG. 13. 1985-91 typical rear bumper assembly

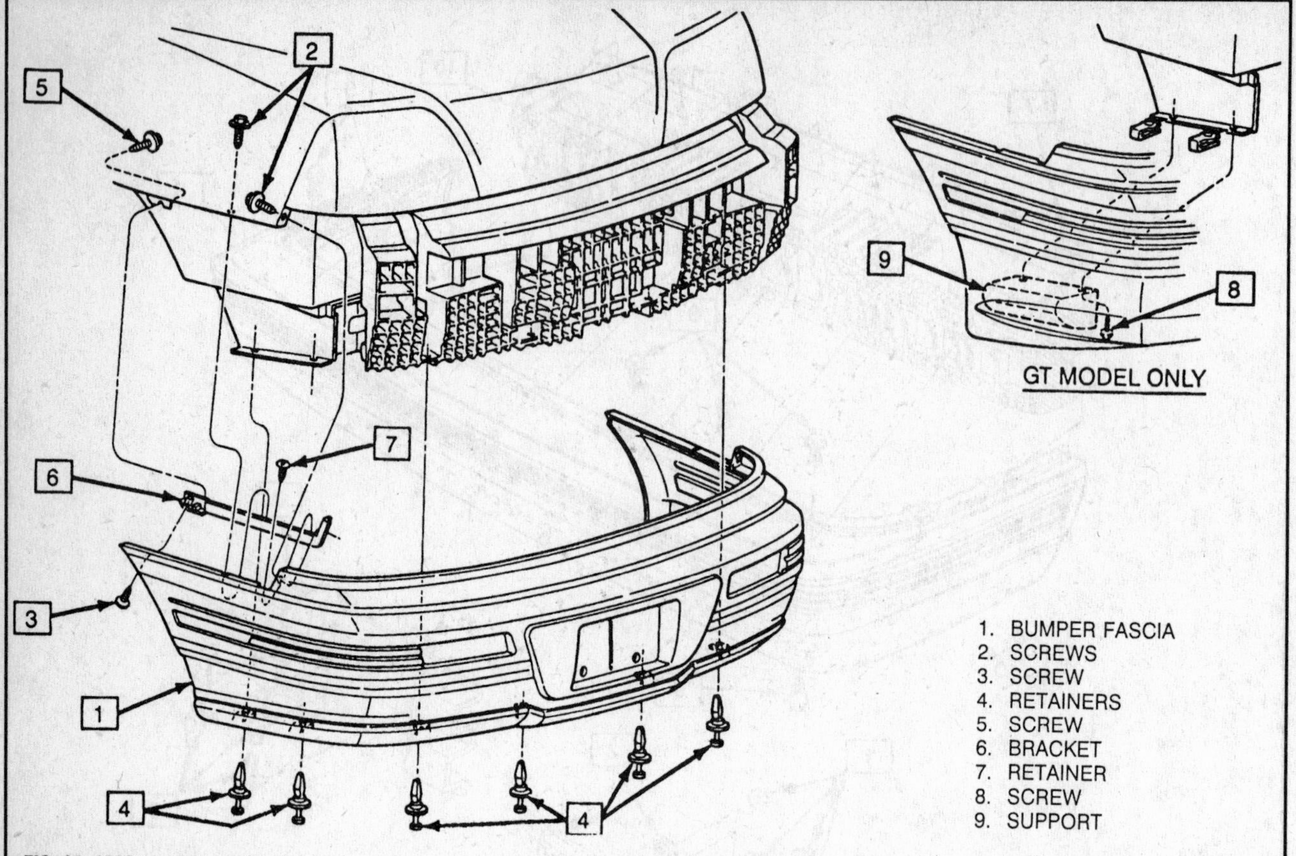

GT MODEL ONLY

1. BUMPER FASCIA
2. SCREWS
3. SCREW
4. RETAINERS
5. SCREW
6. BRACKET
7. RETAINER
8. SCREW
9. SUPPORT

FIG. 14. 1992 rear bumper fascia

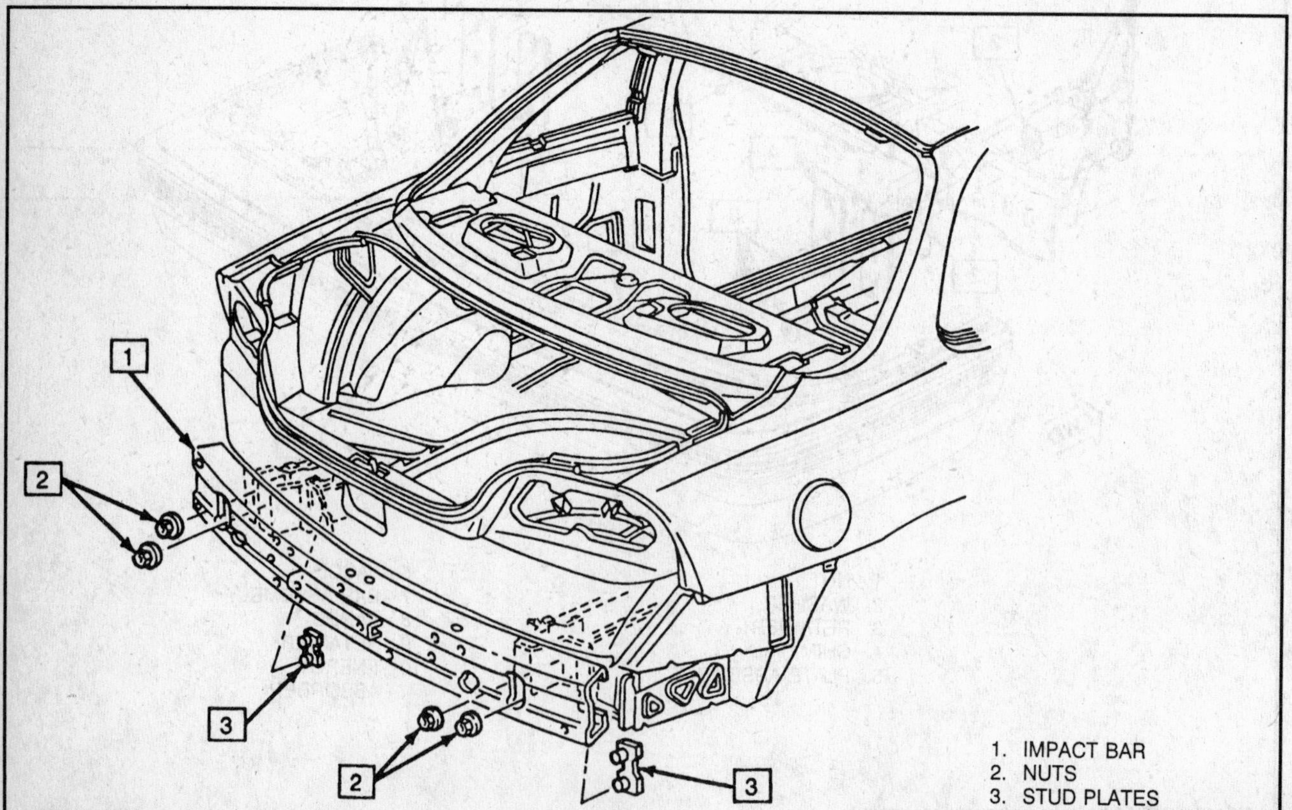

1. IMPACT BAR
2. NUTS
3. STUD PLATES

FIG. 15. 1992 rear bumper impact bar

Grille

➧ SEE FIGS. 16–20

REMOVAL & INSTALLATION

1985-91 Vehicles Except 1989-91 Grand Am

1. Remove the screws from the grille.
2. Remove the grill assembly.

To install:

3. Installation is the reverse of the removal procedure.

1989-91 Grand Am

To remove grille, just release the tabs and pull grille outward. Installation is done by inserting grille and locking tabs.

1992 Achieva and Skylark

1. Remove the screws along the top of the grille.
2. Pull out on the grille to release the lower tabs.

To install:

3. Installation is the reverse of the removal procedure.

On the 1992 Grand Am, the grille is part of the bumper fascia.

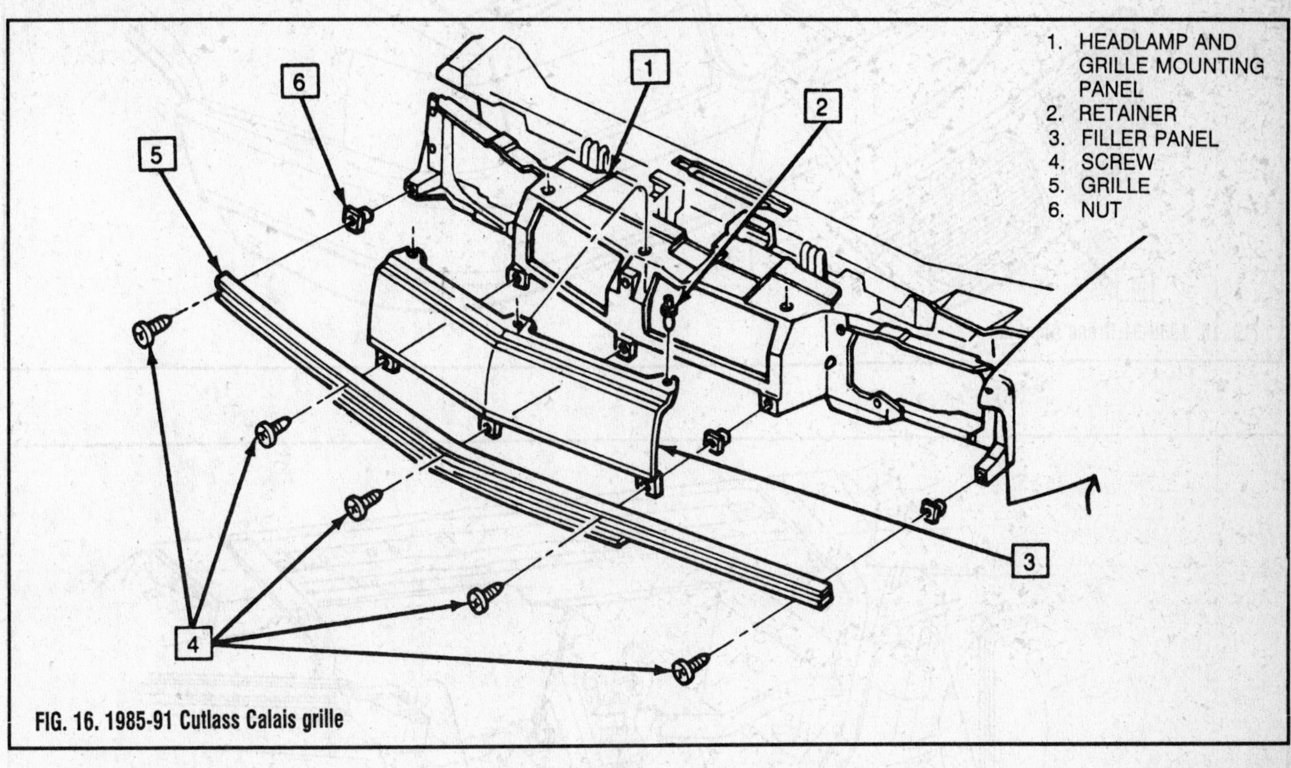

FIG. 16. 1985-91 Cutlass Calais grille

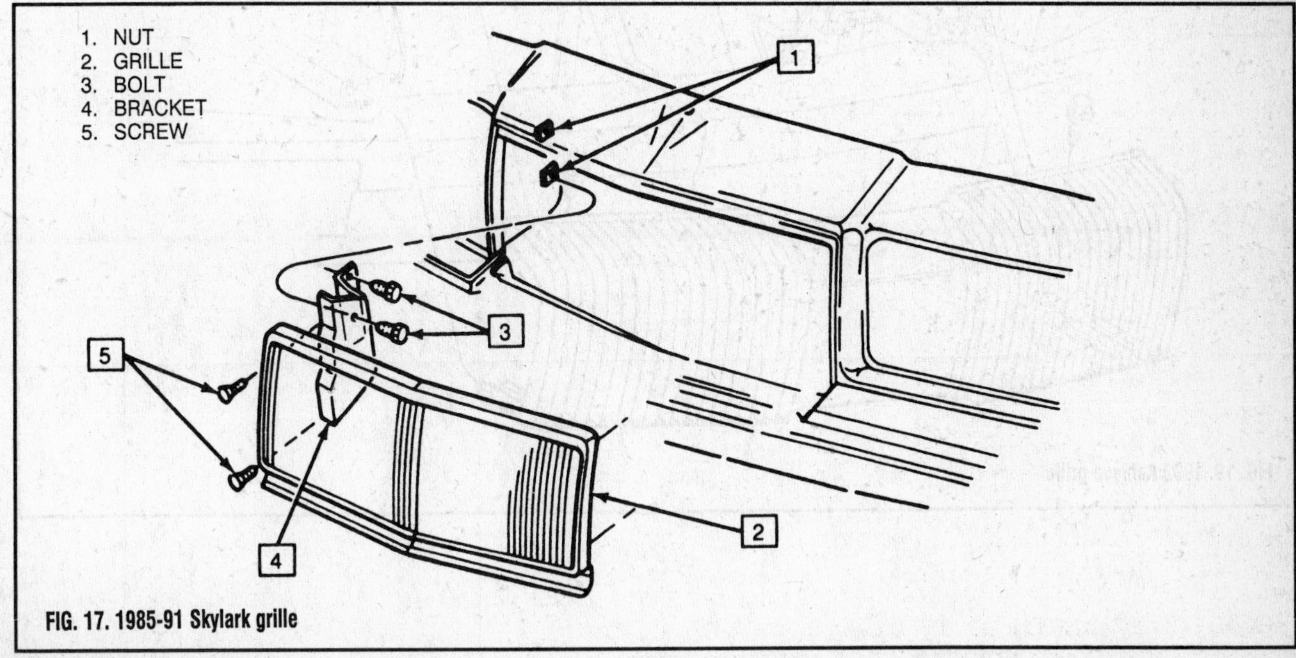

FIG. 17. 1985-91 Skylark grille

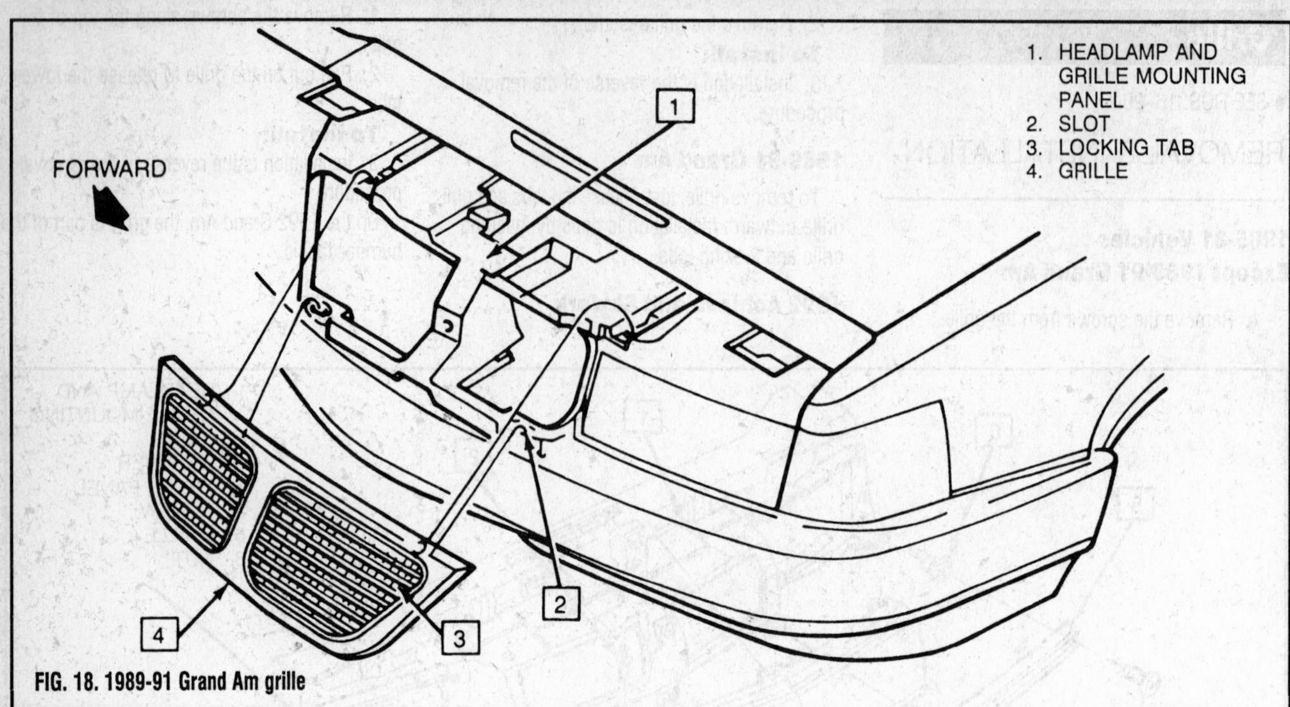

FIG. 18. 1989-91 Grand Am grille

FIG. 19. 1992 Achieva grille

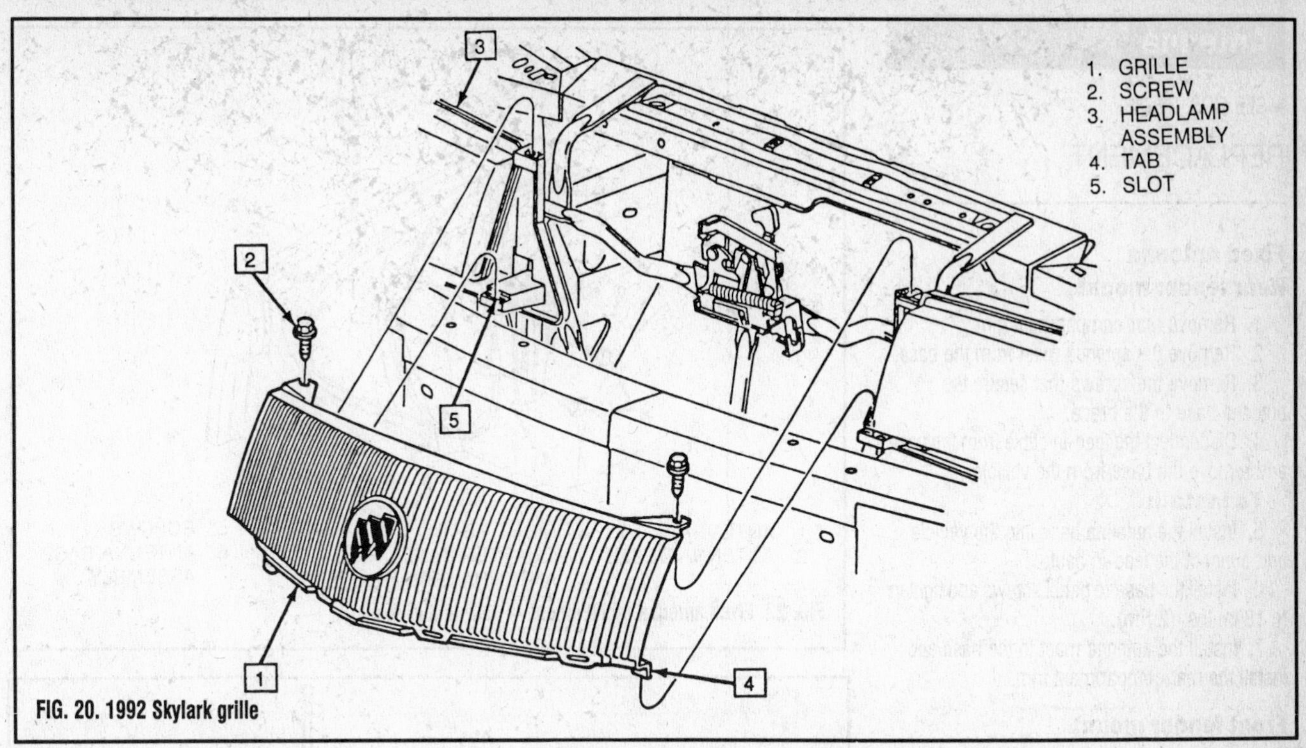

FIG. 20. 1992 Skylark grille

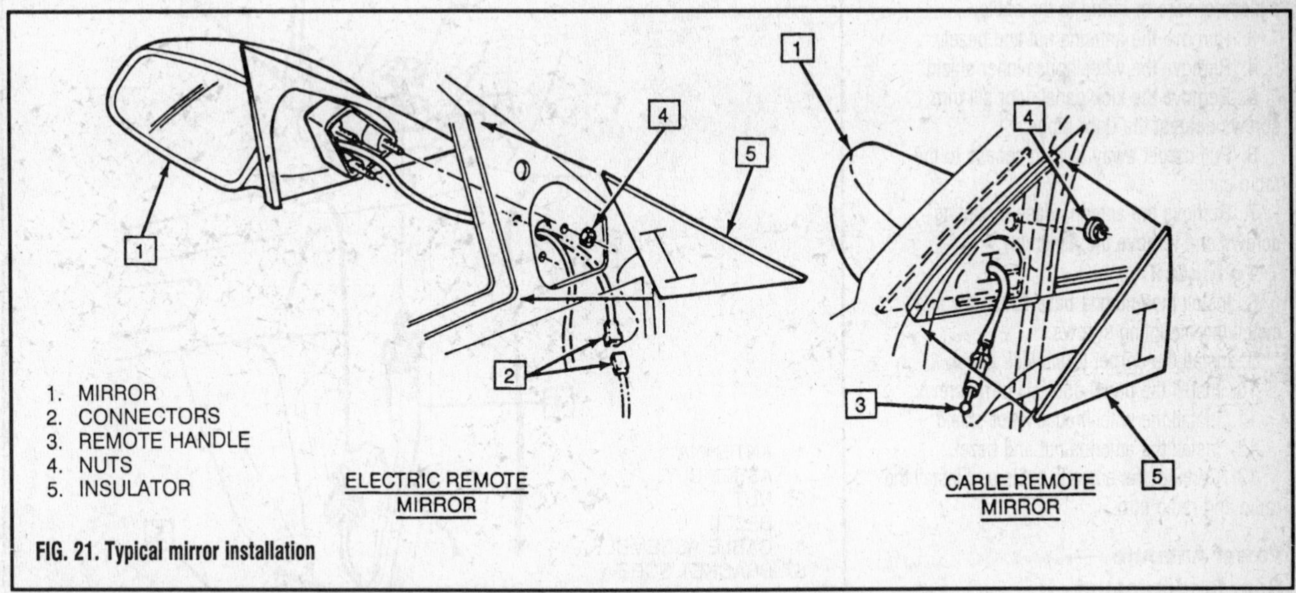

FIG. 21. Typical mirror installation

Outside Mirrors

➧ SEE FIG. 21

REMOVAL & INSTALLATION

1. From inside of door remove the retaining screw.
2. Remove the outside mirror escutcheon by pulling inward.
3. Remove mirror control handle and remove escutcheon.
4. If equipped with power mirrors, disconnect the electrical connector.
5. Remove the gasket and the retaining nuts.
6. Remove the mirror from the door.

To install:

7. Install the mirror to the door and tighten the nuts to 45 in. lbs. (5 Nm).
8. Install the gasket and if equipped with power mirrors connect the electrical connector.
9. Slide the escutcheon onto handle shaft and install handle onto shaft.
10. Snap escutcheon into place and install the screw.

Antenna

SEE FIGS. 22–25

REPLACEMENT

Fixed Antenna

Rear fender mount

1. Remove rear compartment trim.
2. Remove the antenna mast from the base.
3. Remove the screws that secure the antenna base to the brace.
4. Disconnect the lead-in cable from the base and remove the base from the vehicle.

To install:

5. Install the antenna base into the vehicle and connect the lead-in cable.
6. Install the base to panel screws and tighten to 18 in. lbs. (2 Nm).
7. Install the antenna mast to the base and install the rear compartment trim.

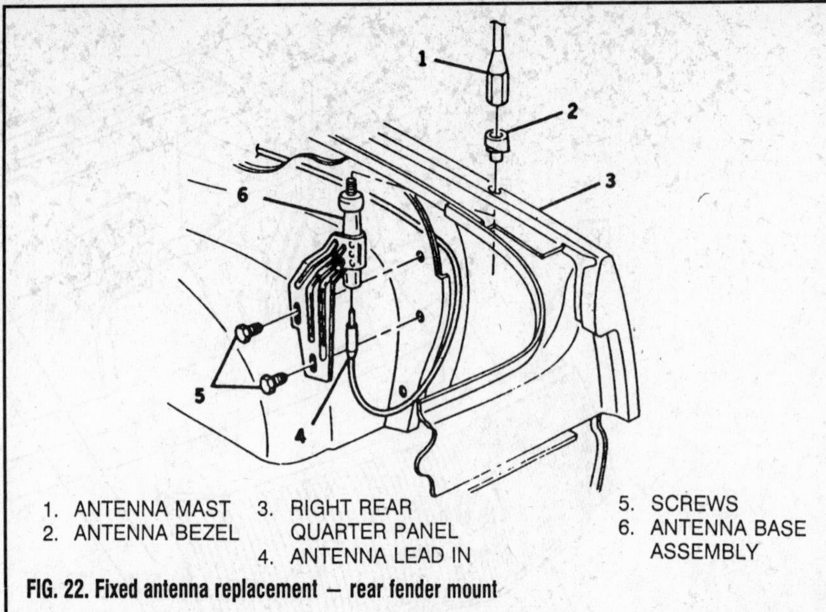

FIG. 22. Fixed antenna replacement — rear fender mount

Front fender mount

1. Remove the radio trim and the radio.
2. Disconnect the antenna cable and connect a piece of wire or string to the cable.
3. Remove the antenna nut and bezel.
4. Remove the wheelhouse inner shield.
5. Remove the kick panel door sill trim screws nearest the door hinge.
6. Pull carpet away to gain access to the radio cable.
7. Remove the antenna base mounting screws and remove the assembly.

To install:

8. Install the antenna base assembly and install the mounting screws.
9. Install the carpet to the kick panel.
10. Install the panel door sill trim screws.
11. Install the wheelhouse inner shield.
12. Install the antenna nut and bezel.
13. Connect the antenna cable and install the radio and radio trim.

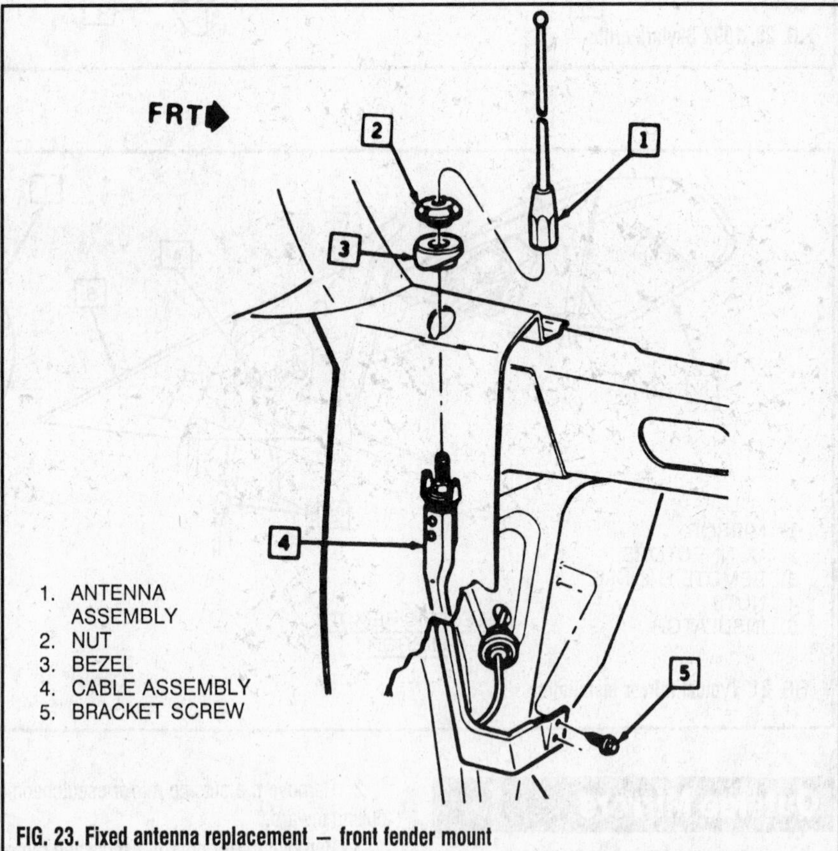

FIG. 23. Fixed antenna replacement — front fender mount

Power Antenna

Rear fender mount

1. Disconnect the negative battery cable.
2. Remove the rear compartment trim.
3. Disconnect the relay connector from the antenna assembly.
4. Remove the screws that secure the antenna assembly to the brace.
5. Remove the antenna insulator and disconnect the lead-in cable from the antenna assembly.
6. Remove antenna assembly from the vehicle.

To install:

7. Connect the lead-in cable to the antenna assembly.
8. Install the base to panel screws and tighten to 18 in. lbs. (2 Nm).
9. Install the antenna insulator and connect the electrical connector to the antenna.
10. Install the rear compartment trim and connect the negative battery cable.

Front fender mount

1. Disconnect the negative battery cable.
2. Remove the right side, under dash, inner panel, sound insulator.

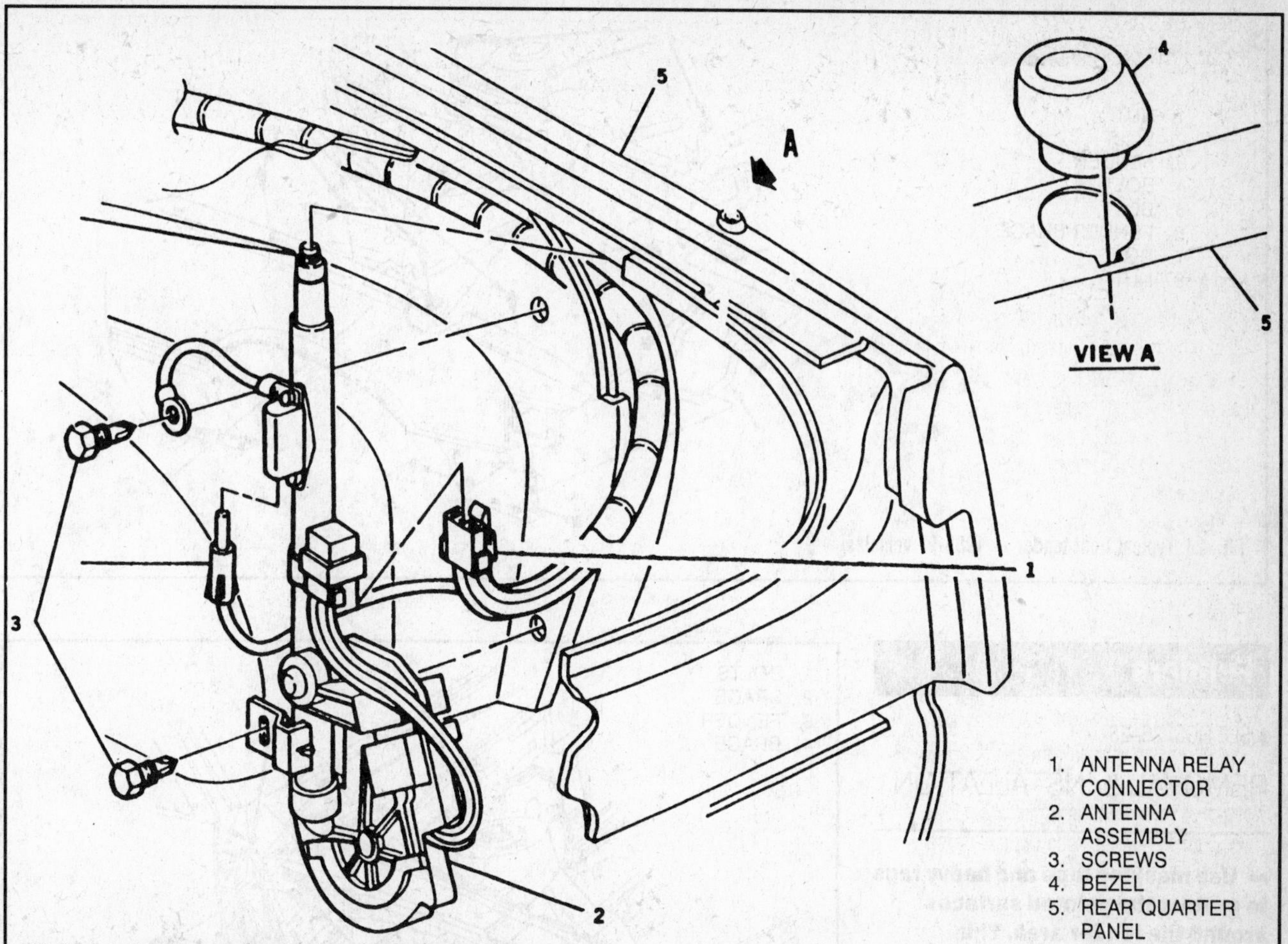

5
A
4
VIEW A
1
3
2

1. ANTENNA RELAY CONNECTOR
2. ANTENNA ASSEMBLY
3. SCREWS
4. BEZEL
5. REAR QUARTER PANEL
6. ANTENNA LEAD

FIG. 24. Power antenna replacement — rear fender mount

3. Disconnect the antenna lead-in cable from extension cable.
4. Disconnect the antenna wiring connector.
5. Remove the grommet from the right cowl.
6. Remove the screws from the right inner fender splash shield.
7. Remove the screws from the antenna motor bracket.
8. Remove the nut and bezel holding the antenna to the fender and remove the assembly from the vehicle.

To install:

9. Install the antenna assembly to the vehicle and install the nut and bezel to the antenna.
10. Install the screws to the antenna motor and bracket.
11. Connect the wiring connector.
12. Connect the antenna lead-in cable to the extension cable.
13. Install the right side sound insulator.
14. Connect the negative battery cable.

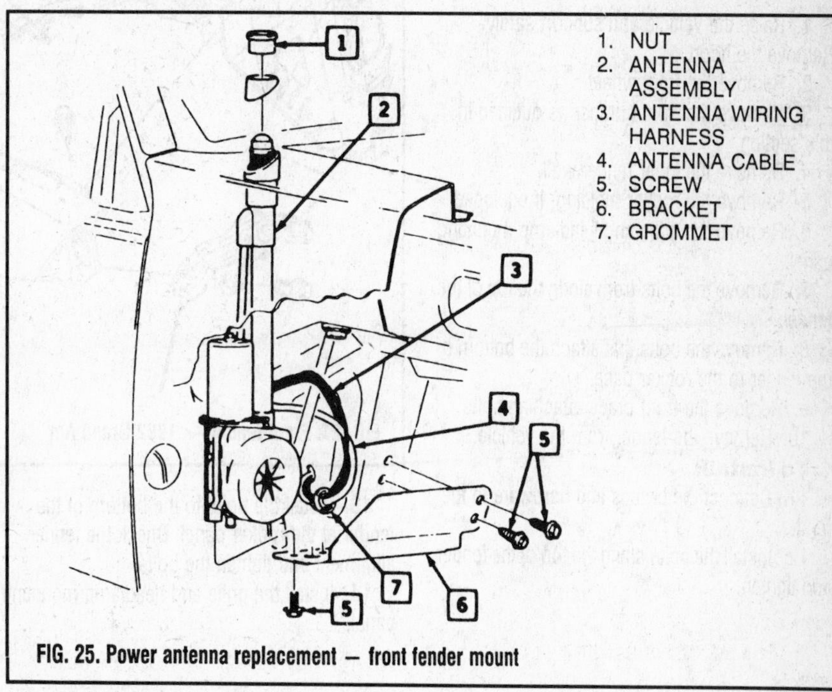

FIG. 25. Power antenna replacement — front fender mount

1. NUT
2. BOLT
3. FENDER
4. BOLT
5. BOLT
6. FENDER BRACE
7. BOLT
8. NUT

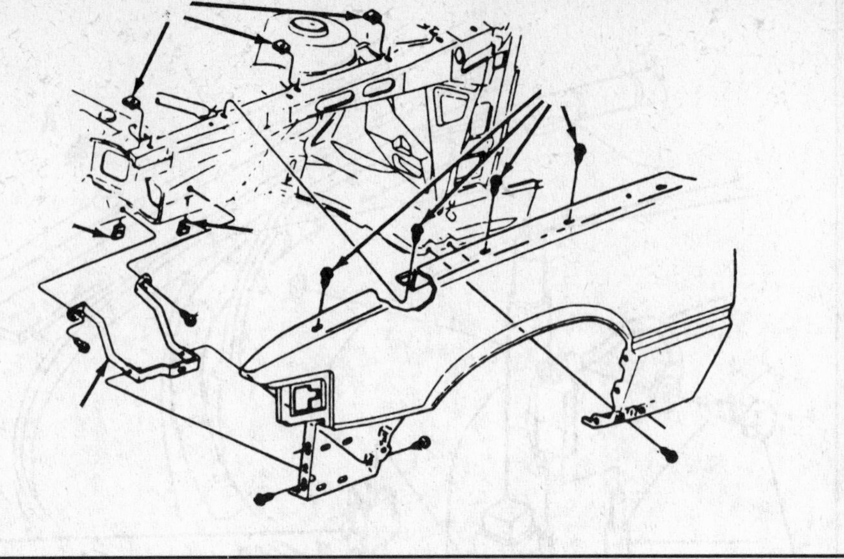

FIG. 26. Typical front fender — 1985-91 vehicles

Fenders

➧ SEE FIGS. 26–28

REMOVAL & INSTALLATION

➡ Use masking tape and heavy rags to protect the painted surfaces around the fender area. This procedure will help avoid expensive paint damage during fender removal and installation.

1. Raise the vehicle and support safely. Remove the hood.
2. Remove the front wheel.
3. Remove the front bumper as outlined in this section.
4. Remove the inner fender well.
5. Remove the rocker molding, if equipped.
6. Remove the grille and headlamp mounting panel.
7. Remove the bolts from along the top of the fender.
8. Remove the bolts that attach the bottom of the fender to the rocker panel.
9. Remove the front brace attaching bolts.
10. Remove the fender from the vehicle.

To install:

11. Connect the braces and hardware to the fender.
12. Install the bolts along the top of the fender and tighten.

1. BOLTS
2. BRACE
3. FENDER
4. BRACE

FIG. 27. Front fender — 1992 Grand Am

13. Install the bolts to the bottom of the fender at the rocker panel. Check the fender alignment and tighten the bolts.
14. Install the grille and headlamp mounting panel.
15. Install the front bumper and wheel well.
16. Connect all electrical connectors.
17. Install the front wheel and install the hood. Slowly lower the hood and check alignment. Realign if necessary.

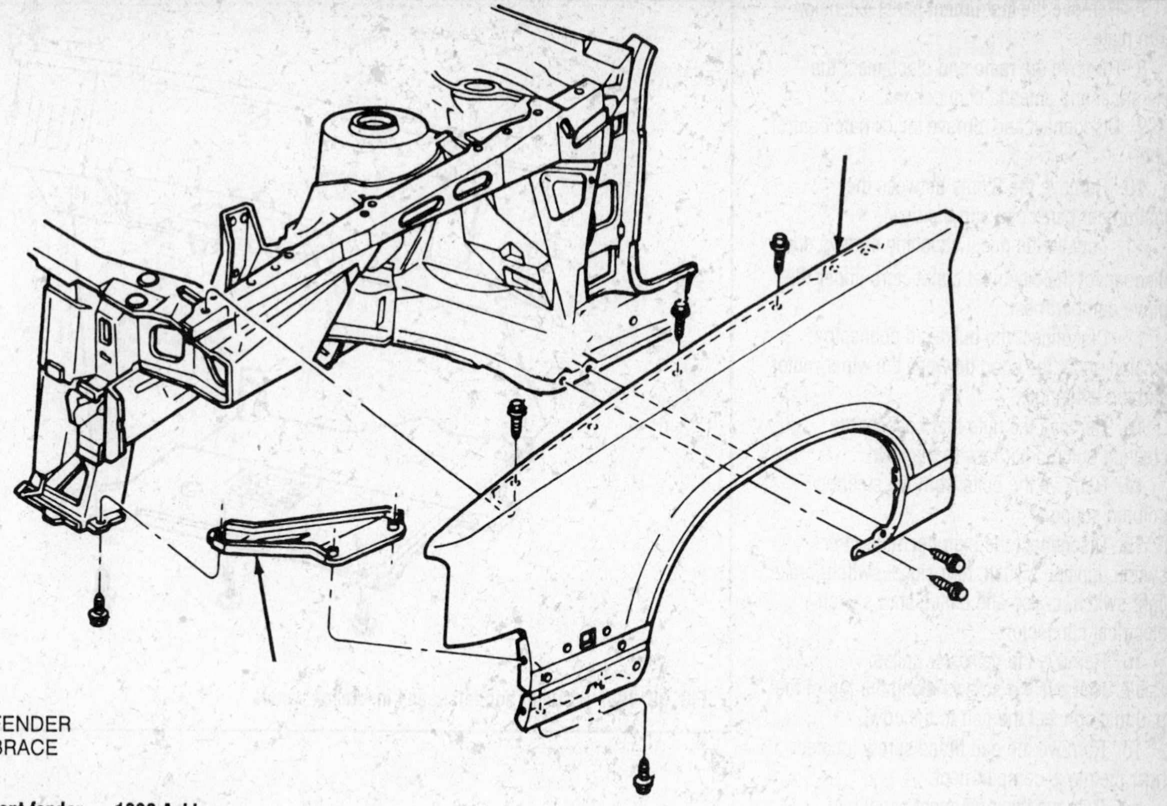

1. FENDER
2. BRACE

FIG. 28. Front fender — 1992 Achieva

INTERIOR

Instrument Panel and Pad

➧ SEE FIGS. 29–40

REMOVAL & INSTALLATION

➡ On some models the center console must first be removed.

1985-91 Vehicles

1. Disconnect the negative battery cable.
2. Remove the left side sound insulator.
3. Remove the right side sound insulator.
4. Remove the steering column opening trim plate.
5. Remove the instrument cluster trim plate.
6. Open the glove compartment door and remove glove compartment.

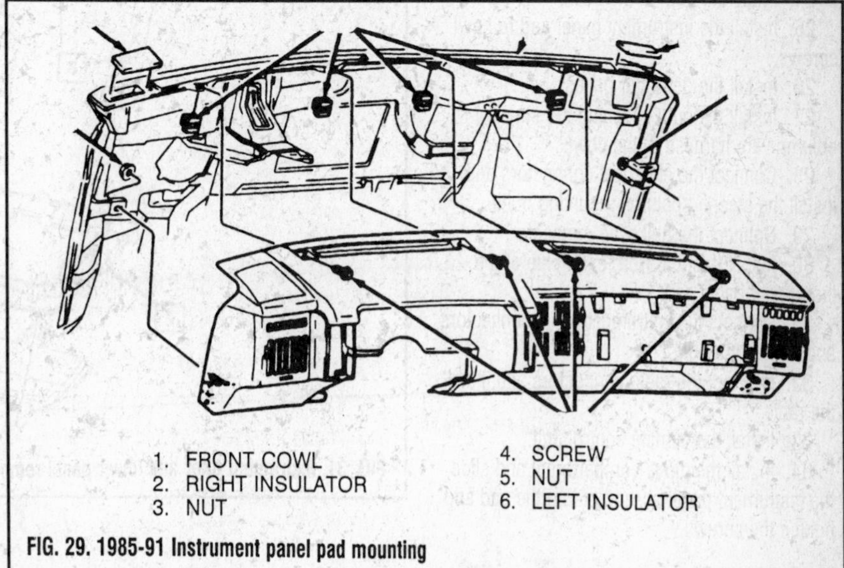

1. FRONT COWL
2. RIGHT INSULATOR
3. NUT
4. SCREW
5. NUT
6. LEFT INSULATOR

FIG. 29. 1985-91 Instrument panel pad mounting

7. Remove the instrument panel extension trim plate.
8. Remove the radio and disconnect the electrical and antenna connections.
9. Disconnect and remove the climate control unit.
10. Remove the 2 nuts between the instrument panel pad and the cowl.
11. Loosen the panel attaching screws and disconnect the electrical connectors under the glove compartment.
12. Disconnect the bulkhead connector located under the hood between the wiper motor and the left fender.
13. Remove the nuts that connect the steering column harness to the cowl.
14. Remove the bolts from the steering column support.
15. Disconnect the high beam dimmer switch, ignition switch, turn signal switch, brake light switch, cruise and clutch start switch electrical connectors.
16. Remove the defroster grilles.
17. Remove the screws along the top of the pad that connect the pad to the cowl.
18. Remove the pad brace screw located near the glove compartment.
19. Remove the instrument panel pad.
20. Disconnect the antenna lead from the pad and disconnect the defroster hoses.
21. Disconnect the body electrical lead from the right side of the instrument panel.

To install:

22. Connect the defroster hoses and body electrical lead.
23. Connect the antenna lead to the instrument panel pad.
24. Place the pad on the cowl.
25. Install the instrument panel pad to cowl screws.
26. Install the defroster grilles.
27. Install the nuts attaching the steering column wire harness to the cowl.
28. Connect the electrical connectors and install the steering column mounting bolts.
29. Connect the bulkhead connector.
30. Install the nuts from each side of the instrument panel pad.
31. Connect the instrument panel connectors and tighten the bolts.
32. Connect the radio connectors and install the radio.
33. Install the climate control unit.
34. Install the glove compartment and slide the instrument panel assembly into the pad and tighten the screws.

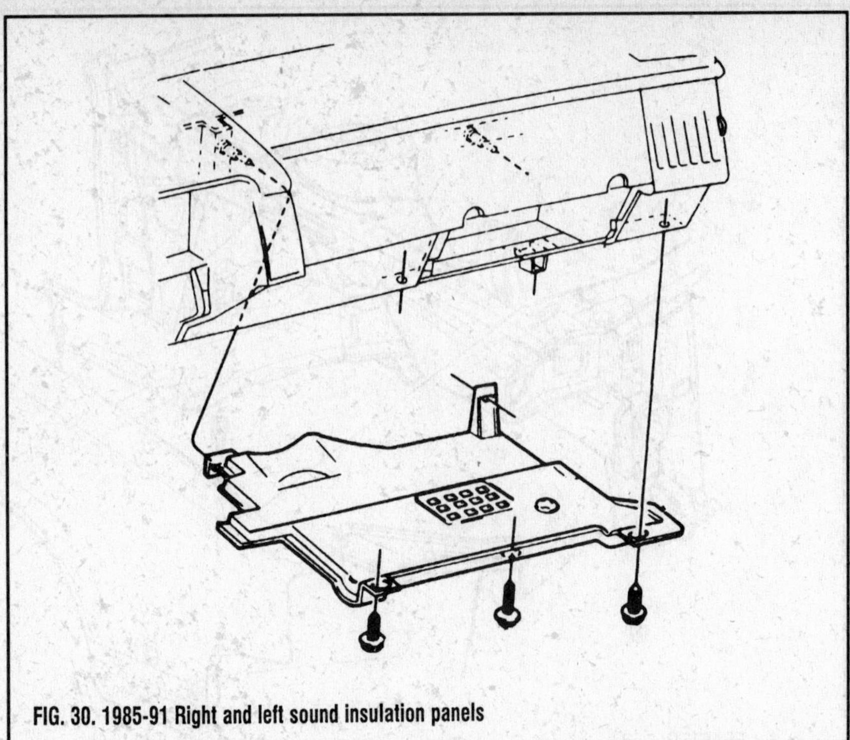

FIG. 30. 1985-91 Right and left sound insulation panels

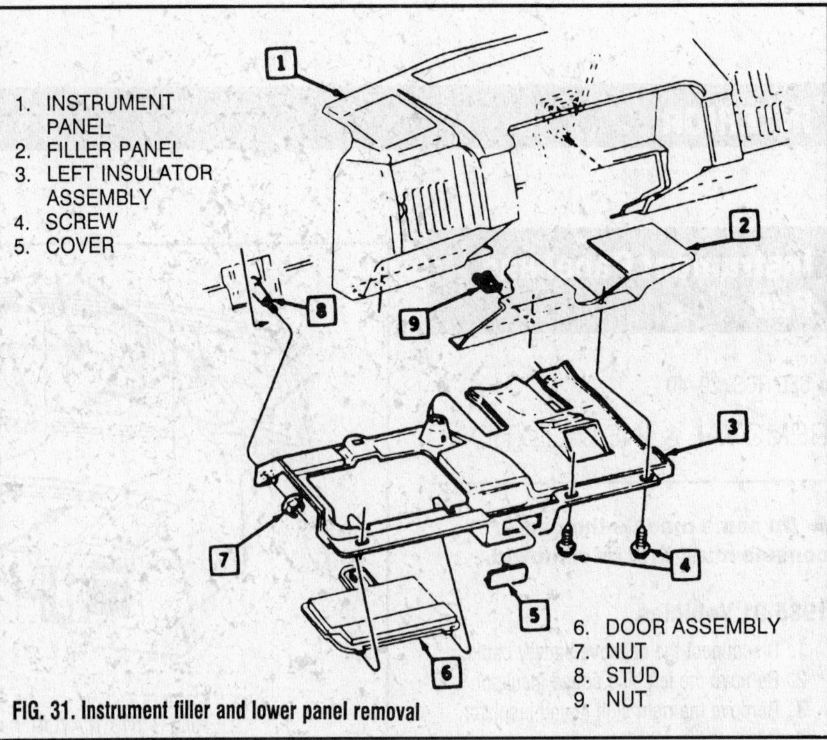

FIG. 31. Instrument filler and lower panel removal

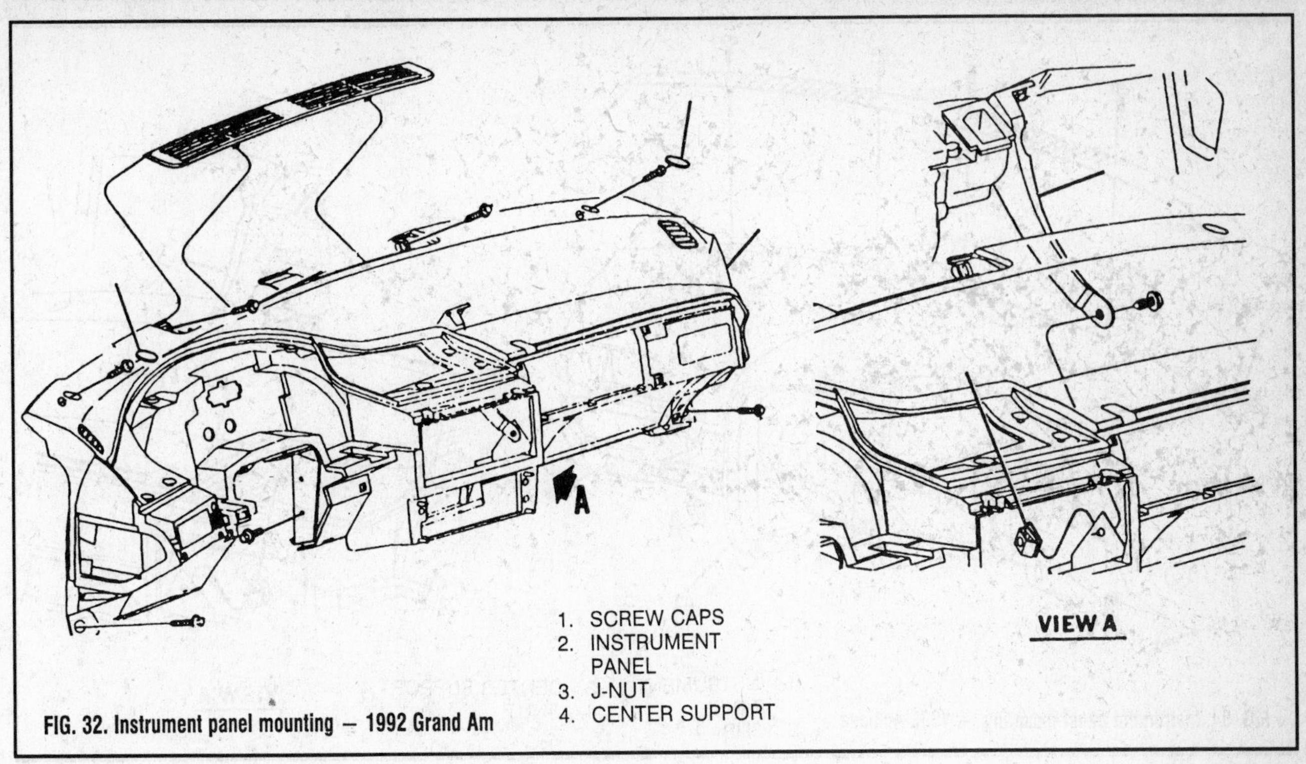

FIG. 32. Instrument panel mounting — 1992 Grand Am

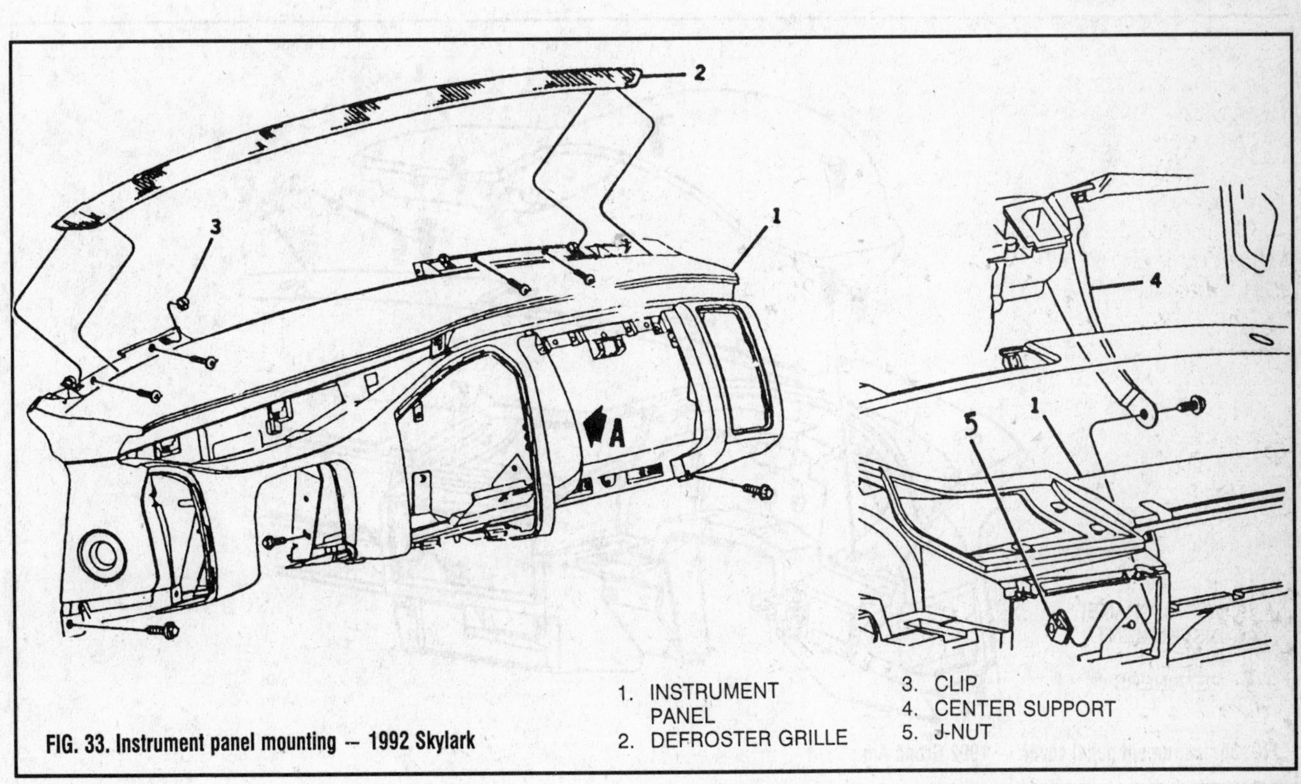

FIG. 33. Instrument panel mounting — 1992 Skylark

1. INSTRUMENT PANEL
2. CLIP
3. CENTER SUPPORT
4. J-NUT

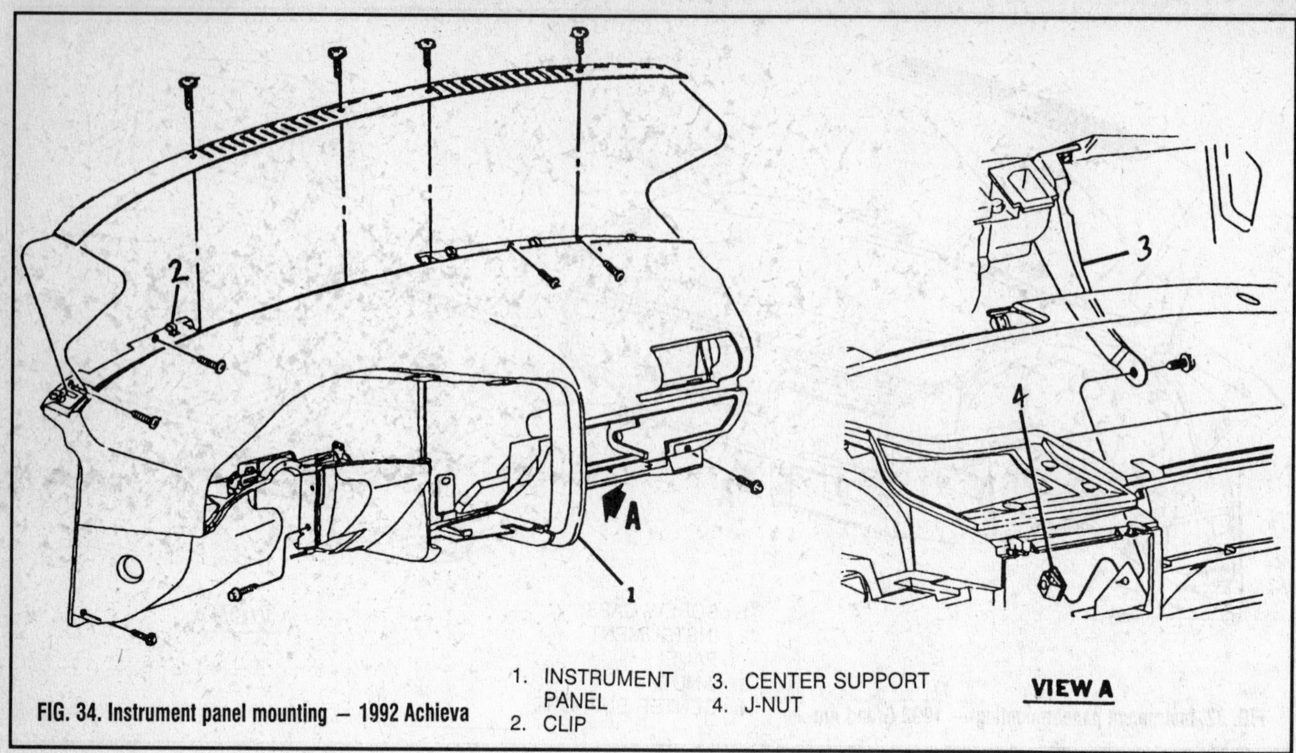

FIG. 34. Instrument panel mounting – 1992 Achieva

1. I/P TRIM PANEL
2. INSTRUMENT PANEL
3. RETAINERS

FIG. 35. Instrument panel cover – 1992 Grand Am

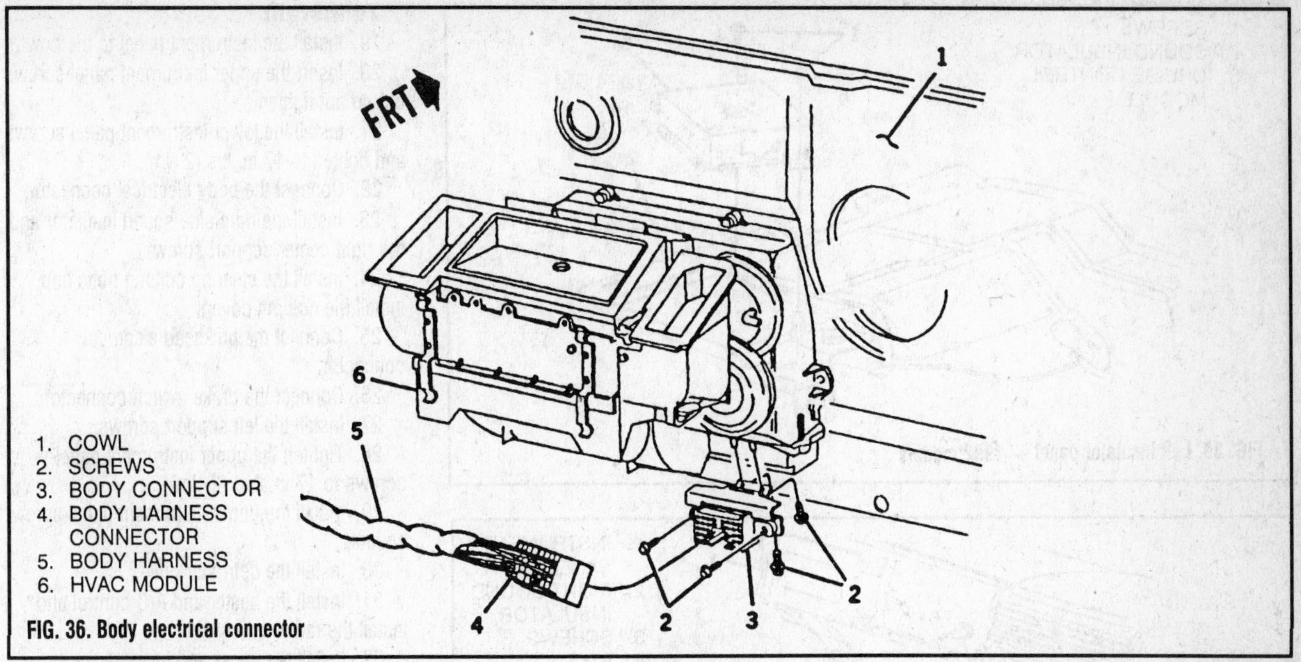

FIG. 36. Body electrical connector

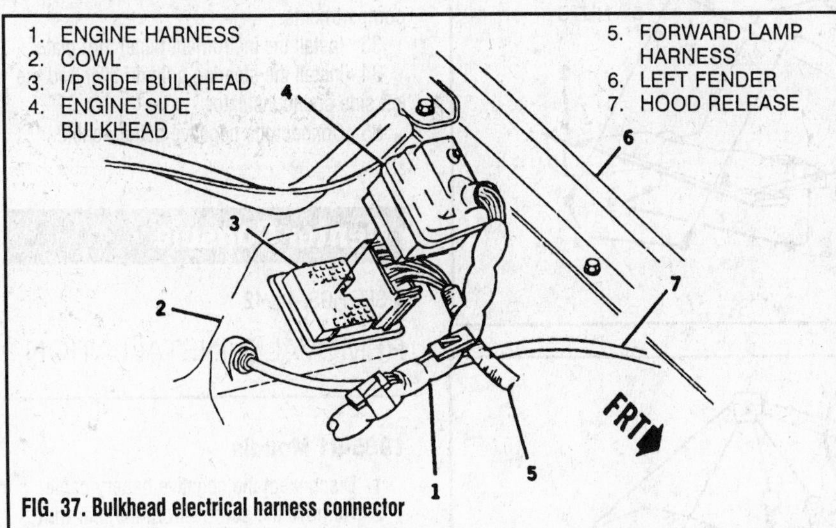

FIG. 37. Bulkhead electrical harness connector

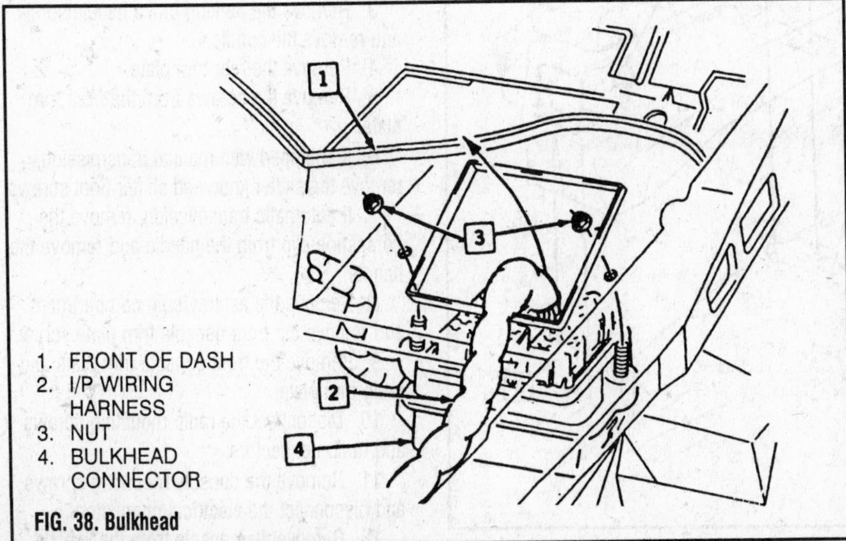

FIG. 38. Bulkhead

35. Install the instrument panel trim plate.
36. Install the steering column trim plate.
37. Install the left and right side sound insulation panels.
38. Connect the negative battery cable.

1992 Vehicles

1. Disconnect the negative battery cable.
2. Remove the left side sound insulator.
3. Remove the steering column filler.
4. Remove the instrument panel cover.
5. Remove the left side instrument panel trim plate.
6. Remove the upper glove compartment screws and remove the compartment.
7. Remove the lower glove compartment screws and remove the compartment.
8. Remove the radio from the vehicle.
9. Remove the heater and A/C control.
10. Remove the defroster grille.
11. Remove the upper instrument panel screw covers and remove the screws.
12. Remove the left side lower support screw.
13. Disconnect the brake switches.
14. Disconnect the bulkhead harness under the hood.
15. Remove the upper and lower steering column covers. Remove the steering column bolts.
16. Remove the right side center support screw at the glove compartment opening.
17. Remove the right sound insulator panel and right side 23 pin electrical connector.
18. Remove the lower instrument panel screws and remove the instrument panel from the vehicle.

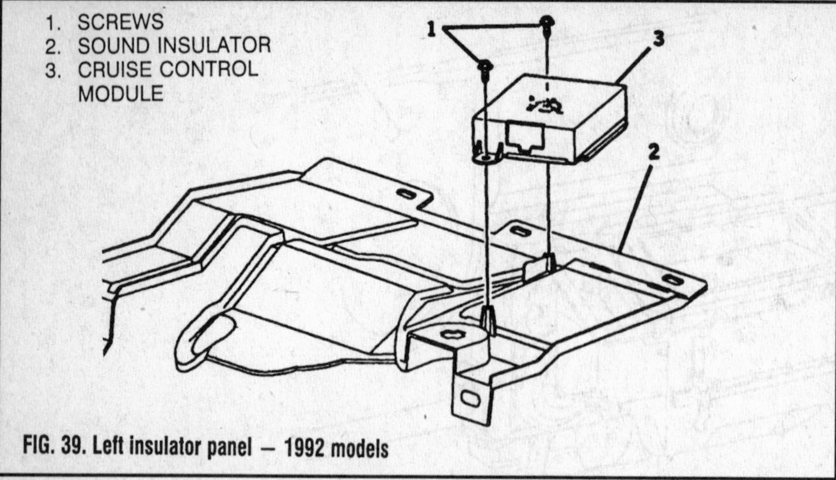

FIG. 39. Left insulator panel — 1992 models

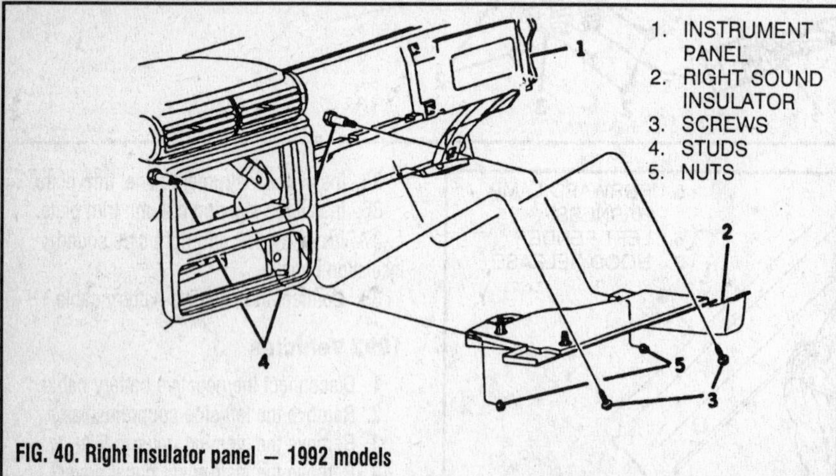

FIG. 40. Right insulator panel — 1992 models

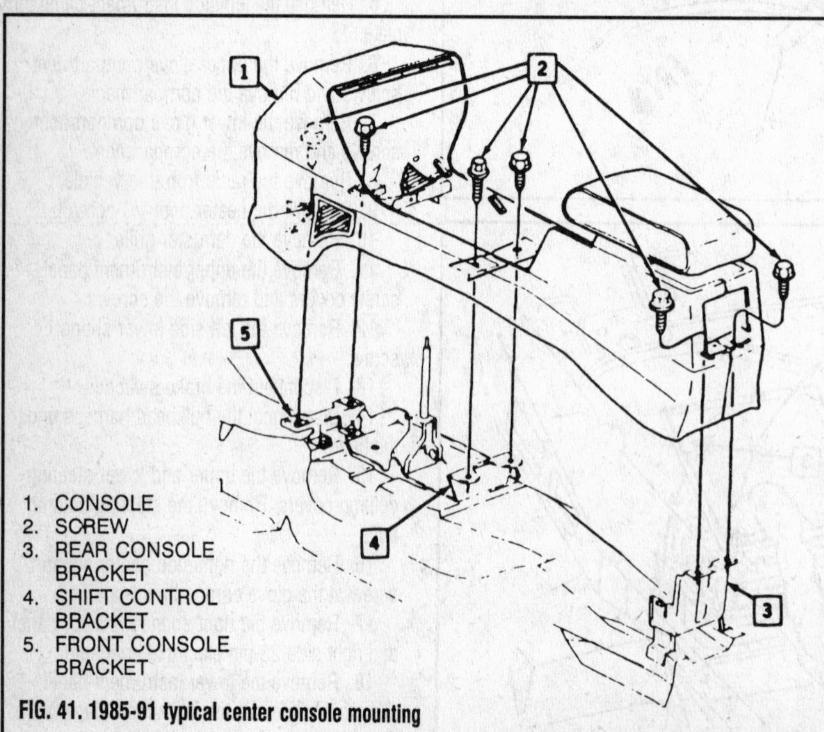

FIG. 41. 1985-91 typical center console mounting

To install:

19. Install the instrument panel to the cowl.
20. Insert the upper instrument panel screws but do not tighten.
21. Install the lower instrument panel screws and tighten to 17 in. lbs.(2 Nm).
22. Connect the body electrical connector.
23. Install the right side sound insulator and the right center support screw.
24. Install the steering column bolts and install the column covers.
25. Connect the bulkhead electrical connector.
26. Connect the brake switch connectors.
27. Install the left support screws.
28. Tighten the upper instrument panel screws to 17 in. lbs. (2 Nm).
29. Install the upper instrument panel screw covers.
30. Install the defroster grilles.
31. Install the heater and A/C control and install the radio.
32. Install the upper and lower glove compartments.
33. Install the instrument panel trim plate.
34. Install the steering column filler and the left side sound insulator.
35. Connect the negative battery cable.

Center Console

➧ SEE FIGS. 41–42

REMOVAL & INSTALLATION

1985-91 Models

1. Disconnect the negative battery cable.
2. Remove the screws from the rear trim plate.
3. Remove the parking brake handle screw and remove the handle.
4. Remove the rear trim plate.
5. Remove the screws from the front trim plate.
6. If equipped with manual transmission, remove the shifter knob and shifter boot screws.
7. If automatic transmission, remove the horseshoe clip from the handle and remove the handle.
8. Remove the ashtray/coin compartment and remove the front console trim plate screw.
9. Remove the front console trim plate and radio trim plate.
10. Disconnect the radio mounting screws and radio connectors.
11. Remove the console mounting screws and disconnect the electrical connectors.
12. Remove the console from the vehicle.

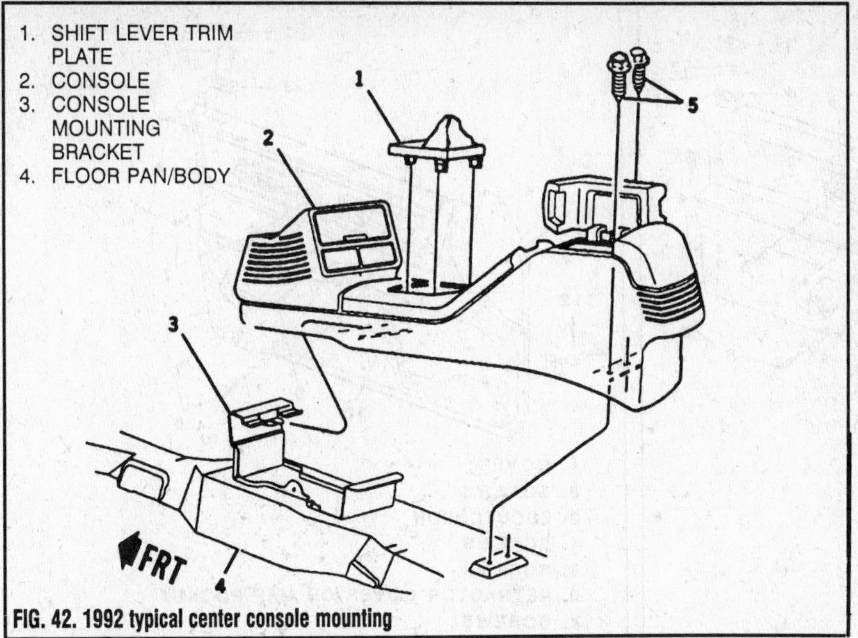

FIG. 42. 1992 typical center console mounting

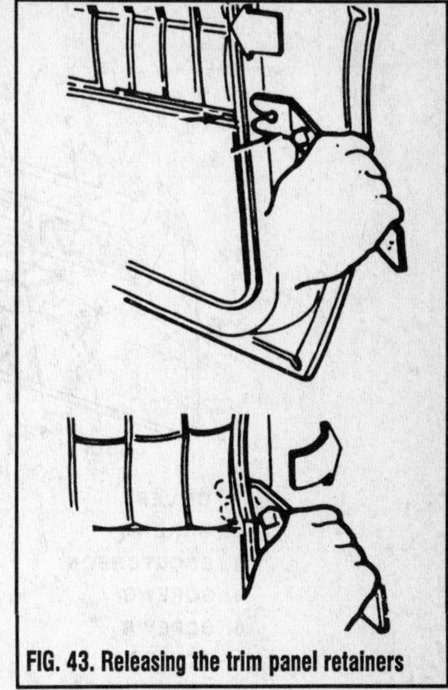
FIG. 43. Releasing the trim panel retainers

To install:

13. Install the console and console mounting screws.
14. Connect the radio connectors and install the radio screws.
15. Install the radio trim plate.
16. Install the front console trim plate screws.
17. Install the ashtray/coin compartment.
18. Install the shifter knob.
19. Install the rear trim plate and parking brake handle.
20. Connect the negative battery cable.

1992 Models

1. Remove the shift lever handle.
2. Carefully pry trim plate upward to disengage clips and remove trim plate.
3. Remove the console compartment.
4. Remove the screws at the rear compartment.
5. Pull console towards the rear and disconnect electrical connectors.
6. Remove the console from the vehicle.

To install:

7. Installation is the reverse of the removal procedure.

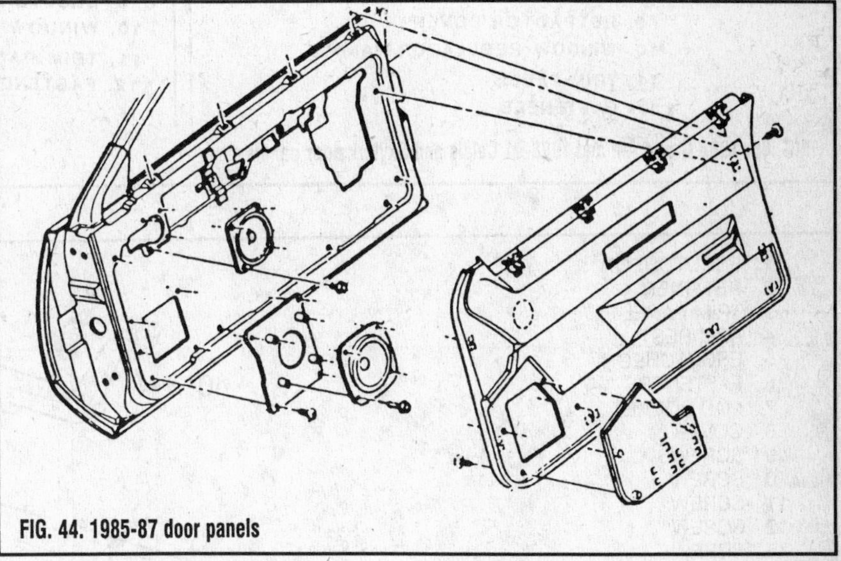
FIG. 44. 1985-87 door panels

Door Panels

➧ SEE FIGS. 43–49

REMOVAL & INSTALLATION

1. Remove outside mirror escutcheon and seat belt escutcheon.
2. Remove the center door panel screw.
3. Remove reflector from door by disconnecting clips with thin blade screwdriver.
4. Remove the screw from behind the reflector base.
5. Remove the screws at the lower front corner of the door panel.
6. Remove window crank handle using special remover tool.
7. Separate the door panel from the door using a door panel removal tool. Pull door panel outward to separate studs from the retainers.
8. Slide seat belt through slit in bottom of trim panel.
9. Lift up on bottom of trim panel to disengage the door panel hooks from the slots.
10. Disconnect any electrical connectors to switches on the door panel.
11. Remove the trim panel from the vehicle.

To install:

12. Connect any electrical connectors to switches on the door panel.
13. Slide the door panel hooks into the slots and push down to engage.
14. Slide the seat belt through the slits in the door panel.
15. Align the studs to the retainers and push inward so the clips engage.
16. Replace all of the screws that were removed. Install the reflector.
17. Install the inside pull handle and window crank handle.
18. Install the outside mirror escutcheon and seat belt opening escutcheon.

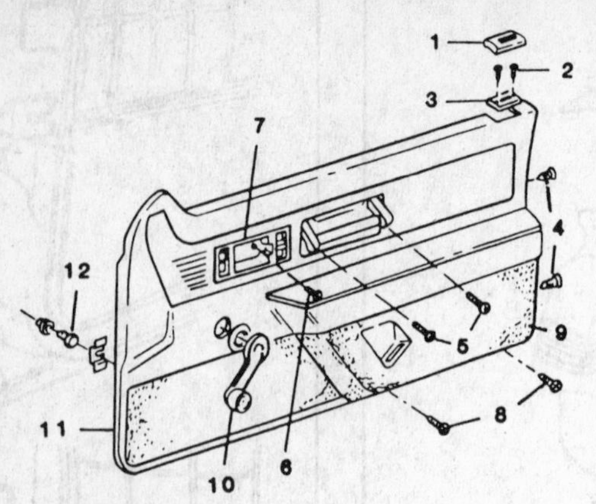

1. COVER
2. SCREWS
3. ESCUTCHEON
4. SCREWS
5. SCREWS
6. SCREW
7. ESCUTCHEON
8. SCREWS
9. RETRACTOR COVER
10. WINDOW REGULATOR HANDLE
11. TRIM PANEL
12. FASTENERS

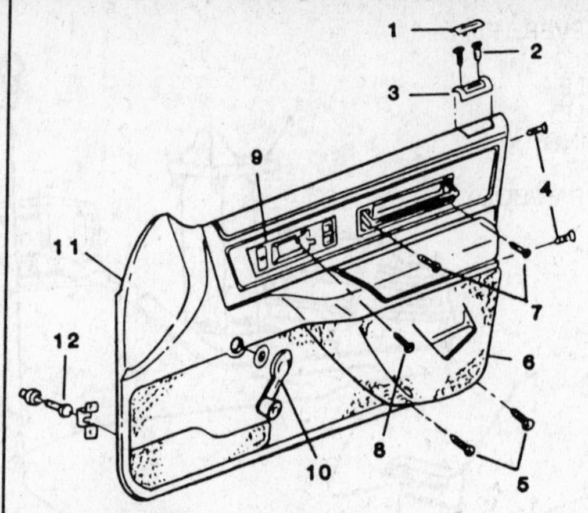

1. COVER
2. SCREWS
3. ESCUTCHEON
4. SCREWS
5. SCREWS
6. RETRACTOR COVER OR MAP POCKET
7. SCREWS
8. SCREWS
9. ESCUTCHEON
10. WINDOW REGULATOR HANDLE
11. TRIM PANEL
12. FASTENER

FIG. 45. 1988 Grand Am and 1988-91 Calais and Skylark door panels

1. ESCUTCHEON
2. RETAINER
3. TRIM PANEL
4. ARM REST
5. ESCUTCHEON
6. FASTENERS
7. MAP POCKET
8. COVER
9. SCREWS
10. SCREW
11. SCREW
12. SCREW
13. SCREWS
14. RETRACTOR COVER
15. SCREWS

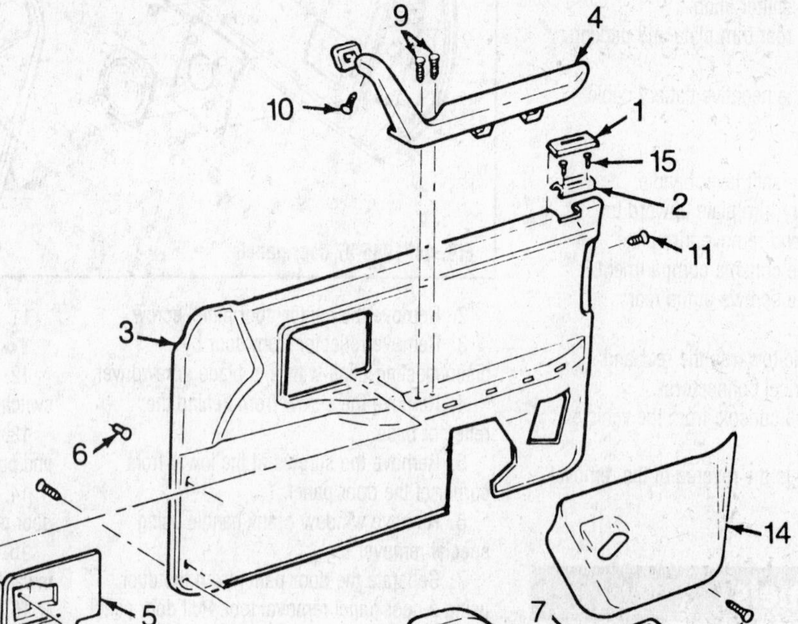

FIG. 46. 1989-91 Grand Am door panel

1. TRIM PANEL
2. ESCUTCHEON
3. SCREW
4. SCREW
5. REFLECTOR
6. CLIPS
7. SCREWS
8. STUD
9. RETAINER
10. HOOK
11. SLOTS
VIEW A
VIEW B
SECTION A-A
SECTION B-B
VIEW C
1
2
3
4
5
6
7
8
9
10
11
12
A
B
C

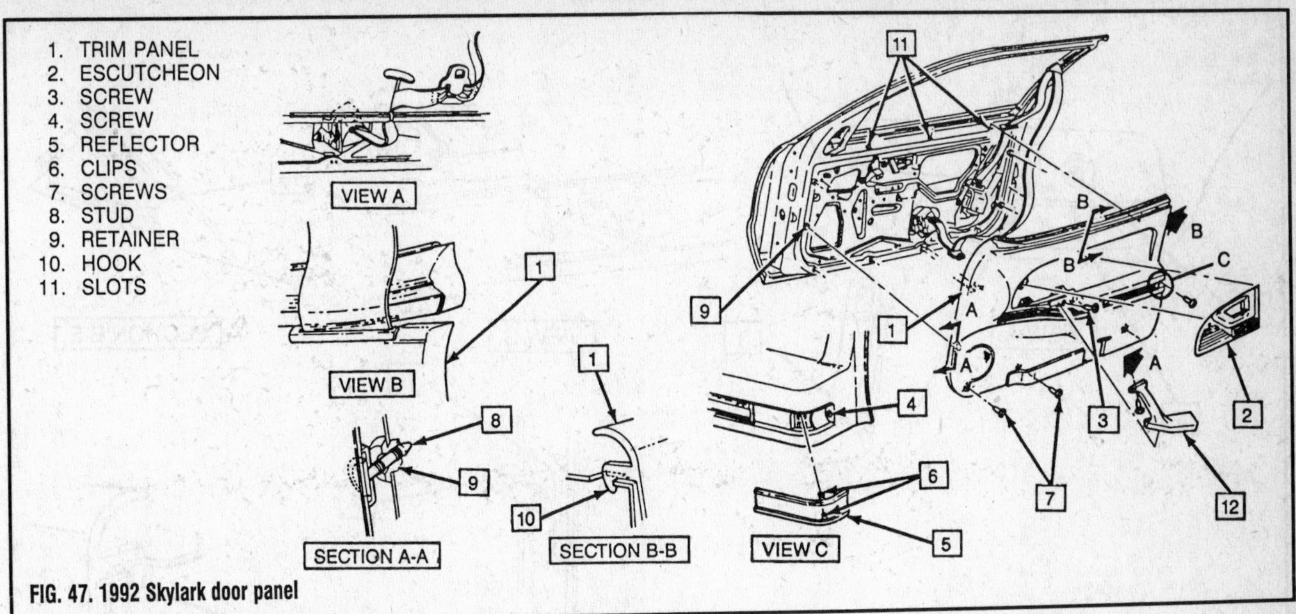

FIG. 47. 1992 Skylark door panel

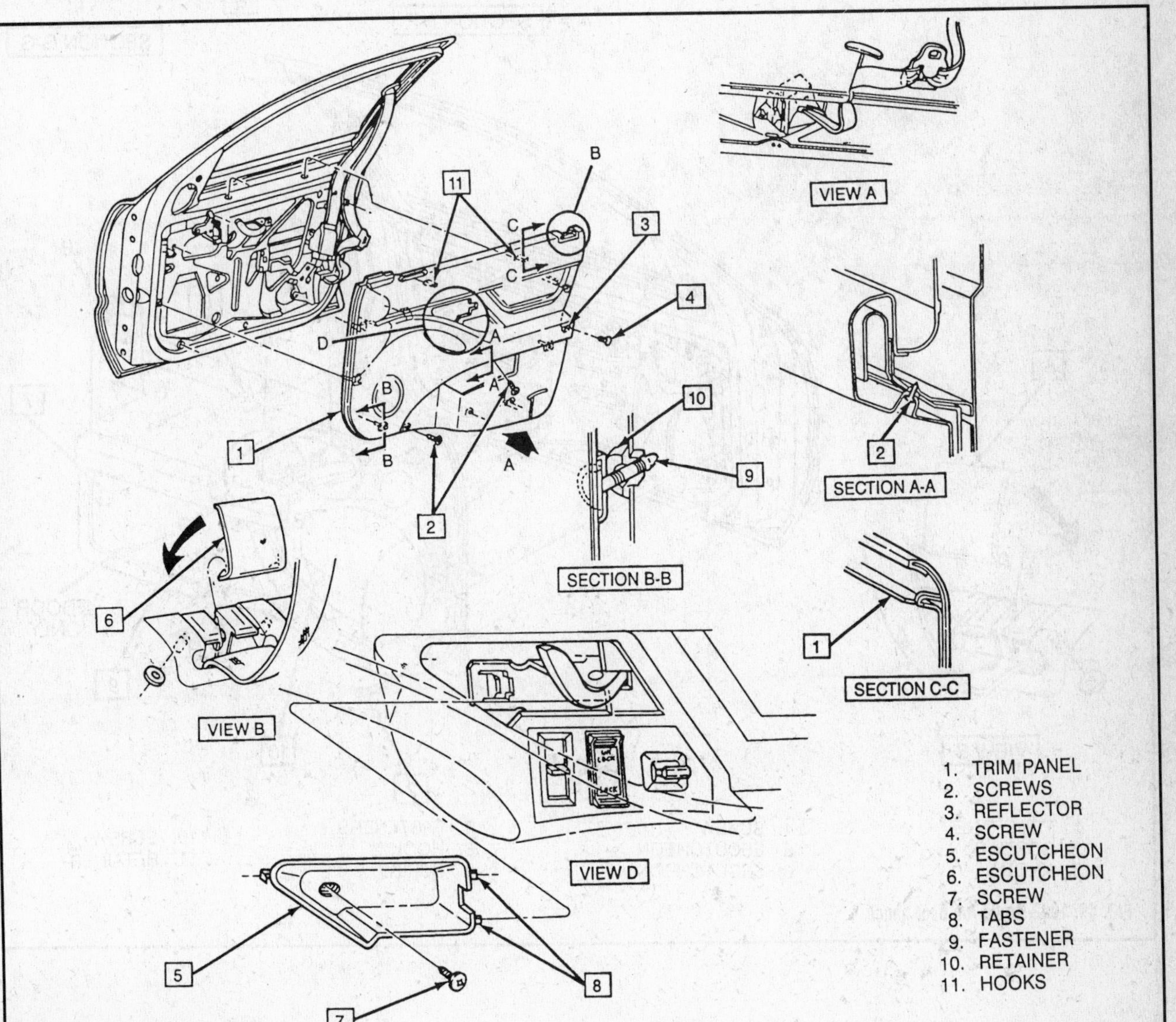

VIEW A
SECTION A-A
SECTION B-B
SECTION C-C
VIEW B
VIEW D
1. TRIM PANEL
2. SCREWS
3. REFLECTOR
4. SCREW
5. ESCUTCHEON
6. ESCUTCHEON
7. SCREW
8. TABS
9. FASTENER
10. RETAINER
11. HOOKS
1
2
3
4
5
6
7
8
9
10
11
A
B
C
D

FIG. 48. 1992 Achieva door panel

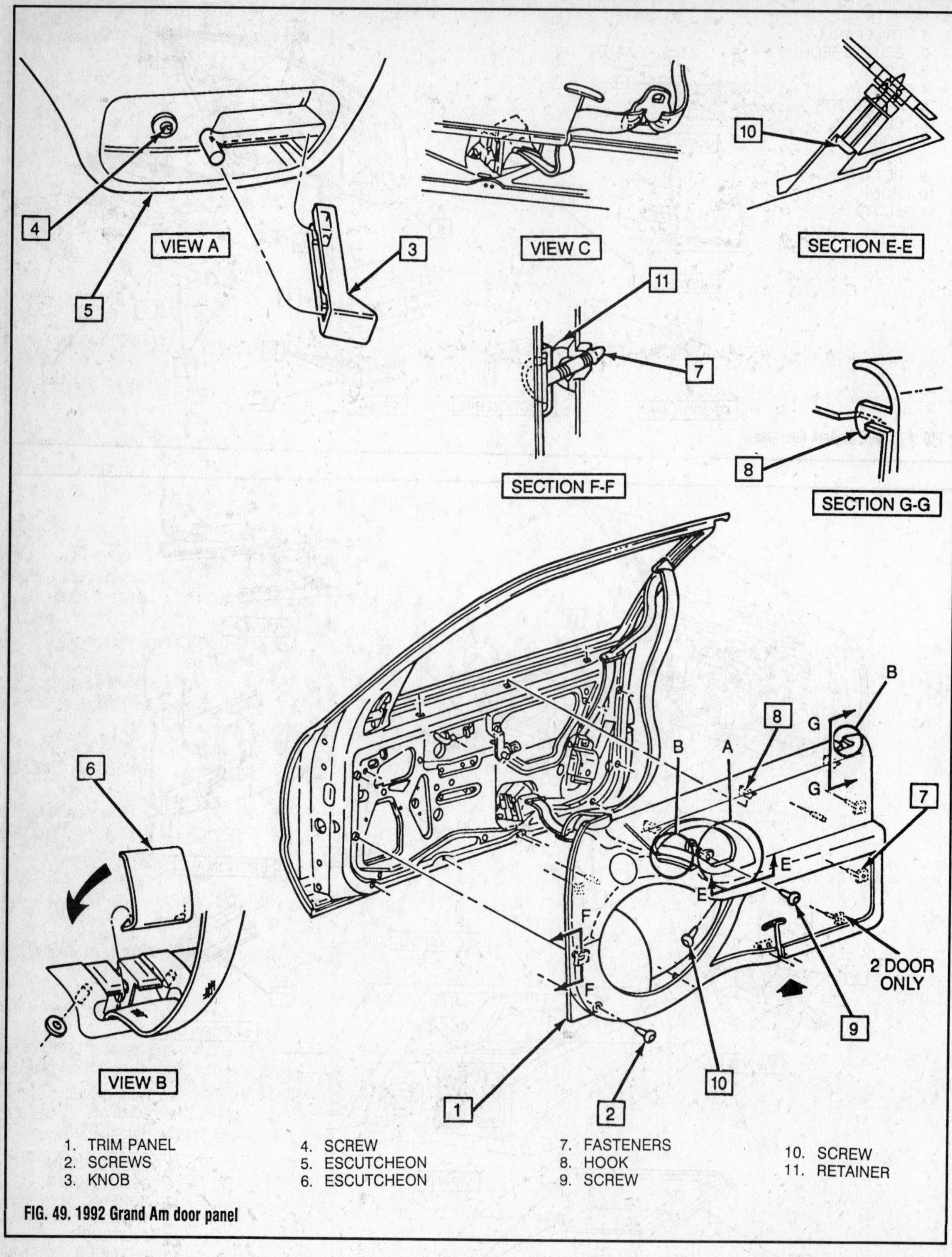

1. TRIM PANEL
2. SCREWS
3. KNOB
4. SCREW
5. ESCUTCHEON
6. ESCUTCHEON
7. FASTENERS
8. HOOK
9. SCREW
10. SCREW
11. RETAINER

FIG. 49. 1992 Grand Am door panel

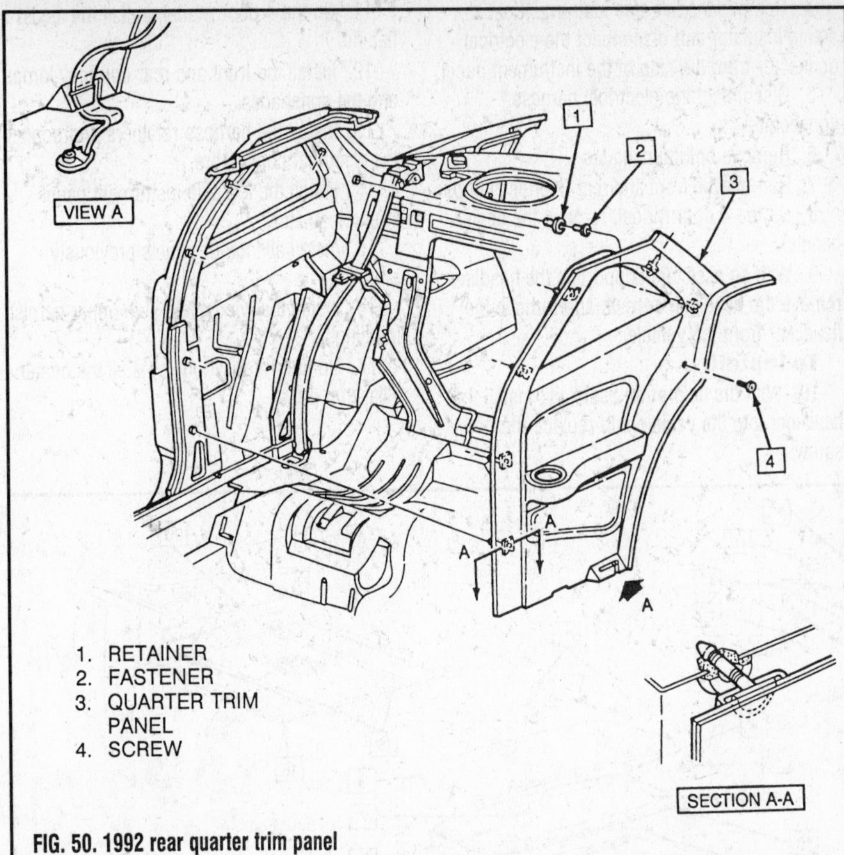

FIG. 50. 1992 rear quarter trim panel

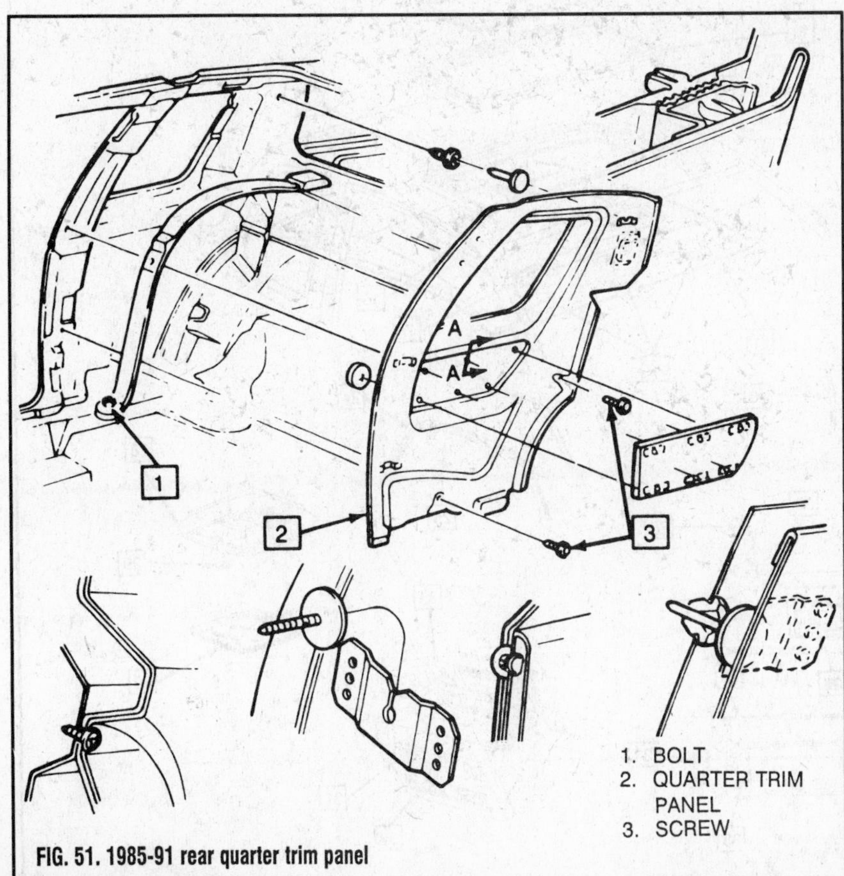

FIG. 51. 1985-91 rear quarter trim panel

Interior Trim Panels

➧ SEE FIGS. 50–51

REMOVAL & INSTALLATION

Upper and Lower Inside Door Trim Panels

1. Remove the inside door panel as detailed above.
2. Remove the nuts securing the trim panel to the door panel.
3. Separate the trim panel from the door panel.
4. Installation is the reverse of the removal procedure.

Rear Quarter Interior Trim Panel 2-door

1. Remove the rear seat back and rear seat cushion
2. Disconnect carpet retainer by removing the screws and lifting up on carpet retainer.
3. Remove windshield side upper molding by grasping molding and pulling down to disengage molding.
4. Remove the trim panel screws.
5. Pull outward on the trim panel to disengage the fasteners from the retainers.
6. Remove the seat belt from the slit in the panel and remove the panel.

To install:

7. Install the seat belt through the slit in the panel.
8. Align the fasteners to the retainers and push in on panel to engage.
9. Install the panel screw.
10. Install windshield side upper molding.
11. Install carpet retainers and install rear seat back and cushion.

Rear Quarter Interior Trim Panel 4-door

1. Remove rear seat cushion and rear seat back.
2. Remove the panel screws and remove trim panel by pulling downward to disengage clips.

To install:

3. Install the trim panel by aligning tabs and retainers and pressing upward until secure.
4. Install panel screws and install rear seat back and rear seat cushion.

Headliner

➧ SEE FIGS. 52–53

REMOVAL & INSTALLATION

1. Pull inward on inside upper garnish molding to release tabs from the retainers and remove the moldings from the vehicle.
2. On the 2 door model, remove the rear quarter trim panel. On the 4 door model, remove the center pillar trim panel.
3. On the 4 door model, remove both the upper and lower quarter trim panels.
4. Remove the left side instrument panel sound insulator and disconnect the electrical connector from the side of the instrument panel.
5. Disconnect the electrical harness connectors.
6. Remove both sunshades.
7. Remove the front and rear courtesy lamps.
8. On the 4 door model, remove the assist handle.
9. With an assistant supporting the headliner, remove the headliner screws and remove the headliner from the vehicle.

To install:

10. With the help of an assistant, install the headliner into the vehicle and replace the screws.
11. On the 4 door model, install the assist handle.
12. Install the front and rear courtesy lamps and the sunshades.
13. Install the harness retainers and connect the electrical connectors.
14. Install the left side instrument panel sound insulator.
15. Install all interior panels previously removed.
16. Install the windshield side upper garnish moldings.
17. On the 4 door model, install the center pillar trim panel.

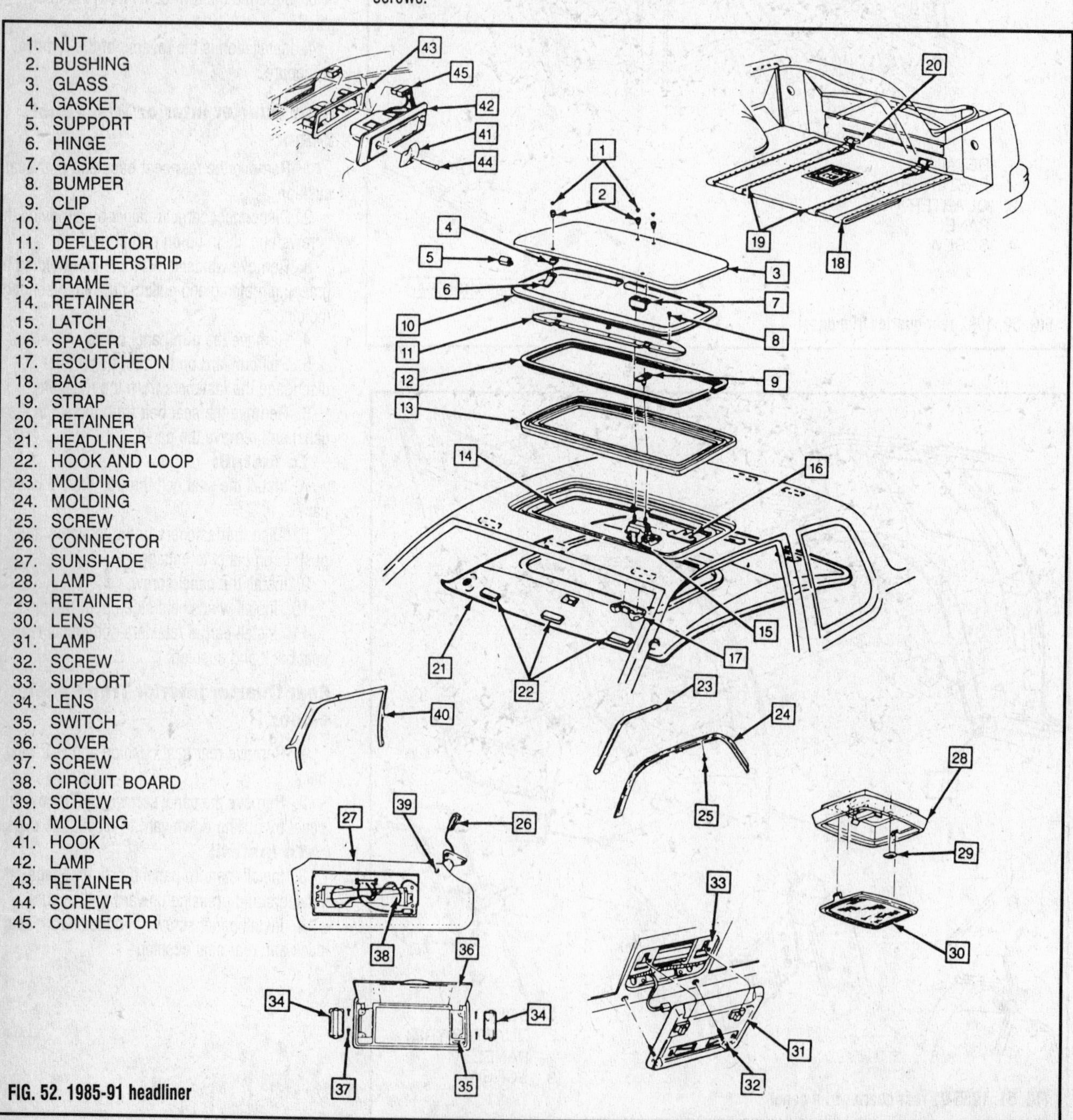

FIG. 52. 1985-91 headliner

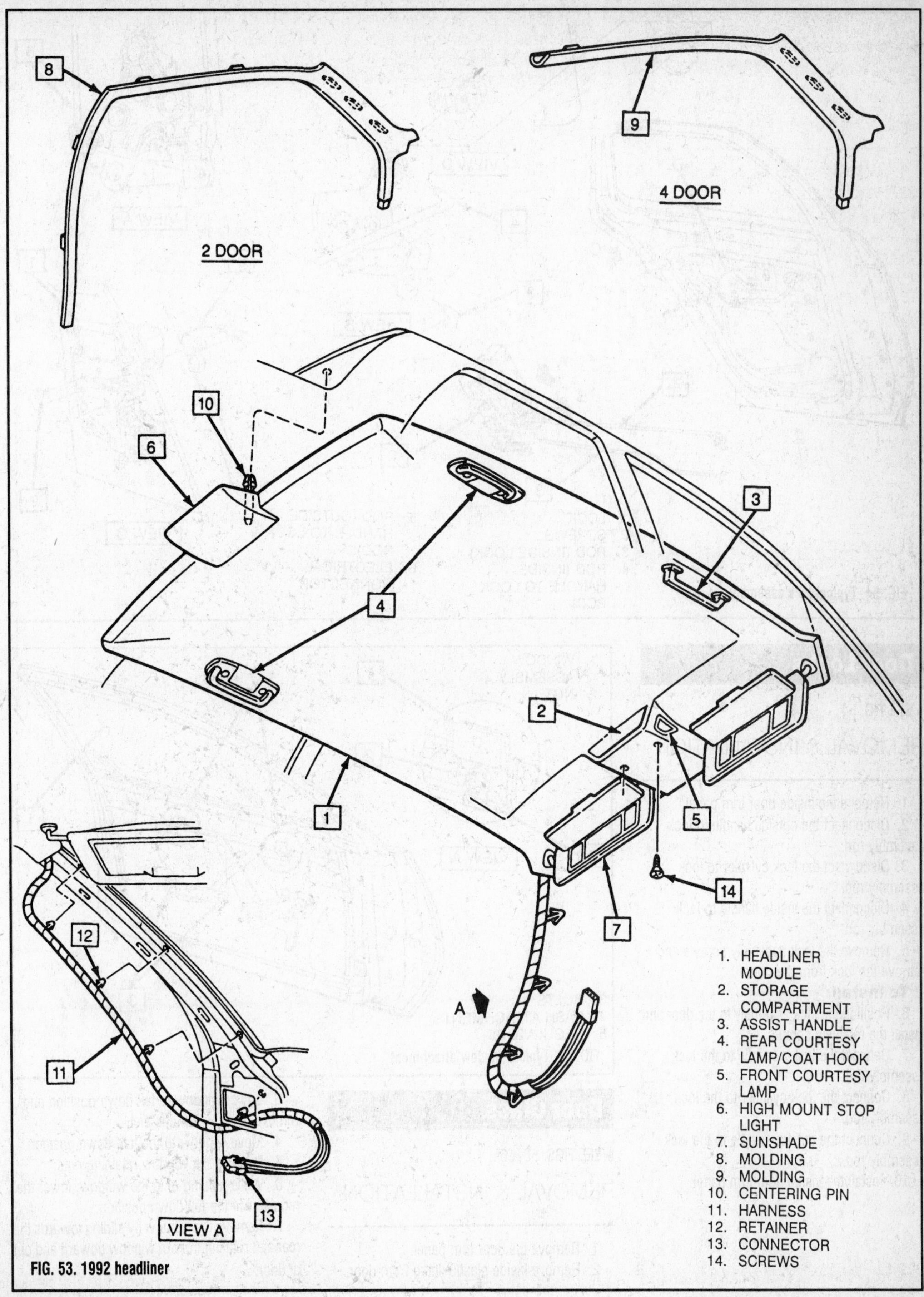

FIG. 53. 1992 headliner

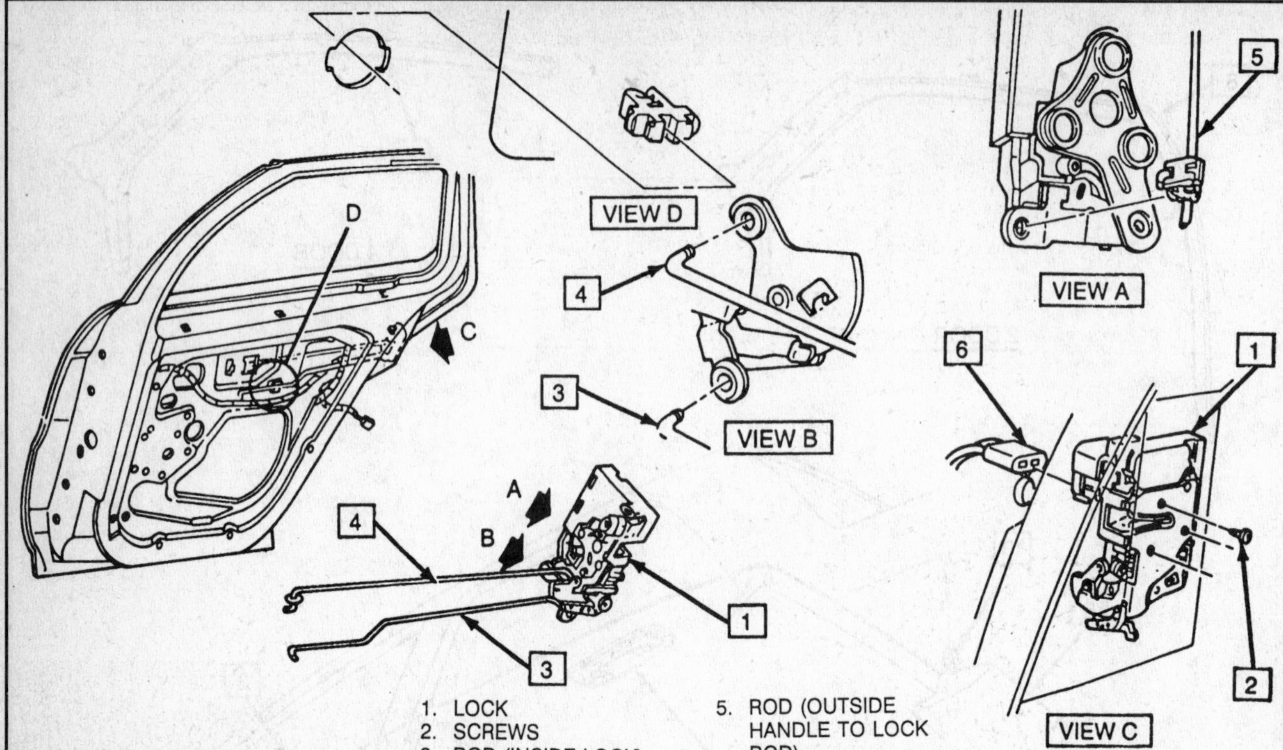

1. LOCK
2. SCREWS
3. ROD (INSIDE LOCK)
4. ROD (INSIDE HANDLE TO LOCK ROD)
5. ROD (OUTSIDE HANDLE TO LOCK ROD)
6. ELECTRICAL CONNECTOR

FIG. 54. Typical lock assembly

Door Locks

➧ SEE FIG. 54

REMOVAL & INSTALLATION

1. Remove the inside door trim panel.
2. Disconnect the outside handle to lock assembly rod.
3. Disconnect the lock cylinder to lock assembly rod.
4. Disconnect the inside handle to lock assembly rod.
5. Remove the lock assembly screws and remove the lock from the door.

To install:

6. Position the lock assembly to the door and install the retaining screws.
7. Connect the inside handle to the lock assembly rod.
8. Connect the lock cylinder to the lock assembly rod.
9. Connect the outside handle to the lock assembly rod.
10. Install the inside door trim panel.

1. WINDOW ASSEMBLY
2. NUT
3. BOLTS
4. SASH ATTACHMENT
5. REGULATOR

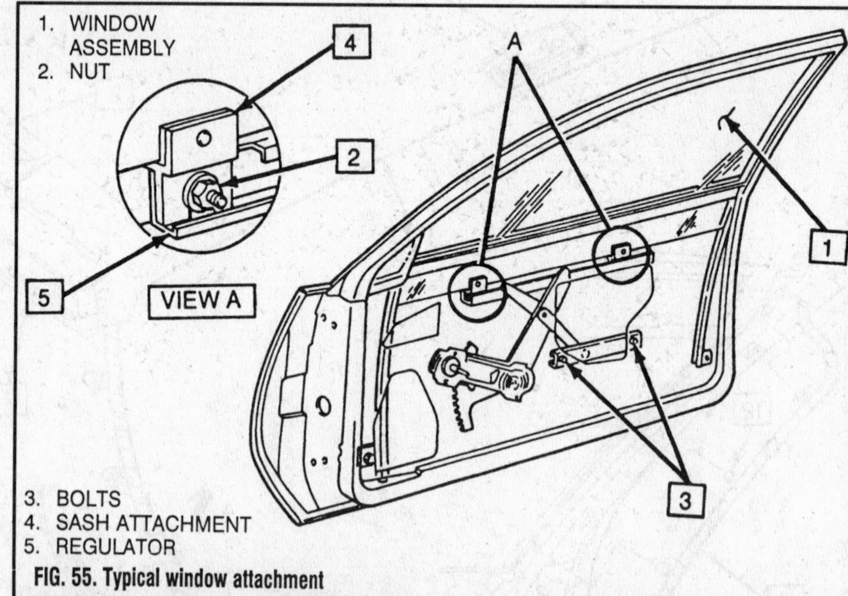

FIG. 55. Typical window attachment

Door Glass

➧ SEE FIGS. 55–56

REMOVAL & INSTALLATION

1. Remove the door trim panel.
2. Remove inside plastic lining from door.
3. Lower window to full down position and remove window run channel.
4. Move window to the half down position.
5. Remove the window retaining nuts.
6. While holding onto the window, lower the regulator to the full down position.
7. Remove the window by sliding towards the rear and rotating front of window upward and out of door.

To install:

8. Install the window to the door and align regulator with the glass.
9. While holding onto window move regulator to half up position.
10. Install the nuts. Roll the window to the full up position.
11. Install the rear run channel.
12. Install the plastic door lining and secure with waterproof adhesive.
13. Install the door trim panel.

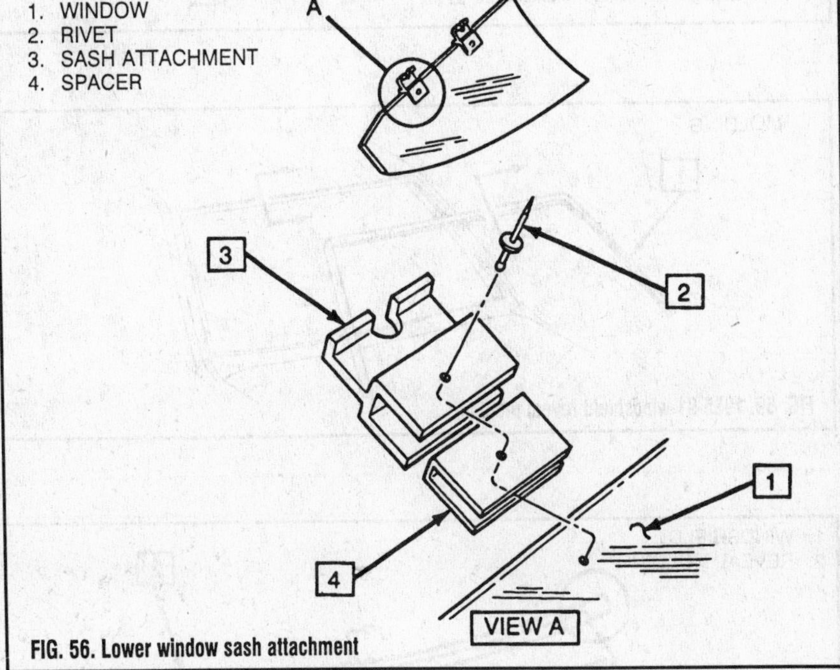

FIG. 56. Lower window sash attachment

Window Regulator

➧ SEE FIG. 57

REMOVAL & INSTALLATION

1. Remove the door trim panel.
2. Remove the inside plastic door liner.
3. Remove the door window assembly- refer to previous section.
4. Remove the bolts securing the regulator to the door.
5. Remove the nuts securing the upper regulator guide.
6. Using a 1/4 in. drill, drill out the regulator rivets.
7. Disconnect the electrical connector if power windows.
8. Remove the regulator through the large access hole in door.

To install:

9. Install the regulator to the door and connect the electrical connector if power windows.
10. While holding the regulator to the inner door panel insert the rivets.
11. Install the regulator bolts and upper guide nuts. Tighten the nuts to 44 in. lbs. (5 Nm)
12. Install the door glass, and inside door plastic panel.
13. Install the inside door trim panel.

Electric Window Motor

REMOVAL & INSTALLATION

1. Remove the window regulator assembly from the door as previously described.

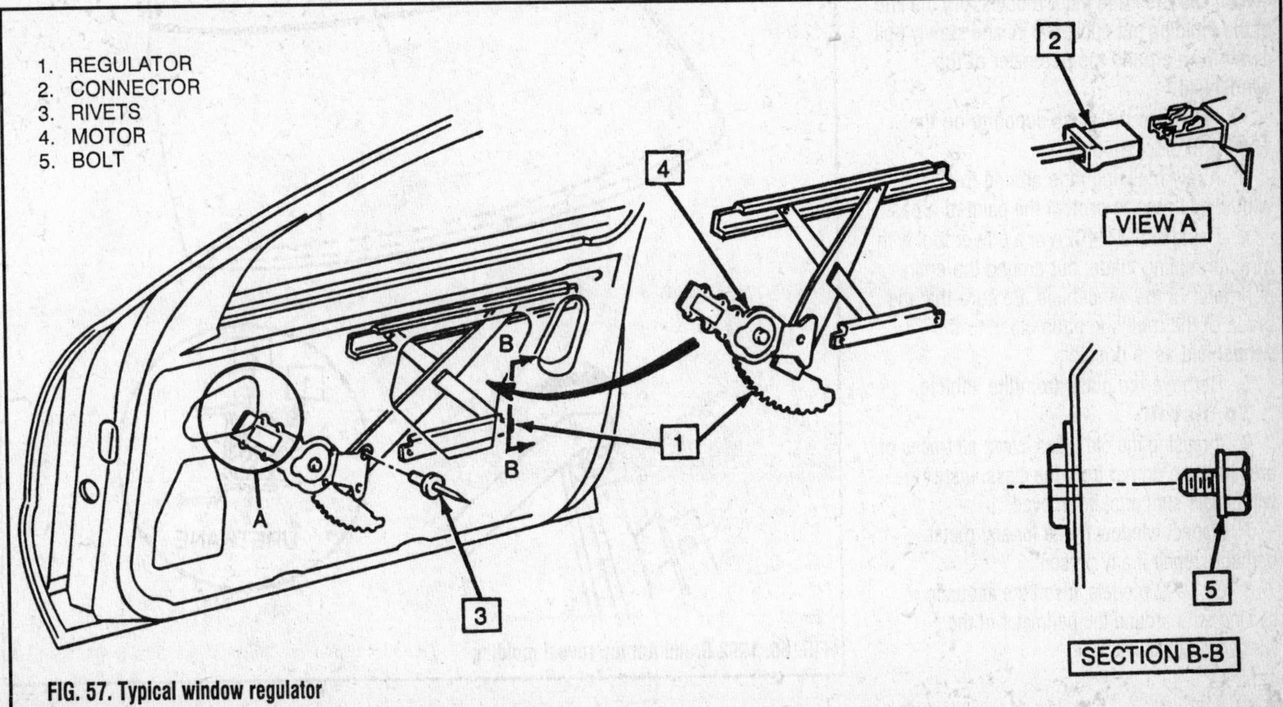

FIG. 57. Typical window regulator

2. Remove the motor from the regulator by drilling out the attaching rivets with a 3/16 in. drill bit.

To install:

3. Connect the window motor to the regulator with 3/16 in. rivets.
4. Install the window regulator assembly.

Windshield and Rear Window

➧ SEE FIGS. 58–66

REMOVAL & INSTALLATION

➡ The windshield is a very delicate and expensive piece of glass. During the procedure the glass can break very easily. Removal and installation is recommended to be performed by a qualified glass installation shop.

1. Remove the wiper arms and the shroud top vent grille panel.
2. Remove the reveal moldings from around the glass. To do this follow the steps below:
   a. On 1992 models, remove the screws securing the side reveal moldings and slide the molding down to disengage it from the top molding.
   b. Grasp the end of the top molding and slowly pull away from the body.
   c. On 1991 and older models, pry the end of the molding out approx. 3 in. and slowly pull away from around the perimeter of the windshield.
   d. Remove the glass supports on the 1991 and older models.
3. Apply masking tape around the windshield area to protect the painted areas.
4. Using tool J24402A or a power tool with a reciprocating blade, cut around the entire perimeter of the windshield. Be sure that the blade of the tool is kept as close to the windshield as is possible.
5. Remove the glass from the vehicle.

To install:

6. If reusing the old glass, clean all traces of urethane and primer from the glass. Install the windshield supports, if removed.
7. Inspect window frame for any metal damage, repair if any present.
8. On 1992 models, insert the acoustic sealing strip around the perimeter of the windshield opening.

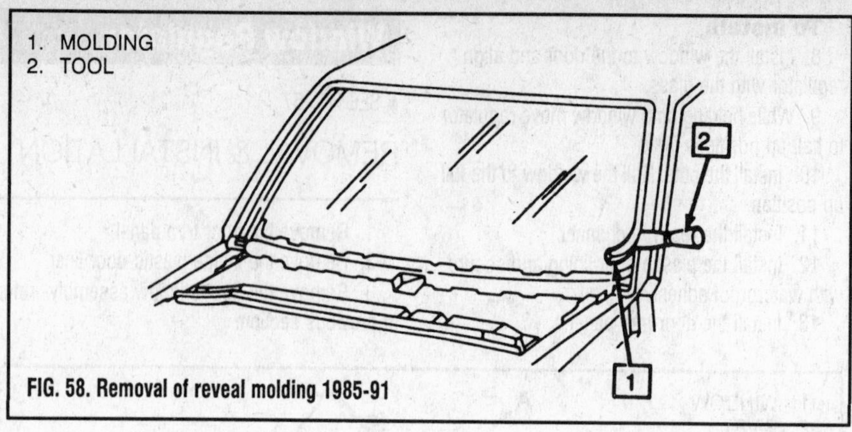

FIG. 58. Removal of reveal molding 1985-91

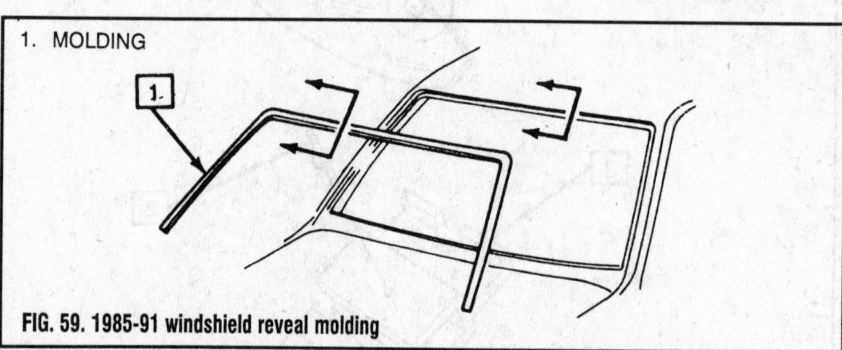

FIG. 59. 1985-91 windshield reveal molding

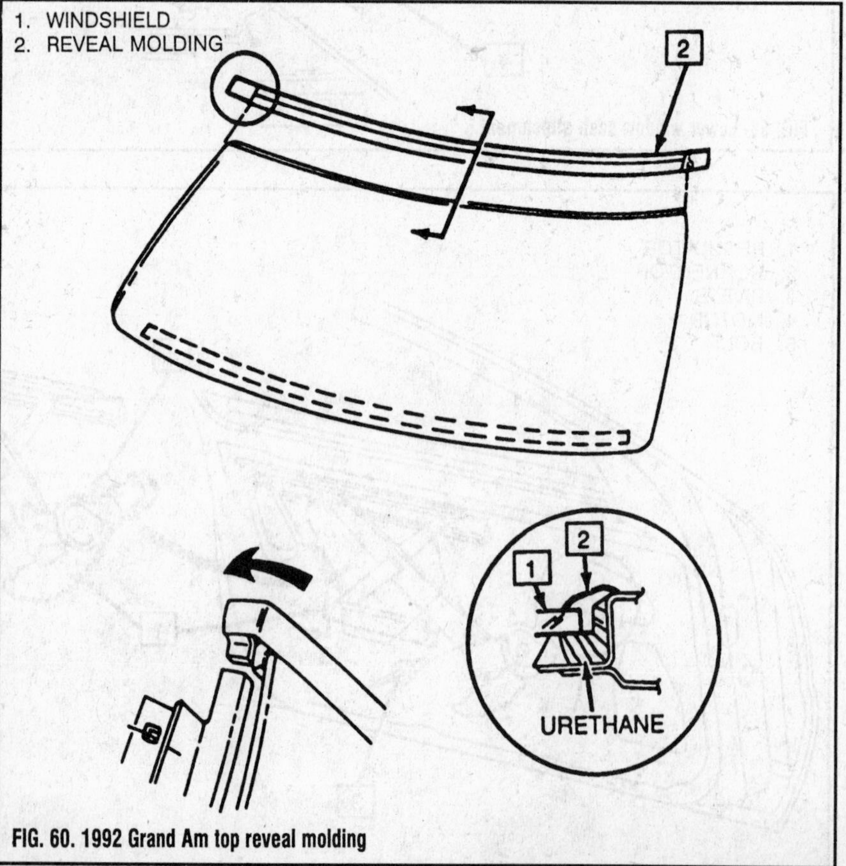

FIG. 60. 1992 Grand Am top reveal molding

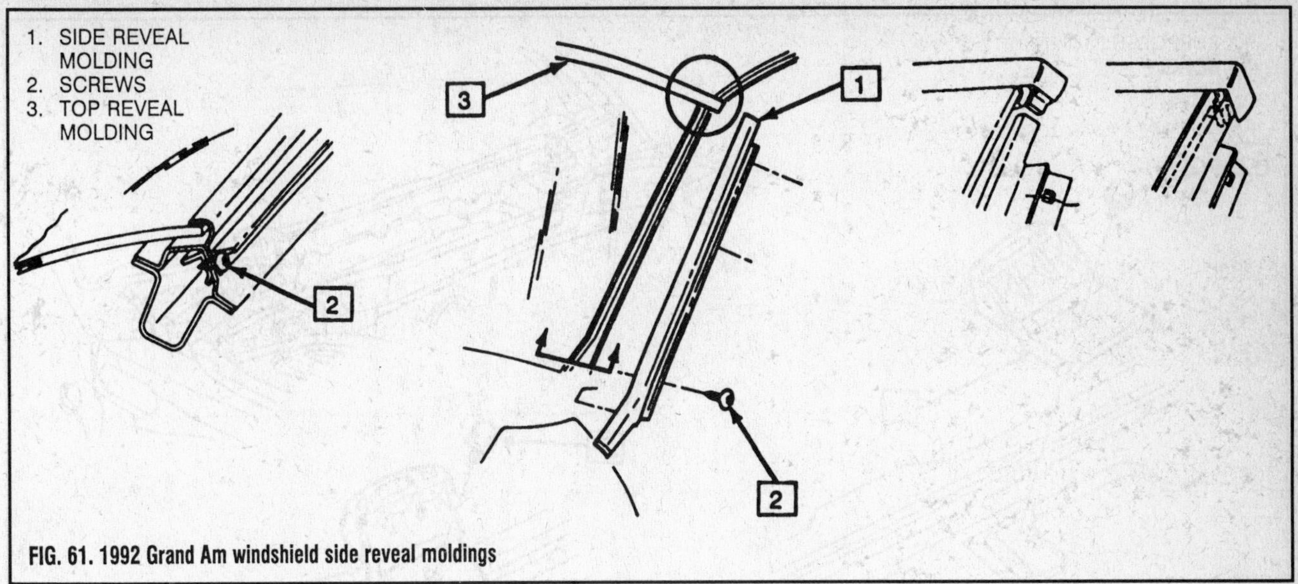

FIG. 61. 1992 Grand Am windshield side reveal moldings

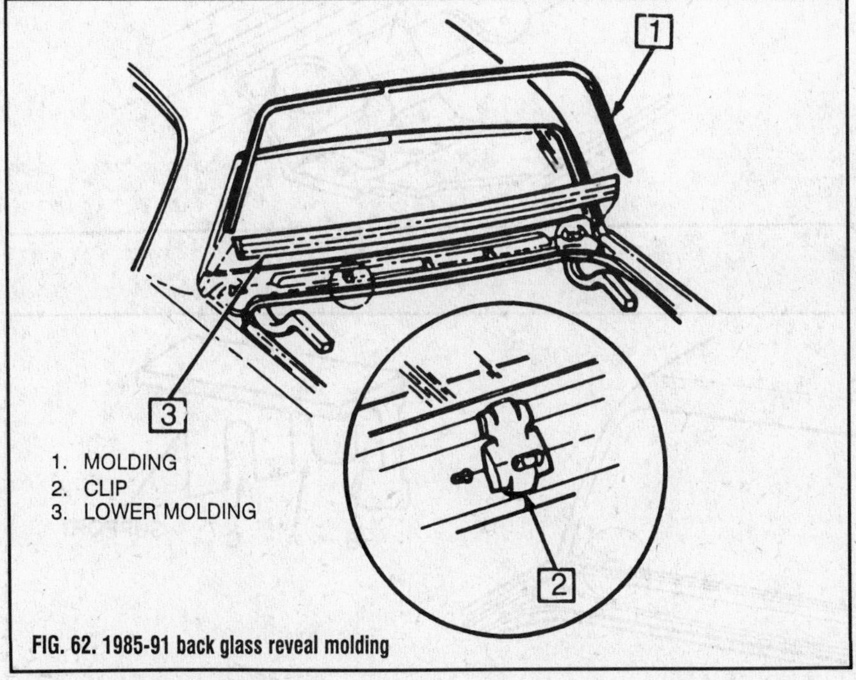

FIG. 62. 1985-91 back glass reveal molding

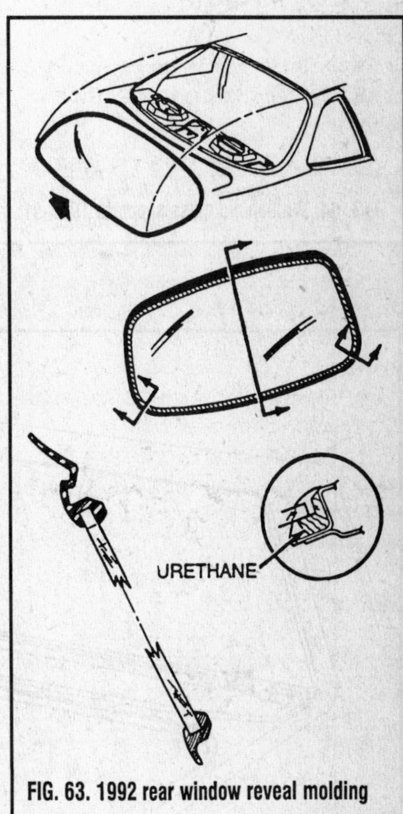

FIG. 63. 1992 rear window reveal molding

9. Apply the clear primer to the perimeter of the windshield and apply a smooth continuous bead of adhesive around the glass. Replace spacers, if removed.
10. With the aid of an assistant, install the windshield into the vehicle.
11. Check windshield alignment and reposition if needed.
12. Press firmly on the glass to set adhesive. Smooth the adhesive out around the windshield to ensure a watertight seal.
13. Water Test the seal with soft spray. Do not direct hard spray at fresh adhesive.
14. Install all reveal moldings and vent grille panel if removed. Connect the rear window defroster connectors, if disconnected.

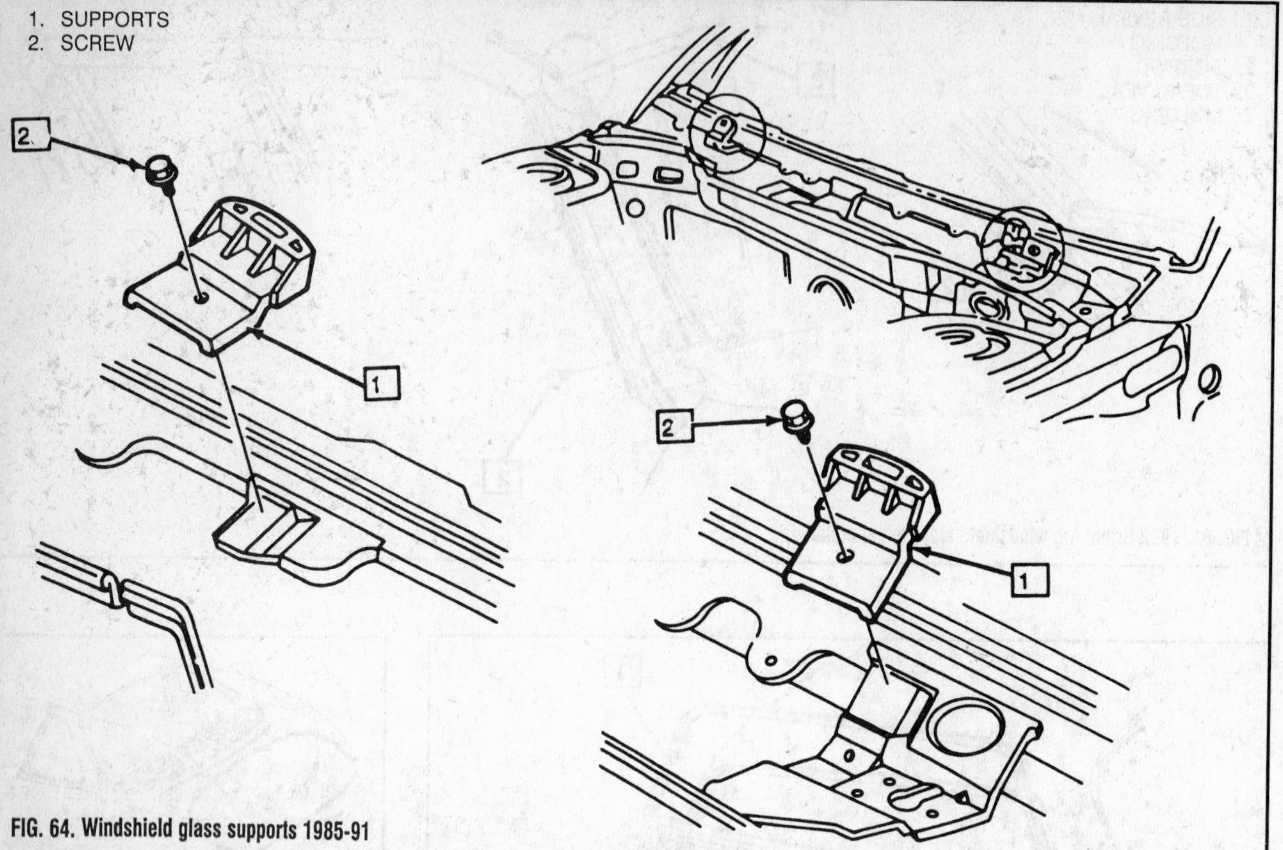

1. SUPPORTS
2. SCREW

FIG. 64. Windshield glass supports 1985-91

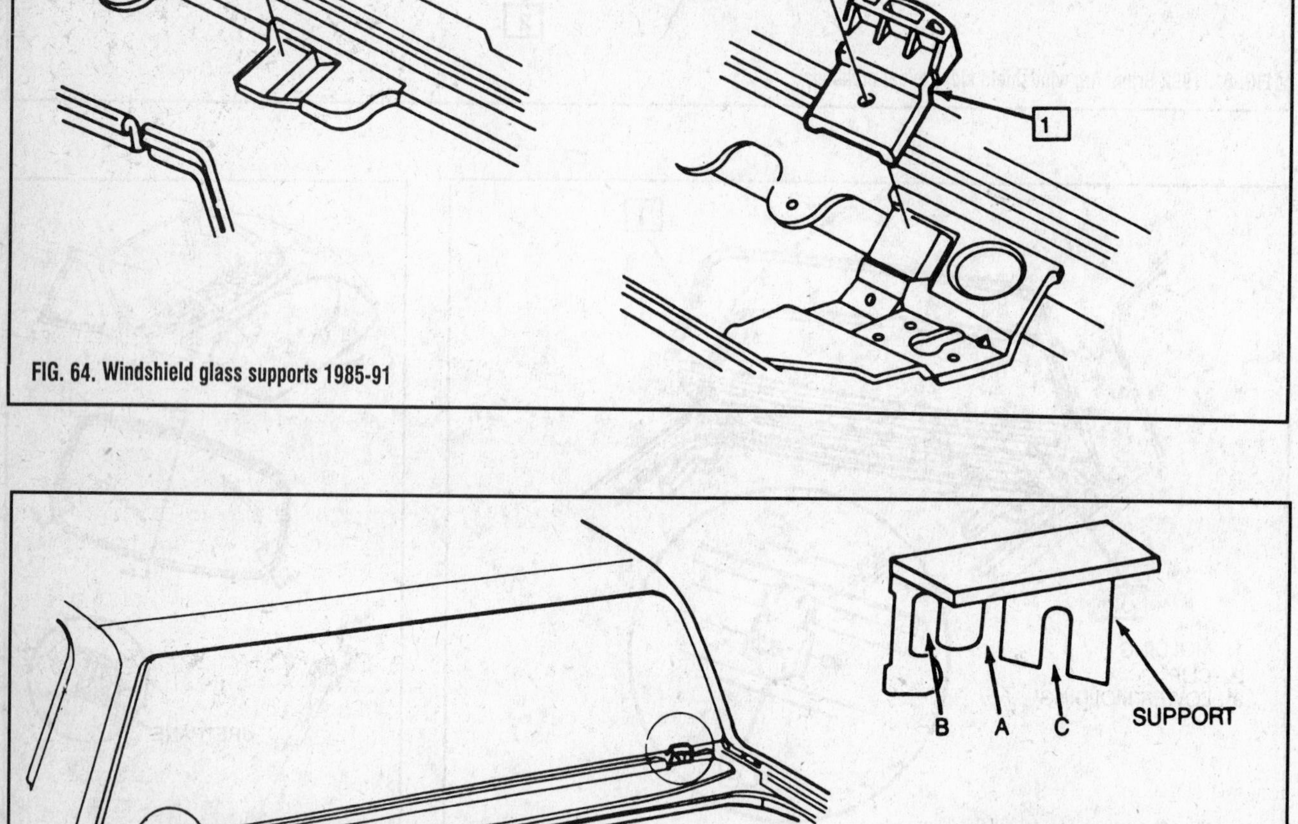

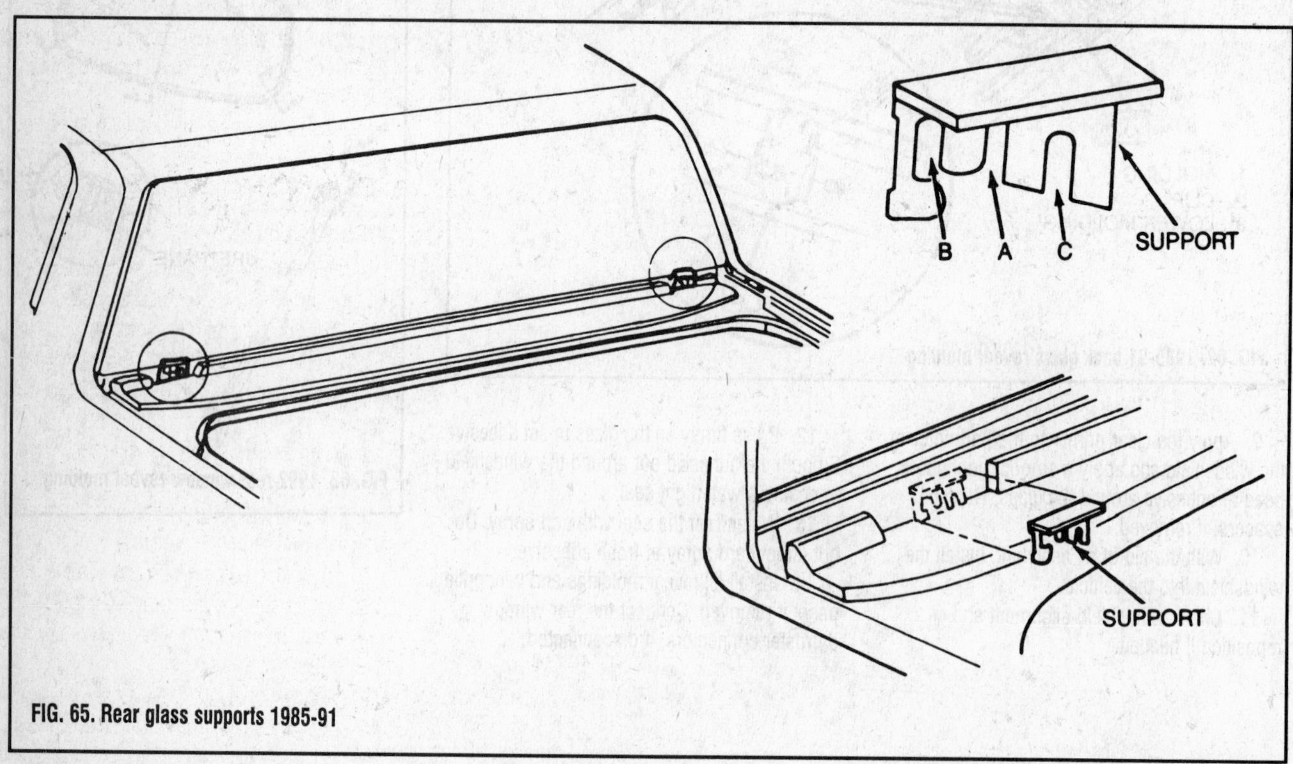

FIG. 65. Rear glass supports 1985-91

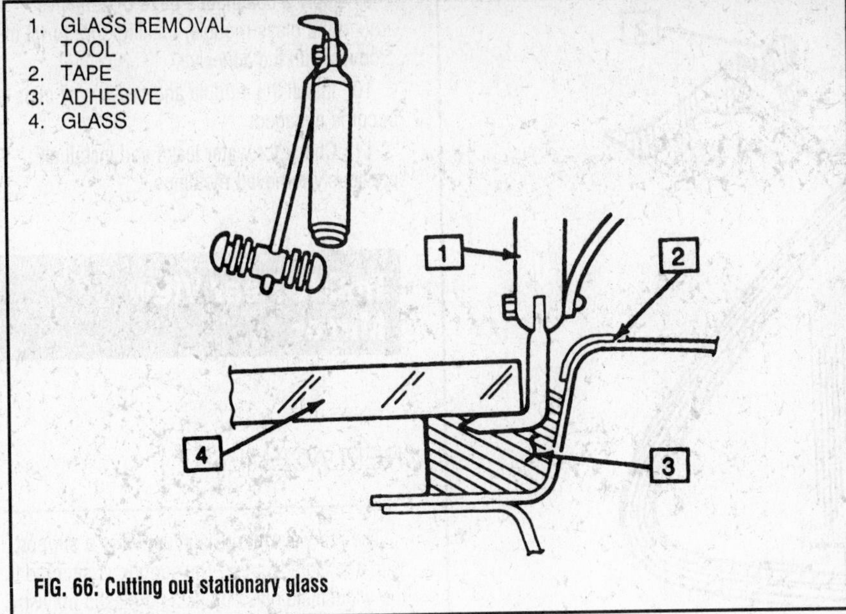

FIG. 66. Cutting out stationary glass

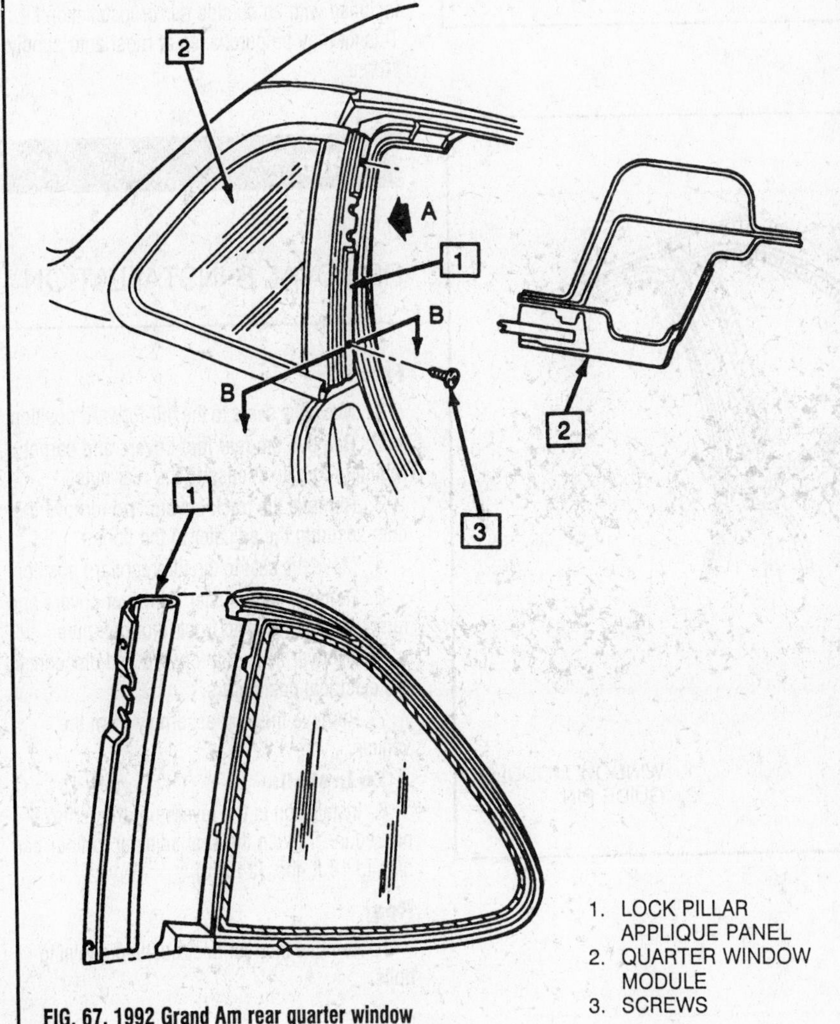

FIG. 67. 1992 Grand Am rear quarter window

Rear Quarter Window 2-Door

➧ SEE FIGS. 67–72

REMOVAL & INSTALLATION

1992 Models

1. Remove the screws securing the body lock applique panel to the door frame and remove the panel.
2. Remove the upper and lower quarter trim panels.
3. Using tool J24402A or a power tool with a oscillating blade, cut around the entire perimeter of the window. Be sure that the blade of the tool is kept as close to the window as possible.
4. Remove window from the vehicle. Clean all traces of adhesive from the window and from the frame.

To install:

5. Apply black primer from urethane adhesive kit around the pinch weld flange.
6. Using a caulking gun, apply a smooth, continuous bead of adhesive material around the entire mounting surface of the window.
7. Place the window into the opening and press firmly to set the glass.
8. Check quarter window for any water leaks by spraying water onto window area while having an assistant watching inside for leakage.
9. Remove any excessive urethane from around the window.
10. Install the upper and lower quarter trim finish panels.
11. Install the body lock pillar applique panel.

1985-91 Models

1. Apply tape to body of vehicle around the rear quarter window to protect the body.
2. Remove the roof drip molding.
3. Remove the screws from the quarter window reveal molding frame, at the body lock pillar.
4. Using a putty knife carefully release the molding from the retainer clips.
5. Carefully cut the urethane bond between the reveal molding and the glass.
6. Apply tape to the inside and outside of the glass to minimize scattering of broken glass.
7. Break the glass with a hammer and cut the module from the vehicle.

To install:

8. Apply the black primer to the pinch weld flange and apply the clear primer to the perimeter of the quarter window. Allow the primer to dry for approx. 5 minutes.

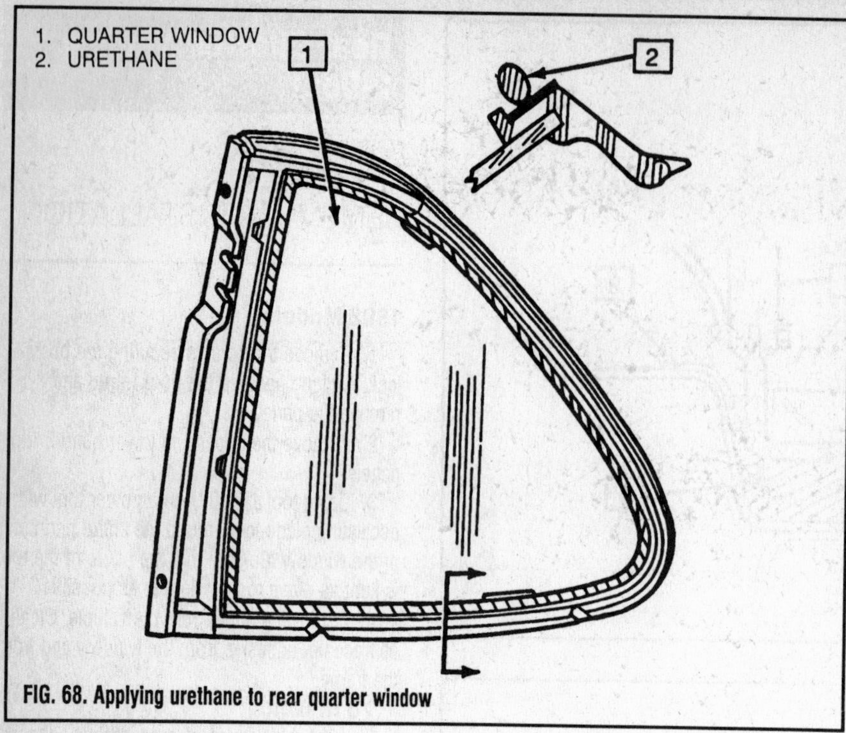

FIG. 68. Applying urethane to rear quarter window

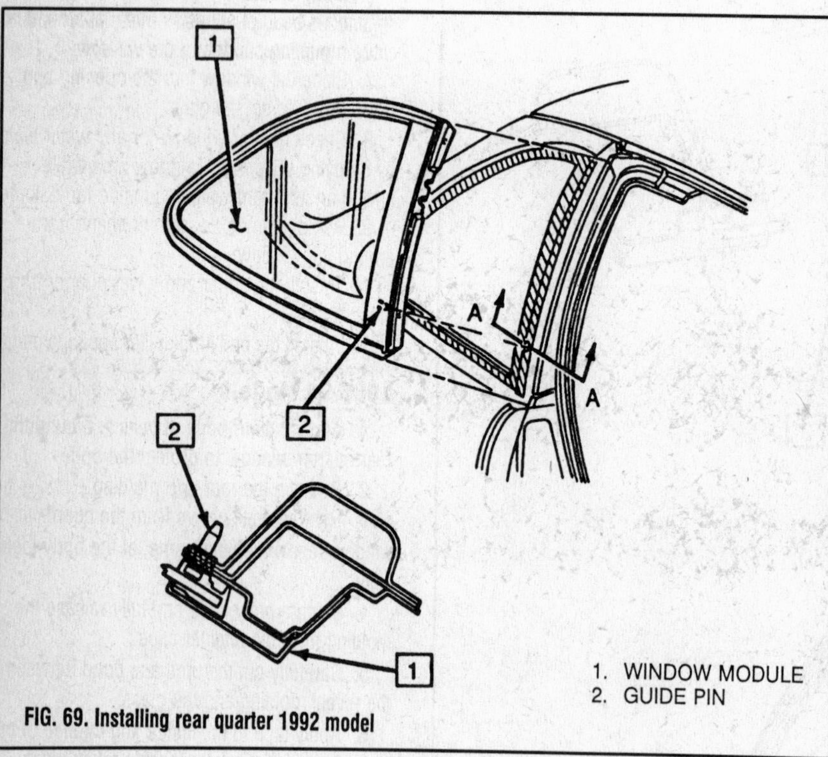

FIG. 69. Installing rear quarter 1992 model

9. Apply a continuous bead of adhesive around the glass module, making sure to fill the grooves with the adhesive.

10. Install the module and press until clips become engaged.

11. Check for water leaks and install all previously removed moldings.

Inside Rear View Mirror

REPLACEMENT

The rearview mirror is attached to a support with a retaining screw. The support is secured to the windshield glass by using a plastic polyvinyl butyl adhesive. To reinstall a mirror support arm to the windshield, follow the instructions included with an outside mirror installation kit. This kit may be purchased at most auto supply stores.

Seats

REMOVAL & INSTALLATION

Front

1. Move the seats to the full-forward position.
2. Remove the rear foot covers and carpet retainers to gain access to the rear nuts.
3. Remove the track covers and remove the nuts securing the adjuster to the floor.
4. Move the seat to the full-rearward position.
5. Remove the adjuster front foot covers and remove the adjuster to front floor pan nuts.
6. If power seats, tilt forward and disconnect the electrical connectors.
7. Remove the seat assembly from the vehicle.

To install:

8. Installation is the reverse of the removal procedure. Tighten the seat adjuster to floor pan nuts to 18 ft. lbs. (24 Nm)

Rear

1. Remove the rear seat cushion retaining bolts.

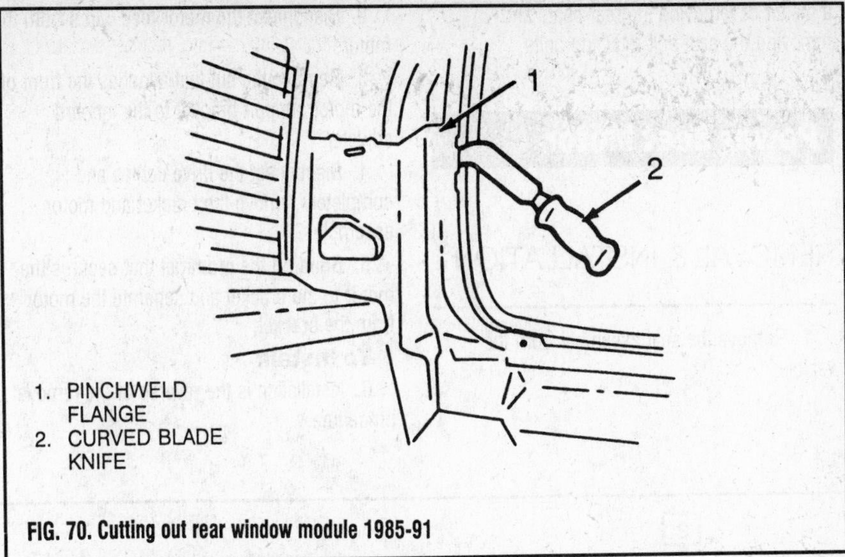

FIG. 70. Cutting out rear window module 1985-91

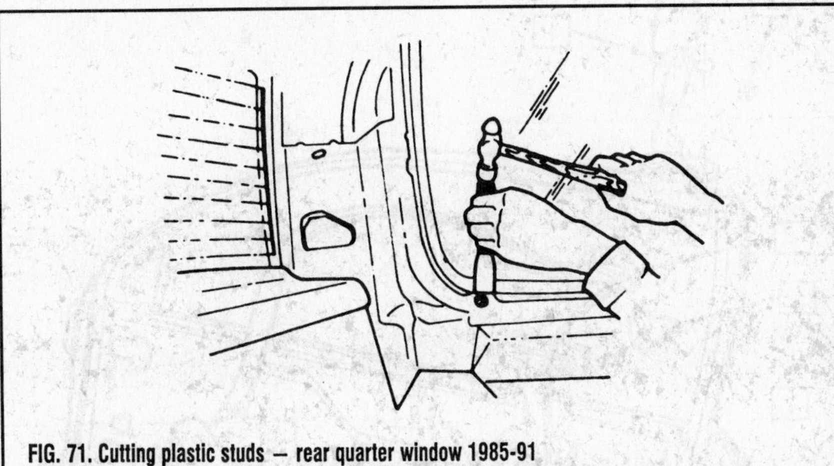

FIG. 71. Cutting plastic studs – rear quarter window 1985-91

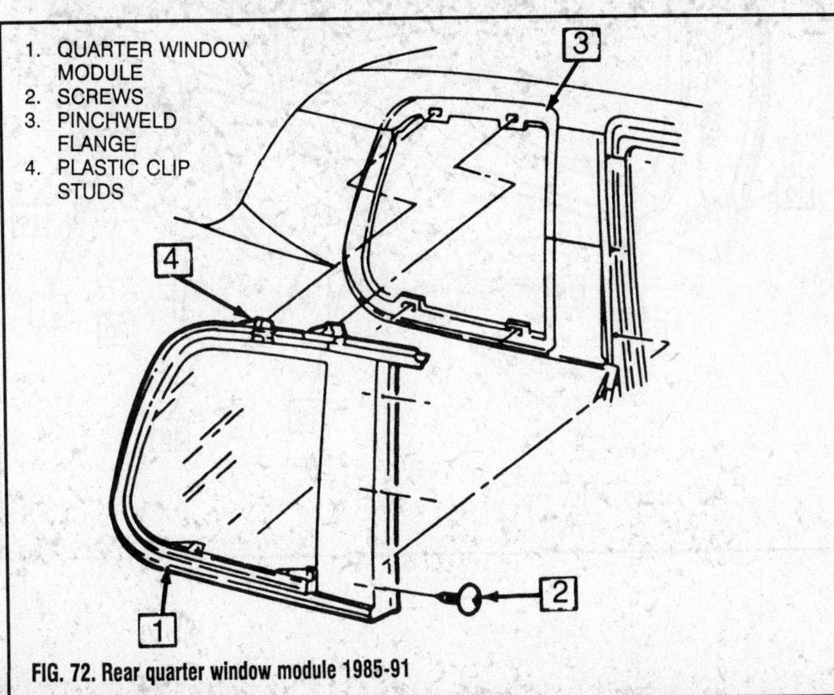

FIG. 72. Rear quarter window module 1985-91

2. Lift up on rear seat cushion and pull out.
3. Remove the rear seat back bottom bolts.
4. Lift up bottom of seat to disengage the back upper frame bar hangers, and remove the rear seat back.

To install:

5. Installation is the reverse of the removal procedure.

Seat Belts

➧ SEE FIGS. 73

REMOVAL & INSTALLATION

Passive Restraint Front Seat Belt System

1. Remove the front courtesy lamp fuse.
2. Remove the door trim panel.
3. Disconnect the solenoid connectors from the seat and shoulder belt retractor units.
4. Remove the anchor plate cover and remove the nut connecting the upper guide loop.
5. Remove the safety belt retainer from the door.
6. Remove the top screw from the shoulder safety belt retractor.
7. Remove the nuts from the seat and shoulder safety belt retractors.

To install:

8. Insert the retaining tab of the seat belt into the inner door panel while seating the bottom of the retainer over the stud.
9. Place the lap belt retractor on the inner door panel studs. Install the nuts and tighten.
10. Install the seat belt retainer and install the retaining screws.
11. Install the anchor plate to the upper guide loop and install the nut.
12. Install the anchor plate cover.
13. Connect the solenoid electrical connectors.
14. Install the door trim panel and the courtesy lamp fuse.
15. Inspect seat belt operation.

Active Restraint Front Seat Belt System

1. Remove the carpet retainer.
2. Remove the windshield upper side garnish molding.
3. Remove the rear seat back and rear seat cushion.

4. Remove the shoulder belt guide cover and upper bolt.

5. Remove the outboard belt assembly lower bolt.

6. Remove the inner quarter trim panel.

7. Using tool J23457 remove the retractor bolts and anchor bolts as required.

To install:

8. Installation is the reverse of the removal procedure.

Rear Seat Belts

Rear seat belt removal and installation is only a matter of removing the rear seats and removing the seat belt retaining bolts.

Power Seat Motor

REMOVAL & INSTALLATION

1. Remove the seat assembly from the vehicle.

2. Disconnect the motor feed wires from the motors.

3. Remove the nut that attaches the front of the motor support bracket to the inboard adjuster.

4. Disconnect the drive cables and completely remove the bracket and motor assembly.

5. Grind off the grommet that secures the motor to the bracket and separate the motor from the bracket.

To install:

6. Installation is the reverse of the removal procedure.

1. INTERLOCK RETAINER
2. SCREW
3. NUT
4. UPPER GUIDE LOOP
5. ANCHOR PLATE COVER
6. SCREW
7. SEAT BELT RETAINER
8. SCREWS
9. COMFORT LOCK RELEASE CABLE
10. COMFORT RELEASE
11. NYLON NUT
12. SPLITTER BOX COVER
13. LATCH PLATE
14. SOLENOID
15. SCREW
16. SHOULDER BELT RETRACTOR
17. NUT
18. SOLENOID
19. COVER
20. SEAT BELT RETRACTOR
21. NUT

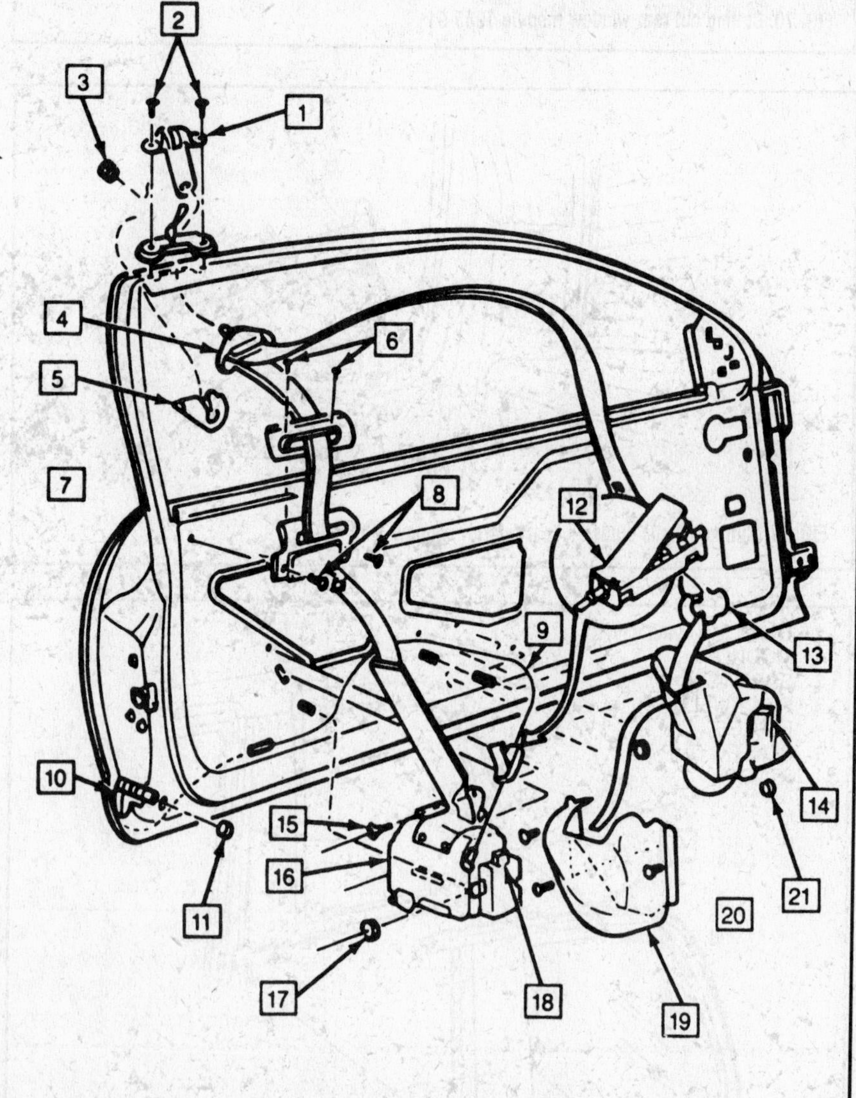

FIG. 73. Typical front seat belt system

How to Remove Stains from Fabric Interior

For best results, spots and stains should be removed as soon as possible. Never use gasoline, lacquer thinner, acetone, nail polish remover or bleach. Use a 3′ x 3″ piece of cheesecloth. Squeeze most of the liquid from the fabric and wipe the stained fabric from the outside of the stain toward the center with a lifting motion. Turn the cheesecloth as soon as one side becomes soiled. When using water to remove a stain, be sure to wash the entire section after the spot has been removed to avoid water stains. Encrusted spots can be broken up with a dull knife and vacuumed before removing the stain.

Type of Stain	How to Remove It
Surface spots	Brush the spots out with a small hand brush or use a commercial preparation such as K2R to lift the stain.
Mildew	Clean around the mildew with warm suds. Rinse in cold water and soak the mildew area in a solution of 1 part table salt and 2 parts water. Wash with upholstery cleaner.
Water stains	Water stains in fabric materials can be removed with a solution made from 1 cup of table salt dissolved in 1 quart of water. Vigorously scrub the solution into the stain and rinse with clear water. Water stains in nylon or other synthetic fabrics should be removed with a commercial type spot remover.
Chewing gum, tar, crayons, shoe polish (greasy stains)	Do not use a cleaner that will soften gum or tar. Harden the deposit with an ice cube and scrape away as much as possible with a dull knife. Moisten the remainder with cleaning fluid and scrub clean.
Ice cream, candy	Most candy has a sugar base and can be removed with a cloth wrung out in warm water. Oily candy, after cleaning with warm water, should be cleaned with upholstery cleaner. Rinse with warm water and clean the remainder with cleaning fluid.
Wine, alcohol, egg, milk, soft drink (non-greasy stains)	Do not use soap. Scrub the stain with a cloth wrung out in warm water. Remove the remainder with cleaning fluid.
Grease, oil, lipstick, butter and related stains	Use a spot remover to avoid leaving a ring. Work from the outisde of the stain to the center and dry with a clean cloth when the spot is gone.
Headliners (cloth)	Mix a solution of warm water and foam upholstery cleaner to give thick suds. Use only foam—liquid may streak or spot. Clean the entire headliner in one operation using a circular motion with a natural sponge.
Headliner (vinyl)	Use a vinyl cleaner with a sponge and wipe clean with a dry cloth.
Seats and door panels	Mix 1 pint upholstery cleaner in 1 gallon of water. Do not soak the fabric around the buttons.
Leather or vinyl fabric	Use a multi-purpose cleaner full strength and a stiff brush. Let stand 2 minutes and scrub thoroughly. Wipe with a clean, soft rag.
Nylon or synthetic fabrics	For normal stains, use the same procedures you would for washing cloth upholstery. If the fabric is extremely dirty, use a multi-purpose cleaner full strength with a stiff scrub brush. Scrub thoroughly in all directions and wipe with a cotton towel or soft rag.

Hood, Trunk Lid, Hatch Lid, Glass and Doors

Problem	Possible Cause	Correction
HOOD/TRUNK/HATCH LID		
Improper closure.	• Striker and latch not properly aligned.	• Adjust the alignment.
Difficulty locking and unlocking.	• Striker and latch not properly aligned.	• Adjust the alignment.
Uneven clearance with body panels.	• Incorrectly installed hood or trunk lid.	• Adjust the alignment.
WINDOW/WINDSHIELD GLASS		
Water leak through windshield	• Defective seal. • Defective body flange.	• Fill sealant • Correct.
Water leak through door window glass.	• Incorrect window glass installation. • Gap at upper window frame.	• Adjust position. • Adjust position.
Water leak through quarter window.	• Defective seal. • Defective body flange.	• Replace seal. • Correct.
Water leak through rear window.	• Defective seal. • Defective body flange.	• Replace seal. • Correct.
FRONT/REAR DOORS		
Door window malfunction.	• Incorrect window glass installation. • Damaged or faulty regulator.	• Adjust position. • Correct or replace.
Water leak through door edge.	• Cracked or faulty weatherstrip.	• Replace.
Water leak from door center.	• Drain hole clogged. • Inadequate waterproof skeet contact or damage.	• Remove foreign objects. • Correct or replace.
Door hard to open.	• Incorrect latch or striker adjustment.	• Adjust.
Door does not open or close completely.	• Incorrect door installation. • Defective door check strap. • Door check strap and hinge require grease.	• Adjust position. • Correct or replace. • Apply grease.
Uneven gap between door and body.	• Incorrect door installation.	• Adjust position.
Wind noise around door.	• Improperly installed weatherstrip. • Improper clearance between door glass and door weatherstrip. • Deformed door.	• Repair or replace. • Adjust. • Repair or replace.

TORQUE SPECIFICATIONS

Component	U.S.	Metric
Bumper impact bar to vehicle bolts	22 ft. lbs.	30 Nm
Bumper impact bar to vehicle nuts	26 ft. lbs.	35 Nm
Door hinge bolts	36 ft. lbs.	48 Nm
Front seat mounting bolts	18 ft. lbs.	24 Nm
Hood and trunk bolts	20 ft. lbs.	27 Nm
Rear seat cushion mounting bolts	12-14 ft. lbs.	16-20 Nm
Seat belt retaining bolts	25-30 ft. lbs.	34-41 Nm
Seat belt retractor to door nuts	18-27 ft. lbs.	24-32 Nm
Seat belt upper guide loop nut	16-22 ft. lbs.	22-30 Nm
Top Fender bolts	106 in. lbs.	12 Nm
Trunk lock bolts	53 in. lbs.	6 Nm

GLOSSARY

AIR/FUEL RATIO: The ratio of air to gasoline by weight in the fuel mixture drawn into the engine.

AIR INJECTION: One method of reducing harmful exhaust emissions by injecting air into each of the exhaust ports of an engine. The fresh air entering the hot exhaust manifold causes any remaining fuel to be burned before it can exit the tailpipe.

ALTERNATOR: A device used for converting mechanical energy into electrical energy.

AMMETER: An instrument, calibrated in amperes, used to measure the flow of an electrical current in a circuit. Ammeters are always connected in series with the circuit being tested.

AMPERE: The rate of flow of electrical current present when one volt of electrical pressure is applied against one ohm of electrical resistance.

ANALOG COMPUTER: Any microprocessor that uses similar (analogous) electrical signals to make its calculations.

ARMATURE: A laminated, soft iron core wrapped by a wire that converts electrical energy to mechanical energy as in a motor or relay. When rotated in a magnetic field, it changes mechanical energy into electrical energy as in a generator.

ATMOSPHERIC PRESSURE: The pressure on the Earth's surface caused by the weight of the air in the atmosphere. At sea level, this pressure is 14.7 psi at 32°F (101 kPa at 0°C).

ATOMIZATION: The breaking down of a liquid into a fine mist that can be suspended in air.

AXIAL PLAY: Movement parallel to a shaft or bearing bore.

BACKFIRE: The sudden combustion of gases in the intake or exhaust system that results in a loud explosion.

BACKLASH: The clearance or play between two parts, such as meshed gears.

BACKPRESSURE: Restrictions in the exhaust system that slow the exit of exhaust gases from the combustion chamber.

BAKELITE: A heat resistant, plastic insulator material commonly used in printed circuit boards and transistorized components.

BALL BEARING: A bearing made up of hardened inner and outer races between which hardened steel balls roll.

BALLAST RESISTOR: A resistor in the primary ignition circuit that lowers voltage after the engine is started to reduce wear on ignition components.

BEARING: A friction reducing, supportive device usually located between a stationary part and a moving part.

BIMETAL TEMPERATURE SENSOR: Any sensor or switch made of two dissimilar types of metal that bend when heated or cooled due to the different expansion rates of the alloys. These types of sensors usually function as an on/off switch.

BLOWBY: Combustion gases, composed of water vapor and unburned fuel, that leak past the piston rings into the crankcase during normal engine operation. These gases are removed by the PCV system to prevent the buildup of harmful acids in the crankcase.

BRAKE PAD: A brake shoe and lining assembly used with disc brakes.

BRAKE SHOE: The backing for the brake lining. The term is, however, usually applied to the assembly of the brake backing and lining.

BUSHING: A liner, usually removable, for a bearing; an anti-friction liner used in place of a bearing.

BYPASS: System used to bypass ballast resistor during engine cranking to increase voltage supplied to the coil.

CALIPER: A hydraulically activated device in a disc brake system, which is mounted straddling the brake rotor (disc). The caliper contains at least one piston and two brake pads. Hydraulic pressure on the piston(s) forces the pads against the rotor.

CAMSHAFT: A shaft in the engine on which are the lobes (cams) which operate the valves. The camshaft is driven by the crankshaft, via a belt, chain or gears, at one half the crankshaft speed.

CAPACITOR: A device which stores an electrical charge.

CARBON MONOXIDE (CO): A colorless, odorless gas given off as a normal byproduct of combustion. It is poisonous and extremely dangerous in confined areas, building up slowly to toxic levels without warning if adequate ventilation is not available.

CARBURETOR: A device, usually mounted on the intake manifold of an engine, which mixes the air and fuel in the proper proportion to allow even combustion.

CATALYTIC CONVERTER: A device installed in the exhaust system, like a muffler, that converts harmful byproducts of combustion into carbon dioxide and water vapor by means of a heat-producing chemical reaction.

CENTRIFUGAL ADVANCE: A mechanical method of advancing the spark timing by using fly weights in the distributor that react to centrifugal force generated by the distributor shaft rotation.

CHECK VALVE: Any one-way valve installed to permit the flow of air, fuel or vacuum in one direction only.

CHOKE: A device, usually a movable valve, placed in the intake path of a carburetor to restrict the flow of air.

CIRCUIT: Any unbroken path through which an electrical current can flow. Also used to describe fuel flow in some instances.

CIRCUIT BREAKER: A switch which protects an electrical circuit from overload by opening the circuit when the current flow exceeds a predetermined level. Some circuit breakers must be reset manually, while most reset automatically

COIL (IGNITION): A transformer in the ignition circuit which steps up the voltage provided to the spark plugs.

COMBINATION MANIFOLD: An assembly which includes both the intake and exhaust manifolds in one casting.

COMBINATION VALVE: A device used in some fuel systems that routes fuel vapors to a charcoal storage canister instead of venting them into the atmosphere. The valve relieves fuel tank pressure and allows fresh air into the tank as the fuel level drops to prevent a vapor lock situation.

COMPRESSION RATIO: The comparison of the total volume of the cylinder and combustion chamber with the piston at BDC and the piston at TDC.

CONDENSER: 1. An electrical device which acts to store an electrical charge, preventing voltage surges.
2. A radiator-like device in the air conditioning system in which refrigerant gas condenses into a liquid, giving off heat.

CONDUCTOR: Any material through which an electrical current can be transmitted easily.

CONTINUITY: Continuous or complete circuit. Can be checked with an ohmmeter.

COUNTERSHAFT: An intermediate shaft which is rotated by a mainshaft and transmits, in turn, that rotation to a working part.

CRANKCASE: The lower part of an engine in which the crankshaft and related parts operate.

CRANKSHAFT: The main driving shaft of an engine which receives reciprocating motion from the pistons and converts it to rotary motion.

CYLINDER: In an engine, the round hole in the engine block in which the piston(s) ride.

CYLINDER BLOCK: The main structural member of an engine in which is found the cylinders, crankshaft and other principal parts.

CYLINDER HEAD: The detachable portion of the engine, fastened, usually, to the top of the cylinder block, containing all or most of the combustion chambers. On overhead valve engines, it contains the valves and their operating parts. On overhead cam engines, it contains the camshaft as well.

DEAD CENTER: The extreme top or bottom of the piston stroke.

DETONATION: An unwanted explosion of the air/fuel mixture in the combustion chamber caused by excess heat and compression, advanced timing, or an overly lean mixture. Also referred to as "ping".

DIAPHRAGM: A thin, flexible wall separating two cavities, such as in a vacuum advance unit.

DIESELING: A condition in which hot spots in the combustion chamber cause the engine to run on after the key is turned off.

DIFFERENTIAL: A geared assembly which allows the transmission of motion between drive axles, giving one axle the ability to turn faster than the other.

DIODE: An electrical device that will allow current to flow in one direction only.

DISC BRAKE: A hydraulic braking assembly consisting of a brake disc, or rotor, mounted on an axle, and a caliper assembly containing, usually two brake pads which are activated by hydraulic pressure. The pads are forced against the sides of the disc, creating friction which slows the vehicle.

DISTRIBUTOR: A mechanically driven device on an engine which is responsible for electrically firing the spark plug at a predetermined point of the piston stroke.

DOWEL PIN: A pin, inserted in mating holes in two different parts allowing those parts to maintain a fixed relationship.

DRUM BRAKE: A braking system which consists of two brake shoes and one or two wheel cylinders, mounted on a fixed backing plate, and a brake drum, mounted on an axle, which revolves around the assembly. Hydraulic action applied to the wheel cylinders forces the shoes outward against the drum, creating friction, slowing the vehicle.

DWELL: The rate, measured in degrees of shaft rotation, at which an electrical circuit cycles on and off.

ELECTRONIC CONTROL UNIT (ECU): Ignition module, amplifier or igniter. See Module for definition.

ELECTRONIC IGNITION: A system in which the timing and firing of the spark plugs is controlled by an electronic control unit, usually called a module. These systems have no points or condenser.

ENDPLAY: The measured amount of axial movement in a shaft.

ENGINE: A device that converts heat into mechanical energy.

EXHAUST MANIFOLD: A set of cast passages or pipes which conduct exhaust gases from the engine.

FEELER GAUGE: A blade, usually metal, of precisely predetermined thickness, used to measure the clearance between two parts. These blades usually are available in sets of assorted thicknesses.

F-HEAD: An engine configuration in which the intake valves are in the cylinder head, while the camshaft and exhaust valves are located in the cylinder block. The camshaft operates the intake valves via lifters and pushrods, while it operates the exhaust valves directly.

FIRING ORDER: The order in which combustion occurs in the cylinders of an engine. Also the order in which spark is distributed to the plugs by the distributor.

FLATHEAD: An engine configuration in which the camshaft and all the valves are located in the cylinder block.

FLOODING: The presence of too much fuel in the intake manifold and combustion chamber which prevents the air/fuel mixture from firing, thereby causing a no-start situation.

FLYWHEEL: A disc shaped part bolted to the rear end of the crankshaft. Around the outer perimeter is affixed the ring gear. The starter drive engages the ring gear, turning the flywheel, which rotates the crankshaft, imparting the initial starting motion to the engine.

FOOT POUND (ft.lb. or sometimes, ft. lbs.): The amount of energy or work needed to raise an item weighing one pound, a distance of one foot.

FUSE: A protective device in a circuit which prevents circuit overload by breaking the circuit when a specific amperage is present. The device is constructed around a strip or wire of a lower amperage rating than the circuit it is designed to protect. When an amperage higher than that stamped on the fuse is present in the circuit, the strip or wire melts, opening the circuit.

GEAR RATIO: The ratio between the number of teeth on meshing gears.

GENERATOR: A device which converts mechanical energy into electrical energy.

HEAT RANGE: The measure of a spark plug's ability to dissipate heat from its firing end. The higher the heat range, the hotter the plug fires.
HUB: The center part of a wheel or gear.

HYDROCARBON (HC): Any chemical compound made up of hydrogen and carbon. A major pollutant formed by the engine as a byproduct of combustion.

HYDROMETER: An instrument used to measure the specific gravity of a solution.

INCH POUND (in.lb. or sometimes, in. lbs.): One twelfth of a foot pound.

INDUCTION: A means of transferring electrical energy in the form of a magnetic field. Principle used in the ignition coil to increase voltage.

INJECTION PUMP: A device, usually mechanically operated, which meters and delivers fuel under pressure to the fuel injector.

INJECTOR: A device which receives metered fuel under relatively low pressure and is activated to inject the fuel into the engine under relatively high pressure at a predetermined time.

INPUT SHAFT: The shaft to which torque is applied, usually carrying the driving gear or gears.

INTAKE MANIFOLD: A casting of passages or pipes used to conduct air or a fuel/air mixture to the cylinders.

JOURNAL: The bearing surface within which a shaft operates.

KEY: A small block usually fitted in a notch between a shaft and a hub to prevent slippage of the two parts.

MANIFOLD: A casting of passages or set of pipes which connect the cylinders to an inlet or outlet source.

MANIFOLD VACUUM: Low pressure in an engine intake manifold formed just below the throttle plates. Manifold vacuum is highest at idle and drops under acceleration.

MASTER CYLINDER: The primary fluid pressurizing device in a hydraulic system. In automotive use, it is found in brake and hydraulic clutch systems and is pedal activated, either directly or, in a power brake system, through the power booster.

MODULE: Electronic control unit, amplifier or igniter of solid state or integrated design which controls the current flow in the ignition primary circuit based on input from the pick- up coil. When the module opens the primary circuit, the high secondary voltage is induced in the coil.

NEEDLE BEARING: A bearing which consists of a number (usually a large number) of long, thin rollers.

OHM:(Ω) The unit used to measure the resistance of conductor to electrical flow. One ohm is the amount of resistance that limits current flow to one ampere in a circuit with one volt of pressure.

OHMMETER: An instrument used for measuring the resistance, in ohms, in an electrical circuit.

OUTPUT SHAFT: The shaft which transmits torque from a device, such as a transmission.

OVERDRIVE: A gear assembly which produces more shaft revolutions than that transmitted to it.

OVERHEAD CAMSHAFT (OHC): An engine configuration in which the camshaft is mounted on top of the cylinder head and operates the valves either directly or by means of rocker arms.

OVERHEAD VALVE (OHV): An engine configuration in which all of the valves are located in the cylinder head and the camshaft is located in the cylinder block. The camshaft operates the valves via lifters and pushrods.

OXIDES OF NITROGEN (NOx): Chemical compounds of nitrogen produced as a byproduct of combustion. They combine with hydrocarbons to produce smog.

OXYGEN SENSOR: Used with the feedback system to sense the presence of oxygen in the exhaust gas and signal the computer which can reference the voltage signal to an air/fuel ratio.

PINION: The smaller of two meshing gears.

PISTON RING: An open ended ring which fits into a groove on the outer diameter of the piston. Its chief function is to form a seal between the piston and cylinder wall. Most automotive pistons have three rings: two for compression sealing; one for oil sealing.

PRELOAD: A predetermined load placed on a bearing during assembly or by adjustment.

PRIMARY CIRCUIT: Is the low voltage side of the ignition system which consists of the ignition switch, ballast resistor or resistance wire, bypass, coil, electronic control unit and pick-up coil as well as the connecting wires and harnesses.

PRESS FIT: The mating of two parts under pressure, due to the inner diameter of one being smaller than the outer diameter of the other, or vice versa; an interference fit.

RACE: The surface on the inner or outer ring of a bearing on which the balls, needles or rollers move.

REGULATOR: A device which maintains the amperage and/or voltage levels of a circuit at predetermined values.

RELAY: A switch which automatically opens and/or closes a circuit.

RESISTANCE: The opposition to the flow of current through a circuit or electrical device, and is measured in ohms. Resistance is equal to the voltage divided by the amperage.

RESISTOR: A device, usually made of wire, which offers a preset amount of resistance in an electrical circuit.

RING GEAR: The name given to a ring-shaped gear attached to a differential case,or affixed to a flywheel or as part a planetary gear set.

ROLLER BEARING: A bearing made up of hardened inner and outer races between which hardened steel rollers move.

ROTOR: 1. The disc-shaped part of a disc brake assembly, upon which the brake pads bear; also called, brake disc.
2. The device mounted atop the distributor shaft, which passes current to the distributor cap tower contacts.

SECONDARY CIRCUIT: The high voltage side of the ignition system, usually above 20,000 volts. The secondary includes the ignition coil, coil wire, distributor cap and rotor, spark plug wires and spark plugs.

SENDING UNIT: A mechanical, electrical, hydraulic or electromagnetic device which transmits information to a gauge.

SENSOR: Any device designed to measure engine operating conditions or ambient pressures and temperatures. Usually electronic in nature and designed to send a voltage signal to an on-board computer, some sensors may operate as a simple on/off switch or they may provide a variable voltage signal (like a potentiometer) as conditions or measured parameters change.

SHIM: Spacers of precise, predetermined thickness used between parts to establish a proper working relationship.

SLAVE CYLINDER: In automotive use, a device in the hydraulic clutch system which is activated by hydraulic force, disengaging the clutch.

SOLENOID: A coil used to produce a magnetic field, the effect of which is to produce work.

SPARK PLUG: A device screwed into the combustion chamber of a spark ignition engine. The basic construction is a conductive core inside of a ceramic insulator, mounted in an outer conductive base. An electrical charge from the spark plug wire travels along the conductive core and jumps a preset air gap to a grounding point or points at the end of the conductive base. The resultant spark ignites the fuel/air mixture in the combustion chamber.

SPLINES: Ridges machined or cast onto the outer diameter of a shaft or inner diameter of a bore to enable parts to mate without rotation.

TACHOMETER: A device used to measure the rotary speed of an engine, shaft, gear, etc., usually in rotations per minute.

THERMOSTAT: A valve, located in the cooling system of an engine, which is closed when cold and opens gradually in response to engine heating, controlling the temperature of the coolant and rate of coolant flow.

TOP DEAD CENTER (TDC): The point at which the piston reaches the top of its travel on the compression stroke.

TORQUE: The twisting force applied to an object.

TORQUE CONVERTER: A turbine used to transmit power from a driving member to a driven member via hydraulic action, providing changes in drive ratio and torque. In automotive use, it links the driveplate at the rear of the engine to the automatic transmission.

TRANSDUCER: A device used to change a force into an electrical signal.

TRANSISTOR: A semi-conductor component which can be actuated by a small voltage to perform an electrical switching function.

TUNE-UP: A regular maintenance function, usually associated with the replacement and adjustment of parts and components in the electrical and fuel systems of a vehicle for the purpose of attaining optimum performance.

TURBOCHARGER: An exhaust driven pump which compresses intake air and forces it into the combustion chambers at higher than atmospheric pressures. The increased air pressure allows more fuel to be burned and results in increased horsepower being produced.

VACUUM ADVANCE: A device which advances the ignition timing in response to increased engine vacuum.

VACUUM GAUGE: An instrument used to measure the presence of vacuum in a chamber.

VALVE: A device which control the pressure, direction of flow or rate of flow of a liquid or gas.

VALVE CLEARANCE: The measured gap between the end of the valve stem and the rocker arm, cam lobe or follower that activates the valve.

VISCOSITY: The rating of a liquid's internal resistance to flow.

VOLTMETER: An instrument used for measuring electrical force in units called volts. Voltmeters are always connected parallel with the circuit being tested.

WHEEL CYLINDER: Found in the automotive drum brake assembly, it is a device, actuated by hydraulic pressure, which, through internal pistons, pushes the brake shoes outward against the drums.

MASTER
INDEX